Encyclopedic Dictionary
of Archaeology

Encyclopedic Dictionary
of Archaeology

Compiled by

Barbara Ann Kipfer, Ph.D.

Kluwer Academic / Plenum Publishers
New York   Boston   Dordrecht   London   Moscow

Library of Congress Cataloging-in-Publication Data

Kipfer, Barbara Ann.
  Encyclopedic dictionary of archaeology/by Barbara Ann Kipfer.
    p. cm.
  Includes bibliographical references.
  ISBN 0-306-46158-7
  1. Archaeology—Dictionaries. I. Title.

  CC70 .K56 2000
  930.1′03—dc21
                                                                99-053995

ISBN 0-306-46158-7

© 2000 Kluwer Academic / Plenum Publishers
233 Spring Street, New York, N.Y. 10013

http://www.wkap.nl/

10 9 8 7 6 5 4 3 2 1

Printed in the United States of America

Preface

Archaeology is the study of human life and activities through material remains. It is used to uncover the history of prehistoric times and peoples without written records. Part of archaeology is creating written records about a time without written records or with incomplete written records. The *Encyclopedic Dictionary of Archaeology* was written to prepare the author for work as an archaeologist who helps others research, write, and edit their data and who writes useful books and publications for other archaeologists.

An archaeologist's work involves locating, collecting, cleaning, sorting, identifying, and measuring objects found in and on the earth and sea. The ultimate goal of the archaeologist is to reconstruct the culture that produced the objects. Therefore, a vital part of an archaeologist's work is writing up and presenting the data and the reconstruction based on the data.

The scientific and technical tools and techniques or archaeology have increased tremendously. The *Encyclopedic Dictionary of Archaeology* provides the student, layperson, and professional archaeologist with clear definitions of complex terms and procedures. It contains descriptions of various types of dating, excavation, tools, and artifacts as well as key individuals in the history of archaeology. It also covers terms borrowed from anthropology, computer science, botany, demography, economics, geography, geology, mathematics, pathology, statistics, surveying, physics, biology, and chemistry. This dictionary has been complied with the aim of introducing anyone who is interested in modern archaeology to the terminology, concepts, and basic aims of the techniques.

This is a general and specialized dictionary of archaeology; cultures and artifacts are described as well as terms describing techniques applied to archaeological material. This book will come as a welcome repository of all the fascinating discoveries in the various fields of research, from the antiquity of the Far East, Europe, and the Middle East to Pre-Columbian cultures of the Americas. For the general reader, the volume is not only a ready reference, but a fascinating home library or bedside book to enrich one's comprehension of human beginnings and subsequent civilizations. The dictionary is comprehensive, with coverage of the whole world beginning with the first hominids of some 3 million years ago and continuing through protohistoric and historical archaeology. One finds here an entry for every site that has contributed uniquely to the essential body of information on which the current major classifications and interpretations of prehistory are based—and for major artifact types and major cultures and their phases and subdivisions. The *Encyclopedic Dictionary of Archaeology* has been carefully constructed to provide balance and depth of treatment.

One of the biggest difficulties in compiling a work of this sort lies in deciding what to put in and what to leave out. I have made no attempt to filter or skip any branch of archaeology. Technical terms have been included but described in a nonintimidating fashion. The dictionary, however, contains enough information to be of value to serious students and to professional archaeologists who seek information outside their specialty.

It has not been possible, however, to include all of the terms of Egyptology or of other very specialized areas. I leave that to various large volumes published on those specific areas of interest.

The entries include synonyms, providing a cross-reference within the dictionary and to other sources. The bibliography includes all of the references used in preparing the text.

A special feature of this work is the chronology of the story of writing and archaeological decipherment from Egyptian hieroglyphs to Linear B. Decipherments are by far the most glamorous achievements of scholarship as there is magic involved in unknown writings of the remote past. This recounting of the evolution of writing and the history of archaeological decipherment is a valuable addition to this dictionary.

Archaeology continues to develop at a fast rate. Certainly during the compilation of this dictionary, further improvements in techniques, newly discovered radiocarbon dates, and new terms have arisen. Further refinements and new data will undoubtedly appear. It is clearly impossible to include a reference to every fact or term of archaeological importance in the world. In North America alone, more than a half-million archaeological sites have been recorded, tens of thousands have been excavated, and thousands of named artifact types and culture complexes have been described in the literature. This is still the largest collection of archaeological terms described in a one-volume reference.

Interest in archaeology is more keen and widespread now than at any time in the past, so much so that the dividing line separating the specialist and the general reader is narrowing. Newspaper articles and books keep the reader informed of the latest archaeological techniques and discoveries. The result is that the intelligent amateur wants to know more and more and is sometimes prepared to wrestle with serious professional works, which the *Encyclopedic Dictionary of Archaeology* also is.

The *Encyclopedic Dictionary of Archaeology* is more modern and comprehensive than any other work of reference in the field available in one volume. It contains over 7,000 entries covering themes, concepts, and discoveries in archaeology and is written in non-technical language and tailored to meet the needs of archaeologists and students as well as the general reader. Every effort has been made to make the dictionary an authoritative, up-to-date, and useful compendium of basic information about archaeology.

* * *

I have benefited greatly from the writings of all the archaeologists and scientists from whose works this dictionary has been distilled: they will doubtless recognize their contributions. It is important that a professional lexicographer write wholly new entries, but it is essential to rely on the works of other lexicographers for information. Many dictionaries, encyclopedias, reference manuals, atlases, and the like of archaeology were consulted for this compilation.

How to Use
This Dictionary

Spelling and Transliteration

The most consistent transliteration has been attempted from other languages, including the use of Pinyin for Chinese names. The spelling that is most familiar to Western readers has been chosen, with synonyms and alternative names offered for all entries that have them.

Dating

The dictionary employs the lowercase "bc" and "bp" to indicate uncalibrated radio-carbon dates. The small capital letters "AD," "BC," and "BP" are used for dates thought to represent "real" or calendar years, including corrected radiocarbon dates, dates derived from documentary sources, and dates derived from laboratory methods other than radio-carbon and not requiring calibration.

Archaeological Abbreviations

AA	*American Anthropologist*		**HSA**	*Highway Salvage Archaeology*
AAA	American Anthropological Association		**ht**	height
AAn	*American Antiquity*		**I**	*Inksherds*
AAS	American Antiquarian Society		**int**	interior
ACRA	American Cultural Resources Association		**IR**	Investigation Reports (National Park Service, Washington, D.C.)
AG	*The American Geologist*		**JAS**	*Journal of Archaeological Science*
AIA	Archaeological Institute of America		**JFA**	*Journal of Field Archaeology*
AJPA	*American Journal of Physical Anthropology*		**JHAA**	*Journal for the History of Astronomy, Archeoastronomy*
AJS	*American Journal of Science*			
AMNH	American Museum of Natural History		**JNWA**	*Journal of New World Archaeology*
AmS	*American Scientist*		**L**	length
An	*Anthropologica*		**mat'l, matl**	material
Ar	*Archaeology*		**N**	*Nature*
ArcA	*Arctic Anthropology*		**N**	north
arch	archaeology		**NAA**	*North American Archaeologist*
Arch	*Archaeometry*		**NaH**	*Natural History* (American Museum of Natural History, New York)
Arcl	*The Archeolog*			
AS	*The American Scholar*		**NG**	*National Geographic* (National Geographic Society, Washington, D.C.)
ASAJ	*ASA Journal*			
beg	beginning		**no**	number
BLM	Bureau of Land Management		**NPSPA**	National Park Service Publications in Archaeology (Washington, D.C.)
c., ca	about			
CAn	*Current Anthropology*		**orig**	original
CEHP	Conservation, Environment, & Historic Preservation		**prel**	preliminary
			PSM	*Popular Science Monthly*
CJA	*Canadian Journal of Archaeology*		**ref**	reference
disp	disposal		**rt**	right
E	east		**S**	*Science*
elev	elevation		**S**	south
est	estimate		**SA**	*Scientific American*
ext	exterior		**SA**	*State Archaeologist*
fr	from		**SAA**	Society for American Archaeology
GM	*Geoscience and Man*		**SCA**	*Smithsonian Contributions to Anthropology* (Smithsonian Institution, Washington, D.C.)
GR	*Geographical Review*			
GSA	Geological Society of America			
HE	*Human Ecology*		**SEA**	*Southeastern Archaeology*
horiz	horizontal		**sect**	section

SHPO State Historic Preservation Officer
SOPA Society of Professional Archaeologists
surf surface
TAPS *Transactions of the American Philosophical Society* (Philadelphia)

USGS U.S. Geological Survey
vert vertical
W west
W width
WA *World Archaeology*

Contents

Aa

Aachen: A city in northwestern Germany, which is the site of a palace complex of Carolingian buildings, particularly a chapel built by Odo of Metz for Charlemagne between 790–805. Aachen was the capital of Charlemagne's kingdom, and the Palatine Chapel (also called Palace Chapel or Octagon), was part of the Cathedral of Aachen. This complex served as Charlemagne's court and national church of the empire. The chapel is the only surviving structure and the most important surviving example of Carolingian architecture. The chapel contains Charlemagne's marble-slab throne, which was used for the coronation of 32 Holy Roman emperors from 936–1531. Odo of Metz modeled it after the Byzantine-style Church of San Vitale at Ravenna (*syn.* French Aix la Chapelle, Dutch Aken)

abacus: In architecture, a crowning rectangular block or topmost stone on the cap of a pillar or column capital, providing support to an architrave or arch. (*syn.* Plural abaci, abacuses)

Abada, Tell: A 'Ubaid site in Iraq with important architecture of the 'Ubaid and Uruk periods.

Abbasids: The second of two Arab dynasties of the Muslim Empire of the Caliphate (caliphs = rulers) and descended from al-Abbas, uncle of the Prophet Muhammad. It overthrew the Umayyad caliphate in AD 750 and was based in Baghdad until 1258 when it was sacked by the Mongols. The end of the Umayyad dynasty meant a shift in power from Syria to Iraq. The Abbasids' settlement in Baghdad marked the beginning of the golden age of Arabic literature. The Abbasids, of great intellectual curiosity, adapted elements of earlier high cultures and incorporated them into their own.

Abbevillian: The name for the period of the earliest hand ax industries of Europe, taken from Abbeville, the type site near the mouth of the River Somme in northern France. The site is a gravel pit in which crudely chipped oval or pear-shaped hand axes were discovered, probably dating to the Mindel Glaciation. This was one of the key sites that showed that humans were of great antiquity. Starting in 1836, Boucher de Perthes excavated the pits, and the significance of these discoveries was recognized around 1859. Abbeville was one of the rich sources for Palaeolithic tools discovered in Europe. In 1939, Abbé Breuil proposed the name Abbevillian for both the hand ax and the industry, which preceded the Acheulian in Europe. (*syn.* Abbevillean, Chellean, Abbeville)

abbey: A place where monks or nuns live, work, and worship. An abbey usually consisted of a group of buildings housing a monastery or a convent and an abbey church or a cathedral. Monasticism originated in the Middle East during the second half of the 4th century and spread to Byzantium, France, Greece, and Italy, where it developed independently from monasticism in Britain. Excavations have shown considerable variation in the layout of abbeys depending on the different monastic orders. They range from beehive cells and oratories of Early Celtic abbeys to the Cistercian plan with cloisters, domestic ranges, and a large church. Before the 10th century, monasteries were the principal artistic, economic, and educational centers of the Christian world. An abbey was thus the complex of buildings that served the needs of these self-contained religious communities. The first European abbey was Montecassino in Italy, founded in 529.

Abdul Hosein, Tepe: An aceramic Neolithic site in Iran's Zagros Mountains with mud-brick structures, chipped and ground stone tools, clay figurines, and evidence of barley and emmer cultivation.

Abingdon: The type site for a Neolithic pottery c. 3900–3200 BC, found in a causewayed camp about 15 km south of Oxford, England. The pottery is fairly heavy and formed into round-bottomed bowls with frequent-stroke decoration and sometimes with handles.

Abejas phase: The first important agricultural phase in the Tehuacan Valley of Mexico, dating 3500–1500 BC, after the introduction of maize.

Abercromby, Lord John (1841–1924): A Scottish antiquary who studied the British Bronze Age and introduced the term *beaker* for decorated handleless drinking vessels. He created the A-B-C beaker classification.

Abeurador, Balma: An Epipalaeolithic to Late Neolithic cave site in France with 10 layers of human occupation from c. 9000–2500 BC.

Abkan: A stone industry of southern Nubia, which was probably the work of indigenous peoples who were ancestral to the Nubian A Group. These peoples maintained trade contact with southerly regions of the Nile Valley during the 4th millennium BC.

aboriginal: The indigenous or native group of a particular region, and its culture.

abrader: A stone tool with abrasive qualities, such as pumice or sandstone, used in grinding, smoothing, sharpening, or shaping tools or other objects. (*syn.* abrading stone)

abri: French word meaning *shelter*, used to refer to the Palaeolithic shallow rock caves or shelters found in the limestone region of southern France. The abri was the living site in the front of a cave under a shelf of overhanging rock.

Abri Pataud: Site of a rock shelter near the village of Les Eyzies (Dordogne) in the Vézère Valley of southwestern France. It has a very rich Upper Palaeolithic sequence of more than 14 main culture layers with radiocarbon dates from c. 32,500 BC, beginning with Aurignacian deposits containing saucerlike living hollows with central hearths. The Aurignacian levels are followed by Perigordian and Proto-Magdalenian and probably Proto-Solutrean levels. Art objects have been found, as well as a skeleton in a top layer. The various hearths and living areas may suggest different social groups inhabiting the area.

Absolon, Karel (1887–1960): A Czech archaeologist who excavated at Dolni Vestonice, Ondratice, Pekarna, Byci Skala, and other Palaeolithic sites.

absolute age: The amount of time elapsed, with reference to a specific time scale, since an object was made or used.

absolute dating: The determination of age with reference to a specific time scale, such as a fixed calendrical system or in years before present (BP), based on measurable physical and chemical qualities or historical associations such as coins and written records. The date on a coin is an absolute data, as are AD 1492 or 501 BC. (*syn.* chronometric dating; absolute dates; absolute chronology; absolute age determination) (*ant.* relative dating)

absolute pollen counting: The determination of the number of grains of each pollen type per unit weight (grains/gram) or unit volume (grains/cm^3) of sample. Variation in the rate of sedimentation sometimes makes the number of years represented uncertain; absolute counts for different samples may therefore not be compatible. Pollen analysis is then calibrated with radiocarbon dating to create pollen influx rates figured by the number of grains of each pollen type accumulating on a unit area of lake or bog surface in one year (grains/cm^2/year) for each sample.

Abu Ballas: A site in the Western Desert of Egypt, occupied 8500–5000 years ago.

Abu Gurab: A site on the west bank of the Nile between Giza and Saqqara, originally called the Pyramid of Righa and containing the remains of a sun temple erected by the 5th Dynasty King Nyuserra (2445–2421 BC) whose pyramid is at Abusir, just to the south. The building of a sun temple to Ra in addition to a royal pyramid complex was customary in the 5th Dynasty. Abu Gurab is the best preserved of the two surviving examples (Userkaf's temple at Abusir is the other). Reliefs from the temple were sent to museums in Germany, but a number of them were destroyed during World War II. (*syn.* Abu Ghurob)

Abu Hureyra, Tell: A small tell on the Euphrates River, 120 km east of Aleppo in Syria. The site was excavated in 1972–1973 before flooding by the Tabqua/Tabqa Dam. Two major phases of occupation were found: Mesolithic or Epi-Palaeolithic (early 9th millennium BC) to a Pre-Pottery Neolithic B Culture in the 6th millennium. There was a long period of abandonment in the 7th millennium and then a final abandonment c. 5800 BC. The site depicted a transition from gathering to cultivation, including large quantities of einkorn wheat, and from hunting to herding (sheep and goats, also gazelle and onager). The Neolithic settlement was of enormous size, larger than any other recorded site of this period—even Çatal Hüyük. In the uppermost levels, a dark burnished pottery appeared.

Abu Ruwaysh: The Egyptian site of the unfinished pyramid of the 4th Dynasty ruler Djedefra (Redjedef) (c. 2566–2558 BC), the third of the seven kings of that dynasty. The pyramid, situated northwest of Giza on the west bank of the Nile, appears unfinished because the walls of the mortuary temple next to it were hastily made of mud brick instead of the usual cut stone. The complex was deliberately ransacked as Djedefra was involved in a dynastic struggle. An Early Dynastic (c. 2925–c. 2575 BC) private cemetery has also been found at Abu Ruwaysh. (*syn.* Abu Rawash; Abu Roash)

Abu Salabikh, Tell: A site of southern Mesopotamia with evidence of Early Dynastic III and Uruk times. Many texts, including the earliest-known literary works of Sumerian literature. I. J. Gelb proposed the name "Kish civilization" to identify this culture of the mid-3rd millennium.

Abu Simbel: The site of two rock-cut temples of the Egyptian king Rameses II (1279–1213 BC), located southeast of

Aswan, formerly Nubia. The facade of the largest temple is dominated by four 20-meter-high (67 feet) seated figures of Rameses, and the main part of the temple is cut into the solid rock of the hillside, penetrating it about 55 meters. The temples were salvaged in the 1960s from the rising waters of the Nile, caused by the erection of the Aswan High Dam. The temples were discovered by the traveler Jean-Louis Burckhardt in 1813 and cleared by the Egyptologist Giovanni Battista Belzoni four years later. There are also reliefs illustrating the king's life, accomplishments, and military campaigns in Syria and Nubia; small figures representing Rameses' queen, Nefertari, and their children; and graffiti providing important evidence of the early history of the alphabet. The temple was built so that, on certain days of the year, the first rays of the morning sun would penetrate its length and illuminate the shrine in the innermost sanctuary. The smaller temple was dedicated to Nefertari for the worship of the goddess Hathor. Between 1964–1968, a UNESCO- and Egyptian-sponsored project began with a team of international engineers and scientists and funds from more than 50 countries to uncover and disassemble both temples and reconstruct them on high ground 60 meters (200 feet) above the riverbed. (*syn.* Abu sunbul)

Abu Sir: An ancient site between Giza and Saqqara where several 5th Dynasty (c. 2494–2345 BC) kings built their pyramids, a sun temple, a number of mastaba tombs, and Late Period (747–332 BC) shaft tombs. The pyramids were poorly constructed; those of King Userkaf and King Neuserre have been excavated. (*syn.* Abusir)

abutment: The part of a structure, as a pier or buttress, from which an arch rises or springs and which directly receives the pressure.

Abydos: An ancient Egyptian site, which was a pilgrimage center for the worship of the god Osiris and the chosen burial place of the pharaohs of the 1st Dynasty. Located on the west bank of the Nile, it flourished from the Predynastic period until Christian times (c. 4000 BC–AD 641). The earliest significant remains are the tombs of the Protodynastic and Early Dynastic periods (c. 3100–2686 BC). From the 2nd Dynasty, the royal graves were at Saqqara. (*syn.* Ancient Abdjw)

Abydos, Tablets of: Two hieroglyphic inscriptions containing the names of Egyptian kings, found on the walls of a small temple at Abydos, Egypt. The first inscription has the names of the kings of the 12th and 18th Dynasties, and it is now in the British Museum. The second inscription begins with Menes, one of the first kings of Egypt, and has a complete list of the first two dynasties as well as a number of names from the 3rd, 4th, 5th, 6th, 9th, 10th, and 11th Dynasties. It was discovered in 1864 by Auguste Mariette, who published the book *Abydos* in 1869.

Acacus: A region of the central Sahara (now southwestern Libya) known for rock shelters with occupation deposits and rock paintings. Pottery was made from about 7000 BC, the earliest of the so-called Aquatic Civilization typified by wavy-line decoration. The skull of a shorthorn ox and traces of sheep and goat supply evidence for animal domestication as early as c. 4000 BC. Rock paintings of oxen predate c. 2700 BC. (*syn.* Tadrat Acacus)

Academy: In ancient Greece, the academy or college of philosophy developed by Socrates and Plato, located just northwest of Athens. Plato acquired property there about 387 BC and used it as a training ground and as a place to teach. At the site had been a park and gymnasium sacred to the legendary Attic hero Academus. The term *academy* was not applied during Plato's time but rather by his successors until the time of Cicero (106–43 BC). The academy was organized for worshiping the Muses, and instruction included mathematics, dialectics, natural science, and political science. It was closed by the emperor Justinian in AD 529. (*syn.* Greek Academeia, Latin Academia)

accelerator mass spectrometric technique: A relatively new method of radiocarbon dating in which the proportion of carbon isotopes is counted directly (as contrasted with the indirect Geiger counter method) by using an accelerator mass spectrometer. The method drastically reduces the quantity of datable material required. (*syn.* AMS technique; AMS radiocarbon dating)

accession number: The number assigned to an object in an archaeological collection which identifies its origin; part of the catalog number.

acculturation: The adoption of a trait or traits by one society from another and the results of such changes. This is a consequence of contact between cultures, usually with one being dominant, and is a process by which a group takes on the lifeways, institutions, and technology of another group. There are two major types of acculturation: free borrowing, where one society selects another culture's elements that it integrates in its own way, and directed change, where one group establishes dominance through military conquest or political control. Although directed change involves selection, it results from the interference in one cultural group by members of another. In anthropology, the change is considered from the point of view of the recipient society. (*ant.* diffusion)

accumulation model: The theory that cultural changes occur gradually as a society accumulates behavioral traits.

aceramic: Without pottery, or not using pottery. This term is applied to periods and societies in which pottery is not used, especially in contrast to other periods of ceramic use and with neighboring ceramic cultures. Aceramic societies may use bark, basketry, gourds, leather, and so on for containers.

Aceramic Neolithic: The early part of the Neolithic period in Western Asia before the widespread use of pottery (c. 8500–6000 BC) in an economy based on the cultivation of crops or the rearing of animals or both. Aceramic Neolithic groups were in the Levant (Pre-Pottery Neolithic A and B). Zagros area (Karim Shahir, Jarmoan), and Anatolia (Hacilar Aceramic Neolithic). Aceramic Neolithic groups are more rare outside Western Asia.

Achaeans: An ancient Greek people, described by Homer, who lived on the mainland and western isles of Greece, Crete, Rhodes, and other isles except the Cyclades. This distribution coincides precisely with the Mycenaeans of the 14th–13th centuries BC. They have also been identified both with the Ahhiyawa, mentioned by the Hittites as a western neighbor and by Herodotus as descendants of earlier Achaeans, and with the Akawasha, described by the Egyptians as part of the Peoples of the Sea. Achaea was the ancient name for Greece. The Achaean League was a 3rd century BC confederacy of 12 cities of the northern Peloponnese. (*syn.* Greek Achaios)

Achaemenids: The Persian dynasty, descendants of Achaemenes (c. 700 BC), which ruled from Cyrus the Great to Darius III (c. 550–331 BC). Cyrus II (559–530 BC) overthrew the Median empire to found a Persian empire, conquering Lydia, Babylonia, the Iranian plateau, and Palestine. His son, Cambyses II, added Egypt in 525 BC. The throne then passed to Darius, who set up an efficient administration of an empire then extending from the Nile to the Indus. This empire for the first time united all the peoples of the East—from Thrace and Egypt to the Aral Sea and the Indus Valley—and had as its capitals Parsargadae, Susa, and Persepolis. At Marathon in 490 BC, Darius failed to conquer the Greeks, as his son Xerxes failed at Salamis in 480. Their successors, notably Artaxerxes, fought to consolidate a waning empire. The Achaemenids were finally overthrown in 332 BC by Alexander the Great. The period is an important one in Iranian civilization. It was marked by contacts between the classical civilizations of Europe and the East and the appearance and spread of Zoroastrianism, at its time the most advanced religion outside Judaism. The Achaemenids' most famous monuments are the work of Darius: his capital of Persepolis, outstanding for its architecture and monumental reliefs, and his trilingual rock-cut inscription at Behistun for the key it gave to the translation of the cuneiform script. Other surviving Achaemenid monuments include the tomb of Cyrus the Great at Pasargadae and the rock-cut tomb of Darius at Naqsh-i Rustam near Persepolis. (*syn.* Achaemenid dynasty, Achaemenid)

Achenheim: A French site with Lower Palaeolithic arti-facts, Mousterian-type tools from the Riss glaciation, and Upper Palaeolithic materials.

Acheulian: (uh'-shool-ee-un) A European culture of the Lower Palaeolithic period named for Saint-Acheul, a town in northern France, the site of numerous stone artifacts of the period. The conventional borderline between Abbevillian and Acheulian is marked by a technological innovation in the working of stone implements, the use of a flaking tool of soft material (wood, bone, antler) in place of a hammer stone. This culture is noted for its hefty multipurpose, pointed (or almond-shaped) hand axes, flat-edged cleaving tools, and other bifacial stone tools with multipole cutting edges. The Acheulian flourished in Africa, western Europe, and southern Asia from over 1 million years ago until less than 100,000 and is commonly associated with *Homo erectus*. This progressive tool industry was the first to use regular bifacial flaking. The term Epoque de St Acheul was introduced by Gabriel de Mortillet in 1872 and is still used occasionally; but after 1925 the idea of epochs began to be supplanted by that of cultures and traditions, and it is in this sense that the term *Acheulian* is more often used today. The earliest assemblages are often rather similar to the Oldowan at such sites as Olduvai Gorge. Subsequent hand ax assemblages are found over most of Africa, southern Asia, and western and southern Europe. The earliest appearance of hand axes in Europe is still referred to by some workers as Abbevillian, denoting a stage when hand axes were still made with crude, irregular devices. The type site, near Amiens in the Somme Valley, contained large hand ax assemblages from around the time of the penultimate interglacial and the succeeding glacial period (Riss), perhaps some 200,000 to 300,000 years ago. Acheulian hand axes are still found around the time of the last interglacial period, and hand axes are common in one part of the succeeding Mousterian period (the Mousterian of Acheulian tradition) down to as recently as 40,000 years ago. *Acheulian* is also used to describe the period when this culture existed. In African terminology, the entire series of hand ax industries is called Acheulian, and the earlier phases of the African Acheulian equate with the Abbevillian of Europe. (*syn.* Acheulean, Acheulian industry)

achieved status/achieved leadership: An individual's social standing and prestige or leadership gained through accomplishments and abilities rather than inheritance. (*ant.* ascribed status)

acinaces: A short sword or scimitar, often very short and worn suspended from a belt around the waist, and used by Eastern horse-riding people of antiquity, especially the Medes, Persians, and Scythians. (*syn.* akinakes)

acisculus: A small pick used by stonecutters and masons in early Roman times.

aclis: A small javelin or harpoon, consisting of a thick, short pole set with spikes. This massive weapon resembles a trident or angon. (*syn.* aclyx, aclys)

acoustic vases: Large earthenware or bronze vases used to strengthen actors' voices and placed in bell towers to help boost the sound of church bells. A church in Westphalia contains fine 9th-century Badorf Wares, and larger Relief-Band Amphorae were used in 10th- and 11th-century churches. (*syn.* acoustic vessels)

acquisition: The first stage of the behavioral processes (followed by manufacture, use, deposition), in which raw materials are procured.

acratophorum: A Greek and Roman table vessel for holding pure wine, as opposed to the crater that held wine mixed with water. This vessel was often made of earthenware and bronze, although some were gold or silver.

acrolith: A Greek statue, of which the head and extremities were of stone or marble and the trunk crafted of wood that was either gilt or draped. The acrolith period was the infancy of Greek plastic art.

Acropole of Susa: A site in southwestern Iran including a large cemetery and platform from Susa's initial occupation, dating to the end of the 5th millennium BC. The site is divided into Acropole 1 and 2; Acropole 1 provided a sequence of 27 levels up to the Akkadian period. Some levels contain evidence of the development of writing: tablets marked with numbers, tokens in envelopes, and tablets of the Proto-Elamite script.

acropolis: (Greek *akros* [high, top] and *polis* [city]) The highest part, or citadel, of an ancient Greek town. The palaces and temples were situated on the acropolis, which was the most strongly defended part of a city. The best-known example is the Acropolis of Athens, where a number of temples were erected in the fifth century BC. Acropolises were also built on hills in Italy and in the Greek colonies of Asia Minor. (*syn.* akropolis)

acroteria: The pedestals, often without bases, placed on the center and sides of pediments for supporting a statue. Also, a decoration (often a statue) or ornament mounted with plinth on the pinnacle and gable ends (the horizontal coping or parapets) of a classical building. (*syn.* acroterion, acroters, acroterium, akroterion)

activation analysis: Method to determine the elements of a material by inducing radioactive reactions to produce radiation characteristic of material composition.

activity: Used to describe the customary use of a given artifact, such as food preparation.

activity area: A place where a specific ancient activity was located or carried out, such as food preparation or stone toolmaking. The place usually corresponded to one or more features and associated artifacts and ecofacts. In American archaeology, the term describes the smallest observable component of a settlement site. See data cluster.

activity set: A set of artifacts that reveal the activities of an individual.

actualistic study: Detailed observation of the actual use of archaeological artifacts, ecofacts, and features, used to produce general analogies for archeological interpretation.

AD: Used as a prefix to a date, it indicates years after the birth of Christ or the beginning of the Christian calendar. Anno Domini means "In the year of our Lord." The lower case "ad" represents uncalibrated radiocarbon years, and "AD" denotes a calibrated radiocarbon date or a historic date that does not need calibration. There is no year 0; 1 BC is followed by AD 1. (*syn.* ad)

adaptive strategy: Research into the effects of demography, ecology, economics, and technology on human behavior.

Addaura: A cave in Monte Pellegrino near Palermo, Sicily, with engravings from the Upper Palaeolithic period. The main scene is of human figures and seems to depict an initiation or circumcision. It is attributed to the Romanellian culture of 11,000 years ago.

additive technology: The manufacturing processes in which material is added to an original mass to form an artifact. Ceramic production and basketmaking are additive technologies.

Adena: A widespread Native American culture of the Early Woodland period in the Ohio Valley (United States) and named after the Adena Mounds of Ross County. It is known for its ceremonial and complex burial practices involving the construction of mounds and for its high level of craftwork and pottery. It is dated from as early as c. 1250 BC and flourished between c. 700–200 BC. It is ancestral to the Hopewell culture in that region. It was also remarkable for long-distance trading and the beginnings of agriculture. The mounds (e.g., Grave Creek Mound) are usually conical; they became most common around 500 BC. There was also cremation. Artifacts included birdstones, blocked-end smoking pipes, boat stones, cord-marked pottery, engraved stone tablets, and hammer stones.

Adlerberg: An Early Bronze Age culture in southwest Germany considered to be a variant of the Unetice culture. There were a number of flat inhumation cemeteries in which the burials included copper and bronze daggers and pins, flint tools, and one-handled pottery cups.

Adlun: A Palaeolithic site between Sidon and Tyre on the Lebanese coast with evidence of Amudian industry and Jabrudian occupation. (*syn.* Abri Zumoffen)

adobe: Spanish term for sun-dried mud brick; also the name for a structure built from this material. These buff or brown mud bricks were not fired, but hardened and dried in the sun. The material was also used as mortar, plaster, and amorphous building material for walls. Adobe structures are found in the southwestern United States and Mexico where there is heavy-textured clay soil and a sunny climate. These structures were often houses, temples, and large, solid platforms in the shape of truncated pyramids. (*pron.* uh'-doh-bee)

Adrar Bous: An informative site on the Tenere Desert in Niger where excavations revealed a long succession of prehistoric occupation. The first was a Levalloiso-Mousterian settlement. By early in the 4th millennium BC, food production techniques are attested. A skeleton of a domestic shorthorn ox dates to 3700 BC, as does remains of small stock that was herded. Cereals, such as sorghum, were possibly cultivated.

Adria: A town in northeastern Italy founded by the Etruscans or the Veneti, which flourished as a port on the Adriatic Sea in the 6th and 5th centuries BC. It was an intersection of Etruscan and Greek trade, linking Etruria, the Po Valley, and northern Europe. The silting up of the Po and Adige deltas caused the sea to recede from the town. There is evidence of a canal being dug around the 5th century BC. (*syn.* Latin Atria or Hadria)

ad sanctos: The custom of arranging to be buried in or beside a church. Around 313 AD when Constantine's edict granted tolerance to Christians, miniature temples were erected over tombs of martyrs. This was the start of funerary basilicas adjacent to towns from the 4th century onward. It was believed that burial near the tombs of saints guaranteed protection in the next world. This gave rise to the custom of burial in or close to a church.

Adulis: A seaport on the Red Sea coast of Ethiopia, near modern Massawa. It was the principal port of Axum on an important trade route. It may have been established in Ptolemaic times during the Pre-Axumite period, although excavations have yielded material belonging to the AD 3rd century or later.

adytum: In classical architecture, an enclosed room that formed the innermost sanctuary of a temple. It was entered via the opisthodomos and was to the rear of the cella. (*syn.* adyton)

adz: A cutting tool, similar to an ax, in which the blade is set at right angles to the handle or haft. One of the earliest tools, it was widely distributed in Stone Age cultures in the form of a hand-held stone chipped to form a blade. By Egyptian times, it was made of stone, metal, or shell and had acquired a handle. It is distinguished from the ax (working edge parallel with haft) by its asymmetrical cross-section. This carpenter's tool was used for rough dressing of timber and possibly for tree felling and for hollowing out a dugout canoe. The adz also was used in the ritual ceremony of Opening of the Mouth in Egypt; touching it to the mouth of the mummy or statue of the deceased was thought to restore the senses. (*syn.* adze)

Adzhi-Koba: A Palaeolithic cave site in the Ukraine with an assemblage of Middle Palaeolithic artifacts and an Upper Palaeolithic occupation with artifacts similar to those of Syuren' I.

aedicula: In Roman architecture, a small shrine usually projecting from an inside wall. Two columns supported a miniature architrave and a pediment. Many wall painting of Pompeii included aediculae. (*syn.* plural aediculae)

Aegina: An Early Bronze Age island site between Piraeus and the Peloponnese with a temple of the Doric order and also the temple of Aphaia, whose decoration depicted the two sackings of Troy.

Aeginetan marbles: Archaic Greek sculpture discovered in the temple of Pallas Athene at Aegina, an island in the Saronic group of Greece. The sculptures are in the Glyptothek at Munich, Germany. Aegina's period of glory was the 5th century BC, which left a legacy of sculpture.

aegis: A shield or defensive armor in ancient mythology. This Greek word for *shield* has been used to describe the representation of a necklace on the head of a deity.

Aegyptiaca: A term sometimes applied to Egyptian objects found outside the borders of Egypt.

aeolian: Of or pertaining to the wind. This adjective is used to describe deposits or materials moved or affected by the wind or processes related to the wind. Aeolian deposits can bury archaeological materials intact or with little disturbance. Aeolian erosion can collapse and displace archaeological materials. Aeolian particle movement can alter archaeological material through abrasion. (*syn.* eolian)

Aeolic order: An architectural order of northwestern Turkey and the island of Lesbos, with an ornate capital formed by two volutes separated by a spreading palmette. The echinus is below the volutes and is often formed by water lily leaves.

aeolipilae: A Greek metal vase with a narrow opening. It was filled with water and placed on a fire to make the chimney draw better or to indicate the wind's direction. (*syn.* aeolipylae, eolipyle)

Aeolis: A group of ancient cities of northwestern Asia Minor (west coast of Anatolia), which were founded at the end of the 2nd millennium BC by Greeks. The earliest settlements, on the islands of Lesbos and Tenedos and on the mainland between Troas and Ionia were formed from migrations during 1130–1000 BC. At the end of the 6th century, after fighting between Greece and Persia, Darius I incorporated Aeolis into a province of the Persian Empire. (*syn.* Aeolia)

aerial archaeology: The study and location of archaeological sites and features through the use of aerial observation, photography, and surveys.

aerial photographic map: A map of a site, feature, or region made through aerial photography. Professional photographic and cartographic techniques make possible the preparation of contour maps and three-dimensional models of surfaces.

aerial photography: A technique of photographic observation and survey of the ground from an aircraft, spacecraft, or satellite, which provides detailed information about sites and features without excavation. It is most important for locating archaeological sites before destruction of the landscape through building, road construction, or modern agricultural practices. When viewed from the air, sites may be revealed as crop marks, soil marks, shadow marks, or frost marks. For example, the plan of a site, ditches, walls, pits, and so on can be reflected in the way crops grow (crop marks), or a pattern of dark occupation soil may show against a lighter topsoil, or stone from walls may be just under the surface (soil marks). Oblique aerial photos, from lower altitudes, detect shadows created by earthworks and permit more detailed interpretations of known sites (shadow marks). Variations in the amount of frost retained on the ground may indicate the presence of buried archaeological features (frost marks). Although these can sometimes be recognized on the ground by careful field walking and contour planning, much larger areas can be examined from the air, and overall patterns are clearer. An ancient site may not be visible every year in aerial photographs, as local climatic variation affects the nature of the feature fillings; a site may be seen only once in 10 or 20 years. The use of false-color infrared photography has increased the versatility of aerial photography, and the development of photogrammetry allows the accurate mapping of both archaeological and geographical information. Recording of thermographic and radar images complements photographic methods. Aerial photography has proved to be one of the most successful methods of discovering archaeological sites. Large areas of ground can be covered quickly, and the ground plan of a new site can be plotted from the photographs. Features can be revealed in extraordinary detail by these means. The pioneers of this technique were O. G. S. Crawford and Major Allen in Britain and Père Poidebard in Syria, although its first use goes back to 1906 at Stonehenge. (*syn.* air photography, aerophotography, aerial reconnaissance)

aerial thermography: A technique of aerial reconnaissance that detects differences in retention and radiation of heat in ground surfaces.

aerobic: An environmental state requiring or using free oxygen in the air for metabolic purposes and that, therefore, causes decay in organic structures. Many materials, including plants, leather, flesh, food remains, and clothing, disintegrate in aerobic conditions.

aes: Latin term of antiquity used to denote brass, bronze, copper, or any alloy of these, as *aes candidum*, a brass alloyed with silver.

Afanasievo culture: A Neolithic culture of the Yenisei Valley of southern Siberia. The people, who were stock breeders and hunters, probably moved into the area in the late 3rd millennium BC. Excavations uncovered burials under kurgans (low mounds), surrounded by circular stone walls. There were stamped dentate pottery, stone, bone, and bronze tools, and some copper ornaments with the burials. The Afanasievo people were the first food producers in the area, breeding cattle, horses, and sheep; they also practiced hunting. The Afanasievo culture was succeeded by the Andronovo culture in the mid-2nd millennium BC.

Afontova: Upper Palaeolithic sites of a culture located in south-central Siberia of c. 20,000–10,000 BP. Artifacts included wedge-shaped microcores, microblades, and scrapers. Reindeer, woolly mammoth, and arctic fox were common.

African food production: Research into the beginnings of food production in Africa has shown that the intensive use of cereals and experimentation with crops began at a rather early date, maybe as far back as the 16th millennium BC in Upper Egypt and Nubia. The best-documented example is at Wadi Kubbaniya where there is evidence of the earliest instance of plant cultivation anywhere in the world, which confirms that this was a native African achievement. Food production was generally not practiced in North Africa before about the 5th millennium BC. Most of the indigenous species such as finger and bulrush millet, sorghum, yams, African rice, teff, enset, and noog were brought under cultivation between the 4th and 2nd millennia BC. South of the equator in Africa the advent of food production did not occur before the beginning of the Iron Age.

African Red Slip ware: A type of red gloss pottery made in North Africa from the 3rd–6th centuries AD. The pottery had stamped decoration and was widely distributed.

Afunfun: Early copper-working sites of Niger from the 2nd millennium BC.

Agade: An ancient city of southern Mesopotamia, founded by Sargon (2334–2279 BC) as his capital. Its location is uncertain. (*syn.* Akkad)

agate: A common semiprecious silica mineral and a variety of chalcedony that occurs in bands of various colors and is somewhat transparent. It is essentially a variety of quartz and was engraved in antiquity. Its name comes from a corruption of the word *Achates*, a river of Sicily, where Pliny said the mineral was first found.

Agate Basin: A Palaeoindian site in Wyoming with evidence of the killing and butchering of animals. Artifacts included a distinctive point, scrapers, and eyed bone needles. The complex dates to 10,500–10,000 BP.

Age of Discovery: A time of Western expansion through European exploration, discovery, and enlightenment about the world, which occurred from about the 15th through the 18th centuries, c. 1515–1800.

age profile: A pattern of the distribution of an animal population's ages as the result of death by natural causes. This mortality pattern is based on bone- or tooth-wear analysis. It demonstrates a "natural" age distribution in which the older the age group, the fewer the individuals it has. (*syn.* catastrophic age profile)

agger: A technical term of ancient Roman roadwork for an earthen mound, embankment, or rampart of a camp, formed by the earth dug out of a ditch. Most Roman roads were built on a slightly raised causeway, mainly to provide drainage. This bank of earth was used for protection from flooding, as the foundation for a road, or for warfare purposes. *Agger* is also a general term for a mound formed by a dike, quay, roadwork, or earthwork. An agger can often be traced even if the surfacing material has been covered or laid bare.

aggregate analysis: The analysis of debitage using size as the prime criterion. (*syn.* mass analysis)

Aggsbach: An Upper Palaeolithic site on the Danube River in Austria with artifacts (end scrapers, backed blades, retouched blades) and faunal remains (woolly mammoth, reindeer, giant deer) dating to 25,700–22,450 BP, the Early Gravettian.

aging of skeletal material: The age at death of ancient skeletal material may be estimated in a number of ways. (1) Epiphyseal fusion. A growing bone consists of a central part (diaphysis) and the ends (ephiyses). At adulthood, the epiphyses fuse to the diaphysis, and the average at which this occurs is known for humans and most domestic animals. The stage of epiphyseal fusion may therefore be used as a guide to the age at death. (2) Dental eruption. The average age for each stage of the eruption of teeth in humans and most domestic animals is well established. The state of dental eruption may therefore be used to estimate the age at death. (3) Dental attrition. Given a standard diet, teeth wear at roughly the same rate, and tables of rate of wear have been established for humans. For other animals, this method must be calibrated by dental eruption. (4) Dental microstructure. The counting of incremental structures in teeth may allow estimation of age at death. (5) Pubic symphysis. In humans, the joint surfaces of the pubic symphysis change progressively with age and can be used to determine the age of humans at death. (6) Antlers. In deer, the development of antlers is roughly related to age.

agora: In ancient Greek cities, an open space, serving as a commercial, political, religious, and social center. The word, first found in Homer, was applied by the Greeks of the 5th century BC in regard to this feature of their daily life. It was often a square or rectangle, surrounded by public and/or sacred buildings and colonnades. The colonnades, sometimes containing shops (stoae), often enclosed the space, which was decorated with altars, fountains, statues, and trees. There were several kinds of agora: (1) archaic, where the colonnades and other buildings were not coordinated, such as Athens; (2) Ionic, more symmetrical, often combining colonnades to form three sides of a rectangle or square, often with two or more courtyards, such as Miletus and Magnesia. In a highly developed agora, like that of Athens, each trade or profession had its own quarter. The agora also served for theatrical and athletic performances until special buildings and places were made for those purposes. Under the Romans, it became a forum where one side was a vast basilica and the rest colonnades. (*syn.* plural agorae)

Agordat: A town in western Eritrea, Ethiopia, with four village sites from around the 3rd millennium BC. Surface artifacts, such as stone maceheads and ground stone axes seem related to the Nubian C Group of the Nile Valley. Other artifacts suggest an early practice of food production that may have been passed from the Nile Valley to the Ethiopian highlands.

Agrelo culture: The Agrelo culture was centered in northwestern Argentina and dates from AD 1–1000. The type site is just south of Mendoza and features distinctive deep, widemouthed pottery with parallel stepped incised lines, punctations, and fingernail impressions, typical of southern Andean tradition. Pottery spindle whorls, crude figurines, labrets, club heads, triangular projectile points, and beads of stone have been found. Pit inhumations were marked by stone circles. The Agrelo represents the agriculture–pottery threshold in this semiarid area. Nearby coastal pottery styles (Cienega, El Molle) may be precursors to Agrelo.

Agrigento: A wealthy, flourishing Greek and Roman city near the southern coast of Sicily, Italy, originally a colony of Gela and founded by Greeks about 580 BC. The plateau site of the ancient city has extraordinarily rich Greek remains. There are extensive walls with remnants of eight gates and the remains of seven Doric temples, but there has been illegal construction in which the ruins were quarried, so little is standing where some of the buildings once were. Agrigento was sacked by the Carthaginians in 406 BC, a disaster from which the city never really recovered. It was refounded by

Timoleon, a Greek general and statesman, in 338 BC, but Agrigento was on the losing side for most of the Punic Wars. Agrigento returned to some commercial prosperity when textiles, sulfur and potash mining, and agriculture expanded. It was abandoned once again in the Christian era although areas were used as Roman and Christian cemeteries and catacombs. There is some evidence for pre-Greek settlement, possibly Neolithic, (*syn.* formerly Girgenti, Greek Acragas or Akragas, Latin Agrigentum; also Agrigagas)

A Group: A term created by the American archaeologist George Reisner to refer to a seminomadic Nubian Neolithic culture of the mid-4th to early 3rd millennium BC. The term has evolved into a *horizon* because there was also a C Group, and the term misleadingly suggested that there were two separate ethnic groups rather than two phases of Nubian material culture. Traces of the A Group, which may have evolved from the Abkan culture, survive throughout Lower Nubia. An important site is Afyeh near Aswan, Sayala, and Qustul. There is evidence among the grave goods that the A Group was engaged in regular trade with the Egyptians of the Predynastic and Early Dynastic periods. The A Group was eventually replaced by the C Group during the Old Kingdom. The existence of a B Group has now been rejected. (*syn.* A Horizon, A-Group)

Aguada: A culture of northwestern Argentina during the period AD 700–1000, located on the western slopes of the Andes and noted for the fine quality of its arts. Decorated copper and bronze plaques and polychrome yellow and black pottery with designs of cats, dragons, humans, birds, warriors, weaponry, and trophy heads are characteristic and reflect a possible influence from Tiahuanaco. Decapitated burials are a further indication that warfare was a dominant preoccupation at Aguada. Its sudden disappearance from the archaeological record in AD c. 1000 was probably the result of invasion from the east.

Aha (c. 3100 BC): One of the earliest 1st Dynasty rulers of a unified Egypt, whose name means "The Fighter." Funerary remains at Abydos, Saqqara, and Naqada attest to his reign, and Flinders Petrie's excavation at Umm el-Qa'ab (Early Dynastic cemetery at Abydos) in 1899–1900 revealed objects bearing the name Aha in Tomb B19/15. However, the earliest of the elite tombs at north Saqqara of the 1st and 2nd Dynasties also contained jar sealings from that time. Evidence suggests that Narmer was Aha's father and that one of the two was also called Menes.

Ahar: A site in Rajasthan, western India, belonging to the Chalcolithic Banas culture and dated c. 2500–1500 BC. The people cultivated cereal, hunted deer, and used copper and a variety of pottery, including Black and Red Ware. During a second period of occupation later in the 1st millennium BC, Northern Black Polished Ware appeared.

Aharoni, Yohanan (1919–1976): An Israeli archaeologist who worked at Arad, Lachish, and Beersheba.

Ahhotep I (c. 1590–1530 BC): New Kingdom queen who played an important part in wars of liberation leading to indigenous Egyptian rule. She was involved in the transition from the Second Intermediate Period to the New Kingdom, when the Hyksos rulers were expelled from Lower Egypt. She was the daughter of the 17th Dynasty ruler Senakhtenra Taa I, the wife of Seqenenra Taa II, and mother of Ahmose I (and maybe of Kamose).

Ahichchatra: A large ancient city of northern India, near Bareilly in the Ganges plain, occupied from the mid-1st millennium BC to AD c. 1100. The ramparts were built c. 500 BC, and there were nine building levels before its abandonment. Painted Gray Ware was the first pottery found; later there was Northern Polished Black Ware.

Ahmose I (reigned c. 1550–1525 BC): The founder of the 18th Dynasty and the prince of Thebes who drove the Hyksos from Egypt, invaded Palestine, and established the New Kingdom. He was the son of the Theban 17th Dynasty ruler Seqenenra Taa II and Queen Ahhotep and came to the throne of a reunited Egypt after he and his predecessor Kamose expelled the Asiatic rulers from Egypt. Ahmose I was responsible for reactivating the copper mines at Sinai, resuming trade with Syrian cities, and restoring temples. He was succeeded by his son Amenhotep I in 1555 BC. (*syn.* Amosis)

Ahmose II (reigned 570–526 BC): King of the late 26th Dynasty and originally a general in Nubia who came to the throne after his defeat of King Apries (589–570 BC). Ahmose was sent to pacify mutineering troops when they proclaimed him king. He fought Apries in a civil war and killed him in battle, although later giving him a royal burial. His reign was a time of great prosperity in Egypt. (*syn.* Amasis, Amosis II)

Ahmose Nefertari (c. 1570–1505 BC): An influential New Kingdom royal woman, whose political and religious titles (like her grandmother Tetisheri and mother Ahhotep I) reflect new roles adopted by women in the early 18th Dynasty. She was the first royal woman to have a title meaning "God's wife of Amun" and was the mother of Amenhotep I and wife of Ahmose I. She seems to have outlived both and contributed to the quarrying and building projects of her husband.

Ahrensburg: A village near Hamburg, Germany, with two Late Palaeolithic sites, Meiendorf and Stellmoor. Stellmoor dates to 8500 BC and is attributed to the Ahrensburgian culture. Tanged points, which were possibly arrowheads, and pine arrow shafts with bowstring notches give evidence for the use of the bow and arrow. The Ahrensburgians mainly hunted reindeer. (*syn.* Ahrensburgian)

Ahrensburgian: An Epipalaeolithic culture of the Late Glacial period in northern Germany and the Low Countries, c.

8850–8300 BC. The small tanged points, pine arrow shafts, abundant reindeer bones, barbed harpoons, and antler adzes of Stellmoor characterized the culture.

ahu: The name of a rectangular stone platform, the largest with stepped sides, which was a focus of court rituals in prehistoric Eastern Polynesian temples (marae). Most of these platforms are found in the Society Islands and on Easter Island, where ahu were statue foundations.

Ahualulco: A large, multiple-circle ceremonial complex in western Mexico with ball courts and elite residences, of c. 200 BC–AD 900/1000. It is part of the shaft tomb culture.

Ai: An ancient Canaanite town near Bethel supposedly destroyed by the Israelites and Joshua. There is a triple circuit of walls from the Early Bronze Age, c. 2900–2500 BC and imposing ruins of a temple and another large building in it. The Bronze Age site is now called at-Tall, and there was a brief reoccupation in the 12th–11th centuries BC. (*syn.* at-Tall)

Ai Bunar: A site with three copper mines, located near Stara Zagora in central Bulgaria. The open-cast mining of malachite ore beds dates to the 4th millennium BC (Karanovo VI period) and was later used in the Late Bronze Age. Quantities of this ore have been discovered in settlements in Moldavia and the Ukraine (Cucuteni-Tripolye culture). (*syn.* Aibunar)

Aichbühl: The site of a Middle Neolithic settlement (end of 3rd millennium BC) on the shores of Lake Federsee in southern Germany. There are foundations of about 25 rectangular houses around the lake. They were built of timber, usually divided into two rooms, and most contained a hearth and clay oven. A large central building was likely used for communal purposes, and there are some storage structures. Small polished stone hatchets, bone implements, shoe last adzes, and unpainted pedestal pottery bowls were among the artifacts.

'Aijul, Tell el-: A tell near Gaza in Palestine, which was excavated by Flinders Petrie in 1930–1934 and 1938 and found to be Middle Bronze Age, although cemeteries of the Chalcolithic and Intermediate Bronze Age were discovered nearby. The town had walls, a plastered Hyksos-type glacis, and a fosse. Five successive palaces were excavated within the walls, and hoards of gold jewelry were found.

Ai Khanum: A Hellenistic city, occupied between 400–100 BC, at the confluence of the Oxus and Koktcha Rivers in Afghanistan. The city includes a citadel, acropolis, and lower town with an administrative center. The administrative center was an imposing complex with a courtyard and a peristyle. Nearby is a funerary chapel known from an inscription as the Temenos of Kineas. Kineas may have been the city's founder, shortly after Alexander the Great conquered the region in 329 BC. The city may have been Alexandria's Oxiana.

'Ain Ghazal: An early farming village in the Jordan Valley, occupied around 8000 years ago. Its clay female figures may be evidence of an early fertility cult.

Ain Hanech: A site in Algeria, which offers some of the earliest evidence of human occupation in northern Africa. Stone tools, including choppers and multifaceted spheroids, were dated to 1–1.5 million years ago. Mammal fauna of Villafranchian type was associated with the tools.

Ain Mallaha: A large village of the early Natufian period near Lake Huleh in Upper Jordan. The three phases contain 50 large circular houses and open areas with storage pits. The well-built houses suggest a permanent occupation. The economy was probably based on the hunting and herding of gazelle and other large animals, fishing, and harvesting cereals. Many houses had paved stone floors and a central stone-lined hearth. (*syn.* Eynan)

Ainu: The native people of Hokkaido, Sakhalin, and the Kuril Islands, Japan, who are physically different from their Mongoloid neighbors. They once lived by hunting, trapping, and fishing and also grew buckwheat. In the 1940s, they numbered about 17,000. Ainu appear to be descendants of the early Caucasoid peoples who were once spread over northern Asia. They did not undergo the sociocultural changes of the Yayoi and Kofun periods. The Ainu were pushed northward over the centuries by the Japanese. Intermarriage and cultural assimilation have made the traditional Ainu almost extinct. Their most important ritual, the Bear Ceremonial, find parallels in Okhutsk ceremonialism.

aisle: A name derived from the French for "wing," describing the areas of a church, basilica, or temple between the arcade or arches or columns and the outer wall on both sides of the nave. It is also used to describe the wing of a building and the side passages of a Roman house.

Ajanta: A site of Buddhist rock-cut cave temples and monasteries in central India. The group of some 30 caves from the 1st century BC to the 5th century AD is celebrated for its wall paintings depicting Buddhist legends and the Buddha's incarnations. There are two types of caves, caityas (sanctuaries) and viharas (monasteries).

Ajdabiya: A town in northeastern Libya near the Gulf of Sidra, the site of Roman and Byzantine colonization, a caravan junction from Egypt to the Maghreb, and a trans-Saharan route from the Sudan during the early Middle Ages. There are ruins from the earlier colonization and two important monuments from the period 912–1051—an early congregational mosque and a *qasr* (fort). (*syn.* Ajdabiyah, Agedabia)

Ajuerado phase: The earliest phase of pre-village, pre-agriculture in Tehuacan Valley, Mexico, from c. 7200–7000 BC, typified by hunting and gathering.

Akashi: A site near Kobe City, Japan, where fossil human bones were found in 1931. The bones have been dated to the Holocene.

Aker: An earth god of the Early Dynastic period in Egypt, most often represented as a form of double sphinx of two lions back to back. Aker's symbolism was closely associated with the junction of the eastern and western horizons in the underworld.

akh: In Egyptian religion, the spirit of a deceased person and one of the five principal elements considered part of a complete personality—the other four being the ka, ba, name, and shadow. Akh is a state in the afterlife, both immortal and unchangeable, and the result of the successful reunion of the ba with its ka. The akh enabled the soul to temporarily assume any form it desired, for the purpose of revisiting the earth or for enjoyment in the next world.

Akhenaten (reigned 1353–1336 BC): The heretic pharaoh of Egypt's 18th Dynasty, who reigned with his queen Nefertiti toward the end of the New Kingdom. He was the son of Amenhotep III and Queen Tiy. During his reign, he attempted to replace Egypt's religions with worship of Amen-Ra, the sun disk, represented by the god Aten (or Aton). The art and literature of Egypt were also marked by rapid change during his reign. He set the tone for a new era by establishing a temple at Karnak dedicated to Aten and moved the capital from Thebes to modern Tell el-Amarnà in Middle Egypt, calling the city Akhetaten. His religious reforms were fanatical, foreign affairs were neglected, and his reign saw the collapse of the Egyptian Asiatic empire built by earlier rulers. His successor and probable brother, Tutankhamen, returned Egypt to the worship of Amen-Ra and the capital to Thebes. Later rulers attempted to remove all record of Akhenaten's heresy and name. Akhenaten has been controversial both in ancient and modern times. (*syn.* Amenhotep IV, Akhnaton, Ikhnaton, Neferkheperure Amenhotep, Greek Amenophis)

Akhmim: A site on the east bank of the Nile opposite modern Sohag, the capital of the ninth nome of Upper Egypt during the Pharaonic period, c. 3100–332 BC. The earliest surviving remains are Old and Middle Kingdom rock-cut tombs. The city originally included a number of temples dedicated to Min, but few stone buildings have survived because of plundering. Colossal statues of Rameses II and Meritamun have been excavated. (*syn.* ancient Ipu, Khent-Mim)

Akjoujt: A site in southern Mauritania, which appears to have been an early copper-working center in Africa, from c. 5th century BC or earlier. It is one of the few Saharan or sub-Saharan areas where there may have been a Copper Age preceding the Iron Age. Arrowheads, spearheads, axes, pins, and some decorative items of copper are attributed to this period.

Akkad: Ancient region in what is now central Iraq, which was the northern (or northwestern) division of ancient Babylonian civilization. It is an archaeologically unlocated site, in or near Babylon roughly where the Tigris and Euphrates Rivers are closest to each other. The name Akkad was taken from the city of Agade, which was founded by Sargon in about 2370 BC. Sargon united various city-states in the area, and his rule encompassed much of Mesopotamia, creating the first empire in history. (*syn.* Agade)

Akkadian: A Semitic-speaking dynasty founded by Sargon the Great (Sharrukin, 2334–2279 BC) c. 2370 BC with Akkad (or Agade), an unidentified site, as his capital. Under Sargon and his grandson, Naram-Sin, the dynasty established an empire that included much of Mesopotamia and neighboring Elam to the east. The dynasty saw three major developments: the beginning of the absorption of the Sumerians by the Semites, a trend from city-state to the larger territorial state, and imperial expansion. It is considered the first empire in history. Akkadian also refers to the Semitic dialects of Old Akkadian (3rd millennium) and Assyrian and Babylonian (2nd and 1st millennia). The Amarna Letters (diplomatic correspondence between Egypt and the Levant in the mid-14th century BC) are written in Babylonian, a late form of Akkadian. Akkadian was written in a cuneiform script borrowed from Sumerian and was the lingua franca of the civilized Near East for much of the 2nd millennium. It replaced Sumerian as the official language (although Sumerian was still used for religious purposes). Akkadian was gradually replaced by Aramaic.

Ak-Kaya: A group of Middle Palaeolithic sites in the Crimea, Ukraine, with Ak-Kaya and Zaskal'Naya artifact assemblages, including bifacial foliates, Prondnik knives, and Bockstein knives.

Akrotiri: The site of a Bronze Age town on Thera/Santorinin in the Aegean, buried by a volcano in the 16th century BC. Excavation has revealed houses with polychrome frescoes. There is evidence of links with Minoan Crete.

alabaster: A term used by Egyptologists for a type of white, semitransparent or translucent stone used in statuary, vases, sarcophagi, and architecture. It is a form of limestone (calcium carbonate), sometimes described as travertine. It was used increasingly from the Early Dynastic period for funerary vessels as well as statuary and altars. Alabaster is found in Middle Egypt, a main source being Hatnub, southeast of el-Amarna. The sarcophagi of Seti I (British Museum) is a fine example. An alabaster (also alabastron or alabastrum) is also the name of a small vase or jar for precious perfumes or oils made of this material. It was often globular with a narrow mouth and often without handles. (*syn.* Egyptian alabaster)

alabastron: A Greek container made of alabaster but sometimes clay, used for unguents.

Alaca Hüyük: (ah-lah'-jah) A tell site in north-central Turkey, near Boghaz Köy and 150 kilometers east of Ankara, occupied in the 4th, 3rd, and 2nd millennia BC. Its Chalcolithic and Copper Age phases include a cemetery of 13 extremely rich tombs from c. 2500 BC (Early Bronze Age II). The burials were single and double inhumations in rectangular pits, with fine metalwork including copper figurines (thought to be mounts from funeral standards), sun discs, ornaments, weapons, jugs and goblets, diadems, bracelets, and beads. The quantity of gold and copper implies that this was a royal cemetery. The tombs were lined with rough stone, and skulls and hooves of animals were hung from the wooden beams as part of the funeral rite. The site was later reoccupied under the Hittites, who erected a monumental gateway with two great stone sphinxes. It has been tentatively identified as the Hittite holy city of Arinna.

Alaka culture: A preceramic shell midden culture on the northwest coast of Guyana, which may date to c. 2000 BC. Located in the mangrove swamps, the middens have been grouped into the Alaka Phase. The culture relied on shellfish gathering, with some grinding stones, choppers, manos, and metates. Some crude ceramics in the later stages represent intrusive cultures and the passing of Alaka.

Alambra-Mouttes: An early Middle Cypriote site in eastern Cyprus with rectangular stone houses.

Alamgirpur: The easternmost site of the Harappan civilization, northeast of Delhi, in the Ganges Valley. It was a small Late Harappan settlement. After a gap of unknown duration, there were later occupations, with Painted Gray Ware and iron use.

Alapraia: The use of a group of Copper Age rock-cut tombs near Lisbon, Portugal. It consists of simple chambers entered through smaller vestibles and includes ritual objects such as clay sandals, clay lunulae, so-called pinecones, and beaker pottery.

Alashiya: A site mentioned in texts of the 2nd millennium BC as a source of copper; assumed to be Cyprus. The texts also record the workings of the Sea Peoples c. 1200 BC.

Alaska Refugium: A large area of interior Alaska, not glaciated during the latter part of the Pleistocene. It was connected to Beringia and eastern Siberia, allowing access for people between Asia and North America.

Alba Fucens: An ancient fortified Roman colony, at the foot of Mount Velino, Italy. It was originally a town of the ancient Marsi people, but was occupied by Latin colonists c. 302–303 BC. It was situated on a hill with three distinct summits, which were enclosed in its walls, much of which are still standing. Remains of the forum with a temple and various buildings of the time of Sulla are there, including a basilica, curia, macellum, theater, and amphitheater. This colony was important during the civil wars of the 1st century BC, and state prisoners of Rome were often held there. (*syn.* modern Albe)

Albani stone: A pepper-colored stone used in ancient Roman buildings before the introduction of marble. The stone may have come from two volcanic craters that formed the modern Lake Albano, southeast of Rome.

Albany industry: A stone industry of southernmost Africa, dated between the 11th and 6th millennia BC. It preceded the appearance of backed-microlith Wilton industry, and its assemblages. Boomplass and Robberg being the most notable, contain flake scrapers. Some archaeologists have grouped this industry under the name Oakhurst Complex, as there are possible related and contemporary industries as far as southern Namibia and Zimbabwe. The appearance of the Albany industry coincides with the Post Pleistocene rise in sea level, and there is evidence that marine food was increasingly exploited by the culture.

albarello: A late medieval (15th–18th centuries) Near East, Spanish, and Italian apothecary pottery jar. It was made in the form known as majolica or with a fine tin glaze over typically blue designs imitating the forms of Arabic script. Its basic shape was cylindrical but incurved and wide mouthed for holding, pouring, and shelving. The jars average 7 inches high (18 centimeters) and are free of handles, lips, and spouts. A piece of paper or parchment was tied around the rim as a cover for the jar. Drug jars from Persia, Syria, and Egypt were introduced into Italy by the 15th century, and luster-decorated pots influenced by the Moors in Spain entered through Sicily. Spanish and Islamic influence is apparent in the colors used in the decoration of early 15th-century Italian albarellos, which are often blue on white. A conventional oak-leaf and floral design, combining handsomely with heraldic shields or with scrollwork and an inscribed label, frequently occurs. Geometric patterns are also common. By the end of the 18th century, albarellos had yielded to other containers. Albarellos have occasionally been found in Britain and the Netherlands. (*syn.* plural albarelli)

albarium: A white lime coating or type of stucco used in Roman times, to cover brick walls after cement was applied. The mixture contained chalk, plaster, and white marble.

Albright, William Foxwell (1891–1971): American orientalist and linguist who worked in Palestine, including Beit Mersim.

album: In Roman and Greek antiquity, a blank tablet on which praetors' edicts and other public notices were recorded for public information. It was also a space on the surface of a wall, covered with white plaster, on which were written such announcements or advertisements. Afterward, this term was extended to denote any kind of white tablet bearing an inscription.

Alcalà: A cemetery in southern Portugal containing corbel-vaulted tombs of megalithic tradition from the early metal ages. Like Los Millares, it was once thought to be an Aegean colony.

Alchi: A town in Ladakh, Tibet, where a number of "nomads' tombs" were discovered and excavated between 1900–1910 by A. H. Francke. Each tomb contained from 3 to 20 long-headed skulls, many small handmade pottery vessels filled with bones, and grave goods, including bronze beads, pendants, bracelets, and bronze vessels. There was also pottery decorated with dark-red incised or zigzag patterns and possibly stylized leaves or grass. Other examples were found at Teu-gser-po and Ba-lu-mk'ar.

alembic: A round apparatus formerly used in distilling, consisting of a cucurbit or gourd-shaped vessel containing the substance to be distilled and the upper part, the alembic proper, which was a head or cap. The beak or downward-sloping spout of the apparatus conveyed the condensed product to another vessel.

Aleppo: A city in northern Syria, which stands on the site of an ancient, as yet unexcavated, city. On the route between the Euphrates and the Orontes Rivers, the ancient site is mentioned in texts from the 2nd millennium onward as the capital of the Amorite kingdom of Yamkhad in the 18th century BC. It subsequently came under Hittite, Egyptian, Mitannian, and again Hittite rule during the 17th–14th centuries. It was known to the Hittites as Halpa. The city was conquered by the Assyrians in the 8th century BC and then controlled by the Achaemenian Persians from the 6th–4th centuries BC before the Seleucids took it over, rebuilt it, and renamed it Beroea. Aleppo was very important during the Hellenistic period for its position along trade routes. The city became part of the Roman province of Syria in the 1st century BC. Conquered by the Arabs in 637, it reverted to its old name of Halab. (*syn.* Arabic Halab, Turkish Halep)

Aleutian Tradition: The later marine mammal-hunting culture of the Aleutian Islands, off southwest Alaska, which separates the Bering Sea from the Pacific Ocean, originating approximately 5000 BP.

Alexander the Great (356–323 BC): Alexander the Great (Alexander III), king of Macedonia, began his career of conquest in 335 BC. He overthrew the Persian Empire and laid the foundation for the territorial kingdoms of the Hellenistic world. Born in Macedonia in 356 BC, he was the son of Philip II and Olympias. He was taught by the great philosopher Aristotle from the age of 13 to 16. Alexander took power in Macedonia and mainland Greece in 340 BC when Philip left to attack Byzantium. By 332 BC, his arrival in Egypt ended the Persian occupation, and he had already conquered much of western Asia and the Levant before his arrival in Egypt. In Egypt, Alexander made sacrifices to the gods at Memphis and visited the oracle of Amun-Ra where he was recognized as the god's son, thus restoring the true pharaonic line. He founded the city of Alexandria and then left Egypt in 331 BC to continue his conquest of the Achaemenid Empire. His empire stretched from India to Egypt. After his death from a fever in 323 BC, his kingdom quickly dissolved.

Alexandria: The Greek city founded by Alexander the Great in 332 BC, capital of the Ptolemy dynasty, located on a narrow strip of land in the Nile Delta of Egypt. Alexandria was placed on the earlier Egyptian settlement of Raqote, of which pre-Ptolemaic seawalls are the only archaeological traces. The great city soon replaced Memphis as the capital of Egypt and is famed for its lighthouse (Pharos, one of the Seven Wonders of the World, built by Sostratos of Knidos between 299–279 BC; destroyed in AD 1326 by an earthquake), the jetty of Heptastadion, the royal palaces, and the Museion, a library and institution of scientific and philological research. It was composed of quarters: Egyptian, Greek, Jewish, and Kings. The city became the center of trade and culture in the eastern Mediterranean. The Ptolemies ruled over Egypt until 30 BC. (*syn.* Raqote)

Alexandrinum: A type of mosaic used especially for Roman rooms, notably in the 9th century. It used tiny, geometrically shaped pieces of colored stone and glass paste that were arranged in intricate geometric patterns dotted with large disks of semiprecious stones. It often was of only two colors, red and black, on a white ground.

Alfred Jewel: An elaborate gold ornament, an example of 9th century Anglo-Saxon craftsmanship, found at Somerset, England in 1893 (now in the Ashmolean Museum, Oxford). It consists of an enameled plaque with an oval portrait in different-colored cloisonné, enhanced with filigree wire and backed by a flat piece of gold engraved with foliate decoration. Engraved around the frame are the Old English words that translate as "Alfred ordered me to be made," assumed to refer to King Alfred.

Alfred the Great (849–899): King of Wessex, 871–899, a Saxon kingdom in southwestern England. He prevented England from being conquered by the Danish and promoted literature, learning, and literacy—helping to begin an artistic renaissance that flourished for two centuries. Our knowledge of him is known from the Anglo-Saxon Chronicle, begun during his reign, c. 890, and the biography written by his friend and teacher Asser. Alfred succeeded to the throne in 871 and fought off invading Danes before being forced to flee in 877. He returned to drive the invaders from his kingdom. Alfred also established the first English fleet and organized a chain of fortified towns on the southern coast for protection. (*syn*. Aelfred)

Aleria: An island colony in eastern Corsica, founded from Phocaea (Turkey) in the 6th century BC. There are similarities with Etrusca in the tombs, and Etruscan artifacts were found.

Alesia: An Iron Age site where the last Celtic stand against the Roman invasion in 52 BC took place. It is an oppidum with remains of Caesar's siege works.

Al Hiba: The site of the city of Lagash, one of the ancient Mesopotamian centers of the city-state of Lagash, dating from Early Dynastic to Old Babylonian times. It was absorbed into Ur and eventually declined in importance.

alidade: An instrument used in topographic and planimetric surveying, mapping, and planning with the plane-table method. It consists of a telescopic sight with stadia hairs mounted on a graduated metal ruler. This term is also used for any sighting device used for angular measurement. The device has a prismatic eyepiece and a spirit level for the plane-table. Some include compasses, and most modern models can measure angles up to 30 degrees.

alignment: An arrangement of single or multiple rows of standing stones (menhirs) at a site once occupied by humans. They are found mainly in Brittany and the British Isles' highland zones and are often aligned on cairns, henge monuments, or stone circles. Others are found in Corsica. The rows do not provide much dating evidence, but they were probably set up in the 2nd and 3rd millennia BC (Neolithic, Bronze Ages).

Ali Kosh: An early farming site near Deh Luran in southwestern Iran, occupied c. 7500–5600 BC. It was the first excavated farming site where significant quantities of plant remains were collected by using the flotation technique, a landmark in the study of farming origins. The earliest phase, named Bus Mordeh and dated c. 7500–6750 BC, is characterized by simple mud-brick buildings and a combination of wild and domesticated foods, some herding, and the catching of fish. The succeeding phase, Ali Kosh and dated c. 6770–6000 BC, had similar plants and animals, hunting and fishing, but a decline in wild plant foods, which points to more successful cereal cultivation. The buildings were much more substantial in this period. The final phase, Muhammed Jaffar and dated c. 6000–5600, saw the introduction of pottery and ground stone. The evidence shows some strain of overexploitation, and by the mid-6th millennium BC, the area was abandoned. The site illustrates the transition from food gathering to food production and the improvement of house-building quality.

Alishar: A tell southeast of Boghazköy in central Turkey, which yielded many occupation levels from Chalcolithic (late 4th millennium) to Phrygian (1st millennium BC). The lowest stratum had eight Chalcolithic levels. The Early Bronze Age levels are characterized by painted pottery with a buff or light red burnish and some geometric patterns in dark brown or buff. There was some trade with Assyria early in the 3rd millennium BC. A *karum* was discovered when some Cappadocian tablets were recovered. There may have been a hiatus in occupation in the Hittite period (later 2nd millennium). (*syn*. Alisar, Alisar Huyuk)

Allahdino: A village site in Pakistan near the Indus Delta. It was an agricultural community of the Harappan civilization.

All Cannings Cross: An Early Iron Age site in Wiltshire, southern England. The settlement contained rectangular houses and evidence of iron smelting. Fine hematite-coated bowls with horizontal furrows above the carinations have been found.

allée couverte: One of the two types of French megalithic tombs, the other being the passage grave. The tomb is a long rectangular monument, sometimes with a covering mound. There is no division between passage and chamber, although some have a small antechamber. They date from the 3rd millennium BC and are found mainly in Brittany and the Paris basin. (*syn*. gallery grave)

Allen's Rule: A biological generalization about body proportions and climate, which says that mammals living in colder environments have stockier bodies and shorter limbs to reduce heat loss. A related rule, Bergmann's Rule, states that body weight tends to a minimum in warmer regions, increases to a certain threshold as temperature declines, and then falls off again as temperature falls further.

Allerød oscillation: An interstadial (transient) period of glacial retreat at the close of the Würm Glacial Stage in Europe, dated to c. 12,000–11,000 years ago. This temporary increase in warmth allowed forests to establish themselves for a time in the ice-free zones. Radiocarbon dates show that similar conditions prevailed in North America at about the same time. This period was followed by another cold, glacial advance. (*syn*. Allerod interstadial)

alliance theory: A term emphasizing the marital bond and relations between groups and a structural explanation for marriage, exchange, and exogamy. Its theorists analyze the rules that determine which people a person may marry and which people he or she may not.

alloy: Any of a number of substances that are a mixture of two or more metals, such as bronze (copper and tin), brass (copper and zinc), or tumbaga (copper and gold). An alloy has properties superior to those of the individual metals. Alloys are not simple mixtures, but complex crystalline structures that may differ considerably from any of their constituents. Slight alterations of the proportions of the metals can bring significant changes in the properties of the alloy.

Alloys containing only two major metals are known as binary alloys, and those with three as ternary alloys. Gold is alloyed with various metals; when mixed with mercury it is called an amalgam, and with silver, native gold. Bronze was the most important alloy in antiquity. The term is also used to describe the technique of mixing the metals.

alluvial fan: A deposited land form, usually by valleys or mountain fronts where tributary streams connect to larger valleys or lowlands. An alluvial fan is created by the accumulation of alluvium that spreads, or fans. Alluvial fans are important settlement sites because they are well-drained landscapes where resources are easily accessible.

alluvium: (uh'-loov-ee-um) The detrital material (clay, gravel, organic material, sand, silt, soil) eroded, transported, and deposited by rivers and streams. It is very fertile and was used by early farmers. Although the largest areas of alluvium are flood plains and deltas, alluvium may also occur where a river overflows its banks, and it is an important constituent of shelf deposits. (*syn.* alluvial deposit, alluvion)

Almagro Basch, Martin (1911–1984): A Spanish archaeologist who worked on megaliths, on the dating and interpretation of prehistoric Spanish cave art, and on the site of Ampurias/Emporion.

Almeria: A coastal province of southeastern Spain with a Neolithic culture in the 5th and 4th millennia BC (c. 5500–4300 BC). The village of El Garcel is typical of the hilltop agricultural communities with circular huts of wattle and daub (with hearths and storage pits), plain baggy pottery, and trapezoidal flint arrowheads. The pottery was of a western Neolithic tradition, possibly deriving from North Africa. Single and multiple burials were in dry stone cists under round mounds, which are thought to be ancestral to the corbel-vaulted tombs of the Copper Age. (*syn.* Almerian)

Al Mina: A site on the coast of Syria near the mouth of the Orontes River, which was a Greek settlement before the end of the 9th century BC and may have been Poseideion. Material from the 8th–4th centuries BC has been found, indicating further links between Greece and the Near East. Al Mina was sacked and destroyed by Ptolemy of Egypt in 413 BC.

Almizaraque: A native site in southeast Spain relating to the Copper Age Los Millares culture. Oval houses were surrounded by ditches, and there is a nearby megalithic tomb, similar to those of Los Millares. Beaker pottery appears in later phases. (*syn.* Almeria)

alpaca: A domesticated South American camelid noted for its soft wool.

Alpera: Well-preserved paintings on the back wall of a shallow rock shelter of Cueva Vieja in southeast Spain. They belong to the Spanish Levant cycle, c. 8000–5000 BC (Mesolithic) and depict a group of women, hunters or warriors with bows and arrows and feather headdresses, deer, ox, and possibly dogs. (*syn.* Albacete)

alphabet: A set of written symbols or characters used to represent the sounds of a language. Each character in an alphabet usually represents a single sound rather than a syllable or group of vowels or consonants. The first alphabets were devised around the eastern shores of the Mediterranean around 1700–1500 BC. The Phoenicians developed what is known as North Semitic, considered the ancestor of all modern alphabets. However, Semitic language scripts used only consonants. The Greeks then added vowels when they adopted an alphabet in c. 8th century BC. The number of letters in an alphabet varies from 20–30 to hundreds for hieroglyphic and cuneiform scripts to thousands for Chinese in which every sign is an ideogram.

Alsónémedi: A large cremation cemetery 30 kilometers south of Budapest, Hungary, of the Bronze Age Nagrév group. It is near a large inhumation cemetery of the Late Copper Age's Baden culture.

Altai: The mountain range and region of southern Siberia, which has yielded important prehistoric remains. Rising above 4,000 meters, this area has Palaeolithic deposits (Ulalinka Creek) and a late glacial occupation (Ust' Kanskaia Cave). Some food-producing cultures appeared c. 3rd millennium BC, and metallurgy entered c. 2nd millennium, when copper ore was exploited. Pastoral nomadism and horseback riding were introduced in the 1st millennium BC. Rich burials indicate a society of social differentiation and a warrior elite that acquired precious goods from far-flung regions. In the 4th–2nd centuries BC, iron gradually replaced bronze. Altai groups are also characterized by animal art styles, similar to the Scythians who occupied the steppes of southern Russia to the west.

Altaic: A language family in the subdivision of the Ural-Altaic. It includes Turkic, Mongolian, Manchu, Tungusic, Korean, and Japanese. These languages are distributed in an arc across northern Eurasia.

Altamira: One of the most important painted Palaeolithic caves (as is Lascaux in France) and one of the earliest discovered (1879). The site is in the Cantabrian Mountains of northeast Spain, and the 280-meter-long cave is famous for its polychrome animals, which include deer, bison, and wild boar painted in red, black, and a range of earth colors. Most art in the cave was produced by Solutrean and Magdalenian peoples, with one layer radiocarbon-dated to c. 13,000 BC. The most famous panel is of 15 bison, along with deer and horses. There is also a hall with black paintings, and symbols are found in several parts of the cave. The paintings' authenticity was challenged until 1902, when Emile Cartailhac finally accepted that they were genuine.

altar: A surface on which a sacrifice is offered or which is used as a center of worship. It began, in primitive times, as a rock or heap of stones or rocks and evolved into large, ornate altars in churches. Small domestic altars have also been used in houses. (*syn.* khat)

Altar de Sacrificios: The Maya site at the junction of the Pasion and Chixoy Rivers in Peten, Guatemala, occupied from c. 1000 BC (Middle Pre-Classic) until AD c. 950–1000 (beginning of Postclassic). Early remains are of Xe pottery and formal architecture (thatch-and-pole) dated to c. 500 BC. The site flourished owing to its position on water routes, and eventually plazas, a ball court, and a temple pyramid were built. There is evidence of intrusion of a group (probably Putun) around AD 800–850 and a second invasion c. 910. After this, the site declined in power and was eventually abandoned.

Altheim: A small site near Landshut, Bavaria (Germany), which has three concentric rings of ditches and palisades. It is also the name of the Late Neolithic–Copper Age culture of the upper Danube basin.

Altin-Depe: A large Chalcolithic and Bronze Age site in southern Turkmenistan, similar to Namazga-Depe. The urban phase of the early 2nd millennium BC has a large artisans' quarter where there is evidence for specialized pottery production. The residential quarter has rich grave goods, including jewelry of precious and semiprecious stones and metals and imported materials. There is a complex of monumental structures similar to the ziggurats of Mesopotamia, with three main periods of construction. The settlement declined early in the 2nd millennium BC and was abandoned mid-millennium. (*syn.* Altin-depe)

altiplanos: Wide mountain basins found at high elevations in the Central Andes (3,000–4,000 miles), with cool, moist climates.

Altithermal: A warm, dry postglacial period in the western United States approximately 5600–2500 BC. Coined by Ernst Antev in 1948, the term describes a time during which temperatures were warmer than at present. Other terms, like Long drought, are used. (*syn.* Climatic Optimum, Thermal Maximum, Long Drought; Great Drought; Holocene climatic optimum)

altitude: The distance an object or surface lies above a datum plane, usually sea level. It is one of the three dimensions defining the spatial location of artifacts.

Altmühlian: A late Middle Palaeolithic industry of central Europe dating to the middle of the last glacial period. It is characterized by Blattspitzen, side scrapers, and retouched blades.

Alto Salaverry: A Late preceramic site on the north coast of Peru with the first sunken circular structure, which eventually was used in other ceremonial sites of the Initial Period.

Altun Ha: A Classic Maya site in Belize, about 35 miles (56 kilometers) north of Belize City, which dates to the Middle Pre-Classic period. It is known for caches of obsidian and jade. The land was poor for agriculture, but marine resources were exploited, and the small center was quite wealthy. There is evidence of long-distance contact with Teotihuacan before the site was abandoned, like other Maya ceremonial centers, AD c. 900.

alveolus: The sockets in the jawbone in which the roots of teeth are set.

Amapa: A site in Mexico dating from AD 250–700, occupied again from 900–1200. Metal artifacts were produced from 900, suggesting a connection with Mesoamerican cultures of the time.

Amara: The site of two Nubian towns about 180 kilometers south of Wadi Halfa, one east and one west of the Nile. Amara West was a walled colony founded by the Egyptians c. 1295–1069 BC when much of Nubia was regarded as Egypt. Amara East has a temple dating to c. 300 BC–AD 350 but few other remains.

Amarnà, Tell el-: The site of the ruins and tombs of the city of the 18th Dynasty pharaoh Akhetaton in Upper Egypt, 44 miles (71 kilometers) north of modern Asyut and 280 kilometers south of Cairo. Akhenaten (Amenhotep IV) built the city in about 1348 BC as his capital and the center of his reformed religion and worship of Aten. The city consisted of a group of palaces, temples, and residential quarters (and rock-cut tombs) inhabited only about 25–30 years. It was abandoned less than 4 years after Akhenaten's death, and the capital returned to Thebes. Tell el-Amarnà's remains have preserved the record of this short, fascinating period of history during which a correspondence in cuneiform between the Egyptian pharaoh, kings of the Hittites and of the Mitanni, and governors of Egyptian possessions in western Asia took place. There is Mycenaean pottery, linking the site to the Aegean, and statuary that differed from the traditional art of pharaonic Egypt. The art of this brief monotheistic period was realistic and unrestrained, in contrast with the stereotyped art styles of other periods in ancient Egypt. It is one of the best-preserved examples of an Egyptian settlement of the New Kingdom. (*syn.* Akhetaten; El-Amarna; Tall al-Amarna; el-Amarna)

Amarna Letters: An important cache of diplomatic documents from Tell el-Amarnà, discovered in 1887, a correspondence in cuneiform between the Egyptian pharaoh, kings of the Hittites and of the Mitanni, and governors of Egyptian possessions in western Asia. This discovery led to further excavations, which revealed a number of clay cuneiform tablets. There are 382 known clay tablets, most of which derive from the "Place of the Letters of Pharaoh," a building identified as the official records office in the city.

Amarna period: A phase in the late 18th Dynasty, including the reigns of Akhenaten, Smenkhkare, Tutankhamun, and Ay (1379–1352 BC), when important religious and artistic changes took place. The name is derived from the site of Akhenaten's capital at Tell el-Amarnà.

amateur: A person actively interested in archaeology but who has not received advanced academic training in the field; also one who has studied but does not pursue work in the field.

amber: Fossilized pine resin, a transparent yellow, orange, or reddish-brown material from coniferous trees. It is amorphous, having a specific gravity of 1.05–1.10 and hardness of 2–2.5 on the Mohs scale, and has two varieties—gray and yellow. Amber was appreciated and popular in antiquity for its beauty and its supposed magical properties. The southeast coast of the Baltic Sea is its major source in Europe, with lesser sources near the North Sea and in the Mediterranean. Amber is washed up by the sea. There is evidence of a strong trade in amber up the Elbe, Vistula, Danube, and into the Adriatic Sea area. The trade began in the Early Bronze Age and expanded greatly with the Mycenaeans and again with the Iron Age peoples of Italy. The Phoenicians were also specialist traders in amber. The soft material was sometimes carved for beads and necklaces.

Ambrona: A Lower Palaeolithic site in Soria, central Spain, first discovered before World War II. Ambrona probably dates 300,000–400,000 years ago, from the end of the Mindel Glacial period. Its occupants hunted elephants, deer, and bovines although the horse was the most common animal in the area. There are stone hand axes, scrapers, and cleavers of the Acheulian type, and like some African sites, they were made from chalcedony, quartzite, quartz, and limestone. Points were fashioned from young elephant tusks. Pieces of charcoal show that fire was used.

ambulatory: A sheltered walkway, often found in temples, cloisters, and churches; a space between the colonnade and the main structure of a temple.

Amekni: A site in southern Algeria dating to c. 7th millennium BC, with pottery similar to wavy-line ware of Early Khartoum. There is no evidence of food production or of fishing in this early settlement.

Amen: The god of Thebes (Upper Egypt) who came into prominence with the dynasties of the Middle and New Kingdoms. Many pharaohs from the 11th Dynasty onward included his name in theirs, such as Amenemhet and Tutankha-

men. Amen was associated with the ram, although represented in human form, and sometimes incorporated with the sun god Ra. (*syn.* Amon, Amun)

Amenemhet: The name of four 12th Dynasty pharaohs, under whom the Middle Kingdom of Egypt reached its peak of development, c. 1938–1756 BC. The name meant "Amun is at the head." They included Amenemhet I (1938–1908 BC), (Sesostris I or Senwosret, 1918–1875 BC). Amenemhet II (1876-1842 BC), (Sesostris II, 1844–1837 BC), Amenemhet III (1818–1770 BC), (Sesostris III, 1836–1818 BC), and Amenemhet IV (c. 1770–1760 BC) (also Sebeknefru, 1756–1750 BC, the first attested female monarch). (*syn.* Ammenemes)

Amenhotep: The name of four pharaohs of the 18th Dynasty of Egypt, 1390–1353 BC, Amenhotep III (Amenhotep the Magnificent) was the most powerful, reigning 1514–1593 BC. He was preceded by Amenhotep I (1514–1493 BC) and Amenhotep II (1426–1400 BC) and succeeded by Amenhotep IV (1352–1336 BC), who was better known by his adopted name of Akhenaten. The name meant "Amun is content." Amenhotep I, the founder of the dynasty, extended Egypt's boundaries in Nubia (modern Sudan). Amenhotep III devoted himself to promoting diplomacy and to extensive building in Egypt and Nubia. Amenhotep IV tried to establish the monotheistic cult of Aten. (*syn.* Amunhotep, Amenophis)

Amenhotep son of Hapu (c. 1440–1360 BC): A high official during the reign of Amenhotep III of Egypt whose offices included chief royal architect. In this capacity, he probably supervised the construction of Amenhotep III's mortuary temples at Thebes near modern Luxor, the building of another temple in Nubia (modern Sudan), the extraction of stone for sculpting reliefs, and the commissioning of royal statues such as the Colossi of Memnon. Amenhotep III even ordered the building of a small funerary temple for Athribis, his honorary designation, next to his own temple, which was a unique honor for a nonroyal person in Egypt. (*syn.* Athribis, Huy)

American Anthropological Association: A professional organization for anthropologists with a special division for archaeologists. The association publishes *American Anthropologist* and *Anthropology Newsletter*. The Archaeology Division publishes the monograph series *Archaeological Papers of the AAA*. (*syn.* AAA)

Americanist archaeology: Archaeology evolving in and practiced in close association with anthropology in the Americas.

American Palaeo-Arctic Tradition: A tradition that includes several complexes and cultures dating to c. 11,000–6500 bp in the Arctic and Subarctic. These complexes are characterized by microblades, bifaces, and burins. Denali Complex is an example.

American Society of Conservation Archaeologists: A professional organization for archaeologists especially committed to the conservation of cultural resources. (*syn.* ASCA)

Amerind: An abbreviated term for American Indian, used to distinguish American aborigines from inhabitants of India. (*syn.* Amerindian)

Amersfoot interstadial: An interstadial of the Weichselian stage, which has radiocarbon dates between 68,000–65,000 bp, but is possibly earlier.

amino acid dating: A method of absolute (chronometric) dating, which is hoped to fill the gap between radiocarbon dates and potassium-argon dates. It is used for human and animal bone and other organic material. Specific changes in its amino acid structure (racemization or epimerization), which occur at a slow, relatively uniform rate, are measured after the organism's death. The basis for the technique is the fact that almost all amino acids change from optically active to optically passive compounds (racemize) over time. Aspartic acid is the compound most often used because it has a half-life of 15,000–20,000 years and allows dates from 5,000–100,000 years to be calculated. However, racemization is very much affected by environmental factors such as temperature change. If there has been significant change in the temperature during the time in which the object is buried, the result is flawed. Other problems of contamination have occurred, so that the technique is not fully established. It is fairly reliable for deep-sea sediments as the temperature is generally more stable. (*syn.* amino-acid dating; aminostratigraphy; amino-acid racemization, amino acid racemization)

Amlash: A site in northwest Iran, southwest of the Caspian Sea, dating to the late 2nd millennium BC. Rich burials in tombs have produced gold and silver vessels, pottery figurines, animal-shaped pottery rhytons (ritual vessels)—material similar to that at Marlik Tepe.

Ammut: Goddess of the Egyptian netherworld, also called "Devouress of the Dead" or "Great of Death." She is often depicted with the head of a crocodile, foreparts of a lion or panther, and rear of a hippopotamus. She is purported to eat the heart of anyone judged unworthy to be admitted to the netherworld. (*syn.* Ammit)

Amorgos: An island in the eastern Cyclades, Greece, which was prosperous in the Early Bronze Age and had three cities, Arcesine, Minoa, and Aegiale. There is an important cemetery on the island with single burials in cist graves, accompanied by copper weapons and pottery. Fine carved stone figurines of Early Cycladic type have also been found, usually made of marble and some being almost life size.

Amorites: A branch of the Semites who were nomads in the Syrian desert and who overthrew the Sumerian civilization of Ur c. 2000 BC and dominated Mesopotamia, Syria, and Palestine until c. 1600 BC. In the oldest cuneiform sources (c. 2400–2000 BC), the Amorites were equated with the West, although their true place of origin was most likely Arabia, not Syria. They founded a series of kingdoms throughout Mesopotamia and northern Syria, the most important being Babylon and Assur. Their arrival in Palestine was at the transition from the Early Bronze to the Middle Bronze Age. The Amorites became assimilated into the population and culture of the regions where they settled. Eventually, the Amorites settled and amalgamated with the Canaanites of the Middle and Late Bronze Ages. During the 2nd millennium BC, the Akkadian term *Amurru* referred not only to an ethnic group but also to a language and to a geographic and political unit in Syria and Palestine. In the dark age between c. 1600–1100 BC, the language of the Amorites disappeared from Babylonia and the mid-Euphrates; in Syria and Palestine, however, it became dominant. In Assyrian inscriptions from about 1100 BC, the term *Amurru* designated part of Syria and all of Phoenicia and Palestine but no longer referred to any specific kingdom, language, or population. (*syn.* Amurru)

Ampajango: A site in Catamarca Province, northwest Argentina, with a river terrace containing a complex of bifacial tools dating c. 10,000 BC.

amphiprostyle: A Greek or Roman temple having two open porticoes (proticum and posticum), one in the rear and one in the front, but without columns on the sides. The construction never exceeded four columns in the front and four in the rear. The porticoes were constructed to project beyond the cella (main body) of the building.

amphitheater: A large-scale Roman arena open to the elements and surrounded by tiers of seats. Amphitheaters were constructed for exhibiting gladiatorial and other public spectacles (military displays, combats, and wild beast fights) to the populace. The earliest were oval and built of wood, later changing to stone construction. Rome's Colosseum has tiered galleries two to three stories in height and has provision for covering the arena with shades to protect against rain or sun. Roofing of so wide an expanse was beyond Roman technology. The arena of the Colosseum had a false timber floor, below which was a labyrinth of service corridors. The animal cages were situated here, linked with pre-tensioned lifts and automatic trapdoors so that participants and animals could be sent up to the floor of the arena with speed and precision. Somehow, Roman engineers staged the grand opening by flooding the arena for a full-scale sea battle. Amphitheaters accommodated a great number of spectators (possibly more than 50,000 at the Colosseum). The Romans derived their ideas from the classic Greek theater and stadium, and the model was widely copied throughout the Roman Empire. The amphitheater could be erected on any terrain, even inside an urban center. An early example of the Republican period is at Pompeii; the Colosseum is of the Imperial model. The fortress of Caerlon and the towns of Caerwent, Cirencester, Colchester, Dorchester, Richborough, and Wroxeter are some British sites with amphitheaters. (*syn.* amphitheater)

amphora: A large Greek or Roman earthenware storage jar, with a narrow neck and mouth and two handles ("two eared"; each called an anem) at the top. The body of the jar is usually oval and long, with a pointed bottom. It was used for holding or transporting liquids, especially wine or oil, and other substances such as resin. Its shape made it easy to handle and ideal for tying onto a mule's or donkey's back. They were often placed side-by-side in upright positions in a sand-floored cellar. Sinking it into the sand or ground kept the contents cool. Amphorae were also made of glass, onyx, gold, stone, and brass, and some had conventional jar bottoms with a flat surface. The container would be sealed when full, and the handle usually carried an amphora stamp, impressed before firing, giving details such as the source, the potter's name, the date, and the capacity. Amphorae were probably not normally reused. (*syn.* plural amphorae, amphoras)

ampulla: A small Greek or Roman globular flask or bottle with two handles and a short, narrow neck. It was used for holding oil for bathers (called ampulla oleria) or wine, oil, vinegar, and other beverages for table use (then called ampulla potaria). These small containers were usually in the form of a globe or bladder, although sometimes shaped like a lentil with rounded sides.

Ampurias: An ancient Greek trading settlement in Spain, 40 kilometers northeast of present-day Gerona. It was originally a colony of Marseilles (Massalia), founded in the early 6th century BC. The town allied with Rome in the 3rd century BC, and it became a Roman colony under Augustus (27 BC– AD 14). Ampurias was probably most prosperous between the 5th–3rd centuries BC, when it established extensive trading across the Mediterranean. Its commercial achievements were marked by the minting of coinage. After Roman presence increased and the harbor began to silt up, the town declined. The end came with the destruction by the Franks in AD 265. (*syn.* Emporion)

Amratian: An Egyptian predynastic culture, centered in Upper Egypt and named for the site El Amrah (or al-'Amirah; c. 4500–4000 BC) near Abydos. Numerous sites, dating to c. 3600 BC, have been excavated. They reveal an animal husbandry and agricultural life similar to the preceding Badarian culture. There are large cemeteries, like that at Naqada, which imply that the settlements were permanent and large.

Many of the dead were buried crouched, with rich grave goods. Flint was quarried for the variety of finely worked daggers, points, and tools. Copper came into use for beads, harpoons, and pins. There was trading with Ethiopia, the Red Sea region, and Syria, based on the finds. Several pottery wares, in a range of shapes, were made: black-topped red ware from the Badarian period onward and white cross-lined (red ware painted in white) later. (*syn.* Naqadah I)

Amri: A site in the Indus Valley in Pakistan, probably dating to the early 3rd millennium BC. It was the first site to be recognized as belonging to the Early Harappan period when excavated by Majumdar in 1929. Its name has been given to a style of hand- and wheel-made painted pottery found in its Chalcolithic levels and on tells over much of Sind and up into the hills of Baluchistan. The tall globular beakers of fine buff ware are painted with geometric designs in black between red horizontal bands. Chert and some copper were used for tools, and the architecture was in mud brick. Fractional burial was the practice for the dead. Periods I and II represent the pre-Harappan settlement of agricultural farmers, who kept cattle, sheep, goats, and donkeys, but also hunted (or herded) gazelle. In the later part of Period II, Harappan ceramics appear alongside Amri wares; Period III represents a full, mature Harappan occupation. The culture was gradually succeeded by that of the Indus civilization. The uppermost levels contained Jhukar and Jhangar material.

Amsadong: A Korean Chulmun culture site near Seoul with pit houses, net weights and sinkers, and querns, dating to 4490–1510 BC. It is the type site of Classic Chulmun pottery.

Amudian: A culture and industry close to the Sea of Galilee near Tiberias, Israel. There are several important caves, including Emireh, the type site of the Emiran, and Zuttiyeh, the type site of the Amudian. These demonstrate the early occurrence of Upper Palaeolithic blades and burins even earlier than the Mousterian and its flake tools. The Amud cave is Mousterian or Emiran, and in 1961 the skeletal remains were found of two adults and two children estimated to have lived about 50,000–60,000 years ago (remains held in the Rockefeller Archaeological Museum, Jerusalem). They consist of a skeleton of an adult male about 25 years old, a fragment of an adult jaw, and skull fragments of infants. The skeleton has an exceptionally large brain (1800 cc). The remains suggest that they are part of a group known as Near Eastern Neanderthal type. This group represents a mixture of West Asian features similar to those of fossils found in 1957 in Iraq, estimated to date from about 46,000 years ago, and those of the Upper Palaeolithic people who lived in southwestern France and the Middle East from about 10,000 to 35,000 years ago. These findings provide more evidence that Neanderthal people were a highly varied species who lived in much of the Northern Hemisphere, except the New World.

Amudian material has been recognized at the cave of et-Tabun (Mount Carmel) and at sites like Jabrud, Adlun, and the Abri Zumoffen in the Levant. It has been suggested that the Amudian may have been ancestral to subsequent Upper Palaeolithic industries of the Middle East, hence the name "pre-Aurignacian," which has sometimes been given to industries of Amudian type. (*syn.* Amud)

amulet: Small good-luck charms, often in the form of gods, hieroglyphs, and sacred animals and made of precious stones or faience. They were especially popular with Egyptians and other Eastern peoples, worn both in life and placed in burials or in mummy wrappings. Amulets were supposed to afford protection and may have been thought to imbue the wearer with particular qualities. Some superstitiously thought amulets could heal diseases or help the wearer avoid them. (*syn.* meket, nehet, sa, wedja, periapta)

Amun: The supreme god of the Egyptian pantheon, who was established by the 11th Dynasty at Thebes. The name means "hidden" or "secret." Amun was frequently identified with Ra, the sun god of Heliopolis, and called Amun-Ra. His temple at Karnak is the best surviving example of a religious complex of the New Kingdom. His wife was Amaunet, and he is depicted in male human form. Amun's supremacy was challenged only during the reign of Akhenaten. (*syn.* Amun-Ra)

'Amuq: A swampy plain in northern Syria east of Antioch (Antakya) at the foot of the Amanus Mountains and beside the Orontes River at the northeast corner of the Mediterranean Sea. Its important sites include Tayanat (Neolithic–Chalcolithic), Atchana (Copper Age–Hittite), and Antioch (Hellenistic and Roman). The plain is rich in tell settlements of the prehistoric and later periods. The basic prehistoric sequence for the area has phases designated by letters: 'Amuq A represents the Early Neolithic.

Amurian: A variant of the *Homo sapiens* who inhabited northeast Asia at the end of the Pleistocene, perhaps ancestors of Native Americans. Present-day Ainu of Japan are a remnant of these people.

Amur Neolithic: A number of Neolithic cultures recognized near the Amur River in eastern Siberia. They are mainly defined by the presence of pottery. In the Middle Amur region, the earliest phase is known as the Novopetrovka blade culture. Later is the Gromatukha culture, with unifacially flaked adzes, bifacially flaked arrowheads, and laurel-leaf knives and spearheads. Settlements on Osinovoe Lake, which are characterized by large pit houses, date to around the 3rd millennium BC. Millet was cultivated, representing the first food production in the area, and there was fishing. A fourth Neolithic culture in the area, dating to the mid-2nd millennium BC, was a combination of farming and fishing by people who moved there from the Lower Amur

area. The Neolithic of the Lower Amur is known from sites such as Kondon, Suchu Island, and Voznesenovka. Fishing provided the economic basis for the establishment of unusually large sedentary settlements of pit houses—a situation paralleling the examples from the northwest coast of North America. In the 1st millennium BC, iron was introduced and fortified villages constructed. In Middle Amur, millet farming became the lifestyle.

Amvrosievka: An Upper Palaeolithic site in southern Ukraine with a large number of bison bones and artifacts of microblades and laterally grooved bone points. The site is dated to 15,250 bp.

amygdaloid: Almond shaped; a term used to describe elongated ovate or cordiform biface tools.

An: The supreme Sumerian god of life and fertility. An was later replaced by Enlil and Marduk, but was always considered the ultimate source of authority. Identified with the city of Uruk, his Akkadian equivalent was Anu.

'Anaeho'omalu: A site on Hawaii dating to the 10th century AD as a fishing camp and later a settlement. It has one of the largest petroglyph fields in the Hawaiian Islands with over 9,000 figures.

anaerobic: Without air; the opposite of aerobic. This term is used to describe environmental conditions where oxygen is not present and where decay of organic material is partially or completely stopped. Anaerobic conditions are usually waterlogged but may also occur when a layer of clay, plant, or animal remains is sealed. The remains survive much better than under normal conditions because there is insufficient oxygen for bacterial or fungal growth. The organic materials reach a state of equilibrium beyond which they do not decay.

anaglyph: A term describing any work of art that is carved, chased, embossed, or sculptured—such as bas-reliefs, cameos, or other raised working of a material. Materials that are incised or sunken are called intaglios or diaglyphs. The Egyptians also used the term *anaglyphs* for a kind of secret writing.

analogy: An anthropological practice using reasoning based on the assumption that if two things are similar in some respects, then they must be similar in other respects. Ethnographic information from recent cultures is then used to make informed hypotheses about archaeological cultures and to compare societies and culture traits of recorded societies with those of prehistoric sites. Analogy is the basis of most archaeological interpretation (see general and specific analogy).

analysis: A stage in archaeological research design involving isolating, describing, and structuring data, usually by typological classification, along with chronological, functional, technological, and constituent determinations. The research involves artifactual and nonartifactual data. The method evolved from the tendency to formalize the archaeological process, especially through the work of L. R. Binford, D. L. Clarke, and J. C. Gardin. Computer science and mathematics are used to elaborate the means for transforming simple descriptions of archaeological data into cultural, economic, and social reconstructions of earlier societies. This type of research attempts to provide archaeology with a theoretical framework based on scientific method. (*syn.* analytical archaeology)

analytical type: The method of defining arbitrary groupings of artifacts. Analytical types consist of groups of attributes that define artifacts for comparing sites in space and time. They do not necessarily coincide with actual tool types used by prehistoric people.

Ananino: An Iron Age culture of the mid-1st millennium BC in the Volga basin of Russia with strong connections with the Scythians to the south.

Anapchi: A 7th-century palace site of the Silla Kingdom in Korea. Artifacts include dugout boats, Buddhist images, pottery and metal vessels, and inscribed wooden tablets.

Anasazi: A major cultural tradition of canyon dwellers found in southwestern United States between AD 100–1600—mainly in the four corners area of northeastern Arizona, northwestern New Mexico, southeastern Utah, and southwestern Colorado. These Native Americans began settlements with the cultivation of maize. Pottery was unknown at the beginning, but basketry was well developed; hence the name "Basket Maker" is given to these early stages. By the 6th century, there were large villages of pit houses with farming and pottery, which evolved into the full Anasazi tradition. The first pueblos and kivas were constructed and fine painted pottery made. The next few centuries (the Pueblo I–III periods) were a time of expansion during which some of the most famous towns were founded (Chaco Canyon) and fine polychrome wares produced. At this time, the Mogollon people to the south adopted the Anasazi way of life, and their Hohokam neighbors were also influenced, perhaps suggesting that the Anasazi actually migrated to these areas. In such an arid environment, farming was always vulnerable to fluctuations in climate and rainfall, and these factors caused considerable population movement and relocation of settlements during the 11th–13th centuries, with the virtual abandonment of Chaco Canyon in 1150 and the plateau heartland by 1300. From 1300 until the arrival of the Spanish in the 16th century, the Anasazi culture and population dwindled, and the homeland in northern Arizona was abandoned. Then, with the encroachment of nomadic Apache and Navajo tribes and with the arrival of Europeans from the south and east, Anasazi territory decreased further. However, some pueblos have continued to be occupied until the present day. The generally accepted chronological framework of three Basket-

maker and five Pueblo stages was first proposed at the 1927 Pecos Conference. Although exact links are uncertain, it is clear that modern Pueblo Indian people are descended from Anasazi ancestors. The name Anasazi is derived from a Navajo word meaning "enemy ancestors" or "early ancestors" or "old people."

Anat: A deity of Egypt introduced from Syria-Palestine. The cult of Anat is first attested in Egypt in the late Middle Kingdom (c. 1800 BC).

anathermal: A period of cool climate in the area of North America, which occurred from about 7000–5000 BC. This was Ernst Antev's name for the first of the Neothermal periods, and it is thought to have started cool before becoming somewhat warmer.

anathyrosis: In Greek architecture, the technique of matching two adjoining blocks or column drums by hollowing out the center and having the blocks make contact only at the edges.

Anatolia: A mountainous region of present-day Turkey, bounded by the Pontine Mountains and the Zagros Mountains. There are a number of early sites dating c. 7000 BC as the rainfall was adequate for dry farming. The area was also important for sources of obsidian, which was exploited from the Upper Palaeolithic onward and was extensively traded in the Neolithic. The area was an important center in the Neolithic and Chalcolithic, with sites like Çatal Hüyük and Can Hasan. It was less important in the Bronze Age but later became the homeland of the Hittite Empire in the 2nd millennium BC.

Anau: A tell site in the Kara Kum oasis of southern Turkestan, first excavated in the 1880s and again in 1904. Its name has been given to a Chalcolithic culture of the 5th and 4th millennia BC, which parallels that of the sites of Sialk and Hissar (Hassuna) in Iran, especially with connections in pottery styles. Characteristic finds include fine pottery with geometric painted decoration and simple copper tools. There was a farming subsistence economy, and metal ores were probably imported from the south.

Anbangbang: A large rock shelter of sandstone in North Australia dating to the Pleistocene. Occupation increased from 6000 bp.

ancestor busts: Small painted apelike busts that were the focus of ancestor worship in Egypt's New Kingdom. Many were of limestone or sandstone, with some smaller examples made of wood and clay.

anchor ornament: An anchor-shaped terra cotta object with a perforation through the shank. These were widespread in the Early Bronze Age of Greece and appear later in Sicily and Malta. Grooving, as if from thread wear, suggests that these objects may have been part of looms.

Ancón Yacht: A site in the Ancón Valley on Peru's coast, just north of Lima. There is a high shell mound with deep stratified layers containing baskets, chipped leaf points, cultivated plants, shell fishhooks, string, twined cloth and baskets, and wooden tools. The site dates between 2500–2000 BC.

Andean chronology: The chronological systems of the Central Andes area with two main stages. Preceramic and Ceramic. The Ceramic is broken down into Initial Period, 1900–1200 BC, Early Horizon 1200–300 BC, Early Intermediate Period 300 BC–AD 700, Middle Horizon 700–100, Late Intermediate Period 1100–1438/1478, and Late Horizon 1438–1532. These horizon periods are times of widespread unity in cultural traits. Intermediate periods are times of cultural diversification.

Andean Hunting–Collecting tradition: A tradition dating 6000–4000 BC, characterized by seasonal changing of residence and a trend toward specialization in certain regions of the Andes.

Andenne ware: A medieval glazed ware made around Andenne on the River Meuse. The potters produced ordinary unglazed wares as well as finer pitchers and bowls. The glazed wares were widely traded in western Europe from the late 11th century to the 14th century.

Andersson, Johan Gunnar (1874–1960): Swedish geologist who laid the foundation for the study of prehistoric China. In 1921, at a cave near Peking, he demonstrated the presence of prehistoric material in that country. He is remembered for his work on the Yang Shao Neolithic culture (dating between 5000–3000 BC) on the middle Yellow River and the Pan Shan cemeteries further west in Kansu. He also carried out the first excavations (1921–1926) at the Palaeolithic cave site at Choukoutien (Zhoukoudian). Andersson started Sweden's Museum of Far Eastern Antiquities.

andesite line: The line dividing the Pacific between the Asiatic and Pacific plates through Polynesia. The rocks to its west are continental rocks, including andesitic basalts. To the east are coral atolls and volcanic islands of olivine basalts and other rocks.

Andrae, Walter (1875–1956): A German scholar and archaeologist who excavated the major Mesopotamian city of Assur, capital of Assyria, between 1903–1914. His high-quality excavations exposed major buildings, including a series of temples of the Early Dynastic Period, which predated the Temple of Ishtar.

Andronovo culture: A culture of southern Siberia, between the Don and Yenisei Rivers, dating to the 2nd millennium BC. The culture was relatively uniform in this large area, and agriculture played a large role. Wheat and millet were cultivated, and cattle, horses, and sheep bred. The people of this metal-using culture (ores from the Altai), which succeeded the Afansievo, lived in settlements of up to 10 large log cabin-like semisubterranean houses. Bowl- and flowerpot-shaped vessels were flat bottomed, smoothed, and decorated with geometric patterns, triangles, rhombs, and meanders. Burial was in contracted position either in stone cists or enclosures with underground timber chambers. The wooden constructions in rich graves may have designated social differentiation. The Andronovo complex is related to the Timber Grave (Russian Srubna) group in southern Russia, and both are branches of the Indo-Iranian cultural block. The Andronovo were the ancestors of Karasuk nomads who later inhabited the Central Asiatic and Siberian steppes.

Anedjib (c. 2925 BC): Egyptian ruler of the late 1st Dynasty who is thought to have been buried in Tomb X in Abydos, the smallest of the Early Dynastic royal tombs in the cemetery of Umm el Qa'ab. (*syn.* Adjib, Andjyeb, Enezib)

Aneityum: A volcanic island of Melanesia with more than 800 agricultural sites from 1,000 years ago.

Ang-ang-hsi: A group of Neolithic sites in Manchuria, which demonstrate strong connections with the Novopetrovka and Gromatukha cultures of the Middle Amur in eastern Siberia, especially in stone tool technology. Animal, fish, and mollusk remains occur on the sites.

Anghelu Ruju: A Copper Age necropolis in Alghero, northwest Sardinia. It contained 36 rock-cut tombs, some very elaborate in plan and decorated with carved bulls' heads. The tombs were used for multiple burials and contained material of the Ozieri culture (copper and silver objects) as well as Ozieri and Beaker pottery.

Angkor: Archaeological site in northwestern Cambodia, which was the capital of the Khmer Empire in Kampuchia and founded in AD c. 9. The name, from Sanskrit *nagara* means "royal city, the capital." As the capital of the Khmer empire from the 9th–15th centuries, its most imposing monuments are Angkor Wat, a temple complex built in the 12th century by King Suryavarman II (reigned AD 1113–c. 1150), and Angkor Thom, a temple complex built about 1200 by King Jayavarman VII (AD 1181–c. 1215). These monuments were lost in jungle and rediscovered in the last century. In total, there are more than 250 monuments, built almost exclusively in sandstone. The Thais conquered Angkor in 1431, and it was abandoned.

Angkor Borei: The site of the capital of the kingdom of Funan toward the end of the 6th century. The rich archaeological site is located south of Phnom Penh, near the Vietnam border, in Cambodia. It appears as Na-fu-na in Chinese writings and is identified with Naravaranagara. There is much stone statuary.

Angkor Thom: The site of a temple complex in the northwestern plain of Angkor built about 1200 by King Jayavarman VII (AD 1181–c. 1215). In the Khmer language, the name means "the big capital," and it served intermittently as the capital of the Khmer Empire from the 11th century onward. It is surrounded with walls and moats of 4-by-4 kilometers, and the temple-mountain Bayon is in the center.

Angkor Wat: A huge stone stepped pyramid, the best-known monument of Angkor (Cambodia), the largest religious structure in the world. The three-storied construction is surrounded by a moat and surmounted by five vast towers, which symbolized the five peaks of Mount Meru. It was built by Suryavarman II (AD 1113–1150) over a 25-year period as his own mausoleum (temple-mountain). The name in Khmer means "the capital (which has become a Buddhist) monastery." Angkor Wat is considered to be the highest expression of Khmer classic architecture and relief sculpture.

Angles: A Germanic people from the Baltic coast of Jutland (Schleswig, Denmark) who, with the Saxons, were the main settlers of Britain in the 5th century AD after the Roman withdrawal. There is evidence in the late 4th century of their pottery at a number of late Roman settlements in England. They crossed the North Sea to settle in the eastern parts of England, and the cultures mixed to become known thereafter as Anglo-Saxons. They gave their name to England, its people, and their language as well as to East Anglia.

Angles-sur-l'Anglin: A site in west-central France of a rock shelter with Upper Palaeolithic art, the Rocaux Sourciers (Angles). The back wall has fine bas-relief carvings, and there is a frieze of female figures dominating the shelter. Several animal carvings were found. Occupation dates to Middle and Late Magdalenian, and the art is dated to c. 11,000 BC.

Anglian: Quaternary glacial deposits found in East Anglia, England. Other possibly related and isolated patches exist elsewhere in Britain, but they are older than the extreme range of radiocarbon dating, and palaeomagnetism shows them to be younger than 700,000 bp. This period is sometimes equated with the Elster Glacial maximum and dated to c. 300,000–400,000 years ago. During the Anglian-Elsterian glaciation in Europe, a large ice-dammed lake formed in the North Sea, and large overflows from it initiated the cutting of the Dover Straits. In East Anglia, the deposits are stratified below Hoxnian and above Cromerian interglacial deposits, and Acheulian and Clactonian artifacts are found in the sediments. Most evidence of human activity in Britain and Europe is later than this time. Anglian is more often used to describe the group of deposits or the one glaciation (antepenultimate) of that time. (*syn.* Anglian-Elsterian)

Anglo-Saxons: The name of the combined cultures, the Angles and the Saxons, who left their North Sea coastal homelands in the 5th century AD and moved to eastern England after the breakdown of Roman rule. The name

derives from two specific groups—the Angles of Jutland and the Saxons from northern Germany. Some other Germanic peoples took part in the migrations, such as the Jutes and the Frisians, and they are sometimes included under this name. The language, culture, and settlement pattern of medieval and later England can be traced directly to the Anglo-Saxons. The movement to the area probably began in the 4th century when barbarian Foederati went to serve in the Roman army in Britain. The main immigration began in the middle of the 5th century. Bede, writing in the early 8th century, gives the only reliable historical record for this period, although incidental information can be found in Old English literature, particularly in the poem of Beowulf. The English kingdoms took shape by the late 6th century. Archaeologically, there are three periods: the Early or Pagan Saxon period until the general acceptance of Christianity in the mid-7th century; the Middle Saxon period until the 9th century; and the Late Saxon period until the Norman invasion of 1066. The earliest period's remains are mainly burial deposits, often cremation in urns or inhumation in cemeteries of trench graves or under barrows. Grave goods often include knives, sword or spear, shield boss, and brooches, buckles, beads, girdle hangers, and pottery—depending on the gender. Most archaeological evidence comes from the cemeteries, including the exceptional ship burial at Sutton Hoo. Churches were built in the Middle and Late Saxon periods, including Bradford-Upon-Avon and Deerhurst. Important monuments of the Middle and Late Saxon periods are the royal palaces at Yeavering and Cheddar. The Late Saxon period, after the Viking invasions, saw the growth of the first towns in Britain since the Roman period, following the establishment of Burhs in response to the Scandinavian threat. There was wide-ranging trade, developed coinage, and improved pottery manufacture and metalworking. The separate British kingdoms (most important: Mercia, Northumbria, and Wessex) eventually became a unified England with a capital at Winchester in Wessex. The Anglo-Saxons were responsible for the introduction of the English language and for the establishment of the settlement patterns of medieval England.

Anglo-Saxon Chronicle: A chronological account of events in Anglo-Saxon and Norman England, a compilation of seven surviving annals that is the primary source for the early history of England. Believed to have been started around 870, during the reign of King Alfred (871–899), it was mostly finished by 891 although further accounts were added until 1154. The annals were probably written in the monasteries of Abingdon, Canterbury, Peterborough, Winchester, and Worcester. They include vivid accounts of the Viking raids, Alfred's reign, and the period of anarchy under Stephen. The Anglo-Saxon Chronicle also included the Venerable Bede's *Historia ecclesiastica gentis Anglorum*, genealogies, regnal and episcopal lists, some northern annals, and some sets of earlier West Saxon annals. The compiler also had access to a set of late 9th-century Frankish annals. The completeness and quality of the entries vary for different periods; the Chronicle has sparse coverage of the mid-10th century and the reign of Canute, for example, but is an excellent authority for the reign of Aethelred the Unready and from the reign of Edward the Confessor until the annals end in 1154. The Chronicle survived in seven manuscripts (one of these being destroyed in the 18th century) and a fragment, which are generally known by letters of the alphabet. The oldest, the A version, was written in one hand until 891 and then continued in various hands. The B and C versions are copies made at Abingdon from a lost archetype. B ends at 977, whereas C, which is an 11th-century copy, ends, mutilated, in 1066. The D and E versions share many features. D, which was written up until 1079, probably remained in the north, whereas the archetype of E was taken south and continued at St. Augustine's, Canterbury, and was used by the scribe of manuscript F. The extant manuscript E is a copy made at Peterborough, written in one stretch until 1121. It is the version that was continued longest. The F version is an abridgment, in both Old English and Latin, made in the late 11th or early 12th century, based on the archetype of E, but with some entries from A, and it extends to 1058. The fragment H deals with 1113–14 and is independent of E.

Aniba: The site of a cemetery and settlement in Lower Nubia, founded as an Egyptian fortress in the Middle Kingdom (2055–1650 BC). It is near the gold-mining region of Nubia. (*syn.* ancient Miam)

Animal Style: A term describing a type of art whose themes were animals and that arose among nomads of the Eurasian steppes, including the Scythians, who moved from southern Russia into the territory between the Don and the Danube and even made incursions into the Near East. During the 6th–4th centuries BC, this style appeared on shaped, pierced plaques made of gold and other materials, which showed running or fighting animals (reindeer, lions, tiger, horses) alone or in pairs facing each other. The animal style had a strong influence in western Asia during the 7th century BC. Ornaments such as necklaces, bracelets, pectorals, diadems, and earrings making up the Ziwiye treasure (found in Iran near the border of Azerbaijan) show evidence of highly expressive animal forms. The most popular themes are antlered stags, ibexes, felines, birds of prey and the animal-combat motif, which shows a predator, usually bird or feline, attacking a herbivore. The joining of different animals and the use of tiny animal figures to decorate the body of an animal are also characteristic. Animal bodies were often contorted—bodies curved into circles and quadrupeds were shown with hindquarters inverted.

ankh: The Egyptian hieroglyphic sign for "life," consisting of T-shape surmounted by a loop. It represents a sandal strap or the handle of a mirror. The ankh is commonly shown being carried by deities and pharaohs and was widely used as an amulet. Temple reliefs frequently included scenes in which a king was offered the ankh by the gods, thus symbolizing the divine conferral of eternal life. It was used in some personal names, such as Tutankhamen. The motif was adapted by Coptic Christians as their cross.

Anlo: A site in Holland with a long sequence of occupation, starting with the Funnel Beaker culture. It was followed by a cattle enclosure during the Late Neolithic (protruding foot beaker) people, then a cemetery of five flat graves with foot beakers and bell beakers with cord ornament. The next phase was a settlement with late varieties of Beaker pottery, followed by a Middle Bronze Age plow soil, and a Late Bronze Age urnfield.

annealing: The treating of a metal or alloy with heat and then cold. After casting metal, it may be necessary to further process it by cold working, hammering, and drawing the metal—either to produce hard cutting edges or to produce beaten sheet metal. Hammering makes the metal harder, although more brittle and subject to cracking, because it destroys its crystalline structure. Annealing, the reheating of the metal gently to a dull red heat and allowing it to cool, produces a new crystalline structure that can be hammered again. The process may be repeated as often as is necessary. The final edge on a weapon may be left unannealed as it will be harder and last longer.

ansa: Latin term for handle or anything handlelike, such as an eyelet, haft, or hole. Any vessel or vase with large ears or circular handles on the neck or body is said to have ansae. (*syn.* plural ansae)

ansa lunata: A handle or handles on a vessel or vase going in two opposite directions or in two diverging projections. The term describes Terramara pottery of the Apennine culture and vessels of central Europe of the Middle to Late Bronze Age.

Anse au Meadow, L': A site on the northern peninsula of Newfoundland, which is the only known Viking settlement in the New World. The Norse explorers were the first Europeans to reach what is now America in AD c. 1000, as is recorded in the Icelandic sagas and recently confirmed by the archaeological discovery of the site at L'Anse-aux-Meadows. Excavations revealed traces of turf-walled houses similar to those at Viking sites in Greenland and Iceland. Also found was a spindle whorl, iron nails, and a smithy with pieces of bog iron and several pounds of slag—all of Norse origin. Radiocarbon dates range from AD 700–1080 with a concentration around 1000, which is the period that, according to the sagas, Norsemen led by Leif Eriksson sailed west from Greenland

and explored the coast of America, which they named Vinland.

anta: A short wall at a right angle to the long walls of a classical temple's cella. This term is also used for a Portuguese chambered tomb (5th millennium BC).

antefix: Ornamental tiles fixed to the eaves and cornices of ancient Greek and Roman buildings to decoratively conceal the ends of the rain tiles. The term also refers to vertical ornamental heads of animals (etc.) That were the spouts of the gutters. (*syn.* adj. antefixal)

antelope: The name for numerous species of deerlike ruminant horned bovid. The main characteristics are cylindrical annulated horns and a lachrymal sinus. There are "true" antelopes, "bush" antelopes, "capriform" (goatlike) antelopes, and "bovine" (oxlike) antelopes. The name is most popularly associated with the "true" antelopes. The term first came through Greek and Latin to describe creatures roaming the banks of the Euphrates. The attributes of the antelope caused it to become a heraldic animal, and it served as the symbol of the 16th Upper Egyptian nome (province). Three species of antelope are known from ancient Egypt (*Alcephalus buselaphus*, *Oryx gazella*, and *Addax nasomaculato*).

Antequera: The site of a town in Málaga province, in the autonomous community (region) of Andalusia, southern Spain, northwest of Málaga, at the foot of the Sierra del Torcal, which is famous for its three Neolithic (Copper Age) chambered tombs (dolmens): the Cuevas de Menga, de Viera, and El Romeral. They are partially cut into the hillside, but each is constructed differently. The Cueva de Menga has a huge orthostat chamber c. 5 meters wide, 3 meters high, and 1.45 meters long, roofed by five large capstones supported by three central pillars and dry stone walls. Scenes with human figures are carved on its walls. The Cueva de Romeral has a magnificent corbel vault nearly 5 meters high, dry stone tholos, and a passage over 30 meters long. The Cuevas de Viera has a long orthostat-lined passage with porthole slabs and a small square chamber. A cemetery of rock-cut tombs of the Bronze Age imitating the tholos form is nearby. (*syn.* Roman Anticaria, Moorish Madinah Antakira)

anthracology: The study of human interactions with the plant environment. Wood charcoal from archaeological sites is studied by microscope and statistically analyzed.

anthropogenic soil: Soil that has been influenced by human activity—indicated by a concentration of phosphorus, organic matter, debris, or artifacts. The different soil and sediment components are physically mixed through cultivation, deforestation, or construction.

anthropoid: Of human form; humanlike. Taken from the Greek term for man shaped, the term is used to describe sarcophagi and coffins and other artifacts of human shape. The term is also used to describe a being that is human only in form or an anthropoid ape (gibbons, orangs, chimpanzees, gorillas). (*syn.* anthropomorphous)

anthropological archaeology: The tradition of archaeology derived from, and most strongly oriented toward, the larger field of anthropology.

anthropological linguistics: The study of human language and its applications for cultural behavior.

anthropology: The study of humankind, its culture and evolution, both extant and extinct. The subdisciplines include physical anthropology, archaeology, anthropological linguistics, cultural anthropology, and social anthropology. Archaeology is sometimes regarded as a separate field rather than as a branch of anthropology. Social anthropology concentrates on patterns of behavior and institutions. Physical anthropology studies the physical (biological) characteristics of animals.

anthropometry: A subdiscipline of physical anthropology, which involves the measurement of the human body to determine its average dimensions and the proportion of its parts at different ages and different races, classes, or cultures. The measurement of the dimensions of humans. (*syn.* n. anthropometer, anthropometrist; adj. anthropometric, anthropometrical; adv. anthropometrically)

anthropomorph: A representation of the human form in art, such as those found on ancient pottery. Also, a figure, object, or rock art with or using a human shape. The term also refers to the attribution of human features and behaviors to animals, inanimate objects, or natural phenomena. (*syn.* anthropomorphic figure; anthropomorphism (n.); anthropomorphous (adj.))

antico rosso: Ancient marble of a deep red or green tint. It is the material of many ancient Egyptian and early Greek sculptures. These green and red marbles (antico rosso and lapis lacedaemonius) were obtained from the southern Peloponnese.

antimonial bronze: A bronze containing antimony in combination, as a third constituent. It may have been added to the original copper ore in the alloy to improve the hardening qualities. It is used this way in, and included in the names of, many minerals, such as antimonial arsenic, copper, and nickel.

antimony: A brittle metallic substance that has been used in the preparation of yellow pigments for enamel and porcelain painting. It forms a fourth constituent in alloys, along with nitrogen, phosphorus, arsenic, bismuth, and others in forming triads and pentads. (*syn.* adj. antimonial)

Antioch: An ancient city of Phrygia near the Orontes River and modern Yalvaç in Turkey. It was founded in 300 BC by

Seleucus I (c. 358–281 BC) after the death of Alexander the Great and was one of the two capitals of the Parthian Empire. It became a Roman city in 64 BC at the hands of Pompey and served as a capital of the province of Syria. As one of the three most important cities of the Roman world, Antioch peaked under Hadrian as a civil and military administrative center, then suffered Persian invasions during the 3rd century AD. It was rebuilt by Diocletian and successive emperors from the 4th century AD. The plain of Antioch was occupied from the Neolithic onward. Its ruins include a large rock cutting, which may have held the temple of Men Ascaënus, the local Phrygian deity. (*syn.* Antiochia, Antioch Pisidian, Antiocheia Pisidias, Caesarea Antiochia)

antiquarian: An amateur interested in ancient artifacts, who studies or collects objects of antiquity. The term also refers to amateurs who dig up artifacts unscientifically. Antiquarianism is the study of the ancient past and its customs and the relics of the ancient past. (*syn.* antiquary; antiquarianism)

antis, in: Used of a temple building in which the lateral walls of the cella extend to form part of the facade, enclosing the sides of the pronaos.

antler: The name given to the bony processes growing on the forward heads of animals of the deer family; also a branch of an antler—bonelike material grown and shed annually. Antlers indicate the sex of the species; for example, only male red deer, fallow deer, and elk (moose) have antlers. They may also indicate whether a site is occupied seasonally as they are naturally shed in the winter, except for female reindeer who shed their antlers in spring. Antlers were a valuable material for making tools in ancient times.

antler sleeve: A section of deer antler carved into a cavity or hole at one end to hold a stone ax head. The piece was either set into a socket in a haft or perforated to attach to the haft. This material was used for its resilience and shock-absorbing value in tool making. Roughly trimmed antler "picks" have been used in construction and flint mining.

Antonine Wall: A defensive fortification on the frontier of the Roman Empire in Scotland, built by the governor Lollius Urbicus for the emperor Antoninus Pius AD c. 142–145. It spans the distance between the Firth of Forth and the Firth of Clyde in Scotland, running for 36.5 miles (58.5 km) with 19 forts on its line and others forward and to the rear. The wall, mainly turf built, was 14–16 feet (4.5 m) wide and probably 10 feet (3 m) high with a ditch 40 feet (12 m) wide and 12 feet (4 m) deep in front of the wall and a military road behind it. The forts are 2 miles (3 km) apart. The wall was probably a last attempt by the Romans to secure the Scottish Lowlands, and it provided defense beyond Hadrian's Wall, which was around 100 miles (160 km) to the south. The work was carried out by men from the legions stationed in Britain and was probably completed section by section by different work groups who marked their handiwork with decorative plaques. Crop marks reveal some evidence for the temporary camps for the builders. The wall was abandoned temporarily in AD c. 155–158 during the northern revolt and permanently before the end of the century when the garrison withdrew to Hadrian's Wall. Rough Castle is a well-preserved fort site, and other traces of the wall remain.

Antonine Column: An important monument in Rome. It is a lofty pillar ornamented with a series of bas-reliefs sent up in spirals from the base to the summit. The bas-reliefs represent the victories of the emperor Marcus Aurelius Antoninus.

Anu: The Mesopotamian sky god, whose seat was at Uruk. Anu was part of the ruling triad with Bel (Enlil) and Ea (Enki). In the city of Uruk, there was a series of seven superimposed temples dedicated to Anu. Anu was the god of kings and the yearly calendar, but he had only a small role in Mesopotamian mythology. (*syn.* Sumerian An)

Anubis: The Egyptian god of the dead, in the form of a wild dog or jackal-headed man. Anubis guarded the tombs and the underworld and presided over mummification and embalming. In the Early Dynastic period and the Old Kingdom, he enjoyed a dominant position but was later overshadowed by Osiris. (*syn.* Inpw, Anpu)

Anuket: Goddess of Sehel, the Nile cataract region near Aswan. She is generally represented as a woman holding a papyrus scepter and wearing a tall plumed crown. (*syn.* Anqet, Anukis)

Anuradhapura: Sinhalese kingdom centered at Anuradhapura in Sri Lanka and its capital from the time of the introduction of Buddhism in the 3rd century BC until the site was abandoned in the 10th century AD after many incursions by the Tamils of South India. The South Indians gained control of the kingdom several times—in the 2nd, 5th, and again in the late 10th century AD, after which Anuradhapura was finally abandoned as the Sinhalese capital in favor of Polonnaruva. There was also internal warring by clans trying to establish separate dynastic lines. The most important Anuradhapuran dynasties were the Vijayan (3rd century BC–1st century AD) and the Lamakanna (1st–4th centuries AD and 7th–10th centuries). Buddhist monuments include palaces, monasteries, and stupas, many of which have been conserved and restored. During its 1,000 years of existence, the kingdom of Anuradhapura developed a high degree of culture. Among the most famous monuments are the Thuparama stupa, the Ruvanveli dagaba (an enormous stupa), and the Lohapassada monastery. The kingdom also developed a remarkably complex system of irrigation, considered by many scholars to be its major achievement.

anvil stone: A stone on which other stones or materials (such as food) are placed and crushed with a stone tool.

Anyang: A city in the Honan province of China, which was the last capital of the Shang (Yin) Dynasty, occupied in the 12th and 11th centuries BC. It was founded c. 14 BC and overthrown by the Chou in 1027 BC and was the seat of 12 kings who ruled for 273 years, a time referred to as the historical Anyang period. Anyang is one of the most extensively excavated sites, beginning in 1928. The buildlings had rammed earth floors, and many sacrifices of men and animals and chariot burials were found under them. Deep storage pits held oracle bones with inscriptions in an archaic form of Chinese, but the most important finds came from the cemeteries, which included royal tombs. At least as early as the Song dynasty (960–1279), Anyang was known as a source of bronze ritual vessels. Very large cruciform shaft tombs were found near the village of Houjiazhuang. There were eight large tombs in the western part of the Xibeigang cemetery and five more in the east. Excavation has shown that rows of satellite burials in the eastern section were not laid down at the time of the royal entombments but instead were later sacrifices offered to the tombs' occupants; these burials correspond with the oracle texts descriptions of victims sacrificed, sometimes by the hundreds, to the reigning king's ancestors. The only intact royal tomb yet discovered is that of Fu Hao, which is not in the Xibeigang cemetery but across the river at Xiatoun. Later excavations have established that Anyang was heir to the flourishing civilization of the Erligang Phase. (*syn.* An-yang, Yinxu)

Anyathian: A Pleistocene industry of stone tools in terrace deposits of the upper Irrawaddy River in Burma. The culture was characterized by primitive pebble tools (choppers, choping tools) and poor flakes made of silicified tuff and fossil wood. The earliest assemblages may be of Middle Pleistocene date, and the industry may have continued into the early Holocene. The Early Anyathian had single-edged core implements associated with crude flake implements. In the Late Anyathian, smaller and better made core and flake artifacts are found.

Anza: A large settlement of the First Neolithic and Early Vinca periods of Macedonia near the Bregnalnica River. Excavations have revealed a four-phase occupation c. 5300–4200 BC. There was cultivation of emmer and wheat as well as some herding. The architecture was mud brick walls and wattle-and-daub timber-framed houses. The artifacts are similar to those found in northern Greece and the Anatolian Late Neolithic. (*syn.* Anzabegovo)

Aosta: A Roman colony and stronghold of the Salassi, which lies at the foot of the Italian Alps. The Romans subdued a Celtic tribe in 25 BC, and Augustus founded a Roman town (Augusta Praetoria) there in 24 BC. The remains of the rectangular circuit of walls, gates, forum, theater, amphitheater, and an Augustan triumphal arch are on the site. (*syn.* Augusta Praetoria)

Apadana: Great reception hall found in Persian royal palaces.

Apamea: A city in Hellenistic Phrygia on the Orontes River, partly covered by modern Dinar. Originally a Macedonian colony founded by Antiochus I Soter in the 3rd century BC, it became a Seleucid city superseding Celaenae and commanding the east-west trade route. In the 2nd century BC, Apamea passed to Roman rule and became capital of the Syria Secunda province. It was a great center for Italian and Jewish traders but declined by the 3rd century AD, and trade was diverted to Constantinople. The Turks captured the town in 1070, and it was devastated by an earthquake in 1152. (*syn.* Apameia; Apamea ad Maeandrum)

Apedemak: A lion-headed deity with cult centers at Musawwarat el-Sufra and Naqa in Sudan.

Apennine culture: The Bronze Age culture of the Italian peninsula, lasting from c. 2000–800 BC. The culture's pottery was distinctively dark, highly burnished, and decorated with incised and punctuated bands filled with white inlay. The handles, often single, were elaborate and included crested, horned, and tongue types. The people seemed to depend on pastoral economy and stock breeding in the mountains that give the culture its name. Trade and a more mixed economy is evidenced at some sites—Ariano, Liparis, Luni, Narce, and Taranto—and the culture had some influence from the Balkans. Some inhumation cemeteries are known, but burials are rare. Bronze tools, although in use, are rarely found until very late in the period. (*syn.* Apennine Bronze Age)

Apepi: An evil serpent or snake god, whose name was adopted by at least one Hyksos pharaoh (Apopis I, c. 1585–1542 BC) who ruled a large area of Egypt in the Second Intermediate Period. The deity symbolized the forces of chaos and evil. Apophis is represented on funerary papyri and on the walls of royal tombs in the Valley of the Kings as the eternal enemy of the sun god Ra. (*syn.* Apopis, Apophis)

Aphrodisias: A Pre-Classical and Classical city on the Meander River of southwest Turkey with extant remains of the Roman period, including an agora, odeum, temple of Aphrodite, and baths. There was also an abundance of free-standing statues. The Pre-Classical mounds show Late Neolithic occupation and a sequence of Late Chalcolithic to Late Bronze Age artifacts.

Apis: In ancient Egypt, the sacred bull worshiped at Memphis. Revered at least as early as the 1st Dynasty (c. 2925–2775 BC) and sacred to Osiris, Apis came to prominence during the Greco-Roman period. Apis was probably at first a fertility god concerned with grain and herds. It served as the ba (physical manifestation) of the god Ptah and was also associated with Sokaris. (*syn.* Egyptian Hap, Hep, Hapi)

apodyterium: An apartment or undressing room in the Roman baths.

Apollo 11 Cave: A cave in southern Namibia near the confluence of the Orange and Great Fish Rivers, which has a long sequence of industries dating from the Middle Stone Age. There is a series of detached rock slabs with rock paintings dating between 28,450–26,350 years old, among the oldest dated paintings in the world and the oldest dated rock art of southern Africa. Later horizons in the Apollo 11 Cave show a scraper-based industry in the 13th–8th millennia BC related to the Albany industry of southern Cape Province. Microlithic findings begin in the 8th millennium BC.

appendicular skeleton: The bone of the appendages, that is, arms, legs, tail.

applied archaeology: The use of archaeological methods and techniques to obtain information about contemporary society and to save sites from being destroyed.

appliqué: Decoration or ornament applied to or laid on another material, such as metal on wood or embroidery on cloth.

Apries (589–567 BC): The fourth king of the Saite 26th Dynasty who succeeded his father, Psamtik II (also Psamtek; 595–589 BC) and ruled from 589–570 BC. Apries received many Jewish refugees into Egypt after Judah fought Babylon. He was able to take the Phoenician port of Sidon but lost in his attack on Cyrene in Libya. As a result, the Egyptian army mutinied and selected its general Ahmose as king. Apries was imprisoned but escaped and was later murdered. (*syn.* Egyptian Haaibra Wahibra; Ouaphris; Hebrew Hophra)

apron: The lip or exposed portion of a prehistoric cave or rock shelter, the soil of which typically contains durable cultural materials such as flaked stone and ceramic artifacts.

apse: Semicircular end of a Classical building or Christian church.

Apulia: An area of southeastern Italy, which produced figure-decorated pottery in the 5th–4th centuries BC and was strongly influenced by the Greeks. Apulian pottery was decorated in the red-figured technique, although there was also plain wares. (*syn.* Puglia)

Aq Kupruk: A rock shelter (Aq Kupruk II) and open site (Aq Kupruk III) on the Balkh River in northern Afghanistan. It is one of the richest Palaeolithic sites in that area. Aq Kupruk II had a single Late Palaeolithic deposit with a blade industry (including microliths) with a radiocarbon date of c. 14,600 BC. Aq Kupruk III had two deposits, one with artifacts similar to II and a lower one without microlithics. The presence of domesticated sheep and goats at Aq Kupruk has been dated to 8000 BC and that of cattle to about 6000 BC. Sickle blades, peaked stone hoes, chisels, hand mills, and pounders suggest the collection and preparation of wild grains, if not cultivation.

Aqab, Tell: A prehistoric site of Syria with an unbroken sequence from the Early Halaf to the 'Ubaid period.

Aqar Quf: The settlement site of the Kassite city of Dur-Kurigalzu in northern Babylonia (Iraq) dating c. 1400–1150 BC. There was a ziggurat and temple complex.

'Aqrab, Tell: A tell site on the Diyala River east of Baghdad, Iraq. There was a flourishing city in the 3rd millennium BC, and excavations revealed a temple of the Early Dynastic period. The temple was dedicated to Shara, patron god of the city of Umma.

Aquatic Civilization: This term has been used to describe a widespread series of cultures in the high lake and river areas of the southern Sahara and Sahal between the 8th and 3rd millennia BC (also 10,000–8000 BP). Barbed bone harpoon heads and pottery with parallel wavy lines reveal some similarities between the regions. First investigated at early Khartoum, sites of this type are now known as far to the southeast as the Lake Turkana basin in Kenya. To the west, related material is found as far as Kourounkorokale in Mali. The greatest significance of the "aquatic civilization" lies in the settled lifestyle of its people, for this led to the subsequent adoption of food production. Artifacts include bone harpoons. (*syn.* Aqualithic)

aqueduct: Any channel or artificial conduit constructed to supply water to an area from a source some distance away. The term is most commonly applied to large arched bridges built by the Romans to carry water over valleys and through ravines and used for baths, street cleaning, and public mains. Aqueducts generally entered a city near its gateway and terminated at a distribution junction (castellum) where the public and private supplies would be drawn. There are some remains, such as Pont-du-Gard near Nîmes in France and Segovia in Spain. The longest was 82 miles (132 km) at Carthage. Aqueducts often discharged into reservoirs. (*syn.* (from *aqua*, water, and *duco*, to lead))

Aquileia: A former city founded as a Roman colony in 181 BC, now a village in northeastern Italy near the Adriatic coast northwest of Trieste. Founded to prevent barbarian invasions, Aquileia became a trade and commercial center along the route north and east into the Black Sea area. By the 4th century, it became capital of the regions of Venetia and Istria. The city fell to the Huns and was sacked in 452. It also once served as an episcopal see of the Roman Catholic Church.

Arad: A city in southern Israel west of the Dead Sea, named for Biblical Arad and having ruins visible at Tel 'Arad, just a few miles northeast. First excavated in 1962, Arad had three separate phases of occupation. The first settlement was in the Chalcolithic period with a walled city at the beginning of the 3d millennium BC, which was destroyed by c. 2700 BC. Imported Egyptian pottery was found in that phase. A resettlement occurred in the Early Bronze I and II phases, and a succession of walled citadels and a temple have been found as well as ostraca (inscribed pottery). The last period of occupation was confined to a citadel on the highest part of the earlier town, occupied from the 12th–11th centuries BC. It served as a southern frontier post of the kingdom of Judah. There was a sanctuary for the worship of Yahweh. There were also citadels on this site in the Hellenistic and Roman periods. The Book of Numbers (21:1–3) tells how the Canaanite king of Arad fought the Israelites during the exodus from Egypt, but his cities were "utterly destroyed" by Israel's armies. The city's name appears on the Temple of Amon, al-Karnak, Egypt, in the inscription of Pharaoh Sheshonk I, first ruler of the 22nd Dynasty (reigned c. 945–924 BC).

Aramaean: A branch of the confederacy of Semite tribes who moved from the Syrian desert, conquered the Canaanites, and established themselves in their own city-states in c. 16–12 BC. The foremost of these states was Aram of Damascus, a large region of northern Syria, which was occupied between the 11th–8th centuries BC, and also Bit-Adini, Aram Naharaim, and Sam'al (Sinjerli). In the same period, some of these tribes seized large areas of Mesopotamia. By the 9th century BC, the whole area from Babylon to the Mediterranean coast was occupied by the Aramaean tribes known collectively as Kaldu (also Kashdu), the biblical Chaldeans. Assyria, nearly encircled, attacked the armies of the Aramaeans, and one by one the states collapsed under the domination of Assyria in the succeeding centuries. The destruction of Hamath by Sargon II of Assyria in 720 marked the end of the Aramaean kingdoms of the west. Those Aramaeans along the lower Tigris River remained independent somewhat longer, and in 626 BC, a Chaldean general (Nabopolassar) proclaimed himself king of Babylon and joined with the Medes and Scythians to overthrow Assyria. In the Chaldean Empire, the Chaldeans, Aramaeans, and Babylonians became one group. Their North Semitic language, Aramaic, became the international language of the Near East by the 8th century BC, replacing Akkadian. Aramaic was written in the Phoenician script and was the diplomatic and vernacular speech of the Holy Land during the time of Christ. It was replaced by Arabic after the Arab Conquest, but is still spoken in some remote villages of Syria. In the Old Testament, the Aramaeans are represented as being related to the Hebrews and living in northern Syria around Harran from about the 16th century BC. Few specifically Aramaic objects have been uncovered by archaeologists. (*syn.* (fr Greek Aramaios, "Syria") adj. Aramaic)

Arambourg, Camille (1885–1969): Palaeontologist and professor who carried out excavations and surveys in Africa, especially in Maghreb, Ain Hanech, Ternifine, Omo-Turkana, and Omo Valley. The Omo remains, a group of hominid fossils, the oldest of which are about 3 million years old, were found by Arambourg, Yves Coppens, F. Clark Howell, and others on an expedition in Ethiopia's Omo River region in 1967–1974. These fossil finds represented a breakthrough in the study of early hominids as they were the first discoveries of such early date. The earliest previously uncovered fossils dated to 1,750,000 years. Arambourgh also found *Homo erectus* (Alanthropus) remains at an Acheulian site at Ternifine.

Araouane: A basin site of former lakes in western Mali dating to 8,000–9,000 years ago.

Ara Pacis: A monumental altar in Rome, dedicated in 9 BC, possibly identified with the emperor Augustus.

Arapi: A Neolithic–Early Bronze Age settlement site/mound in Thessaly, Greece. It was first occupied in the Aceramic Neolithic and is characterized by polychrome decorated pottery.

Aratta: A site name, mentioned in a Sumerian epic, supposedly involved in long-distance trade with Mesopotamia during the 3rd millennium BC.

Arauqinoid or Araquinoid: A ceramic series created to compare the cultures of the Venezuela/Antilles area, which flourished in the Middle Orinoco River region from AD c. 500–1500. Soft-textured gray vessels tempered with spicules of freshwater sponge and geometric incised designs on the interior beveled rims of bowls were characteristic. Collared jars with appliquéd human faces and coffee-bean eyes were also common, and pieces of griddles have been found at most sites. The series replaces the Saladoid and Barrancoid in some areas. (*syn.* Arauqin)

Arawak: A number of linguistically associated native groups—the Antillean Arawak or Taino—who inhabited the villages of the Greater Antilles and parts of mainland South America. They were slash-and-burn agriculturists who cultivated cassava and maize. The people were arranged in social ranks and were ruled by chiefs whose religion centered on a hierarchy of nature spirits and ancestors. Pottery of Saladoid type is found from western Venezuela to the West Indies, and in the northern islands there is a ceramic continuity from Saladoid ware to insular Arawak. The Arawak were driven out of the Lesser Antilles by the Carib shortly before the appearance of Columbus and the Spanish, but they still numbered in the millions at that time. Because the Arawakan language is not found to the north or in Mesoamerica, it is likely that these people came to the islands from the south.

arbitrary level: In an excavation, the basic vertical subdivision of an excavation unit, defined metrically, such as in 5-, 10-, or 20-centimeter levels. These levels are prescribed when natural layers of stratification are lacking or not easily recognizable. (*ant.* natural layers)

arbitrary sample unit: A subdivision of data in a defined area of excavation, such as a sample unit that is defined by a site grid, which has no specific cultural relevance. (*ant.* nonarbitrary sample unit)

arboreal: Concerning trees. In pollen analysis, arboreal pollen types are distinguished from shrub pollen and herbaceous pollen.

archaeo-: Of or relating to archaeology; ancient, original, or primitive. (*syn.* (Greek for "ancient" or "beginning"))

archeoastronomy: The study of the relation between prehistoric knowledge of astronomical events through calendars, observatory sites, and astronomical images in art and past cultural behavior. The field includes the study of mathematical correlations between archaeological features and the movements of celestial bodies. Some sites (Stonehenge, New Grange) show a definite interest in simple solar observations. Ancient astronomical knowledge can be inferred through the study of astronomical alignments and other aspects of these archaeological sites. (*syn.* astroarchaeology)

archaeobotany: The study of botanical remains at archaeological sites. The field examines the natural surroundings of flora as well as the human-controlled flora on sites. The terms palaeoethnobotany, palaeoentomology, and palaeobotany are sometimes used interchangeably in the literature of archaeology. (*syn.* palaeoethnobotany, paleoethnobotany, paleoentomology, palaeoentomology)

archaeofauna: Any assemblage of animal remains recovered from a single archaeological context. (*syn.* archeofauna)

archaeography: The systematic description of archaeological objects over time made by nonprofessionals (travelers, traders, diplomats, etc.) who are often in situations where they view sites and antiquities in a much better state of preservation than that in which they are today. These accounts, either in writings or drawings, are valued in archaeological studies. (*syn.* archeography)

archaeological: Of, relating to, or concerning archaeology. (*syn.* archeological)

archaeological chemistry: The application of chemical theories, processes, and experimental procedures to obtaining archaeological data and to solutions of problems in archaeology. This field includes laboratory analysis of artifacts and materials found in archaeological context. (*syn.* archeological chemistry)

archaeological chronology: Establishment of the temporal sequences of human cultures by the application of a variety of dating methods to cultural remains. (*syn.* archeological chronology)

archaeological conservancy: Any private, nonprofit organization working to save archaeological sites from destruction. This is done primarily by purchasing threatened sites and protecting the sites until they can be turned over to responsible agencies such as national parks. (*syn.* archeological conservancy)

archaeological culture: Constantly recurring artifacts or group of assemblages that represent or are typical of a specific ancient culture at a particular time and place. The term describes the maximum grouping of all assemblages that represent the sum of the human activities carried out within a culture.

archaeological data: Material collected and recorded as significant evidence by an archaeologist. Archaeological data fall into four classes: artifacts, ecofacts, features, and structures. (*syn.* archeological data)

archaeological geology: The use of geological techniques and methods in archaeological work. It is different from geoarchaeology in that the latter is a subfield of archaeology focusing on the physical context of deposits.

Archaeological Institute of America: A professional organization whose membership is predominantly specialists in Old World archaeology. The AIA publishes the popular magazine *Archaeology* and the scholarly *American Journal of Archaeology*. (*syn.* AIA)

archaeological method: Any of a variety of means used by archaeologists to find, recover, analyze, preserve, and describe the artifacts and other remains of past human activities. (*syn.* archeological method)

archaeological reconnaissance: A systematic method of attempting to locate, identify, and record the distribution of archaeological sites on the ground by looking at areas' contrasts in geography and environment. (*syn.* archeological reconnaissance)

archaeological record: The surviving physical remains of past human activities, which are sought, recovered, analyzed, preserved, and described by archaeologists in an attempt to reconstruct the past. (*syn.* archeological record)

archaeological sequence: A method of placing a group of similar objects into a chronological sequence, taking into account stylistic changes that occurred over time.

archaeological site: Any concentration of artifacts, ecofacts, features, and structures manufactured or modified by humans. (*syn.* site; archeological site)

archaeological theory: Any theoretical concepts used to assess the framework and meaning of the remains of past human activity. Such a theory is used to guide a reconstructtation of the past by looking beyond the facts and artifacts for explanations of prehistoric events.

archaeological unit: An arbitrary classification unit set up by an archaeologist to separate one grouping of artifacts from another in space and time.

archaeologist: A professional scholar who studies and reconstructs the human past through its physical remains. An archaeologist's work involves the scientific finding, collecting, cleaning, sorting, identifying, and measuring objects found in or on the earth or sea. The motive is to record and interpret ancient cultures rather than to collect and display artifacts for profit.

archaeology: The scientific study and reconstruction of the human past through the systematic recovery of the physical remains of human life and cultures. Artifacts, structures, settlements, materials, and features of prehistoric or ancient peoples are surveyed and/or excavated to uncover history in times before written records. Archaeology also supplements the study of recorded history. From the end of the 18th century onward, archaeology has come to mean the branch of learning that studies the material remains of humans' past. Its scope is, therefore, enormous, ranging from the first stone tools made and fashioned by humans over 3 million years ago in Africa, to the garbage thrown into our trash cans and taken to city dumps and incinerators yesterday. The objectives of archaeology are to construct cultural history by ordering and describing the events of the past, to study cultural process to explain the meaning of those events and what underlies and conditions human behavior, and to reconstruct past lifestyles. Among the specialties in the field are archaeobiology, archaeobotany, archaeozoology, and social archaeology. Modern archaeology, often considered a subdiscipline of anthropology, has become increasingly scientific and relies on a wide variety of experts such as biologists, geologists, physicists, sociologists, anthropologists, and historians. The methods appropriate to different periods vary, leading to specialized branches of the subject, such as classical, medieval, industrial, archaeology (*syn.* archeology (from "archaia," ancient things, and "logos," science, knowledge, or theory))

archaeology of cult: The study of the materials for changes in patterns in response to religious beliefs.

archaeomagnetic dating: A chronometric method used to date objects containing magnetic materials—especially for buried undisturbed features such as pottery kilns, earthen fireplaces, and brick walls—which can be compared to known schedules of past magnetic alignments in a region and fluctuations in the earth's magnetic field. Clay and rocks contain magnetic minerals, and when they are heated above a certain temperature, the magnetism is destroyed. On cooling, the magnetism returns, taking on the direction and strength of the magnetic field in which the object is lying. Therefore, pottery that is baked in effect "fossilizes" the Earth's magnetic field as it was at the moment of the pottery's last cooling (its archaeomagnetism or remanent magnetism). In areas where variations in the Earth's magnetic field are known, it is possible to date a pottery sample on a curve. This method yields an absolute date within about 50 years. (*syn.* archaeomagnetic intensity dating, archaeomagnetism, palaeointensity dating, archaeomagnetic age determination)

archaeometric: Relating or referring to the use of scientific techniques from fields such as chemistry, geology, physics, and other sciences for the analysis of archaeological data. (*syn.* archaeometry, archeometry)

archaeometry: The large field of work that entails the physical and/or chemical analyses (measurement) of archaeological substances, their constituents, ages, residues, and so on. (*syn.* archaeological science)

archaeozoology: The study of animal remains, especially bones, from archaeological contexts, including the identification and analysis of faunal species as an aid to reconstructing human diets, determining the impact of animals on past economies, and understanding the environment at the time of deposition. Animal remains are collected, cleaned, sorted, identified, and measured for their study and interpretation. The study of bones involves calculations of minimum numbers of individuals belonging to each species found; their size, age, sex, stature, dentition; and whether the bones have any marks from implements implying butchering and eating. Archaeologists attempt to answer questions such as how many species of domesticated animals there were, how far wild animals were exploited, and how many very young animals there were to determine kill patterns and climate changes, in what way animals were butchered, what the sex ratios were, what breeding strategies were used, and if there were any animals of unusual size. By analyzing remains from different parts of a site, it may be possible to understand some of the internal organization of the settlement, while a comparison between sites in a region may show areas of specialization. (*syn.* zooarchaeology)

archaic: A term used to describe an early stage in the development of civilization. In New World chronology, the period just before the shift from hunting, gathering, and fishing to agricultural cultivation, pottery development, and village settlement. Initially, the term was used to designate a nonceramic-using, nonagricultural, and nonsedentary way of life. Archaeologists now realize, however, that ceramics, agriculture, and sedentary life are all found, in specific settings, in contexts that are clearly Archaic but that these activities are subsidiary to the collection of wild foods. In Old World chronology, the term is applied to certain early periods in the history of some civilizations. In Greece, it describes the rise of culture from c. 750 BC to the Persian invasion in 480 BC. In Egypt, it covers the first two dynasties, c. 3200–2800 BC. In Classical archaeology, the term is often used to refer to the period of the 8th–6th centuries BC. The term was coined for certain cultures of the eastern North American woodlands dating from c. 8000–1000 BC, but usage has been extended to various unrelated cultures that show a similar level of development but at widely different times. For example, it describes a group of cultures in the Eastern United States and Canada, which developed from the original migration of humans from Asia during the Pleistocene, between 40,000–20,000 BC, whose economy was based on hunting and fishing, shell and plant gathering. Between 8000–1000 BC, a series of technical achievements characterized the tradition, which can be broken into periods: Early Archaic 8000–5000 BC, mixture of Big Game Hunting tradition with early Archaic cultures, also marked by postglacial climatic change in association with the disappearance of Late Pleistocene big game animals; Middle Archaic tradition cultures from 5000–2000 BC; and a Late Archaic period 2000–1000 BC. In the New World, the lifestyle lacked horticulture, domesticated animals, and permanent villages. (*syn.* Archaic, Archaic period, Archaic tradition)

archaic maiolica: A series of jugs and bowls of the early 13th to late 16th centuries in Tuscan Italian towns. They were decorated with geometric motifs, leaves, and other forms outlined in brown and set into green or brown backgrounds. They were sold as far as Spain, North Africa, and northern Europe. There seems to be a connection to earlier Byzantine and Persian products.

archaistic: Imitatively archaic; affectedly and deliberately antique.

Archanes: A Minoan site on Crete with a 16th century BC palatial structure, cemetery complex, and artifacts of gold, ivory, and marble. (*syn.* Arkhanes)

Archéodrome de Beaune: A museum of reconstructed buildings and experimental archaeology founded in 1978 in Côte d'Or, France. There is a Palaeolithic encampment, a Neolithic house, and Roman siege works.

archetype: An abstract classification that assumes an "ideal" form or structure of all morphological beings, of which the various species are considered as modifications.

architrave: In Greek and Roman architecture, that part of an entablature that rests immediately on the abacus on the capital of a column or pilaster. It is also the term used for the horizontal beam between columns, or between a column and a wall, which supports a ceiling. A third definition is a collective name for the various parts that surround a doorway, arch, or window (jambs, lintel, moldings). (*syn.* epistyle)

Arctic Small Tool tradition: The first coastal dwellers of the true Arctic regions who appeared before 2200 BC and who had a hunting tradition and a distinctive set of stone tools, weapon tips, and adzes of small size (hence the name). Their sites stretched from the Bering Sea across the north Canadian coast as far east as northernmost Greenland, although there is no evidence of sleds or boats. Within a century or two of 2000 BC, they also expanded southward in Alaska to the Alaska Peninsula and south along the northeastern American coast to the Gulf of St. Lawrence. The Denbigh Flint Complex (or Arctic Denbigh culture, named for the type site Cape Denbigh, Alaska) is the characteristic tool assemblage. It included small chipped stone artifacts derived from Neolithic eastern Siberia—such as blades, microblades, burins, scrapers, large bifacial projectile points. There was no pottery, and the economics were balanced between products of the land (caribou, lake and river fish, musk ox) and sea mammals. Approximate dates range from 4000–1000 BC, and this tradition is thought to be associated with ancestral Eskimo. In Canada and Greenland, the Small Tool people gradually developed into the Dorset culture. In Alaska, the Small Tool people disappeared and were replaced by 400 BC by people of the Norton culture who used Siberian-type pottery.

arcosolium: A type of tomb in Roman catacombs as well as pagan and Christian burial places, consisting of an arched cell or niche, with a semicircular vaulted ceiling.

Arcy-sur-Cure: A series of caves southeast of Paris with Upper Palaeolithic art, of which the Grotte du Cheval, Grotte del Hyene, and Grotte du Renne are archaeologically the most important. The early occupation levels are of the Riss period with Mousterian (Neanderthal remains), Chatel-Perronian, Aurignacian, later Perigordian levels.

ard: An ancient light plow with a simple blade that was used to scratch the surface of the soil rather than to turn furrows. It was drawn by animals or man and grooved the ground, but it had no mold board or colter and therefore did not turn over the soil. With this type of plow, cross-plowing was usually necessary, with a second plowing at right angles to the first.

Ardagh Chalice: A large, two-handled silver cup decorated with gold, gilt bronze, and enamel, one of the finest examples of early Christian art from the British Isles. Discovered in 1868 along with a small bronze cup and four brooches in a potato field in Ardagh, Ireland, the chalice may have been part of the buried loot from a monastery after an Irish or Viking raid. The outside of the bowl is engraved with the Latin names of some of the Apostles. There are similarities between the letters of the inscription and some of the large intiials in the Lindisfarne Gospels, which probably dates from about AD 710–720. Thus, the Ardagh Chalice is thought to date from the first half of the 8th century. The chalice displays exceptional artistic and technical skills applied to a variety of precious materials. So far, its manufacture has not been attributed to a particular workshop, but the chalice does have similarities to the celebrated Tara brooch and the Moylough belt-reliquary. It is now housed in the National Museum of Ireland at Dublin.

area excavation: A method of excavation in which the full horizontal extent of a site is cleared and large areas are opened while preserving a stratigraphic record in the balks between large squares. A gradual vertical probe may then take place. This method is often used to uncover houses and prehistoric settlement patterns. Area excavation, which involves the opening up of large horizontal areas, is used especially where single-period deposits lie close to the surface. It is the excavation of as large an area as possible without the intervention of balks and a grid system. This technique allows the recognition of much slighter traces of ancient structures than do other methods. On multiperiod sites, however, it calls for much more meticulous recording because the stratigraphy is revealed one layer at a time. (*syn.* extensive excavation, open excavation, open-area excavation)

arena: The central area of an amphitheater, usually strewn with sand, where the spectacles and combats took place. The surface was coated with sand to absorb the blood of the wounded or slain, and also to give a uniformity to the floor and to conceal trapdoors and other devices. The term is also used, by extension, for a whole amphitheater. (*syn.* (from Latin "sand"))

Arenal: A Preceramic site and culture dating between 6500–6000 BC on the central coast of Peru, south of Lima. The culture was characterized by large diamond-shaped chipped points, which indicated a hunting lifestyle.

Arene Candide: A cave site at Finale Ligure on the Italian Riviera whose excavation revealed a stratigraphy extending from the Upper Palaeolithic through Epi-Palaeolithic, to Early, Middle, and Late Neolithic, as well as poor levels from the Bronze and Iron Ages up to the Roman period. There were some rich burials in the first, second, and fourth levels. The 1940s excavations by Bernabò Brea helped him make important interpretations of the Neolithic period in the Mediterranean.

Arezzo vases: Red-clay Arretine pottery of which many fine examples have been found in or near the town of Arezzo in Tuscany, an important Etruscan city. The red-lustered ware was ornamented in relief and shows evidence of Greek origin.

Argar, El: An Early Bronze Age settlement near Almeria in southeast Spain, which is the type site of a culture of the 2nd millennium BC. The settlement was fortified and contained rectangular stone houses, although little has been recovered as the site is not as well preserved as the Argaric sites Ifre and El Oficio. The settlement also contained 950 interments, with the earliest in cists and the later ones jar burials. Grave goods in the cist burial phase included daggers, halberds, and wrist guards. In the jar burials, there were faience, swords and axes of copper or bronze, and gold and silver ornaments. Silver was more common in this area than anywhere else in Europe at the time. The pottery of this culture was plain burnished, with simple shapes. The Agaric culture, which developed trading with eastern Mediterranean centers, reached its peak between 1700–1000 BC and spread through the central, southern, and Levantine regions and to the Balearic Islands. The area may owe its origin to immigration from western Greece.

argillite: A compact metamorphic rock formed from silt stone, shale, or clay stone and intermediate in structure between shale and slate. It is cemented by silica but has no slaty cleavage.

Argissa: An important Neolithic site in Thessaly, northern Greece, which has given much information on the early phases of the Greek Aceramic Neolithic period. In the Argissa Magula near Larissa, there have been early Prepottery Neolithic finds of probably the 6th millennium BC. Timber-framed huts consisted of shallow mud-walled pits that were likely roofed with branches. Obsidian was already being traded, and flint tools were made. The earliest known domesticated cattle date from about 6000 BC at Argissa (and Nea Nikomedeia) in Greece, in association with cultivated einkorn, emmer wheat, barley, millet, and lentils. Sheep, goats, and pigs were also kept. The site was occupied throughout the Neolithic and well into the Bronze Age.

Argos: City in the northeastern Peloponnese of Greece, just north of the head of the Gulf of Argolis. The name was applied to several districts of ancient Greece, but it is most often used to describe the easternmost part of the Peloponnesian peninsula, and the city of Argos was its capital. Homer described it as the fertile plain inhabited by Agamemnon, Diomedes, and other heroes in the *Iliad*. The site was probably occupied since the Neolithic/Early Bronze Age and was very prominent in Mycenaean times (c. 1300–1200 BC). Argos was probably the base of Dorian operations in the Peloponnese c. 1100–1000 BC and from then on was the dominant city-state of Argolis until it allied itself with Sparta after the Peloponnesian War in 420 BC. In 392, it broke with Sparta to unite with Corinth in the Corinthian War. Argos later joined the Achaean League (229), and Argos became its center after the Roman conquest and destruction of Corinth (146). The city flourished in Byzantine times and did not decline until around AD 1204. One tyrant, Pheidon, is thought to have introduced primitive coinage and a weights and measures system. Archaeological excavations began in 1854 on the Argive Heraeum, and Argos was famed for its connection with the goddess Hera. There was a natural sanctuary there long before the Dorians came c. 1100–1000 BC. The shrine is reported to be of extreme antiquity. The statue of Hera for a new 5th-century temple was done by the celebrated sculptor, Polycleitus, whose work was said to rival that of Pheidias, the sculptor of the Parthenon. There is material evidence of Neolithic and Early and Middle Bronze Age, a Mycenaean cemetery with chamber tombs, Geometric and Archaic features, and ruins of the Classical and Roman city. The Larisa hill was evidently the Mycenaean acropolis and citadel, holding a classical temple. There was also a Roman theater and small odeum. The site is mostly covered by the modern city. (*syn.* Árgos (meaning "agricultural plain"))

Arica: A site in the Tarapacá region on the north coast of Chile at the foot of El Morro. Preceramic shell mounds were excavated at Quiani, Pichalo, and Taltal, which were dated between AD 1200–1450. The city of Arica was founded as San Marcos de Arica in 1570 on the site of a pre-Columbian settlement; it belonged to Peru until 1879, when it was captured by Chile. Arica is near the Peru border and is the northernmost Chilean seaport.

Arikamedu: A site on the Madras coast of southern India near Pondicherry, excavated by Mortimer Wheeler. It was an important trading post of the Romans after the mid-1st century BC, although black-and-red ware found there began well before the period of Roman contact. A town with warehouses in an industrial quarter was built. Black-and-red Iron Age wares associated with Arrentine ware of the 1st century AD, Mediterranean amphorae, and imperial Roman coins were found by Wheeler. Other excavations have found Roman pottery, beads, intaglios, lamps, and glass, which indicate continuous occupation. Graffiti on pottery indicate the presence of Indian traders.

Ariusd: A Late Neolithic settlement (c. 3000 BC) found on a site in Romania's Upper Olt Valley. The regional painted ware is a variant of the Cucuteni–Tripolye culture. At the site, there are at least seven occupation horizons, some with gold jewelry and copper artifacts. The seventh level was a Late Copper Age assemblage of the Schneckenberg type. (*syn.* Erosd)

Arka: An Upper Palaeolithic cave site in northeast Hungary dating to 18,600–17,000 bp. The artifacts include end scrapers, burins, and retouched blades of the Gravettian, and there are some faunal remains.

Arkin: A Stone Age site near Wadi Halfa in the Nubian Nile Valley. There are factory sites for roughouts of foliate points of the Later Mousterian tradition, which are probably con-

temporary with factories at nearby Khor Musa. The artifacts show affinities with Saharan Aterian artifacts.

Arles: A city in southern France on the left bank of the Rhône, once a colony founded by Caesar (46 BC) and with an amphitheater and cryptoporticus dating from 1st century BC. Very little is known of the Celto-Greek settlement, traditionally colonized by the Phocaeans. Marius constructed the Fossae Marianae, a naval canal linking Arles with the sea, in 104 BC. Arles from then on was a service port and naval shipyard. Caesar used it as his naval base in 49 BC when attacking Marseilles (Massilia). Two aqueducts were built to bring water from the Alpilles. Constantine the Great (AD 306–337) adopted the city as one of his capitals. It was a mint in late Roman times, and an imperial Roman theater and the largest amphitheater north of the Alps were located there. In the 1st century AD, St. Trophime founded the bishopric, which remained until 1790. (*syn.* Latin Arelate)

Arlit: A Tenerian site to the west of the Air Mountains of Niger, dated to c. 5500 BP.

Armant: A site in Upper Egypt on the west bank of the Nile, southwest of Luxor, which was the original capital of the Theban nome until the 11th Dynasty. Excavations have revealed extensive cemeteries and areas of Predynastic settlement. Thutmose's annals on the walls of the temple of Karnak describing 20 years of military activity in Asia are supplemented by stelae from Armant. (*syn.* ancient Iunu-Montu, Hermonthis)

armor: Protective clothing with the ability to deflect or absorb arrows, bullets, lances, swords, or other weapons during combat. There are three main types: (1) armor made of leather, fabric, or mixed materials reinforced by quilting or felt; (2) mail, of interwoven rings or iron or steel; and (3) rigid armor of metal, plastic, horn, wood, or other tough material, including plate armor of the Middle Ages. Armor was used by primitive warriors well before historical records were kept. The first armor was likely made of leather hides and included helmets. In the 11th century BC, Chinese warriors wore five to seven layers of rhinoceros skin. Greek heavy infantry wore thick, multilayered linen cuirasses in the 5th century BC. Armor is found along with arrows, clubs, hammers, hatchets, and other weaponry and is often ornamented. Roman defensive armor, the shield, and thorax, were called hopla, and people wearing them were called hoplites. (*syn.* arms, armour, body armor)

Arnhem Land: A region of the Northern Territory of Australia with a complete sequence dating back more than 50,000 years. There is rock art of the Pleistocene and even earlier paintings of land animals and Mimi figures.

aroids: The edible tubers of the Aracae family, important in prehistoric Oceanic, South Asian, and Southeast Asian subsistence. The species is grown in irrigated terraces or fields or cultivated in pits cut to groundwater. Aroids were cultivated by at least 3000 BC and spread from India to Egypt and Africa by the late 1st millennium BC.

Arpachiyah: A tell site in Iraq near Mosul on the Tigris inhabited in the Halaf and Ubaid periods (mid-6th to early 4th millennia BC). The Halaf settlements yielded a long pottery sequence and circular buildings with some rectangular antechambers, on cobbled streets. The function of these buildings is unknown. The site appears to have been a specialized artisan village making fine polychrome pottery. In addition to the painted polychrome wares, other finds include steatite pendants and small stone discs with incised designs, probably early stamp seals. There was pottery of northern Ubaid style and fine Halaf pottery, and stone amulets and figurines. (*syn.* Arpachiyah, Tell)

Arras: The site of an Iron Age cemetery in Yorkshire, England, with at least 90 burials, some barrows covering the burials and some with chariots. There are several related sites (Danes' Graves) in east Yorkshire with similar grave goods, which define the Arras culture along with the burials. Material dates the Arras culture to c. 5–1 BC, and the Arras people seem to have been intruders from the continent. Their artifacts suggest links with the migrations of the Parisii from eastern France and the Rhineland. The chariot gear includes a distinctive three-link horse bit. (*syn.* Aras)

Arretine Ware: A type of bright-red, polished pottery originally made at Arretium (modern Arezzo) in Tuscany from the 1st century BC to the 3rd century AD. The term refers to ware made of clay impressed with designs. The ware was produced to be traded, especially throughout the Roman Empire. It is clearly based on metal prototypes, and the body of the ware was generally cast in a mold. Relief designs were also impressed with stamps in the desired patterns and then applied to the vessels. The quality of the pottery was high, considering its mass production. However, there was a gradually increasing roughness in the forms and decoration over the four centuries of production. After the decline of Arretium production, terra sigillata was made in Gaul from the 1st century AD at La Graufesenque (now Millau) and later at other centers in Gaul. Examples have come from Belgic tombs in pre-Roman Britain and from the port of Arikamedu in southern India. The style changes and the potters' marks stamped on the vessels made these wares a valuable means of dating the other archaeological material found with them. (*syn.* terra sigillata ware; Samian ware)

Arretium: An Etruscan and Roman city, and capital of Arezzo province, in Tuscany, southeast of Florence. Known in antiquity for the fine workmanship of its city walls and its red-clay Arretine pottery, the site flourished as a commune in the Middle Ages before falling to Florence in 1384 and later

becoming part of the grand duchy of Tuscany. Remains of the city walls, closely constructed of stone and lightly fired brick, have been found. The quantity of bronze and the mass production of the pottery indicate a considerable degree of industrialization. Arretine ware, a glossy red tableware both plain and relief decorated, originated at Arretium in the 1st century BC. (*syn.* modern Arezzo)

arris: The sharp ridge or edge formed by the junction of two smooth surfaces, especially on the midrib of a dagger or sword, or in moldings. (*syn.* plural arris, arrises)

arrowhead: A small object of bone, metal, or stone, formed as the pointed end of an arrow for penetration and often found at sites of prehistoric peoples. The earliest known are Solutrean points of the Upper Palaeolithic. Arrowheads are often the only evidence of archery because the arrow shaft and bow rarely survive. The term *projectile point* is generally preferable because it avoids an inference about the method of hafting and propulsion. Most often, arrowheads were placed in a slot in the shaft, tied, then fixed with resin. (*syn.* projectile point, arrow-head)

arrow straightener: A stone with a regular, straight groove on one face. It is thought to have been used to smooth wooden shafts of arrows, so the name is misleading.

arroyo: A dry gully or steep-sided bed of a seasonal stream. The term is also used for a rivulet or stream.

arsenic: A semimetallic substance of steel-gray color, which forms a link between the metals and nonmetallic materials. It is found together with copper in some ore deposits, appearing as arsenical copper (copper alloyed with arsenic). This substance was valued and deliberately produced to improve casting properties and hardness, but was not important after the development of tin bronze (tin alloyed with copper). It gave a very hard cutting edge to tools and weapons.

arsenical bronze: Bronze (copper and tin alloy), which contains arsenic as a third constituent in a small proportion of 2–3%. Arsenic was deliberately added for its hardening effect on the alloy.

arsenical copper: Copper is alloyed with arsenic. This substance was easier to cast than copper alone and was stronger and harder. It was widely used before the introduction of tin bronze (tin alloyed with copper). (*syn.* arsenical bronze)

Arslan Tash: The site of the ancient city of Hadâtu, a provincial capital of the Assyrian kings in northern Syria, first excavated by the French in 1928. There was a central tell surrounded by a circular wall and a palace and temple containing fine ivories, dating from the beginning of the 8th century BC.

Arslantepe: A Chalcolithic to Roman site in eastern Anatolia with monuments of the Syro-Hittites (early 1st millennium BC) and earlier settlements of the Late Uruk period (mid-4th millennium BC).

Artenac: A cave site in Charente, France, which is the type site of the Artenacien culture. Artifacts include copper beads, flint daggers, and fine pottery with beaked handles. There are simple megalithic tombs and burial caves, dating to c. 3000–2000 BC.

Arthur (c. 5th century AD): The legendary British king who is described in medieval romances as the leader of a knightly fellowship called the Round Table. It is said that he rallied the British against the Anglo-Saxon invaders; behind the legend there may be a sub-Roman warleader who filled such a role. Although his name does not survive in contemporary records, he may have led the British at the battle or siege of Mount Badon, which stopped the Saxon advance AD c. 490 for some 50 years hence. All the historical references to him in the chronicles of Bede, Gildas, Nenius, Geoffrey of Monmouth, and others were written between 100 and 600 years after the event, so they are considered unreliable for archaeologists. The search probably started with the monks of Glastonbury, who in 1191 claimed to have found the burial of King Arthur and Queen Guinevere inscribed with the words, "Here lies Arthur in the Isle of Avalon buried." Various locations as far apart as Cornwall and Scotland are claimed as the site of Mount Badon; the refortified Iron Age hillfort of Badbury Rings in Dorset seems the most credible possibility. The site of Arthur's court at Camelot may be the historical site of South Cadbury. Excavations carried out at South Cadbury revealed an important fortified settlement of the 5th and 6th centuries, which could have been the center from which British resistance to the Saxons was organized.

articular surface: The portion of a bone connecting with other bones.

articulated: A term indicated that the bones of a skeleton are in the same relative position to one another as they were when the person or creature was alive. If a skeleton is articulated, it is assumed that it was put into its final resting place while there were still ligaments and flesh to hold it together. (*syn.* noun articulation)

artifact: Any object (article, building, container, device, dwelling, ornament, pottery, tool, weapon, work of art) made, affected, used, or modified in some way by human beings. It may range from a coarse stone or a needle to a pyramid or a highly technical accomplishment—and these objects are used to characterize or identify a people, culture, or stage of development. The most common artifacts are pieces of broken pottery, stone chips, projectile points, and tools. The environment may play a part in the nature of an artifact if it has been seriously altered by people through fire, house and road construction, agricultural practices, and so on. Therefore, the line is sometimes hard to draw between a natural object and one used by people, but there is no doubt when it can be shown that people shaped it in any way, even if only accidentally in the course of use. Artifacts are individually assignable to ceramic, lithic, metal, organic, or other lesser-used categories. A sociotechnic artifact is a tool that is used primarily in the social realm. A technomic artifact is a tool that is used primarily to deal with the physical environment. (*syn.* artefact)

artifact type: A description of a category of artifacts that share a set of somewhat variable attributes, such as spoons or tables. An artifact type occurs together in the majority of cases. (*syn.* artefact type)

Arundel marbles: A collection of marbles and ancient statues taken from Greece and Asia Minor at the expense of Thomas Howard, Earl of Arundel (1585–1646) and given to Oxford University in 1667, which came to be known as the Arundel (or Oxford) marbles. (*syn.* Oxford marbles)

Aryan: A people of the Rigveda who invaded Iran and India from the northwest in the 2nd millennium BC and who then spread east and south over the succeeding centuries. Their language was an early form of Sanskrit, an Indo-European tongue. By c. 500 BC, Aryan speech was probably established over much of the area in which Indo-Aryan languages are now spoken (the Indian subcontinent). Archaeologists have not found much to attribute to the Aryans except for some Painted Gray Ware. It is theorized that the Aryans may have been responsible for, or contributed to, the downfall of the Indus (Harappan) civilization. (*syn.* Arya; Aryans)

aryballos: There are two uses for this term—one for a small Greek vase, one for a large Inca pottery jar. The Greek flask was one handled, normally globular (quasispherical or pear-shaped), with a narrowing neck. It was used mostly for oil, perfume, unguent, or condiments and stood about 2–3 inches (5–8 cm) high. Aryballoi were originally made at Corinth from about 575 BC. There were painted patterns on them until 550 BC, and sometimes patterns were engraved. The Inca version was a large jar with conical base, tall narrow neck, and flaring rim. It was used for carrying liquids, designed to be carried on the back by a rope passed through two strap handles low on the jar's body and over a nubbin at the base of the jar neck. (*syn.* aryballus; from Greek "bag, purse")

arystichos: A Greek or Roman vessel for drawing water, especially from amphorae. (*syn.* ephebos, aruter, arusane, arustis, oinerusis)

Asana: A seasonal Preceramic site in the Andes of southern Peru dating to 7800 BC, with possibly the earliest domestic structures in the Andean region. A ceremonial complex dating to 2660 BC with altars, clay-lined fire basins, and surface hearths has also been found.

Ascalon: A Philistine city on the southern coast of Palestine, southwest of Jerusalem. Excavations have uncovered remains of the Roman period, with some small areas of Philistine levels. Egyptian texts describe Ascalon as one of the cities that revolted against Rameses II. During the Roman period, Ascalon was the birthplace of Herod the Great. It flourished during that time and was occupied in the Byzantine and Arab periods. (*syn.* Askalon, Askelon)

ascribed status/leadership: An individual's social standing or leadership, which was inherited or assigned from his or her parents or other relatives, by sex, or some other fixed criterion.

ash: Volcanic material of less than 4 millimeters in diameter, which falls quickly and can bury sites, preserving the stratigraphy, people, and artifacts. Ash is also the soft, solid remains of burned organic material as from cremation.

Ashdod: A Palestinian site of a Canaanite city of the Late Bronze Age, probably destroyed by the Sea Peoples. It was one of the cities of the Philistine Pentapolis.

Ashkelon: A city of the Philistines on the coast of Palestine near Gaza. Under Roman levels are Philistine deposits, and there is a destruction level, the work of the Peoples of the Sea c. 1200 BC, separating these levels from the underlying Late Bronze Age of the Canaanites.

ashlar construction: The construction of square blocks of hewn stone laid in regular courses for the facings of walls. It was dressed for building good, smooth-surfaced walls. (*syn.* achelor, astler, estlar)

ash mound: A site type found in India where the remains of Neolithic cattle pens of the 3rd millennium BC created by regular fires burning palisades enclosing cattle.

Ashoka (d. 238 BC?): The last major emperor of the Mauryan empire of India in the 3rd century BC. He started out as a bloody tyrant, but underwent a spiritual crisis and became a Buddhist, furthering the expansion of that religion throughout India. His reign was c. 265–238 BC but has also been given as c. 273–232 BC. His kingdom included most of modern Pakistan and India, except the extreme south. Many monuments survive from his period: stupas, rock-cut temples, and commemorative pillars. A series of inscriptions, enshrining Buddhist teaching, survives on rock faces and stone pillars in various parts of the empire. (*syn.* also Asoka, Asokan)

ash tuff: Rock formed from solidified volcanic ash, which often is re-formed after the eruption and deposited elsewhere by water runoff. It is an excellent stratigraphic indicator and, because of the presence of very small crystals, is used to obtain potassium–argon dates. (*syn.* tuffa)

Ashurbanipal (fl. 7th century BC): The last of the great kings of Assyria (668–627 BC), who established the first systematically organized library in the ancient Middle East, a huge collection of Assyrian clay tablets in his palace and that of his grandfather, Sennacherib. The library has been extremely valuable in revealing the art, science, and religion of ancient Mesopotamia. Approximately 20,720 tablets and fragments have been preserved in the British Museum. This collection was assembled by royal command, whereby scribes searched for and collected or copied texts of every genre from temple libraries. Theses were added to a core collection of tablets from Ashur, Calah, and Nineveh itself. The major group includes omen texts based on observations of events; on the behavior and features of men, animals, and plants; and on the motions of the Sun, Moon, planets, and stars. There were dictionaries of Sumerian, Akkadian, and other words, all important to the scribal educational system. Ashurbanipal also collected many incantations, prayers, rituals, fables, proverbs, and other "canonical" and "extra-canonical" texts. The traditional Mesopotamian epics—such as the stories of Creation, Gilgamesh, Irra, Etana, and Anzu—have survived mainly owing to their preservation in Ashurbanipal's library. Handbooks, scientific texts, and some folktales show that this library, of which only a fraction of the clay tablets has survived, was more than a mere reference library. Assurbanipal's many brilliant military campaigns served only to hold what had been already won by previous kings, although Egypt regained its independence and Elam was only retained by complete devastation. (*syn.* Assurbanipal, Asurbanipal, Assurnasirpal)

Ashurnasirpal II (fl. 8th century BC): King of Assyria 883–859 BC, who consolidated the conquests of his father, Tukulti-Ninurta II, and commanded the last period of Assyrian power before the establishment of the New Assyrian Empire. His military expeditions took him as far as the Mediterranean, and, according to his own testimony, he was a brilliant general and adminsitrator. He set the standards of military achievement and brutality, which made the Assyrians feared throughout the Near and Middle East. The details of his reign are known almost entirely from his own inscriptions and the reliefs in the ruins of his palace at Calah (now Nimrud, Iraq). He refounded Calah as a military capital beside Assur and Nineveh. By 879 BC, the main palace in the citadel, the temples of Ninurta and Enlil, shrines for other deities, and the city wall had been completed. Botanic gardens and a zoological garden were laid out, and water supplied by a canal from the Great Zab River. His son and successor, Shalmaneser III (858–824 BC) expanded the empire. (*syn.* Assurnasirpal II)

Asia: A Late Preceramic site on the south-central coast of Peru with a series of mounds and burials with evidence of trephination.

Asiab, Tepe: A semipermanent settlement in the Zagros region of western Iran, dated between 7100–6750 BC, belonging to the Karim Shahir culture. There is evidence of tool manufacture, settlement patterns, and subsistence methods, including the crude beginnings of the domestication of both plants and animals in this site as well as nearby sites at Guran, Ganj-e Dareh, and Ali Kosh. Burials have been excavated, covered in red ochre.

Asikli Hüyük: An Aceramic Neolithic site in central Anatolia, near an obsidian source (Ciftlik) and probably involved in extracting and trading the material. Radiocarbon dates of unstratified contexts at the site are c. 7000–6650 BC. It may have been contemporary with Hacilar.

Asine: A pre-Classical Greek settlement and port on the east side of the Akritas in the Argolid Gulf. It was originally settled by the Argives after the First Messenian War (c. 735–715 BC). There is evidence of Early, Middle, and Late Helladic settlement and of Hellenistic city walls remains. It was reoccupied during the Middle Ages by refugees from the north who gave it the name of their former village. (*syn.* modern Koróni)

askos: An assymetric vessel, often squat and duck shaped, with an off-center mouth, convex top, and single arching handle. It was originally shaped like a leather bottle (*uter*) for holding water, oil, or wine. Some example have two mouths, one for filling and one for emptying, and others are quite unbalanced and have strange mouths. It later assumed the form of an earthenware pitcher. Askoi were popular in the Aegean from the Early Helladic to the Classical period. (*syn.* Greek "bag")

Asmar, Tell: The ancient city of Eshnunna on the Diyala River of Iraq, inhabited from the Uruk to the Old Babylonian period. Excavations here have provided the archaeological definition of the Early Dynastic and Akkadian periods. In the early 2nd millennium BC, Tell Asmar was the center of the kingdom of Eshnunna. (*syn.* Eshnunna)

aspartic acid racemization: A method for determining the absolute age of bone tissue by discovering the process of cumulative change in the form of amino acids, beginning at the death of an organism.

aspect: A characteristic or component that constitutes one of the traits of a culture or community. The term also describes a group of components that display a great many of the specific elements (traits) of a culture.

Aspero: A Late Preceramic site on the north-central coast of Peru, dating to 4360–3950 BP. It is one of the largest Pre-ceramic settlements known in the Andes, and it had a complex social hierarchy. Six platform mounds and other structures include rooms with artifacts, textiles, plant material, clay figurines, and feathers.

Asprochaliko: A large Palaeolithic rock shelter near Ioánnina, in Epirus, northwest Greece. There are Mousterian phases, an earlier one with carefully retouched tools and use of the Levallois technique, and a later phase with small tools. The Upper Palaeolithic levels of backed blades include one radiocarbon dated to c. 26,000 BC (24,000 ± 1000 BC). In the final stage (11,700 ± 260 BC), geometric microliths and microburins appeared alongside the backed blades. Occupation ended around 9000 BC. (*syn.* Asprochalico)

ass: The wild ass was distributed widely in North Africa and Asia. In Asia, it was domesticated as a draft animal c. 3000 BC. The modern donkey derives from an animal of Ethiopia and the Sudan, which the Egyptians imported from the 2nd millennium on. The earliest evidence for the African ass is an Egyptian tomb relief of 1650 BC. Remaining populations can be found in Iran (called the onager), northwest India (called the ghorkar), and Mongolia (called the kiang). Asiatic wild asses as a group may also be called onagers, kemiones, or half-asses. Artistic representation of the domestication of asses has been found, but little osteological evidence. The ass arrived in Europe during medieval times. The domestic ass, or donkey, may be hybridized with the horse: A male ass crossed with a female horse produces a mule, and a female ass crossed with a male horse produces a hinny, and both hybrids are sterile.

assemblage: A group of objects of different or similar types found in close association with one another and thus considered to be the product of one people from one time. Where the assemblage is frequently repeated and covers a reasonably full range of human activity, it is described as a culture; where it is repeated but limited in content, for instance, flint tools only (a set of objects in one medium), it is called an industry. When a group of industries is found together in a single archaeological context, it is called an assemblage. Such a group characterizes a certain culture, era, site, or phase, and it is the sum of all subassemblages. Assemblage examples are artifacts from a site or feature.

assessment: An aspect of cultural resource management in which the surface of a project area is systematically covered by pedestrian survey to locate, document, and evaluate archaeological materials therein. (*syn.* archaeological assessment)

association: The co-occurrence of two or more objects sharing the same general location and stratigraphic level and thought to have been deposited at approximately the same time (being in or on the same matrix). Objects are said to be in association with each other when they are found together in a context that suggests simultaneous deposition. Associations between objects are the basis for relative dating or chronology and the concept of cross-dating as well as interpretation—cultural connections, original function. Pottery and flint tools associated in a closed context would be grounds for linking them into an assemblage, possibly making the full material culture of a group available. The association of undated objects with artifacts of known date allows the one to be dated by the other. When two or more objects are found together and it can be proved that they were deposited together, they are said to be in genuine or closed association. Examples of closed associations are those in a single interment grave, the material in a destruction level, or a hoard. An open association is one in which this can only be assumed, not proved. Artifacts may be found next to each other and still not be associated; one of the artifacts may be intrusive. (*syn.* associated)

Assur: A solar deity who was the chief god of the city of Assur and the kingdom of Assyria. With the latter's conquests, Assur assumed leadership of the Assyrian pantheon and supremacy over the other gods of Mesopotamia. The deity was conceived in anthropomorphic terms. The image of the deity was fed and clothed and was responsible for fertility and security, and represented as a winged sun disc. Assur is also the name of the ancient religious capital of the Assyrian empire in northern Mesopotamia, on the bank of the River Tigris at modern Qalaat-Shergat, which was a great trading center and the burial place of the kings even after the government moved to Nineveh. First recorded in the 3rd millennium BC as a frontier post of the empire of Akkad, it then became an independent city-state and finally the capital of Assyria. After Assyria's collapse in 614 BC, it failed to survive but was briefly revived under the Parthians. Areas of the palaces, temples, walls, and town have been cleared, and a sondage pit was cut beneath the Temple of Ishtar (pre-Sargonid) to reveal the 3rd- and early 2nd-millennium levels (the first use of this technique in Mesopotamian excavation). Sumerian statues were found—among the earliest evidence of Sumerian contact outside the southern plain. For over 2,000 years, successive kings built and rebuilt the fortifications, temple, and palace complexes: Inscriptions associated with these monuments have helped in the construction of the chronology of the site. Three large ziggurats dominated the city with the largest being 60 meters square (completed by Shamsi Adad I c. 1800 BC). It was originally dedicated to Enlil, but later to Assur; the dedication of the other temples also changed through time. Representations on cylinder seals suggest that many buildings might have had parapets and towers. Assurnasirpal II (883–859 BC) moved the capital to Calah, and by 614 BC the city of Assur had fallen to the Median army. (*syn.* Ashur)

Assyria: The name of three different empires dating from about 2000–600 BC, the city-state of Assur, and the people inhabiting this northeastern area of Mesopotamia. Originally Semitic seminomads in northern Mesopotamia, the Assyrians finally settled around Assur and accepted its tutelary god as their own. After the fall of the 3rd Dynasty of Ur (2004 BC), Assyria seems to have become an independent city-state and important as middleman in international trade. In its period of greatness, 883–612 BC, there was continuous war in Assyria to keep the empire's lands, which at their widest extended from the Nile to near the Caspian, and from Cilicia to the Persian Gulf (part of Egypt, much of the area to the west as far as the Mediterranean, Elam to the east, and parts of Anatolia to the north). Its greatest kings were all warriors, Ashurnasirpal II, Shalmaneser III, Tiglathpileser III, Sargon II, Sennacherib, and Ashurbanipal, who made the name of Assyria feared throughout the ancient world through their military skill and brutality. The main achievements in Assyria, outside warfare, were in architecture and sculpture, particularly the protective winged creatures that guarded all palace entrances, and the magnificent reliefs of battles, hunts, and military processions that adorned the walls. Assurnasirpal II (883–859 BC) transferred the center of government to Calah (Nimrud). The fortunes of the empire rose and fell under the kings of the 9th–7th centuries: Assurbanipal (668–627 BC) reconquered Egypt, but in 614 BC the empire fell when the Medes invaded Assyria, captured Calah, and destroyed Assur. (*syn.* Assyrians)

Assyrian: One of the two main dialects of ancient Mesopotamia, used in the north. A Semitic language very close to Babylonian, from which it is thought to have diverged at the end of the 2nd millennium. Assyrian probably disappeared with the destruction of Assyria in the 7th century BC. Old Assyrian cuneiform is attested mostly in the records of Assyrian trading colonists in central Asia Minor (c. 1950 BC; the so-called Cappadocian tablets) and Middle Assyrian in an extensive Law Code and other documents. The Neo-Assyrian period was the great era of Assyrian power, and the writing culminated in the extensive records from the library of Ashurbanipal at Nineveh (c. 650 BC).

Assyriology: The study of the history, language, and antiquities of ancient Assyria and Babylonia in northern Mesopotamia, principally through cuneiform lists. Assyriologists have reconstructed chronological sequences for Assyria through limmu (eponym) lists found by excavators. (*syn.* Assyriological adj., Assyriologist n.)

Astarte: The goddess of the ancient Near East who was the chief deity of many important sites and the fertility goddess of the Phoenicians and the Canaanites. She is sometimes equated with Egyptian Isis, Babylonian Ishtar, Carthaginian Tanit, and Greek Aphrodite, Cybele, and Hera. She originated in Syria as a war goddess and probably was introduced into Egypt in the 18th Dynasty (1550–1295 BC). Astarte was usually portrayed as a naked woman on horseback wearing a headdress or bull horns. (*syn.* Asherah, Ashtoreth, Ashtart)

astronomy: Most ancient civilizations studied the skies for astronomical knowledge. Archaeologists have studied ancient people's knowledge of astronomy in prehistoric Europe through monuments and in Central America through inscriptions and documents. Studies of prehistoric astronomy in Europe have concentrated on the megalithic monuments and stone circles, which have been proved to incorporate alignments of the sun, moon, and brighter stars—especially significant points in their cycles. Solar alignments occur at New Grange and Stonehenge, lunar orientations at the Recumbent Stone Circles of Aberdeenshire and the Carnac stones in Brittany. Many theories are discussed as to the accuracy of measurements and the degree of astronomical understanding achieved by early societies. The ability to predict astronomical events would have enhanced political power, which has been suggested in Mesoamerica. The ability to predict events by governing elite class increased their credibility as able rulers. The Mesoamerican people put great emphasis on the calendar and astronomy and were able to make extremely accurate measurements of the solar year, the appearance of eclipses, and the phases of the Moon. Buildings seen as observatories occur at Chichen Itza and at Palenque, and the Dresden codex is a detailed collection of calculations tracing the eclipses of the Moon and Sun and the cycles of Venus and possibly Mars and Jupiter. The Maya were even aware of the impreciseness of the 365-day year in their Calendar Round and added a correction factor to account for the quarter-day per year discrepancy. The cycle of the Moon was calculated with amazing accuracy (29.5302 days compared with the actual figure of 29.5306). The cycle of Venus (calculated at 583.92 days) was also pinpointed as accurately as measurements taken by modern astronomical methods. The ancient astronomers' awareness of long-term astronomical phenomena was astonishing.

Asturian: A macrolithic industry of the Mesolithic in northern Spain, discovered from shell mounds at cave mouths. It followed the Azilian and is characterized by a long pointed unifacial quartzite pick. It dates to the 9th and 8th millennia BP.

Asuka: A culture and period in Japanese history during which the development of art, the introduction of Buddhism from Korea, and the adoption of a Chinese pattern of government were important. Located in the southwestern part of the Nara Basin (Yamato Plain), the culture flourished from AD 552–645. In art history, the Asuka culture refers to early Buddhist art and architecture in the Northern Wei style. In chronology, the Asuka period refers more to the reign of

Soga family during which Buddhism was promoted and a formal administrative structure with diplomatic relations was introduced. Many temples and palaces are surviving examples of Asuka architecture, sculpture, and painting.

Aswad, Tell: An Aceramic Neolithic site in Syria's Damascus basin, occupied c. 7800–6600 BC. There is evidence of early farming (plant cultivation including barley, cereals, emmer wheat, lentils, peas, pulses).

Aswan: A city in Upper Egypt, on the first cataract of the Nile, where the Aswan High Dam has been erected. The ancient site included important antiquities such as the temples (Abusimbel), the rock-cut tombs of Qubbet el-Hawa, and structures on the island of Elephantine (modern Jazirat Aswan), which have been rescued from flooding by international groups who also explored those structures that could not be saved. There are local quarries on the eastern bank on the Nile, which supplied granite for many ancient Egyptian monuments and which are still in operation. Aswan was the southern frontier of pharaonic Egypt. Aswan later served as a frontier garrison post for the Romans, Turks, and British. (*syn.* Swenet, (Greek) Syene, Assuan, Assouan)

Asyut: Capital of the Asyut muhafazah (governorate) and the largest settlement of Upper Egypt, midway between Cairo and Aswan on the west bank of the Nile. It was a center of worship for Wepwawet, the jackal-headed god. In the Middle Kingdom, it was the capital of the 17th nome (province) of Upper Egypt. It was commercially important as a terminus of caravan routes across the deserts. In Hellenistic times it was known as Lycopolis ("Wolf City"), referring to the worship of the jackal-headed god. (*syn.* ancient Djawty, Lycopolis, Syut, Asiut, Assiout)

Aszód: A Late Neolithic site (4th millennium BC) in the Zagyva Valley, 30 kilometers east of Budapest, Hungary. There are remains of a settlement with 40 rectangular houses containing rich assemblages and a cemetery with rows of graves. There are varying degrees of wealth in the grave goods. Aszód is a rare example of a site east of the Danube River with a western Hungarian material culture.

Ataki I: An Upper Palaeolithic site on the Dnestr River in the Ukraine with four occupation levels dating as far back as 15,000–16,000 BP

Atchana, Tell: A mound on the Amuq plain of northern Syria (southeastern Turkey), next to the River Orontes and identified as the ancient city of Alalakh with occupation levels from the 4th–late 2nd millennia BC. Seventeen building phases spanned c. 3400–1200 BC, including a long Copper Age, a period as an independent state, and one as a provincial capital of the Hittites. There was a mix of cultural influences from Mesopotamia and the Aegean. Atchana was wealthy from trade and from the timber of the Amanus

Mountains. Woolley discovered the remains of a small king-dom of largely Hurrian population. In level VII, dated to the 18th and 17th centuries BC, the palace of Yaram-Lim II (Yamhad) demonstrated an early form of Syrian architecture in which stone, timber, and mud brick were all used. Another palace was excavated in level IV, of the late 15th and early 14th centuries, belonging to Niqmepa, with rooms around a central court and a large number of tablets in Akkadian cuneiform. The tablets describe trading with cities such as Ugarit and the Hittite capital Hattusas, involving food prod-ucts such as wheat, wine, and olive oil. Later in the 14th century, the city fell to the Hittites and became a provincial capital of the Hittite empire. It was eventually abandoned after destruction c. 1200 BC, perhaps at the hands of the Peoples of the Sea. (*syn.* ancient Alalakh)

Aten: The deity represented in the form of a sun disk and introduced as the sole god by the heretic pharaoh, Akhenaten (Amenophis IV, 1353–1336 BC) during the 18th Dynasty of Egypt, c. 1350 BC. Akhenaten built the city of Akhetaton (now Tell el-Amarna) and established a temple at Karnak dedicated to Aten's worship. The sun god was depicted as the solar disk with rays terminating in human hands. (*syn.* Aton, Yati)

Aterian: A stone tool culture of the Middle and Late Pal-aeolithic, widespread in the late Pleistocene in northern Af-rica. Centered on the Atlas Mountains, but with extensions into Libya and deep into the Sahara, the Aterian people were among the first to use the bow and arrow. It appears to have developed, perhaps initially in the Maghreb of Algeria and Morocco, from the local Mousterian tradition. Aterian as-semblages, named after Bir el Ater in Tunisia, are marked by the presence of varied flake tools, many of which possess a marked tang. Some tools (such as side scrapers and Levallois flakes) resemble Mousterian types, but the tanged points and bifacially worked leaf-shaped points appear distinctively At-erian. The leaf-shaped blades, however, have been likened to Solutrean blades, and it has often been suggested that the Aterians may have entered the Iberian Peninsula during Solutrean times. The date at which the Aterian first appeared is not well attested, but may have been c. 80,000 BC. The Aterian occupation came to an end c. 35,000 BC as the Sahara became drier and unsuitable for human settlement.

Athabascan: Native Americans who speak languages of the Athabascan or Dene language family. The Northern variety is in Alaska and the Yukon; the southern variety, including the Apache and Navajo, are in the U.S. Southwest. The groups diverged around AD 500.

Athens: Important classical Greek city-state with evidence for continuous occupation from the Late Neolithic. Because of its continuous occupation and the resulting disturbance of the earlier levels, its history is told from the time of the

Mycenaeans in the Late Bronze Age. The citadel on the Acropolis was walled early in its history. It is the capital of Greece and generally considered to be the birthplace of Western civilization. Athens is best known for its temples and public buildings of antiquity. The Parthenon, a columned, rectangular temple built for the city's patron goddess, Ath-ena, is considered to be the culmination of the Doric order of classical Greek architecture. Also located on the Acropolis are the Erechtheum, originally the temple of both Athena and Poseidon, and the Propylaea, the entrance of which is through the wall of the Acropolis. At the foot of the Acropolis, to the south, are the theaters of Herodes and Dionysus, while to the northwest is the Agora, the ancient marketplace of the city. The Kerameikos cemetery documents the city's Iron Age (c. 11–8 BC), after which archaeology and history combine to tell of its brilliance through the Classical period. Athens sup-posedly rivaled Knossos and later resisted successive waves of Dorian invaders. It is still not clear how far Athens, perhaps the base of the very early Ionian colonies, managed to ride out the dark age that followed the collapse of My-cenaean civilization. There is evidence of a cultural and commercial renaissance in the 7th and 6th centuries BC. A major component of this socioeconomic revolution was the borrowing of the Phoenician alphabet for the writing of Greek. Commercial success brought rapid economic growth and a population explosion. New ideas were imported, and political upheaval led to experiments in government, such as democracy. Athens resisted Persian invaders and developed a prestige that allowed the establishment of the Delian League and the extension of her political power—the Athenian em-pire. In the years 447–431 BC, under Pericles, vast sums were spent on public works, such as the new group of buildings on the Acropolis including the Parthenon. Pericles would not grant the Hellenes the freedom requested by Sparta, which led to the Peloponnesian War (431–404 BC) after which Athens was a dependent of Sparta. Escape from Spartan imperialism in the 4th century BC was threatened by Philip of Macedon and Alexander the Great. By the end of the century, Macedon dominated, and Athens did not achieve indepen-dence until 228 BC. Rome then intruded in the 2nd and 1st centuries, and Athens was sieged and plundered by Sulla. During the Imperial period, Athens was confined to a role as a cultural center and seat of learning for the rich—which lasted into the 6th century AD, when the edict of Justinian in 529 closed down the schools of philosophy. By the Byzantine period, Athens had become a modest provincial town. Athens' ruins will be difficult to protect from the corrosive atmosphere and millions of visiting tourists. (*syn.* Athínai (modern Greek), Athenai (ancient Greek))

Athenian pottery: Pottery produced in Athens from the Late Geometric period of monumental craters and amphorae through the Hellenistic period. The best known is the figure-decorated pottery of the Archaic and Classical periods, which was widely exported along with plain wares.

Athribis: An important Egyptian city in the Nile delta with, to this point, only the remains of a Greco-Roman settlement. (*syn.* Tell Atrib)

Atlantic period: In Europe, a climatic optimum following the last Ice Age. This period was represented as a maximum of temperature, and evidence suggests it was warmer than average for the interglacial. It seems to have begun about 6000 BC, when the average temperature rose. Melting ice sheets ultimately submerged nearly half of western Europe, creating the bays and inlets along the Atlantic coast, which provided a new, rich ecosystem for human subsistence. The Atlantic period was followed by the Subboreal period. The Atlantic period, which succeeded the Boreal, was probably wetter and certainly somewhat warmer, and mixed forests of oak, elm, common lime (linden), and elder spread northward. Only in the late Atlantic period did the beech and hornbeam spread into western and central Europe from the southeast. (*syn.* Atlantic phase, Atlantic climatic period)

Atlantic Bronze Age: A Late Bronze Age metalworking industry, which developed on the west coast of France (Brittany to Gironde) c. 1000—500 BC and spread to southern England and Iberia. The unifying factor of these areas was very active trading along the Atlantic seaways. The period is known from a large number of hoards with typical products being the carp's tongue sword, end-winged ax, hog-backed razor, and bugle-shaped object of uncertain function. The tradition flourished west of the area dominated by the central European Urnfield cultures. (*syn.* carp's tongue sword complex)

Atlantis: An earthly paradise described by Plato in two of his dialogues, "Timaeus" and "Critias." In "Timaeus," quoting the Athenian lawgiver Solon, Plato described a circular island that developed a high level of civilization but that degenerated and sank into the sea (because of earthquakes) as punishment. Atlantis was a rich island whose powerful princes conquered many Mediterranean lands until they were finally defeated by the Athenians and their allies. It was described as existing 9,000 years before Solon's birth—an unlikely dating. Although its location is unknown, it is supposed to have existed between Africa and the New World (west of the Straits of Gibraltar) and was said to be larger than Asia Minor and Libya combined. Some have suggested that it was a vanished Minoan civilization on ancient Thera that was destroyed c. 1470 BC. Many other interpretations have been offered, including that Plato's Atlantis is a philosophical abstraction. In the "Critias," Plato supplied a history of the ideal commonwealth of the Atlantians. (*syn.* Atalantis, Atlantica)

atlas: In Greek architecture, male figures that were so called for the story of the Titan Atlas, in which humans were used instead of columns to support entablatures, balconies, or other projections. Such figures are posed as if supporting great weights, just as Atlas bore the world. The female counterpart is the caryatid, but it is not similarly posed. The earliest known examples of true atlantes occur on a colossal scale in the Greek temple of Zeus (c. 500 BC) in Sicily. Atlantes were used only rarely in the Middle Ages but reappeared in the Mannerist and Baroque periods. (*syn.* atlantes (plural) telamon (Latin), caryatid (female))

atlatl: (at'-lat-ul) A New World version of a spear-throwing device, used by the Aztecs and other peoples of the Americas. It consisted of a wooden shaft used to propel a spear or dart, and it functioned like an extension of the arm, providing more thrusting leverage. Atlatl weights are objects of stone fastened to the throwing stick for added weight. These may be perforated so that the stick passes through the artifact, or they may be grooved for lashing to the stick. In western North America, it was the main hunting weapon from about 6500 BC until AD 500. (*syn.* spear thrower)

Atlitian: An Upper Palaeolithic assemblage named for the type site, Atlit, in the Mount Carmel region of Israel. There are several layers with Aurignacian-like assemblages, and this culture followed the Antelian (formerly Middle Aurignacian). It was among the assemblages that preceded various Mesolithic developments in the Middle East.

atomic absorption spectrometry: A method of analysis used to determine the chemical composition of metal artifacts—especially copper—and nonmetallic substances such as flint. It measures energy in the form of visible light waves and is capable of measuring up to 40 different elements with an error rate of around 1%. It is not a completely nondestructive technique, because a small sample must be removed from the artifact (between 10 mg. and 1 g., depending on the concentration of the elements). The sample is first dissolved and then atomized in a flame. A beam of light, of carefully controlled wavelength, is shone through the flame to a detector on the other side. The light takes a defined wavelength corresponding to the emission wavelength of the chosen element. The atoms of that element in the sample therefore absorb a proportion of the light, measured with a photomultiplier, and a comparison of the intensity of the light with that which has not gone through the sample shows the extent of the absorption, thus providing an estimate of the amount of the chosen element in the specimen. One of the method's drawbacks is that a separate measurement (and a different hollow cathode lamp) is necessary for each element, so that analysis for a large number of elements is time consuming. There are also problems of contamination with the high dilutions necessary for elements present in high concentrations, so that the method is used for the analysis of minor elements and trace elements rather than for major elements. The results are generally more accurate than those obtained using optical emission spectrometry, and the technique's use will probably increase, especially for the identification of sources of metal ores through the recognition and quantification of the trace elements. (*syn.* AAS)

Atranjikhera: A site in the Uttar Pradesh, northern India, with a series of occupation levels. The earliest level contained ochre-colored pottery. It was followed by a level with black and red ware, followed by a series of layers with painted gray ware, which also produced iron tools and weapons. The radiocarbon dates so far recorded are unreliable.

Atrides: A dynasty that may have reigned in Mycenae toward the end of the 2nd millennium BC, which was said to dominate some other Greek principalities.

atrium: The entrance court or hall of a Roman house with a central roof opening (compluvium) and a pool or basin (impluvium draining into a cistern) in which to collect rainwater. The term is perhaps derived from Atria, an Etruscan city of Tuscany, in which such structures were first built. The different apartments or rooms of the house surrounded this central courtyard. The atrium was a most important and interesting part of a Roman mansion. Greek influence is also visible in the use of tetrastyle (four columns to support the roof), and peristyle in some examples. The walls of the atrium would be decorated, sometimes with painted panels or family portraits, and a shrine to the lares and penates (household gods, also probably of Etruscan derivation) is sometimes found. Above the atrium were typically grouped the cubicula (bedrooms), and beyond lay the tablinum (family room and study), triclinium (dining room), and hortus (garden). There are many examples of atriums at Pompeii. An atriolum is a small atrium.

Attic: Pertaining or relating to Athens and the surrounding area of Attica. The particular dialect of Greek spoken and written in classical Athens, especially in the 5th century BC. This dialect was originally only one of a number of differing regional forms, but has come to be regarded as standard classical Greek. Attic is the language of dialogue in tragedy. Thucydides and Plato wrote in Attic Greek.

attribute: A distinct, individual characteristic of an artifact, which cannot be further subdivided and distinguishes it from another. An attribute is used to classify artifacts into groups and describes objects in terms of their physical traits such as color, design pattern, form, shape, size, style, surface texture, technology, and weight. Attribute analysis is a method of using these characteristics to statistically produce clusters of attributes in identifying classes of artifacts.

attritional age profile: The distribution of ages in an animal population, which is the result of selective hunting or predation. A mortality model based on bone or tooth wear is used to figure out attritional mortality victims (those dying from natural causes or from nonhuman predation) or by hunting or predation of the most vulnerable individuals—generally, the young and the old.

Atum: A creator god and solar deity of Heliopolis. Atum's myth merged with that of the sun god Ra (Re), to form the god Ra-Atum (or Re-Atum). Atum came into being before heaven and earth were separated, rising up from Nun (the waters of chaos) to form the Primeval Mound. He was identified with the setting sun and was shown as an aged figure who had to be regenerated during the night, to appear as Khepri at dawn and as Re at the sun's zenith. Atum was often identified with snakes and eels, typical primeval beings. (*syn.* Tem, Tum (means "the all"))

Atwater, Caleb (1778–1867): An American archaeological pioneer with his work on the mounds of the Midwest.

Aubrey, John (1626–1697): An antiquarian and writer who studied and wrote detailed accounts of the monuments at Avebury and Stonehenge. He was the first to recognize the circle of 56 pits now known as the Aubrey holes within the bank at Stonehenge. His literary and scientific interests won him a fellowship of the Royal Society in 1663. After his death, some of his antiquarian materials were included in *The Natural History and Antiquities of … Surrey* (1719) and *The Natural History of Wiltshire* (1847).

auger: A tool used to probe into the ground and extract a small sample of a deposit without performing actual excavation. Its applications in archaeology are as a means of sampling and understanding the geological environment of a site and also for extracting peat for pollen analysis. There are various types of augers, which can be manual or power driven. Simple augers bring up samples on the thread of a drill bit. More elaborate ones open a chamber to collect a core after the drill has bored to an appropriate depth. Augering is generally restricted to the earliest stages of archaeological reconnaissance to determine the depth and characteristics of deposits. (*syn.* augering (n))

Augst: The site of a Roman colony and frontier post founded in 44 BC in Switzerland, which flourished under Hadrian until the time of an attack by the Alamanni in AD 260. There is no evidence of occupation before 15 BC. The site has one of the most complete Roman city layouts north of the Alps with a theater, forum, curia, basilica, theater complex, baths, and city walls. The Romans enlarged the old Celtic settlement, improved water supplies, and constructed the arenas and theaters. Villas were built, providing the bases for agricultural exploitation and for spreading of Roman influence into the surrounding countryside. (*syn.* Augusta Raurica, Roman Augusta Rauricorum)

Au Lac: A kingdom in northern Vietnam, founded by a warlord, Thuc Phan, who united Van Lang, a state he conquered, with his kingdom in 258 BC and called the new state Au Lac—which he then ruled under the name An Duong. Au Lac existed only until 207 BC when it was incorporated by a former Chinese general, Trieu Da, into the kingdom of Nam Viet. The end of Au Lac marks the end of legendary history and the beginning of Vietnamese history, as recorded in Chinese historical annals. (*syn.* Au-lac)

Aulnat: An important Iron Age settlement site in Puy-de-Dome, France, dating to the 3rd century BC, with evidence of gold, silver, bronze, coral, glass, bone, and textiles. It was abandoned soon after the Roman conquest.

aumbry: A recess or small cupboard in a wall, used as a repository or place for keeping things. (*syn.* ambry, aumbrie, aumery, almery)

Aurignacian: A series of Upper Palaeolithic cultures in Europe that existed from about 35,000 to 20,000 years (dates also given as 38,000–22,000 years) ago. They were characterized by their use of stone (flint) and bone tools, the refinement of those tools, and the development of sculpture and cave painting. The culture is named for the type site Aurignac, in southern France, where such artifacts were discovered. In France, it is stratified between the Châtelperronian and the Gravettian (and before the Solutrean and the Magdalenian), but industries of Aurignacian type are also found eastward to the Balkans, Palestine, Iran, and Afghanistan. At Abri Pataud, there is a radiocarbon date of pre-31,000 BC for the Aurignacian, but there are possibly earlier occurrences in central and southeast Europe (Istállóskö in Hungary, Bacho Kiro in Bulgaria). There is still considerable dispute about the extent to which the Aurignacian is contemporary with the cultures of the Perigordian group in southwest France. The sites are often in deep, sheltered valleys. Split-based bone points, carinates (steep-end scrapers), and Aurignac blades (with heavy marginal retouch) are typical of Aurignacian. Aurignacian is also important as the most distinctive and abundantly represented of the early Upper Palaeolithic groups. (*syn.* Aurignac (adj))

auroch: The name of an extinct species of wild ox (*Bos primigenius*), the ancestor of present-day domestic cattle, which became extinct in the 17th century AD. It was described by Caesar as Urus, and it inhabited Europe and the British Isles in ancient times and survived in most recent times in Lithuania, Poland, and Prussia. The name has often been applied erroneously to another species, the European bison, which still exists in the Lithuania forests. It was probably domesticated in some places, such as in eastern Hungary, during the 4th millennium BC.

Australian Core Tool and Scraper Tradition: A late Pleistocene and Holocene stone tool industry of mainland Australia and Tasmania with artifacts dating from 30,000 BC (at Lake Mungo). The industry was characterized by high-domed chunky cores (called horsehoof cores) and steep-edge flake scrapers. The industry has close parallels in the islands of Southeast Asia.

Australian Small Tool Tradition: A mid-Holocene tool industry of the Australian Aborigines, which appeared some 3,000–4,000 years ago when those peoples began to use a new ensemble of small, flaked stone tools (although adze flakes first appeared possibly 2,000 years earlier). The types consisted of backed blades and flakes, unifacial and bifacial points, and small adze flakes. There are some regional distributions of tools, including Bondi points, geometric microliths, Pirri points, and Tula adzes. All except the Bondi points and geometric microliths were still in use as parts of wooden weapons and tools at the time of European contact. The industry has close parallels in the islands of Southeast Asia, especially in the microliths of southwestern Sulawesi from 4000 BC.

Australopithecus: A name for an early genus believed to be related to humans. The species *Australopithecus africanus*, first known from southern and eastern Africa, was small in size—probably under 4 feet tall—and had a brain in the same size range as the chimpanzee and gorilla, but with massive jaws and teeth. The posture and teeth settings were, however, clearly human. The main fossils from South Africa are said to be 2½ to 3 million years old, but fossils from Laetoli near Olduvai are around 3¾ to 5 million years old and are regarded as either an early form of africanus or an ancestral species. At least one other species, *Australopithecus robustus*, has been included in the genus. This form was heavier and stockier with giant molar teeth but small front teeth. Fossil human remains from Olduvai and Koobi Fora in Kenya called *Homo habilis* are often regarded as a late form of *Autralopithecus africanus* or an early form of *Homo erectus*, and they date from 1½ to 2 million years ago. Australopithecus became extinct about 900,000 years ago. There are at least five known species in this genus. Some fragments from Lothagam at c. 5.5 million years may also be Australopithecus. The word *Australopithecus* means "southern ape," and these hominids were so named (in 1924 at Taung,) because their fossils were found first in southern Africa. (*syn.* australopithecine; abbreviation is A.)

Austro-Asiatic: A family of about 150 languages, which includes Vietnamese, Munda (eastern India), Mon (southwest Burma), Khmer (Kampuchea), and several minor language groups including Nicobarese, and Aslian of peninsular Malaysia. Vietnamese, Khmer, and Mon are culturally the most important of these and have the longest recorded history. Khmer is spoken primarily in Cambodia, Mon in Thailand and Myanmar (Burma). Vietnamese and Khmer, with the largest number of speakers, are the national languages, respectively, of Vietnam and Cambodia. Austro-Asiatic was once the main linguistic family of mainland Southeast Asia and eastern India, but its speakers have become geographically split into the Tibeto-Burman, Thai, and Austronesian languages.

Austronesian: The major language family of the islands of Southeast Asia and the Pacific (including Taiwan, the Philippines, Malaysia, Indonesia, parts of southern Vietnam, Madagascar, Melanesia [excluding much of New Guinea], Micronesia, and Polynesia). The family is divided into (1) Western Austronesian, or Indonesian, containing about 200 languages, and (2) Eastern Austronesian, or Oceanic, with about 300 languages. Proto-Austronesian probably started in southern China or Taiwan before 3000 BC. Austronesian speakers were the first humans to settle the Pacific islands beyond western Melanesia. Austronesians were the most widely spread ethnolinguistic group on earth, with the distance from Madagascar to Easter Island being 210 degrees of longitude. (*syn.* Malayo-Polynesian)

authority: Ability to persuade others, by argument or example, to accept one's decisions.

Autun: An Augustan Roman city in central France whose remains include city walls with two Augustan gates, a theater, and a temple of Janus. It was a fortified town built for Augustus in the last decade BC as a replacement capital for the Celtic tribe of the Aedui. The city was also known as a center of learning and for its schools of rhetoric. The city was ruined when it supported Claudius II in AD 269. (*syn.* Augustodunum)

Auvernier: A Neolithic and Late Bronze Age lake dwelling on the northern edge of Lake Neuchâtel, Switzerland, with Cortaillod, Horgen, and Corded Ware materials as well as Hallstatt (c. 1100–750 BC).

Avaris: The capital of the Hyksos in Egypt, possibly the site of Tell Ed-Daba.

Avdeevo: An Upper Palaeolithic site near Kursk in Russia with a single occupation between 11,950–22,700 BP. There were pits and hearths and artifacts of shouldered points and animal and Venus figurines. Woolly mammoth dominates the large faunal assemblage.

Avebury: A site in Wiltshire, England, at which stands one of Britain's finest megalithic monuments (known as henges) and one of the largest ceremonial structures in Europe. It was build in the Neolithic c. 2000 BC at a place where the ridgeways of southern England meet, a natural site for tribal gatherings. It consists of a large bank with internal ditch (1.2 km long) with four equally spaced entrances. Inside the ditch was set a circle of 98 sarsen stones, weighing as much as 40 tons each. In the center were two smaller stone circles, each c.

100 meters in diameter. The north circle contains a U-shaped setting of three large stones, and the southern inner circle once had a complex arrangement of stones at its center. The Ring Stone, a huge stone perforated by a natural hole, stood within the earthworks and main stone circle at the southern entrance. The southern entrance leads to two parallel rows of sarsens forming an avenue 15 meters wide and 2.5 kilometers long, which ends at a ritual building (the so-called Sanctuary) on Overton Hill. Traces of a second avenue remain on the opposite side of the monument. From the bottom of the ditch came sherds of Neolithic Windmill Hill, Peterborough, and Grooved Ware styles, while higher up were fragments of South British (Long Necked) Beaker and Bronze Age pottery. Burials with Beaker and Rinyo-Clacton wares have been excavated at the bases of some of the stones. Near the southern end of the Avenue was an occupation site with Neolithic and Beaker sherds. The complex geometry of the site is studied, especially the possible astronomical alignments built into it. The circles at Avebury and the wooden structure on Overton Hill were all probably built at the same time by Neolithic communities.

Avebury, Lord (formerly Sir John Lubbock) (1834–1913): British archaeologist whose book *Prehistoric Times* (seven editions between 1865–1913) achieved bestseller status. An early convert to Charles Darwin's theory of evolution, Lord Avebury popularized prehistory both as a term and a subject. He introduced the words "Palaeolithic" (old) and "Neolithic" (new), thereby expanding the three-age system (Thomsen and Worsaae) to a four-age system, dividing the Stone Age into old and new periods. He also interpreted cultural change as evidence of invasion from the east and the development of society as the result of economic advance.

Aveline's Hole: A cave site in Somerset, England, with a Creswellian Epipalaeolithic industry and a Magdalenian-style harpoon.

Awdaghast: The site of a trading center in southern Mauritania at the southern end of the main caravan route across the Sahara to Ghana. In the closing centuries of the 1st millennium AD, much gold was probably exported northward along this route. (*syn.* Tegdaoust)

awilum: The class of citizens in Mesopotamia who owned land in their own right and were freemen not dependent on the palace or on the temple, according to Hammurabi's Law Code. The populace was divided into awilum, muskenum, and wardum. The wardum was any slave in bondage who could be bought and sold, with a possibility of regaining freedom under certain conditions as a debtor-slave. The muskenum were, under King Hammurabi at least, persons employed by the palace who could be given land but did not own it. The classes awilum and muskenum were not mutually exclusive. Still unanswered is the question of which segment of the population could be conscripted to the wardum. (*syn.* ["man" in Akkadian])

awl: A small tool consisting of a thin, tapering, sharp-pointed blade of bone, flint, or metal used for piercing holes, making decorations, or in assisting basket weaving. (*syn.* piercer, pricker, bodkin)

ax: One of the last major categories of stone tool to be invented, around the end of the last Ice Age in the Palaeolithic. A flat, heavy cutting tool of stone or metal (bronze) in which the cutting edge is parallel to the haft and which might have the head and handle in one piece. Its main function was for woodworking (hewing, cleaving, or chopping trees), but it was also used as a weapon of war, as the battle ax. There are many forms of ax, depending on the different materials and methods of hafting. The word *ax* is now used instead of celt. *Hand ax* is used to denote the earlier implement, which was not hafted. In Mesolithic times, stone axes were usually chipped from a block of flint and could be resharpened by the removal of a flake from the end. In the Neolithic, axes were polished and often perforated to aid hafting. Axes are now usually iron with a steel edge or blade and fixed by means of a socket in the handle. Smaller, lighter ones are called hatchets. (*syn.* axe)

ax factory: An often isolated outcrop of high-quality rock in Europe. During the Neolithic period, these sources were exploited for the production of polished stone axes, and this became an important industry of the time. The tools were roughly flaked at the factory sites and traded, either as blanks or as finished axes. There were many ax factories in Britain's highlands, northern Ireland, and northwest France. Microscopic analysis is used to identify the rocks by their distinctive crystalline structure, which has enabled the trading networks to be reconstructed. (*syn.* axe factory)

ax-hammer: A tool consisting of an ax and a hammer combined, such as a shaft-hole ax having a hammer knob in addition. It was primarily a weapon of war, combining the functions of battle ax and mace. (*syn.* axe-hammer, axe-adze, hammer-axe)

axial skeleton: The bones of the trunk and head.

Axum: A kingdom formed from at least the 1st century AD in southwestern Ethiopia, which developed into an empire including northern Ethiopia, Sudan, and southern Arabia. It is also the name of a city there, in existence since the 3rd century AD, which rose to be the center of the kingdom. The culture incorporated elements from pre-Axumite cultures of the area. It was the first state in eastern Africa to make gold, silver, and copper coins, which is evidence of economic prosperity from international trade (possibly in ivory). The history of Axum is reflected in the inscriptions and religious symbols on those coins, which run approximately from the 3rd–7th centuries. Axum adopted Christianity in the 4th century. There is archaeological evidence for large multistory stone buildings and a series of monolithic funerary stelae up to 33 meters high. Axum was finally conquered by the Axumites in the 4th century, although it achieved political control over parts of southern Arabia in the 6th century. Thereafter it declined and was sacked in the 10th century. (*syn.* Aksum)

Ay (fl. 14th century BC): King of Egypt (reigned 1323–1319 BC), who rose from the ranks of the civil service and the military to take the throne after the death of Tutankhamen (1333–1323 BC) and was the last king of the 18th Dynasty. Ay became King Tutankhamen's closest adviser and helped him reconcile with the priesthood of Amon, which Akhenaten had persecuted. A ring with Ay's and Tutankhamen's widow's (Ankhesenamen) names, seen in 1932 in Cairo, has been evaluated to mean that Ay became king through marriage with the heiress. Ay's original wife remained his chief queen, as depicted on his royal tomb. (*syn.* Kheperkheprure Ay)

Ayacucho complex: A valley in southern Peru, north of the city of Ayacucho, with a series of caves—notably Pikimachay (Flea) Cave and Jayamachay (Pepper) Cave—which were the site of a complex of unifacial chipped tools (basalt and chert core tools, choppers, unifacial projectile points) and bone artifacts (horse, camel, giant sloth) dating between 15,000 and 11,000 BC. A human presence has been suggested in the Ayacucho Basin at that time, which would correspond with the "first wave" of immigration to the New World. Succeeding levels contain burins, blades, fishtail points, and manos and metates. Gourds, squash, cotton, lucuma, and seed plants such as quinoa and amaranth, were cultivated in the Ayacucho Basin before 3000 BC, corn and beans within the next millennium. There were also ground stone implements for milling seeds. It has been claimed that llamas and guinea pigs were domesticated in the complex.

Ayampitin: A site in Cordoba, northwestern Argentina, which has evidence of a transition from big game hunting to a more specialized hunting and gathering economy. The assemblage contains crude, large bifacial willow-leaf projectile points, lithic hunting tools, and tool-making debris in association with manos and milling stones, dating between 8,000–12,000 years ago.

Ayia Irini: A site on the island of Kea in the Aegean, occupied in the Bronze Age (2nd millennium BC). There was a fortified town with links to Minoan Crete. A temple had very large female terra-cotta figures.

Ayia Triadha: A Minoan palace in southern Crete, built c. 2200 BC and inhabited until its destruction c. 1450 BC. Connected by road to the palace at Phaestus, one room in the palace contained numerous clay tablets with Linear A inscriptions.

Ayios Epiktitos-Vrysi: A Neolithic site in northern Cyprus of the late 5th millennium BC with a perimeter wall and ditch protecting semisubterranean houses.

Aylesford: A cemetery of cremation burials of the 1st century BC discovered in the 1880s in the county of Kent, England. It was excavated by Sir Arthur Evans, who identified the grave goods as belonging to the Iron Age Belgae. It is thought to represent the arrival of Belgic peoples fleeing from Gaul in advance of Caesar's army. Aylesford and Swarling are now the type sites of that culture in southeastern England. There was urned cremation in flat graves and the use of wheel-thrown pots with pedestal bases and horizontal cordon ornament. Brooches (fibulae), wooden stave-built buckets, and bronze have also been found. The culture survived for a time after the Roman conquest in AD 43.

Aymara: A large South American tribal group occupying the Titicaca Plateau (central Andes) in the Late Intermediate period—and the language spoken by this group. The Aymara language is still spoken in some parts of Peru, Bolivia, and Argentina. The Aymara "kingdoms"—Canchi, Colla, Lupaca, Collagua, Ubina, Pacasa, Caranga, Charca, Quillaca, Omasuyo, and Collahuaya—fought among themselves but also shared cultural characteristics. Some of these characteristics appear to have been incorporated into the Inca political system, such as class stratification, a powerful ruling class, and *chullpa* burials. The peoples lived by cultivating tubers and herding alpaca and llama.

ayllu: Quechua term used in Peru and Bolivia for a social and administrative unit made up of related families and owners of land cultivated in common.

Ayutthaya: A town in south-central Thailand founded c. 1350 by Ramathibodi I in his attempt to unify the countries of Siam and Lopburi. It became the capital of the powerful Thai kingdom of the same name for more than 400 years until its destruction by invading Myanmar in 1767. Much architecture, art, and literature was destroyed in the sacking. The seat of government was moved south to Bangkok. Located on an island formed by the Lop Buri River at the mouth of the Pa Sak River, its hundreds of brick monuments have been recently restored. (*syn.* Ayut'ia, Ayuthya, Phra Nakhon Si Ayutthaya, Ayuthia, or Ayuthaya; Krung Kao ["ancient capital"])

Azelik: A series of sites in Niger, which have yielded evidence of metalworking at a very early date, possibly in the late 2nd millennium BC for copper smelting. There may have been a brief "Copper Age" (as at Akjoujt) before the adoption of iron, which was rare in sub-Saharan Africa.

Azilian: A Mesolithic (or Epi-Palaeolithic) culture of southwest France and northern Spain, which seems to follow the Late Magdalenian of the area. It falls within the Late Glacial period and may be correlated with the Allerod oscillation of the 10th millennium BC (c. 9000–8000 BC). The culture was characterized by flint microliths, pebbles painted with schematic designs, small thumb scrapers, fish hooks, and flat bone antler harpoons. It is named for Le Mas d'Azil, a massive cave region in southern France where such artifacts were first discovered in 1889. The Azilians were food gatherers who had domesticated the dog. The Oban and Oransay cultures are degenerated Azilian.

Azmak, Tell: A tell site in southern Bulgaria of the Neolithic and Copper Age. Several settlement horizons, building levels of early Neolithic Karanovo I culture, building levels of Karanovo V and VI cultures, and building phases of Early Bronze Age Karanovo VII culture have been unearthed. The layouts of the villages may yield architectural detail for the whole sequence. (*syn.* Asmaska Moghila)

Aztec: The last pre-Columbian group to enter the Valley of Mexico after the collapse of the Toltec civilization in AD c. 12. The Aztecs built a magnificent capital at Tenochtitlán and were later conquered by the Spaniards (1521). They called themselves the Mexica or Tenochca and were the dominant political group of the Late Post-Classic period. The people spoke Nahuatl. Their origin is obscure, partly because of the deliberate destruction of their own records, but tradition says that in AD 1193 the last of seven Chichimec tribes left Aztlan, a mythical birthplace somewhere north or west of Mexico, and filtered south. For a while, they lived around Lake Texococo, but in 1345 they were allowed to found Tenochtitlán (under present-day Mexico City) on some unoccupied islands. By 1428, Tenochtitlán, Texococo, and Tlacopan formed an independent state, which controlled most of present-day Mexico from the desert zone in the north to Oaxaca in the south, with extensions as far as the Guatemalan border—all through military expansion. By inclination and training, the Aztecs were militaristic, and a person's status depended on his success as a warrior. The chief god of the Aztecs, Huitzilopochtli, was a war god who required the blood of sacrificial victims, and only constant warfare supplied the altar of the god. Human sacrifice was necessary also to ensure the daily rising of the sun. Other major deities were Huitzilpotchtli (the warrior god and chief deity of Tenochtitlán), Texcatlipoca (god of night, death, and destruction), Xipe Totec (god of spring and renewal), and Quetzacoatl, the plumed serpent (god of self-sacrifice and inventor of agriculture and the calendar). Tenochtitlán became a great imperial city, so large that it could not be self-sufficient but had to rely on tribute from its provinces. Luxury goods and necessities were brought to the city, and craftsmen produced jewelry, turquoise mosaics, featherwork, and carved stone. Mold-made clay figurines were common, and black-on-orange pottery was decorated with geometrical designs and stylized creatures. Little architecture or painting survived the Spanish conquest of 1521. Copies of several books have been preserved (such as the Dresden Codex). Aztec society was set in a clearly defined hierarchical class system. At the top was the ruling class (*pipil*) from whom and by whom the emperors were chosen. The mass of the population were freeman (*machuale*), and under them were the serfs (*mayeques*) and at the bottom the slaves. Most people were of the landholding group called the *calpulli*, which had its own internal hierarchy. Change of social class was possible through state service in the military and sometimes through merchant activ-ity. The merchants (*pochteca*) served as early-reconnaissance and espionage groups. The arrival of the Spaniards and the fall of Tenochtitlán after a 90-day siege marked the end of Aztec dominance. (*syn.* Mexica, Tenochcas)

Azykh Cave: A Palaeolithic site in Azerbajdzhan with a unique pebble-tool industry and some faunal remains. There are upper layers with large bifaces and sidescrapers of the Acheulian, associated with Middle Pleistocene fauna. A Middle Palaeolithic/Late Pleistocene assemblage contains a Merck's rhinoceros, and cave bear remains overlie Lower Palaeolithic industry remains.

Bb

ba: In ancient Egyptian religion, one of the principal aspects of the personality—the soul—along with *ka* and *akh*. The ba, which was freed from the body at death, stood for the mobility of the soul in the underworld and its ability to return to earth. It was often represented as a bird or human-headed bird. Graves were often provided with narrow passages for visitation by the ba.

Ba and Shu: Ancient kingdoms ruling the area of modern Szechwan. Pa came into being in the 11th century BC and established relations with Shu in the 5th century BC. Shortly before 316 BC, the state was conquered by the Ch'in and incorporated into the Ch'in Empire. In the middle of the 3rd century BC, the Pa region became part of the kingdom of Shu and was totally independent of north and central China. Ba and Shu cultural remains are similar, especially the boat-coffin burials on river terraces and tanged willow-leaf bronze swords. The central region of Szechwan is still sometimes known as the Pa region. (*syn.* also Pa and Ch'u; Pa-Shu)

Baal: A god worshipped in many ancient Middle Eastern areas and the most important deity of the Canaanites. He was first mentioned in inscriptions of the Middle Bronze Age, mid-2nd millennium BC, and was depicted as a young armed warrior with bull's horns coming from his helmet. He was the fertility deity and also the lord of life and of rain and dew. Baal was later worshipped by the Phoenicians and at Carthage. An important temple dedicated to Baal has been excavated at Ugarit, which is where the first tablets bearing his name were discovered. (*syn.* "lord" or "owner")

Baalbek: Important town and agricultural center in Lebanon and the site of the magnificent ruins of a Roman town. Baalbek was first known at the time of the Greek conquest of Syria (332 BC). After the death of Alexander the Great (323 BC), the region fell to the Ptolemaic dynasty of Egypt, under which the town was called Heliopolis, probably after its Egyptian namesake. It achieved importance in late Hellenistic and Roman times, especially as a holy city. Among the ruins are the temples of Jupiter and Bacchus. In 200 BC, it was taken by the Seleucids' Antiochus the Great, and it was a Seleucid possession until the dynasty's fall in 64 BC, when it was again under Roman control. Baalbek has been an Arab city since AD 637 (*syn.* Ba'labakk [Arabic], Heliopolis [Greek])

Babadag: A tell site and culture of the Late Bronze Age, located in Rumania. Several occupation levels have been identified, all of which are associated with rich assemblages of bones, bronze tools, carbonized cereals, iron tools, and pottery.

Babadan A: A Palaeolithic site in Japan dating between 50,000–70,000 bp. The lithic culture includes choppers.

Babylon: One of the most famous cities of antiquity, the capital of southern Mesopotamia (Babylonia) from the early 2nd millennium to the early 1st millennium BC and capital of the Neo-Babylonian (Chaldean) Empire in the 7th and 6th centuries BC. It was located about 80 kilometers south of Baghdad, Iraq, on the Euphrates River. Babylon was occupied from the 3rd millennium BC, but it first reached prominence under King Hammurabi (reigned c. 1792–1750 BC), who made it the capital of his empire. (Hammurabi is best known for his code of laws.) Babylon was destroyed by the Hittites c. 1595 BC and ruled by the Kassites until c. 1157 BC. The city had frequent wars with Elam and Assyria during several short-lived dynasties until the 11th and last dynasty (626–539 BC), when the city was at its highest development and largest size. This last dynasty—that of Nebuchadnezzar—was instrumental in destroying Assyria, and it conquered lands from the Persian Gulf to the Mediterranean before being overthrown by Cyrus in 539 BC. It continued in existence through the Achaemenid period, although with much reduced importance, until its abandonment in AD after the Muslim conquest. The city itself covered around 200 hectares and had a population of about 100,000. Excavations beginning at the turn of the 20th century revealed the city's plan and scanty remains of the ziggurat, the original Tower of Babel. The high water table, which has risen in the last few millennia, allowed those excavators (R. Koldewey from 1899–1917) access only to buildings of the Neo-Babylonian period. The ruins, including temples (some for Marduk, the city's patron deity), fortifications, palaces, and the substructure of the Hanging Gardens, have not held up well over time, especially owing to brick robbing. The finest surviving monument is the Ishtar Gate and Procession Street. Important buildings excavated include Nebuchadnessar's palace, close to the Ishtar Gate, a huge building with many rooms arranged around five different courtyards. Another huge palace of Nebuchadnezzar's reign (605–562 BC)—the "Summer Palace"—was constructed to the northwest of the Inner City and was enclosed by a triangular outer wall. (*syn.* Bab-ilu [Babylonian], Bab-ilim [Old Babylonian], Bavel or Babel [Hebrew], Atlal Babil [Arabic])

Babylonia: An ancient region occupying southern Mesopotamia between the Tigris and Euphrates Rivers (southern Iraq from Baghdad to the Persian Gulf), whose capital was Babylon for many centuries. The term *Babylonia* also refers to the culture that developed in the area from its original settlement c. 4000 BC and the language of cuneiform script. Before Babylon's rise to political prominence (c. 1850 BC), the area was divided into Sumer (in the southeast; the world's earliest civilization) and Akkad (in the northwest) during the third millennium BC. The region was one of the richest agricultural areas of the ancient world.

Bacho Kiro: A cave in central Bulgaria with Mousterian levels and Upper Palaeolithic levels—some with Aurignacian features. The earliest Upper Palaeolithic levels seem to be c. 43,000 BC.

bacini: Pottery vessels ranging in date from the 11th–15th centuries and found in northern Italy, especially in medieval churches. They were placed in walls of churches, over church doorways, and in church towers, for decorative purposes. These Italian vessels were imported from the Byzantine and Arabic world, but later Italian maiolicas were made as bacini. Bacini were probably also used in southern Italian, Greek, and western European churches. Some were painted and incised; some were monochromic; others had fantastic designs.

backed blade: In stone toolmaking, a small blade with one edge blunted by further chipping along one edge. This retouching technique was used so that the blade could be fitted snugly into a haft, to provide a finger-rest, or so that it could be held in the hand without cutting the fingers.

backfill: Excavated earth put to one side at an archaeological site, which is later used to refill the excavation. The purpose of backfilling may be to prevent erosion or vandalizing. (*syn.* backfill [v.], back-filling [n.]; backdirt)

Bacsonian: An early Holocene stone tool industry (c. 8000–4000 BC) of Indochina (esp. northern Vietnam). It is often regarded as a variant of the Hoabinhian industry of Southeast Asia. The Bacsonian industry is characterized by edge-ground pebble tools and ground-stone axes and adzes, and some sites have cord- or basket-marked pottery.

backstrap: A simple loom known in Pre-Columbian America and still used in western Mexico, Guatemala, and other places in Central America. A continuous warp thread passes between two horizontal poles, one attached to a support and the other to a seated weaver, who adjusts the tension by moving forward or backward. The Navajo Indians wove blankets on a two-bar loom for centuries. Throughout the Caroline Islands (except Palau), strips of banana and hibiscus fiber are woven on backstrap looms.

Bactria: An ancient country (satrapy) lying in a fertile region between the mountains of the Hindu Kush (Paropamisus) and the Amu Darya (ancient Oxus River) in what is now part of Afghanistan, Uzbekistan, and Tajikistan. Bactria was especially important between c. 600 BC–AD 600, as a center for meeting and trading between the East (China) and West (Mediterranean). It was a satrapy of the Achaemenid Empire and was conquered by Alexander the Great in 329 BC. Many Greeks settled in Bactria in the Seleucid period that followed. Consequently, Greek influence on the culture of central Asia and northwestern India was considerable, especially in art, architecture, coins, and writing. Bactria's capital was Bactra (also called Bactra-Zariaspa; probably modern Balkh, ancient Vahlika). (*syn.* Bactriana, Zariaspa)

Bactrian Bronze Age: A culture of northwest Afghanistan with pottery, seals, metal work, ornamented stone vessels, stone statuettes, and so on. It was identified by materials looted from graves and appeared in Baluchistan and the Iranian plateau as far west as Susa.

Badari, el-: An area of Upper Egypt between Matmar and Qau where a Predynastic culture existed. Numerous cemeteries (Mostagedda, Deir Tasa, and the cemetery of el-Badari) and a settlement site at Hammamia have been found. (*syn.* Badari, al-)

Badarian: An Upper Egyptian, Predynastic culture of the later 5th millennium BC, named for the type site of el-Badari, on the east bank of the Nile River. It also extended over much of Middle Egypt. Excavations during the 1920s revealed settlements and cemeteries dating to about 4000 BC (Neolithic). Their fine pottery, black-topped brown ware (later red), was very thin-walled, well-baked, and often decorated with a burnished ripple. This effect was apparently produced by firing the pot inverted to prevent the air from circulating inside and over the upper rim, keeping these areas black, whereas the base and lower wall were externally oxidized to brown or a good red color. Other remains include combs and spoons of ivory, slate palettes, female figurines, and copper, shell, and stone beads. Badarian materials have also been found at Jazirat Armant, al-Hammamiyah, Hierakonpolis (modern Kawm al-Ahmar), al-Matmar, and Tall al-Kawm al-Kabir. Flinders Petrie and other archaeologists found large numbers of graves with artifacts in 1893–1894 and divided the culture into two phases: Naqada Culture I and Naqada Culture II.

Baden: A third millennium Copper Age culture over much of central Europe (the Carpathian basin: northern Yugoslavia, all of Hungary, most of Czechoslovakia, southern Poland, and parts of Austria and Germany). Ancient Baden was occupied by Celts and then by Germanic peoples and was conquered by Rome in the 1st century AD. A successor to the Lengyel culture, the Baden culture produced metal tools including ax-hammers and torcs of twisted copper wire. The pottery was plain and dark, but some had channeled decoration and handles of Ansa Lunata type. The horse was domesticated, and carts mounted on four solid disk-wheels were used. The Baden culture had contacts with the Early Bronze Age cultures of the Aegean. It was named for the town of Baden, near Vienna. A radiocarbon chronology has divided the Baden culture into three phases: Early (2750–2450 BC), Classic (2600–2250 BC), and Late (2400–2200 BC). The most complete sequences are in Hungary and Czechoslovakia. The culture was remarkable at the time because it had a highly dispersed settlement pattern and a central cemetery pattern. (*syn.* Baden-Pécel; Ossarn or Pecel culture; Channeled Ware or Radial-decorated pottery culture)

Bader, Otto Nikolaevich (1903–1980): A Russian archaeologist who worked on sites from the Palaeolithic to the Iron Age, including Kapovaya Cave and Sungir.

Badorf ware: A type of pottery of the 8th–9th centuries in the hills of Cologne, Germany. The globular pitchers and bowls of the Carolingian period are the best known. Badorf-ware kilns have been excavated at Bruhl-Eckdorf and Walberberg, and products have been found in the Netherlands, eastern England, and in Denmark. In the 9th century, the pots began to be decorated with red paint. Gradually, new forms and styles known as Pingsdorf Wares evolved.

Baghdad: The present-day capital of Iraq, a site 330 miles northwest of the Persian Gulf at the intersection of historic trade routes (Khorasn Road, part of the Silk Route), which was the foremost city of ancient Mesopotamia. Archaeological evidence shows that the site of Baghdad was occupied by various peoples long before the Arab conquest of Mesopotamia in AD 637, and several ancient empires had capitals there. The true founding of the city dates from 762 when the Abbasids moved the Islamic capital there. It was the Islamic capital from the 8th–13th centuries. Abbassid Baghdad is buried beneath the modern city. There was a palace, a congre-

gational mosque, ministries, and barracks, surrounded by walls and a moat. In the late 8th and early 9th centuries, Baghdad was large and at its height economically; it was considered the richest city in the world. The caliph abandoned Baghdad in favor of Samarra from 836–892. The city was burnt by the Mongols in 1258, rebuilt and sacked by Timur in 1400. The glory of Baghdad is written about in *The Thousand and One Nights*.

bag wear: The damage that can occur to artifacts and ecofacts during excavation, transportation, and cataloging.

Bahariya Oasis: A fertile depression in the northeast Libyan Desert about 200 kilometers west of the Nile. Archaeological remains date mainly from the early New Kingdom to the Roman period (c. 1550 BC–AD 395). (*syn.* al-Bahriyah Oasis)

Bahía: A phase in Ecuador's culture, dating c. 500 BC–AD 500, discovered on La Plata Island (Manabi). Large pyramidal platform mounds, helmeted figurines, spouted jars, and incised pottery have been found, along with evidence of polychrome painting and metallurgy. Houses with saddle roofs (low, downward-curving roof ridges), pottery head/neck rests, figurines with one leg crossed over the other, Pan pipes graduated toward the center, and ear plugs shaped like golf tees were unique to the culture—but they have parallels in southeast Asia. It has been suggested that they were introduced into Ecuador by voyagers from across the Pacific. Particularly elaborate anthropomorphic vessels give information on dress and ornamentation (nose discs and tusk-like pendants). Bahía was a well-developed sociopolitical and religious unit. The La Plata Island site was probably a ceremonial center as there is little evidence of daily living. Unfortunately, many sites have already been lost to modern development.

Bahrain: An island in the Persian Gulf, which has been identified with the ancient land of Dilmun (Telmun) of about 2000 BC, a prosperous trading center linking Sumeria with the Indus Valley. Written records of the archipelago exist in Assyrian, Persian, Greek, and Roman sources. Burial mounds in the north of Bahrain Island suggest a period of Sumerian influence in the 3rd millennium BC. There are densely packed fields of tumuli in Bahrain and at several places on the adjacent mainland. They are associated with densely packed complexes of cist burials. Excavation has shown the island to be an important link in the sea trade between that region and the Indus civilization. Two important sites in the north of the island belong to the "Dilmun period": a walled town at Qala'at al-Bahrain and a complex temple building at Barbar. Among the finds of this period are circular steatite stamp "Persian Gulf" seals, related to Indus Valley seals, but probably made locally.

Baikal Neolithic: The Neolithic period of the Lake Baikal region in eastern Siberia. Stratified sites in the area show a long, gradual move from the Palaeolithic to the Neolithic stage, starting in the 4th millennium BC. The Postglacial culture was not "true" Neolithic in that there was farming, but it was Neolithic in the sense of using pottery. It was actually a Mongoloid hunting-and-fishing culture (except in southern Siberia around the Aral Sea) with a microlithic flint industry with polished-stone blade tools together with antler, bone, and ivory artifacts, pointed- or round-based pottery, and the bow and arrow. Points and scrapers made of flakes of Mousterian aspect and pebble tools showing a survival of the ancient chopper–chopping tool tradition of eastern Asia have also been found. There was a woodworking and quartzite industry and some cattle breeding. The first bronzes of the region are related to the Shang period of northern China and to the earliest Ordos bronzes. The area covers the mountainous regions from Lake Baikal to the Pacific Ocean and the taiga (coniferous forest) and tundra of northern Siberia. A first stage is named for the site Isakovo and is known only from a small number of burials in cemeteries. The succeeding Serovo stage is also known mainly from burials with the addition of the compound bow backed with bone plates. The third phase, named Kitoi, has burials with red ochre, and composite fish hooks possibly indicate more fishing. The succeeding Glazkovo phase of the 2nd millennium BC saw the beginnings of metal using, but generally showed continuity in artifact and burial types. Some remains of semisubterranean dwellings with centrally located hearths occur, together with female statuettes in bone.

Baile Herculane: A large cave site in Rumania where flint implements from the Paleolithic period (about 2,500,000 years ago) and Neolithic objects were found. There is important Palaeolithic, Mesolithic, Neolithic, and Copper Age stratigraphy making up three main occupation horizons: Upper Palaeolithic levels corresponding to the Würm II phase and defined by a quartzite industry with end scrapers; a late Mesolithic level with microlithic flints, crude quartzite tools, and Danube fish bones; and levels of Late Copper Age occupation.

Baker's Hole, Northfleet: A Lower Palaeolithic site in Kent, England. It was a factory producing Levallois flakes.

Bakong: The earliest surviving temple mountain in southeast Angkor, Cambodia, the first Cambodian temple to be built primarily of stone (sandstone) rather than brick. It was built by King Indravarman I (reigned AD 877–c. 890) and was probably finished in 881. The central tower of the pyramidal structure is 34 meters high. At the summit of the central shrine was a linga, the phallic emblem sacred to Shiva. Around the base of the terraced pyramid stood eight large shrines inside the main enclosure, with a series of moats, causeways, and auxiliary sculptures guarding the approaches to the exterior. Bakong became the model for many larger royal temples at Angkor. These served as monuments to the greatness of their patrons and, subsequently, as their tombs.

baktun: A unit in the Classic Maya long count equaling 144,000 days or about 400 years.

Bakun, Tall-e: A prehistoric tell site near Persepolis in south-central Iran, occupied continuously from c. 4200 to c. 3000 BC. The site, the oldest yet discovered in that area of Iran, was first excavated in 1928. It consisted of 12 mud-brick buildings with one to seven rooms each. Bakun was occupied by an agricultural community that made fine painted pottery related to Susa A wares. Vessels included conical bowls and goblets with a large variety of geometric patterns and animal motifs. Other finds include flint implements, stamp and button seals, vessels of calcite, and many animal and human figurines. The pottery is especially important for the study of early Iranian art. (*syn.* Baken, Tall-I)

Balakot: A settlement site on the coast west of Karachi, Pakistan, dating to the 4th millennium BC. The Balakotian ceramic was followed by Harappan levels. Resources were fish, cattle, sheep, and goats.

Balanovo: A cemetery site in south-central Russia dating to the early 2nd millennium BC near several short-lived settlement sites confined largely to the main river valleys. The regional culture made Corded ware. The cemeteries mainly used flat inhumation rites, including double burials and some rich graves with copper battle axes. Corded beakers, stone battle axes, and fired clay model wheels are characteristic finds.

Balawat: The site of ancient Imgur-Enlil, east of Mosul in northern Iraq. Excavators have found the palace of Shalmaneser II and a pair of great bronze gates (now in the British Museum). These huge wooden gates were part of a set of three with evidence of the campaigns of Assurnasirpal II and Shalmaneser III. They were decorated with horizontal bands of metal 11 inches high, each modeled by a repoussé process, with a double register of narrative scenes. The bronze doors from the Assyrian town portray the course of Shalmaneser's campaigns and undertakings in rows of pictures. Balawat was the country retreat of the Assyrian kings in the first half of the 9th century BC. (*syn.* Tell Balawat)

Balearic Islands: A group of islands including Majorca (Mallorca), Minorca, Ibiza, and Formentera, off the east coast of Spain. Various civilizations left their marks on the islands, although the prehistoric talayotic civilization (so-called from its rough stone towers called *talayots*) seems to have continued without modification for 2,600 years. Their position in the Mediterranean laid them open to continuous influence from eastern civilizations, as is found in archaeological finds. Bronze swords, single and double axes, antennae swords, and heads and figures of bulls and other animals were found. Native talayotic pottery was consistent until the Roman occupation. The most interesting period was the Bronze Age with three important monuments: the Naveta, Talayot, and Taula. The islands were successively ruled by Carthaginians, Romans, Vandals, Moors, and Spaniards.

Bali: An island of Indonesia east of Java. The earliest inscriptions date from the end of the 9th and the 10th centuries, and Buddhism and Shaivite Hinduism have been practiced since the 7th century.

balk: A strip of unexcavated earth left in place between excavated units, pits, or trenches for the purpose of revealing the stratigraphy of an excavation for as long as possible. The balk provides a constant reference to the original pre-excavation level of the site and also carries all sections along or across the site. In an excavation carried out according to the grid method, 25% of the site may consist of balks. Balks may also serve to facilitate access to different areas of the excavation. (*syn.* baulk)

Balkh: A village in northern Afghanistan, which was formerly Bactra, the capital of ancient Bactria. A settlement existed at the site as early as 500 BC, and it was associated with Zoroaster until captured by Alexander the Great in c. 329 BC. It was then made the capital of the Greek satrapy of Bactria, but in succeeding centuries it fell to various nomadic invaders, including the Turks and Kushans, until it was decisively taken by the Arabs in the 8th century. Balkh then became the capital of Khorasan. Under the Abbasids and Samanids, it was a capital and a center of learning known as the "Mother of Cities." Balkh was completely destroyed by the Mongols under Genghis Khan in 1220. It lay in ruins until its capture by Timur in the 15th century. The alleged discovery of the tomb of Ali, the Prophet Muhammad's son-in-law, in neighboring Mazar-e Sharif (1480) once again reduced Balkh to insignificance. Balkh was incorporated into Afghanistan in 1850. Balkh was a caravan city on the Silk Route and a major outpost of Buddhism. Very little is known about the pre-Islamic city. (*syn.* Vazirabad, Bactra)

Ballana and Qustul: Two Nubian necropolis sites on opposing sides of the Nile, 15 kilometers south of Abu Simbel and now submerged under Lake Nassar. Ballana was the type site of a period that lasted from the decline of the Meroitic empire to the arrival of Christianity (AD c. 350–700). Some pictographic writing dating c. 3400–3100 BC was discovered on pottery, slate palettes, and stone at Qustul. Qustul may have been one of the earliest places of state formation in the world when rulers of the A-Group culture adopted symbols of kingship similar to those of contemporary kings of Egypt's Naqadah II–III periods.

ball court: The structure on which the ball game was played in Pre-Columbian Mesoamerica. It was shaped like a capital I with exaggerated end pieces, and in the Post-Classic period stone rings or macaw heads were fixed to the side walls. Aztec records say that the team that passed the ball through one of these rings won the game outright. (*syn.* ballcourt, ball court)

ball game: The ritual and sporting activity played throughout Pre-Columbian Mesoamerica, especially in Mexico and Guatemala from the Pre-Classic period. (Stone reliefs at Dainzu and the possible remains of a ball court at San Lorenzo Tenochititlan indicate that the game existed as early as Pre-Classic times.) It may have originated among the Olmecs (La Venta culture, c. 800–400 BC) or even earlier and spread to other cultures, including Monte Albán and El Tajín; the Maya (called pok-ta-pok); and the Toltec, Mixtec, and Aztec. In Aztec times, it was a nobles' game and was often accompanied by heavy betting. Various myths mention the ball game, sometimes as a contest between day and night deities. It is still played in isolated regions. The players, who were sometimes heavily padded, were allowed to use only their hips and thighs in propelling a rubber ball around the court. The ball court itself was shaped like a capital I with exaggerated end pieces, and in the Post-Classic period stone rings or macaw heads were fixed to the side walls. Aztec records say that the team that passed the ball through one of these rings won the game outright. Tlachtli is the name of the court itself, but also for the game. Tlachtli and ollama are Nahuatl words. There was considerable diversity in the rules both over time and across cultures. Death through injury was not unusual, and the loss of a game could sometimes result in the sacrifice of the losing team. There is a considerable inventory of artifacts associated with the ball game, including hachas, palmas, court markers, elbow stones, and yokes. (*syn.* ballgame, ball game; ollama, pok-ta-pok)

ballista: An ancient heavy missile launcher designed to hurl javelins or heavy balls on the principle of a crossbow. The smaller ballista was just that—a large crossbow fastened to a mount. It was also used to hurl iron shafts, Greek fire, heavy darts, and so on during sieges. The huge, complicated Roman ballista, however, was powered by torsion derived from two thick skeins of twisted cords through which were thrust two separate arms joined at their ends by the cord that propelled the missile. The largest ballistas were quite accurate in hurling 60-pound weights up to about 500 yards. The catapult was yet another machine used for firing bolts and other arrow-like missiles. The two terms are often used interchangeably. (*syn.* balista)

balneum: A small Roman bathhouse that may be attached to a private house.

Balof Cave: A rock shelter in New Ireland, Oceania, dating to c. 5000 BC, with a preceramic industry of obsidian and bone points. The site has one of the earliest dates for human settlement in Oceania east of New Guinea.

balustrade: A row of ornamental supports for a railing or low colonnade. The term also applies to an enclosure or parapet composed of ballisters or other materials designed to prevent falls from elevated architectural elements such as roofs and balconies.

Bambandyanalo: A hill that forms the eastern boundary of K2 in Transvaal, South Africa, where a site dates to the 11th–12th centuries AD—the southern African Iron Age.

Bambata Cave: A large cave of southwestern Zimbabwe, where excavations have revealed a long sequence of occupation over the past 50,000 years. The site gives its name to a stone industry and pottery type, but they are widely separated periods. There are rock paintings on the cave walls, and sheep bones, found in the same archaeological levels as pottery, have been dated to 150 BC. The Bambata industry, dated between the 50th–20th millennia used prepared cores to produce (unretouched) flakes for scrapers and slender unifacial or bifacial lances or spear points. Its distribution extended north to Zambia and south to the Orange Free State and perhaps the Cape. Bambata pottery ware is known only from contexts of the 1st millennium AD in Zimbabwe. It is elaborately decorated with stamped designs.

Bambuk: An area of alluvial gold fields in Guinea, near the headwaters of the Niger and Senegal Rivers. The gold, traded to trans-Saharan markets, contributed to the wealth of the empires of Ghana and Mali, which had an intermediate position between Bambuk and the markets.

Bampur: A site in southeastern Iran with a series of prehistoric mounds and a medieval fort. There is a pottery sequence from the mid-3rd millennium to c. 1900 BC, which exhibits links to pottery from Afghanistan and Umm an-Nar Island in the Persian Gulf.

banana: A giant edible fruit-bearing herb of the genus Musa, which has hundreds of varieties in cultivation. Consumption of the banana is mentioned in early Greek, Latin, and Arab writings, and Alexander the Great saw bananas on an expedition to India. Just after the discovery of America, the banana was brought from the Canary Islands to the New World, where it was first established in Hispaniola and soon spread to other islands and the mainland. Linguistic evidence supports the probability that bananas were being cultivated by Austronesians in Southeast Asia by 3000 BC.

Banas: A Chalcolithic culture of Rajasthan, India, of the 3rd and 2nd millennia BC. Archaeological evidence indicates that early humans lived along the banks of the Banas River (and its tributaries) about 100,000 years ago. The sites at Ahar, Gilund, and Kalibangan reveal Harappan (Indus) and post-Harappan culture (3rd–2nd millennia BC) with black-and-red

ware, often with white painted designs, and other related red wares. Copper and bronze were very common, and agriculture was attested. The Ahar occupation lasted c. 2200–1500 BC. Pottery fragments at Kalibangan are carbon dated to 2700 BC.

Banaue: A region of rice and house terraces in northern Luzon, the Philippines, which dates to c. 1000 BC. It belonged to the Ifugao people, and the terraces extend in giant steps up mountain sides.

Banawali: A site in northern India with occupation between 2500–1500 BC. The earliest settlement had pottery similar to Early Harappan. A second phase was urban with residential blocks on regular streets and Mature Harappan-type pottery. The third phase had pottery comparable to Late Harappan wares (Bara ware, Late Siswal ware, ochre-colored pottery).

Ban Chiang: A settlement site in northeast Thailand with burial deposits from 3600 BC–AD 1600, was occupied from c. 4500 BC. Rice was grown and bronze cast, according to the earliest records. Iron and rice paddy field cultivation began in the 2nd millennium. The basal burials are associated with incised and cord-marked pottery, copper and bronze artifacts. Levels dated to the late 2nd and 1st millennia BC have produced a variety of curvilinear painted red-on-buff pottery, together with iron, and bones of water buffalo. However, there is disagreement over the dating of Ban Chiang, especially for the bronze, iron, and painted pottery. (*syn.* Ban Chiang Hian)

band: A term in cultural anthropology describing the simplest type of human social organization consisting of a small number of nuclear families (30–50 people) who are informally organized for subsistence and security purposes. Bands are egalitarian and based mainly on kinship and marriage, and the division of labor is based on age and sex. Bands may also be integrated into a larger community, usually called a tribe. Bands exist in sparsely populated areas and use primitive technologies (and are often hunters and gatherers)—ranging from the desert-dwelling Australian Aborigines, the Pygmies of the Congo rain forests, and the Kaska Indians of the Yukon. Bands often moved seasonally to exploit wild (undomesticated) food resources.

Bandkeramik: A pottery of the Danubian I culture, a Neolithic culture that existed over large areas of Europe north and west of the Danube River c. 5th millennium BC. The pottery consists of hemispherical bowls and globular jars, usually round based and strongly suggesting copies of gourds. The name refers specifically to the standard incised linear decoration, which was pairs of parallel lines forming spirals, meanders, chevrons, and so on. There was farming of emmer wheat and barley and the keeping of domestic animals such as cattle. The most common stone tool was a polished stone adze. The people lived in large rectangular houses in medium-sized village communities or in small, dispersed clusters. (*syn.* Linearbandkeramik, LBK, Linienbandkeramik [German])

Ban Don Ta Phet: A burial site near U Thong, Thailand, dating to c. 400–200 BC, with etched stone and beads from India and other evidence of long-range trade by sea and land routes. Local wares were iron tools and cast-bronze bowls.

Bandung microliths: A Mid-Holocene obsidian industry of west Java's Bandung Plateau. It was characterized by small backed flakes and other tools.

Banjica:: A settlement on the slopes of the Avala Hill in Belgrade, Serbia. One of the horizons has been dated to c. 3760 BC. The culture is Vinca, and some complete house plans have been recovered with details of food preparation, weaving, and working pits. Pottery with incised signs might indicate ritual activities.

Ban Kao: A burial site in western Thailand, which spanned 2500–1600 BC. There is elaborately shaped unpainted pottery with a range of bone, shell, and stone artifacts.

Ban Nadi: A settlement site near Ban Chiang, Thailand, occupied from c. 1500 BC–AD 250. It was the location of tin-bronze production after 500 BC, with axes, projectile points, and jewelry. Iron was smelted and forged for bangles, hoes, knives, and spearheads from c. 100 BC to AD 200. The bronze wares were bowls, bracelets, and lead-bronze bells.

banner stone: A stone atlatl—a throwing-stick weight—put on the shaft to give great propulsion to a thrown dart. The stone is perforated for hafting and often has a bipennate, "butterfly," or banner-like appearance. (*syn.* [also bird stone, boat stone] bannerstone)

Banpo: (Pan-p'o) The site of an early Yangshao Neolithic village, now a museum at Xi'an, China, in the basin of the confluence of the Yellow River (Huang Ho), the Fen Ho, and Kuei Shui. Radiocarbon dates range from c. 4800–4300 BC. The settlement was about 50,000 square meters and included a cemetery and pottery kilns outside a ditch that surrounded the residences. Dogs, cattle, sheep, chicken, and pigs were domesticated, and millet, rice, kaoling, and possibly soybeans grown. The horse and silkworm may also have been raised. Unpainted pottery was cord marked or stamped, and fine "ceremonial" pottery vessels were painted in black or red with some simple geometric patterns and drawings of fish, turtles, deer, and faces. There were some elaborately worked objects in jade as well as everyday objects made from flint, bone, and ground stone. Sites with similar remains have been excavated at nearby Jiangzhai, Baoji Beishouling, and Hua Xian Yuanjunmiao. These sites all exhibit the first evidence of food production in China.

Banshan: (Pan-shan) Site of a Neolithic cemetery in the Tao River valley of China, the type site of the Banshan (or Pan-shan) culture, which belongs to the western or Gansu branch of the Yangshao Neolithic. Banshan is best known for its painted pottery first found in a grave in 1923. Pan-shan ware is generally considered to date from between 2500–2000 BC, but it may extend as far back as 3000 BC or be as late as c. 1500 BC (Shang dynasty). Most pottery is unglazed urns or reddish brown with painted designs in black and brown, probably applied with a brush, consisting of geometric patterns or stylized figures of people, fish, or birds. The wares were probably shaped on a slow or hand-turned wheel. The handles are set low on the body of the urns, and the lower part of the body is left undecorated—like Greek Proto-Geometric funerary ware. The site was an important find because of the lack of Neolithic Chinese pottery up to 1923. A late stage of Banshan is named after the site of Machang. (*syn.* Pan-shan)

Banteay Srei: A small, beautiful sandstone monument in Angkor, Cambodia, built in 967. Episodic relief (relief panels illustrating various aspects of the royal mythology) sculpture first appears on Banteay Srei. The relief revolves around a series of Indian legends dealing with the cosmic mountain Meru as the source of all creation and with the divine origin of water. The chief artistic achievement of its sophisticated architecture is the way in which the spaces between the walls of the enclosures, the faces of the terraces, and the volumes of the shrine buildings are conceived and coordinated. It seems to have been influenced by the architecture of the Hindu Pallava dynasty in southeastern India. (*syn.* [Khmer "the citadel of the ladies"])

Ban Tha Kae: A prehistoric site in central Thailand near copper sources with a long sequence from Neolithic through Iron Ages, paralleling Khorat sites.

Bantu: A Niger-Congo language family, with approximately 60,000,000 speakers of more than 200 distinct languages, who occupy almost the entire southern projection of the African continent (roughly from the bulge downward). The classification is linguistic as the cultures of the Bantu speakers are extremely diverse. The languages are closely interrelated, indicating expansion of the population from a single source, probably the eastern Nigeria/Cameroon area. Throughout the region, these first farming settlements are marked by a common pottery tradition, the "Early Iron Age" complex.

Baoji: (Pao-chi) An area situated on the north bank of the Wei River, a strategic and transportation center since early times, controlling the northern end of a pass across the Tsinling Mountains. There are Neolithic remains, which may be antecedents of the Banpo culture. Western Zhou bronzes have been found in the Baoji area. Tombs of the 19th century BC contained ritual vessels and the earliest known evidence of silk embroidery. (*syn.* Pao-chi)

Baphuon: Temple mountain built by the Baphuon of Uda-yadityavarman II (reigned AD 1050–1066) in Angkor, Cambodia, unfortunately almost completely destroyed. It was a vast sandstone monument 480 yards (440 m) long and 140 yards (130 m) wide, approached by a 200-yard (180-m) causeway raised on pillars. Its ground plan shows a fully articulated structure, and it was the immediate prototype for the great Angkor Wat. It was, at the time, the most massive artificial mountain of classical Cambodia and the second largest monument after Angkor Wat.

Baradostian: An Upper Palaeolithic flint industry following the Mousterian in northern Iraq and Iran, with the type site in a cave at Shanidar. It has radiocarbon dates c. 30,000 BC and may have begun as early as 36,000 BC. The Baradostian was replaced by a local Upper Palaeolithic industry called the Zarzian (12,000–10,000 BC), probably caused by the extreme cold of the last phase of the Würm glaciation. The Zarzian marks the end of the Iranian Paleolithic sequence that preceded various Mesolithic developments in the Middle East.

bar and dot notation: A Mesoamerican counting system in which a bar stands for 5 and a dot for 1. A stela at Chiapa de Corzo, dating to 36 BC, is the earliest example. The system came into use throughout Mesoamerica and is closely associated with the development of Maya and Zapotec writing.

baray: Large rectangular water reservoirs of the Angkor period in Khmer.

Barbar: A site and culture of northern Bahrain with a sequence of square temples built on an oval platform, dating from the late 3rd to mid-2nd millennia BC. The culture had distinctive pottery and seals and included sites at Qal'at al Bahrain, Bahrain Tumulus Fields, and others from Failaka to Qatar.

barbican: An outer fortification or defense of a city, castle, fort, or settlement, especially a double or single tower erected over a gateway or bridge. It often served as a watch tower. The term was also used for a temporary wooden tower or bulwark. (*syn.* antemural)

barbotine: A primitive technique of decorating pottery by adding thick slip to the surface of a pot before firing. The term also refers to the creamy mixture of kaolin clay itself, for pottery ornamented with barbotine, and to the technique of applying incrustation of this mixture to a ceramic surface for decorative effect. The slip was not applied evenly, but formed a thick incrustation in patches or trails. On certain types of pottery, such as the Nene Valley ware, the barbotine decoration may form a picture or a pattern. Sometimes the result is simply a roughened surface, rather like icing on a cake. The method was particularly popular in Roman Gaul and Britain.

Barca: A Bronze Age settlement of the Otomani culture in eastern Slovakia. Twenty-three large houses with hearths have been found.

bar chart: A statistical method of representing numerical data in a diagram by rectangles of equal width but of varying height or length, drawn side by side along an axis. An assemblage of different types of flint tool can be represented with bars on the horizontal scale, and the actual numbers or percentage of the total of each type recorded on a vertical scale. The bar chart gives an immediate visual representation of the components of the assemblage. A bar chart differs from a histogram, the latter representing different measurements of the same attribute, and therefore the horizontal scale is not arbitrary but ordered.

Barche di Solferino: A Bronze Age Polada culture settlement on Lake Garda, northern Italy, dating to the 2nd millennium BC. Finds include wooden vessels, wheels, and a dugout canoe—all preserved by the mud. The houses were raised off the ground with timbers.

bar-gorget: A bar-like ornament, usually of polished stone and perforated, worn around the throat.

Barkaer: A site of the final Early Neolithic (Phase C, TRB culture) in northeast Jutland, Denmark. There was a cobbled street, two timber buildings (80 m long and divided into 26 single rooms), which were at first thought to be houses but which may have been burial structures. Offerings in the pits below the buildings included amber beads, copper objects, and pottery.

bark shrine: A type of small temple in the shape of a Nile boat, with the prow and stern decorated with the aegis of a god. The cabin contained the cult image of the deity. The term also refers to a small temple, attached to the main Egyptian temples of the Late and Greco-Roman periods. These were where the god of the main temple was "born," or, if the main temple was dedicated to a goddess, the bark shrine was where she bore her child. (*syn.* mammisi, bark)

barley: A hardy group of staple cereals (genus Hordeum), cultivated in all parts of the world and since at least 7000 BC in the Near East, at least as early as wheat. The two-row barley, *Hordeum distichum*, was derived from the wild *H. spontaneum*, distributed from the Aegean to the Hindu Kush. It is recorded from Jarmo and spread as far as Neolithic Switzerland before being replaced by the second group. Six-row barleys, *H. hexastichum*, arose from *H. distichum* in cultivation. Its distribution extended from China to Egypt and Switzerland, and it is still occasionally grown. Modern barleys are all *H. tetrastichum*, a development from hexastichum recorded as early as the Neolithic in Britain and Denmark. All the domestic barleys are closely related, and their nomenclature is jumbled. Barley is used as food (in the

United States and Great Britain) and in the preparation of malt liquors and spirits.

Barlovento: A site on the Gulf coast of Colombia, dating to 1500–1000 BC, with distinctive pottery with wide-lined incised curvilinear designs.

Barnenez: A Neolithic site in Brittany with radiocarbon dates in the 5th millennium BC. It consists of two long cairns, one with 11 passage graves placed side by side. The graves display a range of architectural techniques, using both large megalithic slabs and drystone walling; some chambers had corbelled vaults. Its dates may make it one of the earliest megalithic tombs in Europe.

barracks: A set of buildings erected or used as dormitories for troops. The Romans set up long, narrow buildings, and each held a centuria (80–100 men) and its centurion. When cavalry was in camp, each building then held two *turmae* or 62 men and their *decurions*.

Barrancoid subtradition: A ceramic tradition possibly originating on the Caribbean coast of Colombia and established in the Orinoco Delta by c. 1000 BC. It spread down to the coast and (at the turn of the millennium) east and west to Guyana and Colombia. The pottery is skillfully modeled with biomorphic ornamentation and broad-lined incised patterns. The type site is Barrancas. (*syn.* Barrancas; Neo-Indian epoch)

barrel vault: A semicylindrical roof, used especially for lids of Egyptian Old Kingdom sarcophagi and which may have been used for mastaba superstructures.

barrio: A ward, neighborhood, or quarter of a city, town, or settlement in a Spanish-speaking country or region, as in the Andes. The term may also refer to a rural settlement.

barrow: A round or elongated mound of earth or stones used in early times to cover one or more burials; a grave mound. The mound is often surrounded by a ditch, and the burials may be contained in a cist, mortuary enclosure, mortuary house, or chamber tomb. There are two types, the long (elongated) and the round barrow (also known as tumulus). The former were built in the Late Stone Age, the latter in the Bronze Age, although burial under a round mound was occasionally practiced during the Roman, Anglo-Saxon, and Viking periods. The long barrow was a tribal or family burial vault built of stone slabs, some weighing many tons, and covered with earth or stones. The large, round barrows were often communal. They are often found in prehistoric sites in Britain—earthen (or unchambered) long barrows from the Early and Middle Neolithic (Windmill Hill culture). Other long barrows were constructed over megalithic tombs of gallery grave types. Most of the British round barrows incorporate circles of stakes. Bowl barrows—simple round mounds, often surrounded by a ditch—were the most common form, used throughout the Bronze Age and sporadically

also in the Iron Age. The Wessex culture of the southern English Early Bronze Age was characterized by special types of barrows: bell, disk, saucer, and pond barrows. Bell barrows have relatively small mounds and a berm or gap between the mound and the ditch; disk barrows are very small mounds in the center of a circular open space, surrounded by a ditch; saucer barrows are low disk-like mounds occupying the entire space up to the ditch; while the oddly named pond barrows are not mounds at all, but circular dish-shaped enclosures surrounded by an external bank. The related term *cairn* is used to describe a mound constructed exclusively of stone. Barrow burials occur also in Roman and post-Roman times: One of the most famous of all barrows in Britain is that covering the Anglo-Saxon boat burial at Sutton Hoo. (*syn.* burial mound; tumulus; burial cairn)

barter: A type of direct exchange of different goods, not using any sort of currency, in which each party tries to get an advantage, however slight.

Barumini: The site of a *nurage* (towerlike monument) in southern Sardinia with a radiocarbon date of c. 1800 BC, which remained in occupation until the Roman period after being temporarily deserted in the 6th century BC. It began as a single tower c. 17 meters high and was later surrounded by a perimeter wall with a complex of smaller towers and a village of stone huts. (*syn.* su Nuraxi)

basal grinding: The grinding of projectile points at their base and lower edges (so that the lashings will not be cut); a Paleo-Indian cultural practice. Basal thinning obtains the same result through the removal of small chips instead of grinding.

basalt: A type of very hard, dark, dense rock, igneous in origin, composed of augite or hornblende containing titaniferous magnetic iron and crystals of feldspar. It often lies in columnar strata, as at the Giant's Causeway in Ireland and Fingal's Cave in the Hebrides. It is greenish- or brownish-black and much like lava in appearance. It is also abundant in Egypt and Greece.

Basarabi culture: An Iron Age culture of cemeteries and settlement sites over much of Romania with its type site on the Danube. It is a local version of the Hallstatt culture, dating to 975–850 BC.

Basin of Mexico: A basin enclosed by mountains with cultural remains as early as 19,000 BC at Tlapacoya and 15,000 BC at Tlatilco. The Basin contains the current capital, Mexico City, Mexico, the remains of the Aztec capital of Tenochtitlán, and the cities of Cuicuilco and Teotihuacán. Dry farming, swidden agriculture, *chinampas*, and irrigation have been used to cultivate the area. Important periods in the area's prehistory were from c. 100 BC–AD 650 and from AD 1200–1520, before the Spanish conquest.

basilica: Originally a royal palace that consisted of a large oblong building or hall with double colonnades and a semicircular apse at the end, used for a court of justice and place of public assembly. It formed one side of the forum or marketplace. The term owes its original meaning to the fact that in Macedonia the kings, and in Greece the archon Basileus, dispensed justice in buildings of this description. The Romans, who adopted the basilica from those countries, used it as a court, a branch of the forum, and so on. The first basilica was built at Rome, 182/184 BC. One such building is the Basilica of Maxentius, which has survived in the ruins of the Forum in Rome. Its aisled-hall plan was adopted by many early Christian churches. The form of construction remained popular for a variety of religious purposes in Rome, Ravenna, and North Africa from the 4th–12th centuries. Constantine, the first Christian emperor, constructed several basilican churches in the 4th century, including the first St. Peters. (*syn.* [Greek "royal building"])

Basse-Yutz: Bronze wine flagons found in Moselle, France, with coral and enamel inlay of c. 400 BC. The pair is thought to have come from a Celtic chieftain's grave.

Basket Maker: Two early chronological periods of the early Puebloans or Anasazi–AD 100–500, followed by the Modified Basket Maker period, 500–700. The people lived in the Four Corners area (northwestern New Mexico, southwestern Colorado, southeastern Utah, and northeastern Arizona) of the United States. The origin of the Basket Maker Indians is not known, but it is evident that when they first settled in the area they were already excellent basket weavers and that they were supplementing hunting and wild-seed gathering with the cultivation of maize and pumpkins. They lived either in caves or out in the open in shelters constructed of a masonry of poles and adobe mud. Both caves and houses contained special pits, often roofed over, used for food storage. The Basket Makers were among the first village agricultural societies in the Southwest. Three Basketmaker stages were recognized at the 1927 Pecos Conference of Southwesternists: Basketmaker I (hypothetical); Basketmaker II (AD 1–450), which was a large base camp and widely scattered seasonal camps where the preferred container was the basket; and Basketmaker III (450–700/750) in which there were small villages of pit houses in well-watered valley bottoms. Specialized structures such as wattle-and-daub storage bins and large rooms for communal activity (possibly early kivas) also began to occur more frequently in the latter stage. (*syn.* Basketmakers)

basketry: A class of artifacts created by the practice of weaving containers from vegetable fibers, twigs, or leaves. It was known in Mexico before 7000 BC and in Oregon before 8000 BC, and the earliest recorded examples in the Old World are from the Fayum in Egypt c. 5200 BC. Taking into consideration the perishability of basketry, even these may be comparatively late in the history of the technique. Basketry is not preserved in the same quantities as pottery and stone vessels. (*syn.* cordage)

Basques; Basque: A people living in both Spain and France in areas bordering the Bay of Biscay and encompassing the western foothills of the Pyrenees Mountains. The Basques are distinguished partly by an unusual pattern of blood groups, very high in the Rhesus negative factor, and by their language, quite unrelated to any other known one. They probably represent one of the people who inhabited Europe before the arrival of the Indo-Europeans. Basque is the only remnant of the languages spoken in southwestern Europe before that region was Romanized. The origin of the Basque language remains a mystery. It has been hypothesized that Basque had a genetic connection with the now-extinct Iberian and that both languages evolved from the Hamito-Semitic (Afro-Asiatic) language group—but there is another theory that the similarities between the two arose from geographic proximity. Although Basque and Iberian are similar, the knowledge of Basque could not help decipher ancient Iberian inscriptions discovered in eastern Spain and on the Mediterranean coast of France. Basque is also linked with Caucasian, an ancient language spoken in the Caucasus region. (*syn.* Spanish Vasco, or Vascongado, Basque Euskaldunak or Euskotarak)

Basra: The second-largest city and principal port of Iraq, which from ancient times was a center of commerce, finance, letters, poetry, and science. It was founded as a military encampment by the second caliph, 'Umar I, in 638 about 8 miles (13 km) from the modern town of az-Zubayr, southeastern Iraq. Its proximity to the Persian Gulf and its location on the west bank of the Shatt al-Arab give it easy access to both the Tigris and Euphrates Rivers and to eastern frontiers. The first architecturally significant mosque in Islam was constructed there in 665. From the late 9th century, Basra suffered a series of disasters and gradually declined. The Zanj (Negro slaves who worked in the fields and plantations of southern Iraq) revolted in 869–873 and sacked the city, and in 923 it was plundered by the Qarmarthians. In 1050, parts of the city were in ruins. (*syn.* Arabic Al-Basrah)

bas-relief: A low relief technique of sculpture or carved work in which the figures project less than half of their true proportions from the surface on which they are carved. The term also describes sculptures or carvings in low relief. Mezzo-relievo means projecting exactly half; alto-relievo more than half. (*syn.* low-relief, basso-relievo; low relief)

Bastam: A Urartian settlement in northwest Iran with a citadel of monumental buildings (palaces). Several Urartian texts and sealed bullae kept records of goods stored and traded. Urartian and past-Urartian pottery has been chronologically classified.

Basta, Tell: The site of a temple and town in the eastern Nile Delta, about 80 kilometers northeast of Cairo, which flourished from the 4th Dynasty to the end of the Roman period (c. 2614 BC–AD 395). The main monument at the site is the red granite temple of the cat goddess Bastet. (*syn.* ancient Per-Bastet, Bubastis)

Bastet: The ancient Lower Egyptian goddess worshiped in the form of a lioness, and later a cat. Bastet's form was often changed after the domestication of the cat around 1500 BC. Her principal cult center was Bubastis in the Nile River delta, but she also had an important cult at Memphis. In the Late and Ptolemaic periods, large cemeteries of mummified cats were created at both sites, and thousands of bronze statuettes of the goddess were put there as votive offerings. Her cult was carried to Italy by the Romans, and traces have been found in Rome, Ostia, Nemi, and Pompeii. (*syn.* Bastis, Bast, Ubasti)

Bat: A goddess of the seventh Upper Egyptian nome, usually represented by a cow's head with curling horns. The earliest depiction may have been the pair of heads at the top of the Narmer palette (c. 3100 BC).

Batalimo: A site in the Central African Republic with a large Neolithic tool assemblage of flakes, side scrapers, flaked axes, and elaborately decorated pottery.

Batán Grande: A large architectural complex of South America located in the Lambayeque Valley of north coastal Peru. The site has more than 30 huge platform mounds with an estimated 750,000 burials—most of them looted by treasure hunters who have taken immense quantities of gold, silver, copper, and bronze objects. Occupation at Batán Grande went from the Formative (Cupisnique) to the Inca period. The site was the capital of a powerful state between AD 850–1300. With Batán Grande, Cerro de los Cementerios was a copper-processing area, linked to the Cerro Blanco mine by a prehistoric road. Excavations have revealed metal artifacts, smelting furnaces, grinding slabs, crushed slag, and pottery blow tubes.

Bat Cave: A cave in southern New Mexico's Carlsbad Caverns National Park, notable for its evidence of prehistoric plant cultivation. The site of Bat Cave has produced specimens of a type of primitive corn that is also known from the Flacco phase in Tamaulipas at 2000 BC but that is here in association with a Chiricahua assemblage from which Cochise materials (maize and squash) have been dated at about 1000 BC. Evidence of beans (dated to 1000–400 BC) was found in association with San Pedro materials. Early levels indicate the use of primitive pod corn (dated c. 3500 BC), but a cultivated form of maize was in use by 2500 BC, the earliest date for cultigens in the American Southwest. During the summer, a colony of several million bats inhabits the cave.

Bath: A site of hot mineral springs (120°F [49°C]), which attracted the Romans after their invasion of Britain, who founded Bath as Aquae Sulis, dedicated to the deity of Sul (Minerva). From the late 1st century AD onward, the springs became the center for a complex of lavish monumental buildings. These include the temple of Sulis Minerva and an extensive collection of baths, the most notable being the vaulted Great Bath. (*syn.* [Aquae Sulis])

baths, Roman: The Roman baths featuring a combination of steaming, cleaning, and massage appeared wherever the Romans made conquests. In Rome itself, the aqueducts fed sumptuous baths such as those of Caracalla, which covered 28 acres (11 hectares). From the 1st century BC onward, the Romans built establishments called *balneae* or, later, thermae, incorporating suites of rooms at different temperatures. A typical installation would include a *tepidarium* (warm room, probably without bath), a *caldarium* (hot, with plunge bath), a *frigidarium* (cold, also with bath), and an *apodyterium* (changing room). Elaborate examples might also include a *laconicum* (room with dry heat), a swimming bath, an exercise area (*palaestra*), gardens, and a library. These complexes were important social meeting points and were not limited to high society. Most large private houses from the 2nd century BC onward had their own bath suite. The four large series of baths at Rome were built by Titus, Trajan, Caracalla, and Diocletian. Baths existed as early as the 4th century BC. (*syn.* bathhouse)

bâton de commandement: A name given to perforated batons made of antler rod of the Upper Palaeolithic period in western Europe, from the Aurignacian period (30,000 years ago) through the Magdalenian. They have a hole through the thickest part of the head and are usually 30 centimeters long, but are often broken. The perforation is smooth and round, and highly decorated examples come from the Magdalenian culture. Their use is unknown.

batter: The slope of a wall, pier, terrace, or bank, from the perpendicular; a receding slope. The term also refers to the slope of a structure built specifically to increase the stability of a wall; usually subterranean. This functional and decorative technique was regularly employed for the walls of mastaba tombs as well as the enclosure walls of Egyptian temples, where it was associated with pan bedding and sectional construction. Inclination is expressed as one foot horizontally per vertical unit (in feet). (*syn.* batter [v.])

battering ram: An ancient military "engine" used for smashing in doors and battering down walls. It consisted of a beam of wood with a head of iron—originally a ram's head. It had a roof to protect those working it from the missiles of the garrison.

Battersea Shield: A Late Iron Age parade shield found in the River Thames at Battersea, England. It was a fine example of insular Celtic Art, with an elongated bronze body with rounded ends and decorated in relief and with red glass inlay.

battle ax: A type of prehistoric stone weapon, designed as a weapon of war. It is always of the shaft-hole variety and frequently has a hammer, knob, or point at the end opposite from the cutting edge. In stone, it is common throughout most of Europe in the Late Neolithic and Copper Age and often associated with corded ware and beakers. (The term Battle Ax culture is often used as a synonym for Corded Ware or Single Grave culture.) Further east, more elaborate ones of copper or gold were more ceremonial than functional. The Vikings made iron battle axes and used them well into the Middle Ages. The pole ax is distinguished from the battle ax by a spike on the back of the ax. (*syn.* battleaxe, battle-axe)

Battle Ax culture: A number of Late Neolithic cultural groups in Europe, which appeared between 2800–2300 BC. So-named for their characteristic shaft-hole polished stone battle ax, the people were also known for their use of horses. Their place of origin is not certain, but it was most likely east rather than west of their area of spread. It was a homogeneous culture with central European trade links, and it remained in some areas through the Stone and Bronze Ages. In central Europe, the Beaker folk came into contact with the Battle Ax culture, which was also characterized by beaker-shaped pottery (although different in detail). The two cultures gradually intermixed and later spread from central Europe to eastern England. The Battle Ax people were also responsible for the dissemination of Indo-European speech. (*syn.* Battle-Axe culture; Single-Grave culture; Single Grave culture; Battle Ax culture, Corded Ware culture)

battleship curve: A lens-shaped seriation graph formed by plotted points representing artifact type frequencies. The rise in popularity of an artifact, its period of maximum popularity, and the artifact's eventual decline can be plotted, as well as its origin and disappearance. (*syn.* battleship-shaped curve)

Batungan: Cave sites in the central Philippines dating to at least 900 BC, with flaked stone tools and pottery, some decorated with stamped patterns. There is a possible connection with the pottery of Taiwan, with Kalanay/Sulawesi, and with Lapita ware.

Baturong Caves: Rock shelter sites in north Borneo dating to c. 17,000–12,000 BP, with a stone industry characterized by long knives. It succeeded the Tinkayu industry and preceded the Madai Caves.

Bayeux Tapestry: A medieval embroidery depicting the Norman Conquest of England in 1066, which is considered a remarkable work of art and important as a source for 11th-century history. It consists of a roll of unbleached linen worked in colored worsted with illustrations and is about 70 meters long and 50 centimeters deep. The work was probably commissioned by Bishop Odo of Bayeux, a half-brother of William the Conquerer, and took about 2 years to complete. It was likely finished no later than 1092. The tapestry depicts the events leading up to the invasion of England by William, Duke of Normandy, and the Battle of Hastings on 14 October 1066, when the English King Harold was defeated and killed. Although not proved, the tapestry appears to have been designed and embroidered in England. The themes are enacted much like a feudal drama or chanson de geste. The technical detail and iconography of the Bayeux Tapestry are of great importance. For instance, the 33 buildings depicted offer views of the contemporary churches, castles, towers, and motte and bailey castles. The battle scenes give details of the infantry and cavalry formations, Norman armor and weapons, and clothing and hairstyles of the time. The invasion fleet is "Viking double enders" (clinker-built long boats, propelled by oars and a single mast). The tapestry was "discovered" in the nave of Bayeux Cathedral in France by the French antiquarian and scholar Bernard de Montfaucon, who published the earliest complete reproduction of it in 1730. It narrowly escaped destruction during the French Revolution, was exhibited in Paris at Napoleon's wish in 1803–1804, and thereafter kept in the Bayeux public library.

Bayon: An enormous sandstone monument in northwest Angkor, Cambodia, built c. 1200 by the Buddhist king Jayavarman VII (1181–c. 1220), the last great ruler of the Khmer Empire. It was his temple-mountain and the center of his restored capital Angkor Thom. Bayon had a central circular sanctuary, situated in two bas-relief covered galleries, which vividly depicted the king's battles with Cham forces. Bayon was a distinctively Mahayana Buddhist central pyramid temple designed to serve as the primary locus of the king's royal cult and also as his own personal mausoleum.

BC: An abbreviation used to denote so many years "Before Christ" or before the beginning of the Christian calendar. The lower case *bc* represents uncalibrated radiocarbon years; the capitals BC denote a calibrated radiocarbon date or a date such as a historically derived one, that does not need calibration. There is no year 0: 1 BC is followed by AD 1. (*syn.* bc, BCE, B.C.E.)

BCE: Before the common era; before the Christian era. Dates are often listed as BCE (Before the Common Era = BC) and CE (Common Era = AD). In the Gregorian calendar, eras are designated BCE (before the Common Era or Christian Era) and CE (Common Era or Christian Era), terms equivalent to BC (before Christ) and AD (Latin: anno Domini). (*syn.* B.C.E.)

be: An administrative unit of Japan's Yamato state in the 5th–6th centuries AD. It consisted of the craftspeople and palace service people and their goods and services.

bead: A small, circular, tubular, or oblong ornament with a perforated center; usually made from shell, stone, bone, or glass.

beaker: A simple pottery drinking vessel without handles, more deep than wide, much used in prehistoric Europe. The pottery was usually red or brown burnished ware, decorated with horizontal panels of comb- or cord-impressed designs. It was distributed in Europe from Spain to Poland and from Italy to Scotland in the years after 2500 BC, and the international bell-beaker is particularly widespread, although uncommon in Britain. In Britain, there are local variants, the long-necked (formerly A) beakers of eastern England and the short-necked (formerly C) beakers of Scotland. There are local developments elsewhere, such as the Veluwe beakers in Holland. Beaker vessels are commonly found in graves, which were often single inhumations under round barrows; commonly associated finds include copper or bronze daggers and ornaments, flint arrowheads, stone wrist guards, and stone battle axes. In many northern and western areas, users were the first to introduce copper metallurgy. The widespread distribution of beaker finds has led to the frequent identification of a Beaker people and speculations about their origins. (*syn.* bell beaker [see also funnel beaker, protruding foot beaker])

Beaker people: A widespread Late Neolithic European people of the third and second millennia BC named after the characteristic bell-shaped beakers found buried with their dead. These people spread a knowledge of metalworking in central and western Europe from c. 2500–2000 BC. They first came to Britain between 1900–1800 BC in successive waves, via Holland, from the Rhineland. Their origins are uncertain, with theories of their being the Battle Ax people from south Russia, the Spanish Megalithic people from Almeria, or people from Portugal and Hungary. They were copper and bronze workers and famous for their great collective tombs. The assemblages of grave goods—decorated pottery, fighting equipment (arrowheads, wrist guards, daggers)—were characteristic of the people, who lived in small groups mainly by major river routes as they were known traders. Burial was by contracted inhumation in a trench, under a round barrow, or as a secondary burial in some form of chamber tomb. Each burial was accompanied by a beaker, presumably to hold drink, probably alcoholic, for the dead person's last journey. (*syn.* Beaker Folk, Beaker culture; Bell Beaker culture)

beans: The seeds or pods of certain leguminous plants of the family Fabaceae and important to people since the beginning of food production. Most modern beans are of the genus Phaseolus, different species of which occur wild in the two hemispheres. Their cultivation commenced at an early date in both. These species all originated in Mexico and South America, spreading to the Old World after Columbus. The earliest finds of cultivated Phaseolus beans are from 6th millennium BC Peru and Mexico. *Vicia faba*, the ancestor of the broad bean, was confined to the Old World and was already being grown in the Neolithic Near East. Later in the Neolithic, the species appeared in Spain, Portugal, and eastern Europe. During the Bronze Age, the field bean grew in southern and central Europe, and by the Iron Age it reached Britain.

bear: A large carnivore of the family Ursidae, closely related to the dog (family Canidae) and raccoon (Procyonidae). The bear is the most recently evolved of carnivores, and it appears to have diverged from the dog family during the Miocene. It evolved through such forms as the Pliocene Hyaenarctos (of Europe, Asia, and North America), into modern types such as the black and brown bear (Ursus). Today's bears are of three groups: the brown bears, the black bears, and the polar bear. Occasional finds of fossil polar bear bones outside the Arctic Circle are presumably related to the presence of pack ice and ice shelves at the edges of ice sheets during glaciations. Brown bears existed in Europe and Asia during the late Quaternary period. One very large variant evolved in Europe, the Cave Bear, whose fossils are quite common in Quaternary cave deposits.

Beazley, Sir John Davidson (1885–1970): A British antiquarian who identified much Athenian pottery by the names of the craftsmen who made it.

bec: A Palaeolithic flake boring tool that was retouched on one edge to form a point.

bed: The smallest division of sediment or rock of a stratigraphic series, greater than 1 centimeter thick. It is distinguished from overlying and underlying beds by well-defined divisional or bedding planes.

bedding trench: A trench or slot dug into the ground to receive the foundations of walls or into which timber is laid so that wall posts can be inserted securely.

Bede the Venerable, Saint (AD 672/3–735): Anglo-Saxon theologian, historian, and chronologist who is known for his prolific writings, including *Historia ecclesiastica gentis Anglorum* (Ecclesiastical History of the English People), an important source for the history of the conversion to Christianity of the Anglo-Saxon tribes. Divided into five books, it recorded (in Latin) events in Britain from the raids by Julius Caesar (55–54 BC) to the arrival in Kent (AD 597) of St. Augustine. For his sources, Bede claimed the authority of ancient letters, the "traditions of our forefathers," and his own knowledge of contemporary events. (*syn.* Baeda, Beda)

bedrock mortar: A deep basin set in granite or other large rock outcroppings, formed by the grinding or crushing of foods with stone. A flat or shallow surface of this same type is called a bedrock grinding slick.

Bedsa: A rock-cut Buddhist temple in Deccan, India, dated 1st century BC. Its interior is elaborately decorated, and the pillars have vase-shaped bases and bell-shaped capitals surmounted by sculpted human and animal groups. In front of the temple is a facade and a large entrance with decorated pillars.

beehive tomb: An architectural structure of the Mycenaean civilization, a pointed dome built up of overhanging (corbeled) blocks of conglomerate masonry cut and polished, often with an alley or approach and a great door. The rich or noble of the Bronze Age were buried in these sometimes enormous, perfectly proportioned vaults although they were built in the Shaft Grave period as well, perhaps first in Messenia in the 16th century and then in Greece by the middle of the 15th century. The tholos tomb has three parts: a narrow entranceway, or dromos, often lined with fieldstones and later with cut stones; a deep doorway, or stomion, covered over with one to three lintel blocks; and a circular chamber with a high vaulted or corbeled roof, the thalamos. Most tholos tombs have collapsed, often when the lintel cracked and gave way, and their contents have largely been looted. (*syn.* tholos)

Beersheba: A site in southern Israel, which was a frontier post in ancient Palestine. The earliest occupations were in the 12th and 11th centuries BC, but the first town belonged to the period of the United Monarchy (10th century). The 8th century BC town wall with a great gateway flanked by double guard chambers and external towers has been excavated. There was also a 15-meter ring road inside the wall, which divided the inner and outer towns. Beersheba may have been the administrative center of the region, and there are indications of storerooms, which may have contained the royal stores for the collection of taxes in kind (grain, wine, oil, etc.). The town was destroyed in the mid-7th century BC. Beersheba is first mentioned as the site where Abraham, founder of the Jewish people, made a covenant with the Philistine king Abimelech of Gerar (Genesis 21). Isaac and Jacob, the other patriarchs, also lived there (Genesis 26, 28, 46).

beetle: Any member of the insect order Coleoptera, with at least 250,000 species (the largest order in the animal kingdom), characterized by their special forewings, which are modified into hardened wing covers (elytra) that cover a second pair of functional wings. The order includes some of the largest and smallest insects and is the most widely distributed insect order. Beetles can be found in all environments except Antarctica and the peaks of the highest mountains. Most feed either on other animals or on plants, but some eat decaying matter. Many beetles are very dependent on particular features of their environment; some, for example, live only in the bark of a particular tree. It is this "particularity" that makes beetles useful for reconstructing ancient environments. Parts of the tough beetle exoskeleton may be well preserved in acidic or waterlogged conditions (as in peats, silts, and lake clays). The temperature preferences of beetles may be determined from the fossils, making it possible to reconstruct climatic changes. Beetles can also be used to investigate changes in vegetation, living conditions, and food-storage problems.

Begram: A site in eastern Afghanistan north of Kabul, which has been identified as Kapisa, the capital of several Indo-Greek rulers of the 3rd and 2nd centuries BC and the Kushan summer capital from the 1st century BC to the 3rd century AD. It was important for its placement on the caravan route between India and the West. Excavations have yielded fragmentary ivory furniture, per-Islamic footstools of Indian origin (both c. 1st century AD), as well as painted glass from Alexandria; plaster matrices, bronzes, porphyries, and alabasters from Rome; carved ivories from India; and lacquers from China. The Persian Sasanians established control over parts of Afghanistan, including Begram, in AD 241. (*syn.* Bagram; Kapisa)

behavioral archaeology: The study of the relation between material culture and human behavior and the impact of humans and nature on material culture by interpreting its original use.

behavioral processes: Human activities including acquisition, manufacture, use, and deposition behavior, producing tangible archaeological remains.

Behbet el-Hagar: A town in the north-central Nile Delta, which flourished in the 30th Dynasty (380–343 BC) and the Ptolemaic period (332–30 BC). The site is dominated by the remains of a large granite temple of Isis. (*syn.* Per-hebyt, Iseum)

Behistun: A rock face on the Kermanshah-Hamadan road in Iran on which Darius I (Darius the Great, reigned 521–485 BC) recorded his victories that gave him the Achaemenid Empire in 522–520 BC. The bas-relief—400 feet above the road—shows Darius, under the protection of the god Ahuramazda, receiving his defeated enemies. The inscriptions were carved in the cuneiform script and repeated in the Old Persian, Elamite, and Babylonian languages. The rock face below them was then cut back to the vertical to prevent any attempt at defacement. In total, the area covered by the inscriptions and the relief panel was about 25 feet high and 50 feet wide. In 1833, Sir Henry Rawlinson went to Iran and became extremely interested in Persian antiquities and in deciphering the cuneiform writing at Behistun. Between 1835 and 1847, Rawlinson went through the intense work of copying the inscription from harrowing positions above the road. It enabled him subsequently to understand the cuneiform script and to decipher the languages of the inscription.

In 1837, he published his translations of the first two paragraphs of the inscription. After having to leave the country because of problems between Iran and Britain, Rawlinson was able to return in 1844 to obtain impressions of the Babylonian script. As a result, his *Persian Cuneiform Inscription at Behistun* was published (1846–1851)—containing a complete translation, analysis of the grammar, and notes. The accomplishment yielded valuable information on the history of ancient Persia and its rulers. With other scholars, he succeeded in deciphering the Mesopotamian cuneiform script by 1857. This provided the breakthrough to the decipherment later of other languages in the cuneiform script, including Sumerian. (*syn.* Bisitun, Bisotun)

Beidha: A site in south-central Yemen near Petra, first occupied in the Early Natufian and Aceramic Neolithic. It is situated on a high plateau and, until the unification of the two Yemen states in 1990, was part of North Yemen (San'a), although it lay near the disputed frontier with South Yemen. At first it was a semipermanent camp for those who lived off goat and ibex. Beidha was reoccupied c. 7000 BC by a Pre-Pottery Neolithic A (PPNA) group, who lived in a planned community of roughly circular semisubterranean houses. They domesticated goats and cultivated emmer, wheat, and barley. There was a succeeding PPNB phase in which the buildings changed to complexes of large rectangular rooms, each with small workshops attached and with plastered floors and walls. Burials without skulls were found, and there was also a separate ritual area away from the village. Finds from the site include materials from great distances, including obsidian from Anatolia and cowries and mother-of-pearl from the Red Sea. (*syn.* Bayda', Al-, Beida)

Beijing: The modern capital of China. More than 2,000 years ago, a site just outside present-day Peking was already an important military and trading center for the northeastern frontier of China. The Shang civilization reached this area in the early part of the dynasty and a grave of c. 14th century BC at Pinggu Liujiacun contained bronze ritual vessels and a bronze ax with a blade of forged meteoritic iron. There have been many early Zhou finds, notably at the cemetery site of Fangshan Liulihe. In 1267, during the Yüan (Mongol) dynasty (1206–1368), a new city built on the site (called Ta-tu) became the administrative capital of China. During the reigns of the first two emperors of the Ming dynasty (1368–1644), Nanking was the capital, and the old Mongol capital was renamed Pei-p'ing ("Northern Peace"); the third Ming emperor, however, restored it as the imperial seat of the dynasty and gave it a new name, Peking ("Northern Capital"). Peking has remained the capital of China except for a brief period (1928–49) when the Nationalist government again made Nanking the capital (then Chungking during World War II). (*syn.* Pei-ching, Peking)

Beikthano: A Buddhist religious and settlement site in central Burma of the early- to mid-1st millennium AD.

Beit el-Wali: A rock-cut temple on the west bank of the Nile (Lower Nubia), which was dedicated to Amun-Ra and built during the reign of Rameses II (1279–1213 BC).

Beit Mersim, Tell: A tell in the low hill country southwest of Hebron, on the west bank of the Jordan in Palestine. It was a fortified town of biblical times. William F. Albright uncovered successive occupation layers from the 3rd millennium BC (end of the Early Bronze Age) to the Babylonian destruction of c. 588 BC. It was a small walled town, and its finds helped Albright establish a chronology of the Levant from 2300–588 BC through the detailed analysis of Palestinian pottery. Excavations showed that the Canaanite town of the 14th–13th centuries had been destroyed by the Israelites toward the end of the 13th century and that the town was finished off by the Babylonians. (*syn.* Debir, Kirjath-Sepher [biblical], Lo-Debar, Tall Bayt Mirsham)

Belbasi: A cave on the southern coast of Anatolia, which gave its name to a late Palaeolithic culture. The tool kit includes tanged arrowheads, triangular points, and obliquely truncated blades. There are rock engravings in shelters such as Beldibi, the only known cave art in western Asia.

Beldibi: A rock shelter that gave its name to a Mesolithic or "Proto-Neolithic" culture succeeding the Belbasi culture in southern Anatolia. Phases contained imported obsidian and early forms of pottery. There is no evidence of food production or herding. Bones of deer, ibex, and cattle occur, and subsistence was likely assisted by coastal fishing and the gathering of wild grain.

Belgae: Any of the inhabitants of Gaul north of the Sequana and Matrona (Seine and Marne) Rivers of mixed Celtic and Germanic origin, first described by Julius Caesar in the mid-1st century BC. Their origins on the continent can be traced back to the La Tène period in the 5th century BC, and evidence suggests that the Romans penetrated into those areas about 150 BC. In Caesar's day, they held much of Belgium and parts of northern France and southeast England. The Belgae of Gaul formed a coalition against Caesar after his first Gallic campaign but were subdued the following year (57 BC). During the first half of the 1st century BC, Belgae from the Marne district had crossed into Britain and had formed the kingdom that in 55 BC was ruled by Cassivellaunus. After further Gallic victories (51–41 BC) by Caesar, other settlers took refuge across the Channel, and Belgic culture spread to most of lowland Britain. The three most important Belgic kingdoms, identified by their coinage, were centered at Colchester, St. Albans, and Silchester. Archaeologically, the Belgae can be identified with the bearers of the Aylesford-Swarling culture, otherwise known as Iron Age C. Coinage, the heavy plow, and the potter's wheel were introduced by the Belgae. They lived in large fortified settlements called *oppida*, and amphorae and Italian bronze vessels have been found in their richly furnished tombs.

Bel'kachi I: A settlement site on the Aldan River in central Siberia, occupied during the Neolithic (c. 4th millennium BC). Finds include the earliest pottery in Siberia, a hand-molded, sand-tempered ware decorated with net or mat impressions. There was a succeeding phase, often known as the Bel'kachinsk culture (3rd millennium BC), which had a distinctive pottery, decorated with impressions from a cord-wrapped paddle. In that area during the Late Neolithic (2nd millennium BC), check-stamped ware, made by beating with a grooved paddle, appeared. Changes in stone and bone tools occurred during the development of the Neolithic, but throughout the economic basis remained hunting and fishing.

bell: The earliest bell founding (i.e., the casting of bells from molten metal) is associated with the Bronze Age. The ancient Chinese were superb founders, their craft reaching an apex during the Chou dynasty (c. 1122–221 BC). Characteristic were elliptical temple bells with exquisite symbolic decorations cast onto their surfaces by the cire perdue, or lost wax, process. Bells had an important ceremonial role in ancient China during the Chou Dynasty. The earliest Chinese bells, of the Shang Dynasty (c. 1600–1123 BC), were mounted mouth upward and struck. Later bells hung mouth downward.

Bell Beaker: A type of pottery vessel found all over western and central Europe from the final Neolithic or Chalcolithic, c. 2500–1800 BC. The culture's name derives from the characteristic pottery, which looks like an inverted bell with globular body and flaring rim. The beakers were valuable and highly decorated. They are often associated with special artifacts in grave assemblages, including polished stone wrist guards, V-perforated buttons, and copper-tanged daggers.

Bellows Beach: A coastal occupation site on Oahu, Hawaii, which has produced some of the earliest occupation dates (AD 600–1000) of the island group. The assemblage is of Early Eastern Polynesian type: shell fishhooks, stone adzes, and bones of dog, pig, and rat.

belt hook: Small decorative and functional objects used as garment hooks in China, Korea, and other Far Eastern areas as early as the 7th century BC. Belt hooks have been found in Han tombs in southwestern China, but this luxury item was most in vogue during the Warring States period (5th–3rd centuries BC). These belt hooks were inlaid with gold or silver foil, polished fragments of turquoise, or more rarely with jade or glass; sometimes they were gilded. Most examples are bronze, often lavishly decorated with inlays, but some are made of jade, gold, or iron. The belt hook consists of a bar or flat strip curving into a hook at one end and carrying at the other end, on the back, a button for securing it to the belt. The hooks vary widely in size, shape, and design, and although contemporary sculptures sometimes show them at the waists of human figures, some examples are far too large to have been worn, and their function is unclear. Textual evidence hints that the belt hook was adopted by the Chinese from the mounted nomads of the northern frontier of inner Asia, perhaps along with other articles of the horseman's costume. They were probably worn by both men and women. (*syn.* toggle)

Belverde: A Bronze Age site of the Apennines near Cetona in Tuscany, Italy. There are indications that it may have been a ritual site, with rocks carved to form tiers of seats and other shapes. Complete pottery vessels filled with acorns, beans, and carbonized grain were placed into fissures in the rocks, perhaps as offerings to a deity.

Belzoni, Giovanni (1778–1823): Italian excavator of Egyptian sites, who is known as a picturesque and unscrupulous collector of Egyptian antiques as well as a pioneer in Egyptology. Belzoni sought antiquities both for himself and for the British Consul-General on behalf of the British Museum, whose collection he enhanced enormously. His discoveries were numerous, ranging from the colossal sculpture of the head of Ramses II ("the Young Memnon") at Thebes; in the nearby Valley of the Kings, the tomb of Seti I and the aragonite sarcophagus (for Sir John Soane's Museum, London). Although he managed to take an obelisk from the Nile island of Philae (Jazirat Filah), near Aswan, it was taken from him at gunpoint by agents working for French interests. He explored Elephantine (Jazirat Aswan) and the temple of Edfu (Idfu), cleared the entrance to the great temple of Ramses II at Abu Simbel, was the first to penetrate the pyramid of Khafre at Giza, and identified the ruins of the city of Berenice on the Red Sea. His methods were unnecessarily destructive by modern archaeological standards. He died in western Africa as he began a journey to Timbuktu. An account of his adventures was published in the year of his death, *Narrative of the Operations and Recent Discoveries within the Pyramids, Temples, Tombs and Excavations in Egypt and Nubia* (2 vols., 1820).

benben stone: A cult object made of stone, found at Egyptian sites such as those for the sun god Re at Heliopolis. The sacred stone symbolized the Primeval Mound and perhaps also the petrified semen of the deity. It served as the earliest prototype for the obelisk and possibly even the pyramid. It was probably constructed in the early Old Kingdom, c. 2600 BC.

bench: An eroded terrace with an alluvial cut surface, on bedrock in a valley. The term also refers to an eroded land form with a wave-cut surface in coastal areas and in wave-swept sea cliffs (also called wave-cut platform). (*syn.* wave-cut platform)

Benfica: A site in Angola with many shell middens, stone artifact assemblages, and Early Iron Age pottery dated to the 2nd century AD.

Benghazi/Banghazi: Seaport city of northeastern Libya, the de jure capital, which was founded by the Greeks of Cyrenaica as Hesperides (Euesperides) in the 6th century BC. It was replaced in the mid-3rd century by a new city, named Berenice by the Egyptian pharaoh Ptolemy III in honor of his wife. It continued in occupation until the 10th or 11th century AD and was ultimately replaced by the city of Benghazi, remaining a small town until it was extensively developed during the Italian occupation of Libya (1912–1942). Excavations offer evidence of Classical and Hellenistic levels and the refurbishing of the enclosing walls during Justinian's time (reigned AD 527–565). (*syn.* ancient Euesperides; later Berenice; Italian Bengasi)

Beni Hassan: A Middle Kingdom archaeological site, on the eastern bank of the Nile, Egypt, about 150 miles south of Cairo. The site is known for its rock-cut tombs of the 11th and 12th-Dynasties' (2125–1795 BC) officials of the 16th Upper Egyptian (Oryx) nome, or province. Some of the 39 tombs are painted with scenes of daily life and important biographical texts. The governors of the nome, whose capital was Menat Khufu, ancestral home of the 4th-Dynasty pharaohs, administered the eastern desert. The tomb of one, Khnumhotep II, contains a scene showing Semitic bedouin merchants in richly colored garments entering Egypt. A rock-cut shrine of Pakhet, known as Speos Artemidos, built by Queen Hatshepsut and Thutmose III of the 18th Dynasty, lies 1 mile north, in an ancient quarry, with a smaller shrine of Alexander II nearby. There are some small tombs dating back to the 6th Dynasty (2345–2181 BC). (*syn.* Bani Hasan, Beni Hasan)

Benin City: Capital and largest city of Edo state, Nigeria, which rose to prominence in the 13th century. A series of massive city walls, over 100 kilometers in length, was constructed. The Portuguese first visited in 1485, and the city was burned down and ransacked for nearly 2,500 of its famous bronzes in 1897 when the British occupied the city. Benin City is known for the fine practice of the ancient method of cire perdue ("lost-wax") bronze castings, mostly relief plaques and near life-size human heads produced over a long period. Traces of the old wall and moat remain. (*syn.* Edo)

Bennett, Wendell Clark (1906–1953): American archaeologist who excavated many important sites in Peru from the 1920s–1950s. His studies of Peruvian ceramics produced many of the early sequences on the Peruvian coast and the central highlands, which was considered a major breakthrough in Andean archaeology.

bentonites: A clay formed by the decomposition of volcanic ash, having the ability to absorb large quantities of water and to expand to several times its normal volume.

Benty Grange helmet: An Anglo-Saxon ceremonial helmet found in 1848 at a burial site in Benty Grange. Unlike the Sutton Hoo helmet, which has similarities to Swedish helmets, the Benty Grange example was undoubtedly of native workmanship. It is an elaborate object combining the pagan boar symbol with Christian crosses on the nail heads.

Beowulf: A heroic poem, considered the highest achievement of Old English literature and also the earliest European vernacular epic. Preserved in a single manuscript (Cotton Vitellius A XV) from AD c. 1000, it deals with events of the early 6th century and is believed to have been composed between 700 and 750. It did not appear in print until 1815. Beowulf is one of the earliest, longest, and most complete examples of Anglo-Saxon verse. Although originally untitled, it was later named after the Scandinavian hero Beowulf. Its themes are essentially the conflict between good and evil and the nature of heroism; fantasy and reality are intertwined as the hero Beowulf fights Grendel and other semimythological monsters. There is no evidence of a historical Beowulf, but some characters, sites, and events in the poem can be historically verified. Perhaps Beowulf's greatest contribution to archaeology is the light the poem has shed on the funerary customs displayed in the Sutton Hoo ship burial. The opening passages describe how the dead King Scyld Scefing was borne out to sea in a ship; jewels were placed on his chest, armor and treasure heaped around his body, and a standard was hoisted overhead.

Berdyzh: An Upper Palaeolithic site in Belarus with radiocarbon dates of 23,430–15,000 BP. On the Sozh River, there are faunal remains of woolly mammoth and mammoth-bone houses.

Berekhat Ram: An Acheulian site in the Golan Heights, Israel, which yielded waste flakes, a few bifaces, Levallois flakes, and side scrapers.

Berelekh: The most northern Palaeolithic site in the world, at 71 degrees north in northeastern Siberia, containing a bed of over 8,000 mammal bones, including woolly mammoth, of c. 14,000–12,000 years ago. There is also an Upper Palaeolithic level dating to 13,400–10,600 bp and assigned to the Dyuktai culture.

Berenice: Three different sites: a town on the coast of Cyrenaica, Libya, which was the site of Euhesperides; a port on the Egyptian coast of the Red Sea founded by Ptolemy II, especially important in the 1st and 2nd centuries AD; and Pella, Jordan, which was once known as Berenice.

Bergen: Port city of southwestern Norway, originally called Bjørgvin, and founded in AD 1070 by King Olaf III. About 1100, a castle was built on the northern edge of the Vågen harbor, and Bergen became commercially and politically important; it was Norway's capital in the 12th and 13th centuries. Excavations in the Bryggen, the harbor area, have revealed a sequence of levels that illustrate the area's evolution from the 11th century onward. The levels have been accurately dated by a series of fires, which occurred at various stages of Bergen's history. Waterlogged conditions have preserved many of the timber buildings, streets, and quays. The 11th-century houses and warehouses were on piles and had sills at ground level, while jetties became popular in the Hanseatic period (14th and 15th centuries). The excavations revealed a remarkable collection of imported pottery from all over Europe as well as quantities of leather and wooden objects. Parts of three trading ships or freighters were also found, their timbers having been reused in the buildings.

Beringia: The part of the continental shelf that connects northeast Asia with present-day Alaska. These were the polar continental shelves that escaped glaciation during the ice ages but that were exposed during periods of low sea level, which facilitated migration of people to North America from Asia, and in the Laptev and East Siberian Seas. When exposed at the time of the last glacial maximum, Beringia was a large, flat, vegetated land mass. In 1993, investigations of the climatic interstadial of 11,000–12,000 years ago in Beringia (now submerged under the Bering Strait) and the way it provided for the peopling of the New World from Asia were reported.

Beringian tradition: A culture in existence approximately 12,000 years ago between Siberia and temperate Alaska. The term was used by H. West to cover various Alaskan and Siberian archaeological formations, which had developed from the Siberian Upper Paleolithic period, an area now largely submerged under the Bering Strait. Chronologically these formations lie between the middle of the Holocene period (c. 35,000–9/10,000 BP), depending on the area. West's categorization includes the Bel'kachi, Diuktai, and Lake Ushki cultures in Siberia and the Denalian culture and America Paleo-Arctic formations in Alaska and the Yukon. Although Alaska is generally thought to be the gateway through which humans entered the New World, the earliest undisputed evidence for people there dates later than 12,000 years ago, well after the climax of the last major glacial advance but while glaciers still covered much of Arctic Canada. Artifacts of 11,500 to 9,000 years ago are known from a number of Alaskan sites, where hunters of caribou (and, in one case, of an extinct form of bison) manufactured blades. (*syn.* American Paleo-Arctic)

Bering Land Bridge: The present-day floor of the Chukchi and Bering Seas, which emerged as dry land during Late Pleistocene glacial advances. It is the only route for faunal exchange between Eurasia and North America as it united Siberia and Alaska. It seems to have been breached only in the past 2.5 million years, with the earliest immigrants crossing it about 40,000–15,000 years ago. These people were part of a migratory wave that later reached as far south as South America (about 10,000 years ago). During the Ice Age, the sea level fell by several hundred feet, making the strait into a land bridge between Asia and North America, over which a considerable migration of plants and animals, as well as people, occurred. That period also allowed the transit of cold water currents from the Pacific into the Atlantic.

berm: The flat ground or space between the vallum (ditch) and the fort (walls) surrounding the central mound of a barrow. An example is the stone part of Hadrian's Wall where the berm was about 20 feet wide; it was less wide at the turf wall.

Bernal Garcia, Ignacio (1910–1992): A Mexican archaeologist known for his work at Monte Albán, Dainzú, Teotihuacán, and other Oaxacan sites.

Bernam-Sungkai: A peninsular area of Malaysia with stone slab graves during a metal age around 300 BC.

Bersu, Gerhard (1889–1964): A German archaeologist who emigrated to Britain in the 1930s and introduced methods such as area excavation of settlement sites, as at Little Woodbury and on the Isle of Man.

Bes: A minor god of ancient Egypt, appearing only in the New Kingdom, represented as an ugly dwarf. The name Bes is now used to designate a group of deities of similar appearance. Bes, associated with music and childbirth, was intended to inspire joy or to drive away evil spirits. He was also popular with the Phoenicians.

beta-ray backscattering: A nondestructive physical method of chemical analysis, which, although limited in its application, has been used successfully to determine the lead content of glass and glaze. A specimen is subjected to a beam of electrons from a weak radioactive beta source, and some electrons are absorbed while others are "backscattered" from the surface of the sample and can be counted with a Geiger counter. The percentage of electrons backscattered depends on the atomic number of the elements making up the surface layer of the artifact. Therefore, if an element with a high atomic number is known to be present (e.g., lead), an estimate can be made of its concentration. The equipment cannot distinguish between high concentrations of elements with medium atomic numbers and low concentrations of elements with high atomic numbers. The equipment cannot sense very small amounts of an element. Factors such as the thickness of a glaze affect the amount of backscattering. The technique carries advantages in its cheapness and portability of the equipment and is considered a useful technique for analyzing material like glass.

betel nut: The nut or fruit of the Areca palm, which is chewed in tropical Asia, Melanesia, and New Guinea as a stimulant. It was misnamed by Europeans because it is chewed with the betal leaf; hence, betel palm is the Areca palm from which the nut is obtained. Archaeological occurrences include Spirit Cave (c. 10,000–7,000 BC), eastern Timor (early Holocene), and several sites in the Philippines, where teeth stained by the nut have been found from c. 3000 BC.

Bethel: The site of the ancient city of Palestine, just north of Jerusalem, occupied before 2000 BC to the 6th century BC. Bethel was important in Old Testament times and was associated with Abraham and Jacob. Excavations have been carried out by the American School of Oriental Research and the Pittsburgh-Xenia Theological Seminary. The most important levels were of the Late Bronze Age, a particularly well-built town of the Canaanites, which was violently destroyed early in the 13th century BC, probably by the Israelites. After the division of Israel, Jeroboam I (10th century BC) made Bethel the chief sanctuary of the northern kingdom (Israel), and the city was later the center for the prophetic ministry of Amos. The city apparently escaped destruction by the Assyrians at the time of the fall of Samaria (721 BC), but was occupied by Josiah of Judah (reigned c. 640–c. 609 BC). (*syn.* Luz, Baytin [modern])

Beth-Shan: A very large tell of northeastern Israel, site of one of the oldest inhabited cities of ancient Palestine. Overlooking the town to the north is Tel Bet She'an (Arabic Tall al-Husn), one of the most important stratified mounds in Palestine. It was excavated in 1921–1933 by the University of Pennsylvania, which discovered that the lowest strata date from the late Chalcolithic period in the country (c. 4000–3000 BC) through Bronze Age and Iron Age levels and upward to Byzantine times (c. AD 500). Buildings, including temples and administrative buildings, span the Egyptian period—the earliest from the time of Thutmose III (ruled 1504–1450 BC), and the latest dating to Rameses III (1198–1166 BC). Important stelae (stone monuments) show the conquests of Pharaoh Seti I (1318–1304 BC) and the worship of the goddess Astarte. During the Hellenistic period, the city was called Scythopolis; it was taken by the Romans in 64 BC and given the status of an imperial free city by Pompey. In 1960, a finely preserved Roman amphitheater, with a seating capacity for about 5,000, was excavated. The city was an important center of the Decapolis (a league of 10 Hellenistic cities) and under Byzantine rule was the capital of the northern province of Palaestina Secunda. All these periods were also represented in the surrounding cemeteries. It declined

after the Arab conquest (AD 636) (*syn.* Bet She'an, Baysan [Arabic], Beisan [modern]; Scythopolis)

Beth-Shemesh: A Palestinian site of the Middle Bronze Age, possibly a Hyksos fortified settlement and later a Late Bronze Age and Philistine town.

Betovo: A Middle Palaeolithic site near Bryansk, Russia, with artifacts (denticulates) and faunal remains (snow lemming) that indicate a cold interval such as early in the last glacial.

betyl: A sacred stone, often a standing stone fashioned into a conical shape.

beveled-rim bowl: A widespread, crudely made conical pottery vessel formed in a mold and having a sloped rim, characteristic of the Late Uruk period in Mesopotamia. (*syn.* beveled rim bowl)

Bewcastle Cross: A runic standing cross monument in the churchyard of Bewcastle, Northumberland, northern England, dating from the late 7th or early 8th century. Although the top of the cross has been lost, the 15-foot (4.5-m) shaft remains, with distinct panels of the figures of Christ in Majesty, St. John the Baptist, and St. John the Evangelist, while on the back there is an inhabited vine scroll. Like the Ruthwell Cross, that at Bewcastle has a poem inscribed in Runic script. The worn inscription suggests that the monument was a memorial to Alchfrith, son of Oswiu of Northumbria, and his wife Cyneburh (Cyniburug). It is one of the finest examples of Early Christian Northumbrian art.

Beycesultan: A tell on the upper Meander River of southwestern Anatolia (western Turkey), which has yielded evidence from the Chalcolithic to Late Bronze Age and of a culture contemporary with the Hittite Empire. It is thought to have been the capital of the 2nd-millennium BC state of Arzawa. From the Chalcolithic, there was a cache of sophisticated copper tools and a silver ring, the earliest known use of that metal. Buildings that were religious shrines have been uncovered, almost unknown in Anatolia at those times. Rectangular shrine chambers were arranged in pairs, with ritual installations recalling the Horns of Consecration and Tree, or Pillar, cults of Minoan Crete. A palace building at the same site, dating from the Middle Bronze Age (c. 1750 BC), Beycesultan's most prosperous period, had reception rooms at first-floor level, also in the Minoan manner. In common with most other Bronze Age buildings in Anatolia, its walls were composed of a brick-filled timber framework on stone foundations. The private houses of this period at Beycesultan were all built on the megaron plan. The whole settlement and a lower terrace on the river were enclosed by a perimeter wall. The town was violently destroyed, and although it was rebuilt, it remained relatively poor into the Late Bronze Age.

B Group: A term no longer used to describe the final stages of the Neolithic A Group in Nubia (c. 2800–2300 BC), before the beginning of the C Group phase. In soils, the B horizon lies immediately beneath the A horizon and may reach a depth of 65 to 90 centimeters (26 to 35 in). It is a zone of more moderate weathering in which there is an accumulation of many of the products removed from the A horizon. (*syn.* B Horizon)

Bhaja: A rock-cut cave monastery, famous for its temple with internal stupas set in a kind of sanctuary, from the 2nd–1st centuries BC. The temple is decorated with sculpture in bas-relief, which is some of the earliest Buddhist work.

Bharhut: A village, about 100 miles southwest of Allahabad, India, famous for the ruins of a Buddhist stupa built in the time of Ashoka (c. 250 BC). Originally built of brick, it was enlarged during the 2nd century BC and surrounded with a stone railing with four stone gateways (*toranas*) placed at four cardinal points. An inscription on these gateways assigns the work to King Dhanabhuti in the rule of the Shungas (i.e., before 72 BC). The railing is decorated with scenes from the Jataka stories. The sculptures adorning the shrine are among the earliest and finest examples of the developing style of Buddhist art in India. Discovered in 1873, the stupa's sculptural remains are now mainly preserved in the Indian Museum, Calcutta, and in the Municipal Museum (Allahabad).

Bhimbetka: A large series of Palaeolithic to present-day rock shelters with rich deposits and rock art, close to Bhopal, India. A succession of Acheulian hand axes, cleavers, and Levallois tools are followed by Middle Palaeolithic blades, Upper Palaeolithic bladelets, and then a Mesolithic industry bladelet and grinding lithic assemblage, and finally by copper tools and Chalcolithic pottery. The Mesolithic industry has dates of 6000–1000 BC, and the rock art is of the Mesolithic and later. The rock art is painted in a range of colors, and there are human and animal figures, in hunting, warfare, or ritual scenes. Petroglyphs have been found in a shelter.

biased sample: Sampling technique in which certain units have more chance of inclusion than others.

Bible: The holy book of the Jewish (Old Testament only) and Christian (Old and New Testaments) faiths. The Old Testament is a collection of writings first compiled and preserved as the sacred books of the ancient Hebrew people. As the Bible of the Hebrews and their Jewish descendants down to the present, these books have been perhaps the most decisive single factor in the preservation of the Jews as a cultural entity and Judaism as a religion. The Old Testament and the New Testament—a body of writings that chronicle the origin and early dissemination of Christianity—constitute the Bible of the Christians. The Old Testament, written in Hebrew, represents a history of the Jewish people, beginning with the creation of the world. The New Testament records the life and teachings of Christ. Much early archaeological work in the Near East was designed to illustrate or defend the biblical account. Today the Bible is used as a historical resource and is recognized as a collection of legends, myths, and stories collected long after events described in it. Archaeology has lent support to some biblical accounts, and the Bible has provided information on aspects of society such as marriage customs, inheritance, and land ownership, which are difficult to recreate from archaeological evidence.

Biblical archaeology: The branch of historical archaeology devoted to the discovery and investigation of the places and artifacts recorded by the Bible and to the study of Biblical times and documents. Biblical archaeology, culminating perhaps in the discovery of Masada, the Judaean hill fortress where the Jews made their last stand against the Romans in the revolt of AD 66–73 and mainly excavated in 1963, has given a new perspective to the Old Testament and to studies of ancient Judaism. The value of archaeology and of topographical and linguistic studies for biblical history is well understood.

bibliotheca: The Latin term for a library or collection of books or manuscripts. The most celebrated library of antiquity was founded by the Ptolemies at Alexandria, destroyed by the Arabs in AD 640.

Bibracte: An Iron Age Gallic town and *oppidum* in central France. It was the capital of the Aedui tribe at the time of Caesar and the site where he defeated the Helvetii tribe, the climax of his first campaign in Gaul (58 BC). Augustus moved the inhabitants to his new town Augustodunum (Autun), about 30 kilometers away, in 12 BC. Excavations in the 19th century revealed remains of both the Iron Age settlement and the Roman period, including a large temple, houses, and metalworking workshops. Imported objects such as coins, amphorae, and black and red glaze pottery dating to before the Roman conquest have been found, indicating that Bibracte was a major trading and production center in the late Iron Age. (*syn.* modern Mont Beurvray)

bichrome ware: Pottery having a two-color design or decoration.

bi disk: A flat jade disc with a small hole in the center, made in ancient China for ceremonial purposes, possibly symbolizing heaven. Bi disks have also been described in ancient Chinese texts as a symbol of rank. Jade disks and disklike axes have been found in 4th- and 3rd-millennia BC graves at east-coast Neolithic sites such as Beiyinyangying. Polished stone disk segments are known still earlier at Banpo. (*syn.* bi)

bier: The movable wooden framework or platform on which a corpse is laid, sometimes with grave goods, before burial. It is used to carry the body to the grave.

biface: A type of prehistoric stone tool flaked on both faces or sides, the main tool of *Homo erectus*. The technique was typical of the hand ax tradition of the Lower Palaeolithic period and the Acheulian cultures. Bifaces may be oval, triangular, or almond shaped in form and characterized by axial symmetry, even if marks made by use are more plentiful on one face or on one edge. The cutting edge can be straight or jagged and the tool used as a pick, knife, scraper, or even weapon. Only in the most primitive tools was flaking done to one side only. (*syn.* bifacial; handaxe; coup-de-poing)

biface thinning flake: A flake that has been removed from a biface through percussion as part of the reduction process. These flakes typically were removed from an unfinished biface (or blank) to make it thinner.

bifacial blank: A biface in the early stages of production, displaying only percussion flaking and no evidence of pressure flaking. In many cases, blanks were traded and/or transported from their area of origin and subsequently used as bifacial cores from which flake blanks were detached for production of dart or arrow points.

bifacial core: A core that has had flakes removed from multiple faces; may be mistaken for a large biface blank.

bifacial foliate: A class of artifact made up of leaf-shaped stone tools with complete or nearly complete flaking on both sides.

biga: In Roman antiquity, a chariot drawn by two horses.

big game hunting tradition: Any of several ancient North American cultures based on hunting herd animals such as mammoth and bison; the first indigenous cultural complex of the continent. It may have developed from an earlier hunting culture whose people arrived in North America between 20,000–40,000 years ago in an interstadial (break) in the Wisconsin Ice Age. It is also probable that this culture derived from a migration across the Bering Land Bridge c. 13,000–14,000 BC. The remains of these cultures have been found mainly in the North American plains as well as in the eastern and southwestern regions of North America. Lanceolate projectile points, such as Clovis and Folsom, characterize the tradition. The big game hunting tradition began to decline or change after 8000 BC. (*syn.* Big Game Hunting culture)

Big Horn Medicine Wheel: A medicine wheel in the Big Horn Mountains of Wyoming, which consists of a D-shaped stone cairn from which 28 individual stone spokes radiate. The outer circumference has six smaller cairns. The feature may be astronomically aligned.

Bigo: A great earthwork site in western Uganda associated with the Chwezi people. The massive linear earthworks, over 6½ miles long (10 km), is a ditch system, some of it cut from rock, enclosing a large grazing area on a river bank. It may

have been both a royal capital and a cattle enclosure. Its construction would have required considerable labor and supports a distinction between cultivators and a pastoral aristocracy, which later became typical of this area. Radioactive carbon dating suggests Bigo was occupied from the mid-14th to the early 16th centuries. The site has also yielded early 13th–15th centuries AD roulette-decorated pottery, characteristic of the later Iron Age over much of East Africa.

billabong: In Australia, a branch of a river or waterhole in a watercourse, which fills when flooded during the rainy season, forming a blind channel, backwater, or stagnant pool. It dries up in the dry season.

Bilzingsleben: A travertine site in Germany at which Middle Pleistocene specimens of skull fragments and teeth show resemblances to *Homo erectus*. Excavations have turned up thousands of stone tools of a Lower Palaeolithic Clactonian-type culture. An interglacial environment is indicated with a date in the penultimate or Holstein interglacial, perhaps some 250,000–350,000 years ago.

Binford, Lewis R. (1930–): An influential contemporary American archaeologist, considered by many to be the father of the new archaeology. His books include *In Pursuit of the Past* (1983), *Bones: Ancient Men and Modern Myths* (1981), *An Archaeological Perspective* (1972), and *New Perspectives in Archaeology* (1968).

bioarchaeology: A subdiscipline of biology, which integrates the concepts of human biology with those of anthropological archaeology.

biocultural anthropology: A subdiscipline of anthropology and research strategy, which integrates physical anthropology and archaeology to investigate prehistoric biological systems.

biogeography: A subdiscipline of biology, which studies, and attempts to explain, the geographical distribution of living things, animal and vegetable.

biological environment: Those elements of the habitat consisting of living organisms; the living component of the total environment.

biomass: The total weight of the plant and animal life (organic substances and organisms) existing at a given time in a given area.

biome: A complex (biotic) community of plants and animals established over a large geographic area and characterized by the distinctive life forms of certain species that live in harmony together and have a certain unity. The biome is a plant-plus-animal formation that is composed of a plant matrix together with all the associated animals. The term specifically applies to such a community in a prehistoric period. Examples are the oak/deer biome or the spruce/moose biome of North America.

biosphere: The regions of the earth's crust and atmosphere occupied by living organisms; also, all of the earth's living organisms interacting with the physical environment.

biotope: The smallest subdivision of a habitat, constituting a specific plant and animal grouping and a high degree of uniformity in the subdivision's environmental conditions.

bioturbation: The alteration of a site by nonhuman biological agents, such as burrowing rodents.

bipedalism: Having two feet or, specifically designating a life form that uses its two hind feet for walking or running. The term also describes the method of movement marked by habitual walking on two legs. Bipedalism is a fundamental feature used to define hominids. (*related word* bipedal)

bipennis: An ax with a double blade or edge, used as an agricultural implement, an adze, or a military weapon. It was used by the Amazons, Scythians, and Gauls. (*syn.* bipenne)

bipolar percussion: A type of percussion that involves the placement of raw material (usually small rounded or oval cobbles) on an anvil stone and striking it from the top.

Birch Creek: A series of rock shelters in Idaho with occupation from 8500 BP to historic times. The sites have been important in determining the culture and linguistics (Shoshonean) of the Rocky Mountain area.

bird bones: The identification of bird bones preserved on archaeological sites is a very specialized skill. Interpretation may be carried out in terms of diet and reconstruction of the ancient environment.

Bird, Junius Bouton (1907–1982): An American archaeologist who worked in South America at Fell's Cave (Tierra del Fuego) on establishing the presence of Palaeo Indians of the continent. He also worked in northern Chile's Atacama region and Huaca Prieta in Peru, where he established the Preceramic period of that area. His specialty was the study of textiles.

Birdlip: A Celtic site near Gloucester, England, dated to the 1st century BC. There are four cist graves, one with a woman's skeleton together with bronze bowls, gold and silver bracelets, a bronze brooch, and a bronze mirror with incised and enamel decoration.

birdstone or bird-stone: A class of prehistoric stone objects of undetermined purpose, usually resembling or shaped like a bird; carved bird effigies. Polished stone weights occurred in the cultures of the Archaic tradition (8000–1000 BC) and later cultures in the Eastern Woodlands of North America. They were probably attached to throwing sticks or *atlatls* to add weight and leverage. (*syn.* bannerstone, boatstone)

Bir Kiseiba: A site in southern Egypt's Sahara with early ceramics and cattle bones dating to c. 9500 BP.

Birrigai: A rock shelter in the highlands of the Australian Capital Territory with occupation in the last glacial maximum, starting c. 2100 bp.

Birsmatten: A site in the Bern district of Switzerland, Basis-Grotte, that has one of the longest known sequences of Mesolithic deposits. There are several levels of Sauveterrian and Tardenoisian occupation and extensive human remains.

Bir Tarfawi: A late Aterian site in the western Egyptian desert, dated to about 42,000 BC. The shores of a shallow lake were settled by hunters.

Biskupin: An Early Iron Age defended settlement of the Lusatian culture of c. 550–400 BC, on a former island in Lake Biskupin, northwest Poland. The island site was ringed by a breakwater of piles and fortified by a rampart of timber compartments filled with earth and stones. Inside were more than 100 wooden cabins, which were all erected within a year, arranged along parallel streets made of logs. Up to 1,200 people may have been housed there. Workshops for craftsmen in bone, bronze, and horn have been excavated. Waterlogged ground preserved the structures.

Bismarck Archipelago: A series of islands off Papua New Guinea with sites of the Lapita cultural complex and Pleistocene rock shelters. Occupation goes back more than 30,000 years, and obsidian was brought there 20,000 years ago. New fauna was brought by humans in the Late Pleistocene and mid-Holocene.

bison: The name of two species of wild oxen, the European bison or wisent and the American bison or buffalo. Only a small number of European bison now exist, bred from zoo specimens, and in a protected state in forests of Lithuania. Two further species, now extinct, inhabited Europe and Great Britain for much of the Quaternary period. The great steppe wisent was present during both interglacials and cold periods. The smaller wood wisent was present in Europe only during interglacials. Sometimes these animals are called aurochs. In North America, a number of species preceded today's bison. One species, popularly called buffalo, formerly roamed in vast herds over the interior of the continent, mainly in the Rocky Mountains.

bison jump: A steep or other natural feature used to kill stampeding buffalo.

bît hilani: An architectural type with a pillared porch, usually of wood. A bît hilani is a wooden-pillared portico of one to three columns at the top of a short flight of steps at the entry to reception suites. At one end of the portico there was a staircase to an upper story, leading to a reception or throne room. There was usually an adjoining staircase to the roof and a varying number of retiring rooms. This was a standard palace unit, first found at the Syrian site of Tell Atchana, dated mid-2nd millennium BC. It was adopted by the Syro-Hittites and Assyrians. Another fine example of a bît hilani is the Kaparu Palace at Tall Halaf. (*syn.* bit hilani)

bit, horse: The domesticated horse was probably first controlled with a simple halter. Bit, the mouthpiece of a horse's bridle, consisting of a bit mouth and adjacent parts to which the reins are attached. Bits with cheek-pieces of antler did not appear in central Europe until after 1800 BC, and they were later replaced by bronze bits. Bits without a cheek-piece, in two-piece or three-piece form, were introduced in the Iron Age.

bivalve mold: In metalworking, a form of mold with two halves pegged together and used for casting metal objects. The mold could be made of clay, metal, or stone. The mold would be parted to release the cast object once the metal cooled. It was a reusable mold more complicated than an open mold.

Black-and-red ware: Any Indian pottery with black rims and interior and red outside, caused by firing in the inverted position, which was made beginning in the Iron Age. Characteristic forms include shallow dishes and deeper bowls. This pottery first appeared on late sites of the Indus civilization and was a standard feature of the Banas culture. This ware has been found throughout much of the Indian peninsula with dates of the later 2nd and early 1st millennia BC. In the first millennium, it became widespread in association with iron and megalithic monuments. In the Ganges Valley it postdates ochre-colored pottery and generally precedes painted gray ware. (*syn.* black and red ware)

Black Death: A particularly severe outbreak of plague, which crossed Europe between AD 1347 and 1351, probably a combination of bubonic and pneumonic plagues. It took a greater toll of life than any other known epidemic or war up to that time. A rough estimate is that 25 million people in Europe died from plague during the Black Death. The population of western Europe did not reach its pre-1348 level until the beginning of the 16th century.

Black Earth: A distinctive area of Russia where the soil coloration resulted from intensive settlement activity and major deposits of iron ore.

black-figure: A type of Greek pottery that originated in Corinth c. 700 BC and was popular until red-figure pottery, its inverse, began c. 530 BC. This style consisted of pottery with one or more bands of human and animal figures silhouetted in black against a tan or red ground. The red color is probably taken when the pot is fired. The delineation of the figures was often heightened by the use of incised lines and the addition of white or purple coloring. The figures and ornamentation were drawn on the natural clay surface of a vase in glossy

black pigment; the finishing details were incised into the black. The first significant use of the black-figure technique was on Proto-Corinthian style pottery developed in Corinth in the first half of the 7th century BC. The Corinthian painter's primary ornamental device was the animal frieze. The Athenians, who began to use the technique at the end of the 7th century BC, retained the Corinthian use of animal friezes for decoration until c. 550 BC, when the great Attic painters developed narrative scene decoration and perfected the black-figure style. There were also studios producing black-figure ware in Sparta and eastern Greece. (*syn.* black-figure ware; black-figured [adj.])

black-glazed: A style of pottery decoration in which plain wares were given a black sheen, which continued well into the Hellenistic period—especially in Athens from the 6th–2nd centuries BC. These wares were often made alongside figure-decorated pottery, and from the 5th century BC, the pottery frequently had stamped decoration. In the 4th century BC, rouletting was also used. (*syn.* black-glossed)

Blackwater Draw: The deeply stratified type site for the Clovis point and Llano complex, located near Clovis, New Mexico, with evidence of occupation from the earliest Paleo-Indian through the Archaic period. Clovis points have been found associated with mammoth bones, and Folsom points have been found with bison bones. Also found: Agate Basin points, Cody complex points, a Frederick point, and tools of the Archaic period. Blackwater Draw is also used to evaluate the chronological sequences at other sites. The Blackwater Draw Museum exhibits 12,000-year-old artifacts from the area's archaeological sites.

blade: A long, narrow, sharp-edged, thin flake of stone, used especially as a tool in prehistoric times. This flake is detached by striking from a prepared core, often with a hammer. Its length is usually at least twice the width. The blade may be a tool in itself, or it may be the blank from which a two-edged knife, burin, or spoke shave is manufactured. This term, then, is used by archaeologists in several ways: (1) It can refer to a fragment of stone removed from a parent core. The blade is used to manufacture artifacts in what is known as the "blade and core industry." (2) That portion of an artifact, usually a projectile point or a knife, beyond the base or tang. (3) In certain cultures, small artifacts are called microblades. It was a great technological advance when it was discovered that a knapper could make more than one tool from a chunk of stone. The Châtelperronian and Aurignacian were the earliest of the known blade cultures associated with the arrival of modern humans. Industries in which many of the tools are made from blades became prominent at the start of the Upper Palaeolithic period. A typical blade has parallel sides and regular scars running down its back parallel with the sides. A "backed blade" is a blade with one edge blunted by the removal of tiny flakes. Blades led to another invention—the handle. A handle made it easier and much safer to manipulate a sharp, two-edged blade. (*syn.* blade tool; blade-~ [used attributively])

blank: A partly finished stone artifact that has been roughly worked into a shape but that must be further chipped to a suitable size and form to become a tool. This is an intermediate manufacturing stage in the production of stone tools, where the tools are given the rough shape at a quarry or workshop and often taken elsewhere for completion. Blanks were presumably made in quantity because they were easier to carry from place to place than were heavy lumps of stone.

blanket peat: Peat that forms in areas of high rainfall, which are not dependent on groundwater but receive all their moisture from the atmosphere. This peat can form on higher ground like plateaus. In periods of climatic change, blanket peat alters its nature, such as by developing tree cover in drier periods and then recurring as a bog when rainfall increases. In a peat bog of this type, there may be well-preserved evidence of human activity and organic material in the drier times, which is later covered by renewed peat growth.

Blattspitzen: A category of stone artifact with complete or nearly complete flaking on both sides and points at one or both ends, found in some late Middle and early Upper Palaeolithic industries of central and eastern Europe.

bleeper: A surveying instrument that is a type of proton gradiometer, working on the same principle as the magnetometer. When two detector bottles are used, one near ground level and one about 2 meters above, small magnetic anomalies underground affect the lower, nearer bottle more strongly than the upper. The signals from the two get out of step, and their sound signal is broken into a series of bleeps. It is unaffected by large-scale disturbance, an advantage over the magnetometer, and it is much simpler, cheaper, and more portable than either magnetometer or gradiometer.

Blegen, Carl William (1887–1971): An American archaeologist who worked at Troy, Korakou, Prosymna, and Pylos in Greece.

block statue: A type of Egyptian sculpture introduced in the Middle Kingdom (2055–1650 BC); it represents the subject squatting on the ground with knees drawn up close to the body, under the chin. The arms and legs may be wholly contained in the simple cubic form, with the hands and feet protruding discretely. The 12th-Dynasty block statue of Sihathor in the British Museum is the earliest dated example. The block statue of Queen Hetepheres, in the Egyptian Museum at Cairo, is also one of the earliest examples of this type.

bloom: The spongy mass of material made up of iron and slag, produced from the initial smelting of iron ore. The slag and impurities are mostly driven off in preliminary forging. To produce useful iron, bloom must be hammered at red heat to expel the stone and to add a proportion of carbon to the metal. The term also refers to a mass of iron after it has undergone the first hammering or to an ingot of iron or steel, or to a pile of puddled bars, passed through one set of "rolls," made into a thick bar, and left for further rolling when required for use.

blowout: An area in the earth that has become concave or depressed by a wind removal or erosion of sandy or soft, light soils. The topsoil and, perhaps, some of the lower soils, are so removed, especially in arid regions. A blowout resembles the crater of a volcano. Sometimes when earth is removed in this way, archaeological sites are revealed.

Bluefish Caves: Caves discovered in 1975 in the northern Yukon, Canada, which may be the oldest archaeological site in North America. There are deposits of the late glacial period and some artifacts associated with woolly mammoth, Dall sheep, reindeer, and other vertebrates. The radiocarbon dates of bone fragments range from 25,000–12,000 bp. Evidence of human occupation is from at least 13,000–10,000 bp. There was a wedge-shaped microcore, microblades, and burins similar to those from Siberia of the same time. The lowest levels of 20,000 bp have debitage flakes and large numbers of cut and butchered animal bones.

bluestone: A bluish-gray combination of dolerite, rhyolite, and volcanic stone used in the second phase of building Stonehenge. The source seems to be the Preseli Hills of South Wales, 215 kilometers away.

Boat ax culture: A culture of eastern Scandinavia found in the Late Neolithic Period, c. 2000 BC, which was an outlier of the European Battle Ax cultures. This single-grave culture spread rapidly through Sweden, Finland, and the Danish islands. The people displayed the aspects of a homogeneous culture, with central European trade links. Its characteristic weapon is a slender stone battle ax shaped like a simple boat with upturned ends. The term "Boat ax culture" is sometimes used for the east Scandinavian variant of the Single Grave or Corded Ware culture in which these axes occur. (*syn.* Boat-axe culture, Boat Axe culture)

boat burial: A type of burial during the Late Iron Age in which a body or its cremated remains were placed in a boat, which was then covered by a mound of earth. This was a north European practice, common in Scandinavia and Britain from AD c. 550 to 800. This pagan ritual was widely adopted by the Vikings and practiced to a lesser extent by the Anglo-Saxons and Germans. In Norway alone, there are 500 known boat burials, and many more from the rest of Scandinavia and other Viking colonies. To seafaring people, ships were a means of transport, a way of life, and symbols of power and prestige. The Anglo-Saxon poem *Beowulf* describes the belief that the journey to the afterlife could be achieved in a vessel. In Anglo-Saxon Britain, there are three 7th-century examples in Suffolk, including the rich burial of Sutton Hoo. The best-known after Sutton Hoo are the 9th-century barrows of Oseberg and Gokstad in Norway, and the 10th-century barrow at Ladby in Denmark. Burial in churchyards became customary in the 11th century in those areas. (*syn.* boat grave)

boatmaking: Boatmaking and navigation has been important to people for thousands of years—for communication, transport, and fishing. There is much evidence of dugout canoes from Mesolithic times onward, the earliest being at Perth and in Denmark. Neolithic people used skiffs as well as dugout canoes. Plank boats appeared in the Middle Bronze Age. In the Roman period, boats started being made with nails. Seagoing vessels existed, but there is not much evidence except for skin boats, like the Irish curragh. Classical writers describe plank-built boats with sails of leather on the Atlantic before the Romans arrived. Full documentation begins only with the Vikings. The Americas have yielded two regional pre-conquest types of craft: the reed *caballitos* of the Peruvian coast and Lake Titicaca, and the seagoing balsa rafts from the Gulf of Guayaquil. The oldest boat in Europe was found on the Tay. It is a dugout canoe used by Maglemosian immigrants from Denmark 10,000 years ago.

boat-shaped buildings: In Scandinavia and other parts of Europe, there is evidence of a variety of longhouse with bowed sides during the Viking period. The finest examples have been excavated at 11th-century Viking camps such as Trelleborg in southern Jutland. A reconstructed example there has walls made of halved tree trunks set in rows, with the curved face outward as in stave churches. A series of angled posts around the outside acted as buttresses and gave additional support to the gabled roof with its curved ridge. The roof may have been covered in wooden shingles, thatch, or turf. There is considerable variation in boat-shaped houses, depending on the function and location. Two British examples are a boat-shaped building in Hamwih and another in Bucken.

boatstone: A boat-shaped stone *atlatl*—a throwing-stick weight—put on the shaft to give great propulsion to a thrown dart. Unlike the banner stone, it was apparently lashed to the stick shaft. (*syn.* [see banner stone, bird stone])

Bocca Quadrata: A Middle Neolithic culture of northern Italy characterized by pottery vessels with rounded bodies and square mouths, decorated with incised geometric motifs. (*syn.* Square Mouth)

Bockstein: A series of cave sites in Germany with artifacts and faunal remains of the Middle and Upper Palaeolithic and many Micoquian-style chert bifaces dated to the end of the last interglacial, as well as Bockstein knives.

Bodh Gaya: A site in northeast India, famous as the scene of the Buddha's enlightenment. It was there, under the bodhi (Bo) tree that Gautama Buddha (Prince Siddhartha) became the Buddha. Archaeological remains include an Asokan pillar, erected by Emperor Asoka in 249 BC, and a railing surrounding the tree beneath which the Buddha meditated for 6 years before his enlightenment was erected in the 1st century BC.

bodkin: A sharp, slender instrument for making holes or for other functions. It may be shaped like a dagger, stiletto, or hairpin. The term is also used for a blunt needle with a large eye for drawing tape or ribbon through a loop or hem.

Bodrogkeresztur: The site of a Middle Copper Age cemetery and culture in eastern Hungary, c. 3900–3500 BC. It is the type site for an occupation that made Linear pottery and used metal battle axes and ax-adzes of shaft-hole type. The cemetery has at least 50 inhumation graves. The Bodrogkeresztur culture represents the first peak of metallurgical development in Hungarian prehistory, defined by large-scale production of gold ornaments and heavy shaft-hole copper tools. The occurrence of Translyvanian gold, Slovakian copper, and flint from Poland suggests long-distance exchanges.

bog: A type of wetland ecosystem characterized by wet, spongy, poorly drained peaty soil. The term also describes the communities of plants growing on acid waterlogged ground, as opposed to fen. Three main types of bog exist: valley bogs that remain waterlogged owing to the concentration of drainage into a valley; raised bogs that form as large pillows of peat and are kept waterlogged by high rainfall; and blanket bogs that form through the growth of the organic horizons of gleyed podzols.

bog body: A human body preserved in waterlogged conditions such that skin and hair often survive even though most internal organs and bones decay. Clothing also sometimes survives in such circumstances.

bog burial: Areas where human bodies are found in peat bogs in Scandinavia and northern Europe, including more than 160 from Denmark, and which are remarkably well preserved. The chemicals in the peat preserve the bodies, which allows archaeologists to study aspects of past life, including the soft tissues of the bodies themselves and the contents of the stomachs. Burials and ritual deposits were interred in these bogs in antiquity, especially during the Bronze and Iron Ages.

Boghazköy: The site of the Hittite capital of Hattusas, excavated by Hugo Winckler in the early 20th century, which yielded thousands of cuneiform tablets from which much of Hittite history was reconstructed. The capital is on a rock citadel near the Halys River in central Turkey, and the site had been occupied since Chalcolithic times. In c. 1500 BC, it became the citadel of Hattusas. As the Hittites' power grew, so did their capital, all within a massive defensive wall of stone and mud brick. Six gateways were decorated with impressive monumental carved reliefs, showing a warrior, lions, and sphinxes. Four temples have been excavated within the walls, each grouped around an open porticoed court. Two buildings housed the archives with over 10,000 tablets inscribed in cuneiform script and the Hittite language. A cemetery close to the city held large numbers of cremation burials, a surprisingly early occurrence of this rite. The city fell at the same time as the empire, c. 1200 BC. Little is known of the Chalcolithic or Hittite Old Kingdom phases on the site; excavation has in the main concentrated on the monuments of the New Kingdom city. (*syn.* Boghaz Keui, ancient Hattusas, Bogazkoy, Boghaz Koy)

bog iron: A workable, porous type of brown hematite (impure hydrous oxide) found in bogs (and also in marshes, swamps, peat mosses, and shallow lake beds). This deposit is formed when iron-bearing surface waters come into contact with organic material and iron oxides are precipitated through oxidation of algae, iron bacteria, or the atmosphere. It is frequently found in areas with subarctic or arctic climatic conditions. (*syn.* lake ore, limnite, marsh ore, meadow ore, morass ore, swamp ore, bog iron ore)

bog oak: The wood of an oak tree killed by waterlogging but then preserved in a black state in the peat bog, which formed as a result of the wet conditions.

bog sacrifice: Human bodies, animals, and artifacts that were deliberately deposited in peat bogs and other watery places, most notably in Denmark, but also elsewhere in northwestern Europe.

Bohunice: A Middle Palaeolithic site in Moravia, Czech Republic. There are artifacts—side scrapers, denticulates, burins, and laurel-leaf points—and some faunal remains that date to the early cold maximum of the last glacial.

Bohunician: A late Middle Palaeolithic culture of Moravia, Czechoslovakia, with artifacts including side scrapers, end scrapers, bifacial foliates, denticulates, burins, and laurel-leaf points.

Boian: A Neolithic culture (c. 7000–3500 BC, some say Middle Neolithic c. 4200–3700 BC) in the lower Danube Valley of southern Romania and characterized by terrace-floodplain settlements, consisting at first of mud huts and later of fortified promontory settlements of small tells. The Boian phase was marked by the introduction of copper axes, the extension of agriculture, and the breeding of domestic animals. The distinctive Boian pottery was decorated by rippling, painting, and excised or incised linear designs with white paste. Intramural burial is most common, but occasional large inhumation cemeteries are known. By spreading northward into Transylvania and northeastward to Moldavia, the Boian culture gradually assimilated earlier cultures of those areas. Flourishing exchange networks are known to involve Prut Valley flint, Spondylus shells from the Black Sea, and copper.

bolas stone: Weighted balls of stone, bone, ivory, or ceramic, which are either grooved or pierced for fastening to rawhide thongs and used to hunt prey. The bolas, still found today among some of the peoples of South America and among the Eskimo, usually consists of two or more globular or pear-shaped stones attached to each other by long thongs. They are whirled and thrown at running game, with the thongs wrapping themselves around the limbs of the animal or bird on contact. Bolas stones have been found in many archaeological sites throughout the world, including Africa in Middle and Upper Acheulian strata. (*syn.* bolas; bola; plural bolases)

Bolling interstadial: An interstadial of the Weischselian cold stage, dated to between 13,000–12,000 bp.

Bologna: A city in the Po Valley of northern Italy, originally the Etruscan Felsina, which was occupied by Gauls in the 4th century BC and became a Roman colony and municipium (Bononia) c. 190 BC. Traces of street plans survive, as do cemeteries with trench-type inhumation and cremation. Finds include sandstone grave stelae and many grave goods. Before the Etruscan inhabitation, there were villages of the Apennine culture, which were succeeded by the Villanovan. During that time, the city was a bronzeworking and trade center. It was then subject to the Greeks, then the papacy, then occupied by the Visigoths, Huns, Goths, and Lombards after the barbarian invasions. After a feudal period, Bologna became free in the early 12th century. (*syn.* Bononia; Felsina)

bolt: An iron arrow or missile, especially stout and short with a blunt or thickened head, discharged from a crossbow or other engine. (*syn.* quarrel)

bombylos: A Greek or Roman vase so-called from the gurgling noise that the liquid made when pouring out the narrow neck. (*syn.* bombyle)

Bonampak: A small, Late Classic Period (AD c. 800) Maya site and ceremonial center in Chiapas, a satellite of Yaxchilán, located on a tributary of the Usumacinta. The discovery in 1946 of the magnificent murals in the rooms of an otherwise modest structure astounded the archaeological world. From the floors to vault capstones, its stuccoed walls were covered with highly realistic polychrome scenes of a jungle battle, the arraignment of prisoners, and victory ceremonies. These scenes shed an entirely new light on the nature of Maya society, which up until then had been considered peaceful. These murals are the most complete graphic portrayal of Maya life known. Hieroglyphs also occur frequently, and the whole collection is seen as a continuous narrative. (*syn.* Bonompak)

Bondi point: A small, asymmetric-backed point, named for Bondi, Sydney, Australia, which is a component of the Australian Small Tool tradition. It is usually less than 5 centimeters long and is sometimes described as a backed blade. Some examples suggest that the points were set in wooden handles or shafts. It occurs on coastal and inland sites across Australia, usually south of the Tropic of Capricorn. The oldest examples come from southeast Australia, dating from about 3000 BC, and the most recent are 300–500 years old. The Bondi point was not used by Aborigines when Europeans arrived.

bone: The connective tissues of the body, consisting of crystallite minerals and collagen. After death, the proteins slowly decompose, and the remaining minerals are subject to solution in acid soil conditions. Bones are preserved on a wide variety of archaeological sites. From early prehistory, the bones, horns, or antlers of animals that men hunted or kept provided them with a vital source of raw material for constructing artifacts. There are many types of bone. There are a variety of relative age determination techniques applicable to bone material, including measurements of the depletion of nitrogen (bone dating) and the accumulation of fluorine and uranium.

Bone Age: A loosely defined prehistoric period of human culture characterized by the use of implements made of bone and antler; not part of the Three Age system.

bone dating: Any of a series of methods of analyzing bone samples, especially by measuring fluorine, uranium, nitrogen—also called the FUN technique—or by using stratigraphy. Human remains may be compared with animal bone or fossils found in the same strata. Relative dates may be obtained from time-related chemical changes that occur in bone, especially in fluorine, uranium, and nitrogen. Still, the most commonly used is radiocarbon dating because both the collagen and mineral components of bone are datable.

bone measurement: The measurement of bones to compare size and shape of different individuals. The dimensions of skeletal structures can be taken by using a variety of calipers and other measuring equipment. Multivariate analysis is one method of comparison, which helps to identify and distinguish bones by species and sex and to study the genetics of groups of animals. Much work has been done in human skull measurement to investigate genetic relations of ancient populations.

Bonneville: A time in the late Pleistocene epoch about 30,000 years ago when a prehistoric lake formed covering an estimated 20,000 square miles (52,000 sq km), over much of western Utah and parts of Nevada and Idaho in the United States. These conditions existed during the interval of the last major Pleistocene glaciation. Lake Bonneville shrank rapidly in size and, by 12,000 years ago, had permanently shrunk to a point where it had become smaller than the Great Salt Lake. (*syn.* Bonneville period)

Book of Kells: One of the earliest illuminated manuscripts of Europe, a masterpiece of the ornate Hiberno-Saxon style. It was probably begun in the late 8th century at the Irish monastery on the Scottish island of Iona, and after a Viking raid the book was taken to the monastery of Kells in County Meath, where it may have been completed in the early 9th century. The monastery of Kells was founded by the monks of Iona when they fled the Vikings in 806. The book's contents include gospels, prefaces, summaries, and concordances, as well as legal documents relating to the abbey. A facsimile of the manuscript was published in 1974.

Book of the Dead: The modern name given to a collection of ancient Egyptian mortuary texts made up of spells or magic formulas, placed in tombs and believed to protect and aid the deceased in the hereafter. The collection, literally titled "The Chapters of Coming-Forth-by-Day," received its present name from Karl Richard Lepsius, German Egyptologist, who published the first collection of the texts in 1842. It was probably compiled and re-edited during the 16th century BC, and over half of the collection is made up of the Coffin Texts dating from c. 2000 BC and the Pyramid Texts dating from c. 2400 BC. The Book of the Dead had numerous authors, compilers, and sources. Scribes copied the texts on rolls of papyrus, often with illustrations, and sold them to individuals for use in burials. Many copies of the book have been found in Egyptian tombs, but none contains all of the approximately 200 chapters. The choice of spells varies from copy to copy.

boomerang: A curved wooden throwing stick with a biconvex or semioval cross-section, distributed widely over Australia except for Tasmania, and used for hunting and warfare. The boomerang had marked regional variations in design and decoration. Returning boomerangs were used in Australia as playthings, in tournament competition, and by hunters to imitate hawks for driving flocks of game birds into nets strung from trees. The returning boomerang was developed from the nonreturning types, which swerve in flight. Boomerangs excavated from peat deposits in Wyrie Swamp, South Australia, have been dated to c. 8000 BC. Boomerang-shaped, nonreturning weapons were used by the ancient Egyptians, by Indians of California and Arizona, and in southern India for killing birds, rabbits, and other animals.

Boomplaas: A cave in the Folded Mountain belt of the Cape Province, South Africa, containing a long sequence of Upper Pleistocene and Holocene deposits. The earliest occupation was probably around 80,000 years ago. There was a long "Middle Stone Age" sequence and then occupations attributed to the Robberg, Albany, and Wilton industries.

Boreal: A climatic subdivision of the Holocene epoch, following the Pre-Boreal and preceding the Atlantic climatic intervals. Radiocarbon dating shows the period beginning about 9,500 years ago and ending about 7,500 years ago. The Boreal was supposed to be warm and dry. In Europe, the Early Boreal was characterized by hazel pine forest assemblages and lowering sea levels. In the Late Boreal, hazel–oak forest assemblages were dominant, but the seas were rising. In some areas, notably the North York moors, southern Pennines, and lowland heaths, Mesolithic people appear to have been responsible for temporary clearances by fire and initiated the growth of moor and heath vegetation. (*syn.* Boreal Climatic Interval)

bored stone: A rounded stone of various sizes with a bored hole in the middle, found in central and southern Africa and dating back 40,000 years. Some were used as weights on digging sticks.

Borg-in Nadur: A fortified Bronze Age acropolis in southeast Malta and also the name of its culture on the island. The settlement was surrounded by walls of cyclopean masonry and had enclosed oval huts. The discovery of a sherd of Mycenaean pottery points to long-distance trading contacts. Bronze Age tools and weapons have been found at Borg in-Nadur.

Boriskowskij, Pavel Iossifovitch (1911–1991): A Russian archaeologist who worked at Palaeolithic sites in Amvrosievka, Bol'shaya Akkarzha, Kostenki, and Pushkari. He worked on the social aspects of the Middle/Upper Palaeolithic transition from a Marxist perspective.

Borneo: The largest island of Southeast Asia, first mentioned in Ptolemy's *Guide to Geography* of AD c. 150. Joined to mainland southeast Asia during the low-sea-level Pleistocene period, archaeological sequences have been found in the Niah Caves of Sarawak and the Madai-Tingkayu region of Sabah. The Niah Great Cave sequence suggests the presence of a population of early Australoids from about 40,000 years ago, and evidence from all sites indicates that the ancestors of present-day Borneans arrived around 3000 BC, possibly from the Philippines. Although traces of *Homo erectus* from 2 million years ago were found on neighboring Java, so far no evidence has been found of *Homo erectus* in Borneo. Roman trade beads and Indo-Javanese artifacts give evidence of a flourishing civilization dating to the 2nd or 3rd century BC. A Sanskrit inscription dated to AD c. 400 is the earliest histori-cal document on the island. Three rough foundation stones with an inscription recording a gift to a Brahman priest, found at Kutai, date from the early 5th century AD and provide evidence of a Hindu kingdom. The first recorded European visitor was the Franciscan friar Odoric of Pordenone, who visited on his way from India to China in 1330.

Borobudur: A huge Mahayana Buddhist monument in central Java, Indonesia, northwest of Yogyakarta, constructed between about AD 778–850 under the Sailendra dynasty and the Sanjaya kings. It is the largest Buddhist monument in the world. The Borobudur is in the form of a stepped pyramid, constructed of 2 million cubic feet of volcanic stone around and over a natural hill, and consists of six square and three circular superimposed terraces, crowned by a large stupa. There are 504 statues of the Buddha, 1,300 reliefs, and 72 stupas on the Borobudur. (*syn.* Barabudur)

borrow pit: A prehistoric pit from which mud, clay, or earth was taken for building purposes. The term also refers to an excavated area where material has been dug for use as fill at another location.

Borsippa: An ancient Babylonian city southwest of Babylon, Iraq. It is the site of the highest surviving ziggurat (154 ft/47 m), built by Nebuchadrezzar (reigned 605–562 BC) and dedicated to its patron god, Nabu. Borsippa's proximity to Babylon led to its being identified with the Tower of Babel, and it became an important religious center. The incomplete and now ruined ziggurat was excavated in 1902 by the German archaeologist Robert Koldewey. Hammurabi (reigned 1792–1750 BC) built or rebuilt the Ezida temple at Borsippa, dedicating it to Marduk. Borsippa was destroyed by the Achaemenian King Xerxes I in the early 5th century BC and never fully recovered. (*syn.* modern Birs, Birs Nimrud)

Boscoreale: The site of two villas in suburbs of Rome, near Pompeii, with important and sumptuous artifacts and painted rooms dating c. 40 BC. These villas included possessions of the great patrician families of Rome, such as paintings illustrating Dionysiac mysteries, jewels, and magnificent gold and silver household furnishings. The *cubiculum* of one villa at Boscoreale is preserved in the Metropolitan Museum of Art in New York City, and other items are kept at the Louvre. Many of the rich hoards were accidentally saved by the volcanic catastrophe of AD 79.

Boserup, Ester (1910–): A Danish economist who created an "optimistic" model that proposes that population pressure produces technological responses. She wrote *Population and Technological Change*, published in 1981.

boshanlu: (po-shan-lu) A Chinese incense burner (*lu*) with a lid designed to represent mountain peaks, such as Boshan, a mountain in Shangdong province. These are stemmed bowls of pottery or bronze with perforated conical lids. Most examples date from the western Han period. One from the tomb of Liu Sheng (d. 113 BC) at Mancheng is inlaid with gold.

bossed bone plaque: Objects of unknown function made from long animal bones and carved with a row of bosses—circular, square, or oval ornamental motifs. Examples from Lerna, Troy, and Altamira date to the late 3rd millennium BC. The finest also have engraved decoration. A series from Castelluccio, Sicily, with outliers in Italy and Malta, are curved in cross section and dated just before 2500 BC.

Bosumpra: A cave site near Abetifi, Ghana, which yielded one of the first scientifically excavated assemblages of West African Neolithic industry. Radiocarbon dating has shown that occupation began around the middle 4th millennium BC and continued for at least 3,000 years. Throughout the sequence, a microlithic chipped-stone industry was associated with simple pottery and with ground-stone ax- or hoe-like implements.

botany: The scientific study of the structure, growth, and identification of plants.

bothros: In Greek archaeology, a pit used for storage or rubbish disposal.

Botta, Paul-Emile (1802–1870): French consul in Mosul, Iraq, and archaeologist whose discovery of the palace of the Assyrian king Sargon II at Dur Sharrukin in 1843 started the large-scale field archaeology of ancient Mesopotamia. He was seeking the vanished cities of Assyria, known at that time only from the accounts of ancient writers and from biblical references. Botta revealed the remains of the great palace of Sargon II (721–505 BC), with its famed winged figures, relief sculptures, and cuneiform inscriptions—but he mistakenly thought he had found ancient Nineveh. The remains tended to disintegrate quickly after being unearthed, and one shipment of antiquities was sunk in transit, but another reached Paris and the Louvre. He published *Monuments of Nineveh …* in 1849–1850, with beautiful illustrations by E. N. Flandin. Later, Botta devoted himself to deciphering cuneiform.

Bouar: A city of the Central African Republic where, about 2,500 years ago, farming people set up numerous series of megalithic monuments consisting of standing stones—which weighed several tons—associated with tumuli. The cooperation necessary to make and position these monuments suggests that they were built by fairly large social units.

Bouärd, Michel de (1909–   ): A French archaeologist who worked in medieval studies, especially on earthworks as fortifications. Bouärd also investigated ceramics and other aspects of medieval material culture and made advances in archaeological laboratory research.

Boucher (de Crèvecoeur) de Perthes, Jacques (1788–1868): French archaeologist and writer who was the first to develop the idea that prehistory could be measured on the basis of periods of geological time. In 1837, in the Somme Valley, he discovered flint hand axes and other stone tools along with the bones of extinct mammals in deposits of the Pleistocene epoch (or Ice Age, ending about 10,000 years ago). Boucher de Perthes was the first to draw attention to the Stone Age's revolutionary significance, because at the time, 4004 BC was still believed to be the year of the creation. His claims that these objects were the tools of ancient man and that they occurred in association with the bones of extinct animals were ridiculed. In 1859, Boucher de Perthes's conclusions were finally upheld by a group of eminent British scientists, including Charles Lyell, Hugh Falconer, John Preswich, and John Evans, who visited the excavated sites. His archaeological writings include *De la Création: essai sur l'origine et la progression des êtres* (1838–1841) and *Antiquités Celtiques et antédiluviennes* (1847–1864). (*syn.* Boucher de Perthes)

Boudicca (d. AD 60): Ancient British queen of the Iceni tribe of Norfolk who led a revolt against Roman rule in AD 60. After suffering many cruelties to her family, herself, and her tribe at the hands of the Romans, Boudicca raised a rebellion throughout East Anglia. She and her followers burned Camulodunum (Colchester), Verulamium (St. Albans), the mart of Londinium (London), and several military posts, massacred approximately 70,000 Romans and pro-Roman Britons; and destroyed the Roman 9th Legion. The Roman governor Paulinus regained the province in a battle during which 80,000 of the rebelling tribesmen were killed and after which Boudicca took poison or died of shock. (*syn.* Boadicea)

Bougon: A cemetery site of megalithic tombs at Deux-Sèvres, France, with radiocarbon dates to the mid-5th millennium BC, making the tombs among the oldest chambered tombs in Europe. There is pottery from the Early Neolithic and Late Neolithic/Early Bronze Age.

boulder: A rock size that is a subdivision of gravel clasts, 256 millimeters or larger in diameter (Wentworth-Udden classification).

boulder clay: A clayey deposit of the Ice Age, which contains boulders. Also, the clay of the Glacial or Drift period.

bouleuterion: The Greek structure for meetings of the city council (*boule*), a rectangular building, often with a D-shaped hall with a curved side with rows of seats. Athens' bouleterion was built c. 500 BC, and a Hellenistic example at Miletus dates to c. 170 BC. The structure was the model for Roman Senate buildings (curia).

boundary: A zone of vertical change from one soil horizon to another. Boundaries are described in vertical distance—as abrupt, clear, or gradual—and the horizontal character as being smooth, wavy, or irregular.

Bouqras: 7th-millennium BC Pre-Pottery Neolithic village near the River Euphrates in Syria. The first occupation phase had two levels with rectangular mud-brick houses. The next four levels had more solid mud-brick houses, some with plastered floors, benches, and pillars. The economy was based on hunting of wild animals, except in the final phase when sheep and cattle were bred. Sickle blades, pounders, and querns were used for wild or cultivated plants in the first phase. Artifacts include a white ware, made of mixed lime and ash and used to cover baskets, producing watertight vessels. Obsidian occurs in large quantities, indicating extensive trade networks linking Bouqras with the source sites in Anatolia.

Boussargues: A village site in France with pottery of the Chalcolithic Fontbouisse culture, c. 2500 BC. There are apsidal (having one end rounded) houses surrounded by a wall with projecting huts or towers of dry stone.

bout coupé: In British archaeology, a well-made cordiform or subtriangular refined biface from northwest Europe. It may be a diagnostic Mousterian tool.

bow: An offensive weapon for shooting arrows or missiles and used in hunting and war. It generally consists of a strip of bendable wood or other material with a string stretched between its two ends. The arrow or missile is shot by the recoil after retraction of the string. The weapon was first used in the Upper Palaeolithic by the Gravettians. Some Mesolithic examples have been preserved in peat bogs, but often all that remains is an arrowhead or wrist guard.

bowsing: A technique used to locate features beneath the surface, such as buried chambers or ditches, by thumping the ground and sensing the differences between compacted and undisturbed earth. A resulting resonant sound may indicate a buried chamber or pit. It is an unsophisticated but effective method of searching for earthworks at archaeological sites, especially in chalk subsoil. Wooden mallets or lead-filled tools are examples of implements used. The verb *bose* or *bowse* means to test the ground for the presence of buried structures by noting the sound of percussion from a weighted striker. (*syn.* bosing)

box flue: A brick of four terra-cotta tiles, which were joined together to conduct the furnace-heated air of a Roman (hypocaust) heating system. The tiles were joined at the edges and open at the top and bottom. The air was directed through them up the walls to escape at the eaves. The exposed faces of the box-flue tiles were often decorated in relief to provide a key for the wall plaster that normally covered them.

Boxgrove: An Acheulian site in West Sussex, England, with biface manufacturing, lithic tools, and debitage.

Boyne: The site of prehistoric ritual monuments and Neolithic passage graves in the valley of the River Boyne, Ireland, dating to the 4th millennium BC. The complex includes five henges, a number of mounds, and the three great passage graves of Newgrange, Dowth, and Knowth. These megalithic tombs are set in round mounds and are usually on hilltops or grouped in cemeteries. These structures are notable for their size, their decoration, and the architectural expertise involved. The term *Boyne culture* is sometimes used to describe the material found inside passage graves all over Ireland. Its characteristics are highly decorated Carrowkeel pottery, bone pins with poppy- or mushroom-shaped heads, pendants, and beads. (*syn.* Boyne Valley tombs)

BP: The abbreviation for *Before the Present*, used especially in radiocarbon dating. The fixed reference date for *Before the Present* has been established as AD 1950. Thus, 4250 BP would mean 4,250 years before 1950, or 2300 BC. The year 1950 was the latest that the atmosphere was sufficiently uncontaminated to act as a standard for radiocarbon dating. The lower case *bp* represents uncalibrated radiocarbon years; the small capitals BP denote a calibrated radiocarbon date, or a date derived from some other dating method, such as potassium-argon, that does not need calibration. (*syn.* Before Present, BP)

brachycephalic: Being short or broad headed, that is, having a cephalic index of 80–84.9. The maximum width of the cranium is 80% or more of the maximum length. In ethnology, this term denotes skulls of which the breadth is at least four-fifths of the length. (*syn.* brachycranic) (*ant.* dolichocephalic)

bracteate: A coin, medal, dish, or ornament made of thin, beaten metal—usually gold or silver. These items were often disk shaped—hollow on the underside and convex on the upper.

Bradford-on-Avon: A parish in Wiltshire, England, the site of a monastery that existed in the late 7th century and the Saxon Church of St. Lawrence, dated in the early 8th century and discovered and carefully restored in 1856. St. Lawrence Church is possibly the finest and best-preserved Anglo-Saxon church in England.

Bradshaw figures: Small, red painted figures in scenes of the Kimberley region of Western Australia, named for Joseph Bradshaw who discovered them.

Brahmagiri: A settlement site and cemetery dating from at least the 2nd millennium BC in southern India. Wheeler found a Chalcolithic level (c. 2800–1250 BC) with abundant microliths, polished stone axes, and crude burnished gray pottery, an Iron Age level (1st millennium BC) with black-and-red ware, 300 tombs, stone circles, and ossuaries for bones, and a level from the 1st century AD with rouletted ware and traces of Roman contact. Bone points and some evidence of a stone-blade industry have also been found. There are many cattle bones, but also sheep and goats. The culture seemed to continue with little change for many centuries.

brain endocast: A cast of the cranial cavity (inner surface of the cranium) to produce an accurate image and approximate shape of the brain. These are made by pouring latex rubber into a skull. The fossil record can yield endocranial casts and, from them, possible brain volumes—especially of early man. (*syn.* endocranial cast)

Brak, Tell: A tell on the upper Khabur River in Syria, which had an Akkadian fortress and garrison and was occupied from at least the Halaf and Ubaid periods until the mid-2nd millennium BC. On the Syrian-Iraqi border, it was a powerful fortress on the imperial line of communication, and its most important remains are the four "Eye Temples" of the Jemdet Nasr period, c. 3000 BC. They are so-called for the large number of small, flat alabaster figurines of which the eyes are the only recognizable features. Eye temples were decorated with clay cones, copper panels, and goldwork, in a style very similar to that found in the contemporary temples of Sumer. Halaf, Ubaid, and Uruk sherds have been found. When the site became a frontier post of the kingdom of Akkad, a palace was built here by Naram-Sin c. 2280 BC, and it became a depot for the storage of tribute and loot. The city was plundered after the fall of the Akkadian Empire, but the palace was rebuilt in the Ur III period by Ur Nammu. A Roman fort was built there later. (*syn.* Brak, Tall Birak at-Tahtani)

Branc: A cemetery site in southeastern Czech Republic of the Early Bronze Age where the burials were differentiated according to sex and the orientation was reversed from contemporary sites. At Branc, 81% of females were on their left side and 61% of males on their right. These mostly simple rectangular pits, sometimes with a wooden lining, of 308 inhumation graves spanning 200–400 years of the early Unetician culture were also analyzed for their grave goods. In the graves, there was clear evidence of community differentiation, with some individuals having more elaborate grave goods than others (on the basis of the rarity of the raw materials used and the time needed to produce the goods). This suggests that there would be leading families and that wealth and status would tend to be inherited (ascribed), and there is evidence that each member of the community was placed according to lineage, sex, and age.

Brandberg: A mountain massif in central Namibia with Stone Age and Iron Age material, including 43,000 important cave art paintings. The "White Lady of the Brandberg," romanticized by Abbé Breuil, is the most celebrated.

brass: The general name for alloys of copper with zinc or tin, with the proportions about 70–90% copper and 10–30%

of the other base metal. It is possible that owing to difficulties in introducing the zinc ore calamine into the melt, brass appeared later in use than bronze (copper and tin) and other copper alloys. Mosaic gold, pinchbeck, prince's metal are varieties of brass differing in the proportions of the ingredients. Corinthian brass is an alloy of gold, silver, and copper.

Brassempouy: A series of early Upper Palaeolithic deposits in southwest France near Brassempouy, famous for carved ivories and broken statuettes of "Venus" or "Lady." These statues are thought to be the work of Cro-Magnon artists.

Brauron: The temenos of the goddess Artemis Brauronia in Attica, Greece. There are remains of a Doric temple and stoa with dining rooms.

breadfruit: The fruit of a tree in the South Sea islands, about the size of a melon, whose whitish pulp (with the consistency of new bread) requires cooking before it can be eaten. The tree was probably first cultivated from the Philippines to New Guinea and attained great economic importance in the Polynesian Islands, especially the Marquesas and Tahiti, about 1500–2000 years ago. The fruit was also dried or allowed to ferment and could then be stored for several years in underground pits. In 1788, Captain William Bligh was attempting to take breadfruit saplings from Tahiti to the West Indies when the famous mutiny on HMS Bounty occurred. (*syn.* bread-fruit)

Breasted, James Henry (1854–1935): American Egyptologist, archaeologist, and historian who excavated Megiddo (Armageddon), established ancient Egyptian historical periods, and founded the University of Chicago's Oriental Institute (1919). Breasted promoted research on ancient Egypt and the ancient civilizations of western Asia, compiled a record of every known Egyptian hieroglyphic inscription, and published a translation of these in a five-volume work, *Ancient Records of Egypt* (1906). He led expeditions to Egypt and the Sudan (1905–1907) and copied inscriptions from monuments that had been previously inaccessible or were perishing. The Oriental Institute is a renowned center for the study of the ancient cultures of southwest Asia and the Middle East. His other books included *History of Egypt* (1905), *Ancient Times* (1916), and *Development of Religion and Thought in Ancient Egypt* (1912). His excavation at Megiddo uncovered a large riding stable thought to have been King Solomon's, and his excavation at Persepolis yielded some Achaemenid sculptures.

breccia: A deposit of angular composite stone fragments held together by a matrix of natural cement, such as sap, lime, or calcium-charged water. Its occurrence indicates a previous cold phase in the climate, because the rock is detached either by frost or by alternating heat and cold. Many caves occupied by early people, such as Dordogne in southwest France, have layers of breccia crammed with bones, tools, art objects. This conglomerate was used by ancient peoples for architecture and sculpture. It is the opposite of conglomerate, in which the fragments are rounded and water worn. Osseous or bone breccia is breccia in which fossil bones are found.

Breitenbach: An Upper Palaeolithic site in eastern Germany with artifacts including end scrapers, burins, and several bone points of the Aurignacian. Faunal remains are woolly mammoth and reindeer.

Breuil, Abbé Henri (1877–1961): A French archaeologist who was regarded as an authority on prehistoric cave paintings of Europe and Africa. He devoted much of his life to studying examples of prehistoric art in southern France, northern Spain, and southern Africa. Breuil was a fine draftsman, and his greatest contributions were in the recording and interpretation of cave art in more than 600 publications. He proposed a series of four successive art styles, based on the superposition of paintings found in many caves, and held the view that the purpose of the paintings was sympathetic magic, to ensure success in hunting. Breuil fit the Aurignacian culture into its right place in the French Palaeolithic sequence and was responsible for working out the chronologies of French Upper and Middle Palaeolithic periods. (*syn.* Breuil, Henri-Édouard-Prosper)

brick: An important building material of individual blocks of clay or mud, some with tempering of sand or straw. Bricks, which are not always rectangular, may be baked in a kiln to terra cotta or sun dried—which is referred to as mud brick or adobe. The chief building material throughout the Near East has always been mud brick. Bricks can be used as dating criteria, especially when they bear stamped inscriptions. Decorative glazed bricks first appeared in Assyrian times, as at the Ishtar Gate in Babylon.

brick relief: A technique of sculpture in which subjects are put in bas-relief on a brick surface or wall.

bridge: A structure forming a road over a river or allowing passage between two points above the ground. A bridge can be a simple plank or single arch or an elaborate architectural structure supported by arches, chains, girders, piers, and so on. The first bridges were natural, such as arches of rock. The first manmade bridges were flat stones or tree trunks laid across a stream to make a girder bridge. Three types of bridge—beam or girder, arch, and suspension—have been known and built from the earliest times.

bridging argument: In middle-range research, any logical statements linking the static archaeological record to the past dynamics that produced it. Contemporary observations, especially through ethnoarchaeology and experimental archaeology, are generally used to define these links.

bristlecone pine: A small pine tree, approximately 15–40 feet (5–13 m) high, which is the oldest living tree in the world. It is native to the Rocky Mountains of the United States, at elevations above 7,500 feet (2,300 m), has the longest life span of any conifer. A stand of this tree in eastern Nevada is known to have several trees over 3,000 years old, and one of them is thought to be about 4,900 years old. The combination of these and some well-preserved dead examples has allowed a dendrochronological key to be built, has changed some of the assumptions underlying radiocarbon dating, and has provided calibration for radiocarbon dates going back about 7,000 years.

Britannia: The name given to England, Wales, and lowland Scotland by the Romans when they occupied it as a province from AD 43 to 410. In 197, the province was divided into two, then into four parts c. 300, and in 369 into five provinces.

British Mountain culture: A Late Palaeolithic culture of the Northwest Arctic in Yukon, near the border of Canada and Alaska. Artifacts, such as percussion flakes, share traits of European and Asian Levallois-Mousterian stone tool kits and are possibly 18,000 years old.

Brno: The traditional capital of Moravia in the southeastern Czech Republic, which was inhabited in prehistoric times, according to archaeological evidence. Important sites surround and are in the town, including a burial covered in red ochre, mammoth tusks, and ornaments, which has proved to be one of the earliest Upper Palaeolithic burials known. Traces of Neanderthal man were found in a cave called Svéduv stul ("Swedish Table"), and a camping ground of the Cro-Magnon mammoth hunters (30,000 BC) was discovered at Dolni Vestonice, 20 miles (30 km) south. There are also traces of Celts and other tribes and many Slav settlements from the 5th and 6th centuries.

Broadbeach: A burial site along the coast south of Brisbane, Queensland, Australia. Excavations uncovered 200 burials over a span of 1,300 years, with wide variations in burial practices, possibly related to age, sex, and status. Red ochre was present in nearly all graves, while grave goods included bone, shell, and stone artifacts and tools.

Broad Spectrum Revolution: A theory that there was a subsistence change in western Asia involving a wide range of foodstuffs, including small mammals, invertebrates, aquatic resources, and plants in the Late Pleistocene—a prelude to the "Neolithic revolution." (*syn.* Kebaran Complex, Natufian)

broch: A prehistoric circular towerlike building of dry stone, which was peculiar to the north and west of Scotland. The hollow walls, which contained chambers and stairways, were built of dry masonry, and the tower was usually 13–20 meters in diameter and tapered inward in the upper courses. The walls may be up to 20 feet (4 meters) thick. Over 400 are known in Scotland, and the structures served as fortified homesteads. They originated in the mid-1st millennium BC, but most date from the beginning of the Christian era. The Broch of Mousa on Shetland is the best-preserved and most famous example. They are always in a strong defensive position, close to the sea.

Broederstroom: An Early Iron Age village site in Pretoria, South Africa, from the mid-1st millennium AD. Its remains, including 13 circular houses, gives a fairly complete picture of life at the time. There was iron smelting and herding of cattle, sheep, and goats. Broederstroom pottery suggests connections with contemporary people to the northwest.

Broken Hill: A cave and mine site in central Zambia in which a complete skull was found, which is attributed to Rhodesian man (*Homo sapiens rhodesiensis*) and has characteristics similar to Neanderthals. The skull was found on a ledge in 1922 and has no definite evidence of a date, but the artifacts in the Bone Cave were of the Middle Stone Age (Charaman industry). Dating by amino-acid racemization indicates an age of more than 100,000 years. Mining operations have exposed a long series of stone industries extending from the Acheulian to the Charman. Over 25% of the species represented by the associated faunal remains are now extinct.

Brommian: An Allerod and Dryas culture of Denmark, southern Sweden, and northern Germany and Poland of c. 10,000 BC. It resembles the Hamburgian and is characterized by the Lyngby point and Lyngby reindeer-antler ax/club.

Brongniart, Alexandre (1770–1847): French mineralogist, geologist, and naturalist, who first arranged the geologic formations of the Tertiary period (from 66.4–1.6 million years ago) in chronological order and described them. Brongniart helped introduce the principle of geologic dating by the identification of distinctive fossils found in each geological stratum.

bronze: An alloy of copper and tin that is harder than copper. Bronze was made before 3000 BC, although it was not used in tools and weapons for some time. The proportions of copper and tin varied widely (67–95% copper in surviving artifacts), and the addition of zinc, nickel, lead, arsenic, or antimony is also known. Adding tin to copper makes casting easier and the edges of tools and weapons harder. The main disadvantage was the comparative scarcity of tin. A higher percentage of tin produces potin or speculum. The Bronze Age of the Three Age system began in Eurasia when it replaced copper as the main material for tools and weapons. It was then replaced by the more common and efficient iron, but was still used for decorative purposes. Modern bronze also contains zinc and lead.

Bronze Age: The second age of the Three Age system, beginning about 4000–3000 BC in the Mideast and about 2000–1500 BC in Europe. It followed the Stone Age and preceded the Iron Age and was defined by a shift from stone tools and weapons to the use of bronze. During this time, civilization based on agriculture and urban life developed. Trading to obtain tin for making bronze led to the rapid diffusion of ideas and technological improvements. The Iron Age began about 1500 BC in the Mideast and 900 BC in Europe. Bronze artifacts were valued highly and became part of many hoards. In the Americas, true bronze was used in northern Argentina before AD 1000, and it spread to Peru and the Incas. Bronze was never as important in the New World as in the Old. The Bronze Age is often divided into three periods: Early Bronze Age (c. 4000–2000 BC), Middle Bronze Age (c. 2000–1600 BC), and Late Bronze Age (c. 1600–1200 BC), but the chronological limits and the terminology vary from region to region.

bronze mirror: Any of the smooth-faced bronze discs of eastern Asia in the late 2nd millennium BC. These cast-decorated items became important to the Han dynasty elite in China. In Korea and Japan, they were used for rituals or ceremonies.

brooch: An ornamental pin or piece of decorative metalwork attached by a pin, either a fastener or ornament, and found from c. 1400 BC. Brooches developed from the Roman fibula, which was similar to a safety pin, and were first made at La Tène on Lake Neuchâtel, Switzerland. Their styles vary especially in the twistings of the spring and may be used to date other finds. There were long brooches, rosette or circular brooches, and penannular types.

Brørup interstadial: An interstadial of the Weichselian cold period, radiocarbon dated to between 63,000 and 61,000 bp, but it may be earlier.

brown earth: Brown forest soils that result from prolonged forestal conditions and that develop under mature deciduous woodland. Brown earths are thought to have covered most of the British Isles and temperate Europe under the great forests that existed during the middle of the present Interglacial. The soil type is penetrated by tree roots and actively worked by earthworms to a considerable depth. The top is well-mixed mineral material and humus. As a result of woodland cover being removed repeatedly, these soils are rare today. (*syn.* brown forest soil, brown earths)

Bruniquel: A cave and rock shelter in southwest France with Magdalenian deposits, including the remains of two or three well-preserved skulls and skeletal parts and fragmentary remains of over a dozen more individuals. These are attributed to Cro-Magnon people. Carved bone and antler artifacts are also known.

Brynzeny: A cave site in Moldova with Palaeolithic, Mesolithic, and earlier artifacts. An unusual find was a carved and decorated woolly mammoth tusk.

Brythons: A combination of Nordic and Alpine peoples who arrived in southeast England about 550 BC. They introduced iron and gave their name to Britain. During the Roman occupation, England was inhabited by Celtic Brythons, but the Celts withdrew before the Teutonic Angles, Saxons, and Jutes into the mountainous areas of western and northern Britain and to Ireland. (*syn.* Britons)

Brzesc Kujawski: A large settlement site in central Poland of the Lengyel culture of the early 4th millennium BC. There were about 60 trapezoidal longhouses, smaller areas of one or more house clusters, and a large inhumation cemetery with double graves, animal burials, and rich copper grave goods. There were four phases of occupation.

Bubalus period: The earliest phase of rock art in northern Africa, between 12,000–8,000 BC, in which large-scale carvings of animals appeared. These early engravings—in southern Oran, in Algeria, and in Libya—reflect a hunting economy based on the now-extinct giant buffalo *Homoioceras antiquus* or *Bubalus antiquus* (hence the name).

Bubanj: A Late Neolithic culture of late 4th to early 3rd millennia BC in the Morava Valley of eastern Yugoslavia, close to Nis. The site, on a gravel terrace of a river, was first excavated in the 1950s, and the culture is derived from the Vinca and closely related to the Salcuta in Romania. The main periods recognized include the early Neolithic Starcevo with graphite painted ware and Vinca-like dark burnished ware; a phase of Baden pottery; and an Early Bronze Age occupation. (*syn.* Bubanj-Hum)

Bubastis: An Egyptian site in the southeastern Nile Delta with monuments of the 22nd Dynasty. (*syn.* Tell Basta)

bucchero: A fine gray pottery, with a black or gray shiny surface, which was produced principally in Greek-speaking or Etruscan areas between the 8th and 5th centuries BC. Shapes and decoration styles varied greatly—incised, stamped and applied were employed. This earthenware pottery was common in pre-Roman Italy between the 7th and early 5th centuries BC. The shiny surface was produced by polishing, and the color achieved by firing in an atmosphere charged with carbon monoxide instead of oxygen ("reducing firing"). The light, thin-walled bucchero sottile, considered the finest, was made in the 7th and early 6th centuries, and the shapes were derived largely from Oriental models. In the 6th century, the Greek influence changed the forms to alabastrums, amphorae, kraters, kylikes with incised, modeled, or applied birds and animals in friezes or geometric schemes. Greek black pigment was used, and human and animal figures were painted on the surface of bucchero in black, red, and white. Technique and workmanship declined from about the mid-6th century onward, when bucchero sottile was replaced by bucchero pasantë, a heavy, complex thick-walled ware that was decorated with elaborate reliefs.

Buccino: A series of sites near Buccino, southwest Italy, with a cemetery of rock-cut tombs of the Copper Age with radiocarbon dates of c. 3350–2500 BC. There is also an Early Bronze Age settlement of the Apennine culture surrounded by a stone wall and containing rectangular stone-built huts.

Buchau: A Late Bronze Age settlement site in southern Germany with two Urnfield period occupations. There were single-room buildings and a larger two-roomed building in one occupation; the second settlement had nine complexes of large multiroom houses with outbuildings. (*syn.* Wasserburg Buchau)

Buchis: In ancient Egyptian religion, a sacred bull of Luxor that was the incarnation of the war god Mont. Buchis was believed to be the principal physical manifestation (ba) of Ra and Osiris. It was represented as a white bull with black markings or as the solar disk with two tall plumes between two horns. According to legend, his hair grew in the opposite direction from that of ordinary animals and changed color every hour. Particular bulls were worshipped as Buchis and were mummified and buried with honors on their deaths.

bucranium: In Roman times, an ox skull that was carved in relief and was part of the decoration of a building.

Buda industry: A Lower Palaeolithic industry of Hungary characterized by the production of chopping tools on pebbles and flake tools.

Budakalász: A Baden culture cemetery near Budapest, Hungary, where a very early four-wheeled wagon was found in a grave.

Buddhagupta stone: A Sanskrit language inscription of c. 5th century AD in western Malaysia, reflecting trade by Buddhists of Southeast Asia. Related inscriptions have been found in Borneo and Brunei.

Bug/Dniester: A complex of sites in two river valleys in Russia from the 5th millennium BC. Each phase is typified by short-lived sites on river terraces, occupied year round for 5–10 years. There was hunting, fishing, and shell collecting, and some domestication of pigs, cattle, and einkorn wheat. Pointed-base pottery evolved there. (*syn.* Bug-Dniester)

Buhen: An ancient Egyptian fort site of Lower Nubia, near Wadi Halfa, where the ruins of an Egyptian colony of the Middle Kingdom are located. Pharaoh Snefru (c. 2575 BC) raided Nubia and established an Egyptian outpost at Buhen on the west bank of the Nile at the north end of the Second Cataract, and it endured for 200 years. Graffiti and inscribed seals at Buhen document Egyptian presence until late in the 5th Dynasty (c. 2325 BC). It was a center for Egyptian mining expeditions and for securing Egyptian control of trade in gold and other commodities. Buhen was probably abandoned in the face of immigration from the south and the desert.

Bukhara: A city in Uzbekistan in the Bukhara oasis founded no later than the 1st century AD and an important trade and craft center before the Arab conquest in AD 709. It was the capital of the Samanid dynasty in the 9th–10th centuries, and later seized by the Qarakhanids and Karakitais before falling to Genghis Khan in 1220 and to Timur (Tamerlane) in 1370. The best-known monument is the Mausoleum of Ismael the Samanid, built shortly before the ruler's death in 907. The oldest surviving mosque is the 12th-century Masjid Magoki Attari. (*syn.* Buchara, Bokhara)

Bukit Tengku Lembu: A rock shelter site in Malaysia with remains related to the Ban Kao Neolithic and black ware that may be Indo-Roman rouletted ware.

Bükk: A rugged mountain range in northern Hungary, which gave its name to a Middle Neolithic pottery culture of the late 5th millennium BC. There are a number of cave sites with evidence of seasonal occupation and use of rocks for tools. There are hoards of axes and flint blades as well as painted and incised pottery. Obsidian was also exchanged even though there are volcanic tuffs, lavas, and postvolcanic hot springs.

bulbar scar: The irregularly shaped scar on the bulb of percussion of a struck flint flake. It marks the place where a small piece of flint is dislodged during fracture. The bulbar surface is the surface on which the bulb of percussion occurs. This fracture pattern is evident by a bruised striking platform at the point of impact with shock waves radiating from it and, on the resultant flake, a bulb of percussion and bulbar scar. When these features are present, it is possible to distinguish human workmanship from natural breakage caused by heat or frost.

bulb of percussion: In flint making, a swelling or bulb left on the surface of a blade or flake directly below the point of impact on the striking platform—in other words, a swelling on a flake or blade at the point where it has been struck to detach it from a core. On the flake or blade struck off, there is a rounded, slightly convex shape around this point, called the bulb of percussion, and on the core there is a corresponding concave bulb. The point and the bulb of percussion are rarely present if a flake has been struck off naturally, as by heat or frost. Thus the presence of a bulb of percussion makes it possible to distinguish human workmanship from natural breakage. (*syn.* bulb of force)

Bulk provenience: The location (provenience) of a group of similar objects by type of material and by level or surface.

bulla: A hollow lump of clay made as an Etruscan ornamental pendant or in the Near East as a container for tokens representing goods traded. A bulla was round or oval and often was decorated with filigree or granulation on the edges or with seal impressions. There was a removable loop from which the pendant was hung, which may also have acted as a stopper for the bulla if it contained a liquid, as perfume. (*syn.* plural bullae)

bundle burial: A secondary burial practice in which the bones of the deceased are collected after the flesh has decayed and then are re-buried in a nonarticulated pile, vessel, bundle, or other grave.

Buni: An important early Indonesian port in west Java, along the spice trade route in the first centuries AD. The burial site yielded crucibles, bronze items, and Indo-Roman rouletted ware.

Buret: A site in southern Siberia, western Turkistan, which was occupied in Late Palaeolithic times. It is known for mammoth-tusk figurines of women, which resemble Paleolithic statuettes from Europe and the Middle East. The nude ones probably served as fertility symbols or as representations of the great goddess, whose cult was widespread. Of five found at Buret, the most unusual is a clothed woman wearing a one-piece trouser suit with a hood attached to it, comparable to those still worn by present-day Eskimos.

Burgaschi-See Sud: A lake settlement site of the Neolithic Cortaillod culture in Switzerland, dated to the mid-4th millennium BC. The organic remains are well preserved as on other Cortaillod sites. The most important hunted fauna were red deer, roe deer, aurochs, and wild boar. Domesticated cattle, sheep, goat, and pig were kept. Artifacts include copper beads.

burh: An Anglo-Saxon stronghold or fortification; a term used for the defended settlements built by King Alfred of Wessex as a system of defense in the 9th century (known as the burghal system). Threatened by Viking (Danish) incursions, Alfred (and later his successors) built small fortified towns where the population could take refuge when threatened. Excavations in many burhs, such as Wareham, Tamworth, Wallingford, Devon, Bury, and Cricklade, show wide palisaded banks and v-shaped ditches with turf and timber revetments. Many of the burhs were also developed as market towns, and gridded streets were laid out in a number of them. (*syn.* burg)

burial: Inhumation or cremation—the laying of a body in the ground, in a natural or artificial chamber, or in an urn after burning. In collective burial, a single chamber is used for more than one corpse. A primary burial is one for which a burial monument such as a barrow was erected. The term *secondary burial* is used for the practice of collecting the bones of a skeleton after the flesh has decayed and placing them in some form of ossuary. In fractional burial, only some of the bones are so collected and interred. Archaeologists can learn a great deal about prehistoric societies by studying skeletons and the way they were buried. In some cultures, bodies were buried stretched out; in others, they were placed in the ground in a fetal or flexed position. In still other societies, the dead were exposed on platforms or in charnel houses; when the flesh had decayed or been scavenged, the disarticulated bones were made into a bundle and buried. Sometimes bodies were cremated and the remains buried. Goods interred with a burial give many clues to the social position of the person and his or her culture, and the study of bones can reveal sex, age, and information about nutrition and disease. The earliest deliberate burial of the dead was that of Neanderthal people of Palaeolithic times 100,000 years ago. They were buried in the cave in which the family continued to live. Food and tools were buried with them, proof of the belief in an afterlife. Neolithic people buried their dead in the long barrow, a communal tomb. Inhumation was followed by cremation in the Late Bronze Age.

burial mound: A large artificial hill of earth and stones built or placed over the remains of the dead at the time of burial. In England, the equivalent term is barrow; in Scotland, cairn; and in Europe and elsewhere, tumulus. In western Europe and the British Isles, burial cairns and barrows date primarily from the Neolithic period and Early Bronze Age (4000 BC– AD 600).

Burial Mound Builders: A term used to describe the prehistoric Native Americans who constructed the burial and temple mounds that are widespread east of the Mississippi River. It was once thought to be a distinctive group of peoples, but now the mounds are assigned to the Hopewell and Adena cultures. Burial mounds were characteristic of the Indian cultures of east-central North America from about 1000 BC to AD 700. The most numerous and grandly conceived ones, found in the Ohio and Mississippi River Valleys, were large conical or elliptical mounds surrounded by extensive earthworks.

Burial Mound Period: The penultimate period of eastern North American prehistoric chronology, from 1000 BC to AD 700. Formulated in 1941 by J. A. Ford and Gordon Willey, the total chronology, from early to late, is Paleo-Indian, Archaic, Burial Mound, and Temple Mound. The Burial Mound period I (1000–300 BC) covers the period of transition from Late Archaic to Early Woodland ways of life and is associated especially with the Adena culture. Burial Mound II (300 BC–AD 700) is associated especially with Middle and Late Woodland groups, especially Hopewell.

burial orientation: The direction or alignment of the body at the time of burial, especially the direction toward which the head is positioned. Burial orientation may vary according to the culture involved.

burial urn: A vessel in which the cremated ashes of one or more individuals are placed.

buried soil: Any ancient land surface buried and undisturbed under a structure or in a deposit, such as peat. Buried soil reflects the nature of the soil, at least at a very local level, at the time the structure was erected or the natural deposit laid down. Buried soil may be analyzed for faunal, insect, molluscan, and pollen remains, which give information about the environment of the period. Such soils are frequently preserved under barrows, mounds, or ramparts, or buried in the fill of a ditch. (*syn.* paleosol)

burin: A specialized engraving tool with a chipped flint or stone shaft that is cut or ground diagonally downward to form a diamond-shaped point at the tip. The angle of the point affected the width and depth of the engraved lines. The shaft of the tool was fixed in a flat handle that could be held close to the working surface. A burin had a wide rounded end for bracing against the palm of the hand, and the point was guided by thumb and forefinger. A blade or flake could be formed into any one of about 20 varieties of the tool. In its most characteristic form, the working tip is a narrow transverse edge formed by the intersection of two flake scars produced by striking at an angle to the main axis of the blade. Sometimes one facet is made by simply snapping the blade or by truncating it with a steep retouch. Burins were used to carve or engrave softer materials such as antler, bone, ivory, metal, or wood. This tool was characteristic of the Upper Paleolithic (especially Magdalenian) in the Old World and of some Early Lithic and Mesolithic cultures of the New World. (*syn.* graver)

Burma/Myanmar: Burma was the name of this Southeast Asian country when it was under British control; the name *Myanmar* was adopted in 1989. The first human settlements in Myanmar appeared some 11,000 years ago in the middle Irrawaddy River Valley. A group of people known as the Pyu, who spoke a Tibeto-Burman language, began establishing city-kingdoms in northern Myanmar between the 1st century BC and AD 800. To the south of the Pyu were the Mon, a people speaking an Austro-Asiatic language, who established a port capital at Thaton.

burnish: A polish given to the surface of an artifact, either to improve its appearance and make it more valuable or to compact it (as with clay) to make it less porous. A pot is polished, often using a spatula of wood or bone, while it is still in a leathery "green" state, before firing. After firing, the surface is extremely shiny. Often the whole outer surface of the pot is thus decorated, but in certain ceramic traditions there is "pattern burnishing" where the outside and, in the case of open bowls, the inside are decorated with burnished patterns in which some areas are left matte. In stroke burnish, the surface is completely polished, but the marks of the burnisher, a pebble or bone slip, remain distinct. On bronze, it was done to improve the appearance; even mirrors could be produced in this way. A burnisher is a metal instrument used by engravers to soften lines or efface them.

Burrill Lake: A rock shelter on the southeast coast of New South Wales, Australia, with deposits dated to the Pleistocene, c. 18,000 BC. Stone artifacts included flake scrapers and dentated saws. Around 3000 BC, Bondi points and other tools of the Australian Small Tool tradition appeared.

Burrup Peninsula: A rich archaeological area on the northwest coast of Western Australia with more than 10,000 engravings on rocks, including geometric figures of humans and animals. Artifacts and features include quarries, shell middens, standing stones, and dry-stone walls and terraces. The site dates range from 6700–200 bp.

Burzahom: A Neolithic site in the Vale of Kashmir with phases of occupation dating from c. 3050 BC to the 3rd–4th centuries AD. Deep pit dwellings are associated with ground stone axes, bone tools, and coarse gray burnished pottery. These characteristics and the absence of blades, use of pierced rectangular knives, and association of dog skeletons with human burials, all seem to point to connections with central and northern Asia, such as Mongolia, rather than with the rest of the Indian subcontinent. Hunting seems to have been the main basis of the economy. Phase II had houses of mud and mud brick, and Phase III had a group of large stones arranged in a rough semicircle.

Bush Barrow: The site of a rich grave under a barrow that belonged to the Wessex Culture of southern England. The single male inhumation included a bronze axe, two bronze daggers, and a stone macehead.

Butana: Seven sites in eastern Sudan, dating to 5500–4500 BP, with ceramics and stone artifacts. The cultural group belonged to the Kassala phase.

butcher marks: Marks made on animal bone by stone tools during butchering. These marks are used to associate humans with animal remains for a relative date. The marks are classified according to form and function as cut marks, chop marks, and scrapes. (*syn.* cut marks, chop marks, scrapes)

Butmir: A Late Neolithic settlement near Sarajevo in Bosnia, which gave its name to a culture, although the type site is not characteristic of the entire Butmir culture. The site represents a classic or late phase, defined by richly decorated ceramics (with incised meander designs) and a wide range of fired clay anthropomorphic figurines of various physical types, costume, and pathological condition. The culture was related to the Vinca culture. The Butmir culture includes the Middle and Late Neolithic of central Bosnia, in the period c. 4350–3700 BC.

Butser: An experimental farm and museum in Hampshire, England. Iron Age plant cultivation, animal husbandry, and architecture are tested and studied.

button: Small, usually disklike, pieces of bone, metal, stone, or other solid material, with holes or a shank through which they are sewn on to garments. Buttons are used to fasten or close a garment and are sometimes purely decoration. They are known from the Copper Age onward in Europe, developing in the Mediterranean area and being spread along with beakers. The ancient Greeks and Etruscans fastened their tunics at the shoulders with buttons and loops. The presence of buttons implies a tailored garment, as draped ones were better fastened with a pin or fibula.

Byblos: An ancient seaport on the Mediterranean coast just north of Beirut, Lebanon, and one of the oldest continuously inhabited towns in the world. Papyrus received its early Greek name (byblos, byblinos) from its being exported to the Aegean through Byblos. The English word Bible is derived from Byblos as "the (papyrus) book." Excavations revealed that Byblos was occupied at least by the Neolithic period (c. 8000–4000 BC) and that an extensive settlement developed during the 4th millennium BC. Byblos was the main harbor for exporting cedar and other valuable wood to Egypt from 3000 BC on. Egyptian monuments and inscriptions on the site describe close relations with the Nile Valley throughout the second half of the 2nd millennium. During Egypt's 12th Dynasty (1938–1756 BC), Byblos became an Egyptian dependency, and the chief goddess of the city, Baalat, with her well-known temple at Byblos, was worshiped in Egypt. After the collapse of the Egyptian New Kingdom in the 11th century BC, Byblos became the most important city of Phoenicia. Byblos has yielded almost all the known early Phoenician inscriptions, most of them dating from the 10th century BC. The crusaders captured the town in 1103, but they later lost it to the Ayyubids in 1189. The ruins today consist of the crusader ramparts and gate; a Roman colonnade and small theater; Phoenician ramparts; three major temples; and a necropolis. (*syn.* modern Gebeil, Gubla, Jubeil, Gebail, Jubayl, Jebeil; ancient/biblical Gebal; adjective Jiblite [Kubna, ancient Egyptian; Gubla, Akkadian])

Byci Skála: A prehistoric cave site near Brno, Czech Republic, with artifacts and faunal remains of the Middle and Upper Palaeolithic and the Hallstatt (Early Iron Age). There are sidescrapers and burins, numerous bronze objects, inhumation burials, and cremated bones. Several burials included wagons with iron tires, likely to have belonged to high-status people.

Bygholm: A site in Jutland, Denmark, with copper finds dating to c. 4000 BC, among the earliest metal objects in Denmark.

Bylany: A large village settlement of the Danubian culture in the loess lands of the Bohemian plain of the Czech Republic. This large site had many phases of occupation, including some by people who made stroke-ornamented pottery. There were timber-framed longhouses in the three main phases of the Linear Pottery sequence. Subsistence was based on emmer wheat cultivation and cattle husbandry.

Byzantine empire: The eastern half of the Roman Empire, based in Byzantium (later Constantinople, now Istanbul), an ancient Greek settlement on the European side of the Bosporus. It was inaugurated in AD 330 by the Emperor Constantine I, who transferred the capital of the Roman Empire to Byzantium. The empire survived the collapse of the Western empire until it was overrun by the Ottoman Turks in 1453. Originally a Greek colony at the entrance to the Black Sea, a typical Roman town was then laid out over it. Remains of the imperial palace lie south of the former Greek city nucleus. The land walls, giving the city an area greater than that of Rome, were built by Theodosius II (AD 408–450) and are among the best-preserved ancient fortifications anywhere. In the 7th century BC, Dorian Greeks founded the settlement of Byzantium on a trapezoidal promontory on the European side of the Bosporus channel, which leads from the Mediterranean to the Black Sea and separates Europe from Asia. Septimus Severus (AD 193–211) was responsible for restoring the city, re-walling it, and beginning the construction of the limestone racecourse, the Hippodrome. In AD 368, Valens raised his still impressive aqueduct. In 413, Theodosius II built the colossal surviving walls of stone and brick-faced concrete, with 96 variously shaped towers, and the principal entrance at the Golden Gate. The Eastern Christian Empire preserved much of Greek and Roman culture and introduced eastern ideas to the west. Byzantium was essentially a Christian church state, preserving its religion against the onslaught of Islam, despite the Arab encroachments on Palestine, Syria, and northern Africa during the 6th–7th centuries AD. The Byzantine period is the period, about the 6th–12th centuries AD, when its style of architecture and art developed. Byzantine architecture is noted for its Christian places of worship, with a cupola, or dome, an almost square ground plan in place of the long aisles of the Roman church, and piers instead of columns. The apse always formed part of Byzantine buildings, which were richly decorated, and contained much marble. St. Sophia (532–537), St. Mark's (Venice, 977), and the Cathedral of Aix-la-Chapelle (796–804) are of pure Byzantine style. Byzantine painting preceded and foreshadowed the renaissance of art in Italy. Mosaics and icon painting are perhaps the supreme achievements of Byzantine art. (*syn.* Byzantium)

Byzovaya: An Upper Palaeolithic site in Russia, the northernmost Palaeolithic site in Europe (65°) and probably occupied before the last glacial maximum (before 25,000 bp).

Cc

caatinga: A type of forest consisting of dry, thorny shrubs and stunted deciduous trees found in Brazil, especially in the northeast. (*syn.* thorn forest)

Caballo Muerto: A complex of monuments of the Initial Period and Early Horizon on the north coast of Peru. There are 17 mounds on the Moche Valley site, with the most complex structure at Huaca de los Reyes. It is a multilevel, U-shaped complex decorated with relief friezes, while inside is a series of structures, stairways, pillared halls, and a courtyard.

Cabalwanian industry: A stone industry of flakes in Luzon, the Philippines, thought to be early Holocene.

Cabenge: A site in southwest Sulawesi, Indonesia, with late Pliocene fauna. Stone tools are found in association with bones. Toalian tools in the area include large core tools of the chopper/chopping tool tradition.

cacao: The tropical American tree and its fruit from which cocoa and chocolate are made. Chocolate was the favored drink of the nobility of many Mesoamerican cultures. It grows only in tropical lowlands and was therefore considered a luxury item by the Aztec and Maya. Depictions on Izapan sculpture give its first use as the Pre-Classic period. The Codex Mendoza indicates that the beans were a medium of exchange and tribute in Aztec times. Cocoa beans were taken to Europe in the 16th century, where cocoa and chocolate were developed.

Cacaxtla: A group of platforms, palaces, and ceremonial buildings occupied between AD 400–1100 in the area of modern Tlaxcala, Mexico. Some structures have well-preserved frescoes, painted murals, and plaster reliefs from the 8th and 9th centuries depicting dancers and elaborately dressed warriors, with day glyphs and numbers associated with Mexican gods such as Quetzalcóatl and Tlaloc. The style of painting shows a strong influence from both Maya and Teotihuacán art. In the pottery, Teotihuacán wares predominate, although there are also links with the Gulf Coast and the Puebla-Oaxaca. (*syn.* modern Tlaxcala)

caccabus: A type of Greek or Roman pot or vessel for cooking any kind of food. It was made of bronze, silver, or earthenware and had a variety of forms. The most common shape was like an egg with a top opening that was closed with a lid; the vessel rested on a trivet (tripus).

cache: A collection of similar items and/or ecofacts deliberately hidden for future use. Caches are often discovered in burials or in caves and usually consist of ceremonial and ritual objects or emergency food supplies.

Cachi: Archaeological complex dating from 3000–1750 BC in the Ayacucho Valley of Peru. It showed the first evidence of an economic system in which products of lower elevation villages and camps (corn, beans, squash, gourd, chile, coca) were exchanged for potatoes, quinoa, and camelids of the seasonally nomadic herders of the higher elevations.

cadastre: A public record of the extent, value, and ownership of land in a district for purposes of taxation. (*syn.* cadaster)

Cadbury: Three hill forts in Somerset, the most important being South Cadbury, which has been equated with the Camelot of King Arthur. Excavation has shown that it was indeed occupied in the 5th century AD. There are also extensive remains of pre-Roman Iron Age occupation and a settlement of the Neolithic. (*syn.* Cadbury castle)

cadus: A large Greek or Roman earthenware jar, which was a wine jar but also used as a measure for liquids. An ordinary cadus was about 3 feet high and broad enough in the mouth to allow the contents to be baled out.

caelatura: From the Latin word meaning "to emboss, engrave," a general term for working in metal by raised work or intaglio, such as engraving, carving, chasing, riveting, soldering, or smelting. Similar work on wood, ivory, marble, glass, or precious stones was called *sculptura*.

Caeretan ware: Archaic pottery of Etruria, probably made at Cerveteri. It was black-figured style.

Caerleon: A town and archaeological site in Wales in which the Romans established a legionary fortress dating to AD 74–75 when the conquest of the Silures of Wales began. The foundation of the fortress is set on a terrace along the Usk, and it is one of three major legionary fortresses—the other two being at Chester and York. Originally built of timber and earth, it had been largely rebuilt in stone (253–255) before the Roman garrison left during the abandonment of the province. Evidence has been found for centurion houses, workshops, barracks, stores, ovens, hospital, baths, and latrines. There is also an amphitheater, two bath buildings, and extensive cemeteries in an associated settlement. The fortress was occupied, probably by a nonmilitary population, until the 370s. Caerleon, traditionally a seat of the legendary King Arthur, was a Welsh princely capital until the Norman Conquest (1066). (*syn.* Isca)

Caesarea: An ancient port and administrative city of Palestine on the Mediterranean coast of present-day Israel. It is often called Caesarea Palaestinae or Caesarea Maritima to distinguish it from Caesarea Philippi. It was originally an ancient Phoenician settlement known as Straton's (Strato's Tower) and was rebuilt and enlarged by Herod the Great around 22–10 BC. Herod renamed it for his patron, Caesar Augustus, and also rebuilt the harbor, which traded with his newly built city at Sebaste (Augusta) or ancient Samaria. There were Hellenistic-Roman public buildings and an aqueduct. After Herod died, it became the capital of the Roman province of Judaea in AD 6. An inscription naming Pontius Pilate is one of the best known finds from the site. Jewish revolts and later Byzantine and Arab rule caused the city's decline. (*syn.* Cherchel, Caesarea Palaestinae, Caesarea Maritima, Straton's Tower, Strato's Tower)

Cagayan Valley: A broad valley in northern Luzon, the Philippines, with several sites at which some evidence has been found of a pebble and flake industry with Middle Pleistocene fauna including elephants, Stegodon, rhinoceros, and bovids.

Cahokia: The largest and most impressive town of the Middle Mississippi culture, on the Illinois bank of the river near East St. Louis. Cahokia Mounds State Historic and World Heritage Site, the location of this large prehistoric Indian city, is to the northeast. It constituted probably the largest pre-Columbian (c. AD 900–1300) community north of Mexico in the Mississippi floodplain. The scale of public works in the culture can be estimated from remains of the largest of the Mississippi earthworks, Monk's Mound near Cahokia, which measures 1,000 feet (300 m) long, 700 feet (200 m) wide, and 100 feet (30 m) high—larger than the Great Pyramid of Egypt. The magnitude of such public works and the distribution of temples suggest a dominant religious cult, a series of priest-rulers who commanded the services of a large population, and the establishment of artist–craftsman guilds. In addition to large-scale construction, there is evidence of long-distance trade, elaborate ceremonial activity, and possibly astronomical observation. There were around 10,000–38,000 inhabitants and a town of warehouses and workshops, residential housing arranged along a grid of streets, open plazas, and 100 manmade mounds (burial and platform types). One of the smaller mounds contained rich burials, including a corpse wrapped in a robe sewn with more than 12,000 shell beads; caches of arrowheads, polished stone, and mica; and his retainers—6 men at his side and 53 women in a mass grave nearby. Artifacts include flint hoes, shell and limestone-tempered pottery, and engraved stone tablets sometimes etched with the motifs of the Southern Cult.

Cahuachi: A large ceremonial site that was the principal center of the Nasca culture of Peru. There are 40 adobe mounds, likely to have been used only for religious ceremonies. It was built in the Early Nasca period but was used through Late Nasca and the Middle Horizon.

Cai Beo: A site in north Vietnam with a sequence from the late Hoabinhian stone tools to edge grinding (c. 5000 BC) to Neolithic polished stone adzes (c. 4500 BC).

cairn: (kayrn, kern) A pyramid of rough stones, raised for a memorial or mark of some kind, usually over a burial but also as a landmark or monument. A cairn could also indicate where something valuable was stored. In America, a cairn is a structure of rounded stones. The word is often used as a synonym for *barrow* in areas where burial mounds were normally of stone. In Scotland and Ireland, the custom was for friends to add a stone to the pile when they passed a cairn. (*syn.* barrow)

Cairo: The capital of modern Egypt, which has more than 400 registered historical monuments—the largest number of any African or Middle Eastern city—dating from AD 130. The ancient metropolis has stood for more than 1,000 years on the same site. The Pyramids of Giza stand at the southwestern edge of the Cairo metropolis. The Egyptian (National) Museum in Cairo specializes in antiquities of the Pharaonic and Greco-Roman periods. It contains more than 100,000 items, including some 1,700 items from the tomb of Tutankhamen, such as the solid-gold mask that covered the pharaoh's head. Other treasures include reliefs, sarcophagi, papyri, funerary art and the contents of various tombs, jewelry, and ornaments of all kinds. (*syn.* Arabic Al-Qahirah)

Cajamarca: An ancient Inca city, the site of the capture, ransom, and execution of the Inca chief Atahuallpa by the conquistador Francisco Pizarro in 1532. In the north Peruvian highlands, Cajamarca developed a strong regional civilization and was a provincial capital, flourishing between AD

200–1476. Cajamarca pottery is slip painted with linear running patterns (cursive) or with stylized creatures and animal heads in brownish black over a cream background. It was a cultural center during the Early Intermediate period. The cemetery, Nievería, has Huari-related artifacts. The Spanish capture ended the Inca period and Andean prehistory. (*syn.* Cajamarquilla)

Caka: A Late Bronze Age urnfield cemetery in Slovakia with some high-status burials that included bronze breastplates.

calabash: The hollow shell of a gourd or pumpkin or the fruit of the calabash tree, used as a storage or drinking vessel. Such a shell was used for household utensils, water bottles, kettles, musical instruments, and so on. It is round or oval and hard enough to be used in boiling liquids over a fire.

calamus: A reed or cane used by early writers, especially as an implement for scribes working on clay. Calami were usually made from reeds in Mesopotamia, but also from wood, and the point was sharpened to form a triangle. The pressure of the calamus on the clay produced the cuneiform script. Pressing lightly or firmly made longer or shorter lines. (*syn.* plural calami)

calcareous concretions: A rounded mass of mineral matter occurring in sandstone, clay, and so on—often in concentric layers around a nucleus.

calcium carbonate: A natural calcium–carbon–oxygen combination that occurs in limestone, chalk, marble, dolomite, eggshells, pearls, coral, stalactites, stalagmites, and the shells of many marine animals. Calcite is often the adhesive in composite rocks. The most abundant dissolved solid in dry land groundwater is calcium carbonate. When deposited, this mineral forms the hard, calcareous cement known as caliche. Caliche is a crust of calcium carbonate often present in semiarid or arid areas, either on top of or in the soil. (*syn.* calcite)

calculi: In antiquity, small stones or pebbles used for calculation.

caldarium: The heat room of a Roman bathhouse. An attached plunge bath made it very humid.

caldera: A large, bowl-shaped volcanic depression leading to the expulsion of a large quantity of molten rock (magma). The depression is more than 1 kilometer in diameter and surrounded by faults with instabilities that can bring about a renewal of volcanic activity. Calderas usually, if not always, form by the collapse of the top of a volcanic cone or group of cones because of removal of the underlying body of magma. Subsequent minor eruptions may build small cones on the floor of the caldera. These may later fill with water, as did Crater Lake in Oregon.

calendar: A cyclical system of measuring the passage of time. The day is the fundamental unit of computation in any calendar. Most ancient civilizations (and perhaps some non-literate prehistoric societies) developed calendrical systems to mark the passage of time, and various methods have been employed by different peoples. Where these were both carefully calculated and written down, as in Egypt, Mesopotamia, and Mesoamerica, they are of considerable assistance to archaeologists for dating purposes. In the Americas, the origins of calendrics are still obscure, but evidence from Monte Albán suggests that the 52-year Calendar Round was known by the 6th century BC. The Long Count system was in use by c. 1st century BC if not before. Ancient Near Eastern calendars varied from city to city and from period to period. In most cities, the year started in the spring and was divided into 12 or 13 months. In some places, the months were of fixed length; in others, they were lunar months starting at the first sighting of the crescent of the new moon. As there are more than 12 lunar months in a solar year, additional, or intercalary, months were included so that every third year contained 13 months. The earliest Egyptian calendars were based on lunar observations combined with the annual cycle of the Nile inundation, measured with nilometers. On this basis, the Egyptians divided the year into 12 months and three seasons: *akhet* (inundation), *peret* (spring/crops), and *shemu* (harvest). The Egyptians had 30-day months and 5 intercalary days in their solar or civil calendar. For agricultural purposes and for determining religious festivals, they used a different calendar based on observations of Sirius, the dog star. The calendar in use in ancient Mesopotamia and the Levant was lunar, based on 12 months of 30 days each. This produced a year of only 354 days, about 11 days short of the true solar year; the necessary correction was made by the addition of 7 months over a period of 19 years. This type of calendar is still used in both Judaism and Islam for religious purposes, although many countries now also employ the Gregorian solar calendar for secular purposes. The origin of the calendric system in general use today—the Gregorian calendar—can be traced back to the Roman republican calendar, which is thought to have been introduced by the 5th king of Rome, Tarquinius Priscus (616–579 BC). This calendar was likely derived from an earlier Roman calendar—a lunar system of 10 months—that was supposedly devised about 738 BC by Romulus, the founder of Rome. In the year 46 BC, Julius Caesar corrected the calendar by having a year of 345 days (known as the *ultimus annus confusionis* or 'the last year of the muddled reckoning'). He then adapted the Egyptian solar calendar for Roman use, inserting extra days in the shorter months to bring the total up to 365, with the addition of a single day between the 23rd and 24th February in leap years. This calendar, known as the Julian Calendar, remained in use until the time of Gregory XIII in 1582, who made a further correction (of 11 days) and instituted the calendar in general use today. Very useful to Mesoamerican archaeologists is the Maya Long Count or Initial Series, which was a means of recording absolute time. Its starting date of 3113 BC (using the Goodman–Thompson–Martinex correlation) marks some mythical event in Maya history and itself stands at the beginning of a cycle 13 Baktuns long. A Baktun at 144,000 days is the largest unit of time in the calendar and is further divided into smaller units: the Katun (7200 days); the Tun (360 days); the Uninal (20 days); and the Kin (a single day). Thus Long Count dates are expressed in terms of these units in a five-place notation. Therefore the date 9.18.0.0.0. indicates the passage of 9 times 144,000 plus 18 times 7,200 days since the initial date of 3113 BC. In cultural contexts, however, the dates are inscribed as a series of hieroglyphs that incorporate numeration via bars (units of five) and dots (units of one). Short count dating replaced the Long Count after AD 900, and the Katun replaced the Baktun as the largest unit. It is less precise, however. (*syn.* calendrics)

Calendar Round: A ritually and historically important calendar used throughout Mesoamerica in which the solar calendar of 365 days ran in parallel with a sacred 260-day ritual calendar of named days. The Calendar Round is a 52-year cycle, because both calendars begin on the same day only once every 52 years. Coefficients for days and months were expressed by bar-and-dot numerals, a system that is first known in Monte Albán I and that became characteristic of the Classic Maya. The basic structure of the Mayan calendar is common to all calendars of Mesoamerica. To identify a date of the Calendar Round, they designated the day by its numeral and name and added the name of the current month, indicating the number of its days that had elapsed by prefixing one of the numerals from 0 through 19. A date written in this way occurs once in every Calendar Round, at intervals of 52 years. It is the meshing of the two Mayan calendars, the Tzolkin and the Haab. (*syn.* Calendar Round)

Calendar Stone: A 20-ton, 4-meter-wide carved monolith commissioned by the emperor Axayacatl in 1479, which symbolizes the Aztec universe. The population of central Mexico believed that they were living in the fifth epoch of a series of worlds (or suns) marked by cyclical generation and destruction. The central figure of the stone is this fifth sun, Tonatuih. Surrounding this are four rectangular cartouches containing dates and symbols for the gods Ehecatl, Texcatlipoca, Tlaloc, and Chilchihuitlicue, who represent the four worlds previously destroyed, and the dates of the previous holocausts—4 Tiger, 4 Wind, 4 Rain, and 4 Water. The central panel contains the date 4 Ollin (movement), on which the Aztecs showed that they anticipated that their current world would be destroyed by an earthquake. In a series of increasingly larger concentric bands, symbols for the 20 days

of the month, precious materials, and certain stars are represented. The outermost band depicts two massive serpents whose heads meet at the stone's base. The Calendar Stone is in the Museo Nacional de Antropologia (National Museum of Anthropology) in Mexico City.

calendrical age determination: An absolute dating technique used when an object has been inscribed with a date from an ancient calendrical system or is associated with calendrical inscriptions that can be correlated with a modern calendar.

calendrics: The decipherment and study of calendars.

calibration: A method used to obtain the most accurate dating, especially applied to radiocarbon dating. The term refers to the adjustment of dates in radiocarbon years by means of the dendrochronological data so that a date in calendar years is achieved. Fluctuations in the amount of carbon 14 in the atmosphere mean that radiocarbon dating is not completely accurate. By obtaining radiocarbon dates for wood of known dendrochronological date, a correction factor can be introduced to calibrate radiocarbon dates. Uncalibrated dates are raw dates in radiocarbon years. Accurate calibration of radiocarbon dates is not possible before 6285 BC. (*syn.* calibrated dates)

caliche or caliché: (kuh-lee-chee) An encrustation or deposit of hard, calcareous cement made up of nitrates, sulfates, halides, and sand. It appears on the surface of materials such as bone, ceramic, or stone after they have been buried or exposed to moisture for an extended time. These layers of calcium carbonate (lime accumulation) are often present in semiarid or arid areas, either on top of or in the soil—as in the desert basins of southern Arizona.

Calico Mountains: A site in the Mojave Desert of California where lithic debris lies in the former Lake Manix. These artifacts (blades, flakes) may have been buried in fan despoits and date to c. 200,000 BP. If this date is accurate, the site is the earliest Lower Palaeolithic settlement known in the New World.

caliph: Any of the successors of Muhammad (Mohammed) as rulers and religious leaders of the Muslim community, the most powerful being those of the Umayyad and 'Abbasid dynasties. A caliphate is the Islamic empire ruled by a caliph. When Muhammad died (8 June, 632), Abu Bakr succeeded to his political and administrative functions as khalifah rasul Allah, "successor of the Messenger of God," but it was probably under 'Umar ibn al-Khattab, the second caliph, the that the term *caliph* came into use as a title of the civil and religious head of the Muslim state. Abu Bakr and his three immediate successors are known as the "perfect" caliphs. There were then 14 Umayyad caliphs and 38 'Abbasid caliphs, whose dynasty fell to the Mongols in 1258. There were titular caliphs from 1258–1517, when the last caliph was captured by the Ottoman sultan Selim I. The Ottoman sultans then claimed the title and used it until it was abolished by the Turkish Republic in 1924. (*syn.* calif, khalifah)

calix: A chalice or cup-shaped vase used as a drinking goblet. It had two handles and was mounted on a stand.

Calixtlahuaca: A site in Toluca Valley, Mexico, with a ceramic sequence from Teotihuacán times until the Aztec conquest and some evidence of the Preclassic. It was occupied from AD 1200–1472 by a Nahua group (Matlatzincas) who were enemies of the Aztecs and who were conquered by them between AD 1474–1510. The Temple of Quetzalcóatl, a circular structure, was built up three times.

callaïs: A greenish decorative stone occasionally used for beads from the Late Neolithic to Early Bronze Age in western Europe.

Callanish: An important group of Bronze Age megalithic monuments on the island of Lewis in the Outer Hebrides. Equal in importance to Stonehenge, the Callanish megaliths are aligned to make a rough Celtic cross 405 feet (123 m) north to south and 140 feet (43 m) east to west and may be tied to astronomy. In the middle is a small passage grave under a round cairn. Several smaller stone circles in the area align with Callanish.

Calowanie: An Upper Palaeolithic site in eastern Poland with artifacts dating to 11,500 BP and overlying layers dating to c. 11,000–10,000 BP.

calpulli: Corporate group in Aztec society, which functioned above the level of the household. *Calpullis* had social, political, and economic functions. They occupied whole villages or neighborhoods of towns and cities; members corporately held rights to farm plots as long as they continued to use them.

calvarium: The skull minus the facial bones.

Camare: An assemblage of artifacts including choppers, scrapers, leaf points, and other tools from the surface of the high terraces in Rio Pedregal, Venezuela. Dating indicates the site may have been inhabited 15,000 years ago.

cambium: A viscid substance lying under the bark of trees, consisting of cellular tissue in which the annual growth of wood and bark takes place.

Cambodia: Neolithic peoples inhabited present-day Cambodia during the 2nd and 1st millennia BC. Stone tools have been found in terraces of the Mekong River in possible association with tektites from a shower that fell c. 600,000 to 700,000 years ago. In western Cambodia, there is an important Hoabinhian sequence from the cave of Laang Spean, dating to 4300 BC. A major Neolithic mound site at Somrong Sen yielded an elaborate assemblage, which seems to predate

100 BC. Khmer civilization developed over several distinct periods, starting with the Hindu-Buddhist kingdoms of Funan and Chenla in the 1st century AD, which extended into the 8th century. (*syn.* Kampuchea)

Camden, William (1551–1623): A renowned British antiquary who was among the first to describe antiquities found in Britain. His book *Britannia* (1586) described the archaeological past of all the British Isles to Norman times and was the first comprehensive topographical survey of England.

camel: A large hornless ruminant quadruped with a humped back, long neck, and cushioned feet. It is domesticated as the main beast of burden in arid regions of western Asia and northern Africa. There are two distinct species, the Arabian or one humped, and the Bactrian or two humped. A lighter and faster variety of the Arabian is known as the dromedary. The Bactrian was fully domesticated by the 1st millennium BC, and evidence of their existence dates to the first half of 3rd millennium BC. There are four camelids found in the Andes of Peru—the vicuna, guanaco, llama, and alpaca. The first two are wild, the last two domesticated. Cave excavations yielded bones from c. 8000–1000 BC with herding evidence c. 3000–2000 BC and pack animal use between AD 600–1000.

cameo glass: A Roman artifact of layered, multicolored glass with the effect of a cameo cut from onyx. The Portland Vase in the British Museum is an important example.

camp: A term used to describe any ditched or embanked enclosure—from the Neolithic causewayed camps to Iron Age hill forts and Roman fortifications. Used to describe ancient works, it usually means the entrenched and fortified site in which an army lodged or defended itself. The Roman army erected temporary fortifications called camps when on campaigns.

Campania: A area of southern Italy along the Bay of Naples, which was the location of the Greek colony Cumae and was once controlled by the Etruscans. Campanian pottery was made before the middle of the 4th century BC at both Cumae and Capua.

campo santo: In Spanish, "holy field" or a cemetery or burial ground associated with a church.

Canaanite: The original pre-Israelite inhabitants of an area encompassing all of Palestine and Syria, sometimes including all land west of the Jordan River and the coast from Acre north. The names Canaan and Canaanite occur in cuneiform, Egyptian, and Phoenician writings from about the 15th century BC as well as in the Bible. They were the branch of the Semites who may have been partly related to the Hyksos, who occupied the Levant from the Middle to the Late Bronze Age, c. 2000–1200 BC. In the south, they were displaced by the Israelites and Philistines; in the north, they were the ancestors of the Phoenicians. Their main significance in history lies in their role as middlemen and traders, through whose hands passed cultural influences between Egypt, Mesopotamia, and the Hittites. Canaanite sites include Lachish, Megiddo, Byblos, and Ugarit. The Canaanites were responsible for the invention of the first alphabetic writing system. (*syn.* Canaan)

Canario: The name of a site, culture, and people in the Canary Islands. The population is thought to have been of Cro-Magnon origin and may possibly have come from central and southern Europe via northern Africa. The people left alphabet-like engravings and characters whose meanings are obscure. This aboriginal group had brown complexion, blue or gray eyes, and blondish hair, and these characteristics still persist in a large number of present inhabitants of the islands. The name Canarios is now applied to all present residents.

candelabra model: One of the theories of human development in which modern humans are thought to have descended from *Homo erectus* in Africa, Europe, and Asia. The opposing theory, known as the Noah's Ark model, holds that modern humans originated in one single area of Africa. (*syn.* regional continuity theory)

candelabrum: A candlestick, often an ornamental one, or any kind of stand by which a light can be supported. The term also refers to a chandelier. (*syn.* pl. candelabra)

candi: Late 1st–early 2nd millennia AD funerary temples in Java in which Hindu and Buddhist religions were combined with local cults.

Can Hasan: The site of a number of tells in southern Turkey. Can Hasan III was an aceramic Neolithic settlement c. 6500 BC. There were at least seven structural phases, with dark burnished pottery in several levels and painted pottery in one. The villagers were agriculturists, growing einkorn and emmer, lentil, and vetch in the earlier phases. The main Can Hasan mound was occupied in the late Neolithic and Chalcolithic periods.

cannibalism: The eating of human flesh by people. This is done either out of dire need or for ritual purposes, when parts of deceased relatives or enemies may be eaten so that their power can be magically acquired. Disarticulated bones of humans, as well as of animals, found in the ditches of Neolithic camps, are thought to be suggestive of cannibalism. Its existence in Paleolithic cultures is suggested by the lengthwise splitting of long bones so as to extract marrow from them. In Mesoamerica, there is evidence of the practice among hunter-gatherers at the start of Holocene through the 1st millennium BC in farming villages. There were many written documents concerning cannibalism from the Aztecs of the 15th century AD. To the Aztecs, the human flesh sacrificed and offered to the gods became a sacred food.

canopic jar: Ancient Egyptian funerary ritual objects: Four covered vessels of wood, stone, pottery, or faience were used to hold the organs removed during mummification. The embalmed liver, lungs, stomach, and intestines were placed in separate canopic jars. The jars or urns were then placed beside the mummy in the tomb, to be reunited in spirit, subject to the appropriate spells and rituals having been performed. The earliest canopic jars came into use during the Old Kingdom (c. 2575–2130 BC) and had plain lids. During the Middle Kingdom (c. 1938–1600 BC), the jars were decorated with sculpted human heads, probably depicting of the deceased. Then from the 19th Dynasty until the end of the New Kingdom (1539–1075 BC), the heads represented the four sons of the god Horus (Duamutef, Qebehsenuf, Imset, Hapy). In the 20th Dynasty (1190–1075 BC), the practice began of returning the embalmed viscera to the body. The term appears to refer to a Greek demigod, Canopus, venerated in the form of a jar with a human head. (*syn.* canopic vase, canopea)

Canterbury: A site on the River Stour in southeast England occupied since pre-Roman times. Lying at the intersection of important land routes, Canterbury already had a sizable Belgic settlement before the arrival of the Romans in AD 43. The town was refounded soon after the invasion as Durovernum, the tribal capital of the Cantiaci, around AD 49. Traces have been found of a theater (c. 210–220), a forum, houses, streets, and a stone wall with earth bank added as fortification c. 270–290. There is some evidence of Christian occupation from the 4th century, but the settlement declined sharply after 400, probably following the withdrawal of Roman forces. Archaeological investigations in Canterbury have contributed to an understanding of the secular occupation in Roman towns after the imperial withdrawal from Britain. Excavations have also been carried out on a group of churches, which may date to the late 6th or 7th century: St. Augustine's Abbey, St. Martin's, and St. Pancras. Canterbury was an important medieval town, and there is a medieval cathedral, an impressive circuit of town walls, a large 12th-century castle, and some of the best preserved timber-framed buildings in England. (*syn.* Durovernum Cantiacorum)

cantharus: In Greek antiquity, a large, two-handled drinking cup. This type of pottery cup was made in Greek-speaking areas and in Etruria between the 8th and 1st centuries BC and had a deep bowl, a foot, and pair of high vertical handles. It was often consecrated to personifications of Bacchus. (*syn.* kantharos)

Cape Coastal Ware: A Stone Age pottery style from the coast of southern Namibia to eastern Cape Province, South Africa, after c. 1600 BP. It is characterized by point-based pots.

Cape Gelidoniya: The site of a Bronze Age shipwreck off

the southwestern coast of Turkey between Rhodes and Cyprus, from the 13th century BC. A small merchant ship was carrying copper and bronze ingots, still wrapped in basketry. Excavation also produced a structural plan of the ship, including evidence of a grill of twigs on the bows to keep water off the deck—a technique still in use today. The finds included pottery and three scarabs.

Cape Krusenstern: The site of a national monument on the coast of the Chukchi Sea with a horizontal stratigraphy covering the whole of north Alaskan prehistory. Located on 114 ridges along ancient beach lines, the monument's remarkable archaeological sites illustrate the cultural evolution of the Arctic people, dating back some 4,000 years and continuing to modern Eskimos. There are campsites of 10 successive cultures, beginning with the Denbigh Flint Complex, followed by the Old Whaling culture, then by the Eskimo cultures known as Trails Creek-Chloris, Chloris, Norton, Near Ipiutak, Ipiutak, Birnirk, Western Thule, and late prehistoric. On the terrace behind the beaches were two more phases (Palisades I and II), which go back to c. 8000 BC. The stratigraphy is visible as a sequence of strips, roughly parallel to the shoreline, with the oldest, Denbigh, being farthest from the present-day shoreline. This horizontal sequence, in combination with the vertical stratigraphy of Onion Portage, forms the most reliable chronological framework in western Arctic prehistory.

Capelitti: A cave site in the Aures Mountains of eastern Algeria, which has evidence of early North African pastoralism by a "Capsian Neolithic" population. Sheep and/or goats appear to have coincided with the beginning of pottery making from the 5th millennium BC. By the 3rd millennium, small domestic cattle are also attested.

capital: In architecture, the feature that most readily distinguishes the Classical "order": the top member of a column, pier, anta, pilaster, or other columnar form, which supports a horizontal member (entablature) or arch above. A capital is usually made of wood or stone, and it was decorated according to the Corinthian, Doric, or Ionic order.

Capitolium: The principal hill at Rome and the one that acted as its religious center. The hill was the fortress and asylum of Romulus's Rome. The northern peak was the site of the temple of Juno Moneta and the citadel. The southern crest, sacred to Jupiter, became, in 509 BC, the site of the temple of Jupiter Optimus Maximus, the largest temple in central Italy. The Roman Senate held its first meeting every year because of the "divine guidance" it received at the site. (*syn.* Capitoline)

Cappadocian trade: The trade that was carried out between Assyria and the region of Cappadocia in the 2nd millennium BC. Trade was mostly in tin and textiles shipped via Assur from the east and south, in exchange for copper from Ana-

tolia. There are many cuneiform tablets documenting this Mesopotamian trading system.

Capsian and Capsian Neolithic: A Mesolithic/Stone Age (8000–2700 BC) cultural complex prominent in inland northern Africa near the present border between Tunisia and Algeria. Its shell midden sites are in the area of the great salt lakes of what is now southern Tunisia, the type site being Jabal al-Maqta.' The tool kit of the Capsian is a classic example of the industries of the late Würm Glacial period, and it is apparently related to the Gravettian stage of Europe's Perigordian industry (which dates from about 17,000 years ago). However, it occurs in Neothermal (postglacial) times, and, like its predecessor, the Ibero-Maurusian industry (Oranian industry), the Capsian was a microlithic tool complex. It differed from the Ibero-Maurusian, however, in having a far more varied tool kit with large backed blades, scrapers, backed bladelets, microburins, and burins in its earlier phase and a gradual development of geometric microliths later. These became its leading feature by the 6th millennium BC. Shortly after 5000 BC, pottery and domesticated animals were introduced. Some North African rock paintings are attributed to people of the Capsian industry. The Capsian Neolithic, with pointed-base pottery and a stone industry, lasted from c. 6200–5300 BP, in the Atlas Mountains of Algeria and the northern Sahara. The name derives from Capsa, the Latin form of Gafsa, a town in south-central Tunisia where such artifacts were first discovered. Hunting and snail collecting seem to have formed the basis of the economy. Human remains from Capsian sites are mostly of Mechta-Afalou type. (*syn.* Capsian industry)

capstone: A stone slab placed horizontally over a series of other stones, at the top of an arch, often as a roof. Some are large blocks used to span the walls of dolmens, cists, passage graves, and other megalithic chamber tombs.

Capua: An ancient city of Italy, founded around 600 BC by the Etruscans, whose people spoke the Oscan dialect of Italic. There had been an early Iron Age settlement in the 9th century BC. After the period of Etruscan domination, it fell to the Samnites c. 440 BC. Capua supported the Latin Confederacy in its war against Rome in 340 BC. After Rome's victory in the war, Capua became a self-governing community, and its people were granted limited Roman citizenship. In 312 BC, Capua was connected with Rome by the Appian Way, and its prosperity increased to make it the second most important in Italy. During the Second Punic War (218–201 BC), Capua sided with Carthage against Rome. When the Romans recaptured the city in 211 BC, they deprived the citizens of political rights. Spartacus, the slave leader, began his revolt at Capua in 73 BC. Although it suffered during the Roman civil wars in the last decades of the republic, the city prospered under the empire until 27 BC. The Vandals sacked Capua in AD 456, and

Muslim invaders destroyed everything except the church of Sta. Maria in 840. Capua was famous for its bronzes and perfumes. There are ruins of a theater, amphitheater, baths, ceremonial arch of Hadrian, and a mithraeum with painted frescoes. The Etruscan artifacts include characteristic pottery, bronzes, and tombs, and an important document of the Etruscan language—the Capua Tile, an inscription of some 62 lines, which was either religious or ritual text. (*syn.* modern Santa Maria di Capua Vetere; Casilinum)

caravanserai: In the Middle East, a public building that served as an unfurnished inn or staging post for sheltering caravans and other travelers. It was usually constructed outside the walls of a town and was a quandrangular enclosure with massive walls, with small windows near the top and small air holes near the bottom. A heavy-doored gateway was the entrance, and it was secured from within by massive iron chains. Refreshments were available to the travelers. (*syn.* khan; caravansary)

carbon-14: A naturally occurring radioactive isotope of carbon with a half-life of 5,730 (± 40 years) years and a mass number of 14, commonly used in radiocarbon dating archaeological materials and in demonstrating the metabolic path of carbon in photosynthesis. Its known rate of decay is the basis of radiocarbon dating. Willard Libby discovered natural carbon-14. Libby showed the essential uniformity of carbon-14 in living material and went on to measure the radiocarbon level in organic samples dated historically—materials as old as 5,000 years from sources such as Egyptian tombs. Libby's conclusion, with allowance for radioactive decay, was that over the past 5,000 years the carbon-14 level in living materials has remained constant within 5% precision of measurement. His work made this dating method available to scientists. (*syn.* radiocarbon, C14)

carbon-14 dating: The occurrence of natural radioactive carbon in the atmosphere allows archaeologists the ability to date organic materials as old as 50,000 years. Carbon-14 is continuously produced in the atmosphere and decays with a half-life of 5,730 years (± 40 years). Unlike most isotopic dating methods, the carbon-14 dating technique relies on the progressive decay or disappearance of the radioactive parent with time. This is now a common method for estimating the age of carbonaceous archaeological artifacts. The radioactivity of an artifact's carbon-14 content determines how long ago the specimen was separated from equilibrium with the atmosphere–plant–animal cycle. The method is based on the principle that all plants and animals, while they are alive, take in small amounts of carbon-14, and when they die, the intake ends. By measuring the loss rate of the carbon 14, the age of the object can be established. Measurement of the carbon-14 activity in a cypress beam in the tomb of the Egyptian Pharaoh Snefru, for example, established the date of the tomb as c. 2600 BC. (*syn.* radiocarbon dating)

carbonization: The burning or scorching of organic materials, such as plants, seeds, or grains, in conditions of insufficient oxygen, which results in their preservation. Charcoal is a widely known example. (*syn.* adj. carbonized, charring)

Carcassonne: A city in southwest France occupied as early as the 5th century BC by the Iberians and then by the Gallo-Romans. Its inner rampart was built in AD 485. The site is one of the best-preserved examples of a medieval fortified town in Europe with an inner wall and citadel dating from the 11th–13th centuries. The site was extensively restored in the 19th century, and the church of Saint Vincent and the cathedral of Saint-Michel, both 13th century, survive.

Carchemish: An ancient city-state near modern Jarabulus, Syria. The site was a strategic crossing at the Euphrates River for caravans in Syrian, Mesopotamian, and Anatolian trade. The great tell of Carchemish was excavated by David G. Hogarth and later by Sir Leonard Woolley and was first occupied in the Neolithic Period. Halaf ware from the Chalcolithic (5th millennium BC) was found as well as later finds of Uruk–Jamdat Nasr pottery, a product of Sumerian cities in the southern Euphrates Valley of c. 3000 BC. There were also tombs from the end of the Early Bronze (c. 2300 BC) and the Middle and Late Bronze Age (c. 2300–1550, c. 1550–1200 BC). Written records about Carchemish first appear in the Mari letters—royal archives of Mari, c. 18th century BC. At that time, the city was a center for trading wood and shipped Anatolian timber down the Euphrates. The large fortified citadel was important under the empire of the Hittites (14th century BC) and remained so after the fall of the empire, during the period of Syro-Hittite city-states (12th–8th centuries BC). The monumental city gates, temples, and palaces all bore considerable numbers of carved reliefs and inscriptions of the period. The Hittite hieroglyphic inscriptions were of great importance in helping to piece together the city's history down to its annexation by Assyria in 716 BC. (*syn.* Europus)

Cardial Ware: An impressed ware of the Early Neolithic in the western Mediterranean (Sardinia, Corsica, Liguria, Provence, and Spain). Soft clay was impressed with the serrated edge of the cardium (cockle) shell, from which it received its name. (*syn.* Cardial pottery)

cardo: The term for the second major road of a Roman town, fort, or camp—the main north-south axis. The term seems to originate with Roman agricultural surveying practice, where cardo denotes the principal north-south axis of the site, about which other measurements "hinge." When a site is divided, the cardo is used with the other principal axis, the *decumanus* (east-west) to sectioned into squares. From the 4th century BC, this system was adopted for the Roman grid system used for army camps and new towns. The technique was taken from the Etruscans and the Greeks, both of whom used grid town planning. The cardo maximus was the main north-south road. (*syn.* pl. cardines)

Carib: American Indian people who inhabited the Lesser Antilles and parts of the neighboring South American coast at the time of the Spanish conquest. They were warlike immigrants from the mainland who drove the Arawak from the Lesser Antilles. They were notorious for eating captives (the word "cannibal" is a corruption of the Spanish *Caribal*). They were skilled pottery makers and agriculturists but were mostly concerned with warfare. They were a maritime people who carried out long-distance raids with large dugout canoes. The Carib language was spoken only by the men; women spoke Arawak.

carination: A sharp break or angle in the curve of the profile of a container or vessel, which resulted in a projecting angle or arris. On ancient jars or pots, it appeared as a sharply angled shoulder dividing the neck from the body of the vessel. It has been considered to be a purely stylistic feature derived from metal prototypes, but it may also be that carination had a practical function—for example, for retaining dregs from a liquid while pouring.

Carmel, Mount: Site of a series of prehistoric limestone caves near Haifa, Israel, with deposits from the Acheulian and Mousterian. The name is derived from Hebrew *kerem* ("vineyard" or "orchard") owing to the mountain's fertility in ancient times. There is a cemetery in the Skhul cave, whose occupants' skeletal remains were between Neanderthal and modern man. The caves' Upper Palaeolithic sequence ends with the Natufian. Sanctified since early times, Mount Carmel is mentioned as a "holy mountain" in Egyptian records of the 16th century BC and was a center of idol worship as well as being sacred to the early Christians.

Carnac: A village in western France near the Atlantic coast, the site of more than 3,000 prehistoric stone monuments of the alignment type. These menhirs are arranged in three groups of 10–13 parallel rows, which ended at semicircles or rectangles of standing stones. The single stone menhirs and multistone dolmens were made from local granite and are worn by time and weather and covered in white lichen. The area also has a series of long cairns of mid-Neolithic to Early Bronze Age, which covers funerary chambers and secondary cists. The grave goods included polished axes of rare stones such as jadeite and fibrolite, stone boxes containing charcoal, cattle bones, and pottery. The area was clearly an important ritual center, venerated by the Bretons until fairly recent times, and adopted by the Romans for religious purposes. Christians added crosses and other symbols to the stones. In 1874, James Miln uncovered the remains of a Gallo-Roman villa 1 mile east of the village. The Musée Miln-Le Rouzic in Carnac has an important collection of artifacts.

Carnarvon Gorge: An area of Queensland, Australia, known for its stenciled rock art as well as engravings and paintings. Cathedral Cave has occupation deposits.

carnelian: A reddish-brown semiprecious stone used for beads, seal stones, and jewelry in antiquity. The Indus Valley civilization, Greeks, and Romans valued the stone. It is a translucent variety of the silica mineral chalcedony. Carnelian is usually found in volcanic rocks, such as the Deccan Traps of western India. Engraved cornelians in rings and signets have offered information about the manners and customs of ancient Greeks and Romans. (*syn.* cornelian)

Carolingian: A term referring to the time and place of Charlemagne (Charles the Great), who called himself the "king of the Franks and Lombards" from AD 768–814. In an archaeological and architectural sense, Carolingian describes the period AD c. 750–900. The Carolingian kingdom of Italy occupied the northern and central peninsula down to Rome, except for Venice and Benevento. The cultural revival of the Carolingian period, stimulated by Charlemagne, was a renovation and renaissance of the arts and education.

carp's tongue sword: A type of bronze sword used in the Late Bronze Age in western Europe—mainly in northwest France and southern England—in the early 1st millennium BC. It had a broad slashing blade, a long projecting point for thrusting, and a flange hilt.

Carrowmore: A cemetery site in Sligo, Ireland, with megalithic tombs consisting of circular boulder kerbs and boulder-built chambers. The radiocarbon date is c. 4500 BC, which would make these the earliest chambered tombs of Ireland.

carrying capacity: The maximum population of a species that can be supported by a particular habitat or area with the food potentially available to it from the resources of the area, including the most unfavorable period of the year. The carrying capacity is different for each species in a habitat because of the species' particular requirements for food, shelter, and social contact and because of competition with other species that have similar requirements. Studies of both human and animal groups suggest that few populations reach such a theoretical maximum level, but adjust themselves to a size that allows a margin for fluctuations in the actual food production in the area. In archaeological terms, carrying capacity is the size and density of ancient populations that a given site or region could have supported under a specified subsistence technology.

cart: A two-wheeled vehicle drawn by a draft animal, used throughout recorded history for the transportation of goods and people. The cart, usually drawn by a single animal, was used by the Greeks and the Assyrians by 1800 BC. However, such vehicles could have been used as early as 3500 BC as an extension of the invention of the wheel. Bronze Age finds in Heathery Burn (England) included four nave bands for a four-wheeled cart. La Tène two-wheeled chariots are found from the third century BC.

Cartailhac, Émile (1845–1921): A French prehistorian sometimes called one of the founders of archaeology in France. He edited the journal *Matéreaux pour l'histoire primitive et naturelle de l'homme* and wrote books on French and Mediterranean prehistory, including *La Caverne de Font-de-Gaume …* (1910; The Cave of Font-de-Gaume …), with Henri Breuil. He is best remembered for his long refusal to accept the authenticity of cave art, denouncing such archaeologists as Marcellino de Sautuola. After visiting the Spanish site of Altamira with the Abbé Breuil, Cartailhac changed his opinion and in 1902 published an article subtitled "Mea culpa d'un sceptique," in which he admitted the antiquity of the cave paintings. He then helped to convince many scholars that cave paintings were indeed genuine and the earliest manifestations of art in the world.

Carter, Howard (1874–1939): British archaeologist who made one of the richest and most celebrated contributions to Egyptology: the discovery in 1922 of the largely intact tomb of King Tutankhamen. At 17, Carter joined a British-sponsored archaeological survey of Egypt. He received his training as an excavator and epigrapher from some of the most important Egyptologists of the late nineteenth century, including Gaston Maspero and Flinders Petrie, with whom he worked at el-Amarna in 1892. He made drawings of the sculptures and inscriptions at the temple of Queen Hatshepsut in Thebes and then served as inspector-general of the Egyptian antiquities department. While supervising excavations in the Valley of the Kings in 1902, he discovered the tombs of Hatshepsut and Thutmose IV. Around 1907, he began his association with the 5th Earl of Carnarvon, a collector of antiquities who asked Carter to supervise excavations in the valley. On 4 November 1922, Carter found the first sign of Tutankhamen's tomb, and three days later he reached its sealed entrance. For the next 10 years, Carter supervised the removal of its contents, most of which are now in the Cairo Museum. His patient and long unrewarded study of the Valley of the Kings brought to light the only largely unrobbed Egyptian pharaoh's tomb and the richest treasure ever to be discovered.

Carthage: A great city of antiquity founded, according to tradition, on the north coast of Africa by the Phoenicians of Tyre in 814 BC and now a suburb of Tunis. However, Phoenician occupation on the site is archaeologically attested only about 1 century later. The *Aeneid* tells of the city's founding by the Tyrian princess Dido, who fled from her brother Pygmalion (a king of Tyre). Until around 500 BC, Carthage

was one of three great mercantile powers in the central Mediterranean, together with the Etruscans and Western Greeks. Much of Carthage's revenue came from its exploitation of the silver mines of North Africa and southern Spain, begun as early as 800 BC, and from its role as a middleman in trade. Carthage was for many years in conflict with the Greeks, especially in Sicily. Carthage lost both Sicily and Sardinia to Rome in 241 BC at the close of the First Punic War. From an enlarged domain in southern Spain, the Carthaginian general Hannibal in 218 BC led his army across the Alps to victories in Italy. When Hannibal returned to Africa, he was defeated at Zama in 202 BC. Although humiliated, Carthage survived until it was destroyed by Rome in 146 BC, after having fought the three Punic Wars of the 3rd and 2nd centuries. Carthage was then reconstructed as a Roman city by Julius Caesar and Octavian. The Roman city prospered by shipping grain and olive oil to Italy. Carthage replaced Utica as the capital of the African province, and it became the second largest city in the western part of the empire, after Rome itself. The Phoenician/Punic remains include the citadel, Byrsa, the sanctuary of Tanit, and two manmade harbors (all pre-146 BC); the Roman remains are the Antonine Baths, odeum, theater, circus, amphitheater, aqueduct, and areas of streets and houses. Also on the Byrsa site stood an open-air portico, from which the finest Roman sculptures at Carthage have survived. The standard of living in Carthage was probably far below that of the larger cities of the classical world. In Roman times, beds, cushions, and mattresses were luxuries. The Punic language and its distinctive alphabet remained in use long after the city's destruction. After the breakup of the Roman empire, the Vandals took Carthage in 439 and stayed in control until the Byzantine invasion in 533. Carthage was the capital of the Byzantine Empire in Africa until the Arab takeover of 698. (*syn.* [adj. Carthaginian, Punic] Carthago; Kart-Hadasht)

cartonnage: An Egyptian mummy case made of layers of papyrus or linen soaked in gesso plaster and shaped around an embalmed body, much like papier maché, and then decorated with paint or gilding when dry. The term also refers to the material used thus and for mummy masks, anthropoid coffins, and other funerary items made in the same manner. (*syn.* cartonage)

cartouche: (kar'-toosh) The name given to the oval or oblong figures in Egyptian hieroglyphics, which enclosed characters representing royal or divine names or titles. The term is also used for the amulet of similar design worn in ancient Egypt as a protection against the loss of one's name (i.e., one's identity). In architecture, the term refers to the ornamentation in scroll form, applied especially to elaborate frames around tablets or coats of arms. By extension, the word is applied to any oval shape or even to a decorative shield, whether scrolled or not. Detailed examples of cartouches show that the sign represents a length of knotted rope, looped so that it is neverending; it thus symbolizes cyclical return. The French word *cartouche*, meaning "gun cartridge," was originally given to the royal frame by Napoleon's soldiers, because of its cartridge-like shape. (*syn.* shenu)

carved tree: A tree with designs, often geometric, cut into the bark. Carved trees occur in Australia and in the Chatham Islands. (*syn.* dendroglyph)

caryatid: A supporting base or column of a structure shaped in the form of a woman. Most often, a caryatid supported a porch, entablature, or colonnade and was in the form of a draped woman bearing the structure on her head. The best known caryatids are those of the Erechtheum at Athens (420–415 BC), and other examples include part of three small buildings (treasuries) at Delphi in Greece (550–530 BC). The figures' origin can be traced to mirror handles of nude figures carved from ivory in Phoenicia and draped figures cast from bronze in archaic Greece. Caryatids were used in the Roman emperor Hadrian's villa at Tivoli, the Villa Albani at Rome, two colossal figures at Eleusis, in Marcus Vipsanius Agrippa's Pantheon, and in the colonnade surrounding the Forum of Augustus at Rome. The male counterparts of caryatids are called "atlantes." (*syn.* pl. caryatides; korai)

Casas Grandes: A culture, river, and site in Chihuahua, northern Mexico. The town's name, Spanish for "great houses," refers to the extensive, multistoried ruins of a pre-Columbian town, which was probably founded in 1050 and burned around 1340, after which the abandoned valley lands were occupied by the Suma, who migrated from the east. Ruins of this type are common in the valleys of the Casas Grandes and its tributaries. The earliest culture, called the Viejo, was characterized by Mogollon-type pottery and pithouse dwellings. The following period, the Medio, had adobe houses. A third period, the Tardio, came after AD 1300 and was heavily influenced by Mesoamerica. The area was settled by the Spaniards in 1661/1662 and is now a national monument under the jurisdiction of the National Institute of Anthropology and History.

Cascioarele: A small settlement on an island in the Danube River, southern Rumania. Excavations have revealed occupation layers of the Middle Neolithic, c. 3900–3700 BC, and Late Neolithic, c. 3700–3500 BC. A complete village plan has been found in the later occupation, with one large central structure surrounded by six smaller structures. The finds have ritual implications and technological importance. There is evidence of heavy reliance on wild animal meat.

casemate wall: A defensive wall consisting of parallel walls with a space or internal chambers in the thickness of the wall. Sometimes the chambers were rooms; sometimes they were filled with debris or left empty.

Cashel: A rock in Tipperary, Ireland, which rises dramatically 358 feet (109 m) above the surrounding plain. On the summit of this limestone outcrop is a group of ruins, including the remains of the town's defenses, St. Patrick's Cathedral, the bishop's castle, and an ancient cross. The rock was the stronghold of the kings of Munster from the 4th century. St. Patrick consecrated Cashel as a bishopric c. 450. In 1101, the rock was given to the church by King Murtagh O'Brien. (*syn.* Rock of Cashel)

Caskey, John (1908–1981): An American archaeologist who served as director of the American School of Classical Studies at Athens and worked at Lerna and Ayia Irini.

Caso y Andrade, Alfonso (1896–1970): Mexican archaeologist and government official who explored the early Oaxacan cultures and who excavated Tomb Seven at Monte Albán, the earliest-known North American necropolis. His discovery and analysis of the burial offerings at Tomb Seven proved that Monte Albán had been occupied by the Mixtec people after they had displaced the Zapotecs before the Spanish conquest. Caso found evidence of five major phases, dating back to the 8th century BC, and established a rough chronology through comparisons with other sites. Caso also deciphered the Mixtec Codices. He made important contributions to regional archaeology and to the interpretation of Mixtec manuscripts, Mexican calendars, and dynastic history in general. He held posts as head of the Department of Archaeology at the National Museum, director of the museum, and director of the National Institute for Indian Affairs.

Cassibile: A Late Bronze Age settlement and cemetery containing 2,000 rock-cut chamber tombs near Syracuse in southeast Sicily. It is the type site of a Late Bronze Age phase—Pantalica II—of the early 1st millennium BC. The Pantalica culture was characterized by large urban settlements. Artifacts include a distinctive buff painted ware with plume or "feather" motifs, c. 1250–1000 BC, and a number of typical bronze types, including stilted and thick-arc fibulae and shaft-hole axes.

Cassivellaunus (fl. 1st century BC): A powerful British chieftain who was defeated by Julius Caesar during Caesar's second raid of Britain in 54 BC. Cassivellaunus is the first man in England whose name we know, and he led his tribe, the Catuvellauni, a group of Belgic invaders from the River Marne area. He used guerrilla tactics and chariot warfare successfully until Caesar captured the fortified settlement, identified as present-day Wheathampstead, Hertfordshire. Cassivellaunus agreed to provide hostages and pay an annual tribute to Rome, but there is no evidence that he kept these promises. His son was Cunobelin, the "Cymbeline" written about by Shakespeare. (*syn.* Cassivelaunus)

Cass ny Hawin: A Mesolithic settlement site on the Isle of Man with stone tools, including microliths.

Castanet: An Upper Palaeolithic rock shelter at Castel-merle, southwest France. There were two Aurignacian levels with art objects of carved or painted stone. The art from Castanet and neighboring Blanchard rock shelter is amongst the earliest known, dating c. 33,000 BC.

caste: Social class with clearly delineated boundaries; one is usually born into a caste and ascribed social and economic roles on the basis of caste affiliation. It is difficult or impossible to ascend from one caste to a higher one.

Castelluccio: An Early Bronze Age settlement and cemetery of rock-cut tombs near Syracuse, Sicily. Excavated by Orsi in 1891–1892, the cemetery contained several hundred tombs used for collective burial. One tomb had a carved facade, and several were closed by slabs with carved double spirals. The characteristic pottery was a buff ware painted with black or green lines and designs. Pottery shapes included splay-necked cups and pedestaled bowls. There were also bossed bone plaques, showing connections with the Aegean world well before 2000 BC.

casting: Casting consists of pouring molten metal into a mold, where it solidifies into the shape of the mold. The process was well established in the Bronze Age (beginning c. 3000 BC), when it was used to form bronze pieces. It is particularly valuable for the economical production of complex shapes, from mass-produced parts to one-of-a-kind items or even large machinery. Three principal techniques of casting were successively developed in prehistoric Europe: one-piece stone molds for flat-faced objects; clay or stone piece molds that could be dismantled and reused; and one-off clay molds for complex shapes made in one piece around a wax or lead pattern (cire perdue). Every metal with a low enough melting point was exploited in early Europe, except iron and steel, for casting artifacts.

casting jet: A plug of metal knocked out after an artifact is cast, which fits exactly into the opening (aperture or gate) of a mold. When casting metal into a bivalve or composite mold, the aperture through which the metal is poured into the mold becomes filled up with molten metal, and this plug of metal cools and hardens with the object. When the finished artifact is removed from the mold, the casting jet is still attached; in most cases it is knocked off and the scar polished down, the metal plug being melted down for reuse. In some cases, however, it may be left on, particularly on neck rings and bracelets. Examples are sometimes in founders' hoards.

casting-on technique: A method used in a secondary stage of making metal objects for adding handles, legs, and hilts to complex artifacts. A clay mold is placed around part of an existing object, and molten metal is then poured in and fuses onto the original object.

casting seam: The place where a small amount of molten metal runs into the joint between the surfaces of the parts of the casting mold. In a bivalve or composite mold, this seepage results in a visible seam when the object is removed from the mold. It is usually filled and polished off; unfinished objects are often found with a visible seam or ridge.

castle: A medieval European structure, generally the residence of a king or a lord of the territory. The word *castle* is derived from Latin *castellum*, a fortified camp, and there are various linguistic forms, including chateau, *castello*, *castrum*, and burg. These medieval strongholds developed rapidly from the 9th century. The word is sometimes applied to prehistoric earthworks, such as Maiden Castle, England. Castles developed with the feudal system, which installed a societal classification in which land and other privileges were granted in return for military service. Castle architecture had three essential elements: a tower (keep or donjon), residence for the noble, and a fortified enclosure wall. The first late Carolingian types were likely modeled on the fortified homesteads of the Slavs, and in the 10th century the manor or principal house was then set up on a raised mound in the enclosure. This "motte and bailey" type was introduced to France in the 11th century. The Normans then carried it to the British Isles and southern Italy and also built stone keeps within their enclosures. Later 12th-century castles in France and England have large stone walls, gateways modeled on Arabic and Byzantine forts, and massive circular central keeps. Multiple walls with strengthened gateways are an invention of the mid-13th century. The introduction of the cannon and other firearms in the 15th and 16th centuries made castles vulnerable to attack. Castle architecture was revised with low walls, which could be defended all around by artillery, the guns mounted on bastions and redans.

Castor ware: A distinctive pottery named after a Roman settlement site on the north bank of the Nene in Northamptonshire. Castor ware is a slate-colored pottery, which commonly had hunting scenes of dogs, boars, and so on, on the outer surface, applied by squeezing paste from a bag or applying by brush. The E barbotine hunt cups were a highlight of the native Romano-British potters' craft.

castro: Portuguese term for a fortified site, ranging from the small walled citadels of the Copper Age (e.g., Vila Nova de Sao Pedro) to the hillfort settlements of the Celtic Iron Age.

casual find: A nonscientific discovery of an archaeological object, as by an explorer or hunter.

catacomb: A subterranean cemetery of galleries or passages with side niches (loculi) for tombs. Catacombs consisted of galleries, burial niches, and chambers cut into the rock; the walls and ceilings were decorated with pagan and Christian motifs. The term was first applied to the subterranean cemetery under the Basilica of San Sebastiano (on the Appian Way near Rome), which was reputed to have been the temporary resting place of the bodies of Saints Peter and Paul in the last half of the 3rd century. By extension, the word came to refer to all the subterranean cemeteries around Rome, although the type is widely known elsewhere, especially around the Mediterranean. Their subterranean nature is explained by the need for security and secrecy on the part of the Christian religion that was banned in many places.

Catacomb Grave culture: The second in the Kurgan culture series, after Yamnaya and before Srubnaya, in southern Russia and the Ukraine between the Dniepr and Volga Rivers. It is dated between c. 2000–1500 bc (Bronze Age). The graves are not true catacombs but rather burials in which the skeleton and grave goods are put in a side wall niche of a shallow shaft. The shaft is filled in and then covered with a barrow.

catafalque: A decorated wooden platform on which a sarcophagus was temporarily placed before burial. These ornate funereal structures were often mounted on a stage to support a coffin for a lying-in-state.

Çatal Hüyük: (cha'-tahl) One of the world's earliest towns, a huge Neolithic site in south-central Turkey's Konya Plain. At least 14 levels have been excavated so far with radiocarbon dates from 6500 bc to 5400 bc, without undisturbed deposits being reached. Cereals were cultivated, cattle and sheep were bred, and hunting took place. Pottery had apparently only just been introduced. Trade in such materials as obsidian and seashells was extensive. There were flaked stone tools and polished obsidian mirrors. The mud-brick buildings were rectangular with access possible only through the roofs. Built-in furniture included benches and platforms. Early evidence of religious beliefs has been found at the mound of Çatal Hüyük. Shrines were very frequent, with huge figures of goddesses in the posture of giving birth, leopards, and the heads of bulls and rams modeled in high relief on the walls. Other shrines contained elaborate frescoes of the hunting of deer and aurochs, or vultures devouring headless human corpses. Stone and terra-cotta statuettes found in these shrines represent female figures, sometimes accompanied by leopards and, from the earlier levels of excavation, a male either bearded and seated on a bull or youthful and riding a leopard. The main deity of these people was evidently a goddess. The dead were buried beneath plastered platforms in the shrines or under the floors of the buildings. Evidence suggests both craft specialization and social stratification.

catalog, catalogue: An inventory of archaeological data in which an artifact is labeled with a reference number and described in detail. The catalog number is the unique number assigned to each individual item—or group of items—in an archaeological collection.

cataract: Any rocky areas of rapids interrupting the flow of the Nile River, caused by granite abruptly interspersed in the Nubian sandstone belt. There are six numbered and several minor cataracts between Aswan and Khartoum, which are hazards to navigation. The 2nd Cataract, the most formidable, was impassable except during the annual inundation. Cataracts 1–4 and the Dal Cataract were political frontiers at different times.

catastrophe theory: A mathematical theory and branch of geometry, which demonstrates ways in which a system can undergo sudden large changes as one or more of the variables that control it are continuously changed. The theory explains change through a succession of sudden catastrophes: A small change in one variable can produce a sudden discontinuity in another. Archaeologists use the theory to show that sudden changes can stem from comparatively small variations. It has been used to explain the dramatic change in settlement patterns and the collapse of Maya and Mycenaean civilizations brought about by comparatively small changes without large causes such as invasions or natural disasters. (*syn.* catastrophism)

catchment: The resource area of an archaeological site; the geographical area in which the inhabitants of a village or camp obtain resources. (*syn.* catchment area)

catena: A sequence of soils formed by the same parent material but from different landscape positions have taken on differing characteristics. Seeing these differences may assist in interpretation of archaeological sites.

Cathedral Cave: A site rich in rock art in Carnarvon Gorge, Australia, with evidence of occupation from about 3500 bp and with stone and bone artifacts.

Catherwood, Frederick (1799–1854): The first great explorer of Mesoamerica who, along with John Lloyd Stephens, explored the Maya lowlands, made drawings that provided insights into the culture, and detailed the Maya glyphs.

cation-ratio dating: A method of direct dating rock carvings and engravings, potentially applicable to Palaeolithic artifacts with a strong patina caused by exposure to desert dust. The technique is based on the principle that cations of certain elements are more soluble than others; they leach out of rock varnish more rapidly than the less soluble elements, and their concentration decreases with time. A cation is an ion carrying a positive charge, which moves toward a negative electrode/cathode during electrolysis. (*syn.* cation ratio dating)

cattle: Domesticated bovine farm animals of the genus Bos raised for their meat or milk or for draft purposes. Wild cattle or aurochs (*Bos primigenius*) were present from the Middle Pleistocene; they were widely distributed and are beautifully portrayed in Palaeolithic cave art. The earliest evidence of domestication (*Bos taurus*) comes from northern Greece before 6000 BC (Nea Nikomedeia in Macedonia, Argissa in Thessaly, and Knossos in Crete) and from c. 5800 BC at Çatal Hüyük (Anatolia). Thereafter, different breeds were developed, notably *B. longifrons* in southwest Asia and Europe, and the humped zebu, *B. indica*, in India. The last record of *Bos primigenius* was AD 1627 in Poland, the animal was uncommon long before then. (*syn.* live stock)

Caton-Thompson, Gertrude (1888–1985): A British archaeologist who worked in Egypt, northern Transvaal, and the Arabian peninsula. She showed that the Great Zimbabwe site was of African construction.

cauldron: A large metal vessel for cooking, usually with a round base, heavy flange rim, and handles for suspending it over a fire. Examples date from the European Late Bronze Age, with especially important ones from Urartu. In the Iron Age, they were sometimes made of silver, but they were usually made of sheet bronze riveted together and had two to four handles. Cauldrons were a sign of great wealth or power.

cause: In the archaeological sense, any event that forces people to make decisions about how to deal with a new situation.

causeway: A pathway or road, often paved but not macadamized. It was often a raised road across a low or wet place or body of water—as from the Nile River to a pyramid across the desert plateau. The term was used for Roman roads, especially military ones, and was also applied to piers that extended into rivers or the sea.

causewayed camp: A hilltop entrenchment characteristic of Neolithic times, 4th millennium BC, especially in southern Britain. The hilltop was enclosed by a series of concentric ditches, one to four in number, with internal banks, not continuous, but interrupted by solid causeways (undisturbed lanes of earth). Pottery, animal bones, and domestic garbage stratified in the ditches show that the camps were used during the entire Neolithic period. A common theory about the camps is that they were used as meeting places at intervals by the population of a wide area.

Cavdar: A tell site in western Bulgaria of the first temperate Neolithic, dating to c. 5100–4700 BC. There are Kremikovci occupation levels and one Karanovo level. The inhabitants grew emmer wheat and barley and raised cattle. Kremikovci painted wares include a rich polychrome assemblage dating to the end of the Early Neolithic. (*syn.* Cevdar)

cavea: The concave-shaped auditorium of an ancient open-air theater, which was often a semicircle of stone benches rising in tiers. A cavea might be divided, depending on the size of the building, into one to three distinct tiers, called upper, lower, middle (summa, ima, media cavea).

cave art: Any paintings, engravings, or designs on cave walls, humans' oldest surviving art, especially that by Palaeolithic and Pleistocene people found in southwest France, northeast Spain, and elsewhere in Europe. Other sites have been discovered in Portugal, Italy, Greece, and the Ural Mountains; the only known Russian site is Kapovo Cave. The subject matter of cave art is predominantly animals, especially mammoth, horse, ox, deer, and bison; human figures are relatively uncommon. There are also numerous signs and symbols. The artists used a range of reds, blacks, yellows, and browns derived from ochres and other naturally occurring mineral pigments (iron oxide and manganese dioxide). The purpose and meaning of cave art are still obscure. In France and Spain, the caves are mainly in the limestone of the Perigord and Pyrenean regions, and the most famous are Altamira, Lascaux, Niaux, and Pech Merle. Occupational evidence is rarely found with the art.

Cave Bay Cave: A rock shelter on Hunter Island off Tasmania, Australia, with three occupations around 23,000, 7000, and 2500 bp. The site shifted to a marine economy in the early Holocene, but was abandoned in mid-Holocene.

cave bear: An extinct species of bear that lived 300,000–10,000 years ago in Europe and the Mediterranean. They could be up to 8 feet long and about twice the weight of modern European brown bears. They were vegetarian.

cave dwelling: Natural prehistoric living places inside caves or rock shelters, often inhabited by Palaeolithic people. Cave dwellings were inhabited more often during colder periods by hunters and gatherers. (*syn.* n. cave-dweller or cave-man)

cave earth: A layer of earth forming the old floor of a cave before the depositing of stalagmite. The term also describes cave deposits of shattered boulders and pebbles that occur from frost and weathering.

Cave of Hearths: A cave in northern Transvaal, which yielded the right side of a *Homo sapiens* child's jaw, of Rhodesioid type, dating from about 50,000 years ago. It is located close to the Makapansgat site, the oldest cave site known in Africa. Both offer extremely early evidence of the use of fire by man in Africa and tools of the transitional Acheulian-Fauresmith type. The earliest deposits of the Cave of Hearths are Acheulian, followed by a long period of abandonment. There was a long succession of Pietersburg industries and some signs of typological continuity between the Acheulian and the Pietersburg assemblages. The Pietersburg industry was succeeded by an assemblage of subtriangular points and flake scrapers similar to the Bambata industry of Zimbabwe.

cavetto: A hollow concave molding projecting from the tops of Egyptian cornices, pylons, altars, walls, doorways, flat-topped stelae, and false doors and whose profile is the quadrant of a circle. It was probably derived from the appearance of the tops of fronds of vegetation. (*syn.* cavetto cornice)

Cayla de Mailhac: A site in southwestern France with a settlement and a series of cemeteries of Late Bronze and Early Iron Ages c. 700–100 BC. Occupation began with an urnfield culture. Iron became common in a second phase, and a cart burial from La Redorte shows similarities to the Hallstatt Iron Age cultures. Phase III is dated to the second half of the 6th century BC by imports of Greek black figure ware and Etruscan pottery. The settlement of Phase IV was enclosed by a rampart and had houses of sun-dried brick. Datable material included Greek red figure pottery and fibula brooches of Hallstatt/early La Tène types. The last phase was of the La Tène culture.

Cayönü Tepesi: A site on a tributary of the Tigris River in eastern Turkey with occupation dating from c. 7500–6500 BC. There are impressive architectural remains with stone foundations and evidence of a farming and hunting community. The latest phase included domesticated sheep and goats. Einkorn wheat was cultivated as well as emmer wheat, peas, and lentils. Another important feature of this site was the very early appearance of simple copper objects, derived from nearby Ergani Maden. Also, clay bricks, baked figurines, and pottery have been found.

Ceahlau-Cetatica: An Upper Palaeolithic site in eastern Romania with artifacts of bifacial foliates, side scrapers, and end scrapers. Upper levels of backed blades are from the Gravettian.

Cederberg: A range of the Cape Fold Mountains near Cape Town, South Africa, known for rock paintings from the Later Stone Age onward.

Celadon ware: A type of Chinese pottery with a pale green glaze—either porcelain or stoneware. It was the earliest tinted Chinese pottery, dating from the Sung Dynasty AD 960–1279. The main kilns were in Yao-chou in Shensi Province, Lin-ju in Honan Province, Li-shui, and Lung-ch'uan in Chekiang Province. (*syn.* celadon)

Celebes: An Indonesian island east of Borneo, which has produced the oldest Buddhist image known in the archipelago, dated to the 4th century. Celebes lies between the two shelves of the Australian and Asian continents. A broad central area is made up of igneous rocks with a band of volcanic detritus (tuff) that is more than 65 million years old. The earliest traces of human habitation on Celebes are stone implements of the Toalian culture. (*syn.* Sulawesi)

cella: In Classical architecture, the body of a temple—the inner room or main hall where the principal statue or symbol of the god was worshiped. This inner sanctum, as distinct from the portico, was a simple room, usually rectangular, with the entrance at one end and with the side walls often being extended to form a porch. In larger temples, where the cella was open to the sky, a small temple was sometimes placed within. (*syn.* naos)

celt: (selt) A New Stone Age tool, usually a polished, ungrooved ax or adze head or blade that would be attached to a wooden shaft. The tool, often shaped like a chisel and made of stone or bronze, was probably used for felling trees or shaping wood. Great numbers of celts have been discovered in the British Isles and Denmark, and they were traded widely. Bronze Age tools of similar general design are also called celts.

Celtic art: An art style of the European Iron Age, c. 500 BC, developed presumably by Celtic peoples. It originated on the middle Rhine River, extending to the upper Danube and the Marne. Its finest specimens are from the British Isles in the first century BC and AD. It appears most commonly in bronzework or other metals, weapons and horse gear, eating and drinking vessels, personal ornaments, and monumental stone carvings. It seems likely that the craftsmen worked under the direct patronage of the chieftains. Techniques employed were decoration in relief, engraving, and inlay. Stylistically, Celtic art combines elements taken from the classical world, from the Scythians to the east, and from the local earlier Hallstatt Iron Age. The art developed into several styles in continental Europe (Early, Waldalgesheim, Plastic, and Sword styles) but came to an end with the Roman occupation. In Ireland, the art style returned after the Roman withdrawal. (*syn.* La Tène art)

Celtic fields: A term used for small plots with low earthen banks formed around them, which were field systems of pre-Roman times in Britain and northwest Europe. These date to the Early Bronze Age (1800 BC), so that it is a misnomer to attach "Celtic" to them. Traces of these systems may still be visible where later agriculture has not removed them. The oldest examples in Britain are blocks of arable land (sometimes associated with farmsteads, hollow ways, stockades, and enclosures) divided into a patchwork of more or less square units. They are defined by lynchets at the upper and lower edges and by slightly raised ridges at the sides. Similar fields are known from Scandinavia and the Netherlands.

Celts: (kelts) An important people of central and western Europe. Greek and Roman writers recorded them as having lived in the final centuries BC, and their existence is first attested c. 500 BC, but they were around long before that. They were a fierce warrior race distinguished by three factors: their language, their beliefs, and their material culture. They are known to have invaded Italy and sacked Rome itself in the early 4th century BC, while in the following century groups of Celts invaded Greece, sacking Delphi, and others invaded Anatolia. Their language belonged to the Indo-

European family and divided into two branches at an early date (3rd–2nd millennia BC), respectively represented by the Welsh and Irish Gaelic languages. Original homelands appear to have been on the western and central mainland of Europe: France, Germany, Bohemia, Austria, and Switzerland. By the mid-1st millennium BC, they also lived in Iberia (Spain and Portugal), Britain, Ireland, the Low Countries south of the Rhine Delta, and Italy north of the River Po. In Britain, they were defeated by the Romans in AD 43. Archaeologically, in central Europe there were aristocratic burials of the Hallstatt culture, often containing wagons or horses. Archaeological cultures do not necessarily coincide with ethnic or linguistic groups, and it is preferable to use the cultural terms Hallstatt and La Tene when describing archaeological remains. (*syn.* adj Celtic; Gaels; Goidels; Galatians; Gauls)

cemetery: A place set apart for burial or entombment of the dead.

cenotaph: Greek for "empty tomb," the term describing a tomb built as a memorial for ceremonial purposes and never intended for the interment of a body. Greek writings indicate that the ancients erected many cenotaphs, including one for the poet Euripides in Athens, but none of these survive. The subsidiary pyramids of the 4th–6th Egyptian Dynasties are probably cenotaphs. At the Abydos cenotaph, chapels for private individuals are characteristic of the Middle Kingdom, and there are royal cenotaph temples of the Middle and New Kingdoms. The term also refers to a monument raised to a Roman citizen who had been drowned at sea or who, from any other cause, failed to receive burial.

cenote: A type of natural well or reservoir, common in the Yucatán Peninsula, Mexico, formed when a limestone surface collapses, exposing water underneath. Cenotes are the major source of water in Yucatán, and they are associated with the cult of the rain gods, or Chacs. In ancient times, especially at the Maya site of Chichén Itzá, precious objects, such as jade, gold, copper, and incense—and human beings, usually children—were thrown into the cenotes as offerings. A survivor was believed to bring a message from the gods about the year's crops.

Cenozoic: (sen'-uh-zoh-ik) The most recent geological era in the earth's history, in which mammals came to dominate animal life. The Cenozoic began 66.4 million years ago and extends to the present; it began when Asia acquired its present appearance and mammals came to dominate animal life. The most important tectonic event in the Cenozoic history of Asia was its collision with India some 50 million years ago. This collision took place some 1,250 miles farther south of the present location of the line of collision along the Indus-Brahmaputra suture behind the main range of the Himalayas. The Cenozoic includes the Tertiary and Quaternary periods.

centaur: In Greek mythology, a race of creatures, part horse and part man, dwelling in the mountains of Thessaly and Arcadia. Centaurs had a human head and arms and upper body, and the four legs and lower body of a horse.

centralization: Evolutionary process whereby wealth, power, political decision making, and social prestige are concentrated in the hands of fewer and fewer subgroups or individuals in a society.

centrally based wandering model: A model for hunter-gatherer cultures centered around base camps.

central place theory: In geography, a theory concerning the size and distribution of central places (settlements) in a system or region. The primary purpose of a settlement or market town, according to central place theory, is the provision of goods and services for the surrounding market area. Such towns are centrally located and may be called central places. As applied to archaeology, the theory states that human settlements space themselves evenly across a landscape as a function of the availability of natural resources, communication and transportation routes, and other factors. Eventually, these evolve into a hierarchy of settlements of different size that depend on one another. Central place theory attempts to illustrate how settlements locate in relation to one another, the amount of market area (goods and services) a central place can control, and why some central places function as hamlets, villages, towns, or cities. The theory was first developed by the German geographer Walter Christaller. Christaller's theory concentrated on centers of different order, because in a complex system some larger centers offer more specialized services to a wider area; there may indeed by many levels of such centers in a complex settlement hierarchy. Christaller's model has been modified by other geographers, especially August Losch. The theory may suggest ways in which factors have affected the settlement pattern. Central place theory has found useful applications in archaeology as a preliminary heuristic device. (*syn.* central-place theory)

centuriation: The practice of dividing the territory surrounding a new Roman colony to match the city's grid plan of square blocks, normally 2,330 feet (710 m) on a side. The centuriation process was done for land distribution to the settlers and also for inventory. Signs of it were first detected in northern Africa from the 1830s, through surviving crop marks and roads, and have been found, mainly through air photography, in Trier and Homs (Syria) and large areas of northern Italy and Tunisia.

cephalic index: A measurement technique used to define

the relation between the length and breadth of a human skull. The breadth of the skull is expressed as a percentage of the length, and the ratio is figured as the maximum breadth to the maximum length, measured from a pint just above the eyebrow ridges, multiplied by 100. This produces an index that defines the skull as round headed (brachycephalic; a reading above 80), long headed (dolichocephalic; a reading below 75), or in between (meso- or mesaticephalic; a reading between 75–80). It is an important anthropological tool although it is now recognized that other methods of measurement are needed to compare skull shapes adequately.

ceque: Any of 41 imaginary lines radiating outward from the Temple of the Sun in Inca city of Cuzco, Peru. The lines go to the edges of the valley, and along each was a series of *huacas* or shrines at which offerings were made. The huacas and ceques combined to total the 328 days of the Inca calendar.

ceramic analysis: Any of various techniques used to study artifacts made from fired clay to obtain archaeological data. Color is objectively described by reference to the Munsell soil color charts. Examination under the microscope may reveal the technique of manufacture and allow the identification of mineral grains in the tempering, which identify the area of manufacture. Refiring experiments often show how the original baking was done.

ceramic artifact: Any artifact made of fired clay, belonging to pottery, figurine, or other ceramic industries.

ceramic petrology: The study of the composition, texture, and structure of the minerals in the clay from which pottery is manufactured. The purpose of ceramic petrology is to locate the source of the clay from which the pot was made. Ceramic petrology involves either heavy mineral analysis or petrologic microscopy, both of which require samples to be removed from the pot. Neutron activation analysis is also used. Results from these studies have far-reaching consequences for the study of early economic systems. Not only has it been shown that pottery and its contents were transported over long distances in antiquity, but also that the specialized manufacture and marketing of pottery started as far back as the first agriculture in Europe.

ceramics: The art or process of making useful and ornamental articles from clay by shaping and then hardening them by firing at high temperatures. Ceramics are generally known as pottery, but the term also refers to the manufacture of any product from a nonmetallic mineral by firing at high temperatures. The exceptional porcelain and stonewares of China are very well known, from as early as the Yang-Shao Neolithic culture, c. 4500 BC. (*syn.* pottery)

ceramic sociology: A field of study involving the reconstruction of past social systems from the distributions of stylistic attributes of pottery in time and space.

ceramique oncteuse: A type of medieval pottery of western Brittany, made from the 10th–18th centuries. It is typically very soft and uses talc as the tempering material. This unusual pottery was a distinctive product of the Breton culture.

ceremonial center: In the prehistoric New World, a complex of buildings that served as the focus of religious and governmental activities, differing from a village or town. These buildings were used at prescribed times by the peoples lived in dispersed areas. Permanent residence was restricted to very few people on these sites, usually the elite and their retainers. Sites such as Teotihuacan, Tikal, and Monte Alban have been interpreted as ceremonial centers. However, subsequent fieldwork beyond the major architectural features has shown that many sites were directly associated with large populations and thus has challenged the original premise of their being ceremonial centers. Other more valid examples may be La Venta and San Lorenzo.

ceremonial object: Any artifact associated with a ritual or ceremony or that functions only in a symbolic sense, as opposed to a tool or other practical device.

Ceren, Joya de: A Maya settlement located in San Salvador, which was buried by the eruption of the Laguna Caldera in AD 684. There is a farmhouse of the 5th century AD preserved under the ash, with bodies huddled in one room and the contents still in excellent condition.

Cernavoda: A cemetery site of the Late Neolithic near the Black Sea coast of Rumania dating to the mid-4th millennium BC. Over 300 inhumations are known, occurring in groups, some with rich grave goods of the Hamangia culture. There is also a Late Copper Age site dating to the 3rd millennium BC, which ranges over the Black Sea coast of Rumania and Bulgaria. The latter had short-lived occupation sites and is associated with the Ezero group.

Cernica: A Neolithic site of the late 5th millennium BC in Rumania. There is a settlement and cemetery with over 350 graves, some with richer grave goods of marble, shell and bone beads, and some copper ornaments.

Cerny: An Early Neolithic culture of the Paris and Loire regions of France, c. 4400–4000 BC. Cerny followed Villeneuve-St.-Germain and preceded the Chasséen. It was characterized by round-based vessels with impressed decoration or applied cordons.

Cerro Blanco: A site in the Nepena Valley on the central coast of Peru, which has a massive platform of conical adobes and stones. This temple complex supports rooms with walls covered by Chavín decoration, including eyes and feline fangs, modeled in mud plaster in low relief and painted red and greenish yellow.

Cerro de las Mesas: A site in southern Veracruz, Mexico, in the plains of the Papaloápan River, which is a hybrid site of the Pre-Classic and Classic periods. Dozens of earthen mounds are scattered over the surface in a seemingly haphazard manner, and the archaeological sequence is long and complex. The site reached its apogee in the Early Classic, when the stone monuments for which it is best known were carved. Most important are a number of stelae, some of which are carved in a low-relief style recalling Late Formative Tres Zapotes, early lowland Maya, and Cotzumalhuapa. Cerro de las Mesas pottery, deposited in rich burial offerings of the Early Classic, is much like that of Teotihuacan, with slab-legged tripods. Potters made large, hollow, handmade figures of the gods, and the most spectacular discovery on the site was a cache of 782 jade objects, many of Olmec workmanship. Cerro de las Mesas is famous for Remojadas-style pottery figurines, found in great quantity as burial goods. Because the Classic occupation contains abundant Teotihuacan materials and two Maya Long Count dates (AD 468 and AD 533), it is usually interpreted as a redistribution point for materials from both Mexico and the Maya lowlands.

Cerro Sechin: A Pre-Columbian temple site in the Casma Valley on the north-central coast of Peru, dating to c. 1800–900 BC (Initial Period, pre-Chavín) and known for its unusual large stone sculptures. These carvings are in a style unlike anything else reported in Peru, executed by deep-line incisions of warriors and dignitaries in regalia on dressed and carved stone slabs. Most of the figures represent humans. The site has one of the earliest appearances of monumental art in Mesoamerica.

Cerveteri: One of the most important cities in Italy, north of Rome, whose earliest occupation was the Iron Age Villanovan of the 9th–8th centuries BC. It flourished from the 7th–5th centuries as one of the 12 major cities of the Etruscan federation. Two necropolises from this period have been identified, with evidence for pit, trench, and chamber tombs. Accumulating wealth is reflected in the grandeur of many surviving tombs. There were two ports, Pyrgi and Alsium, the former with evidence of temples, which have provided scholars of the Etruscan language an important piece of evidence—a text on gold laminae. The city lost importance during the Roman period, and by the early empire was reported to be no more than a village. (*syn.* ancient Caere; Roman Caere vetus, Etruscan Xaire, Greek Agylla)

cesium magnetometer: A measurement tool used to detect large structures underground and their magnetic fluctuations by measuring the effects of transitions between atomic energy levels. It is considered more efficient than a proton magnetometer, which does the same thing.

cestrum: A type of ivory graver used in encaustic painting on ivory, with one pointed end. (*syn.* viriculum)

C Group: A culture of Nubia between the Old and New Kingdoms (c. 2494–1550 BC). The indigenous C Group people were subjected to varying degrees of social and economic influence from their powerful northern neighbors. (*syn.* C Horizon, C-group)

chacmool: A Mesoamerican life-sized sculpted stone figure representing a reclining human with head turned to one side, knees drawn up, and hands holding a shallow receptacle flat on the stomach. This was a widespread art form in the Post-Classic Period, especially at the Toltec sites of Tula and Chichen Itza and at Aztec and Tarascan sites. It is located at the entranceways to temples and was probably a repository for offerings.

Chaco Canyon: An alluvium-filled 20-kilometer stretch of canyon in northwest New Mexico, occupied by the Anasazi during Pueblo I and II, AD c. 850–1150. Now a national park, it contained spectacular pueblos, including Pueblo Bonito (c. 919–1130), which housed some 1,200 people. There were at least a dozen pueblo-like towns and hundreds of small villages. During a period of increased rainfall between 950–1150, several other pueblos were constructed in the Canyon, with fields, irrigation canals, an elaborate road system, and signal stations for long-distance trade. The entire complex of ruins has been studied with the aid of photogrammetry, including infrared air photography, satellite photographs, image enhancement, and computer mapping. When the climate started to become drier, in c. 1150, the main occupation of Chaco Canyon ended.

Chagar Bazar: A tell site on a tributary of the River Khabur in northeast Syria with levels from the 5th millennium BC (Halaf period) to the mid-2nd millennium BC. It gradually grew in size and importance and during the reign of the Assyrian king, Shamsi Adad I (early 2nd millennium BC) was an administrative center. Excavated by Sir Max Mallowan from 1935–1937, it yielded an important sequence of prehistoric wares, particularly Halaf and Samarra. There was iron (from the 28th c. BC) and copper, too. (*syn.* Tell Chagar Bazar)

chain mail: A type of protective body armor in the form of interlinked metal rings, worn by European knights and other military men throughout most of the medieval period. An early form of mail, made by sewing iron rings to fabric or leather, was worn in late Roman times and may have originated in Asia, where it was worn for many centuries. (*syn.* mail)

Chaironeia: A Middle Neolithic settlement on a mound in Boeotia, Greece, with distinctive red-on-cream pottery. The site has a stone lion that guards the tomb of Thebans killed in a battle in 338 BC. (*syn.* Chaeronea)

Chaiya: The location of two sites in Thailand: Wat Wiang of the late 1st–early 2nd millennium and Ban Phum Rieng. Wat

Wiang is a moated settlement with inscriptions connecting the town with Grahi, Srivijaya, and Tambralinga.

Chalandriani: An Early Bronze Age settlement and cemetery in the Cyclades Islands off Greece, dating to the 3rd millennium BC. The settlement was surrounded by stone defenses with six semicircular bastions; inside were a number of small rooms, separated by narrow paths. The cemetery of around 500 tombs, each containing one or two bodies, had artifacts of the so-called Keros-Syros culture, including the highly decorated dishes known as frying pans.

Chalcatzingo: A large Olmec site and trade center in Mexico with many rock carvings.

chalcedony: A fine-grained hard stone, a variety of the silica mineral quartz. A form of chert, it is found in a variety of milky or grayish colors with distinctive parallel bands of contrasting color. In antiquity, chalcedony was the stone most used by gem engravers for beads, seals, and sometimes as a substitute for flint. The agate, carnelian, jasper, and onyx are some of the varieties still cut and polished as ornamental stones.

Chalcidian ware: Black-figured pottery found in Etruria and the Chalcidian colony of Rhegium (modern Reggio) in Italy. The style included lettering of the inscriptions as part of the decoration.

Chalcolithic: Literally, the "Copper Stone Age," a period between the Neolithic (Stone Age) and the Bronze Age, from 3000–2500 BC, in which both stone and copper tools were used. It was a transitional phase between Stone Age technology and the Bronze Age and was marked by an increase in trade and cultural exchanges. The term is much less widely used than other divisions and subdivisions of the Three Age system, partly because of the difficulty in distinguishing copper from bronze without chemical analysis, partly because many areas did not have a Chalcolithic period at all. (*syn.* Chalcolithic period; Eneolithic, Copper Age)

Chaldea: A land in southern Babylonia (modern southern Iraq) frequently mentioned in the Old Testament and first described by the Assyrian king Ashurnasirpal II (reigned 884/883–859 BC). Its more important rulers were Nabopolassar, Nebuchadnezzar, and Nabonidus, who ruled an empire from the Persian Gulf between the Arabian desert and the Euphrates Delta. In 625, Nabopolassar became king of Babylon and inaugurated a Chaldean dynasty that lasted until the Persian invasion of 539 BC. The prestige of his successors, Nebuchadrezzar II (reigned 605–562) and Nabonidus (reigned 556–539), was such that "Chaldean" became synonymous with "Babylonian," and Chaldea replaced Assyria as the main power in the Near East. "Chaldean" also was used by several ancient authors to denote the priests and other persons educated in classical Babylonian astronomy and

astrology and to denote the Aramaean tribe, named for Kaldu, which first settled in this area in the 10th century BC. (*syn.* Chaldaea; Chaldaeans)

chaltoon: A series of underground chambers found in areas of Mesoamerica, used principally for storage. Shaped like bottles, they may also have been used as seat baths or burial chambers. (*syn.* choltun, chultun)

Cham: A linguistic and ethnic group of the Austronesian family, which once controlled the central coast of modern Vietnam as the state of Champa.

chamber tomb: A prehistoric tomb, often megalithic in construction, that contained a large burial chamber. Such a vault was usually used for successive burials over a long period. The term is also used for a rock-cut tomb, especially the shaft-and-chamber tomb, with a similar burial rite. Chamber tombs were built in many parts of the world and at many different times. The European varieties were called court cairn, dolmen, entrance grave, gallery grave, giants' grave, hunebed, passage grave, portal dolmen, tholos, transepted gallery grave, and wedge-shaped gallery grave. Many were rectangular chambers cut into the side of a hill and approached by a long entrance passage (dromos), especially in the Aegean. (*syn.* chambered tomb)

Champa: An ancient kingdom formed in AD 192, during the breakup of the Han Dynasty of China, corresponding roughly to present central Vietnam. Although the territory was at first inhabited mainly by wild tribes that struggled with the Chinese colonies in Tonkin, it gradually came under Indian cultural influence. Champa artifacts include well-developed sculpture and reliefs from the 7th century and impressive architecture from the 9th century. The kingdom was slowly absorbed into Vietnam and by the end of the 17th century had ceased to exist.

Champ Durand: A Neolithic fortification in Vendée, France, and associated material of the Late Neolithic, including Peu-Richardien decorated pottery of c. 3300–3000 BC.

champlevé: An enameling technique or an object made by the process, a form of inlay in which the pattern was cut out of the metal to be ornamented. The pattern was then filled with enamel frit and fused in an oven or filled with polished stones or shells. Champlevé can be distinguished from the similar technique of cloisonné by a greater irregularity in the width of the metal lines. It developed as a Celtic art in western Europe in the Roman period and was copied by the Anglo-Saxons. In the Rhine River Valley and in Belgium's Meuse River Valley, champlevé production flourished especially during the late 11th and 12th centuries. It was often used in the decoration of the escutcheons on hanging bowls. (*syn.* champ-levé)

Champollion, Jean-François (1778–1867): French historian and linguist who founded scientific Egyptology and played a major role in the deciphering of Egyptian hieroglyphics by deciphering the Rosetta Stone. A masterful linguist, Champollion started publishing papers on the hieroglyphic and hieratic elements of the Rosetta Stone in 1821–1822, and he went on to establish an entire list of hieroglyphic signs and their Greek equivalents. He was first to recognize that some of the signs were alphabetic, some syllabic, and some determinative (standing for a whole idea or object previously expressed). His brilliant discoveries met with great opposition, however. He became curator of the Egyptian collection at the Louvre, conducted an archaeological expedition to Egypt, and received the chair of Egyptian antiquities, created specially for him, at the Collège de France. He also published an Egyptian grammar and dictionary, as well as other works about Egypt.

Chanapata: A culture of the Cuzco area in the Peruvian Andes, c. 1000–200 BC. The type site has dark-hued or red pottery with incised, punctated, relief-modeled decoration, and a burnished or brushed finish.

Chancay: In central Peru, a distinctive type of pottery made by the Chancay people between AD 1000–1500 (from Late Intermediate Period). It is black on white with parallel or checkered design, sometimes with biomorphic figures or painted in soft colors. The most common forms were tall, two-handled, egg-shaped collared jars; bowls and beakers with slightly bowed sides; and large figurines. The pottery is associated with large effigy figurines, dolls, and lacelike textiles. Chancay weaving was considered excellent.

chancel: The part of a church for the choir, often near the altar and on the east side. At one time, only clergy and choir members were permitted in the chancel and it was often set off by a railing or screen.

Chancelade: Magdalenian rock shelters in Dordogne, France, with hearths, harpoons, and mobiliary art. The ochre-covered burial of "Chancelade man," found in 1888, was a *Homo sapiens sapiens*. (*syn.* Raymonden)

Chan Chan: An ancient pre-Inca city on the northern coast of Peru, the capital of the Chimú kingdom, AD c. 1200–1400. The ruins cover nearly 14 square miles (36 square km) and are in good condition because there is no rain. The buildings were made of adobe brick, and there are 10 walled citadels (quadrangles), each containing pyramidal temples, cemeteries, gardens, symmetrical rooms, and reservoirs. These quadrangles were probably the living quarters, burial places, and warehouses of the aristocracy. Most of the city's population (40,000–200,000 total) lived outside the quadrangles in modest quarters. The Chimú kingdom was the chief state in Peru before the establishment of the Inca empire, and its economy was agricultural. The Chimús produced fine textiles and gold, silver, and copper objects. Between 1465–

1470, the Chimú came under Inca rule. Chan Chan was one of the largest Pre-Columbian cities in Peru. (*syn.* Chanchan)

Chandoli: A site in southern India occupied in the 2nd millennium BC. Ground stone axes, copper flat axes and antenna swords/daggers, and pottery of Malwa type have been found as well as urn burials.

Ch'ang-An: An ancient site in China, formerly the capital of the Han, Sui, and T'ang Dynasties, located near the modern city of Sian. It was first used by the western Chou Dynasty (1027–771 BC). Han-yuan Palace contains the tombs of the T'ang imperial family. In the T'ang period, Ch'ang-An was the eastern terminus of the Silk Route and one of the world's great cities. The site of the Qin capital Xianyang is near Xi'an, and the Western Zhou capitals Feng and Hao are supposed to have been in this area as well, possibly lying within the boundaries of the modern Ch'ang-An district southwest of Xi'an. (*syn.* Ch'ang-an, Chang'an)

Chang'an: The capital of both the early Han and Tang Dynasties of China, both walled cities located adjacent to each other. There was a grid street layout and gate wall enclosure in the Tang period. The royal palace was positioned in the north for the first time, and Chang'an became the model for urban development in 7th century AD Japan and Korea. (*syn.* Ch'ang-an)

Changsha: City and capital of Hunan Province, China, where Neolithic sites have been investigated since 1955. Isolated finds hint at Shang and Western Zhou settlement in this area. Over a thousand Chu burials have been excavated, with the richest being the early 2nd century BC tombs at Mawangdui. Artifacts form the Chu capital at Jiang-ling are comparable in date and importance. (*syn.* Ch'ang-sha)

Chanhu-Daro: A city of the Harappan civilization of the 3rd millennium BC, located in the Indus Valley south of Mohenjo-Daro in modern Pakistan. First excavated in the 1930s, it was characterized by a gridiron street plan and drainage system typical of Harappan towns. Evidence was found for the processes of sawing, flaking, grinding, and boring of stone beads. Occasional copper or bronze weapons of "foreign" type are found in late contexts at Chanhu-daro. Excavation also showed that, like Mohenjo-Daro, Chanhu-Daro had been inundated by floods: It was twice destroyed and subsequently rebuilt on a different plan. After the end of the Indus Valley civilization, it was reoccupied by the Jhukar culture. (*syn.* Chanhudaro, Chanhu-daro)

Chania: The site of a Minoan administrative center, Kydonia, in western Crete. No palace has been found at the Bronze Age settlement, but Linear A and Linear B inscriptions have been discovered. (*syn.* Khania, Kydonia)

channeled: The decoration of an artifact with grooves or broad incisions.

channel flake: The long, thin blade of stone removed longitudinally from the base of a fluted Paleo-Indian projectile point by percussion or pressure from the center line of either face. The smooth depression it leaves behind is known as a flute or channel.

Chansen: A settlement site of central Thailand, which traded with India during the first two centuries AD and with Funan sites till the 5th–6th centuries.

chape: The metal mounting, trim, or case of the upper end of a sword scabbard, protecting the tip.

characterization: Methods of examining and identifying characteristic properties of the constituent material of traded goods for identifying their source of origin. This study is mostly done on clay, metal, and stone and involves petrographic thin-section analysis. (*syn.* characterization studies)

Charaman: A stone industry of Zimbabwe and parts of southern and central Zambia where it was the local successor of the Sangoan. Many Charaman assemblages come from surface or river-gravel occurrences, as at Victoria Falls. There are many scrapers, subtriangular points, and other flake tools. Charaman deposits have been found in cave sites, such as Broken Hill, which yielded the remains of *Homo sapiens rhodesiensis*. (*syn.* Proto-Stillbay, Charama)

Charavines: A lake dwelling in Isère, France, which is underwater but well preserved. There were timber houses, and dendrochronology dates the first village to 2740 BC. There are finely flaked flint daggers with coiled willow handles.

charcoal identification: A method of studying charcoal, frequently found in archaeological contexts, to identify the type of tree from which it came. Charcoal is partly burned ("charred") wood, consisting mostly of carbon, sometimes found in situ as burned timbers of buildings and other structures or in hearths, but more frequently widely disseminated through deposits. Its transverse, radial, and tangential sections are examined, as each type of wood has a characteristic structure. The main value of charcoal identification is for showing the use of different resources by ancient people. Charcoal survives because carbon cannot be used by organism decomposition.

Charentian: A Mousterian (Middle Palaeolithic) culture of at least two types, Quina and Ferrassie, of the Charente region of France. Dominance racloirs (side scrapers), Quina retouch, and hand axes have been found. The Charentian seems to originate in the penultimate glacial period and has a distribution across Europe and Russia.

chariot: A light vehicle of war, usually carrying two people, a warrior and a driver. Examples have been found from the Uruk period in Mesopotamia, and the chariot was shown on the standard of Ur. It first appeared in the Near East in the 17 century BC, associated with the immigrant peoples who became the Hyksos, Kassites, and Hurri. Its arrival in Egypt can be fairly reliably dated to the Second Intermediate Period (1650–1550 BC). The Aryans carried it to India, and in China it formed the core of the Shang army. The Mycenaeans introduced it to Europe, where it spread widely and rapidly. It revolutionized warfare by allowing warriors to be transferred rapidly from one part of a battlefield to another. It was mainly for aristocrats, which explains its popularity as a funeral offering. Burials of complete chariots with horses and charioteers have been excavated in Shang China (1200 BC), in Cyprus from the 7th century BC, and among the La Tène Celts. The earliest Celt chariot burials are in the Rhineland and eastern France with dates around 500 BC, and later burials are in east Yorkshire and Europe as far east as Hungary, Bulgaria, and southern Russia. The chariot was replaced by the mounted warrior or knight when horses of sufficient strength had been bred in the late and post-Roman periods.

Charlemagne (c. 742–814): The king of the Franks from AD 768–814, who conquered the Lombard kingdom in Italy, subdued the Saxons, and annexed Bavaria to his kingdom. He is one of the greatest historical and legendary heroes, son of Pepin the Short, who restored the kingdom's laws and economy and re-established the institutions of the Western Church. Charlemagne was an able military leader, fighting campaigns in Spain and Hungary, uniting into one superstate almost all the Christian lands of western Europe. In 800, he also became emperor. His patronage and accomplishments became known as the Carolingian Renaissance. (*syn.* Carolus Magnus, Charles the Great, Charles I of the Holy Roman Empire, Charles I of France)

charred, charring: Converted to charcoal or carbon usually by heat, organic materials may be preserved. Partial burning reduces the materials to a carbon-rich residue. In the case of wood, this residue is charcoal. Many organic materials may not retain their structure and become an amorphous residue. Charred remains are preserved on archaeological sites because carbon is relatively inert in the soil and the microorganisms that normally break down organic material are unable to make use of this form of carbon. Charred remains are a particularly good material for radiocarbon dating.

Charsada: A site in Pakistan, which was the capital of the Achaemenid satrapy of Gandhara. There is a series of mounds, up to 20 meters high, concealing the caravan city of Pushkalavati, with occupation from the 6th century BC to the 2nd or 1st century BC. Excavations near the largest mound, Bala Hisar, identified the defenses overrun by Alexander the Great in 327 BC, a rampart and ditch. A separate mound nearby, Shaikhan, was an Indo-Greek city of the second century BC. (*syn.* Pushkalavati, Peukolaotis)

Chartres: A city in northern France, which was the site of an important pilgrimage church since the Carolingian period (mid-13th century). Chartres was named after a Celtic tribe, the Canutes, who made it their principal Druidic center. It was attacked several times by the Normans and was burned by them in 858. A series of fires destroyed Notre Dame, but after 1145 it was reconstructed as one of Europe's greatest Gothic cathedrals.

chasing: A technique for the decoration of metalwork by engraving on the outside of the raised surface. The metal is worked from the front by hammering with tools that raise, depress, or push aside the metal without removing any from the surface. Chasing is the opposite of embossing, or repoussé, in which the metal is worked from the back to give a higher relief. Strictly, chasing refers to line decoration applied to the face of repoussé work with a tracer, but the term is frequently used more generally to describe any hammered or punched decoration on metal.

Chassey: A Middle Neolithic culture found over most of France, named for the Camp de Chassey, which appeared c. 4300 BC. By this time, Chassey pottery had superseded impressed ware in the south, and the new style is found in caves, village sites, cists, pit graves, and megalithic chamber tombs. The earliest Chassey pottery is often decorated with scratched geometric patterns, whereas the later wares are more plain and have pan-pipe (*flûte de pan*) lugs. In north and central France, the culture appeared c. 3800. In many areas, the Chassey people were the first Neolithic farmers. The pottery and flintwork of the Paris basin differ in many ways from those of the Midi. One distinctive form of vessel, the vase support with scratched decoration, is confined to the Paris basin and western France. Both cave and open settlements were occupied. (*syn.* Chasséen culture)

Chateau Gaillard: A 12th-century castle built by Richard the Lion-Heart on his return from the Third Crusade in 1196. Sitting on the Andelys cliff overlooking the Seine River in France, substantial portions of it still stand. Château Gaillard, the strongest castle of its age, guarded the Seine River Valley approach to Normandy. It was successfully besieged by Philip II in 1204. The French isolated the fort with a double ditch, then collapsed part of the châtelet and penetrated the main fortress through the latrines. (*syn.* [French: "Saucy Castle"])

Chateauneuf-les-Martigues: A large rock shelter northwest of Marseilles in southern France, with a series of deposits from the Upper Palaeolithic to the Neolithic. There was impressed ware and a radiocarbon date in the early 6th millennium BC. It was probably the site of the Roman camp, Maritima Avaticorum. (*syn.* Martigues)

Châtelperronian: An Upper Palaeolithic culture and earlier stage of the Perigordian, concentrated in the Périgord region of France but believed to have originated in southwestern Asia. It is distinguished from contemporary stone tool culture complexes by the presence of curved-backed knives (knives sharpened both on the cutting edge and the back). It is the earliest known blade culture. The Châtelperronian has radiocarbon dates of 31,690 BC ± 250 and 31,550 ± 400 at Grotte du Renne (Arcysur-Cure, Yonne), but it may have started as early as 35,000–34,000. This cave site culture is also characterized by bone tools and weapons (made of ivory or reindeer antler) and flint knives. (*syn.* Chatelperonian, Chatelperron, Chatelperronian, Lower Périgordian; formerly Lower Aurignacian)

Chatham Islands: Ten islands in the South Pacific, 860 kilometers east of New Zealand, which were settled by Polynesians from New Zealand about AD 1000–1200. The culture was a fishing and collecting population until European contact (1791). The original inhabitants, called Moriois, died out following contact with Europeans and conquest by New Zealand Maoris in 1835. Areas of limestone indicate that the islands may once have been part of New Zealand. There are no indigenous mammals, and the reptiles are of New Zealand species.

Chavín de Huántar: The area of the great ruin of the earliest highly developed culture in pre-Columbian Peru, which flourished between about 900 and 200 BC and may have originated c. 1200 BC. During this time, Chavín art spread over the north and central parts of what is now Peru. It is not known whether this was the actual center of origin of the culture and art style. The central building at Chavín de Huántar is a massive temple complex constructed of dressed rectangular stone blocks, with interior galleries and bas-relief carvings on pillars and lintels. The principal motifs of the Chavín style are human, feline, and crocodilian or serpentine figures. Carved stone objects, fantastic pottery that demonstrates the most advanced skill, stone construction, and remarkably sophisticated goldwork have been found. Chavín pottery is known from the decorated types found in the temple and in graves on the northern coast, where it is called Cupisnique. Until the end of the period, the ware was monochrome—dull red, brown, or gray—and stonelike. Vessels were massive and heavy, and the main forms are open bowls with vertical or slightly expanding sides and flat or gently rounded bases, flasks, and stirrup-spouted bottles. The surface may be modeled in relief or decorated by incision, stamping, brushing, rouletting, or dentate rocker stamping. Some bowls have deeply incised designs on both the inside and outside faces. Its art style was never surpassed in the complexity of its iconography. The buildings, which show several periods of reconstruction, consist of various temple platforms containing a series of interlinked galleries and chambers on different levels. In the oldest part of the complex is a granite block, the Lanzón, on which is carved a human figure with feline fangs and with snakes in place of hair. Relief carvings in a similar style decorate the lintels, gateways, and cornices at the site, and human and jaguar heads of stone were on the outside wall of one of the platforms. On the coast, where stone is scarce, the highland architecture is replaced by work in adobe. Further south, the Paracas culture shows strong continuing Chavín influence. (*syn.* Chavín)

Cheddar: A site in Somerset County, England, where a gorge and caverns have offered up human remains and artifacts (stone and bone tools) dating back to the Stone Age. The Gough's Cave finds probably date from 8,000 to 10,000 BC. Cheddar cheese was first made there at or before the beginning of the 12th century and was aged in the caves. (*syn.* adj. Crewellian, Cheddarian)

Chedworth: A site in Cotswold, southern England, with the ruins of a large Roman villa, one of the best-preserved in Britain. The villa was typical of the last years of the Roman occupation. Three phases have been found, AD c. 100–150, early 3rd century, and early 4th century.

cheek piece: A plate or rod of bone, bronze, leather, or another metal, which is attached to the lower rim of a helmet to protect the wearer's cheeks. It is also the name of an attachment from a horse bit to the reins.

Cheetup: A rock shelter in Western Australia with deposits from the Late Pleistocene; cycad plants date to 13,200 bp.

Chelford: An interstadial of the Devensian cold stage (the last glaciation), of c. 61,000 BP according to radiocarbon dating—although it could be older.

Chellean: An early Stone Age industry (Lower Palaeolithic) characterized by crudely worked hand axes. The implements from the type site Chelles-sur-Marne, near Paris, France, which gave the industry its name, are now grouped with the Acheulian industry. The term Chellean, in the sense of earliest hand ax culture, has been replaced by Abbevillian industry. The industry was so-named in the 1880s, replacing the term Acheulian, which was eventually reinstated. (*syn.* Chellian)

chemical analysis: The main use of chemical analysis in archaeology has been the identification of trace, major, and minor elements characteristic of particular sources of raw materials such as obsidian. The methods include x-ray fluorescence spectrometry, optical emission spectrometry, atomic absorption spectrometry, spectrographic x-ray diffraction, and neutron activation analysis. This information can be useful in the study of technology, trade, and distribution.

Chenes: One of the three architectural styles of the Lowland Maya area of north-central Yucatán, AD c. 600–1000, overlapping the Classic and Post-Classic periods. Chenes is a flamboyant style of building distinguished from the Rio Bec and Puuc by its concentration on towerless, low, single-story buildings. Maya architects constructed frontal portals surrounded by the jaws of sky serpents and faced entire buildings with a riot of baroquely carved grotesques and spirals. The best example is at Hochob.

Cheng-chou: The site of the Shang Dynasty capital from 1500–1200 BC, in Honan Province, China, on the Yellow River. Following villages of the Yang Shao and Lung Shan cultures, four phases of Shang occupation have been traced. Cemeteries of pit graves have been found, and a rectangular wall enclosed an area divided into different quarters. Outside this city, in addition to remains of large public buildings, a complex of small settlements has been discovered. Since 1950, archaeological finds have shown that there were Neolithic settlements in the area. The site remained occupied after the Shang Dynasty moved its capital again; Chou (post-1050 BC) tombs have also been discovered. It is thought that in the Western Chou period (1111–771 BC) it became the fief of a family named Kuan. In AD 605, it was first called Cheng-chu. (*syn.* Cheng Chou, Chengxian)

Chenla: A kingdom of the Khmers of the 6th–8th centuries AD in what is now southern Laos. It expanded to absorb the territories formerly occupied by Funan (now Cambodia). At the beginning of the 8th century, it split into "Water Chenla" and "Land Chenla." Chenla ceased to exist when the kingdom of Angkor was established in 802. From local inscriptions, remarkable sculptures, architectural remains, and Chinese sources, it is clear that it was an Indianized kingdom. There was an important cult site called Wat Phu (Laos).

Cheops (fl early 26th century BC): The second king of the 4th Dynasty (c. 2575–2465 BC) of Egypt who erected the Great Pyramid of Giza. It is the largest of the three pyramids, the length of each side at the base averaging 755¾ feet (230.4 m) and its original height being 481⅖-feet (147 m). Cheops/Khufu reigned c. 2570 BC. His sons, Djedefre (Redjedef) and Chephren (Khafre), succeeded him. (*syn.* Kheops, Khufu, Khufwey, Khnomkhufwey)

Chephren (fl late 26th century BC): The fourth king of the 4th Dynasty (c. 2575–2465 BC) of Egypt, Cheops' (Khufu) son. Chephren erected the second pyramid of the Giza group as well as the Great Sphinx. He reigned c. 2540 BC. The middle pyramid measures 707¾ feet (216 m) on each side and was originally 471 feet (143 m) high. Many consider the Great Sphinx to bear Chephren/Khafre's features. (*syn.* Khafre, Khephren, Khafra, Souphis)

Chernigov: A town on the River Dniepr in western Russia, whose archaeology suggests a 7th-century origin, although the site was first mentioned in 907 as founded by the Swedish Vikings. It was one of the chief towns of Kievan Rus and center of a princedom. Its Spassky Cathedral dates from 1024. It was principally a trading town on the north-south route across eastern Europe between the Black Sea and Baltic areas. (*syn.* Cernigov)

chert: A coarse type of siliceous (silica) rock, a form of quartz, used for the manufacture of stone tools where flint was not available. It is of poorer quality than flint, formed from ancient ocean sediments, and often has a semiglassy finish. It is pinkish, white, brown, gray, or blue-gray in color. Flint, chert, and other siliceous rocks like obsidian are very hard and produce a razor-sharp edge when properly flaked into tools. This crystalline form of the mineral silica is found as nodules in limestones. Varieties of chert are jasper, chalcedony, agate, flint, and novaculite. Chert and flint provided the main source of tools and weapons for Stone Age man. (*syn.* hornstone, phthanite)

Chesowanja: A site in Kenya, dated 1.4 million years ago, which has produced very early evidence of fire in association with tools. If it was man-made, as opposed to a natural cause such as lightning, then there is the question as to which hominid was responsible: *Homo erectus* or *Austrlopithecus robustus.*

Chester: The site of the Roman headquarters of the 20th Legion. It was an important Roman town but was deserted by the early 5th century. There are a number of Roman remains, including the foundations of the north and east walls. Modern Chester overlies the massive Roman camp (castra) of some 24 hectares, sited strategically on the River Dee. Perhaps already a small fort by AD 60, the fortress and an aqueduct were firmly established in 76–79. Outside the fortifications lay a civilian settlement, an amphitheater, cemeteries, and quarries. Roman abandonment came about 380. (*syn.* Roman Deva, Castra Devana)

chevaux de frise: A form of defense consisting of closely spaced stakes, spikes, or stones placed on end, which served to impede or break up a cavalry charge. Chevaux de frises are sometimes found as the outer defense of hill forts in prehistoric Europe.

Chevdar: An early Neolithic tell site in Bulgaria. It was the target of one of the earliest uses of flotation in European archaeology, on soil samples from floors and ovens. (*syn.* Cevdar)

Chiao: A former independent kingdom of Nam Viet, which became the Chinese province of Chiao, later incorporated into the Han Empire in 111 BC. The province of Chiao consisted of nine commanderies, six of which correspond to the present Chinese provinces of Kwangtung and Kwangsi and the island of Hainan, while the other three formed the northern half of present Vietnam, which gained independence from China in 939. (*syn.* Giao Chi, Giao Chau, Giao, Chiao-Chih, Giao-chi)

Chiapa de Corzo: A site on the Grijalva River in Chiapas, Mexico, with one of the longest occupational sequences in Mesoamerica, c. 1500 BC to the present. It flourished in Late Pre-Classic to Early Classic times, with adobe construction, ceramics and figurines, and then pyramids dating to 550 BC and residential complexes of cut stone to 150 BC. The style and iconography of certain artifacts indicate contact with Izapa and Kaminaijuyu in the Late Pre-Classic. Hundreds of broken sherds tell of trade contact with sites in the Penen and with Monte Alban and Teotihuacan in the Early Classic.

Chibcha: A South American people who lived in the high valleys around the modern cities of Bogota and Tunja in Colombia. They had a population of more than 500,000 and were more centralized politically than any other South American people outside the Inca Empire. Each of the many small districts had its own chief, and they belonged to several lesser states that in turn were allied to two major states, each headed by a hereditary ruler. The arrival of the Spanish cut short the Chibchas' development, and their political structure was crushed in the 16th century. Their language was no longer spoken by the 18th century. Archaeological evidence is of a scattered rural population who cultivated highland crops and traded salt and emeralds for cotton, gold, and luxury goods. Gold, copper and tumbaga (a copper-gold alloy) were also worked in a variety of techniques. The ceremonial coating of the chief's body with gold leaf may well be the origin of the El Dorado legend. Chibcha's ceremonial practice centered around sun worship and included human sacrifice. (*syn.* Muisca)

Chicanel: A phase of the Lowland Maya Pre-Classic, the Late Formative culture of Petén, dating from 300 BC to AD 150. It was characterized by architectural and ceramic traits that convey the rise of the Classic Maya civilization: temple-pyramids, corbelled arches, and painted murals. The sites are quite uniform, and there was a variety of ceramic forms. Chicanel pottery includes dishes with wide, grooved rims, bowls, and vessels resembling ice buckets. Figurines are absent. Temple platforms (e.g., Uaxactún) were built by facing a cemented-rubble core with thick layers of plaster. At Tikal, a huge Maya ceremonial center, the acropolis was begun in Chicanel times, and white-stuccoed platforms and stairways with polychromed masks were much like Uaxactún. There is also a huge site, El Mirador, in the northern part of Petén. The El Mirador construction dwarfs even that of Tikal, although El Mirador flourished only through the Chicanel phase. Chicanel-like civilization is also known in Yucatán, where some temple pyramids of enormous size are datable to the Late Formative. Another important site is the cave of Loltún in Yucatán.

Chichén Itzá: The site of a ruined ancient Mayan city in south-central Yucatán state, Mexico. Chichén Itzá was founded in about the 6th century AD, presumably by Mayan peoples of the Yucatán Peninsula who had occupied the region since Pre-Classic, or Formative, period times (1500 BC–AD 300). The only source of water in the region is from wells (Mayan cenotes) formed by the collapse of portions of the limestone formation of the area. Two big cenotes on the site made it a suitable place for the city and gave it its name, from *chi* ("mouths"), *chen* ("wells"), and Itzá, the name of the tribe that settled there. There are traces of early occupation at the site, but the oldest surviving buildings are in the Puuc style of the 8th–early 10th centuries. In the 10th century, after the collapse of the Maya cities of the southern lowlands, Chichén Itzá was invaded—probably by the Toltecs. New buildings have their closest parallels at Tula, and offerings thrown into the Sacred Cenote, or Well of Sacrifice, show widespread trade contacts. Chichén Itzá was the dominant power in Yucatán until about 1200, when it was superseded by Mayapán. At the center of the site is the Castillo or temple-pyramid of Kulkulkan, the Maya equivalent of Quetzacóatl; this is linked by a causeway to the nearby Sacred Cenote. Other major structures include the temple of the Warriors (in front of which stands a Chacmool), large "dance platforms," the Group of a Thousand Columns, the temple of the Jaguars, and the largest Ball Court in Mesoamerica. Bas-relief carvings on a massive skull rack (*tzompantli*) show the ball game to be associated with scenes of sacrifice. Relief carvings with themes of conquest and violence abound, and representations of Maya warriors submitting to Toltec warriors have been found on gold discs recovered from the Sacred Cenote.

Ch'i-chia culture: A late Neolithic culture in northwest China dating from c. 1700 BC, which shows North Eurasian influence. Descendant of earlier painted pottery Neolithic cultures, it is characterized by the use of amphora-like jars with loop handles and comblike designs and by copper tools (axes and rectangular knives). The culture survived into historic times, and remains from as late as the 1st century BC have been found. Evidence of the culture was first found in Ch'i-chia-p'ing in the early 1920s by the Swedish geologist Johan Gunnar Andersson. In the 1950s, important finds were located in nearby Yang-wa-wan and Ts'ui-chia-chuang by the Chinese archaeologists Pei Wen-chung and Hsia Nai. The Ch'i-chia people lived in large villages in terraces along the Huang Ho (Yellow River) and buried their dead in pits. (*syn.* Qijia)

Chichimec: A collective name applied to various barbarian tribes who invaded the valley of central Mexico from the northwest from c. 7th–13th centuries AD in periodic waves and migrations. The Aztec, or Mexica, were one of the competing Chichimec tribes. Some of these groups, who may have been farmers, may have entered the Valley of Mexico after the fall of Teotihuacán, and there is a Chicimec constitu-

ent in Toltec culture. The Chichimec period proper, however, begins after the destruction of Tula and the decline of Toltec influence in about AD 1200. In 1224, a band of Náhuatl-speaking Chichimecs entered the northern part of the Valley and established a kingdom at Tenayuca. After their arrival, the barbarians settled down again to farming life, became civilized, and were eventually absorbed into the Aztec confederation. In the north, some independent Chichimecs maintained their nomadic and hunting way of life until the Spanish conquest. The Chichimecs are also associated with the introduction of the bow and arrow into the Valley of Mexico. Their language, also called Chichimec, is of the Oto-Pamean language stock.

Chicoid: One of the two ceramic series (the other, Meillacod) that seem to have developed out of the Ostinoid series. They originated near the type site of Boca Chica, Dominican Republic, and then influenced much of the eastern Antilles. The Chicoid materials represent the ball game, Zemis, and include a variety of wood and stone carvings, and a strong Barrancoid influence is evident in the ceramics (modeled ornamentation and incision). The series first appears in AD c. 1000 and continues until European contact. (*syn.* Boca Chica)

chiefdom: A form of sociopolitical organization in which there is a chief who is the central authority over a social ranking or hierarchy. Individuals' status is determined by birth and closeness of relationship to the chief. The chief occupies a central role socially, politically, and economically. The central authority enables considerable human effort to be mobilized and directed, often into the building of large public works such as monuments or irrigation systems and in the establishment of mechanisms for distributing goods and services. A chiefdom generally has a permanent ritual and ceremonial center, as well as being characterized by local specialization in crafts.

chief steward: In Egypt's New Kingdom and Late Period, the title of the administrator of an estate of the temple of a god, the king or his mortuary temple, a member of the royal family, or even a private individual. Because of the economic importance of the function, chief stewards were very influential. One, Senenmut, combined the offices of Chief Steward of Amun, of Queen Hatshepsut, and of Princess Neferure. He designed and built Queen Hatshepsut's temple near the tomb of Mentuhotep II at Deir al-Bahri. Amenhotpe Huy, the brother of Ramose, was Chief Steward of Memphis in the reign of Amenophis III. (*syn.* steward)

Chien ware: A dark brown or blackish glazed Chinese stoneware made for domestic use, mainly during the Sung Dynasty (960–1279) and into the early 14th century. Within its limited palette, Chien ware has a range of variations. By careful control of the kiln temperatures, streaking and iridescent patches were formed on the glaze to make the "hare's fur" and "oil spot" glaze, which were the most prized. Large deposits of kiln wastes have been found at Chien-yang and Chien-an in Fukien Province. Tea bowls are by far the most common, although not the only, form of Chien ware that survives. Used by Ch'an (Zen) Buddhist monks, the highly esteemed tea bowls were carried back to Japan by Japanese monks who had visited China to study Buddhism. Until the late 16th century, Chien ware was the type of tea bowl preferred for the highly ritualized Japanese tea ceremony. (*syn.* Chien Yao, Jian Yao, Temmoku ware, Tenmoku ware)

Chiflet, Jean-Jacques (1588–1673): Philip IV's (Spain) surgeon who was entrusted with studying and reporting on objects found in the tomb of Childeric I (AD 481/482), Clovis's father, discovered at Tournai in 1653. *Anastasis Childerici I*, printed in 1655, may be regarded as the earliest scientific archaeological publication.

Chifumbaze: An Early Iron Age complex found over a wide area of eastern/southeastern Africa, dating from 2,500 years ago until the 11th century AD. The sites have evidence of metallurgy and manufacture of pottery. The complex is divided into the Urewe or Eastern Stream tradition and Kalundu or Western Stream tradition.

Chihua: Phase of 4300–3000 BC, in the Ayacucho basin of Peru, where transhumance and agriculture may have been introduced. The beginning of agriculture in the highlands preceded settled village life, in contrast to Peruvian coastal lifeways.

Chilca: A site in the coastal valley south of modern Lima, Peru, where excavations have revealed settlements dating to the Pre-Ceramic period c. 4200 BC. The Chilca Monument was originally a summer camp and later, owing to an increasingly warm climate, became favorable for a subsistence pattern called *encanto*. There are remains of conical huts of cane thatched with sedge. The dead were buried wrapped in twined-sedge mats and the skins of the guanaco. The *lomas*, patches of vegetation outside the valleys that were watered at that season by fogs, began to dry up. The lomas had provided wild seeds, tubers, and large snails; and deer, guanaco, owls, and foxes were hunted. The camps were eventually abandoned c. 2500 BC in favor of permanent fishing villages. Dolichocephalic human remains date to this period but appear ultimately to have been replaced by brachycephalic types some time after 2500 BC.

Childe, Vere Gordon (1892–1957): Australian-born British historian whose study of European prehistory in the 2nd and 3rd millennia BC brought his development of the diffusionist theory, which was to explain the relation between Europe and the Middle East. Childe introduced the concept of the archaeological culture. The Diffusionist view interpreted all major developments in prehistoric Europe in terms of the spread of either people or ideas from the Near East. Childe was professor of prehistoric archaeology at the University of Edinburgh and then director of the Institute of Archaeology, University of London. His many publications include *The Dawn of European Civilization* (1925; 6th ed., 1957), *The Danube in Prehistory* (1929), *The Bronze Age (1930), Man Makes Himself* (1936), *What Happened in History* (1942), and *Society and Knowledge* (1956).

Chimú: South American Indians who created the largest and most important political system in Peru before the Inca, and who developed large-scale irrigation systems. The distinctive pottery of the Chimú aids in dating Andean civilization in the late periods along the north coast of Peru. The black pottery had molded reliefs with some vessels in the shape of people, animals, houses, and everyday items. The stirrup-spout and spout-and-bridge vessels are the most common forms. There were also objects of silver and gold. The Chimú expanded by conquest, and the state began to form. According to legend, the political entity was the creation of Ñançen-pinco (reigned AD c. 1370) but archaeology shows that Chimú material culture developed out of the terminal Moche (Mochica) culture of the north coast from c. 850/900 onward. Chanchan was the capital, a vast settlement of giant rectangular enclosures. In 1465–1470, however, they were conquered by the Inca, who absorbed much of the culture, including their political organization, irrigation systems, and road engineering.

chinampa: A system of cultivation on small, stationary, artificial islands made of vegetation and mud in shallow freshwater lakes, created in the Valley of Mexico (Xochimilco). These very fertile fields were created by massive Aztec reclamation projects and consisted of little islands, each averaging 6 to 10 meters (19.7 to 32.8 feet) wide and 100 to 200 meters (30.5 to 656.2 feet) long, with fertilization from organic wastes in mud and aquatic life. Periodic renewal of this mud layer created a permanent supply of fertile soil so that as one crop was harvested it could be immediately replaced with another. Much of the Aztecs' Tenochtitlan used such intensively farmed, reclaimed land. The champas were normally separated by a system of canals, which allowed both access and water circulation. (*syn.* chinampas; floating garden)

China Lake: Prehistoric sites along the Mojave Desert in southern California, including flakes, mammoth remains, and so on, and thought to have been occupied c. 12,000 BP.

Chincha: A powerful ancient state on the southern coast of Peru, primarily from the study of historical sources, and which flourished during the Late Intermediate Period, c. 1000–1478. Chincha reached the height of its power in the early 15th century when it also controlled part of the Pisco Valley, and it retained a certain prestige under the Inca after their conquest of the area in 1476. The main city was La Centinela, which included pyramids, platforms, and courts surrounded by storerooms and dwellings of the nobility. Chincha prospered through trade (black ware pottery and some polychromes) with the adjacent highlands and northern coastal areas, and there were about 30,000 households. Other sites include the administrative complex at Tambo de Mora (probably the capital) and La Cumbe. The Chincha vanished within the first three decades of the Spanish invasion.

Chinchorro: A site on the coast of northern Chile where the earliest intentionally mummified humans have been found, dating to c. 7000 bp. The bodies were disemboweled, skinned, and covered with clay, and clay masks were placed on the faces.

Chindadn point: A small teardrop-shaped bifacial point found in central Alaska and dating to c. 12,000–10,000 bp; they are diagnostic of the Nenana complex.

Chin Dynasty: A Chinese dynasty (AD 1115–1234) founded by the Jurchen tribes of Manchuria, who were formerly vassals of the Khitans or Liao Dynasty (AD 916–1125). They overran most of northern China and captured the Sung capital of K'ai-feng, forcing the Chinese to move their capital south to Hang-chou in 1126. The empire covered much of Inner Asia and all of North China. (*syn.* Jin, Juchen, Jurchen, Ju-Chen, Ruzhen, Jurched, Jurchid)

Ch'in Dynasty: Dynasty of 221–206 BC, which unified China into a single empire. The Ch'in, from which the name China is derived, established the approximate boundaries and basic administrative system that Chinese dynasties were to follow for the next 2,000 years. The dynasty was originated by the state of Ch'in, one of the many small feudal states into which China was divided between 771–221 BC. In 247, the boy king Chao Cheng came to the throne, and he completed the Ch'in conquests and created the Ch'in Empire. Chao Cheng proclaimed himself Ch'in Shih huang-ti ("First Sovereign Emperor of Ch'in"). To rule the vast territory, the Ch'in installed a rigid, authoritarian government; the dynasty standardized the writing system, standardized the measurements of length and weight and the width of highways, abolished all feudal privileges, built the Great Wall, and in 213 ordered all books burned except those on utilitarian subjects. Excavations have found examples of the standard weights and measures imposed on China. There is also a spectacular large group of lifesize pottery figures of warriors, horses, and chariots found in an area adjacent to the tomb of the first Ch'in emperor, Ch'in Shih huang-ti. (*syn.* Kin, Qin)

Ch'ing Dynasty: The last imperial dynasty of China AD 1644–1911/12), Manchu in origin. Under the Ch'ing, the territory tripled in size, and the population grew from 150,000,000 to 450,000,000. An integrated national economy was established. There are some elaborately constructed tombs. Ch'ing porcelain is technically masterful, but Ch'ing artists were individualistic and innovative. (*syn.* Qing, Manchu dynasty)

Ch'ing-lien-kang culture: The name given an Eastern Neolithic culture of China, c. 4000–3000 BC, found in the provinces of southern Shantung, Kiangsu, and northern Chekiang. Painted pottery with flowerlike designs had certain affinities with pottery from the western Neolithic Yang-Shao culture. Pottery on high pierced stands, fine flat polished axes, and decorative pendants in jade have also been found.

Chiot pottery: Archaic pottery of the Greek island of Chios, although it may also have been made at Naucratis. The pots and chalices had a cream slip and glazed interior. Decoration on the exterior was scenes with figures; inside were floral patterns.

Chiozza: A Neolithic settlement site in Emilia in northern Italy, of the later 5th or early 4th millennium BC. Structural remains are oval and circular pits. The pottery was square mouthed, and the term Chiozza is sometimes used for this type of pottery or its latter phase.

chip carving: A technique of decoration with the use of an ax, hatchet, mallet, and/or chisel, which probably originated in the Roman and Celtic world. The technique was adapted by Germanic woodcarvers to make animal ornaments and by metalsmiths of the Migration period. This excised decoration was done by cutting from the surface triangular and rectilinear small chips. The end result was a pattern of combined V-shaped incisions, with a glittering faceted appearance. It is found in woodwork and pottery, when it has to be done before the clay is fired. False relief is a special version of this technique. Examples are the Tassilo Chalice (Kremsmünster Abbey, Austria) and the Lindau Gospels book cover (Pierpont Morgan Library, New York City) (*syn.* chip carving)

chippable: Of a stone, capable of being worked to produce a tool or other such artifact. Chipped-stone artifacts are the class of lithic artifacts produced by fracturing flakes from a core. (*syn.* chipped-stone)

chipped stone tool: Any tool produced by flaking or chipping of pieces from a stone core to produce an implement.

chipping floor: A workshop area characterized by debris from the manufacture of chipped stone tools. In the process of flaking stone tools, large quantities of waste chips are produced. Stone Age chipping floors are often found with finished tools and indications of other activities.

Chirand: A site on the lower Ganges River in northeast India with five periods of occupation: Neolithic (Chirand I), Chalcolithic (Chirand II A–B), Northern Black Polished Ware (Chirand III), early 1st millennium AD, and medieval.

Chirand I dated to the early 2nd millennium BC and perhaps the 3rd.

Chiricahua: The second of three chronological stages of the Cochise culture in southern Arizona and New Mexico, with dates clustering between 4000–500 BC. The appearance of distinctive, side-notched projectile points indicates an interest in hunting although a mixed food-gathering economy is indicated by assemblages commonly including cobble manos, shallow basin grinding slabs, choppers, and scrapers. There were large base camps, storage pits, and outlying specialized-activity camps that show some permanence. There is evidence from Bat Cave in New Mexico of the cultivation of primitive maize.

Chiripa: An early village site on the southern end of Lake Titicaca in Bolivia, dating to the Early and Middle Horizon. Late Chiripa pottery of the Early Horizon period (1800–200 BC) is decorated with cream on red color zones, separated by incised lines. Early pottery is a cream-on-white ware, decorated with geometric designs. The common form is a flat-bottomed, vertical-sided open bowl. The artistic style is linked to Pucara and Tiahuanaco. There is a series of rectangular rooms, some with underfloor stone-lined graves, arranged around a rectangular plaza. An unusual feature is the storage space between the double walls of some structures.

Chiriquí: An area of Panama known for its fine gold objects and elegant pottery, with dates from AD 1100 to the Spanish conquest, although it may have begun centuries earlier in the highlands. The pottery is often decorated with negative painting or modeled animals. Some large stone sculptures from Penonomé, in Chiriquí, suggest the use of stone in large structures, but apparently all these structures were destroyed in the years after the Spanish Conquest.

chi-square test: A statistical test that is used to measure the significant differences between sets of observed values and those that would be expected and to determine whether the deviation from what was expected is more than random chance suggests. It can be used for many different archaeological observations, such as examining the existence of an association between settlement distribution and distinct ecological zones in a region, or between different fabrics and decorative styles in pottery production. From the data, the number expected in each zone on a random distribution can be calculated by proportion, and the deviation between expectation and observation measured. It is then possible to assess whether the observed data could have arisen by chance, or whether some other factor is affecting it. Karl Pearson developed the test.

Chivateros: A stratified, ancient quarry/worship site just north of Lima, Peru—an area of coastal *lomas* (areas of fog vegetation). Excavations revealed a lithic flake industry as early as the Late Pleistocene, dating between 9,000 to 11,000 years ago. Wood fragments helped define a Chivateros I period of c. 9500–8000 BC. There is also a red zone with some flint chips, which, by comparison with artifacts of the nearby Oquendo workshop, date to pre-10,500 BC. The whole industry is characterized by burins and bifaces with the upper level (Chinateros II) containing long, keeled, leaf-shaped projectile points that resemble points from both Lauricocha II and El Jobo. Dating has been aided by the deposition of both loess and salt crust layers, which suggest alternating dryness and humidity and which can be synchronized with glacial activity in the Northern Hemisphere.

chlorite: A soft gray, green, or black silicate mineral used for seals and vessels, also called steatite. Chlorite is a common rock-forming mineral in clastic sediments and in hydrothermally altered igneous rocks; chlorites are widespread and important constituents of such metamorphic rocks as green schists or chlorite schists. (*syn.* steatite, soapstone)

chocolate flint: A high-quality flint of the Holy Cross Mountains in Poland, used for artifacts from the Mesolithic to Early Bronze Age. It is homogeneous and has excellent flaking qualities.

Choga Mami: A settlement site of the Samarra culture in southeast Iraq with radiocarbon dates of the late 6th millennium BC. There are several occupation phases from the Samarran to the 'Ubaid culture. Cattle, sheep, and goats were raised, and wheat, barley, and flax cultivated with the aid of irrigation. The site has buildings of mud brick; houses were rectangular and had ranges of rooms, in two or three rows. A mud-brick tower guarded the entrance to the settlement. Artifacts include Samarran painted pottery and elaborate female figurines of clay.

Choga Mish: A site in southwest Iran occupied in the 6th millennium BC. The earliest layers have painted pottery related to that from Muhammed Jaffar, followed by pottery of Tepe Sabz and Susiana A.

Choga Zanbil: An ancient Elamite site located near Susa in southwestern Iran. It is especially known for its remains dating to the Middle Elamite period (c. 1500–1000 BC), when the Elamite ruler Untash-Gal built a magnificent ziggurat, temples, and a palace. The remains of the ziggurat, the largest one known, are 335 feet (102 m) square and 80 feet (24 m) high, less than half its estimated original height. Other palaces, a reservoir, and the fortification walls have been excavated in the city, which was lavishly laid out but never completed. There is also a variety of small artifacts, including an excellent collection of Middle Elamite cylinder seals, and evidence of glass and glazes. (*syn.* Dur-Untash, Choga Zambil, Chogha Zambil, Dur Untashi)

Choisy-au-Bac: A settlement site at the confluence of the Oise and Aisne Rivers in France, occupied from the Late Bronze Age to Hallstatt D in three main phases. There are bronze-working debris and iron-working furnaces.

Chojnice-Pienki: A late Mesolithic culture in Poland, overlapping in space and time with the Janislawice culture during the late Boreal and Atlantic climatic periods. It is characterized by trapeze-shaped projectile points.

chokkomon: In Japanese archaeology, a design of shattered spirals engraved on artifacts of the Kofun period.

Chokurcha: Middle Palaeolithic cave sites in the Crimea, Ukraine. One had three occupation levels associated with woolly mammoth, steppe bison, and wild ass, and the artifacts were side scrapers and bifacial foliates. The other cave had wild ass, side scrapers, and some mobiliary art.

Cholula: One of the great cities and religious centers of ancient Mexico, first occupied c. 800–300 BC. Cholulu, Nahuatl for "place of springs," was a town dedicated to the god Quetzalcoatl and is known for its many domed churches, which the Spanish built on top of the natives' temples. Cholula was a major center of the pre-conquest Mesoamerican Indian culture as far back as the Early Classic period (AD 100–600) and reached its maximum growth in the Late Classic period (900–1200). It came within the orbit of the Teotihuacán civilization, during which time a major pyramid was built and then enlarged three times to produce the largest pyramid in Mesoamerica (177 ft or 55 m high). Tunneling has revealed the older pyramids nesting inside the final version. Around AD 1300, Cholula became a center of the Mexteca-Puebla culture. Cholula polychrome wares were highly prized by the Aztecs. When the Spaniards reached Cholula, they found a splendid city dominated by the ruins of the Great Pyramid. The Cholulans, who were makers and traders of textiles and pottery, were Nahuatl speakers and at the time of the conquest owed a nominal allegiance to Montezuma. Cholula was one of the independent Post-Classic centers to survive after the fall of Teothihuacan.

Chondwe: Early Iron Age site in Zambia, dating to the 4th–5th centuries AD. There is evidence linking it with the Lusaka area and other areas to the west, for small-scale exploitation of the region's copper deposits, and some regional trade.

chopper: Any large, simple stone or pebble tool with a single, transverse cutting edge. It was used for hacking, breaking, or chopping and was especially characteristic of Middle Pleistocene, pre-Acheulian industries of the Old World, such as Choukoutien, the Clactonian in England, and the earliest levels of Oldowan industries. This crude tool was made by striking a limited number of flakes from the edge of a cobble or fist-size rock to produce a coarse cutting edge. It persisted until the Neolithic. (*syn.* chopping tool)

Choris: An early form of the Norton tradition of Western Arctic prehistory, dating to c. 1500–500 BC. The type site is at Kotsebue Sound. Cape Krusentern, Point Barrow, and Onion Portage are other Arctic sites with the characteristic coarse stamped pottery. Tool assemblages are diverse with some of polished slate. Oil lamps first appear in Choris times.

Chotnica: Tell settlement site of the Late Neolithic, c. late 5th–early 4th millennium BC, in northern Bulgaria. The cultures found represent regional variants of Rumanian groups of the lower Danube Valley. There are three main occupation horizons: I, with pits and post holes and a rich pottery assemblage; II, Boian level with ceramics; and III, a complete village plan with over 15 houses. A hoard of more than 44 gold ornaments was found in the third horizon. (*syn.* Hotnica)

Chou: The dynasty that ruled ancient China from 1122–256/255 BC), establishing the political and cultural characteristics that would be identified with China for the next 2,000 years. Some date the dynasty to 1027–1050 BC. The Chou coexisted with the Shang for many years, just west of the Shang territory in what is now Shensi Province. At various times, they were a friendly tributary state to the Shang, alternatively warring with them. The Chou overthrew the Shang in 1027 BC, and the dynasty was itself destroyed by the Ch'in in 256. Its capital in the Western Chou period was at Tsung Chou in Shensi, moving to Loyang in Honan in 771, to begin the Eastern Chou period. The archaeological evidence comes mainly from the excavation of tombs. Iron came into use c. 500 BC, both forged and cast. Bronze remained the material for weapons, and the Chou bronzes are the most famous of their artworks. The sword, crossbow, and use of roof tiles were other technological innovations of the dynasty. (*syn.* Chou Dynasty, Zhou)

Choukoutien: A type site near Peking, China, of an Upper and Middle Paleolithic culture. It is the place where 40 of the first skeletons of *Homo erectus* were found—in limestone fissures of Middle Pleistocene deposits, probably of Mindel date, some 500,000 years old. The find also yielded extinct animals; flake, core, and chopping tools of quartz and sandstone; and traces of fire. From another area came skeletons of *Homo sapiens* with stone and bone tools of the Upper Palaeolithic. (*syn.* adj. Choukoutienian)

chous: A Greek or Roman measure of liquids, containing one eighth of a Roman amphora, or about 7 pints. It was also equal to 12 Greek cotyle. (*syn.* congius)

Christy, Henry (1810–1865): English archaeologist and ethnologist who journeyed from Mexico's Toltec remains to Hudson's Bay to the caves of southern France and who supported other excavations after a successful banking career. He assisted French archaeologist Edouard Lartet in his investigation of the series of Palaeolithic caves in southwest

France, including Laugerie Haute, La Madeleine, Les Eyzies, and Le Moustier. With Christy, Lartet went on to show that the Stone Age included successive phases of human culture. Their research was published as *Reliquiae Aquitanicae* (Aquitanian Remains) in 1865–1875 with money left by Christy in his will. Christy left Palaeolithic material to be divided between France and Britain, and his trustees presented the rest of the ethnological collection to the British Museum together with money for future acquisition. The Christy Collection now contains about 30,000 specimens.

chromatography: A technique of separating colored substances and analyzing their chemical structure by chromotographic adsorption. Differences in the rate of movement along a liquid or solid column are noted and used for the identification of organic substances. Archaeologically this can be useful for identifying sources, as for amber. There are several methods of chromatography, but particularly used in archaeology are paper and gas. In the former, a solution of the substance to be examined is placed at the end of a piece of filter paper; the end is then dipped into a solvent, which moves the constituents of the sample along the paper by capillary action. Different substances reach different points on the filter paper and, by comparison with reference substances, can be identified. Gas chromatography is done by introducing the mixture into a column of material. The mixture is carried through by gases, and measurements of the gas coming through over time are made by a gas detector. The use of gas chromatography in the study of amber has shown that different sources produce different chromatograms.

chronology: Any method used to order time and to place events in the sequence in which they occurred. A sequential ordering that places cultural entities in temporal, and often spatial, distribution. It involves the collection of dates or successive datings establishing the position in time of a series of phenomena such as the phases of a civilization or the events of the history of a state. A chronology is relative/floating when only the order of a succession of facts is known, but not their dates, and absolute when the opposite is true. For periods or areas for which no textual evidence is available, relative chronologies have to be established, and these are mostly based on pottery sequences and typology. Relative chronology is also based on the application of the principles of stratigraphy and cross-dating. The discovery of inscribed monuments and calendars associated with dated astronomical observations contributed to the development of an Egyptian chronology, and it has served as a framework—through cross-dating—for all other Near Eastern chronologies. Inscribed Egyptian objects found in Near Eastern contexts have allowed the latter to be dated. Absolute chronology is based on scientific methods such as radiocarbon dating, thermoluminescence dating, and archaeomagnetism.

Dates are often calibrated with dendrochronological dates. For dates after 1500 BC, an absolute chronology is not likely to change by more than 10 years.

chronometric date: A date indicating that a measured value of time (years, centuries) has elapsed since a past event occurred.

chronometric dating: Any technique of dating that relies on chronological measurement such as calendars, radiocarbon dates, and so on, and that gives the result in calendar years before the present, or BP. Most of these techniques produce results with a standard deviation, but they have a relation to the calendar, which relative dating techniques do not. Among the most useful chronometric dating techniques are radiocarbon dating, potassium argon dating, and thermoluminescence dating. Dendrochronology, the relation of dated ancient trees with live trees, has no standard deviation and is the most accurate of all, although not universally applicable. Chronometric dating has developed in the last 30 years and has revolutionized archaeology. (*syn.* absolute dating; chronometry)

chryselephantine statue: A type of figurine sculpture made of ivory and gold. The flesh was of ivory and the drapery of gold. These were produced in ancient Egypt, Mesopotamia, and Crete, and in Greece from the 6th century BC. They were often colossal cult figures placed in the interiors of major temples, such as that of Athena by Pheidias, which stood in the Parthenon on the Akropolis at Athens and was 40 feet high, and that of Zeus, 45 feet high, also by Pheidias, in the temple of Olympia.

chthonic: Of the underworld; term used to describe phenomena relating to the underworld and the earth, including deities such as Geb, Aker, and Osiris.

Ch'u: One of the most important independent states of south-central China between 770–221 BC, during the second half of the Chou Dynasty. It emerged in the fertile Yangtze River Valley just outside the Chinese culture of the time. It was a great military threat to other Chinese states as the state was barbarian in origin. Ch'u began to expand rapidly into China proper, conquering much of present-day Honan province, and its people soon began to acquire Chinese speech and customs. From the 8th century until its destruction by Qin in the 3rd century BC, Chu was the largest and most powerful of the Eastern Zhou states. Artifacts include casting of fine inlaid bronzes, weapons, ritual vessels, bells, and drums, and mirrors, and the state was known also for lacquer and silk. Lacquered objects range from containers to wooden effigies, musical instruments, coffins, and other wooden tomb furniture. Sites were discovered near Tung-t'ing (Yungmeng) Lake and in Xiasi and Xinyang, but Ch'u remains are most densely concentrated at Jiangling in southern Hubei and Changsha in northern Hunana. The Ch'u capital was at Jiangling from 689–278 BC, when the city fell to Qin. The Ch'u court retreated to the Huai Valley and stayed there until its final overthrow in 221 BC. Archaeological and historical sources show it to have been a distinctive, highly civilized cultural and political entity. (*syn.* Ch'u state; Chu)

Ch'ü-chia-ling culture: Neolithic culture of central China in the middle and lower Yangtze River Valley in the 4th and 3rd millennia. It followed the Yang-Shao culture and preceded the Lung-Shan culture and shared a significant number of traits with the Ta-hsi culture. There was cultivation of rice, flat polished axes, ring-footed vessels, goblets with sharply angled profiles, ceramic whorls, and black pottery with designs painted in red after firing. Characteristic Ch'ü-chia-ling ceramic objects include eggshell-thin goblets and bowls painted with black or orange designs; double-waisted bowls; tall, ring-footed goblets and serving stands; and many styles of tripods. The whorls suggest a thriving textile industry. The chronological distribution of ceramic features suggests a transmission from Ta-hsi to Ch'ü-chia-ling, but the precise relation between the two cultures is not known.

Chuera, Tell: Important site in north Syria with buildings of the Early Dynastic period and distinctive temples. A late 3rd millennium BC processional way is lined with stelae.

chullpa: A burial tower commonly found in the southern Peruvian Andes, especially around Lake Titicaca, just before and after the Inca conquest. It was cylindrical, rectangular, or square and made of stone or adobe. Cruder chullpas are associated with pottery derived from the final Tiahuanaco styles, but chullpas made of dressed stone are often of Inca date.

Chulmun: A postglacial hunter-gatherer and agricultural culture of the Korean peninsula, from the 7th–2nd millennia BC, that produced a Neolithic textured-surface pottery (Chulmun "comb-patterned"). The people began to cultivate millet by the end of the period, and the pottery was succeeded by Mumun pottery. Shortly thereafter, rice was introduced. Chulmun sites are Amsadong, Tongsamdong, and Osan-Ri.

chultun: A bottle-shaped underground cistern found at some sites in the Maya lowlands. They were probably used for water or food storage.

Chumash: Culture of a late prehistoric and historic Native American people originally living along the coast of southern California and speaking a Hokan language. Chumash also occupied the three northern channel islands off Santa Barbara. The major Chumash groups were the Obispeño, Purisimeño, Ynezeño, Barbareño, and Ventureño, Emigdiano, and Cuyama. The Chumash were skilled artisans, made wooden-plank canoes and vessels of soapstone, as well as a variety of tools out of wood, whalebone, and other materials. They produced basketry, did rock painting, and started the practice of clamshell-bead currency in the area. The Chumash were among the first native Californians to be encountered by the Spanish explorer Juan Rodriguez Cabríllo, who visited the islands in 1542–1543.

Ch'un-ch'iu: A term for the Spring and Autumn period, 772–479 BC. It also refers to the "Spring and Autumn [Annals]," the first Chinese chronological history, said to be the traditional history of Lu, as revised by Confucius. It is one of the Five Classics of Confucianism. The name, which is actually an abbreviation of "Spring, Summer, Autumn, Winter," derives from the custom of dating events by season as well as by year. The work is a complete account of significant events that occurred during the reign of 12 rules of Lu, the native state of Confucius. The account begins in 722 BC and ends shortly before Confucius' death (479 BC). It is interpreted by Confucian scholars in their commentaries. (*syn.* Chun Qiu)

Chün ware: A Chinese stoneware of the Northern Sung period (AD 960–1126) with a pale blue opalescent or translucent green glaze, at the kilns near Lin-ju-hsien and at Kung-hsien in Honan Province in China. Another well-known class has a red or flambé glaze and consists of flowerpots, bulb bowls, elegant shallow dishes, water pots, and small boxes. (*syn.* Jun)

Chuquitana: A Late Preceramic site on the coast near Lima, Peru, occupied between 1800–1600 BC. The ruins reveal eight complexes of approximately 25 rooms, each built of stone. The complexes were rebuilt five or six times. Artifacts of shell, bone, stone, wood, and polished dried clay figurines have been found as well as evidence of woven cotton textiles. (*syn.* El Paraiso)

church: A building used for collective Christian worship, the performance of ceremonies, pilgrimages, and the veneration of relics. The earliest churches were hidden in caves and catacombs. With the official acceptance of Christianity in the 4th century, larger buildings were built specifically for communal worship. In the early Christian period, baptisteries, martyria, and covered cemeteries often remained separate at the side of the building. Although the usual form of churches has been the hall or axial plan, other forms have also been used: circular, polygonal, or cross shaped. The plan and appearance of a church are determined by its liturgical and ceremonial functions and by other symbolic and spiritual considerations.

Cibola: A mythical gold-rich land sought by the Spanish conquistadors in the 16th century, legendary cities of splendor and riches. The fabulous cities were first reported by Álvar Núñez Cabeza de Vaca who, after being shipwrecked off Florida in 1528, wandered through what later became Texas and northern Mexico before his rescue in 1536. In 1540, Francisco Vázquez de Coronado was sent to search for the cities; he found only a group of Zuni pueblos, although he explored as far north as modern Kansas. (*syn.* Seven Golden Cities of Cibola)

cicatrization: The process of healing over a wound by a scab, which leaves a scar/cicatrice on the skin.

Ciempozuelos: A Copper Age cemetery site near Madrid, Spain, which has given its name to a late variety of Spanish beaker of the 2nd millennium BC. Artifacts come mainly from pit tombs or cist burials. The Ciempozuelos beakers and other pottery are of high quality with a red or brown burnished slip and complex incised decoration. Most of the burials were flexed inhumations in cists.

Cimmerians: An ancient nomadic people of the Russian steppes, north of the Caucasus and Sea of Azov, driven out by the Scythians into Anatolia toward the end of the 8th century BC. As they retreated, they destroyed Phrygia, Lydia, and the Greek cities on the coast and then caused havoc in Anatolia. Their decline soon began, and their final defeat may be dated c. 637 or 626, when they were routed by Alyattes of Lydia. Their relatives, the Thracians, retreated similarly into the Balkans. The Cimmerian origin is uncertain, but they may have been responsible for the Catacomb and Kuban cultures, c. 1700 BC onward. The Cimmerians' destruction across southwestern Asia has been detected archaeologically at many sites. Our knowledge of them has come from the writings of Herodotus and the Assyrian records. (*syn.* Thraco-Cimmerian)

cinerarium: A place for depositing the ashes of the dead after cremation. Also, a niche in a tomb for holding an urn of ashes or a sarcophagus.

cinerary urn: A sepulchral vessel or urn used to preserve the ashes of the dead after cremation.

cinnabar: A red, crystalline form of mercuric sulphide, a naturally occurring and most important ore of mercury. It was used as a pigment for painting sculptures, pottery, and figurines by the Romans, Olmecs, and others.

cippus: A small, low column or pillar of stone, usually rectangular or cylindrical and with moldings at the top and bottom instead of a capital and a base. Often inscribed, it is normally associated with burials or tombs and used as a landmark, memorial, or sepulchral monument. (*syn.* pl. cippi)

Circea: A settlement site of the Early Neolithic Cris in the Olt Valley of southwestern Rumania, dating from the late 6th to mid-5th millennia BC. Four main occupation phases have been found, all of which are defined by rich painted ware assemblages. Level I has some of the earliest white-on-red painted pottery of the First Temperate Neolithic, and the latest level has polychrome painted pottery of Starcevo-Cris.

circle: A series of stones set up in a ring, the commonest prehistoric monuments of England, such as those at Avebury and Stonehenge. Most were of stone, although some were of wood or a combination of the two. They vary greatly in size, from a few feet in diameter, to those that are ¼ mile in diameter with huge monoliths of 60 tons. Some circles have monoliths in the center, and some smaller circles have burials in the center.

circumpolar cultures: A group of related cultures in the most northerly (Arctic) regions of Europe, including Siberia and North America. These peoples lived north of the region where settled farming life was possible. Although contemporary with Neolithic and Bronze Age communities farther south, the circumpolar tribes remained seminomadic hunters and gatherers. They adopted pottery from the farming peoples and their trade connections, making egg-shaped bowls with pitted or comb-stamped decoration. Characteristic tools were hunting and woodworking equipment, often of ground slate. Rock carvings and artifacts attest the use of skin boats, skis, and sledges, which suggest long-distance trade— especially of amber. The sites and cemeteries are usually close to water. Fishing was an important activity, and they exploited food sources such as elk, reindeer, and seal. (*syn.* Arctic Stone Age)

circus: A large building in Roman antiquity, generally a long oblong or oval, used for horse and chariot racing and public spectacles. The audience sat in rising tiers of seats around the track, and the races were run around a central island. Rome's Circus Maximus, the largest and best known, was originally built by Tarquinius Priscus, but enlarged various times until the late Roman period. It is essentially a Roman development from the Greek stadium or hippodrome.

Cirencester: A site in Gloucestershire, southwest England, where the Romano-British Corinium, the capital of the Dobuni tribe, was located. At the junction of important Roman and British routes, a cavalry fort was erected during AD 43– 70, and by the 3rd century the town walls enclosed c. 100 hectares. Remains in those walls include an amphitheater and many rich villas. Occupation continued well into the Anglo-Saxon period. Excavations have revealed much of the layout of the town and the plan of the forum and basilica, a market hall, shops and houses. Cemetery finds have shown that the skeletons contained high levels of lead, supporting the view that lead poisoning contributed to the decline of the Roman Empire. The town was the largest in Roman Britain after London and was probably a capital in the 4th century. The Corinium Museum houses a Roman collection. Saxons captured the town in 577, and it later became a royal demesne (dominion or territory). (*syn.* Corinium Dobunnorum)

cire perdue: A metalworking technique used to cast figurines and statues. A model of the object to be cast is made in wax, solid if the object is to be of solid metal, or made around a clay core if it is to be hollow. The wax model is covered with clay, and the whole is heated to allow the wax to melt and run off; this leaves a space into which molten metal is poured. After it has cooled, the outside clay is knocked off, the inner core may be removed, and remaining is a metal version of the original wax model. The technique is common on every continent except Australia and dates from the 3rd millennium BC, having gone through few changes since then. Because the "mold" cannot be used again, each version of an object made using this technique is unique, and the process is more time consuming than making a complex mold and reusing it. However, more detail can be accomplished with the cire perdue process. (*syn.* lost wax process)

Cishan: An early Neolithic millet-cultivating site in China. Features include pit houses, storage pits, and burials with artifacts including querns, ground-stone sickles, tripod vessels, and bone and stone fishing and hunting implements. Animal domestication is also attested to at the site, dating to the early 6th millennium BC. (*syn.* Tz'u-shan)

Cistercian ware: A lead-glazed English earthenware of the 15th–16th centuries. The earthenware is dark red with a black or brown metallic-appearing glaze and was called Cistercian because it was first excavated at Yorkshire Cistercian abbeys. The pottery forms were mainly drinking vessels, tall mugs, trumpet-shaped tygs (with two, four, or eight handles), and tankards. The majority of the ware is undecorated, but some examples are distinguished by horizontal ribbing or by white slip ornamentation consisting of roundels or rosettes. Potteries producing these wares were at Abergavenny, Monmouthshire; Tickford, Debryshire; and Wrotham, Kent.

cistern: An artificial reservoir or receptacle, such as an underground tank, for holding water or another liquid. It was especially used for catching and storing rainwater.

cist tomb or cist grave: A prehistoric coffin containing either a body or ashes, usually made of stone or a hollowed-out tree, of Europe and Asia. The grave might be lined with stones and covered with slabs or enclosed on four sides by stone slabs standing upright and closed with a lid (dolmen). Cists were for one or several burials and could be totally or partly buried. *Cist* has also been used in a more general sense to refer to the stone burial place itself. The term also referred to a storage place for sacred objects. (*syn.* slab tomb, kist, stone chest)

citadel: A stronghold; any strongly fortified structure, especially in a city. (*syn.* acropolis)

city-state: A political system consisting of an independent city having sovereignty over contiguous territory and serving as the center of political, economic, and cultural life. The term originated in England in the late 19th century and has been applied especially to the cities of ancient Greece, Phoenicia, and Italy and to the cities of medieval Italy. Its ancient name, polis, was derived from the citadel (akropolis) that was its administrative center. City-states differed from tribal or national systems in size, patriotism, and desire for independence. The origin of city-states probably occurred between 1000–800 BC in Greece, the Aegean islands, and western Asia Minor. As they grew, their people emigrated and created city-states on the coasts of the Mediterranean Sea and the Black Sea, mainly between 750–550 BC. A city-state had its own government and was not subject to any outside authority. (*syn.* polis)

ciudadela: Large rectangular enclosures (literally, "citadels") found in Mesoamerica and thought to have been the dwellings of the ruling classes and their retainers. The enclosures, surrounded by tapering adobe walls, contained courts, storerooms, administrative structures, and platform burials. Some may have been the palaces of the Chimu kings; the number of recognizable ciudadelas agrees with the number (10) of known Chimú rulers. Ciudadelas have been found in the ancient Andean city of Chan Chan, and it has even been suggested that they were the palaces of successive rulers, maintained by their descendants in the way that those of deceased Inca were maintained in Cuzco.

Ciumesti: A small number of Mesolithic and Neolithic settlement sites in northwest Rumania. Late Mesolithic, Early Neolithic Cris, and later Neolithic Linear Pottery sites have been found. The chipped stone assemblages are distinguished by a high percentage of obsidian, procured from the Tokaj Mountains some 180 kilometers away in northeastern Hungary.

Cividale: A site, Cividale del Friuli, in northeast Italy, with fine surviving examples of Lombardic architecture from the 8th century. There is an octagonal baptistery, the chapel (Tempietto) of a nunnery, and the altar of the church of S. Martino. The national archaeological museum contains Gothic and Lombard antiquities.

civilization: Complex sociopolitical form defined by the institution of the state and the existence of a distinctive great tradition.

Civita Castellana: A site near Rome, originally the capital of the Faliscans, the 9th-century BC Falerii Veteres. It was reputedly founded by the Pelasgians from Argos. The Faliscans were a tribe belonging to the Etruscan confederation against Rome. The city was destroyed by the Romans in 395 BC and again in 241 BC. Faliscan vases have been found in its rich necropolis. (*syn.* Falerii)

civitas: A term used in the later Roman Republic and under the Roman Empire for a favored provincial community. Some were exempted from tribute payment and Roman judicial jurisdiction. Others received grants of self-government and were not subject to military occupation. The term also referred to citizenship in ancient Rome.

Clactonian: An early flake-tool culture of Europe, dating from the early Mindel-Riss (Great Interglacial) of the Pleistocene epoch, which occurred from 1,600,000 to 10,000 years ago. It was named after discoveries at Clacton-on-Sea, Essex, England. A kind of concave scraper, perhaps used to smooth and shape wooden spears, is typical of the Clactonian industry. Apart from the tip of a wooden spear, the artifacts consisted of trimmed flint flakes and chipped pebbles, some of which can be classified as chopper tools. Handaxes were absent. The Clactonian seems therefore to have coexisted with Early Acheulian. Some believe that the two industries are quite distinct, while others maintain that both assemblages might have been made by the same people, and that the Clactonian could in theory be an Acheulian industry from which hand axes were absent because such tools were not needed for the jobs carried out at a particular site. Clactonian and related industries are distributed throughout the north European plain, and Clactonian tools are similar in appearance to those produced in the Soan industry of Pakistan and in several sites in eastern and southern Africa. The Tayacian industry of France and Israel is believed to be a smaller edition of the Clactonian.

Clairvaux-les-lacs: Neolithic village sites occupied from 3700–2400 BC in Jura, France. Many buildings, organic remains, and some pottery (Burgundian Middle Neolithic) have been found.

Clarke, David Leonard (1937–1976): British archaeologist; founder of analytical archaeology, who died tragically young after making notable contributions to the use of computers in archaeology, demonstrated by his study of beakers, and to a reassessment of archaeological methodology. His book *Analytical Archaeology*, published in 1968, emphasized the need for an explicit theory and a more rigorous methodology in archaeology.

clan: A group or tribe of persons from one common family, united by a chieftain. A clan develops for social and security reasons, and membership of a clan is defined in terms of actual or purported descent from a common ancestor. The descent is unilineal—derived only through the male (patriclan) or the female (matriclan). Normally, but not always, the clans are exogamous, marriage within the clan being forbidden and regarded as incest. Clans may segment into subclans or lineages.

class: A general group of artifacts, like "hand axes," which can be broken down into specific types, like "ovates," etc.

classic, Classic, Classical: A general term referring to the period when a culture or civilization reaches its highest point

of complexity and achievement. In a broader sense, the term often describes the whole period of Greek and Roman antiquity with the following breakdown: Early Classical Period 500–450 BC, High Classical Period 450–400 BC, and Late Classical 400–323 BC. Specifically, the term describes, in New World chronology, the period between the Formative (Pre-Classic) and the Post-Classic, which was characterized by the emergence of city-states. During the Classic stage, civilized life in pre-Columbian America reached its fullest flowering, with large temple centers, advanced art styles, and writing. It was originally coined for the Maya civilization, initially defined by the earliest and most recent Long Count dates found on Maya stelae, AD 300–900. A division between Early and Late Classic was arbitrarily set at AD 600, but because in some areas, such as Teothihuacán, great civilizations had already collapsed, some scholars regard this date as marking the end of the Classic Period. By extension, the word came to be used for other Mexican cultures with a similar level of excellence (Teotihuacán, Monte Albán, El Tajín). In these areas, the cultural climax was roughly contemporary with that of the Maya, and the term Classic took on a chronological meaning as well. The full Maya artistic, architectural, and calendric-hieroglyphic traditions took place during the Early Classic. Tikal, Uaxactún, and Copán all attained their glory then. In the Late Classic, between AD 600–900, ceremonial centers in the Maya Lowlands grew in number, as did the making of the inscribed, dated stelae and monuments. The breakdown of the Classic Period civilizations began with the destruction of the city of Teotihuacán in about AD 700. Some date the Classic period to AD 300–900. (*syn.* Classical Age, Classic Period)

classical archaeology: A field in historical archaeology specializing in the study of Old World Greek and Roman civilizations, their antecedents and contemporaries.

classic orders of architecture: The Grecian Doric, Ionic, and Corinthian and the Roman Tuscan, Doric, Ionic, Corinthian, and Composite orders as defined by the particular type of column and entablature in one basic unit. A column consists of a shaft together with its base and its capital. The column supports a section of an entablature, which constitutes the upper horizontal part of a classical building and is itself composed of (from bottom to top) an architrave, frieze, and cornice. The form of the capital is the most distinguishing characteristic of a particular order. The five major orders are Doric, Ionic, Corinthian, Tuscan, and Composite. (*syn.* order of architecture)

classification: The ordering of archaeological data that share certain attributes or characteristics into groups and classes; the divisions arrived at by such a process. Classification is the first step in the analysis of archaeological data—

when particles or objects are sorted or categorized by established criteria, such as size, function, material, or color.

clast: An individual grain of a rock that becomes part of a sediment. Archaeological debris often consists of rocks or grains resulting from the breakdown of larger rocks. A clastic deposit is made up of fragments of preexisting rock. (*related word* clastic)

claw beaker: Elaborate glass beakers dating from AD c. 500 onward in Early Saxon graves and Frankish burials. Also called Rüsselbecher, the beakers have two superimposed rows of hollow, trunklike protrusions curving down to rejoin the wall of the vessel above a small button foot. In form, they are similar to free-standing conical beakers, but they are embellished by a series of unusual clawlike protrusions. In many cases, the glass is tinted brown, blue, or yellow. The beakers were probably made in Cologne or Trier, Germany. (*syn.* elephant's trunk beaker, Rüsselbecher)

clay: Soil particles of less than 0.005 millimeters in diameter or rock composed mainly of clay particles. There are ceramic clays, clay shales, mud stones, glacial clays, deep-sea clays, and soils—which are plastic when wet and hard when dry. No other natural material has so wide an importance or such extended uses as does clay. The use of clay in pottery making antedates recorded human history, and pottery remains provide a record of past civilizations. As building materials, bricks (baked and as adobe) have been used in construction since earliest times.

clay tablet: The main writing material used by the scribes of early civilizations. Signs were impressed or inscribed on the soft clay, which was then dried in the sun. The ancient Sumerians, Babylonians, Assyrians, and Hittites wrote on tablets made from water-cleaned clay. A common form was a thin quadrilateral tile about five inches long, which, while still wet, was inscribed by a stylus with cuneiform characters. By writing on the surface in small characters, a scribe could copy a substantial text on a single tablet. For longer texts, several tablets were used and then linked by numbers or catchwords. Book production on clay tablets probably continued for 2,000 years in Mesopotamia and Asia Minor. Either dried in the sun or baked in a kiln, clay tablets were almost indestructible. The latter process was used for texts of special value, legal codes, royal annals, and epics to ensure greater preservation. Buried for thousands of years in the mounds of forgotten cities, they have been removed intact or almost so in modern archaeological excavations. The number of clay tablets recovered is nearly half a million, but there are constantly new finds. The largest surviving category consists of private commercial documents and government archives. When the Aramaic language and alphabet arose in the 6th century BC, clay tablet use declined because clay was less suited than papyrus to the Aramaic characters.

clearing excavation: Any excavation designed primarily to reveal the horizontal and, by inference, functional dimensions of an archaeological site—such as the extent, distribution, and patterning of buried data.

cleaver: A heavy, large core or flake tool of the Palaeolithic period, typically having a wide, straight cutting edge at one end, like a modern ax head. Technologically it is related to the hand ax and is often found as a component of Acheulian (esp. Upper Acheulian) hand ax industries. The sharp transverse cutting edge was almost always notched by use but never sharpened. Along with bifacial tools, it was one of the main instruments of *Homo erectus*. It is found mainly in Africa, where much of the flake surface is left unretouched. The axlike knife was used since the Middle Pleistocene era to cut through meat.

Cleland Hills: A rock-art site in central Australia, west of Alice Springs. In addition to "Panaramitee" motifs, there are deeply engraved and weathered heart-shaped "faces" with concentric circle "eyes."

Cleopatra: The name given to seven Ptolemaic queens of Egypt. The last of these, Cleopatra VII (69–30 BC; reigned 51–30 BC), was the most illustrious.

cliff dwelling: The "apartment houses" of masonry built by the Pueblo/Anasazi people of the American Southwest during Pueblo III times, or Classic Pueblo, located in rock shelters on the sides of canyon walls. These prehistoric houses were built along the sides or under the overhangs of cliffs, primarily in the Four Corners area where the states of Arizona, New Mexico, Colorado, and Utah meet. Mesa Verde National Park's Cliff Palace (CO) and Pueblo Bonito (NM) had about 200–800 rooms each. After this period, the Pueblo/Anasazi moved farther south and built the pueblo villages that they still inhabit. When the ancestors of the Pueblo/Anasazi people became sedentary and began to cultivate corn, they also began to build circular pits as storage bins. When the bins were later reinforced with stone walls and covered with roofs, some people began to use the enclosures as houses. Their use of hand-hewn stone building blocks and adobe mortar was unexcelled even in later buildings. Ceilings were built by laying two or more large crossbeams and placing on them a solid line of laths made of smaller branches. The layers were then plastered over with the adobe mixture. Some of the structures were several stories high, creating a row of terraces that gives the structure the appearance of a ziggurat (ancient Babylonian temple tower). The rooms were about 10 by 20 feet (3 by 6 m). Ground-floor rooms were entered by ladder through a hole in the ceiling; rooms on upper floors could be entered both by doorways from adjoining rooms and by a hole in the ceiling. Each community had two or more kivas, or ceremonial rooms. The Pueblo/Anasazi began to build these cliff dwellings around AD 1000. The cliffs offered natural protection against attack, and many smaller communities combined to form the large towns in the cliffs. Toward the end of the 13th century, the cliff dwellings were deserted by the inhabitants. Two factors were involved: a severe drought between 1272–1299 and possibly internal turmoil between tribes. Smaller pueblos were created in the south near better water sources.

Cliff Palace: An important site in Mesa Verde, Colorado, which was constructed by the Anasazi (Pueblo) in a large cliff overhang. It is a multistory pueblo with more than 200 rooms and 23 kivas, abandoned at the end of the 13th century AD, along with the rest of Mesa Verde, after being occupied a very short time.

CLIMAP: One of two projects (including COHMAP) aimed at producing paleoclimatic maps showing sea-surface temperatures in different parts of the globe at various periods: CLIMAP stands for Climate Long-range Interpretation, Mapping, and Prediction, and COHMAP is the Cooperative Holocene Mapping Project. CLIMAP was an attempt to specify in detail the condition of the Earth's surface, most notably the oceans, at the climax of the Wisconsin glaciation 18,000 years ago. It also included a series of mathematical modeling exercises aimed at defining the atmospheric circulation present at that time. Evidence for the most recent 18,000 years of Earth history is more diverse than that available for earlier epochs. Paleolimnological and paleoecological data (lake sediments and peat deposits, interpreted chiefly for their pollen contents) have resulted in remarkable advances in climatic knowledge. COHMAP was a later exercise designed to unravel the history of deglaciation of North America and Eurasia, the recolonization of the northern land surfaces by plants and animals, and the equivalent changes in the tropics and the Southern Hemisphere. (*syn.* Climate: Long-range Interpretation, Mapping, and Prediction)

climate: The condition of the atmosphere at a particular location over a long period; the sum of the atmospheric elements that, over short periods, make up weather. These elements are solar radiation, temperature, humidity, precipitation (type, frequency, and amount), atmospheric pressure, and wind (speed and direction). Climate is now considered as part of a larger system that includes not only the atmosphere but also the hydrosphere (all liquid and frozen surface waters), the lithosphere (all solid land surfaces, including the ocean floors), the biosphere (all living things), and extraterrestrial factors such as the Sun.

clinker-built: A shipbuilding technique in which the hull is formed by overlapping planks caulked together, and then the internal frame is added. This method of construction was used in Northern Europe from c. 350 BC (the earliest known vessel, from Halsnoy) into the 20th century. The Sutton Hoo

ship of the c. 6th century AD and Viking ships of Oseberg and Gokstad (8th–9th centuries) are examples.

Cloggs Cave: A limestone cave in northeastern Victoria, Australia, with human occupation deposits dating from c. 16,000–7000 BC. Ochre and hearths as well as stone tools of the Australian Core Tool and Scraper tradition have been found, and the tools resemble similar Tasmanian artifacts. Bones of extinct animals found in deposits that are more than 20,000 years old and are separate from the human deposits. Australian Small Tool tradition artifacts were excavated from the late Holocene deposits in a rock shelter outside the main cave.

cloisonné: A technique of decorative enameling in which different colors of a pattern are separated by thin strips of metal. It consists of soldering to a metal surface, thin metal strips bent to the outline of a design and filling the resulting spaces, called "cloisons" (French for "partitions," or "cells") with vitreous enamel paste. The object is fired, ground smooth, and polished. Sometimes metal wire is used in place of gold, brass, silver, or copper strips. It was used in Anglo-Saxon England and by Germanic metalsmiths to decorate polychrome jewelry and metalwork. The technique is somewhat similar to champlevé, but it allows more intricacy of design. Among the earliest examples of cloisonné are six Mycenaean rings of the 13th century BC. The great Western period of cloisonné enameling was from the 10th–12th century, especially in the Byzantine Empire. In China, cloisonné was widely made during the Ming (1368–1644) and Ch'ing (1644–1911/12) Dynasties. In Japan, it was especially popular during the Tokugawa, or Edo (1603–1868), and Meiji (1868–1912) periods.

cloister: A type of court or quadrangle surrounded by covered walkways, much like the atrium of a Roman house. Cloisters are usually attached to abbeys with one of the sides bounded by the church; also attached to cathedral churches or colleges. The walls were often adorned with frescoes, and the court (cloister garth) contained a fountain and trees. The term is also used for the walkways or alleys themselves.

closed association: The relation of two or more objects that are found together and that can be proved to have been deposited together.

closed site: An archaeological site located in a pyramid, chambered tomb, barrow (burial mound), sealed cave, or rock shelter.

closed system: A system that is isolated and internally self-regulating, receiving no feedback or information from external sources, or matter, light, heat, or energy from its environment.

Clovis: A Paleo-Indian culture located on the plateau of Arizona, New Mexico, and western Texas and beginning sometime before 10,000 BC. It is so named from its first important site near Clovis, New Mexico. The culture is generally considered to be ancestral to the later Folsom complex, and it, like Folsom, was part of the big-game hunting tradition. It is characterized by distinctive, fluted, lanceolate stone projectile points, believed to be the oldest of their type. In Arizona, Clovis projectile points have been found in association with mammoth bones. The most problematical Clovis find comes from a site in Texas where a Clovis point was found in hearths with a radiocarbon date of 37,000+ years. The type site for this complex is Blackwater Draw, and its artifacts are of the Llano complex.

Clovis point: A distinctive, fluted, lanceolate (leaf-shaped) stone projectile point characteristic of the early Paleo-Indian period, c. 10,000–9000 BC, and often found in association with mammoth bones. It is named for Clovis, New Mexico, where it was first found. The concave-based projectile point has a longitudinal groove on each face running from the base to a point not more than halfway along the tool. The base of a Clovis point is concave, and the edge of the base is usually blunted through grinding, probably to ensure that the thongs, attaching the point to the projectile, were not cut. It is assumed to have been a spear because of its size; the length of points varies from 2–4 inches (7–12 cm), and their widest width is 1–1½ inch (3–4 cm). Clovis points and the artifacts associated with them (grouped together as the Llano complex) are among the earliest tools known from the New World and have been found over most of North America, with a few outliers as far south as Mexico and Panama. It is the earliest projectile point of the big game hunting tradition of North America. From these points came the later, more sophisticated points, such as the Folsom. (*syn.* Clovis spear point)

Clusium: An ancient Etruscan town on the site of modern Chiusi, in Tuscany, Italy. Clusium enjoyed good agricultural fertility, deposits of iron and copper ore, natural hot springs, and a key position on trade routes. Settlement appears to be unbroken and successful from the first Villanovan dwellers onward. It was founded in the 8th century BC on the site of an older Umbrian town known as Camars. In the early 6th century BC, it allied with Arretium (Arezzo) as part of the 12-city Etruscan confederation. At the end of the 6th century BC, Clusium's king, Lars Porsena, attacked Rome and may even have captured the city in an attempt to restore the power of the Tarquins there. In 391 BC, Clusium allied with Rome against invading Gauls. Like other Etruscan cities, Clusium was surrounded by cemeteries and tombs. Excavation of Clusian tombs, mostly cut into the soft tufa rock, has yielded earthenware funerary (canopic) jars, as well as ceramic human figures and Greek and locally made pottery. There is evidence for persistence of the cremation rite, seen in the wide variety of cinerary urns, canopic jars, and characteristic

hollow seated figures made from pietra fetida limestone. Clusium also had a reputation for fine bronze and stone craftsmanship. The decorations on sarcophagi in the tombs are a major source of inscriptions in the Etruscan language. (*syn.* Clusius, Chiusi)

cluster analysis: A multivariate statistical technique that assesses the similarities between units or assemblages, based on the occurrence or nonoccurrence of specific artifact types or other components within them. It also involves comparing the distances between points or objects, whose dimensions are measurements or scores for a number of variables. Cluster analysis results are normally plotted as a "dendrogram," a treelike representation of the distances between objects in hyperspace. Items that are closer together are deemed to be more closely related. Cluster analysis is most often done on a computer.

Clyde-Carlingford tombs: A series of megalithic chamber tombs in southwestern Scotland and northern Ireland with some radiocarbon dates before 3000 BC, an early stage of the Neolithic. They are sometimes described as segmented gallery graves, because they have subdivided rectangular chambers. Another important characteristic was a concave or semicircular forecourt. In some of the Irish examples, this was oval or circular, and they are described as court cairns. The overlying cairns are long and either oval, rectangular, or trapezoidal in shape. Collective inhumation was the normal practice, although cremation sometimes occurred in Ireland.

Cmielów: A Funnel Beaker culture settlement site in the Holy Cross Mountains of Poland. There were mines of banded flint, which were used to make cores and axes, and evidence of copper metallurgy.

coal: One of the most important of the primary fossil fuels, a dark-colored, carbon-rich material that occurs in stratified, sedimentary deposits. Two major periods of coal formation are known in geologic history. The older includes the Carboniferous and Permian periods (from about 350,000,000–250,000,000 years ago). Much of the bituminous coal of eastern North America and Europe is Carboniferous in age. Most coals in Siberia, eastern Asia, and Australia are of Permian origin. The younger era began in the Cretaceous period (about 135,000,000 years ago) and culminated during the Tertiary period (about 65,000,000–2,500,000 years ago). From this era came nearly all the world's lignites and sub-bituminous (brown) coals.

Coalbrookdale: The site of the first cast-iron bridge, spanning the River Severn at Coalbrookdale, Shropshire, England, now a British national monument and considered the birthplace of the Industrial Revolution. Abraham Darby pioneered the smelting of iron with coke here in 1709, and the bridge was by Thomas Pritchard and erected by John Wilkinson and Abraham Darby in 1777–1779.

coarse ware: A classification of sandy, rough pottery including castor ware, new forest ware, and rustic ware.

cobble: A rounded stone worn smooth by the action of water and used as a core for a stone tool; thus "cobble tool."

Cochise: An ancient North American Indian culture that existed 9,000–2,000 years ago, in Arizona and western New Mexico. The culture was named for the ancient Lake Cochise (now Willcox Playa, Arizona), near which important finds were made. The Cochise, a local variant of the Desert culture, contrasted with the big game hunting cultures to the east (Clovis, Folsom) and was based on gathering and collecting wild plant foods. In later stages, there is evidence of the development of agriculture. The Cochise culture has been divided into three developmental periods. The earliest stage, Sulphur Spring, dates from 6000 or 7000 BC to about 4000 BC and is characterized by milling stones for grinding wild seeds and by various scrapers, but no knives, blades, or projectile points. Its type site has been associated with mammoth and extinct horse remains, and there are some indications of hunting. During the second stage, Chiricahua, lasting from 4000 to perhaps 500 BC, appearance of projectile points seems to indicate an increased interest in hunting, and the remains of a primitive form of maize in Bat Cave (NM) suggest the beginnings of farming. In the final or San Pedro stage, from 500 BC to the beginning of the Christian era, milling stones were replaced by mortars and pestles (mano and metate), and pit houses (houses of poles and earth built over pits) appeared. During the San Pedro stage, pottery appeared in the area of the Mogollon Indians. The poorly understood Cazador phase may bridge the long hiatus between Sulphur Springs and Chiricahua, but the evidence so far in inconclusive.

Coclé: A region in Panama where the type site of Sitio Conte has yielded deep rectangular tombs with grave goods of a rich ceramic and metallurgical tradition of AD 500–1000. The Coclé region was strongly influenced by the Quimbaya style. It is particularly known for its striking gold pieces set with precious stones, including emeralds, quartzes, jaspers, opals, agates, and green serpentines. The extremely fine polychrome pottery is characterized by decoration of intricate geometric patterns and by stylized biomorphic forms. Gold- and tumbaga-working techniques, probably imported from Columbia, include cire perdue casting. Some association with Tairona is recognized in some artifacts, especially in the wing-shaped pendants. In addition to the grave goods, there are indications that wife and servant sacrifice took place at the death of an important person.

coconut: The nut or seed of the coco palm, whose white flesh may be eaten. It was probably cultivated in Southeast Asia by 3000 BC and then spread by Austronesians through the Pacific and eventually to central America, India, and East Africa. Charred fruits occur in western Melanesian sites back to c. 3000 BC. The coconut must always have been of importance in coastal tropical economics owing to its enormous range of uses. It has high salt tolerance, and the seed (the coconut itself) is easy to transport.

codex: Any handwritten manuscript, either Christian or in Mesoamerica before the Spanish conquest. In Mesoamerica, these documents were written and painted in hieroglyphic or pictographic characters on bark paper or animal skin, and they contain information about pre-Columbian and postconquest life. The surviving codices, of which there are four, were folded concertina-fashion, like a map. The information concerned astronomy, religious ceremonies, calendrics, genealogy, or simple accounting. The best surviving example is the Dresden Codex. A number were commissioned by the Spanish, and some are copies of earlier works, including the Mayan Book of Chilam Balam, the Popol Vuh, and the Aztec tribute lists of the Mendoza Codex. Those written postconquest might resemble a book in format. The early Christian gospel books were produced in monasteries in the post-Roman era, including the Codex Sinaiticus, Alexandrinus, and Vaticanus. (*syn.* pl. codices [from "caudex," trunk of a tree])

Cody complex: A North America flint industry with a late Plato tool assemblage representing the last of the plains-based hunting groups. First identified in Cody, Wyoming, it dates to c. 7500–5000 BC. There are Eden and Scotsbluff varieties of finely worked lanceolate blades and projectile points and a unique asymmetrical knife with a shoulder on one side (the Cody knife), usually found with bison remains.

Coedès, George (1886–1969): A French scholar of classical Southeast Asia who spent most of his career in Indochina and Siam. He is best known for *Angkor: An Introduction* (1963; reissued 1986). He published more than 300 papers and discovered the Indonesian empire of Srivijava in 1918.

coevolution: The recent theory that life and climate interact and that they have mutually altered each other over geologic history. The term was coined by the American biologists Paul R. Ehrlich and Peter H. Raven to describe the process whereby two or more species depend on the interactions between them. The coevolution of life and climate during the past 4,000,000,000 years of the Earth's history is an expression for the complex mixture of forces causing climatic change. The theory suggests that changes in social systems are best understood as mutual selection among components rather than a linear cause-and-effect sequence. For example, it has been argued that the origins of agriculture can best be understood by exploring the evolutionary forces affecting the development of domestication systems. Viewed this way, domestication is not seen as an evolutionary stage, but rather as a process and is the result of coevolutionary interactions between humans and plants. (*syn.* coevolutionary perspective)

coffin: Any box or chest, usually rectangular or anthropoid in shape, in which a corpse or mummy is enclosed for burial. Clay, stone, metal, and wood are among the materials used. Primitive wooden coffins, formed of a tree trunk split and hollowed out, are still in use among some aboriginal peoples. The term *sarcophagus* is used only for the stone outer container that encases one or more coffins. From the Latin word for "basket," *cophinus*. (*syn.* sarcophagus)

Coffin Texts: A collection of ancient Egyptian funerary texts consisting of spells or magic formulas that are intended to aid the deceased in their passage to the hereafter. The text was painted on or in burial coffins from the First Intermediate period (c. 2130–1939 BC) and the Middle Kingdom (1938–c. 1600 BC). Many of the Coffin Texts were derived from the Pyramid Texts, a sequence of often-obscure spells carved on the internal walls of the Old Kingdom pyramids, but were used by private individuals. More than 1,000 spells are known. The Coffin Texts combined with the Pyramid Texts were the primary sources of the Book of the Dead, which was in prominent use during the New Kingdom and Late period. These three collections represent the main body of Egyptian religious literature.

cognitive archaeology: The study of past mental processes, ideological systems, and thought patterns from the archaeological record—often through the symbols left behind on material remains. (*syn.* structural archaeology)

cognitive concept of culture: A model of culture consisting of a set of meanings (categories and relations) people construct for making sense of their lives. It is used in archaeological interpretation for both synchronic and diachronic descriptions of cultural meaning.

cognitive map: An interpretive framework of the world that, it is said, exists in the human mind and affects actions and decisions as well as knowledge structures.

cognitive-processual approach: An alternative to the functional-processual approach, this theory is concerned with the cognitive and symbolic aspects of early societies and the role of ideology as an organizational force.

cognized model: A representation of reality, which is based in part on idealized expectations about the real situation.

coil building: A method of pottery making in which a rope of clay is coiled around a flat base and continued up to form the walls of a pot. The layers of clay are pressed together, and the inside and outside smoothed off to remove the lines between the coils. Frequently this is not done completely, and the coils may still be visible. Pottery often breaks along the coil lines. (*syn.* coiling, coil-built pottery)

coiled: Concerning a method of basketry based on a spirally coiled foundation, especially that made with a vertical stitch or weft. A basket is said to be coiled when a long bundle of fibrous material is laid up, spiral fashion. Each coil is sewn by a slender splint to the coil below it. The basketmaker would pierce the fiber bundle with a bone awl and pass the splint through the hole thus made. In ceramics, coiling is a construction technique where the vessel is formed from the base up with long coils or wedges of clay shaped and joined together. (*syn.* coiled basketry)

coin: A piece of metal or, rarely, some other material (such as leather or porcelain) certified by a mark or marks on it as being of a specific value. Coinage is considered to be any standardized series of metal tokens, their specific weights representing specific values, and usually stamped with designs and inscriptions. Coins or coinlike objects were first issued by the Lydians of Anatolia in the late 7th century BC, made of the gold-silver alloy electrum. Their use was adopted in the Far East, then around the Mediterranean, and has since spread throughout the world. Early coins were used for specialized, prestigious purposes and not for everyday exchange. The early Greek coins were also made of electrum, silver, or gold; the first Roman coins were produced in the early 3rd century BC and were also made of precious metals. Later in that century, the first bronze coin was introduced. These material remains are self-dating, although they do not always "date" the materials they are found with as they may have been traded, handed down through generations, or displaced in the stratigraphy of a site.

Colchester: A district and borough northeast of London, England, which was the capital of the pre-Roman Belgic ruler Cunobelinus by AD 43, formerly an Iron Age Celtic settlement (*oppidum*) surrounded by dikes. Although it burned down in AD 60, Colchester soon became one of the chief towns in Roman Britain, and there are surviving walls and gateways from this period. Some of the masonry of the temple to Claudius survives in the foundations of the Norman castle. (*syn.* Camulodunum, Camolodunum; Colneceaste; Colcestra)

cold hammering: A technique for making metal artifacts in which the metal is shaped by percussion without heating. Most metals, such as copper, bronze, gold, and silver, are soft enough to be worked while cold. Operations such as hammering and beating could be carried out without any heating to make the metal softer. These softer metals, however, cannot be cold-worked indefinitely because the metal becomes brittle and eventually fractures. It can be counteracted by gentle heating called annealing. Annealing allows crystals in the metal to recrystallize and distribute the stress that has built up. Cold working can then go on until the metal becomes brittle again. Metallographic examination, the study of crystal structures, can give information about the cold working and annealing processes in the last stages of the making of an artifact. Pure gold is one of the few metals that can be cold worked indefinitely without annealing. (*syn.* cold working)

collagen content: Collagen is a protein abundant in living bone, which contains about 4% nitrogen. Collagen survives long after death, and the collagen content of a bone, measured by the amount of nitrogen present, yields information as to its relative date. The rate of decay varies with temperature and other aspects of the environment, but collagen dating can give only relative dates for different bone samples from a particular site. The test is used mainly in association with the fluorine test and radiometric assay, as in the cases of Piltdown and Swanscombe Man. (*syn.* collagen dating)

collared urn: A type of urn used in the British Early Bronze Age, also called an "overhanging rim urn." It has a developed rim, which may be straight, convex, or slightly concave in profile. Decoration is normally on the rim or the upper half of the vessel. Collared urns often contained cremation burials, although some have been found in domestic contexts.

collecting: Any nonscientific removal of archaeological materials from a site by nonresidents. Although collectors were important to the origins of archaeology, they are now a major cause of the destruction of the world's cultural resources.

collective tomb: A chamber tomb of Neolithic times, either rock cut or megalithic, built to contain many burials, often successive depositions spread over a long time. By 4000 BC, the first big collective tombs were built from boulders in Spain.

collector system: A lifeways system in which people obtain food in bulk and store it.

Colless Creek: A rock shelter site of northwest Queensland, Australia, with a rich artifact assemblage. Occupation was before 17,350 bp—possibly 30,000 years ago.

colluvial: A deposit resulting from soil erosion, usually at the foot of a slope, and containing rock detritus or talus. At the bottom of slopes, soils lose their structure and become eroded owing to clearance of forest, plowing, or cultivation. Colluvial material typically gathers in the dry valleys of chalklands and also at the foot of escarpments or valley sides. (*syn.* colluvium)

Co-loa: A place believed to have been the capital of Vietnam's legendary Au Lac Dynasty, c. 258–207 BC. It is about 20 kilometers northwest of Hanoi, and there are three walls that surrounded the city in a spiral. In AD 939, the kingdom of Nam Viet centered in the Red River Valley at Co Loa. Ngo Quyen drove the Chinese out of the area and founded his own

dynasty, which endured only until 954. Historical sites include the Co Loa citadel. (*syn.* Co Loa)

Cologne: A site on the left bank of the Rhine, West Germany, colonized by the Roman general Agrippa in 53 BC. A fortified settlement was established c. 38 BC, and it became a Roman colony in AD 50. It was named Colonia Claudia Ara Agrippinensium, shortened to Colonia. It became the capital of the province of Lower Germania, which was an important commercial center. After AD 258, it was, for a time, the capital of an empire making up Gaul, Britain, and Spain. In 310, Constantine the Great built a castle and a permanent bridge to it across the Rhine. About 456, it was conquered by the Franks, and it soon became the residence of the kings of the Ripuarian part of the Frankish kingdom. Ceramics and glass were manufactured in Cologne in Roman times. Traces of the Roman period survive, including the principal elements of the street plan, town walls and gates, Roman and Gallo-Roman temples, water installations, Rhine port, bridges and fort, pottery and glass factories, and villas and cemeteries. In the 5th century, the Roman town was overrun by the Franks. During the Frankish and Carolingian periods and much of the Middle Ages, Cologne was a major bishopric and a leading commercial and cultural center. Spectacular Frankish royal graves dating to the mid-6th century have been uncovered. (*syn.* [Roman] Colonia Agrippinensis, Colonia Claudia Ara Agrippinensium, Colonia)

colonia: A Roman settlement in conquered territory, a name first used in the later Republican and imperial Roman periods for a township, often of retired veteran soldiers, strategically placed to defend imperial interests. Its self-governing constitution imitated that of Rome, and the citizens had either full (Roman) citizenship or limited (Latin) citizenship. After the 2nd century BC, colonia became the highest rank that a community could attain. It involved a transfer of Roman citizens to a settlement to administer it in collaboration with the magistrates of the capital. In exchange for a commitment to provide military aid, its citizens acquired the right to trade and contract marriages with Roman citizens. In the Greek world, a colony was a city founded by a contingent of Greek citizens in a foreign territory for agricultural and/or commercial purposes. (*syn.* colony)

colonial archaeology: A branch of historical archaeology dealing with the colonial period in America history, from the discovery of America to the establishment of the United States, generally, the 16th through the 18th centuries.

Colonial Williamsburg: A restoration of a large town of the early colonial area, which was first settled in 1633 as Middle Plantation. The restoration was begun in 1926, and the more than 3,000 acres of land have nearly 150 major buildings restored or reconstructed. The exhibition buildings, which include the Capitol and Governor's Palace, are furnished as they were in the 18th century, and the entire area is landscaped as it was in colonial times. This living history museum has been reconstructed partly with the aid of archaeological research.

color-coated ware: A way of referring to many kinds of pottery in the Greek and Roman periods, which were given an extra surface coating, usually slightly glossy and most often red. Research suggests that the coating was made from fine clay particles suspended in water with a peptizing agent added.

Colosseum: The original name and modern nickname for the giant Flavian Amphitheater in Rome, whose construction began during the reign of the emperor Vespasian (AD 69–79), between 70–72. The name apparently derived from an adjacent colossal statue. It was officially dedicated in AD 80 by Titus in a ceremony that included 100 days of games. In AD 82, Domitian added the uppermost story. Unlike earlier amphitheaters, which were nearly all dug into hillsides for extra support, the Colosseum is a freestanding structure of stone and concrete, measuring 620 by 513 feet and seating 50,000 spectators. It was the scene of thousands of hand-to-hand combats between gladiators, of contests between men and animals, and of many larger combats, including mock naval engagements. It has been damaged by lightning and earthquakes, but especially by vandalism; all the marble seats and decorative materials have disappeared.

Colossi of Memnon: Two colossal seated statues of Amenhotep III (1390–1352 BC), carved from quartzite sandstone, which are located at the eastern end of the site of his much-plundered mortuary temple in western Thebes; each of the figures is flanked by a representation of Tiy. The two remaining statues are 70 feet (21 m) high, each hewn from a single block of stone. The more northerly of these was partly destroyed by an earthquake in 27 BC, resulting in a curious phenomenon. Every morning, when the rays of the rising sun touched the statue, musical sounds like the twang of a harp string were heard. This was supposed to be the voice of Memnon responding to the greeting of his mother, Eos. After the restoration of the statue by the Roman emperor Septimius Severus (AD 170), the sounds ceased. The sounds came from air passing through the pores of the stone, caused by the change of temperature at sunrise, and the masonry patching caused the "singing" to cease. These statues once flanked the gateway in front of the temple pylon but now sit alone in the middle of cultivated fields.

colossus: A gigantic statue or image of the human form, usually of a king but also of private individuals and gods. They are typically set up outside the gates or pylons of temples. The term was originally applied by Herodotus to sculptures of Egypt. The most famous is the bronze statue of Apollo at Rhodes, one of the seven wonders of the world, reputed to have stood at the entrance to the harbor and claimed by Pliny to have been 90 feet tall. (*syn.* pl. colossi, colossuses)

Colt Hoare, Sir Richard (1758–1838): British antiquary who established the techniques of archaeological excavation in Britain. He excavated a large number of barrows (mostly on Salisbury Plain), classified and published his findings. He also recorded many other monuments of the area. However, at the time there was no means of dating the material he found.

columbarium: A term from Roman antiquity for a subterranean sepulcher with wall niches or pigeonholes for cinerary urns. The term was also used for the recesses themselves. This type of burial was typically afforded to the large staff of slaves and freedmen. Originating as variants of traditional Etruscan and republican Roman house tombs, columbaria were usually rectangular brick structures built around an open court, the walls of which contained niches for the urns. Some columbaria were elaborate and held numerous inscriptions, stucco paintings, and mosaics, which provide information about the lower classes. Some of the best examples of columbaria are those in the great necropolis beneath the Basilica of San Sebastiano in Rome. In Hadrian's time (AD 117–138), inhumation replaced cremation, and columbaria became obsolete. (*syn.* pl. columbaria)

column: In architecture, a cylindrical or slightly tapering support or pillar for some part of a building, usually made of stone or wood. There were "classic orders" of columns, which had specific shapes for the base, shaft, and capital that supported the entablature. In Gothic and Norman architecture, the column was the pillar or pier supporting an arch. A column may also stand alone, as Trajan's Column in Rome. A circuit of columns, enclosing an open space in the interior of a building, was called a peristyle.

Columnata: A site in the Atlas Mountains of northern Algeria with several Mechtoid-type human burials dated to 8300–7300 BP.

comb: A toothed object of wood, bone, horn, or metal, with a number of uses—for hair dressing, carding wool, currying horses, compacting the weft in weaving, decorating pottery, or an ornament to keep the hair in place. As used for combing the hair, but not wearing, combs were found in Pompeian and Egyptian tombs and in early British, Roman, and Saxon barrows.

Combe Capelle: A rock shelter in Dordogne, France, with Châtelperronian, Aurignacian, Gravettian, and Solutrean industries as well as a burial of a *Homo sapiens sapiens*.

combed ornament: Any pottery decorated by drawing a toothed instrument across the surface of the soft clay or colored slip. The pottery was often decorated by the application of two or more different-colored slips that were either brushed or combed to produce the effect of marbled paper, a broad band of parallel incisions, often wavy. (*syn.* combed ware)

Combe-Grenal: A rock shelter site on the Dordogne River in southwest France, near the town of Domme. There are 64 archaeological levels, including nine bottom levels of the Acheulian industry dating from the end of the Riss glaciation, followed by a series of 55 Mousterian levels. Occupation ended just before the end of the Mousterian period, and there is a radiocarbon date of just over 37,000 BC from Level 12, near the top of the deposit. The site has the largest number of cultural levels of any Palaeolithic site known to date. The 55 Mousterian levels have formed the basis for the analysis of the Mousterian into five main types. A burial pit has been recognized in the Mousterian levels with some human bones. The site has fauna and pollen evidence from all levels. (*syn.* Combe Grenal)

comet: A celestial body moving around the Sun in an elliptical orbit and often seen as a starlike nucleus with a train of light or "tail" following it. Comets were often mentioned in ancient records, as in the Bayeux Tapestry. Their occurrences can be calculated by astronomers, as can eclipses, and ancient reports can thus be exactly dated, a useful check on the recorded chronology.

comitium: In Roman architecture, a building near the forum, used for voting and other political matters.

Commagene: An area in ancient Syria at the junction of the Taurus Mountains and the Euphrates River—a strategic position between the Roman and Parthian Empires from which obsidian was exported from c. 8000 BC. Commagene broke from the Seleucid Empire about 162 BC, and its king, Antiochus I (c. 69–34 BC) helped it rise in importance. Antiochus built his spectacular mausoleum on the peak of Nimrud Dag. Commagene was annexed by Rome in AD 17 and was later incorporated into the Roman province of Syria. (*syn.* Kommagene)

commandery: In ancient China, a military and administrative unit during the Han Dynasty (206 BC–AD 220), which governed newly conquered areas. It was run by a commander.

community: The tangible remains of the activities of the maximum number of people who occupied a settlement during a time period. A biological community is an interacting population of various kinds of individuals (species) in a common location.

compartmented seal: The typical, usually metal, seal of the Bronze Age in western Central Asia and northern Afghanistan. Most often round, the seals' motifs were geometric or of objects of nature.

compass map: A map of a region or site created by using a compass to control geographical direction and, usually, pacing or tape measures to control distances, but not elevation.

complex: A group of artifacts and traits that regularly appear together in two or more sites in a restricted area over a period and that are presumed to represent an archaeological culture. A complex could be a characteristic tool or type of pottery, or it could be a pattern of buildings that occur together. A complex is a chronological subdivision of different artifact types and implies a culture, whereas an assemblage is merely a collection of contemporaneous specimens. (*syn.* cultural complex)

compluvium: In Roman architecture, the central opening in the roof over the middle of the atrium in a house. The impluvium was directly below.

component: A culturally homogeneous stratigraphic layer in a site that belongs to one culture and is interpreted as the remains of a single people during a relatively brief time. At a particular site, there may be present several components, recognized by critical changes in the artifact assemblages. A number of similar and contemporary components make up a phase. (*syn.* focus; phase)

composite: The fifth of the classical orders of architecture, a blend of the Ionic and Corinthian styles (specifically, the Ionic grafted on the Corinthian). Examples are the arches of Septimus Severus, Titus, and Bacchus and baths of Diocletian. (*syn.* composite order of architecture)

composite bow: An archer's bow made of more than one material—as wood and fiberglass—to combine properties of strength, durability, and power. In early times, a bow of wood was reinforced on one side by layers of animal sinew and on the other side by animal horn.

composite mold: A kind of mold for making metal objects, which can have three or more pieces. It may be a simple bivalve mold with the addition of a third part—a plug, which forms a socket in the artifact when it is removed.

composite soil: A soil profile that forces its features on more than one parent material. (*syn.* welded soil, superimposed soil, polypedomorphic soil)

compound tool: Any tool made of two or more different materials, such as a bone harpoon with stone points and barbs set in it, or a wooden arrow with a shaped stone point. (*syn.* composite tool)

compression rings: The faint lines on the dorsal side of a flake, indicating the direction of force.

computerized axial tomography: a method of obtaining cross-sectional images or "slices" of internal bodily structures. A body or mummy is passed into a scanner, and the computer-enhanced tomography, x-raying of deep internal structures, is executed. (*syn.* CAT scanner; computer axial tomography; computer tomography)

computer simulation: Reconstruction of the past based on the production of computerized models. The computer model describes ancient conditions and variables, and those are used to generate a sequence of events that are compared against the known archaeological record. The computer imitates the dynamic behavior of an explicit model and helps scientists examine how such systems respond to changing conditions; it also refines and tests hypotheses about the past. In an example of a study of hunter-gatherers, the effect of various changes in the natural environment on such factors as the population settlement pattern or subsistence could be monitored; or the growth of a settlement system could be studied under different conditions of population, economy, technological or environmental change. The relation between the various elements in the cultural system must be specified, and then any variety of actual conditions can be simulated. The data used could be derived from observations and the simulation used to examine the effect of different assumptions; the results could then be compared with the observed data to test their validity. (*syn.* computer simulation studies)

Conca d'Oro: A Copper Age site on the plain around Palermo, northwest Sicily, where a number of rock-cut shaft-and-chamber tombs (a forno or oven-shaped type) have been found dating to the 3rd millennium BC. They were used for collective burial, and the associated grave goods include pottery vessels and some metal tools and weapons. There is local incised pottery and a local imitation known as the "Carni beaker," as well as imported Beaker pottery of west Mediterranean type.

conchoidal: A characteristic shell-like fracture pattern that occurs in siliceous rocks, such as obsidian, chert, and flint. The fracture has smooth shell-like convexities and concavities. (*syn.* conchoidal fracture)

conchology: The science or study of shells and shellfish; also the collection of shells.

Conchopata: A Middle Horizon site in the Ayacucho Valley near Huari, Peru, which was probably a religious shrine. Two large offering deposits of Huari ceramics have been found, including large beaker-shaped urns and painted face-neck jars, intentionally smashed, which have a distinctive polychrome decoration that is clearly Tiahuanaco influenced, including iconography similar to that of the Gateway of the Sun.

concretion: a mass of mineral matter found generally in rock of a composition different from its own and produced by deposition from aqueous solution in the rock. It is usually formed around a nucleus that may consist of archaeological

debris. Concretions form under certain conditions, and the study of their characteristics may aid reconstruction of the environmental conditions of the time.

cone mosaic: A type of wall decoration used in the Uruk (VI–IV) and Jemdet Nasr periods of southern Mesopotamia. Stone or baked clay cones were stuck into the surface of building facades to produce a colored mosaic geometric pattern. Examples have been found in the Eanna section of Warka.

cone of force: A cone-shaped area on a stone core and its associated flake, which results when force is applied to separate the flake.

conflict theories: Theories that trace the origin of the state to warfare or intragroup conflicts.

cong: A tubular jade object, circular on the inside and enclosed in a rectangular body, made in various sizes and used for ritual purposes in ancient China. Cong were described in ancient Chinese texts as symbols of rank and were used as ritual objects primarily in the Shang (18th–12th century BC) and Chou (1111–255 BC) Dynasties. They have been found in graves, arranged with bi disks around the corpses of the elite. The cong is thought to have symbolized Earth or possibly to have been an astronomical instrument. (*syn.* ts'ung)

conjoining: The refitting or rejoining of artifact or ecofact fragments, especially those of struck stone flakes to recreate the original core. Such studies allow definition of cumulative features, such as the lithic artifact and debitage scatters. The technique may allow reconstruction of ancient manufacture and use behavior. (*syn.* refitting; rejoining)

conjunctive approach: A methodological alternative to traditional normative archaeology, developed by Walter W. Taylor in 1948. In it, the full range of a culture system is to be taken into consideration in explanatory models, with explicit connection of archaeological objects in their cultural contexts. Ancient behavior is reconstructed by defining functional sets of archaeological data.

conquest: Aggressive movement of human groups from one area to another, resulting in the subjugation of the indigenous society. It is also described as the acquisition of territory by the victorious state in a war, at the expense of the defeated state. An effective conquest takes place when physical appropriation of territory is followed by subjugation (legal process of transferring title).

conquistador: The Spanish word for "conqueror," any one of the leaders in the Spanish conquest of America, especially of Mexico and Peru, in the 16th century.

conservation archaeology: A subfield of archaeology which focuses on the preservation of archaeological resources and explicitly recognizes archaeological sites as nonrenewable resources. This branch of archaeology seeking to preserve the archaeological record from destruction, by protective legislation, education, and efforts such as the Archaeological Conservancy. (*syn.* cultural resource management)

consistency: A property of soil that is defined by cohesion and adhesion—or by resistance to deformation. Consistency varies greatly with soil water and clay content.

Constantinople: The capital, once Byzantium, chosen by the Roman emperor Constantine I (reigned AD 306–337). He built the Great Palace, which has since been enlarged and altered. Constantinople was the principal residence of Byzantine emperors until about the end of 11th century AD. Constantine's choice of capital had profound effects on the ancient Greek and Roman worlds. It displaced the power center of the Roman Empire, moving it eastward, and achieved the first lasting unification of Greece.

constituent analysis: Any technique used to reveal the composition of artifacts and other archaeological materials by examining their constituent parts. This type of analysis is useful in determining raw material sources for the reconstruction of ancient exchange systems.

construct: The most basic level of archaeological theory, referring to concepts through which time, space, form, and function are perceived and interpreted.

constructed feature: A feature deliberately built to provide a setting for one or more activities, such as a house, storeroom, or burial chamber.

contact: The interface of surfaces between two successive stratigraphic levels, either vertical or horizontal. Various geological criteria are used to distinguish between two contact types: conformable and unconformable. Conformable contacts are deposit conditions not significantly different or interrupted from an adjacent unit. Unconformable contacts are surfaces of no deposit or erosion in an adjacent unit.

contact period: The period in the history and culture of the Americas when the first impact of the Europeans was made.

contamination: Materials that are not part of a natural archaeological deposit or assemblage but that have intruded or altered the deposit or assemblage. The term is often applied to samples taken for radiocarbon dating, which have been affected by their environment, for example by humus, which also contains carbon, and may be much younger than the sample, thus resulting in an inaccurate age determination.

context: The time and space setting of an artifact, feature, or culture. The context of a find is its position on a site, its relation through association with other artifacts, and its chronological position as revealed through stratigraphy. Certain features or artifacts may be normally associated with particular contexts; for example, a pottery type may be found in the context of certain burials. If such an artifact is found out of context, it may suggest the previous presence of a burial, the robbery of a burial, or a place of manufacture of the pots that accompanied burials. An artifact's context usually consists of its immediate matrix (the material surrounding it—e.g., gravel, clay, or sand), its provenience (horizontal and vertical position in the matrix), and its association with other artifacts (occurrence together with other archaeological remains, usually in the same matrix). The assessment of context includes study of what has happened to the find since it was buried in the ground. (*syn.* archaeological context)

context, systematic: Artifacts and features as they functioned in the behavioral system that produced or used them.

contextual seriation: A seriation technique, also called sequence dating, pioneered by Sir Flinders Petrie in the 19th century, in which artifacts are arranged according to the frequencies of their co-occurrence in specific contexts—usually burials. This relative dating method, based on shared typological features, enabled Petrie to establish the temporal order of a large number of Egyptian graves. (*syn.* sequence dating)

continental plates: Giant slabs of the Earth's crust, which are believed to move slowly in relation to one another. An example of a continental plate is the North American Plate, which includes North America as well as the oceanic crust between it and a portion of the Mid-Atlantic Ridge. The other type of plate is oceanic.

contingency table: A table for classifying elements of a population according to two variables—recording the relation between two classes of items, each entry counting the number of specific occurrences of the possible combinations. The rows correspond to one variable and the column to the other. The classes compared in such a cross-tabulation might be, for instance, sites in different ecological zones, artifacts in different contexts, or the coincidence of different decorative traits and fabric types in a pottery assemblage. Various statistics can be calculated from such a table, especially to test the significance of the observed correlations; the chi-square test is often used to do this.

contour fort: A fort on a hill in which the defensive bank and ditch follow the contour so as to enclose the entire hilltop.

contract archaeology: Archaeological work conducted under the direction and regulations of governments or other agencies, especially under the aegis of federal or state legislation, and often in advance of highway construction or urban development. Archaeologists are contracted to undertake research to protect cultural resources.

control pit: A preliminary excavation pit dug to determine the nature of a site and to establish the techniques needed for actual excavation. (*syn.* test pit, sondage)

convergence: Term used to describe the appearance of similar traits in different areas or at different times or in different contexts, as a result of parallel or converging evolution. For example, a rocker pattern was used for decorating pottery in widely separated contexts. (*syn.* convergent evolution) (*ant.* diffusion)

Coobool Creek: A site of Australian Aboriginal skeletal remains in New South Wales, found in the Wakool River, from the mid- to late Holocene.

Cook, Captain James (1728–1779): English navigator who made three voyages of exploration in the Pacific from 1769–1779, making many discoveries in Polynesia, Melanesia, and Australia. Although Cook was not the first European to discover most of the islands he visited, his accounts of the native peoples at the crucial point of first European contact are by far the most important in maritime history. His journals are used constantly by archaeologists who work in the Pacific region.

Cook Islands: An extensive island group in the central Pacific whose traditions and linguistic patterns indicate that they were initially settled by Polynesians from Tonga and Samoa, some of whom later colonized New Zealand. Remains show a highly organized society by about AD 1100, although the area was probably settled 1,500 years ago. Archaeological excavations have been undertaken on Rarotonga, Aitutaki, and Penrhyn, and many islands of the group have well-preserved examples of Polynesian temples (Marae).

copal: Incense used in Maya rituals, obtained from the resin of various tropical trees.

Copán: A ruined ancient Mayan city, in extreme western Honduras near the Guatemalan border, one of the largest and most impressive sites of that civilization. Copán was an important Maya city during the Classic period (AD 300–900), peaking in the 8th century with as many as 20,000 people. The site has stone temples, two large pyramids, several stairways and plazas, and a ball court for tlachtli. Most of these structures center on a raised platform called the Acropolis and are constructed in a locally available greenish volcanic tuff. Copán is particularly known for the ornate stone carving on the buildings and the portrait sculptures on its many stelae. The Hieroglyphic Stairway, which leads to one of the temples, is beautifully carved with 2,500 hieroglyphics on the risers of its 63 steps. During the Classic period, there is evidence that astronomers in Copán calculated the most accurate solar calendar produced by the Maya up to that time. The site's ruins were discovered by Spanish explorers in the early 16th century and rediscovered by the American traveler

John Lloyd Stephens in 1839, who "purchased" the site for $50. Since then, much of the beautiful carving has deteriorated, but the highly detailed pen-and-ink drawings of his colleague Frederick Catherwood still survive and are a great source of iconographic detail. Restoration work revealed much of Copán's political and dynastic history through the decipherment of hieroglyphic inscriptions on its monuments. A dynasty of at least 16 kings ruled Copán from about AD 426–822; the Maya had completely abandoned the site by about 1200. Finds date from the Late Prehistoric period (c. 300 BC–250 AD).

Coppa Nevigata: A small prehistoric mound site on the coast of southeast Italy, first occupied in the Early Neolithic. The first occupants were shellfish gatherers who used impressed cardial ware pottery and had a microlithic flint industry as early as the 6th millennium BC. A later occupation belongs to the Apennine Bronze Age.

copper: A ductile, malleable metallic element used in many functional and decorative artifacts. It was one of the first metals to be exploited by man because, like gold, it can be found in native form, pure and requiring no smelting. It is most frequently obtained from a variety of ores: carbonate (malachite), oxides, and sulphides. Shaping could be done by simple hammering, which served also to harden the metal. "Pure" copper may contain up to 1% of impurities, and the concentrations of these impurities may indicate the source of the ore. Arsenical copper alloys (2–3% arsenic) have some advantages over pure copper in ease of casting and in the hardness of a hammered edge. In the New World, cire perdue casting of copper is first recorded in the Paracas culture of Peru, and by the European conquest, the technique was practiced from the southwest United States to Argentina. Copper occurs fairly widely in the Old World and was first used in Western Asia before 8000 BC as a substitute for stone, although it did not come into common use until after 4000 BC. Metallurgy dawned in Egypt as copper was cast to shape in molds (c. 4000 BC), was reduced to metal from ores with fire and charcoal, and was intentionally alloyed with tin as bronze (c. 3500 BC). The earliest surviving examples from Egypt are small artifacts such as beads and borers of the Badarian period, c. 5500–4000 BC. Great copper hoards occur in the Ganges-Yamuna alluvial plain and just south of the lower Ganges and elsewhere in India and Pakistan.

Copper Age: An intermediate period between the Neolithic and the Bronze Ages, characterized by the use of copper tools. According to the principles of the Three Age system, it should strictly mean the period when copper was the main material for man's basic tools and weapons. It is difficult to apply in this sense as copper at its first appearance was very scarce, and experimentation with alloying seems to have begun early on. The alternative names of Chalcolithic and

Eneolithic imply the joint use of copper and stone. In many sequences, notably in Europe and Asia, there is a period between the Neolithic and Bronze Age, separated from each by breaks in the cultural development, in which copper was coming into use, and *Copper Age* is the best term to use. In Asia, the age saw the origins of civilization, and in Europe the great folk movements of the beaker and corded ware cultures, and perhaps the introduction of the Indo-European languages. The period lasted for almost 1,000 years in southeast Europe, from 3500 BC. (*syn.* Chalcolithic, Eneolithic)

coprolite: Fossilized or desiccated human or animal feces. The study of these remains can provide information about the human or animal activity in that particular locale, such as diet and disease; the study of these remains is called coprology. Coprolites survive only in exceptional circumstances—arid, frozen, and occasionally waterlogged deposits. They can be reconstituted by the addition of chemicals like trisodium phosphate and can then be analyzed for their plant and animal remains. This gives additional insight into what was being eaten on a site, because the evidence from pollen analysis, or flotation, suggests only what was being grown.

coprology: The study of coprolites, which consists of the examination of fossil excreta, the extraction and identification of the constituents, and the analysis of the results in terms of diet and disease. (*syn.* related field)

Coptic period: Chronological phase in Egypt lasting from the end of the Roman period, AD c. 395, until the Islamic conquest, AD c. 641. It is also described as the "Christian" period and is roughly equivalent to the Byzantine period elsewhere in the Near East.

Copts: The Christian population of Egypt whose church rituals and traditions date from before the Arab conquest of the 7th century. Their art is largely borrowed from Syria, Sassanian Persia, and the Egyptian past, sometimes using Christianized symbols from ancient Egyptian religion. Although the Coptic Church survives, Copts made little contribution to art after the 9th century when Islamic art merged with it. Many Copts preserve in their facial and body features the characteristics of the people of Pharaonic Egypt. The Copts are most numerous in the middle Nile Valley muhafazat of Asyut, al-Minya, and Qina. About one fourth of the total Coptic population lives in Cairo.

coracle: Primitive, light, small bowl-shaped boats with a wattle frame of grasses, reeds, or saplings covered with hides. They were first known and are still used in Wales and along coastal Ireland, usually with a canvas and tar covering. The term also refers to an Old English boat of wickerwork covered with hides. Native Americans used the similar bull boat, covered with buffalo hides, on the Missouri River, and the *corita*, often sealed with bitumen, on the Colorado. (*syn.* curragh)

corbel vault: In architecture, a simple form of vault in which the stones are overlapped on one another and topped with a capstone. As distinguished from the true arch, it has no keystone and is not self-supporting; the thrust must be take up by massive walls. The corbel vault is therefore suitable for spanning only limited spaces. In the Mayan style, corbel vaults can support a roof or upper story. Corbel vaults and arches were useful in cultures that had not yet developed curving arches and other ceiling structures. (*syn.* corbelled vault)

corbelling, corbeling: A technique of roofing in stone-built chambers whereby successive courses of bricks or slabs are allowed to project a little further inward than the course below until a curved or domed ceiling is achieved. The Maya used this method to create a corbelled "false" arch, or vault, with the earliest expressions in Late Chicanel tombs at Tikal and Altar de Sacrificios. The technique was also used in the megalithic tradition in Europe in some of the passage graves, such as New Grange and Maes Howe, and in the tholos tombs of the Mycenaean world. Babylonian architecture made wide use of corbel arches. (*syn.* corbeled roof)

Corbridge: A Roman fort site in northeast England, on the River Tyne, dating to AD 79–80. It burned and was rebuilt in c. 105, but was neglected when Hadrian's Wall with its own forts was built not far to the north. When the Roman frontier was pushed farther north in 139, the fort was reconstructed in stone, and later, when the frontier fell back to Hadrian's Wall once again, Corbridge flourished as a market town and military supply depot. Remains of military quarters, granaries, and temples may still be seen. (*syn.* Roman Corstopitum)

cordate: Of or pertaining to a refined heart-shaped biface with a flat profile, characteristic of the Mousterian in western Europe.

Corded Beaker culture: A Late Neolithic culture in central and northern Europe from c. 2800 BC, named after a characteristic cord-marked decoration found on pottery. The Corded Beaker culture belongs to the so-called Battle-Ax cultures of Europe. There were two phases of new burial rites, with individual rather than communal burials and an emphasis on burying rich grave goods with adult males. The first phase, characterized by Corded Ware pottery and stone battle axes, is found particularly in central and northern Europe. The second phase, dated to 2500–2200 BC, is marked by Bell Beaker pottery and the frequent occurrence of copper daggers in the graves; it is found from Hungary to Britain and as far south as Italy, Spain, and North Africa. At the same time, there was an increase in the exchange of prestige goods such as amber, copper, and tools from particular rock sources.

corded ware: A Late Neolithic pottery ware decorated with twisted cord ornament found over much of north and central Europe in the 2nd half of the 3rd millennium BC. The commonest shapes are the beaker and the globular amphora. The ware is always associated with primitive agriculture, and the stone battle ax and usually with single burial under a small barrow or kurgan. The ware may derive from Denmark, central Germany (Saxo-Thuringia), eastern Poland, or the Ukraine. The culture received its name from the characteristic pottery. Some groups also had metal artifacts. There is some evidence that Corded Ware people had domesticated horses and wheeled vehicles, and they are sometimes interpreted as nomadic groups—possibly Indo-European speaking—who spread across northern Europe from the east. Closely related are the Globular Amphora and Funnel Beaker cultures. (*syn.* Corded Ware)

Cordilleran: The ice mass that covered the coastal mountains along the Pacific Ocean coast of North America from northern Washington state into southern Alaska. At its maximum extent, about 20,000 years ago, it connected with the Laurentide ice sheet to the east and with the Pacific Ocean to the west and reached a thickness of some 3 kilometers (1 mi). The Cordilleran Geosyncline is a linear trough in the Earth's crust in which rocks of Late Precambrian to Mesozoic age (roughly 600 million to 66 million years ago) were deposited along the western coast of North America, from southern Alaska through western Canada and the United States, probably to western Mexico. The eastern boundary of the geosyncline extends from southeastern Alaska along the eastern edge of the Northern Cordillera and Northern Rocky Mountains of Canada and Montana, along the eastern edge of the Great Basin of Utah and Nevada, and into southeastern California and Mexico. The Old Cordilleran culture appeared in the Pacific Northwest about 9000 or 10,000 BC and persisted until about 5000 BC in some areas. Subsistence was based on hunting, fishing, and gathering. Simple willow-leaf-shaped, bipointed projectile points are characteristic artifacts. (*syn.* Cordilleran ice sheet; Laurentide)

Córdoba: A site in southern Spain, probably Carthaginian in origin, and occupied by the Romans in 152 BC. It declined under the rule of the Visigoths from the 6th to the early 8th centuries AD. In 711, Córdoba was captured and largely destroyed by the Muslims. It recovered under 'Abd ar-Rahman I, a member of the Umayyad family, who made Córdoba his capital in 756. 'Abd ar-Rahman I founded the Great Mosque of Córdoba, which was later enlarged and completed about 976. The city quickly rose to become one of the finest in Europe, rivaled only by Baghdad and Constantinople. In the 10th century, one of the rulers of Córdoba built a pleasure city outside its walls known as Medina al Zahara; this is now an archaeological site.

cordon: In ceramics, a strip of clay added around the outside surface of a pot before firing for decoration or handling. The cordon(s) may be decorated in some way, for example with fingertip or stick impressions. On wheel-turned pots, cordons may be created by pushing the clay out in a narrow ring from inside, achieving a similar effect. In metalworking, a cordon is formed in much the same way as on a wheel-turned pot, that is, by the repoussé technique.

cord ornament: Pottery decoration produced by impressing a twisted cord into the surface of the soft clay. Sometimes short individual motifs were produced by wrapping a cord around a stick (Peterborough ware), or part or the whole of a vessel was wrapped closely in cord (Corded Ware and some varieties of Beaker).

core: A piece of stone used as a blank from which flakes or blades were removed by prehistoric toolmakers. Usually it was the by-product of toolmaking, but it may also have been shaped and modified to serve as an implement in its own right. An object, such as a hand ax, chopper, or scraper, made in this way is a core tool. Cores were most often produced when hit by a pebble, antler, or bone hammer. (*syn.* nucleus)

core borer: A hollow tubelike instrument used to collect samples of soils, pollens, and other materials from below the surface. The cylinder of soil that is collected is called the core. The core is undisturbed, and the sediment contacts, soil boundaries, and structures are intact and can be described accurately.

core-formed glass: A type of glass made by twisting melted glass around a core, often with different colors. This technique was used especially in the Classical and Hellenistic periods of the eastern Mediterranean.

coregency: A term applied to the periods during which two rulers were simultaneously in power, usually with an overlap of several years.

core sampling: A subsurface detection technique using a hollow metal tube driven into the ground to lift a column of earth for stratigraphic study. This technique is used in underground or undersea exploration. A core sample is a roughly cylindrical piece of subsurface material removed by a special drill and brought to the surface for examination. Such a sample reveals the properties of underground rock, such as its porosity and permeability, and allows investigation of the features of a given stratum. (*syn.* coring)

core tool: A stone tool, such as a hand ax, chopper, or scraper, formed by chipping away flakes from a core. These tools, often large and relatively heavy, were characteristic of the Palaeolithic culture. They were made by using a pebble, antler, or bone hammer. (*syn.* core, core-tool)

Coricancha: The principal religious site of the Inca in their capital of Cuzco, Peru, called the "enclosure of gold." There are temples dedicated to the sun, stars, rainbow, thunder, and moon. The walls were once covered with sheets of gold, and life-sized statues in gold and silver were found there. Coricancha was thoroughly plundered during the Spanish Conquest.

Corinth: An ancient city of Greece, located where the Peloponnese meets the isthmus that connects it to the Greek mainland. The city has an exceptionally high akropolis on Acronocorinth Hill and profited from having ports on both the Corinthian and Saronic Gulfs. The site was occupied from before 3000 BC, but its history is obscure until the early 8th century BC, when the city-state of Corinth began to develop as a commercial center. There is evidence of a Neolithic and an Early Bronze Age settlement at Corinth, both of considerable size. There is little evidence of Mycenaean settlement, however, and the next major settlement belonged to the Dark Age, c. late 10th century BC. Corinth was a very important city throughout the Archaic, Classical, and Hellenistic periods. Corinth's political influence was increasd through territorial expansion in the vicinity, and by the late 8th century it had secured control of the isthmus. The Corinthians established colonies at Corcyra and Syracuse, later making them dominant in trade with the western Mediterranean. From c. 720–570 BC, Corinthian painted vases in the black-figure technique (which the Corinthians invented) were exported all over the Greek world. Workshops dating to this period have been excavated in the potters' quarter at Corinth, producing both pottery and terra-cottas. Corinthian pottery provides the most useful dating method available to archaeologists studying this period. Northwest of the agora stand seven Doric columns, which are the remains of the temple of Apollo (c. 550 BC). Callimachus is said to have invented the Corinthian column capital here c. 450–425 BC. Corinth was involved in most of Greece's political struggles and in 146 BC was destroyed by the Roman general Lucius Mummius. In 44 BC, Julius Caesar re-established Corinth as a Roman colony. Many of the visible remains date from the classical Greek and especially the early Roman periods, including a Roman agora (marketplace), the Odeon, the Pirene fountain, the Glauke fountain, temples, villas, baths, pottery factory, gymnasium, basilica, theater, and an amphitheater. Parts of the classical fortifications on the akropolis survive. In the later medieval period, it then passed from Frankish to Venetian and eventually to Turkish hands. Substantial buildings from all these periods have been found in excavations since 1896. Modern Corinth was founded in 1858, 3 miles north of the ancient town, after an earthquake leveled the latter.

Corinthian order: An architectural style characterized by columns with a diameter-to-height ratio of one-to-ten, and an enlarged capital (uppermost part) decorated with sculptured foliage, often acanthus leaves. It originated in Greece, was extensively used by the Romans, and is related to the Ionic order. The innovation is traditionally ascribed to Callimachus of Corinth, c. 450–425 BC. The style was incorporated in the so-called "composite" order—a combination of four-sided Ionic and Corinthian. The earliest-known Corinthian capital was inside the temple of Apollo at Bassae. (*syn.* Corinthian column, Corinthian style)

Corinthian pottery: A widely distributed pottery made at Corinth and found throughout the Mediterranean, from the late 7th century BC until the mid-6th century BC. This important stage of vase painting included "naturalistic" designs of animals, maenads, and satyrs and the invention of black-figure technique and some new shapes, such as the aryballos and alabastron. Proto-Corinthian pottery, most of which is miniature in size, was the first to be decorated in the black-figure painting technique: figure silhouettes drawn in black and filled in with incised details.

cornelian: A translucent, semiprecious variety of the silica mineral chalcedony, which owes its red to reddish brown color to hematite (iron oxide). It is found in India, Brazil, Australia, Africa, and the Nile Valley. It was highly valued and used in rings and signets by the Greeks and Romans. (*syn.* carnelian)

cornice: The uppermost projecting element of the entablature of a Classical building, immediately below the roof line. It is located above the triglyphs and metopes in the Doric order, or above the frieze in the Ionic order.

corn mummy: A type of anthropomorphic funerary object made of soil mixed with grains of corn, which was usually wrapped in linen bandages and had a face mask.

correlation: The use of various methods, often multiple methods, to demonstrate the equivalence of stratigraphic units. This term refers to the relation of one stratigraphical unit to another, by petrological, osteological, lithographic, cultural, chronological, or palaeontological means. For example, stratigraphic units may be correlated by using palaeontological criteria, absolute dating methods, relative dating methods, cross-dating methods, and position relative to the glacial-interglacial cycle by examining physical and biological attributes. Correlation of fossil inclusions is a principle of stratigraphy: that strata may be correlated based on the sequence and uniqueness of their floral and faunal content.

corrugation: A technique of decorating pottery in which the individual coils are not smoothed on the outside, thus forming an overlapping surface. Corrugation improves a pot's heat conductivity.

Cortaillod: A Neolithic village site of pile dwellings on the edge of Lake Neuchâtel, and the type site of the oldest Neolithic culture in western Switzerland, with a starting date of c. 3800 BC and lasting to after 2500 BC. Cortaillod is noted for the fine preservation of wood, cloth, and plant remains, and for its plain round-based pottery of Western Neolithic type. A large number of wooden and birch-bark utensils and containers have been found as well as organic remains, including fruits and nuts, cereals, pulses, and flax. The houses were built on wooden frames with walls of clay set on closely spaced timbers; the roof was probably thatched. The inhabitants practiced mixed farming, hunting, and fishing. The round-based dark burnished pottery demonstrates connections with the Chassey culture of France.

Cortes de Navarra: An Urnfield settlement site of the Late Bronze and Early Iron Ages near Sargossa in the Ebro Valley of northern Spain. Narrow, rectangular mud-brick houses were arranged in rows on terraces, and the site is actually a tell. Some archaeologists regard the appearance of such traits in southern France and northern Spain in the early 1st millennium BC as indicating the movement of Celtic groups into the area.

Cortés, Hernán (or Hernando Cortez) (c. 1485–1547): The Spanish conqueror of the Aztec Empire and founder of the colony of New Spain. After arriving in 1519, he founded the city of Veracruz and marched to Tenochtitlán. He captured Montezuma, the Aztec ruler, was later driven out, but returned to conquer and destroy the city in 1521.

cortex: A tough covering or crust on an unmodified stone cobble or newly exposed flint nodule and tabular flint. It is formed by weathering and is usually discarded during the knapping process.

cortical flake: A flake with its dorsal aspect completely covered by cortex. (*syn.* primary flake)

Cosa: A town on the west coast of Italy, north of Rome, which was a Latin colony founded in 273 BC. There is well-preserved massive polygonal masonry surviving in the city walls, the forum, basilica, citadel, capitol, baths, and temples—as well as remains of the grid street plan. The site was abandoned in 1st century BC. (*syn.* modern Ansedonia)

cosmetics: The earliest cosmetics known to archaeologists were in use in Egypt in the 4th millennium BC, with evidence among funerary artifacts of eye makeup and scented unguents. Both Egyptian men and women used oils, perfumes, and eye paints. By the start of the Christian era, cosmetics were in wide use in the Roman Empire.

costrel: A type of medieval pottery flask, of which the majority were made of leather and have not survived. Merovingian and Carolingian pottery costrels tend to be roughly round in shape, with a slight neck for a stopper. The best known is the Zelzate costrel, made in the "Badorf-type" industries of the central Rhineland, which contained a Viking-period hoard dating to 870.

Cotofeni: A late Eneolithic/Late Copper Age culture in the eastern Balkans, mainly in southern Rumania, and dating to the 3rd millennium BC. The sites were small, short-lived settlements suggesting agriculture and fishing as well as movement for seasonal reasons. Most burial sites used inhumation rites, although cremation is found. Cotofeni sites have a rich pottery assemblage with handled mugs and pitchers with lentil-impressed decoration.

Cotte de Sainte Brelade, La: A Palaeolithic cave site in Jersey, the Channel Islands, which also has pre-Mousterian and Mousterian levels. Human remains include large teeth and a piece of a child's skull presumed to be Neanderthal. There is also evidence that at La Cotte de Sainte Brelade rhinoceroses and mammoths were driven over a cliff edge.

cotton: A plant cultivated for its hairy flowering heads, from which come fibers widely used in textiles. The earliest cotton yet found comes from the site of Mehrgarh in Pakistan, where it was probably being cultivated before 4000 BC. The earliest records of cotton in the New World come from the Tehuacan Valley of central Mexico, c. 4300 BC, and from pre-ceramic villages on the Peruvian coast from 3300 BC. It was grown in northeast Mexico by c. 2000 and was introduced into the southwestern United States in the 1st millennium BC. In the Old World, the first known occurrence is in the Indus Valley civilization where cotton was used for both string and textiles at Mohenjo-Daro by 2750 BC. The first record in African archaeology goes back only to the culture of Meroë in the fifth century BC. Actual cotton fabrics appeared at Mohenjodaro around 2500 BC.

Cotzumahualpa, Santa Lucia: The site of a localized culture of the Late Classic period on the Pacific slopes of Guatemala. It was known for its unique style of stone sculpture, depicting scenes of deities gazing upward, skulls, serpent heads, and human sacrifice—all enclosed in cartouches. There was also San Juan plumbate pottery.

Cougnac: A Palaeolithic cave site in Quercy, France, known for its paintings of megaloceros and ibex. The radiocarbon dates are 13,050–12,350 bc.

Council on Underwater Archaeology: A professional organization for archaeologists specializing in nautical archaeology; affiliated with the Society for Historical Archaeology. (*syn.* CUA)

counterscarp bank: The facing wall on the forward (outer, downhill) side of a defensive ditch, often faced by brick or stone for ease of maintenance. The scarp was the main fortress wall of a hill fort or earthwork site. The term also describes the side of the vallum and ditch farthest away from the camp and facing in toward it. (*syn.* counterscarp)

court cairn: A type of Neolithic (c. 3500 BC) chamber tomb common in southwest Scotland and northern Ireland. Its features include an elongated rectangular or trapeze-shaped cairn with an unroofed semicircular forecourt at one end. The courtyard gives access to the burial chamber proper, which is normally a gallery with two or more chambers separated by jambs, or by a combination of jambs and sills. This basic form sometimes called a "horned cairn" has many variants. In the "lobster-claw" or "full court" cairns, the wings of the facade curve around until they almost meet at the front of the tomb to enclose a circular or oval forecourt. Sometimes a cairn contains more than one tomb, or there are subsidiary chambers. Court cairns continued to be used until the end of the Neolithic period around 2200 BC. The later court cairns share many features with the Severn-Cotswold tombs of southwest Britain and with the transepted gallery graves near the river Loire. (*syn.* Clyde-Carlingford tomb)

Covalanas: An Upper Palaeolithic painted cave in the Canabrian region of northern Spain. The style, including a finger-blob technique, suggests that it belongs to a primitive stage of cave art, possibly preceding the Solutrean.

cover sand: A deposit or sediment of wind-blown sand, which is formed by the carrying of sand grains from glacial outwash deposits or from the shore by wind gusts. In areas where this occurs, the deposits may wipe out evidence of previous occupation—but they may also preserve artifact associations if the deposition is thick and rapid. If it happens slowly, the archaeological material may eventually end up several kilometers from its source. (*syn.* coversand, blow sand)

Coveta de l'Or: A cave site in eastern Spain near Valencia with Early Neolithic cardial (impressed) ware pottery, bones of domestic animals, and remains of cultivated emmer and bread wheats. Large, deep pottery jars may have been used for grain storage. The radiocarbon dates are of the mid-5th millennium BC. (*syn.* Coveta del Or)

cowrie: A variety of spiral shell from marine snails of the genus Cypraea, in which the opening is reduced to a slit running the length of one side. The humped, thick shell is beautifully colored (often speckled) and glossy; the apertural lips, which open into the first whorl in the shell, are rolled inward and may be fine toothed. Its popularity in antiquity seems to depend on its use as a symbol of the female vulva. It was widely traded, larger species being imported into Europe from as far as the Red Sea. A cowrie-shaped amulet, known from Predynastic Egypt, was called a cowroid. (*syn.* cowry)

Coxcatlán phase: Occupation phase of Mexico's Tehuacán Valley from c. 5500–4500 BC. Maize first appeared, although wild and semidomesticated plants were still eaten along with small game.

Coyotlatelco: A ceramic horizon of the Early Post-Classic period beginning in central Mesoamerica after the fall of Teothihuacán. It was a distinctive red-on-buff painted ware and appeared in the early phases of both Tula and Cholula; it is a forerunner of the late Mazpan style.

Cozumel: An island located less than 20 miles off the east coast of the northern Yucatán Peninsula in Mexico, which was a trading port and pilgrimage spot for the Maya. Its earliest artifacts date to c. 1000 BC, but its rise began from 300 BC (Late Pre-Classic or Formative period), and its major period of occupation was the Post-Classic, c. 800–1000. Cozumel was a major link in the long-distance trading network, which the ancient Maya operated between Honduras and the Guatemalan highlands to the south, around the Peninsula, to Tabasco, Campeche, and Veracruz in the west. It was also a place of pilgrimage to the Mayan mood (and childbirth) goddess Ix Chel. Its ceremonial architecture, however, is considerably more modest that the great Classic centers of the mainland. Cozumel is the putative starting point for the Itza migrations into the northern Yucatán. The Spanish explorers discovered it in 1518.

crackle porcelain: A type of china with glaze that has been purposely crackled or covered with a network of fine crackle in the kiln. It is caused by the shrinking of the glaze as the vessel cooled after firing and was often the only ornament on the exquisite ware. The Chinese made many variations of this porcelain, some rare and valuable. In some examples there is engraved decoration under the glaze. The low-fired Ju stoneware is distinguished by a seemingly soft, milky glaze of pale blue or grayish green with hair-thin crackle. A variant with strongly marked crackle became known as ko ware as it was made by the elder brother (*ko*) of the director of the Lungch'üan factory. (*syn.* cracklin)

cranial: Of or pertaining to the cranium or skull. A cranial skeleton is the bones of the head, including the mandible. The cranium is the bones of the skull, not including the mandible.

crannog: An artificial island in a lake, bog, or march, which forms the foundation for a small settlement and on which a fortified structure is usually built. This structure was typical of prehistoric Ireland, Scotland, and the Isle of Man, especially during the first century AD. The island was constructed from brush wood, stones, peat, and timber and usually surrounded by a wooden palisade. Most crannogs probably represent single homesteads. The oldest examples in Ireland have yielded early Neolithic material (Bann flakes), and others have Beaker pottery. Most of them, however, are of Late Bronze Age, Iron Age, Early Christian, or medieval. The most interesting is that in Lough Cur in Limerick.

crater: A large, wide-mouthed two-handled Greek or Roman bowl or vase, usually made of pottery or metal. It is characteristic of Greece in the Mycenaean and Classical periods, and such bowls were used to serve wine, mixed with water in varying proportions, into individual drinking cups, and handed out at banquets and sacrifices. The word is Greek for "mixing bowl." There is a classification of four types: column crater, volute crater, calyx crater, and bell crater, which take their names from the characteristic shape either of the handle or of the body of the vase.

Crawford, O. G. S. (1886–1957): British archaeologist who made many contributions to the development of the field— including being the first exponent of the mapping of distributions, of air photography, of field archaeology, of the national mapping of antiquities, and of enlightening the public. He was the editor of the popular journal *Antiquity* for its first 31 years and Archaeological Officer of the Ordnance Survey, where he was largely responsible for the high standard of mapping of archaeological sites in Britain.

crazing: In lithics, a cross-hatched pattern of fractures, observable on the surface of a stone, as the result of excessive temperature exposure. In ceramic analysis, it is a situation in which differential shrinkage causes the surface of the vessel to crack while the remainder of the vessel wall remains undamaged.

cremation: The practice of burning the dead. The practice of cremation on open fires was introduced to the Western world by the Greeks as early as 1000 BC. There is much variation in the disposal of the ashes, one distinctive practice being to place them in a cinerary urn for burial. Primary cremation is the burning of the deceased on a pyre in the grave. Secondary cremation is the practice of removing the remains of the deceased from the pyre to a grave. The cremation pit is a depression in which the remains of a cremation are buried.

crepido: In Roman antiquity, a kind of base or stand on which another object rests, and by analogy the embankment of a quay, a dike, or jetty. Also used for the raised causeway for foot passengers at the side of a road or street (as in Pompeii) or for the platforms or stages around a great altar.

crescent: A crescent-shaped bifacially flaked stone tool generally restricted to the Paleo-Indian period and almost always found in association with extinct Pleistocene lakes. They were possibly used for hunting large shorebirds. (*syn.* Great Basin Transverse point)

Creswell Crags: The type site of the Creswellian culture, a gorge about 1,500 feet long near Creswell, England, which has caves that have yielded one of the most important British series of extinct vertebrate remains, accompanied by implements of Palaeolithic hunters. The Creswellian culture is regarded as a variant of the Magdalenian culture of southwestern France and occurred during the final stages of the Würm glaciation. Finds include flint tools of Mousterian, "proto-Solutrean," Creswellian, and Mesolithic types, as well as harpoons and a bone fragment with an engraved horse's head in Late Magdalenian style. Mammal remains

include reindeer, woolly rhinoceros, mammoth, and wild horse. The Creswellian culture never used the stone ax, but their tools were a Gravettian-type of blunted-back blade showing development in manufacture over a long period. Creswell Crags was first excavated in 1875.

Creswellian: A Late Upper Palaeolithic culture found at Creswell Crags and in caves in Wales and southern England. It is regarded as a variant of the Magdalenian culture of southwestern France and occurred during the final stages of the Würm glaciation. The characteristic tools are large trapezes, obliquely blunted-back blades, and small backed blades. Later cultural traditions such as the Federmesser, Creswellian, and Ahrensburgian (c. 20,000–10,000 BP) formed the basis for the cultures of the succeeding Mesolithic period.

Crete: The fifth largest island in the Mediterranean, lying south of Greece, where the first flowering of the Greek Bronze Age culture took place (c. 2600–2000 BC). There is no evidence that humans arrived on Crete before 6000–5000 BC. By 3000 BC, however, a Bronze Age culture—the Minoan civilization, named after the legendary ruler Minos—had developed. Strongly influenced by Eastern ideas, in its first centuries this culture produced circular vaulted (tholos-type) tombs and some fine stone-carved vases, but about 2000 BC the inhabitants began to build palaces on the sites of Knossos, Phaestus, and Mallia. This was called the first palace period (Middle Minoan, 2000–1700 BC) and the second palace period (1700–1400 BC), during which the population greatly increased and large settlements were built. The Minoan civilization was centered at Knossos and reached its peak in the 16th century BC, trading widely in the eastern Mediterranean. It produced striking sculpture, fresco painting, pottery, and metalwork. By about 1500 BC, Greek mainlanders from Mycenae began to influence Minoan affairs, but Crete suffered a major earthquake (c. 1450) that destroyed Knossos and other places. The Mycenaeans took power until the Iron Age (1200 BC). Eventually, the Dorians moved in and gained power. Crete is the source of many myths, legends, and laws. The Romans came and by 67 BC had completed their conquest of the island.

Crickley Hill: A Neolithic causewayed camp and Iron Age hill fort in Gloucestershire, southwest England. The site was used for several centuries, and the ditches and banks were refurbished several times. The final Neolithic phase had deeper quarry ditches and a rampart faced with drystone walling at the front and a timber stockade at the back and a wooden fence on the top. There were two gateways, and evidence of burning and large numbers of flint arrowheads indicate that the site was attacked and burnt down around 1500 BC. There is also a stone circle erected in the Late Neolithic. The site was abandoned for nearly 2 millennia, when it was once again used for a defended settlement. Two phases of Iron Age occupation are represented, probably falling between 700–500 BC. The earlier phase was characterized by rectangular houses and square storage huts, while the second phase had one large round house, smaller round buildings, and more small square huts, perhaps granaries. The site was burned down again c. 500 BC and never re-occupied.

Cris culture: An Early Neolithic culture of Romania and Moldova, part of the complex of Balkan Early Neolithic cultures. Cris settlements were flat and open.

critical theory: A theoretical approach that was an attempt to adapt Karl Marx's ideas to an understanding of events and circumstances of 20th-century life. The relations between the assumptions and discoveries of a scholarly discipline and its ties to modern life are subject to examination, automatically relating the questions, methods, and discoveries of a science such as anthropology to those of the anthropologist's own culture. The theory claims that all knowledge is historical. (*syn.* Critical Theory)

Cro-Magnon: A population of anatomically modern *Homo sapiens* dating from the Upper Palaeolithic period (c. 35,000–10,000 years ago), first found in 1868 in a shallow cave at Cro-Magnon in the Dordogne region of southern France. French geologist Louis Lartet uncovered five archaeological layers, and the race of prehistoric humans revealed by this find was called Cro-Magnon and has since been considered, along with Neanderthals, to be representative of prehistoric humans at that time. It was also the first discovery of remains of *Homo sapiens* in a deposit containing Upper Palaeolithic tools. The skeletons had been carefully buried, covered with red ochre, and necklaces laid beside them. They were the earliest known modern humans in Europe, who were characterized by the long skull and high forehead, a tall erect stature, and the use of blade technology and bone tools. They were associated with the Aurignacian culture, which produced the earliest European art. Unlike Neanderthal man, the remains are hardly different from modern man. (*syn.* Cromagnon)

Cromerian: An interglacial stage of northern Europe correlated with the Günz-Mindel Interglacial, part of the series of interglacials recognized in Britain: the Pastonian (oldest), Beestonian, and Cromerian. The Cromerian stage is a group of Interglacial deposits of the Quaternary system, which are stratified under Anglian glacial deposits and above an extensive sequence of earlier Quaternary deposits. The type site of the stage is at West Runton, Norfolk. In northwest Europe, a group of deposits represents several interglacials and intervening cold stages, and these deposits are stratified below Elster glacial deposits and above a sequence extending back into the Pliocene.

cromlech: (kam-leck) A term used in Wales for any megalithic tomb. In Britain, the term refers to a circle of upright stones of prehistoric times. The enclosure was formed by menhirs, huge stones planted in the ground in a circle or semicircle. These enclosures were consecrated places used as burial grounds. The former usage is now obsolete in archaeological literature but has persisted in Welsh folk usage. (*syn.* dolmen)

crop mark: Variations in the color or growth of surface vegetation, which indicate the outline of buried archaeological features, such as walls, pits, or buildings; visible by aerial observation or photography. These indications are revealed by the abnormal growth of overlying crops. Buried archaeological features such as wells stunt crop growth; ditches increase crop growth. Buried pits and ditches may retain moisture better than the surrounding subsoil, and during a dry spell plant growth is often enhanced over such features.

cross-bed: A sedimentary structure with fine strata (laminae) in a bed, which are inclined relative to the bounding beds. Orientation of cross-bedding can be used to reconstruct past depositional environments that may have related archaeological deposits.

crossbow: A bow made with a crossbow parallel to the arrow and operated by a mechanical trigger release. It was likely invented by the Chinese in the late Chou Dynasty (c. 400 BC) for defending their cities. The best-preserved examples were in Ch'u state. Chinese skill in bronze casting enabled them to make the accurate trigger of several interlocking parts for the weapon's effectiveness. Cast-bronze trigger mechanisms are commonly found in late Eastern Zhou burials along with inlaid bronze bow fittings and bronze arrow points. It was the most important weapon of the Middle Ages; its earliest appearance in Europe was in Italian cities during the 10th and 11th centuries.

cross-dating: A correlation dating technique that can yield a relative or absolute age or chronology. The basis of cross-dating is the occurrence of finds in association. The assumption is that a particular type of artifact, for example a type of sword, when found in an undated context, will bear a similar date to one found in a dated context, thus enabling the whole of the undated context to be given a chronological value. The method is based on the assumption that typologies evolved at the same rate and in the same way over a wide area or alternatively on assumptions of diffusion. Many of the chronologies constructed before the advent of chronometric dating techniques were based on cross-dating. New techniques such as radiocarbon dating showed some of the links established by cross-dating to be invalid, so that the method has become somewhat discredited. However, its use is still helpful where recognizable products of dateable manufacture are found in undated contexts with no possibility of using a chronometric dating technique. In the absence of geochronology, two cultural groups can be proved contemporary only by the discovery of links between them. If in Culture A an object produced by Culture B is found, A must be contemporary with, or later than, B. The term cross-dating ought strictly to be used only when an object of Culture A is also found in proved association with Culture B, when overlap of at least part of the time span of each is proved. Items having an established date, such as dated coins or buildings or ceramics of known manufacture, are most often used. By itself, a cross-dated chronology does not give absolute dates, but it may be calibrated by reference to other dating methods. A type of cross-dating has always been used in geology, and stratigraphical sequences are often correlated by the assemblages of fossils they contain; this is known as biostratigraphy. The archaeological versions of cross-dating may have been developed directly out of the geological method and may have been based on a false analogy between biological fossils and archaeological artifacts. (*syn.* cross dating)

cross-laminae: A sedimentary structure in which laminae are deposited at an inclined angle to the main depositional surface (bedding plane). The constituents and orientation of cross-laminae can be used to reconstruct past depositional environments.

cross-over immunoelectrophoresis: One of the several techniques used in protein residue analysis. (*syn.* CIEP)

Cross River: A river valley in western Africa, mostly in southeastern Nigeria, where more than 300 huge anthropomorphic monoliths were found, probably dating from the 16th century AD.

cross-sectional trenches: A type of excavation in which a set of superimposed strata are cut across by deep trenches that expose the history of deposition. (*syn.* slot trenches)

Crow Creek: A settlement site in South Dakota from the Initial Coalescent period of the Plains Village Indians with more than 500 human skeletons from a massacre.

crucible: A small, coarse pottery (or other refractory material) vessel used for holding molten metal during smelting, testing, or casting. It is usually easily recognizable from the effects of the high temperatures to which it has been subjected, as well as from its shape and thickness. Crucibles were probably so named from the Latin word crux, "cross" or "trial."

crucible smelting: A technique of separating copper from ore by heating the ore in an open vessel, designed to withstand very high temperatures, rather than in a closed furnace.

cruciform chamber: A megalithic tomb, characteristic of the passage-tomb tradition in Ireland, in which a passage, a chamber, and three apses form a cross-shaped structure.

cruck: A simple timber-framed building, known from the 13th century onward, which is easily constructed and most commonly used for barns, farm buildings, and dwellings. Curved timbers are part of the construction—the longitudinal supports take the form of a series of curved, triangular trusses, connected by purlins and provided with vertical in-filled walls.

Crvena Stijena: A prehistoric cave site near the Adriatic coast in Montenegro. Artifacts and faunal remains date back to the last glaciation, and deposits include the Palaeolithic, Mousterian, Upper Palaeolithic (Aurignacian), Early and Late Mesolithic (with microlithic flint industries and a large faunal sample of red deer and chamois), Early Neolithic (with Impressed Ware and Danilo-Kakanj pottery, also macrolithic flint industry), Late Neolithic (Danilo culture), and a Late Bronze Age level (with Hallstatt A–B metalwork).

cryoturbation: The disturbing or mixing of soil by frost action and the freezing of the active layer of permafrost late in the melting season. The soil in regions close to an ice sheet contains a good deal of water, and when it refreezes after the seasonal thaw the pressure of growing ice crystals tends to rotate and rearrange the stones. The presence of such a structured soil indicates former cold climatic episodes.

crypt: A vault or subterranean chamber, especially one beneath the main floor of a church or other building, and used as a burial place. In the catacombs, it was a tomb in which a number of bodies were interred together. Early Christians called their catacombs crypts; when churches came to be erected over the tombs of saints and martyrs, subterranean chapels, known as crypts or confessiones, were built around the actual tomb. The most famous of these was St. Peter's, built over the circus of Nero, the site of St. Peter's martyrdom. By the time of the emperor Constantine the Great (306–337), the crypt was considered a normal part of a church building. (*syn.* crypta)

cryptoportico: In Roman architecture, an underground corridor, usually in the substructure of a large building complex.

Ctesiphon: Ancient city founded by the Parthians, located on the Tigris River southeast of modern Baghdad, Iraq. It served as the winter capital of the Parthian Empire and later of the Sasanian Empire. The site is famous for the remains of a gigantic vaulted hall, the Taq Kisra, which is traditionally regarded as the palace of the Sassanian king Khosrow I (reigned AD 531–579) and Shapur I (reigned AD 241–272). The hall has one of the largest single-span mud-brick arches in the world. (*syn.* Tusbun, Taysafun)

cubiculum: In Roman architecture, the bedchamber of a house. The term also refers to a chamber in a catacomb used for rites of the dead.

Cucuteni-Tripolye: A Neolithic culture of southeastern Europe, distributed throughout the Ukraine (Tripolye culture) and Moldova and Romania (Cucuteni culture), which arose about 3000 BC. The type site of the Cucuteni is in the Siret Valley of Romania, and the type site of the Tripolye is near Kiev in the Ukraine. The Cucuteni is divided into stages: Pre-Cucuteni, Cucuteni A, AB, and B, dating c. 4200–3000 BC. Tripolye is divided into five phases—A, B1, B2, C1, and C2—the latest dating to the full Early Bronze Age in the 3rd millennium BC. The late Cucuteni-Tripolye phase is regarded as the local climax of Neolithic cultural development. It produced fine wares (red or orange, as decorated with curvilinear designs painted or grooved on the surface) on a large scale and long chipped-stone blades. The people also mastered metallurgical techniques such as alloying, casting, and welding. There was a subsistence economy depending on fruits and the earliest recorded domestication in Europe of the horse. The villages consisted of long, rectangular houses, although the Tripolye people practiced shifting agriculture and frequently moved.

Cuello: A small Maya site in northern Belize, with one of the longest and most complete sequences covering the whole of the Pre-Classic period of Lowland Maya culture. It is the earliest-known ancient Maya site. A major discovery was of an early (Swasey) stage, c. 2500–1200 BC, below Middle and Late Formative structures, with maize cultivation and a unique, fully developed ceramic complex of great variety. The site has long stratigraphic and ceramic sequences covering the period from the Early formative to the Early Classic (AD 300).

cuesta: A gentle slope, inclined plain, or long, low ridge with a relatively steep drop; a hill or ridge with one steep face (escarpment) and one that is gently sloping.

Cueva Morin: A Palaeolithic cave site of northern Spain with seven Mousterian levels, a lower Perigordian layer dated to 36,350 bp, and Aurignacian levels with dwellings and burials. It was one of the first Spanish sites excavated by scientific methods.

Cuicuilco: A Late Pre-Classic ceremonial site, at the southern end of ancient Lake Texcoco near Mexico City, with the first stone monument (pyramid) on the Mexican plateau. Cuicuilco was one of the largest and most important centers of the period—possibly an early rival of Teotihuacán. Early large-scale construction in the form of adobe and stone-faced platforms took place around 600–200 BC. The pyramid is a truncated cone, with a clay-and-rubble core; the rest is made of sun-dried brick with a stone facing. Rising up in four tiers, the Cuicuilco pyramid is faced with broken lava blocks, and the summit is reached by ramps on two sides. The site was covered by volcano lava around AD 300–400, forcing total abandonment. Lava from the volcano covers all of Cuicuilco,

including the lower part of the round pyramid. The Cuicuilco-Ticomán culture succeeded the Middle Formative villages of the valley but retained many of their traits, such as the manufacture of solid handmade figurines.

cuirass: A piece of armor to protect the torso, both front and back, and often molded to the contours of the body. Originally made of thick leather, it was variously made of laminated linen, sheet bronze, iron, or scales of horn, hide, or metal. In Homeric and Hellenistic times, it was made of bronze. Cuirasses of leather as well as iron were worn by officers in the armies of the Roman Empire. Later made of steel, the cuirass was forerunner to body armor worn to deflect bullets.

Cuiry-lès-Chaudardes: An Early Neolithic site of the Paris Basin's Linear Pottery culture, occupied c. 4800 BC. There were timber longhouses, pits, potsherds decorated in Bandkeramik, grindstones, flint tools, and waste flakes.

Cu Lao Rua: A late Neolithic to early Bronze Age site near Saigon, Vietnam, with shouldered polished stone adzes.

cultigen: A variety of species of plant that is known only in cultivation, such as maize. A cultigen evolves after a series of cumulative changes brought about by human selection (intentional or otherwise) has acquired certain characteristics that make it better suited to being cultivated and/or productive. Another example is cultivated wheat, the grains of which, unlike those of wild wheat, do not scatter once they have reached maturity, but remain attached to the ear.

cultivation: The raising of plants by humans for their use; deliberate propagation of a species primarily for its fruit, seed, leaf, or fiber. Cultivation greatly increased and stabilized human food supply. The change from food gathering to food production has been called the Neolithic Revolution and was one of the most important advances in human development. The first among Old World crops were wheat and barley, developed as cultivated species c. 7th millennium BC. To these were added oats and rye in Europe, millet in Asia, and sorghum in Africa. In the Americas, the process was equally slow. First crops included beans, cotton, gourds, maize, manioc, potatoes, and squashes.

cult temple: A temple for worship of a god with images of deities, where the followers worshiped daily. The cult temple achieved its most highly developed form in the great sanctuaries erected over many centuries at Thebes—especially the Luxor Temple, started by Amenhotep III of the 18th Dynasty.

cultural adaptation: The whole of the adjustments of a human society to its environment. It is the process of change undergone by a community to better conform with environmental conditions or other external stimuli.

cultural anthropology: A subdiscipline of anthropology emphasizing nonbiological aspects—the learned social, linguistic, technological, and familial behaviors of humans; a term used in the Americas. Two important branches of cultural anthropology are ethnography (the study of living cultures) and ethnology (which attempts to compare cultures using ethnographic evidence). In Europe, the field is referred to as social anthropology. In the United States, prehistoric archaeology is usually considered a subdivision of cultural anthropology.

cultural chronology: The ordering of past material culture into a meaningful time sequence.

cultural diffusion: In anthropology, the transmission or borrowing of certain culture traits from the group of origin into a foreign group; usually technological elements rather than those of social organization. This term defines the spread of ideas, traits, or people from one area to another— not necessarily implying the movement of people, because trade and the adoption of new ideas from neighboring cultures are reasonable explanations of diffusion. The diffusion of new ideas can come, however, from the peaceful or war-like expansion of a population into new territory. The theory of diffusion was used in the past to explain the beginning of most new ideas: it was assumed that technological skills such as metalworking, or the building of large monumental structures, could only have begun in one place, whence they diffused to other areas. It is now clear, through the use of new dating techniques, that independent invention was certainly possible and probable for many new ideas. (*syn.* diffusion)

cultural drift: A gradual cultural change owing to the imperfect transmission of information between generations; it is analogous to genetic drift in biology.

cultural ecology: A term describing the dynamic relation between human society and its environment, in which culture is viewed as the primary adaptive mechanism in the relation.

cultural environment: Those elements of the habitat created or modified by human cultures; a component of the total environment as seen by cultural ecology.

cultural evolution: A subdiscipline of anthropology emphasizing the systematic change of cultural systems through time. The theory is that societal change can be understood by analogy with the processes underlying the biological evolution of species, which argues that human cultures change gradually throughout time as a result of a number of cultural processes.

cultural group: A complex of regularly occurring associated artifacts, features, burial types, and house forms making up a distinct identity.

cultural intervention: The introduction of new cultural forms to a society, by either accident or design.

cultural layer: The deposition of materials from settlements or other prehistoric areas of activity, which accumulate over a relatively continuous time. Several such layers create a stratigraphic and chronological sequence.

cultural materialism: A research strategy that assumes that technological, economic, and ecological processes are the components of every sociocultural system. Developed by Marvin Harris, an anthropological historian, who saw functionalism in the social sciences as being similar to "adaptation" in biology. His work on the surplus controversy and ethnoenergetic exchange in primitive cultures led him to comparisons with medieval European economies, in which he saw two distinct types, feudalism and manorialism.

cultural processes: Sets of interrelated changes occurring through time, operating very broadly in geographical, social, and temporal terms over the course of a culture's history.

cultural processual approach: A deductive approach to archaeological research that is designed to study the changes and interactions in cultural systems and the processes by which human cultures change throughout time. A cultural process is the cumulative cause and effect of the mechanisms and interactions in a culture producing stability and/or change. The delineation of cultural process is one of the goals of archaeological research. Processual archaeologists use both descriptive and explanatory models based on functional, ecological, or multilinear cultural evolutionary concepts of culture. (*syn.* cultural process)

cultural relativism: The belief that all cultures are unique and thus can be evaluated only in their own terms and that cross-cultural comparisons and generalizations are invalid or inappropriate.

cultural resource management: A professional area of archaeology that focuses on the protection of archaeological sites from urban development, energy exploration, or natural processes. It is the legally mandated conservation, protection, and management of sites and artifacts as a means of protecting the past. Safeguarding the archaeological heritage is done through the protection of sites and salvage archaeology (rescue archaeology). This branch of archaeology is also concerned with developing policies and action in regard to the preservation and use of cultural resources. (*syn.* CRM)

cultural resources: Sites, structures, landscapes, and objects of some importance to a culture or community for scientific, traditional, religious, or other reasons. The remains that compose our nonrenewable heritage from the past, including both the archaeological and historical records.

cultural revival: Reacceptance of cultural forms or ideas that had fallen into disuse.

cultural selection: The process that leads to the acceptance of some cultural traits and innovations that make a culture more adaptive to its environment; somewhat akin to natural selection in biological evolution. The process leads to differential retention of cultural traits that increase a society's potential for successful cultural adaptation, while eliminating maladaptive traits.

cultural system: The nonbiological mechanism that relates the human organism to its physical and social environments. It is a perspective that thinks of culture and its environment as a number of linked systems in which change occurs through a series of minor, linked variations in one or more of these systems.

cultural tradition: Any distinctive toolkit or technology that lasts a long time, longer than the duration of one culture, at one locality or several localities. The term also refers to cultural continuity in social attitudes, customs, and institutions.

cultural transformation: A change in the archaeological record resulting from later human behavior, such as digging a rubbish pit into earlier levels.

culture: In a general sense, the whole way of life of humans as a species. In a more specific usage, it is the learned behavior, social customs, ideas, and technology characteristic of a certain people or civilization at a particular time or over a period (such as Eskimo culture). In this sense, a culture is a group of people whose total activities define what they represent and whose activities are transmitted to others in the group by social (mainly linguistic)—as opposed to genetic—means. Culture includes the production of ideas, artifacts, and institutions. In a more restricted sense (as in the term "blade culture"), culture signifies the artifacts or tool- and implement-making tradition of a people or a stage of development. Similar or related assemblages found in several sites in a defined area during the same period, considered to represent the activities of one specific group of people, is a culture. Cultures are often named for a particular site or an artifact. The word *culture* in archaeology means a collection of archaeologically observable data; it is defined as the regularly occurring assemblage of associated artifacts and practices, such as pottery, house-types, metalwork, and burial rites, and regarded in this sense as the physical expression of a particular social group. This usage is especially associated with Gordon Childe, who popularized this concept as a means of analyzing prehistoric material. Thus the Bandkeramik culture of Neolithic Europe is a hypothesized social group characterized by its use of a particular type of pottery, houses, and so on. The term, in reference to the specific elements of material culture, is most often used in the Old World.

culture area: Major anthropological subdivisions of the North American continent, characterized by relatively uniform environments and relatively similar cultures. It is a geographical region in which general cultural homogeneity is to be found, defined by ethnographically observed cultural similarities in the area. A culture area is also a geographic area in which one culture prevailed at a given time. This concept was devised as a means of organizing museum data. Examples are the Southwest, the Northwest Coast.

culture center: The center of a culture area, so designated because it best represents the essential qualities of the culture.

culture change: Any significant modification in the essential structure and elements of a culture over a period.

culture complex: An integrated group of cultural traits functioning as a distinct system in a culture area.

culture core: Technological, organizational, and ideological features most directly related to meeting the most important material needs of a society.

culture-historical approach: An approach to archaeological interpretation, which uses the procedure of the traditional historian; the organization of the archaeological record into a basic sequence of events in time and space. This approach assumes that artifacts can be used to build a generalized picture of human culture and descriptive models in time and space, and that these can be interpreted. It is the reconstruction of the prehistoric past based on temporal and spatial syntheses of data and the application of general descriptive models usually derived from a normative concept of culture and induction. Culture history is the chronological arrangement of the time phases and events of a particular culture. (*syn.* culture history; culture historical approach)

culture sequence: The order in which cultures or assemblages from different cultures follow one another. In successive levels of a stratified site, the oldest is usually at the lowest level.

Cumae: An ancient city, probably the oldest Greek mainland colony in the west, and home of the Sibyline Oracle (Greek prophetess), described by Virgil in the opening of the sixth book of the *Aeneid*. Located on a hill on the Italian coast west of Naples, it was founded about 750 BC by Greeks, although there were earlier Bronze and Iron Age settlements, too. Cumae came to control the most fertile parts of the Campanian plain and fought mainly with the Etruscans during the last half of the 6th century and the first half of the 5th. The Samnites, however, overwhelmed Cumae in 428/421 BC, and the city was dominated by Rome from 338 BC. In 1205 it was destroyed, but remains of fortifications and graves from all periods have been found on the city's akropolis hill and elsewhere on the site. It is probably through Cumae that a Chalcidaean version of the Greek alphabet was transmitted to the Etruscans in the 7th century BC and thence eventually to the Italian peninsula.

cumulative diagram: A technique of graphic representation, which makes it possible to assess the degree of similarity between collections of tools or groups of sites. Along the horizontal x-coordinate are arranged the tools or characteristics in question, in accordance with a defined order corresponding to the "type list" of the collections or sites. On the vertical y-coordinate, their relative frequency is plotted. The diagram appears as series of steps, each of which conveys the relative numerical importance of each tool or characteristic, added to the relative frequency of the elements that precede it in the type list. (*syn.* cumulative graph; cumulative percentage frequency graph; ogive)

cumulative feature: A feature that has been formed without deliberate construction or constraints. The feature results from accretion, for example, in a midden, or subtraction, for example, in a quarry.

cumulative recording: Excavating and recording a trench in three dimensions, using both horizontal and vertical observations to reconstruct events at the site.

cumulative section: A record of a stratigraphic sequence in which each layer is drawn and then removed, rather than left standing as a reference and drawn in its entirety at the end of the excavation.

cuneiform: The characteristic wedge-shaped writing of western Asia, used for over 3,000 years, emerging in the 4th millennium BC in southern Mesopotamia as a system of accounting during the Uruk period. It consisted of triangular markings pressed on a clay tablet with a split reed. The word itself comes from Latin *cuneus* meaning "wedge shaped," "wedge." The pictographic script of the Uruk period, the oldest known in the world, was reduced to angular forms to make it more suitable for impressing in wet clay with a split reed. The nature of the script was very like that of the Egyptians, with ideographs, phonograms, and determinatives. The script was used for a number of languages (Sumerian, Akkadian, Elamite, Hittite, Old Persian), even being adapted to serve as an alphabet at Ugarit. The first success in its decipherment was by Georg Grotefend, a German philologist, in 1802. In inscriptions from Persepolis, he recognized the names of Darius and Xerxes and the Old Persian word for *king*. In 1844–1847, further progress came, through the recording and study of Darius's rock inscriptions at Behistun by Henry Rawlinson. He was able to translate the Old Persian version; Westergaard in 1854 tackled the Elamite text, and Rawlinson, with others, cracked the Babylonian in 1857. This was much the most important of the three as it led directly back, through the many cuneiform inscriptions at that time coming to light, to the first written records, those of ancient Sumer. Cuneiform texts have been found in Egypt at el-'Amarna, and on various objects of the Persian period. In the Near East, cuneiform tablets from Egypt have been found at Bo-gazkoy in Anatolia and Kamid el-Loz in Syria. A consonantal alphabet developed at Ugarit, which vanished with the town at beginning of the 12th century BC; and syllabary script was used solely by Achaemenid Persians to transcribe their language from the 6th–4th century BC.

Cunningham, Sir Alexander (1814–1883): British general and archaeologist who excavated many sites in India, including Sarnath and Sanchi, and served as the first director of the Indian Archaeological Survey. He published an annual report, listing and describing the principal monuments of ancient India for the first time. His writings include *The Bhilsa Topes* (1854), the first serious attempt to trace Buddhist history through its architectural remains; *The Ancient Geography of India* (1871), the first collection of the edicts of the 3rd-century BC Indian emperor Ashoka; and *The Stûpa of Bharhut* (1879).

Cunnington, William (1754–1810): British antiquary who, like his contemporary Colt Hoare, recorded and excavated many barrows and other prehistoric monuments in southern England, especially on the Salisbury Plain. His excavations were of good quality for the time.

cup-and-ring mark: The commonest form of rock carving in the British Isles, consisting of a cup-like depression surrounded by one or more concentric grooves. Cup-and-ring marks are found on standing stones, singular or in stone circles, and on the slabs of burial cists, as well as on natural rock surfaces. In its classic form most cup-and-ring art belongs in the Bronze Age, but the motif occurs on passage graves, for example in the Clava tombs and on the capstones at Newgrange, where it may show links with similar rock carvings in northwest Spain. The marks are also found in Ireland and Scotland and can be dated to the Neolithic period of the 4th–3rd millennia BC. (*syn.* cup mark, cup and ring mark)

cupellation: A process in metallurgy, the separation of gold or silver from impurities by melting the impure metal in a cupel (crucible) and then directing a blast of hot air on it in a special furnace. The impurities, including lead, copper, tin, and other unwanted metals, are oxidized and partly vaporized and partly absorbed into the pores of the cupel. It is used to obtain silver by separating it from the lead with which it is naturally associated in argentiferous lead ores, or to obtain gold from the naturally occurring alloy of argentiferous gold (electrum).

Cupisnique: A style of pottery of the north coast of Peru during the Early Horizon, and a local variant of Chavín culture. It is most often associated with graves and is characteristically a polished gray-black ware with globular bodies, stirrup spouts, and relief decoration. Early Cupisnique tends to be strongly modeled by plastic manipulation of the surface. In later phases, red and black banding, separated by incision and life modeling, especially stylized felines, appear. The style dates from 900–200 BC and gave rise to three other styles: Salinar, Gallinazo, and Vicus.

curaca: A rank in the Inca Empire. Different grades of curaca were the chiefs of provinces or villages, in charge of between 100 and 10,000 people.

Curacchiaghiu: A rock shelter in southern Corsica, France, with a sequence of deposits from Mesolithic and Neolithic occupation levels dating to the 7th millennium BC—the earliest evidence of man in Corsica. The Early Neolithic levels (6th millennium BC) had pottery with punctated and incised decoration a lithic industry with geometric trapezes on hard rock and obsidian imported from Sardinia.

curation: Deliberate attempts by prehistoric peoples to preserve key artifacts and structures for posterity. These artifacts are reused and transported so often that they are rarely deposited in contexts where their original locations of manufacture and use are known. (*syn.* curated technology)

curia: The meeting place at Rome for the Senate, near the Comitium and the Forum, built by Caesar, starting in 44 BC. The term also refers to similar meeting places for assembles built in other Roman towns and colonies, which were also placed adjacent to the forum. They had tiers of marble bench seats around a large D-shaped or rectangular room. Rebuilt many times, this building now survives in a version restored by Diocletian in AD 303.

currency bar: A strip of iron about 1½ inches wide and 2–3 feet long and pinched up at one end, which served as a unit of currency in Britain during the late Iron Age, before the introduction of coins by the Belgae. The bars may have originated as sword blanks or roughouts. Their distribution was mainly in Dorset and the Cotswolds, with some in the Severn basin.

cursive: Rapid, handwritten forms of a script, used chiefly to describe special forms of hieratic and demotic. Cursive hieroglyphs are special simplified sign forms, similar to hieratic, written in ink and used for religious texts and for the initial training of scribes. The form died out in the 1st millennium BC.

cursus: A Neolithic ritual monument consisting of a long, narrow enclosure or avenue delineated by banks and external ditches. William Stukeley coined the term for the Stonehenge example, which is more than 3 kilometers long. These monuments clearly represent a very considerable investment of labor for Neolithic communities, but their function remains unknown. This type of monument is found only in Britain and belongs to the later part of the Neolithic. The Dorset Cursus (the longest known example) in Cranborne Chase is 6 miles long, 100 yards wide, flanked by banks and external ditch, and is the largest prehistoric monument in Britain.

Cut mark: Any microscopic scratch on the surface of an animal bone, with distinctive V-shaped grooves. The marks indicate meat and muscle were removed from the bone using stone flakes.

cutting tool: Any tool used for cutting, gouging, shaving, piercing, scraping, and sawing.

Cuvier, Georges (1769–1832): French zoologist who was the founder of comparative anatomy and paleontology. He was an expert on fossil bones and one of the most influential proponents of "catastrophism." Although Cuvier's theory of catastrophism did not last, he based the science of palaeontology on a firm, empirical foundation. He introduced fossils into zoological classification, showing the progressive relation between rock strata and their fossil remains, and demonstrated, in his comparative anatomy and his reconstruction of fossil skeletons, the importance of functional and anatomical relations.

Cuzco: The political and religious capital of the Inca Empire, located in the southern highlands of Peru. Although previously occupied, the site was first settled by the Inca in Late Intermediate period, AD c. 1200. After 1438, Pachacuti planned and rebuilt a city metropolis. It was a ceremonial center rather than a population center and stood at the intersection of the four administrative quarters of the empire (called Tawantinguyu). There were great palaces around the Huacapata (Holy Place), the Sunturhuasi, a tower that stood in the square, and the Sun Temple (Coricancha/Curicancha). The city was planned on a grid system, and cyclopean masonry walls of some streets, such as Callejon de Loreto, still exist, as do those of the nearby fortress of Sacsahuaman. A system of stone conduits brought residents water from various river sources. (*syn.* Cusco)

Cycladic: Concerning the Bronze Age of the Cyclades, Aegean Islands, equivalent to Helladic on the Greek mainland and Minoan in Crete. It is usually divided into three major divisions: Early (c. 3000–2000 BC), Middle (c. 2000–1550 BC), and Late (c. 1550–1050 BC). In the earlier Bronze Age, Cycladic culture seems to be largely independent, but in the late Middle Cycladic to early Late Cycladic, Minoan influence becomes important. After c. 1400 BC, mainland (Mycenaean) influence replaces the Minoan, and many islands were colonized by the Mycenaeans. Colin Renfrew has proposed an alternative Early Cycladic subdivision into Grotta-Pelos, Keros-Syros, and Phylakopi I—a culture sequence.

cyclic agriculture: A term describing a hypothetical process that may have existed among early agriculturists. Before the use of fertilizers and other efficient farming methods, cultivated land around a settlement lost its fertility over time and eventually becomes unproductive unless it was allowed to lie fallow for a while. An early farming site might have been exploited for a decade and then left while the inhabitants founded a new settlement not too far away, farming that area for a decade before moving on again. Its use is suspected in certain areas, such as in eastern Europe.

cyclopean masonry: A style of masonry that calls for large, close-fitting, irregularly shaped stones, used typically in Mycenaean fortifications. The massive stone wall's gaps between the inner and outer faces of the huge stone boulders were filled with small stones and clay. It was named after the Greek mythical character Cyclops, thought by the Greeks to have built the walls of Tiryns, which are constructed in this fashion. The technique occurs widely elsewhere in the Mediterranean (Nuraghe, Naveta, Talayot, Torre) and was sometimes employed by the Inca and other Andean peoples. (*syn.* cyclopean construction, cyclopean wall, cyclopean monuments, Pelasgian)

cylinder hammer technique: A stone-flaking technique using a bone, antler, wood, or other relatively soft material as a hammer to remove small, flat flakes from a core during flint knapping. These flakes have a characteristically long, thin form with a diffuse bulb of percussion. (*syn.* soft hammer technique, bar hammer technique)

cylinder seal: A cylinder engraved with a design, scene, and/or inscription, which was impressed onto the plastic clay when the cylinder seal was rolled over a clay tablet. This was the standard seal form of the Mesopotamian civilization, starting in the Uruk period. The incised stone cylinder was rolled over a soft surface so that the design appeared in relief. These seals were used to mark property and to legalize documents. Dating is based on changes in the design carved on the seal as well as the seal's size and proportion.

cylindrical tripod vase: A ceramic form popular in the Early Classic period in Mesoamerica and an important artifact of Teotihuacán. It is cylindrical in shape and stands on three slab or cylindrical legs and frequently has a knobbed lid. (*syn.* cylindrical vase)

cymbium: A small Greek boat-shaped drinking cup of methal or clay with two handles.

Cypriot: Of or pertaining to the Bronze Age culture of Cyprus. It is divided into Early Cypriot (c. 2500–1900 BC, Middle Cypriot (c. 1900–1650 BC, and Late Cypriot (c. 1650–1050 BC). The Sea Peoples may have been responsible for the destruction of a number of sites c. 1200 BC. The Mycenaean Greeks subsequently settled on Cyprus. (*syn.* Cypriote)

Cypro-Minoan: The syllabic script used in Cyprus from the 15th century BC, falling into disuse before being revived in the 8th century BC. It was used to write Greek until the 3rd century BC. It has similarities to Minoan Linear A and may have come from Crete. Inscriptions appear on baked clay tablets, bronze votives, ivories, and seals. It has not been deciphered.

Cyprus: The third-largest island in the Mediterranean, on its east end. Cyprus was inhabited as early as the late Neolithic age (mid-6th millennium BC) and by the late Bronze Age (c. 1600 BC–c. 1050 BC) had become a trading center, visited and settled by Mycenaeans and Achaeans, who introduced Greek culture and language. By 800 BC, Phoenicians had begun to settle there. By the 7th century BC, a number of Cypriot kingdoms had achieved great wealth and influence. It was finally taken over by the Ptolemys of Egypt and then annexed by Rome in 58 BC. Initially, its most important center was Enkomi; later Salamis.

Cyrene: A Greek colony in Libya founded c. 630–650 BC by settlers from Thera; it was located halfway between Egypt and Tunisia on the African coast. Its fertile soil made it a great African city in Roman times. Cyrene was also famous in antiquity for its horses and the production of the plant silphium, which was used by the Greeks to prepare certain medicines. The extensive remains still visible today are mostly Roman, laid out on an Hellenistic plan. Evidence exists for earlier buildings, including the 6th-century BC temple of Apollo with stone columns and mainly mud-brick walls. Imported Greek pottery of the Archaic period has been found in the sanctuary of Demeter.

Cyrus the Great (590/580 BC–529/530 BC): The first great Achaemenid king, who founded the Achaemenid Empire after overthrowing the Medes and expanding westward through the mountains into Anatolia and eastward across the Iranian plateau into Central Asia. His capital was at Pasargadae (Persia), where his tomb survives. He is remembered as a tolerant and ideal monarch who was called the father of his people by the ancient Persians and described in the Bible as the liberator of the Jews captive in Babylonia. His successors extended the kingdom into Egypt, western India, and Macedonia.

cyst: A box-shaped burial structure made of stone slabs (especially slate, schist, or granite) set on edge. Cysts may be either sunk below ground level or built on the land surface, in which case they are covered by a protective barrow. The body, in a crouched position, was buried, or an urn, containing cremation ashes, and funerary furniture were placed and buried. The name comes from the Greek word *kiste*, meaning chest or box. (*syn.* cist, cist grave)

Dd

Dabar Kot: A large tell site in the Loralai Valley in north Baluchistan, Pakistan. It was a trading post of the Indus civilization, probably occupied first from the 5th millennium BC; later occupied by other cultures. The later levels have produced material of Harappan type associated with local artifacts such as figurines of Zhob type.

Dabban: An early blade-and-burin industry of Cyrenaica, Libya, dating to 40,000–14,000 years ago. It is thought to be the oldest dated blade-and-burin industry of Upper Palaeolithic type and is recorded from only two sites: Hagfed ed-Dabba and the Haua Fteah. The Dabban is clearly related in some way to the broadly contemporary Upper Palaeolithic complex of Europe and the Near East with backed blades, burins, and end scrapers being its most characteristic artifacts. Its origins are still unknown. Dabban occupation of Haua Fteah continued until c. 12,000 BC.

dabber: A tool used in etching to distribute the etching ground over a plate of metal in the first process of engraving and, in printing from copper plate engraving and woodcuts, to spread the ink.

Da But: A marine shell midden near Thanh-hoa in northern Vietnam, which has produced a mixed Bacsonian and Neolithic stone industry together with ochre-stained burials and pottery. It has been dated to c. 4000 BC.

Dacia: A Roman frontier province north of the Danube in the area of the Carpathian Mountains and Transylvania, in present-day western Romania, spanning AD c. 106–270. The Dacians were agricultural and worked their rich mines of gold, iron, and silver. As a people, they first lived south of the Danube and traded with the Greeks. They were a threat to the Romans from 112 BC, extending their kingdom. The Dacian Wars (AD 85–89) took place under the emperor Domitian, and then the Romans under Trajan reopened hostilities in AD 101–106, finally taking the country. The Dacian Wars were commemorated on Trajan's Column in Rome. The Romans exploited the Dacian mines, constructed roads, and made Sarmizegethusa and Tsierna (Orsova) colonies. The new province was divided under Hadrian: Dacia Superior was Transylvania, and Dacia Inferior was the region of Walachia. Marcus Aurelius made the provinces a single military region in about AD 168; but the province was abandoned by Aurelian in 270.

dado: In Classical architecture, the plain lower portion between the base and cornice of the pedestal of a column. The term also referred to the lower portion of a wall, distinctively decorated, paneled, or painted, up to 2–3 feet above the floor. Internal walls were so treated between the 16–18th centuries, although toward the close of that period the dado was left plain and merely defined by a rail along the wall.

Dadunzi: A Neolithic site in Pei Xian, Jiangsu province, China, with three mail levels named after the nearby sites of Qinlian'gang, Liulin, and Huating. The lowest (Qinglian'gang) level at Dadunzi yielded a radiocarbon date of c. 4500 BC. In the middle (Liulin) level, extraordinary painted pottery was found with the usual undecorated pots native to the local Qinglian'gang tradition. Both the shapes and the painted designs copy the Yangshao pottery of Miaodigou; radiocarbon dates suggest that the Liulin phase belongs in the 4th millennium BC. Some graves of the Liulin phase at Dadunzi contained sacrificed dogs. At Dawenkou in Shangdong, where the lower level belongs to the Huating phase, pigs appear instead, and the graves often take the form of a stepped pit—significant as forerunners of characteristic Shang burial practices. Perforated tortoise shells from Liulin graves may likewise foreshadow tortoise plastrons in Shang oracle bones. (*syn.* Ta-tun-tzu)

daga: A puddle clay used to plaster the walls and floors of houses in the Iron Age settlements of sub-Saharan Africa.

dagger: A short stabbing knife that, in ancient and medieval times, was not very different from a short sword. From about 1300, the European dagger was differentiated from the sword. In earliest antiquity, it was made of flint, copper, bronze, iron, or bone. It is difficult to distinguish it from an inoffensive knife blade. Prehistoric daggers were made in flint by the Beaker Folk in the Neolithic-Early Bronze Age, about 1900 BC. Bronze daggers, tanged for wooden hilt, were imported by Beaker Folk from western Europe between 1900–500 BC. The fully developed style of the Iron Age came to be in the lst century BC. In copper, it was ancestral to the rapier, sword, spear, and halberd.

dagger ax: A bronze Chinese weapon in use from the Shang Dynasty (c. 1500 BC) to the Han Dynasty (206 BC–AD 220). The earliest forms were broad and mounted at right angles to a wooden shaft through which the tang projected. Later forms had a slender blade, which extended down the shaft at right angles to the main point to prevent it from snapping. (*syn.* ko)

Dahe: A Neolithic village site, now preserved as a museum, at Zhengzhou in China. Several Yanshao levels are overlaid by Hougang II and Shang remains; radiocarbon dates range from c. 3700–3050 BC. The upper most Yanshao level is a late stage of the Miaodigou I culture; the expected painted pottery is found alongside unpainted pots, including ding and dou shapes, that recall the Huating-Dawendou phase of the Qinglian'gang culture. This pottery may represent the beginnings of a westward movement of east-coast influences that eventually transformed the Yangshao tradition, giving rise to the Hougan II culture. (*syn.* Ta-ho)

Dahshur: An Egyptian royal necropolis, a group of five pyramids making up the southern end of the Memphite necropolis, the nucleus of which is Saqqara (Saqqarah) on the west bank of the Nile. The most prominent of the surviving monuments at Dahshur are the two pyramids of the first 4th Dynasty pharaoh, Snefru (reigned 2575–2551 BC), of the Old Kingdom. The earliest is called either the Blunted, Bent, False, or Rhomboidal Pyramid, and it represents the first attempt to build a true pyramid. It is the only Old Kingdom pyramid with two entrances. The second of Snefru's pyramids at Dahshur is called the North Stone Pyramid. Other major monuments are of Amenemhat II, Senwosret III, and Amenemhat III of the Middle Kingdom's 12th Dynasty (1938–1756 BC), and they are not as well preserved. The subsidiary tombs of Princess Khnemet and Princess Iti near Amenemhat II's pyramid yielded the Dahshur Treasure of jewelry and other personal items.

Daima: A series of large mounds in northeastern Nigeria, which constitute the remains of early farming villages on the southern flood plain of Lake Chad and were occupied from about 600 BC–AD 1200. For the first 5 centuries, the Daima people only had polished stone axes and tools of bone, plus stone grinders and querns. There is pottery present from the first occupation and evidence of domesticated cattle, sheep, and goats. Cultivation of sorghum was important, as were hunting and fishing. Iron was introduced in the 1st–6th centuries AD. Some centuries later, however, Daima became part of a more wide-ranging trade system.

Daimabad: A site in western India with five phases from the 3rd and 2nd millennia BC known for copper hoards.

Dainzú: A site in central Oaxaca, Mexico, dating to c. 300 BC, with bas-relief carvings similar to the Danzantes at Monte Albán.

Dakhla Oasis: One of a chain of oases located in the Libyan Desert, west of the Egyptian city of Luxor. The main pharaonic sites in Dakhla include a town site of the Old Kingdom (2686–2160 BC) and its associated cemetery of 6th Dynasty mastaba tombs, near the modern village of Balat. (*syn.* ad-Dakhilah Oasis)

Dalles: A series of sites along the Columbia River on the Oregon/Washington border, going back to 10,000 BC. The salmon of the river are thought to have made the area important.

Dalmatia: A Roman province on the east coast of the Adriatic, roughly corresponding to modern Yugoslavia. The Roman expansion began c. mid-2nd century BC and ended around the 9th century AD when the area became the province of Illyricum. The fall of the Dalmatian capital, Delminium, in 155, brought Roman civilization to the country. On the collapse of the Western Roman Empire, Dalmatia fell under the power of Odoacer in 481 and later under that of Theodoric. It was a battlefield during the wars between the Goths and the Byzantine emperor Justinian I and valuable to Rome for its mineral deposits, land routes and harbors, and legendary soldiers. Illyricum was soon subdivided into two provinces, known by the Flavian period as Dalmatia and Pannonia. The name Dalmatia probably comes from the name of an Illyrian tribe, the Delmata, an Indo-European people who overran the northwestern part of the Balkan Peninsula beginning about 1000 BC.

Dálriada: A kingdom founded by Fergus and his brothers when they led the Scots from Ireland to the northeast coast of Scotland in the 5th century AD, roughly the modern county of Argyll (Argyllshire). It was ruled from the rock fortress of Dunadd, a nucleated fortified citadel dating to around 500. It consists of a dry-stone central stronghold with two outer walled enclosures. In about 843, Kenneth MacAlpin extended his rule over the Picts to lay the foundations of the kingdom of Scotland. Dálriada was important for its Celtic church under St. Columba and for the island of Iona, which was a base for the conversion of northern Britain to Christianity. The Dálriada introduced the Picts to their version of the Ogham script as well as the Scottish/Gaelic language.

Dalton: A complex of the late Paleo-Indian and Archaic periods of the midwestern and eastern United States, associated with the Dalton projectile point class. The point was varied owing to reuse and resharpening. The Dalton sites indicate that hunting deer was important. Brand in northeast Arkansas and Stanfield-Worley Bluff in Alabama are the best-known sites.

damascening: The art of incrusting one metal on another, in the form of wire, which by undercutting and hammering is completely attached to the metal it ornaments. The process of etching slight ornaments on polished steel wares is also called damascening. Although related to pattern welding, this technique used in the manufacture of sword blades probably developed independently. First a high-carbon steel is produced by firing wrought iron and wood together in a sealed crucible; the resulting steel, or wootz, consists of light cementations in a darker matrix, and this, together with a series of complicated forging techniques at relatively low temperatures, produced the delicate "watered silk" pattern with the alternating high- and low-carbon areas. Damascene steel was very strong and highly elastic. (*syn.* damaskeening).

Damascus: A rich oasis at the inland end of a pass in Syria and the modern capital of Syria. Damascus was occupied by the 3rd millennium BC, but the settlements of the prehistoric, biblical, and Roman periods underlie the modern and medieval city and are therefore not readily available for excavation. Excavations have demonstrated that an urban center existed in the 4th millennium BC at Tall as-Salhiyah, southeast of Damascus. Pottery from the 3rd millennium BC has been found in the Old City. Before the 2nd millennium BC, an intricate system of irrigation for Damascus and al-Ghutah had been developed. Egyptian texts and references in the Bible attest the city's importance in international trade from the 16th century BC; it appears as Dimashqa in the Tell el-Amarna documents. The Aramaeans conquered Damascus in the late 2nd millennium BC, and it was subsequently annexed by the Israelites (10th century BC) and later the Assyrians (8th century BC). By 85 BC, it had become the capital of the Nabatean kingdom; by 64 BC, it was a Roman city of commercial and strategic importance, and subsequently a major Byzantine garrison. Damascus was captured by the Arabs in 635 and chosen as their capital by the Ummayads, who formed the first Islamic dynasty and ruled from 661–750. Its most famous Islamic monument is the Great Mosque of the caliph al-Walid, built in 706–714/715. Among ancient cities of the world, Damascus is perhaps the oldest continuously inhabited. Its name, Dimashq in Arabic (colloquially ash-Sham, meaning "the northern," as located from Arabia), derives from Dimashka, a word of pre-Semitic etymology, suggesting that the beginnings of Damascus go back to a time before recorded history.

Damb Sada'at: A prehistoric site in the Quetta Valley of western Pakistan, which was occupied during the 3rd millennium BC. Well-built mud-brick houses consisting of several small rooms, copper tools, and wheel-turned pottery painted in black designs on a buff or greenish ground known as Quetta ware have been excavated. (*syn.* Quetta)

Dambwa: An Early Iron Age division of the Chifumbaze complex, of the 5th–8th centuries AD, in the Zambezi Valley and northwest Zimbabwe.

Damous el Ahmar: A cave site with Capsian Neolithic industry in Algeria.

Danebury: An Iron Age hill fort in Hampshire, England, dating to the 6th century BC. The defenses were built with a timber-laced rampart, remodeled twice, and the main gateway is just as old. Within the ramparts, there was a permanent settlement. By the 4th century, rows of four- and six-post structures flanked the roads but were later replaced by circular houses. The site was abandoned c. 100 BC.

Danevirke: A 5th-century line of earthwork fortifications that cut across the base of the Jutland peninsula, forming the southern boundary of Viking Age Denmark (now in Germany). Timbers in its construction have been dated to about 737 AD, but these were likely replacement timbers, making the first building phase still earlier. It is puzzling archaeologically because the traces of only one large timber hall have been found, associated with enormous quantities of imported luxury items including a great deal of Western European glass. Godfrey, king of Denmark, who halted Charlemagne's march northward, began the construction of the Danevirke. (*syn.* Danekirke)

Danger Cave: A cave site of long occupation in western Utah, dated to 11,500–11,000 BC and having one of the most complete inventories from the Desert tradition. Artifacts include leaf-shaped projectile points, baskets, manos, metates. The last occupation dates to after 2000 BC.

Daniel, Glyn Edmund (1914–1986): A British prehistorian who studied the megaliths of Europe and developed the study of the history of archaeology. He popularized the discipline through his writings.

Darius I (550–486 BC): The king of Persia from 522–486 BC, one of the greatest rulers of the Achaemenid Dynasty, who was known for his great building projects and his administrative abilities. Darius extended his kingdom to India and Thrace and attempted several times to conquer Greece; his fleet was destroyed by a storm in 492, and the Athenians defeated his army at Marathon in 490. The details of his accession, which extinguished the rule of the senior branch of his family, are clouded by the fact that we have only his side of the story, notably in his great inscription at Behistun. His change of the royal capital from Pasargadae to Persepolis was important in his accession. His tomb survives, carved in the cliff face at Naqsh-i-Rustam, near Persepolis. (*syn.* Darius the Great)

Dar Tichitt: A series of very early Neolithic farming sites on the southern fringes of the Sahara Desert in southern Mauritania. The first village settlements of the Naghez phase, 1200–1000 BC, had circular compounds connected by wide paths. Fishing, hunting, and gathering wild grasses were the village's subsistence. During the Chebka phase, 1000–700 BC, lakes dried up, so that animal husbandry increased and millet was cultivated. The Akanjeir phase, 700–300 BC, saw further climatic deterioration, ending permanent settlement.

Dart, Raymond Arthur (1893–1988): A South African professor of anatomy who discovered the first Australopithecine fossil, in 1924.

Darwin, Charles (1809–1882): The founder of modern evolutionary biology, who developed the theory of the origin of species by means of natural selection. His *Origin of Species by Means of Natural Selection or the Preservation of Favored Races in the Struggle for Life* was published in 1859. His theory explained the origin of plant and animal species through a process of natural selection that tends to perpetuate adaptive variations. Its relevance for archaeology was to further the acceptance of the antiquity of man. In his book, *The Descent of Man* (1871), he speculated that our closest relatives in the animal world were chimpanzee and gorilla and that Africa was our likely homeland.

Dasas: The inhabitants of northwestern India at the time of the Indo-European migrations, described in the *Rig-Veda* as having dark faces and snub noses, speaking unintelligibly, and worshipping strange gods, but living in fortified cities (*pur*) and being very rich, especially in cattle. The Dasas are often identified with the inhabitants of the towns of the Indus Valley culture.

Dashly: An area of southern Bactria, Afghanistan, with Bronze Age, Achaemenid, and Classical sites. There are major architectural ruins from these periods.

data: Relevant observations made on artifacts, serving as the basis for study and discussion. Factual information (as measurements or statistics) used as a basis for reasoning, discussing, or calculation.

data acquisition: A stage in archaeological research design in which data are gathered, normally by three basic procedures—reconnaissance, surface survey, and excavation.

data cluster: Archaeological data found in association and in primary context and used to define areas and kinds of ancient activity. Such information may be divided into composite, differentiated, and simple data clusters.

data pool: The archaeological evidence available in a given data universe, conditioned by both behavioral and transformational processes.

data processing: A stage in archaeological research design usually involving, in the case of artifacts, cleaning, conserving, labeling, inventorying, and cataloging.

data universe: A defined area of archaeological investigation, bounded in time and space, often a geographic region or an archaeological site.

dating: The process by which an archaeologist determines dates for objects, deposits, buildings, and so on, in an attempt to situate a given phenomenon in time. Relative dating, in which the order of certain events is determined, must be distinguished from absolute dating, in which figures in solar years (often with some necessary margin of error) can be applied to a particular event. Unless tied to historical records, dating by archaeological methods can be only relative—such as stratigraphy, typology, cross-dating, and sequence dating. Absolute dating, with some reservation, is provided by dendrochronology, varve dating, thermoluminescence, potassium-argon dating, and, most important presently, radiocarbon dating. Some relative dating can be calibrated by these or by historical methods to give a close approximation to absolute dates—archaeomagnetism, obsidian hydration dating, and pollen analysis. Still others remain strictly relative—collagen content, fluorine and nitrogen test, and radiometric assay. Other methods include coin dating, seriation, and amino-acid racemization. The methods have varying applications, accuracy, range, and cost. Many new techniques are being developed and tested. (*syn.* chronology)

datum point: The point on an archaeological site from which all measurements of level and contour are taken. It is the reference point used for vertical and horizontal measurement. It can be chosen at random, at a place from which all or most of the site can be seen, and should be tied in to the national standard, usually sea level, by reference to the nearest survey point. Depths of features, of objects found in features, or simply of contours, are leveled in with reference to the datum point and are usually recorded as being a certain height "below local datum." Should variations in contour or the extent of the site prove too great for a single datum point, another can be used as long as it is leveled in with reference to the first. A site grid and excavation units are laid out or measured with reference to this point. (*syn.* datum)

daub: Clay smeared onto a structure of timber or wattle (interwoven twigs) as a finish to the surface. It is normally added to both faces of a wall and is used to keep out drafts and give a smooth finish. The material usually survives only when baked or fire hardened, as would be the case if a structure burned down. It can usually be recognized by the impressions of the wattle found on its inner face. It was used by both Indians and European settlers in North America to construct houses.

Davis, Edwin Hamilton (1811–1888): An American antiquary who studied the Ohio mounds and earthen enclosures with E. G. Squier.

Dawenkou: A Middle Neolithic site in Shandong Province, China, which gave its name to a culture of c. 4500–2700 BC. There is elaborately shaped pottery and increasingly rich burials. (*syn.* Ta-wen-k'ou)

Dazaifu: The remains of a frontier administrative center near Fukuoka, Japan. Established just after Japan's defeat in the Korean campaign of 663, Dazaifu remained an important outpost of the government in the western frontier for the next few centuries and was the bureaucratic gateway from Kyushu to the continent. The Dazaifu area, with administrative buildings and temples, has been excavated.

Dead Sea Scrolls: Ancient Hebrew manuscripts recovered from five cave sites in which they had been hidden at the northwest corner of the Dead Sea. They are believed to be the religious writings of the Essenes, a sect who in the 1st century BC and 1st century AD dwelt in a monastery at Khirbet Qumran. This material, first found in 1947, is extremely relevant to the origins of Christianity. The library included all the Old Testament texts as well as sectarian works. The scrolls, together with the excavations at Qumran, have provided much information about the beliefs and way of life of the Essenes. It is thought that the library was hidden in the cave in anticipation of the destruction of Khirbet Qumran by the Romans, which occurred in 67–73 AD. The manuscripts of leather, papyrus, and copper are among the more important discoveries in the history of modern archaeology. Their recovery has enabled scholars to push back the date of the Hebrew Bible to no later than 70 AD and to reconstruct the history of Palestine from the 4th century BC to 135 AD.

Deagan, Kathleen (1948–): A leading contemporary Americanist archaeologist, specializing in the excavation and analysis of Spanish colonial period sites in the American Southeast and the Caribbean.

Debert: A Clovis site in Nova Scotia, Canada, dating to 11,000–10,000 BP. Artifacts, hearths, and faunal evidence are on the site.

debitage: The waste by-products—chips or debris—resulting from the manufacture of stone tools, found in large quantities in a tool-making area. Study of debitage can reveal a good deal about techniques used by knappers. Certain waste flakes have a characteristic appearance and indicate the tools that were made or prepared at a site even when the tools themselves are absent.

Déchelette, Joseph (1862–1914): French archaeologist and author of monographs on Mont Beuvray (Bibracte) and decorated pottery vases of Roman Gaul and a four-volume manual of prehistoric archaeology (*Manuel d'archéologie préhis-torique, Celtique, et Gallo-romaine*, 1908–1915), which greatly influenced protohistoric studies in France. His works are considered some of the finest in the history of European archaeology. The author was killed in World War I after only two volumes had been published; Albert Grenier completed his work.

declination: The difference between true and magnetic north. In astronomy, the angular distance of a body north or south of the celestial equator.

decumanus: East-west street of a Roman camp or town. The square grid layouts of the two were basically identical, and the decumanus usually ran from the gate in the middle of one wall to the gate opposite. The decumanus maximus was the main east-west street. The main transverse street was known as the *cardo*; the administrative block or forum was at the intersection of the two. Other decumani parallel to the decumanus maximus cross the transverse cardines to divide the area into insulae. (*syn.* decumanus maximus)

deduction: A process of reasoning sometimes used in archaeology, which goes from the general to the specific, or, from a lucky guess to a provable fact. It involves generating hypotheses and then testing them with data. Deductive research is cumulative and involves constant refining of hypotheses. In deductive arguments, the conclusions must be true, given that the premises are true. It is the opposite of inductive approaches, which proceed from specific observations to general conclusions. (*syn.* deductive strategy)

deductive nomological explanation: A formal method of explanation based on the testing of hypotheses derived from general laws. A general law is established, the ramifications are deduced, and the ramifications are then used to explain a specific set of data. Some archaeologists believe that this is the appropriate way to explain cultural processes. (*syn.* D-N; deductive-nomological reasoning; deductive reasoning)

deep sea cores: A technique used in the analysis of data from oceanic sediments in which the material retrieved by the core yields information on temperature changes in the ocean through time. These changes, suggestive of climatic variation, help to chart the progress of glaciation, and, because they can be dated, the technique assists in the establishment of a chronology for the Quaternary. The cores, some 5 centimeters in diameter and up to 25 meters deep, are extracted from the ocean floor. The sediments they contain have a high percentage of calcium carbonate content made up of the shells of small marine organisms, and these sediments build up very slowly, from 10–50 millimeters per 1,000 years, but their sequence is uninterrupted. Because these organisms have different temperature preferences depending on species, the relative abundance of the various species changes as the temperature alters. Variations in the ratio of two oxygen isotopes in the calcium carbonate of these shells give a sensitive indicator of sea temperature at the time the organisms were alive. Through the identification of the species, and by the use of oxygen isotope analysis, a picture can be built up of variations in temperature over the millennia. Various forms of dating (radiocarbon dating, ionium dating, uranium series dating, palaeomagnetism, protactinium/ionium dating) can be used on the carbonate in the shells, so that absolute dates can be given to the different levels in the core. Thus dates emerge for glaciations and interglacial periods, which can assist in the age determination of archaeological material found in association with these glacial phases. Problems with the technique are the difficulty of correlating oceanic temperature changes with continental glacial and interglacial phases and the disturbance by animals living on the ocean bottom. The piston corer was developed in 1947. (*syn.* deep sea core dating, deep-sea core)

de facto refuse: (dee-fak'-to) Artifacts left behind when a settlement or activity area is abandoned.

De Geer, Baron Gerhard (Jakob), Friherre (1858–1943): Swedish geologist, originator of the varve-counting method used in geochronology, first published in a paper entitled, "A Geochronology of the Last 12,000 Years." De Geer observed that lake beds consist of couplets of laminated sediments (varves), light-colored silt layers alternating with strata of darker clay. These represent annual accumulations and thus provide a means for dating the sediments simply by counting the number of varves present.

Deh Luran: The site in Iran where Frank Hole and Ken Flannery studied the origins of food production. They excavated at Tepe Ali Kosh, Tepe Sabz, and Choga Sefid to create a cultural sequence from around 8000 BC through the Uruk period to historical times.

Deichmann, Friedrich Wilhelm (1909–   ): A German archaeologist who made contributions concerning Early Christian architecture in the Mediterranean. His detailed studies of features and styles were published in *Frühchristliche Bauten and Mosaiken von Ravenna* (1958) and *Ravenna, Hauptstadt des spätantiken Abendlandes*, 2 vols. in 5 (1969–1989).

Deir el-Bahri: A Theban religious and funerary site on the west bank of the Nile in Upper Egypt, opposite Luxor. In a bay of the cliffs, two great funerary temples were erected. That of Mentuhotep I of the 11th Dynasty (Middle Kingdom, c. 2033–1982 BC) consisted of a chamber tomb and a pyramid set in elaborately planned colonnades and terraces. That of Queen Hatshepsut, on a similar plan but without the pyramid, belongs to the 18th Dynasty (New Kingdom, c. 1480 BC). It is famous for a series of reliefs including one portraying a trading expedition to the Land of Punt and the transport of an obelisk. (*syn.* Deir el-Bahari, Deir el Bahari)

Deir el-Medina: Settlement site on the west bank of the Nile opposite Luxor, situated in a bay in the cliffs midway between the Ramesseum and Medinet Habu. It is the site of the village of the workmen who built the tombs in the Valleys of the Kings during the New Kingdom. The inhabitants were stonecutters, masons, plasterers, scribes, draftsmen, and artists who excavated and adorned royal and private tombs in the Theban necropolis from the early 18th Dynasty until the end of the New Kingdom. The site produced a large number of documents, mainly on ostraka.

deity: An ancient god who was worshipped. The god chosen was often an appropriate god for the purpose behind the prayer of the worshiper.

Dejbjerg: A bog site in west Jutland where two pre-Roman Iron Age vehicles were found, believed to be imports from southern Gaul. They were decorated with open work bronze, bronze masks, bosses, and lattice work. The wheels had iron tires and pegs of hard wood to act as ball bearings.

Delos: A small island in the Aegean, in the middle of the Cyclades, the birthplace of Apollo and Artemis. There was an important sanctuary that contained a colossal marble kouros and a sanctuary of Artemis with a temple. There are four main groups of ruins on the western coast: the commercial port and small sanctuaries; the religious city of Apollo, a hieron (sanctuary); the sanctuaries of Mount Cynthos and the theater; and the region of the Sacred Lake. There is evidence for some late Neolithic and some Mycenaean settlement; it was inhabited from the late 3rd millennium BC. Sometime early in the 1st millennium BC, its association with the worship of Apollo was established. The island became a populous religious and political center, with an oracle that was perhaps second only to Delphi. Delos was also chosen as the headquarters and treasury for the important maritime alliance against the Persians, the Delian League (487 BC). Tine streets, Greek and oriental temples, meetinghouses for the merchant guilds, a unique colonnaded ("hypostyle") hall, and splendid houses were built. Rome took the island in 166 BC, and eventually it was abandoned. Excavations have been conducted since 1873 by the French School of Athens.

Delphi: An important sanctuary site in central Greece, where the Delphic oracle was located. Situated at the foot of Mount Parnassus, Delphi was thought (by the Greeks) to lie at the center of the earth. The setting has a striking backdrop of cliff face, rock fissures, and springs. The sanctuary of Apollo held the oracle, which was frequently consulted by all Greek city-states at the start of a new enterprise. In addition to answering consultations by states and individuals (the answers were often couched in obscure hexameter verses, which had to be figured out by the questioner), Delphi was a religious and festival center for the Greek city-states belonging to the Amphictyonic League. The Pythian Games, held at Delphi, became a great national festival. Along a Sacred Way were placed some 20 temple-like treasuries (thesauroi), erected by member states to house valuable offerings. Above, on a terrace supported by a wall of unusual polygonal masonry, stood the great temple of Apollo, containing in a holy of holies (adyton) a navel-shaped stone (omphalos) marking the center of the earth, and a rock fissure from which emanations were supposed to inspire the Pythian priestess. The virgin priestess would fall into a trance to give five (inarticulate) answers to male priests (women were not admitted). The temple was reconstructed after earthquake damage in c. 350 BC, and a theater and stadium were added. After c. 300 BC, the oracle began a slow decline in authority, and Roman rule brought further deterioration and then plundering. The oracle was finally closed by Emperor Theodosius in AD 390 as anti-Christian.

Delphic Oracle: The most famous ancient oracle, located at Delphi on the slopes of Mt. Parnassus above the Corinthian Gulf. Traditionally, the oracle first belonged to Mother Earth (Gaea) but later was either given to or stolen by Apollo. At Delphi, the medium was a woman over fifty, known as the Pythia, who lived apart from her husband and dressed in a maiden's clothes. Although the oracle, at first called Pytho, was known to Homer and was the site of a Mycenaean settlement, its fame did not come until the 7th–6th centuries BC, when Apollo's advice or sanction was sought by lawmakers, colonists, and cult founders. The Pythia's counsel was most often used to predict the outcome of wars or political actions. Consultations were normally restricted to the seventh day of the Delphic month, Apollo's birthday, and were at first banned during the three winter months when Apollo was believed to be visiting the Hyperboreans in the north, although Dionysus later took Apollo's place at Delphi during that time. The usual procedure required a sponsor and the provision of a *pelanos* (ritual cake) and a sacrificial beast that conformed to rigid physical standards. The Pythia and her consultants first bathed in the Castalian spring; afterward, she drank from the sacred spring Cassotis and then entered the temple. There she apparently descended into a basement cell, mounted a sacred tripod, and chewed leaves of the laurel, Apollo's sacred tree. While in this drugged state, the Pythia would speak, often unintelligibly. Her words, however, were not directly recorded by the inquirer; instead, they were interpreted and written down by the priests in what were often very ambiguous words.

Delta: The greater part of Lower Egypt, the Nile Delta north of ancient Memphis, which is in marked contrast with Upper Egypt's valley. Although it has equally important history, its remains are now lost, buried beneath many meters of the silt that has accumulated since ancient times. The lowercased term refers to any flat alluvial tract built up by the deposition of silt at the mouth of a river. The name derives from the fact that the Nile fans out into several tributaries as it approaches the Mediterranean, creating a triangular area of fertile land shaped like the Greek letter delta.

deme: In ancient Greece, a country district or village, as distinct from a polis, or city-state. Demos also meant the common people like the Latin plebs. In Cleisthenes' democratic reform at Athens (508/507 BC), the demes of Attica (the area around Athens) were given status in local and state administration. Males 18 years of age were registered in their local demes, thereby acquiring civic status and rights. These local communities retained a basic political and social importance well into the 5th–6th centuries.

demography: The study of the distribution, density, and vital statistics of populations. The statistical study of populations with reference to the natality, mortality, migratory movements, age, and sex, among other social, ethnic, environmental, and economic factors indicates the processes that contribute to population structure and their temporal and spatial dynamics. (*syn.* population estimation)

demotic: The Egyptian cursive script for secular/everyday use and civil records, derived from hieroglyphs by way of hieratic. Although more easily written, its structure was identical with that of the original hieroglyphic. It first appeared in the 7th century BC, surviving until the 5th century AD. It was used for the central of the three inscriptions on the Rosetta Stone. The term comes from the Greek *demotika*, "popular script" or "script in common use," also known as *enchorial*, "of the country."

Denalian culture: A prehistoric culture or complex of central Alaska (the Tangle Lakes) dating to c. 10,500–700 BC. Similar to the Siberian Dyuktai (Diuktai) culture and defined by H. West in 1967, it is characterized by wedge-shaped microcores, microblades, burins, and bifacial points, scrapers on flakes, and large blades. (*syn.* Denali complex)

Denbigh Flint complex: An Arctic Small Tool tradition flint industry found at Cape Denbigh, Iyatayet, Cape Krusenstern, Onion Portage, and other Alaskan sites. The typical artifacts are finely worked microblade tools (bladelets, small crescents), burins, and bifacially pressure-flaked points. The Denbigh complex had developed by c. 3200 BC. The Arctic Small Tool tradition spread eastward over the whole Arctic zone from Alaska to Greenland and contributed to the earliest Eskimo cultures. Land mammals seem to have been the primary focus of subsistence activity.

Dendra: A Bronze Age cemetery in Greece with a Middle Helladic tumulus. Mycenaean tholos tomb (15th–14th centuries BC), and rich chamber tombs. The associated settlement may be the Mycenaean citadel of Midea. (*syn.* Dhendra)

Dendera: A site in Upper Egypt with a well-preserved temple of Hathor from the Middle Kingdom and frequently added to by later rulers up to the Roman emperor Trajan. It was the site of the ancient capital of the sixth Upper Egyptian nome, located near modern Qena, close to the mouth of the Wadi Hammamat route to the Red Sea, making it an important center in Dynastic times. The Dendera necropolis of mastaba tombs ranges in date from the Early Dynastic (Old Kingdom) period to the First Intermediate period. (*syn.* Iunet, Tantere, Tentyris)

dendrochronology: An absolute chronometric dating technique for measuring time intervals and dating events and environmental changes by reading and dating the pattern (number and condition) of annual rings formed in the trunks of trees. The results are compared with an established tree-ring sequence for a particular region with consideration to annual fluctuations in rainfall, which result in variations in the size of the rings laid down by trees on the outside of their trunks. These variations, given favorable conditions, form a consistent pattern; and sections or cores taken from beams in ruins have been matched to provide a long chronology over large areas. The method is based on the principle that trees add a growth ring for each year of their lives and that variations in climatic conditions affect the width of these rings on suitable trees. In a very dry year, growth is restricted, and the ring is narrow, while a wet and humid year produces luxuriant growth and a thick ring. By comparing a complete series of rings from a tree of known date (for example, one still alive) with a series from an earlier, dead tree overlapping in age, ring patterns from the central layers of the recent tree and the outer of the old may show a correlation, which allows the dating, in calendar years, of the older tree. The central rings of this older tree may then be compared with the outer rings of a yet older tree and so on, until the dates reach back into prehistory. Problems arise when climatic variation and suitable trees (sensitive trees react to climatic changes, complacent trees do not) are not present to produce any significant and recognizable pattern of variation in the rings. Another problem is that there may be gaps in the sequences of available timber, so that the chronology "floats," or is not tied in to a calendrical date or living trees: It can only be used for relative dating. Also, the tree-ring key can go back only a certain distance into the past, because the availability of sufficient amounts of timber to construct a sequence obviously decreases. Only in a few areas of the world are there species of trees so long lived that long chronologies can be built up. This method is especially important in the southwestern United States, Alaska, and Scandinavia, dating back to several thousand years BC in some areas. Dendrochronology is of immense importance for archaeology, especially for its contribution to the refining of radiocarbon dating. Because timber can be dated by radiocarbon, dates may be obtained from dendrochronologically dated trees. It has been shown that the radiocarbon dates diverge increasingly from cal-

endrical dates provided by tree rings the farther back into prehistory they go, the radiocarbon dates being younger than the tree-ring dates. This has allowed the questioning of one of the underlying assumptions of radiocarbon dating, the constancy of the concentration of C14 in the atmosphere. Fluctuations in this concentration have now been shown back as far as dendrochronological sequences go (to c. 7000 BC), and thus the dating technique is serving the further research on another. In 1929, A. E. Douglass first showed that this method could be used to date archaeological material. The long-living Bristlecone Pine (*Pinus aristata*) of California has yielded a sequence extending back to c. 9000 bp. In Ireland, oak preserved in bogs has produced a floating chronology from c. 2850–5950 bp. (*syn.* tree-ring dating)

dendrogram: A diagram in the form of a schematized tree with many branching lines at one end and uniting into a single trunk at the other—used to record the analysis of tree-ring widths for a sample(s). It is then compared to a master chronology in dendrochronology studies.

Denekamp Interstadial: A warm period during the Middle pleniglacial phase of the last (Weichselian) glaciation (cold stage) in Europe. It is dated to around 28,000 BC (30,000 bp).

Denisova Cave: A Palaeolithic site in the Altai region of Siberia with at least 16 cultural layers. It is an important site for the study of the Middle to Upper Palaeolithic transition in northern Asia.

denticulate: An artifact (flake or blade tool) with several small tooth-like (dentate or serrated) notches on the working edge.

dentition: The general characteristic arrangement, type, and number of teeth in animal (vertebrate) species. The study of dentition is an important part of the discipline of archaeozoology. It is used to identify animal remains and can also be used to determine age in both man and animal, either from the state of eruption and replacement of milk teeth or from the amount of wear. Its study may also tell us something about the animal's diet.

depletion gilding: A New World metallurgical technique in which tumbaga (copper and gold alloy) metal artifacts were treated with chemicals that removed much of the copper from the surface, leaving a finish that looks like pure gold.

deposition: Any of the various processes by which artifacts move from active use to an archaeological context, such as loss, disposal, abandonment, or burial. It is the laying, placing, or throwing down of any material. In geology, it is the constructive process of accumulation into beds, veins, or irregular masses of any kind of loose, solid rock material by any kind of natural agent (wind, water, ice). The transformation of materials from a systemic to an archaeological context is directly responsible for the accumulation of archaeological sites, and it constitutes the dominant factor in forming the archaeological record. Deposition is the last stage of behavioral processes in which artifacts are discarded. (*syn.* depositional process)

depositional environment: Any stratum or unit making up a separate layer of material at an archaeological site; the total of sedimentary and biological conditions, factors, and processes that result in a deposit(s). A depositional history is the order in which objects are deposited at a site.

Dereivka: A Late Neolithic settlement site located on the River Omifinev in the Ukraine and dated to the 3rd millennium BC. A site of the Sredni Stog culture includes a cemetery of the Mariupol type, with over 100 extended inhumations arranged in groups. Adjacent to the cemetery is the settlement with Dnieper-Donets pottery, traces of dwellings, hearths, and other features. (*syn.* Dereivca)

descent reckoning: The rules by which people in a particular culture determine membership in defined kin groups.

Desert culture: A hunting-and-gathering way of life adapted to the post-Pleistocene conditions of the arid and semiarid zones of the American West from Oregon to California, with extensions into similar areas of Mexico. Agriculture was unknown or unimportant, and the small nomadic bands lived by collecting wild plants and hunting game. The concept was devised by J. Jennings at Danger Cave. Typical artifacts include grinding stones, basketry, small projectile points, and spear throwers. There is an absence of ceramics. The mode of subsistence was established c. 9000 BC and lasted until agriculture had developed sufficiently to permit settled life. In Mexico, farming villages were widespread by 2000 BC. In the southwestern United States, this did not occur until the last few centuries BC. (*syn.* Desert tradition)

desert pavement: Terrain that is thickly covered—or paved—with small rocks. Vegetation is scarce, so that soil, sand, and gravel have not been held in place. Wind and rain leave only rocks too large to move. This type of terrain is part of many southwestern U.S. archaeological finds.

desert varnish: A chemical dark-colored crust or film of iron and manganese oxides (usually with some silica) deposited on exposed rocks, artifacts, and petroglyph surfaces. Of bacterial origin, this varnish becomes polished by wind abrasion and can be used in cation ratio dating; its organic matter can be analyzed by accelerator mass spectrometer radiocarbon dating.

determinative: An indication of which category of objects or beings is in question. In hieroglyphic writing, an ideographic sign next to a word phonetically represented, for the purpose of defining its meaning.

detritus: Debris or droppings created by detrition. Matter produced by the wearing away of exposed surfaces, especially gravel, sand, clay, or other materials eroded and washed away by water.

Developed Oldowan: A series of Early Stone Age industries of the Oldowan Industrial Complex seen at Olduvai Gorge and other African sites, dating c. 1.6–0.6 million years ago. They differ from the classic Oldowan industry in the types of stone artifacts. (*syn.* Developed Oldowan A, Developed Oldowan B, Developed Oldowan C)

Devensian: The final continental glacial advance, dating to c. 115,000–10,000 BP, especially referring to a group of British deposits, stratified above Ipswichian Interglacial deposits. Much of northern England, Scotland, and Wales is covered by a blanket of Devensian tills, sands, and gravels, and these sediments were deposited by the ice sheet. South of the ice-sheet margin is a series of related pro-glacial and periglacial deposits. Most of the Devensian stage can be dated by using radiocarbon, and by this means it has been correlated with the Wichselian in northwest Europe and the Wisconsin in North America. All these formations represent one cold stage and directly preceded our present period of predominantly warm climate (the Flandrian or Holocene). Not all of the Devensian deposits are strictly glacial; some contain abundant fossils that indicate warmer interstadial periods. Three interstadials have been defined in Britain: the Chelford Interstadial (c. 61,000 bp); the Upton Warren Interstadial complex (45,000–25,000 bp), and the Windermere Interstadial (13,000–11,000 bp). Levallosian, Mousterian, and Upper Palaeolithic artifacts are found in Devensian deposits, and bones of *Homo sapiens* have been found in Devensian cave sediments. (*syn.* Weichselian, Devensian glaciation, Weichsel glaciation)

Deverel-Rimbury culture: A Bronze Age culture of southern Britain of the 15th–12th centuries BC. It was named after two sites in Dorset and was characterized by Celtic fields, nucleated small farmsteads, and palisaded cattle enclosures and by urn cremations, either in flat urnfields or under low barrows. The distinctive pots were globular vessels with channeled or fluted decoration and barrel- or bucket-shaped urns with cordoned ornament. It is thought that the people came from France and were great farmers, introducing the plow into England. The square lynchets, which can be seen today, are the result of their plowing. (*syn.* Deverel-Rimbury people)

deviation-amplifying system: A system that continues to change as a result of positive feedback.

deviation-counteracting system: A system that reaches equilibrium as a result of negative feedback.

Devil's Lair: A limestone cave near the southwest coast of Western Australia, containing deep, well-preserved organic and stone deposits dating from 27,000–10,000 BC. It is one of the longest occupation sequences in Australia, with well-defined hearths and occupation floors and a rich faunal assemblage. The stone assemblage included cores, scrapers, denticulate flakes, retouched flakes, and adze flakes of chart or quartz. Undersea-drill cores from the nearby continental shelf have produced the same Eocene chert from a zone that would have been exposed during Pleistocene low sea levels. Three unifacially incised limestone plaques (10,000–18,400 BC) and a piece of artificially perforated marl have been interpreted as ritual items or adornments. Bone tool artifacts included points dating to c. 27,000 BC and beads of macropod (kangaroo/wallaby) fibulae between 13,000–10,000 BC, claimed to be the oldest known ornaments in Australia.

Devon Downs: A limestone shelter in cliffs beside the lower Murray River in South Australia with a deposit rich in faunal material as well as stone and bone tools and dating to c. 4000 BC. It was the first systematic archaeological excavation in Australia (1929). Interpretation of the stratigraphy and stone tool sequence at two sites introduced concepts of antiquity and cultural change in Aboriginal prehistory, which had previously been denied in Australian anthropology.

dew pond: Hollowed-out areas in hilltop camps, usually covered with hay and clay as an insulator. Condensation of the moisture in the air resulted and collected as a pond.

Dhang Rial: A mound in southern Sudan with a two-part Iron Age sequence starting in AD 500, with an earlier ceramic Stone Age occupation.

Dhar Tichitt: An area of south-central Mauritania (Africa) on the southern edge of the Sahara Desert with evidence of local beginnings of cereal cultivation in the 2nd millennium BC in the form of plant impressions on pottery. Wild sorghum and bulrush millet are indigenous to the area. At the time, there were extensive lakes at Dhar Tichitt for fishing, and by c. 1500 BC the inhabitants had domestic cattle and goats. By the 4th century BC, bulrush millet clearly formed the staple diet of the inhabitants of the area.

Dhimini: A small fortified Late Neolithic settlement site in Thessaly, Greece. In the multiple walls and elaborate system of fortifications were a large megaron palace and smaller buildings. The typical pottery was elegant bichrome with spirals and meanders painted in black or white on a yellow or buff ground. Two tholos tombs date from the Mycenean period.

Dhlo Dhlo: A later Iron Age site located northeast of Bulawayo, Zimbabwe, and the 17th–19th century AD capital of the Torwa state. Occupation probably began during the 16th century, marked by elaborately decorated dry-stone terrace-retaining walls surrounding extensive house platforms. The foundation of the site is comparable to stone structures at Khami and Naletale. Dhlo Dhlo appears to have

had access to imported luxury goods from coastal trade. (*syn.* Danangombe)

diachronic: Referring to two or more reference points in time, especially as they pertain to phenomena as they occur or change over time; a chronological perspective. The term refers to actions or things, as in the study of artifacts in a region as they change across sequential periods. (*syn.* diachronous) (*ant.* synchronous)

diadem: A plain or decorated headband or crown of man-made or natural materials, usually as a badge of status or office.

diagnostic trait: Any cultural trait that helps to distinguish one group of people from another. A diagnostic trait appears in one group but not in another with which it might be confused.

diagnostics: Artifacts that can be used as index fossils in a cultural context.

Diaguita: Indian peoples of South America, formerly inhabiting northwestern Argentina and the Chilean provinces of Atacama and Coquimbo. They are characterized by distinctive ceramic complexes. Two principal subgroups have been defined—the Argentinian, on the eastern side of the Andes, and the Chilean, on the western side—which have some cultural traits in common: funerary practices, use of bronze, and probably language. The Calchaquí, the Argentinian subgroup, farmed terraced fields, built irrigation canals, and kept herds of llama. They did loom weaving of llama-wool textiles, which they dyed; made baskets; and had a rather elaborate ceramic industry. Metallurgy was also known. Religious beliefs involved shamanistic practices for the cure of illness felt to be caused by witchcraft. Polychrome funerary urns were used for burial for children; adult burials were stone-lined pit inhumations. The Chilean Diaguita ceramics are, on the whole, smaller and more delicately decorated. Influence from the north (Tiahuanaco in the early stages and Inca later) is also apparent. Petroglyphs are common throughout the Diaguita area. The earliest date for Diaguita is AD c. 900, and it continued until the Spanish Conquest.

diamicton: A sediment or soil texture larger than sand-sized clasts. It is a matrix of sand, silt, and clay, and many are glacial debris-flow and colluvial deposits. (*syn.* diamict)

Dian: A Bronze age culture on Lake Dian in China, dating to the late 1st millennium BC. It is characterized by bronze drums resembling those of southeast Asia's Dong Son culture. (*syn.* Tien)

Diana: A site on the island of Lipari, of the Aeolian Islands north of Sicily, which has given its name to a local Late Neolithic culture with date in the early 4th millennium BC. Diana had a very distinctive pottery with a glossy red slip and splayed lugs or tubular handles, found also on Sicily and mainland Italy. The culture is associated with the last phase of intensive exploitation of the Lipari obsidian source.

Dian kingdom: A Bronze Age culture and barbarian kingdom in southwest China centered on Lake Dian in Yunnan province. According to Chinese sources, the Dian royal house traced its descent from a Chu general who invaded Yunnan in the late 4th century BC and remained to rule the local tribes. In 109 BC, Dian surrendered to Han armies; a generation later, the kingdom was destroyed after a revolt. The highly distinctive culture is known mainly from cemetery sites, especially Shizhaishan, where the burials date from the Han occupation. Earlier burials of the period c. 600–300 BC have been excavated at Dapona and Wanjiaba. Many of the objects unearthed at Shizhaishan were imports from China: coins, mirrors, belt hooks, silk, crossbow mechanisms, and a gold seal from the Han court that reads "Seal of the King of Dian." Other finds seem to be local adaptations of prototypes originating in the state of Chu. There was active trade with the southern Zhou states of Shu and Ba before the Han Dynasty. (*syn.* Tien)

diaspora: The dispersion of people, either forced or voluntary, from a central area of origin to many distant regions. In particular, the dispersion of Jews among the Gentiles after the Babylonian Exile or the aggregate of Jews or Jewish communities scattered "in exile" outside Palestine or present-day Israel.

diatom: Microscopic, unicellular algae, which grow in marine or fresh water and secrete silica skeletons (microfossils) that are distinct by species. Their chances of survival are enhanced because of the silica and their deposition in anaerobic conditions. Diatoms can be sampled through deep sea or lake cores. Different species are associated with different habitats, so that examples in archaeological deposits can yield information on the changing environment, particularly at coastal sites.

diatom analysis: A method of environmental reconstruction based on plant microfossils. Diatoms are unicellular algae, whose silica cell walls survive after the algae die, and they accumulate in large numbers at the bottom of both fresh and marine waters. Their assemblages directly reflect the floristic composition of the water's extinct communities, as well as the water's salinity, alkalinity, and nutrient status.

diatomite: Microfossils formed from the silicate exoskeletons of diatoms found in marine or fresh water. Different species are associated with different habitats, so that examples in archaeological deposits can yield information on the changing environment.

Didyma: A temple site in Miletus, Turkey, dating to the 8th century BC. The reconstructed Hellenistic temple included a naiskos inside the adyton.

Die Kelders: A cave in South Africa with Middle Stone Age remains and a shell midden of the Later Stone Age, plus some of the earliest Late Stone Age pottery in southern Africa.

Dieng: A complex of Hindu temples of the 8th–9th centuries AD, built around the volcanic hot springs of north-central Java.

differential access to key resources: Situation in which different individuals or groups in a society do not share equal access to necessary resources.

differential fluxgate gradiometer: A magnetic surveying instrument used in subsurface detection, which records changes in the intensity of a magnetic field. Readings can be obtained continually rather than as individual spot measurements of a proton magnetometer. However, it is an expensive alternative to the proton gradiometer. Its electronics involve two detectors with mu-metal strips of a staff that is carried vertically; an initial pure sine-wave voltage is applied, and the difference in intensities observed between the two detectors corresponds to disturbance in the magnetic field cause by baked clay or buried features. These differences are displayed on the instrument's meter. (*syn.* fluxgate gradiometer, differential fluxgate magnetometer, magnetometer)

differential heat analysis: A remote sensing technique in which the variability in heat absorption and dissemination is used to plot hidden archaeological features. In analytical chemistry, this technique is used for identifying and quantitatively analyzing the chemical composition of substances by observing the thermal behavior of a sample as it is heated. (*syn.* differential thermal analysis)

differentiated data cluster: A method of clustering data that are heterogeneous and patterned in regard to two or more activities reflective of age or sex differences; for instance, a house floor with cooking utensils and hunting weapons in primary context.

differential reproduction: The measure of fitness calculated by the relative rates at which different individuals produce live offspring.

diffusion: The process whereby cultural traits, ideas, or objects are spread or transmitted from one culture or society to another. It may be carried by folk movement, war, trade, or imitation. Diffusion has played a major part in human development by spreading ideas and techniques more rapidly than they could have spread had they been independently invented. Primary diffusion occurs when people migrate and take their habits with them. When ideas or customs, but not the people who have them, move, it is secondary diffusion. The spread of agriculture in North America was secondary diffusion. The burden of proof is on the diffusionist to show that the trait is the same in the two areas, that communication between the two was possible, and that there are no difficulties in the relative dates. In a great number of cases these criteria can be met, and diffusion is an important explanatory concept in culture history. The theory was popularized by V. G. Childe, who said that all the attributes of civilization from architecture to metalworking had diffused from the Near East to Europe. (*syn.* cultural diffusion; diffusionism; diffusionist approach; diffusionist)

dig: An archaeological excavation or the site that has been or is being excavated. (*syn.* diggings)

diggings: Excavated materials or the site that has been or is being excavated.

digging stick: A straight, often pointed, wooden tool for loosening or digging up the ground. It was used in food-gathering economies to turn up roots or burrowing animals, and in Neolithic communities for cultivation, until displaced by the hoe and later (in the Old World) by the plow. It could be made more efficient by adding a perforated stone as a weight onto the shaft near the lower end.

Dilmun: A region and island situated in the Gulf, probably Bahrain, the western shore of the Gulf and the island of Failaka in Kuwait, which was an important trading center during the 3rd millennium BC. The name appeared in Meso-potamian texts of the Early Dynastic, Akkadian, and Ur III periods; the epic hero Gilgamesh visited Dilmun in his search for immortality. The name Dilmun appears in economic documents with which the cities of Magan and Meluhha traded. From the Mesopotamian documents, it seems that Dilmun served mainly as an entrepot for trade between the Indus Valley civilization and Mesopotamia, but it is also recorded as exporting dates and pearls of its own. (*syn.* Tilmun)

Dimolit: A Neolithic open settlement site in northern Luzon, the Philippines, dating from c 2500 BC. The occupation had pottery, flakes with edge gloss, postholes of small square houses, and items paralleled in Taiwanese Neolithic sites.

Dinas Powys: An Iron Age hill fort near Cardiff, Wales, which was refurbished in the sub-Roman and medieval pe-riods. Traces of hearts, a collection of Mediterranean impor-ted pottery, and metalworking debris such as molds, fur-naces, and ovens have been found.

ding: A Chinese tripod bowl with solid legs. From the Neolithic it was made of ceramic, and from the Shang period it occurred in bronze; there were also quadrapods. (*syn.* ting)

Dingcun: Middle Palaeolithic sites in Shanxi Province, China, with human remains, flake tools, points, and stone balls. It is the type site of the culture. (*syn.* Ting-ts'un)

dingo: A native Australian dog, which was the only terres-trial nonmarsupial carnivore and one of the few pre-European placental mammals in Australia. Introduced during the Holo-cene, the earliest dates are between 3500–3000 bp in Wom-bah, New Tasmania. At present, the dingo's external origins are unknown, but the answer may bring to light human migrations and contacts between Australia and Asia in the mid-Holocene. The dog most closely resembles Indian mid-Holocene dogs.

dinos: A Greek round-bottomed cauldron that would be placed on a tripod or stand, probably used for mixing wine.

diorite: A dark, granular igneous (crystalline) rock consist-ing essentially of the minerals plagioclase feldspar and horn-blende or biotite. (*syn.* black granite)

Diprotodon: A very large Australian herbivorous marsu-pial, now extinct, of the group that includes kangaroos, koalas, and wombats. It was characterized by two prominent incisors on the lower jaw. It is the largest of the extinct Australian species of Pleistocene megafauna.

diptych: Double-leafed tablets of metal, ivory, or wood, attached by strings or hinges. Diptychs are common in Chris-tian archaeology, often as alterpieces or paintings composed of two leaves that close like a book.

direct age determination: The determination of the age of archaeological data by analysis of an artifact, ecofact, or feature.

direct historical analogy: Analogy using historical records or historical ethnographic data.

direct historical approach: The technique of working backward in time, from the present into the past, from historic sites of known age into earlier times. This method of chrono-logical ordering is based on the comparison of historically documented or contemporary artifacts with those recovered from archaeological contexts. An analogy or homology is made by using historical records or historical ethnographic data for the site and the surrounding region. This technique was developed by W. D. Strong in the 1930s.

direct percussion: A technique used in the manufacture of chipped-stone artifacts in which flakes are produced by strik-ing a core with another stone or a hammer stone or by striking the core against a fixed stone or anvil to dislodge a flake. The method is less precise in its results than indirect percussion. (*syn.* free-hand percussion)

Diring: A Neolithic site in northeast Siberia with burials of the Ymyakhtakh culture and an assemblage of quartzite cores, pebble tools, and flakes.

disarticulated: Bones out of their natural arrangement.

discard rate: The typical rate at which a group or society disposes of its unwanted objects; plentiful, easily replaced items tend to have a higher discard rate than rare or highly durable ones.

discoidal nucleus technique: A method of core knapping used during the Middle Palaeolithic by which flaking was done until the core was too small to use. The Beaker People, in particular, made circular, oval, or oblong, thin flakes of stone with this technique, which is very similar to the Levallois technique.

disconformity: A geological term referring to a weathered surface of a soil or rock stratum covered by an overlying stratum. This type of unconformity separates two parallel strata, is characterized by the weathered surface of the older stratum, and indicates a lapse of time before the deposition of the younger stratum. Its recognition is important in site stratigraphy.

discriminant analysis: A technique of multivariate analysis in which new variables are calculated from the original, large number of variables, and this function is combined with classification. Discriminant functions are especially calculated to show up differences between previously defined groups of items (e.g., artifacts from several different sites), whereas principal components do not make any distinction between groups. The object of the classification is to see how widely separated the multivariate distributions of a number of previously defined groups of items are in hyperspace. The results are presented as a classification results table in which the known grouping of items is compared with the most likely grouping, calculated from the variables supplied from the analysis. An example of useful classification would be comparing groups of skulls from different sites on the basis of their measurements.

disk-core method: A technique in the making of stone tools in which a core is trimmed to a distinctive disk shape and flakes are then chipped off for tools.

Dissignac: A Neolithic burial mound in Loire-Atlantique, France, with two passage graves, microliths, Early Neolithic pottery, and a paleosol with pollen of cultivated cereals dated to c. 4000 BC.

dissociation: The principle that states that artifacts deposited together in a certain location were not necessarily used together at that location.

distal: Located away from the point of origin or attachment or a central point. In anatomy, the part of a long bone (leg or arm) farthest from the body; the opposite end is the proximal.

distance-decay function: A mathematical expression of the inverse ratio between the quantity of a substance and the distance from its source; the rate at which interaction declines as the distance from the source increases. This function is a specific example of linear regression analysis and can be used to describe the relation between the amount of a given commodity found at any point and the place from which it was exported. The patterns and mathematical expressions help to distinguish different forms of trade and exchange. In general, distance-decay varies with the value of the object traded, with the richer items spreading farther from the source. (*syn.* distance decay)

distribution: Simply, the spatial location of archaeological sites or artifacts. More specifically, a definition of the spatial location of artifacts, structures, or settlement types over a landscape. Analysis of the distribution of a particular artifact type may lead to conclusions about the nature of the industry or culture that produced or used it. The distribution of objects is studied by the plotting of an artifact's find places on a distribution map. This is the visual representation of the distribution of some archaeologically significant trait or traits. The relation of the find-spot symbols to the natural environment may reveal something about communication networks, economic subsystem, cultural or technological entities. The distribution map should show the extent of a culture for which the traits are distinctive, outlying occurrences being explained by diffusion, especially if spread along natural routes. The origin of more localized traits may be defined. The overlaying of one trait on another may suggest association or sequence, while mutually exclusive distributions can imply contemporaneity. The emphasis is on individual parts of archaeological deposits rather than on the site as a unit (*syn.* distributional archaeology)

disturbance: The changing or altering of an archaeological context by the effect(s) of an unrelated activity at a later time. Examples include dam building, farming, and heavy construction, as well as noncultural activities such as freeze thaw cycles, landslides, and simple erosion. Disturbance is also the nonscientific removal of an artifact from its archaeological context. (*syn.* disturbance process)

distyle: Of a Classical building, having two columns on the facade.

ditch: A common feature of archaeological sites in association with defensive structures, as a means of drainage, or as a construction trench. A ditch was usually dug outside the walls of forts, fortresses, and so on, as part of the defenses, and was often filled with water. Ditches allowed to erode, without much interference, go through three phases of infilling. Primary fill accumulates as the sides of the ditch collapse. Vegetation then begins at the bottom of the ditch, and the secondary fill starts to build up. This material has a much finer texture than primary fill. The rate of secondary fill deposition is related to soil erosion in the surrounding area. If the land by the ditch is plowed, thick colluvial deposits, called tertiary fill, may bury the secondary fill.

divination: The practice of foretelling the future by various natural, psychological, and other techniques. It is found in all civilizations—both ancient and modern, primitive and sophisticated—and in all areas. In the Western world, the primary form is the use of horoscopic astrology or horoscopes. There is no scientific evidence that divination indeed foretells the future.

divine kings: In Egypt, a pharaoh was accorded divine status, although most rulers in the Near East claimed to be merely the priests or agents of the gods. In some societies, especially in ancient kingdoms or empires, the king was regarded as a god or identified with some god. In early Egypt, the divine king would be identified with the sky-god (Horus) and with the sun god (Re, Amon, or Aton). Similar identifications were made in early China and early Erech in Mesopotamia. The first king has been regarded as a god and his successors as sons of the god in a number of societies—in Africa, Polynesia, Japan, Peru, Egypt, Mesopotamia, and Canaan. Some early kings such as Gilgamesh were deified after death; many kings of the late 3rd and early 2nd millennia BC claimed to be gods in their lifetimes. (*syn.* reth)

Divostin: A Neolithic site in Serbia with occupations of the Early Starcevo and Vinca cultures dating from c. 5250–4960 (Starcevo) to c. 3900–3300 BC (Vinca). Excavation uncovered seven complete house plans of the Late Vinca village, including one house containing 100 pots. The subsistence economy was based on cattle husbandry and agriculture. Cult objects included a model ritual scene and many fired clay anthropomorphic figurines.

Diyala: One of the main tributaries of the Tigris River, east of Baghdad, Iraq, where four sites were excavated: Tell Asmar (Eshnunna), Khafajah (Khafaje), Ischali, and Tell Aqrab of the Jemdet Nasr and Early Dynastic periods. The work allowed the establishment of a pottery sequence for this part of Mesopotamia, from the late 4th to the early 2nd millennia BC, and the investigation of a number of important buildings of the periods.

djed pillar: In Egypt, a widely found amulet of roughly cruciform style with at least three crossbars. It seems to have been a fetish from prehistoric times and came to represent the abstract concept of stability. Like the ankh, it was commonly used in friezes and painted inside the base of coffins.

Djeitun: A Neolithic site of a 6th millennium BC (and possibly late 7th) culture of Turkmenia characterized by mudbrick architecture of one-roomed houses with lime-plastered floors. Both floors and walls were sometimes painted. The subsistence economy was based on cereal agriculture (barley, wheat), accompanied by the rearing of sheep, cattle, and goats and the hunting of gazelle, onager, wild pig, and smaller animals. The Djeitun culture had a microlithic flint industry and chaff-tempered pottery, decorated with simple painted designs. The culture was the earliest Neolithic of central Asia.

Djer (c. 3000 BC): An early king of the 1st Dynasty of Egypt, who was probably third in the sequence of rulers beginning with Narmer—as listed on a clay seal impression from his tomb in the royal cemetery at Abydos. He may also be the same as Iti, mentioned in the king list in the temple of Sety I at Abydos.

Djet (c. 2980 BC): A ruler of the 1st Dynasty who was probably buried in Tomb Z at Abydos, which was first excavated by Emile Amélineau and Flinders Petrie at the beginning of the 20th century. (*syn.* Wadj)

Djoser (fl. 27th c. BC; c. 2667–2648 BC): The second king of the 3rd Dynasty (c. 2650–2575 BC) of Egypt, who undertook the construction of the earliest important stone building in Egypt. His reign was marked by great technological innovation. He and his architect/minister, Imhotep, who was himself deified, constructed the Step pyramid at Saqqara, which was not only the first pyramidal funerary complex but also the earliest example of large-scale stone masonry in Egypt. He was effectively the founder of the Old Kingdom. (*syn.* Zoser, Netjerykhet)

DNA: The basic material of chromosomes, which carries the hereditary instructions (the "blueprint") that determine the formation of all living organisms. Genes, the organizers of inheritance, are composed of DNA. Analysis of the DNA of different primate groups has been used to determine the evolutionary line of modern humans. DNA techniques have also been used to show how long various regional human populations have been separated from one another. DNA analysis of blood residue, both human and animal, on prehistoric tools and weapons may provide information on the evolutionary relations of a range of animal species and between prehistoric and modern humans. (*syn.* deoxyribonucleic acid)

Dnieper-Donets: A 3rd- and 2nd-millennia BC Late Neolithic culture of the Ukraine. Large numbers of small settlements are known with evidence of hunter-gatherer subsistence. Large quantities of comb-pricked pots were found, but grave goods were rare except for copper rings and tooth necklaces. Extended inhumation was the norm; the physical type in these burials is identified as Cro-Magnon. (*syn.* Dnepr-Donets)

Dobranichevka: An Upper Palaeolithic site in central Ukraine with a date of 12,700 bp. Remains include woolly mammoth associated with mammoth-bone houses, pits, hearths, and debris.

doctrine of uniformitarianism: A theory that asserts that the processes now modifying the earth's surface are the same processes as occurred in the geological past. This principle provided the cornerstone of modern geology.

Dodona: An oracle for the god Zeus in northern Greece. The temenos contained bronze dedications, and the remains include a theater and Hellenistic stadium.

dog: The first domesticated animal species; the earliest known site is the Upper Palaeolithic cave of Palegawra in Iraq, with a date of c. 10,000 BC. Other early evidence is from the Mesolithic in Star Carr c. 7500 BC, from Turkey c. 7000 BC, and in America in a Late Pleistocene deposit at Jaguar Cave, Idaho. A number of different types of dogs can be recognized from depictions in Egyptian tombs. All domestic dogs appear ultimately to have been derived from the wolf. The dog is found in hunter-gatherer communities as well as early farming communities.

dog-leash technique: A method of defining an archaeological recovery area by attaching a rope to a centrally located marker stake and tracing the boundary in a circle.

dogu: A type of clay figurine, most often depicting a pregnant female, made in Japan during the Jomon period, c. 5th–4th millennia to c. 250 BC. The function of these figurines is unknown, but it is generally believed that they were a fertility symbol. They are reminiscent of the rigidly frontal fertility figures produced by other prehistoric cultures. Archaeological evidence suggests they were aids in childbirth as well as fertility symbols. They are also found in simulated burials, indicating some ceremonial function. Fired at a low temperature, they often have crumbly surfaces, and many are painted red.

Doian: A stone industry found exclusively in the southern and eastern areas of Somalia and northeastern Kenya in East Africa. Doian assemblages contain pressure-flaked small points, backed microliths, and flake scrapers. A post-Pleistocene age is possible but not yet determined. (*syn.* Eibian)

Doigahama: A Yayoi cemetery site in Yamaguchi prefecture, Japan. The remains of at least 200 men and women of various ages were found buried in pits, in extended or flexed position. Apart from personal ornaments of glass, stone, and shell, the burials were sparsely furnished, unlike the Middle Yayoi burials, such as Sugus, in Kyushu. The body type is different from the Palaeoasiatic Jomon.

Dölauer Heide: A Neolithic settlement in southeastern Germany of the Funnel Beaker culture. Excavations revealed fortifications of bank-and-ditch systems, a palisade, and a number of barrows—all on a hilltop.

dolerite: A fine- to medium-grained, dark gray to black intrusive igneous rock with the composition of basalt. It is extremely hard and tough and is commonly quarried for crushed stone (trap). It is used for monumental stone and is one of the dark-colored rocks commercially known as black granite. Diabase is widespread. (*syn.* diabase)

dolichocephalic: A term in physical anthropology meaning long and narrow headed. On the cephalic index, the cranium has a maximum width of 75% or less of the maximum length, or a cephalic index greater than 75. (*syn.* dolichocranic)

dolium: A large Greek or Roman coarse earthenware vessel with a wide mouth and spherical form. It was used to store wine and oil; later, smaller vessels were produced. (*syn.* culeus)

dolmen: In antiquity (especially in France), a word for a megalithic tomb consisting of orthostats and capstone or for megalithic chamber tombs in general. This was usually a stone structure consisting of upright columns supporting a slab roof known from Neolithic times. In English archaeological literature *dolmen* should be used only for tombs whose original plan cannot be determined or for tombs of simple unspecialized types, which do not fit into the passage grave or gallery grave categories; it is also used for relatively small, closed megalithic chambers, such as the dysser of Scandinavia. The name was probably derived from Cornish *tolmen* (stone table). The word has a second meaning as the enclosure for burial in a jar of the Yayoi period in Japan, consisting of a single large stone slab supported on a ring of stones. A third meaning is as a megalithic stone burial feature in western China and the coastal Yellow Sea area, dating to the last millennium BC, of which there are three forms—raised table, low table, and unsupported capstone.

dolmen deity: A symbol of mysterious personage or divinity who peers from megalithic and rock-cut tombs of western Europe. She is sometimes represented by nothing but a pair of eyes or eyebrows, the oculus motif. Breasts and necklaces are female attributes often shown. The most detailed representation is on the French statue Menhir.

Dolní Vestonice: An Upper Palaeolithic camping site in southern Moravia for mammoth hunters of the loess country. Excavation has revealed various phases of occupation, represented by houses, hearths, flint tools (burins, scrapers, backed blades), ornaments of mammoth ivory, animal figurines of baked clay. Venus figurines, faunal and human remains. The main occupation level dates from 25,000 BP, the beginning of the last glacial maximum (the end of an interstadial period). The culture has been called Pavlovian or eastern Gravettian.

Domesday Book: A survey of land ownership in England after the Norman Conquest. The Anglo-Saxon Chronicle describes how in 1085 it was decided to make a record of the number of hides in land existing in each English shire and to establish the amount and value of acreage and livestock possessed by individual landowners. The idea was to create a new rating system that would protect and enlarge the king's revenue. The resulting document—a two-volume survey of land ownership arranged under tenurial rather than territorial headings—is the great testament of feudal England. The Domesday Book is of fundamental importance to both historians and archaeologists of the Late Saxon and early Norman periods, as it gives the names and sizes of villages, farms, manors, churches, and other properties that existed at the time as well as certain sales and transactions.

domestication: The adaptation of an animal or plant through breeding in captivity for useful advantage to and by humans. Early agriculturists controlled fauna through selection and breeding so that animals might produce more of what man needed than did their wild forebears. The definition includes the taming of cats and dogs as house pets, as well as the care and control of cattle, sheep, goat, pig, horse, llama, camel, guinea pig, and so on. It included breeding for produce such as milk, meat, hides, and wool and the training of animals for draft and carrying. This selection by man resulted in osteological changes in the animals, so that in general domesticated animals can be distinguished by their remains from their wild ancestors. The process of domestication was a slow one, dogs likely being the first in Mesolithic times. Sheep were likely domesticated by 9000 BC in Iraq. Goats, cattle, and pigs followed in the next 3,000 years, all in southwest Asia. The horse appears in the 2nd millennium, and the camel in the 1st. In the New World, domesticable animals were far fewer, notably the dog, llama, and guinea pig. The change involved, from hunting and gathering to food production, was one of the most important in human development. Adaptations made by animal and plant species to the cultural environment as a result of human interference in reproductive or other behavior are often detectable as specific physical changes in faunal or floral ecofacts. (*syn.* domestic animals)

Domica: A cave site in eastern Slovakia with linear pottery culture of the Bükk group.

domus de janas: The Sardinian name for a kind of rock-cut chamber tomb, often with many interconnecting rooms, found on the island from the Copper Age and Early Bronze Age. The term means "house of the fairies" and describes often complex, multichambered tombs.

Dongbei: The northeastern part of present-day China, including the Manchurian Basin and Bohai Bay. The region is often treated separately from the archaeology of the North China Plain and includes Liaoning, Heilongjiang, and Jilin provinces. (*syn.* Tung-pei)

Dong-dau: The second Bronze Age phase of North Vietnam (*bronze moyen*), dated to the second half of the 2nd millennium BC. Its bronzes contain about 20% tin, and forms and casting methods are ancestral to those of the classic Dong-Son (*bronze final*) phase and succeeded Phung Nguyen in c. 1500 BC. Dong-dau is the site that gave its name to this period. (*syn.* Dong Dau)

Dong-son: A classic Bronze Age site in north Vietnam and its culture, dating c. 500 BC to AD 100. It was preceded by the Go Bong (c. 2000–1500 BC), Dong-Dau (c. 1500–100 BC),

and Go Mun (c. 1000–500 BC) phases of the Vietnamese Bronze Age. The Dong-son culture thus overlaps the Chinese conquest of northern Vietnam in 111 BC. Characteristic are large incised cast-bronze drums, bronze situlae (buckets), bells, tools, and weapons from elaborate boat burials and assemblages in lacquered wood coffins. Dong-son drums of presumed Vietnamese manufacture were traded through wide areas of Southeast Asia and southern China as far as New Guinea, and the Dong-son bronze-working tradition was by far the richest and most advanced ever to develop in Southeast Asia. Iron was used for tools. There is evidence for developing urbanism in defensive earthworks and wet rice cultivation. Major sites include Chao Can, Viet Khe, Lang Ca, and Co Loa. (*syn.* Dong Son)

Don Noi: A Neolithic site in Thailand where stone working was done near chalcedony quarries, dating to the 3rd millennium BC. Tools made included flaked adzes.

Dong Zuobin (1895–1963): Chinese archaeologist who specialized in oracle bone inscriptions from the Shang dynasty (1400–1100/1027 BC). He tried to reconstruct the bones' context and to establish criteria for determining fakes. He found 10,000 complete or fragmentary oracle bones.

Dorak: A site of northwest Anatolia (western Turkey), south of the Sea of Marmora, reported to have two looted "royal tombs" of the Copper Age comparable to, but far richer than, those of Alaca Hüyük. The material, which was photographed, drawn, and described by J. Mellaart, vanished immediately after his report—creating controversy and doubt that the tombs even existed.

Dorestad: The trading center of the Frisians in the Netherlands, from which they controlled the old Rhine, the Vecht, and the Lek until the course of the river changed. Excavations have located an earthwork defense of this medieval site and have produced enormous quantities of occupation debris including large amounts of imported Rhenish and local pottery, wine casks from the Mainz area, Niedermendig lava querns, and stone mortars made in eastern Belgium. There is also evidence of industrial activities like weaving, shipbuilding, bone and metalworking. Dorestad is the best-excavated and finest example of a Carolingian emporium and illustrates the scale of commerce between the imperial estates in the Rhineland and other North Sea communities. (*syn.* Duurstede)

Dorians: Peoples who invaded southern Greece from the north around the end of the 2nd millennium BC (1100) after the decline of the Mycenaeans. Some speculate that the Dorians were responsible for the Mycenaeans' overthrow. It has proved difficult to recognize their products in the archaeological record and therefore it is hard to discover their origins. In Classical times, the important Dorian dialect was spoken through much of the Peloponnese, the southern Aegean islands, and the southwest coast of Asia Minor. They also introduced the use of iron for swords. The invading Dorians had a relatively low cultural level, however, and after sweeping away the last of the declining Mycenaean and Minoan civilizations, they led the region into a dark age from which the Greek city-states did not emerge until almost 3 centuries later.

Doric order: A style of architecture used on mainland Greece and in the western Mediterranean with the plainest of capitals and a simple column with no pedestal or base and a distinctive echinus and abacus. The order was distinguished by being the earliest and simplest. The fluted columns had a diameter-to-height ratio of one to eight, and the frieze was alternating triglyphs (triple groove) and metopes (brow). It was named after the tribe of the Dorians. (*syn.* doric, Doric style, Doric column)

Dörpfeld, Wilhelm (1853–1940): A German archaeologist who excavated many important prehistoric and Classical sites in the Greek world. He worked first under Ernst Curtius on the excavations of Olympia and then assisted Heinrich Schliemann on his third and fourth seasons at Troy, bringing to this work the careful digging and recording techniques worked out at Olympia. After Schliemann's death, he continued work at Troy, then later worked on the Ionian island of Leukas, off the west coast of Greece, which, contrary to most other authorities, he believed to be Homer's Ithaca, home of Odysseus.

Dorset: A prehistoric Eskimo culture that settled in the eastern Canadian Arctic and Greenland around 1000 BC and lasted until AD 1000 when it was replaced by the Thule culture. The earliest manifestation, known as pre-Dorsen (in some areas as Sarqaq), is represented at sites on Baffin Island and dates from c. 2400 BC. The Dorsen subtradition developed from the pre-Eskimo Arctic Small Tool tradition. A typical site of the late Dorset subtradition is Port aux Choix 2 in western Newfoundland with house and storage pits. The people hunted sea mammals and caribou. The tradition had a stone tool assemblage of end scrapers and spear points and was also known for beautiful carvings of animals and humans in bone, ivory, and wood. (*related word* Dorset tradition)

Dos Aguas: A rock shelter with paintings of the Spanish Levantine (Mesolithic) type situated in Valencia, Spain. Hunters of food and marine shellfish can be seen in cave art at Dos Aguas. More than 7,500 figures painted by these hunters and gatherers are known from all over the eastern and southern peninsula, dating from 7000–3500 BC. Located in the open air, usually beneath rock overhangs or in protecting hollows, are animated representations of people dancing, including two women in voluminous skirts at Dos Aguas.

Dosariyah: A Saudi Arabian site representing the 'Ubaid

influence in the Persian Gulf. There is 'Ubaid pottery and chipped stone.

Dos Pilas: The largest Maya city of the Petexbatun part of Guatemala during the Late Classic period. The tomb of a Late Classic ruler was discovered, which included a spectacular headdress.

dotaku: A type of bronze bell made in Yayoi period Japan, which was cast from melted bronzes, some heavily decorated. The bells may have been used in agricultural fertility rituals.

Douar Doum: A site near Rabat, Morocco, with some of the earliest stone tools in Africa. The tools are in rough stone and include a variety of pebble tools, but no hand axes. They are typical of the Oldowan or pebble culture of Africa and are contemporary with the Moulouyan dunes, about 2 million years old or more.

double ax: A shaft-hole cutting tool, which has two opposed (symmetrical) blades and is made of copper or bronze. With two cutting edges, it did not have to be sharpened as often as a single ax. The best-known examples are from Minoan Crete, where it was a practical tool and a cult symbol. The stone battle ax is occasionally found in this form. (*syn.* double axe)

Dougga: A Numidian settlement, the best-preserved ancient Roman city in modern Tunisia, located near modern Tabursuq, west of the ancient road between Carthage and Theveste. It was a dependency of Carthage until the 3rd century AD. Thugga's most notable pre-Roman ruin is a 2nd-century BC mausoleum, built in honor of a Numidian prince. It is a three-story building topped by a pyramid, and the mausoleum contained a bilingual Phoenician and Numidian inscription. It represented a combination of the Egyptian pyramidal funerary building and the Hellenistic Greek temple. Thugga was made a municipium by the Roman emperor Septimius Severus (reigned AD 193–211), and an arch erected in his honor is one of the outstanding Roman remains. Other important buildings dating to Roman times include a forum, baths, villas, capitol, circus, temples, an aqueduct (and system of water cisterns), and a theater. (*syn.* Thugga)

Douglass, Andrew Ellicott (1867–1962): An American astronomer who developed the dendrochronology dating method. He outlined the method as early as 1901, but it was not until 1929 that he was able to publish an unbroken sequence of tree rings for the Southwest United States, extending back from the present day to the early years of the present era. This provided a dating method for the southwestern Pueblo villages.

Dowris: A site in Ireland where a hoard of over 200 bronzes of the Irish Late Bronze Age have been dated to the 8th century BC. Implements of the Dowris A phase (c. 1000–c. 800 BC) include many gold ornaments and a series of bronzes showing great proficiency in casting and sheet metalwork.

Ireland was at this time in contact with Mediterranean and Nordic lands. Bronze cauldrons and V-notched-shields demonstrate western links, while U-notched shields, bronze buckets and horns, pins with sunflower-shaped heads, and the use of conical rivets show connections with northern and central Europe. Ireland did not enter the Iron Age until just after 400 BC (i.e., during the La Tène period), although a few swords and axes show contact with Hallstatt Iron Age cultures. Dowrin B and C were the final Irish bronze industries (c. 800–400 BC) contemporary with the first part of the continental Iron Age.

dowsing: A technique for discovering buried features or materials by the use of a Y-shaped hazel wand or bimetal strip—a practice similar to water divining. Supposedly the location of subsurface features may take place by employing a twig, copper rod, or pendulum and observing the discontinuous movements of these "instruments."

Drachenloch: A cave site in western Germany with purported evidence of a Middle Palaeolithic cave bear cult: a stone cist with bear skulls and bones. According to the Nibelungen legends, the Drachenloch in the hill sheltered the dragon slain by the hero Siegfried. (*syn.* Dragon's Cave)

drachma: A Greek silver coin equivalent to six obols. In Athens, drachma were often decorated with Athena's head and her owl.

Dragendorff, Hans (1870–1941): A German scholar who in 1895–1896 published a scheme of classification for the shapes of Terra Sigillata or Samian ware.

dragon: A legendary monster usually depicted as a huge-bat-winged, fire-breathing, scaly lizard or snake with a barbed tail. In general, in the Middle Eastern world, the dragon was symbolic of the principle of evil. In the Far East, the dragon was prestigious and considered a beneficent creature. The Chinese dragon, *lung,* represented yang, the principle of heaven, activity, and maleness in the yin-yang of Chinese cosmology. From ancient times, it was the emblem of the Imperial family, and until the founding of the republic (1911) the dragon was on the Chinese flag.

drained fields: Intensive form of agriculture in which fields are created by draining plots of swampy land.

Drakensberg: A South African mountain range forming the southern and eastern boundary of Lesotho, where there is an abundance of Stone Age rock paintings.

Dralang: A Megalithic site in southwestern Tibet with a large, tablelike stone structure and other large standing stones in the monument. There were pits for human sacrifices, also.

drift: Any debris transported or deposited by or from glacial ice and melt water; a glacial deposit laid down by ice or water in glacial streams, lakes, or arctic oceans. The term *drift* remains in common usage and includes alluvium, pro-glacial deposits, till, and ice-contact stratified drift.

dromos: The corridor-like entrance passage leading into Minoan-Mycenaean tholos and chamber tombs. It is from the Green word meaning "course" or "avenue." Also, the term refers to an avenue leading to the entrances of Egyptian temples; that leading to the great temple of Karnac contained 660 colossal sphinxes, all of which were monoliths.

Druids: A powerful Celtic priesthood of the Gauls and Britons from the 1st century BC through the 1st century AD. They led the resistance to the Romans, and when they were finally defeated in AD 78 they were exterminated, partly because of human sacrifices that they carried out. The Druids believed in reincarnation, worshiped the moon and heavenly bodies, and built circular temples in forest groves. Archaeologically, the only material definitely attributed to them is a hoard of bronze and iron at Llyn Cerrig Bach in Anglesey. It is not held that they built Stonehenge or Avebury.

Dry Creek: The most important prehistoric site in Alaska, in the foothills of the Alaska Range in the south-central region. The lowest layer is assigned to the Nenna complex, the middle microblade assemblage to the Denali complex (10,690 bp), and the upper side-notched points are classed as Northern Archaic (4670–3430 bp).

Dryas: A series of cold climatic phases in northwestern Europe, during a time when the North Atlantic was in almost full glacial condition. Dryas I was c. 16,000/14,000 BP, Dryas II (Older Dryas) was c. 12,300–11,800 bp, and Dryas III (Younger Dryas) was c. 11,000–10,000 bp. It is named after a tundra plant. The increasing temperature after the late Dryas period during the Pre-Boreal and the Boreal (c. 8000–5500 BC, according to radiocarbon dating) caused a remarkable change in late glacial flora and fauna.

duat: An Egyptian term for the land of the dead, which was thought to be similar to Egypt itself, lying under the earth, and entered through the western horizon.

Dublin: The modern capital of Ireland (Eire) was founded by the Vikings, or Norsemen, in the 9th century (c. 831) and built on the ridge above the south bank of the river, the same spot where Dublin Castle was built. Throughout much of the Middle Ages it remained one of the foremost sea ports in the British Isles. Viking Dublin was a prosperous settlement, and excavations begun in the 1960s revealed a wealth of archaeological evidence for that period. From prehistoric times, people have dwelt in the area about Dublin Bay, and four of Ireland's five great roads converged near the spot called Baile Átha Cliath ("The Town of the Ford of the Hurdle"). Remarkable waterlogged conditions have preserved organic material from levels dating to between the 9th–14th centuries. The footings of wattle-and-daub and timber-framed buildings have been recovered, with door posts, screens, and hearths, as well as timber streets. There is also abundant evidence of the crafts and industries from the Hiberno-Scandinavian and Anglo-Norman periods—woodworking, metalworking, hooping, comb making, leather-working, and cobbling.

Dubois, Eugène (1858–1940): A Dutch palaeoanthropologist and anatomist who discovered Java man, the first known fossil of *Homo erectus*, in 1891. Dubois named the fossils *Pithecanthropus erectus* to indicate an intermediate phase in the evolution then believed to proceed from simian ancestors having the upright posture of modern man. For years there was much controversy over his finds, until they were re-examined in 1923.

Dudesti: The type site of a Middle Neolithic culture of southeastern Romania, of the late 5th millennium BC. Contemporaneous with the Vadastra, Vinca A/B, and Karanovo III, Dudesti sites are typically short-lived occupations, defined by storage pits and postholes. Most sites are limited to the first terraces of major river valleys. The largely undecorated pottery is derivative of the dark burnished ware tradition of the south Balkans.

Duff, Roger Shepherd (1912–1978): A New Zealand archaeologist known for *The Moa-Hunter Period of Maori Culture* (1950) and for being a pioneer of Polynesian archaeology. He worked at Wairau Bar, classified Polynesian and Southeast Asian stone adzes, and proved the Polynesian origin of the first inhabitants of New Zealand.

dugout canoe: A simple canoe made from a single tree hollowed out by burning or chopping.

Dumuzi: A shepherd god of Sumerian myth, husband of Inanna. Dumuzi is Tammuz in later western Asian myth.

dun: A Scottish/Irish term for a fortified stone dwelling place. There are large duns of hill-fort type and small defended homesteads. Some examples, of both ring fort and promontory fort types, have galleries or passages with the drystone enclosure wall. The oldest duns belong to the late Iron Age, but they continued to be built into the early Christian and medieval periods.

Dunadd: A site in Argyllshire, Scotland, which was a fort of the Kingdom of Dalriada, taken by the Picts in AD 683 and 736. A main citadel connected to a middle courtyard by a stone wall has been located. The most important finds from Dunadd are several carved stones and imported Mediterranean pottery.

Dundo: A town of northeastern Angola with mines where alluvial deposits were worked for diamonds. A sequence of stone industries includes an Acheulian occupation succeeded by Sangoan and then Lupemban industries, the last being dated to before 30,000 BC. The Lupemban continued until c. 13,000 BC. From c. 12,000 BC, Tshitolian industries devel-

oped and continued until after the introduction of ironworking around the beginning of the Christian era.

Dunhuang: A site in northwestern China with many Buddhist sculptures, frescoes, and Mogao grottoes. It was a Chinese frontier outpost at a place where the Silk Route branched before crossing Central Asia. It was established as a Han military commandery in 111 BC, and many documents and manuscripts dating from the Han Dynasty have been found there. There is a complex of nearly 500 Buddhist cave temples with well-preserved paintings and sculptures. A Buddhist library walled up in a cave around 1035 and rediscovered in 1900 contained thousands of manuscripts written in Chinese and various Central Asian scripts, some with dates ranging from 406–996. Among the material in the British Museum is the oldest extant printed book in the world, a Chinese translation of the Diamond Sutra, a Buddhist text, dated AD 868. Many other manuscripts and paintings obtained by Aurel Stein are kept at the British Museum. (*syn.* Tun-huang)

Dura-Europus: A ruined Syrian city in the Syrian desert, on the middle Euphrates River, originally a Babylonian town (Dura), but rebuilt as a military colony about 300 BC by the Seleucids and given the second name of Europus. About 100 BC, it fell to the Parthians and became a prosperous caravan city. It was annexed by the Romans in AD 165 and was a frontier fortress. Shortly after AD 256, it was overrun and destroyed by the Sasanians. The remains at Dura-Europus give an unusually detailed picture of the everyday life there; and the inscriptions, reliefs, and architecture give much information about the mixing of Greek and Semitic cultures. Two structures dating to the 3rd century AD contain extensive wall paintings. There also is an irregular enceinte (enclosure), a city grid system, and many sanctuaries and temples dedicated to the many deities of the mixed population. (*syn.* Dura Europos, Doura-Europus)

Durrington Walls: A Neolithic (late 3rd millennium BC) henge monument in Wiltshire, England, with a large twin entrance, first occupied by people who made pottery of the Windmill Hill, Grooved Ware, and Beaker styles. Inside, the excavators found remains of two large circular timber structures, each of which had evidence for several different phases of construction.

Dürrnberg bei Hallein: An Iron Age salt mining center in Austria from the 5th century BC. It eclipsed the mining complex at Hallstatt. There are many wealthy burials and artifacts linking the site with other parts of central Europe and the Mediterranean.

Duruthy: A rock shelter in southwest France, occupied from the early Magdalenian to the Azilian, including the Chalcolithic. Some Magdalenian layers have been dated to the 14th millennium bp. It is characterized by portable art.

Duvanli: A tumulus cemetery in Thrace (modern Bulgaria) of the 5th century BC, with imported Athenian pottery and items of Greek gold-figured silver plate.

Dvaravati: A Buddhist kingdom in present-day Thailand and an early Mon state, first mentioned in Chinese sources as T'o-lo-po-ti in the middle of the 7th century AD. Although few records have survived, its capital may have been at Nakhon Pathom, and its territory must have included almost all present Thailand. There are architectural remains, terracotta modeling, stucco relief sculpture, and Buddhist statuary in bronze and stone. The kingdom came to an end when the Khmers incorporated the area in the empire of Angkor in the 11th century AD.

Dvuglazka Cave: A Palaeolithic and Mesolithic site on the Tolchei River in south-central Siberia. Artifacts—Levallois cores, denticulates, and scrapers—are found with sheep and other mammal remains. It was the northernmost Middle Palaeolithic site in Asia.

dyad: A pair of statues, often carved from the same block of material, either representing a man and his wife or depicting two versions of the same person. (*syn.* pair-statue)

Dynastic Period: A period of ancient Egypt's history tied to a framework of 30 dynasties (ruling houses) of kings, or pharaohs, who ruled from the time of the country's unification into a single kingdom in c. 3100 BC until its conquest by Alexander the Great in 332 BC. The two Predynastic kingdoms of Upper and Lower Egypt were united by the legendary king Menes, possibly to be identified with the historical King Narmer. The Dynastic Period was followed by a Greek Period when the country was ruled by the Ptolemys, descendants of Alexander the Great's general. The Ptolemaic Period and Egypt's independence were brought to an end in 30 BC when Queen Cleopatra VII died and the country was absorbed into the Roman Empire. The political history, largely derived from written sources, has a detailed and, for the most part, precise chronology. From the 21st Dynasty onward, Egypt's cohesion broke, and from the 11th–7th centuries BC, Libyan, Asian, and Nubian contenders vied with Egyptians for control of the state. The divine ruler, the pharaoh, was ultimately responsible for the complex bureaucracy and was also the figurehead of the official religion, the personification of the sun god Ra, counterpart of Osiris, the god of the land of the dead. Because of their belief in the afterlife, the royal tombs of the pharaohs in particular reflect the great wealth and concentration of resources at the pharaoh's disposal. Much of our information about ancient Egyptian history comes from the records that were carefully maintained by the Egyptians themselves, notably by the priests who were regarded as the guardians of the state's accumulated wisdom. (*syn.* Dynastic Egypt)

dynasty: Any line of rulers whose right to power is inherited; usually a line of kings, related by blood, who succeed one another on a throne. Egyptian history was divided into 31 dynasties by Manetho in the 3rd century BC when he wrote a history of Egypt. The dynasties of Mesopotamia were distinguished by their places of origin rather than their relationships, such as those of Ur and Larsa. In China, the dynasties were longer lived and often encompassed only regions, those of Shang and Chou spanning twelve centuries. The term is sometimes used for rulers from a single city or ethnic group.

dyss: The Danish name for the earliest type of megalithic chamber tomb found in Scandinavia in the Early neolithic. The oldest dysser are rectangular slab cysts roofed with capstones and containing one to six skeletons. The burial chamber is covered with a mound that rises to the height of the capstone and has a retaining curb of stones. Dysser are associated with an early phase (C) of the TRB culture. Similar but less massive cysts were built by other TRB groups elsewhere in northern Europe. (*syn.* pl. dysser)

Dyuktai: An Upper Palaeolithic culture of northeast Siberia with the type site being the Dyuktai Cave at the confluence of the Dyuktai and Aldan Rivers. It is characterized by bifacial tools of various shapes, burins on flakes and blades, blades, and microblades. The industry was associated with mammoth, bison, and horse bones and is similar to the Denali complex of Alaska. The cave's earliest occupation dates to c. 33,000 BC, and the culture seems to have ceased c. 10,000 BC. The people who first migrated into North America may have been from this cultural group, and it may be ancestral to the earliest lithic technologies, in particular the bifacially flaked points, of North America. (*syn.* Diuktai, Dyuktai Cave)

Dzhruchula: Middle Palaeolithic cave in the Greater Caucasus of Georgia, with two main cultural layers. Tools are scrapers and points, and the newer assemblage has Levallois technique tools and blades.

Dzibilchaltún: A large Maya ceremonial site in the northwest Yucatán Peninsula, one of the largest Mayan cities ever built, covering 50 square miles and having a maximum population of over 50,000 around AD 1000. Its occupation was continuous from 500 BC to the late Classic and Early Post-Classic, from AD 600–1000, but the population dropped to less than 10% of its former size from AD 1000–1200. Its earliest occupation is denoted by Mamon ceramics and Chicanel structures. The site centers around the Cenote Xlacah, with major plazas, the Temple of Seven Dolls, pyramids, platforms, and numerous causeways (*sache*) converge in the middle of the site. It may have been the capital of the Maya civilization.

Dzierzyslaw: An Upper Palaeolithic site in Poland with an assemblage of scrapers and laurel-leaf points of the Szeletian and probably dating to the middle of the last glacial period.

Ee

Ea: Mesopotamian/Sumerian (Enki) god of water and a member of the triad of deities completed by Anu (Sumerian An) and Bel (Enlil). From a local deity worshipped in the city of Eridu, Ea evolved into a major god, Lord of Apsu, the fresh waters beneath the earth. Ea, the Akkadian counterpart of Enki, was the god of ritual purification.

Eanna sounding: A test excavation in the Eanna district of Warka for study of the origins of writing in southern Mesopotamia. The site has an 18-level sequence from the 'Ubaid (XVIII–XV), Early Uruk (XIV–IX), Middle Uruk (VIII–VI), Late Uruk (V–IV), Jemdet Nasr (III), and Early Dynastic (II–I) periods. Cylinder seals, sealings, and written texts from Mesopotamian administrations were found here for the first time.

ear-flare: A large circular ear ornament, flared like the bell of a trumpet, which was often made of jade. The ear-flare was an elaborate form of ear spool.

Earlier Stone Age: The first stage of the Stone Age in sub-Saharan Africa, dating from more than 2.5 million years ago to c. 150,000 years ago. The earliest artifacts are representative of the Oldowan Industrial complex, which was succeeded by the Acheulian Industrial complex between c. 1.5 million–150,000 years ago.

Early Bronze Age: A period in the Levant dating to c. 3200–1950 BC, just before Egypt's Archaic period. Increasing urbanization was shown by the building of walled towns.

Early Dynastic period: A chronological phase in southern Mesopotamia between c. 2900–2330 BC, ending with the founding of the Dynasty of Akkad. It was also known as the Pre-Sargonid period. The Sumerian city-states flourished under their separate dynastic rulers—Ur, Umma, Kish, and Lagash. The period is 3100–2450 BC on what is called the "high chronology" (the other being the "medium chronology"). The term itself is derived from the Sumerian king list, which implied that Sumer was ruled by kings at this stage,

although archaeological evidence for the existence of kingship is meager before the middle of the period. Traditionally, it is divided by archaeologists into three subdivisions—ED I, II, and III—each of approximately 200 years duration. The Royal Tombs of Ur belong the ED III period. The Early Dynastic phase shows clear continuity from the preceding Jemdet Nasr and represents a period of rapid political, cultural, and artistic development. In this period, the pictographic writing of the earlier period developed into the standardized cuneiform script. This period represents the earliest conjunction of archaeological and written evidence for the history of southern Mesopotamia. (*syn.* Archaic Period)

Early Horizon: A period during which the Chavín culture flourished in the central Andes of South America and was integrated into the northern highlands and coastal region of Peru, c. 900–1 BC (also said to be c. 1200–300 BC). It is one of a seven-period chronological construction used in Peruvian archaeology. It coincides with the duration of the Chavín style and its derivatives, such as Cupisnique. Following this, there was regional differentiation culminating in the complex cultures of the Early Intermediate period.

Early Intermediate period: A period of development of distinctive regional cultures in the central Andes of South America, AD c. 1–600 (also said to be AD c. 300–600). The period was characterized by nationalism, full population, first large-scale irrigation works in coastal valleys, inter-regional warfare, construction of forts, craft specialization, social class distinctions, rise of the first great Peruvian cities. Two of the better-known cultures are the Moche and Nasca civilizations. The Middle Horizon emerged from these expansions.

Early Khartoum: A base camp site in modern Khartoum, which provided the first clear picture of the so-called Aquatic Civilization. The site had traces of sun-dried daub suggesting the presence of temporary structures. Fishing with bone-headed harpoons was the economic basis of the settlement.

Other artifacts include chipped and ground stone and pottery with wavy-line decoration. Dates of 6th or 5th millennium BC seem probable; similar harpoons at Tagra, to the south, are dated to c. 6300 BC.

Early Later Stone Age: An informal designation for the microlithic late Pleistocene Stone Age industry of some sites in South Africa. One such site is Border Cave, characterized by small backed pieces, bone points, ostrich eggshell beads, and incised bone and wood. (*syn.* ESLA)

Early Lithic: A term applied to the earliest stage in New World history, when man first appeared and started hunting and gathering. The period is characterized by large projectile points and percussion-chipped stone tools suitable for the slaughter and butchering of big game. (*syn.* Paleo-Indian)

Early Man Shelter: An Australian rock shelter at Cape York, with patinaed Panaramitee-style paintings and engravings of humans, animals, tracks, and abstract motifs. Charcoal from occupation deposits covering wall engravings yielded radiocarbon dates between 10,000–13,000 bp. The shelter also contained the oldest known remains of *Sarcophilus harriisii* (Tasmanian devil) in tropical Australia: it is now found only in Tasmania. Bone tools are present that are 3000–6000 years old.

early-stage biface: A biface in the initial step of manufacture, usually with sinuous edges and simple surface topography.

ear spool: An ornament worn in the ear lobe, sometimes of such weight that the ear might be stretched to shoulder length.

earth: A general term used to describe mixed material dug from an excavation. Earth is not really the same as soil, which has a more precise definition, although earth may include material from soils in addition to material from other sources.

earthenware: Ceramics fired at temperatures high enough for vitrification to begin.

earth lodge: In American Midwest and East cultures, any wood structure with an earthen covering used for shelter and ceremonies. They have hard-packed floors and/or postholes, which are the remains of wall and roof supports. (*syn.* earthlodge)

earth sciences: Sciences concerned with the study of formation processes that affect the earth's surface.

earthwork, earthworks: Any early structure built from a mound or bank of earth, often created as fortification. In the plan of earthworks, the heads of the line of "tadpoles" are the top or highest point.

earthworm: Any of nearly 2,000 species of terrestrial worms, which act as one of the main agents by which plant litter, humus, and minerals are incorporated and mixed in soil. Earthworms are responsible for the maintenance and stability of various types of soil, especially the brown forest soils. The character of a soil may change markedly if the plant litter made by the vegetation changes to a kind that is unpalatable to earthworms. The effects of earthworm sorting may be seen on archaeological sites in the blurring of layers and the development of worm-sorted layers in the top of buried soils. Earthworms usually remain near the soil surface, but they are known to tunnel as deep as 6 feet during periods of dryness or in winter. Indirectly they provide food for man by aerating the soil, promoting drainage, and drawing organic material into their burrows, where it decomposes faster, thus producing more nutritive materials for growing plants. (*syn.* angleworm)

Easter Island: The easternmost inhabited island of Polynesia, a small volcanic one, about 2,500 miles from South America and 1,250 miles from Pitcairn Island, its nearest inhabited Polynesian neighbor. It was settled by the Polynesians early in the 1st millennium AD and developed a horticultural economy. By AD 700, the inhabitants built large stone platforms (*ahu*), some of cut stone, and between AD 1000–1700 these platforms supported rows of huge stone statues (*moai*), some with separate top knots. Shaped by stone tools, as there is no metal on the island, from quarries in volcanic craters, there are about 300 platforms and about 600 statues. By about 1700, the warrior chiefdoms were fighting, and all the statues were toppled from their pedestals. The platforms were used for human burial in stone chambers inserted into the stonework. There is a village of stone houses and many petroglyphs. The Europeans discovered Easter Island in 1722, after which the culture and population grew. The islanders also carved on wooden boards in an undeciphered script, Rongorongo. Easter Island culture represents the cultural development of an isolated human community. (*syn.* Rapa Nui)

Eastern Chin Dynasty: A phase of the Chin Dynasty, the ruling house of Chinese origin controlling southeastern China from AD 317–420 when northern China was under the rule of Turkic tribes. There are numerous tombs and Yueh Ware. It was one of the Six Dynasties of China.

Eastern Gravettian: An Upper Palaeolithic industry across central and eastern Europe during the last glacial maximum, c. 30,000–20,000 BP. Assemblages include shouldered points, backed blades, and some Venus figurines.

East Greek pottery: A type of pottery produced during the Archaic period in the Greek islands and on the western coast of Turkey, at Chios, Samos, Ephesus, Miletus, Clazomenae, and Rhodes.

Eastern Zhou [Chou] period: The latter part of the Zhou Dynasty, from 770 BC to the extinction of the Zhou royal house in 256 BC. The term also refers to the period up to the founding of the Qin Dynasty in 221 BC.

East Rudolf: An important site on the northeastern shore of Lake Turkana (Lake Rudolf) in northern Kenya for research into earliest man, with major contributions to knowledge of the Australopithecines and Hominids (*Australopithecus boisei*, *A. africanus*, and *Homo habilis*). There are sediments rich in fossils and volcanic layers of the 1–3-million-year time range. (*syn.* Koobi Fora)

East Spanish rock art: An art style of southeastern Spain, found on the walls of shallow rock shelters and probably of the Mesolithic period. The subjects are lively scenes from everyday life, with warriors, hunters, dancers, and animals. The style is unlike that of cave art, the figures being small and painted in solid colors with no attempt at light and shade.

Ebbsfleet: A small valley in southern England with an important series of loams and gravels spanning the last two glacial periods and intervening interglacial. Stone tools included Levallois flakes, but only a few hand axes and other tool types were found. The area has also given its name to a decorated pottery style of the Neolithic period. The first Jutes, Hengist and Horsa, landed at Ebbsfleet in the Isle of Thanet in AD 449.

Ebla: A site on the River Orontes in northern Syria (now Tell Mardikh), which was the seat of a powerful state in the mid-3rd millennium BC, although occupied from the 4th millennium onward. It fell to Akkad c. 2250 but continued to flourish. The remains and a large archive of over 15,000 cuneiform texts and fragments in a palace complex showed a high level of wealth and culture. The archive yielded evidence of a previously unknown language, a Semitic tongue now labeled Eblaite, and the history of a powerful state of the 3rd millennium BC. The tablets also record many Semitic names used in the Old Testament of the bible, suggesting that Eblites and Israelites interacted. Ebla was important under a dynasty of Amorites in the 2nd millennium, before being destroyed c. 1600 BC by the Hittites. The city was clearly an important commercial center, exporting woolen cloth, wood, and furniture to Assur in Mesopotamia and Kanesh in Anatolia. The culture was contemporary with the late Early Dynastic city-states and early Akkadian rulers of southern Mesopotamia. (*syn.* Eblaite, Tell Mardik Ebla, Tell Mardikh)

Eburran: An East African obsidian industry of the central Rift Valley, Kenya, previously known as the Kenya Capsian and before that as the Kenya Aurignacian. Its time span is the 13th–8th millennia BC. The assemblages, as recovered from Gamble's Cave and Nderit Drift, include large backed blades, crescentric microliths, burins, and end scrapers. (*syn.* Kenya Capsian, Kenya Aurignacian)

echinus: In architecture, the top of classical column shafts, which form part of the capital. In the Doric order, it is a convex section immediately below the abacus. In the Ionic order, it is between the volutes of the capital and is often decorated with an egg-and-dart pattern.

echo sounding: An acoustic underwater survey technique used to trace the topography of submerged land surfaces. It is a method in which a sound pulse travels from the vessel to the ocean floor, is reflected, and returns. By calculations involving the time elapsed between generation of the pulse and its return and the speed of sound in water, a continuous record of sea floor topography can be made. Echo sounding depends on timing the lapse between the transmission of a short loud noise or pulse and its return from the target—in this case the bottom of the sea or lake. Most echo sounders perform these calculations mechanically, producing a graphic record in the form of a paper chart. Misleading reflections caused by the presence of undersea canyons or mountains, plus variations in the speed of sound through water caused by differences in temperature, depth, and salinity, limit the accuracy of echo sounding.

ecofact: Any flora or fauna material found at an archaeological site; nonartifactual evidence that has not been technologically altered but that has cultural relevance, such as a shell carried from the ocean to an inland settlement. Seeds, pollen, animal bone, insects, fish bones, and mollusks are all ecofacts; the category includes both inorganic and organic ecofacts.

ecological community: The different biotic species of a specific region and the network of interrelations that exists among them.

ecological determinants approach: A research strategy in settlement archaeology emphasizing the location of human settlements in response to specific ecological factors; the study of changes in the environment determining changes in human society. (*syn.* ecological determinism)

ecology: The study of entire assemblages of living organisms and their physical milieus, which together constitute an integrated system. In archaeology, ecology seeks to reconstruct the past environment of man and his impact on it. The term encompasses the relation of plants and animals with their environment—climate, geology, soils, vegetation, other animals, manmade structures. Environmental archaeology is concerned with the ecology of man, but also with the ecology of other animals and plants living in the same environment.

economic specialization: Situation in which necessary or useful economic tasks are not equally shared by all members of society, making individuals or groups economically interdependent.

economic symbiosis: Economic interdependence of population units in a region for the good of all.

economy: The structure of economic life in a country, area, or period; the provisioning of human society with food, water, shelter, and so on.

ecosystem: The complex of living organisms, their physical environment, and all their interrelations in a particular unit of space; the total living community of a single environment—the flora, fauna, insects, and man himself—and the interactions of the constituent parts as well as their relation with the nonliving environment. The flow of energy through an ecosystem leads to a clearly defined structure, biotic diversity, and system of exchange cycles between the living and nonliving parts of the ecosystem.

ecotone: A transition zone between habitats of two different plant communities, such as forest and grassland; the dividing line between two different ecological communities. It has some of the characteristics of each bordering community and often contains species not found in the overlapping communities. An ecotone may exist in a broad or narrow area. The influence of the two bordering communities on each other is known as the edge effect. An ecotonal area often has a higher density of organisms of one species and a greater number of species than are found in either individual community. Some organisms need this transitional area for activities such as courtship, nesting, or foraging for food.

edaphic: Of or pertaining to the soil; resulting from or influenced by the soil rather than the climate. Edaphic factors are those ecological factors associated with the properties of soil and underlying rock, which, along with climate, determine the characteristics of the surrounding plant and animal life.

ed-Daba, Tell: A site in the eastern Nile delta of Egypt, probably the ancient city of Avaris, a Palestinian Middle Bronze Age occupation.

Edfu: An Upper Egyptian site dominated by a large, well-preserved temple dedicated to the hawk god Horus. It was constructed under Ptolemaic kings between 237–57 BC and is the most complete surviving example of an ancient Egyptian temple. To its west are the tombs of the Old and Middle Kingdom and the tell of the ancient town. The site was occupied continuously from at least the Old Kingdom until Greco-Roman times. (*syn.* ancient Djeb, Apollonopolis Magna)

edge angle: The angle of the cutting edge of a stone (or other material) tool. The edge angle often indicates the purpose for which the tool was used. Edge-water analysis is the microscopic examination of the working edges of tools. (*syn.* edge-angle)

edge-ground stone tool: A tool classification of Pleistocene northern Australia and New Guinea, and Southeast Asia, made up of hatchets, flakes, and other tools. Important sites include Nawamoyn, Malangangerr, Arnhem Land, Cape York, New Guinea Highlands. Edge-ground tools do not appear until the late Holocene elsewhere in Australia; they are completely absent from Tasmania. In Southeast Asia, the classification includes flaked stone tools sharpened by grinding or polishing the cutting edge only. They existed in the Bacsonian and Hoabhinian periods.

edge-modified flake: A flake with evidence of modification along one or more edges, whether by natural forces, human use, or bag wear.

Eemian: The last Interglacial of northern Europe, after the Saalian and before the Weichsel Glaciation, from c. 125,000–115,000 BP. This group of Quarternary Interglacial deposits is found right across Europe from the Netherlands to Russia and contains fossils that indicate warm conditions. In the Netherlands and northern Germany, the rising sea level caused the deposition of Eemian marine sediments. Evidence from bore holes indicates that the Eemian may represent two or even three interglacial stages. Levalloisian and Mousterian artifacts are found in Eemina deposits. The Riss-Würm in Alpine regions, the Sangamon in North America, and the Ipswichian in Britain are its equivalents. (*syn.* Eemian Interglacial)

effigy: An image or representation, usually depicting people or animals, often made of pottery or stone—such as a ceramic vessel. Such vessels were typical artifacts of the Mississippian period in North America, AD c. 75–1540. (*syn.* effigy vessel)

effigy mound: A Late Woodland culture in the upper Mississippi Valley characterized by low but very long burial mounds, built mainly between AD c. 700–800. The largest effigy mound is located in southern Ohio and is in the form of an uncoiling snake holding an egg-shaped object in its mouth. Most effigy mounds have been found in the shape of birds and others in the shape of animals. Bundled, flexed, and cremated burials are common, with certain locations in the life-form mounds being preferred (e.g., the head, heart, and hips). Grave goods, if they occur at all, are very simple. Although it is known that most of the effigy mounds are burial sites, some are not, and their significance remains a mystery. The Effigy Mound culture has been dated from AD 300 to the mid-1600s. (*syn.* Effigy mound culture)

effigy pipe: Small stone pipes carved in one piece and polished, representing birds, fish, and other animals, particularly from the Hopewell culture of the Eastern Woodlands of the United States during 300 BC–AD 200. In other areas and periods of the United States, larger stone effigy pipes were carved in a variety of zoomorphic and human forms, such as the human effigy pipes of Adena Mound, Ohio.

Efimenko, Pyotr Petrovich (1884–1969): A Russian archaeologist who made important contributions to the development of Palaeolithic archaeology, promoting the study of sociological aspects from a Marxist viewpoint. He made the first discovery of a Palaeolithic longhouse (Kostenki) and later published a major work on Palaeolithic prehistory, *Primeval Society.*

egalitarian society: Collective term for bands and tribes, societies in which all members have equal access to basic resources. Leadership is situational and attainable by achievement within the confines of age and sex.

Egolzwil: A series of Neolithic sites around former Lake Wauwil in Switzerland, from the earliest phase of the Neolithic in that area. Most of them belong to the Cortaillod culture and have well-preserved organic material. The site of Egolzwil 4 had 10 rectangular wooden houses placed close together. Food remains include cereals, lentils, beans, flax, wild strawberries, and chestnuts; animal remains include both domesticated and wild animals, and duck, salmon, perch, and carp from the lake. The earliest settlement, Egolzwil 3, dated to the late 5th or early 4th millennium BC.

Egtved: A Middle Bronze Age burial in east Jutland, Denmark, in an oak tree trunk coffin under a circular tumulus. The cremated bones of a child were also in the coffin with a woman's body, clothing, and bronze ornaments preserved by waterlogged conditions. She was wearing a woolen jacket and skirt and was covered by an oxhide shroud; bronze bracelets and a bronze belt disc also survived. The grave also contained a birchbark box containing an awl and a hairnet.

Egyptology: A branch of archaeology specializing in the investigation of ancient Egyptian civilization, especially the study of pharaonic Egypt (c. 4500 BC–AD 641) and its relics. Some scholars date the beginning of the discipline to September 1822, when Jean-François Champollion wrote his "Lettre a Dacier relative a l'alphabet des hierglyphes phonetiques," in which he demonstrated that he had deciphered the hieroglyphic script. Others say Egyptology began when the scholars accompanying Napoleon Bonaparte's invasion of Egypt (1798–1801) published the *Description de l'Égypte* (1809–28), which made large quantities of source material about ancient Egypt available to scholars.

Ehringsdorf: A Middle Pleistocene site in eastern Germany near Weimar. A badly broken skull and other human remains have been found with stone tools resembling the Mousterian. The fossil man is of generalized Neanderthal type, and the artifacts include scrapers, points, and bifaces, which were typical of the Middle Palaeolithic. Often ascribed to the last interglacial (about 120,000 years ago), the remains have also been dated by the uranium series method to about 225,000 years ago.

Eibian: A microlithic Later Stone Age industry in East Africa, characterized by pressure-flaked points and other tools and dating to the late Pleistocene. (*syn.* Doian)

Eilsleben: A settlement site of the Linear Pottery culture in eastern Germany. The fortified area was surrounded by a rampart and ditch system.

Ein Gev I: A site on Lake Kinneret in Israel with semisubterranean pit structures and a Kebaran lithic assemblage. There are blades, mortars, pestles, and grinding stones.

einkorn;: A variety of wheat (*Triticum monococcum*) cultivated in Neolithic times. It has pale red kernels and is a hulled grain (i.e., the glume remains on the grain after threshing), found at farming sites of the 8th and 7th millennia BC. Like the other cereals, it could be used for breadmaking or for porridge. It probably originated in southeastern Europe and southwestern Asia, and is still grown in mountainous parts of southern Europe as grain for horses.

Ekain: A Magdalenian cave site in northern Spain with fine cave art. The material of the Aurignacian and early Magdalenian dates from 16,500–15,400 bp, but the art is assigned to around 12,050 bp.

ekphora: In Greek antiquity, a funeral procession of chariots and mourners. Ekphorai are depicted on ceramic monumental funerary markers in Athens, dating to the 8th century BC.

el-Ajjul, Tell: A cemetery site in Palestine of the Early to Middle Bronze Age, with graves including copper daggers. Tell el-Ajjul has large palaces, and much gold jewelry and seals have been found in excavations.

Elam: An ancient kingdom of southwest Iran with its capital at Susa and other centers at Anshan and Dur-Untash. This broad valley of the Karkeh and Karun Rivers was geographically an extension of the southern plain of Mesopotamia. Early on, it adopted writing and devised its own pictographic script (proto-Elamite) to suit its language; later it used Akkadian cuneiform. Politically the two regions were usually bitterly opposed, and the Elamites overthrew the 3rd Dynasty of Ur shortly before 2000 BC and raided as far as Babylon in the later 13th century BC. The Golden Age of Elamite civilization was c. 1300–1100 BC, reaching its peak under Untash-Gal (c. 1265–1245 BC), the builder of Choga Zambil. Raids into Mesopotamia brought the downfall of the Kassite Dynasty there in 1157BC. The period was also remarkable for glass technology and bronze casting (cire perdue). Elam was absorbed into the Achaemenid Empire in the 6th century BC, after falling to the Assyrians when Ashurbanipal sacked the city of Susa. Little is known about the Elamite language, which is not related to any known tongue and is still not fully deciphered. (*syn.* Elamite)

Elands Bay: A cave site on the coast of Cape Province, South Africa, with Middle Stone Age material.

Elandsfontein: A farming site in southern Cape Province, South Africa, which has produced several Palaeolithic cultures and a human skull somewhat like that of Broken Hill. The skull ("Saldanha" cranium) is believed to be associated with late Acheulian tools and is considered to be of late Middle Pleistocene age. Traces of Middle Stone Age and Late Stone Age artifacts and pottery were also found.

Elateia: An important Neolithic settlement site in Central Greece, with the most complete stratified sequence of Greek Neolithic pottery deposits for the region. Radiocarbon dates place its beginnings c. 5500 bc. A series of pottery styles has been recognized, starting with undecorated dark- and light-surfaced wares, later replaced by black polished and polychrome painted wares. Certain coal-scuttle shaped vessels on four legs, presumably for ritual use, show connections with the Danilo culture of Yugoslavia. Rectangular houses were built of timber with earthen floors. (*syn.* Drakhmani; Drachmani)

el-Bersheh: A rock-cut tomb site of Egypt's Middle Kingdom.

El Beyed: Late Acheulian site in Mauretania, Africa, with hand axes, Levallois cores, and angular blades.

El Castillo: Cave site in northern Spain, spanning the entire Palaeolithic. Its earliest Aurignacian material has been dated to c. 38,700 bp. There are engravings and paintings of the Upper Palaeolithic, c. 20,000–10,000 bc, in the caves.

Ele Bor: A rock shelter site of northern Kenya first occupied in the Middle Stone Age. There was a backed-microlith industry used by the inhabitants and by the following group of the Aquatic Civilization. Domestic sheep/goats and camel were present in small numbers from about the 3rd millennium bc, at which time pottery also came into use. The climate at the time was somewhat moister than that of the present. With the subsequent drier climate, cereal use was abandoned, but both hunting and small-scale pastoralism continued into the present millennium.

electrolysis: A cleaning technique used in archaeological conservation. Artifacts are placed in a chemical solution, and by passing a weak current between them and a surrounding metal grill, the corrosive salts move from the cathode (object) to the anode (grill), removing any accumulated deposit and leaving the artifact clean. The process of electrolysis works by passing an electric current through a substance to effect a chemical change. The chemical change is one in which the substance loses or gains an electron (oxidation or reduction).

electromagnetic surveying: A geophysical surveying method used to locate archaeological features and differences in sediment or soil textures. A pulsed induction meter or soil conductivity meter generates electromagnetic waves at the surface of the earth, penetrating it and inducing currents in conducting ore bodies, thereby generating new waves that are detected by instruments at the surface or by a receiving coil lowered into a bore hole. This technique works only at a very shallow level, and no electromagnetic instrument is as accurate as a resistivity meter or proton magnetometer. (*syn.* electromagnetic prospecting)

electronic distance measuring devices: Any surveying or mapping instrument using electronics and infrared or laser beams in measuring and calculating distances, points, and angles. Such devices often work with computers. (*syn.* EDM)

electron microscopy: A technique used to study materials at extremely high magnification by using electrons instead of light. It is useful for identifying a range of things, including bone diseases and residues on the edges of used stone tools.

electron probe microanalysis: A physical method of chemical analysis, which can determine the constituent elements in metal, stone, glass, pigments/stains, and pottery/ceramics. The technique is slightly destructive, requiring the removal of a small sample from the artifact. An electron beam is used to excite the atomic electrons, and the result is the emission of secondary x-rays with characteristic wavelengths for the elements concerned. The beam can be focused onto a very small area of the specimen and can be moved around to sample different points: Thus the method is particularly useful for the study of surface enrichment in metals and of pigments. It can be used with samples as small as 10–11 cubic centimeters and is similar to x-ray fluorescence spectrometry (XRF). (*syn.* electron probe microanalyzer)

electron spin resonance dating: A dating method using the residual effects of electron's changing energy levels under natural irradiation of alpha, beta, and gamma rays. The technique enables trapped electrons in bone and shell to be measured without the heating that thermoluminescence requires; the number of trapped electrons indicates the age of the specimen. There are a number of factors that may cause errors with the method. Precision is difficult to estimate and varies with the type of sample. (*syn.* ESR)

electrum: A natural or artificial alloy of gold and silver (at least 20%) from which artifacts were once made; also used to make the first known coins in the Western world. Most natural electrum contains copper, iron, palladium, bismuth, and perhaps other metals. The process of extracting the silver from the gold is complex; it was used particularly for decorative vessels. Electrum's color was whiter and more luminous than that of gold, and its metal was supposed to ward off poison. In the ancient world, the main source was Lydia, in Asia Minor, where the alloy was found in the area of the Pactolus River (modern Turkey).

element: A substance that cannot be broken down any further, made up of atoms with the same atomic number. It joins with other elements to form compounds. Common examples are hydrogen, gold, and iron. The term also means, in faunal analysis, the specific part of the animal (e.g., humerus).

elephant: Either of two species of the family Elephantidae, characterized by their large size, huge head, columnar legs, and large ears. The Indian elephant was regularly employed for show and war as early as the Bronze Age in China. Wild herds survived in the Near East into the 1st millennium BC, when they were hunted to extinction for their ivory, and in North Africa, where they supplied Hannibal with his war elephants. Forms now extinct, especially the mammoth, were an important source of food in the Palaeolithic period and are portrayed in cave art. Living elephants are now confined to Africa. The African elephant formerly occupied a far larger area, as is attested by skeletal evidence and cave paintings in North Africa. The reduction in its range is probably due to the combined effects of climatic change, human hunting, and cattle grazing. The straight-tusked elephant, *Elephas antiquus*, apparently adapted to the open deciduous woodlands of interglacials in Europe, but became extinct at the end of the Ipswichian Interglacial. Dwarf forms of the straight-tusked elephant evolved on islands of the Mediterranean.

Elephantine: An island in the Nile just above Aswan, Egypt, which was the traditional southern boundary between Egypt and Nubia during the Old and Middle Kingdoms. It had famous granite quarries whose stone was used extensively throughout ancient Egypt. Two temples recorded by the archaeologists of Napoleon's expedition have since disappeared. Remains show continual occupation from the Archaic period to the Greco-Roman period.

Eleusis: Important Greek town just west of Athens, famous for the Eleusinian mysteries celebrated in honor of Demeter and Persephone. Occupation is attested from the early Bronze Age, and the sanctuary was in use from at least Mycenaean times. The site's most famous monument, the *telesterion* (hall with rock-cut seats), was built in late 6th century BC. It was a temple of unusual design, dedicated to Demeter, with rare features such as a lantern over the *anaktoron* (holy of holies) and builtin seating in the main hall. The Romans built the prophylaea. Alaric and his hordes (Goths) devastated the area, and the edicts of the emperor Theodosius led to its abandonment.

elevation drawing: A two-dimensional rendering of a feature, viewed from the side, showing details of surface composition.

Elgin, Lord (1766–1841): British diplomat known for obtaining permission to remove the marble metopes from the Parthenon in Athens to London. Since 1816, these sculptures, known as the Elgin marbles, have been housed in the British Museum. The removal of these sculptures from their source has often been criticized as part of a movement by European social elite to acquire Classical art for decorations and museums.

El Guettar: Aterian site in southern Tunisia associated with a Mousterian-type industry of scrapers and other stone tools. Its climate has preserved many animal fossils.

el-Hammamiya: Site in Upper Egypt with a settlement sequence from the Badarian to the Gerzean.

el-Hesy, Tell: Palestianian site important from the Middle Bronze Age through the Iron Age. It was here that Sir Flinders Petrie carried out his pioneering work on stratigraphy.

El Inga: An early Preceramic Paleo-Indian site in Ecuador at a height of 9,100 feet in Rio Inga gorge. There is an obsidian workshop and hunting campsite with an estimated date of 10,000 BC. Fishtail stemmed points show technological similarities to the Clovis/Folsom points of Fell's Cave. The variety of point styles and tool types suggests that several cultures may be represented, covering over 5,000 years of intermittent occupation and giving evidence for humans' southward passage through South America.

El Jobo: A series of preagricultural hunting sites in northwest Venezuela where Pleistocene tools have been found on old river terraces. There is a distinctive leaf-shaped spear point (the Jobo point), which has also been found at mammoth-kill sites in neighboring parts of Venezuela, where radiocarbon dates confirm a late Pleistocene age (13,000–7000 BC). The crude chopping tools from El Jobo may belong to an earlier period. Some archaeologists prefer to see the complex as a local development unassociated with the movement of big game hunters into South America.

El Juyo: An Upper Palaeolithic cave site of northern spain with much faunal evidence from the Solutrean and Magdalenian (14,440 bp) phases. It seems that red deer were hunted by driving rather than stalking.

Elkab: Upper Egyptian site on the east bank of the Nile, consisting of prehistoric and pharaonic settlements, rock-cut tombs of the earth 18th Dynasty (1550–1295 BC), and remains of temples dating from the Early Dynastic period (3100–2686 BC) to the Ptolemaic period (332–30 BC). The most substantial remains are the massive mud-brick enclosure walls of the towns and the temple of Nekhbet. It is the type site of El-Kabian, a microlithic Epipalaeolithic industry dated to c. 6000 BC. (*syn.* Nekheb, El-Kab)

El Khril: Capsian Neolithic site near Tangier in northern Morocco. The pottery is of cardial type, similar to contemporary Iberian wares, and is associated with evidence for the herding of small animals.

el Khiam: A site in Palestine with distinctive points of the PPNA lithic industry. The point is a truncated and symmetrically notched bladelet with a tip formed by marginal retouching.

el-Lahun: An Egyptian site at the entrance to the Faiyum, important in the Middle Kingdom (c. 1938–1600 BC). There is the pyramid of Senwosret (Sesostris) II and the burial of Princess Sat-Hathor-Iunet with rich grave goods. The pyramid was unusual in that the entrance to the burial chamber was not on the north side of the pyramid but on the south. The pyramid was robbed in antiquity, but a treasure of jewelry was discovered in the tombs of the princesses, located in the pyramid-enclosure wall. Technically and artistically, the collection rivals all other Middle Kingdom objects of its type. Hieratic papyri dealing with a variety of subjects have been recovered at the site. (*syn.* el-Kahun; al-Lahun; Kahun; Illahun)

Elliot Smith, Sir Grafton (1871–1937): Australian-born anatomist who, with his student W. J. Perry, espoused a theory called "hyper-diffusionism," which said that all civilizations, if not all cultures (including the New World) originated from ancient Egypt. He was involved in the examination of the remains from Piltdown, and it has been suggested that he may have been involved in the forgery.

Ellora: A site in central India with a series of magnificent rock-cut Buddhist, Jain, and Hindu temples, mainly of the Gupta period AD c. 320–540. Many of them have fine sculptures. The most remarkable of the monuments is the monolithic Kailasa Temple, cut from a single outcropping of rock. It is extensively carved with sculptures of Hindu divinities and mythological figures and dedicated to Shiva. It was built in the 8th century.

elm decline: A phase in the history of northern European vegetation recognized through pollen analysis and dated by radiocarbon to c. 4000 BC. It marked a sudden and marked decline in elm pollen in contrast with other tree pollens. In some areas, it was accompanied by a drop in frost-sensitive species such as ivy and mistletoe, while in many others it coincided with the appearance of plants associated with human settlements (plantain and nettles). It is now attributed to disease from beetles causing Dutch elm disease, although other explanations for the decline include climatic change and human interference.

Elmenteitan: A Pastoral Neolithic stone industry of early East Africa in a restricted area on the west side of the central Rift Valley in Kenya. Typical artifact assemblages include large double-edged obsidian blades, plain pottery bowls, and shallow stone vessels. Domestic cattle and small stock were herded. The dead were cremated, as at the mass-burial site at Njoro River Cave (c. 1000 BC), one of the earliest Elmenteitan sites. The industry continued into the 1st millennium AD. The name also applies to the Pastoral Neolithic and Iron Age pottery tradition associated with the stone artifacts.

El Mirador: Late Preclassic site of northern Petén, Guatemala, which was one of the earliest urban centers in the Maya lowlands. El Mirador's architectural complex dwarfs that of Tikal, although El Mirador was only substantially occupied through the Chicanel phase. It declined around 2300 bp.

El Niño: A periodic climatic phenomenon in which unusually warm ocean conditions occur along the tropical west coast of South America. The tropical water flows south, causing heavy rains and ecological destruction from Ecuador to Chile. The phenomenon can also affect the equatorial Pacific and occasionally Asia and North America.

Eloaua Island: A Melanesian island with two oldest Lapita sites, dating to 3450–2350 BP. There are house posts, plant remains, Lapita pottery, and evidence of shell artifact making as well as obsidian from Talasea and Lou.

El Oficio: A settlement site of the Argaric Early Bronze Age in Almeria, northeast Spain. The site was surrounded by a thick defensive wall and had rectangular stone houses. Several hundred burials were found, some under the floors of houses. Social class is very marked at El Oficio, where the richest women were adorned with silver diadems, while their male consorts had bronze swords, axes, and polished pottery.

elouera: A backed flake with triangular sections, like orange segments, which have polish from worked wood along the straight edge. These artifacts are part of the Australian Small Tool tradition.

El Paraiso: A large ceremonial site in the Chillón Valley on the central coast of Peru, dating to the Late Preceramic and Initial periods. It has a massive architectural complex of six to seven mounds, courts, and rooms interconnected by corridors. Five to six building phases are evident in the constructions of fieldstone masonry laid in clay. No pottery or maize has been found, but twined and woven textiles are common in burials, and domesticated beans and squash remains have also been recovered. (*syn.* Chuquitanta)

El Riego phase: The occupation phase of c. 7000–5500 BC in Tehuacán Valley, Mexico, with a hunter-gatherer society. Squash, chili peppers, and avocados may have been domesticated by the very small population.

Elsloo: A settlement and cemetery of the Neolithic Linear Pottery culture of southern Netherlands. Longhouses of various types have been found, as in the other Dutch sites of this culture (Geleen, Sittard, Stein). Elsloo has been organized into six main chronological phases. The grave goods have provided information about the Linear Pottery social stratification.

Elster/Elsterian: A north European Middle Pleistocene cold stage with at least one glacial advance. It began c. 450,000–400,000 BP and ended c. 300,000 BP with the Holsteinian Interglacial. The British equivalent is the Anglian cold stage; the Alpine is the Mindel and the North American equivalent is the Kansas.

El Tajín: The major ceremonial site of the classic Veracruz civilization on the Gulf Coast of Mexico. The first construction goes back to 100 BC, and building was continuous until c. AD 1200 when the site was burned and abandoned. The principal structure is the pyramid of niches with 365 square niches built into the sides, corresponding to the 365 heads on the temple of Quetzalcoatl at Teotihuacán. There are several ball courts and a series of carved reliefs depicting mythological and ritual themes in which ballplayers have an important role. Another part of the site is Tahin Chico, containing chambered buildings on low substructures. The people of El Tajín maintained trade contacts with Teotihuacan and the Maya states. The art style of the site was subject to many influences including Mayan, Izapan, and Olmec, but Teotihuacán influence dominates the early period. The artifact most commonly associated with Classic Veracruz culture is the hollow, clay, "smiling face" figurine. El Tajín's final destruction was probably at the hands of the Chichimecs. (*syn.* Tajín)

Els Tudons: A stone-built tomb of Naveta ("little boat") type on the island of Minorca (Menorca), Spain. It contains a two-storied chamber originally housing the remains of many individuals and is built of cyclopean masonry. Like the other navetas on the island, Els Tudons belongs to the Talayotic culture of the Bronze Age, c. 1500–800 BC. (*syn.* Es Tudons).

eluvial horizon: A soil horizon from which minerals, humus, or plant nutrients have been lost. It has lost the material in solution or suspension by pedogenesic processes. The most common eluvial horizon is E.

el-Wad: Cave site on Mount Carmel, Israel, with an industry of the Middle Upper Palaeolithic, containing Mousterian tools and Emiran points. That level was followed by Aurignacian-like Upper Palaeolithic levels, Atlitian layers, and Natufian levels.

el-Yehudiyeh, Tell: Camp site of the southeastern Nile Delta in Egypt, surrounded by a glacis. Just north is a Jewish temple and town founded during the reign of Ptolemy VI.

emblem glyph: Symbols standing for royal lineages and their domains in the Maya civilization; a Maya glyph identifying a place or polity. Each of the principal Maya cities had its own hieroglyph, which appears in inscriptions of all kinds. All such emblem glyphs share the same prefix, but the main element varies from one city to another. Many of these glyphs can now be linked to specific sites; others have still to be identified. They were first discovered in 1958.

emblema: A center panel with figure representations of people, animals, or other scenes in relief in a Hellenistic or Roman mosaic. Emblemata were usually executed in opus vermiculatum, very fine work with tiny tesserae (stone, ceramic glass, or other hard cubes), and surrounded by floral or geometric designs in coarser mosaic work. Although some emblemata were large scenes with several figures, most were small and portable. They were also used to decorate the insides of bowls, attached by solder. The first known emblema dates from about 200 BC. (*syn.* plural emblemata)

Emery, Walter Bryan (1903–1971): British Egyptologist noted for his careful surveying and study of prospective sites. He discovered galleries of the Bucheum in Armant, burials of Nubian X-group kings, queens, and nobility of 4th–6th centuries AD, and at Saqqara, excavated many Archaic period mastabas. His most important discovery was a row of 1st-Dynasty tombs attributable to kings or nobles. He excavated at Thebes' West Bank, Nubia's Buhen, and Ballana and Qustul.

emic: A term referring to anthropological concepts and distinctions that are considered meaningful, accurate, or appropriate to the participants in a given culture. It involves an analysis of linguistic or behavioral phenomena in terms of the internal structure of a particular culture.

Emirean: An early Upper Palaeolithic industry of the Levant region, named for the Emireh Cave at the north end of the Sea of Galilee (Israel), which yielded tools and triangular arrowheads with a base tapered by means of bifacial retouches (Emireh points). It is the earliest stage of the Upper Palaeolithic recognized in the eastern Mediterranean region. The Emiran is believed to date from about 30,000 BC and may be transitional from the Mousterian. (*syn.* Emiran)

Emishi: The farming population of the Tohoku region (the northern districts of Honshu) of Japan. (*syn.* Ezo)

emmer: A primitive variety of wheat, similar to einkorn. It was cultivated by early farmers and is a hulled species (i.e., threshing does not remove the glumes from the grain). It is found in archaeological contexts in its wild and cultivated forms from the eighth millennium BC onward. It is still grown in mountainous parts of southern Europe as a cereal crop and livestock food. It is thought to be the ancestor of many other varieties of wheat.

empirical: Based on practical experience and observation of physical evidence.

emporium: A place that served as a center of commerce and is characterized by a wide range of goods. They were often located at seaports where imported merchandise was warehoused and sold. The remains of the ancient emporium of Rome have been discovered on the banks of the Tiber. (*syn.* plural emporia)

emulation: A process of imitation, which is a frequent feature accompanying competition. Customs, buildings, and artifacts in one society may be adopted by neighboring ones through imitation, which is often competitive in nature.

en: A Sumerian word meaning "high priest," "ruler," or "lord"—a title used by the rulers of early Sumerian cities, especially Uruk. *Ensi* was a Sumerian title used by rulers of some city-states, and meant "governor." Entu-priestess is the Akkadian version of the Sumerian term for high priestess.

enamel: A comparatively soft glass, a compound of flint or sand, red lead, and soda or potash. The materials are melted together, producing an almost clear glass, with a slightly bluish or greenish tinge (flux or frit). The degree of hardness of the flux depends on the proportions of the components in the mix. Enamels are called hard when the temperature required to fuse them is very high, and it does not decompose as soft enamel would. Soft enamels require less heat to fire them and consequently are more convenient to use, but they do not wear as well. Enamel was first used in the Bronze and Iron Ages. It was often melted and united with gold, silver, copper, bronze, and other metals in a furnace. Enamel is colored white by oxide of tin, blue by oxide of cobalt, red by gold, green by copper. Different kinds of enamel are: (1) inlaid or incrusted, (2) transparent, showing designs on the metal under it, (3) painted as a complete picture. The various techniques practiced by craftsmen in the past differ mainly in the methods employed in preparing the metal to receive the powdered enamel. Some of those methods are cloisonné, champlevé, encrusted enameling, and painted enamels.

Encanto: A series of sites on the central coastline of Peru, including Chilca, which constitute a cultural phase when people began to exploit maritime resources and practice cultivation, c. 3750–2500 BC. Stone artifacts include milling stones, small percussion-flaked projectile points, and simple scrapers as well as bone and wooden tools are typical. The changing subsistence patterns resulted from the decreasing availability of lomas vegetation.

encaustic: An ancient method of painting, recorded by Pliny, of fixing pigments with heated wax. It was probably first practiced in Egypt about 3000 BC and is thought to have reached its peak in Classical Greece, although no examples from that period survive. Pigments, mixed with melted beeswax, were brushed onto stone or plaster, smoothed with a metal spatula, and then blended and driven into the wall with a heated iron. The surface was later polished with a cloth. It was particularly used for the Fayum mummy portraits of Roman Egypt. Leonardo da Vinci and others attempted unsuccessfully to revive the technique. North American Indians used an encaustic method whereby pigments mixed with hot animal fat were pressed into a design engraved on smoothed buffalo hide. (*syn.* [from Greek "burnt in"])

enculturation: The process of learning whereby an individual acquires the beliefs, customs, values, and behaviors appropriate to a specific culture.

endocast: An internal cast, as of the inside of the human skull. A cast of the cranial cavity showing the approximate shape of the brain. (*syn.* endocranial cast)

endblade: A small blade tool, often bipointed and used to tip bone and antler arrowheads. Triangular end blades were probably used to tip harpoon heads.

endogamy: The practice of marrying a person within one's own social unit, such as a clan or tribe.

end scraper: A stone tool formed by chipping the end of a flake of stone, which can then be used to scrape animal hides and wood. Its steeply angled (acute) working edge was used to flense or soften hides and to dress skins. It appeared in Europe during the Upper Palaeolithic period. The tool differed from side scrapers in that it had a rounded retouched end and was often made on a blade. A side scraper had a retouched working edge along the long edge of the flake. (*syn.* endscraper, grattoir)

Eneolithic: A period in the Near East and southeastern Europe when copper metallurgy was being adopted by Neolithic cultures, in the 4th and 3rd millennia BC. The period is called the Chalcolithic in the Near East and the Copper Age in other areas. (*syn.* Aeneolithic, Chalcolithic, Copper Age)

Engaruka: An Iron Age site on the western side of the Eastern Rift Valley in northern Tanzania with the remains of an Iron Age irrigation system of the 14th century AD. It was an important and concentrated agricultural settlement, occupied for over a thousand years. Water from streams flowing into the valley was dispersed through an elaborate network of stone-lined furrows to serve a large number of small stone-terraced fields. Sorghum was one of the crops cultivated. However, its pottery does not seem to have been related to those types that became widespread in the 1st millennium AD. It is assumed that its inhabitants were Cushitic speakers.

Enki: The third, with An and Enlil, of the great Sumerian gods, associated with water and purification. (*syn.* Ea [Akkadian])

Enkomi: An important Bronze Age settlement on Salamis Bay in Cyprus. It was first founded in the Middle Bronze Age (2nd millennium BC) and flourished as a result of its copperworking, trading the metal widely through the east Mediterranean. After the collapse of Late Bronze Age Greece, Mycenaeans seized the town in the 13th century BC. About 1200, it was destroyed again, probably by the Peoples of the Sea, but continued with declining prosperity for another 2 centuries before being abandoned in favor of Salamis. There are major Cyclopean fortifications and fine ashlar architecture. Enkomi may have been Alashiya, the ancient capital of Cyprus.

Enlil: The chief god of the Sumerian pantheon, the patron god of Nippur and most important god of the Sumerians until ousted by Marduk in the late 2nd millennium BC. His particular domain was the air, sky, and the storm ("Lord Wind"). He was the son of Anu and inherited his father's title of "father" or "king" of the pantheon. Like Anu, he is credited with giving kingship to man, and the Tablet of Destiny, through which the fate of man and gods was decreed, also belonged to Enlil. The god was thought to have been responsible for the downfall of Akkad.

ennead: Groups of nine deities, nine being the "plural" of three (in Egypt the number three symbolized plurality in general), but some enneads had more than nine gods. The earliest and principal ennead was the Great Ennead of Heliopolis. This was headed by the sun god and creator Re or Re-Atum, followed by Shu and Tefnut, deities of air and moisture; Geb and Nut, who represented earth and sky; and Osiris, Isis, Seth, and Nephthys. Enneads are associated with several major cult centers. (*syn.* pesedjet)

Ensérune: Iron Age *oppidum* (promontory fort) in Hérault, southern France, first founded in the 6th century BC. It had defenses of cyclopean masonry and well laid-out stone houses, both of which are very similar to those found on Greek settlements in the area. Large storage jars and silos excavated into the tufa were probably for grain or water. Nearby is a large cremation cemetery of the 3rd century with inurned burials. A major reconstruction took place in c. 200 BC and then again in the 4th century.

entablature: In architecture, the horizontal moldings and bands supported by and located immediately above the columns of Classical buildings. The term also refers to similar structural supports in non-Classical buildings. The entablature is usually divided into three sections: the lowest band, or architrave, which originally took the form of a simple beam running from support to support; the central band, or frieze, consisting of an unmolded strip with or without ornament; the top band, or cornice, constructed from a series of moldings that project from the edge of the frieze. The styles of the entablature are different for the main orders of architecture: Doric, Ionic, and Corinthian. In the Doric order, it includes the architrave above which were placed the alternating triglyphs and metopes. In the Ionic order, a continuous frieze was placed above the architrave.

entasis: In architecture, the exaggerated convex curve of a column, spire, or similar upright member, intended to give the optical illusion of straight sides. Almost all Classic columns use entasis. It was exaggerated in Doric work. Entasis is also occasionally found in Gothic spires and in smaller Romanesque columns.

entrance grave: A type of megalithic chamber tomb characterized by a chamber without separate passage, under a round barrow. It shares features of both passage grave and gallery grave. The round mound is in the passage grave tradition, but there is no clear distinction between the entrance passage and the funerary chamber, hence the alternative term, undifferentiated passage grave. The chamber form is similar to that of the gallery grave. Entrance graves are found in southern spain, Brittany, southwest Ireland, and the Channel Isles. (*syn.* undifferentiated passage grave)

Entremont: An important *oppidum* near Aix-en-Provence, France, a Celto-Ligurian structure built in the 3rd century BC (middle La Tène culture). It was the capital of the Salyes until destroyed by the Romans c. 125 BC. Entremont had a sanctuary with sculptured figures, and finds include heads and torsos carved in the round, and four-sided limestone pillars with severed human heads and skulls carved in relief. It had ramparts built of large stone blocks, with watch towers, and inside were streets, houses of dry stone, drainage and water systems, all laid out on a rectilinear system.

entrepôt: An intermediary trading town or city, often a port, strategically situated for the redistribution of goods from a variety of sources.

envelope: A hollow clay ball of spherical, ovoid, or oblong shape holding tokens and usually bearing seal impressions. Clay envelops, dating from 3500 BC, have markings corresponding to the clay shapes inside. Moreover, these markings are more or less similar to the shapes drawn on clay tablets that date back to about 3100 BC. These markings are thought to constitute a logographic form of writing consisting of some 1,200 different characters representing numerals, names, and such material objects as cloth and cow. Tokens placed in an envelope might have constituted a sort of "bill of lading" or a record of indebtedness. To serve as a reminder of the contents of the envelope, so that readers need not break open the envelope to read the contents, corresponding shapes were impressed on the envelope. If the content was marked on the envelope, there was no need to put the tokens in an envelope at all; the envelope could be flattened into a convenient surface and the shapes impressed on it. Now that there was no need for the tokens, their message was simply inscribed into the clay. These shapes, drawn in the west clay with a reed stylus or pointed stick, are thought to constitute the first writing.

environment: The complex of physical, chemical, and biological factors that act on an organism or an ecological community and ultimately determine its form and survival. The pace of environmental change quickened dramatically with the introduction of agriculture from 7,000 years ago onward: Forests were cut down, and cultivation led to soil degradation and erosion. New species were introduced, both as crops and weeds, and the relentless growth of population ensured that human activities made an ever-increasing impact on the landscape.

environmental archaeology: A subfield of archaeology, which is the study of the environment in archaeological contexts. It includes not only the study of past flora (pollen analysis, palaeobotany, palaeoethnobotany, archaeobotany), and fauna (archaeozoology), but also that of insects (insect analysis), fish (fish bone analysis), and snail shells (molluscan analysis). All are studied in an attempt to recover the total environment of a past society and to understand human impact on, and changes to, that environment. It is a field in which interdisciplinary research involves archaeologists and natural scientists. Many disciplines are involved in this study: climatology, Quaternary geology, soil science, palaeobotany, zoology, and human biology.

environmental indicator(s): A method in which species of plants and animals are used to indicate a feature of the environment. If the modern environmental requirements are known, the presence of preserved remains of the same species in ancient deposits and soils may suggest that similar conditions prevailed in the past. Many such indicator fossils are used to reconstruct temperature. However, the absence of an environmental indicator does not imply lack of the conditions that it is supposed to indicate. The method is reliable only when whole communities, including many different species, all indicate the existence of a particular environment.

Eocene: (ee'uh-seen) A major geological epoch of the earth's history—the second division of the Tertiary period (Cenozoic Ear), which began about 57.8 million years ago and ended about 36.6 million years ago. It follows the Paleocene epoch and precedes the Oligocene epoch. The Eocene is often divided into Early (57.8 to 52 million years ago), Middle (52 to 43.6 mya), and Late (43.6 to 36.6 mya) epochs. The name Eocene is derived from the Greek eos ("dawn") and refers to the dawn of recent life; during the Eocene, all the major divisions, or orders, of modern mammals appeared.

eolian: (ee'-ohl'yun) Of or pertaining to the wind. This adjective is used to describe deposits or materials moved or affected by the wind or processes related to the wind. Aeolian deposits can bury archaeological materials intact or with little disturbance. Aeolian erosion can collapse and displace archaeological materials. Aeolian particle movement can alter archaeological material through abrasion. (*syn.* aeolian)

eolith:: (ee'-uh-lith) Any naturally shaped or broken stone, once considered to be the oldest artifacts of early man. They consist of crudely chipped flakes and cores from pre-Pleistocene or very early Pleistocene deposits. It is now accepted that eoliths were not made by humans but chipped by natural agencies as far back as 500,000 years BC. Most eoliths were frost-split chunks with irregular chipping around the edge. Eolithic is a term sometimes used by archaeologists for the earliest stage of human culture before the Paleolithic,

characterized by very primitive stone tools, especially of flint. It means "Dawn of the Stone Age." (*syn.* dawn stone)

Ephesus: A major port on the west coast of Asia Minor (Turkey), originally an Ionic city of which only a few fragments survive. The city walls are Hellenistic, but the majority of the remains date from the Roman period, when the city was one of the richest and most important in Asia. The temple of Artemis and many important public buildings have been found, including agoras, baths, the library of Celus, arcaded streets, market buildings, gymnasia, stadium, and a theater. The temple, one of the Seven Wonders of the World, was burned in 356 BC. The town was situated strategically in the delta area of the River Cayster, and there is some evidence for occupation from Mycenaean times. Tradition, however, describes the settlement as founded from Athens by King Androklos.

Epi-Acheulian: A term used to describe stone industries from the early Middle Palaeolithic, which combine some very rare Acheulian-type bifaces with an already well developed tool kit based on flakes.

epicanthic fold: The skin and flesh immediately above the upper eyelid; a fold of skin across the inner corner of the eye (canthus). The epicanthal fold produces the eye shape characteristic of persons from Asian (Mongoloid) geographic areas; it is also seen in some American Indians and occasionally in Europeans (e.g., Scandinavians and Poles). (*syn.* epicanthal fold, Mongolian eye fold)

Epicardial: An Early Neolithic pottery style of c. 5300–4600 BC, which was developed from the Cardial style in southern France. The decoration is incised.

epichysis: A Greek or Roman wine pot or vessel with a long neck and handle, used for pouring wine into cups.

Epidauros: A Classical Greek city with the sanctuary of the healing god Asklepios, in the Peloponnese. The lower city and harbor are now submerged, but sections of cyclopean wall are still visible. Epidauros was famous for the sanctuary, especially from the 4th century BC onward. There were two Doric cult buildings and a fine Doric rotunda with labyrinth. There were baths, a stadium, hospitals and sanitaria, and a magnificent 4th-century BC theater, which is exceptionally well preserved.

epigraphy: The study of ancient inscriptions and letter forms on buildings, statuary, tablets, and other durable materials and objects (such as wood, bone, pottery, stone). An expert in such studies is an epigrapher or epigraphist. Such tests are often the only surviving records of extinct cultures and chronicle ancient events, beliefs, and lists of kings. Epigraphy encompasses inscriptions from the earliest complex societies to those of modern states. Epigraphy sometimes does not include the study of texts painted on ceramics or written on papyrus or wood, which are regarded as within the studies of ceramics and papyrology, respectively. Epigraphy deals both with the form of the inscriptions and with their content: study of the form enables assessment of the development of language and the alphabet; their content is, however, usually more important for the light thrown on the social, political, religious, and economic life of the ancient world. The science includes decipherment, translation, explanation, and evaluation of the inscriptions. (*syn.* epigrapher)

Epigravettian: The late glacial industries of Italy from 20,000–8000 bp, which evolved into the Mesolithic. It is divided into early (20,000–16,000 bp), evolved (16,000–14,000 bp), and final (14,000–8,000 bp) phases. Epigravettian was followed by the Sauveterrian and Castelnovian in the 7th millennium BC. Epigravettian cultures developed contemporaneously in various parts of Europe, notably the Creswellian in Britain. (*syn.* Epi-Gravettian)

epi-Palaeolithic cultures: The final Upper Palaeolithic industries that emerged at the end of the final glaciation; the continuation of Palaeolithic (Old Stone Age) cultures after the end of the last Ice Age, followed by Neolithic. In the Levant, it was c. 20,000–10,000 BP. (*syn.* Epipalaeolithic, Epipaleolithic)

epiphysis: The articulating end of a long bone or vertebra, which in an adult is fused with the shaft or main part of the bone, but which is a separate bony mass in the early years of life. For both human and animal bones, therefore, the state of fusion of the epiphyses can be used to determine the age of the skeleton if it is under 20 years old (human) or 3–4 years (domestic animals). (*syn.* plural epiphyses)

Epi-Pietersburg: A Middle Stone Age industry of southern Africa, which succeeded the Pietersburg and has radiocarbon dates of 80,000–49,000 years ago.

Episkopi-Phaneromeni: A Middle or Late settlement site of Cyprus, occupied c. 1600–1500 BC, with a Middle Cypriot chamber tomb cemetery.

epistemology: Study or theory of the nature and grounds of knowledge, especially by using scientific reasoning to evaluate its validity.

eraillure scar: The small flake scar on the dorsal side of a flake next to the platform. It is the result of rebounding force during percussion flaking.

Erbil: Ancient Assyrian city buried beneath a modern town in Iraq, on the summit of a large tell. Because there has been little excavation, it is known mainly from texts, which describe a temple dedicated to Ishtar, a cult center second only to Assur. The earliest records referring to Arab'ilu belong to the late 3rd millennium BC. (*syn.* Arab'ilu)

Erd: A Middle Palaeolithic Mousterian site in Hungary. The faunal remains suggest that it was occupied before the last glacial, and the tools are mainly scrapers.

Erech: Biblical name for the ancient Mesopotamian city of Uruk.

Erechtheum: A temple on the Akropolis at Athens, dedicated to Erechtheus, the legendary king of the city. It was built in c. 421–407 BC and is remarkable for its caryatid porch and the complexity of its plan. It is a large and complex rectangular building in the Ionic style, built of white Pantelic marble and dark Eleusis stone. (*syn.* Erechtheion)

erectine: A term used for a now-extinct member of the genus Homo, including *Homo erectus*, who lived in Africa, Asia, and Europe during the Lower and Middle Pleistocene. Erectines walked upright, may have used fire, and are often associated with the Acheulean industries, especially with hand axes.

Erevan Cave: A Middle Palaeolithic site in Armenia with occupations during cool climatic conditions. Artifacts include side scrapers, and faunal remains are from rhinoceros, horse, elk, and red deer.

Eridu: A tell site at Abu Shahrain, identified as the ancient Eridu, the oldest city of Sumer—possibly the oldest in history. Occupation began in the 'Ubaid period, the earliest phase of which is named after this site, in the mid-6th millennium BC. A series of temples of the 'Ubaid and Uruk periods have been found, decorated with typical Sumerian buttresses and niches in the walls. Its long succession of superimposed temples portrayed the growth and development of an elaborate mud-brick architecture. A palace of the Early Dynastic period c. 2500 BC has also been excavated. The city was important throughout Mesopotamian history as a religious center and sanctuary of Enki (Ea). Outside the temple precinct, a large cemetery of the late 'Ubaid period was found, containing around 1,000 graves. Grave goods include painted pottery vessels, terra-cotta figurines, and baked clay tools, such as sickles and shaft-hole axes. The site declined in importance with the rise of Ur under its 3rd Dynasty (c. 2100 BC) and was occupied until around c. 600 BC. (*syn.* Abu Shahrain)

Erimi: A deeply stratified site in southern Cyprus, which has produced evidence of a sequence of pottery styles covering most of the 4th millennium BC. It is the type site for the Chalcolithic I Erimi culture, characterized by red-on-white pottery. The houses were first cut into rock, but later were circular huts of wattle and daub on stone foundations. The site is best known for its single copper chisel, the earliest evidence on Cyprus for the use of the metal from which it derives its name. (*syn.* Erimi-Bamboula)

Er Lannic: The site of two Neolithic stone circles on an islet in France, now partly submerged. There were stone-built cists or hearths, polished stone axes, and pottery.

Erligang phase: A stage of the early Bronze Age in north China seen in two strata at Zhengzhou Erligang, classified archaeologically as Middle Shang. The phase preceded the Anyang period (c. 1300–1030 BC), and radiocarbon dates are c. 1600–1550 BC. The massive rammed-earth fortification, 118 feet wide at its base and enclosing an area of 1.2 square miles, would have taken 10,000 men more than 12 years to build. Also found were ritual bronzes, including four monumental tetrapods; palace foundations; workshops for bronze casting, pot making, and bone working; burials; and two inscribed fragments of oracle bones. The Erligang phase may correspond to the widest sway of the Shang Empire and is known for its highly developed bronze-casting industry. Some Chinese archaeologists call the phase Early Shang. (*syn.* Erh-li-kang)

Erlitou: Type site of the Erlitou phase in Henan province, north China. The Erlitou phase represents the earliest known stage of the Chinese Bronze Age of c. early 2nd millennium BC. The earliest bronze ritual vessels yet known from China, along with bronze blades and fine jades, were also found. Two palace compounds have been excavated. The Erlitou remains provide the fullest evidence now available for the emergence of the Shang civilization from its local forbears. (*syn.* Erh-li-t'ou)

Ermine Street: A major Roman road in England, between London and York. Doubtless following more ancient tracks, it was most likely established soon after the Roman invasion of Britain in AD 43. It retained its importance until modern times.

erosion: The wearing away or loosening and transportation of soil or rock by water, wind, and ice. A group of processes is involved in the physical breakdown or chemical solution, removal, and transportation of the materials. Erosion can be accelerated by activities on the landscape. Three forms that can have significant impact on the archaeological record are soil erosion, gully erosion, and wind erosion. (*syn.* weathering)

error factor: The measurement error inherent in every chronometric dating technique, indicating the range of accuracy of the estimated date; usually expressed as plus or minus a certain number of years.

Ertebølle: The final Mesolithic culture of the west Baltic coastal region and coastal kitchen midden culture of Scandinavia. The type site is a coastal shell mound in Jutland, Denmark, dated to c. 3900–3250 BC. Pollen analysis places the start of the culture in the Atlantic period, after c. 5000 BC. The later phases of Ertebølle are marked by the introduction of pottery and polished stone axes, perhaps as a result of contact with the newly arrived Neolithic farmers to the south.

escarpment: A natural steep landmark or massive fault block. This land form consists of a steep slope that marks an abrupt change in altitude between two adjacent land surfaces. This long cliff or steep slope separates two comparatively level or more gently sloping surfaces and is a result of erosion or faulting. The term also refers to the side of the vallum sloping into the fossa, or ditch, nearest to a fort(ification). (*syn.* scarp)

Eshnunna: An ancient city under the mound of Tell Asmar, northeast of Baghdad, Iraq. It was a city-state in the Early Dynastic period (early 3rd millennium BC), with shrines, sculpture, palaces, and private houses. It became politically important in the 19th and 18th centuries BC, when it was involved in a struggle for power with Assur, Mari, Elam, and Babylon. It is rarely mentioned in history after its conquest by Hammurabi of Babylon, c. 1761 BC. (*syn.* Tell Asmar)

Esh Shaheinab: The type site for the Khartoum Neolithic in the Sudan, dated to the second half of the 4th millennium BC. Fishing was evidently of major importance and was conducted both by means of shell fishhooks and with harpoons whose barbed bone points were pierced for attaching a line. Edge-ground axes and adzes were made of bone and stone. The microlithic stone industry and the pottery were very similar to those from Early Khartoum. Domestic stock has radiocarbon dates of 5300 BP.

Eskimo: The aboriginal cultural group of the Arctic regions of North America, which evolved between 2000–100 BC. The Eskimo way of life and the distinctive tool types can be traced back into the Arctic Small Tool tradition. Other traits seem to have been adopted by the Alaskan Eskimos from Siberian tribes. The group is characterized by uniformity in culture, language, and physical stock. The Eskimo call themselves Inuit, because "Eskimo" is a derogatory Algonquin word meaning "eater of raw flesh." (*syn.* Inuit)

Esna: A site on the west bank of the Nile in Upper Egypt. The main surviving remains are the sacred necropolis of the Nile perch and the Greco-Roman hypostyle hall of the temple dedicated to the ram-god Khnum, which was started as early as 170–164 BC. (*syn.* ancient Iunyt, Ta-senet, Latopolis)

Es-Skhul: Cave site in Israel's Mount Carmel complex. It has Natufian, Upper Palaeolithic, and Levallois-Mousterian occupation levels and skeletal remains dating to c. 100,000 BP, thought to be ancestral to European Cro-Magnons.

Estaqueria: Middle Horizon site in the Nasca Valley of Peru's south coast, with an adobe compound and large cemeteries.

Este: An ancient town on the edge of the Po plain near Padua, Italy. It has given its name to a rich Iron Age culture, the Atestine, of the 9th century BC. Profiting from its position, it flourished down to the invasion of the Celts in 4th century BC and is particularly famous for its fine red and black cordoned vases, its magnificent situla art, and much fine sheet bronze work. The area was annexed by Rome in 184 BC.

etched carnelian bead: Beads with an etched decoration created with heat after a design in an alkali or metallic oxide paste has been painted. It was developed by the late Harappan period in south Asia and continues to be used.

ethnicity: The national, cultural, religious, linguistic, or other attributes that are perceived as characteristic of distinct groups. The term also refers to the existence of ethnic groups, including tribal groups.

ethnoarchaeology: The study of contemporary cultures with a view to understanding the behavioral relations that underlie the production of material culture. It is the use of archaeological techniques and data to study these living cultures, especially current or recent aboriginal groups such as the Inuit or Bushmen. It is a relatively new branch of the discipline, followed particularly in America. It seeks to compare the patterns recognized in the material culture of archaeological contexts with patterns yielded through the study of living societies. The ethnoarchaeologist is particularly concerned with the manufacture, distribution, and use of artifacts, the remains of various processes that might be expected to survive, and the interpretation of archaeological material in the light of the ethnographic information. Less materially oriented questions such as technological development, subsistence strategies, and social evolution are also compared in archaeology and ethnology under the general heading of ethnographic analogy. Lewis Binford's study of the Nunamiut Eskimo is one of the best known studies in ethnoarchaeology.

ethnocentrism: The belief that one's own ethnic group is superior to all others. Observational bias in which other societies are evaluated by standards relevant to the observer's culture.

ethnographic parallel: A contemporary culture or behavior that, by the use of analogy and homology, is considered to be similar to another in history and therefore sheds light on the latter. It is the use of both material and nonmaterial aspects of a living culture to form models to test interpretations of archaeological remains. (*syn.* ethnological parallel; ethnographic analogy)

ethnographic present: That point in time when a traditional culture came into contact with individuals from literate culture and was documented by them.

ethnography: The description and analysis of contemporary cultures, which is based almost entirely on in-depth fieldwork. The formulating of generalizations about culture and the drawing of comparisons are components of ethnography. It is part of the subdiscipline of cultural anthropology. An important technique is participant observation, whereby the anthropologist lives in the society being studied. Ethnography provides data to archaeologists through analogy and homology. An ethnographic study is that of the cultural characteristics of a particular ethnic or social group. (*syn.* ethnographic study)

ethnohistory: The study of non-Western cultures by using evidence from documentary sources and oral traditions. In areas where prehistoric and nonliterate cultures have survived into historical times, it is possible to reconstruct history before contact with literate populations through the study of myth and oral traditions, collected ethnographically. In Central America, the aboriginal written records are used in conjunction with the early European records, archaeological investigations, and oral tradition to reconstruct prehistoric life.

ethnology: The use of ethnographic data to study contemporary cultures; one of the four subdisciplines of cultural anthropology. The study of the varieties of the human race in a comparative analysis to understand how they work and why they change. Ethnology is a term more widely used in Europe and encompasses the analytical and comparative study of cultures in general, which in American usage is the academic field known as cultural anthropology (in British usage, social anthropology). (*syn.* cultural anthropology)

ethnos: The ethnic group, defined as a firm aggregate of people, historically established on a given territory, possessing in common relatively stable peculiarities of language and culture, and also recognizing their unity and difference as expressed in a self-appointed name (ethnonym).

ethology: The study of animal behavior, which can offer hypotheses for human behaviors. The ethologist is interested in the behavioral process rather than in a particular animal group and often studies one type of behavior (e.g., aggression) in a number of unrelated animals.

etic: Referring to the perspective of the observer; a view external to the culture being studied. It is applied to concepts and distinctions that are meaningful and appropriate to the community of scientific observers.

Etiolles: A Magdalenian site just south of Paris, France, with successive occupations dating to 12,000 bp. There is an abundance of flint and flint knapping areas, hearths, and debitage.

Etowah: A large temple mound site in northern Georgia, of the Mississippian tradition and dating from the Temple Mound II period AD c. 1200–1700. A fortified farming village with three temple mounds appears to have functioned mainly as a ceremonial center. In North America, only Monk's Mound at Cahokia contains a greater volume than Etowah's 20-meter-high mound. The artifacts include Lamar pottery (an elaborately stamped or incised utilitarian ware), under-lifesize stone statues of humans usually in a sitting or kneeling position, and Southern Cult paraphernalia.

Etruria: The area to the north of Rome, bounded by the Tiber and Arno Rivers and the Tyrrhenian Sea. The Etruscans inhabited the area and colonized Aleria, the Po Valley, and parts of Campania. The area is rich in gold, iron, and bronze. The dead were buried in underground tombs or tumuli and were accompanied by a range of funerary goods. The tombs are an important source of Athenian pottery.

Etruscan: The people who occupied north-central Italy (ancient Etruria, modern Tuscany) in the 1st millennium BC. They can first be recognized in the 8th century BC, distinguished from their predecessors the Villanovans by the wealth and oriental appearance of their tombs. They developed a high level of civilization very quickly, with extensive trade contacts with Greece and Carthage and across the Alpine passes to central Europe. Their cities were large and rich: Populonia, Vetulonia, Tarquinia, and Caere (Cerveteri) near the coast, and Veii, Clusium (Chiusi), and Perusia (Perugia) inland. Etruscan influence spread widely, through Rome itself down to Campania in the south and north to the Po Valley, and the civilization reached its height in the 6th century BC. Conflict with the Celts in the north and Rome in the south led to conquest by the latter, beginning with Veii in 396 BC and completed early in the 2nd century BC. The Etruscans' own writings, in an alphabet borrowed from the Greeks, can be transliterated, but little of their non-Indo-European language can be translated. Etruscan tombs show their genius; the finest are mounds covering a burial vault, as in the cemeteries of Tarquinia and Cerveteri. The values may be elaborately frescoed with scenes from life, mythoiogy, or the rites associated with death. Also remarkable is a tomb at Cerveteri, the walls of which are covered with stucco reliefs of everyday objects. There is a high preponderance of imports, especially metalwork and Athenian pottery. Typical products of the Etruscans are decorated bronze mirrors, bucchero pottery, and sophisticated filigree jewelry. The influence of the Etruscans on Roman civilization was enormous. Rome is indebted to the Etruscans not only for its early kings, such as the notorious Tarquin, but virtually for the total infrastructure of its civilization. Roman culture is essentially the continuation of Etruscan under another name and language. Among areas of continuity are religion (e.g., Etruscan haruspex and Roman augury), political and social organization, strategic arts, architecture, art, drama, theater, and civil engineering (notably hydraulics, such as aqueducts and drainage systems). The origin of the Etruscans has been a subject of debate since antiquity. Herodotus, for example, argued that the Etruscans descended from a people who invaded Etruria from Anatolia before 800 BC and established themselves over the native Iron Age inhabitants of the region, whereas Dionysius of Halicarnassus believed that the Etruscans were of local Italian origin.

eustasy: Changes in sea level on a global basis, usually as the result of a major event such as the end of a glaciation. In such a case, a eustatic rise owing to the melting of the glaciers can be expected in a postglacial period. These sea-level movements can be independent of any change in the height of the land, but isostasy can happen contemporaneously as a result of the same phenomenon. This worldwide alteration in sea level is independent of any isostatic movement of the land. At the end of a glaciation, melting of the water previously held in the ice sheets raises sea levels (eustatic rise), and a high level can often be correlated with an interglacial period or with the postglacial phase. Such fluctuations have occurred through the Quaternary, because of changes in the extent of ice sheets and thus in the volume of water locked up as ice. The larger the ice sheets, the less water available to the sea, and sea level is lower during glacials than during interglacials. Evidence exists for a whole series of eustatic sea level fluctuations, but the most widespread is the "high stand" in c. 120,000 bp, just before the start of the last cold stage, when sea levels were between 2–10 meters higher than at the present day. During the maximum extent of the ice sheets of the last cold stage, eustatic sea level was much lower than that of today. Large areas of continental shelf were exposed, some being occupied by the ice sheets themselves. Recovery of sea level at the end of the last cold stage is relatively well known from deposits in the Netherlands, Scandinavia, and Scotland, but is complicated by isostatic changes. The North Sea and English Channel flooded, separating Britain from the Continent, by about 7000 bp. Ireland became a separate island at about the same time. Scandinavia had a complicated series of different seas and lakes, until a sea similar to today's Baltic became established around 7000 bp. The main factors that influence sea level are global ice volumes, plate tectonics, changes in ocean volumes and dimensions, and the movement of mantle material. (*syn.* adj. eustatic)

Eutresis: A settlement site in Boeotia, central Greece, first occupied in Middle, Late, and sub-Neolithic, but the most important occupation was in the Bronze Age beginning c. 3450 BC. The Middle Helladic seems here to have carried on late, unaffected by the Late Helladic of the Mycenaeans elsewhere. The site was inhabited continuously until the 13th century BC, when it was extensively fortified and subsequently abandoned. It was reoccupied in the Classical and Hellenistic periods. Eutresis is the type site for the Early Helladic I Eutresis culture.

Evans, Sir Arthur (1851–1941): A British scholar and archaeologist who contributed much to the study of Greek archaeology with his excavations at the Minoan palace of

Knossos. His first interest was in coins and hieroglyphic seals, and it was the latter that drew his attention to Crete. He began excavations at Knossos in 1899 at his own expense, and in the next 35 years laid bare not only this Bronze Age palace of the Minoans, but in effect their whole civilization. Careful cross-dating with Egypt allowed him to put dates to his sequence, making it a vitally important link in the dating of prehistoric Europe before the discovery of radiocarbon. Although he was unable to decipher the Minoans' three written scripts, his detailed study of them gave the necessary basis for later work, culminating in the reading of Linear B by Michael Ventris in 1952. He was largely responsible for demonstrating the existence of a pre-Mycenaean Aegean civilization, for naming it Minoan (after the legendary King Minos of Crete), and for revealing most of its characteristics. He was the son of Sir John Evans.

Evans, Clifford (1920–1981): American archaeologist working in the Amazon with his wife, Betty Meggers. They investigated Ecuador, Venezuela, British Guiana, and Brazil and provided the chronology and cultural definitions of prehistoric cultures of the region.

Evans, Sir John (1823–1908): British scholar, collector, and antiquary; the father of Sir Arthur Evans. Sir John conducted detailed studies of pre-Roman coinage and the stone and bronze implements of Britain. He was actively concerned in the controversies over the authenticity of the hand ax and the eolith. He published three major works on British prehistoric artifacts.

"Eve" theory: The hypothesis that all modern humans are descended from a common first mother who lived in southern Africa about 200,000 years ago. The "Eve" theory is similar to the Noah's Ark model and is based on genetic research showing that as modern humans spread throughout the world, they rarely, if at all, interbred with existing, but more archaic, humans, such as the Neanderthals. The "Eve" theory does not imply a creationist view, only that there has been a chance survival of a single line of mitochondrial DNA.

evolution: A theory of biology about the gradual or rapid change of the form of living organisms throughout time that reflects adaptive change; it is the theory that all forms of life derive from a process of change via natural selection. Its great exponent was Charles Darwin, whose *The Origin of Species* appeared in 1859. It had an immediate impact on prehistory and the question of the antiquity of man. The Darwinian idea—of species generally over-reproducing themselves and only the better-fitted surviving to pass on their superior adaptation to the next generation—has been modified and amplified in the 20th century by new knowledge of genetics and especially of mutation and recombination of genes. The newer view is often called Neo-Darwinism. Darwin's work laid the foundations for the study of artifact typology, pi-

oneered by such scholars as Pitt-Rivers and Montelius. The idea that the animals and plants of today originated from ancestors of a different kind goes back at least to early Greek philosophers.

evolutionary archaeology: An explanatory framework for the past that accounts for structure and change in the archaeological record in much the same way as biological evolution.

excavate: To dig out and remove archaeological materials from a site; to carry out the process of excavation.

excavation: The systematic and scientific recovery of cultural, material remains of people as a means of obtaining data about past human activity. Excavation is digging or related types of salvage work, scientifically controlled so as to yield the maximum amount of data. It is the main tool of the archaeologist. The excavation of a site, however, involved the destruction of the primary evidence, which can never be recovered. Excavation should therefore never be undertaken lightly or without an understanding of the obligations of the excavators to the evidence they destroy. The first decision is whether to excavate a site at all, a question of particular interest when sites are being rapidly destroyed by farming methods and road and town building. The nature and scale of the undertaking is the next decision. If time and/or money is short, sampling of the site may be all that is possible. If a large-scale excavation is to be undertaken, the approach will be area (open excavation, grid method, quadrant method, rabotage, or sondage. Removal of the topsoil is carried out by either hand or machine. After an initial plan has been made of all visible features before excavation, digging proceeds according to the dictates of the site: Sections may be taken across areas of feature intersection or across individual features. A permanent record of the whole process should be kept: plans, drawings, notes, photographs. Excavation is only the first part of the process. For years, excavation was regarded as merely a method of collecting artifacts. Pitt-Rivers in Britain and Petrie in the Near East first placed emphasis on evidence rather than artifacts, not on what is found but where it was found relative to the layers of deposit (stratigraphy) and to other objects (association)—the context. Excavators can justify destruction only if it is done with meticulous care so that every artifact, be it an ax or a posthole, is discovered and if possible preserved; if it is recorded accurately enough for all information to remain available after the site has disappeared; and if this record is quickly made available by publication. In short, excavation is the digging of archaeological sites, removal of the matrix, observance of the provenience and context of the finds therein, and the recording of them in a three-dimensional way.

excavation unit: A basic area that is often the first space opened in an excavation; usually a trench, a standard-sized square (grid), or a defined feature such as a house floor.

exchange: A system that promotes the transfer of goods and services between people, either individuals or societies. The term *trade* may be used to mean the same, but it often refers more specifically to the formalized economic relations of modern societies. Three different forms of exchange can be found: reciprocity, redistribution, and market exchange. There are also different spatial patterns of traded items, which can reveal the mode of exchange. In "down-the-line" exchange, a commodity is passed successively from one group to another even farther away from its source. The pattern shows a distinct decline in the quantity of the item as distance from the source increases; the higher the value of the item, the further it reaches. In "directional exchange," where a commodity is traded directly from its source to a distant point without any intermediate exchange, the pattern of decreasing quantities with increasing distance is distorted with a local concentration. Primitive forms of exchange include barter, gift exchange, potlatch, and silent trade. (*syn.* directional trade; exchange system)

exchange system: Any system for exchanging goods and services between individuals and/or societies. This term also refers to the trade or transfer of ideas.

excised decoration: Pottery decoration produced by cutting strips or shapes out of the soft clay surface before firing. The resulting hollows, notches, or cavities were often inlaid with a white paste to contrast with the dark pot surface. Incised decoration has narrow lines; excised has wide lines.

execration text: Curses written on clay figurines, statuettes, or pottery jars/vessels, listing the names of the enemies of Egypt—places, groups of people, or individuals regarded as hostile or evil. These texts were ritually smashed and then buried as part of a magical process of triumphing over the persons or places listed.

exogamy: The practice of marrying outside one's particular social group or range of kinship. The term also refers to a rule requiring marriage outside a social or cultural unit.

experimental archaeology: The reconstruction and reproduction of past behavior and processes to obtain or evaluate archaeological data and test hypotheses about the way people dealt with subsistence and technology. The experiments involve such activities as creating and using stone tools, duplicating prehistoric methods of farming, building, and travel. The term is normally used only for those experiments that deal with material culture, such as industry, the building of structures, mining, and crop processing. The more theoretical aspects, such as ideas about the development and organization of society, are generally thought of as a part of pro-

cessual archaeology rather than experimental. Reconstructions can be based on excavated ground plans, and some of these have been deliberately burned or left to decay, so that an idea can be gained of what the archaeologist might expect to find later. Boats have been built and sailed, food has been cooked in earth ovens and eaten, stone monuments have been laboriously erected, and trumpets and stringed instruments have been made and played. Although past events are not exactly repeatable, experimental simulation can prove very instructive and is being increasingly used. One of the earliest examples was General Pitt-Rivers' observations of the rate and duration of ditch silting on his excavations at Cranbourne Chase in the 19th century.

experimental hypothesis: A specific hypothesis, deduced from a generalization or general law, which can then be directly tested against data.

explanation: The end product of scientific research. In archaeology, explanation describes what happened in the past, and when, where, how, and why it happened.

extraction locus: Any place where large amounts of material are extracted or processed, such as a quarry, clay pit, or kill site.

Eyasi: A late Middle Pleistocene site in northern Tanzania with faunal remains including archaic *Homo sapiens* and extinct mammal species as well as artifacts.

Eynan (Ain Mallaha): An early Natufian village beside Lake Huleh in northern Palestine. Excavations revealed three occupations starting with the 10th millennium BC. There were 50 semisubterranean stone-lined circular huts, some with hearths and storage bins. Large storage pits and burials were outside the structures. Among the burials, one was more elaborately equipped and might have been a village headman. Eynan had a bone tool industry, bone and stone artwork, and stone vessels. (*syn.* Ein Mallaha)

Ezero: Eneolithic and Early Bronze Age site in central Bulgaria, which lends its name to a culture of the lower Danube basin and the Black Sea coast of Bulgaria. There were two building phases of the Veselinovo culture (Karanovo III) dated c. 4320 BC, a level with Karanovo IV pottery, eight building levels of the Copper Age (Karanovo V–VII) dated c. 3630 BC, and nine building levels of the Early Bronze Age. The Bronze Age levels have radiocarbon dates of c. 2500–2200 BC, and the pottery has affinities with the Early Bronze Age of Troy. Ezero had a very rich bone, antler, and stone industry and provides the most detailed chronology for southeastern Europe for the period.

Ff

fabatarium: A large Roman earthenware vessel in which bean flour (*puls fabacia*) was served, boiled with water or broth and forming a kind of polenta.

Faboura: A shell collection in Senegal, dated to 1900–1300 BP. These *Arca senelis* bivalve shells are linked to the Manding people.

fabric: The material of which pottery is composed; the body of processed clay and temper additives in ceramics.

fabricator: A flint implement or piece of stone or bone used in the manufacture of other flint tools. Often rod shaped and worn heavily on one end, it is used to chip flakes from a stone core.

façade: The principal face or front of a structure, often toward a street or other open place. It is often visually impressive. (*syn.* facade)

facies: Any subgroup of elements in an industry or main culture tradition, distinguished from the whole on the basis of some aspect of appearance or composition. A major division of a cultural sequence, such as the Mousterian culture of the European Palaeolithic, is often described as having different facies—for example, the Quina Mousterian or the Mousterian of Acheulian tradition—although these may reflect different industries or cultures. It is also a geological term used to describe the characters of any part of a formation that is differentiated by its appearance or composition, especially by the fossils it contains, its constituent rocks, or its texture. The term has also been applied to pedology (soil).

factor analysis: A multivariate mathematical technique that assesses the degree of variation between artifact types and is based on a matrix of correlation coefficients that measure the relative association between any two variables. This statistical technique calculates the relative importance of a set of factors that together are assumed to influence some observed set of values or properties.

factorium: A vessel containing exactly a factum, or quantity of grapes or olives to be placed under the press (torcular) in one making.

Fafos: An early Vinca settlement in Serbia with several occupation levels with pits and postholes. The site is characterized by particularly rich ritual artifacts, including fired clay figurines in the local Kosovo style.

faience: A name used for the medieval pottery of Faenza in northern Italy, one of the chief seats of the ceramics industry in the 16th century; it was an early maiolica. It is also used for the tin-glazed earthenware made in France, Germany, Spain, and Scandinavia as distinguished from Faenza maiolica, and that made in the Netherlands and England, which is called delft. Most accurately, it is the primitive form of glass developed in Mesopotamia in the 3rd millennium BC and then, almost as early, in Egypt; it is sometimes called Egyptian faience. It is a substance composed of a sand and clay mixture baked to a temperature at which the surface begins to fuse to a bluish or greenish glass. It was colored with copper salts to produce a blue-green finish and used especially for beads and figurines, particularly in the second millennium BC. Its main use in the Bronze Age was for beads, seals, figurines, and similar small objects. The glazed material could be made of a base of either carved steatite (soapstone) or molded clay with a core of crushed quartz (or quartz and soda-lime) fired so that the surface fuses into a glassy coating. Examples occur also in Bronze Age contexts in Europe, including the Wessex Culture. (*syn.* faïence, fayence; frit, paste)

Faiyum: A fertile area of the Egyptian Sahara, which receives water from an arm of the Nile. It was important during the Neolithic and developed only during the Middle Kingdom and the Greco-Roman period.

Faiyum "A": The earliest-known phase of the Predynastic sequence of Lower Egypt with settlements in the northern Faiyum area. The economic base was agriculture, although there was much hunting of large mammals (elephant, hippopotamus).

Fajada Butte: A geological feature in Chaco Canyon, New Mexico, with two vertical slabs of rock through which the light of the summer and winter solstices creates carved spiral designs. This "sun dagger" has been interpreted by some as a solar observatory.

Fakheriyah, Tell: Perhaps the site of Washukanni, the capital of the kingdom of Mitanni in northern Mesopotamia, on the River Khabur. Tablets, statues, ivories of the 2nd millennium BC have been found. (*syn.* Washukanni)

fall-off analysis: The study of regularities in the way in which quantities of traded items found in the archaeological record decline as the distance from the source increases. This may be plotted as a fall-off curve, with the quantities of material (Y-axis) plotted against the distance from source (X-axis).

fallow period: The time allowed for a field to rest, when no crops are grown on it.

fallowing: Practice of letting agricultural fields lie unused through one or more planting seasons to restore their fertility.

false color infrared photography: A technique of aerial photography used in archaeology, especially in the Americas. Infrared film reacts to the varying water absorption qualities of different features, thus allowing changes in vegetation, the occurrence of buried features filled with disturbed soil, the presence of otherwise invisible roadways to be detected. The false color refers to the accentuation of specific features in red, pink, yellow, blue, and so on, which emphasize the contrasts but which are not the true colors of the features. This technique often achieves greater resolution than conventional photography because the wavelengths are unaffected by atmospheric haze. (*syn.* false-color satellite imagery)

false entrance: An elaborate architectural element of Egyptian tombs and mortuary temples, which was a dummy entrance where the true entrance would normally be. The false entrance was for show; it served as the focal point of a tomb and had a door carved or painted, presumably through which the ka could enter and leave at will when partaking of funerary offerings. These first appeared in tombs of the Old Kingdom (2686–2181 BC). The term also refers to a phenomenon found in megalithic tombs in the British Isles, where an apparent entrance to a chamber, often leading from a forecourt, is in fact a dummy, and the real chambers open not from the end but the side of the mound. (*syn.* false door)

false relief: A form of excised or impressed decoration on pottery in which two rows of inward pointing triangles are cut from, or impressed on, the pot surface. The zigzag running between them then appears to be in relief, although it is actually no higher than the surface of the pot.

Fara: The site of the ancient Sumerian city of Shuruppak, in southern Mesopotamia, occupied during the first half of the 3rd millennium BC. It has yielded tablets and seal impressions of Early Dynastic period II–III. (*syn.* Shuruppak)

Far'ah, Tall al-: Ancient site in southwestern Palestine, located on the Wadi Ghazzah near Tall al-'Ajjul, in modern Israel. It has Chalcolithic remains of the 4th millennium BC (pottery, stone objects) and was important in Early Bronze Age periods I and II when it was walled. Some scholars believe that the site is ancient Sharuhen, an important Egyptian (Hyksos) fortress during the late 17th–early 16th centuries BC. According to the Egyptian account, after the collapse of Hyksos rule in Egypt, Sharuhen managed to withstand a siege by anti-Hyksos Egyptians for 3 years. Excavations have revealed city levels and tombs dating from c. 1900–1200 BC. In the 9th century BC, it might have been Tirzah, capital of King Omri before he moved to Samaria. It was destroyed by the Assyrians in 722 BC. (*syn.* Tell el Far'ah; el-Fara, Tell; Beth-pelet; Sharuhen)

Farafra Oasis: A fertile depression in the Western Desert of Egypt, west of modern Asyut. The smallest of the major Egyptian oases, it is first mentioned in texts dating to the Old Kingdom (2686–2181 BC), and by the 19th Dynasty (1295–1186 BC) it was said to have been inhabited by Libyans. (*syn.* ancient Ta-iht, al-Farafirah Oasis)

Far'ah, Tell el-: Two tells of this name, excavated in Palestine, inland from Gaza. The northern tell had a 4th millennium BC Chalcolithic settlement with circular, semisubterranean dwellings and an Early Bronze Age occupation. It later became an Israelite town; for a few years in the 9th century BC, the northern tell was the capital of Israel (Tirzah), before Omri moved to Samaria. The southern tell may have been a Hyksos fortification. Its remains include a large building of the Late Bronze Age and Remains of the Philistines from the Iron Age. The most impressive material came from five rich Philistine tombs containing characteristic Philistine decorated pottery, native Late Bronze Age undecorated wares, bronze bowls, daggers and spears; an iron dagger and an iron knife were also found, among the earliest finds of this metal in Palestine. (*syn.* el-Fara)

Fara'in, Tell el-: A series of three mounds including two towns and a temple complex in the northwestern delta of the Nile. Identified as ancient Buto by Flinders Petrie, it was occupied from late Predynastic times until the Roman period, c. 3300 BC–AD 395. (*syn.* ancient Pe and Dep, Per-Wadjyt, Buto)

Faras: A former capital of the Nubian kingdom of Nobatia, located on the border of modern Egypt and Sudan on the west bank of the Nile. It was first established as a small Egyptian fortress in the Middle Kingdom (2055–1650 BC) and continued in use in the 18th to 19th Dynasties (1550–1186 BC) with the construction of five Egyptian temples. (*syn.* ancient Pachoras)

fardo: In Peruvian archaeology, the "package" formed by a human mummy wrapped together with various funerary offerings (amulets, etc.), usually in several yards of material. Often a false head of wood or straw or metal mask was fixed to the top of a fardo.

Farfa: A rich Benedictine monastery of the early Middle Ages, located northeast of Rome, Italy. Founded c. 680–700, its scriptorium was famous, and it has undergone several rebuildings and ambitious additions.

Fatimid: An Islamic dynasty that seized power from the earlier Abbasid Dynasty in Tunisia in 909. The Fatimids subsequently conquered Egypt in 969, which they then dominated for some 2 centuries. Much Fatimid architecture survives, including great mosques, palaces, and elaborately decorated chamber tombs.

Fat'janovo: A cemetery site on the upper Volga in central Russia, with a regional culture on the edge of a broader corded-ware complex. In the cemetery, the dead were buried with spherical amphorae with cord ornament, model wheels of terra-cotta, stone battle axes with drooping blades, and copper trinkets. Although the tombs are not covered by mounds, the Fat'janovo culture is a late (Copper/Early Bronze Age) subgroup within the main Single-Grave/Battle ax tradition. (*syn.* Fatyanovo)

fauna: Animals.

faunal analysis: The study of animal remains in an archaeological site, as by identifying bones or shells, examining butcher marks, and so on. The analysis is used to determine past hunting and dietary practices.

faunal association: A relative age determination technique based on archaeological associations with remains of extinct species.

faunal dating: A method of relative dating based on observing the evolutionary changes in particular species of mammals, so as to form a rough chronological sequence.

faunal ecofacts: Ecofacts derived from animals, including bones, teeth, antlers, and so forth. They are usually subdivided into human remains and nonhuman ecofacts.

faunalturbation: A disturbance of the soil surface by animals, especially by the burrowing and tunneling of gophers, mice, rabbits, and so on.

Fauresmith: An older term used to refer to the final Acheulian phase in the southern African interior. It was a Stone Age industry with tools representing a development from the final Acheulian hand ax tradition; the hand axes were small, well finished, and pointed. At Saldanha, Fauresmith artifacts were

likely contemporary with a Neanderthal-like skull similar to the one from Broken Hill.

Fayyum, al- or Fayum: A large fertile depression in the Libyan Desert, southwest of Cairo near the west bank of the Nile, with two prehistoric cultures dating to c. 5000 BC and c. 4500 BC. These early settlements were of the first food-producing peoples of Egypt. Emmer and barley were cultivated and cattle, sheep, and pigs bred. Saw-edged sickle flints, mat-lined silo pits, and saddle querns have been found, and ax heads were of flaked flint or ground pebbles. Hollow-based flint arrowheads, bone dart tips, stone mace heads, and bone harpoons were used for hunting and fishing. Artifacts of special note include a threshing flail and a wooden sickle set with flint teeth. Pottery was in use, and beads of ostrich eggshell and seashells of both Mediterranean and Red Sea types were imported. Lake Qarun had fish, which were a delicacy for Egyptians throughout the ages. In the Middle Kingdom (c. 2000 BC), the pharaohs (Amenemhet III) engaged in huge irrigation and drainage schemes, and the area was famous for orchards and gardens. After a period of decline, the Ptolemies in turn took an interest in the area, establishing a number of small towns there; the papyrus archives have survived in great quantity and excellent state of preservation. The region incorporates archaeological sites dating from the late Palaeolithic to the late Roman and Christian periods (c. 8000 BC–AD 641), including Shedet (later Crocodilopolis), chief center for worship of the crocodile god Sebek, near which al-Fayyum town now lies. (*syn.* Fayoum, Fayum region, ancient Ta-she, She-resy, Moeris)

feature: A nonmoveable/nonportable element of an archaeological site. It is any separate archaeological unit that is not recorded as a structure, a layer, or an isolated artifact; a wall, hearth, storage pit, or burial area are examples of features. A feature carries evidence of human activity, and it is any constituent of an archaeological site not classed as a find, layer, or structure.

fecundity figure: A type of offering bearer depicted on Egyptian temple walls, mostly seen as personifications of geographical areas, the inundation, or abstract concepts. The male figures have heavy, pendulous breasts and bulging stomachs, their fatness symbolizing the abundance they bring with them.

Feddersen Wierde: Terp settlements of the North Sea German littoral, occupied from c. 1st century. There was leather and bone working in "industrial" areas, and the buildings were of an aisled longhouse type. There seems to have been foreign trade in the early 5th century.

Federmesser: Small backed blades, about the size and shape of penknife blades, which were the most distinctive artifacts of the Final Glacial peoples of the north European plain during the Allerød Oscillation (c. 9850–8850 BC).

Similar bladelets occur in the related Creswellian culture of Britain, and the blades are very similar to the Azilian point. They are backed blades tapering to a point and were probably used as arrowheads. They tend to have curved or angled backs unlike the earlier Gravette points.

feedback: A concept in archaeological applications of systems theory reflecting the continually changing relation between cultural variables and their environment. It is the modification, adjustment, or control of a process or system by a result or effect of the process—especially by a difference between a desired and an actual result.

Fell's Cave: An Early Preceramic (Palaeo Indian) cave site in Chile (Pantagonia) dating to 9050–8770 bc. The Pleistocene bones of horse and ground sloth are found together with crude chopping tools, bone awls, disks of lava, and pressure-flaked fluted, stemmed fishtail projectile points. Radiocarbon dates at Fell's Cave and Palli Aike suggest that humans had spread south to the Straits of Magellan by the 9th millennium BC.

fen: A community of plants growing in basic or neutral waterlogged conditions, as opposed to a bog. This wetlands community, characterized by alkaline conditions, grows in zones between fresh water and land, as along lake margins. Fens represent a stage in the progressive colonization of shallow water; this plant succession continues with the colonization by trees (the "carr" stage) followed in some areas by the growth of a raised bog on top of the fen and carr. This low land is subject to frequent inundations and is a very good source of artifactual information.

Fengate: A series of farmsteads in England dating from the Middle Neolithic to the end of the Middle Bronze Age and then reoccupied in the Early Iron Age.

Fenbitou: A site and Neolithic culture on the southwestern coast of Taiwan, dating to 2400–1800 BC. (*syn.* [Feng-pi-t'ou])

Fernando Po: An island off the coast of Equatorial Guinea, once called Formosa, of particular archaeological interest. A Neolithic technology existed and continued until the early centuries of the 2nd millennium AD, presumably owing to the absence of sources of metal. A similar situation existed in the Canary Islands. This site in western Africa lies in a strategic situation from which the Niger mouths and the Slave Coast could be watched. (*syn.* Bioko, Formosa)

Ferrières: A Late Neolithic dolmen (passage grave) in Hérault, southern France, and the type site of the culture that existed c. 3200–2800 BC. Its pottery is characterized by incised-line and geometric motif decoration. The earlier variety belongs to the Neolithic period, and the later style is contemporary with the Copper Age pottery of Fontbouïsse. Ferrières pottery has been found in caves, village sites, passage graves, and cremation cemeteries. (*syn.* Ferrières-les-Verreries)

Fertile Crescent: The region in the Middle East where the civilizations of the Middle East and the Mediterranean basin began. The term was invented by the American Orientalist James Henry Breasted in 1916. It applied to the crescent-shaped area of cultivable land between the highland zones and the West Asian desert, stretching from Egypt through the Levant to southern Anatolia and northern Mesopotamia, and eastward to the flanks of the Zagros Mountains. Conditions in this area were favorable for the early development of farming, and all the earliest farming communities were thought to lie within it. The Fertile Crescent in its wider extension corresponds exactly to the region described in the Hebrew traditions of Genesis; it also contains the ancient countries— Babylonia, Assyria, Egypt, Phoenicia—from which the Greek and Roman civilizations evolved. The belief that the earliest culture known to mankind originated in the Fertile Crescent has been confirmed by radiocarbon dating since 1948. It is now known that incipient agriculture and village agglomerations there must be dated back to about 8000 BC, if not earlier, and that irrigation was used almost immediately.

fetish: An inanimate object associated with a spiritual being or magical powers and worshiped by primitive peoples. A fetish differs from an idol in that it is worshiped in its own character, not as the image or symbol of a deity.

feudalism: A hierarchical political and economic system of the Middle Ages in which land was granted in return for military or labor services and the peasantry was ruled by a class of landowners. Several of the great civilizations of the world have passed through a feudal period in the course of their history—in many countries of Europe and in Japan. The origins of European feudalism were in the early Frankish kingdom of the 8th century; feudalism spread with Frankish conquests. (*syn.* feudal system)

fiber-tempered pottery: Any clay pottery to which grass or root fibers have been added as a tempering material. This ware is the earliest pottery in Caribbean South America and the oldest pottery in the United States, making its appearance in Archaic shell mounds in Georgia and Florida before 2500 BC.

fibula: In antiquity, a clasp, buckle, or brooch of various designs, usually shaped like a modern safety pin. It was often used for fastening a draped garment such as a toga or cloak, made of bronze, gold, silver, ivory, and so on, and consisted of a bow, pin, and catch. It is the Latin word for "brooch" and is so named for the outer of two bones of lower leg or hind limb, which together with the tibia resemble an ancient brooch. The earliest examples date to around 1300 BC. There are two main families of fibulae. In the south, they were made in one piece, starting with the Peschiera or violin bow form in northern Italy and Mycenaean Greece. From this developed the arc fibula north of the Mediterranean and the harp and spectacle fibulae in the eastern Alps in the years around 1000 BC. From the Certosa form was derived the long series of La Tène Iron Age varieties. Even wider variation is found among the succeeding Roman fibulae, leading to the final forms in the Saxon and Migration periods. Around the same time, there was an apparently independent development in northern Europe of the two-piece variety. Fibula types include violin bow, arc, elbowed, serpentine, dragon, harp, disk with "elastic bow," leech, boat, two-piece fibula, spiral, La Tène I, III. Fibula terms include catchplate, pin, spring, bow, stilt, elongated catch plate, disk catch plate, knobbed (Certosa) catch plate. Although primarily functional, fibulae were often also highly decorated items of personal adornment, sometimes inlaid with glass and precious stones. An enormous number of different types of fibulae were made, and they can often be a useful guide to dating. (*syn.* pl. fibulae)

ficron: A long pointed, roughly worked biface with slightly concave sides and a detailed tip. It may have preceded the Micoquian biface.

field archaeology: The study of archaeological remains through observation and interpretation of what is in the "field" without recourse to excavation. Some features are readily seen and identifiable and others must be sought out or are found only by chance disturbance. The technique is associated with O. G. S. Crawford, who demonstrated its methods and value. The three stages are observation (link with air photography), interpretation, and accurate recording. (*syn.* archaeological field survey; humps and bumps archaeology)

field notes: A written account of archaeological research, usually kept by each investigator, recording all stages of research design, but especially the conduct of data acquisition. It is the written record containing firsthand, on-the-spot observations. Field notes are considered primary field data.

field operations journal: A running record of activities and finds during an archaeological excavation.

field walking: Systematic exploration of an area by a team of investigators, walking, collecting, and recording surface artifacts or noting earthworks and other phenomena.

fieldwork: Any form of archaeological research or exploration carried out in an actual setting in the natural environment—excavation, surveying, field walking—rather than in a laboratory, museum, or other such facility. Some archaeologists call everything they do outdoors "fieldwork," but others distinguish between fieldwork and excavation. Fieldwork, in the narrow sense, consists of the discovery and recording of archaeological sites and their examination by methods other than the use of the shovel and the trowel. (*syn.* field study)

Fiesole: A chief city of the Etruscan confederacy, near Florence, with important Roman remains. It probably dates from the 9th–8th centuries BC, but its first record (as Faesulae) is in 283 BC, when it was conquered by the Romans. In 80 BC, it was occupied by the dictator Lucius Cornelius Sulla, who built the town. Traces of an Etruscan temple dating to the 3rd century BC survive, but the town was taken by barbarians in AD 405. It later declined and was superseded by Florence. (*syn.* Faesulae)

figurine: A small carved or sculpted figure of a human or animal, usually of clay, stone, wood, or a metal. A figurine's purpose is often religious, either as an object of worship itself or as a votive offering to a god. They were made in prehistoric Europe from the Upper Palaeolithic onward, although they became less common in the Bronze Age.

Fiji: An archipelago in eastern Melanesia. Archaeological evidence shows that Fiji was settled by Austronesian-speaking peoples in the late 2nd millennium BC, and the inhabitants developed pottery by about 1300 BC. A rich archaeological sequence begins with the Lapita culture from about 1300 BC and progresses through successive ceramic phases to a period of earthwork for construction and warfare, starting after AD c. 1100. Fijians are a Melanesian/Polynesian population, and their islands formed the main bridgehead for the Polynesian settlement of western Polynesia soon after 1300 BC. Fiji is the most easterly point in Oceania to have maintained production of pottery throughout its prehistory. The Dutch navigator Abel Tasman explored the islands of Vanua Levu and Taveuni in 1643.

Fikellura ware: An Archaic East Greek black-figure pottery style. It has been found in the Fikellura cemetery on Rhodes; the source of the clay was Miletus.

filigree: A technique of decorating jewelry with gold, silver, or electrum soldered onto metalwork. It consists of creating a fine open metalwork pattern from wire that is soldered together and to the main body of the piece. The wire can be plain or decorative. For goldwork, the solder was normally a gold-copper alloy (82% gold, 18% copper), which had a lower melting point than pure gold. The word is derived from the Italian *filigrana*, which is *filum* and *granum* or "granular network." It was first developed in the Near East and was often used in combination with granulation. The technique had been mastered by the Early Dynastic Sumerian craftsmen of the 3rd millennium BC, and fine jewelry decorated in this way appears in the Royal Tombs of Ur. Anglo-Saxon and Germanic metalworkers greatly developed the technique. (*syn.* filagree, filigraine)

Filimoshki: A Pleistocene site on the Zeya River in eastern Siberia, with flaked quartzite cobbles recovered from alluvium and classified as Lower Palaeolithic tools.

Filitosa: A fortified promontory settlement in Corsica, France, dating to the Chalcolithic or Early Bronze Age c. 2500–2000 BC. There is a tower (*torre*)—a dry-stone tower fortified by a wall of cylopean masonry; inside are three buildings. The walls incorporate statue-menhirs, which show warriors armed with daggers and swords. There is a radiocarbon date of c. 1500 BC for one of the three torri inside the defenses.

Final Neolithic: A transition phase where copper and bronze came into use, but stone was still most important.

find: An act or instance of discovering archaeological remains, the remains discovered, or the location where this discovery occurs.

find-spot or find spot: The location where an archaeological find is discovered. (*syn.* find-place)

Fine Orange Pottery: A high-quality orange ware, often decorated with incised, molded, or black-painted patterns; a late Classic (and post-Classic) pottery type of the lowland Maya area of Mesoamerica. Found at sites under the influence of Teotihuacán, it comes from the Tabasco-Campeche region (Usumacinta drainage).

Finglesham: An early Saxon cemetery in Kent, used between the early 6th and mid-7th centuries. The large inhumation cemetery has produced an impressive collection of material including a pattern-welded sword, garnet-inlaid bird brooches made in Kent, radiate brooches from the continent, and a richly decorated square-headed brooch. Wooden boxes with bronze binding, strings of beads, corroded buckets, and bone objects of the period were also found. Some of the female burials seem to have been interred alive.

Fiorelli, Giuseppe (1823–1896): Archaeologist who took over the early excavations at Pompeii, from 1860–1875, and was one of the first to apply the methods of stratigraphy and area excavation on a large scale. Through his training school at Pompeii, he passed on his methods to many other archaeologists. He also developed a technique for taking plaster casts of the hollows in the hardened ash and cinders, thus creating impressions of the dead and other vanished creatures and objects.

fire: The natural product of combustion, seen in the form of flame and smoke. The use of fire was a major landmark in man's adaptation to the cooler environment of the earth; it is often considered the single most important discovery by early man. Man probably knew how to make fire between 500,000–800,000 years ago in Europe or Asia. The ability to make fire efficiently and at will rather than merely catching it from natural sources may date from less than 200,000 years ago. Fire is first found on occupation sites of the Lower Palaeolithic period, approximately half a million years ago, although true hearths do not become typical until the penulti-

mate glacial period, perhaps 200,000 years ago. Hearths and thick deposits of burnt material are typical of the last glacial period, by which time it is likely that the two main methods of making fire (the friction method of rubbing or rotating sticks to generate heat and the percussion method of striking sparks with iron and flint) were both in use.

firedog: An instrument consisting of an iron bar held horizontally at one end by an upright support, used to ensure the proper burning of a fire. A pair of these was put at each side of the hearth or fireplace to support burning wood; the end of a log could rest on the crosspiece, which was supported by two uprights. Decorative iron examples come from La Tene Iron Age contexts, mostly in graves. In a kitchen fireplace, the upright support might hold a rack in front for the spit to turn in. (*syn.* andiron)

fire effected: Of stone, showing the effects of having been heated, as in cooking. (*syn.* fire-cracked)

fire hardening: The exposure of a wooden implement to fire to dry out the wood but not char it. The tool becomes harder and more useful.

fire hearth: A flat piece of wood on which a stick (drill) is twisted vigorously to start a fire.

fireplace: A place for building a fire, especially a semiopen space with a chimney; housing for an open fire in a dwelling. These are used for heating and cooking. Very early medieval fireplaces had semicircular backs and hoods, and there was no chimney; the smoke passed out through an opening in the wall. By the 11th century, chimneys were added. Early fireplaces were made of stone; later, brick became the more popular material. (*syn.* fire-place, hearth)

fire setting: The softening or cracking of the working face of a lode of quarrying stone, to facilitate excavation, by exposing it to a wood fire built against it. The fire shattered the outcrops of rock.

firestarter: A wood tool having a base with drilled holes and a stick that is rubbed through the holes in the base to produce enough friction to give a spark. (*syn.* firestarter kit)

First Intermediate Period: Chronological phase (c. 2130–1938 BC) between the Old Kingdom (2575–2130 BC) and the Middle Kingdom (1938–1600 BC), which appears to have been a time of relative political disunity and instability. The period includes the 9th Dynasty (c. 2130–2080 BC), 10th Dynasty (c. 2080–1970 BC), and 11th Dynasty (c. 2081–1938 BC). (The period corresponds to Manetho's 7th to 10th Dynasties and the early part of the 11th Dynasty.) After the end of the 8th Dynasty, the throne passed to kings from Heracleopolis, who made their native city the capital. Major themes of inscriptions of the period are the provision of food supplies for people in times of famine and the promotion of irrigation works. In the 10th Dynasty, a period of generalized conflict focused on twin dynasties at Thebes and Heracleopolis. The 11th Dynasty made Thebes its capital. In the First Intermediate Period, monuments were erected by a larger section of the population, and, in the absence of central control, internal dissent and conflicts of authority became visible in public records. Nonroyal individuals took over some of the privileges of royalty, notably identification with Osiris in the hereafter and the use of the Pyramid Texts. These were incorporated into a more extensive corpus inscribed on coffins—the Coffin Texts—and continued to be inscribed during the Middle Kingdom.

First Temperate Neolithic: A term sometimes used to describe the earliest farming cultures in the temperate zone of Europe (and sometimes in other areas). In southeast Europe from c. 5400–4500/4300 BC, there was the Starcevo (eastern and northern Yugoslavia), Körös (eastern and southwest Hungary), Cris (west and lowland Rumania), Kremikovci (northwest Bulgaria), and Karanovo (central and southern Bulgaria). The regional groups are differentiated by their individual painted wares, but the group of cultures is unified by nonceramic traits such as miniature polished bone spoons, fired clay lip plugs, rod-head figurines, and stamp seals. The vast majority of early FTN sites are located in the major river valleys of the Balkans, either as tell settlements or as short-lived flat sites. Hoe or digging-stick agriculture combined with cattle husbandry was the economic base of most FTN settlements. (*syn.* FTN)

fishbone analysis: The study of the remains of fish on archaeological sites, in the form of bones, otoliths, and scales. The latter survive only occasionally in anaerobic conditions, while otoliths have not, to date, been frequently recorded. Fish have markedly different skeletons from mammals. Many fishbones are so small that they appear only in sieving, and the bones commonly preserved are the jaws and some other head bones and the vertebrae. They usually accumulate in refuse deposits and may be interpreted in terms of diet and fishing on the site or in the area that supplied it. Identification of species through comparison with modern fishbones is becoming easier as larger collections of comparative material are built up. When a species has been identified, it can lead to evidence for the hydrological conditions around the site; also, the occurrence of the remains of marine species on an inland site has implications for the movement of groups or a trade in fish. A combination of species identification and aging of fish through study of the otoliths can lead to assumptions about the seasonal occupation of certain settlement sites and the subsistence economy of the associated groups.

Fishbourne: A Roman site in Sussex, England, best known for the palace/villa of Cogidubnus of the 1st century AD. The site began as a coastal depot with granaries and was replaced

by a residential area and then by extensive building. The palace, built in AD c. 70–75, was one of the most lavish of the time in the empire, with a formal garden court, suites of mosaic-floored rooms, stucco moldings, painted wall plaster, and a complete set of baths. Cogidubnus was the British king of the tribe of the Regni. The site lies near to Chichester, which was first a fort and then Civitas, capital of the Regni. Alterations and rebuilding took place during the 2nd century, after the death of Cogidubnus, and sometime in the last 3rd–early 4th centuries there was a fire that caused unrepairable damage.

fish hook: Artifact of two basic types: bait hook and lure hook. Varied in form throughout the Pacific, they are made of bone, shell, tortoise shell, or wood.

fishing: The catching of fish as a source of food did not become important until quite late in human evolution. Some fish remains are found on early Palaeolithic sites, such as Olduvai. Fish and other seafood were more important for coastal peoples and for those closer to the poles. In the Mesolithic, from c. 6000 BC on, fishhooks and nets were made, and boats are likely to have come into general use.

fishtail point: A fluted and stemmed, fishlike stone tool of South America, dating to c. 11,000–8000 bc. The complex has some similarities to the Clovis of North America and is representative of the Palaeo Indian time in South America.

fission track dating: A chronometric dating technique based on the natural, spontaneous nuclear fission of uranium 238 and its byproduct, linear atomic displacements/tracks. The basis for this technique is that a uranium isotope, U238, as well as decaying to a stable lead isotope, also undergoes spontaneous fission. One in every 2 million atoms decays in this way. Fission is accompanied by an energy release that sends the resulting two nuclei into the surrounding material, the tracks causing damage to the crystal lattice. These tracks can be counted under a microscope after the polished surface of the sample has been etched with acid. The concentration of uranium can be determined by the induced fission of U235 by neutron irradiation of the sample. Because the ratio of U235 to U238 is known and is constant, a comparison of the number of tracks from natural fission and the number from induced fission gives the age of the sample. Although the method has been limited in its archaeological use so far, it has already proved a useful check method for potassium-argon dating for volcanic deposits at Olduvai Gorge, Tanzania. Obsidian, tephra beds, mineral inclusions in pottery, and some manmade glasses have also been dated. A further use of the method is based on the fact that fission tracks disappear if the substance is heated about 500 degrees or so: Thus a date achieved for clay (like a hearth), pottery, or obsidian that had been burnt gives the date of burning or firing, because previous fission tracks would have disappeared. (*syn.* fission-track dating; fission track age determination)

Five Dynasties period: In Chinese history, time between the fall of the T'ang Dynasty (AD 907) and the founding of the Sung (Song) Dynasty (960), when five would-be dynasties followed one another in quick succession in North China. The era coincides with the Ten Kingdoms—the 10 regimes that dominated separate regions of South China—during the same period.

Flag Fen: A Late Bronze Age settlement site on the Cambridgeshire fens (island) of England. It was reached by a timber track from the mainland at Fengate and was occupied c. 1000–700 BC. Artifacts include flint tools, a bronze dagger, shale bracelet, wooden items, and pottery.

flake: A thin, broad piece of stone detached from a larger mass for use as a tool; a piece of stone removed from a larger piece (core or nucleus) during knapping (percussion or pressure) and used in prehistoric times as a cutting instrument. Flakes often served as "blanks" from which more complex artifacts—burins, scrapers, gravers, arrowheads—could be made. Waste flakes (debitage) are those discarded during the manufacture of a tool. Flakes may be retouched to make a flake tool or used unmodified. The process leaves characteristic marks on both the core and flake. This makes it comparatively easy to distinguish human workmanship from natural accident. (*syn.* flake tool)

flaked stone: Any object made by one of the various percussion or pressure techniques of stone tool technology. Tools produced by the removal of flakes (or chips, commonly referred to as debitage) from the stone to create a sharp surface. Projectile points, bifaces, unifaces, and cores are common flaked stone artifact types. (*syn.* chipped stone, flaked stone tool, flaked stone artifacts)

flaker: Any pressure-flaking tool, often made from bone or antler, used to detach flakes from stone material in knapping; an implement for flaking flint.

flake scar: A mark or trace on a stone showing the point of attachment of a flake that has been removed; the point where a flake has been chipped off in the making of a tool.

flake scatter: A quantity of stone flakes loosely discarded during toolmaking, often found in a semicircle pattern where work was done.

flaking: The process of making stone tools by removing flakes from a larger mass, by percussion or pressure from another tool. Percussion flaking is done by striking the stone to be chipped with another stone or bone. Pressure flaking is done by pressing a blunt-pointed tool of antler or bone against the edge to be worked. Flaking is feasible with materials that are glassy in nature and fracture evenly (as obsidian,

flint); it is not feasible with materials such as granite or sandstone, which in general are ground.

Flandrian: Of or pertaining to the period since the retreat of the ice sheet and the rise of sea level at the end of the last glaciation in northwestern Europe. The Flandrian can be dated by radiocarbon and ranges from 10,000 bp (the end of the Devensian) up to the present day. These deposits represent the latest Quaternary interglacial stage, equivalent to the Holocene epoch. The Flandrian includes sediments similar to those of previous interglacials, deposits on archaeological sites that contain Mesolithic, Neolithic, Bronze Age, Iron Age, Roman, Dark Age, medieval, and more recent artifacts.

flange: The transverse flattening of an edge—making a projecting flat rim, collar, or rib on an artifact. It was used to strengthen an object, to guide it, to keep it in place, or to allow its attachment to another object. The external ledge of a pottery bowl is often termed *flange*.

flat grave: Any burial consisting of a simple oval or rectangular pit containing an inhumed individual. The pit was infilled but not marked by a mound or other earthwork. The genuine Urnfield tradition was flat graves. In the Hallstatt, cremation was practiced in cemeteries of flat graves.

Flavian: The period of rule of the Roman emperors Vespasian (69–79), Titus (79–81), and Domitian (81–96)—AD 69–96—members of the Flavia gens.

Flemish black ware: A type of later medieval pottery known from paintings of the Renaissance period. Some of the wares were well decorated, but most Flemish wares were coarse black wares with pinched bases. They emerged from a Roman tradition of pottery making in Flanders.

flesher: A tool used for fleshing hides. In antiquity, it was often a long, broad-edged tool of bone, antler, or stone used to scrape or rub hides free of fat, sinew, hair, and other unwanted matter.

flexed burial: A method of burial in which the body is interred in a fetal position.

flexible rule: A tool used to draw curved lines or to outline the shape of an object so that its form can be drawn.

flint: A type of hard stone, often gray in color, found in rounded nodules and usually covered with a white incrustation. A member of the chalcedony group of water-bearing silica minerals, it was found from early use to fracture conchoidally and was ideal for making stone tools with sharp edges. It is chemically a quartz, but has a different microcrystalline structure. It can therefore be flaked readily in any direction and so shaped to many useful forms. It occurs widely, and where available was the basic material for man's tools until the advent of metal; it is the commonest "stone" of the Stone Age. The only types of stone preferred to it were obsidian and the tougher rocks used for ground tools in the Neolithic. The term is often used interchangeably with chert and also as a generic term denoting stone tools in the Old World. Nodules of flint occur commonly as seams in the upper and middle chalk of northwest Europe. During the Neolithic and Copper Ages of Europe, flint workers recognized that flint from beds below ground were of superior quality to surface flint, especially for the manufacture of large tools such as axes. These beds were exploited by sinking shafts and then excavating galleries outward. Flint mines are known from many areas of Europe, and good examples occur in Poland (Krzemionki), Holland, Belgium (Spiennes), and England (Grimes Graves). (*syn.* chert, firestone)

flintknapping: The technique of striking flakes or blades from a large flint stone (core or nucleus) and the shaping of cores and flakes into tools. The most commonly used stone was flint (chert), a hard, brittle stone, commonly found as nodules in limestone areas, which breaks with a conchoidal fracture. Flintknapping began with the simple striking of one stone against another. Later methods include the use of antler and wooden strikers for both direct and indirect percussion and bone and antler pressure-flaking tools. (*syn.* flint-knapping, knapping)

floating chronology: A chronometrically dated chronology not yet tied in to calendar years. A floating chronology is a decipherable record of time that was terminated long ago. The most common floating chronologies occur in dendrochronology where climate affects the growth of the rings and sequences are local. Local sequences cannot always be tied to the master sequences established in certain areas from the present day back into prehistory, and therefore the local sequences "float" until some link with a known historical data is found. Similarly, in magnetic dating, many of the sequences float until some independently dated sites can be entered on the curve. The term is also used in reference to varve chronologies.

flood: The Bible and Sumerian and Babylonian myths recorded a catastrophic flood sent by the gods to destroy humankind. With the assistance of the gods, one man (variously called Noah, Ziusudra, or Utnapishtim) and his family survived by building a boat. The discovery of the legend by George Smith in 1872 in Ashurbanipal's library at Neneveh, in cuneiform tablets of the epic of Gilgamesh, was very close in details to the Old Testament story of Noah. It is assumed by many that the stories derive from a common source. At Ur in 1929, Leonard Woolley revealed a depth of 2.5 meters of silt separating the 'Ubaid and Uruk levels, a deposit he could account for only by just such a flood. It should be noted, however, that flood levels have been found at other sites whose dates can be more appropriately equated with Noah's.

Today, many archaeologists believe that the various flood stories do not represent the record of a single event, but rather a whole series of natural disasters that affected the low-lying alluvial plain of southern Mesopotamia. (*syn.* Flood)

floodplain: A land form created by deposits in a river valley that floods. As the flood waters recede, the suspended sediment is deposited as alluvium and causes slow vertical accretion. Floodplains are often made up of secondary features such as individual flood basins, abandoned channels, secondary flood channels, tributary stream courses, and natural levees. They are prime agricultural land and archaeological deposits may be well preserved in the subenvironments. (*syn.* flood-plain)

flora: Plants or vegetation.

floral analysis: The study of plant remains from an archaeological site, including identification, association with artifacts and food processing, and so on.

floral ecofacts: Ecofacts derived from plants. They are subdivided into microspecimens (pollen, opal phytoliths) and macrospecimens (seeds, plant fragments, impressions).

floralturbation: The disturbance of the soil surface by plants, especially by tree fall and by root growth or decay.

Florence: Florence is a city in central Italy, founded as a Roman military colony about the 1st century BC. It achieved preeminence in commerce and finance, learning, and the arts during the 14th–16th centuries. Discovery of Villanovan material suggests earlier occupation, perhaps from the 8th–9th centuries BC. Remains of the Roman period include bath buildings, theater and amphitheater, and a temple to Isis. (*syn.* Roman Florentia, modern Italian Firenze)

florescence: In archaeology, what is considered the peak period of a culture—the state or period of flourishing—particularly in material aspects such as art and architecture.

Florisbad: A spring deposit in the Orange Free State, South Africa, which preserved a human cranium of *Homo sapiens sapiens*. Its brow ridges, while pronounced, are markedly less prominent than those of the (presumably earlier) skull from Broken Hill in Zambia. The Florisbad specimen is dated to c. 50,000 bc (late Middle Pleistocene) and appears to be associated with a Middle Stone Age industry of Pietersburg type.

flot: A term from the technique of flotation; it is used to describe the material that floats on water or other media during the flotation process. Flot can be plant remains such as seeds and charcoal, insect remains, shells, as well as miscellaneous intrusive material like plant roots that are sorted from the sample before analysis.

flotation: A technique developed to assist in the recovery of plant, insect, and molluscan remains from archaeological deposits; a method of screening in which minute pieces of flora are separated from the soil by agitation with water. The technique works on the principle that organic material such as carbonized seeds, snailshells, and beetle wing cases have a lower specific gravity than inorganic materials such as soil and stone and thus float on the top of a suitable liquid medium while the rest sink. Water is commonly used for flotation, although there are disadvantages: It has a fairly low specific gravity, and heavier material such as fruit stones sink. Other media have been used, such as carbon tetrachloride solution or zinc chloride solution. Flotation of samples by hand is called wet sieving. Samples of material are slowly poured into water, any lumps are broken up, and the flot is drawn off with a sieve. The method is more controlled than flotation by machine, and the recovery rate is better. For large-scale excavations, machines are used. Operating principles vary: Samples are poured into a large container of water, or water and paraffin, which is agitated by air injection or by currents of inflowing water. The addition of a flocculating agent increases surface tension, although not all machines are "froth flotation" machines. The flot is carried off the surface through a mesh or series of meshes to allow preliminary sorting. Samples retrieved are sent away for specialist identification and analysis by an archaeobotanist.

fluorine dating: A relative dating technique used on bone. Bone absorbs fluorine from groundwater at a rate proportional to the time since burial—if groundwater migration rates remain constant. Fluorine concentrations are chemically analyzed by the gradual combination of fluorine in groundwater with the calcium phosphate of the buried bone material. Bones from the same stratigraphical context can be dated relatively by comparison of their fluorine content. The Piltdown forgery was finally exposed by this method. (*syn.* fluorine test)

flute: A channel or grove running up a pillar or running up the center of a projectile point made of stone. In architecture, a flute resembles half of a flute split longitudinally, with the concave side outward. In referring to projectile point artifacts, the mark is a distinctive longitudinal groove left on the point after removal of a channel flake. It is characteristic of Folsom and Clovis points.

flûte de Pan: A type of suspension lug found on pottery of the Chassey, Cortaillod, and Lagozza cultures. Several vertical clay tubes, of width suitable to take a suspension cord, are set side-by-side on the wall of the vessel. The lug resembles a pan pipe or a section of corrugated cardboard.

fluted point: A projectile point with a distinctive longitudinal groove left after removal of a channel flake; a long, medial channel notched to the base of a flake. The channeled flake is removed from one or both faces by striking the specially prepared base sharply with a piece of wood or bone.

The sharp ridges of the flutes were ground smooth near the base of the point, to prevent them from cutting the bindings when the point was inserted into a notched foreshaft. These points have extreme symmetry, careful flaking, and the removal of a long, parallel and shallow flake from one or both sides. Fluted points, such as the Clovis and Folsom projectile points are characteristic of the Palaeo Indian peoples of North America. (*syn.* fluted projectile point)

flying buttress: An arched supporting pier outside a building, which takes most of the weight of the roof, allowing the walls to have windows rather than only supporting the roof. It is a prop or stay, usually held by part of the arch, springing from a support and abutting the structure. (*syn.* arch-buttress)

focus: A group of components that share high frequencies of similar cultural traits. The components are probably not identical but should have a sufficient number of significant traits in common to indicate a relation. (*syn.* phase)

fogou: A type of Iron Age structure found in Cornwall, England, and also in Scotland, Ireland, and Brittany. It is constructed like a gallery, partially or mostly underground, and is usually covered by a mound of earth and stone slabs. It is generally found near a settlement and may have been used as a storeroom or as a refuge, or both. Many date to the 2nd and 1st centuries BC, and the earliest are from Brittany, c. mid-1st millennium BC. (*syn.* fougou; souterrain)

folk traditions: Local traditions and beliefs associated with small-scale egalitarian societies or the nonelite antecedents of complex societies, usually expressed in media other than writing.

Folsom: A village in northeastern New Mexico, which lends its name to the remains of a prehistoric culture first found there and especially to its characteristic projectile point (Folsom point). It was a Stone Age culture, characterized by refinement of fluted projectile points, marking a significant advance over the projectile points of the earlier Clovis culture. The culture is believed to be 10,000 to 13,000 years old (11,000–10,200 BP). It was the scene of one of the first New World discoveries of artifacts associated with extinct fauna (the remains of 23 extinct giant bison). Folsom points are usually dated between c. 9000–8000 BC. Folsom points are slightly different from Clovis: They are smaller, with their widest dimension near the middle rather than toward the base, more concave base than Clovis, and the edges of Folsom points were retouched. Another site, Blackwater Draw, has its Folsom layer dated to 8340 BC. (*syn.* Folsom culture)

Folsom point: A distinctive Palaeo Indian fluted projectile point with a single flute on each face and fine pressure flaking. Found in sites around Folsom, New Mexico, from c. 9000–8000 BC (alternatively 11,000–10,200 BP), they differ from Clovis points in the length of the flute, which extends over most of the point's side. Folsom points are smaller, with their widest dimension near the middle rather than toward the base, more concave base than Clovis, and the edges of Folsom points were retouched. (*syn.* Folsom projectile point)

Fontbouïsse: A Chalcolithic (Copper Age) settlement site in Gard, France, which has given its name to a style of pottery decorated with channeled decoration usually arranged in metopic or concentric semicircle patterns. Fontbouïsse ware is widespread in southern France, occurring in chamber tombs, village sites, burial caves, natural rock clefts, and small cremation cysts. It is also the name of a cultural group known for its dry-stone houses, megalithic tombs and caves used for burials, and associated with extensive flint mining and the first evidence of copper working in the area.

Fontbrégoua: Cave site in southern France with Epipalaeolithic and Neolithic occupations, dating to c. 8000 BC. Hunting and gathering remains are hazelnuts and plants; there was domestic livestock and pottery of the Cardial and Epicardial phases. Neolithic remains include pits of human bones with cut marks and pits of butchered animal bones, possibly evidence for cannibalism. There are also Middle Neolithic Chasséen, Late Neolithic, and Bell Beaker artifacts.

Font de Gaume: A painted cave close to Les Eyzies in the Dordogne region, southwest France. Excavations have revealed archaeological levels deep in the interior, spanning several earlier Upper Palaeolithic phases, but the polychrome paintings of bison and other animals date from the late Magdalenian at the end of the Palaeolithic (c. 14,000–10,000 BC). (*syn.* Font-de-Gaume)

Fontéchevade: A French cave site in the Charente region, dated to the Riss glaciation. It has fragments of a human skull in association with chopping tools of Tayacian or Clactonian character dating from the Riss or Riss-Würm Interglacial period. The Fontéchevade skull has been classified as pre- or early Neanderthal. The upper levels are Middle and Upper Palaeolithic material.

food chain: The set of relations among plant and animal species in an ecosystem through which energy is channeled. (*syn.* food web)

food-producing revolution: A term used to describe the development of farming and animal husbandry and the beginning of settled village life. The first indications of the beginning of the revolution from food gathering to food producing are found in approximately 9000 BC. The change is associated with great improvements in making stone tools. Digging sticks and the first crude plows, stone sickles, querns that ground grain by friction between two stones, and irrigation techniques for keeping the ground watered and fertile— all these became well established in the great subtropical river valleys of Egypt and Mesopotamia before 3000 BC. The coming of the Iron Age to southern Africa almost 2,000 years ago brought with it the food-producing revolution. Agriculture combined with pastoralism supported much larger settled communities than had been possible and enabled more complex social and political organizations to develop. (*syn.* Neolithic Revolution)

food vessel: One of the two main cultures of the Bronze Age; the name given to a series of pottery vessels in northern Britain, Scotland, and Ireland. It was a prototype derived from that of the Beaker Folk and other Neolithic cultures. The food vessel culture people were hunters and farmers, raising sheep and growing corn. They also sold bronze and other metal goods made in Ireland. They buried food vessels with their dead (inhumation, in crouched positions, buried in cists under cairns or barrows). In the graves, too, are found the crescent-shaped necklaces of jet and shale beads and gold necklaces of the same shape (lunula) from Ireland. There are also bronze halbards, axes, daggers, earrings of gold and bronze, bone hairpins, and plano-convex flint knives. The culture is dated to 2000–1600 BC. (*syn.* food vessel culture)

foot survey: Archaeological reconnaissance on foot; the direct observation of a surface by walking over it. It is often carried out with a set interval between members of the survey team, and surface features and artifacts are plotted on a site map. Excavation is determined from this primary information. (*syn.* ground survey)

foraging system: The movement of people to search for resources.

foramen magnum: A large oval opening in the base of the skull through which the medulla oblongata passes, linking the spinal cord and brain. Its position is an indication of posture. If the foramen magnum is far forward on the skull base, it indicates an upright posture, like that of humans, with the head balanced on top of the spine. In four-footed animals, the head hangs from the end of the vertebral column, and the foramen magnum is placed posteriorly. In apes, with the assumption of semierect posture, the foramen moved partially downward and forward. In human evolution, the foramen magnum has continued to move forward as an aspect of adaptation to walking on two legs, until the head became balanced vertically on top of the vertebral column.

foramina: Any of a wide variety of holes in bones for nerves, blood vessels, and so on.

ford: A shallow part of a body of water that may be crossed; the commonest route across a river is often a ford.

Ford, James Alfred (1911–1968): American archaeologist who worked mainly in southeastern United States and developed the technique of seriation of chronological ordering. He established the archaeological sequence of ceramic typology, seriation, and stratigraphy of coastal Peru. Ford argued that archaeological types were imposed on data by the classifier.

foreshaft: The front part of something, as of a projectile point. (*syn.* fore-shaft)

forest clearance: The cutting down of natural vegetation before the planting of crops or grazing of domestic animals. Early on, clearings would be produced by the slash and burn method. Evidence for this process is provided by pollen analysis, in the form of a sharp decline in the proportion of tree pollen, corresponding with a rise in the pollen of grasses, including the cereals, and weeds of cultivation, especially plantains and goosefoots.

forging: In metalworking, the heating of a metal to soften it and then working it by hammering. It is a process used for the working of iron and steel after smelting. Although copper and other metals can be worked "cold" with occasional annealing, this procedure is not suitable for iron and steel. Forging involves the heating of the bloom to red heat and hammering. This would be carried out on a flat anvil with a hammer to remove impurities and the remains of slag. The resulting bars of iron could then be thinned down and hammered into shape again, continuously heating the iron and hammering while red hot. During the forging process, iron can be bent, flanges or other features introduced, or sheet metal produced.

form: The physical characteristics—size, shape, composition, arrangement—of any archaeological find or any component of a culture. Form is an essential part of attribute analysis; in archaeological research, the first objective is to describe and analyze the physical attributes of data to determine distributions in time and space. This process leads to form classifications. For example, the shape of a pot or other tool directly reflects its function. (*syn.* formal difference, formal dimension, form attribute, form analysis, form type)

formal context: The affinity of an object to a general class of objects sharing general characteristics of form.

formation process: The total of the processes—natural and cultural, individual and combined—that affected the formation and development of the archaeological record. Natural formation processes refer to natural or environmental events that govern the burial and survival of the archaeological record. Cultural formation processes include the deliberate or accidental activities of humans. On a settlement site, for example, the nature of human occupation, the activities carried out, the pattern of breakage and loss of material, rubbish disposal, rebuilding, or reuse of the same area all influence the surviving archaeological deposits. After the site's abandonment, it is further affected by such factors as erosion, glaciation, later agriculture, the activities of plants and animals, as well as the natural processes of chemical action in the soil. Reconstruction of these processes helps to relate the observed evidence of an archaeological site to the human activity responsible for it. (*syn.* site formation process)

Formative: A cultural stage in North America when agriculture and village settlement were developed, accompanied by pottery, weaving, stonecarving, and ceremonial objects and architecture. In the New World, especially Mesoamerica, it is also called the Pre-Classic period and preceded the Classic Period. The period was also characterized by initial complex societies (chiefdoms) and long-distance trade networks. In Mesoamerica, it is divided into Early (2000–1000 BC), Middle (1000–300 BC), and Late (300 BC–AD 300). In Andean, South America, the period is usually framed within the period 1800–1 BC and includes the Initial period and Early Horizon. It begins with the introduction of ceramics. This occurred c. 7600 bp in Amazonia and c. 5200 bp in northwest Columbia. (*syn.* Pre-Classic-Formative period; Preclassic)

formulation: The first stage in archaeological research design, involving definition of the research problem and goals, background investigations, and feasibility studies. It is the process of making decisions about a research project before formal research design.

formula dating: Absolute dating using artifact attributes, especially applied to pipe stems and ceramics.

fort: A fortified place or position prepared for defensive or protective purposes and usually surrounded by a ditch, rampart, and parapet. Forts were first built on hilltops, from late Neolithic to Roman times. Even farmhouses had earthworks of ditch, rampart, and wooden stockade built against raiding parties. At first, stockades were built on hilltops without massive earthworks. The origins of fortification in the Greek and Roman world were probably influenced by eastern Mediterranean civilizations and arose in the major cities of the Greek Bronze Age. In ancient days, fortifications hindered the best attacking troops for months and even years. (*syn.* fortress, fortification)

Fort Ancient: A series of cultures along the Ohio River and its tributaries, dating to AD 900–1600. There were developed agriculture, platform and burial mounds, and palisaded houses with a Mississippian influence.

Fort Harrouard: A Middle Neolithic fort in Eure-et-Loire, France, occupied until the Gaul-Roman period. There was a Chasséen phase with decorated vase supports and terra-cotta female figurines, an Artenacien occupation, and evidence of metallurgy in the Middle and Late Bronze Age (crucibles, molds, etc.).

Fort Rock Cave: An ancient Pleistocene site in Oregon dated to over 13,000 BP and associated sites with a long sequence of occupation in the same lake basin. Deposits of pumice from an eruption of nearby Mount Mazama in c. 5000 bc provided excellent chronological control for these sites. Associated artifacts, including a mano and metate, projectile points, and other stone artifacts, indicate an early hunting and gathering subsistence pattern for this period. Later contexts contain artifacts of the Desert Tradition. Occupation continued into historic times, but looting has caused the archaeological record to be unreliable after c. 1000 BC. (*syn.* Fort Rock Basin)

forum: The administrative center and marketplace of a Roman town, usually placed at the intersection of the main streets, the decumanus and cardo. The square served as a meeting- and/or marketplace; it corresponded to the Greek agora. Public notices were displayed on the basilica. Inside the basilica, the court of law met, functions of the town hall were carried out, and businessmen discussed deals. The forum was the main shopping center, with rows of shops having colonnades in front, most having fronts open to the forum. The main baths and temples were adjacent to the forum. The Roman Forum (Forum Romanum) was important from the time of the republic onward, and various emperors built fora of their own: Caesar, Augustus, Vespasian, Nerva, and Trajan. Most include a temple (sometimes the capitolium), peristyle courtyard, basilica, comitium, and curia. (*syn.* pl. fora)

forum ware: A distinctive green glazed pottery found in the 19th-century excavations of the Forum in Rome. This ware has since been found on many sites close to Rome and in settlements of all types in southern Etruria. Typically there are pitchers, often with incised wavy-line decoration around the body of the pot. The ware belongs to the late 6th or early 7th century, a phase of Late Roman activity.

Fosse Way: A Roman road in England, from Devon to Lincoln (southwest to northeast), marking the line originally chosen by the invading Romans as the frontier of the new province before AD 47. The road was needed to link a line of forts. The line, however, proved unsatisfactory, and the frontier was soon pushed northward, leaving Fosse Way to serve as a major cross-country trunk route of the expanded province.

fossil: In palaeontology, the organic remains, impression, imprint, traces, or mineral replacement of an animal or plant organism of a past geologic age preserved in the strata of the earth's crust. Only a small fraction of ancient organisms are preserved as fossils, and usually only organisms that have a solid and resistant skeleton are preserved.

fossil beach: A former beach, now situated above sea or lake level. Vertical displacement may be caused by isostatic crust changes or eustatic sea-level fluctuations. (*syn.* raised beach)

fossil cuticles: The outermost layer of the skin of leaves or blades of grass, made of cutin, a very resistant, protective material that survives in the archaeological record often in feces. Cuticular analysis is useful to palynology in environmental reconstruction.

fossil ice wedges: Soil features caused when the ground freezes and contracts, opening up fissures in the permafrost that fill with wedges of ice. The fossil wedges are proof of past cooling of climate and of the depth of permafrost. Foliated ground ice, or wedge ice, is the term for large masses of ice growing in thermal contraction cracks in permafrost. (*syn.* foliated ground ice, wedge ice)

fossiles directeurs: Classes of lithic artifacts associated with specific periods and archaeological cultures of the European Palaeolithic. (*syn.* type fossils)

fossil ivory: Ivory furnished by the tusks of the mammoth preserved in great quantity in Siberian ice. It is the material of which nearly all ivory turners' work in Russia is made. The ivory has not undergone any petrifying change like other fossils, and it can be used for artifact manufacture as easily as tusks from living animals.

foundation deposit: A collection of objects buried in the walls or under the floors of a building to ensure the goodwill of the gods to the householder(s).

Fourneau du Diable: A cave in the northern part of the Dordogne, southwest France, occupied during the Upper Palaeolithic, with Perigordian, Solutrian and Magdalenian deposits. It is one of only two sites where Solutrian art is well exemplified.

Four Sons of Horus: The Egyptian gods who protected the internal organs of the deceased. From the 19th Dynasty, canopic jars' lids were shaped like the heads of these gods. Wax figures of these deities were often placed within the mummy wrappings; sometimes the appropriate figure was placed with the wrapped, prepared internal organ, which was specifically under its protection.

Fox, Sir Cyril (1882–1967): British archaeologist who made important contributions to the development of field archaeology in the 1920s–1930s. With Wheeler, he led the development of excavation techniques in Britain, and he is also remembered for his geographical approach to archaeological problems, as in his *Archaeology of the Cambridge Region* (1923) and *Personality of Britain* (1932) in which he described the concept of a division of Britain into highland and lowland zones.

Franchthi Cave: A prehistoric cave site on the Bay of Argos in the Peloponnese of Greece with dates to c. 22,000–10,300 BP. An Epipalaeolithic occupation (c. 10,000 BC) was succeeded after an interval by a Mesolithic (c. 7500–6000 BC) with dozens of burials and some possible cremations. Excavations at the Franchthi Cave showed that boats already sailed to the island of Melos north of Crete for obsidian by about 13,000–11,000 BC and that the cultivation of hybrid grains, the domestication of animals, and organized community tuna hunts had already begun, marking the transition from hunting and gathering. A little later, the first pottery appeared. Late Upper Palaeolithic artifacts included small backed blades and geometric microliths.

Frankfort, Henri (1897–1954): A Dutch-American archaeologist who completed a well-documented reconstruction of Early Dynastic Mesopotamian culture, established the relation between Egypt and Mesopotamia, and discovered much new information on both civilizations. A historian, he worked at Abydos, Amarnà, Armant in Egypt, and in Iraq as head of the University of Chicago's Diyala project. He published important works on pottery and cylinder seals as well as a study of kingship, religious attitudes, and art in western Asia and Egypt.

Franks: A Germanic-speaking people who invaded the western Roman Empire in the 5th century AD. Dominating present-day northern France, Belgium, and western Germany, the Franks established the most powerful Christian kingdom of early medieval western Europe. The name France (Francia) is derived from their name. They originally settled to the east of the Rhine and expanded west from the later 3rd and early 4th centuries. The Frankish kingdom was increased in size by Clovis (481–511) to occupy much of Roman Gaul, but reached its greatest extent under Charlemagne. The archaeology of the Franks is best known from their cemeteries and the goods interred in them. Many Roman manufacturing industries were preserved by the Franks, but they introduced Germanic craftsmanship, arts, and building techniques.

Fraser River: A complex of sites in the Fraser River delta in British Columbia, Canada, showing the sequence of the Northwest Coast tradition of three periods: Early 1000 BC–AD 1; Intermediate AD 1–1250; and Late from AD 1250. Three culturally distinct areas (the Canyon, the Plateau, and the Delta) contain evidence of the differing influences on the Northwest Coast tradition materials. Canyon sites provide evidence of a long occupation covering Big Game Hunting tradition, Old Cordilleran culture, and Archaic. Taken together, the sites indicate a movement from inland to the coast beginning c. 2000 BC.

Fremont culture: An agricultural Puebloan people found throughout much of present-day Utah between AD 400–1350. There is some similarity to the Anasazi in pottery types and pit house architecture. Hunting and gathering was most important, supplemented by the growing of maize, beans, and squash.

frequency difference: A method of defining variation in associated artifacts by differences in their rate of distribution at various sites.

frequency seriation: A relative age determination technique in which artifacts or other archaeological data are chronologically ordered by ranking their relative frequencies of appearance. It is based on the idea that an artifact type first steadily grows in popularity and then steadily declines.

Frere, John (1740–1807): A British antiquary who first recognized the antiquity of Palaeolithic flint artifacts. His flint weapon finds in the Hoxne brick-earth pit in Suffolk in association with bones of extinct mammals in an undisturbed deep stratum was reported in 1797. Frere recognized that the implements were manmade, "fabricated and used by a people who had not the use of metals," and suggested that they should be referred to "a very remote period indeed; even beyond that of the present world." His ideas were in advance of his time, and his conclusions were ignored largely because they contradicted the accepted Creation date of 4004 BC.

fresco: A method of painting on the plastered surface of a wall or ceiling before the plaster has dried so that the colors become incorporated in it. The term refers to any painting done on freshly laid wet plaster and left to dry with the plaster; the painting becomes part of the wall. It was usually executed with mineral and earth pigments on a freshly laid ground of stucco. Lime, which is part of fresco, was found in nearly all the colors of Pompeii.

frieze: A decorative band or feature, as a long band of relief sculpture decorating the upper stonework of a temple. It is the zone above the epistyle, decorated with triglyphs and metopes in the Doric order or sculpture or dentils in Ionic order architecture. This type of band of decoration on a wall or vessel may be painted or in bas-relief.

frigidarium: The cold room of a Roman bath house with a cold plunge bath. It was located close to the apodyterium.

Frisians: A Germanic people inhabiting the North Sea coastal plain and islands between the Rhineland and the Elbe (Frisia) in the early centuries BC and AD. Their coastal settlements were on artificial mounds known as *terpen*. The Frisians were involved in the invasion of England by the Anglo-Saxons in the 5th century AD. They controlled the trade of the North Sea from the port of Dorestad at the mouth of the Rhine, which became a target for Viking raids. Frisia was absorbed into the Frankish kingdom, its conquest being completed by Charlemagne. Archaeological evidence of these trading ventures is seen at Dorestad, where extensive excavations have been done. Evidence in the mounded villages show signs of long-distance trade contacts, suggesting that the Frisians linked the Rhineland to the northern world from the beginning of the Roman period until modern times.

frit: The vitreous compound from which soft porcelain is made; the fusible ceramic mixture used to make glazes and enamels for dinnerware and metallic surfaces. In the manufacture of glaze, the oxides are normally suspended in water for application, but some compounds (e.g., potassium and sodium) are very water soluble and if applied directly would be absorbed into the pot. Therefore, the raw materials are fused together under heat to form an insoluble glass known as frit. The frit is powdered, suspended in water, and applied to the pot.

Fromms Landing: A limestone shelter site in the Lower Murray River Valley of South Australia with human occupation from c. 3000 BC and deposits spanning 5,000 years. The evidence parallels the nearby sequence of Devon Downs and includes stone artifacts (Pirri points and microliths) and a well-preserved dingo skeleton dated to 1000–1200 BC.

frontlet: The forehead of an animal, as the upper skull and antlers of a deer or stag.

frost marks: Variations in the amount of frost retained on the ground, which indicates the presence of buried archaeological features, detected primarily by aerial photography. The differential retention of frost in hollows and over different types of material can reveal the features of an archaeological site.

froth flotation: Flotation in which the separation is enhanced by using a liquid to which a frothing agent, such as a detergent, has been added and bubbling air through it, forming a froth in which certain lightweight materials collect. Soil samples agitated in froth flotation, such as seeds and charcoal fragments, can be more easily separated from the matrix by this method.

frying pan: A term used to describe any shallow circular vessel or bowl with a decorated base found in the Early Bronze Age of the Cyclades, especially the Cycladic Grotta-Pelos and Keros-Syros cultures. Made of clay, the handle was split into two knob-like projections, and the stamped or incised decoration often included spirals. The vessel's purpose is unknown, perhaps ritual but not for cooking. It has been suggested that when filled with water it was used as a mirror. The resemblance to a frying pan is superficial and certainly misleading.

Fuchsberg: A Neolithic pottery style of the Danish Early and Middle Neolithic, c. 3400 BC. It was characterized by rich incised decoration and has been found at Sarup and Toftum.

Fudodo: Middle Jomon site in Japan with an impressive oval pit building, which was likely a communal gathering place or workplace.

Fuegian tradition: A primitive people inhabiting the South American archipelago of Tierra del Fuego from c. 2000 BC. The culture, a coastal tradition of the Alacaluf tribes, was often called the Shell Knife culture. It was based on the exploitation of marine resources and operative on the south-ern coast and offshore islands of southern Chile. The beginning of the tradition was marked by a change from land-oriented hunting and gathering; bone and stone tool technology persisted well into historic times. The primitive cultures of the Ona and Yámana (Yahgan) of Tierra del Fuego are so similar that anthropologists traditionally group them with the neighboring Chono and Alakaluf of Chile into this one "Fuegian culture area." The Ona inhabit the interior forests and depend heavily on hunting guanaco (a small New World camel). The Yámana are canoe-using fishermen and shellfish gatherers. They are all nomadic and are sparsely scattered over the landscape and poor in material culture. (*syn.* Shell Knife culture)

Fufeng: A district north of the Wei River in central Shaanxi province, China, rich in Western Chou/Zhou (1122–771 BC) remains. The area was the center of Chou power for several generations preceding the founding of the Chou Dynasty, and the dynastic capital Zong Zhou may also have been here. Excavations have revealed a palace complex dating from the early and middle Western Chou. A hoard of 103 ritual vessels and bells is the single most important find of Western Chou bronzes ever made; the contents of the hoard span nearly the whole of the Western Chou period. (*syn.* Fu-feng)

Fu Hao (fl. 12th c. BC): A consort of the late Shang king, Wu-ting, the fourth Shang ruler of Anyang. Fu Hao is mentioned in many oracle bone texts and on bronze ritual vessels. Her tomb, discovered at Anyang Xiaotun in 1976, is the only royal tomb of the Shang period found intact and the only one whose occupant could be identified (by the 500 bronze vessels). The tomb was a small pit without entrance ramps, but its furnishings were very rich. Besides the bronze ritual vessels, 200 bronze weapons and tools, 600 jades and stone carvings, 500 objects of carved bone and ivory, 4 bronze mirrors, 7,000 cowrie shells (used as money), and 16 sacrificial victims were revealed. The discovery has an important bearing on the chronology of Shang art and the periodization of oracle bone texts.

Fujinoki: A mounded tomb in Nara Prefecture, Japan, of the late 7th century AD, with a stone sarcophagus full of horse paraphernalia and gilt-bronze ornaments.

Fujiwara: The site of the first urban capital of the Chinese Chang'an model in Nara Prefecture, Japan, built in AD 694. It was abandoned after only 20 years for Heijo.

Fukui: A deep stratified rock shelter in Nagasaki Prefecture, Japan, of the Late Palaeolithic and yielding Initial Jomon pottery (with geometric designs) together with obsidian microliths. The stone tools from the oldest layer, dated older than 31,900 years, are among the earliest evidence of human occupation of Japan. Microblades continue into the two early ceramic layers, suggesting a continuity in stone tools when pottery making began in Japan. The older ceramic layer, dated to 10,650 bc, contained linear-relief pottery, while the younger one, dated to 10,450 bc, included fingernail-impressed ware. The ceramics have been dated by radiocarbon to 12,700 BP, the earliest occurrence in the world of ceramic vessels.

fulcrum: In Roman antiquity, the curved raised end of a Roman banquet couch.

full-time specialist: A nonfood producer who earns a living by an occupation other than farming and who must exchange goods or services for food.

Funan: The Chinese name for an early kingdom of Southeast Asia, founded in the 1st century AD and recorded as a trading partner of China from at least the 3rd century AD. Located in the lower Mekong region of Cambodia and southern Vietnam, this Indianized state was strategically situated on the trade routes between India and China. It was conquered by the Khmer state of Chenla in the 7th century. There is abundant information about the material culture of Funan from excavations, notably those of Oc-eo, thought to have been its main port, and from Angkor Borei.

function: The purpose or use of a component in a culture. The second goal of archaeological research is analysis of data and their relations to determine function and this to reconstruct and create synchronic descriptions of ancient behavior. It is a model of culture that is keyed to the functions of its various components, which unite into a single system or structure. (*syn.* functional concept)

functional attribute: Any characteristic of an object that indicates its function, such as its form or a residue from an activity for which it was used.

functional type: Classification based on cultural use or function rather than on outward form or chronological position.

F-U-N dating or F.U.N. dating: A collective term for the techniques of fluorine, uranium, and nitrogen dating. It is a relative dating technique, which compares concentrations of fluorine, uranium, or nitrogen in various samples from the same matrix to determine contemporaneity. (*syn.* F-U-N method)

funeral urn: The receptacle in which the ashes are placed after cremation. (*syn.* funeral pot)

funerary cones: Egyptian solid pottery cones, 10–30 centimeters in length, which were placed at the entrances to tombs, often with the name and titles of the deceased on the flat, circular end. Found mainly in the Theban area of Middle Kingdom to Late Period dates (2125–332 bc), these cones were originally inserted in the brick-built tomb facade or tomb pyramid to form horizontal rows. Most belong to the New Kingdom and the bulk of them to the 18th Dynasty (1550–1295 bc).

funerary cult: Any of a number of ongoing rituals, with their associated offerings, performed for the benefit of the deceased at the tomb or in a funerary temple. Cults were mainly made up of relatives or specially appointed priests. Funerary or mortuary temples were the shrines for the funerary cults of dead kings.

funerary monument: In many cultures and civilizations, the tomb was superseded by, or coexisted with, monuments or memorials to the dead. This foreshadowed a general revival of the Greek practice of erecting funerary monuments, rather than tombs, during Hellenistic times.

funerary offering: Any items provided initially by mourners and later, magically, through inscriptions and pictures in the tomb. Funerary offerings are "essential" for the well-being of the *ka* in Egyptian tradition. Funerary offerings present rich documentary evidence of a culture.

funerary texts: The Egyptians' compositions—mainly the Coffin Texts and the Pyramid Texts—relating to death and the afterlife. They probably originated in preliterate oral tradition. The earliest such writings are the Pyramid Texts, the first examples of which were inscribed in the 5th Dynasty pyramid of Unas (2375–2345 BC) at Saqqara. These texts were prepared by the officiants in temple cults. Most of the vast corpus of funerary texts is magical in character, with spells and formulas. The Coffin Texts, combined with the Pyramid Texts from which they were derived, were the primary sources of the Book of the Dead, which was in prominent use during the New Kingdom and Late period.

funnel beaker: A vessel with a globular body and expanded neck, characteristic of the Early and Middle Neolithic culture of northern Europe. The funnel beaker is not directly related to the bell beaker of central and western Europe. The complex culture represents the first agriculturists in Scandinavia and the north European plain, appearing from 3500 BC onward. It is named after the characteristic pottery, which is often found in megalithic tombs in northern Germany. (*syn.* funnel-necked beaker culture; funnel [neck] beaker; Trichterbecher or TRB)

Fustát, al-: The capital of the Muslim province of Egypt during the Umayyad and 'Abbasid caliphates, and under succeeding dynasties, until captured by the Fatimid Jawhar in 969. Founded in 641 by the Muslim conqueror of Egypt, 'Amr ibn al-'As, on the east bank of the Nile, south of modern Cairo, al-Fustát was the earliest Arab settlement in Egypt and site of the province's first mosque, Jami' 'Amr. It was burnt to the ground in 1168; it was rebuilt by Saladin, who joined it with Cairo. Fustát ware is a style of pottery originating from al-Fustát. Characteristic qualities are white glaze and pigments from lemon to intense copper in color. Some pieces are incised and covered with transparent glaze. (*syn.* Al-Fostát)

futhark: The writing system of uncertain origin used by Germanic peoples of northern Europe, Britain, Scandinavia, and Iceland from about the 3rd century to the 16th or 17th century AD. Runic writing appeared rather late in the history of writing and is clearly derived from one of the alphabets of the Mediterranean area. It has angular letter forms, which were written from right to left like the earliest alphabets. It is so named from its first six symbols. (*syn.* runic alphabet)

Füzesabony: The third stage of the early Hungarian Bronze Age, named after the Tószeg Tell in Heves. The Füzesabony culture of the 21st–19th centuries BC is the Hungarian version of the Transylvanian/Rumanian Otomani culture. Most known settlements are unfortified tells with wattle-and-daub timber-framed houses, sometimes with plank and beam floors. There are large cemeteries, usually with inhumation burial. Notable finds are antler cheek pieces for horse bits.

fynbos: The vegetation of the Cape Floristic Kingdom of Cape Province, South Africa, which has an unusually high number of species but is treeless and almost grassless. Its shrub-filled area has been important for approximately 125,000 years.

Fyrkat: A great circular fortress in northern Jutland dating to the mid-10th century AD. Fyrkat, close to the open sea, is now generally believed to have been a royal center rather than an encampment for warriors. Like the other Trelleborg-type fortresses, the site was probably abandoned early in the 11th century as the Danish kings founded new towns and built small palaces in them.

Gg

Gabillou: An Upper Palaeolithic cave site in Dordogne, southwest France, with Magdalenian levels, including numerous engravings. The engravings are among the finest and most delicate ever found from the Palaeolithic period.

Gades: A city of southwestern Spain, which was prosperous in antiquity for more than a millennium as a commercial port. It was founded by Phoenicians from Tyre around 1100 BC, but a date in the 7th or 8th century BC is perhaps more plausible. Prosperity declined with the rise of nearby Hispalis (Seville) in the 2nd century AD. Trade and fishing are reported on early coins; trade was strongly associated with the area's metallurgy. By the 1st century BC, Gades seems to have had a significant market in tin mining and the tin trade. It defected from the Carthaginian side to Rome in 206 BC. It was known to the Romans for its gaiety and exotic pleasures. (*syn.* Phoenician Gadir, modern Cádiz)

gadroon: A decorative pattern used in the ornamentation of gold and silver metalwork and pottery, consisting of an embossed tear shape. A gadroon is one of a set of convex curves or arcs joined at their ends to form this pattern, usually one of a series radiating from the base of a work.

Gagarino: An Upper Palaeolithic site in the Don River basin in European Russia. The artifacts, including shouldered points and Venus figurines, have been assigned to the Kostenki Willendorf culture or the Eastern Gravettian as the dates are 30,000–21,800 bp. The people were mammoth hunters who also carved bone and ivory.

Galindo: A Middle Horizon site in the Moche Valley of coastal Peru. The small local group of people may have been under control of the Huari Empire, but the valley was largely abandoned by the Moche culture by this time.

gallery grave: A tunnel-shaped megalithic tomb of Europe, characterized by a rectangular chamber with no separate entrance passage. The structures therefore resemble a megalithic corridor under an elongated mound, although sometimes they are cut in the rock. Gallery graves are frequently but not always found under long barrows; they may be subdivided (segmented) or have additional side chambers (transepted). They are sometimes associated with elaborate facades and forecourts. Local variants are distributed in Catalonia, France, the British Isles, northward as far as Sweden, as well as in Sardinia and south Italy. Most of the tombs were built during the Neolithic period from the early 4th millennium BC on and were still in use during the Copper Age when Beaker pottery was introduced; the Sardinian examples belong to the full Bronze Age. Many contain multiple burials. (*syn.* allée couverte)

Gallery Hill: A site in Western Australia with petroglyphs of tracks, circles, animals, and some human figures. Later pecked engravings show a wide range of subjects, including anthropomorphs.

Gallinazo: A pottery style and culture of the first phase of the Early Intermediate Period, flourishing c. 200 BC–AD 200 on the north-central coast of Peru (Virú Valley). Together with the slightly earlier Salinar, the Gallinazo culture is seen as transitional from Chavín-associated groups, such as Cupisnique, to the rise of the Moche state. It is related to the contemporary Recuay style of the highlands. The best-known Gallinazo pottery is black-on-orange negative resist decorated ware. The type site appears to have been a ceremonial center with a nucleus of adobe mounds and walled courtyards. Residential apartment complexes are scattered over an area around the center; it was abandoned some time after the rise of Moche.

Gallurus Oratory: A boat-shaped oratory on the Dingle peninsula in Kerry, Ireland, one of the few examples of pre-11th century Irish ecclesiastical architecture to have survived. It seems to have belonged to a building tradition that falls between the beehives of the 6th and 7th centuries and the first stone churches of the 11th and 12th centuries. The building is constructed of large, flat corbelled stones, with inward-sloping walls apexing in a gable at each end.

Gamberian: A distinctive Early Holocene industry of coastal southeast South Australia and southwest Victoria, with retouched flint flake tools.

Gamble's Cave: A cave in the central Rift Valley of Kenya with a long sequence attributed to the Eburran industry (formerly known as the Upper Kenya Capsian), followed by Elmenteitan assemblages.

Gamio, Manual (1883–1960): Mexican archaeologist, one of the first to work in Mesoamerica and to excavate using metric stratigraphy. He carried out a monumental study of the populations of Teotihuacán Valley and set up a ceramic sequence for the Valley of Mexico.

Gandhara: A culture of the 2nd and 1st millennia BC in the valleys of northwestern Pakistan—and the Achaemenid (Persian) satrapy of this name. This culture was important in passing Persian ideas on to the civilizations of the Ganges Valley. It also introduced Hellenistic art styles to India. Western influence is also apparent in the grid town planning found at the Gandharan cities of Charsada and Taxila. Characteristic burials are in tombs consisting of two small chambers, one on top of the other; the lower chamber contained both the burial (inhumed or cremated) and the grave goods, while the upper chamber was empty. The population, which bred livestock and carried out agriculture, were accomplished metalworkers, producing tools, weapons, and ornaments of copper, bronze, gold, silver, and iron. The pottery in the grave goods was mostly a red or gray plain burnished type. (*syn.* Gandhara grave culture complex)

Ganges civilization: A city-state civilization by the 7th–6th centuries BC, characterized by extensive urban settlement and a developed social organization. The state engaged in long struggles for power, which ended in the 4th century BC with the establishment of the Mauryan Empire. Much of the information about the Ganges civilization comes from literary sources. Archaeological excavations have usually been on a small scale. Cities were large and usually fortified, often with massive mud ramparts. The characteristic pottery is northern black polished ware.

Gangetic hoards: Hoards of copper objects found in the Ganges basin in India. The main types of objects are flat and shouldered axes, bar chisels, barbed harpoons, antenna-hilted swords, hooked spears, and anthropomorphic objects. Associations with ochre-colored pottery suggest a date of the 2nd millennium BC.

Ganj Dareh, Tepe: A small mound in the Kermanshah region of western Iran, which has yielded five occupation levels with radiocarbon dates ranging from 8400–6800 BC. The lowest level had no permanent architecture, only shallow pits and hollows. The next level had mud-brick structures, mostly very small adjoining cubicles, perhaps used for storage. Subsequent phases include wattle-and-daub rectilinear structures and a wide range of unfired clay objects. Animal and human figurines suggest that the stone industry remained largely the same throughout. (*syn.* Ganj Dareh)

Gaocheng: Area in southern Hebei province, China, with widely scattered Shang remains. At Taixicun, the main occupation postdates the Erligang phase and has one radiocarbon date of c. 1500 BC. The site is dominated by three large rectangular Hangtu platforms and a large house foundation with sacrificial burials. Other graves yielded bronze ritual vessels, fragments of lacquer, and a bronze ax with a blade of meteoritic iron. Evidence suggests that it may be the location of a Shang capital occupied after Zhengzhou but before Anyang. (*syn.* Kao-ch'eng)

Garagay: An Initial period site occupied into the Early Horizon period, near Lima, Peru. There is a large U-shaped ceremonial formation and central mound estimated at 3000–1800 BC. There are Chavín-like clay figurines and pottery.

Garcel, El: A Middle Neolithic hilltop settlement in Almeria, southeast Spain, the type site of the earlier phase of the Almerian culture, c. 5th millennium BC. Excavations have produced evidence of wattle-and-daub round houses, storage pits, undecorated round- and pointed-based pottery and, before the end of the settlement, copper slag, suggesting the local development of metallurgy. (*syn.* El Garcel)

Gargas: A cave in southern France (Hautes-Pyrénées) containing important examples of Late Palaeolithic mural art, paintings, and engravings dating from the Aurignacian period, the oldest phase of European Stone Age art. The site was first known for its Ice Age fauna. There are approximately 150 engravings of animals and 250 red or black hand prints. A curious feature of these silhouettes is that many are representations of multilated hands with one or more finger joints missing, most frequently the last two joints of the last four fingers. The significance of the hand prints and the missing fingers is unknown. The cave was occupied from at least the Middle Palaeolithic, and the animal engravings are attributed to the Gravettian.

garrison state: A fortified state organized to serve primarily its own need for military security; also a state maintained by military power and established in a strategic position. The garrison states of the Zhou feudalistic network were protected by walled cities and ruled by kinsmen and allies through marriage with the Zhou royal house.

Garrod, Dorothy A. E. (1892–1968): A British archaeologist known for work on the Palaeolithic of England and Gibraltar and for extensive excavations at Mount Carmel, Palestine, uncovering skeletal remains of primary importance to the study of human evolution. Some authorities believe that these remains represent an intermediate stage between Neanderthal man and modern man. She and Dorothy Bate found a long sequence of Lower Palaeolithic to Epipalaeolithic cultures in several caves. Garrod also worked in southern Kurdistan, Bulgaria, France, and southern Lebanon. She was the first woman professor at Cambridge University.

Garstang, Professor John (1876–1956): British archaeologist prominent in Near Eastern archaeology, including his major excavations at Mersin (Turkey), Sakje Geuzi (Syria), Jericho (Palestine), Meroe (Sudan), Beni Hassan, Esna, and Abydos (Egypt). He made major contributions to the development of Near Eastern prehistory.

Gash: A series of sites in the Atbara region of Sudan with a food-producing economy and human burials indicating a social hierarchy. The main site is Mahal Teglinos.

gastrolith: A stone or pebble ingested by a fish, reptile, or bird for the purpose of grinding food to aid digestion.

Gatecliff Shelter: A prehistoric archaeological site in Monitor Valley of central Nevada with deposits spanning the last 7,000 years.

Gatung'ang'a: An early Iron Age site in the eastern highlands of Kenya, c. second half of the 1st millennium AD. The pottery has similarities with Kwale ware.

Gaudo: A Chalcolithic cemetery site in Campania, Italy, with 3rd millennium BC rock-cut tombs; the type site of the Campanian Gaudo culture. The tombs produced up to 25 disarticulated skeletons each and great quantities of highly burnished unusual pots, especially asymmetric straight-necked flasks (sometimes called askoi as they approximate the form of an askos). There were also cups, open dishes, lids, and double vessels. This group has parallels with Central Italian Rinaldone. There are flint arrowheads and daggers; metalwork is rare, but some copper daggers and awls occur and a few small silver objects.

Gaul: A Roman province formed by modern-day France and parts of Belgium, western Germany, northern Italy, and Switzerland. Cities were Nîmes, Autun, Arles, Orange, Trier, and Frejus. Caesar's conquests (58–51 BC) and Augustus's organization (30 BC–AD 14) resulted in four Gallic provinces: southern or "senatorial" Narbonensis, the "imperial" Aquitania, Lugdunensis, and Belgica. The region was inhabited by the ancient Gauls, a Celtic race, who lived in an agricultural society and were divided into several tribes ruled by a landed class. (*syn.* Gallia)

Gaviota: The name of a final preceramic phase, 2000–1750 BC, of the central Peruvian coast. There was sedentary agricultural village life and early construction of large ceremonial centers.

Gavrinis: A Neolithic rectangular cairn on an island in the Gulf of Morbihan, France, with one of the most elaborately decorated passage graves in Europe. The designs pecked into the walls include representations of polished stone axes as well as abstract patterns. The radiocarbon date is c. 3400 BC.

Gawra, Tepe: A tell site east of the Tigris River near Khorsabad, Iraq, occupied from the 6th–2nd millennia BC. The earliest material was of the Halaf period, while the succeeding period shows increasing contacts with the southern Mesopotamian 'Ubaid culture. It was a northern outpost of the 'Ibaid culture in the 5th–4th millennia. Three temples facing onto open courtyards show resemblance to works at Eridu and Warka. There is evidence for surprisingly extensive trade. Neolithic settlers used undecorated pottery and Halaf pottery. The succeeding period is contemporary with the Uruk and Jemdet Nasr periods to the south; this is often described as the Gawra period (late 4th millennium BC). In this period, there is abundant evidence for differential wealth and social position, seen in the grave goods. Several temples of the period have an unusual form with separate portico. The most distinctive building of this phase, however, is a circular structure known as the Round House.

Gaza: A Palestinian site under modern Gaza; the southernmost city of the Philistine Pentapolis. Philistines, Egyptians, and Peoples of the Sea occupied the site. The earliest evidence comes from two cemeteries, one to the north and one to the east of the main mound, with shaft graves containing pottery and daggers of the late 3rd millennium BC. On the tell itself, the earliest excavated remains are of the Middle Bronze Age (2nd millennium BC); earliest of all was a cemetery, underlying a large building interpreted by Flinders-Petrie as a palace of the Middle Bronze Age II period. This was succeeded by four other large buildings, of the later Bronze Age and early Iron Age. There are famous mosaics in the synagogue from c. 6th century AD and the Great Mosque, originally a cathedral of the 12th century AD.

Gdansk: A city situated on the mouth of the Vistula River in Poland, which evolved from the 12th century AD to become one of the most important trading centers of eastern Europe. A collection of Byzantine silks was an important archaeological find.

ge: A dagger-ax, the characteristic weapon of the Chinese Bronze Age during the Shang Dynasty and then made from iron from the Zhou Dynasty onward. The dagger-shaped bronze blade, usually with a flat tang but occasionally with a shaft hole, was mounted perpendicular to the wooden shaft. The blade had a crosspiece parallel to the shaft to help hold it in place. Bronze Age blades and nonfunctional jade replicas of blades often appear as mortuary gifts in Shang tombs. The earliest ge yet known have come from Erlitou, c. mid-2nd millennium BC. In the Eastern Zhou period, the ge was sometimes combined with a spear, the ge blade at right angles to the spearhead, to form a ji. The ji was in existence by the late 6th or early 5th century BC. They are chopping implements. (*syn.* ko)

Geb: The god of the earth, whose sister was the sky goddess Nut; they were of the second generation in the Ennead (group of nine gods) of Heliopolis. He was the third divine ruler among the gods; the human pharaohs claimed to be descended from him. He was the father of Osiris, Isis, Seth, and Nephthys.

Gebel Barkal: A mountain in Upper Nubia, which was a center of worship for Amen in the New Kingdom. A temple built by Ramesses II was extended by other rulers. There are nearby pyramids related to the Meroitic period.

Gedi: An early Swahili coastal town on the East African coast of Kenya. Gedi was probably founded around AD 1300 and enjoyed prosperity into at least the 16th century owing to the Indian Ocean trade and increased exploitation of Zimbabwean gold. The ruins of the houses and great mosque are well preserved.

Geissenklösterle: A cave in Baden-Württemberg, Germany, with Middle Palaeolithic, Aurignacian (36,000–34,000 bp), Gravettian (23,000 bp), Magdalenian, and Mesolithic material. The Aurignacian levels have ivory figurines and an ivory bas-relief of a human.

Gela: A colony in southern Sicily founded by Cretan and Rhodian colonists c. 688 BC, whose inhabitants founded Acragas (now Agrigento) in c. 581 BC. Gela was prosperous under the tyrant Hippocrates of Gela (498–491 BC), and his powerful successor, Gelon, who transferred his capital and half of the Gela population to Syracuse in 482 BC. Gela was refounded in 466 BC, but it was destroyed by the Carthaginians in 405 BC and abandoned by order of Dionysius I the Elder of Syracuse. It was refounded in the 4th century and again in 1233 by Frederick II and known as Terranova di Sicilia until 1928.

Geleen: A settlement of the Neolithic Linear Pottery culture in southern Holland, c. 6500 BP, which has produced house types similar to those of other Dutch sites of this culture, including Elsloo, Sittard, and Stein.

Gelidonya: A cape in southwest Turkey off which a Bronze Age merchant ship foundered in the 13th century BC. It was discovered in 1960, providing a classic example of underwater archaeology and useful information on the Mycenaeans. Its cargo consisted of pottery, bronze tools, and oxhide-shaped ingots of copper and tin from Cyprus.

gelifluction: A geologic process occurring when the active layer of permafrost moves under the influence of gravity. The soft flowing layer is often folded and draped on hillsides and at the base of slopes as solifluction, or gelifluction, lobes.

Gelifluction can cause destruction or redistribution of archaeological deposits.

gem: Any precious or semiprecious stone; this group also includes some animal and vegetable products with precious characteristics, such as amber, pearls, and coral. Conventionally, the following are classified as precious stones: diamonds, rubies (corundum), emeralds (beryl), and sapphires (corundum). Sometimes chrysoberyl, topaz, and zircon are added because of their hardness, refraction, and transparency index. Deeply engraved semiprecious or precious stones were used as seals. Engraved stones (intaglios) were found in the Middle Minoan period in Crete, but the technique of working stones fell out of use until the 7th century BC. In the 6th century BC, the scarab form of seal was introduced from Egypt, which developed into the Classical Greek gemstone technique.

gene: The basic unit of hereditary information that occupies a fixed position on a chromosome and is governed by the specific sequence of the genetic markers in the DNA of the individual concerned. Genes achieve their effects by directing the synthesis of proteins.

general analogy: An analogy used in archaeological interpretation based on broad and generalized comparisons that are documented across many cultural traditions. The broadest level of archaeological theory, referring to frameworks that describe and attempt to explain cultural processes that operated in the past. (*syn.* general theory)

general evolution: The long-term "progressive" change characteristic of human culture in general, as opposed to the short-term, localized social and ecological adjustments that cause specific cultures to differ from one another as they adapt to their own unique environments (specific evolution). It is the overall advance or progression stage by stage, as measured in absolute terms; the evolution from heterogeneity toward homogeneity.

general systems theory: A theory that human society can be studied as a system broken down into many interacting subsystems, or parts. It is the premise that any organization may be looked at to discover how its parts are related and how changes in either parts or their relations produce changes in the overall system. In archaeological terms, the system might be the whole of a society's culture, or some part of it such as the economy, or even a single settlement. Systems can be regarded as either open or closed; the latter have no input of energy or matter from the outside, tend to reach a state of stable equilibrium in which small changes can be offset, and eventually stagnate and disintegrate, while open systems have an input of energy from the outside, reach a state of unstable equilibrium in which any small change can produce significant transformations in the system as a whole, and are characterized by growth and change. The process by which a system tends to maintain equilibrium in the face of changed surroundings is termed homeostasis, while morphogenesis is the process by which the structure is changed or elaborated. (*syn.* cybernetics)

Genoa: A major medieval port that probably began as a Ligurian village on the Sarzano Hill overlooking the natural port (today Molo Vecchio). It prospered through contacts with the Etruscans and the Greeks and as a flourishing Roman municipium, became a road junction, military port, and a market of the Ligurians. After the fall of the Roman Empire and the invasions of Ostrogoths and Lombards, Genoa existed in comparative obscurity as a fishing and agrarian center with little trade. In medieval times, it competed with Venice, Pisa, and Florence for the trade of the Mediterranean. Eastern spices, dyestuffs and medicaments, western cloth and metals, African wool, skins, coral, and gold were the main articles of diversified international commerce. The medieval city wall enclosed a substantial area and dates to the 12th century. The notable project at the Cloister of San Silvestro, for example, revealed well-preserved buildings and a rich range of pottery from many parts of Italy and Spain.

genome: The collection of genes in the nucleic-acid core of a virus or the complete set of genetic material—the chromosomes and the genes they contain—that makes up any organism and determines hereditary features.

geoarchaeology: The techniques of geology applied to archaeological issues, such as dating methodology, mineral identification, soil and stratification analysis; the investigation of the relation between archaeological and geological processes. It is an ecological approach to archaeology with the goal of understanding the physical context of archaeological remains and the emphasis on the interrelations among cultural and land systems.

geochemical analysis: An investigatory technique that involves taking soil samples at regular intervals from the surface of a site and measuring their phosphate content and other chemical properties to determine the natural separation and concentration of elements by Earth processes.

geochronology: The study of Earth history by correlating archaeological events to the timing and sequencing of geological events. Specifically, it is the dating of archaeological data in association with a geological deposit or formation, such as the dating of Pleistocene human remains in the context of glacial advances and retreats. The term is applied to all absolute and relative dating methods that involve the Earth's physical changes, like radiocarbon dating, dendrochronology, archaeomagnetism, fluorine testing, obsidian dating, potassium argon dating, thermoluminescence, and varve dating. (*syn.* geological dating)

geofact: Any mineral or rock resource found in an archaeological site; it can reveal evidence of a nearby quarry, and so on.

geoglyph: (jee-uh-glif) Any ground-constructed example of rock art, such as intaglios or rock alignments, straight lines, geometric shapes, and other representative designs found on the desert plain. Geoglyphs can be formed by piling up materials on the ground surface or by removing surface materials, and most suggest a largely ceremonial function. (*syn.* Nasca lines; Nazca Lines)

Geographical Society Cave: An Upper Palaeolithic site in eastern Siberian with faunal remains dating to 32,570 bp. The artifacts include pebble cores, flakes, and a scraping tool.

Geographic Information Systems: Computer-generated mapping systems that allow archaeologists to plot and analyze site distributions against environmental and other background data derived from remote sensing, digitized maps, and other sources. It is computerized technology for storage, analysis, and display of geographically referenced information. (*syn.* GIS)

geography: One of the oldest sciences; the descriptive study of the Earth's surface and of its exploitation by life forms. From Greek *geo*, "earth" and *graphein*, "to write," geography describes and analyzes the spatial variations in physical, biological, and human phenomena that occur on the surface of the globe and their interrelations and patterns.

Geoksyur: An oasis in the ancient delta of the Tedjen River in southeast Turkmenia, first settled in the early Chalcolithic period, designated Anau I or Namazga I. The earliest sequence of 10 levels spans the later 5th and 4th millennia BC. Typical settlements were small villages of mud-brick houses, although the central settlement of Geoksyur itself seems to have been much larger. The exploitation of this oasis indicates the existence of a developed agricultural economy involving the cultivation of both wheat and barley with the help of irrigation. The area gives its name to a style of painted pottery of the Namazga III period (late 4th millennium BC), with densely packed, repeated geometrics.

geology: The study of the physical, chemical, and biological processes and products of the Earth; simply, the study of the history of the Earth and an understanding of the time scale over which humans developed. Geology's aims overlap considerably with those of archaeology, particularly in the prehistoric periods. For example, work on the stratigraphy of the Quaternary to provide a geological chronology for the study of the reconstruction of environmental changes throughout the Quaternary forms an essential background to all archaeology. The palaeontology of fossil hominids and the other animals that lived at the same time is another area in which geology and archaeology overlap. The geological methods of dating such as radiocarbon, palaeomagnetism, and potassium-argon form the basis of most prehistoric chronologies. Geophysical techniques are used for the location of sites, and petrology traces the origins of stone implements and inclusions in pottery.

geomagnetic reversals: An alternation of the Earth's magnetic polarity in geologic time. It is an aspect of archaeomagnetism especially relevant to the dating of the Lower Palaeolithic, involving complete reversals in the Earth's magnetic field.

geomagnetism: The study of the source, configuration, and changes in the Earth's magnetic field and the study and interpretation of the remanent magnetism in rocks induced by the Earth's magnetic field when the rocks were formed (paleomagnetism). The geological variant of archaeomagnetism.

geometric: A style of decoration with repeated geometric motifs—circles, squares, triangles, lozenges, and running linear patterns—flourishing in Greece c. 900 –700 BC. The term is also applied to such design on wall painting, for textiles. The style derived from the triangular, circular, meander, zigzags, rhomboids, and other linear decoration on Greek pottery of this period. In classical Greek art history, the term is used specifically of the early phases of vase painting as, for example, Protogeometric (c. 1050–900 BC), Geometric (c. 900–750 BC), and Late Geometric (c. 750–700 BC). When the term is applied to the period of Greek history in which the decoration flourished, it is often extended to 1100–700 BC, after the fall of Mycenaean civilization and marking the transition from Bronze to Iron Age. The first phase, called Protogeometric (1100–900) corresponds to the "dark ages" when Greek culture was inward looking and very poor. Its final phase, Late Geometric (770–700) coincided with the resumption of relations with Asian cultures and the beginning of colonization of the northern, southern, and western shores of the Mediterranean. (*syn.* Geometric)

Geometric pottery: The well-fired, stamp-impressed pottery characteristic of c. 2000 BC–AD 300 sites in south and southeastern China. The "Geometric pottery cultures" seem to have grown out of local Neolithic predecessors and characterize the protohistoric Wucheng, Hushu, and Maqiao cultures of the region.

geomorphology: A branch of geology (or geography) concerned with the form and development of landscapes. It includes specializations such as sedimentology. Cultural remains are part of landscapes of the past.

geophysical prospecting: The location and recording of buried sites by detecting variations in the magnetic properties or resistance to an electrical current of the soil. Many archaeological surveying techniques designed to identify features without excavation use instruments that measure physical properties of surface materials.

geophysics: The study of the physical properties of the Earth—structure, composition, and development—such as magnetism, radioactivity, vulcanism. Its applications to archaeology have been to provide dating methods (geochronology) and techniques for exploration (magnetometer and resistivity survey). Some dating techniques, such as palaeomagnetism, are based on geophysical properties of the Earth. It is a subdiscipline of both geology and physics.

georadar: A technique used in ground reconnaissance, similar to soil-sounding radar, but with a much larger antenna and more extensive coverage.

geosol: A unit of classification for a sediment or rock body with one or more soil horizons. A geosol is a recognized soil or palaeosol.

Gerasa: A major Roman city of Judea (modern Jordan), founded by the Seleucids. Extensive remains include colonnaded street, forum, stadium, triumphal arch, theater, and temples to Athena and Zeus. Gerasa was one of the 10 cities of the Decapolis league. (*syn.* Jerash)

Gergovia: An Iron Age *oppidum* and capital of the Averni, in Puy de-Dôme, France. Vercingetorix, the Gallic chief, took refuge there in 52 BC and repulsed Julius Caesar's attempts to capture the site—the first outright defeat of Caesar in Gaul. It is a historic monument.

Gerzean: A late predynastic culture of Upper Egypt, successor of the Amratian, c. 4000–3500 BC. It is named after the site of El Gerza or Gerzeh in the Fayum and is well represented at the cemetery of Naqada in Upper Egypt; another important site is Herakonpolis. Flintwork included ripple-flaked knives, and there was metalworking as copper was coming into use for axes, daggers, and so on. Faience was introduced, and ground stone vessels were popular and very finely worked. Typical pottery is a light-colored fabric in shapes imitating stone vessels, decorated with red painted designs. These include imitations of stone markings, geometrical patterns, and designs taken from nature. Ships were common, especially the papyrus-bundle craft used on the Nile. There is much evidence of contact with southwestern Asia (in wavy-ledged handles on jars, cylinder seals, representations of mythical animals, the use of mud-brick in architecture, and possibly writing). These seem to have led to the advances that brought Egypt to the level of unified civilization at the start of the Dynastic period c. 3200 BC. (*syn.* Nagada II)

gesso: Material consisting of a layer of fine plaster to which gilding was often attached by using an adhesive. It was a fluid, white coating composed of plaster of Paris, chalk, gypsum, or other whiting mixed with glue, applied to smooth surfaces such as wood panels, plaster, stone, or canvas to provide the ground for tempera and oil painting or for gilding and painting carved furniture and picture frames. In Medieval and Renaissance tempera painting, the surface was covered first with a layer of gesso grosso (rough gesso) made with coarse, unslaked plaster, then with a series of layers of gesso sottile (finishing gesso) made with fine plaster slaked in water, which produced an opaque, white, reflective surface. (*syn.* gypsum, chalk)

Getae or Getian: A tribal name for peoples in the territories of modern Romania and Bulgaria during the later Iron Age. They are often referred to as Thraco-Getians or Geto-Dacians and were strongly influenced by both Celts and Scythians. Their culture developed from the 4th century BC until their conquest by Rome in AD 106. It is a local version of La Tène. (*syn.* Geto-Dacians, Thraco-Getians)

Gezer: An important Biblical tell site of Palestine near Jerusalem, occupied from the Chalcolithic (5th millennium BC) to the Byzantine period. The first fortified town belonged to the Middle Bronze Age (early 2nd millennium BC); an important discovery of this phase was a "High Place" (ceremonial meeting place) consisting of a row of 10 tall monoliths. To the Iron Age belong the remains of a gateway built by Solomon. Succeeding levels show a decline, with destruction attributed to Assyrians and later, Babylonians. The city became important again in the Hellenistic period. The most noteworthy finds were a potsherd with one of the earliest uses of the alphabet (18th–17th centuries BC) and the Gezer calendar (11th–10th centuries BC), the oldest known inscription in Early Hebrew writing. The city was particularly prosperous during the 2nd millennium BC and is mentioned in Egyptian texts from the 15th century onward.

Ghana: The earliest and one of the most important of the West African empires, on the border of southern Mauretania and Mali and dating from at least the 8th century AD. It may have arisen as an organization of agricultural people who fought Saharan nomads. This early Sudanic state was well established when it was first visited by Muslims from north of the Sahara. Its capital is believed to have been at Kumbi Saleh, where ruins of a large stone-built town have been investigated. Ghana also controlled the trading center at Awdaghast, at the southern end of the one of the major trans-Saharan caravan routes. The stage regulated and profited from trade in gold, ivory, and salt. From the 11th century, Arabic written accounts are an important source for the history of ancient Ghana; late in that century, the state was conquered by the Almoravids, who imposed Islam. Ghana was effectively eclipsed by Mali during the 13th century.

Ghar Dalam: A cave site in southern Malta near Birzebbuga which has lent its name to the island's earliest Neolithic phase. The culture, dated to the late 5th millennium BC, is characterized by evidence of domesticated animals and cultivated plants and by the use of Impressed Ware similar to that

of contemporary eastern Sicily (Stentinello). There was obsidian from Lipari. The earliest archaeological remains date from about 3800 BC. Neolithic farmers lived in caves like those at Dalam or villages like Skorba (near Nadur Tower).

Ghar-i Kamarband: Cave site near the southeast corner of the Caspian Sea in northern Iran with occupation levels spanning the late Palaeolithic to the early farming period c. 10,000–5000 BC. After c. 6000 BC, there is evidence of increasing sheep and goat, possibly indicating domestication, and evidence of harvesting of wild cereals. Pottery appears c. 5300 BC; shortly afterward, the cave was abandoned. (*syn.* Belt Cave)

Ghar-i Khar: Cave site in the mountains of western Iran, occupied from the Middle Palaeolithic onward. The Upper Palaeolithic industry is similar to the Baradostian at Shanidar Cave. The cave has also yielded a Neolithic level with pottery, probably associated with a food producing community. (*syn.* Dopnkey Cave)

Ghassul: Chalcolithic site northeast of the Dead Sea in the Jordan Valley with four major occupations indicated—most notably the culture of the 4th millennium BC known from the sites of Teleilat Ghassul and Nahal Mishmar. The houses were of pisé (simple mud-brick on stone foundations) and had elaborate polychrome frescoes. A wide range of well-made pottery shapes were in use, which were found on many other Palestinian sites. Carbonized date and olive stones are among the earliest evidence for the cultivation of these fruits. Burials were in cists, made of stone slabs and covered by stone cairns. The culture exploited copper early on and was the last period of large-scale stone tool use in Palestine. (*syn.* Teleilat, Teleilat el Ghassul; Ghassulian)

Ghazni: A major pre-Islamic site and Afghanistan's only remaining walled town, dominated by a 150-foot citadel built in the 13th century. The ruins of ancient Ghazna include two 140-foot towers and the tomb of Mahmud of Ghazna (971–1030), the most powerful emir (sultan) of the Ghaznavid dynasty. Ghazni's early history is obscure; it probably existed at least since the 7th century. Early in the 11th century, under Mahmud of Ghazna, the town became the capital of the vast empire of the Ghaznavids, Afghanistan's first Muslim Dynasty. Excavation has revealed part of the palace of Musud III, which contemporary writers described as filled with booty from India. The central courtyard contains a magnificently carved inscription, in Persian rather than the customary Arabic—one of the oldest examples of Persian epigraphy. (*syn.* Ghazna)

Ghirshman, Roman (1895–1979): Ukrainian/French developer of archaeological work in Afghanistan and Iran, who led a rescue mission in Luristan and carried out excavations at Tepe Sialk near Kashan. After World War II, he headed the

French excavations at Susa in Southwestern Iran. He also worked at Tello, Giyan, Sialk, and Choga Zanbil.

ghost wall: The outline of a wall that has been removed so that the building materials may be used elsewhere. (*syn.* shadow wall)

Gi: A site in northwest Botswana with Middle and Later Stone Age remains, including a microlithic industry associated with game trap pits.

Giant's Grave: Local name for the megalithic chamber tombs of the island of Sardinia during the mid-2nd millennium BC. The burial chamber is of gallery grave type and is set in an elongated cairn with a retaining wall. The cairn covers a long burial chamber of cyclopean construction with a corbelled roof. Some giants' tombs have curved or horned facades enclosing a forecourt. They belong to the Nuraghic Bronze Age culture. (*syn.* Italian Tomba di Giganti)

Gibraltar: A promontory on the southern tip of Spain known for its cave sites with remains of Neanderthal man and stone tools of the Middle and Upper Palaeolithic. The first Neanderthal skull ever found came from Forbes Quarry in 1848. A second, juvenile, Neanderthal was found in 1926 at Devil's Tower. The third, with the Mousterian and Upper Palaeolithic, is Gorham's Cave.

Giglio Island: A mountainous volcanic island off the coast of Etruria, which has an archaic Etruscan shipwreck with a cargo of amphorae filled with olives, ingots, and perfumed oil in Corinthian and Etruscan aryballoi.

gilding: The art of decorating with a thin layer of gold paint or gold leaf. The term includes the application of silver, palladium, aluminum, and copper alloys.

Gilf el Kebir: A plateau of Nubian sandstone in the Sahara Desert of southwest Egypt with Late Acheulian artifacts and Neolithic material (stone tools, grinding stones, bone, pottery) and prehistoric rock engravings.

Gilgamesh: The hero of the best-known Sumerian epic, a famous figure of the early 3rd millennium BC in Mesopotamia. Gilgamesh was considered half god, half man in the literature. The Gilgamesh epic is an Akkadian poem written on 12 tablets, which describe his reign as ruler of Uruk and his search for immortality; it includes the story of the Flood. The historical figure was named as a ruler of Warka in the Sumerian king list. He is now thought to have been a real king of the First Dynasty of Uruk (Early Dynastic III phase, c. 2650–2550 BC). The epics credit him with the construction of two temples and the city wall at Uruk, and archaeological excavations have shown that these are real structures. Out of the nine Sumerian epics known, four are about Gilgamesh and cover a wide variety of topics, including man and nature, love and adventure, and friendship and combat. The desire for immortality carries Gilgamesh to the mythical land of Dilmun and brings him into contact with the Babylonian/Sumerian Noah-figure, Utanapishtim.

Gilimanuk: A settlement and burial site in western Bali, Indonesia, of the early 1st millennium AD. There are extended burials, jar burials, and stone sarcophagi and burial goods including bronze, iron, and glass and stone beads of local and imported origin.

Gilund: A site in Rajasthan, western India, along the banks of the Banas and its tributaries of the Harappan (Indus) and post-Harappan cultures of the 3rd and 2nd millennia BC. Archaeological evidence indicates that early humans lived there some 100,000 years ago. It became a substantial farming village, with four major phases of occupation. Pottery types include black and red ware and a fine black, red, and white polychrome ware.

gisant: In sepulchral sculpture, an effigy representing the person in death; especially, an effigy depicting the deceased in a state of advanced decomposition. It was popular in 15th- and 16th-century northern Europe. The gisant was often placed below a portrait, or orant, effigy, which represented the person praying or kneeling, as in life. It was a reminder of the transitory nature of life.

Giyan, Tepe: A long-lived tell site south of Hamadan, western Iran, going back to late Halaf c. mid-5th millennium BC. Excavations provided the cultural sequence that was the standard for Luristan for some time. The five-phase sequence continued into the Iron Age and had a series of painted pottery styles. In the 2nd millennium, the native painted pottery was replaced by the gray monochrome ware believed to be associated with the first Indo-European-speaking Iranians. Its highest level shows it to have been an outpost of Assyria, with a palace of the 8th century BC.

Giza: The site of the pyramid complexes of the Egyptian kings Khufu, Khafre, and Menkaure, on the west bank of the Nile opposite modern Cairo. It is most famous for the Great Pyramid of Khufu, two only slightly smaller pyramids, the Great Sphinx (statue of a human-headed lion) and its temple, and the tomb of Hetepheres, erected in the 4th Dynasty, c. 2600–2500 BC. The Great Pyramid is 481 feet (146.6 m) high and covers 13.1 acres. The earliest known monument is Mastaba V, which probably dates to the reign of the 1st Dynasty ruler Djet (c. 2980 BC). The royal pyramid cemetery derived from earlier tomb types as seen at Saqqara. Elaborate measures were adopted to prevent disturbance of the royal burials, but all the pyramids were looted in antiquity.

Gla: A Mycenaean site in Boeotia, Greece, which was fortified in the 13th century BC and had a Mycenaean palace. Formerly the site of Lake Copais, other structures include granaries. The citadel was burnt and abandoned late in the 13th century BC.

glacial: Any of a number of cold climatic periods in which there was widespread ice and cold climate flora and fauna.

glacial eustacy: The theory that the adjustments in sea levels and the Earth's crust result from expansion and contraction of Pleistocene ice sheets. It has been suggested based on observed patterns of Cretaceous rocks and physical calculations that, as the Earth's continents move about, the oceans bulge out at some places to compensate, and thus sea-level rise is different from ocean basin to ocean basin.

glacial maximum: The peak of an ice age, when the ice sheets are at their greatest extent and temperatures at their lowest. The last glacial maximum occurred between 20,000–15,000 years ago. At the maximum of the last ice age, more than 30 percent of the Earth's land surface was covered by ice.

glaciation: The process by which land is covered by continental and alpine glacier ice sheets or the period of time during which such covering occurred; several glaciations are required to make up an ice age (as the Pleistocene). The land is subject to erosion and deposition by this process, which occurred repeatedly during the Quaternary; the process modifies landscapes and affects the level of ocean basins. These periods of colder weather are also called glacials, and the warmer periods between them interglacials. At the onset of colder weather, water is taken up into the ice sheets and glaciers, causing a drop in sea level. Landscapes covered by ice can be recognized by the smooth rock surfaces and the U-shaped valleys formed by the ice-sheets and glaciers and the rock rubble carried along in them. As the climate warmed, the glaciers retreated, the ice melted, and the sea level rose. The ice also deposited various forms of boulder clays and banks of debris at the sides and ends of glaciers, known as moraines. Beyond the limits of glaciers and ice sheets, extensive layers of outwash sands and gravels were deposited; where these deposits occur in lakes they are called varves. The periglacial zone around the margin of an ice sheet has permanently frozen subsoil and is occupied by cold-loving plants and animals. Erosion was mainly brought about by solifluxion. The low temperatures and the constant freezing and thawing also affect the soil; these frost effects are called cryoturbation. Particularly characteristic are ice wedges, polygonal cracks in the ground frequently recognizable in air photographs. They were caused by the shrinking of the ground at low temperatures and the filling of the cracks with water, which subsequently expanded on freezing to open the crack still further. The last two million years have been marked by a series of such glaciations. Broad correlations between the glaciation schemes in different parts of Europe and North America exist. Four Ice Ages have been figured; in Europe, the First Glaciation was at a climax 550,000 years ago. This gradually gave way to the First Interglacial (Günz–Mindel) Period lasting about 60,000 years in which warm conditions again prevailed. The Second Glaciation came along with its climax 450,000 years ago, and the Second Interglacial Period (Mindel–Riss) followed, lasting 200,000 years. The Third Glacial Period (Riss) climax 185,000 years ago was relieved by 60,000 years of interglacial warmth. The Fourth (Würm) and last Ice Age was at its height 72,000 years ago. The term has also commonly been used to describe the periods of generally cold climate, which occurred at intervals during the Quaternary period. It is, however, now clear that ice sheets grew only during parts of these so-called "glacials" (e.g., the Devensian). For this reason, the term *cold stage* is preferable. (*syn.* glacial)

glacis: The open, smooth slope below the outer rampart of a fortification at the base of a defensive wall, where the attackers are exposed to the missiles of the defenders, particularly characteristic of the Middle Bronze Age in the Levant.

Gladkaia I: A Neolithic occupation site in eastern Siberia, dating to c. 2nd millennium BC. The population of Gladkaia I lived by hunting and fishing and used pottery and tools made of obsidian.

Glanum: A settlement site in southern Gaul (France), originally founded by the Greek colonists of Marseilles, with three phases of occupation—native Ligurian, Hellenistic, and Roman. With Romanization from the 1st century BC, Glanum became a prosperous provincial town with baths, forum, temples, shrines, a triumphal arch, and the so-called mausoleum of the Julii. German attack in AD 270 brought an end to the occupation of the site. (*syn.* St. Rémy de Provence)

Glasinac: A mountain valley near Sarajevo in Bosnia where there are several thousand tumuli of the Late Bronze and Early Iron Ages (10th–1st centuries BC) containing more than 10,000 cremation burials. Inhumation was the dominant rite, and some graves were very richly equipped. The metal and ceramic objects show connections with Greece, Italy, and the Danube Valley.

glass: A hard, amorphous, inorganic, usually transparent, brittle substance made by fusing silicates, sometimes borates and phosphates, with certain basic oxides and then rapidly cooling to prevent crystallization. It was first developed from faience about 4,000 years ago in the Near East, but was rarely used for anything larger than beads until Hellenistic and Roman times. Glass bottles in Egypt are represented on monuments of the 4th Dynasty (at least 2000 BC). A vase of greenish glass found at Nineveh dates to 700 BC. Glass is in the windows at Pompeii, and the Romans stained it, blew it, worked it on lathes, and engraved it. Natural glasses, such as obsidian, are rare, but cryptocrystalline materials, with fine crystal structures somewhat like glasses, are relatively common (e.g., flint).

glass layer counting: A dating technique for glass based on the idea that the layers present in the surface crust of ancient glass were added annually and that counting them would yield a chronometric date. Research showed different numbers of layers on different parts of the same piece, and for some pieces of known date, not enough layers to suggest annual growth. Therefore, an understanding of the processes that lead to the formation of the layers is necessary before the technique can be used with any confidence.

Glastonbury: A lake village in Somerset, England, which has yielded more data than any other site about life in the British Iron Age. The village was built on a wooden platform keyed to the underlying peat and was enclosed by a timber palisade. Inside were more than 90 round huts with clay and plank floors. They had central hearths for the fires. Cobbled paths and alleyways ran between the huts. Preservation was so good that the excavators recovered baskets, iron objects (including currency bars and tools with their original hafts), dugout canoes, fragments of spoked wheels, lathe-turned bowls, basins and tubs decorated with La Tène art motifs, farming and fishing gear, basketry and wickerwork, and evidence of potting, weaving, and metalworking from the village. Occupation started from the 3rd/2nd to the 1st century BC, just before the Roman conquest. On the high ground nearby is an Iron Age earthwork, Roman pottery, and a Dark Age structure dated to the 6th century AD. Glastonbury, like Cadbury Castle, is linked in folklore with King Arthur. A rotary quern was invented here and eventually became universal. The Benedictine Abbey of St. Mary at Glastonbury was perhaps the oldest (AD c. 166) and certainly one of the richest in England.

glaze: A type of slip applied to pottery, which produces an impermeable and glassy surface when fired at high temperatures. It is usually produced by coating pottery with powdered glass and reheating it to a temperature where the glass begins to fuse. Glaze is a vitreous substance, and, like glass, glaze is made from silica; this substance melts only at a temperature higher than that which would melt the pot, so a flux must be added to make it useable. Silica is present in most pottery, so in these cases only the flux—an oxide of sodium, lead, or potassium—needs to be added, and a colorant if required, usually in the form of a frit crushed and suspended in water. The pot is then fired at a temperature suitable for melting the glaze (somewhere between 900°–1200° C depending on the constituents), which runs into an even layer all over the pot. It was known in ancient Egypt where a mixture of fine sand, quartz, or crystal dust was used with an alkaline base (soda, potash). Glaze or couverte can be identified in the Persian faiences and Flemish stoneware. In the Hellenistic period, lead glaze was invented, in which lead monoxide replaced soda or potash. A large variety of glazes may be used, varying in color, texture, and suitability for different types of pottery. (*syn.* enamel, couverte)

gley horizon: A soil horizon characterized by blue, gray, or olive coloring owing to excessive moisture in anaerobic conditions; a waterlogging of soil. Gleying may result from a raised water table or from impeded drainage in the soil profile; the latter condition occurs in some podzols. Gley horizons and gley soils are conducive to preservation of organic remains. (*syn.* gleying)

gleying: The process of waterlogging of soil in which iron is bacterially reduced under anaerobic conditions. Gleying may result from a raised water table or from impeded drainage in the soil profile—especially in bogs, fens, flood plains, lakes, and swamps. The soil is blue, gray, or olive in coloring and forms gley horizons. (*syn.* gley horizon)

Glob, Peter Vilhelm (1911–1985): A Danish archaeologist who wrote *An Archaeological History from the Stone Age to the Vikings* (also published as *Danish Prehistoric Monuments*, 1971; originally published in Danish, 1942), *The Mound People: Danish Bronze-Age Man Preserved* (1974, reissued 1983; originally published in Danish, 1970), and *The Bog People: Iron Age Man Preserved* (1969, reissued 1988; originally published in Danish, 1965). His writings focused on the bog bodies of Tollund and Grauballe; he was also Director General of Museums and Antiquities in Denmark.

Global Positioning System: A satellite-based system used in determining the location of archaeological sites by triangulation from orbiting satellites. The Global Positioning System has 18 satellites, six in each of three orbital planes spaced 120 degrees apart. The GPS is designed to provide fixes anywhere on Earth to an accuracy of 20 meters and a relative accuracy 10 times greater. (*syn.* GPS)

globular amphora: A type of pottery vessel that has given its name to a Late Neolithic or Copper Age culture of the 3rd millennium BC through much of Germany, Poland, and western Russia. The amphora itself is bulbous in shape with a narrow neck and small handles (for hanging) and appeared with the eastern wing of the European funnel-necked beaker culture, differentiated from the western part. Some examples are undecorated, which others have incised, stamped or cord-impressed ornament on the upper part of the vessel. There are individual burials in stone cists under barrows, accompanied by the globular amphora. The culture is closely linked to the TRB culture and may be a parallel development to the Single Grave/Corded Ware group in Scandinavia of 2600–2200 bc. (*syn.* Globular Amphora culture)

gloss: A type of surface treatment of pottery frequently mistaken for glazing. It involves the application of a slip to the surface, but the slip is made of very fine clay containing an unusually high proportion of the mineral illite, which results in a glossier, shinier surface then normal slip after firing.

glottochronology: The science of the comparative study of the vocabularies of languages for measuring linguistic change through absolute time. By studying the rate of change, the length of time (time depth) during which two related languages developed independently may be calculated. Glottochronology relies on statistical comparison of the basic vocabulary shared by two or more related languages and on the assumption that the rate of vocabulary replacement is constant over sufficiently long periods. It is a way of arriving at a date of separation between two languages that have a common origin by studying the extent to which they have diverged from each other and provides archaeologists with approximate dates for the origination of subcultures diverging from each other. For instance, in Alaska the great difference between the Aleut language and the other Eskimo languages is thought to have been the result of the cultural isolation of the Aleuts from the 3rd millennium BC onward. It is a controversial method. (*syn.* lexicostatistics)

Gloucester: A Roman colonia of Glevum in southwest England, founded by the emperor Nerva, AD 96–98. The Abbey of St. Peter built by King Osric of Northumbria was founded in 681, and it became the capital of the Anglo-Saxon kingdom of Mercia. It achieved reasonable prosperity and had a colonnaded forum, a basilica, and houses with mosaic floors. (*syn.* Roman Glevum)

Glozel: A site in Allier, France, with an assemblage of pottery, clay tablets, bricks, terra-cottas, and glass that has been claimed as evidence of civilization in France before Greek and Roman contact. These items have been dismissed as forgeries, but some items tested by thermoluminescence indicate a date range of 700 BC–AD 100. The discrepancy between the archaeological and scientific evidence has yet to be resolved.

glume: A floral ecofact; the casing holding the wheat kernel.

glyph: (glif) A symbol in a writing system; a painted or incised conventionalized sign. These individual images or design elements make up systems such as hieroglyphics, pictographs, or petroglyphs. Glyphs range from concrete images, such as an animal or a house, to abstractions, such as the use of a footprint to indicate travel, to signs representing the sound of words. In the Mesoamerican system, a glyph may represent an idea, word, sound, syllable, or a combination of them.

glyptics: The arts of carving gems and hard stones. In the ancient East, the term also describes the engraving of seals. (*syn.* sigillography; glyptic arts)

Gnathian ware: A pottery fabric of the Hellenistic period (4th–3rd centuries BC) in southern Italy. Produced originally at Apulia, the pots are decorated with a black-glossed technique with simple designs in yellow and white. It is the western equivalent of West Slope ware. It is unlike other south Italian pottery and was widely exported.

Gnedovo: A site outside Smolensk on the River Volga, where excavations have revealed one of the largest Viking Age grave fields of Russia. Most of the grave mounds contained cremations associated with oval brooches and other objects dating from the 9th and 10th centuries. The burial area itself seems to be associated with a very large Baltic trading center.

Gniezno: An early medieval town of western Poland, established during the 960s when Mieszko I united bands of Slavic tribes to form the Polish state. Excavations have been carried out on the earliest timber fortress. The old town has many buildings, including the cathedral, which has 12th-century carved bronze doors. By the 10th century, the town had become a key center of the early Polish state.

goat: A member of the genus *Capra*, different from the *Ovis* genus (sheep) in differences in scent glands, the presence of a beard, and the scimitar-like horns sweeping back from the forehead. Goat bones first appear in Middle Paleolithic levels of caves. The first evidence for possible human management is at Shanidar Cave, Kurdistan, where there are high proportions of juvenile goats and sheep around c. 8500 BC. Domesticated bones are recorded from such early sites as Jericho, Jarmo, and Çatal Hüyük. Goats seem to have been imported into Europe already domesticated; they appear in the Aegean before 6000 BC. For archaeologists, goats may be hard to differentiate from sheep, especially in the skeleton.

Gobedra: A small rock shelter near Axum in northern Ethiopia, which has yielded a stratified sequence covering the last 12,000 years. The earliest occurrence was of large blades, followed c. 8000 BC by an industry dominated by backed microliths. Pottery first appeared at a level tentatively dated to the 3rd millennium BC. The seeds of cultivated finger millet (*Eleusine coracana*) are dated to between 7,000–5,000 years ago. This find, if correctly associated with these dates, would be the earliest-known evidence for an indigenous African crop. The latest stone industry was a specialized one of small steep scrapers.

Gobi: The great desert of east-central Asia that stretches across vast lands in the Mongolian People's Republic and the Inner Mongolia region of China. Mesolithic and Neolithic material was discovered, proving that climatic conditions were much less extreme in the past. Finds included many microliths, together with polished stone axes and coarse pottery. The items show influences from Siberia and, to a lesser extent, China. The ancient Silk Road traversed the southern part of the Ala Shan Desert and crossed the Ka-shun Gobi as it skirted north and west around the Takla Makam

Desert. The Gobi region first became known to Europeans through the vivid 13th-century descriptions of Marco Polo.

Godin Tepe: A site in the Kangavar Valley of Luristan, western Iran, with continuous occupation from the early 5th millennium to c. 1600 BC (late Iron Age), when it was abandoned following an earthquake and not reoccupied for around 800 years. The cultural sequence provides the framework for the cultural history of this section of the Zagros Mountains. The earliest two building levels are associated with straw-tempered, poorly fired pottery and a stone industry. Most interesting is Godin V of the late 4th millennium BC in which Late Uruk materials (bevel-rimmed bowls, pottery, seal styles, tablets) are found. In Godin II, c. 750 BC, the site was a fortified town of the Medes, and an important building with three colonnaded halls and a throne room has been excavated. A stain on an amphora has revealed the world's earliest wine c. 3500 BC.

Gogoshiis Qabe: A rock shelter of southern Somalia with Middle and Later Stone Age sequences and early Holocene burials. These graves, associated with lesser kudu horn cores, represent the earliest evidence of intentional grave goods in East Africa. (*syn.* Gure Makeke)

Gokomere: An Early Iron Age site in south-central Zimbabwe, occupied between the 5th–7th centuries AD, which is also the name of an Early Iron Age industry. Its characteristic pottery is accompanied by copper and iron fragments.

Gokstad Ship: A Viking ship unearthed in Sandefjord in 1880 under a large tumulus on the Oslo Fjord, Norway. Much of its original timber was preserved by the clay in which it was set. In the middle of the ship, a special platform had been constructed to hold the funerary chamber, which contained the skeleton of a man (possibly King Olaf of Vestfold who died in 890) surrounded by weapons, slaughtered animals, and other objects. The ship is the ultimate Viking war machine—a slender oak-built vessel made for strength and speed, propelled by a large square sail and 16 pairs of oars. It would have been equally navigable in open seas or in shallow inland waters; in 1893, a replica successfully crossed the Atlantic.

Golasecca: An Iron Age culture whose type site is a cemetery in Lombardy, Italy. Occupied from the 9th century BC to the 3rd century BC, it is an urnfield cemetery with some burials accompanied by wheeled vehicles. Some contain rich grave goods of metal, showing connections both with the Hallstatt Iron Age culture of central Europe and with the Etruscans in central Italy.

gold: A chemical element; a dense, lustrous, yellow precious metal with several qualities that have made it exceptionally valuable throughout history. It is attractive in color and brightness, durable to the point of virtual indestruc-

tibility, highly malleable, and usually found in nature in a comparatively pure form. It was one of the first metals to be exploited by man. Early working was basically by hammering, to which more complicated techniques like casting, soldering, granulation, and filigree were later added.

gold-figured: A Greek technique of decorating silver plate with gold foil, especially on cups, phialae, and kantharois. Detail is incised in the gold foil, and the decoration is similar to the red-figured technique used particularly on Athenian pottery.

Goljamo Delcevo: A Neolithici and Copper Age tell site of the Cuceteni Tripolye culture in northeast Bulgaria. The settlement with adjoining cemetery is dated pre-4000–3600 BC and has 16 occupation layers with many complete house plans. There is a system of rectangular fortifications with palisades. In the small Copper Age cemetery of 30 graves, contracted inhumation is the norm, with occasional cenotaph graves. (*syn.* Golyamo Delchevo)

Gombe Point: A site overlooking the Congo River in Kinshasa, where the first stratigraphic succession of stone industries in central Africa was described. These are considered local variants of the Lupemban-Tshitolian sequence of west-central Africa. Although apparently stratified, the succession is now believed to have suffered a considerable degree of postdepositional mixing. (*syn.* Kalina Point)

Gomolava: A large, frequently occupied, double-tell site on the Sava River in Serbia. On both tells, the prehistoric sequence goes from the Late Neolithic to the Middle Ages. The Late Neolithic occupation belongs primarily to the Vinca culture, with houses, pits, and a cemetery with copper grave goods. The subsistence economy of most levels indicates reliance on einkorn wheat, flax, and cattle husbandry.

Go Mun: A site in north Vietnam, which has given its name to the third phase of the Bronze Age of the area, dated to c. 1200–600 BC, following Dong Dau and preceding Dong Son. There was a range of bronze tools, weapons, ornaments, and polished stone adzes. The phase fell within the Phung-Nguyen culture.

Gönnersdorf: An Upper Palaeolithic site on the Rhine River in northwest Germany, known for its many Late Magdalenian engraved schist plaques with radiocarbon dating of 12,600 BP. A volcanic eruption preserved the site during the Allerød.

Gontsy: An Upper Palaeolithic site in the Ukraine on the Udaj River, one of the earliest Palaeolithic discoveries of Europe. It has a radiocarbon date of 13,400 BP and fauna of woolly mammoth.

Gonur-depe: A site in Turkmenia with a fortress of the Gonur phase between the Kelleli and Togolok phases, c. late

3rd–early 2nd millennia BC. There are Murghab seal-amulets with rich iconography.

Gonvillars: A Neolithic cave site in France with a Bandkeramik camp from c. 5000 BC. There was hunting, pottery, domesticated animals, and cultivated cereals. This was followed by Rössen occupation c. 4000–3500 BC.

Goodwin, Astley John Hilary (1900–1959): The first archaeologist in sub-Saharan Africa, who wrote (with C. Van Riet Low), *The Stone Age Cultures of South Africa* (1929) in which they classified the southern African Stone Age into Earlier, Middle, and Later stages, which is still used today.

Gordium: The capital of the Phrygians in the 8th century BC, on the bank of the Sakarya River in central Anatolia (now Turkey). Gordion was surrounded by a massive mud-brick wall and a monumental gateway and was dominated by about 10 important buildings built on the megaron plan, and a palace complex. Outside the city gate was a cemetery of nearly 80 large tumuli, which has yielded rich finds from the 8th–6th centuries BC. The great royal tomb investigated was once identified as King Midas, who allegedly committed suicide when the Cimmerian nomads sacked the city in 685 BC. The tomb also contained inscriptions in the Phrygian script, nine tables and two screens of wood, three bronze cauldrons, 166 other bronze vessels, and 146 bronze fibulae. Traces of linen and woolen textiles were found on the bed, and traces of purple cloth were also found on the throne in another rich tumulus. Occupation of the site continued into Roman times. (*syn.* Gordion)

gorget: A flat artifact made of stone or another material and worn as an ornament over the chest. It may also have been a protective piece for the throat region. These ornamental collars were common in the prehistoric U.S. Southeast and Midwest.

gorgoneion: The mask of the gorgon, the mythical monster whose glance could turn people to stone, which became a symbol to ward off evil. It was widely used on Athenian pottery and on Roman cineraria. It was on the center of the pediment of the temple of Artemis on Corfu.

Gorman, Chester F. (1938–1981): An American archaeologist who specialized in early metallurgy and horticulture in Thailand and who worked at Spirit Cave and Ban Chiang.

Gornja Tuzla: A tell settlement in Bosnia and Hercegovina of the Starcevo, Early and Late Vinca, and Late Copper Age periods. Pottery typology and radiocarbon dates are c. 4690 BC for Starcevo and c. 3760–3630 BC for Late Vinca. There was sporadic occupation interspersed with long breaks. In the Late Vinca levels, evidence of copper smelting is known. The area has long been associated with deposits of rock salt.

Gorods'ke: The latest phase of the Cucuteni-Tripolye culture development dated to the late 3rd millennium BC and centered on Volhynia, northeast of the Carpathians. Most settlements are located on high plateaus above river valleys, with rich household assemblages of bone and stone work. Metal is plentiful in Gorods'ke cremation cemeteries; some metal tools and weapons indicate a date in the Early Bronze Age.

Gorodtsov, Vasili Alekseevich (1860–1945): Russian archaeologist who developed the Bronze Age chronology for Russia, focusing on formal typology. He also wrote syntheses of Russian prehistory and worked at Gontsy, Il'Skaya I, and Timonovka.

Gorodtsov culture: An early Upper Palaeolithic culture of the Kostenki-Borshchevo sites in European Russia with assemblages c. 30,000–25,000 bp. The artifacts include end scrapers and Middle Palaeolithic side scrapers as well as bone tools.

Gortyn: Ancient Greek city of western Crete, considered the most important city of Classical Greek and Roman Crete. Although unimportant in Minoan times, Gortyn displaced Phaestus as the dominant city in the Mesara. It shared or disputed control of the island with Knossos until the Roman annexation in 67 BC. It controlled the sea route between east and west through its ports of Matalon and Leben. The great civic inscription, or "code," of Gortyn, dating to c. 450 BC, was discovered in 1884; it is the most extensive monument of Greek law before the Hellenistic Age. The Gortynian Law Code was incorporated by the Romans into the back wall of an odeum when this was being reconstructed in AD 100 under Trajan. The Code, written boustrophedon (alternatively from left and right), contains rules of civil law concerning such matters as family, adultery, divorce, property, mortgage, and the rights of slaves. Later excavations disclosed most of the plan and public buildings of the Roman city, which was the administrative capital of the Roman province of Crete and Cyrenaica; identifiable are a preaetorium, agora, and odeum. The acropolis appears to have Neolithic and Late Bronze Age evidence, and there are traces of a temple of the 8th–7th centuries BC. Homer refers to the city and describes it as walled, although no walls survive. A votive deposit associated with an altar on the slope of the hill contained a wide selection of objects from all periods from Late Minoan III to Roman. Gortyn maintained its importance through early Christian times, becoming an early Byzantine religious center. (*syn.* Gortyna)

Gothic: A style of painting, sculpture, architecture, and music characteristic of western and central Europe during the Middle Ages. Gothic art evolved from Romanesque art and lasted from the mid-12th century to as late as the end of the 16th century in some areas. The term *Gothic* alluded to the barbarian Gothic tribes that had destroyed the Roman Empire and its classical culture in the 5th century AD. It was a slightly derogatory term until the 19th century.

Goths: A Germanic people whose two branches, the Ostrogoths and the Visigoths, for centuries harassed the Roman Empire. According to their own legend, the Goths originated in southern Scandinavia and crossed in three ships under their king Berig to the southern shore of the Baltic Sea, where they settled after defeating the Vandals and other Germanic peoples in that area. The split into two groups took place AD c. 200. Those Goths living between the Danube and the Dnestr Rivers became known as Visigoths, and those in what is now the Ukraine as Ostrogoths. Under their king Alaric, the Visigoths sacked Rome in AD 410. Later they moved to southern France and settled in Aquitaine before seizing control of Spain. The Ostrogoths helped defeat the Huns in Italy in 454. Under Oadacer and Theodoric, there was a period of comparative peace until they were challenged and defeated by Justinian. (*syn.* Ostrogoth, Visigoth)

Gough's Cave: An Upper Palaeolithic cave site in Somerset, England, with flint, bone, and antler artifacts and animal bones with butchery marks. Human bones also show deliberate cut marks, signifying cannibalism.

gourd: The *Lagenaria siceraria*, a plant of the melon family, grown solely for its hard rind, which was much used for making vessels and containers. In some areas, the shapes of pots can be explained as copies of gourd vessels, such as in Danubian I. Attested in South America and Thailand (Spirit Cave) before 7000 BC, the plant is perhaps the most widespread of all the ancient cultigens. Thought to be of African origin, the dates and routes of its spread are unknown.

Gournia: A Late Bronze Age Minoan town on eastern Crete, which dates from the Neopalatial period c. 1600–1450 BC. A small palace was built on the site in Middle Minoan III, c. 1600 BC, showing features copied from the palaces of Knossos and Mallia. Through the Late Minoan period, from c. 1550, the town grew up around it, with modest houses and narrow curving streets, and the palace was turned into small domestic dwellings.

Grachwil: A series of Hallstatt barrows in Berne, Switzerland, with rich grave goods including a fine imported Greek bronze hydria of the early 6th century BC.

Gradesnitsa: A Late Neolithic village site of the Gumelnita culture in northwest Bulgaria with Karanovo I and Copper Age layers. Excavations have revealed complete early Neolithic house plans, succeeded in the Copper Age by a large village of three occupational phases with houses arranged in streets. In a Copper Age ritual assemblage is a house model inscribed with signs and the so-called Gradesnitsa plaque—a fired clay disc covered in elaborate incised symbols—similar to the one found at Tartaria.

gradiometer: A geophysical device used to conduct surveys by measuring the gradient in a magnetic or gravitational field. This instrument is used to identify shallowly buried features and structures. (*syn.* proton gradiometer, fluxgate gradiometer, differential fluxgate gradiometer)

gradualism: The view that changes occur slowly and cumulatively rather than rapidly and disjunctively.

graffiti: Writing placed on walls or other objects; any figures or inscriptions scratched into a surface, often indicating the maker or owner. It is any casual writing, rude drawing, or marking on the walls of buildings, as distinguished from a deliberate writing known as an inscription. Graffiti are found in great abundance, as on the monuments of ancient Egypt. Graffiti are important to the palaeographer as illustrating the forms and corruptions of the various alphabets used by the people and may guide the archaeologist to the date of the building. Graffiti are important to the linguist because the language of graffiti is closer to the spoken language of the period and place than usual written language. Graffiti are also invaluable to the historian for the light thrown on everyday life of the period and on intimate details of customs and institutions.

Graig Llwyd: A Neolithic ax factory and stone quarry in north Wales with fine-grained igneous rock. The axes date from c. 4000–2500 BC and were widely traded; they have been found as far away as southern England, Yorkshire, and east Lothian.

grain impression: A cereal grain that has been incorporated by chance in an artifact, such as pottery, bricks, or daub. The impression left in the clay may be clear enough for identification to be possible and thus provide useful evidence of the crops in cultivation at the time. On firing, or as a result of decomposition of time, the organic material is lost, but its outline remains, often in great detail. Casts of these impressions are taken by using latex rubber, and the original plant or animal may be identified. Before the widespread sieving and flotation of deposits began to yield large amounts of environmental evidence, these grain impressions were an important method of getting information on farming practices.

Graman: A series of rock shelters in a valley of the Northern Tablelands of New South Wales, Australia, with human occupation dated between c. 3000–1000 BC. Stone artifacts included some of the earliest Bondi points and geometric microliths, grinding slabs, adze flakes, awls, perforated pendant fragments, and bone points.

Granada: Kingdom and city important from the 13th century in Spain. Although its origins go back to the early years of the Moorish occupation in the 8th century, Granada rose to importance after the mid-13th century, when it became the capital of a new state founded by Muhammad I (1232 –1273).

The kingdom included, principally, the area of the modern provinces of Granada, Málaga, and Almería. The city was dominated by the fortified citadel and Alcazaba, Medinat-al-Hamra, now known as the Alhambra. The Alhambra was defended by a massive towered enceinte enclosing a series of magnificent palaces linked by courtyards and gardens, much of which still remains. Apart from the Alhambra, Granada also preserves many examples of Islamic architecture in the older quarters of the city. Granada was the site of an Iberian settlement, Elibyrge, in the 5th century BC and of the Roman Illiberis. As the seat of the Moorish kingdom of Granada, it was the final stronghold of the Moors in Spain, falling to the Roman Catholic monarchs Ferdinand II and Isabella I in 1492.

Gran Chichimeca: The northern frontier of Mesoamerica inhabited by the Chichimecs before they moved south. The Chichimecs were true hunters and gatherers who were mainly migrants. The term Chichimeca was also applied to agricultural but less civilized peoples (e.g., Otomí, central Mexico) and thus an unsophisticated, rustic lifestyle. Because the northwestern portion of Mesoamerica was occupied by such people, the legends of north-south migrations of invaders probably refer to movements of agricultural rather than hunting and gathering peoples. The term is also used to refer to the southwestern United States.

Grand Pressigny: A complex of flint quarries in Indre-et-Loire, France, whose products were widely traded throughout western Europe in the Late Neolithic and Copper Ages. The distinctive caramel-colored flint was exported in the form of blocks and unfinished blanks. The exploitation of Grand Pressigny flint took place c. 2800–2400 BC.

grange: A type of medieval manor house controlling the estates belonging to a monastery. Granges were first created in the 12th century in several countries of western Europe. The farms were run by monks with the assistance of lay servants, and their purpose was to produce food for the church as well as for sale in the marketplace. Granges range in form from the elaborate monumental farm complexes of the Loire Valley (Parcay-Meslay), to the elegant Piedmont farms of Renaissance Italy and the hill farms of the Pennines in England.

granite: A granular igneous rock composed essentially of the minerals quartz, orthoclase feldspar, and mica. It is the most common plutonic rock of the Earth's crust, formed by the cooling of magma at depth. Primarily gray in color, the crystalline rock is used mainly for building, paving, and tombstones.

granulation: A technique used in the decoration of jewelry by soldering it with grains of gold, electrum, or silver. Tiny spherical drops of metal were soldered onto a background, forming the required pattern and giving it a granular texture.

The drops may have been made by heating a gold wire until a drop formed, or by melting gold and slowly pouring it into cold water. As also for filigree, the solder was normally a gold copper alloy with a lower melting point than gold. First used as early as the 3rd millennium BC, it was widely known in western Asia and Egypt. The ancient Greeks perfected the technique, but by the 5th century BC granulation had been largely replaced by filigree in Greek work. The art of granulation probably reached its peak with the Etruscans between the 7th and 6th centuries BC, in the elaborately granulated and embossed earrings, pronged shoulder clasps for clothes, and beads found in Etruscan tombs. Granulation was particularly important in India and Persia after contact with the Roman Empire.

graphite painting: A surface treatment for pottery involving the application of powdered graphite before firing. As in hematite coating, the mineral may have been applied by mixing with a slip and applied as "paint." The resulting surface is silvery gray and shiny.

grass-marked pottery: Pottery either marked or tempered with grass. In western Britain, there are examples of pottery covered with "grass" impressions from Ulster, the Hebrides, and Cornwall, especially around the 5th–6th centuries AD. The term also refers to crude handmade ware made in various parts of Frisia in the Migration period and in certain parts of southern England in the Early Saxon period in which ferns and other organic material were used as tempering. (*syn.* grass-tempered pottery)

grattoir: (gra-twah'; gwa-twahr') A flaked stone scraping tool, usually flint, in which the working edge is at the end of the blade or flake and lies across its long axis. It is characteristic of the Upper Paleolithic and was probably used to work wood and clean hides; from the French *gratter* "scratch, scrape." (*syn.* end scraper)

Grauballe Man: A Danish bog burial in central Jutland of the Roman Iron Age with a radiocarbon date of AD c. 310. Grauballe Man was naked, and his neck had been cut almost from ear to ear. His skin was particularly well preserved by the peat. His last meal had consisted of a gruel made of 63 different types of identifiable seeds.

Grave Creek Mound: The largest cone-shaped earth mound in the New World, found in northern West Virginia, of the Adena culture. The mound is about 19 meters high, and the base is 73 meters, and it was the center of a complex of smaller mounds and earthworks, constructed during the 3rd and 2nd centuries BC.

grave goods: Valuables deposited with a corpse in a grave; the artifacts associated with a burial or cremation, usually meant to be helpful in the afterlife (such as jewelry, weapons, or food). They may also represent personal possessions or offerings to the dead person's spirit. (*syn.* grave-goods)

gravel: Any stone that is greater than 2 millimeters in diameter. Gravel may be classified as granule, pebble, cobble, and boulder gravel. The term also refers to a sedimentary deposit consisting mainly of gravel-sized clasts.

Graveney Boat: A well-preserved Anglo-Saxon timber boat found in 1970 in the Graveney marshes in Kent, England. It is the only vessel of this period from the British Isles, which has left more than an impression in the soil. Radiocarbon and dendrochronology have effectively dated it to the late 9th century AD. The well-constructed Graveney Boat was a cross-Channel cargo; it has been restored and is in the National Maritime Museum in Greenwich, England.

graver: A stone tool manufactured from a flake by chipping (pressure-flaking) it on two edges at one end so as to leave a sharp point. Gravers were to cut or score soft materials such as bone, shell, wood, and antler and perhaps for punching leather and other purposes. The term also refers to a type of metalworking tool that includes a number of subtypes, although all are hand held, hard, and sharp and are used to cut or engrave metal. Such a graver has a metal shaft that is cut or ground diagonally downward to form a diamond-shaped point at the tip. The angle of the point affects the width and depth of the engraved lines; the point is guided by thumb and forefinger. (*syn.* burin)

Gravettian: An Upper Palaeolithic industry named after the site La Gravette in the Dordogne of southwest France and characterized by well-developed blade tools of flint and female figurines of ivory. This advanced industry succeeded the Aurignacian and preceded the Solutrean, c. 28,000–20,000 BP. In France it is known as the Upper Périgordian (Périgordian IV), and the Gravettian appears to have developed in central Europe, expanding to the east and west. The small, pointed blades with straight blunted backs are called Gravette points. Most of the French sites are caves, but possibly related industries, known as Eastern Gravettian, are distributed through the loess lands of central Europe and Russia at the camp sites of mammoth-hunters; other sites are in Spain, Belgium, Czechoslovakia, and Italy. The Gravettians invented the bow and arrow, blunted-back knives of flint, and the tanged arrowheads. They are famous, too, for their cave paintings. Other artifacts include bone or ivory spears and, in eastern Europe, numerous other bone tools incised with an elaborate geometric pattern.

Gravisca: A port of Tarquinia in Etruria where excavations have yielded large quantities of Greek pottery and a Greek stone anchor.

gravity model: A theory, derived from Newton's law of universal gravitation, that the degree of interaction between two communities is directly proportional to their proximity to each other. The model has been tested with data from modern societies and is valid for a wide range of types of interaction, such as migration, travel, and communication. The model can also be reformulated to determine when the balance of interaction swings from one location to another.

Graziosi, Paolo (1906–1988): An Italian archaeologist who concentrated on rock art studies in Italian and North African excavations. He discovered the art at Levanzo and published *L'Arte dell'Antica Eta della Pietra* (1956).

Great Basin: A natural region of western North America, with rugged north-south mountains and broad valleys, covering 190,000 square miles. It is bordered by the Sierra Nevada Range on the west, the Wasatch Mountains on the east, the Columbia Plateau on the north, and the Mojave Desert on the south. Most of Nevada, the western half of Utah, and portions of other states lie within its boundaries. (*syn.* Great Basin Desert)

Greater Peten: A major architectural style of the Classic Maya lowlands, especially the use of polychrome painted stucco on wall surfaces.

Great Interglacial: A major division of the Pleistocene epoch, the warm interval between the Mindel and the Riss Glaciations c. 400,000–200,000 years ago. (*syn.* Hoxnian, Mindel-Riss)

Great Langdale: A Neolithic ax factory in Cumbria, northwest England, with high-quality stone quarried at several sites and traded over very wide areas of England by the Peterborough people, c. 4000–3000 BC.

Great Rift Valley: The main branch of the East African Rift system, an ancient geological feature where the action of earthquakes and volcanoes created ideal conditions for burying and preserving bones. Many early hominid fossil sites have been discovered in the Great Rift Valley. In the north, the rift is occupied by the Jordan River, the Dead Sea, and the Gulf of Aqaba. It continues southward along the Red Sea and into the Ethiopian Denakil Plain to Lakes Rudolf (Turkana), Naivasha, and Magadi in Kenya. It continues through Tanzania southward through the Shire River Valley and Mozambique Plain to the coast of the Indian Ocean near Beira, Mozambique. (*syn.* Rift Valley)

Great Serpent Mound: Large ritual earth mound in Ohio with the form of a curved serpent holding either an egg or a frog. The mound is associated with a nearby burial mound of the Adena culture.

Great Silla Dynasty: First unification of Korean peninsula under single rule (AD 668–935). The Unified Silla period produced more granite Buddhist images and pagodas than any other period, and the T'ang Dynasty of China exerted considerable influence over the culture. (*syn.* Unified Silla period)

Great Tombs period: A period in Japanese history, 4th–7th century AD, known for round tombs covered by a mound with a square platform off to the side, making a keyhole shape. Towards the end of the period, tombs, were very large and surrounded by a moat, and earthenware figures and models (Haniwa) were placed in a series of concentric rings around the tomb. Inside was a chamber of stone slabs, probably adopted from cist tombs of northeast Asia. Burial goods included bronze mirrors, Chinese-type swords, *magatama* (fine polished stone ornaments), and Sue Ware pottery. (*syn.* Kofun)

Great Tradition: Set of elite values and behaviors that emerge from folk traditions during the evolution of complex societies and that are expressed in distinctive rituals, art, writing, or other symbolic forms.

Great Wall of China: A monumental building project that created a wall running (with all its branches) about 4,000 miles (6,400 km) west to east from Bohai Bay to a point deep in central Asia, the Tarim Basin. Parts of the vast fortification date from the 4th century BC. In 214 BC, the first emperor of a united China (Shih Huang-ti of the Qin Dynasty) connected a number of existing defensive walls into a single system fortified by watchtowers, which served both to guard the rampart and to communicate with the capital, Hsien-yang, by signal—smoke by day and fire by night. The enemy against whom the Great Wall was built were the Hsiung-nu, the nomadic tribes of the northern steppes. The wall was originally made of masonry and rammed earth and was faced with brick on its eastern portion. It was substantially rebuilt in later times, especially in the 15th and 16th centuries. The basic wall is generally about 30 feet high, and the towers are about 40 feet high.

Great Zimbabwe: A Late Iron Age site in southeastern Zimbabwe, by far the largest and most elaborate of the dry-stone constructions to which the term *dzimbahwe* is applied. After an Early Iron Age phase of AD 500–900, the main sequence of occupation began around 1000 when Shona speakers occupied Zimbabwe Hill and began building stone walls around 1300. Great Zimbabwe was the capital of the Shona empire from AD 1270–1450, which stretched from the Zambezi River to the northern Transvaal of South Africa and eastern Botswana. There was a class system, and the kings accumulated wealth through trade, attested by items such as glass vessels and beads, pottery, and porcelain. Gold was the principal export; Great Zimbabwe appears to have been at the center of a network of related sites through which control was exercised over the gold-producing areas. Archaeologically, the culture is called the Zimbabwe tradition and is divided into Mapungubwe, Zimbabwe, and Khami phases. In the 15th century, the site declined with trade and political power shifting to the north near the Zambezi Valley.

greave: A piece of armor designed to protect the part of the leg below the knee. It originally covered the shin only, but in medieval Europe there was also a closed greave, which protected both the shin and the calf.

Grebeniki culture: A Late Mesolithic culture situated between the Carpathians and the Dniestr Valley in the Ukraine c. 6000 BC. It was succeeded by the Bug-Dniestr complex c. 5500 BC.

Greek fire: Any of several flammable materials used in warfare in ancient and medieval times. Ancient writers refer to flamming arrows, firepots, and such substances as pitch, naphtha, sulfur, and charcoal, but true Greek fire was evidently a petroleum-based mixture. It was evidently invented during the reign of Constantine IV Pogonatus by a Greek-speaking Syrian refugee from the Arab conquest of Syria. It could be thrown in pots or discharged from tubes and was difficult to put out when alight.

Green Gully: A Pleistocene site in southern Victoria, Australia, occupied between 15,000 and 4000 BC. Stone tools include large side-trimmed and concave flakes similar to those in Tasmania and at Kenniff Cave of the same period, and bipolar cores. Bones of two individuals, one male and one female, were found combined in a grave and were dated by radiocarbon on collagen to 4500 BC.

Greenland: The world's largest island; the Inuit are believed to have crossed from North America to northwest Greenland, using the islands of the Canadian Arctic as stepping stones in a series of migrations that stretched from 4000 BC to AD 1000. Several distinct cultures are known, including the Sarqaq (c. 1400–700 BC), Dorset (c. 800 BC–AD 1300), and others such as the Dundas (Thule) and Inugsuk. The Icelandic sagas and histories tell of failed attempts to colonize Greenland in the 970s and of the exiled Erik the Red's eventual success in 985. Archaeologists have located several early farmsteads, where the occupants began some cultivation and animal farming, supplementing their diets by hunting and fishing. Erik's own farm at Bratthalio consisted of a main longhouse with thick walls of stone and turf. Inside there was a central conduit and animal stalls with partitions made of whale scapulae. There were also four barns and outbuildings and the remains of a small U-shaped chapel with a wooden gable, which was built by Erik's wife after her conversion to Christianity around 1000. From Greenland, voyages were made to the coast of America, and Erik's son was one of the first explorers to reach "Vinland," which was probably Maine.

greenstone: A loosely applied term for a variety of metamorphosed basic igneous rocks of a green color: serpentine, olivine, jade, jadeite, nephrite, chloromelanite, and so on. The general term is useful, because ancient man used these materials interchangeably, mainly for high quality or ceremonial polished stone axes, figures, and other objects. Jade was particularly popular in China and Middle America and considered to have magical properties. Greenstone was important in southeastern Australia and in New Zealand. The green color comes from the minerals chlorite, hornblende, or epidote.

gray ware: The typical household and ceremonial ceramic ware of Monte Albán and the Valley of Oaxaca, Mexico, made from a fine gray paste in the middle Pre-Classic period. Gray ware occurs throughout Monte Albán's occupation, with some variations in shape and ornamentation. In the latter periods in the Oaxaca sequence, after the collapse of Monte Albán, Mixtec gray ware was distributed through the Valley. The Zapotecs' merge with the Mixtecs is suggested by the correlation between the distribution of the Mixtec ceramics in Zapotec households, c. AD 1250–1521. (*syn.* grayware)

grid: A system of perpendicular lines and equally spaced points to form a rectangle, which is used as a frame of locational reference on archaeological sites. A grid is usually defined by its distance and direction in reference to a datum point. Excavations units are often planned and recorded by grid. Grids are often aligned with either the anticipated site layout or with a land form on which the site sits. Many archaeological sites are surveyed by measuring from a grid enclosing the site. It is a rectilinear system of X, Y coordinates, which is established over the area to be excavated so that spatial control can be maintained. (*syn.* grid unit)

grid amplitude: A method of defining the location of features and artifacts on a site by plotting from a reference point oriented to magnetic north or some other known point. Meridian lines run north-south and baselines run east-west on a grid square.

griddle: A flat ceramic plate used in the final stage of detoxifying manioc. After grating and pulping, thin disks of manioc are baked on the griddle into a kind of unleavened bread. Although there are other methods of preparation, use of the griddle is especially common in northeastern South American contexts, where the artifact signifies agricultural practice.

grid layout: The practice of dividing an archaeological site into squares for ease of recording features and objects during excavation. The term also refers to the two-dimensional intersecting network defining the squares in which archaeologists dig, usually set out with strings, stakes, and a transit. Often a square trench is cut in each grid square, separated by a balk from each neighboring trench. Each square is suitable for excavation by two or three people. Advantages of the method are the creation of a number of readily available

sections on the site, the ease of spoil removal (along the balk), and the control that can be exercised over excavators. On open sites with little stratigraphy above the rock surface, the method is often unnecessary. The balks in the grid method may also obscure many of the important stratigraphical relations or make impossible the recognition of structures. This technique allows the fast recording of very large areas, but is not as accurate as triangulation for the pinpointing of small objects and features. The use of grid planning and triagulation together often satisfies most of the combined needs of speed and accuracy. (*syn.* grid system, grid method, box system, grid planning)

Grimaldi: A site on the Italian Riviera near the French border with caves and rock shelters of Middle and Upper Palaeolithic flint industries, mainly Aurignacian and Gravettian assemblages (also termed Grimaldian industries). The caves also have elaborate *Homo sapiens sapiens* burials with grave goods including Venus figurines, backed blades, and objects of adornment. The Grotte du Prince yielded a pure Mousterian deposit. There is no Magdalenian in Liguria, where the Grimaldian persists until the end of the Palaeolithic period.

Grimes Graves: The oldest known Neolithic flint mine in England, in Norfolk, with the remains of around 350 mine shafts. The high-quality flint had three banks: floor stone, wall stone, and top stone. The products, mainly ax blades, were roughly chipped to shape at the site and were then traded in semifinished condition. The miners used flint tools, deers' antlers as picks or wedges, and animal shoulder blades as spades. Excavation was probably by wooden shovel (a product of the polished ax and chisel) or possibly the shoulder blades of oxen. It is estimated that 50,000 picks made of red-deer antler were used during the 600 years of activity in the mine, which began about 2300 BC. In one shaft, the miners made a chalk statuette of a fat pregnant woman and a phallus of chalk; this practice, a fertility cult, was perhaps used to bring fruitful results in further mining. There are differing dates for the use of the mine shafts. (*syn.* Grime's Graves)

Grimston: A Neolithic long barrow in Yorkshire, England, which is the type site of the Grimston-Lyles Hill pottery ware. The pottery is characterized by plain, round-bottomed carinated bowls with an everted rim but without handles. It was current across most of Britain c. 4500–3300 BC. Some variants, as at Ebbsfleet in Kent, made more use of decoration. (*syn.* Hanging Grimston)

grinding stone: Any lithic (stone) artifact used to process plant for food, medicines, cosmetics, or pigments. The grinding was done on a flat or concave surface.

Grivac: A large open site of the Starcevo and early Vinca periods in Serbia with rectangular houses dated to c. 4375–

3980 BC for Vinca and c. 5300 BC for the architectural remains of the Starcevo. The Starcevo occupation is the earliest radiocarbon date yet known from the Serbian Neolithic.

gród: Any of numerous early medieval fortified enclosures of east-central Europe. They have earthen ramparts, often with wooden reinforcement. Large ones are in Gniezno and Mikulcice, and Poland has the most enclosures of this type. (*syn.* pl. grody; Burgwalle, Herrenburgen, hradiste)

Gródek Nadbuzny: A Neolithic settlement of the Funnel Beaker culture of southeast Poland with evidence of copper metallurgy.

grog: Fragments of old or wasted pottery or firebricks, which are ground up and added to clay as filler material to help reduce plasticity. Grog is used in the manufacture of refractory products (as crucibles) to reduce shrinkage in drying and firing.

Groitzsch: A series of Upper Palaeolithic sites in eastern Germany, dating to around the end of the Pleistocene. Burins and end scrapers are assigned to the Magdalenian.

groma: A Roman surveying instrument that traced right angles. It was made of a horizontal wooden cross pivoted at the middle and supported from above. From the end of each of the four arms hung a plumb bob. By sighting along each pair of plumb bob cords in turn, the right angle could be established. The device could be adjusted to a precise right angle by observing the same angle after turning the device approximately 90 degrees. By shifting one of the cords to take up half the error, a perfect right angle would result. It was used for laying out the grid patterns of towns and forts, for road construction, and for centuriation.

grooved decoration: Pottery decoration in which broad lines are drawn on the firm but unbaked pot surface. No clay is removed, as it is in excised decoration, nor is the surface itself broken, as with incised decoration.

Grooved Ware: A pottery style of the British Late Neolithic, widely distributed c. 2750–1850 BC. The characteristic vessel is flat based with straight vertical or outward sloping walls. It was formerly known as Rinyo-Clacton after two widely separated find spots (Clacton in Essex and Rinyo in the Orkney Islands). Throughout eastern and southern England, where it is particularly frequent on henge sites (Stonehenge and Durrington Walls), it is decorated with shallow grooving or sometimes with applied cordons. A Scottish group, where appliqué cordons were much used in addition, is represented in Orkney at sites like Rinyo and Skara Brae. It is also found in settlement sites and in chambered tombs. (*syn.* Rinyo-Clacton)

Grotefend, Georg Friedrich (1775–1853): German-language scholar who made the first major breakthrough in the decipherment of the ancient Persian cuneiform script. He presented a paper on his work in 1802, but it was not published, and his work was largely ignored. He was not particularly versed in Oriental languages, but was good at solving puzzles. Knowing that the inscriptions dated from about the 5th century BC and were associated with the sculptures of kings, he concluded that the recurrence of certain symbols signified "king" and "king of kings." Eventually he was able to connect the names of Darius and Xerxes with the terms of royalty. A third name proved to be that of Hystaspes, the governor of Parthia and father of Darius I. Of the 13 symbols he deciphered, 9 were correct. He also published works on two ancient Italic dialects, Oscan and Umbrian. An account of his work is found in C. W. Ceram's *Gods, Graves, and Scholars* (1967).

Grotta dell'Uzzo: A cave site of northwest Sicily with Mesolithic (c. 8000–6500 BC) and Early Neolithic (c. 6000 BC) deposits. The Early Neolithic contained cardial impressed ware, domesticated animal bones, and traces of wheat and barley. It was followed by Middle Neolithic layers with Stentinello and painted Masseria La Quercia ware and then dark Diana wares of the Late Neolithic. It may be one of the earliest Neolithic sites of the central Mediterranean.

Grotta Guattari: A cave site southeast of Rome where the skull and jawbone of a Neanderthal man were found, dating to 57,000–51,000 BP.

Grotta-Pelos: A culture of a series of archaeological sites in the Cyclades (Early Cycladic I), c. 3200–2700 BC. (*syn.* Pelos-Lakkoudes)

Grotte des Enfants: An Upper Palaeolithic cave of the Grimaldi complex with three Cro-Magnon burials.

Grotte Vaufrey: A cave site in Dordogne, France, with stratigraphy from Mindel/Riss to early Würm, including an occurrence of the Mousterian. The span is c. 246,000–74,000 BP.

ground-penetrating radar: A remote sensing device used in subsurface detection, which transmits a radar pulse into the soil and records differential reflection of the pulses from buried strata and features. When a discontinuity is encountered, an echo returns to the radar receiving unit, where it is recorded.

ground reconnaissance: A collective name for a variety of methods for identifying archaeological sites, including consultation of documentary sources, place-name evidence, local folklore and legend, but primarily the visual inspection from groundwork of a potential site.

groundstone: A class of lithic (stone) artifacts produced by abrasion—grinding or pecking—and formed into a tool or vessel. Granite, pumice, and steatite fall into this class. Manos, metates, mortars, and pestles are common groundstones artifacts. Groundstone tools used to crush, pound, grind, or otherwise process materials are also commonly referred to as "milling implements" (*syn.* ground stone; polished tool; ground-stone artifact, ground stone tool)

ground survey: A surface survey technique using direct observation to gather archaeological data that are present on the ground surface. The term includes mapping and surface collection of artifacts.

ground truth: The determination of the causes of patterns revealed by remote sensing, such as by examining, on the ground, features identified by aerial photography.

Grubenhäuser: Characteristic "sunken" huts of the Germanic peoples during the Migration period and up to c. 1000, so-called for their sunken floors. They were usually rectangular and had a superstructure supported on two, four, or six posts. The sunken hut was usually roofed by a leanto structure supported by one or three posts at either end and a simple ridge post creating a tentlike structure. It seems that many of these buildings had floors, with the sunken area being a kind of shallow cellar. Grubenhäuser have been found in the Low Countries, Britain, France, often alongside rectangular buildings and farmhouses. These sunken huts apparently date back to the Roman period in North Germany and Frisia. Dienne-sur-Meine in France has many post-Carolingian examples of Grubenhäuser. In England, the first sunken huts were probably employed as short-term dwellings by the migrants. It was a significant type of building distinguishing early medieval settlements in western Europe. (*syn.* Grubenhauser)

Gua Cha: A large limestone rock shelter in central Malaysia, occupied from c. 10,000/8000 BC and AD 1000. The lowest level is Hoabinhian, spanning 8000–1000 BC, with burials. Neolithic burials with southern Thai/Ban Kao pottery affinities span c. 1000 BC–AD 1000. Stone tools span the transition. A similar sequence is found at Kota Tongkat, and Gua Cha's Neolithic sequence relates to the ancestry of the present orang asli (Austro-Asiatic-speaking aborigines) of central Malaya.

Gua Kechil: A limestone rock shelter in central Malaysia, with remains related to the Ban Kao Neolithic, like other sites such as Gua Cha. This site also had a late phase of the Hoabinhian with cord-marked pottery. The Neolithic assemblage dates to c. 2800 BC.

Gua Lawa: A limestone rock shelter near Sampung in eastern Java, whose sequence may show a transition from a Preceramic assemblage of small hollow-based stone arrowheads to a Neolithic assemblage with cord-marked pottery and many bone and antler tools.

Gubs Shelter: A Palaeolithic rock shelter in the northern Caucasus of European Russia. A Middle Palaeolithic assemblage contained side scrapers. Upper Palaeolithic layers have

end scrapers and backed blades. The sequence probably dates to the last glacial.

Gudea (fl. 2100 BC): A ruler of Lagash in the post-Akkadian period, c. 2125 BC, known from the numerous inscribed statues of him at Tello. These are among the best-known objects of Sumerian art.

Gudenus Cave: A prehistoric cave site on the Danube River in Austria, with artifacts and faunal remains starting with the Middle Palaeolithic (side scrapers, bifaces, cave bear, woolly mammoth, reindeer). There is an Upper Palaeolithic/Magdalenian assemblage and a Neolithic.

Gudnja: A cave site in a steep valley in southern Dalmatia, Croatia. The occupation levels discovered include Early Neolithic Impressed ware; Middle Neolithic Danilo culture; Late Neolithic regional variant of the Hvar culture; and Copper Age. This site has yielded the first radiocarbon dates for the Dalmation Neolithic: the Impressed ware occupation dates to c. 5200–4600 BC, the Danilo levels to c. 4600–4450 BC.

gui: In Chinese religion, a troublesome spirit that roams the world, causing misfortune, illness, and death. These were believed to be the spirits of individuals who were not buried properly or whose families neglected to make proper memorial offerings. The term also refers to a Chinese Neolithic tripod pottery pitcher, first made with solid legs and then acquiring bulbous hollow-shaped legs, and to an early Chinese bronze ritual bowl with handles. The latter often bore writing as well as complex designs. The bronze gui was known in the Shang period but was especially common in Western Zhou. These items were used in protective rituals as talismans devised to ward gui away from the family abode. (*syn.* kuei)

Guilá Naquitz: A Preceramic site in the eastern Valley of Oaxaca, Mexico, with indications of a gradual transition from the Early Hunting to the Incipient Cultivation period as early as 8900 BC. It is one of the most thoroughly researched preceramic sites of Mesoamerica.

guilloche: A decorative chain pattern, often looking like regularly interlaced ribbons, reproduced on a plane surface. It has often decorated tableware.

Guinea Neolithic: A series of industries in the coastal regions of West Africa during the last 10,000 years. Backed microliths akin to those manufactured in earlier times are associated with pottery and with ground stone ax- and hoe-like implements. One of the few well-described and dated occurrences is at Bosumpra near Abetifi in Ghana, where the occupation is dated between the 4th–2nd millennia BC. Because most of these peoples were nonliterate, there are few records up to AD c. 1000, when Arab historians began describing the western African region. By that time, it already had centralized states, agriculture, and long-distance trading routes.

Guitarrero Cave: A stratified cave site of long occupation in the Callejón de Huaylas in northern Peru. It was occupied in the Preceramic period (c. 12,500–6,000 years ago) and continued through later ceramic periods, showing domesticated lima and common beans by c. 8000 BC. A wide variety of artifacts, lithic and organic, in Guitarrero I (10,610 to 360 bc) contains flaked tools similar to the Ayacucho complex and Tagua-Tagua. Stemmed points similar to those in Lauricocha II were found in the same level. There is evidence that the site was occupied by hunter gatherers and that the subsistence was transhumance. Some human bones, if dated correctly, represent the earliest human remains yet found in South America. Guitarrero II has produced a series of radiocarbon dates covering the period c. 8500–5700 BC and contains bone and wood artifacts, basketry, loosely woven textiles, and the willow-leaf projectile point.

gully: An eroded land form, which is a trench with steep side walls and a head wall cut into the land by an accelerated stream of water. The process of erosion can remove large quantities of sediment and destroy archaeological deposits. Some deep gullies have been used as settlement sites.

Gumanye: A Late Iron Age site in southern Zimbabwe, AD c. 1000–1100. It gives its name to a facies of the Kutama tradition. It marks a clear break with the preceding Early Iron Age with the appearance of Shona people at Great Zimbabwe.

Gumelnita: A Late Neolithic/Copper Age culture of eastern Romania, Bulgaria, and northern Greece (eastern Balkans) c. 3800–3000/2500 BC. There were permanent villages of rectangular houses forming low tells, use of copper and gold, and a flourishing painted pottery. The pottery was often decorated with graphite designs. Gumelnita can be derived from the Hamangia, Boian, and Maritza cultures that preceded it in this area. The culture parallels the partitioning of the closely related Karanovo V and VI culture in Bulgaria. The Gumelnita represents the climax of the Neolithic sequence in south Romania. (*syn.* Gumelnitsa, Gumeilnita)

Gundestrup: The find spot of a great silver cauldron of late pre-Roman Iron Age in a bog in northern Jutland, Denmark, which was clearly a votive offering. On the 12 plaques that decorate both the inside and outside of the bowl are scenes from Celtic mythology. The cauldron was probably manufactured in Romania or Bulgaria or possibly Thrace during the 2nd or 1st century BC.

Günz/Mindel: A major division of Pleistocene time and deposits in the Alpine region of Europe and one of the divisions of the geological system that recognized the number of Pleistocene glaciations. The Günz-Mindel Interglacial

preceded the Mindel Glacial stage and followed the Günz Glacial state and was a time of relatively moderate climatic conditions between two periods of glacial advance. The Günz-Mindel Interglacial is correlated with the Cromerian Interglacial stage of northern Europe and the series of interglacials recognized in Britain: the Pastonian (oldest), Beestonian, and Cromerian. The Günz-Mindel Interglacial is also broadly equivalent to the Aftonian Interglacial stage of North America.

Günz glaciation: The first major Alpine glacial advance and first major Pleistocene glaciation (ice age), which started c. 590,000 years ago and lasted until the end of the Mindel Glaciation. The Günz preceded the Günz-Mindel Interglacial and followed the Donau-Günz Interglacial, both periods of relatively moderate climatic conditions. The Günz is correlated with the Baventian stage of marine deposits of Great Britain and the Menapian Glacial stage of northern Europe. It is broadly equivalent to the Nebraskan Glacial stage of North America. (*syn.* Günz Glacial stage)

Guo Moruo (1892–1978): Important person in Chinese archaeology, who used a Marxist interpretation of history in all his work. He produced a monumental study of inscriptions on oracle bones and bronze vessels, *Liang Chou chin wen tz'u ta hsi t'u lu k'ao shi"h* (1935, new ed. 1957; *Corpus of Inscriptions on Bronzes from the Two Chou Dynasties*). He was the leading authority on Shang bone inscriptions and on bronze from the Chou period, using these first written texts as a basis for his study of Chinese society. In this work, he attempted to demonstrate, according to Communist doctrine, the "slave society" nature of ancient China. His research work on bronzes from the Chou period, carried out at the same time as B. Karlgren's, consisted of making a chronological classification of the bronzes based on their inscriptions and using their typology as a secondary procedure. He reconstructed the development of these bronzes and defined the basis on which research being carried out today still rests. After 1949, Guo held many important positions in the People's Republic of China, including the presidency of the Chinese Academy of Sciences.

Gura Baciului: An Early Neolithic site of the Cris culture of Transylvania similar to Karanovo I, Sesklo, and Anza settlements. Obsidian from Hungarian sources is a major component of the lithic assemblage.

Guran, Tepe: A site in western Iran with at least 21 occupation levels dated c. 6500–5500 BC. In the earliest aceramic levels, there were remains of wooden huts, probably from a semipermanent winter camp. In later levels with pottery, there are mud-brick houses and evidence of farming, goat domestication, and barley cultivation.

Gussage All Saints: An Iron Age settlement in Dorset, England, with evidence of metalworking—bronze fittings for chariots and harnesses. It may have been an area of vehicle production.

Guti: A 3rd millennium BC tribe of the Zagros Mountains, which invaded Mesopotamia c. 2230 BC and brought the downfall of the Akkadian empire. Their original home was probably Luristan or Hammadan. The Gutian, or post-Akkadian, period in Mesopotamia was a time of political fragmentation (there is evidence of independent rulers in various parts of Babylonia, such as Gudea at Lagash), and the period only lasted for about 40 years (until c. 2130 BC) before the people of Ur-Nammu (Uruk) took over the region. The Guti, from their home in the Zagros, continued to menace the subsequent dynasties and kingdoms, but they were never able to take control of southern Mesopotamia again. (*syn.* Gutians)

gutta: A series of peglike features, shaped like a frustrum of a cone, on the underside of mutules and triglyphs on classical buildings of the Doric order. (*syn.* pl. guttae)

gutturnium: A narrow-necked Roman water jug or pitcher. It was an elegant vessel, used by slaves for pouring water over the hands of guests before and after a meal.

guttus: A narrow-necked Roman cruet or oil flask, by which liquids could be poured out drop by drop; used in sacrifices.

Guweicun: A late Eastern Zhou cemetery site in Hui-hsien, China. Three large shaft tombs have north and south entrance ramps and are similar in construction to far earlier Shang tombs. The largest of the three was marked at ground level by a low mound edged with large stones, a new feature modeled on works of the northern nomads. A number of cast-iron tools—plowshares, picks, hoes, shovels, axes, and chisels—were found in the tomb. (*syn.* Ku-wei-ts'un)

Gvardzhilas-Klde: An Upper Palaeolithic cave site in the Greater Caucasus of Georgia. Artifacts include backed blades, Gravettian points, needles, and harpoons.

Gwisho: A series of mounds and hot springs in western Zambia with evidence of intense Late Stone Age (Zambian Wilton) occupation from about 5,000–3,500 years ago. The sites are of particular importance because of the preservation of organic materials in the spring deposits. Grass-lined hollows have been interpreted as sleeping places. Among the wooden artifacts in the assemblage were bows, arrowheads, fire drills, and digging sticks. The microlithic chipped stone industry is of the Zambian Wilton type. Graves at the sites yielded some 35 Khoisan skeletons. The economy was based on hunting game but also on a variety of vegetables.

Gwithian: A Middle Bronze Age farming site in Cornwall, England, with prehistoric and medieval remains. There are houses of the Beaker period, field systems of the Middle Bronze Age, and small square fields of Celtic type. The sites of the post-Roman period include a small settlement of circular dry stone huts, a shell midden, and a late Saxon chapel. There are also sub-Roman (400–950), early Christian (550–850), and Late Saxon (850–1050) levels, which have been determined by the pottery. Gwithian ware and Mediterranean imports mark the first phase, and Grass-Marked pottery, the second. The chapel of St. Gocanius is one of the few pre-Conquest buildings in Cornwall (c. 9th–10th centuries).

gymnasium: An area in ancient Greek cities used as a sports ground. It could be within or outside the city and normally had a palaestra, running track, dressing rooms, bathrooms, and other rooms for exercise and ball games. It was for men only, except at Sparta, and was also a center of education (philosophy, literature, and music). The Academy of Plato and the Lyceum of Aristotle were both gymnasia. The combination of health for the body and education for the mind might have represented an ideal to the Greeks. The literal meaning of the word *gymnasion* was "school for naked exercise," and every important city had one. (*syn.* pl. gymnasia)

gypsum: A soft white stone, hydrated calcium sulfate mineral, which was a primary or secondary mineral of limestone, shale, marl, and clay. Combined with sand, water, and organic materials, it was used to make plasterlike materials used in cements, coatings, casts, molds, and sculptures. The dense, fine-grained variety is alabaster and was used in architecture. The fibrous massive variety is used for ornaments and jewelry. Nowadays, gypsum is used in the manufacture of plaster of Paris.

Hh

Ha'amonga: A massive coral trilithon (archway) at Ha-
hake, Tongatapu (Tonga) with a lintel resting in two notched
uprights. According to tradition, it was erected around AD
1200 by the Tui Tonga Dynasty's chief. The monument is
unique in the Pacific region. (*syn.* Ha'amonga-a-Maui)

Habasesti: A stratigraphic settlement site of the Late Neolithic Cuceteni culture, in north Moldavia, Romania. The
main settlement level (Cucuteni A3), has a radiocarbon date
of c. 3130 BC. A village of almost 70 houses is on a promontory site, which is defended by a ditch and palisade. Rich
polychrome painted ware and a group of large copper bossed
pendants, with affinities in Denmark and Austria, have been
found.

habiline/habilis: An early member of the genus Homo,
including *Homo habilis*, known from fossils in Africa dating
from 2 million to about 1.5 million years ago. There is much
disagreement about the evolutionary place of this species, but
H. habilis is generally accepted as the earliest member of the
genus Homo, following Australopithecus and preceding
Homo erectus. Habilines made crude stone tools. Their skeletal remains were first discovered in 1959–1960 in northern
Tanzania.

Habiru: A nomadic people, largely Semitic, whose name
means "outsiders." This name was applied to nomads, fugitives, bandits, and workers of inferior status; the word is
etymologically related to "Hebrew," and the relationship of
the Habiru [and the Hyksos people that included the Habiru]
to the Hebrews has long been debated. The Habiru appear to
have established a military aristocracy in Palestine, infiltrat-
ing the area during the Middle Bronze Age, bringing to the
towns new defenses and new prosperity (as well as Egyptian
culture) without interrupting the basic character of the local
culture. The Habiru survived the destruction of Megiddo,
Jericho, and Tell Beit Mirsim, which followed the Egyptians'
expulsion of the Hyksos from Egypt into Palestine at the end

of the Middle Bronze Age (c. 1550). They were ancestral to
the Israelites. (*syn.* Khabiru, 'Apiru, Hapiru)

habitat: The physical environment where a plant or animal
naturally or normally lives and grows. An area in the biome
where different communities and populations flourish, each
with specific locales.

habitation site: A general term for any area that has evidence of a domestic activity, such as food preparation. Any
site where people lived in the past.

HABS/HAER survey: Historic American Buildings Sur-
vey/Historic American Engineering Record, standards for
historic surveys of buildings in the United States.

Habuba al-Kabira: A fortified site on the Euphrates River
in Syria, representing an outpost of Uruk culture in the 4th
millennium BC, probably as a trading center. There was a
large walled town with pottery, seals, and numerical tablets
that are southern Mesopotamian in character. (*syn.* Habuba
Kabira)

hachure: In map making and drawing, short lines laid down
in a pattern to indicate the direction of slope on the survey of
an earthwork. The hachure points downhill, and its length is
related to the steepness of the slope.

Hacilar: (haj'-i-lar) A small but important site in the lake
region of southwest Turkey, with Late Neolithic and early
Chalcolithic (c. 5600–4500 BC) levels. The aceramic early
levels have some radiocarbon dates in the 7th millennium BC.
The houses were of mud brick or wood and daub on stone
foundations, with an upper story of wood. They were finished
internally in plaster, rarely painted. Crops included barley,
emmer, and lentils, and bones of sheep, deer, and cattle were
also found. The site was abandoned and then reoccupied in
the Late Neolithic, early in the 6th millennium BC, when it
had more substantial houses, monochrome red to brown
pottery, and some use of copper. Querns, mortars, and
braziers were fitted into mud plaster floors, while recesses in

the walls acted as cupboards. The kitchen was separated from the living rooms, and upper stories were used as granaries and workshops. Female figurines of a unique style were also made. The latest phase of this period was burnt c. 5400 BC, and when the site was reoccupied it was smaller; this settlement was also burnt c. 5050–5000 BC. The Hacilar (Chalcolithic) period had a fortified settlement, characterized by boldly painted red on white pottery.

hacksilver: The fragments of ornaments and ingots in Viking silver hoards, having been deliberately cut up to be weighed out for the purpose of making payments, before the use of coins as money.

Hadar: A site in northeast Ethiopia where remains of Australopithecus 3.5 to 2.5 million years old have been found, named by their finders *A. afarensis*. The best-known specimens are an almost half-complete skeleton known as Lucy and fragments of at least thirteen individuals found together. Claims of stone tool making at about 2.7 million years ago have also been made.

Haddenham: A Neolithic long barrow in Cambridgeshire, England, important for its being an example of the type of wooden structures that may have existed in nonmegalithic long mounds of northern Europe. The site was covered by fen peat, thus preserving the original barrow in waterlogged conditions.

Hadra ware: A kind of Hellenistic pottery first found in the Hadra cemetery at Alexandria. It was a burial container inscribed with the name of the deceased and often had the date painted or incised on the shoulder.

Hadrian's Villa: An imperial country residence built AD c. 125–134 at Tivoli near Rome by the emperor Hadrian. This villa is considered the epitome of architecture and elegance in the Roman world. The imperial garden city included baths and bath buildings, libraries, sculpture gardens, theaters, alfresco dining halls, pavilions, and private suites. Significant portions of the complex have survived to modern times. Hadrian himself was unable to enjoy his villa for long, as he died in 138.

Hadrian's Wall: The best known of the Roman frontier works, built in northern Britain on orders of the emperor Hadrian in AD 122–127. Stone-walled ditches facing north and a military zone behind are protected by an earthwork to the south. It ran for 80 Roman miles (about 73 mil/117 km) from the Solway Firth (Bowness) to the Tyne (Wallsend). The wall itself is 12–15 meters wide, with small forts (mile castles) with two turrets between built into it every 1 mile (1.5 km), and 16 Roman forts along it. Some parts were originally constructed in turf, but in time (by about 160) the whole structure was completed in limestone. To the south of the wall, another great ditch with wide-spaced banks, the vallum,

follows roughly the same line, perhaps marking the limit of the military zone. Although the whole work, with outlying forts and service roads, was a most impressive undertaking, it could serve its purpose of excluding the barbarians only when adequately manned. It was overrun in 197, rebuilt by Severus, overrun again in 296, and restored by Constantius Chlorus, overrun again in 367, and rebuilt by Count Theodosius, and finally abandoned by AD 400. Antoninus built a second wall (the Antonine Wall) about 100 kilometers (62 mil) to the north along the line between Forth and Clyde Rivers. This second line of fortification lasted only AD c. 145–160.

Hafit: A mountain ridge in southeast Arabia with Jemdet Nasr-type pottery in cairns. There are other Mesopotamian ceramics and local materials in the early–3rd millennia BC burials. It is evidence of Mesopotamian contact with the ancient Magan culture and provides the name for the earliest Bronze Age cultural period in the area.

haft: The handle of a compound weapon or a tool–such as an adze, awl, ax, or knife.

Haftavan Tepe: A tell site in northwest Iran occupied off and on from the Early Bronze Age to the Sassanian period. The earliest occupation is dated to the 6th millennium BC, but its most important material comes from the Elamite period of the 15th–13th centuries BC. A royal tomb of c. 1500 BC containing 21 skeletons, some covered in red ochre, is an early example of a vaulted tomb. This tomb was connected by a stairway to the main temple, which contained many simple burials, some in urns. Fragments of inscribed stelae in cuneiform in the 14th-century BC Elamite language have provided details of the temple economy. In the 8th century BC, the mound became an Urartian citadel with an attached lower town. It was destroyed either by Sargon II in 714 BC or by the Cimmerians. The site was reoccupied in the Sassanian period: A town wall and numerous graves of this period are known. (*syn.* Haft Tepe)

Hafun/Hafun Point: A peninsula on the eastern coast of Somalia with the best archaeological evidence yet available from the East African coast south of the Red Sea for early trade contact with the Mediterranean world at the beginning of the Christian era. No permanent settlement is attested, but burials contain imported pottery, some of it Hellenistic. The earliest written accounts of the East African coast occur in the *Periplus Maris Erythraei*—apparently written by a Greek merchant living in Egypt in the second half of the 1st century AD—and in Ptolemy's Guide to Geography, the East African section of which, in its extant form, probably represents a compilation of geographic knowledge available at Byzantium in about 400. The *Periplus* describes in some detail the shore of what was to become northern Somalia. Ships sailed from there to western India to bring back cotton cloth, grain, oil, sugar, and ghee, while others moved down the Red Sea to the East African coast bringing cloaks, tunics, copper, and tin. Aromatic gums, spices, tortoise shell, ivory, and slaves were traded in return. (*syn.* Xaafuun)

Hagar Qim: The site of one of the largest of the Maltese temple complexes, in southwest Malta. It contains three separate temples, constructed over a considerable period. The buildings have numerous altars of various shapes and a variety of niches and recesses. Many of the stones have pitted decoration. A cult centering around rock-cut collective tombs has been dated 2400 BC.

Hagia Sophia: In Constantinople (now Istanbul), a splendid cathedral built under the direction of the Byzantine emperor Justinian I. It is a unique building and one of the world's great monuments. The domed basilica was built in an amazing 6 years, completed in AD 537. The architects were Anthemius of Tralles and Isidore of Miletus. Constantinople was the capital of the Eastern Roman Empire at the time. For many years the Hagia Sophia was unsurpassed in size, and the interior still retains much of its original elegant appearance. Its lower walls are faced with polished multicolored marbles, and the vaults, domes, and pendentives are covered with brilliant Byzantine mosaics set in their background of gold. (*syn.* Church of the Holy Wisdom)

Hagia Triada: A Minoan palace in southern Crete, built c. 2200 BC and inhabited until its destruction c. 1450 BC. Connected by road to the palace at Phaestus, one room contained numerous clay tablets with Linear A inscriptions. The small town around it continued later, and it is to Late Minoan III that the site's most famous find belongs. This is a pottery coffin painted with scenes associated with funeral ritual, the pouring of libations, bringing of offerings, and so on. Also well known is the Harvester Vase, a stone rhyton portraying in low relief a delightful and vigorous scene of a procession of celebrating harvesters. (*syn.* Ayia Triadha)

Haguenau: A Bronze and Iron Age cemetery of burial mounds in Bas-Rhin, France. The richest mounds date to c. 1500–1350 BC when the area was under the influence of the Tumulus culture of southern Germany. There were heavy palstaves and pottery with geometric excised decoration.

Haithabu: A medieval Danish trading settlement on the Jutland Peninsula in northwest Germany of the 7th century AD, important in the southeast Baltic region. Its trade included slaves, furs, textiles, iron, and weapons; it was one of the earliest Scandinavian urban centers. In the early 9th century, King Godfred of Denmark built the Danewirk, an earthwork barrier, along the base of the peninsula south of Hedeby to protect it from Frankish incursions. (*syn.* Hedeby)

Hajdúsámson: A level of Hungarian and Rumanian metalwork hoards (Apa-Hajdusamson horizon) dated to the later Early Bronze Age, c. 1700–1500 BC. The bronze solid-hilted swords, disk-butted and shaft-tube axes, and daggers are often richly decorated, but the gold working is even finer. The horizon includes many small ornaments (disks, rings, bracelets) as well as unique pieces such as the Persinari sword and the Bihar cups. The unique pieces were probably the products of a single workshop in Transylvania.

Haji/haji: An unglazed Japanese earthenware, developed in the Tumulus/Kofun period of the 4th century AD, derived from the Yayoi tradition and influenced by Sue-ware shapes in the 5th century. Early Haji pottery is characterized by the appearance of ceremonial vessels that are homogenous throughout a wide area, along with domestic vessels made in local styles. After the wheel-made, kiln-fired Sue pottery was introduced in the 5th century, only domestic vessels were made in Hajii ware, and from the 8th century onward Hajii pottery, too, was made on the potter's wheel. A rust-red earthenware, Haji ware is baked in oxidizing fires. Shapes unknown to the Yayoi culture appeared in Haji ware, however, such as small, globular jars and wide-rimmed pots. Although the surfaces of Haji pieces are finely finished, both their form and firing lack the refinement of Yayoi pottery.

Hajjar bin Humeid: A site of pre-Islamic occupation in southwest Arabia with a number of strata and a ceramic sequence from the 1st millennium BC through the mid-1st millennium AD.

Hajji Muhammed: A small early 5th-millennium BC site near Uruk in southern Mesopotamia, which has given its name to a type of painted pottery and an early phase of the 'Ubaid culture (Ubaid 2). The pottery is painted in dark brown or purplish black in a geometric style. Hajji Muhammed pottery is found also at Eridu in layers stratified between the earliest Eridu pottery and the fully developed 'Ubaid culture. It is found over southern Mesopotamia, as far north as Ras Al-Amiya. The architecture was wattle and dabu. (*syn.* Hajjii Mohammad)

Hakataya: A pottery-making tradition of the American Southwest, which includes groups of regionally distinct cultures of the southwestern plateau and Colorado River basin, such as Cerbat, Prescott, Cohohina, and Sinagua. There is considerable disagreement about the real extent and cultural affiliations of the tradition, and dates start around AD 500. As with other Southwest traditions (e.g., Anasazi, Mogollon), the Hakataya is thought to have emerged from the Desert tradition. (*syn.* Patayan)

Halaf: A large tell site on the Khabur River in northeastern Syria near the Turkish border, which is the type site of an important stage of north Mesopotamian development, roughly 6th millennium BC to the beginning of the 5th (5050–4300 BC). The distinctive pottery, known as Halaf ware, was exceptionally fine, a thin hard ware in a wide range of competent and attractive shapes bearing brilliant carpet-like designs painted in black, red, and white on the buff surface. Simple steatite stamp seals were coming into use, which imply the development of personal property. In the villages, the typical dwelling was a round house with a vaulted dome (tholos), constructed of mud brick, sometimes on stone foundations. The Halaf culture was succeeded in northern Mesopotamia by the 'Ubaid culture. It was the seat of an Aramaean kingdom and then a provincial capital of the Neo-Assyrian empire. In 808 BC, Adad-nirari III of Assyria sacked the city and reduced the surrounding district to a province of the Assyrian Empire. The Assyrian archives provide valuable details of the administrative affairs of the time. It was the Old Testament 'Gozan' to which the Israelites were deported in 722 after the capture of Samaria. (*syn.* Guzana; Halafian; Tell Halaf)

Halaf culture complex: A material culture with a distinctive painted pottery style, centered at Tell Halaf. It is divided into Early, Middle, and Late phases from the late 6th to early 5th millennia BC (5050–4300). The pottery is decorated with geometric, floral, and some nature motifs. The Late Halaf pottery includes a polychrome painted ware. Well-known sites include Tell Aqab, Arpachiyah, and Yarim Tepe.

Hala Sultan Tekke: A Late Cypriot settlement supporting copper trade in the Aegean, Anatolia, Syria, and Egypt. It was abandoned in the 11th century BC, possibly because an earthquake destroyed its harbor.

Halawa Valley: A valley on eastern Molokai, Hawaiian Islands, which has been the focus of intensive archaeological research. Major sites include one of the earliest Hawaiian settlements at the valley mouth (c. 600–1200), and inside the valley are many irrigated taro terraces that document intensification of cultivation and perhaps political development at a late stage of Hawaiian prehistory (after 1500).

halberd: A weapon with a pointed or V-shaped blade mounted at right angles to its haft (handle), yet with its flat surface in the same plane as the shaft, and used with a chopping motion. In bronze, it was popular in the European Early Bronze Age (mainly in Ireland and central Europe) and appears again in the Chinese Bronze Age.

Halfan: A Nubian stone industry and culture, named after the settlement of the Wadi Halfa, dating from c. 23,000–17,000 BC. Its sites, characterized by tools made on small blades, appear to have been camps of hunters and fishermen.

half-life: The time taken for half of a given amount of a radioactive substance to decay into a nonradioactive substance. It is also defined as the time taken for half the quantity of a radioactive isotope in a sample to decay and form a stable element. It is the basis of radiocarbon and other radiometric dating methods. This decay rate, expressed as a statistical constant, is different for each isotope. If a sample, such as a piece of wood, has half of the original amount of radiocarbon remaining, then a time equivalent to the half-life has passed since the wood died. The half-life of radiocarbon is 5,730 ± 40 years, while the half-life of radioactive potassium, used in potassium–argon dating is 1.3 billion years. The half-life in effect determines the general age range over which a radiometric dating method is potentially useful. (*syn.* half-value period, radioactive half-life)

half-timbered: Constructed of wood framing with spaces filled with masonry, or by stone, rubble, or mud brick.

Halicarnassus: A Greek city on the west coast of Turkey (once Asia Minor), the birthplace of the 5th-century BC historian Herodotus. Having belonged to the Delian league, its peak period was as capital city of Mausolus (satrap), who ruled Caria from 377–353 BC. He built walls, public buildings (agora, theater), and the famous mausoleum (one of the Seven Wonders of Ancient World) as his funerary temple, of which nothing now remains but fragments preserved in the British Museum. Halicarnassus' sack by Alexander the Great in 334 BC is the last major event on record. Virtually all traces of ancient Halicarnassus have now unfortunately disappeared under modern Bodrum. Some sections of the city wall survive, and the site of the mausoleum, the tomb of Mausolus, is known. (*syn.* Bodrum)

Hallstatt: A site on Lake Hallstatt in the Austrian Alps with a cemetery of over 3,000 cremation and inhumation graves with great quantities of local and imported grave goods. There were prehistoric salt mines in the area. Hallstatt is also a late Bronze Age and early Iron Age cultural tradition, c. 1200–600 BC, in continental temperate Europe. The term also refers to a cultural period of the Late Bronze Age and Early Iron Age in central Europe, divided into four phases, Hallstatt A, B, C, and D. In central European archaeology, the terms Hallstatt A (12th and 11th centuries BC) and Hallstatt B (10th–8th centuries BC) are used as a chronological framework for the urnfield cultures of the Late Bronze Age. The first iron objects north of the Alps appear at the close of this period, and the Iron Age proper begins with the Hallstatt C (or I) stage of the 7th century BC. The area of fullest development is Bohemia, upper Austria, and Bavaria, where hill forts were constructed and the dead were sometimes interred on or with a four-wheeled wagon, covered by a mortuary house below a barrow. Sheet bronze was still used for armor, vessels, and decorative metalwork, but the characteristic weapon was a long iron sword (or bronze copy). These swords are found as far afield as southeast England, in the so-called Iron Age A cultures. During the Hallstatt D (or II) period, in the 6th century, the most advanced cultures were found further west, in Burgundy, Switzerland, and the Rhineland. Wagon burials were still prominent, and trade brought luxury objects from the Greek and Etruscan cities around the Mediterranean. By the close of this period in the mid-5th century BC, elements of Hallstatt culture were found from southern France to Yugoslavia and Czechoslovakia. The Hallstatt precedes the La Tène period; the Hallstatt Iron Age culture certainly developed from the Urnfield Bronze Age groups. (*syn.* Hallstatt period)

Hallur: A prehistoric site in southern India, which has produced evidence of a Neolithic-Chalcolithic culture of the 2nd millennium BC, characterized by one-roomed circular houses, burnished gray ware, an abundant ground stone industry, and a few copper objects. A later level has black and red ware, iron objects, and a radiocarbon date of c. 1100–1400 BC. Three periods have been defined: Hallur IA, IB, and II.

halophytic: Plants (such as saltbush, sea lavender) that can tolerate the absorption of a certain amount of mineral salts present in the soil in which they grow. These salts impregnate the plant tissues. Halophytes usually have a physiological resemblance to a true xerophyte.

Hal Saflieni: A large rock-cut hypogeum on Malta, which was constructed by the same population that built the Maltese temples, and is a complex of many small rock-cut chambers, on three different levels, linked by a series of halls, passages, and stairways. Many of the chambers are elaborately decorated, often with carved features imitating wooden structures such as beams and lintels; other chambers have painted decoration, usually on the ceilings. Most of the chambers had been used for burial, and it has been calculated that some 7,000 individuals were buried in the whole hypogeum, over a period of some centuries. The hypogeum may also have been used as a temple as some places without burials were set aside for ritual. Artifacts include highly decorated pottery and a series of female figurines. The earliest chambers date to the 5th millennium BC.

Hama: A city in central Syria on the Orontes River, an important prehistoric settlement that became the kingdom of Hamath under the Aramaeans in the 11th century BC. It fell under Assyrian control in the 9th century BC, later passing under Persian, Macedonian, and Seleucid rule. A Neolithic occupation comparable to that of Mersin was succeeded by a village with Halaf pottery. Later levels continued through to the Iron Age, when it was an inland site of the Phoenicians. During the 2nd millennium BC, Hama was a large town, but it does not appear in ancient documents until c. 1000 BC, when it became capital of an Aramaean kingdom. Excavations revealed a fine palace of this period, with evidence of ivory carving. The Arabs took the city in the 7th century AD. (*syn.* ancient Hamath; Epiphaneia)

Hamada, Kosaku (1881–1938): A Japanese art historian and archaeologist who was important in the development of archaeology in Japan. He realized the importance of the links between the Japanese archipelago and the main continent (Korea and China). He established the first formal course in archaeology in Japan.

Hamangia: A Late Neolithic culture of the Black Sea near the mouth of the Danube (Romania and Bulgaria), which was contemporaneous with the early periods of the Boian and Maritsa cultures. The culture was rather short lived c. 4000–3700 BC, and was succeeded by the Gumelnita culture. It is regarded by some as a branch of the Impressed Ware culture, arriving by sea from the Aegean before 4300 BC. Noteworthy are its spondylus shell bracelets and its famous terra-cotta and marble figurines.

Hambledon Hill: A Neolithic causewayed camp and Iron Age hill fort in Dorset, England. The causewayed camp of the 3rd millennium BC had pits of pottery, flint tools, and bone. Human skulls had been placed at regular intervals along the ditch bottom. The disarticulated human remains of the camp may reveal exposure of corpses. A long barrow was nearby on the same hilltop. Much later, in the first millennium BC, there was an impressive Iron Age hill fort on another ridge of this three-spurred hill.

Hamburg: A city in northern Germany whose history begins with the Hammaburg, a moated castle of modest size, built in about AD 825 on a promontory between the Alster and Elbe Rivers. Archaeologists have located the fortified Carolingian monastic nucleus, which, according to the 9th-century chronicler Rimbert, was attacked by the Danes in 845.

Hamburgian: A Late Upper Palaeolithic culture of north Germany and the Low Countries, contemporary with the Magdalenian of France, c. 13,000–11,750 BP. It was the culture of the first people to colonize north Germany and the Low Countries after the final retreat of the Pleistocene ice sheets had made the area available for settlement. The Hamburgians may have been the descendants of Eastern Gravettian or peripheral Magdalenian groups. They were reindeer hunters whose tools are small, single-shouldered points, harpoons, end scrapers, microburins, and *zinken* (small beaked borers used for working antler).

hammerstone: A hard stone used as a hammer during the knapping of flint and other stone, for processing food, breaking up shells or bones, and so on.

Hammurabi (1792–1750 BC): The sixth king of the first Amorite dynasty of Babylon and one of the best known of the Mesopotamian kings. In c. 1783 BC, he began the series of campaigns that extended his empire from Mari and Nineveh to the Persian Gulf. He is best remembered for his Code of Laws, which had an emphasis on retaliation and an eye for an eye. The Code of Hammurabi also yielded detailed evidence on the structure of contemporary society. His 43-year reign saw the final extinction of Sumer as a political power. His empire declined soon after his death, until it was taken by the Hittites and Kassites c. 1595 BC. The lasting achievement of Hammurabi's rule was that the important part of Mesopotamia, which had been in the south from the beginning of the 3rd millennium BC, was shifted to the north, where it remained for more than 1,000 years. (*syn.* Hammurapi)

Handan: The capital of the Eastern Chou (Zhou) state of Caho from 386–228 BC. The area was already settled in Shang times (c. 1766–1122 BC) and first mentioned in about 500 BC, but became a center of trade and was famed for luxury and elegance as the capital. In 228, it was attacked and taken by the armies of the Ch'in Dynasty (221–206 BC) and became a commandery. Under the Han (206 BC–AD 220), it became the seat of an important feudal kingdom, Chao-kuo. The remains of the walls and foundations of buildings of both the Chao capital and the Han city still remain to the southwest of the modern city. A cemetery north of the walled city contained six chariot burials and 12 rich tombs, five with human sacrifices. (*syn.* Han-tan)

hand ax: A large bifacially worked core tool, normally oval, pointed, or pear shaped, and one of the most typical stone tools of the Lower Palaeolithic. It is the diagnostic implement of certain Lower Palaeolithic industries (Abbevillian, Chellean, Acheulian), and one variety of the Mousterian. In spite of the name, it was not an ax at all and probably served as an all-purpose tool. The oldest and crudest hand axes have been found in Africa; the finer, Acheulian, tools are known from most of Africa, Europe, southwest Asia, and India. It was used for chopping, chipping, flaking, cutting, digging, and scraping. Hand axes first appear between 1 and 2 million years ago, and they were common in assemblages for about a million years. (*syn.* hand-ax, handaxe; biface)

hand stencil: An impression of a hand produced by spraying thick paint (often made from white clay or red or yellow ocher) through a blowpipe around the edges of a hand placed against a rock surface. Many hand stencils are found in caves.

handstone: A hand-held milling stone used to process materials on a metate. (*syn.* mano)

Han Dynasty: A historical dynasty and period in China, after the collapse of the brief rule of the Ch'in (Qin) Dynasty, from 206 BC to AD 220. This dynasty took over the control of a unified China and had two main periods: Western (Early) Han (206 BC–AD 8) and Eastern (Late Han (AD 25–220), separated by the Wang Meng (Wangman) of AD 9–25. The Western Han capital was Chang'an, and the Eastern (Late) Han (AD 25–220) was Lo-Yang (Luoyang). Next to the rich tombs at Mawangdui and Mancheng, perhaps the most revealing Han archaeological finds are a number of tombs whose wall paintings, decorated tiles, and stone reliefs form

the earliest substantial corpus of Chinese pictorial art. The Han Dynasty started iron and salt monopolies, extended itself through the commandery system, opened trade to the West via the silk route, and began the tradition of court histories.

Hane: An Early Eastern Polynesian dune site on Ua Huka Island, the Marquesas. It has documented aspects of Marquesan prehistory from initial settlement (c. AD 300) to European contact. It is a crucial site for documenting early human dispersal into eastern Polynesia.

hanging bowls: Thin bronze shallow bowls found in Anglo-Saxon graves up until the 7th century, an important part of a Celtic metal-working tradition, which has its origins in the Roman and pre-Roman Iron Age. They have three equally spaced suspension rings, fixed to the bowl by escutcheons usually decorated with colored enamel and millefiori.

Hang Gon: A prehistoric bronze-working site in southern Vietnam from the late 1st millennium BC. It overlapped the Cu Lao Rua and had urnfield remains.

Hanging Grimston: A long barrow on Yorkshire Wolds, England, of the British Earlier Neolithic of the 4th millennium BC. It gave its name to the Grimston-Lyles Hill pottery, whose characteristic vessel was the round-based carinated bowl with everted rim.

hang-t'u: A type of rammed-earth construction of walls and foundation platforms for buildings developed by the Chinese from the Late Neolithic (Longshan) period and Shang Dynasty (c. 1600–1027 BC), notably at An-Yang. It was also used for shaft tombs in the Shang and Zhou (Chou) periods. Earth was packed between wooden forms in successive thin layers, each layer being pounded down before the next was added. Hangtu walls have been found at only two Late Neolithic sites, Chengziyai and Hougang. Much of the Great Wall of China was originally built of rammed earth. (*syn.* hangtu)

haniwa: Unglazed earthenware funerary sculptures or cylinders of the Kofun period (4th–7th centuries AD) in Japan. They were erected on, around, or inside mounded tomb surfaces and often had representations of horses, animals, birds, humans, and houses. They are considered to have developed out of the tall stands for Late Yayoi ritual vessels of the 3rd century.

Hapy: The Egyptian god of the inundation (flooding of the Nile), often depicted with a baboon head.

Harappa: One of the twin capitals of the Indus civilization, located in Pakistan and northwest India, c. 2300–1750 BC. Excavation has revealed a pre-Indus occupation related to that of Kot Diji and perhaps the Zhob Valley. There was a brick-walled town with pre-Harappan material, rare Indus inhumation cemetery, granaries, and cemetery of dismembered burials with non-Indus pottery, dating from reoccupation, possibly by Aryans. Mohenjo-Daro and Harappa are remarkable for their town planning and public and private systems of hygiene and sanitation. Unfortunately, the site was largely destroyed during the last century by the extraction of bricks for ballast for the Lahore-Multan railway, then under construction.

Harappan civilization: One of the great civilizations of antiquity, located in Pakistan and northwest India in the 3rd millennium BC. Nearly 300 settlements of the civilization are known: two large cities (Mohenjo-Daro and Harappa), and a number of smaller towns and villages (Chanhu-Daro, Judeirjo-Daro, Kalibangan, and Lothal). The Harappan civilization was characterized by a high level of architectural, craft, and technical achievement. We know little of the political, social, and economic structure of the civilization because, although it was literate, the script remains undeciphered. Like other early civilizations in Mesopotamia and Egypt, the Harappan civilization was based on the cultivation of cereal crops (plus rice and cotton), probably with irrigation. Among the most distinctive achievements of this civilization are architecture and town planning, with the use of the true baked brick for building, and cities and towns laid out on a grid street plan, perhaps the earliest examples of town planning in the world. Among crafts, the most outstanding were the seals, mostly made of steatite and decorated with carefully executed incised designs. The Harappan civilization came to an end early in the 2nd millennium, either as a result of environmental factors (excessive flooding) or as a result of invasions by Aryan intruders. It is divided into three phases—Early, Mature (Urban), and Late (Post Urban) and emerged from the Punjab and Baluchistan regions. (*syn.* Indus Valley civilization)

hard-hammer percussion: The use of a hammer stone to remove flakes during knapping, Hard hammer flakes are short and deep with a prominent bulb of percussion. (*syn.* hard hammer technique)

hardness: The resistance of a mineral or metal to scratching, indentation, abrasion, or cutting. There are scales and tests of hardness, including the Mohs scale, using specific minerals numbered in order of hardness with which other substances are compared. There is also the diamond pyramid scale and the Brinell hardness scale. The Brinell method involves the forcing of a ball of hardened steel of known diameter into the sample to be tested for a standard length of time under standard pressure. The softer the metal under test, the greater the diameter of the resulting depression, which is measured with a micrometer. Such tests allow conclusions to be drawn about past metalworking techniques and their efficiency. There are more than 30 different hardness tests.

hard water effect: A potential source of artifact contamination in radiocarbon dating. When material that is radiocarbon

dated has been buried, groundwater may have percolated into it. Groundwater frequently contains dissolved calcium carbonate, after it has passed through limestones. Such carbonate may crystallize in the sample to be dated. As a result, carbon from a source very much older than the sample may be included. Dates from material that has been contaminated in this way will be too old. Samples such as wood and charcoal may be treated with hydrochloric acid to dissolve the crystallized carbonate, thus eliminating the problem. Shell samples, which are themselves made of calcium carbonate, cannot be so treated. If the hard water effect is suspected and corrections are not made, the dates should be reported as maximums only.

Hargeisan: A stone industry of northern Somalia with production of large blades from prismatic cores, which appears to predate the local appearance of microlith industries. It may be related to the Eburran occupation of the central Kenyan Rift Valley between the 11th and 8th millennia BC.

Harifian: A hunter-gatherer culture of the Negev and Sinai. The people lived in the desert and in seasonal camps and had a Late Natufian lithic industry. The Harif point was an obliquely truncated bladelet with a pointed base formed by microburin technique and a steep retouch.

Harmal, Tell: An administrative center, Shaduppum, of the kingdom of Eshnunna of the Old Babylonian period, on the outskirts of Baghdad, Iraq. It was a walled settlement (Shaduppum) from the early 2nd millennium BC, with several temples, residential buildings, and a collection of literary, scholarly, and administrative texts on tablets. The Laws of Eshnunna are inscribed on two broken tablets, which are not duplicates but separate copies of an older source. The laws are believed to be about two generations older than the Code of Hammurabi; the differences between the two codes help illuminate the development of ancient law. (*syn.* Shaduppum; Tall Abu Harmal)

harpoon: A spearlike missile with a detachable head, often consisting of a pointed shaft with backward-pointing barbs. It was often loosely hafted so that it would separate from its shaft after the point had struck its target. The appearance of this weapon is associated in particular with the Magdalenian culture; it was particularly popular during the Upper Palaeolithic and Mesolithic and was used for hunting or fishing. An attached line was used to retrieve the catch. Some anthropologists refer to all barbed bone or antler points as harpoons.

Harran: An ancient city of northern Mesopotamia mentioned in Hittite, Old Testament, and Assyrian texts, now a village in southeastern Turkey. The town was located on the road that ran from Nineveh to Carchemish. It is frequently mentioned in the Bible; Abraham's family settled there when they left Ur of the Chaldeans. It was the scene of a disastrous defeat of the Roman governor Crassus by the Parthians (53

BC) and of a later defeat of the emperor Galerius by the Persian king Narses (AD 297). (*syn.* Haran, (Roman) Carrhae)

Harris lines: A term for stress lines on human bones. These are alternating patterns of arrested (abnormal) and normal bone growth resulting from stress, such as starvation and disease.

Harris matrix: A system devised by E. Harris for representing a site's stratigraphy in schematic form, emphasizing the chronological relations between the various deposits. It is a method of summarizing the vertical and horizontal interrelations of all the layers and features on a site in a diagrammatic form.

Harshaf: An ancient Egyptian and Greek ram-headed god whose cult center was at Herakleopolis Magna. A shrine was built in the 1st Dynasty (3100–2890 BC) according to the Palermo Stone. Harshaf was a fertility god. (*syn.* Arsaphes; Harsaphes)

Hasanlu: A tell site on Lake Urmia, northwest Iran, with a sequence beginning in the late 7th millennium BC. Much information has been gained on the early Ceramic Neolithic phase of the late 7th to mid-6th millennia BC. The citadel dates from the 10th century BC and is surrounded by a lower town. Four buildings on the citadel, facing onto a court and linked to a higher court with further buildings, have been interpreted as a palace complex. In c. 800 BC, Hassanlu was destroyed. One of the skeletons held a magnificent gold bowl decorated with mythical scenes in relief. The bowl is related artistically to the finds from Marlik and Ziwiyeh. Other rich finds of gold, silver, electrum, glass, and ivory have been made at Hasanlu.

Hascherkeller: A Late Bronze Age and Early Iron Age site of the Hallstatt period in Bavaria, Germany. The farmsteads enclosed by earthworks showed pottery and bronze-casting activities in the 1st millennium BC. It is typical of the period in central Europe before the emergence of large centers of production and commerce.

Hassi Mouilah: An Algerian Capsian Neolithic site of c. 5300 BP with point-based pots with impressed decoration, projectile points, geometric microliths, ostrich eggshell, and amazonite beads.

Hassuna: A prehistoric tell site near Mosul in northern Iraq with a sequence of a pre-Samarran culture in northern Mesopotamia. The site has given its name to the pottery present in its lowest levels, dated to the 6th millennium BC, and a culture complex. This pottery may be related to that of the upper levels at Jarmo and is widely distributed. It was usually a buff ware in simple shapes, sometimes burnished, sometimes painted or incised with simple geometric patterns. In higher levels, it was replaced by Samarra ware. Evidence from Yarim Tepe, another important Hassuna site, indicates that people were already experimenting with metallurgy and that pottery making was a specialist activity (with true pottery kilns). The appearance of stamp seals suggests the importance of private ownership. There were several Halaf levels and 'Ubaid levels. Subsistence was based on cereal cultivation and herding cattle, goat, and sheep. The material culture used copper, turquoise, and carnelian beads. (*syn.* Tell Hassuna)

hasta: A spear or shaft used for thrusting, or as a missile for hurling from the hand, or as a bolt from an engine. The hastile is the shaft of the spear.

Hastinapura: A site on the upper Ganges in India, which revealed important prehistoric stratigraphy. The lowest level, with ocher-colored pottery, was followed by painted gray ware and mud-brick walls. Over this, there was a settlement of mud-brick houses with northern black polished ware and coinage of the later 1st millennium BC. Over this were levels as late as the 15th century AD.

Hathor: Ancient Egyptian cow goddess, represented in either human or animal form, who was the goddess of the sky, women, fertility, and love. Her associations and cult centers were among the most numerous and diverse of any of the Egyptian deities. Hathor's worship originated in predynastic times (4th millennium BC).

Hatnub: A site in Upper Egypt, southeast of El-Amarna, with alabaster (travertine) quarries and a seasonal workers' settlement from as early as the Old Kingdom until the Middle Kingdom. There are inscriptions on stelae and graffiti on the quarry walls.

Hatra: An ancient city between the Tigris and Euphrates Rivers in northern Iraq, founded as a military outpost by the Arsacids (Parthians) during the 1st century BC. It soon became the center of the small state of Araba and was an important caravan city. Temples were built for the Sumero-Akkadian god Nergal, to Hermes (Greek), to Atargatis (Aramean), to al-Lat and Shamiya (Arabian), and to Shamash, a sun god. Hatra defied many Roman invasions. It was destroyed by the Sassanians AD c. 241. Ruins include town walls, gates, a large palace, houses, and tombs, with striking stone statues and reliefs and Aramaic inscriptions. (*syn.* present day al-Hadr)

Hatshepsut (1473–1458 BC): A queen of Egypt, reigning c. 1479–1457 BC in the 18th Dynasty. She was the daughter of Thutmose I (1504–1492 BC) and Queen Ahmose Nefetari and was married to her half-brother Thutmose II (1492–1479 BC). A strong ruler, she sent a trading expedition to Punt, as recorded in detail in her funerary temple. She was succeeded by her son Thuthmose III. Her reign was marked by peace, prosperity, and artistic achievement. Her funerary temple at

Deir El-Bahir at Thebes is one of the most original and beautiful in Egypt. (*syn.* Hatchepsut)

Hattusas: The ancient name for Boghaz Köy, the capital of the Hittites, who established a powerful empire in Anatolia and northern Syria in the 2nd millennium BC. (*syn.* Boghaz Köy; Hattusa, Hattusha, Khattusas, Bogazköy)

Hatvan: The type site, northeast of Budapest, Hungary, of the second stage of the Hungarian Early Bronze Age (which is defined by Tószeg). The Hatvan culture occurred between the Nagyrév culture and the Füzesabony, c. early 2nd millennium BC. Many of the sites are tells in the Great Hungarian plain, although enclosed hilltop sites are known in the Carpathian foothills. Cremation burials in pits were frequent. Hatvan settlements commonly produce large numbers of fired clay zoomorphic figurines and vases, as well as model cartwheels.

Haua Fteah: A large cave site in Cyrenaica, Libya, with the most complete sequence, back to c. 78,000 BC, of Upper Pleistocene and Holocene industries known from a single site in North Africa. The oldest flint industry is a Libyan variant of the Pre-Aurignacian (Libyan Amudian) and is followed successively by Levalloiso-Mousterian (60,000 years ago), Dabban (40,000 years ago), Oranian (18,000 to 16,000 years ago), Libyco-Capsian, and finally (from c. 6800–6400) by Neolithic with pottery and domesticated animals. Based on the striking of parallel-sided blades from prismatic cores, the earliest stage has clear affinities with broadly contemporary industries in Syria, Lebanon, and Israel. Its makers exploited both large game animals and seafood resources. There was a return to blade technology with the Dabban industry, and the beginning of the Dabban occupation of Crenaica seems to have coincided with the onset of very arid conditions in the Saharan regions to the south. The Oranian had small backed bladelets.

Hawaiian Islands: A series of islands in the north-central Pacific Ocean (Kauai, Oahu, Maui, Molokai, and Hawaii, plus many smaller islands) first settled by Polynesians in the mid-1st millennium AD. The area has many temple remains (Heiau), dwelling sites, and ancient horticultural systems. The finds document the development of the populous and highly stratified society observed by Captain Cook in 1778.

Hawara: A royal necropolis in Egypt's southeastern Al-Fayyum region, known as the site of the second pyramid of King Amenemhat III (reigned 1818–1770 BC). The pyramid is dated to c. 1844–1797 BC, and it has a very large mortuary temple attached. Amenemhat III brought economic prosperity by building a system to regulate the inflow of water into Lake Moeris. As part of this great work, the labyrinth described by the Greek historian Herodotus was probably built nearby. Amenemhet erected two colossuses of himself nearby, also described by the Greek historian Herodotus.

Hayonim Cave: A prehistoric site in Israel with the earliest occupation in the cave having Mousterian artifacts and bones. There is an Aurignacian layer with flint and bone tools, Kebaran deposits, and several Natufian layers.

Hazleton: A Neolithic chambered long Severn-Cotswold barrow in Gloucestershire, England, with two megalithic chambers. The radiocarbon dates were c. 4700 BC.

Hazor: A large Palestinian tell site in northern Israel, occupied from the Early Bronze Age until the Hellenistic period. In the Middle Bronze Age, c. 1700 BC, it was a large town with a citadel and surrounded by a rampart with sloping plaster ramp, of the type associated with the Hyksos. In c. 1220 BC, the Canaanites were driven from the city by the Israelites, reputedly under Joshua. In the 10th century BC, the city was rebuilt by Solomon, who constructed a monumental gateway. This city was destroyed by the Assyrians c. 734 (or 732) BC; however, the citadel continued to be used into the Hellenistic period.

header and stretcher: In architecture, a header is a brick or stone laid in a wall with its end toward the face of the wall; a stretcher is a brick or stone laid with its length parallel to the face of a wall.

headhunting: The practice of removing and preserving human heads. Headhunting arises in some cultures from a belief in the existence of a material soul. Headhunting may go back to Palaeolithic times, as in deposits of the Late Palaeolithic Azilian culture found at Ofnet in Bavaria. In Europe, the practice survived until the early 20th century in the Balkan Peninsula.

Head-Smashed-In: A bison kill site in southern Alberta, Canada, with evidence of use from 3700 BC.

Healy Lake: A prehistoric site in Tanana Valley, Alaska, with four cultural layers starting c. 11,000–10,000 bp. That layer contained Chindadn points and microblades.

hearth: Any place where a pit was dug and a fire built, sometimes identified by charcoal, baked earth, ash, discoloration, or an outline of stones or clay footing. The site of an open domestic fire might have served as a kiln or oven. Hearths often appear in one layer of soil after another as an archaeologist digs down through a site, and they are an indication of a succession of camps or habitations. Charcoal from a hearth can be dated by the radiocarbon method. Baked clay in a hearth can be dated by the palaeomagnetic method. Burnt earthen rims may provide oxidized material for archaeomagnetic dating. The hearth is often centrally located and has a variety of shapes and sizes.

Heathery Burn: A cave site in Durham, England, which had the remains of a Late Bronze Age occupation by metalsmiths. There was much pottery, animal bones, and bronzes.

The cave may have been a hunting shelter in the 8th century BC.

Heavenly Horse, Tomb of the: A 5th century AD mounded tomb of the Silla Kingdom in Kyongju City, Korea. There was an internal wooden chamber with a lacquered wooden coffin of a male dressed in gold crown and with very rich grave goods.

heavy mineral analysis: A method of analysis carried out on artifacts such as potsherds to identify the materials used; the shard is crushed and put into a viscous fluid in which the heavier minerals sink to the bottom. It is used to determine the geological source of the sand inclusions in the clay of the pot and therefore the probable area of manufacture. The method involves the crushing of 10–30 grams of pottery and the floating of the resulting powder on a heavy liquid such as bromoform with a specific gravity of 2.85. Heavy minerals like zircon, garnet, epidote, and tourmaline sink, while quartz sand and clay float: it is the heavy minerals (separated, identified, and counted under a low-power microscope) that characterize the parent formation and enable the source of the sand to be identified.

heddle loom: A specialized loom that lifts some of the warp (lengthwise) threads so that the weft (crosswise) threads can be passed through the warp easily and quickly. The heddles are short lengths of wire or flat steel strips used to deflect the warp to either side of the main sheet of fabric. Originally, heddles were movable rods, but later cords, wires, or steel bands were used. They are supported by the loom's harness, and each has an eyelet through which the warp threads pass. The heddle is considered to be the most important single advance in the evolution of looms in general. (*syn.* heald loom)

Hedeby: An important Viking settlement in northern Germany and one of the earliest Scandinavian urban centers, established in the late 8th century. It is situated on a fjord, defended by a large earth rampart. Between 800–1050, Hedeby was a major trading center, and many imported luxury goods have been found, especially in graves. Excavation has revealed many wooden buildings, well preserved in waterlogged conditions, and evidence of industrial and commercial activity. It served as an early focus of national unification and as a crossroads for Western-Eastern European and European-Western Asian trade. (*syn.* Haithabu, Haddeby)

Heekeren, H. Robert Van (1902–1974): Dutch archaeologist who spent his career in Indonesia and wrote two important books—*The Stone Age of Indonesia* (1957, 1972) and *The Bronze-Iron Age of Indonesia* (1958). Van Heekeren excavated on Sulawesi and Java.

Heh: The Egyptian god of infinity or infinite space, usually represented as a kneeling man either holding a notched palm rib in each hand or wearing a palm rib or sun disk on his head. (*syn.* Neheh)

heiau: A prehistoric Hawaiian stone temple, akin to the Marae of eastern Polynesia. Most heiau are complex arrangements of walls, terraces, and platforms. Holo-Holo-Ku Heiau is one of the oldest examples.

Heijo: The site of an 8th century AD palace and the capital of the Ritsuryo state in Nara Prefecture, Japan. The seat of the government from 710–784, the grid city plan includes remains of some 500 buildings, including royal residences, administrative quarters, warehouses, and workshops. Of particular interest are over 20,000 inked thin rectangular pieces of wood (*mokkan*), which served as office memoranda and labels attached to tributes from the provinces. (*syn.* Nara Palace)

hei tiki: A Maori neck pendant, often of greenstone, in the shape of a human.

Heket: An Egyptian goddess represented in the form of a frog, standing for rebirth and new life. Heket's strongest association was with childbirth, particularly the final stages of labor. (*syn.* Heqat)

Helgö: A small island in Lake Malaren in Sweden, which was a migration period trading and industrial post in the 1st millennium AD. There are several important artisans' (brooch, bead) houses spanning the 5th–6th centuries up to the 9th century. Exotic finds include a 7th-century Buddha from Kashmir, a Coptic ladle, a number of gold coins, and Rhenish pots. The molds and debris from the brooch making provide a great deal of new information about the development of this craft up to the beginning of the Viking period. Helgö was probably abandoned before the end of the 9th century.

Heliopolis: An important ancient Egyptian city, which was the major cult center of the sun god Re (Ra), just east of Cairo. The oldest obelisk in existence—that of King Senwosret (Sesostris) I—remains on the site. The two obelisks of Thutmose III, called Cleopatra's Needle, are now in London and New York. It was the capital of the 15th nome of Lower Egypt, but was important as a religious rather than a political center. Its great temple of Re, built c. 2600 BC during the early Old Kingdom, was second in size only to that of Amon at Thebes. In the New Kingdom, the temple of Re-Horakhte became the repository of royal records. (*syn.* Tell Hisn, ancient Iunu, On, Baalbek)

Helladic: The Bronze Age culture of central and southern mainland Greece, with three main divisions: Early (c. 3000–2000 BC), Middle (c. 2000–1550 BC), and Late (c. 1550–1050 BC). It is equivalent to Cycladic in the Cyclades and Minoan in Crete; Late Helladic is equated with the period of the Mycenaean civilization. Each of the three periods is subdivided into three phases designated by Roman numerals. (*syn.* Helladic culture)

Hellenistic period: Period of widest Greek influence, the era between the death of Alexander the Great (323 BC) and the rise of the Roman Empire (27/30 BC), when a single, uniform civilization, based on Greek traditions, prevailed all over the ancient world, from India, in the east, to Spain, in the west. During these three centuries, Greek culture crossed many political frontiers and spread through many cities founded at that time, especially the new capitals of Alexandria, Antioch, and Pergamum. A common civilization became established throughout the known world for the first time, one that integrated the cultural heritage of each region and subsequently left a deep impression on the institutions, thought, religions, and art of the Roman, Parthian, and Kushan empires. Hellenistic cultural influence continued to be a powerful force in the Roman and Parthian Empires during the early centuries AD. A common form of the Greek language, Koine [Greek: "common"] developed, which was largely indebted to Attic Greek. The term *hellenistic art* is applied to the post-classical material outside this geographic area, such as in Etruria or southern Italy. (*syn.* Hellenistic and Roman period; hellenistic)

Hellespont: The former name of the Dardanelles, the narrow strait in northwestern Turkey, linking the Aegean Sea with the Sea of Marmara. This narrow sea channel divides Europe from Asia Minor at the northeast corner of the Mediterranean. The strait holds a significant place in history. Both Troy and Byzantium owed their importance to their location at the entrance to the Black Sea. The Hellespont is the scene of the Greek legend of the two lovers Hero and Leander. The ancient city of Troy defended the Dardanelles from its strategic position at the southwest end (Asian side). In 480 BC, the Persian army of Xerxes I crossed the strait by a bridge of boats; and Alexander the Great did the same in 334 BC on his expedition against Persia.

Hell Gap: A Plano tradition complex of the Paleo-Indian period occupied from c. 11,200–8000 BC (complex 10,000–9500 BP) and centered on a well-preserved, deeply stratified site in eastern Wyoming. Hell Gap is also the name of a projectile point type of the Plano tradition.

helmet: Protective headgear that goes back almost as far as evidence for warfare. The basic function was to protect the head, face, and sometimes the neck from the cutting blows of swords, spears, arrows, and other weapons. The Assyrians and Persians had helmets of leather and iron, and the Greeks created bronze helmets, some of which covered the entire head, with only a narrow opening in front for vision and breathing. The Romans developed several forms of helmets, including the round legionary's helmet and the special gladiator's helmet, with broad brim and pierced visor, giving

exceptional protection to head, face, and neck. The troops on the Royal Standard of Ur wear leather helmets. The Blue Crown worn by the pharaoh in the New Kingdom of Egypt was a war helmet. One type covered with boar's tusks was current among the Mycenaeans. More obviously for parade than war are the bronze examples from the European Late Bronze and Iron Ages. Among the Villanovans, the cinerary urn was often covered with the helmet of the dead warrior. Several fine examples from Britain are decorated with Celtic art. The New World has yielded helmets made of gold and wood encrusted with turquoise mosaic. The term *helm* was applied by both Saxons and Normans, in the 11th century, to the conical steel cap with a nose guard, the common headpiece of the day. "Helmet" is the diminutive of helm.

Helwan: A prehistoric and pharaonic settlement near the eastern bank of the Nile by Cairo. The name is sometimes applied to the material from the neighboring Neolithic site of El Omari. (*syn.* Hulwan)

hematite: A heavy, deep red iron oxide commonly used by the Indians as decorative body paint and pictographs. Steel-gray crystals and coarse-grained varieties are known as specular iron ore; thin scaly types are called micaceous hematite. Much hematite occurs in a soft, fine-grained, earthy form called red ocher or ruddle. Red ocher is used as a paint pigment; a purified form, rouge, is used to polish plate glass. The most important deposits of hematite are sedimentary in origin, and the largest deposit is in the Lake Superior district in North America. (*syn.* bloodstone, red hematite, red iron ore, red ocher, rhombohedral iron ore, haematite)

hematite coating: A surface treatment for pottery involving the application of powdered hematite iron ore before firing. Hematite may have been mixed with a slip and then applied, or painted on as a suspension in water. When fired the surface normally appears red, although under reduced firing conditions it may turn black. (*syn.* haematite coating)

Hembury: A Neolithic causewayed camp in Devon, England, with radiocarbon dates showing occupation from 4200–3900 BC. It has given its name to the plain pottery (also called Windmill Hill pottery) of the earliest Neolithic in southern England, round-bottomed bowls frequently with lug handles. An Iron Age hill fort was later built, and postholes of a circular Neolithic house have been found beneath the Iron Age gate. The Neolithic deposit included greenstone and flint axes and charred spelt wheat—by far the earliest occurrence of this type of wheat in Britain.

Hemudu: An Early Neolithic site in Zhejiang Province, China, dating back to the late 6th and early 5th millennia BC. Two radiocarbon dates of c. 5000 and c. 4800 BC are the earliest yet for rice cultivation, and it is the type site of the southern rice-growing regime (millet was grown in the north). Pigs, dogs, and water buffalo were domesticated.

Hoes or spades made from cattle scapulae have been found in large quantities; stone tools were few and crude. Timber houses show the use of a mortise-and-tenon technique. The low-fired handmade pottery includes shallow Ding tripods. It was succeeded by the Qingliangang culture in the Early Neolithic and by the Daxi, Qujialing, and Liangzhu cultures in the Middle Neolithic, c. 3800–2800 BC. (*syn.* Ho-mu-tu)

henge: A circular, prehistoric religious enclosure constructed of wood or stones and enclosed by ditches, banks, and walls—and found only in the British Isles. Henge monuments are characteristic of the megalithic period in southern and eastern England in particular. To the west and north, henges often enclose a stone circle. There are 13 such examples, including Avebury and Stonehenge. The circular area is delimited by a ditch with the bank normally outside it. Class I henges have a single entrance marked by a gap in the earthworks, while those of Class II have two such entrances placed opposite each other. Avebury had four entrances. Many henges have extra features such as burials, pits, circles of upright stones (Avebury, Stonehenge), or of timber posts (Durrington Walls, Woodhenge). Henges are often associated with Late Neolithic pottery of grooved ware, Peterborough and Beaker types, dating from the centuries after 2500 BC. Occasional examples were still in use in the Bronze Age, such as Stonehenge. Henges are believed to have been focal points for "ritual" activity, but there is much controversy over their design. They range in size from c. 30 meters to more than 400 meters in diameter (Avebury, Durrington Walls). (*syn.* henge monument)

Hengelo interstadial: A Continental Middle Pleniglacial interstadial of the Weichselian cold stage, starting around 39,000 BP. It occurred during the final glaciation between the Moershooft and Denekamp interstadials.

Hengistbury Head: An Upper Palaeolithic/Creswellian site with flint artifacts with thermoluminescence dates of c. 12,500 bp. There is also a nearby Mesolithic site with evidence of flint knapping. The site became important c. 100 BC (Iron Age) as a trading center with continental Europe; Roman wine amphorae were among the imports.

heqin: A system of reverse tribute used in the Han Dynasty of China. Lavish goods were given as a reward for voluntary tributes and loyalty to the Han. (*syn.* [ho-ch'in])

Herakleopolis Magna: An ancient Egyptian site that was the capital of the 20th nome of Upper Egypt and the cult center for the god Harsaphes. Its peak came when it was the capital of the 9th and 10th Dynasties of the First Intermediate Period (2181–2055 BC). The city was lost by the clan when Mentuhotpe II of the 11th Dynasty attacked in 2040 BC. There is an Old Kingdom shrine, temple of Harsaphes, and necropolis of Herakleopolis at Gebel Sedment. (*syn.* Ihnasya el-Medina; ancient Henen-nesw; Ninsu, Nen-nesut)

Herat: A town and province in western Afghanistan, important in pre-Islamic times and sometimes identified as the capital of the Achaemenid satrapy of Aria and the Hellenistic city of Alexandria Ariana. The principal monuments of Herat were built in the reigns of the Timurid rulers Shah Rukh (1405–1447), the son of Timur, and Husaid Baikara (1469–1506). (*syn.* Harat)

Herculaneum: An ancient city of Campania, Italy, buried in AD 79 by the same volcano that took Pompeii. Already damaged by Vesuvius in AD 63, Herculaneum was home to 5,000 people. It had modern houses, tastefully decorated, and it was wealthier than Pompeii. In the destruction of AD 79, the town was covered in liquid mud which subsequently solidified after percolating and filling structures. It tended to preserve organic materials, especially timber. The houses are remarkable for the preservation of internal and external structures in timber and, in some cases, of furniture and fittings. Also found are papyri and a library containing the works of Epicurus. Herculaneum probably started as an Archaic Greek foundation. (*syn.* modern Ercolano)

herm: A statue in the form of a square stone pillar topped by a bust or head, especially of Hermes.

Hermopolis Magna: An ancient pharaonic capital in northern Egypt, of the 15th Upper Egyptian nome. It was the cult center of Thoth, of which there are remains of his great temple, and had its necropolis at Tuna el-Gebel. The earliest dates of the stone structures are from the Middle Kingdom. There is also the remains of a Roman basilica. (*syn.* el-Ashmunein; ancient Khmun)

hero cult: In ancient times, the worship of a god of partly human and partly divine origin, such as the worship of the hero Hercules. Hero-cult worship was the forerunner of the worship of living rulers, a feature of Hellenistic and Roman times. The hero cult invested a dead man with divine qualities of intelligence and strength, which made him worthy of being honored by a cult. The founders of the city-states (such as Theseus at Athens) were often heroized. One basis for belief in heroes and the hero cult was the idea that the mighty dead continued to live and to be active as spiritual powers from the sites of their graves. Another source of the cult of heroes was the conception that gods were often lowered to the status of heroes. One of the best-known heroes is Heracles, who became famous through his mighty deeds. (*syn.* heroization)

Herodium: A Palestinian site with a fortress built by Herod the Great (37–4 BC) and the site of his tomb. It was a stronghold for Jewish rebels against the Roman rule.

Herodotus (c. 484–c. 430/420 BC): Greek traveler and historian born at Halicarnassus in Asia Minor, who wrote the first great narrative history of the ancient world (*History*, mainly about the Greco-Persian wars). Herodotus' work remains the leading source of original information not only for Greek history of 550–479 BC, but also for much of that of western Asia and of Egypt at that time.

heröon/Heroon: A space, building, and so on, dedicated to the cult of a hero, often built around his tomb or a cenotaph. War memorial; hero cult or heroic shrine.

Herpaly: A regional variant of the three Late Neolithic cultures (Tisza, Herpaly, Czöszhalom) of the Great Hungarian Plain, c. 4000–3400 BC. The Herpaly culture, distributed in the northern Alföld zone, is characterized by tell settlement. Throned figures and anthropomorphic and zoomorphic figurines indicate ritual activities.

Hertzian cone of force: The cone shape in which the energy of a projectile impact in high silica content stone radiates through the structure of the stone.

Herzfeld, Ernst (1879–1948): A German archaeologist/Orientalist who excavated in the Middle East before World War II, particularly at Persepolis, Samarra, and Tall-1 Bakun. He also wrote *Zoroaster and His World* (1947, reprinted 1974).

Hesi, Tell el-: A tell site in southern Palestine occupied from the Early Bronze Age, c. 2600 BC, to the Hellenistic period/Iron Age. Its excavation by Sir Flinders Petrie and F. J. Bliss were the first stratigraphic excavations in the area and lent much information on pottery typology and successive building levels. Their work began the establishment of an absolute chronology for Palestinian prehistory, through the discovery of imported, datable Egyptian objects in association with local material.

Hetepheres I (c. 2600 BC): An Early 4th Dynasty queen (Old Kingdom), who was the principal wife of Snefru (2613–2589 BC), the mother of Khufu (2589–2566 BC), and probably also the daughter of Huni, last ruler of the 3rd Dynasty. Her unmarked tomb, inside Khufu's pyramid complex at Giza, has been found. At the bottom of a deep stone-filled shaft was found the queen's empty sarcophagus, surrounded by furniture and articles of jewelry attesting to the high artistic and technical ability of 4th-Dynasty craftsmen.

Heuneburg, the: An Early Iron Age fortified site and hill fort of the Hallstatt period on the upper Danube in Baden-Württemberg, Germany. The site was the center of the dominant Celtic chiefdom in southwest Germany c. 600–500 BC. Wine amphorae and Attic black-figure pottery were imported from the Greek city of Massalia, demonstrating Heuneburg's wealth. There are nearby princely burials of the same date, including the rich Hohmichele tumulus. This covered a timber mortuary house containing the body of an archer accompanied by a wooden wagon and precious offerings. The site has five main building phases, the most remarkably of which was the second, when the traditional timber-framed construc-

tion was replaced by a Greek type of construction, with a bastioned wall built of mud brick on stone foundations.

heuristic: Pertaining to, involving, or serving as an aid to learning, discovery, or problem solving by experimental and especially trial-and-error methods.

hexastyle: Of a Classical building, having six columns on the facade.

Hiba'al-: An Egyptian settlement site important in the 21st Dynasty (1075–c. 950 BC) where there is a poorly preserved temple of Amun (of the crag), built by Sheshonq I (945–924 BC). The fortress town was the northern frontier of the Theban priests' domain (much of the Nile Valley) during the Tanite 21st Dynasty. (*syn.* ancient Teudjoi; Ankyronpolis; el-Hiba)

Hierakonpolis: An important Predynastic and Archaic settlement and necropolis in southern Upper Egypt (Luxor). The town's population was in excess of 5,000, and it was particularly associated with the god Horus. In protodynastic times, Hierakonpolis was the capital of southern Egypt. Discoveries of this period are stone palettes, votive objects, and mace heads, with carving illustrating the rise of the kings to the divine status they enjoyed in pharaonic times. A series of successive shrines dates from early Archaic/late Predynastic. (*syn.* Kom e-Ahmar; ancient Nekhen)

hierarchy: Any organization of a group of items into a series of classes ranked from high to low, each successively higher class having fewer members. In a social hierarchy, the ranking would reflect differences in power, prestige, or access to economic resources. In a settlement hierarchy, the individual sites might be organized on the basis of population size or number of functions fulfilled into a series of classes such as town, village, and hamlet.

hieratic: A cursive form of the Egyptian hieroglyphs developed for everyday use in handwritten documents. It arose from the use of brush pen or papyrus for business and similar nonmonumental purposes, starting at the end of the Early Dynastic period (c. 2686 BC). It was gradually replaced by demotic starting in the 7th century BC, but survived for religious use to the end of paganism in Egypt. The word comes from Greek *hieratika*, "sacred." Hieratic signs lost the pictorial character of hieroglyphs and were often joined together. Hieratic was written in one direction only, from right to left. In earlier times, the lines had run vertically and later, about 2000 BC, horizontally. Subsequently, the papyrus scrolls were written in columns of changing widths. There were ligatures in hieratic so that two, but no more than two, signs could be written in one stroke. As a consequence of its decreased legibility, the spelling of the heiratic script was more rigid than that of hieroglyphic writing. Variations from uniformity at a given time were minor; but, during the course of the various periods, the spelling developed and changed. As a result, hieratic texts do not correspond exactly to contemporary hieroglyphic texts, either in the placing of signs or in the spelling of words. Hieratic used diacritical additions to distinguish between two signs that had grown similar to one another because of cursive writing. In the life of the Egyptians, hieratic script played a larger role than hieroglyphic writing and was also taught earlier in the schools. The latest hieratic texts are from the end of the 1st century or the beginning of the 2nd century AD. Hieratic should not be confused with "cursive hieroglyphs," which were used for most of the pharaonic period in such religious writings as the Coffin Texts and the Book of the Dead.

hieroglyphics: (hi'row-glif'-ik) A pictorial script used by ancient Egyptians from the beginning of the 3rd millennium BC until the end of the 4th century AD. A hieroglyph was a single character or pictorial element used in hieroglyphics. Literally, in Greek, it means "sacred carved letters." The script consisted of three basic types of signs: phonograms, logograms, and "determinatives," arranged in horizontal and vertical lines. The script was used for funerary and monumental inscriptions as well as more strictly religious ones. The script's development seems to have been so rapid that it may have been in some sense an imitation of the earliest writing of Mesopotamia in its Uruk phase. In both scripts, three classes of symbol were used, each a single picture or geometric figure. Pictograms or ideograms represented whole words in pictorial form. Phonograms represented the sounds of words, the picture of an object pronounced in the same way as the desired word being used in its place (this was made easier by the fact that the vowels were disregarded). Determinatives told the reader the class of word spelled by the phonograms, necessary where these were ambiguous. Often all three classes of symbol were used in conjunction. No attempt was made in its long history to simplify the system, even when the more cursive forms of it, hieratic and demotic, were introduced. More loosely, the term has been applied to other pictographic writing systems, particularly those of Minoan Crete, the Hittites and the Maya. Many of the symbols consist of a conventionalized picture of the idea or object they represent. Egyptian hieroglyphs were deciphered by Jean-François Champollion in 1822, through his study of the bilingual inscriptions on the Rosetta Stone and an obelisk from Philae. Some 700 signs were employed. (*syn.* hieroglyphic; hieroglyph)

Higgs, Eric Sidney (1908–1976): A British archaeologist who pioneered the technique of site catchment analysis, started the study of palaeoeconomy, and did innovative work on the origins of agriculture.

high-energy societies: Societies characterized by high per-capita consumption of energy, mostly through nonfood sources. Industrial societies, with their reliance on fossil fuels, are high-energy societies.

higher-order central place: A large and functionally diverse community in a regional hierarchy of communities differentiated by number, size, and function.

Highland zone: A settlement and geographic area corresponding to northern England, the Pennines, Wales, Devon, and Cornwall.

High Lodge: A British Palaeolithic site in Suffolk, where distinctive tools were found including classic Quina-type scrapers similar to those of the Charentian culture of France. At first it was believed to have had three industries: Acheulian ovate biface, a crude flake industry, and a Mousterian. Dates of 450,000–500,000 years ago now suggest that the assemblage may be similar to material from Clacton and Swanscombe.

hilani: A pillared porch; a structure consisting of a columned portico, a long reception room with an adjoining staircase to the roof, and a varying number of retiring rooms. This architectural unit was much employed by the Syro-Hittites in the early 1st millennium BC and was copied by the Assyrians. The earliest known examples are from Tell Atchana. A striking example is the Kaparu Palace at Tall Halaf. (*syn.* bit-hilani; bit hilani)

Hili: A number of small settlement sites in southeastern Arabia. Hili 8 provided the architectural and ceramic sequence for the Bronze Age of the region, c. 3000–1800 BC. The occurrence of domesticated sorghum is among the earliest known. Burials, ceramics, and stone vessels have been excavated.

hill figure: A type of monument found on the chalk downs of southern Britain where a human or horse figure is cut into the hillside and stands out white against the green turf. The oldest figure, the White Horse of Uffington, may date to the Late Iron Age. The Cerne Abbas giant in Dorset is of the Roman period, and the Long Man of Wilmington may be either Roman or Saxon. All the others are of more recent date and are usually commemorative or purely ornamental than religious in nature.

hill fort: Any well-fortified structure located on a hilltop and enclosed by at least one wall of stone and earth, commonly referring to sites of the Late Bronze Age or Iron Age. The earliest date to c. 1000 BC. Some hill forts contain houses and were perhaps royal residences or, in the case of large forts of *oppidum* type, true towns; others seem to lack permanent buildings and were probably refuges where the people and flocks from the surrounding area took shelter in times of crisis. At first, they were usually promontory forts, but in the last four centuries BC the true hill fort, with defense works following the contours, became the predominant form. From about the second century BC until the Roman conquest, hill forts were common throughout Celtic lands. In Britain, most of the great forts were built during the 2½ centuries before the conquest of AD 43, but in Ireland and highland Britain, hill forts continued to be built and used for several more centuries. They are found throughout much of Europe, except in Russia and Scandinavia. In size, hill forts ranged from less than 1 acre to several hundred acres. (*syn.* hill fort)

hillslope: The flanks of valleys and the margins of eroding uplands, the major zones where rock and soil are loosened by weathering processes and then transported down gradient, often to a river channel. They are produced by erosion and deposition and are unstable.

hinge fracture: A feature of a struck flint flake, which occurs either through an error in striking technique or because of the conchoidal nature of a particular piece of flint. Instead of coming to a sharp, thin end, the struck flake ends in a rounded, smooth, turned-out edge.

Hippodamian planning: A rectangular town layout used by Hippodamos of Miletus in the 5th century BC. Miletus, in western Turkey, existed until Roman imperial times, and Piraeus in Greece is another example.

hippodrome: An ancient Greek stadium for horse and chariot racing. The typical hippodrome was dug into a hillside, and an embankment was created for supporting seats on the opposite side. The hippodrome was oblong, with one end semicircular and the other square (resembling a U with a closed top). There were tiered seats along the length and curve; at the straight end, dignitaries occupied seats. A low wall (*spina*) ran most of the length of the stadium and divided the course. The spina was decorated with monuments and had sculptures that could be tilted or removed to keep spectators informed of the laps completed by the racers. It is much the same as a stadium, but intended rather for horse than foot racing. The hippodrome was the initial model for the Roman circus, which likewise concentrated on chariot races. (*syn.* hippodromus; (Roman circus))

Hispaniola: The second largest island of the West Indies of the Greater Antilles, which since the 17th century has been divided between Haiti and the Dominican Republic. (*syn.* formerly Espanola)

Hispano-Moresque pottery: A tin-glazed, lustrous, highly decorated earthenware made by Moorish potters in Spain in the late medieval period, chiefly at Málaga in the 15th century, and in the region of Manises, near Valencia, in the 16th century. They tend to be plates and jugs with bold semi-abstract designs painted on a creamy background and with a gold luster finish. These wares were much in demand throughout Europe, and, judging from finds in northern Europe, they were widely traded. The tin glaze was applied over a design usually traced in cobalt blue; after the first firing, the luster, a metallic pigment, was applied by brush over the tin glaze, and the piece was fired again. Imitation of this pottery in Italy led to the development of Italian maiolica ware.

Hissar, Tepe: A tell site near Damghan in northern Iran, occupied from the 5th to the early 2nd millennia BC. Before 2500 BC, earlier than elsewhere in Iran, the painted pottery tradition was replaced by one of gray monochrome ware. This is usually held to mark the first movement of Indo-European speaking peoples from central Asia into Iran. The settlement was destroyed somewhere between c. 1900–1600 BC. Evidence from the later 4th–early 3rd millennia BC suggests a Proto-Elamite phenomenon manifested in pottery, seals, and tablet blanks. There are more than 1,600 prehistoric burials and a Sussanian palace on the site, which has an interesting pottery sequence and metal objects.

Hissarlik: A small site above the Scamander Plain, Turkey, with massive ruins that Heinrich Schliemann established to be the ruins of ancient Troy (1877–1890). It is set on a plain overlooking the southern entrance to the Dardanelles in northwestern Anatolia. The series of seven Bronze Age settlements (with subphases) date from the late 4th millennium BC to the 12th century BC. The famous "treasure of Priam," a hoard of precious metal and semiprecious stone objects, came from one of the Troy II levels. The settlement was ended by massive fires. (*syn.* Hisarlik/Troy)

histogram: A graphical representation of a distribution function by means of rectangles whose widths represent intervals into which the range of observed values is divided and whose heights represent the number of observations occurring in each interval. For example, if measurements of length have been taken for bronze spearheads from one particular area and period, the measurements are represented by marking off intervals of lengths on the horizontal axis and counting the number of spearheads falling into each division. These numbers are marked off on the vertical axis. To compare one set of data with another or others, a cumulative version of the histogram may be used, where the succeeding values are added to the preceding: These are called cumulative frequency polygons and are useful for comparative work, but are difficult to use if single histograms need to be extracted. A useful way to assess the density of rocks is to make a histogram plot of the statistical range of a set of data. The representative value and its variation can be expressed as follows: (1) mean, the average value; (2) mode, the most common value (i.e., the peak of the distribution curve); (3) median, the value of the middle sample of the data set (i.e., the value at which half of the samples are below and half are above); and (4) standard deviation, a statistical measure of the spread of the data (plus and minus one standard deviation from the mean value includes about two-thirds of the data).

historic archaeology: A branch of archaeological study and interpretation that deals with literate societies—the objects and events since the beginnings of recorded history. In North America, historically documented research is directed at colonial and postcolonial settlement, analogous to the study of medieval and postmedieval archaeology in Europe. (*syn.* historical archaeology; historic sites archaeology)

historical particularism: A school of anthropological thought associated with the work of Franz Boas and his students (including Ruth Benedict, Margaret Mead, and A. L. Kroeber), whose studies of culture emphasized the integrated way of life distinctive of a people. It is a detailed descriptive approach to anthropology designed as an alternative to the broad generalizing approach favored by other anthropologists, and the research is based on particular cultural traits and elements.

historical record: The written texts produced by past human societies, which are sought, recovered, studied, and interpreted by historians to reconstruct the past.

historic period: Any past period that can be studied from its written documents.

historiographic approach: A form of explanation based primarily on traditional descriptive historical frameworks.

historiography: The writing of history, with particular reference to the examination and evaluation of primary source material. Historiography is also the study of the development of historical method. The study is based on the critical examination of sources, the selection of facts from the authentic materials, and the synthesis of facts into a narrative.

history: The study of the past through written records, which are compared, judged for truth, placed in chronological sequence, and interpreted in light of preceding, contemporary, and subsequent events.

Hittite: A people of obscure origin who infiltrated Anatolia and the Levant from the north during the later 3rd millennium BC. In the Old Kingdom (c. 1750–1450), they established a state in central Turkey with its capital first at Kussara, then at Boghazköy. They overran north Syria c. 1600 and pushed on as far as Babylon. Under the empire (1450–1200), a more stable state was built up over most of Anatolia and north Syria, displacing the kingdom of the Mitanni and successfully challenging Assyria and Egypt. The end came quite suddenly in the Late Bronze Age c. 1200 BC, notably by movements of the Peoples of the Sea and Anatolian groups from the north. The Hittite outposts in north Syria, however, survived as a chain of Syro-Hittite or neo-Hittite city-states—Karatepe, Sinjerli, Sakçe Gözü, Malatya, Atchana, and Carchemish—down to their final annexation by the Assyrians in the 8th century BC. They are also known for their metal working. They exploited and traded copper, lead, silver, and also iron; indeed, they were among the first peoples to use iron and for a period maintained a virtual monopoly in the new metal. Their language, Hittite and Hieroglyphic Hittite, is Indo-European, the earliest to be recorded. Hurrian, the language of the Hurri, was non-Indo-European, as of course was the Akkadian much used for commercial and foreign correspondence. The Akkadian cuneiform script was generally used too, although for monumental purposes local hieroglyphs were preferred. The discovery of the Hittite language was the major advance this century in the field of Indo-European languages—with archives yielding thousands of tablets in many languages. The great period of the empire was 14th–13th centuries BC when a vast amount of material was recorded—some in the important sister Anatolian languages of Palaic and Luvian. (*syn.* Hatti, Kheta)

Hiw-Semaina region: A group of Predynastic, Pharaonic, and Roman-period sites on the eastern bank of the Nile in Upper Egypt. (*syn.* Diospolis Parva)

Hjortspring: A peat bog on the Danish island of Als where a votive deposit with a boat or war canoe was deposited in c. 200 BC (pre-Roman Iron Age). With the boat were many shields, spears, and swords. The boat was plank built, sewn together without the use of nails, with room for about 50 oarsmen. The bow and stern were upturned and had ramlike projections. There were also everyday items such as bowls, boxes, and smith's tools.

Hoabinhian: A little-known Mesolithic or Neolithic culture (early to mid-Holocene stone tool industry) of southeast Asia (type site is Hoa Binh, Vietnam) dating from 10,000–2000 BC. There are many chipped, pecked, and polished stone axes found in piles of shells. Its importance lies in its position between the earliest centers of rice growing in India and China, and in the part it must have played in diffusing the knowledge of agriculture into Indonesia and the Pacific. The Neolithic assemblages have pottery and ground-stone tools for several millennia after 6000 BC. It is best described as a technocomplex with successive cultural accretions; the Hoabinhian cannot be regarded as an archaeological culture of chronological horizon. The majority of Hoabinhian sites found to date are in rock shelters and coastal shell middens. The three recognized phases are archaic with unifacially worked pebble tools, intermediate with smaller pebble tools and bifacial working and edge grinding, and late characterized by some pottery, smaller scrapers, grinding stones, knives, piercers, polished stone tools, and shell artifacts. (*syn.* Hoabinh)

hoard: Any collection of objects buried at one time; a deliberate deposit of complete and/or broken objects buried in the ground for subsequent recovery or as a symbolic act. A hoard often included valuables or prized possessions. Many hoards represent the personal property of individuals, buried for safety at a time of threat. Hoards are a useful source of evidence for archaeologists, because they provide considerable quantities of material and, except in the case of some votive hoards, the material represents a true association. Various classes are distinguished according to their method of accumulation. A personal hoard consists of an individual's personal property buried for safety and not recovered. A merchant's hoard contains new objects ready for sale. A founder's hoard by contrast contains obsolete, worn-out, or miscast objects, and frequently cake metal as well, all of it awaiting melting down and recasting. A votive hoard is rather different in that the objects were deposited, possibly over a long period, in temples or caves, buried, or thrown into water as religious offerings, with no intention of recovery. A hoard of loot is self-explanatory. Bronze Age hoards provide much of the evidence for the period.

Hochdorf: An Iron Age tumulus in Baden-Württemberg, Germany, from the 6th century BC (late Hallstatt). One burial chamber had very rich grave goods, including Mediterranean materials, a Greek bronze cauldron, gold-covered shoes, and bronze couch.

Hod Hill: An Iron Age site in Dorset, England, with evidence of circular huts defended by huge ramparts. The site was attacked by the Romans in AD 44. The fortification seems to have been damaged by fire AD c. 52–53 and not reused.

hoe: One of the oldest tools of agriculture, a digging implement consisting of a blade set at right angles to a long handle (haft). Early hoes had stone or wooden blades. Examples made from antler go back to the Mesolithic. Most early hoes were used by the farming peoples of the Neolithic. Hoes succeeded the digging stick and gave rise to the plow. The digging stick, precursor of most agricultural hand tools, was simply a sharpened branch sometimes weighted with a stone. (*syn.* mattock)

Hoëdic: A small island off the southern coast of Brittany, France, with a Mesolithic settlement and cemetery with 14 individuals accompanied by antlers. The artifacts were of Tardenoisian type, and the whole site was a Mesolithic midden, although there are remains of domestic sheep. The radiocarbon date is 4625 BC.

hogback: A type of house-shaped tomb, with a curved ridge, which originated in the areas of Scandinavian settlement in northwestern England in the 10th century AD. They take the form of rectangular blocks with pitched roofs and are usually decorated with designs. (*syn.* hog-back tombs)

Hohenasperg: An Iron Age *oppidium* on a 6th century BC site of the Hallstatt D period. Hohenasperg was a commercial center whose finds included many luxury items from Greece.

Hohlenstein-Stadel: A cave in Baden-Württemberg, Germany, with occupation during the Mousterian, Aurignacian (with an ivory anthropomorphic statuette of 31,750 bp), Magdalenian (14th millennium bp), and Mesolithic.

Hohmichele, the: A rich Hallstatt grave near the Heuneburg hill fort on the Danube in southern Germany. The barrow was one of the satellite graves around the hill fort and covered a central grave and 12 secondary burials of the 6th century BC Iron Age. The central grave was robbed in antiquity, but it had been an inhumation grave in a wood-lined chamber, which acted as the display area for the wealth of the deceased. The walls seem to have been draped in textiles with thin gold bands, and the deceased, dressed in finery including silk, was placed on a bed next to a four-wheeled wagon. It is the earliest documented occurrence of silk in Europe. The objects implied wine-drinking ceremonies, and there is furniture directly imported from the south (central Europe).

Hohokam: A prehistoric tradition of southern Arizona, which began as a sedentary farming culture around 300 BC and existed until AD 1400/1450. It was a cultural unit in the Cochise subculture, and it had large villages, canal irrigation, and pottery making. The finest craft products were shell jewelry and objects of carved stone. Diagnostic traits include small villages of shallow, oblong pit houses with no formalized community plan, cremation of the dead, plain gray or brown paddle and anvil-smoothed pottery (or sometimes painted red on buff). The tradition is divided into Pioneer (AD 150–550), Colonial (AD 550–900), Sedentary (AD 900–1100), Classic (AD 1100–1450), and Post-Classic (AD 1450–1700). Between AD 550–1200, renewed Mexican contacts brought foreign elements to the Hohokam: courts for the ball game, platform mounds, new types of maize, slab metates, mosaic mirrors, exotic symbolism from Mexican religion, and the use of copper bells. From about 1100, certain groups began to construct pueblos under Anasazi influence. After 1400/1450, the Hohokam territory along the Gila and Salt Rivers seems to have been partially abandoned. Their cultural heirs are the Pima and Papago Indians. Snaketown is an important Hohokam site.

hokei shukobo: Burial precincts of the Yayoi and Kufun periods of Japan. There are coffin and pit burials of adults and jar burials of children.

Hokuriku: An industrial region of Japan on northern Honshu Island, consisting of Niigata, Toyama, Ishikawa, and Fukui prefectures. Hokuriku's traditional industries included the manufacture of silk, timber products, lacquer ware, and agricultural tools.

Holmes, William Henry (1846–1933): American archaeologist who extinguished the more bizarre theories of the origins of humans in North America and who helped establish professional archaeology in the United States. Holmes opposed a popular belief that there was a period in New World prehistory comparable to Upper Palaeolithic (Old

Stone Age) Europe. His 1903 monograph on ceramics laid the foundation for the culture history of the eastern United States. He was curator of the Field Museum of Natural History in Chicago and the Smithsonian Museum in Washington D.C. His other published works include *Handbook of Aboriginal American Antiquities* (1919).

Holocene: The present geological epoch, which began some 10,000 (bp) years ago (8300 BC). It falls within the Quaternary period (one of the four main divisions of the Earth's history) and followed the Pleistocene Ice Age. The Holocene is marked by rising temperatures throughout the world and the retreat of the ice sheets. During this epoch, agriculture became the common human subsistence practice. During the Holocene, *Homo sapiens* diversified their tool technology, organized their habitat more efficiently, and adapted their way of life. The Holocene stage/series includes all deposits younger than the top of either the Wisconsinian stage of the Pleistocene Series in North America and the Würm/Weichsel in Europe. (*syn.* Recent, Postglacial)

Holstein: North European Middle Pleistocene warm phase occurring between the Elsterian and Saalian cold stages, c. 300,000–200,000 BP. These deposits are stratified above Elster glacial deposits and are overlain by Saale glacial deposits. The Alpine equivalent is the Mindel-Riss and the North American equivalent is the Yarmouth. In Britain, it was the Hoxnian. (*syn.* Holsteinian Interglacial)

Holy Cross Mountains: Low mountains in central Poland, important sources of flint during the Mesolithic, Neolithic, and Early Bronze Ages and a center for iron metallurgy during the Iron Age.

home: A permanent shelter or living place. In the Stone Age, man was a hunter gatherer and nomad, sheltering wherever he/she could. The earliest known "homes" of the Upper Palaeolithic are the Creswell Crags caves, dating back to Mousterian times around 115,000 BC.

homeostasis: A term used to describe a relatively stable state of equilibrium or a tendency toward such a state between the different but interdependent elements or groups of elements of an organism, population, or group. In systems thinking, it is used to describe the action of negative feedback processes in maintaining the system at a constant equilibrium state.

Homer (9th/8th/7th century BC?): A Greek writer of which little is known other than that his name is attached to the two great epic poems of ancient Greece, the *Iliad* and the *Odyssey*. Homeric archaeology is the study of the poems attributed to Homer, attempting to match the description of an object, building, social structure, or custom in the poems to the archaeological record. Heinrich Schliemann is the best-known Homeric archaeologist, having discovered Troy.

Hominidae: The family to which humans (Homo) and Australopithecines belong; the family includes both extinct and modern forms of man. Humanlike ancestors are split into four main groups: Australopithecus, *Homo habilis*, *Homo erectus*, and *Homo sapiens*. In most modern classifications, the Great Apes are included in the family. Hominids reached their greatest diversity about 2 million years ago with as many as five species present, including the oldest species of Homo, *Homo habilis*. (*syn.* hominids; hominoid)

Homo: The Hominid genus to which humans belong. The genus includes modern man (*Homo sapiens*), Neanderthal Man (*H. neaderthalensis*), and *Homo erectus* (Pithecanthropus).

Homo erectus: "Upright man," an extinct form of *Homo sapiens* who evolved 1 million years ago, just before Neanderthal man. This species had a larger brain and was bigger than *Homo habilis*, with a muscular, stocky body and heavy face with thick brow bones. It is thought that *Homo erectus* made Acheulian stone artifacts and spread around Africa. He gradually evolved into archaic *Homo sapiens* about 500,000 years ago. The best known discoveries are from the Far East (Java, Choukoutien, Yuanmou), but skeletal remains have been found in East Africa (Olduvai), in North Africa (Ternifine, Sidi Abderrahman), and in Europe (Mauer Jaw, Vértesszöllös). At Choukoutien, there was proof that he knew the use of fire. This ancestor of modern humans evolved from Australopithecus, and his brain was about two-thirds the size of contemporary humans'. (*syn.* [obsolete Peking man], Pithecanthropus, Pithecanthropus erectus)

Homo habilis: "Handy man," the oldest species of the genus Homo. It was small built but had a larger brain than the Australopithecines and was a toolmaker. Fossils have been found in East and South African dating to 2.2–1.6 million years ago at the famous sites of Koobi Fora and Olduvai Gorge. Dr. Louis Leakey, who found fossils at Olduvai Gorge, said that the habilis skeletons showed certain features (e.g., greater brain size, opposable thumb, shape of skull) that distinguished them from those of other Australopithecus forms and placed them closer to the line of descent leading to *Homo erectus* and the advanced forms of man. *Homo habilis* is regarded as a possible ancestor of *Homo erectus* or *Homo sapiens*; others believe it should be included in the species *Australopithecus africanus* or *Homo erectus* or be regarded as transitional from one to the other.

Homolka: A Late Neolithic fort site in Bohemia of the Rivnac culture.

homology: A type of reasoning by analogy, where two phenomena separated in time are similar because of a historic or genetic connection. In biology, similarity of the structure, physiology, or development of different species of organisms based on their descent from a common evolutionary ancestor.

Homology is contrasted with analogy, which is a functional similarity of structure based not on common evolutionary origins but on mere similarity of use.

Homo sapiens: The modern human species, possibly evolving out of Neanderthal man, with the archaic *Homo sapiens* dating to between c. 100,000–33,000 years ago (*Homo sapiens neanderthalensis*) and the oldest-known anatomically modern *Homo sapiens* fossils dating between 130,000–80,000 years ago. Modern man—a large, erect, omnivorous terrestrial biped—first appears in the fossil record during the late Upper Pleistocene around 35,000 BC. It is still controversial how Neanderthals were replaced by the modern *Homo sapiens*. The oldest fossils come from sites in Africa and the Near East. In Eurasia, the oldest flint industries associated with *Homo sapiens* are always of Upper Palaeolithic blade-and-burin type. Modern man's technology replaced that of the Mousterian period.

homostadial: Archaeological cultures that represent similar levels or technological advance with other cultures, regardless of a difference derived in absolute dating methods. This is the principle behind the Three Age system.

homotaxial: Archaeological cultures or strata that have the same relation to one another but are not necessarily contemporaneous. Objects are homotaxial if they appear in the same relative position in different sequences. The assumption that they are therefore contemporary is usually valid in geology, with its enormous time spans, but certainly not in archaeology, where time lag must be allowed for.

Honam: A district of South Korea, which includes the North and South Cholla provinces.

Hong Kong: An island country with evidence of human habitation from Neolithic times. The excavated artifacts suggest an influence from northern Chinese Stone Age cultures, most notably the Lung-shan. Before the British occupation, Hong Kong Island was inhabited only by a small fishing population. Hong Kong was firmly incorporated in the Chinese cultural sphere in the late Chou and Han Dynasties (late 1st millennium BC). The earliest sites in Hong Kong date from about 3500 BC and belong to Yueh coastal Neolithic. There was geometric-stamped pottery during the 2nd millennium BC.

Hongshan: A site in Liaoning Province, China, and the name of a Neolithic culture dated to c. 3500–3000 BC. Hongshan had elaborate jade animal ornaments, large temple sites, female figurines, and masks. (*syn.* [Hung-shan])

Hopewell: An agricultural subculture of the Woodland Stage complex settling in Ohio and Illinois around 100 BC and lasting to AD 500. It was one of the most advanced Indian cultures of North America, with conical or dome-shaped burial mounds, large enclosures with earthen walls, and fine pottery with corded or stamped decoration. Farming was practiced, and trade brought exotic raw materials from many parts of the continent. Hopewell is noted for its minor art objects, such as carved platform pipes, ornaments cut out of sheet copper or mica, Yellowstone obsidian, distinctive broad-bladed points, and ceremonial obsidian knives—often found in rich burials of the Hopewell rulers. Between 200 BC–AD 600, the "Hopewell Interaction Sphere" flourished in the Midwest, which constituted Hopewell religious cults and distinctive burial customs associated with a widespread (through trading) art tradition. The culture, which had both agriculture and hunting gathering, succeeded the Adena culture. (*syn.* Hopewellian culture)

hopper mortar: A mortar whose sides are formed by a bottomless basket attached to the stone.

Horgen: A Middle and Late Neolithic culture with its type site on Lake Neuchâtel in Switzerland. The pottery consists of rough bucket-shaped vessels with decoration limited to a few appliqué cordons. The bucket shapes and ornament resemble that of the French Seine–Oise–Marne culture. Horgen succeeded the Cortaillod (in western Switzerland) and the Pfyn. Horgen pottery is found on settlement sites and also in Megalithic tombs, and the culture dated to c. 3400–2800 BC. There was a decline in the use of copper.

horizon: Any artifact, art style, or other cultural trait that has extensive geographical distribution but a limited time span. The term, in anthropology, refers to the spread of certain levels of cultural development and, in geology, the layers of natural features in a region; in soil science, a horizon is a layer formed in a soil profile by soil-forming processes. The main meaning, however, refers to a phase, characterized by a particular artifact or artistic style that is introduced to a wide area and that may cross cultural boundaries. Provided that these "horizon markers" were diffused rapidly and remained in use for only a short time, the local regional cultures in which they occur will be roughly contemporary. The term is less commonly used now that chronometric dating techniques allow accurate local chronologies to be built. Examples of art styles that fulfill these conditions are called a horizon style—such as Tiahuanaco or Chavín. (*syn.* horizon style)

horizontal exposure: The excavation of a site to reveal its horizontal extent. Such an excavation is designed to uncover large areas of a site, especially settlement layouts. (*syn.* horizontal (area) excavation)

horizontal stratigraphy: Chronological sequences based on successive horizontal displacements, such as sequential beach terraces. Stratigraphy is by definition obtained from superposed deposits, but other circumstances can be treated in the same way. For example, the oldest burials are likely to be those nearest the settlement, the top of a hill, or some other favored position. The later ones will be progressively further out as the cemetery expands. The concept can be a helpful tool in the interpretation of a site.

horn: One of a pair of bony processes that grow from the head of many hoofed mammals. They are usually permanent hollow sheaths of keratin present in both sexes of cattle and their relatives. Antlers are also horns.

horn core: The hard, bony inner portion of animal horn; the bony projections from the skull that support horns. The horn itself forms a tight sheath around the core, which is removed for horn working. Some archaeological sites have large accumulations of horn cores related to a horn-working industry. (*syn.* horn core)

horns of consecration: A common religious symbol of the Minoans, based on the horns of a sacrificed bull. It frequently topped walls or shrines in the palace of Knossos or was found in sanctuaries and other buildings and was made of alabaster or other stone. Horns of consecration also appear in artistic depictions. (*syn.* sacral horns)

horreum: A Roman granary; a large building placed next to the principia in forts. The roof tiles were heavy to prevent fire, and the floor was raised to allow ventilation and prevent entry by rodents. The walls were strengthened by buttresses to prevent collapse. A space in front of the doors allowed carts to load or unload at the door. Their large size and frequency in the empire testify to their importance. Extensive examples remain at Ostia. (*syn.* granary; pl. horrea)

horse: A large solid-hoofed herbivorous mammal domesticated since prehistoric times and used as a beast of burden, a draft animal, or for riding. During ancient cold periods, horses also occupied the open vegetation that then existed in northern and western Europe. At some sites, horse bones formed a major part of Palaeolithic hunters' diet. The animals were widespread in temperate regions during the Pleistocene. With the end of the last glaciation, they disappeared from northwest Europe and became restricted to the temperate grassland and dry shrubland of Central Europe and Asia. In America, they were hunted to extinction, to be reintroduced only in recent centuries. In the steppes, the horse was domesticated much later than cattle, sheep, and so on. The first evidence for possible manipulation of horse by man occurs in the 4th and 3rd millennia BC in sites of the Tripoyle culture and related cultures of the Ukraine. It spread rapidly through the Near East when northern peoples like the Hurri, Hyksos, Kassites, and Aryans, particularly after the invention of the chariot in Syria. The domesticated horse was introduced into Egypt from western Asia in the Second Intermediate Period (1650–1550 BC) at roughly the same time as the chariot. Only later, as a heavier stock was bred, did the practice of riding become important. Its use for commercial draft and general

agricultural purposes came much later still. Today's horses all seem to represent one species, *Equus caballus.*

horsehoof cores: A steep-edged, often large, domed core with flat based striking platforms, heavily step-flaked around their margins. Both very large and smaller varieties are found commonly on Pleistocene sites in most areas of Australia and on some mid-Holocene sites, and they are considered characteristic of the Australian Core Tool and Scraper tradition. They were chopping tools mainly used in woodworking. The step-flaking could have resulted from repeated striking to remove flakes.

Horsham: A site in southern England where a number of Mesolithic flints have been found, including a hollow-based point sometimes called a Horsham point. It was once considered characteristic of a Horsham culture or group.

Horus: An Egyptian god in the form of a falcon, recognized in Hierakonpolis and Edfu as contemporary with and opponent of Seth. The falcon's eyes stood for the sun and the moon. He later was considered the son of Isis and Osiris, with the reigning pharaoh being his incarnation. Horus is one of the oldest gods of Egypt, attested from at least as early as the beginning of the Dynastic period (c. 2775 BC). He could also be a falcon-headed human in form. Horus appeared as a local god in many places and under different names and epithets: for instance, as Harmakhis (Har-em-akhet, "Horus in the Horizon"); Harpocrates (Har-pe-khrad, "Horus the Child"); Harsiesis (Har-si-Ese, "Horus, Son of Isis"); Harakhte ("Horus of the Horizon," closely associated with the sun god Re); and, at Kawn Umbu (Kom Ombo), as Haroeris (Harwer, "Horus the Elder"). Horus was later identified by the Greeks with Apollo. (*syn.* Harmakhis, Harakhte, Harsiesis, Kawm Umbu, Haroeris, Harpocrates, Harsomtus, Horemakhet, Ra-Horakhty; Hor; Har)

Hoshino: A Palaeolithic site in Tochigi Prefecture, Japan, with many cultural strata providing the stone tool chronology for the Kanto region. Tools, mostly of chert, were recovered from more than 13 layers, and choppers, scrapers, and flakes in the lowest layers are 40,000 to 50,000 BP according to radiocarbon and fission track ages of pumice beds between the layers. Blades and bifacial points in the top layers date to between 21,000–10,000 years ago. The dates are considerably older than most of the Japanese Palaeolithic sites, lending support to the idea that the archipelago was occupied in the Middle Pleistocene.

Hötting: A late Bronze Age urnfield culture of the North Tyrol and Upper Australia. The Hötting people controlled the huge copper mines of Mitterberg and were probably the principal suppliers of the metal throughout the east Alpine region.

Hou-kang: The type site of a Neolithic culture (also called

Honan Lung-shan, Henan Longshan) in Honan province, China, the first to show Yangshao, Honan Longshan, and Shang remains in stratigraphic succession. Other cultural sites are Xiawanggang and Dahe. The radiocarbon dates obtained from Hou-kang are c. 4400–4200 BC for the Banpo-type Yangshao level and c. 2350 BC for the Honan Lung-shan level. (*syn.* Hougang)

Houhanshu: A history of the Later Han Dynasty and peoples of peripheral regions of East Asia, the *Chronicles of the Later Han*, compiled in AD 398–445 from the Weizhi.

Hou-ma: An ancient city of China with extensive remains of an Eastern Chou city, possibly the site of Xintian, capital of the Chin state from 584–453 BC. Pollen analyses from western and southern Shansi reveal that several cereal plants were grown there as early as the 5th–3rd millennium BC. During the Hsi (Western) Chou period (1111–771 BC), the fief of Chin (now a colloquial and literary name for Shansi) was established in the area of Hou-ma along the Fen River. Several thousand stone and jade tablets were found at the site, inscribed with the texts of alliances between various Eastern Chou states, and date chiefly from the early 5th century BC. A very large foundry complex has been uncovered with over 30,000 fragments of clay molds and models for casting ritual vessels. Chariot fittings, weapons, belt hooks, coins, and other bronzes were distributed over the site in such a way as to suggest separate specialized workshops. The mold fragments show that Hou-ma used the section-mold method perfected in Shang foundries a thousand years earlier, as opposed to the cire perdue method. (*syn.* Houma; modern Ch'u-wu)

hourglass perforation: A type of perforation found in many prehistoric stone artifacts in which holes are drilled from opposite sides of the artifact. The perforation tends to be biconical or hourglass in form. (*syn.* hour-glass perforation)

household: A social unit made up of those living together in the same dwelling. (*syn.* household unit)

household archaeology: A branch of settlement archaeology specializing in the study of the activities and facilities associated with ancient households or houses.

household cluster: A term used to describe a set of features associated with one house structure. Components include a house, a few storage pits, graves, a rubbish area, perhaps an oven or hearth, and activity areas. It is an arbitrary archaeological unit defining artifact patterns reflecting the activities that take place around a house and assumed to belong to one household. (*syn.* household unit)

housemound: A type of low earth platform used by the ancient Maya Indians as a foundation for a house.

house of the dead: A type of wooden building above a tomb or connected to a grave, widespread in Denmark and Ger-

many, but also found in other areas of northern Europe during the Neolithic period.

Housesteads: The best-preserved fort along Hadrian's Wall in Britain; one of the best examples of a permanent military camp there, with its defenses, street plan, administrative buildings, and barrack blocks. There was also a small civil settlement for traders, and so on, at its gates. It is roughly midway along the Wall's length, in Northumberland. At Housesteads, archaeologists have uncovered a market where northern natives exchanged cattle and hides for Roman products. This allowed Roman wares and Roman cultural influences to make their way north. (*syn.* ancient Vercovicium, Borcovicium; Dorcovicus)

Howiesonspoort: A Middle Stone Age industry of southern Africa's Cape Province. It is characterized by the appearance of small blades, standardized backed tools (e.g., segments), and some unifacial and bifacial points at a time when most stone industries were still based on the production of flakes struck from discoidal cores. The radiocarbon dates are greater than 40,000 years old. In addition to the type site, the industry has been investigated at Klasies River mouth, Epi-Pietersburg, and Montagu Cave. (*syn.* Howiesons Poort)

Hoxne: A site in Suffolk, England, where John Frere discovered Stone Age implements (hand axes) among some fossilized bones of extinct animals in 1797. At that time, it was believed that the Earth had been created in 4004 BC. In reporting his findings, Frere suggested that the remains came from a time considerably earlier than that. His report was politely received, but it was not until 1956 that it was demonstrated that the lake clays had a distinctive Hoxnian pollen diagram, and the Acheulian hand axes were associated with this.

Hoxnian: An interglacial stage of Great Britain correlated with the Needian Interglacial of the Netherlands, the Holstein Interglacial of northern Europe, the Mindel-Riss Interglacial of classical Alpine Europe and is also considered to be approximately contemporaneous with the Yarmouth Interglacial of North America. It is named after the site of Hoxne where deposits are older than the extreme range of radiocarbon dating (70,000 bp). Some Hoxnian deposits are stratified above Anglian glacial deposits, others below Wolstonian glacial deposits. Acheulian and Clactonian artifacts are found in Hoxnian deposits. In addition, parts of hominid skull have been found in Hoxnian gravels at Swanscombe.

Hsia: The name of the first Chinese dynasty of the 1st millennium BC. Seventeen Hsia kings are listed in the Shih-chi, a comprehensive history written during the 1st century BC.

Hsin-tien culture: A culture of northwest China in c. 1500 BC, based on farming and using handmade pottery and copper tools. The pottery was often painted with rudimentary scrolls.

Hsiung-nu: A nomadic people who at the end of the 3rd century BC formed a great tribal league that was able to dominate much of Central Asia for more than 500 years. They appeared in historical records about 500 BC. China's wars against the Hsiung-nu, who were a constant threat to the country's northern frontier throughout this period, led to the Chinese exploration and conquest of much of Central Asia. This pastoral people wore bronze plaques decorated with animals as harness and belt ornaments.

huaca: A Quechua word meaning "holiness," "sacredness," or "sanctity" and referring to ancient mounds, ruins, tombs, or their contents, in Latin America. Diverse in nature, they range from portable amulets to large natural phenomena such as caves or stones piled in a field (*apachitas*) to stepped pyramids and were thought by the Inca, Quechua, or Aymara to have magical or religious powers. Huaca means spirits that either inhabit or actually are physical phenomena such as waterfalls, mountains, or manmade shrines. The term is also used to refer to sacred ritual or the state of being after death. (*syn.* guaca; wak'a)

Huaca La Florida: A large monumental site near Lima, Peru, or the early Initial period, c. 1700 BC. Its construction may have begun in the Late Preceramic; it was probably used for only a few centuries and abandoned.

Huacaloma: An Initial period and Early Horizon site in the Cajamarca region of Peru. The ceremonial architecture reached its climax in the late Early Horizon and Early Intermediate periods.

Huaca Prieta: A Late Preceramic site on the desert coast of north Peru with a radiocarbon date of c. 2300 BC and probably occupied from c. 3500–1800 BC. It was the first pre-ceramic village to be excavated in the country and one of the first sites dated by the radiocarbon method. Evidence of a sedentary life is seen in subterranean houses, gourd containers, and reliance on sea food, wild plants, and cultivated beans, peppers, and squashes—the earliest agriculture in South America. The people made patterned cotton textiles by twining without the aid of a loom and also produced basketry. (*syn.* Huaca Prieta de Chicama; Chicama)

Huai style: A type of bronze decoration used in the 6th–3rd centuries BC by the Eastern Chou. Cast in relief, the decoration was dense arrays of hooks and curls. The style is found by and named for the Huai River. In its early manifestations, the Huai style might be viewed as a Yangzi-region counterpart to the Liyu designs of North China. The most outstanding Huai-style designs, including extraordinary examples from Sui Xian, belong to the 5th century. This term is sometimes used for a period style applicable to the whole of China for the years c. 650–200 BC.

Huai Yai: A site in central Thailand, a center of copper and bronze production in the 2nd and 1st millennia BC. It was also a center for making polished stone adzes and stone bracelets.

Huamanga: A cultural phase, AD 900–1100, In Ayacucho, Peru, which follows the downfall of the Huari Empire. It is characterized by crude polychrome pottery.

huang: A flat semicircular or arc-shaped jade pendant known from Heolithic sites in China and made throughout the Bronze Age.

Huanghe: The Chinese name for the Yellow River in northern China. (*syn.* [Huang-ho] Yellow River)

Huang-tao ware: A type of Chinese stoneware made in the T'ang Dynasty (AD 618–907) in the Honan province. It is glazed in black or brown and splashed with an opalescent bluish or gray contrasting glaze.

Huánuco Pampa: An Inca provincial capital in the Peruvian Andes. The main town included a high-status residence, military garrison, and a compound probably for the "Chosen Women." A Spanish census report allowed the archaeologists to identify the villages occupied by the various conquered groups who paid tribute to the Incas at Huánuco. Each local group had its own style of pottery and architecture, which did not occur in the Inca town. Imperial Inca styles of pottery and building were confined to Huánuco.

Huari: An empire and large city in the central Peruvian Andes near Ayacucho, dating from AD 600–1000 (Middle Horizon). The local culture first came under Tiahuanaco influence, and Huari acted as a secondary center from which a modified version of the Tiahuanaco art style was spread to the Pacific coast and into the northern Andes. As many as 100,000 people lived in the capital, and the empire included most of Peru. There was polychrome pottery; early ceramics (Chakipampa A) date to the Early Intermediate period and are seen as a blend of Huarpa (a black-on-white geometric style) and Nasca styles. The later Chakipampa B style shows a strong Tiahuanacan influence. Structures include huge rectangular compounds with multi-story and subterranean masonry. Unlike Tiahuanaco, there are no megalithic structures, and although there is some dressed stone work, cobbles of unformed stone are also widely used. The Huari empire collapsed and was abandoned c. 800 (Early Intermediate period), after which the regional traditions began to reassert themselves in art and politics, with the eventual emergence of new states (Chimú, Cuismancu, Chincha). The Huari were also skilled in metalwork. The well-to-do were buried in stone tombs. (*syn.* Wari)

Huaricoto: A ceremonial site in the northern highlands of Peru of the Late Preceramic, Initial period, and Early Horizon. It includes a small artificial mound of 13 superimposed constructions. Its ritual chambers with hearths are similar to the Kotosh Religious tradition.

Huashan: A site in southwest China with the world's largest rock art panel. It is a limestone cliff along the Zuojiang River with over 1,800 red paintings of anthropomorphs and zoomorphs. The art was done between 2,170–2,115 years ago between the Early Warring States period and the Eastern Han Dynasty.

Huasteca: An area on the northeastern fringe of Mesoamerica in northern Veracruz and Tamaulipas provinces of Mexico, and the Maya-speaking group that lived there. The people were hunter gatherers, and the area has an archaeological sequence from the Early Preclassic to the Aztec conquest and Spanish contact. The cultural climax of the Huasteca occurs in the Early Post-Classic. The largest of the Huasteca centers (Las Flores, Tamuin) contain only moderately sized pyramids surrounded by a number of house mounds. The monumental sculpture is of relatively poor quality. The hallmarks of the Huastec culture are structures on a round plan, a black-on-white hard paste pottery, and carved shell ornaments.

Huelva: A town in southwest Spain in which a large hoard of Late Bronze Ages bronzes, dated 8th–6th centuries BC, was found. Probably the cargo of a wrecked merchant ship, it included a remarkable range of types: carp's tongue sword, an Irish lunate spearhead, and a Cypriot type of elbowed fibula. It was originally a Carthaginian trading station and afterward a Roman colony (Onuba).

Humaitá: A lithic tradition of southeastern Brazil, dated to the 5th millennium BC and continuing into the Christian era. The earliest artifacts are rough unifacial flakes and some bifacial boomerang shapes, flake knives, choppers, and scrapers—all for hunting. Bifacial projectile points begin to appear more in the 3rd millennium BC and semipolished axes and grooved bola stones were added in c. 2000–1000 BC. The complex had no pottery.

humanism: A system of thought or action that emphasizes the importance of intuition and feelings in the acquisition of knowledge rather than a scientific focus.

humus: Decomposed organic matter that becomes incorporated into soil. Litter from plants (organic matter) on or near the surface of the Earth is slowly broken down by soil organisms (decomposed and oxidized) into fine particles, which may then be incorporated into the soil by earthworms and other soil organisms. It may be combined with the products of the decomposition of various rocks and then forms the soil in which plants grow.

Hunam-ri: A Mumun pottery site in Korea with pit houses dated to between 3280–2520 bp. The houses yielded carbonized rice, foxtail millet, barley, sorghum, and soybeans—probably the earliest agricultural remains on the peninsula. (*syn.* [Hunamni])

hunebed: The Dutch name (literally "Hun's grave") for a local variety of megalithic chamber tombs in the northern Netherlands and northern Germany. The tombs are built of large stones and consist of a round or oval mound surrounded by a curb and covering a rectangular burial chamber with its entrance on one of the long sides. A few examples have an entrance passage, giving them a T plan, which suggests an association with the passage graves of Denmark. The Danish tombs are slightly later than the oldest Dutch ones, but in both places they were built by the TRB culture during the Neolithic in the 4th and 3rd millennia BC.

Huns: A nomadic pastoralist people who invaded southeastern Europe AD c. 370 and over the next 70 years built up an enormous empire there and in central Europe. Originating from beyond the Volga River after the middle of the 4th century, they first overran the Alani, who occupied the plains between the Volga and the Don Rivers, and then quickly overthrew the empire of the Ostrogoths between the Don and the Dnestr. Around AD 376, they defeated the Visigoths living in what is now approximately Romania and then became one of the many "barbarian" tribes who threatened the Roman Empire during the 4th and 5th centuries. There is little archaeological evidence attributed to the Huns, but they are remembered in the literature as being fearsome and bloodthirsty. During the 5th century, the Romans adopted a policy of employing "barbarian" mercenaries to defend the Empire against potential invaders, so the Huns were used to defend eastern Gaul from the Burgundians. The most notable period for the Huns was under their leader Attila, who invaded Gaul in 451. Visigothic and Roman forces joined to defeat Attila near Troyes, and after Attila's death the Huns were never again a major force in European history.

hunter gatherer: A way of life in which subsistence is based on the hunting of animals and the collection of wild plants rather than settled agriculture. It is a collective term for the members of small-scale mobile (to be near seasonally available wild foods) or semisedentary societies, and the organizational structure is based on bands with strong kinship ties. This way of life is believed to have lasted for over 3 million years during the Palaeolithic and Mesolithic periods. It survived down to recent times over considerable areas: Australia until the Europeans, South Africa until the Portuguese and Bantu, America until the Europeans settled, and Siberia.

Huon Peninsula: An area of the northeast coast of Papua New Guinea with coral-reef formations of the Pleistocene. Waisted axes have been found beneath volcanic ashes dating to c. 40,000 bp.

Hureidah: A site in Yemen, southwestern Arabia, with a temple to the god Sin. The temple of dressed stone blocks on a plastered rubble platform has a tentative date of 7th–6th centuries BC.

Hurri/Hurrian: A people who appeared in northern Mesopotamia and Syria at the end of the 3rd millennium BC and by c. 1600 BC had established a number of kingdoms in the area. They may have come from the Caucasus or Armenia, and some evidence suggests a connection with the Kura-Araxes culture. They had a pantheon, distinct from that of their neighbors, which was recorded in the rock sanctuary of Yazilikaya by the Hittites. Their language—non-Semitic and non-Sumerian—is known from a number of religious texts and a letter among the archives of Tell el-Amarnà. It is not related to any of the major language families. They came into contact with the Hittites, Assyrians, and Egyptians in the second half of the 2nd millennium BC. The Syrian part of their territory was absorbed into the Assyrian Empire, but the district of Urartu remained independent until much later. The name Mitanni has come to be applied to an Indo-Iranian element in the population, which was aristocratic and probably responsible for introduction of horses and chariots into the Near East. The language is not related to any known linguistic group, but is close to Urartu (Armenian). It is an agglutinative language, with a series of suffixes being added to nouns and verbs to express grammatical inflections. (*syn.* Hurrian)

Hushu: A site and culture of the Jiangsu province in China, characterized by geometric pottery and bronze implements, tools, and vessels and contemporary with the Shang and early Chou bronze cultures.

hut circle: A circle of earth or stones along the circumference of a previously existing hut. A circular depression, wall, or ring of boulders, marking the footing of a vanished hut.

Huxley's Line: The biological and geographical divide between Bali and Lombok and Borneo and Sulawesi, west of the Philippines and marking the boundary of the East Asian faunal zone during the Pleistocene periods of low sea level. It is often confused with Wallace's Line, which follows the same course but runs south, not west, of the Philippines. Huxley's Line also marks the limit of settlement by hominids before the emergence of anatomically modern humans (c. 50,000 years ago).

hüyük: A Turkish work for artifical mound, equivalent to the Arabic "tell."

Hvar: An island with a large number of Late Neolithic and Copper Age sites, off the Dalmation coast and part of present-day Croatia. The caves yielded striking Late Neolithic pottery—dark burnished ware with red crusted decoration. Hvar has been continuously inhabited since early Neolithic times, and an ancient wall surrounds the old city of Hvar. Since the vast majority of Hvar sites are caves, the economy was likely based on fishing and shell collecting. In 385 BC, Greek colonists founded Dimos (presently Hvar) and Pharos (Stari Grad), and in 219 BC, the island became Roman. Slavs fleeing the mainland in the 7th century AD settled on the island. The pottery is found in neighboring areas of the mainland, where it is known as the Lisicice style. The island's occupation probably began in the 4th millennium BC. (*syn.* Dimos)

hydration rim: A surface layer on obsidian artifacts, which can be measured as a dating technique.

hydria: A form of Greek water pot; a large jar or pitcher for carrying water with two or three handles. The body was bulbous, the neck round. It was wider and usually lower than the amphora and it had a well-defined foot and neck. There were two horizontal loop handles on the body for carrying and one vertical handle from the rim to the shoulder for pouring.

hydroceramic: Designating porous, unglazed pottery in which liqudis were cooled or filtered. (*syn.* hydro-ceramic)

hydrology: The scientific study of water, its properties and laws, and its distribution over the Earth's surface.

hyena: A carnivorous quadruped of a family related to the dog, although the skull resembles the Felidae or cat family. It has powerful jaws, neck, and shoulders but its hind quarters are low and relatively undeveloped. Three species survive today: the striped hyena (*Hyaena striata*), the brown hyena (*Hyaena brunnea*), and the spotted hyena or tiger wolf (*Hyaena crocuta*). Most hyenas live in Africa, although there are some in Asia. Remains of extinct hyena have been found in caves of the Old World. The "laughing" hyena is the spotted hyena. (*syn.* hyaena)

Hyksos: A nomadic desert tribe of Palestine whose name means "rulers of foreign lands" and who infiltrated Egypt during the Second Intermediate Period (1800–1650 BC). They infiltrated the Eastern Delta during the Middle Kingdom, and from 1630 to 1521 BC they dominated the Nile Valley from their capital of Avaris in the Delta. They became powerful enough to form the 15th Dynasty; traditionally they also formed the 16th Dynasty. Their breaking of Egyptian isolation opened the way for the flowering of culture in the New Kingdom, which immediately followed their expulsion by Ahmose. Ahmose was the founder of the 18th Dynasty, and the end of the Hyksos rule marked the beginning of the New Kingdom. The Hyksos were responsible for the introduction of the horse and chariot, and perhaps the upright loom, olive, and pomegranate. They made improved battle axes and fortification techniques. The name Hyksos was used by the Egyptian historian Manetho (fl. 300 BC), who, according to the Jewish historian Josephus (fl. 1st century AD), translated the word as "king-shepherds" or "captive shepherds." (*syn.* Heka Khaswt, Hycos, Poimenes, Mentiou Sati, Asia Shepherds, Scourges)

hyoid: A horseshoe- or U-shaped bone situated between the chin and the thyroid cartilage and making up part of the larynx in the throat. It is the only human bone that does not connect with another bone. In man, it is embedded horizontally in the root of the tongue and held in place by several ligaments. In most other mammals, it is larger and more complicated than in man.

hypaethral: In architecture, designating a building that is open to the sky and has no roof, as the kiosk of Trajan at Philae, Egypt. It especially referred to temples, the cella of which had no roof or a partial roof. On the roofs of Egyptian temples, hypaethral temples are arranged with regard to astronomical observations, by which the calendar was regulated.

hypocaust: A Roman heating system in which a floor of tile and concrete, sometimes with mosaic, was supported on low tiled pillars to allow the hot air from a furnace to circulate beneath it. Warm air, heated in an outside stoke hole, circulated under the raised floor and also often entered a room through vents above floor level. The gases escaped up box flue tiles at intervals around the walls, thus also warming them. This heating system in baths (thermae) and houses gave a central-heating effect. Examples are found from about 100 BC onward.

hypogeum: A rock-cut underground chamber or vault, often used for a series of inhumations. They are a principal part of Egyptian architecture of every period. (*syn.* pl. hypogea)

hypostyle hall: In temples, a columned hall or court situated between the sanctuary and the open court behind the pylon. The term comes from the Greek for "under pillars." These halls are the outermost, and grandest, parts of the main structures of temples, frequently added after the rest, and often exhibit an elaborate symbolism. They were used extensively in ancient Egypt—the temple of Amon at Karnak—and in Persia in the ruins at Persepolis. (*syn.* hypostyle)

hypothesis: A proposition or theory, often derived from a broader generalization or law, that postulates relations between two or more variables, based on assumptions but not yet proved. It must be tested on independent evidence; discarded hypotheses are signs of growth and advance. (*syn.* pl. hypotheses)

hypothesis testing: The process of examining how well various hypotheses explain the actual data, eliminating those that are invalid and identifying those that best fit the observed phenomena. A successful hypothesis is found to be the best approximation of truth given the current state of knowledge. In archaeology, the primary standard for accepting a hypothesis is compatibility with available data and other criteria include predictability, parsimony, completeness, and symmetry.

hypotheticodeduction: A type of scientific reasoning in which a hypothesis is made, predictions are deduced, and then the hypothesis tested for accuracy against archaeological data. Deductive reasoning is used to find and verify the logical consequences. Developed by Sir Isaac Newton in the late 17th century, it is a procedure for the construction of a scientific theory that will account for results obtained through direct observation and experimentation and that will, through inference, predict further effects that can then be verified or disproved by empirical (observed or experienced) evidence derived from other experiments. (*syn.* hypothetico-deductive explanation, hypothetico-deductive reasoning)

Hypsithermal: A Holocene climatic optimum in the Eastern Woodlands, equivalent to the Altithermal segment of the Holocene Epoch (Holocene is 10,000 years ago–present), dated on the basis of pollen studies. The Hypsithermal climatic interval began about 9,000 years ago and ended about 2,500 years ago. It has been divided into smaller units beginning with the Boreal. The Hypsithermal follows the Pre-Boreal and precedes the Sub-Atlantic intervals. It was a time of comparatively warm climatic conditions, which resulted in the elimination of many cooler plant and animal refuges and the extinction of some species. In many parts of the world, pine forests gave way to forests dominated by oak during the Hypsithermal. Mesolithic and Neolithic cultures are contemporaneous with Hypsithermal events in both the New and Old Worlds.

Hyrax Hill: A site located on Lake Nakuru in central Kenya with Later Stone Age material and a pastoral Neolithic settlement. The earlier settlement is attributed to the East African Pastoral Neolithic complex. The second phase is of the Iron Age and includes a series of so-called Sirikwa Holes, which are interpreted as semisubterranean cattle pens constructed by Nilotic-speaking peoples. There is also a cemetery of stone-covered flexed burials.

Ii

Iberians: A prehistoric people of southern and eastern Spanish coastal regions of the 1st millennium BC who later gave their name to the whole peninsula. In the 8th–6th centuries BC, waves of Celtic peoples migrated to the region. By the time of the Greek historian Herodotus (mid-5th century BC), "Iberian" applied to all the peoples between the Ebro and Huelva Rivers, who were probably linguistically connected and whose material culture was distinct from that of the north and west. There was a common script of 28 syllabic and alphabetic characters somewhat derived from Greek and Phoenician, and a non Indo-European language that cannot yet be translated. Notable among their products are their jewelry and statues, of which the Lady of Elche is the most famous. The Iberians' origins are obscure, perhaps North African. They disappeared as a separate group under the Roman occupation, partly by fusion with the Celts of the interior, partly through displacement of their language by Latin. The Iberian economy had a rich agriculture and mining and metallurgy.

Ibero-Maurusian: A stone tool culture characterized by small backed bladelets and found across the North African coast from at least 22,000–10,000 years ago (the late Würm (last) glacial period). It followed the Aterian in the Epipalaeolithic of Maghreb in North Africa and preceded the Capsian. The culture was related to Cro-Magnon, a group of people known as the Mechta-el-Arbi race, living along the Mediterranean from Tunisia to Morocco and also Libya. Linked to the sea, there are huge shell mounds of mussels, oysters, and arca. Associated with these are pottery and limited stone tool industry, in conjunction with hearths, sometimes still marked by supporting stones. Extensive cemeteries have been investigated, as at Taforalt, and also at Afalou bou Rhummel and Columnata in Algeria. Burials were sometimes decorated with ocher or accompanied by food remains or horns of wild cattle. The industry does bear a close resemblance to the late Magdalenian culture in Spain, which is broadly contemporary (c. 15,000 BC). There is evidence suggesting that the Ibero-Maurusian industry is derived from a Nile River valley culture known as Halfan, which dates from c. 17,000 BC. (*syn.* Iberomaurusian; Mouillian; Oranian)

ibex: A sturdy wild goat of the mountains of Europe, Asia, and northeast Africa, with large, recurved horns and a beard. They were often depicted by Upper Palaeolithic artists.

Iblis, Tal-i: A prehistoric mound of Kirman, Iran, occupied off and on in the 5th through 1st millennia BC. The earliest occupation, dating to the early 5th millennium BC (Tal-i Iblis O), is characterized by coarse-tempered red burnished ware made into a variety of simple forms. In the next phase, dated to the late 5th millennium BC (Tal-i Iblis I), small quantities of painted ware, in maroon or black on a buff ground, appear in a settlement of mud-brick houses, each consisting of a central area of storerooms, surrounded by living rooms with red plaster floors. This layer also produced abundant evidence of copper working and smelting. The finds suggest that the communities of Iran were at least as developed as those of Mesopotamia, if not more so, in the practice of metallurgy. The exploitation of copper and steatite and trade in these commodities to the civilizations of southern Mesopotamia and Susiana in the 4th and early 3rd millennia BC allowed Tal-i Iblis to grow to urban or protourban status. Clay tablets inscribed in the Proto-Elamite script demonstrate the connections that linked Iran to western countries by the early 3rd millennium BC.

Ice Age/ice age: A period of intense cold and the expansion of glaciers, resulting in a lower sea level. Such periods of large-scale glaciation may last several million years and drastically reshape surface features of entire continents. In the past, there were many ice ages; the earliest known took place during Precambrian time dating back more than 570 million years. The most recent periods of widespread glaciation occurred during the Pleistocene epoch (1,600,000 to 10,000 years ago). A lesser, recent glacial stage called the

Little Ice Age began in the 16th century and advanced and receded intermittently over three centuries. Its maximum development was reached about 1750, at which time glaciers were more widespread on Earth than at any time since the principal Quaternary Ice Ages. The idea of an ice age in the geological sequence is usually credited to Jean Louis Agassiz, a Swiss naturalist, who suggested it c. 1837. Agassiz conceived a worldwide cold period when areas as far apart as North America and Germany had been glaciated. (*syn.* glaciation; glacial age)

ice cores: Borings taken from the Arctic and Antarctic polar ice caps, containing layers of compacted ice, useful for the reconstruction of paleoenvironments and paleoclimatology and as a method of absolute dating. Continuous cores, sometimes taken to the bedrock below, allow the sampling of an ice sheet through its entire history of accumulation. Because there is no melting, the layered structure of the ice preserves a continuous record of snow accumulation and chemistry, air temperature and chemistry, and fallout from volcanic, terrestrial, marine, cosmic, and manmade sources. Actual samples of ancient atmospheres are trapped in air bubbles in the ice. This record extends back more than 300,000 years.

ice-free corridor: An area that was never glaciated, located between the Cordilleran and Laurentide glacial systems in North America. The corridor runs down the eastern slope of the Rockies. It provided access to the continent's interior at the end of the Pleistocene.

Iceland: An island country founded during the Viking age of exploration (late 9th century) and one of the most active volcanic regions in the world. The country was rich in fertile land and natural resources, and independent farmers, mainly coming from Norway, flourished. There was much trade with the Viking world. The details of Iceland's history and way of life have come down through their poetry and chronicles but mostly through the unique medieval prose form known as the saga. The sagas first emerged in the 12th century and increased in craftsmanship and output through the 13th century. They tell of family feuds, murderous intrigues, and voyages. The sagas are regarded as among the finest literary achievements of the Middle Ages.

ice wedge: Large masses of ice growing in thermal contraction cracks in permafrost. In periglacial conditions, alternating freeze and thaw can lead to the formation of vertical, narrow, and deep wedges of ice in gravels. After melting, these tend to fill with sediment, forming a cast of the ice wedge seen as dark bands, easily confused with manmade features, in aerial photographs. Casts of fossil ice wedges are one of the few true indicators of former permafrost conditions. Fossil ice wedges of this kind are seen in many sections of sand and gravel deposits in Europe. They have been used to reconstruct the extent of the periglacial zone that devel-oped around the Devensian and Weichselian ice sheets. (*syn.* ice-wedge; foliated ground ice)

ichneumon: A small carnivorous mammal and species of mongoose that kills snakes and destroys crocodile eggs. The ichneumon and the shrewmouse were both associated with the sun god. Ichneumons in particular were often buried in the Late and Greco-Roman periods, and many bronze statuettes of them are known. The creature is also portrayed in a number of Egyptian Old Kingdom tombs such as that of the 5th Dynasty noble Ty (c. 2400 BC).

Icknield Way: An early Neolithic trackway across England from Norfolk to Wiltshire, connecting camps on the hilltops. It ran from Avebury and Stonehenge to the coast of Norfolk, the site of the major flint mines known as Grime's Graves. In parts, the track is doubled above and below the spring line of the escarpment, suggesting seasonal variation in use.

iconography: The art of representing or illustrating by means of pictures, images, or figures; a symbolic and metaphorical representation of a particular subject. It is sometimes considered a component of cognitive archaeology, in which artistic representations that usually have an overt religious or ceremonial significance are studied. Iconography is also the study of statues and images, bas-reliefs, busts, medals, and so on. The earliest iconographical studies were published in the 16th century. Extensive iconographical study did not begin in Europe until the 18th century, however, when, as a companion to archaeology, it consisted of the classification of subjects and motifs in ancient monuments. (*syn.* icon)

Idaean Cave: A sacred cave on Mount Ida in central Crete, one of those claimed to be the birthplace of Zeus. Votive offerings were made here by the Minoans, as it was an important cult center. There was a large rock shaped into a stepped altar. A magnificent series of decorated shields of the 8th and 7th centuries BC, showing artistic influence from Syria and Assyria, was also on the site.

idealist explanation: Any rationalistic account of human goals and of the universe in general. A form of explanation stressing the search for insights into the historical circumstances leading up to an event by studying the ideas and motives of the individuals involved.

ideational strategy: A research perspective that defines ideas, symbols, and mental structures as driving forces in shaping human behavior.

ideofact: Archaeological material resulting from past human ideological activities. Any object whose function is to express or symbolize the beliefs of a people rather than to serve practical or social needs.

ideofunction: The use of an object for ideological purposes; for example, the wearing of a special garment as part of a religious ceremony. (*syn.* adj. ideofunctional)

ideogram: A single written symbol representing a concept, idea, or object without signifying a spoken sound—such as the Chinese characters and most Egyptian hieroglyphics. Ideograms were the next stage in the development of writing after pictographs. (*syn.* ideograph; logogram; pictogram; ideographic writing)

ideographic writing: A form of figurative writing, derived from pictographic writing (which refers only to objects); its symbols (ideograms) can also express an abstract concept or idea.

ideological systems: A component of culture based on the use of ideas or beliefs as part of their cultural adaptation; the knowledge or beliefs used by human societies to understand and cope with their existence. (*related word* ideology)

ideotechnic: The properties of an artifact that definitively reflect the mental, cognitive component of culture.

idiographic: Concerning individual or unique events and the specific histories of people, including unique processes, facts, and idiosyncrasies.

idiolect: The linguistic system of one person; individual variation in pronunciation or the use of language or dialect.

Idojiri: A group of about 50 Middle and Late Jomon sites in Nagano Prefecture, Japan. The sites are large clusters of substantial pit houses. The pottery has molded rim ornamentation, and there are figurines and ceremonial stone arrangements. It is thought that the inhabitants practiced plant cultivation, nut collecting, and hunting.

Ife: An important town in southern Nigeria, which dates to the 1st millennium AD. Ife has yielded a magnificent series of life-size brass/bronze and terra-cotta human heads and figures, which may have been inspired by the earlier Nok tradition and are dated from AD 1100–1450. The metal employed in the cire perdue (lost wax) process by which the bronze figures were made appears to have been derived from a northerly origin or from trans-Saharan trade. The architecture was of sun-dried brick.

Igbo Ikwu: A site in southeast Nigeria dating to the 9th century AD, with rich Iron Age deposits and bronze objects. It has yielded remarkable evidence for artistic and technological development and accumulation of wealth in that part of West Africa during the closing centuries of the 1st millennium AD. A corpse was interred in a deep pit, sitting on a stool surrounded by extensive regalia; the burial chamber was then roofed over, and the bodies of attendants were placed above it. Further offerings were deposited nearby, most notably the delicate and intricate cire perdue bronze castings of vases, bowls, and items of personal adornment. Domestic pottery and enormous numbers of glass beads were also in the deposits. (*syn.* Igbo Ukwu)

Ignateva Cave: A cave site in the southern Urals of Russia with microliths and faunal remains from the late Upper Palaeolithic. There are also numerous schematic cave paintings. The upper layer has Iron Age remains. (*syn.* Yamazy-Tash)

Ile Carn: Early Neolithic passage grave in Brittany, of drystone walling with a corbelled vault to the chamber and dated to c. 3270 bc. Inside were only a few sherds and flint flakes.

Ileret: A site on the east side of Lake Turkana in Kenya, which has yielded important archaeological sites from the Pleistocene and one from the late 3rd millennium BC. Domestic cattle and sheep make this one of the earliest sites in East Africa with evidence for pastoralism. Associated pottery and stone bowls serve as a link with Pastoral Neolithic sites of significantly later date in the Rift Valley highlands to the south. The site of Koobi Fora is very important for its finds of early Hominid fossils and stone artifacts from 2.5–1 million years ago. (*syn.* Koobi Fora)

Illapa: One of the divisions of the temple of the Sun (the sun god was Inti) among the ancient Inca, literally meaning "thunder."

Illinoian: A glacial stage of the Quaternary in North America, followed by the Sangamon Interglacial and following the Yarmouth. The Illinoian ice sheet covered a small area of southeastern and extreme eastern Iowa, and in so doing it diverted the Mississippi River and created a valley along its western front that can still be seen. It consists mainly of tills, the products of large ice sheets, and has been split into three substages, the Liman, Monican, and Jubileean. It is unclear how many cold stages the Illinoian deposits represent, but there may be more than one. The Illinoian Glacial Stage ended with a cool, moist period that gradually became drier and then warmer. The Illinoian has never been dated satisfactorily but it is roughly contemporary with the Riss and Saale Glacial Periods.

illuminated manuscript: Handwritten books that were decorated with gold or silver, brilliant colors, or elaborate designs or miniature pictures. Although various Islamic societies practiced this art, Europe had the longest and probably the most highly developed tradition of illuminating manuscripts. These medieval handwritten books were usually done on parchment or vellum. The illustrations themselves fall into several categories: miniatures (small paintings incorporated into the text or border or occupying a whole page), decorated monograms or initial letters, and decorative borders. Before the year 1000, the books most commonly illustrated in this way were gospels or psalters. The origins of manuscript illumination are thought to lie in 5th-century Coptic Egypt. It is now thought that illuminated manuscripts were relatively few in number even at the time they were produced. Very few religious or classical texts survive. After the development of printing in Europe in the second half of the 15th century, illumination was superseded by printed illustrations.

illuvial horizon: A soil horizon resulting from the deposition of minerals, humus, or plant nutrients, washed down from higher up in the profile. The most common illuvial horizon is the B horizon. Its opposite is the eluvial horizon.

Illyria: A location described in classical writing, inhabited from about the 10th century BC by the Illyrians, consisting of the northwestern part of the Balkan Peninsula. West of the Vardar and Morava Valleys, south of the Roman province of Pannonia and west of Moesia, at its height Illyria extended from the Danube River southward to the Adriatic Sea and from there eastward to the Sar Mountains. The Illyrians, descendants of the hallstatt culture, were divided into tribes, each a self-governing community with a council of elders and a chosen leader. The last and best-known Illyrian kingdom had its capital at Scodra (modern Shkodër, Albania). One of its most important rulers was King Agron (second half of the 3rd century BC), who, in alliance with Demetrius II of Macedonia, defeated the Aetolians (231).

Ilopango: The site of catastrophic volcanic eruption in south-central El Salvador in the late Pre-Classic period, AD c. 260. At least two volcanic events occurred close together, and the effects devastated a large area, forcing the local populations of early Maya to migrate north and east into the lowlands of central Guatemala and Belize. This sudden influx of migrants may have given rise to the improved agricultural methods that mark the beginning of the Classic Maya civilization. Archaeological evidence at Barton Ramie (and at Altar De Sacrificios) indicates a period of noticeable environmental and demographic change at that time.

Il'skaya I: A Middle Palaeolithic site in the northern Caucasus, Russia. There are numerous occupation horizons with remains of steppe bison and side scraper artifacts.

Imhotep (fl. 27th century BC): Vizier, sage, astrologer, and architect of the first pyramid, the Step Pyramid of Djoser (2630–2611 BC), the second king of Egypt's 3rd Dynasty. He was chief minister to Djoser and was later worshiped as the god of medicine in Egypt and Greece (Asclepius). Manetho credits him with the invention of building in dressed stone, and he is considered the designer of the first temple of Edfu, on the upper Nile, and the architect of the step pyramid built at the necropolis of Saqqarah in the city of Memphis. (*syn.* Imouthes)

impasto: A type of early pottery of Etruria, made from unrefined clay and fired to a dark brown or black, especially during the Villanovan period. Some were biconical urns and hut models and were used for cremations. Impasto is also a paint that is applied to a canvas or panel in quantities that make it stand out from the surface. It was used frequently to mimic the broken-textured quality of highlights—the surfaces of objects that are struck by an intense light.

implementation: The second stage in archaeological research design; it involves obtaining permits, raising funds, and making logistical arrangements.

impluvium: In Roman architecture, a cistern or tank for collecting rainwater, situated in the atrium under an opening in the roof (compluvium). (*syn.* pl. impluvia)

impressed decoration: A type of pottery decoration produced by pressing something into the surface of the clay when it is still soft. Stamped decoration is a special form of this, in which a stick or bone is previously carved to give the impression of its design. Intermediate in form are the impressions of natural objects like bird bones or serrated sea shells. There are a number of cultures that made pottery with impressed designs. (*syn.* impressed pottery cultures)

Impressed Ware: The earliest Neolithic pottery of the Mediterranean area, with decoration impressed into the clay by sticks, combs, fingernails, or seashells, from before 6000 BC to around 4000 BC (although until later in North Africa). The pottery itself was characterized as having simple round-bottomed shapes. The serrated edge of the cardium shell was particularly popular in the western area, and it is also known as Cardial Ware. Before c. 5000 BC, the ware is found mainly in caves or rock shelters or shell midden sites, where it is associated with hunting gathering and breeding of sheep. Around 5000 BC, crop cultivation was introduced, and large settled villages sprang up. Other types of pottery are found alongside Impressed Ware at this stage, including fine red painted ware in Italy, Stentinello Ware in Sicily, and Ghar Dalam ware in Malta, which represent specialized versions of Impressed Ware. The pottery style may have originated in Asia Minor or even Yugoslavia (Starcevo culture).

Inamgaon: A site in Pune of west-central India, which includes the 2nd millennium BC Malwa and Jorwe cultures of the northern Deccan. The Malwa phase had large rectangular, wattle-and-daub structures. By late Jorwe times, the structures were mainly small round wattle-and-daub huts. The area provides one of the clearest pictures of the region after the demise of the Indus civilization.

Inanna: A Sumerian deity, the goddess of love and war, storehouse and rain. She was the daughter of Nanna/Sin, sister of Enmerkar, and associated with Warka. She is equivalent to the Akkadian Ishtar. She is sometimes the daughter of the sky god An, sometimes his wife; in other myths, she is the daughter of Nanna, god of the moon, or of the wind, Enlil. She is sometimes referred to as the Lady of the Date Clusters.

Inariyama: A keyhole-shaped kofun (tumulus) in Saitama Prefecture, Japan. There are at least three other kofun by the same name in different parts of Japan. The one in Saitama has two moats around a mound. An x-ray examination revealed an inscription with 115 characters on an iron sword. It referred to a person called Wakatakeru, who is likely to be Emperatro Yuraku of the Yamato court, with a date of 471/531.

Inca: South American Indians who, at the time of the Spanish conquest in 1532, ruled an empire that extended along the Pacific coast and Andean highlands from the northern border of modern Ecuador to the Maule River in central Chile. The Inca established their capital at Cuzco (Peru) in the 12th century. They began their conquests in the early 15th century and within 100 years had gained control of an Andean population of about 12,000,000 people. These Quechua-speaking tribes' origins are uncertain. Their vast empire had a centralized organization, and at its head was the ruler, "Son of the Sun," worshiped as a god in his own lifetime. As a divine king, he was above the law, and as a despotic ruler, he was very much the political head of the state. Administration was in the hands of officials drawn from the Inca nobility and from the chiefs of conquered tribes. An efficient road system, along which relays of messengers could travel 250 kilometers in a day, ensured that Cuzco was kept informed of developments all over the empire. These same roads allowed Inca forces to be quickly moved into any province that showed signs of rebellion. This centralization was both the strength and the weakness of the Inca state. The unifying force was the ruler in person, and the death of Huayna Capac precipitated a crisis. Civil war broke out when two of his sons, Huascar and Atahuallpa, disputed the succession. Atahuallpa won the war, but before he could consolidate his position he was seized and murdered by Francisco Pizarro's Spaniards in 1532. Without a leader, the Inca system could not function. Most of the empire was quickly brought under Spanish control, but an independent Inca group held out in the Urubamba valley until 1572. Viracocha Inca was the creator, culture hero, and supreme deity of the Inca, but the religion embraced a pantheon of gods of nature. The most actively worshiped were the Sun and, by extension, the emperor, who was considered the son of the Sun. The temple of the Sun, built at the pre-Incan ceremonial center of Pachacamac, suggests some incorporation of earlier religions. Archaeologically, the Inca culture is characterized by fine-quality stone masonry, agricultural terraces, mass-produced and standardized pottery forms (aryballus), and metal objects. The considerable architectural skill of the Inca is reflected in Cyclopean masonry, although many buildings were constructed using rectangular dressed stone blocks as well as adobe. The basic dwelling unit was a cluster of single rooms arranged around a rectangular courtyard and was most often enclosed by a wall. Writing was unknown, but the quipu was used for keeping records. Agriculture was based on plant foods, especially potato, manioc, quinoa, and maize. Domesticated animals included dog, llama, cava (guinea pig), and alpaca. Fine textiles were woven by using a simple backstrap loom. The civilization was the largest and most powerful political unit in all of prehistoric America. It has been argued that the whole of Inca achievement relied heavily on a variety of political, societal and religious infrastructures already in place before their ascendancy.

Inca Pirca: A site in Ecuador with a unique oval platform faced with cut stone. On its summit was a gable-roofed building. It may have had a religious use or could have been a castle or guardhouse.

incense burner: Any container, often of bronze or pottery and fitted with a perforated lid, in which incense is burnt. The burning of incense as part of ritual life was a widespread practice in Mesoamerica, from as early as the Pre-Classic period, as well as in Europe and the East. In Mesoamerica, there was considerable variety in form, from the simple small candelero (Teotihuacán) to the highly elaborate incensarios of Palenque and Mayapan. *Copal*, the Maya word for pine resin, was widely traded as incense; it appears in the Aztec tribute lists in the Codex Mendoza. In China during the Han dynasty (206 BC–AD 220), a type of vessel known as a hill censer was used. Incense burners of the Ming Dynasty (1368–1644) were made in two basic forms: a square vessel on four feet, fitted with two handles and a pierced lid; and a circular tripod vessel, also fitted with a perforated lid.

incense cup: A small subsidiary vessel found with Middle Bronze Age burials and placed beside food vessels or urns in southern England. It is found with the skeleton or cinerary urn in the barrows of the Wessex culture, c. 1700 BC. The name is an archaeological label only, arising from the holes some of these vessels have through their walls, as their use is actually unknown. (*syn.* pygmy vessel)

Inchtuhil: An unfinished Roman fort in Tay, Scotland, built by Agricola during his Scottish campaigns of the early 80s AD. The fort was constructed largely of earth and timber and had 64 barracks, a commandant's house, officers' quarters, and a hospital. About 87–88, the fort was systematically dismantled as part of a planned withdrawal.

incised decoration: A type of pottery decoration in which the soft surface of the clay is cut with a sharp instrument. The term also refers to decoration scratched into the surface of other artifacts and structural features. Incised decoration has narrow lines; excised has wide lines. (*syn.* incision)

incised slate: A flat, unshaped stone tablet containing motifs inscribed by a human hand.

included fragments: A principle of stratigraphy in which fragments, material, or debris from an older bed may be incorporated in a younger bed, but not vice versa.

Independencian: A culture sited in Independence Fjord in northeast Greenland, with two Paleo-Eskimo formations, Independencian I and Independencian II. The first may be the earliest manifestation of Arctic microlithic tradition in the eastern Arctic. There were fairly standardized and precisely shaped tools, a fine saw edge on bifacial artifacts, and an absence of polished stone and adze blades. Some of the dwellings are arranged axially with slabs of stone placed vertically around a central hearth and spaces on each side where food could be stored.

independent invention: A theory that a few of the total mass of cultural traits possessed and shared by the peoples of the world have been invented more than once. The theory maintains the likelihood that ideas such as the invention of copper and iron working or the erection of particular types of monumental building were invented in more than one place at the same or different times, opposing the theory of diffusion. New chronometric dating techniques have shown the probability of independent invention for at least some of these ideas. (*syn.* parallelism)

index fossil: A fossil with widespread geographical range but restricted in time to a brief existence. In archaeology, it is a theory that proposes that strata containing similar fossil assemblages tend to be of similar age. This concept enables archaeologists to characterize and date strata in archaeological sites by using diagnostic artifact forms, making an animal species the basis for dating by faunal association. Artifacts that share the attributes of index fossils are useful in the cross-dating and correlation of deposits that contain them and in the construction of chronologies. (*syn.* index fossil concept; index species)

Indianization: The transplantation by peaceful means of the Indian civilization in Europe and other parts of Asia; the process of making Indian in character or composition, as by the replacement of foreigners by native-born Indians in positions of authority. The expansion of the Indian culture was founded on their concept of royalty and characterized by Hindu or Buddhist cults, mythology and cosmology, and use of the Sanskrit language. The process began around the beginning of the Christian era, lasted for several centuries, and created so-called Indianized kingdoms or civilizations that declined in the 13th or 14th century. (*syn.* Hinduization)

Indian Knoll: A shell mound site in Kentucky with over 1,100 burials, many with exotic grave goods. This Archaic midden is dated c. 4000–2000 BC.

indigo: A substance obtained as a blue powder from plants of the genus Indigofera, a plant cultivated since ancient times in Africa. It is produced by the decomposition of the glucoside indican. It is the essential component of indigo blue.

indirect age determination: The determination of the age of archaeological data by association with a matrix or object of known age. When Object A is found clearly associated with Object B, whose data is known, the date of B is given to A. (*syn.* indirect dating)

indirect percussion: A technique of stone-tool manufacture in which flakes are removed from a flint core in a way that causes less wasteful shatter of the material than direct percussion. The hammer or hammer stone does not strike the flint but rather a wood, antler, or bone punch, usually with a prepared edge, so that the manufacture of flakes is more controlled.

Indo-Aryan: Languages of the Indo-European family used by those settled in eastern Iran and Afghanistan, probably in the 3rd millennium BC. Some of these people, who called themselves Aryans, seem to have gradually worked their way into the Indian world. In the first millennium BC, these groups of Indo-Aryans seem to have been responsible for the diffusion of the Vedic culture and of Sanskrit throughout northern India.

Indo-European: A group of languages from which most modern European languages are derived, as well as Indian Sanskrit and the Farsi language of Iran. It is assumed that the dispersal of these languages must have occurred through large-scale migrations of people. Attempts have been made to identify the carriers of Indo-European languages with groups recognizable in the archaeological record. When the groups were literate or recorded in other people's documents, as with the Hittites and the Luwians in Asia Minor, it is possible to establish that the groups were indeed Indo-European speakers. One school maintains that the original homeland was in the south Russian steppes in the 5th millennium BC and that people spread into Europe with the Single Grave, Corded Ware, and Globular Amphorae groups. Indo-European was first recognized by Sir William Jones in 1786. It includes most of the modern European languages (Romance, Germanic, Slavic, Baltic, Greek, Albanian) and modern Indo-Iranian (Persian, Hindi).

Indonesia: The most southerly and largest portion of island Southeast Asia. It is divided by the Huxley/Wallace Line into westerly Sunadaland and easterly Wallacea, the former being settled by *Homo erectus* (Java man) by 2 million years ago. Around 40,000 years ago, people moved across Huxley's Line to reach Australia and New Guinea (early Australoid populations). Small flake and blade industries popped up in eastern Indonesia and Australia after 4000 BC, and the spread of Neolithic cultures correlated with Austronesian expansion after 3000 BC. Bronze metallurgy spread in the 1st millennium BC.

Indrapura: A city and dynasty in Cambodia that was the first capital of King Indravarman II (the sixth in Champan history) before he founded the kingdom of Angkor. It served in that capacity from 875–986, when the capital was then transferred to Vijaya, farther south.

induced polarization technique: A technique similar to resistivity surveying used for the location of archaeological features. It involves the measurement of transient induced polarization voltage, which results from the passing of direct current through the ground via electrodes. The method requires the presence of an electrolytic solution, and thus it is the greater or lesser water content of the features, in contrast to the surrounding soil, that allows its detection. A ditch would have a high induced polarization response, while a wall would have a low one.

induction: A method of reasoning in archaeology in which one proceeds from the specific to the general so that the conclusions contain more information than the premises do. (*syn.* inductive research)

inductively coupled plasma emission spectrometry: A technique used to identify trace elements in stone, pottery, and metal artifacts in an attempt to trace the components' origins. It is based on the same basic principles as optical emission spectrometry, but the generation of much higher temperatures reduces problems of interference and produces more accurate results. (*syn.* ICPS)

Indus civilization: The earliest known urban culture of the Indian subcontinent, identified in 1921–1922 by its two capitals—Harappa and Mohenjo-Daro—both in modern Pakistan. It was also the most extensive of the three earliest civilizations, the other two being Mesopotamia and Egypt. It was one of the greatest civilizations of antiquity, but its origins are obscure. By around 2300 BC, the Indus civilization was fully developed and in trading contact with Sargonid Sumer. Radiocarbon dates from several sites support an origin c. 2600 BC and suggest that by 2000 BC the civilization was in marked decline. The Indus River seems to have played a significant part, as many sites show deposits left by frequent catastrophic floods. Exploitation of the vegetation, particularly for the baking of enormous quantities of brick, caused the decline of the countryside. The final collapse seems to have been due to hostile attack. A few inhumation cemeteries have been found associated with the gridiron-plan cities, and there were also elaborate drainage systems. The site of Mohenjo-Daro had a great bath, assembly hall, and other monumental buildings. There was widespread use of an undeciphered hieroglyphic script and standard weights and measures. The economy was based on mixed agriculture, and humped cattle were the most important domestic animals. The pottery was mass produced and plain. Artistically the finest products were square steatite seals, carved with local or mythical animals and brief inscriptions. The civilization's effect on the later culture and religion of India seems to have

been considerable. (*syn.* Indus Valley civilization, Harrapan civilization)

industrial archaeology: The archaeological study of the period and sites of the Industrial Revolution and later. It involves the discovery, recording, and study of the material remains of past industrial activities, covering ways of making, transporting, and distributing things.

industry: A frequently repeated assemblage of a particular material or function, such as flake industry or flint industry. Such an assemblage of artifacts including the same types so consistently suggests that it is the product of a single society. The term also describes a large grouping of artifacts that is considered to represent or identify a particular people or culture, such as the Acheulian industry. If more than one class of objects (e.g., flint tools or bronze weapons) is found, it is a "culture."

inevitable variation: The premise that all cultures vary and change through time without specific cause and in a cumulative manner, a general and unsatisfactory descriptive model sometimes implied in the culture historical approach.

infrared absorption spectrometry: A technique used to identify mineral and chemical composition artifacts, either to determine their nature or to identify their source. A small sample is taken from the object and is ground finely before being subjected to infrared radiation. Constituent atoms in the specimen vibrate at characteristic frequencies; if the frequency is the same as that of the radiation, the radiation will be absorbed, while if frequencies do not match, the radiation will pass through the sample. A measurement of the amount of absorption at each wavelength leads to the identification of the minerals and chemical compounds present. Although the method can be used for both inorganic and organic materials, it tends to be used alongside x-ray diffraction for inorganic substances, where it is more sensitive to poorly crystallized minerals. It is most useful for organic materials such as amber, as the organic compounds in the amber absorb different wavelengths of infrared radiation passed through them. (*syn.* infra-red absorption spectrometry)

infrared photography: A technique of aerial photography for detection and recording on film of infrared radiation reflected from the sun. Direct infrared-recording aerial photography shows up ground features of differential infrared reflection but similar light reflection and cuts through haze and mist.

infrastructural determinism: A research strategy used by cultural materialists, in which priority is assigned to modes of production and reproduction. Technological, demographic, ecological, and economic processes are the most important elements for satisfying basic human needs (the "independent variable"); the social system is the dependent variable. These primary elements lie at the causal heart of every sociocultural system. Domestic and political subsystems (the "structure") are considered to be secondary. Values, aesthetics, rituals, religion, philosophy, rules, and symbols (the "superstructure") are tertiary. (*syn.* infrastructure)

Ingaladdi: A sandstone rock shelter in the Australian Northern Territory known for two well-separated stone industries and for art. The upper levels date 3000 bp and contained an Australian Core Tool assemblage with points and tula adze flakes. The unifacial points included some with denticulated margins and others classed as Pirri points. Rock paintings included Wandjina style mythical beings, animals, men on horseback, and revolvers. Fragments of Panaramitee-style engravings were found in layers dated 5000–3000 BC. Following a sterile layer, the lower layers contained large flake scrapers, horsehoof cores, and engraved sandstone fragments of 7000–5000 bp.

Ingombe Ilede: An Iron Age site in southern Zambia, occupied in the 14th–15th centuries AD by peoples who engaged in extensive trade in copper and gold. Elaborate graves contained metal bangles, ingots, iron hoes and gongs, bundles of copper wire, woven cotton cloth, marine gastropod shells, gold beads, and imported glass beads. This evidence for development of trade in the Zambezi Valley coincides in date with the decline of Great Zimbabwe.

ingot: A shaped or cast mass of unwrought metal resulting from smelting or other extraction process. Ingots are often of a standard weight, sometimes of a guaranteed purity. Examples include the ingot of the Mycenaeans (c. 30 kg of copper) in the shape of an oxhide, the bronze ingot torc of the European Bronze Age, the iron currency bar of the English Iron Age, and the Roman lead pig stamped with the smelter's name.

inhumation: The practice of burying the dead, contrasting with cremation and exposure. Burial may be in a dug grave or in a natural or built chamber—and may be simple or elaborate. Terms commonly used to describe it are extended (with spine and leg bones more or less in a straight line); flexed (with the leg bones bent, but by less than 90 degrees); or crouched (with the hip and knee joints bent through more than 90 degrees). Extended burials may be supine (on the back), prone (on the face), or on the side. Primary inhumation is the initial burial of a deceased individual. Secondary inhumation is the practice of removing the remains of the deceased individual from the pyre to the grave. (*syn.* burial; grave burial)

Initial Period: The period of 1800–900 BC marking the introduction of pottery in Andean South America. It was also the time when agriculture and animal husbandry began to be the subsistence base for most cultures in the area. It is one of a seven-period chronological construction used in Peruvian archaeology. Its close is marked by the occurrence of Chavín materials and the abandonment of many of the coastal centers. Many of the traits that make up the Peruvian cultural tradition such as intensive agriculture, the widespread use of textiles, monumental ceremonial architecture, and larger and more numerous population centers, occurred during this period.

inorganic ecofacts: Ecofacts (faunal or flora material) derived from nonbiological remains (matter other than plant or animal), including soils, minerals, and the like.

inorganic materials: Material that is neither animal or plant; inanimate or artificial material.

inscription: Something that is inscribed; the act of inscribing. It is writing or any type cut into or raised on a hard surface—clay, wood, stone, metal—and therefore endures. Inscriptions on coins, medals, seals, currency notes, and so on may be done with symbolic picture writing, abbreviations, or phonetic alphabets.

insect analysis: Any studies of insect remains in an attempt to reconstruct past environments. Pollen analysis and molluscan analysis can reveal information on climate, the environment, and, sometimes, human activities. Insect remains are usually found in the form of the exoskeleton, parts such as the wing cases of beetles, and they always come from anaerobic deposits such as ditches, wells, pits, and peat bogs; many of the parts of insects that are species distinctive do not survive in archaeological deposits. They can be separated from the soil sample by flotation. Insects respond more quickly than plants to climatic change and may therefore assist in the identification of microclimatic phases. Insects also have habitat preferences, which are helpful in identifying specific environments.

in situ: (in si'-choo) Latin for "in place." In the normal or natural or original position or place—describing an artifact encountered during excavation or survey.

instrument map: An archaeological map made by use of surveyors' instruments, allowing for accurate control over distance, direction, and elevation.

insula: In Roman antiquity, a block in the grid pattern of a Roman city; a block of buildings in a Roman camp or town planned on the grid principle. The term refers to an area of a town, typically enclosed by four streets, and probably corresponding to a smaller subdivision on the familiar cardo/decumanus grid—or a large tenement-type house or apartment block, as seen at Roman Ostia. (*syn.* pl. insulae)

intaglio: (in-tal'-yo) A gemstone into whose surface a decoration is cut and this technique of decoration. This prehistoric incised carving was also done on precious metal. The design was especially used on seal stones, which were sometimes set into rings and used as personal seals. The engraved subject is sunk beneath the surface, thus distinguishing it from a cameo, which is engraved in relief.

Intef (fl. 21st–20th century BC): Name taken by three rulers of the 11th Dynasty of Thebes (2081–1939 BC), particularly Intef II, also called Wahankh Intef (fl. 21st century BC), the third king of the dynasty. During his long reign, he successfully warred against the allies of the Heracleopolitans—rulers of Middle and Lower (northern) Egypt composing the 9th and 10th Dynasties. These three kings were buried in rock-cut tombs in the el-Tarif region in western Thebes. The others were Intef Sehertawy and Intef III Nakhtnebtepnefer. (*syn.* Inyotef)

Integration Period: The last stage of Ecuadorian prehistory, from about AD 500 to the Inca conquest (1550), characterized by greater cultural uniformity over wider areas. There is evidence for urban centers, class distinction, intensive agriculture, and high-quality metallurgy throughout the region. The absorption of Ecuador into the Inca Empire was the culmination of this trend. It is part of the chronological continuum—Formative, Regional Development, Integration—formulated by Betty Meggers. (*syn.* Late Period)

interaction sphere: Any regional or interregional exchange system, such as the Hopewell interaction sphere.

Intercultural Style: A style of decoration of stone vessels, normally made of chlorite, found in Iran, Mesopotamia, and the Persian Gulf in the second half of the 3rd millennium BC. Vessels and other objects made of chlorite, steatite, serpentine, and other soft stones shared a rich iconography. A production center was discovered at Tepe Yahya. (*syn.* Intercultural style carved chlorite)

interface: The point of contact between two layers or features in an excavation, stratigraphically important. An example is the point between the fill of a buried ditch and the soil through which it was dug.

interglacial: A warm period between two glaciations with little or no glacial ice and marked by warm climate processes, deposits, flora and fauna, and increased soil formation. The ice sheets diminish in area, and the improved climate allows the growth of temperate types of vegetation. The last 10,000 years (the Holocene) is probably an interglacial. During the Quaternary, interglacials have been considerably shorter than glacials. (*syn.* adj interglacial)

interior flake: A flake having no cortex. (*syn.* tertiary flake, noncortical flake)

interlace: A pattern of ornamentation that consists of twisted and plaited ribbons making geometric patterns or of intertwined strands extending from animal and plant motifs. In the 7th and 8th centuries, interlace ornament was refined and used to great effect by Celtic and Anglo-Saxon metal-workers, sculptors, and manuscript illuminators. This artistic tradition was also prominent during the Viking period.

Intermediate Periods: One of the three periods in Egyptian history when the country was divided into regional potentates instead of united. These periods occurred between the Old Kingdom, Middle Kingdom, New Kingdom, and Late Period. The First Intermediate Period was 2130–1938 BC, the Second Intermediate Period was 1630–1540 BC, and the Third Intermediate Period was 1075–656 BC. In Andean/Peruvian archaeology, there were also Intermediate Periods. The Early Intermediate Period (200 BC–AD 600) was characterized by the rise of the first great city-states, such as Moche and Nasca. The Late Intermediate Period (AD 1000–1476) was characterized by the presence of numerous fractionalized corporate units that arose after the decline of Tiahuanaco and Huari, such as Chimu and Aymara.

interment: The practice or act of burying the dead. (*syn.* burial)

interpretation: A stage in archaeological research design at which the results of analyses are synthesized and attempts made to explain their meaning, allowing a reconstruction of the past.

interstadial: A brief period of milder climate in a longer, cooler glacial period (between two cold periods during a major glaciation). Although it is similar to an interglacial period, it is too cold or too short to allow for growth of vegetation. Examples are the Devensian, Weichselian, and Wisconsin.

intervallum: The space between two ramparts or palisades. The term also referred to the roadway inside a fort, at the foot of the wall.

Inti: In Inca religion, the sun god, believed to be the ancestor of the Incas. Inti was the head of the cult, and his worship was imposed throughout the empire. He was represented in human form with his face as a gold disk from which rays and flames extended. The temple of the Sun was called Inti-huasi (house of the Sun) with seven principal divisions; *inti* or sanctuary (center of temple), *mama-quilla* (moon), *cayllur* (stars), *illapa* (thunder), *ckuichi* (rainbow), *huilacuma* (chief priest), and the dwelling of the priests. Inti's sister and consort was the moon, Mama-Kilya (or Mama-Quilla), who was portrayed as a silver disk with human features. (*syn.* Punchau; Apu-Punchau)

Intihuasi Cave: An Argentinian site with long occupation and clear chronological continuity and similar to the Desert Tradition. Its lowest level, dated to c. 6000 BC, contains willow-leaf points and other hunting tools in association with manos, milling stones, and ground-stone ornaments. Other levels contain medium-sized triangular points, bone projectile points, and a ceramic level (AD c. 750).

intramural: Pertaining to graves located in the confines of a settlement. Graves outside a settlement are extramural.

Inuit: The eastern Arctic peoples descending from the Thule culture, a prehistoric maritime society, whose subsistence was based on hunting. The origins of the Inuit living in the territories, largely in the coastal areas, are obscure. They now constitute about one third of the territorial population. (*syn.* Eskimo)

inundation: A term used to describe the annual flooding of the Nile River in Egypt, which has not taken place since the completion of the Aswan High Dam in 1971.

invent: To create a new artifact.

involution: A structure that develops in the active layer of the Periglacial (permafrost) zone. Cryoturbation (seasonal freezing) causes movement in the layer and sorting of its component materials. Involutions help to define the area of ancient periglacial zones, but their action can cause disturbance or mixing of archaeological deposits. Involutions may also be confused with archaeological features.

Inyanga: A series of mountains that separate Zimbabwe from Mozambique, which has evidence of a prolonged sequence of Iron Age occupation. Early Iron Age settlement, related to that at Gokomere, is attested at several sites around Ziwa Mountain. Between the 16th and 18th centuries and perhaps earlier, extensive irrigation works were built. Other stone structures date from the same period, including semi-subterranean structures interpreted as stock pens.

Iol: An ancient seaport of Mauretania, located west of what is now Algiers in Algeria on the North African coast. Iol was originally founded as a Carthaginian trading station, but it was later renamed Caesarea and became the capital of Mauretania in 25 BC. The city was famous as a center of Hellenistic culture, and under the Romans it became one of the most important ports on the North African coast. It was colonized by Claudius in AD 40. Remains include the city wall, theater/amphitheater, circus, baths, and a lighthouse. (*syn.* Cherchell, Sharshal, Caesarea)

Iona: An island of the Inner Hebrides off the coast of Scotland. In 563, it was granted by Connal of Dálriada to St. Columba for the founding of a monastery. It was the base from which the Celtic church, under Columba, Aidan, and their successors, converted northern Britain to Christianity. Lindisfarne was its most important daughter house. The remains of the monastery are earthworks that include a distinctive rectangular vallum or ditched enclosure surrounding the complex. The standing buildings belong to the later medieval Benedictine abbey. The island also has a fine collection of 8th-century standing crosses. In the early 9th century, the Vikings caused the Columban monks to abandon their monastery, and many returned to Ireland.

Ionic order: In architecture, one of the orders of ancient Greece, also found in cities of western Turkey and the islands of the eastern Aegean. The elegantly designed column has a capital formed by two sets of volutes, which looked like a pair of formalized ram's horns. Between the volutes was an echinus decorated with an egg-and-dart pattern. The entablature allowed for a continuous frieze, which could be decorated in relief. The diameter-to-height ratio was between one-to-eight and one-to-ten. In classical architecture, the Ionic order emerged after the Doric, perhaps from about 570 BC. Unlike the Doric, the Ionic capital has four distinct sides, only two of which are intended to be conspicuous. (*syn.* Ionic column, Ionic style, Ionic)

Ipiutak: An Eskimo/Inuit culture of northwestern Alaska, probably dating from the 2nd to the 6th century AD. The type site at Point Hope is the largest Eskimo/Inuit village ever discovered in Alaska. The village had about 600 houses and many burials accompanied by finely carved bone and ivory objects. The art style includes animal forms, which show links with Siberia and northern Eurasia. The people were sea and land hunters and expert stone workers with no pottery. A Siberian origin has been suggested, based on similarities in burial practices and ceremonialism, animal carvings and designs, and some use of iron; there seem to be links with the Kachemak culture. It has also been suggested that the culture developed from the Choris-Norton-Near Ipiutak subtradition, intermingled with Northern Maritime and Siberian influences. Ipiutak is particularly important for its demonstration of the continuing influence of Siberian cultures on the Eskimo/Inuit tradition. It is the most recent variation of the Norton tradition, a series of Arctic Alaska cultures dating from 1000 BC–AD 1000. Projectile points and other stone implements are similar to those of the preceding Norton culture.

Ipswichian: The last interglacial of Britain, equivalent to the Eemian Interglacial of North Europe, with its type site at Bobbit's Hole, Ipswich. The Alpine equivalent is the Riss-Würm, and the Sangamon is the North America equivalent. The deposits indicate warm conditions with evidence of vertebrate fossils. One radiocarbon date of 174,000–30,000 BP has been found. Levalloisian and Mousterian artifacts are found in Ipswichian deposits. (*syn.* Eemian)

Ipswich ware: A pottery ware made in the 7th–9th centuries at Ipswich, England, where kiln debris has been found. The cooking pots and undecorated pitchers were distributed widely in East Anglia, while stamp-decorated pitchers were traded as far as York and Richborough. This ware makes it possible to identify sites of the Middle Saxon period.

iron: A ductile, malleable, magnetic metallic element, used to make artifacts of both practical and decorative function. Its oxide form, hematite, is found naturally, and the technique of ironworking was mastered around 1500 BC by the Hittites.

Iron began to spread and replace bronze for basic tools and weapons—the start of the Iron Age. Early in the 1st millennium BC, iron industries were established in Greece and Italy, and by 500 BC, iron had replaced bronze for the manufacture of tools and weapons throughout Europe. The pre-Columbian New World, however, did not develop iron technology. Iron smelting is more complicated than processing copper or tin; the first smelt gives only slaggy lumps, the bloom. Hammering at red heat is then required to expel stone fragments and combine carbon with the iron to make in effect a steel, but the resulting metal is far superior to copper or tin. The two basic methods of working iron are by forging—hammering into shape at red heat—and casting. The Chinese used the latter method as early as the 5th century BC, but it was not employed in Europe until the Middle Ages. The first evidence of iron smelting in Egypt dates to the 6th century BC. Large-scale steel manufacture depends on the production of cast iron, which in Europe dates only from the 14th century AD. The West did not enter the "Age of Steel" until the 19th century with the invention of the Bessemer and Siemens processes, which are industrial processes for obtaining liquid metal of any desired carbon content by the decarburization of cast iron. Steel was made in China within a few centuries of the first known use of smelted iron. In principle, modern techniques descended from China's casting techniques.

Iron Age: The period during which people used iron, beginning about 3,000 years ago, following the Stone Age and Bronze Age in the Three-Age system. In this period, tools, implements, and weapons were first made of iron. Iron had many advantages over bronze, so that its spread was rapid. The Iron Age began at different times in different parts of the world according to the availability of iron ore and the state of knowledge. In Europe, the earliest iron appears around 1100 BC. The traditional timing of the transition from bronze to iron is placed in the early 1st millennium BC. The age began about 1500 BC in the Middle East, about 900 BC in southern Europe, and after 400 BC in northern Europe. In most of Asia, the Iron Age falls entirely within the historic period. In America, iron was introduced by the arrival of Europeans; in Africa, it began before the earlier metal ages. The southern African Iron Age is divided into the Early Iron Age, AD 200–1000, and the Late Iron Age, AD 1000 until the 19th century. The term is general and arbitrary. There is evidence that meteorites were used as a source of iron before 3000 BC, but extraction of the metal from ores dates from about 2000 BC.

iron making, direct process: The technique of smelting iron ore in a furnace with charcoal and limestone to produce a spongy, low-carbon form of iron known as a bloom. This ductile material can be forged into tools and weapons.

iron making, indirect process: The technique of smelting iron ore in a furnace at a very high temperature to yield a molten, high-carbon form of iron. The high-carbon content makes it too brittle for most direct uses, and it must undergo a secondary process, oxidization, to make it more ductile. It can then be forged into weapons and tools. The indirect process of iron making was developed in China early in the first millennium BC. The Chinese made iron artifacts, heating blooms in a fire and hammering the red-hot metal to produce the desired objects; iron made in this way is known as wrought iron.

ironstone: A hard sedimentary rock rich in iron, especially a siderite in a coal region. This ore of iron, commonly a carbonate, has clayey impurities. Ironstone china is a hard heavy durable white pottery developed in England early in the 19th century.

Iroquois: North American Indian tribes speaking a language of the Iroquoian family—the Cayuga, Cherokee, Huron, Mohawk, Oneida, Onondaga, Seneca, or Tuscarora. The Iroquois occupied territory around Lakes Ontario, Huron, and Erie, in present-day New York state and Pennsylvania and southern Ontario and Quebec. It was a very important culture, dating from the middle of this millennium. The people lived in longhouses, practiced agriculture, fished, hunted, and engaged in much warfare.

Isaac, Glynn Llywelyn (1937–1985): Palaeoanthropologist who studied the early Pleistocene of East Africa. He is credited with developing new approaches to the interpretation of very early archaeological remains.

Isbister: A Neolithic chambered tomb on the island of South Ronaldsay, Orkney, Scotland, dating to c. 3150 BC. Remains of 342 people were found in the chambers, mostly as disarticulated bones that were sorted.

Ischia: A volcanic island off Campania, southern Italy, with some Mycenaean pottery, which had an 8th century BC European colony before Cumae. The clay of Ischia is believed to have been used by the ancient potteries of Cumae and Puteoli (Pozzuoli).

Isernia: A Lower Palaeolithic site in central Italy with many disarticulated animal bones associated with stone tools and dating to c. 730,000 BP. In modern times, it originated as Aesernia, a town of the Samnites and later became a Roman colony. (syn. La Pineta)

Isfahan: A city in Iran, which was a Parthian provincial capital and possibly occupied throughout the Sassanian period, the central province of the ancient pre-Islamic Iranian empires. The Great Mosque of Isfahan was one of the most influential of all early Seljuq religious structures; it was probably completed around 1130 after a long and complicated history of rebuildings. The best known Safavid monuments are located at Isfahan, where 'Abbas I built a whole new city. 'Abbas expressed his new role by moving his capital in about 1597–1598 to Isfahan. According to one description, the city contained 162 mosques, 48 madrasahs, 1,802 commercial buildings, and 283 baths. Most of these buildings no longer survive, but what remains constitutes some of the finest monuments of Islamic architecture.

Ishango: A Stone Age midden on the shore of Lake Edward in eastern Zaire, dated to 20,000 BP. It has a long sequence of occupation and represents the southernmost known manifestation of the so-called African Aquatic civilization. A crude stone industry with rare backed microliths was accompanied by bone harpoon heads. There was no pottery.

Ishtar: In Mesopotamian religion, the goddess of war, love, and procreation. She was the Akkadian counterpart of the West Semitic goddess Astarte. Her husband was Tammuz. Part of her cult worship probably included temple prostitution, and her cult center, Erech, was filled with courtesans and harlots. She was popular throughout the ancient Middle East. (*syn.* Inanna)

Isimila: A site in southern Tanzania that may have been occupied about 250,000 years ago. The most distinctive tools are hand axes and cleavers of African Acheulian type, but two other assemblage types are found, one with picks and the other with small retouched tools.

Isin: An ancient Mesopotamian city, probably the origin of a large mound near Ad-Diwaniyah, in southern Iraq. An independent dynasty was established at Isin about 2017 BC by Ishbi-Erra, who founded a line of Amorite rulers of whom the first five claimed authority over the city of Ur to the south. The fifth of the rulers of Isin, Lipit-Ishtar (reigned 1934–1924 BC), is famous for having published a series of laws in the Sumerian language anticipating the code of Hammurabi by more than a century. About 1794 BC, Isin lost its independence to Larsa and later to Babylon. The city revived between about 1156 and 1025 under its 2nd dynasty, a number of whose kings exercised authority over Babylonia (southern Iraq) after the Kassite period.

Isis: Important Egyptian goddess, wife of Osiris and mother of Horus. She was anthropoid in form and goddess of the Moon. She was a powerful magician and also venerated as the ideal mother. She became the symbolic mother of the Egyptian king, who was himself regarded as a human manifestation of Horus. She had important temples throughout Egypt, as at Philae and Behbet el-Hagar, and in Nubia. By Greco-Roman times, she was dominant among Egyptian goddesses. Several temples were dedicated to her in Alexandria, where she became the "patroness of seafarers." From Alexandria, her cult spread throughout the Mediterranean, including Greece and Rome. In Hellenistic times, the mysteries of Isis and Osiris developed; these were comparable to other Greek mystery cults. (*syn.* Aset, Eset)

Isle Royale: An island in Lake Superior where there are 10 sunken ships dating from the mid-1800s on. The cold freshwater has preserved the wrecks well.

isochronous: Formed during the same span of time. Isochronal means uniform in time, having equal duration, recurring at regular intervals.

isolate: One or two artifacts occurring by themselves and not associated with an archaeological site; generally thought to represent items lost or discarded by people as they moved through an area.

isolated data: A single object that is found without association to any other artifact or feature, typically lost during travel or moved by a relic hunter. Any unassociated archaeological remains.

isometric drawing: Projections in which the plan and the elevations are combined to give a "three-dimensional" view, on which correct measurements can be taken either in any direction (isometric) or along two or three axes (axonometric). The three-dimensional rendering, usually of a feature or a site, is used to record and reconstruct the results of archaeological research. In contrast to perspective drawings, isometric drawings maintain a constant scale in all three dimensions. (*syn.* isometric and axonometric projection)

isostasy: An alteration in the height of the land relative to the sea; the distribution of mass in the Earth's crust is balanced by large-scale topography. These variations are not necessarily associated with changes in sea level (eustasy), but a major event such as glaciation can affect both land and sea. The weight of ice sheets can cause a lowering in the height of the land, but a thaw at the end of a glaciation frees the land of this pressure and it rises. Continental crust behaves like a body "floating" on the denser underlying layers. Loading of one area may cause downwarping of the crust, which is compensated by uplift elsewhere. Removal of the load causes the crust to readjust to its former state. It is a theory that the condition of approximate equilibrium in the outer part of the Earth is approximately counterbalanced by a deficiency of density in the material beneath those masses, while a deficiency of density in ocean waters is counterbalanced by an excess in density of the material under the oceans. This phenomenon has occurred during the Quaternary, owing to the development of large ice sheets. The enormous weight of ice caused downwarping of the continental crust beneath. At the ice-sheet margins, there was a compensatory uplift. On the melting of the ice sheets, the crust readjusted by uplift in the areas directly underneath and by downwarping at the edges. This process is continuing today, for example, in northern Europe. (*syn.* isostatic uplift)

isostatic: Pertaining to changes in the altitude of the Earth's crust relative to the sea—shifts in the crustal mass in compensation for loading and unloading of the crust.

isothermic line: A line on a map linking locations of equivalent temperature at a given time.

isotope: Atoms of the same elements, but with different

atomic masses owing to having different numbers of neutrons in the nuclei, and having similar chemical properties. Many of these forms of elements with a specific number of electrons (such as carbon 14 or potassium 40) are unstable and decay into different elements, releasing their surplus electrons. Radiocarbon, potassium-argon, fission track, and thermoluminescence dating all rely on this phenomenon in different ways.

isotopic analysis: Any dating technique relying on the phenomenon of isotopal decay—analyzing the ratios of the principal isotopes. The analysis of isotopes—any of two or more species of atoms of a chemical element with the same atomic number and nearly identical chemical behavior but with differing atomic mass or mass number and different physical properties.

isotopic fractionation: The enrichment of one isotope relative to another in a chemical or physical process. Two isotopes of an element are different in weight but not in gross chemical properties, which are determined by the number of electrons. It can be predicted theoretically and demonstrated experimentally, however, that subtle chemical effects do result from the difference in mass of isotopes. Isotopes of an element may have slightly different equilibrium constants for a particular chemical reaction, so that fractionation of the isotopes results from that reaction. One of the assumptions of radiocarbon dating is that carbon 12, carbon 13, and carbon 14 are passed around the carbon cycle at similar rates. The three isotopes are chemically very similar, but slight differences among them may cause them to be taken up at different rates by some plants and animals. This isotopic fractionation may cause inaccuracies in radiocarbon dating. Both carbon 12 and carbon 13 are stable isotopes, and their ratio should therefore remain constant throughout life and after death. If the ratio has changed from the expected value, then fractionation has occurred. Once the degree of fractionation is known, it can be corrected for mathematically by the laboratory.

isotopic replacement: A chemical process that creates inaccuracies in radiocarbon/radiometric dating. An isotope in a sample is exchanged with an isotope of the same element that is a different age. This can occur in fossil shells whose C14 isotope in the calcium carbonate may be replaced during recrystallization by different carbon isotopes dissolved in the surrounding groundwater.

Israelites: A branch of Semitic people of nomadic origin, who emerged in the Levant at the start of the Iron Age, c. 1200 BC. This emergence is identified with a shift of settlement, small villages dispersed in upland regions replacing urban life. They are said to have been led by Moses from Egypt to the Promised Land of Palestine. They conquered the Canaanites and the Philistines in some areas and created a powerful monarchy, with its capital at Jerusalem, in the 10th century BC. The Canaanites retained control of the coastal area, however. Shortly thereafter, the Israelite kingdom split into the kingdoms of Israel and Judah, later to be destroyed, respectively, by the Assyrians in 722 BC and the Babylonians in 587 BC. Although there exists a wealth of documentary evidence for the Israelites in the Bible, they are difficult to identify in the archaeological record. The major building works of the united kingdom belong to the reign of Solomon.

Istállóskö: An Upper Palaeolithic cave site in the Bükk Mountains of northern Hungary. The lower Aurignacian assemblage with split-base bone points but few stone tools had a radiocarbon date of 42,350 bp, one of the oldest Aurignacian occupations in Europe. The upper layer is Aurignacian of c. 31,000 bp with a bone flute, burins, end scrapers, and bone points.

isthmus: A narrow strip of land connecting two large land areas otherwise separated by the sea. The two most famous are the Isthmus of Panama, connecting North and South America, and the Isthmus of Suez, connecting Africa and Asia. Historically the Isthmus of Corinth was of major importance because it connected what otherwise would be the island of the Peloponnese with the rest of the Greek peninsula.

Isturitz: A cave system in the Pyrenees-Atlantiques of southeast France with one of the longest sequences of Palaeolithic strata yet known. Several Mousterian levels were overlaid by a long sequence of Upper Palaeolithic levels. Human remains were found, and numerous portable art objects and wall engravings have been recovered, mainly in the Magdalenian levels. There are also intact Magdalenian hearths on the floor of the lowest tunnel, the Erberua. (*syn.* Isturitis)

Itazuke: An early agricultural village in Fukuoka Prefecture, Japan, the type site for Early Yayoi pottery. The site had extensive paddy field remains. The pottery was associated with wooden hoes and semilunar stone harvesting knives. There are also Early Yayoi graves and Middle and Late Yayoi occupation levels. Other artifacts recovered from the site include spindle whorls and bronze weapons. (*syn.* Itatsuke)

ivory: Material from enlarged teeth (or tusk) of certain mammals, used for various tools and artifacts from the Upper Palaeolithic. The tusks of elephants, mammoths, and walruses have been prized throughout prehistory and history.

Iwajuku: The first Palaeolithic site discovered in Japan, with layers 20,000 and 15,000 years old. Excavation there provided the first convincing evidence that the Japanese islands were occupied by humans during Palaeolithic times. Among the finds are elongate blades, choppers, and scrapers in the oldest layer and thin small blades in the second. Other crude "tools" estimated to be over 50,000 years old have been found.

Iwo Eleru: A rock shelter in the forest zone of southwestern Nigeria, which has yielded the longest dated sequence of microlithic artifacts found in West Africa. Occupation was established by 12,000 years ago, and the chipped stone industry continued for as long as 8,000 years with only minor changes. From the lowest horizon, a human burial, described as showing Negroid physical features, was recovered, and it is the oldest Nigerian skeleton yet uncovered. In about the mid-4th millennium, ground stone artifacts and pottery came into use. There is some evidence for the beginning of agriculture around that time.

Iximché: A Maya site in Guatemala of the Post-Classic period. A burial, dating to less than 100 years before the Spanish conquest (when the site was the capital of the Cakchiquel Maya), has the largest cache of gold items found in the Maya area.

Izapa: Large, important ceremonial site and type site of a culture in Chiapas, Mexico, built about 3,500 years ago (Middle–Late Preclassic). Izapa is famous for its art style, which is distributed in Chiapas and parts of Guatemala. The relief art, carved on altar stones and stelae, was influenced by the Olmec and Maya traditions. The style falls mainly within the Late Pre-Classic period (300 BC–AD 300), intermediate in time between Olmec and Maya. Dates were written in the long count system; a pure Izapan stele from El Baul, Guatemala, carries a figure equivalent to AD 36. Most of its 80 temple pyramids, courts, and plazas were built in the Late Pre-Classic. The center's economic base may have been cacao, which is featured in Izapan iconography.

Izmir: City on the west coast of Turkey, one of the oldest cities of the Mediterranean world, of almost continuous historical importance during the last 5,000 years. Excavations indicate settlement contemporary with that of the first city of Troy, dating from the 3rd millennium BC. Greek settlement is first attested by pottery dating from c. 1000 BC. According to the Greek historian Herodotus, the Greek city was founded by Aeolians but soon was seized by Ionians. By the 7th century, it had massive fortifications and blocks of two-storied houses. Captured by Alyattes of Lydia c. 600 BC, it disappeared for about 300 years until it was refounded by either Alexander the Great or his lieutenants in the 4th century BC at a new site on and around Mount Pagus. It soon emerged as one of the principal cities of Asia Minor and was later the center of a civil diocese in the Roman province of Asia, vying with Ephesus and Pergamum for the title "first city of Asia." Smyrna was one of the early seats of Christianity. Capital of the province of Samos under the Byzantine emperors, Smyrna was taken by the Turkmen Aydin principality in the early 14th century AD. It was annexed to the Ottoman Empire c. 1425. Although severely damaged by earthquakes in 1688 and 1778, it remained a prosperous Ottoman port with a large European population. The city's landmarks include the partly excavated remains of its agora and the ancient aqueducts of Kizilçullu. The archaeological museum has a fine collection of local antiquities. (*syn.* Smyrna)

Izumi, Seiichi or Izumi Shimada (1918–1970): Japanese archaeologist who worked in Peru, excavating at Kotosh near Huanuco. A cultural peak was reached in the valleys of Pacasmayo, Chicama, and Moche on the northern Peruvian coast. A large proportion of this area has been grouped by archaeologists into a Moche culture, although some of the territory encompassed by these valleys was not part of the polity called Moche. Izumi referred to this kind of control as "horizontally discontinuous territoriality."

Jj

Jabrud: A site of three rock shelters in Syria, each with long series of Palaeolithic industries, as well as some Natufian and Neolithic material. Jabrud is the type site of the Jabrudian industry, which is broadly contemporary with the Amudian and Late Acheulian of the Middle East. The Jabrudian is distinguished by well-made, tick side scrapers of Mousterian type and some bifacial blades similar to those of the Amudian as well as hand axes. At Jabrud, the industry bears a strong resemblance to some Mousterian industries from France. The dating probably falls within the Riss-Würm Interglacial or the first Würm Interstadial. It marks one of the ways in which the transition from Lower Palaeolithic to Middle Palaeolithic cultures occurred in the Levant, about 150,000 BP, a kind of final Acheulian. (*syn.* Yabrud)

jacal: A type of house construction in which walls were made of poles coated with mud plaster. Often called adobe, the term also refers to the dried mud itself. (*syn.* adobe)

jade: A name applied to two distinct minerals, nephrite and jadeite; a general term for a semiprecious stone used in East Asia from the Neolithic onward. Jade, in the form of polished axes, was traded in Neolithic Europe but was chiefly known from contexts in China and Mesoamerica. It is too hard to be cut or flaked, but may be worked by abrasion. The most highly prized of the two minerals is jadeite.

jadeite: A rare mineral, the mostly highly prized of the two distinct minerals that may be called jade. Much jadeite is green, but it varies widely in color. It is a stone carved by Mesoamericans into ornaments and statuary. Many prehistoric artifacts in Europe are made from jadeite, but no suitable European resources are known today. Sources of jadeite are known in Burma, Mexico, and California.

Jaguar Cave: Cave in Tennessee with aboriginal footprints and charcoal dating to 4700 BP. It is also the name of a cave site in Idaho, dating to the 9th and 10th millennia BC, with early evidence of the dog.

Jaina: An island north of Campeche, Yucatán, in the Gulf of Mexico, which was an important Late Classic Maya necropolis. It is known for its high-quality portrait ceramic figurines. There are two minor ceremonial centers at Zayosal and El Zacpool, built of uncut stone and stucco. Burials are commonly flexed, wrapped, and sprinkled with cinnabar; a jade bead was commonly put in the mouth to serve as currency in the next world. Some cremations and urn burials also occur.

Jam: A remote valley in western Afghanistan where a spectacular tower, inscribed with the name of the Ghorid ruler Ghiyath al-Din Muhammad b. Sam (1153–1203) was discovered. The tower is 65 meters high and built of brick, with an octagonal base and four cylindrical tiers, each narrower and shorter than the one below. The fourth tier is a circular arcade supporting a dome. It is usually identified as a minaret (one of the tallest in existence) and may have belonged to the "lost" Ghorid capital, Firuzkuh.

Jamestown: The first permanent English settlement in the United States, in present-day Tidewater, Virginia. It was founded in 1607 by 105 settlers and served for a time as the capital of Virginia. James Fort, as it was first called, was built 15 miles inland from the Chesapeake Bay, on a swampy island in the James River on the site of previous native occupation. Many structures have been found as well as a huge inventory of 17th-century artifacts. The earliest settlers subsisted by fishing, trade with natives, and farming of both local (maize, squash, pumpkin) and imported staples. Houses from that time were of wattle and daub with thatched roofs, giving way later to structures of locally made brick. Pottery and glassmaking were other local industries. In 1699, Williamsburg became the capital of the colony, after which Jamestown went into decline and was ultimately abandoned. The excavations have documented early colonial life.

Janislawice: Type site of the Janislawice culture, a late Mesolithic people inhabiting east-central Europe, in central

Poland. There is a Mesolithic burial, dated to the Atlantic climatic period of c. 6000–4000 BC, with grave goods.

Jankovich: Prehistoric cave site near the River Danube, north-central Hungary, with a Middle Palaeolithic assemblage of bifacial foliates and side scrapers. An Upper Palaeolithic assemblage, Neolithic, and Bronze Age artifacts were also found.

Japanese periodization: A classification used by archaeologists and historians: Jomon 10,000–300 BC, Yayoi 300 BC–AD 300, Kofun 300–710, Nara 710–794, Heian 794–1183, Medieval (Kamakura, Muromachi, Momoyama) 1183–1603, Feudal (Edo/Tokugawa) 1603–1868, Meiji 1868–1914, Taisho 1914–1925, Showa 1925–1988, and Heisei 1989–present.

jar burial: Any inhumation burial in a pottery vessel. Urn burial, in contrast, requires a much smaller pot. The use of jar burial occurred in the Mediterranean area, going back to the Early Bronze Age in Anatolia.

Jarlshof: A settlement site at the southern tip of the Shetland Island, Scotland, with a settlement from the early 2nd millennium BC. This early occupation was a Late Neolithic village comparable to Skara Brae, and it was followed after an interval by oval houses of the Late Bronze Age, a roundhouse and wheelhouse with Souterrain of the Iron Age, a Viking settlement, and continuous occupation throughout the Dark Ages. It was named after a house in a Sir Walter Scott novel. Some of the most interesting artifacts recovered from the Norse levels are a series of slates incised with drawings of animals and abstract decorations.

Jarmo: A small aceramic Neolithic to ceramic Neolithic village site in the foothills of the Zagros mountains of northern Iraq. Jarmo was used to explain the origins of food production by Robert Braidwood, as the site dated to the later 7th millennium BC and there was carbonized wheat and barley. Its radiocarbon dates place it among the world's earliest food-producing settlements. Goat and dog bones show domestication. The first 11 of its 16 levels had no pottery, although clay-lined pits were baked in situ. Square houses of pisé were built with clay ovens and grain pits, which included flint and obsidian chipped stone tools, stone bowls, and clay figurines. Flaked and ground stone were freely used for tools and utensils. It is the type site of the Jarmoan culture.

Jarrow: The site of twin monasteries that were important in the Middle Anglo-Saxon period in England. One was the home of the Venerable Bede. Both monasteries suffered seriously during the Viking raids of the 9th century. At Jarrow, there was evidence for glassmaking and other crafts. The earliest colored window glass known in Europe comes from these excavations and bears out Bede's statement that

Benedict Biscop brought glaziers from Gaul to work on his churches.

jasper: A high-quality chert or agate often used as raw material for the manufacture of stone tools. It is an opaque, fine-grained or dense variety of the silica mineral that is mainly brick red to brownish red. Jasper has long been used for jewelry and ornamentation; it has a dull luster but takes a fine polish. Its hardness and other physical properties are those of quartz.

Jastorf culture: Iron Age culture of the southern Baltic during the late Hallstatt (600–300 BC), with some of the earliest iron metallurgy of the area. It extended from Lower Saxony through Pomerania.

Jaszdozsa: An Early Bronze Age tell settlement near Szolnok, Hungary. Occupation layers of the Hatvan and Füzesabony groups have been found, with well-preserved domestic architecture.

Java: A major island of Indonesia, best known for its remains of *Homo erectus* dating from 1,000,000–500,000 BP. Neolithic and Bronze Age cultures are known. The colonization of Java apparently took place from mainland Southeast Asia, and domestic agriculture is known to have been practiced there as early as 2500 BC. Indian traders began arriving in Java from about the 1st century AD, and the resulting Hindu Indian influence developed in the kingdom of Mataram in the 8th century AD.

Java man: The remains of *Homo erectus* found in Java, probably dating from c. 1 million to 500,000 BP, by E. Dubois in 1891. Dubois, however, originally classified his find as *Pithecanthropus erectus*. Other fossils from Sangiran and the remains of an infant from Modjokerto indicate that *H. erectus* occupied Java during the middle Pleistocene epoch.

Jaywa: A Preceramic phase, 7100–5800 BC, in the Ayacucho basin of the central Andes, Peru. Nomadic groups of hunters and gatherers used a distinctive tool kit of stemmed and pentagonal projectile points.

Jazdzewski, Konrad (1908–1985): Polish archaeologist who worked at Brzesc Kujawski and Leg Piekarski and was director of the Museum of Archaeology and Ethnography in Lodz.

Jebel et Tomat: A settlement site in central Sudan with evidence of sorghum cultivation by the 3rd century AD. The site was occupied through the first five centuries of the Christian era by mixed-farming people who supplemented their rare iron tools by continuing the production of chipped stone artifacts.

Jebel Irhoud: A site in northern Morocco where Levalloiso-Mousterian artifacts were recovered in association with fossil human remains of Neanderthal type. ESR dates range from over 80,000–150,000 BP.

Jebel Moya: A mountain with many graves in southern Gezira of Sudan, probably occupied c. 4000 BP. The pottery resembles that of the Nubian C group. A later occupation has Meroitic traits.

Jebel Uweinat: A mountainous region of the eastern Sahara, where Libya, Sudan, and Egypt meet. The many rock shelters had prehistoric occupation, with abundant rock art. The art is of particular interest for its representations of various creatures, including giraffe and ostrich, which are tethered. It was a focal point for Neolithic herders around 6200 BP.

Jefferson, Thomas (1743–1826): The third president of the United States and considered by many to be the father of American archaeology because of his meticulous excavation of a Virginia burial mound. Jefferson was the first person, in North America or anywhere, to undertake (1784) excavations of a prehistoric site as a means of understanding the people who built it. He wanted to find out why the burial mounds on his land had been built. One mound he excavated carefully with trenches, noting that in a number of levels skeletons had been placed in the ground and covered—producing a mound 12 feet (4 m) high. In observing the different levels, he was anticipating the stratigraphical method that became common practice in Europe and America only at the end of the 19th century. Worsaae's work in Denmark came a half-century later, and the wider adoption of stratigraphical excavation methods was 100 years later.

Jellinge: A site in East Jutland, in Denmark, which seems to be the remains of a 10th-century royal palace and an important burial ground. Among the groups of remarkable monuments are the two largest barrows in that country. The barrows are traditionally held to be that of the Viking king Gorm (d. c. AD 950) and Thyra, his queen. In the cemetery area stand fifty bauta stones forming a boat-shaped outline and two fine rune stones outlining the exploits and Christian conversion of Gorm and Harald Bluetooth. One of the stones depicts the oldest crucifixion scene in Denmark, and on the other is a magnificent lion—inspiring the term Jellinge Style. (*syn.* Jelling)

Jellinge style: An art style that takes its name from the Viking site at Jellinge. Much Anglo-Saxon and Scandinavian art from the 9th century until the mid-11th century is characterized by animal ornament and zoomorphic motifs, which are usually disjointed, stylized, and abstract. This type of decoration was most often applied to jewelry, sculptured crosses, and sculptured stones.

Jemdet Nasr: A small site between Baghdad and Babylon, near Kish, Iraq, which has given its name to a period of Mesopotamian chronology and its black-and-red painted pottery ware. The period of 3100–2900 BC was characterized by writing in pictographs, pottery with painted designs or plum-red burnished slip, and plain pottery with beveled rims. Cylinder seals were squat and plain, and drills were used in making the designs. The period is characterized by increasing populations, the development of more extensive irrigation systems, towns dominated by temples, increased use of writing and cylinder seals, more trade, and craft specialization. The period—equivalent to Uruk III of the Eanna sounding sequence—was followed immediately by the Early Dynastic period of Sumer. A building of Jemdet Nasr date may be the oldest palace discovered in southern Mesopotamia. (*syn.* Jamdat Nasr)

Jenne-jeno: A now-abandoned section of the trading center of Jenne in Mali, established by about the 3rd century BC. By late in the 1st millennium AD, Jenne-jeno had grown into a major urban center, and it was important in trade for another 1,000 years. Metal was one of the main commodities involved. The city itself was the center of a fertile and prosperous region that cultivated indigenous African rice. A series of elaborate anthropomorphic clay statuettes date from the early centuries of the 2nd millennium AD. (*syn.* Djenne; Jeno)

Jenness, Diamond (1886–1969): Canadian archaeologist and ethnologist who pioneered the archaeology of the Arctic and who first described the Dorset culture, which predated the Thule.

Jennings, J. D. (1909–   ): American anthropologist and archaeologist who has researched the archaic civilizations, or "desert cultures," of the semiarid western areas of North America of the past 10,000 years. Work at Danger Cave, Utah, dating to c. 9000 BC, confirmed survival of the earliest ways of life in the American West until historic times.

Jericho: An important site in the Jordan Valley of Israel with a continuous sequence from the Natufian to the Late Bronze Age. Camping occupation of the Mesolithic c. 9000 BC developed into the pre-pottery Neolithic c. 8350–7350 BC when there was a walled town of mud-brick houses, which is among the earliest permanent settlements known. There was at least one massive stone tower. To the succeeding PPNB levels dated 7250–5850 BC belongs the series of famous plastered skulls. In c. 1580, the Hyksos settlement, with its tombs, plastered glacis, woodwork, basketry, pottery, and bronze, was destroyed by the Egyptians. The Late Bronze Age town captured by Joshua's Israelites has left very few traces. There was some reoccupation during the Iron Age. (*syn.* Tell es-Sultan)

Jerzmanowician: An early Upper Palaeolithic industry of Poland characterized by foliated bifacial points, retouched blades, and denticulates. The type site is Nietoperzowa Cave at Jermanovice near Cracow in Poland. (*syn.* Jermanovician)

Jerusalem: City in the Judaean hills, Israel, occupied for more than 4,000 years and now the capital of Israel. Many excavations have taken place since the 1860s, but because of the long history of destruction and rebuilding on the site, it has been difficult to reconstruct the development of the city. Sporadic traces of 4th- and 3rd-millennium BC occupation occur, but the first substantial settlement with a town wall belongs to the Late Bronze Age of the 2nd millennium BC. Jerusalem was captured by the Israelites under David in c. 996 BC and extended to the north by Solomon, who built a temple and palace. Few early buildings survive with the exception of the rock-cut water tunnel constructed by Hezekiah in the late 8th century BC. The city fell to the Babylonians in 587 BC and was rebuilt after 538 BC. The present plan of the city, excluding the two ridges to the south, goes back to Herod the Great (37–34 BC) and the rebuilding under Hadrian. It became a Hellenistic city under Antiochus IV and was Romanized in the 1st century BC. The Jewish revolt of AD 70 inspired Titus to destroy the city. Under Constantine, it gained new importance as a Christian center and was destroyed once more in AD 614, by the Persians. Jerusalem is venerated by Jews, Christians, and Muslims. The Dome of the Rock (AD 685–692) is the most striking Islamic building in Jerusalem.

jet: A hard black dense form of coal, a lignitic fossil wood. It was used for decorative purposes (beds, buttons, etc.) in the British Bronze Age as it accepts a strong polish and has good workability. Ornaments of jet are found in ancient tumuli. A well-known British source of jet is at Whitby in Yorkshire.

Jetis: Geological formation on the Brantas River of east Java with remains of early Pleistocene fauna and *Homo erectus* remains (Mojokerto child) dating c. 1.5 million years BP and earlier. (*syn.* Djetis)

Jevisovice: Late Neolithic site in Moravia of the Funnel Beaker and Baden cultures, used as a guide to the Late Neolithic and Eneolithic of the Carpathian Basin.

jewelry: Decorative objects made mainly for the adornment of the body. The art of jewelry making originated in prehistoric times when primitive people used objects from the animal world—such as horn, shell, and feathers—to adorn themselves. Cave paintings and carvings show figures decorated with bracelets, necklaces, and headdreses. Brooches, or fibulae, were used to fasten clothes and were made of bronze or silver, and some were enameled. There were also finger rings and earrings.

Jhukar: A site in Sindh, Pakistan, lending its name to a Late Harappan culture of Chalcolithic times (2nd millennium BC). The culture, which succeeded the Indus civilization on certain sites in Sindh (type site of Chanhu-daro; Amri) has material showing a mixture of elements from the Indus, Baluchistan, and the Middle East. There were compartmented seals, copper dress pins, and a shaft hole ax. The pottery is that of the Mature Harappan. Certain copper or bronze weapons and tools are comparable to examples from Iran and Central Asia.

Jiangling: A county sea of the Ch'in Dynasty (221–206 BC) in third century BC China. Western Chou, Eastern Zhou, and Han remains as well as burials containing painted lacquers are of interest. Chiang-ling was also a center of a handicraft–textile industry, which was developed on a large scale by the Chi'ing Dynasty in the 18th century, Chiang-ling satins being especially famous. (*syn.* Chiang-ling)

Jincamocco: Middle Horizon site of the central highlands of Peru with Huari-style architecture. It was an administrative center of the Huari from AD 650–800.

Jincun: A village near Luoyang, China, where rich tombs yielded 5th–2nd century BC carved jades and inlaid bronze ritual vessels, many of which are now in Western collections. The name Jincun is often applied to a style of Eastern Chou bronze decor, also called the inlay style, characterized by inlays of gold, silver, malachite, turquoise, jade, and glass. (*syn.* Chin-ts'un)

Jingdezhen: The site of ancient kiln works in Jiangxi Province, China, where porcelains were made from the end of the Tang Dynasty in the late 10th century AD. (*syn.* [Ching-te-chen])

Jinniushan: Early and Late Palaeolithic site in Liaoning Province, China, with scrapers, bipolar flakes, and *Homo sapiens* remains. (*syn.* [Chin-niu-shan])

Jomon: The earliest major postglacial culture of hunting and gathering in Japan, 10,000–300 BC, divided into six phases. This early culture, its relics surviving in shell mounds of kitchen midden type around the coasts of the Japanese islands, had pottery but no metal. The pottery was heavy but elaborate, especially in the modeling of its castellated rims. The term Jomon means "cord marked," indicating the characteristic decoration of the pottery with cord-pattern impressions or reliefs. One of the earliest dates in the world for pottery making has been established as c. 12,700 BC in Fukin Cave, Kyshu. Other artifacts, of stone and bone, were simple. Light huts, round or rectangular, have been identified. Burials were by inhumation, crouched or extended. The Jomon was succeeded by the Yayoi period. There are over 10,000 Jomon sites divided into the six phases: Incipient (10,000–7500 BC), Earliest (7500–5000 BC), Early (5000–3500 BC), Middle (3500–2500/2000 BC), Late (2500/2000–1000 BC), and Final (1000–300 BC). Widespread trading networks and ritual development took place in the Middle Jomon. Rice agriculture was adopted during the last millennium BC. The origins of

Jomon culture remain uncertain, although similarities with early cultures of northeast Asia and even America are often cited. (*syn.* Jomon Period).

Jones-Miller: Site in northeast Colorado of the Hell Gap complex, used as a bison kill and butchering site. There were also stone tools and bone artifacts dating to c. 8000 BC.

Jordanów: A settlement and cemetery site in Silesia, southern Poland, the type site for a subgroup of the Late Neolithic Lengyel culture. Its pottery is incised or painted, and copper objects were beginning to be used—among the earliest known from north of the Carpathians. The settlement had timber houses that were trapezoidal in plan. (*syn.* Jordansmühl; Jordanów Slaski; Jordanova)

Jorwe: A small Chalcolithic site in southern India, consisting of several mounds and representing a single-period material culture in the second half of the 2nd millennium BC. There was a wheel-made red ware painted in black, including distinctive long-spouted vessels. Jorwe had a rich copper tool industry in addition to stone toolmaking, and it seems to be related to the Malwa complex farther north.

Judea: A Roman province in Palestine annexed by Pompey in 64 BC. It was first ruled by Herod the Great, but later by Roman procurators, of whom Pontius Pilate is best known. Its chief city was Jerusalem.

Judeidah: A tell site in the Amuq plain of northern Syria. Its lowest level, XIV, was of the Neolithic Mersin type, with a long series of succeeding deposits.

Judeirjo-daro: A town of the Harappan civilization in Kachi province, Pakistan, probably the third largest settlement of this civilization, after Mohenjo-daro and Harappa. Surface investigation suggests that both pre-Harappan and mature Harappan phases are represented on the site.

Juodkrante: A site of the Baltic Early Bronze Age, in western Lithuania, and dated to the mid-2nd millennium BC. An amber-processing workshop was found with half-finished pendants and beads.

Jute: A branch of the Germanic peoples who, with the Angles and Saxons, invaded Britain in the 5th century AD. There is evidence that their home was in the Scandinavian area (probably Jutland). According to the Venerable Bede, the Jutes settled in Kent, the Isle of Wight, and parts of Hampshire. There is archaeological evidence to confirm Bede's statement that the Isles of Wight and Kent were settled by the same people, and their presence in Hampshire is confirmed by place names. The proximity of their settlements to the continent led to a development of cross-Channel trade and close cultural links with the Franks of the lower Rhine. One result was the increase in wealth of Kent, as typified by the justly famous garnet-inlaid jewelry. Their capital was in Canterbury.

Ju ware: The most highly prized of all Chinese ceramics. Ju wares were produced exclusively for the Northern Sung emperor Hui-tsung from about 1107–1127. The original kiln site, Ch'ing-liang-ssu, yielded 37 examples. The undecorated bluish- or greenish-gray glaze of Ju wares is cloudy and opaque, often with a pale blue or lavender tinge and fine irregular crackle. This glaze typically covers a gray stoneware body that has a simple, exquisitely elegant shape. (*syn.* Ru)

Juxtlahuaca Caves: A cave site in Guerrero, Mexico, containing the earliest polychrome painting in the New World. Done in the Olmec style, they are dated to c. 3,000 years ago and are found nearly a mile inside a mountain. Similar cave paintings have been found in nearby Oxtotilan.

Kk

K2: Late Iron Age site in northern Transvaal, South Africa, occupied in the 11th–12th centuries AD. It is the name of the initial phase of the Leopard's Kopje Complex of the Limpopo Valley, characterized by bone and ivory working.

ka: The spiritual double of a living human being, created at the time of birth in Egyptian belief and coming into its own in the afterlife. The ka could be released during life in dreams, but was finally released at death. It was symbolized by a pair of upraised arms and received mortuary offerings, including food for daily provision. The ka was considered to be the essential ingredient that differentiated a living person from a dead one and is therefore sometimes translated as "sustenance."

Kabáh: A Maya Late Classic center in Yucatán, Mexico, which peaked from the 8th–10th centuries AD before being abandoned. Its ceremonial architecture includes the Kodz Pop, a building covered with long-nosed masks. There is a paved causeway (*sacbe*) from it to Uxmal, a Puuc city.

Kabambian: Iron Age industry of southeastern Zaire, which succeeds the Kisalian and is best known from numerous graves, especially at Sanga. The industry is dated between the 14th–18th centuries AD and is marked by an abundance of copper cross-shaped ingots (croisettes), of standardized weights, which may have served as a medium of exchange.

Kachemak stage: A marine mammal-hunting culture found around the Kachemak Bay of the southern Kenai Peninsula in central southern Alaska. It is divided into three phases, the oldest of which may date back as far as the 8th century BC and the most recent lasting until historic times. The first phase was the most distinctly Eskimo in character. Stone (including slate) implements in the early period were usually retouched; later they were ground. Round or oval stone lamps and realistic human figures of carved stone have been found. Copper tools and pottery appeared in the third stage. Rock paintings were mainly representations of men and animals. Burials have the body in a crouched position, with associated grave goods. During the final stage, artificial bone or ivory eyes were placed over those of the deceased. There may have been cultural connections with eastern Asia, with adjacent land areas, and with Kodiak Island. (*syn.* Kachemak culture)

Kadero: Important Khartoum Neolithic site on the edge of the old Nile flood plain, which has provided information on the early development of food production in the central Sudan. Kadero was an extensive village inhabited during the second half of the 4th millennium BC. Herding was mainly of cattle, with some sheep and goats. There were many grindstones, and grain impressions on the pottery indicate the presence of wild panicum, sorghum, and finger millet. Burials included stone mace heads, palettes, carnelian bead necklaces, ivory bracelets, pottery, and ocher.

Kadesh: A site strategically placed on the River Orontes in Syria, famous for the inconclusive battle between Ramesses II of Egypt and Muwatallis of the Hittites c. 1286 (1275 in some accounts) BC. Both sides claimed the victory, but it was actually a truce. Kadesh is mentioned for the first time in Egyptian sources when Thutmose III (1479–1426 BC) defeated a Syrian insurrection by the prince of Kadesh at Megiddo in Palestine. Kadesh remained an outpost of Egyptian influence until it came under Hittite rule (c. 1340 BC). The invasion of the Sea Peoples in c. 1185 BC was the demise of Kadesh. (*syn.* Qadesh, modern Tell Nebi Mend, Tall An-Nabi Mind)

Kadiri: The western, Hinduized kingdom in eastern Java, established about the 11th century. According to the "Pararaton" ("Book of Kings"), the king of eastern Java, Airlangga, divided his kingdom between his two sons before he died in 1049: The western part was called Kadiri, or Panjalu, with Daha as its capital, while the eastern part was called Janggala. Originally called Panjalu, it became better known by the name of Kadiri and soon absorbed Janggala, thus becoming in fact the successor to the kingdom of Airlanga.

The kingdom of Kadiri lasted until 1222, when it was succeeded by that of Tumapel/Singhasari. (*syn.* modern Kediri)

Kafiavana: A rock shelter in the New Guinea Highlands, with a sequence that starts with edge-ground axes (adzes) and flake tools of early Australian type (c. 11,000 BC), then documents trade in coastal shells (from c. 8000 BC), and the appearance of pigs (by 3500–4000 BC). The deposits contain bone tools and a rich faunal assemblage. Pigs, which were not native, occur from about 6500 bp.

kaizuka: The term for shell midden in Japanese. It existed in the Jomon and early Yayoi periods.

Kakanj: The type site for a Middle Neolithic regional group in north-central Bosnia, located near Visoko and dated c. 4700–4300 BC. The culture is typified by fine monochrome wares and decorative elements with affinities in the coastal Danilo culture. There are working pits, flint production areas, and a rich bone-working assemblage.

Kakóvatos: The site of a Mycenaean settlement in Messenia, Greece (in Triphylia). There are three tholos tombs that have been excavated. It was once thought to be the site of Homeric Pylos.

Kalabsha: The site of an unfinished, free-standing temple in Lower Nubia, south of Aswan. Dedicated to the local god Mandulis, the complex was built in sandstone masonry and consisted of a pylon, forecourt, hypostyle hall, two vestibules, and a sanctuary. It dates to the early Roman period c. 30 BC, although the colony itself dates to Amenhotep II (1427–1400 BC). (*syn.* ancient Talmis)

Kalambo: An Early Iron Age group in northern Zambia, taking its name from the 4th century AD village at Kalambo Falls. It is of the Chifumbaze complex. A prepared-core industry existed by c. 36,000 BC, and a true backed microlith assemblage appeared by 20,000 BC. The shift to a microlithic industry was accompanied by a change in faunal remains indicating a new preference for hunting small solitary creatures. The site also contains a large series of rock paintings, probably of later Iron Age date. (*syn.* Kalemba)

Kalambo Falls: A site on the Zambia–Tanzania border at the southeast corner of Lake Tanganyika, which has yielded one of the longest archaeological sequences (100,000 years) in sub-Saharan Africa and important pollen and radiocarbon data. The ancient lake deposits preserved objects from the Stone and Iron Ages. The oldest deposit contained Late Acheulian tools, dating to the late Middle Pleistocene. Wooden objects, food remains, and evidence that people were already using fire have been found. Pollen preserved in the deposits indicates that the local late Acheulian climate was cooler and wetter than that of today. The sequence continued with Sangoan (radiocarbon dated to 50,000–40,000 BC), followed by Early Middle Stone Age (Lupem-

ban, 30,000 BC) industries related to those of the Congo, then Magosian, and a microlith-using Late Stone Age culture of Wilton type, and finally (from mid-4th century AD) remains of early agricultural and iron-using peoples who were probably of Bantu stock. Early Iron Age occupation of the Kalambo basin appears to have been established by the 4th century AD and to have continued through much of the 1st millennium.

Kalanay: A cave site on Masbate Island in the central Philippines, which has produced incised and impressed pottery of a type found widely in Southeast Asia and South Vietnam from c. 500/400 BC to AD 1500. Kalanay is one of the type sites for the "Sa-Huynh-Kalanay" pottery complex (Sa-Huynh of coastal Vietnam). There are metal period jar burials from the late 1st millennium BC or later.

Kalavasos: A site in southern Cyprus, which began with an Aceramic Neolithic I settlement in the 7th millennium BC. Another area had a Chalcolithic site of the early 4th millennium BC. Another, occupied c. 1325–1225 BC, is an extensive Late Cypriot town. Copper and gypsum are mined at Kalavasos.

Kalhu: The site of the Black Obelisk, Assyrian monument of King Shalmaneser III (reigned 859–824 BC). It is the most complete Assyrian obelisk yet discovered, decorated with cuneiform inscriptions and reliefs recording military campaigns and other triumphs, including payment of tribute by King Jehu of Israel (reigned 842–815). The 6-foot (1.8-meter) black basalt piece was discovered in 1845 at ancient Kalhu, south of Mosul, Iraq, by Austen Henry Layard and is now in the British Museum. Kalhu was an imperial Assyrian city on the River Tigris with a citadel (Nimrud) and arsenal at Fort Shalmaneser. Middle Assyrian texts found there established the existence of the town in the later 2nd millennium BC. It was made the imperial seat by Assurnasirpal II (883–859 BC). Sargon II (721–705 BC) moved the imperial seat to Khorsabad, and after that, Kalhu was a provincial capital. Occupation continued until the Hellenistic period. (*syn.* Kalakh; biblical Calah; modern Nimrud)

Kalibangan: A site in India near the extinct Ghaggar/Hakra River with Early and Mature Harappan settlements. A Chalcolithic settlement similar to Kot Diji and the site underlying the Indus city at Harappa has given radiocarbon dates of c. 2750 BC. An intact plowed field has been discovered, indicating that the plow was already in use before the main Harappan period. About 2450, a small town of the Indus civilization was built over it, which flourished to c. 2150 BC. In the Mature Harappan period, the site consisted of a citadel and a lower town, both defended, and laid out in the normal Indus Valley grid pattern.

Kalomo: A Late Iron Age industry in southern Zambia, dating from the end of the 9th till the 13th century AD. The industry probably developed from an Early Iron Age ancestor in the valley and spread to the plateau. The people were subsistence farmers, herding cattle and small stock, cultivating a variety of food crops, making pottery and a few metal tools, and occupying villages beside river valleys or on artificially built mounds.

Kalumpang: A Neolithic site in Sulawesi, which, along with Minanga Sipakko, has produced late Neolithic assemblages of polished stone adzes, ground slate projectile points, and pottery. Some aspects of the artifacts are similar to Taiwanese Neolithic and Lapita wares of Oceania.

Kalundu: A mound site near Kalomo in southern Zambia with an Early Iron Age tradition of the Chifumbaze complex of the same name dating to the 5th–9th centuries AD.

Kamabai: Rock shelter site in Sierra Leone with levels dating from 4500–600 BP, the Later Stone Age through the Guinea Neolithic to the Iron Age.

Kamares Cave: A sacred cave of the Minoans on the slopes of Mount Ida overlooking Phaestos in Crete. The artifacts include Middle Minoan polychrome pottery, 2000–1550 BC, painted in red, orange, and white on black ground, called Kamares ware. (*syn.* Kamares)

Kambuja: The Khmer kingdom founded in Cambodia by Jayavarman during the pre-14th century phase known as Angkor. It is the ethnic name of the people of the first kingdom of the Khmers. Jayavarman was Cambodia's first nationally oriented king. (*syn.* Kambuja-desa)

Kamegaoka: A waterlogged Jomon site in Aomori prefecture in northern Honshu, Japan, best known for its Final Jomon deposits with elaborate pottery and lacquered wooden dishes. The Kamegaoka complex, named after the site, is characterized by the distinctive pottery style, production of hollow figurines, stone and bone personal ornaments, making salt from sea water, and fishing and sea-mammal hunting with harpoons. It was partly contemporary with the Early Yayoi culture. (*syn.* Obora culture, Kamegaoka culture)

Kamennaya Mogila: A Mesolithic or Aceramic Neolithic site in the southern Ukraine, similar to that of the Bug-Dniestr culture at Soroki.

Kamid al Loz, Tell: A site in Lebanon, Kumidi, that was the seat of a state during the Late Bronze Age (mentioned in the Amarná archive). Settlement began in the late Neolithic and continued to Byzantine times. In the Middle Bronze Age and Late Bronze Age, it was a walled town with a palace and temples. Its location made it strategically important. (*syn.* Kumidi)

Kamikuroiwa: A Jomon rock shelter on Shikoku, Japan, with pottery radiocarbon dated to the late 11th millennium BC, similar to that at Fukui and Sempukuji. It is associated with bifacial points rather than with microblades. Incised flat pebbles representing human females were also found—the earliest portable art found in Japan. The 20 human and two dog burials in one of the upper layers are among the oldest Initial (Incipient) Jomon burials.

Kamilamba: Named after a site in the Upemba depression of the valley of the upper Lualaba in southeastern Zaire, this is the initial phase of the local Early Iron Age, precursor of the Kisalian. Dated to between the 5th and 8th centuries AD, it is poorly illustrated by the research so far undertaken, but the associated pottery shows affinities with that from settlements of the same age in the Copperbelt area farther southeast.

Kaminaljuyú: A large and important Maya site near Guatemala City, which originally contained over 200 mounds, strongly influenced by Teotihuacán during the Early Classic. As the greatest of the early centers in the highland Maya zone, Kaminaljuyú has a history of occupation dating back to c. 1800 BC, but it reached its first climax during the Miraflores phase in the centuries after 300 BC. Its earliest occupation during the Early to Mid-Pre-Classic has Olmec-influenced artifacts such as the "squashed frog" motif, kaolin pottery, and pits reminiscent of those at Tlatilco. About 200 burial sites from the Late Formative period, 300 BC–AD 100, have been uncovered, and there are carved stelae in the Izapa manner and a hieroglyphic script unlike that of the lowland Maya. There are also courts for playing the ball game *tlachtli*. Because of the lack of stone suitable for construction, pyramids and other structures at Kaminaljuyú were built of adobe and later of other perishable materials. After a period of decline, the site was revived in c. 400 when it became an outpost of the Teotihuacán civilization. Kaminaljuyú controlled the obsidian production along the Pacific. Its decline took place after the Late Classic Period AD c. 600–900. Evidence suggests that various Mexican dynasties ruled over the Maya population until the Spanish conquest.

Kamoa: A site on the Kamoa River in southeastern Zaire, the first place in central Africa at which Acheulian artifacts were found, revealing human occupation in the region back to the Earlier Stone Age. The culture evolved through the Later Stone Age.

Kamose (fl. 17th–16th centuries BC): The late king of the Theban 17th Dynasty (c. 1630–1540 BC) of Egypt, successor of Seqenenra Taa II (Seqenenre) (c. 1560 BC) and predecessor of Ahmose I (1550–1525 BC), the first 18th Dynasty ruler. He started hostilities with the Hyksos, the west Semitic invaders who had seized part of Egypt in the 17th century BC. Following the death of his father, Seqenenre, Kamose became ruler of the southernmost third of Egypt. Most scholars agree that he did not rule for more than 5 years.

Kampong Sungei Lang: A site near Klang, Malaysia, with a metal age boat burial dated to c. 300 BC. The grave goods include two Dong Son bronze drums, Mutisalah beads, and iron implements. It may be contemporary with the Bernam-Sungkai slab graves.

kana: The Japanese writing system, developed in the 9th century AD from simplified Chinese characters. There are two types of kana (hiragana and katakana) syllabaries, each with symbols for 46 basic sounds and each of which independently represents all the sounds of the language. Although each derives its simple elements from Chinese characters, the two serve different purposes and differ stylistically. Katakana symbols, which are more angular, are used for foreign words, telegrams, and some children's books and often for advertising in print media, television, and billboards. Hiragana, a cursive, graceful writing system, is used in modern Japanese primarily to perform grammatical functions. In theory, any sound in Japanese can be written using one of the kana systems, but in practice, a combination of the two, together with Chinese characters, is used.

Kandahar: A site near the crossing of the Arghandab in southern Afghanistan. The city was included in the Achaemenian Empire by Darius I, was taken by Alexander the Great in 329 BC, was surrendered by Seleucus I to Candra Gupta in 305 BC, and dignified by a rock inscription in Greek and Aramaic by his grandson Ashoka, and thereafter was successively held by Greco-Bactrians, Parthians, Sakas, Kushans, and Sasanians. The town seems to have been occupied continuously until the 18th century, and a large barrow cemetery belongs to the Islamic period. (*syn.* Qandahar)

Kandanda: A site on the upper Zambezi River in Zambia, with a prepared-core industry that included rare bifacial hand axes, which continued to a remarkably late date. It was replaced by a microlithic industry probably around 1000 BC.

Kaneaki: A heiau of Molokai, Hawaii, with six construction phases starting from AD 1460.

Kanem: African trading empire ruled by the Sef (Sayf) Dynasty that controlled the area around Lake Chad from the 9th to the 19th centuries. Its territory at various times included what is now southern Chad, northern Cameroon, northeastern Nigeria, eastern Niger, and southern Libya. Kanem-Bornu was probably founded around the mid-9th century, and its first capital was at Njimi. Toward the end of the 11th century, Kanem-Bornu became an Islamic state. Because of its location, it served as a point of contact in trade between North Africa, the Nile Valley, and the sub-Sahara region. (*syn.* Kanem-Bornu)

Kangaroo Island: An island off South Australia with Kartan sites showing previous Aboriginal occupation, although it was uninhabited at European contact. These sites may be late Pleistocene, but material found at Cape du Couedic is dated to around 7000 bp.

Kanjera: A site near Kanam in western Kenya with hand axes of probably Acheulian type in the Middle Pleistocene deposits. Very fragmentary remains of skulls are probably post-Pleistocene.

Kansai: A region of ancient cities to the west (*sai*) of the mountain barrier (*kan*) near Mount Fuji, the birthplace of the earliest Japanese state and one of Japan's traditional cultural areas. It is an area of historically dense population and until well into the 20th century was the most industrialized and economically advanced part of Japan. It was an early medieval administrative district of west-central Japan, roughly the same as the modern Kinki district. The Keihanshin Industrial Zone corresponds to the Kansai.

Kansanshi: An ancient copper mine near the modern Solwezi in central Zambia's Copperbelt. Small-scale exploitation of the copper deposit appears to have begun during the early Iron Age of the second half of the 1st millennium AD. Large-scale workings are not attested before the 14th or 15th century.

Kansyore ware: A comb-stamped pottery found at several pre-Iron Age sites around Lake Victoria in East Africa in the first millennium BC. The makers of Kansyore ware appear to have been hunter gatherers, makers of a backed microlith industry.

Kantarawichai: A large late prehistoric or early historic moated site between Non Chai and Ban Chiang Hian in Khorat, Thailand.

kantharos: In Greek antiquity, a large, two-handled drinking cup. This type of pottery cup was made in Greek-speaking areas and in Etruria between the 8th and the 1st centuries BC and had a deep bowl, a foot, and a pair of high vertical handles. It was often consecrated to personifications of Bacchus. Early examples are often stemmed. In the 4th and 3rd centuries BC, it became one of the most popular types of drinking vessel in the Greek world. (*syn.* cantharus)

Kanto: Modern administrative district of eastern Honshu Island, Japan. It consists of Tokyo-Yokohama Metropolitan District and Gumma, Saitama, Kanagawa, Tochigi, Ibaragi, and Chiba (prefectures).

kaolin: A fine white porcelain clay formed by the weathering of volcanic rocks. Kaolin is named after the hill in China (Kao-ling) that yielded the first clay of this type sent to Europe. This soft white clay is an essential ingredient in the manufacture of china and porcelain and is widely used in the making of paper, rubber, paint, and many other products. (*syn.* china clay)

Käpää: A site of the late Mesolithic Narva culture, stratified in a peat bog in Estonia. The thin occupation deposits on slight wooden platforms have radiocarbon dates of c. 2900–

2400 BC. A rich assemblage of bone tools is associated with fragmentary Narva pottery.

Kaposwa: A late Holocene microlithic Later Stone Age industry at Kalambo Falls in northern Zambia.

Kapovaya: A painted cave in the southern Urals of European Russia, important for cave art that is otherwise unknown in central and eastern Europe. The rare examples of east European Palaeolithic cave art include representations of woolly mammoth and woolly rhinoceros and geometric figures. A cultural layer with stone artifacts and ornaments is dated to the Upper Palaeolithic. (*syn.* Kapovo, Shul'gantash)

Kapwirimbwe: An Early Iron Age village site near modern Lusaka, Zambia, dated to about the 5th century AD, which gives its name to a tradition of the Chifumbaze complex. The elaborately decorated pottery is similar to that from contemporary Copperbelt sites. Iron working was a major industry. A late phase, 9th–11th centuries AD, is represented at the Twickenham Road site.

K-Ar dating: Absolute dating technique that traces the transformation of one isotope into another—potassium (K) into argon (Ar). Its range is 100,000 years to 1.3 billion years.

Kara-Bom: Palaeolithic site in the Altai region of Siberia with artifacts including Levallois cores, retouched blades, denticulates, and end scrapers probably dating to the early Upper Palaeolithic.

Karako: A village site in Nara prefecture, Japan, of the Yayoi culture that is the type site for the western Yayoi pottery chronology. Over 100 dwelling and storage pits contained pottery covering the whole span of the Yayoi period in this area. Organic materials were well preserved, including baskets, wooden agricultural tools, a bundle of rice plants, melon seeds, nuts, and bones of wild board, deer, dogs, and cattle. A bronze bell casting mold indicated craft production.

Karanis: Classical term for the site of Kom Aushim, in Faiyum (Fayyum), Egypt, which yielded over 5,000 papyri and ostraka. These are a major source of information about the economy and administration of Roman Egypt during the 2nd–4th centuries AD. (*syn.* Kom Aushim)

Karanog: A large town and necropolis located in Lower Nubia, south of Aswan, which flourished in the Meroitic and post-Meroitic periods c. 300 BC–AD 550. By at least as early as the third century BC, Karanog had developed into a major town.

Karanovo: A tell site in eastern Bulgaria, which has given the basic chronological sequence from the Early Neolithic, and much of the Eneolithic, to the Bronze Age, 7th–mid-2nd millennia BC, of the eastern Balkans. There were seven major phases of occupation. Karanovo I is the earliest Neolithic and forms part of the complex of cultures that include Starcevo,

Cris, and Körös. The architecture was wattle and daub and eventually the 50 to 60 early, scattered, square huts were replaced by rectangular, larger, plastered, and painted ones. Karanovo II also represents the First Temperate Neolithic level. Karanovo III has Middle Neolithic Veselinovo levels, with dark burnished and carinated pottery. Level IV is the Kalojanoven level, and V represents Marica levels, with graphite painted wares and excised pottery—both are contemporaneous with the Late Neolithic Vinca culture of the western Balkans. Level VI is the main Eneolithic Gumelnita occupation with graphite painted wares and copper metallurgy. Level VII is the Early Bronze Age level. Almost all the period designations have become known as cultures in their own right (e.g., the Karanovo III culture).

Karari: Earlier Stone Age industry of the Oldowan Complex at Koobi Fora in Kenya, dating to 1.5–1.25 million years ago. There are many artifact types, including bifaces.

Karasuk: A Bronze Age culture that succeeded the Andronovo culture in southern Siberia in the late 2nd millennium BC. The three main, basically successive, yet often overlapping cultures were the Afanasyevskaya, Andronovo, and Karasuk. The Karasuk culture developed when a gradual change was made from settled communities to seasonal transhumance. Two settlements of large pit houses are known and many cemeteries of stone cists covered by a low mound and set in a square stone enclosure equipped with round-bottomed pots; many of these are in the Minusinsk Basin. The Karasuk people were farmers who concentrated on sheep and cattle breeding. They also practiced metallurgy on a large scale; the most characteristic artifact is a bronze knife or dagger, with a curved profile and a decorated handle, related to China's An-Yang bronzes. They produced a realistic animal art, which probably contributed to the development of the later Sytho-Siberian animal art style. Remains of bridles mark the beginning of horse riding on the Siberian steppe. The character of their material culture came from exchange with the centers of Far Eastern metallurgy. The Karasuk culture originated and spread its influences farther to western Siberia and Russian Turkistan than did the Andronovo. Trade relations extended to central Russia. Chronology of this period is based on comparisons with northern Chinese bronzes. The Karasuk period persisted down to c. 700 BC.

Karatepe: An 8th century BC Neo-Hittite fortified palace on the Ceyhan River in southwestern Anatolia (Turkey), founded by Asitawandas, king of the Danunians, c. 740 BC. A series of carved reliefs and inscriptions on two monumental gateways tell a great deal about classical Hittite, Assyrian, Phoenico-Egyptian, and Syro-Hittite. The gateway inscriptions are bilingual Phoenician-Luwian (Hittite) hieroglyphics, which were instrumental in the decipherment of the Luwian writing system and the understanding of the Hittite language. The Assyrians probably destroyed the city in about 700 BC, when the last remaining principalities in the region were subjugated.

Karbuna: One of the earliest hoards discovered in the Balkan Neolithic of the Cucuteni-Tripolye culture in Moldova. The Karbuna hoard of 852 objects was discovered in a Tripolye A-B1 pot, and it includes some of the earliest cast copper items and shell, marble, and bone jewelry. The date of deposition is disputed at c. 3800/3500 BC, and the hoard has been interpreted as either a shaman's kit or as a communal ornament collection.

Karim Shahir: A hilltop site near Kirkuk in northern Iraq occupied in the period when the transition was beginning from hunting and gathering to farming. Its material is closely related to that of Zawi Chemi Shanidar, and the culture is dated c. 9000–7000 BC. There is no evidence of architecture, so that the site was probably seasonal. Artifact evidence suggests an increased dependence on plant resources: blades with the silica sheen often described as "sickle gloss," pierced stone balls that might have been weights for digging sticks, and stone axes.

Karkarichinkat (Nord and Sud): Mounds in the Tilemsi valley of Mali, Africa, occupied by herder-fishermen between c. 3900–3300 BP.

Karlgren, Bernhard (1889–1978): Swedish archaeologist was the first person to reconstruct the phonology of Chinese characters in use around AD 600 and then in earlier periods. He reconstructed the vowel system of Old Chinese to account for the language in *Classic of Poetry* (800–600 BC). He studied numerous fundamental texts of the pre-Han period and succeeded in assessing their authenticity and in translating them into English and providing commentaries. In the field of early bronzes, he laid the foundations for an analytical method, the principles of which are still valid.

Karli: A village in west-central India with a rock-cut Buddhist temple (*chaitya*) of the 2nd century AD. The chaitya, the largest and most elaborate of the cave temples of Hinayana Buddhism, is about 45 feet to the crown of its teak-ribbed vault.

Karmir-blur: Urartian city near modern Erevan, Armenia, with a citadel and walled residential area, mainly occupied in the 7th century BC. There were pre-Urartian graves and a Hellenistic occupation. It may have replaced Erebuni as the Urartian seat in the 8th century.

Karnak: A huge complex of religious buildings in the northern part of Thebes, the ancient capital of Upper Egypt (modern Luxor), with a great temple to Amen (Amon) and a series of subsidiary structures. Recent excavations indicate that occupation began in the Gerzean period (c. 3200 BC), when a small settlement was founded on the eastern bank of the Nile floodplain. The village has given its name to the northern half of the ruins of Thebes. There is a smaller complex of the goddess Mut, consort of Amen (built largely by Amenhotep III, whose architect was commemorated by statues in the temple), and one to the god Montu/Mont, predecessor of Amen. Between these two precincts lay the largest of all Egyptian temples, and one of the largest in the world, the great temple of the state god, Amen (Amon-Re). It is a complex of temples, added to and altered at many periods. A series of processional gateways link the temple with that of Mut to the south, and farther, by way of the avenue of sphinxes, with the temple at Luxor 2 miles (3 km) away. (*syn.* ancient Ipet-isut; al-Karnak)

Karolta: A site in northwest South Australia with petroglyphs in Panaramitee-style engravings. Dates range from 31,600–1400 bp.

karst: An irregular limestone region with sinkholes, underground streams, and caverns. Karsts owe their existence to the removal of bedrock in solution and to the development of underground drainage without the development of surface stream valleys. Karst is characterized by the formation and growth of cavities resulting from chemical weathering and erosion in regions of carbonate and evaporite rocks. Karsts show much variation and are usually described in terms of a dominant land form. Most important are fluviokarst, doline karst, cone and tower karst, and pavement karst. Approximately 15% of the Earth's land surface is karst. The most extensive karst area of the United States occurs in the limestones of Mississippian age (about 325,000,000–345,000,000 years old) of the Interior Low Plateaus. Karst also occurs in the limestones of Ordovician age (about 430,000,000–500,000,000 years old) in Kentucky and Tennessee.

Kartan culture: A group of stone assemblages with heavy core tools found on Kangaroo Island and the nearby peninsulas of South Australia, a variant of the Australian Core Tool and Scraper tradition. Kangaroo Island, now separated from Australia by a 15-kilometer strait, was joined to the mainland during the Pleistocene. There were no Aboriginal inhabitants at the time of European contact. Radiocarbon estimates of 14,000 BC have been obtained for a possibly subsequent small scraper industry in Seton rock shelter on Kangaroo Island. Kartan tools include unifacially flaked pebble choppers, large steep-edged flake scrapers, waisted ax blades, and large horsehoof cores (mean weights of 500 g), sometimes associated with small quartz flakes. The proportion of core tools in the assemblage is much higher than in other Pleistocene sites.

Kar-Tukulti-Ninurta: A city across from Assur on the Tigris River, a cult and royal residence of the Middle Assyrian king Tukulti-Ninurta I (1238–1197 BC). This king asserted Assyrian supremacy over King Kashtiliash IV, ruler of the Kassites to the southeast, and subjugated ancient Armenia to the northeast and, for a time, Babylonia. After constructing this new capital, he was slain by his son. There is a large palace complex, a temple of Assur, and domestic architecture.

karum: An Akkadian word meaning "quay" or "harbor," a place where trade occurs. It was extended to the marketplace by the quay and hence to a trading post and the corps of merchants of a city. The term also referred to the organization of merchants in the area, which were self-governing. An example is Kanish.

Kas: Site of a Bronze Age shipwreck off Cap Uluburun, Turkey, which was probably going to the Aegean when it sank in the 14th century BC. Objects found in 1982 in the shipwreck include the first known gold scarab of the Egyptian queen Nefertiti. Other items are copper, tin, and glass ingots, bronze tools and weapons, jewelry for the Near East, Egypt, and the Aegean; and pottery from Cyprus, Canaan, and Mycenae. The ship's contents reveal a tight web of interconnections in the later 14th century among Mycenaean Greece, Cyprus, Egypt, Palestine, Syria, and Africa. (*syn.* Kas-Ula Burun)

Kasori: A Middle or Late Jomon plaza-type shell midden village in Chiba prefecture, Japan. There were at least 47 pit houses in a circular plan, with shell deposits around the rim. It is the type site for Kasori Jomon ceramics.

Kassala: A cultural phase of the eastern Sudan including the Butana, Gash, and Mokram groups.

Kassites: A people of the central Zagros Mountains who occupied Babylon after the Hittite raid c. 1595 BC and who had a distinctive culture and language. Their occupation ended with the city's conquest by Assyria and Elam c. 1157 BC. The Kassites may or may not have been Indo-Europeans, but their rulers were probably Indo-Aryan aristocracy who taught them horse breeding and riding, which they introduced into Mesopotamia. One important source of information on the Kassites was the Amarna correspondence on foreign relations of the 14th century BC. The Kassites used distinctive boundary stones called *kudurru*. The Kassite rule represents the longest episode of political integration in the history of southern Mesopotamia. Important sites are Aqar Quf, Warka, and Nippur.

Kastri: A site on the island of Kythera, Greece, of an Early Helladic settlement later colonized by the Minoans in c. 2500 BC. Kastri prospered from trade between Crete and Laconia. The site of Delphi was occupied by the modern village of Kastri until 1890, when the village was moved to a site nearby and renamed Delphi. There is another Kastri on the island of Syros.

Kastritsa: An Upper Palaeolithic cave site in northwest Greece with occupation beginning c. 22,000–11,000 bp. Arti-facts include backed blades, shouldered points, bone points, and decorated pebbles.

Katoto: An Iron Age cemetery on the Lualaba River, southeastern Zaire, probably dating to around the 13th century AD, contemporary with the Iron Age Kisalian tradition. The collective graves were accompanied by rich and varied grave goods including pottery, copper, and iron artifacts, notably an iron gong of a type that serves as a symbol of political authority in central African societies. The presence of sea shells and imported glass beads indicates links with the Indian Ocean coast. (*syn.* Katotan)

katun: A period in the Classic Maya Long Count equal to 7,200 days (about 20 years). It is also the chronological unit making up the Short Count. The celebration of katuns was a major ritual of kingship in the Classic period.

Katuruka: An Early Iron Age site in Buhaya, northeastern Tanzania. The pottery appears to be of the Urewe type known from other parts of the Lake Victoria basin. There is also evidence of sophisticated iron-smelting technology during the last few centuries BC. It is the oldest-known evidence for ironworking in central and southern Africa.

Kaupangr: A city in Norway founded in 997 by King Olaf I Tryggvason; he built a church and a royal residence, Kongsgård, there. The pottery, glass, and coins from the excavations indicate that the site flourished in the 9th century. Like Hedeby and Birka, Kaupangr seems to have maintained extensive contacts with the Franks and Slavs as well as links with the Arab world. (*syn.* Trondheim)

Kauri Point: A Maori Pa near Tauranga, New Zealand, which has revealed several phases of Classic Maori ditch and bank fortification from AD 1500–1750. The interior of the pa contained large numbers of sweet potato storage pits. The swamp preserved many artifacts, including wooden combs.

Kasusambi: A site in the Ganges Valley of northern India, which was a great urban center in the early historical period. Its earliest wall, of mud brick faced with baked brick 12 meters high, was built about 500 BC. Within it is a Buddhist monastery of the fifth century BC where, according to an inscription, the Buddha himself stayed for a time. Of the same period is a building interpreted as a palace, with walls of stone rubble. The site has provided important information about the origins and development of the Gangetic Iron Age urban civilization. The earliest levels contain pottery related to the Ochre Colored pottery horizon and dated to the mid-2nd millennium BC. The second level has black-and-red, red, gray, and black wares, and iron objects also appear, in the second quarter of the 1st millennium BC. There was Northern Black Polished ware in the third level of around 500 BC. (*syn.* Kaushambi)

Kauthara: One of the four small states, named after regions of India—Amaravati (Quang Nam); Vijaya (Binh Dinh); Kauthara (Nha Trang); and Panduranga (Phan Rang)—of Champa (now southern Vietnam). Champa was formed in AD 192 during the breakup of the Han Dynasty in China. The states' populations remained concentrated in small coastal enclaves. To this period belong several brick sanctuaries in the Nha-trang area, notably that of Po Nagar. Nha-trang dates to the 3rd century AD, when, as part of the independent land of Kauthara, it acknowledged the suzerainty of Funan.

kava: An intoxicating drink prepared from the crushed, chewed, or pounded aromatic roots of the Polynesian shrub *Piper methysticum* or *Macropiper latifolium*. Kava was drunk at ceremonial events in Fiji and other parts of central and eastern Oceania. The term also refers to the plant and the root. (*syn.* kaava, cava, kawa)

Kawa: An ancient Egyptian colony in Kush, Sudan, on the east bank of the Nile, with a temple complex in the heartland of the Nubian Kerma (Karmah) culture. The Egyptian king Amenhotep I (1514–1493 BC) conquered it when he destroyed the Cushite state. The temple complex was built by Amenhotep III (1390–1353 BC). The temple, however, was destroyed by his successor, Akhenaton, but it was later restored by Tutankhamen (reigned 1333–23 BC). The Romans sacked the city in 23 BC.

Kawakiu Bay: Site in western Molokai, Hawaii, with large midden deposits and stone structures from a fishing community, dated to AD 1750.

Kawela: A valley in Molokai, Hawaii, with a well-preserved pre-European settlement from the last 1 or 2 centuries before contact.

Kaya: A confederation of polities (tribal league) on the southern Korean coast formed before the 3rd century AD. The Kaya confederation developed trade largely by sea with the Chinese capital at Lo-yang and with Wae, Japan. The people of Kaya are thought to have been closely related to the tribes that crossed over from Korea to Japan a century or two before this period, and Kaya frequently sought aid from the Japanese in its feuds with its larger Korean neighbors (Silla, Paekche). There are cist burials or mounded tombs containing multiple cist burials. Artifacts include gray stoneware, the first made in Korea, which preceded the Sue ware of Japan. The Kaya people invented a unique musical instrument, the *kayagum*. Silla subjugated the confederation between the years of 532–562.

Kayatha: A site with three Chalcolithic cultures on the Malwa plateau of central India. The first, dated to the second half of the third millennium BC, was characterized by Kayatha ware of violet-painted brown slip and incised and red-painted buff wares. The second phase had pottery similar to the Banas culture, white painted black-and-red ware, dated to

the early 2nd millennium BC. The last phase, of the second quarter of the 2nd millennium, belonged to the Malwa culture. There was also an Iron Age level.

Kayenta: A regional variation of the Anasazi people, located in northeast Arizona, especially in the Pueblo II stage of AD c. 1250–1300. Kayenta has specific pottery types and architectural techniques. As seen at the Navajo National Monument, the principal dwellings of the Kayenta, the construction of the cliff dwellings was apparently the result of their evolution from hunters and gatherers to sedentary farmers. They probably moved to the mesas to the south because of climatic changes involving erosion and water shortages, which made farming impossible.

Kazanlik: A large Neolithic, Copper Age (Eneolithic), and Early Bronze Age tell in the Valley of Roses, southern Bulgaria. The stratigraphy includes a Karanovo I occupation; Veselinovo occupation levels; Karanovo V–VI layers (with a stone wall enclosing the site at the end of this period), and an Early Bronze Age occupation. The Kazanluk Tomb, discovered in 1944 on the outskirts of town, is a Thracian burial tomb of an unknown ruler from the 4th or 3rd century BC. The fine murals that decorate the entire tomb distinguish it from 13 similar known examples. (*syn.* Kazanluk)

KBS: An Earlier Stone Age industry (and site) of the Oldowan industrial complex at Koobi Fora, Kenya, dating to 1.8 million years ago. The site has stone artifacts and animal bones that are an important source of information on early hominids.

Kebarian: A stone-tool culture in Kebara (Kebareh) Cave of Mount Carmel, Israel. It is from the early Levantine Epipalaeolithic (c. 20,000–14,500 BP), after the local Upper Palaeolithic. The nomadic hunter gatherers worked with wild cereals, and the flint industry was characterized by bladelets and microlithis modified to form backed and pointed pieces and by mortars and pestles. (*syn.* Kebaran)

Kechi Beg: A 3rd-millennium BC site in the Quetta Valley of western Pakistan, which has given its name to a fine buff-colored pottery painted in black and solid bands interspersed with delicately painted patterns. Red paint was also used to produce a polychrome effect.

Kehe: Early Palaeolithic site in Shanxi Province, China, of the heavy tool tradition of Lantian and Dingcun. (*syn.* [K'o-ho])

Keilor: A site near Melbourne, Australia, with a cranium with modern features found in alluvial sediments and dated to c. 13,000 bp. It resembles the Green Gully skull found 3 kilometers away. Other finds include stone flakes and hearths possibly 30,000 years old and the bones of extinct megafauna. The earliest levels have a minimum estimated date of 36,000 BP.

Kellia: The site of a large Coptic monastic settlement from the 4th–8th centuries AD in the western Nile Delta of Egypt. The pottery makes up an important ceramic assemblage of the Late Roman period of Egypt.

Kel'taminar: Culture complex at Khoresmia and Kyzyl Kum in Kazakhstan, Uzebkistan, and Turkmenia. The foraging-herding culture made pottery, some worked copper and turquoise, and existed c. 5th–3rd millennia BC (Mesolithic to the early Bronze Age). The culture may have affected the subsequent Srubnaya and Andronovo cultures. (*syn.* Kel'teminar)

Kemet: A name used by the ancient Egyptians in referring to Egypt itself. The literal meaning of Kemet is "black land," a reference to the fertile Nile silt, which was annually spread across the land by the inundation.

kendi: A spouted water container made in southeast Asia during the late 1st and early 2nd millennia AD.

Kenniff Cave: A sandstone rock shelter in south-central Queensland, Australia, one of the oldest sites yet discovered in the continent and containing one of the longest and most complete technological sequences for any Australian site. The basal strata contain an industry of core and flake scrapers dated by radiocarbon to c. 14,000–13,000 BC. These tools were later joined by small blades, microliths, delicate points, woodworking flakes, and (around 2400 BC) by backed blades. Stone tools from the base to the 3000 BC levels also included steep-edge flake scrapers and cores, including horse hoof cores. Between 3000–500 BC, there occurred an unusually wide range of Australian Small Tools, including Pirri points, geometric microliths, Bondi points, and Tula adze flakes, as well as grinding stones. Ocher pellets, some use striated, were scattered through all levels. There is stenciled art going back 19,000 years. It was the first evidence of Pleistocene occupation in Australia, establishing the two-phase sequence in current use for the continent.

Kensington Stone: A stone slab found on a Minnesota farm in 1898 with an inscription in runes purporting to record the arrival of a party of exploring Vikings. An object of controversy from the start, it is now dismissed as a forgery, despite recent confirmation of the Viking visits to the eastern American coast. This supposed relic of a 14th-century Scandinavian exploration of the interior of North America is a 200-pound slab of graywacke inscribed with runes (medieval Germanic script). The inscription, dated 1362, is purported to be by a group of Norwegian and Swedish explorers from Vinland who visited the Great Lakes area in that year. The stone is housed in a special museum in Alexandria, Minnesota, and a 26-ton replica stands in nearby Runestone Park.

Kent's Cavern: A cave site at Torquay, Devon, England, occupied around 400,000 years ago. The main occupation is of the Middle and Upper Palaeolithic periods and includes artifacts of the Mousterian, Aurignacian, "proto-Solutrean," and Creswellian culture, as well as harpoons and a needle of Magdalenian appearance. The sequence compares closely with that from Creswell Crags—those being the two oldest human homes in England. A human skull 20,000 years old, remains of saber-toothed tiger, cave lion, and bear, rhinoceros, mammoth, wolf, elk, and hyena have all been found ossified in the cave. A rostro-carinate dating back 500,000 years was found in the lowest layers under the stalagmites. There was also Lower Palaeolithic occupation with rather crude implements including bifaces.

Kenyon, (Dame) Kathleen Mary (1906–1978): British archaeologist who made major contributions to the understanding of the history of Palestine—especially through work at Jericho and Jerusalem. The work at Jericho established the existence of an aceramic Neolithic (PPNA/B) and an Epipalaeolithic subsistence on wild cereals in the 9th–8th millennia BC.

Kephala: A Late (Final) Neolithic settlement and cist grave cemetery on the Cycladic island of Kea, dated to the mid-4th millennium BC. The cemetery contained graves made of small flat stones in circular or rectangular constructions, each with a number of burials. Children were commonly buried in pottery jars (pithoi). The typical pottery was covered with a red slip and decorated by patter burnishing. Evidence for copper smelting was found, one of the earliest occurrences in the Aegean. There is evidence of close links between Kephala and sites in Attica (Athens, Thorikos).

Kerameikós: The most prestigious cemetery and pottery workshop region of Athens, including a multiple burial of Spartans from the 5th century BC. Many tombs were marked by stelae with relief decoration. There was a precinct for the Messenians, one for some immigrants from Heraclea on the Black Sea, and one for those from Sinope, also in the Black Sea region.

kerb: The term for a retaining wall built around the edge of a cairn or barrow; a circle of stones bordering a burial mound. (*syn.* kerbstone circle)

Kerbschnitt: The technique of carving or decorating wood by use of an ax or hatchet. (*syn.* chip carving, chip-carving)

Kerinci: Highland region of west-central Sumatra with obsidian microliths similar to Tianko Panjang of the mid-Holocene and Dong Son bronze items of the later centuries BC.

Kerma: The site of a capital of an independent Nubian/ Kushite kingdom, which became prominent after a northward retreat of the Egyptians during the 13th Dynasty, c. 1700 BC. On the third Nile cataract in Upper Nubia (Sudan), it came into existence during the Egyptian Old and Middle

Kingdoms (2686–1650 BC) and is the type site for the Kerma culture (c. 2500–1500 BC), probably identified with the Egyptians' "land of Yam." Kerma traded widely, and great wealth was accumulated. There was a high level of craftsmanship, especially in pottery. The rulers of Kerma, together with the bodies of many retainers, were buried under huge grave mounds. There were also sacrificial human interments. This royal necropolis of the kings of Kush probably dates to the Second Intermediate Period c. 1633–1550 BC. The only substantial surviving building is a large mud-brick "Western Deffufa."

Kerma ware: Distinctive thin-walled pottery with a black-and-red finish, produced by the Kerma culture in various shapes.

Kernonen: A burial mound of the Armorican Early Bronze Age Tumulus culture c. 2000–2500 BC, in Finistère, France. The circular stone cairn covered a rectangular dry-stone chamber. Grave goods include fine flaked flint arrowheads, amber beads, bronze axes and daggers, and wooden hilts decorated with gold nails.

kernos: A Green cult vessel—dish, bowl, or jar—made of terra-cotta or stucco-covered sun-baked brick and used for the offering of first fruits. The jar held small cups around its lip, and examples are found from the Bronze Age onward.

kero: A large wooden flared beaker, painted with black, white, and light red designs of pumas, condors, and other creatures on a dark red ground color. Keros decorated with incised geometric patterns were used in Inca times, but examples with scenes painted in lacquer are of post-Conquest date. In pottery, the shape started earlier and was especially popular in the Tiahuanaco culture.

Kéros-Syros: Cultural phase of two islands in the Cyclades, corresponding to Early Cycladic II, c. 2700–2300 BC, in traditional chronology. An open-air sanctuary filled with marble figurines on the island of Kéros (Káros) is assignable to the Early Bronze Age.

Kesslerloch: Magdalenian reindeer-hunting cave site in Switzerland, occupied during a cold phase of the final glaciation. There are bone harpoons and spear throwers, art objects such as an engraving of a rutting reindeer, and a stone tool kit of borers.

Ketrosy: Middle Palaeolithic site on the Dnestr River, Ukraine, dating to an interstadial preceding the early cold maximum of the last glacial. There are side scrapers and denticulates among the tools.

kettle drum: Large bronze drums, also known as Dong Son drums (northern Vietnam), first produced more than 2,000 years ago and found throughout southeast Asia (with the exception of the Philippines and the island of Borneo). These drums are generally associated with wealth, power, and fertility and were important in rituals. (*syn*. Dong Son drums)

keyhole tombs: Mounded tombs of the Kofun period in Japan. The ground plan was shaped like a keyhole, and they are assumed to be tombs of rulers or the elite in the 4th–5th centuries AD.

Khabur River: An important tributary of the Euphrates River in eastern Syria. Its basin was a strategic area for communications between Mesopotamia, Syria, and Anatolia (Turkey), and it contains such important sites as Tell Halaf, Chagar Bazar, and Tell Brak. It has given its name to a distinctive painted ware found in northern Mesopotamia and north Syria in the early 2nd millennium BC. Pottery of this type also occurs at Kultepe in Anatolia, indicating wideranging trade at the time.

Khafajah: A group of tells on the Diyala River in east-central Iraq with the best evidence for the threefold subdivision of the Mesopotamian Early Dynastic period (3rd millennium BC). The stratified ceramic sequence from Jemdet Nasr to the late Early Dynastic times, combined with the findings from Tell Asmar, provided this information. A temple with 10 building levels of the Jemdet Nasr and Early Dynastic periods was dedicated to the moon god Sin. A second Early Dynastic rectangular mud-brick temple faced onto a square court around which were grouped storehouses and priests' quarters. There were a number of burials beneath the floors of residential housing. (*syn*. ancient Tutub; Khafadje)

Khafre (fl. late 26th century BC): Son of Khufu (2589–2566 BC), the fourth ruler of the 4th Dynasty (2575–2465 BC, of the Old Kingdom) and builder of the second of three pyramids at Giza. The complex includes the Valley Temple and the Great Sphinx, whose features are presumably Khafre's. He succeeded to the throne after the death of his half-brother Djedefre (Redjedef, 2566–2588 BC), who had constructed his pyramid at Abu Roash. (*syn*. Chephren, Rakhaef; Khafra, Souphis)

Khami: A microlithic Later Stone Age industry of the Matobo Hills of southwest Zimbabwe, dating back 8,000 years. It is also the name of the capital of the Torwa state, built in the 15th century AD after the decline of Great Zimbabwe, and occupied until the mid-17th century when the capital was moved. It is also the term for the third phase of the Zimbabwe tradition, which continued to the early 19th century. (*syn*. Matopo industry)

Kharga Oasis: The southernmost and largest of the major Egyptian western oases, which is located in the Libyan Desert about 175 kilometers east of Luxor. There are traces of Middle Palaeolithic (Mousterian) occupation at Kharga, and its material culture was closely connected with that of the Nile Valley throughout the pharaonic period. This oasis is of approximately the same age as the Epi-Levalloisian sites of the Sebilian and the Fayyum Depression. (*syn.* al-Wahat al-Kharijah; al-Kharijah)

Kharosti script: A writing system used in northwestern India before about AD 500; one of the two main early Indian scripts. The earliest extant inscription in Kharosti dates from 251 BC and the latest from the 4th–5th century AD. The system was probably derived from the Aramaic alphabet while northwestern India was under Persian rule in the 5th century BC. Aramaic, however, is a Semitic alphabet of 22 consonantal letters, while Kharosti is syllabic and has 252 separate signs for consonant and vowel combinations. A cursive script written from right to left, Kharosti was used for commercial and calligraphic purposes. It was influenced somewhat by Brahmi, the other Indian script of the period, which eventually superseded it. The name Karoshti literally means "asses' lips" and is said to refer to the similarity of the highly curvilinear script to the movement of asses' lips.

Khartoum Neolithic: Industry of Sudan dating to c. 5200 BP, characterized by domesticated animals, pottery, and a special adze.

Khasekhemwy (fl. 27th century BC): The sixth and last king of Egypt in the 2nd Dynasty (c. 2775–2650 BC), who ended the internal struggles of the mid-2nd Dynasty and reunited the country. He was the last Abydene/Abydos ruler. Probably starting from a base at Hierakonpolis, Khasekhemwy extended his control over the whole kingdom. His monuments refer to his unification of Upper and Lower Egypt, and other inscriptions suggest that he raided Nubia; his name has been found in Lebanon, probably indicating trade with the Syrians. Annals of the Old Kingdom record great technological advances that were made during his last 6 years. Khasekhemwy was an ancestor of the 3rd-Dynasty king, Djoser. (*syn.* Khasekhem; Khasekhemui; Khesekhem)

Kheit Qasim: Three sites in east-central Iraq. Kheit Quasim I has a large Early Dynastic cemetery of brick tombs with multiple inhumations, unusual for southern Mesopotamia. Kheit Qasim III was a small 'Ubaid site.

kheker frieze: The name of a decorative motif common in ancient Egyptian architecture from at least as early as the 3rd Dynasty (2686–2613 BC): rows of knots in decorative carved or painted friezes around the upper edges of buildings.

Khepri: The ancient sun god, conceived as a great scarab beetle rolling the sun across the heavens, whose cult was centered at Heliopolis. This deity is sometimes depicted in tomb painting and funerary papyri as a man with a scarab as a head or as a scarab in a boat held aloft by Nun. This was just one of the sun god's manifestations: Khepri was the morning form, then Re-Harakhty, and Atum, the evening form.

kher: The term for a quarter of tombs—the whole number of burial places of a hypogea, an underground chamber or vault.

Khirbet al-Mafjar: A palatial complex just outside Jericho in the Jordan Valley, attributed via epigraphy to the Umayyad caliph Hisham (724–743). There was a south building, two-story mansion, a mosque, and a bathhouse (with elaborate domes and vaults) supplied by an aqueduct; and a north building, a khan or guesthouse. The buildings are particularly important because they are closely datable in a period when the Hellenistic traditions of art and architecture were being transformed for Muslim patrons and also because they yielded rich collections of stucco, wall paintings, and mosaics.

Khirbet Kerak: A Palestinian site on the southwest shore of the Sea of Galilee, settled from the Early–Middle Bronze Ages and occupied again from the Hellenistic to the Byzantine periods. In the 4th–3rd millennia BC, it was a small walled town that lent its name to a distinctive pottery ware (Khirbet Kerak ware, c. 3400), which has been found on many sites throughout the Near East, from Judeidah in the Amuq to Lachish in the south. This highly burnished ware with red or black slip is often incised or ribbed in decoration. Its origins lie in the southern Caucasus (it was related to Early Transcaucasian wares), from which it was likely carried south by an emigration of the ancestors of the Hittites. The pottery belongs to the EB III phase and has a wide distribution in Syria and Palestine. It is usually thought to have originated in northeast Anatolia and may have been distributed either by emigration or by trade. The town of the mid-3rd millennium BC contains a massive public building, probably a religious structure, that includes eight circular stone structures all enclosed by a massive outer rectangular wall. (*syn.* ancient Beth-yerah; Tell Beth Yerah)

Khirokitia: An Early Neolithic settlement in southern Cyprus, first occupied in the aceramic Neolithic I of the 7th millennium BC. It was abandoned and reoccupied in Neolithic II, later 5th millennium BC. The settlement, surrounded by a massive wall, consisted of roundhouses of mud brick on stone footings. Hearths and benches were found inside, and some houses had burials with grave goods (especially stone bowls) underneath the floors. There was a fine stone industry, using Anatolian obsidian and flint for tools, local andesite for both tools and containers, and Levantine carnelian for beads. The site has given its name to the Early Neolithic culture of the island.

Khmer: The ethnic name of a linguistic group inhabiting Cambodia, southern Vietnam, and parts of Thailand. Late in the 6th century AD, they annexed the declining Funan Empire of south Cambodia and extended westward. The Khmer were linguistically related to the Mon and at the height of their power ruled most of Thailand and southern Laos. The empire had its capital at Angkor in Kampuchea, and it was destroyed by the Thais in about AD 1400. Khmer was one of the most impressive civilizations of southeast Asia, known for spectacular and monumental religious architecture.

Khnum: The ancient Egyptian god of fertility, associated with water and procreation. Khnum was worshiped from the 1st Dynasty, c. 2925–2775 BC, into the early centuries AD. He was represented as a ram with horizontal, twisting horns or as a man with a ram's head. Khnum was believed to have created humankind from clay like a potter, and his first main cult center was Herwer. From the New Kingdom (1539–1075 BC) on, however, he became the god of the island of Elephantine and the area of the First Cataract of the Nile River. There he formed a triad of deities with the goddesses Satis (Satet) and Anukis. Khnum also had an important cult at Esna, south of Thebes. (*syn.* Khnemu)

Khoikhoin: A Stone Age pastoral people of southwestern Africa during the last 2,000 years. The first European explorers found them in the hinterland, and they now live either in European settlements or on official reserves in South Africa or Namibia. Khoikhoin (meaning "men of men") is their own name for themselves; Hottentot is the term fashioned by the Dutch (later Afrikaner) settlers, probably in imitation of the clicks in their language. They may be descended from Bantu speakers of northern Botswana. They have cattle, sheep, and goats and make pottery. (*syn.* Khoi, Khoikhoi, Khoekhoe; Hottentots)

Khoisan: Collective term for the Khoikhoin and San peoples of southern Africa and their languages. The Khoisan languages are click languages spoken in southern Africa. The term Khoisan was created to refer to the related peoples known as Bushmen and Hottentots (i.e., the Khoisanid peoples) under a common name and has become increasingly accepted since its creation is 1928. The word is derived from Khoikhoi and San, the names of the peoples called, respectively and pejoratively, Hottentots and Bushmen.

Khok Charoen: Prehistoric cemetery in Pa Sak Valley of central Thailand, which dates to c. 1000 BC and has polished stone adzes and stone ornaments, but no metal has been found.

Khok Phanom Di: Prehistoric settlement in south-central Thailand with radiocarbon dates of c. 2000–1400 BC, although no metal has been found. It had a rich pottery making and exporting tradition. The burials indicate social hierarchy.

Khons: An ancient Egyptian moon god in the form of a young man. Khons was regarded as the son of the god Amon and the goddess Mut. In the period of the late New Kingdom, c. 1100 BC, a major temple was built for Khons in the Karnak complex at Thebes. Khons was also associated with baboons and was sometimes assimilated to Thoth, another moon god associated with baboons. (*syn.* Khonsu, Khensu, Chons)

Khorat: A saucer-shaped low plateau in northeast Thailand occupying 60,000 square miles and drained by the Chi and Mun Rivers. Rice agriculture began before the 4th millennium BC. The plateau's development is divided into General Period A, c. 3600–2000 BC; General Period B, c. 2000–800/400 BC; General Period C, c. 800/400 BC–AD 300/500; and General Period D, AD c. 300/500–1300. The initial settlement had polished stone adzes and stone and shell jewelry indicating some trade. The second period was the transition to the use of tin-bronze and production of bronze using imported metals. In the third period, iron replaced bronze, and wet rice cultivation was established. The fourth period saw an expansion of settlements, formation of small states, long-distance trade, and some Indianization. (*syn.* Korat plateau)

Khor Musa: A site of Middle Palaeolithic occupation in the southern Nile Valley of Egypt in the Second Cataract. It has given its name to the final phase of the Nubian "Middle Stone Age" for other sites close to the River Nile and contemporary with, or following, the Aterian. The site had Levallois flakes, denticulates, and burins. It seems probable that the Khormusan industry was broadly contemporary with the Dabban of Cyrenaica, belonging to the period following c. 40,000 BC when increased aridity rendered the Sahara uninhabitable. Faunal remains from Khormusan sites indicate fishing and the hunting of land animals. (*syn.* Khor-Musa)

Khorramabad: A valley of the Luristan section of Iran with a series of Middle and Upper Palaeolithic sites (Gar Arjeneh, Ghamari, Kunji, Pa Sangar, Yafteh). There is a sequence of Mousterian, Baradostian, and Zarzian industries that span the Late Pleistocene, similar to Shanidar. (*syn.* Khurramabad)

Khorsabad: The site of the ancient city of Dur-Sharrukin, near Mosul, Iraq. It was a short-lived capital of Assyria. Founded by the Neo-Assyrian king Sargon II in 717 BC, it included a magnificent palace in a city, but it did not survive its founder's death in 705 BC. It was built by Sargon to replace Nimrud. However, after Sargon's death, his son Sennacherib moved the capital to Nineveh. It has yielded a rich collection of sculptured slabs and cuneiform inscriptions now in the Louvre in Paris, although much was lost in the Euphrates while being transported to France. The most impressive remains lie on the citadel—several temples, a ziggurat, and a royal palace. (*syn.* ancient Dur-Sharrukin, Fort of Sargon)

Khotylevo: Palaeolithic sites on the Desna River in the Ukraine. In the Middle Palaeolithic level, there are Levallois cores and bifaces. In the Upper Palaeolithic level, there are Venus figurines.

Khryashchi: Palaeolithic site on the Northern Donets River in Russia dating to the late Middle Pleistocene. The artifacts include flake and core tools.

Khuan Lukpad: An industrial and trading settlement in Krabi, Thailand, where glass and stone beads and tin were made. Roman and Indian seals, Middle Eastern glass, and glazed stonewares date to the early–mid-1st millennium AD.

Khufu (fl. early 26th century BC): The second king (pharaoh) (reigned 2589–2566 BC) of the Egyptian 4th Dynasty (c. 2575–2465 BC), during the Old Kingdom, and the successor of Snefru (2613–2589 BC). His name is an abbreviation of the phrase Khnum-kuefui ("Khnum protects me"). He was the builder of the Great Pyramid at Giza, the largest of the ancient pyramids. The pyramid covers a ground area of 53,000 square meters and rises to a height of 148 meters, reflecting a complex and efficient organization of which the pharaoh was the head. Two of his sons, Djedefre (Redjedef) and Khafre, succeeded him. (*syn.* Cheops, Khufwey, Khnomkhufwey)

Khyan (c. 1600 BC): A 15th Dynasty Hyksos ruler of Lower Egypt, whose "throne name" was Seuserenra. Unlike the other Hyksos pharaohs, who commissioned very few architectural or sculptural monuments, Khyan was responsible for the decoration of religious structures at Gebelein and Bubastis. (*syn.* Seuserenra)

Kian ware: A white ware made at Yung-ho near Kian/Chi-an in Kiangsi, often in the forms of bowls decorated with leaves, medallions, birds, or plants. It could be black glazed and was made during the Sung Dynasty (AD 960–1279). This ware appears to be an imitation of Ting. (*syn.* Chi-an)

Kidder, Alfred Vincent (1885–1963): A pioneering American archaeologist working in the U.S. Southwest. He carried out stratigraphical and seriation excavations, notably of the Pueblo at Pecos, New Mexico, and combined stratigraphy with pottery typology to produce the first synthesis of southwestern prehistory. It has since been refined by dendrochronology, but it still provides the framework: Kidder's research forms the basis of nearly all later studies in the area. He later did archaeological surveys and excavations for the Maya program of the Carnegie Institution of Washington. He worked at Kaminaljuyú and Uaxactún. He was hailed for his multidisciplinary approach to archaeology and for changing American archaeology from antiquarianism to scientific discipline.

Kietrz: A large urnfield cemetery of the Lusatian culture of Silesia, Poland, containing over 3,000 graves. Some appear to have had mortuary structures erected above them.

Kiev: An important medieval Russian city, capital of the Ukraine, on the eastern bank of the Dnepr River. In the 10th century, small hamlets were built with sunken-floored workshops, merchant houses, and artisans' dwellings. A fortified town with churches and palaces grew through the 11th century. Kiev had developed into an important political and trade center on the route from the Baltic to Byzantium. The influence of Byzantium is apparent on local monumental architecture of the 11th–14th centuries. It was sacked by the Mongols in the 13th century.

Kiik Koba: A Middle Palaeolithic cave site in the Crimea, Ukraine, occupied in Mousterian times. Some Neanderthal remains have been found, including foot bones and hand bones, but no complete skulls were recovered. Evidence of cold climatic conditions and artifacts such as side scrapers and bifacial folitates have been found. (*syn.* Kiik-Koba)

Kili Ghul Mohammed: A prehistoric site just north of Quetta in western Pakistan, with four phases of occupation. The first has 4th millennium BC dates, farming, and cultivation of cereal crop but no pottery. In the second level, crude hand-made pottery was introduced, and mud brick was used for building. In the third level, black-on-red painted wares and some wheelmade wares occur; in phase four, the beautiful Kechi Beg ware and copper tools appear.

Killke: A culture and ceramic pottery style of the Cuzco basin of Peru, from the Late Intermediate period, AD c. 1000–1438. It immediately preceded the Inca style ceramics. Killke pots have globular bodies, white or buff slip, and simple black (or black and red) geometric patterns.

kill site: Any archaeological site that was primarily used for killing and butchering animals. It is recognized by its distinctive location, tools assemblages, or animal bone evidence. These sites are also recognized through taphonomy. (*syn.* kill-site)

kiln: A chamber built for the firing (baking) of pottery, used from prehistoric times. These, usually dome-shaped, structures are designed to produce the high temperatures needed for the industry. In a pottery kiln, the pots were often stacked upside down on a shelf. An opening for draft was left at the top, and a flue provided at the side. Fuel was piled in and around the kiln, and when the heat was at its greatest, the openings were shut to preserve the temperatures and fire the pots inside with temperatures of 800–1000 centigrade achieved. Other versions were used for glassmaking or the parching of corn. The kiln, like the potter's wheel, implies craft specialization and appears only at advanced stages of economic development.

kiln site: Centers for the production of glazed stonewares during the early 2nd millennium AD on mainland Asia. The best known were at Phnom Kulen and Buriram (Angkor), Go Sanh (Champa), and Kalong and Sukhothai (Thailand). There were also sites in north Vietnam and Burma.

Kilu: Limestone shelter on Buka Island, Northern Solomons, Melanesia, with occupations from 28,000–20,000 bp, 9000–6500 bp, and c. 2500 bp. This establishes Late Pleistocene occupation of the islands, suggesting open-sea voyages.

Kilwa: A major trading city of the East African coast, on an island off Tanzania. For 3 centuries before the arrival of the Portuguese in 1500, it was the leading entrepot on the east African coast. It was first occupied in the 9th century AD, with the earliest settlement being a village of thatched, timber-framed houses. The only industries were iron working and the manufacture of shell beads. Small quantities of pottery from western Asia and, toward the end of the period, chlorite schist from Madagascar indicate commercial activity on a modest scale. Prosperity began c. 1200, marked by the introduction of coins, widespread use of masonry, and the construction of the mosque. In the 14th century, the sultan built a spectacular palace, known as Husuni Kubwa, just outside the town. The establishment of a wealthy Islamic community is identified with the arrival of the so-called Shirazi dynasty which, according to tradition, came from the Persian Gulf. In the 14th and 15th centuries, Kilwa controlled the coast far to the south and grew even more wealthy through its control of the trade in Zimbabwean gold. The arrival of the Portuguese in the Indian Ocean at the end of the 15th century heralded Kilwa's decline.

Kimberley point: A pressure-flaked bifacial point with serrated margins and long, shallow surface scar beds, found in the Kimberley region of western Australia and neighboring areas of the Northern Territory and northwest Queensland. South of the Kimberleys, the point was a trade item and was used as a surgical knife. The points were made at the time of European contact, when bottle glass and porcelain were adapted for the industry.

Kimhae: Shell midden site of the Proto-Three Kingdoms time on the southern Korean coast and the type site for a category of pottery. Stoneware and/or earthenware were made from the 1st–4th centuries AD.

kin: The term for a single day in the Classic Maya Long Count.

Kinai: Core region of Honshu island, Japan, consisting of Yamato, Kawachi, Izumi, Settsu, and Yamashiro—which now make up parts of Nara, Osaka, and Kyoto Prefectures.

Kingdoms, Old, Middle, and New: The names traditionally applied to the three peak periods of development in the history of ancient Egypt, separated by times of decline and disorder. The Old Kingdom included the 3rd–6th Dynasties, c. 2700–2200 BC; the Middle Kingdom was the 11th–13th Dynasties, 2100–1650 BC; and the New Kingdom consisted of the 18th–20th Dynasties, 1580–1075 BC.

king list: A term used for any text recording the names and titles of the rulers of Egypt or Mesopotamia and the length of their reigns. The most important include the Sumerian King List, which recorded the dynasties ruling southern Mesopotamia from the mythical period before the Flood to the Isin-Larsa period, and the Assyrian King List, which listed the rulers of Assyria from before 2000 BC to the Late Assyrian period. There were also lists in Egypt, which incorporate information on principal events of individual reigns. Virtually all of the surviving examples are found in religious or funerary contexts and often relate to the celebration of the cult of royal ancestors, whereby each king established his own legitimacy and place in the succession by making regular offerings to a list of the names of his predecessors. The lists are often surprisingly accurate, although they are also noticeably selective, regularly omitting certain rulers who were considered to have been in any way illegitimate or inappropriate, such as Akhenaten (1352–1336 BC).

kin group: A group of people related by blood rather than, for example, age or gender.

Kingsborough, Lord (1795–1837): An English nobleman who published the Dresden Codex in *Antiquities of Mexico* (1830–1848). He erroneously attributed the codex to the Aztecs. His mission had been to prove that the civilized peoples of Mexico and Central America descended from the 10 lost tribes of Israel. (*syn.* Edward King, Viscount Kingsborough)

King's Lynn: A town and seaport in Norfolk, England, which grew in importance from the 12th century. It was mostly involved with North Sea trade and specialized in exporting the wool and agricultural produce of the fens to Flanders and the Baltic countries. There are remains of the old wall, including the 15th-century South Gate, the Customs House (1683), and several merchants' homes. St. George's Guildhall (1406) is one of the largest and oldest examples of a merchant guildhall in England.

Kinki: District of Japan including Hyogo, Kyoto, Shuga, Mie, Nara, Osaka, and Wayakama Prefectures.

kinship: Socially recognized relationships based on real or imagined descent and marriage patterns. Kinship ties impose mutual obligations on all members of a kin group.

Kintampo Neolithic: An industry of Ghana in West Africa with the first evidence of animal husbandry and food production, dated to 3600 BP. This savanna woodland and forest margin in the basin of the Black Volta River also had ceramics, flaked stone tools, and scored stone rasps that may have been used for grating or grinding. (*syn.* Kintampo)

kiosk: A small, open circular temple with supporting pillars, used as a way station for statues of gods during festivals when they left their main temples. The term also applied to the summer palaces of Turkism sultans. The best-known examples are that of Senusret I (1965–1920 BC) at Karnak and that of Trajan (AD 98–117) at Philae. The term is sometimes used for a small sunshade or pavilion for the use of a king or official.

Kirillovskaya: Upper Palaeolithic site in Kiev, Ukraine, with a radiocarbon date of 19,200 bp and many woolly mammoth remains.

Kisalian: An Iron Age industry of southeastern Zaire, which succeeded the Kamilambian c. 8th century AD. There is a large cemetery site at Sanga on the shore of Lake Kisale, with numerous objects in ceramics, iron, copper, and ivory and items suggesting east African coastal trade. The industry reached its full development in the 10th–14th centuries. The funerary practices indicate the beginning of a hierarchical society in central Africa.

Kisapostag: An Early to Middle Bronze Age culture of western Hungary and Slovenia typologically contemporaneous with the late Unetice and Hatvan cultures. This Danube Valley culture dates to the early 2nd millennium BC, with a number of cemeteries in which inurned cremation is the characteristic rite. Kisapostag arsenical copper work is relatively rich and has typological affinities with the Unetice metalwork of Bohemia.

Kisese: A number of sites with rock paintings in the Kondoa region of central Tanzania. There is a long sequence of Later Stone Age microlithic stone assemblages dating from 19,000 BP. The paintings are of animals and anthropomorphs.

Kish: An Early Dynastic city-state of ancient Sumer near Babylon, spread over a series of tells. Occupation began in the Jemdet Nasr period, succeeded by Early Dynastic levels containing the remains of a royal Sumerian palace. There are also Neo-Babylonian forts, temples, tombs, and a Parthian fort and buildings. Although the supremacy passed to Ur c. 2600 BC, Kish remained in occupation through to the Sassanian period in the early centuries AD. In the Early Dynastic levels, there are rich burials including cart burials similar to those at Ur and Susa. The importance of Kish is seen in texts where it was said to play a pivotal role in regional political affairs. The city may have been the center of a cultural tradition distinct from that farther south in Mesopotamia.

Kiskevély: Cave site near Budapest, Hungary, with Middle Palaeolithic tools of the Last Glacial Gravettian as well as Neolithic remains.

Kissonerga-Mosphilia: Chalcolithic settlements on Cyprus with circular stone structures from the mid-4th to mid-3rd millennia BC.

Kissonerga-Mylouthkia: Early Chalcolithic site in western Cyprus of the mid-4th millennium BC.

kitchen-garden agriculture: A kitchen garden in which plants (as vegetables or herbs) for use in the kitchen are cultivated. Cultivation of garden and tree crops in plots next to dwellings was important to the Maya. Clear areas near residential Maya mounds may be kitchen gardens.

kitchen midden: A mound or deposit that is formed from the accumulation of domestic refuse, including cooking and eating equipment, food, and garbage, Some of these mounds are of seashells left by some foodgathering peoples. The term was first used in Danish to describe the middens of the Ertebolle culture and is also used as an adjective for the people who create middens. In Scandinavia, there are many mounds of shellfish debris. (*syn.* midden; shell midden)

Kition: An important Late Cypriot settlement in southern Cyprus, first occupied in the 13th century BC. The copper trade supported it until it was destroyed c. 1200 BC, possibly by the Sea Peoples. In the 11th century BC, possibly because of an earthquake, it was abandoned but then recolonized by the Phoenicians about 800 BC. The colony was a dependency of the mother city, Tyre. The Phoenicians rebuilt two temples and stayed until 312 BC. (*syn.* Citium)

kiva: A specialized room or chamber, often semi- or completely underground, of the ancient southwestern U.S. pueblo villages, used for ceremonies or other community activities. They often contain benches and fire pits and are generally circular, sometimes rectangular. They were used primarily by men and were entered by a projecting ladder through an opening in the flat roof. The word means "old house" in Hopi, and the structure may have derived from circular pit houses of Basketmaker cultures, 100 BC–AD 700.

Kivik: A site in southern Sweden with one of the largest grave mounds in Scandinavia, c. 70 meters in diameter. The barrow covers a central cyst made of slabs with carvings on their inner faces. The designs include processional scenes, a chariot with rider, ships, horses, fish, axes, sun wheels, and human figures. The contents of the tomb were plundered at the time of discovery in 1748, but the carvings that remain are of Middle or Late Bronze Age style and may date to about the 12th century BC.

Kizilkaya: A mid- to late-6th millennium BC Neolithic culture of the Taurus Mountains above Antalya, in southern Turkey. The culture is known mostly for its pottery, which shows links both with that of Early Neolithic Çatal Hüyük and that of Late Neolithic Hacilar; it may fit chronologically between the two.

Klasies River Mouth: A complex of caves and overhangs on the south coast of South Africa (Cape Province). It provides one of the most complete sequences available for the area, including sea-level changes of the Late Pleistocene— for at least the last 60,000 years. A long development of the "Middle Stone Age" shares some features with the Pietersburg industries and is interrupted by a phase attributed to Howiesons Poort. This is followed by Later Stone Age deposits containing three painted stone slabs and burials with shell beads dating to 5,000 years ago. The site has some of the oldest-known remains of anatomically modern *Homo* *sapiens*, dating to 100,000 years ago. There are indications of cannibalism in the Late Pleistocene and exploitation of the marine resources around 120,000 years ago.

Klein Aspergle: The site of a rich Celtic burial of the early La Tène period in Ludwigsburg, Württemberg, Germany. Funerary offerings included an Etruscan bronze vessel, a native copy of an Etruscan beaked flagon, gold mounts for a pair of drinking horns, and two imported Attic cups dated around 450 BC. In the same village is a slightly earlier tumulus burial, of the late Hallstatt D period, with imported ivories (including a sphinx) as well as bronzes.

Klepsydra/klepsydra: A spring on the northwest slope of the Akropolis of Athens. It is also the name of a Greek water clock with one basin draining into a second basin at a lower level.

kleroterion: An ancient machine used to decide who would serve on a jury in courts of law. There are surviving examples, such as the one from the Agora at Athens. Different colored balls would drop when tickets were inserted; the color determined acceptance or rejection.

kline: A Greek couch with a headboard and sometimes a footboard, used for reclining during the symposium. Their placement in dining rooms is revealed on archaeological sites by the placement of entrance doors.

knapping: The working of stone by applying force to its surface—by percussion or pressure—to produce a tool. A knapper is one who manufactures stone artifacts, especially by chipping. This technique of striking flakes or blades from a hard, brittle rock, such as flint or obsidian, is done by means of short, sharp blows delivered with a hammer of stone, bone, or wood. Knapping was used to fashion stone tools and weapons, such as blades and arrowheads, in the Harappan culture of the Indus Valley and was also applied to making beads from agate and carnelian.

Kniegrotte: Upper Palaeolithic cave site on the Orla River of eastern Germany, radiocarbon dated to 13,582–10,175 bp. Artifacts include burins, borers, and harpoons from the late Magdalenian.

Knossos: A well-known palace site on the island of Crete, inhabited almost continuously from 6000 BC when the first Neolithic settlement was constructed. It was the location of the chief palace of the Minoans, near Herakleion at the center of the north coast of Crete. The Neolithic settlement was succeeded by an Early Minoan one, but little is known about this phase. The site was leveled for the palace at the beginning of the Middle Minoan period, c. 2000 BC. Around the palace were the main buildings, the throne room, reception halls, shrines, magazines, and the domestic quarter of at least three stories. Large banks of rooms of various types were arranged around a central courtyard, giving rise to the story of the labyrinth. Unlike the other Cretan palaces, Knossos

survived the violent eruption of Santorini/Thera c. 1450 BC, but came under new rulers, Mycenaeans. The palace was opulent, and the frescoes show the bull sports that took place in or near the palace, the courtiers who watched them, others in ceremonial procession carrying offerings, and the priest-king himself. Clay tablets with inscriptions in Linear A and B show the careful accounting that supported this show. From them, too, we learn that in the last phase of occupation the rulers of the palace were Greek. Knossos likely governed much of Crete. The palace site was finally destroyed probably c. 1375 BC, although Knossos remained prosperous and powerful, emerging as one of the foremost Greek city-states on Crete. (*syn.* Cnossus)

Knovíz culture: A Bronze Age urnfield culture of Bohemia, Thuringia, and Bavaria, following the decline of the Tumulus Bronze Age, c. 1400–900 BC. Except for the burial rite, the Knovíz culture is similar to that of the neighboring Milavce group. The Knovíz group is one of the exceptions to the normal urnfield rite in that inhumation is more frequent than cremation burial. Few large settlement sites are known, the bulk of material deriving from small farmsteads with pits and postholes and cemeteries. Hengiform monuments and horseshoe-shaped enclosures are occasionally associated with Knovíz pottery. The vessel form is the Etagengefass, with a large bulging body and a smaller bottomless pot fused on top of it to form the neck. (*syn.* Knovís)

Knowth: One of the largest Neolithic burial grounds on the River Boyne in County Meath, Ireland. It is a circular burial mound containing two passage graves entered from opposite sides. The first is a large but simple passage grave, with several decorated stones but no evidence of corbelling. The second tomb, also a passage grave, has a corbel-vaulted burial chamber with three niches. One of these contained a stone basin ornamented with grooves and circular designs, and there is further carving on the walls of the tomb itself. The central mound was surrounded by at least 15 smaller tombs, each under its own cairn, and these "satellite" tombs included both entrance graves and passage graves of cruciform plan. Knowth is one of the three principal elements of the Boyne Valley megalithic cemetery, dating from the 4th millennium BC. Knowth was later reoccupied in the early historic period when Souterrains were constructed in the mound. Excavations have also revealed the remains of the Early Christian royal center here, belonging to the Northern Brega known from the Irish annals.

Kobystan: The site of rock art in Azerbaijan on the eastern end of the Caucasus Mountains, Mesolithic and Neolithic, Bronze Age and medieval. Hunting-gathering peoples used a microlithic tool kit and eventually made pottery.

Kodak: Middle Palaeolithic site on the Dnepr River in the Ukraine with side scrapers, woolly mammoth, and reindeer.

Kodiak tradition: A culture centered on Kodiak Island and the adjacent mainland of southeast Alaska from 5000 BP. Polished slate was used for artifacts, and there were sea mammal, fish, and caribou hunting. It was later influenced by the Thule culture.

kodja: A type of flaked stone hatchet of southwest Australia, made with two stones hafted in a ball of resin on the end of a stick, known for 2,000–3,000 years. One stone is used for pounding, and the other is sharp for chopping.

Koenigswald, Gustav Heinrich Ralph von (1902–1982): A Dutch-German palaeoanthropologist who discovered hominid remains in Java at Ngandong and at Sangiran. At Sangiran were Pithecanthropus remains, assigned to the Homo genus by Koenigswald. He also found *Meganthropus palaeojavanicus* on Java. He discovered the first specimens of Gigantopithecus, a genus of large fossil ape, in Chinese drugstores, where they were known as "dragon's teeth."

Kofun: The name of the protohistoric tomb period of Japan, AD 300–710, and the type of tumulus used for the burials. Large tombs that were built were covered with artificial hillocks about 8 meters high, with burial chambers about 2 meters underneath the top surface. The burial chamber, enclosed with stones, contained coffins and various funerary offerings. The period when tombs of this kind were built in abundance was characterized by Haji ware and Sue ware. It is divided into Early, 4th century; Middle, 5th century; and Late, late 5th–7th centuries. The Kofun period falls between the Yayoi period and the fully historic Nara period and partially overlaps the Asuka and Hakuho periods of art historians. In their writings, the Kojiki and Nihon Shoki texts, the culture was explained. Early kofun were built by modifying natural hills, as were Late Yayoi burial mounds. Haji pottery, used throughout the Kofun period, is very similar to Yayoi pottery, and farmers lived in the same kinds of houses, using very similar tools. Technical advances over the Yayoi period include irrigation canals and dams. There were also silversmiths who made the ornaments deposited in kofun, and professional potters began making Sue pottery in the 5th century. Those in the fertile and well-protected Yamato Basin actively sought new technical and administrative skills on the continent, and thus artisans came to make new kinds of pottery, ornaments, and weapons. Yamato leaders gained control over much of Japan in the 7th century and moved the capital to Heijo in 710. The magnificent kofun tombs indicate that the Yamato court based in the Yamato area (the present Nara Prefecture) succeeded in bringing almost the whole of Japan under its control. (*syn.* Great Burial Period, Tumulus Period)

Koguryo: Protohistoric people of eastern Manchuria of the 4th century AD, related to the Puyo and known as horse riders and for their mural tombs.

Kojiki: The oldest extant comprehensive history of Japan, a chronicle compiled in AD 712 under the Ritsuryo state. The

effort to compile and edit legends and genealogies into a coherent account exemplifies the supremacy of the ruling Yamato house. Written in an old Japanese using the linguistically incompatible Chinese characters, the account begins with a creation myth and covers the events up to the early 7th century. Together with the Nihon Shoki, it provides protohistoric data for the Kofun period. (*syn.* Records of Ancient Matters)

Kok Charoen: A site in central Thailand, dating to the 2nd and 1st millennia BC, which yielded occupational remains and more than 60 burials furnished with pottery similar to that of Non Nok Tha. It is considered to be the largest Neolithic burial site so far discovered in Southeast Asia.

Kökénydomb: Neolithic settlement of the Tisza culture of Hungary. The rectangular houses were decorated with elaborate incised decoration. Clay pedestals, or altars, are among the ceramics.

Ko Kho Kao: Port on the west coast of Thailand with Middle Eastern glass and Chinese glazed stonewares from the late 8th and 9th centuries AD. It was probably linked by an overland route to Laem Pho.

Kokkinopilos: A series of Palaeolithic sites on the Louros River in northern Greece. There are artifacts dating to the early last glacial, Middle Palaeolithic artifacts including Levallois cores, side scrapers, and bifacial foliates. A surface collection of Mousterian types has also been found.

Kokorevo: Six Upper Palaeolithic sites on the Yenisei River in southern Siberia. Radiocarbon dates put Kokorevo I–IV between 15,900–12,940 bp. There are wedge-shaped microcores, microblades, side scrapers, and retouched blades. Level I is Kokorevo culture, II and III are Afontova culture. The Kokorevo culture is dated to c. 20,000–10,000 BP and included end scrapers.

Koldewey, Robert (1855–1925): German architect and archaeologist who worked in Anatolia, the eastern Mediterranean (Assus, Lesbos), and especially Mesopotamia. He excavated at Al Hiba, Fara, Assur, and Babylon, uncovering the Ishtar Gate, the temple of Marduk, a ziggurat, and palace of Nebuchadnezzar. He began digging on March 26, 1899, and continued to work there with little interruption for the next 18 years. He believed he had found the remains of the Hanging Gardens of Babylon, one of the Seven Wonders of the World, when he uncovered an arched structure with a well nearby. His work revealed the destroyed capital of Hammurabi, the capital of the Neo-Babylonian empire (7th–6th centuries BC), and remains from Seleucid-Parthian and Sassanian periods. This work marked the beginning of scientific archaeology in Near East. The results were published in Koldewey's book *The Excavation at Babylon* (1914) as well as in reports over the years.

Köln-Lindenthal: A settlement site of the Linear Pottery culture outside modern Cologne, Germany. Köln-Lindenthal is recognized as a typical Danubian site with seven widely separated phases of occupation covering the Danubian I and II periods. It was the site of one of the earliest attempts to uncover a settlement plan. Post structures were identified as longhouses made of mud plaster, but was unusual because of being encircled by a ditched enclosure.

Kolomiishchina: Settlement site of the Cucuteni-Tripolye culture in western Ukraine, dated to the late 4th to early 3rd millennia BC. The earlier of two occupations contains Tripolye B2 pottery associated with a small number of houses. In the second phase, a more formal circular village plan of some 25 houses is laid out. This village is dated to the earlier Bronze Age Tripolye C1 phase; the pottery in the houses shows affinities with the Corded Ware and Yamnaya styles.

Kolomoki: Large multimound site in southern Georgia, United States, which includes burial mounds and a platform mound from the latter half of the 1st century AD. It seems to have thrived in the period between the decline of the Woodland tradition and the emergence of the Mississippian. Elaborately worked funerary vessels and grave goods such as copper ornaments and shell beads attest to ceremonial burial practice. There are indications of a chiefdom organization.

Kolonna: Aegean island site of Aegina, occupied since the late 4th millennium BC. The Bronze Age settlement combined Helladic, Cycladic, and Minoan cultural traditions. The name of the site is derived from a single intact column of the 6th century BC temple of Apollo.

kom: A term generally referring to the mounds made up of the ruins of ancient settlements. Its meaning is similar to the Arabic word "tell," although the latter is more commonly applied to the higher settlement mounds of the Levant and Mesopotamia.

Kom Abu Billo: The site of a pharaonic and Greco-Roman town in the western Nile Delta. It derives its name from that of the snake goddess Renenutet, whose cult was celebrated in the area. An early Ptolemaic temple remains, dedicated to the goddess Hathor. (*syn.* Terenuthis)

Kom el-Hisn: The site of ancient Imu, in the western Nile Delta. (*syn.* ancient Imu)

Kommos: Minoan settlement on the southern coast of Crete, possibly the harbor town for the palace of Phaistos. In the 10th century BC, a temple was built on the ruins of the Minoan town.

Kom Ombo: The site of a unique double temple of the Ptolemaic and Roman periods, which is dedicated to Sebek (Suchos), the crocodile god, and to Horus, the falcon-headed god. Ombos was important for its strategic location, commanding both the Nile River and the routes from Nubia northward to the Nile River valley. The site dates from at least the 18th Dynasty (1550–1295 BC), and the ancient town was especially prosperous under the Hellenistic Ptolemaic Dynasty (304–30 BC), when it was the capital of the separate nome (province) of Ombos. There are also a number of Upper Palaeolithic sites with chronologically overlapping industries—the Sebekian, Silsillian, and Sebillian—from c. 15,000–9500 BC. This riverine plain had extensive exploitation of wild grasses during the period of 12,000–10,000 BC. (*syn.* ancient Ombos, Kawm Umbu)

Komornica culture: Early Mesolithic assemblages of the area between the Oder and Bug drainage systems in north-central Poland. It is contemporaneous with the Maglemosian culture of Denmark of the 7th–8th millennia BC.

Kongemose: Mesolithic culture of southern Scandinavia centered on the type site lake settlement of Kongemosen in Zealand. It dates to the late Boreal and early Atlantic, c. 5600–5000 bc, between the Maglemosian and Ertebolle. Artifacts include geometric art, large blades, axes, and bone points.

Königsaue: Middle Palaeolithic site near Halle, Germany, dating to the early glacial. There were side scrapers and small hand axes.

Kon-Tiki: A replica of a balsa raft constructed by Thor Heyerdahl in 1947 to test the hypothesis that South American Indians could have drifted into Polynesia. This was the type of raft used in the 16th century AD along the coasts of Ecuador and northern Peru. He sailed the raft from South America to the Tuamotu Archipelago to show that Indians could have reached Polynesia. Archaeological evidence, however, has shown that any contacts were only of a minor nature.

Koobi Fora: The site of important hominid finds and stone artifacts on the northeastern shore of Lake Turkana (formerly Lake Rudolf), in northern Kenya, dating between 2.5 and 1 million years ago. Fragmentary remains of more than 150 hominids, including *Australopithecus boisei*, *A. africanus*, and *Homo habilis* were found. At least two lineages seem to be represented in the period between 1 and 1.5 million years ago, *Homo erectus* and *Australopithecus robustus/boisei*. Earlier fossils may be of the *Homo habilis* type. Stone tools are found at several levels from the KBS tuff at about 1.8 million years ago up to some levels where axes appear in small quantities. The large-brained skull number 1470, dated to c. 2 million years ago, was found here. Richard Leakey worked at the site from 1969.

Koolan 2: Rock shelter in West Kimberley, western Australia, where marine resources were used in the Late Pleistocene and Early Holocene. With a radiocarbon date of 27,300 bp, it is the oldest coastal site in Australia.

Koonalda: Large limestone cave site beneath the Nullarbor Plain, south Australia, with radiocarbon dates of c. 20,000–

13,000 BC. Parietal art in the form of "finger" groves on soft limestone and scratches and engravings on harder rock have been dated by covering rock fall to at least 18,000 BC. They cover several thousand square feet, and it is possible that their significance lies in their placement at specific points in the cave. (*syn.* Koonalda Cave)

Koongine: Limestone cave in southeast south Australia, occupied from 9000 bp for 1,000–2,000 years. The stone assemblage gives an Early Holocene date for the Gambieran industry. It was reoccupied only within the last 1,000 years.

Koori: The name used by nontraditional Aboriginal people of southeast Australia for themselves. (*syn.* Koorie)

Kootwijk: A Migration period settlement in central Holland dating from between the later 7th–later 10th centuries. There was evidence of 45 post-built houses, 177 sunken huts, 14 animal sheds, and three grain silos. At its largest, Kootwijk probably had more than 15 farm units.

Koptos: Town site in Upper Egypt just below Luxor, at the entrance to the Wadi Hammamat (the road to the Red Sea), existing since early dynastic times. It was important for nearby gold and quartzite mines in the Eastern Desert, worked during the 1st and 2nd Dynasties, and as a starting point for expeditions to Punt. The town was associated with the god Min, whose temple ruins remain, and the goddess Isis, who, according to legend, found part of Osiris' body there. Destroyed in AD 292 by Diocletian, it later became a Christian community. This valley also served as the principal trade route between the Nile Valley and the Red Sea. (*syn.* Qift, ancient Kebet, Qebtu)

Korakou: Bronze Age site of Corinthia, Greece, which became the basis of the classification of Helladic pottery developed by Carl Blegen and Alan Wace. It is the type site for the Early Helladic II Korakou culture.

kore: A type of freestanding statue of a maiden—the female counterpart of the kouros, or standing youth—that appeared with the beginning of Greek monumental sculpture in about 660 BC and remained to the end of the Archaic period in about 500 BC. It evolved from a highly stylized form to a more naturalistic one. The statue was usually draped, carved from marble, and painted in its original form. These are often dedications in sanctuaries and some are found in funeral contexts. Important series were in the temple of Hera on Samos and on the Akropolis in Athens. (*syn.* pl. korai)

Korean periodization: Classification of the eras of Korea by archaeologists and historians. The major divisions following the Palaeolithic are Chulman, 7000–1000 BC; Bronze Age, 700 BC–AD; Iron Age, 400 BC–AD 300; Proto-Three Kingdoms, AD 0–300; Three Kingdoms, 300–668; United Silla, 668–935; Koryo, 935–1392; Yi, 1392–1910; Japanese Colonial, 1910–1945; and Modern, 1945–present.

Korman' IV: Palaeolithic and Mesolithic site on the Dnestr River in the Ukraine with 16 occupation levels. The Middle Palaeolithic levels seem to date to warm intervals during the last glacial. Upper Palaeolithic levels are radiocarbon dated to 30,000–10,000 bp.

Korolevo: Palaeolithic site on the Tisza River in the eastern Carpathian basin of the Ukraine with 13 layers, the lowest of which are dated to the late Lower Pleistocene, c. 730,000 BP. The artifacts and dating show Korolevo to be one of the oldest occupations and having one of the most important Palaeolithic cultural sequences in Europe.

Körös: Early Neolithic culture of southern Hungary, which belongs to the complex including Karanovo I, Cris, and Starcevo cultures. The Körös variant is distinguished by its footed vessels and relative lack of painted wares. It is believed to have been the precursor of the Linear Pottery culture that developed on the Hungarian Plain.

Korpach: Upper Palaeolithic site on the Prut River of Moldova, with its lowest layer dated to 25,250 bp. The assemblage has tools of the Middle and Upper Palaeolithic.

Korucu Tepe: Mound of the Altinova Plain of eastern Anatolia where 12 phases of occupation began with the Early Chalcolithic, c. 4500 BC. The Korucu sequence, which runs to the Early Iron Age c. 800 BC, is used for regional comparative chronology. There is some connection with the Halaf and Kura-Araxes cultures and a late Uruk connection.

Koryo Dynasty: Kingdom of Korea from AD 918–1392; the dynasty lasted from 935–1392. It turned to Buddhism in adversity, built many temples, and made exquisite celadon objects. Koryo's close cultural ties with China during the Sung period (960–1279) resulted in direct influences from the advanced Chinese urban culture. The peace of the realm was often disrupted by invaders from Manchuria, first Khitan, then Juchen, and finally the Mongols. In 1232, the Koryo court fled to Kanghwa Island off the west coast of Korea, leaving the country to Mongol devastation and control. The art of Koryo never again equaled its pre-Mongol achievements. It is from the name Koryo that the Western word Korea is derived.

Kosipe: The oldest site with human occupation in New Guinea, lying in the Papuan Highlands, and dating to c. 26,000 bp. The artifacts include waisted stone tools (axes) and tanged tools. Such tools continue to occur in other Highland sites (especially Kiowa) until about 3000 BC.

Kostenki: Group of 25 Upper Palaeolithic sites on the Don River in Russia. The most important are Kostenki I, XIV, VIII, XII, II, XI, and XVII. The Early Upper Palaeolithic occupations, associated with the remains of horse and other mammals, began by 25,000 bp. Other sites dated to c. 36,000–26,000 bp with assemblages assigned to the Strelets culture and Spitsyn culture. Other layers from c. 32,000–26,000 are of the Strelets and Gorodtsov cultures. The industries of 25,000–10,000 bp have mammoth-bone houses, hearths, and some portable art. Skeletons of Cro-Magnon type but mainly immature have been found at sites II, XIV, and XV. Kostenki I has produced more of the Venus figurines than any other site in Europe. (*syn.* Kostenki-Borshchevo)

Kostenki-Willendorf culture: Upper Palaeolithic culture of central Europe and the Russian plain dating to c. 30,000–20,000 bp. This culture is based on assemblages containing backed blades, shouldered points, and Venus figurines among the art objects. It is generally equated with the Eastern Gravettian industry.

Koster: A site of long occupation in west-central Illinois, known as one of the first multidisciplinary endeavors of new archaeology; the findings serve as a benchmark for defining the Archaic period in the Midwest. The site is unusual for its long stratigraphic sequence of Archaic and Woodland settlements, dating from c. 8700 bp to AD 1000. Hunter gatherers and, later, farmers, settled at this location on the Illinois River to exploit the fertile river bottom. The site served variously as a workshop for stone tools, as a deer-butchering camp, and possibly as the site for one of the earliest villages in North America. Stone-ground adzes, manos, and metates are dated c. 6400 BC. In later levels, there is evidence of increased hunting efficiency (the replacement of the atlatl by the bow and arrow) and of agriculture (squash and pumpkin), and possibly Mississippian association. The site also contributed to the methodology of excavation, including approaches to deeply buried sites and the use of flotation as a technique.

Kostolac: Eneolithic site in the Carpathian basin of Serbia and name of a culture considered a variant of the Baden culture.

Kostrzewski, Józef (1885–1969): Polish archaeologist who excavated at Biskupin and other important sites. He founded the department of archaeology at the University of Poznan.

Koszider: Three large hoards found at Dunapentele-Kosziderpadlá, on the Danube south of Budapest, Hungary. The contents were characteristic of an early phase of the Tumulus culture of the (Early) Bronze Age and serve to document the expansion of that culture (Romania, Czechoslovakia, Poland, Germany) c. 1400 BC. Similar hoards with ivy-leaf pendants, spiral anklets with rolled ends, shaft-hole battle axes decorated with spiral and geometric patterns, belt plates, flanged axes, plastaves, solid-hilted daggers, socketed axes, and tanged sickles have been found in east-central Europe from the Baltic to the Sea of Azov and mark the Koszider horizon throughout the region. (*syn.* Kosziderpadlás)

Kota Batu: The capital of the Muslim Sultanate of Brunei in northern Borneo, dating from the 10th–13th centuries AD.

There was a defended palace and sumptuous court and large quantities of imported Chinese and Thai pottery dating from about 1380–1580. The palace was on the bank of the Brunei River, and most of the town's inhabitants appear to have lived in pile dwellings built over the estuarine waters. It replaced Santybong as the major port by the 15th century.

Koto Tampan: Site in peninsular Malaysia with a pebble and flake industry dating to 31,000 BP in the Upper Palaeolithic. In northern Malaya, a large series of choppers and chopping tools made on quartzite pebbles and found in Middle Pleistocene tin-bearing gravels have been referred to collectively as the Tampanian, because they come from Kota Tampan in Perak.

Kot Diji: A tell site of the Indus Valley, east of Mohenjo-Daro in Pakistan, which has given its name to one of a group of pre-Harappan cultures in the area (variant of Nal-Amri). Radiocarbon dates suggest early 3rd millennium BC for the settlement, which was eventually destroyed and replaced by a settlement of the Indus civilization. The Kot-Dijian pottery was a thin pinkish ware decorated with horizontal black lines, perhaps related to that of the Zhob Valley. Comparable wares have been found in pre-Indus levels at Harappa and Kalibangan in Punjab.

Kotosh: Major Pre-Columbian ceremonial site in the north-central highlands of Peru, near Huánuco, coming into use during the Late Preceramic period and continuing until after the end of the Chavín culture during the Early Horizon, AD c. 1. It is known for its temple structures, the earliest of which have interior wall niches and mud-relief decorative friezes and date to the end of the Late Preceramic period (c. 2000–1800 BC). In the earliest levels (Mito) are remains of a platform on which stood the temple of the Crossed Hands. Stone tools, some similar to Laurichocha II and III, and other artifacts appropriate to an Archaic subsistence pattern also occur in this phase. The next (Wairajirca) period has a radiocarbon date of 2305 ± 110 BC and saw the introduction of the first pottery, a gray ware with incised designs and post-fired painting in red, white, or yellow. In the following (Kotosh) stage, there is evidence of maize cultivation, and the pottery, with grooved designs, graphite painting, and stirrup spouts, has Chavín-like features. Radiocarbon dates suggest that this period is centered on c. 1200 BC and was closely followed by a pure Chavín stage with the typical pottery and ornament. Next in sequence came levels (Sajarapatac and San Blas phases) with white-on-red pottery, and the uppermost strata (Hiqueras period) were characterized by red vessels, rare negative painting, and copper tools.

kotyle: A Greek drinking cup with two horizontal handles. (*syn.* skyphos)

Kouklia-Palaepaphos: Southern Cyprus site occupied from the 3rd millennium BC, which became a major center in the Late Cypriot period. It was settled by Greek colonists in the Mycenaean period. Besides the Evreti cemetery, there was an ashlar temple built c. 1200 BC for Aphrodite's cult. Palaepaphos was capital of one of the Cypriot kingdoms in 498 BC when it was attacked by the Persians. The Cinyrad Dynasty ruled Palaepaphos until its final conquest by Ptolemy I of Egypt (294 BC). (*syn.* Old Paphos, Palaipaphos)

Koumbi Saleh: Site north of Bamako, Mali, which may have been the capital of the ancient Ghana Empire in the 11th century. Ghana was a great trading empire that flourished in western Africa from the 9th through the 13th centuries. The city had a large urban settlement, two cemeteries, and a mosque. In its boundaries there were—as was the custom of the early kingdoms of the western Sudan—two cities, one of which was occupied by the king, the other by Muslim traders. The mosque's foundation was built in the 9th century AD. Ghana's power declined during the 11th century after nearly 20 years of attacks from the Almoravids, a Berber military and religious order from the Sahara, devoted to converting nonbelievers to Islam. (*syn.* Kumbi)

Kourion: One of the capitals of the six ancient Greek kingdoms on Cyprus, a small port in the southwest part of the island. It was overwhelmed by a great earthquake on 21 July, 365. Excavations at the village have revealed many details of the disaster. (*syn.* Curium)

kouros: A Greek statue of a youth or a standing nude male youth, of the Archaic period. The large stone figures began to appear in Greece about 615–590 BC. They were used as funerary markers or dedications in sanctuaries. They are usually larger than lifesize, made of marble, bronze, or alabaster, and could be painted. They are thought to have been influenced by Egyptian sculpture; the first appearance of such monumental stone figures seems to coincide with the reopening of Greek trade with Egypt c. 672 BC. The kouros remained a popular form of sculpture until about 460 BC. (*syn.* kore (female); plural kouroi)

Kouroukorokale: Rock shelter near Bamako in Mali, West Africa, containing a microlithic and harpoon industry. The crude stone industry was accompanied in the second phase by barbed bone harpoon heads. The site may indicate a westerly representative of the heterogeneous complex of harpoon-fishing adaptations, which is attested in the southern Sahara between the 8th–3rd millennia BC. Economy for the first phase was fishing, mollusks, and hunting; for the second it was mainly hunting and gathering.

Kow Swamp: Large cemetery site in Murray Valley, Victoria, southern Australia, dated to between 15,000–9000 bp. More than 40 crania and mandibles show marked robusticity of the frontofacial regions combined with more modern, but still thick-boned, posterior areas of the crania. There is evidence of artificial deformation. Kow Swamp stone tools consisted of a few small quartz flakes and bipolar cores, similar to finds of the same age at Green Gully. Kow Swamp had the largest single Late Pleistocene population in the world.

Krak des Chevaliers: The greatest fortress built by European crusaders in Syria and Palestine, one of the most notable surviving examples of medieval military architecture. Built at Qal'at al-Hisn, Syria, near the northern border of present-day Lebanon, Krak occupied the site of an earlier Muslim stronghold. It was built by the Knights of St. John (Hospitallers), who held it from 1142–1271, when it was captured by the Maluk sultan Baybars I. It has two concentric towered walls separated by a wide moat and could accommodate 2,000 men. It is one of the few crusader castles to have been systematically excavated and restored.

Kraków-Spadzista: Three Upper Palaeolithic sites in Kraków, Poland, including Eastern Gravettian artifacts from 23,040–20,600 bp and an Aurignacian assemblage.

Kraków-Zwierzyneic: Palaeolithic site in Kraków, Poland, including Middle Palaeolithic assemblages of the last interglacial and subsequent cooler periods. The Upper Palaeolithic assemblages of the Aurignacian date to the interstadial preceding the last glacial maximum.

Krapina Cave: Middle Palaeolithic site north of Zagreb, Croatia, dating to around the last interglacial. The industry was dominated by side scrapers. Over 650 skeletal fragments of archaic *Homo sapiens* have been found. These include the skeletal fossils of at least 13 adults and children and are estimated to derive from the early last glacial period, about 40,000 to 75,000 years ago. They are identified as being transitional from Neanderthal to modern man. The evidence suggests cannibalism or funerary ritual.

Krasnyj Yar: Upper Palaeolithic site in south-central Siberia, occupied from around the last glacial maximum of 25,000–14,000 bp. The artifacts include wedge-shaped microcores, microblades, points, and end scrapers.

krater: Ancient Greek vessel used for diluting wine with water. It usually stood on a tripod in the dining room, where wine was mixed. Kraters were made of metal or pottery and were often painted or elaborately ornamented. In Homer's *Iliad*, the prize offered by Achilles for the foot race at Patroclus' funeral games was a silver krater. The Greek historian Herodotus described many enormous and costly kraters dedicated at temples or used in religious ceremonies. Kraters are large, with a broad body and base and usually a wide mouth. They may have horizontal handles placed near the base or vertical handles rising from the shoulder. Among the many variations are the bell krater, confined to red-figure pottery, shaped like an inverted bell, with loop handles and a disk foot; the volute krater, with an egg-shaped body and handles that rise from the shoulder and curl in a volute (scroll-shaped form) well above the rim; the calyx krater, the shape of which spreads out like the cup or calyx of a flower; and the column krater, with columnar handles rising from the shoulder to a flat, projecting lip rim. Some were fitted with a strainer. (*syn.* crater; bell krater; volute krater; calyx krater; column krater)

Krefeld-Gellep: A large Roman and Frankish cemetery located on the lower Rhine in Germany. Among the 2,000 excavated burials in the cemetery, one grave of outstanding wealth dated to about AD 630 contained a gilded helmet, a sword inlaid with precious stones, three spears, a dagger, ax, and shield. There were other items of silver, gold, and bronze. The personal apparel included a garnet-inlaid purse and gold belt buckle and ring. The occupant may have been a chieftain or the founder of a settlement.

Kremikovci: Early Neolithic culture of the Balkans, on the Bulgarian border in Macedonia. It is contemporaneous with the Karanovo I culture of southern Bulgaria, Starcevo culture of Serbia and Bosnia, Körös culture of southern Hungary, and Cris culture of Romania. The ceramics are white-on-red or black-on-red painted decoration.

Kremlin: The fortified citadel of medieval Russia. The term also applies to those in medieval Slavic towns. The most famous and best preserved is the one in Moscow, which is a rare stone-built example. In it are a variety of palaces, churches, and state buildings in a range of styles spanning the 14th–18th centuries. Archaeological work has revealed that in 1156 Prince Dolgoruky built the first fortifications—ditches and earthen ramparts topped by a wooden wall with blockhouses. The origin of the word kremlin is disputed; some authorities suggest Greek words for "citadel" or "steepness," others, the early Russian word *krem*, meaning a conifer providing timber suitable for building. The fortified enclosure of the Kremlin was the symbol of first Russian and later Soviet power and authority. Its crenellated red brick walls and 20 towers were built at the end of the 15th century by Italian builders hired by Ivan III the Great.

Krems: An Upper Palaeolithic site on the Danube in northeast Austria, dating to around 35,200 bp. The Krems-Hundssteig locality has revealed a very rich Aurignacian-like assemblage in which numerous bladelets, end scrapers, retouched blades, and "Krems" points were found. A female figurine of green serpentine was dated to 31,790 bp. (*syn.* Krems-Hundssteig)

krepidoma: The term for the base or foundation of a Classical building, often stepped.

Krivodol group: Eneolithic regional culture of northwest Bulgaria, c. 3000–2800 BC, with a settlement at Zaminets.

Kroeber, Alfred Louis (1876–1960): American anthropologist who made great contributions to American Indian ethnology; to the archaeology of New Mexico, Mexico, and Peru; and to the study of linguistics, folklore, kinship, and social structure. He was one of the small group of scholars whose work laid the basis of New World archaeology as a scientific discipline. His first work was in preparing a typological seriation of potsherds from Zuñi sites of the American Southwest, and his work, together with that of Kidder and Nelson in the same area, showed how archaeological methods could reveal time depth and cultural change in North America. From 1921, Kroeber applied the same techniques to Max Uhle's Peruvian collections. He worked out a scheme for Peruvian archaeology, which formed the basis of all studies of the subject for the next 20 years. Kroeber explored much of the Peruvian coast, especially the Nasca Valley, where he made the first-ever stratigraphic excavation of a Peruvian midden. Kroeber continued to write about the ethnology of North American Indians and also concentrated on theoretical aspects of anthropology, in particular the processes of culture change. His *Configurations of Culture Growth* (1945) sought to trace the growth and decline of all of civilized man's thought and art. *The Nature of Culture* (1952) was a collection of Kroeber's essays published on such topics as cultural theory, kinship, social psychology, and psychoanalysis.

Kromdraai: Plio-Pleistocene cave site in Transvaal, South Africa, where the first robust Australopithecine was found in 1938. It is one of three neighboring South African sites (Sterkfontein, Swartkrans) where important fossil hominid remains have been found.

krotovina: A soil feature made up of an animal burrow filled with soil or sediment. That soil or sediment is often different from the material around the burrow and is derived from overlying soil horizons or sediment strata.

Krzemionki: Middle and Late Neolithic flint mine of the Holy Cross Mountains of central Poland. It was used by the Funnel Beaker and Globular Amphora cultures.

kshemenitsa: A term for a dense scatter of flint artifacts and debitage on a Late Palaeolithic or Mesolithic site in Eastern Europe, indicating a flint-working site.

Kuala Selinsing: A coastal site in northern Perak, peninsular Malaysia, which has produced remains of pile dwellings probably built over a mangrove swamp, burials in canoe-like coffins, pottery similar to Pontian, Indian seals, Chinese stonewares, and remains of a bead industry from the 1st millennium AD. The site may have been a small trade station between AD 600–1100. (*syn.* Tanjong Rawa)

Kuan ware: Fine Chinese stoneware of the Sung Dynasty, AD 960–1279, characterized by a wash of brown slip and by glazes varying from pale green to lavender blue. A wide-meshed crackle is brought out by the application of brown pigment. First made in North China, Kuan ware was produced from about 1127 at Hang-chou, Chekiang province, in the south. (*syn.* Guan)

Kuban culture: A regional variant of the earlier Bronze Age "North Caucasian" culture group, located in the Kuban Valley of southwestern Russia, dated to the mid-2nd millennium BC. It was also the name of an industrial complex of the late Bronze Age to early Iron Age, dated to the early 1st millennium BC, in the same area. That culture was distinguished by rich kurgan graves, use of the battle ax, and a range of metal objects including the "Pontiac" hammerheaded pin. The heavy concentration of Caucasian bronzes in the amber source zone of east Prussia indicates an extensive amber trade. (*syn.* Koban culture)

Ku Bua: Settlement of the Dvaravati period in south-central Thailand near the mouth of the Mae Klong River. Remains of Dvaravati architecture include stupa bases at Ku Bua, some of which have elephants supporting their bases, following a pattern that originated in Ceylon. A moat dates to the Khmer period, AD c. 1000.

Kudaro: Two cave sites in the Greater Caucasus Mountains of Georgia with Acheulian layers associated with Middle Pleistocene vertebrates and bifaces, choppers, and side scrapers. Some Middle Palaeolithic artifacts are associated with Late Pleistocene vertebrates and points and side scrapers. There are also late Upper Palaeolithic and Mesolithic remains.

kudurru: An Akkadian term meaning "frontier," or "boundary," for a type of boundary stone used by the Kassites of Mesopotamia. It was a stone block or slab that served as a record of a grant of land made by the king to a favored person. The original kudurrus were kept in temples, while clay copies were given to the landowners. On the stone were engraved the clauses of the contract, the images of symbols of the gods under whose protection the gift was placed, and the curse on those who violated the rights conferred. The kudurrus are important not only for economic and religious reasons but also as almost the only works of art surviving from the period of Kassite rule in Babylonia, c. 16th–12th centuries BC. The word also means "son," as in personal names such as Nabu-kudurri-usur (Nebuchadnezzar). The term also applies to the 3rd millennium cuneiform documents in southern Mesopotamia that record land transfers.

Kufa: Before the founding of Baghdad, one of the largest and most important towns in Iraq. It was founded as a garrison by the caliph Omar I in 638. In 749, it served briefly as the capital of the Abbasids, before they founded Baghdad. Kufa became a large commercial and intellectual center, but a series of incursions by the Qarmathians caused extensive damage, and by the 14th century it was almost deserted. The mosque, built in 670, was a stone structure with columns 15 meters high supporting the roof without the use of arches.

Kufr Nigm: Cemetery site of the Archaic period in the eastern Nile Delta of Egypt. There are ceramic jars incised with the name of Narmer.

Kujavish grave: A distinctive type of grave of central Poland during the middle part of the local Neolithic/TRB culture. Each tomb consists of a triangular or trapeze-shaped mound, which covers a single flat grave containing an extended inhumation burial. The chamber or a trench was usually stone built, covered by long trapezoidal barrows, and sometimes surrounded by a stone curb. Very few of these tombs had more than one burial. (*syn.* Kujavian grave)

Kuk: A site complex in the New Guinea Highlands, near Mount Hangen, which has produced several systems of swamp-drainage ditches, going back to about 7000 BC. A drain and evidence of clearance took place then, and a sequence of field systems was made from about 6000 bp to the present. The findings have great significance because they appear to document a totally independent origin of horticulture in the New Guinea Highlands, quite separate from any Austronesian influence. There is also a 30,000-year-old hearth.

Kukuba: The oldest known limestone shelter in lowland New Guinea, dating to c. 4000 bp.

Kulèn: An administrative capital established in 802 by Jayavarman II, the founder of the Angkor kingdom. It was a rather unsuitable place for a capital, but it was a mountain, and the peoples of Southeast Asia have always believed that gods and spirits dwell on mountaintops. The site may have been chosen so that he could claim the title of "King of the Mountain" (i.e., universal ruler), which seems to have been that of the kings of Funan before him. There are the ruins of several monuments on this hill, and it also served as a quarry for the sandstone used in a number of monuments of Angkor, notably Angkor Wat. (*syn.* Phnom Kulèn, Mahendraparvata)

kula ring: A system of ceremonial, noncompetitive, exchange practiced in Melanesia to establish and reinforce alliances. This exchange system began among the people of the Trobriand Islands of southeast Melanesia, in which permanent contractual partners traded traditional valuables by following an established ceremonial pattern and trade route. In this system, described by the British anthropologist Bronislaw Malinowski, only two kinds of articles, traveling in opposite directions around a rough geographical "ring" several hundred miles in circumference, were exchanged. These were red shell necklaces and white shell bracelets. Kula objects, which sometimes had names and histories attached, were not owned to be used but rather to acquire prestige and rank. Malinowski's study of this system was influential in shaping the anthropological concept of reciprocal exchange.

The partnerships between men, involving mutual duties and obligations, were permanent and lifelong. The network of relationships based on the kula served to link many tribes by providing allies and communication of material and non-material cultural elements to distant areas.

Kulichivka: Upper Palaeolithic site near Kremenets, western Ukraine, the lowest level dating to the interstadial before the last glacial maximum, with tools of the Middle and Upper Palaeolithic. The Upper Palaeolithic level dates to 25,000–10,000 bp.

Kulli: An important Chalcolithic culture and pottery style of south Baluchistan. The pottery is mainly buff and wheel-made, painted in black with friezes of elongated humped bulls, cats, or goats and spiky trees between zones of geometric ornament. Clay figurines of women and bulls are found in this culture, as are copper tools and ornaments of lapis lzauli, bone, and other materials. The culture is further distinguished from those of Amri-Nal in the same area by the practice of cremation burial; an important cemetery was excavated at Mehi. Mud-brick architecture and small tell sites are common to the two cultures. There are signs of Indus civilization influence on later Kulli material with carved stone vessels identical with examples from Early Dynastic Mesopotamia, dating to the early 3rd millennium BC.

Kulna Cave: Cave site in Moravia, Czechoslovakia, with lower levels of the last interglacial and early glacial with a Middle Palaeolithic industry. The Middle Palaeolithic industry probably dates to the early last glacial. There are also Late Upper Palaeolithic/Magdalenian, Neolithic, Iron Age, and newer remains.

Kulp'o-ri: Middle Palaeolithic site in North Hamgyong, Korea, with the first evidence of Palaeolithic dwellings in Korea.

Kültepe: A tell site in Cappadocia, central Turkey (Anatolia), a center of the Assyrian merchant colony, or *karum*, of Kanesh (Kanish). It was a Bronze Age city at which a colony of Assyrian merchants set up the trading organization, the karum, to control and foster the trade, especially of metals, between Anatolia and Mesopotamia. It is the best documented of these sites, with correspondence written in Assyrian cuneiform on clay tablets and constituting the oldest surviving records from Turkey. Nearly 15,000 cuneiform tablets, known as "Cappadocian," relate day-to-day activities and business transactions. Supplemented by the evidence from the houses and burials revealed by excavation, the tablets throw invaluable light on the country immediately before the rise of the Hittites. The karum was destroyed by fire in the early 1st millennium BC, and the trading colony ceased to exist. Excavations in the karum have revealed houses, separated by streets and alleys, and workshops, which suggest that it was also important as an industrial center for metalworking. The associated city had a double fortification and enclosed a palace complex and other public buildings, including temples. (*syn.* ancient Kanesh)

Kulupuari: Site on the Kikori River, Gulf Province, Papua New Guinea, with the earliest evidence of sago palm exploitation and coastal trading before 1300 bp.

Kumadzulo: An Early Iron Age village site near Victoria Falls, southern Zambia, dated between the 5th–7th centuries AD. Kumadzulo has preserved the remains of several rectangular pole and clay houses of unusually small size. There was herding of domestic animals, and the presence of grindstones and iron hoes indicates that food crops were cultivated.

Kumbi: A site in Ghana whose extensive ruins have been identified as the capital of the 11th century. Excavations have revealed the presence of a stone-built mosque and two-story houses with storerooms. Pottery and glass indicate trans-Saharan trade with North Africa. It was the last of the capitals of ancient Ghana, a great trading empire that flourished in western Africa from the 9th through the 13th centuries. At the height of its prosperity, before 1240, it was the greatest city of western Africa with a population of more than 15,000. In its boundaries there were—as was the custom of the early kingdoms of the western Sudan—two cities, one of which was occupied by the king, the other by Muslim traders. (*syn.* Koumbi Saleh, Kumbi Saleh)

Kumtepe: A site in northwestern Turkey, overlooking the Dardanelles, close to Troy. Excavations have demonstrated three phases of Early Bronze Age occupation, all earlier than the first settlement at Troy, and probably dating to the earlier 4th millennium BC.

Kunda culture: The eastern Baltic variant of the Baltic Boreal and Atlantic climatic periods, c. 7000–5000 BC, a Mesolithic culture named after the site of Kunda-Lammasmagi in Estonia. Most Kunda settlements are located at the edge of the forest, near rivers, lakes, and marshes. There was hunting of elk and seal and fishing. Bone and antler tools were decorated with simple geometric motifs. The Kunda culture was followed by the Narva culture, with the appearance of pottery and food production.

Kuntur Wasi: A site near Cajamarca in the northern highlands of Peru, of the Chavín culture of the Early Horizon period c. 800 BC. The central structure was a stone-faced, triple-terraced pyramid, surmounted by a temple or temples. Three-dimensional statues and other carved stone are executed in the Chavín style with the characteristic feline motif common. Other associated features, however, such as ceramics, appear to be a mixture of Chavín and later styles, suggesting that the site may extend beyond the Early Horizon. (*syn.* La Copa)

Kura-Araxes culture: Culture complex of Early Bronze Age sites of Transcaucasia, eastern Anatolia, and northwest Iran, probably of the later 4th through later 3rd millennia BC. The complex is characterized by black or red highly burnished pottery. There were portable hearths and some circular houses. (*syn.* Eastern Anatolian Bronze Age, Transcaucasian Early Bronze Age)

kurgan: The Russian word for a burial mound (barrow or tumulus) covering a pit grave, mortuary house, or catacomb grave. It is mainly connected with Eneolithic and Bronze Age burial practices. The earliest kurgans appeared during the 4th millennium BC among the Copper Age peoples of the Caucasus and soon afterward in the south Russian steppe and the Ukraine. Shortly after 3200 BC, the kurgan cultures began influencing most of east, central, and northern Europe. The local Late Neolithic and Copper Age communities adopted such new traits as globular amphora vessels, corded ware, asymmetrical stone battle axes, domesticated horses, and burial of a single body (often sprinkled with ocher) in a pit or mortuary house, covered by a barrow. After c. 2500 BC, several regional kurgan-derived cultures can be recognized. In Russia, the kurgan tradition persisted late and was still practiced by the historical Scythians and Sarmatians of the steppe zone. Three forms of kurgan burial can be identified: Yamnaya (pit-grave) burial, dated c. 2400–1800 BC; Katakombnaja (catacomb-grave) burial, dated c. 2300–1800 BC; and Srubnaya (timber grave) burial, dated c. 1600–900 BC.

Kurgan cultures: A seminomadic pastoralist culture that spread from the Russian steppes to Danubian Europe about 3500 BC. By about 2300 BC, the kurgan people arrived in the Aegean and Adriatic regions. They buried their dead in deep shafts in artificial burial mounds, or barrows. The word *kurgan* means "barrow," or "artificial mound," in Turkic and Russian. The first kurgan culture was the Yamnaya, or Pit-Grave, culture. Then came the Catacomb Grave culture, and finally the Srubnaya (Timber-Grave) culture.

Kurgus: Site in Nubia where Thutmose I (c. 1493–1482 BC) and Thutmose III (1479–1426 BC) both carved inscriptions on boulders marking the southern frontier of Egypt. After Thutmose I destroyed the Karmah state, he inscribed a rock as a boundary marker, later confirmed by Thutmose III, near Kanisa-Kurgus, north of the fifth cataract. He then executed a brilliant campaign into Syria and across the Euphrates, where he erected a victory stela near Carchemish. (*syn.* Kanisa-Kurgus; Kanisa Kurgus)

Kurru, el-: A site in Upper Nubia with a royal necropolis of the Napatan period, c. late 9th–mid-7th centuries BC. The site was first used from c. 1000 BC onward for the tumulus burials of the rulers of the kingdom of Kush (Kerma culture). These were replaced by steep-sided pyramids after the conquest of Egypt by the Napatan kings. (*syn.* Kurru)

Kurtén, Björn (1924–1988): Finnish palaeontologist who studied Pleistocene mammals of the Holarctic, contributing to our knowledge of their environments and of human palaeoecology.

Kush: An Egyptian term for Upper Nubia and the independent states of the region during periods of Egyptian weakness. It is the name applied to the area that during and after the pharaonic period, was subject to Egyptian cultural and/or political influence. Kush's main period of independence began c. 9th century BC. In the 8th century, the kings of Kush conquered Egypt and ruled briefly there as the 25th Dynasty, being expelled southward after the Assyrian invasion of Egypt in 671 BC. In their homeland, the Kushites' capital was established first at Napata near the fourth Nile cataract, then moved to Meroe about 600 BC. There the capital was better situated to exploit trade routes eastward to the Red Sea and Ethiopia as well as those of the Nile Valley. Timber was also more plentiful and was used to fuel the Meroitic iron industry, which probably began on a small scale in about the 6th century BC. The kingdom of Kush survived until AD 350, when the final collapse of Meroe was probably due to an invasion from Axum (Aksum). (*syn.* Cush)

Kushan: A ruling line descended from the Yüeh-chih, a people that ruled over most of the northern Indian subcontinent, Afghanistan, and parts of Central Asia during the first 3 centuries of the Christian era. It began as a nomadic tribe in the 2nd century BC. Under Kaniska I (fl. 1st century AD) and his successors, the Kushan kingdom reached its height. It was considered one of the four great Eurasian powers of its time (the others being China, Rome, and Parthia). The Kushans were instrumental in spreading Buddhism in Central Asia and China and in developing Mahayana Buddhism and the Gandhara and Mathura schools of art. The Kushans became affluent through trade, particularly with Rome. After the rise of the Sasanian dynasty in Iran and of local powers in northern India, Kushan rule declined. (*syn.* Kusana)

Kutama: Early to Late Iron Age tradition of southern Africa during the late 1st millennium AD. It includes the Gumanye, Harare, K2, Leopard's Kopje, Mambo, Mapungubwe, and Woolandale pottery groups.

Kutei: Region of eastern Borneo that has yielded several 5th century AD Sanskrit inscriptions that resemble Hindu. It was written for local rulers and on 9th–10th century statuary similar to that of Java.

Kutikina: Limestone cave of southwest Tasmania occupied from 20,000–15,000 years ago. It established the Pleistocene occupation of the area. (*syn.* Fraser Cave)

Kuyavian long barrow: Earthen long barrows of the Funnel Beaker culture in northern Poland from c. 3000 BC. They are usually surrounded by a curb of large boulders and are sometimes megalithic. They have a trapezoidal plan, normally have single primary burials, and are related to the Hunebeds of northern Germany and Holland.

Kwale: Site in southeast Kenya that has given its name to the Early Iron Age industry of that area and northern Tanzania. It was a branch of the Eastern Stream or Urewe tradition of the Chifumbaze Early Iron Age complex, starting in the 2nd century AD. The highly characteristic pottery, Kwale ware, occurs far down the east African coast in Mozambique and eastern Transvaal, where it is dated to the 4th century AD.

kyathos: A Greek or Etruscan dipper of silver, bronze, or clay, which consists of a small bowl at the end of a long handle.

kylix: A Greek stemmed drinking cup or chalice, usually made of clay or metal. The term was originally used for a cup of any form, but modern scholars restrict it to shallow two-handed stemmed forms. This wide-bowled drinking cup with horizontal handles was one of the most popular pottery forms from Mycenaean times through the classical Athenian period. There was usually a painted frieze around the outer surface, depicting a subject from mythology or everyday life, and on the bottom of the inside a painting often depicting a dancing or drinking scene. (*syn.* cylix)

Ll

La Adam cave: Mesolithic cave site on the coast of the Black Sea in Romania.

Laang Spean: Cave site in western Cambodia, occupied between c. 7000–500 BC, which has yielded a Hoabinhian sequence with an appearance of ground stone tools and pottery by perhaps 4300 BC. Succeeding layers contain more elaborate pottery and flaked stone tools.

Labastide: Magdalenian cave in Hautes-Pyrénées, France, with many engraved figures and a large polychrome horse painting. There are hearths and engraved stones in the cave, which is dated to 12,310 BC.

labret: A lip plug or ornament inserted in an incision in the lower lip, often made of shell, bone, ivory, metal, stone, wood, or pottery. Sometimes a succession is worn, each larger than the predecessor. Labrets indicated the eminence of the wearer, for instance, women of high rank of the northwest coast of North America. Although styles vary and labrets were particularly popular in Mesoamerica, they occur in artifact inventories from the Arctic to the Andes. (*syn.* labrum)

labyrinth: A building of considerable size, usually underground, containing streets and crossroads, like the catacombs. It was the name given by the ancient Greeks and Romans to buildings, entirely or partly subterranean, containing a number of chambers and passages that rendered egress difficult. Later, especially from the European Renaissance onward, the labyrinth or maze occurred in formal gardens, consisting of intricate paths separated by high hedges. (*syn.* maze)

La Chapelle: Mousterian cave site in Corrèze, southwest France. In 1908, a skeleton of Neanderthal man was found buried in a level of Mousterian (Quina) type. The La Chapelle man was deformed pathologically by chronic osteoarthritis and other degenerations often found with old age today. Middle Palaeolithic stone tools were also found. (*syn.* La Chapelle-aux-Saints)

La Chaussée-Tirancourt: Late Neolithic allée couverte (gallery grave) of c. 2900 BC in Somme, France. It was used until c. 2000 BC, and remains of over 350 people have been preserved.

Lachish: Palestinian Biblical site, a Chalcolithic and Early Bronze Age cave dwelling, after which the caves were used for burials and a settlement founded. A massive plastered glacis of Hyskos type belonged to the Middle Bronze Age settlement, but was destroyed by the Egyptians c. 1580 BC. The Canaanites built three successive temples in the 15th–13th centuries BC. Lachish was sacked in 701 BC by the Assyrians, noted in the palace reliefs in Nineveh. It fell to the Babylonians in 588 BC. There were later levels of Achaemenid and Hellenistic date. The site is most famous for three vital groups of inscriptions, including a dagger dated to the 18th or 17th century BC with four symbols engraved on it—one of the earliest alphabetic inscriptions known. Lachish has also produced a group of incised pottery vessels associated with the temple at the foot of the mound and dated to c. 1400 BC, and a group of incised potsherds found in a guardhouse by the gate and dating to the period immediately before the Babylonian destruction. (*syn.* Tell Duweir, Tell ed-Duweir)

Laconian pottery: Spartan pottery made in the 6th century BC, characterized as black figured and black glossed. The fabric was widely exported—to Cyrenaica, Etruria, and the Greek colonies in Italy.

La Cotte de Saint-Brelade: Cave site on Jersey in the Channel Islands, with prehistoric remains of Palaeolithic man, and there is abundant evidence of the Neolithic and Bronze ages. There are Acheulian bifaces, Mousterian artifacts, and Neanderthal teeth. Jersey was linked to the continent in times of low sea level.

lacquer: The resin of the sumac tree, used as a coating to harden and strengthen manufactured items. This varnishing substance was used from prehistoric times and was indigenous to southern and central China. Applied in many coats to a core made of wood, fabric, paper, baskets, leather, ceramics, and so on, it forms a tough and durable protective surface, resistant to water and capable of a high polish. In China, lacquered vessels were made as early as the Shang Dynasty. Lacquer is often colored red or black. (*syn.* lacquer ware)

Laem Pho: Port city in Thailand with Middle Eastern glass vessel and Chinese glazed stoneware artifacts from the late 8th and 9th centuries AD. It may have been linked by an overland trade route to Ko Kho Kao.

laeti: A term used for a class of non-Roman cultivators under the later Roman Empire (3rd century AD onward), who occupied lands for which they paid tribute. These barbarians were settled as farmers by the Roman government, in areas deserted after intrusive raids. They also had an obligation, inherited by their descendants, to perform Roman military service. (*related word* adj. laetic)

Laetoli: A site just south of Olduvai in northern Tanzania where Australopithecine fossils have been found dating to about 4–3.5-million years ago. The fossils are attributed to *Australopithecus afarensis* or *A. africanus*. Of particular interest are 3.8-million-year-old lines of footprints left in muddy ash, apparently by a family of these creatures, found in 1978 by Mary Leakey. The site is part of the same group of Pleistocene and Pliocene deposits as the Olduvai Gorge site. In the upper Ngaloba beds, stone tools have been recovered that have been attributed to the African Middle Stone Age cultural complex, and they resemble tools recovered from the upper Ndutu beds at nearby Olduvai Gorge. (*syn.* formerly Laetolil)

La Ferrassie: A rock shelter in the Dordogne, southwest France, with Middle Palaeolithic material and burials of several Neanderthal. Occupation began in the Mousterian period, to which belong two Neanderthal adults and five children, buried in shallow trenches. There are several layers of "Ferrassie," a subdivision of the Charentian Mousterian tradition, with Levallois flaking. There is a long series of Upper Palaeolithic levels, including Châtelperonian, Aurignacian, and finally a thin Gravettian level. The stratification has contributed to an understanding of the Upper Palaeolithic sequence in France.

La Florida: The name given by Spanish explorer Ponce de León to the land he discovered in the Easter season (Pascua Florida = Feast of Flowers) in 1513. The Spanish used the term to refer to the land they claimed in the North American Southeast.

La Galgada: Late Preceramic and early Initial period site in the northern highlands of Peru, similar to Kotosh with a series of temple structures. Temple structures were filled, sometimes used as tombs, and covered before the construction of subsequent temples. The latest ceremonial structures are in U-shaped configurations.

Laga Oda: A rock shelter near Harar in southeastern Ethiopia, with occupation beginning around the 14th millennium BC. The industry of small blades and numerous backed elements continued into the 2nd millennium AD. The site also contains rock paintings depicting humans, cattle, and fat-tailed sheep.

Lagash: One of the most important capital cities of ancient Sumer, located midway between the Tigris and Euphrates Rivers in southeast Iraq. The city was founded in the prehistoric Ubaid period, c. 5200–3500 BC and was still occupied as late as the Parthian era, 247 BC–AD 224. In the Early Dynastic period, the stele of the Vultures was erected to celebrate the victory of King Eannatum over the neighboring state of Umma. Control of Lagash fell to Sargon of Akkad (reigned c. 2334–2279 BC). Lagash revived about 150 years later, prospering under Gudea, although the city-state was nominally subject to the Guti, a people who controlled much of Babylonia from about 2230–2130. Lagash was endowed with many temples, including the Eninnu, "House of the Fifty," a seat of the high god Enlil. French excavators found at least 50,000 cuneiform texts, which have proved one of the major sources for knowledge of Sumer in the 3rd millennium BC. Dedicatory inscriptions on stone and on bricks also have provided the chronological development of Sumerian art. The ancient name of the mound of Telloh was actually Girsu, while Lagash originally denoted a site southeast of Girsu, later becoming the name of the whole district and also of Girsu itself. The site continued into Old Babylonian times, although after its absorption into the Ur III state, it declined in importance. (*syn.* Al Hiba, modern Telloh)

lagena: A Greek or Roman earthenware vessel with a globular body, used for holding wine, vegetables, or fruit.

Lagoa Santa caves: A system of caves in Minas Gerais, Brazil, occupied from the late Pleistocene, with human remains, stone tools, and remains of extinct mastodon and sloth. Dated to 15,300 bp is an industry of quartz flakes. The Cerca Grande complex of 10,000–8000 bp had small rock-crystal flakes, axes, bone projectile points, hammer stones, and a cemetery of 50 flexed inhumations. There are hundreds of rock paintings from the Planalto tradition of 7000–3000 bp.

La Gorge-Meillet: Rich Iron Age chariot burial of the Marnian culture, Marne, France. The body of a youth was accompanied by a sword, bronze helmet, gold items, spearheads, wheelmade pottery vessels, and an Etruscan bronze flagon. It is dated to La Tène c. 475–450 BC.

Lagozza: Late Neolithic lake village settlement in Lombardy, Italy, dated to c. 3600 BC. Remains of wooden pile dwellings exist in the type site of the Lagozza culture, characterized by finely made black-burnished carinated bowls. Decoration is rare, consisting of radiating lines on the lower walls or scratched cross-hatched triangles. Instead of proper handles, simple and multiple perforated lugs were used, including the flûte de pan. The culture is related to, and possibly derived from, Chassey (France) and Cortaillod (Switzerland). Spindle whorls and loom weights show textile production. The culture was established in the north and spread slowly down the Adriatic side of Italy to the Marche and Ripoli in the Late Neolithic and to Ariano by the Copper Age, surviving there to give rise to the Apennine culture of the Bronze Age. Copper axes are among the earliest copper items of northern Italy. (*syn.* Lagozza di Besnate)

lagynos: Greek or Roman jug with a low, squat body, vertical neck, rounded mouth, and single strap handle.

Lahun, el-/al-: An Egyptian site at the entrance to the Faiyum (Fayyum), important in the Middle Kingdom (c. 1938–1600 BC). There is the pyramid of Senwosret (Senusret/Sesostris) II (1880–1874 BC) and the burial of Princess Sat-Hathor-Iunet with rich grave goods. The pyramid was unusual in that the entrance to the burial chamber was not on the north side of the pyramid but on the south. The pyramid was robbed in antiquity but a treasure of jewelry was discovered in the tomb of the princess, located within the pyramid-enclosure wall. Technically and artistically, the collection rivals all other Middle Kingdom objects of its type. Hieratic papyri dealing with a variety of subjects have been recovered at the site. Excavation of the village and necropolis, which was also inhabited during the Second Intermediate Period (c. 1630–1540 BC), revealed a remarkable degree of town planning. (*syn.* Illahun; Kahun)

Lake Arumpo: Large dry lake bed, formerly a Pleistocene lake, in western New South Wales, Australia. A radiocarbon date of 33,600 BC has been determined for an occupation layer containing shells and charcoal fragments.

Lake Besaka: A series of sites in southeastern Ethiopia where, in the mid-2nd millennium BC, local stone industries made a variety of scrapers. Stone bowls, akin to those of the East African Pastoral Neolithic sites far to the south, also occur.

Lake Condah: Complex of stone structures in southwest Victoria, Australia, including fish traps and huts, postdating the Late Pleistocene c. 4000 bp. Fish-trap systems characterize the Holocene and may have been part of ceremonial gatherings.

lake dwelling: A type of Neolithic settlement common in prehistoric Europe in areas with many lakes, such as Switzerland, Germany, and north Italy. Such a settlement was formerly on the edge of a lake but is now buried by lake shore sediment or is underwater. These should properly be labeled lakeside villages, because in most cases they were constructed on the shore and not on stilts over the water, as was formerly believed. They were, however, frequently constructed on timber platforms, and subsequently rising water levels in the lakes have preserved these platforms and much other wooden material, as well as artifacts of other organic substances. Cultures in which lake villages were common include Chassey, Cortaillod, Horgen, and Polada. (*syn.* lake village)

Lake George: Lake of southeast New South Wales, Australia, with a pollen sequence for the Pleistocene. A date of 120,000 BP is used to postulate the arrival of humans in Australia; however, it is controversial.

Lake Hauroko burial: Site of a 17th-century AD burial of a Maori woman on an island in Lake Hauroko, southwestern South Island, New Zealand. When found, the skeleton was still sitting on a bier of sticks and wrapped in a woven flax cloak with a dog skin collar with feather edging.

Lake Mangakaware pa: A Maori lake-edge fortification (*pa*) in the Waikato District, North Island, New Zealand. The site has produced one of the most complete Classic Maori settlement plans known, dated AD 1500–1800, with remains of palisades, a central open space (*marae*), and many wooden objects.

Lake Mungo: A dry lake with an associated lunette in the Willandra Lakes, a complex of former Pleistocene lakes in western New South Wales, Australia. Excavation of the lunette has produced the best authenticated series of radiocarbon dates for the earliest evidence of human occupation of Australia, and the remains of a cremated human female date to c. 26,000 bp, the oldest evidence of cremation in the world. The remains of a man in an extended inhumation covered with red ocher is dated to c. 30,000 bp. Stone tools belong to the Australian Core Tool and Scraper tradition, and there are artifact scatters, freshwater shell middens, and hearths dated by thermoluminescence to 31,400–36,400 years ago. The Willandra Lakes started to dry up c. 13,000 BC. The appearance of grinding stones in this period suggests adaptation to wild grain exploitation. Intensive occupation ceased with increasing aridity, although sporadic visits occurred during the Holocene. (*syn.* Mungo)

Lake Ngaroto pa: A lake-edge fortification (*pa*) of Classic Maori date in the Waikato District, North Island, of New Zealand. This is one of the largest and deepest sites in the Waikato, 5400 square meters in area, with deposits up to 3 meters deep. It is an artificial mound built up from repeated construction of sandy living floors.

Lake Nitchie: Ancient lake bed in western New South Wales, Australia, with a shaft burial of a very tall man wearing a necklace of 159 pierced teeth of the Tasmanian devil—about 47 of the now-extinct animals. The burial was dated to c. 6500–7000 bp.

Lake Sentani: A lake in northeastern Irian Jaya, northern New Guinea, known for a range of tools and weapons of bronze and brass found in burial mounds. These artifacts are undated, but could represent a metallurgical industry established by Indonesian traders in recent centuries. New Guinea has no other ancient metallurgical traditions. The items included socketed axes and spearheads.

Lalibela: A religious and pilgrimage center of north-central Ethiopia, capital of the Zague Dynasty for about 300 years. It was renamed for its emperor, Lalibela (reigned c. 1185–1225), who according to tradition built the 11 monolithic churches for which the location is famous. The churches were hewn out of solid rock entirely below ground level in a variety of styles. They retain representations of many features known also from the architecture of Axum (Aksum) in earlier times. The expert craftsmanship of the Lalibela churches has been linked with the earlier church of Debre Damo near Aksum. Emperor Lalibela had most of the churches constructed in his capital in the hope of replacing ancient Axum as a city of Ethiopian pre-eminence. Recent restoration indicates that some of them may have been used originally as fortifications and royal residences. (*syn.* Roha)

Lalla: A pre-Capsian bladelet industry and site in Tunisia, possibly earlier than Iberomaurusian.

La Madeleine: A Dordogne rock shelter in France, extremely rich in mobiliary art, which is the type site for the Magdalenian—the final West European Upper Palaeolithic industry. First excavated by Edouard Lartet and Henry Christy, the Magdalenian dated from approximately 16,000–10,000 BC. Very numerous carved art pieces have been found with the stone and bone tools.

La Marche: Palaeolithic cave site in the Vienne region of France with more than 1,500 engraved stone slabs with figures of humans and animals. It has been dated to 14,280 bp, early mid-Magdalenian.

lamassu: The colossal stone, part human, part animal, figures carved on the doorways of Assyrian and Achaemenid buildings, as at Nineveh. These were guardian figures.

Lamb Spring: Palaeo-Indian site in Colorado with camel bones dated to c. 13,000 BP. There are also mammoth, bison, and horse bones and later Palaeo-Indian components.

La Micoque: A rock shelter near Les Eyzies in the Dordogne, southwest France, with a series of the Lower-Middle Palaeolithic levels. The uppermost contained hand axes in the type assemblage of the Micoquian industry, while the five lower levels are the type series of the Tayacian.

lamina: A flat, sheetlike stratum of sediment (clay, fine sand) defined by stratification planes less than 1 centimeter apart. The term "stratum" identifies a single bed, or unit, normally greater than 1 centimeter in thickness and visibly separable from superjacent (overlying) and subjacent (underlying) beds. "Strata" refer to two or more beds, and the term "lamina" is applied to a unit less than 1 centimeter in thickness. The term is also used for a sample of clay that has been cut in section and placed between two plates of glass, enabling a petrographic analyst to read and determine through a microscope the constituent ingredients of a piece of ceramic. (*syn.* pl. laminae)

laminating: The production of a high-quality metal tool or weapon by repeatedly forging out a blank form, folding the metal over, and forging it again so that qualities of malleability and hardness can be combined.

Laming-Emperaire, Annette (1917–1977): French prehistorian specializing in prehistoric rock art, who found and studied sites in Chilean Pantagonia—Englefield, Ponsonby, Munición—and in Brazil, José Vieira and several sambaquis (shell middens). She also excavated at Marassi (Tierra del Fuego), Lapa Vermehla, and Lagoa Santa.

Lamoka culture: An inland site of the late Archaic period located in the Finger Lakes region of central New York, dating c. 2500–1800 BC. It is characterized by narrow-stemmed points of a type usually associated with coastal areas and by a well-developed industry in worked bone. Other traits include houses framed with upright poles, beveled adzes, atlatl weights, manos and metates, and fishing gear.

lamp: A device for producing illumination, consisting originally of a vessel containing a wick soaked in combustible material. The lamp was invented by at least 70,000 BC and was originally a hollowed-out rock filled with an absorbent material soaked with animal fat and lit. Simple saucers of stone or chalk for this purpose go back to the Upper Palaeolithic. In pottery, the use can rarely be proved unless a special spout or pinched lip was provided to support the wick or signs of burning have survived at the rim. In ancient Greece, lamps did not begin to appear until the 7th century BC, when they replaced torches and braziers.

Lancefield: A small swamp in south-central Victoria, Australia, containing bones of an extinct megafauna representing an estimated 10,000 individuals, dated to c. 24,000 BC. Six species are represented, but *Macropus titan*, a giant kangaroo, predominates. A few stone tools have been found in the bone beds indicating that humans and megafauna were contemporary in the area, probably for 7,000 years. Cut marks on some bones have been interpreted as the teeth marks of the carnivorous predator *Thylacoleo carnifex*, an extinct marsupial carnivore. (*syn.* Lancefield Swamp)

lance head: A large, flat missile point of stone, bone, ivory, or metal—larger than an arrowhead and smaller than a spear head. It is assumed to have armed a light lance or javelin and was mounted on a long shaft for hunting or war.

lanceolate: Shaped like a lance head, referring to projectile points tapering to a point at the apex and sometimes at the base. The term is often applied to flaked stone blades of laurel-leaf form and much like spear heads.

Lan Chang: The earliest kingdom of Laos, founded in 1353, the establishment of an eastern branch of the Thai people in a territory that belonged to the declining Khmer Empire of Angkor. The kingdom was formed by the union of the principalities of Muang Chawa (present-day Luang Prabang) and Wian Chan (present-day Vientiane). It flourished until it was split into two separate kingdoms, Vien Chang and Luang Prabang, in the 18th century. Conflict with its Myanmar (Burmese) and Thai (Siamese) neighbors forced the kingdom's rulers to transfer the capital from Luang Prabang to Vientiane in 1563, but the kingdom maintained its power and was at the height of its glory in the 17th century. (*syn.* Lan Xang)

Landa, Bishop Diego de (1524–1579): Spanish Franciscan priest and bishop of Yucatán who is best known for his classic account of Mayan culture. His book *Relacion de las Cosas de Yucatan* is the primary resource for interpretation of Maya archaeology. Especially important was the calendar section, recorded day and month names, and rudimentary explanation of Katun. Landa was sympathetic to the Mayan people, but he abhorred their human sacrifices. Landa, in his religious zeal, ordered all icons and Mayan books to be burned. At the same time he wrote his comprehensive work on Mayan culture, his orders to destroy all icons and hieroglyphics obliterated the Mayan language forever, helping to undermine and destroy the civilization he so vividly described. Yet his book, which was not printed until 1864, provided a phonetic alphabet that made it possible to decipher about one third of the Mayan hieroglyphs, and many of the remainder have since been deciphered.

land form: A natural feature of a land surface; a feature of the Earth created by an erosional or depositional process or series of processes. Land forms together make up a landscape.

landnam: A Danish word meaning "land taking," used to describe a common form of early agriculture in which an area of woodland was cleared and cultivated (which has been identified in the pollen record). The land was later abandoned and was taken over by weeds, finally reverting to woodland. Its regeneration began with the birch, a rapid colonizer of areas cleared by fire. Landnam has been recognized in pollen analysis by changes in the pollen spectra: the drop in tree pollen, the appearance of grass and plantain pollens, a subsequent increase in the latter, and an eventual reappearance of the tree pollen. Landnam range in date from Neolithic to Bronze Age.

Landsat: The Earth Resources Technology Satellites, any of a series of unmanned U.S. scientific satellites that produce small-scale images of vast areas of the earth's surface and are used to study regional patterns of use of land and other resources.

landscape: An aggregate of land forms in a region; the collection of land forms particular to a region at a particular time.

landscape archaeology: The study of individual features including settlements seen as single components in the broader perspective of the patterning of human activity over a wide area. It is the recovery of the story of an area of countryside using all possible techniques—surface scatters, field and other boundaries, standing buildings, as well as excavation. This approach in archaeology emphasizes examination of the complete landscape, focusing in dispersed features and on areas between and surrounding traditional sites as well as on the sites themselves. (*syn.* total archaeology)

langi tombs: Large square or rectangular earthen burial mounds on the island of Tonga of the Tui Tonga Dynasty. They have terraced sides faced with slabs of cut coral limestone. Some contain burial chambers, also built of coral slabs. According to tradition, langi were the burial places of the Tongan ruling aristocracy. Most are associated with the ceremonial center at Mu'a on Tongatapu.

Langkasuka: An early Indianized state in the Pattani region of peninsular Thailand. The name first appears (as Lang-ya-hsiu) in a Chinese source of the 6th century AD, asserting that it was founded 400 years earlier; its name reappears in later Malayan and Javanese chronicles. Langkasuka was the most important of the Indianized states and controlled much of northern Malaya. Malaya developed an international reputation as a source of gold and tin, populated by renowned seafarers. Between the 7th and 13th centuries, many of these small, often prosperous peninsular maritime trading states may have come under the loose control of Shrivijaya, the great Sumatra-based empire.

Langmannersdorf: Upper Palaeolithic site in Austria with layers dating to the last glacial maximum, c. 20,580–20,260 bp. The Aurignacian assemblage has burins and end scrapers.

language: The overall manner of speaking that reflects general shared speech patterns. It is a system of conventional spoken or written symbols by means of which human beings, as members of a social group and participants in its culture, communicate. Ancient Egyptian is probably the second oldest written language in the world, being preceded only by Sumerian in western Asia.

Lan Na: An ancient northern Thai principality, centered around present Chiang Mai. Founded in the late 13th century, it was also called Yonaratha or Yonakarattha or Bingarattha in the Pali chronicles. Recently the name has also been used to designate a Palaeolithic industry discovered in northern Thailand (the "Lannathian"). Lan Na—with Chiang Mai as its capital—became not only powerful but also a center for the spread of Theravada Buddhism to Tai peoples in what are now northeastern Myanmar, southern China, and northern Laos. Under Tilokaracha (ruled 1441–1487), Lan Na became famous for its Buddhist scholarship and literature.

L'Anse-Amour: Burial site on southern Labrador's (Canada) coast with a skeleton dated to c. 5000 BC. The grave goods include a walrus tusk, stone spear points, and antler harpoon head. It is a complex burial for the time and the oldest burial mound in North America.

L'Anse aux Meadows: A site on Epaves Bay, northern Newfoundland, Canada, with evidence of a Viking settlement founded in the late 10th century AD. There are remains of Scandinavian-style turf-built houses and other artifacts of European origin: iron rivets, slag, a ring-headed bronze pin, and a soapstone spindle whorl. Supporting documents, such as Groen-lendingabok, Erik's Saga, and the map of Sigurthur Stefansson, also indicate that around 1000 Norse sailors journeyed to a land west of Greenland, which they called Vinland. The site has produced a series of radiocarbon dates that cluster around AD 1000. (*syn.* L'Anse-aux-Meadow)

Lantian: Early Palaeolithic site in Shensi Province, China, with *Homo erectus* remains at Gongwangling and Chenjiawo dated to c. 700,000 bp (Middle Pleistocene). Lantian Man is the hominid species identified by Chinese archaeologists; the remains (both female) are as old as Java man, an early form of *Homo erectus*, and older than Peking man, another form. It was named *Sinanthropus lantianensis*, classified by most scholars as *Homo erectus*. The core tools are of the heavy-tool tradition of Palaeolithic China, and stone implements from a third site in Lan-t'ien may be contemporary with the human fossils. (*syn.* [Lan-t'ien])

Laodicea: The ancient name of several cities of western Asia, mostly founded or rebuilt in the 3rd century BC by rulers of the Seleucid Dynasty, and named after Laodice, the mother of Seleucus I Nicator, or after Laodice, daughter or niece of Antiochus I Soter and wife of Antiochus II Theos. It became one of the greatest cities of the Seleucid kingdom. The cities aided in the Hellenization of western Asia and subsequently in the spread of Christianity in the region. The most important of the cities was Laodicea ad Lycum (near modern Denizli, Turkey); its church was one of the seven to which Saint John addressed the Revelation. Laodicea ad Mare (modern Latakia, Syria) was a major seaport.

lapis lazuli: A semiprecious stone of an intense blue color, very popular in the ancient Near East for decorative inlays, beads, seals, and so on. It is a metamorphosed form of limestone, rich in the blue mineral lazurite, which is dark blue in color and often flecked with impurities of calcite, iron pyrites, or gold. Its main source was Badakhshan, northern Afghanistan, and Iran, from which it was traded as far as Egypt. The Egyptians considered that its appearance imitated that of the heavens; therefore they considered it to be superior to all materials other than gold and silver. They used it extensively in jewelry until the Late Period (747–332 BC), when it was particularly popular for amulets. One of the richest collection of lapis lazuli objects was found in the burials at Tepe Gawra. It has also been found at Ovalle, Chile. (*syn.* khesbed)

Lapita: A major Oceanic culture complex, named after the type site of Lapita, New Caledonia. It is defined by a distinctive type of pottery with dentate-stamped banded decoration in geometric patterns, appearing c. 3500 bp. It appeared throughout much of the western Pacific, including Fiji and Samoa. Most Lapita sites are on offshore islands, and assemblages include elaborate shell tools and ornaments, the use of obsidian, and stone adzes. The obsidian and pottery style suggest long-distance trade. The culture is almost certainly associated with ancestral Polynesians moving eastward from islands of Southeast Asia (perhaps from the Philippines), through previously inhabited Melanesia, to the hitherto empty islands of Tonga and Samoa in western Polynesia. The culture therefore represents the origin of the Polynesians before their settlement of geographical Polynesia. It is thought to be associated with the spread of Austronesian speakers into the western Pacific.

La Quina: Middle and Upper Palaeolithic rock shelter complex in Charente, southwest France, and the name of a subdivision of the Charentian Mousterian tradition. The stone tool industry produced thick scrapers with a very curved cutting edge and stepped, splintered retouches. Another industry had many thin scrapers produced by Levallois technique. Human remains include 27 of Neanderthal type.

Lara Jonggrang: A monument of the Prambanan group in the region of Yogyakarta in central Java, Indonesia, built in the early 10th century by King Dhaksa, a king of Mendang-Mataram (Hindu-Mataram) as the funerary temple of his predecessor, King Balitung. The largest monument of the group, it is particularly known for its lively Brahmanic relief scenes. It was built to worship the Hindu god Shiva (Siva) and is the largest Shiva temple in Indonesia. Restoration of the Lara Jonggrang, which had been partly damaged, was completed in 1951. (*syn.* Lara Yonggrang)

La Riera: Prehistoric cave site in Asturias, Spain, with a large number of stone artifacts and faunal evidence of the Upper Palaeolithic (Solutrean and Magdalenian). There was an Azilian shell midden and Asturian levels; its occupation spans c. 20,500–6500 bp.

Larisa: Mousterian site in northern Greece and a Final Neolithic culture with a black polished pottery. In antiquity, Larissa was the seat of the Aleuad clan, founded by Aleuas, who claimed descent from Heracles. The poet Pindar and the physician Hippocrates died there. In 357 BC, the last Aleuads called in Philip II of Macedonia against the tyrants of Pherae, and from 344 to 196 Larissa remained under Macedonia. Rome then made it capital of the reorganized Thessalian League. The emperor Justinian fortified the city, whose name means "citadel." (*syn.* Larissa)

larnax: A Minoan-Mycenaean clay or terra-cotta coffin. This kind of coffin, resembling a rectangular wooden chest, enjoyed a brief popularity in the eastern Greek region c. 530–460 BC. The sarcophagus was often crudely painted on the sides with funerary or religious scenes. "Clazomenian" examples were painted in imitation of contemporary vase styles. The term was also used for a closed box, seen in a royal tomb at Vergina, and in art. A third use of the term was for a bathtub made of a fabric containing straw. (*syn.* plural larnakes)

Larnian culture: A Mesolithic culture, named after Larne, Ireland, and found only on sites close to coasts and estuaries in western Scotland and eastern Ireland. It is characterized by shell middens, and the early tool kits include leaf-shaped points made on a flake, the oldest unambiguous implement in Ireland, and scrapers. Some are dated to 6000 BC. Later assemblages contain more flakes than blades and include tranchet axes and very small scrapers. More recent work casts doubt on the antiquity of the people who were responsible for the Larnian industry; association with Neolithic remains suggests that they should be considered not as Mesolithic but rather as contemporary with the Neolithic farmers. The Larnian could then be interpreted as a specialized aspect of contemporary Neolithic culture. Lake and riverside finds, especially along the River Bann, show a comparable tradition. A single radioactive carbon date of 5725 ± 110 BC from Toome Bay, north of Lough Neagh, for woodworking and flint has been cited in support of a Mesolithic phase in Ireland.

Larsa: The most important city of southern Mesopotamia during the early Old Babylonian period, one of the city-states of Sumer. It was located on the Euphrates River between Ur and Babylon, southeast of Uruk, southern Iraq. Archaeological remains are found in a group of tells, although most of its history has been recovered from documents from other sites. It emerged as a city-state during the Early Dynastic period, and its period of greatness was in the early 2nd millennium BC, when it contested the supremacy of Mesopotamia with Isin, Assur, and Eshnunna. The first great ruler was Naplanum (reigned c. 2025–2005 BC), who was succeeded by 13 kings. Its greatest ruler, Rim Sin, destroyed Isin c. 1794 BC but was himself overthrown by Hammurabi of Babylon c. 1763. Remains include a ziggurat, a temple to the sun god, and a palace of Nur-Adad (c. 1865–1850 BC), as well as many tombs and other remains of the Neo-Babylonian and Seleucid periods. The documented settlement history of the site ranges from the late 3rd millennium (Ur III) to the mid-1st millennium (Neo-Babylonian) BC. (*syn.* modern Senkera or Tall Sankarah)

Lartet, Edouard (1801–1871): A French scholar, one of the pioneers of Palaeolithic archaeology, known as the founder of the science of palaeontology. He proposed a classification scheme for the Palaeolithic period based on animal bones: the Cave Bear period; the Woolly Mammoth and Rhinoceros period; the Reindeer period; and the Aurochs or Bison period. He collaborated with Henry Christy in excavating many of the well-known rock shelter sites of southern France and was one of the first to recognize in situ mobiliary art; the publication of these objects from well-excavated contexts made it easier for scholars to accept the authenticity of cave art. With Christy, he carried out the first systematic study of south French caves and excavated many of the most famous sites in the Dordogne (Laugerie-Haute, Le Moustier, La Madeleine). Their results appeared in several important articles, and also, during the decade 1865–1875, in the volumes of *Reliquiae Aquitanicae.*

Las Bocas: A site in Puebla, Mexico, known for its hollow figurines and other pottery in the Olmec style, at the eastern entrance to the Morelos Plain. Las Bocas is noticeably similar to a site at the other end of the plain, Chalcatzingo, and is thought to have been one of a series of Olmec trading stations. Burials similar to those at Tlatilco further confirm the Olmec connection.

Lascaux: A Magdalenian cave in the Dordogne, southwest France, with a spectacular collection of Palaeolithic paintings and engravings. After the cave had been opened to visitors, the delicate atmospheric balance was disturbed, and the paintings were attacked by fungus; it was closed to the public in 1963. A small number of archaeological finds from inside the cave probably date to the early Magdalenian, including lamps. A Neanderthal skeleton was found a few hundred meters away at Regoudou. There are 600 paintings of aurochs, horses, deer, and signs, accompanied by 1,500 engravings dominated by horses. Some of the paintings in the rotunda, especially the bulls, approach life size, which is unusual in cave art. A number of paintings are in two contrasting colors, red iron oxide and black manganese dioxide. It was probably never inhabited, but was used from c. 15,000 BC. A nearby facsimile cave, Lascaux II, is now open to the public.

Las Haldas: Initial period ceremonial site on the north-central coast of Peru. The earliest ceramics have yielded radiocarbon dates of about 1800 BC. There is a stepped pyramid, three plazas, smaller mounds, and sunken courts along a linear axis.

Lashkari Bazar: The site of a large royal palace erected in the 11th and 12th centuries, on the Helmand Rud, near the site of Bust in Afghanistan. Lashkari Bazar was the winter retreat of the rulers of Ghazni. It was conquered by the Arabs c. 661, and the 10th-century writer Ibn Hauqal described it as a large and wealthy town. Apart from the tell, the principal monument is a ceremonial arch of the Ghorid period. The palace complex at Lashkari Bazar extends northward from Bust for more than 5 kilometers and was founded by the Ghaznavid sultan Mahmud (998–1030), who with his son Masud I (1030–1041) built the so-called South Palace. Later rulers added two other palaces. The complex also contained barracks and a bazaar. Lashkari Bazar was sacked by the Ghorids in 1151; it was restored by them, then destroyed by the Khwarezmshah or the Mongols in the early 13th century. Excavations revealed elaborate wall paintings in the South Palace and a fine stucco Mihrab in an adjacent mosque.

Lasithi: A plain on Crete, which has been occupied since the Neolithic and which was intensively used by the Minoans.

Last Glacial Maximum: The geological period dating between 25,000–14,000 bp, during which global temperatures reached the lowest levels of the Upper Pleistocene (127,000–10,000 bp). Massive continental ice sheets formed in the northern hemisphere, and sea levels fell worldwide. The people were anatomically modern and conducted industries of the Upper Palaeolithic in unglaciated parts of the Old World. (*syn.* Late Pleniglacial)

Late Bronze Age: A period of the Levant, following the expulsion of the Hyksos, during which the Egyptians invaded and the Canaanite cities were under Egyptian control. It is divided into LBA I, c. 1550–1400 BC; LBA IIa, c. 1400–1300 BC; and LBA IIb, c. 1300–1200 BC.

late glacial period: The closing stages of the Pleistocene Ice Age, when the glaciers had begun their final retreat and when much of northern Europe was tundra. This period lasted from c. 13,000–8500 BC. The substages in northern Europe are the Oldest Dryas (13,000–10,450), the Bølling oscillation (10,450–10,050), the Older Dryas (10,050–9850), the Allerød oscillation (9850–8850), and the Younger Dryas (8850–8300). Cultures of the late glacial period include Ahrensburgian, Creswellian, Federmesser, and Hamburgian.

Late Horizon: A division of time in central Andean chronology, AD 1450–1533, which corresponds to the Inca Empire's expansion from Cuzco. It is the most recent and briefest period of a chronological construction of Peruvian archaeology. The early date marks the point at which territorial expansion was virtually complete; the late date marks the passing of control to the Spanish under Pizarro. Archaeologists have come to distinguish the various peoples and civilizations by descriptive terms—the Late Preceramic, the Initial (or Lower Formative) Period, the Early Horizon, the Early Intermediate Period, the Middle Horizon, the Late Intermediate Period, and the Late Horizon. (*syn.* Upper Formative; Inca Period)

Late Intermediate Period: A division of time in central Andean chronology, AD 1000–1450, which was a period of regional diversification on the coast and in the highlands. New styles, cultures, and kingdoms arose after the collapse of the Middle Horizon empires. The period began with the dying out of the signs of unity imposed by Huari. Warfare, secularization of urban centers, and rectangular enclosure plans were prominent. The cultures and styles were Chimú, Chancay, Pachacamac, Chincha, Ica; Cajamarca, Chanca, Killke, Lucre, Colla, Lupaca. The various empires that developed during the Late Intermediate Period were conquered by the Inca Empire.

La Tène: The site of a great Iron Age votive deposit in the shallow water at the east end of Lake Neuchâtel, Switzerland. Excavations revealed wooden piles, two timber causeways, and a mass of tools and weapons of bronze, iron, and wood (swords, fibulae, spearheads, etc.). Some of these objects bore curvilinear patterns which are the hallmark of La Tène (Celtic) art everywhere from central Europe to Ireland and the Pyrenees. La Tène has given its name to the second major division of the European Iron Age, which followed the Hallstatt period over much of the continent and lasted from the mid-5th century BC until the Celts were subdued by Roman conquest c. 50 BC. Settlement was characteristically in hill forts, and, from the 3rd and 2nd centuries BC, massive *oppida* occur. As in the Hallstatt culture, there is a notable distinction between the markedly wealthy burials of chieftains and their associates, and burials of other members of society. The highest development, and the birth of the art style, took place in west-central Europe from the Rhineland to the Marne. Contact with the Greek and Etruscan worlds brought wine, metal flagons, and Attic drinking cups into lands north of the Alps, and La Tène art shows links with that of the Scythians to the east. In Britain, contact with the continental La Tène cultures is shown by chariot burials and the presence of La Tène art motifs on metalwork and pottery. British cultures showing La Tène influence are sometimes grouped in an Iron Age B complex. In Ireland, which the Romans never invaded, a Celtic culture and an art style with La Tène elements persisted into the Early Christian period. It is subdivided into La Tène I c. 480–220 BC, La Tène II c. 220–120 BC, and La Tène III, c. 120–Roman conquest (at different times in different areas). (*syn.* La Tene period)

Late Period: A phase of Egyptian history, c. 664–332 BC, including the 26th–31st Dynasties, stretching from the end of the Third Intermediate Period to the arrival of Alexander the Great. Shabaqo (716–702 BC), the second ruler of the Kushite 25th Dynasty, exerted Nubian influence by moving the administrative center back from Thebes to Memphis. In writing, the demotic script, the new cursive form, was introduced from the north and spread gradually through the country. Hieratic was, however, retained for literary and religious texts, among which very ancient material, such as the Pyramid Texts, was revived and inscribed in tombs and on coffins and sarcophagi. The Late Period also saw the greatest development of animal worship in Egypt.

lateral excavation: The excavation or opening up of large areas so that subsurface features and architecture are broadly exposed. (*syn.* extensive excavation)

laterite: A soil layer that is rich in iron oxide and derived from a wide variety of rocks weathering under strongly oxidizing and leaching conditions. It forms in tropical and subtropical regions where the climate is humid.

Later Stone Age: The third and final phase of Stone Age technology in sub-Saharan Africa, dating from about 30,000+ years ago until historical times in some places. There was much art and personal decoration, evidence of burials, and some microlithic stone tools in assemblages. Pottery and stone bowls appear during the last 3 millennia as the lifeways changed to herding from nomadic hunting and gathering. The large number of distinctive Later Stone Age industries that emerged reflect increasing specialization as hunter gatherers exploited different environments, often moving seasonally between them, and developed different subsistence strategies. As in many parts of the world, changes in technology seem to mark a shift to the consumption of smaller game, fish, invertebrates, and plants. Later Stone Age peoples used bows and arrows and a variety of snares and traps for hunting, as well as grindstones and digging sticks for gathering plant food; with hooks, barbed spears, and wicker baskets, they were also able to catch fish and thus exploit rivers, lake shores, and seacoasts more effectively. The appearance of cave art, careful burials, and ostrich eggshell beads for adornments suggests more sophisticated behavior and new patterns of culture. These developments apparently are associated with the emergence between 20,000 and 15,000 BC of the earliest of the historically recognizable populations of southern Africa: the Pygmy, San, and Khoi peoples, who were probably genetically related to the ancient population that had evolved in the African subcontinent.

Laterza: A cemetery of rock-cut tombs near Taranto, southeast Italy, which has given its name to a local Copper Age culture of the 3rd millennium BC. The tombs were used for collective burial and contained grave goods including a few copper weapons, tools, and ornaments, bifacially worked flint arrowheads, and a variety of decorated pottery bowls and cups, some of which appear to be ancestral to the Apennine pottery of the Bronze Age. Other Laterza burial sites are known; these include rock-cut tombs and stone cists and possibly megalithic tombs.

late-stage biface: A biface in the final step of manufacture, usually with relatively straight edges and complex surface topography.

Late Woodland period: A period AD c. 400–1000, in the American Midwest, when populations spread west to the eastern slopes of the Rockies and were in contact with eastward-moving Puebloan people. A favorable agricultural period was indicated by the marked increase in village size and in population density. Areas along major streams were occupied by various interrelated cultural groups collectively known as the Plains Mississippian cultures. Part of this complex was connected to the developing Mississippi complexes to the east by diffusion and, to some degree, by a migration of such groups as the Omaha and Ponca from the St. Louis area by about AD 1000. It follows the Middle Woodland era but lacks the elaborate Hopewellian artifacts and structures.

Lathrap, Donald Ward (1927–1990): American archaeologist who studied South and Central America and who proposed that the lowland Amazon regions supported complex societies and civilizations before those elsewhere on the continent. He published *The Upper Amazon* in 1970.

Latians: The ancient people of Latium; an Iron Age people of the region just south of Rome. Their cremation cemeteries are known particularly from the Alban Hills and from Rome itself. The Latians seem to have developed from the Pianello urnfielders, notably those who buried their dead in the cemetery at Allumiere and were certainly the ancestors of the Romans. The first huts on the Palatine Hill were built by these people in the 9th century BC. Latium was an ancient area in west-central Italy, originally limited to the territory around the Alban Hills, but extending by about 500 BC south of the Tiber River as far as the promontory of Mount Circeo. (*syn.* Latin)

latifundia: Large planned agricultural estates geared to efficient production and high profits through the use of cheap, usually slave, labor. The estates were owned by the Roman upper classes and were first created toward the end of the Roman Republic. The land was confiscated by Rome from conquered communities beginning in the early 2nd century BC. They were common throughout the western part of the Empire in the early centuries of the first millennium AD. Although strictly a Roman term, its use extends to any agricultural estates, as in South America, where production is at an industrial level. It occurred in classical Greece in the 5th century BC, and later, in the Hellenistic Age from 323 BC, large estates were held by rulers, ministers, and other rich people and by some great temples. Upper-class Romans who owned latifundia had enough money to improve their crops and livestock, displacing the small farm as the regular agricultural unit by the 3rd century AD. As the Empire declined and disappeared in the West (5th century AD), the latifundia assumed great importance not only as economic but also as local political and cultural centers. (*syn.* singular latifundium)

Latin script: Writing using a–z. Based on older forms, it developed during the Roman Empire and is used today in most countries of Europe, the Americas, Africa, Oceania, and some Asian nations.

latte: Double rows of large stone pillars with capstones that formed the foundation of structures, especially in the Mariana Islands, Micronesia, about 1,000 years ago. The latte stones of this area are now thought to have been piles for raised houses, perhaps for chiefs and wealthy men, because the latte sites are relatively few for the reported population. Burials were sometimes placed between the pillars.

Laugerie-Haute: A rock shelter in the Dordogne near Les Eyzies, France, which has yielded the richest Upper Palaeolithic sequence ever recorded. It starts with Upper Périgordian (Gravettian), followed by "proto-Magdelenian," final Aurignacian, several rich layers of Early, Middle, and Late Solutrean, and finally by Early Magdalenian. A number of radiocarbon dates are available, in the range c. 20,000–16,000 BC for Solutrean and Initial Magdalenian levels. (*syn.* Laugerie; Laugerie Haute)

Lauicocha Caves: A series of caves of long occupation in the central Peruvian highlands, mainly summer hunting camps, the associated winter locus being the lowlands, during the Archaic. The earliest period of occupation was c. 8000–6000 BC; this level is characterized by stemless triangular points and stemmed diamond-shaped points. A number of burials indicate a dolichocephalic population. The willow-leaf points of Lauricocha II (6000–4000 BC) show strong similarities to points at Chivaterros, El Jobo, and Ayampitim and are associated with knives, scrapers, and other hide-working implements. Later levels contain small points and then ceramics.

Laurel culture: An Initial Woodland culture, dating c. 200 BC–AD 700, located in northern Michigan, northern Ontario, northern Minnesota, south-central Manitoba, and east-central Saskatchewan. Artifacts include togglehead antler harpoons, cut beaver incisors, copper tools and beads, and grit-tempered pottery with stamping and incising. Laurel sites also have burial mounds.

laurel-leaf point: A distinctive long, thin leaf-shaped Solu-

trean flake tool made with delicate workmanship. The largest was found in Volgu, France. The points were made during the Upper Palaeolithic in Europe. (*syn.* laurel-leaf blade)

Laurentian: Important Late Archaic tradition in northern New York and Vermont and the upper St. Lawrence valley, c. 4000–1500 BC. Characteristic artifacts are broad-bladed, notched projectile points; bifaces, scrapers, and polished-stone tools (celts, gouges, plummets, slate knives, or points). The tradition has phases such as Brewerton, Vergennes, and Vosburg. (*syn.* Lake Forest Late Archaic)

Laurentide: The ice mass that covered most of Canada and parts of the United States, including the Great Lakes area and northern New England, during the Pleistocene epoch. It originated in northeastern Canada during the Wisconsin Glacial and then spread south and west. At its maximum extent, about 20,000 years ago, it was connected with the Cordilleran ice sheet to the west and covered an area of more than 13,000,000 square kilometers (5,000,000 sq. mi). In some areas, its thickness reached 2,400–3,000 meters (8,000–10,000 ft). The system began to recede about 14,000 BP. (*syn.* Laurentide ice sheet)

Lauricocha: Area of several preceramic cave sites in the highlands of central Peru. The earliest level, dating c. 8000–6000 BC, yielded the skeletons of people who hunted deer and guanaco with spears tipped with leaf-shaped points. The sites represent seasonal hunting camps. A second phase, dated c. 6000–4000BC, had better-made points of willow leaf shape. The second culture at Lauricocha was replaced by a third one with smaller leaf- and diamond-shaped points, which lasted until 1500 or later; the latter part of this period overlaps with the earliest farming villages on the Peruvian coast, where points of Lauricocha type have been found. Fourth and fifth stages represent pottery-using cultures. Other caves in the area have engravings, some of which include motifs used by about 1000 BC on pottery at Kotosh. Occupations extend into the Initial period.

Laurion: A hilly region of Attica, Greece, which was important for silver mines from the Bronze Age in the 1st millennium BC. The region developed into a principal mining area, especially from about 483 BC until the end of the 5th century BC. The mines may have been worked as early as 1000 BC, but in 483 BC Athenians exploited the veins to finance construction of a large fleet, which then defeated the Persians at Salamis in 480. Production remained low until after 350, and the mines were closed in the 2nd century AD. The mines were state property, rented out to individual contractors, and worked by slaves. The area has ancient mine shafts, processing areas, surface mining structures, water cisterns, and ore washeries. The Laureot Owls, Athenian silver coinage attributed to the mines, were circulated throughout the classical world, but by Roman times the mines lay neglected because of competition from the gold and silver mines in Macedonia and pirate raids on the Laurium mines. About the beginning of the Christian Era, the silver was exhausted. (*syn.* Roman Laurium)

Lausitz: A northeasterly group of the European Urnfield cultures, occurring in East Germany, Poland, and parts of Czechoslovakia, which emerged c. 1500 BC and survived well into the Iron Age c. 300 BC. Fortified settlements occur, seen in the well-preserved site at Biskupin. The dead were cremated and placed in urns and buried either in urnfields or under barrows. The good-quality pottery was often decorated with graphite painted designs and plastic ornament. The bronze industry, of general Urnfield type, flourished; iron was introduced from the Hallstatt Iron Age culture from the later 7th century BC. Historic Lusatia was centered on the Neisse and upper Spree Rivers, in what is now eastern Germany, between the present-day cities of Cottbus (north) and Dresden (south). (*syn.* Lusatia, Lusatian)

Laussel: A rock shelter near Les Eyzies in Dordogne, southwest France, with a long sequence of Mousterian and Upper Palaeolithic levels. The site is best known for its bas-relief carvings, especially the female figure holding a horn or "cornucopia."

lava: Molten rock (magma) poured out onto the Earth's surface at temperatures from about 700 to 1,200 degrees centigrade (1,300 to 2,200 F) from an active volcano. Lava is well adapted to ornamental carving.

La Vache: Magdalenian cave site in Ariège, French Pyrenees, with occupation and portable art dating to the 11th millennium BC. Art objects use the same pigment mixtures as Niaux.

La Venta: The most important Olmec ceremonial center, located in Tabasco, Mexico, and built around 1000 BC. The site occupies a small island, entirely surrounded by swamps, and lacking both farmland and building stone. The principal monument is a huge lobed pyramid of clay, the tallest of the Olmec sites, and subsidiary structures include platforms and courtyards. La Venta is famous for its Preclassic stone sculpture, buried pavements of serpentine blocks brought from about 100–160 kilometers away, and offerings of carved jade including six jadeite axes. The important buildings were constructed from c. 1000–600 BC; the site grew in importance after the abandonment of San Lorenzo, especially during the Middle Formative period, c. 850–750 BC. The end of La Venta was violent, possibly caused by a conflict between the carrying capacity of the area and the large number of workers needed to construct the site's structures.

La Victoria: An early Pre-Classic village site located on the Pacific coastal region of Ocos in Guatemala. The site's earliest phase dates to c. 1300 BC and contains Olmec or Olmec-influenced pottery, some of which has been traded to other areas of Mesoamerica. The later Conchas Phase, 800–300 BC, contains sherds of a unique striped design that has also been found in Ecuador, indicating probable ocean trade.

Lavo: Ancient town of south-central Thailand founded in the 5th–7th centuries and later incorporated into the Khmer Empire of Angkor in the 10th or 11th century. It became an important provincial capital. One of Thailand's major historical sites, the city retains numerous buildings from the early periods. The Prang Sam Yod (Three-Spired Sanctuary), the symbol of the Lop Buri region, was built by the Khmers. Other places of interest include the temple complex of Wat Phra Si Ratana Maha That (1157) and the remains of the Nakhon Kosa temple. It later became an active center in the kingdom of Ayutthaya (founded 1351) and was the summer capital of the Ayutthaya king Narai (reigned 1657–1688). Thereafter the city declined, and many of its buildings decayed. (*syn.* Lopburi, Lop Buri)

law codes: Any systematic and comprehensive written statement of laws compiled since ancient times, recording judgments and appropriate penalties for various crimes. The oldest extant evidence for a code are tablets from the ancient archives of the city of Ebla (Tell Mardikh, Syria), which date to around 2400 BC. The best known ancient code is that of the Babylonian king Hammurabi of the 18th century BC. Roman legal records began in the 5th century BC, but there was no major codification of Roman law until that of the emperor Justinian in the 6th century AD. The Burgundians, Visigoths, and the Salian Franks also made codes of law. During the later Middle Ages in Europe, maritime customs laws were also drawn up.

law of cross-cutting relationships: A principle of stratigraphy that says a feature that cuts across or into a bed or stratum must be younger than that bed or stratum.

law of evolutionary potential: The group with the more generalized adaptation has more potential for change than does the group with the more highly specialized adaptation.

law of superposition: The principle that states that, in any pile of sedimentary rocks that have not been disturbed by folding or overturning, the strata on the bottom will have been deposited first. This is the principle that the sequence of observable strata, from bottom to top, reflects the order of deposition, from earliest to latest. Older beds or strata are overlaid and buried by progressively younger beds or strata.

Layard, Sir Austen Henry (1817–1894): British excavator and explorer—one of the earliest in Mesopotamia. His most important discoveries were at Nimrud, which he identified wrongly as Nineveh. The Assyrian winged bulls and reliefs he excavated from the massive palace complexes are now in the British Museum. At Nineveh proper (modern Kuyunjik), he recovered a library of cuneiform tablets from Sennacherib's palace. His book on his finds, *Nineveh and its Remains* (1849), ranks as one of the first archaeological bestsellers. He also excavated at Assur, Babylon, and Nippur.

layer: A unit of stratigraphy, greater than 1 centimeter thick, often part of a bed. Layers are identified by archaeologists, and the boundaries between them are often well marked, where deposition of one layer is separated from the next by a clear interval or change in texture, color, or mineralogy. Some are not clearly demarcated as deposition of one layer may merge with another so that boundaries between them are unclear, or a layer may change in composition from place to place. (*syn.* strata, stratum)

Lazaret: Acheulian cave site near Nice, France, with some evidence of hutlike structures and an assemblage dated to Riss III with pointed bifaces and choppers.

Lchashen: Bronze Age site by Lake Sevan, Armenia, with pit graves under stone cairns. There are traces of wheeled wagons, carts, and chariots.

leaching: To dissolve or subject to the action of percolating liquid—as water; such as water seeping through the soil and removing the soluble materials from it.

lead: A soft, silvery-white or grayish metal that is very malleable, ductile, and dense and is a poor conductor of electricity. Known in antiquity and believed by the alchemists to be the oldest of metals, lead is highly durable and resistant to corrosion, as is indicated by the continuing use of lead water pipes installed by the ancient Romans. In antiquity, galena (from which silver may also be extracted) was the main source of lead in the Old World, although anglesite and cerussite were also exploited. Lead was used to make patterns for casting, to "wet" bronze and ease its casting; in making glazes; and, alloyed with tin, to make soft solder for joining metals and pewter for tablewares as well as for pipes, roofing, and so on. The first evidence for lead extraction in parts of Europe is the addition of the metal to bronze during the Late Bronze Age.

lead bronze: An alloy of copper and tin with lead, often 60–70% copper, up to 2% nickel, up to 15% tin, and lead. The presence of lead, which remains free in the alloy as opposed to becoming part of the crystalline structure, increases the fluidity of the metal in its molten state and makes the casting of finely detailed objects easier. It is used as a bearing metal.

lead glaze: A type of glaze found on European pottery and the soft-fired earthenware of the Han Dynasty of China. It was probably invented by the Greeks and/or Romans by the 3rd century BC, involving either dusting the unfired vessel with galena (lead ore) or dipping it into a mixture of lead ore and water. The glaze fuses in one firing. The natural color of lead glaze has a yellowish tinge; after the 13th century,

copper ore was often added to give a greenish-gray effect. In China, it was used for vessels and miniature ceramic sculptures in funerary deposits. (*syn.* lead-glazed ware)

lead isotope analysis: A technique based on the relative abundance of lead isotopes, which differ according to the origin of the lead, allowing scientists to pinpoint the source of a piece of lead once the ratios of the isotopes have been determined. A mass spectrometer is used on a small sample to determine the ratio of the isotopic concentrations, which are similar in different regions if the geological time scale is similar. The method can be used to identify sources of lead impurities in other metals as well as in glass and glaze.

leaf-shaped: Of a tool, pointed at the ends and with convex sides, as on a willow leaf. The term is applied to an arrowhead, the blade of a slashing sword, or the flattened bow of a fibula, and other tools that have been retouched on both faces to produce a flattish effect. Many Upper Palaeolithic tools are named after leaves (Solutrean laurel leaf). Some Middle Palaeolithic industries are characterized by the presence of bifaces, others by the presence of leaf-shaped objects. Mousterian industries producing leaf-shaped items in central and eastern Europe. (*syn.* foliated; foliate)

Leakey, Louis Seymour Bazett (1903–1972): Kenyan-born British archaeologist and anthropologist whose brilliant career was devoted to the recovery and interpretation of the bones and tools of early man and his forebears in East Africa. His name is particularly associated with Olduvai Gorge and *Homo habilis*, and his work was extended and continued by his wife Mary and son Richard. As a geologist and palaeontologist, he clarified the palaeoclimatic scale of the Pleistocene. His intensive early hominid research in East Africa included finds of *Australopithecus boisei* (Zinjanthropus) and *Homo habilis*, dating to c. 1.75 million years ago. These discoveries proved that man was far older than had previously been believed and that human evolution was centered in Africa, rather than in Asia, as earlier discoveries had suggested. Leakey was also noted for his controversial interpretations of these archaeological finds. He was also instrumental in persuading Jane Goodall and Dian Fossey to undertake their pioneering long-term studies of chimpanzees and gorillas, respectively, in those animals' natural habitats. Leakey wrote *Adam's Ancestors* (1934; rev. ed., 1953), *Stone-Age Africa* (1936), *White African* (1937), *Olduvai Gorge* (1952), *Mau Mau and the Kikuyu* (1952), *Olduvai Gorge, 1965–61* (1965), *Unveiling Man's Origins* (1969; with Jane Goodall), and *Animals of East Africa* (1969). (*syn.* L. S. B. Leakey)

Leakey, Mary Douglas (1913–1996): English-born archaeologist and palaeoanthropologist who made several of the most important fossil finds subsequently interpreted and publicized by her husband, the noted anthropologist Louis

Leakey. She discovered the skull of *Proconsul africanus*, an apelike ancestor of both apes and early humans that lived about 25,000,000 years ago. At Olduvai Gorge, she found the skull of an early hominid *Australopithecus boisei* (Zinjanthropus). At Laetoli, she discovered several sets of footprints made in volcanic ash by early hominids who lived about 3.5 million years ago. The footprints indicated that their makers walked upright; this discovery pushed back the advent of human bipedalism to a date earlier than had previously been suspected by the scientific community. Among Mary Leakey's books were *Olduvai Gorge: My Search for Early Man* (1979) and the autobiographical *Disclosing the Past* (1984).

Leakey, Richard (1944–): Kenyan physical anthropologist and palaeontologist, son of Louis and Mary Leakey, responsible for extensive fossil finds of human ancestral forms in East Africa. His investigations suggested that relatively intelligent, tool-using ancestors of true man lived in eastern Africa as early as 3,000,000 years ago, or almost twice the time span of previous estimates. Leakey uncovered some 400 hominid fossils, making Koobi Fora the site of the richest and most varied assemblage of early human remains found to date in the world. Leakey proposed controversial interpretations of his fossil finds. In two books written with science writer Roger Lewin, *Origins* (1977) and *People of the Lake* (1978), Leakey said that about 3 million years ago, three hominid forms coexisted with one another: *Homo habilis*, *Australopithecus africanus*, and *Australopithecus boisei*. Leakey contended that a relatively large-brained, upright, bipedal form of the species Homo lived in eastern Africa c. 2.5–3.5 million years ago. He also wrote *The Making of Mankind* (1981).

Leang Burung: Rock shelter site in southwestern Sulawesi, Indonesia, with deposits postdating Ulu Leang. Shelter I has produced a late Toalian assemblage with microliths, Maros points, and pottery dating to the 2nd and 1st millennia BC. However, Shelter 2 produced a much older stone tool assemblage, late Pleistocene, with possible early Australian and also Levalloisian technological affinities, dating back to c. 30,000–17,000 BC.

Leang Tuwo Mane'e: Rock shelter on the coast of Karakellang, Talaud Islands, northeastern Indonesia, which has produced a preceramic small blade industry, c. 3000 BC, followed by the appearance of a Neolithic assemblage by about 2000 BC, probably introduced from the Philippines.

leather-hard: A stage in the manufacture of ceramic artifacts between forming and firing when the clay is sufficiently dry to lose plasticity but still can be polished to compact its surface.

Lébous: A Chalcolithic settlement in St.-Mathieu-de-Tréviers, Hérault, France, which was a fortified village of the Copper Age Fontbouïsse people. The site is surrounded by a stone wall with towers at intervals and has a radiocarbon date of 2410 ± 250 BC.

Le Croy point: An Early Archaic bifurcate, chipped-stone projectile point of the U.S. Southeast, small or medium sized with a short triangular blade. The type is dated c. 6500–6000 BC and is found in Ohio and Tennessee river drainages and north to the Great Lakes. (*syn.* LeCroy)

Lefkandi: Important settlement site on Euboea, an island in the Aegean, occupied from the later 3rd millennium until the end of the 2nd millennium BC. Early levels have Anatolian-type pottery. At Toumba, there is an artificial tumulus covering an apsidal structure, which is surrounded by a peristyle of wooden columns, c. 1000 BC. The rich burial of a man and woman may have been a shrine for a hero cult. Artifacts link this site to the eastern Mediterranean: The large bronze vessel in which the man's ashes were deposited came from Cyprus, and the gold items buried with the woman are of sophisticated workmanship. Remains of horses were found as well; the animals had been buried with their snaffle bits. The grave was in a large collapsed house, whose form anticipates that of the Greek temples 2 centuries later. This burial and finds at other cemeteries further attest contacts between Egypt and Cyprus between 1000–800 BC.

legion: A military unit forming the backbone of the Roman army, nominally composed of 6,000 soldiers, and divided into 10 cohorts, with each cohort containing 6 centuria. The centurion thus nominally commanded about 100 men, and there were 60 centurions in a legion. Each was based at a legionary fortress, a larger and more permanent version of the Roman military camp. Numbers in a legion changed again under the Empire, and from Diocletian onward (284–316 AD), the legions were increased in number but reduced in size. Each legion was given the standard of the eagle, an identifying number, and an honorific title, often based upon the name of the founder.

Leg Piekarski: A rich burial site in west-central Poland, dated to the 1st–2nd century AD, referred to as "princes' graves." There are elaborate silver and bronze vessels among the grave goods. The burials are evidence of the emergence of local hereditary chiefdoms at that time.

Lehringen: A Middle Palaeolithic site near Bremen in north Germany (Lower Saxony), where organic muds revealed a pollen diagram of the last interglacial. In these muds, a yew wood spear broken into several pieces was found. It passed between the ribs of the skeleton of an elephant of *Elephas antiquus* type. The tip was finely shaved to a point and fire hardened; the spear was evidently used for thrusting.

Leibig's law: Rule stating that the numbers of a population are regulated by the essential resource in shortest supply.

Leilan, Tell: Site on the Wadi Jarrah, northwest Syria, identified as Shubat Enlil, the capital of Shamshi-Adad I, 1813–1781 BC. Occupation began in the early 4th millennium and extended to the 2nd millennium BC. The sequences include 'Ubaid, Uruk, Ninevite 5, and an occupation with Khabur ware. In the 3rd millennium BC occupation, a walled lower town covered a large area, and there was an upper town and possibly a *karum*. Documents have been recovered that should help shed light on developments in the area as well as Shamshi-Adad's empire. (*syn.* Shubat Enlil; Tall Leilan)

leilira: Large pointed or rectangular blade, which may be retouched to form a point or scraper-like tool. It could be hafted as a spear head or fighting pick or used as a knife. It is associated with the Australian Small Tool tradition in northern Australia.

Leisner, Georg (1871–1957) and Leisner, Vera (1885–1972): Team of German archaeologists who studied megalithic tombs in Iberia. They published a series of monographs, *Die Megalithgräber der Iberischen Halbinsel* (1942–1965).

leister: A two-pronged forklike fish spear made of two bone or antler heads with barbs pointing inward and backward. They are recorded from Mesolithic and lakeside Neolithic settlements, and are in present-day use by the Eskimo, mainly for salmon.

Lejre: A reconstruction of a working prehistoric farm near Roskilde in Denmark. It is one of the most ambitious and informative examples yet of experimental archaeology.

lekane: In Greek antiquity, large open basin, usually with two horizontal handles, used in the common household. It was probably multipurpose in function. Some had a cover or lid.

lekanis: In Greek antiquity, a shallow basin, usually with two horizontal handles and fitted with a lid that would be reversed to act as a stemmed plate. There are red-figured examples decorated with scenes of women.

Leki Male: A complex of tumulus burials of the Unetice culture of southern Poland. The central burials are in stone cists with wood ceilings, covered with stone. Grave goods include bronze axes, daggers, and halberds, gold ornaments, amber ornaments, and pottery. These are similar to burials of the Wessex culture.

lekythos: In ancient Greece, a pottery oil flask used at baths and gymnasiums and for funerary offerings. The flask has a long, cylindrical body gracefully tapered to the base and a narrow neck with a single loop-shaped handle. The body was often covered with white slip and then painted in polychrome. (*syn.* lecythus; plural lecythi or lekythoi)

Leland, John (c. 1506–1552): An early notable antiquarian who, in his official capacity as King's Antiquary to King Henry VIII, toured England and Wales describing places of antiquarian interest, including prominent prehistoric sites. He intended to write a book ("History and Antiquities of the Nation") that would provide a topographical account of the British Isles and the adjacent islands and to add a description of the nobility and of the royal palaces. He died, however, before these works were prepared.

Lelang: One of the Han colonies established in the Korean peninsula, a Chinese commandery established in 108 BC. Lelang survived as an outpost of the Chinese empire until 313 AD. Tombs contained Han lacquers, bronze mirrors, and gold filigree work. Some of the lacquers carry dated inscriptions, the dates ranging from 85 BC–AD 102, indicating that they were made in Sichuan in western China. (*syn.* [Lo-lang; Korean: Nangnang])

Le Lazaret: A cave site on the coast close to Nice, France, with deposits from before the last interglacial, with Acheulian tools and interspersed beach deposits. Human remains of two children and one adult are known, and it has been claimed that large huts were constructed inside the cave. The assemblage is dated to Riss III and includes pointed bifaces and choppers. (*syn.* Lazaret)

Lelesu: Early Iron Age tradition of the Chifumbaze complex in central Tanzania.

Le Mas d'Azil: Huge river tunnel and limestone grottoes in Ariège of the French Pyrenees with occupation from the Aurignacian to the Bronze Age. The Magdalenian level has portable art dated to the 12th millennium BC. The Azilian material, between the Palaeolithic and Neolithic, included perforated barbed points and painted pebbles. The site is rich in Palaeolithic remains.

Lemba-Lakkous: Chalcolithic settlement of the mid-4th to mid-3rd millennia BC in western Cyprus. Circular huts of stone and pisé were accompanied by pit grave burials.

Le Moustier: A cave near Les Eyzies in the Dordogne region of France, the type site of the Mousterian or Middle Palaeolithic. The type artifacts from the Mousterian consist of points and side scrapers, in addition to a few hand axes (especially heart- or triangular-shaped forms), and the secondary working is coarse. Upper Palaeolithic levels cover the Mousterian levels in both the classic shelter and the lower shelter. From the lower shelter came a Neanderthal skeleton of nearly mature age.

Lengyel: A late Danubian culture with the type site in western Hungary and many regional variants in Hungary, parts of Austria, and much of Czechoslovakia and Poland. It is closely linked to the Tisza culture of the Hungarian plain, and it may have been from this area that the Lengyel people adopted painted pottery and the occasional use of copper (some of the earliest use in temperate Europe). With the

Rössen and Tisza culture, it is a descendant of the Linear Pottery culture. The Lengyel culture is divided into two main phases: the Painted Lengyel, defined by white, red, and yellow crusted wares and dated c. 4000–3500 BC, and the Unpainted Lengyel, characterized by knobbed and incised pottery and dated c. 3500–3000 BC. The type site was a settlement adjoining a cemetery of some 90 inhumation graves. Sites have trapezoidal longhouses and some defensive works.

Leopards Hill: A cave in south-central Zambia, east of Lusaka, with a dated sequence from c. 20,000 BC through a Nachi-Kufan I phase and successive stages, to the appearance of the local Early Iron Age in about the 5th century AD.

Leopard's Kopje: A site near Khami, southwestern Zimbabwe, and the name of a later Iron Age industry that developed in c. 10th–11th century AD. At the type site, large circular houses were excavated. During later phases, from about the 14th century, gold mining and building with stone occurred. The complex covered adjacent areas of the northern Transvaal, South Africa. There was trade with the East African coast, class distinction, and the development of sacred leadership leading up to the Zimbabwe culture. (*syn.* Nthabazingwe)

lepaste: A large vessel shaped like a cylix but resting on a broad stand, used for holding pure wine.

Lepenski Vir: A hunter-fisher village settlement on the banks of the Danube in Serbia. Trapezoidal houses (often with red plastered floors), stone hearths filled with fish bones and other refuse, and a remarkable group of stone sculptures—by far the earliest monumental sculpture in Europe—were part of an advanced Mesolithic economy. Many carved stone human heads were found, often with "fishy" features. Radiocarbon places the site in the 7th millennium BC. The site was later occupied by a Starcevo village. The most significant aspect of Lepenski Vir is the degree of cultural elaboration achieved by sedentary fisher hunters at a time when agriculture was gradually becoming established in other areas of southeast Europe.

Le Placard: Cave site in the Charente region of France with Solutrean and Magdalenian levels with much industry and art material. Included in the artifacts were well-carved batons de commandement and other decorated, carved objects as well as engravings on the walls.

Lepsius, Karl Richard (1810–1884): German Egyptologist who led the Prussian expedition and survey of Egyptian monuments in 1842–1845. He also worked in Sudan and Palestine, sending some 15,000 antiquities and plaster casts back to Prussia. He published the results of the expedition in a 12-volume work, *Denkmäler aus Aegypten und Äthiopien* (1859), which still provides useful information for archaeologists. He is credited with virtually recreating Egyptology as a subject after the premature death of Jean François Champollion, by doing further work on the decipherment of Egyptian hieroglyphic writing.

Leptis Magna: A principal city of Roman North Africa (now Libya), the largest city of the ancient Tripolis. The original settlement was by the Phoenicians during the 6th century BC, then by Carthaginians and Numidians, later becoming Romanized under Emperor Augustus and colonized by Emperor Trajan; it was the birthplace of Septimius Severus. Among the ruins are a theater, forum, basilica curia, circus, gate, arches, amphitheater, and the hunting baths—particularly well preserved after the 7th-century decline (following Arab conquest) by desert sand. The earliest remains are from the Augustan age, and the site is important as evidence for the early development of Roman North African provincial architecture. (*syn.* Lepcis, Lepcis Magna; Punic Lpdy or Lpqy or Lpqi, modern Labdah)

leptolithic: Describing industries with many blades and blade tools, especially end scrapers, burins, and backed blades, typical of the Upper Palaeolithic. The term leptolithic, literally "of small stones," has sometimes been used specifically to refer to this type of stone technology, without any dating connotation or evolutionary position.

Lerici periscope: A subsurface detection probe fitted with a periscope or camera and light source, used to examine subterranean chambers—most often Etruscan tombs. The Lerici Foundation of Milan and Rome has had great success with this method since the development of the periscope, first used in 1957 in an Etruscan tomb in the cemetery of Monte Abbatone. The periscope is inserted into the burial chamber and can photograph the walls and contents of the whole tomb. (*syn.* Nistri periscope)

Lerma point: A projectile point made before 7000 BC in Tamaulipas and Puebla, Mexico. It is laurel leaf shaped and similar to those found in the Great Basin of the United States.

Lerna: Long-lived coastal settlement site near Argos in the Peloponnese, southern Greece. Middle and Late Neolithic villages were succeeded by a fortified township of Early Helladic II (c. 3000 BC, Early Bronze Age). At this stage it was a fortified township, surrounded by a stone wall with D-shaped bastions. Houses, built of mud brick on stone foundations, include a building known as the house of tiles, roofed with stone and terra-cotta tiles—a very early appearance of this roofing technique. Around 2400–2200 BC, it burnt down and was rebuilt in Early Helladic III (Middle Bronze Age), when the first pieces of Minyan Ware appear; the radical cultural change suggests the burning was intentional. Scattered imports from Crete assist in the dating. Two rectangular-shaft royal graves contemporary with the Shaft Grave B circle at Mycenae, c. 1600 BC (Middle Helladic), were the latest material on the site.

Leroi-Gourhan, André George Léandre (1911–1986): French prehistorian who prepared important works on Palaeolithic art. He worked at Les Furtins, Arcy-sur-Cure, and Pincevent, pioneering techniques of horizontal excavation, the study of occupation floors, and ethnological reconstruction of prehistoric life. He published *Treasures of Prehistoric Art* (also published as *The Art of Prehistoric Man in Western Europe*, 1967; originally published in French, 1965), a magnificently illustrated volume on the art of the Cro-Magnon peoples and *The Dawn of European Art: An Introduction to Palaeolithic Cave Painting* (1982; originally published in Italian, 1980), a well-illustrated technical discussion.

lesche: In Greek antiquity, an enclosed area for sitting and talking, and possibly dining. The lesche was primarily a local club, which served meals to strangers as well as to its local members.

Les Combarelles: A long narrow cave just outside Les Eyzies in the Dordogne, southwest France, where thousands of superimposed engravings from the late Aurignacian through the middle Magdalenian periods were discovered. The engravings are dominated by horses, bison, bear, reindeer, mammoth, and andropomorphs. They are assigned to the mid-Magdalenian, c. 14,000–12,000 BC. The number of engravings suggests that the cave long served as the center of a hunting cult. Scholars rank Les Combarelles as one of the finest products of the Ice Age.

Les Eyzies: Village near the center of the Dordogne, southwest France, the site of many Palaeolithic cave and rock shelter sites left by prehistoric man in the limestone zone called the Perigord. The chateau and National Museum contain many important finds, and underneath it there is a small Magdalenian and Azilian site, Grotte des Eyzies.

Les Fouaillages: Neolithic cairn on Guernsey, Channel Islands, with pottery of Cerny type dated to c. 4300 BC. It covered a megalithic cist on one end, a closed megalithic cist in the middle, and a passage grave on its widest end.

Les Furtins: Mousterian cave site in Saone-et-Loire, France, with evidence of a possible cave bear cult.

Lespugue: Series of cave sites in Save Gorge, Haute-Garonne of the French Pyrenees, with occupation from the Aurignacian to the Magdalenian. A famous ivory Venus was associated with Gravettian material.

Let: A settlement of the Early Neolithic Cris culture, the Romanian regional variant of the First Temperate Neolithic, with later Boian and Gumelnita occupation levels. It is dated to the early 5th millennium BC and is a rare example of a multilevel Cris site, with three occupation horizons, each characterized by differing styles of painted wares.

Le Tillet: Site of Palaeolithic industries at Seine-et-Marne, France, including Acheulian and a Mousterian assemblage with bout-coupé bifaces.

letter: A type of writing preserved in the archaeological record: Sometimes the originals have survived in the form of papyri, ostraca, and wooden boards, but in many cases stelae, inscriptions, or temple archives incorporate transcriptions of letters. Letters were also written to the dead; relatives of deceased often sought to communicate to them by writing letters, asking for help or forgiveness.

Leubingen: An early Bronze Age chieftain's burial of the Unetice culture of Saxony, Germany. It consisted of a leanto wooden mortuary chamber under a stone cairn, itself covered by a barrow. Inside was the burial of an extended elderly male and, placed at right angles across him, a second body, of an adolescent, perhaps female. Grave goods included a series of gold ornaments (pins, spirals, hair rings, beads, earrings, and an arm ring), bronze daggers, axes, halberds, and chisels, stone tools, and pottery.

Levalloisian: (luv'-uh-loz'-ee-un) Pertaining to the Levallois technique or describing tools made by this method of producing flint flakes from a prepared core. It is also the name of the middle Palaeolithic culture or industry of the second interglacial in France, characterized by the introduction and refinement of flake tools. The name is derived from Levallois-Perret, a town near Paris, where such artifacts were first discovered. (*syn.* Levallois; Levalloisian flake technique)

Levallois technique: (lah-val-wah') A distinctive method of stone toolmaking in which flakes are removed by percussion from a preshaped core, with little other modification. This prepared-core knapping technique allows the removal of large flakes of predetermined size and shape. The face of the core is trimmed to shape to control the form and size of the intended flake. Characteristically, the preparatory flaking is directed from the periphery of the core toward the center. The residual core is shaped rather like a tortoise, with one face plane and the other domed, while the flake shows the scars of the preparatory work on one face and is plane on the other. It is named for Levallois-Perret, a suburb of Paris, where such artifacts were first discovered. The Levallois technique was known from the Acheulian period and was employed by certain late Lower Palaeolithic hand ax makers, and throughout the Middle Palaeolithic by some Mousterian communities. It lasted into the Upper Palaeolithic of the Levant and in the Epi-Lavalloisian industries of Egypt. (*syn.* Levallois facies)

Levalloiso-Mousterian: A term used for the Mousterian cultures found at Mount Carmel, Jebel Qafzeh, Shanidar Cave, and other east Mediterranean sites. It was once thought that Levallois flakes signified a Levalloisian culture, whereas side scrapers indicated a Mousterian culture, and when the two were found together the phenomenon was called Levalloiso-Mousterian. The idea of such a hybrid culture is now generally rejected.

Le Vallonet: A cave on the Mediterranean coast of Provence, France, which has yielded what may be the oldest tools in Europe. In sediments with fauna of Upper Villa-Franchian type were five pebble tools and four flakes. Both the animal bones and the tools suggest a correlation with the early part of the Olduvai sequence.

Levant: Historically, the countries bordering the eastern Mediterranean shores. The term is also associated with Venetian and other trading ventures as at Tyre and Sidon as a result of the Crusades. It was applied to the coastlands of Asia Minor and Syria, sometimes extending from Greece to Egypt. It was also used for Anatolia and as a synonym for the Middle or Near East. The term is from the French *lever*, "to rise," a reference to where the sun rises.

Levantine art: Rock art found mainly in eastern Spain and dating to the Neolithic period. Small red-painted deer, ibex, humans, and so on were used in hunting scenes. The art was once assigned to the Mesolithic.

Levanzo: A small island off western Sicily, Italy, where fine engravings of animals have been found in a cave, Grotta Genovese. It belongs to the Upper Palaeolithic Romanellian group of c. 10,000 BC and depicts horses, deer, cattle, and humans.

level: An instrument used in surveying, which takes vertical measurements and which is much used in excavation for the recording of site contours and accurate depths of features, especially for making maps and identifying the location of artifacts. There are several types of leveling instruments, the Y or dumpy level, the tilting level, and the self-leveling level. Each consists of a telescope fitted with a spirit level and generally mounted on a tripod. It is used in conjunction with a graduated rod placed at the point to be measured and sighted through the telescope. The theodolite (q.v.), or transit, is used to measure horizontal and vertical angles; it may be used also for leveling. The differences between the types are in the ease of leveling: The first has a single spirit level for the whole instrument, the second a separate spirit level for spindle and telescope with a tilting mechanism and adjustable screw on the telescope, and the third an optical part operated by a pendulum so that the line of sight is always horizontal. After establishing a datum point, the instrument is sighted on a leveling staff or rod, which is marked in a graduated scale, metric or imperial. The difference in level between the telescope and the base of the rod can be read off on this scale, and the result subtracted from the height of the level itself above ground; the final figure gives the real height, or depth, of the feature above or below the ground at instrument point. Subtracting the stadia rod reading from the height of the level above the ground surface gives the difference in height between ground surface at the instrument station and the ground surface at the datum point. A series of levels taken across a site will give contours, while excavated features and small finds can be leveled in with greater accuracy than with tapes from a hypothetical ground surface. The term is also used to refer to the actual height measurements taken with such an instrument. More generally, archaeologists often use the term *level* interchangeably with layer. In excavations, the remains are divided into levels that contain the buildings and objects belonging to a phase.

level bag: A paper sack, usually containing archaeological objects from a single horizontal level in a single excavation square. Finds are usually grouped by type (by artifact classes, bones, plant remains, charcoal) and put into labeled (plastic) bags inside the level bag.

leveling: To establish the height above the site datum of a number of points (spot heights), which will either record the level of the surface of a feature or layer or enable a contour survey to be constructed. It also means to find the heights of different points in a piece of land, especially with a surveyor's level. (*syn.* leveling)

levigated: Purified by sedimentation. When clay is mixed with water and allowed to stand, the coarser grains settle to the bottom, and water and any vegetable impurities can be strained off the top. The layer between gives a particularly fine clay for delicate or high-quality pottery. Levigation is the process of producing fine clay for high-quality pottery by water purification. (*syn.* levigation (noun))

Lévi-Strauss, Claude (1908–   ): French anthropologist and founder of structuralism, a name applied to the analysis of cultures, viewed as systems, in terms of the structural relations among their elements. Structuralism has influenced social science, philosophy, comparative religion, literature, and film. According to Lévi-Strauss's theories, universal patterns in cultural systems are products of the invariant structure of the human mind. Structure referred exclusively to mental structure, although he found evidence of such structure in his far-ranging analyses of kinship, patterns in mythology, art, religion, ritual, and culinary traditions.

Levkas: One of the Ionian Islands off the west coast of Greece, which was once believed to be Homer's Ithaca, home of Odysseus. Mycenaean remains at Nidhri on the east coast testify to early occupation and convince some scholars that Leucas, not Ithaca, was the home of Odysseus. The cave of Chirospilia has yielded Neolithic material, but more important are the Early and Middle Bronze Age cemeteries. The former included the rites of jar burial and partial cremation under barrows. Two groups of tombs of the Middle Bronze Age contained some Minyan Ware and show some links with the shaft graves of Mycenae and with burial mounds in Albania. In the mid-7th century BC, Corinthian colonists established themselves just south of the present capital and dug a canal through the isthmus. Under Roman rule in the 2nd century BC, a stone bridge, of which there are some remains, was constructed to the main island. In 167, the Romans made Levkas a free city. (*syn.* Leucas)

lexicostatistics: A method for estimating the approximate date when two or more languages separated from a common parent language by using statistics to compare similarities and differences in vocabulary. It is the study of linguistic divergence between two languages, based on changes in a list of common vocabulary terms and the sharing of common root words. This science comparatively studies the vocabularies of languages and measures linguistic change through absolute time. By studying the rate of change, the length of time (time depth) during which two related languages developed independently may be calculated. Lexicostatistics relies on statistical comparison of the basic vocabulary shared by two or more related languages and on the assumption that the rate of vocabulary replacement is constant over sufficiently long periods. It is a way of arriving at a date of separation between two languages that have a common origin by studying the extent to which they have diverged from each other, and it provides archaeologists with approximate dates for the origination of subcultures diverging from each other. For instance, in Alaska the great difference between the Aleut language and the other Eskimo languages is thought to have been the result of the cultural isolation of the Aleuts from the 3rd millennium BC onward. It is a controversial method. (*syn.* glottochronology)

ley line/ley-line: A hypothetical straight line connecting prehistoric sites, frequently regarded as the line of an ancient track and credited by some with paranormal properties. The term also refers to the alignment of diverse features, usually taken from small-scale maps rather than from the ground, assumed to have some ancient esoteric significance. (*syn.* ley)

Lhokseumawe: Marine shell middens of the mid-Holocene on the coast of northeast Sumatra. There are Hoabinhian stone tools, especially sumatraliths.

li: A cooking vessel common in the Chinese Neolithic and Bronze Ages in both pottery and bronze. It is a small tripod bowl with hollow legs, characteristic of the Henan and Shaanxi Longshan cultures (Hougang II, Kexingzhuang II), which in Shang and Chou times was copied in bronze. The Xian steamer was a perforated bowl set atop a li and first appeared in Henan Longshan pottery and bronze in the Shang period.

lian: Chinese term for a lacquered wooden box in which toilet necessities or food such as cooked cereals was kept.

Liang-chu: A Middle and Late Neolithic culture in central southern China, with its type site in Jiangsu Province, originating c. 3000 BC. Its painted pottery succeeded the Yang-Shao culture and preceded or was contemporary with the Longshan culture; Liangzhu is a continuation of the Maji-

bang culture of the same region and is of Hemudu lineage. The jade industry was very advanced, with intricate incising and relief carvings of the *taotie* motif. It was a rice-growing culture. (*syn.* Liangzhu)

Liao Dynasty: A dynasty formed by the nomadic Khitan tribes (907–1125) in much of present-day Manchuria (Northeast Provinces) and Mongolia and the northeastern corner of China proper. There were elaborate chambered tombs.

libation: A Greek or Roman offering of wine to the gods; an act of pouring liquid as a sacrifice to a deity. It was poured from a phiale or patera, which was filled by an oinochoe.

Libby, Willard Frank (1908–1980): An American physicist and chemist who received the Nobel Prize for developing the radiocarbon-dating technique.

library: Collection of books used for reading or study, or the building or room in which such a collection is kept. Libraries originated in the 3rd millennium BC, when records on clay tablets were stored in a temple in the Babylonian town of Nippur. In the 7th century BC, the Assyrian king Ashurbanipal assembled and organized a collection of records, of which some 20,000 tablets and fragments have survived. The first libraries as repositories of books were those of the Greek temples and those established in conjunction with the Greek schools of philosophy in the 4th century BC. Important libraries of the ancient world were those of Aristotle, the great Library of Alexandria with its thousands of papyrus and vellum scrolls, its rival at Pergamum, which included many works on parchment, the Bibliotheca Ulpia of Rome, and the Imperial Library at Byzantium set up by Constantine the Great in the 4th century AD. China also has a long tradition of record keeping and book collecting, in private libraries as well as in centralized government libraries. Extant Greek and Roman literary works were preserved alongside the early Christian literature in Constantine's library and, beginning in the 2nd century, in libraries of monasteries. The loss of the Great Library at Alexandria, which was burned to the ground in the late third century AD, was devastating. The Alexandria library had probably been established by Ptolemy I Soter (305–285 BC), who also founded the Museum ("shrine of the Muses"), initially creating both institutions as annexes to his palace. Later in the Ptolemaic period, another large library was created, probably in the Alexandria serapeum, but this too was destroyed in 391 AD.

Libyans: A people of the Old and Middle Kingdoms living in the Western Desert, beyond Egypt's frontiers. They seem to have been seminomadic pastoralists. The Libyans ruled Egypt during the 22nd and 23rd Dynasties. (*syn.* Tjehenu, Tjemehu, Meshwesh, Libu)

Li Chi (1896–1979): Chinese archaeologist responsible for establishing the historical authenticity of the semilegendary Shang Dynasty of China (c. 1766–1122 BC). He supervised numerous excavations at Anyang (An-yang), working to identify the features distinguishing the Shang civilization from previous Neolithic cultures. More than 300 tombs, including four important royal burial sites, were uncovered and carefully studied. Some 1,100 skeletons and oracle bones, unquestionably linked with the Shang period, were recovered. Li Chi created a typology of bronzes based on their shapes, of ceramic sherds, and bone hairpins. Following the Japanese invasion of China and the expulsion of the Chinese Nationalists from the mainland, many of Li's Anyang remains and notes were lost. After escaping to Taiwan, he established the first archaeology and anthropology department at a Chinese university (National University in Taipei). He published a number of books, including *The Beginnings of Chinese Civilization* (1957). (*syn.* [Li Ch'i])

lienzo: In ancient Mesoamerica, a lengthy document made of animal skin or cloth, similar to a codex. The difference is that a lienzo is rectangular or irregular and a codex is a long scroll. The lienzo is often a map depicting elite land holdings. The surviving specimens were prepared after the Spanish Conquest.

Lifan: Type site northwest of Chengdu, China, of a local culture of western Sichuan province. It was characterized by slate cist burials and grave goods that suggest that the culture flourished in the late Eastern Chou and early Han periods. It seems to have had wide-ranging contacts, including metropolitan China (western Han coins), the Xindian culture of Gansu (pottery shapes), the Ordos region (small animal bronzes), and perhaps even Western Asia (glass beads). (*syn.* Li-fan)

lifeway/lifeways: A traditional way or manner of living of a culture. The settlement pattern, population density, technology, economy, organization of domestic life, kinship, social stratification, ritual, art, and religion of a culture. (*syn.* cultural form; life-way)

ligature: A printed or written character consisting of two or more letters or characters joined together. Two or more signs joined as one—ff, fi, ffi are examples of phonographic ligature. The signs for percent and for fractions are logographic ligatures, and the sign & was once a xenographic ligature.

Lightfoot, Dr. John (1602–1675): The master of St. Catharine's and vice-chancellor of Cambridge University, who in 1642 declared that humans, heaven, and earth all were created by the Trinity on October 23, 4004 BC, at 9 o'clock in the morning.

Lima culture: An Early Intermediate period (c. 200 BC–AD 600) culture of the central coast of Peru. Its major population centers were Cajamarquilla and Pachacamac. There are ceramics (Maranga, Interlocking style) showing the influence of the Moche culture. Changes in the pottery style during the Middle Horizon (AD 600–1000) indicate influence from the Huari Empire.

limes: The Latin word for "path," in ancient Rome, the strip of open land along which troops advanced into unfriendly territory. The word, therefore, came to mean a Roman military road, fortified with watchtowers and forts. Finally, limes acquired the sense of frontier, either natural or artificial; towers and forts tended to be concentrated along it, and the military road between them was often replaced by a continuous barrier. Its use as a term for the frontier zone of the Roman Empire, under direct military rule, was particularly used of the Rhine and Danube Rivers in central Germany, adopted as the frontiers of the Roman Empire (from AD 9). This was later extended into the Black Forest area by Hadrian and Antoninus Pius. The Alemanni broke through the limes in c. 260, and the Roman frontier was withdrawn to the Rhine and Danube once more. The limites in Great Britain were Hadrian's Wall between the Rivers Tyne and Solway and, farther north, the turf wall of Antoninus Pius between the Rivers Forth and Clyde. Limes were also created in Anatolia, Syria, and North Africa. (*syn.* plural limites)

Lime Springs: Site in northeast New South Wales, Australia with evidence of diprotodon, protemnodon, and other megafauna in association with artifacts. Kartan material is dated to 19,300 bp.

limited-area reconnaissance: A method of comprehensively inquiring about a site, supported by actual substantiation of claims that sites exist by checking the ground.

limonite: Limonite is the catchall name widely applied to hydrous iron oxide minerals. It is more specifically an impure hydrated iron oxide varying in color from dark brown to yellow, colloidal or amorphous in character.

Lincoln: An important Roman colony in eastern England on the main Roman route north. The site is on the intersection of two principal Roman roads, the Fosse Way and Ermine Street, and shows earlier traces of Iron Age occupation. Roman use was possibly from as early as AD c. 43, and by c. 60 a turf and timber fortress was built for the 9th Legion. By about the end of the 1st century, a colonia was established with stone walls and tower defenses. Industrialized pottery production is probable, and remains survive, mostly from the 3rd and 4th centuries, of walls, baths, mosaic floors, and a stone sewage system. Evidence for an aqueduct seems to show an uphill gradient, which may imply the use of pumps. Three Roman gateways still exist, including Newport Arch. (*syn.* Roman Lindum)

Lindenmeier: Folsom site in eastern Colorado with occupation c. 11,000 BP, also with Archaic and Late Archaic components. It was a kill, butchering, and camp site and may have been a seasonal meeting and camping place for hunting groups. The Folsom is characterized by a distinct leaf-shaped projectile point and a variety of scrapers, knives, and blades. It marked the first association in the Americas of manmade artifacts with the bones of long-extinct mammalian forms

Lindenschmit, Ludwig (1809–1893) and Wilhelm (1806–1848): Brothers who attributed burials they excavated at Selzen near Mainz to great invasions and the Franks. They used comparative methods and made proper use of terminus post quem provided by dates on coins.

Lindholme Hoje: A site on the northern shore of Limfjord in Jutland, used as a gravefield from the prehistoric period until the Viking era, including a Viking ship cemetery. In the 11th century it was overlaid by a Viking village, which functioned as a small trading and industrial settlement. One interesting find was a spoked wagon wheel. The settlement went out of use around 1100 owing to the silting up of the fjord and continual sand drifts. (*syn.* Lindholm Hills)

Lindisfarne: Island off the coast of Northumberland, northeast England, where in 634, Saint Aidan and other monks from Iona founded a monastery. It became a center for producing illuminated manuscripts (Lindisfarne Gospel, c. 700) and works of art of the Northumbrian school. In 793, it was subjected to the first Viking (Danes) raid on England, and the monastery functioned only intermittently afterward. There are no traces of the earliest buildings; the church, cloister, ranges and walls visible today all date to the Norman Benedictine abbey. Lindisfarne's past is reflected in the manuscripts that have survived, Saint Cuthbert's coffin, and some carved sculpture. It was connected to the coast of Northumberland only at low tide. (*syn.* Holy Island)

Lindisfarne Gospel: Manuscript illuminated at Lindisfarne in the late 7th or 8th centuries in Hiberno-Saxon style (Celtic-Germanic). It is one of the most splendid Early Christian manuscripts from the British Isles and is housed in the British Museum. It was the first great Anglo-Saxon work of this kind. Attributed to the Northumbrian school, the Lindisfarne Gospels show the fusion of Irish, classical, and Byzantine elements of manuscript illumination.

Lindner Site, Nauwalabila: Painted sandstone shelter in Arnhem Land, northern Australia, dating to 20,000 years ago. The lowest levels have Australian Core Tool and Scraper tradition artifacts of older than 18,000 bp. There are edge-ground tools dating c. 14,000 bp, Australian Small Tool tradition points of about 6000 bp, and then adzes of about 3500 bp.

Lindow Man: A body found in a peat bog of Cheshire, England, possibly a ritual sacrifice with radiocarbon dates of the 1st–2nd centuries AD. Parts of other bodies have been found there.

lineage: Descent in a line from a common progenitor; a group of individuals tracing descent from a common ancestor. A kinship that traces descent through either the male (patrilineal) or female (matrilineal) members.

linear: A term describing a script composed of simply drawn lines with little attempt at pictorial representation, especially a form of cursive in which the hieroglyphs were sketched by outline only.

Linear A: A syllabic script created by the Minoans and used in Crete and on other Aegean islands of Greece during the Neopalatial (early palace) period, c. 1700–1450 BC (also c. 2000/1900–1400 BC). The script has never been deciphered. It was inscribed on clay tablets as administrative records, as well as on stone (religious) vases and bronze double axes. Sir Arthur Evans named the Linear A and B scripts to distinguish them from the hieroglyphic that preceded them; Linear A is the earlier of the two. Each is a syllabary and was written with a sharp point on clay tablets. Linear A is of the Middle Minoan III–Late Minoan I. It is in some ways similar to Linear B and has pictograms reduced to formal outline patterns. Linear A tablets have been found in the palaces of Crete itself and also on the Cycladic islands of Melos, Keos, Kythera, Naxos, and Thera.

Linear B: A syllabic script used in Minoan Crete and Mycenaean Greece from c. 1450–1200 (also c. 1500–1100) BC. Michael Ventris deciphered it in 1952 as an early form of Greek. It was created at Knossos when the Mycenaeans took control and spread to mainland Greece. It was used mainly at the palace sites of Mycenae, Pylos, Thebes, and Tiryns. Most of the Linear B writings are on clay tablets but also on terracotta jars that were traded throughout the Aegean region. The writings are administrative/economic in nature, and their decipherment has thrown much light on the continuity between Bronze Age and classical Greece. They are from the Late Minoan II in Crete and Mycenaean III A–B on the mainland. It is probable that when the Mycenaeans overran the Minoans they adopted the script used on Crete, Linear A, and adapted it for writing the Greek language; many signs were added to the existing Linear A signs.

linear earthwork: An earthwork, dike, ditch, or bank that is created in a straight line, not curving around to form an enclosure. Such earthworks were of various lengths and created for various purposes. Some Bronze and Iron Age examples may be ranch boundaries with no defensive value, but later in the Iron Age and the post-Roman Dark Age may be either boundary markers or defense works. Many of these later dikes cut across communication routes or lines of easy access, and would have been an effective obstacle against chariots or wheeled vehicles. (*syn.* dyke, dike)

Linear Elamite script: A syllabic script used in Elam for inscriptions c. 2200 BC. The earliest Elamite writings are in a figurative or pictographic script and date from the middle of the 3rd millennium BC. Documents from the second period, which lasted from the 16th to the 8th century BC, are written in cuneiform; the stage of the language found in these documents is sometimes called Old Elamite. The last period of Elamite texts is that of the reign of the Achaemenid kings of Persia (6th–4th centuries BC), who used Elamite, along with Akkadian and Old Persian, in their inscriptions. The language of this period, also written in the cuneiform script, is often called New Elamite.

Linear Pottery culture: The earliest Neolithic culture of central Europe, western Ukraine to eastern France, between c. 4500–3900 BC. It is so named after curvilinear incised patterns that make its pottery so recognizable. This was the first farming culture in central Europe, based on grain cultivation and domesticated livestock, lasting to 3200 BC on its periphery. The Linear Pottery core area stretches from eastern Hungary to the Netherlands, including settlement concentrations in the Pannonian Basin, Bohemia, Moravia, central Germany, and the Rhineland. A second rapid expansion occurred eastward around the northern rim of the Carpathians, from Poland to the Dniepr. Linear Pottery is characterized by incised and sometimes painted pottery (¾ spherical bowl) with linear designs (curvilinear, zigzag, spiral, and meander patterns), polished stone shoe-last adzes, and a microlithic stone industry. Small cemeteries of individual inhumations are common as are longhouses with rectangular ground plans. The remarkable uniformity that characterized the Linear Pottery culture in its core area broke down after c. 4000 BC, and the cultures that emerged—Tisza, Lengyel, Stroke-Ornamented Ware, Rossen, and so on—were more divergent in characteristics. It is most possible that the culture derived from the Körös culture of the northern Balkans. (*syn.* Linearbandkeramik; LBK; Danubian I)

linear regression analysis: A statistical procedure for determining the relation between two variables. It has many applications in archaeology, as in the study of variations in population or the size of clay-pipe stems through time, or the relation between the quantity of an item and the distance from its source. One variable (e.g., time or distance) is regarded as independent, while the second is dependent on it; from a set of known observations, it is possible to estimate the relation between the two. Thus, given the population figures for different times in a region, it would be possible to predict the population for any other date. The method assumes that there is a linear relation between the variables and uses only one variable to explain all the variation in the other; these can be serious limitations.

line level: A small spirit bubble designed for suspension from a string; often used to lay in horizontal lines across an archaeological site. It is not as accurate as transit-defined vertical provenience.

lingling-o: A kind of knobbed earring made of jadeite, glass, or metal and typical of Sa Huynh in Vietnam. It is also found in the neighboring islands and was possibly traded in Southeast Asia.

linguistics: A subdiscipline of anthropology that emphasizes the relations between cultural behavior and language. It is the study of human speech including the units, nature, structure, and modification of language.

lintel: A horizontal stone slab, beam, or wooden block forming the top of a door or window; a horizontal architectural member spanning and usually carrying the load above an opening.

Linyi: An ancient Indochinese kingdom founded in AD 192 in the southern Shandong province, China, and lasting to the 17th century AD. In the past decade, at least 10 important Western Han tombs have been excavated in this district, some richly furnished with paintings on silk and lacquers comparable to those from Mawangdui. One tomb contained nearly 5,000 inscribed bamboo slips that preserve the texts of a number of late Eastern Chou philosophical works and military treatises, including the Sun Zi bing fa ("Master Sun on the Art of War"). The kingdom later became known as the Indianized kingdom of Champa, which was eventually absorbed by Vietnam. (*syn.* Lin-i; Lin-yi; Champa)

lion: A large, powerfully built cat of the family Felidae, and the second largest of the big cats (after the tiger), now found wild only in Africa south of the Sahara. A few hundred live in Gir Forest National Park in Gujarat state, India. It has been, since earliest times, one of the best known of wild animals. During the late Pleistocene epoch (1,600,000 to 10,000 years ago), lions had an extremely wide geographic distribution and ranged over all of North America and Africa, most of the Balkans, and across Anatolia and the Middle East into India. They disappeared from North America about 10,000 years ago, from the Balkans about 2,000 years ago, and from Palestine during the Crusades. It is possible that the connection between the king and the lion stemmed from the hunting of these animals by the tribal chiefs of the Predynastic period in Egypt.

Lipari: An acropolis site on Lipari Island of the Aeolian Islands off the north coast of Sicily. Occupation started in the Neolithic c. 4000 BC, when obsidian was exploited. In the Bronze Age, Lipari became an important trading center. Mycenaean pottery has been found dating to 1500–1250 BC. The remains of Hellenistic buildings indicate its importance in Classical times. The volcanoes have created one of the finest stratigraphies of archaeological deposits anywhere.

Later in prehistory, Lipari remained important because of its strategic position, which allowed communities positioned there to control trade routes through the Straits of Messina and up the west coast of Italy. The site was abandoned some time in the 9th century BC and not reoccupied until the foundation of a Greek settlement by a mixed group of Cnidians and Rhodians in the early 6th century BC.

Lisht, el-/al-: Royal necropolis of Egypt's earliest 12th Dynasty rulers, Amenemhat I and Senwosret (Senusret/Sesostris) I (c. 1985–1920 BC), located on the west bank of the Nile, about 50 kilometers south of Cairo. It was close to the now unknown capital of the time, Iti-Tawy (Itj-towy). Found in Senwosret's pyramid complex were 10 larger-than-life-size statues of the king. (*syn.* Lisht)

Lisicici: A Late Neolithic culture in southern Bosnia, dated to the 4th millennium BC. There are few structural remains, and the ceramic assemblage shows affinities with the Dalmatian Late Neolithic Hvar culture.

lithic/Lithic/-lithic: Pertaining to or describing a stone tool or artifact. The capitalized term describes the first developmental period in New World chronology, preceding the Archaic period and characterized by the use of flaked stone tools and hunting and gathering subsistence. The combining form means relating to or characteristic of a (specified) stage in humankind's use of stone as a cultural tool and to form the names of cultural phases, such as Neolithic, Mesolithic. Lithics is the process or industry of making stone tools and artifacts. (*syn.* lithics)

lithic experimentation: Experimenting with the manufacture of stone tools, a useful analytical approach to the interpretation of prehistoric artifacts.

lithic scatter: A common class of sites where tools were made or repaired, resulting in a large number of flakes (and typically few other artifacts) at a site.

lithofacies: A part of sediment or rock that is different in composition or character, such as grain size. Characteristics of sediment are closely related to their depositional environment. Lithofacies is a lateral, mappable subdivision of a designated stratigraphic unit, distinguished from adjacent subdivisions on the basis of lithology—or a facies (appearance and characteristics of a rock) characterized by particular lithologic features.

lithofacies analysis: A technique used to identify and interpret depositional environments in which archaeological deposits are found. The lithofacies are determined by geometry, vertical sequences, and lateral associations. Lithofacies models or maps, generalized summaries of sediment characteristics of specific depositional environments, serve as guides to interpretation. Such a map shows variation in the overall lithologic character of a given stratigraphic unit and its changing composition throughout its geographic extent.

lithology: The description of rocks on the basis of such characteristics as color, mineral composition, and grain size. Also, the physical character of a rock. (*syn.* adj. lithologic, lithic)

lithophone: Naturally occurring stones, often stalactites or stalagmites, which were struck to make music since Palaeolithic times. Such sets of struck sonorous stones (individually called phonoliths) were found from the South Seas and South America to Africa and the Far East. Large stones were used in some Vietnamese temples, and one of the oldest surviving lithophones was discovered there. Remains of other ancient stones come from Chinese archaeological digs, and such instruments are mentioned in sources as early as the Chou Dynasty (c. 1122–256/255 BC). (*syn.* stone chimes; phonoliths)

Little Salt Spring: A prehistoric site in Florida with hearths, a boomerang, projectile point, and shell of an extinct giant land tortoise from the Palaeoindian period (12,000–8500 BP). There was an Archaic occupation (6800–5200 BP) with burials of 1,000 individuals preserved in peat.

Little Tradition: Folk elements that survive alongside the great tradition.

Little Woodbury: A palisaded Iron Age farmstead, south of Salisbury in Wiltshire, England, whose excavation set new standards in British Iron Age studies. It consisted of a circular post-built house surrounded by corn-drying frames, granaries, and storage pits, all enclosed in a wooden stockade. It was probably occupied from the 4th–2nd centuries BC.

Liulige: (Liu-li-ko) A town in Hui Xian, Hunan Province, China, where many burials of the Shang and Eastern Chou periods have been excavated. The Shang burials, some containing bronze ritual vessels, belong to the Erligang phase. Eastern Chou finds date from the 7th–2nd centuries BC and include one of the largest of Chinese chariot burials—a single pit containing 19 chariots.

living archaeology: The study of the living patterns of existing hunter-gatherer and farming societies whose traditions extend from ancient predecessors, such as the Australian Aborigines.

living floor: A layer of human occupation; this generic and imprecise term is applied to an assumed level of occupation in an archaeological site. It includes any surface that indicates use as a house or camp area, as evidenced by signs of cooking, sleeping, or working at household tasks. The area can be in a cave or structure or out in the open—anywhere everyday human activities took place. Ancient living floors have occasionally been preserved through the accumulation of soil and debris over them. (*syn.* living surface)

livre de beurre: Distinctive blade cores of Grand Pressigny (France) flint, which are yellow and resemble slabs of butter.

Liyu: A village near Hunyan in northern Shanxi, China, where a large hoard of bronzes of the 6th and 5th centuries BC was found. The name Liyu has since been applied to a style of decoration shared by many bronzes from the hoard and characterized by an interlace of dragons whose ribbon-like bodies are textured with fine meander and volute patterns. Its borrowings from steppe art are common to much Chinese art of the period.

Ljubljanko Blat: A marsh near Ljubljana in Slovenia, on which a number of Late Neolithic and Eneolithic village sites have been found. The material includes copper and molds for casting it. The culture is related to others throughout the East Alpine area, such as Vucedol, and was in contact with northern Italy.

llama: South American member of the camel family, Camelidae, a domesticated animal exploited by the ancient Andean civilizations as a beast of burden and, to a lesser extent, for its meat and wool. It is smaller in size than a camel and lacking a hump. Its wild ancestor, the guanaco, is still found in the Andes. The center of domestication was probably the highlands of southern Peru, Bolivia, and north Chile, perhaps as early as the 6th millennium BC. The first clear evidence of its domestication (dating to the Initial period) comes from ceremonial burials in the Viru Valley and from remains at Kotosh. Able to carry loads of up to 60 kilograms over difficult terrain, the llama gained economic importance as the basic unit of transportation of goods in the Inca Empire and was also maintained purely as a form of wealth, with the state owning huge flocks. Sacrifice (sometimes in the hundreds) was quite common.

Llano: The earliest Palaeoindian Big Game Hunting culture, from the plains of New Mexico, 10,000–9000 BC. Best known is the type site of Blackwater Draw; other sites were located in what was once boggy lake shore. Its chief diagnostic trait is the presence of Clovis materials, especially the fluted point, in association with mammoth remains. Evidence of the culture exists throughout North America: as far south as Iztapan, Mexico, as far north as Worland, Wyoming, and possibly as far east as Debert, Nova Scotia. The large plateau of Llano Estacado covered eastern New Mexico and the Texas Panhandle. (*syn.* Llano tradition)

loam: A texture of soil used to describe a mixture of less than 52% sand, 28–50% silt, and 7–27% clay. Loams are agriculturally productive and have good drainage qualities. There are other loamy textures with different percentages of the materials. (*syn.* loehm, lehm)

locational analysis: Any of a set of techniques borrowed from geography to study the relation between a site or sites and the environment. The relation between sites can be examined in different ways: nearest-neighbor analysis, network analysis, rank-size rule, central place theory, and site catchment analysis. Locational analysis is the search for additional information from the geographical placing and spacing of sites, the significance of which can sometimes be tested mathematically.

Loch Lomond stadial: A widespread but short interval of renewed glacial activity and cold climatic conditions in the British Isles. This event occurred about 11,000 years ago, some 2,000 years before the dissipation of the ice sheet. It is a stadial of the Devensian cold stage during which small glaciers were formed in the high mountains of Wales and the Lake District and an icecap was formed over the highlands of Scotland. The Loch Lomond Stadial may be correlated with Godwin's Pollen Zone III and the Younger Dryas (Scandinavia). (*syn.* Younger Dryas)

lock rings: Small penannular (almost complete ring) ornaments of gold or bronze popular in the Early to Middle Bronze Age in northern Europe. They are thought to have been used as hair ornaments. (*syn.* lock-ring)

Lockshoek: A nonmicrolithic Later Stone Age industry of the Oakhurst complex in interior South Africa, c. 12,000–8000 BP. It was contemporary with the Albany industry of Cape Province. (*syn.* formerly Smithfield A)

loculus: In Roman antiquity, a small chamber or cell in an ancient tomb for the reception of a body or urn. It was generally made of stone.

locus: A predicted archaeological site locality; a center of cultural activity. The term is also applied to a distinct portion of an archaeological site, typically separated from other parts of the site by space devoid of cultural materials. Many open-air sites consist of various loci spread over a relatively large area. (*syn.* pl. loci)

Loddekopinge: Settlement near Lund in southern Sweden, dating to the Viking period. Excavations have shown that in the 9th–10th centuries this was probably the site of a fair, to which traders came. Loddekopinge expanded to a considerable size before it was superseded by Lund.

Lödöse: Small settlement and trading site in southwest Sweden, and the forerunner of Gothenburg. Finds include a range of later medieval pots imported from Britain, western France, and Denmark at the time of the Hanseatic League.

loess: A wind-borne rock dust (very fine sediments, silt) carried from outwash deposits and moraines and laid down as a thick stratum during periglacial conditions in the steppe country surrounding the ice sheets. Wind erosion was widespread in the periglacial zone that surrounded the large Quaternary ice sheets. Material was picked up by the wind from the large expanses of proglacial deposits at the ice sheet margins. Because of its exceptional fertility, areas of loess were chosen for settlement by early agriculturists. In central and eastern Europe, as well as Asia and North America, there are notable concentrations of sites on loess. It provided good grazing for the animals on which Palaeolithic people fed, was rich in nutrients for plants, and was later settled by Neolithic farmers who found it easy to till with primitive equipment. It is an essentially unconsolidated, unstratified calcareous silt; commonly it is homogeneous, permeable, and buff to gray in color and contains calcareous concretions and fossils. Loess is important archaeologically as soil erosion in these regions during the Holocene caused substantial redeposition of this silt, often burying (deeply) and preserving archaeological sites. In semiarid regions, people such as the Pueblo Indians made houses and fortresslike closed edifices from loess-based adobe.

Loftus, Sir William K. (1821?–1858): British geologist and one of the early excavators in Mesopotamia. He worked at Susa, Uruk, Ur, Larsa, Nineveh, Nimrud, and other sites in Mesopotamia. The main objective of the excavations was to collect antiquities, some of which were transported back to the British Museum.

logogram: A written or pictorial symbol intended to represent a whole word. Writing systems that make use of logograms include Chinese, Egyptian hieroglyphic writing, and early cuneiform writing systems. No known writing system is totally logographic; all such systems have both logograms and symbols representing particular sounds or syllables. A logogram represents a frequently recurring word or phrase, differing from a determinative in that it furnishes additional information instead of classifying information already given. Many scripts contain a class of logograms, such as $, =, +, and numeric signs in English. Abbreviations, although composed of phonograms, are logographic in function. (*syn.* logograph)

lomas: Patches of vegetation outside valleys, which were seasonally watered by fogs. The Peruvian coast was covered with areas of this type of vegetation, which could live off the moisture from the fog in the air. Lomas were created as a result of climatic shift at the end of the Pleistocene. Lomas culture was developed in these areas by hunters who turned to exploitation of this vegetation as their economic basis. They set up seasonally occupied camps during the winter months. The lomas provided wild seeds, tubers, and large snails; deer, camelids (probably guanaco), owls, and foxes were hunted. Milling stones, manos, mortars, pestles, and projectile points frequently occur in the assemblages. Around 2500 BC, a further climatic change made much of the lomas dry up, and the area became a desert. Lomas sites were abandoned in favor of permanent settlement at the littoral zone along the coast, where maritime resources were exploited. The de-

posits are not thick enough to show stratification, but they have been arranged in chronological order by comparing the implement types and noting their distribution in the shrinking patches of vegetation.

Lombards: A tribe of Germanic descent that conquered northern Italy in the late 6th and early 7th centuries. The region was weak from the Gothic wars and made vulnerable by the death of the Emperor Justinian (565). Having swept through Venice, Milan, Tuscany, and Benevento, King Alboin established Pavia, on the Ticino River, as the capital of the newly created Lombard kingdom in 572. Although their territorial expansion extended as far south as Benevento, the Lombards never managed to gain complete control of the peninsula. Many major Byzantine cities fell to them, but the Eastern Empire maintained a firm hold in the coastal ports of Ravenna and Venice. The Lombards' impact was considerable, and they imposed distinct cultural traditions on Italy's decaying classical past. They made rich inlaid gold jewelry, fine sculpture, and created new architectural design which played a significant part in the development of the Romanesque style. The Lombard settlement seems to have been largely to the north of the Po River, the area with the majority of Lombard place names and Germanic-style archaeological finds, mainly from cemetery sites. The Lombard language seems to have disappeared by the 8th century, leaving few loanwords in the Italian language. When the Franks invaded, Lombards and Romans moved together still more as a conquered, by now "Italian," people.

London: Important port and capital town of Roman Britain by about AD 100, probably replacing the originally intended capital at Clochester. The site, on a previously unoccupied gravel plateau on the north side of the River Thames, was probably chosen as the lowest crossing point at the time of the Roman invasion in AD 43. Use began as a supply depot and a trading center as it was a convenient starting point for the growing network of Roman roads. Burnt and ravaged by Boudicca in 60–61, the town soon revived, and capital status brought a large forum (Leadenhall Market), governor's palace (Canon Street), and a legionary fort (area of London Wall). Although damaged by fire again in c. 125–130, the settlement continued to consolidate its position, and a wall was added to protect it between 183–217. Continuous occupation since the Roman period has prevented much extensive excavation. The Museum of London holds marble heads of Mithras, Serapis, and Minerva from the Mithraeum, and the British Museum holds the Tomb of Julius Alpinus Classicianus, procurator of Britain after Boudicca's revolt. A section of wall may be seen in Trinity Place near the Tower of London, and the Mithraeum has been reconstructed to the west of its original site, in front of Temple Court, Queen Victoria Street. (*syn.* Roman Londinium)

long-barrow/long barrow: An elongated mound covering a burial chamber, typical of the Early and Mid-Neolithic periods in Europe. Barrows of the Neolithic period were long and contained the various members of a family or clan. In southern England, the burial chamber consists of a megalithic tomb. (*syn.* portal tomb, court tomb)

long-branch: One of the two main versions of the Scandinavian runic alphabet used during the Viking Age; the other is short-twig. (*syn.* Danish runes)

Long Count system: A means of recording time in the Mesoamerican Preclassic period, the only one to refer to an initial fixed date, which was perhaps the equivalent of 3113 BC. Passage of time recorded in decreasing units equaling x times 144,000 days (day is *kin*), x times 72,000 days, x times 360 days, x times 20 days, and x times 1 day. In the Maya lowlands in the south, the Long Count system was used between AD c. 300–900, but Mayas are not thought to have invented this system of calculation. The units of measure are *kin, uinal, tun, katun,* and *baktun*—mainly progressing by 20s.

longevity: The expectation of the life span of a person, culture, and so on. Human's expectation of life is one of the simplest ways of measuring the ability to cope with the surroundings. It can rarely be calculated for an ancient population because usually too few skeletons are found to provide an adequate statistical sample for skeletal analysis. Even then the results may be biased, because infants often failed to qualify for ceremonial burial and so may not be represented. The age distribution of even a few skeletons, however, may give useful results.

longhouse/long house: In Neolithic times, an elongated (oblong) wooden post house that appeared in central Europe with the first farming communities in the Early Neolithic Bandkeramik cultures, about 4500–3000 BC, as well as the later Iron Age, about 100 BC–AD 500, of north-central Europe. It also applies to the Late Woodland cultures of northeast North America, about AD 1300–1600, especially the Iroquois and Huron. Life in the longhouse had ended by 1800, but the meeting room of the contemporary tribe continues to be called the longhouse. In North American antiquity, longhouses were divided into living quarters for a number of groups. In Europe, structures may have been multipurpose buildings for dwellings and livestock stables. Among the most famous are those of the Linear Pottery culture, which reached lengths of up to 40 meters. Archaeologically, the two halves of the longhouse are often distinguished by the existence of a hearth in the living quarters, a central drain, and sometimes stalls in the byre. The purpose of the European longhouse was to keep stock during the wet winter months and at the same time to provide dwelling for the farmers. In Upper Palaeolithic times, the longhouse was an elongated above-ground structure of up to 100 meters in length, with a central series of hearths. The walls and roofing were probably supported by wooden poles and large mammal bones. Remains of these have been found in Kostenki, Pushkari, and Avdeevo.

Longmen: A series of Chinese cave temples carved into the rock of a high river bank south of the city of Lo-yang, in Honan Province. The temples were begun late in the Northern Wei Dynasty (386–535), in the Six Dynasties period, and construction continued sporadically through the 6th century and the T'ang Dynasty (618–907). Following the transfer of the Northern Wei capital to Lo-yang in 494, a new series of Buddhist cave temples was begun. Construction of temples and images was most active during the first three decades of the 6th century and again in the T'ang Dynasty from about 650–710. The site is dominated by a colossal seated image of the Buddha Vairocana carved under T'ang imperial patronage in 672–675. (*syn.* Lung-men)

longphort: A term used in 9th-century Ireland for the first winter base camps of the Vikings, forts along the shore for the protection of their ships. (*syn.* longfort)

Longshan: Collective name of the regional cultures of the Late Neolithic in northern China of the 3rd to mid-2nd millennia BC. The term refers to the culture of the Chengziyai type site, often distinguished as the Classic Longshan or Shandong Longshan, which may have survived to a time contemporary with the bronze-using Shang civilization. The Longshan period encompasses first metal use, warfare, compressed earth walled sites of Hangtu construction, abundant gray pottery, rectangular polished stone axes, and the delicate wheel-turned black-burnished pottery of intricate shapes. A method of divination involving the heating of cattle bones and interpreting the cracks began here. In Honan, where its distribution overlaps that of the Yang Shao culture, Longshan is stratified above the former and below Shang material. Lungshanoid is another term used to describe these Neolithic cultures. (*syn.* Lung Shan; Lung-shan; lungshanoid)

loom: A device used for weaving cloth. Normally the variety of loom used can be deduced from surviving fragments of the resulting cloth. The cloth shows, for example, that the horizontal loom was the more usual in ancient Egypt, the vertical loom in Syria and Mesopotamia. In Europe, the vertical loom with weighted warps was standard. The weights—disk shaped, quoit shaped, or pyramidal—are frequently found on sites from the Late Neolithic to the Bronze Age and reappear with the Anglo-Saxons. In the Americas, the most common form was the belt or backstrap loom, in which a continuous warp thread passed between two horizontal poles. One was attached to a support while the other was attached to the seated weaver, who could adjust the tension of the warps simply by leaning forward or backward. The earliest evidence of the use of the loom, 4400 BC, is a representation of a horizontal two-bar (or two-beamed—i.e., warp beam and cloth beam) loom pictured on a pottery dish found at al-Badari, Egypt. Loom weights have been found at archaeological sites dating from 3000 BC, but this type of loom may have originated even earlier. By about 2500 BC, a more advanced loom was apparently evolving in East Asia.

looting: Any unscientific and illegal act of plundering archaeological sites for profit. Looters destroy evidence that archaeologists rely on to understand the past.

Lopburi: Settlement in central Thailand occupied from the Copper Age and in a region of copper and bronze production during the 2nd and 1st millennia BC. Some sites made copper and iron into the Khmer occupation. Lopburi, already a provincial capital, became a major center during the 11th–13th centuries AD and gives its name to the Khmer-influenced art of that time. It was the summer capital of the Ayutthaya king Narai (reigned 1657–1688). Thereafter the city declined, and many of its buildings decayed. (*syn.* Lop Buri; Lavo)

Los Millares: Important Chalcolithic settlement and cemetery in Almeria, southeast Spain, of c. 2400 BC, and located on a spur between the River Andarax and a stream. In the settlement are circular houses, outside there are forts, megalithic walls, and a cemetery with over 80 passage graves (circular tholos type). The rich grave goods included bone idol figurines, copper axes and daggers, pottery with double-eye motifs, and ivory and ostrich-eggshell artifacts. The site typifies "Millaran culture" of the mid-3rd millennium BC in southern Spain and Portugal, with the emergence of ranked societies whose power may have been based on the control of water supplies and sources of metal ores.

loss rate: The pattern of loss for a cultural object; large objects are less subject to loss than small ones, and valuable items are more likely to be searched for than items considered to have little value.

lost-wax: A method of casting metals in which the desired form was carved in wax, coated with clay, and baked; the wax runs out through vents left in the clay for the purpose, and molten metal is then poured through the same vents into the mold. When the metal is cool, the clay is broken off to reveal the metal casting. Each mold can be used only once. The technique was first developed in the 4th millennium BC in the Far East, especially by the Shang bronze workers of China. It was also used for gold in South America and Mesoamerica. The method was used for casting complex forms, such as statuary. (*syn.* cire perdue, lost-wax casting; lost wax process, lost-wax casting technique)

Lothagam: A site at the south end of Lake Turkana (formerly Lake Rudolf) in northern Kenya, with jaw fragments of what is thought to be a hominid from deposits some 5–6 million years old. It may be Australopithecus.

Lothal: A Harrapan town, one of the most important of the southern Indus civilization sites, at the head of the Gulf of Cambay, northwestern India. Besides typical Indus structures like a walled citadel, granary, drainage system, and a grid street plan, it had a dock faced with baked brick. There were residential and craftworking (shell, bone, bead, copper, gold) areas. The site was important for its sea trade, as shown by the discovery of a Dilmun seal from the Persian Gulf. There were also contacts with the Chalcolithic cultures of the Deccan peninsula and the practice of rice cultivation, which had been introduced from farther east. There was much local non-Harappan pottery in the Mature Harappan levels. Radiocarbon dates place it in the later 3rd millennium BC (c. 2400–2100 BC).

lot number: The number assigned to an archaeological collection that identifies an aspect of context in a collection; part of the catalog number.

lotus: The lotus is a genus of the pea family (Fabaceae or Leguminosae), containing about 100 species distributed in temperate regions of Europe, Asia, Africa, and North America and is any of several different plants. In ancient Egypt and Buddhist Asia, it is a water lily, the bud and flower of which were much used as motifs in the arts.

Lough Gur: A series of 16 Neolithic and Early Bronze Age settlement sites around the shores of a lake in Limerick, Ireland, one of the greatest concentrations of sites in Ireland. There were rectangular Neolithic houses, some associated with Beaker pottery. Some are enclosed by a double ring of stones, dated to c. 2600 bc. There are also megalithic chambered tombs, and stone circles nearby. Ritual or funerary monuments include menhirs, a wedge-shaped gallery grave, a flat-topped cairn with urn burials, and a circle of contiguous stones that yielded Late Neolithic and Early Bronze Age pottery. There are also several cashels and a crannog.

Lou Island: An island in the Manus, Admiralty Islands, which was an important source of obsidian for the Bismarcks and the western Pacific and first appeared about 3000 bp. The Manus group was settled after an open sea voyage around 5000 bp. The short-lived occupation sites and obsidian workshops are buried by volcanic ash.

Loulan: A Chinese military outpost in eastern Turkestan (modern Sinkiang), founded in the mid-3rd century. Documents of the 3rd and 4th centuries and silk fabrics have been found there, including Chinese textiles of Han date and a piece of silk tapestry dating c. 200/100 BC–AD 100–200. (*syn.* Lou-lan)

loutrophoros: In Greek antiquity, a container with a slender ovoid body, long neck, flaring mouth, and two long handles.

They were used from the 6th century BC for ritual purposes at weddings and funerals. The shape also appears in relief on the round on Attic Grave stelae.

Lovcicky: Late Bronze Age settlement of the Velatice group in southern Moravia of the Urnfield period.

Lovelock Cave: A Late Archaic site in the Humbolt Lake region of west-central Nevada, occupied as early as 7000 BC. Located near a desert marsh, it has yielded details of prehistoric desert adaptations over a long period. A dating scheme covering the period 2500 BC–AD 500 has been developed. The pits and artifacts indicate that the site was a cache or storage place rather than a living community.

Lowasera: A beach site on the eastern shore of Lake Turkana (formerly Lake Rudolf) in northern Kenya, formed between the 9th–4th millennia BC. The site was occupied from at least the 7th millennium BC by people who produced both microlithic and macrolithic implements and depended for their livelihood on fish caught by means of barbed bone harpoons similar to those from Early Khartoum. The early pottery at Lowasera was of wavy-line style; the later pottery was undecorated. Occupation continued until after the retreat of the lake at the end of the 4th millennium BC.

low-energy societies: Societies in which most energy comes from food and there is little dependence on nonhuman forms of energy.

Lower Egypt: The northern part of Egypt, land around the Nile Delta and Memphis, from modern Cairo to the Mediterranean coast. This geographic and cultural division of Egypt was bounded generally by the 30th parallel north in the south and by the Mediterranean Sea in the north. The boundary between Lower and Upper Egypt was somewhere between Lisht and Meidum on the west bank of the Nile. On the east bank, the second nome of Upper Egypt existed farther to the north. Characterized by broad expanses of fertile soil, Lower Egypt contrasts sharply with Upper Egypt, where the centers of habitation along the Nile valley are close to the desert. Lower Egypt in late Predynastic times constituted a political entity separate from Upper Egypt. Menes (fl. 3100 BC) joined the two regions, using the royal title, "King of Upper and Lower Egypt."

Lower Nubia: The part of the Nile Valley south of the traditional border of Egypt at Aswan as far as the second cataract of the Nile River. The region of Lower Nubia, basically between the first and second Nile cataracts, saw one of the earliest phases of state formation in the world when rulers of the A-Group culture, who were buried in a cemetery at Qustul, adopted symbols of kingship similar to those of contemporary kings of Egypt of the Naqadah II–III period. Lower Nubia is now one of the most thoroughly explored archaeological regions of the world. Most of its many tem-ples have been moved, either to higher ground nearby, as happened at Abu Simbel and Philae, or to quite different places, including various foreign museums.

lower-order central place: A small and functionally simple community in a regional hierarchy of communities differentiated by number, size, and function.

Lower Palaeolithic: The earliest part of the Palaeolithic period, beginning about 2.5 million years ago and lasting to about 100,000 years ago. It was characterized by the first use of crude stone tools, the practice of hunting and gathering; and the development of social units, settlements, and structures. It was the era of the earliest forms of humans. The phases of the Palaeolithic have been subdivided based on artifact typology; the Lower Palaeolithic is the period of early hominid pebble tool and core tool manufacture. In China, the Early Palaeolithic ran from 1,000,000–73,000 BC. (*syn.* Lower Paleolithic)

Lower Sonoran Agricultural Complex: A zone of high temperatures and tolerant crops in the southwest United States. The Lower Sonoran zone, in the southern sections of the Rio Grande and Pecos valleys and in New Mexico's southwestern corner, usually occurs at altitudes below 4,500 feet. It includes nearly 20,000 square miles of New Mexico's best grazing area and irrigated farmland. Utah's 4,000 plant species represent six climatic zones, from the arid Lower Sonoran in the southwestern Virgin Valley to the Arctic on mountain peaks.

Loyang: Ancient city in northwestern Honan Province, China, near the south bank of the Yellow River. It was important in history as the capital of nine ruling dynasties and as a Buddhist center. Lo-yang is divided into an east town and a west town. Lo-i (modern Lo-yang) was founded at the beginning of the Chou Dynasty (late 12th century BC), near the present west town, as the residence of the imperial kings. It became the Chou capital in 771 following the loss of Tsung Chou in Shensi, and was later moved to a site northeast of the present east town; it was named Lo-yang because it was north (yang) of the Lo River, and its ruins are now distinguished as the ancient city of Lo-yang. Traces of its rammed earth walls and one of its cemeteries of pit graves have been found. Bronzes and pottery recovered from some 270 tombs excavated at Luoyang Zhongzhoulu supply a valuable artifact sequence, spanning the entire Eastern Chou period. Particularly rich finds from Jincun, just northeast of the modern city, belong to the latter part of Eastern Chou; lesser tombs from the end of Eastern Chou and the Han period have been excavated at Shaogou. During the Qin and Western Han Dynasties, the capital returned to Shaanxi, but Luoyang was again the capital during the Eastern Han Dynasty and, for the last time, from AD 494–535, when the Northern Wei emperors ruled there. It finally fell to the Ch'in in 256. (*syn.* Lo-yang; Luoyang; formerly Honan-Fu; Honan)

Luangwa tradition: A Late Iron Age complex of central, eastern, and northern Zambia in the 2nd millennium AD with a distinctive pottery style. It appeared as a break from the Chifumbaze complex in the 11th century, originated in Zaire, and has continued into recent times. The term (also Luangwa variant) is also used for Earlier Stone Age Sangoan collections from eastern Zambia. This facies of the Sangoan industry is found in gravel deposits of the Luangwa and tributary valleys of eastern Zambia and is marked by large picks and other core tools made from water-rounded cobbles.

Lubaantun: A site in the Maya Mountains southeastern periphery, which was a small Classic and Late Classic Maya center in southern Belize. It was built in the early 8th century and consists largely of ceremonial buildings. There was a sizable population and flourishing market system. Its proximity to one of the few areas where cacao grows suggests that control of this much sought-after commodity was its major economic base and may be the reason why such a considerable investment of labor was made in building the site. It was fairly short lived and abandoned some time between 850–900, probably as part of the general Maya collapse.

Lucania: Area of ancient Italy south of Campania and next to the Tyrrhenian Sea. It was made up of several Greek colonies, including Paestum. This ancient territorial division of southern Italy corresponds to most of the modern region of Basilicata, with much of the province of Salerno and part of that of Cosenza. Before its conquest by the Lucanians, a Samnite tribe, about the mid-5th century BC, it formed part of the Greek-dominated region of Oenotria. Recent discoveries include the elaborately painted graves at Paestum, a city taken by the Lucanians about 400. Although they allied with Rome in 298, the Lucanians opposed and were defeated by Rome in the Pyrrhic War (280–275), the Second Punic War (218–201), and the Social War (90–88).

Lucanian pottery: Red-figured pottery made in Lucania from the late 5th and through the 4th centuries BC. There are links with Apulian pottery.

lucerna: A oil lamp or lantern of terra-cotta or bronze. One side had a handle, the other had one or more places for wicks. The oil was poured in through an opening in the center.

Lucy: A small 3-million-year-old Australopithecine, generally attributed to *Australopithecus afarensis*, found at Hadar in Ethiopia. It is the most complete specimen of an australopithecine found.

lug: Ear-shaped protuberances, sometimes flattened, added to the wall of a pot to assist in holding it. They may or may not be perforated. The hole was designed to take a cord or thong only and it was not a true handle.

lugal: A Sumerian word for "king." In the Early Dynastic period, the rulers of Lagash called themselves "king" (lugal), although the city itself never was included in the official Sumerian canon of kingship. The lugal may originally have been a war leader.

Luka Vrublevetskaya: Eneolithic settlement of the Cucuteni-Tripolye culture in the Ukraine. Pit dwellings include hearths and female figurines.

Lukenya Hill: An inselberg (boulder-hill) in southern Kenya, southeast of Nairobi, with material from the Middle Stone Age to the Late Iron Age. Numerous rock shelters and other sites have preserved this long sequence of prehistoric occupation. A backed microlith industry was established by the 16th millennium BC and probably long before. A fragment of human skull associated with this industry displays modern Negroid features.

Lumbini: A grove near the southern border of modern-day Nepal, India, where, according to Buddhist legend, Queen Maha Maya stood and gave birth to the future Buddha. Archaeological finds include Northern Black-Polished ware, which was in use during the period of the Buddha's lifetime. In c. 249 BC, the emperor Asoka made a pilgrimage to Lumbini and set up a commemorative pillar, which still survives. It is still a popular Buddhist pilgrimage place.

lunate: A crescent or half moon-shaped flint with the inner edge untrimmed and the thick, rounded edge having small chips removed; used as an arrowhead.

Lund, Peter W. (1801–1880): Danish naturalist who excavated more than 800 caves in Brazil. His finds of fossilized animals were used by Darwin in his evolution research. The discovery of human bones in association with animal remains from the Pleistocene led him to suggest in 1844 that these animals might have been contemporary with an "antediluvian" man.

Luni: An Apennine village with longhouses cut into soft rock, a small but prosperous Roman town on the Ligurian coast of north Italy. It specialized in the trade of marbles quarried at Carrara. There is evidence of its Late Roman trading contacts with North Africa and the Eastern Mediterranean, and there are imported soapstones and lead coins of the 7th–9th centuries.

lunula: A crescent-shaped sheet of gold, probably worn as a collar or chest ornament in the Early Bronze Age, possibly for rituals. Their incised geometric decoration is similar to that on bell beakers. They originated with the food vessel people of Ireland, Scotland, and perhaps Wales in the Early Bronze Age, and were traded not only to southern England but also across to northern Europe. The decoration has led to the suggestion that it imitates the multiple-strand necklaces of jet and amber that are also found during the Early Bronze Age. (*syn.* pl. lunulae)

Lupembian/Lupemban: A stone industry of the Lower Palaeolithic of west-central Africa, developed from a Sangoan predecessor and characterized by tools appropriate for rough woodwork. Lupemban is found in northern Angola and southern Zaire, and an important dated site is at Kalambo Falls on the Zambia/Tanzania border. In contrast with the Sangoan, Lupermban assemblages are marked by the fine quality of their bifacial stone-working technique on elongated double-ended points, large side scrapers, and thick core axes. The industry spans from before 30,000 BC until c. 15,000 BC.

lur: A Late Bronze Age, large bronze musical horn or trumpet, having a double curve and a disk-shaped, permanent mouth. The long curving tube was cast in sections by the lost-wax (cire perdue) method and fit together, ending in a flat metal disk decorated with raised embossing. Lurer come from the peat bogs of Scandinavia and are almost always found in pairs, suggesting that they were votive offerings. Lurer are among the most elaborate products of the European bronzesmith; experiments have shown that they have a surprisingly large musical range. (*syn.* pl. lurer; lure)

Luristan: A region of the central Zagros Mountains on the border of west-central Iran, where a distinctive bronze-working industry flourished 2600–600 BC. It is characterized by horse trappings, utensils, weapons, jewelry, belt buckles, and ritual and votive objects of bronze—which became most distinctive around 1000 BC. Scholars believe that they were created either by the Cimmerians, a nomadic people from southern Russia who may have invaded Iran in the 8th century BC, or by such related Indo-European peoples as the early Medes and Persians. The immigrants grafted onto a population of Kassites who had already developed a bronze industry around 2000 BC. Important Luristan sites are Tepe Giyan and Tepe Djamshidi, Tepe Ganj Dareh, Tepe Asiab, Tepe Sarab, Tepe Guran, and especially Tepe Sialk. Many bronzes were placed into museum collections as a result of persistent looting of tombs from the 10th–7th centuries BC. Iron also appears at an early date in the Luristan tombs.

Luristan bronze: Any of the horse trappings, utensils, weapons, jewelry, belt buckles, and ritual and votive objects of bronze probably dating from roughly 2600–600 BC, which have been excavated in the Harsin, Khorramabad, and Alishtar Valleys of the Zagros Mountains in the Lorestan region of western Iran, especially at the site of Tepe Sialk. Their precise origin is unknown. Scholars believe that they were created either by the Cimmerians, a nomadic people from southern Russia who may have invaded Iran in the 8th century BC, or by such related Indo-European peoples as the early Medes and Persians. The term denotes a broad region of

this metalwork and therefore has little cultural historical meaning. (*syn.* Lorestan)

Lusatian culture: A Late Bronze Age and Early Iron Age (Hallstatt period) culture of Poland and eastern Germany, an urnfield culture that had formed by c. 1500 BC. Larger settlements, such as Biskupin, Senftenberg, and Sobiejuchy, are fortified. The culture is noted for its bronzework and its fine dark pottery, sometimes graphite burnished and generally decorated with bosses and fluted ornament. Iron tools were adopted in the north throughout the earlier Iron Age. In some classifications, the Middle Bronze Age "pre-Lausitz" phase is considered the first stage of the Lusatian culture proper. (*syn.* Lausitz culture; Lusatia)

lustral basin: In Minoan architecture, a sunken room reached by a short flight of steps and often screened off by a parapet. They were either bathrooms or used for ritual purification.

Luwian: An extinct Indo-European language primarily of the western and southern part of ancient Asia Minor of the 2nd and 1st millennia BC, especially important to Arzawa. It was closely related to Hittite, Palaic, and Lydian and was a forerunner of the Lycian language. Knowledge of Luwian comes from cuneiform tablets discovered in the ruins of the Hittite archives at Bogazköy (modern Turkey). The pioneering work on Cuneiform Luwian was done by Emil Forrer in 1922. In addition to Luwian passages in the cuneiform tablets, a number of instructions occur in a hieroglyphic system of writing that originated with the early Hittite stamp seals of the 17th and 18th centuries BC. Hieroglyphic Luwian (often called Hieroglyphic Hittite) texts have been found dating from as late as the last quarter of the 8th century BC. The language was deciphered in the 1930s. More was learned about the meaning of the writing after the discovery of the Karatepe bilingual inscriptions, written in both Hieroglyphic Luwian and Phoenician. The Lycian language of about 600–200 BC, written in an alphabetic script, is believed to be descended from a West Luwian dialect. Luwian was probably the language of the Trojans during the Trojan War. The language survived in southwest Turkey until the Roman period. (*syn.* Luvian, Luish)

Luxor: The modern town now covering the site of ancient Thebes (Upper Egypt), connected with Karnak by a processional route. In the southern part of the town is the temple of Luxor, built under Amenhotep III (reigned 1390–1353 BC) and Ramesses II. The Great Temple of Amon was originally built for the festival of Opet. When Thebes declined politically, Luxor remained the populated part of the town. (*syn.* El-Aksur, Al-Uqsur)

Lycia: Ancient kingdom of southwestern Anatolia (Turkey), located on the Mediterranean coast between Caria and Pamphylia and extending to the Taurus Mountains, with its capital in Xanthos. In the Amarnà letters of the 14th–13th centuries BC, the Lycians are described as living between the Hittites on the north and the Achaean Greeks on the coast. They participated in the Sea Peoples' attempt to invade Egypt in the late 13th century. Nothing more is known of the Lycians until the 8th century BC, when they reappear as a thriving maritime people in cities of the Lycian League. The kingdom eventually fell to Cyrus' general Harpagus. Under Achaemenian Persia and later under the rule of the Romans, Lycia enjoyed relative freedom and was able to preserve its federal institutions until the time of Augustus. It was annexed to Roman Pamphylia in AD 43 and became a separate Roman province after the 4th century. Archaeological discoveries made on sites at Xanthus, Patara, Myra, and other of its cities have revealed a distinctive type of funerary architecture. The people spoke a dialect of Indo-European Luwian. Sir Charles Fellows discovered the ruins of the cities of Lycia. (*syn.* Lycians; Luka)

Lydenburg: An Early Iron Age site in eastern Transvaal, South Africa, occupied from AD 400–600. The culture of this name made fired-clay human heads of up to lifesize. They are thought to have been used in rituals.

Lydia: A small kingdom that appeared in western Anatolia (Turkey) in the 1st millennium BC, known to the Assyrians as Luddu. The land extended east from the Aegean Sea, occupying the Hermus and Cayster River valleys. By about the 7th century BC, Lydia was important in trade between the Aegean and the oriental civilizations. Its capital at Sardis became rich, exploiting the gold of the nearby Pactolus River; the Lydians are said to be the originators of gold and silver coins. In the mid-7th century, the kingdom was overrun by the Cimmerians, but re-emerged powerfully. The kingdom was most powerful under Alyattes (c. 619–560 BC), who extended his rule in Ionia. The legendary rich king Croesus (560–546 BC) was ruler when Lydia was finally overcome by the Achaemenids (c. 546–540). Sardis subsequently became the western capital of the Persian Empire, linked to Susa by a royal road. The Lydians are known for two achievements in particular: mastery of fine stone masonry, witnessed in the akropolis wall at Sardis and in the Pyramid Tomb and the Tomb of Gyges in the royal cemetery, and the invention of a true coin currency, which was adopted by both the Greeks and the Persians. The Lydians were a commercial people, who, according to Herodotus, had customs like the Greeks and were the first people to establish permanent retail shops. Sardis was captured by Alexander the Great in 334 BC and became a Greek city. (*syn.* Lydians)

lydion: In Greek antiquity, a type of pot for perfumes. Numerous examples have been found in Lydia, western Turkey, and Athens.

Lyell, Sir Charles (1797–1875): Scottish geologist largely responsible for the general acceptance of the view that all features of the Earth's surface are produced by physical, chemical, and biological processes over long periods of geological time (uniformitarianism). Lyell's achievements laid the foundations for evolutionary biology as well as for an understanding of the Earth's development. His work had a bearing on the development of archaeology at two points. His *Principles of Geology* (1830–1833) established the view that the Earth had been in existence for very much longer than the 6,000 years allowed by the biblical chronology and laid open the way for the later acceptance of the antiquity of man. In 1859, publication of Darwin's *Origin of Species* gave new impetus to Lyell's work. Lyell's *The Geological Evidence of the Antiquity of Man* (1863), tentatively accepted evolution by natural selection.

Lyles Hill: An enclosed Neolithic settlement and cairn in Antrim, Ireland, which has, with Grimston, given its name to a pottery ware widespread in Britain—the Grimston–Lyles Hill style. The pottery was made during the British Middle Neolithic, c. 4th millennium BC.

lynchet: A bank of earth that accumulates on the downhill side of an ancient plowed field as the disturbed soil moves down the slope under the action of gravity. It is a small-scale terracing effect visible particularly in ancient field systems, which is caused by accumulation of soil against an obstruction such as a field boundary. Field boundaries, such as banks or walls, become enlarged and overlaid by material loosened in the cultivation process. A corresponding erosion from the downslope side of the boundary creates a negative lynchet. Lynchets are conspicuous in the square Celtic fields (Bronze Age to Romano-British in date) and in the long rectangular fields, the so-called strip lynchets, laid out on sloping terrain in post-Roman and medieval times. (*syn.* terracette)

Lyngby: A site in Jutland, Denmark, which has given its name to a kind of small bone implement (ax) made of antler stem and branch and beveled to form a sharp edge. The tools date to c. 9000–8000 BC. (*syn.* Lyngby tools)

Lyons: A major Roman provincial town (colonia) in southern France, once the capital of the three imperial provinces of Roman Gaul and birthplace of the Emperor Claudius. Lugdunum was founded in 43 BC, shortly after the conquests of Julius Caesar, in an area of two previous Gallic settlements. The site was important as the center of Agrippa's road system and for commercial traffic on its two rivers. The town was built on the grid plan and was prosperous until AD 197. A large number of monumental remains and other Roman evidence have been found, including the Forum Vetus, the theater, and the odeum. As many as four aqueducts existed, and there are examples of the use of siphons. An industrial area in the Quai de Serin shows potters' kilns and glass and bronze foundries. Lugdunum was clearly an important center for the manufacture and distribution of imperial pottery. (*syn.* Lugdunum)

Mm

Maadi: Egyptian Late Predynastic settlement site, south of Cairo, occupied c. 3200–3000 BC, immediately preceding the Archaic period. The settlement, consisting of wattle-and-daub oval and crescent-shaped huts, as well as large subterranean houses, flourished from Naqada I to II. There are large pottery jars and storage pits, imports of the Gerzean of Upper Egypt and of Early Bronze Age Palestine.

Maa-Palaekastro: Site of a fortified settlement on the west coast of Cyprus, first occupied in the 13th century BC, possibly by the Sea Peoples. An ashlar structure may have been their sanctuary. In the 12th century BC, the settlement was destroyed by fire, then taken over for a period by the Mycenaean Greeks.

Maat: The ancient Egyptian goddess of truth and order, whose symbol was the ostrich feather. She represented order, balance, correct attitudes and thinking, morality, and justice. It was the feather of Maat against which the heart of the deceased was weighed. The power of Maat was said to regulate the seasons, the movement of the stars, and the relations between men and gods. It was central to the ideas about the universe and the Egyptians' code of ethics.

Maba or Mapa: Site in Guangdong (Kwangtung) Province, China, where fossils falling between *Homo erectus* and *Homo sapiens sapiens* were discovered from the Middle Palaeolithic. Called Mapa man, it is believed the skull predates or is contemporaneous with Neanderthal man of Europe. It has been suggested this skull represents one member of an extinct population contemporaneous with, but distinct from, the Neanderthal peoples of Europe and western Asia. (*syn.* [Ma-pa])

macaroni style: In art, Late Palaeolithic finger tracings in clay, the oldest form of art known. Innumerable examples appear on the walls and ceilings of limestone caves associated with human habitation in France (Pech Merle) and Spain, the oldest dating from about 30,000 BC. They range from simple scratchings and jumbled lines to deliberate meanders and arabesques and outline drawings of animals and are so-called because they look like pieces of macaroni. It is thought that these macaroni, like the numerous foot- and handprints pressed into the clay of the caves, were inspired by animal tracks. (*syn.* macaroni)

Macassans: Indonesian traders, particularly from Sulawesi, who visited tropical Australia during the Indonesian monsoon season. They collected and processed sea slugs (trepang, bêche-de-mer, sea cucumber), an important ingredient in their cooking. Archaeological evidence consists of stone structures used to support boiling vats, scatters of Indonesian potsherds, ash concentrations from smokehouses, graves, and living tamarind trees descended from seeds brought by the trepangers. Their cultural legacies to the Aborigines included metal tools, dugout canoes, vocabulary, art motifs, song cycles, rituals, and depictions of Macassan praus in rock paintings and stone arrangements. Macassan voyagers to Australia arrived around AD 1700 and continued until the end of the 19th century.

mace: A small clublike weapon, usually of stone, crafted to fit snugly in the hand, for pounding. It often had a perforated head and was attached to a shaft of wood (or ivory or horn), often tapering toward the end that was gripped. Many mace heads have been excavated from Predynastic and Early Dynastic cemeteries in Egypt. In medieval times, it was made of iron and used for breaking defensive armor.

macehual: In the Aztec period, commoners who made up the bulk of the population and who cultivated land held by his or her descent group. The macehual class was further differentiated into class levels. Certain occupations were accorded higher prestige than others (merchants, lapidarians, goldsmiths, and feather workers are mentioned, and the list probably included stone sculptors); and all urban occupations were assigned higher status as compared with rural farming.

macellum: In Roman antiquity, a marketplace for perishable foods consisting of shops around a colonnaded court; the center building was either round or octagonal. Some more sophisticated examples have individual architectural features associated with them, such as (at Leptis Magna and Pompeii) a porticoed-enclosed rectangular courtyard, with one or two colonnaded pavilions in the central area. At Pompeii, shops under the portico face inward into the market and also outward into the surrounding streets. At Rome, the Macellum Magnum erected by Nero was apparently a grand-scale example, doubling both the portico and the pavilion into two-storied structures.

MacEnery, Reverend J. (17??–d. 1841): A Roman Catholic priest who excavated at Kent's Cavern, England, and discovered Palaeolithic flint tools alongside the bones of extinct animals in an undisturbed stratum. He concluded that man and these ancient animals must have coexisted, but these views found little acceptance at the time. MacEnery died without publishing his results; William Pengelly did publish the report of MacEnery's excavations (1869).

Machalilla: A series of early Formative period sites on the coast of Ecuador of c. 2000 BC, known chiefly through ceramics—the distinctive Machalilla ceramic complex. Traded sherds found in both Valdivia C and Late Tutish-Canyno contexts suggest mid- to late 2nd millennium BC. Machalilla ceramics, in contrast to Valdivian, are painted (red banded and black on white), and figurines are rare and crudely made. Wattle-and-daub fragments in middens indicate that houses existed, but no foundations have been defined.

Machang: Late Neolithic culture of northwestern China belonging to the western or Gansu branch of the Yangshao Neolithic. It was contemporaneous with Longshan cultures of the east dating to 2800–1800 BC and seems to be a late stage or outgrowth of the Banshan culture and precedes Qijia. Machang pottery is a cruder form of Banshan ware. (*syn.* Ma-ch'ang; Ma-chia)

Machu Picchu: An Inca site northwest of Cuzco, Peru, discovered in 1911 by Hiram Bingham, ingeniously situated on a hill crest in the Andes overlooking a drop of 1,500 feet on either side. This ancient fortress city contains some fine, well-preserved stone buildings and is located in a mountain saddle between two peaks at a height of 7,710 feet (2350 m), 2,000 feet above the Urubamba River. The shrines and buildings are numerous and of unusual design, requiring much engineering skill and fine stone masonry. Many structures are arranged around courts in enclosures and with patios on terraces; the majority are single or back-to-back one-roomed buildings with niches symmetrically arranged on inside walls. Walls are inclined, and doors, niches, and windows are trapezoidal in form. There are 16 finely carved fountains beside the main thoroughfare. The temple and citadel were once surrounded by terraced gardens connected by more than 3,000 steps. One of the most striking buildings was the

astronomical observatory. Machu Picchu was a walled fortified city with a steep stone stairway to its single entrance and was approached via a stone roadway connected to Cuzco. Excavations revealed an unusual number of female skeletons buried in caves on the steep rocky slopes, suggesting that the site may have been the refuge of the Chosen Women (Virgins of the Sun). A pre-Incan presence is suspected from a number of green schist "record stones" found in the oldest part of the site. The Incas thrived from c. 1400–1540 AD.

MacNeish, Richard "Scotty" (1918–): American archaeologist who pioneered research on the evolution of agriculture and who studied the earliest human migrations into the New World. He suggested a human presence as early as 15,000 BC in the Ayacucho Basin, which would correspond to the traditional "first wave" of immigrants into the New World.

macroband: An anthropological term used to describe a group of several, usually related families who set up seasonal hunter-gatherer camps, used as a model of prehistoric societies. There can be more than one camp in the region exploited by each macroband, which moves from one area to another to exploit seasonal food resources. At some times of the year, the macroband splits into microbands.

macrofauna: Large animals; cf. microfauna.

macrofloral remains: Those plant remains from archaeological sites that are visible to the naked eye, primarily seeds and charcoal.

macrofossils: Large-scale floral or faunal remains recovered from an archaeological excavation; cf. microfossils.

macrolith: Any large stone tool; cf. microlith.

macropod: A grazing Australian marsupial with short forelimbs and long hind limbs adapted for hopping. It has a long, muscular tail, like that of the kangaroo, the wallaby, and the tree kangaroo. "Macropodidae" is the kangaroo family.

Madagascar: An island in the Indian Ocean off the east coast of Africa, which was one of the last major tropical land masses to be settled by man. There is no evidence for human presence before the 1st millennium AD. It is generally accepted that the island's first settlers came from Indonesia, perhaps from Borneo. Later, probably in about the 11th century AD, Bantu-speaking immigrants from east Africa also arrived.

Madai Caves: A series of caves in eastern Sabah, northern Borneo, Malaysia, which form a large complex like those of Niah, Sarawak. The largest cave is Agop Atas, and it has produced an industry of early Australian type dated to 8,000 years ago, with a pottery sequence dated from 500 BC to the present. It, along with Agop Sarapad, was inhabited from c. 9000–5000 BC by hunters using pebble and flake tools. After a 4,000-year gap, the caves were reused between c. 2000–500 BC by people using stone flake tools and pottery. The caves were abandoned again and later reused in the early 1st millennium AD.

Mad'arovce: Early Bronze Age regional group of the central Danube basin in western Slovakia and dated to the mid-2nd millennium BC. A large number of sites are hilltop settlements fortified by earthen banks or ditches. Tell-like multiphase settlements are also known from lowland valleys, often with rich assemblages of dark burnished pottery. Mixed burial rites, sometimes inhumation, sometimes cremation, are known from the medium-sized lowland cemeteries. The culture emerged toward the end of the neighboring Unetice culture and may have been a late subgroup of that culture.

Maes Howe: A magnificent passage grave in Orkney, Scotland, roofed by corbelling and covered by a circular cairn surrounded by a ring ditch. Its unusual plan is a squared burial chamber with three rectangular cells opening from it through doorways placed about 1 meter above the level of the chamber floor. Nothing was found inside the tomb, but scratched on the wall is a 12th-century AD inscription in runes stating that the grave was looted by Vikings who carried off a great treasure. However, radiocarbon dates average c. 2700 BC.

Maeva: A complex of 25 Polynesian *marae* (stone temples) on the island of Huahine, Society Islands, Polynesia. Many of the *ahu* and pavements have been restored. It is one of the most visible and impressive marae complexes in Polynesia.

Magadha: Ancient kingdom of India, situated in what is now west-central Bihar state, in northeastern India, in a strategic position in the Ganges River valley. It was the nucleus of several larger kingdoms or empires between the 6th century BC and the 8th century AD. It first flourished under Chandragupta and, later, Asoka, becoming the center of the vast and powerful Mauryan Empire. Many sites in Magadha were sacred to Buddhism. Toward the close of the 12th century, Magadha was conquered by the Muslims.

Magan: A semilegendary land described in Mesopotamian (Sumerian) texts of the Early Dynastic, Akkadian, and Ur III (c. 3000 BC) periods as a prosperous seafaring and trading nation. It was very important as a producer of copper for Persian Gulf trade. Sumer traded with Magan, and it was probably situated somewhere in the southern part of the Persian Gulf, either in Baluchistan (on the Iranian side) or in Oman (on the other side), or possibly both. Archaeologists working at the site of Umm An-nar, a small island off the west coast of Abu Dhabi, have suggested that it might be Magan.

magatama: Term meaning "curved bead/jewel," a jade or jasper pendant made since the Neolithic but especially during the Jomon, Yayoi, and Kofun periods. These comma-shaped beads (with a perforation at the thick end) have been found in 4th–7th century AD tombs in Korea and Japan. They purportedly had magic properties. In the Tumulus/Kofun period (3rd–6th centuries) of Japan, it was an imperial emblem. Many of these beads decorated the gold crowns of Silla (Korea). Its form may derive from prehistoric animal-tooth pendants. (*syn.* kogok)

Magdalenian: (mag'-duh-lee'-nee-un) The final major European culture of the Upper Palaeolithic period, from about 15,000–10,000 years ago; characterized by composite or specialized tools, tailored clothing, and especially geometric and representational cave art (e.g., Altamira) and by beautiful decorative work in bone and ivory (mobiliary art). The people were chiefly fishermen and reindeer hunters; they were the first known people to have used a spear thrower (of reindeer bone and antler) to increase range, strength, and accuracy. Magdalenian stone tools include small geometrically shaped implements (e.g., triangles, semilunar blades) probably set into bone or antler handles for use, burins (a sort of chisel), scrapers, borers, backed bladelets, and shouldered and leaf-shaped projectile points. Bone was used extensively to make wedges, adzes, hammers, spear heads with link shafts, barbed points and harpoons, eyed needles, jewelry, and hooked rods probably used as spear throwers. They killed animals with spears, snares, and traps and lived in caves, rock shelters, or substantial dwellings in winter and in tents in summer. The name is derived from La Madeleine or Magdalene, the type site in the Dordogne of southwest France. Its center of origin was southwest France and the adjacent parts of Spain, but elements characteristic of the later stages are represented in Britain (Creswell Crags) and eastward to southwest Germany and Poland. The Magdalenian culture, like that of earlier Upper Palaeolithic communities, was adapted to the cold conditions of the last (Würm) glaciation. The Magdalenian has been divided into six phases; it followed the Solutrean industry and was succeeded by the simplified Azilian. Magdalenian culture disappeared as the cool, near-glacial climate warmed at the end of the Fourth (Würm) Glacial Period (c. 10,000 BC), and herd animals became scarce. (*syn.* Age of the Reindeer)

Magdalenska Gora: Early Iron Age (Hallstatt period) complex of tumuli of the early La Tène period, located near Smarje/Sticna, in Slovenia. The cemetery included large barrows into which as many as 40 burials are inserted. The rich grave goods include weapons, armor, helmets, horse trappings, jewelry, and bronze vessels, including a complete bronze situlae—all from the 7th century BC.

Magellan periods: A chronological sequence covering 8000 BC–AD 1000, constructed on the basis of assemblages from Fell's Cave and the Palli Aike Cave in Patagonia, South

America. The sequence is divided into five phases, describing a series of hunting and marine adaptations. The earliest assemblage (Magellan I) contains fishtail projectile points, signifying Palaeo-Indian activity. Horse and sloth bones and the remains of three partly cremated Dolichocephalic humans, found in association with these points, have produced a single radiocarbon date of c. 8700 BC. A shift to willow-leaf points occurred in Magellan II c. 8000–4000 BC, which coincides with the disappearance of Pleistocene megafauna and widespread climatic change. Magellan IV–V are ill defined but represent a continuing hunting strategy blending into a period of ceramic use. (*syn.* Magellan complex)

Maghzalia, Tell: Aceramic Neolithic site in northern Iraq's Sinjar region. It provides evidence of the introduction of sedentary communities and farming in northern Mesopotamia. There were rectilinear structures with stone foundations and a lithic industry similar to other sites in the Zagros and Syro-Palestine. (*syn.* Maghzaliyah)

magic bricks: A set of four mud bricks that were often placed on the four sides of an Egyptian tomb during the New Kingdom, 1550–1069 BC, to protect the deceased from evil.

Maglemosian: The first Mesolithic culture of the north European plain, found in Scandinavia, the northern Balkans, northern Scotland, and northern England, and lasting from c. 9000/8000–5000 BC. The way of life was adapted to a forest and river/lakeside environment. Much has been preserved in waterlogged deposits. Thus more is known about the Maglemosian industry than about other tool industries of the same period. The tool kit included microliths, woodworking tools such as chipped axes and adzes, picks, barbed points, spear heads of bone or antler, and fishing gear. Wooden bows, paddles, and dugout canoes have been found, and the dog was already domesticated. The Maglemosian industry was named after the bog (*magle mose*, "big hog," in Danish) at Mullerup, Denmark, where evidence of the industry was first recognized. The Maglemosian industry was also highly artistic, with decorative designs on tools and decorative objects, such as pendants and amulets. (*syn.* Maglemosan)

Magna Graecia: A group of ancient Greek cities along the coast of southern Italy; a general term for the Greek cities of southern Italy and Sicily. An important center of the Greek civilization, it was the site of extensive trade and commerce and the seat of the Pythagorean and Eleatic systems of philosophy. Euboeans founded the first colonies, Pithecussae and Cumae, about 750 BC, and subsequently Spartans settled at Tarentum; Achaeans at Metapontum, Sybaris, and Croton; Locrians at Locri Epizephyrii; and Chalcidians at Rhegium (Reggio di Calabria). After the 5th century, attacks by neighboring Italic peoples, strife among cities, and malaria caused most of the cities to decline in importance.

magnetic: Of or pertaining to magnetism, the ability to be magnetized or affected by a magnet, or relating to the Earth's magnetic field. Magnetism is a class of physical phenomena associated with the motion of charge, the attraction for iron observed in lodestone and magnets. It is associated with moving electricity, exhibited by electric currents, and characterized by fields of force. It can be an electric current in a conductor or charged particles moving through space, or it can be the motion of an electron in atomic orbit.

magnetic dating: Any theoretically chronometric dating technique that uses the thermoremanent magnetism of certain types of archaeological material. These methods use the known changes that have taken place in the direction and intensity of the Earth's magnetic field. Magnetic minerals present in clay and rocks each have their own magnetic orientation. When heated to the so-called blocking temperature, the original magnetic orientation of the particles is destroyed, and they take on the orientation of the Earth's magnetic field in a fixed alignment—which does not alter after cooling. These methods are most suitable for kilns and hearths. Once the direction of the archaeological sample has been determined, it may be possible to date it by fitting it to the secular variation curve established for the local area. There is no universal curve, because not only does the Earth's main field vary, but there are also local disturbances. Because the dating of the curve has to be constructed through independent dating techniques, and these are not available for every area, there are not established curves for every region. As a dating technique, it is strictly limited to those areas where dated curves have been established. A more recent dating technique using thermoremanent magnetism is palaeointensity dating (archaeomagnetic intensity dating). The principle is that the thermoremanent magnetism in burnt clay is proportional to the intensity of the magnetic field acting on the clay as it cools down. The measurement of its intensity, and a comparison with the intensity revealed by reheating in today's magnetic field, gives a ratio for the past and present fields, which can be used to establish a curve of variation in the Earth's magnetic field intensity. The method promises to be useful because direction in situ is not required, and it can therefore be used for pottery and other artifacts as well as hearths and kilns. (*syn.* palaeomagnetic dating)

magnetic reversals: A change in the magnetic direction of the Earth. It was discovered that volcanic lava flows, which like kilns and fired clay record the magnetism at the time they were hot, retained measurable magnetization in a reversed direction. Over the last 4 million years, magnetic direction changed at least 10 times. It switched to normal, as we know it, about 700,000 years ago. The direction of the dipole component reverses, on an average, about every 300,000 to 1,000,000 years. This reversal is very sudden on a geologic time scale, apparently taking about 5,000 years. The time between reversals is highly variable, sometimes occurring in less than 40,000 years and at other times remaining steady for as long as 35,000,000 years. No regularities or periodicities have yet been discovered in the pattern of reversals. A long interval of one polarity may be followed by a short interval of opposite polarity. These reversals have proved an important dating aid to archaeology.

magnetic surveying: A technique for the location of archaeological features adapted from techniques used in geological surveying. It is based on the fact that features with thermoremanent magnetism, like hearths or kilns, or features with a high humus content, like pits or ditches and iron objects, distort the Earth's magnetic field from the normal. Instruments such as the proton magnetometer or the differential fluxgate gradiometer are used to measure those disturbances, and by plotting the results, a map of the features can be built. The ways in which the different types of feature distort the magnetic field vary, although they can all be picked up on the same instrument. Hematite or magnetic, present in most clays, has a small magnetic effect when unburnt, because grains point in random directions and cancel each one another. Once heated to about 700 degrees (C) or more, the grains line up, increasing the magnetic effect and causing an anomaly in the magnetic field. This thermoremanent magnetism is also the basis for magnetic dating. The presence of modern iron as in wire fences can cause problems with this technique of location; if the area to be surveyed is clearly crossed with power lines or fenced with iron posts, a resistivity survey may be more suitable. The method of surveying used requires a grid to be measured out on the site and readings to be taken at regular intervals. The nature of the site may prevent such a grid being laid out, for instance, if it is heavily wooded, and magnetic survey may not be possible on these sites. It is one of the most commonly used geophysical surveying methods. (*syn.* electromagnetic surveying)

magnetic susceptibility: A property of soil and sediment, measured as a ratio of intensity of magnetization of the material to the strength of an applied magnetic field. Topsoil often has a somewhat enhanced "magnetic susceptibility" owing to magnetic minerals in the material, especially compared with the subsoil. The filling of a ditch or a pit has greater susceptibility than the surrounding area because of higher humus content and perhaps the presence of burnt occupation material. On the basis that contrast between feature and surroundings locates the features, walls and other stone settings can also be located because they have less susceptibility than the area around them; that is, they exhibit a reverse anomaly.

magnetite: A strongly magnetic form of iron ore, a major constituent of magnetitite and a common accessory mineral in igneous rocks. In the Mesoamerican region, magnetite was commonly mined and polished to make mirrors and compasses. It frequently has distinct north and south poles and has been known for this property at least since 500 BC. (*syn.* lodestone, magnetic iron ore)

magnetometer: A geophysical instrument that measures the intensity and sometimes direction of the Earth's magnetic field. It is used in electromagnetic surveying to identify changes in the field in soil or sediment that might be caused by subsurface features, hearths, kilns, or metal artifacts. When a current is passed through a coil in a bottle of water or alcohol, the protons of the hydrogen atoms align themselves to its magnetic field. When the current is cut off, the protons realign themselves according to the Earth's field, its strength being indicated by the frequency of their gyration on realignment. This sets up a weak current, which is transmitted back from the bottle to the instrument and there registered on dials. The resulting figures are plotted to reveal anomalies in field strength—usually caused by buried iron, kilns, hearths, or pits or ditches. These features can thus be rapidly located without disturbance of the ground, and excavation can be directed to the most promising areas. Magnetrometry is the use of a magnetometer for mapping subsurface anomalies. There are a number of designs, but two are particularly widely used. The proton magnetometer makes an absolute measurement of field strength, but is intermittent in operation: each reading is initiated by the push of a button and takes some seconds to appear on the display of the instrument. Fluxgate magnetometers work on a different principle and give a continuous reading, which makes surveying less time consuming. Most fluxgate machines do not however measure field strength directly, but rather are gradiometers, measuring the vertical gradient of the Earth's magnetic field, that is, how fast the field strength changes with vertical distance from the Earth's magnetic field. Gradient measurements can also be used in archaeological surveys and have an advantage over absolute measurements. The Earth's field strength varies continuously during the day at any one location. Absolute measurements taken at different times have to be calibrated for this effect if they are to be comparable. Gradient measurements are not affected by this diurnal drift in field strength and so do not need to be calibrated. Proton gradiometers are also available. The fluxgate, differential fluxgate, and proton gradiometer take continuous measurements of relative vertical change in the intensity of field strength. (*syn.* proton magnetometer)

Magosian: A stone industry found in eastern and southern Africa, dated to c. 10,000–600 BC. The diagnostic tools include small points, microliths, and small blades, as well as Middle Stone Age artifacts. An advanced Levallois technique was employed for the production of flakes for the manufacture of other tools, together with a punch technique for the production of microlithic artifacts. Projectile points were produced by pressure flaking. The culture may have been transitional between the Middle and Later Stone Ages. The type site is Magosi in Uganda. Other sites in central and southern Africa that are dated to the Pleistocene epoch (1,600,000–10,000 years ago) are often considered to represent the same material culture and hunting and gathering adaptation.

maguey: A fiber obtained from the fleshy-leafed agave plant of tropical America and used for rope and cordage. Native Americans ate both the flower head, which they harvested after it had bloomed, and the heart of the maguey, which they prepared by digging up the entire plant and roasting it in earth ovens for 24–72 hours.

Mahaiatea: The largest *marae* (stone temple) constructed in Tahiti, Society Islands, Polynesia. It was an 11-stepped pyramidal *ahu* covering 81 by 22 meters, 13.5 meters high. Constructed by the chieftainess Purea of Papara district in 1767, it now has only a few foundation fragments surviving.

Mahdiya: The first capital of the Fatimids, c. 902, who later conquered Egypt (969) and thereafter ruled from Cairo. Mahdiya occupied a narrow peninsula with a double wall and a single imposing entrance, the Sqifa al-Kahla. The other important Fatimid monument is the mosque of Obeid Allah, built c. 912, with a monumental entrance, a courtyard with single arcades on all four sides, and a sanctuary with a T-shaped arrangement of nave and transepts. Its plan anticipates the Fatimid mosque at Ajdabiyah and the mosques of Cairo. Other Fatimid buildings at Mahdiya include part of the palace of Obeid Allah and a naval dockyard.

Maheshwar: A central Indian site in western Madhya Pradesh state, just north of the Narmada River—the ancient site of the capital of a Haihaya king, Arjuna Kartavirya (c. 200 BC), mentioned in the Sanskrit epics *Ramayana* and *Mahabharata*. On the opposite bank of the Narmada lies the early site of Navdatoli, where painted pottery and other artifacts have been excavated.

Maiden Castle: One of the largest and most famous Iron Age hill forts in Britain, located in Dorset, England. The oldest structure on the hilltop is a Neolithic causewayed camp (c. 2000–1500 BC), followed after an interval by an earthen long barrow, which is partly built over the ditches of the earlier camp. Occupation resumed in the Early Iron Age (c. 5th century BC) with the construction of a hill fort (c. 250 BC), which was later extended to fortify the entire hill. Maiden Castle was at that time a permanent settlement with stone and wooden huts linked by surfaced trackways. Sometime before 50 BC, the site came under the control of the Belgae and became the tribal capital of the Durotriges, with

coinage and imported Gallo-Roman luxuries. During the Roman conquest, the fort was sacked by Vespasian's legion (AD 43–44), and the slain defenders were buried in a cemetery near the east gate. The Romans moved the remaining population to a new site at Durnovaria (Dorchester), and the hillfort was abandoned until the 4th century AD when a Romano-Celtic temple was built there.

Maikop: The site of one of the richest Eneolithic kurgan burials ever discovered, located in the northern Caucasus Mountains of Russia and dating to the late 3rd millennium BC. The barrow covered a timber mortuary house divided into three sections. In the central area was a royal burial of a man sprinkled with ocher and laid under a canopy with gold and silver supports. The corpse was accompanied by copper tools and weapons, gold ornaments, gold vessels and figurines, rich textiles, carnelian and turquoise jewelry, wooden carts or wagons, and silver vases engraved with animal scenes. The metalwork shows links with Mesopotamia and southwest Asia. The Maikop burials have given their name to the Maikop culture and its walled settlements.

Mailhac: A series of important Late Bronze Age and Iron Age sites near Narbonne in southwest France, dating from the 8th–1st centuries BC. The sites include a defended hilltop settlement (Le Cayla) and a series of urnfield cemeteries (Le Moulin, Grand Bassin I and II). The earliest phase has an urnfield-type cemetery, wooden houses, and evidence of farming supplemented by hunting. In the second phase (early 6th century BC), Hallstatt influences include iron and a chieftain's wagon burial (La Redorte). Greek and Etruscan imports appear in both graves and occupation deposits in this and in the succeeding phase. Occupation ended early in the 1st century BC with a burning, probably a Roman punitive action after threatened uprisings in the area.

Mailu: An island off the southeast coast of New Guinea, important in Papuan trading as "middle man" between *kula* and *hiri*. The Mailu people made shell valuables and pottery. Dates go back 1,500 years.

Mainz: An imperial Roman legion base and settlement in west-central Germany, a port on the left bank of the Rhine opposite Wiesbaden and the mouth of the Main River. It was the site of a Celtic settlement where the Romans established (14–9 BC) the military camp, known as Mogontiacum (Moguntiacum) after the Celtic god Mogo. A fort was built of timber, then renewed in stone somewhere between AD 50–100. Between the fort and the river grew up a civilian settlement with a port, which, under Domitan, was to become capital of Germania Superior (Upper Germany). Surviving remains include a great column of the god Jupiter with reliefs of 28 deities, evidence for a Flavian aqueduct, portions of the late Roman wall, and some civil and military cemeteries. (*syn.* Roman Mogontiacum)

Maiolica: Tin-glazed earthenware—a distinctive kind of colorful, decorated earthenware that is tin enameled and glazed—usually of Italian, Spanish, or Mexican origin. This earthenware was introduced by Moorish potters from the island of Majorca in the 15th century. Distinguishing features of Maiolica ware are coarseness of ware, intricacy of pattern, occasionally prismatic glaze. Made of potter's clay mixed with marl and sand, it is soft or hard according to the nature of the composition and the degree of heat under which it is fired in the kiln. Soft wares are either unglazed or lustrous, glazed, or enameled. The maiolica painter's palette was usually restricted to five colors: cobalt blue, antimony yellow, iron red, copper green, and manganese purple; purple and blue were used, at various periods, mainly for outline. A white tin enamel was also used for highlights or alone on the white tin glaze in what was called bianco sopra bianco, "white on white." The Italian lustrous ware is properly Maiolica and originated in Faenza, Deruta, Urbino, Orvieto, Gubbio, Florence, and Savona. (*syn.* Majolica; faience; delft)

maize: A tall cereal grass widely grown in Mexico, South America, and the United States, which originated as a staple food in Mexico about 9,000 years ago. A field of maize is a milpa. No wild maize appears to exist today. The plant originated in the Central Mexican highlands, where pollen belonging to maize, or one of its near relatives, has been found in cores from Mexico City, dated to between 60,000–80,000 bp. The earliest macrofossils of maize appear in the Tehuacan Valley in Mexico between 7000–5000 BC. These early finds have very small cobs and kernels, and it has been suggested that they come from wild maize. Archaeologically, the oldest cultivated maize in Mexico is from the Coxcatlan period in the Tehuacan Valley (4800–3500 BC), and maize appears in the caves of Tamaulipas, northeast Mexico, around 3200 BC. In South America, the oldest direct evidence comes from the Valdivia culture of Ecuador, around 3000, although maize phytoliths were found in the preceding Vegas period, c. 6000 BC. It was in fairly general use in the southwestern United States by 1000 BC, although it did not reach the eastern woodlands until about the time of Christ. It was an important early domesticated food plant in the New World and one of the trio that provided a balanced diet for early American farmers (the other two being beans and squash). (*syn.* corn)

Majapahit: The last Indianized kingdom in Indonesia; based in eastern Java, it existed between the 13th and 16th centuries. The founder of the empire was Vijaya, a prince of Singhasari, who escaped when Jayakatwang, the ruler of Kadiri, seized the palace. From 1292, it developed into the most powerful empire of the archipelago for two centuries until its decline in the face of the advance of Islam. The apogee of Majapahit was reached by King Hayam Wuruk and his prime minister, Gajah Mada (1350–1389), when the kingdom's suzerainty was extended to its farthest limits.

Majiabang: A Neolithic site and culture of Jiaxing, China, near Shanghai. The people were descendants of the 5th millennium BC Ho-mu-tu in the region south of the Yangtze near Shanghai. The early phase yielded a radiocarbon date of c. 4000 BC. It had close ties with the Ch'ing-lien-kang culture in southern Kiangsu, northern Chekiang, and Shanghai. The successor to the Majiabang culture is the 3rd millennium BC Liangzhu culture. The earliest examples of jade from the lower Yangtze River region appear in the latter phases of Ma-chia-pang culture (c. 5100–3900 BC). (*syn.* Ma-chia-pang)

Majiayao: Type site and culture of the late 4th to early 3rd millennia in eastern Kansu, eastern Tsinghai, and northern Szechwan, China. Majiayao is regarded as the earliest stage of the western or Gansu branch of the Yanshao Neolithic. Majiayao pottery designs, perhaps the finest known from the Chinese Neolithic, are painted in black only; most derive from running spiral patterns, although in some of the more attenuated and asymmetrical designs the spirals are well concealed. Thirty percent of Ma-chia-yao vessels were decorated on the upper two thirds of the body with a variety of designs in black pigment; multiarmed radial spirals, painted with calligraphic ease, were the most prominent. (*syn.* Ma-chia-yao)

Majninskaya: Upper Palaeolithic site on the Uj River near its confluence with the Yenisei in Siberia. The occupations dated from c. 19,000–9000 bp. Artifacts include wedge-shaped microcores, side scrapers, end scrapers, bone points, and an anthropomorphic figurine.

Makaha Valley: An important valley on western Oahu, Hawaii, which has been the scene of intensive settlement archaeology to document cultural developments from AD 1100–1800. There are agricultural terraces, habitation sites, and *heiau*. The valley contains well-preserved dry-land cultivation systems in its lower portion and wet taro terraces for root crops in its upper section.

Makapansgat: A limeworks cave at the entrance to the Makapan Valley in northern Transvaal, South Africa, with important samples of *Autralopithecus africanus* and other fossil animal remains (antelope, baboon). Perhaps the best-known so-called archaeological evidence from the South African cave sites came from Makapansgat. There are no typical stone tools, but many bone and horn fragments are alleged to have been modified as tools, the so-called "osteodontokeratic" (bone-tooth-horn) culture. The hominid remains may date from about three million years ago. The nearby Cave of Hearths has Acheulian and later deposits. (*syn.* Makapans)

Makarovo: Four Upper Palaeolithic sites on the Lena River in south-central Siberia. Makarovo II dates between c. 11,400–11,950 bp and contains microblades. Makarovo III's assemblage includes side scrapers, end scrapers, and choppers. Makarovo IV has points, side scrapers, and end scrapers believed to predate the last glacial maximum.

makers' marks: Manufacturing marks etched or stamped onto mass-produced ceramics, glassware, and metals. (*syn.* hallmarks)

Makwe: A rock shelter in eastern Zambia, near Mozambique, with occupation during the last four millennia BC evidenced by a stone industry of backed microliths. Traces of mastic provided evidence of the way these implements had been hafted.

malachite: A minor ore but a widespread mineral of copper; basic copper carbonate, green in color. It was first employed as a cosmetic and ointment for the eyes, to cut down the glare of the sun and to discourage flies. The discovery that metal could be obtained from it was probably accidental, and then it was used as a source of copper. The extensive deposits in Sinai were much exploited in antiquity. It was also used for oils and watercolors and encrusted on other materials as ornament.

malacology: The study of mollusks as indicators of past diet and environmental conditions.

Malakunanja 2: Sandstone shelter in Arnhem Land, northern Australia, with a sequence similar to the Lindner site/Nauwalabila I. Dates show human occupation in the area between 50,000–60,000 years ago.

Malambo: A village site south of Barranquilla on the Gulf coast of Colombia with distinctive pottery with incised, punctated, and "adorno" (appliqué) modeled decoration dating 1120 BC to AD 100. Pottery griddles indicated that manioc or cassava was grown.

Malangangerr: Rock shelter in Arnhem Land, northern Australia, with occupation 25,000 years ago. Evidence from 20,000-year-old levels established the presence of edge-ground tools in the Pleistocene of the area.

Malatya: The Tell of Arslantepe near the upper Euphrates in central Turkey, an important site of the Syro-Hittites of the early 1st millennium BC. It is best known for the reliefs on its Lion Gate and the colossal statue of one of its kings. (*syn.* ancient Milid; Eski)

Malaya Sya: Upper Palaeolithic site in western Siberia on the Belyj Iyus River with artifacts and faunal remains dating from 34,500–20,370 bp, predating the last glacial maximum. Artifacts include large retouched blades and end scrapers.

Malaysia: A country of Southeast Asia, composed of two noncontiguous regions—peninsular (west) Malaysia and east Malaysia. It has been inhabited for at least 6,000 to 8,000 years. There was a Pleistocene assemblage (Kota Tampan), but the first coherent and widespread industry is the Hoabinhian (Gua Cha, Gua Kechil). The Neolithic culture was well established by 2500–1500 BC. Neolithic assemblages of probable Thai origin appear in north and central Malaya after 2800 BC (Gua Cha, Gua Kechil). Small Malayan kingdoms existed in the 2nd or 3rd centuries AD, when adventurers from India arrived and initiated more than 1,000 years of Indian influence.

Malkata: A settlement and palace site at the southern end of western Thebes, opposite modern Luxor, dating to the early 14th century BC. Essentially the remains of a community that grew up around the Theban residence of Amenhotep III (1390–1352 BC) and Queen Tiy. The ruins indicate it must have been one of the finest buildings in western Thebes.

Mali: A landlocked country in western Africa, one of the early African Sudanic states, which rose to prominence in the 12th–13th centuries. It effectively took over control of the Bambuk goldfields from ancient Ghana—as well as links with the trans-Saharan trade. By the 14th century, its rulers controlled an extensive stretch of territory, including the Songhai country of the middle Niger, and Mali's ruler made the pilgrimage to Mecca. The empire declined in the late 15th century after its overthrow by Songhay. Mali was occupied in the Palaeolithic and Neolithic, with remains including Asselar man, a human skeleton found north of Timbuktu in 1927, and rock paintings and carvings.

Malian: Ancient Anshan, located in the Kur River drainage of Fars, southwest Iran, a center of Elam. This tell site was occupied from the 5th millennium BC, and many buildings of the Proto-Elamite and Middle Elamite periods have been discovered. In the 3rd and 2nd millennium BC, the city was clearly a major trading center, with much imported as well as local material. It traditionally warred with southern Mesopotamian states. Its sequence extends to the early 1st millennium AD. Its most important occupations were the Banesh, c. 3400–2800 BC, and Kaftari, c. 2200–1600 BC. (*syn.* Malyan, Tal-i; Tal I Malyan; Anshan)

Maliq: A settlement site of the Neolithic, Copper, and Bronze Ages, located in south-central Albania. There are two late Neolithic building levels with rectangular houses with reed on plaster floors set on timber beams, associated with rich painted pottery. Incised and channeled ware is found in the Late Copper Age.

Mallia: A palace and town of the Minoans on the north coast of Crete, east of Knossos. The large palace has a central court and was built in the Middle Minoan and Late Minoan I periods (c. 1900–1450 BC) although rebuilding was needed after an earthquake c. 1700 BC. The final destruction is dated c. 1450 BC, probably by the eruption of Thera. Among notable individual finds are a great bronze sword and a battle ax carved in the form of a leopard. There are two large Proto-palatial complexes, the Agora and Quartier Mu. (*syn.* Malia)

Mallowan, Sir Max Edgar Lucien (1904–1978): British archaeologist who worked in the Middle East, excavating at Arpachiyah, Chagar Bazar, Tell Brak, and Nimrud (Kalhu). He also served as director of the British School of Archaeology in Baghdad and ran the British Institute of Persian Studies. He was married to Agatha Christie.

Mal'ta: Upper Palaeolithic and Mesolithic site in south-central Siberia. There are traces of a dwelling and a burial of a young person of possibly mongoloid affinities, as well as several art objects. The Upper Palaeolithic level is dated to the beginning of the last glacial maximum, c. 24,000–23,000 bp. The artifacts include prismatic cores, retouched blades, and end scrapers.

Malta: A Mediterranean island south of Sicily with a settlement of the impressed ware culture at Skorba dated to c. 4900 BC. Further immigrants arrived from Sicily c. 3500. These people from c. 4000–2400 BC erected a startling and unique series of megalithic temples, some 30 still surviving, of sophisticated plan and construction. They are among the oldest human monuments in the Mediterranean basin. The major temple complexes, most of which contained two or three separate temples, were built in several phases over a long period. The temples are built of local limestone in Cyclopean masonry and are characterized by a series of apsidal courts or chambers arranged on either side of a central corridor opening from a monumental facade. The whole structure is enclosed by a solid outer wall and the space between this and the building itself filled with stone and earth rubble. They have a number of installations, which are presumably ritual, including altar-like constructions, niches, and porthole openings. The temples are unique in form and construction and are in any case too early to be derived from any east Mediterranean stone architecture. They are now seen as a local development. The people of this time were succeeded by warlike immigrants, possibly from western Greece or Carthage (8th–7th centuries BC), who dug an urnfield into the ruins of the temples and built villages on naturally defended hilltops; it is to this period that the mysterious "cart ruts" belong. The island was finally brought under the control of the Phoenicians in the 9th century BC and conquered by Rome in 218 BC.

Malthi: Bronze Age acropolis in Messenia, Greece, a Middle Helladic site. It was fortified and had houses. There are two tholos tombs at the foot of the acropolis.

Malthus, Thomas Robert (1766–1834): English economist and demographer, best known for his theory that population growth overran available food resources unless it was controlled by catastrophes such as war, epidemics, or natural disasters—or by limits on reproduction.

Maluquer de Motes, Juan (1915–1988): Spanish archaeologist known for his work on the megaliths of Navarre and excavations at Cortes de Navarra.

Malwa: A plateau of northwestern Madhya Pradesh in India, which is also the name of a Chalcolithic culture of the early 2nd millennium BC. Important sites include Navdatoli, Nagda, and Kayatha (Ujjain). The characteristic pottery (Malwa ware) is a red-slipped, black painted ware on a red or cream ground in geometric, plant, and animal motifs. There was also black-painted cream-slipped, black-and-red painted, Jorwe, and Lustrous Red wares. The people cultivated crops, kept animals, and made objects of copper and stone.

mama-quilla/Mama-Quilla: One of the divisions of the temple of the Sun (Inti); dedicated to the moon. The moon was portrayed as a silver disk with human features. (*syn.* Mama-Kilya)

Mambo: A Late Iron Age phase of the Leopard's Kopje complex of southern Zimbabwe. It is dated to the 10th–11th centuries AD.

mammisi: An independent religious building usually associated with the larger cult temples of the Late period (Graeco-Roman) of Egypt, 747 BC–AD 395. This term, invented by the Egyptologist Jean-François Champollion, described the buildings attached to temples at Edfu, Dendera, and Philae. The buildings were often placed at right angles to the main temple axis. The Ptolemaic mammisi usually consisted of a small temple, surrounded by a colonnade with intercolumnar screen walls, in which the rituals of the marriage of the goddess (Isis or Hathor) and the birth of the child god were celebrated. (*syn.* birth-house)

mammoth: A large extinct species of elephant (Mammuthus), which became adapted to Ice Age conditions in the northern hemisphere about a quarter of a million years ago. It was perhaps the largest animal hunted by Palaeolithic man. It is possible that they were killed by spearing, as no pit traps have ever been found near their carcasses. At Gravettian hunters' campsites in Moravia and the Ukraine, large numbers of mammoth bones have been found, and houses were even built from them. The woolly mammoth spread across Eurasia into North America and became extinct c. 11,000–10,000 BC. They were frequently depicted in Palaeolithic art, and complete carcasses have been found in Siberia and Alaska. They subsisted mainly on open grassy vegetation. The two main species were woolly mammoth and the Columbian mammoth.

mammoth-bone house: A kind of dwelling built by people of the Upper Palaeolithic in central and eastern Europe between c. 25,000–12,000 bp, especially in areas where wood was scarce. The remains of such a structure would typically have a circular or oval arrangement of woolly mammoth bones and tusks, with a central hearth and occupation debris. The bones and tusks were the structure's support. External to the structure may be hearths, pits, and debris. Examples are found in Poland and the former Soviet Union. Mammoth bones were used to build the winter structures for some of these peoples and mammoth fat used to keep the fires burning.

Mamon: A phase of the Pre-Classic in the Lowland Maya area dated c. 550–300 BC, first defined at Uaxactún and Tikal. Some artifacts of stone and obsidian are included in the complex, but it is principally characterized by monochrome pottery with a "waxy" feel to it. The flat-bottomed bowl was a common shape. Figurines are also characteristic.

Mamutowa: Palaeolithic cave site in southern Poland on the Kluczwoda River. Middle Palaeolithic artifacts include side scrapers, and the early Upper Palaeolithic industries were Aurignacian and Jerzmanowician, probably dating to the interstadial before the last glacial maximum. In the upper layers are Gravettian artifacts from the last glacial maximum.

Man-ch'eng: Site in Hebei Province, China, where two Early Han Dynasty tombs are cut into a rock cliff—the tombs of Liu Sheng (c. 113 BC), Prince of Chung-shan, and his wife Dou Wan. Numerous grave goods, 2,800 items, including jade, gold, silver, iron, glass articles; inlaid and gilded vessels, earthenware, lacquer ware, silk fabrics, and fine weapons, are in the chambered tombs behind sealed doors. Both tombs were provided with large stores of food and wine and escorts of chariots and horses. The bodies of Liu Sheng and Dou Wan were dressed in shrouds made of jade plaques sewn together with gold thread, the first of some dozen jade shrouds thus recovered from Han tombs. (*syn.* Mancheng)

Manching: Large *oppidum* of the late Iron Age in Bavaria, Germany, near Ingolstadt, dated to the La Tène period, c. 200 BC. It was one of the largest oppida in Europe. Manching, at that time adjacent to the Danube, may have been a regional market. The defense was an elaborate construction consisting of 4-mile-long walls built of timber and stones and including four gateways. The organization of the settlement was pre-planned, with streets up to 30 feet wide and regular rows of rectangular buildings in front of zones containing pits and working areas; other areas were enclosed for granaries or horse stalls. The site was divided into work areas for particular crafts, such as wood, leather, and ironworking. Coins were minted and used on the site. There is evidence of a violent end to the settlement c. 50 BC.

Manda: The site of a Swahili city-state apparently established in the 9th century and distinguished for its seawalls of coral blocks, each of which weighs up to 1 ton. Located in the Lamu Archipelago off the coast of Kenya, it had numerous stone-built (and wattle-and-daub) houses. Trade, which seems to have been by barter, was considerable, with the main export probably of ivory. Manda had close trading

connections with the Persian Gulf—Siraf in particular. It imported large quantities of Islamic pottery and, in the 9th and 10th centuries, Chinese porcelain. There is evidence of a considerable iron-smelting industry at Manda.

Mandu Mandu Creek: Rock shelter in Northwest Cape, western Australia, with occupation between 25,000–19,000 bp. It was abandoned and not reoccupied until c. 2500 bp.

Manetho (c. 305–285 BC): An Egyptian priest and historian who wrote a history of his country in the 3rd century BC. Although the work is lost, quotations from it in later writings are extremely important for reconstructing the dynastic lists of the pharaohs. The history was probably written in Greek for Ptolemy I (305–282). He provided the basis for the relative chronology of Egypt before the invasion of Alexander the Great. The fragments of his work confirmed the succession of kings where the archaeological evidence was inconclusive, and Manetho's division of the rulers of Egypt into 30 dynasties is still accepted.

Mangaasi: A long-lived pottery tradition of central Vanuatu, Melanesia, dated to between c. 700 BC–AD 1600. It had incised and applied relief and is quite different from the ancestral Polynesian Lapita pottery. It was a Melanesian tradition, with parallels in the northern Solomons and New Caledonia.

manioc: A starchy root plant native to the tropical lowland zone of South America, where it was cultivated along with other root crops. Its origin may have been in Venezuela before 2500 BC, and it became established in the Andes and reached the Peruvian coast before 2000 BC. Manioc can grow under various conditions, but only in the lowland forest did manioc retain its position as the main food plant. On archaeological sites, large clay disks are often interpreted as griddles on which were baked flat cakes made of a flour prepared by roasting grated manioc roots and juice-catching pots for the prussic acid they contain. The plant underwent elaborate an detoxification process (including grating, pulping, draining, and finally cooking) before consumption. It was the staple diet throughout most of Amazonia and the Caribbean at the time of European contact. Manioc is the source of tapioca. (*syn.* cassava, yuca)

mano: A one- or two-handled ground stone tool used with a metate (quern) for grinding vegetable material such as maize, seeds, nuts, pigments. The mano dates to the Archaic Indian period, the word coming from Spanish mano de piedra, "hand stone"—referring to the upper stone, which is usually cylindrical or ovoid in shape. The underlying smooth stone slab is the metate. It is a hallmark artifact, defining the economic or subsistence base of prehistoric societies. Its forms very considerably, from a barely modified cobble to a long cylinder similar to a rolling pin. (*syn.* handstone)

manor: A political, economic, and social system by which the peasants of medieval Europe were dependent on their land and on their lord. Its basic unit was the manor, a self-sufficient landed estate, or fief, that was under the control of a lord who enjoyed a variety of rights over it and the peasants who were serfs. It was the focus of the feudal societies that developed in western Europe from the 8th–9th centuries. Well-known examples are 10th–12th-century sites of Goltho in Lincolnshire and Sulgrave in Northamptonshire for the Anglo-Norman period, and Wintringham, Lincolnshire, and Hound Tor, Devon, for the later Middle Ages. Houses of feudal lords from the 11th and 12th centuries in northern and western France have been excavated as well as small castles inside fortified villages, as at Rougiers in Provence or in Renaissance villages in Tuscany. (*syn.* manorial system, seignorialism, seignorial system)

mansiones: In the Roman Empire, hostelries called mansiones were situated along the Roman road system to accommodate travelers on government or commercial business. They were a kind of Roman lodging house. In the Roman Empire, communications were carried along main roads, and the houses were used for overnight stays. They were spaced 1 day's journey apart. They usually had a defended post, with a ditch, rampart, gatehouses with guardrooms for the road police, and a canteen or taberna. Between these rest houses were mutationes with stables for changing horses and a taberna for refreshing the riders. (*syn.* mansionis)

mantelet: Great wicker or wooden shields, sometimes mounted on wheels, used in sieges by archers as a protective screen.

manufacture: The second stage of behavioral processes, in which raw materials are modified to produce artifacts.

manuport: Any artifact or natural object that is transported, but not necessarily modified, and deposited by humans. Examples include seashells found inland or water-rolled pebbles away from any river.

Maoris: The descendants of the Polynesians who settled in New Zealand, arriving about AD 900 from central Polynesia, possibly from the Cook or Society Islands. The traditional Maori social organization consists of members of each tribe (*iwi*) who recognized a common ancestry and common allegiance to a chief or chiefs (*ariki*). The most important social groups were the *hapuu* (subtribe), the primary landholding group and the one within which marriage was preferred, and the extended family (*whaanau*).

mapping: The scaled recording of the horizontal position of exposed features and, in some cases, artifacts and ecofacts, using standardized symbols. It is one of the two basic ground survey methods used in surface survey of archaeological sites, the other being surface collection.

Mapungubwe: Late Iron Age hilltop site in northern Transvaal, South Africa's first urban center. It has given its name to the southern facies of Phase B of the Leopard's Kopje complex, and it was occupied between AD 1220–1270. The material from the earliest levels is very similar to that from the nearby site of Bambandyanalo. Mapungubwe was a forerunner of the developments at Great Zimbabwe and may have been the capital of a state that controlled trade with the East African coast. In Mapungubwe and Great Zimbabwe, a wealthy and privileged elite built with stone and was buried with gold and copper ornaments, exotic beads, and fine imported pottery and cloth. Their homes, diet, and ostentatious burials are in stark contrast to those of the common folk. The 13th-century burial of an important official uncovered at Mapungubwe was accompanied by a gold-covered statue of a rhinoceros, a golden staff, and other artifacts—one of the earliest indications of gold mining in southern Africa. The Mapungubwe gold was panned from alluvial deposits.

marae: A stone temple of eastern Polynesia, made of courtyards and a stone platform or *ahu*, where ceremonies took place. The court was walled, paved, or terraced. Marae are among the important remains on Easter Island, the Hawaiian Islands (especially Heiau), and the Tuamoto, Society, Cook, Austral, and Marquesas Islands. Ancestral forms probably go back to Early Eastern Polynesian settlement, AD c. 500. Figures of the gods were kept at the marae, often in special wooden containers housed in portable shelters. Large numbers of thin, tall wooden slabs were set up on the marae; they were carved with openwork geometric designs and topped with figures of birds, human beings, or spiked projections. Marae are especially characteristic of AD 1200–1800. The term *marae* also refers to an open space in a village in Tonga, Samoa, or New Zealand. (*syn.* malae)

Marajó Island, Marajoara: A large island at the mouth of the Amazon River in Brazil with numerous artificial mound sites. Small ones served as house platforms, and larger ones contained urn burials. The pottery has sophisticated polychrome designs and is similar to that of Pre-Columbian Andean cultures. Radiocarbon dates suggest that the Marajoara style began no later than the 5th century AD and lasted until 1300 AD. The largest center, Os Camutins, has 40 mounds. It is the world's largest fluvial island (one produced by sediments deposited by a stream or river), and half of it is flooded during the rainy season. (*syn.* Marajó)

Marathon: A coastal plain on the northeast coast of Attica, Greece, famous for the battle between the Persians and Athenians in 490 BC and for news of the battle being taken by the runner Pheidippides from Marathon to Athens—about 25 miles. The defeat of the Persians is commemorated by the Soros, the large mound where the Athenians were buried, and the tomb of the Plataeans, which seems to be the grave of the

Greek allies. Their fine black- and red-figure ware were grave goods. There are many other tombs: an Early Helladic cist grave cemetery, Middle Helladic tumuli, and a Mycenaean tholos tomb with two horses as grave offerings. The area shows evidence for some kind of occupation from Neolithic times, through Helladic, continuously to Classical.

marble: A granular limestone or dolomite (a rock composed of calcium-magnesium carbonate) that has been recrystallized under the influence of heat, pressure, and aqueous solutions. This polished stone was used for sculpture and decoration and for architecture from the 7th century BC onward. Most used were fine white marbles of Greece, although colored marbles were used in Hellenistic architecture. Roman marble, principally from Carrara quarries at Luna, became popular in the 1st century BC.

Marca Huamachuco: Large Early Intermediate period and Middle horizon site located in the northern highlands of Peru near the ruins of Viracochapampa. It was the center of a major polity, the site consisting of a complex of circular and rectangular multistory buildings of cut stone and surrounded by a stone wall. The center appears to have been important as early as Huari times and seems to have had some Chimu affiliations. It survived long enough to have been remodeled by the Inca.

Marcavalle: An Early Horizon period pottery style of Cuzco, Peru, overlapping with and from which Chanapata style derived, c. 1200 BC.

marching camp: Temporary military camps set up by the Roman army. When it was on the move, this was its systematic procedure for overnight and short-stay stops. Surveyors laid out a suitable and reasonably flat rectangular site, tent positions were planned and marked, usually surmounted by a palisade of stakes. These distinctive enclosures may be identified by aerial survey. Roman marching camps exist at Culter, Kintore, and Ythan Wells in Scotland.

Marchiori: A ceramic complex from the mouth of Amazon with unusual geometric incised and painted motifs on white background, dating from 2500 BC.

Mardikh, Tell: Large fortified site in northern Mesopotamia, southwest of Aleppo, Syria, which was ancient Ebla. Important Middle Bronze Age remains, including the city gate and fine sculpture have been found. Ebla was previously known from cuneiform texts, including inscriptions of the kings of Akkad and Gudea of Lagash. Its large palace was destroyed by Naram-Sin c. 2240 BC. The library of the place contained around 16,630 tablets and fragments with commerical, administrative, financial, lexical, historical, literary, and agricultural texts in cuneiform in a hitherto unknown northwest Semitic language called Eblaite. The discovery of the Eblaite tablets has aided comparative studies of Semitic languages and has also aided modern studies of the unrelated Sumerican language. (*syn.* ancient Ebla)

Marduk: The god of Babylon who in the 13th–12th centuries BC ousted Enlil as the most prominent god in the Sumerian pantheon. He became the ruler of the gods rather than just their head, which represented a shift in the relationship between the gods—paralleling the rise in power of the Mesopotamian kings. Marduk's seat was at Babylon; Marduk's chief temples at Babylon were the Esagila and the Etemenanki, a ziggurat with a shrine of Marduk on the top. Originally he seems to have been a god of thunderstorms. (*syn.* Bel)

margin: The edge of a stone tool or flake.

marginal: In anthropology, a term referring to traits or cultures that are either at a great distance from the center of development or simple in comparison to more complex developments elsewhere. The term is comparative and has no meaning except with reference to a specified center.

Mari: A city and kingdom of Mesopotamia, on the right bank of the Euphrates near the Syrian-Iraqi border. It was the chief city of the middle Euphrates until its destruction by Hammurabi c. 1759 BC. It was founded in the early 3rd millennium BC and was occupied until the late 1st millennium BC. Major temple and palace complexes and major archives belong to the third quarter of the 3rd millennium and to the early 2nd millennium. The great palace was repeatedly enlarged during its 400-year period of use; during the reign of Zimri-Lim, its last king, it had 300 rooms, and its archives contained about 25,000 cuneiform tablets informative about international politics of the period and the administrative and economic organization of the kingdom. A room near the archive has been interpreted as a school—the only one known from Mesopotamia. The Palace is also famous for its mural decorations: Both representational pictures and geometric designs were painted directly on a thin layer of mud plaster, representing a new and impressive school of decoration. Among the important Early Dynastic buildings are six temples dedicated to Ishtar, goddess of love. Mari stood on the Euphrates River at a point where three trade routes met; tin, copper, silver, lapis lazuli, timber, and textiles were traded. (*syn.* modern Tell Hariri)

Marianas Islands: An island group in western Micronesia with a sequence starting with settlement around 1500 BC, by island people in southeast Asia. They made a distinctive red-slipped ware (Marianas Redware phase), sometimes incised with lime-filled decoration, closely related to Philippine wares. By AD 800, a plain, unslipped ware was in use, and stone architecture had developed. Parallel rows of upright pillars topped with hemispheric capstones (halege) were erected. The pillars were supports for structures called *latte* (after which term the culture is named), which may have served as houses or canoe sheds. Each village had from one to several latte structures. Stone and shell tools were used, and the betel nut was chewed, as shown by extended burials most often located between the rows of latte.

Marib: Site in northern Yemen on the Wadi Dhana, associated with Sabaean kingdom of the south Arabian civilization. It was the capital of the kingdom of Saba.' A dam was built across the wadi in the mid-1st millennium BC and used until the mid-1st millennium AD. The temple of Haram Bilqis (Awwam) still stands. The temple of Almaqah, also in Marib, had an unusual shape, that of an ellipse with a major axis about 345 feet long, with a strong wall about 28 feet high, built of fine limestone ashlars. A small temple, in front of which were eight standing pillars, includes a gallery supported by pillars around a rectangular court; it served as a peristyle to the main temple, in the wall of which it was inserted.

Mariette, François Auguste Ferdinand (1821–1881): French Egyptologist who excavated many of the major Egyptian sites and monuments and founded the Egyptian Antiquities Service and what was to become the Cairo Museum (National Museum of Egyptian Antiquities). He excavated the Saqqara Serapeum and found the burials of the Apis bulls and the jewels belonging to Rameses II. He also uncovered sites at Giza, Abydos, Thebes, Edfu, Elephantine, and the Delta. He is buried in sarcophagus in front of the Cairo Museum.

Marinatos, Spyridon Nikolaou (1901–1974): Greek archaeologist who came up with the theory that the end of the Minoan civilization in the Aegean could have been caused by the volcano on the island of Thera in 1500 BC. He also discovered the buried Bronze Age port city at Akrotiri on Thera. Among the finds made at the site were the finest frescoes discovered in the Mediterranean region to that time, surpassing even those found at Knossos in Crete. He was the discoverer of the site of the battle of Thermopylae (480 BC) and the burial ground associated with the battle of Marathon (490 BC). He wrote *Crete and Mycenae* (1959).

Maritsa culture: Late Neolithic culture of the eastern Balkans, contemporary with Vinca C, between 4000–3700 BC. It is characterized by the materials from Karanovo's Layer V, with dark pottery whose surface tended to be covered by either incised or excised lines, which were filled with white paint after firing.

Mariupol: Neolithic cemetery of the Dnepr-Donets culture on the Sea of Azov in southern Ukraine. Burials included flint tools, pendants, and beads of animal teeth, bone, and shells. Nonlocal stone beads were also found. (*syn.* Zhdanov)

market: A mode of exchange in which the price of a commodity is fixed by the relative proportions of supply and demand. The term may also be applied more specifically to the place where people come together for transactions of this sort or the occasion on which they do so. A degree of social control is necessary, for instance, to guarantee access to the market and the security of traders, but prices are fixed independently. It usually involves a system of price making through negotiation. Market has the variable meanings of (a) a process of buyer–seller exchange, (b) the demand for something; and (c) a kind of economy. (*syn.* market exchange)

marking: Notations on tokens and envelopes. Some of the envelopes have markings corresponding to the clay shapes inside. Moreover, these markings are more or less similar to the shapes drawn on clay tablets that date back to about 3100 BC and that are unambiguously related to the Sumerian language. These markings are thought to constitute a logographic form of writing consisting of some 1,200 different characters representing numerals, names, and such material objects as cloth and cow.

Markleeberg: Lower Palaeolithic site outside Leipzig, Germany, where gravel pits have gravels earlier than the Saale ice maximum advance in the region. They contain a cold-indicating fauna of early penultimate glacial date and numerous stone artifacts, especially Levallois flakes, side scrapers, and hand axes. Artifacts and faunal remains are buried in the riverine gravels, probably deposited during the late Middle Pleistocene.

marl: A soil of fine-grained minerals, mainly composed of clay and carbonate of lime. The term is applied to a great variety of sediments and rocks with a considerable range of composition. Calcareous marls grade into clays. Marl is valuable as a fertilizer and in making bricks.

Marlik Tepe: Early Iron Age royal cemetery of the late 2nd millennium BC southwest of the Caspian Sea in northern Iran. Its tombs included a wealth of gold and silver vessels, jewelry, and weapons. Some graves had rectangular stone slabs on which the body with its grave goods was laid and then covered with earth. Characteristic decoration was in relief and with mythical animal and human figures. Marlik Tepe may represent an early phase in the development of the art of the Medes.

Marnian: An Iron Age/La Tène culture of northeastern France, which occupied a region centered on the Marne Valley. It was characterized by chariot burials from c. 475–325 BC. The people may have invaded or traded with Britain in the 3rd and 2nd centuries BC. There were close connections between the Marne region groups and the Arras culture of eastern Yorkshire. (*syn.* Marnians)

Maroni-Vournes: Site of a major Late Cypriot settlement in southern Cyprus, first occupied c. 1600 BC. A grand ashlar structure dates from the 13th century BC.

Maros point: Small hollow-based stone projectile points, often with serrated edge retouch, characteristic of a mature phase of the Toalian industry of southwestern Sulawesi, India, c. 6000 BC into the 1st millennium BC. They were part of a mid-Holocene stone flake and blade industry.

Marpole culture: An archaeological complex in Canada, dating c. 500 BC–AD 1500; the type site is at the mouth of the Fraser River in British Columbia. Its distinctive traits include flaked-stone points, microblades, ground-slate points, and fish knives, and disc beads of shell and shale. Antler was used for barbed points and harpoon making. There were midden burials, some with plentiful grave goods. It probably evolved from the Locarno Beach culture.

Marquesas Islands: An island group of Eastern Polynesia, first settled AD c. 300.

Marrakesh: A city built in southern Morocco, founded in 1062 by Yusuf ibn Tashufin of the dynasty of the Almoravids. It served as the Almoravid capital until it fell to the Almohads in 1147. It was the capital of the Almoravids from 1062–1147 and then of the Almohads from 1147–1248. Marrakesh contains one major Almoravid monument, the al-Barudiyin Qubba, a domed mausoleum built in 1109 or 1117. Of the Almohad period, there are city walls and the Kutubiya Mosque; its famous minaret was built in 1199. (*syn.* Marrakech)

Marsa Matruh: Harbor site on the Mediterranean coast in northwestern Egypt, which was the site of the Ptolemaic city of Paraetonium. It was the capital of Sicca. (*syn.* ancient Paraetonium)

Marseilles: City on the coast of southern France, an important Mediterranean port founded in either c. 600 or 540 BC, according to tradition. Originally it was a colony of Phocaea in western Turkey. By c. 535 BC, the inhabitants were prosperous enough to dedicate a treasury at the sanctuary of Delphi in mainland Greece. Even under Roman rule, the port was fairly independent and maintained its Greek culture. There are remains of Roman docks. (*syn.* Greek Massalia; Roman Massilia)

Marshall, Sir John (1876–1958) (DISPUTED d. 1959): British archaeologist who worked in India as director-general of Archaeological Survey in India and who played a part in revealing India's long prehistory. He excavated at Harappa and Mohenjo-Daro and at sites of the Indus civilization. He also discovered much about the preceding Calcolithic cultures. He was interested in Alexander's campaign and in Graeco-Buddhist monuments at Sanchi and Taxila.

Marshalltown trowel: Renowned trowel made in Iowa, used by many archaeologists. The city is the future site of the Archaeological Hall of Fame.

Martin's Hundred: Site settled near Jamestown and Williamsburg, Virginia, on the James River, by English colonists in 1619. Excavations have revealed a massacre by the Indians in 1622 and early colonial life in North America. The center of the plantation was Wolstenholme Towne.

Marxist archaeology: The use of the writings of Karl Marx and Friedrich Engels, which depict a materialist model of social change, to understand past societies. Change in a society is seen as the result of contradictions arising between the forces of production (technology) and the relations of production (social organization). Such contradictions are seen to emerge as a struggle between distinct social classes. Marxist archaeology is built on the notion that an understanding of who has power and how that power is exercised are vital elements in explaining social change.

Mary Rose: A Tudor warship, the flagship of Henry VIII's fleet, which sank in the Portsmouth Harbor, off the south coast of England, on its maiden voyage in 1545. The exploration, excavation, and recovery of the ship is the largest underwater archaeology project ever undertaken. By the time the ship was raised in October 1982, the project had already cost $4 million. The Mary Rose excavation has yielded remarkable information about Tudor military and daily life. It has also provided the opportunity for the development of new equipment and techniques for underwater archaeology.

Marzabotto: An Etruscan occupation site, 25 kilometers from Bologna, northern Italy, in the Reno Valley. It was probably set on an important Etruscan trade route. Its 6th-century BC phase was characterized by plain, primitive dwellings with evidence of metalworking. In a 5th-century BC stage, the city appears to have been laid out afresh on a grid system, with blocks of houses on carefully paved streets. The town shows sophisticated drainage, both road and domestic. There were workshops, foundries, and kilns bordering the principal street. Its akropolis showed evidence of three temples. Marzabotto's occupation, and possibly destruction, by the Boii in the 4th century BC seems to have brought an end to the settlement.

Masada: Palestinian site with a great rock fortress-palace complex built by Herod the Great (37–4 BC). It lies west of the Dead Sea, where the last survivors of the first Jewish rebellion (Zealots) of AD 70 defied the Roman army (AD 66–73), and whose siege works can still be traced. Although first fortified by the Hasmonean king Alexander Jannaeus (ruled 103–76 BC), Herod was the chief builder of Masada. His constructions (37–31 BC) included two ornate palaces (one of them on three levels), heavy walls, and aqueducts, which brought water to cisterns holding nearly 200,000 gallons. After Herod's death (4 BC), Masada was captured by the Romans, but the Jewish Zealots took it by surprise in AD 66.

A synagogue and ritual bath discovered there are the earliest yet found in Palestine.

Maskhutah, Tell el-: Ancient Egyptian city located near Ismailia in al-Isma'illyah muhafazah (governorate). Mentioned in the Bible (Exodus 1:11) as one of the treasure cities built for the pharaoh by the Hebrews, it was known to have been enlarged by the Ramesside pharaohs, especially by Ramses II (reigned 1279–1213 BC), in whose reign the Exodus of the Hebrews may have taken place. The site has yielded sphinxes and statues of Ramses II and the best preserved of the trilingual stelae that commemorated Darius I the Great's completion of the Nile–Red Sea Canal. It was the capital of the eighth nome of Lower Egypt during the Late Period (747–332 BC). It was a site of pharaonic storehouses built by the Hebrews under Egyptian bondage. (*syn.* Tall al-Maskhutah; ancient Per-Atum, Per Tum; biblical Pithum)

Maspero, Gaston Camille Charles (1846–1916): French Egyptologist who succeeded August Mariette as director of the Egyptian Antiquities Service and who edited the first 50 volumes of the immense catalog of the collection there. He excavated numerous sites from Saqqara to the Valley of the Kings. At Deir el Bahari (Dayr al-Bahri), he came on a fabulous collection of 40 royal mummies, including those of the pharaohs Seti I, Amenhotep I, Thutmose III, and Ramses II, in inscribed sarcophagi, as well as a profusion of decorative and funerary artifacts. Maspero's intensive study of these findings was published in *Les Momies royales de Deir-el-Bahari* (1889; *The Royal Mummies of Dayr al-Bahri*). He also published an account of the Nubian monuments threatened by construction of the first Aswan dam. He helped found the Egyptian Museum in 1902. During his second tenure as director general (1899–1914), Maspero regulated excavations, tried to prevent illicit trade in antiquities, sought to preserve and strengthen monuments, and directed the archaeological survey of Nubia. His writings include *Histoire ancienne des peuples de l'Orient classique*, (1895–97; *Ancient History of the Peoples of the Classic Orient*), *L'Archéologie égyptienne* (1887; *Egyptian Archaeology*), *Les Contes populaires de l'Égypte ancienne* (4th ed. 1914; *Popular Tales of Ancient Egypt*), and *Causeries d'Égypte* (1907; *New Light on Ancient Egypt*).

massebah: A standing stone or group of stones in the Levant similar to a dolmen. There was probably a cult purpose when erected by Canaanites (as at Gezer, Hazor). When set up by the Israelites, it was likely commemorative.

mastaba: The Arabic word for "bench," a mud-brick superstructure of Egyptian tombs, mainly of the Archaic period and Old Kingdom, including the royal tombs of the 1st and 2nd Dynasties. It was a low, rectangular building with a flat roof and vertical or slightly inclined walls that enclosed the shaft to the underground burial chamber. Later versions were reinforced with stone and grew more elaborate. It often contained a chapel, a statue of the deceased, and sometimes large numbers of rooms. The pyramids were a direct development from the mastaba. At first, kings as well as their nobles and officials were buried in mastabas, but from the 3rd Dynasty, pharaohs had pyramids, and the mastabas of their eminent subjects were built around the pyramids.

mastodon: Any of the various now-extinct species of large mammals related to elephants. They looked like a stocky, long elephant, with long reddish-brown hair and shorter, straighter tusks than the mammoth. The American mastodon (*Mammut americanum*), is classified as a browser from its low-crowned teeth, as opposed to the woolly mammoth (*Mammuthus primigenius*), which because of its high-crowned teeth, is classified as a grazer. It lived on spruce and pine. The mastodon had large hemispherical cusps on the surface of each molar tooth. They first appeared in the early Miocene and continued in various forms through the Pleistocene epoch (from 1,600,000–10,000 years ago). In North America, mastodons probably persisted into post-Pleistocene time and were contemporaneous with historic North American Indian groups. Mastodons had a worldwide distribution; their remains are quite common and are often very well preserved. Hunting may have led to their extinction.

mastos: A breast-shaped drinking cup, usually with one horizontal and one vertical handle. In Athens, black-glossed and figured-decorated examples have been found.

Maszycka Cave: Cave site near Krakow, Poland, on the Pradnik River, with an Upper Palaeolithic assemblage assigned to the Magdalenian c. 17,500–16,500 BP. Human skeletal remains of 16 people are associated with the layer. The uppermost layer contained Neolithic remains.

mataa: Large-stemmed obsidian spear point that was shaped and hafted by inhabitants of Easter Island. It is of the period of internal wars, 18th–19th centuries AD.

Matacapan: Site on the southern Gulf Coast of Mexico near the Tuxtla Mountains, with a sequence beginning in the Early Pre-Classic. Its Early Classic settlement was influenced by Teotihuacán and contains a barrio (neighborhood) in the Central Mexico architectural style and was part of the Teotihuacán trade network.

Mataram: Dynasty founded by King Sanjaya in the 8th century AD in the southern part of central Java, Indonesia. The state dominated during the 8th–10th centuries AD and was ruled by the Shailendra dynasty. Major sites are the stupa of Borobudur, a temple complex in Dieng, and numerous funerary temples (*candi*) as at Prambanan. It is also the name of a large kingdom that lasted from the late 16th–18th centuries in Java. (*syn.* Mendang-Mataram)

Matarrubilla: A large passage grave near Seville, southern

Spain, built during the Copper Age. The tomb was built mainly of dry stone walling, and the chamber was roofed with a corbelled vault. A number of crouched inhumations were discovered, with rich grave goods including an ivory necklace and a clay sandal.

matchlock: A device for igniting gunpowder in firearms, developed in the 15th century, a major advance in the manufacture of small arms. The matchlock was the first mechanical firing device. It consisted of a type of musket that used an attached burning taper to light the gunpowder. A match would fire the priming powder in the pan attached to the side of the barrel. The flash in the pan penetrated a small port in the breech of the gun and ignited the main charge.

Matenbek: Limestone shelter near Matenkupkum, Bismarck Archipelago, Melanesia, with occupation from c. 19,000 bp. A later occupation began c. 8000 bp. Obsidian from Talasea appears as well as phalanger (possum) introduced during the Pleistocene.

Matenkupkum: Cave site in New Ireland, Bismarck Archipelago, Melanesia. Marine resources were used c. 32,000 bp. A stone assemblage includes unretouched flakes. Obsidian from Talasea appears c. 12,000 bp.

Matera: A small city in southern Italy, northwest of Taranto, which formed part of the duchy of Benevento and of the principality of Salerno. It was occupied successively by the Normans, the Aragonese, and the Orsini. In the old part of the city, people inhabited cavelike houses cut into the rock with only an opening for the door, a system dating from prehistoric times. The name is also applied to a Middle Neolithic ware from many sites in its neighborhood, notably the ditched villages of Murgecchia and Murgia Timone and a cave site, the Grotta dei Pipistrelli. A dark burnished ware with curved bowls and straight-necked jars, it is characterized by rectilinear geometric designs scratched after firing and filled with an inlay of red ocher. A quite different ware, thin, buff colored, and painted with broad bands of scarlet, is sometimes included in the term.

material culture: The artifacts and ecofacts used by a group to cope with the physical and social environment. Material culture includes the buildings, tools, and other artifacts that constitute the material remains of a former society—its technology and artifacts combined. Material culture thus embraces folk architecture, folk arts, and folk crafts. For example, the construction of houses, the design and decoration of buildings and utensils, and the performance of home industries, according to traditional styles and methods, make up material culture. The distinction is made between those aspects of culture that appear as physical objects and those aspects that are nonmaterial. It is the major source of evidence for archaeology.

Matola: Early Iron Age shell midden site near Maputo on the coast of southern Mozambique. Its pottery is used to define the Matola section of the first Iron Age farmers in the area. The pottery recovered is remarkably similar to that from Kwale near the Kenya coast far to the north. There may have been an extremely rapid southward spread of Early Iron Age cultural traits along the eastern coast of Africa between the 3rd–5th centuries AD.

Matopo: Microlithic Later Stone Age industry of the Matopo Hills, southwestern Zimbabwe, dated to 6000 BC. The hills are associated with folklore and tradition, some being venerated as dwelling places of the spirits of departed Ndebele chiefs. The hills contain gigantic caves with Khoisan paintings, and there are Stone and Iron Age archaeological sites. (*syn.* Southern Rhodesian Wilton; Khami industry)

matri-: A prefix meaning "mother" or "maternal." *Matriarchal* means characterized by family authority resting with the woman's family. *Matrilineal* means descent reckoned through the female line only. *Matrilocal* refers to married couples living with or near the wife's mother.

matrix: The soil or physical material in which an excavation is conducted or in which artifacts or fossils are embedded or supported. The term also refers to the surrounding deposit in which archaeological finds are situated. Originally the term described the grains in sediments or rocks that are finer than the coarsest material in the sediment or rock. Matrix is the material in which cultural debris is contained. (*syn.* plural matrices or matrixes)

Matt-painted pottery: Middle Helladic pottery with simple decoration in manganese-based purple-black paint on a pale ground. Matt-painted pottery has been found in the nearer islands and even as far as Crete and the Anatolian coast.

Matupi: Cave site in northeastern Zaire in the Ituri forest, containing a long sequence of predominantly microlithic Later Stone Age industries extending back to c. 40,000–3000 BP. It represents one of the earliest such occurrences in sub-Saharan Africa. The appearance of true backed microliths is dated before 19,000 BC. The levels of c. 21,000–12,000 BP have decorated bored stones and drills.

Maudslay, Alfred Percival (1850–1931): British soldier who was one of the first people to visit and make a scientific record of the great Maya sites. Inspired by travelers' accounts of the ruins, he visited Guatemala and the neighboring republics and by 1894 had made seven expeditions. He made photographs, casts, plans, and drawings at such sites as Quirigua, Palenque, and Chichén Itzá. He was also the first archaeologist to see the important ruins of Yaxchilan. He published the results of his journeys as part of a series entitled *Biologia Centrali-Americana*, or *Contributions to the Knowledge of the Flora and Fauna of Mexico and Central America* (1889–

1902). Maudslay's work was accurate and objective; his records are still a valuable source of information. The texts he transcribed formed the basis of early studies of Maya hieroglyphs.

Mauer jaw: A large broken lower jaw of *Homo erectus* or pre-Neanderthaler type found in the Mauer sands near Heidelberg, Germany. It is dated to either the Mindel Glaciation or the Günz-Mindel Interglacial—probably the latter. No tools were recovered from the stratum, but there was associated fauna (elephant, rhinoceros, bear, horse, sabertoothed cat). Although it dates from perhaps 400,000 years ago, it is not very different from the Neanderthals of c. 50,000 years ago. (*syn.* Heidelberg jaw)

Mauern: The Weinberg caves at Mauern in Bavaria, southern Germany, which have revealed two Mousterian levels, the upper one with many leaf points. Above these is an Upper Palaeolithic level.

maul: A heavy, massive, long-handled hammer dating to the Archaic Indian period.

Mauna Kea: The highest mountain in Polynesia and a dormant volcano on north-central Hawaii Island. It has very extensive prehistoric basalt adze quarries, mostly between 3350–3780 meters (12,400 feet) above sea level. The sites include workshops, rock shelters, stone-walled enclosures, and religious shrines. Radiocarbon dates from the shelters range from AD 1400–1650. The dome of the volcano is 30 miles (48 km) across, with numerous cinder cones, and is the site of a major astronomical observatory.

Maungaroa Valley: Area on Raratonga, Southern Cook Islands, with a well-preserved Polynesian settlement. The *marae* and paved house platforms were arranged in four places and dated between AD c. 1600–1823.

Maupiti burial site: An early Eastern Polynesian burial site on Maupiti, Society Islands, dated to AD 800–1200. There are 16 flexed and extended burials with grave goods of adzes, pendants, pearl-shell fishhooks paralleling the Hane in the Marquesas, and elsewhere in the Society Islands at Vaito'otia (at Huahine) and in New Zealand. (*syn.* Maupiti burial ground)

Mauriwi: The early inhabitants of New Zealand, in the 19th–20th centuries, who were probably conquered by the Maori.

Mauryan empire: An ancient Indian state, c. 321–185 BC, centered at Pataliputra (modern Patna) near the junction of the Son and Ganges rivers. After Alexander the Great's death in 323 BC, Candra Gupta (Chandragupta) founded the dynasty that encompassed most of the subcontinent except for the Tamil south. He drove the Greeks out of India and established the Mauryan Empire as an efficient and highly organized autocracy with a standing army and civil service. The

Buddhist Mauryan emperor Ashoka (reigned c. 265–238 BC, or c. 273–232 BC) is well known, especially from the stone edicts that he had erected throughout his realm, which are among the oldest deciphered original texts of India. The dynasty subsequently declined and was deposed by Sunga in 187 BC. (*syn.* Mauryas)

mausoleum: A storage structure for the dead, which was above ground; a large, impressive sepulchral monument. The original mausoleum was the gigantic tomb of Mausolus, ruler of Caria, in southwest Asia Minor, built at Halicarnassus c. 353–350 BC. It was considered one of the seven wonders of the ancient world. The word later came to be used for any tomb built on a monumental scale, such as those of Augustus in the field of Mars and Hadrian on the banks of the Tiber (now the Castel Sant' Angelo, Rome). As one of the Seven Wonders of the World, it was famous not only for its vast dimensions, but also for the refinement of its decoration and sculptures. Attributed to the architect Pythius, it seems to have been constructed entirely of white marble and reached a total height of some 40 meters. It consisted of a massively broad and high plinth, surmounted probably by a temple with Ionic peristyle, topped by a pyramid, and the whole capped with a gigantic chariot and horse group. Some time before the 15th century, it collapsed from earthquake damage. The colossal statues identified as those of Mausolus and Artemisia were brought to the British Museum, together with sculpture and frieze details. Probably the most ambitious mausoleum is the white marble Taj Mahal at Agra, in India, built by the Mughal emperor Shah Jahan for his favorite wife, who died in 1631. Other famous mausoleums are those of Vladimir Lenin and Napoleon III. (*syn.* Greek mausoleion)

Mawangdui: Site in Hunan Province, China, near Chang-Sha (Changsha City), of three Early Han Dynasty tombs with features of both shafts and mounded tombs. Tomb No. 2 belonged to the first marquis of Dai (d. 186 BC), a high official of the Han administration. Nos. 3 and 1 are apparently the tombs of his son (d. 168 BC) and wife (d. shortly after 168 BC). In construction and contents, the three tombs are far different from Han princely burials in the north and reflect the lingering traditions and material culture of the Chu kingdom, which had fallen to Qin less than a century earlier. Each tomb takes the form of a massive compartmented timber box at the bottom of a deep stepped shaft; the shaft was filled in with rammed earth, and a mound was raised over it. The contents of Tomb No. 1 were very well preserved: The body of the wife of the marquis was wrapped in silk and laid inside four richly decorated nested coffins. The 180 dishes, toilet boxes, and other lacquer articles, silk clothing, offerings of food, musical instruments, small wooden figures of servants and musicians, and a complete inventory of the grave goods written on bamboo slips depict extreme wealth. Tomb 3 was furnished in the same fashion as Tomb 1, but contained more silk paintings, three rare musical instruments, and an extraordinary collection of manuscripts, some on silk and some on bamboo slips, including some of the earliest known maps from China, treatises on medicine and astronomy, comet charts, and important literary texts (the Daoist/Taoist classic "Dao De jing" ["Tao te ching"], the "Yi jing" ["Book of Changes"]). The contents of Tomb 2 are comparable to those of Tomb 1 but are poorly preserved. (*syn.* Ma-wang-tui)

Maxton: Early Iron Age site in central Zimbabwe of the 11th century AD; also the name of the late phase culture. The sites are often on hilltops with stone walls.

Maya: Very important culture of Mesoamerica, one of the major Classic civilizations, which occupied the peninsula of Yucatán and Belize, the lowland jungle south of it, and the highlands of Guatemala and western Honduras. The civilization developed from other pre-Classic cultures by about 200 BC and continued until being conquered by the Spaniards in AD 1541. By c. 200 BC, at sites like Tikal and Uaxactún, the first pyramids were being built. Population increase and the introduction of new ceramic and architectural forms are accompanied by an artistic transition from Olmec through Izapan to Mayan. The classic Maya civilization dates to AD c. 292, the earliest Long Count date found on stele 29 at Tikal. The Early Classic period (200–600) was the golden age of the lowland culture, and the great centers acted as foci for administration, religion, and the arts. Architecture, sculpture, and painting were highly developed; records were kept in hieroglyphic writing, and elaborate ceremonies were carried out in the temples on top of the pyramids. A class of astronomer-priests observed the sun, moon, and planets and evolved a calendrical system more accurate than the Julian calendar used in Christian Europe. In mathematics, the priests used a vigesimal system with the concept of zero and with a positional notation. The Classic Maya culture is characterized by an immense investment of labor in construction of ceremonial architecture, the erection of stelae, and a growing differentiation between the elite and the peasant population. The Maya practiced swidden agriculture as well as intensive agriculture, terracing and raised fields, and aboriculture. Polychrome pottery is a hallmark of the Maya Lowland Classic culture. The Late Classic period (AD c. 600–900) shows development in sculpture and architecture—and regional styles can be recognized. Northern Yucatán began to come into its own at sites like Chichén Itzá and Uxmal, where fine buildings in the Punc style were erected during the 7th–9th centuries. The later part of this period witnessed the end of civilization in the lowlands; the great centers were abandoned during the 9th and early 10th centuries. The Post-Classic period, c. 900 to the Spanish conquest, had strong Mexican influence, particularly at Chichén Itzá where build-ings were constructed in the Toltec style of central Mexico, and the art shows representations of Toltec warriors overpowering Maya chiefs. During the collapse in the southern lowlands, centers in the northern lowlands began to grow, AD c. 800–1000. The South's decline may have played a role in the North's prosperity. Sometime around 1200, the Itzá were driven from their capital, and Mayapán became the leading city of Yucatán. In about 1440–1450, Mayapán was overthrown, and there followed a time of disunity and warfare, which lasted until the Spaniards conquered Yucatan in 1541. The Maya kingdoms of highland Guatemala were subdued in 1525, but in the lowlands the descendants of the exiled Itzá held out until 1697. The collapse of Maya culture (in c. 900) is a puzzling phenomenon, and its relative suddenness still remains without satisfactory explanation. There are no Long Count dates after 900, after which time lowland populations dwindled by as much as 90 percent. The term Maya also refers to a culture area and is typically divided into the lowland and highland Maya. Descendants of the Maya still occupy the region. (*syn.* Classic Maya)

Maya calendar: A method employed by the Maya of measuring the passage of time, made up of two separate calendar systems: the Calendar Round, used for everyday pourposes, and the Long Count, used for the reckoning of historical dates. Maya chronology consisted of three main elements: a 260-day sacred year (*tzolkin*) formed by the combination of 13 numbers (1 to 13) and 20 day names; a solar year (*haab*), divided into 18 months of 20 days numbered from 0 to 19, followed by a five-day unlucky period (*Uayeb*); and a series of cycles—*uinal* (20 *kins*, or days), *tun* (360 days), *katun* (7,200 days), *baktun* (144,000 days), with the highest cycle being the *alautun* of 23,040,000,000 days. All Middle American civilizations used the two first counts, which permitted officials accurately to determine a date within a period defined as the least common multiple of 260 and 365: 18,980 days, or 52 years. The Classic Maya Long Count inscriptions enumerate the cycles that have elapsed since a zero date in 3114 BC. Thus, "9.6.0.0.0," a katun-ending date, means that nine baktuns and six katuns have elapsed from the zero date to the day 2 Ahau 13 Tzec (9 May, AD 751). To those Initial Series were added the Supplementary Series (information about the lunar month) and the Secondary Series, a calendar-correction formula that brought the conventional date in harmony with the true position of the day in the solar year.

Mayapán: A Late Post-Classic Maya center in west-central Yucatán, Mexico. The walled town covered 4.2 square kilometers and contained 3,600 houses, as well as temples that are rather poor copies of those at Chichén Itzá. This dense concentration of housing represented something new in Mayan architecture, and walls are found at other sites of the period. The population ranged from 6,000–15,000. After the decline of Chichén Itzá in about AD 1200, Mayapán became the dominant city in northern Yucatán and was able to extort tribute from several neighboring states. Among the major features are a central temple-pyramid complex dedicated to Kulculkan (the Mayan name for Quetzacoatl). The most characteristic artifact is the highly elaborate *incensario* (incense burner). The end of this relatively short-lived center was precipitated by internal dissension resulting in the summary execution of the ruling elite, and it was finally sacked in a local uprising in c. 1400; abandonment followed shortly thereafter in c. 1450.

mayeque: In the Aztec period, a landless, rural tenant farmer. These serfs were attached to private- or state-owned rural estates.

Mayor Island: Important source of obsidian in New Zealand, in the Bay of Plenty, North Island. It was traded throughout New Zealand.

Maysar: An Umm An-Nar settlement in southeastern Arabia with Bronze Age copper smelting. It was the chief product of ancient Magan. There is also evidence of Bronze Age agriculture and burial patterns; Iron Age settlements, fortifications, and burials. (*syn.* Samad)

Mazapan ware: A ceramic style developing out of Coyotlatelco and first appearing in association with major architecture at Tula, Mexico, in the Post-Classic Toltec phase (9th–12th century AD). The orange-on-buff (or red-on-buff) pottery was decorated by straight or wavy parallel lines produced by multiple brushes.

McBurney, Charles Brian Montagu (1914–1979): British prehistorian who worked at Haua Fteah cave in northern Africa and at La Cotte de St Brelade, Jersey. He wrote *France Before the Romans* (1974).

McKean Complex: A Middle Plains Archaic complex dating to c. 5000–3000 BC and occupying parts of the northwestern Plains of North America. Its type site is in northeast Wyoming and has a McKean projectile point—a stemmed, lanceolate form.

McKellar hypothesis: A principle stating that very small items, when no longer useful, are discarded at their original location rather than disposed of elsewhere; thus such an item found at a specific site can be presumed to have been actually used at that site. The hypothesis was formulated by Judith McKellar, American archaeologist.

Meadowcroft: A rock shelter in Pennsylvania with a long series of stratified deposits spanning the period from at least 14,000 BC up to the 18th century AD—Palaeo-Indian, Archaic, Late prehistoric, and historic periods. The site was occupied intermittently by groups representing all the major cultural stages in northeastern North America. Charcoal samples in the lowest stratum have yielded dates in the range 35,000–19,500 BC, although there was no association with cultural material. Flint tools bear a resemblance to finds at Blackwater Draw and Lindenmeier. The evidence from Meadowcroft established beyond reasonable doubt the presence of a human population south of the ice masses in the Late Pleistocene. Meadowcroft provides some of the earliest reliable evidence of man in North America. (*syn.* Meadowcroft rock shelter)

me'ae: A ceremonial structure of the southern Marquesas Islands, Polynesia, including complex, irregular groups of terraces with platforms (*pa'epa'e*). Mortuary me'ae were built in secluded places and used stone-lined pits for burials. Public me'ae were associated with tohua.

mealing bin: A small adobe- or stone-lined pit in which was placed a metate, used for grinding maize.

mean: In mathematics, a quantity that has a value intermediate between those of the extreme members of some set. In archaeological technique, it is a measure of central tendency in a distribution. The arithmetic mean is the sum of all values, divided by the number of cases. Other measures of central tendency include the mode—the most commonly occurring value—and the median—the value in the middle of the distribution's range.

mean ceramic date: A statistical technique devised by Stanley South for pooling the median age of manufacture for temporally significant pottery types at American Colonial sites. It is especially applicable to 18th-century sites, where many distinctive ceramic types may be expected to occur in large numbers. The mean ceramic date is found by multiplying the sum of the median dates for the manufacture of each ceramic type of the frequency of each ceramic type and dividing this figure by the total frequency of all ceramic types. The median date for each type is arrived at from documentary evidence. One shortcoming is the supposition that the median date coincides with the period of maximum use; another is the use of a count of sherds rather than whole vessels. (*syn.* mean ceramic dating; mean ceramic dating formula)

meander: Any running design consisting of a single line or band twisting regularly. The spiral meander is a simple running spiral, the square meander a rectilinear form of the same thing. The earliest known examples of finger painting are the prehistoric decorative and figurative "meanders" traced on walls of the Altamira caves in Spain.

Meare: A lakeside village of the Iron Age on the Somerset Levels in southwest England, with groups of mounds similar to those at nearby Glastonbury. The settlement consisted of about 40 round houses built on desiccated peat, with timber and brushwood floors. It was surrounded by a palisade and occupied from the 3rd century BC to the 1st century AD. The pottery dates from about 60 BC until about the time of the

Roman invasions of the 1st century AD. The site was re-occupied during the 4th century. The Abbot's Tribunal, Glastonbury, houses some of the objects discovered during excavation.

Mecca: A caravan town on the route from southern Arabia to Palestine, the most holy city of Islam; it was the birthplace of the Prophet Muhammad, the founder of Islam, and is a religious center to which Muslims attempt a pilgrimage, or hajj, during their lifetime. Located in the Sirat Mountains in western Saudi Arabia, the focal point of the pilgrimage is the sanctuary that contains the Ka'bah which, according to Islamic tradition, Abraham and Ishmael built as the house of God. The Ka'bah was built before the advent of Islam in the 7th century and has been destroyed and rebuilt several times. Now entirely of stone, it was embellished (according to Mas'udi) with mosaic brought from a church at San'a in Yemen. The town was located about midway between Ma'rib in the south and Petra in the north, and it gradually developed by Roman and Byzantine times into an important trade and religious center. The holy book of Islam, the Qur'an, was revealed to the Prophet partly on Mount Arafat, just outside Mecca. (*syn.* Mekka, Makkah, ancient Bakkah, Macoraba)

Mechta-Afalou: The name given to a modern human physical type represented in the archaeological record of the Maghreb, especially on Ibero-Maurusian sites and associated with bladelet industries in the Nile Valley. Cemeteries such as those at Columnata and Afalou bou Rhummel have yielded large numbers of skeletons. The people were of medium height, robustly built, and with a mean cranial capacity of around 1650 cc. Remains from earlier periods suggest that the Mechta-Afalou population was of stock indigenous to northwestern Africa. Mechtoid-related forms are restricted to the western and central Sahara during the last 10,000 years and are considered a North African branch of Cro-Magnon man. (*syn.* Mechta Afalou)

Mechta-el-Arbi: Important Upper Capsian site in Algeria with remains of humans of the same name, considered a North African branch of Cro-Magnon man.

Medamud: The site of an ancient town located northeast of the Karnak temple, at the northernmost edge of Thebes. It is dominated by a temple of the falcon god Montu, which dates back at least to the Middle Kingdom (2055–1650 BC), although the nucleus of the complex is of the 18th Dynasty (1550–1295 BC) and the outer sections are Greco-Roman in date (332 BC–AD 395). (*syn.* ancient Madu)

Medemblik: A town on the Zuyder Zee, Netherlands, with a monastery known to have existed from Carolingian times up to the later medieval period. Occupation material suggests that there was an ancillary settlement from the later Merovingian era during the 8th and 9th centuries. Documents state that Pepin the Short incorporated Medemblik in a grant of land given to the Bishop of Utrecht. (*syn.* formerly Medemelach)

Medes: An Indo-European speaking people, related to the Persians, who settled in northwest Iran after moving southward through the Zagros from a still undetermined region during the Iron Age. Between the 8th–6th centuries BC, they played an active part in the complicated power politics of the Middle East, their greatest achievement being the destruction of Assyria in 614–612, under Cyaxares. They migrated to Iran at the same time as the Persians and at first were the more powerful of the two peoples. Although the initiative was seized by the Persians under Cyrus, the Medes remained ruling partners in the Achaemenid Empire he set up, and the peoples were subsequently united by marriage connections. The Persian king Cyrus II the Great overran the Medes in the mid-6th century BC. The Medians are well illustrated in the friezes of Persepolis. Their capital was at Ecbatana (modern Hamadan). Median sites have been excavated at Godin Tepe, Baba Jan, and Nush-i Jan. By tradition, the Medes are credited with the invention of trousers. (*syn.* Medians)

medial: The middle portion of an artifact or faunal element.

median historic date: The intermediate age of occupation for a known-age site.

Medicine Lodge Creek: A deeply stratified site located in the Big Horn Mountains of Wyoming, with a date range of c. 8000 BC to historic times. Evidence of a diversified subsistence base of small game hunting and gathering occurs at a time when the Big Game Hunting tradition was still widely practiced in the Great Plains. Manos, metates, and remains of fish, gopher, and rabbit were found at levels dated from 7500–6500 BC. Lanceolate projectile points, similar to those found at Mummy Cave, also fall within this date range, but stemmed points typical of the Archaic fall slightly later at c. 6300 BC.

medicine wheel: A kind of site in the northwest North American Plains, composed of stone alignments set in radiating spokes, often with central and peripheral cairns. Medicine wheels served a number of purposes and some are as old as 5500 BP. In southern Montana is a medicine wheel that is a prehistoric relic constructed of rough stones laid side by side, forming a circle 70 feet (20 m) in diameter with 28 spokes leading from the center hub, which is about 12 feet (3.5 m) in diameter.

medieval archaeology: A branch of historical archaeology studying the period in Europe between the Middle Ages and the Renaissance—AD c. 500–1500.

Medina: An oasis town in western Saudi Arabia, 447 kilometers (278 mi) from Mecca, known as Yathrib before Muhammad's residence there. Medina is second only to Mecca as the holiest place of Muslim pilgrimage. It is venerated by all Muslims as the place to which the Prophet Muhammad fled from Mecca in 622. This event (the Hijrah/Hegira/higira) marks the beginning of the Islamic era and the Muslim calendar. Muhammad built himself a house consisting of a walled compound containing a courtyard, living quarters, and a double portico. The Prophet and his followers worshiped here, and the building, with its large courtyard and covered hall, became the prototype of congregational mosques, such as those at Samar-Ra. Soon afterward, Muhammad drove out the Jews who had controlled the oasis. Thereafter known as Medina, the city prospered as the administrative capital of the steadily expanding Islamic state, a position it maintained until 661, when it was superseded in that role by Damascus. The House of the Prophet was rebuilt in 707–709 by the caliph al-Walid, who inserted a niche (the mihab) in the end wall of the portico to indicate the direction one must face while praying. (*syn.* ancient Yathrib)

Medinet Habu: Temple complex dating from the New Kingdom to the Late Period, c. 1550–332 BC, at the southernmost part of the necropolis region of western Thebes, Upper Egypt, opposite modern Luxor. The well-preserved mortuary temple of Ramesses III (1187–1157 BC) with scenes of the king's campaigns against the Sea Peoples and the Libyans is the most impressive monument. It was situated in a fortified enclosure wall, with remarkable entrance towers, imitating Syrian migdol fortresses, on the east side. A royal palace was attached at the south of the open forecourt of this temple, which was also dedicated to the god Amon. Ramesses III's walls had enclosed a small temple called Djeser-Iset that was dedicated to Amon and had been built by the earlier pharaohs Hatshepsut and Thutmose III. Medinet Habu was at one time the most important administrative center in the Theban area. In the first millennium BC, a town called Djeme developed in the fortifications of the temple; a settlement survived there into the Coptic period. (*syn.* ancient Djamet; Djeme; Madinat Habu)

Medinet Maadi: A site in the southwestern Fayyum region where a temple of the cobra goddess Renenutet (harvest deity) was founded during the reigns of Amenemhat III and IV, c. 1855–1799 BC. (*syn.* ancient Dja; Narmouthis)

medithermal: The last of the divisions of the Neothermal (postglacial) period, dating from about 4,000 years ago to the present.

Medvednjak: A pair of Neolithic settlement sites on adjoining hills, north of Smederevska Palanka in northern Serbia. The first site is dated to the earliest Vinca phase; the second has two occupations of the Early Vinca and Late Vinca (Vinca culture c. 4500–3500 BC). Complete house plans from the latest level indicate rectangular houses, and assemblages have ritual finds and evidence of spinning, weaving, food storage, and grinding.

megafauna: The large, Ice Age big-game fauna in North America, now extinct. These Late Pleistocene food sources included mammoths, mastodon, giant bison, sloths, camels, and diprotodons. The term also covers extinct larger species of quite small animals, such as giant beavers. The late Pleistocene extinction of megafauna did not occur synchronously nor was it of equal magnitude throughout the world. Considerable doubt exists about the timing of the megafaunal extinction on various land masses. Evidence suggests that the earliest mass megafaunal extinctions occurred in Australia and New Guinea about 30,000 or more years ago. Eighty-six percent of the Australian vertebrate genera whose members weighed more than 40 kilograms became extinct. Much smaller extinction events occurred in Africa, Asia, and Euope earlier in the Pleistocene, removing very large species such as rhinoceroses, elephants, and the largest artiodactyls. Other mass megafaunal extinction events occurred on the Eurasian tundra about 12,000 years ago (affecting mammoths, Irish elk, and woolly rhinoceroses); in North and South America, they occurred about 11,000 years ago (affecting a wide variety of species, including elephants, giant sloths, lions, and bears). These extinctions have removed 29% of the vertebrate genera weighing more than 40 kilograms from Europe and 73% of such genera from North America. Until 1,000 to 2,000 years ago, the megafauna of large, long-isolated land masses such as New Zealand and Madagascar survived. Gigantic birds such as the elephant birds of Madagascar and the moas of New Zealand disappeared in the past few thousand years.

megalith: From the Greek *megas* "large" and *lithos* "stone," the term for a large stone and also for structures or arrangements of large stones (menhirs, stone circles, and alignments). The term is used especially for the monuments of northern and western Europe from the Mesolithic period, such as Stonehenge and Carnac in France of the late Neolithic culture of western Europe. Such a stone was sometimes freestanding, sometimes part of a structure. The term could also refer to a large tomb that used megaliths to create passages and chambers in which burials of one or more people could be placed, such as the passage graves of Brittany. Some authorities have used the term in a still wider sense to cover monuments built of cyclopean masonry such as the Maltese temples, the Nuraghi of Sardinia, and the Navetas of Minorca. Various types of megalithic monuments have also been found in parts of Asia, Oceania, and Africa. The migration theories based on megalithic monuments are now discounted. It is now accepted that the practice of erecting these monuments arose independently in different times and places and for different reasons. (*syn.* megalithic; megalithic tomb; megalithic monument)

megalithic art: Neolithic engravings found on megalithic stones of chambered tombs and menhirs. Motifs include the concrete and the abstract. The art is associated with passage graves. Examples are Gavrinis, Knowth, and Newgrange. Megalithic art objects often suggest a highly developed cult of a spirit world connected with the remains of the dead. (*syn.* stone art)

megalithic culture: In India, an Iron Age culture of the south from the 1st millennium BC or earlier, which lasted into the early 1st millennium AD. The grave forms include urn burials and various cist, pit, and rock-cut graves. Stone alignments are also associated, and graves generally contain burnished black-and-red ware, iron tools, weapons, horse, and household equipment.

megalithic yard: A unit of measurement, 0.829 meters or 2.72 feet, deduced from the layout of stone circles and alignments in Britain and Brittany.

Megaloceros: An extinct giant elk of the Pleistocene ("giant deer"), whose best-known species *M. giganteus* was abundant in Ireland, Europe, and western Asia. It had the largest antlers of any deer known—some 13 feet (4 m) across. Its remains are sometimes found in Palaeolithic assemblages, and there are rare depictions in cave art. It became generally extinct in c. 10,500 BP, although some may have survived to 700–500 BC. (*syn.* Irish elk)

Meganthropus: The name given to a large-toothed hominid of the Djetis deposits of central Java, Indonesia, which have been related to the Astralopithecines or to *Homo erectus* or *Homo habilis*. They are known only by mandible fragments. (*syn.* Meganthropus palaeojavanicus)

megapode: A member of a family of stocky, chickenlike birds (order Galliformes, family Megapodidae) found in Australia and the islands of the southwestern Pacific, which build huge mounds of decaying vegetable matter in which to incubate their eggs. Most of the 12 species rely on fermenting plant matter to produce heat for incubation, but some use solar heat, and others the heat produced by volcanic action. (*syn.* mound builder, incubator bird)

Megarian bowl: A handleless hemispherical Greek drinking cup made in molds and often decorated in relief and finished in the black-glossed technique. Widespread in the Hellenistic period from the 3rd century BC, they developed into the red-glossed Arrentine wares. The type was first recognized at Megara and was made until the 1st century AD. They were imitations of gold and silver vessels and served as the first form of "book illustration." They often bear on their exteriors scenes in relief from literary texts that are sometimes accompanied by Greek quotations. They likely served as models for Roman artists who created the first "true" book illustrations.

megaron: In Aegean (ancient Greece and the Middle East) architecture, a hall consisting basically of a rectangular or apsidal-ended room with the side walls projecting beyond the forward end to form a porch, which may be pillared. There was often a large, round central hearth in the hall and extra rooms at the rear end, between the same side walls. It was usually entered through the shallow porch at the one end. The form is recorded at Troy in the later 4th millennium BC and continued to be used in Turkey until much later. It appears as early as the Sesklo period in Greece but is best known in the great painted halls of Mycenaean princes. This architectural unit formed the main hall of a Mycenaean house or the central block of a Mycenaean palace. It also became an important element in the Classical temple. A typical megaron plan is that of the palace of Nestor at Pylos, where the large main unit apparently served as royal living quarters. It faced onto the usual courtyard, which was entered through a decorative gateway with fluted columns on either side. (*syn.* Megaron)

megger: An instrument for measuring high electrical resistance in megohms. (*syn.* megohmmeter)

Megiddo: A large tell on a natural hill in northern Palestine, a Biblical city. A town in the Early Bronze Age was built in the early 4th millennium BC and the site was sporadically occupied since the Neolithic and Chalcolithic. It became a great fortified center through its strategic position on the land route from Egypt to Mesopotamia and on the route that connected Phoenician cities with Jerusalem. Megiddo was captured by the Egyptian king Thutmose III about 1468 but survived frequent sackings down to c. 350 BC. Notable finds include a hoard of 400 Phoenician ivories, a rock-cut shaft and a 65-meter passage to give the Canaanites access to a spring from inside the walls—all from the 13th century BC. To the 9th century BC belong a series of palace, shrine, and stable buildings created by the Israelites. The town was destroyed at the end of the 8th century BC, and, although rebuilt, it declined into insignificance by the Hellenistic period. (*syn.* Tell Megiddo)

Mehi: A tell site of the Kulli culture in southern Baluchistan (Pakistan) with a settlement and cremation cemetery. Grave goods include copper tools, beads, and terra-cotta figurines of females, bulls, and birds. The tell also yielded Indus civilization material such as carved stone vases. A number of steatite bowls imported from Tepe Yahya around 2800 BC have been found.

Mehrgarh: Important site of a series of settlements of the Neolithic and Chalcolithic periods in Baluchistan, western Pakistan, important as the earliest farming site known in the area, perhaps dating from the 8th–6th millennia BC. The earliest phase was aceramic, and the evidence at Mehrgarh provides a clear picture of an early agricultural settlement exhibiting domestic architecture and a variety of well-established crafts. The use of seashells and of various semiprecious stones, including turquoise and lapis lazuli, indicates the existence of trade networks extending from the coast and perhaps also from Central Asia. Subsequent phases in the 5th, 4th, and 3rd millennia show a developing society, characterized by craft specialization (with specialist production of pottery figurines and beads of semiprecious stones) and extensive trade networks linking Baluchistan with eastern Iran and southern Turkmenistan. Although no Harappan civilization phase is represented here, the culture of Mehrgarh provides a plausible local antecedent for this civilization. It was probably occupied until the beginning of the Mature Harappan in the 3rd millennium BC. (*syn.* Mehrgahr)

Meidum: Ancient Egyptian site of the remains of the first true Egyptian pyramid complex, near Memphis on the west bank of the Nile River in the Fayyum region. It is the earliest-known pyramid complex with all the parts of a "normal" Old Kingdom (c. 2575–c. 2130 BC) funerary monument. These parts included the pyramid itself, a mortuary temple, and a sloping causeway leading to a valley temple built near the Nile River. The pyramid is usually ascribed to King Huni (c. 2650–2575 BC), last king of the 3rd Dynasty, but completed by his successor Snefru. The pyramid is also associated with mastabas of the early 4th Dynasty. (*syn.* Maydum, Medum)

Meiendorf: A site close to Hamburg, northern Germany, in a glacial "tunnel valley," with late glacial occupation in peat deposits, with numerous remains of reindeer and stone and bone tools of Hamburgian type. The Hamburgian was Late Upper Palaeolithic, c. 13,000–11,750 BP.

Meillacoid phase: One of two ceramic series (the other being Chicoid), which emerged from the Ostinoid series. Originating in Haiti, it remained largely confined to the western Greater Antilles. Sites are usually village shell middens, but are often close to good agricultural land. The characteristic pottery is thin and hard but with a rough surface texture and simple incision, sometimes combined with appliquéd strips. The dates are usually within AD 850–1000, although some sites in central Cuba endured to as late as 1500. (*syn.* Melliac)

Meipin: The Japanese name for a type of bottle with narrow neck, high shoulders, and pinched-in base. Meipin were originally a Chinese creation, popular in the Sung, Yuan, Ming periods and beginning of T'sing. The shape spread to Korea (Koryo celadons) and to Japan. Some were made in kilns. (*syn.* Meiping (Chinese))

Meir: Important group of decorated rock-cut tombs in Middle Egypt, about 50 kilometers northwest of modern Asyut. The tombs belonged to the local monarchs of the late Old–Middle Kingdoms, dating to the 6th–12th Dynasties (2345–2181 and 1985–1795 BC).

Mejiro: A rock shelter near Old Oyo, southwestern Nigeria, where a microlithic industry occurs, without associated pottery. It is one of relatively few presumed prepottery "Late Stone Age" occurrences yet known in Nigeria.

Melanesia: The region including New Guinea, the Bismarck Archipelago, the Solomons, Vanuatu, New Caledonia, Fiji, and minor intermediate groups. Early Australoid settlers reached New Guinea when it was joined to Australia, by at least 30,000–40,000 years ago, and the New Guinea highlands have a long, stable archaeological sequence extending into the Holocene (Kospie, Kiowa, Kafianvana). The highlands may also have seen an independent development of early Holocene horticulture (Kuk). The Bismarcks and Solomons (Kilu) seem to have been occupied by c. 30,000 bp. Settlement of the rest of Melanesia may have occurred as part of the expansion of Austronesian speakers in the Pacific. Major archaeological entities include the Lapita culture and the Manaasi pottery tradition.

Melka Kontoure: A site in Ethiopia some 50 kilometers south of Addis Ababa, with many archaeological levels dating from over 1.5 million years ago at the base to late Pleistocene times. Its long stone artifact sequence included Oldowan, Acheulian, Middle Stone Age, and Microlithic Later Stone Age. A few hominid fragments have been found, but it is the long succession of artifact assemblages and living floors that make the site important.

Melkart: One of the Phoenician gods of Solomon's temple in Jerusalem; chief deity of Tyre and its colonies Carthage and Gadir. (*syn.* Melqart, Tyrian Baal Malku)

Melkhoutboom: Cave in eastern Cape Province, South Africa, with Later Stone Age material spanning the last 15,000 years. There is an excellent plant collection from the last 7,500 years; Late Stone Age people relied heavily on plant foods, the remains of which have been well preserved at this site. (*syn.* Melkhoutboom Cave)

Melos: One of the Cyclades in the Aegean, famous as a major source of obsidian, whose trade brought wealth to the island. It was used extensively for chipped stone implements in Aegean prehistory from as early as the 10th millennium BC. The island, however, was not inhabited until the 4th millennium BC. At Phylakopi, three successive settlements were discovered, of roughly Early Cycladic II, Middle Cycladic, and Late Cycladic, respectively. They show increasing influence from the Minoans of Crete, so much so that the third settlement is better regarded as a provincial Minoan town than a native Cycladic one. Nevertheless, the island maintained close contact with the Greek mainland, and with the collapse of Crete it came fully into the sphere of the Mycenaeans. The classical polis, destroyed by Athens in 416 BC, centered on the fortified acropolis of ancient Melos.

melting: The point at which a metal liquifies. This point must be reached if a metal object is to be cast. In antiquity, gold, silver, copper, iron, and lead were all melted and cast. Melting points are as follows: tin, 232°C; lead, 327°C; silver, 960°C; gold, 1063°C; copper, 1083°C; iron 1525°C.

Meluhha: The ancient Akkadian name for the Indus region. It was a land that traded with the city-states of Sumer, to its west, and appeared in Mesopotamian texts of the Akkadian and Ur III periods. The land was described as a source of gold and is usually identified as the area of the Harappan civilization in western India and Pakistan during the 3rd and 2nd millennia BC. In the 1st millennium BC, Meluhha refers to Nubia, to the south of Egypt. Literary references to Meluhhan trade date from the Akkadian, Ur III, and Isin-Larsa Periods (i.e., c. 2350–1800 BC), but as texts and archaeological data indicate, the trade probably started in the Early Dynastic period (c. 2600 BC). During the Akkadian period, Meluhhan vessels sailed directly to Mesopotamian ports, but by the Isin-Larsa period, Dilmun (modern Bahrain) was the entrepôt for Meluhhan and Mesopotamian traders. By the subsequent Old Babylonian period, trade between the two cultures evidently had ceased entirely.

Memphis: The capital of Egypt in the Archaic period and Old Kingdom (c. 2575–c. 2130 BC), and thereafter one of the most important cities of the Near East. Located in Lower Egypt, it stood near the key point where the Nile begins to divide its waters at the head of the delta, 15 miles south of Cairo. The only surviving remains are the cemeteries west of the city, most notably the pyramids and Great Sphinx of Giza. The main pyramid fields are Abu Ruwaysh, Giza, Zawayet el-Aryan, Abu Sir, Saqqarah (Saqqara), and Dahshur. It is said to have been founded by the 1st Dynasty ruler Menes c. 2925 BC and was the seat of the creator god Ptah. During the New Kingdom (1539–1075), Memphis probably functioned as the second, or northern, capital of Egypt. Despite the rise of the god Amon of Thebes, Ptah remained one of the principal gods of the pantheon. The Great Temple was added to or rebuilt by virtually every king of the 18th dynasty. Chapels were constructed by Thutmose I and Thutmose IV and by Amenhotep III. Amenhotep III's son, the religious reformer Akhenaton, built a temple to his god, Aton, in Memphis. A number of handsome private tombs dating from this period in the Memphite necropolis testify to the existence of a sizable court. In 332 BC, Alexander the Great used Memphis as his headquarters while making plans for his new city of Alexandria. From the Fifth Dynasty onward, there was a very marked reduction in the size of the royal tombs, together with the use of materials and techniques that involved a lesser expenditure of effort and resources in their construction. By the First Intermediate period, the construc-

tion of monumental tombs seems to have stopped. (*syn.* Men-nefer)

Menelaion, the: The main Mycenaean site in Laconia, Greece, with two mansions of the 15th and 14th centuries BC. In the 8th century BC, the cult of Menelaus and Helen was established, leaving the remains of their Classical shrine. The administrative center of Mycenaean Sparta was probably in the Párnon Mountains at the site.

Menes (fl. c. 2925 BC): The first king of unified Egypt, who, according to tradition, joined Upper and Lower Egypt in a single, centralized monarchy. Manetho, a 3rd-century-BC Egyptian historian, called him Menes; the 5th-century-BC Greek historian Herodotus referred to him as Min; and two native king lists of the 19th Dynasty (13th century BC) called him Meni. Modern scholars have inconclusively identified the traditional Menes with one or more of the archaic Egyptian kings bearing the names Scorpion, Narmer, and Aha. In addition to crediting Menes with the unification of Egypt by war and administrative measures, tradition attributes to him the founding of the capital, Memphis, near modern Cairo. According to Greek tradition, the pharaoh founded the 1st Dynasty, c. 2925 BC. To the ancient Egyptians, he was the first human ruler. According to Manetho, Menes reigned 62 years and was killed by a hippopotamus. (*syn.* Mena, Meni, Min)

menhir: A single, vertical standing stone; any prehistoric structure consisting of a tall, upright megalith (huge stone). The name is from the Old Breton *men*, meaning "stone," and *hir*, meaning "long." Menhirs occur in all parts of the world where megalithic monuments are known, but they are particularly profuse in prehistoric Europe. Menhirs are difficult to date, but in Ireland and southwest England a few examples mark burials dating from the Neolithic to the Middle or Late Bronze Age. A similar or slightly earlier date is attested for some of the Breton menhirs. In all these areas, a few of the stones bear cup marks. Such a megalith is often isolated, erected by a family or tribe as a memorial stone for some deceased hero or some great event. It may have been a religious object for worship like the American Indian totem pole. Others are associated with dolmens, tumuli, and circles of stones. Menhirs may occur singly, in rows (alignments), or in enclosures (stone circles). Anthropomorphic examples are known as statue-menhirs.

Menkaure (fl. late 26th century BC): Egyptian king of the 4th Dynasty (Old Kingdom) and builder of the third, and smallest, pyramid at Giza. He was the firth or sixth king of the dynasty (c. 2575–2465 BC), the son of Khafre (2558–2532 BC) and grandson of Khufu (2589–2566 BC), the builders of the two other pyramids at the site. In the funerary complex were found some of the finest sculptures of the Pyramid Age, including a slate statue group of Menkaure and his sister-wife Khamerernebti II. (*syn.* Menkaura, Mycerinus, Menkure)

mensuration: Any act of measuring; measurement. The earliest standard measurements appeared in the ancient Mediterranean cultures and were based on parts of the body, or on calculations of what man or beast could haul, or on the volume of containers or the area of fields in common use. The Egyptian cubit is generally recognized to have been the most widespread unit of linear measurement in the ancient world. It came into use around 3000 BC and was based on the length of the arm from the elbow to the extended finger tips. It was standardized by a royal master cubit of black granite, against which all cubit sticks in Egypt were regularly checked. One of the earliest known weight measures was the Babylonian mina, although the two surviving examples vary widely— 640 grams (about 1.4 pounds) and 978 grams (about 2.15 pounds).

mentalist approach: Any approach to archaeology (including postprocessualism) which stresses the importance of symbolism, ideology, and meaning.

Mentuhotep II (fl. 19th century BC): A king of Egypt's 11th Dynasty (ruled 2008–1957 BC), who, starting as the ruler of southernmost Egypt in about 2008, reunified the country by defeating his rivals and ushered in the period known as the Middle Kingdom. His reign heralded a return to political stability after the comparative confusion and decentralization of the First Intermediate period. It was also the birth name held by two other Theban kings of the 11th Dynasty and one of their ancestors. Mentuhotep II's funerary temple at Deir el-Bahri, on the west bank at Thebes, may have influenced Queen Hatshepsut, who later built on same site. (*syn.* Nebhapetre)

Mercia: One of the kingdoms of central Anglo-Saxon England; it held a position of dominance for much of the period from the mid-7th to the early 9th century. Mercia originally included the border areas (modern Staffordshire, Derbyshire, Nottinghamshire, and northern West Midlands and Warwickshire) that lay between the districts of Anglo-Saxon settlement and the Celtic tribes they had driven to the west. It later absorbed the Hwicce territory (the rest of West Midlands and Warwickshire, eastern Hereford and Worcester, and Gloucestershire) and spread also into what was later Cheshire, Salop (Shropshire), and western Hereford and Worcester. Mercia eventually came to denote an area bounded by the frontiers of Wales, the River Humber, East Anglia, and the River Thames. Its most famous kings were Penda (632–654), Aethelbald (reigned 716–757), and Offa (757–796). During this time, the important Mercian School of manuscript illumination and sculpture developed. Thereafter, it declined and disappeared under the encroachments of the Danes and of Wessex.

Merenptah (d. 1204 BC?): The 13th son of his long-lived father, Ramesses II, Merneptah was nearing 60 years of age at his accession in about 1213. Because of the extraordinary length of the reign of Ramesses II (1279–1213 BC), at least twelve of his sons died before him, including Khaemwaset, who was for several years the appointed heir. Early in Merneptah's reign, his troops had to suppress a revolt in Palestine by the cities of Ashqelon, Gezer, and Yenoam. Merneptah's greatest challenge, however, came from the Libyans who were encroaching on Egyptian lands. About 1209, Merneptah learned that some Sea Peoples, who were roving the Middle East, had joined and armed the Libyans and with them were conspiring to attack Memphis and Heliopolis. He is responsible for the great victory over the Libyans and Sea Peoples, in which they lost nearly 9,400 men. Merneptah ordered the carving of four great commemorative texts in celebration. One of these, the famous "Israel Stela," refers to the suppression of the revolt in Palestine. It contains the earliest-known reference to Israel, which Merneptah counted among the peoples that he defeated. Hebrew scholars suggest that the circumstances agree approximately with the period noted in biblical books from late Exodus to Judges. A fragmentary stela from the Sudan also suggests that the king quelled a rebellion in Lower Nubia, probably after his Palestinian exploits. (*syn.* Meneptah, Merenptah)

Meretseger: The Theban cobra goddess, whose cult was centered on the mountain that dominates the Valley of the Kings. Her cult is primarily attested during the New Kingdom (1550–1069 BC).

Merida: A Roman colony in Spain, founded by the Romans in 25 BC as Augusta Emerita. As the capital of Lusitania (roughly equivalent to modern Portugal), it became one of the most important towns in Iberia and was large enough to contain a garrison of 90,000 men. It prospered anew in the 7th century under the Visigoths. Roman buildings survive: theater, amphitheater (both built by Agrippa), circus, temples, aqueducts, and a Roman bridge of 64 arches. There is a temple of Diana, an arch of Trajan, aqueducts and conduits, a group of structures devoted to Mithras and other mystery cults, and a number of rich houses with colonnaded courts and mosaics (including the so-called Creation of the Universe). Gold tesserae are found, and some of the sculptures, especially Roman marble portraits, are of fine quality. (*syn.* Emerita Augusta, Roman Augusta Emerita)

Merimde Beni Salama: Site on the west bank of the Nile Delta, Egypt, representing one of the earliest cultures of Egypt, similar to that of the Fayyum (Faiyum). It yielded a radiocarbon date of 5060 BC and was occupied for about 600 years, probably c. 4900–4300 BC, by a population up to 16,000. Three occupation phases showed progressively more substantial shelters, beneath which the dead were buried in a crouched position. Barley and emmer, cattle, sheep, and pigs are attested. Sickle flints and hollow-based arrowheads, pyriform and spherical mace heads, sling stones, fishhooks, spindle whorls, and simple stone ax heads have been found. The pottery was poor, plain, straw tempered and often covered with a slip. It is the earliest evidence for fully sedentary village life in the Nile Valley. The Merimda phase of the Lower Egyptian Predynastic period appears to have been roughly contemporary with the late Badarian and Amratian phases in Upper Egypt. (*syn.* Merinde, Merimda Beni Salama)

Meroe: A site in Upper Nubia, a city-state in the Sudan, which succeeded Napata (original capital of kingdom of Kush/Cush) as the capital of a vigorous state flourishing from 750 BC–AD 350. The 25th, or "Ethiopian," dynasty of ancient Egypt is believed to have retired to Kush after 656 BC and established itself at Meroe. After the sack if Napata in c. 590 by the Egyptian pharaoh Psamtik II, Meroe became the capital of the kingdom. It is the type site of the Meroitic period (c. 300 BC–AD 350) and located on the east bank of the Nile in the Butana region of Sudan. Dependent on the Nile, the kingdom lay in a triangle of land at the confluence of Nile and Atbara. It was the center of the Kushite kingdom in the 5th century BC. Meroe was able to exploit a region of considerable agricultural potential with fairly regular, if not abundant, rainfall. There was also a supply of timber adequate to fuel the smelting of the local iron deposits. By the beginning of the Christian era, if not before, the iron industry had been developed on a considerable scale. Meroitic architecture included temples in the Egyptian style and royal pyramid tombs (e.g., Musawwarat es-Sufra). Egyptian influence gradually diminished; Egyptian hieroglyphs were abandoned in about the 2nd century BC in favor of a local script. The Meroitic language thus recorded cannot at present be understood. The tenuous nature of the link with Egypt is to be appreciated by considering the trade route, which it appears did not follow the inhospitable Nile Valley, but ran along the Red Sea coast. From about the beginning of the Christian era, this route was increasingly endangered by local development, notably the rise of the kingdom of Axum. By the 3rd century AD, Meroe was in decline; its final collapse came with the conquest by Axum early in the 4th century. The chief features are palaces and a great temple of Amon.

Merovingian: A dynasty of Frankish rulers and their kingdom, from AD c. 476–750, recognized as the "first race" of the kings of France. Named after its founder, Merovech, the Merovingians ruled France from the time of Childeric I to that of Charles Martel. Merovingian is a term used to describe Frankish archaeology of the 6th to mid-8th centuries AD. The area was that of western Rhineland to the Atlantic coast of France and embraces a number of kingdoms such as Austria, Neustria, and Burgundia. The Merovingian kings consolidated power and brought Christianity to the Frankish kingdom (modern France and the Rhineland) after the fall of the Roman Empire in Gaul and laid the political and artistic foundation for the Carolingian Empire that followed. Merovingian art is characterized by a mixture of the Roman classical style with native Germanic-Frankish artistic traditions, which favored abstraction and geometric patterning. The Merovingian script is the writing of the pre-Carolingian hands of France, which were derived from Latin cursive script in the 7th and 8th centuries.

Mersin: The tell site of Yümük-Tepe on the southern coast of Turkey (Anatolia) with 33 major levels, the bulk of which are Neolithic and Chalcolithic. The lowest levels were of an Early Neolithic characterized by monochrome impressed wares and radiocarbon dated to 6000 BC. A long series of Chalcolithic levels were tied into the Mesopotamian sequence (Hassuna, Halaf, Ubaid, etc.) by imported sherds. Occupation resumed in the Middle Bronze Age until the Iron Age. The Iron Age levels have ceramic evidence of contacts with the Aegean world. There are also Byzantine and medieval (AD c. 1500) occupations.

mesa: A steep-sided, flat-topped hill, tableland, or mountain. A mesa is an isolated and relatively flat-topped natural elevation usually more extensive than a butte and less extensive than a plateau. The term is also applied to a broad terrace with an abrupt slope on one side. In the U.S. Southwest, mesas were often used for settlements in Pre-Columbian times.

Mesara: Large, fertile southern plain of Crete, exploited since the later Neolithic. The Minoan palace of Phaistos and Gortyn, the capital of the Roman province of Crete and Cyrenaica, are the two main archaeological sites. The tholoi, or beehive tombs, were developed on the Mesara plain.

Mesa Verde: A large flat-topped mountain in southwest Colorado, which was an area of Anasazi occupation beginning in AD c. 600. The structures are among the most spectacular in the American Southwest: cliff dwellings that are large Pueblo III multiroom apartment dwellings. The most famous is the Cliff Palace, made up of 200 rooms and 23 kivas built of dressed stone blocks. The popoulation rose steadily until 1200, after which date came decline and total abandonment of the area by c. 1300.

Mesoamerica: A geographical and cultural area from central Honduras and northwest Costa Rica north through Mexico and including Tamaulipas and Sinaloa—roughly between central Mexico and Costa Rica—the location of several notable Pre-Columbian civilizations. It is the area in Central America in which various Classic and Post-classic civilizations developed, including Olmec, Teotihuacán, Aztec, and Maya. The culture area was originally defined on the basis of shared traits such as the developments of agriculture, urbanization, and elaborate ceremonial practice. An immense environmental diversity is enclosed in the area. In recent years the term has been applied to the geographic area alone, without being limited by the defining traits named above. The culture began with village life more than 4,000 years ago.

mesocephalic: A physical anthropological term meaning "medium headed" or "intermediate," that is, the maximum width of the cranium being between 75–80% of the length.

Mesolithic: A period in human history beginning with the retreat of glacial ice c. 8500 BC and the changing climatic conditions following it; a development in northwestern Europe that lasted until about 2700 BC. This Middle Stone Age followed the Upper Palaeolithic and preceded the Neolithic. It was a period of transition in the early Holocene between the hunter-gatherer existence and the development of farming and pottery production. Glacial flora and fauna were replaced by modern forms, and the flint industries are often distinguished by an abundance of microliths. The equipment was designed for fishing and fowling as well as hunting and often included many tiny flints, or microliths, that were set in wooden shafts and hafts, and stone axes or adzes used for woodworking. Forests grew in Europe, and people modified their lives accordingly. In the Near East, which remained free of ice sheets, climatic change was less significant than in northern Europe, and agriculture was practiced soon after the close of the Pleistocene. In this area, the Mesolithic period was short and poorly differentiated. In Britain, the Mesolithic-Neolithic transition did not come until around 4000 BC. The dog was domesticated during the Mesolithic. The term is used widely only in European prehistory. (*syn.* mesolithic, Epipalaeolithic, Middle Stone Age)

Mesopotamia: Term meaning "land between the (two) rivers," the area between the Tigris and Euphrates Rivers in western Asia (modern Iraq), which encompassed various ancient kingdoms. This land was the home of the world's earliest civilization, that of the Sumerians, and of the later Babylonian, Akkadian, and Assyrian civilizations. The chronology of the prehistoric periods is based on radiocarbon dates; the historical periods' chronology is based on a combination of documentary sources and calendrical information. The area was the focus of the development of complex societies until the collapse of Mesopotamia at the end of the 1st millennium BC. The geography of the area allowed the development of husbandry, agriculture, and permanent settlements. Trade with other regions also flourished; irrigation techniques were created as well as pottery and other crafts; building methods based on clay bricks were developed; and elaborate religious cults evolved. The birth of the city took place in the 4th millennium BC, and the invention of writing occurred about 3000 BC—both in Sumer. Excavations of

Sumerian cities (Eridu, Kish, Uruk, Isin, Lagash, Ur) have yielded thousands of clay tablets inscribed with cuneiform writing. Sargon, the king of Akkad, fought wars of conquest from the Mediterranean to the Zagros and ruled over history's first empire. The Akkadians were a Semitic people, and their Akkadian language became the common vocabulary. The Akkadian ruled only about 2 centuries. After that, Ur (c. 2112–2004 BC), the parallel dynasties of Isin and Larsa (to c. 1763 BC), and then Babylon were the powers. The outstanding ruler of Babylon was Hammurabi (c. 1792–1750 BC), who is best known for the code of laws he had inscribed on a great stela. From about 1600–1450 BC, Babylonian culture declined as the Hurrians and the Kassites migrated into Mesopotamia and established themselves as rulers. Some time after 1500 BC, the Mitanni kingdom extended its rule over much of northern Mesopotamia. The language of the kingdom was Hurrian, but its rulers may have been of Aryan origin. Toward the end of the 15th century BC, the city of Ashur in northern Mesopotamia, a region that came to be known as Assyria, began its rise. By 1350 BC, the Assyrian empire was well established, and its kings conquered large areas from the Mitanni kingdom, the Kassites, and the Hittites. Another Babylonian dynasty, known as the 2nd Dynasty of Isin, revived the greatness of the Old Empire under Nebuchadrezzar I (c. 1119–1098). Assyria reached new heights of power under Tiglath-pileser I (c. 1115–1077) and Ashurnasirpal II (883–859). Between 746–727 BC, the Neo-Assyrian Empire formed and subdued the Aramaeans who had settled much of Babylonia and then conquered Urartu, Syria, Israel, and other areas. The empire reached its zenith after conquering Egypt in 671 and then the reign of Ashurbanipal (668–627), but its rapid decline came soon after attacks by the Medes, Scythians, and Babylonians. The Assyrian Empire was crushed in 609. Babylon's Nebuchadrezzar II (605–561) is best known for his destruction of Jerusalem in 588/587 and his forcing of thousands of Jews into the "Babylonian exile." The Neo-Babylonian Empire ended in 539, when Nabonidus surrendered to Cyrus II of Persia. Under the Persians and Alexander the Great, Babylon was a rich capital. The Seleucid kings ruled Mesopotamia from about 312 BC until the middle of the 2nd century BC. In the 2nd century BC, Mesopotamia became part of the Parthian Empire. Human occupation of Mesopotamia began some time around 6000 BC. The prehistoric cultural stages of Hassuna-Samarra' and Halaf succeeded each other here before there is evidence of settlement in the south (Sumer). There, the earliest settlements, such as Eridu, appear to have been founded around 5000 BC, in the late Halaf period. From then on, the cultures of the north and south moved through a succession of major archaeological periods that in their southern forms are known as 'Ubaid, Warka, Protoliterate, and Early Dynastic, at the end of which—shortly after 3000

BC—recorded history began. The historical periods of the 3rd millennium are, in order, Akkad, Gutium, 3rd Dynasty of Ur; those of the 2nd millennium are Isin-Larsa, Old Babylonian, Kassite, and Middle Babylonian; and those of the 1st millennium are Assyrian, Neo-Babylonian, Achaemenian, Seleucid, and Parthian.

Mesozoic: The second of the Earth's three major geologic eras of Phanerozoic time and the interval during which the continental land masses as known today were separated from the supercontinents Laurasia (North America and Eurasia) and Gondwana by continental drift. It occurred before the Cenozoic and after the Palaeozoic and was marked by the development of the ancestors of the major plant and animal groups that exist today and the extinction of the dinosaur, suddenly at the end of the Cretaceous Period. It lasted from about 245 to 66.4 million years ago and included, in order, the Triassic Period, the Jurassic Period, and the Cretaceous Period.

mesquite pod: The edible, bean-like seed vessel harvested from the mesquite tree (genus Prosopis) of southwestern United States, central America, and South America. Native Americans cooked the sugary pods into a syrup; the seeds could also be roasted and eaten.

Messene: Ancient Greek city in southwest Peloponnese, Greece, founded in 369 BC after the defeat of Sparta by Athens. The site includes Megalopolis, Mantineia, and Argos; the summit of Mt. Ithómi served as the akropolis. The classical city withstood several Macedonian and Spartan sieges. After the Battle of Chaeronea in 338 BC, it was absorbed into the domain of Philip II of Macedonia, and it remained important under the Romans. The Hellenistic agora, theater, stadium, temple of Artemis, city walls, and council chamber have been excavated. (*syn.* Messini)

Mestizo: A person of mixed blood—particularly used to denote mixed European and Native American ancestry. (*syn.* mestizo)

metal artifact: Any artifact made from metal, including copper, bronze, iron, gold, silver, tin, and lead.

metal detector: A geophysical instrument used in electromagnetic surveying to locate metal on the surface, hidden under vegetation, or shallowly buried. Some metal detectors can be programmed to detect only artifacts of a certain alloy.

metallographic microscopy: The microscopic examination of metal artifacts with the aim of studying their manufacturing technqiues rather than their composition. A sample is taken from the artifact, preferably a cross-sectional slice, and it is highly polished. The surface is then etched to dissolve some of the metal, leaving visible its internal structure for examination under a metallurgical microscope. This uses reflected light, which emphasizes the uneven surfaces re-vealed by the etching process and caused by such features as the boundaries between grains of metal. The size and shape of the grains or dendrites in a metal (crystalline structure), as well as other details of microstructure, can yield information on casting methods or postcasting working. The technique can be used on both ferrous and nonferrous metals. (*syn.* metallographic examination)

metallurgical analysis: The study of metals. Metal artifacts and the tools or waste products of their manufacture are examined to reconstruct manufacturing processes, the source of raw materials, and the usage. This may be done by the various techniques of chemical analysis or may involve metallographic examination under a microscope. In the case of copper, bronze, and other nonferrous metals, such analysis may yield information about alloys, casting, cold working, and annealing. For iron and steel, there may be information about forging, carburization, quenching, and tempering.

metallurgy: The art of working metals. Various techniques include annealing, repoussé, cire perdue, cold working, casting, forging, carburization, quenching, tempering, soldering, smelting, welding, and creation of alloys.

Metaponto: Greek colony in southern Italy with Hippodamian planning. Two temples of the Doric order may have been for Hera and Apollo Lycaeus. (*syn.* Metapontum)

metate: A ground-stone slab with a concave upper surface used as a lower millstone against which another stone is rubbed to grind vegetable material such as cereal grains, seeds, nuts. A metate is one of a two-part milling apparatus—the other part being with a mano (handheld upper grindstone). Metates are found in agricultural and preagricultural contexts over much of the world and are often made of volcanic rock in Mesoamerica. It is a Spanish term for the smoothed, usually immobile, stone with a concave upper surface and is mostly associated with the grinding of maize. It is a hallmark artifact in the definition of prehistoric subsistence patterns. (*syn.* lower grindstone, concave quern, stone saddle quern)

methodology: Working concepts or approach, whether consciously adopted or otherwise acquired. A methodology can be a body of methods, rules, and postulates employed by a discipline. An archaeologist analyzes the principles or procedures of inquiry in a particular endeavor.

metope: In architecture, the space between two triglyphs of a Doric frieze often adorned with carved work. It is the part of the entablature of a building of the Doric order placed between triglyphs. The frieze in buildings using the classical Doric order is usually composed of alternate triglyphs (projecting rectangular blocks, each ornamented with three vertical channels) and metopes (spaces).

metrical signs: A term denoting a sign for units of measurement, like $. It is a subclass of logographic signs.

Metsamor: Sites in Armenia near Yerevan with Kura-Araxes and Late Bronze to Early Iron Age occupations. The latter indicates the existence of pre-Urartian states in Transcaucasia. Objects inscribed in Mesopotamian cuneiform and Egyptian hieroglyphics have been found in the graves dating to the 15th–14th centuries BC. These imply long-distance contacts with southern civilizations.

Mezhirich: Upper Palaeolithic site at the Rosava and Ros' Rivers in the Ukraine with occupation from c. 17,855–12,900 bp. Mammoth-bone houses with associated pits, hearths, and debris concentrations have been found. There are stone and nonstone artifacts and art objects.

Mezin: Upper Palaeolithic site in the Desna Valley in the Ukraine with a radiocarbon date of 15,100 bp. Art material with squared key pattern carving was made, including an ivory wrist band. There are at least two mammoth bone houses with associated pits and hearths.

Miao-ti-kou: Important site of the Middle Neolithic Yang-shao culture in China. It was occupied periodically, suggesting slash-and-burn agriculture. In the upper level, dated c. 2800 BC, fine pottery was made with designs of arcs and dots, showing some connection with earlier Yanshao cultures (e.g., Banpo) but the Miaodigou painted designs, monochrome or painted in black over a red or white slip, are entirely abstract. The most sophisticated Miaodigou patterns have running spiral designs and close affinities with Majiayao in Gansu. The second level, dated c. 3900 BC, has unpainted pottery and includes many shapes virtually unknown to the Yanshao tradition, such as tripods with solid or hollow legs. (*syn.* Miaodigou)

mica: Any of a group of hydrous potassium, aluminum silicate minerals that occur in a glittering, scaly form; widely prized for ornament in prehistory.

Michelsberg: A Middle Neolithic culture of Belgium, northeastern France, the Rhineland, and parts of Switzerland, from c. 4500–4000 BC. It occupies a frontier zone on the borders of the Danubian culture, TRB culture, and western Neolithic complex and shares traits with all three. The type site is a hilltop enclosure in Baden-Württemberg, Germany There are many regional subgroups. The Belgian one has leaf-shaped arrowheads, antler combs, flint mines, and enclosures similar in construction to causewayed camps and may have had links with the Windmill Hill culture of Britain. In the Rhineland and Low Countries, the culture was closely related to the Funnel-Necked Beaker culture and a successor to the Röessen culture. Pottery forms include pointed- and round-based vessels with flaring rims and flat pottery disks (plats à pain), which were probably lids. One innovation was

the use of deep mines for flint (Spiennes in Belgium, Rijckholt in Netherlands) where axes were made. Contacts by the Michelsberg with late Mesolithic hunter gatherers north of the loess zone gave rise to semiagricultural communities, as evidenced by relics from about 4000 BC found in the Netherlands delta at Swifterbant in Flevoland and Hazendonkborn and Bergschenhoekborn in Zuid-Holland.

Micoquain: Final Acheulian phase defined on the basis of assemblages from La Micoque, near Les Eyzies, France. Sites are in central Europe, including some in the former Soviet Union. The characteristic artifact is a pointed-pyriform (pear-shaped) or lanceolate (tapering) biface with a well-made tip.

microband: A modern anthropological term describing a very small band of a few people, perhaps a single family, who carries out collecting and hunting activities together seasonally and who may belong to a macroband which it rejoins at other seasons of the year for greater efficiency when there is a lot of seasonal food.

microblade: A small, narrow stone blade, ranging from less than 5–11 millimeters wide and about 15–45 millimeters long. They were often made from a conical or wedge-shaped microcore, often punch struck or pressure flaked. Microblades were often retouched into various forms of microliths. Microblades are found in the Upper Palaeolithic industries of Eurasia and in the Upper Palaeolithic of Siberia, but are also characteristic of the Mesolithic and later industries of the circumpolar regions. Examples are the Eastern Gravettian, Dyuktai culture, and the Arctic Small Tool tradition.

microburin: A microlith produced by notching and snapping a blade; a small piece of stone snapped off a microlith that is a byproduct of the manufacture of microliths. A blade is notched and then snapped off where the chipping has narrowed and weakened it. One piece becomes a microlithic tool, while the residue (the microburin) still shows traces of the original notch and fracture. Certain trapeze-shaped microliths were made from the central part of a double-notched blade, in which case both ends have the appearance of microburins. This procedure allowed the maker to obtain a strong head with a sharp point by breaking up flint blades after making a notch in them—a practice widespread in Mesolithic as a means of manufacturing arrowheads. The name originates from the errroneous belief that these pieces were the same as burins. (*syn.* microburin technique)

microclimate: The specific and uniform local climate of a small site or habitat brought about by hills, slopes, woodland, lakes, or other features of the landscape. These features modify the general climate of the region. The term is also applied to any climatic condition in a relatively small area, within a few meters or less above and below the Earth's surface and within canopies of vegetation. The microclimates of a region are strongly tied to the average moisture, temperature, and winds of the climate and to latitude, elevation, and season. Weather and climate are sometimes, in turn, influenced by microclimatic conditions, especially by variations in surface characteristics. Wet ground, for example, promotes evaporation and increases humidity. The drying of bare soil, on the other hand, creates a surface crust that inhibits ground moisture from diffusing upward, which promotes the persistence of dry atmosphere. Microclimates control evaporation from surfaces and influence precipitation and so are important to the hydrologic cycle (the circulation of the Earth's waters). The effect of soil types on microclimates is considerable. Also strongly influencing the microclimate is the ability of the soil to absorb and retain moisture, which depends on the composition of the soil and its use.

microenvironment: A small or relatively small, uusally distinctly specialized and effectively isolated habitat—as a forest canopy. It is a characteristic biotic assemblage, often exploited as a distinctive ecological niche. These minimal subdivisions of the environment allow alternative opportunities for exploitation.

microfauna: Small animals, such as rodents and insectivores, as compared with macrofauna. Besides referring to the small or strictly localized fauna, as of a microenvironment, the term is applied to minute animals, especially those invisible to the naked eye. (*syn.* adj. microfaunal)

microflake: A tiny scar on the surface of a stone tool, which may indicate use of a specific type, such as for cutting or scraping. Microflaking is minute edge flaking that occurs when stone tools are used.

microfloral remains: Those plant remains from archaeological sites that are visible only with the aid of magnification, primarily pollen and phytoliths. The term is also applied to any small or strictly localized flora, as of a microenvironment.

microlith: Any of various very small stone tools varying in size from 1–5 centimeters—mainly thin blade or blade fragments with sharp cutting edges, usually geometric in shape and set into a wooden handle or shaft or the tip of a bone or antler as an arrow point. They were shaped by abrupt retouch into various shapes like triangles and crescents. Microliths were produced during the Later Upper Palaeolithic and Mesolithic and were either struck as blades from very small cores or were made from fractured blades using the microburin technique. They are characteristic, for example, of Azilian culture of the Mesolithic. Microliths represent both a versatile and an economic use of raw material: just as blades yield more cutting edge than flakes per unit weight of raw material, so bladelets improve yet further this advantage, by a factor of something over 100 compared with core tools. (*syn.* pigmy stone)

Micronesia: An ethnographic and geographic region including the Palau, Marianas, Guam, Nauru, Caroline, and Marshall Islands and Kiribati. The Palaus and Marianas were probably settled from the Philippines after 2000 BC, and each has a ceramic sequence throughout prehistory. The eastern groups, mainly atolls, were settled later, perhaps from a Lapita source in Melanesia, and pottery production died out after initial settlement (as in Polynesia). Physically and linguistically, the Micronesians are close cousins to the Polynesians although their Polynesian ancestors appear to have moved through Melanesia rather than Micronesia.

micropolish: Any edge or surface abrasion and gloss that increases from tool use. It is sometimes evident only when stone tools are studied under high-powered microscopy.

microscarring: Minute patterns of edge damage on a stone tool, often suggesting how that tool was used.

microtoponymy: The extension of toponymy—place-name research—to uninhabited places such as fields, small parts of forests. Hodonymy is the study of the names of streets, roads, and so on. Hydronymy is the study of the names of bodies of water, and oronymy concerns names of mountains.

microwear: The patterns of edge damage on a stone tool, providing archaeological evidence of the ways in which that tool was used. Microscopic scratches and polish on the surface of stone tools or hominid teeth might reveal how various tools were used or what types of food certain hominids ate. (*syn.* microscarring)

microwear analysis: The study of the patterns of wear or damage on the edge of stone tools, which provides valuable information on the way in which the tool was used.

midden: Any large refuse heap, mound, or concentration of cultural debris associated with human occupation. The term includes such materials as discarded artifacts (e.g., broken pots and tools), food remains, shells, bones, charcoal, and ashes—and may include the material in which the debris is encapsulated and modification of this matrix. Midden debris usually contains decayed organic material, bone scrap, artifacts (broken and whole), and miscellaneous detritus. Middens are a valuable source of archaeological data. The long-term disposal of refuse can result in stratified deposits, which are useful for relative dating. Sometimes the midden is a dump or trash pile separate from the residential area, but more commonly among hunters and gatherers the houses are on top of the midden itself. Some of the largest shell middens were accumulated by shore dwellers in Mesolithic Denmark. (*syn.* kitchen midden)

Middle Assyrian: A period in the history of the Assyrian

Empire extending from the 14th–12th centuries BC. In the Late Bronze Age, Assyria was dominated by the Mitanni state, but in the 14th century BC, Assyria became dominant. Ashur-uballit I created the first Assyrian Empire and initiated the Middle Assyrian period. With the help of the Hittites, he destroyed the dominion of the Aryan Mitanni (a non-Semitic people from upper Iran and Syria) and ravaged Nineveh. Later, allied with the Kassite successors in Babylonia, Ashur-uballit ended Hittite and Hurrian rule. By intermarriage he then influenced the Kassite dynasty and eventually dominated all of Babylonia, thus paving the way for the Neo-Assyrian mastery during the Sargonid dynasty (12th to 7th centuries). The succeeding Assyrian kings expanded the empire through northern Mesopotamia and the mountains to the north and briefly occupied Babylonia. Several kings weakened Assyria, but then others brought back its dominion. Middle Assyrian is also the name of a form of cuneiform that was used extensively in writing law code and other documents. Middle Assyrian laws were found on clay tablets at Ashur (at the time of Tiglath-pileser I, 1114–1076 BC).

Middle Awash: River valley of northeast Ethiopia with rich hominid fossil finds as well as archaeological sites dating from the Miocene to the Holocene. Australopithecine fossils from c. 4.5–2.5 million years ago (mainly *A. afarensis*) and some of the oldest-known stone artifacts in the world (flaked cobble Oldowan Complex, c. 3–2.5 million years ago) were found there.

Middle Bronze Age: In the Levant, the period of sophisticated urban civilization of the Canaanites, MBA I, c. 1950–1800 BC and MBA II, c. 1800–1550 BC. The Middle Bronze Age provides the background for the beginning of the story of the Old Testament. The archaeological evidence for the period shows new types of pottery, weapons, and burial practices. It was an urban civilization based on agriculture. There was much contact with the Phoenicians and the Egyptians during this time. The destruction of Megiddo, Jericho, and Tell Beit Mirsim, which followed the Egyptians' expulsion of the Hyksos into Palestine, occurred at the end of the Middle Bronze Age. (*syn.* MBA)

Middleburg: A town on the island of Walcharan in the southwestern Netherlands, probably founded as a refuge for the Flemish population in the times of Viking raids. Many of this type of refuge were probably planned by Baldwin of Flanders in the 890s. Middleburg consisted of a simple circular fortress with a massive rampart and ditch. The symmetry of these early fortresses is fossilized in the street plan of modern Middleburg. Excavations show the town was founded about 1000, from which time it developed as a regional center.

Middle Egypt: Geographical term loosely applied to the area south of Luxor, especially to sites around Beni Hasan and Tell el-Amarna, generally from Lisht to Panopolis. In Ptolemaic times, a heptanomis of seven nomes was formed in Middle Egypt.

Middle Horizon: A division of time in Andean/Peruvian South America c. AD 600–1000, used to refer to the first imperialistic domination of area under the unifying forces of Tiahuanaco and Huari (Wari) cultures. It was the time of the first large-scale imperial expansions. During the first half of the Middle Horizon, in central Peru, the Huari came to control the highlands and possibly the coast. The remains of large groups of food-storage buildings in the Huari strongholds suggest military activity like that of the late Inca. Huari is closely linked in its art style to the monuments of the great site of Tiahuanaco, located on Lake Titicaca, Bolivia. Tiahuanaco expanded over the altiplano and adjacent regions of Bolivia, southern Peru, and northern Chile. The principal buildings of Tiahuanaco include the Akapana Pyramid, a huge platform mound or stepped pyramid of earth faced with cut andesite; a rectangular enclosure known as the Kalasasaya, constructed of alternating tall stone columns and smaller rectangular blocks; and another enclosure known as the Palacio. They practiced the raised-field system of agriculture. Some Tiahuanaco effigy vessels have been discovered at Huari, but otherwise they seem to have been independent entities. In the second half of the Middle Horizon, the political and economic systems slowly collapsed. The decline of these two states was followed by a period of more localized political power. The Late Intermediate period began about AD 1000.

Middle Kingdom: A period in Egyptian history including the 11th through 13th Dynasties, c. 2008–1630 BC. This phase began with the reunification of Upper and Lower Egypt by the 11th Dynasty king Mentuhotep II (Nebhapetre), ushering in years of stability and prosperity. It is usually divided into two phases, the early Middle Kingdom (late 11th and early 12th Dynasties) and the late Middle Kingdom (from the reign of Senusret III to end of 13th Dynasty).

Middle Mississippi culture: A part of the Woodland culture in the central Mississippi valley and its tributaries, which came into existence around AD 700 and lasted until the historical 16th–17th centuries. The most notable features are elaborate pottery, large and often fortified villages, and ceremonial centers with temple platforms and courtyards. From its origin, these cultures spread outward until they had overrun most of the eastern United States. In the north, the Mississippi culture encroached on and blended with the Woodland cultural tradition. Important sites are Etowah (Georgia), Moundville (Alabama), Spiro (Oklahoma), and Cahokia (Illinois).

Middle Missouri Tradition: One of three broad cultural traditions (along with Central Plains and Coalescent), which constitute the Plains Village Indian or Plains Village Pattern of c. AD 1000–1500. There were many permanent farming village sites along the central Missouri River trench in North and South Dakota. The culture is characterized by a specially developed strain of cold-resistant, quick-maturing maize, by the bison scapula hoe, and by permanent dwellings in the form of the semisubterranean timber-and-earth lodge. Often palisaded and constructed on high promontories overlooking a river, villages of over 100 dwellings are quite common. Ceramics, although Woodland derived, bear evidence of some Mississippian influence, such as shell tempering. The tradition disappeared, owing to drought and/or alien incursions, by 1500. Historic tribes such as the Mandan, Arikara, and Hidatsa are thought to be the cultural heirs to the tradition. (*syn.* Plains Village Indian)

Middle Palaeolithic: The intermediate part of the Palaeolithic period, from about 100,000 years ago to about 35,000 years ago. It was characterized by the development of a variety of stone tools and the first symbolic use of artifacts and sites. It ended with the extinction of the Neanderthals. The Middle Palaeolithic is equivalent to the Middle Stone Age in sub-Saharan Africa. The Middle Palaeolithic makes up the Mousterian, a portion of the Levalloisian, and the Tayacian, all of which are complexes based on the production of flakes, although the hand ax tradition survived in many instances. Middle Palaeolithic assemblages first appear in deposits of the third interglacial and persist during the first major oscillation of the Fourth Glacial (Würm) stage. Associated with the Tayacian, in which the artifacts consist of very crude flakes, remains of modern man (*Homo sapiens*) have been found. Mousterian man, on the other hand, is of the Neanderthal race. It is in the Mousterian levels of the caves and rock shelters of central and southern France that the earliest evidence of the use of fire and the first definite burials have been discovered in western Europe. The artifacts consist of (1) the prepared striking-platform-tortoise-core (Levalloisian) tradition; (2) the plain striking-platform-discoidal-core technique of Clactonian tradition; and (3) a persistence of the bifacial core tool, or Acheulean tradition. (*syn.* Palaeolithic)

middle-range research: A set of frameworks or theories that allow the construction of accurate statements of past behavior based on the analysis of the contemporary archaeological record. It applies to any investigation aimed at linking the static data from the archaeological record with the dynamic processes that formed it. The frameworks link the archaeological record and the original activites that produced that record, allowing archaeologists to make inferences about past human behavior. It is considered by some to be the key to a scientific understanding of the archaeological record. (*syn.* Middle Range Theory, middle-range theory)

Middle Stone Age: The second part of the Stone Age in sub-Saharan Africa, dating from c. 150,000–30,000 years ago and roughly equivalent to the Middle Palaeolithic elsewhere in the Old World. Assemblages are characterized by flakes made by preparing the core; there were many shapes and sizes of these artifacts. The characteristic tools are made on flakes produced by a developed Levalloisian technqiue, including slender unifacial and bifacial lances or spear points for stabbing or throwing. In the final stages of the Middle Stone Age, known as the South African Magosian, microlithic elements appear. Middle Stone Age assemblages are associated with anatomically modern *Homo sapiens* in southern Africa. People continued to live in open camps, while rock overhangs were also used for shelter. Middle Stone Age bands hunted medium-size and large prey. Sometimes they collected tortoises and ostrich eggs in large quantities, as well as seabirds and marine mammals that could be found along the shore. The rich archaeological deposits of Klasies River Mouth Cave preserve the earliest evidence in the world for the use of shellfish as a food source.

Middle Woodland period: A term sometimes used to describe the time during which the Hopewell culture flourished throughout the American Midwest, from roughly 50 BC to AD 400.

Midland: Palaeo-Indian complex of the North American plains simillar to the Folsom but the point is different. The type site is the Scharbauer site near Midland, Texas, although the culture is best represented at Hell Gap. A skeleton (Midland Man) of a young woman dating to 10,000 BP from Scharbauer was one of the earliest acceptable human remains in North America. The Midland point is an unfluted Folsom point.

midrib: The raised midline or thickening of the centerline of a bronze weapon, such as a dagger, to add strength and reinforce the blade.

Midwestern Taxonomic System: A hierarchical framework devised by William McKern in 1939 to systematize historical sequences in the Great Plains area of the United States, using the general principle of similarities between artifact assemblages. It was used to organize artifacts and sites in North America before World War II and is still in widespread use in modified form. One occupational unit of a particular culture was called a component. Related components were grouped into a focus, representing a culture unit approximating a tribe. Related foci constituted a pattern, and related patterns constituted a base, the highest level in the system. Classification was based strictly on similarities between compared units without regard to their respective ages. Many of the names of cultures are still called foci, and the standard definition of a component is a single unit of occupation. Most units formerly called foci are now called phases, which have temporal as well as descriptive meaning. (*syn.* midwestern taxonomic system; McKern taxonomic system)

Migdal temples: Tower-fortress temples typical of the Middle Bronze Age in the Levant.

migration: Movement of human populations from one area to another, usually resulting in cultural contact.

Migration Period: The period of large-scale movement of peoples in western Europe during the 4th, 5th, and 6th centuries AD—including the Anglo-Saxon settlement of England. These movements are associated with the collapse of the Roman empire. Barbarians from beyond the Roman frontiers settled in many of the former provinces. The Migration period is often extended to cover the period from the 3rd century AD to the accession of Charlemagne in AD 800.

Mikhajlovka: A settlement of the Late Neolithic and Bronze Age, located in the lower Dnepr Valley near Nikopol, Ukraine. Three main occupation horizons have been distinguished, the first a Cucuteni-Tripolye culture, the second the Sredni Stog culture, and the last the Catacomb Grave culture. Near the settlement was a flat cemetery of pit graves (Yamnaya burial rite). (*syn.* Mikhailovka, Mykhailvka)

Mikulcice: A site situated on the Morava River in the Czech Republic, a settlement of Great Moravia and the earliest Slavic state polity. It is a complex site with stratified deposits going back to the late 6th century, when it was one of the earliest Slavic fortified centers. The stronghold consisted of a central nucleus in a plank-built palisade, with an additional suburb of workshops and houses. Mikulcice was an important metal production center, famous for elaborate bronze and gilded spurs. In Midulcice's second phase during the early 9th century, the defenses were refurbished in stone and timber, and a stone church was built. In the latter part of the 9th century, a stone-built palace and a number of other churches were built. These churches display an enormous variety of designs and include several rotunda buildings. Greater Moravia fell in AD 907.

Milan: A city founded by the Gauls about the year 600 BC as Mediolanum, which became the capital of a Celtic tribe known as the Insubres. At the time of the Roman conquest, 222 BC, Mediolanum, was already one of the most powerful cities of the region on the Roman side of the Alps known as Cisalpine Gaul. Under the emperor Augustus, it became a part of the 11th region of Italy, acquiring increasing prestige and economic power until it became the second city of the Western Roman Empire after Rome itself. In the 3rd century AD, following the division of the empire by Diocletian, it was the residence and main administrative center for one of the two emperors. Constantine the Great declared it the seat of the Vicar of Italy. In the year 452, Attila the Hun devastated the city, and in 539 the Goths destroyed it. The city sprang back to life by the second half of the 10th century. It was the principal road center of northern Italy and is the site of the imperial palace, Augustan and later walls, theater, amphi-

theater, circus, Constantinian baths, and early churches. (*syn.* Mediolanum)

Milavce: The type site of a southeastern Bohemian culture stemming from the Tumulus Bronze Age but showing elements of the new urnfield rite. This Middle Bronze Age site was related to Knoviz, and most of the cremations were urnless except for one richly furnished grave with ashes in a wheeled cauldron of cast bronze. (*syn.* Milavec)

Milazzo: A town founded in 716 BC by colonists from Zankle (Messina). It was taken by the Athenians in 426 BC and by the Syracusan tyrant Agathocles in 315 BC. The consul Gaius Duilius won the first Roman naval victory over the Carthaginians in the bay in 260 BC. It is located on the northeast coast of Sicily, facing the Aeolian Islands, and demonstrates close cultural connections with the prehistoric sequence on these islands. It was occupied throughout the Bronze Age; the Middle Bronze Age culture had a cemetery of pithos burials (with the dead placed in large jars in the crouched position) while the succeeding Late Bronze Age phase (Ausonian culture) had a cemetery of urnfield type, characterized by cremations in urns and bronzes of local Urnfield (Proto-Villanovan) type. The old town on a hill above is partly surrounded by Spanish walls from the 16th century and contains a 13th-century Norman castle.

Mildenhall: A town in Suffolk, England, famous for the treasure of silver making up the household silver of a wealthy Roman family near the remains of a 4th-century Roman building. The silver was richly decorated with figured reliefs, and the 34 pieces include a large dish depicting the head of Oceanus, ringed by friezes of sea and other deities reveling; two smaller platters with Bacchic scenes; a niello dish with geometric design; a covered bowl with centaurs; goblets; ladles and eight spoons, five with Christian inscriptions. Possibly the owners buried their family plate in the troubled days of the Anglo-Saxon invasions. The collection is now in the British Museum in London. (*syn.* Mildenhall Treasure)

milecastle: A fortlet (small fort) set at intervals of 1 Roman mile along a major well-defended frontier—such as Hadrian's Wall. They measured 60–70 by 50–60 ft. A roadway passed through the center of the milecastle and through the wall itself, with gateways at both entrances. There were two barrack buildings parallel with the road. In one corner, next to the wall, was a stairway up to the wall top; in the other was the cookhouse. It is estimated that 30–100 men could be accommodated in each milecastle. (*syn.* mile fort, mile castle)

milestone: Roman road markers—cylindrical blocks of stone usually about 6 feet (1.8 m) high—recording the distance from a central point in the province or a local center. These were placed along all principal roads, and instances are found from about 250 BC onward. The stone was typically inscribed to give the distance in (Roman) miles to the nearest major town and commonly a date of installation, expressed in terms of Republican magistracies, or the years of an Emperor's reign. They often bore the title of the emperor or consul under whose direction the road was laid out or repaired.

Miletus: Greek settlement at the mouth of the Meander valley in Turkey (western Anatolia), inhabited from the 2nd millennium BC. By the beginning of the 1st millennium BC, it was an Ionian Greek city, colonizing Black Sea and Egyptian Delta areas in the 7th and 6th centuries BC. Miletus played an important role in the founding of the Greek colony of Naukratis in Egypt and founded more than 60 colonies on the shores of the Black Sea, including Abydos, Cyzicus, Sinope, Olbia, and Panticapaeum. Before 500 BC, Miletus was the greatest Greek city in the east. Miletus produced the classical historian Hecateus and the town planner Hippodamus. It was destroyed by the Persians in 494 BC, and the new layout reflected Hippodamian planning. The city came under Athenian, Persian, Greek and (in 129 BC) Roman control. Impressive ruins survive nearby of the rebuilt Hellenistic Greek oracular temple of Apollo and a Roman theater. The harbor mouth was guarded by statues of lions. Subsequently, the harbor silted up and Miletus declined, but occupation continued into the early Byzantine period. In AD 263, it survived an attack by the Goths and was refurbished by the emperor Diocletian. New Byzantine churches and monumental buildings were eventually erected within its boundaries. In the 10th century, the citadel was destroyed by an earthquake but was again rebuilt over the ancient ruins. The ruins occupy the former peninsula extending northward from the hill of Kalabak Tepe. Only one temple, from the 6th century BC, survives in part on Kalabak Tepe. To the south there are extensive remains of the classical city from the 5th century BC to Roman imperial times. The Hellenistic council house has some of the earliest known examples of true pilasters.

Millares, Los: A walled township, with projecting bastions and four outlying forts, near the coast in Almeria, southeast Spain. The cemetery includes 100 megalithic tombs. The pottery, of the Millaran culture, consisted of plain ware, including troncoconic vessels and carinated forms, and also much decorated ware. Symbolism appears on the decorated ware and on other pottery, stone, and bone. Arrowheads were bifacially worked, leaf shaped, rhomboid, and barbed and tanged, and copper was in common use. The settlement was townlike, with rows of stone houses, alleys, and a central communal place within the walls. An artificial watercourse may have led to the settlement. There was specialization of production between households. This culture was succeeded by that represented by Beakers.

millefiore: A type of multicolored glass and the technique that creates it—literally meaning "a thousand flowers." One millefiore method is to take a cane of glass, encase it with several layers of glass of different colors, and then heat the whole, and roll it on a corrugated surface, thus compressing the colors at certain points and producing a rod with a flowerlike section. Small slices can be cut off this rod and inlaid into the object to be decorated. Another method is to lay thin glass rods of different colors into a pattern, fuse them together, draw them out, and cut them in slices in the same way. The effect is mosaic. The technique was developed by Anglo-Saxon glass- and metalworkers. Some of the finest examples of the millefiore technique can be seen adorning the Sutton Hoo discoveries—the brilliant reds and blues on the purse lid and shoulder clasps. (*syn.* millefiori)

millet: Any of various grasses used as forage or cereals, probably first cultivated in Asia or Africa about 4,000 years ago. Four cereals are grouped under this name. *Panicum miliaceum* was the most important, first recorded at Jemdet Nasr in Mesopotamia. It was widely grown in Neolithic Europe and was the staple crop in early China. *Setaria italica* was possibly developed in southern Europe, and even there was never as common as panicum. It was also known in China in the Neolithic. Grains of the Setaria genus were an important item of diet in parts of Mexico as early as c. 6500 BC. Eleusine and Pennisetum are of more recent origin, largely confined to tropical Africa, and introduced thence to India. Millets are an important food staple in much of Asia, Russia, and western Africa. In the United States and western Europe, they are used chiefly for pasture or to produce hay, although they were major grains in Europe during the Middle Ages. The millets are high in carbohydrates, with protein content varying from 6 to 11% and fat varying from 1.5 to 5%. They are somewhat strong in taste and cannot be made into leavened bread. They are mainly consumed in flatbreads and porridges or prepared and eaten much like rice.

milling stone: Any stone slab or basin that is used to process seeds, nuts, and other such foods by rubbing, grinding, or pounding them against this object with another stone. (*syn.* grinding stone; metate)

milpa: An agricultural technique whereby forest vegetation is cut down annually and burned in place to prepare fields for crops—slash-and-burn agriculture. Its derivation is from a term referring to the cultivation of maize fields, usually for only a few years, by swidden agriculture. Depictions on Maya frescos and codices, coupled with ethnographic evidence of modern-day methods of cultivation in the Maya Lowlands, gave rise to the theory that milpa agriculture was the basis of Maya subsistence. Exhaustion of the land by its indiscriminate practice was long held to be a factor in the Maya collapse. (*syn.* milpa agriculture)

Mimbres: Regional variant of the Mogollon culture, centered in south-central New Mexico, and dated to AD 1000–1200. The Mimbres people are particularly renowned for the black-on-white painted pottery bowls, which they made especially to be put in burials. The pottery is decorated with abstract designs and with pictures of people, bears, rabbits, and other animals. Farmers grew maize and gathered beans and acorns and hunted deer, antelope, and rabbits. The culture also evidences a strong Anasazi influence.

Mimi style: A style of art associated with the Pirri culture of Arnhem Land in which plain red stylized human figures showing vigorous movement are depicted. The thin, sticklike human figures are a feature of the Arnhem Land rock art of northern Australia. The paintings are thought to be about 3,000 years old, earlier than x-ray art. (*syn.* Mimi figures)

Min: An Egyptian fertility god and symbol of the harvest, who was also worshiped as the Lord of the Eastern Desert. His cult originated in Predynastic times (4th millennium BC). His cult was strongest in Coptos and Akhmim (Panopolis), where festivals were held celebrating his "coming forth" with a public procession and presentation of offerings.

Mina: A pottery style found in coastal shell mounds in Brazil near the mouth of the Amazon, with a radiocarbon date around 3880 BC. It is among the oldest pottery in the New World.

Minaean: One of the kingdoms of southern Arabia in the 1st millennium BC, contemporary with the Sabeans, Qatabaneans, and Hadramis. The Minaean kingdom lasted from the 4th to the 2nd century BC and was predominantly a trading organization that, for the period, monopolized the trade routes. The people seem to be loosely associated with the 'Amir people to the north of the Minaean capital of Qarnaw (now Ma'in), which is at the eastern end of the Wadi Al-Jawf and on the western border of the Sayhad sands. The Minaeans had a second town surrounded by impressive and still extant walls at Yathill, and they had trading establishments at Dedan and in the Qatabanian and Hadramite capitals. The overwhelming majority of Minaean inscriptions come from Qarnaw, Yathill, and Dedan. (*syn.* Minaeans, Ma'in)

Mina Perdida: Ceremonial platform mound site in the Lurin Valley of Peru, dated to the early Initial Period.

Minatogawa: Late Palaeolithic site in Okinawa Prefecture, Japan, with skeletal remains dating to c. 16,000 to 18,000 bp.

Mindel glaciation: The second major Pleistocene glaciation of Alpine Europe, which ended with the onset of the Holsteinian Interglacial. It was the second major Ice Age in the Pleistocene period, shown in Quaternary deposits in the Alps and the valleys of south German rivers. The Mindel consists of moraine and related river terraces of proglacial deposits. The Mindel Glacial Stage is part of the early geo-logic scheme (c. 1900) that first recognized the importance of multiple episodes of Pleistocene glaciation. The stage, a period of relatively severe climatic conditions and glacial advance, preceded the Mindel-Riss Interglacial and followed the Günz-Mindel Interglacial, both periods of relatively moderate climatic conditions. The Mindel Glacial Stage lasted from about 750,000 to 675,000 years ago. At least two periods of glacial advance, separated by a moderate period, are recognized in the Mindel. (*syn.* Mindel Glacial; Mindel Glacial Stage)

Mindelheim: A Hallstatt C cemetery west of Munich in West Germany, dated to the 7th century BC. The grave goods include distinctive melon-shaped urns and wide open bowls, heavily decorated with incised geometric designs, as well as the long sword type to which the site has given its name. Mindelheim swords are made of bronze or iron and are around 90 centimeters long, with a leaf-shaped blade and a pommel on the hilt.

Mindel-Riss: The interglacial stage that followed the Mindel Glacial Stage, a separation between the Mindel and Riss Glacials in Alpine Europe. (*syn.* Mindel/Riss)

mineral: A solid homogeneous crystalline chemical element or compound that results from the inorganic processes of nature. The term includes any of various ground substances such as stone, coal, salt, sulfur, sand, petroleum, water, or natural gas. Each of these naturally occurring substances has a characteristic chemical composition expressed by a chemical formula.

Ming Dynasty: Major late dynasty of China AD 1368–1644, succeeding the Mongol Yüan Dynasty (1280–1368). The period is known for painting and decorative arts, porcelain, lacquer, cloisonné, and textiles. The burial sites of the Ming emperors are near modern Beijing. The Ming extended the Chinese Empire into Korea, Mongolia, and Turkistan on the north and into Vietnam and Myanmar (Burma) on the south, exercising more far-reaching influence in East Asia than any other native rulers of China.

mingqi: A Chinese term used to describe small objects, sometimes imitating objects of daily life or buildings. They were placed in tombs as offering and were of fairly early origin, some from the Shang period.

minimum number of individuals: The minimum number of individuals represented in a given faunal or human bone collection; determined from the number in the largest category of skeletal elements recovered. It is a method of assessing species abundance in faunal assemblages based on a calculation of the smallest number of animals necessary to account for all the identified bones. It is usually calculated from the most abundant bone or tooth from either the left or right side of the animal. (*syn.* MNI)

mining: The creation of a pit or excavation in the earth from which mineral substances are taken. The colonization of the northern European plain and the introduction of the plow in the third millennium BC first necessitated the mining of flint to produce supplies of stone to make axes for clearing the forest. The first systematic mining in Classical times was carried out in the silver mines of Athens.

Minoan: The Bronze Age civilization of Crete, a name coined by Sir Arthur Evans, derived from the legendary ruler of Knossos, Minos. The civilization is divided into three phases: Early (c. 3000–2000 BC), Middle (c. 2000–1550 BC), and Late (c. 1550–1050 BC). Each had three subdivisions marked with Roman numerals. They stand out as the first civilized Europeans, with a highly sophisticated way of life and material equipment, and were surprisingly modern. They probably represented a fusion between Anatolian immigrants and the native Neolithic population, with some trading contacts through the east Mediterranean. In the Middle Minoan period, urbanization became apparent, towns appeared and, a Minoan specialty, the first of the great palaces at Knossos, Mallia, and Phaestos. Overseas trade was greatly expanded, too. The height of its development was in the 18th–15th centuries BC. By about 1580 BC, Minoan civilization began to spread across the Aegean to the neighboring islands and to the mainland of Greece. Minoan cultural influence was reflected in the Mycenean culture of the mainland, which began to spread throughout the Aegean about 1500 BC. The palaces were destroyed c. 1450, probably by the cataclysmic eruption of Santorini/Thera—or by conquerors from the mainland. After that, Greek-speaking Mycenaeans gained control of Knossos and Crete; only Knossos was reoccupied on a significant scale. The final fall of Knossos, c. 1400 BC, marked the end of Crete's period of greatness. Their Linear A script has not been deciphered, but Linear B has been successfully translated as an early form of Greek, written in a syllabary. Linear B belongs only to the period of mainland domination and is therefore more relevant to Mycenaeans than Minoans. Minoan pottery is among the most artistic of any place or time, using abstract cuvilinear, floral, and marine designs. Craftsmen reached high levels of technical skill and aesthetic achievement in pottery, metalwork, stonework, jewelry, and wall painting (the palaces are lavishly decorated with frescoes). Vessels, figurines, and magnificent seal stones were also carved in stone and bronze, and gold objects made. There were many bull sporting events. Cult activities normally took place either in hilltop shrines, often in caves, or in small shrines in the palaces and often involved animals, including goats and especially bulls. There is an alternative division of the Minoan civilization into Prepalatial (Early Minoan I–III), Protopalatial (Middle Minoan I–II), Neopalatial (Middle Minoan III–Late Minoan IIIA1), and Postpalatial (Late Minoan IIIA2–IIIC).

Minshat Abu Omar: A Predynastic and Early Dynastic/Archaic cemetery site located in the northeastern Delta, Egypt, which, like the roughly contemporary settlement of Maadi, shows evidence of trade with southern Palestine. Grave goods (ceramic and stone vessels, slate palettes, jewelry, copper tools) included imports from Palestine and Upper Egypt.

Minusinsk Basin: A steppe region on the upper Yenisei River in southern Siberia, surrounded by forested mountains. Very large numbers of burial mounds of different periods exist in the area, and some 40,000 bronze objects survive in collections—presumably only a fraction of the number originally present. There were many mines in the basin, worked as early as the 14th century BC.

Minyan Ware: A distinctive Middle Helladic pottery—a gray or yellow wheelmade ware of high quality first appearing at Troy VI and in Greece c. 19th century BC. It was the first wheelmade pottery to be produced in Middle Bronze Age Greece. It was ancestral to Mycenaean pottery and may represent a movement of new peoples into the Aegean area, the first Greek speakers. Traditionally, it has been associated with an apparently violent end to the Early Helladic culture, c. 2000–1900 BC and the arrival of Greek-speaking peoples in the Aegean. The term was coined by Heinrich Schliemann. The ware had a soaplike feeling, and its forms were modeled after metal objects.

Miocene: A geological epoch of the Tertiary period in the Earth's history, in which many of the great mountain chains were formed and mammals came to dominate animal life. During this epoch, many mammals of modern form, such as dogs, horses, and humanlike apes, evolved. The Miocene occurred after the Oligocene and before the Pliocene and is dated between 25–5 (23.7–5.3) million years ago. It is often divided into the Early Miocene epoch (23.7 to 16.6 million years ago), the Middle Miocene epoch (16.6 to 11.2 million years ago), and the Late Miocene epoch (11.2 to 5.3 million years ago). The Miocene may also be divided into six ages and their corresponding rock stages: From oldest to youngest these ages or stages are the Aquitanian, Burdigalian, Langhian, Serravallian, Tortonian, and Messinian.

Miraflores: A complex of cultural materials that define a phase from 100 BC to AD 200 of highland Mayan sites in the Late Pre-Classic period. It is the Late Formative period of the valley of Guatemala. Characteristic artifacts include engraved soft stone and monochrome ceramic vessels, as well as "mushroom stones" (hollow stones set in an annular base and capped with mushroom-shaped covers, which may have been used in rites with hallucinogenic mushrooms). A strong Izapan influence is evident. The huge Miraflores mounds located at Kaminaljuyú contained log tombs of incredible richness. In one, the deceased was accompanied by sacrificed followers or captives. As many as 340 objects were placed with him, including jade mosaic masks, jade ear spools and necklaces, bowls of chlorite schist, and pottery vessels of great beauty.

Mirgissa: Fortified site of the Middle Kingdom (2055–1650 BC), located in Lower Nubia, at the northern end of the second cataract of the Nile. The site has been submerged beneath Lake Nasser since the completion of Aswan High Dam in 1971. It was the major commercial center known in ancient times as Iken. (*syn.* ancient Iken)

Miriwun: A rock shelter in the Ord River valley, Kimberley, western Australia, now inundated by the Argyle Dam and submerge by Lake Argyle. Occupation deposits date from 16,000 BC. Artifacts from the early phase include adze flakes, small denticulated flakes, thick notched flakes, pebble tools, irregular blade cores, and amorphous cores. Late phase tools, c. 1000 BC, included unifacial and bifacial points, many denticulated, with the earlier tool types continued alongside.

mirror: A polished metal artifact with functional and symbolic uses. It was made in the Iron Age, and the backs were decorated in beautiful La Tène designs. It was also made in Egypt from at least the Old Kingdom (2686–2181 BC). In China, mirrors were thought to have magical powers to influence the spirits and were therefore frequently buried in tombs from the late Chou Dynasty (1072–221 BC) until the T'ang Dynasty (AD 618–906). Made of bronze, they were cast with elaborate decoration on the reverse of a highly polished convex surface. In Japan, many round imported mirrors and their domestic copies are found in Yayoi and Kofun graves. In Greek and Roman world, mirrors were of polished tin and bronze, decorated, and with handles of bone or ivory. Celtic Britain had fine bronze mirrors of c. 100 BC–AD 100.

misericorde: A narrow-bladed dagger of the 14th century, which was pushed through the eye slits or between the armor plates of a knight immobilized on the ground by the weight of armor, and so gave the coupe de grace.

Mi-so'n: A site in the northern part of Champa, in the present province of Quang-nam, central Vietnam, which has given its name to the earliest style in Cham art, dating from the 7th century. It is also important for inscriptions of the 5th century, attesting to the oldest known royal linga in Southeast Asia. Goldwork and silverwork of the Cham culture are preserved from the 10th century. It is exemplified by a crown and heavy jewelry made for a lifesize statue found in the ruin of a temple at Mison. (*syn.* Mison)

Mississippian: A group of cultures that arose in southeastern North America—especially the central and lower Mississippi Valley—after AD 700 into the historic period. It spread over a great area of the Southeast and the midconti-

nent, in the river valleys of what are now the states of Mississippi, Alabama, Georgia, Arkansas, Missouri, Kentucky, Illinois, Indiana, and Ohio, with scattered extensions northward into Wisconsin and Minnesota and westward into the Great Plains. It stands in contrast to the Woodland tradition with three new traits—building of rectangular, flat-topped mounds as bases for temples; burial mounds becoming less prominent; and radical pottery changes (pulverized shell rather than grit used for temper). New pottery shapes and forms, such as olla, and new types of decoration (burnishing, painting) appeared. Maize became the predominant crop, accompanied by beans and squash, which supplemented hunting and gathering. The largest of the earthworks is Monks Mound, in the Cahokia Mounds near Collinsville, Illinois. The Mississippian is divided into the periods Temple Mound I (AD 700–1200) and Temple Mound II (AD 1200–1700). It was the last major cultural tradition in prehistoric North America. By the late 17th century, all the major centers had been abandoned. (*syn.* Mississippi tradition)

mit'a: A tax or duty exacted from the people of the Inca Empire by the state, payable in the form of labor.

Mitanni: A kingdom in northern Mesopotamia and Syria, which arose in the foothills between the Tigris and Euphrates c. 1500 BC, the most important of the 2nd millennium BC Hurrian kingdoms with Indo-European elements in its elite society and rulers. Its capital of Wassukkanni has not been identified. At its height, the empire extended from Kirkuk (ancient Arrapkha) and the Zagros Mountains in the east through Assyria to the Mediterranean Sea in the west. It flourished for a little over a century and treated on near-equal terms with Egypt and the Hittites, until overthrown by the Hittites c. 1370 BC and then the Assyrians. (It had formed a buffer zone between the kingdoms of the Hittites and the Assyrians.) Its people were mainly Hurri, but its ruling dynasty, from the form of their names and more especially from the gods they invoked in an extant treaty, were Indo-Europeans related to the roughly contemporary Aryans of India. Mitannian style was associated with works of northern Syria and Iraq from the 16th–14th centuries BC and even later, for the style survived after the fall of the Mitanni Empire.

Mitathal: Prehistoric site in Haryana, India, with a double mound consisting of two occupational periods. Mitathal I has pottery similar to the Early Harappan site of Kalibangan. Mitathal II has the same pottery with Mature Harappan changes, also seen in other artifacts and in the town layout.

Mithraeum: A small Roman temple used for worship in the eastern cult of Mithras (Persian mystery god), often in the form of a basilica. They were very popular with the Roman army, and many fort sites have Mithraea nearby. The usual layout is that of a central nave flanked by two side aisles. At the far end of the nave, a type of reredos often depicts Mithras in his act of slaying the bull, and the building itself apparently represents the cave of the original story. Symbolism shows the coming of new life from the blood spilt, and the conquering of evil (of which the scorpion is sometimes the agent). The side aisles are typically raised to form reclining couches for the taking of the sacred banquet. Some examples show more elaborate architecture, such as the addition of apse and colonnades, as at Walbrook in London. (*syn.* pl. Mithraea; Mithraic sanctuaries)

Mithras: A Persian demigod who achieved independence and importance during the Roman Empire, and best known as the savior deity of the Roman mystery cult of Mithraism. Especially in military circles, his worship challenged early Christianity. He is portrayed as a young man in a Phrygian cap, usually in the act of kneeling on the back of a bull to dispatch it by a sword thrust in the neck. A Mithraeum is a building, often semisubterranean, containing a passage between broad shelves on which the worshipers reclined during the ceremonies. The end wall may hold a fresco or relief of Mithras himself. From the 1st century BC onward, he begins to appear in the Roman world as the god of a mystery cult. His disciples, who were exclusively men and often limited to the ranks of soldiers and businessmen, were promised life and happiness after death. As in other mystery cults, the rites were kept secret, and truth and benefits came only to initiated believers, who had to pass through a sequence of seven grades of initiation. These were the stages of the Raven (Corax), Bride (Nymphus), Soldier (Miles), Lion (Leo), Persian (Perses), Runner of the Sun (Heliodromos), and Father (Pater). The disciple also underwent baptism, took part in re-enacting the sacred meal, and bore the seal of his discipleship on his body. Mithraism expanded rapidly from the second half of the 1st century AD.

mitigation: In archaeology, measures taken to minimize destruction on archaeological sites.

Mitla: A site in central Oaxaca, Mexico, which was first occupied in the centuries before 800 BC, after which it became an outpost of Monte Albán civilization. It is generally believed that Mitla (Nahuatl: Place of the Dead) was established as a sacred burial site long before the Christian Era, probably by the Zapotecs, whose influence was predominant until about AD 900. Between 900–1500, the Mixtecs moved down from northern Oaxaca and took possession of Mitla; it is the Mixtec influence that is most pronounced in the existing ruins. Its ceramics date from Monte Albán I (900–300 BC), but there is no structural evidence until Monte Albán III (AD 200–1521). After the parent site was abandoned in the 8th–10th centuries AD, a fortification wall was built at Mitla, and pyramids were constructed there. The town became an important religious center, and there are five clusters of columned, flat-roofed palace structures (Grupo de las Co-

lumnas [Columns Group], Grupo de los Adobes [Adobe Group], and Grupo del Sur [Southern Group]). Major construction in the Early Post-Classic coincides with the abandonment of Monte Alban, suggesting that it became a new locus for the Zapotec. At the time of the Spanish Conquest, Mitla was said to be the residence of the Zapotec high priest. Certain frescoes were painted in pure Mixtec style, although Mitla itself may have remained under Zapotec control.

mitmaq: A Quechua term for a group of itinerant people who frequently moved over long distances. The Inca used the establishment of colonies as a strategy for breaking up disloyal groups among rebellious ones; mitmaq were also used to colonize newly reclaimed land and to make it productive.

Mito: An early preceramic occupation, c. 2000–1800 BC, associated with the Crossed Hands and Nichitos temples at the site of Kotosh in the Higueras Valley of central Peru.

mitochondrial DNA: The genetic material inside the mitochondrian, an energy-producing unit of a cell, which has been studied to calculate the antiquity of modern humans. Some mtDNA studies suggest that modern humans arose first in Africa around 200,000 years ago. Investigations of human mitochondrial DNA reveal that the variation among modern human populations is small compared, for example, with that between apes and monkeys, which points to the recency of human origin. Research also points out that there is a distinction between African and other human mitochondrial DNA types, suggesting the substantial antiquity of the African peoples and the relative recency of other human populations. (*syn.* mtDNA)

Mixtec: A linguistic and cultural group of the Oaxaca state of southern Mexico, especially the Mixteca Alta region. The Mixtecs and Zapotecs struggled for power in Oaxaca, and Early Mixtec dynasties date to the 7th century AD. The people were mainly skilled craftsmen—known for their metalwork, painting, stone carving, and turquoise mosaic—living in this mountainous country. Several books/codices have survived, and they trace the history and politics of the Mixtec dynasties before the Spanish Conquest. During the Post-Classic period, they ventured into Zapotec territory and occupied much of the Valley of Oaxaca (Monte Albán, Mitla). The influence of Mixtec art is apparent as far north as Cholula, in the state of Puebla, where a regional Mixteca-Puebla style came into being and was in turn one of the formative influences on Aztec art. Many of the finest objects from Aztec territory were probably the work of Mixtec artisans. The polychrome pottery had a lacquerlike polish and brilliant colors. Parts of the Mixteca were conquered by the Aztecs in the early 16th century, but in the south some Mixtecs remained independent until the arrival of the Spaniards. Their capital was at Tilantongo.

Mladec point: A point made from bone, antler, or ivory with an elongated oval shape. It has been found at Aurignacian sites in central Europe.

Mlu Prei: Prehistoric sites in north-central Cambodia, including O Yak, O Pie Can, and O Nari, occupied in the transition between the Neolithic to bronze and then iron. There were polished stone adzes, flaked side scrapers, and bone projectile points during the Neolithic. Bronze items and clay crucibles followed and then the iron axes and other artifacts.

Mnevis: In ancient Egyptian religion, the sacred bull regarded as the ba ("power" or physical manifestation) of the sun god at Heliopolis. As one of several sacred bulls in Egypt, he was most closely associated with the sun god Re-Atum. There was only one Apis, Buchis, or Mnevis bull at any one time. Although not attested until later, the cult of Mnevis probably dated to the 1st Dynasty (c. 2925–2775 BC) or earlier. The Mnevis bull was either black or piebald in color, and in sculptures and paintings he was represented with a solar disk between his horns. (*syn.* Mer-wer, Menuis, Nemur, Merwer)

MNI: The minimum number of individuals represented in a given faunal or human bone collection; determined from the number in the largest category of skeletal elements recovered. It is a method of assessing species abundance in faunal assemblages based on a calculation of the smallest number of animals necessary to account for all the identified bones. It is usually calculated from the most abundant bone or tooth from either the left or right side of the animal. (*syn.* minimum number of individuals)

moai: Colossal stone figure found on Easter Island, carved between AD c. 600–1500. There are 800–1000 known figures, quarried from the volcanic tuff at Rano Raraku. They can be up to 10 meters tall and weigh 28 tons. Many were put in ahu on the coast, on top and facing inland. The moai were probably ancestor figures. Most of the moai were knocked over during internal strife on the island. The term moai also refers to small wooden statues of uncertain religious significance, also carved on Easter Island. The figures are of two types, moai kavakava (male) and moai paepae (female). They were sometimes used for fertility rites but were more often used for harvest celebrations. During the time between these public festivals, the statues were wrapped in bark cloth and kept in private homes.

Mo'alla, el-: A rock-cut cemetery of the First Intermediate Period (2181–2055 BC), located on the east bank of the Nile, about 24 kilometers south of Luxor.

moa: Any of several extinct, ostrichlike flightless birds native to New Zealand and constituting the order Dinornithiformes. Moas (a Polynesian term) ranged in size from a turkey to an ostrich. Moa hunting was once an economic mainstay of the Archaic Maoris, even though large concentrations occurred only in certain regions, especially east coastal South Island. Early Polynesian peoples hunted moas for food; they made spear points, hooks, and ornaments from their bones and water carriers from their eggs. Although the larger moas probably had become extinct by the end of the 17th century, a few smaller species may have survived into the 19th.

moated site: A class of sites in places like Thailand, Cambodia, England, Ireland, and Flanders. In the first two, they are known from protohistoric and early historic sites and are settlements encircled by one or more irregular moats. In England, Ireland, and Flanders, they were built during the late medieval period. There was a tradition of building defensive moats around castles and manorial establishments, and it was taken up by wealthy farmers later. In marshy areas, a moat provided an extra means of drainage when the climate was deteriorating and acted as a source of both dry-season water and edible aquatic flora and fauna.

mobile: Any settlement pattern in which social groups move from place to place in a given territory, building camps at each site.

mobiliary art: A general term used to describe the small and portable objects produced by artists during the Upper Palaeolithic period. These included carved or engraved stone, bone, ivory, or antler, and small crudely fired clay models. Artifacts include figurines, artists' trial pieces, decorated weapons, tools, and ornaments. The distribution extends from Siberia to Spain. Cave art covers the paintings, engravings, and reliefs found on the walls of caves and rock shelters of the same period. Unlike wall art, which is difficult to date, mobiliary art is usually found in archaeological layers and can therefore be dated. The earliest pieces probably date to about 35,000 years ago, and they continued being made throughout the Upper Palaeolithic to c. 10,000 BC. (*syn.* home art; French art mobilier; chattel art)

Moche: The major culture of the northern coast of Peru during the Early Intermediate Period. It originated in the Moche and Chicama Valleys and later spread by conquest as far south as the Santa and Nepeña Rivers. The culture developed around the start of the Christian era and lasted until AD c. 700. Dominant during the Early Intermediate period (c. 400 BC–AD 600), it is best known for its irrigation works, its massive adobe temple platforms, and its pottery. Especially famous are the modeled vessels and portrait head vases, and the jars, often with stirrup spouts, painted in reddish brown with scenes of religion, war, and everyday life. The pottery sequence has five phases, which are identified by the details of the spout formation on the stirrup-necked bottles, and they are used for relative dating of the sites (AD c. 300–700). The

Moche culture was the major contributor to the subsequent Chimú culture of the north coast. Huge structures at the ceremonial center include a large, terraced, truncated pyramid, Huaca del Sol, and the smaller Huaca de la Luna, on top of which is a series of courtyards and rooms, some with wall paintings. Huaca del Sol was perhaps the largest single construction of the prehistoric Andean region. Grave goods in gold, silver, and copper display a fairly advanced metalworking technology. Archaeologists excavated a site called Huaca Rajada and found the elaborate, jewelry-filled tomb of a Moche warrior priest. Several more burial chambers containing the remains of Moche royalty have been excavated, all dating from about AD 300, whose finds greatly aided the understanding of Moche society, religion, and culture. Incised lines on lima beans have recently been interpreted as a form of nonverbal communication similar in concept to the quipu. Developing out of Cupisnique, Gallinazo, and Salinar, Moche survived into the Middle Horizon but appears ultimately to have been overtaken by the Huari culture. In the last phase (Moche V), the southern part of the Moche territory was abandoned, and a new capital established in the north, at Pampa Grande. (*syn.* Mochica)

Mochlos: An island on the northern coast of Crete, once a peninsula where an Early Minoan cemetery of house tombs and a Middle–Late Minoan settlement have been found. Communal tombs at Mochlos had rectangular compartments or rooms and flat roofs, such as those in contemporary houses. Some of the finest jewelry was found in communal tombs at Mochlos as well as stone vases dating to c. 2000–1700 BC. The hairpins with flower heads are reminiscent of jewelry from the royal tombs at Ur in Mesopotamia. After the eruption of Thera c. 1500 BC, Mochlos was never inhabited again.

mode: The most specific category of classification for artifacts, representing items in the same type and variety that share further common attributes. Modes are single or multiple attributes whose frequencies change through time and space. They are useful in constructing culture history.

model: A device used by archaeologists to aid the interpretation of data; models consist of hypothetical reconstructions of dynamic processes partly based on material remains and partly testing the validity of interpretations of material culture. They are idealized representations of the real world, used to demonstrate a simplified version of some of its characteristics. Models vary in complexity and can be physical representations or literary descriptions. A physical model of a site or landscape might explain some feature of its function or organization; such models at full scale are well known in experimental archaeology. A simple model might be a map showing, for example, the distribution of sites in a region or a scatter diagram showing the relation between two measured variables. Models need not be based on specific archaeological data, but can be derived from a number of sources: Invented data can be generated by computer simulation; geometrical and mathematical models can also be used, such as central place theory or the rank-size rule in the study of regional settlement, or catastrophe theory in the study of cultural collapse. General systems theory can also be a source of systems models designed to show a simplified version of the working of a complex social or economic organization. The term *model* can also be used in a less specific sense for any general mode of thought in which archaeologic research is conducted, for example, descriptive, historical, or ecological. Models may also be diachronic or synchronic. The concept of formulating a model, testing it, and refining it, is frequently applied in a nonmathematical way, and this is the way in which it is most often used in archaeology. In this sense, it is either synonymous with *hypothesis* or refers to a number of interlocking hypotheses.

modeling: A ceramic vessel construction technique where a mass of clay is handworked into a rough approximation of the vessel through punching, pinching, and/or drawing.

modified diffusionism: A form of diffusionist theory, espoused by V. Gordon Childe and others, that allowed for some local cultural evolution.

modius: A tall cylindrical container, which was also the largest Roman measure of capacity. In Classical art and Egyptology, the term is used also to describe a cylindrical headdress commonly worn by such deities as the hippopotamus goddess Taweret.

Moesia: Province of the Roman Empire in the lower Danube area, extending from Serbia to the mouth of the Danube and between Dacia and Thracia. Moesia was conquered by Marcus Licinius Crassus in 30–28 BC and became a Roman province in AD 15. In the 1st century AD, a series of defensive walls and forts in southern Romania were built to guard the Moesia–Dacia frontier. Moesia was fairly prosperous because of the wheat from the Black Sea area. Agriculture and fruit growing fluorished, and there was mineral wealth in the Balkan Mountains. The province suffered heavily from barbarian invasions in the 3rd century AD, and when Dacia was abandoned about 270, its inhabitants were largely transferred to Moesia. Moesia remained part of the Eastern Roman Empire until the 7th century.

Moershoofd interstadial: An Interstadial of the Weichselian cold stage. It is dated to c. 50,000–43,000 bp.

Mogollon: A prehistoric civilization that existed from before 500 BC to approximately AD 1400 in southeastern Arizona and southwestern New Mexico in the Mogollon highlands. Its roots lie in the Cochise version of the Desert Culture in this area, but the Mogollon folk were settled agriculturists who lived in villages of pit houses; they were also strongly influenced by the Anasazi and Hohokam. Evidence of maize and bean horticulture found at Bat Cave dates to earlier than 2000 BC, but unequivocally characteristic traits, such as plain brown pottery, do not appear until 300 BC. Although the tradition was agriculturally based, hunting and gathering continued to play some part in subsistence activities. Before AD c. 1000, typical communities were small villages of pit houses, located in easily defensible positions such as high mesas. Larger villages often included a communal assembly building (possibly early kiva) and sometimes fortifications. From AD c. 1000, the Mogollon people came under the influence of their northern neighbors, the Anasazi, and began to build pueblos. To this late period belongs some of the finest pottery of the American Southwest, Mimbres ware, painted with stylized black animals on a white background. The culture is chronologically divided on the basis of architectural and pottery changes (Pine Lawn period, about 200 BC–AD 500; Georgetown period, 500–700; San Francisco period, 700–900; Three Circle period, 900–1050; and Mimbres period, 1050–1200). Unlike the Anasazi culture, the Mogollon culture did not survive as a recognizable group of modern Native Americans. Remnants of the Mogollon may have merged with Anasazi peoples to become what is known as the Western Pueblo people. The tradition has a number of regional variants: Mimbres, Pine Lawn, Upper Little Colorado, Forestdale, and Point of Pines.

Mohenjo-daro: One of the two capitals of the Indus civilization, the best known of the Mature Harappan cities, located in the Sind region on the right bank of the Indus in Pakistan. Radiocarbon dates and corroboration with Mesopotamian data date the capital to about 3000–1700 BC. The city, covering approximately 2.5 square kilometers, was laid out on a grid plan, the oldest recorded. The larger blocks, separated by broad streets with elaborate drains, were subdivided. It was the largest of all the Indus Valley sites, and like other Indus Valley settlements, Mohenjo-Daro consists of two parts: a lower town in the east, overlooked by a high artificial mound or citadel on the west side. Traces of mud and baked brick defenses have been found. Within these, an assembly hall, "college," great bath, and granary were excavated. Numerous craft installations were in the lower town, for pottery, bead making, shell working, dyeing, and metalworking. Artifacts provide the basic definition of the Mature Harappan material culture for pottery styles, seals, weights, bead forms, metal forms, figurines, and so on. There are many flood deposits, which many times overwhelmed the city. Mohenjo-daro was abandoned c. 1700/1600 BC, apparently after a massacre, as in the latest layers groups of skeletons were found lying in houses and in the streets. The other capital, Harappa, was 400 miles away. (*syn.* Mohenjo-Daro)

Mohs scale: A scale from 1 to 10 used to determine the hardness of minerals, talc being 1 and diamond being 10. It is a rough measure of the resistance of a smooth surface to

scratching or abrasion, expressed in terms of a scale devised in 1812 by the German mineralogist Friedrich Mohs. The Mohs hardness of a mineral is determined by observing whether its surface is scratched by a substance of known or defined hardness. To give numerical values to this physical property, minerals are ranked along the Mohs scale, which is composed of 10 minerals that have been given arbitrary hardness values. The scale contains the following minerals, in ascending order of hardness: 1. talc, 2. gypsum, 3. calcite, 4. fluorite, 5. apatite, 6. orthoclase, 7. quartz, 8. topaz, 9. corundum, and 10. diamond. If a mineral is scratched by orthoclase but not by apatite, its Mohs hardness is between 5 and 6.

moiety: A division of a society into two distinct social categories or groups, often on the basis of descent; one of two basic complementary tribal subdivisions. Moieties are groups that are exogamous (i.e., marriage between members of the same moiety is forbidden), of unilineal descent, and in some sense opposed. Sometimes the term *moiety* is used more loosely to refer simply to one of two divisions of a society, regardless of descent or marriage regulation.

Moi fort: Small circular earthen-walled enclosures set in series along the foothills of the middle Mekong valley in Cambodia. They are considered late Neolithic, c. 2500–2000 BC, with polished stone adzes and no metal. (*syn.* Cham fort)

Mojokerto: The find spot in eastern Java, Indonesia, of a skull of an archaic *Homo erectus* child, dated to c. 1.5 million years BP or before. Believed to be the oldest hominid fossil in Southeast Asia, the Mojokerto child has also been classed as *Pithecanthropus robustus* and *P. modjokertensis*. (*syn.* Modjokerto)

mokkan: In Japan, wooden tablets from the Han Dynasty Chinese sites. There were used for keeping track of taxes, work, and so on, and there are thousands in the Heijo Palace and other administrative offices. The United Silla of Korea and Ritsuryo state in Japan, c. 8th century AD, adopted their use.

Mokram: A people that succeeded the Gash in eastern Sudan c. 3300 BP. There was domesticated stock, sorghum, and possibly settlement hierarchy.

Mokrin: The type site of an earlier Bronze Age group in the lowland Banat, dated to the early 2nd millennium BC. Located near Kikinda (north Yugoslavia), it has a large cemetery with over 300 graves. The graves are organized in 11 lines radiating from the central area, a possible indication of family groupings. Some rich graves have gold ornaments and imported metal objects.

mold: A matrix for casting metal. Molten metal poured into a concavity will solidify into a corresponding shape. The concavity has only to be given the shape of the required artifact. Such molds can be made of stone, pottery, or metal with a melting point higher than that of the alloy being cast. Molds were also used for making figurines and relief-decorated pottery. The simplest type of mold is a one-piece or open one, from which the casting emerges with one flat face, requiring further hammering to give it a symmetrical form. Two-piece molds allowed bifacial tools and weapons to be cast—a third piece, or core, being added if a socket was required. These technical advances had been made before the end of the Early Bronze Age. Multipiece molds were used in Shang China. Molds were used to produce the elaborate asymmetrical vessels of the Mochica and Chimú styles. The earliest molds for casting metal were made of stone. During the Late Bronze Age, piece molds began to be formed of clay. (*syn.* mould)

molding: A ceramic vessel construction technique where a flat, circular mass of clay is pressed into a concave mold or placed over the top of a convex mold.

molecular clock: A method of tracing evolutionary lines based on the changes in the protein structure and DNA of living organisms, which take place over long periods. By establishing the degree of difference between the proteins of two species, it is possible to calculate how long ago they shared a common ancestor. Studies of molecular evolution rates have led to the proposition that macromolecules may serve as evolutionary clocks. If the rate of evolution of a protein or gene was approximately the same in the evolutionary lineages leading to different species, proteins and DNA sequences would provide a molecular clock of evolution. The sequences could then be used not only to reconstruct the topology of a phylogeny (the sequence of branching events) but also the time when the various events occurred.

Molfetta: Middle Neolithic settlement on the Italian Adriatic coast near Puglia, Italy—in the "Pulo di Molfetta"—by an enormous collapsed cave. A Neolithic village and cemetery beside this provide a type site for the south Italian impressed ware, for which radiocarbon dates around 5200 BC have been obtained. In about 1600 BC, a Bronze Age people, bringing an early version of the Apennine culture, occupied the floor of the depression and caves in its walls. It was originally a circular cave over 100 meters across. An Early Neolithic village had small round huts with stone footings and wattle-and-daub walls.

molinology: The description and study of watermills and windmills.

molluscan analysis: The analysis of molluscan remains, of both marine and land species, as part of the examination of the human environment. A mollusk/mollusc is any of a large phylum (Mollusca) of invertebrate animals (as snails, clams, or squids) with a soft unsegmented body usually enclosed in a calcareous shell. Edible species yield information on the subsistence economy of certain groups; in most cases it is the

shells that survive. The analysis of marine mollusks involves separation of the shells from the sample by wet sieving and the identification of varieties. The occurrence of mounds of discarded shell debris in shell middens also allows for a clear understanding of the collecting patterns, seasonal use, and preferences of man in the marine region. Land snails are increasingly used as an adjunct to pollen and insect analysis in attempts to reconstruct past environments.

mollusk: Any of a large phylum (Mollusca) of invertebrate animals (as snails, clams, or squids) with a soft unsegmented body usually enclosed in a calcareous shell. Often occurring in calcareous deposits, they may give useful information if associated with archaeologic remains. A group may give an indication of environmental conditions and general climatic conditions. More tentatively, a deposit containing mollusks may be dated against the geological scale. The phylum Mollusca is divided into five classes: Amphineura (chitons), Gastropoda (snails and slugs), Scaphopoda (elephant's tusk shells), Lamellibranchiata (bivalve mollusks, such as mussels, clams, oysters), and Cephalopods (octopus and squids). With the exception of the gastropods, most of these groups are aquatic; shells of gastropods and lamellibranchs are frequently found on archaeological sites. Shells also remain from the exploitation of these animals for food, most often found in middens found near coastal sites. Land snails are increasingly used as an adjunct to pollen and insect analysis in attempts to reconstruct past environments. (*syn.* mollusc, snail shell)

Molodova: A group of Palaeolithic and Mesolithic sites on the Dnestr River in western Ukraine—with Moldova V consisting of 12+ archaeological levels spanning from c. 45,000–7000 BC according to radiocarbon evidence. The occupation was not continuous. There are many Middle Palaeolithic artifacts and associated faunal remains, and most of the levels date to the interstadials before the beginning of the last glacial. Upper Palaeolithic assemblages have a large number of burins. The sites provide a complete dated sequence of Upper Palaeolithic occupation in the Ukraine.

Molodova culture: Upper Palaeolithic culture of the western Ukraine, found in the 5th level of Moldova. The early phase, c. 30,000–25,000 bp, has burins, large retouched blades, and end scrapers; later phases, c. 23,000–12,000 bp, also had backed blades and points.

Moloko: Late Iron Age complex in Transvaal, South Africa, AD c. 1200–1300. Another phase started AD c. 1600 and had many stone settlements.

Momil: A site on Sinu River in western Colombia, which has two ceramic periods—Momil I, 1000–500 BC, and Momil II, 500 BC–AD 1. The site is also significant for its evidence of the transition from manioc to maize farming. Momil I had stone tools, both percussion and pressure flaked, incised and stamped pottery, and circular-rimmed griddles. Momil II had troughed metates, similar to those used in Mesoamerica. New vessel forms, hollow figurines, and the earliest known occurrence of negative resist painting in Colombia also appear.

Mon: A people in mainland southeast Asia speaking an Austro-Asiatic language akin to Khmer, who formed the earliest states in the lower Irrawaddy valley of Burma, the Chao Phraya valley, Khorat, and the peninsular regions of Thailand. Their origin is unknown, but archaeological evidence indicates that at the beginning of the Christian Era the Mons must have occupied a large territory stretching from Lower Burma into the southern part of the Indochinese peninsula. Also called Hanthawaddy Kingdom, the Mon kingdom was powerful in Myanmar (Burma) from the 9th to the 11th and from the 13th to the 16th centuries and for a brief period in the mid-18th century. The capital of the Mon probably was the port of Thaton, which was located northwest of the mouth of the Salween River. The Mon center eventually shifted to Pegu, located on the Pegu River, about 50 miles from present-day Rangoon. The Mon culture was not abandoned or displaced, and the Mon blended the old with the new. The Mons are now only a small ethnic minority centered around the eastern shore of the Gulf of Martaban.

Mondsee culture: A Copper Age/Eneolithic culture of Upper Austria's Alpine foothills, noted for its villages of pile dwellings and for its decorated pottery with white-inlaid circles and stellar designs. The Mondsee people were the first to smelt the local copper ores and manufacture copper artifacts on a large scale in the region.

monetized economy: Any prehistoric economy based on money; the use of money to purchase goods and services.

Mongch'on: Walled site on the Han River in Seoul, Korea, dating from the late 3rd–late 5th centuries AD. It was probably an economic and administrative center of Paekche state.

Mongol: The powerful Mongol, or Yüan, Dynasty (AD 1279–1368) was established by Kublai Khan, the grandson of Genghis Khan. In trying to bring southern China under their control, the Mongol armies invaded and sacked the Burmese capital at Pagan. The term also refers to any member of an Asiatic ethnographic group of closely related tribal peoples who live on the Mongolian plateau and shared a common language and nomadic tradition. Their homeland is now divided into the independent nation of Mongolia and Inner Mongolia, an autonomous *ch'ü* (region) of the People's Republic of China.

Mongoloid: A major race of humankind to which American Indians, Eskimos, and Aleuts belong. This human populations (local races and microraces) is located in east, southeast, and east-central Asia. Mongoloid peoples are also found on many of the islands off the Asian mainland (e.g., Japan, Indonesia, the Aleutian Islands) and in the North American Arctic (the Eskimo). (*syn.* Mongoloid geographic race, Asian geographic race)

Monitor Valley: A high-altitude area in the central Great Basin (Nevada); the location of Gatecliff Shelter.

Mon-Khmer: An Austro-Asiatic linguistic family of southern Asia, including Mon, Khmer, and a number of languages of mountain populations in the Indochinese peninsula as well as in India. Mon-Khmer languages constitute the indigenous language family of mainland southeast Asia. They range north to southern China, south to Malaysia, west to Assam state in India, and east to Vietnam. The most important Mon-Khmer languages, having populations greater than 100,000, are Vietnamese, Khmer, Muong, Mon, Khasi, Khmu, and Wa. There are 130 languages in total.

monocausal explanation: An explanation of culture change (e.g., for state origins), which lays stress on a single dominant explanatory factor or "prime mover."

monolith: A single great stone often in the form of an obelisk, menhir, or column or in another form of monument or sculpture. The term also refers to any object formed of a single block of stone. (*syn.* menhir)

Monreale Cathedral: A magnificent cathedral, in northwestern Sicily, Italy, constructed between 1174–1189 by William II, the third Norman king of Sicily. Little now remains of the monastic buildings except the splendid cloister (with 216 marble columns) adjacent to the cathedral. The cathedral is one of the richest and most beautiful churches in Italy, combining Norman, Byzantine, Italian, and Saracen styles. Particularly notable is the interior mosaic decoration, one of the most extensive in existence. The subjects of the mosaics include an Old Testament cycle, the miracles of Christ, the life of Christ, and the lives of the saints Peter and Paul. It was created by a group of craftsmen trained in Byzantium.

monstrance: An ornamental vessel of gold, silver, silver-gilt, or gilded or silvered copper, in which the eucharistic host is carried in processions and ceremonies. The decoration often represents a sun with rays, in the center of which is a lunule or glass box in which the consecrated wafer is carried and exposed on the altars of churches. The earliest do not date before the 12th century. First used in France and Germany in the 14th century, monstrances were modeled after pyxes or reliquaries, sacred vessels for transporting the Host or relics. The Host was shown in a glass cylinder mounted on a base and surmounted by some sort of metal crown. In the 16th century, the monstrance took its present shape: a circular pane of glass set in a cross or surrounded with metal rays. The Host is placed in a holder called a lunette, which fits into an opening behind the glass. (*syn.* expositorium; ostensorium)

monotheistic, monotheism: Recognizing only one god; the belief or doctrine that there is only one god.

Montagu Cave: An Early Stone Age rock shelter located in the Cape Province of South Africa, about 150 kilometers east of Cape Town. This site is one of the very few African caves to have preserved traces of Acheulian material. Later horizons include one containing an industry that has been variously attributed to the Hoiesonspoort and to a Pietersburg variant.

Mont Bégo: Glaciated valleys on the slopes of Mont Bégo in the Maritime Alps of France, which contain 150,000 protohistoric rock art engravings, especially in Vallée des Merveilles and Fontanalba. Dates are the Early Bronze Age and as recent as the Middle Ages.

Montbolo, Balma de: Cave with Neolithic and Chalcolithic deposits in the Pyrenees Orientales, France. The cave is located halfway up a rock face, and its Neolithic assemblage has simple globular vessels with tubular lug handles that fall between Early Neolithic cardial ware and Middle Neolithic Chasséen. The layer is dated to 4500 BC; Chalcolithic burials are c. 2100 BC.

Monte Albán: A major ceremonial center of the Zapotec people in Oaxaca, Mexico, built around 900 BC on top of an artificially flattened mountain. Monte Albán (I = 900–300 BC) was probably created to serve as the capital of the entire valley, which had previously been divided among several states. It was an immense complex of monumental construction, with a huge plaza (300 × 200 m) dominated by three central mounds. The plaza was flanked on the east and west by temples, pyramids, and platform mounds; on the northern and southern extremities are more complexes of monumental building, including a ball court. There are also underground passageways. By the end of Period I, the city had between 10,000–20,000 inhabitants living in houses on hill-slope terraces around a nucleus of ceremonial and governmental buildings. Hieroglyphic writing was in use, with bar-and-dot numerals, and dates were expressed in terms of the calendar round. More than 300 carved slabs (*danzantes*) depict naked and contorted figures who may be captives, and inscriptions definitely recording conquests occur soon afterward. In Late I/Early II, the city was surrounded by a defense wall. Period I includes the appearance of Gray Ware and Olmec-influenced monumental art. Period II is characterized by contact with Maya lowland centers and later, by the increasing influence of Teotihuacán. Period IIIA (the 3rd–5th centuries AD) is marked by increased contact with Teotihuacán, reflected in pottery (thin orange ware, cylindrical tripod vases), tomb frescoes, Talud-Tablero architecture, and stela inscriptions. Monte Albán reached the height of its power in Period IIIB, AD 500–900, during which elaborate funerary urns in Gray Ware made their appearance and when the site reached its peak population of 50,000 to 60,000 people. Most of the surviving buildings belong to this time. During Monte Albán IV, AD 900–1521, building ceased. After 900, the centers of power moved elsewhere, and Monte Albán was considerably depopulated. It was essentially abandoned. In Period V, Monte Albán was of only secondary importance as a city and a political force. Mixtec art styles make their appearance in the valley, and Monte Albán was used as a cemetery, with earlier Zapotec tombs reused for the Mixtec dead. One of the richest discoveries in ancient Mexico was Tomb 7, with over 500 precious offerings in Mixtec style gold and silver ornaments, fine stonework, and a series of bones carved with hieroglyphic and calendrical inscriptions.

Monte Circeo: An isolated promontory on the southwestern coast of Italy, south of Rome, with several caves containing prehistoric remains. The numerous coastal grottoes have yielded many traces of Stone Age settlement. Fossellone Cave has several early Upper Palaeolithic levels, and Grotta Guattari had a Neanderthal skull and three lower jaws in Mousterian deposits.

Montelius, Oscar (1843–1921): Swedish archaeologist who constructed a chronology for prehistoric Europe and who developed typological schemes for the European Neolithic and Bronze Ages. He divided European prehistory into numbered periods (four for the Neolithic, five for the Bronze Age), and to these periods he gave absolute dates by extending cross-dating from Egypt across Europe. Montelius believed in the diffusionist view (called ex oriente lux) that all European culture in later prehistoric times was derived from the ancient civilizations of Egypt and the Near East. Still controversial is his theory, the "Swedish typology," suggesting that material culture and biological life develop through essentially the same kind of evolutionary process. He published *Om tidsbestämming inom ronsåldern* (1885; "On Determining the Periods Within the Bronze Age"), *The Civilization of Sweden in Heathen Times* (1888), and *Die älteren Kulturperioden in Orient und in Europa* (1903–23; "The Older Cultural Periods in the Orient and Europe"). (*syn.* Gustav Oscar Augustin Montelius)

Monteoru: A fortified hilltop near Bucharest, which is the type site of a Middle to Late Bronze Age culture, c. 2000–1600 BC, covering much of eastern Romania. This culture of the Sub-Carpathian zone was of local origin, but absorbed influences from both the south (notably faience in trade) and the steppes. It had a rich, varied collection of pot and metal forms. The site had a citadel with a long occupation and four large grave groupings in an adjoining cemetery. The citadel was fortified by box-like ramparts and stone walls, with house platforms in the interior. The burial rite is predominantly contracted inhumation, with pottery, bronze jewelry, and stone or faience beads as grave goods.

Montespan: Palaeolithic cave site in Haute-Garonne, French Pyrenees, which has a deep central cave with traces of probable (middle) Magdalenian engravings on the walls. There is also a series of clay statues and bas-reliefs. The cave is famous for a modeled clay body of a life-sized bear or bear cub, probably originally covered with a bear pelt and apparently speared in ritual ceremonies.

Montet, Pierre (1885–1966): French Egyptologist who worked at Tanis and Byblos. He conducted major excavations of the New Empire (c. 1567–525 BC) capital at Tanis, in the Nile Delta, discovering, in particular, funerary treasures from the 21st and 22nd Dynasties. At his first major excavation at Byblos (modern Jubayl, Lebanon), one of the oldest continuously inhabited towns in the world, he found what was then believed to be the earliest alphabetical writing and published his researches in *Byblos et l'Égypte* (1928). He published *La Nécropole royale de Tanis*, (3 vol., 1947–60; "The Royal Cemetery at Tanis") and *Everyday Life in the Days of Ramesses the Great* (1958) and *Eternal Egypt* (1964).

Monte Verde: Early Preceramic site in southern Chile, c. 13,000 bp, one of the few pre-Clovis occupations in the New World. There are huts with shallow clay-lined pits and tools of wood, bone, or stone. There was a dated layer with evidence of occupation c. 33,000 bp, but that is disputed.

Mont Lassois: Iron Age hill fort in Cote-d'Or, France, on a route from the River Seine to the Mediterranean. Occupation is dated to the 6th century BC (Hallstatt D), the residence of a Celtic chieftain. The hillfort of Vix seems to have been the center of political authority and extensive trade relations. The rich Celtic and Greek artifacts found there, including Massiliote wine amphorae and Attic black-figure ware, as well as those from the nearby tumulus burials near the villages of Vix and Sainte-Colombe-sur-Seine, indicate trade between the Celts and the Greeks.

Montu: Falcon-headed god of war, usually represented with a headdress consisting of a sun disc and two plumes. He was the god of the 4th Upper Egyptian nome, whose original capital of Hermonthis (modern Armant) was replaced by Thebes during the 11th Dynasty (2081–1939 BC). The cult is attested in the Theban region and in major temples from the Middle Kingdom to the Roman period. From the 30th Dynasty (380–343 BC), the bull had an elaborate cult and important temple complexes at Karnak in Thebes and at Hermonthis, Al-Tud, and Al-Madamud. (*syn.* Mont, Monthu, Mentu)

monumental: A term describing the more prestigious or public form of a script as distinct from its cursive form.

monumental architecture: Large buildings such as temples, palaces, and pyramids, readily identifiable in the archaeological record and assumed to have been built by means of the collective labor of many people.

Moore, Clarence Bloomfield (1852–1936): American archaeologist considered one of the forefathers of Americanist archaeology. He worked on the southeastern coast of North America with major contributions at Moundville, Alabama, and Poverty Point, Louisiana.

Moose Mountain: A medicine wheel in southern Saskatchewan, Canada. There is a central cairn surrounded by an ellipse of stones; radiating from the center are five stone lines, each ending in a small stone cairn. There are radiocarbon dates of c. 2600 BP and 1700 BP.

Mootwingee: A rich rock-art site near Broken Hill, western New South Wales, Australia. Human and animal figures in the Panaramitee style were engraved on rock surfaces. Other motifs include emus and eggs, kangaroos, sets of animal and human tracks, and radiating lines. Other finds include body part stencils and artifacts.

moraine: Generallly, a bank or layer of mud, gravel, and stones deposited by an advancing or retreating glacier. The term described a family of depositional land forms created by glacier ice. There are five common types: end or terminal moraine, recessional moraine, ground moraine, hummocky/ablation/medial moraine, and lateral moraine. The material, which ranges in size from blocks or boulders (usually faceted or striated) to sand and clay, is unstratified when dropped by the glacier and shows no sorting or bedding.

Morgan, Lewis Henry (1818–1881): A founder of American anthropology (scientific anthropology), known especially for establishing the study of kinship systems and for his comprehensive theory of social evolution. He put forth the scheme of development as being savagery to barbarism to civilization. His work directly affected the application of the theory of evolution to the discipline of anthropology. Morgan's theory of cultural evolution was published in *Ancient Society, or Researches in the Lines of Human Progress from Savagery Through Barbarism to Civilization* (1877). This was the first major scientific account of the origin and evolution of civilization, with illustrations of developmental stages drawn from various cultures.

Moriori: The native Polynesian inhabitants of the Chatham Islands, east of New Zealand. The Moriori, who were heavily dependent on marine resources, are thought to have settled the islands from New Zealand about AD 1400. They were conquered, enslaved, and assimilated by Maori immigrants in the mid-1800s.

Morley, Sylvanus Griswold (1883–1948): American archaeologist known for his work on the Mayan civilization. His major contribution relates to carved Mayan inscriptions, which he catalogued, reproduced, and partially translated. His interpretation was that the Classic Maya were not urban dwellers, but farmers who occupied the ceremonial centers only on religious holidays.

morphological type: A descriptive and abstract grouping of individual artifacts whose focus is on overall similarity rather than specific form or function. The shape, size, and superficial characteristics of artifacts, features, structure, sites, and so on, provided by measurements (including weight) that permit comparative statistical analysis of attributes and frequencies. (*syn.* morphology)

Morse, Edward Sylvester (1838–1925): American zoologist who introduced archaeology to Japan by excavating the Omori shell midden. He was the first to use the term "Jomon" ("cord mark") for the Neolithic earthenware pottery whose surface decoration consists of impressions of twisted cords.

mortar: Part of an ancient device for processing plant foods; usually used with a pestle. It was a stone or wooden receptacle with a cup-shaped depression. Mortars were frequently made of special rocks, which might be traded over considerable distances. The mortars of the medieval period in Europe have been studied at length; the first stone mortars occur in 8th century Dore-Stad and have origins in the Moselle Valley, while the French Carolingians at this time were using pottery mortars.

mortarium: A Roman grinding bowl, or mortar; a culinary pottery form. Examples are often stamped with a maker's name, and some sophisticated versions have been found.

mortice: A hole, groove, or slot, usually rectangular, cut into a timber beam or plank, to take a tenon, which is a projection cut on the end of another beam and inserted into the mortice so that they can be joined together.

Mortillet, Gabriel de (1821–1898): French prehistorian who, after being a student of Edouard Lartet, proposed an alternative to Lartet's Palaeolithic classification scheme. For the palaeontological criteria of Lartet, he substituted archaeological ones based on tool forms rather than faunal remains. He extended into prehistory the geological system of periods, or epochs, each characterized by a limited range of type fossils. Each period had "type names" after a "type site" where the diagnostic material was well represented—such as Mousterian, Aurignacian, and Solutrean. By 1869, de Mortillet's scheme for the Stone Age had the following subdivisions: Thenaisian (for the now discredited eoliths), followed by Chellean, Mousterian, Solutrean, Aurignacian, Magdalenian, and (for the Neolithic) Robenhausian, named after a lake village—although alterations and additions (Acheulian) were made later. With further modifications, this classification was widely adopted and remained the standard terminology for European archaeology until well into the 20th century. De Mortillet saw his epochs as periods of time or as stages of development with a universal validity, and his scheme was basically a refinement of the Three Age System. He did not allow for purely local variants in a single epoch; he divided the Palaeolithic into periods, not cultures or traditions. This is no longer accepted, and de Mortillet's epochs are now thought to represent cultures and to have local validity only. The practice of using type site names, however, proved so useful that it became standard practice. He founded, in 1864, one of the earliest archaeological journals, *Matériaux pour l'histoire positive et philosophique de l'homme*. His classifications were published in *Le Préhistorique: antiquité de l'homme* (1882; "The Prehistoric: Man's Antiquity") and in subsequent revisions. (*syn.* Mortillet, (Louis-Laurent-Marie) Gabriel de)

mortuary cult: A group providing regular funerary offerings for the eternal well-being of the deceased and in hopes of partaking in the salvation offered by the deity. The mortuary cults of many peoples indicate that the dead were imagined as actually residing in their tombs and able to receive the offerings of food and drink made to them; some graves in ancient Crete and Ugarit (Ras Shamra) were equipped with pottery conduits, from the surface, for libations.

mortuary enclosure: Any structure made of earth, stone, or wood, used for the storage of bodies before their collective burial. Remains of such enclosures are sometimes found under barrows.

mortuary house: A wooden or stone copy of an actual dwelling, buried under a barrow or kurgan, and used as a tomb for the dead. There is sometimes an overlap between the definitions of mortuary house and mortuary enclosure, but very different ritual ideas may be involved. A mortuary house often contains only a single corpse and serves primarily as a sepulcher rather than as a charnel house in which bodies were accumulated. Grave goods might be included, and, in some instances, an earthen mound (barrow) was raised over the mortuary structure.

mortuary priest: In ancient Egypt, a person or persons appointed to bring daily funerary offerings to a tomb; known as the "servant of the ka." An endowment of lands and estates during the life or after the death of the deceased provided the offerings, which then reverted to the priests.

mortuary temple: An Egyptian temple, located close to a royal tomb, where the mortuary cult of a king was carried out. It was a center for the performance of rites for the benefit of the dead king and a depository for offerings of food, and so on. It was originally part of the funerary complex; in the New Kingdom, it came to be separated from the tomb, often by miles. In the Old and Middle Kingdoms (c. 2575–2130 BC and 1938–1060 BC), the mortuary temple usually adjoined the pyramid and had an open, pillared court, storerooms, five elongated shrines, and a chapel containing a false door and an offering table. In the New Kingdom (1539–1075 BC), the kings were buried in rock-cut tombs, but separate mortuary temples were built nearby. All were provided with a staff of priests and assured of supplies through endowments of estates and lands to ensure religious services and offerings in perpetuity.

mosaic: A technique of decoration used mainly on floors or walls, involving the setting of small colored fragments of stone, tile, mineral, shell, or glass, each called a tessera (plural tesserae), in a cement or adhesive matrix. Mosaic also refers to a tesselated area, often of complex designs and, possibly, inscriptions. Mosaic floors were made from small squares, triangles, or other regular shapes up to 1 inch in size. They were laid in cement to form designs, figures of animals, or classical figures representing the seasons, and so on. Old limestone would be used for white, and various reds, browns, or grays came from baked clays. Glass, too, was sometimes incorporated. The earliest known mosaics date from the 8th century BC and are made of pebbles, a technique refined by Greek craftsmen in the 5th century BC. Greek mosaics were simple pebble floors and then became more complex and sophisticated under Macedonian kings. Mosaics are known from Pompeii and Rome, Tivoli, Aquileia, and Ostia—as well as Africa, Antioch, Sicily, and Britain. Under the Roman Empire, the achievements of the 5th–6th century Byzantine artists at Ravenna are impressive. An excellent collection of mosaics from Pompeii may be seen in the Museo Nazionale at Naples, and a good selection of Imperial Roman provincial work may be seen at the Museum of Le Bardo, outside modern Tunis, Tunisia. Pre-Columbian American Indians favored mosaics of semiprecious stones such as garnet and turquoise and mother-of-pearl. These were normally used to encrust small objects such as shields, masks, and cult statues. Mosaic as an art form has most in common with painting. It represents a design or image in two dimensions. It is also, like painting, a technique appropriate to large-scale surface decoration. (*syn.* mosaic work)

Moshebi's Shelter: A rock shelter site in eastern Lesotho, close to the borders of Natal and the Cape Province of South Africa, with two early industries attributed to the "Middle Stone Age." The later of these contains a number of large backed crescent-shaped pieces and other tools, which suggest a possible connection with the Howiesons-Poort industries. The later industries are of backed microlith type. At a level dated to the 1st millennium AD, pottery is first represented, as are pressure-flaked tanged arrowheads.

mosque: Any house or open area of prayer in Islam. The earliest mosques were simple enclosures, imitating the courtyard of the Prophet Muhammad's house at Medina of the 7th century AD. Most mosques have large areas, partly covered and partly open, where the community meets for prayer.

Mosques usually, but not always, face Mecca, the direction of which (*qibla*) is indicated by a niche (*mihrab*) at the center of the end wall. To the right, there is a stepped pulpit (*minbar*). Outside the mosque, the most prominent feature is the minaret(s) (*manar*), usually towers, from which the muezzin gives the call to prayer. Schools and libraries are frequently attached to mosques. In some cases a *maktab* (elementary school) is attached to a mosque, mainly for the teaching of the Qur'an, and informal classes in law and doctrine are given for people of the surrounding neighborhood. (*syn.* Arabic: masjid)

Mössbauer spectroscopy: A technique used in the analysis of artifact composition, particularly iron-bearing minerals in pottery. It involves the measurement of the gamma radiation absorbed by the iron nuclei, which provides information on the particular iron compounds in the sample, and hence on the conditions of firing when the pottery was being made. Samples are bombarded with gamma rays and a record made of the detected amount of absorption by iron nuclei. The use of this method of physical analysis has been confined mainly to the examination of iron compounds, although other uses have been suggested. The Mössbauer effect of recoil-free emission and absorption of gamma rays occurs only with a limited number of isotopes, of which one of the iron isotopes is useful in archaeological contexts. Because of its sensitivity to short-range crystalline order, the technique is better for examining poorly crystallized iron-bearing minerals than is x-ray diffraction. This type of spectroscopy is also used for the study of nuclear hyperfine structure, chemical shifts, and chemical analysis.

Mossgiel: The find site of a skeleton with robust cranial morphology on the western plains of New South Wales, Australia. Radiocarbon dating of bone gave an estimate of about 4000 BC.

motif: A single repeated design (or color); an element in a (usually) complex design. It may be nonrepresentational or pictorial.

motte: An elevated mound of earth, part of the motte-and-bailey castle, which was crowned with a timber palisade and surrounded by a defensive ditch that also separated the motte from a palisaded outer compound, called the bailey. Access to the motte was by means of an elevated bridge across the ditch from the bailey. This structure appeared in the 10th and 11th centuries between the Rhine and Loire Rivers and eventually spread to most of western Europe. The motte was usually made of earth, but sometimes of stone. Attached to it might be one or more baileys, which are enclosures surrounded by ramparts or stone walls. Motte should not be confused with moat; the latter was a ditch. The motte was formed from the soil originally dug from the ditch. It was the mound on which the wooden castle of the motte and bailey was built in early Norman times. Motte-and-bailey was the type of wooden castle first erected by Norman conquerors, and it was an expedient, quickly erected, medieval fortification. Several classic examples of motte and bailey castles are illustrated in the Bayeaux tapestry, with wooden towers and palisades on top of the motte. (*syn.* motte and bailey, motte-and-bailey castle)

Motupore: A site on an offshore island near Port Moresby, Papua New Guinea, with an excavated sequence from AD 1100–1700, ancestral to the present Austronesian-speaking Motu inhabitants of the region. The sequence documents the development of the specialized ethnographic Motu trading system, in which pottery, shell beads, and marine resources were exchanged for sago and wallaby meat from adjacent Papuan Gulf communities.

Motya: One of the three principal centers of Carthaginian Sicily (the other two were at Panorums (Palermo) and Soloeis (Soluntum)). It was a Phoenician harbor town on a tiny island off the extreme west of Sicily. The settlement was founded in the 8th century BC and was joined to the mainland by a causeway. Excavations have revealed stretches of walls with gates and towers, an artificial dock (cothon), a temple, a sanctuary (tophet), houses, and cemeteries. Much Greek pottery has also been found at Motya. After the destruction of the city by Dionysius the Elder of Syracuse in 397 BC, the inhabitants left to colonize nearby Lilybaeum. (*syn.* modern San Pantaleo)

moufflon: A wild sheep of southwest Asia, *Ovis orientalis*, found from Cyprus through Syria to Iran. It was the breed first domesticated, being found at Zawi Chemi Shanidar c. 9000 BC and at Jarmo 6000. Later it was largely replaced by the urial. A second species of moufflon, *O. musimon*, still occurs wild on Corsica and Sardinia, but is probably descended from escaped domesticates. The males have large curling horns.

mound: A gradual accumulation of debris on which a continuously occupied settlement is built, or which is the by-product or remains of some activity. The term can mean (1) a constructed earthwork or fortification, especially one with a geometric or animal form (also called effigy mound), (2) a low, isolated, rounded natural hill, usually of earth, (3) a structure built by fossil colonial organisms, (4) prehistoric refuse heap consisting chiefly of the shells of edible mollusks (also called shell mound), or (5) an artificial construction commonly used for human burial (also called burial mound) or as a foundation for a temple or dwelling. (*syn.* tuft)

mound architecture: The use of elevated mounds of earth or stone as the foundation for buildings, platforms, temples, and pyramids, which were often made of adobe (mud brick).

Mound Builder People: A mythical, non-Native American people, c. 500 BC to AD c. 100, postulated as being responsible for constructing the thousands of burial mounds with extensive enclosures of banked earth in the east-central and southeast United States.

mounded tomb: A type of elite burial used in east Asia, built with monumental earthen or stone-piled mounds that contained burial facilities. The burials ranged from wooden chambers, clay enclosures, to brick or stone megalithic chambers. There were round and square mounds, and Japan's were keyhole shaped. The tombs provide the source of data for the Three Kingdoms period of Korea and the Kofun of Japan. One of the earliest mounded tombs of China was that of the First Emperor of Qin, and the Ming tombs are some of the latest. Prestige grave goods are found in all. Haniwa ("circle of clay"), unglazed terra-cotta cylinders, and hollow sculptures, were arranged on and around the mounded tombs (kofun) of the Japanese elite dating from the Tumulus period (AD c. 250–552). The first and most common haniwa were barrel-shaped cylinders used to mark the borders of a burial ground. Later, in the early 4th century, the cylinders were surmounted by sculptural forms such as figures of warriors, female attendants, dancers, birds, animals, boats, military equipment, and houses. It is believed that the figures symbolized continued service to the deceased in the other world.

Moundville: Mississippian site in Alabama composed of 20, mostly platform, mounds, with over 3,000 burials. The site reached its peak c. 1250, and it was probably part of a chiefdom. There is much evidence for the Southern Cult.

Mount Camel: Archaic midden on North Island, New Zealand, dating to AD 1150–1260.

Mount Carmel: A group of Palaeolithic caves in Israel, on biblical Mount Carmel, which have between them yielded a long stratigraphy. The most important of these sites are el Wad, es Skhul, Tabun, and Nahal Oren. The sequence began with coarse flake tools of Tayacian type, followed by Acheulian handax industries. Associated (and perhaps interstratified) with the final Acheulian were Jabrudian artifacts and eventually blade tools of Amudian type. The next industry, the Levalloiso-Mousterian, was represented at two caves, Tabun and es Skhul, and was associated with human remains whose evolutionary position is controversial. The sequence continued with the so-called Emiran industry, followed by the Palestine Aurignacian (also called Antelian), by a blade/scraper/burin industry (the Atlitian), and finally by Natufian. The el Wad has a sequence of Upper Palaeolithic deposits with important Natufian levels at the top and on the plateau outside and numerous associated burials.

Mount Do: A site near Thanh-hoa in northern Vietnam, which has yielded a pebble and flake industry with a few bifaces. Chellean (early Acheulian) affinities have been suggested. (*syn.* Nui do)

Mount Mazama ash: Volcanic ash (or tephra) originating from the eruption of Mount Mazama (Crater Lake, Oregon) nearly 7,000 years ago (6,600 years ago). Undisturbed beds of Mazama ash provide important contextual dates for archaeological sites throughout the northwestern United States and southwestern Canada. The eruption also produced Crater Lake in Oregon. Great thicknesses of pumice were deposited on the flanks of Mount Mazama, while finer material was blown over great distances by the winds. The widespread distribution of the Mazama Ash has made it useful in archaeological studies as a horizon, or time, marker. Studies of sediments formed in relation to the ash deposits suggest that the ash formed at a time when generally drier climates prevailed in the regions in which the ash occurs. The mineralogical composition of the ash is distinctive and allows it to be distinguished from other volcanic ash deposits. (*syn.* Mazama Ash)

Mount Sandel: Mesolithic site in Londonderry, Ireland, with circular wooden hut foundations with central hearths. There was a lithic industry of microliths, tranchet axes, and polished stone axes.

Mount William: A greenstone ax quarry and workshop in Victoria, Australia. It was the center of an exchange network in Victoria, South Australia, and southern New South Wales. Mount William is the highest peak in western Australia (3829 feet).

Mousterian: A Middle Palaeolithic culture that is defined by the development of a wide variety of specialized tools made with prepared-core knapping techniques, such as spear points. It is named for the first such artifacts recovered from the lower rock shelter at Le Moustier, Dordogne, France. Stone tools, scrapers, and points found in the cave came to be recognized as the flint industry present throughout Europe during first half of the last glaciation (Würm) and associated with Neanderthal. The earliest Mousterian goes back to the Riss Glaciation, but most of it comes into the late middle Würm Glaciation, giving a total life span from 180,000 BC until c. 30,000 BP. Flintwork of Mousterian type (with racloirs, triangular points made on flakes, and—in some variants—well-made hand axes) has been found over most of the unglaciated parts of Eurasia, as well as in the Near East and North Africa (in the latter two areas, it constitutes the Middle Palaeolithic). Three major regional variants have been identified—West, East, and Levalloiso-Mousterian, each with subgroups. In certain industries, called Levalloiso-Mousterian, the tools were made on flakes produced by the Levallois technqiue. It was a progressive stage in the manufacture of stone tools. Mousterian peoples mainly lived in cave mouths and rock shelters. (*syn.* Mousterian industry)

Mousterian of Acheulian Tradition: A Mousterian variant found in southwest France. Its Type A is characterized by bifaces, backed knives, denticulates, and scrapers. Type B had fewer bifaces and more Upper Palaeolithic burins and awls. (*syn.* MAT, MTA)

Movius, Hallam Leonard (1907–1987): American prehistorian who worked in Northern Ireland, southeast Asia, and Abri Pataud, France.

Msecké Zehrovice: Iron Age settlement in Bohemia, dated to the La Tène C–D period, c. 150–50 BC. There is evidence of iron and shale working. A bust of a Celt with curled mustache and wavy hair is the site's best-known find.

Mshatta: Among the most famous pre-Islamic secular palaces, located in Jordan. Although only the main building was finished, it consisted of a square enclosure with a single gate in the south side. The interior was divided into three parallel strips running from north to south. There was a triple arch leading to a long basilical hall and a square, triple-apsed throne room, reminiscent of the bishop's palace at Bosra in Syria, which is attributed to the 6th century. The main entrance and other parts of Mshatta were faced with richly carved stone reliefs. The palace is attributed to the Umayyad caliph Walid II (743–744), and presumably work stopped when he died. The Mshatta throne room does have a number of Sasanian elements, and Iranian brickwork appears.

Mu: A mythical, sunken continent supposed to have been in the Pacific Ocean.

Mu'a: The main ceremonial and residential center of the ruling dynasties of Tongatapu, Tonga, held by tradition to have been in use from the 11th century AD. The site has a core area of 400 × 500 meters defended by an earthwork and contains numerous house platforms and tombs (Langi). According to tradition, it became the residence of the Tui Tonga Dynasty about AD 1200, and the defenses were built about AD 1400.

Muang Fa Daet: Settlement in the upper Chi valley, Thailand, the largest moated site in the Khorat. Its three concentric moats and reservoir dated to the Khmer of the late 1st millennium AD. There was farming, trading, bronze working, and ironworking. Its material culture resembles Dvaravati.

Muang Sima: Settlement in the Mun valley, Khorat, Thailand, occupied by the early 1st millennium AD. The moated site was the center of a small Indianized state known from an inscription as Sri Canasa.

Mucking: A settlement and cemetery site in Essex, one of the largest and most extensively excavated Early Saxon sites in England. It is situated on the high gravel terraces of the Thames estuary, and more than 100 sunken huts as well as at least two hall houses have been found. The main occupation debris from the site consists of clay loom weights; handmade, grass-tempered pots, and some fine metalwork. The cemeteries contain a mixture of inhumation and cremation burials, including some wealthy graves that possess a full range of Early saxon jewelry and weapons.

mud brick: A brick dried in the sun rather than baked, used for construction in dry climates, such as the Middle East, Africa, Asia and Mesoamerica. In a dry climate, where fuel for baking brick is scarce, bricks were and are commonly sun dried only. A building constructed of these can expect only a limited life, perhaps 30 years. When it collapses, new brick is brought in for any new building, which is superimposed on the leveled ruins of the old, with the floor at a correspondingly higher level. It is this process that largely explains the great height and bulk of Near Eastern tells. The two principal building materials used in ancient Egypt were unbaked mud brick and stone. Mud brick was used even for royal palaces, fortresses, the great walls of temple precincts and towns, and subsidiary buildings in temple complexes. The first fired bricks appeared about 3000 BC (in Mesopotamia). (*syn.* adobe, pisé, mud-brick)

Mudejar: A unique style of art and architecture, part Gothic, part Islamic, which developed in the Iberian peninsula during the Moorish occupation of the 12th–15th centuries. The style, marked by the frequent use of the horseshoe arch and the vault, distinguishes the church and palace architecture of Toledo, Córdoba, Seville, and Valencia. Many of the greatest Mudejar buildings were constructed by Moorish workmen for Christian masters and were executed in brick, tile, and wood. One of the finest examples is the great Mudejar palace of the Alcazar in Seville.

Mud Glyph Cave: Rich prehistoric art site in Tennessee with "galleries" of incisions in mud on cave walls. The designs are anthropomorphic and zoomorphic. There are abstract designs like those on contemporary artifacts. The cave site was used from AD 420–1750, mainly in the 12th–16th centuries.

Muge: Mesolithic shell mounds (*concheiros*) in Portugal, dated between 7350–5150 bp (Atlantic period). There was a microlithic industry, quartzite pebbles and grindstones, and bone points and axes of red deer antlers. There are more than 230 burials—individuals with at least some Cro-Magnon characteristics, called Cro-Magnoids. It is an important European Mesolithic funerary assemblage.

muller: A small grinding stone, often for use with pigments but also grains, ores, and drugs. In painting, it is an instrument used in conjunction with a slab to grind artists' colors by hand. From ancient Egyptian times until the 18th century, porphyry (a rock of feldspar crystals) was used.

Müller, Sophus (1846–1934): Danish prehistorian and palaeontologist who succeeded Christian Jurgensen Thomsen as director of the National Museum of Denmark in 1865. In the field, Müller improved the techniques of excavation, particularly in recognizing stratigraphic relations. Müller developed new techniques of excavation and monument preservation and supported the principle of the influence of Mediterranean civilization on northern Europe. He built detailed typological sequences and cross-dated them by reference to the historical calendars of the Near Eastern civilizations. He was aware of the possibility of variation in culture among contemporary groups and suggested, for instance, that there were several contemporary versions of the Neolithic of northern Europe. During the late 19th century, he discovered the first of the Neolithic battle ax cultures in Denmark.

Mullerup: The type site in Denmark for the Maglemosian tool culture of northern Europe, situated in the Magle Mose (or "big bog") in Zealand. The Maglemosian is one of the Mesolithic cultures characterized by stone microliths (tiny stone blades, edges, and points) used as arrowheads or set into the cutting edges of mattocks, axes, and adzes, and many bone and wood tools are known. It belongs to the early postglacial period or Boreal time, c. 9000–5000 BC.

Mulloy, William Thomas (1917–1978): American archaeologist who developed the cultural chronology of the northwest plains, especially at Pictograph Cave in Montana. He also worked on Easter Island on orongo, ahu, and their moai.

multidimensional scaling: A multivariate statistical technique, which aims to develop spatial structure from numerical data by estimating the differences and similarities between analytical units. Points or items are distributed in a hyperspace, whose dimensions are a large number of variables, and can be similarly distributed in a space of fewer dimensions. The points, originally randomly distributed, are moved about in the new space until the distances between points are similar in proportion to those between points in the original hyperspace. For example, a group of artifacts, about which a large number of characteristics and measurements have been recorded, can be represented by a two-dimensional plot. The reverse is also possible: Distributions in a space of few dimensions can be "unfolded" into a space of many more dimensions. (*syn.* MDSCAL, multidimensional scaling)

multidirectional core: A core that has had flakes removed from two or more directions.

multifaceted platform: A platform with more than one plane of detachment, such as on the margins of some bifaces or multidirectional cores.

multilinear cultural evolution: A theory of cultural evolution that sees each human culture evolving in its own way by adaptation to diverse environments. It is sometimes divided into four broad stages of evolving of social organization: band, tribe, chiefdom, and state-organized society. It is often defined by these four general levels of complexity rather than seeing all societies as pursuing a single course.

multiple working hypotheses: The simultaneous testing of alternative hypotheses to minimize bias and maximize the chances of finding the best available choice.

multiplier effect: A term used in systems thinking to describe the process by which changes in one field of human activity (subsystem) sometimes act to promote changes in other fields and in turn to act on the original subsystem itself. An instance of positive feedback, it is thought by some to be one of the primary mechanisms of societal change.

multivallate: Having more than one rampart or protective barrier.

multivariate: Having or involving a number of independent mathematical or statistical variables. In reference to analysis or explanation, it is a perspective that views several interacting variables simultaneously rather than focusing on one variate at a time, as in univariate analysis. This approach is used to generate explanations of culture change, such as the origin of the state, which, in contrast to monocausal approaches, stresses the interaction of several factors operating simultaneously. Some multivariate techniques (e.g., cluster analysis and discriminant analysis) analyze the distribution of the items under study in hyperspace, reporting their results as a table or plot. Other techniques (e.g., principal components, discriminant functions, multidimensional scaling) mathematically reduce the number of dimensions of the space. Typically, a multidiminesional distribution may be reduced to two or three dimensions, after which it may be plotted or analyzed by conventional statistics. (*syn.* multivariate explanation, multivariate analysis, multivariate techniques)

Mumba-Höhle: Rock shelter in northern Tanzania, a deeply stratified site spanning much of the last 125,000 years. It contains material from the Middle Stone Age to the Iron Age.

mummification: The technique of preserving a body whereby the viscera and brain are extracted from the dried body before embalming it in sodium carbonate and finally wrapping it in bandages and a canvas shroud. This treatment of a cadaver, the mummy, has the aim of preserving a lifelike appearance and was used by the Egyptians since the Old Kingdom. The preservation of the body was an essential part of ancient Egyptian funerary practice, because it was to the body that the ka would return to find sustenance. If the body had decayed or was unrecognizable, the ka would go hungry, and the afterlife would be jeopardized. Mummification was therefore dedicated to the prevention of decay. In the New Kingdom, the new technqiues of removal of internal organs (although in a late period they were replaced after treatment), use of effective desiccating agents, and subcutaneous padding made mummification possible on a large scale. Sacred animals and birds were also mummified. Mummification was accompanied by elaborate rituals. Among the many other

peoples who practiced mummification were people living along the Torres Strait, between Papua New Guinea and Australia, and the Incas of South America. The term is also applied to bodies accidentally preserved in this way in other parts of the world, as in desert regions of Peru and Andean caves.

mummy: The dead body of a person or animal preserved according to the rites practiced in ancient Egypt. After removal of the organs to separate canopic jars, the body was treated with resin (natron) to dry it out thoroughly. It was then wrapped tightly in linen bandages, accompanied by jewelry, religious texts, and unguents of various kinds. Human mummies were then generally enclosed in cartonage, wooden, stone, or gold cases of human form, before being placed in the tomb. All stages of the procedure were accompanied by elaborate rituals, culminating in the ceremony of the "opening of the mouth," which symbolically restored to the completed mummy the faculties of life. The practice arose from the accidental preservation of bodies by desiccation in the desert sand, giving rise to the idea that such preservation was necessary to the survival of the dead man's soul. It continued until the end of pharaonic times. The name derives from *moumiya*, or bitumen, with which the Persians mistakenly thought the bodies were coated.

Mummy Cave: A deeply stratified site in northwest Wyoming, containing 38 distinct cultural levels from which a series of radiocarbon dates was taken. There is evidence of intermittent occupation from at least 7300 BC–AD 1580. Subsistence activities were not based on the big game hunting tradition normally associated with the Plains area, but was a general hunting and gathering lifestyle. The cave is named for the desiccated body of an adult male who died there some 1,200 years ago.

mummy label: A type of identification tag used during the Greco-Roman period, when corpses were regularly being transported from the home to the cemetery or back to their village. The tags were made of wood and, occasionally, stone. Mummy labels were inscribed with short ink texts in Greek or demotic, giving name, age, hometown, and destination of the deceased. (*syn.* Greek tabla)

Mumun: A Korean term meaning "no decoration" for the plain pottery of the peninsula, which succeeded Chulmun pottery from c. 1500 BC–AD 300. It was the dominant pottery type from the Bronze Age through the Proto-Three Kingdoms period.

Mundigak: Tell site near Kandahar in Afghanistan with an important cultural sequence from the 5th–2nd millennia BC. By the later 3rd millennium BC, it was a major urban center with a large colonnaded "palace" and other monumental structures in a walled citadel. Pottery and other artifacts of that time indicate interaction with Turkmenistan, Baluchistan, and the Early Harappan Indus region. It was closely related to the city of Shahr-I Sikhta, also on the Helmand River but in Iran. It is likely that the wealth of Mundigak, as of Shahr-I Sokhta, was based largely on trade in lapis lazuli and perhaps also copper. The Chalcolithic levels contained mud brick and black-on-buff painted pottery and had a radiocarbon date of 3400 ± 300 BC.

Munhata: A site occupied in the PPNB phase, located on a high terrace of the River Jordan in Israel, with a radiocarbon date of c. 7200 BC. Several different building phases are documented, and the architecture is characterrized by plastered areas and raised stone platforms; earlier rectangular buildings were later replaced by round ones. Sickle blades, querns, grind stones, and pestles suggest that wild cereals were harvested. After a hiatus in occupation, there were three ceramic phases: the Yarmukian, with semisunken round huts; the Munhata phase with similar structures; and the Wadi Rabah phase with rectangular houses.

municipium: A Roman term of political classification, for a community incorporated into the Roman state after the dissolution of the Latin League. Initially, inhabitants of these municipalities were considered Roman citizens without voting rights. As the Italian provinces were incorporated into the Roman state, residents of the municipia were registered in the tribes and accorded full political rights. These cities maintained a certain amount of autonomy and were permitted to have their own governments; there was a uniform pattern of local government under four magistrates. However, the municipia remained under the jurisdiction of Rome in matters of foreign policy, and they supplied Rome with troops and were not permitted to mint money. By the 1st century BC, all Latin and Italian communities became municipia. Later, municipium status was granted widely in the western provinces. (*syn.* plural municipia)

Munsell soil color charts: A color identification system for sediment, soil, chert, pottery, and rock; an aid used in the physical examination and recording of objects where color is thought to be an essential or at least a significant aspect of the analysis. Devised by Albert H. Munsell, the three factors of hue, value, and chroma are taken into consideration; all rated on a scale of 0–10 and expressed quantitatively. Hue describes the colors of the spectrum present, value their concentration, and chroma their purity. The color of soil or, for example, pottery, can be matched in the chart and given a value, so that anyone with a similar set of charts can understand the exact color of the material. The method allows direct comparison of colors without physically moving the material and is clearly preferable to the use of such subjective descriptions as "reddish-brown" or "yellowish-gray." The charts are contained in a loose-leaf notebook with pages of hundreds of standardized color chips, each perforated with a hole through which the color of the soil or other material can be compared with the standard sample. (*syn.* Munsell Color Chart)

Münsingen-Rain: Iron Age cemetery near Berne, Switzerland, with more than 200 graves of the early and middle La Tène periods (to c. 200 BC). The graves are scattered along a ridge, and the cemetery has a horizontal stratigraphy with the oldest tombs at the north and the more recent ones at the southern end. Grave goods include swords, spears, fibulae, and a necklace of amber beads.

Munyama Cave: A cave on Buvuma Island in Lake Victoria, Uganda, with a backed microlith industry extending back to c. 15,000 BC. Small backed bladelets were the most common implements, with end scrapers and some geometrical backed microliths. Backed microlith industries of comparable antiquity are known in east Africa at Nasera, Lukenya Hill, and Matupi.

Muqdam, Tell el-: Large settlement site in the central Nile Delta, Egypt, which was probably the center of the 23rd Dynasty (818–715 BC). The site is still dominated by the remains of the temple to the local lion god Mihos. (*syn.* ancient Taremu; Leontopolis)

mural: A work of art on a wall or ceiling surface.

mural tomb: Mounded tombs of East Asia, which have painted frescoes on the walls of the interior stone chamber. These tombs are associated with Koguryo, but also occur in China and Japan. The murals are genre paintings, portraits, and directional deities of the Chinese tradition.

murex: A mainly tropical marine snails of the family Muricidae (subclass Prosobranchia of the class Gastropoda); the elongated or heavy shell is elaborately spined or frilled. Found in the Mediterranean, the seashell provided the purple dye for which the Phoenicians were famous (royal Tyrian purple). It also was used on the painted pottery of the Minoans.

Mureybet: A site in the curve of the Euphrates 80 kilometers east of Aleppo in Syria, occupied in the late-Epipalaeolithic (Natufian) and Aceramic Neolithic (to PPNB), from c. 8500–6800 BC. The Natufian level had a date of 8640 ± 140 BC. Einkorn was the staple of the villagers' diet, possibly cultivated. It is an important site for understanding the emergence of food production and village life on the middle Euphrates. (*syn.* Mureybit, Mureybat)

murus gallicus: A type of rampart used in Europe during the La Tène Iron Age; coined by Julius Caesar to describe the defenses of the Celtic *oppidum* of Avaricum (Bourges). The ramparts were made of earth and stone with horizontal timber lacing and held together with iron nails. The spaces of the beams were filled by stone walling. It was often used at great Iron Age hill forts of Europe during prehistory.

Muryong: Early 6th century AD king of Paekche (reigned 501–523) with a mounded tomb in Kongju, Korea. Bricks with molded decoration were used to build the chamber. Burial goods found include a bronze chopstick, spoon set; toiletry items, glass sculptures, and a plaque identifying the king.

Musang Cave: Cave in northern Luzon, the Philippines, with an early flake industry c. 12,000–9000 BC. There is also a Neolithic assemblage dated to c. 3500 BC (or later).

Musawwarat es-Sufra: Meroitic site in Upper Nubia with a colonnaded temple, complex of monumental stone buildings, and elephant pens.

Muselievo: Palaeolithic site on the Osm River near its confluence with the Danube in Bulgaria. Artifacts include bifacial foliates and side scrapers; the layer is estimated to date to the early cold maximum of the last glacial.

Musengezi: Late Iron Age group of the Luangwa Tradition, 13th century AD, known from burial caves in northern Zimbabwe.

museum: An institution that collects, studies, exhibits, and conserves objects for cultural and educational purposes; literally, a temple (or seat) of the muses. The term was first applied to an establishment founded by Ptolemy I, called Soter, at Alexandria in Egypt, in the late 3rd century BC.

muskenum: One of the three classes of people in Hammurabi's Code, probably a servant of the state; the other two were *awilum* and *wardum*. The muskenum were, under King Hammurabi at least, persons employed by the palace who could be given land to work without receiving it as property. The classes awilum and muskenum are not mutually exclusive: a man in high palace office could fairly easily purchase land as private property, whereas the free citizen who got into debt as a result of a bad harvest or some other misfortune could become part of the servant class.

Mushroom Rock: Painted sandstone shelter in Cape York, Australia, first occupied in the Late Pleistocene. There is the earlier Australian Core Tool and Scraper tradition and the later Australian Small Tool tradition.

Musingen: A cemetery of the Early and Middle La Tène Iron Age in Berne, Switzerland. The more than 200 graves were commonly lined with stone and contained coffins. The typology of the grave goods, especially the brooches, has provided the basis for the detailed subdivision of the La Tène period in this area.

Mut: In Egyptian religion, a sky goddess and great divine mother. Mut may have originated either in the Nile River delta or in Middle Egypt. During the 18th Dynasty (1539–1292 BC), she became the companion of the god Amon at Thebes, forming the theban triad with him and Khons, who was said to be Mut's son. The name Mut means "mother," and her role was that of an older woman among the gods. She was associated with the uraeus (rearing cobra), lionesses, and royal crowns. She was also identified with other goddesses, mainly Bastet and Sekhmet. At Thebes, the principal festival of Mut was her "navigation" on the distinctive horseshoe-shaped lake, or Isheru, that surrounded her temple complex at Karnak. Mut was usually represented as a woman wearing the double crown (of Upper and Lower Egypt) typically worn by the king and by the god Atum. She was also occasionally depicted with the head of a lioness.

mutationes: Roman horse-changing stations between rest houses. A supply of post horses was kept to replace tired animals. There was also a taberna to refresh the tired traveler. (*syn.* mutatio)

mutisalah: Small opaque reddish glass bead used in the late 1st millennium BC at maritime southeast Asia sites. It was probably made in southern India.

mutule: Projecting flat slab under the cornice in Classical structures of the Doric order.

Mwanganda: An elephant butchery site in northern Malawi, undated, but containing scrapers and core axes. The site is of interest as preserving in situ the debris of a single, clearly defined, activity. It has been attributed to the Lupemban industry.

Mycenae: The chief city of the Mycenaeans of Bronze Age Greece, overlooking the plain of Argos (Argolid) in the eastern Peloponnese. Inhabited in the Early Helladic period, 2500–1900 BC, it was taken over c. 1900 BC by Greek-speaking invaders. After existing as a minor Middle Helladic site, it rose to prominence by the 15th century BC. In the Late Helladic, c. 1400–1250 BC, it was surrounded by massive walls of cyclopean masonry and entered by the monumental Lion Gate. Little remains of the palace on the acropolis, although some houses lower on the slope have survived. Just inside the gate was the Shaft Grave Circle A, with six tombs yielding a great treasure of metalwork of high quality and artistic skill—weapons, drinking vessels, jewelry, face masks—and pottery dating to the 16th century BC. Stelae, carved with chariots, hunting scenes, and spirals in relief stood over the graves. A second shaft grave circle was found outside the city, slightly earlier in date and less rich. Later members of the royal family were buried in the nine great tholos tombs, which include the magnificent Treasury of Atreus. The city escaped the disasters of the 13th century better than others, but Mycenae fell in c. 1200 BC, attributed to the Dorians. Mycenae is famous in Homer as the home of Agamemnon, leader of Greek heroes at Troy. It emerged from the Dark Ages as a minor town.

Mycenaeans: Inhabitants of Mycenae, the civilization of

late Bronze Age Greece, set in the Argolid. Their name for themselves was Achaeans, and their achievements were remembered in the legends of the classical Greeks. Their forebears probably arrived in Greece around 2000 BC, bringing Minyan ware and an Indo-European language with them. Mycenaean civilization arose in the 16th century BC by the sudden influx of many features of material culture from the Minoans. Later traditions speak of the arrival of new rulers from the east. By c. 1450 BC, the Mycenaeans were powerful enough to take over both Knossos and the profitable trade across the east Mediterranean, especially in Cypriote copper. Trade was extended also to the central Mediterranean and continental Europe, where Baltic amber was one of the commodities sought. The peak of their power lasted only a century and a half until natural and unnatural disaster struck. The Trojan War at the end of the 13th century points to unrest east of the Aegean. There is evidence of increasing depopulation of southern Greece about the same time, paving the way for invasion by the Dorians. At home, the Mycenaeans dwelt in strongly walled citadels containing palaces of the megaron type, exemplified at Mycenae, Tiryns, Thebes, and Pylos. To these were added the more Minoan features—frescoes, painted pottery, skillfully carved seals, artistic metalwork, clay tablets. Their writing, Linear B, was an adaptation of the Minoan script, presumably first made by the mainlanders who had occupied Knossos, for the writing of their own, Greek, language. (Linear B was deciphered by Michael Ventris.) The Mycenaeans contributed greatly to the economy and technology of Late Bronze Age Europe and to the population of the east Mediterranean coasts after the Egyptian defeat of the Peoples of the Sea, and they also left a legacy in their language and literature to their descendants in Greece. The civilization collapsed in c. 1200 BC. (*syn.* Mycenaean)

Mykerinus (fl. late 26th century BC) or Menkaure: Egyptian king of the 4th Dynasty (Old Kingdom) and builder of the third, and smallest, pyramid at Giza. He was the fifth or sixth king of the dynasty (c. 2575–2465 BC), the son of Khafre (2558–2532 BC) and grandson of Khufu (2589–2566 BC), the builders of the two other pyramids at the site. In the funerary complex were found some of the finest sculptures of the Pyramid Age, including a slate statue group of Menkaure and his sister-wife Khamerernebti II. (*syn.* Menkaura, Mycerinus, Menkure)

Mylasa: A town in Asia Minor possibly founded by Mausolus, ruler of Caria (377–353 BC). Hellenistic and Roman site with Corinthian-style temple of Zeus, temple of Augustus and Rome, and ceremonial arch. (*syn.* Milas)

Mylonas, George (1898–1988): Greek archaeologist who excavated at Ayios Kosmas, Eleusis, Mycenae, and Olynthus.

Myrina: City on the western coast of Turkey with Hellenistic cemeteries containing hundreds of terra-cotta figurines.

Myrtos: An Early Minoan settlement in southern Crete, occupied c. 2600–2200 BC. It was a village of irregularly grouped buildings on a sloping hillside. There is evidence of relatively complex economic organization, attested by seals and sealings and by evidence of craft specialization. The economy may have been based in part on cultivation of the olive. A Neopalatial country house, built c. 1550 BC, was destroyed by fire c. 1450 BC.

Myrtou-Pigadhes: Site of a Late Cypriot settlement and sanctuary in northern Cyprus, built c. 1400 BC. The sanctuary was used until c. 1175 BC and contained an ashlar altar with horns of consecration.

Nn

Nabataean: A rich merchant Semitic people who established a kingdom south and east of Edom—ancient Midian—on a trade route from the Red Sea to the Mediterranean, by the 6th century BC. The Nabataeans infiltrated Edom and forced the Edomites into southern Palestine. They made Petra (in Jordan) their capital in c. 312 BC, but they also controlled Bosra and Damascus at the height of their power. The city prospered as the center of the spice trade. The Khirbet Tannur temple, the Wadi Rum temple, watchtowers, and an elaborate hydraulic network are attributed to them. During 64–63 BCE, the kingdom of Nabataea was conquered by the Romans under Pompey, who restored the Hellenistic cities destroyed by the Jews and set up the Decapolis. The country remained independent but paid imperial taxes. The kingdom was annexed by the Romans in AD 106 as "Provincia Arabia Petraea" (Palaestina Tertia).

Nabonidus (d. 538 BC): The king of Babylonia from 556–539 BC, when Babylon fell to Cyrus, king of Persia. After a popular rising led by the priests of Marduk, chief god of the city, Nabonidus, who favored the moon god Sin, made his son Belshazzar co-regent and spent much of his reign in Arabia. Returning to Babylon in 539 BC, he was captured by Cyrus' general Gobryas and exiled. He was the last king of the Neo-Babylonian Empire and is often considered to be the first archaeologist because he searched the ruined temples of ancient Babylon to answer questions about the remote past. (*syn.* Nabu-na'id)

Nabta Playa: A low-lying lake basin near the Egypt/Sudan border in the desert west of the Nile. Extensive scattered prehistoric occupation is attested from c. 8100 bp, with assemblages of wild plant foods and ceramics. Settlement later concentrated in larger sites adjacent to the lake-shore. Pottery and concave-based arrowheads show affinities to those from Early Khartoum and the Fayyum, respectively. Cattle, probably domestic, were in the faunal remains. Sheep and goats were present by 6700 bp. Seeds were well preserved and include two kinds of barley, doum palm, date palm, possible sorghum, and several weed species indicative of the presence of cultivation. The degree of continuity from earlier times illustrated by this Neolithic phase is noteworthy, as is the early documentation of food production. A large aggregation site of 7000–6000 BP has associated megaliths.

Nachikufan: Backed microlith industries of northern Zambia of the Later Stone Age, named after Nachikufu Cave. The complex, once regarded as a single local tradition (Nachikufan Industrial Complex), was of long duration and divided into three successive phases. The first phase, Nachikufan I, is now seen as a widespread industry, characterized by the presence of large numbers of small pointed backed bladelets, of early date; it extends back as early as c. 20,000 BP at such sites as Kalemba and Leopard's Hill, until 12,000 BP. There were also various scrapers and examples of bored stones. The later phases are more restricted geographically and form part of a general continuum of variation among the backed-microlith industries of south-central Africa during the last 7–8 millennia BC.

Nag el-Deir: Cemetery site in northern Upper Egypt situated on the east bank of the Nile south of Akhmim and spanning the Predynastic period to the Middle Kingdom (c. 4000–1650 BC). (*syn.* Naga-el-Der)

Nagyrév: The type site for a regional group of the Hungarian Early Bronze Age; the initial culture in the tripartite sequence distributed in the lowlands of northern Hungary, dated to c. 2300–1500 BC. This first phase shows connections with the Beaker and Vucedol cultures, while the later phase is contemporary with early Unetice. The Nagyrév precedes the Hatvan and Füzesabony. Most known settlement sites are tells surrounded by enclosing banks and ditches. Timber-framed houses are common, although some clay houses are found at Tószeg. Rich grave goods are rare, occurring predominantly in the Budapest area. A universal pottery form is the one- or two-handled cup with tall funnel neck in black burnished ware.

Nahal Mishmar: Site in Palestine in a cave on the Judean desert, containing 630 Chalcolithic copper ritual objects from the Ghassulian culture, including 240 mace heads, 80 scepters, and 10 crowns. They have incised and solid decorative elements.

Nahal Oren: Cave and open terrace site on the western slope of Mount Carmel, Israel, occupied from the early Upper Palaeolithic (Kebaran, c. 16,300–13,850 BC) to the early Aceramic Neolithic (PPNA) and PPNB (Pre-Pottery Neolithic B). Natufian levels show a strong bias toward the selective hunting, or possibly herding, of gazelle, and this continued through the PPNA levels. There was a growing assemblage of processing tools such as mortars, suggesting that plant gathering was becoming more important. The material culture included chipped stone tools, ground stone tools, bone tools, stone vessels, and art objects. Natufian and PPNA buildings were roundhouses with central fireplaces. In the PPNB, there were rectangular houses with paved floors; these were sited on the artificial terrace outside the cave, constructed in the Natufian phase. A cemetery of early Natufian date is associated with the site: Bodies were buried individually, usually tightly flexed with knees drawn up to the chin; old mortars were used as grave markers. Grave goods include carved stone and bone work; the most notable example was a gazelle's head.

Nahua: The tribal population of Central Mexico, originating from the north. The last and best known were the Aztecs. The language of the Aztecs, Nahua, is spoken by all the Nahua peoples in a variety of dialects.

Náhuatl: A Uto-Aztecan language; the language spoken by the Aztecs and many other Mexican tribes. Related languages are distributed sporadically from the northwestern United States to Panama. Still widely spoken in the Basin of Mexico, it is the source of a number of words current in the English language, such as tomato and chocolate. It is also the source of the widely used New World term for spear thrower, atlatl. Groups speaking Nahuatl migrated into Mesoamerica from its northern frontier, Gran Chichimec.

naiskos: A small Greek temple or shrine.

Naj Tunich: Cave in southeastern Guatemala with Maya cave art of the 8th century AD. There are 100 paintings and some petroglyphs, mostly hieroglyphic texts and human figures.

Nakamine: Palaeolithic site in Miyagi Prefecture, Japan, with stone tools between layers dated to 300,000–150,000 bp, possibly an Early Palaeolithic occupation of the islands.

Nakbe: Urban center of the Maya in the dense tropical forest of northern Guatemala, 13 kilometers away from El Mirador,

to which it was joined by a causeway. It was one of the earliest ceremonial centers of the Maya. There are two main clusters of platforms and mounds, including a 50-meter-high pyramid. Thought to have been typical of the architecture of the period known as the Late Formative, or Late Pre-Classic (300 BC–AD 100), the huge stone pyramids, temples, and other relatively tall buildings characteristic of the construction at Nakbe have been carbon dated to 600–400 BC (corresponding to the Middle Formative). Although remains have been unearthed from almost every period of Mayan culture at Nakbe, it was not important after the beginning of the Late Formative period.

Nakhon Pathom: Large protohistoric and early historic site in the lower Chao Phraya valley of central Thailand. It is thought to have been the capital of the state of Dvaravati for a while. According to local tradition, it is the oldest city in Thailand—said to be more than 2,000 years old—and was visited by the Buddha. Artifacts have been found there dating from the 6th century AD. Phra Pathom, the highest stupa in Thailand, rises to 380 feet (116 m).

Nakhon Si Thammarat: Walled town of Nakhon Si Thammarat, one of Thailand's oldest cities, which lies near the coast of the Gulf of Thailand. Founded more than 1,000 years ago, it was the capital of a powerful state that controlled the middle portion of the peninsula; it was often called Ligor until the early 20th century. (*syn.* Ligor)

Nal: A cultural group named after the site of Sohr Damb (Red Mound), near the village of Nal in central Baluchistan, Pakistan. It is related to the Kulli culture further south and is dated to the first half of the 3rd millennium BC. Both settlements are associated with water-control systems, which allowed exploitation of alluvial plains for agriculture. The Chalcolithic population used copper for many tools and weapons, as well as ground stone. They made beads from agate and perhaps also lapis lazuli. The fine buff pottery, some wheelmade, is decorated with geometric patterns in black paint; red, blue, green, and yellow pigments were often applied after firing. Some traits in the pottery, a glazed steatite seal, and many faience beads point to contact with the Indus civilization. Many burials were excavated on the type site, belonging to a period later than the settlement. The rite employed was fractional burial, the graves containing fragmentary skeletons together with quantities of distinctive pottery.

Namazga-depe: Large Chalcolithic and Bronze Age settlement in southern Turkmenia (western Central Asia) on the north slope of Kopet Dagh. The Namazga phases I–III are assigned to the Chalcolithic period, while Namazga IV and V belong to the Bronze Age—the Eneolithic (c. 4800–3000 BC) and Bronze Age (c. 3000–1500 BC); the sequence covers Anau IA Neolithic to the beginning of the Iron Age. The site was urban in character with a high population concentration and separate artisans' quarters, producing evidence of specialist production of bronze, gold, and silver goods, and wheelmade, kiln-fired pottery. The "proto-civilization" of southern Turkmenia in the later 3rd millennium BC was characterized by two large towns—Namazga-depe and Altin-Depe—and a number of smaller settlements such as Ulug-depe. Other features include a wide-ranging trade network and an incipient writing system with repetitive symbols incised on flat clay figurines. This civilization never reached the levels achieved by the fully fledged civilizations of Mesopotamia, Egypt, and the Indus Valley. There was a marked decline in the early 2nd millennium BC, possibly owing to environmental changes, and a collapse in its final "tower" phase in the late 3rd or early 2nd millennium BC. Altin-depe was abandoned while Namazga-depe survived only as a small village.

Nam-Viet: An ancient kingdom that made up the southern Chinese provinces Kwangtung and Kwangsi and northern Vietnam and came into being in 207 BC, when a Chinese official declared himself king of the southern province of Nan Hai. To that he added the conquered kingdom of Au-Lac; its capital was near present Canton. The expansion of the Han empire put an end to the existence of Nam-Viet in 111 BC. (*syn.* Nam Viet, Nan Yue)

Nana Mode: An Iron Age village site in the Central African Republic, dated to about the 7th century AD. Excavations have revealed pottery decorated by a carved wooden toothed wheel or disk. It has been suggested that this type of pottery may have been made by speakers of an Ubangian language.

Nan Madol: Town and ceremonial center built in a shallow tidal lagoon off the shore of Ponape in the Caroline Islands; it is the largest single complex of ancient stonework in Oceania, making up about 70 hectares with 92 rectilinear basalt and coral platforms. The most famous structure is the burial platform of Nan Douwas, which contains four pit tombs with prismatic basalt enclosure walls up to 8.5 meters high. The whole complex is traditionally associated with the Sau Deleur rulers of Ponape and was presumably constructed several centuries ago.

Nanna: The Sumerian moon god; also known as the Akkadian/Semitic Sin. With his consort Ningal, he was the patron deity of Ur, where his temple and ziggurat were built. Nanna was intimately connected with the cattle herds that were the livelihood of the people in the marshes of the lower Euphrates River, where the cult developed. (*syn.* Akkadian Sin)

naology: The study and science of temples.

naos: A shrine, usually monolithic, in which the image of an Egyptian deity was kept, especially in temple sanctuaries. A small wooden naos was normally placed inside a monolithic one in hard stone; the latter are typical of the Late Period and are sometimes elaborately decorated. The largest naoi are those where a temple's main cult statue was kept, in the sanctuary. A naos generally took the form of a rectangular chest or box hewn from a single block of wood or stone and could also be used as a container for a funerary statue or mummified animal. Egyptian naophorous statues portrayed the subject holding a shrine, sometimes containing a divine image. The term is also used for the interior apartment of a Greek temple (a Greek temple placed in a temenos) or the cella of the Roman temple. In Classical architecture, it is the body of a temple (as distinct from the portico) in which the image of the deity is housed. In early Greek and Roman architecture, it was a simple room, usually rectangular, with the entrance at one end and with the side walls often being extended to form a porch. In larger temples, where the cella is open to the sky, a small temple was sometimes placed within. In the Byzantine architectural tradition, the naos was preserved as the area of a centrally planned church, including the core and the sanctuary, where the liturgy is performed. (*syn.* temple sanctuary; naoi = plural)

Napata: District of Upper Nubia on the Dongola reach of the Nile, southwest of the fourth cataract, which has given its name to the Napatan period. The district includes the sites of Kurru, Gebel Barkal, Nuri, and Sanam. Napata was settled in the mid-15th century BC as a southern outpost of the Egyptian Empire, the seat of a kingdom (called Kush by the Egyptians) to which it gives its name. It flourished from the late 9th–early 3rd centuries BC. Napata's main feature, the hill of Barkol, was regarded from the Egyptian New Kingdom (1521–1075 BC) as a holy mountain, the seat of the god Amon; under it lie the ruins of several temples. A stela of Thutmose III (reigned 1479–1425), on which a fort is mentioned, has been found there, and Amenhotep II (reigned c. 1426–1400 BC) sent an Asian prisoner to be hanged on its walls.

Naples: Naples was founded about 600 BC as Neapolis ("New City") by Greek settlers, close to the more ancient Palaepolis. Both towns were extensions of Greek colonies on the nearby island of Pithecusa (now Ischia) and at Cumae on the adjacent mainland. The principal Greek city of Campania, southern Italy, it was of only modest size and importance during the Roman period. Earlier occupation of this fertile location, framed an one edge by Mount Vesuvius and by the sulphurous plains of the "Phlegraean Fields" on the other, is extremely likely. It was taken over by the Romans in 326 BC. Among the traces that still survive of the Greco-Roman city, stretches of Greek city walling have been identified in several areas and a portion of 7th–6th century BC necropolis located in the Pizzofalcone region. A 700-meter tunnel on the Via Puteolana, joining Naples and Puteoli, was originally constructed by Augustus' architect, Cocceius. Under the Empire, Naples and its environs served as a center of Greek culture and erudition and as a pleasure resort for a succession of emperors and wealthy Romans, whose coastal villas extended from Misenum on the Gulf of Pozzuoli (the ancient Puteoli) to the Sorrentine peninsula. The Museo Archeologico Nazionale contains an extensive collection of Campanian antiquities and much material from Pompeii and Herculaneum. (*syn.* Neapolis)

Naqada: A site in Upper Egypt, which produced the first evidence of the Neolithic in Egypt and provided the framework for the Predynastic sequence of the area. Its large Predynastic cemetery yielded some 2,000 burials of the Amratian and Gerzean periods. Naqada I was the Predynastic culture of ancient Egypt, and Naqada II had new features accounted for by direct imports and by increasing cultural contact with the rest of the Near East, particularly Mesopotamia. (*syn.* ancient Nubt, Ombos; Nagada)

Naram-sin: Akkadian king who reigned c. 2254–2218 BC, the grandson of Sargon and the last great ruler of the Akkadian Empire.

Nara period: A period in Japanese history, AD 710–794, named after the new capital of Nara (or Heijo as it was then known), to which the court moved from Fujiwara. The capital was established there to secure greater centralized power. The palace buildings—the *dairi* (the Imperial living quarters), buildings for ritual, and governmental buildings for administrative business—were arranged in a plan imitating that of the T'ang capital of Ch'ang-an. No palace building is in existence now; but the lecture hall (*Kodo*) of the Toshodai Temple in Nara, believed to have originally been the Chosuden (for court officials' important ceremonies) of the Heijo Palace, is suggestive of palace architecture of the time.

Narce: A settlement site on the Treia gorge near Calcata in Lazio, Italy, surrounded by an extensive necropolis, and probably inhabited from the 12th century BC. Occupation was mainly by Faliscans, an Indo-European Italic group, and it is therefore associated with their centers at Falerii and Capena. The town prospered under Etruscan domination in the 7th and 6th centuries BC. Material evidence seems in general to follow a local (Faliscan) cultural sequence. Evidence survives for fortification walls, pit and trench burials, and chamber tombs with monumental doorways. Occupation continued to the 4th–3rd centuries BC.

Narmer (c. 3100 BC): One of the first pharaohs of Egypt, perhaps to be equated with Menes who founded the 1st Dynasty c. 3200 BC and mythical founder of Memphis (and united Egypt). He ruled in Upper Egypt in the late Pre-Dynastic Period and is best known from the "Main Deposit" of ritual objects at Hierakonpolis. The most important record

of him, indeed one of the first from Egypt, is a slate palette on which he is shown in the White Crown of Upper Egypt conquering his enemies on one side, and in the Red Crown of Lower Egypt reconstructing the land on the other. The Narmer Palette is in the Egyptian Museum at Cairo. Narmer is thought to have been buried in Tomb B17–18 in the Umm el-Qa'ab royal cemetery at Abydos. (*syn.* Menes)

Narosura: Important Pastoral Neolithic settlement site near Narok in southern Kenya, occupied between the 9th–5th centuries BC. Postholes suggest the presence of semipermanent structures of some kind, and the site appears to have covered an area of at least 8,000 square meters. A backed microlith industry in obsidian was accompanied by ground stone axes, burins, stone bowls, and pottery with comb-stamped and incised decoration of a type also found on many other Pastoral Neolithic sites and known as Narosura ware. The animal bones recovered were of mainly domestic species; there is no conclusive evidence for the practice of agriculture.

Narva: A Neolithic culture and its type site in the eastern Baltic coast region (Estonia, Latvia, Lithuania; parts of Poland, Belarus) and dated to the 4th–3rd millennia BC. Similar in type to the ancestral Kunda culture, the Narva economy was based on hunting and fishing, with more tools of bone and antler than stone. Simple pointed-based pottery (with straight or S-profiles) and oval bowls was made. Important sites are Osa, Sarnate, Sventoji, and Narva-town. (*syn.* Narva culture)

Nasbeh, Tell en-: A site near Jerusalem, occupied throughout the Iron Age. Noteworthy were its massive rubble walls, 4 meters thick, with projecting towers and a very strong gateway. It is the probable site of biblical Mizpah. (*syn.* Tell en-Nasbeh; Tall al-Nasbeh; Tel Mizpe)

Nasca: Major culture of the southern coast of Peru during the Early Intermediate period, c. 200 BC–AD 600, developed out of Paracas. The principal Nasca site is at Cahuachi on the Nasca River, with a great adobe temple atop a mound, some walled courts and large rooms, and a number of smaller constructions. The earliest pottery, of roughly the 2nd century BC, still shows Paracas influence in the iconography and the use of up to 16 colors, but the paint was not put on before firing. Typical Nasca pottery with designs of fish, birds, severed heads, human figures, and demons, shows a long internal development. The final Nasca substyle incorporates patterns taken from the art of Huari, and this contact was soon followed by invasion. Stylistically, the Nasca ceramics have been divided into nine phases. With the expansion of the Huari Empire of the coast around the 7th century AD, Nasca culture came to an end and was replaced by a local version of Huari. To the Nasca period belong some (or all) of the desert markings, the so-called "Nasca lines," made by scraping away the weathered surface of the desert to expose the lighter material beneath. Motifs include lines, geometrical patterns, and a few animal or bird forms. The dead were buried in large cemeteries, mainly near Cahuachi. Nasca survived into the Middle Horizon, when it became fused with the more dominant Huari and Tiahuanaco styles. (*syn.* Nazca)

Nasca lines: In the Peruvian desert or Nasca region of the southern coast, geometric and geomorphic patterns created by the removal of surface stones to reveal the pale earth beneath. The lines were made by clearing the surface of small red/brown stones and exposing the lighter-colored soil underneath. The straight lines radiate to points in small hills and suggest a ceremonial function. The straight lines date to the Early Intermediate as well as to later periods. Maria Reiche, a researcher, believes that the figures represent constellations and the straight lines have astronomical significance. Others believe the lines pointed toward sacred places. The Nasca lines are virtually indecipherable from ground level, but are plainly visible from the air. The lines have been preserved by the extreme dryness of the climate of the region. (*syn.* geoglyphs; Nazca lines)

Nasera: Boulder hill in northern Tanzania with a deep deposit of Middle and Later Stone Age material. (*syn.* Apis Rock)

Nasik: A town in western India, an important religious center attracting thousands of pilgrims annually because of the sanctity of the Godavari River and because of the legend that Rama, the hero of the Ramayana epic, lived there for a time with his wife Sita and his brother Laksmana. Nasik is the site of the Pandu (Buddhist) and Chamar (Jaina) cave temples dating to the 1st century AD.

Natal Early Iron Age: A South African province of Natal, which has traces of the furthest southeastern extension of the Early Iron Age complex of sub-Saharan Africa, which has been linked with the dispersal of peoples speaking Bantu languages. Evidence for Early Iron Age settlement is found in the fertile areas of the lower river valleys and dates from about the 4th century AD. Closely related sites are known from the Transvaal, as at Broederstroom and Lydenburg.

natatio: The swimming pool in a Roman bath complex.

National Register: A federally maintained list of archaeological, architectural, historical, and cultural sites of local, state, or national significance.

nation-state: A political unit consisting of a number of diverse cities and their hinterlands, organized into a single state with a unified set of laws and system of government. The most important type of political system in the modern world is the nation-state. The world today is divided territorially into more than 176 states, in each of which a national government claims to exercise sovereignty and seeks obedience by its citizens.

Native American Grave Protection & Repatriation Act: A 1990 law establishing procedures for protecting and determining disposition of Native America human remains, funerary objects, sacred objects, and objects of cultural patrimony that are intentionally excavated or inadvertently discovered on federal or tribal lands. It also establishes procedures for conducting summaries and inventories and repatriating human remains, funerary objects, sacred objects, and objects of cultural patrimony in museum or federal agency collections. (*syn.* NAGPRA)

Native American: Aboriginal inhabitants of North America, usually recognized in two groupings. The first and larger group, called Native Americans (or American Indians), is further divided geographically into North American, Middle American, and South American Indian peoples. The second group consists of a number of Arctic peoples, most of whom are variously called Eskimos or Inuit, but also including such other groups as Aleuts. (*syn.* Indians)

native copper: Metallic copper found unadulterated in nature, especially in nuggets, which can be worked by hammering, cutting, and annealing.

natron: A naturally occurring salt consisting of sodium carbonate and sodium bicarbonate, found in Egypt and used as a cleansing agent for washing clothes, bodies, and teeth. It was also used as a preservative during mummification and in purification rituals. It was subject to a royal monopoly in the Ptolemaic period (332–30 BC).

Natsushima: An initial Jomon period shell midden near Tokyo, Japan, dated to 7290–7500 BC. The dated layer contained deep conical bowls with cord marks, bones of domestic dogs, bone and stone arrowheads, grinding stones, partially ground pebble axes, bone fishhooks, and eyed needles.

Natufian: The final Epipalaeolithic (Mesolithic) culture complex of the Levant, dated to c. 12,500–10,000 BP, with its type site at Wadi an-Natuf in Palestine. Hunting and gathering were still the basis of subsistence, but some Natufian communities had adopted a settled mode of life, and the period saw the development of cereal grain exploitation. They built first permanent village settlements in pre-agricultural times in Palestine (Mallaha) and on the middle Euphrates in Syria (Mureybet, Abu Hureyra). A series of burials was excavated at Mount Carmel; one important site is Wad Cave with a large cemetery, querns, sickles. The shrine at the base of the tell at Jericho was built during the Early Natufian phase, and the descendants of the Natufians built the earliest Neolithic town at the site. The characteristic tool kit includes geometric microliths, sickles, pestles, mortars, fishing gear, and ornaments of bone and shell. Generally, Natufian sites demonstrate greater diversity in economy and more permanent settlement than earlier cultures.

natural levee: Elongate narrow ridges that form adjacent to channels when the largest particles of the suspended load are deposited as soon as the river leaves the confines of its channel. It is a depositional land form, which is created as channels overflow their banks.

natural levels: Excavation units corresponding to levels defined by stratigraphy, as opposed to arbitrary levels.

natural secondary context: A secondary context resulting from natural transformational processes such as erosion or animal or plant activity.

natural selection: The mechanism that leads to differential survival and reproduction of those individuals suited to a given environment in contrast to others less well adapted. It is the process that results in the adaptation of an organism to its environment by means of selectively reproducing changes in its genotype or genetic constitution. Natural selection enhances the preservation of a group of organisms that are best adjusted to the physical and biological conditions of their environment and may also result in their improvement in some cases.

natural transformations: Changes in the archaeological record resulting from natural phenomena that occur after the artifacts are deposited in the ground.

natural type: An archaeological type coinciding with an actual category recognized by the original toolmaker.

Naukratis: An ancient Greek town in the Nile River delta, on the Canopic (western) branch of the river. An emporion ("trading station") with exclusive trading rights in Egypt, Naukratis was the center of cultural relations and trade between Greece and Egypt in the pre-Hellenistic period. It was established by Milesians in the 7th century BC and flourished throughout the classical period. There was a shared administrative building called the Helleneion. It declined after Alexander's conquest of Egypt and the foundation of Alexandria (332 BC). There is evidence for the minting of silver and bronze coins and for the existence of a new building program under the early Ptolemies. By Roman imperial times, the site may have been abandoned. Dedications to deities and Greek pottery have thrown light on the early history of the Greek alphabet and the commercial activity of various Greek states, especially in the 6th century BC. It was mentioned by Herodotus as the chief point of contact between Egypt and Greece until the Hellenistic period and rise of Alexandria. (*syn.* Kom Gi'eif, Naucratis)

Navajo: Athabascan language group people of the U.S. Southwest. Their intrusion from northwestern subarctic areas of Canada, AD c. 900–1200, helped bring about the abandonment of Pueblos in the Anasazi subarea. They were probably aided by groups of Apache Indians, also Athabascans, moving into the Southwest at that time. The Navajo speak an Apachean language, which, like the language of their Apache cousins, is classified in the Athabascan family.

Navan: Iron Age royal residence in County Meath, Ireland, with a roundhouse and stockage occupied c. 700–100 BC. In c. 100 BC, a large circular timber building with banked and ditched enclosure was built. It was later burned and covered by a monumental cairn. The Iron Age occupation is identified with Emhain Macha, ancient royal seat of Ulaid, and the Irish king Tuathal. (*syn.* Teltown Hill)

Navdatoli: Important prehistoric site on the Narbada River of central India, made up of four separate mounds, with Lower and Middle Palaeolithic, Chalcolithic, Iron Age, and medieval occupations. The Chalcolithic, dated to the 2nd millennium BC, had four phases with a pointed black-and-red ware and black-painted cream slip ware in the first phase, then Jorwe ware, and finally painted Malwa ware. Its rectangular houses were of timber and bamboo, with lime-coated clay or dung floors. Simple copper and microlithic stone industries were employed. Only wheat was recorded from the lowest level, but from the second phase rice was also known. The site was abandoned in the 1st millennium AD, and its role as a trading center was assumed by Maheshwar on the opposite side of the river.

nave: The central and principal part of a Christian church. It extended from the entrance (the narthex) to the transepts (transverse aisle crossing the nave in front of the sanctuary in a cruciform church) or, in the absence of transepts, to the chancel (area around the altar). More simply, the middle part or body of a church between the aisles, extending from the choir to the principal entrance.

naveta: A type of megalithic chamber tomb shaped like an upturned boat with rounded prow and squared stern, peculiar to the island of Minorca and dating to the earlier part of the Bronze Age c. 2200–1500 BC. Navetas found on the Balearic Islands date from c. 1500–800 BC. Each had an elongated U-shaped plan, a vault roofed by corbelling, and a flat or slightly concave façade. The gallery-shaped burial chamber is approached by a corridor through the thickness of the wall, and there is occasionally a porthole slab partially blocking it. The best preserved example is Els Tudons.

Naville, Henri Edouard (1844–1926): Swiss Egyptologist who worked at Abydos, Deir el-Bahri, and in the Delta at Bubastis.

Náxos (Greece): The largest of the Greek Cyclades Islands in the Aegean Sea and an important center for the so-called Cycladic culture of the Aegean Early Bronze Age, late 4th–2nd millennia BC. Mycenaean, Protogeometric, and Geometric periods are also well represented. In the period of classical Greece, Naxos had a relatively insignificant political history, and is better known for its wines and as a center of worship of the god Dionysus. Náxos marble was used for the sculpture of monumental figures, and the island also supplied the emery with which to polish the marble. The Cycladic period has left numerous graves and examples of the characteristic Cycladic idols. An isolated marble door frame on the Palatia hill is the cella door of a 6th-century BC temple, while near Sangri lies the site of a square temple. For the ancient quarries, there is no lack of evidence, particularly for the practice of cutting large statues in situ. There are several unfinished figures, notably a colossal archaic statue, male and with beard—possibly a representation of Dionysius. During the 6th century BC, the tyrant Lygdamis ruled Náxos in alliance with the tyrant Peisistratus of Athens. In 490, the island was captured by the Persians and treated with severity; Náxos deserted Persia in 480, joining the Greeks at the Battle of Salamis and then joining the Delian League. After revolting from the league in 471, Náxos was immediately captured by Athens, which controlled it until 404. In the 8th century, Náxos is said to have combined forces with Chalcis in a colonizing initiative to Sicily, where a colony of the same name was founded. In AD 1207, the Venetians captured Náxos, initiating the duchy of Náxos.

Naxos (Sicily): The earliest Greek colony in Sicily, founded by Chalcidians under Theocles (Thucles) about 734 BC. It lay on the east coast, south of Tauromenium, on what is now Cape Schisò. The adoption of the name of Naxos, after the island in the Aegean Sea, indicates there were Naxians among its founders. It soon founded other colonies at Leontini and Catana. After 461 BC, Naxos was in opposition to Syracuse, allied with Leontini (427) and Athens (415). In 403 BC, it was destroyed by Dionysius I, tyrant of Syracuse, and its territory given to the Sicels. Its Greek exiles at last found refuge in 358 at Tauromenium. Scanty traces of its walls are to be seen; there is evidence in the area for Neolithic huts, Bronze Age settlement, and a sanctuary area assigned to Aphrodite. Pottery is often distinctive in style, with Euboean and Cycladic reminiscences, and a potters' quarter (vicinity of Colle Salluzzo) with kilns, depositories, and antefix molds. Naxos coins (6th–5th centuries BC) carry a bearded Dioynysus with ivy, vine, and grape decoration, while later examples have his companion in revelry, Sinenus, who is also on the local terra-cotta antefixes.

Nderit Drift: Site on the Nderit River south of Lake Nakuru, Kenya, which preserves a long sequence of archaeological deposits that illustrate the precursors of the Pastoral Neolithic complex. A blade industry of the 11th millennium BC is regarded as a probable ancestor of the Eburran (Gambles's Cave).

Nderit ware: First discovered at Stable's Drift on the Nderit River, south of Lake Nakuru in the central Rift Valley of Kenya, Nderit ware is a widespread variety of pottery, which may predate the florescence of the Pastoral Neolithic in the area. It is one of several distinct pottery wares associated with the Pastoral Neolithic in Kenya and northern Tanzania. It is characterized by finely executed, wedge-shaped decoration, apparently made by means of repeated impressions of a pointed object such as obsidian; it is also often deeply scored on the inside surface of the vessel. In northern Kenya, the pottery occurs at least as early as the 3rd millennium BC. Farther to the south, Nderit ware occurs only with other pottery traditions. (*syn.* Gumban A)

Ndondondwane: Early Iron Age village of the mid-8th century AD in central Natal, South Africa. Remains of structures that may have been stockages were accompanied by waste from the making of ivory bangles and pieces of large ceramic sculpture. The site has the earliest date for domesticated chicken in southern Africa.

Neanderthal man: An early form of *Homo sapiens* that inhabited much of Europe and the Mediterranean area during the late Pleistocene Epoch, about 100,000 to 35,000 years ago. Neanderthal remains have also been found in the Middle East, North Africa, and western Central Asia. This type of fossil human is a subspecies of *Homo sapiens* and is distinguished by a low broad braincase, continuous arched brow ridges, projecting occipital region, short limbs, and large joints; his brain was as large as modern man's. His flint work, which in North Africa and Eurasia was of Middle Palaeolithic (Mousterian) type, was technically more advanced than anything that had gone before (scrapers and points), and the careful burial of dead with funerary offerings provides the oldest surviving evidence for religious beliefs. Neanderthals mainly lived in caves. They used fire and hunted small and medium-sized animals (e.g., goats, deer) and scavenged from the kills of large carnivores. The oldest skeletal remains belong to the Riss–Würm Interglacial Period, but Neanderthal man persisted through the earlier stage of the succeeding Würm Glaciation until he was replaced by modern man. This replacement probably took place between 40,000–35,000 BC, but the scarcity of skeletal evidence from the period makes it impossible to give a more precise date. The manner of this replacement is also in doubt. Neanderthal man is sometimes classified as a distinct species of the genus Homo, but has also been considered as falling within the same species as *Homo sapiens*, whose ancestor he may have been. The species is named after its type area in Neanderthal, a valley near Düsseldorf in Germany, where skeletal remains of this type of human were first found in 1856. (*syn.* Neandertal, *Homo neanderthalensis*, *Homo sapiens neanderthalensis*, Neanderthals)

Nea Nikomedeia: An Early Neolithic tell settlement in Macedonia in northern Greece. From a large structure (shrine?) in the center of the mound, there were terra-cotta female figurines thought to have been used in rituals. The remains of rectangular mud houses, a number of crouched burials, and plain and painted pottery, frogs carved from greenstone, flint blades, and many ground stone axes have been found. Radiocarbon dates of c. 6200–5300 BC were obtained. The earliest known domesticated cattle date from about 6000 BC at Nea Nikomedeia, in association with cultivated einkorn, emmer, and barley. (*syn.* Nea Nikomidhia)

nearest-neighbor analysis: A method of analyzing the extent to which two-dimensionally located points are randomly distributed; a measure of the relation between a cluster of points in a pattern based on the expected value and the observed value. The statistic equals observed value divided by expected value. This method of analyzing the degree of dispersion in a distribution pattern was first developed by plant ecologists studying the concentration of certain species. A nearest-neighbor index (usually denoted by the symbol R), is calculated from the ratio of the average observed distance from each point in the pattern to its nearest neighbor, to the average distance expected if the pattern were randomly distributed, which depends solely on the density of the pattern being studied. The index R varies from 0.00 for a totally clustered pattern through 1.00 for a random distribution to a maximum of 2.15 for a completely regularly spaced pattern. The index is influenced by the size of the study area chosen; it is therefore essential to select a relevant framework for the distribution being studied. With any boundary, however, it is possible for the index to be distorted by the "boundary effect" to give a figure closer to the maximum than would be justified; this arises because the nearest neighbors of points near to the boundary may in fact lie beyond the boundary and hence not be properly counted, thus increasing the figure for the observed mean distance. It is also essential that the points in the pattern being analyzed are of the same date and similar function, and that the pattern should be complete. The index R describes only a part of the total pattern and can serve as a useful basis for asking more detailed questions about the factors that underlie the observed pattern. The technique has been useful to archaeologists studying the distribution of sites over a landscape and their relation to one another. (*syn.* nearest-neighbor statistic)

Near Oceania: Those islands of the Pacific Ocean that can be reached by watercraft without going out of sight of land— basically the Indonesian archipelago, the Philippines, New Guinea, and the Solomon Islands.

Nebo: Late Neolithic site of the Butmir culture, near Travinik, central Bosnia, and dating to the early 4th millennium BC. Excavations indicated two occupation phases in the Classic and Late Butmir periods. The large quantities of manufacturing debris on the site may be interpreted as workshop debris from stone and bone tool production.

Nebuchadnezzar II (604–562 BC: The most famous of the kings of Babylon, the second of that name. His father, Nabopolassar, ejected the Assyrians to restore Babylon's independence and to found Chaldaea or the Neo-Babylonian Kingdom in 626 BC. Nebuchadnezzar extended these conquests to the Mediterranean, capturing Jerusalem twice, and on the second occasion, 586 BC, sacking it and deporting its people to exile "by the waters of Babylon." It was under his rule and that of a successor, Nabonidus (556–539 BC), that the civilization of Babylon reached its highest level. Nebuchadnezzar II was a great royal figure and is well known from the Bible accounts of his activities in Judea and Samaria. The Neo-Babylonian Empire did not long survive his death. Nabodinus fought with the Marduk priesthood at Babylon and Cyrus conquered Babylonia in 539 BC, freeing the Jewish captives. (*syn.* Nebuchadrezzar, ancient Nabu-kudurri-usur)

Necho: The name of two rulers of Egypt's 26th Dynasty. Necho I (fl. c. 672–664 BC), was governor of Sais and the first of the Saite pharaohs. Necho's ancestor was probably a prince of Libyan descent of the 24th Egyptian Dynasty. Necho II (Wehemibra) (fl. 6th–7th century BC) was king of Egypt (reigned 610–595 BC), and a member of the 26th Dynasty, who unsuccessfully attempted to aid Assyria against the Neo-Babylonians and later sponsored an expedition that circumnavigated Africa. He was the third Saite pharaoh and successor to Psamtek I. (*syn.* Nekau)

Necker Island: Small barren and isolated island off the western end of the Hawaiian chain, containing a very large number of prehistoric sites (including 33 Heiau; houses, cultivation terraces) for its size. Small stone figures, representative of ancestral Polynesian carving, are among the earliest sculpture from Hawaii. The island may have been visited sporadically from the main Hawaiian islands or it is possible that it had a resident population of Hawaiians who died out, unable to return to their homeland. The island, the most northerly of the chain, was uninhabited on European discovery.

necropolis: A cemetery or burial place, often near a town, the Greek word for "a city of the dead." It refers to Egyptian cemeteries from all periods and includes the Valley of the Kings, Giza, and Saqqara. *Necropolis* normally describes large and important burial areas that were in use for long periods, *cemetery* smaller and more homogeneous sites; cemeteries may also be subdivisions of a necropolis.

Nectanebo: Name employed by the Greek historian Manetho to refer to two Egyptian rulers of the 30th Dynasty (380–343 BC), who actually held two different "birth names": Nakhtnebef (Nectanebo I) and Nakhthorheb (Nectanebo II). Nectanebo I (fl. 4th century BC) was the first king (reigned 380–362 BC) of the 30th Dynasty of Egypt; he successfully opposed an attempt by the Persians to reimpose their rule on

Egypt (373 BC). Nectanebo II (also fl. 4th century BC) was the third and last king (reigned 360–343 BC) of the 30th Dynasty of Egypt; he was the last of the native Egyptian kings.

Nefertari (c. 1300–1250 BC): The principal wife of Rameses II (1279–1213 BC), often depicted at his side for at least the first 20 years of his reign. The smaller temple at Abu Simbel (in Nubia) was dedicated to her and the goddess Hathor. Rameses also built a magnificent tomb for her in the Valley of the Queens (in Thebes). She was probably the only royal wife, apart from Tiy, to be deified in her lifetime.

Nefertem: In ancient Egyptian religion, the youthful god of the lotus blossom, who is represented by the blue lotus (*nymphaea cerulea*) and depicted as a man with a lotus-flower headdress. He also had a warlike aspect and could be depicted as a lion. Nefertem was mentioned in the Pyramid Texts (c. 2350 BC), but he became more prominent during the New Kingdom (1539–c. 1075 BC) and later. (*syn.* Nefertum, Nefertemu)

Nefertiti (c. 1380–1340 BC): The principal wife of the 18th Dynasty ruler Akhenaten (1352–1336 BC) during the "Amarna period" and queen of Egypt. She may also have been daughter of Ay (1327–1323 BC), who later succeeded Tutankhamun (1336–1327 BC) on the throne. She supported her husband's religious revolution and is thought by some to have adhered to the new cult of the sun god Aton even after the king began to compromise with the upholders of the old order. Nefertiti is best known for her portrait bust, found at Tell el-Amarnà (ancient Akhetaton), the king's new capital. She also appears prominently at her husband's side in reliefs found at Tell el-Amarnà. Nefertiti had six daughters, two of whom became queens of Egypt. In the 12th year of Akhenaton's reign, or possibly later, Nefertiti either retired after losing favor with the king or, less likely, died. Objects belonging to her have been found at the northern palace in Amarnà, suggesting that she may have retired there. However, some scholars associate her with the monarch named Smenkhare who briefly succeeded Akhenaten. (*syn.* Nefertiit, Nofretete)

negative bulb of percussion: A small depression on a core below the striking platform, produced by the force that detached a flake.

negative feedback: In systems thinking, a process that acts to counter or "dampen" the potentially disruptive effects of external inputs, acting as a stabilizing mechanism. In other words, a response to a system that lessens the chance of change.

negative painting: A technique of pottery decoration used in many parts of the Americas in which a design area is covered with a paint-resistant substance (wax, gum, clay) and then dipped in paint or dye, dried, and fired. The pot might be either smoked or dipped into a black wash. The dark coating is unable to reach those areas of the surface protected by the resistant substance, and when the resistant substance is removed, the pattern stands out in the original color against the black background. (*syn.* resist dyeing; resist-dye)

Neith: Ancient Egyptian goddess who was the patroness of the city of Sais in the Nile River delta. Neith was worshiped as early as Predynastic times (c. 3000 BC), and several queens of the 1st Dynasty (c. 2925–2775 BC) were named after her. She also became an important goddess in the capital city of Memphis. Her principal emblem was a pair of crossed arrows shown against the background of a leather shield. Another emblem was a bow case, which the goddess was sometimes depicted wearing on her head in place of a crown. She was usually depicted as a woman wearing the red crown associated with Lower Egypt, holding crossed arrows and a bow. In mythology, she was the mother of the crocodile god Sebek, and later of Re. The worship of Neith was prominent in the 26th Dynasty (664–525 BC), when Egypt's capital was located at Sais. She is associated with funerary rituals and war. (*syn.* Neit)

Nekhbet: In Egyptian religion, vulture goddess who was the protector of Upper Egypt and especially its rulers. Nekhbet was portrayed as spreading her wings over the pharaoh while grasping in her claw the cartouche symbol or other emblems. She also appeared as a woman, often with a vulture's head, wearing a white crown. Nekhbet's cult was at al-Kab (Eileithyiaspolis), but she was also the goddess of Hierakonpolis (Nekhen), the ancient town opposite al-Kab, on the west bank of the Nile River.

Nelson, Nels (1875–1964): American archaeologist born in Denmark, who had a profound effect on 20th-century North American archaeology. Working primarily in the Southwest, Nelson is best known for his contributions to the stratigraphic method of excavation, especially in his work in the Galisteo Basin of New Mexico.

Nelson Bay: Cave on the Robberg Peninsula in southern Cape Province, South Africa, with a Middle Stone Age layer and Later Stone Age industries.

Nemi, Lake: Site in the Alban Hills, near Rome, Italy, where the remains of two ships belonging to the emperor Caligula were found. These two Roman galleys rested on the lake bottom on the west side and were raided continually, with the ships finally raised in the 1920s. They were pleasure ships of the period of the emperor Caligula, one measuring 210 by 66 ft, the other 233 by 80 ft. Many of the objects found on the ships are in museums in Rome, but the ships were unfortunately burned by the retreating German army on 31 May, 1944. Other excavations led to the discovery of the temple, one of the richest in Latium. The remains of the temple precinct—a large platform, the back of which is formed by a wall of concrete, with niches, resting against the cliffs—are situated a little above the level of the lake, on the northeast.

nemset vessel: A type of spouted vase or lustration vessel usually used in Egyptian ritual contexts such as the opening of the mouth ceremony, which was a ritual intended to instill life into funerary statues or mummies.

Nenana Complex: Prehistoric culture (or complex) in south-central Alaska dated to c. 12,000–10,500 bp. It is characterized by small bifacial projectile points (Chindadn points). It is the earliest dated set of archaeological finds in Alaska.

Nene Valley ware: A type of Roman pottery made by an organized industry on the banks of the River Nene west of Peterborough, by the Roman town of Water Newton (ancient Durobrivae), England, from the 2nd–4th centuries AD. (It was formerly known as Castor Ware.) The commonest shapes are drinking vessels and tumblers, made of a light clay with a dark slip, sometimes with a white decoration. Decoration was by applied scales, rouletting, or barbotine. Barbotine ornamentation is applied to pottery by squeezing a bag containing thin clay slip in the same way as a cake is iced today. It may be applied by brush or spatula as well. The best known are the Hunt Cups, showing dogs pursuing deer or hares, but human scenes also occur. It is a local ware, made in imitation of the dark, glossy Rhenish wares, and was perhaps the first fine ware to be produced locally in Roman Britain. (*syn.* Castor Ware)

Nenumbo: Lapita site dating to c. 1100 BC in the Main Reef Islands of the Santa Cruz group. Artifacts include obsidian shell ornaments from Talasea and Lapita pottery.

neo-: A prefix meaning "new" or "different in form," as in "Neolithic." As a hyphenated prefix, it is used to describe the reappearance of a culture after a period of decline, such as neo-Babylonian, neo-Hittite.

Neoanthropus: The Greek name for the major group to which *Homo sapiens* belongs as opposed to Paleoanthropus (paleos = old) to which *Homo neanderthalensis, Pithecanthropus erectus*, and Sinanthropus belong. Neoanthropus developed in Africa and later in Asia.

Neo-Assyrian: A political period of the Assyrian Empire in the Iron Age, an extension of the Middle Assyrian. It lasted from Assurnasirpal II (883–859 BC) until Sargon, Sennacherib, Esarhaddon, and finally, Assurbanipal (668–627 BC). The Assyrian Empire was destroyed by the Babylonians and Medes in 612 BC. The Neo-Assyrian period was the great era of Assyrian power, and the writing culminated in the extensive records of the library of Ashurbanipal at Nineveh (c. 650 BC). Neo-Assyrian is also the name of the cuneiform script of the time.

Neo-Babylonian: A political and economic period of weakness during the early 1st millennium BC, which ended with the absorption of Babylonia into the Neo-Assyrian Empire by 688 BC. A rebellion in the 620s evicted the Assyrians, and in alliance with Medes, the Babylonians destroyed the Assyrian Empire in 612 BC. Persia's Cyrus invaded and occupied Babylon in 539 BC.

Neogene period: The upper division of the Tertiary system including the Miocene and Pliocene periods; latest of the two divisions of the Cenozoic Era (66.4 million years ago to the present). The Neogene includes the Miocene and Pliocene epochs (23,700,000–1.600.000 years ago) and is considered by some to encompass the time up to the present. The Neogene, which means "new born," was designated as such to emphasize that the marine and terrestrial fossils found in the strata of this time were more closely related to one another than to those of the preceding period called the Paleogene. The term *Neogene* is widely used in Europe as a geologic division, but it is generally not employed in North America, where the Cenozoic Era is simply divided into the Tertiary Period (66,400,000–1,600,000 years ago) and the Quaternary Period (1,600,000 years ago to the present).

Neolithic: The period of prehistory when people began to use ground stone tools, cultivate plants, and domesticate livestock, but before the use of metal for tools. It is the technical name for the New Stone Age in the Old World following the Mesolithic. In the Neolithic, villages were established, pottery and weaving appeared, and farming began. The Neolithic began about 8000–7000 BC in the Middle East and about 4000–3000 BC in Europe. It was followed by the Bronze Age, which began about 3500–3000 BC in the Middle East and about 2000–1500 BC in Europe. The criteria for "defining" the Neolithic have become progressively more difficult to apply as both food production and metal-working took a long time to develop. In Britain, the Neolithic has other more specific characteristics: the use of pottery and of ground stone (besides the long-employed flaked stone), and the appearance of construction works like the long barrow, causewayed camp, and megalithic tomb. Elsewhere, however, some Mesolithic cultures made use of pottery, in Japan for example; and certain so-called pre-pottery, Neolithic groups had none, as at Jericho. If the term *Neolithic* is to be retained at all, it must be based on the appearance of food production (especially cereal grains), sometimes called the Neolithic revolution, commencing in southwest Asia 9000–6000 BC. This might be considered the most important single advance ever made by people because it allowed them to settle permanently in one spot. This in turn encouraged the accumulation of material possessions, stimulated trade, and by giving a storable surplus of food allowed a larger population and craft specialization. All these were prerequisite to further human progress. The Neolithic was followed by the Mesolithic period, the Chalcolithic, or the Bronze Age, depending on the terminology used in different areas and the nature of the archaeological sequence itself. The Neolithic followed the Palaeolithic Period. (*syn.* neolithic, New Stone Age)

Neolithic Revolution: A term coined by V. G. Childe to describe the origin and consequences of farming—the development of stock raising and agriculture—allowing the widespread development of settled village life (c. 9000–6000 BC in Asia). This group of cultural processes marked the transition from an economy based on hunting and gathering to an agricultural economy. These processes were linked with development of village life and production of artifacts such as pottery and weaving. (*syn.* Neolithization)

Neopalatial: The period of the New or Second palaces of Minoan Crete. It is also known as Minoan III–Late Minoan IIIA1, c. 1700–1375 BC, in traditional chronology.

Neothermal: Postglacial times, a period of time from about 11,000 years ago to the present.

neoteny: The retention of juvenile or fetal features into adult life. Neoteny entails the maturation of a larva's reproductive capabilities without the accompanying development of its external morphological features. This phenomenon occurs in some aquatic salamanders and is due to delayed somatic development. It is thought to be an important mechanism in evolution, having facilitated certain crucial changes such as the emergence of the first chordates. Modern man has a number of features that seem to be neotenous, at least in relation to the apes and to the kind of common apelike ancestor we are thought to have. Neoteny is one possible mechanism to explain the emergence of modern morphology, perhaps from a Neanderthal-like ancestor.

nephrite: The more common form of jade, an iron calcium magnesium silicate of the amphibole mineral group. It is whitish to dark green in color, although it can be blue and black, prized as an ornamental stone for carving and jewelry. Jadeite is tougher and more compact. Sources of the material are known in China, Siberia, Pakistan, New Zealand, the Philippines, New Guinea and Australia, Poland, the Swiss Alps, Italy and Sicily, and North and South America.

Nephthys: Egyption goddess, sister of Isis, Osiris, and Seth, whose wife she was in the Osiris legend. With Isis, referred to one of the "two kites," screeching birds that sounded like mourning women. She was a protectress of the head. She was a goddess in the Great Ennead of Heliopolis, but seems to have no cult center or temple of her own. She was said to be the mother of Anubis from a union with Orion, and the daughter of Nut.

net sinker: A term applied loosely to any perforated stone or terra-cotta object, which may have been used to keep a fishing net vertical in the water. They are found all over the world.

network analysis: The study of any network or system of links, sites, points, and nodes, especially a communication system such as roads. The way in which the network is organized is studied rather than the actual lengths of the links, to determine the degree to which an efficient system has been evolved. Roman roads, for instance, are particularly suitable for this sort of analysis, and the changing patterns demanded by military and civilian usage can be distinguished. The analysis is aimed at understanding the reasons for a particular network configuration, which may be economic, geographical, or social.

neutron activation analysis: A physical method of chemical analysis used to determine the composition of various substances such as flint, obsidian, pottery, coins, found in archaeological contexts. It can be totally nondestructive to the sample and involves the excitation of the atomic nuclei rather than the atomic electrons. The specimen is bombarded with neutrons, which interact with nuclei in the sample to form radioactive isotopes that emit gamma rays as they decay. The energy spectrum of the emitted rays is detected by a scintillation or semiconductor counter. Constituent elements and concentrations are identified by the characteristic energy spectrum of emitted rays and their intensity. The time between the neutron activation of the sample and the measurement of the gamma rays depends on the half-lives of the radioactive isotopes, which may range from seconds to thousands of years: Often a few weeks may be necessary before measurement takes place. Neutron activation analysis has an advantage over x-ray fluorescence spectrometry because it analyzes the whole specimen as opposed to the surface only. Care must be taken that the neutron dose is not so great as to make the specimen radioactively unsafe for handling. The method is particularly useful for the identification of trace elements; however, it is not universally applicable because some elements have too short a half-life for measurement, and others do not form radioactive isotopes. The method is accurate to about plus or minus 5%. Neutron activation analysis of certain Hopewell artifacts made of obsidian has proved that the source of the obsidian was in what is now Yellowstone National Park. (*syn.* NAA)

neutron scattering: A remote sensing technique involving the placing of a probe into the soil to measure the relative rates of neutron flows through the soil. A beam of neutrons is aimed at the target material, and the resultant scattering of the neutrons yields information about that material's atomic structure. Because stone produces a lower count rate than soil, buried features can often be detected.

Nevali Cori: Prehistoric site on the Euphrates River near Samsat, Turkey, with an Aceramic Neolithic settlement revealing information about the PPNB complex. There is a series of buildings with stone foundations and broken stelae. Later occupation included Halaf period and Early Bronze Age I.

Nevasa: Prehistoric site on the northern Deccan plateau in western central India with a Middle Palaeolithic industry, a regional Chalcolithic with Jorwe ware of the later 2nd millennium BC, and a settlement of the late 1st millennium BC with wares of late Iron Age southern India. Another phase shows trade with Rome by the early 1st millennium AD. Glass beads and bangles characteristic of the Hindu culture of about 200 BC have been discovered in Nevasa excavations.

new archaeology: A movement that began in America in the 1960s, aimed at making archaeology more scientific, now more often called processual archaeology. It was suggested that explanations be based on carefully designed models of human behavior and emphasized the importance of understanding underlying cultural processes. This new approach was controversial and is commonly associated with Lewis R. Binford and his students. Binford's *New Perspectives in Archaeology* in 1968 stressed the following ideas: the use of new techniques such as the computer for statistical and matrix analyses of data and the concept of the ecosystem for the understanding of the economic and subsistence bases of prehistoric societies; an evolutionary view of culture; the use of models of cultures, viewed as systems, incorporating the evolutionary view of culture; and a close relation between archaeology and anthropology. Although the proponents of the new archaeology have been criticized by more traditionally minded scholars, their basic principles are now widely accepted. (*syn.* New Archaeology; processual archaeology)

New Britain: The largest island of the Bismarck Archipelago, southwestern Pacific, in Papua New Guinea. Archaeological discoveries include stone pestles and mortars like those from the New Guinea Highlands, an undated industry of waisted flaked tools from Kandrian, and the first discovered Lapita site, Watom Island. The Talasea obsidian source, the most important in the southwestern Pacific and quarried since at least 9000 BC, is on New Britain. The island was probably settled by Papuan speakers from New Guinea before 9000 BC.

New Caledonia: A French overseas territory in the southwestern Pacific, the largest island of southwest Melanesia, with an Austronesian-speaking population and an archaeological record going back to Lapita settlement, about 1300 BC. The island is well known for its prehistoric and ethnographic systems of terraced wet taro cultivation and also has the richest assemblage of rock carvings in Oceania.

Lapita, on the Foué Peninsula on New Caledonia Island, is the type site for Lapita ware, which indicates an Austronesian presence in the area about 2000–1000 BC.

New Forest ware: One of the pottery wares of southern Roman Britain in the late 3rd–4th centuries AD, produced by craftsmen in the New Forest area. Decoration is scarce, consisting of white slipped scrolls or rosette stamps or stamped-on designs. Vessel shapes included cups, flagons, and mortaria. It was of two kinds: one a hard gray ware, with a painted, white ornamentation and a dark purple glaze and the other a creamy ware with a red slip. It had limited distribution, no farther than 80 kilometers from the kilns.

Newgrange: The most famous and splendidly decorated of the Irish passage graves, part of the Boyne Valley cemetery, in Meath County. The kidney-shaped mound, dated to c. 3100 BC, is over 100 meters in diameter and 13 meters high. The cairn itself was carefully made of alternate layers of stones and turf. A curb of large stones carved with wavy lines, lozenges, triangles encloses the base of the mound. On either side of the entrance the green curbstones were topped by a retaining wall of white quartz. Some distance from the original base of the mound is a surrounding circle of free-standing stones. The burial chamber, cruciform in plan, is roofed by corbelling and has three subsidiary cells; the tomb has a very long passage, 19 meters in length, built of orthostats. Midwinter sunrise shines through an opening above the door to illuminate the central chamber, the clearest example of an astronomical orientation recorded from a European prehistoric monument. Many stones of both chamber and passage carry pecked designs including an unusual triple spiral. Excavation has shown that the upper surfaces of the capstones had drainage channels, as well as art that would have been invisible once the overlying cairn had been built. Traces of cremation burials were found in the cells of the chamber, and soil from a habitation site, possibly close to the tomb, had been used to pack the interstices of the passage roof. There are two radiocarbon dates around 3200 BC. The site was reoccupied after the tomb builders had left it and the cairn had begun to slump by a group that used Late Neolithic and Beaker pottery. (*syn.* New Grange)

New Guinea: The largest island of Oceania, in the eastern Malay Archipelago, north of Australia. New Guinea was joined to Australia in low sea-level periods of the Pleistocene and was probably first settled by early Australoids at the same time as its larger neighbor. New Guinea archaeology examines the highlands, which is totally Papuan speaking, and also the coasts, which is mixed Papuan and Austronesian. The highland prehistoric sequence is totally aceramic. Stone mortars and pestles, many elaborate in shape, are also found in the highlands. The New Guinea coasts have sequences only back to 3000–2000 years ago as earlier sites were probably drowned by rising sea levels. The best-reported are Collingwood Bay and south coastal Papua, both with pottery. Some coastal groups had developed elaborate trading networks by the time of European contact. Almost the whole of New Guinea is occupied by speakers of Papuan languages, the original settlers of the island, who live mainly in the interior and southern sections. Ethnic composition is complex among the Papuans, who speak some 700 different languages.

New Guinea Highlands: An area of Oceania that was unknown until the 1930s and whose population is Melanesian speakers of Papuan languages. Its prehistory goes back at least 26,000 years, and it supported agricultural systems dating back at least 6,000 years.

New Kingdom: A period of Egyptian history including the 18th–20th Dynasties, c. 1550–1070 BC. It was the period following the expulsion of Asiatic Hyksos rulers and the subsequent reunification by Thutmose I–IV, Amenhotep, Akhenaten, Tutankhamun, and Ramesses I–XI. The Egyptian army pushed beyond the traditional frontiers of Egypt into Syria-Palestine. The Theban conquerors established the 18th Dynasty (1550–1295 BC), creating a great empire under a succession of rulers bearing the names Thutmose and Amenhotep. The newly reunified land had a stronger economy, supplemented by resources of empire in Nubia and western Asia. To this period belongs much of the monumental architecture of Egypt. From the beginning of the New Kingdom, temples of the gods became the principal monuments; royal palaces and private houses, which are very little known, were less important. Temples and tombs were stone with relief decoration on their walls and were filled with stone and wooden statuary, inscribed and decorated stelae (free-standing small stone monuments), and, in their inner areas, composite works of art in precious materials.

Newstead: A Roman fort on the Tweed near Melrose, first built by Agricola AD c. 81. There were rebuildings in c. 86, 145, and 158, enlarging and strengthening it to hold a garrison of a thousand men. It remained the main base for the Roman army of occupation in the Scottish lowlands as long as this region was held. (*syn.* ancient Trimontium)

New World: The Western Hemisphere, the continental land mass of North and South America. The term often includes the neighboring islands. (*syn.* western hemisphere)

New Zealand: The southernmost and (except for Chatham Islands) only temperate land mass to be settled by Polynesians/Maoris. Beginning in AD c. 900, the lifestyle was predominantly horticultural on the North Island, but was hunting and gathering on the colder South Island. Language, economy, and technology are almost fully Polynesian. There are two archaeological phases: Archaic, c. 900–1300, and Classic, c. 1300–1800. The Classic is associated with many earthwork fortifications, a rich woodcarving tradition, and development of the chiefly society observed by Captain Cook in 1769.

Nezwiska: A site of the Linear Pottery Culture in the Ukraine.

Ngamuriak: Neolithic site in southwestern Kenya with stone tools and pottery of the Elmenteitan tradition, c. 2000 BC. The earliest evidence for humped cattle in eastern Africa was found there as well as obsidian obtained from the Rift Valley, more than 100 kilometers away, used to make tools.

Ngandong: Terrace site in the Solo River valley in Java, Indonesia, which had remains of Pleistocene fauna and advanced *Homo erectus* (Solo Man) of c. 200,000 years ago. Solo Man has features of earlier Java Man and has also been regarded as a tropical Neanderthal. Faunal associations are Upper Pleistocene, and age estimates range from 60,000–300,000 years. There was a stone industry of choppers and retouched flakes, but it may not be associated with Solo Man.

Ngilipitji: Quartzite quarry in eastern Arnhem Land, northern Australia. Products include Leilira blades.

Nhunguza: Later Iron Age site in northern Mashonaland, Zimbabwe, where a large clay structure has been interpreted as a courthouse, with open yard and audience chamber.

Niah: A limestone massif with a number of caves, which have produced material of all periods from Palaeolithic to AD c. 1300 in Sarawak, north Borneo. It is one of the major prehistoric deposits of island southeast Asia with human remains. The most important site, the Great Cave, has deposits that may be of Middle Palaeolithic age, but a later stratum (dated around 38,000 BC) yielded a *Homo sapiens* skull, which is probably the oldest yet known in the region. Other deposits include a series of flexed, seated, and fragmentary burials dated to 12,000–1500 BC and extended burials in wooden coffins or mats of the last two millennia BC. There are also jar burials and cremations from c. 1500 BC to AD 1000. There was distinctive pottery c. 2500 BC, Neolithic polished stone adzes, and metal by the 1st millennium AD. (*syn.* Sarawak, Niah Caves)

Niaux: One of the greatest Palaeolithic painted caves, in Ariège in the Pyrenees, southwest France. No trace of occupation has been found in the huge cave. The paintings are in black; bison and horse are the animals most frequently depicted. The "Salon noir" has six panels of black bison, horse, ibex, and deer figures, which were probably sketched in charcoal and then painted with different pigments. A new gallery discovered in 1970 has hundreds of Palaeolithic footprints. Much of Niaux's art is late Magdalenian (11th millennium BC).

niche: In ecology, the smallest unit of a habitat that is occupied by an organism. *Habitat niche* refers to the physical space occupied by the organism; *ecological niche* refers to the role it plays in the community of organisms found in the habitat (sometimes referred to as an animal's profession). *Niche* is also the functional role of an organism in a community; not only where that organism lives, but also what it does and eats, how it responds to the environment, and how it is constrained by other species and external forces.

Nichoria: Mycenaean settlement in Messenia, Greece, with a 15th century BC structure that may have been an early palace. There were at least two tholos tombs. (*syn.* Nikhoria)

niello: Powdered sulfides of copper, silver, and lead, heated and used to make a bluish-black plastic substance applied to metalwork. The material was soft; it was cast into the cut-out pattern on the object and polished flat. It was used particularly to decorate the inlaid daggers of shaft grave circles at Mycenae. The art of chasing out lines or forms and inlaying a black composition was probably well known to the Greeks. The Byzantines compounded silver, lead, sulfur, and copper and laid it on the silver in a powder, then put it through a furnace, where it melted and incorporated with the solid metal. Germanic and Anglo-Saxon metalworkers also used the technique. Objects decorated with niello, called nielli, are usually small in scale. During the Renaissance, at the height of its popularity, the technique was widely used for the embellishment of liturgical objects and for the decoration of cups, boxes, knife handles, and belt buckles. (*syn.* nigellum; Tula work)

Nietoperzowa Cave: Prehistoric cave site northwest of Kraków, southern Poland. There are Middle Palaeolithic assemblages of side scrapers correlating to the end of the Middle Pleistocene, last interglacial, and early glacial. Upper Palaeolithic levels contain laurel-leaf points of the Jerzmanowician industry, with one radiocarbon date of 38,500 bp. There are Neolithic and later remains in the top layer. (*syn.* Jerzmanowice)

Nihewan: Formation in Hebei Province, China, thought to be 1 million years old and containing northern China's earliest Palaeolithic tools of quartzite choppers and flakes. Mammal fauna is of the Lower Pleistocene and may be an early form of horse. (*syn.* [Ni-ho-wan])

Nihon shoki: The second-earliest surviving chronicle of Japan, the "Chronicle of Japan," completed in 720. The work began in the 7th century with the same objectives as for Koji-ki, but the Nihon Shoki is a more lengthy and scholarly attempt written in Chinese, the official written language of the day. It was compiled as part of the Ritsuryo state's effort to legitimize the ruling dynasty. Numerous documents, including Chinese and Korean sources, were clearly consulted and often cited. Beginning with a slightly different version of a creation myth from the one related in Koji-ki, the chronicles end with the events at the very end of the 7th century. The accounts include imperial genealogies, legendary events, and reign chronicles. They have been used in archaeological studies of the protohistoric Kofun period. (*syn.* Nihongi)

Nile: The longest river in Africa and the world, stretching for 6741 kilometers, rising in the highlands south of the equator and flowing northward through northeastern Africa to drain into the Mediterranean Sea. Its waters and fertile flood plain allowed Egyptian civilization to develop in the deserts of northeastern Africa. The Nile River basin covers about one tenth of the area of the African continent. Three rivers flow in from the south: the Blue Nile, White Nile, and Atbara. The southern section between Aswan and Khartoum is interrupted by six "cataracts" consisting of a series of rapids and corresponding to the land of Nubia. The first use of the Nile for irrigation in Egypt began when seeds were sown in the mud left after the river's annual floodwaters had subsided, and it has supported continuous human settlement for at least 5,000 years.

Nilometer: A device to measure the Nile's height, usually consisting of a series of steps (staircase) against which the increasing height of the inundation could be measured. The most famous are on Elephantine Island at Aswan and on Roda Island in Cairo; surviving Nilometers are also associated with the temples at Philae, Edfu, Esna, Kom Ombo, and Dendera.

Nîmes: Colony founded by the emperor Augustus in southern Gaul (France), originally a Celtic settlement (capital of the Volcae Arecomici). It became a colony in 121 BC, and the walls and gates were built by Augustus; in Roman times it was one of the richest towns of Gaul. Remains include an amphitheater designed by Titus Crisius Reburrus, which holds 24,000 people; the Maison carrée, a temple from the 1st century BC, and part of the colony's aqueduct, Pont du gard, built by Agrippa. The Maison carée was a rectangular temple 82 ft (25 m) long by 40 ft (12 m) wide, dedicated to Gaius and Lucius Caesar, adopted sons of the first Roman emperor Augustus, and is one of the most beautiful monuments built by the Romans in Gaul, and certainly the best preserved. The Tour magne, on top of a hill just outside the city, is the oldest Roman building, 92 ft high, but probably originally higher. Its original function is not known, but it was incorporated into the Roman wall in 16 BC. Nîmes seems to have achieved its greatest prosperity somewhere around the end of the 2nd century AD. In the 5th century, Nîmes was plundered by the Vandals and the Visigoths. It was later occupied by the Saracens (Arabs), who were driven out in 737. (*syn.* Roman Nemausus)

Nimrud: Assyrian capital of Kalhu (Calah), founded in 883 BC by Ashurnasirpal II (883–859 BC) over the ruins of an earlier city built by Shalmaneser I (1274–1245 BC) in the 13th century BC. It is located by the Tigris River, south of modern Mosul (Iraq) in Mesopotamia. It was the third capital city, with Assur and Nineveh, of Assyria. The statues and inscriptions found by Sir Austen Henry Layard were some of the first archaeological discoveries to stir the public imagination. Its wall was some 8 kilometers in circuit, enclosing at one corner a citadel that contained a ziggurat, temples, and palaces. The palaces have yielded the richest finds, enormous stone winged bulls, reliefs, and exquisite carved ivories that once adorned the royal furniture. Another rich collection of ivories was found in the arsenal of Shalmaneser III in the outer town. Some of the ivories show traces of the fire that accompanied the overthrow of the city by the Medes in 612 BC. Unlike many of the cities of Mesopotamia, Nimrud was not a long-lived site occupied from the prehistoric period. Its heyday continued until c. 710 BC when the capital was transferred first to Khorsabad and subsequently to Nineveh. Many of the sculptures were brought back to England by Layard and are now in the British Museum. (*syn.* ancient Kalhu, biblical Calah)

Nineveh: Large walled city, a capital of the Assyrians from the end of the 8th century BC, located across the Tigris River from Mosul, Iraq. The site was occupied from the earliest times, with pottery from the Hassuna phase on. The site today consists of two main mounds, Kuyunjik (the citadel) and Nebi Yunus (the arsenal). It was occupied from the 6th millennium BC (a test pit beneath the temple of Ishtar, the goddess of fertility, produced material of Hassuna type at the bottom) until it was destroyed by the Medes late in the 7th century BC. Ninevite ware (or Ninevite V) represents the comparatively backward culture of the north, contemporary with the Early Dynastic of Sumer. Little of importance is recorded of the site until it became a joint capital of Assyria, with Assur and Nimrud, in the early 1st millennium. Sennacherib was responsible for making it a capital, and his great palace has splendid carved reliefs. To this period belong the site's other spectacular monuments, the palaces with their elaborate architecture, carved reliefs, and cuneiform inscriptions. The most important finds were probably the two libraries of clay tablets found in the palaces of Sennacherib (704–681 BC) and Assurbanipal (668–627 BC). The city was destroyed by Medes in 612 BC. A lifesize bronze head of an Akkadian king, possibly Sargon (founder of the Akkadian Empire), dated to the later 3rd millennium BC, was found there. (*syn.* modern Kuyunjik)

Ninevite 5: The period or horizon from c. 2900–2500 BC in northern Mesopotamia, characterized by distinctive painted and incised and excised pottery. The name derives from the site of Nineveh where it was first excavated. The term also refers to the pottery itself.

Ninstints: Village site on Anthony Island, off British Columbia, Canada, with fine in situ examples of Northwest Coast architecture and monumental art. There are standing superstructures, living floors, and mortuary poles, some dating to the early 1800s. The earliest occupation is dated to AD 360, and the village was abandoned in 1888. It was occupied by the Haida.

Nintoku: The 17th emperor of Japan (5th century AD) and the name of the keyhole-shaped mounded tomb, the largest in Japan, used as his mausoleum in Osaka Prefecture. It is the largest tomb of the Tumulus period, a 5th-century structure surrounded by three moats and occupying some 80 acres (32 hectares).

Nippur: A city and important cultural center at the heart of Sumer of southern Mesopotamia (now Iraq), first occupied in 'Ubaid times and inhabited into the 1st millennium AD. Nippur played a special role in the life of Sumer as a religious city, center of the worship of Enlil. Lying between the Tigris and Euphrates Rivers, its remains include the temple of Enlil and its ziggurat, a sequence of Early Dynastic temples, Old Babylonian residences, and Uruk pottery of the 4th millennium BC. Its fame rests primarily on the discovery of cuneiform tablets of the sacerdotal library, which have yielded more of the literary tradition of the Sumerians than any other Mesopotamian site. The tablets range in date from the late 3rd millennium to the later 1st millennium BC and include administrative, cultic, economic, and literary texts. There is an extremely detailed sequence of pottery covering most of the pre-Islamic period of southern Iraq, much from the Inanna temple precinct. (*syn.* modern Nuffar)

Nishapur: One of the most important towns of Khorasan in the early Islamic period (now in Iran); for a short period in the 9th century, it replaced Marv as the regional capital. The town was a major commercial center, noted for its textiles. Nishapur became a capital again in 1037 under Tughril Beg, the first Salijuq ruler. His successor, Malik Shah, made the city a center of learning, the home of Omar Khayyam, among other famous scholars. It declined in the 12th century as a result of earthquakes (in 1115, 1145). In 1221, Nishapur was sacked by the Mongols and never regained its former prominence. The most important contribution of the Samanid age (AD 819–999) to Islamic art is the pottery produced at Nishapur. The ceramics were of bold style and showed links with Sassanian and Central Asian work. The style originated in Transoxania, an ancient eastern district of Iran, and showed such specific characteristics as black and ocher birds with dashes of white and green. There was also a rougher type portraying human and animal figures against an ornamental background. (*syn.* Neyshabur)

Nishiyagi: Site dating to the Palaeolithic in Hyogo Prefecture, Japan, where wooden boards are preserved by waterlogging and dated to 50,000–70,000 bp.

NISP: In faunal analysis, the number of identified specimens in a collection. (*syn.* number of identified specimens)

Nissan Island: Melanesian island with a sequence of Lapita and pre-Lapita (c. 5000 bp, Aceramic Neolithic). The pre-Lapita deposits contain obsidian from Talasea, indicating long-distance sea voyages.

Nitovikla: Site of a fortress in eastern Cyprus built in the Middle Cypriot period.

Nitra: A fortified site where excavations have revealed traces of the 9th-century stronghold and a large cemetery of the Linear Pottery culture of southern Slovakia. In Nitra's walls there were workshops producing relics and metalwork that were distributed to other Slavic sites. The cemetery's artifacts and remains have provided data on mortality, age, and sex during the Early Neolithic. Grave goods included spondylus shell ornaments and shoe-last axes. (*syn.* Neutra, Nyitra)

Nitriansky Hrádok: A multiple-phase defended settlement site of the Boleráz culture, a transition from the Eneolithic to Early Bronze Age, located on the banks of the River Nitra, western Slovakia. It dates to the late 3rd–early 2nd millennia BC. There was a double ditch and timber-framed rampart; the tell-like accumulation of material includes antler cheek pieces for horse bits.

nitrogen dating: A relative dating technique used on bone, based on the gradual reduction of nitrogen in bone as collagen is broken down into amino acids and leached away. Bone collagen decomposes, releasing nitrogen, at a fairly uniform slow rate. Nitrogen is present in bone in a proportion of approximately 4%. The relative ages of bones in similar burial environments can be compared by looking at the remaining nitrogen content; it is relative because the rate of decline is affected by local environmental factors such as temperature or chemical constituents in the find deposit. Nitrogen concentrations are determined by chemical analysis. (*syn.* nitrogen test)

Njoro River Cave: One of the earliest well-documented Pastoral Neolithic sites in southern Kenya, of the Elmenteitan industry and dated to c. 12th century BC. It was a cemetery for cremated burials, each interment being accompanied by a stone bowl, mortar, and pestle, as well as by numerous hard stone beads and pendants. A finely decorated wooden vessel and a gourd were also preserved.

Nkope: Early Iron Age site near the southern end of Lake Nyasa, which has given its name to the variant of the Early Iron Age complex represented in southern Malawi and eastern Zambia from about the 4th–11th centuries AD. It is a branch of the Eastern Stream or Urewe Tradition of the Chifumbaze Complex. It is thought that a migration from Nkope resulted in the appearance of the Gokomere Complex in Zimbabwe AD c. 500.

Nkudzi: Later Iron age cemetery site on the southwestern shore of Lake Malawi (formerly Lake Nyasa), probably dating to the late 18th–early 19th centuries AD. The abundant grave goods may reflect the material culture in the area at a time of increasing slave raiding and coastal trade.

Noah's Ark model: A theory that modern humans originated in a single area of Africa and spread throughout the world, replacing other, more archaic, human types. This view is supported by the so-called "Eve" theory, which postulates that all modern humans are descended from a common mother. The opposing hypothesis is often called the candelabra model. (*syn.* replacement hypothesis)

Noailles: The Grotte de Noailles, close to Brive, Corrèze, southwest France, which has given its name to a small multiple burin—an Upper Palaeolithic flake tool retouched to give several chisel-like edges. The Noailles burin distinguishes a facies of the Upper Perigordian or Noaillian, dating to c. 27,000 bp. (*syn.* Noailles burin)

nock: One of the notches cut in either of two tips of horn attached to the ends of a bow for holding the bowstring or a groove into which the bowstring is inserted on an arrow. The term is also used for the part of an arrow having a notch for the bowstring and for the notch itself.

nodule: A hard mass of mineral, usually rounded, found in various forms in soil created by the deposition of minerals from solution. The way nodules are formed can assist in palaeoenvironmental reconstruction and in determining the age of the conditions under which they formed. Nodules are often elongate with a knobby irregular surface; they usually are oriented parallel to the bedding. Chert and flint often occur as dense and structureless nodules of nearly pure silica in limestone or chalk, where they seem to be replacements of the carbonate rock by silica.

Nogliki I: A Neolithic settlement of pit houses in the northeast of Sakhalin, an island off the east coast of Siberia, north of Japan. Its time placement is defined by the presence of pottery rather than the practice of farming.

Noin Ula: A range of hills in northern Mongolia near Lake Baikal, where a rich burial site, possibly of the Xiongnu nobility of the 1st century AD, has been excavated. To the north of Ulaanbaatar on the Selenge River, Noin Ula had horse burials, and the furnishings of one tomb were especially lavish. The prince for whom it was made must have been in contact with China, for his coffin was apparently made for him there, as were some of his possessions buried with him—a lacquer cup inscribed with the name of its Chinese maker and dated 5 September AD 13. His horse trappings were elaborately decorated and the saddle covered with leather threaded with black and red wool clipped to resemble velvet. The magnificent textiles in the tomb included a woven wool rug lined with thin leather, with purple, brown, and white felt appliqué work. Other textiles were of Greco-Bactrian and Parthian origin. Some objects are similar to ones from Pazyryk in the Altai. The tombs, which were plundered in antiquity, take the form of wooden burial chambers in deep shafts over which earthen barrows were raised. (*syn.* Noin-ula)

Noirmoutier: An island that lies off the coast of western France just south of the mouth of the Loire, first colonized by Philibert monks in the 6th–7th centuries. The monastery became an important producer of salt during Carolingian times. From 842, the Vikings raided the island repeatedly, forcing the monks to flee inland with the remains of Saint Philibert. There they constructed the church of St. Philibert de Grandieu, one of the finest examples of French 9th-century architecture.

Nok culture: A valley in central Nigeria (Benue Plateau) associated with the first iron-smelting people of west Africa and an Early Iron Age culture characterized by distinctive broken terra-cotta human and animal figures, some of them life sized. Shallow pits with low surrounding walls served as furnaces for the smelting of iron. The terra-cotta figures are associated with an agricultural fertility cult; the detailed and accomplished modeling pays particular attention both to attributes such as beads as well as to physical peculiarities or deformities. Other artifacts of the Nok culture include iron tools, stone axes, and other stone tools, and stone ornaments. Nok sites at Taruga and Samun Dukiya date to c. 5th–3rd centuries BC. The culture may have continued to the 2nd century AD in some places. The work was possibly ancestral to the medieval sculpture of Yoruba and Ibo. (*syn.* Nok figurine culture)

nomadic: A term used to describe the movement of whole social groups who utilized different parts of a given territory in different seasons, usually summer and winter pastures, and built camps for those periods.

nomarch: Governor of the ancient Egyptian administrative division called the nome. The district governor was appointed as a delegate by the pharaoh and tended to be an autonomous chieftain in troubled periods. Nomarchs often built lavish tombs for themselves.

Nombe: A rock shelter in Simbu Province, Papua New Guinea, in the New Guinea highlands, with evidence of occupation going back 25,000 years. Excavation has revealed a rich cultural sequence from the late Pleistocene to the present, and the basal levels contain waisted axes, pebble tools, and several extinct animals, including Protemnodon and Thylacine.

nome: An administrative unit or province of ancient Egypt, each consisting of a town or group of villages with its own guardian deity, district governor (nomarch), and symbol or

standard. There were 42–44 such provinces in Egypt, varying over the course of the centuries, which ancient Egyptians called *sepat*. The system of division into provinces existed at least from the Old Kingdom (c. 2575–2130 BC) and continued until the Muslim conquest (AD 640). In the Graeco-Roman period, whose temples are the source of the surviving lists of nomes, there were 22 nomes in Upper Egypt and 20 in Lower Egypt. In Ptolemaic times, a "heptanomis" of seven nomes was formed in Middle Egypt. The Nile valley south of Ombos was sometimes regarded as one with the province of Nubia. The nomarchs were appointed as delegates by the pharaoh and tended to be autonomous chieftains in troubled periods.

nomoli: Figures carved in soapstone by the Mende in Sierra Leone, which were set up in shelters to protect the crop. The figures are similar in style and are thought to be similar in date to ivories carved in the 16th century for Portuguese traders in the adjacent Sherbro area.

nomothetics: The search for general laws and principles of human behavior. The opposite of nomothetic is idiographic. (*syn.* nomothetic)

nonarbitrary sample unit: A subdivision of the data universe with cultural relevance, such as sample units defined by data clusters in remains of rooms or houses.

Non Chai: Late prehistoric settlement in the Chi valley, Khorat, Thailand, settled c. 600 BC. Local pottery was traded to the Songkhram basin c. 200–100 BC. The site was abandoned by AD 300.

noncortical flake: A flake having no cortex. (*syn.* interior flake, tertiary flake)

Non Dua: Late prehistoric moated site in southern Khorat, Thailand, and occupied from c. 600 BC to AD c. 800.

Non Nok Tha: Extensively excavated prehistoric site in north-central Thailand (Khorat region), with burials spanning the period c. 3500 BC to late 1st millennium AD. There is evidence for possible 4th–3rd millennia BC domestication of cattle, pig, and dog; the cultivation of rice, and the use of copper and bronze. Non Nok Tha and Ban Chiang may have the earliest evidence for bronzeworking in the world. Unlike Ban Chiang, the site appears to have been abandoned before iron was in general use.

Non Pa Wai: Prehistoric copper-extracting and -smelting sites in Khao Wong Prachan valley, Khorat, Thailand. There are crucibles, tuyères, ore, cup molds for ingot casting, and clay bivalve molds for bracelets; ax, spear, and arrowheads. The site is dated c. 1500–250 BC.

non-probabilistic sampling: A nonstatistical sampling strategy (in contrast to probabilistic sampling), which concentrates on sampling areas on the basis of intuition, historical documentation, or long field experience in the area. It is the acquisition of sample data based on informal criteria or personal judgment. It does not allow evaluation of how representative the sample is with respect to the data population. (*syn.* nonprobabilistic sampling)

non-site archaeology: The recovery and analysis of unclustered physical remains produced by human activities. Non-site archaeology generally concentrates on remains recovered in a surface or plot zone context. It is an approach, especially in archaeological survey, where the unit of analysis is the artifact rather than the site. Practitioners document the distribution of humanly modified materials across the landscape. (*syn.* off-site archaeology; landscape archaeology)

Nora: A Phoenician colony on the promontory of Cape Pula, Sardinia, southwest of Cagliari, probably of the 8th century BC. Tradition ascribes its founding to Iberians from Tartessus. From the end of the 6th century BC, Sardinia came under Carthaginian control, and from 238 BC under Roman, becoming a province in 227 BC. Nora seems to have enjoyed particular prosperity under Roman rule, rivaled only by Cagliari (municipium Iulium). After the Roman annexation of Sardinia, Nora was its capital in the republican period and later became a municipium (Romanized community) under the Empire (after 27 BC). Decline appears to have come with the 4th century AD. Excavations have uncovered a Sardinian *nuraghe* (towerlike monument), a Punic necropolis, a Hellenistic *tophet* (shrine), a temple to Tanit and one to Juno, a nymphaeum, a theater with a mosaic-surfaced orchestra, an aqueduct, and Roman bath buildings (also with mosaic). The northwest shore was lined with a series of luxury houses, including the so-called house of the Atrium.

Nordic tribes: Peoples from the Baltic who arrived in Britain in Neolithic times, who originated from southern Russia. They settled in western areas of England and were one of the two main Neolithic groups.

Noricum: Iron Age polity (kingdom) in the eastern Alps, with its seat in Magdalensberg, Austria. The region included modern central Austria and parts of Bavaria. Earlier Illyrian in culture, the region came under Celtic influence from the 3rd century BC, and the name Noricum is thought by some to derive from the Celtic Norici centered around Noreia. Becoming a Celtic kingdom, with reasonably friendly relations with Rome, it became a province about 15 BC. With wealth derived from its mineral resources (iron and gold), it was able to develop a markedly Romanized culture (evident from Latin legends on coins and other Latin inscriptions). Five of its communities were made into Roman municipia by the emperor Claudius (reigned AD 41–54), and the province supplied many soldiers for legions and the Praetorian Guard. The capital was at Virunum in the Klagenfurt area. The area was subdivided into two provinces by the emperor Diocletian

AD c. 300; Roman rule finally collapsed with German incursions in the 5th century. It was linked to the Italian peninsula through trade; mining and ironworking were important.

Normans: Vikings, or Norsemen, who settled in France; the population of the duchy of Normandy in northern France, a mixed race descending from the Franks and 10th-century Norse settlers of Denmark, Norway, and Iceland. In AD 1066, their leader, William of Normandy, conquered England, then Wales, Scotland, and Ireland. The Normans also conquered Sicily and southern Italy in a volatile period that began in 1063. These military feats were consolidated by the strength of the Norman feudal aristocracy and their skill in erecting strong, expedient fortifications ranging from motte and bailey earthworks to substantial stone castles. The Normans were also the main force behind the Crusades, which began in the 11th century AD. They promoted the French language and French culture and the Romanesque style of architecture. By 1200, the Norman conquerors had been absorbed into the countries they ruled, but many of their institutions lasted into the late Middle Ages. Despite their eventual conversion to Christianity, their adoption of the French language, and their abandonment of sea roving for Frankish cavalry warfare in the decades following their settlement in Normandy, the Normans retained many of the traits of their piratical Viking ancestors. They were restless, reckless, and loved fighting; they extended the practice of centralized authoritarian rule, feudalism, cavalry warfare, and religious reform.

normative: Relating to a view of human culture stressing shared, homogeneous culture; important to defining cultural units in time and space. It argues that an individual society has a uniform and standard way of doing things and that these norms are represented by particular homogeneous patterns in the archaeological record. It is a descriptive approach to culture, used in an archaeological interpretation of both synchronic and diachronic descriptions of cultural forms. (*syn.* normative view, normative approach, normative concept of culture)

Norsuntepe: Prehistoric site on the upper Euphrates River in eastern Anatolia with a sequence of occupation from the Chalcolithic to Iron Age times. Early levels show connections with Halaf and 'Ubaid. Architecture became more elaborate, and there is a probable copper foundry and copper workshops through the Early Bronze Age levels (mid-4th millennium BC). The copper production relied on Ergani copper sources and fed the demands of southern Mesopotamia.

Northern Archaic Tradition: Culture of the North American arctic and subarctic dating to c. 6000–4000 bp. The characteristic artifact is the side-notched point. Assemblages also contain oval bifaces, end scrapers, and notched pebbles. The tradition was defined at Onion Portage in the Denbigh

Flint Complex and postdates the American Paleo-Arctic Tradition. The peoples are thought to have come there from the south; they hunted terrestrial mammals such as caribou and developed their own styles of artifacts. They showed a preference for expanding northern forests, and, although they left traces outside the forest limits in a few places, they generally avoided the now-deglaciated coasts of Canada's far north. (*syn.* Northern Archaic tool tradition)

Northern Black Polished Ware: A fine gray metallic ware with a glossy black surface characteristic of the Iron Age civilization of northern and central India, dating to c. 500–100 BC. It is a hard, wheelmade ware, mainly bowls and dishes. The surface is made with an alkali flux and fired in a reducing atmosphere. It succeeds Painted Gray Ware in the Ganges sequence and is the main pottery type associated with the Ganges civilization. It characterizes the urban kingdoms of early historical India. (*syn.* Northern black polished ware; NBP, NBPW)

Northern zone: Steppe region south of the Gobi Desert along the northern edge of agricultural China, including Inner Mongolia, the Ordos, and southern Dongbei regions. This zone had several nomadic Bronze Age cultures during the 1st millennium BC.

Northumbria: One of the most important kingdoms of Anglo-Saxon England, lying north of the Humber River. During its peak period, it extended from the Irish Sea to the North Sea, between two west-east lines formed in the north by the Ayrshire coast and the Firth of Forth and in the south by the Ribble/Mersey River and the Humber. It resulted from the union of Deira, with its capital at York, and Bernicia, based on Bamburgh, under Edwin in AD 622. After the conversion of King Edwin in 626 and the establishment of many major monasteries in the region, Northumbria became a center of missionary activity and a leading center for the production of Christian art. In the later 7th–8th centuries, despite political decline, it was the scene of a cultural renaissance, attested by the history of Bede, the illuminated manuscripts of Lindisfarne, and so on. Schools of art and monumental architecture also flourished. Archaeologically, its most important site is Yeavering, a series of palaces built by Edwin and his successors in northern Northumberland. The cultural life and the political unity of Northumbria were destroyed by the arrival of the Danes.

Northwest Coast tradition: A series of prehistoric groups of the northern California coast, Oregon, Washington, British Columbia, and southeastern Alaska, with origins in the Fraser River delta and clearly established by 1000 BC. Their subsistence was based on hunting and gathering of riverine and marine food sources (mollusks, salmon, halibut, sea mammals). Characteristics in the archaeological record include bone and slate hunting tools, stone effigy carving, and

woodworking tools. Totem poles and elaborately carved long houses are still a cultural feature in the area.

Northwest microblade tradition: An interior sub-Arctic cultural sequence of Alaska, Yukon, and Northwest Territories of Canada, dating from c. 6500–3500 BC, although in western Canada it survived until c. 1000 BC. It is characterized by small stone blades, burins, bifacial knives, and lanceolate projectile points. It is possible that the Athabascan population of the interior western sub-Arctic may have started arriving in North America considerably earlier than the Eskimos. The Athabascans, the historical tribes of the Denetasiro tradition, were specialized fishers, hunters, and trappers in the forests of the Northwest. It is the first construct assimilating all the northwestern interior microblade industries into one culture unit.

Northwest Riverine tradition: A series of cultures that reached maturity in the interior of Oregon, Washington, and British Columbia, and in Idaho at the beginning of this millennium. The Columbia-Snake, Fraser-Thompson, and Klamath Rivers run through it, and it is where the Old Cordilleran tradition arose. It is characterized by pebble choppers, leaf-shaped flaked stone projectile points, stone hammers, stone bowls, tubular pipes, stone slubs, and fine stone carving. It is an integrative concept created by G. R. Willey in an effort to characterize all of Plateau prehistory between AD 500–1850. (*syn.* Plateau tradition)

Norton: A series of Arctic Alaska cultures, mainly coastal, dating from c. 500 BC–AD 1100, with the first pottery of the region. The Choris culture, the earliest manifestation, has pottery that is Asiatic in origin, fiber tempered with linear- and check-stamp decoration. Sometimes designated Palaeo-Eskimo, the Norton tradition embraces the cultural continuum Choris-Norton-Ipiutak. The Norton aspect of this continuum is typically represented by the presence of poorly fired, check-stamped pottery and tools of crude appearance, made from basalt rather than chert. Polished slate implements and oil lamps appear as well as points, tips, side blades, discoidal scraper bits, broad flat labrets, and toggling harpoon heads. Cape Denbigh, Cape Krusenstern, and Onion Portage, for example, all have a Norton component. The extent to which the Norton tradition was ancestral to any of the Eskimos is open to interpretation, although the Yup'ik Eskimo are likely descendants of Norton people. (*syn.* Norton tradition phase)

Nové Kosariská: Early Iron Age complex of tumuli near Bratislava, Slovakia, dated to the Hallstatt C and D periods. The tumuli have elaborate central timber-lined chambers with cremation burials in different vessels—20–80 per tumulus.

Nové Mesto: Upper Palaeolithic site in western Slovakia with a Middle Pleistocene layer with some flakes, Middle

Palaeolithic artifacts of side scrapers and a laurel-leaf point, and artifacts of the Eastern Gravettian.

Novgorod: Early city in northwest Russia, about 160 kilometers south of St Petersburg and founded in the 9th century AD. Waterlogged conditions have preserved intact a complete sequence of medieval wooden buildings and streets dating from the foundation of the city up to the 18th century. Dendrochronology has made it possible to accurately date the layers of timber streets superimposed on top of one another as well as their relations to the log cabins either side of them. There are small factories with tools for metal, wood, leather, and glass working. Also found were medieval textiles and a collection of 700 birch-bark documents, which have proved invaluable in understanding the history, trading relations, and feudal estates of the town. The fortified kremlin at Novgorod dates from the 11th century and is one of the earliest to have been given a stone enceinte. Novgorod controlled a vast territory in the 14th–15th centuries, extending to the Arctic Ocean and beyond the Ural Mountains.

Novo Mesto: Early Iron Age settlement and complex of tumuli in Slovenia and dated to the Hallstatt D (5th century BC). A stone wall encircled the settlement, and 10 tumuli have been excavated. Bronze situlae, breastplates, and helmets and objects of Baltic amber have been found.

Novye Ruseshty: Neolithic and Eneolithic site in Moldova, starting with the Linear Pottery culture and then the Cucuteni-Tripolye culture. (*syn.* Novi Rusesti)

Noyen-sur-Seine: Middle Neolithic system of palisades cutting across a meander of the River Seine in France. There are hearths, storage pits, pottery, and female terra-cotta figurines. Peat deposits preserved organic remains from c. 7000–5000 BC, such as a dugout canoe and basket fish traps.

Ntereso: Site of a fishing settlement related to the Kintampo industry, located to the east of that industry's main area of distribution, in the valley of the White Volta, northern Ghana. Bifacially flaked arrowheads, small axes, bone harpoon heads, and fish hooks may have affinities with sites far to the north, in the southern Sahara. The site dates to the late 2nd millennium BC.

Nubia: That area south of ancient Egypt proper, which extends from the Nile Valley from Aswan and the first cataract as far south as the Khartoum district in the Sudan, east to the Red Sea and west to the Libyan Desert. It was conventionally divided into Upper and Lower Nubia. Most of the Egyptian section was submerged under Lake Nasser since the Aswan High Dam completion in 1971. Defined as a "corridor to Africa," Nubia was a crucial trading conduit from the 4th millennium BC until the Middle Ages. The southern part of it to the southern end of the second cataract of the Nile was called Cush (Kush) under the 18th-Dynasty pharaohs of ancient Egypt and Ethiopia by the ancient Greeks. The northern part of the region, up to the first cataract of Aswan, was called Wawat. (*syn.* ancient Yam, Irem, Ta-sety, Kush)

Nubian A Group: The name conventionally given to the earliest fully food-producing society known in the archaeological record of Nubia, late in the 4th millennium BC. The "A Group" people probably had an indigenous Nubian ancestry, but were evidently in regular trade contact. The A Group is known mainly from graves, as from the excavated cemetery at Qustul, and adopted symbols of kingship similar to those of contemporary kings of Egypt of the Naqadah II–III period. It was one of the earliest phases of state formation in the world. Some settlement sites have been investigated, as at Afyeh near the first cataract where rectangular stone houses were built, as well other rural villages. Sheep and goats were herded, with some cattle, while both wheat and barley were cultivated. Luxury manufactured goods imported from Egypt included stone vessels, amulets, copper tools and linen cloth. (*syn.* Nubian A-Group culture)

Nubian C Group: The conventional designation of the indigenous population of Nubia in the late 3rd millennium BC. There is disagreement as to the extent to which these people were the direct descendants of the preceding Nubian A Group population. There are apparent connections between the C Group and contemporary peoples inhabiting the Red Sea hills, east of the Nile. Livelihood depended to a large extent on their herds of small stock and cattle. Settlement sites investigated consist mainly of circular houses with their lower walls of stone. In later C-Group times, more elaborate buildings were erected, and there was an increase in the quantity of luxury goods imported from Egypt. Both these developments reached their peak at Karmah. Egypt no longer controlled Lower Nubia, which was settled by the C Group and formed into political units of gradually increasing size; relations with this state deteriorated into armed conflict in the reign of Pepi II. Karmah was the southern cultural successor of the Nubian A Group and became an urban center in the late 3rd millennium BC remaining Egypt's chief southern neighbor for 7 centuries. (*syn.* Nubian C-Group culture)

Nubian rescue campaign: An international movement, coordinated by UNESCO between 1960–1980, to limit the loss of archaeological data as a result of the building of the Aswan High Dam and the subsequent flooding of much of Lower Nubia by Lake Nasser. The movement wanted to survey and excavate as many of the sites as possible and dismantle and re-erect the most important temples—Abu Simbel, Philae, and Kalabsha.

nuclear area: A location where large, complex societies occur at different times, such as the valley of central Mexico. The term is also defined as the focus of activity in a site, such as a camp or village around which hunting or agricultural activity takes place.

Numantia: A Bronze Age, Hallstatt, and Celtic site on the upper Duero (Douro) River in Spain near modern Soria, scene of heroic Celtiberian resistance to Rome in 133 BC. Founded on the site of earlier settlements by Iberians who penetrated the Celtic highlands about 300 BC, it later formed the center of Celtiberian resistance to Rome, withstanding repeated attacks. Scipio Aemilianus (Numantinus) finally blockaded it (in 133 BC) by establishing 6 miles of continuous ramparts around it. It eventually buckled, its destruction ending all serious resistance to Rome in Celtiberia. Numantia was later rebuilt by the emperor Augustus, but it had little importance. Archaeologists have found siege camps and 13 Roman camps.

nucleus: The block of primary material from which flakes have been removed by percussion for use in tools. The nucleus is what is left after the stone has been worked on and often bears characteristic signs of the method used. (*syn.* core)

number of identified specimens: A gross counting technique used in the quantification of animal bones. The method may produce misleading results in assessing the relative abundance of different species, because skeletal differences and differential rates of bone preservation mean that some species are represented more than others. It is a largely outdated measure of sample size in archaeological fauna. (*syn.* NISP)

numerical taxonomy: A set of mathematical procedures for grouping individual items into classes. The technique used is cluster analysis, which produces groupings of items based on their degree of similarity. There are different ways of measuring the similarity between items and different techniques of producing clusters from such measurements. Agglomerative techniques start with the most similar items and repeatedly add new members to existing clusters as the standard of similarity is lowered; divisive methods, on the other hand, start with the entire collection to be classified and repeatedly subdivided into smaller groups on the basis of certain attributes. The results of the analyses can be shown in the form of a dendrogram, but the interpretation of the groupings produced depends on a detailed assessment of the archaeological data itself. Numerical taxonomy is also the multivariate analysis of many measurable features (taxonomic characters) to produce a biological classification. Because of the complexity of the analysis, the use of a computer is virtually mandatory. No attempt is made, as in evolutionary taxonomy, to weight characters on the basis of their presumed roles in natural selection. For this reason, numerical taxonomy produces a classification that reflects "phenetic distances," that is, degrees of similarity. Such classifications are rejected by

many conventional taxonomists who feel that the relations expressed in a classification should be strictly evolutionary. The numerical evaluation of the affinity or similarity between taxonomic units and the ordering of these units into taxa on the basis of their affinities are used often in archaeology. (*syn.* cluster analysis; taximetrics)

Numidia: Under the Roman Republic and Empire, a part of Africa north of the Sahara, the boundaries of which at times corresponded roughly with those of modern Algeria and western part of Tunisia, excluding the area of Carthage. Its earliest inhabitants were divided into tribes and clans and were racially indistinguishable from the other Berber inhabitants of early North Africa. From the 6th century BC, points along the coast were occupied by the Carthaginians, who by the 3rd century BC had expanded into the interior as far as Theveste (Tébessa). Numidians were frequently found in the Carthaginian armies by that time. Their leader, Maninissa (240–148 BC), was largely responsible for the spread of Phoenician culture into this area, and by skillful management of his link with Rome he was able to bring greatly increased prosperity and stability to his community. After 146 BC, thousands of Carthaginians fled to Numidia after the destruction of Carthage. This kingdom, formed by nomads, was converted into a Roman province (Africa Nova) in 46 BC, and its chief city was Cirta. Numidia seems to have grown wine and olives very successfully on the plain, and horses and sheep were reared on higher ground. Caesar formed a new province, Africa Nova, from Numidian territory, and Augustus united Africa Nova ("New Africa") with Africa Vetus ("Old Africa," the province surrounding Carthage); but a separate province of Numidia was formally created by Septimius Severus. There are remains at Lambaesis, Timgad, and Theveste.

Nun: The oldest of the ancient Egyptian gods and father of Re-Atum, the sun god. He personified the original formless ocean of chaos from which the Primeval Mound of the sun god Re-Atum arose. (*syn.* Nu)

Nunamira Cave: Limestone cave in southwest Tasmania, Australia, with rich Pleistocene deposits. It was occupied c. 30,500 bp and abandoned c. 12,000 years ago. (*syn.* Bluff Cave)

nuraghe: A type of tower built of cyclopean masonry and peculiar to Sardinia from c. 1500 BC until the Roman conquest of the island c. 800 BC. They are circular stone defensive towers with corbel-vaulted internal chambers of the Middle and Late Bronze Ages. The walls of the tower slope inward toward the top, and there are commonly two or more stories. Each floor consists of a single round room roofed by corbelling and sometimes provided with lateral cells. The turrets were as high as 30–60 feet, and some nuraghi contain stones of 100 cubic feet each in their structure. The more complex examples consist of several towers, courtyards, and curtain walls, and many nuraghi (e.g., Barumini) are surrounded by substantial outer fortifications with further stone towers. Nuraghi continued to be built during the Phoenician and Carthaginian occupation of the island, right down to the Roman conquest. There are thousands of nuraghi in Sardinia, and they remain a prominent feature of the island's landscape today. The Nuraghic culture is associated with a flourishing bronze industry, which in its later stages produced a series of attractive figurines and votive models. The megalithic tombs known as "tombe di giganti" belong to the monuments including sacred wells. The Corsican *torre* (torri) and Balearic Island *talayots* share many architectural features with the nuraghi of Sardinia. (*syn.* plural nuraghi; nurhag; Nuraghic culture)

Nuri: Site in Upper Nubia, the successor to Kurru as the main royal pyramid cemetery of the Napatan kings of the mid-7th to early-3rd centuries BC. It is about 25 kilometers southwest of the fourth Nile cataract and a few kilometers to the northeast of Napata (a principal political center of Kush/Cush). The largest pyramid, that of the king Taharqa (reigned 690–664 BC), is situated there. Royal burials continued to take place at Nuri until 315 BC.

Nus-i Jan: Median site in the Malayer valley of Luristan, western Iran, which had a small fortified settlement in the late 8th century BC. Its architecture revealed Median cultic practices. A later Parthian settlement was also on the site.

Nut: In Egyptian religion, a goddess of the sky, vault of the heavens, often depicted as a woman arched over the earth god Geb. On 5 special days preceding the New Year, Nut gave birth successively to the deities Osiris, Horus, Seth, Isis, and Nephthys. These gods, with the exception of Horus, were commonly referred to as the "children of Nut." In the Heliopolitan doctrine of the Ennead, she was considered the daughter of Shu and sister-wife of Geb.

Nuzi: A provincial center with Old Akkadian, Old Assyrian, and Middle Assyrian/Hurrian levels ('Ubaid to Sassanian times), near Kirkuk (ancient Arrapha) in northern Mesopotamia (Iraq). A palace and private houses of the 15th–14th centuries BC were excavated, and finds include some 20,000 Old Akkadian clay tablets of the 23rd century BC. There is material from a mid-2nd millennium occupation associated with the kingdom of Arrapkha and with the Mitanni. Texts recovered provide the richest available documentation of the Mitanni Empire. During the 2nd half of the 2nd millennium BC, Nuzi was known as Gasur. Its distinctive type of pottery (Nuzi ware) dates to the time of association with the Mitanni and is found at other sites such as Tell Atchana from the mid-2nd millennium BC. (*syn.* modern Yorgan Tepe)

Nydam: A bog in Schleswig, southern Jutland, which yielded a rich votive deposit of the Roman Iron Age. The main finds were more than 100 iron swords (some with damascened blades, others stamped with the maker's name), and a wooden boat some 21 meters long. The boat was clinker built, had no mast or sail, and was provided with 15 rowlocks on each side. The bow and stern post were upturned, and the vessel was steered by an oar. It is now a famous exhibit, the Nydamboot (Nydam boat). This 4th-century Viking ship was discovered in 1863 in the Nydam marsh. It was one of the most important archaeological finds of the Migration Period. The boat is believed to have been typical of the vessels used by the Anglo-Saxon migrants coming to England in the 5th century. Its construction, however, would have made this a dangerous journey, and it is likely that its use was confined to the tideless sea of the Baltic.

nymphaeum or nymphaion: An ancient Greek and Roman sanctuary consecrated to water nymphs. It was an elaborately decorated public drinking fountain—a semicircular monumental Classical fountain house. It often had niches filled with sculpture. The nymphs were associated with a range of natural features such as water, mountains, and trees. Nymphaea were often erected near the head of a spring. The nymphaeum served as a sanctuary, a reservoir, and an assembly chamber where weddings were held. The rotunda nymphaeum, common in the Roman period, was borrowed from such Hellenistic structures as the Great Nymphaeum of Ephesus. Nymphaea existed at Corinth, Antioch, and Constantinople; the remains of about 20 have been found in Rome; and others exist as ruins in Asia Minor, Syria, and North Africa. The word *nymphaeum* was also used in ancient Rome to refer to a bordello and to the fountain in the atrium of the Christian basilica. (*syn.* nympheum)

Oo

Oakhurst: Cave in the southern Cape Province of South Africa with Later Stone Age material, including a microlithic industry of Wilton type overlying material without backed microliths and where large quadrilateral flakes and informal scrapers were used exclusively (c. 12th–9th millennia BC). This material is ascribed to the Albany or Oakhurst industry (formerly Smithfield A). Some include this industry with the Lockshoek and Pomongwe industries in the Oakhurst Complex.

oasis: A fertile patch in a desert. There are five major oases in western Egypt: Siwa, Bahariya, Farafra, Dakhla, and Kharga. Except for some Old Kingdom and First Intermediate settlements in Dakhla, most of the oases were probably not occupied until the 1st millennium BC. Two thirds of the total population of the Sahara are sedentary peoples living in oases, and these areas have vegetative growth. In all Saharan oases the date palm constitutes the main source of food, while in its shade are grown citrus fruits, figs, peaches, apricots, vegetables, and cereals such as wheat, barley, and millet. (*syn.* plural oases)

oat: An edible starchy grain of the oat plant (species *Avena sativa*), a cereal widely cultivated in the temperate regions of the world. "Wild oats" are present at early Neolithic sites of the Near East, dating to c. 6000 BC. Cultivated oats first appeared in Bronze Age Europe.

Obanian culture: A group of kitchen midden settlements of the western Scottish coast, a Late Mesolithic culture (c. 3065–3900 BC) named from Oban in Argyll. The sites are rock shelters and shell middens on postglacial raised beaches. Diagnostic tools include barbed spears, some limpet picks, scoops, and antler harpoon heads.

obelisk: Ancient Egyptian monolithic monument, consisting of a stone pillar with tapering square section and a pyramid top (pyramidion; Egyptian *benbenet*). They were erected for religious or monumental purposes and frequently bear carved inscriptions in hieroglyphs. Old Kingdom examples were squat and closely related to the pyramids, both being solar symbols. They were set up in pairs outside the entrances to some Old Kingdom tombs and outside temples; a single obelisk in east Karnak was the object of a cult. Later ones, such as Cleopatra's Needle, one of a pair erected by Thothmes III at Heliopolis, were much more slender. They were derived ultimately from the ancient benben stone in the temple of the sun god at Heliopolis. This stone was believed to be that on which the rays of the rising sun first fell, sacred at least by the 1st Dynasty (3100–2890 BC). Obelisks were usually cut from hard stone, particularly red granite from Aswan. The largest surviving examples (30 m high, 450 tons) were products of the New Kingdom. The earliest surviving obelisk dates from the reign of Sesostris I (1918–1875 BC) and stands at Heliopolis, where once stood a temple to Re. (*syn.* Egyptian tekhen; needle)

object clustering: An approach to typology based on clusters of human artifacts that are seen as specific classificatory types.

objet d'art: An object of artistic value.

Oblazowa: Upper Palaeolithic cave site in southern Poland on the Bialka River. Artifacts include an end-scraper, blades, and polished woolly mammoth tusk.

oblique flaking: A flaking technique in which the flake scars appear from left to right diagonally across the face of an artifact.

oblique photographs: In aerial photography, taken from an angle (neither perpendicular nor parallel) so as to reveal elevation and contours.

obol: Greek silver coin, six of which equaled a drachma.

Obre: A complex of Neolithic settlements on the Bosnia River near Sarajevo, Bosnia. Obre I has four occupation horizons, the first with Starcevo pottery, dating c. 4500–4200 BC. It has rectangular houses similar to those at Karanovo I and Anza, arranged in rows. Obre II represents the most complete development of the Butmir culture yet discovered, with nine habitation horizons in three main periods (dated c. 4250–3950 BC, c. 3900 BC, and c. 3800 BC). This 1300-year cut through the Bosnian Neolithic sequence provides details on the evolution of timber-framed architecture, subsistence economy, and exchange systems. The pottery is interpreted as reflecting possible transhumant pastoralism.

obsidian: A jet-black to gray, naturally occurring volcanic glass, formed by rapid cooling of viscous lava. It was often used as raw material for the manufacture of stone tools and was very popular as a superior form of flint for flaking or, as it is easily chipped, to form extremely sharp edges. Obsidian breaks with a conchoidal fracture and is easily chipped into precise and delicate forms. It was very widely traded from the anciently exploited sources in Hungary, Sardinia, Lipari in Sicily, Melos in the Aegean, central and eastern Anatolia, Mexico, and so forth. Chemical analysis of their trace elements now allows most of the sources to be distinguished (especially by neutron activation and x-ray fluorescence spectrometry), so that the pattern of trade spreading out from each can be traced. Two dating methods have been applied to obsidian: obsidian hydration dating and fission track dating. In Europe, obsidian was exploited extensively from c. 6000–3000 BC; after 3000 BC, it generally went out of favor for everyday purposes (perhaps as a result of competition from metal tools), but it continued to be used for prestige objects in some areas, especially by the Minoans and Mycenaeans. Obsidian has been quarried and traded by western Melanesians since at least 19,000 bp, with the earliest-used and most important source being that at Talasea on New Britain. Obsidian was also an important trade item in Mesoamerica. (*syn.* hyalopsite, Iceland agate, mountain mahogany)

obsidian hydration: The absorption of water on exposed surfaces of obsidian. In each specific environment, the surface of an obsidian artifact absorbs water at a steady rate, forming the hydration layer. The thicker the layer, the older the artifact. If the local hydration rate is known and constant, this phenomenon can be used as an absolute age determination technique through measurement of the thickness of the hydration layer.

obsidian hydration dating: A method of dating in which the age of an obsidian artifact is established by measuring the thickness of its hydration rim (layer of water penetration) and comparing that with a known local hydration rate. The hydration layer is caused by absorption of water on exposed surfaces of the rock. The surface of obsidian starts to absorb water as soon as it is exposed by flaking during manufacture of an artifact. The layer of hydrated obsidian is visible when a slice of the artifact is examined under an optical microscope at a magnification of times 500. Hydration varies geographically, and several factors such as climate, chemical environ-

ment, and physical abrasion also affect the thickness of the layer, so that most studies are locally or regionally based. Obsidian may also be dated by the fission track dating technique. Dates have been obtained in Japan extending back as far as c. 25,000 BC. (*syn.* obsidian hydration layer dating, obsidian dating)

obsidian sourcing: A method to fingerprint unknown obsidian samples and compare them with known sources, to determine the source of the unknown sample.

occupation layer: A layer in which an original deposit is preserved as it existed when the site was abandoned. The term describes any layer of in situ accumulation of domestic refuse and other debris resulting from occupation of an area of a site by humans. (*syn.* living floor)

occupation span: The time during which a site is occupied by humans.

occupation surface: Any surface used for human activities, such as a room floor, a stairway, or a walkway. (*syn.* occupation floor)

Ocean Bay tradition: A culture of the southern coast of Alaska, dated from c. 4000–1000 BC, a marine mammal-hunting tradition. The principal excavated sites are Sitkalidak Roadcut (Kodiak Islands) and Takli Island.

Oc-eo: Protohistoric site in southern Vietnam in the Mekong Delta, thought to have been the main port of the kingdom of Funan, built on a Neolithic site. This port settlement, which flourished amid a complex of other settlements connected by canals, was not only an extraordinarily rich emporium dealing in articles from as far as Rome and inner Asia, but it was also a local manufacturing center producing its own jewelry, pottery, and other trade goods. In addition to objects of local production, a large amount of traded goods from India and China, western Asia, and even the Mediterranean, dated to between the 2nd–7th centuries AD, has been found. These finds include Roman coins of Antoninus Pius and Marcus Aurelius of the 2nd century AD; Chinese bronzes; Indian beads, seals, and other jewelry. (*syn.* Oc Eo)

ocher: Soft varieties of iron oxide (hematite, limonite, goethite), which were ground and used with other materials in prehistory to take pigment. Ocher occurs naturally and was much used for coloring matter, as in cave art, pottery painting, and personal decoration. Red ocher was certainly used ceremonially to give an impression of life to the corpse during funerary rites. There are many records from the Upper Palaeolithic onward of ocher staining of skeletons. It was mixed with earth, clay, blood, or grease to make the paint. Ocher was used as crayons or powder in the Aurignacian period for paintings on walls of caves or on bone or stone artifacts. It was mainly yellow, brown, black, orange, and red (hematite). (*syn.* ochre)

Ocher-Colored Pottery: An Indian pottery type, a distinctive ceramic of the post-Harappan upper Ganges Valley. It is a thick and usually badly fired and badly preserved red ware with an ocher wash, and its importance lies in the fact that it serves to bridge the gap in the later 2nd millennium between the Harappan material of the Indus civilization and the black-and-red and painted-gray wares of the Iron Age. The earliest date for the ware comes from Jodhpura in Rajasthan, c. early 3rd millennium BC, but in the upper Ganges Valley it has early 2nd millennium BC dates. It has been found in association with a harpoon of Gangetichoard type at Saipai and with Gangetic hoards. (*syn.* Ochre Colored Pottery; OCP)

Ocsöd-Kovashalom: Late Neolithic site of the Tisza culture, on the Körös River in eastern Hungary. There are many settlement features, including ovens, storage pits, rubbish pits, and burials.

oculus: The central opening at the top of a dome, such as in the Pantheon at Rome. The term is also used for a small window that is circular or oval in shape, such as an oeil-de-boeuf window. A third meaning is a decorative and religious motif symbolizing an eye, consisting of paired circles or spirals, as on the Spanish symbolkeramik. The design was widespread in western Europe in the 4th–3rd millennia BC. It occurs in the Spanish Copper Age, for instance at Los Millares, and is also found in Ireland and northern Europe in the late Neolithic. The capital of every Ionic column features a characteristic pair of volutes, or spiral scrolls, at the center of each of which is an eye, or disk, also known as on oculus.

OD: Datum against which height and depths are measured. (*syn.* ordnance survey)

Odderade Interstadial: An interstadial of the Weichselian Cold Stage, dated by radiocarbon to c. 58,000 bp, but it may be earlier. The beginning of the Weichsel has been placed at about 70,000 years ago.

odeon: A Greek or Roman concert hall with tiered seating, built on a circular plan, and covered with a roof. It was probably used for concerts and speeches. The earliest is that constructed by Pericles at Eleusis (Athens) in 435 BC. Roman examples exist at Pompeii, Lyons, and Pula. An important example is that of Agrippia in the Agora at Athens; it differed from later odeums in its square shape and pointed roof. (*syn.* odeion, odeum)

Odmut: Cave site on the Piva River, Montenegro, occupied during the Mesolithic, Neolithic, Copper Age, and Bronze Age. The first levels were dated c. 8100–6650 BC, with a hunting economy based on ibex exploitation. There was an Early Neolithic Impressed Ware level, dated c. 5035–4950 BC. Undated levels contained pottery with Danilo and Kakanji affinities; Final Neolithic black burnished ware; and Late Copper Age pottery. A radiocarbon date of c. 1710 BC accompanied Early Bronze Age pottery.

oecus: A reception room in a private Greek or Roman residence (domus).

Oelknitz: Upper Palaeolithic site on the Saale River, eastern Germany, dated to 12,542–11,750 bp. There are backed blades, end-scrapers, burins, bone points, and Venus figurines. The assemblage is assigned to the Magdalenian.

oenochoe: A wine jug from the classical period of Greek pottery, a graceful vessel with delicately curved handle and trefoil-shaped mouth. It was used to take the wine from the crater and distribute it into cups (especially at symposiums) and is the vase carried by goddesses and used for libations in conjunction with a phiale. It was made from precious metal, bronze, or clay. The oenochoe was revived during the Renaissance and again during the Neoclassical period of the 18th century. (*syn.* oinochoe)

Oenpelli Shelters: A group of five sites in Arnhem Land, northern Australia (Padypadiy, Nawamoyn, Malangangerr, Tyimede I and II). Similar tool assemblages dating from 20,000–3000 BC appeared at Malanganerr, Nawamoyn, Tyimede II—thick flake scrapers with steep edges, horse-hoof cores, stone hammers, grinders, and waisted or grooved ground-edge axes. The ground-edge axes found at Malangangerr and Nawamoyn in levels dated to 20,000–16,000 BC are the oldest examples of edge-grinding known in Australia. The sudden appearance of estuarine species in shell middens of 5000–4000 BC in the Malangangerr and Nawamoyn deposits reflects rising sea levels. About 2000 years later, at all five sites, small stone points and scrapers appeared and continued until the present. There is also much bark painting in the area.

Offa's Dyke: A linear earthwork, some 270 kilometers long, built by King Offa of Mercia (reigned 757–796) as a frontier between his Anglo-Saxon kingdom and the kingdom of Powys. It is a large earthen bank and quarry ditch and runs almost continuously between Treuddy and Chepstow, close to the border of England and Wales. Offa's reign is also noteworthy for the close connections he established between Mercia and the Carolingian Empire (his daughter married one of Charlemagne's sons) and for the introduction of regular coinage based on pennies.

offering table: An important element of the Egyptian private tomb throughout the pharaonic and Greco-Roman periods. It was usually placed in an accessible location, such as the chapel, so that offerings could be brought to it by the funerary priests or relatives of the deceased.

offertory: In Egyptian archaeology, an offering made to the gods. As an artifact, it could take on various forms: outstretched hands supporting a cup; or spoons of ivory, wood, or bronze, the handle of which is formed by a human figure.

offset planning: A technique used in small-scale excavations to measure the plans of features. A point is measured with reference to a baseline, which is frequently the edge of an excavation trench. The measurement requires the formation of a right angle at the point at which the tapes meet; this can be achieved by using a T-square or by constructing a right-angled triangle with a tape by using the Pythagoras theorem.

off-site archaeology: The recovery and analysis of unclustered physical remains produced by human activities. Nonsite archaeology generally concentrates on remains recovered in a surface or plow zone context. It is an approach, especially in archaeological survey, where the unit of analysis is the artifact rather than the site. Practitioners document the distribution of humanly modified materials across the landscape. (*syn.* non-site archaeology, landscape archaeology)

off-site data: Unclustered physical remains produced by human activities; evidence from a range of information, including scatters of artifacts and features such as plow marks and field boundaries. These data can provide important evidence about human exploitation of the environment.

Ofnet: A cave near Nordingen in Bavaria, best known for the composite burial of 33 skulls of early Mesolithic date. Some earlier Palaeolithic deposits are also present in this and the nearby Klein Ofnet cave. In deposits of the Late Palaeolithic Azilian culture found at Ofnet, carefully decapitated heads were buried separately from the bodies, indicating beliefs in the special sanctity or importance of the head.

Ogdoad: A group of eight deities or eons (four male-female pairs) associated with Hermopolis, who symbolize the state of the world before creation. The group's composition varies, but its classic form is: Nun and Naunet, primeval waters; Huh and Hauhet, endless space; Kuk and Kauket, darkness; Amun and Amaunet, what is hidden. The priests at Hermopolis Magna, the principal cult place of Thoth, identified these eight as the primeval actors in a creation myth.

ogham: A Celtic script used for writing in northwest Europe, probably created in the 2nd–3rd centuries AD, and used for writing Irish and Pictish languages. The alphabet has 20 letters represented by tally marks on either side of or crossing a horizontal baseline. The script is better suited for carving on stone (or possibly wood) than for writing in ink. It is believed to have originated in Ireland or south Wales as a secret script, and it spread throughout the Celtic areas for use on memorial stones. It is also found associated with the symbols and carvings of the Picts, who used it until the 9th century. Ogham is used on memorial pillar stones in the Celtic regions of Britain, usually consisting of no more than the name and descent of the dead man. It was often the custom, particularly in the south and west in Wales and Cornwall, to provide a translation in Latin minuscule, and this has proved important for the translation and dating of ohgam. Of the more than 375

ogham inscriptions known, about 300 are from Ireland. (*syn.* Ogam, ogam, Ogham, ogum; Pictish symbol stones)

Ohaba-Ponor: Palaeolithic cave site in the southern Carpathian Mountains of Romania. There is a Middle Palaeolithic layer with side scrapers and points and a small Upper Palaeolithic layer.

oinochoe: A wine jug from the classical period of Greek pottery, a graceful vessel with delicately curved handle and trefoil-shaped mouth. It was used to take the wine out of the crater and distribute it into cups (especially at symposiums) and is the vase carried by goddesses and used for libations in conjunction with a phiale. It was made from precious metal, bronze, or clay. The oinochoe was revived during the Renaissance and again during the Neoclassical period of the 18th century. (*syn.* oenochoe)

Ojin (fl. 4th–5th c. AD): The 15th emperor of Japan, given in the traditional list for the 3rd–4th century AD. It is also the name of the keyhole mounded tomb, the second largest in Japan, used as his mausoleum at Habikino near Osaka. Ojin is believed to have consolidated imperial power, championed land reform, and promoted cultural exchanges with Korea and China. It is said that highly skilled weaving techniques were brought from Korea during his reign. Chinese scholars introduced Confucianism and the Chinese writing system into the country, thus marking the beginning of Japanese cultural growth.

Okhotsk: A late prehistoric deep-sea fishing culture of the coastal areas of northern and eastern Hokkaido, Sakhalin, and the Kurile Islands, Japan. It coexisted with the Satsumon culture from about AD 800–1300, and then disappeared. The hunter-fishermen also kept pigs and lived in distinctive hexagonal pit houses.

Okladnikov, Aleksei Pavlovich (1908–1984): Soviet archaeologist working in Siberia and Central Asia. He discovered the Neanderthal burial at Teshik Tash in Uzbekistan and worked at the Palaeolithic sites of Ust'-Kan Cave, Ulalinka, Makarovo, Krasnyj Yar, and Buret.' He wrote the classic *Yakutia Before Its Incorporation into the Russian State* (1970, originally published in Russian, 2nd ed., 1955).

Okvik: Eskimo site of the Thule tradition of the Punuk Islands in the Bering Sea. It dates to c. 300 BC and has artifacts of the art style that developed through the succeeding Old Bering Sea and Punuk phases of the Northern Maritime subtradition. The earliest and finest statuettes of which there is knowledge are assigned to the Okvik culture; Okvik art is concerned primarily with the representation of the human figure, differing in that respect from the contemporary or slightly later Old Bering Sea culture, where the main interest is animals, such as reindeer, elks, bears, and seals. There were also decorated ivory tools such as harpoons and extensive use of polished slate and organic artifacts.

Old Babylonian period: Chronological period of c. 2000–1600 BC when there were competing kingdoms in southern Mesopotamia, which were eventually conquered by Hammurabi of Babylon. The kingdoms included Isin and Larsa, important during the first half of the period, and the large kingdom created by Hammurabi, which flourished in the second half. The period was a time of increasing intellectual endeavors in literature, astronomy, mathematics, law.

Old Bering Sea Culture: An Eskimo subculture in northern Alaska and northeast Siberia between 1500–2000 years ago and best known for its ivory objects. The earliest sites were in Bering Strait area, and the major type site is on St. Lawrence Island. It is an early manifestation of the western Arctic Thule tradition, often linked with the possibly contemporaneous Okvik culture. Although both share similar traits—a highly evolved art style, polished slate tools, and pottery—the relation between the two is still uncertain. The art style appears to have flourished between AD 100–500. (*syn.* Old Bering Sea stage)

Oldbury: Rock shelter in Kent, England, with a collection of tools of Mousterian or Acheulian type tools. These tools, including bifaces and flake tools, are more abundant than in any other British Mousterian site. It is one of the few areas of Britain with caves suitable for occupation during the Palaeolithic.

Old Copper Culture: A series of late Archaic complexes in the upper Great Lakes area of the United States and Canada, which settled there approximately 5,000 years ago. This culture of hunters and fishermen did not have pottery and agriculture, but the people mined native copper around Lake Superior and used it to make tools. The metal was worked by hot and cold hammering and by annealing. Characteristic copper implements were spear points, knives, awls, and *atlatl* weights. Its best-known assemblages are from Osceola and Ocanto. Later cultures did not develop metal technology, but reverted to stone use. There is general agreement that 1500 BC represents the terminal date.

Old Cordilleran Culture: A late Pleistocene cultural tradition based on the hunting of small game and the collection of wild foods in the mountain and plateau region of western North America, especially Oregon and Washington, between c. 9000–5000 BC (or later). The diagnostic tool is the leaf-shaped Cascade point, a distinctive bipointed lanceolate point. It was usually accompanied by scraping tools (chopper tools, bolas) and occasionally by milling stones (burins). The type site is Five Mile Rapids, Oregon (9800 BP). It may have been contemporaneous with the Big Game Hunting tradition. The culture has a terminal date of c. 7000 BP, and it may have cultural ties to the San Dieguito. (*syn.* Old Cordilleran)

Old Crow: Series of sites along the Old Crow River in the northern Yukon, Canada, with bones of extinct Pleistocene animals and one tool (a flesher made of caribou bone), which once had a radiocarbon date of c. 27,000 ± 2000 BC. It is now dated to 1350 bp. Dating of other artifacts could show Old Crow to be among the earliest sites in the western hemisphere, going back some 40,000 years. (*syn.* Old Crow Flats)

Older Dryas: A stadial of the Weichselian Cold Stage, dating to between c. 12,000–11,800 bp.

Oldishi: Kenyan Pastoral Neolithic pottery tradition. There are southern, eastern, and northern facies; Narosura Ware belongs to the southern facies.

Old Kingdom: A period in Egyptian history including the 3rd through 8th Dynasties, c. 2575–2130 BC. It preceded the Middle Kingdom and is marked by the building of colossal stone pyramids. Most of the royal pyramid complexes and private mastaba tombs of the Memphite necropolis were built during this time. The first significant ruler of the 3rd Dynasty was Djoser Netjerikhet (2667–2648 BC), whose Step Pyramid still dominates the skyline of northern Saqqara. Also, the term refers to one of the two main periods of Hittite history, covering c. 1700–1500 BC (the New Kingdom, or Empire, was c. 1400–1180). With the end of the 8th Dynasty, the Old Kingdom Egyptian state collapsed. (*syn.* Pyramid Age)

Oldowan: An Earlier Stone Age industry and complex seen at Olduvai Gorge in Tanzania and other African sites, dating from c. 2.5 million to about 1.6 million years ago (and later). It includes the earliest tool kits, flake and pebble tools, used by hominids (*Homo habilis*). Robust australopithecines were present at the same time and at the same sites, however. These simple stone tools were flaked in one or two directions and are characterized by the production of small flakes removed from alternate faces along the edge of a cobble. In its pure form, hand axes are absent. Oldowan tools were made for nearly 1 million years before gradual improvement in technique resulted in a standardized industry known as the Acheulian. (*syn.* Oldowan industry)

Old South American Hunting tradition: A tradition dating from between 10,000–7000 BC, characterized by its "fish-tailed" fluted stone projectile points and leaf-shaped lanceolate points. The points' origin may be related to North American pressured flaked points of Clovis and Folsom. Old South American Hunting tradition gave rise to the Andean Hunting and Collecting tradition.

Olduvai: A site in northern Tanzania, which is one of the most important sites for the understanding of both human evolution and the development of the earliest tools. Olduvai gorge is 30 miles long, located on the volcanic belt of the Great Rift Valley. Louis and Mary Leakey uncovered numerous hominid remains, animal bones, and stone artifacts from c. 1.9 million years to less than 10,000 years ago. Living floors and camp sites with pebble tools, choppers, and a few artifacts made of flakes go back to the earliest date as do the bones of two primitive forms of hominid, *Homo habilis* and *Australopithecus robustus* (Zinjanthropus). Crude hand axes have been dated to c. 1.2–0.5 million years ago and are accompanied by several hominid fossils of *Homo erectus* and *Homo sapiens*. Acheulian tools are found with Neanderthal remains, and later beds contained a Kenya Capsian industry. No site in the world has produced a longer sequence of stone tool assemblages and of hominid fossils. (*syn.* Olduvai Gorge)

Old World: The Eastern Hemisphere, with special reference to Europe, Africa, and Asia; the part of the world known to Europeans before contact with the Americas. (*syn.* eastern hemisphere)

Oleneostrovski Mogilnik: Large Mesolithic cemetery on Lake Onega in northern Russia, with thousands of artifacts from the excavated graves.

Oligocene: Major worldwide division of the Tertiary period, which began about 36.6 million years ago and ended about 23.7 million years ago. It follows the Eocene Epoch and precedes the Miocene Epoch. The term *Oligocene* is derived from Greek and means the "epoch of few recent forms," referring to the sparseness of the number of modern animals that originated during the Oligocene. Many large mountain systems and herbivorous mammals began to develop, however. During this epoch, many of the older types of mammals became extinct, and the first apes appeared. The largest land mammal of all time, Baluchitherium, is known from Asia, and the first mastodons are known from Egypt. In North America, primitive horses were evolving, including three-toed forms such as Mesohippus and Miohippus. Pigs and peccaries first appeared in the early Oligocene of Europe and reached North America late in the epoch. The earliest apelike form, Parapithecus, is known from Oligocene deposits in Egypt, which have also yielded remains of several kinds of Old World monkeys. The earliest New World monkeys are known from late Oligocene deposits in South America. (*syn.* Oligocene Epoch)

olive: Subtropical, broad-leaved, evergreen tree and its edible, oil-producing fruit. It was recorded from El Garcel in Spain in the Neolithic, and the edible olive was grown on the island of Crete about 3500 BC; the Semitic peoples apparently cultivated it as early as 3000 BC. Olive oil was prized for anointing the body in Greece during the time of Homer; and it was an important crop of the Romans c. 600 BC. Later, olive growing spread to all the countries bordering the Mediterranean.

olive jar: A type of pottery vessel used to ship olives and wine (and other commodities) from Spain; commonly found in Spanish colonial archaeological sites.

olivella: A genus of marine univalve shell commonly used as raw material for the manufacture of beads and ornaments. It is a small spiral shell.

Oliviense: A flake industry of the terraces in the Caleta Olivia and Bahia Solano region of southern Argentina. It was originally believed to be Late Pleistocene, but may actually be more recent.

olla: A ceramic vessel generally used to store and cool water—globular shaped, narrow mouthed. It resembled flower pots, but had swelling sides, flaring necks and rims, and was covered with a lid.

Ollantaytambo: Inca site in Urubamba Valley, near Cuzco, Peru. It was a planned, trapezoidal town with ceremonial and domestic architecture. It was a royal estate for Inca Pachacuti and then used as a fort when the Spanish arrived. Architecturally, the Incas surpassed all others in their use of intricately cut, giant-size stone blocks, as displayed at Ollantaytambo.

Olmalenge: Kenyan Pastoral Neolithic pottery tradition. There is a northern facies in the Turkana region and a southern facies in Nakuru Basin.

Olmec: The first complex civilization of Mesoamerica and its distinctive art style, beginning in the Early Preclassic (c. 1200 BC) and ending c. 400 BC. The farming population built and supported great ceremonial centers (La Venta, San Lorenzo, Tenochititlan, Tres Zapotes), importing tons of serpentine and basalt from outside the region. The Olmecs were great stonecarvers whose products ranged from basalt heads almost 2 meters high to small jade figurines in which the attributes of a baby-faced human being merge and blend with those of a jaguar to form a composite monster (were-jaguar). Carvings in this distinctive style have been discovered over much of Mexico and as far south as El Salvador and Costa Rica. They are also noted for a distinctive black, white-rimmed kaolin pottery. Olmec figurines and pottery have been found at various sites in central Mexico, and contacts were strong with the cultures of Oaxaca before the construction of Monte Albán. The Olmec are also known for art in jadeite and shell and the first hieroglyphic writing system. The Olmec golden age was the early part of the 1st millennium BC. They developed many of the religious traditions that were to sustain the Maya and other Mesoamerican civilizations such as Teotihuacán. They are not to be confused with historic Olmecs, who were a later group and may have helped destroy Teotihuacán, and whose tyranny was responsible for the migration of many Mesoamerican peoples. (*syn.* Tenocelome, La Venta)

Olorgesailie: Important Lower Palaeolithic site south of Nairobi in southern Kenya; the area of Mount Olorgesailie was where the Rift Valley was first recognized. It had an informative Earlier Stone Age Acheulian industry with hand axes, cleavers, and other stone artifacts dating to 900,000–700,000 years ago. Baboons were hunted in large numbers.

Olsen-Chubbuck: A bison kill site in Colorado on the North American plains, which revealed many details of Palaeoindian hunting and butchering techniques. It is about 8,500 years old, of the Firstview Complex of the Plano tradition.

Olszanica: Linear Pottery culture settlement in southern Poland near Kraków dating to the late 5th millennium BC. There were 13 longhouses, one of high status, and obsidian and Bürk pottery from Hungary.

Oltome: Kenyan Pastoral Neolithic pottery tradition. Kansyore ware may be a facies.

Olympia: Principal sanctuary of Zeus in Greece and the site of the original Olympic Games, a Panhellenic sanctuary in the western Peloponnese of Greece. It originated in the Greek Bronze Age and has a 7th-century BC temple of Hera and a 5th-century BC temple of Zeus. Traces of the circular building of Philip of Macedon and buildings associated with athletes and games—gymnasium, palaestra, bouleuterion, Leonidaeon, and running track—have been found. The workshop of the sculptor Pheidias, who made the statue of Athena at Athens and that of Zeus at Olympia, has been located. Perhaps first attracting use as an earth shrine and oracle, the site shows signs of continuous occupation from early in the 3rd millennium BC. The Games were celebrated on a 4-year cycle, the Olympiad, which came to form the basis of a Greek system of dating. The first Olympiad is dated to 776 BC, but tradition places the commencement of the Games in the 9th century, with ascriptions variously to Heracles or Pelops as founder. The Games showed an unbroken record of celebration from 776 BC to 393 AD, when Theodosius I abolished them.

Olynthus: Ancient city of northern Greece, captured and destroyed by Philip of Macedon in 348 BC. Some late Neolithic settlement is followed after a gap by Iron Age occupation by Thracian tribes, perhaps from about 1000 BC. The 5th–4th centuries BC saw the classical Greek town caught up in alliances, misalliances, intrigues, and wars. The town, from c. 430 BC, had a road system and Hippodamian-planned house blocks. Many of the houses show an internal courtyard, sometimes colonnaded, and a south-facing dining room. In some cases, a second story is reached by a wooden staircase from the courtyard. The roof is typically pitched and tiled. There are important examples of pebble mosaic floors, some with mythological scenes, and of a bathroom with pottery tub. Inscriptional evidence from the houses gives information of their sale, rental, and mortgage. The houses have produced several coin hoards. The city also provides a ter-

minus ante quem for the development of black-glossed pottery.

Omari, el-: A site south of Cairo, Egypt, on the east of the Nile Delta, showing primitive Neolithic material closely comparable to that from Merimde. This phase of the Lower Egyptian Predynastic period, consisting of several Predynastic settlements and cemeteries clustered around the Wadi Hof, was transitional between the Merimde and Maadi. (*syn.* Omari)

Omo: A river basin in Ethiopia north of Lake Turkana, where fragmentary remains of Australopithecus and early Homo have been found. The same deposits have produced flakes of imported quartz, 2.4–2 million years old, the oldest securely dated artifacts. The site is of outstanding importance as a basis for dating other sites throughout Africa, because its time scale is unusually well fixed by palaeomagnetic studies, potassium argon dates, and faunal comparisons.

Omori: A late to Final Jomon shell midden near Tokyo, Japan. Edward S. Morse conducted the first scientific excavation of an archaeological site in Japan here in 1877. "Jomon" is the Japanese translation of the term "cord mark" used by Morse to describe the pottery from the site.

omphalos: The "navel" of the earth, marked by a stone shaped like a Christmas pudding, decorated by a network of woolen ribbons and located at Delphi in the temple of Apollo. It supposedly marked the exact center of the universe.

onager: A subspecies of the wild ass of Asia that ranged in the steppes from northwest Iran to Turkmenistan. Pale colored and small, it has a short erect mane and fairly large ears. It was domesticated in ancient times but was replaced by the domestic horse and donkey. It is now found in limited numbers and is close to extinction.

Ondratice: Middle Palaeolithic site northeast of Brno in Moravia, Czechoslovakia. There are end scrapers and side scrapers of Middle and Upper Palaeolithic types.

Ongbah Cave: Cave site in west-central Thailand near Three Pagodas Pass with a Hoabinhian period occupation c. 9000 BC. There are some 3rd–2nd century BC burials, iron implements, bronze bangles. stone beads, and parts of Dong-Son cast bronze drums.

Onion Portage: Important site in northwest Alaska containing one of the continent's longest stratigraphies; occupied from at least 8500 BP by a number of Eskimo–Siberian–Indian subcultures (American Palaeoarctic, Northern Archaic, Arctic Small Tool traditions, Inuit cultures). The oldest industries, called Akmak and Kobuk, are thought to last from c. 9000 BC until the mid-7th millennium BC and include chipped tools (blades, bifaces, and associated cores), which are closer to Siberian types than to those of temperate America. The Kobuk (6200–6000 BC) contained similar tools but of limited variety. After a long hiatus in occupation, the Palisades II industry (4850–3350 BC, variously 4000–2000 BC) shows links with the archaic cultures of the forest zone to the southeast, as does the succeeding Portage complex (3350–3000 BC, variously 2600–2200 BC). Next came tools of the Denbigh Flint Complex (3200 BC, variously 2200–1800 BC), followed by Chloris (1500–500 BC) with the oldest pottery in the Arctic, then a local version (Norton) of Ipiutak (AD 400–800), by a forest-adapted Indian culture called Itkillik Complex (AD 500–1000), and finally by an Arctic Woodland Culture facies of the Thule tradition. The excellent vertical stratigraphy of this site makes it the major reference for all western Arctic chronologies, especially when taken together with the horizontal stratigraphy of Cape Krusenstern.

onomasticon: A Greek thesaurus of terms, a type of ancient text consisting of lists of various categories of names, from plants and animals to cities or professions. The onomastica were presumably intended to serve both as repositories of knowledge and as training exercises for scribes. (*syn.* plural onomastica)

Onuris: An Egyptian deity associated with war and hunting, whose name means "he who brings back the distant one," referring to his principal mythical role in which he returned from Nubia with his consort, the lioness goddess Mehit. (*syn.* Anhur, Inhert)

opal phytolith: Microscopic silica bodies that form in living plants, providing a durable floral ecofact that allows identification of plant remains in archaeological deposits. (*syn.* plant opal phytolith, phytolith)

open association: An assumed relation between two or more artifacts that are found together, when it cannot be proved that they were deposited together.

open excavation: The opening up of large horizontal areas for excavation, used especially where single period deposits lie close to the surface. It is the excavation of as large an area as possible without the intervention of balks and a grid system. This technique allows the recognition of much slighter traces of ancient structures than other methods. On multiperiod sites, however, it calls for much more meticulous recording because the stratigraphy is revealed one layer at a time. In this method of excavation, the full horizontal extent of a site is cleared, and large areas are open while preserving a stratigraphic record in the balks between large squares. A gradual vertical probe may then take place. This method is often used to uncover houses and prehistoric settlement patterns. (*syn.* area excavation; open-area excavation, extensive excavation)

Opening of the Mouth: The ancient Egyptian ceremony performed at the funeral to restore the senses of the deceased. Part of the reanimation rite, the ritual opening of the mouth

was an important element of the ceremony so that the mummy might breathe and eat.

open mold: An early and simple mold developed for casting metal tools and weapons and, later, glass and brick. It consisted of a single block of stone, or occasionally clay, with the shape of the required artifact cut into it. Only very simple objects can be cast in this way, especially when one surface must be flat. The molds continued in use after more sophisticated versions had been developed, mainly for the manufacture of blanks for coins. The molds were probably not technically open, because this would result in oxidation of the surface of the metal, so that probably a flat stone or other cover was placed over the mold during cooling. Glass was cast in open molds by the Egyptians as early as 5 BC. (*syn.* open mould)

open site: A term for any archaeological site not located in a cave or rock shelter. (*syn.* open-air site)

open system: In archaeology, cultural systems that interchange energy, matter, or information with their environment. The system changes because of sources either internal or external to the system.

openwork: Decorative technique in which gaps or interstices are left around a pattern, sometimes to be filled in with a different material. It is also any work constructed so as to show openings through its substance; work that is perforated or pierced.

operational model: A representation of reality that is based on observation of how the component parts of the real situation operate.

opisthodomos: An entrance room or rear porch for the adyton of a Classical temple, at the rear of the temple and entered through two columns placed between stub walls. The pronaos is the front porch.

Oplontis: Seaside city destroyed by the eruption of Vesuvius in AD 79. Torre Annunziata was again destroyed by Vesuvius in 1631 and since rebuilt. (*syn.* Torre Annunziata)

Opole: A series of centralized territories and the name of a city and province in southwestern Poland. Opole the city began as the home of the Slavic Opolanie tribe; the earliest mention of it was in the 9th century. In 1202, it became the capital of the Opole principality, which included the entire Upper Silesia region. The town passed to Bohemia (1327), the Habsburgs (16th century), and Prussia (1742) and was returned to Poland in 1945. Each Opole (the territory) was dominated by a fortified timber citadel, which often had large and complex defenses; examples are at Leczyic and Szeligi.

oppidum: A Roman term, coined by Caesar, for the fortified Celtic towns he found in his campaigns in Gaul in 58–51 BC. The Roman oppidum was a town that served as administrative center for its surrounding area, or, in the provinces, was a community of Roman citizens, either Italian immigrants or enfranchised natives. The term is now used for comparable sites in Celtic territory, from Spain and Britain to the Carpathians. Celtic oppida of the 2nd and 1st centuries BC were large permanent settlements, usually of hill-fort type, the first true towns in Europe north of the Alps. Oppida also served as centers for trade, industry, market, craft production, and religion. (*syn.* plural oppida)

optical emission spectrometry: A physical technique used to analyze the trace elements in artifacts, especially stone, metal, glasses, and ceramics. It involves the excitation, by means of an electric discharge or a laser beam, of the atoms in the sample, and the analysis of the constituent wavelengths of the light released when the atoms relax. The wavelengths, separated by the use of a prism or diffraction grating, are each characteristic of individual elements, and the intensity of the light of particular wavelengths indicates the concentration of each element. Optical emission spectrometry has been used with great success to establish the sources of obsidian artifacts in the Near East and Mediterranean. Generally, this method gives an accuracy of only 25% and has been superseded by inductively coupled plasma emission spectrometry (IPS). Between 5–100 micrograms of material are needed. (*syn.* OES)

optical square: A surveying instrument, used for setting out right angles on the ground.

optimal foraging theory: The theory that an animal's efficient foraging behavior should maximize an animal's net rate of food intake. It is a theoretical perspective used in evolutionary biology, which attempts to develop a set of models to apply to a broad range of animal species based on theories of optimal net rates of energy gain.

opus caementicium: Roman concrete work; the mortar of lime, sand, water, and pozzolana was mixed with stones and broken brick to form a true concrete.

opus incertum: A Roman construction technique involving walls of very small rough stones, not laid in courses, but held together by the mortar or attached to a concrete core. This technical term was also used by Vitruvius c. 30 BC to describe the irregular patchwork stone surface that was commonly applied to Republican-period walls, as a decorative facing for the concrete inner core. Opus incertum was the most common facing for ordinary concrete walls of the 2nd and 1st centuries BC. The face of the concrete was studded with three- to four-inch irregularly shaped pieces of stone, usually tuff.

opus mixtum: A Roman construction technique using mixed brick and stone facing popular under the later Roman Empire and especially under Diocletian (AD 284–305).

opus quadratum: A Roman construction technique using squared blocks, the equivalent of ashlar masonry. It was ordinary stone walling and was used as a facing especially for important public buildings under the earlier Empire—for example, the exterior of the Colosseum. They were fairly large squared blocks laid in regular courses as headers (stone or brick laid with its end toward the face of the wall) and stretchers (stone or brick laid with its length parallel to the face of the wall).

opus reticulatum: A Roman construction technique consisting of blocks laid on a concrete core so that the edges are placed on a diagonal and produce a criss-cross pattern. It is a technical term used by Vitruvius c. 30 BC to describe the diamond pattern of square stones that was often used as a decorative facing to an inner rough concrete core. Opus reticulatum came into vogue in the 1st century BC and remained until the time of Hadrian (AD 117). The construction was like that of opus incertum, but the pieces of stone were pyramid-shaped with square bases set diagonally in rows and wedged into the concrete walls.

opus sectile: A Roman construction technique using thin pieces of marble of different colors in geometric, floral, or figured designs as part of floors or wall surfaces. Latin for "sectioned work," this technical term was used by Vitruvius, c. 30 BC. Shell or mother-of-pearl was sometimes used instead of marble. Opus sectile began in the Hellenistic world, perhaps first in Italy, and continued as a European decorative tradition. Opus sectile first appeared in Rome in Republican times as pavement in simple geometrical and floral designs. From the 1st century AD, there was also a regular production of small pictures of the opus sectile type. The technique was most popular in Rome c. 200 BC–AD 400. Geometrical opus sectile continued to be the major form of floor decoration in Italian churches throughout the Middle Ages and Renaissance.

opus signium: A Roman construction technique of crushed brick set in mortar, a kind of waterproof plaster, used to seal walls and floors in bath complexes. The mix was essentially a lime mortar with an aggregate of coarse pieces of broken terra-cotta. This Latin technique term was used by Vitruvius c. 30 BC.

opus tessellatum: Mosaic technique that involves the use of tesserae (small cubes of stone, marble, glass, ceramic, or other hard material) of uniform size applied to a ground to form pictures and ornamental designs. Opus tessellatum was the most commonly used technique in the production of Hellenistic, Roman, early Christian, and Byzantine mosaics. Opus tesselatum came to be used for entire mosaic floors in most areas of the eastern Mediterranean by at least the beginning of the 2nd century BC. The earliest mosaics in opus tessellatum were composed of stone and marble tesserae, but, in the course of the 2nd century, tesserae of colored glass were introduced. In the Hellenistic period (3rd to 1st centuries BC), pictorial mosaics were made in opus tessellatum; more commonly, however, opus tessellatum was reserved for decorative borders surrounding emblemata, or central figural panels executed in opus vermiculatum, a finer mosaic work using much smaller tesserae. In the 1st century AD, figural opus tessellatum was increasingly used to cover whole floors. With the widespread use of monumental wall mosaics, opus tessellatum entirely replaced opus vermiculatum, being much better suited, with its large tesserae and rougher visual effect, for viewing at a distance. Glass tesserae were used almost exclusively for these wall mosaics, and glass opus tessellatum remained the common mosaic technique throughout the Middle Ages.

opus testaceum: A Roman construction technique using brick- and tile-faced concrete, which was by far the most common material for walling during the Empire. Triangular tiles were used with their points turned into the concrete and their long sides showing, thus giving the appearance of a wall built of thin bricks. Bonding courses of bipedales were employed at intervals of 2–3 feet.

opus vermiculatum: Mosaic technique used in Hellenistic and Roman times, in which part or all of a figural mosaic is made up of small, closely set tesserae (cubes of stone, ceramic, glass, or other hard material) that permit fine gradations of color and an exact following of figure contours and outlines. The word *vermiculatum* (''wormlike'') refers to the undulating rows of tesserae in this work. Opus vermiculatum was generally used for emblemata, or central figural panels, which were surrounded by geometrical or floral designs in opus tessellatum, a coarser mosaic technique with larger tesserae; occasionally opus vermiculatum was used only for faces and other details in an opus tessellatum mosaic. The earliest known example of opus vermiculatum, c. 200 BC, is an emblema showing a personification of the city of Alexandria. By the 1st century BC, Romans had adopted the technique or imported Greek artists to do it; a number of fine opus vermiculatum pieces from this period have been found at Pompeii.

oracle bones: The bones (usually shoulder blades) of oxen or tortoise undershells used in the Shang culture of northern China for divination. Used to divine messages from ancestors, they are inscribed with the question, answer, and/or name of the diviner. Oracle bones ordinarily record a question addressed by a Shang king to his deceased ancestors, or the response to the question, or even the ultimate outcome of the matter divined. The subjects of divination included a limited range of royal concerns. The Anyang kings asked chiefly about war, hunting, rainfall, harvests, sickness, their consorts' childbearing, the fortune of the coming week, and,

above all, sacrifices. Oracle bones originated in the Lung-Shun culture and have been discovered at the Chou site of Qishan and the Shang site of Anyang, dating to the late 2nd millennium BC. Anyang was the last capital of the Shang Dynasty; apart from the far more limited corpus of inscriptions on bronze ritual vessels, the oracle texts are the only documents left by the Shang civilization. The depressions were made in a bone, and then a heated point was applied to cause the bone to crack. Divination proceeded by interpretation of these cracks. The inscriptions are the earliest examples of the fully developed form of Chinese characters. Those deciphered from Anyang have helped reconstruct the Shang kinship system and aspects of the culture. These inscriptions preserve the earliest known Chinese writing and sometimes, by naming kings and ancestors, confirm the historical basis of early legends. A few examples have been found at Neolithic sites such as Kexingzhuang (Dadunzi). The divination practice is called *scapulimancy* (scapulae are shoulder blades).

oral tradition: Historical traditions, often genealogies, passed down from generation to generation by word of mouth. It is the handing down of this information by word of mouth or by example from one generation to another without written instruction.

Orange: A *colonia* in southern France, established under Augustus' rule (27 BC–AD 14), which became a prosperous city. In the pre-Roman period, the area was occupied by rich, powerful Celtic tribes who appreciated its strategic position on the Rhône River. The semicircular theater, probably built during the reign of Augustus, is the best preserved of its kind. The tiered benches, which rise on the slopes of a slight hill, originally seated 1,100. The magnificent wall at the back of the theater is 334 feet (102 m) long and 124 feet (38 m) high. An imposing statue of Augustus, about 12 feet (3.7 m) high, stands in the wall's central niche. Orange also has the triumphal arch of Tiberius (AD c. 20), one of the largest built by the Romans; standing c. 61 feet (19 m) high, its sculptures show the victories of Julius Caesar. A lime kiln near the theater has produced fragments that document various local land surveys and, in particular, describe the terms of confiscation and redistribution that were applied at the time of the original founding of the colonia. In the 5th century, Arausio was pillaged by the Visigoths. (*syn.* Roman Arausio)

Orangia: Middle Stone Age site in the Orange River valley in the extreme south of the Orange Free State, South Africa. The artifacts are analogous to those of the Pietersburg complex to the north. It is the type site of an early Middle Stone Age Pietersburg-like flake-blade industry. It is now inundated by a dam.

Oranian: North African culture of late Upper Palaeolithic type, with many backed blades and some microliths. A few inland sites are known, but most are concentrated along the

Mediterranean littoral from Cyrenaica (the Haua Fteah) to Morocco. The time range is c. 12,000–8000 BC. It is contemporary with the Capsian, although the Capsian sites are all inland, whereas the Oranian has a coastal distribution. Both are microlithic tool complexes that persisted after the introduction of Neolithic traits into the area. (*syn.* Ibero-Maurusian)

orchestra: The dancing floor area for the chorus between the stage and the audience in an ancient theater. It was the lowest part of the Greek and Roman theaters and contained an altar, on which sacrifices to Bacchus were sometimes made. When permanent theaters were built, the orchestra was where the acting took place; actors gained access by means of a *parados.*

Orchestra Shell Cave: Cave near Perth, western Australia, occupied at least 6,500 years ago. The finger markings resemble those in Koonalda Cave.

Orchomenos: Important Bronze Age site in Boeotia, central Greece, home of the legendary King Minyas. Extensive remains of the Early and Middle Helladic periods survive, although the Mycenaean levels are badly eroded. A large frescoed Late Helladic structure is probably a palace, and to the east lies the tholos tomb known as the treasury of Minyas. About 20 kilometers to the east is the huge Mycenaean fortress of Gla, defended by walls of cyclopean masonry 6 meters thick. This fortress and a number of subsidiary forts must have defended the eastern approaches to the Copais basin, which, according to ancient literary tradition, was drained and cultivated by the people of Orchomenos in Mycenaean times. There are impressive fortifications of the Classical city and a 4th century BC theater. Linear B has been found in inscriptions on pots and jars at Orchomenos.

order: Any of several styles of classical or Neoclassical architecture, defined by the particular type of column and entablature used as a basic unit. A column consists of a shaft together with its base and its capital. The column supports a section of an entablature, which constitutes the upper horizontal part of a classical building and is itself composed of (from bottom to top) an architrave, frieze, and cornice. The form of the capital is the most distinguishing characteristic of a particular order. There are five major orders: Doric, Ionic, Corinthian, Tuscan, and Composite—as established by Vitruvius (1st century AD). (*syn.* order of architecture)

Ordos: The desert region in the northward loop of the Yellow River (Huang Ho) in northern China, the location of the Palaeolithic Ordos culture. From the 8th century BC, the region was inhabited by seminomadic tribes, among them the Hsiung-Nu, threatening the Chou Dynasty and the Han Dynasty. Broad bronze daggers, curved knives, pole finials, harness ornaments, and animal-style bronze belt plaques are characteristic of the 1st millennium BC ("the Ordos bronzes").

The pictorial or narrative compositions common among these plaques, many including human figures, are typical also of Sarmatian metalwork. The distinctive metal culture of the Ordos reaches back as far as the latter part of the 2nd millennium BC, a date fixed by the discovery at Anyang of knives with animal-head pommels closely related to Ordos types. Owing to its position on the northern frontier of China, the Ordos was probably the main channel by which Chinese influences were transmitted to the steppes; it was also the route by which foreign elements reached China, especially during the Eastern Chou and Han Dynasties. An Upper Palaeolithic site (Sjara Osso Gol) yielded a microlithic industry. In the 1970s and 1980s, Chinese scientists unearthed more than 20 human fossils 30,000–60,000 years old at Hsiao-ch'iao-pan in the Sjara-Osso River valley. The terms *Ordos man* and *Ordosian culture* are applied to their findings. The area is now referred to as the Northern Zone. (*syn.* Northern Zone)

ore: A mineral or mineral aggregate containing a prized constituent, usually a metal, for which it is mined and worked.

organic artifact: Artifact made of organic materials—living organisms, including wood, bone, horn, fiber, ivory, or hide. (*syn.* organic material)

organic ecofact: Ecofact derived from the remains of living organisms.

Orientalizing: The period in the 8th and 7th centuries BC, during which Scythian-Iranian Oriental objects with their animalistic motifs were spread and consequently imitated throughout the Mediterranean countries, especially in Greece and Italy. It is also the style of Greek art in that period, a decorative scheme found especially on pottery. The style was probably the result of renewed contact with Syria, Phoenicia, and Egypt. It is an art history term also used of various periods and cultures in antiquity when a "western" production shows evidence for influence from the Near, Middle, or Far East. An example would be the borrowing by Greek black-figure vase painters of numerous abstract, vegetable, and animal motifs from Syrian and Phoenician art. From about 650 BC on, the Greeks began to visit Egypt regularly, and their observation of the monumental stone buildings there was the genesis of the ultimate development of monumental architecture and sculpture in Greece. The Egyptians worked in hard stone instead of the limestone, clay, or wood to which the Greeks had been accustomed. The Greeks learned the techniques of handling the harder stone in Egypt, and at home they turned to the fine white marble of the Cyclades islands (Paros, Naxos) for their materials. It was at this time that the first truly monumental examples of Greek sculpture appeared. The period in Greece continued through the 7th century BC and saw the rise of narrative in Greek art. (*syn.* orientalizing)

Orissa: A constituent state off eastern India, well known for its Jaina rock-cut temples, dating from the 1st century AD. Over the centuries, the land now called Orissa has passed under the names of Utkala, Kalinga, and Odra Desha, names originally associated with particular peoples.

Ornament Horizon: A brief period in the Middle Bronze Age of southwest Britain marked by the occurrence, in hoards, of tools and bronze ornaments that owe their inspiration to types current in north Germany and Scandinavia from c. 1400 BC. These "foreign" objects include torcs, coiled finger rings, ribbed bracelets, knobbed sickles, and square-mouthed socketed axes. In Devon, Somerset, and Sussex, hoards of the Ornament Horizon also contain native spear heads, palstaves, and quoit-headed pins. This influx seems to have given a boost to the native bronze industry.

Orongo: A ceremonial village of 48 stone houses with corbelled roofs on the rim of Rano Kau volcanic crater on Easter Island. Famous as the gathering place for the annual "birdman" ceremony, which took place on the island, the Orongo village was probably built in the 16th century AD, and the ceremony itself continued until c. 1878. Adjacent to the village are rock carvings (petroglyphs) of birdmen holding eggs. The corbelled houses are unique in Oceania, and South American parallels have been claimed for them.

Oronsay: Island of the Inner Hebrides, Scotland, with coastal Late Mesolithic shell midden sites dated to c. 3700–3200 BC. Small groups of people likely moved between the sites.

orthostat: A large vertical stone slab supporting the capstone or roof of a chamber or passage in a megalithic tomb. Also a large vertical stone slab facing a wall in Near Eastern royal architecture, often decorated with sculpture. (*syn.* adj. orthostatic)

Ortoire: A cultural phase in Trinidad dated to c. 800 BC, recognized by crude chipped stone tools, net sinkers, and grinding stones.

Osa: Late Mesolithic and Early Neolithic settlement located in Latvia (formerly part of Russia). The Mesolithic levels had a rich bone and antler industry with radiocarbon dates of c. 5200–4800 BC. An Early Neolithic occupation contained Osa type pottery and similar bone tools, with radiocarbon dates of 3950–3800 BC. There was also a thin layer of the Pit-Comb Ware group, with a radiocarbon date of c. 2050 BC.

Osan-ri: Early Neolithic site in Kangwondo Province, Korea, with 7th millennium BC dates for Chulmun pottery. (*syn.* Osanni)

oscillum: In Roman architecture, an ornament of marble suspended from the architrave of a peristyle in a house. Some are circular with reliefs cut on both faces; others are theatrical masks.

Oseberg ship: Important Viking ship burial, discovered in 1903 in south Norway in a peat mound. It was found with most of its timbers intact and its main burial chamber still filled with most of its contents. Among the objects in the chamber were the skeletons of a man (AD c. 850–900), dogs and horses, a chest containing oil lamps and personal items, a wooden bed, and a sledge. Now reconstructed in the Oslo Ship Museum, the Oseberg ship is a fine example of a large, sophisticated Viking warship. The ship itself was plank built and had a pronounced keel, a large mast, and a beautifully carved stern. It shed much light on everyday life of the Vikings.

Oshara tradition: A Southwestern Archaic tradition of the Four Corners region of the southwestern United States. It was an Archaic hunting and gathering culture from c. 5500 BC to AD c. 400. There are five phases based on projectile point form, artifact assemblages, and socioeconomic organization. These phases are Jay, c. 5000–4800 BC, and Bajada, c. 4800–3300 BC of the Early Archaic, with nomadic bands of foragers and hunters; the San Jose Phase, c. 3300–1800 BC; the Armijo Phase, c. 1800–800 BC, with maize horticulture introduced; and the En Medio Phase, c. 800 BC–AD 400, which encompassed the Basketmaker II Phase of the Anasazi culture.

Osirid pillar: A square pillar with one of its faces carved in the form of a colossal statue of the god Osiris or a dead king. The pillar, most likely in an open court or portico, was not a weight-bearing element. Most are mummiform.

Osiris: The ancient Egyptian god of death, represented as an anthropoid figure with mummy body. He was a brother and husband to Isis and the father of Horus. Through them, he was linked to the vegetation cycle myth. Slain by his brother Seth in the autumn, his dismembered and scattered remains were collected by Isis, reassembled, and returned to life as Horus in the spring. His chief sanctuary was at Abydos. Originally he was identified with the deceased king, but eventually, any dead person came to be referred to as "an Osiris," a dweller in the land of the dead. He was one of the most important deities of ancient Egypt.

Oslonki: Lengyel culture settlement in north-central Poland, c. 3500–3300 BC. It has trapezoidal longhouses and numerous burials with many copper artifacts.

Osorkon: Libyan name held by five rulers of the 21st–23rd Dynasties as their birth name or nomen. The fifth king of the 21st Dynasty, Osorkon I (ruled c. 979–973 BC), was of Libyan descent and probably was an ancestor of the 22nd Dynasty, which followed a generation later. From his time to the 26th Dynasty, leading Libyans in Egypt kept their Libyan names and ethnic identity.

ossification: The fusion of a limb bone with its articular end, which implies calcification of soft tissue into bonelike material.

ossuary: A charnel house used for multiple, mainly secondary, inhumations. It was also the name for a sarcophagus of earthenware, stone, or marble, in which the vessel containing the cremated ashes of the dead was placed. It may be either a small portable article for a single interment (larnax, pithos, urn) or a cave or built structure to take a number of burials (chamber tomb, tholos). (*syn.* ossarium, ossuarium; osteotheke)

osteoarchaeology: A branch of archaeology that deals with human anatomy, particularly the bones in archaeological deposits.

osteodontokeratic: Literally "bone-tooth-horn," referring to the controversial tool "technology" of some early hominids. When there is no sign that a people used wood or stone for tools and when it is supposed that the people did make tools of bones, teeth, and horns, their culture is said to be osteodontokeratic. The term is based on an assemblage of fossilized animal bones found at Taung by Raymond Arthur Dart in South Africa, where the first specimen of *Australopithecus africanus* was found, and at Makapansgat, where other specimens of *A. africanus* were found. Dart proposed that these fossils were tools used by *A. africanus*, an early hominid species. He postulated that teeth were used as saws and scrapers, long bones as clubs, and so on. He explained his theory on the basis of the fact that certain bones turned up regularly, while others were rarely found. Later research, however, cast doubt on the general interpretation of altered-bone remains as tools. More likely, the accumulation studied by Dart resulted from the natural breakdown of skeletons, predators, and damage to the bones by falling stones.

osteology: The study of bones; a branch of anatomy dealing with bones.

Ostia: Major Roman port and colony at the mouth of the Tiber River, founded in the 4th century BC. Toward the end of 4th century BC, a rectangular fort was constructed, securing Rome's interest in trade routes through Ostia; the town was for a long time effectively the port of ancient Rome. It grew until 78 BC when it was destroyed in the Roman civil wars. It was later rebuilt by Sulla with a forum and capitolium. Claudius (AD 41–54) and Trajan (AD 98–117) had two harbors built at Portus, immediately north of Ostia. The 2nd century AD proved to be a period of unprecedented prosperity, which has left the most plentiful traces in today's ruins. The new harbors were largely administered through Ostia, and presumably much of the workforce chose to live at Ostia. Large brick apartment blocks were built in the 1st–2nd centuries AD. They were of three, four, and five stories; the floors in these buildings were paved with mosaic, and the walls elaborately painted. The second century also saw the construction of an aqueduct, imperial suites of public baths, and synagogue. The need for depositories and warehouses (*horrea*) became very important. The increase in trade brought prosperity to many areas of the city. In a double colonnade behind the theater, a large number of small offices housed agencies for all the major shipping destinations and types of trade. In the city, over 800 shops are known. Third century AD political instability at Rome combined with an economic recession brought a general decline in shipping. Constantine preferred Portus to Ostia, so that the city became a seaside resort with expensive houses. Even so, the area declined under barbarian raids in the 5th century. It was abandoned after the erection of Gregoriopolis, site of Ostia Antica, by Pope Gregory IV (827–844). The Roman ruins were quarried for building materials in the Middle Ages and for sculptors' marble in the Renaissance. Archaeological excavation was begun in the 19th century under papal authority, and about two thirds of the Roman town can now be seen. (*syn.* modern Ostia Antica)

Ostionoid, Ostiones: One of three associated ceramic series in the Greater Antilles area. Seen as transitional to Chicoid and Meillacoid, the Ostionoid appears in AD c. 650 in Puerto Rico, where it overlays Saladoid materials. Vessels are generally smooth, finished in red monochrome slip, often with plain tabular lugs. The introduction of items like petalloid celts, potter stamps, and zemis indicates external influence, possibly Mesoamerican. Agriculture activity is indicated by the presence of griddles used in the preparation of manioc.

ostrakon: A potsherd or, more rarely, a flake of stone, bearing an inscription in ink or paint. In Greece, they were employed for voting; in Egypt, for memoranda, business accounts, writing exercises, jottings, artists' sketches, and list making. They commonly consisted of personal jottings, letters, sketches, or scribal exercises, but also were often inscribed with literary texts. They could be fragments from inscribed jars (e.g., a wine jar inscribed with the details of a vintage). Ostraca are known from all periods, but 19th- and 20th-Dynasty examples are commonest (up to 20,000 have been found) in Egypt. Most of the Egyptian examples are in hieratic or demotic, but there are also cursive hieroglyphic texts and numerous pictures, including drafts of hieroglyphic inscriptions. The term is derived from the classical Greek voting practice of *ostrakismos* (ostracism), a 5th-century BC political move in which each citizen could write on a potsherd the name of someone whom he wished to see banished. If sufficient votes were cast against one person (the number seems to have been 6,000), the person named would be banished for 10 years. The usage of inscribed sherds seems to have spread to Egypt with the Greek conquest. Ostraca from the New Kingdom are especially numerous. Deir el-Medina's ostraca are a great source of evidence for the life of its workmen's village and community. (*syn.* pl. ostraca; ostracon (pl. ostraka))

Ostrów Lednicki: An island in Lake Lednika, Poland, with an important medieval site. The earliest 9th-century settlement was fortified with a rampart in the early 10th century. At the end of the 10th century, a grandiose citadel, one of the official residences of the Polish rulers, was built. The official secular and religious buildings inside the stronghold consisted of a stone-built palace with an inner courtyard. The wooden dwellings and workshops were concentrated outside.

Otakanini: A Maori *pa* (hill fort) on a small island in Kaipara Harbor, North Island, New Zealand. The site has three defensive phases from the 14th–18th centuries AD, and after 1500 its inner citadel was defended by palisades and large raised fighting platforms. Cultural affiliations are Classic Maori.

otolith: Small, dense calcareous concretions from the middle ear region of fish, quite commonly found on archaeological sites. Otoliths are species distinctive and can therefore be used for identification purposes in the analysis of fish remains from a site. They also grow in annual rings and can thus be used to age the fish and to indicate seasonal use of the site. Otoliths are normally recovered by wet sieving of deposits.

Otomani: An Early Bronze Age culture of eastern Hungary, northwestern Romania, and eastern Slovakia, dating to the period 2000–1600 BC and showing connections with Unetice. It is the equivalent of the Hungarian Füzesabony group in the central Hungarian sequence. A high proportion of Otomani settlements are artificially or naturally fortified (Barca, Spissky Stvrtok), often by the use of water, and tells are frequent. The type site, near Marghita, is a citadel overlooking the eastern edge of the Hungarian plain. The ceramics feature large, pointed bosses. Black burnished ware with bossed decoration on one-handled cups is the most frequent pottery type. Bronze artifacts are elaborately ornamented.

Otranto mosaic: A Romanesque cathedral in Apulia, southeastern Italy, with a mosaic pavement covering the nave and aisles. Laid between 1163–1166, it was designed by a priest named Pantaleon and shows certain similarities to the Bayeux tapestry. The central theme is the history of the universe. Similar mosaics existed at other Apulian Romanesque cathedrals, but this splendid work is the only one to have survived.

Ottonian: The successors to the Carolingians, the empire of Otto emperors, AD 936–1024. As inheritors of the Carolingian tradition of the Holy Roman Empire, the German emperors also assumed the Carolingian artistic heritage, the conscientious revival of late antique and Early Christian art forms. Ottonian art later developed a style of its own, particularly in painting, ivory carving, and sculpture; there was a hieratic quality in some art, especially manuscript painting.

The architecture consisted of fortress-like basilicas with massive walls, groups of towers, and tiny windows. The achievements of Ottonian artists provided the background and impetus for the Romanesque style.

Otzaki: An Aceramic Neolithic–Early Bronze Age tell (or *magoula*) settlement in Thessaly, Greece. Early Neolithic pre-Sesklo occupation with Impressed Ware was succeeded by Middle Neolithic Sesklo painted pottery. Houses were of mud brick and rectangular, some having stone footings and internal buttresses. The megaron type appears late in the period.

'Oueli: Small mound near Larsa with a sequence of 'Ubaid deposits dating from c. 5800–5500 BC onward. Decorated ceramics resemble Samarran pottery. 'Oueli has provided the first stratigraphic evidence of early settlement on the southern Mesopotamian alluvium.

Ounan Point: Pointed bladelet with basal stem used in North African Late Pleistocene and Holocene, such as in Ounanian and Early Neolithic industries of the Eastern Sahara.

ovate: A refined Acheulian biface with an egg-shaped outline and a flat or twisted profile; some have a tranchet finish.

Ovcarovo: A tell settlement and two cemeteries in northeast Bulgaria, with an Early Neolithic occupation with pits and postholes stratified beneath 13 Copper Age habitation levels, dated to much of the 4th millennium BC. There is an initial rectangular wooden palisade enclosure; some of the houses were two storied. Many ritual objects were incised with simple signs. Both cemeteries date to the Copper Age.

oven: A closed structure, in contrast to a hearth, resembling a kiln but designed for cooking food. Sometimes the fire was lit in the chamber and removed before the food could be put in. More elaborate versions have the firebox and cooking chamber separate.

overburden: Soil and rock overlying a bed of clay or other base to be dug, excavated, mined, or quarried.

Owasco tradition: The precursor to the Iroquois culture in New York state, dated to AD c. 1000–1300. It is characterized by ceramics with cord-wrapped paddles, smoking pipes with straight stems, and the growing of corn, beans, and squash. The elongated houses were ancestral to the Iroquois longhouse.

Owo: Ancient Yoruba kingdom and city in southwest Nigeria with terra-cotta sculptures dated to the early 15th century AD. The city of Owo, near the frontier with the Edo-speaking peoples, developed an art style and a whole culture that is a blend of Yoruba and Benin traditions. Ivory carving is especially important, and wooden heads of rams and of humans with rams' horns are used on ancestral altars.

oxidizing atmosphere: A term used in relation to pottery technology, describing certain firing conditions involving a gaseous atmosphere in which an oxidation reaction (the oxidation of solids) occurs. If a kiln is being fired with food, dry fuel and with plenty of draft, the carbon in the fuel is converted into carbon dioxide, and there is oxygen in the atmosphere. This oxidizing atmosphere causes pottery to be fired to a red or orange color whether it has a slip or not. The opposite phenomenon, a reducing atmosphere, produces black pottery. Much pottery, however, varies in color over its surface because of changing conditions during the firing process.

Oxus Treasure: A collection of Persian art of the Achaemenid period (6th–4th centuries BC) now in the British Museum, London. It was discovered in 1877 on the bank of the Oxus River near the present Afghanistan-Russian border. This large hoard of gold and silver metalwork included a variety of jewelry, ornamental plaques, figurines, chariot models, and vessels. One of the armlets consists of a circular gold band with its two ends meeting in the form of finely worked griffins.

oxygen isotope analysis: Isotope analysis looking at the O18/O16 ratio in materials. The method can be used to classify glass types and to analyze mollusk shells to try to reconstruct their original environment and thus source. It is also used to interpret deep sea cores. The basis for this technique is the fact that the ratio of two of the stable isotopes of oxygen varies according to the material in which it is found. The oxygen is released from the sample and is converted to carbon dioxide; the oxygen isotopic ratio is determined after ionization in a mass spectrometer. Variations in the isotopic ratios for the raw materials can lead to a classification of types and even, in some cases, to the suggestion of a source for the raw materials. The technique is also used to analyze mollusk shells in an attempt to reconstruct the original aquatic environment. Because temperature variations are correlated with changes in atmospheric O18/O16 ratios, oxygen isotope analysis has also been used to identify seasonal changes in ice cores, to interpret temperature variations during speleothem precipitation, and to examine isotopic variations in tree ring climates. Foraminifera sampled from deep sea cores have revealed fluctuations in the O18/O16 ratio. These present evidence for glacial-interglacial cycles in the form of continental ice volume change. (*syn.* oxygen isotope examination)

Oxyrhynchus: Ancient Greco-Roman town west of the Nile on the left bank of the Bahr Yusuf in Middle Egypt, best known for its papyri texts. Oxyrhynchus was a regional capital, which was reasonably prosperous in the Roman period and developed into a church and monastic center during the Coptic period. A large number of fragmentary papyri were written or copied, and these texts are now of central importance in the reconstruction of the manuscript tradition of a number of major classical authors, including Homer, Pindar, and Aristotle. Also included are previously lost works or sections of works, such as Menander and Callimachus. They were uncovered, first by B. P. Grenfell and A. S. Hunt (1897–1907), and later by Italian scholars early in the 20th century. The papyri—dating from about 250 BC to AD 700 and written primarily in Greek and Latin but also in demotic Egyptian, Coptic, Hebrew, Syriac, and Arabic—include religious texts (e.g., miracles of Sarapis, early copies of the New Testament, and such apocryphal books such as the Gospel of Thomas) and also masterpieces of Greek classical literature. The works of the so-called Oxyrhynchus historian were also found. (*syn.* Arabic Bahnasa)

Oyu: City on Akita Prefecture, Japan, with two Late Jomon period stone circles. They have associated sundial arrangements and have been found to contain burials in shallow pits under the alignments.

Ozark: A cultural area named after the Ozark Hills of Arkansas, Oklahoma, and Missouri. An Archaic culture, called Grove phase and dating before 5000 BC, was probably ancestral to the Bluff-Dweller sites of the Ozark area. Occupied in this millennium, it consists of rock shelters, caves, and open sites. Baskets and extensive remains were preserved because of the dryness of the cave sites.

Ozette: A coastal settlement in Washington state occupied for c. 1000 years by ancestors of the present-day Makah Indians; a prehistoric culture of the Northwest Coast tradition. Ozette suffered a disaster 2 centuries ago when longhouses and individual dwellings were buried by mud slides and preserved in perfect condition for archaeologists to investigate in the 1970s. The over 60,000 artifacts recovered, including whale-hunting paraphernalia, weaving equipment, and wooden boxes and bowls, constitute the assemblage.

Ozieri Culture: Late Neolithic culture of Sardinia, known from caves and open villages, and dated to the late 4th and 3rd millennia BC. It produced elaborately decorated, high-quality pottery. Classic Ozieri decorated ware has been dated to c. 4100–3500 BC at the Grotta di Filiestru (Bonu Ighinu). There are rock-cut tombs with Beaker pottery and occasionally copper and silver objects and marble figurines.

Pp

pa: A Maori term for a fortified village. Excavated examples, mostly in the North Island of New Zealand, are of Classic Maori date. Most are defended by ditch-bank combinations or scarped terraces (Kauri Point, Otakanini, Tirimoana), but some were built up from swamps and defended by multiple rows of palisades (Lake Mangakaware, Lake Ngaroto).

Pacariqtambo: Region south of Cuzco, Peru, where the Inca royal dynasty originated according to oral tradition. The original Inca were four brothers Ayar and their four sister-wives.

Pacatnamú: Middle Horizon and Late Intermediate period site in Jequetepeque Valley in Peru. Located on a promontory, it has large defensive walls and more than 50 truncated pyramid complexes. The large site may represent the southernmost Moche V polity. The site was abandoned at the end of the Middle Horizon and then again when the Chimu expanded into the region.

Paccaicasas: The earliest stone tool complex of the Ayacucho Valley, in the central highlands of Peru, which may represent humans' earliest presence in South America. Radiocarbon dates of 17,260 BC and 12,730 BC were obtained from sloth bone found in association with crude stone tools and flakes of volcanic tuff. Choppers, bifacial tools, and waste flakes are therefore dated between 18,000–12,000 BC. (*syn.* Paccaicasa)

Pachacamac: A large Pre-Columbian ruin in the Lurin Valley on the central coast of Peru. The earliest major occupation and construction of Pachacamac date to the Early Intermediate Period (c. 200 BC–AD 600) by the Early Lima culture (Maranga, Interlocking style). The terraced adobe pyramid and temple known as the temple of Pachacamac belong to this time and culture, and Pachacamac's fame as the seat of an oracle probably began in the Early Intermediate Period. During the Middle Horizon (AD 600–1000), it continued as a major center and place of pilgrimage and was probably the principal establishment of the Huari Empire on the coast. In late Pre-Columbian times, the Inca constructed the temple of the Sun and the oracle of Pachacamac. The temple's buildings contained richly appointed female mummies, some of which bear evidence of ritual stragulation. The shrine and temple were sacked by Francisco Pizarro's soldiers during the Spanish conquest in 1532. Huari influence is seen on the polychrome pottery, AD c. 800–1000.

Pachamachay: Preceramic cave site in the central highlands of Peru, a base camp with a date of 11,800 bp. Occupation was highest between 9000–2000 bp.

Pacheco: Middle Horizon site of the Nasca Valley in Peru. A major Huari offering deposit was found with hundreds of smashed polychrome vessels.

Pacific Littoral tradition: A tradition developed c. 4000–1800 BC on the Peruvian coast. Settled communities lived off maritime resources and cultivated cotton and gourds for materials for the fishing industry. Bone, wood, shell, and stone were worked. There were textiles, an early art style, and temple platforms in ceremonial centers.

Pacitanian: A pebble and flake tool industry with a small percentage of bifaces found in valleys in south-central Java, Indonesia. The region is known as Pacitan or Patjitan. The chopper and chopping tools were of a middle and Late Pleistocene time. These tools were also a small part of a late Pleistocene and early Holocene industry. (*syn.* Patjitanian; Pacitan, Patjitan)

pack-rat midden: Any collection of artifacts or objects concealed at some point by a pack rat (also wood or trade rat) and remaining in an assemblage at that location. Pack rats are so-called because they collect various bits of material to deposit in their dens. They sometimes pick up shiny objects in camps and may at the same time leave something they were carrying, thus giving the impression that they are "trading" one item for the other.

Padah Lin: A cave site in east Burma, with early hunter-gatherer remains dating to c. 11,000 BC, among the earliest-known Hoabinhian assemblages.

paddies: Fields for the intensive cultivation of rice, flooded naturally or by irrigation. Wet land on which rice is grown. (*syn.* singular paddy)

paddle-and-anvil: A pottery-making method in which a wooden paddle and a stone or ceramic disk are used to smooth and shape a coiled pot. The paddle was used to strike the exterior surface of the vessel as a convex stone or clay anvil was held against the corresponding interior surface. (*syn.* paddle-and-anvil technique)

Padina: Settlement site in Serbia on the River Danube with two major occupations: "pre-Neolithic" c. 7400–5800 BC, and a Neolithic c. 5100–4600 BC. The "pre-Neolithic" was contemporaneous with Lepenski Vir I and II. The Neolithic level contained Starcevo pottery. Unlike at Lepenski Vir, the Padina site revealed the association of trapezoidal houses with both Mesolithic finds and Starcevo pottery. Large numbers of burials occur between the houses at Padina during both occupations: The skeletal type is Cromagnoid (i.e., the descendants of the local Palaeolithic stock).

Padre Island: Site off the coast of Texas with the remains of three Spanish treasure ships that wrecked in 1554. The ships have been scientifically excavated.

Paekche: Early state on the Korean peninsula, AD c. 300–662, which succeeded Mahan and competed with Koguryo and Silla. Its first capital was near Mongch'on Fortress near Seoul, then Ungjin (Kongju) and Sabi (Puyo). There are stone-stepped and earthen mounded tombs. A gridded city was built in the 7th century.

pa'epa'e: In the Marquesas Islands of Polynesia, elaborate, well-built, rectangular house platforms.

Paestan pottery: South Italian pottery made at Paestum, some signed by the craftsmen, starting in the mid-4th century BC.

Paestum: A Greek coastal colony in Lucania, southwest Italy, c. 600 BC. It is known for three almost complete Doric temples of the 6th and 5th centuries BC, a forum (3rd century BC), amphitheater, shrine, temple of Peace, and a number of smaller temples. The temples were dedicated to Argive Hera, Poseidon, and Athena. There is some occupational evidence for both Palaeolithic and Neolithic, and there is a Copper Age necropolis at Contrada Gaudo, just north of the classical town. Traditional sources ascribe the Greek colony to Sybaris, and proto-Corinthian pottery suggests the date of 600 BC. Some of the local tombs were decorated with murals; the famous "Tomb of the Divers" with "Etruscan"-style painted decoration is from the 5th century BC. After many years' resistance, the city came under the domination of the Luca-

nians sometime before 400 BC, after which its name was changed to Paestum. Alexander, the king of Epirus, defeated the Lucanians at Paestum about 332 BC, but the city remained Lucanian until 273, when it came under Roman rule and a Latin colony was founded there. Paestum was still prosperous during the early years of the Roman Empire, but the gradual silting up of the mouth of the Silarus River eventually created a malarial swamp, and Paestum was finally deserted after being sacked by Muslim raiders in AD 871. The abandoned site's remains were rediscovered in the 18th century. (*syn.* Greek Poseidonia)

Paffrath ware: Hard-fired ware with a black finish, made from the 10th–11th centuries until the 13th century at Paffrath, near Cologne, Germany. The best-known products of this center are the so-called handled ladles—small cooking pots or bowls with a curved handle.

Pagan: A city in northern Burma, close to the confluence of the Irrawaddy and the Chindwin, formed in 849 by the union of 19 villages and originally called Arimaddanapura. It is a Buddhist religious center, and the rulers of the Pagan dynasty (1044–1287) erected around 5,000 Buddhist monuments (temples and stupas) made of baked brick, which contributed to the deforestation of the area now known as the "Dry Zone" of Burma. Until its conquest by the Mongols in 1287, Pagan was the capital of an expanding Burman kingdom, which included the Mon country to the south and areas inhabited by Thai peoples in the East. (*syn.* Arimaddanapura)

Paglicci: Prehistoric cave site on the Gargano peninsula on the Adriatic coast of Italy. Excavations have yielded a long sequence of Upper Palaeolithic levels of Gravettian or Epi-Gravettian type dating from c. 24,700–20,000 bp. There are engraved objects from several levels, a few cave paintings, and two burials covered by ocher.

pagus: A term for the smallest unit of land in the territorial system of Italy: a country area, not a village or town, and distinguished from *oppidum* and *vicus*. The inhabitants of this "locality" were called *pagani*.

Paiján: Preceramic tradition of the north and central coast highlands of Peru. The Paiján tradition probably postdates the Palaeoindian Fishtail Point tradition, and its characteristic points are triangular with a long narrow stem. The tradition may have been the first to exploit maritime resources on the Peruvian coast.

Painted Gray ware: A pottery type characteristic of Iron Age sites in northern India, with its center of distribution in the eastern Punjab and central Ganges Valley. It was a fine, wheelmade, thin-walled ware with a gray surface decorated with simple designs of circles and pot hooks, made before 500 BC. The designs were in red or black paint. The forms that occur most frequently are a shallow dish and a deeper bowl. The pottery occurs in deposits of the later 2nd millennium and early 1st millennium BC. Many authorities believe that Painted Gray ware was the pottery used by the early Aryans in India.

painting: Artwork first found on rocks in Europe and Africa, created with charcoal, lime, and iron oxide of various colors mixed with animal fat or marrow. European paintings are in caves and date to early Aurignacian times 70,000–80,000 BC; if created purely for art, they would not have been done in the depths of the caves. It is thought that they must have been of religious, magical, or ritual significance. There is proof that schools of painting were held in some caves. Polychrome paintings were made at the peak of Palaeolithic art, mid-Magdalenian times, about 10,000 BC.

Pair-non-Par: An engraved cave near Bordeaux, western France, with one Mousterian and several Upper Palaeolithic levels. The engravings are possibly Aurignacian; also found were a flute and human remains.

palace: A term derived from Middle English *palais*, from Old French, from Latin *palatium*, from *Palatium*, the Palatine Hill in Rome where the emperor's residences were built. It is often the term for the official residence of a chief of state (as a monarch or a president).

Palaeoanthropus: The name of the group to which *Homo neanderthalensis*, *Pithicanthropus erectus*, and Sinanthropus belong.

Palaeoasiatic: A theoretical early "race" of *Homo sapiens* in northeastern Asia. This race included the postglacial Chulmun and Jomon inhabitants of Korea and Japan and the modern Ainu. The far northeastern region of Siberia is the home of the so-called Palaeoasiatic peoples, including the Chukchi, Koryak, Itelmen, and Yukaghir. The term also refers to a language group; the languages of the indigenous peoples of the Eurasian Arctic and subarctic can be grouped into four classes: Uralic, Tungusic, Turkic, and Palaeoasiatic.

palaeoeconomy: A school of archaeological thought concerned with long-term determinants of human behavior. E. S. Higgs wrote *Palaeoeconomy* in 1975.

palaeoenvironment: The ancient environment, which can be reconstructed by using techniques such as archaeozoology and palynology.

palaeosol: A fossil soil preserved in a sequence of deposits. It comes from a period when cold conditions had improved enough for vegetation to colonize and for a soil to be formed. Palaeosols are widespread in the Pleistocene loess sequences of the Netherlands, Germany, and Denmark. The interstadials of the Weichselian have been reconstructed from the northern European palaeosol and loess succession; extensive palaeosols also characterize interglacials and interstadials of

North America. It is a source of much palaeoenvironmental information. (*syn.* paleosol)

palaestra: In Greco-Roman times, an open-air courtyard surrounded by a colonnade (or porticos) and used for wrestling, gymnastics, and military training. This building consisted of a large central sand-covered courtyard surrounded by changing rooms and washrooms. It is from the Greek word for "area of wrestling" or "wrestling school"; it was often part of a gymnasium complex, which would include a stadium. It might also be connected to thermae.

palafitta: The Italian name for villages of pile dwellings in the northern part of the country. Most of these lakeside villages belong to the Neolithic period and earlier part of the Bronze Age. Later changes in water levels have caused many of these villages to become submerged. (*syn.* pl. palafitte)

Palaikastro: Minoan settlement site on the island of Crete, a Neopalatial town with no palace yet discovered. Palaikastro in eastern Crete was an important town with blocks of houses marked by colored stone foundations, narrow streets with drains, and pottery of exceptional quality.

Palanga: A find spot on the Baltic coast of Poland, with a stray find of a perforated amber disc pendant. The disc is a skeuomorph of a bone type more common in central Europe and the south Russian steppe zone. It was dated to the earlier Bronze Age c. 2nd millennium BC.

Palatine: Principal of the seven hills of ancient Rome, and the favored location in the later Republic and the Empire for magnificent private houses and sumptuous residences of the emperors. It is a four-sided plateau rising 131 feet (40 m) south of the Forum in Rome and 168 feet (51 m) above sea level. It has a circumference of 5,700 feet (1,740 m). The city of Rome was founded on the Palatine, where archaeological discoveries range from prehistoric remains to the ruins of imperial palaces. The modern use of "palace" is commonly traced back to this period. Tradition said the Palatine Hill was the site of the earliest Roman occupation, associated with mythical Romulus and Remus. Augustus was born on the hill and started a fashion for imperial residence by buying and enlarging the house of Hortensius. This trend was followed with zest by later emperors, and Domitian took over most of the hill for his amazingly extensive Domus Augustiana. Later structures included a special emperor's box overlooking the Circus Maximus, and the Septizonium, a monumental facade built solely to screen the southeast corner of the palace. (*syn.* Palatine Hill)

Palau Islands: An island group and independent republic in western Micronesia, perhaps settled from the Philippines c. 2000 BC. Its prehistory includes a continuous pottery sequence to ethnographic times. There are large-scale terraced, horticultural, and defensive hilltop sites. Glass beads and bracelet segments are characteristic artifacts.

Palegawra: Late Palaeolithic site in northern Iraq occupied by Zarzian hunters c. 12,000–10,000 BC.

Palenque: A Maya center in Chiapus, Mexico, which reached its height during the Late Classic, coming into power when Teotihuacán declined. There are inscribed monuments erected between AD 630–810, after which the site was abandoned. The buildings have fine relief decoration modeled in stucco or carved on limestone panels, and they are known for unusual features (pillar and lintel doorways, mansard roofing). A richly furnished tomb of the Classic period was found underneath the pyramid of the temple of the Inscriptions, equally important as Tutankhamun's in Egypt (jade ornaments, a number of sacrificed retainers, and a massive, elaborately carved sarcophagus). A subterranean vaulted aqueduct joins the central palace complex, with its unique four-story tower, to the eastern terraces where the temples of the Foliated Cross, the Cross, and the Sun are situated. Palenque was the westernmost of the great Classic Maya sites. It was among the first major centers to suffer in the general Mayan collapse; it was abandoned in 810.

paleo-: A combining form meaning old, ancient, or prehistoric; involved or dealing with ancient forms or conditions and former geologic time periods. Special sciences are devoted to palaeoastronomy, paleobotany, paleoecology, paleoethnobotany, paleozoology, and so on. (*syn.* palaeo-, pale-, palae-)

paleoanthropology: The study of human origins and evolution as revealed by fossil remains; the study of the archaeology of the earliest human beings. Fossils are assessed by the techniques of physical anthropology, comparative anatomy, and the theory of evolution. It is a branch of anthropology. (*syn.* human paleontology; palaeoanthropology)

Paleo-Arctic tradition: A tradition grouping industries of the Early Holocene in the western Arctic, including American Paleo-Arctic and Siberian Paleo-Arctic, which are derived from the Siberian Upper Paleolithic. Common features are blades and microblades, small wedge-shaped cores of "campus" type, various kinds of bifaces in varying degrees foliated, end scrapers, and often burins of thick flakes.

paleoautopsy: The technical analysis of a human burial by a trained physical anthropologist specializing in paleopathology. (*syn.* palaeoautopsy)

paleobotany: The study of ancient plant life and the remains of ancient or extinct plants. This includes material that has no direct connection with humans and their activities and is thus less specific to archaeology than palaeoethnobotany or archaeobotany. Much of human material equipment came, however, from vegetable matter. This material is occasion-

ally preserved by desiccation, waterlogging, or charring—or by fossilization. From these sources, various useful results have been obtained, notably in ascertaining the early history of cultivated crops. Paleobotany provides information about the climate and environment and about materials available for food, fuel, tools, and shelter. Paleobotany is a branch of paleontology, and it includes pollen analysis, palynology, reconstruction of climatic sequences for interglacial periods, study of seeds, and study of plant remains. (*syn.* palaeobotany; prehistoric botany)

Paleocene epoch: The earliest geological epoch and division of the Tertiary period, beginning about 66.4 million years ago and lasting about 8.6 million years (c. 65–55 million years ago); it precedes the Eocene epoch and follows the Cretaceous period. During this epoch, there was major development of primitive mammals. The earliest known primates date from the Paleocene. (*syn.* Palaeocene)

paleoclimatology: The scientific study of the extended climatic conditions of past geologic ages. The study of past climates, using information such as vegetation and sedimentary records, geomorphology, and animal distribution. Paleoclimatologists study the changing relation between the Earth and the Sun and the changes in the planet itself. It is a branch of paleontology. (*syn.* palaeoclimatology)

paleodemography: The study of ancient human population and population changes and the study of mortality patterns in antiquity. It aims to reconstruct the demography of ancient populations on the basis of archaeological evidence by using bone remains and the traces left by occupation. It is a branch of paleontology. (*syn.* palaeodemography)

paleoentomology: The study of botanical remains at archaeological sites. The field examines the natural surroundings of flora as well as the human-controlled flora on sites. The terms *palaeoethnobotany* and *palaeobotany* are sometimes used interchangeably in the literature of archaeology. (*syn.* archaeobotany, paleoethnobotany, palaeoethnobotany, palaeoentomology)

paleoenvironmental reconstruction: The determination of the prehistoric environment of an archaeological site, using the methodologies of geology, botany, palynology, and archaeozoology. The paleoenvironment is the ancient environment. (*syn.* palaeoenvironmental reconstruction)

Paleoeskimo: The earliest prehistoric Eskimo people, before the beginning of whale hunting; later whale-hunting people are called Neoeskimo. (*syn.* Palaeoeskimo)

paleoethnobotany: The study of botanical remains at archaeological sites; the analysis and interpretation of interrelations between people and plants from evidence in the archaeological record. The field examines the natural surroundings of flora as well as the human-controlled flora on sites. The terms *archaeobotany*, *palaeoentomology*, and *palaeobotany* are sometimes used interchangeably in the literature of archaeology. (*syn.* archaeobotany, palaeoethnobotany, palaeoentomology, palaeobotany)

paleoethnography: The study of extinct lifeways. The study and systematic recording of prehistoric human cultures; a branch of paleontology. (*syn.* palaeoethnography; paleoethnology; palaeoethnology)

paleoethnology: Ethnology is a science that deals with the division of human beings into races and their origin, distribution, relations, and characteristics. It is anthropology dealing chiefly with the comparative and analytical study of cultures— more commonly called cultural anthropology. Paleoethnology is the study of the behavior of vanished peoples. Now renamed, it is the ethnological study of prehistoric peoples based solely on archaeological evidence.

Paleogene: The lower division of the Tertiary system including the Palaeocene, Eocene, and Oligocene periods. The older of the two stratigraphic divisions of the Cenozoic era (which began about 66.4 million years ago and extends to the present). The Paleogene, whose beginning coincides with that of the Cenozoic era, lasted about 42.7 million years and was followed by the Neogene period. The Paleogene, which means "ancient born," includes the Paleocene (Palaeocene), Eocene, and Oligocene epochs. The term *Paleogene* was devised in Europe to emphasize the similarity of marine fossils found in rocks of the first three Cenozoic epochs, as opposed to the later fossils of the Neogene period. In North America, the terms *Paleogene* and *Neogene* are not widely used, and the Cenozoic is divided only into the Tertiary period (c. 66.4 million–1.6 million years ago) and the Quaternary period (c. 1.6 million years ago to the present). Thus, the Paleogene period may also be considered to be roughly equivalent to the first two thirds of the Tertiary period. (*syn.* Palaeogene)

paleography: Ancient writing or forms of writing, as in documents and inscriptions; also, the study of ancient writings.

Paleo-Indian or Palaeoindian: One of the prehistoric people who migrated from Asia and settled throughout the Americas no later than 10,000 BC. They existed as big-game hunters from about 10,000 BC to about 6000 BC in the Great Plains and eastern North America. (The other tradition at the time was the Desert-culture peoples of the western basin-range region.) Some regard the term as referring to all hunting groups involved with now-extinct mammals, in which case the peoples who hunted the species of bison that became extinct about 4500 BC would also be classified as Paleo-Indians. The oldest remains of the Paleo-Indian tradition are found on sites where large Pleistocene mammals were killed and butchered. The most distinctive artifact type of this horizon is the Clovis Fluted projectile point, which was accompanied by side scrapers. Paleo-Indians are most frequently associated with mammoth, although associations with extinct species of bison, horse, and camel have also been reported. The term also refers to the earliest period in New World chronology, representing the time up to the development of agriculture and villages. In yet another sense, it refers to the period in archaeology (also called Early Lithic) beginning with the earliest stone tools, about 750,000 years ago (*syn.* Paleoindians; Early Lithic)

Paleolithic or Palaeolithic: (pay'-lee-uh-lith'-ik) The more technical name for the Old Stone Age, a division of prehistory covering the time from the first use of stone tools by humans, c. 2.5 million years ago, to the retreat of the glacial ice in the northern hemisphere c. 10,000–8500 BC. It began in the Pliocene epoch and was followed by the Mesolithic. It is the Old World equivalent, although with a much greater extension back in time, of the Paleo-Indian or Early Lithic stage of New World development. The Paleolithic was characterized by the making of chipped or flaked stone tools and weapons and by a hunting and food-gathering way of life. It is usually divided into Lower, Middle, and Upper (or Late) Paleolithic—mainly based on artifact typology. The subdivisions are characterized this way: Lower Paleolithic, c. 2.5 million–200,000 BC, the earliest forms of man (Australopithecus and *Homo erectus*), and the predominance of core tools of pebble tool, hand ax, and chopper type; Middle Paleolithic, c. 150,000–40,000 BC, the era of Neanderthal man and the predominance of flake-tool industries (e.g., Mousterian) over most of Eurasia; and Upper Paleolithic (starting perhaps as early as 38,000 BC–c. 10,000 BC), with *Homo sapiens sapiens*, blade-and-burin industries, and the development of cave art in western Europe. During this stage, man colonized the New World and Australia. The main Palaeolithic cultures of Europe were, in chronological order: (1) Pre-Abbevillian, (2) Abbevillian, (3) Clactonian, (4) Acheulian, (5) Levalloisian, (6) Mousterian, (7) Aurignacian, (8) Solutrean, and (9) Magdalenian. The term was introduced in 1865 by John Lubbock in *Prehistoric Times*. The Palaeolithic was originally defined by the use of chipped stone tools, but later an economic criterion was added, and the practice of hunting and gathering is now regarded as a defining characteristic. (*syn.* Old Stone Age)

Paleolithic art: The art of the last Ice Age. It is divided into: (1) portable or mobiliary art, (2) deep engravings or bas-reliefs on large stones, and (3) cave art or parietal art. Portable or mobiliary art is known in a variety of forms from Spain to Siberia; engravings are found mainly in southwestern France, and cave art in France, Italy, and Spain. Art of similar antiquity is known on other continents.

paleomagnetism: The magnetic polarization acquired by the minerals in a rock at the time the rock was deposited or solidified. The permanent magnetism in rocks, resulting from the orientation of the Earth's magnetic field at the time of rock formation in a past geological age. It is the source of information for the paleomagnetic studies of polar wandering and continental drift. The field of paleomagnetism involves techniques for determining the age of rocks by analyzing the magnetic field polarity of certain minerals in the rock, and its importance in archaeology lies in its use as a dating method. The ancient orientation and intensity of the Earth's magnetic field are preserved by the magnetization of iron oxides in rocks and sediments and archaeological materials (archaeomagnetism). Ancient direction and intensity of the Earth's magnetic field may be preserved in three ways: (a) thermoremanet magnetism (TRM) works through the alignment of the magnetic domains in iron minerals when heated to above the Curie point and subsequently cooling; (b) detrital remanent magnetism works through the alignment of clay particles sinking down slowly through still lake or deep ocean water; a block of sediment is magnetized in the direction of the Earth's field at the time when it was deposited; and (c) sun-dried bricks as the bricks become magnetized in the current direction and intensity of the Earth's field. By using igneous rocks, independently dated by potassium/argon, and kilns, hearths, pots, and so on, dated archaeologically, it has been possible to reconstruct something of the history of the Earth's magnetic field. Palaeomagnetism proper is done by studying reversals in the magnetic field of the Earth, the youngest reversal dating to 700,000 bp. Measurement of the declination and inclination of the magnetic poles as it affects materials of different ages can be used to build regional chronologies. Palaeomagnetic dating has also been successfully applied to lacustrine deposits, deep sea cores, and volcanic rocks. (*syn.* palaeomagnetism, remanent magnetism; paleo-magnetism, palaeo-magnetism; archaeomagnetism)

paleometallurgy: The study of ancient metallurgy from its beginnings up to the industrial age, examining and interpreting the remains of old metal-working equipment and sites. Paleometallurgists look at the areas where metal was extracted, where ore was treated, and the workshops of goldsmiths, silversmiths, bronze and ironworkers. (*syn.* palaeometallurgy)

paleontology: The study of the forms of life existing in former geologic periods, as represented by their fossils. It is the science of life of the geologic past and involves examination of the remains, origin, and evolution of plant and animal fossils. Fossils may provide palaeoenvironmental information. Human paleontology is the study of the origins of man himself. (*syn.* palaeontology)

paleopathology: The study of human ills, diseases, diet, traumatic injuries, and so on, by examination of human and animal remains. Such studies can determine life expectancy and population statistics and contributory reason for the success or failure of a particular population. Most of the material studied is osteological, although soft tissue may be analyzed when preserved, as in mummification or bog preservation. Some of man's ills—fractures, malnutrition, dental decay, and some diseases—leave their mark on bones. Where bones survive, evidence can be recovered that may reveal much about the conditions in which people lived and died. Congenital malformations may show relations between skeletons; diseases such as arthritis, tuberculosis, syphilis, and leprosy can be identified, as well as such conditions as bone fracture through injury. Evidence of war wounds and cannibalism are also sought. The following groups of diseases have been regularly diagnosed in skeletons (both human and animals) from archaeological sites: (1) dental diseases; (2) diseases of the joints; (3) trauma (fractures and other injuries); (4) dietary deficiency diseases; (5) tumors; (6) inflammatory diseases: general inflammation and more specific conditions such as tuberculosis, leprosy, and syphilis in man; (7) congenital deformities; and (8) endocrine disturbances. Study of the relative frequency of different diseases yields information about both the medical history and the biology of ancient populations. (*syn.* palaeopathology, paleophysioanthropology)

paleopedology: The study of the creation, character, stratigraphy of buried fossil soils (palaeosols), which includes material in both geological and archaeological contexts and their geomorphic, temporal, and palaeoenvironmental significance. Soil scientists can assist archaeologists by explaining the natural and man-influenced processes on sites, such as the manner of filling of certain types of feature. Information may be deduced about climatic and environmental variation, which can lead to conclusions about the manipulation of the land by man. (*syn.* palaeopedology)

paleoserology: The study of ancient man by blood groups; a branch of serology dealing with human sera and their properties. Results have been obtained from mummified and frozen bodies, with research concentrating on family groupings among mummified remains, although diseases may also be studied (palaeopathology) through the examination of blood. Further results have come from testing the spongy bone tissue of skeletons. (*syn.* palaeoserology)

Paleozoic: (payl'-ee-uh-zoh-ik) Major interval of geologic time extending from 540–245 million years ago. It is the first era of the Phanerozoic Eon. It is a geological era in the Earth's history before the Mesozoic and after the Precambrian, marked by the development of fishes, land plants, insects, reptiles, and fernlike trees. The early Paleozoic (probably the first 130 million years) was characterized by widespread ups and downs of the Earth's crust, which resulted in mountain building and geosynclines (downward flexing) in parts of North America, Europe, and Asia. Great seas were formed in the southern areas of the emergent land masses. Much of North America was covered by a warm shallow sea with many coral reefs. The late Paleozoic, which extended from about 410 to 245 million years ago, saw tremendous changes wrought in the Earth. Both plant and animal life flourished in the great, warm, shallow seas, and the various convolutions of the Earth laid down extensive mineral deposits. Much of the copper, gold, lead, zinc, and other minerals mined today derive from Devonian times in the late Paleozoic. Huge swampy forest regions covered much of the northern continents, and these were repeatedly and suddenly invaded by the seas, which buried the vegetation, then covered it with silt. When the sea subsequently withdrew, the forests revived and were again buried in rhythmic cycles that are now evident in deposits called cyclothems. Heat and pressure transformed the buried vegetation into oil and coal. During the Devonian Period, animal life emerged from the ocean, and various species adapted themselves to breathing air and moving about on land. This happened by way of the amphibians, which evolved in the Carboniferous and Permian periods, and were succeeded by reptiles. The late Paleozoic also saw the beginning of insect life—and fishes and land plants underwent rapid development. (*syn.* Palaeozoic)

Palermo: Major city of Sicily, on the northwest coast of the island, which has been continuously occupied for 2½ millennia. The Phoenicians established a port at the site by the 8th century BC, and from the 5th century BC the city was controlled by Carthage. The Romans captured Palermo in 254 BC. The city decayed under Roman rule but prospered after AD 535, when the Byzantine general Belisarius recovered it from the Ostrogoths. The island remained in Byzantine hands until the Islamic offensive in 831. Palermo was prosperous when it fell to the Norman adventurers Roger I and Robert Guiscard in 1072. The ensuing era of Norman rule (1072–1194) was Palermo's golden age, particularly after the founding of the Norman kingdom of Sicily in 1130 by Roger II. Palermo became the capital of this kingdom and has some notable buildings from the Norman and succeeding periods. It continues to be Sicily's chief port and center of government.

Palermo Stone: A slab of black basalt bearing a record of the first five Egyptian dynasties (Old Kingdom), compiled in the 5th Dynasty, c. 2400 BC. It is one of the basic sources of information about the chronology and cultural history of Egypt during the first five dynasties (c. 2925–c. 2325 BC). Named for the Sicilian city in which one slab is stored, the diorite stela is one of six existing fragments that probably originally stood in Egyptian temples; other slabs are now in London and Cairo. It is inscribed on both sides with horizontal lines of hieroglyphic text, the top row listing the names of predynastic rulers. The following rows, each headed by the name of a different king, are divided into compartments, each compartment signifying 1 year. In the compartments, the hieroglyphs always list one or more memorable events of that year. Thus the original monument was apparently a year-by-year record of all the kings from the 1st–5th Dynasties, although the last name preserved on the stone is that of Neferirkare, the third of the nine kings of the 5th Dynasty.

Pales, Léon (1905–1988): French prehistorian who did pioneering work in palaeopathology. He studied cave footprints and spent 25 years deciphering engraved slabs from La Marche.

palette: A small slab of stone for grinding and mixing substances like paint or cosmetics. A series from early Egypt, as that of Narmer, is important because the relief decoration provides valuable evidence of the art and history of the country at the beginning of Dynastic times, c. 3000 BC. The term is also used to describe scribal palettes. Cosmetic/ceremonial palettes were usually of silt stone (greywacke) and are found in grave goods as early as the Badarian period (c. 5500–4000 BC). Scribal palettes, long rectangular pieces of wood or stone (averaging 30 cm long, 6 cm wide), had a shallow central groove or slot to hold reed brushes or pens and circular depressions for cakes of pigment. The order of colors was white, then yellows, reds, blues, to black.

palisade: A continuous wall or fence of stakes, especially for defense; a series of long, strong stakes pointed at the top and set close with others as a defense. They were usually set in a continuous foundation trench or on the tops of vallums, embankments, or ramparts surrounding a fort.

Palliser Bay: An area at the southern limit of New Zealand's North Island with Archaic Maori sites associated with sweet potato cultivation, attesting a fairly large horticultural population between AD 1100–1400. After 1450, the area became depopulated, because of environmental degradation and an adverse climatic change. Settlements and burials have been excavated.

palmate stone: A large spatulate stone object about 2 feet (61 cm) long, shaped like a hand with extended fingers, believed to be a ceremonial representation of a device worn by ball-game players in Mesoamerica and dating to the Classic Period. It rested on a yoke, which fitted around the waist and projected upward to protect the chest. Probably of wood or leather with carving on both sides, they may have been trophies, religious symbols, or for burial purposes. The center for these puzzling stone carvings seems to be the coastal Veracruz area. (*syn.* palma)

Palmela: A cemetery of four Copper Age (Chalcolithic) rock-cut tombs in Setúbal, Portugal, near Lisbon. Each has a kidney-shaped chamber, originally used for collective inhumation, entered by a long passage or through a hole in the roof. The cemetery forms the type site of a culture flourishing in central Portugal c. 3800–3200 BC. A variety of amuletic objects in stone includes decorated plano-convex or cylindrical stylized human figurines, crescents, model hoes or adzes, and a pair of sandals from Alapraia. Stonework follows Neolithic traditions, but adds deeply concave-based arrowheads. The tombs were rich in Beaker material, including 50 beakers with copper knives and fragments of gold foil. Pottery, too, follows on from the Almeria culture, although foreign elements have been connected with the dark-slipped Urfirnis ware of Greece. There is also a distinctive type of arrowhead with near-circular copper blade and long tang, the Palmela point. The settlements are likely a variant of the Vila Nova de São Pedro culture.

palmette: A decorative motif suggestive of a palm; a stylized palm frond used to decorate Greek and Roman art.

Palmyra: Syrian city on the caravan route from the eastern Mediterranean to the Euphrates; an ancient oasis town. Occupation was probably continuous since the 3rd millennium BC, but the town achieved prominence in the 1st century BC by exploitation of the caravan trade. Under the Roman influence of Septimus Severus, it gained the status of a colony. A temple to Baal (Bel) dedicated in AD 32, colonnaded streets, agora, senate house, and headquarters building or fort by Diocletian have been found. Communal tower tombs (hypogea) were marked by relief plaques naming the deceased. Its monuments blend Greek, Roman and Parthian traditions and art.

palstave: A Middle Bronze Age form of ax with side flanges, stop-bar (or -ridge), and sometimes one or (rarely) two loops attached—found in Europe. Its features made for more secure hafting of the ax blade by preventing lateral movement and haft splitting. This development lead to the socketed ax. It was used by the Celtic nations in war for battering the armor of the enemy.

palynology: The study of fossil and living spores (of lichens and mosses) and pollen (of flowering plants); the technique through which the fossil pollen grains and spores from archaeological sites are studied. The examination of their production, dispersal, and applications is an aid to the reconstruction of past vegetation and climates and to developing relative chronologies. Each kind of flowering plant produces pollen that is unique, and pollen grains have tough coverings that can last a long time. The resilient exine of the pollen and spores is preserved in anaerobic environments, such as lakes and bogs, and some acidic and dry soils, as in caves. Palynology helps archaeologists find out what plant resources were available to ancient peoples and what the climate was at those times. Palynology was developed by the Swedish botanist Lennart von Post. (*syn.* pollen analysis)

Pampa de las Llamas or Moxeke: Major Initial Period ceremonial center on the north-central coast of Peru. The site is on a linear axis with the large mound of Moxeke at one end and Huaca A at the other. There are small U-shaped structures parallel to the central axis.

Pampa Grande: Middle Horizon, Moche V site in the Lambayeque Valley, northern Peru, dated c. 1000 BC and occupied for a relatively short time. It was a large urban center and probably the relocated capital, after the abandonment of Huacas del Sol and Luna, of the Moche polity in its closing phases. Highly differentiated architecture is scattered over the area, and structures include masonry platforms, truncated adobe pyramids, small agglutinated rooms, and an extensive network of corridors and large storage rooms. A variety of human face motifs on molded and handmade neck jars may have socioeconomic significance in identifying either the contents or the owner. Stone tools were used in metalworking, and small utilitarian artifacts in copper have also been found.

Panaramitee style: An art style found in many parts of Australia, involving rock engravings featuring circles and tridents (possibly kangaroo and emu tracks) and dating to Pleistocene times. It is found at Panaramitee in the Flinder Ranges, South Australia, and arid regions in South Australia, New South Wales, north Queensland, and the Northern Territory; isolated examples have also been found in northern Tasmania and near Sydney. Engravings were found at Ingaladdi dating to 5000–7000 bp, at Early Man Shelter c. 13,000 bp, and at Karolta c. 30,000 years old. The style involves the pecking on rock surfaces by indirect percussion of clusters of hundreds of small figures, usually about 10 centimeters tall, in outline or infilled forms. The designs include dots, spirals, mazes, and crescents, human footprints, lizards, radiating lines, and tectiforms (roof shapes). The art is thought to be of considerable antiquity on the basis of still inconclusive evidence of patination, distribution in both Australia and Tasmania, and the absence of stone tool types belonging to the post-2000 BC Australian Small Tool tradition. (*syn.* Panaramitee art)

pan bedding: An Egyptian construction technique, usually in mud brick, consisting of curved courses. It is most often seen in temple enclosure walls from the Late Period (747–332 BC) onward, which are usually built in sections and with a pronounced batter.

Panduranga: A state of the kingdom of Champa on the coast of southern Vietnam. It became the center of Champan activity from the mid-8th century onward. (*syn.* Phan Rang)

pan-grave culture: Material culture of a group of seminomadic Nubian cattle herders who entered Egypt in the late Middle Kingdom (2055–1650 BC) and during the Second Intermediate Period (c. 1633–1550 BC). They were well attested in Eastern Desert, the characteristic being shallow circular pit graves with black-topped pottery, the "pan graves" of Upper Egypt and Lower Nubia. Their material culture was similar to the C-Group. The people were mercenaries during this period of Egyptian history and during the New Kingdom, when they were called the Medjay. (*syn.* Pangrave culture)

Panhellenic: A term meaning "all Greek," referring to regional sanctuaries that attracted dedications from within the Greek world.

Panlongcheng: Chinese archaeological site from about the middle of the Shang Dynasty period (18th–12th centuries BC). The site, located near the confluence of the Yangtze and Han-shui Rivers in central Hupei, consists of five graves and two storage pits. It is thought to be the southernmost outpost of the political system in the 15th–13th centuries BC. Palatial foundations, elite burials with Erligang-style bronze ritual vessels, and a hang-tu city wall have been excavated. There are poor burials, pottery, stone tools, and other bronze items. The earliest wood carvings yet found in China were at Panlongcheng. (*syn.* P'an-lung-ch'eng)

Pannonia: Province of the Roman Empire, corresponding to present western Hungary and parts of eastern Austria, Slovenia, and northern Yugoslavia (Vojvodina) incorporated into the Roman Empire in AD 10. (Roman conquest began there about 35 BC under Octavian.) Pannonia was a prosperous Roman frontier province with numerous villas. The principal town was Aquincum (part of modern Budapest). The emperor Trajan divided the province about AD 106. The western and northern districts constituted Pannonia Superior, which was the focal point of the Roman wars with the Marcomanni during the reign of Marcus Aurelius (161–180). The southern and eastern districts were organized as Pannonia Inferior under Diocletian (284–305). Pannonia Superior was divided into Pannonia Prima and Pannonia Ripariensis (or Savia), and Pannonia Inferior was divided into Valeria and Pannonia Secunda. Pannonia was the birthplace of several Roman emperors of the 3rd century, and the province provided large numbers of troops for the Roman army. The grave barbarian threat in the 4th century AD forced the Romans to withdraw after 395. The Pannonians were mainly Illyrians, but there were some Celts in the western part of the province.

P'an-p'an: One of the earliest Indianized kingdoms of Southeast Asia, with ambassadors to China between the 5th–7th centuries. Its name is known only from Chinese sources, and its exact location is unknown, but it is thought to have been situated on the Malay Peninsula.

panpipe lug: A type of handle found on Neolithic pottery of the Chassey, Cortaillod, and Lagozza cultures in France, Switzerland, and northern Italy. It consisted of cylindrical vertical lugs placed side by side, thus slightly resembling the panpipe. The panpipe, a wind instrument, was widespread in Neolithic and later cultures, especially in Melanesia and pre-Columbian South America. (*syn.* pan-pipe lug)

Pan-p'o-ts'un: Chinese Neolithic Yang-Shao culture site of c. 4500 BC with slash-and-burn agriculture, domesticated animals, and handmade painted pottery.

Pan Shan: A branch of the Yang-Shao culture of Neolithic China with a distinctive painted pottery, c. 2500–2000 BC. There are extensive cemeteries in the hills of the upper Yellow River basin in Kansu province, which yielded great quantities of the pottery with inhumation burials. The most common were large globular urns painted with bold spiral or other curvilinear designs or lozenges in red, black, purple, or brown. The "death pattern" consists of a red band between two black ones internally fringed. The geometric patterns or stylized figures are of men, fish, and birds; there is no glaze. Coiling was common, but some of the wares were probably shaped on a slow, or hand-turned, wheel. The handles are set low on the body of the urns, and the lower part of the body is left undecorated—as with most Greek Proto-Geometric funerary ware, to which there is a certain likeness. Striking parallels have been found in Turkestan, the Caucasus, and the Ukraine. (*syn.* Pan-shan, Banshan)

Pantalica: A Late Bronze Age to Early Iron Age site inland from Syracuse in southeast Sicily, occupied c. 13th–8th centuries BC. The 5,000 rock-cut tombs that honeycomb the hillside have yielded great quantities of material. Pottery and metal goods from the tombs indicate trading contacts with both mainland Italy and the Aegean. The characteristic local pottery is wheelmade, red slipped, and burnished. Four phases run from contemporary with Late Mycenaean c. 1200 BC to well after the first Greek colonies formed in the 8th century BC. At least one public building has been exposed: a large stone-built structure described as an *anaktoron* or palace.

Pantano Longarini: A large wreck of the 5th–7th centuries found in the sea off Pantano Longarini in southeast Sicily. The vessel would have been about 45 meters long and 9 meters wide; the structural details of the boat have contributed to the study of Byzantine ship building.

Pantelleria: Small island in the central Mediterranean between Sicily and Tunisia. A fortified Neolithic village c. 3000 BC has been excavated, with remains of huts, pottery, and obsidian tools. Of volcanic origin, it has a source of obsidian that was exploited in prehistory. There are tombs, known as *sesi*, similar to the *nuraghi* of Sardinia, made up of rough lava towers with sepulchral chambers in them. After a considerable interval of no habitation, the Phoenicians established a trading station there in the 7th century BC. Later controlled by the Carthaginians, it was occupied by the Romans in 217 BC. Under the Roman Empire, it served as a place of banishment.

Pantheon: A temple dedicated to a group of gods or collective divinities; the term also refers to the group of gods. The first Pantheon was built by Agrippa in 27–25 BC and rebuilt by Hadrian sometime between AD 118–128, and was one of the most remarkable buildings of Rome. The rotunda was roofed by a dome, fronted by a portico and entrance hall, of brick-faced concrete and of a height equal to its internal diameter, c. 145 ft. The sophistication of the domed, coffered ceiling was important in the development of Roman architecture. The term has another meaning: a building serving as the burial place of or containing memorials to the famous dead of a nation. (*syn.* pantheon)

Papuan languages: A group of over 700 languages of New Guinea and adjacent parts of eastern Indonesia and Melanesia. Today these languages are spoken by about 2.9 million people, and the family is perhaps the most diverse in the world. The Papuan languages presumably descend from the languages of the first settlers of Melanesia c. 30,000–40,000 years ago, and some linguists claim to be able to trace population expansion and migrations in the New Guinea region from about 15,000 years ago. (*syn.* Non-Austronesian languages, NAN languages)

papyrus: A reed of the sedge family, growing in Mediterranean lands, particularly in Egypt along the banks of the Nile. It is the flexible writing material produced from the plant. By splitting and opening out its stems, laying them together in two layers at right angles to each other, then beating them together, activating the plant's natural starch to form an adhesive—an inexpensive writing material was created. Examples preserved by the dry climate of Egypt and other regions in tombs, caves, and so on, have yielded invaluable evidence on the ancient history of the area. *Papyrus* is the Latin form, from which our word "paper" derives. Its stems were also bound together in bundles to make lightweight boats. Used first in Egypt, it later replaced clay tablets in the Near East when the Aramaic alphabet replaced the cuneiform script. Unlike engraved clay tablets, papyrus allowed a light, cursive script, thus encouraging the spread of a technique that was originally very restricted and specialized. The earliest papyrus dates to the 1st Dynasty, the latest to the Islamic Period, when the plant died out in Egypt. (*syn.* Cyperus papyrus)

papyrus column: In Egyptian religion, an amulet that conveyed freshness, youth, vigor, and the continuance of life to its wearer. It is also the name of the mighty columns erected at Karnak, 134 in total, 12 of which formed the higher central aisle (76 ft/23 m) of the hypostyle hall.

Paracas: Large ceremonial area and major Early Horizon culture on the south coast of Peru, showing direct influence from Chavín—especially in the pottery (called Ocucaje in the Inca Valley). The pottery is a highly individual polychrome ware with designs executed in resinous paint applied after the pot was fired, including paint-filled incisions of Chavinoid deities. The early period pottery was not well fired. Desert conditions have preserved all kinds of organic materials, including fine textiles, in rich burials. The best-known graves belong to the closing stages of the culture and are of two types: deep shafts leading into underground chambers with several mummy bundles (Paracas Cavernas), and pits or abandoned houses filled with sand and containing more than 400 mummy bundles (the type site, Paracas Necropolis). The people also engaged in artificial deformation of the skull by binding the head in infancy. Much of the material from the necropolis belongs to the earliest stage of the Nasca culture, which developed out of Paracas in about the 2nd century BC. The paracas culture's earlier phase, called Paracas Cavernas, is dated 900 BC–AD 1; the Paracas cultures of the middle Early Intermediate Period (c. AD 1–400) are referred to as the Paracas Pinilla and the Paracas Necrópolis phases. There are no large temple structures at the type site.

paradigm: A conceptual framework for a scientific discipline; a set of assumptions, methodologies, and objectives that determine a scientific investigation. It is a strategy for integrating a research method, theory, and goals. Examples in archaeology are postprocessual archaeology, behavioral archaeology, and culture history. A paradigmatic classification is one based on an equal weighting of attributes, so that each class is defined by a cluster of unique attributes and is not dependent on the order in which the attributes were defined.

parados: An entrance or exit used by actors to reach or leave an orchestra in a theater; the area between the seats and the skene.

parallel: A second, and presumed significant, occurrence of a trait under consideration, implying derivation or contact; a secondary occurrence similar enough to show resemblance.

páramos: A biome of wet grasslands or forests at high elevations with alpine-type vegetation characterized by tussock grasses and cushion plants. (*syn.* páramo)

Paranthropus: A fossil hominid genus initially assigned by Robert Broom to the form of australopithecine found at Kromdraai and Swartkrans, South Africa. The remains are known as *Australopithecus robustus* to scholars who do not consider it a separate genus from other australopithecines. It was a large and heavy species, one of the oldest and most primitive forms of man. (*syn.* Australopithecus robustus)

paraskenia: In a Greek theater, the side wings of the

skene—which was originally a mask-changing building and developed into an edifice decorated with columns, with three doors used for entrances and exits and the appearance of ghosts and gods.

Pararaton: A Javanese chronicle dating from the end of the 15th century, containing detailed biographies of kings and persons of their entourage and accounts of the scandals and dramas of the court. (*syn.* Book of Kings)

parchment: Writing material made from the skin of calves, sheep, or goat, which gradually replaced papyrus during the late Roman Empire, resulting in the book (codex) replacing the scroll. The name apparently derives from the ancient Greek city of Pergamum (in Turkey), where parchment is said to have been invented in the 2nd century BC. It is less fragile and could also be reused after the original text had been erased by scraping (called palimpsests). The finer kind of parchment known as vellum is from the skins of calves, kids, and dead-born lambs. In the 4th century AD, vellum or parchment as a material and the codex as a form became dominant, although there are later examples of rolls, and papyrus was occasionally used for official documents until the 10th century. Paper then took over from the 14th century.

Parian: A white, semitransparent marble used for sculpture and quarried from subterranean pits on the north side of Mt. Marpessa, a chief source of wealth for ancient Páros, an island of the Cyclades, Greece. It was particularly prized as its large crystals absorb light and glow in the sun.

Parian Chronicle: A document inscribed on Parian marble in the Attic Greek dialect and containing an outline of Greek history from the reign of Cecrops, legendary king of Athens, c. 1582 BC, down to the archonship of Diognetus at Athens (264 BC). The author recorded the dates of festivals and when they were established, the introduction of various kinds of poetry, and the births and deaths of the poets. One large fragment is at the Ashmolean Museum (among the so-called Arundel Marbles), Oxford; another is in the Paros Museum. (*syn.* Marmor Parium)

parietal art: Literally, "art on walls," a term used to designate art on the walls of caves and shelters, extended to cover art on any nonmovable surface (large rocks, blocks, ceilings, floors).

Parisi: An Iron Age tribe of invaders from the River Seine who settled in Yorkshire, England, about 250 BC. They brought La Tène culture, a warrior aristocracy, the use of chariots, and weapons of war. They had poor pottery, indicating few women. Many prehistoric remains have been discovered in Yorkshire, the most prominent being the hill forts. The Romans found the region inhabited by the Brigantes and, in the eastern portion, by the Parisi. The Romans established control over the region in the 1st century AD.

Parmana: An area of the Middle Orinoco drainage, Venezuela, which shifted from root crops to seed crop cultivation (mainly maize) between 800–400 BC. The cultivation of maize gave rise to an increase in population and provided the basis for the emergence of chiefdom-led societies.

parodos: In Greek theater, the chorus entrance. In the earliest times, the actors and the chorus entered together from this main approach.

paroikoi: The dependent peasants or tenants of a Byzantine monastic economy. An estate, *pronoia*, was granted by the emperor and tied to military obligation. The recipient of a pronoia was entitled to all the revenues of his estate and to the taxes payable by his tenants—the paroikoi—on condition of equipping himself as a mounted cavalryman with a varying number of troops. He was in absolute possession of his property until it reverted to the crown upon his death.

Paroong Cave: A limestone cave in the Mount Gambier district, South Australia, with deeply incised or pounded motifs of Karake style, possibly from the Pleistocene.

Parpalló Cave: A cave in the province of Valencia, Spain, with a sequence of Solutrean and other Upper Palaeolithic deposits. There is a Gravettian layer with backed blades, burins, and end scrapers, followed by a sequence of Solutrean levels with barbed and tanged points. Four Magdalenian levels had stone, bone, and antler artifacts (microliths, needles, harpoons). Over 5,000 small stone plaques, engraved and painted with animal figures, were found in the Palaeolithic levels; a Mesolithic phase had microburins.

Parrot, André (1901–1980): Mesopotamian archaeologist who worked at Mari, Baalbek, Byblos, Tello, and Larsa. Much of his time was spent at Mari, which dates to 3100 BC, and he was also in government museum service (including director of the Louvre). He wrote a history of Mesopotamian archaeology.

Parthenon: The famous temple of Athena on the Akropolis at Athens, considered the finest example of the Doric order of architecture. It was built by Ictinus and Callicrates, 447–432 BC, as the centerpiece of Pericles' grand scheme for the Akropolis, under the supervision of the sculptor Phidias, who contributed the great statue of Athena. The material is Pentelic marble (from Mount Pentelikon, north of Athens). Much of the sculptured decoration may be seen in the British Museum, London (the so-called Elgin marbles). After the classical period, the building survived various conversions to the function of church and mosque, until wartime in 1687 when the temple exploded into two ruined halves. Other sculptures from the Parthenon are now in the Louvre Museum in Paris and in Copenhagen, and many are still in Athens.

Parthian: A steppe people from east of the Caspian Sea who entered northeastern Iran and set up a kingdom at the expense of the Seleucid Empire and Bactria. The Parthian Empire existed from 247 BC–AD 224. The earliest Parthian capital was probably at Dara; two of the later capitals were Nisa and Hecatompylos. Between 160–140 BC, Mithridates I extended the Parthian state into an empire, incorporating Iran and most of Mesopotamia, which survived 350 years of almost constant conflict with the Seleucids and later the Romans until its overthrow by the Sassanians in the early 3rd century AD. When flourishing, the Parthians established an oriental empire with Greek civilization grafted on. Their culture and location were an important intermediary between the Near and Far East, and they controlled most of the trade routes between Asia and the Greco-Roman world. The silk road to China was opened under Mithradates II (124/123–87 BC). The Parthians were also famous for their superlative horsemanship. (*syn.* Parthia, Parthava (modern Khorasan))

partially cortical flake: A flake possessing some cortex on its dorsal aspect. (*syn.* secondary flake)

particle accelerator: A device that produces a beam of fast-moving, electrically charged atomic or subatomic particles, used mainly in nuclear physics, to increase the velocities of atomic fragments such as electrons, protons, and ions. Particle accelerators are used in a certain form of radiocarbon dating.

particle size analysis: A technique for analyzing the grain sizes of archaeological or geological sediments, used to discover the manner and process of their deposition. The technique also allows the accurate description of a deposit and comparison with other sediments. There are several methods of particle size analysis. Dry sieving, the sifting of deposits through various sizes of mesh so that particles are grouped into sizes, is suitable for larger grains from pebbles to coarse sand. Light or electron microscopy is used for finer grains of sand, silt, and clay. Sedimentation, the counting of grains dispersed in liquid as they fall to the bottom of a container, is suitable for the finest grains of silt and clay. A combination of methods is frequently used. The analysis may yield information on whether the deposit is wind or water borne, how much it has weathered, and to what extent it has been affected by man. Particles are classified into a number of size grades, normally under such headings as boulders, pebbles, stones, gravel, sand, silt, and clay; sand is often further subdivided. The mixture of particle size grades found in a material is known as the texture. (*syn.* particle-size analysis, size analysis, size-frequency analysis, grain size analysis)

particularism: An interpretative framework that characterized American archaeology in the early 1900s, whereby individual cultures were documented without comparative reference to others. This school of anthropological thought is associated with Franz Boas and his students (including Margaret Mead and A. L. Kroeber), whose studies of culture emphasized the integrated way of life distinctive of a people. Boas concentrated on describing the particular characteristics of a given culture with a view toward reconstructing the historical events that led to its present structure. Hypotheses about evolutionary development and the influence of one culture on another were considered secondary to the study of particular societies. Boas urged the historical method, based on the description of particular culture traits and elements, and rejected the assumption of a single standard of rationality to which all cultures could be compared. (*syn.* historical particularism)

part-time specialist: A food producer who also specializes in nonfood goods or services.

Pasargadae: The first dynastic capital of the Achaemenian Empire, situated northeast of Persepolis in modern southwestern Iran. Traditionally, Cyrus II the Great (reigned c. 559–529 BC) chose the site because it lay near the scene of his victory over Astyages the Mede (550 BC). The buildings are scattered over a wide area; they include two palaces, a gatehouse, and a square stone tower, as well as a religious area with a large fire altar. Trilingual inscriptions in Elamite, Babylonian (Akkadian), and Old Persian, all in the cuneiform script, occur on the palaces and gatehouse. Southwest of the palaces is the tomb of Cyrus, almost intact: an impressive rectangular stone chamber with a gabled roof, set on a high stepped plinth. At the extreme southern edge of the site, an impressive rock-cut road or canal indicates the course of the ancient highway that once linked Pasargadae with Persepolis. After the accession of Darius I the Great (522 BC), Persepolis replaced Pasargadae as the dynastic seat.

Pasemah Plateau: A plateau in southern Sumatra with a series of impressive prehistoric megalithic monuments—massive slab graves and a rich collection of lifesized anthropomorphic carvings. The large stones are roughly carved into the shape of animals, such as the buffalo and elephant, and human figures—some with swords, helmets, and ornaments and some apparently carrying drums. They are stylistically similar to those of Iron Age burials of the last centuries BC, and remote connections with the Dong Son culture of northern Vietnam and the megalithic cultures of south India are likely. (*syn.* Pasemah)

Paso: A shell mound on the shore of Lake Tondano in northern Sulawesi, which is the best-preserved pre-Neolithic midden to be excavated in Indonesia. Dated to c. 6500 BC, there are obsidian flake tools and bone points pre-dating the Toalian. Its inhabitants lived on shellfish and hunted the local fauna. Paso provides an important terminus post quem for the small flake and blade industries and Neolithic cultures (after 3000 BC) that later appear in the region.

passage grave: A category of megalithic or chambered tomb in which there is a burial chamber and a separate passage into the tomb; the chamber is reached from the edge of the covering mound via a long passage. It includes the earliest known megalithic graves of Europe, dating from about 5000 BC (in Brittany). The diagnostic features are a round mound covering a burial chamber (often roofed by corbelling) approached by a narrower entrance passage. The distinction between passage and funerary chamber proper is very marked. The origin of the passage grave is unclear. Passage graves occur throughout the area where megalithic tombs occur in Europe, but have a predominantly western distribution. In some areas, passage graves were still being constructed in the Bronze Age. (*syn.* passage tomb)

Passo di Corvo: A large Middle Neolithic settlement site on the Tavoliere plain in Puglie, southeast Italy, with a radiocarbon date of 5200 BC. The site is concentrically ditched (known as a villaggio trincerato) and has about 100 circular hut enclosures. The site has produced evidence of a mixed farming economy and abundant pottery of various types, including Impressed Ware and a variety of red painted wares.

Passy-sur-Yonne: Middle Neolithic long mound cemetery in Yonne, France, with associated pottery and a date of c. 3800 BC.

paste: The clay substance of pottery, excluding temper/filler additives.

paste texture: In ceramic analysis, the appearance of the ceramic paste as determined by clay particle size.

Pasteurs des Plateaux: The general name for the Late Neolithic and Copper Age peoples who lived on the uplands of Languedoc, southern France, c. 2500 BC, and who made pottery of the Ferrières and Fontbouisse styles.

pastoralism: An economy based on livestock raising, in which the bulk of the food supply is derived from domesticated animals, often in the form of secondary products such as milk, yogurt, and cheese.

Pastoral Neolithic: A complex of cultures that appeared in southern Kenya and northern Tanzania about 3500 BC; a general term for the pre-Iron Age food-producing societies of East Africa. It remains unknown whether they also cultivated plants. The earliest sites are on the plains of northern Kenya and date to the mid-3rd millennium BC. About 1,300 years ago, they were absorbed or replaced by iron-using pastoralists and mixed farmers. Disposal of the dead was by burial beneath a stone cairn or between rocks. Stone platters, bowls, and pestles occur on most sites. Settlements show a great range of size, as does the relative importance of herding cattle and small stock in comparison with hunting. Pastoral Neolithic settlement is attested as far to the south as the Serengeti Plain of northern Tanzania. The subdivision of the Pastoral Neolithic in the East African highlands is not clearly defined. Pastoral Neolithic traditions recognized, although not well

defined chronologically, are: Elmenteitan, Kansyore, Narosura, Nderit, Njoro River Cave, Oldishi, Olmalenge, and Oltome. (*syn.* Pastoral Neolithic of East Africa)

Patayan: Culture of the lower Colorado River, northwestern Arizona, occupying the area by AD 100 until 1500—a division of the Hakataya Culture. These people of Yuman speech included the tribes of Hazasupai, Mojave, and Walapai. They had three provinces: Cerbat, Prescott, and Cohonina. They farmed alluvial flood plains, hunted, and gathered foods. Between 1000–1500, pottery spread over a much wider area and was influenced by Hohokam; the vessels had red-on-buff designs and stucco finishing. (*syn.* Hakataya; Patayan Division)

patera: In Roman antiquity, a rounded bowl, often of bronze, usually with a long handle and used for pouring libations. The dish was also used in sacrifices.

pathology: The study of diseases or abnormalities.

patina: (pa-tee'-nuh, pat'-i-nuh) The outermost layer of an artifact, which may differ in color, texture, luster, or substance from the inner part of the artifact because of physical, biological, or chemical alteration caused by environmental conditions. The term also refers to any thin, colored film or layer formed on the surface of flint or other rock as a result of alkaline conditions. It is a porous bluish or white weathering, possibly becoming stained with brown or yellow because of contacts with iron compounds in percolating water. Similarly, the green patina on bronze objects is a product of corrosion. The amount of patination is sometimes used as a very rough indication of age; the longer the exposure, the deeper is the patination. (*syn.* patination)

Patjitanian: A Middle Pleistocene chopper–chopping tool culture from Java characterized by coarse flakes in the shape of cleavers, known from a very prolific site in south-central Java. In the Patjitanian, the main types of implements consist of single-edged choppers and chopping tools that occur in association with primitive flakes with unprepared, high-angle striking platforms. There are also pointed, bifacial implements that have been described as crude hand axes.

Patna: A city in northeast India, founded as Pataliputra in the 5th century BC by Ajatashatru, king of Magadha. His son Udaya (Udayin) made it the capital of Magadha, which it remained until the 1st century BC. The second Magadha dynasty, the Maurya, ruled in the 3rd and early 2nd centuries BC until the city was sacked in 185 by Indo-Greeks. The Shunga Dynasty followed, until about 73 BC. Pataliputra remained a center of learning and in the 4th century AD became the Gupta capital. It declined and was deserted by the 7th century. The city was refounded as Patna in 1541 and again rose to prosperity under the Mughal Empire. Part of the ancient city's rampart (reinforced with timber) and a large pillared hall survive. This hall, with its 80 pillars, has frequently been compared to similar halls found in Achaemenid Persia, and it has been suggested that some Achaemenid craftsmen fled to India after the defeat of the Persians by Alexander the Great. (*syn.* ancient Pataliputra)

patri-: A prefix meaning "father" or coming through the male line of a family.

patterns of discard: A term referring to remains left for investigation after natural destructive forces have affected artifacts and food remains abandoned by their original users.

pattern welding: A post-Roman period technique of ironworking used particularly in the manufacture of weapons, mainly swords, developed to overcome the problems of brittleness caused by trying to diffuse carbon into iron. It produced blades that were both strong and decorative. In the manufacture of a sword, for example, the central part would typically be a core of carbon steel, with soft iron welded to it. Wire and strip metal, sometimes in varying combinations of type and color, were welded together and hammered out to produce a blade with patterned effect. The pattern derives from the difference in the carbon content between the uncarburized cores and the carburized surfaces of the welded strips, which is exposed during the forging and grinding of the weapon. A sword of this quality could have taken some 75 hours to make. The finest examples have been attributed to Frankish workshops, although notable examples are also known from Anglo-Saxon and Viking contexts. (*syn.* pattern-welding)

patu: A Polynesian/Maori short clublike weapon, made of a variety of materials including wood, bone, stone, and whalebone (paroa). Finds on the Society Islands that are similar to the Maori patu suggest they may have been part of the Early Eastern Polynesian assemblage of New Zealand's first settlers.

Paviland Man: A buried Cro-Magnon in Paviland Cave, South Wales, the earliest-known British ceremonial burial. He was coated in red ocher to simulate life and had ivory objects, beads, bangle, awls, and shellfish and a mammoth's head buried with him—proof of a belief in an afterlife. The material in the caves has been dated from c. 38,000–10,000 years ago (Aurignacian, Creswellian). The skeleton has a radiocarbon date of 26,350 bp. (*syn.* Paviland Cave)

Pavlovian: An Upper Palaeolithic culture found in central and eastern Europe, with the type site at Pavlov in southern Moravia, Czechoslovakia. There, a large settlement of Upper Palaeolithic mammoth hunters left skeletal remains, hut plans, and numerous art objects. The artifacts include small retouched blades, Gravette points, and animal figurines assigned to the Eastern Gravettian. The radiocarbon dates are 26,730–26,000 bp.

Payne, Humfry (1902–1936): English archaeologist who directed the British School at Athens from 1929–1936. He prepared a definitive study of Archaic Corinthian art, *Necrocorinthia*, in 1931, in which a vast body of important information on archaic vase painting and other arts practiced at Corinth was gathered and classified. He also compiled an illustrated catalog of the Archaic sculpture from the Akropolis in Athens, *Archaic Marble Sculpture from the Acropolis* (1936).

Pazyryk: A group of some 40 barrows in the Altai Mountains of central Asia in Kazakhstan, dating to the 5th–3rd centuries BC. They consist of pits some 6 meters square covered with low cairns. The construction and altitude have combined to keep their contents frozen, and they are thus remarkably well preserved. There is a rich collection of clothing and felt hangings decorated with animal art, dismantled four-wheeled wagons, and artifacts of wood, leather, skin, and wool. There are mummified remains in several tombs; one man was covered with tattoos. Many horses, with bridles, saddles, and saddlecloths, had been buried in neighboring chambers. The burials clearly belonged to the rulers of a nomadic people of the eastern steppes related to the Scythians. The site is perhaps the richest source of information about the customs and artifacts of the Scythians before their westward migrations into western Asia and Europe. (*syn.* Pazirik)

peak sanctuary: Minoan cult location in the mountains of Crete. These sanctuaries had deposits of votive offerings but no monumental architecture.

peat: An accumulation of dead organic matter, mostly from plants, which becomes preserved mainly by the exclusion of oxygen. It is dark brown or black and partially decomposed, being preserved under anaerobic conditions in an environment of excessive moisture. Peat forms mostly in bogs and fens; the importance of peat to archaeology lies in its preservation of palaeobotanical (palaeoenvironmental) evidence, which can be used to reconstruct the ancient environment. The remains can often be radiocarbon dated. Vast beds of this organic fuel occur in Europe, North America, and northern Asia but are worked only where coal is deficient. Peat deposition is the first step in the formation of coal.

pebble: A size of gravel between 4–64 millimeters in diameter, according to the Wentworth–Udden classification. Pebbles are shaped by the action of waves, torrents, or rivers and are marked by splintering or rounded through rubbing. Tools such as the chopper and polyhedra (with several sides) were fashioned from pebbles. The pebble tool industries that preceded the Acheulian were based on tools made from pebble-sized clasts—which provided a cutting edge (chopper) or a faceted sphere (polyhedron) formed by the removal of one or several pieces (flakes).

pebble tool: A simple form of stone cutting tool, the oldest type of tool made by forerunners of modern humans. The tool consists of a rounded stone struck a number of blows with a similar stone used as a pounder, which created a serrated crest that served as a chopping blade. The core is only slightly altered by striking off a few small flakes. The most typical are choppers and chopping tools. These tools could be used as crude hunting knives, to grub roots, and for other purposes. The oldest examples are perhaps 2 to 2½ million years old, from sites like the Omo Valley and Hadar in Ethiopia. Those found in large numbers in Olduvai Gorge, in Tanganyika, are universally accepted as eoliths, dating back man's history to 1,000,000 years ago. By a process of refinement, these pebble tools developed into the hand axes of Africa, Europe, and southwest Asia, and into the chopping tools of the Far East. (*syn.* pebble chopper)

Pécel: A Late Eneolithic (Copper Age) culture, a regional variant of the Baden group (southwestern Hungary), in southeast and central Europe in the 3rd millennium BC. Although some settlement sites are known, the majority of Pécel sites are cemeteries with cremation and inhumation burial.

Pech de l'Azé: Palaeolithic tunnel cave and shelter in the Dordogne, southwest France, with six Acheulian levels dating to the Riss Glaciation, then six Mousterian levels dated to the Würm Glaciation. Occupation is dated to c. 232,000–53,000 years ago.

Pech Merle: Cave site in Quercy, France, with Palaeolithic paintings and engravings of three phases from 20,000–10,000 BC. It was not inhabited, but there are animal figures, dots, and signs.

Pecica: A Geto-Dacian walled city during Burebistas' reign (82–44 BC), in western Romania, near Arad. It was a long-lived tell settlement of the Bronze Age. At least 16 occupation horizons have been distinguished, with one of the clearest sequences of pottery development in the Banat. A large collection of stone molds for metallurgy was found, along with inhumation cemeteries containing rich grave goods of gold, bronze, and faience and amber beads.

pecking: A technique of shaping, or producing a design on, stone by hammering. The surface is crushed, usually with a stone hammer, and the dusty fragments swept aside. Incising or pecking designs into rock was practiced by Native American peoples.

Pecos classification: A. V. Kidder's classification of Southwestern prehistory based on his Pecos excavation; a culture stage sequence devised at the first Pecos Conference of 1927 in an attempt to organize prehistoric material of the American Southwest. It is now restricted to the Anasazi tradition, including Basketmaker I–III and Pueblo I–V. Architecture and ceramics define the stages.

Pecos Conference: A convention of southwestern archaeologists established in 1927 by A. V. Kidder in an attempt to organize prehistoric material of the American Southwest. The conference, to determine a uniform cultural chronology and a relatively consistent terminology, is still held today.

Pecos, New Mexico: An Anasazi pueblo in the American Southwest, which was occupied for much of the past 2,000 years. It provided the first stratigraphic sequence for American Southwest prehistory as a result of A. V. Kidder's excavations.

pectoral: A decorative and/or protective plate that covers the chest. It is also a plate forming the front of a cuirass that covers the chest.

pedestal: The base of a structure, especially one supporting a statue or monumental column. It has three parts: the base or foot next to the ground, the dado or die forming the center, and the cornice or surbase moldings at the top. A second architectural definition is the support or foot of a late classic or neoclassical column. The term also refers to any upright column of sediment that is left standing as the surrounding archaeological excavation continues, to reflect the stratigraphy of the site or to hold a specific artifact in place.

pedestrian survey: A method of examining a site in which surveyors, spaced at regular intervals, systematically walk over the area being investigated. (*syn.* pedestrian tactic, surface survey, fieldwalking)

pediment: A low-pitched gable forming the top section of the facade of a classical Greek or Roman temple; a triangular recess usually found at both ends of classical temples and treasuries and often filled with sculpture. In the classical temple, the outline of the triangle is formed by horizontal and "raking" cornices, which carry decorative moldings. The vertical "back wall" (tympanum) is often decorated with painting, relief, or sculpture. Each of the three corners was also faced with a special "corner piece" (acroterion). It is located above the entablature.

pedogenesis: The interaction of the physical, chemical, and biological factors, processes, and conditions that cause a soil to evolve into a soil horizon.

pedology: The study of soils and their structure, especially the creation, characteristics, distribution, and uses of soils. Archaeology depends on identification of soils to come up with the proper interpretation of the context and integrity of deposits. This scientific discipline is concerned with all aspects of soils, including their physical and chemical properties, the role of organisms in soil production and in relation to soil character, the description and mapping of soil units, and the origin and formation of soils.

pedoturbation: Any of the various processes by which soils are disturbed, mixed, sorted, and so on, such as by the burrowing of animals.

Pedra Furada: Large painted sandstone rock shelter in Piauí region of Brazil with hearths of c. 47,500 bp. The rock art is dated from 12,000–17,000 bp. There was some post-Palaeoindian occupation. (*syn.* Toca do Boqueirao do Sitio da Pedra Furada)

peer-polity interaction: A term describing the full scope of competitive exchanges taking place—imitation, emulation, competition, warfare, the exchange of material goods and information—between autonomous sociopolitical units, generally in the same geographic region.

Pefkakia: Late Neolithic–Bronze Age settlement mound in Thessaly, Greece. It has been important in reconstructing the Thessalian cultural sequence.

Pei Wenzhong (1904–1982): Chinese archaeologist who studied Palaeolithic sites and was a pioneer of taphonomic studies of bone breakage. (*syn.* [Pei, Wen-chung])

Peiligang: Neolithic sites in Henan Province, China, and the name of the earliest millet-based culture of northern China. It includes or parallels Cishan, Laoguantai, and Lijiacun. (*syn.* [P'ei-li-kang])

Pejeng: Site in Bali with a large bronze drum dating to the early 1st millennium AD, a local variant of the Dong Son drum tradition. The style was ancestral to the moko drums of eastern Indonesia.

Pekárna: Cave site in Brno, Moravia, Czechoslovakia, with assemblages of the Eastern Gravettian, Middle Palaeolithic, Magdalenian, and Neolithic. The Magdalenian layers contained end scrapers, borers, bone and antler points, a harpoon, and art objects.

Peking man: An obsolete name for a variety of *Homo erectus* found at Zhoukoudian cave (Choukoutien), southwest of Beijing (Peking). The braincase was thick, with a massive basal and occipital torus structure and heavy brow ridges. The remains of over 40 fossil humans were found there. These Chou-k'ou-tien fossils are dated to the Middle Pleistocene, about 900,000–130,000 years ago. Peking man postdates Java man and is considered more advanced in having a larger cranial capacity, a forehead, and nonoverlapping canines. (*syn.* Pekin man, Sinanthropus)

pelike: In Greek antiquity, a large wine container with two vertical handles—a type of amphora where the greatest diameter was below midpoint. It was probably used at a symposium.

Pella: The ancient capital of King Archelaus of Macedonia at the end of the 5th century BC (until 168 BC) and birthplace of Alexander the Great. It is in northern Greece, northwest of Thessaloníki. The city flourished under Philip II, but, after the defeat of the last Macedonian king by the Romans (168 BC), it became a small provincial town. Excavations have revealed houses with colonnaded courts and rooms with mosaic floors made with small natural pebbles of various colors, dating from the late 4th century BC. The town had a rectangular grid plan; under the streets are terra-cotta pipes for distributing fresh water. (*syn.* Bounomos)

pemmican: Preserved buffalo meat that was dried in strips by Native Americans. It could be cut up and mixed with melted fat to be eaten. Across the subarctic, people preserved meat by drying and pounding it together with fat and berries to make pemmican.

penannular: A term referring to an artifact in the form of a ring, but with a small break at one point, used particularly for forms of brooch and torc. It means "not a complete ring." The penannular brooch was characteristic of Irish production; generally of great size and probably worn on the shoulder with the pin pointing upward, it was decorated with interlaced patterns. It was the most common type of dress fastener of the sub-Roman period; it remained popular in Celtic regions of Britain up until the 10th century. There is an extensive typology for these ornaments, and they vary in appearance from plain bronze or iron rings to elaborately inlaid and gilded examples such as the Tara brooch, which was made around AD 700 in Ireland.

Pendlebury, J. D. S. (1904–1941): An archaeologist who worked in Egypt, notably on the site of Tell el-Amarna, and then moved to the Aegean, attracted by the ancient Egyptian imports to that region, which are vitally important for cross-dating. His most famous book, *The Archaeology of Crete*, was published in 1939. Pendlebury also wrote *Tell el-Amarna* (1935), a summary up to that date.

peneplain: A large land surface of slight relief shaped by erosion; a region that is almost a plain.

penetrating excavation: An excavating technique that exposes the vertical face of a site. This type of excavation is designed to reveal the vertical and temporal dimensions in an archaeological deposit—the depth, sequence, and composition of buried data.

Pengelly, William (1812–1894): A British geologist and archaeologist who did cave excavation and demonstrated the antiquity of Palaeolithic artifacts by showing that stone tools made by humans were contemporary with remains of extinct animals. At Kent's Cavern, he was able to confirm the conclusions of Reverend J. MacEnery that flint tools were associated with the bones of extinct animals. Although this association was not widely accepted, he continued to find further proof with work at Windmill Cave, Brixham (Devon). He gained academic support, and, in 1859, John Evans and several of Britain's leading geologists joined him in contradicting the 4004 BC date for the creation of man. The discoveries of Jacques Boucher de Pethes in the Somme Valley in France corroborated Pengelly's findings and were used to demonstrate the antiquity of man in 1859, the same year that saw the publication of Darwin's revolutionary *Origin of Species*.

Peninj: A site west of Lake Natron, 50 miles (80 km) north of Olduvai in Tanzania, where an almost perfectly preserved fossil hominid jaw with a complete set of adult teeth was found. The specimen was assigned to *Australopithecus boisei*, c. 1.5 million years old. The artifacts belonged to the Acheulian industry, including stone cleavers and hand axes. (*syn.* Peninj mandible, Natron mandible)

Penmaenmawr: Neolithic stone-ax-making site in England, with the remains of a Bronze Age stone circle located on the crest of a hill above the town. The axes were bartered over a large area in England.

Pentelic marble: White marble quarried from Pentelikon (Mount Pentelicus) Mountain in Attica, Greece, and used for public buildings such as the Parthenon. This excellent marble was used for most of the buildings and sculptures of Athens in the 5th and 4th centuries BC. Phidias, Praxiteles, and other Greek sculptors executed their principal works in Pentelic marble. In classical times, the peak had 25 quarries on the south slope.

Peoples of the Sea: Any of the groups of aggressive seafarers who invaded eastern Anatolia, Syria, Palestine, Cyprus, and Egypt toward the end of the Bronze Age, especially in the 13th century BC. They are considered responsible for the destruction of the Hittite Empire, among others. Because of the abrupt break in ancient Near Eastern records as a result of the invasions, the precise extent and origin of the upheavals remain uncertain. Principal evidence is based on Egyptian texts and illustrations; other important information comes from Hittite sources and from archaeological data. The peoples were of mixed origin, and tentative identifications of the people are: Pulesati/Pelset/Peleset = Philistines; Luka/Lukka = Lycians; Akawasha/Ahhiyawa/Ekwesh = Achaeans; Danuna = Danaoi; Sherden/Sherdana/Shardana = Sardinians; Shekelesh/Sicels/Sikels/Siculi = Sicilians; Tursha/Tyrsi/Teresh/Tyrrhenians (Tyrsenoi) = Etruscans. The Philistines, who perhaps came from Crete, were the only major tribe of the Sea Peoples to settle permanently in Palestine. (*syn.* Sea People(s), Peoples of the Islands in the Midst of the Sea)

Pepi: Birth name (nomen) held by two 6th-Dynasty rulers: Pepy I Meryra (c. 2321–2287 BC), the third king of the 6th Dynasty, and Pepy II Neferkare (c. 2278–2184 BC), the fifth king. Pepi II was a son of Pepi I and was born late in his father's reign. (*syn.* Pepy)

Perachora: A Greek sanctuary dedicated to Hera and located on a promontory on the bay of Corinth. The Early Iron Age sanctuary had offerings of ivory.

perceived environment: The physical environment as perceived by a human society, not by archaeologists.

percussion marks: Distinctive, striated pits on the surface of an animal bone indicating the bone was broken by human hands using a hammer stone.

percussion technique: Any of the methods used to strike a flake from a core in the making of stone tools; the reduction of a stone core by hitting it with a hammerstone or bone. Direct percussion is hitting a core with a hammer. Indirect percussion uses a punch between the core and the hammer. Anvil percussion (block on block) is the striking of a core against a fixed hard stone anvil. Bipolar percussion involves resting the core on an anvil and striking it with a hammer, making a flake with a bulb of percussion on each end. (*syn.* percussion method, percussion flaking)

percussor: A hammer stone, bone, and so on, used to strike a stone in a percussion technique.

perforation: A form of self-sacrifice widely practiced by the cultures of Mesoamerica. Historical sources, such as the Codex Mendoza, indicate that the Aztec frequently engaged in penitential exercises by causing self-inflicted wounds with maguey thorns. Artifactual evidence in the form of plant thorns, stingray spines, and pointed instruments has been found with great frequency at sites of almost all the Mesoamerican cultures, including Classic Maya, Olmec, and Teothihuacan. The ear, leg, arms, hands, penis, and tongue seem to have been the most frequently perforated organs. (*syn.* bloodletting)

Pergamum: Capital of a Hellenistic kingdom of the same name in Anatolia (Turkey) dating to 283–133 BC. The site is fine example of Hellenistic town planning with buildings terraced up to the palace and the akropolis. There was monumental planning and design and sculpture in the baroque style culminating in the frieze of the altar of Zeus. In 133 BC, Attalus III bequeathed his kingdom to Rome, which made it the province of Asia. The Attalid kings had invested much of their wealth in Pergamum, making it a center for literature, the arts, and the sciences; their library rivaled Alexandria with 200,000 volumes (many written on parchment). The Attalid dynasty fortress and palace stood on the peak of the hill, while the town itself occupied the lower slopes. Under the Roman Empire, the city was situated on the plain below. In the Roman period, there was extensive new building and rebuilding. Hadrian restyled the round, domed temple of Asklepios and built a temple of Trajan. (*syn.* Pergamon)

Periam: A tell site near Arad, Romania, the type site of the Early-Middle Bronze Age culture, dated to the mid-2nd millennium BC. It is the Romanian aspect of the Periam–Mokrin–Szöreg group. It is largely contemporaneous with the Otomani or Füzesabony culture. A culture layer yielded a rich collection of domestic pottery and bone work, discovered mostly in large storage pits. The material belongs to the first stage of the Pecica culture, which is named after another settlement near Arad, and which lasted from the 25th–18th centuries BC. Both sites yielded metal objects of Early Bronze Age type and provided much information about the Bronze Age in this area. (*syn.* Perjamos, Periamus, Perjámos)

Peribsen (c. 2700 BC): Egyptian king of the 2nd Dynasty (c. 2775–2650 BC), who promoted the cult of the god Seth over that of Horus, the god favored by his predecessors. His tomb was located in Seth's district in Upper Egypt, at Abydos (Tomb P in the Umm el-Qa'ab cemetery). The supremacy of Horus was restored after his death. (*syn.* Sekhemib)

Pericot Garcia, Luis (1899–1978): Spanish archaeologist known for his work at Parpalló Cave and on northeastern Spanish megaliths.

periglacial: A term describing cold-climate processes and land forms, an environment with severe frost in nonglacial conditions and much ground ice, mass movements, and strong winds. It applies to the region surrounding a glacial area and regions immediately beyond the ice front during a glaciation. In a periglacial zone, part of the ground is perennially frozen. This so-called permafrost layer is covered by a layer that thaws and freezes seasonally, the active layer. Such seasonal changes give rise to several processes, some of which sort the constituents of the active layer and are collectively known as cryoturbation. A variety of land forms, including involutions, ice wedges, and pingos, are formed in the active layer and permafrost. Hill slopes become mantled with frost-shattered rubble that moves downslope during cycles of freezing and thawing. Rivers are usually seasonal in the periglacial zone, and erosion by frost action is dominant. Wind erosion and deposition are often important factors and caused the formation of the huge deposits of loess and cover sands in Europe and Asia. The periglacial zone is of interest because it would have been the environment in which man lived for long periods during the Devensian/Weichselian Cold Stage. During the coldest periods of the Quaternary (the last 1,600,000 years), the periglacial zone was enlarged to approximately twice its present size.

Périgordian: A French classification for the Upper Palaeolithic tradition of western Europe, from its identification with the Périgord region of southern France. The flint industry sequence begins with the Chatelperronian (or Early Périgordian) from which, according to some, developed the first of the "Upper Périgordian" industries (Gravettian, or Périgordian IV). The later stages are represented by industries with Font Robert points and Noailles burins, and finally by the Proto-Magdalenian. The Périgordian tradition comes to an end in western Europe with the intrusion of a new Solutrean style of flint work. No known site has a complete and unbroken "Périgordian" sequence, and in many caves the Lower and Upper "Périgordian" levels are separated by strata of the intrusive Aurignacian industry, which must represent a break of several thousand years. The French scheme requires the Périgordian and Aurignacian people to have lived side by side with each other for millennia without any apparent contact between them. In the 1930s, Denis Peyrony advocated the view that the Aurignacian or early Upper Palaeolithic in France consisted of a true Aurignacian and a separate line of cultures, the Périgordian, beginning before the Aurignacian but coexisting alongside it down the time of the Solutrean. It is not known what kind of man was responsible for the Périgordian, but it is usually assumed that it was Cro-Magnon man, at least in the latter part. A Neanderthal-like skull has been found with the Early Périgordian, or Chatelperronian. Art is found in a few later Périgordian contexts. The Périgordian scheme is not now widely accepted as it is based on artifact typology rather than stratigraphic evidence.

perimortem: The term used to refer to events or processes that occurred to an individual's body when it cannot be determined whether it was before or after death.

period: Any specific interval of time in the archaeological record, such as the Upper Palaeolithic period. This term is often confusingly used interchangeably with phase and stage. A period is a true time division of the history of a large region (such as the Valley of Mexico or southern China) and does not necessarily imply any developmental characteristics. In archaeological context, it is a major unit of prehistoric time, usually containing several phases and pertaining to a wide area. It is a convenient term used to discuss the history of a complex area.

peripheral chopper: A pebble tool worked on both faces and often irregular in shape. The cutting edge can go around the periphery, or there may be a break; it can be plano-convex in section. It differs from a biface in that it is often not axially symmetric and in the undifferentiated position of the cutting edge. It is characteristic of the Oldowan and Acheulian complexes.

peripteral: A temple surrounded by a single row of columns, having a row of columns on all sides. An architectural term denoting a building surrounded by an external colonnade, such as Mammisi. The Theseum in Athens is a Doric peripteral temple, with 13 columns at the sides and 6 at the ends.

perishable: Any artifact made from organic material that ordinarily would decay but for some reason was preserved. Such artifacts include basketry, cordage, and leather.

peristalith: A ring or curb of stones surrounding a cairn or barrow.

Peristeria: Early Mycenaean settlement, c. 1550–1400 BC, in Messenia, Greece. It was one of the most prosperous and powerful settlements. Four tholos tombs contained rich offerings; the East House may have been a palace.

peristyle: The screen of pillars surrounding a temple, forming colonnades along its sides. These colonnades are found on the exterior of buildings, as in the classical Greek temple, and also in the courtyard of a Hellenistic or Roman house. A peristyle court is a court with a roof around the sides supported by rows of columns and an open space in the center. The peristyle of the domus, typified by that of the house of the Vettii at Pompeii, contained the private living quarters of the family; clustered around its colonnaded court were the oecus (reception room), cubiculai (bedrooms), alae (recesses for private talk), and tricliniai (dining rooms). (*syn.* peristyle court)

permafrost: Permanently frozen subsoil with a temperature below 0 degrees (32°F) continuously for 2 or more years. The permafrost line is a line demarcating regions where the subsoil is permanently frozen. Permafrost is overlaid by a surface layer that is subject to thawing during the warmer seasons of the year. This zone of seasonal freezing and thawing is termed the active layer. Permafrost is related to the tree line, because the frozen ground prevents tree roots from penetrating deeply and inhibits the subsurface drainage of melt water. Permafrost is estimated to underlie 20% of the Earth's land surface and reaches depths of 1,500 meters (5,000 feet) in northern Siberia. It occurs in 85% of Alaska, more than half of Russia and Canada, and probably all of Antarctica. Permafrost has preserved the carcasses of extinct Ice Age mammals; one or two almost complete, frozen mammoths dating from at least 10,000 years ago have been reported from Siberia.

per nefer: Egyptian for "house of beauty" or "good house," the place where part of purification and mummification procedures or rituals took place.

pernette: Small terra-cotta tripod used to stack vases in the kiln so as to prevent them sticking to one another during firing.

Persepolis: The capital of the Achaemenid Empire, in the Zagros Mountains of Iran, founded by Darius shortly after 518 BC; it was destroyed by Alexander the Great in 330 BC. The ceremonial palace was built by teams of workers and craftspeople from all parts of the empire. It replaced the earlier capital, Pasargadae, and was in many ways modeled on it, although incorporating many architectural and artistic innovations. It consists of a stone terrace platform on which were erected a series of monumental palaces and audience halls, as well as other buildings, constructed over a period of some 60 years. It is the showpiece of Achaemenid art, consisting of a series of great palaces and columned reception halls (apadana). Monumental stairways are flanked by lines of reliefs showing Median and Persian nobles, tribute bearers from all quarters of the empire, servants preparing banquets; in the treasury, reliefs depicted the enthroned ruler himself. The records and stylistic details attest the employment of Medes, Syrians, Urartians, and Ionian Greeks among others. The two largest buildings, the Apadana of Darius and the Throne Hall of Xerxes, occupied the center of the terrace and divided it into two functional halves. The northern area was military and mainly the work of Artaxerxes I, while the southern area contained the palaces of Darius and Xerxes, the harem, and treasury areas. Just north of Persepolis is Naqsh-i Rustam, where four monumental tombs were carved in the cliff face; these are the tombs of Darius I and three of his successors (probably those of Xerxes I, Artaxerxes I, and Darius II). They are also decorated with relief carvings and bear trilingual inscriptions in Elamite, Babylonian (Akkadian), and Old Persian. There are also late 2nd millennium BC Middle Elamite and early 1st millennium AD Sassanian inscriptions. (*syn.* modern Takht-i Jamshid; Parsa)

Persian Gulf trade: The maritime trading of the 3rd and early 2nd millennia BC between Mesopotamia and Dilmun, Magain, and Meluhha. The busiest Mesopotamian sites were Lagash and Ur, and the other three places' names are known from cuneiform texts. Combined with archaeological information, these data allow scholars to determine that Dilmun corresponds to the Barbar culture of the Persian Gulf, Magain relates to Umm an-Nar in southwest Arabia, and Meluhha is identified with the Harappan culture area.

Persian: An Indo-European people who moved into northwest Iran from Turkestan about 1000 BC and finally settled in the province of Pars/Parsa (modern Fars). They twice built great empires through the Middle East, under the Achaemenids (559–330 BC) and under the Sassanians (AD 224–651). Their neighbors were the Medes. The Achaemenid Empire dominated much of western Asia until it fell to Alexander the Great in the late 4th century BC. The use of the name was gradually extended by the ancient Greeks and other Western peoples to apply to the whole Iranian plateau. (*syn.* Persia)

perspective drawing: A three-dimensional rendering, usually of a feature or a site, used to record and reconstruct the results of archaeological research. Geometric perspective is a drawing method by which it is possible to depict a three-dimensional form as a two-dimensional image that closely resembles the scene as visualized by the human eye. Perspective drawings and photographs are easily interpreted because they closely resemble visual images.

Peschiera: Bronze Age lake village at the southern end of Lake Garda in northern Italy, with close connections to the Terramara culture. Late Bronze Age metalwork of c. 1250–1100 BC, pottery, artifacts, and timber piles have been recovered. In particular, a knife or dagger with a forked end to its flanged hilt is called after the site, as is sometimes the violin-bow fibula—to which the site has lent its name.

pestle: Club-shaped (oblong, cylindrical, or subcylindrical) implement or stone used for pounding, crushing, or grinding substances in a mortar.

Petén: A geographical and cultural part of the Maya lowlands in Mesoamerica, including much of the southern Yucatán. The center of the Mayan Old Empire, Tikal, Uaxactún, and the Altar de Sacrificios are in Petén.

Peterborough Culture: Neolithic culture grafted onto the native Mesolithic culture, one of the two major Neolithic groups of England (with the Windmill Hill people). They lived in villages and on seashores, grew grain and raised cattle, and hunted with square-tipped arrowheads. They also used axes and microlithic sickles.

Peterborough Ware: A poorly made, elaborately decorated pottery of the British Late Neolithic, found in southern England. The ornament consists of pits, bone, and wooden stick impressions and "maggot" patterns made by impressing a bit of whipped cord into the soft clay. The earliest (Ebbsfleet) substyle developed from Grimston-Lyles Hill ware c. 3500 BC and consisted of round-based vessels with fairly restrained ornament. The later variants have more complicated decoration and show the influence of Beaker pottery: The second (Mortlake) substyle still occurs on round-based vessels, but in the final (Fengate) substyle the pots are flat bottomed and have many features that lead on to the collared urns of the Bronze Age. These vessels were probably intended for everyday domestic use.

Petersfels: A cave site in Baden, southern Germany, with Upper Palaeolithic occupation and rich Magdalenian occupation with jet artifacts, harpoon heads, burins, awls, backed bladelets, and decorated batons-de-commandement.

Petit-Chasseur, Sion: Late Neolithic and Chalcolithic burial complex in Valais, Switzerland, with one large megalithic chamber and other smaller tombs. Many stelae have been found in tombs that have triangular daggers on them, paralleling those in northern Italy in the 3rd millennium BC.

Petra: A city in Jordan, which was the capital of the Edomite and Nabataean kingdoms on the main route between the Dead Sea and Red Sea, important (especially for trade) during the Hellenistic period. Set deep in the mountains with main access through a cleft in the rock called the Siq, Petra is best known for its buildings, temples, and tombs cut in multicolored sandstone. It also had an elaborate system of dams, waterworks, and cisterns. A theater and temple belong to the Roman period (after AD 106). Little is known of the later history of Petra, although a Crusader fort survives.

Petralona: Middle Palaeolithic cave site near Thessalonika, Greece, with a series of occupations probably from the early last glacial to the early Middle Pleistocene. A virtually complete skull is now seen to be close to *Homo sapiens*, c. 400,000 years old. Other artifacts include scrapers, chopping tools, and spheres of the early Mousterian.

Petrarch (1304–1374): An Italian poet, often considered the first humanist and perhaps the most influential individual of the early Renaissance. In 1337, he visited Rome for the first time, to be stirred among its ruins by the evident grandeur of its past. He provided a strong impetus for archaeological research by looking to antiquity for moral philosophy; his humanism led to a rediscovery of the past. (*syn.* Francesco Petrarca)

petraria: A type of heavy siege engine that hurled stones at castles with the effect of modern shrapnel. Trebuchet was the largest of the petrariae, or siege engines. It consisted of a long beam, up to 50 feet long, with massive weights of 8–9 tons at one end. It rested on a crossbeam, and the long arm was hauled down by a rope attached to the end and wound onto the windlass. (*syn.* pl. petraria)

Petresti culture: A Late Neolithic and Eneolithic culture of Transylvania, northwestern Romania, and dated to the early 4th millennium BC. Petresti settlement pattern is tell based, with most occupations preceded by Early Vinca levels. The defining characteristic is a wide range of painted wares, bichrome and trichrome in style, and decorated with brown parallel lines in elaborate patterns. The culture is contemporaneous with the early stages of Cucuteni-Tripolye to the east and Gumelnita to the southeast.

Petrie, Sir William Matthew Flinders (1853–1942): An English Egyptologist and a leading figure in the development of archaeology; he developed the technique known as sequence dating. He was self-taught and, in 1880, went to Egypt to draw up plans and take measurements of the pyramids (Tanis, Naucratis, Daphnae, Hawara, Kahun, Medium, el-Amarna, Nagada, Abydos, Memphis, Sedment, Qau). He is recognized as the first scientific excavator in Egypt, and he wrote many books on general topics, tools and weapons, ancient weights and measures, and Egyptian architecture; in all, he published more than 1,000 books and articles. His work was summarized in *Seventy Years in Archaeology* (1931). At Tell el-Hesi in 1890, the importance of stratigraphy in the excavation was for the first time fully appreciated. At Naqada in 1894, his discovery of the predynastic cemetery led him to devise the technique of sequence dating, a form of seriation. Sequence dating used the pottery types found in the nearly 3,000 graves of the Naqada cemeteries. His other achievements in Egypt included a survey of the Giza pyramids, excavation at Tell el-Amarna, and the discovery of the Greek city of Naukratis. After 1926, he concentrated on Palestine, for example, at Tell el-Ajjul.

petroform: A row of rocks or boulders configured on the ground in the shape of an animal, mythological figure, and so on.

petroglyph: Any design, picture, or writing carved or chipped into a rock surface. The technique involved in producing the petroglyph usually was incising, carving, pecking, or pounding. (*syn.* petrogram)

petrographic: Having to do with the microscopic analysis of geological structures. A petrographic microscope is an instrument that employs polarized light that vibrates in a single plane. (*syn.* petrological)

petrological identification: The study of the mineral constituents of stone with a petrological microscope, involving the examination of thin sections of stone artifacts to determine the provenience of the rock used to make them. A number of artifacts containing minerals can be investigated in this way: pottery, stone axes, querns, building stones. The technique is based on the optical behavior of polarized light as it passes through the thin section of stone. Minerals refract the light in different ways because of their different crystal lattice configurations, allowing their identification. Detailed petrological analysis of the material of Neolithic polished stone axes has enabled archaeologists to establish the location of prehistoric ax factories and trade routes. It is also now possible to study the prehistoric distribution of obsidian through petrological analysis. Spectrographic analysis is an extension of the technique. (*syn.* petrological analysis, petrological microscopy)

petrological microscopy: The petrological microscope is used in the examination of thin sections of stone artifacts or pottery (ceramic petrology), to identify, and eventually locate, the geographical source of the rocks or minerals present. A slice, approximately 1 millimeter thick, is removed from the artifact, ground until completely smooth, placed on a slide, and then the other side is ground to produce an almost transparent slice that can then be examined under the microscope. The microscope has a polarizer and an analyzer that transmits the light vibrating in one direction only; the reaction of various minerals to this type of light allows their identification because minerals refract the light in different ways because of their different crystal lattice configurations.

petrology: The study of rocks, usually by microscopic and spectrographic analysis. Because most rocks are composed of minerals, petrology is strongly dependent on mineralogy. Fields of specialization in petrology correspond to the afore-

mentioned three major rock types—igneous, sedimentary, and metamorphic.

Peu Richard: Late Neolithic enclosure in Charente, France, a settlement with concentric rock-cut ditches and the type site of the Peu-Richardien culture of western France. The pottery is ornamented by incised channeled decoration or narrow appliqué cordons, with some use of the tunnel handle, and including oculi or double-eye motifs. Peu Richard ware is dated c. 3500–2800 BC and occurs in megalithic tombs of dolmen and passage grave types. Settlements were generally on hilltops and, like the type site, surrounded by ditches. (*syn.* Peu-Richard)

pewter: A tin-based alloy used as a material from which domestic utensils were fashioned. The alloy is often 100 parts of tin to 17 of antimony, or 89 tin, 7 antimony, and 2 copper. Tin and zinc, and lead and tin are sometimes used to make pewter. The use of pewter dates back at least 2,000 years to Roman times. Ancient pewter contained about 70% tin and 30% lead. Such pewter, also called black metal, darkened greatly with age, and the lead leached out in contact with acidic foods. (*syn.* black metal)

Peyrony, Denis (1869–1954): French prehistorian who discovered the cave art at Font de Gaume, Bernifal, and Teyjat and excavated at La Ferassie and Laugerie Haute. He proposed the Périgordian system and founded the prehistory museum of Les Eyzies. The La Ferassie skeletons are hominid fossils found in a rock shelter grave site north of Bugue, Dordogne, by R. Capitan and D. Peyrony between 1909–1921, but not fully reported until 1934. The fossils of La Ferassie are estimated to date from about 60,000 years ago and are associated with the Mousterian stone tool industry.

PF beaker: Abbreviation of protruding foot beaker. (*syn.* protruding foot beaker)

Pfupi: Term used for Later Stone Age material in southwest Zimbabwe. The terms *Khami* or *Matopo* are now more generally used.

Pfyn: Middle Neolithic culture of northeast Switzerland, with a number of lake dwellings and related to the Michelsberg culture of Rhineland. Pottery was round and flat based, and there are also copper objects and crucibles.

Phaistos: The site of a Bronze Age palace of the Minoans in south-central Crete, constructed c. 1900 BC, destroyed by an earthquake c. 1700 BC, rebuilt, and succumbing to final destruction c. 1450 BC from the eruption of Thera. Its plan follows closely the pattern of other Minoan palaces—a large central court with large reception rooms, domestic quarters, and extensive magazines grouped around it. In the Late Minoan period, although occupation continued, power and wealth passed to Hagia (Ayia) Triada, just to the west. Finds include a series of Middle Minoan Kamares Ware vases and the intriguing Phaistos Disk, a unique clay disk with stamped inscriptions in a spiral on each face. It comes from a deposit dated c. 1700 BC, which makes it contemporary with the different—but equally undeciphered—Linear A script. Phaistos is the second largest of the Minoan palaces, after Knossos, and has a rather similar early history. (*syn.* Phaestos, Phaestus)

Phaistos disk: A unique clay disk with stamped inscriptions in a spiral on each face of its 16-centimeter diameter, found in 1908 at Phaistos, Crete. It is made of baked clay and on either side is an inscription, which consists of signs impressed on the wet clay with a punch or stamp. The Phaistos disk is therefore the "world's first typewritten document" in the words of John Chadwick. There are 242 signs arranged into 61 groups demarcated into boxes by lines. The signs appear to be written from the outer edge and spiral inward in a clockwise direction. The disk came from a deposit dated c. 1700 BC, which makes it contemporary with the Linear A script. At this time, however, it appears not to be Linear A but may be an Anatolian script. (*syn.* Phaestos disk)

Phalaborwa: An area of the eastern Transvaal, South Africa, with a copper and iron ore mining town and a long Iron Age sequence dated to the 8th century AD. Mining began during the final centuries of the 1st millennium AD, and from the 11th century onward the later Iron Age occupation appears to belong to a single developing tradition, perhaps related to the Sotho groups. Agriculture on terraced hillsides and the herding of domestic cattle formed the basis of the subsistence economy. There are hundreds of sites where ore was smelted and then worked into tools and ornaments. (*syn.* Palabora)

pH analysis: A technique used for measuring the pH (acidity/alkalinity)—hydrogen ion concentration of a soil or sediment. The results of the test may suggest what type of remains are to be expected on a site. In an acid soil, bone, shell, and carbonate lithic debris do not survive, but pollen grains do; in an alkaline soil, there are only rare occurrences of pollen, but calcareous material should be more plentiful. The pH is tested by moistening a sample of soil with neutral distilled water and dipping indicator paper into it. The resulting color, which depends on the pH content, can be matched against prepared charts of known pH values. (*syn.* pH test)

pharaoh: The title of the rulers of ancient Egypt, who combined the roles of king and god. It is used today as a synonym for the king of ancient Egypt. Much expense of labor, money, and treasure was involved in their funeral rites, exemplified by the pyramids and the tombs such as that of Tutankhamen. Each line of kings formed a dynasty, of which there were 31 in all, the peaks of power and development being known as the Old, Middle, and New Kingdoms. The term originally and literally meant the "great house" or house of the king,

the royal palace. From the time of the New Kingdom (starting in the 18th Dynasty, 1539–1292 BC), the term came to be used for kings of Egypt. Pharaoh was never formally the king's title. (*syn.* Pharaoh)

Pharaonic period: The entire history of Egypt from the establishment of the monarchy in 2925 BC to the invasion of Alexander in 332 BC.

Pharos: One of the Seven Wonders of the World and the most famous lighthouse in antiquity, built on the island of Pharos in the harbor of Alexandria. It was a technological triumph and is the archetype of all lighthouses since. Built by Sostratus of Cnidus for Ptolemy II of Egypt in c. 280 BC, it is said to have been more than 350 feet (110 m) high). The lighthouse was surmounted by a huge statue, probably representing either Alexander the Great or Ptolemy I Soter. Pharos appeared in the list of wonders in the 6th century AD, and it was known to still be standing in the 12th century. By 1477, it was in ruins.

phase: A term generally referring to an archaeological unit defined by artifacts and cultural traits that distinguish it from other units. It is an archaeological unit defined by characteristic groupings of culture traits that can be identified precisely in time and space. It lasts for a relatively short time and is found at one or more sites in a locality or region. Therefore, it is an interval of time in the archaeological record, especially a relatively limited time in a specific locality or region and often used to represent a distinct prehistoric people. The archaeologist abstracts the phase from a number of components that occupy a certain area in space and the same span in time and that share many or most of their distinctive features. These components may represent units as small as tribal camps or as large as cities. It is similar to "focus" in the Midwestern Taxonomic System and to "culture" in the Old World.

phaskon: Greek vessel of a flattened ovoid form, with a long spout, and a handle at the top, like the askos.

phenotype: A biological type determined by the visible characters common to a group as distinguished from their hereditary characters. It is all the apparent characteristics of an organism, such as shape, size, color, and behavior, which result from the interaction of its genotype (total genetic heritage) with the living environment. The common type of a group of physically similar organisms is sometimes also known as the phenotype. Individuals of different genotypes can thus manifest similar phenotypical characteristics.

phiale: In Greek antiquity, a shallow dish used either for drinking or for pouring libations.

Phigalian marbles: Sculptured friezes in the British Museum, from the temple of Apollo Epikourios, at Bassae near ancient Phigalia in Arcadia. There are 23 slabs in high relief,

11 representing the battle between the Centaurs and the Lapithae, and the rest the contest of the Greeks and Amazons. It is attributed to the last quarter of the 5th century BC.

Philae: An island in the Nile at Elephantine near Aswan, the site of one of the finest surviving temples of the Ptolemaic period. The most important of the complex of temples is that of Isis to whom the island was considered sacred. The earliest standing monument dates from the reign of Nectanebo I (380–362 BC). Other buildings were erected by the Ptolemaic kings and early Roman emperors. During the Nubian Rescue Campaign, the temples of Philae were dismantled and re-erected on the island of Agilkia. Inscriptions in Greek and hieroglyphs on a commemorative obelisk at Philae supplemented the evidence of the Rosetta Stone to give Champollion the key to the ancient Egyptian writings.

Philia: Type site for the Chalcolithic III culture in northern Cyprus, mid-3rd millennium BC. It is characterized by red polished pottery.

Philippi: Old Thasian settlement in Kavála, Greece, which Philip II of Macedon fortified in 356 BC to control the neighboring gold mines. In 42 BC, Philippi was the site of the decisive Roman battle in which Mark Antony and Octavian (later the emperor Augustus) defeated Brutus and Cassius, the leading assassins of Julius Caesar. Located in Thrace, it was the object of an unsuccessful attempt at colonization by Thasos in the 6th century BC and for a time was known as Crenides and Daton. After his victory, Mark Antony established Philippi as a colonia for his veterans, and the two gained strategic importance from Phillipi's position and proximity to the port of Neapolis. Philippi was important in the early history of Christianity, as is shown by the prominence given to the story of Saint Paul preaching there in AD 49 and being consequently imprisoned and also by extensive early Christian building. Among the ruins are walls, akropolis, forum, gymnasium, macellum, baths, and theaters.

Philippines, the: An archipelago of about 7,100 islands and islets lying about 500 miles (800 km) off the southeastern coast of Asia. A firm archaeological sequence began there c. 30,000 years ago, at Tabon Cave on Palawan Island. There are Late Pleistocene stone industries, the spread of a small flake and blade technology after 5000 BC (Holocene), and the arrival and rapid spread of Austronesian-speaking horticulturists after 3000 BC. Rich jar-burial assemblages occur in the islands from about 1000 BC; bronze and iron appear later. Chinese traders visited and lived on the islands from about AD 1000. Indian culture reached the archipelago during the 14th–16th centuries via Indonesian kingdoms, notably the Java-based kingdom of Majapahit. This is particularly noticeable in Philippine languages and literatures where Sanskrit loanwords and ancient Indian motifs abound. At the beginning of the 15th century, Filipinos were primarily shift-ing cultivators, hunters, and fishermen with animistic beliefs. Islam was introduced later in the same century, followed by Ferdinand Magellan's discovery of the Philippines in 1521.

Philistines: One of the Peoples of the Sea who, repulsed from Egypt c. 1200 BC, drove the Canaanites from southern Palestine (its name derived from their name) and settled there, marking the beginning of the Iron Age in that region. They were a warlike, seafaring people and adopted the culture of the Canaanites, but introduced a new type of pottery decorated with metopes and bird designs. The Philistine tombs at Tell Fara contained iron weapons and pottery coffins with anthropoid lids. Ashkelon, Ashdod, Gaza, Gath, and Ekron were their five chief cities. The Philistines were eventually absorbed by the Israelites under David c. 1000 BC. They are known mainly from documentary sources, appearing in Egyptian records as one of the Peoples of the Sea, and in Biblical accounts as a people who drove the Canaanites out of the coastal plain and eventually became part of the Israelite kingdom. (*syn.* (Egyptian) Pulesati)

philyra: Strips of papyrus used for making a sheet of writing paper; 10–12 strips of payrus were first glued together lengthwise, and then a sufficient number of strips were fastened crosswise underneath to double the thickness of the surface. (*syn.* philura)

Phimai: Moated settlement in the Mun Valley, Khorat, Thailand, occupied before 600 BC. It became a major iron-working and trading center between c. 200 BC–AD 300. Phimai Black Pottery is found in large quantities. A temple made of sandstone was built by the Khmer kings Jayavarman VI (1080–1107) and Dharanindravarman I (1107–1112) of Angkor; it is in the Angkor Wat style. It was a commercial, administrative, and religious center under the Khmer rule.

Phocaean ware: Roman red-glossed pottery made from the 4th–7th centuries AD on the west coast of Turkey. It was widely distributed in the eastern Mediterranean.

Phoenician: A Semitic people who lived in the coastal area of Lebanon and Syria from about 1000 BC, the cultural heirs of the Canaanites. They flourished as traders from their ports of Tyre, Sidon, and Byblos. They are credited with founding Carthage and inventing the alphabet; the Greek, Roman, Arabic, and Hebrew alphabets are all derived from the Phoenician. Even after their incorporation into the Babylonian Empire in 574 BC, they continued to influence politics in the Near East through their fleets, in the west through their powerful colony of Carthage. They also established colonies in Utica, north Africa, Gades in Spain, Motya in Sicily, Nora and Tharros in Sardinia, and other settlements in Malta and Ibiza. Culturally their role as merchants and middlemen was uninterrupted until they were absorbed into the Hellenistic and Roman world. They are reputed to have circumnavigated Africa. They developed the alphabet to assist their commercial activities. They are not well known archaeologically in their homeland, although there has been some exploration of their major sites; they have left few lasting memorials in the form of great works of art or monumental architecture. The Phoenicians engaged in a series of three Punic Wars with the Romans, which led to their ultimate defeat and incorporation into the Roman world in the 2nd century BC. (*syn.* Phoenicia)

phoneme: In linguistics, a term for a unit of speech that is recognized as significant in a particular language. It is the smallest unit of speech distinguishing one word (or word element) from another, as the sound *p* in "cap," which separates that word from "cab" and "can." In Chinese, speakers hear and use aspirated and unaspirated *p* as separate sounds, but English speakers do not.

phonetic: A term describing signs that express the sounds as opposed to logographic or ideographic signs and determinatives. (*syn.* phonographic)

phonogram: The same or different forms used to represent sounds; a character or symbol used to represent a word, syllable, or phoneme.

phosphate analysis: The examination of phosphates from decayed organic matter; a technique for detecting the presence of phosphate in soil and for using phosphorus concentrations to determine human settlements and activity in sites. Phosphate is a natural constituent of soil; however, it is concentrated by animals' bones, excrement, and food refuse. The technique has been employed particularly in the study of cave deposits (to show human or animal occupation), settlement sites (to identify the uses to which different areas were put), and burials (to show the former existence of bodies completely decayed). Once phosphate is in the soil, it is usually converted into an insoluble form, so that it does not tend to move down profile or to be redistributed sideways in the soil. For this reason, settlements and farms tend to leave high concentrations of phosphate in the soil, which often remain stable over long periods, sometimes thousands of years. Much preliminary work must be done on the distribution and range of naturally occurring phosphorus because variations are caused by vegetation abundance and type and by soil horizon. (*syn.* phosphate surveying, phosphorus survey)

photogrammetry: A technique for mapping of areas by using photographs taken directly from above. Although used mainly in map making, it can also be used for the planning of archaeological sites. For large-scale map making, the photographs are taken from the air, a sequence along each flight path with each exposure overlapping the next by 60%. Adjustment is made so that the photographs can be laid side by side in a mosaic, with common reference points lying over each other. They are then converted into maps by the use of multiple projectors. A similar technique can be used to plan smaller scale features such as excavations. The camera can

be mounted on a rigid frame and moved along so that it takes overlapping vertical photographs. It can greatly speed up the mapping of complicated features. Many of today's maps are largely produced by this method.

photography: The recording of archaeological data on photographic film, especially during data acquisition, processing, and analysis.

photomicrograph: A photograph of an object or part of an object taken at high magnification to reveal details of form and structure. Many of these are taken automatically for documentation purposes during the use of such instruments as the scanning electron microscope, the petrological microscope, binocular microscope, and the optical microscope. Photomicrographs can reveal the detailed structure of palaeobotanical remains, the presence of different tempering materials in pottery, analysis of thin sections, the use-wear on artifacts, or the details of structure in metals, which can help to identify metalworking procedures.

Phrygian: A people who moved from Thrace into central Anatolia (Turkey) after the collapse of the Hittite Empire by the mid-12th century BC. They founded a kingdom under Midas, which covered most of Anatolia and lasted c. 750–680 BC, with the capital at Gordium (Gordion). After they were destroyed by the Cimmerians, the Phrygian culture continued under the rule of Lydia into Classical times in Anatolia. Noteworthy are elaborate monuments carved in rock faces, once considered tombs but now interpreted as religious centers. Rich burials were placed under great tumuli. The richly painted pottery is related to that of the contemporary Greeks. They are said to have invented embroidery. (*syn.* ancient Muski; Phrygia)

Phu Lon: A metal-extracting and -working site near the Mekong River in Khorat, Thailand, used between 1750–1425 and 300–275 BC.

Phung-nguyen: Site of a transitional Late Neolithic–Early Bronze Age culture of the Red River valley of northern Vietnam, dated c. 2300–1500 BC. Pottery has elaborate incised and stamped decoration, and some appears to have been wheel made and kiln fired. Artifacts include polished stone adzes. It preceded the Dong Dau culture. (*syn.* Phung Nguyen)

Phu Wiang: An area and culture in Khorat, Thailand, with prehistoric sites inhabited between c. 3000–2500 BC. It was a transitional Neolithic–Early Bronze Age phase.

phylactery: General term that included any kind of amulet worn about the person as a protection against dangers. The name phylactery is derived from the Greek *phylakterion*, meaning amulet.

Phylakopi: Bronze Age settlement on the island of Melos in the southern Aegean. The site was important because of the exploitation of the source of obsidian on the island. There were three successive cities of the Early, Middle, and Late Cycladic—the third with ties to Minoan Crete and Mycenaean Greece. Excavations have provided one of the main sources of information about the Cycladic Bronze Age. The Early Cycladic Grotta-Pelos culture was followed by the Middle Cycladic town of c. 2000 BC. That town was destroyed in the 18th century BC, but was rebuilt and flourished again, coming increasingly under Minoan influence until the collapse of Minoan power in the mid-15th century BC. Subsequently, mainland Mycenaean influence dominated Phylakopi. The administrative center seems to have been a megaron; a Mycenaean cult center has also been found.

physical anthropology: A subdiscipline of anthropology that views humans as biological organisms, studying human biological or physical characteristics and their evolution. Study includes fossil human beings, genetics, primates and blood groups. It is one of the two major subdivisions of anthropology.

physical environment: Nonbiotic elements of the habitat created or modified by natural forces; a component of the total environment as seen by cultural ecology.

phytolith: Microscopic silica bodies that form in living plants, providing a durable floral ecofact that allows identification of plant remains in archaeological deposits. It is a fossilized part of a living plant that secreted opal silica bodies, and it is found in the cells of certain plants, especially grasses and cereals. These silica bodies are often able to survive after the organism has decomposed or been burned. They are common in ash layers, pottery, and even on stone tools used to cut the stems of silica-rich plants (e.g., cereals). Different plants produce phytoliths with different characteristic shapes and sizes, although not all are unique to specific species. These can be detected by an electronic scanning microscope. (*syn.* opal phytolith, plant opal phytolith)

Pianello: A site near Ancona, near the Italian Adriatic coast, with a large urnfield cemetery of c. 1100 BC. It is the type site of a group scattered through much of Italy and often labeled Proto-Villanovan. The ashes, sometimes accompanied by an arc fibula or quadrangular razor, were buried in a small biconical urn and covered with inverted bowls used as lids. (*syn.* Proto-Villanovan)

Piano Conte: Copper Age culture of Lipari, traces of which have also been found on the Italian mainland, perhaps from trade in obsidian with Lipari. This early 3rd millennium BC culture had many fine tools of flint, but copper was still rare. The pottery was distinctive, decorated with close-set grooves, making a corrugated effect.

piazza: An open square, especially in Italian towns, often surrounded by buildings. The term is also used for an arcaded and roofed gallery, generally supported by pillars, and form-ing a vaulted promenade. The term is sometimes applied to the archways of a colonnade.

Picene: Early Iron Age inhabitants of the Marche on the Adriatic coast of Italy. There are rich inhumation cemeteries of the 9th–6th centuries BC and evidence of trading with Greeks as early as the 7th century BC. There is much evidence of trade with communities on the other side of the Adriatic, in modern Yugoslavia, and with central Europe. They likely were warlike, with artifacts including armor, weapons, and ornaments of bronze or iron. Finds also include numerous fibulae, torcs, bracelets, girdles, ornamental pendants, and amber. They had two main centers, one at Novilara in the north, and another around Belmonte and Fermo farther south. In 268 BC, their territory was annexed by Rome. (*syn.* Piceni, Picenes)

Picosa culture: Late Archaic culture that began c. 3000 BC in the American Southwest and is considered by some to be ancestral to the Anasazi, Hohokam, and Mogollon traditions. It was located in southern California, southern Nevada, Arizona, and southwestern New Mexico, as well as the Four Corners region.

Pictish symbol stones: Pictish symbol stones are a unique class of sculptured monument of the Pictish people in the Post-Roman period. The Picts occupied Scotland north of the Forth and possessed a distinctive culture, seen particularly in their carved symbol stones. The stones are roughly divided into three chronological categories. The Class I stones (5th–7th centuries) are rough-hewn, undressed blocks or pillars, inscribed with pictorial symbols of spiral creatures, such as fishes and birds. They are also decorated with strange geometric shapes as well as inanimate objects like mirrors and combs, grouped together in various combinations. Class II (8th–10th centuries) stones are regularly dressed slabs with the same range of carvings but with the addition of new Christian elements and humans in animated scenes. Class III stones (from the 9th century) are, in most cases, free-standing crosses decorated with a combination of a distinctive form of interlace as well as some elements of the older motifs. Some bear Ogham inscriptions in which it has recently been shown that three languages were in use, two Celtic and one pre-Indo-European. From these memorial stones, we know something of the Pictish royal succession.

pictograph: Any design, picture, or drawing painted on a surface (usually rock/stone) and used to represent a thing, action, or event. Pictographs are believed to be the earliest form in the development of writing (pictography). It represents a form of nonverbal communication used by nonliterate people. (*syn.* petrograph, pictogram)

Pict: An ancient people who lived in eastern-northeastern Scotland, known as the "Painted People," probably referring to a custom of body painting or tattooing. Probably descendants of pre-Celtic aborigines or from the Bay of Biscay, where they had helped Caesar defeat the Veneti, the Picts were described in AD 297 by a Roman writing of the "Picts and Irish [Scots] attacking" Hadrian's Wall. They were the principal enemies of Rome in north Britain. Then or soon after, they developed two kingdoms north of the Firth of Forth, which became a united "Pict-land" by the 7th century. In 843, Kenneth I MacAlpin, king of the Scots, became also king of the Picts, uniting their two lands in a new kingdom of Alba, which evolved into Scotland. The Pictish kingdom is known for its symbol stones and crosses. Their name for themselves was Cruithni. There is little archaeological material that can be confidently attributed to the Picts except for the symbol stones. (*syn.* Cruithni, Cruithne; Painted People, Pictae)

picture-stone: A term used to describe the unique series of engraved memorial stones (*bildstenar*) that were raised on the Baltic island of Gotland (off Sweden) between the 5th–11th centuries AD. The Kylver Stone, found in a Gotland tomb, is a limestone slab that bears a 5th-century runic inscription and provides the oldest extant record of the Germanic runic series.

piece mold: In metalworking, a clay mold made of separate pieces fitting together and used for casting intricately shaped objects. (*syn.* piece mould)

pie chart: A type of visual representation of quantitative data, involving a circle representative of the total of units and marking off segments like slices in the proportions of the percentages of different categories. The size of each slice of the pie is proportional to the number of data values in the corresponding class.

Piedmont Tradition: Late Archaic tradition in northeast North America. It is characterized by stemmed projectile points and lithic assemblages.

Piedras Negras: Classic Lowland Maya site located on steep terraces on the Usumacinta River, Guatemala. There were ball courts, temple pyramids, courtyards, and ceremonial sweatbaths (temescales). It is best known for the finely carved stone monuments in the form of hieroglyphic inscriptions on lintels, stelae, and wall panels. These art works were the main source in Tatiana Proskouriakoff's study for showing that certain hieroglyphs recorded historical rather than ceremonial events. Military themes occur frequently in the art; the seashells are from both the Pacific and Gulf coasts, and obsidian and jade attest to widespread trading. The terminal Long Count date for the site is AD 795.

Piestina: Neolithic settlement site on a tributary of the Aiviekste River in Russia, dated to the 3rd millennium BC. The various levels are associated with vegetable- and shell-tempered coarse wares, with barbotine, incised and cord

ornament, termed the Piestina style. A rich assemblage of amber buttons, pendants, rings, and beads is present, as well as stone, bone, and antler tools and weapons.

Pietersburg: A term for south African early Middle Stone Age artifact assemblages of the late Middle or early Late Pleistocene, occurring mainly in the Transvaal although related material is also found farther south. It belongs to the general group of industries based on the removal of flakes from prepared cores but is differentiated from other contemporary industries of this type by the presence of large numbers of long parallel-sided flake-blades (many of which have minimal retouch or use damage on the sides). The best sequence showing the development of the Pietersburg industry is at the Cave of Hearths in the northern Transvaal. The chronology is still poorly defined, but is roughly 60,000–20,000 BC or after.

Piette, Edouard (1827–1906): French prehistorian who excavated many caves in the Pyrenees and was the first to recognize the Azilian culture, bridging the gap between the Palaeolithic and Mesolithic. He was a pioneer in accepting the authenticity of Altamira's art and worked at Le Mas D'Azil and Brassempouy. He amassed the greatest collection of Palaeolithic portable art for the French government. He was the author of various classificatory schemes for prehistory, subdividing the Palaeolithic period into three, the Amygdalithic, Niphetic, and Glyptic periods (approximately equivalent to the Lower, Middle, and Upper Palaeolithic), but this system was never very widely adopted.

pig: A wild and domestic descendant of the wild boar, *Sus scrofa scrofa*, of continental Europe and southern Asia. Wild pigs formed part of the diet of Palaeolithic and Mesolithic hunters. The first records for wild pigs are from the Belt Cave in Iran, Jarmo in Iraq, and Tespesi in Kurdistan in the 7th millennium BC. Modern pigs derive from *Sus scrofa vittatus*, native to southeastern Asia and bred in China since the Neolithic. Wild pigs are believed to have been introduced on Christopher Columbus' second voyage in 1493 brought to the mainland in the early 1500s.

Piki: An archaeological phase occurring in Ayacucho basin in central Andes, Peru, with artifacts dating c. 5800–4550 BC.

Pikillacta: Middle Horizon site near Cuzco, Peru, which was a Huari administrative center. There are many small ovoid structures on the site.

Pikimachay Cave: Preceramic cave site in the Ayacucho basin of central highland Peru. At one time, it was believed to have the longest stratigraphy in the New World with remains 25,000 years old. These pre-Clovis phases have been largely discounted as having human occupation. A long preceramic occupation did begin c. 9000 BC. (*syn.* Pikimachay)

Piklihal: Site in southwest India's eastern Karnata, with a series of Neolithic and Megalithic Grave period occupations. The Neolithic settlements began c. 2100 BC and may be associated with the Deccan ash mounds. There was hand-made pottery in the early Neolithic, changing to wheel made and resembling the late Jorwe pottery. The Megalithic had pottery in the 1st millennium BC to the early 1st millennium AD—black-and-red wares, white-painted black-and-red wares, russet-coated ware, rouletted ware, and red polished ware.

pilaster: A rectangular column attached to a wall, partly embedded in it, with one fourth or one fifth of its thickness projecting. In classical architecture, a pilaster normally observes the form of one of the architectural orders, such as Ionic or Corinthian, and supports roof beams. The anta of ancient Greece was the direct ancestor of the Roman pilaster. In ancient Roman architecture, the pilaster gradually became more and more decorative rather than structural. The fourth-story wall of the Colosseum in Rome contains examples of the Roman use of pilasters. These pillar-like structures were also found in the inside walls of Anasazi kivas.

pile dwelling: Platforms raised on posts above open water or on damp ground at water's edge; a type of Neolithic settlement found commonly in prehistoric Europe in areas with many lakes, such as Switzerland, Germany, and north Italy. Such a settlement was formerly on the edge of a lake but is now buried by lake shore sediment or underwater. They should properly be labeled lakeside villages, because in most cases they were constructed on the shore and not on stilts over the water, as was formerly believed. They were, however, frequently constructed on timber platforms, and subsequently rising water levels in the lakes have preserved these platforms and much other wooden material, as well as artifacts of other organic substances. Cultures in which lake villages were common include Chassey, Cortaillod, Horgen, and Polada. (*syn.* lake dwelling)

pilgrim: A person journeying to foreign lands or one who travels to a holy place.

pillar crypt: In Minoan architecture, a basement room with one or two pillars. Some were incised with sacred symbols.

Piltdown Man: A set of skull fragments presented in 1913 as an apelike jaw and claiming to be the missing evolutionary link between ancient and modern humans, but revealed to be an elaborate hoax. It was supposedly found at a site near Lewes in Sussex. In 1953, analysis by fluorine test and other methods showed that the skull was indeed that of *Homo sapiens* combined with the jaw of a modern orangutan. Between 1953 and 1955, it was shown that these objects were mostly doctored fakes and had all been introduced to the site. (*syn.* Piltdown)

pin: One of the simplest artifacts, consisting of a narrow metal or bone shaft with a point at one end and usually some sort of decorative head at the other. Its function was to secure garments (ancestral to the fibula) or, sometimes, the hair. Their decorative heads were highly variable and nonfunctional, and therefore a culturally significant feature.

Pincevent: Large Upper Palaeolithic/Late Magdalenian open-air site east of Paris at the confluence of the Seine and Yonne. The project pioneered large-scale horizontal excavation in the western Europe Palaeolithic as well as the plotting and refitting of flint fragments as an aid to reconstructing the living conditions. Artifacts and debris of flint (including conjoined flints) and bone are found from 10,000–9000 BC in at least 15 occupations. Over 100 tent/hut habitations and 20 large hearths have been found.

pinger: An underwater survey device for producing pulses of sound—for marking an underwater site or detecting an underwater object. It is more powerful than sidescan sonar, capable of probing up to 60 meters below the seabed. (*syn.* boomer profiler)

pingo: An ice-cored mound that develops in the active layer and permafrost of the periglacial zone. These conical mounds can be up to 40 meters high and 600 meters wide. Layers of ice may separate out by percolation of water, or form by the injection of water-charged sediment from below. When a pingo melts, its center collapses, leaving behind a circular "rampart" of material (a circular ridge with a central basin, often filled with peat). Pingo ramparts have been used to reconstruct the extent of the periglacial zone that developed around the Devensian/Weichselian ice sheets.

Pinsdorf ware: Hard-fired pots made in the villages in the Vorgebirge Hills, west of Cologne and Bonn in Germany. The earliest example is the Wermelskirchen coinhoard pot, dated to AD c. 960. Pingsdorf ware is characteristically decorated with red paint and commonly occurs as pitchers with thumb-impressed ring bases; smaller pots, including money-boxes and toys, were also made. The products were exported to all parts of the Rhineland, as well as Britain and Scandinavia.

pintadera: A small object, usually of terra-cotta, consisting of a decorative stamp with a knob at the back for holding. The stamping surface is flat, concave, or convex. It has been suggested that they served to apply pigments to the human skin in repeat patterns as an alternative to tattooing. They are found in the Late Neolithic of central Europe and Italy, and pintaderas of both stamp and roller types occur widely in American cultures.

Pinto tradition: Culture of southern California deserts with characteristic Pinto points, a heavy, often crudely made projectile point with triangular blade, narrow stem, and indented base. Artifacts also include plano-convex bifaces, scraper planes, choppers, hammer stones, and flat grinding slabs. Pinto was dated c. 5000–2000 BC and the sometimes related Gypsum (in the Pinto/Gypsum Complex) c. 1500 BC–AD 600). (*syn.* San Dieguito-Pinto, Pinto/Gypsum Complex)

Piotrovsky, Boris B. (1908–1992): Russian archaeologist who excavated Urartu (Armenia), the citadel of Karmir-Blur (ancient Teishebaini). He wrote on the Scythians in Caucasus and Transcaucasia. *Urartu* (1967) offers a popular survey of the kingdom's art, while his *The Ancient Civilization of Urartu* (1969) is an illustrated political and cultural history.

pipe-stem dating: A method of calculating the date of American Colonial assemblages based on the variation in hole diameters in clay pipe stems. J. C. Harrington first drew attention to the fact that there is a general reduction in hole size from 1620–1800. Lewis Binford then developed a regression equation, thus: $[y = 1931.85 - 38.26x]$ where y is the mean date for the group and x is the mean pipe-stem diameter for the sample. ("A New Method of Calculating Dates from Kaolin Pipe Stem Samples," Lewis R. Binford.) The formula works well for the period 1680–1760, but fails to produce satisfactory results for post-1780 assemblages.

Piraeus: The main port of Athens, fortified in the 5th century BC and linked to Athens by long walls for a 10-mile corridor to the sea. At Piraeus, three harbors were used— Peraiki, Munychia, and the Great Harbor of Kantharos (Cantharus). The Athenian statesman Themistocles persuaded his colleagues about 493 BC to fortify and use Piraeus for the new Athenian fleet. Soon after 460, the long walls from the base of Munychia to Athens were built, thereby ensuring communications between Athens and its port in the event of a siege. Under Pericles' program of public works in the middle of the 5th century BC, the town was laid out by Hippodamian planning. Sections of the walling, traces of trireme (warship) sheds, and a small Hellenistic theater may be seen. The Spartans captured Piraeus at the close of the Peloponnesian War and demolished the long walls and the port's fortifications in 404 BC. They were rebuilt under the Athenian leader Conon in 393 BC. In 86 BC, the Roman commander Lucius Cornelius Sulla destroyed the city, and it was virtually deserted until its revival in 1834.

Pirak: Prehistoric site on the Kacchi Plain, Baluchistan, Pakistan where a post-Harappan cultural sequence has at least seven phases over the 2nd millennium and early 1st millennium BC. The sequence is characterized by a painted pottery with a geometric style with earlier monochrome painted decoration becoming bichrome in later times. There is evidence of intensified agricultural production, and the horse and camel appear. Between 1200–1100 BC, iron came into use, the earliest occurrence in India.

Pirri graver: An Australian tool type with extensive flaking on one face and an underside curvature as well as retouched cutting edge on the narrow end. They are up to 80 millimeters long and seem to correspond to that of the Tula. (*syn.* pirri graver)

Pirri point: An Australian stone tool type, a symmetrical leaf-shaped point, up to 7 centimeters long, unifacially flaked all over its dorsal surface. The striking platform and bulb of percussion are sometimes removed to produce a rounded, thinned butt. Pirri points have been found distributed widely in inland Australia from South Australia to the Northern Territory and northwestern Australia. A component of the Australian Small Tool tradition, the Pirri point dates from about 3000 BC. The aboriginal term *pirri* means "wood-engraving tool." (*syn.* Pirri culture, pirri point)

piscina: In Roman architecture, a large decorated basin used as a fish pond or as a swimming bath and sunk into the floor of a room in a Roman villa. During the Middle Ages, a piscina was a pool or tank in which fish were stored by monastic communities, for whom fish was a diet staple.

pisé: A term describing walls made of mud or clay, not formed into separate bricks but shaped, rammed, or piled up into walls in situ. The clay dries hard in the sun, but the resulting walls would not survive heavy rainfall. It was much used in the ancient Near East. (*syn.* terre pisée, pisé-work)

piston corer: A device for extracting columns of sediment from the ocean floor. Deeper cores are taken by the piston corer, which can take samples as long as 20 meters. In a piston corer, a closely fitted piston attached to the end of the lowering cable is installed inside the coring tube. When the coring tube is driven into the ocean floor, friction exerts a downward pull on the core sample. The hydrostatic pressure on the ocean bottom, however, exerts an upward pressure on the core that works against a vacuum being created between the piston and the top of the core. The piston, in effect, provides a suction that overcomes the frictional forces acting between the sediment sample and the inside of the coring tube. The hydraulic piston corer is used by deep-sea drilling ships and can take undisturbed cores of lengths up to 200 meters. Dates for the different layers are obtained by radiocarbon, palaeomagnetism, or uranium series methods.

pit: An area (hole, shaft, cavity) dug out by humans for storage, food preparation, refuse disposal, and so on. These include storage pits/silos, rubbish dumps or "borrow pits," and remains of pit dwellings. When left undisturbed by man, pits erode and fill, in a sequence similar to ditches. Frequently they have been used for waste disposal and contain large quantities of food debris and rubbish from hearths.

Pitcairn Island: One of the isolated islands of eastern Polynesia, settled by Polynesians AD c. 1100, but abandoned when mutineers from HMS Bounty arrived in 1790. Pitcairn is one of many isolated Polynesian islands with a "lost" population. Their is evidence of occupation in stone platforms with anthropomorphic statues, petroglyphs, and stone fishhooks and adzes—resembling New Zealand Archaic assemblages. Its current population is descended from the mutineers of the British ship HMS Bounty and their Tahitian Polynesian consorts.

Pit-Comb Ware: A coarse pottery with deep, round-based bowls decorated with pits and comb impressions and used in the circumpolar cultures of the forest zone of northeast Europe. The area includes that around the southern Baltic and the glacial outwash of central and eastern Poland. Its makers were probably hunters and fishers, making little use of the techniques of food production, although adopting such Neolithic traits as pot making and ax grinding. There are few sites and little data. (*syn.* Pit-Comb ware)

Pit Grave culture: Late Neolithic culture of the lower Volga and Don steppes, the forerunner to Corded Ware, Single Grave, or Kurgan culture. It appears on Ukrainian steppes in the 3rd millennium BC, with fortified villages and burials in pits under barrows. (*syn.* Yamnaya Kultura; Pit-Grave culture, Yamnaya culture)

Pithecanthropus: The former genus name assigned to fossil hominids including Java man and Peking man, both now classified as *Homo erectus.*

Pithekoussai: A volcanic island off the northern part of the Bay of Naples, and the site of arguably the earliest Greek colony in the western Mediterranean. Lying on sea trade routes to Italy and especially Etruria, the colony was established by Euboean Greeks from Chalcis and Eretria, c. 775–750 BC. The Monte Vico region shows occupational evidence going back to the Bronze Age, and the akropolis shows also Bronze Age and Iron Age material. The island had good agricultural land and rich deposits of potters' clay, and it became the principal supplier to Campania. There was also a wide variety of metalworking. A large necropolis has inhumation and cremation burials containing oriental trinkets, Egyptian scarabs, and varied imported and local pottery, including inter alia, a Rhodian cup bearing one of the earliest examples of the Greek alphabet, a Chalcidian version written from right to left. This cup, bearing the Greek inscription in the Euboean script "I am the cup of Nestor," can be securely dated to before 700 BC. Cumae, a mainland Italian offshoot of the island settlement of Pithekoussai, was founded c. 750 BC. (*syn.* ancient Aenaria, Inarime; modern Ischia)

pithos: A large Greek earthenware storage jar with a narrow neck, used for oil, wine, or grain. They were used on occasion for jar burial in the Aegean area. (*syn.* pl. pithoi)

pit house: A subterranean or semisubterranean dwelling found in the American Southwest—the earliest manmade dwellings there. It usually had an underground floor and aboveground earthen or brush walls supported by interior posts and was the primary habitation structure of individual families of basketweaving cultures. These structures may be round, oval, or square to rectangular, but usually have a straight entrance. Most were roofed with thatch and supported by posts. Often, all that remains on an archaeological site is a large, shallow pit. Its most popular period was AD 200–900, and it evolved into the kiva. (*syn.* pithouse; pit dwelling)

pito: Mexican name for the pipe of the Aztecs, which resembled a flageolet. It was made of red clay and had four finger holes.

Pitted-Ware culture: In Sweden and Finland, a series of foraging groups during the 3rd–1st millennia BC, part of the circumpolar complex of Holocene foragers. Amber ornaments were made widely, and communities depended on seals and pigs for subsistence.

Pitt-Rivers, General Augustus Lane-Fox (1827–1900): British scholar and pioneer in archaeological excavation and recording, working on prehistoric and Romano-British sites in England. His large-scale excavations unearthed villages, camps, cemeteries, and barrows at sites such as Woodcutts, Rotherley, South Lodge, Bokerly Dyke, and Wansdyke. From his study of firearms, he realized that something analogous to evolution can be traced in artifacts as well as in living organisms, with the same gradual developments and occasional degenerations. He assembled an ethnographical collection arranged by use rather than by provenance, a practical example of typology. He helped to advance excavation to a scientific technique with precise work, total excavation of sites, meticulous recording of detail, and full and rapid publication. His work on his own estate, Cranborne Chase, was published in five volumes entitled *Excavations in Cranborne Chase* (1887–1903). He stressed stratigraphy and precise recording of all finds and is often called the "father of British archaeology."

pixel: A picture element, the minimum unit recorded electronically by the Landsat satellites. A pixel is any of the small discrete elements that together constitute an image—as on a television screen or as any of the detecting elements of a charge-coupled device used as an optical sensor.

Pizarro, Francisco (1475–1541): Spanish explorer and adventurer who came to Peru in 1532 looking for gold and destroyed the Inca Empire. The Inca wrongly believed the Spanairds to be gods returning as prophesied in legends. He founded Lima.

Place, Victor (1818–1875): French consul in Mosul and excavator of Khorsabad (the first archaeological excavations in Mesopotamia), succeeding Paul-Emile Botta. His finds were lost in shipment down the Tigris.

place-name: A place-name is a word or words used to

indicate, denote, or identify a geographic locality such as a town, river, or mountain. Toponymy divides place-names into two broad categories: habitation names and feature names. A habitation name denotes a locality that is peopled or inhabited, such as a homestead, village, or town. Feature names refer to natural or physical features of the landscape. The study of place-names plays a vital role in medieval studies. The form of the name often indicates a Celtic, Latin, or Germanic origin, and its prefix or suffix may suggest the type of settlement, for instance, hamlet, village, riverside place, woodland settlement, and so on. Two basic assumptions are that every place-name has a meaning, including place-names derived from personal names; and place-names describe the site and record some evidence of human occupation or ownership. Toponymy can uncover important historical information about a place, such as the period the original language of the inhabitants lasted, settlement history, and population dispersal.

Plain of Jars: A site complex of mainland southeast Asia in northern Laos with about 250 stone burial jars, up to 3 meters high, together with other megalithic monuments (menhirs) and pottery jar burials. The jars contained few remains as the bones appear to have been cremated. Artifacts on the burial and ceremonial sites include bronze and iron with local and possible Indian affinities. The sites appear to predate Hindu/ Buddhist influence, c. 300 BC–AD 300. (*syn.* Xiang Khouang, Xiangkhouang)

Plains Village tradition: Name given to a group of cultures of the central and eastern plains of North America between AD 900–1850, particularly in Kansas, Nebraska, and South Dakota. Contemporaneous with Mississippian tradition of Eastern Woodlands, it represents a fusion of that tradition with the Plains variant of the Woodland tradition. The Plains Village tradition was characterized by large habitation structures in settlements that were often fortified. Subsistence dependent on hunting, farming along rivers, beans/squash/ maize, and the pottery was related to Mississippian and had incised decoration and rim adornment. When drought forced abandonment of the central plains, the inhabitants moved to the Middle Missouri area (North, South Dakota) and formed the Coalescent tradition. (*syn.* Plains Village Indian)

Plainview: The name of a Plano projectile point that has parallel sides and a concave base and the name of the type site in Texas as well as the complex. The complex is associated with the point and nondiagnostic stone and bone tools.

plaited: Basketry made with both a horizontal and a vertical stitch or weft—like a braid. The weave is basically the same in both directions. (*syn.* plaited basketry)

plan drawing: A two-dimensional rendering at a constant scale, showing the horizontal dimensions of archaeological data.

plane table: Portable surveying instrument that consists of a drawing board and a ruler (alidade) mounted on a tripod and used to sight and map topographic details and to plot survey lines directly from field observations. This piece of equipment is much used in earlier surveying and map making. One end of the alidade is held on the point on the map representing the point of operation, and the other is directed at a marker on the point to be plotted. This gives the angle from the point of operation, and distance can be plotted directly along the ruler after scaling down from the original measurement. The technique has been replaced mainly by photogrammetry. (*syn.* plane-table)

planimetric map: Map used to record details of an archaeological site(s) or features but which contains no topographic information.

Plano: Widespread late Palaeo-Indian tradition in North America from 10,000–7000 BP. In the west, it is characterized by bison hunting and diverse projectile point styles; complexes include Agate Basin, Hell Gap, Cody, and Frederick. The characteristic unfluted leaf-shaped projectile point appears to have developed from Llano and Folsom types. These many styles or types have been identified by such local names as Plainview, Angostura, Milnesand, Agate Basin, and Scottsbluff, and their primarily hunting culture may be included in the term Plano. The Plano complex or culture type was a direct descendant of the fluted-blade early American hunters. As the climate moderated, peoples of the Late Plano complex moved north into Saskatchewan and Alberta with the grazing game animals and, by 3000 BC, had reached the Arctic tundra zone in the Northwest Territories of Canada. It is the most recent of the three major Palaeo-Indian cultures.

planoconvex: Pertaining to an artifact with one flat and one convex side. (*syn.* plano-convex)

plano-convex brick: A sun-dried or kiln-fired rectangular brick with a flat under surface and a domed upper surface, used in the Early Dynastic period of southern Mesopotamia. They often had thumb-impressed holes on the domed surface. They were used with mud mortar in vertical courses inclined in alternating directions to create a herringbone pattern.

Plano point: Name of projectile points developed out of the Clovis and Folsom points of the Big Game Hunting tradition, after 8000 BC in North America. Unfluted, large lanceolate stone forms were made by pressure flaking techniques. The two main types of Plano points are Plainview of 7800–5100 BC and Parallel, which are longer, more slender, and more finely made.

plantago: A weed of cultivation, which appears strongly in the pollen record as a result of the clearing of previously wooded land. There are several varieties, and their presence is taken by archaeologists to imply cereal cultivation. The greater plantain (*Plantago major*) provides seed spikes for bird food. Ribwort and hoary plantain (*P. lanceolata* and *P. media*, respectively) are troublesome weeds. Psyllium and *P. ovata* have been useful in medical science.

plant domestication: The process of hereditary reorganization of wild plants into domestic and cultivated forms according to the interests of people. The cultural selection of useful fruits resulting in new plants that depend on human beings for their existence. The first attempts at domestication of plants were made in the Old World by peoples of the Mesolithic Period. Domestication of vegetatively reproducing plants, such as those with tubers, probably preceded domestication of the seed plants—cereals, legumes, and other vegetables.

plant macrofossil: Preserved or carbonized plant parts recovered from archaeological sites and large enough to be observed without a microscope.

planum: An excavation method in which horizontal slices are removed either from the whole site, or from specific features, to reveal a succession of plans.

plan-view: The view from overhead looking down, commonly used in maps.

plastered skull: Skulls found at Jericho, Israel, which were covered in plaster and painted as well as decorated with cowry shells in the orbits. They were found in PPNB contexts at several sites in Syro-Palestine.

plate armor: Protective armor in the form of sheet iron fittings (metal plates) tailored to the shape of the body and strapped in position. This type of armor was current in 15th–16th century Europe. The knights of the European Middle Ages wore this armor, composed of large steel or iron plates that were linked by loosely closed rivets and by internal leathers to allow the wearer maximum freedom of movement. (*syn.* plate armour)

platform: The place on a core or flake where it was struck by a hammer.

platform burial: The practice of placing a corpse on an artificial, above-ground structure; the body was sometimes retrieved at a later date for interment.

platform mound: A platform of earth and stone, usually rectangular in shape and flat topped, that forms a base for the construction of a building, such as a palace or temple. The buildings served as habitation and/or ceremonial structures.

plating: The coating of a metal or other material such as plastic or china with a hard, nonporous metallic surface to improve durability and beauty. Gold, silver, stainless steel, palladium, copper, and nickel are formed by dipping an object into a solution containing the desired surface material, which is deposited by chemical or electrochemical action. Although much plating is done for decorative purposes, still more is done to increase the durability and corrosion resistance of softer materials.

platinum: A very heavy, precious, silver-white metal that is soft and ductile and has a high melting point and good resistance to corrosion and chemical attack. It is found in the Transvaal, South Africa, among other places.

playa: A shallow basin-like area in which surface water collects, found mainly in arid regions. It is often the sandy, salty, or mud-caked floor of a desert basin with interior drainage, usually occupied by a shallow lake during the rainy season or after prolonged, heavy rains. The word also refers to the lake itself. (*syn.* takyr, sabkha, kavir)

Playa Hermosa: A site on the central Peruvian coast north of Lima, which has yielded an assemblage of preceramic period tools, textiles, and evidence of cultivated corn, lima beans, chili peppers, c. 2300–2100 BC.

plaza: An open square in ancient cities of the New World, similar to the Roman forum, which was the focus for meetings and events. It is usually an unroofed, but architecturally enclosed, space, around or in which are placed platform mounds and their associated buildings, such as palaces and temples.

Pleistocene: A geochronological division of geological time, an epoch of the Quaternary period following the Pliocene. During the Pleistocene, large areas of the northern hemisphere were covered with ice, and there were successive glacial advances and retreats. The Lower Pleistocene began c. 1.8 million years ago, the Middle Pleistocene c. 730,000 years ago, and the Upper Pleistocene c. 127,000 years ago; it ended about 10,000 years ago. Most present-day mammals appeared during the Pleistocene. The onset of the Pleistocene was marked by an increasingly cold climate, by the appearance of Calabrian mollusca and Villafranchian fauna with elephant, ox, and horse species, and by changes in foraminifera. The oldest form of man had evolved by the Early Pleistocene (Australopithecus), and in archaeological terms the cultures classed as Palaeolithic all fall within this period. By the mid-Pleistocene, *Homo sapiens* evolved in Africa and Europe. *Homo sapiens* spread to Asia and the Americas before the end of the epoch. There were mass extinctions of large and small fauna during the Pleistocene. In North America, more than 30 genera of large mammals became extinct within a span of roughly 2,000 years during the late Pleistocene. Of the many causes that have been proposed by scientists for these faunal extinctions, the two most likely are changing environment with changing climate, and the disruption of the ecological pattern by early humans. The Pleistocene was succeeded by the Holocene or present epoch. (*syn.* ice age, Ice Age, Iluvium; Quaternary; Great Ice Age; Pleistocene Epoch)

Pleistocene Series: A division of the Quaternary System defined by its deposits. It is a worldwide division of rocks deposited during the Pleistocene Epoch (1,600,000–10,000 years ago). It overlies rocks from the Pliocene Epoch (5.3–1.6 million years ago) and is itself overlain by rocks of the Holocene Series; together these two latter divisions make up the Quaternary System. These deposits contain evidence of humans and their development throughout glacial and inter-glacial conditions. By international agreement, the global stratotype section/point for the base of the Pleistocene Series is in the Vrica section in Calabria, Italy. The Pleistocene's boundary with the Pliocene occurs just above the position of the magnetic reversal that marks the Olduvai Normal Polarity Subzone, thus allowing the worldwide correlation of Pleisto-cene rocks with reference to the magneto-stratigraphic time scale.

plinth: In architecture, the foot or lowest member of a base of a column, pedestal, or wall; a block on which the moldings of an architrave or trim are stopped at the bottom.

Pliocene: The latest geological epoch of the Tertiary period; the epoch dating between c. 5 million years ago and the beginning of the Pleistocene (c. 1.8 million years ago). During the Pliocene, mammals such as the elephant, horse, ox, and deer appeared, in addition to ancestors of man. It followed the Miocene. There was a separation of the Homo genus and the Australopithecus genus, the first worked tools, and the first camps. It is often divided into the Early Pliocene Epoch (5.3 to 3.4 million years ago) and the Late Pliocene Epoch (3.4 to 1.8 million years ago). The Pliocene is also subdivided into two ages and their corresponding rock stages—the Zanclean and the Piacenzian.

Plio-Pleistocene: The later part of the Pliocene and the early part of the Pleistocene, c. 5–1 million years ago. The early Plio-Pleistocene *Homo habilis* appears to be more closely related to *Homo sapiens* than is *Homo erectus*.

Plocnik: A settlement site on the Morava River in southern Serbia. Its name is coupled with that of Vinca to describe the Late Neolithic culture of the area c. 3950–3300 BC. There is Late Vinca pottery in two occupation levels and Bubanj-Hum pottery in the topmost level. Four hoards of copper tools and ornaments have been found in correspondence to the Bubanj-Hum assemblage (late 4th millennium BC). They represent one of the earliest metal hoards in the Yugoslavian Copper Age.

ploshchadki: In Russian antiquity, house floors that had a layer of clay covering a base of horizontal logs and often hardened by fire. They are characteristic of the Cucuteni-Tripolye culture and also occur in the Gumelnita, Petresti, and Vinca cultures extending into southeastern Europe in the Late Neolithic. (*syn.* ploshchadi)

plow: A tool designed to be drawn through the ground to break it up for cultivation, often powered by a yoke (or more) of oxen, other animals, or men. The earliest type of plow, developed from the hoe and digging stick, is the ard or scratch plow, which stirs the soil without turning it. Cross-plowing, the result of a second plowing at right angles to the first, is usually necessary. This type was of Near Eastern origin c. 4th millennium BC. The later plow, heavier and wheeled, did not appear until the early centuries AD. It is more suited to the heavier soils of Europe. Prehistoric America, lacking suitable draft animals, did not have a plow. The 18th-century addition of the moldboard, which turned the furrow slice cut by the plowshare, was an important advance. The plow is considered the most important agricultural implement of history, used to turn and break up soil, to bury crop residues, and to help control weeds. (*syn.* plough)

plow marks: Marks left in buried soil indicating that the land has been plowed at some remote time, giving evidence of ancient agricultural activity. Plow marks have been found, for example, under several British Neolithic monuments and are valuable evidence for ancient clearance and cultivation. They are identified by sharp physical discontinuities in soil color and texture as seen in excavation profiles or plan-view. (*syn.* plough marks, plowmarks, plow scars)

plowwash: A sediment caused by farming activities in breaking up the soil on hills or slopes. The cultivation of soil for crops, or the intensive pasturing of animals, causes a change in the structure of the soil, which may result in poor drainage; combined with the lack of vegetation, it caused the soil to move downhill. (*syn.* ploughwash)

plow zone: The top layer of the soil to the depth at which a plow penetrates and disturbs archaelogical deposits.

Plumbate Ware: A fine pottery made on the Pacific coast of Mesoamerica, near the Mexico–Guatemala border, during early Post-Classic and Pre-Columbian times. It was traded over a wide area, from Nayarit in northwest Mexico to Costa Rica in the south and was present in all but the lowest levels in the Toltec center at Tula. The glazed appearance of the surface of Plumbate Ware is due to the unusual composition of the clay from which it is made and to the carefully controlled firing conditions. There was a high percentage of iron compounds and, on firing, the ceramic surface acquired a hard, lustrous vitrified surface, often with metallic shine. Its original point of manufacture was on the Pacific coast of Mesoamerica in the vicinity of Izapa.

Plussulien: Neolithic quarry in Côtes-du-Nord, France, mined from c. 4000–2000 BC, for making polished stone axes of dolerite. Artifacts include hammer stones, grinders, and much toolmaking debris as well as hearths.

pluvial: A wet climatic episode or rainy season in a normally arid area. It is marked by changes in lake levels, which produce fossil beaches, among other evidence, and by changes in flora and fauna. In lowland and subtropical regions that were never covered by Pleistocene ice sheets, alternations in climate were expressed as changes in rainfall. The changes accompanying the increased precipitation led to increased human occupation in areas that otherwise are not as attractive.

ply: The strand(s) of material used in the construction of cordage.

PMT: A high-quality, glossy photo reproduction of a figure. (*syn.* photometric transfer)

Pnyx or pnys: An ancient Greek open-air auditorium for public (popular) assemblies; the site in Athens (a hill to the west of the Akropolis) where the Ecclesiae were held. It was a semicircular rising ground, with an area of 12,000 square yards, leveled with a pavement of large stones, and surrounded by a wall, behind which was the bema or platform from which speakers addressed the people. It was used from the 6th century BC and remodeled in the 4th century BC.

pochteca: In Aztec society, the class of long-distance merchants who traveled to foreign lands to trade and to spy. It was a hereditary guild of armed merchants who traveled into distant lands looking for luxury goods to bring back to the royal house. Quite often, the pochteca would seize lands of hostile peoples through which they passed, or they would provoke incidents that led to the intervention of the regular Aztec army.

poculum: A Roman cup or glass for drinking, distinct from the crater for mixing, and the cyathus for drawing wine from a bowl.

Pod Hradem: Upper Palaeolithic cave site in Moravia, Czechoslovakia. There are laurel-leaf points of the Szeletian and an early Upper Palaeolithic industry of retouched blades, dated to the middle of the last glacial.

podium: In architecture, any of various elements that form the "foot," or base, of a structure, such as a raised pedestal or base, a low wall supporting columns, or the structurally or decoratively emphasized lowest portion of a wall. The podium formed a sort of shelf or seat around a wall. The term *podium* is also used for raised platforms in general, as for speakers, and for a low basement. The architectural podium is usually designed with a modeled base and plinth at the bottom; a central surface known as a die, or dado; and a projecting cornice, or cap. Major Roman examples can be seen in the Maison carrée (c. 12 BC) in Nîmes, France, and the temple of Fortuna Virilis (c. 40 BC) in the Forum Boarium at Rome. (*syn.* plural podiums, podia)

podsol: A soil type characteristic of coniferous woodland, heath, tundra, or moorland—leached, acid soils formed under conditions of very cold climate's forest vegetation cover.

The fauna produce phenols that are washed into the horizons and disperse the clay/humus complexes. Minerals, humus, and nutrients are washed down the profile and become deposited as illuvial horizons of humus and iron oxides. The latter is often called the "iron pan." A bleached, sandy eluvial horizon is left at the top of the profile. Podsols develop naturally in areas of high annual rainfall, but most of the large areas of podsols in the uplands and lowland heaths of the British Isles were probably at least initiated by man's clearance of woodland during the present interglacial. (*syn.* podzol, podsol soil, podzol soil)

point: A category of stone artifacts consisting of pointed tools flaked on one or both sides. A weapon or tool having such a part and used for stabbing or piercing, such as arrowhead, spear head.

point bar: A channel bar of mud to coarse conglomerate forming on the convex side of a channel bend owing to reduced flow velocity. This land form is the most common type of lateral accretion: a depositional alluvial land form on and behind the convex bank of meandering streams. It is formed and modified as the stream floods and the meander bend moves. Over a period of years, point bars expand laterally as the opposite bank is continually eroded backward. The bars progressively spread across the valley bottom, usually as a thin sheet of sand or gravel containing layers that dip into the channel bottom.

point of percussion: The point at which a core is struck with a hammer stone to remove a flake. The point of percussion is a visible excrescence on the core, a small scar on the struck flake. The bulb of percussion surrounds it.

point provenience: The location (provenience) of a specific object at an exact point on a site.

Polada: An Early Bronze Age lake dwelling site near the southern end of Lake Garda in Lombardy, Italy, the type site of the Polada culture, c. 2200–1600 BC. The culture was characterized by a coarse undecorated ware forming deep carinated cups and various simple jars. The strap handles were often surmounted by knobs. Flat and slightly flanged axes were made of bronze. Antler was much used, and objects and vessels of wood survive on waterlogged sites. A variety of settlement types occur, including hill sites and lake villages like Polada itself. The Polada people were accomplished metalworkers, producing a range of tools and weapons showing strong connections with Unetice and other Early Bronze Age groups north of the Alps. The Polada culture also has features derived from Beaker assemblages, such as wristguards and v-perforated buttons.

Polesini: Upper Palaeolithic site near Rome with thousands of stone tools and faunal remains, but best known for engraved mobiliary art dated to the 11th millennium bp.

Poliochni: A settlement site on the island of Lemnos in the northern Aegean, first occupied in the Final Neolithic. Its seven successive phases span the Neolithic to Middle Bronze Age, parallel to the first six cities of Troy. Its Neolithic cities, equipped with stone baths, represented the most advanced Neolithic civilization yet found in the Aegean. The Copper Age city was dated to c. 5000 BC. In the Early Bronze Age (c. 3000 BC), it was a fortified township with stone defenses, one of the largest in the Aegean, with houses laid out along streets and evidence of the practice of metallurgy. An associated cemetery of inhumation burials has many with rich grave goods. There was a catastrophic destruction, although the site was later reoccupied.

polis: An ancient Greek city-state—a state incorporating a city, smaller towns, and villages. The polis centered on one town, but included the surrounding countryside. The town contained a citadel on raised ground (akropolis) and a marketplace (agora). The city-state in Greece probably originated from the natural divisions of the country by mountains and the sea and from the original local tribal (ethnic) and cult divisions. There were several hundred poleis. (*syn.* plural poleis)

polished stone adze: A chopping or cutting tool, beveled on one side and characteristic of the Neolithic in Southeast Asia. It appeared as early as 6000 BC in some places and continued in use into the 1st millennium AD in places with little metal. They were generally flaked to shape from a large core, then ground and polished. Traded forms were roughed-out blanks that would be polished later. The form was a simple quadrangle. By the Late Neolithic, a decrease in the proportion of stone axes to adzes suggests the increasing dominance of permanent agriculture.

polished tool: Any artifact made by the pecking or grinding of hard stones. The Neolithic Period was the first widespread used of polished rock tools, notably axes, with the adoption of a new technique of stoneworking. The revolutionary method used to create polished tools was essentially a finishing process that slicked a chipped tool by rubbing it on or with an abrasive rock to remove the scars of the chipping process that had produced the rough tool. Not only was the edge keener, but the smooth sides of the edge also promoted deeper penetration, with the added advantage of easier tool extraction from a deep wedged cut. (*syn.* ground stone tool)

polity: A politically independent or autonomous social unit, whether simple or complex. In the case of a complex society, such as a state, it may include many dependent components. The term was used by Colin Renfrew to describe small-scale, politically autonomous early states, as in Mycenaean Greece and Etruscan Italy.

Polivanov Yar: Neolithic settlement site of the Cucuteni–Tripolye culture in the Ukraine. Found were smelted copper ingots suggesting trade contacts with the Carpathian–Balkan region.

Poljanica: A Copper Age tell in northeastern Bulgaria, dated to the mid-4th millennium BC, with many occupation levels. Eight levels have 10–15 complete houses densely packed in a triple palisade. Poljanica resembles a Roman fort in outward appearance, and the name is also applied to the Early and Middle Eneolithic culture of northeast Bulgaria, related to the Boian and Marica cultures. (*syn.* Polyanitsa)

pollen analysis: The study of pollen grains in soil samples from an archaeological site, which provides information on ancient human use of plants and plant resources. This technique, which is used in establishing relative chronologies as well as in environmental archaeology, was developed primarily as a technique for the relative dating of natural horizons. Pollen grains are produced in vast quantities by all plants, especially the wind-pollinated tree species. The outer skin (exine) of these grains is remarkably resistant to decay, and on wet ground or on a buried surface, it is preserved, locked in the humus content. The pollen grains of trees, shrubs, grasses, and flowers are preserved in either anaerobic conditions or in acid soils. Samples can be taken from the deposits by means of a core or from individual layers at frequent intervals in a section face on an archaeological site. The pollen is extracted and then concentrated and stained and examined under a microscope. Pollen grains are identifiable by their shape, and the percentages of the different species present in each sample are recorded on a pollen diagram. A comparison of the pollen diagrams for different levels in a deposit allows the identification of changes in the percentages of species and thus changes in the environment. As a dating technique, pollen has been used to identify different zones of arboreal vegetation, which often correspond to climatic changes. The technique is invaluable for disclosing the environment of early man's sites and can even, over a series of samples, reveal man's influence on his environment by, for example, forest clearance. The sediments most frequently investigated are peat and lake deposits, but the more acid soils, such as podsols, are also analyzed. Radiocarbon dates may be taken at intervals in the sequence, and it is possible to reconstruct the history of vegetation in the area around the site where the samples were taken. Palynology plays an important role in the investigation of ancient climates, particularly through studies of deposits formed during glacial and interglacial stages of the Pleistocene epoch. (*syn.* palynology)

pollen core: A stratified sample of soil or sediment, taken to recover the plant pollen, and hence to discover changes in the local vegetation over time. A column of soil or peat is extracted from the ground, containing a continuous record of pollen grains representative of changing vegetation over a period—and the deeper the core, the older the pollen.

pollen diagram: A diagram produced after the analysis of the pollen from a column of peat or other soil. Pollen diagrams consist of a number of graphs, showing the fluctuations of different pollen types through a sediment or soil. The vertical axis of the diagram represents depth through the deposit and is therefore roughly related to time, as the deeper layers are the oldest. Each small graph represents the changing frequency of one pollen type, either as a percentage (proportional pollen counting) or as an absolute frequency (absolute pollen counting). It is often possible to split the diagram up into a number of pollen zones, each dominated by high frequencies of a particular pollen type or types. (*syn.* pollen spectrum)

pollen influx: An estimate of the number of pollen grains incorporated into a fixed volume of sediments over a particular time. If the pollen influx is known, the number of years contained in a certain volume of sediment can be estimated.

pollen zones: A series of divisions that can be drawn across a pollen diagram on the basis of fluctuations in pollen types. Each pollen zone is dominated by high frequencies of a particular pollen type or types. In recent years, many palynologists have abandoned general zonation schemes and instead have divided their pollen diagrams into "pollen assemblage zones" (p.a.z.). These are based simply on the pollen fluctuations seen in each particular diagram and can therefore take account of local variation in the history of vegetation.

Polo, Marco (1254–1324): Venetian adventurer and traveler who journeyed from Europe to Asia in 1271–1295, and wrote *Il milione* ("The Million"), known in English as the *Travels of Marco Polo*, a geographical classic.

Polonnaruwa: A town in north-central Sri Lanka (Ceylon), that was an ancient Ceylonese capital. Polonnaruwa became the residence of Ceylon's kings in AD 368 and succeeded Anuradhapura as the capital in the 8th century when the latter was captured by the Tamils. The most impressive surviving monuments belong to the later 12th and 13th centuries and include a series of colossal sculptured figures and a number of temples and monasteries in the Great Quadrangle. (*syn.* Polonnaruva)

polychrome pottery: Pottery that is decorated in more than two colors, but the term is also applied to pottery with more than one color. (*syn.* sensu stricto)

polyhedron: A six-sided pebble or piece of stone, which has been totally or partly reshaped by chipping of the surface in a number of directions; it resembles a ball. It was first created in pre-Acheulian and Acheulian and Middle Palaeolithic times and used as percussion tools, throwing weapons, and nuclei for flakes.

Polynesia: A vast region of scattered islands in the central Pacific occupied by closely related ethnic groups, falling mostly in a triangle made up of the Hawaiian Islands, New Zealand, and Easter Island. Western Polynesia was settled by Austronesian speakers from Southeast Asia (Lapita culture) around 1500 BC, and migrations progressed throughout the triangle until New Zealand was reached AD c. 900. The Polynesians are a homogeneous population in terms of language and social organization, which developed into powerful chiefdoms in the larger islands. The Polynesian economy was based on tuber and fruit horticulture. Pottery production ceased in Western Polynesia AD c. 300 and was never present in most eastern island or in New Zealand. Western Polynesia consists of Tonga, Samoa, and Tuvalu; eastern Polynesia includes the Society, Cook, Austral, Marquesas, Tuamotu, and Hawaiian Islands, Easter Island, and New Zealand.

Polynesian Outliers: Communities occupying the 19 small islands to windward (east) of the large Melanesian islands of the Solomons, New Hebrides, Vanuatu, New Caledonia, and on the southern fringes of Micronesia. Archaeology and linguistics suggest settlement by a back-movement from western Polynesia (Samoa, Futuna, Ellice) perhaps starting in the 1st millennium AD. Archaeological evidence indicates that by 1300 BC islands in northern Vanuatu were settled by the makers of the distinctive Lapita pottery from Melanesian islands to the west. (*syn.* Polynesian outliers)

polyphone: A phonetic sign that may stand for two or more different sounds, like the English *c* or *a*; the opposite of homophone.

polypod bowl: A bowl that stands on two, three, or four small legs—found especially in Middle American archaeology. The form was also popular among the southwestern groups of the Beaker folk and in related central European wares.

polythetic definition: A group or class consisting of a large number of its members who share most of the characteristics. Although the group or class shares a number of common characteristics, none of them is essential for membership.

Pomongwe: A cave in Matopo Hills near Bulawayo, Zimbabwe, with fine rock paintings, especially of giraffe. The cave has a long sequence of stone industries, and the name Pomongwe also refers to a Later Stone Age industry of southwestern Zimbabwe dated between 10,800–9400 bp. At the very bottom of the deep archaeological deposits at Pomongwe are a few artifacts possibly of Sangoan type. Later occupations are attributed successively to the Charaman, Bambata, Tshangula, and Wilton industries. Interstratified between the last two is the Pomongwe culture's assemblage, containing utilized flakes and crude scrapers with virtually no other stone implements. Some see it as a regional industry in the Oakhurst Complex.

Pompeii: A Roman town lying at the foot of Mount Vesuvius in Campania, Italy, which was covered with volcanic ash in an eruption in AD 79. Much of the town has been uncovered since excavations began in the mid-18th century. The uncovering of the city offers much evidence for prosperous provincial urban life in the 1st century AD. It was a port and principal city on the Bay of Naples as early as the 8th century BC. In 89 BC, Pompeii was taken by the Roman general Sulla and became subject to Rome. A new suburb was laid out next to the old town before an earthquake in AD 62; much rebuilding in Roman imperial style was done before the final disaster. A Doric temple of the 6th century BC together with Attic Black-Figure ware suggests a strong Greek presence, and association with Cumae, Naples, and Paestum is probable; Etruscan influence is also very likely. The deposits from Vesuvius in AD 79 were first small pumice and then ash, followed by poisonous gas and rain. Of all the numerous surviving buildings, Pompeii is perhaps most celebrated for its atrium-style private houses, often having fine gardens and decorated inside with elaborate mosaics and mural panels. The amphitheater is probably the earliest stone-built example in existence. There were two theaters, a palaestra, civic buildings, workshops, at least three major public bath complexes, and nine temples. In particular, the temple of Isis reflects the popularity of the personalized Oriental mystery cults under the early Roman Empire. Pompeian life is further documented by the frequent painted and inscribed notices, or graffiti, which are to be found on both internal and external walls. They often refer to local elections and to events taking place at the amphitheater. There was also a gambling den and brothel. Outside the city gates were cemeteries and large villas. During the eruption, both human beings and animals were covered by the deposit, forming paralyzed shapes. Casts made from these give a startling impression of the original victims. There are ancient accounts of the earthquake by Seneca, Tacitus, and Pliny the Younger. Also destroyed were the cities of Herculaneum and Stabiae. The ruins at Pompeii were first discovered late in the 16th century by the architect Domenico Fontana. Excavation of the buried cities began first at Herculaneum, in 1709. Work did not begin at Pompeii until 1748, and in 1763 an inscription ("rei publicae Pompeianorum") was found that identified the site as Pompeii.

Po Nagar: Literally, "Lady of the City," a well-preserved cluster of four Cham shrines dedicated to Shiva and erected or rebuilt between the 7th–12th centuries. It was at a site during the kingdom of Champa, on the coast of southern Vietnam. It is also known for its Sanskrit inscriptions recording the late 8th-century raids by seamen from Java who destroyed several temples. (*syn.* Nha Trang)

Pong Tuk: Site on the Mae Kong River in Thailand where a late-Roman bronze lamp, c. 5th–6th centuries AD, was found.

It was similar in form to ceramic lamps at other sites in the vicinity.

Pont du Gard: A stretch of Roman aqueduct, 40 kilometers long, in the form of a three-storied arched bridge over River Gard near Nîmes, France. It was probably built by Agrippa c. 19 BC to take water some 49 meters above the river to Nîmes. This notable Roman architectural work has three tiers of arches rising to a height of 155 feet (47 m).

Pontian: Site in peninsular Malaysia where a Southeast Asian-type boat burial of the early centuries AD was found in association with pottery similar to that of Kuala Selinsing.

Pontic ware: Black-figured pottery made in Etruria during the Archaic period, possibly influenced by the techniques of Attica, Corinth, and Ionia.

Pontnewydd Cave: A cave site in north Wales occupied in the Lower Palaeolithic period by a stone industry of Upper Acheulian type, including artifacts made using the Levallois technique. Middle Pleistocene hominid remains are dated to 170,000–230,000 BP. The only other site in Britain to have produced hominid remains of this early period is Swanscombe.

population: In sampling methods, the sum of sample units selected in a date universe; a group of individual persons, objects, or items from which samples are taken for statistical measurement.

population, biological: The number of individuals of a species living in a restricted area, or the total number or combined weight of members of a plant species present in a given area. It is also defined as a group of organisms of a single species that at a given time are capable of interbreeding.

population, cultural: A specific society, such as the Shoshone or Arikara.

population estimation: The determination by archaeologists of the suspected population of an ancient culture. Estimates of the number of inhabitants of a settlement can be attempted on the basis of the number of houses, number of burials, or population density—but these estimates involve many assumptions.

population, statistical: A set of variates (counts, measurements, or characteristics) about which relevant inquiries can be made.

porcelain: Vitrified pottery with a white, fine-grained body that is usually translucent, as distinguished from earthenware, which is porous, opaque, and coarser. Porcelain is a fine form of pottery that is fired to a very high temperature to vitrify the clay. The name is derived from Portuguese *porcellana* ("little pigs," the name given to cowrie shells by early traders). Porcelain was developed by the Chinese from a long tradition of making stoneware in white clay. In the T'ang

Dynasty (AD 618–906) came proto-porcelains, followed by true porcelain in the Sung Dynasty (AD 960–1279). The three main types of porcelain are true, or hard-paste, porcelain; artificial, or soft-paste, porcelain; and bone china.

porphyry: A hard stone much used in Egyptian sculpture and sarcophagi, quarried in the eastern Egyptian desert. The volcanic rock is red, green, and black and is capable of taking a fine polish. It was a constituent element in the river pebbles used in the Hoabinhian industry. (*syn.* porphyrite)

portal dolmen: A form of megalithic chamber tomb found mainly in Ireland, but with outliers in Wales and Cornwall. It had an above-ground chamber consisting of a heavy capstone supported by three or more uprights in a way that made the capstone slope down from front to back—becoming narrower and lower toward the rear. It was approached through two tall portal slabs which formed a miniature porch or forecourt. The entrance to the chamber is often blocked by a slab, which may reach right up to the capstone. The scarce grave goods are similar to those from the court cairns, and both types of tomb are early in the Neolithic period, with dates close to 3800 BC. (*syn.* portal tomb)

Port Arthur: A penal complex on the Tasman Peninsula, Australia, used from 1830–1877. Historical archaeologists have studied it extensively. The partially restored ruins of the penal colony, including a church built by convicts, and the spot called "Isle of the Dead" (with unmarked convict graves), are now tourist attractions.

Port aux Choix: Archaic cemetery site in northwest Newfoundland, Canada, dated between the late 3rd–late 2nd millennia BC. The 100 burials had grave goods of ocher, polished slate, barbed bone points, toggled bone harpoon beads, shell beads and combs, needles, knives, and scrapers.

Portchester: The site of extensive Saxon occupation, a shore fort in Hampshire, southern England. There was some use of the site from the 1st century AD, although the Roman stone, flint, and tile walls are from a late 3rd century AD occupation. That lasted until AD 370 when the troops were shifted to nearby Bitterne (Roman Clausentum). The fort was deserted until Henry I constructed a keep in the northwest corner c. 1120, and a Romanesque church was built in 1133. A castle was built in 1160–1172 by Henry II. (*syn.* Roman Portus Adurni)

Port Essington: A pioneering example of historical archaeology in the northern territory of Australia. There are surviving structures of a Victoria military settlement of 1838–1849 when the British tried to settle tropical Australia. There is evidence of Aboriginal presence at the site. Relics of the settlement are preserved in the Cobourg Marine Park.

port-hole slab: A stone slab with a (usually) circular hole, often forming the entrance to a megalithic chamber tomb.

Sometimes the hole is square, or the entrance is made from two slabs set side by side with notches cut from their adjoining edges. These are found from western Europe to India. The holes are usually large enough to allow the passage of a human and generally served to provide restricted entrance to a tomb or part of a tomb.

Porticello: Site of a shipwreck in the Straits of Messina between Italy and Sicily, c. 440–430 BC. The cargo included lifesize bronze statuary, amphorae, ingots, inkpots, and fine pottery.

portico: In Greek and Roman architecture, colonnaded porch, annex, or entrance of a building, such as a palaestra. It could also be a covered walkway supported by regularly spaced columns. Porticoes formed the entrances to ancient Greek temples.

port of trade: Any town or city whose specific function is to act as a meeting place for foreign traders. It serves as a center for transshipment and storage of goods; the site is characterized by facilities for storage. Ports of trade, such as Tyre and Sidon, may have been important models of early long-distance trade.

positive feedback: A term used in systems of thinking to describe a response in which changing output conditions in the system stimulate further growth in input; one of the principal factors in generating system change or morphogenesis. It is a response to changing conditions that acts to stimulate further reactions in a system.

positive painting: The direct application of a design by use of pigments, as in painting pottery.

positivism: A philosophical position holding that all natural and social phenomena can be understood by determining their origins and causes. Developed by Auguste Comte in the 18th century, it emphasizes the testability of statements and the separation of data from the theories that explain them. It is the primary theoretical basis of the new archaeology.

Post-Classic or Postclassic: The final Pre-Columbian period in New World cultural history, following the collapse of Classic period civilizations, from 750/900 until AD 1520. The period is characterized by metalworking, complex urban societies, advanced commerce, militarism, imperialism, and secularism. It is traditionally dated from the fall of the Classic Maya in 900, but the collapse did not occur simultaneously throughout Mesoamerica.

postcranial skeleton: All bones other than those of the cranial skeleton.

Postglacial period: A period occurring following a glacial episode, especially that from the end of the Pleistocene Ice Age, c. 8300 BC to the present. The substages in northern Europe are: pre-Boreal (c. 8300–7700 BC), BOREAL (7700–

5550 BC), Atlantic (5550–3800 BC), Sub-Boreal (3800–1200 BC), and Sub-Atlantic (1200 BC to present). (*syn.* postglacial)

posthole: A hole dug or bored into the ground for holding an upright post. Once the post is installed, the remaining area of posthole is backfilled with earth and sometimes stronger packing material like stone. To archaeologists, postholes are the outline of a deteriorated post, indicating the former location of some structure. Even when the wood has decayed and the hole silted up or the post has been extracted, the existence of a posthole can be recognized by differences between the color and texture of its fill and those of the earth into which it was dug. A pattern of postholes may provide the only evidence for the size and shape of houses and other wooden structures. They can reveal that a settlement was surrounded by a palisade and presumably had enemies. (*syn.* post mold, post hole, post-pipe, post-pit)

postmortem: The term used to refer to events or processes that occurred to an individual's body after death.

Postoloprty: Neolithic site of the Lengyel culture in Bohemia, Czechoslovakia, where sites of several other periods are known. The Neolithic settlement dates from the 4th millennium BC and has a timber-framed trapezoidal longhouse with an antechamber and four domed ovens and bedding trenches.

Postpalatial: In Minoan Crete, the period after the destruction of the palaces, a part of the chronological system for the area devised by Platon. It is the same as Late Minoan IIIA2–IIIC, c. 1375–1100 BC, in traditional chronology.

postprocessual archaeology: A relatively new school of archaeological thinking that uses the ideational strategy and cautions against the shortcomings of scientific methods and the new (or processual) archaeology. It was formulated in reaction to the perceived limitations of functional-processual archaeology and pushes for an "individualizing" or "idiosyncratic" approach that is influenced by structuralism, critical theory, and neo-Marxist thought. It emphasizes social factors in human societies, both the active role of individuals as decision makers and the meaning-laden contexts in which decisions are made. It is based on the notions that culture must be understood as sets of symbols that evoke meanings and that these vary depending on particular contexts of use and the histories of artifacts and the people who use them. (*syn.* post-processual explanation, postprocessual approach)

potassium-argon dating: An isotopic method of dating the age of a rock or mineral by measuring the rate at which potassium 40, a radioactive form of this element, decays into argon. It is used primarily to measure lava flows and tuffs and ocean floor basalts. Potassium, which is present in most rocks and minerals, has a single radioactive isotope, K40. This decays by two different processes in calcium 40 and argon 40. Although 89% decays to calcium 40, it is not suitable for measurement because most rocks contain calcium 40 as a primary element, and the amount caused by the decay of K40 cannot be determined. The remaining 11% decays into the gas argon 40, and this can be measured, along with the amount of potassium in the sample, to get a date. Dates produced by using this technique have been checked by fission track dating. The technique is best used on material more than 100,000 years old—such as the dating of layers associated with the earliest remains of hominids, notably in the Olduvai Gorge. Lava flows embedded with the deposits containing archaeological material have been dated. (*syn.* K-A dating; potassium argon dating)

potato: One of the 150 tuber-bearing species of the genus Solanum (family Solanaceae). The potato is considered by most botanists a native of the Peruvian-Bolivian Andes and is one of the world's main food crops. At the time of the Spanish conquest, potatoes were grown all over the highlands from Colombia to Chile. Unlike maize, the potato flourishes at high altitudes and was the basic staple of many of the societies of the Altiplano, such as Tiahuanaco. (*syn.* common potato, white potato, Irish potato)

pot boilers: The name given to stones, often flint, which have been heated in a fire and have a white or grayish cracked appearance. They are thought to have been used to heat water for cooking purposes.

pothole: A depression or pit left by a pothunter.

pothunter or pot-hunter: Any person who collects archaeological objects or excavates sites in an unscientific manner for personal gain and whose actions result in the destruction of surrounding data. Pothunting is illegal artifact collection.

potin: A bronze alloy with a high tin content, between standard bronze and speculum. It was used particularly for a type of coinage current in western Europe and in India in the first centuries BC and AD with a tin content between 7–27%.

potlatch: The ceremonial distribution of property and gifts to affirm or reaffirm social status, unique to Native Americans of the Northwest Pacific coast in the 19th century.

pot lid: A small portion (flake) of stone that may "pop off" a core during heat treatment because of rapid heating or excessive temperature, creating many small flake scars on the surface.

Potocka Cave: Upper Palaeolithic site in Slovenia's mountains with artifacts and faunal remains of the last glacial. The assemblage includes side scrapers, end scrapers, and retouched blades of the Aurignacian.

potsherd: Any pottery fragment—piece of broken pot or other earthenware item—that has archaeological significance. Often abbreviated to sherd, potsherds are an invaluable part of the archaeological record because they are well preserved. The analysis of ceramic changes recorded in potsherds has become one of the primary techniques used by archaeologists in assigning components and phases to times and cultures. (*syn.* sherd, shard)

potter's comb: An implement with serrated edge capable of producing an impressed decoration on pottery. A marbled effect was sometimes achieved (as in Chinese pottery of the T'ang Dynasty) by mingling, with a comb, slips of contrasting colors after they had been applied to the vessel. Potter's combs were made of stone, bone, shell, or wood.

potter's wheel: A wheel rotating horizontally, which assists a potter in shaping clay into vessels. The development of the slow, or hand-turned, wheel as an adjunct to pottery manufacture led to the kick wheel, rotated by foot, which became the potter's principal tool. The potter throws the clay onto a rapidly rotating disk and shapes his pot by manipulating it with both hands. By the Uruk phase in Mesopotamia, c. 3400 BC, the fast wheel was already in use. It spread slowly, reaching Europe with the Minoans c. 2400 BC, and Britain with the Belgae in the 1st century BC. Its presence can be taken to imply an organized pottery industry, often also using an advanced type of kiln.

pottery: One of the oldest of the decorative arts, consisting of objects made of clay and hardened with heat. The objects are commonly useful. Earthenware is the oldest and simplest form of pottery; stoneware is a pottery compound that is fired at a sufficiently high temperature to cause it to vitrify and become extremely hard; and porcelain, finer than stoneware and generally translucent, is made by adding feldspar to kaolin and then firing at a high temperature. Its raw material is common, shaping and baking it are simple, and it can be given an infinite variety of forms and decorations. Pottery sherds, almost indestructible, are one of the commonest finds and are very important to archaeologists. It is often one of the clearest indicators of cultural differences, relations, and developments, and its techniques of manufacture can be comparatively easily recovered by ceramic analysis. It can be shown whether it was modeled, coil built, or wheel made. The nature of its fabric, ware, or body can be identified, as can any surface treatment such as slip, paint, or burnish. The wide range of methods of decoration can also be studied. As the date of manufacture can usually be fixed, pieces of pottery give clues to archaeologists as to the date of other finds at the site. Petrological analysis of inclusions has been used to trace the source of pot clays and thus reconstruct ancient trade in pottery. Archaeologists usually call fired pot clay the "fabric" of a piece of pottery. Texture, mineralogy, and color of fabric may be used to describe and classify pottery.

Poverty Point: A site in northern Louisiana with a spectacular group of late Archaic sites, c. 1300–400 BC, in the Wood-

land stage. The site consisted of six concentric octagons, each formed of earthern ridges that seem to have been used as dwelling areas. There are also two mounds, and from the larger one the vernal and autumnal equinoxes can be observed directly over the center of the village. Artifacts include numerous clay balls used for cooking in lieu of heated stones, microliths, stone smoking pipes and vessels, clay figurines, and fiber-tempered pottery sherds. The clay balls are found in thousands, both here and at other sites in the Lower Mississippi valley. A high level of social organization is indicated by the presence of earthworks like that at Poverty Point, but there is very little evidence of the practice of agriculture.

Poznan: A city in west-central Poland, one of the centers of the early Polish kingdom established under Mieszko I during the second half of the 10th century. Beginning as a small stronghold in the 9th century, Poznan became the capital of Poland (with Gniezno) and the residence of Poland's first two sovereigns. The first Polish bishopric was founded here in 968. A 10th-century rampart and many relics of the Slavic period have been found.

pozzolana: Volcanic ash or dust found in central Italy, especially near Pozzuoli. It was used to fortify Roman concrete and line water channels. The Romans used it from the 2nd century BC onward. The natural properties of this and related materials may well have been of central importance in the Romans' rapid development of the technology of concrete buildings in the late Republican and early Imperial periods. (*syn.* pozzuolana)

praenomen: An Egyptian king's first cartouche name, which he adopted on his accession. It is a statement about the god Re, later with additional epithets, such as Menkheprure (Tuthmosis IV) "Re is enduring of manifestations." It is also the term for the given name or forename of a Roman personal name; the family name was the nomen. (*syn.* throne name)

praetorium: A Roman commander's house in a fort or fortress, rectangular in shape with a central court surrounded by a verandah onto which all rooms opened. Outside the house, but attached to it, was the private bathhouse. The term eventually meant any large house or palace.

Praia das Macas: Two Chalcolithic chambered tombs near Lisbon, Portugal. In its first phase, there was a simple rock-cut tomb, and subsequently a passage grave with partially corbelled chamber was added. The rock-cut tomb contained decorated slate plaques and other material of Late Neolithic or early Chalcolithic type with a date of c. 2300 BC. The later tomb, which blocked the entrance to the earlier tomb, contained about 150 burials, Beaker pottery, Palmela points, and a tanged dagger. Its date is 1690 BC.

Prairie phase: Early Woodland-Middle Woodland group in southwestern Wisconsin, dated to AD 100. Prairie Ware, sandy-paste vessels with incised, corded, and fingernail-punctated decoration, was associated with it.

Prambanan: A complex of Hindu and Buddhist temples on a plain near Yogyakarta, Java, built in the late 8th and 9th centuries AD. These stone monuments were built by the rulers of Mataram and include Loro Jonggrang, Candi Sewu, and Plaosan; their many inscriptions are a rich source of historical information. (*syn.* Prambanan Group)

preaching cross: A class of monumental sculpture unique to the British Isles, developed from the 7th century onward. The tall, tapering cross shaft rested on a plinth or base and carried a three-armed cross head. Both the cross and the shaft were usually ornamented with Christian figures and other decorative motifs. They may be Celtic interpretations of Mediterranean crosses and Iron Age stelae. (*syn.* standing cross)

Preah Vihear: A large mountaintop temple built by the Khmer king Suryavarman, located on the border of Thailand and northern Cambodia. It has been described as one of the most beautiful natural sites of the whole of Asia.

Pre-Axumite period: A term applied to the developed societies of south Arabian origin in the northern part of the Ethiopian plateau, c. 5th century BC– 1st century AD. South Arabian elements assimilated through influence of the kingdom of Sheba into a culture developed from the Neolithic. Texts engraved on stone using south Arabian script have been found. There is evidence of influence from Meroe, with Ethiopia as a crossroads for trade, traffic, and culture. These societies provided the base from which the kingdom of Axum rose to prominence during the first centuries AD.

Pre-Boreal: A division of Holocene chronology, which began about 10,000 years ago and ended about 9,500 years ago. The Pre-Boreal Climatic Interval preceded the Boreal Climatic Interval and was a time of increasing climatic moderation. Birch-pine forests and tundra were dominant. It is a subdivision of the Flandrian Interglacial and represents the start of the Flandrian. (*syn.* Pre-Boreal Climatic Interval)

preceramic: Before ceramics, referring to a period antedating the use of ceramics or pottery.

Preceramic Period: The earliest of a seven-period chronological construction used in Peruvian archaeology, c. 9000–1800 BC, starting with the first human occupation and ending with the introduction of ceramic artifacts. It is usually subdivided into six periods and is characterized by a variety of subsistence patterns and by a lack of ceramics. The first two periods (up to 8000 BC) represent a subsistence based on hunting. The third period, c. 8000–6000 BC, is seen as transitional from hunting to hunting and gathering. Period four c.

6000–4000 BC, had cyclical, seasonal migration. In Preceramic V, c. 4000–2500 BC, the lomas dried up, and people tended to be sedentary; agriculture supplied an increasing part of the diet. Large habitation sites, ceremonial centers, and agriculture appear increasingly in Preceramic VI, c. 2500–1800 BC. There are lithic complexes in the Early Preceramic, followed by an Archaic Period with foraging populations and the beginning of domestic and ceremonial architecture. The preceramic was followed by the Initial Period.

Pre-Classic or Preclassic period: A period in Mesoamerican archaeology during which agriculture formed the basis of settled village life, c. 2000 BC–AD 250. The earliest writing—glyphs in Mesoamerica began in this period. The Olmec was the first culture to appear in the Preclassic. A similar level was attained in Peru at about the same time (Chavín). In many other areas, life remained on a Formative level until the Spanish conquest. The final phase of the Pre-Classic cultures of the central highland forms a transition from the village to the city, from rural to urban life. (*syn.* Formative period)

Pre-Columbian: A term used to describe the period in the Americas before European contact. Pre-Columbian civilization refers to the aboriginal American Indian cultures that evolved in Mesoamerica and the Andean region before Spanish exploration and conquest in the 16th century.

Predionica: Late Neolithic settlement of the early Vinca culture in southern Serbia. The first of three occupation horizons has a radiocarbon date of c. 4330 BC. Monumental fired-clay figurine heads have been discovered, which were made by abstract modeling with plastic features reinforced by incised lines.

Predmostí: Palaeolithic site near Prerov in northeastern Moravia, Czechoslovakia. Over 20 skeletons of males, females, and children were found in a large communal grave, associated with an Eastern Gravettian layer. The age of the grave is probably around 26,870 BC. Some of the males had marked Neanderthaloid features, but the overall morphology was Cro-Magnon. Middle Palaeolithic artifacts, probably of the Early Glacial and Upper Palaeolithic (Aurignacian, Eastern Gravettian) levels have been found. There are ivory and bone tools, pendants, and portable art.

Pre-Dorset: A term for a group of Arctic cultures and complexes characterized by microblades, knives, scrapers, and burins and coming before the Dorset culture (c. 3000 BP). They hunted seal, walrus, and some land animals and originated in the 5th millennium BP. Pre-Dorset is part of the Arctic Small Tool tradition.

predynastic period: The period before recorded history in Egypt and before it became a unified state in c. 3100 BC. The term *predynastic* denotes the period of emerging cultures that preceded the establishment of the 1st Dynasty in Egypt. In the late 5th millennium BC, there began to emerge patterns of civilization that displayed characteristics deserving to be called Egyptian. The accepted sequence of predynastic cultures is based on the excavations of Sir Flinders Petrie at Naqadad, al-ʻAmirah (el-ʻÂmra), and al-Jazirah (el-Gezira). Another somewhat earlier stage of predynastic culture has been identified at al-Badari in Upper Egypt. Until recently, most of our knowledge of predynastic Egypt was derived from the excavation of graves. Predynastic communities appeared in the section of the Nile Valley immediately south of Asyut. Large settlements were established, notably that at Hierakonpolis. Some time after 5000 BC, the raising of crops was introduced, probably on a horticultural scale, in small, local cultures that seem to have penetrated southward through Egypt into the oases and the Sudan. The food-producing economy was based on the cultivation of emmer wheat and barley and on the herding of cattle and small stock, together with some fishing, hunting, and use of wild plant foods. Highly specialized craftsmen emerged to build vessels, make copper objects, weave linen, and make basketry and pottery. A series of small states arose, until around 3100 BC; the unified kingdom of Ancient Egypt came into being. (*syn.* Pre-Dynastic Egypt; Predynastic)

Pre-Eskimo archaeology: The study of the time before man emerged or entered the New World via the Bering Strait, c. 20,000–40,000 years ago.

prefecture: An administrative division of a Chinese or Japanese province; Japan has urban and metropolitan prefectures.

preform: A bifacially flaked piece of stone that exhibits both percussion and pressure flaking, and that usually is triangular in shape, indicating that it was being fashioned into a projectile point or knife.

prehistoric archaeology: The branch of archaeology that deals with the times before the beginnings of recorded history. The area of archaeology concerned with preliterate or nonliterate societies, in contrast to historical archaeology. In North America, prehistoric archaeology is considered part of the discipline of anthropology.

prehistory: Any period for which there is no documentary evidence and the study of cultures before written history or of more recent cultures lacking formal historical records. In the strict sense, *history* is an account of the past recovered from written records, but such an account can be prepared from other sources, notably archaeology. The term *prehistory* was coined by Daniel Wilson in 1851 to cover the story of man's development before the appearance of writing. It is succeeded by protohistory, the period for which we have some records but must still rely largely on archaeological evidence to give us a coherent account. Prehistory differs from history in dealing with the activities of a society or culture, not of

the individual; it is restricted to the material evidence that has survived. (*syn.* prehistoric period)

pre-Neanderthal: A term used to refer to the Acheulian industry people, who are believed to have developed into the Neanderthals.

Prepalatial: In Minoan Crete, the period before the construction of the palaces, a part of the chronological system for the area devised by Platon. It is the same as Early Minoan I–II, c. 3000–2000 BC, in traditional chronology.

prepared-core technique: A method of stone-tool production whereby cores themselves are shaped to produce flakes of a desired form, instead of the flakes being shaped after their removal from the core.

Pre-Pottery Neolithic: Early phases of the Neolithic of the Near East/Levant, characterized by the practice of agriculture and permanent settlement before the use of pottery. Two phases of the Pre-Pottery Neolithic have been identified: the PPNA phase, with radiocarbon dates in the range 8500–7600 BC; and PPNB, dated c. 7600–6000 BC. Recent work suggests a third phase, the PPNC, dated to 6200–5900 BC.

Pre-Pottery Neolithic A: A Palestinian village-based culture dated 8500–7600 BC, first defined at Jericho. It is derived from the Natufian culture, making use of and developing Natufian architecture (roundhouses). It offers evidence of the first attempts at agriculture in the Near East, although still in a hunting context. (*syn.* PPNA)

Pre-Pottery Neolithic B: Levantine culture pre-dating the use of pottery, dated 7600–6000 BC, and first defined at Jericho. It originated in Syria and is characterized by rectangular buildings with lime-coated or plastered floors, by the cultivation of cereal crops, and by the beginnings of small-animal husbandry. Toward the end, it saw the first expansion of agriculture and the spread of Neolithic culture beyond its semiarid zone toward the temperate coastal regions of Syria (Ras Shamra) and the desert oases. Pottery began to appear sporadically. (*syn.* PPNB)

pre-projectile point complex: A term applied to a complex consisting of the earliest archaeological evidence of humans on the North American continent. It is characterized by the lack of stone projectile points, which can be dated.

pressure flaking: A method for the secondary working of flint tools involving the use of a hard object against a stone core or mass to remove flakes. The roughed-out form of the tool is sharpened and finished by exerting pressure with a bone, antler, stone, or stick on the edge to remove small thin chips. By using a short, pointed instrument to pry, not strike, the tiny flakes leave only the smallest scars. As the least violent and most advanced of the methods of working stone, it gave the craftsman the ultimate in control for the removal of materials in the shaping of an implement. Fine-edged weapons, such as daggers, arrowheads, and spear heads, can be produced by using this technique. This technique was first widely used in the Solutrean c. 18,000 BC and is associated with some New World points. (*syn.* pressure-flaking; pressure technique, pressure method)

pre-state society: Any small-scale society without highly stratified class structure.

prestige goods: Exchange goods, often limited in range, to which a society ascribes high status or value. Examples are amber, copper, glass beads, and marine shells. High-prestige goods served to enhance the political value of the trade to local elites who directed and controlled it.

Prezletice: Lower Palaeolithic site just outside Prague, Czechoslovakia, with mammals of Cromerian type dated c. 0.7 million years old. Artifacts pre-date the Middle Pleistocene; the assemblage includes chopping tools, crude bifaces, and flakes.

Priene: Small Hellenistic Greek town in Asia Minor, important as a settlement of the 4th century BC. The lower city was laid out in a Hippodamian grid pattern. There was an akropolis, city walls, agora, bouleuterion, pyrtaneion, stadium, gymnasium, theater, and temples. It is important for these examples of 4th-century BC and Hellenistic urban architecture. Priene was probably one of the very early Ionian Greek colonies.

primary burial: The initial or direct inhumation of the fully articulated corpse. (*syn.* primary inhumation)

primary classification: Any classification based on directly observable attributes, often carried out by archaeologists in the field.

primary context: An undisturbed associated, matrix, and provenience; the condition when they have not been disturbed since the original deposition of archaeological data.

primary cremation: The burning of a dead person on a pyre in the grave.

primary flake: An unretouched flake of stone from which smaller flakes are removed during knapping. A flake with its dorsal aspect completely covered by cortex. (*syn.* cortical flake)

Primary Neolithic: A term used to describe the earliest British Neolithic cultures, such as the Windmill Hill culture. These cultures were thought to be intrusive early farming groups.

primary refuse: Unwanted objects or materials found in the context where they were used and discarded.

primary silt: The initial silt from the top and sides of a newly dug feature (ditch, gully, pit, etc.) that falls naturally to the bottom. It occurs as a result of the immediate weathering

of the sides and top because of wind or the action of precipitation. Unless the feature was cleaned of this material in antiquity, it may be recognized in many archaeological features, and any material found in it may date from around the time of the original digging. However, a more ancient artifact lying on the ground surface close to the lip of the ditch may tumble into the fill when the edges of the trench crumble and collapse. (*syn.* rapid silt)

primate: Member of the order of mammals that includes monkeys, apes, and humans. The mammalian order includes two suborders: the prosimians (lemurs, lorises, and tarsiers) and the anthropoids (monkeys, apes, and humans). According to fossil records, primates originated in the Late Cretaceous (97.5–66.4 million years ago) as forest-dwelling creatures. Evidence that modern man is a descendant of these early primates was first provided by Charles Darwin in his *Origin of Species* (1859).

prime mover: A concept in the study of the origins of civilization, meaning a single, primary cause generating urban societies. This includes crucial factors that stimulate cultural change: the causal variable in a simple, direct, and inevitable relation, resulting in a particular effect. Many theorists considered irrigation a prime mover of Egyptian civilization.

Primeval Mound: In Egyptian antiquity, the hill that emerged from the primeval waters of Nun, which was the principal symbol of the act of creation. The Memphite god Tatjenen was a personification of the hill itself. It is the site of creation claimed by all temples and recorded especially in the temple of Edfu, which was guarded by two lords, the Companions of the Most Divine Heart. (*syn.* High Dune)

primitive valuables: A term describing the tokens of wealth and prestige, often especially valued items, that were used in the ceremonial exchange systems of nonstate societies. Examples include the shell necklaces and bracelets of the kula system.

principal component analysis: A technique of multivariate analysis designed to reduce redundancy in a body of data and to clarify underlying structural relations. New variables are calculated in a way that most of the variation in the original distribution is contained in the first few components. The principal components may then be plotted or analyzed by conventional means. It can be calculated by computer. (*syn.* principal components)

principal investigator: The archaeologist who prepares the research design and manages its execution. (*syn.* PI)

probabilistic sampling: An archaeological sampling method based on formal statistical criteria in selecting sample units to be investigated. It is designed to draw reliable general conclusions about a site or region, based on small sample areas, and allows evaluation of how representative the sample is with respect to the data population. Four types of sampling strategies are recognized: (1) simple random sampling; (2) stratified random sampling; (3) systematic sampling; (4) stratified systematic sampling.

probe: A tool consisting of a metal rod or tube pushed into unexcavated deposits to locate as yet unexposed hard features such as walls, floors, or bedrock. It is also used for exploring subsurface stratigraphy and is less expensive than a core but works down only a few meters. (*syn.* soil probe)

problematic: Any object that presents a problem that archaeologists admit they cannot solve.

problem orientation: The question or issue that a particular archaeological research effort is designed to address.

process: Cultural change that takes place as a result of interactions between a cultural system's elements and the culture's environment. (*syn.* cultural process)

processional way: A route, often stone or brick paved, along which the statues of the gods were carried at festivals. The term is used particularly for the road leading from the Temple of Marduk to the Ishtar Gate and Akitu House temple in Babylon. About 615 BC, the Chaldeans connected the city's temples to the royal palaces with a major Processional Way, a road in which burned bricks and carefully shaped stones were laid in bituminous mortar. In ancient Egyptian towns, there is evidence of the use of paved processional roads leading to the temples. In architecture, the ambulatory is a continuation of the aisled spaces on either side of the nave around the apse or chancel to form a continuous processional way.

processual archaeology: A branch of archaeology that seeks to understand the nature of cultural change by a study of the variables that cause it, usually in a manner characteristic of "new archaeology." After scientific observation, questions are formulated, hypotheses are formed to answer the questions and are then tested against the data. The ultimate aim is the formulation of laws. This approach stresses the dynamic relation between social and economic aspects of culture and the environment. The earlier functional-processual archaeology has been contrasted with cognitive-processual archaeology, where the emphasis is on integrating ideological and symbolic aspects. (*syn.* new archaeology)

procurement: Any process by which materials are obtained from the environment, such as the collecting of plant foods. Much of animal evolution involves adaptation for the procurement of food.

profile: A vertical wall, section, or face of an excavation pit that exposes the lateral relations, archaeological features, structures, stratigraphy—and their relations. By extension, a profile is a record or graphic representation of these, including color, soil type, features, and content. Soil profiles consist of a number of layers, or horizons, which result from soil-forming processes. (*syn.* section)

profile drawing: A two-dimensional graphic representation similar to a section drawing except that features are depicted in outline without showing their internal composition. (*syn.* profile view)

proglacial: Land forms and deposits just beyond the margin of glacial ice; the deposition or environments at the edge of an ice sheet or glacier. This includes lakes, streams, loess, and periglacial features. Melt water released from the glacial mass carries loads of material eroded by the ice, and this material is deposited in the proglacial area.

prognathic: A term in physical anthropology referring to the forward projection, beyond the vertical plane, of the alveolar process and mandible (mouth area). This protruding form contrasts with orthognathic, or straighter faced, appearance.

progress: A philosophical position holding that change in natural or social phenomena implies increase in complexity or sophistication and gradual betterment.

projectile point: The general term for the stone, bone, or wooden tip of a projectile—the point that is attached to a weapon such as an arrow, dart, lance, or spear. Among such points are arrowheads, which are usually of small size, and dart and spear points, which may be quite large. Such tools are valuable in reconstruction of culture history.

Prolom II: Middle Palaeolithic cave site in the Crimea, Ukraine, occupied from possibly early in the last glacial. Artifacts include side scrapers, bifacial foliates, and worked bone and are assigned to the Ak-Kaya culture.

Promontory culture: A culture sometimes identified with the Fremont culture in northern Utah which is now considered an early phase of the late prehistoric groups that followed the Fremont. The people hunted bison and lived in caves.

promontory fort: A defended area on the top of a hill, spur, or cliff, with the defensive works blocking the easiest approach along the neck of the peninsula. The other sides would rely chiefly or soley on their natural defenses.

promontory peg: A type of carved wooden artifact, probably used as the trigger for a snare, and first recognized at the Promontory Caves, northwest of Salt Lake City, Utah.

pronaos: In Greek architecture, the room or shallow porch in front of the sanctuary (naos) of a temple; the vestibule in front of the cella. The cella of a Greek temple was entered through this and the cult-statue approached.

prondnik: A type of stone artifact that is an asymmetrical scraping tool flaked on both sides and found on some late Middle Neolithic sites of Central Europe.

prone: A term used to describe the position of a burial where the body is lying flat on the stomach or with the face down.

proportional pollen counting: A type of pollen analysis carried out by determining the proportion of different pollen types in each sample. Proportions are usually expressed as percentages of total tree (arboreal) pollen. This method is fairly quick as only a fraction of the grains present in a sample need be counted. Its main disadvantage is that percentages can never indicate actual numbers of grains falling to earth, which is solved by Absolute Pollen Counting.

propylaeum: The entrance gate to a classical temenos, temple, or other sacred enclosure; the gateway that stands in front of a pylon. At the Akropolis in Athens, the monumental Propylaia (Propylaeum) was built in 437 BC on the same orientation as the Parthenon. This monumental entrance had various forms generally involving a colonnade (of four columns) positioned in front of an entrance cut into a continuous enclosure wall. The propylaeum may have columns both outside and inside the enclosure wall. (*syn.* pl. propylaea; propylon)

proscenium: A single-story structure located in front of the skene and protruding into the orchestra of a Classical theater. It was often faced with half-columns and was probably used as a raised stage. It was the frame or arch separating the stage from the auditorium, through which the action of a play was viewed. In the ancient Greek theater, the proscenium originally referred to a row of colonnades, supporting a raised acting platform (logeion), and afterward to the entire acting area. (*syn.* proskenion)

Prosek, Frantisek (1922–1958): Czechoslovakian archaeologist who specialized in the Palaeolithic and was instrumental in establishing the stratigraphic position in the Szeletian industry in Central Europe.

Proskouriakoff, Tatiana (1909–1985): Mesoamerican archaeologist and epigrapher born in Siberia, who worked to decipher the Maya glyphs. She established the use of stelae to document dynastic sequences and deciphered glyphs of conflicts, adding substantially to an understanding of the Maya civilization. She wrote *An Album of Maya Architecture* (1963, 1978).

prospect: A site where stone was tested for suitability, whether the stone was used or not.

prostyle: A facade composed solely of free-standing columns.

protein residue analysis: The recovery and identification of proteins preserved in or on archaeological materials.

protein sequencing: The analysis of the sequence of the amino acids that make up a protein. Comparison of the sequences in different species is one way of working out their degrees of interrelations. Protein sequencing is one of several molecular methods developed for estimating genetic change during evolution.

Protemnodon: An extinct species of giant kangaroo. It has been found in several Australian and New Guinean sites. It lived during the Pleistocene.

prothesis: In Greek antiquity, the lying-in-state of a corpse. It is depicted in pottery scenes and on ceramic monumental funerary markers as having occurred mainly at home, particularly in the 8th century BC.

proto-: Indicating an early developmental stage of the main root word, such as prototype, proto-Villanovan, protohistoric. It means "beginning" or "giving rise to."

Protoclassic period: In Mesoamerica, the period at the end of the Preclassic and immediately before the Classic period, c. 50 BC–AD 250. It refers to the cultures of the Maya area, which were transitioning between Preclassic and Classic.

Proto-Elamite: The earliest texts written in an undeciphered script by the civilization of Elam in the late 4th to early 3rd millennia BC. Like the early Sumerian writing, Proto-Elamite is pictographic, and it may well be derived from the slightly earlier Sumerian script. Many of the Proto-Elamite clay tablets bear numerical symbols only, and it is assumed that it was used for accounting and trade. Proto-Elamite tablets have been found over a surprisingly wide area of modern Iran: Warka, Susa, Godin, Sialk, Tepe Malyan, Tepe Yahya, Acropole, Sialk, and Shahri-I Sokhta and are usually associated with a distinctive ceramic assemblage and style of seal.

Proto-geometric: A type of Greek painted pottery and the period of its making, c. 1050–900 BC, which succeeded the Mycenaean. The style emerged at Athens and then other regions. Decoration was severely geometric and included concentric circles and the use of zigzags and triangles. (*syn.* Protogeometric)

protohistoric archaeology: The study of the period just before the beginning of recorded history. Protohistory is the earliest historic periods—those with minimal documentary evidence.

protohistory: The period in any area following prehistory and preceding the appearance of coherent history derived from written records. It is a transitional period between prehistory and recorded history, for which both archaeological and historical data are employed. There are several more detailed definitions, such as (1) a time when nonliterate aboriginal peoples had access to European goods but had not had face-to-face contact; (2) periods during which historical documentation is fragmentary or not directly from the society being studied; and (3) the period of AD 1250–1519 in Mesoamerica, which followed the Postclassic and ends just before the Spanish conquest (there are historic documents for this period). (*syn.* protohistoric era, protohistoric period)

proto-maiolica: A type of tin-glazed wares made in Sicily and southern Italy from shortly before 1200 until the 15th century. The appearance of these wares coincided with the importation of tin-glazed pottery from North Africa, particularly the Maghreb. The jugs and bowls were usually painted with various animals or coats-of-arms in the variety of colors before glaze was applied. The best-known proto-maiolicas are from northern Apulia; they were traded extensively to local villages and across the Adriatic to Yugoslavia.

protome: Decorative motif in the form of a human or animal head.

Proto-Neolithic: A transitional period between the hunting-and-gathering cultures of the Epipalaeolithic and the farming cultures of the Aceramic Neolithic (c. 9300–8500 BC). The term is used variously, but here it includes the Pre-Pottery Neolithic A of the Levant and the early stages of the adoption of characteristic Neolithic traits such as animal and plant domestication and the manufacture of pottery.

proton gradiometer: An instrument used in magnetic surveying for detecting the presence of magnetic anomalies; it takes continuous measurements of relative vertical change in intensity of field strength. There are two decorator bottles filled with water or alcohol placed at either end of a staff two meters long and held vertically during operation. Protons that form the nuclei of hydrogen atoms in the liquid gyrate or precess; the frequency of precession is identical in the two bottles if no anomaly is present. Any disturbance in the magnetic intensity caused, for example, by a buried feature, results in a different frequency in the two bottles.

proton magnetometer: An instrument used in magnetic surveying for detecting changes in magnetic field intensity; it takes intermittent measurements of absolute field strength. The detector consists of a bottle of alcohol or water around which is wound an electrical coil of 1,000 turns. The protons, which form the nuclei of hydrogen atoms in the liquid, spin and gyrate in their attempt to align themselves in the direction of the Earth's magnetic field intensity. A current of 1 amp is passed through the coil for 3 seconds, which aligns the majority of the protons in the direction of the magnetic field thus produced. When this current is cut off, the protons attempt to realign in the direction of the Earth's magnetic field; the speed of gyration, or frequency of precession, is amplified and measured in the instrument. This measurement reflects any alteration in the magnetic intensity caused by the presence of fired structures, soil disturbances (e.g., pits, ditches, etc.), or iron objects. It is a highly sensitive magnetometer, used in subsurface detection to record variations in the Earth's magnetic field caused by buried iron, kilns, hearths, pits, or ditches. (*syn.* proton precession magnetometer)

Protopalatial: In Minoan Crete, the period of the Old or First palaces, a part of the chronological system for the area devised by Platon. It is the same as Middle Minoan I–II, c. 2000–1700 BC, in traditional chronology.

Protosesklo: A term used for the Greek Early Neolithic period or the Early Neolithic in Thessaly.

Proto-Three Kingdoms: The protohistoric period of the Korean peninsula, AD c. 1–300, which preceded the Three Kingdoms period of Koguryo, Silla, and the Paekche. Archaeological finds of the period are mainly from Lelang and Koguryo in the north and Samhan in the south. Bronze and iron were used, and iron was made at shell midden sites on the southern coast. In actuality, the Three Kingdoms period was c. 57 BC–AD 668. (*syn.* Late Iron Age, Lelang)

prototype: A prototype is the first in a series of artifacts, the earliest form of some type that later develops—such as the first of a new type of pottery. A prototype is a model after which objects are copied: The prototype for a clay wine jar could be a metal wine jug of similar shape.

protoworld language: A single, original language, hypothesized to have been spoken by the first modern humans in Africa, from which all modern languages may have evolved. It has been suggested that linguistic traces of this language have survived into the present.

protruding foot beaker: The typical vessel of the Late Neolithic in the Netherlands with radiocarbon dates from c. 3200–2400 BC. The basic form has a splayed neck, S-shaped profile, and flat everted base. It has cord ornament, dentate spatula impressions, or herringbone incisions. The vessel also defines the culture, which had burials in either a single flat grave or a pit under a barrow, and used the battle-ax. The culture represents the Dutch branch of the widespread corded ware–battle-ax complex, or single-grave cultures. In the Netherlands, there is some hybridization between the Protruding Foot Beaker culture and the Bell Beaker.

provenience: The source, origin, or location of an artifact or feature and the recording of same. It is the position of an archaeological find in time and space, recorded three-dimensionally. The horizontal reference system is usually some form of grid tied to a reference datum; the vertical dimension is reference to a vertical datum. (*syn.* provenance)

provenience lot: A defined spatial area, in either two dimensions (for surface data) or three dimensions (for excavated data), used as a minimal unit for provenience determination and recording.

proximal: The part of a long bone (arm or leg), which is nearest the body; the opposite end is the distal. The term also means close to the center or to the point of attachment and can refer to geological features as well as anatomical features.

proximal shoulder angle: A term describing the shape of the base on a projectile point, based on the angle formed by the hafting notch and the axis of the shaft.

prytaneion: In Greek antiquity, a building for the prytaneis, the administrative officials/inner executive council of a Greek city-state; the town hall of a Greek or Hellenistic city-state. Its origin may be in palaces of tyrants or kings, combining official with residential functions. In Athens, it had a central courtyard with rooms around it; the so-called tholos, a round building used as an office, was nearby. At Athens, for example, a group of 50 prytanies ("presidents, chiefs"), elected by lot and serving for short periods in rotation, acted as committee to the boule ("council"). Ambassadors, distinguished foreigners, and citizens who had done signal service were entertained there. Prytanea are attested at Sigeum in the Troas from the 6th century BC and at various dates in Cyzicus, Erythrae, Priene, Ephesus, Epidamnus, Rhodes, and Olympia. (*syn.* prytaneium, prytaneum; Greek prytaneion)

Przeworsk culture: Late Iron Age culture in the Vistula and Bug drainages in southeast Poland of the La Tène period. It is known mainly from graves, which have metal artifacts and fibulae.

Psamtek: Birth name given to three kings of the 26th (or Saite) Dynasty (664–525 BC): Psamtek I Wahibra (reigned 664–610 BC), who expelled the Assyrians from Egypt and reunited the country, founded the 26th Dynasty. Psamtek II Neferibra (reigned 595–589 BC), conducted an important expedition against the kingdom of Cush. Psamtek III Ankhkaenra (reigned 526–525 BC) was the last king of the dynasty and failed to block the Persian invasion of 525 and was later executed for treason. (*syn.* Psammetichus, Psamtik)

psephoperibombetrios: In Geek antiquity, a type of drinking cup with a hollow rim into which pellets were inserted. When it was shaken, it may have attracted attention for more wine or was used to accompany the symposium's music. There are 4th century BC kantharoi examples.

pseudo-archaeology: The use of selective archaeological evidence, real or imagined, to promulgate nonscientific, fictional accounts of the past. (*syn.* pseudoarchaeology)

psuedo-artifact: Any object that appears to be a manmade tool, but actually has been molded by natural forces.

pseudo-isodomic: A Greek masonry style with squared blocks placed in alternating wide and narrow layers.

Psusennes: Birth name taken by two kings of the 21st Dynasty, who ruled from Tanis in the Delta at the start of the Third Intermediate Period: Psusennes I Aakheperra Setepenamun (ruled c. 1045–c. 997 BC) and Psusennes II Titkheperura Setepenra (ruled c. 964–c. 950 BC). (*syn.* Pasebakhaenniut)

Ptah: In Egyptian religion, the creator god and maker of things, the patron of crafts and craftsmen, represented as a mummy. His chief cult center was at Memphis, capital of Egypt from the 1st Dynasty; he was worshiped from earliest times and throughout the Dynastic period. The Greeks identified Ptah with Hephaestus (Vulcan), the divine blacksmith. With his companions Sekhmet and Nefertem, he was one of the Memphite Triad of deities. As a mortuary god, Ptah was often fused with Seker (or Soker) and Osiris to form Ptah-Seker-Osiris. (*syn.* Phthah)

Ptolemaic Egypt: Term describing Egypt during the Hellenistic era, when it was ruled by the dynasty of the Macedonian general Ptolemy I Soter (reigned 305/304–283/282 BC) and his descendants. The Ptolemaic period was a large-scale experiment in bureaucratic centralism and mercantilism. Egypt was ruled by Ptolemy's descendants until the death of Cleopatra VII on 12 Aug. 30 BC.

Ptolemy: Name held by a succession of 15 Hellenistic rulers of Egypt from 305/304 to 30 BC. The Ptolemaic period is often taken to include the brief preceding Macedonian phase (332–305 BC), encompassing the reigns of Alexander the Great (332–323 BC), his half-brother Philip Arrhidaeus (323–317 BC), and his son Alexander IV (317–310 BC). Ptolemy I Soter (b. 367/366 or 364 BC–d. 283/282, Egypt), Macedonian general of Alexander the Great, became ruler of Egypt (305/304–283/282 BC) and founder of the Ptolemaic dynasty. The dynasty reigned longer than any other dynasty and only succumbed to the Romans in 30 BC after Cleopatra VII's death.

Puabi or Pu-abi (c. 2900–2334 BC): A queen of Ur buried in Grave 800 of the Royal Cemetery (Sumeria) around the middle of the 3rd millennium BC, whose tomb contained the bodies of more than 60 attendants. In the grave was the skeleton of Puabi, adorned with ornaments of gold, silver, and lapis lazuli, and an attendant. In the entrance shaft were skeletons of richly adorned women and men, as well as a sledge and the skeletons of the two oxen, which had pulled it. Rich grave goods included many vessels of gold, silver, and copper, a gaming board, and a silver harp inlaid with shell and red and blue stone. (*syn.* Shubad; Shub-Ad)

Puamau Valley: A valley on eastern Hiva Oa, Marquesas Islands, Polynesia, containing a group of anthropomorphic stone statues up to 2.5 meters high. This is the biggest group of large statues in Polynesia outside Easter Island.

public archaeology: A branch of archaeology dealing with the impact of construction and development on archaeological sites and laws enacted to lessen the threat. In the United States, it has helped create the industries of salvage archaeology and cultural resource management (in England, rescue archaeology).

publication: The final stage of archaeological research design, with the preparation of reports of the data and interpretations resulting from archaeological research.

Pucara: A major urban center of the Early Intermediate period, near the Peruvian shore of Lake Titicaca. The important buildings included a walled sanctuary, monumental U-shaped sunken court surrounded by structures, and walls of dressed stone slabs. The city is best known for its carved stone statues and its polychrome pottery with designs, including the divided eye motif found later at Tiahuanaco. The pottery is typically black and yellow on red with color zones separated by incised lines, possibly related to the ceramics of the late Paracas culture. Radiocarbon dates indicate occupation from 200 BC–AD 200. There are subterranean burial vaults. The site was abandoned before the zenith of Huari, and the art style is almost certainly a precursor to Tiahuanaco.

Puducun: A village in Chang'an Xian, China, near the modern city of Xi'an. Western Zhou bronzes include a vessel dated by its inscription to the reign of the fifth Zhou king Mu Wang (10th century BC). (*syn.* P'u-tu-ts'un)

Pueblo or pueblo: In its capitalized form, a term for a stage in various chronologies of the American Southwest, typically spanning the time period from AD 700 to the 1700s and to a specific Native American group, culture, or site of this time. These Native Americans are believed to be the successors of the prehistoric Anasazi, Hohokam, and Mogollon. The lowercased form is a term for village, applied to the sites in the American southwest where the Pueblo lived. Often these were apartment-like complexes of rectangular living rooms, built close together and often arranged in several stories or terraces, made of wattle and daub. This building style is especially associated with the Anasazi tradition. The chronological period followed the Basketmaker and was divided into five stages at the 1927 Pecos Conference: Pueblo I (700–850/900), Pueblo II (900–1100/1150), Pueblo III (1100/1150–1300), Pueblo IV (1300–1600), and Pueblo V (1600–1700s).

Pueblo Bonito: Major Anasazi town (pueblo) located in Chaco Canyon National Monument, northwest New Mexico. Enclosed by high walls, it is a self-contained complex of some 800 contiguous rooms (300 on the ground floor), rising 4–5, stories with 32 kivas (two great kivas) and two large open plazas. Construction started in 919 (Pueblo II) and was completed in the latter half of the 11th century. The overall D-shaped plan, however, appears to have come about through accretion rather than deliberate planning. The sealing of some outside windows and entrance ways took place in Pueblo III, a period generally noted for the rise of defensive sites. Pueblo Bonito was abandoned by c. 1200.

Puerto Hormiga: A shell midden site on the Caribbean coast of Colombia, which offers evidence of a pottery-making culture as early as 3000 BC. Fiber-tempered pottery

in an Archaic context from the site has radiocarbon dates between 3880–3310 BC (also 3090–2552 BC), one of the oldest wares in the Americas, rivaled only by the Valdiva of Ecuador and the Mina of Brazil. Much of the pottery's decoration was by impression, incision, or punctation.

Pujo: A place name found on silver seals of the tombs near the Han-Dynasty Lelang commandery on the Korean peninsula. It may refer to a place in eastern Korea around the time of the establishment of Lelang.

pulsed induction meter: An instrument used in electromagnetic surveying, mainly for the detection of metals, although on a limited scale; it can be used to locate archaeological features. The instrument has a transmitter coil, which sends pulses of magnetic field to the ground: The continuous rising and falling of the field produces eddy currents in metal objects and magnetic fields in susceptible soil. These are detected by a receiver coil. Only shallow features can be satisfactorily located, and it can be used to find metals, graves, and pottery. (*syn.* pulse radar)

Pulumelei: Site of a massive stone platform, 50 by 60 meters by 12 meters high, on Savai'i Island, Samoa. The Pulumelei is perhaps the largest surviving man-made stone structure in Polynesia, and it may once have supported a large community house or temple. The site is undated, but probably postdates AD 1000.

puna: The highest ecozone of the Andes, where camelids are herded and wild camelids are hunted. There is little agriculture and few permanent settlements. Remains of preceramic hunter-gatherer groups have been widely found.

Punapau: A volcanic crater on Easter Island, which was the quarry for the red tuff topknots (*pukao*) or *scoria* (volcanic rock) originally placed on the heads of the Easter Island statues. All statues and topknots were deliberately toppled during tribal wars before 1860. These were later placed on some major moai. (*syn.* Puna Pau)

punch: A pointed tool, usually of bone, stone, or wood, used to perforate a material such as hide or shell.

punctuated equilibria: A principal feature of the evolutionary theory propounded by Niles Eldredge and Stephen J. Gould, in which species' change is represented as a form of Darwinian gradualism, "punctuated" by periods of rapid evolutionary change. It is a revision of Darwinian theory proposing that the creation of new species through evolutionary change occurs not at slow, constant rates over millions of years but rather in rapid bursts over periods as short as thousands of years, which are then followed by long periods of stability during which organisms undergo little further change.

Punic wars: Three wars between the Roman Republic and the Carthaginian (Punic) Empire, which resulted in the destruction of Carthage. These wars between Rome and Carthage took place in the 3rd–2nd centuries BC. The first (264–241 BC) was fought to establish control over the strategic islands of Corsica and Sicily. After the second (218–201 BC), Carthage was forced to pay an indemnity and surrender its navy, and Spain and the Mediterranean islands were ceded to Rome. The third war (149–146 BC) resulted in the final destruction of Carthage, the enslavement of its population, and Roman hegemony over the western Mediterranean. Of a city population that may have exceeded a quarter of a million, only 50,000 remained at the final surrender. The city was razed, and the territory was made a Roman province under the name of Africa.

Punt: A district bordering the mouth of the Red Sea in eastern Africa, probably close to the Sudan/Eritrea border, from which Egyptian naval expeditions brought myrrh trees, gold, ivory, from at least the 5th Dynasty (2494–2345 BC) onward. The most famous of these expeditions is recorded at Deir el-Bahri in the funerary temple of Queen Hatshepsut of the 18th Dynasty, c. 1478 BC. (*syn.* Pwenet)

Puntutjarpa: A rock shelter in the Warburton Ranges of the western desert, western Australia, with occupation from c. 8000 BC. It is part of the "Australian desert culture" with stone tools in the earliest levels consisting of small stone scrapers (microadze flakes or thumbnail scrapers), large flake scrapers, and horse hoof cores. Larger adze flakes and seed grinders appeared around 5000 BC. Microliths (Bondi points and crescents) were present from 2000 BC. The earlier tool types persisted until the present, with the late addition of flake knives and hand axes. The preponderance of adze flakes showed the significance of woodworking in the desert culture.

puquio: Semisubterranean aqueducts (35 or an original c. 40) in the Nasca region of Peru. Each puquio works as a horizontal well, tapping ground water and directing it through a subterranean tunnel or open trench to a small reservoir. Evidence indicates that the construction was done c. 6th century AD by the Nasca culture.

Puritjarra: Sandstone shelter in Cleland Hills, Australia, which was used by at least 22,000–18,000 bp. Other intensive occupation occurred c. 15,000 and 12–13,000 bp. Stone assemblages include small elongated flakes and larger flakes. The findings demonstrate occupation of the arid zone before the last glacial maximum.

Purron phase: In the Tehuacán Valley, Mexico, a phase, c. 2300–1500 BC, with food collecting and plant cultivation. The dates fall between the end of the Abejas and the start of the Ajalpan phases. In the Purron phase, the first pottery was produced in vessel forms that duplicate earlier stone vessels.

Pusan: A region of the South Korean peninsula with a well-excavated prehistoric sequence. The first period, Chodo, is not dated but may be contemporary with the Early Jomon of Japan. The Chodo culture is ceramic and classed as Neolithic. The second period, Mokto, has a radiocarbon date of c. 3950 BC. The third period, Pusan, is radiocarbon dated to c. 3000 BC and was succeeded by the Tudo period characterized by "comb-pattern" ware. Trade with Japan is documented by imported obsidian and by glycemeris shell bracelets. (*syn.* Busan)

Pushkari I: Upper Palaeolithic site above the Desna River in the Ukraine with a radiocarbon date of 16,775 bp. There is a small longhouse, three hearths, pits, and debris and woolly mammoth in the fauna.

Puskaporos: Rock shelter in the Bükk Mountains of northeast Hungary, with Middle Palaeolithic, Late Upper Palaeolithic, and Neolithic assemblages and faunal remains.

Putnam, Frederic Ward (1839–1915): Curator of the Peabody Museum of American Archaeology and Ethnology, Harvard University, from 1875–1909. He was a leader in the founding of anthropological science in the United States. He was important as an archaeologist who classified and described finds and as an administrator and archaeological sponsor. In fieldwork, he depended on scientific techniques for surveying, excavating, drawing cross-sections of excavations, and plotting finds. He did studies of the mounds of the Midwest United States and of the antiquity of humans on the continent, which he believed to predate the end of the last glaciation. In 1891, Putnam began organizing the anthropological section of the World's Columbian Exposition of 1893 in Chicago. That collection became the basis of Chicago's Field Museum of Natural History. He was the curator of anthropology at the American Museum of Natural History following that, and in 1903 he went to the University of California, Berkeley, to organize both the new department of anthropology and the anthropological museum. Putnam published more than 400 zoological and anthropological articles, reports, and notes and was also a founder and the editor of the periodical *American Naturalist*.

Putun: A Chontal-speaking group of the delta regions of Campeche and Tabasco on the Gulf of Mexico. Expert seamen and skilled merchants, their material culture shows some connection with Central Mexico. Their influence spread throughout the Yucatán Peninsula in the Late Classic Period. It seems likely that they were, in fact, the Itza of historical record.

Puuc: Region in the north-central region of the Yucatán, Mexico, with a distinctive Maya architectural style of AD 600–900, the last variant of the Classic Maya culture. Its main characteristic is the use of veneer masonry to cover rubble and concrete walls, and the prefabrication of sculpted elements assembled to form patterns and masks. The style was florid, with alternating zones of plain and elaborately decorated carving; fret and lattice designs and round columns are common, with many low, single-story residential buildings. These mosaics are found at Uxmal, one of the best-known Puuc centers. Puuc architecture has also been found at Labná, Kabah, and Sayil. The style spread all over the northern Yucatán, and there are some structures at Chichen Itza. Puuc sites are thought by some to represent a lowland Maya "New Empire" with its apogee in the 9th–10th centuries, a time during which the great Petén, or Central Subregion, centers were in decline or had collapsed.

Pu'uhonua: An ancient Hawaiian "city of refuge" located at Honaunau on the west coast of the island of Hawaii. The site has three heiau on a rocky peninsula with a 4-meter-high stone wall. The complex was traditionally first built around 1450 and served as a refuge to which fugitives could flee for divine protection. One of the original temples was still in use in 1823.

Puyo: An ethnic group in the northern Manchurian basin of the Han Chinese times. The Paekche and Koguryo political elite claimed ancestral affiliation to the Puyo. It is also the name of a modern city that was the last Paekche capital.

Pyla-Kokkinokremos: Late Cypriot settlement in south Cyprus, occupied in the late 13th century BC possibly by the Sea Peoples. Massive fortifications were built, but the site was abandoned for Kition (Citium). Ancient Kition was founded by the Mycenaeans in the 13th century BC.

pylon: A monumental gateway to Egyptian temples or palaces built in stone and usually decorated with relief figures and hieroglyphs. It was the usual entrance from the Middle Kingdom to the Roman period (c. 2055 BC–AD 395). The Egyptians made frequent use of them, usually in the form of foreshortened pyramids to mark the entrances of tombs. A pylon consisted of a pair of massifs (massive towers) flanked by a smaller gateway. All the wall faces were inclined; the corners were completed with a torus molding and the top with torus and cavetto cornice. The interior of a pylon contained staircases and chambers. Pairs of colossal statues and obelisks were often erected in front of the pylon. Pylons are the largest and least essential parts of a temple; some temples have series of them (e.g., 10 at Karnak). Rituals relating to the sun god were evidently carried out on top of the gateway. (*syn.* bekhenet)

Pylos: A palace and town of the Mycenaeans, traditionally ruled by Nestor, and overlooking Navarino Bay on the west coast of the Peloponnese in Greece. It is perhaps the best preserved of all mainland palaces, built in the 14th century BC. A megaron with frescoed walls and painted floor opened onto a courtyard, around which were the domestic quarters, storerooms, guard chamber, and the archives room. The 1,200 tablets in the archive were baked by the fire that destroyed the palace in the 13th century BC and have been of enormous value in deciphering the Linear B script. The tablets indicate that the ruler of Pylos exercised control over much of Messenia.

pyramid: A monumental tomb in the shape of a pentahedron, a square base and four straight sides converging to an apex, built by the ancient Egyptians in stone or brick to cover or contain the burial chamber of a pharaoh. Its origin lay in the mud-brick mastaba of the Archaic period, which in the Old Kingdom became more elaborate with the use of stone, regular shape, and larger size. It evolved from the step pyramid as seen at Sakkara, Dahshur, and Meidum. The pyramid is the central monument in a pyramid complex and was the preferred tomb in the Old and Middle Kingdoms (3rd–12th Dynasties). The largest and most famous is the Giza group, and Khufu's is the biggest with a 230-meter-long base and original height of 146 meters. The elaborateness of the funerary ritual, witnessed by the mortuary temples attached to all pyramids, had the same purpose, of guaranteeing the eternal well-being of the deceased. This sepulchral chamber having been connected with the upper world by a passage sloping downward from the north, the graduated structure was regularly built over it, the proportions of the base to the sides being constantly preserved. The building was continued during the lifetime of its destined tenant and covered and closed immediately on his death. The construction of the pyramids as early as the 26th century BC was an extraordinary achievement of engineering and architecture. The tradition of the pyramid as a royal tomb was revived by the kings of Napata and Meroe. In Mesopotamia, Mesoamerica, and South America, pyramids were used as temple-platforms. There are over 80 pyramids in Egypt and ancient Nubia (Sudan).

pyramid complex: The structures associated with royal pyramids of the Old Kingdom and Middle Kingdom in Egypt. The major elements were: the valley temple, the causeway, the mortuary temple, the royal pyramid, a subsidiary/satellite pyramid(s), subsidiary burials of members of the extended royal family and officials of the king, and pits containing full-size boats. The valley temple often had a quay on the River Nile and was probably the site of mummification ceremonies for kings. The causeway was an enclosed passageway from the valley temple to the mortuary temple and used as the way to the tomb during the royal funeral. It may have also been the slipway for transporting blocks in construction of the pyramid. During the Old Kingdom, the essential components were the pyramid itself, containing or surmounting the grave proper and standing in an enclosure on high desert ground; an adjacent mortuary temple; and a causeway leading down to a pavilion (usually called the valley temple), situated at the edge of the cultivation and probably connected with the Nile by a canal. About 80 royal pyramids have been found in Egypt.

pyramidion: The capstone of a pyramid or top of an obelisk. The pyramidion was decorated and became a symbolic object in its own right, being used also on the small brick pyramids of private tombs of the New Kingdom.

Pyramid Texts: In Egypt, 800 spells or "utterances" carved on the walls of burial chambers of pyramids of the 5th–8th dynasties, the earliest Egyptian funerary texts. They were later used by private individuals for most of Egyptian history. Some texts may relate to the king's burial ceremonies, but others are concerned with temple ritual and many other matters. They have been found in nine pyramids of the late Old Kingdom (2375–2181 BC) and First Intermediate period (2181–2055 BC).

Pyu: An ethnolinguistic group, now extinct, with a Tibeto-Burman language, calling themselves Tirchul. They were probably related to the Burmese. Their kingdom of P'iao in the Irrawaddy Basin was first mentioned in the 3rd century by Chinese sources and probably existed from the 1st century BC–9th century AD. Chinese historical records noted that the Pyu claimed sovereignty over 18 kingdoms, many of them in the southern portions of Myanmar. By the 12th century, the Pyus were absorbed by the Burmans.

pyxis: In Greek antiquity, a cylindrical canister-like vessel with a flat shoulder and lid, used to hold trinkets. The name is more loosely applied to lidded boxes in Greek archaeology.

pyrotechnology: The intentional use and control of fire by humans.

Qq

Qa'a (c. 2890 BC): The last ruler of the 1st Dynasty (3100–2890 BC), who was probably buried in Tomb Q at Abydos. (*syn.* Ka'a)

Qadan: Nubian stone industry belonging to the period of high water levels in the Nile Valley before 9000 BC. There are various local stone tool assemblages, and the Qadan people evidently fished, hunted, and consumed large quantities of wild grains.

Qafzeh: Rock shelter in Israel, which yielded adult's and children's remains thought to be archaic or proto-Cro-Magnon. Flint tools are dated to c. 95,000 BP, and animal teeth are 100,000 BP.

Qairawan: Important caravan city in north-central Tunisia on the east-west route between Egypt and the Maghreb. Founded in 670 on the site of the Byzantine fortress of Kamouinia, it has four major 9th-century structures: the Great Mosque, the Mosque of Three Doors, and two massive cisterns. The Great Mosque bears the name of Uqba b. Nafi, the conqueror of North Africa, who built the first mosque at Qairawan in 670. The mosque was rebuilt again by the Aghlabid ruler, Ziyadat Allah, and his successors, beginning in 836. The 9th-century mosque, much of which survives, influenced Islamic architecture in the Maghreb. The mosque of Three Doors (Jami Tleta Biban) has a square sanctuary with nine domes and was built in 866. As a result of Bedouin incursions in the 11th century, the decline of steppe cultivation in favor of nomadic life, and the rise of Tunis as capital, Qairawan declined into an isolated market town for nomads. (*syn.* Al-Qayrawan)

Qal'a of the Banu Hammad: Site in northeast Algeria founded in 1007 as a new capital by Hammad, the grandson of Ziri, builder of the first Sanhaja center at Ashir. The major monuments include the Manar Palace, Lake Palace, and the mosque.

Qala'at al Bahrain: Tell site on the northern coast of Bahrain, with an archaeological sequence for the central Persian Gulf region from the mid-3rd millennium BC to medieval times. The Barbar culture had seals, sealings, Indus weights, and cuneiform texts. It was followed by a Kassite period settlement and then towns of the 1st millennium BC, including a Sassanian fortress.

Qal'at Sharqat: Modern name of Assur, capital of Assyria in northern Mesopotamia. (*syn.* Ash Sharqat)

Qaluyu: A site and cultural phase of the Early Horizon period in the northern Titicaca area of Peru. The pottery had incisions or simple painted geometric motifs in red on cream.

Qandahar: Site in Afghanistan with Classical associations, containing pottery of the Timurid period, late 14th–15th centuries AD. (*syn.* Arachosia)

Qantir: Site of an ancient Egyptian harbor town in the eastern Delta near modern el-Khatana. It was the ancient Egyptian capital in the 15th, 19th, and 20th Dynasties. It was likely first founded in the Old Kingdom, but then was overrun by the Palestinians c. 1700 BC. Refounded by Seti I (1290–1279 BC), it was transformed into a new royal residence and seat of government by his successor Rameses II (1279–1213 BC). (*syn.* ancient Per Ramessu; Pi Ramesse, biblical Raamses, Khata'na, Tall Ad-Daba'a)

Qasr al-Hayr East: An Islamic site in Syria with two fortified buildings and a bathhouse. There were towers and a monumental gate as this was the site of a rural princely complex dating from AD 710–750, erected by Umayyad princes. An inscription from the mosque, now lost, gives the date 728–729 and refers to the site as a town. Although the principal occupation belongs to the 8th century, Qasr al-Hayr enjoyed revival in the 11th and 12th centuries.

Qasr es-Sagha: Egyptian site in northern Fayyum with an undecorated temple, probably of the Middle Kingdom.

Qasr Ibrim: Site of a Lower Nubian fortified settlement, now located on a headland in Lake Nasser. Its occupation was almost continual and mainly military from as early as the New Kingdom. A Roman garrison has been excavated. It was abandoned in AD 1812. (*syn.* ancient Pedeme, Primis)

Qataban: One of the kingdoms of southern Arabia in the 1st millennium BC, contemporary with the Minaeans, Sabaeans, and Hadramis. Its capital city was Timna'. Its heartland was at Wadi Bayhan.

Qatna: A fortified city east of Homs in Syria with evidence of 3rd millennium BC occupation. The fortifications of freestanding glacis (bank) belong to the Middle Bronze Age in the early 2nd millennium BC and were probably constructed by the Hyksos. (*syn.* Qatanum)

Qermez Dere: Late Epipalaeolithic to early Aceramic Neolithic site in northern Iraq with seven phases of occupation defined. The lithic industry is similar to those west on the Euphrates River (Mureybet). It is the beginning of documented habitation on the north Mesopotamian plain. Views on the earliest Neolithic in Iraq have undergone radical revisions in the light of discoveries made at Qermez Dere, Nemrik, and Maghzaliyah.

Qijia: Protohistoric culture of northwest China, successor to the Yanshao, and named after the site of Qijiaping in the Tao River valley. Qijia is contemporaneous with the Longshan and early Shang cultures of c. 2000 BC. Qijia pottery is sometimes painted and often seems to copy metal vessels. Many simple tools and ornaments of copper have been found at Qijia sites, along with some lead and tin bronze. Four radiocarbon dates for the Qijia culture lie in the range c. 2250–1900 BC. It was succeeded in the late 2nd or 1st millennium BC by several primitive Chalcolithic cultures. (*syn.* Ch'i-chia)

Qilakitsoq: Site on the western coast of Greenland, with mummified remains dating AD c. 1425–1525. There were facial tattoos on five of the adults, and the people were of the Thule culture.

Qin: Name of an Eastern Zhou state centered in the Wei River valley of Shaanxi province, China, and of the dynasty (221–206 BC) founded after the Qin state had conquered and absorbed the various states ruling the rest of China. The first emperor of the dynasty, Qin Shihuangdi, established his capital at Xianyang near Chang'an. He was the first emperor of a united China and was buried in a large mounded tomb near Xian City. A terra-cotta army of over 7,000 lifesize soldiers protected him in three long pits. The Qin Dynasty was known for the standardization of weights and measures as well as for coinage and the development of a state infrastructure. Although short lived, it was the first dynasty to unite under a single rule most of the area since regarded as belonging to China proper. (*syn.* Ch'in)

Qing: The name of the Manchu dynasty that ruled China from 1644 to 1911. (*syn.* Ch'ing)

Qingliangang: A Neolithic culture and site of the 5th millennium BC in Huaian Xian, northern Jiangsu Province, China. It succeeded Hemudu and merged with Dawenkou. It had unpainted openwork ceramics with pedestals. (*syn.* Ch'ing-lien-kang)

Qin Shihuangdi (fl. 247 BC-d. 210 BC): A boy king (Chao Cheng) who came to China's throne and completed the Ch'in conquests and in 221 created the Ch'in Empire. He proclaimed himself Ch'in Shih Huang-ti ("First Sovereign Emperor of Ch'in") and instituted a rigid, authoritarian government. During the Ch'in Dynasty, the writing system was standardized along with weights and measures and coinage. The Great Wall was also built. Rebellion erupted after Shihuangdi's death in 210 BC. In 206, the dynasty was overthrown and replaced by the Han Dynasty (206 BC–AD 220). His tomb is the focal point of a vast mausoleum complex that includes a buried army of 7,000 lifesize terra-cotta figures. (*syn.* Ch'in Shih Huang-ti; Qin Shi Huangdi; Chao Cheng)

Qishan: A site in Shaanxi Province, China, where the Zhou people established their dynasty and capital before they overthrew the Shang Dynasty in 1027 BC. A large palace complex included inscribed oracle bones antedating the founding of the dynasty. The tiled roofs of the buildings are the earliest known (11th century BC) of this standard feature of later Chinese architecture. There are also *hangtu* foundation platforms for palace buildings. Many bronze ritual vessels have been found in the Qishan area, mostly Western Zhou in date. (*syn.* Ch'i-shan)

quadrantal: An ancient square vessel used as a measure, the solid contents of which were exactly equal to an amphora.

quadrant method: A procedure for excavating a circular feature such as a mound, barrow, or pit, by laying out trenches. Material is extracted from four quarters of the feature, starting with the two opposite each other and ending with the other two. The quadrants are slightly offset, so that the outer face of the east balk of one is continuous (in reverse) with the outer face of the east balk of its opposite, going through the center of the feature. After the recording of the sections, the balks may be removed, and the rest of the center excavated. Before the complete removal of the feature, this method allows a look at all four quarters, at two complete cross-sections, and at part of the center, allowing a better interpretation of the stratigraphy of the site.

quadrat: A usually rectangular plot used for ecological or population studies; unit of spatial analysis used to divide an area into cells for analysis.

Quanterness: A passage grave on Orkney, north Scotland, of the Maes Howe or Quanterness/Quoyness type and dated to c. 3000 BC. Like other such tombs, it had been used for collective burial, but the number of bodies found here was unusually high: remains of 157 individuals were found, and the tomb may originally have housed 400. Radiocarbon dates indicated it may have represented an extended family over a period of nearly 1,000 years. The long, low passage led to the principal rectangular-plan chamber, which had a corbel-vaulted roof. It is dry stone and covered by a large circular cairn.

quantitative archaeology: Archaeological techniques dependent on counting, measuring, and the use of statistical methods and computers.

Quanzhou: Late 13th century AD Song Dynasty shipwreck at Houzhou, China. It was a 24-meter-long keeled ship with 13 compartments. The acquisition and preservation of this massive artifact was spectacular; it is on display in a Chinese museum. (*syn.* C'üan-chou)

quarry: An open excavation usually for obtaining building stone, slate, or limestone. In archaeological terms, it is a cumulative feature resulting from the mining of mineral resources or a place where stone was removed from a larger source, for instance, to subsequently manufacture tools.

quartz: A hard mineral of many varieties, which consists primarily of silica or silicon dioxide. Quartz has been important from the earliest times; crystals of it were known to the ancient Greeks as "krystallos." It is typically colorless to white, with some minor impurities that turn it into many different colors. Quartz has great economic importance. Many varieties are gemstones, including amethyst, citrine, smoky quartz, and rose quartz. Sandstone, composed mainly of quartz, is an important building stone. Large amounts of quartz sand are used in the manufacture of glass and porcelain and for foundry molds in metal casting. Quartz is the second most abundant mineral in the Earth's crust after feldspar.

quartzite: Metamorphic rock based on sandstone and consisting mostly of quartz; it is a dense, hard rock that fractures concoidally. Flaked tools were made of quartzite when there was no chert or flint, and it was important for heavy monumental building stone. Pebbles of it were made into hammer stones and hand axes.

Quaternary: Major geochronological subdivision, which includes the Pleistocene (c. 1.8–2.45 million years bp) and Holocene (c. 10,000 BC) epochs and marked by the appearance of near-humans and *Homo sapiens*. It is the second period of the Cenozoic geologic era, following the Tertiary, the youngest of the 11 periods in Earth history. These terms may also be applied to groups of deposits, which are described as the Quaternary "System" and the Pleistocene or Holocene "Series." The base of the Quaternary System is defined by basal deposits that overlie Pliocene deposits. The Quaternary was marked by repeated invasions of vast areas of mid-latitude North America and northwestern Eurasia by ice sheets, the period is frequently referred to as the Great Ice Age. (*syn.* Quaternary era; Quaternary Period; Quaternary System)

Quechua: Prehistoric Andean province and the language used by its Inca empire people; it became the official Inca language. Several dialects are still spoken in Peru and Bolivia, and it was used for government and all communications between provinces under Inca rule. The term *Quechua* also refers to the Andean ecozone in which maize and other grains were grown in hillside terraces. (*syn.* Quichua; Runa Simi)

quenching: In metalworking, rapid cooling, as by immersion in water, brine, or oil, of a metal object from the high temperature at which it has been shaped. The resulting metalwork is softer than when allowed to cool slowly, important for iron and steel as quenching produces a different structure, much harder and more brittle. Quenched steel can then be made less brittle by heating gently.

Quentovic: A port and trading center on the English Channel in the Early Medieval period, which had a toll and a mint. Its coins were first minted in the early 7th century, and during the 8th–9th centuries its mint was one of the most important in the Carolingian Empire. Despite its prominence, the location of the site has not been found. Most historians believe that it lies near Etaples, on the coast at the mouth of the Canche. Quentovic was attacked by the Vikings several times, but its demise is usually attributed to the 10th century when other more fortified sites were preferred to it.

quern: (kwurn) Large ancient grinding stone for grain or corn. A rough but hard stone was necessary to avoid grit in the flour. Its earliest (Neolithic before 5600 BC) form was the saddle quern, where material was ground with a hand stone (or muller) on an immobile concave stone. It was later replaced by the rotary quern (by Roman times), where one stone is rotated on another by hand, animal, or wind power. Lava was widely traded for this purpose. (*syn.* saddle quern, rotary quern, true quern)

Quéroy: Cave site in Charente, France, with deposits from the early Middle Neolithic to the La Tène Iron Age. Late Bronze Age sherds of c. 800 BC had incised symbols, and similar signs are on potsherds in other parts of France. They are a form of protowriting.

Quetta: A city and adjacent valley in western Pakistan, with tell sites that produced a chronological sequence for the region. A pre-pottery occupation with domestic animals was dated c. 5000 BC and was followed by creamy handmade and basket-marked pottery, later joined by red and black painted ware in the later 3rd millennium BC. Mud brick and stone blades were used, but copper appeared only at the very end. The most important sites are Kili Gul Mohammad, Damb Sada'at, and Kechi Beg. The Quetta sequence is particularly useful because it links prehistoric sites in Pakistan with those of Afghanistan, like Mundigak, and Iran, such as Tepe Hissar and Tepe Sialk. The name Quetta ware is given to a black on buff wheel-turned ware, which is found in Damb Sadaat II.

quetzal: Any of several birds belonging to the genus Pharomachrus of the trogon family, a bird of Central America. Its distinctive and brightly colored plumage was highly valued in ancient Mesoamerica. The Aztec emperor Moctezuma's headdress, given as a gift to the Spanish conquistador Hernan Cortéz, was made mainly of brilliant green quetzal feathers. It is the national bird of Guatemala.

Quetzalcóatl: The Náhuatl name for the principal Aztec god of Late Postclassic Central America, usually depicted as a feathered serpent. He was the god of self-sacrifice, patron of the arts and crafts, and inventor of agriculture and the calendar. In another form, he was also the wind god and god of the morning and evening star. The name was also used as the official title of high priest among Aztecs. His cult can be recognized in the Classic period at Teotihuacán, at Tula, Cholula, and at many Mexican sites. He was an important figure in the early Toltec pantheon (becoming identified with a local ruler), and his effigy appears in the Maya territory after the Toltec invasion of Chichén Itzá. According to legend, Quetzalcóatl was driven away from Mexico, but before leaving he gave a promise to return. For a while, the Aztecs believed that the invading Spaniards were the god and his followers returning to fulfill this prophecy—a belief leading to the downfall of the Aztec empire.

Quiani: A shell mound south of Africa, on the northern Chilean coast, c. 4000 BC, with shell fishhooks and leaf points.

quid: A cut or wad of something chewable, such as the fibrous remains of rhizomes that were chewed by many hunting-gathering peoples.

Quimbaya: A late prehistoric culture of western Colombia, South America, dated AD 300–1600. It is known for its fine goldwork—flasks, helmets, jewelry, pins, and so on. It represents some of the most advanced metallurgical techniques in the prehistoric New World. Pottery with negative painting and incision, and sometimes modeled, belongs to the final centuries before the Spanish Conquest. The Coclé region in Panama was strongly influenced by the Quimbaya style. It is particularly known for its striking gold pieces set with precious stones, including emeralds, quartzes, jaspers, opals, agates, and green serpentines.

quinoa: A pigweed (*Chenopodium quinoa*) of the high Andes, whose seeds are ground and widely used as food in Peru. It was cultivated at high elevations in Andean prehistory.

quinquereme: A Roman and Hellenistic warship, which was larger and more powerful than its predecessor, the trireme. Quinqueremis is a galley with five banks of oars.

Quinzano: A quarry near Verona, Italy, with several lower and Middle Palaeolithic levels and a human occipital skull bone of Neanderthal type. There was an open settlement of the Square-Mouthed Pottery Neolithic culture and a cemetery of crouched inhumations. The name Finale-Quinzano is sometimes given to a variant of square-mouthed pottery named after this site and Arene Candide.

quipu: A mnemonic device used by the Inca for keeping accounts and records. It consisted of a number of thick cords of various thicknesses and colors, on which numbers and other data were indicated by knots of different sizes and positions on the strings. Based on a decimal system, the color of the cord, as well as the size, configuration, and placement of each knot had a special meaning. So complex was the system that a special class of workers, *quipu-camayoq* (quipucamoyac), kept the imperial records on quipu. The Incas did not have writing, but quipus could also be used as aids in recording historical or liturgical information accumulated by the government. A modified form is still used by some Andean herdsmen.

Quiriguá: Small Maya center in the southern Guatemala lowlands, an important Classic period site with the tallest sandstone stelae known. The tallest, Stela E, is almost 11 meters high. There are also giant boulder sculptures of mythical monsters and animals in Southern Regional style. It was probably at least partly controlled by Copán. The terminal Long Count date of 810 is carved on a lintel of the main building.

Quishqui Puncu: The preceramic site of Calleyon de Huaylas in Peru, which has yielded artifacts and fine leaf points that date from c. 4000 BC.

Qujialing: Type site in Jingshan Xian, Hubei province, China, of a rice-growing Neolithic culture of the middle Yangtze region. Radiocarbon dates from various sites range from c. 3100– 2650 BC. Qujialing's closest affiliations seem to be with the east-coast Neolithic cultures of the lower Ynazi. During the 4th and 3rd millennia BC, the Ta-his and Ch'ü-chia-ling cultures shared a significant number of traits, including rice production, ring-footed vessels, goblets with sharply angled profiles, ceramic whorls, and black pottery with designs painted in red after firing. Characteristic Ch'ü-chia-ling ceramic objects not generally found in Ta-hsi sites include eggshell-thin goblets and bowls painted with black or orange designs; double-waisted bowls; tall, ring-footed goblets and serving stands; and many styles of tripods. There are indications of a thriving textile industry. The chronological distribution of ceramic features suggests a transmission from Ta-hsi to Ch'ü-chia-ling, but the precise relation between the two cultures has been much debated. (*syn.* [Ch'ü-chia-ling])

Qumran: A site near the Dead Sea in Israel, where the first Dead Sea Scrolls were found, leading to excavation of the headquarters of a religious community and of a large cemetery at Khirbet Qumran, both of the Greco-Roman period. The Essenes, a Jewish sect living there from c. 1st century BC to the 1st century AD, left their religious writings in caves during the time that the Romans put down the Jewish Revolt. Discovered in 1947, the scrolls are dated to the last two centuries BC and the 1st century AD.

Qurum: Sites on the coast of Oman, Arabia, with evidence of mid-Holocene hunting-gathering/maritime people. There are extensive cemeteries on the sites. (*syn.* Ras al Hamra)

Quyn-van: Shell midden in northern Vietnam, which has produced a flaked stone industry together with pottery, grind stones and contracted burials dated c. 3000 BC. It could be a late and specialized coastal variant of the Hoabinhian.

Rr

Ra: The supreme god of ancient Egypt before his displacement by Amen (Amun). He was sun god and deity of the city of Heliopolis, whose cult is first attested in the name of the 2nd Dynasty ruler Raneb (c. 2865 BC). Ra is depicted as a hawk-headed man with a sun disc on his head. He was especially important during the Old Kingdom's 4th and 5th Dynasties. In the New Kingdom, Ra was attested in the composite deity Amen-Re, state god of the empire. (*syn.* Re)

rabotage: The process of carefully scraping a horizontal surface to reveal features in it distinguished by color differences. It is particularly useful in sandy soils and gravels, revealing surprising detail.

rachis: A floral ecofact: the elongated axis of an inflorescence or an extension of the petiole of a compound leaf that bears the leaflets. An example is the stem connecting the wheat kernel to the shaft.

Rachmani: Neolithic and Bronze Age settlement mound in Thessaly, Greece. The Final Neolithic is characterized by red, pink, and white pottery. (*syn.* Rakhmani)

racloir: A large scraper that has the retouched working edge along the long edge of the flake. The racloir is one of the most characteristic Mousterian implements and may have served as both knife and (side) scraper. (*syn.* sidescraper)

radiate: An imperial Roman coin on which the emperor is shown wearing a radiate or pointed solar crown, especially in the 3rd century AD.

radioactive decay: The regular process by which radioactive isotopes break down into their decay products with a half-life specific to the isotope in question. This process transmutes an isotope of one element into an isotope of another; for instance, potassium 40 to argon 40 or uranium 235 to lead 207.

radiocarbon: An unstable (radioactive) isotope of carbon with atomic mass 14, produced in the atmosphere by cosmic radiation. It is the basis for radiocarbon dating, the method most frequently used in archaeology. It acts like C12, being taken into the organic compounds of all living matter. The proportions of radioactive and inert carbon are identical throughout the vegetable and animal kingdom's carbon cycle. When organic matter dies, it ceases to exchange its carbon, as carbon dioxide, with the atmosphere, so that its C14 dwindles by decay and is not replenished. Determination of the radioactivity of carbon from a sample reveals the proportion of C14 to C12, and this, in turn, through the known rate of decay of C14, gives the age of, or more accurately the time elapsed since the death of, the sample.

radiocarbon age: The most likely statistical age of an object dated by radiocarbon. This date comes from the laboratory and is expressed in radiocarbon years before the present (calculated as the age before 1950 AD) with a plus or minus factor; for instance, 3618 ± 120.

radiocarbon dating: A radiometric dating technique for determining the age of carbon-bearing minerals, including wood and plant remains, charcoal, bone, peat, and calcium carbonate shell, back to about 50,000 bp. The technique is based on measuring the loss of radiocarbon (carbon 14) that begins disintegration at the death of the object containing the carbon at a known rate. It is one of the best-known chronometric dating techniques and the most important in archaeology presently. It can be used for dating organic material up to 75,000 years old. It is based on the theory of Willard F. Libby (1947); his radioactive-carbon dating provided an extremely valuable tool for archaeologists, anthropologists, and earth scientists. When organic matter dies, it ceases to exchange its carbon, as carbon dioxide, with the atmosphere, so that its C14 dwindles by decay and is not replenished. Determination of the radioactivity of carbon from a sample reveals the proportion of C14 to C12, and this, in turn, through the known rate of decay of C14, gives the age of, or more accurately the time elapsed since the death of, the sample. Two things in the method have to be allowed for: first, the "date" given is never exact. The ± figure, which should always be quoted, is a statistical one and means that there is a 2 to 1 chance that the correct date lies within the bracket. Second, the rate of decay of C14 is based in all published examples on a half-life of 5,730 ± 40 years (after 5,730 years, one half of the C14 will have disintegrated; after another 5,730 years, one half of the remainder, and so on). Correction tables are used to correct "raw" radiocarbon dates (quoted as years ad or bc) into true dates (AD or BC). The method yields reliable dates back to about 50,000 bp and under some conditions to about 75,000 bp. One of the basic assumptions of the technique is that the amount of radiocarbon in the atmosphere has remained constant through time. It has now been established, with the dendrochronological sequence for the bristlecone pine, that the C14 concentration has fluctuated. The reasons for the fluctuation are not yet fully understood. The calibration of radiocarbon dates is therefore necessary to achieve an approximate date in calendar years. Dates quoted in radiocarbon years, before calibration, are written bc or bp (before the present), as opposed to calibrated dates, written BC or BP. The original half-life for radiocarbon of 5,568 ± 30 years has been revised to 5,730 ± 40 years, although dates are normally published according to the old half-life to avoid confusion (the date can be adjusted for the new half-life by multiplying the old date by 1.029). All radiocarbon dates are quoted with a standard deviation. Ideally, a series of dates should be obtained for any deposit, as a series may cluster around a central point. New refinements continue to improve the technique's accuracy as well as to extend the range of dates that can be achieved. A previous limit of 50,000 years on the age of material that could be dated, set by the limits on the ability of the proportional counter used to record beta particle emissions, has been extended to 70,000 years by the use of isotopic enrichment, the artificial enrichment of the C14 to C12 ratio. (*syn.* radioactive carbon dating, radiocarbon age determination, carbon-14 dating; radiochronometry)

radiography: The physical technique of producing a photographic image of an opaque specimen by transmitting a beam of x-rays through it onto an adjacent photographic film; the image results from variations in the thickness, density, and chemical composition of the specimen. The technique is used to study details of structure, decoration, or composition invisible to the naked eye. X-rays are normally used, although gamma-rays may be employed in circumstances where an x-ray tube is difficult to manipulate. Differential absorption of the rays denotes variations in composition, and these are shown on the film as contrasting light and dark tones. This form of examination works well on iron objects where rust and corrosion products prevent proper study of the object. Radiography is also used in the study of biological material, such as bone and mummies. Radiography has also been used to examine sedimentary structures. Microradiographic tech-

niques have been developed to examine the atomic structure of crystalline substances. (*syn.* x-radiography; also X-ray microscopy and microradiographic techniques)

radioimmunoassay: A method of protein analysis in which it is possible to identify protein molecules surviving in fossils that are thousands and even millions of years old.

radiometric dating: Dating by measuring processes that involve the decay of radioactive isotopes and yielding absolute age estimations. Radiocarbon, potassium/argon, and uranium series dating employ the known rate of decay, expressed by their half-lives. Fission track dating similarly employs spontaneous nuclear fission, which also occurs at a known rate. (*syn.* radiometric assay; radiometrics)

Radomyshl': Upper Palaeolithic site in European Russia with a pit, hearths, and woolly mammoth remains. Artifacts are tool types characteristic of both Middle and Upper Palaeolithic, and the radiocarbon date is 19,000 bp.

Rahman Dehri: Site in the western Punjab, Pakistan, with a culture of 3400–2500 BC leading up to the Mature Harappan civilization. Early levels have a regional painted pottery; the ceramics became Kot Diji style. There are graffiti on sherds, possibly an antecedent to the Harappan script.

raised beach: An ancient or previous shoreline from a period when the land level was lower than it is today in relation to the sea level. This geological feature is produced by changing sea levels through time, and although it may now be some distance from the sea, a raised beach shows where the original coastline was. Changes in relative heights of land and sea can often be correlated with fluctuations in the Pleistocene climate. (*syn.* fossil beach)

Rajagrha: Indian city of the Ganges civilization and capital of the kingdom of Magadha. The earliest surviving remains are ramparts of rubble masonry, probably of the 6th century BC. The city was often visited by the Buddha, and a series of elliptical structures may be the remains of his monastery. One of the towers on Baibhar Hill (Vaibharagiri) has been identified as the Pippala stone house in which Buddha lived. It is also said to have been the residence of the legendary Magadha emperor Jarasandha of the Hindu epic "Mahabharata." (*syn.* modern Rajgir)

Rajghat: City of the Ganges civilization, India, in Uttar Pradesh, with the earliest occupation characterized by Black and Red ware and the beginnings of iron technology. There are eight phases starting with that in c. 800 BC. The settlement of this period was surrounded by a massive brick rampart. After c. 700–600 BC. Northern Black Polished ware and copper coins appear. (*syn.* Old Banaras)

Ramesses or Ramses or Rameses: The name of two pharaohs of Egypt of the 19th Dynasty and nine of the 20th Dynasty; therefore the period was called Ramesside. The most important of these rulers were Ramesses I Menpehtyra (1292–1290 BC), Ramesses II Usermaatra Setepenra (or Ramesses the Great) (1279–1213 BC), and Ramesses III Usermaatra Meryamun (1187–1156 BC). Ramesses II's victory at Kadesh, however doubtful, at least stabilized his frontier with the Hittites for many years. He also carried out much temple building in Egypt and Nubia, including his funerary temple at Thebes (Ramesseum). After Ramesses II's marriage to the Hittite king's daughter, his reign saw the florescence of Egyptian art and monumental architecture, most notably at the great temple of Abu Simbel. Ramesses III saved the country by defeating invasions of the Peoples of the Sea and the Libyans c. 1170 BC.

Ramesseum: The mortuary temple of Ramesses II (1279–1213 BC), located on the west bank of the Nile at western Thebes, opposite modern Luxor. The temple is famous for its 57-foot seated statue of Ramesses II. The walls of the Ramesseum are decorated with reliefs, including scenes depicting the Battle of Kadesh, the Syrian wars, and the festival of Min.

rampart: An earthwork built to defend a site, such as a fort. It was the mound of earth on the inner side of the ditch or an elongated bank, often forming an enclosure. Often a palisade of stakes was on top. A rampart made it difficult to attack a castle or fort. Combinations of ramparts and ditches made up the defenses of hill forts in prehistoric Europe. Roman legion camps were always built with a rampart of ditches, earth walls, and wooden palisades, in which the space was divided into headquarters, supply, and troop areas. Indications of the construction of the rampart may occur as tip lines or turf lines, which may represent pauses in the work or different phases of building. Buried soils are frequently found underneath mounds and ramparts, a source of information for environmental archaeology.

Rana Ghundai: A tell in the Loralai Valley of north Baluchistan with a stratigraphic sequence beginning with handmade pottery and chipped stone tools (4th millennium BC). This was followed by a level with black-on-red painted Zhob wares.

rancheria: In the southwestern United States and Mesoamerica, a family household unit or settlement. It is also a place, hut, or house where rancheros live.

Rancho La Brea: Quaternary site (Le Brea Tar Pits) near Los Angeles, with very large numbers of vertebrate remains dating c. 40,000–11,000 BP, buried in tar pits (asphalt deposits of ancient tar seeps). The tar pits contain the fossilized skulls and bones of prehistoric animals that became entrapped in the sticky seepage of the pits. The remains of such Pleistocene mammals as imperial mammoth, mastodon, saber-toothed cat, giant ground sloth, and camel have been recovered.

There are some artifacts, including manos and wooden spear points. (*syn.* La Brea Tar Pits)

random sampling: A sample drawn at random from a population, each member of it having an equal or other specified chance of inclusion. This sampling technique is based on a totally random selection of sample units to be investigated, with each unit having an equal chance of being selected. (*syn.* random sample)

ranging pole: In surveying, a rod or pole for setting a straight line, for sighting points and lines, or for showing the position of a ground point. The pole, often 6–8 feet long, is graduated for measuring vertical distances and is frequently included in photographs of an excavated site. (*syn.* range rod, line rod, lining pole, range pole, ranging rod, sight rod)

Ranis Cave: Site near the River Saale in eastern Germany, starting with Middle Palaeolithic material, then Upper Palaeolithic dating to the middle of the last glacial maximum. Late Upper Palaeolithic, Bronze Age, and historic remains have also been found at the site. (*syn.* Ilsenhöhle)

Ranjpur: Prehistoric site in northwest India with evidence of the Mature and Late Harappan, divided into five periods from c. 3000 BC. The Mature Harappan had baked bricks, drains, graffiti on pottery, stone weights, terra-cotta cakes, beads, and pottery. New elements appear in the material culture—animal motifs on painted pottery and Lustrous Red ware. The latter became common, and black-and-red ware appeared in the Late Harappan at Lothal, Rodji, and Ranjpur.

rank: The position held by an individual on the basis of his or her status in a society where statuses are not all equal, but are graded into a hierarchical structure. A society with such inequalities of status is called a ranked society. A rank is a distinct class or level in a hierarchy.

ranked society: A society in which all statuses are not equal, but rather there exists a hierarchical structure. There is unequal access to the higher status categories, and thus many people who are qualified for high-status positions are unable to achieve them. In these societies, individuals are ranked vis-à-vis one another in terms of kinship status and social prestige, which are largely ascribed. Fewer positions of authority exist than there are individuals capable of filling them.

rank-size rule: A general relation between the size of a settlement and its rank in a set of settlements. If sites are ranked in order of size on a logarithmic scale, the population of the Nth rank city will be 1/Nth the size of the largest; thus the 3rd site will be 1/3 the size of the largest. The rule works best in areas of complex economic and political organization, with comparatively long histories of urban development. It has been suggested that this relation represents a natural balance of settlement growth. Roman walled towns fit the rule well. However, this is often not the case because in many newer, developing countries the chief city or capital is larger than expected (primate city) because of historic factors.

Rano Raraku: An extinct volcanic crater on Easter Island, which served as a quarry for the stone statues (*moai*) erected in rows on the many *ahu* on the island. The rock is a soft tuff, and the main usage of the two quarries, one inside and one outside the crater, dates to between AD c. 1000–1500. The site is filled with almost 400 unfinished statues and with many finished erected moai. Thousands of basalt hand-held picks were discarded at the site.

rapier: A long, pointed two-edged sword used for thrusting or cutting; an offensive weapon of bronze distinguished from the sword by the slenderness of its blade. It developed in the Middle Bronze Age by lengthening of the dagger and was replaced by the slashing sword in the Late Bronze Age of central and northwest Europe. In its later form, it was a light, slender sharp-pointed sword for thrusting only. (*syn.* tuck)

Raqqa: City in northern Syria on the Euphrates River, founded by the 'Abbasid caliph al-Mansur and reputedly having gates modeled on those of Baghdad. Raqqa is on the site of an ancient Greek city, Nicephorium, and a later Roman fortress and market town, Callinicus. It flourished again in early Arab times when the 'Abbasid caliph Harun ar-Rashid built several palatial residences there and made it his head-quarters against the Byzantines. The surviving part of the Baghdad gate shows that it had a four-centered arch surmounted by a band of three-lobed niches resting on engaged colonnettes. The congregational mosque, also attributed to al-Mansur, was a rectangular building with a sanctuary of three arcades. Raqqa ware is 12th- and 13th-century earthenware with painted ornament under thick alkaline glaze. (*syn.* Ar-Raqqah, Rakka; Ar-Rashid)

rareca: Peruvian aqueducts, distinct from the subterranean aqueducts called *huircas* or *pinchas*.

Ras al-Amiya: A site near Kish in southern Mesopotamia (modern Iraq), which consisted of a small mound with pottery of Hajji Muhammad type, now regarded as an early phase of the 'Ubaid culture of the earlier 5th millennium BC. Architectural remains included rectangular houses arranged around courtyards.

rath: A type of small ring fort found in Ireland and southwest Wales. The fort, rarely more than 60 meters in diameter, was enclosed by a bank with an outer ditch. Rath is generally used to describe a fort with earthen banks, while a stone-built fort is described as a cashel. The oldest forts belong to the late Iron Age/Roman period of 1st century BC–4th century AD in Wales, and in Ireland they are from the 5th–10th centuries AD. Some of these raths were reused by the Normans as the foundations for small motte and bailey castles, while others continued to be occupied until the postmedieval period.

Ravenna: City on the Adriatic Sea in northern Italy, which became a Roman city in 49 BC and the base of Adriatic fleet. The earliest inhabitants of Ravenna were probably Italic peoples who moved southward from Aquileia about 1400 BC. According to tradition, it was occupied by the Etruscans and later by the Gauls. It was selected by the Roman emperor Honorius as his capital in AD 402 because of its security. Ravenna was important in history as the capital of the Western Roman Empire in the 5th century AD and later (6th–8th centuries) of Ostrogothic and Byzantine Italy. During Theodoric's reign (498–526), the emperor constructed new churches and public buildings, decorated in styles that blended the Eastern and Western art styles of the time. The mosaics inside the buildings are the finest collection anywhere in the Byzantine world and were extremely influential in determining art styles throughout much of Europe and the East in the early Middle Ages. One of the earliest of Ravenna's extant monuments is the mausoleum of Galla Placidia, built in the 5th century AD by Galla Placidia, the sister of the emperor Honorius.

Rawlinson, General Sir Henry Creswicke (1810–1895): A British diplomat who was one of a group of scholars whose work on the trilingual inscription at Behistun (Iran) was instrumental in the decipherment of the cuneiform (leading to the decipherment of Old Persian and Akkadian) languages of western Asia. He copied the Behistun inscription, deciphered it, and published the translation of the Persian text in 1851 and of the Babylonian in 1857. Rawlinson also encouraged much archaeological research and excavation in Mesopotamia.

Re: The supreme god of ancient Egypt before his displacement by Amen (Amun). He was sun god and deity of the city of Heliopolis, whose cult is first attested in the name of the 2nd Dynasty ruler Raneb (c. 2865 BC). Ra is depicted as a hawk-headed man with a sun disc on his head. He was especially important during the Old Kingdom's 4th and 5th Dynasties. In the New Kingdom, Ra was attested in the composite deity Amen-Re, state god of the empire. (*syn.* Ra)

Real Alto: A village of the Valdivia culture of Ecuador, near the coast, occupied from c. 3500–3000 BC. It had a formal layout, with an open plaza surrounded by elongated mounds of household rubbish. Excavation revealed large timber and thatch houses, one mound with offerings, and a second with elaborate high-status burials. There is evidence for the emergence of an early complex social organization.

reave: A long low bank or wall found at Dartmoor, England. These Bronze Age stone boundary walls may designate the territorial extent of individual communities.

rebus: A mode of expressing words and phrases by pictures of objects whose names resemble those words or the syllables of which they are composed. These are signs that are a sort of punning logogram in which the picture of something easy to draw represents something that is difficult to draw but whose name sounds the same. The Sumerian example most often cited is an arrow (*ti*) used to stand for life (also ti). An English example of a rebus message would be the picture of a bee followed by the picture of a well sent to an invalid to wish him a quick recovery (be well). Several rebuses may be combined to make a phrase or sentence. Literary rebuses use letters, numbers, musical notes, or specially placed words to make sentences. Complex rebuses combine pictures and letters. An early form of rebus occurs in picture writings, where abstract words were represented by pictures of objects pronounced the same way—as in Egyptian hieroglyphs and early Chinese pictographs.

recalibration: Correction process carried out on radiocarbon dates to adjust them to calendar years by using results gained from dendrochronology.

Recent: The epoch of geologic time in the late Quaternary following the Pleistocene; referred to as Holocene in several European countries. It is the present geological epoch, which began some 10,000 (bp) years ago (8300 BC). The Recent epoch is marked by rising temperatures throughout the world and the retreat of the ice sheets. During this epoch, agriculture became the common human subsistence practice. During the Recent epoch, *Homo sapiens* diversified his tool technology, organized his habitat more efficiently, and adapted his way of life. The Recent stage/series includes all deposits younger than the top of either the Wisconsinian stage of the Pleistocene Series in North America and the Würm/Weichsel in Europe. (*syn.* Holocene)

reciprocity: A form of primitive exchange in which goods are transferred between individuals or groups of the same status without any central control, usually in a balanced and mutually beneficial manner. A mode of exchange in which transactions take place between individuals who are symmetrically placed, that is, they are exchanging as equals, neither being in a dominant position. The exchange was often an expression of the social obligations between the parties. In a family, generalized reciprocity occurs where there is giving with no expectation of immediate return. Between families in a community, balanced reciprocity may occur, with both parties expecting give-and-take of goods to be of approximately equal value. The items exchanged may be utilitarian goods, foodstuffs, or prestige materials. Negative reciprocity occurs when both sides attempt to receive more than they give. (*syn.* reciprocal exchange)

reclamation: Any of various processes by which artifacts move from an archaeological context to an active status, or are "reclaimed," as when a later society makes use of objects deposited earlier. It is the transition of cultural materials from the archaeological record back into the systemic context, such as the scavenging of archaeological artifacts for reuse by both nonindustrial and industrial peoples. The act of archaeological excavation is actually reclamation. (*syn.* reclamation process)

reconnaissance: A broad range of techniques involved in the location of archaeological sites, such as surface survey and the recording of surface artifacts and features, the sampling of natural and mineral resources, and sometimes testing of an area to assess the number and extent of archaeological resources. (*syn.* reconnaissance survey)

recording unit: A specific location or feature that is defined as an entity for the purpose of recording archaeological data.

recovery: The act or process of obtaining artifacts from a site for the purpose of deriving archaeological data. (*syn.* archaeological recovery)

recovery theory: Any of the various principles that archaeologists employ in the process of recovery, such as where and how to search for sites and how to excavate those sites.

recovery unit: A defined area from which archaeological materials are recovered, such as an excavation pit.

Recuay: Pre-Columbian culture and site near present-day Recuay in the Callejón de Huaylas Valley of the northern highlands of Peru. The Recuay culture dates to the Early Intermediate period, c. 200 BC–AD 600 and was contemporaneous with the Moche culture on the north coast. Recuay is known for its distinctive pottery, which features a type of decoration in three colors (black, red, white) and a style of modeling with small figures of men, jaguars, llamas, and other animals attached to the vessel. The vessels were found in underground galleries and box-shaped tombs. The style, also called Huaylas, shows contact with the Moche and Gallinazo styles. Recuay stone carving (called Aija) is related to that of the Pucará and Tiahuanaco cultures. It is characterized by the stiff, blockish quality that is widespread throughout the Peruvian Highlands. (*syn.* Huaylas)

recurrence surface: A division in peat stratigraphy, which separates well-humified peat from unhumified peat. Recurrence surfaces are found in raised bogs and blanket bogs, which are nourished only by rainfall. It has therefore been suggested that recurrence surfaces are due to a change to a damper climate. Recurrence surfaces of many dates have been found, often several in one bog, although not so many fitting into one age range. During the late prehistoric and early historic phases of the past 6,000 years, the peat bogs of northern Europe appear to have undergone a number of desiccations (warm, dry summers), revealed in the bog cores as dry, often wooded, surfaces. The dry phases were generally followed by wet conditions in which peat accumulation was rapid. These overlying layers of renewed peat growth are also known as "recurrence horizons." (*syn.* recurrence horizon)

Redcliff: Series of fossil cave fillings in a limestone quarry of central Zimbabwe. There are Middle and Later Stone Age assemblages and Iron Age Gokomere pottery.

red-figure or red-figured: A technique of decorating pottery in which the area of the figure is left empty (reserved) and the detail is painted in. The red of the clay contrasts with the black. It is an important phase in Greek vase painting, the inverse of black-figure style, and it started in Athens in the late 6th century BC and was popular to the 4th century BC. Other local schools also developed in the late 5th century, especially in southern Italy, and continued until c. 300 BC. It was also produced at Corinth. (*syn.* Red-Figure ware)

Red Hills or red hills: A local name for the mounds of burned clay, ash, and coarse pottery that dot the coasts of eastern England. They mark the sites at which salt was obtained by artificial evaporation of sea water during the later Iron Age and the Romano-British period.

redistribution: A mode of primitive exchange in which the operation was directed and controlled by some central organizing authority; a complex process that was a critical part of the evolution of civilization. Goods are received or appropriated by the central authority, and subsequently some of them are sent by that authority to other locations. It might involve the physical collection and pooling of locally produced items and their subsequent reallocation or merely control the flow without central collection. Storage facilities and a system of record keeping are often associated with the central power. The goods exchanged may be local products, which would permit some degree of craft specialization, because the specialists can depend on the central authority for the supply of all necessities. The products received in return for these exports may be treated as prestige items and made available to only a restricted number of the local people in the upper levels of the social hierarchy. Redistribution is often associated with societies organized as chiefdoms with a central authority and marked differences in social ranking. (*syn.* redistributive exchange)

red polished ware: A fine red ware with red or orange slip that is highly burnished. It was made in southern Asia in the first three centuries AD. It is often thought to be an imitation of the Roman Arrentine ware. The characteristic and most widely dispersed type of pottery of the Roman Empire was the red, polished Arretine ware. Most Inca pottery is also red polished ware.

red-slipped: Any pottery to which a slip, a thin layer of fine clay, is applied to pottery before firing by dipping the pot into a thick liquid mixture of clay and water. Slip decorates the fabric, often chosen to bake to a color such as red, yellow, or black, and makes the pot more watertight by clogging the pores of the earthenware.

reducing atmosphere: A term for pottery-firing conditions in which the supply of air is limited or the fuel damp. The fuel does not totally burn under these circumstances, and the gases contain carbon monoxide rather than oxygen. This generally results in black-surfaced pottery as opposed to the red produced in an oxidizing atmosphere, although shades of color may vary if the conditions during firing are not stable. Native Americans and Mesoamericans understood the effect of a reducing atmosphere, so that gray and black pots are found as well as the red and brown ones fired in an oxidizing flame.

reduction: A South American Indian settlement directed by Jesuit missionaries, existing as a Spanish colonial policy that brought dispersed Indian populations into mission settlements. The term also means the removal of mass from a stone.

refitting: The reassembling of stone debitage and cores to reconstruct ancient lithic technologies. It is any attempt to put stone tools and flakes back together again, which provides important information on the processes involved in the knapper's craft. The refitting or conjoining of artifact or ecofact fragments, especially those of struck stone flakes to recreate the original core, allows definition of cumulative features, such as the lithic artifact and debitage scatters. The technique may allow reconstruction of ancient manufacture and use behavior. (*syn.* conjoining; rejoining)

reflex bow: A small but powerful bow made such that, until strung, the ends of the bow project forward rather than backward. The simple bow, made from a single piece of wood, was known to Neolithic hunters; it is depicted in cave paintings by 30,000 BC. The first improvement was the reflex bow, a bow that was curved forward, or reflexively, near its center so that the string lay close against the grip before the bow was drawn. This increased the effective length of the draw because it began farther forward, close to the archer's left hand.

refuse: Any materials or remains left behind or discarded by humans. (*syn.* trash, garbage)

region: A geographically defined area containing a series of interrelated human communities sharing a single cultural-ecological system.

Regional Development Period: A term used in Ecuadorian archaeology for the period 500 BC–AD 500, when local adaptation led to the proliferation of regional cultures. The continuum Formative, Regional Development, Integration Period has also been applied to neighboring parts of South and Central America. Some of the Ecuadorian coastal variants produced fine pottery, elaborate figurines, and many small art objects. There are hints of Asiatic influence in the cultures of Bahia and Jama-Coaque, which occupied the coast land from La Plata island to Cape Francisco. The period is characterized by changes in sociopolitical organization and art styles and technology, which gave rise to region-wide rather than purely local cultures.

regional map: Any map designed to depict the distribution of archaeological sites in regions.

regional survey: A broad survey that includes the total environmental setting around an archaeological site.

regional system: Any system of time divisions such as those used in the Americas, based on major technological or social changes that produced regional cultures rather than local ones.

regnal year: A year reckoned from the date or anniversary of a monarch's accession to the throne, for instance, "in his eighth regnal year." At times, documents were dated by a king's regnal year. Before the time of Alexander the Great, the first regnal year was the new year following the king's accession.

Reichenau: Small island in the Untersee, the western arm of Lake Constance (Bodensee) in Baden-Württemberg Land (state), southwestern Germany, known for the Benedictine monastery founded there in 724 and secularized in 1803. It was an important Carolingian and Ottonian period monastery. Reichenau was the artistic and literary center of southwestern Germany during the 9th–11th centuries.

reindeer: Arctic deer domesticated in some polar regions, which ranged from Spitsbergen and Scandinavia to eastern Siberia. They are also native to North America and are divisible into two types: the northern, or barren ground caribou of the tundra and taiga, and the woodland caribou of Canadian forests. Both types of reindeer are game animals valued for meat, hide, and antlers. A number of hunting peoples living in Europe during the later part of the ice ages seem to have specialized in hunting reindeer, for its bones are much more common than those of other animals on these sites. This is true of a few Mousterian levels, but it is almost the rule for Late Palaeolithic sites of the Magdalenian and Solutrean. Reindeer are likely to have lived in large herds, but we do not know whether they migrated widely in western Europe as they do today in the Arctic. (*syn.* caribou)

Reinecke, Paul (1872–1958): German archaeologist who was responsible for many typological studies and is best known for his subdivision of the central European Bronze and Iron Ages (with phases denoted by letters). His system involved eight phases: Bronze A to D (Early and Middle Bronze Age) and Hallstatt A to D (Late Bronze Age and Early Iron Age). It is still widely used today, although often in modified form. It was largely based on the typology of hoard finds in southern Germany.

Reingraberfeld: A term for a classic form of graveyard found in France, the Low Countries, and western Germany in the 5th–7th centuries. It is normally found by a river on a south-facing slope, usually some distance from a settlement. Bodies were buried in individual trenches in neat rows (no sarcophagi or coffins). The men were traditionally buried with one or more weapons, and the women with their brooches, hairpins, and other furnishings. (*syn.* Reihengraberfeld)

Reisner, George Andrew (1867–1942): American Egyptologist who set new standards in Egyptian archaeology with his meticulous excavation methods, which were then comparable only with those of the British archaeologist Flinders Petrie. He carried out long-term excavations at Giza, Nag ed-Der, Kerma, and Deir el-Ballas. He directed a campaign in Nubia to survey threatened monuments and conducted excavations at Samaria in Palestine and in Sudan (Kerma, Meroe, Gebel Barkal). In Egypt, he excavated many tombs (Pyramid of Menkaure, tomb of Hetepheres) and the Valley Temple of Mycerinus at Giza.

relational difference: A method of defining variation in artifacts according to which other artifacts they are found with. A characteristic of an artifact based on the other artifacts it is found in association with. (*syn.* relational dimension)

relative age determination: The determination of a chronological sequence without reference to a fixed time scale. Relative age refers to chronological relations among relatively younger and older things, even though no actual dates may be available. (*syn.* relative age)

relative chronology: A time scale developed by the law of superposition or artifact ordering. It is the establishment of a chronology in which occurrences can be placed in the correct sequence relative to one another or to some known succession of events. Stratigraphy is the study of the relative chronology of the Earth's strata. (*syn.* stratigraphy)

relative dating: Dating methods where phases or objects can be put into a sequence relative to one another, but not tied to calendrically measured time. It is the sequencing of events or materials relative to another but without linkage to ages in years bp (before the present) or calendar years. A relative date is a date that can be said to be earlier than, later than, or contemporary with an event but that (unlike an absolute date) cannot be measured in calendar years. When archaeologists say that Event A occurred before or after Event B, they have a relative date for A. Before the advent of chronometric dating techniques, all dating was relative except where links with historical events could be proved. Some of these techniques, mainly stratigraphy and seriation, are still useful where chronometric dates cannot be obtained. Theoretically, floating chronologies that cannot be tied to an absolute date (e.g., certain dendrochronological sequences) are relative chronologies even though the techniques are essentially chronometric. (*syn.* relative dates; relative dating techniques)

relic: Any object surviving from an earlier culture, especially a valuable or symbolic object. In religion, a relic is the mortal remains of a saint and includes any object that has been in contact with the saint. Christianity was governed throughout the Middle Ages by the belief that spiritual virtue could be transmitted through relics of a person who in life was blessed with miraculous powers. Coffins and small objects such as combs, jewelry, and clothing were commonly sanctified and subsequently housed in beautiful reliquary caskets or shrines. Ecclesiastical centers with a collection of relics would be visited by large number of pilgrims, especially on saints' days, when the objects were put on special display and sometimes paraded.

relict soil: Soil formed on a pre-existing landscape but not subsequently buried under younger sediments. It must be taken into account that relict soils may represent a wide range of periods.

relief: Any sculpture in which the figures project from a supporting background or flat surface. Reliefs are classified according to the height of the figures' projection or detachment from the background. In a low relief, or bas-relief (basso-relievo), the design projects only slightly. In a high relief, or alto-relievo, the forms project at least half or more of their natural circumference from the background. Middle relief, or mezzo-relievo, falls roughly between the high and low forms. A variation of relief carving, found almost exclusively in ancient Egyptian sculpture, is sunken relief (also called incised relief), in which the carving is sunk below the level of the surrounding surface and is contained in a sharply incised contour line. Intaglio, likewise, is a sunken relief but is carved as a negative image like a mold instead of a positive (projecting) form. (*syn.* raised bas-relief; relievo)

relief-bank amphora: A distinctive, large storage jar made in the Rhineland in the 7th century, mainly at Badorf pottery centers. Each was strengthened with clay straps or bands and often used to carry Rhine wine to other countries. As a result, there are many amphorae sherds at sites in Britain, the Netherlands, and Scandinavia. The Badorf amphorae were probably made only until the 11th century, but similar forms were by then being produced in the new pottery centers at Andenne and Limburg.

relieving compartment: An empty room or other rough construction placed in a wall above an arch or opening to relieve it of much of the weight. The empty room would reduce the pressure from above.

religion: A framework of beliefs relating to supernatural or superhuman beings or forces that transcend the everyday material world. Prehistoric man was also religious—burying tools and food with the dead—obviously believing in a life hereafter.

reliquary: A portable shrine, box, or casket in which the relic(s) of a saint or other holy person were kept. A reliquary made to be worn around the neck was called an encolpium or phylacterium.

Remedello Sotto: A village and cemetery in Lombardy, Italy, or the Chalcolithic Remedello culture of the Po Valley and the Veneto in the 3rd millennium BC. Its famous cemetery of 117 tombs is the type site of a Copper Age culture. Skeletons were crouched in trench graves, accompanied by bifacially flaked fling daggers, traingular copper daggers, halberds, axes, and awls in copper, and barbed-and-tanged flint arrowheads. Pottery was scarce and variable. Sherds of beakers have been found associated with this material with a date c. 2500 BC. (*syn.* Remedellian)

Remojadas: A Classic Period center with distinctive pottery, dating to the Late Formative and lasting until the Early Postclassic, southeast of El Tajin near Veracruz, Mexico. Best known are the mold-made "smiling face" figurines and small wheeled animals. The figurines were turned out in incredible quantities for use as burial goods. Ball-game players and warriors are frequent subjects of the figurines, but women and children are also common. Locally available natural outcrops of asphalt were used as paint to highlight some features of the figurines. Examples of wheeled animals have been found as far afield as Nayarit and El Salvador. Farther down the Gulf coast plain, the Remojadas tradition of hollow pottery figurines continued to be active in the Late Classic, with a particularly large production of the mysterious smiling figures of dancing boys and girls, which were intended as funerary offerings.

Remote Oceania: The small islands of the Pacific, which can be reached only by sailing out of sight of land, including all the islands east of a line stretching from the Philippines to the Solomons.

remote sensing: The nondestructive techniques used in geophysical prospecting and in generating archaeological data without excavation. It is a general term for reconnaissance and surface survey techniques that leave subsurface archaeological deposits undisturbed. Reconnaissance and site survey methods use such devices as aerial photography and pedestrian survey to detect subsurface features and sites. It includes the detection of hidden archaeological features such as walls, pits, or roads by means of sound or radar impulses passed through the ground.

Renaissance: The period in European civilization immediately following the Middle Ages, conventionally held to have been characterized by a surge of interest in classical learning and values. It was the rebirth of European intellectual curiosity about the natural world and the role of humans in it, originating in the 15th century in Italy. Changing social, political, and economics conditions, as well as the rediscovery of Classical texts, were basic to this rebirth.

rendsina: A soil type characteristic of chalk or limestone subsoils; any of a group of dark grayish brown intrazonal soils developed in grasslands on soft calcareous marl, soft limestone, or chalk. Rendzinas are one of a group of soils known as primitive soils. Unlike mature soils, which have three or more horizons in their profile, rendzinas have only a mixed mineral/humus horizon, which rests directly on the weathered parent material. They represent an early stage in soil development. This fertile lime-rich soil is characterized by a dark friable humus-rich surface layer above a softer pale calcareous layer. (*syn.* rendzina)

replicability: The ability of different scientists using the same methods of observation or experimentation to achieve the same results. Also, the state or property of being experimentally replicable.

Repolust Cave: Palaeolithic cave site on the Mur River in southeast Australia, with artifacts and faunal remains of a warm interval. There is an undated assemblage of Lower or Middle Palaeolithic side scrapers, and so on.

repoussé: A jewelry-making and metalworking technique whereby a design is raised or embossed by hammering or punching out the metal from behind. Repoussé is usually done on bronze, but also on gold and silver. It consists of hammering up the design from the back of the object by using round-edged punches. The surface of the raised design can then be decorated. Further work on the design can be done by using chisels and punches on the front of the sheet—a technique known as chasing.

Repton: The church of St. Wystan at Repton in Derbyshire, England, with parts of the upstanding masonry belonging to the pre-Conquest period. There is an 8th–9th century crypt, the only English example of that date supported on four central columns. Repton is known to be the burial place of the Mercian kings, and recent excavations have found evidence of a mausoleum outside the main building, as well as evidence of the Viking encampment of 867.

Republic Groves: Archaic cemetery in Florida, with well-preserved human and animal bone, stone artifacts, and burial goods.

rescue archaeology: The branch of archaeology devoted to studying artifacts and features on sites imminently threatened by development in the form of the construction of dams, buildings, highways, and so on. Threats to archaeological remains occur in the form of road building, road improvement, new building of houses, offices, and industrial complexes, the flooding of valleys for reservoirs, and improved

farming techniques involving the use of deep plowing. The rescue, or salvage, archaeologist, is concerned with the retrieval of as much information as possible about the archaeological sites before they are damaged or destroyed. Frequently, time is too short and funds are too limited for anything but a brief survey. (*syn.* salvage archaeology, cultural resource management; rescue projects)

rescue project: Any attempt by cultural resource management to study artifacts and features imminently threatened by development.

research design: A carefully formulated and systematic plan for executing archaeological research. Systematic planning of archaeological research usually includes (1) the formulation of a strategy to resolve a particular question; (2) the collection and recording of the evidence; (3) the processing and analysis of these data and its interpretation; and (4) the publication of results. It begins as a statement outlining these four key elements as a blueprint of archaeological research: statement of perspective, synthesis of the existing database, research domains, and relevant research strategy. Research design is carried out to ensure the efficient use of resources and to guide the research according to the scientific method.

research proposal: A formally presented research design or strategy describing an intended project and its predicted results.

reserve head: A type of funerary sculpture of the Egyptian Old Kingdom, found mainly in tombs at Giza, and considered by some to be true portraits of the deceased. They consist of a limestone human head, usually with excised (or unsculpted) ears and enigmatic lines carved around the neck and down the back of the cranium. (*syn.* portrait head)

residence rule: A description of the household location of newly married couples in a given society, usually distinguished between actual and ideal patterns of behavior. In Australia's aboriginal society, residence rules generally required women to move into the groups and territories of their husbands after marriage.

residential group: Physical gathering of people at the domestic, territorial, or community level.

resistivity: The resistance of soil or buried features to the passage of an electrical current, measured during geophysical surveying. Different materials offer varying resistance to electrical currents, depending on the amount of water present. Resistivity is a method used to identify underlying deposits without excavation.

resistivity meter: A geophysical instrument used to measure the electrical resistivity of the Earth to identify buried features and structures. Because the resistivity of the soil changes with humidity, humus content, and so on, the machine can detect pits, ditches, roads, floors. This is generally done through an array of four electrodes, pushed into the ground surface. Despite their name, resistivity meters do not actually measure resistivity, but ground resistance. Resistivity is this resistance, standardized for the distance between the electrodes in the ground. The instrument consists of a source of electricity (a handle-operated dynamo in the megger earth tester, batteries in the tellohm, a transistor oscillator in the Martin-Clark meter) and a meter to record the results. All systems employ four steel probes connected by cable to the meter, two to carry the activating current, two to pick up the current passing through the ground. Also, the resistance between two roving probes is now compared with that between two distant static ones. Different spacing between the probes is employed in different conditions; where the probes are spaced equally, as in the Wenner configuration, features up to a depth equal to the probe separation can be detected. Anomalous readings may indicate the presence of archaeological material. (*syn.* resistivity detector)

resistivity surveying: A geosurvey technique that measures the electrical resistance of the ground for the location of buried features and structures. Any electrical exploration method in which current is introduced in the ground by two contact electrodes and potential differences are measured between two or more other electrodes. It relies on the principle that different deposits offer different resistance to the passage of an electric current, depending largely on the amount of water present. A damp pit or ditch fill offers less resistance, stone wall foundations more, than the surrounding soil. It is one of the most commonly used and least expensive geophysical surveying methods. Readings are taken in a grid pattern of points all over a suspected site. Variation of resistance through a site is caused mainly by differences in the amount of water contained in pore spaces of deposits and structures. The outline of features may be seen if the readings are plotted as a plan. Although the technique is generally known as "resistivity surveying," most archaeological surveys use only the ground resistance (in ohms). It compares well with magnetic surveying, as the instruments are simple and cheap and also because modern features such as power cables, iron scrap, and standing buildings do not affect the readings. (*syn.* resistivity survey)

resource-stress model: The control of stress caused by food shortages by rectifying behavior in response to changing conditions.

reticulated work: In masonry, it is a type of facing used on ancient Roman concrete or mortared rubble work walls. It appeared during the late Roman Republic and succeeded the earliest type of facing, an irregular patchwork called opus incertum. Reticulated work looks like a diagonal checkerboard with its square stones set lozenge fashion, separated by relatively fine joints. In porcelain production, it is a technique in which the outer side is entirely cut out in geometric patterns, honeycomb, circles intercrossed and superimposed to a second vase of similar or of cylindrical form. (*syn.* reticulated porcelain; opus reticulatum)

retouch: The working of a primary flake, usually by the removal of small fragments, to form a tool; to thin, sharpen, straighten, or otherwise refine an existing stone tool for further use. It is the work done to a flint implement after its preliminary roughing out to make it into a functional tool. In the case of a core tool, such as a hand ax, retouch may consist of roughly trimming the edge by striking with a hammer stone, but on smaller, finer flake or blade tools it is usually carried out by pressure flaking. It is done two ways, either by blows that knock small flakes off an edge (percussion retouch) or by pressure to force the flakes off (pressure retouch). The different types of retouch are also described as backing or blunting retouch, and invasive or normal retouch. Invasive retouch can be steep or shallow, depending mainly on the kind of edge being retouched; this retouch can also be scaly in character. Backing is most often applied to blades and may have been done to blunt the back or to bring its end to a stout point. Evidence suggests that it may have been done to regularize the blade edge to facilitate fixing by resin "maxtic" to a bone or wood shaft. Such a strip of mastic was found in Lascaux, France. Notching or toothing is another form of retouch, and the removal of spalls or slivers as in the burin technique could be regarded as a further form of retouch or modification. Retouch is one of the most obvious features distinguishing a manmade from a naturally struck flint. (*syn.* secondary working; secondary flaking)

re-use process: The transformation of materials through successive states in the behavioral system. Potsherds, for example, are sometimes ground up to be used as temper in making new vessels.

revetment: A retaining wall that supports an earthwork structure or fortifications, or holds the sides of a bank in place. It often has a facing such as concrete, stone, or wood.

Rhapta: On the east African coast, called Azania, the chief town, which may lie buried in the Rufiji Delta of present-day Tanzania. Rhapta's main imports were metal weapons and iron tools—suggesting iron smelting. According to the Periplus of the Erythraean Sea, who wrote in the first few centuries AD, this was the southernmost port of the East African coast to which voyagers from the Mediterranean world at that time penetrated. From documentary evidence, it is possible that Rhapta was located in the general vicinity of the modern Dar es Salaam, perhaps in the delta of the Rufiji River.

rhinoceros: Any of five species of large hoofed mammals found in eastern and southern Africa and in tropical Asia. The term *rhinoceros* is sometimes also applied to other, extinct members of the family Rhinocerotidae. Five species of rhinoceros have survived until recently: the Great Indian rhino (*Rhinoceros unicornis*), the Javan rhino (*R. sondaicus*), the Sumatran rhino (*Dicerorhinus sumatrensis*), the white, or grass rhino (*Ceratotherium simum*), and the black, or browse rhino (*Diceros bicornis*). Like the elephant, these species have presumably been restricted both by intensified desertification and the interference of man. The closely related woolly rhinoceros evolved late in the Quaternary period and was adapted to cold, open conditions. It became common across Europe and northern Asia during times of colder climate, but became extinct before 10,000 BC. (*syn.* pl. rhinoceroses, rhinoceri)

Rhodes: Large Ionian/Aegean island, prosperous in Classical times as it was on trade routes from Greece to Egypt and the East. Minoan remains at Ialysus are evidence of early Cretan influence. With the collapse of the Minoan civilization (c. 1500–1400 BC), Rhodes became a powerful independent kingdom with a late Bronze Age culture. Rhodes was occupied by Dorians, mainly from Argos, c. 1100–1000 BC. The Rhodian cities of Lindus, Ialysus, and Camirus, along with Cos, Cnidus, and Halicarnassus, belonged to the Dorian Hexapolis (league of six cities) by which the Greeks protected themselves in Asia Minor. The cities of Rhodes traded throughout the Mediterranean and founded colonies in Italy, Sicily, Spain, and Asia Minor. Rhodes supported Rome during its war with Philip V of Macedonia. The island steadily declined after Rome made Delos a free port c. 166 BC. During the triumvirate of Antony, Octavian, and Lepidus (43 BC), the conspirator Gaius Cassius plundered Rhodes for refusal to support him. Although it continued for another century as a free city, it never recovered its former prosperity; in about 227 BC, a severe earthquake devastated the island. Excavations have unearthed a stadium, odeum, temples, and city walls. At its wealthiest and most powerful in the period c. 323–166 BC, Rhodes developed a new form of house whose colonnaded court (peristyle) had one row of columns higher than the others; provided a grand entrance to the Lindos akropolis sanctuary of Athena; and produced sculptures of quality, including a colossus overlooking the harbor (which fell in the earthquake of 227 BC). Rhodes became important again during the Crusader period, when it was chosen for an important military base.

Rhône culture: After the melting of the glaciers, Neolithic cultures established themselves in parts of the Rhône and Rhine valleys. The Rhône culture is the Swiss and east French counterpart of the Early Bronze Age cultures of central Europe. The metalwork and pottery are similar to those of the Straubing group in Bavaria.

rhyolite: An igneous rock that is the volcanic equivalent of granite; a constituent element in Hoabinhian pebble tools.

rhythmite: A sedimentary structure of rhythmically paired laminations or beds. The flat-lying, fine-grained bottom-set beds of many large former glacial lakes filled in and buried all of the pre-existing relief and are now exposed, forming perfectly flat lake plains. Cuts into these sediments often reveal rhythmically interbedded silts and clays. Some of these so-called rhythmites have been shown to be the result of seasonal changes in the proglacial environment. If such lacustrine deposits have annual silt and clay "couplets," they are known as varves.

rhyton: A Greek vessel of earthenware, metal, or stone, and sometimes in the form of an animal head. It was a deep vessel with a single handle intended for the pouring of libations or liquid offerings to the gods and spirits of the dead. The mouth at the upper end is often balanced by a hole at the lower end. It is presumed that the covering of this aperture by the celebrant would control the pouring of the libation until the right moment in the ceremony. Rhytons were often made of precious materials and in elaborate forms. They are typical of the Minoans, Mycenaeans, classical Greeks, and the Achaemenid Persians. It is technically a ritual vessel, found from the Bronze Age onward.

rice: Edible starchy cereal grain and the plant by which it is produced. The origin of rice culture has been traced to India. Rice culture gradually spread westward and was introduced to southern Europe in medieval times. Roughly one half of the world population, including virtually all of East and Southeast Asia, is wholly dependent on rice as a staple food. The earliest datable record is from Chirard in the Ganges Valley, before 4500 BC. By the third millennium, it was widely grown in south China, and it was likely domesticated at Hemudu by the early 5th millennium BC. Its original center of cultivation could lie anywhere between the two areas. The earliest cultivated rice may have been grown in natural swamps or middens, but by at least 2,000 years ago many parts of southeast Asia were developing terraced or wet-field cultivation. (*syn.* Oryza sativa)

Richborough: The site of a Roman port in Kent, England, just north of Sandwich. After the Roman invasion of Britain in AD 43, Richborough/Rutupiae was established to guard the Wantsum Channel separating the island of Thanet from the rest of Kent. Extant remains of Richborough Castle include the north wall of a Saxon shore fort, possibly built in the 3rd century. The fort was equipped with a military bath suite, of which the hypocaust survives, and an external amphitheater. Close by is the site of the landing of the Saxon leaders Hengist and Horsa in AD 449. It is also starting point for the Roman road, Watling Street, to Chester via London. The site is now 5 kilometers inland and no longer on the coast, following silting of the Wantsum Channel. (*syn.* ancient Rutupiae)

Richey-Roberts Clovis Cache: Clovis site in Washington

state with just 30 artifacts and bone and antler fragments. There are several hypotheses about the site's function.

ridge and furrow: A pattern of parallel ridges resulting from the plowing of strip fields in medieval and later open field systems. The fossilized remains of ancient plow marks are a common sight in England, having the appearance of long, rounded parallel ridges with alternating ditches. There is no absolute dating for the ridge and furrow field; a few contentious examples could be Roman in date, while others are as late as the 17th and 18th centuries.

ridgeway: An ancient communications route following the line of an upland ridge. These are tracks along the watersheds from hill fort to hill fort, used by prehistoric man. Often there is no artificially constructed roadway, but some routes became Roman roads or medieval droveways. The dates of the finds extend back beyond the Middle Ages. Important British ridgeways are the Jurassic Way along the limestone ridge from Dorset to Lincolnshire, the Icknield Way in the Chilterns, and the Pilgrims' Way along the North Downs.

riemchen: A rectangular, square-sectioned brick used in the Late Uruk period of Mesopotamia. It was used to build bonded walls and to make patterns on the facades of public buildings. (*syn.* Riemchen)

Rigveda: A collection of hymns forming part of the ancient sacred literature of India known as the Vedas. It was the earliest and most important of the Vedas, the religious writings of the Aryans at the time of their conquest of northwest India. It contains over a thousand poems of great variety of content, written in Sanskrit. It can be dated loosely to the second half of the 2nd millennium BC. It probably assumed its present form c. 1000 BC and was transmitted orally, with great accuracy, for many centuries. It is the oldest literary document of India. The Rigveda is of the greatest importance to philologists studying Hinduism and its immediate predecessor, Vedism. Its interest to archaeologists is in the information on the Aryan invasions of the 2nd millennium BC and the nature of early Indo-European societies in India. (*syn.* Rgveda)

Rikhta: Middle Palaeolithic site in central Ukraine, with undated artifacts, including bifacial foliates.

Rillaton: A gold cup found in a Wessex culture grave in Cornwall, southwest England, from the Bronze Age. It is one of the finest pieces of Wessex Culture craftsmanship—made of sheet gold, strengthened with corrugations, and with an S-shaped profile and a single handle. The burial was a stone cist beneath a burial mound. The cup is dated to c. 1650–1400 BC. (*syn.* Rillaton cup)

Rim: A site in northern Burkino Faso, Africa, with three phases dating c. 12,000–1,000 years ago. The second phase, a backed microlith industry lacking pottery and ground stone

artifacts, is dated to 3600 bp. From the mid-2nd millennium BC, both these elements are present. Stone tool technology continued until around 1,000 years ago, after the first local appearance of metal implements.

Rimini: A harbor town on the Adriatic Sea in northern Italy. It originally belonged to the Umbro-Etruscan civilization and was occupied in 268 BC by the Romans. A Latin colony was established there, and as the junction of the great Roman roads the Via Aemilia and the Via Flamina, it became a Roman municipium. It was later sacked by the dictator Sulla. Rimini passed to the Byzantines and from them to the Goths, from whom it was recaptured by the Byzantine general Narses, and then to the Lombards and Franks. It has one of earliest Roman triumphal arches, built in 27 BC. (*syn.* Ariminum)

rimsherd: A fragment of the rim of a pottery artifact.

Rinaldone: A cemetery in Lazio, Italy, the type site of a Copper Age culture lying between those of Remedello and Gaudo, and showing some connections with both. There are collective burials in rock-cut tombs or single or collective burials in trench graves—with crouched skeletons, pottery, flat copper axes, halberds, and daggers, stone battle axes, fine flint daggers, and numerous barbed-and-tanged arrowheads. The dark burnished ware has bottle shapes with lug and tunnel handles. It dates from c. 3000–2200 BC.

Ringkloster: Unusual Late Mesolithic (Ertebolle) site in Denmark, about 10 kilometers inland but with evidence of contact with the coast.

ringwork: A circular entrenchment, the most modest form of medieval castle, originating in Germany in the later 10th century. Excavations of several of the hundreds of 10th–13th-century ringworks have shown them to be fortified manors. The first ringworks in England were constructed just before the Norman Conquest; after the Conquest, hundreds of ringworks were erected to defend timber and masonry buildings. (*syn.* ring-work)

Rinyo-Clacton: The name formerly used for a Late Neolithic pottery style of Britain now known as Grooved Ware. It was so-called after two widely separated findspots (Clacton in Essex and Rinyo in the Orkney Islands).

Rio Bec: Southernmost of a trio of architectural styles in the lowland Maya Classic Period, based on the heavy use of uncut stone and stucco. Large towers imitating the steep stepped temple-pyramids of such centers as Tikal consist entirely of fill that has been plastered over. The style included mosaic facades rather than the modeled stucco of the Greater Peten group. The best example of Rio Bec architecture is at Xpuhil in Campeche. (*syn.* Rio Bec-Chenes)

Rio Claro: Early stratified site in the highlands of São Paulo state, Brazil. The sequence begins with crude choppers dating c. 20,000 years ago and ends with large stemmed points c. 6000 BC.

Rio Seco: Large preceramic site of c. 2500 BC on the north-central coast of Peru with two large pyramids, rectangular ground level, and subterranean structures. It dates to the Pre-Ceramic Period VI, and the earliest structures were an isolated group of house compounds. Some of these were later filled with rubble, and two pyramids were built over them. These were subjected to further reconstructions. Caches of offerings were buried in shell refuse around the bases of the pyramids. Rio Seco had a population of 500 to 1,000 at its height and was abandoned before the onset of the Initial Period.

Riparo de Romito, Papasidero: Cave site in Italy near Cosenze, with Gravettian, Epigravettian (18,700 bp), and Romanellian (10,960 bp) material.

Riparo Tagliente: Rock shelter in Italy's Verona region with Mousterian, early Aurignacian, and final Epigravettian (13,300–12,000 bp) material. The Epigravettian had animal and abstract engravings on stone.

Ripiceni-Izvor: Prehistoric site in eastern Romania, starting with a Lower Palaeolithic containing flakes. Six overlying levels are assigned to the Middle Palaeolithic and have side scrapers and bifacial foliates, of at least c. 46,400–40,200 bp. There are also Aurignacian, Gravettian, and post-Palaeolithic assemblages.

Ripoli: A village of Middle to Late Neolithic hut foundations (*fondi di capanne*) and some crouched burials in Aburzzi, Italy. It has given its name to the Ripoli Trichrome Painted ware of the central Italian Middle Neolithic, c. 4500–3500 BC. Ripoli ware has a buff fabric painted with geometric designs in black, separated from areas painted red by a pair of lines enclosing a row of dots. The usual shape is a round-based cup with straight vertical wall and single handle, sometimes with a pair of curious projections from the top. The Ripoli pottery is one of a series of Italian trichrome painted wares, including the Capri style and the Scaloria style. There are connections with Danilo across the Adriatic. Notable among the flintwork are tanged and single-barbed arrowheads.

rippled decoration: A technique of pottery burnish in which the whole surface is worked into ripples, in extreme examples approaching fluting.

Riss glaciation: The third major glaciation of the Pleistocene in Alpine Europe; the penultimate Alpine glacial advance. It started 250,000 years ago and lasted over 100,000 years. The Riss, during which mountain glaciers descended from the highlands, followed the Mindel-Riss Interglacial Stage and preceded the Riss-Würm Interglacial Stage, both periods of relatively moderate climatic conditions. The Riss

is correlated with the Gipping Glacial Stage of Great Britain and the Saale Glacial Stage of northern Europe. Like the Saale, the Riss Glacial Stage included two major phases of ice advance separated by a period of more moderate conditions. The Riss Glacial Stage is roughly contemporaneous with the Illinoian Glacial Stage of North America. (*syn.* Riss Glacial Stage)

Riss-Würm Interglacial Stage: Major division of the Pleistocene in Alpine Europe, a period of relatively moderate climatic conditions, followed the Riss Glacial Stage, and preceded the Würm Glacial Stage, both periods of deteriorating conditions. The Riss-Würm is correlated with the Eemian Interglacial Stage of northern Europe and the Ipswichian Interglacial Stage of Great Britain. It is broadly equivalent to the Sangamon Interglacial Stage of North America.

rite of intensification: A ritual that symbolizes group concerns and solidarity, especially at critical times.

rite of passage: A ritual symbolizing a transition in the life of an individual and his or her altered relationships to others.

ritsuryo: Code of laws adopted in Japan in AD 702, marking the shift from yamato at ritsuryo state administration. The ritsuryo system refers to the government structure defined by ritsu, the criminal code, and ryo, the administrative and civil codes. Such a system had long been in force in China, and the Japanese ritsuryo was an imitation of the lü-ling of T'ang China and incorporated many of its original articles. The Ritsuryo state used the T'ang Dynasty model of capital city, from which trunk routes radiated. These formed the focus of regional administrative districts, which were further divided into provinces with provincial capitals. In this system, the emperor was an absolute monarch, and the people were divided into two classes, freemen and slaves.

ritual: The performance of ceremonial acts prescribed by tradition or by sacerdotal decree is a specific, observable mode of behavior exhibited by all known societies. Rituals are connected with some magic or religious practice. (*syn.* rite)

ritual vessel: Any object made and intended for the worship of ancestors, who are often named in inscriptions on the object, which is usually bronze. Many were specially cast to commemorate important events in the lives of their possessors. The vessels were also meant to serve as heirlooms. Although ritual vessels are found in many parts of ancient world (rhytons or libation vessels of Greek Bronze Age), they were particularly important in China—used for sacrifices of food and wine offered to ancestors. The bronze ritual vessel is the characteristic artifact of the Chinese civilization. Many are found in the tombs of the Shang and Chou Dynasties, made almost exclusively by casting. Beginning in the Anyang period (c. 1300–1030 BC), vessels were often cast with inscriptions dedicating them to the service of deceased ancestors; hence the sacrificial offerings of wine and food presented in the vessels were connected with the ancestral cult known also from the Anyang oracle bone inscriptions. The practice of providing imposing vessels as mortuary gifts, and perhaps even the ancestral cult itself, originated in the east-coast Neolithic tradition, where some of the Shang vessel shapes have precursors in pottery and where important Shang cultural traits are foreshadowed as early as the 4th millennium BC. The vessel types are known today either by names given them in Shang or Chou times that can be identified in contemporary inscriptions, such as the li, ting, and hsien, or by names, such as yu, chia, and kuang, given them by later Chinese scholars and antiquarians. The vessels may be grouped according to their presumed function in sacrificial rites.

river terrace: A bench or step that extends along the side of a valley and represents a former level of the valley floor. It is the result of alternating period of erosion and aggradation (silting) in a river valley, brought about by oscillations of sea level relative to land. When sea level is low, the gradient of the river is increased, the water flows more quickly, and it cuts away the river bed. During a period of high sea level, the gradient is less, the river flows sluggishly, and gravel is deposited on the valley floor. A second period of erosion will carry away most of this gravel, except at the edge of the valley, where a residual platform, or terrace, may remain. It is often possible to correlate cycles of erosion and aggradation with the fluctuations of Pleistocene climate and thus to work out the relative dating of artifacts incorporated in the gravels of the terraces. Another type of terrace is cut into bedrock and may have a thin veneer of alluvium, or sedimentary deposits. (*syn.* terrace)

Riverton culture: Archaic culture near Vincennes, Indiana, dating c. 1500–1000 BC. It was a hunting-gathering culture with a variety of stone and bone tools. There were year-round settlements and seasonally occupied bases, hunting, and transient camps.

rivet: A small metal rod used to attach a metal blade to its haft (as the handles of bronze daggers) or to fasten two sheets of metal together. Each end of the rivet is burred over (spread and flattened) by hammering after it has been passed through the two elements to be joined. Riveting is also a method of making joints in metalwork. The rivets are short metal rods that pass through holes in the parts to be joined and are hammered down on either side to hold the joint firmly together. In antiquity, riveting was used to make such artifacts as helmets or situlae.

Rivnac culture: Eneolithic culture of Bohemia (now the Czech Republic), with small ditched and palisaded sites (Homolka) of the late 3rd millennium BC. The culture is related to the Baden culture to the southeast.

Rivoli: A series of sites, including hilltop settlements, of Rivoli, near Verona in northeast Italy, which have provided the name for a version of the northern Italian Neolithic Square-Mouthed Pottery culture. As well as the characteristic pottery, the sites have produced pintaderas and a fragment of copper—early evidence of metal working in the area. There is also a castle begun by Victor Amadeus II, king of Sicily and Sardinia, in 1712, on the site of an older structure.

road: A traveled way on which people, animals, or wheeled vehicles move. The earliest roads developed from the paths and trails of prehistoric peoples; their construction was concurrent with the appearance of wheeled vehicles, which was probably in the area between the Caucasus Mountains and the Persian Gulf sometime before 3000 BC. Road systems were developed that connected the civilizations of Mesopotamia and Egypt and facilitated trade. The first major road was the Persian Royal Road, which extended from the Persian Gulf to the Aegean Sea over a distance of 1,775 miles (2,857 km) and was used from about 3500–300 BC. Originally made for the use of troops and their supplies, roads were eventually much used by the civilian population for the carriage of goods. This encouraged free trade and helped the advance of civilization and the subjugation and unification of the tribes. Early roads were about 20 feet wide and had ditches along both sides for drainage purposes. Large stones were laid on the foundation, then smaller ones, or gravel, on top. Traffic and weather blended the road material and helped to form the surface. Some curbs were made to hold the road surface together, and sometimes a line of stone was laid in the middle to help in the binding. The Romans were the first to construct roads scientifically. Their roads were characteristically straight, and the best ones were composed of a graded soil foundation that was topped by four layers: a bedding of sand or mortar; rows of large, flat stones; a thin layer of gravel mixed with lime; and a thin wearing surface of flintlike lava. Roman roads varied in thickness from 3–5 feet, and their design remained the most sophisticated until the modern road-building technology in the late 18th and early 19th centuries. Along the Roman roads were resthouses/mansiones and horse-changing stations/mutationes.

Roaix: Rock-cut tomb (hypogeum) in Vaucluse, France, with hundreds of bodily remains in two layers of c. 2150 BC and c. 2090 BC. The earlier layer had flint daggers and arrowheads, simple pots, and beads of copper, glass paste, green stone, and turquoise. The upper layer had flint arrowheads in some of the skeletons, indicating a war grave.

Robberg: Later Stone Age microlithic industry of southern and eastern Cape Province, South Africa, dated to c. 18,000–12,000 BP. There are many diminutive artifacts with few retouched implements, including bladelet cores, bladelets, scrapers, and backed bladelets. Worked bone and ostrich eggshell beads have also been found. (*syn.* Nelson Bay Cave)

robber trench: A term used to describe a feature created by the robbing of its original filling material. In areas where stone or other building materials are scarce or where a new structure is being built near one that is out of use, a monument's building materials may be plundered. The trench left is usually backfilled by the laborers who have "robbed" a wall either completely or of its facing stone. The trenches where the walls once stood and where the stone has been removed are called robber trenches or ghost walls. Archaeologists should be able to reconstruct a plan of the original structure from careful examination and recording of the robber trenches. (*syn.* ghost wall)

Roc de Sers: A Palaeolithic rock shelter in the Charente, France, with Solutrean and Magdalenian levels, including burials in the latter. A line of limestone blocks carved with bas-relief bison, horse, ibex, and other figures is among the rare examples of Solutrean art.

rock alignment: A design created by an arrangement of rocks, typically found across desert plains; usually the complete image can be discerned only aerially.

rock art: Painting and engraving on rock or cave surfaces, done as decoration, depiction of narratives, or for religious purposes. There are petroglyphs (carvings on rock face), engravings (incisions), and pictographs (paintings on rock surfaces). A great deal of rock art occurs throughout the African continent. In contrast to the painted caves of Europe, African art takes the form of either paintings in rock shelters (not in caves) or engravings on open rock outcrops or boulders.

rock-cut tomb: A chamber tomb cut into solid rock. In Egypt, this method was used during the Middle Kingdom (c. 1938–1600 BC); examples are found in the cliffs along the Nile, burials in the Valley of the Kings, and tombs of the nobles at Luxor. In the New Kingdom (1539–1075 BC), the kings were buried in rock-cut tombs, but separate mortuary temples continued to be built nearby. Rock-cut tombs are either made directly from a cliff face, by cutting a vertical shaft from the surface, or by a sloping or stepped passage (dromos). Rock-cut tombs are particularly common in the Mediterranean region, where they occur from the Neolithic to the Iron Age. They may be used either for single or collective burial.

rocker jaw: Distinctive anatomical feature of Polynesian peoples, where the lower edge of the mandible is convex.

rocker pattern: A type of pottery decoration in which a straight or curved edge is moved across the soft clay by pivoting on alternate corners, the result being a zigzag of curved lines. The technique was discovered and employed in a number of different times and places—the Neolithic impressed ware of the central Mediterranean, the Iron Age of the Sudan and of Manchuria, in North America (Hopewell),

and widely in pre-Classic cultures of Middle and South America.

rock shelter or rockshelter: A natural cave with a roof of overlying rock, which extends beyond the sides of the cave; a cave that is formed by a ledge of overhanging rock. Such a shallow cave or cliff overhang was used by humans as shelter from the elements, especially among hunters and gatherers. The shelter is not deep enough to be classed as a cave. (*syn.* abri)

rock-temple: An Egyptian temple cut into a solid outcrop of rock, particularly in Nubia's sandstone cliffs.

rock varnish: Natural accretions of manganese and iron oxides, together with clay minerals and organic matter, which can provide valuable environmental evidence. When combined with radiocarbon methods, the study of rock varnishes can provide a minimum age for some land forms and even for some types of stone tool that accumulate varnish.

Rocky Cape: Northern Tasmania site with the longest continuous sequence of a coastal midden in Australia. The South Cave was occupied from 8000–3800 bp, and its living floor is dated c. 6800 bp; the North Cave was used from c. 5500 bp.

Rogachev, Aleksandr Nikolaevich (1912–1984): Soviet archaeologist who specialized in the Palaeolithic and the study of stratigraphy and remains at Kostenki-Borshchevo sites. He also excavated at Avdeevo.

Romanelli: A large coastal cave in Apulia, Italy, occupied in the Palaeolithic period. Over a beach of late interglacial date came some Mousterian deposits and a series of Upper Palaeolithic (c. 12,000 BP) deposits of "Romanellian" type. There are engraved art objects in these layers and on the walls, and skeletal material is also found in the Romanellian levels. These include geometric microliths, over 200 plaques with engravings, and meanders and abstract designs engraved on the walls.

Romanesque: A style of architecture that emerged about 1000 and lasted until about 1150, by which time it had evolved into Gothic. It was a hybrid style of architecture and ornament, transitional from the classical Roman to the introduction of the Gothic. It was a combination of horizontal and arched construction, and the ornament included natural and fanciful objects. The term also refers to a style of monumental sculpture and painting.

Roman period: The period of Roman political and military control, generally between 200 BC and AD 400, but varying for different regions, depending on the date of conquest.

Rome, ancient: Historic city of Italy located on the Tiber River in central Italy. The historical site of Rome on the Seven Hills—the Aventine, Caelian, Capitoline, Esquiline, Palatine, Quirinal, and Viminal—was occupied as early as c. 900 BC, but continuous settlement by Indo-European peoples did not take place until the beginning of the 1st millennium BC. By the early 6th century BC, a politically unified city had emerged. The Romans gradually conquered the Italian peninsula, extended their dominion over the entire Mediterranean, and expanded their empire into continental Europe toward the Atlantic. As the capital of this empire, Rome became the site of grandiose palaces, temples, public baths, theaters, stadiums, and other public buildings. The focus of the city was the Forum. Ancient Rome reached the peak of its grandeur and ancient population during the last 1st and early 2nd centuries AD.

Rongorongo: The ancient script of Easter Island, carved in boustrophedon fashion on wooden boards. The script has about 120 pictographic symbols and has not been deciphered or traced to any specific outside source. It survives on 29 pieces of wood. It may be indigenous to the island and may even be of post-European inspiration (it was not recorded until the mid-19th century AD). It does not appear to be a true phonetic writing system. (*syn.* rongorongo)

roomblock: In the U.S. Southwest, a single or double row of rooms made either of wattle and daub or masonry slabs. A roomblock had either a pithouse or kiva, and its rooms were living quarters, storage, or for specialized activities.

Roonka: An open-site burial ground on the Lower Murray River, south Australia, with areas dating to 18,000 bp. It was exclusively a cemetery from 7000–400 bp. From 2000 BC, until the last century it was again a campsite as well as a cemetery with a variety of mortuary practices. Grave goods were found only in shaft graves and included food animals, ocher, bone and shell ornaments, and stone and bone tools.

Rop: A rock shelter on the Jos Plateau of central Nigeria with two main artifact-bearing layers, the first containing large scrapers and backed crescent-shaped implements, but no pottery. The later horizon contained a backed microlithic industry and pottery and dates to 2000 BP.

Roquepertuse: A late Iron Age sanctuary in Bouches-du-Rhône, France, where there was a Celto-Ligurian *oppidum* and famous stone sculptures. These included large human figures seated in a cross-legged position and a portal with niches for the display of severed human heads, as it was the site of a skull or severed-head cult. Many carvings bear traces of their original paint. The sanctuary was probably of the late 3rd or 2nd century BC and was destroyed by the Romans in 123 BC during their conquest of Provence.

Rosellini, (Niccolo Francesco) Ippolito (1800–1843): Italian Egyptologist who accompanied Jean-François Champollion on a Franco-Tuscan expedition to Egypt in 1828–1829. They published *Monuments de l'Égypte et Nubie*. This 10-volume description of the major monuments of Egypt

(1832–1844) was one of the most influential Egyptological publications of the mid-19th century.

Rosetta Stone: A basalt stela discovered at Rosetta, at the western mouth of the Nile, during Napoleon's occupation of Egypt, in 1799. This trilingual inscription on stone, a decree of King Ptolemy V (196 BC), was carved in Greek, Egyptian Demotic, and Egyptian hieroglyphic. It provided Jean-François Champollion with the key to the decipherment of the ancient Egyptian hieroglyphs, thus paving the way to modern Egyptology. The Rosetta Stone is now in the British Museum.

Roskilde: A city in Denmark at the head of the Roskilde Fjord, which was the former seat of Danish kings (c. 1020–1416) and capital of Denmark (until 1443). Underwater excavations have attempted to retrieve a barrier of sunken ships dating to 1000–1050, which was deliberately planned to protect the town from enemy raiders. The ships were reassembled and are now on display in Roskilde Ship Museum. The range of vessels recovered from the fjord includes a knarr, a long-distance sea-going cargo ship built out of pine and oak and propelled by a sail; an oak-built merchant ship; a warship; a ferry or fishing boat; and a Viking longship.

Rössen culture: The successor of the western branch of the Neolithic Linear Pottery culture, with which it has many features in common. Its main distribution was in Rhineland and central and southern Germany, parallel to the Lengyel culture in Czechoslovakia and the mid-Danube. It is characterized by pottery with complex incised geometric motifs and by sites with trapezoidal longhouses. Radiocarbon dates indicate the early 4th millennium BC. It is named after a cemetery site in Halle, with 70 burials accompanied by bone and jet necklaces, shaft-hole-stone axes, and some long trapezoidal ones. (*syn.* Röessen culture)

rosso antico: A salt-glazed red stoneware (red porcelain) produced by Josiah Wedgewood in the 18th century.

rostro-carinate: A term for an eolith shaped like a bird's beak.

Rouffignac: A huge cave in the Dordogne, southwest France, with Mesolithic levels (Sauveterrian and Tardensoisian) at the entrance dating from 9150–8370 bp. Deep inside this large cave system are black paintings and engravings in which mammoth predominates from the Magdalenian. There has been much controversy on which of the cave's paintings and engravings are authentic and which are modern.

roughout: An early stage in the making of bifacially chipped stone tools. Roughouts were often manufactured in quarry areas and later reworked into finished artifacts elsewhere.

rouletting: A technique used to decorate pottery. In Greek pottery making, it began in the early 4th century BC. A strip of metal was applied to the pot as it was turned on the wheel, leaving a band of even decoration on the inside; it was more accurately called chattering. Alternatively, a cogged wheel was rotated over the soft clay of a pot to leave a series of impressed dashes at right angles. That method was used especially on Roman pottery and was found on the exteriors of vessels, especially on the rim. In India, the technique was used on pottery of rougher fabric and on forms derived from Northern Black Polished wares, possibly beginning in the late 1st millennium BC. The Pre-Columbian civilization of the Chavín also used rouletting on its pottery. (*syn.* roulette)

round tower: A form of architecture in which a hollow circular column, 50–150 feet high, is capped by a short, pointed roof of stone. There are many in Ireland (upward of 100), also in Scotland, the Isle of Man, in Denmark, and as part of Windsor Castle in England. Round towers were a feature of Irish monasteries from the Viking period and into the Romanesque. There is usually a single entrance door, about 8–15 feet above the ground, usually five stories high, and each floor was lit by a separate window and had a wooden floor. Because the doors were placed high off the ground, it seems that the main function of the towers was as a refuge from Viking and Irish raiders, but they may also have been used as companiles.

Routsi: Site of a Mycenaean tholos tomb in Messenia, Greece, with grave goods including bronze weapons, gold, amber and glass jewelry, and pottery.

Royal Cemetery: A site in Ur in southern Mesopotamia with 1,500 tombs from the later Early Dynastic to the Ur III period, mostly from c. 2600–2300 BC. The richest tomb belonged to King Meskalamdug and held many precious materials and famous artifacts of the Sumerian civilization. The royal burials were accompanied by soldiers and servants, carts, and horses.

royal titulary: The classic sequence of names and titles held by each of the Egyptian pharaohs, which consisted of five names ("fivefold titulary"). The system was not entirely established until the Middle Kingdom (c. 1938–1600 BC). The five epithets encapsulate Egyptian views on kingship: three stressing the king's role as a god and the other two emphasizing Egypt as divided into two lands, both under the control of the pharaoh. The birth name was usually the last name in the sequence in inscriptions giving the king's name and titles, but it was the only one to be given to the pharaoh as soon as he was born. The other four names were given to the ruler at the time of his installation on the throne.

Roy Mata (b. ?–c. 1265): A great chief of central Vanuatu, especially on the islands of Efate and Retoka, who arrived around AD 1200 and set up a highly stratified society. His death was marked by an elaborate ritual that included the burying alive of one man and one woman from each of the clans under his influence. His grave, on Retoka, has been excavated, and it was surrounded by evidence for the mass sacrifice of 35 retainers, including 11 male-female pairs. Many bodies had ankle, wrist, and neck ornaments of shells and pig tusks. (*syn.* Roymata)

Rozhok I: Middle Palaeolithic site on the Sea of Azov in European Russia, with six cultural levels, dated from the early last glacial. Artifacts include side scrapers and typical Upper Palaeolithic tools.

Ruanga: An Iron Age settlement in northern Mashonaland, Zimbabwe, where a stone building appears to have been occupied by people related to those of Great Zimbabwe.

Rudenko, Sergei I. (1885–1969): Russian archaeologist and ethnographer, who became an expert on the peoples of Siberia and the Volga area. He excavated the frozen tombs at Pazyryk and wrote *Frozen Tombs of Siberia: The Pazyryk Burials of Iron Age Horsemen* (1970).

Rudna Glava: The site of a Late Vinca copper mine, in the limestone hills of northeastern Serbia. The mine, dated to the early 4th millennium BC, employed a mining technique involving the construction of platforms on the steep hillside and followed the vertical veins of malachite down, thereby creating empty "shafts." Sealed deposits of miners' lamps, antler picks, and gabbro mauls have been found at the bottom of abandoned mineshafts, of which there are over 25.

rune: An angular script for carving on wood or stone, developed by Germanic peoples (northern Germany, Scandinavia) around the 4th century AD through contact with Mediterranean alphabets. The early alphabet, with 24 letters divided into three groups of eight, was mainly used for short commemorative or magic protective formulae. A simplified alphabet of 16 characters was developed in Scandinavia from the 9th century, and this was used for more elaborate inscriptions, continuing for a long period in the Middle Ages. The etymology of the word means "secret," "mystery," "counsel," and "charm." It is first recorded in Denmark and Schleswig and spread widely across northern Europe. The voyages of the Vikings later carried it as far as Russia and Iceland, where it remained in use into the Middle Ages. There are no substantiated runic inscriptions from the New World. A rune stone is a free-standing memorial stone with an inscription in runes. Runes are associated with ceremonial artifacts, but are also seen as graffiti. (*syn.* futhark; runic)

rune stone: A free-standing memorial stone with an inscription in runes, developed by Germanic peoples around the 4th century AD. Rune stones from the Viking period are found throughout Scandinavia. (*syn.* runestone, rune-stone)

Runnymede: Site on the River Thames in Surrey, England, with occupation in the Middle Neolithic, c. 3700–3300 BC, and Late Bronze Age, c. 900–700 BC. There are intact hearths from the Neolithic and a roundhouse and two other buildings of the Late Bronze Age.

Rupar: A site in east Punjab, Pakistan, at the foot of the Simla Hills, with vestiges of two phases of the Indus Valley or Harappan civilization. It is stratified below an occupation with Painted Gray ware, which was itself by a level with Northern Black Polished ware.

Ruse: A city of northern Bulgaria, located on a major crossing point of the Danube, which began as a fortified Roman harbor called Sexantaprista ("Sixty Ships") in the 1st century BC. It was destroyed by barbarians in the 7th century. The Ottomans built a new town, Roustchouk, which subsequently bore the names Cherven and Roussé. It is the site of a large tell of the Karanovo V–VI group (4th millennium BC) where 11 Copper Age occupation levels have been uncovered. Interspersed between house levels were over 100 intramural burials. (*syn.* Russe, Roussé, Sexantaprista, Roustchouk)

rustication: In pottery decoration, the roughening of the surface of a pot, which may or may not have an applied slip. The roughening may be achieved by using fingers, fingernails, twigs, and so on, and although it may be pure decoration, in most cases it is probably a device to prevent a greasy pot from slipping through the fingers. On some, a grit such as flint may actually be added to the roughened clay to give additional grip. (*syn.* rusticated)

Rustic Ware: A pottery type made principally in northern Britain, a technique occasionally used on flower pots today. Barbotine is applied to the ware and a finger put on the wet clay and lifted off, so that the clay has finger forms in ridges and then a point. The term also refers to pottery made by Frenchman Bernard Palissy, who from about 1548 produced large earthenware dishes decorated with naturalistic pictures in high relief. The wares were colored with lead glazes, and the rustic ware was imitated by potters in France, Portugal, and England. (*syn.* rustic ware)

Ruthwell Cross: A cross with an important English-language runic inscription, from the Dumfries region of Scotland. The cross, an example of Northumbrian art of the early 8th century, stands more than 18 feet (5.5 m) high. It is carved with Gospel scenes and twining vines, as well as 18 verses of "The Dream of the Rood." The inscription has linguistic significance because it contains six runic symbols indicating guttural sounds, whereas the Scandinavians employed only one or two. Much of the inscription is also copied in Latin. It is now preserved in the interior of the parish church at Ruthwell in Northumberland, northeast England.

rye: A cereal grass and its edible grain, used to make rye bread and rye whiskey. Rye cultivation probably originated in southwestern Asia about 6500 BC, migrating westward across the Balkan Peninsula and over Europe. Today rye is grown extensively in Europe, Asia, and North America. It is mainly cultivated where climate and soil are unfavorable for other cereals and as a winter crop where temperatures are too cool for winter wheat. The plant, which thrives in high altitudes, has the greatest winter hardiness of all small grains, growing as far north as the Arctic Circle.

Rzuczewo: A settlement site and regional group of the Corded Ware/Single Grave complex of the Late Neolithic, located on the shores of the east Baltic in northern Poland and Latvia and dated to the turn of the 3rd millennium BC. At the type site, near Gdansk, large timber-framed houses are known. (*syn.* Haffkustenkultur)

Ss

sa: A hieroglyphic sign meaning "protection," which may have originally represented the rolled-up reed mat that would have sheltered herdsmen or the papyrus "life-vest" for boatmen. The sign was used either as an amulet or a symbol and held by the deities Bes and Taweret.

Saale: A division of Pleistocene deposits and time in northern Europe, which followed the Holstein Interglacial Stage and preceded the Eemian Interglacial Stage. It was the penultimate cold stage in northern Europe, c. 200,000–125,000 BP. The extensive and complex Saale deposits are correlated with the Wolstonian (or Gipping) Glacial Stage of Britain and the Riss Glacial Stage of the European Alpine region. The Saale is roughly contemporaneous with the Illinoian Glacial Stage of North America. The Saale has three complex phases: the Drente, Treene, and Warthe Substages. The Drente and Warthe represent periods of glacial advance, or maxima, whereas the Treene represents an interstadial period of glacial retreat between the early Drente and the late Warthe. In the region of central Europe, the Saale is represented by three glacial maxima separated by two periods, or interstadials, of moderating climatic conditions. One of the main features is a complex series of end moraines, demarcating the maximum extent of ice sheets. These ice sheets flowed out from centers in Scandinavia, across the Baltic Sea, and into northern Europe and Russia. The end moraines are split into two sets: one called the Drenthe moraines (or Dnieper), and the Warthe moraines (Moscow in Russia). These formations are complex and each seems to represent several "pulses" of the ice-sheet edge. The Saale Glacial Stage was named for the German river, a tributary of the Elbe. (*syn.* Saale Glacial Stage, Saalian cold stage)

Sabaean: One of four major peoples/kingdoms of southern Arabia in the 1st millennium BC, contemporary with the Minaeans, Qatabanians, and Hadramites. The Sabaean capital was at Marib (Ma'rib). The people who called themselves Saba' (biblical Sheba) are both the earliest and the most abundantly attested in the surviving written records. Sabaean rulers—who are mentioned in Assyrian annals of the late 8th and early 7th centuries BC—were responsible for impressive cultural and irrigational constructions. Two secondary centers were Sirwah, on a tributary of the Wadi Dhana above the dam, and Nashq (now Al-Bayda'), at the western end of Wadi Al-Jawf.

Sabatinovka: An area in the western Ukraine with several Tripolye sites, the most important being of the early 4th millennium BC and a late Tripolye site yielding a knot-headed copper pin comparable to early Unetice metalwork of the early 2nd millennium BC. A later site forms the eponymous site of the Ukrainian aspect of the Nova Sabatinovka–Bilogrudivka culture, a mid-2nd millennium BC culture found also in north Romania and Podolia. Most settlement sites are unfortified lowland camps, whose large quantities of ash in domestic debris inspired the term *zolniki* (ash pits). Timber-framed houses on stone foundations are organized along streets at some sites. (*syn.* Sabatinivka)

sabbakhin: Arabic word for diggers of sabbakh, nitrogenous earth from ancient sites used as fertilizer. Sabbakh may be mud brick or remains of organic refuse. Sabbakhin are among the chief agents of destruction of ancient sites.

Sabratha: Roman port on the north African coast in Libya, remarkable for its extensive imperial Roman remains. Originally settled by the Phoenicians in the 5th century BC, Sabratha was one of the three cities of Roman Tripolitania. Together with neighboring Oea and Leptis Magna, it made up a trio of wealthy trading cities, the Tripolis, which were important in linking the Mediterranean sea routes to the trans-Saharan caravans. It was first annexed by Rome in 46 BC and subsequently granted colonia status in the 2nd century AD. The city enjoyed great prosperity under the early empire. Sacked by the Austuriani in about 363, Sabratha recovered to have a second period of brief prosperity under Byzantine rule, when new walls enclosing a smaller area were constructed. Urban occupation seems to have been abandoned after the Arab seizure in 643. Among the surviving buildings are the various bath buildings and the Antonine-period theater. (*syn.* Greek Habrotonon, Roman Sabratha)

Sabz, Tepe: Tell site in Khuzestan in southwest Iran, which has given its name to a cultural phase succeeding the Muhammad Jafar phase, c. 5500–5250 BC. It is characterized by the appearance of painted pottery, buff colored with geometric designs executed in black paint. Evidence suggests that irrigation agriculture was practiced, and flax, emmer, barley, and pulses cultivated. By approximately 6000 BC, patterns of village farming were widely spread over much of the Iranian Plateau and in lowland Khuzestan. It has yielded evidence of fairly sophisticated patterns of agricultural life and general cultural connections with the beginnings of settled village life in neighboring areas such as Afghanistan, Baluchistan, Soviet Central Asia, and Mesopotamia.

Saccopastore: Palaeolithic site in a quarry near Rome, Italy, which has yielded two human skulls. These are regarded as early or generalized Neanderthals (Neanderthaloid) and are believed to belong to the last interglacial. The brain sizes of both skulls are smaller than classic Neanderthals. A few Mousterian stone tools were found associated with them.

sacellum: A term for a small enclosure with an altar and consecrated to a divinity. The term also means small monumental chapels in churches. (*syn.* sacred spot)

sacred: Worthy of religious veneration; pertaining to beliefs or propositions so valued that they are unquestioned. Also, of or relating to religion.

sacrifice: Many societies in various parts of the world and at different times have practiced animal or human sacrifice or both. One of the best-known examples in the Old World is the Mesopotamian city of Ur's Royal Cemetery. The Vedic and Hindu religions of India also have a complicated system of sacrifice. In the New World, the practice of animal and human sacrifice was an aspect of almost all Mesoamerican cultures and dates back into the early Formative Period, c. 6000–4800 BC. The extreme expression of sacrifice occurs in the Post-Classic, especially under the Aztec, whose perception of the universe as a continuing battle between the forces of generation and destruction made sacrifice a prerequisite for the continuation of the world. Sacrifice is fundamentally a religious act that has been of profound significance to individuals and social groups throughout history.

Sacsahuamán or Sacsayhuaman: An immense fortified Inca complex, built as an adjunct to the Incan capital at Cuzco, Peru, and begun some time after 1438. Thought to have functioned as a storage center and military garrison in peacetime, it was used as a safe haven for Cuzco residents in times of danger. Its north-facing limestone walls are cyclo-

pean, and the remains of round towers are still visible. They are built on a zigzag sawtooth plan, and the interior structures are built on three rising terraces and include storage and dwelling places, a reservoir and a conduit system. It is said to have been constructed over a period of 80 years with the labor of 20,000 Incans.

saddle quern: Ancient device for milling by pounding, a round stone rolled or rubbed on a flat stone bed. It is the earliest-known example, along with the mortar and pestle, of milling equipment, invented in Neolithic times (before 5600 BC). It consisted of a large, slightly concave lower stone and a smaller upper stone. Grain spread on the surface of the lower stone was ground by being rubbed with the upper stone.

saff tomb: A type of rock-cut tomb of the Theban 11th Dynasty, consisting of a row of openings—or colonnade—in the hillside. These were constructed primarily in the el-Tarif area of western Thebes for the local rulers of the 11th Dynasty (Intef I–III, 2125–2055 BC). The term *saff* (Arabic for "row") refers to the rows of rock-cut pillars that stood around three sides of a large trapezoidal sunk forecourt, forming the distinctive frontage of each of the tomb chapels. Private saff tombs have also been excavated at Armant and Dendera.

sagittal crest: The crest along the top of the skull where the chewing muscles are attached, found only in very large-jawed species. In primates that have large jaws and well-developed chewing muscles (e.g., gorillas, orangutans, and baboons), the parietal bones may be continued upward at the midline to form a sagittal crest. Among early hominids, Paranthropus (also called *Autralopithecus robustus*) sometimes exhibited a sagittal crest.

sago: A food starch prepared from carbohydrate material stored in the trunks of several palms, native from Indonesia to Samoa. This starch can be washed out from the chopped pith of felled trees and then cooked into porridge or cakes. Sago was used and traded widely around coastal New Guinea and the Mouccas Islands. Sago starch was important in early diets in equatorial Indonesia and Melanesia.

Sagvar: Upper Palaeolithic site in Hungary with radiocarbon dates of 18,900–17,760 bp. The artifacts, including end scrapers, are of the Gravettian.

Sagvardzhile: Upper Palaeolithic and Neolithic cave site in western Georgia on the Shavitskhali-Dzevrula River. The Upper Palaeolithic layer includes points and scrapers dating to 30,000–25,000 bp. There are also Palaeolithic remains mixed with Neolithic after redepositing.

Sahel: Grassland zone in the southern Sahara Desert, which is occupied by pastoral peoples. This semiarid region of western and north-central Africa extends from Senegal eastward to the Sudan. It forms a transitional zone between the arid Sahara to the north and the belt of humid savannas to the south. The Sahel ("shore" in Arabic) stretches from the Atlantic Ocean eastward through northern Senegal, southern Mauritania, the great bend of the Niger River in Mali, Burkina Faso (formerly Upper Volta), southern Niger, northeastern Nigeria, south-central Chad, and into the Sudan. (*syn.* Sahil)

Sahul Shelf: The shallow ocean shelf between Australia and New Guinea, at its narrowest under the present Torres Strait; the continental shelf that includes Australia, New Guinea, and Tasmania. The shelf was exposed as dry land at periods of low sea level in the Pleistocene, and New Guinea and Australia share a linked prehistory until the Torres Strait was finally drowned between 6000–4500 BC. (*syn.* Sahul shelf)

Sa-huynh: Iron Age culture and site on the central coast of southern Vietnam, dating mainly from the 1st millennium BC and associated with pottery urn burials and rich artifact assemblages paralleled most closely in the Philippines, north Borneo, and Sulawesi. The culture may be associated with early Chamic (Austronesian) settlement in Vietnam or proto-Cham and appears to be contemporary with, but separate from, the Dong-son culture of north Vietnam. Most assemblages known are from jar burials. Characteristic artifacts include lingling-o earrings and double-headed animal pendants of jadeite. It was active c. 600 BC–AD 100. (*syn.* Sa Huynh)

Sai: Island in Upper Nubia with a cemetery of the Kerma culture.

Sailendra: A Mahayana Buddhist empire established in Java in the 8th century. Its name ("King of the Mountain") has been seen as the claim to "Universal Rulership," taken over from the kings of Funan. In the 9th century, the dynasty left Java for Sumatra where they continued to hold power for several centuries.

St. Albans: A British town was established on the west bank of the Ver in the 1st century BC, and subsequently the Romans built their town of Verulamium on the site. In AD 61, the town was sacked. Ruins of the town wall dating from the 2nd century AD exist. In c. 304, a Roman named Alban, who had converted to Christianity, was taken from the town and killed on the east bank of the Ver. An abbey was later founded on the alleged site of his martyrdom, and the town of St. Albans grew up around the abbey. (*syn.* St. Albans phase)

Saint-Blaise: Site near the mouth of the Rhône in France, with Greek pottery from the 7th century BC. There are also quantities of Etruscan bucchero and the remains of the Hellenistic town.

Saint-Césaire: Prehistoric rock shelter in Charente-Maritime, France, with Aurignacian, Châtelperronian, and Mousterian layers. A Neanderthal skeleton was found in the Châtelperro-

nian level and dated to c. 36,300 BP, perhaps one of the last Neanderthalers.

St. Gall Plan: An important Carolingian document, probably formulated after the Council of Inden in 816 and then sent by the Abbot of Reichenau to Abbot Gozbert of St. Gall. The plan, written in ink on parchment, is an architect's drawing for the rebuilding of the monastic complex. The St. Gall Plan epitomizes an ideal "modern" Carolingian monastic unit, and although it was never fully realized at St. Gall, it remains an important source of reference for architectural historians and archaeologists.

Saint-Michel-du-Touch: Neolithic site with an enclosure of palisades and ditches in Haute-Garonne, France. There are many small structures that may be hut bases or hearths, all dating to the Chasséen, c. 4500–3400 BC. A pit contained two rich burials.

St. Ninian's Isle: An islet in the Shetlands, with the ruins of a small 12th-century chapel with the finest hoard of Pictish metalwork ever found in Britain. The hoard seems to have been deposited at the end of the 8th century, possibly in response to Viking raids, and included such objects as silver bowls, hanging bowls, spoons, sword pommel, thimble-shaped objects, and penannular brooches. The treasure is strong evidence that the tradition of Pictish metalworking continued into the early Christian era. It is now in the National Museum of Scotland in Edinburgh.

Saintonge ware: Major pottery industry in the region of Saintes in western France from the 13th century until recent times. The best known of these wares are the tall jugs with polychrome glazed decoration, which appear to have been traded with western French wine to the English. The jugs exported were only one of the variety of wares made at centers like La Chapelle des Pots, where kilns and workshops have been excavated. Saintonge was originally the territory inhabited by the Santones, a Gallic tribe.

Sais: Site in the Western Nile delta, capital of Egypt during the 26th Dynasty (664–525 BC). It was probably an impressive city; sculptural masterpieces from Sais have come from digging for sebbakh, which destroyed the tell. The remains are mostly covered by the modern village, and date principally to the 8th–6th centuries BC. (*syn.* Sa el-Hagar)

Saite: The 26th Dynasty of Egypt (664–525 BC) is known as the Saite period, as its pharaohs took Sais in the Delta as their capital. It was characterized by a notable revival in Egyptian art and Egyptian nationalism. The Saites were overthrown by the Persian invasion under Cambyses.

Sai Yok: A rock-shelter site in western Thailand with a sequence from a possibly pre-Hoabinhian industry, Hoabinhian, and a Neolithic assemblage of Ban Kao type. The sequence could have the longest record of Hoabinhian development in southeast Asia. The preceramic phase had pebble tools c. 10,000–8000 BC. The term is also applied to the pebble tools.

Sakas: Iranian steppe people from central Asia organized into a confederacy that, like that of the Scythians (to whom they were related), brought together tribes of agriculturists and of nomadic herdsmen. They took part in the great movement of peoples that swept away the Greek kingdom of Bactria in the mid-2nd century BC. After being repulsed by the Parthians, the Sakas settled in Drangiana (Seistan) and in the Indus Valley. They also held Kandahar for a short time.

Sakazhia: Middle and Upper Palaeolithic cave site in western Georgia on the Tskhaltsitela River. Assemblages include scrapers and denticulates from the Middle Palaeolithic and backed blades and points of the Upper Palaeolithic. Skeletal fragments classified as Neanderthal are in one of the lower levels of the Middle Palaeolithic.

Sakçe Gözü or Sakjegeuzu: A tell site in southeast Turkey, occupied in the Early Neolithic (comparable to Mersin) and a palace site of the Syro-Hittites of the early 1st millennium BC. The latter has produced quantities of important reliefs and inscriptions. The Neolithic period had a sequence of wares relating to the Amuq and Halaf pottery styles. The fortification walls, nearly 12 feet thick, were strengthened by projecting external buttresses and by turrets at the corners. The palace was approached through a portico with a beautiful series of sculptures showing strong Assyrian influence. The whole mound was composed of stratified debris of the 5th and early 4th millennia BC. (*syn.* Sakçagöze, Sakje-Gözü)

Saladoid series: A group of related pottery styles found along the Orinoco River in Venezuela and named after the type site at Saladero. Saladoid pottery is thin and fine, painted with white or red designs, especially white on red; the utilitarian wares include flat plates or griddles for making manioc bread. The everted bell, often with tabular lugs, is the favored vessel form. The Saladoid tradition may have begun before 2000 BC and lasted in some areas up to AD c. 1000. Some Saladoid groups migrated to Trinidad, Virgin Islands, and the Antilles during the early centuries AD, and this movement may represent the Arawak colonization of the West Indies. (*syn.* Saladero, Salader)

Salamis (Cyprus): A principal city of prehistoric and classic Cyprus, located on the east coast of the island, north of modern Famagusta. According to the Homeric epics, Salamis was founded after the Trojan War by the archer Teucer, who came from the island of Salamis, off Attica. This literary tradition probably reflects the Sea Peoples' occupation of Cyprus (c. 1193 BC). Later, the city grew because of its harbor; it became the chief Cypriot outlet for trade with Phoenicia, Egypt, and Cilicia. Salamis came under Persian control in 525 BC. In 306 BC, Demetrius I Poliorcetes of

Macedonia won a great naval victory there over Ptolemy I of Egypt. Salamis was sacked in the Jewish revolt of AD 115–117 and suffered repeatedly from earthquakes. It was completely rebuilt by the Christian emperor Constantius II (reigned AD 337–361) and given the name Constantia. Under Christian rule, Salamis was the metropolitan see of Cyprus. Destroyed again by the Arabs under Mu'awiyah (c. 648), the city was then abandoned. There is a large area of surviving ruins and an extensive necropolis to the west. The Mycenaean settlement was probably at Enkomi. Most remarkable are the so-called Royal Tombs, perhaps dating from the Late Geometric period, featuring large dromoi. The burial chambers are constructed of large rectangular blocks and have gable roofs, but were robbed in antiquity. There is an association with horse-and-chariot funerary rites, and horse skeletons still complete with bit in mouth have been discovered. There are also bronze horse accouterments, and cauldrons and tripods, and ivory furniture. One tomb shows evidence for an original upper beehive structure or tholos; other tombs are rock cut and show evidence for rites involving pyres and clay figurines.

Salamis (Greece): An island and town of Attikí, Greece, the site of the straits in which the Greeks won a decisive naval victory over the Persians in 480 BC. The invading forces of Xerxes and the Persians were repulsed. The city was occupied from the Bronze Age, and chamber tombs of the Early Iron Age had remains of the social elite.

Salcuta: A Late Neolithic culture and site of southwestern Romania, c. 3500–2500 BC. It derives from the Vinca culture, with further influence from the Aegean. By its end, copper was coming into use. There are four main occupation phases in the tell stratigraphy. The pottery is typically a dark burnished ware, contemporaneous to the Gumelnita and other Balkan cultures, and crusted painted wares. The Late Copper Age levels are characterized by unpainted pottery with *Furstenstich* decoration and with affinities to Cotofeni and Baden pottery.

Saliagos: Neolithic village on an islet once part of a peninsula joining Paros and Antiparos in the Cyclades of the Aegean. The community that lived here c. 4200–3700 BC lived largely by tunny fishing, although farming was also practiced. Tanged points of Melian obsidian were common, as was painted pottery, with white designs on a dark ground. Parian marble was used to produce stylized fiddle-shaped idols, ancestral to the better known figurines of the later Cycladic Bronze Age.

Salinar: A pottery style that followed Cupisnique in the Chicama and Virú Valleys of north Peru, c. 200 BC–AD 200. It is distinguished by modeled vessels, pots with stirrup spouts, and whistling jars. Some vessels have simple white patterns over a red slip. The transition from Cupisnique is evidenced in a shift from reduced-fired to oxidized-fired ceramics and the introduction of new forms and decorative techniques. Salinar introduces the handle-and-spout vessel, although the Chavinoid stirrup-spout form continues. The characteristic decoration is broad white painted bands and dots, sometimes outlined with incision. Salinar gave way to the Gallinazo and then Mochica styles.

Salinas La Blanca: Early Formative village site on the left bank of the Narajo River near Ocos, Guatemala. The principal features of the site are two low house mounds constructed of clay and household debris and dating to 1000–850 BC. A typical household cluster consisted of the house and outdoor hearth, a number of "borrow pits" (dug to obtain clay) and a sherd-and-shell midden. Large numbers of primitive corncobs indicate some farming.

salvage: An emergency survey and excavation at a site that is threatened by immediate destruction because of human development or natural phenomena.

salvage archaeology: The branch of archaeology devoted to studying artifacts and features on sites imminently threatened by development in the form of the construction of dams, buildings, highways, and so on. Threats to archaeological remains occur in the form of road building, road improvement, new building of houses, offices, and industrial complexes, the flooding of valleys for reservoirs, and improved farming techniques involving the use of deep plowing. The rescue, or salvage, archaeologist is concerned with the retrieval of as much information as possible about the archaeological sites before they are damaged or destroyed. Salvage archaeology is the location, recording (usually through excavation), and collection of archaeological data from a site in advance of highway construction, drainage projects, or urban development. In the United States, the first major program of salvage archaeology was undertaken in the 1930s, before the construction and dam building done by the Tennessee Valley Authority. (*syn.* rescue archaeology; cultural resource management)

Salzgitter-Lebenstedt: Mousterian hunting site in northwest Germany near Hanover, dated to c. 50,000 BP. It yielded reindeer and mammoth remains hunted by Middle Palaeolithic men and an eastern Mousterian assemblage with some western Mousterian artifact forms. Human skull fragments were found, possibly dating from early in the last glacial period.

Salzofen Cave: Cave site in southeast Austria with artifacts of the Middle Palaeolithic and Neolithic.

Samaria: Palestinian site that was the capital of the northern Kingdom of Israel. After a sporadic Early Bronze Age occupation, the city was founded by Omri, king of Israel, in 880 BC, and the earliest, and very fine, buildings and planning are

attributed to him and his son, Ahab. Omri had a palace defended by walls of ashlar masonry. Influence of the Phoenicians is visible, especially in a collection of carved ivories comparable to those of Nimrud. To c. 800 belongs a group of ostraca, throwing light on political conditions and the development of the Hebrew script. The site continued to be occupied after its destruction by the Assyrians c. 721 BC. It regained importance in the Hellenistic, Roman, and Byzantine periods.

Samarkand: City in east-central Uzbekistan, one of the oldest cities of Central Asia. In the 4th century BC, then known as Maracanda, it was the capital of Sogdiana and was captured (329 BC) by Alexander the Great. It benefited from its location in a fertile oasis at the point where the Silk Route from the West divided, one branch proceeding to China and the other to India. Excavations have revealed abundant Graeco-Sogdiana material. A palace of the 6th or 7th century AD yielded wall paintings comparable to the famous paintings from Pendzhikent. (*syn.* Samarqand, Maracanda)

Samarra: Islamic city of the Abbasid dynasty, mid-8th to mid-10th century AD, founded as the new capital in 836 AD on the Tigris River in central Iraq. Its Neolithic culture, 6th millennium BC, was remarkable for its elaborate painted pottery with geometric or naturalistic patterns. At that time, it was characterized by large villages with complex, multiroom buildings, and the introduction of irrigated agriculture and cattle rearing. The pottery, found mainly in the Samarra cemetery, replaced Hassuna ware, on which it marked a considerable advance. It was absorbed by the Halaf tradition, c. 5000 BC. The later site is a rich source of information on early Islamic architecture, public monuments, and town planning.

Samarran culture complex: Cultural phase of east-central Iraq along the Tigris River, which dates to the second half of the 6th and early 5th millennia BC, with sites such as Tell es Sawwan and Choga Mami. There are three phases of the complex: Early Samarran with coarse ware decorated by incision, Middle Samarran with painted pottery using naturalistic scenes and geometric designs; and Late Samarran with more geometric painted pottery and no naturalistic scenes. The Samarrans used irrigation agriculture and herding of animals, both important to the developing Mesopotamian civilizations.

Sambaquí: Shell middens along the Brazilian coast, north of Rio de Janeiro. The oldest debris was left by nonagricultural peoples who used no pottery and who made artifacts of chipped and polished stone (axes, adzes, choppers). The middens are of widely differing ages, from the 6th millennium BC until the centuries before the European conquest. There are also well-finished polished stone effigies (usually of birds or fish), which have a basin-like depression in the back. Probably of ceremonial significance, these effigies are thought to have been used in the ritual taking of snuff. (*syn.* Sambaqui tradition)

Sambor Prei Kuk: Early historic center southeast of Angkor, Cambodia, likely the capital of the pre-Angkor Khmer state of Isanapura (7th–8th centuries AD). (*syn.* Zhenla)

Sambungmachan: The find site on the Solo River, Java, of *Homo erectus* ancestor fossils (specifically a cranium) with Middle or Upper Pleistocene faunal associations. It is perhaps slightly earlier than the population from Ngadndong, further downstream on the Solo River. Some stone tools were found at Sambungmachan, believed to be the first found in the same context as *Homo erectus* in Java. (*syn.* Sambungmatjan)

Samguk Sagi: Historical record of the Three Kingdoms, the earliest surviving history for Korea. It was compiled by Kim Pu-sik in AD 1146 during the Koryo Dynasty.

Samhan: In Korea, the collective name for the Mahan, P'yonhan, and Chinhan protohistoric peoples during the Proto-Three Kingdoms period. Literally, "three Han," these people lived in the southern half of the Korean peninsula. Small polities are thought to have risen into the states of Paekche, Kaya, and Silla from the Samhan.

Samian ware: A distinctive Roman pottery produced mainly in south and central Gaul and the Moselle valley in the first century BC and first three centuries AD; later it was made in Britain (Colchester). It was copied from Italian Arretine ware and was itself widely imitated. It is a red ware with a bright glossy surface, plain or elaborately decorated by means of molds. Its second name derives from the stamp with which the potter frequently added his name to his products. The maker's name was stamped on the pottery, but the decorations, the shape, the fabric all help in dating and tracing its origin. The shapes come from metal prototypes. The forms, decorations, and stamps have allowed a detailed chronology to be established. The wares provide a valuable means of dating the other archaeological material found with them. (*syn.* Terra Sigillata, terra sigillata ware)

Samoa: A major island group in the south-central Pacific Ocean about 1,600 miles (2,600 km) northeast of New Zealand. American Samoa, a dependency of the United States, consists of six islands. Western Samoa, an independent nation, consists of nine islands. The islands were settled by Lapita colonists in the late 2nd millennium BC. There is a pottery sequence through the 1st millennium BC, after which pottery manufacture ceases. On the evidence of adze typology, Samoa may have been the source of the first settlers to penetrate eastern Polynesia, perhaps to the Marquesas, in the early 1st millennium AD. The last 1,500 years of Samoan prehistory are associated with above-ground monuments, including earthwork forts, earth or stone houses, god-house platforms, and agricultural terraces.

Samos: Greek island in the Aegean just off mainland western Asia Minor. There is evidence of Early Neolithic occupancy on the south coast, near Tigáni. About the 11th century BC, the Ionians appeared, and by the 7th century BC the island was one of the leading commercial centers of Greece. The tyrant Polycrates ruled from c. 540 BC, in what was perhaps the golden age of Samos. He ruled in alliance with the Egyptian pharaoh and had a powerful fleet that blockaded the Persian-controlled mainland until his death, c. 522 BC. Samos was part of the Delian League of Aegean states and then eclipsed by Rhodes in Hellenistic times. Ruins include the late 5th-century BC Temple of Hera and sanctuary and an aqueduct tunnel about 3/4 miles (1 km) long. Samos was the birthplace of the mathematician and philosopher Pythagoras.

sample: Any subset of a population; a set of units selected from a population. In statistics, a sample refers to a representative group of objects, cases, or items, selected from a larger population. The degree to which a sample is truly representative is controlled by the size of the sample and biasing factors affecting its selection. The larger the sample and the smaller the bias, the more representative the sample. All groups of archaeological material are samples, selected through preservation and choice of site, of an original population. The term sample is also used to describe the small sections cut from artifacts to do dating and analysis.

sample, quadrat: An archaeological research design in which the sampling element is a square or rectangular grid.

sample, transect: An archaeological research design in which the sampling element is a fairly long linear unit.

sample data acquisition: Investigation of only a portion of the sample units in a population, by either probabilistic or nonprobabilistic sampling.

sample, selection, random: A method of selecting a sample in which every element has a known and equal probability of selection.

sample selection, systematic: A method of selecting a sample in which the first element is drawn randomly and the others are selected at predetermined intervals. Samples are arranged in a regular pattern to ensure even coverage with only the starting point chosen randomly.

sample size: The total number of sample units drawn from a sampling frame or population.

sample unit: The basic unit of archaeological investigation; a subdivision of the data universe. It is an arbitrary or nonarbitrary unit of the data universe, used for sampling archaeological data.

sampling: The process of selecting part of a site for excavation or an area for fieldwork, preferably according to a strategy that allows statistical estimates and generalizations of the relation of the sample to the unexplored parts of the whole site or area. In a way, all archaeological fieldwork and excavation is sampling, because it is impossible to collect all the data from the complex mass of an archaeological site. Selection may be arbitrary or nonarbitrary—perhaps by the need for particular evidence for a specific question (a "judgment sample"); the question itself will be determined by the existing framework of archaeological thought. In a more specific sense, sampling or probabilistic or random sampling uses the theory of probability to make estimates of how closely the observations obtained from the part examined ("sample") represent the characteristics of the whole group being studied ("population"), by using fixed rules of random selection so that each unit is given a known chance of selection. The area under study may be divided into subzones (strata), and each stratum can be sampled separately to give a more precise estimate of the whole population. The choice of sample design, the size of the sample units, and the proportion of the population sampled (the sampling fraction) all affect the result, but even with quite small fractions accurate estimates of the entire population of sites in an area can be obtained. The method is particularly good at estimating the number of different types of sites in the area. Methods are also being developed for the sampling of large groups of artifacts; excavations frequently produce very large quantities of bone or flint, and it has been shown that often it is necessary to study only a small sample of the whole population to obtain a reliable estimate of its character.

sampling element: The object of study in a probability sample.

sampling fraction: The total number of sample units drawn from a sampling frame, expressed as a percentage of the population size.

sampling frame: A list of sample units from which a sample is drawn.

sampling universe: The set of all possible elements to be considered in a probability sample.

Sampung: Area in east-central Java and the name of a mid-Holocene industry characterized by stone points and bone tools. The sites include Gua Lawa, Gunung Cantalan, Petpuruh, Sodong, and Marjan.

Samrong Sen: Late prehistoric settlement site in central Cambodia, c. 1000 BC, with polished stone adzes and bronze implements.

Samuilitsa II: Middle Palaeolithic cave site on the Iskr River in Bulgaria. The layers date back to the early last glacial, and the upper layers are estimated to 42,780 bp. Artifacts include scrapers and bifacial foliates.

San: The hunter-gatherer people of southern Africa who once lived throughout the region and spoke a number of languages before becoming absorbed into agricultural societies. They were a nomadic egalitarian society with small bands of about 20 people. Men hunted with bow and arrow, and women gathered plant foods. Their record provides insights into Later Stone Age remains and rock art. By the late 20th century, many San had become laborers and trackers in settled areas. They are part of the Capoid local race, a subgroup, of the Negroid (African) geographic race (also including the Khoikhoin [Hottentots]). The most striking feature of the San languages is their extensive use of click sounds. (*syn.* Bushmen)

San Agustin: A locality in the south Colombian Andes highland, with a number of cemeteries, house platforms, ancient fields, stone-built chambers underneath mounds, and also a series of more than 300 stone statues representing mythological personages, some of them with jaguar fangs. The mounds commonly have internal stone-lined passageways and chambers, some of which contain sculpture, suggesting their use as places of worship as well as burial. Sculptures are rendered in a variety of techniques but are usually free-standing stelae and can be up to 4 meters high. Although stylistic comparisons are often made with Chavín, these themes have strong parallels in Olmec iconography. Occupation extends from about 700 BC almost to the Spanish conquest. The spectacular stonework falls somewhere between 500 BC and AD 1500. There is also incised and modeled pottery and gold ornaments from the underground burial chambers.

Sanchi: The site of three stupas in central India. They are the Great Stupa, Stupa No. 1, an Ashokan foundation enlarged over the centuries; No. 2, with railing decorations of the late Shunga period (c. 1st century BC); and No. 3, with its single toran (ceremonial gateway) of the late 1st century BC–1st century AD. Other features of interest include a commemorative pillar erected by the emperor Ashoka (c. 265–238 BC); an early Gupta temple (temple No. 17), early 5th century, with a flat roof and pillared portico; and monastic buildings ranging over several centuries. Sanchi sculpture is the early Indian style embellishing the 1st-century BC gateways of the Buddhist relic mound called the Great Stupa. The region of Sanchi, however, had a continuous artistic history from the 3rd century BC to the 11th century AD.

sand: A term describing the size of sediment or soil particles, 0.06–2 mm in diameter (BS 1377). The term has no implication of color, organic content, or any property other than particle size or texture.

Sandai: Chinese for "three periods"; the Xia, Shang, and Chou (Zhou) of protohistoric China.

Sandalja I: Lower Palaeolithic site in Croatia dating to the Lower Pleistocene, with chopping tool artifacts.

Sandia Cave: Type site for a tanged and unfluted projectile point in New Mexico's Sandia Mountains. This cave has yielded artifacts of the so-called Sandia Man (25,000 BC). In Pueblo mythology, the Sandias were sacred, marking the southern boundary of the Tiwa-speaking Indian territory. Sandia points were stratified below Folsom points, but the radiocarbon dates of pre-20,000 BC are often discounted, the true date probably falling in the range 12,000–8000 BC, overlapping with Clovis. Associated fauna of bison, mammoth, and mastodon suggested contemporaneity with the Llano Complex. Sandia Type I has a lanceolate blade without fluting and without the concave base of Clovis/Folsom and a shoulder to one side of the base of the blade, suggesting knife use. Sandia Type II has a rounded base.

San Dieguito complex: Late Palaeo-Indian complex of California, southwestern Nevada, and western Arizona, c. 8000–7000 BC. Characteristic artifacts are leaf-shaped biface points or knives, choppers, scrapers, and hammer stones. It postdates the Clovis in local sequences. This tradition was distinct from the Desert Culture in its reliance on hunting rather than gathering.

Sanga: Important Iron Age cemetery in Upemba depression, southeastern Zaire. The numerous graves that have been investigated are attributed to the Kisalian and Kabambian industries dating from the end of the 1st millennium AD to the last two centuries. Isalian iron and copper objects and pottery are associated with the 11th–12th centuries AD.

Sangamonian: The term in reference to "Age" is a major North American geochronological subdivision of the Pleistocene epoch, from c. 125,000–75,000 bp. The Sangamon includes a range of sediments, including organic sediment, but is represented mainly by a warm climate palaesol, the Sangamon geosol, which overlies Illinoian Age tills and is covered by Wisconsinan Age loess and tills. It appears to represent one single interglacial. As a "stage," it is a chronostratigraphic subdivision of the Pleistocene. (*syn.* Sangamon, Sangamonia Age, Sangamonian Stage)

Sangiran: Important site for Indonesian finds of *Homo erectus* in the Solo River valley of Java. Rich fossil-bearing deposits of both Middle Pleistocene (Trini fauna) and Lower Pleistocene (Djetis fauna) have yielded fossils of more than four hominid individuals from each level, including five skulls from the later level of perhaps c. 0.5–1 million years ago. The name was also used for a stone small-flake industry of the Middle Pleistocene. The human-made flakes are now mainly attributed to the high terrace gravels of the late Pleistocene or the Holocene.

Sangoan: Stone tool industry or complex of Sango Bay in Uganda on Lake Victoria, a mainly Middle Pleistocene series of assemblages containing heavy-duty picks (core axes), hand axes, scrapers, finely flaked lanceolate points, cleavers, and small specialized tools. The Sangoan may have developed from a late Acheulian basis and was roughly contemporary with the Mousterian of Europe, dating to 100,000–20,000 BP. The term is loosely applied to a rather heterogeneous group of industries in eastern and south-central Africa, and perhaps in West Africa. The most informative site for the composition and sequence of Sangoan industries is at Kalambo Falls, Zambia. In several regions of Zaire and neighboring countries, the Sangoan appears to mark the first human settlement of the low-lying country now occupied by the equatorial forest.

San'in: District of Honshu Island, Japan, used in archaeological documents, including parts of modern Kyoto and Hyogo Prefectures, and Tottori and Shimane Prefectures.

San José Mogote: The largest of a number of Zapotec village communities that developed in the Pre-Classic or Formative period in central Oaxaca, Mexico, before 1300 BC. Agriculture was practiced by "pot irrigation," direct watering from a well. There is evidence of Olmec influence, and by c. 900 BC the village had grown to 20 hectares. There were small lower class residences, public buildings, and workshops. Artifacts include debris from "prized" minerals such as ilmenite, hematite, mica, and green quartz, as well as finished goods of Olmec origin. These suggest that San José Mogote was a manufacturing site of shell ornaments and magnetite mirrors and was part of an Olmec-controlled trade system.

Sankalia, H. D. (1908–): Indian archaeologist whose field work and publications have been important to the development of Indian archaeology. Comprehensive surveys and research papers, especially on the prehistory of the Deccan, include "Archaeology in Rajasthan" (1988), "Prehistoric and Historic Archaeology of Gujarat" (1987), "The University of Nalanda" (1972), which recounts the history of one of the most important Buddhist monastic establishments.

Sankisa: Famous Buddhist pilgrimage center in the upper Ganges Valley, India, where the Buddha is said to have descended from heaven. It was visited by the emperor Ashoka in his pilgrimage of 249 BC and retains the commemorative pillar with its elephant capital erected on that occasion. (*syn.* ancient Samkashya)

San Lorenzo Tenochtitlan/San Lorenzo: The oldest-known Olmec center, located in Veracruz, Mexico, and revealing information on Olmec origins. It was a large nucleated village flourishing during the Early Formative. The first phase of occupation (Ojochi, c. 1800–1650 BC) left no architectural traces, but during the next period (Bajío, 1650–1550 BC) a start was made on the artificial plateau with lateral ridges forming the base of most subsequent structures. The Chicarras phase (1550–1450 BC) foreshadows true Olmec in its pottery, figurines, and perhaps also in stone carving. The San Lorenzo phase (1450–1100 BC) marks the Olmec climax at the site, whose layout then resembled that of La Venta. The principal features of the site are a large platform mound and a cluster of smaller mounds surrounding what may be the earliest ball court in Mesoamerica; more than 200 house mounds are clustered around these central features. A system of carved stone drains underlying the site is a unique structural feature. Around 900 BC, the stone monuments were mutilated and buried on the center's collapse. La Venta then came to power. The monuments weighed as much as 44 tons and were carved from basalt from the Cerro Cintepec, a volcanic flow in the Tuxtla Mountains about 50 air miles to the northwest. It is believed that the stones were somehow dragged down to the nearest navigable stream and from there transported on rafts up the Coatzacoalcos River to the San Lorenzo area. The amount of labor involved must have been enormous, indicating a complex social system to ensure the task's completion. Most striking are the "colossal heads," human portraits on a stupendous scale, the largest of which is 9 feet high. After a short hiatus, the site was reoccupied by a group whose culture still shows late Olmec affinities (Palangana phase, 800–450 BC), but was again abandoned until AD 900 when it was settled by early post-Classic (Villa Alta) people who used plumbate and fine orange pottery. The collapse of San Lorenzo c. 1150/1100 BC was abrupt and violent. The population was forced to do its agricultural work well outside the site, which may have contributed to the center's collapse.

San Pedro: The final chronological period of the Cochise culture in the Atacama region of northern Chile, contemporaneous with Tiahuanaco in Bolivia, AD c. 500–1000. Polychrome kero or beaker-shaped vessels are found in graves and typically, tool assemblages contain seed-grinding tools such as manos and metates, mortars and pestles, and a variety of projectile points, including the narrow stemmed, side-notched type, which first appeared during Chiricahua. Pit houses (houses of poles and earth built over pits) are also characteristic. During the San Pedro stage, pottery appeared in the area of the Mogollon Indians. The Cochise tradition may be taken as the base for subsequent cultural developments among various Indians in the Southwest.

Sanskrit: A language of the Indo-Aryan branch of Indo-European, an early Indo-European language used by the Aryans of India, and still in use for Hindu religious texts. It is related to Greek and Latin and was the most important early Indo-European language of northern India, being, for several centuries, the medium for much Hindu and Buddhist religious writing. Vedic Sanskrit, based on a dialect of north-

western India, dates from as early as 1800 BC; it was described and standardized in the important grammar book by Panini, dating from about the 5th century BC. The Rigveda, the oldest religious document of India, was written in an archaic form of Sanskrit in the mid-1st millennium BC. (*syn.* Sanscrit)

Santa Catalina de Guale: Spanish mission site c. 1566–1680 located on St. Catherine's Island in Georgia (US).

Santa Isabel Iztapán: Two mammoth kill sites in southeast Chiapas, Mexico, with human occupation dating 9,250 years ago. At one site, a skeleton, scrapers, knives, and blades of flint and obsidian, as well as a stemmed projectile point of flint, were found. The second mammoth site yielded a chert knife, a leaf-shaped point of flint, and a lanceolate point with a flat base. Similar kill sites were found at San Bartolo Atepehuacan, on the outskirts of Mexico City and at Tepexpan. The site is important as an indicator of the rapidity with which newly arrived (Asian) hunters dispersed southward. Stone tools of both the Big Game Hunting tradition and the Old Cordilleran tradition were found in the same levels, which is puzzling and infers that a combination of hunting techniques was used.

Santa Lucia: An inhumation and cremation cemetery in Slovenia with more than 6,000 graves, dating to c. 9th–2nd centuries BC. The graves' contents showed extensive trade with north Italy and central Europe. The Roman city of Emona (1st century BC) was located there.

Santubong: A complex of sites on the coast of Sarawak, northern Borneo, most dating between 900–1350. It was a major port of that time, probably connected with the Chinese state called Po-ni. There is evidence of iron smelting, large quantities of Chinese pottery, and local pottery of the Tanjong Kubor type.

sanukite: Type of andesite produced by now-extinct volcanoes in the Inland Sea area of Japan. It was used extensively during the Palaeolithic and postglacial (Jomon, Yayoi) for stone tools.

San Vicnezo al Volturno: An important Benedictine monastery in central Italy, founded in the early 8th century and sacked by the Arabs in 881 and eventually abandoned. The site appears to overlie a late Roman complex. A crypt of c. 830 is an example of an important painting technique of the time.

San'yo: District of Honshu Island, Japan, used in archaeological documents, including modern Yamaguchi, Hiroshima, and Okayama Prefectures and part of Hyogo Prefecture.

Sao: Industry in Chari Basin, Chad, associated with mound sites and dating to the late 2nd millennium BC.

Saoura: In the northwest Sahara, a basin with a long sequence from the Oldowan, Acheulian, and Aterian. Called a wadi or *oued*, meaning "ephemeral stream," the Saoura is the longest wadi, running nearly 600 miles south from the High Atlas to the Saharan interior, where it eventually dies out.

Sapalli-depe: Site in southern Uzbekistan, with Middle to Late Bronze Age occupation. Data found there define the Sapalli phase of regional chronology, mid–late 3rd millennia BC. There was a central square fortification and intramural burials with well-preserved organic remains. (*syn.* Sapalli-Tepe)

Saqqara: The site of the principal necropolis of the ancient city of Memphis, near Cairo, Egypt, used from the 2nd Dynasty to the Christian period. There are 15 royal pyramids, mainly of the Old Kingdom (c. 2575–2130 BC), the most being the Step Pyramid erected by Imhotep for Djoser, pharaoh of the 3rd Dynasty, c. 2630 BC. The royal mastaba tombs of the nobility making up most of the cemetery have yielded much evidence on the Archaic period. Also buried here, at the Serapeum, were the sacred Apis bulls. With the passage of time, burial chambers were more massively constructed of stone and eventually hewn from solid rock. There are a large number of important private tombs of the Archaic through the Graeco-Roman periods. (*syn.* Sakkara, Saqqarah)

Sarab, Tepe: Early farming site near Kermanshah in the Zagros Mountains of western Iran, dating c. 6000–5650 BC. The most unusual finds are two female figurines, in the sitting position with bulging thighs and breasts, but without facial features.

sarcophagus: A coffin or sepulchral chest of stone, wood, lead, or terra-cotta, typically carved or inscribed and intended to be exposed to view. In Egypt, it was the outermost container, with one or more wooden coffins and a mummy case within. Greek for "flesh-eater" or "flesh-swallowing," it is also the term for a kind of limestone reputed to consume the flesh of dead bodies. In the Classical world, the term was used for a clay or marble container holding a corpse. Many were elaborately painted and, in the Roman period, elaborately carved.

Sardis: City in western Anatolia (near Izmir, Turkey), associated with Croesus and the Lydians, the capital city of Lydia. The Lydian city, of the 7th–6th centuries BC, had an acropolis and walled lower settlement. From about 560–546 BC, Sardis was ruled by Croesus, who was renowned for his great wealth and was the last king of Lydia. Taken by the Persians (c. 546 BC), Sardis fell in turn to the Athenians, the Seleucids, and the Attalids until bequeathed to the Romans in 133 BC. Among the ruins are the palace of Croesus, temple of Artemis, gold work, and grave mounds of the royal cemetery. It was first occupied in the Early Bronze Age and became the first city where gold and silver coins were minted. Leveled by an earthquake in AD 17, the city was rebuilt and remained one of the great cities of Anatolia until the later Byzantine period. The Mongol Timur (Tamerlane) then destroyed it in 1402. Its ruins include the ancient Lydian citadel and about 1,000 Lydian graves. Excavations of Sardis have uncovered more remains of the Hellenistic and Byzantine city than of the Lydian town described by the Greek historian Herodotus. (*syn.* Sardes)

Sargon (c. 2330–2280 BC): The founder of the Akkadian Empire in the late 24th century BC, the first successful ruler of Mesopotamia. Sargon founded a new capital at Agade, conquering all of southern Mesopotamia as well as parts of Syria, Anatolia, and Elam (western Iran). He established the region's first Semitic dynasty and was considered the founder of the Mesopotamian military tradition. Sargon is known almost entirely from the legends and tales in 2,000 years of cuneiform Mesopotamian history, not from any documents that were written during his lifetime. (*syn.* Sargon of Akkad)

Sarka style: Variant of Linear pottery of western Bohemia, c. 3900 BC, parallel to the Zeliezovce in Slovakia and southern Poland. The vessels are painted in black spirals on buff before firing.

Sarmatian: A people originally of Iranian stock who migrated from Central Asia to the Ural Mountains between the 6th–4th centuries BC and eventually settled in most of southern European Russia and the eastern Balkans. These nomadic tribes were related to the Scythians and became a political and cultural force whose influence extended into central Asia and Transcaucasia, as well as into western Europe where the Sarmatians challenged the Romans before themselves being driven back by the Huns AD c. 370. Sarmatian art was strongly geometric, floral, and richly colored. They made jewelry in the form of rings, bracelets, diadems, brooches, gold plaques, buckles, buttons, and mounts, and exceptional metalwork was found in the tombs, including gold openwork plaques, bronze bracelets, spears, swords, gold-handled knives, and gold jewelry and cups. The Sarmatians were also very experienced in horsemanship and warfare.

Sarmizegethusa: Late Iron Age town of eastern Romania, seat of the Dacian state founded by Burebistas in the 1st century BC. A hilltop citadel is next to a sanctuary area with several shrines and temples. Bronze and iron products and pottery were made in an industrial area. In 101, Trajan led an invasion of Dacia (First Dacian War). The capital of Sarmizegethusa was captured, and Decebalus was forced in 102 to accept Roman occupation garrisons. In 105, Decebalus defeated the occupation forces and invaded Moesia (Second Dacian War). But after Trajan seized Sarmizegethusa a second time (106), the defeated king committed suicide, and in 107 Dacia became a Roman province. (*syn.* Gradistea Muncelului; Varhély)

Sarnate: A settlement site of the Late Mesolithic Narva culture, located in the southeast Baltic province of Latvia. The single culture level has radiocarbon dates of 2950–2250 BC and contains a rich collection of Narva pointed-base pottery and bone implements. A variety of wooden artifacts have been found on the waterlogged site.

Sarnath: Site north of Varanasi, Uttar Pradesh state, northern India, where, according to tradition, the Buddha first began teaching his followers. The emperor Ashoka visited the site on his pilgrimage of 249 BC and erected a stupa and the famous lion-capital memorial pillar. There is also a small temple, also of the 3rd century BC.

Sarnowo: Site of Kuyavian long barrows in north-central Poland, dated c. 3100–2900 BC. Traces of ard marks have been preserved under one of the nine trapezoidal-plan barrows. They belong to the Funnel Beaker culture.

sarsens/sarsen: A type of sandstone of the Marlborough Downs in Wiltshire, England. The sarsens are the remnants of a cap of Tertiary period sandstone, which once covered the area. They were used by the builders of Stonehenge, Avebury, and several megalithic chamber tombs. Stonehenge is almost 30 kilometers from the quarry site. (*syn.* sarsenstones)

Sarup: Neolithic site in Funen, Denmark, with two enclosures—Sarup I of the Fuchsberg phase (Early to Middle Neolithic) c. 3400 BC and Sarup II of c. 120 years later. About 12 Neolithic enclosures like this are known in southern Scandinavia.

Sassanian: The Persian dynasty that overthrew the Parthian Empire in AD 224 and ruled until conquered by Islam in 651. The empire extended from India to Syria, where they fought with the Romans. Remains include rock reliefs, Sassanian metalwork, fine stamp seals, textiles. Archaeologically, they are known from impressive architectural remains of palaces, temples, and fortifications and from the rock reliefs. Important Sassanian sites include Bishapur, Firuzabad, Naqsh-i Rustam, and Siraf.

satellite sensor imagery: A method of recording sites from the air by using infrared radiation that is beyond the practical spectral response of photographic film. The method is useful for tracing prehistoric agricultural system. (*syn.* scanner imagery)

Satet: Goddess associated with the island of Elephantine at Aswan and guardian of the southern frontiers of Egypt. She was Khnum's, the creator god's, companion. She was depicted as wearing the white crown of Upper Egypt, with antelope horns on either side of it. (*syn.* Satis)

Satingpra: Area on the east coast of Thailand with sites from the later 1st and early 2nd millennia AD, including Kok Moh, possibly associated with Langkasuka.

satrapy: One of the administrative units or provinces of the Achaemenid/Persian Empire, such as Ionia, Media, Bactria. Each was ruled by a governor or satrap appointed by the king. Sometimes a satrapy became an appanage of the royal princes. A satrapy would consist of a collection of ethnic groups rather than a piece of land with precise boundaries. Inhabitants had to make payments (tribute) to the empire and provide military services. The division of the empire into satrapies was completed by Darius I (reigned 522–486 BC), who established 20. The satrapal administration was retained by Alexander III the Great and his successors.

Satruper Moor: Region in Schleswig-Holstein, Germany, with sites c. 3500–3000 BC, the transition from foraging to sedentary lifestyle in northern Europe. Some of the sites are of the Ertebolle/Ellerbek culture, with pointed-base pots.

Satsumon: A type of Haji-like incised-motif pottery made in early Hokkaido and northern Honshu, Japan, from c. 4th–14th centuries, and to the culture characterized by this pottery. Satsumon houses are very much like Late Kofun houses. Iron tools were used, and cloth was woven. The Satsumon culture is seen as the transformation of a Jomon-type culture, which continued late in northern Japan, as the result of the contacts with Haji-using people to the south. The people are thought to be the ancestors of the historic Ainu.

sauceboat: In Greek antiquity, a vessel of clay or metal made on mainland Greece or in the Cyclades in mid–late 3rd millennia BC. They seem to have been for drinking rather than pouring.

Sautuola, Marcellino Sanz de (1831–1888): Spanish amateur geologist and archaeologist who excavated Altamira Cave, near Santillana, in northern Spain, which contains the earliest-known (c. 20,000–13,000 BC) examples of Stone Age painting. The colored ceiling paintings in a side cavern, which came to be regarded as the "Sistine Chapel of Prehistory," were the most spectacular. Sautuola had accurate drawings of the paintings prepared and published a book in 1880. He was unable to persuade scholars of the paintings' authenticity and died dishonored and bitter. Not until other similar paintings had been found in southwestern France (1895–1901) was Sautuola's contribution finally vindicated.

Sauveterrian: An Early Mesolithic culture of France and neighboring parts of Europe, following the Azilian in c. 9000 bp. It later spread to Britain and was contemporary with the Later Maglemosian. It is characterized by the lack of woodworking tools and by an abundance of geometric microliths. It is named after rock shelters in Sauveterre-la-Lémance, France. Sauveterrian related to 8000–4500 BC in the southern half of France, and it preceded the Tardenoisian. (*syn.* Sauveterre-la-Lemance)

Sawwan, Tell es-: One of the earliest villages discovered in the plain of Mesopotamia, near Samarra, the best-known Samarran period site. A developmental sequence for the painted pottery was very important as was the uncovering of five architectural levels (pottery plain and crude, then monochrome, then polychrome). There is a large group of burials and evidence of crops, early irrigation, domestication of animals. The radiocarbon dates are in the second half of the 6th millennium BC. The earliest known mold-made bricks are from this site, which also has veined alabaster vessels and figurines. (*syn.* Tall Sawwan)

Saxon: One of the Germanic peoples known collectively as Anglo-Saxons, who took part in the settlement of southern and eastern England in the 5th century AD after the Romans left. Their original home was on the North Sea coast north of the Elbe.

Saxon Shore: A system for defending the coasts of southeast England against raiding Saxon pirates, begun between AD 287–296 and later (AD 367) constituting a separate command under the Count of the Saxon Shore. It consisted of a series of forts at strategic sites from the Wash to Southampton, usually at the mouth of estuaries that served as harbors for attached naval units. Burgh Castle near Yarmouth, Richborough in Kent, and Porchester near Portsmouth are the best preserved of these forts. The forts were massive stone structures, defended by projecting bastions, and characterized by narrow gateways. It was a comprehensive coastal command developed with communications and administration. (*syn.* Latin litus saxonicum)

Sayil: A major Puuc site/Lowland Maya site in Yucatán, Mexico, which peaked during the Late Classic. There is a multistoried palace, chultuns under residences, and palaces used as reservoirs or kitchen gardens. Some of the most famous Mayan architectural monuments are at Sayil.

scaled drawing: Standardized rendering used to record archaeological data, especially during data acquisition. It would include elevation, isometric, perspective, plan, profile, and section drawings.

scanning electron microscopy: A technique used to gain information on the microscopic and submicroscopic structure of a wide range of materials such as ceramics, metals, stone, teeth, hair. It involves a type of electron microscope (SEM) in which a beam of electrons systematically sweeps over the specimen, the electron beam passing through a series of magnetic lenses that demagnify the beam diameter. The backscattered electrons and secondary electrons emitted are detected by means of a scintillation or semiconductor counter. The angle at which the beam hits the surface of the specimen determines the number of backscattered and secondary electrons detected, and thus the pattern of contrast represents the topography and elements of the specimen. The signal from these emissions is processed, and an image of the object is displayed on a screen. Its advantages over transmission electron microscopy include a greater depth of focus at high magnification and its ability to deal with specimens of much greater bulk, making it less destructive. The chemical composition of the material of the surface can also be deduced from the backscattered electrons. No elaborate specimen-preparation techniques are required for examination in the scanning electron microscope, and large and bulky specimens may be accommodated.

scaphium: A Greek vessel, small in size and in the form of a boat (scapha), which was used as a drinking cup and was also sacrificial.

scapula saw: An artifact made from the shoulder blade of a bighorn sheep or antelope.

scapulomancy: Divination method used in ancient China, consisting of the burning of shoulder blades of domesticated animals and interpretation of the cracks caused by the fire. It was widespread in North America and Eurasia. (*syn.* scapulimancy)

scar: In stone tools, this is the negative impression left after the removal of a flake.

scarab: An image or representation of a dung beetle (*Scarabaeus sacer*), very common in ancient Egypt, especially on the Egyptian stamp seal, in use from the Middle Kingdom (1938–c. 1600? BC). The dung beetle was held sacred by the ancient Egyptians as a symbol of the motive power of the sun, which was equated with the beetle's ball of dung. It figured frequently in jewelry and other art forms but is best known as the standard form of Egyptian stamp seals. These are made of stone or faience in the shape of a beetle resting on a flat base, the underside of which is carved with a distinguishing inscription in hieroglyphs and the name and titles of the owner. The back of the seal was the dung beetle form. Scarabs were perforated lengthwise and were worn around the neck or as a finger ring, serving as amulet as well as seal.

scarcement: The setback of a wall or embankment to form a ledge.

Scarlet Ware: A type of red-and-black painted pottery used in the early 3rd millennium BC in the plains of eastern Mesopotamia, of the Early Dynastic period. It was derived from Jemdet Nasr ware. Geometrical designs in black on buff, separated by large areas of red paint, became progressively more elaborate, in later stages including animal and human figures in red outlined in black. There are hints of connections with the wares of Baluchistan, especially in the elongated bulls.

scatter diagram: A visual way of presenting data that might otherwise be offered in numerical form. It consists of the plotting of units as dots against an X and a Y axis representing two attributes, so that relations between attributes as well as relations between units may be shown. When clustering of dots into different groups occurs, it may suggest the presence of different classes. It is also possible to see whether one attribute co-varies with another, seen by the grouping of the dots around the line from bottom left to top right of the diagram.

scavenging: The nonscientific or amateur removal of archaeological materials from a site by later inhabitants or visitors to a site.

sceatta: Small silver coin minted when the Anglo-Saxons reintroduced currency into England in the 7th century. The earliest identifiable ones are of Eorpwald of East Anglia (625–627) and Penda of Mercia (625–654). Our penny may owe its name to the latter. With this change of name, it remained the standard coin from the reforms of Offa of Mercia (757–796) until the 12th century. Sceattas are distinctive because they were made from pellets that were hammered between two dies, not minted from a flattened piece of metal (as after c. 790 in England). The kings of Kent imitated these silver coins in about 690 and issued them with a variety of designs that are collectively known as the primary series of sceattas. The primary series is virtually confined to Kent and ended about 720. The secondary series include a wider variety of designs that occur over a larger area. (*syn.* sceat)

scepter: In antiquity, a long staff similar to the shaft of a spear, carried to lean on when walking. It eventually became the truncheon, a weapon. Ornament was then added to the upper end of the staff, as the scepter became a staff or baton borne by a sovereign as an emblem of authority. (*syn.* sceptre)

Schela: Late Mesolithic and Neolithic site in western Romania of the Iron Gates gorge of the River Danube with radiocarbon dates of 6800–5600 BC. The Schela group is contemporary with the sites of Vlasac, Lepenski Vir, and Padina and includes cave as well as open sites. Burials were located around a hearth, with feet pointing toward it. There was herding and plant gathering to supplement fishing and hunting. Remains of the Neolithic Cris culture were in another layer. (*syn.* Schela Cladovei)

schist hones: Whetstones made of mica schist from the distinctive Eisdorg rocks of southern Norway. They were widely distributed on sites around the North Sea throughout the medieval period. A 9th-century boat carrying these hones was found near Kaupang.

schlepp effect: The result of the butchering process in which the meat is piled on the skin and the lower limb bones, which are used to drag the meat home. When this is done, the upper limb bones are discarded at the kill site, and the lower limb bones are found more commonly at the habitation site.

Schliemann, Heinrich (1822–1890): (shlee'-man) German businessman and archaeologist who discovered and excavated Troy, Tiryns, Mycenae, and Ithaca. Retiring from business a wealthy man at 41, he sought to identify Homer's Troy. He did so, on a site overlooking the Dardanelles with nine superimposed cities containing a startling wealth of material. He was the first to recognize the stratigraphy in a Near Eastern tell (Hisarlik was the first large dry-land manmade mound to be dug); he popularized archaeology; and he set standards of careful observation, recording, and rapid publication. He also worked at Mycenae, where his discovery of the shaft graves and their implications was as important as his work at Troy. Schliemann, together with Wilhelm Dörpfeld, excavated the great fortified site of Tiryns near Mycenae. They revealed the wealth and civilization of the Aegean Bronze Age and gave added support to the reliability of the classical legends. Modern archaeologists have criticized his approaches, but Schleimann remains a pioneer and an extremely important contributor to the study of the Mycenaean civilization. He had long thought that there must have existed in the Mediterranean a civilization earlier than Mycenae and Bronze Age Hisarlik, and he guessed that it might be in Crete. At one time, he wanted to excavate in Crete, but he could not agree to the price asked for the land. The discovery of the pre-Mycenaean civilization of Minoan Crete was left to Sir Arthur Evans, 10 years after Schliemann's death.

Schmidt, Erich (1897–1964): American archaeologist, excavator at Tepe Hissar (1931–1933), Fara (1931), and Persepolis (1934–1939).

Schönfeld group: Late Neolithic group in southeast Germany, which may be a regional variation of Corded ware or related to the Tiefstichkeramik of the late Funnel Beaker culture. The ceramics have distinctive shallow parabolic bowls with incised zigzag line patterns.

Schroda: In northeast Transvaal, South Africa, the 9th century AD capital and religious center of the Zhizo phase of the Early Iron Age. Trade began between the southern African interior and the East African coast, leading to the rise of Mapungubwe and Great Zimbabwe. Evidence shows the site's occupants were rich in both livestock and trade beads.

science: The search for universals in nature by means of established scientific methods of inquiry. Scientific method is an operational series of systematic procedures by which investigators examine natural phenomena and reach reasoned conclusions. Science is a way of acquiring knowledge and understanding about the parts of the natural world that can be observed; any disciplined and highly ordered search for knowledge carried out systematically. A continually self-correcting method of testing and refining the conclusions resulting from observation constitutes the scientific method.

Scoglio del Tonno: Prehistoric site on a promontory projecting into the harbor of Taranto in Puglie, Italy, where a Middle and Late Bronze Age settlement existed. It was first occupied during the Late Neolithic by people using Serra D'Alto ware. It was then abandoned but resettled in the mid-2nd millennium BC by a community of the Apennine Bronze Age culture. A great wealth of material of the 14th–12th centuries BC has been found, including much bronzework and sherds of Late Helladic III pottery, which indicate contact with Mycenaean traders c. 1300 BC. After the collapse of the Mycenaean world, Scoglio del Tonno continued to exist and trade with the Greek world. It survived until the foundation of the Greek colony of Taras in 706 BC. Scoglio del Tonno was destroyed, after excavation, when the port was extended in 1899.

scorper: A small steel metalworking tool with a broad sharp edge used for removing the background from designs on metalwork to allow the pattern to stand out. The tool may also be moved forward or backward through the metal on alternate corners—thus producing a zigzag or tremolo line. It is likely that scorpers had to be of iron or steel to work on bronze, and therefore, they may belong to later stages in the development of metalworking than tracers. In ancient minting, engraving of the details was carried out by the use of scorpers. In wood engraving, scorpers were used for cutting away large spaces after outlining and engraving, so as to leave only the drawing in relief.

Scorpion (c. 3150 BC): Name held by two Protodynastic rulers, one of whom was perhaps buried in Tomb U-j of the Umm el Qa'ab cemetery at Abydos.

scramasax: The single-edged knife often accompanying male Anglo-Saxon burials, a cross between an iron hacking sword and a dagger, with an angled back. It apparently served as general purpose knife or dagger. They commonly occur in Migration period and Anglo-Saxon contexts until about the 10th century. They tended to become increasingly elaborate: Many were finely inlaid with a variety of metals, and some had very distinctive pommels.

scraper: A retouched flake tool with a thick working edge; a flake tool that has been sharpened on one edge and left blunt on other edges to allow grasping, probably used to scrape (dress) animal hides. It is called a side scraper (racloir) or end scraper (grattoir) depending on the sharpened edge; side scrapers use the long side, and end scrapers have the scraping facet on one end. "Thumbnail" scrapers are very small; some cultures used scrapers as big as a fist. Scrapers were also used in woodworking and in shaping bone or ivory. Other types were snub nosed, round/horseshoe. Side scrapers are typical of the Middle Palaeolithic, while end scrapers are typical of the later Palaeolithic. (*syn.* side scraper, end scraper, sidescraper, endscraper)

scratched decoration: Pottery decoration in which lines are drawn with a hard point, probably of flint, on a burnished surface after the pot has been baked. A thin but charac-teristically ragged line results, providing for the inlay of ocher or plaster. The technique was used widely, notably in the Neolithic of Italy (Matera and Lagozza) and France (Chassey).

screening: The passing of excavated matrix through a metal mesh to recover artifacts and larger ecofacts.

scriber: A sharp-pointed metalworking tool used for outlining designs on metalwork before chasing, engraving, or repoussé work. Occasionally, traces of this preliminary work can be seen where subsequent tooling has not completely obliterated it.

script: Any writing system in its totality; a signary and the conventions that govern its use. Scripts may contain several different classes of sign—punctuation, determinative, logographic, and phonetic.

sculpture: An art form including all carved work in wood, ivory, stone, marble, metal, or other material and those works formed in a softer material not requiring carving, such as wax or clay. It includes statuary, carved ornament, glyptics, incised gems, and cameos. The most ancient specimens are carved of the hardest stones (basalt, granite, porphyry) and done before the introduction of steel tools. (*syn.* plastic art)

Scythian: The people of the steppes of southern Russia and Kazakhstan who were nomadic in the mid-1st millennium BC and displaced the Cimmerians in the Eurasian steppes. They were a horse-riding aristocracy and became a settled agricultural population. From the 8th century BC, they generally lived west of the Volga and north of the Black Sea (Royal Scyths). At the beginning of 7th century BC, they also moved into Iran and Anatolia, occupying Urartu territory, and appear in Assyrian records. Later, they returned to south Russia; their burials appear in the Kuban and Pontic steppes. They traded with the Greeks and were skilled artists and metalworkers. Grain from the areas under Scythian control was exchanged for luxury goods. Herodotus, who visited the area c. 450 BC, left much useful information on their customs. Their greatest contribution was their art, the bold and rhythmic animal style of the steppes. Its influence may be seen in the developing Celtic art of Europe and that of Luristan and neighboring areas of Iran and the Indus, where they moved in the late 2nd century BC. They destroyed the Greek kingdoms of Bactria and north India. These movements brought the Saka of the Achaemenid and Indian texts and were soon followed by the Yueh-chi, who gave rise to the Kushana kingdom of the early 1st millennium AD in north India and Afghanistan. The western branch of the Scyths was absorbed by the Sarmatians and finally disappeared under the Gothic invasions of the 3rd century AD. Scythian burials, known from places like Pazyryk, are elaborate and artifacts have animal motifs. (*syn.* Scyth)

Seacow Valley: River valley in Cape Province, South Africa, with more than 14,000 Stone Age sites. The ceramic sequence dates to the millennium before European settlers. There is information about the Stone Age Smithfield hunter gatherers from this area. (*syn.* Zeekoei Valley)

seal: A device for impressing characteristic marks into a soft surface, such as wet clay or wax, to indicate ownership or authenticity. Seals were made of bone, ivory, stone, or wood and had an intaglio design and were in the form of stamps or cylinder seals. The first can have a very wide range of shapes and gives single impressions. The second, characteristic of ancient Mesopotamia, is rolled across the surface to yield a frieze of repeat designs. Their social and linguistic significance is great. They were fundamental in the development of writing system and were a status symbol of authority and sometimes accorded talismanic properties. The use of seals and writing on clay tablets appeared together in Mesopotamia, toward the end of the 4th millennium BC.

Sealand: An area of marshes and lagoons of southern Babylonia (Persian Gulf). In the middle of the 2nd millennium BC, the dynasty of the Sealand controlled much of southern Mesopotamia, but little is known about its rule. Only one of its kings is documented in contemporary texts. Earlier documents referred to the area of the kingdom of Chaldea as the "Sealand."

sea level: The level of the surface of the sea; position of the air–sea interface, to which all terrestrial elevations and submarine depths are referred. Changes in the volume of water held in the sea and relative movements of the land surface, resulting from various types of deformation of the Earth's crust, are important in archaeology. Sea-level fluctuations are shown by deposits and land forms on the coasts of localities. The sea level constantly changes at every locality with the changes in tides, atmospheric pressure, and wind conditions. Longer term changes in sea level are influenced by the Earth's changing climates. The sea level appears to have been very close to its present position 35,000 years ago. (*syn.* mean sea level)

Sea Peoples: A collective term for various peoples who were on the move in the Aegean, Anatolia, and the Levant in the 13th and 12th centuries BC. They were responsible for widespread destruction of settlements in these areas, particularly Ugarit and Alalakh, and, more remotely, for the fall of Mycenaean Greece and the Hittite Empire. Dorians, Aeolians, and Ionians moved into Greece and Aegean islands, probably destroyed the Mycenaean kingdom, and drove the inhabitants eastward (Trojan War, c. 1200 BC). The Thraco-Phrygians were also driven into Anatolia, where they brought about the fall of the Hittite Empire. Homeless peoples swept southward along the coasts of Asia Minor and Syria, burning and looting as they went, and were only stopped by Ramesses III and Merenptah in 1174 BC. It was at this time that the Philistines settled in Palestine. (*syn.* Sea People)

seasonality of occupation: The exploitation of different environments at different times of the year by the same group of people; an estimate of when during the year a particular archaeological site was occupied. Transhumance is one instance of this practice, where high pasture land is grazed in the summer. There was also exploitation of water resources for fish or water birds and the following of wild herds by hunter gatherers. The people usually moved back to their original starting place each year. (*syn.* seasonality)

sebbakh: A term for the deteriorated mud brick of ancient buildings. It was used as fertilizer by Arab peasants, and the practice of digging for it has unearthed many artifacts that are now in museums.

Sechín Alto: Large Initial period ceremonial site on the north-central coast of Peru, possibly the largest site of that time. There are a series of platform mounds and plazas.

secondary altriciality: A unique human phenomenon of brain growth, during which the brain doubles its size in the first year of life. It may have been a feature of our ancestor *Homo erectus.*

secondary burial: The practice of removing the remains of a corpse, which was initially buried or put elsewhere, to another grave or ossuary. (*syn.* secondary inhumation)

secondary classification: A classification based on inferred or analytic attributes, often carried out by technicians in specialized laboratories.

secondary context: A context of an archaeological find that has been disturbed by subsequent human activity or natural phenomena. The provenience, association, and matrix of such archaeological data have been wholly or partially altered by transformational processes after original deposition.

secondary cremation: A burial practice in which the remains of a deceased are removed from the initial burial and placed in a grave or ossuary elsewhere.

secondary flake: A stone flake removed from a larger flake, as in the process of refining for a new use; a flake possessing some cortex on its dorsal aspect. The flakes are removed from an existing stone tool to thin, sharpen, blunt, or otherwise modify it for a specific use. Secondary flaking is the trimming that gives a chipped stone tool its final shape after the primary flaking has produced a blank (blade, flake, or core) of roughly the required form. (*syn.* partially cortical flake, retouch, secondary flaking, secondary retouch)

Secondary Neolithic: A term used to describe a number of Neolithic communities composed entirely of Mesolithic peoples who adopted Neolithic equipment. For example, in Britain this was a group characterized by the use of Peterborough ware or Grooved ware (Rinyo-Clacton ware). Such groups of Mesolithic ancestry had acquired the arts of farming and associated crafts (like pottery manufacture) from Primary Neolithic groups, such as the Windmill Hill culture.

secondary prehistory: The time when literate people came in contact with and wrote about nonliterate peoples. (*syn.* protohistoric)

Secondary Products Revolution: In the Late Neolithic, a series of changes in the culture and subsistence data, which have been interpreted as a shift from floodplain horticulture to a greater reliance on domestic livestock, particularly their "secondary products."

secondary refuse: Unwanted objects or materials that are removed from the site at which they were used and are disposed of at a different location. This often included artifacts, bone, shell, and other habitation debris, discarded away from the immediate area of use.

secondary use: An artifact or feature showing an alternate or later use that differs from its original function. For example, an abandoned well might be used as a refuse pit.

Second Intermediate Period: The time, 1630–1540 BC, when groups of Asiatic people appear to have migrated into the Egyptian Delta and established settlements. The Second Intermediate Period began with the establishment of the 15th Dynasty, called the Hyksos (c. 1630–c. 1523 BC), with its capital at Avaris (Tall ad-Dab'a) in the Delta, and ended with the 17th Dynasty (c. 1630–1540 BC), ruling from Thebes. The Second Intermediate Period was the consequence of political fragmentation and immigration, and the time may have been somewhat impoverished.

section: In excavation, the exposing of a deposit vertically to reveal the stratigraphy of a site or details of a particular feature. A balk is left across a feature or a complex of features, or a hole is cut out of a feature and trimmed to a flat face in which layers and changes in soil color may be examined. Sections automatically occur when the grid method of excavation is used, on all four sides of each trench. The term is also applied to the drawing of the vertical record of the stratification of a site or feature. A section drawing is a two-dimensional rendering, at a constant scale, depicting archaeological data and matrix as seen in the wall of an excavation. Advocates of open-area excavation prefer not to have standing sections on the site; instead of drawing sections after the whole area has been excavated, they record the profile of each deposit as it is excavated and construct what are known as "cumulative" or "running sections." (*syn.* section drawing)

Sedeinga: A religious site in Upper Nubia between the second and third Nile cataracts, north of the temple of Soleb. It consists of the ruins of a temple of Amenhotep III (reigned 1390–1353 BC).

sedentism: A way of life in which people remain settled in one place throughout the year; permanent settlement at one location. It is settlement based in a single location rather than involving moving camp at regular intervals. (*syn.* sedentary settlement, sedentary lifestyle)

sediment: A layer of soil, organic material, or rock particles that are no longer in the place where they were formed geologically but that have been redeposited away from their source. The agents of redeposition can be weathering, erosion, decay, soil-forming processes, and man himself. The material is carried by, suspended in, or dropped by air, water, or ice; or a mass that is accumulated by any other natural agent and that forms in layers on the Earth's surface such as sand, gravel, silt, mud, fill, or loess. Thus an archaeological site is a complicated sequence of various sediments and soils. The study of such sequences is called stratigraphy.

sedimentary structure: The observable properties of sediments: composition, size, shape, orientation, and grain packing. These properties combine to provide data on processes and environment, giving much information about the past.

sedimentation: The process of deposition of a solid material from a state of suspension or solution in a fluid (air, water, ice). It also includes deposits from glacial ice and those materials collected by gravity, or accumulations of rock debris at the base of cliffs. Depending on the conditions of sedimentation, archaeological deposits may be buried intact or with redistribution of the pre-existing material. (*syn.* sedimentary petrology, sedimentology)

sedimentology: A subdivision of geomorphology concerned with the investigation of the structure and texture of sediments, such as the global term for material deposited on the Earth's surface. This scientific discipline is concerned with the physical and chemical properties of sedimentary rocks and the processes involved in their formation, including the transportation, deposition, and lithification (transformation to rock) of sediments.

seed beater: An instrument usually made of wood or reeds, formed into a racketlike shape and used to strike seeds from bushes.

seeds: A variety of seeds may be preserved on archaeological sites by charring, grain impressions, or as a result of waterlogging. They may be the seeds of weed plants, fruits, pulses (see Beans), or the grains of cereals.

Segesta: Ancient city of Sicily, north of modern Calatafimi, which was the chief city of the Elymi. The Elymi may have been of Trojan origin; they are archaeologically indistinguishable in the Early Iron Age (c. 1000–500 BC) from their Sicanian neighbors. Segesta had a Greek culture, but it often sided with the Carthaginians against its Greek neighbors (mainly Selinus). Early in the First Punic War, Segesta massacred the Carthaginian garrison and allied themselves with Rome. It became a free city under Roman rule. Segesta ruins include an unfinished 5th-century BC temple and a Hellenistic theater. The city site is on the plateau adjacent to the theater. The surviving 5th-century temple, which stood outside the original city, is usually seen as a distinguished, but unfinished example; it has a colonnade, but no interior cella. (*syn.* Greek Egesta)

segment: Small stone tool made on a blade or bladelet and shaped like part of a circle; the backing is along a curved arc opposite a straight unretouched edge. It was hafted, possibly as a projectile tip or as part of a cutting tool. Segments occur in some sub-Saharan African Howiesons Poort and Later Stone Age assemblages and are widespread in North Africa. (*syn.* crescent)

segmentary society: Any relatively small and autonomous group, usually agriculturist, who regulates its own affairs. In some cases, it may join together with other segmentary societies to form a larger ethnic unit.

segmented cist: A type of megalithic tomb—cist or burial chamber—divided into compartments by jambs projecting from the walls, or by sill stones (septal slabs) set transversely on edge across the floor. These tombs are sometimes labeled segmented gallery graves. Good examples are in the British Isles among the Clyde Carlingford tombs. (*syn.* segmented gallery grave)

Segovia: A local *oppidum* of central Spain, which was an Iberian settlement from about 700 BC. It was taken in about 80 BC by the Romans and occupied at the beginning of the 8th century AD by the Moors, from whom Alfonso VI recaptured it in 1079. It is famous for its grand-scale aqueduct, attributed to Trajan (AD 98–117). The system brought water from a distance of some 16 kilometers. The masonry bridge (El Puente) was used to span the final depression before the city and is close to 900 meters high. (*syn.* Roman Segobriga)

Sehonghong: In eastern Lesotho, a large rock shelter with a sequence of Stone Age occupation from c. 70,000 BP. There is Middle Stone Age Howiesons Poort material (c. 20,000 BP) and later Stone Age hunter-gatherer remains.

Seibal: A lowland Maya center located in south-central Petén, Guatemala. The site was occupied as early as 800 BC, expanded in size and importance in the Pre-Classic period, and was at its height in the Late Classic, AD 770–900, while the rest of Maya civilization was declining. Archaeologists think that the influx of non-Classic Maya (Putun) from the Gulf Coast prompted its development at that time. The site is dominated by three groups of ceremonial buildings, built around plazas and connected by causeways. Most of the population lived in small house clusters around these nuclei.

Seibal was abandoned by 950, probably as part of the general decline of the Classic Petén centers.

Seine-Oise-Marne (SOM) culture: A Late Neolithic culture of the Paris basin of northeast France c. 3400–2800 BC, named after three rivers. It is best known for its megalithic tombs of gallery-grave type (hypogées), semisubterranean funerary houses, and allées couvertes. The megalithic tombs often include porthole slabs. In the chalk country of the Marne, rock-cut tombs were similarly made, and some have hafted axes or schematized "goddess" figures carved on their walls. Native artifacts include transverse arrows, antler, daggers, and rough, plain flat-based pots of cylinder and bucket shapes. The pottery type is the coarse ware flat-based flower pot. Trade brought copper, Callaïs stone, and beads, and Grand Pressigny flint to the region. The culture seems to have a composite origin, and certain elements of the assemblage occur in other—perhaps unrelated—cultures outside the SOM area proper. The SOM type of megalithic tomb is found from Brittany to Belgium, Westphalia, and Sweden, while similar crude pottery occurs in Brittany, west France, Switzerland (Horgen), and Denmark. (*syn.* SOM)

seismic reflection profiler: An acoustic underwater survey device that uses the principle of echo sounding to locate submerged land forms. The concept is similar to echo sounding: Seismic waves are reflected at interfaces where rock properties change and the round-trip travel time, together with velocity information, gives the distance to the interface. The relief on the interface can be determined by mapping the reflection at many locations. In water depths of 100 meters, this method can achieve penetration of more than 10 meters into the sea floor.

Sekhemkhet (2648–2640 BC): One of the principal rulers of the 3rd Dynasty, whose reign was probably just 8 years. As Djoser's successor, he planned a still more grandiose step pyramid complex.

Sekhmet: In Egyptian religion, a goddess of war and the destroyer of the enemies of the sun god Re. Sekhmet was associated with both disease and with healing and medicine. She was the companion of the god Ptah and was worshiped principally at Memphis. Depicted as a lioness or woman with a lioness head, she was sometimes identified with other Egyptian goddesses such as Hathor, Bastet, and Mut and was probably mother of Nefertem in the Memphite Triad. (*syn.* Sakhmet)

Selinunte: Greek colony in southwest Sicily, traditionally founded by Megara Hyblaea in 651/628 BC. There are a series of temples of the Doric order with relief metopes in some. Fortifications occur on the akropolis, and early material has been found on the temenos of Malophoros. Early Corinthian pottery has been dated based on the colony's foundation.

Sembiran: Port site in north Bali, Indonesia, important on the spice trade route, with remains from the 1st–12th centuries AD. There is Indo-Roman rouletted ware and imported glass beads, among other artifacts.

Semenov, Sergei Aristarkhovich (1898–1978): Russian archaeologist who developed the technique of microscopic analysis of wear patterns on artifacts to determine their function.

Semibratny: The Seven Brothers' tumuli in Kuban, Georgia—rich Scythian burials of the 5th century BC. They included numerous horses, examples of Scythian craftsmanship, and examples of Greek gold-figured silver plate.

Semite: A name applied to the speakers of a set of related languages, who inhabited portions of southwestern Asia since the time of the first cities. Semitic languages are characterized by the importance of the consonants, usually three forming the root of each word. The vowels are omitted altogether in a number of the scripts. The Semites are first recorded on the steppe margins of the Arabian desert, encroaching on the Sumerians to form the kingdom of Akkad c. 2400 BC. The Amorites appear c. 2000 in the same area and in Syria-Palestine, where they settled to become the Canaanites. The Khabiru (Hebrews) appear in the same context. In the 12th century BC, the Amorites were followed by the Aramaeans, particularly in inland Syria. The Phoenicians from the 9th century BC carried their Semitic language over much of the Mediterranean. Arabic and Hebrew are the most important surviving Semitic languages. Most, probably all, alphabetic scripts derive from the Semitic alphabet, created sometime in the 2nd millennium BC. The Semitic script was invented by speakers of some Semitic language, possibly Phoenician, who lived in the northern part of the Fertile Crescent.

Semitic: A group of languages including Akkadian, Eblaite, Canaanite, Amorite, Ugaritic, Phoenician, Aramaic, Hebrew, and Arabic, widely spoken throughout the Near East.

Semna: A fortified town erected on the west bank of the Nile at the southern end of a series of fortresses founded during the 12th Dynasty (1985–1795 BC) in the second cataract area of Lower Nubia. The town was established in the reign of Senusret I (1965–1920 BC), and the forts were probably built to defend the southern limit of Egyptian penetration under the Middle Kingdom. The forts have also been used as trading stations.

sem priest: In Egypt, a priest associated with funerary ritual, especially the Opening of the Mouth ceremony. This person characteristically wore a leopard-skin garment.

Sempukuji: An early Jomon rock shelter site in Nagasaki Prefecture on Kyushu, Japan. There is an association of microblades with linear-relief pottery, found earlier at Fukui,

and an older pottery with discontinuous relief (bean-pattern). Dating puts the site in the late 11th millennium BC, slightly younger than the Fukui date.

Senftenberg: Late Bronze Age fortified site of the Lusatian culture in east Germany.

Sennacherib (d. 681 BC): King of Assyria (705/704–681 BC), son of Sargon II, who made Nineveh his capital, building a new palace, extending and beautifying the city, and erecting inner and outer city walls that still stand. Sennacherib figures prominently in the Old Testament for his attack on Jerusalem. Pestilence prevented his attack on Egypt, which remained free until the reign of his son Esarhaddon. In 689, he conquered and devastated Babylon. He was also credited with building a temple at Athens. (*syn.* Akkadian Sin-Akhkheeriba)

Senwosret, Sesostris, Senusret: The birth name of three kings of Egypt's Middle Kingdom. With the four kings named Amenemhat, they constitute the majority of the 12th Dynasty (c. 1963–1786 BC). They include: Sesostris I (1918–1875 BC), Sesostris II (1844–1837 BC), and Sesostris III (1836–1818 BC)—alternatively listed as: Senusret I Kheperkara (1965–1920 BC), Senusret II Khakheperra (1880–1874 BC), and Senusret III (Khakaura (1874–1855 BC).

septal slab: An upright stone slab set across the floor of a megalithic chambered tomb to divide it into separate compartments (e.g., in a court cairn). They vary in height from low curbs to the full height of the chamber; in the latter case they are sometimes provided with portholes.

Sepulcros de Fosa: Middle Neolithic cemeteries of crouched inhumations in pits or stone cists found in Catalonia, Spain, and dated to the 5th–4th millennia BC.

Seqenenre (c. 1560 BC, fl. 16th century BC): King of Egypt (c. 1545 BC) who, according to tradition, faced unreasonable demands from the Hyksos, the west-Semitic conquerors who had overrun much of Egypt in the 17th century BC. This Theban ruler of the 17th Dynasty began the series of campaigns against the Hyksos rulers in the Delta, which were eventually to culminate in the liberation of Egypt by his son Ahmose I (1550–1525 BC), the first ruler of the 18th Dynasty. He was probably assassinated. (*syn.* Seqenenre Tao)

sequence: A series of periods in the history of a particular culture, each characterized by recognizably different material remains. The term also applies to the arrangement of material culture into a time framework.

sequence comparison: A relative age determination technique based on similarities between newly classified artifacts or features and established chronological sequences of similar materials.

sequence dating: A method developed by Sir Flinders Petrie (for Egyptian predynastic cemeteries) for dating a group of similar objects according to their archaeological sequence. By studying the typology of the changing forms of certain artifacts, they may be set into sequence. Petrie used it to arrange undated graves into a hypothetical (relative) chronological order according to the typology and association of the artifacts found in them (based on a stylistic seriation of Egyptian predynastic tomb pottery). Artifacts found at other sites were then correlated with the sequence and given a sequence date. The technique can be used only to determine whether one type of artifact is earlier or later than another; it cannot show length of time between the two. This type of seriation, when combined with cross-dating, is still useful in the absence of other dating methods.

Serabit el-Khadim: Ancient Egyptian site in southwest Sinai, which had rich deposits of turquoise and copper ore. There is a temple of Hathor (12th–20th Dynasties) with stelae erected by kings and officials doing mining work in the area.

serapeum: Two temples of ancient Egypt dedicated to the worship of the Greco-Egyptian god Sarapis (Serapis). The original elaborate temple of that name was located on the west bank of the Nile near Saqqara and was a monument to the deceased Apis bulls. Although the area was used as a cemetery for the bulls as early as 1400 BC, it was Ramesses II (1279–1213 BC) who designed a main gallery and subsidiary chambers. Under the Ptolemaic Dynasty, the temple was called the Sarapeum. The vast underground galleries at Saqqara housed the 64 embalmed bodies of the Apis bulls. The French Egyptologist Auguste Mariette discovered the ruins, first finding a limestone sphinx almost hidden in the sand in an area northwest of the Step Pyramid of Djoser and uncovering an avenue leading into the Western Desert, at the end of which lay a small temple built by a 30th-Dynasty pharaoh. He also found a large blocked doorway and 24 vaulted burial chambers within. Another important serapeum was built at Alexandria, the new Ptolemaic capital. Ptolemy I Soter (reigned 305–284 BC) selected Sarapis as the official god for Egypt and built the largest and best known of the god's temples. There Sarapis was worshipped until AD 391, when the serapeum was destroyed. In Roman times, other serapeums were constructed throughout the empire. (*syn*. Serapeum, Sarapeum, Sarapieion)

Serapis: A Greco-Egyptian composite god resulting from the fusion of the Egyptian god Osorapis (who, in death, became assimilated to the god Osiris as Osiris-Apis) with attributes of a number of Hellenistic gods, notably Zeus, Helios, Hades, Asklepios, and Dionysos. (*syn*. Sarapis)

serdab: In Egyptian architecture, a chamber found in some mastabas of the Old Kingdom (2686–2181 BC), appearing during the reign of Djoser and widespread in the Giza and Saqqara cemeteries after Menkaure's reign. It consists of a walled-up chamber provided in a mortuary chapel or burial shaft to contain an image or statue of the deceased. Statues of the ka of the deceased were usually placed here. It derives from the Arabic word for "cellar."

Sered'-Macanské vrsky: Mesolithic dune site near Nitra, Slovakia, which is the type site of the Sered' group. The group is distinguished by geometric microlithic tools.

serekh: Hieroglyphic symbol making up the recessed paneling described in modern times as "palace facade" decoration. It is the image of a brick facade to a palace or enclosure, with a rectangular space above. It is believed to have been modeled on the design of the earliest royal residences beginning in the Early Dynastic Period. It is found on mastaba tombs, false door stelae, coffins, sarcophagi, and numerous other funerary and ceremonial contexts throughout Egyptian history. A falcon (the sign for Horus) perches on the top horizontal of the rectangle, which encloses a king's Horus name (the first name in a king's titulary). (*syn*. palace facade decoration)

seria: A type of earthenware vessel used mainly for holding wine and oil—larger than the amphora, smaller than the dolium.

seriation: A relative dating technique in which artifacts or features are organized into a sequence according to changes over time in their attributes or frequency of appearance. The technique shows how these items have changed over time and it is a way to establish chronology. Archaeological material, such as assemblages of pottery or the grave goods deposited with burials is arranged into chronological order. The types that make up the assemblages to be ordered in this way must be from the same archaeological tradition and from a single region or locality. Once the variations in a particular object have been classified by typology, it can often be shown that they fall into a developmental series, sometimes in a single line, sometimes in branching lines more as in a family tree. The order produced is theoretically chronological, but needs archaeological assessment. Outside evidence, such as dating of two or more stages in the development, may be needed to determine which is the first and which the last member of the series. There are several types of seriation: frequency seriation, contextual seriation, evolutionary seriation, and similarity/stylistic seriation—based on different changes. A seriation technique, called sequence dating, based on shared typological features, enabled Sir Flinders Petrie to establish the temporal order of a large number of Egyptian graves.

series: A term used to describe a number of cultures or industries broadly related in time and space and yet discrete entities. Some type of intergroup relation, common ancestry, or similarity of interaction with the environment is implied. In American terminology, *series* is a broad unit of classification embracing a number of related cultures or pottery styles. A series has both duration in time, when one culture or style develops into another, and extent in the space (the area occupied by the various cultures or styles making up the series).

Seriña, Serinya: Cave sites in Girona, Spain, occupied in the Mousterian and Upper Palaeolithic, as well as the Magdalenian and Solutrean. Radiocarbon dates for the Upper Mousterian are c. 40,400 bp and c. 38,500 bp for the Aurignacian.

Serket: Scorpion-goddess who guarded the royal coffin and canopic chest with Isis, Nephthys, and Neith. (*syn.* Selket, Selkis)

serpentine: A magnesium-rich silicate mineral occurring in a number of forms and used for decorative work as they vary widely in color and take on a high polish. Sources are known in the British Isles, Ireland, Canada, United States, New Zealand, and Afghanistan. Serpentine minerals were also used in making fine stone tools and vessels as well as jewelry and architectural decoration. (*syn.* serpentinite)

Serpent Mound: Large ritual earth mound near Locust Grove, Ohio, with the form of a curved serpent holding either an egg or a frog. The mound is associated with a nearby burial mound of the Adena culture. At 405 meters long, 1–2 meters high, it is probably the largest serpent effigy in the world. (*syn.* Great Serpent Mound)

Serra d'Alto: Neolithic village in Basilicata, Italy, on a hill defended by three concentric ditches. It has yielded a distinctive painted pottery of the same name, c. 4500–3500 BC. Geometric designs with diagonal meanders and solid triangles are painted in black or purple-brown on a buff surface. A frequent motif is a zigzag line between parallels ("linea a tremolo marginato"). Jars and handled cups are the standard forms, and the elaborate handles are horizontal, tubular, with zoomorphic additions on the top. In the later phase, a thin and markedly splayed trumpet lug was adopted from the Diana Ware of Lipari. The high quality of the ware and the fact that it most often occurs in graves and other ritual contexts suggest that it was produced for special purposes. It was traded over a wide area, occurring in Sicily, Lipari, Lake Garda, Malta, and in central Italy.

Serraferlicchio: A site near Agrigento in southern Sicily, which has given its name to a style of pottery of the Copper Age (3rd millennium BC). It is found mainly in rock-cut tombs and consists of a bright-red slipped ware decorated with black paint in geometric designs. Characteristic forms are open bowls and a variety of jug and cup shapes.

sese: The name given to the Bronze Age tombs on the Mediterranean island of Pantelleria, between Sicily and Tunisia. The sesi are stone cairns containing 1–11 burial cham-

bers, each consisting of a cell roofed by corbelling and approached by an entrance passage. (*syn.* pl. sesi)

Sesebi-Sudla: A walled settlement in the Upper Nubia's Abri-Delgo, between the second and third cataracts, founded by the 18th Dynasty pharaoh Akhenaten (1352–1336 BC).

Seshat: Goddess of writing and measurement, usually a woman in panther-skin dress and a headdress with a seven-pointed star and a bow. She shared the responsibility of writing with Thoth.

Sesklo: Neolithic tell settlement site near Volos in Thessaly, Greece, first occupied in the 7th millennium (Aceramic Neolithic). It has given its name to a pottery ware known over much of continental Greece in the Middle Neolithic, 6th millennium BC. The pottery's most distinctive feature is a fine white slip painted in red with geometric designs, often in zigzag patterns. The pre-Sesklo that it succeeds was a local branch of the widespread Starcevo culture. The settlement has closely grouped mud-brick houses set on stone foundations, each with a domed oven. There was a large megaron complex on the akropolis, and it was an important settlement through the Bronze Age.

Seth: Egyptian god, brother (and murderer) of Osiris and also brother of Isis and Nephthys. With his consort Sekhet, he was opposed to the trinity of Osiris, Isis, and Horus. He personified evil and was represented with the black head of an unidentified animal. According to legend, his murder of Osiris was avenged by Horus. He was represented as an animal-headed man. (*syn.* Set, Setekh, Suty, Sutekh)

Setouchi: Late Palaeolithic stone-working culture making side-blow flakes using sanukite. They were used for Kou knives (Kou, Osaka Prefecture) and other knives. Setouchi is also the name for the Inland Sea region of western Japan (Okayama, Hiroshima, and Yamaguchi on Honshu, and Kagawa and Ehime on Shikoku).

settlement archaeology: The study of the spatial distribution of ancient activities, the remains of single-activity areas or of entire regions.

settlement pattern: The study of ancient human occupation and activity patterns in a specified area—the distribution of features and sites, buildings, and other constructions in relation to the topography of a given area. Archaeological studies of settlement patterns deal with such matters as urbanization, the relation between town, village, and countryside, and the operation of administrative centers. Findings reflect the relation of the inhabitants with their environment, and the relation of groups with one another in that environment. Factors influencing the pattern of settlement in any area may include the subsistence strategy, the political structure, the social structure, population density, and carrying capacity. (*syn.* settlement pattern study)

settlement system: The entire set of settlements used by a community—for example, all the camps used by a band of hunter gatherers.

Sety: Birth name of two pharaohs of the 19th Dynasty, Seti I (reigned 1290–1279 BC) and Seti II (reigned 1204–1198 BC). Seti I strengthened Egypt's defenses by successful campaigns in Palestine and Syria. Seti did much to promote the prosperity of Egypt: fortified the frontier, opened mines and quarries, dug wells, and rebuilt temples and shrines that had fallen into decay or been damaged. He continued the work begun by his father, Ramesses I, on the construction of the great hypostyle hall at Karnak, which is one of the most impressive monuments of Egyptian architecture. His greatest memorial is his mortuary temple at Abydos; his tomb is the finest in the Valley of the Kings in western Thebes. His son was Ramesses II. Seti II was the successor of his father, Merneptah, and was one of the last rulers of the 19th Dynasty. (*syn.* Seti, Sethos)

Seven Wonders of the World: A list made in the Hellenistic period (2nd century BC) of what were then considered to be the seven greatest wonders (monuments) of the world. These were the Great Pyramids of Egypt; the Hanging Gardens of Babylon; the Temple of Artemis (Artemision) at Ephesus; the chryselephantine statue of Zeus at Olympia; the Colossus of Rhodes; the Pharos lighthouse of Alexandria; and the Mausoleum of Mausolus at Halicarnassus.

severed head cult: Some Celtic groups in Iron Age Europe collected the heads of enemies as charms and status symbols. This practice was elevated to the status of a cult among Celto-Ligurain groups in southern France and at sanctuary sites like Entremont, Glanum, and Roquepertuse, which have stone statuary associated with the cult. The statuary are of carved stone heads, headless torsos, and pillars carved with severed heads, as well as niches for the display of actual severed heads.

Severn-Cotswold tomb: A group of Neolithic burial monuments in southwest Britain around the Bristol Channel—megalithic tombs consisting of a long mound, tapering on one end, with one or more passage graves. In the finest tombs, the funerary area is a long gallery with up to three pairs of side chambers opening from it. In others, the courtyard leads only to a false entrance while the burial chambers open laterally onto the side of the mound. The Severn-Cotswold tombs were built early in the Neolithic period, and there is a radiocarbon date of 3600 ± 130 BC from Waylands Smithy, Berkshire. The West Kennet tomb (3330 ± 150) was constructed at much the same time as the nearby causewayed camp at Windmill Hill. In plan, these graves show a general similarity to the French transepted gallery graves around the mouth of the River Loire. There are two main varieties: axial-chambered tombs, with the passage entrance opening from the center of the broader end of the mound, and lateral-chambered tombs, where two megalithic chambers are entered from opposite sides of the mound. (*syn.* Severn-Cotswold)

Sevier: A Fremont culture variant, in the Great Basin of the United States.

sexual dimorphism: The differences between males and females in shape, size, or color within any population.

sgraffito ware: Sgraffito ware refers to glazed vessels prepared first by incising decoration in the surface and then adding paint in the incisions before the application of glaze. There is a contrast between the brightly colored decoration and the overall color of the glazed vessel. Byzantine sgraffito wares date to the 11th–12th centuries in western Europe. It was not until the 16th–17th centuries that the technique was established in northern Europe. Sgraffito ware was produced by Islamic potters and became common throughout the Middle East. The 18th-century scratch blue class of English white stoneware is decorated with sgraffito patterns. Sgraffito ware was produced as early as 1735 by German settlers in colonial America. Sgraffito is also a form of fresco painting for exterior walls, done in Europe since the Middle Ages. A rough plaster undercoat is followed by thin plaster layers, each stained with a different color. These coats are covered by a fine-grain mortar finishing surface. The plaster is then engraved with knives and gouges at different levels to reveal the various colored layers beneath. It is also a glass-decorating technique.

Shaar ha-Golan: Palestinian type site of a Neolithic culture of the Jordan Valley, the Yarmukian. Its characteristic artifact is a schematic pebble or clay figurine.

Shabaqo (fl. 8th century BC): Cushite king who conquered Egypt and founded its 25th (Ethiopian) Dynasty. He ruled Egypt from about 719/718–703 BC. He had old texts recopied and also revived the practice of pyramid burials. He was interred in a pyramid at Mount Barkal, between the third and fourth cataracts of the Nile. (*syn.* Shabaka, Sabacon)

shabti: Funerary figurine of Egyptian tombs from the Middle Kingdom, usually mummiform in appearance and carrying agricultural tools. It was developed out of the funerary statuettes and models provided in tombs of Old Kingdom. The shabti was intended to serve as a replacement if the deceased was called on to perform manual labor in the netherworld. The finest examples were from the New Kingdom, some of Saite date. Made of wood, stone, terra-cotta, or faience, such statuettes were placed in tombs, often in large numbers. (*syn.* Egyptian ushabti, shawabti)

shadow: In Egyptian antiquity, the shadow was regarded as an essential element of every human being. As with the akh, ba, ka, and name, it was considered necessary to protect it from harm. (*syn.* shade; Egyptian shwt)

shadow marks: Surface shadows of an archaeological site, caused by irregularities in elevation, indicating the presence of submerged features such as earthworks and ditches. These may be revealed through aerial photography. Shadow marks are best seen in the low sun of evenings and early mornings.

shadow sites: Surface shadows on an archaeological site, caused by irregularities in elevation, indicating the presence of submerged features such as earthworks and ditches. Such sites are identified from the air, especially in aerial photography. Shadow sites are best seen in the low sun of evenings and early mornings. Oblique light can show reduced topography of sites invisible from the ground.

shaduf: An irrigation tool invented in ancient times, consisting of a long wooden pole with a receptacle at one end and a counterbalancing weight at the other, for transferring water out of a river or canal. This hand-operated device is still used in India, Egypt, and some other countries to irrigate land. The pole is mounted like a seesaw, a skin or bucket hung on a rope from one end, and a counterweight hung on the other. The operator pulls down on a rope to fill the bucket and allows the counterweight to raise the bucket. To raise water to higher levels, a series of shadufs are sometimes mounted one above the other. (*syn.* shadoof, denkli, paecottah)

shaft-and-chamber tomb: A tomb in which the burials are laid in a side chamber opening from the bottom of a pit.

shaft grave: A grave in which the burial chamber was reached by a vertical shaft, the burials themselves placed at the bottom of a deep narrow pit, used in the early Bronze Age. The tomb was usually rectangular, and the burial chamber was at its base. After the burial was done, the chamber was roofed and the shaft above it filled in. Shaft graves occur in various parts of the world and are not all of the same date. The most famous examples are the richly furnished tombs at Mycenae. At Mycenae, there are Circles A and B, which may have stone markers. The vertical shaft tomb was also characteristic of Bronze Age China, and it was used by the Shang elite of northern China. (*syn.* shaft tomb)

Shaft Grave Circles A and B: Richly furnished tombs at Mycenae made up of circles enclosed by a low stone parapet and containing 30 graves. The offerings suggest that the rulers of Mycenae must have been buried here, probably in the later 17th and 16th centuries BC. The grave goods include gold and silver cups, jewelry, dress ornaments, golden diadems, elaborate hairpins, amethyst beads, amber, and bronze weapons. The great influence of Crete on these graves is visible in the metal cups, faience "sacral knots," appliquéd ostrich eggs, conch shells, gold triple shrine facades, and imported pottery. There is a wealth of local art such as formal gold cups, gold worked in patterns of lions, bulls, and plants, and lions twisted as ornament.

shaft-hole: A hole in an implement or weapon to hold the haft. A shaft-hole ax is an ax head of metal or stone with a hole through it for hafting. Bronze axes and adzes from Mesopotamia of at least 2700 BC are shaft-hole types, the hole for the handle being formed in a mold. This method eliminated lashing the blades and permitted a heavier head than the thin-bladed Egyptian models. Shaft-hole axes and adzes were also being cast in Crete in about 2000 BC. The Beaker folk, Late Neolithic–Early Bronze Age people living about 6,000 years ago in Europe, also used the shaft-hole battle ax.

shaft straightener: An artifact made from a coarse, often volcanic, stone, with a groove used as a rasp to finish spears and arrow shafts. The Mousterian industry used denticulate (toothed) instruments produced by making notches in a flake, which were perhaps used as saws or shaft straighteners.

Shahdad: A series of settlements on an oasis in the Kirman province, Iran, dated from the late 4th millennium BC. A series of floods in prehistoric times destroyed most buildings, but left brick-lined tombs and many artifacts suggesting that Shahdad was an important manufacturing and trading center in the first half of the 3rd millennium BC, contemporary with the Early Dynastic period in Mesopotamia. There were a number of almost lifesize unbaked clay statues found lying in the graves, face to face with the corpses, presumed to be actual portraits of the dead people. Bronze, copper, and silver was locally worked and made into tools, decorated vessels, ornaments, and cylinder seals. Other finds include vessels of steatite and alabaster, and beads of agate, carnelian, and lapis lazuli. A very early form of writing appears on pottery, sometimes incised, sometimes impressed with seals; some 700 different pictographic symbols have been identified, occurring singly or in groups of up to five symbols. The evidence documents the emergence of stratified societies during the 3rd millennium BC.

Shahi Tump: Small tell site in western Baluchistan with a small inhumation cemetery, probably of the 3rd millennium BC. Pottery and other artifacts show connections both with Iranian sites and the Kulli culture of southern Baluchistan. Grave goods included fine gray ware bowls with swastika motifs in soft black paint, rich copper work, a shaft-hole ax, and five compartmented stamp seals. Three phases of use were recognized: two phases of occupation, followed by a phase of use as a cemetery.

Shahr-i Qumis: Parthian city in northeast Iran with occupation of some kind from the Iron Age to the Seljuq period, ended by the Mongol invasion in the 13th century. The size of the Parthian city and its location on a major highway linking Mesopotamia with Central Asia suggest that it might be the

Parthian capital known to the Greeks as Hecatompylos ("The City of a Hundred Gates"). Parthian structures that have been excavated include vaulted mud-brick chambers used for burials and a fortified mansion with six towers, a large courtyard, and a number of long rooms on the ground floor.

Shahr-i Sokhta: Tell site in the Seistan district of eastern Iran, close to the Afghan and Pakistan borders, which was the site of a vast urban center of the late 4th–early 2nd millennia BC. As well as abundant structural remains, enormous numbers of finds have been excavated—thousands of potsherds and stone tools, clay figurines, and animal bones. The wealth of Shahr-i Sokhta was due at least in part to its role in the trade in lapis lazuli between its source in north Afghanistan and the markets of Mesopotamia and Egypt. An industrial area produced thousands of unfinished lapis lazuli beads, as well as flint drills and other tools used in their manufacture. Shahr-i Sokhta also has a huge cemetery, estimated to have contained 200,000 burials. In the early 2nd millennium BC, the course of the Helmand River, on which the city depended, changed; this led to the decline and abandonment of the settlement. The site is still important for understanding the urbanization, production and subsistence techniques, and complex societies of Bronze Age Iran and Afghanistan.

Shalmaneser: Five kings of Assyria bore this name, starting with Shalmaneser I (fl. 13th century BC), king of Assyria (reigned c. 1263–c. 1234 BC) who significantly extended Assyrian power. The second, fourth, and fifth were comparatively unimportant. Shalmaneser III (fl. 9th century BC), king of Assyria (reigned 858–824 BC) was known for his military expansion in campaigns as far as Palestine, the Persian Gulf, Urartu, and Cilicia. These were raids, however, rather than permanent conquests. The raids are graphically recorded on the Black Obelisk at Nimrud and on the bronze gates at Balawat, another of Shalmaneser's palaces. The son and successor of Ashurnasirpal, Shalmaneser III, directed most of his campaigns against Syria.

shaman: A medicine man in societies, often believed to have supernatural powers, who is capable of healing—or harming. A shaman receives an "inner call" to this vocation or receives the office through heredity. The shaman is called on to mediate with the spirit world on the community's behalf in times of sickness. The shaman presides over rituals and may also be responsible for the keeping of laws and the continuity of traditions. Shamanism is the dominant element in the religion of most known arctic and subarctic (Siberian and Ural-Altaic) hunter gatherers. Most shamans are male. This religious ideology may be north Asian in origin.

shaman's bundle: A parcel of sacred objects, often used in magic and/or curing by a shaman, who is a person who is regarded as having healing powers derived from supernatural sources.

Shamarkian: A Nubian microlithic industry of 8,000–6,000 years ago in the Sudanese Nile Valley. The typology of the industry shows certain Saharan affinities. By the 6th millennium BC, some of the toolmakers had adopted a specialized fishing economy using harpoons with barbed bone heads, as seen at Catfish Cave near the second Nile cataract.

Shamshi-Adad I (c. 1813–1781 BC): The first of the great rulers of Assyria, who started a tribe near Mari on the Euphrates River. He created an empire in northern Mesopotamia from the middle Euphrates to the mountains in the east. His capitals were at Assur and Shubat-Enlil. His sons, Ekallatum and Mari, acted as governors—but could not maintain the empire after Shamshi-Adad's death. The remains of Shamshi-Adad's palace were partially excavated, with the most important find at the site being an archive of royal correspondence preserved on more than 1,000 cuneiform tablets. The archives consist mostly of financial and administrative records, with some diplomatic correspondence between the ruler of Shubat-Enlil and neighboring kings. They complement the archives found at the site of the ancient city of Mari in the great palace of Zimrilim.

Sham Wan: Prehistoric site in Hong Kong on a beach ridge on Lamma Island, spanning the Neolithic (c. 3500 BC) through Bronze Age (c. 1500–200 BC) into Tang times. Much of the prehistoric material is associated with that from the neighboring mainland province of Kwangtung.

Shang: The first Chinese dynasty recorded historically, thought to have ruled from the mid-16th to mid-11th centuries BC (some scholars date the Shang dynasty from the mid-18th to the late 12th centuries BC). However, Shang as an archaeological term must be distinguished from Shang as a dynastic one. Earlier stages of the culture known from Anyang have been recognized at sites assigned to the Erligang Phase and, still earlier, the Erlitou phase. So far, virtually no inscriptions have been found at these pre-Anyang sites; even if the date of the dynasty's founding were known, it would be uncertain to what extent these archaeologically defined phases fall in the Shang period. Thus, although the type site of the Erligang phase at Zhengzhou is generally assumed to have been a Shang capital, some archaeologists have argued that the Erlitou phase falls in the time of the Hsia Dynasty, traditional predecessor of Shang. The archaeological classification of Middle Shang is represented by the remains found at Erligang (Erh-li-kang) (c. 1600 BC) near Cheng-chou (Zhengzhou). The Shang replaced the Hsia (Zia) in c. 1500 BC and was overthrown by the Chou in 1027 BC. The Shang Dynasty belongs technically to the advanced Bronze Age—with that metal used for tools (socketed axes, knives, etc.), weapons (halberds, spears, and arrowheads), and for the highly ornamented and artistic ritual vessels. There was a fine white pottery and coarser gray wares, wheel made and occasionally glazed, which clearly derive from the preceding Neolithic pottery. The period's claim to rank as a civilization is supported by the size and complexity of its cities and its use of writing. Two of its capitals have been identified, at modern Cheng-chou and Anyang, both in Honan Province near the middle Yellow River. Rich cemeteries provide much of the evidence, particularly the royal tombs at Anyang. Building was mainly in timber on rammed earth foundations; city walls were also of rammed earth. Burial was by inhumation in pit graves with the skeletons extended, some face down. The pictographic writing appears as occasional inscriptions on the bronzes, much more commonly on the enormous number of oracle bones. The Shang was the second of the Chinese dynasties in the Protohistoric Sandai period. (*syn.* Yin; Shang civilization)

Shangcunling: The site of a large early Eastern Chou cemetery near the city of Sanmenxia in Shan Xian, Honan Province, China. Inscribed bronzes show that members of the royal family of Guo were buried here. Guo was a small state probably founded before the end of the Western Chou period (771 BC) and ending in 655 BC, when its territory was absorbed by the state of Jin. The cemetery includes well-preserved chariot burials and remarkably simple bronze ritual vessels. (*syn.* Shang-ts'un-ling)

Shanidar: A cave in the Zagros mountains of Iraq with a long Palaeolithic cultural sequence including the Mousterian, Baradostian, and Mesolithic. At the base was a Mousterian deposit with several Neanderthal burials (c. 60,000–44,000 BP). The Mousterian was followed by a blade industry of Upper Palaeolithic type—the Baradostian (c. 33,000–27,000 BP), and then, after a hiatus, by the Zarzian (c. 10,000 BC), a Late Palaeolithic industry with many small tools and some true microliths. By the 9th millennium BC, there is evidence for a shift away from hunting toward the gathering of wild plant foods.

Shaqadud: Site in the Sudan with early Khartoum Neolithic material dated to c. 5500 bp. There was also a late Neolithic occupation c. 4200–3600 bp.

shard: Any pottery fragment—piece of broken pot or other earthenware item–that has archaeological significance. Often abbreviated to sherd, potsherds are an invaluable part of the archaeological record because they are well preserved. The analysis of ceramic changes recorded in potsherds has become one of the primary techniques used by archaeologists in assigning components and phases to times and cultures. (*syn.* sherd; potsherd)

shatter: All angular waste resulting from stone toolmaking activities that are not otherwise diagnostic.

shawabti: Funerary figurine of Egyptian tombs from the Middle Kingdom, usually mummiform in appearance and carrying agricultural tools. It was developed out of the funerary statuettes and models provided in tombs of Old Kingdom. The shawabti was intended to serve as a replacement if the deceased was called on to perform manual labor in the netherworld. The finest examples were from the New Kingdom, some of Saite date. Made of wood, stone, terra-cotta, or faience, such statuettes were placed in tombs, often in large numbers. (*syn.* shabti, Egyptian ushabti)

Shechem: Palestinian site and biblical city with its most important period of occupation in the Middle Bronze Age, c. 17th century BC, when it was given a great insloping wall of cyclopean masonry. To the same period belongs a stone plaque bearing one of the earliest known alphabetic inscriptions. The town was destroyed at the end of the Middle Bronze Age and not reoccupied until the 16th century BC. The site included a glacis of the Hyksos period, when it probably controlled the territory from Megiddo to Gezer. It was clearly an important city in the Late Bronze Age, and it figures prominently in the Amarna letters. At that time, fortifications and a temple with a massebah were erected. The town was destroyed in the 12th century BC, and there was another break in occupation until the 10th century BC, when it became an Israelite city and the short-lived capital of the kingdom of Israel. This was destroyed by the Assyrians in 720 BC, after which there was intermittent occupation until its final destruction in 101 BC. The site was replaced by Nablus (Neapolis) in AD 67. There was also some occupation in the Pre-Pottery Neolithic period. (*syn.* modern Balatah, Balata)

sheep: A ruminant (cud-chewing) mammal of the genus Ovis, usually stockier than its relative the goat. Sheep were first domesticated from wild species of sheep by at least 5000 BC, and their remains have been found at numerous sites of early human habitation in the Middle East, Europe, and Central Asia. Domesticated sheep are raised for their fleece (wool), for milk, and for meat. The flesh of mature sheep is called mutton; that of immature animals is called lamb. The moufflon (*Ovis orientalis*) of Syria, Turkey, and Iraq, was the first food animal to be tamed, probably c. 9000 BC. The urial (*O. vignei*) lived further east, between the Caspian and Tibet, and its bones have been identified as dating c. 4900 BC. It was introduced into Europe in the Neolithic. In practice, the bones of sheep and goats from archaeological sites are lumped together by many researchers who do not distinguish between them in archaeological site reports and refer instead to sheep/goat, ovicaprid, caprovine, and so on. Only a few of them, notably the horn cores, are firmly diagnostic. Goats are distinguished from sheep by differences in scent glands, lack of "beard," the number of chromosomes, and the possession of tightly curled horns.

shell: A hard, rigid usually calcareous covering or support of an animal, as a mollusk. Many varieties of shell were used in antiquity, apart from the use of their contents as food. Some were used for tools (oyster, conch), and others were made into jewelry or used for decorative inlays. Others, such as ostrich and smaller seashells, were used to make beads. Shell was perforated and strung on necklaces since at least the Upper Palaeolithic. It is frequently found in tombs, probably symbolizing the resurrection. Shell was traded widely to areas where it was not locally available.

shell midden: An archaeological deposit consisting of a refuse mound of discarded shells, offering evidence of early human use of certain mollusks. These often extensive heaps are the result of many years of exploitation of marine resources as a main or supplementary food source. Shell middens provide information on diet, harvesting techniques, subsistence economy, and seasonality. (*syn.* shell mound)

shengwen: Pottery of early postglacial Cina, predating the Neolithic Cishan and Hemudu wares. It is coarse with a textured surface decoration. (*syn.* [sheng-wen])

Sheshonq: Libyan name held by five kings of the 22nd and 23rd Dynasties (945–715 BC, 818–715 BC, respectively) as their birth name or nomen. Sheshonq I (fl. 10th century BC), was the first king (reigned 945–924 BC) of the 22nd Dynasty of Egypt. (*syn.* Shoshenq, Sheshonk, Shishak)

shield: A piece of armor carried in the hand or on the arm, usually the left, to ward off weapons. Examples from the Bronze and Iron Ages come from bogs and rivers of northwest Europe. In the Bronze Age, shields were circular and made of wood covered with bronze. They had a raised, dome-shaped boss in the center, into the back of which the hand fitted, holding the grip. In the Iron Age, shields were sometimes called bucklers and had become long and rectangular. They were made of bronze and embossed. Some were enameled in La Tène style and lined with wood or leather. Leather shields, with few surviving, are functionally more efficient, and wooden ones are also known, notably in Mexico, where they were decorated with feather mosaic.

shieling: Either a mountain hut used as a shelter by shepherds or a summer pasture in the mountains. The summer pasture to which livestock were driven often had associated huts or temporary accommodation for seasonal use.

shifting cultivation: A primitive and widespread form of agriculture in which forest was cleared, commonly by chopping and burning small trees. It is one of the earliest forms of cultivation. The clearance would be followed by planting of crops in the clearance—seeds planted in holes poked into the ashes—and their harvesting and replanting for a few years. Without fertilizers, however, the land soon loses its nutritional value, and the clearance must be left fallow, to grow over again, while other areas of forest are cleared. A return to the original plot may be made after a reasonable length of time; hence it is also called shifting cultivation and cyclic agriculture. In temperate regions, it is a wasteful method because soil fertility and crop yields, although initially high, decline rapidly, after which a new stretch of forest must be cleared. (*syn.* swidden agriculture)

Shih-chai-shan: One of a group of 1st-century BC sites near Lake Tien in Yunnan Province, southwest China, with the cemetery of a regional Dian bronze culture contemporaneous with the Han Dynasty. The graves have bronze and iron weapons and tools with unique motifs—and bronze cowrie containers and drums. Links with southeast Asia and western areas of China are seen in the Dian drums. (*syn.* Shizhaishan)

Shindo: A small spur projecting into the valley of the Kyi Chu River near Lhasa, Tibet. Three phases have been distinguished. Horizon A had flexed burials in rock-cut pits, accompanied by crude, handmade pottery but no metalwork. Horizon B contained two flexed burials in rock-cut pits with much finer handmade pottery and a few iron artifacts. There was also one larger tomb closed with two carefully dressed stone slabs and containing two skulls, a pile of long bones and vertebrae, three pottery vessels, and a wooden bowl with metal lining. Horizon C consisted of two tumuli built of pebbles, with flexed burials, fine wheel-turned pottery with traces of red decoration, and a few iron artifacts. About 50 meters from this ridge is a boulder with pecked carvings of animals and letters.

Shinto: The native religion of Japan, which is not recorded in literature until the 6th century. The core of belief seems to be that spirits reside in numerous natural phenomena, such as sun, water, fire and mountains, and that it is important to attain ritual purity from pollution. Shinto shrines often have a mirror as the embodiment of the deity.

shipwreck: The remains of sunken ships, which are often investigated by underwater archaeologists.

Shirataki: Palaeolithic sites in Hokkaido, Japan, with a large number of obsidian artifacts dating from about 18,000–13,000 BC, and including large blades, burins, scrapers, and some bifacial points. There are more bifacial points and microblades in a younger group, which dates c. 13,000–10,000 BC. The microblades were made by a special technique, called the Yubetsu technique, where a large biface is made into a core that looks like a tall carinated scraper. The technology is also called Yubetsu, although the type site is Shirataki-Hattoridai. (*syn.* Yubetsu)

Shiyu: Late Palaeolithic site in Shanxi Province, China, with a fossil human occipital bone and a radiocarbon date of c. 28,000 bp. There are small scrapers, points, and microlithic blades and cores. (*syn.* [Shih-yu])

shoe-last adze: A long thin stone adze (chisel-shaped ground-stone tool) employed by the Danubian farmers of the

Early Neolithic, possibly as a hoe for cultivating their fields. It is a common stone tool found in Early Neolithic Linear Pottery contexts throughout Europe. It might also have been used as an adze for carpentry.. (*syn.* shoe-last celt)

Short Count: The 52-year cycle in the Maya system, based on a sequence of 13 *katuns.*

short-twig: One of the two main versions of the Scandinavian runic alphabet (the other, long-branch) in use during the Viking Age, mainly before AD 800. (*syn.* Swedo-Norwegian runes, common runes)

Shortugai: A site with definite links to the Harappan civilization near the Amu River, northeast of Konduz, Afghanistan. The lower two levels had Mature Harappan material (2nd half of the 3rd millennium BC) and an irrigation system; it was probably a trading colony. There was also occupation by the Beshkent culture dated to the 1st half of the 2nd millennium BC.

Shoshone: Native American group that inhabited much of the Great Basin during both historic and prehistoric times.

shouldered adze: Polished stone adze of the Neolithic period, distributed along the coastal area of China from Shantung southward and in central-southern China. It was also prominent in Southeast Asia.

shouldered point: Type of stone point made on a blade, with a notch on one side of the base and flaked partly or wholly on both sides. Shouldered points are characteristic of some Upper Palaeolithic cultures of Europe, such as the Solutrean, Magdalenian, and Eastern Gravettian.

shovel test: A subsurface detection technique using either posthole diggers or shovels to quickly determine the density and distribution of archaeological remains. Also, a shovel-sized sample taken at various intervals across a site. (*syn.* shovel testing)

Showlow: Pueblo site in Arizona, which provided timber to allow the modern dendrochronology sequence to be related to the prehistoric sequence for the first time.

shrine: The innermost element of a temple where the cult image or bark of the deity was placed or the elaborate boxes containing funerary statuary. It was a repository for relics, either fixed, as a tomb, or movable, as a feretory. A shrine can be a case, box, or receptacle, especially one in which sacred relics (as the bones of a saint) are deposited—or a place in which devotion is paid to a saint or deity (sanctuary). A shrine can also be a niche containing a religious image, a receptacle (as a tomb) for the dead, or a place or object worshiped in association. (*syn.* naos, per, sanctuary)

Shriver: Woodland culture site in Missouri with a Folsom occupation and an assemblage of chert flaked tools (which are dated to 10,700–13,000 BP).

Shroud of Turin: A sheet of twill-woven linen cloth on which appears a pale sepia-tone image of the front and back of a naked man about 6 feet tall, alleged to be the actual cloth in which Christ's crucified body was wrapped. The images contain markings that allegedly correspond to the stigmata of Jesus, including a thorn mark on the head, lacerations (as if from flogging) on the back, bruises on the shoulders, and various stains of what is presumed to be blood. Since emerging in 1354, it has been purported to be the burial garment of Jesus Christ; it has been preserved since 1578 in the royal chapel of the Cathedral of San Giovanni Battista in Turin, Italy. (*syn.* Holy Shroud)

Shu: In Egyptian religion, the god of air and sunlight, created solely by Atum. Shu and his sister and companion, Tefnut (goddess of moisture), were the first couple of the group of nine gods called the Ennead of Heliopolis; Nut and Geb were their children. In some Middle Kingdom texts, Shu was given the status of a primeval creator god.

Shub-Ad (fl. 3rd millennium BC): A queen of Ur c. 2600 BC (Early Dynastic period in Mesopotamia, c. 2900–2334 BC), whose tomb was discovered in the Royal Cemetery. The tomb contained the bodies of more than 60 attendants. The queen herself lay on a wooden bier in a stone-built chamber beside that of Abargi, probably her husband. She was wearing a cloak of beads of gold, silver, and precious stones, an elaborate headdress of gold ribbons with gold and lapis lazuli pendants, and large lunate gold earrings. There were also bowls and other vessels of gold, silver, and copper, as well as pottery. In the shaft of the tomb were a wooden sledge with mosaic decoration and two oxen to draw it, an inlaid gaming board, and a magnificent harp inlaid with shell, red, and blue stone. (*syn.* Puabi)

Shuidonggou: Late Palaeolithic site in Ningxia Hui, China, with blade artifacts, assigned to the Ordos culture. (*syn.* [Shui-tung-kou])

Shulaveri-Shomu culture: Neolithic culture based on two sites on the Kura River in Georgia and Azerbaijan. There was coarse pottery decorated by incision or knobs and small round domestic structures. The culture is dated to mid-6th or early-5th millennia BC.

Shulgi (reigned 2094–2047 BC): The son and successor of Ur-Nammu, who founded the Ur III dynasty. He gained control over the economy of the empire and extended his holdings up the Tigris River and through the Zagros Mountains. His most important victory was over Elam. The empire collapsed during the reign of Shulgi's third successor. The empire only existed from c. 2112–2004.

Shungurian: An industry of the lower Omo Valley north of Lake Turkana, Ethiopia, known for its remains of animals and hominids. Several archaeological deposits have been discovered on the site, dating back 2 million years. The industry is based on very small quartz flakes made from a nucleus or from the accidental shattering of pebbles used as percussion tools.

Shuruppak: Ancient Sumerian city-state located south of Nippur in Iraq and originally on the bank of the Euphrates River. Excavations show three levels of habitation extending from the late prehistoric period to the 3rd dynasty of Ur (c. 2112–2004 BC). The most distinctive finds were ruins of well-built houses, along with cuneiform tablets with administrative records and lists of words. Shuruppak was celebrated in Sumerian legend as the scene of the Deluge, which destroyed all humanity except one survivor, Ziusudra. Ziusudra corresponds with Utnapishtim in the Gilgamesh epic and with the biblical Noah. (*syn.* modern Fara, Tall Fa'rah)

Sialk, Tepe: Important tell site near Kashan on the plateau of Iran, with six major phases from the Neolithic to the Iron Age. They are: I, dating to the 6th–5th millennia BC, a simple village of recently settled farmers who used pottery painted with basketry designs and copper only in the form of hammered ornaments; II, a village of mud-brick architecture with very fine pottery elaborately painted with stylized animals; III, pottery made by wheel and kiln and more use of copper; IV, around 3000 BC, the site fell under the influence of Susa and Mesopotamia, the painted ware replaced by monochrome gray or red, much jewelry, and the introduction of proto-Elamite writing. This phase was followed by a break in occupation and the resettlement—represented in cemetery A—is often attributed to intruders from the northeast, who are thought to have been responsible for the introduction of Indo-European languages to this area. The final occupation of Tepe Sialk, represented in cemetery B and dated to the late 2nd–early 1 millennia BC, saw the first use of iron. Around 9th–8th centuries BC, the site was destroyed and abandoned. (*syn.* Siyalk)

Siassi Islands: Islands between New Guinea and New Britain, which were occupied by traders between 1,500–2,000 years ago. Located in the Vitiaz Strait, they sent pottery west and obsidian and sago east.

Sibri: A settlement site with a suggested date of 2000 BC, near Mehrgahr, Pakistan, with a cemetery. Much of the material culture is identical to Central Asian forms—and with "foreign" copper and bronze tools and weapons and typical pottery forms from cemeteries of the Sapalli-Tepe group in Tajikistan and Uzbekistan. The connection of Sibri to these two areas has not yet been worked out.

sica: A curved dagger or scimitar, different from a *pugio*, a straight dagger.

Sicilian pottery: South Italian pottery using the red-figured technique of the late 5th century BC. Production centers included Syracuse, Himera, and Centuripe.

Sicily: The largest island in the Mediterranean Sea with settlement from 10,000 years ago. It was colonized by the Greeks between 8th–6th centuries BC, with cities such as Syracuse, Leontini, Naxos, Megara, Agragas, and Selinus. At the coming of the Greeks, three peoples occupied Sicily: in the east the Siculi, or Sicels, who gave their name to the island but were reputed to be latecomers from Italy; to the west of the Gelas River, the Sicani; and in the extreme west, the Elymians, a people of Trojan origin with their chief centers at Segesta and at Eryx (Erice). Sicily came into conflict with the Phoenician colony of Carthage early on, and in the battle at Himera in 480 BC, the Syracusan fleet (Syracuse was Sicily's capital) beat the Carthaginians. Sicily eventually fell under the control of Romans, becoming the first Roman province, in 227 BC.

sickle: A knife for reaping corn, first used by Neolithic man, made of flint and shaped like a banana. These flint blades were mounted in a wooden or bone haft, as in the Natufian of Palestine. Later sickles were of bronze, and some of terracotta were found in Sumer. In the Bronze Age, a socketed sickle appeared. Since the introduction of iron, the balanced sickle has become the standard form—a deeply curved blade bent back from the handle. Its modern form is a curved metal blade with a short handle fitted on a tang.

sickle gloss: The gloss that occurs on the edge of flint sickle blades, caused by the wear of the blade against the phytoliths in the grasses being reaped. A distinctive shine produced on flint tools that have been used to reap cereal grasses. The polish comes from the abrasive action of silica present in the stems of both wild and cultivated cereals, so that the occurrence of reaping tools with sickle gloss need not by itself imply agriculture. (*syn.* sickle sheen)

sideblade: A narrow flake with a sharp edge on one side, often inserted into bone arrowheads and spear heads.

side-looking airborne radar: An instrument used in aerial reconnaissance to detect large archaeological sites by using an oblique radar image, a remote sensing technique that involves the recording in radar images of the return of pulses of electromagnetic radiation sent out from aircraft. The tool is especially useful because it can penetrate cloud cover and, to a degree, vegetation. This variety of airborne radar employs a large side-looking antenna (i.e., one whose beam is perpendicular to the aircraft's line of flight) and is capable of high-range resolution. SLAR generates maplike images of the ground. (*syn.* SLAR, sideways-looking airborne radar)

Sidemi culture: A culture of the Vladivostok area of eastern Siberia from the late 2nd millennium BC. The population lived in coastal settlements of semisubterranean houses, which are associated with shell middens. Characteristic tools were made of polished slate, although small quantities of iron were also used. The area came under strong influence from

Manchuria and China, and in the 1st millennium AD it formed part of the Po Hai state. (*syn.* Shell Midden culture)

side-notched point: Type of stone point, which is chipped on both faces and has notches on both sides near the base. They are characteristic of the Northern Archaic tradition in North America.

sidescan sonar: A survey method used in underwater archaeology, which provides the broadest view of the sea floor and its texture. An acoustic emitter is towed behind a vessel and sends out sound waves in a fan-shaped beam. These pulses of sonic energy are reflected back to a transducer and recorded on a rotating drum. (*syn.* side-scan sonar, side-scan sonograph, side-scanning sonar)

side scraper: A retouched flake tool with a thick working edge; a flake tool that has been sharpened on one edge and left blunt on other edges to allow grasping, probably used to scrape (dress) animal hides and for working hard materials. It is called a side scraper (racloir) because its sharpened edge is the long side. (*syn.* sidescraper, scraper, racloir)

sidewall: The vertical margin of an archaeological excavation; the vertical side of an excavation pit. It is an important record of site stratigraphy and often provides the axis for measuring artifact provenience. (*syn.* side wall)

Sidi Abd er Rahman/Sidi Abderrahmane: Palaeolithic site close to Casablanca on the Moroccan coast with Acheulian levels. There are abundant stone artifacts and a mandible attributed to *Homo erectus*. These are earlier than the Amirian dune (perhaps 0.5 million years old or "Mindel") and later than the Saletian dune of about 1 million years of age.

Sidon: Ancient city of the Phoenicians on the coast of Lebanon south of Beirut. It shared supremacy with Tyre but was greater importance under the Achaemenid (Persian) Empire, 6th–4th centuries BC. It was destroyed by the Assyrians in 677 BC but rebuilt. Sidon was an important Mediterranean trading center from the Early or Middle Bronze Age. Because the site underlies the modern town, little excavation has taken place. However, a number of burials of various dates have been found both in and around the city, including that of Ahiram, bearing a 10th-century BC inscription, and Greco-Roman coffins of the 5th and 4th centuries BC. (*syn.* Saida; modern Sarda)

sieving: A technique of particle size analysis used to determine the size grades of pebble gravel, sand, and coarse silt in sediment and soils of archaeological deposits. The archaeologist processes all the earth from the site through a fine mesh, then does dry screening in a shaker frame or wet sieving with flowing water. It improves the recovery rate of artifacts. For lighter soils, dry sieving may be effective. Wet sieving is used for more claylike material and for recovering bones, shells, seeds, and other biological remains. The sieved residues are then dried and sorted by hand. The sample is placed on the top sieve of a series of nested sieves. Sieve mesh sizes are standardized. Wet sieving as part of a flotation technique is used to recover small remains from sites.

Sigatoka: A beach-dune site on southwestern Viti Levu, Fiji, which has produced an important but discontinuous pottery sequence from late Lapita, c. 500 BC through a paddle-impressed style of AD 200.

Signal Butte: Great Plains site in western Nebraska occupied from c. 4500 BP until historic times. It is located on a large mesa and played an important role in the initial chronological ordering of the Great Plains. There are lanceolate projectile points resembling the Folsom type in the lowest level. In the second level, there are early Late Archaic materials dating c. 2000 BC. The third level had a component of the Dismal River Aspect, glass beads, aboriginal artifacts, and traded copper, as well an Upper Republican Aspect component.

signaling station: Small forts built at intervals from North Yorkshire to the Wash in Britain, usually on high cliffs and not connected with fortified harbors. Each had a tower about 80 ft high, with sides 40 feet wide and walls 5 feet thick. The tower was surrounded by a wall 6 feet thick and 20 feet away from it, thus forming a courtyard.

signary: The set of signs of all classes in a script, or the set of signs in one of these classes, as in phonetic signary. Signs themselves are representations that are nonfigurative. (*syn.* signs)

Silbury Hill: Largest prehistoric manmade mound in Europe, located in Wiltshire, England, and part of the Avebury complex of Neolithic monuments. It is a huge conical chalk mound, 40 meters high and 160 meters in diameter. No burials have been found in or beneath the mound to this date. It was built in four distinct phases, but apparently continuously as part of a single constructional process, dated c. 2600–2300 BC.

Silchester: An important Roman-British town, which was a node on the Roman road system in Britain, located in Hampshire, England. All that stands now is the impressive wall of the 1st century AD. In it were a forum, inn, church, four temples, two baths, grid street plan, shops, and houses. An amphitheater existed outside the wall. Most of the antiquities recovered from the site are in the Reading Museum; the local Calleva Museum (1957) illustrates the life of the Roman town. (*syn.* ancient Calleva Atrebatum)

silex: A flint or flint stone, often, any kind of hard stone hewn into polygonal blocks. Technically, it is silica or a siliceous material.

silhouette: A stain or shadow left in soils under certain environmental conditions by organic or other objects. Silhouettes of timber, for example, the shadow of a post in a posthole, are relatively common. Where the soil is too acid to preserve bone, the mineral component of bone may result in an iron manganese stain that frequently has the shape of a skeleton.

silk: Thread that can be drawn off the cocoon spun by the grub of the moth *Bombyx mori* and used for weaving fine cloth, which originated in China in the Neolithic period. The silk industry was established by the Anyang period, c. 1300–1030 BC. The Anyang oracle bones include characters for silk, silk fabrics, silkworm, and mulberry tree, and traces of silk fabrics are occasionally found preserved. Silk fabric was used as a writing surface at least as early as the 5th century BC. Both manuscripts and paintings on silk have come from Chu tombs of the 5th century BC and later. Elaborate methods of weaving were developed by the Han Dynasty (206 BC–AD 220), and textiles exported in large numbers along the Silk Route to the Roman world and later to Byzantium. The route is the collective name for several overland and ocean routes for the silk trade from the 1st–8th centuries AD. From Chang'an, capital of the Han Dynasty, the main route went west through the Gansu corridor.

Silk Route: The collective name for several overland and ocean routes for the silk trade between China and the Roman world, and later Byzantium, from the 1st–8th centuries AD. From Chang'an, capital of the Han Dynasty, the main route went west through the Gansu corridor into the Tarim basin at Dunhuang. There it branched into two main routes across the Central Asian deserts. After crossing the Pamirs, the two routes finally rejoined at Merv and continued via Ecbatana and Ctesiphon to Palmyra and the Mediterranean. The institutionalized traffic in silk began in the Han Dynasty (206 BC–AD 220). The cities along the Silk Route flourished despite political changes. From the 9th century onward, trade came increasingly to depend on sea routes, and the main Chinese export was not silk but porcelain. Overland commerce revived only briefly during the continent-wide peace that ensued after the Mongol conquests of the 13th century when Marco Polo followed the Silk Route to the court of the Yuan emperor Kublai Khan.

Silla: A kingdom traditionally dated 57 BC–AD 668, the oldest of the monarchies of the Three Kingdoms period, and including the Unified or Great Silla period of 668–935, the golden age of Korean art. It eventually came to cover most of southeastern Korea east of the Naktong River. The original territory of the Silla kingdom, the modern North Kyongsang province, is a mountain-secluded triangle. Silla was in competition with the Koguryo and Paekche until 668 and had relations with Japan's Yamato. When it unified in 668, its capital remained in Kyongju. At that site are large mounded tombs of the 5th–6th centuries with fine gold work. It became

a gridded city in the 7th century, and the Anapchi pond was built.

silt: Sediment or soil particles ranging from 0.002/0.004–0.05/0.06 millimeters in diameter. Sediments are seldom composed entirely of silt but rather are a mixture of clay, silt, and sand. Silt refers to extremely fine grains of soil or sediment usually carried along in river water. Silt deposits formed by wind are known as loess, a yellow, unconsolidated rock. The term has no implications of color, organic content, or any property other than particle size or texture.

silver: A white, lustrous metal valued for its decorative beauty and electrical conductivity. It is found nearly as early as copper and gold, in the form of beads, trinkets, and display vessels. The main source of this metal in antiquity was the lead ore galena, in which silver sulfide occurs as an impurity. After smelting the ore, silver was recovered by the process of cupellation, where the lead is oxidized, leaving silver unaltered. Silver is soft and could be cold worked, but it was too soft for most purposes and was often alloyed with other metals, even in antiquity.

silver-figured: Technique used to decorate Greek and Etruscan bronze and gold in which silver figures were attached to the other metal or silver foil was placed over relief decoration.

Silver Leaves: Iron Age site south of the Zambezi River in eastern Transvaal, South Africa, dated to the 3rd–4th centuries AD.

sima: The roof gutter of a Classical roof; a row of vertical tiles placed at the edge of the roof above the cornice. It was usually clay, and water was thrown clear of the building by elaborate spouts often shaped like lions' heads.

Similaun Man: Chalcolithic man's skeleton found in the Similaun Pass of the Tirolean Alps, Italy. The well-preserved corpse, clothing, and appointments were probably covered by a glacier c. 5,000–5,500 years ago (radiocarbon 3300 BC). It was the oldest mummified body found intact. (*syn.* Ice Man, Iceman, Otzi)

simple data cluster: Clustered data that are homogeneous in that they have a single function, such as those from an obsidian tool workshop.

simple random sampling: A probabilistic sampling technique in which each sample unit has a statistically equal chance for selection. The areas to be sampled are chosen by using a table of random numbers.

simple tool: An artifact consisting of a single part.

simulation: The use of a model to simulate an observed phenomenon. In modern times, simulation is done by the formulation and computer implementation of dynamic models, such as models concerned with change through time. Simulation is a useful heuristic device and can be of considerable help in the development of explanation. Models can be used in archaeology to simulate, for example, the distribution of a group of artifacts or settlements.

Si Mu Wu fang ding/Ssu Mu Wu: A Late Shang bronze ritual vessel, a tetrapod weighing 1,925 pounds (875 kg), the largest metal casting surviving from Chinese antiquity. Late Shang ritual vessels reveal high technological competence and large-scale, labor-intensive metal production. Said to have been found in the Anyang royal cemetery, this vessel is inscribed with a dedication to an empress and dates probably from the 12th century BC. It is now in the Historical Museum, Beijing. (*syn.* Ssu Mu Wu fang-ting)

Sinai: Triangular peninsula linking Africa with Asia and occupying an area of 23,500 square miles. It lies between the Gulf of Suez and the Suez Canal on the west and the Gulf of Aqaba and the Negev Desert on the east, and it is bounded by the Mediterranean Sea on the north and the Red Sea to the south. Occupied since prehistoric times, the earliest written information about it dates from 3000 BC, when the ancient Egyptians recorded their explorations there in search of copper ores. From very early times, it was an important source of malachite, turquoise, and copper. Certain inscriptions associated with the copper mines are believed to be among the earliest examples of the alphabet, c. 16th century BC.

Sinan: A district in South Cholla Province, South Korea, where a sunken Yuan merchant ship of the 14th century AD was discovered off the coast. The ship's cargo was Chinese porcelain: More than 17,000 pieces have been recovered, mainly celadon and qingbai wares. Dated coins, 18.5 tons, and many metal, stone, wooden, and lacquer objects have also been found.

Sinanthropus: Genus formerly assigned to Peking Man, now classified as *Homo erectus*. (*syn.* Peking man; Pekin man; Lantian man)

Sinda: Late Cypriot settlement site first occupied in the 13th century BC. In eastern Cyprus, it was massively fortified but suffered two major destructions—possibly by the Sea Peoples. It was abandoned early in the 12th century BC.

sinew: Thread or cord made from uncured animal tendon.

sinew frayer: A tool similar in shape to a scraper but with serrated edges, which may have been the forerunner of the saw. Primitive tribes today use similar stones to stroke sinews into fibers for sewing.

single-facet platform: A platform on a biface or core with a single plane of detachment.

Single Grave culture: Late Neolithic cultures of Scandinavia, northern Germany, and the Low Countries, dated to c. 2800–2400 BC. The burial rite was inhumation of a single corpse under or in a round barrow and sometimes laid in a pit

grave or a mortuary house. The burials include the stone battle ax and corded ware beakers. The Single Grave culture has traditionally been regarded as intrusive in northern Europe because of the contrast with the collective burial in megalithic tombs practiced by the earlier Neolithic TRB people in the same area. It is possible that it developed out of the TRB culture and that the changes in the archaeological record at this time can be explained in terms of changing social systems—more complex social structures and the emergence of elites. The burial mounds are sometimes multiphase with the sequence of undergrave, bottom-grave, and overgrave. (*syn.* Single-Grave Culture)

Sinjerli: Site in the foothills of the Anti-Taurus Mountains, south-central Turkey, of a Late Hittite city-state after the downfall of the Hittite Empire (c. 1190 BC). It had grown slowly to importance under the Hittites, flourishing after their downfall as the independent state of Sam'al until annexed by the Assyrians in the 7th century BC and then abandoned. Its fortified citadel contained two palaces, each including the architectural unit known as a *bit hilani* ("pillared porch"). Immediately surrounding the citadel was the city itself, enclosed by a circular fortification wall topped by 100 towers. The palaces and gateways were freely decorated with the reliefs and hieroglyphic inscriptions of the Syro-Hittites. The identity with ancient Sam'al was confirmed by the discovery of a victory inscription of the Assyrian king Esarhaddon from 670 BC. (*syn.* Zincirli Höyük, Zincirli, Zenjirli, Senjirli, Zinjerli; ancient Sam'al)

sintering: A process in which the edges of the clay particles soften and adhere to one another. This process begins at about 350 degrees Centigrade and is completed by 700 degrees Centigrade.

Sipán: A site on the northern coast of Peru, in the Lambayeque region, with a complex of tombs of the Moche culture (Early Intermediate period). There are royal or very lavish tombs, including that of the lord of Sipán, a warrior-priest, with spectacular artifacts. Several more burial chambers containing the remains of Moche royalty have been excavated, all dating from AD c. 300. These finds have greatly aided the understanding of Moche society, religion, and culture.

sipapu: (see-pah-pooh) In a kiva (ceremonial room) of the U.S. Southwest, a hole in the center of the floor that symbolizes the emergence of the spirit into another world—giving access to the lower world in Pueblo mythology. They are sometimes carved through a plank of wood. Sipapus have been identified by homology.

Sippar: Ancient city of Babylonia, southwest of Baghdad, Iraq, an ancient Sumerian city lying on a canal linking the Tigris and the Euphrates. It was an important religious and trading center in southern Mesopotamia. Sippar was subject to the 1st Dynasty of Babylon, but little is known about the city before 1174 BC, when it was sacked by the Elamite king Kutir-Nahhunte. It recovered and was later captured by the Assyrian king Tiglath-pileser I. Under the 8th Dynasty of Babylon (c. 880), Sippar's great temple of Shamash was rebuilt. Tens of thousands of tablets from Old Babylonian and Neo-Babylonian periods have been found. (*syn.* modern Abu Habbah)

Siret, Henri (1857–1933) and Siret, Louis (1860–1934): Belgian amateur archaeologists who worked in the Almeria region of Spain and uncovered Chalcolithic and Bronze Age cultures at such sites as Los Millares, El Argar, and Tabernas.

Sirikwa Holes: Feature of Iron Age sites in the western highlands of Kenya, which consists of circular depressions 5–10 meters in diameter, sometimes encircled by stone walling. They functioned as cattle barns during the first half of the 2nd millennium AD.

Si Satchanalai: Industrial center of the Sukhothai state in northern Thailand, with over 600 kilns for pottery and stoneware. The Chalieng brown-glazed wares, Sukhothai black-on-cream wares, and green-glazed Celadon wares are the best known. They are collectively called Sawankhalok and dated to the 14th–16th centuries AD (although they have earlier phases in some places). (*syn.* Sawankhalok)

sistrum: Ancient Egyptian percussion instrument, a rattle consisting of a wood, metal, or clay frame set loosely with crossbars (often hung with jingles that sound when the instrument is shaken). A handle is attached to the frame. It was sacred to Hathor and used in ceremonial worship of Isis and at funerals. Open-topped, U-shaped sistrums existed by 2500 BC in Sumer. They are still used in Coptic and Ethiopian churches, in western Africa, among two Native American tribes, and in Malaysia and Melanesia. (*syn.* seistron)

Sisupalgarh: Iron Age city in Orissa, eastern India, with black and red ware in its earliest occupation. In the later 1st millennium BC, the city was surrounded by elaborate defensive walls and shows evidence of advanced town planning.

Sitagroi: Settlement mound in eastern Macedonia, northern Greece, which has produced an important stratigraphy for the chronology of the north Aegean. Sitagroi began with a Middle Neolithic occupation dated c. 4500 BC and continued into the Early Bronze Age in the 3rd millennium BC. The site was chosen for excavation to clarify the relations between the cultural sequence in the Aegean and the Balkans during those times. The excavation established that finds of Gumelnita type preceded by a considerable period finds of Troy I type. The site also supports claims for the primacy of southeast European metalworking over that of Anatolia and that copper metallurgy was an independent development in the Balkans.

site: Any location that demonstrates past human activity, as evidenced by the presence of artifacts, features, ecofacts, or other material remains; a single place in which excavation or reconnaissance has revealed objects or data of archaeological interest. The definition implies that such a location was used by humans for a sufficient period to develop features or become a deposit ground for artifacts. Sites can range from small, temporary camps to large, complex cities, from a living site to a quarry site, and from one artifact to many levels of occupation. Major types of sites include domestic/habitation sites, kill sites, and processing/butchering sites.

site catchment: The area surrounding a settlement or camp, habitually used by the inhabitants as a source of materials for food, toolmaking, and the like. It is defined as the total area from which all the animals, plants, and artifacts of which there are remains preserved on the site are derived. Each group of people living on the site is assumed to have had a "territory," the area around the site that they habitually exploited. (*syn.* site territory, catchment area)

site catchment analysis: A method of reconstructing the economy of a site by studying the resources that are available in a reasonable distance, generally 1–2 hours' walking time from the site. The technique was devised by E. Higgs and C. Vita-Finzi for "the study of the relationship between technology and those natural resources lying within economic range of individual sites," an extension of the least-cost principle. The catchment area is defined by drawing a circle around the site; the radius has often been set at 5 kilometers (i.e., an hour's walk) for agriculturists and 10 kilometers (i.e., two hours' walk) for hunter gatherers, figures that represent ethnographically observed averages. In the catchment area, the proportions of such resources as arable or pastoral land are calculated, and from these figures conclusions can be drawn about the nature and function of the site. The technique offers a valuable and reasonable objective method for analyzing relations between site location, technology, and available resources. This type of "offsite" analysis can concentrate on the total area from which a site's contents have been derived. (*syn.* SCA; site-catchment analysis)

site exploitation survey: A method of achieving a fairly standardized assessment of the area habitually used by a site's occupants. (*syn.* SET)

site exploitation territory: The area around a particular site, which would have been most intensively or frequently exploited for resources such as food. It is a central concept in palaeoeconomy.

site-formation processes: The total of the processes—natural and cultural, individual and combined—that affected the formation and development of the archaeological record. Natural formation processes refer to natural or environmental events that govern the burial and survival of the archaeological record. Cultural formation processes include the deliberate or accidental activities of humans. On a settlement site, for example, the nature of human occupation, the activities carried out, the pattern of breakage and loss of material, rubbish disposal, rebuilding, or reuse of the same area all influence the surviving archaeological deposits. After the site's abandonment, it is further affected by such factors as erosion, glaciation, later agriculture, the activities of plants and animals, as well as the natural processes of chemical action in the soil. Reconstruction of these processes helps to relate the observed evidence of an archaeological site to the human activity responsible for it. (*syn.* site formation process; formation process)

site grid: A set of regularly spaced intersecting north-south and east-west lines, usually marked by stakes, providing the basic reference system for recording horizontal provenience (coordinates) in a site.

site map: A map depicting the details of a site, usually made by recording all observable surface features.

site plan: A specially prepared map for recording the horizontal provenience of artifacts, food remains, and features—keyed to topographic maps. Such a map may be designed to depict a specific detail in a site, usually a single feature or group of features.

site structure: The arrangement of the various components of an archaeological site, including artifacts, features, and structures. Site structure analysis identifies how a space was organized and used and how it related to aspects of the cultural system. Site structure analyses are used to make warranting arguments in the context of the archaeological record and are often done in ethnoarchaeological studies.

site survey: The collection of surface data and evaluation of a site's archaeological significance.

Sitio Conte: A Panamanian site, in Coclé province, occupied from AD 200–1300. Its cemetery, used 500–900, had some 60 tombs filled with gold regalia, tools and weapons, ornaments of carved stone or bone, and thousands of pots, some painted in several colors. All these items were decorated with elaborate scroll designs and animal forms. Elements of this Sitio Conte (or Coclé) art style are found at other sites up to the Spanish conquest.

Sittard: Settlement site of the Neolithic Linear Pottery culture in Limburg, the Netherlands. The settlement was surrounded by a palisade and contained a number of timber longhouses. Some of the larger houses were clearly divided into three parts for various purposes.

situla: A bucket-shaped vessel of pottery, silver, or sheet bronze, a Classical container, with a swinging handle across the rim. Examples of bronze from the north Italian Iron Age were particularly elaborately decorated; the style of decoration found on these situlae and other sheet bronze objects is known as situla art. A situla had a short vertical neck, a shallow shoulder, and sloped downward to a narrow base; there were two handles and a lid. It would be used for drawing water from a well. (*syn.* plural situlae)

situla art: Examples of bronze situlae from the north Italian Iron Age, which were particularly elaborately decorated. The embossed or incised decoration is of Early Iron Age date in south-central Europe, the medium for which was usually a bronze shouldered bucket-shaped vessel (situla).

Six Dynasties: The period of Chinese history between the fall of the Han Dynasty in AD 220 and the founding of the Sui Dynasty in 589, during which six dynasties had capitals in the south at Nanjing, while North China was ruled by barbarian dynasties. They were the Wu (222–280), the Eastern Chin (317–420), the Liu-Sung (420–479), the Southern Ch'i (479–502), the Southern Liang (502–557), and the Southern Ch'en (557–589). In the course of the Six Dynasties period, Buddhism came to be firmly established. Six Dynasties tombs have contributed notably to the study of ceramics and early pictorial art. Great advances were made in medicine, astronomy, botany, and chemistry—and major changes took place in the arts and architecture. Wheelbarrows and kites were invented, coal was first used as a fuel, and it was also during the Six Dynasties that the great aristocratic families began to arise in Chinese society.

Six's technique: Technique of decorating Athenian pottery in the 6th century BC, as described by Jan Six. The pottery's black surface was painted in red or white and detail cut through, showing the black surface.

Siwa Oasis: An oasis in the Libyan Desert, west of the Nile, the seat of the oracle temple of Amon, which was already famous in the time of Herodotus and was consulted by Alexander the Great. The fragmentary remains of the temple, with inscriptions dating from the 4th century BC, lie in the ruins of Aghurmi. The oracle fell into disrepute during the Roman occupation of Egypt. Nearby is the ruined temple of Umm Beda (Um Ebeida), and there are also many Roman remains in the vicinity. The earliest remains date to the 26th Dynasty (664–525 BC). Two rock outcrops provide the sites of the old walled settlements of Siwa and Aghurmi, which are veritable fortresses. (*syn.* ancient Sekhet-imit; Ammonium)

Skara Brae: Neolithic village of stone-built houses in Orkney, Scotland, preserved beneath a sand dune with occupation c. 3100–2500 BC. In its latest phase, the village consisted of six or seven houses and a workshop hut, all clustered together and linked by paved alleyways. The associated pottery was of Grooved Ware type. Furniture included beds, hearths, tables, dressers, and cupboards.

Skateholm: Mesolithic fishing sites in southern Sweden (Scania) with domestic areas and over 80 graves. The site is dated to 6000–5500 BP.

skeletal analysis: The examination of surviving human bones for information, such as the racial affinities, the blood group, and so on. The skeleton's sex is shown clearly by the pelvis and, with less certainty, by the skull. The age at death appears from the state of fusion of the long bone epiphyses and skull sutures and the eruption and wear of the teeth. The bones may show signs of injury or disease (palaeopathology). All this information has greater value when many associated skeletons can be studied as a population rather than as individuals.

skeleton: The bony supporting element in the bodies of vertebrate animals. It consists of the axial skeleton—skull (including teeth) and vertebral column—and the appendicular skeleton—ribs, girdles, and limbs. In man, the proportions of various bones are fairly generalized, but in other animals bones may become eliminated, elongated, or strengthened. Only broken fragments of the skeleton usually survive on archaeological sites, except in such cases as deliberate burial. For this reason, human bones are often studied separately from those of other animals. In the case of most animals, the parts that survive are a function of butchery. Identification of species may be possible when there is a considerable number of fragments.

Skellig Michael: The ruins of a Celtic monastery on the east coast of Ireland, one of the best preserved of the early Irish monasteries although possibly of the 8th century. The monastic complex includes two rectangular oratories with fine corbelled roofs, a later chapel, and a series of terrace walls known as the "monks garden"; there are also six beehive huts in which the monks lived. The island suffered Viking raids, but the monastery continued to be used until the 12th or 13th century.

skene: In Greek antiquity, a temporary shop or building but, more commonly, a building behind the playing area, originally a hut for the changing of masks and costumes but eventually became the background for the plays. It was often several stories with a stage placed behind the orchestra. Skenes were first used c. 465 BC. By the end of the 5th century BC, the wooden skene was replaced by a permanent stone structure. In the Roman theater, it was an elaborate building facade.

sketch map: A roughly drawn map with few details. An impressionistic rendering of a region, site, or feature made without instruments, therefore showing no geographical direction or elevation and with distances estimated by pacing. The Incas used sketch maps and cut some in stone to show relief features. Many specimens of early Eskimo sketch maps on skin, wood, and bone have been found. (*syn.* sketch-map)

skeuomorph: An object whose shape or decoration copies the form of the object originally made from another material or by another technique. For example, a pot would be decorated to make it look similar to a vessel of basketry, skin, or other material. In some cases, it is an artifact that represents in decorative form a feature that was originally functional. A decorative bow attached to a shoe is a skeuomorph of the laces once used to tie it; triangular shapes drawn below handles on pottery are skeuomorphs of the metal plates by which the handles on metal prototypes were attached; and the semicircular mark on the back of a teaspoon represents the broadening of the handle where it was soldered to the bowl when it used to be made in two pieces. Frequently, a skeuomorph may yield important information about extinct types, especially when organic materials like basketry are recorded in this way. (*syn.* adj. skeuomorphic)

Skorba: Site on the island of Malta near Nadur Tower, with a temple complex under which earlier deposits have been found. Underneath a small trefoil-shaped temple, dated c. 3000–2600 BC, was a Neolithic settlement of mud-brick houses on stone foundations and an oval hut of the Ghar Dalam (impressed ware) phase (c. 5000 BC). A three-apse temple of the preceding Ggantija phase (c. 3600–3000 BC) was also found as well as an oval-room building of the Red Skorba phase (c. 4300–4000 BC). The latter is thought to have been a shrine, precursor to later temples. The name Skorba has been give to two successive pottery styles. Gray Skorba and Red Skorba, which seem to have developed out of the impressed pottery of the Ghar Dalam phase. The pottery seems related to that of contemporary eastern Sicily.

Skraeling: Norse term for native peoples of Greenland, also known as Inuit, who settled the island in the late 10th century AD. They are probably of the Thule culture.

skyphos: Greek drinking vessel, usually a deep cup with two horizontal handles mounted near the rim.

slag: Partially vitrified waste material created by industrial processes such as smelting, welding, glassmaking, and pottery making. It is the glassy material made up of impurities of metals and ores removed during such processes. It is difficult to distinguish between slags of copper and iron smelting. (*syn.* bloom)

slash and burn: A primitive and widespread form of agriculture in which forest was cleared by chopping and burning small trees. It is one of the earliest forms of cultivation. The clearance would be followed by planting of crops in the clearance—seeds planted in holes poked into the ashes—and their harvesting and replanting for a few years. Without fertilizers, however, the land soon loses its nutritional value and the clearance must be left fallow, to grow over again, while other areas of forest are cleared. A return to the original plot may be made after a reasonable length of time; hence it is also called shifting cultivation and cyclic agriculture. In temperate regions, it is a wasteful method because soil fertility and crop yields, although initially high, decline rapidly, after which a new stretch of forest must be cleared. (*syn.* slash-and-burn agriculture, swidden [North American], shifting cultivation, roza [Spanish American], Brandwirtschaft [German], slash and burn agriculture, swidden agriculture)

slave: People who "belonged" to someone else, who had few rights and were used to perform duties for the "owner." The existence of slaves is known from many civilizations, including ancient Egypt. There, it was a "hereditary profession," included among possessions of kings, high-ranking officials, or temple estates, and better described as serfs (*semedet* or *meret*), allowed to own property but enjoying limited freedom by modern standards. In ancient Italy, there were great numbers of slaves by the 3rd–1st centuries BC, some used in agriculture or serving the administration and others being servants, workers, or craftsmen. It was not unusual for slaves to be freed. In some areas, although they could be sold, punished at will, and could never legally marry, they often held highly responsible posts, such as doctors and estate managers.

Slav: Term used for the ethnic groups speaking related languages in eastern Europe during the second half of the 1st millennium AD. They inhabited an area concentrated in modern Poland, and by the early Middle Ages they were considered a distinct cultural group. The origins of the Slavs are obscure, although they seem to derive from the Iron Age tribes indigenous to the Oder-Vistula area. Prehistorically, the original habitat of the Slavs was Asia, from which they migrated in the 3rd or 2nd millennium BC to populate parts of eastern Europe. Subsequently, these European lands of the Slavs were crossed or settled by many peoples forced by economic conditions to migrate. State-level polities began in Greater Moravia in the 9th century AD and in Poland in the 10th century. They are principally defined by linguistic and place-name evidence rather than by historical or archaeological remains. The *gród* or *hrad* ("castle") was the stronghold of Slav communities. The Slavs are the most numerous ethnic and linguistic body of peoples in Europe, residing also across northern Asia to the Pacific Ocean. Slavic languages belong to the Indo-European family. Customarily, Slavs are subdivided into east Slavs (Russians, Ukrainians, and Belarusians), west Slavs (Poles, Czechs, Slovaks, and Wends, or Sorbs), and south Slavs (Serbs, Croats, Slovenes, and Macedonians).

sleeper beam: A large horizontal timber into which uprights are socketed to construct the frame of a building. In early timber-framed buildings (Roman, Saxon, and medieval), the framing was often erected not on a wall foundation but directly on a horizontal beam resting on or slightly recessed into the ground. Although rarely surviving, its wood often leaves a dark stain in the ground detectable by careful excavation. (*syn.* sill-beam; cill-beam; ground-sill)

sling: A weapon consisting of two thongs attached to a pouch, one of the first missile weapons in warfare. The weapon was whirled and a thong released, hurling a stone from the pouch with considerable velocity. Except in desert areas, such as the Peruvian coast, the sling itself does not survive, but sling bolts or shot of stone, terra-cotta, or lead are present as artifacts. It is rarely found in the same cultural contexts as the bow and arrow. In another type, the sling was attached to a short staff that was held in both hands; it was used for heavier missiles, especially in siege operations during the European Middle Ages.

slip: A form of surface finishing applied to pottery, a mixture of clay and water applied before firing to improve the pot's smoothness and decrease porosity (it makes it more watertight by clogging the pores of the earthenware). Slip often contains the pigment that imparts, after firing, the ground color of the vessel. The slip, being clay based, is subject to the same color variation through different firing conditions (oxidizing or reducing) as the clay itself. Hematite slips, intended to be red, occasionally fire to a shiny black finish in a reducing atmosphere. Slips may or may not be polished after drying, and all sorts of decorative techniques may be used to alter this coating. Used as a decoration, slip is applied fairly thickly to form white or tinted patterns; this technique is called "slip painted." (*syn.* slurry)

slopewash: A type of sediment formed by soil and rubble being moved down hillslopes. The deposit may be caused by solifluxion or by plowwash. The poorly sorted deposit can sometimes carry the remains of archaeological sites downhill with it, resulting in a false location and mixed material.

Slupia Stara: Iron Age site in the Holy Cross Mountains of central Poland, used for metallurgy in the 1st–2nd centuries AD. There are iron smelting furnaces in parallel rows.

small find: A term used to define artifacts that can be picked up and transported, as opposed to features. In different areas, however, the term means different things. In the New World, all artifacts of this sort can be called small finds, while in Britain there can be a distinction between "finds" and "small finds." On a site producing few artifacts, any find may be dealt with as small finds, while on a site producing large quantities of material, a small find is something special, unusual, or unclassifiable.

small mammal bone: The bones of a mammal traditionally defined as one that cannot be seen above long grass. This includes a variety of rodents, lagomorphs (hares and rabbits), insectivores, and carnivores. Bones of these animals are often preserved on archaeological sites. Identification of teeth and jaws of the smaller animals is relatively easy. The composition of small mammal faunas may be interpreted in terms of the environment in and surrounding the archaeological site.

smelting: The separation of metal from ore, usually by heating in a hearth or furnace. It is a major process in metalworking, producing the usable metal for the making of artifacts. After smelting, copper can be cast, and iron can be forged. The main chemical reaction in smelting most of the ores used in antiquity is that of reducing a metal oxide. If the ore was not already in the oxide form, then it was converted by a preliminary process. Careful control of the amount of air entering the furnace would be required for successful smelting. Remains of the smelting process include ingots, slag, tuyères, hearths containing slag and cinder, and more sophisticated furnaces. (*syn.* smelt)

Smith, Charles Roach (1807–1890): The founder in 1843 of the British Archaeological Association, who gave the British Museum 5,000 items from his collection. He also gave artifacts to a private museum at Strood in Kent and published seven volumes of *Collectanea Antiqua* (1848–1880).

Smith, William (1769–1839): British engineer and geologist known for his development of the science of stratigraphy. He collected fossils throughout England and discovered that different exposures of the same stratum contained comparable fossils, eventually leading to the formulation of the index fossil concept. Smith's great geologic map of England and Wales (1815) set the style for modern geologic maps, and many of the names he applied to the strata are still in use today.

Smith, Worthington George (1835–1917): Amateur archaeologist of England who pioneered scientific excavation and detailed recording of Palaeolithic sites, known for illustrations of flint artifacts and conjoining of flint flakes.

Smithfield: A Later Stone Age industry and hunting and gathering culture of southern Africa, originally thought contemporary with the Wilton, but technologically different from it, and now referring to a complex between AD 1300–1700. The culture was on the same level as that of the Mesolithic people of Europe or the modern Kalahari bushmen. The unifying feature of this industry was the almost complete absence of backed microliths and tiny semicircular scrapers.

smoking: A process used at the end of the firing of pottery in which materials that produce a thick smoke are burnt in the kiln or hearth. Smoking alters the appearance of the pottery, coloring it deep black, and makes the objects less porous.

Smolensk: A site in western Russia first mentioned in 863, when it was already a key stronghold controlling the portages between the Dnepr and the Western Dvina rivers and the route between the Moscow region and western Europe. The town also lay on the trade route between the Baltic Sea to the north and Kiev and the Byzantine Empire to the south.

Excavations have begun to increase our knowledge of early medieval Russia. Stone and timber houses and five churches of the Pre-Mongol period have been discovered; colorful frescoes imitating Byzantine silks were found attached to the church walls.

Smyrna: City on the Aegean coast of Asia Minor in western Turkey on the trade routes to Persia, one of the largest late Classical and early Byzantine seaports. Izmir is one of the oldest cities of the Mediterranean world and of almost continuous historical importance during the last 5,000 years. Excavations indicate settlement contemporary with that of the first city of Troy, dating from the 3rd millennium BC. Greek settlement is first clearly attested by the presence of pottery dating from c. 1000 BC. According to the Greek historian Herodotus, the Greek city was founded by Aeolians but soon was seized by Ionians. By the 7th century BC, it had massive fortifications and blocks of two-storied houses. Captured by Lydia (Persians) c. 600 BC, it was refounded by either Alexander the Great or his lieutenants in the 4th century BC at a new site on and around Mount Pagus. It soon emerged as one of the principal cities of Asia Minor throughout the Hellenistic and Roman periods. Izmir was celebrated for its wealth, beauty, library, school of medicine, and rhetorical tradition, and it was one of the early seats of Christianity. (*syn.* ancient Izmir)

snail: A gastropod, especially one having an enclosing shell, into which it may retract completely for protection. Land snail shells are frequently preserved in buried soils, the fills of ditches, and other deposits over limestone subsoils and sometimes fill a gap in environmental reconstruction. Other species are shade-loving snails, open-country snails, and intermediate or catholic species that live in a variety of habitats—including many of the more common species of snail. By means of these categories of snail ecology, the relative frequencies of shell fragments from different species, extracted from deposits and soils, can be used to reconstruct ancient environments.

Snaketown: Large, important Hohokam site in the lower Gila River valley of Arizona, with 1,400 years of continuous occupation beginning c. 300 BC. It is the best documented of all Hohokam villages, with 60 mounds (some rubbish heaps, others platforms) and a ball court, as well as fields, irrigation canals, and more than 200 excavated pit houses. The pottery and shell show craft specialization and contact with Mesoamerican cultures. At its peak, c. 1100, the village had about 1,000 inhabitants, but was abandoned then or soon after. Snaketown followed the standard sequence of Hohokam development, with Mexican influence becoming marked during the final centuries.

Snefru (fl. 26th–25th centuries BC): First pharaoh of the 4th Dynasty (c. 2575–2465 BC) in Egypt, who was deified by the Middle Kingdom and celebrated in later literature as a benevolent and kind ruler. He created a centralized administration that marked the end of the Old Kingdom. The pyramids at Dahshur and the completion of the pyramids at Meidum are attributed to him. After a 24-year reign, Snefru was succeeded by his son, Khufu, the renowned builder of the Great Pyramid at Giza. (*syn.* Snofru, Sneferu)

Snettisham: Site in Norfolk, England, of a hoard of fine late Iron Age metalwork, dated to the 1st century BC. The hoard consisted of around 200 gold, silver, and bronze torcs (neck rings), gold bracelets, and coins. The finest torc was made of eight twisted strands of electrum wire, each strand made of eight strands; the terminals were decorated in relief, and one contained a Gallo-Belgic coin of the late 1st century BC.

Soan: A Lower Palaeolithic pebble tool and chopper industry of the Punjab (Pakistan) and northwest India. After a pre-Soan phase, the Soan proper begins during the second Himalayan interglacial, and its final stage, with an increase in flake tools (including some made by the Levallois technique), is probably contemporary with the early part of the Würm Glaciation of Alpine Europe. There were hand axes and chopper/chopping tools. Some of the material has been re-dated to the Middle Palaeolithic and has questionable archaeological validity.

Sobek: In ancient Egyptian religion, crocodile god whose chief sanctuary in Fayyum province included a live sacred crocodile, Petsuchos. He was portrayed as a crocodile or as a man with crocodile's head and may have been an early fertility god or associated with death and burial before becoming a major deity and patron of kings in the Middle Kingdom (c. 1850–1630 BC). Cemeteries of mummified crocodiles have been found in the Fayyum and at Kawm Umbu. (*syn.* Sebek, Suchos)

Sobekhotep: Birth name held by eight rulers of the 13th Dynasty (c. 1795–1650 BC), most of whom had very short reigns.

Sobekneferu (18th C BC): Female pharaoh, last ruler of the 12th Dynasty, who ruled c. 1760?–1756 BC. (*syn.* Sebeknefru)

Sobiejuchy: Late Bronze Age and Early Iron Age settlement site in north-central Poland of the Hallstatt period and Lusatian culture. It was occupied for about 75 years before being destroyed by fire. Skeletons had arrowheads embedded in the bones.

social anthropology: The British equivalent of cultural anthropology. (*syn.* cultural anthropology)

social organization: The structural hierarchy of a society, first divided into smaller social units, called groups, in which are recognized social positions, or statuses. The term also refers to appropriate behavior patterns for these positions, or roles.

social system: One of the three basic components of culture, the means by which human societies organize themselves and their interactions with other societies.

Society for American Archaeology: Professional organization for archaeologists specializing in New World archaeology. It publishes the scholarly journals *American Antiquity*, *Latin American Antiquity*, and the *Bulletin of the SAA*. (*syn.* SAA)

Society for Historical Archaeology: Professional organization for archaeologists specializing in historical archaeology. It publishes the scholarly journal *Historical Archaeology*. (*syn.* SHA)

Society Islands: A major archipelago in eastern Polynesia in the central South Pacific, divided into the Windward (Tahiti and Moorea) and Leeward (Raiatea, Huahine, Borabora, Tahaa, Maupiti). The islands were settled around AD 500 by Polynesians who developed a number of chiefdoms. The islands were first recorded by Europeans after 1767, when they were claimed for Britain by Captain Samuel Wallis. Important early sites include the Maupiti Burial Ground and the site of Vaito'Otia on Huahine, and later sites are mainly complexes of Marae. The island of Raiatea was regarded as a source of religion and ritual by eastern Polynesians, but by the time of European contact this island had fallen under the control of the neighboring smaller island of Borabora.

Society of Professional Archaeologists: Professional organization for archaeologists specializing in contract archaeology and cultural resource management. Incorporated in 1976, it was created in response to the rapid growth of culture resource management in the United States and Canada. One of its major functions has been to compile and maintain an up-to-date listing of qualified professional archaeologists, and those accepting such certification must subscribe to SOPA's code of ethics, institutional standards, and standards of research performance. (*syn.* SOPA)

sociofact: Archaeological data resulting from past human social activities; an object whose primary function is to express or establish social rank, rather than to serve practical or ideological needs. An example is an ax that is used as a symbol of chiefdom rather than as a weapon.

sociofunction: The use of an object for social purposes, to express social status or organization, such as the wearing of a certain garment to convey high social status.

socket: A hole made in an object to take a haft. It is usually closed at one end, in contrast to a shaft hole, which is open at both. The term also refers to a bronze or iron weapon or tool cast so that it was hollow and open at the butt end to allow a haft to be inserted. (*syn.* socketed implement)

sodalite: A relatively hard mineral that consists of a silicate of sodium and aluminum with some chlorine and is found in various igneous rocks. It was commonly used for ornamental purposes in antiquity, often confused with lapis lazuli, which has a similar color.

sodality: An organized society, a nonkinship organization created for specific purposes that add to the cohesiveness of that society. It is a social group disregarding kinship or lineage and based on a common interest or voluntary participation.

soft hammer technique: The use of a hammer that is softer than the material being hammered or struck. The hammer would be made of angler, bone, wood, or other soft material and used to remove flat flakes from flint. These flakes have a characteristic appearance: long, thin, with a diffuse bulb of percussion. (*syn.* bar hammer technique, cylinder hammer technique)

Sohar: The principal town of the Batina coast of Oman in the Sassanian and early Islamic periods, owing its wealth to maritime trade. In the 3rd century, it became the center of the Sassanian enclave known as Mazun but did not become prominent until the 10th century, when Omani merchants went to China, the East Indies, and Africa. The Buyid rulers of Iran and Iraq attacked and destroyed Sohar in 972–973.

soil: Mineral or organic matter that is unconsolidated and on or near the land surface. A prerequisite for soil formation is the growth of vegetation. Gradual colonization, first by lichens and then by higher plants, causes buildup of organic matter (humus) in the developing soil. Clay minerals form complexes with humus and act as reservoirs of nutrients. Water from rainfall, entering the top of a soil profile, drains down the soil, taking with it nutrients and sometimes parts of the clay/humus complexes. The type of vegetation, the fauna of small animals that live in the soil, the type of parent material, the way in which the clay/humus complexes behave, the amount of rainfall and the quality of drainage all go to determine the type of soil that develops. Soil forms differentiated layers (soil horizons) with respect to the land surface. The study of soils is called pedology. Studies of the way soils have developed may allow a reconstruction of the environmental changes that have taken place. Several complicated soil classification systems exist.

soil analysis: The study of soil and subsoil to determine climate, vegetation, and human disturbance. It is used to assist the interpretation of deposits. Tools are primarily mechanical grading of particle size, determination of soil color, chemical tests like phosphate analysis, and pollen analysis. (*syn.* pedology)

soil conductivity meter: A geophysical instrument used in electromagnetic surveying for the detection of metal, but also for the location of archaeological features such as shallow pits, which have a different conductivity from the surrounding soil. The instrument has a transmitter coil, which is fed with a continuous sinusoidal current, and a receiver coil; they are mounted at right angles to each other at opposite ends of a horizontal bar about a meter long. The instrument is designed to pick up differences in conductivity between features and the surrounding soil, such as the reverse of a resistivity meter. Resistivity surveying is considered more sensitive and versatile.

soil geomorphology: Study of the interaction of pedogenic and geomorphic processes to interpret landscapes. The physical context of archaeological material is determined and evaluated by soil geomorphic techniques.

soil horizon: A layer in a soil developed through the natural weathering of geological and archaeological surfaces. It differs from related layers chemically, physically, or biologically. Sequences of related soil horizons make up the soil profile.

soil mark: Any visible irregularity in the appearance of the soil surface, indicating traces of buried sites or features on the surface of plowed or otherwise disturbed ground. As revealed through aerial photography, a darker area may indicate human wastes, or a lighter area a former road or trail.

soil profile: The vertical sequence of horizons in the soil, which occur not as the result of stratification but as a result of weathering and other processes. The profile provides environmental or palaeoenvironmental information, such as information on vegetation and climate. The term also refers to a vertical section exposed in excavation or naturally that shows horizons and parent material. The soil profile is made up of some or all of the following: the A or humus horizon, the E or leached horizon, the B or (B) horizons or accumulation or chemical weathering, and the C horizon of parent material. Different soil profiles occur in different environmental regions, ranging from rendsinas, through brown earths, to podsols, gleys, and chernozems. The soil profile and the type of vegetation are interdependent, and man's activities have an effect on and are affected by both.

soil resistivity: A remote sensing technique that monitors the degree of electrical resistance in soils—which often depends on moisture content—near the surface. Buried features are usually detected by a differential retention of groundwater.

soil-sounding radar: A method of subsurface detection in which short radio pulses are sent through the soil; the echoes reflect back significant changes in soil conditions.

soil stratigraphy: A branch of stratigraphy in which soils are identified as stratigraphic units with specific chronological ordering. A pedostratigraphic unit is a three-dimensional, laterally traceable, buried sediment or rock with one or more soil horizons. It is not the same as the sequencing of soil horizons in a soil profile.

soil structure: Physical arrangement of sediment into peds (a natural soil aggregate) as the result of pedogenesis (reproduction by young or larval animals). Soil has a "structure" on which its porosity-permeability depends. Soil structure is built up by alternate moistening and drying, and plant roots contribute greatly by opening pores between soil aggregates. The stability of aggregates increases with humus content, especially humus that originates from grass vegetation.

Sokar: God of the Memphis necropolis, often mummiform in appearance, with the head of a hawk. He was possibly patron of craftsmen and a fertility god. (*syn.* Seker)

Sokchang-ri: Palaeolithic site in southern Korea (South Ch'ungch'ong Province) with 12 cultural layers starting c. 20,000 bp. That layer contained obsidian scrapers, rhyolite burins, and prismatic cores. (*syn.* [Sokchangni])

solar boat: In Egyptian mythology, a high-prowed boat in which the sun god was believed to navigate the heavens. Some Pyramid Texts refer to the deceased pharaoh going to join the gods in such a boat. There were two different types: day/mandet, night/mesektet. (*syn.* solar bark, sun boat)

Soleb: Site in the third cataract region of Upper Nubia, capital of Kush, under Tutankhamen. It is known for its sandstone temple built by Amenhotep III (c. 1391–1353 BC), remains of the town of the late 18th Dynasty, and cemeteries of New Kingdom and Neroitic period.

solifluction: The slippage of soil and rock particles because of the freezing and subsequent thawing of the Earth; the process of mass movement of soil and sediment on the thawing of water-laden ground. Many deposits in valleys and on the lower part of hills are due to the land having been glaciated, with the top level thawing in the spring and the water, unable to permeate the still-frozen subsoil, flowing downhill, taking with it chunks of loose material. Full glaciation is not necessary to cause solifluxion; hard winters with frozen earth and occasional thaws can cause minor solifluxion that may add to the accumulation of material. Solifluction can cause artifactual material to be moved from one deposit to another; sometimes whole areas of archaeological sites may be covered with solifluction material. When solifluction can be recognized geologically, it is a valuable indicator of glacial conditions in areas that remained free of ice. (*syn.* solifluxion, sludging, soil flow, soil fluction, soil flowage)

sol lessivé: Soil usually forming in a broadleaf forest and characterized by moderate leaching, which produces an accumulation of clay and some iron, which have been transported (eluviated) from another area by water. The humus formed produces a textural horizon that is less than 50 centi-

meters (20 in) from the surface. Podzolic soils may have laterite in place of the humic horizon or along with it. Sols lessivés are often difficult to identify, but they are the dominant soil type of much of lowland Britain, where forest was cleared to make way for agriculture. (*syn.* podzolic soil, podsolic, lessivé soil)

Solo: River in central and eastern Java with Pliocene and Pleistocene remains and stone tools. The levels include the Pucangan, lower-middle Pleistocene c. 3–2 million years BC; Kabush, middle Pleistocene c. 1.4–0.7 million years BP; Notopuro; and High Solo gravels (High Terrace) of the upper Pleistocene c. 0.5 million years BP (associated with Solo Man).

Solo Man: Advanced hominid, *Homo erectus soloensis*, found at Ngandong and Sambungmacan in the Solo River valley of Java. More archaic than European Neanderthals, it may be later than Peking Man. There were 11 fossil skulls (without facial skeletons) and 2 leg-bone fragments recovered from terraces. Solo man has been thought to date to the Late Pleistocene (c. 15,000–20,000 years ago)—but his age remains uncertain. Others believe Solo man is a regional variant of early *Homo sapiens* populations, also including the Neanderthal peoples of Europe and the Rhodesioid peoples of Africa. The Solo fossils were originally given the genus name Javanthropus.

Solomon (fl. mid-10th century BC): King of the united Israel and Judah who reigned c. 965–928 BC and built at many sites, including his temple at Jerusalem. He is traditionally regarded as the greatest king of Israel.

Solomon Islands: Island nation in the center of Melanesia, southwestern Pacific Ocean. The Solomon Islands were initially settled by 2000 BC, probably by people of the Austronesian language group. The first European to reach the islands was the Spanish explorer Alvaro de Mendaña de Neira in 1568; the islands were named after King Solomon of the Old Testament. Archaeological sequences are best known from the northern and southern extremities of the chain; the Santa Cruz Islands in the south have very fine Lapita assemblages dating to c. 1500–500 BC, and the island of Buka in the north has a continuous sequence from late Lapita (c. 500 BC) through successive localized ceramic phases (similar to the Mangaasi tradition of Vanuatu) to recent times.

Solutrean: A culture of the Upper Palaeolithic period in western Europe, from about 19,000 BC, following the Perigordian and Aurignacian, characterized by the use of projectile points, especially the laurel-leaf blade. From Solutré, a site in central France, it was a short-lived style of toolmaking with particularly fine workmanship. The Solutrean industry, like those of other late Palaeolithic big-game hunters, contained a variety of tools such as burins, scrapers, and borers; but blades that were formed in the shape of laurel or willow leaves and shouldered points are the implements that distinguish the Solutrean. It preceded the Magdalenian in parts of France and Spain. At Laugerie-Haute, unifacially chipped leaf-shaped points in the Early Solutrean show the gradual development of bifacial working, a stage dated c. 19,000–18,000 BC. The Middle phase is characterized by fine large bifacial points and by the introduction of pressure flaking. In the Later Solutrean, this technique was used to produce slim leaf-shaped projectiles and small single-shouldered points. In southeast Spain, this final stage also has barbed and tanged arrowheads. The "laurel leaves" were typical of Middle Solutrean, and "willow leaves" (shouldered points) were from the Later Solutrean. The bone needle with an eye was invented in this period. Many decorated caves in France can be assigned to this period. (*syn.* Solutrian)

Somerset Levels: Low-lying wetland region of Somerset in southwest England, famous for the preservation of remains in peat. Ancient trackways have been revealed and, with techniques such as pollen analysis and radiocarbon dating, it has been possible to establish the sequence of human and climatic development in the area. Permanent settlement occurred only on small "islands" raised above the level of the marsh (e.g., the Iron Age villages of Glastonbury and Meare), but wooden tracks crossed the wet areas. The earliest discovered is the Sweet track dated to the Neolithic c. 3600/2800 BC; after that, tracks continued to be built at various times in the 3rd millennium BC. There was a long hiatus in track construction, perhaps because drier conditions made them unnecessary, but with climatic deterioration in the Late Bronze Age, there was a new phase of track construction c. 900–450 BC (alternatively, c. 1100–500 BC).

Somme Bionne: A chariot burial of the Early La Tène Iron Age, in the Marne area of France, dated to c. 450–420 BC. The burial, presumably of a chieftain, was under a large barrow and contained very rich grave goods, both imported objects and locally manufactured items. The imported items include an Attic Red-Figure kylix and bronze Etruscan beaked wine flagons. (*syn.* Somme-Bionne)

Somme sequence: The valley in France, which was one of the first places where the great antiquity of man was recognized, and which includes the type site of the Acheulian (St. Acheul) and the Abbevillean (Abbeville).

sondage: A deep trench, often of restricted area, to investigate the stratigraphy of a site; an exploratory excavation made to determine whether a thorough excavation is warranted; a genteel term for test pit. A number of sondages may be dug so that the maximum of preliminary information may be gained with the minimum of effort and disturbance. In modern archaeology, this technique of pre-examination of a site is generally replaced by physical methods (e.g., magnetometer survey, resistivity survey), or if applicable, aerial photography, although a more sophisticated version of the technique of sondage digging would be classified as sampling. Sondage may later be enlarged into an area excavation to give more evidence on the cultural levels or building phases disclosed. The term is often associated with the investigation of the deep stratigraphic record of tells in the Near East. (*syn.* test pit)

Sondershausen: Linear Pottery culture cemetery in eastern Germany with spondylus shell ornaments.

Song: Chinese dynasty that ruled the country AD 960–1279 (only in the south after 1127) during one of its most brilliant cultural epochs. During the Song Dynasty, commerce developed; trade guilds were organized; paper currency came into increasing use; and several cities with populations of more than 1 million flourished along the principal waterways and the southeast coast. Widespread printing of the Confucian classics and the use of movable type, beginning in the 11th century, brought literature and learning to the people. The Song Dynasty is particularly noted, however, for the great artistic achievements that it encouraged and subsidized. The capital was at Kaifeng near the Yellow River; during the Southern Song (1127–1279), it was at Hangzhou. The study of antiquities flourished, with large collections of artifacts collected, catalogs published, and epigraphic works compiled. The present-day nomenclature of bronze ritual vessels is owed largely to the work of Song epigraphers. (*syn.* Sung)

Songguk-ri: Bronze Age site in South Ch'ungch'ong Province, Korea, with a stone cist burial containing a Liaoning-type dagger. There are two pit houses dated to the 5th century BC. (*syn.* [Songgungni])

Songhay: West African empire of the 15th–16th centuries, which controlled the great bend of the Niger River in Mali. Songhay was wealthy from Saharan caravan trade. (*syn.* Songhai)

Songon Dagbe: One of over 100 large shell mounds in the Ebrie Lagoon in the Ivory Coast. It is dated to c. 2400 bp.

Sons of Horus: Four deities—jackal-headed Duamutef, falcon-headed Qebehsenuf, human-headed Imset, and baboon-headed Hapy—who were responsible for protecting the internal organs of the deceased in canopic jars. The jars were decorated with sculpted human heads, and from the 19th Dynasty until the end of the New Kingdom (1539–1075 BC), the heads represented the four sons of the god Horus.

Sonviian: Pre-Hoabinhian stone industry in Upper Palaeolithic cave sites around the Red River valley of northern Vietnam. It is regarded as the immediate predecessor (or an early stage) of the Hoabinhian and of late Pleistocene date c. 18,000–9000 BC. It is characterized by unifacially flaked pebbles, some bifacially worked pebbles, choppers, side scrapers, and "round-edged" pebbles. Son Vi is the type site of this industry. (*syn.* Son Vi)

Sopdet: Personification of Sirius, or the dog star—a woman with a star on her head. (*syn.* Sothis, Sirius)

Sopot-Lengyel: Eneolithic culture of the northwest Balkans (north Bosnia and east Slavonia, Yugoslavia) of c. 4300–3700 BC. The pottery of this group shares affinities with the dark burnished ware tradition of the south Balkans and the incised and monochrome tradition of the north Balkans. Few cemeteries are known, but there is plenty of settlement evidence (tells, open sites). It is viewed as a regional variant of either the Lengyel or the Vinca culture. (*syn.* Sopot Lengyel)

Sopron: Early Iron Age cemetery of the Hallstatt C period in western Hungary. Cremation burials under barrows were in urns with incised and unusual human figures. Artifacts from the area indicate Neolithic, Bronze Age, Illyrian, and Celtic settlements before the town's becoming the Roman municipium of Scarabantia.

sorghum: A cereal grain plant, probably originating in Africa, with edible starchy seeds. It was probably first cultivated when increasing dryness began to affect the already numerous human groups, after 7000 BP. This plant with its fine ears of grain needs 500–600 millimeters of water a year. *Sorghum vulgare*, which includes varieties of grain sorghums and grass sorghums, is grown for hay and fodder, and broomcorn, used in making brooms and brushes. Grain sorghums include durra, milo, shallu, kafir corn, Egyptian corn, great millet, and Indian millet. Sorghum is especially valued in hot and arid regions for its resistance to drought and heat. (*syn.* India: jowar, cholam, jonna; West Africa: Guinea corn; China: kaoliang)

Soroki: A complex of short-lived settlement sites of the Late Mesolithic and Early Neolithic, located in the middle Dnestr valley in Moldova. The Mesolithic sites, with radiocarbon dates of c. 5600–5400 BC, have provided data on the late Mesolithic/early Neolithic Bug-Dnestr culture. The earliest occupations are aceramic and had a hunting-fishing economy. Later levels, c. 4800 BC, have pointed-base vessels, hearths, and shallow pits. The subsistence economy is similar to the preceding Mesolithic, with the addition of some cultivated einkorn wheat and some domesticated cattle and pig.

soros: A Greek burial mound, such as the one from the battle of Marathon in 490 BC.

Sothic cycle: In ancient Egypt, the civil year was a quarter of a day too short in relation to the rising of Sothis (Sirius), the dog star, so that the new year advanced by one day ever 4 years; New Year's Day and the rising of Sothis coincided again only after approximately 1,460 years. The period elapsing between each such rising is known as the Sothic cycle. The error with respect to the 365-day year and the heliacal risings of Sirius amounted to 1 day every 4 tropical years, or 1 whole Egyptian calendar year every 1,460 tropical years (4 × 365), which was equivalent to 1,461 Egyptian calendar years. After this period, the heliacal rising and setting of Sothis would again coincide with the calendar dates. The dates for the start of each Sothic cycle are fortunately known because the Roman historian Censorinus fixed the coincidence of New Year's Day and the heliacal rising of Sothis in AD 139. Taking into account a slight difference between a Sothic year and a year of the fixed stars, the years 1322, 2782, and 4242 BC are taken as starting points of a Sothic cycle. Sothis appeared immediately preceding the Nile flood and was important in the Egyptian calendar.

Sotira-Teppes: Southern Cyprus type site of the Neolithic II of the later 5th millennium BC. There were circular and oval stone and mud-brick houses, a simple pit-grave cemetery, and combed ware. A Chalcolithic Philia culture of the mid-3rd millennium BC was also found in nearby Sotira-Kaminoudhia. Small ornaments of picrolite (a type of soapstone) and pottery distinguish the Sotira culture; toward the end of the period, copper came into use. (*syn.* Sotira culture)

Soufli: Aceramic Neolithic-Bronze Age settlement in Thessaly, northern Greece. It had a Larisa phase cremation cemetery and is known for a rare piece of monumental sculpture depicting a more than lifesize woman wearing a skirt and necklace.

Sounion: Promontory in Attica, Greece, on which was the temple of Poseidon, dated to the mid-5th century BC. This classical sanctuary site probably goes back to the 8th–7th centuries BC, and it was traditionally popular as a refuge with runaway slaves. It was fortified in 413 BC by a substantial wall enclosing the headland. A ship shed has been discovered, and there is evidence for houses from the 5th century BC to the Roman period. The marble Poseidon Temple was preceded by a limestone version, which was apparently demolished by the invading Persians in 480 BC. North of the main sanctuary lies a smaller sacred area (temos), which encloses the remains of two temples. The best-known kouros is the colossal figure from the temple of Poseidon at Sounion. (*syn.* Roman: Cape Sunium)

souterrain: A long stone-built gallery with a slab roof, below ground level. It was usually, perhaps in its earliest stages always, associated with a settlement of the Broch culture. Such galleries are widespread in Ireland, Scotland, and the highland zone of Britain, and seem to show an immigration up the Atlantic seaways from western Gaul in the last centuries BC. In Cornwall, they are called *fogous* and considered locally to be refuges of the 2nd–1st centuries BC; in eastern Scotland, they are misleadingly known as Pictish houses. In Brittany, the earliest are of the mid-1st millennium BC. Mainly, they were used for cold storage. (*syn.* fogous)

South Arabian civilization: A series of pre-Islamic kingdoms of the 1st millennium BC through the mid-1st millennium AD in southwestern Arabia (modern Yemen). The most famous of these were the Minaeans, Qatabanians, Sabaeans, and Himyar.

Southeastern ceremonial complex/Southern Cult: A complex consisting of a range of specialized artifacts and motifs found in mortuaries and rich burials at some of the principal sites of the Middle Mississippi culture (Mississippian) in southeastern North America. Beginning AD c. 1200, cult objects include ear spools, ceremonial axes, and disks made of copper or shell—all engraved with symbols of military and supernatural power, such as the cross, the sun circle, the swastika, and the eye-and-hand. Characteristic artifacts such as monolithic ceremonial axes, effigy jars, and worked shell objects have been found in abundance at the major ceremonial centers at Etowah, Georgia; Spiro, Oklahoma; and Moundville, Alabama. The cult's climax occurred between 1200–1400, but it had virtually disappeared by the time of the first European explorers. (*syn.* Southeastern tradition)

Southampton: City and English Channel port in Hampshire, England, where in AD 43 there was a Roman settlement, Clausentum. Inscribed stones, coins, pottery, and other artifacts have been found. Southampton (Hamtun, Suhampton) superseded the Saxon Hamtun and was a royal borough before 1086. (*syn.* Clausentum)

South Cadbury: A site in Somerset, southwest England, that is one of the more important secular Dark Age sites in Britain. It is an Iron Age hill fort with a history of abandonment and refortification throughout the prehistoric, Roman, and medieval periods. The 16th-century antiquarian John Leyland first recognized South Cadbury's links with the Dark Ages and named it as Camelot, thus initiating its romantic associations with the Arthurian legend.

Southern Highveld Settlements: Iron Age farms of the early 2nd millennium AD in Orange Free State and Transvaal, South Africa. There are extensive grasslands on which stone walls enclosed cattle barns and courtyards around houses. They are classified as types (N, V, Z) and associated with the Moloko Complex.

South Italian pottery: Pottery type made by the Greek colonies of southern Italy and Sicily, mainly from the late 5th century BC, with many centers of production.

Sozudai: Palaeolithic site in Oita Prefecture, Japan, where a date of 400,000 bp was claimed based on geology and tool comparisons with Zhoukoudian. A few hundred tools, mostly of quartzite, were recovered from a secondary deposit on a marine terrace, including hand axes, scrapers, and flakes. A date of only 70,000 bp is accepted by many archaeologists.

spacer plate: A specialized flat bead with several parallel perforations intended to hold apart in regular order the threads of a multiple-strand necklace. Sometimes, as in the amber multiperforated spacer plates of the central European and British Bronze Age and the Mycenaeans, the perforations themselves are used decoratively. They were also made of jet or faience. Similar examples found in distant regions are often taken as indicators of long-range trade. (*syn.* spacerplate)

Spanish Borderland: The North American Spanish colonial territories.

Spanish Levant Art: A series of rock shelters in the arid region of the Spanish Levant (Mediterranean Spain), with paintings in red and black from the Mesolithic. The scenes were quite unlike Palaeolithic art, and the depictions offer information about the character of everyday life.

Sparta: A small town in the central Peloponnese, Greece, which in the Classical period created the Peloponnesian League and organized the military forces that broke the Athenian empire and subjugated Athens in 404 BC. It was reputedly founded in the 9th century BC, later the capital of the Laconia district and an important sanctuary dating from the Early Iron Age. Much of our evidence comes from the sanctuary of Artemis Ortheia, where ivory, bone, lead, and ceramic offerings have been found. The sparsity of ruins from antiquity around the modern city reflects the austerity of the military oligarchy that ruled the Spartan city-state from the 6th–2nd centuries BC. The town was finally destroyed by Alaric and the Visigoths in AD 396. (*syn.* Greek: Sparti, historically Lacedaemon)

spatial analysis: The statistical study of concentrations of human activity in a defined space; the systematic study of spatial patterning in archaeological data. Distribution maps showing artifacts or sites have long been used in archaeology, but spatial analysis adds rigorous mathematical and statistical techniques for examining such maps. Techniques adapted from modern geography include locational analysis for the study of settlement patterns and the use of distance-decay functions, linear regression analysis, and trend-surface analysis for exploring the distribution of artifacts.

spatial archaeology: The study of the interrelations of archaeological sites with one another and with their environments, or the distribution patterns of artifacts, using analytical methods derived from geography.

spatial context: The location of an object and its spatial relation to other objects in the archaeological record.

spatial difference: A method used to define variations among artifacts by their location in an activity area.

spatial dimension: A characteristic of an artifact based on its location in an activity area.

spatula: A tool, usually of bone, lime, wood, ebony, turtleshell, consisting of a broad but thin blade. It served many general purposes—spreading, mixing, scooping, lifting—including burnishing pottery, working pelts, spooning flour, and so on.

Spaulding, Albert Clinton (1914–1990): American archaeologist who contributed to the development of modern theory, especially processual archaeology. He advocated the adoption of scientific and quantitative methods.

spear: A pole weapon with a sharp point, either thrown or thrust at an enemy or prey, one of the earliest weapons created by man and dating back to Palaeolithic times. It was originally a sharpened stick, and some were made of stone, shaped and fixed to the shaft by thongs and possibly resins. In the Bronze Age, they were made of that metal and had a tang for riveting the head to the shaft. Later, the tang was replaced by a socket into which the shaft fitted. The Iron Age spears retained this feature and were sometimes decorated with La Tène designs.

spearhead: Bifacially flaked points—or a thrusting blade mounted on a long shaft (spear) as a weapon for war or hunting. Early examples in flint were usually leaf shaped and hafted simply in a cleft in the spear shaft. In the Early Bronze Age, bronze dagger blades were made and ferrules added. The socketed spear head came when these were cast in one piece with the blade.

spearpoint: The tip of a projectile, used for throwing, thrusting, or stabbing.

spear thrower or spear-thrower or spearthrower: A device that increases the power with which a spear can be hurled; a long stick with a hooked end, which holds the butt of a spear. The implement usually has finger grips at one end. The device thus becomes an artificial extension of the thrower's arm, giving him increased leverage and range and allowing the thrower to hurl a spear accurately a much greater distance than he could by unaided hand. Spear throwers were used in Europe during the Palaeolithic and throughout the New World in pre-Columbian times, where they were known as *atlatls*. Spear throwers made of reindeer antler are characteristic of the Magdalenian period in Europe. Similar devices were used in the Arctic, and in Australia, where they are often called *woomeras*. (*syn.* throwing stick, atlatl, woomera)

specchia: A type of Iron Age burial monument found in Apulia, southern Italy. It consists of a stone cairn with a single crouched skeleton in a slab-built cist with traces of an entrance passage, but the name is also given to larger cairns. These large specchie contain neither burials nor offerings, but traces of circular walls have been found in their cairns, and some have external staircases. (*syn.* pl. specchie)

specific analogy: An analogy used in archaeological interpretation based on specific comparisons documented in a single cultural tradition.

specific evolution: The localized social and ecological adjustments that cause specific cultures to differ from one another as they adapt to their own unique environments. The increasing adaptive specializations that improve the chances for survival of species, cultures, or individuals.

specific gravity determination: Specific gravity is the ratio of the density of a substance to the density of pure water taken as a standard when both densities are obtained by weighing in air and in prescribed temperature conditions. The measurement of the specific gravity of a metal artifact can be a useful nondestructive method of determining its composition, if it is a two-component alloy and preferably if one of the alloy components is known. The specimen must be weighed in the air and then suspended in a suitable liquid with a known specific gravity; the result is determined by an equation. Because the presence of a third metal in small amounts upsets the accuracy of the technique, the amount of foreknowledge required is greater than in most of the other methods of determining the chemical composition of objects. Devices used to measure specific gravity are the Jolly balance, the Westphal balance, the pycnometer, and the hydrometer. (*syn.* relative density)

specimen: In faunal analysis, all individual faunal pieces together.

spectrographic analysis: Method for quantitative analysis of small samples of various compounds, which has high accuracy. It involves passing the light refracted from a sample through a prism or diffraction grating that spreads out the wavelengths of trace elements into a spectrum. This enables the identification of different trace elements and depends on the fact that light emitted by any element on volatilization shows a characteristic pattern when split by a prism into its spectrum. The elements present can be measured by the intensity of the lines in comparison with control spectra of known composition produced under the same conditions. A small sample can be used, less than 10 milligrams, making the method particularly suitable for archaeological material. The method has been used especially for metal analysis, giving useful information on technology and sources of the raw materials, and also for glass, faience, pottery, and obsidian.

spectrometry: The analysis of the constituent (and trace) elements of metals, stone, or other materials by the measurement of the wavelengths of light or radiation emitted from them.

specularia: Window panes made with a kind of transparent stone (*lapis specularis*).

speculative period: The period in the history of archaeology in the New World between 1400–1840, characterized by unsystematic and speculative interpretations about the past.

speculum: An alloy of antiquity made of copper and tin containing more than 30% tin. Speculum is hard and brittle because of the formation of intermetallic compounds. It was principally used for certain coins among the Celtic tribes of central and western Europe and for mirrors. The back of the mirrors were decorated with beautiful engraved or enchased designs. (*syn.* speculum alloy)

speech: The ability to communicate or express thoughts in spoken words, one of the attributes of *Homo sapiens*. In prehistoric man, the ability to speak is deduced from the shape of the jaws of fossilized skulls.

speleothem: Mineral deposits that form in a cave after the creation of the cave itself. These deposits are generally composed of calcium carbonate dissolved from the surrounding limestone by groundwater. Carbon dioxide carried in the water is released as the water encounters the cave air; this reduces the water's capacity to hold calcite in solution and causes the calcite to be deposited. These deposits may accumulate to form stalactites, stalagmites, flowstone, cave pearls, and many other formations. Speleothem growth can be dated by the uranium series dating method. Speleothems can potentially bury earlier archaeological deposits. (*syn.* cave deposit)

spelt: A primitive variety of wheat (*Triticum aestivum spelta*) with lax spikes and spikelets containing two light red kernels. It was apparently not cultivated on the earliest of farming sites, but appeared only in the 2nd millennium BC. It is a hulled grain (i.e., grains and glumes do not separate during threshing), and was probably used for bread making, porridge, and even brewing.

speos: In Egyptology, a term for a small rock-cut temple or tomb, the hypogea or subterranean Egyptian temples. Hemispeos were temples built partly above and partly under the ground. A speos was often of some architectural importance.

Speos Artemidos: Rock-cut temple dedicated to the lioness-goddess Pakhet (Pasht), just east of the Middle Kingdom rock-cut tombs of Beni Hasan, Egypt. It was built by Queen Hatshepsut and Thutmose III of the 18th Dynasty; a smaller shrine of Alexander II is nearby.

sphere of exchange: In nonmarket societies, the prestige valuables and ordinary commodities were often exchanged separately. Valuables were exchanged for valuables in prestige transactions. Commodities, however, were unceremoniously exchanged for commodities, in mutually profitable barter transactions.

sphinx: A mythical beast portrayed with the crouched body of a lion and head or face of a man. It is especially known from Egyptian art as a symbol of royal power, and only the pharaoh was depicted in this form. Originally considered by the Egyptians to represent the guardian of the Gates of Sunset, the statues were usually erected to guard tombs or temples from intruders. The largest and most famous of the sphinxes is that of Giza, carved from a knoll left by the quarrying of stone for the Great Pyramid. Its features are those of the pharaoh Chephren (Khafre) of the 4th Dynasty, reigning c. 26th century BC; it is 73 meters long and 20 meters high. Human-headed lions, usually female, were also portrayed by the Hittites and Greeks, and the Romans adopted sphinxes and placed them in the pronaos of their temples. Representations of ram-headed lions are called crio-sphinxes and were associated with the god Amon (Amen); they are of the New Kingdom and found along the roads between the Temple of Luxor and Karnak.

sphyrelaton: A type of bronze hammered statue, made by hammering bronze plates over a core, which were secured by nails. It is an early form of art manufacture in metal, the precursor to the lost wax (cire perdue) technique. The temple of Apollo on Crete (8th century BC) has three statues of this type. The technique was also used to produce colossal statues. Another definition is repoussé work in Minoan or Etruscan art. (*syn.* sphyrelata)

spiculum: The barbed head of an iron arrow or lance. (*syn.* pl. spicula)

Spiennes: A flint-mining site of the later Neolithic Michelsberg culture in Hainaut, Belgium. There are opencast pits and deep shafts with underground galleries. These flint mines are similar to the British Neolithic flint mines and were worked in similar ways, with the use of bone and antler picks. Skeletons of workers killed by falls have been discovered at Spiennes.

Spina: Pre-Roman port on the northern Adriatic, at the mouth of the River Po in Italy. The town was probably Etruscan from the late 6th–early 5th centuries BC. Together with a settlement at Adria, Spina was an important link between the markets of Etruria and the Poplain and Greek shipping in the Adriatic. Cemeteries (Valle Trebba, Valle Pega) have yielded large amounts of Greek pottery, especially Athenian Red-Figure ware, terra-cottas, fine Etruscan bronzes, western Greek and Etruscan jewelry, faience, and amber. The town also kept a treasury at Delphi. The site had palisades, earth ramparts, and a network of canals as well as a grid plan. At its height, it may have shipped agricultural produce and slaves. Soon after 400 BC, Spina was sacked by the Gauls. With the collapse of its market and the silting of its port, it became obsolete.

spindle whorl: A circular object with a central perforation intended to act as a flywheel on a spindle, giving momentum to its rotation—an artifact providing evidence of the spinning of thread. It would maintain the momentum of the spindle rotated by the spinner while the spinner teases more fibers out of a fleece. It can be of stone, bone, or pottery, varying from a flat disk to spherical or pyriform, and from 2.5–10 centimenters in diameter.

spinning: The extrusion of liquid fiber-forming material, followed by hardening to form filaments; a technical process by which fibers are twisted together to make continuous threads. The wool was fixed as a mass on the distaff. A thread was drawn out by one hand and fixed on the spindle. Attached to this last was a stone spindle whorl. As the spindle was spun around, the whorl gave momentum on the flywheel principle. The thread from the distaff was twisted and then wound onto the spindle. Rarely are the threads, or cloth woven from them, found in archaeological contexts, unless preserved by desiccation, waterlogging, or metal corrosion products. Proof of spinning comes more commonly from the discovery of a spindle whorl, loom weight, or comb. Spinning was engaged in during Neolithic times.

spiral: A widely popular artistic motif, consisting of a curve of constantly increasing diameter; any motif that is coiled or curling. A double spiral is one in which two spirals are conjoined at the center. A running spiral is a series of regularly interconnected spirals. (*syn.* spira)

spiral fracture: Type of bone fracture where the breakage curves along and around the shaft. It is seen by some specialists as diagnostic of human use of bones for tools.

Spirit Cave: One of many limestone caves in northwest Thailand, occupied from before 9000 BC until c. 5500 BC, intermittently. It has yielded early evidence of cultivated plants (vegetables, beans, water chestnuts) c. 9000 BC, of Neolithic polished stone tools (ground stone adzes and knives) c. 7000 BC, and of pottery c. 6800 BC. This Hoabinhian site shows the practice of incipient forms of horticulture after hunting and gathering and before dependence on rice as a staple.

spirit path: Rows of stone sculptures facing up the path to Chinese mounded tombs, created from the Han Dynasty to guard or honor the deceased. They are often sculptures of people or animals, from close to lifesize to double lifesize.

Spiro: A site in eastern Oklahoma of the Mississippian tradition (Middle Mississippi) Caddo culture beginning in the 8th century AD as a village of one-room houses, and by 950 had reached its maximum extent with the addition of eight burial mounds. The eight mounds are of various sizes, and one served as a temple mound and burial mound (Craig Mound). In about 1200, Spiro was abandoned as a settlement and became a specialized mortuary and temple complex. To this final period, 1350–1400, belongs the enormous Craig Mound, covering an intact wooden mortuary house. Commoners and servants received only simple burial, but the ruling elite were placed in funerary litters filled with weapons, fabrics, smoking pipes, imported minerals, copper, and shell ornaments decorated with designs of the Southeastern Ceremonial Complex (Southern Cult). Because of its abundance of paraphernalia of the Southern Cult, it is often linked to the centers at Etoway and Moundville, even though it is culturally distinct from them. Many designs on carved shell gorgets and embossed sheet copper ornaments probably came from Mesoamerica, perhaps from the Huastec culture of Veracruz. The site's archaeological value has been considerably diminished, as it was heavily vandalized during a period of commercial exploitation in the 1930s.

Spissky Stvrtov: Early Bronze Age hill fort of the Otomani culture in eastern Slovakia and dated to the mid-2nd millennium BC. A partly encircling stone wall defends the site on the east side, where the main entrance is flanked by towerlike bastions. In the fort interior, 26 houses are arranged around a "village square," and these houses, with stone foundations, sometimes had below-ground chests containing gold and bronze objects. Houses outside this "acropolis" were of simpler construction. This was a fortified site of economic, administrative, and strategic importance. That there was differentiation into an akropolis and a settlement area, with the houses of the akropolis built using a different technique, and the amount of gold and bronze objects hidden in chests under the floors of the houses in the settlement area, suggests that there were economic and social distinctions among the inhabitants. Bronze workshops are known, as well as a ritual area where a rhomboidal stone upright lies near two inurned cremations. (*syn.* Spassky Stvrtok)

Spitsyn culture: Early Upper Palaeolithic culture on the Don River in European Russia, dating to c. 40,000–30,000 bp. Its artifacts include burins, retouched blades and scrapers, bone tools and ornaments.

Split: Roman city on the Adriatic coast of Croatia. Remains survive of part of the Roman town, including the nucleus of the old town, built within the palace of Diocletian, who abdicated the imperial crown in AD 305 (reigned from 285) and lived there until his death in 313. The immense palace has walls 7 feet (2 m) thick and 72 feet (22 m) high on its seaward side and 48 feet (15 m) high on the northern side. Originally it had 16 towers, of which 3 remain, and 4 gates. The walls enclosed colonnaded streets, a vaulted temple, a domed mausoleum, baths, and a residential section. The palace was damaged by the Avars, who in 615 had sacked Salona(e); its inhabitants first fled to the islands but then returned to seek refuge in the palace (c. 620), calling the settlement Spalatum. They built their homes in the palace compound, incorporating its walls and pillars. This should be distinguished from Salona, some 6 kilometers inland, which had been the prosperous capital of the Roman imperial province of Dalmatia, and earlier still, capital of native Illyricum. (*syn.* Spalatum)

spokeshave: A stone tool with a semicircular concavity used for smoothing spears or arrow shafts; a draw knife or small transverse plane with end handles for planing convex or concave surfaces.

Spondylus gaederopus: Mediterranean mussel shell from which ornaments (bracelets, beads, disks) were made, found across the Balkans, up the Danube Valley, and even on the Saale and the Main. It was traded for this purpose into central Europe in the Early Neolithic. Spondylus shell ornaments occurred in contexts of the First Temperate Neolithic and Linear Pottery culture (Czechoslovakia, Germany, the Netherlands). (*syn.* spondylus)

spot: An arbitrary sample unit defined by geographical co-ordinates.

spout and bridge pot: A distinctive closed vessel with two spouts connected by a strap handle, popular in southern coastal Peruvian cultures with antecedents in the Initial Period ceramics of the Hacha complex. Typically it is a closed kettle-shaped vessel, but its defining characteristic is a pair of vertical tubular spouts joined to each other by a strip or bridge. Sometimes, however, one spout terminates as a whistle or as a modeled life figure. It was particularly popular with the Nasca and Chimu but has been found in many other New World contexts (e.g., Paracas). (*syn.* spout-and-bridge vessel)

Spy: The find site of three Neanderthal skeletons in a cave at Spy, Belgium, associated with Middle Palaeolithic stone tools and an extinct subarctic fauna. These complete skeletons were found during excavations of the Mousterian levels. It was only after these discoveries that it was recognized that Neanderthal man was associated with the Mousterian and that Neanderthals were an archaic and extinct human form rather than an abnormal modern human. There was also Upper Palaeolithic material in the cave.

square-mouthed pot: A vessel type in which the circular mouth has been pinched into a squarish form while the clay was still soft, characteristic of the Middle Neolithic of northern Italy, especially at Arene Candide. It is thought to show influence from the Danubian culture of central Europe. There are scattered examples from as far as Crete, Sicily, and Spain. (*syn.* square-mouthed pottery, bocca quadrata)

Squier, Ephraim George (1821–1888) and Edwin H. Davis (1811–1888): Journalist and doctor who made a study of the prehistoric mounds of the eastern United States, *Ancient Monuments of the Mississippi Valley* (1848), the first scientific publication of the Smithsonian Institution. The book contained detailed descriptions and classification of the mounds, but concluded that they were constructed by a lost race of moundbuilders, who had migrated away from the area

(perhaps to Mexico), rather than by the ancestors of the surviving Native Americans of the area. Squier also worked in Central America, Peru, and Bolivia.

Sredni Stog culture: Early Eneolithic culture of the Dnepr basin of the Ukraine, c. late 4th and early 3rd millennia BC, with settlements and cemeteries. It preceded the Yamnaya culture (Late Eneolithic) and was important in the domestication of the horse.

Srikshetra: Ancient name for Prome in lower Burma, the historical center of the Pyus. It became the capital and Buddhist religious center of the state by the same name in the early–mid 1st millennium AD. It was later absorbed by Pagan. (*syn.* Sri Ksetra)

Srivijaya: Ancient Sumatran kingdom centered on Palembang in the Malacca Straits, which came into being at the end of the 7th century and controlled the ports of Sumatra and peninsular Malaysia. Its rise might coincide with the fall of Funan. First mentioned by the Chinese pilgrim I-Ching as an important center of Buddhist learning and a relay station on the way to India, it was strong in the 7th–8th centuries and again in the 10th–13th centuries. Remains have been found at several sites: Muara Jambi, Kota Cina, Lobo Tuwa, Kampong Sungei Mas, Padang Lawas, Muara Takus, and Pengkalan Bujang.

Srubnaya culture or Timber Grave culture: Bronze Age culture of the Volga and Don steppes in southern Russia, following the Yamnaya culture. The burials include horse appointments. The Andronovo complex is related to the Timber Grave group in southern Russia; both represent branches of the Indo-Iranian cultural block. (*syn.* Srubna culture, Timber-Grave culture)

stable isotope analysis: A technique for reconstructing past diets (plant foods) by analyzing the isotopic ratios, particularly carbon and nitrogen, contained in human bone. Human remains are analyzed for a measurement of the ratio between 13 C and 12 C isotopes in ancient human bone collagen. (*syn.* stable carbon isotope analysis)

stadial: A period during glaciation when the temperature was at its lowest and ice sheets and glaciers most extensive. They are separated by warmer interstadial periods. These cold episodes are of relatively short duration. (*syn.* stadia)

stadia rod: A long, brightly colored rod with calibrations for obtaining elevations with a surveying instrument. Stadia is a surveying method for determination of distances and differences of elevation by means of this telescopic instrument having two horizontal lines through which the marks on a graduated rod are observed. (*syn.* stadia)

stadium: In classical Greece, a long narrow track for footraces and other athletic events. It most often is exactly one "stadium" or 600 feet (180 m) long, a Greek measure equaling ⅛ of a Roman mile. It is an open-air construction with seating probably on raised embankments along the two sides and around the turning end. The Greek stadium is the ancestor of the Roman circus. Surviving examples are at Olympia, Delphi, Epidauros, Athens, and Isthmia. Sometimes they were connected with major sanctuaries where athletic games took place, but were also part of the public buildings for a Greek city. The first Greek stadiums were in the shape of a horseshoe. They were sometimes cut into the side of a hill, as at Thebes, Epidaurus, and Olympia, site of the Olympic Games, begun there in the 8th century BC. The Greeks also built hippodrome stadiums similar in layout but broad enough to accommodate four-horse chariot races. (*syn.* Greek stadion)

stage: A level of cultural development characterized by a technology and its associated social and ideological features; a large-scale archaeological unit consisting of a well-defined level of development attained by a particular culture area. The adoption of agriculture, for instance, had profound cultural and social consequences, raising people to a higher stage. This technological subdivision of prehistoric time has little chronological meaning beyond the regional (as it may be continental or global), an example being the Stone Age, although stages are integral parts of the chronological sequencing of culture history.

stained glass: Colored glass used for making decorative windows and other objects through which light passes, created since early Christian times. It was not an important art until about the 12th century.

stake hole: The small hole left in the ground after the removal or decay of a stake or post, which would usually have been part of a structure or fence. The cavity becomes filled with soil of a slightly different color or texture from that into which the stake hole was originally cut, thus allowing its detection by archaeologists. They were put into the ground by hammering. They may be distinguished from postholes mainly by their shape and size. (*syn.* stakehole)

stalled cairn: A type of cairn found in the Orkney Islands, which covers elongated burial chambers in which stone slabs project from the walls. The corpses were laid on the slabs.

Stamford ware: An Anglo-Saxon pottery industry centered around Stamford in Lincolnshire, England, which produced fine glazed ceramics in the 9th–13th centuries. The buff wares included characteristic spouted pitchers and jugs, which were much in demand in England and were sometimes traded abroad.

stamnos: A type of Classical Greek vase, similar in size to the amphora, and likewise used typically for the storage of wine. The stamnos, however, is more squat in form, with two horizontal handles and a round mouth. The shape is popular

with Athenian Red-Figure vase painters in the period from about 525–400 BC and in Etruria in the 4th century BC.

stamped decoration: A technique of ornamentation on the soft clay of a pot by repeatedly impressing a simple design previously carved on a bone or wooden tool. Sometimes a natural object, such as a bird bone, was used for this purpose. It was used generally to decorate plain wares and first appeared on Athenian pottery in the mid-5th century BC. Starting in the 4th century BC, it was used together with rouletting. Figured stamps were also used. Neolithic pots sometimes have stamped patterns.

stamp seal: A small, hard block that has a flat surface engraved with a design that can be transferred to soft clay or wax as a mark of ownership or authenticity. Stamp seals appear in Mesopotamia from the Halafian period in the fifth millennium BC, when they were used to impress ownership marks on lumps of clay which were then attached to goods. In the Bronze Age, it was differently shaped for different cultures: square in the Indus, round in the Persian Gulf (Barbar), and compartmented in central Asia (Bactrian). Stamp seals preceded cylinders and developed over a period of about 1,500 years until largely replaced by the cylinder in the 3rd millennium BC. Seals came into use before the invention of writing for the securing of property, and the method was either to shape clay over the stopper or lid or to make a fastening with cord and place clay around the knot and then impress it with the seal. The sealing of written documents, mainly clay tablets and papyrus scrolls, became regularly established in the latter part of the 3rd millennium BC.

Stanca Ripiceni Cave: Upper Palaeolithic site in eastern Romania, with four cultural layers starting c. 25,000 bp. There are bifaces, scrapers, and burins in the lowest assemblage and geometric microliths in the uppermost assemblage.

standard deviation: The natural statistical distribution of a series of measurements around an arithmetic mean value; a measure of the scatter (variability, dispersion, spread) about the mean in a distribution. In archaeology, it is used in association with chronometric dating techniques like radiocarbon dating, where each measurement is a calculation of date for the sample, and the final date given, such as 2,400 ± 200, is a statistical description of a "real" date. The standard deviation (±) as quoted means that there is a 66% chance of the real date lying within that range (for the above example, between 2,600–2,200). For greater probability, the date must be taken to two standard deviations (there is a 95% certainty that the date lies between 2,800–2,000) or three standard deviations (99% certainty). A single date with a relatively large error is generally of less use than a series of dates from the same context, which may show a clustering around a central date.

standardized form: Any preformatted information sheet

to be completed in the field for recording archaeological data, especially during data acquisition, data processing, and analysis.

standing wave technique: An acoustic method, similar to bosing, used in subsurface detection.

Stanegate: Roman road in northern England from the Tyne at Corbridge to the Solway at Carlisle, whose construction is attributed to Agricola, AD c. 80. Originally a military trunk route, it also had a line of forts spaced at intervals of 1 or ½ day's march. It was superseded by the construction of Hadrian's Wall (122–128), and Stanegate became a service road and its forts used as depots.

Stanwick: Largest late Iron Age earthwork fortification in Britain, in Richmond, Yorkshire, once called the largest "hillfort." It was constructed in the 1st century AD, probably in three phases. Phase I was a hill fort, which was partly demolished in Phase II (c. 50–60) when a larger enclosure was added at the north. In Phase III (c. 72), it was greatly enlarged to enclose the south side. Stanwick was probably a center of the Celtic Brigantes, an Iron Age tribe that always had a strong anti-Roman faction and was in rebellion between AD 50–70. A hoard of Celtic metal objects, mainly chariot gear of the 1st century AD, was found close to the earthworks. The whole complex may have been designed to protect not only the people, but also the livestock—including horses—of a basically pastoralist economy. Some time between 69–72, Stanwick fell to the Romans, and the site was abandoned. It is now thought to be an enclosed private estate or demesne containing residential compounds.

Staraja Ladoga: Major north Russian town founded in the 10th century on the left bank of the River Volkhow, 20 kilometers from its outlet in Lake Ladoga, close to the eastern end of the Baltic Sea. Although Scandinavian material has been found, the Russians firmly contend that the town is Slavic in character and origin, and it is seen by many as the precursor of Novgorod.

Star Carr: Important Earlier Maglemosian lakeside site in Yorkshire, England—a postglacial hunting stand dating to c. 8200 BC. Excavation revealed a small summer habitation site, and because of the fine preservation by organic mud, Star Carr has produced the best collection of flint, bone, antler (barbed points), and wooden objects yet recovered from a British Mesolithic site.

Starcevo: Earliest Neolithic culture of the western Balkans, named for a settlement site on the north bank of the Danube opposite Belgrade, Serbia. It is part of a broad complex of cultures that includes Karanovo I, Kremikovci, Körös, Maritza, and Cris—c. 6000–5000 BC. Settlements in the southern Balkans are generally tells; in Serbia they are usually flat sites. It has given its name to a widespread pottery style, and it seems to represent the earliest farming occupation of the area, although hunting and food gathering remained important. The pottery is often coarse and rusticated, but finer fluted and channeled wares and simple painted ones are found in later levels. A bone spatula, perhaps for scooping flour, is a distinctive type for the culture. It developed into the Vinca culture. (*syn.* Starcevo culture)

Staré Hradisko: Late Iron Age *oppidum* in Moravia, occupied from the mid-2nd century BC and then abandoned a century later. There was manufacturing, including pottery making in kilns.

Staré Mesto: Settlement site ("Old Town") in the March Valley of Poland on the right bank of the Vltava, dating from the 12th century. A fortified citadel with a stone-and-mortar church, and rich graves have been excavated. It was a great industrial center, specializing in gold work.

star mound: In Samoa, a stone or earth structure about 2 meters high and 10–15 meters in diameter, with jutting arms; likely religious structures. By 300 BC, Western Samoa had sizable but nonnucleated settlements, with house and ritual mounds and agricultural terraces, including unique star-shaped mounds and the largest surviving mound in Polynesia, Pulemelei (Palauli district, Savai'i).

Staroselje: Middle Palaeolithic rock shelter in the Crimea, with artifacts (scrapers, bifacial foliates) and faunal remains (arctic fox, reindeer, wild ass). The skeleton of a child and bones of an adult are modern humans, which is problematic in relation to the dates of the artifacts and faunal remains. (*syn.* Starosel'e)

state: A form of social organization characterized by a strong central government, socioeconomic class divisions, and a market economy; the most complex form of social organization. Leadership is not based on kinship affiliation, although it may be. States are frequently marked by an armed force and a bureaucracy for recordkeeping. They often have very large populations, cities, and monumental architecture. Such a society retains many chiefdom characteristics in elaborated form, but also includes true political power sanctioned by legitimate force and social integration through concepts of nationality and citizenship usually defined by territorial boundaries. A distinction can be drawn between primary states, those whose origin is independent of any contact with previously existing states, and secondary states, which arise from influences emanating from already established states. In cultural evolutionist models, it ranks second only to the empire as the most complex societal developmental stage. (*syn.* state-organized society)

stater: A Greek coin of electrum and silver, a standard unit that was equivalent to the Near Eastern shekel and the silver didrachm.

statistics: The science of making valid inferences about the characteristics of a group of persons or objects on the basis of numerical information obtained from a randomly selected sample of the group. Artifacts, ecofacts, features, sites, and so on can be reduced to a series of measurements, analytically determined values, or systematic observations, which can be represented as numbers. The distribution of items with respect to these variables can then be studied. A wide variety of quantities summarizing the distributions may be calculated and compared, possibly determining the degree of similarity between distributions. The use of statistics procedures in archaeology most often involves assumptions because archaeologists are dealing with remains that are only representative of the original population of artifacts, ecofacts, features, sites.

statue menhir: A standing stone carved to represent the human form, sometimes with details of clothing or weapons. Most examples in Europe seem to belong to the Late Neolithic/Copper Age period, and they are concentrated in southern and western France, Iberia, Liguria, Corsica, Sardinia, and Italy (Apulia, northwest Tuscany, and near the Swiss and Austrian borders). Northern Italy also has a more recent group of statue menhirs set up by Ligurian peoples during the Iron Age. Bronze Age examples are also known; most statue menhirs are of men. (*syn.* statue-menhir, stela-menhir, stelae-menhirs)

status: Individual position or rank in society in relation to all other members of the society. This may be determined by one's personal achievements in life (achieved status) or by birth and ancestry (ascribed status).

status, achieved: The social rights and duties attributed to individuals according to achievement rather than inherited social position. An individual would work to gain a particular achieved status.

status, ascribed: The social rights and duties attributed to an individual at birth, regardless of ability or achievement. An individual would be born into a particular class or family to have ascribed status.

stave bow: A simple bow made from a single piece of wood, such as yew.

stave church: A church built of wooden staves, consisting of split logs (upright planks) either set directly into the ground or into a wooden sill (horizontal beam). These were mainly built in Norway from the 11th–13th centuries. (*syn.* stave construction)

steatite: A soft magnesian mineral, white to green massive rock composed mainly of talc. The softness of the stone made it very popular for the carving of artifacts: figurines, vessels, jewelry, decorative stone works, and stamp seals. Its resistance to high temperatures made it particularly suitable for mold making for metal casting. In the Indus civilization, seals of this material were whitened by heating with lime, a process called "glazing." (*syn.* soapstone)

steel: An alloy of iron and carbon in which the carbon content amounts to about 2% or less. Steel appears in the archaeological record during the Iron Age and was usually produced by carburization of wrought iron. In this process, the iron is heated in a hearth with charcoal to about 800 degrees Centigrade. Carbon diffuses into the surface of the metal to make steel. As only the surface is affected, only thin strips of steel could be made by this method. Some Iron Age artifacts are made of such steel strips forged together. Further processes such as quenching and tempering were known from Roman times. Viking swords combined the strength of wrought iron with the hardness of steel, using a technique known as pattern welding.

Stein, Sir Mark Aurel (1862–1943): British archaeologist and explorer born in Hungary, who was a great traveler of central and western Asia (especially Chinese Turkistan), recording an extraordinary number of archaeological sites. He was also Superintendent of the Indian Archaeological Survey (1910–1929).

Steinheim: Site near Stuttgart, Germany, where a human skull was discovered in gravels of the Holsteinian (penultimate) Interglacial some 250,000 or 300,000 years ago. No artifacts were found, but the Steinheim skull is older than any Neanderthal or *Homo sapiens* skeleton and is closer to the Swanscombe skull than to any other specimen. The Steinheim and Swanscombe skulls may belong to a distinct subspecies of Homo, but have also been classified as early Neanderthaloids or primitive *Homo sapiens*.

stela or stele: An upright, freestanding stone monument, often inscribed or carved in relief, and sometimes painted. These pillars or tablets of stone were often used to mark a grave or erected as a monument. Inscriptions may commemorate a victory or a major event or proclaim a formal decree. Stelae are frequently encountered in Maya and Olmec sites of Mesoamerica (often carved with calendrical and hieroglyphic inscriptions), in the Buddhist civilizations of Asia, and in early Greece. The earliest funerary stelae are from a cemetery of 1st- and 2nd-Dynasty kings at Abydos and are located in publicly accessible superstructures of the tombs. Commemorative stelae were erected in temples. Votive stelae recorded an individual's veneration of a particular deity(ies). (*syn.* pl. stelae)

stela cult: The widespread use of inscribed upright stone monuments, one of the most prominent and unique Maya Great Tradition markers.

Stellmoor: Site near Hamburg, north Germany, of late glacial and postglacial date and containing an older Hamburgian level c. 13,000–11,750 BP and a later level of c. 8500 BC, Ahrensburgian, with tanged points. The Ahrensburgian level also had a hoard of pinewood arrow shafts. Both cultures were reindeer hunters.

Stentinello: Neolithic ditched village site at Syracuse in Sicily, the type site of the Sicilian version of impressed ware, which survives later there than elsewhere. Round-based dishes and necked jars have elaborate impressed and, distinctively, intricate stamped designs and multiple excised chevrons filled with white inlay. On some, a pair of stamped lozenges is combined with an applied knob near the lip to suggest a human face. The dates are c. 5600–4400 BC.

Stephens, John Lloyd (1852–1905): American explorer and amateur archaeologist who visited the abandoned Maya lowlands centers with Frederick Catherwood. His documentation was published in books that became bestsellers and did much to arouse popular interest in what was then an almost unknown civilization. The drawings by Catherwood set a new standard of scientific accuracy.

steppe: Vast level and usually treeless tracts in southeastern Europe or Asia or the arid land with vegetation found in regions of extreme temperature range and loess soil. This open grassland region is bounded on the north by forest, on the south by the Black Sea, the Caspian, and the mountains of central Asia. It supported nomadic Pastoralist such as the Indo-Europeans, the Scythians, the Huns, and the Mongols. Their nomadic movements across the steppes spread cultural traits widely. The rich burials from Pazyryk are one of the few examples illustrating their wealth of material culture.

stepped adze: Polished stone adze of the Chinese Neolithic, roughly rectangular in shape, flat on one side with a step on the other. It is also found in Southeast Asia.

step pyramid: A form of Egyptian royal tomb, transitional between the mastaba of the early Archaic period and the true pyramid of the Old Kingdom. Djoser's at Saqqarah is the only completed step pyramid known. The pyramid itself evolved through numerous stages from a flat mastaba (an oblong tomb with a burial chamber dug beneath it, common at earlier nonroyal sites) into a six-stepped, almost square pyramid (a terraced structure rising in six unequal stages to a height of 60 m, its base measuring 120 m by 108 m). The substructure has an intricate system of underground corridors and rooms, its main feature being a central shaft 25 meters deep and 8 meters wide, at the bottom of which is the sepulchral chamber built of granite from Aswan. The Step Pyramid rises in a vast walled court 544 meters long and 277 meters wide, in which there are remnants of other stone edifices.

step trench: Excavation technique in which a series of stair-like cuts are made, often used to uncover sections of a deep deposit, such as a mound tell site. (*syn.* step-trenching)

stereoscope: An optical instrument with two eyepieces for helping the observer to combine the images of two pictures differing slightly in point of view, thereby giving a "solid" effect.

sterile layer: An excavation layer or deposit in which there are no cultural materials or evidence of human occupation or activity. (*syn.* sterile soil)

Sterkfontein: Site near Krugersdorp in Transvaal, South Africa, which is one of the most important hominid sites in southern Africa and dating from c. 2.5 million years ago. From the fossiliferous cave fillings have come the largest collection of Australopithecine fossils in south Africa, especially *Australopithecus africanus* and *Plesianthropus transvaalensis*, *Australopithecus robustus*, *Homo erectus*, and *Homo habilis*. The latter is thought to have made Earlier Stone Age artifacts (Developed Oldowan B or early Acheulian). Sterkfontein is one of three neighboring sites (with Swartkrans and Kromdraai) at which the remains of fossil hominids have been found.

Steward, Julian Haynes (1902–1972): American anthropologist and archaeologist who influenced archaeological theory, emphasizing that the goals of both disciplines were the same: understanding of cultural change and the plotting of that change on spatial and temporal planes. His best-known book was *Theory of Culture Change: the Methodology of Multilinear Evolution* (1955) and he also wrote *Handbook of South American Indians* (1946–1950) and *Irrigation Civilizations* (1955). He carried out fieldwork in the Great Basin, British Columbia, and the Andes, planned and helped establish the Virú Valley project. He worked for the use of evolutionary and ecological thought in anthropology and archaeology; he is known as the founder of the theory of cultural ecology.

Sticna: Early Iron Age fortified settlement site and burial mounds near Ljubljana, Slovenia. Over 6,000 graves are known, in about 140 burial mounds, of the later Hallstatt period. An iron-rich site, it was an iron-smelting and commercial center.

Stillbay: Site on Cape Province, South Africa, with an assemblage of Late Palaeolithic stone tools and dating c. 30,000–50,000 years ago. The stone flake culture reached from Ethiopia to South Africa along the eastern coast and produced a variety of stone tools that are similar to the Mousterian industry of North Africa and Europe. Tools were made generally by the Levallois stone-flaking technique, and the Stillbay industry also included leaf-shaped bifacial points. Some archaeologists now use a series of more local designations, such as Bambata in Zimbabwe, to describe the culture of that time.

Stirling, Matthew Williams (1896–1975): American archaeologist who worked extensively to investigate the Olmec, especially at La Venta, San Lorenzo, Tres Zapotes, and Cerro de las Mesas. At Tres Zapotes, near the Tuxtla Mountains in the old Olmec "heartland," he found its most famous monument, the fragmentary Stela C. On the reverse is a column of numerals in the bar-and-dot system, which he read as a date in the Maya calendar corresponding to 31 BC; this is more than a century earlier than any known dated inscription from the Maya area itself. It was thus highly probable that this calendrical system, formerly thought to be a Maya invention, was developed in the Late Formative by epi-Olmec peoples living outside the Maya area proper. He also found, at La Venta, the tremendous "colossal heads."

stirrup jar: Ceramic jar of medium size having a flat knob connected to the shoulder by two handles, in place of the central mouth. A separate spout was added elsewhere on the shoulder. It was much used by the Mycenaeans and in Minoan Crete for storing or transporting perfume, oil, and so on. (*syn.* false-necked amphora)

stirrup spout: Semicircular tub set vertically, like a croquet hoop, on top of a closed vessel—common in many Peruvian cultures (Moche, Chimu, Chavín, Cupisnique, Nazca) and other parts of the New World. The lower ends open into the body of the pot, and from the apex of the curve rises a single vertical spout. From the side, it looks like a stirrup. It had precursors in the Initial period. In Chavín pottery, for example, the earliest stirrup spouts were relatively small, very thick and heavy, and the spout had a thick flange. As time went on, the stirrups became lighter and the spouts longer; the flange was reduced and finally disappeared. The necks of the flasks underwent similar changes. The Cupisnique stirrup-spouted vessels, some of which were modeled in the form of human beings, animals, or fruits, were the beginning of a north-coast tradition of naturalistic modeling. (*syn.* stirrup-spout vessel)

stoa: A classical Greek building with a long open colonnade, one or two story, for civil, religious, or commercial purpose. It was essentially a long, straight colonnade, with vertical wall (and sometimes rooms) behind and roof over. The colonnade is sometimes doubled, and a projecting wing may be added to either end. They are often found on the edge of an agora or a temenos. Several such buildings are in Athens, from about 650 BC onward, such as the Stoa of Attalus and the Stoa Poikile (c. 460 BC). The popular Hellenistic and Roman philosophy of Stoicism takes its name from the Stoa Poikile, where it was taught. (*syn.* pl. stoae)

stone: A concretion of mineral matter, one of the first materials to be used for making artifacts. Very fine grained or glassy stones, such as flint and obsidian, were mainly shaped by chipping or flaking. Other less brittle stones had to be hammered or chiseled into shape and then polished. Precious and decorative stones were also widely used in antiquity. Petrological analysis of stone has allowed the source materials to be discovered.

Stone Age: The oldest and longest division of the Three-Age System, preceding the Bronze Age and Iron Age, the oldest known period of human culture—characterized by the use of stone tools. This prehistoric age embraces the Palaeolithic (Old), Mesolithic (Middle), and Neolithic (New). These three separate periods are based on the degree of sophistication in the fashioning and use of tools. Metals were unknown, but tools and weapons were also made of wood, bone, and antler. The dates for the Stone Age vary considerably from one region to another, and some communities were still living a Stone Age life until very recent time. In sub-Saharan Africa, the Stone Age is equivalent to the term Palaeolithic and spans c. 2.5 mya until the 19th century AD.

stone-boiling: Cooking that is done by heating stones and placing them in the liquid or substance to be cooked. This type of cooking was often done in baskets or containers that cannot be placed directly in or over a fire.

stone circle: A ring of standing stones, either circular or near-circular, found in the British Isles from the Neolithic and Early Bronze Ages. There are almost 1,000 stone circles, some surrounded by a ditch, with the most famous examples being Stonehenge, Avebury, and Callanish. Two atypical examples are in Brittany. The standing stones that make up these circles are widely spaced; in many examples they are incorporated into a ring bank of smaller piled stones, which has one opening as the entrance. A local variant is the recumbent stone circle of Aberdeenshire, in which the entrance is marked by a large horizontal stone flanked by tall portal stones. A recumbent stone is also a feature of circles in southwest Ireland, but here the two tallest stones are placed diametrically opposite the horizontal stone. Two of the Scottish recumbent stone circles have yielded Beaker pottery, while urn burials in various "standard" circles were of Bronze Age type. Circles are often associated with cairns, menhirs, and alignments. Many have tried to interpret the complex geometric layouts and placement of the stones in an astronomical base. There has been much discussion about the validity of various theories, and there is no agreement on the subject.

Stonehenge: Ancient monument on Salisbury Plain, Wiltshire, England, the remains of four massive trilithons surrounded by concentric circles of megaliths, probably constructed since c. 3200 BC. It was a major Neolithic and Early Bronze Age ritual monument, architecturally unique, surrounded by a whole complex of barrow cemeteries and ritual sites. It had many phases of reconstruction. Apart from a cursus, the oldest structure was a circular earthwork about 100 meters in diameter, consisting of a ditch with an inner bank broken by a single entrance. Just inside the bank was a ring of 56 Aubrey holes (pits), some of which contained cremations. There were further cremations in the ditch and on the inner plateau. The presence of grooved ware pottery, together with radiocarbon dates from a cremation suggest that Stonehenge I belongs to the end of the Neolithic. Phase II occurred in c. 2200–2000 when two concentric rings of sockets were dug at the center of the site for the erection of 80 bluestones imported from the Preseli Hills of southwest Wales. To this period belong the Avenue, two parallel banks and ditches that run from the entrance to the River Avon 3 kilometers away. In Stonehenge's third phase, the bluestones were removed, and Sarsen stones, some weighing over 50 tons, were brought from the downs 38 kilometers away to the north. These blocks, unlike those of any other henge or megalithic tomb, were dressed to shape before erection and were then set up as a circle of uprights with a continuous curving lintel, enclosing a U-shaped arrangement of five trilithons. This phase has been dated 2120 ± 150 BC, and its work was carried out by the bearers of the Wessex culture. At a later stage (phase IIIc), the bluestones were re-erected in their present positions, duplicating the sarsen structure. There is a radiocarbon date of 1540 ± 105 BC for the early part of this final stage, and the whole of Stonehenge III probably falls within the Early Bronze Age. The final stage came in the Middle or Late Bronze Age when the Avenue was extended 2,000 meters east. The function of the monument is usually held to be religious, although it had no connection with the Druids. Theories are that the northeast-southwest axis may suggest some form of sun cult, the stone settings may have been used for astronomical observations in connection with the calendar, and the Aubrey holes for calculating the occurrence of eclipses. It has also been interpreted as the temple of a sun or sky cult. Archaeologists have long been fascinated by this monument, with its evidence of massive manpower input (one calculation suggests 30 million man-hours would have been required for the phase IIIA structure), its architectural sophistication, and astronomical alignments.

stone line: A subsurface sheet of stones one layer thick in a soil that appears as a line parallel to the soil surface. Stone lines of geologic origin may contribute to the formation of ferruginous horizons; they may contain archaeological debris. The interpretation of archaeological debris in a stone line context depends on proper interpretation of the origin of the stone line.

stone setting: A setting of stones marking out a grave, known in various shapes, including ships.

stoneware: Distinctive pottery that has been fired at a high temperature (about 1,200 C/2,200 F) until glasslike and impervious to liquid. Usually opaque, but mainly because it is nonporous, it does not require a glaze. When a glaze is used,

it is decorative only. Stoneware originated in China as early as 1400 BC (Shang Dynasty). The technique made possible the production of durable tablewares.

stone zone: A subsurface bed of stones or stone material in a soil that is larger than one layer thick; it may contain archaeological debris. Similar to stone lines, the origin of a stone zone is necessary for interpretation of the archaeological debris in this context.

stop-ridge: Transverse ridges added to the faces of a flat ax mounted in a right-angled cleft haft to transfer some of the impact from the base of the cleft to the tips. Axes with stop-ridges form an intermediate step in development between the flanged ax and the palstave. The term also refers to a ridge on a celt or pipe, which prevents one part from slipping too far over another. (*syn.* stop ridge)

Strabo (c. 64/63 BC–AD 21/23): Greek geographer and historian whose multivolume "Geography" is the only extant work covering the whole range of peoples and countries known to both Greeks and Romans during the reign of Augustus (27 BC–AD 14).

Stradonice: Iron Age *oppidum* in Bohemia of the 2nd century BC, La Tène period. Fine painted ceramics and coins were made there.

Strandloper: A term, literally "beachcomber," for people thought to have created shell middens along the southern Africa coast. It is also the name of a South African coastal Later Stone Age industry characterized by pottery, large flakes, flaked cobbles, and retouched stone artifacts. It has existed for the last 2,000 years.

Stránská Skála: Lower Palaeolithic cave site in Moravia, Czechoslovakia. Artifacts are earlier than the Middle Pleistocene, including chopping tools and flakes.

Strashnaya Cave: Middle Palaeolithic site in the Altai region of Siberia, with occupation probably before the last glacial. The artifacts are Levallois cores, scrapers, and denticulates.

strata: The definable layers of archaeological matrix or features revealed by excavation; units of sedimentation greater than 1 centimeter thick. A layer in which archaeological material—as artifacts, skeletons, and dwelling remains—is found during excavation. It is the more or less homogeneous or gradational material, visually separable from other levels by a discrete change in the character of the material being deposited or a sharp break in deposition (or both). (*syn.* singular stratum; layers)

Strathclyde: Native Briton kingdom that, from about the 6th century, had extended over the basin of the River Clyde and adjacent western coastal districts, the former county of Ayr. Its capital was Dumbarton, then known as Alclut. Its people were in frequent conflict with the Anglo-Saxons of Northumbria and later the Scots of Dálriada. They were converted to Christianity by Saint Ninian and his successors from the monastery of Whithorn. It became a province of Scotland in 1016/1018.

stratification: An arrangement or deposition of sediment or sedimentary rocks in a sequence of layers (strata); the accumulated sequence of strata on an archaeological site. A succession of layers should provide a relative chronological sequence, with the earliest at the bottom and the latest at the top. Stratification is the basis for stratigraphy.

stratified random sampling: A probabilistic sampling technique used to cluster and isolate sample units when regular spacing is inappropriate for cultural reasons. The region or site is divided into natural zones or strata, such as cultivated land and forest, and units are then chosen by a random-number procedure to give each zone a number of squares proportional to its area, thus overcoming the inherent bias in simple random sampling. In stratified sampling, the population is divided into classes, and simple random samples are drawn from each class. (*syn.* stratified sampling; stratified sample)

stratified society: Society in which competing groups have unequal access to power and/or resources, some groups being subordinate to others. The uppermost stratum is termed an "elite."

stratified systematic sampling: A probabilistic sampling technique that combines elements of simple random sampling, stratified random sampling, and systematic sampling—in an effort to reduce sampling bias.

stratigraphic profile: Drawing of natural and/or cultural deposits of strata of a trench, which can be correlated with the data collections recovered from that trench.

stratigraphy: The study and interpretation of the stratification of rocks, sediments, soils, or cultural debris, based on the principle that the lowest layer is the oldest and the uppermost is the youngest—a major tool in establishing a relative dating sequence. The sequence of deposition can be assessed by a study of the relations of different layers. Dateable artifacts found in layers, and layers or structures that are themselves dateable, can be used to date parts of stratigraphic sequences. An archaeologist has to master the skill to recognize it—to distinguish one deposit from another by its color, texture, smell, or contents; to understand it—to explain how each layer came to be added, whether by natural accumulation, deliberate fill, or collapse of higher standing buildings; and to record it in measured drawings of the section. There can be problems where a feature filled with one type of material cuts into layers of the same material. Unless the later feature is recognized, objects of two different phases may appear to be stratified together. The underlying principles are law of superposition, law of cross-cutting relations, included fragments, and correlation by fossil inclusions. The stratigraphy principle was adopted from geology and is the basis of reconstructing the history of an archaeological site.

stratum: The definable layers of archaeological matrix or features revealed by excavation; units of sedimentation greater than 1 centimeter thick. A layer in which archaeological material—as artifacts, skeletons, and dwelling remains—is found during excavation. It is the more or less homogeneous or gradational material, visually separable from other levels by a discrete change in the character of the material being deposited or a sharp break in deposition (or both). (*syn.* pl. strata; layer)

Straubing: Early Bronze Age regional variant of the Unetice culture in Lower Bavaria, Germany. It is characterized by flat inhumation cemeteries with grave goods such as simple bronze daggers, awls, torcs, cones of coiled wire, and amber beads. It is dated to the early 2nd millennium BC. (*syn.* Straubing group)

stray find: An object of some kind—pottery, metalwork, a coin, and so on—which has not been found in an archaeological context. Stray finds are useful if the total distribution of a particular type of object is required, but the absence of associated material or structures makes their interpretation difficult.

Strelets culture: Upper Palaeolithic culture of the Oka-Don lowland of European Russia, dated to c. 40,000–25,000 bp. The earliest assemblages include Middle Palaeolithic scrapers, points, and bifaces. Later assemblages have scrapers, burins, nonstone tools, and art objects. The diagnostic tool is a small triangular bifacial point with concave base.

Strelice: Small settlement site of the Late Neolithic Lengyel culture in central Moravia, Czechoslovakia, and dated to the mid-4th millennium BC. The rich Middle Lengyel ritual assemblage included a fixed-clay house model showing timber posts and a pitched roof and the largest group of anthropomorphic figurines in Moravia.

stress: Any environmental factor that forces an individual or population out of equilibrium.

Strettweg: Hallstatt burial in eastern Austria of the 7th century BC, famous for a miniature bronze wagon, which is possibly a cult object. The wagon frame has a group of mounted warriors flanking a much larger naked woman, interpreted as a goddess, holding a bowl above her head.

striation: Microscopic scratches, grooves, or channels on stone tools, which often reveal the direction of force and the nature of tool use.

strigil: A narrow curved scraper, made of horn or metal

(bronze, silver), used by Roman and Greek bathers for the cleansing of the skin. A strigil was used to remove olive oil applied after bathing or exercising. Romans used them particularly in the hot room (caldarium), and the task was often performed by slaves. On Athenian pottery, strigils are shown in the hands of athletes. (*syn.* Latin strigilis)

striking platform: The area on a store core, which is struck to remove a flake or blade in toolmaking. Part of the original platform is removed with the detached flake. The platform itself is prepared by the removal of one or more flakes and in the latter case is described as a faceted striking platform. (*syn.* platform)

strip method: A method of excavating whereby a large horizontal area is dug instead of a deep vertical one; clearing excavations in which large areas of overburden are removed to reveal horizontal distributions of data without leaving balks. This excavation layout is designed to investigate a large area for a modest outlay of effort. It has the disadvantage that no longitudinal section is available for study, only transverse ones, and that the site can never been seen in its entirety. It is a little-used method with the introduction of technology. (*syn.* stripping excavations)

Stroke-Ornamented Ware: Early/Middle Neolithic culture of west-central Europe, developed directly out of the Linear Pottery culture, c. 4000–3800 BC. The pottery has zigzag patterns made by a series of distinct jabs rather than continuous lines. Bohemia, southwest Poland, Bavaria, and central Germany were its locale. The culture had longhouses, which were slightly trapezoidal. (*syn.* Stroke-Ornamented Pottery culture; Stichbandkeramik)

Strong, William Duncan (1899–1962): American anthropologist who was a pioneer of Plains archaeology and one of the founders of modern Peruvian archaeology. He excavated extensively on the coast of Nazca, in Pachacamac, Paracas, and Viru Valley. He also worked on the south coast and defined stylistic relations between the various pre-Inca cultures of the area. Strong helped developed the direct historical approach of working back through archaeological sequences from the known historical past.

structural archaeology: A branch of archaeology based on the assumption that codes and rules, beliefs and symbolic concepts, produce human culture systems. It is a research perspective that views culture as the shared symbolic structures that are cumulative creations of the mind and is closely related to postprocessual archaeology. The objective of structural analysis is to discover the basic principles of the human mind as reflected in myth, art, kinship, and language. Structural archaeology is concerned with how people manipulate the meaning of material culture, embedded in structural codes, to make new meanings and statements. (*syn.* structural anthropology, symbolic archaeology, cognitive archaeology)

structuralist approaches: Interpretations that stress that human actions are guided by codes and rules, beliefs and symbolic concepts, and that culture is the cumulative creations of these minds. Structuralist approaches attempt to uncover the structures of thought and to study their influence in shaping the ideas in the minds of the humans who created the archaeological record. (*syn.* structuralism)

structure: A domestic and political system causally conditioned by infrastructure.

stucco: A fine lime plaster used for covering walls and creating interior architectural elements, which is a mixture of gypsum and glue or white marble and pulverized with plaster of lime and mixed with water. This weather-resistant plaster is used as a wall covering and for decorative features such as moldings, friezes, facades, and cornices. The Maya decorated temples and other monumental architecture with stucco masks and figures. Examples of stuccowork also occur in the Aztec architecture of Mexico and the Muslim architecture of North Africa and Spain. In ancient Greece, stucco was applied to both interior and exterior temple walls as early as 1400 BC.

studded: Pottery decorated by the addition of pellets of clay to its surface.

Stukeley, William (1687–1765): British antiquary and field archaeologist whose surveys of the monumental Neolithic Period–Bronze Age stone circles at Stonehenge and Avebury, Wiltshire, led him to elaborate theories relating them to the Druids. His views were widely accepted in the late 18th century, and this misconception about the Druid connection has no data to back it up. His extensive antiquarian travels are recorded in *Itinerarium Curiosum* (1724, "Observant Itinerary").

stupa: A Buddhist monument consisting of a circular or hemispherical mound with a domelike casing of stone, often tiled, and intended to contain relics of the Buddha or of a Buddhist saint. Existing in China, Japan, Korea, India, Java, and Southeast Asia, stupas are often the focus of a monastery. They are surrounded by a decorative railing showing the Buddha's life and mythological figures. The Mauryan emperor Asoka is said to have built 84,000 stupas, including the most famous at Sanchi (Madhya Pradesh, c. 2nd century BC). Hindus of the Jainist sect built stupas commemorating saints.

Sturts Meadows: Site in New South Wales, Australia, of the Panaramitee, with engravings on mudstone outcrops. Radiocarbon dates are c. 10,000 bp.

S-twist: Cordage ply twisted to the maker's right.

style: Any distinctive and therefore recognizable way in which an act is performed and made. In archaeology, stylistic areas are area units representing shared ways of producing and decorating artifacts.

style zone: An area in which the artifacts of various communities show the same stylistic attributes.

stylistic analysis: Artifact analysis focused on form and function as well as the decorative styles used by the makers, used very often for ceramics.

stylistic attribute: Well-defined local variations in artifacts, which may reflect territorial boundaries. Characteristics/attributes of an artifact, which relate to its surface appearance, such as color, decoration, and texture—leading to stylistic classifications. (*syn.* stylistic boundary marker)

stylistic seriation: The organization of artifacts or other data by sequence according to changes over time in their stylistic attributes, a relative age determination technique.

stylistic type: Artifact classes based on stylistic attributes and distinctions.

stylobate: The substructure on which the columns of a temple or other building stand.

stylus: Pointed writing instrument made from a variety of materials: reed stem, bone, ivory, or metal (iron, bronze, silver). The sharpened implement is shaped like a pen with a wedge-shaped tip and one end flattened like a spatula; the latter served either to spread the wax on a writing tablet or to erase by smoothing. The stylus was used in ancient times as a tool for writing on parchment or papyrus. The early Greeks incised letters on wax-covered boxwood tablets by using a stylus. A stylus was also used for impressing cuneiform writing into wet clay tablets, which were then baked. (*syn.* stilus; plural styli, styluses)

Subalyuk: Middle Palaeolithic cave site in the Bükk Mountains, Hungary, predating the last glacial. Artifacts include scrapers and there are skeletal remains with Neanderthal characteristics.

sub-arctic: Concerning the environment immediately outside the arctic circle; the arctic environment south of the boreal tree line. The subarctic, or the physiographic zone called the taiga, is a land of coniferous forest covered with sphagnum moss and traversed by many waterways.

subarea: The subdivision of an archaeological area, usually defined by geographic or cultural considerations.

subassemblage: A grouping or association of artifacts, based on form and functional criteria. A subassemblage is assumed to represent a single occupational group in a prehistoric community.

Sub-Atlantic: Last of the five postglacial climate and vegetation periods of northern Europe, beginning c. 1500 BC (according to pollen analysis, although radiocarbon dates are c. 225 BC). It is a division of Holocene chronology (10,000 years ago–present). The Sub-Atlantic Interval followed the Sub-Boreal Climatic Interval and continues today. It is a subdivision of the Flandrian, thought to be wet and cold, a trend started in the preceding Sub-Boreal period. There was a dominance of beech forests, and the fauna were essentially modern. During the Iron Age, pollen analysis shows evidence of intensified forest clearance for mixed farming. Sea levels have been generally regressive during this time interval, although North America is an exception. (*syn.* Sub-Atlantic Climatic period, Sub-Atlantic Climatic Interval)

Sub-Boreal: One of the five postglacial climate and vegetation periods of northern Europe, occurring c. 3000–1500 BC or, according to some, AD, based on pollen analysis. The Sub-Boreal, dated by radiocarbon methods, began c. 5,100 years ago and ended about 2,200 years ago. It is a division of Holocene chronology (10,000 years ago–present). The Sub-Boreal Climatic interval followed the Atlantic and preceded the Sub-Atlantic Climatic interval. It was characterized by a cooler and moister climate than that of the preceding Atlantic period. It is a subdivision of the Flandrian, starting with the Elm Decline. Frequencies of tree pollen fall, and herbaceous pollen rises, representing man's invasion of the forest in the Neolithic and Bronze Ages. It is correlated with Pollen Zone VIII, and the climate was warm and dry. The Sub-Boreal forests were dominated by oak and ash and show the first evidence of extensive burning and clearance by humans. Domesticated animals and natural fauna were abundant. (*syn.* Sub-Boreal Climatic period, subboreal)

Suberde: Small aceramic Neolithic settlement in the Konya plain of southern Turkey, dated to the later 7th millennium BC. Two occupation levels were recognized, the earlier with traces of hut floors, the latter with building of mud brick and plastered floors. Thousands of animal bones have been found—sheep, goat, cattle, pig—and some harvesting of wild cereals may have occurred.

Submycenaean: A phase between the Late Helladic and the Protogeometric periods on mainland Greece, known from its pottery found in cemeteries in Attica and from sites in central Greece and the Peloponnese. It is dated c. 1050–1020 BC. Pottery was the first art to recover its standards after the Dorian invasion and the overthrow of Mycenae. Athens escaped these disasters and in the ensuing dark age became the main source of ceramic ideas. For a short time, Mycenaean motifs survived on new shapes—the Submycenaean ware. It gave way to the Protogeometric (c. 1020–900 BC) style by converting the decaying Mycenaean ornament into regular geometrical patterns.

subsistence: Means of supporting life, in particular by obtaining food. Subsistence is that part of economy concerned with acquisition, distribution, and production of food.

subsistence economy: The way in which a society exploits its environment to procure food, including acquisition, distribution, and production. There are two broad types of subsistence: exploitation of wild plants and animals or of domesticated plants and animals. There are variations and combinations of these two types. The term can also be used to describe the economic level of those who produce only enough food for their own consumption, without any surplus. (*syn.* subsistence strategy)

subsurface detection: Remote sensing techniques carried out at ground level, and including bosing (or bowsing), augering, coring, Lerici periscope, resistivity detector, magnetometer, and radar techniques.

subtractive technology: Any manufacturing process in which artifacts take form as material is removed from the original mass. Flint knapping is a subtractive technology.

Succase: Settlement site of the Rzucewo culture, a regional variant of the Corded Ware culture dated to the beginning of the 2nd millennium BC and located in Pomerania, Poland. Several occupation layers are represented by overlapping rectangular timber-framed house plans. Microlithic flintwork is found associated with an amber industry.

sudatorium: The hot-air room at the Roman baths and sufficiently hot to produce perspiration.

Sue ware: Bluish-gray high-fired pottery of the Kofun, Nara, and Heian periods in Japan (5th–14th centuries AD), derived from Kaya pottery of the Old Silla period in Korea. A large number of vessels were made on a mechanical wheel and fired in a kiln at about 1,100 degrees Centigrade; the blue-gray color resulted from the oxygen-reduced atmosphere in the kiln toward the end of the firing process. By the 6th century, Sue pottery was mass-produced at many centers, with the emphasis on specialized ceremonial vessels, then on utilitarian pots and dishes for the elite, and finally on storage and cooking pots for the general population. When it was first imported from Korea, it was deposited in mounded tombs of the Kofun period.

sugar cane: Grasses that contain a sweet syrup in their coarse fibrous stems. It is believed that they were first used by man in the New Guinea region in an early phase of Austronesian settlement c. 3000 BC.

Sugu: Site in Fukuoka Prefecture, Japan, with many Yayoi settlements, cemeteries, and workshops. The Sugu site proper is a cemetery containing over 200 jar burials. The most famous burial was that of a probable political leader inside two jars, set mouth to mouth, along with at least 33 imported Chinese bronze mirrors, several bronze weapons, and ornaments of glass, stone, and antler. The fine pottery used in the funerary jars is known as the Sugu type, characteristic of the Middle Yayoi (100 BC–AD 100) of Kyushu. (*syn.* Sugu site group)

Sui Dynasty: Ruling house, AD 581–618, which reunified China after several centuries of fragmentation. Its capital was

at Ch'ang-an, and it laid the foundations for the T'ang Dynasty.

Sukhaya Mechetka: Middle Palaeolithic site at Volgograd on the Volga River (European Russia), occupied from the last interglacial; one of the few last interglacial sites on the Russian Plain. Artifacts are scrapers and bifacial foliates.

Sukhothai: Early Buddhist Thai state in northern Thailand founded in the 13th century, independent of the declining Khmer Empire of Angkor. Its core towns were Sukhothai and Si Satchanalai. Under its greatest king Ram Khamhaeng (c. 1275–1317), the power of Sukhothai expanded over vast areas of the Indochinese and even the Malay Peninsula. In the 15th century, the center of Thai power shifted south to Ayuthya, and Sukhothai ceased to exist as an independent kingdom. It is also known for its glazed stoneware vessels, of the same name, widely exported. The pottery had underglaze decoration in black/brown on a cream slip.

Sulawesi: Largest island of eastern Indonesia, with a possible late Pleistocene industry from Cabenge and with many rock shelters having Toalian assemblages. The Paso shell midden in Minahasa and the Kalumpang Neolithic site are of archaeological interest.

Sulphur Spring: The earliest of three stages of the Cochise culture, named for a cluster of sites in southeast Arizona, and dating from 6000/7000 BC to c. 4000 BC. Evidence of plant food processing (cobble manos) together with split and burnt faunal remains, implies an Archaic lifestyle, although there are almost no projectile points, blades, or knives. Besides milling stones, it is characterized by various scrapers. The remains of food animals indicate that some hunting was done. (*syn.* Sulphur Springs)

Sumatra: One of the Greater Sunda Islands and the second largest island of Indonesia, with Tianko Panjang cave in Jambi Province yielding an obsidian flake industry dating from c. 8000 BC. There is undated cord-marked pottery in the cave's upper layers. The Pasemah megaliths may date from the early 1st millennium AD.

sumatralith: Unifacially worked discoid stone tool, often made from a thin slice of the cortex of a large pebble. It is found in Southeast Asia and northern Sumatra, characteristic of some Hoabinhian assemblages.

Sumer/Sumerian: The earliest documented inhabitants of southern Mesopotamia (southern Iraq), c. 3500 BC, considered the world's first civilization. Located between Babylon and the head of the Persian Gulf, these people spoke a language unrelated to any other known language. Formed originally by the need for irrigation agriculture, they created a social and political organization, their own art, literature, and religious observances and greatly influenced neighboring cultures. Cities appeared, such as Eridu, Lagash, Uruk, and Ur, with craft specialization and accumulation of wealth. Most important was the invention of writing. The cuneiform script developed for writing Sumerian can be read. The political unit was the city-state, in which the patron deity, through the priesthood and temple organization, was the major power in all matters. Secular rulers were required only in time of war. The various city-states were united by a common culture and religion, the patron deities such as Enki, Enlil, Nannar, and the rest being members of a single Sumerian pantheon. Sumer was conquered by the Semites of Akkad under Sargon c. 2370 BC. The Sumerian culture survived this and later foreign conquests with very little change. Some scholars believe that the Sumerians go back much further and may even have been the first sedentary inhabitants of southern Mesopotamia, from about 5500 BC. The Sumerian language had invariable bisyllabic or monosyllabic roots, around which prefixes or suffixes, also invariable, were arranged to express grammatical inflections. The structure of the language must have made it easier to invent writing and, in a second period, the use of syllabic characters. Sumerian was overtaken by Babylonian and ceased to be spoken at the beginning of 2nd millennium BC, but then became a language used for cultural purposes and retained that function until cuneiform writing itself disappeared in the 1st century AD.

Sumerian king list: Cuneiform documents of the early 2nd millennium BC in southern Mesopotamia, which contain historical and mythical summaries of the ruling dynasties. It does not include many important dynasties. The list lacks all mention of the 1st Dynasty of Lagash and the florescence of Uruk at the beginning of the 3rd millennium BC. The list seems to have a political purpose rather than a truly documentary one. This literary composition, dating from Old Babylonian times, describes kingship in Mesopotamia from primeval times to the end of the 1st Dynasty of Isin. The Sumerian king list is a compilation of names, places, and wholly fabulous dates and exploits, apparently edited to show and promote the time-hallowed oneness of kingship in the face of the splintered city-states of the period.

Sumerian question: Academic question of the origins of the Sumerians, culturally and linguistically. Their language has no known relatives and is poorly understood, despite many cuneiform texts found in southern Mesopotamia. Sumerian is the oldest written language in existence.

Sundaland: The enlarged Southeast Asian continental area, which was created when sea levels dropped in periods of glaciation. Much of western Indonesia was then connected to the mainland. Until about 7000 BC, the seas were some 150 feet (50 m) lower than they are now, and the area west of Makassar Strait consisted of a web of watered plains that is called Sundaland. These land connections may account for similarities in early human development observed in the Hoabinhian age, which lasted from about 13,000–5000/4000 BC. The stone tools across Southeast Asia during this period show a remarkable degree of similarity in design and development.

Sunda Shelf: The shallow submarine continental shelf, or platform, that is a southward extension of mainland Southeast Asia. Borneo and parts of Java, Sumatra, Bali, Palawan, and associated islands are eroded metamorphic sections of the shelf left above sea level. These were joined to the Asian continent at times of low Pleistocene sea level. The eastern edge of the shelf (Huxley's Line) may have been the eastern limit of settlement by *Homo erectus*.

sun disk: Decorative symbol for the sun; an ancient Near Eastern symbol consisting of a disk with conventionalized wings emblematic of the sun god (as Ra in Egypt). It was also used frequently throughout the European Bronze Age. (*syn.* sun disc)

Sung Dynasty: Chinese dynasty (960–1279) that ruled the country (only in the south after 1127) during one of its most brilliant cultural epochs. The Sung Dynasty was founded when Chao K'uang-yin, the military inspector general of the Chou Dynasty, last of the Five Dynasties, gained control in a coup. China was reunified after the divisions of the 10th century, and it was a period of great literary and artistic achievement, although constantly threatened by the Mongols. (*syn.* Song Dynasty)

Sungir: Upper Palaeolithic site near Vladimir, European Russia, occupied c. 25,000–20,000 BC. It is by far the most northeastern of the rich Upper Palaeolithic sites of Europe, and there is a strong Mousterian element in the stone artifacts. The skeletons found buried on the site had archaic features such as large brow ridges. The single and double burials are of interest for the numerous beads and other grave goods left with them, allowing the reconstruction of clothing details. Radiocarbon dates range from c. 25,500–14,600 bp. The artifacts have been compared to the Strelets culture assemblages of Kostenki.

Sunium: Promontory at the southern tip of Attica with a temple to Poseidon, c. 440 BC, and a harbor fortified during the Peloponnesian Wars in the late 4th century BC. State-owned silver mines were near Sunium. (*syn.* Soúnion)

sun temple: Religious building constructed by kings of the 5th Dynasty of Egypt for worshipping the sun god Re. They resemble the pyramid complexes of the same period, with valley temple and causeway leading to the upper temple. Six sun temples are known, but only those at Abusir and Abu Gurab have been found. Nyuserre, sixth king of the 5th Dynasty, is primarily known for his sun temple at Abu Gurab (Abu Jirab) in Lower Egypt. The temple plan, like that built by Userkaf (the first king of the 5th Dynasty), consisted of a valley temple, causeway, gate, and temple court, which contained an obelisk (the symbol of Re) and an alabaster altar. Although impressive in size, Nyuserre's pyramid was exceeded both in height and in length by his sun temple, indicating the unusual prominence of the cult of Re during the 5th Dynasty.

superposition: The principle that artifacts found at a lower level of a site predate those at a higher level. The order in which sedimentary layers are deposited, the highest being the youngest.

superstructure: The values, aesthetics, rules, rituals, philosophies, beliefs, religions, symbols, and other forms of knowledge assumed by cultural materialists to be causally conditioned by infrastructure.

supine: A term used to describe the position of a burial where the body is lying on the back with the face upward.

Suppiluliuma I (fl. 14th century BC): Great Hittite king (reigned c. 1380–1346 BC), who dominated the history of the ancient Middle East for the greater part of four decades and raised the Hittite Kingdom to imperial power. Suppiluliumas began his reign by rebuilding the old capital, Hattusas (Bogazköy, Turkey), and consolidating the Hittite heartland. He first subdued almost the whole of Asia Minor and then took advantage of the weakness of Egypt to establish Hittite rule in northern Syria, overcoming the Mitanni. He placed his sons, based in Aleppo and Carchemish, in authority over the Syrian territories. (*syn.* Shuppiluliumash, Subbiluliuma)

surface archaeology: The recovery and analysis of unburied artifacts.

surface collection: Systematic gathering of exposed artifacts or ecofacts. It is one of two basic ground survey methods used in the surface survey of archaeological sites, the other being mapping.

surface enrichment: In metal alloy coinage, an occurrence where the more "noble" metal has a higher observed concentration at the surface of the coin than at the center. A silver-copper alloy has a higher concentration of silver, and a gold-silver alloy has a higher concentration of gold. This phenomenon is important because the composition of coins is used to locate their source and to gain other data.

surface find: An artifact found on the surface of the ground.

surface site: Area where archaeological remains can be found on the surface of the ground.

surface survey: A method of data collection in which archaeological finds are gathered from the ground surface of sites and then evaluated. Surface survey helps to establish the types of activity on the site, locate major structures, and gather information on the most densely occupied areas of the site that could be most productive for total or sample excava-tion. There are two basic kinds of surface survey: unsystematic and systematic. The former involves field walking, scanning the ground along one's path and recording the location of artifacts and surface features. Systematic survey is less subjective and involves a grid system that is walked systematically, thus making the recording of finds more accurate. Surface survey usually includes the mapping of features.

Sur Jangal: Prehistoric site in the Loralai Valley of northern Baluchistan, Pakistan, with three major phases of occupation probably belonging to the later 4th and 3rd millennium BC. Black-on-red painted wares frequently show humped (zebu) and humpless cattle; other artifacts include female figurines of Zhob type.

Surkh Kotal: Site in Afghanistan with important monuments of the Kushans, who in the 1st century AD created an empire extending from Bactria to the upper Ganges. The famous Kushan ruler Kanishka (early 2nd century AD) built the hilltop fortress. The temple contained sculptures in clay and stone, including three statues of gods or kings. Among the inscriptions from the site is a long text in the Bactrian language using cursive Greek letters.

surveying: A means of examining the surface of an archaeological site for the purpose of recording before and during excavation and for creating a preliminary analysis. This method does not destroy remains but enables study through observation and analysis. Surveying often uses geophysical methods, including measurements of variations in the Earth's magnetism. Surveying makes it possible to conduct a rapid study of fairly extensive areas. Increasing use is now being made of electronic surveying equipment and photogrammetry for surveying sites. The term "survey" also refers to the three-dimensional plotting of a site and its features and artifacts. (*syn.* survey)

Susa: Major city of western Asia, in Khuzistan, Iran, with its first four phases paralleling those of Mesopotamia ('Ubaid, Uruk, Jemdet Nasr, and Early Dynastic). It was the capital of Elam in Akkadian times (3rd, 2nd, 1st millennia BC) and again in the first as a capital of the Achaemenid Empire. Susa controlled important east-west trade routes and was the end of the Achaemenid Royal Road from Lydian Sardis. Darius built the citadel c. 500 BC. The tell is made up of four separate mounds: (1) the acropolis, which has produced most of the prehistoric material from the site; (2) the Royal City which has important Elamite remains of the 2nd millennium BC; (3) the Apadana, with a large, impressive Achaemenid palace; and (4) the Artisans' Town, of the Achaemenid period and later. It continued under the name of Seleucia after being captured by Alexander the Great in 331 BC; it later passed to the Parthians and Sassanians. Susa's characteristic early fine ceramic ware had geometric motifs painted in dark colors onto a light background. Among the more important finds of

Susa are the victory stela of Naram-Sin (Akkadian period), many Kassite kudurru, and the law code of Hammurabi (Old Babylonian period), which had been brought to Susa from Babylon after an Elamite raid. Susa was traditionally associated with Anshan (Tepe Malyan) in Fars. (*syn.* Susiana, Shushan, Seleucia)

susi temple: A kind of temple found in Urartu, which is a square, single-chambered towerlike building.

Susquehanna: Late Archaic tradition of northeast North America. It is characterized by stemmed points and knives, which may have evolved from the Piedmont tradition. Susquehanna is also the name of Iroquoian-speaking American Indians who lived in palisaded towns along the Susquehanna River in what are now New York, Pennsylvania, and Maryland. (*syn.* Susquehanna Tradition; Susquehannock, Conestoga)

Susuya: Site in southern Sakhalin, eastern Russia, an island off the coast of Siberia, dating to the last few centuries BC– first few centuries AD. It was the first appearance in that area of a true maritime economy of sea-mammal hunters using efficient harpoons. It is probably a settlement of a group coming from the north. Later, this way of life spread farther south into northern Hokkaido (Japan), where it appears in the Okhotsk culture.

Sutkagen Dor: The westernmost site of the Indus (Harappan) civilization near the shore of the Arabian Sea, west of Karachi, probably a port or trading post supporting the sea trade with the Persian Gulf. It was defended by a massive semidressed stone wall and was divided into a citadel and a lower town; the lower town shows connections with the local Kulli culture.

suttee: The rite in India whereby a widow takes her own life to accompany her deceased husband into the afterlife. The practice is often suggested when a male and female skeleton are found in the same grave, especially if the female is a significantly younger individual and is placed in a subsidiary position in the grave. This former Indian custom involved a widow burning herself, either on the funeral pyre of her dead husband or soon after his death. Sometimes, the wife was immolated before the husband's expected death in battle, and it was then called *jauhar*. Numerous suttee stones, memorials to the widows who died this way, are found all over India, the earliest dated AD 510. (*syn.* sati)

Sutton Hoo: Sixth and seventh century AD burial mounds in Suffolk, England, the richest treasure found in British soil. It was the royal cemetery of the Wuffingas, early Anglo-Saxon kings of East Anglia. The largest of the burial mounds was found to cover a Saxon boat, its form preserved only by the impression left in the sand by its vanished timbers, with the iron bolts still in their original positions. The boat had been propelled by 38 oars; there was no mast. The grave goods include a decorated helmet, sword, and shield; ceremonial whetstone; gold belt buckle; purse and cloak clasps; Millefiori glass; cloisonné garnets; Merovingian gold coins; and Byzantium silver vessels and spoons. It is likely to have been prepared as a cenotaph in honor of Redwald (d. 625), the most important East Anglian king. The treasure shows a higher cultural level and wider commercial contacts than had previously been figured for the early Saxon period in England. This type of funerary ritual is known from Migration period Europe and is described in the Anglo-Saxon poem Beowulf. The ship and artifacts are now housed in the British Museum.

Suvarnabhumi: A site or territory on the mainland of Southeast Asia, possibly identified with the Mon country in southern Myanmar (Burma) and central Thailand, to which the 3rd-century BC Indian emperor Asoka sent the two Buddhist missionaries, Sona and Uttara.

suzerainty: The dominion of a suzerain, a ruler of a dependent state; overlordship. A suzerain was a superior feudal lord to whom fealty is due (overlord) or a dominant state controlling the foreign relations of a vassal state but allowing it sovereign authority in its internal affairs.

Suzuki: Stratified site in Kodaira city, near Tokyo, Japan, with Palaeolithic materials including regularly shaped blades and edge-ground axes dated to c. 30,000 years ago.

Sventoji I: Late Mesolithic–Late Neolithic settlement site in the southeast Baltic area of Lithuania. Two cultural levels include one of the Narva culture with radiocarbon dates of c. 2700–2150 BC and a later occupation of the Rzucewo group of the Corded Ware culture group with a radiocarbon date of c. 1910 BC. The peat bog preserved textiles, wood, nets, oars, cradles, and wooden statues of deities.

Swanscombe, Barnfield Pit: British Lower Palaeolithic site on a terrace of the lower Thames Valley, North Kent, England, with a skull of possibly an archaic *Homo sapiens* with strong Neanderthal features. The skull bones are considerably thicker than those of modern European or Neanderthal skulls; the skull pieces may be the oldest of *Homo sapiens* found in Europe. More recent opinion holds that the skull is non-sapiens and has closer affinities with those of Neanderthal type. There is a succession of artifact-bearing strata of the Mindel-Riss Interglacial Period (400,000–200,000 years ago), with the earliest tools of Clactonian type. Middle Acheulian hand axes and a pointed biface assemblage were found in the Middle Gravel level, and in the Upper Loam level, Middle Acheulian tools of a more evolved form and a refined ovate assemblage. The deposits contain useful environmental evidence, including abundant mollusk and mammal remains and large assemblages of stone tools.

Swartkrans: One of three neighboring South African sites where important fossil hominid remains have been found—a short distance from Sterkfontein and Kromdraai. The valley is the richest hominid site in South Africa, and Swartkrans dates between 1.8–1 million years ago, with remains of possibly over 60 individuals of *Australopithecus robustus*. The Swartkrans artifacts are mainly relatively crude stone chopper cores, flakes, and scrapers made of quartzite and quartz, and some bone tools. The stone tools, including rough hand axes, are attributed to the Developed Oldowan. A second hominid is present, probably *Homo erectus* or *habilis*. Fire-blackened bones of 1.5–1 million years ago may be the oldest known direct evidence for the use of fire.

Swasey: The earliest known stage of lowland Maya culture, dated 2500–1300 BC. Most Swasey sites cluster in north Belize. The site at Cuello, a village of hunters and farmers, provides reasonably complete information. Maize, squash, root crops, and cacao were grown, and timber structures were built on low platform foundations plastered with stucco. The dead were buried with imported seashells and jadeite beads. Swasey pottery developed into the Mamon style of the Maya Middle Pre-Classic period.

sweat house: Special building for taking sweat baths (cleansing one's body by sweating), a common native Californian institution. There was a fire area for heating stones; water would then be poured over the stones to produce steam. It doubled as a community center for prayers and other religious activities. (*syn.* sweat-house)

sweet potato: Food plant native to tropical America and widely cultivated in tropical and warmer temperate climates, not to be confused with the yam. It is reported from sites in Peru as early as 8000 BC. During the mid-1st millennium AD, the sweet potato was carried by prehistoric voyagers into eastern Polynesia and became important in the prehistoric economies of Easter Island, the Hawaiian Islands, and New Zealand. It spread farther after Spanish settlement of the New World; since the 16th century, it has been very important to the New Guinea highlands.

Sweet Track: Neolithic timber track preserved in peat at Somerset Levels, England. It ran for 1,800 meters across swamp from Somerset Levels to Westhay Island and is dated to 3807/3806 BC. It is considered Europe's oldest road.

swidden agriculture: Agricultural technique whereby forest vegetation is cut down annually, let dry, and burned to prepare fields for crops. The method enriches the soil with nutrients from the ash, but the fields are productive for only a few years—at which time it is necessary to change fields. Swidden agriculture is most common to Mesoamerica. The foremost benefit of this procedure is that the plot is relatively weed free at first. (*syn.* swidden farming; slash-and-burn agriculture; swidden; shifting cultivation; swidden cultivation)

Swiderian: Late Upper Palaeolithic industry of Poland, known from sites such as Calowanie and Swidry Wielkie. They are associated with dune deposits dating to the end of the Pleistocene c. 11,000–9000 BP They are characterized by elongated tanged points, burins, and scrapers.

Swiderian point: Type of stone point made on a blade and having a stemmed base flaked on both sides. It is characteristic of the Swiderian industry of Poland (Upper Palaeolithic, c. 11,000–9000 BP).

Swidry: Upper Palaeolithic sites on the Vistula River, Poland, dated to c. 11,000 BP (Pleistocene) and assigned to the Swiderian culture. There are Swiderian points, scrapers, and burins.

Swieciechów flint: Variety of flint found in the Holy Cross Mountains of central Poland, used by the Funnel Beaker culture and distributed over a broad area. It was commonly made into very large blades and axes.

sword: A weapon evolved from daggers in the Bronze Age, becoming longer and made with different kinds of grips. It was used for slashing and thrusting and has a broader blade than a rapier, plus a flanged hilt. Single-edged swords are rare, and they are more often called sabers or falchions. Sword classifications are based on the form of the hilt and the shoulder. It was probably developed in Hungary and then spread to the Aegean, where it is found in shaft graves at Mycenae, c. 1650 BC, and the rest of Europe and western Asia. From then until the development of firearms, it remained one of the main weapons of war.

Sybaris: Ancient Greek city in southern Italy on the Gulf of Tarentum, known for its wealth and the luxury it enjoyed, contributing to the modern meaning of "sybaritic." Founded c. 720 BC by Achaeans and Troezenians, it quickly became prosperous. It was destroyed by Croton (510 and c. 448 BC), and then rebuilt a third time with Athenian help. A new settlement, Thurii, was founded in 443 BC by Pericles of Athens. The Sybarites who were then expelled founded a fourth Sybaris farther south on the Traeis (Trionto) River. After the Punic Wars, a Roman colony named Copia was established at Thurii, and occupation seems to have continued until the 4th century AD. The original Sybaris founded other colonies, notably Paestum. Pottery and structural evidence support occupation from the 8th century BC; from Copia, there remains an early imperial theater and some residences. (*syn.* Thurii, Copia)

syenite: Any of a class of igneous rocks essentially composed of an alkali feldspar and a ferromagnesian mineral; the name was first used by Pliny the Elder.

syllabary: A system of written symbols used to represent the syllables of the words of a language. Writing systems that use syllabaries include modern Japanese, Cherokee, the ancient Cretan scripts (Linear A, Linear B), and various Indic and cuneiform writing systems. Some syllabaries have separate symbols for each possible syllable that may occur in the language; others use a system of consonant symbols that include an inherent vowel. Most languages would require about 80 symbols to cover all syllables in use. The unit of a syllabary is sometimes called syllabogram, which may be of these types: vowel, consonant-vowel, vowel-consonant, consonant-vowel-consonant, or consonant-vowel-consonant-vowel.

syllabic: A term describing scripts, in which each of the signs represents a syllable, as in Linear A and B.

syllabogram: The unit of a syllabary, which may be of these types: vowel, consonant-vowel, vowel-consonant, consonant-vowel-consonant, or consonant-vowel-consonant-vowel. In the Cretan scripts of the 2nd millennium BC, Linear A and B, a sign denoting by means of an arbitrary drawing an open syllable.

symbol: Expression that is arbitrarily associated with what it conveys; an arbitrary or conventional sign used in writing to represent operations, quantities, elements, relations, or qualities.

symbolic anthropology: A research perspective that gives prime attention to the role of symbols in society. Culture is a system of inherited conceptions expressed in symbolic forms, which are used to communicate and develop knowledge and attitudes. The function of culture then is to impose meaning on the world and make it understandable. The role of symbolic anthropologists is to try to interpret the guiding symbols of each culture. In this view, culture becomes a public phenomenon transcending the cognitive realization of any single individual. This field is based mainly on the work of Clifford Geertz.

Symbolkeramik: Pottery ware of the Spanish Copper/Early Bronze Ages of Almeria, as at Los Millares, decorated with stylized designs, especially oculi (rayed sun) motifs. The designs are thought to hold symbolic meanings.

symmetry analysis: A mathematical analytical approach to the decorative style of symmetry. Patterns are divided into two distinct groups or symmetry classes: 17 classes for those patterns that repeat motifs horizontally, and 46 classes for those that repeat them horizontally and vertically. Such studies suggest that the choice of motif arrangement in a particular culture is very important.

symposium: In ancient Greece, a males-only drinking party often after a banquet. The symposium is often a scene on Greek pottery. There was music, conversation, and sex.

syncretism: A process by which two or more deities were fused into the object of a single cult, which was a fundamental aspect of the development of Egyptian religion.

synchronic: Pertaining to phenomena at one point in time, occurring simultaneously or at the same time; referring to a single period. This approach is not primarily concerned with change and often refers to the correlation of events or surfaces of stratigraphic units. (*syn.* synchronous)

synostosis: The joining of separate pieces of bone in human skeletons; the union of two or more separate bones to form a single bone. The precise timing of such processes is an important indicator of age.

synthesis: In archaeology, the assemblage and analysis of data before interpretation.

Syracuse: A Corinthian colony and principal port founded traditionally c. 734 BC on the east coast of Sicily. The earliest occupation was on the island of Ortygia; later settlement was on the mainland in the Achradina area. Early Palaeolithic material occurs in the Great Harbor. Syracuse was the leader of Greek cities in Sicily and had many struggles with Athens and Carthage, becoming capital of Roman Sicily in the 3rd century BC. Siding with Hannibal in the Second Punic War was a mistake, which led to a long siege by Rome. In the early Christian era, Syracuse became something of a religious center, and there are extensive catacombs. From the 5th century onward, the city's civilization disintegrated under the general chaos of the western empire. Surviving remains include the archaic Doric temples of Zeus and Apollo, Temple of Athena, the Greek theater, and a 3rd-century AD amphitheater. Evidence also survives for an extensive fortification system of Epipolae, a triangular-plan rocky plateau that was unified with the city in some 27 kilometers of walling; the fort of Euryalos was at the highest point.

Syria-Palestine: Geographical area of western Asia making up the southern and northern sections of the Levant, bordered by the Sinai Peninsula to the southwest, the Mediterranean to the west, Anatolia to the north, and the Arabian Desert and Mesopotamia to the south and east. This eastern Mediterranean seaboard has parallel ranges of mountains and great river valleys and is part of the same geological fault as the Great Rift Valley in Africa, leading from the Red Sea up to the Dead Sea, the Jordan Valley, and the Sea of Galilee.

system: Any organization that functions through the interdependence of its parts; a regularly interacting or interdependent group of items forming a unified whole.

systematics: In archaeology, the defining of a system of classification for archaeological units for a particular purpose.

systematic sampling: A probabilistic sampling technique, which uses a grid of equally spaced sample units, for example, selecting every other square. It is a refinement of random sampling in which one unit is chosen, then others at regular intervals from the first. The sample incorporates randomness and determinacy by specifying that the random selection of a case example has to occur in a certain group of cases. (*syn.* systematic sample)

systematic settlement survey: The reconnaissance of an archaeological site based on a sampling design, which is intended to ensure that all types of areas in the region are surveyed.

system of communication: The underlying rationale of language, to communicate information among individuals.

systems-ecological approach: An approach to archaeology that involves three models of cultural change: systems models, cultural ecology, and multilinear evolution.

systems thinking: A method of formal analysis in which the object of study is viewed as making up distinct analytical subunits. In archaeology, it is a form of explanation in which a society or culture is seen through the interaction and interdependence of its component parts. These system parameters may include population size, settlement pattern, crop production, technology.

Syuren' I: Upper Palaeolithic cave site in the Crimea, Ukraine, with elements typical of the Middle Palaeolithic and Aurignacian. It is one of the rare Upper Palaeolithic sites of the Crimea.

Szakalhát-Lebo group: Middle Neolithic culture of the Tisza River valley in southeast Hungary, succeeding the Alföld Linear pottery and preceding the Tisza culture, between c. 4100–3800 BC. The occupation includes a level with late Alföld Linear pottery and a level with Szakalhát pottery. The two main pottery decorative styles are wide incised curvilinear and dark burnished. The settlements have small rectangular single-room structures.

Szegar-Tuzkoves: A later Neolithic settlement near Szentes, southeast Hungary. There is an occupation of the Szakalhát (Alföld Linear pottery) of the late 5th millennium BC and a Tisza culture level dated to the 4th millennium BC. Several complete Tisza culture house plans have been excavated, some with bucrania on the gable ends. Also found was the "Sickle God," a complete, seated, fired-clay male figurine carrying a sickle.

Szeleta Cave: Cave site on the Szinva River in the Bükk Mountains of Hungary, occupied from the Middle Palaeolithic. The Upper Palaeolithic with laurel-leaf points and scrapers is dated c. 41,700 bp, and there are Neolithic remains.

Szeletian: Early Upper Palaeolithic industry of central Europe with bifacial foliated points and side scrapers, but it has also been applied to the industries with foliated points, which mark the transition from the Middle Palaeolithic to Upper Palaeolithic periods throughout the eastern part of central Europe. It appears to have developed from the Middle Palaeolithic (Micoquian). The type site is Szeleta Cave in the Bükk Mountains in Hungary. The culture seems to date between 45,000–25,000 BC, the middle of the last glacial. Later assemblages contain end scrapers and retouched blades.

Szelim: Cave site near the Danube River in central Hungary of the Middle Palaeolithic (beginning of last glacial), Late Upper Palaeolithic, and Neolithic.

Tt

taberna: Roman term for a room opening on to a street or on to a portico or stoa, used as a workshop or shop.

tablero-talud: In architecture, a sloped basal apron surmounted by a recessed vertical tablet. The talud-tablero architectural motif is typical of Teotihuacán culture: On each body or tier of a stepped pyramid is a rectangular frontal panel (tablero) supported by a sloping batter (talud). The tablero is surrounded by a kind of projecting frame, and the recessed portion of the panel usually bears a polychrome mural applied to the stuccoed surface.

tablet: Any flat surface for inscriptions, especially those on which cuneiform inscriptions were written. Tablets were normally of clay but were also made of stone or metal. The shape and size varied according to the nature of the inscription and the period when the tablet was inscribed. An impressed tablet is one bearing notations impressed with tokens or the blunt end of a stylus. These tablets were referred to in literature as "numerical tablets" as they noted units of goods. An incised tablet bears notations traced with the sharp end of a stylus. A pictographic tablet is one bearing notations traced with the sharp end of a stylus; these two types of tablets had signs in the shape of the things they represented. The earliest known books are the clay tablets of Mesopotamia (and the papyrus rolls of Egypt) dating from the early 3rd millennium BC. (*syn.* clay tablet)

tablinum: A central room opening off the atrium of a Roman house.

taap knife: A type of saw knife used in Western Australia. It was made of small stone chips mounted in a row on a wooden handle.

Tabon Caves: Large complex of limestone caves in southwest Palawan, the Philippines, which have produced a sequence ranging from c. 22,000 BC to the late metal age. Tabon Cave itself has a flake industry of early Australian type dating from 30,000–9,000 years ago, in association with early Aus-

traloid skeletal remains dated c. 22,000–20,000 BC. A simple blade technology appears in Duyong Cave c. 5000 BC, and other caves continue through the Neolithic (c. 3800–500 BC) and into a rich jar-burial tradition elsewhere in the Philippines. There are also later deposits with Chinese ceramic imports.

Tabun: Cave site on Mount Carmel, Israel, with Neanderthal-like remains and Tayacian, Final Acheulian, Jabrudian, Amudian, and Levalloiso-Mousterian levels. Radiocarbon dates are c. 51,000–38,800 BP.

Taforalt: Large cave in eastern Morocco with a blade industry of c. 22,000 bp (Mousterian) through Aterian to a long succession of Iberomaurusian phases. A large Iberomaurusian cemetery and shell midden have been excavated. The cemetery had 185 people and is of the Mechta-Afalou type (c. 11,900 bp).

Tagalagal: Neolithic site in northeast Niger, dating to c. 9300 bp. Burin-like flakes, arrowheads, and grinding tools have been found, along with ceramics with some of the oldest dates in the Sahara.

Tagar culture: Culture in south Siberia in the region of Minusinsk, c. 700–200/100 BC. The Bronze Age Karasuk culture was replaced by the Tagar culture, which endured until the 2nd century BC, producing an art of animal motifs related to that of the Scythians of southern European Russia. They also had broad daggers. On the Yenisey River, the Tagar culture was replaced by the Tashtyk culture, dating from the 1st–4th centuries AD.

Tagua-Tagua: Lakeside site in central Chile with stone artifacts (unifacial tools, blades) of a Levallois-Mousterian type, and bone tools have been found in association with mastodon, horse, and deer bones, c. 9400 BC or older. The combination indicates a Palaeo-Indian presence at an early date. Butchering scars on bone and other lithic evidence strongly suggest a switch to the Big Game Hunting tradition. (*syn.* Tagua-tagua)

Taharqo (fl. 7th century BC**):** The fourth king (reigned 690–664 BC) of the 25th Dynasty of Egypt, who inherited the throne of Egypt and Nubia from his cousin Shabitqo (or Shebitku, 702–690 BC). He undertook considerable construction at Karnak, Kawa, Medinet Habu, and Sanam; he was buried in a large pyramid at Nuri. (*syn.* Taharka, Taharqa, Tarku, Tarakos, Tirhaka)

taiga: Subarctic boreal forest; open coniferous forest in the northern latitudes. Taiga grows on swampy ground that is commonly covered with lichen. It is the characteristic vegetation of the subpolar region spanning northern Eurasia, between the colder tundra zone to the north and the warmer temperate zone to the south. (*syn.* boreal forest)

Taima-Taima: Site in northwest Venezuela, dated from 12,000–15,000 BP, with bifacial tools, scrapers, blades, and leaf-shaped points. Mastodon bones were also found. It may be a pre-Clovis occupation.

Taino: Arawakan Indians who occupied much of the Greater Antilles, especially Hispaniola, at the time of Columbus's arrival. There were permanent villages of up to 1,000 houses (of logs and poles with thatched roofs), some built on open plazas. Government was by hereditary chiefs and sub-chiefs. There were classes of nobles, commoners, and serfs. Cultivation was based on slash-and-burn techniques, and they were skilled carvers in wood and stone. The characteristic pottery was of the Chi-Coid series. They became extinct within 100 years after the Spanish conquest of the late 15th century.

Taipivai: Valley on the island of Nuku Hiva, Marquesas Islands, Polynesia, famous for a novelized account of the life of its inhabitants, *Typee*, written by Herman Melville in 1846. There are many stone structures, including Vahangeku'a and anthropomorphic stone statues—some of the largest stone structures in the Marquesas. There are also megalithic terraced dance floors (tohua) and temples. (*syn.* Taipivai Valley)

Tairona: Late prehistoric culture of northeast Colombia in the Sierra Nevada de Santa Marta. The Taironas were organized into small political states (chiefdoms) and had one of the most advanced cultures of the Caribbean mainland. Their crafts were ceramic ware (black and red painted with zoomorphic design and appliqué); stone utensils (metates); bone and shell ornaments; and beads, buttons, and jewelry made of gold, copper, and gold-copper alloy (tumbaga). Most sites, like Pueblito and Buritaca-200, have hundreds of stone foundations for circular houses. There are also remains of tombs, stone-built retaining walls, bridges, stairways, roads, agricultural terraces, and irrigation canals. A central feature of most villages was a ceremonial building, usually on a platform-mound, and often of dressed masonry. The town site at Pueblito had all these features and, in addition, paved streets, the remains of large irrigation projects, and urn burials. Specialized funerary vessels were often modeled with life forms similar to Mesoamerican motifs. Populations in the thousands occupied Tairona towns and villages at the time of the Spanish conquest.

Taiwan: Island 100 miles (160 km) off the southeast coast of the China mainland. Taiwan had a native aboriginal population of Malayo-Polynesian ancestry, and it occupies an important position in the prehistory of Southeast Asia. Evidence for pre-Neolithic settlement is from c. 3500 BC, followed by a Neolithic culture (Ta-p'en-k'eng culture). That culture had cord-marked pottery and was related to contemporary rice-cultivating cultures on the adjacent mainland. Linguistically, it represents the earliest recognizable phase of Austronesian language in the islands of Southeast Asia. Later Taiwan Neolithic cultures also show close connections with south China and the Philippines. Major Chinese settlement of the island did not occur until the 17th century AD. (*syn.* Formosa)

Takamatsuzuka: Mounded tomb (tumulus) of the Kofun period, which is about 18 meters in diameter and 5 meters high, dating to the 7th century AD in Nara Prefecture, Japan. Excavation revealed paintings of human and mythological figures and celestial bodies, and murals of Chinese directional symbols, on the walls and ceiling of the burial chamber. Close similarities to the Tang are seen, and a Tang mirror and some gold- and silver-plated ornaments have been found.

Takht-i-Sulaiman: Site in Azerbaijan, northwest Iran, which was an important religious site in the Parthian, Sassanian, and Islamic periods. In the Parthian period, it was surrounded by a mud-brick wall; the Sassanians added a further outer wall of stone. To the Sassanian period belong a palace and a fire temple, which was the focus of a pilgrimage center. The Gushnasp fire was the ancient fire of the Magi (in Media), but it came to be the symbol of the monarchic and religious unity. (*syn.* ancient Shiz; Takht-i-Suleyman)

Talasea: Important obsidian source in western Melanesia, on the north coast of New Britain, occurring from 9000 BC (Late Pleistocene) at Matenkupkum and Matenbek. The obsidian was widely distributed in Lapita times (c. 1500–1 BC) to as far as New Caledonia, 2,600 kilometers away.

talatat: Typical small sandstone building blocks used in Egypt for the temples of Amenophis IV (Akhenaten) at Aten at el-Amarnà and Karnak and other temples of the Amarnà period (c. 1352–1336 BC). It is the Arabic word for three handbreadths, describing the length of these stones that were used for rapid construction. They are often decorated in relief. After return to the orthodox worship of Amen, these monuments were dismantled and their components then used by Akhenaten's successors as rubble core in later buildings. (*syn.* talatate)

talayot: Massive dry-stone towers of the Bronze and Iron

Ages of the Balearic Islands, mainly Majorca and Minorca, c. 1000–300 BC. In its oldest and most simple form, a talayot is a round tower built of large stone blocks. It may be solid or enclose a single cell or chamber roofed by corbelling; there may be niches in the wall. In other examples, the roof is of flat slabs supported by a central pillar. From c. 850 BC, square talayots were also built, and some of these have a second chamber above the one on the ground floor. Many later became the center of a small village of dry-stone houses, enclosed by walls of cyclopean masonry. The architecture shows resemblances to contemporary structures in Sardinia (the *nuraghe*) and in Corsica. The precise function of talayots is unknown, but they could have been used as lookout towers or as refuges in times of trouble. The tower has also given its name to the local Bronze Age culture. (*syn.* Talayotic culture)

Talgai: The site of the first human fossil found in Australia, in southeast Queensland. The cranium belongs to the robust group and has not yet been firmly dated, although sediments in which it was found have been dated to 14,000–16,000 bp. It resembles findings in Kow Swamp. Some estimate the skull to be 25,000 years old. (*syn.* Talgai cranium)

talisman: A charm or fetish thought to produce unusual, extraordinary happenings. The object often bears a sign or engraved character and is thought to act as a charm to avert evil and bring good fortune. A talisman may be worn to protect a person from dangers.

Tall al-Ahmar: The site of the capital of the Aramaean state of Bit-Adini in Mesopotamia. From the 10th century BC, the Assyrian kings controlled the Syrian and Cilician states from this provincial capital and garrison town. (*syn.* Tell Ahmar; Til Barsib (Barsip), Kar-Shulmanashared (Kar-Salmanasar))

talud-tablero: Important architectural features of Mesoamerican stepped pyramids in Mexico. Each terrace consists of a vertical panel with a recessed inset and a sloping batter or apron (talud) surmounted by a horizontal, rectangular panel with insert (tablero). The technique was used primarily at Teotihuacán, where it is the dominant style for temple pyramids, and in a modified form elsewhere—Kaminaljuyu (Palangana Complex) in the Guatemalan highlands, Tikal, and the temple buildings at Chichen Itza.

talus: Rock fragments transported downslope by flowing water or falling off the cliff from which they were wedged by the ice and accumulating as angular debris at the base of steep slopes. A natural slope formed by the accumulation of rock debris.

Tamar Hat: Cave site in Algeria with Ibermaurusian remains c. 20,600 bp and occupation on and off over 5,000 years.

Tamaulipas: A state in northeastern Mexico on the gulf of Mexico, with a series of caves having evidence of incipient agriculture in the Infernillo phase. The earliest period had crude pebble tools (preprojectile points) and was overlain by the Lerma phase c. 7000 BC, which had projectile points similar to those of the Old Cordilleran tradition. Desert Culture materials have been found associated with the earliest known cultivated plants in the New World. Here, in the Infernillo phase, it appears that Native American squash, peppers, and perhaps beans were being cultivated as early as 6500 BC. Manos and metates are found in increasing numbers in later phases, as well as flexed, wrapped burials. An early cereal, the foxtail millet, was probably domesticated around 4000 BC in Tamaulipas, but it was superseded by primitive maize, c. 3000–2200 BC, during the La Perra phase.

Tamaya Mellet: A site west of the Air Mountains in the Tamesna of Niger, Africa, where pottery occurs in one of its earliest known Saharan contexts, c. 7300 BC. The sherds were found in association with barbed bone harpoon heads. Also, bone harpoons associated with lucustrine fauna have been dated to c. 9400 bp.

tambo or tampu: In the Inca road system, a way station; these were set a day's travel apart and had storehouses and resthouses. More elaborate way stations were located 4–5 days' travel apart. A runner (*chaski*) was stationed at each tambo for carrying messages in relays throughout the empire.

Tambo Colorado: Well-preserved Inca walled town in the Pisco Valley, southern Peru, probably an administrative center or military barracks. It is on an important road connecting the coast with Vilcas Guaman. It was constructed in terraces of adobe on stone foundations; traces of red and yellow paint are still visible on the walls. On the southern side is a ceremonial center and associated buildings. It was abandoned shortly after the Spanish conquest.

Tambo Viejo: Large site on the southern coast of Peru occupied in the early Nasca phases of the Early Intermediate period and reoccupied during Inca times.

Tambralinga: Early Indianized state of peninsular Thailand on the Malay Peninsula, which existed in the later 1st and 2nd millennia AD. The kingdom may already have existed in the 2nd century and is attested by 6th-century inscriptions. It was centered around Nakhon si Thammarat and eventually recognized the suzerainty of the Thai Kingdom of Sukhotai.

Tammuz: Consort of the Sumerian goddess Ishtar, who was prominent in the fertility rituals of the Sacred Marriage. On death, he became a god of the underworld. The earliest known mention of Tammuz is in texts dating to the early part of the Early Dynastic III period (c. 2600–2334 BC), but his cult was probably older. The cult is attested for most of the major cities of Sumer in the 3rd and 2nd millennia BC. He was an agricultural deity, viewed as the power of the grain in texts of the Assyrians and Sabaeans. (*syn.* Dumuzi)

Tamworth: The site of a palace built by Offa, 8th-century king of Anglo-Saxon Mercia. In the early 10th century, it was reestablished as a burh town. Parts of the burh defenses and a gate have been found and a mill believed to be part of the 8th-century royal complex. Waterlogged conditions have preserved many of the structures. By Anglo-Saxon standards, the Tamworth mill was large and sophisticated, probably driven by a horizontal wheel.

Tanagra: Site in Boeotia, Greece, where a large cache of finely worked, cast terra-cotta figurines was found in Hellenistic-period cemeteries spanning the period from c. 340–150 BC. There are also Mycenaean chamber tombs in the area. The nearly circular hill of the ancient ruined city was first occupied by the Gephyreans, an Athenian clan. It became the chief town of the eastern Boeotians, with lands extending to the Gulf of Euboea. Tanagra probably assumed leadership of the Boeotian confederacy following the Greco-Persian Wars when it took over the clay-working industry of devastated Thebes.

tang: Narrow projection or prong from the base of a tool or weapon, which could be used to secure it to a handle or shaft.

T'ang Dynasty: One of the greatest Chinese dynasties, ruling from its capital Ch'ang-an (Sian), over a large portion of central Asia from AD 618–907. It succeeded the short-lived Sui Dynasty and developed a successful form of government and administration and stimulated a cultural and artistic golden age. The dynasty reached its peak in the early 8th century. (*syn.* Tang)

tanged point cultures: A term once used for the series of cultures of the Postglacial period, whose tool kits include small tanged or shouldered points, such as the Ahrensburgian and Hamburgian.

Tanis: Most important archaeological site in the northeastern Nile Delta of Egypt and capital of the 14th nome of Lower Egypt in the Late period (747–332 BC) and, at one time, of the entire country. There are massive mud-brick temple enclosure walls built by Ramesside and 21st-Dynasty pharaohs. The site is best known for the rich royal tombs of the 21st and 22nd Dynasties of c. 1070–715 BC, built near the great temple of Amon. Silver coffins, gold masks, and jewelry in gold and silver have been found, and the tombs and some sarcophagi were reused from earlier periods. The Tanite Dynasty is the 21st Dynasty of Egypt (1075–945 BC). The pharaohs of the 22nd Dynasty continued to reside at Tanis until the collapse of their shrinking domain in 712 BC. (*syn.* ancient Djanet; biblical Zoan; modern San al-Hajar al-Qibliyah)

Tanit: Chief goddess of Carthage, equivalent of Astarte, who was a mother goddess, represented mainly by fertility symbols. She was probably the consort of Baal Hammon (or Amon), the chief god of Carthage. Children, probably firstborn, were sacrificed to Tanit. Evidence of the practice has been found, when a *tofet* (a sanctuary for the sacrifice of children) was discovered. (*syn.* Tinith, Tinnit, Tint)

Tanum: Site of prehistoric rock art in Bohuslän, Sweden. The carved designs, especially oared ships, *hällristningar,* are pecked on glacially smooth rock surfaces. Tanum art is mainly from the later Bronze Age. Ancient burial grounds attest to the existence of Stone, Bronze, and Iron Age settlements in Bohuslän, which is also reputedly the scene of the second part of the Old English epic "Beowulf."

Tanutamon (reigned 664–656 BC): Last of the 25th Dynasty pharaohs, successor of Taharqa, who led an invasion of Lower Egypt and captured Memphis. He defeated and killed the Assyrian-backed Saite ruler Nekau I in 664 BC. In 663 BC, the Assyrian king Ashurbanipal drove Tanutamon out, sacking Thebes. (*syn.* Tantamani, Tanwetamani)

t'ao t'ieh: Chinese term for a Neolithic design put on jade objects of the Liangzhu culture and then used on bronze in the Shang period. In the Shang (18th–12th century BC) and Chou (1111–c. 900 BC) Dynasties, it was a zoomorphic monster mask seen full face with a gaping mouth and no lower jaw, the eyes, ears, and horns placed symmetrically on either side of a vertical frontal line. T'ao t'ieh often consisted of two kui (dragons facing each other, also symmetrical, with body in profile, winding tail, and clawed feet). The t'ao t'ieh is the most important of a number of such patterns used to decorate bronze vessels. (*syn.* taotie, t'ao-t'ie)

tapa: Paperlike barkcloth of the Pacific Islands, made by soaking and then beating the inner bark of the paper mulberry tree. It was used for paintings in Oceanic arts.

Taperinha: Shell midden near Santarem, Brazil, with the oldest pottery in the New World—dated to the 8th millennium BP.

taphonomy: The study of the transformation of organic remains after death to form fossil and archaeological remains. The study includes the processes that disturb and damage bones before, during, and after burial—burial, decay, and preservation. The term combines the Greek word for tomb or burial (*taphos*) with that for law (*nomos*). The focus is on an understanding of the processes resulting in the archaeological record.

Taputapuatea: Traditionally, the most sacred marae of eastern Polynesia, on Raiatea, Society Islands. It is associated with the worship of the god Oro. The surviving platform (*ahu*) is 40 meters by 7 meters and is faced with coral slabs. The platform's shell is dated to the 17th century AD.

Tara: Site in Meath County northwest of Dublin, the Hill of Tara, which was the original residence of the pre-Christian and early Christian High Kings of Ireland. The oldest monument is a decorated Neolithic passage grave with radiocarbon dates ranging from 3000–2400 BC, but most of the burial mounds and enclosures are of the early historic period. There was a settlement on the site as early as the 1st century AD, but Tara did not become a political capital until the time of Cormac Mac Airt in the 3rd century. Bronze Age remains from Tara include about 50 single graves with food vessels or urns, mostly with cremations, although one inhumation was accompanied by a rich necklace of copper, jet, amber, and faience beads. Tara became an important settlement site in the Iron Age and early historic period. To this period belong a large hill fort (the Royal Enclosure) and a series of smaller forts and burial mounds. The site was a royal capital when St. Patrick visited it in the 5th century. It remained the seat of the high kingship until about 1000 AD, when it was finally overthrown.

Taranto: A city at the head of the Ionian Sea in southern Italy, first occupied by a Neolithic village with Serra d'Alto ware. This was succeeded by the Apennine culture, to which around 1250 BC was added a colony of Mycenaeans. Trade up the Adriatic continued after the fall of Mycenaean Greece, distributing Terramara bronzework from northern Italy. In the 8th century BC (traditional date 706), Greek settlers from Sparta and Laconia conquered the Messapian village and founded the new Taras on the peninsula. It soon became one of the leading cities of Magna Graecia, and its inhabitants founded several other coastal cities. Taranto reached the peak of power and prosperity in the 4th century BC under Archytas. The city then suffered in a series of wars, culminating in its submission to Rome in 272 BC. During the Second Punic War, it fell into the hands of the Carthaginian general Hannibal but was recaptured and plundered by the Romans in 209. It declined under the Roman Empire. Very little survives today because both the Greek and the Roman towns lie beneath the modern city. Votive and sanctuary terra-cottas and tombs with decorated sarcophagi and funerary couches have been found. (*syn.* Greek Taras, Roman Tarentum)

Tarascan: An independent state of the Late Post-Classic Period centered in the mountains of the Michoacán province of Mexico, one of the very few to successfully resist Aztec incursions. It is also the name of the people there, who were linguistically unrelated to any other Mesoamerican group. Their capital, Tzinzunzan, was built overlooking Lake Patzcuaro and appears to be a ceremonial center consisting of a huge platform mound surmounted by five pyramids. Fine gold and tumbaga jewelry and well-made copper and bronze tools have been found. The Tarascan state, with its later capital of Pátzcuaro, survived into historic times. They reached a level of social and political organization comparable to that of the Aztec and the Maya. (*syn.* Tarascans, Purépecha)

Tardenoisian: A Mesolithic culture of southwest France, which followed the Sauveterrian and which was characterized by the use of small stone tools with geometric shapes (trapeze-shaped chisel-ended arrowheads and small blades). Tardenoisian and similar industries are found from Iberia to central Europe and span the period from the early 6th millennium BC until the arrival of the first Neolithic farmers. Fère-en-Tardenois, in the Paris basin, is the type site of the Tardenoisian. (*syn.* Tardenois)

Tardiguet: Site on the Morocco coast near Rabat, with early stone tools of simple Oldowan type. There are no hand axes; the commonest tools are choppers. They belong to Stage 1 of the Pebble Tool culture and are probably among the earliest cases of toolmaking known.

Tarentum: Colony of ancient Sparta in southeast Italy. It was founded in the late 8th century BC. Excavations have found Mycenaean pottery, tombs of the Archaic period with Greek pottery, and Apulian pottery and terra-cotta figurines produced in the Classical period. Rome put down resistance in Italy and took Tarentum by siege in 272 BC.

taro: Large herbaceous plant of tropical Asian origin, rich in starch and a staple food in the Pacific Islands and Oceania. The tubers are consumed as cooked vegetable and made into puddings and breads and also made into the Polynesian poi, a thin, pasty, highly digestible mass of fermented taro starch. (*syn.* eddo, dasheen)

Tarquinia: Great Etruscan city in Tuscany, Italy, famous for tombs with a series of grave paintings from the 6th–1st centuries BC and the remains of a wall and base of the great central temple of the 4th–3rd centuries BC. Traditionally, the earliest of the cities of Etruria there was an earlier Villanovan settlement (10th–7th centuries BC). It is also important for its contribution to early Rome of that city's early kings, the Tarquins, as well as a cultural and technological heritage. It did not come under Roman control until 353 BC. The Villanovan burials are especially rich in bronze artifacts, particularly horse and chariot items, shields, and helmets. The Etruscan painted tombs are usually approached by steeply descending dromoi, and they show scenes of funeral banqueting and games, and later the demons of the underworld. Sarcophagi mostly have relief decoration. The city shows traces of a grid plan, tufa city wall, and the remains of the 4th–3rd centuries BC temple (Ara della Regina). (*syn.* Roman Tarquinii; Etruscan Tarkhuna)

Tarragona: Important city of Roman Spain, later capital of the province of Hispania Tarraconensis, with the first identifiable occupation by the local Iberians. In 218 BC, it was captured by Roman generals and was transformed into one of the earliest Roman strongholds in Spain. Augustus recuperated there during his Cantabrian wars, where an altar and temple were later dedicated to him. The emperors Hadrian and Trajan endowed Tarragona with power and cultural prestige, while its flax trade and other industries made it one of the richest seaports of the Roman Empire. It prospered until being sacked by the Franks in AD 260. Remains surviving include the Republican-period walling, Augustus' palace, an amphitheater, a section of aqueduct (the Devil's Bridge), and a Romano-Christian cemetery. (*syn.* Kallipolis; Iberian Cissa or Cissis; Carthaginian Tarchon; Roman Tarraco)

Tarsus: Prehistoric settlement in coastal Cilicia, southeast Turkey (Anatolia), the site of the Mound of Gözlüküle (Gözlü Kale). It was occupied from the 5th–1st millennia BC with a sequence paralleling that of Mersin. This included a late Neolithic, Chalcolithic, Early Bronze Age, Middle Bronze Age, Late Bronze Age, Iron Age, and early medieval period occupations. Tarsus' prosperity between the 5th century BC and the Arab invasions in the 7th century AD was based primarily on its fertile soil, its position at the southern end of the Cilician Gates, and the great harbor of Rhegma, which enabled Tarsus to establish strong connections with the Levant.

Tartanga: Site on the lower Murray River, South Australia, with small cores, scrapers, bone points, grinding stones, and tula adze flakes dated to c. 4000 BC. Skeletons of two juveniles found have some cranial features similar to the robust Talgai skull.

Tartaria: Late Neolithic site in Transylvania, Romania, with a Vinca pit containing three controversial clay tablets in a Tordos level. They bear incised signs, are unbaked, and resemble pictographic signs from Jemdet-Nasr and Uruk. However, there is approximately a 1000-year discrepancy between the Tartaria tablets and the later Mesopotamian symbols.

Tartessos: Early trading kingdom at the mouth of the Guadalquivir Valley in southwestern Spain, site of a semimythical city referred to by ancient writers as a source of gold, silver, tin, and lead. Tartessos, in fact, was the late Bronze Age society that included the mines of the Rio Tinto in its territory. There is strong circumstantial evidence in the Huelva hoard, for trading with Sardinia, Sicily, Cyprus, the Phoenicians, France, Brittany, and Ireland c. 800–550 BC. It has given its name to the Tartessian culture of the early 1st millennium BC, which is essentially Phoenician with Etruscan and Greek admixture and whose influence in Spain, on the civilized Iberians of the east coast and the less advanced peoples of the center and north, was considerable. (*syn.* biblical Tarshish, Greek Tarsis; Tartessus)

Taruga: Settlement site on the slopes of the Jos Plateau in central Nigeria of the Iron Age. Terra-cotta figurines of Nok type were found in association with domestic pottery and iron-smelting debris c. 5th–3rd centuries BC. The iron-smelting debris and furnaces are among the oldest discovered in West Africa.

Tarxien: Late Neolithic temple complex in eastern Malta with four temples dated c. 3500–2500 BC. Many stone slabs in the walls and courtyards are decorated with relief carvings. The most remarkable find is the lower half of an enormous statue of a "fat lady," known also from figurines and thought to represent a goddess, and is 2.75 meters high. The temples were abandoned c. 2500 BC. In the ruins, Bronze Age people placed a rich cremation cemetery, dating 2500–1500 BC. The Bronze Age culture is named the Tarxien Cemetery culture after this site.

Tasaday: Small group of forest food collectors isolated in the rain forests of Mindanao, the Philippines, first reported by anthropological investigators in 1971 though authenticity has been questioned. Numbering 25 at the time, the Tasadays have a simple technology and food-gathering strategy. Linguistic studies suggest that they may have descended from an original horticultural population and may have simplified their own culture during about 700 years of isolation. The Tasaday were dressed only in loincloths and skirts made of orchid leaves, used only crude stone tools (axes and scrapers) and wooden implements (fire drills and digging sticks), and had no weapons for hunting or war.

Tasian: Possibly the oldest-known cultural phase in Upper Egypt, c. 4500 BC, known from evidence on the east bank of the Nile River at al-Badari and at Deir Tasa. A settlement of primitive farmers, it is now regarded as at best a local variant of the Badarian culture.

Tasmania: Island that was part of the Australian continent during the late Pleistocene, then separated by rising sea levels that formed the Bass Strait about 9000 BC. Occupation of southwestern Tasmania by 30,000 bp is now well established. At the time of European contact, Tasmanian aborigines had a simple tool kit of stone flakes and core scrapers, pebble choppers, wooden pointed spears, digging sticks, clubs, and throwing sticks. They lacked all the post-Pleistocene tools known on the mainland. At sites on the northwestern tip, deposits are dated to c. 6000 BC with bone points, stone scrapers, and pebble tools. Around 1000 BC, bone points disappeared, and there is evidence of fish exploitation. Pecked engravings at Mount Cameron West resemble the Panaramitee style of central Australia. The arrival of Europeans was disastrous, with Tasmanians becoming almost extinct in the 19th century.

Tassili n'Ajjer: Site in southeast Algeria with famous but undated rock art covering most of the Saharan sequence. The art is in three styles—"archaic" paintings of large animal and human figures and geometric abstract symbols; a "naturalistic" style with humans and animals portrayed in great detail in scenes showing cattle running and herdsmen with bows; and a "cubist" style with dark shapes and light areas.

Stone forms, which were probably used as tomb sculpture, have also been found at the Tassili site. There is much stone painting, but not much stone carving or engraving. Scholars have been unable to decipher the hieroglyphic language that is engraved on the rocks. (*syn.* Tassili-n-Ajjer)

Tassilo Chalice: Copper-gilt chalice of Kremsmünster Abbey, Austria, which survived from AD c. 778–788. It is an outstanding and original object, possibly made by Northumbrian craftsmen, decorated with a combination of Hiberno-Saxon ornament typical of the period. The chalice is cast in bronze overlaid with gilt and silver niello engravings.

Tata: Middle Palaeolithic site on the Danube River in Hungary with artifacts and fauna, including woolly mammoth, horse, and wild ass, and dated to the early last glacial. Tools are side scrapers, bifaces, Upper Palaeolithic tools.

tauf: Arabic term for building out of mud, especially mud mixed with straw applied to the top of the wall and allowed to dry before a further course is added. (*syn.* pisé (French), chineh (Persian))

taula: Bronze Age ritual monument found in the Balearic Islands of Minorca and Majorca from the Talayot culture. A taula may be 4 meters in height and consists of a horizontal block supported either by a monolithic pillar or a column made of several stones. Often surrounded by a U-shaped enclosure wall, it is thought to have had a cult function.

Taung: A fossiliferous deposit in Bophuthatswana, South Africa, with the first Australopithecine fossil found. This early hominid skull of a child, found in 1924, was named *Australopithecus africanus* and dubbed the "Taung baby." The deposit is 2 million years old.

Tautavel: Cave site in the east Pyrenees-Orientales of southern France with Middle Pleistocene/Lower Palaeolithic deposits of pre-Mousterian date with little stratification. The front half of a skull with heavy brow ridges and robust facial features has been found, as well as two lower jaws, one much bigger toothed than the other. They are associated with an archaic Taycian quartz industry. Their date may be c. 320,000–200,000 years ago. (*syn.* Caune de l'Arago)

Tawantinsuyu: The name used by the Incas for their empire, literally "the four inextricably linked quarters." By 1532, the Inca state had incorporated dozens of coastal and highland ethnic groups stretching from what is now the northern border of Ecuador to Mendoza in west-central Argentina and the Maule River in central Chile—at least 12 million people.

Ta-wen-k'ou: Neolithic culture of China, a painted pottery group found mainly in Shantung Province. Dated to c. 3500 BC, it precedes the Lung-Shan culture. There were graveside ritual offerings of liquids, pig skulls, and pig jaws. There were tomb ramps and coffin chambers at Ta-wen-k'ou.

Taweret: Goddess of ancient Egypt, household deity and protectress of fertility and childbirth, associated also with the nursing of infants. She was depicted as having the head of a hippopotamus standing upright, the tail of a crocodile, and the claws of a lion. Taurt was connected in particular with the goddess Hathor. She was also strongly associated with the inundation of the Nile and received particular worship at Jabal al-Silsila, where rituals were performed for the inundation. (*syn.* Taurt, Thoueris)

Taxila: One of the two main cities of the Achaemenid Empire (satrapy of Gandhara), located in Pakistan and flourishing in the 5th–2nd centuries BC. It rose again as an Indo-Greek city from the 1st century BC through the 1st century AD. It was surrendered to Alexander the Great in 327 BC and then destroyed AD c. 500, probably by the White Huns. The extensive remains of Taxila include Bhir mound, which conceals the pre-Hellenistic town of the 6th century BC and later; Sirkap, an Indo-Greek "new town" with a rectilinear grid of streets laid out in the 2nd century BC; and Sirsukh (Sirsuleh), another new town founded by the Kushans in the 1st century AD.

taxon: The scientific classification of an organism.

taxonomy: A classification based on an unequal weighting of attributes that are imposed in a hierarchical order so that the attributes defining each class are dependent on the order in which the attributes were considered. It is a system of classifying artifacts or other cultural material into taxa, based on their similarities. An ordered set of operations results in the subdivision of objects into ordered classifications, and it stems from the general principles that regulate scientific (biological) classification. Taxonomy is the basis of the organization of material culture remains.

Taya, Tell: Tell site in northern Iraq, of a city of the Early Dynastic and Sargonid periods (mid-3rd millennium BC to early 2nd millennium BC) with extensive stone architecture. Unlike most Mesopotamian cities, the building material was not mud brick but stone, which has made it possible to map in considerable detail the 3rd-millennium city's plan. There was also a later Neo-Assyrian, Parthian, and Islamic settlement.

Tayacian: A term sometimes used to describe Lower and Middle Palaeolithic flake industries that lack hand axes, bifaces, and carefully retouched implements. Originally, the term was coined for the industries from the lower levels at La Micoque (Les Eyzies-de-Tayac, the Dordogne, France), but it has subsequently been applied to industries over a wide geographical and chronological range. The layers, which probably belong to the penultimate glacial period, were assigned to a Tayacian culture. The culture is also described as a primitive flake-tool tradition of Israel, believed to be essentially a smaller edition of the Clactonian industry.

Taylor, Walter W. (1913–): American archaeologist who believes in the conjunctive approach to archaeology, emphasizing the connection of objects to their cultural contexts.

Taylour, Lord William (1904–1989): British archaeologist who worked at Mycenae, where he found the cult center, and at Ayios Stefanos. He wrote *The Mycenaeans* (rev. ed. 1983).

Tayma: Iron Age city in Hejaz, Arabia. Nabonidus (r. 555–539 BC) was the last king of the Neo-Babylonian Empire and lived there for 10 years. There are a series of large walled compounds and a small mound in the center of town. There is a cultic area and carved scenes with an iconography derived from the Mesopotamian world. Stelae with Aramaic inscriptions of the 1st millennium BC have been found. As early as the 6th century BC, the Chaldean kings of Babylon maintained Tayma as a summer capital. (*syn.* Tayma')

Te Awanga: Fortified site in Tiromoana, New Zealand, with sweet potato storage pits, possibly with very early dates for the earliest settlement.

technofact: An artifact that was used for a practical function, such as providing food, shelter, or defense, rather than connected to social or ideological activity. The term is also more generally applied to archaeological data resulting from past technological activities.

technofunction: The use of an artifact for practical purposes, such as garments offering warmth or protection. (*syn.* adj. technofunctional or technomic)

technological analysis: The study of technological methods used to make an artifact.

technological attribute: Characteristic(s) of an artifact, which is the direct result of how it was made (manufacturing methods) or of the raw material used (constituents)—which leads to technological classifications. (*syn.* technological type)

technology: One of the three basic components of culture; the systematic study of techniques for making and doing things. It is the means by which humans have developed things to help them adapt to and exploit their environment. By virtue of his nature as a toolmaker, man has been a technologist from the beginning, and the history of technology encompasses the whole evolution of man.

tectonic movements: Displacements in the plates that make up the Earth's crust, often responsible for the occurrence of raised beaches and for seismic and volcanic activity. Plate tectonics is a theory dealing with the dynamics of the Earth's outer shell, the lithosphere. The theory states that the lithosphere consists of about a dozen large plates and several small ones. These plates move relative to each other and interact at their boundaries, where they diverge, converge, or slip harmlessly past one another. (*syn.* plate tectonics)

Tefnut: Egyptian goddess associated with moisture or damp air. She was one of first gods created by Atum along with her brother/husband Shu. Her children were Geb (earth god) and Nut (sky goddess). Shu and Tefnut were the first couple of the group of nine gods called the Ennead of Heliopolis.

Tehuacán Valley: Valley site in Puebla, Mexico, with human occupation from at least 7000 BC. This desert valley, 1,800 meters above sea level, has one of the longest continuous sequences in Mesoamerica (ending AD 1520). The earliest inhabitants were nomadic food gatherers and hunters. Maize was grown by c. 5000 BC, pottery was first made around 2300 BC, and settled village life may go back to the 3rd millennium BC (although it is not well attested before 1800 BC). Incipient agriculture phases gave way to reliance on domesticated foods. From the Pre-Classic period onward, the valley was not as important as the richer and more fertile areas of Mexico. It was, before the Spanish conquest, a center of Mixteca-Puebla culture. The earliest phase is considered part of the Desert tradition. The Ajuereado Phase (before 6500 BC) was characterized by small wandering groups engaged in hunting and gathering. In the El Riego Phase (6500–5000 BC), small groups gathered seasonally into larger groups, and grinding tools, weaving, and some plant cultivation were present. The Coxcatlan Phase (5000–3500 BC) marked the appearance of larger semisedentary groups occupying fewer sites and engaged in agriculture. Artifacts include manors and metates and improved basketry. A significant change in settlement pattern occurs in the Abejas Phase (3500–2300 BC) with pit-house villages occurring along the river terraces as year-round dwellings. New species of plant food, long obsidian blades, and possibly cotton appeared, and there is increased hunting of small game. Pottery, which is a good index of the degree of permanence of a settlement (fragility makes it difficult to transport), was made in the Tehuacán Valley by 2300 BC. The later phases (including Purron, 2300–1500 BC) represent a sedentary life, wide use of ceramics, and domestication of the dog.

Tekkalakota: Neolithic site in the south-central Deccan, India, with two phases of settlement in the early 2nd millennium BC. There are mud/stone floors in circular or rectilinear huts and fractional burials early on, later replaced by extended burials in interconnected vessels for adults, while children were buried in urns. Artifacts include rare metal objects (copper, gold). Three gold ornaments were found, indicating exploitation of local gold deposits. The people produced distinctive burnished gray pottery, smaller quantities of black-on-red painted pottery, stone axes, and bone points, and there is some evidence of a stone-blade industry. (*syn.* Tekkalkota)

Telarmachay: Seasonally occupied preceramic rock shelter in central Peru, dated 9000–2000 bp.

telehistoric site: Prehistoric sites far removed from the origination of written records.

Teleilat Ghassul: Type site of the Ghassulian in the Jordan Valley (Palestine) near the Dead Sea, dated c. 3800–3350 BC. It is known for polychrome geometric and figurative mural paintings in trapezoid-shaped mud-brick houses. The Ghassulian stage was characterized by small settlements of farming peoples whose pottery was elaborate in style and included footed bowls and horn-shaped goblets. The Ghassulians also smelted copper. (*syn.* Tulaylat al-Ghassul)

tell or tepe: A large mound formed by superimposed habitation layers, particularly in the Middle East (Near East). Tells are the result of continuous habitation over a long time span and are important ancient settlement sites. Tells are normally found only in regions where buildings were of mud brick, a material of limited life and too plentiful to be worth salvaging when it collapses. This, coupled with the accumulation of domestic refuse, can build up vast mounds over 100 feet/30 meters. The tells of the Middle East offer valuable stratigraphic evidence. Such mounds incorporate other settlement refuse, graves, and many other materials. [Site names beginning with "Tell" in this dictionary are alphabetized under the second part of the name.] (*syn.* tell mound; tel [Hebrew]; choga, tepe [Persian]; hüyük [Turkish])

Tellem: Pre-Dogon people with large necropolises in Mali, Africa, of the 11th–16th centuries AD. The oldest wood sculptures to survive (dated 15th–17th centuries AD) were found in caves in the Bandiagara escarpment and are attributed to the Tellem. The figures, simplified and elongated in form, often with hands raised, seem to be the prototype of the ancestor figures that the Dogon carve on the doors and locks of their houses and granaries. Cotton and woolen cloth have also been found in the caves.

Tello, Julio César (1880–1947): Peruvian archaeologist who discovered and studied some of the most important sites in Peru; considered with Max Uhle and Alfred Kroeber to be a founder of Peruvian archaeology. His main contributions were the excavation of the Paracas cemeteries and the study of the Chavín, but he also worked at Pachacamac, Cajamarquilla, Huari, Pacheco, Cerro Blanco, Punkuri, Kotosh, Cerro Sechin, and Ancon. He also identified many cultural groups, including the Chavín, Chimu, Huari, and Nazca. Tello founded the National Museum of Anthropology and Archaeology in Lima.

Telloh or Tello: Tell site north of Ur in southern Mesopotamia, long thought to be the city of Lagash but more recently identified as Girsu. Girsu was possibly a religious center in the state of Lagash. It is important for the vast number of cuneiform tablets found there, which depict the economic, social, and political aspects of the Early Dynastic III and Ur III periods in Sumer. There are fine statues of Gudea, governor of Lagash in the 22nd century BC. Most of the finds belong to the 3rd millennium BC, from the Early Dynastic, Akkadian, and Ur III periods. It was occupied from the late 'Ubaid to Old Babylonian times and has a late 1st millennium BC palace. (*syn.* ancient Girsu)

Tembeling: River valley in peninsular Malaysia, with Neolithic and metal age sites.

temenos: In Greek antiquity, the enclosure of a sanctuary, the holy ground belonging to the god and governed by special rules, or the sacred precinct at a cult center—containing the altar, temple, and other features. There might be numerous buildings for the main cult and a series of thesauroi, stoas, and dedications from worshipers. In Egyptian architecture, loosely applied to the area in the enclosure wall of a temple. (*syn.* pl. temenoi)

Temet: Neolithic site in northeast Niger, Africa, dated c. 9500 BP; its stone industry had blades, bladelets, and microliths.

temmoku: Dark brown or blackish Chinese stoneware made for domestic use mainly during the Sung Dynasty (960–1279) and into the early 14th century. The stoneware bowls had a lustrous iron or manganese black or brown glaze. This is a Japanese term applied to Chinese bowls used in the tea ceremony until the late 16th century. Some Japanese bowls are called temmoku solely on account of their similarity of shape and do not have the glaze. These bowls were highly valued when the tea ceremony first started (15th century) and were classified according to seven types of glazing decoration. In China, this stoneware is called Chien ware. (*syn.* temmoku ware, tenmoku)

Temnata Cave: Palaeolithic cave site in central Bulgaria with artifacts and faunal remains, starting with a Middle Palaeolithic assemblage of the last glacial, then Aurignacian and Gravettian. Another Middle Palaeolithic assemblage with bifacial foliates was discovered outside the cave.

temper: Foreign material (sand, plant fibers, grit, shell, crushed rock, broken pottery) added to clay for pottery making to improve its firing qualities and to prevent a vessel from cracking during the drying process. Temper reduces plasticity, which would cause shrinkage or cracking on drying and firing. The study of temper is important for the identification of the place of manufacture of a vessel. (*syn.* grog)

tempering: One of the processes in the manufacture of steel and other metal artifacts, the heat treatment of hardened steels to improve toughness and reduce brittleness. The steel is reheated to a temperature of around 450 degrees Centigrade and then rapidly cooled by quenching.

temple: A building with a religious function, of various shapes and sizes. For the ancient Egyptians and Near Easterners, it was the "house" of a deity or deities, and the most important component was the innermost cult chamber or shrine, where the image of the deity was kept. Temples were not originally intended for worshipers, but as shrines for the gods. In Egypt, they consisted of the following elements: the pylon, an open courtyard with colonnades, the hypostyle hall, and the sanctuary. The sacred precinct of a town, including the temple and associated buildings, was often surrounded by a massive mud-brick wall. In the Classical world, many great temples were built. Because of the importance of temples in a society, temple architecture often represents the best of a culture's design and craftsmanship. (*syn.* templum)

temple mound: A large flat-topped earthen structure, artificially made of earth and stone, designed as a mountain on which to set a temple above the landscape. In Mesoamerica, these structures are terraced or stepped. Some temple mounds also served as tombs and formed the symbolic centers of theocratic government controlled by a priestly class.

Temple Mound Period: Time period from AD c. 800 to European colonization, when Native Americans of the Mississippian tradition built large flat-topped earthen structures (platform mounds) designed to function as artificial mountains elevating their temples above the landscape. This period followed the Burial Mound period and is the most recent period of a chronological construction relating to the whole of eastern North American prehistory (formulated by J. A. Ford and Gordon Willey). The periods are Palaeo-Indian, Archaic, Burial Mound, and Temple Mound. The Temple Mound period is divided into two subperiods: Temple Mound I (AD 800–1200), the establishment and rise of the Mississippian Tradition; and Temple Mound II (AD 1200–1700), the peak and then demise of the Mississippian. (*syn.* Mississippian)

temple mountain: A form of monument that occurred only in Cambodia from the 9th–13th centuries AD. There are a series of artificial mountains on the Cambodian plain at Angkor, each crowned by shrines containing images of gods and of Khmer kings, their families, and their ancestors. The huge platforms of earth on which these buildings were founded are oriented east to west, the main gates facing east. Each king tried to outdo his predecessor in the height, size, and splendor of his temple mountain. The earlier ones are relatively small, although beautiful; the later ones, such as Angkor Wat and the Bayon, are of stupendous size. The design originated from the belief that the main temple of the king, which is the ritual center of the kingdom and eventually becomes his mausoleum, must be situated on a mountain or at least a hill. The architecture of the shrines themselves is relatively simple; it is based on patterns invented in India, although the ornament of the shrines is often highly developed and characteristically Cambodian. On some of the temple mountains, there are relief panels illustrating various aspects of the royal mythology. The earliest surviving temple mountain at Angkor itself is the Bakong, probably finished in 881. (*syn.* temple-mountain)

temporal context: The age or date of an archaeological find and its temporal (time) relation to other objects in the archaeological record.

temporal type: A morphological (structure, form) type that has been shown to have temporal significance. (*syn.* time-marker)

Tenayuca: Site where a group of Chichimec, under the leadership of Xólotl, succeeded in gaining power in the Valley of Mexico, establishing their center there in 1224, now the northern suburbs of Mexico City. Its large pyramid is the best surviving example of pyramids of Chichimec and Aztec type, and it is thought to resemble the Great Temple at Tenochtitlán. It was covered at 52-year intervals by at least six successive pyramid and temple buildings. It consists of two parallel stairways leading to two temples on the top of the one structure, with traces of Talud-Tablero style architecture, indicating Teotihuacán occupation in the Classic Period. An altar decorated with a skull and crossbones motif is similar to one at Tula.

Ténéré Neolithic: Variant of the so-called Saharan Neolithic complex in the Ténéré Desert, which extends from northeastern Niger into western Chad, Africa, dating from 6500–4500 BP. Chipped stone implements include backed microliths, bifacial projectile points, and discoid knives, and the pottery may have connections with contemporary Sudanese Nile valley sites. Rock engravings and rock pictures of animals were also created by the Neolithic (8,000–5,000 BC) inhabitants. A pastoral economy existed as well as hunting; the climatic conditions at the time may have dictated the subsistence. Ténéré is now one of the most forbidding regions of the Sahara, with an extremely hot and dry climate and virtually no plant life. Fossils show that this arid desert was, in the Late Carboniferous period (320–286 million years ago), a sea floor and later became a humid tropical forest. In the Middle Palaeolithic (c. 60,000 BC), human habitation is indicated in this region by flint axes, arrowheads, and stone artifacts. (*syn.* Tenerian)

Tenochtitlán: The Aztec capital, built on islands in Lake Texcoco (AD 1325), which once was the center of the Valley of Mexico; few remains survive underneath present-day Mexico City. The Aztecs built artificial islands and constructed houses, other buildings, and chinampas and then connected them to the mainland by three giant causeways. The population may have been as high as 400,000 people over 5 square miles. Under the ruler Itzcóatl (1428–1440), Tenochtitlán formed alliances with the neighboring states of Texcoco and Tlacopan and became the dominant power in central Mexico. By commerce and conquest, Tenochtitlán came to rule an empire of 400–500 small states—by 1519 some 5,000,000–6,000,000 people over 80,000 square miles. Accounts describe 25 pyramid-temples with nine priests' quarters, seven *tzompantli* (sacrificial racks), two ball courts, and a huge plaza consisting of the Great Temple with the temples of Tlaloc and Huitzilopochtli. The city was taken by Hernando Cortes and the Spaniards in 1519, and by 1522 it was virtually destroyed. The Spaniards built their own city on the site. Some archaeological remains were discovered during the building of a subway in Mexico City.

tenoned: Joined by a knob (tenon) fitting into a socket or mortise. Specifically said of the end of a piece of wood shaped to fit into another piece.

tenoned mosaic: A mosaic design formed when a series of stone sculptures is set into the exterior facade of a masonry building, such as that by the Maya at Copán, in Honduras. The front of the stone was carved with a face or symbol; the middle and rear parts formed a long tenon that anchored the stone in the interior fill of the building. The mosaic design also carried a symbolic message.

teocalli: Nahuatl (Aztec) term for temple; an ancient temple of Mexico or Central America usually built on the summit of a truncated pyramidal mound.

teosinte: Mexican tall annual grass grown as fodder, considered ancestral to domesticated maize.

Teotihuacán: Very important site north of Mexico City, at its peak AD c. 450–650 the largest and most powerful city in Mesoamerica. It had its beginnings as one of a number of small agricultural settlements around the shores of ancient Lake Texcoco. Teotihuacán flourished by c. 300/200 BC, and by AD 100, it had about 40,000 inhabitants. Archaeological work has provided more information about Teotihuacán than about any comparable Mexican site. Teotihuacán maintained extensive political and trade contacts with lowland Mexico and is famed for its enormous public buildings and pyramids. At its heart is a complex of magnificent architecture including the massive pyramid of the Sun and the pyramid of the Moon, the Cuidadela (probably an administrative center), and the Great Compound (probably a marketplace); there are no ball courts. The structures are distributed along a central roadway known as the Street of the Dead. After the destruction of Cuicuilco, Teotihuacán expanded, and people were housed in apartment compounds that exhibit some social differentiation. Many of the inhabitants were craftsmen, and some 500 workshop sites have been identified. Four fifths of those sites were devoted to obsidian working. Teotihuacán controlled the central highlands of Mexico, and was in contact with all the principal centers of civilization (Monte Albán, Tikal, etc.) as far as Belize. The influence of Teotihuacán during the Early Classic was considerable, and most major centers have some Teotihuacán forms. Characteristic of Teotihuacán influence are Talud-Tablero architecture, images of Tlaloc, cylindrical tripod vases, Thin Orange ware, murals, and stylized human face masks. There is very little massive stone sculpture except as architectural embellishments. The end of Teotihuacán came fairly suddenly. A decline in its influence at other sites was evident by c. 600, but the city itself was not destroyed until 750. There is much evidence of burning from that time, indicating that the city may have been sacked—possibly by the Chichimecs. The city was never rebuilt, but a small population remained in the ruined city for more than a hundred years.

tepe: Persian word for "tell" or artificial mound. [In this dictionary, the sites are listed by their second element.]

Tepeu: Late Classic phase dated to AD 600–900, one of two lowland Maya chronological phases or cultures (the other being the Tzakol, Early Classic, AD c. 250). It is defined by a complex of cultural materials, especially the polychrome vase. The typical shape is a tall, cylindrical vessel with a flat base, and it is decorated with life scenes often involving mythological creatures and a band of hieroglyphs. The Tepeu culture saw the full florescence of Maya achievements. It ended with the downfall and abandonment of the central subregion.

Tepexpan: Site of Late Pleistocene occupation in the Valley of Mexico, northeast of Mexico City, with skeletons of two mammoths killed with spears fitted with lancelike stone points and butchered on the spot. They have been given a possible date of 9000/8000 BC. In the same geologic layer, a human skeleton was found—Tepexpan "man." There were no grave goods; the corpse was buried face down with flexed legs and was identified as female. Fluorine analysis has confirmed the date of both skeleton types.

tephra: General term for volcanic ash or any solid material ejected during a volcanic eruption. Tephra beds are ideal stratigraphic markers because they are deposited instantaneously; they may be dated by potassium-argon dating and fission track dating.

tephrochronology: A method for the relative dating of horizons in volcanic regions by identification of different layers of ash (tephra). Tephra layers (beds) are ideal stratigraphic markers because they are deposited instantaneously. Also, the chemical content of tephra (volcanic ash) is unique for each eruption. If artifacts lie below tephra known to have come from a certain eruption, the artifacts predate the eruption. Tephra layers may be dated by potassium-argon dating and fission track dating, and they can sometimes be tied to absolute chronology where radiocarbon dates can be obtained from material contemporary with the deposit. To establish a chronology, it is necessary to identify and correlate as many tephra units as possible over the widest possible area. In the Mediterranean, deep-sea coring produced evidence for the ash fall from the eruption of Thera, and its stratigraphic position provided important information in the construction of a relative chronology. The identification of multiple tephra beds may give bracketing ages for intervening strata. Tephrochronology has also been used to date glacial advances, sea level changes, and alluvial fans. (*syn.* tephrachronology)

tepidarium: In Roman baths, the warm room or chamber, used as a lounge where bathers rested, talked, and gambled, and prepared for the sudatorium. Often a plunge bath was attached to it, adding humidity to the room.

Tequendama Cave: Cave site outside Bogota, in the highlands of southeast Colombia, with preceramic remains dating from 9000–1000 BC. There are large stemmed points in the earliest levels.

terminus ante quem: Latin phrase meaning "the end before which"—the date before which a stratum, feature, or artifact must have been deposited. The term is used either to define a relative chronological date for artifacts or to provide fixed points in a site's stratigraphy. If a deposit can be securely dated by material found in it—for example, a deposit with coins dating to the 2nd century AD found above another layer—then the coins would provide that deposit with a terminus ante quem of the 2nd century AD. In some circumstances, such a "date" may be combined with a terminus post quem from an earlier phase to produce a date range for the intervening deposit. This type of dating is used to show that something cannot be later than, or earlier than, something else. (*syn.* TAQ; t.a.q.)

terminus post quem: Latin phrase meaning "the end after which"—the date after which a stratum, feature, or artifact must have been deposited. The term is used either to define a relative chronological data for artifacts or to provide fixed points in a site's stratigraphy. If a deposit contains datable coins or pottery, then deposits stratigraphically later must be of a later date than that given by such material; the dated layer gives a terminus post quem for the undated deposit. In some circumstances, if combined with a terminus ante quem, the deposit may be dated securely between the two. (*syn.* TPQ, t.p.q.)

Ternifine: Acheulian site in Algeria, east of Oran, with three well-preserved jaws of *Homo erectus* type, along with numerous stone tools including hand axes and cleavers. The fauna is regarded as Middle Pleistocene.

terp: Manmade mound, similar to a tell, found in late prehistoric northwest Europe, created by the continual remaking of clay floors and deposition of rubbish. Terpen were good settlement sites for the Frisians and other Germanic peoples in areas threatened by flooding. The earliest go back to the 3rd century BC, and many remained in use until the Middle Ages. These nucleated settlements were indigenous to the Iron Age and Migration period cultures of the Frisian coastlands. Excavations have shown that terpen were densely populated; they contain large numbers of dwellings, including buildings in which crafts were made. (*syn.* pl. terpen; warf, werft, wurt, wierde, wierden)

Terra Amata: Lower Palaeolithic site in Nice, France, with occupation from the Mindel glaciation c. 380,000 BP through 11 total levels. The levels are ascribed to the Acheulian, but few tools or hand axes have been recovered.

terrace: A bench or step that extends along the side of a valley and represents a former level of the valley floor. Terraces are flat surfaces preserved in valleys, which represent floodplains developed when the river flowed at a higher elevation than at present. Another type of terrace is cut into bedrock and may have a thin veneer of alluvium, or sedimentary deposits. In paired terraces, the terrace features on each side of a valley correspond. A marine terrace is a rock terrace formed where a sea cliff, with a wave-cut platform, is raised above sea level. Any terrace consists of two parts: (1) a tread, which is the flat surface of the former floodplain, and (2) a scarp, which is the steep slope that connects the tread to any surface standing lower in the valley. A simple definition is the previous location of the shore of a body of water or a valley floor on which a stream once flowed. Archaeological deposits associated with terraces are equal in age or younger than the terrace.

terra-cotta: Literally "baked earth" or "baked clay"; fired clay that is incompletely fired and still porous. It is used to make artifacts such as vessels, figurines, tablets, spindle whorls, loom weights, or net sinkers. It is a material from which much ancient pottery and other fired clay objects were made. It is also found as a structural material in hearths and kilns, where the clay of which they were built has been baked in use. A special variety of terra-cotta called "daub" was produced only by accidental burning. Today, the term is applied to statuary, building materials, and so on, rather than the better fired modern pottery.

Terramara: A local name for Middle Bronze Age settlements in the Emilia region of northern Italy's Po Valley—consisting of mounds of dark earth formed by the accumulated rubbish of a permanent settlement occupied for a long period. The habitations were built on pilings and protected by a vallum, or defensive wall, which screened them from floods in a flat countryside with violent seasonal rains. These villages, whose dead were cremated, lasted until the Early Iron Age. The people of the terramara culture migrated to Italy from the Danubian region during the Middle Bronze Age (early 2nd millennium BC) and introduced the rite of urnfield burial into Italy. They were excellent bronze workers whose products were traded over much of Italy. The society was peasant, and its art was limited to the construction of dwellings and to the production and ornamentation of weapons and vases. The pottery is a dark burnished ware with concentric groove decoration, bosses, and horned handles. The Terramara culture strongly influenced the Apennine culture in its last phase. The terramara is considered a forerunner of the Roman street and camp planning and also the medieval castle and village. (*syn.* pl. terremare; Terramara or Terramare)

terra sigillata: A type of fine, mass-produced Roman pottery of the imperial period, usually red glazed or glossed and mold made, to which stamps bearing the name of the potter were applied. Made in several centers, it was exported through western Europe and the Mediterranean; it can be a very accurate chronological indicator. The best known is the plain and relief-decorated pottery of 1st–3rd centuries AD from southern, central, and eastern Gaul (called Samian ware) and also from Italy and Germany. Another type is the Arretine of c. 30 BC–AD 50. Generically related or derivative of terra sigillata are the late Roman Argonne or Marne ware and North African (African Red Slip) and eastern red wares.

Terrasse, Henri (1895–1971): French archaeologist who worked on Hispano-Moorish art from its beginnings to the 13th century. He is known as the discoverer of the Hispano-Maghreb world and a pioneer of systematic research.

terret: A ring through which the driving reins of a chariot or other horse-drawn vehicle are passed.

Tertiary: (tur'-shee-air-ee) The geological period following the Mesozoic (Secondary) era, constituting the first of two periods of the Cenozoic Era, the second being the Quaternary. It includes the Palaeocene, Eocene, Oligocene, Miocene, and Pliocene. It extended from the end of the Cretaceous to the beginning of the Quaternary, from 66.4–1.6 million years ago. The Miocene and Pliocene epochs were important in hominid evolution. Some prefer not to use the term Tertiary and instead divide the interval into two periods, the Palaeogene period (66.4–23.7 mya) and the Neogene period (23.7–1.6 mya). Most of the existing mountain belts and ranges, notably the Andes, the Rockies, the Alps, the Himalayas, and the Atlas Mountains, were formed either partly or wholly during the Tertiary. The emergence and submergence of land bridges between continents, especially between North and South America, Eurasia and Africa, and Asia and North America, critically affected the migration of fauna and flora. The earliest generally accepted hominid fossils, those of Australopithecus, come from rocks of Pliocene age (5.3–1.6 mya) in eastern Africa.

tertiary flake: A flake having no cortex. (*syn.* interior flake, noncortical flake)

Tesetice-Kyjovice: Lengyel culture site in southern Moravia. The circular enclosure had four entrances approximate to the cardinal points of a compass; two concentric palisades were within the enclosure.

Teshik Tash: Middle Palaeolithic cave in Tadjikistan in the west Himalayas, with several Mousterian levels, and the skeleton of a Neanderthal child. The site is dated c. 44,000 BP.

tessellated: A Roman floor or other surface decorated with tesserae; inlaid or mosaic work composed of tesserae.

tessera: A piece of stone, colored glass, or tile used with others to make mosaic patterns on floors, walls, ceilings, and so on. The pieces were set in cement by Roman, and later, craftsmen. Small cubes of up to 1 inch in size were used to make the floors. In the Roman period, tesserae, sometimes inscribed, were in circulation for various purposes. These were small tokens of bronze, lead, terra-cotta, and bone. The earliest tesserae, which by 200 BC had replaced natural pebbles in Hellenistic mosaics, were cut from marble and limestone. Stone tesserae dominated mosaics into Roman times, but between the 3rd–1st centuries BC tesserae of smalto (colored glass) also began to be produced. An important variety of glass tessera, appearing first in Roman mosaics of the 4th century AD, was that made with gold and silver leaf. (*syn.* adj. tessellated; pl. tesserae)

test square: An excavation unit used to sample or probe a site before large-scale excavation or to check surface surveys. Typically a 2-meter square, it is a small exploratory sounding often designed to determine a site's depth and stratigraphy, preparatory to full-scale excavation. (*syn.* test pit; test excavation)

Teti (fl. 23rd century BC): First king of the 6th Dynasty (c. 2325–2150 BC), whose reign does not represent a marked break with the preceding reign of Unas. Around Teti's pyramid in northern Saqqarah was a cemetery of large tombs, including those of several viziers. Together with tombs near the pyramid of Unas, this is the latest group of private monuments of the Old Kingdom in the Memphis area.

tetrapylon: A building or structure with four gates.

tetrastyle: In classical building, having four columns on the facade. Also, in Roman architecture, four columns placed in a square pattern, as at four corners.

Teufelsbrücke: Upper Palaeolithic site on the Saale River in eastern Germany, starting with the end of the Pleistocene. Assemblages with bone points and harpoons are of the late Magdalenian. There is a radiocarbon date of 13,025 bp.

Teuton: Germanic-speaking peoples who moved into north-central Europe after the Celts in the second and first centuries BC.

Téviec: A small island in Morbihan, southern Brittany, France, where the burial of 23 Mesolithic skeletons were found in a Tardenoisian settlement. Grave goods include stag antlers and shell jewelry. There was a shell midden, and the site is dated to c. 6575 bp.

textile: Fabric produced by spinning and weaving fibers, whether of animal or vegetable origin. Fragments may be preserved by waterlogging and tanning, by desiccation, or by corrosion of copper or bronze lying alongside. More commonly, items such as spindle whorls, weaving combs, and loom weights attest their existence.

texture: The size, shape, and arrangement of grains or crystals in rocks and also a property of soil, sediment, or similar material. Soil texture class names are assigned to indicate specific ranges of percentage of sand, silt, and clay. As with particle size, several different systems of texture classification are in use, including the British Standard 1377 system and the United States Department of Agriculture system. For rocks, there are also classification schemes. The texture of artifacts is one property used to help identify the source material, conditions, and environment of deposition or crystallization and recrystallization, and subsequent geologic history and change.

Teyjat: Two Palaeolithic caves occupied in the Magdalenian period in the northern Dordogne, southwest France. One has fine line engravings of animals on blocks of limestone.

Thailand: Archaeological evidence indicates almost continuous human occupation of Thailand for the last 20,000 years. Tai-speaking peoples migrated southward and westward from China around the 10th century AD. Important Hoabinhian sites are Sai Yok, Spirit Cave, Non Nok Tha, and Ban Chiang, which suggest the presence of rice cultivation, cattle domestication, and copper-bronze metallurgy from about 3500 BC, followed by iron metallurgy and wet rice cultivation about 1500 BC. In southern Thailand at Ban Kao and Kok Charoen, Neolithic cultures continued into the 2nd millennium BC. The Bronze and Iron Age remains are related to the Dong-Son culture of Vietnam (1st millennium BC).

Thames pick: A term for a large, coarsely chipped Mesolithic tranchet ax and other long flint tools with tranchet-shaped points found in the River Thames.

Thapsos: Site of a Middle Bronze Age cemetery near Syracuse, Sicily, of nearly 400 rock-cut tombs with dromos entrances. Most have a vertical shaft and were used for collective inhumations. It is the type site of the Thapsos culture, characterized by pottery, bronze swords and daggers, and Mycenaean imports of pottery and faience beads. The local ware has large cups and vases, often on high pedestals and with handles, with decoration in chevrons and cordons. The material is dated c. 1400–1200 BC. Thapsos is a promontory but was once an island. The Thapsos culture follows the Castelluccio culture and is succeeded by the Pantalica culture in the same area.

Tharros: Phoenician colony on the northern Gulf of Oristano, Sardinia. It was built over an earlier Nuraghic occupation and was part of a network of Carthaginian harbors. It prospered between the 6th–5th centuries BC, continuing under Roman rule from 238 BC. It was abandoned after the Byzantine period. From Phoenician times survives the largest tophet on Sardinia, a temple with Doric columns, and remains of the town's water and drainage system. Roman material includes housing in insulae, shops, bath buildings, and aqueduct installations. Two necropoleis date from the 7th century BC, with rock-cut tombs, some having dromoi. (*syn.* present-day S. Giovanni di Sinis)

Thatcham: Mesolithic sites in peat deposits of the Kennet Valley in England, with dates from c. 8000–6000 BC; all seem to contain Maglemosean artifacts.

Thaton: An early Talaing (Mon) capital in Lower Burma, subject to Indian influence from the time of Ashoka. It seems to have been the principal of a number of colonies of Indians from Orissa.

theater: Building or space in which a performance is given to an audience, an important adjunct of most Greek and Roman towns. In ancient Greece, where theater began in the 5th century BC, the theaters of the Classical period were constructed between two hills (essentially D-shaped) so that the audience sat in a tiered semicircular arrangement facing the orchestra circle, in which most of the action took place. (The name *amphitheater* should be used only of a circular or oval structure in which the seating completely surrounds the stage, as in the Colosseum). Greek theater consisted of two main elements: the orchestra, a space for acting and dancing, which was usually circular; and the auditorium, a spectators' area, which was probably no more than a hillside or slope originally. Later, the skene (originally perhaps only a temporary structure for the convenience of performers) was added. Well-preserved examples survive at Epidaurus, Pompeii, and Orange. (*syn.* theatre)

Thebes: Principal city of Upper Egypt, on the east bank of the Nile, which was the capital of the fourth nome of Upper Egypt and, during much of the Middle and New Kingdoms, of the whole country. Its importance lay in its being the seat of Amon (Amun), and the surviving remains include the impressive temples at Karnak and Luxor as well as the tombs and temples of the cemeteries on the west bank, including the Valley of the Kings, Deir El-Bahri, and the Valley of the Queens. Those mortuary temples and tombs were for kings and high officials from the Middle Kingdom to the end of the pharaonic period (c. 2055–332 BC). In contrast with the practice of earlier times, the pharaohs of this time were buried in carefully concealed rock-cut tombs. The only one surviving looters fairly intact was that of Tutankhamun, a comparatively minor ruler of the 18th Dynasty. The height of

Theban prosperity was reached in the 14th century BC in the reign of Amenhotep III, much of whose vast wealth from foreign tribute was poured into the temples of Amon. Thebes is also the name of a site in Greece, the principal city of Boeotia in the Classical and Pre-Classical periods, with a legendary history that predates the Trojan expedition. The ruined 15th-century BC Minoan-style palace at Cadmea had frescoes of Theban women in Minoan dress; some Cretan vases also suggest contacts between Thebes and Knossos in the period 1450–1400 BC. Clay tablets confirmed Mycenaean-Minoan links, and the discovery of Mesopotamian cylinder seals reinforced the theory that Cadmus introduced writing to Greece. Thebes rivaled Argolis as a center of Mycenaean power until its palace and walls were destroyed shortly before the Trojan War (c. 1200 BC). According to tradition, the city was destroyed by the sons of the Seven about whom Aeschylus wrote. (*syn.* ancient Waset, Wase, Wo'se, Nowe, Nuwe)

Thebes-East Bank: This part of Thebes included the main part of the city, now overbuilt by Luxor, and a temple built by Amenhotep III and Ramesses II. Just north was the temple of Karnak.

Thebes-West Bank: This part of Thebes includes the necropolis of the ancient city and the largest group of standing monuments in Egypt. They are mortuary temples and royal/private tombs. The royal and private tombs were mainly dug into cliffs and valleys of the Theban mountain. The mortuary temples were built on the desert plain between the mountain and the cultivated land of the Nile. Mortuary temples include those of Nebhepetre Mmontuhotep, Hatshepsut, Ramesses III, Ramesses II, Seti I, and the Colossi of Memnon. The royal tombs are at el-Tarif, Dra Abu el-Naga, the Valley of the Kings, and the Valley of the Queens.

themata: Large units of the Byzantine armed forces in the period of the 7th–10th centuries AD. Each themata was governed by a *strategos* (general). The original five large thematas were subdivided to form smaller units, while many new thematas were added along the frontier during the period of reconquests by the Byzantines in the late 9th–10th centuries. (*syn.* theme)

theodolite: An instrument used in archaeology for surveying sites, especially for measuring horizontal and vertical angles. The accurate plotting of excavation trenches can be carried out, and it can also be used in place of a level for determining heights and contours. There are different types of theodolites, although all include the focusing telescope, a leveling device, and scales for measuring horizontal and vertical angles. Vertical readings are easier to take on the theodolite than on the transit. The focusing telescope is mounted so that it freely rotates around horizontal and vertical axes; the telescope is usually fitted with a right-angle

prism so that the observer continues to look horizontally into the eyepiece, whatever the variation of the elevation angle. Theodolites are frequently used in archaeology for setting out excavation units, mapping sites and environments, and for topographic mapping.

theory: Any scientific explanation that has been widely tested and accepted; also, plausible or scientifically acceptable general principle or body of principles offered to explain phenomena.

Thera: Volcanic island in the Cyclades and the site of a Mycenaean settlement and a flourishing Bronze Age Minoan town (Akrotiri) on its lower slopes. The inhabitants were driven out by an earthquake c. 1500 BC, and in c. 1470 a catastrophic eruption buried the remains under 30 meters of ash. There were shock waves across the south Aegean Sea, and the extent to which the volcano's eruption contributed to the downfall of the Minoans on Crete is debated. There is, however, a chronological problem: The destruction of the Minoan palaces on Crete seems to have occurred c. 1450 BC, some 50 years after the abandonment of Akrotiri. Based on evidence from a Greenland ice core and from tree-ring and radiocarbon dating, some scholars believe that the destruction occurred earlier, during the 1620s BC. Some tie the events to the legend of Atlantis. Around the beginning of the first millennium BC, Dorian settlers came to Thera. From 308 to 145, the island, a member of the Cycladic League, was a Ptolemaic protectorate. Akrotiri's houses contain some of the finest Minoan frescoes found in the Mediterranean. (*syn.* modern Santorini)

Thericleian ware: A type of decoration of the 5th–3rd centuries BC, used on silver, terebinth wood (pistachio), and clay. It is characterized by ribbing and a black color. Therikles, a Corinthian potter, was said to have developed the technique.

thermae: In Roman architecture, a bath complex with rooms of different temperatures and exercise areas. Such a complex of rooms designed for public bathing, relaxation, and social activity for the ancient Romans. The great imperial thermae are the baths of Titus (AD 81), baths of Domitian (95), Trajan's Baths (c. 100), the baths of Caracalla (217), and the Thermae of Diocletian (c. 302).

thermal analysis: Any technique used to get information on the physical or thermodynamic properties in which heat is involved; in archaeology, especially to obtain information on the firing temperature of pottery and other clay objects. The techniques include boiling, freezing, solidification-point determinations; heat of fusion and heat of vaporization measurements; distillation, calorimetry, and differential thermal, thermogravimetric, thermometric, and thermometric titration analyses. (*syn.* thermoanalysis; thermal prospection)

Thermi: Early Bronze Age settlement on the Aegean island of Lesbos. Excavations revealed five phases of occupation (3000–2750 BC), mainly a settlement of timber houses, later defended by a stone wall. Thermi apparently was settled by Troas, judging from its Troy I-like black pottery. It was destroyed some time before 3000 BC, at approximately the same time as sites such as Troy I in northwest Anatolia and Poliochni on Lemnos. It was later resettled and then destroyed by fire c. 13th century BC.

thermography: Nonphotographic technique that uses thermal or heat sensors from aircraft to record the temperature of the soil surface. Temperatures can be mapped by using thermography to provide a graphic or visual representation of the temperature conditions on the surface of an object or land area. Variations in soil temperature can be the result of the presence of buried structures.

thermoluminescence: Chronometric method of dating ceramic materials by measuring the stored energy created when they were first fired. It is based on the principle that ceramic material, like other crystalline nonconducting solids, contains small amounts of radioactive impurities such as potassium, uranium, and thorium, which emit alpha and beta particles and gamma rays causing ionizing radiation. This produces electrons and other charge-carriers (holes), which become caught in traps in the crystal lattice. Heating of the pottery causes the electrons and holes to be released from the traps, and they recombine in the form of thermoluminescence. The amount of thermoluminescence from a heated sample is used to determine the number of trapped electrons resulting from the absorption of alpha radiation. The quantity of light emitted depends on three factors—the number of flaws in the crystal, the strength of the radioactivity to which it has been exposed, and the duration of exposure. An age determination technique in which the amount of light energy released in a pottery sample during heating gives a measure of the time elapsed since the material was last heated to a critical temperature. The older a piece of pottery, the more light produced. Accuracy for the technique is generally claimed at $\pm$ 10%. It overlaps with radiocarbon in the period for which it is useful, spanning 50,000–300,000 years ago, but also has the potential for dating earlier periods. It has much in common with electron spin resonance (ESR). (*syn.* thermoluminescence dating, thermoluminescent dating; TL)

thesauros: A treasury much like a naiskos and located in a temenos as storage of the valuables of foreign states. There is an elaborate series of thesauroi in Delphi leading up the sacred way. (*syn.* pl. thesauroi)

Thessalonica: Macedonian and Roman city and port in the north of Greece. In Roman times, it was the capital of the province of Macedonia, and it was very important in Byzantine times. Churches and monuments are among its ruins. (*syn.* Salonica)

Thetford: Town in Norfolk, England, which was created by King Alfred in the 9th century. There are well-preserved Saxon defenses, traces of narrow cobbled streets bordered by large and smaller buildings, substantial rectangular timber buildings, industrial workshops. Metal working was carried out, and Late Saxon wheel-made pottery (Thetford ware) was mass produced.

Thiessen polygons: Method of describing settlement patterns based on territorial divisions centered on a single site or feature (locational analysis); the polygons are created by drawing straight lines between pairs of neighboring sites, then at the midpoint along each of these lines, a second series of lines is drawn at right angles to the first. Linking the second series of lines creates the Thiessen polygons. Where the exact boundaries between ancient territories are undetermined, an attempt to reconstruct them can be made if the distribution of focal points (central place), one to each territory, is known. The assumption is that any point depends on the nearest central place. Thiessen polygons are useful for defining theoretical territories related to each center—an area of production, a source of an important material, or a market center. These theoretical territories can be tested by comparison with actual archaeological data such as artifact distributions. (*syn.* Thiessen polygon method)

Thinis: A site in Upper Egypt where the 1st and 2nd Dynasties originated, according to the 3rd-century BC historian Manetho. Thinis is located north of the Predynastic and Early Dynastic cemeteries of Abydos (modern al-Barba). (*syn.* Tjene, This; Thinite period)

Thinite dynasties: The 1st and 2nd Dynasties of Egypt, c. 3100–2686 BC, named by the Egyptian historian Manetho (3rd century BC) for Thinis, a city near Abydos, where some of its kings were allegedly buried. Menes (c. 3100–3040 BC) is considered the traditional founder of the dynasty. (*syn.* Thinite period)

Thin Orange pottery: A thin-walled, orange-fired ware with a distinctive mica schist temper and a decoration of incised and dotted patterns of Mesoamerica. It was introduced in the late Pre-Classic period and widely traded in Mesoamerica during the Classic period. It has been found in Colima, Jalisco, Nayarit, Kaminaljuyú, Copán, Monte Albán, and Teotihuacán. It is regarded as evidence of central Mexican influence, although its probable point of origin is the Valley of Puebla. It should not be confused with the early Post-Classic Fine Orange ware. (*syn.* Thin Orange ware)

thin sectioning: The removal of a very thin slice of material from an object, typically pottery or stone, for the purpose of examination under the petrological microscope. The sample chip may have to be ground down to 0.03 mm before mounting on a slide. The sample must be thin enough to determine the details of crystals and other structures. It is then possible to identify the source of the raw materials from which the object was made. The technique is also applied to soil, bone, and dental tissues. (*syn.* thin-section analysis; thin-section; thin section)

Third Intermediate Period: A chronological phase (1075–656 BC) following the New Kingdom, when Egypt was divided. The north was inherited by the Tanite 21st Dynasty (c. 1075–950 BC), and much of the Nile Valley came under the control of the Theban priests.

tholos: A beehive-shaped tomb built of stone and roofed by corbelling, sometimes royal, characteristic of the Mycenaean civilization. In Greek architecture, the term is generally used for the burial chambers of certain passage graves of similar plan and construction. The round chamber had an attached rectilinear entrance passage, the most famous examples being the treasury of Atreus and the tomb of Clytemnestra at Mycenae. The corbelling is trimmed to form a smooth surface, and the ornamental doorway is approached by a masonry-lined, horizontal passage or dromos. Such a tomb is set partly underground or sometimes built into the side of a hill. In classical archaeology, the term can be applied to either temples or tombs. (*syn.* pl. tholoi; tholos tomb; beehive tombs)

Thomas, Cyrus (1825–1910): American scholar who worked on the mounds of the U.S. Midwest and who demonstrated that they were built by ancestors of Native Americans.

Thompson, Sir John Eric Sidney (1898–1975): English archaeologist and ethnographer who worked in the Maya area. He reconstructed the temple of the Warriors at Chichen Itza and correlated the Mayan and Gregorian calendars (Goodman–Martinez–Thompson correlation between Mayan and Christian calendars, which provided the basis for the chronology of Classic Maya civilization). Thompson was able to extensively decipher early Mayan glyphs, determining that they contained historical as well as ritualistic and religious records. He also worked at Lubaantun, Rio Bec, and Pushilha, and he was the first to establish a chronology for the Belize Valley based on the seriation of ceramics. His books include *The Civilization of the Maya* (1927), *The Rise and Fall of Maya Civilization* (1954), and *Maya History and Religion* (1970).

Thomsen, Christian Jurgensen (1788–1865): Danish antiquary and first curator of the National Museum of Denmark. His main contribution to prehistory was the Three Age system (Stone, Bronze, and Iron Ages), first devised in 1819 as a method of classifying the museum collections, but soon recognized as a tool of enormous value in interpreting the prehistoric past. He is considered the first ethnoarchaeologist and also promoted osteological studies and the chemical analysis of pot residue.

Thorikos: Area of Attica, Greece, a rich source of metallic ores exploited as early as the 3rd millennium BC for copper, lead, and silver. It prospered in the Mycenaean period, which includes two tholos tombs on the akropolis. There is also an elliptical theater from Classical times.

Thoth: Ibis-headed god of ancient Egypt, patron of scribes and learning and later identified with the Greek god Hermes. His main cult centers were Hermopolis Magna and Hermopolis Parva. (*syn.* Djehuty)

Thrace or Thracia: Ancient and modern region of the southeastern Balkans; in ancient times, the part north of Greek settlement extending to the Black Sea. In the 5th century BC, it included modern Bulgaria and Romania. Some Thracians became subject to Persia in c. 516–510 BC. Thrace was assimilated (356–342 BC) by Philip II of Macedon and later provided Philip's son, Alexander the Great, with troops during his conquests. In 197 BC, Rome assigned much of Thrace to the kingdom of Pergamum. In the 1st century BC, Rome became more involved in the affairs of the region, and emperor Claudius I annexed the entire Thracian kingdom in AD 46. Thrace was subsequently made into a Roman province. The emperor Trajan and his successor, Hadrian, founded cities in Thrace, notably Sardica (modern Sofia) and Hadrianopolis (modern Edirne). In about AD 300, Diocletian reorganized the area between the Lower Danube and the Aegean into the diocese of Thrace. Archaeological sites are the homes of Democritus, the 5th-century philosopher, and of Protagoras, a counselor of Alexander the Great; and the Roman highway Via Egnatia.

Three-Age system: The division of human prehistory into three successive stages—Stone Age, Bronze Age, and Iron Age—based on the main type of material used in tools of the period. The system was first formulated by Christian J. Thomsen in 1819 as a means of classifying the collections in the National Museum of Denmark. The scheme became progressively elaborated by dividing the Stone Age into Old and New, the Palaeolithic and Neolithic. A Middle Stone Age or Mesolithic was later added. The further subdivisions Early, Middle, and Late of the Palaeolithic (Lower, Middle, and Upper) were introduced, and a Copper Age was inserted between New Stone and Bronze. The Ages are only developmental stages, and some areas skipped one or more of the stages. At first entirely hypothetical, these divisions were later confirmed by archaeological observations. The Three-Age system established the principle that by classifying artifacts, one could produce a chronological ordering. (*syn.* three-age sequence, Three Age System)

Three Kingdoms: In Korea, the protohistoric kingdoms of Koguryo, Old Silla, and Paekche, which existed independently from AD c. 300–668. In 668, the peninsula was unified under the Silla. The term also refers to the Wei (AD 220–265),

Su Han (AD 221–263), and Wu (AD 222–280) in China of the Kingdoms of the Three Kingdoms/Six Dynasties period. It succeeded the Han Dynasty.

thrusting spear: A handheld spear used for stabbing rather than throwing.

Thule: A prehistoric subculture of the Eskimo, which began in Alaska about AD 900 and spread as far as Greenland by AD 1000. The culture was distributed throughout the northern Arctic from Siberia to Greenland and was ancestral to most of the historic Eskimo cultures of that area. The latest phase in the west dates to c. 1300. Thule people lived in circular houses partially dug into the ground and roofed with whalebones, turf, and stone. Tools are mainly bone, ivory, antler, and polished slate rather than chipped stone, and they made coarse impressed pottery (later replaced by soapstone vessels). They hunted and fished with harpoon points, used skin-covered boats (open ones = umiaks, closed ones = kayaks), and dog sleds for travel across land and ice. Thule was characterized by ornaments of ivory, bone, and stone with simple geometric designs. This was the final Eskimo culture of the Northern Maritime tradition. It either absorbed or supplanted the Dorset culture of the central and east Arctic. The Thule were the Skraelings discovered by the Vikings in the 10th century AD.

Thunderbird: Palaeo-Indian and Archaic campsites at Flint Run, Virginia, with a long-exploited jasper quarry. Core fragments, flakes, and broken or preformed tools show a large flint knapping industry. Occupations began in Clovis times through the Archaic. Postholes in association with living floors dated to c. 9000 BC raises the possibility of this being the site of the earliest house structures in America. (*syn.* Thunderbird site)

Thutmose: The name of four Egyptian monarchs of the 18th Dynasty, early New Kingdom. Thutmose I (ruled 1493–c. 1482 BC), Thutmose II (ruled c 1482–1479 BC), Thutmose III (ruled 1479–1426 BC, and Thutmose IV (ruled 1400–1390 BC). Thutmose III is regarded as the greatest of the rulers of ancient Egypt. Thutmose III brought the Egyptian empire to the zenith of its power by conquering all of Syria, defeating the Mitannians, and penetrating south along the Nile to Napata in the Sudan. He also built a great number of temples and monuments to commemorate his deeds. Thumose I and II actively extended the empire through military campaigns in Palestine and Nubia. (*syn.* Tuthmosis, Tutmose, Tuthmosis)

Tiahuanaco: Large urban and ceremonial site which dominated the Titicaca Basin and the high Andes of Bolivia from c. 100–1250 AD, a major Middle Horizon site and probably the capital of an empire. The central area has principal religious structures on a large rectangular plaza, a large U-shaped mound around a spring, and a monumental Gate of the Sun cut from a single block of stone. The Tiahuanaco

people had trade links with the Amazon jungle and the Pacific coast, exporting potatoes, root crops, and llama products. In the 10th century, Tiahuanaco colonies were established on the coasts of southern Peru and northern Chile. Tiahuanaco's distinctive art and architectural styles influenced the central highlands and southern Peru, northern Chile, Bolivia, and Argentina. Tiahuanacan influence spread over a wide area of the Central Andes and is especially evident because of its unique ceramics. Typically, pottery was pointed black-on-white on a red polished surface, although later styles employed as many as six colors. Geometric designs were common as well as stylized pumas, condors, and serpents. The kero (a flared-rim beaker) is a characteristic form. Articles of bronze, copper and gold suggest that the city may also have been an important metallurgical center. Iconographic links with Huari to the north are such that a strong economic and cultural bond between the two is assumed. Tiahuanaco and Huari together constitute the Middle Horizon style of the Andes. (*syn.* Tiwanaku)

Tianko Panjang: Cave site in central Sumatra with an obsidian microlith industry of c. 9000 BC (e.g., unretouched flakes).

Tibava: Early Copper Age cemetery and settlement of the Tiszapolgár culture, located in the upper Bodrog Valley in eastern Slovakia and dated to the late 4th millennium BC. The site lies near a pass across the Carpathians. The richness of its grave goods shows it was an area of trade; the largest collection of Early Copper Age gold pendants in the Carpathians has been found, as well as south Polish and Volhynian flint nodules and rich copper finds.

Tiefstichkeramik: A style of pottery decoration used by the Funnel Beaker culture of Germany and Holland, c. 3000–2700 BC. The decoration is short, deeply incised bands and zigzags. The style is associated with the hunebed tombs.

Tiekene-Boussoura: Megalithic site in eastern Senegal, of the 6th–8th centuries AD. There are 30 monuments and nine circles of upright stones enclosing multiple burials. The pottery suggests a highly stratified society.

Tiemassas: Site in Senegal, south of Dakar, with extensive undated microlithic industry. There may have been successive occupation phases, including a pre-pottery phase characterized by large backed tools, geometric microliths, and hollow-based and leaf-shaped bifacial projectile points.

Tievebulliagh: Neolithic ax factories near Cushendall, Ireland, where Group IX porcelanite axes were made. These axes are widely found in Ireland and in mainland Britain (western Scotland).

tightly flexed: A term used to describe the position of a burial where the body is positioned with the knees touching the chest and the arms folded close to the body.

Tiglathpileser: Three Assyrian kings bore this name. The first (c. 1115–1077 BC) brought about a brief revival of Assyrian power by his conquests in Syria, Urartu, and Babylon. The second reigned from c. 965–932 BC, but was not significant. Tiglathpileser III (745–727 BC) was the real founder of the later Assyrian Empire; he restored and extended the empire after the 9th century Neo-Assyrian Empire had collapsed. He set up an administration and made military conquests of Syria and Palestine. He also annexed Babylon (Babylonia) as a client state, effectively merging the kingdoms. (*syn.* Tiglath-pileser)

Tikal: Large and important site of the Maya people in the rain forest of Petén, Guatemala, dating to 800 BC. The earliest buildings were constructed in 800 BC when it was a simple farming village. It is the most thoroughly studied of the great lowland Maya sites and peaked AD c. 600–800 in the Classic period (AD c. 300–900), when Tikal was one of the largest and politically most important Maya capitals. Studies of its architecture, tombs, art style, settlement pattern, subsistence and storage, and artifacts have accompanied an extensive mapping project. A population of between 45,000–75,000 occupied 120 square kilometers. Six statuesque limestone temple pyramids, giant paved plazas, shrines, palatial residences, ball courts—in all, 3,000 buildings, hundreds of monuments, stelae, altars are among the ruins. It is also the location of the oldest Maya monument known, AD 292. Archaeologists have been able to work out the dynastic history of Tikal on the basis of stela inscriptions and have identified the tombs of individual listed rulers. Numerous elite burials containing exotic materials, such as jade, obsidian, and stingray spines occur in the Great Plaza and in some of the temple-pyramids. Commoners, by contrast, are usually buried under their houses. Archaeological data confirmed that there were close relations with Teotihuacán during the Early Classic period; Tikal was an important post in the great trading network that Teotihuacán had established in southern Mesoamerica. Like other lowland Maya sites, Tikal was abandoned around AD 900.

tile: Thin, flat slab or block used structurally or decoratively in building.

Tilemsi valley: A tributary valley of the River Niger, which ends at Gao in Mali, Africa. The Tilemsi valley may have been an area where domestic animals were introduced into West Africa by pastoralists who moved south after the desiccation of the Sahara after 4500 BP. (*syn.* Tilemsi)

Tilkitepe: Halaf culture site in eastern Anatolia, the northernmost documented representation of the culture. There was also a Chalcolithic and Early Bronze Age occupation. Obsidian sources are near Lake Van.

till: An aggregate of material—unsorted soil consisting of sand, gravel, clay, and unsorted stones, and deposited directly by a glacier or ice sheet. All grades of particle size may be found. Till is sometimes called boulder clay because it is composed of clay, boulders of intermediate sizes, or a mixture of these. Ice does not sort the material it carries, and the range of particle sizes, as well as the range of rock types, depends on the geology over which the ice sheet or glacier has flowed. There are two types of till, basal and ablation. Basal till is that carried in the base of the glacier and commonly set under it. Ablation till is that carried on or near the surface of the glacier and deposited as the glacier melted. (*syn.* boulder clay)

Tillya-Depe: Iron Age site in southern Bactria, Afghanistan, dating to the first half of the 1st millennium BC. There was a central fortified architectural platform and a group of Kushan "royal tombs" dug after abandonment of the site. The graves were very rich, with gold vessels and jewelry, and were dated to the late 1st millennium BC. Afghanistan's archaeological discoveries are recounted by Viktor Sarianidi in *The Golden Hoard of Bactria: From the Tillya-tepe Excavations in Northern Afghanistan* (1985), an illustrated account of grave goods excavated from an early Kushan princely cemetery.

timber lacing: A technique for strengthening a stone or earthen rampart by means of a timber framework. Timber lacing was used in the second city at Troy and for various Minoan and Mycenaean buildings. In Europe, it was used for defense works from the 10th century BC and also at many of the Iron Age hill fort sites in the Hallstatt and La Tène periods. Timber was occasionally used as a lacing for brickwork, particularly in large-scale work such as the defenses or the granary at Mohenjo-daro.

timber-slot: A trench dug to contain a horizontal beam. (*syn.* timber slot)

time-marker or time marker: A temporally significant class of artifacts defined by a consistent clustering of attributes. (*syn.* horizon marker)

time–space grid: A method synthesizing temporal and spatial distributions of data and used in the culture historical approach based on period sequences in culture areas.

Timmari: Hilltop settlement site and associated cemetery near Matera, Italy, with the main occupation in the Late Bronze Age and Early Iron Age. The Neolithic occupation had Serra d'Alto ware. The associated cemetery is an urnfield of the so-called Proto-Villanovan group. The urns were placed in several layers and sometimes marked by small standing stones; there are some bronzes of Proto-Villanovan type. The cemetery is dated c. 11th–10th centuries BC.

Timna': Two sites: Capital city of the Qatabanian kingdom of southern Arabia and an area of copper-smelting sites in southern Israel. In the 1st millennium BC, Timna' in Arabia was a walled city; it was destroyed c. 1st century AD in a war. The site has produced a number of important inscriptions in the local South Arabian language and script. North of the city is a cemetery site with a series of structures made of stone and mud brick. The tombs have been robbed, but have yielded some sculpture, inscribed tablets, bronzes, pottery, and jewelry. In Israel, the presence of copper (in Palestine) is mentioned in the Bible, and archaeologists have identified remnants of ancient smelting operations, complete with crude furnaces and slag heaps, as being of the Egyptian pharaonic and Solomonic periods. The ancient mines are called Mikhrot Shelomo ha-Melekh—King Solomon's Mines. There is also a temple of the goddess Hathor, showing Egyptian interest in the area during the New Kingdom. (*syn.* Hajar Kohlan)

Timonovka: Upper Palaeolithic sites in European Russia on the Desna River, dated 15,110–12,200 bp. Two mammoth-bone houses exist from the first occupation.

Timor: An island of the Malay Archipelago, eastern Indonesia, possibly a staging point for early migrations to Australia. Timor and neighboring Flores had possible Pleistocene industries. There is some evidence of early Pleistocene land bridges reaching the island from Java. The earliest archaeological dated remains come from caves in east Timor, where flake industries date from c. 11,000 BC and Neolithic cultures appear after 3000 BC.

Timur (1336–1405): Turkic/Mongol conqueror who made Samarkand the capital of a vast nomad empire extending from Mongolia to the Mediterranean, but centered on Iran, Afghanistan, and Soviet central Asia. Many Timurid monuments, built by Timur himself and his grandson, Ulugbek, still survive in Samarkand. The monuments are covered in azure, turquoise, gold, and alabaster mosaics and are dominated by the great cathedral mosque and his mausoleum, the Gur-e Amir. Of Islamic faith, he is remembered for his barbarous conquests and the cultural achievements of his dynasty. (*syn.* Timour, Timur Lenk, Timurlenk, Tamerlane, Tamburlaine)

tin: A malleable, comparatively scarce metallic element, which is used as a constituent in alloys, notably bronze. In the Old World, ancient sources are known in England, Spain, and Bohemia—with others probably in central Italy and eastern Turkey. Although the New World had no Bronze Age, some tin was used in Mexico for vessels and ornaments, and it was alloyed with copper in Middle America and the Andean countries. Tin is extracted from cassiterite.

Ting: A type of cream-colored Chinese porcelain made in China, mainly in the form of tripod bowls, during the Sung AD (960–1279) and Yüan (AD 1280–1368) Dynasties. Ting ware may be either plain or decorated with incised, molded, impressed, or carved designs. Characteristic forms include bowls, cups, and dishes. Fired upside down, many pieces, especially bowls, have an unglazed rim banded with metal. (*syn.* Ting ware; Ding)

Tinkayu: Series of sites on the edge of a now-dry lake near the Madai Caves in eastern Sabah, Borneo. The pebble and flake industry produced many well-made bifacially flaked lanceolate knives and large tabular bifaces of chert—of a kind previously unknown from Southeast Asia. They are dated c. 28,000–17,000 BP. (*syn.* Tinkayu)

tin glaze: The process of adding tin oxide to other ingredients during the glazing of pottery to produce an opaque, white-enameled effect. It was used from c. 1000 BC by the Assyrians; in the 8th–9th centuries AD, Persian and Islamic potters rediscovered the technique, and it was transmitted to Spain, Italy, France, and Holland. Tin glaze was probably first used to hide faults of color in the body, for most clays contain a variable amount of iron that colors the body from buff to dark red. Tin-glazed wares look somewhat as though they have been covered with thick white paint.

Tintagel: Site on the northwest coast of Cornwall, England, with the ruins of a Norman castle stretching across the isthmus. It was built on the site of a Celtic monastery that appears to have existed from AD c. 350–850. Legend has it that King Arthur was born there. The earls of Cornwall occupied the castle in Norman times and built the chapel. Excavations have revealed several complexes of dry-stone buildings, and there are large quantities of sub-Roman imported sherds of Mediterranean origin.

Tintan: Holocene site in northern Mauritania, Africa, with 50 skeletons of the Mechta-Afalou type.

tipi ring: Any circle of stones found in the Northern (Great) Plains of North America, thought to be the remains of weights used to hold up a tipi (tepee).

tipline: Term applied to a feature in places where rubbish has been dumped (pits, ditches, mounds) and the deposit assumes a sloping line as a result of the material slipping until it reaches a point (or angle) of rest. The stratigraphy of such a deposit shows a number of sloping levels, or tip lines, and by studying the direction and disposition of these it is often possible to see how the deposit is accumulated. (*syn.* tip line)

Tirimoana pa: Earthwork hill fort on Hawkes Bay, North Island, New Zealand, with early storage pits for sweet potatoes dated to AD c. 1000. This is evidence that Maoris raised sweet potatoes from their initial settlement of New Zealand. The main ditch and bank defenses with palisades were built between 1400–1600.

Tîrpesti: Settlement site of the Cucuteni-Tripolye culture, located in Moldavia, Romania, and dated to the start of the 4th millennium BC. It is a characteristic promontory site, surrounded by a ditch. The remains of 10 fired clay house floors have been discovered, associated with a rich Pre-Cucuteni III pottery assemblage and figurines.

Tiryns: A fortified citadel of the Mycenaeans in the Argolid, Greece, an important Bronze Age center. The palace of its rulers, a megaron opening onto a porticoed court, was decorated with frescoes after the style of the Minoans. They include one of the best surviving representations of the bull-leaping rite and the fresco of a court lady carrying an ornamental casket. The walls of cyclopean masonry contain corbelled galleries, whose construction as attributed by the ancients to the Cyclopes from Lycia. The settlement was occupied from the Early Bronze Age, but the palace and the massive defensive wall were constructed c. 1400 BC. Excavation also revealed an Early Helladic structure. Tiryns was destroyed c. 1200 BC, like other Mycenaean sites.

Tisza: Late Neolithic culture of eastern Hungary, centered on the middle Danube region east of the River Tisza of the early 4th millennium BC, with tell and horizontal settlements. Characteristic are anthropomorphic vessels and pottery with incised basketry designs or with paint applied after firing. The wide variety of forms included footed and pedestaled bowls. Cereal production was important, as demonstrated by the large quantity of cereal storage jars, fired clay bins, and granaries in the villages. There was domestication of aurochs and intensive cattle husbandry. The culture is contemporaneous with the Lengyel culture of east-central Europe.

Tiszapolgár: The oldest stage of the Hungarian Copper (Eneolithic) Age, c. 3500–3000 BC, and successor to the Tisza culture. It is named for Tiszapolgár-Basatanya, a cemetery in the plain of eastern Hungary with 156 graves containing single inhumations accompanied by pottery, long flint blades, and a few copper objects. The oldest graves belong to the Tiszapolgár phase, while the more recent ones are of the Bodrogkeresztur culture. Most domestic occupations were small-scale and short-lived farmsteads. The pottery is a continuation of the Tisza tradition, but with little or no decoration.

Tito Bustillo: Cave site in Asturias, Spain, with portable and parietal polychrome art of the Upper Magdalenian and engraved stones of that time, c. 14,250 bp.

Titterington culture: A nonceramic Late Archaic culture of the Midwest, c. 2500–1900 BC, with small hunting and processing camps, base settlements, and mortuary sties. The artifacts include bifaces and were not heat treated. (*syn.* Titterington Focus)

Tivoli: Roman city in central Italy, captured by Rome in the 4th century BC and later a fashionable resort with fine villas. It received Roman citizenship in 90 BC. It is important for its architecture. There are remains of wealthy Roman residences, including Hadrian's (AD 118–128)—the largest and most sumptuous imperial villa in the Roman Empire. It contained palaces, libraries, guest quarters, public baths, and two theatres. Among other surviving Roman monuments are two small temples and the great temple of Hercules Victor (Ercole Vincitore), remains of aqueducts, and the poet Horace's Sabine farm. (*syn.* Tibur)

Tiy (c. 1400–1340 BC): Important queen of Egypt, principal wife of the late 18th Dynasty ruler Amenhotep III (reigned 1390–1353 BC). She exerted considerable influence on her husband and son Akhenaten (Amenhotep IV; 1352–1336 BC). (*syn.* Tiye)

Tlaloc: Mesoamerican rain and fertility god, usually depicted wearing a fringed mouth-mask or a spectacle-shaped frame around his eyes, in the art of the Aztec people of Teotihuacán. Under various names, Tlaloc was worshipped by other Mexican tribes: Chac (lowland Maya), Tajin (Totonacs), and Cocijo (Zapotecs). Images of Tlaloc occur in many contexts over a considerable period, such as at Copán, Monte Alban, Kaminaljuyu, and Chichen Itza. During the Classic period, his image appears on pottery, wall painting, and architecture.

Tlapacoya: Site in central Mexico on ancient Lake Chalco, with human remains dated to 21,000 BC. The site has produced important archaeological information from several different periods and environmental data from the Pleistocene onward. There are chipped stone tools with radiocarbon dates of c. 22,000–20,000 BC. Sedentary life occurred between 6000–4500 BC during the preceramic period, and a sequence of Pre-Classic pottery styles has given information on early village life in the Basin of Mexico. The small Pre-Classic village site has an early pyramid and Olmec cultural material.

Tlatilco: Pre-Classic village site just outside present-day Mexico City, dated to c. 1500–1000 BC, with a cemetery of more than 500 graves. The graves had local artifacts and some of the Olmec style, including figurines showing clothing types, hairstyles, skin decoration, and various occupations. Although there is no monumental stone architecture, low earth pyramids and bottle-shaped pits filled with household refuse indicate permanent residence. Located on an exit point on the western side of the valley, Tlatilco may possibly have been one of a number of stations on an Olmec trade route.

tlatoani: The Nahuatl (Aztec) term for ruler, the head of the state. All household heads owed allegiance, respect, and tax obligations to the tlatoani. It was mostly an inherited position; in some areas, succession passed from father to son; in others, the succession went through a series of brothers and then passed to the eldest son of the eldest brother. In still other states, the office was elective, but the choice was limited to sons or brothers of the deceased ruler. The ruler lived in a large, multiroom masonry palace inhabited by a number of wives, servants, and professional craftsmen. He was carried in a sedan chair in public and held considerable power: appointing bureaucrats, promoting to higher military status, organizing military campaigns, and distributing booty and tribute. He also owned private estates with serfs, was the final judge in legal cases, was titular head of the religious cult, and head of the town market.

tlatoque: An Aztec ruler of a city-state in the Basin of Mexico. Such a ruler was supported by the produce grown on communal land and by tributes paid in labor and services. The tlatoque claimed descent from Quetzalcóatl through the Toltecs.

To'aga: Site on the coast of Ofu Island, Samoa, occupied from 3700–3300 BP, possibly Lapita. The succeeding assemblage is c. 2500–1900 BP and has ceramics, shell fishhooks, and ornaments. Much shell and bone have been preserved.

Toalian industry: Mid-Holocene stone flake and blade industry of a number of caves in southern Sulawesi, Indonesia, c. 6000 BC and later. The industry developed out of preceding flake industries and is characterized by small backed flakes and microliths and well-made Maros points. The Toalian industry may have continued into the 1st millennium AD and overlapped with pottery from the late 3rd millennium BC. The earliest traces of human habitation on Celebes are stone implements of the Toalian culture.

Toca de Esperança: Preceramic site in eastern Brazil with a questionable date of 295,000 bp on a level with extinct Pleistocene fauna and crude stone tools.

Tocra: Greek city in Cyrenaica, Libya, founded c. late 7th century BC, with imported Archaic Greek pottery in votive deposits.

Toftum: Neolithic site in Jutland, Denmark, with a causewayed ditch and material from the Fuchsberg phase c. 3400 BC.

toggling harpoon: A type of detachable harpoon head attached to shaft by a line and float.

Togolok: Late Bronze Age sites in the Murghab delta, Turkmenia, with a material culture similar to the Bactrian Late Bronze Age. Togolok is also a chronological phase, c. 2nd quarter of the 2nd millennium BC, with continuity with the preceding Gonur phase.

Togueres: Flood plain area in Mali, Africa, with material from an agricultural fishing people and occupied c. 1000–800 BP (Toguere Galia), c. 1000–500 BP (Toguere Dowpil).

Tohoku: District of northern Honshu Island, Japan, used in archaeological documents, including Aomori, Iwate, Akita, Yamagata, Miyagi, and Fukushima Prefectures.

tohua: In the Marquesas Islands, Polynesia, the large rectangular ceremonial plaza—flat areas surrounded by raised platforms. The grounds were used for ceremonies and daily social gatherings. This complex of structures, often 600 feet (200 meters) or more in length, was generally built on a huge artificial terrace carved out of a slope. Surrounding the plaza atop the terrace were the houses of the tribal chiefs and priests, temples and other sacred structures, and long sheds for spectators. At one end, there was usually a temple with a sacred banyan tree, in which were suspended the packaged bones of the illustrious dead of the tribe. A large example is Vahangeku'a in Taipivai Valley.

Tokai: District of Japan, used in archaeological documents, including modern Tokyo Metropolitan District and Chiba, Ibaragi, Saitama, Kanagawa, Shizuoka, Aichi, and Mie Prefectures.

token: Small artifacts, generally of clay, made into 1 of 16 types: cones, spheres, disks, cylinders, tetrahedrons, ovoids, rectangles, triangles, biconoids, paraboloids, bent coils, ovals, vessels, tools, animals, or miscellaneous. Such objects were used on early Neolithic sites in western Asia as counters to keep records of goods. A plain token was typical of the periods between 8000–4300 BC and after 3100 BC. The shapes are mostly restricted to cones, spheres, disks, cylinders, and tetrahedrons; the surface is usually plain. Complex tokens were typical of the 4th millennium BC temple administration and include all 16 types of tokens. Complex tokens are characterized by an extensive use of markings—linear, punctuated, or appliqué. Researchers (esp. D. Schmandt-Besserat) suggest that tokens were the precursor of writing as they began to be placed in clay bullae (envelopes) that were marked with a cylinder seal representing the content of the bullae. This led to writing pictographs and numbers on a tablet, and then to the writing of words.

Tokharian: Indo-European language that was spoken in northern Chinese Turkistan during the latter half of the 1st millennium AD. Documents from about 500–700 show two dialects: Tocharian A, from the area of Turfan in the east; and Tocharian B, chiefly from the region of Kucha in the west but also from the Turfan area. (*syn.* Tocharian, Tocharish)

Tolbaga: Upper Palaeolithic site on the Khilok River in south-central Siberia, with faunal remains dated c. 34,860 and c. 27,210 bp. Artifacts include retouched blades, side scrapers, end scrapers, points, and burins.

Toldos, Los: Stratified cave in Patagonia, southern Argentina, with a sequence of unifacial tools, fishtail points, and preceramic materials dating c. 10,600–2000 BC.

Tollund Man: Preserved body of an Iron Age man found in peat at Tollund Fen in Denmark; he had been hanged c. 3rd century BC. Tollund Man had been hanged with a leather rope, and his body was dressed only in a cap and belt. His stomach contents were sufficiently preserved for analysis; his last meal was gruel made of various seeds, both wild and cultivated.

Toltec: Important Mesoamerican people of composite origin—a mixture of Chichimec tribes and more advanced groups from Puebla and the Gulf Coast—who controlled central Mexico from AD 900–1100. After absorbing civilized peoples in the Valley of Mexico, the Toltecs produced a warrior-dominated society, worshiped their tribal god Tezcatlipoca, and put emphasis on human sacrifice. In the 10th century, they established their capital at Tula, north of modern Mexico City. The Toltec state ended in the departure of the Quetzalcoatl faction in AD 987. After conquering many Maya cities, this faction established itself at Chichen Itza and transported its architectural style but incorporated Maya features. This group of Toltecs was ousted about 300 years later. Evidence of Toltec influence (e.g., Mazapan ware, metallurgy, imported Plumbate ware, massive architectonic decoration) has been found at many sites, including Chichen Itza, Xochicalco, and Cholula. Numerous fragmented Toltec groups seem to have survived in central Mexico after the destruction of their capital, and their prestige caused many Post-Classic groups to claim them as ancestors, most notably the Aztec.

tomb: A burial structure or chamber; the term is applied loosely to all kinds of graves, funerary monuments, and memorials. In many cultures and civilizations, the tomb was superseded by, or coexisted with, monuments or memorials to the dead. The styles of tombs have undergone different phases of development in various cultures.

Tomskaya: Upper Palaeolithic site in Tomsk, western Siberia, with a small assemblage of burins and retouched blades, c. 18,300 bp. It is a rare kill site in Palaeolithic Russia.

Tonga: An archipelago of 169 islands in the southwestern Pacific Ocean (western Polynesia), inhabited at least 3,000 years ago by Austronesian-speaking peoples who made elaborately decorated Lapita pottery similar to that found on Fiji. It was settled, like neighboring Samoa, by Lapita colonists in the late 2nd millennium BC. Tonga maintains a pottery sequence throughout the 1st millennium BC, after which pottery manufacture ceases. After AD 1000, large monuments appear, which are related to the growth of the powerful centralized chiefdoms.

Tongsamdong: Neolithic shell midden in South Kyongsang Province, Korea, c. 4500–1500 BC, with Jomon pottery and obsidian among the Chulmun material.

tool: Any existing physical object that is in some way fashioned or altered by humans and employed for a specific task or purpose. Tools made of stone included of axes, adzes, arrowheads, spear heads, daggers, knife blades, scrapers, borers, burins, picks. The first tools date to c. 2,600,000 years ago, the beginning of the Palaeolithic Age, and are different-sized pebble tools called choppers. The chopper was the only tool used by man for almost 2,000,000 years, until the appearance of the hand ax, a superior (and sharper) version of the chopper.

tool kit or toolkit: A term for all the tools used by a given culture for its technology (spatially patterned), or for a set of tools used together for a specific task (functionally patterned).

Toolondo: Earth-cut fish-trap system in southwest Victoria, Australia, of unknown antiquity.

topographic map: Map that can be used to relate archaeological sites to basic features of the natural landscape. Topographic maps are cartographic representation of the Earth's surface at a level of detail or scale between that of a plan (small area) and a chorographic (large regional) map. Topographic maps show as accurately as possible the location and shape of both natural and manmade features. They depict topographic (land-form) data in combination with representations of archaeological sites.

topography: Art or practice of graphic depiction on maps or charts of the natural and manmade features of a place or region, especially to show their relative positions and elevations in relief and contour. Another definition is the configuration of a surface including its relief and the position of its natural and manmade features. Detailing of site topography is very important in archaeological site description. A transit, theodolite, and/or level may be used in making a topographic map.

Toprakkale: Site on Lake Van, eastern Anatolia (Turkey), which was the center of the Urartian state, c. 850–600 BC. A large temple complex was an Urartian fortress with storerooms and residential area and finds including bronze, carved ivory, and silk artifacts. There are other temples, storerooms, and so on, in the area in which some wall paintings remain. The walls of Toprakkale, erected in the 8th century BC, were of cyclopean masonry and sloped slightly inward, perhaps as a defense against earthquakes. Artifacts show a high level of artistic achievement, in bronze, gold, silver, and ivory. Excavations have also uncovered a basalt floor inlaid with limestone and marble, parts of a decorated marble frieze, and brilliantly polished red pottery vessels. Toprakkale is also the name of a fine burnished red ware of the Urartian period. (*syn.* Topra Kaleh)

torc: A neck ring, of gold or bronze, and penannular in shape (an almost-complete ring). Examples are made of spirally twisted metal and appeared in the Early Bronze Age of central Europe and continued to the Roman occupation, being particularly popular among the Celts. Very common in the La Tène Iron Age, examples of gold, silver, and electrum occur in graves and hoards. (*syn.* torque)

Torcello: Island and flourishing ancient city in the Laguna Veneta (Venice Lagoon), Italy. Founded in AD 452 by refugees from Altino on the mainland, Torcello was the head of an association of the communes of the lagoon until the seat of government was moved to the Rialto in 811. Excavations revealed an important glassmaking center and the remains of a 6th–7th century kiln that was producing a great range of glass tablewares.

Tordos: A site on the Mures River in Transylvania, Romania, with archaeological finds dating from the Middle Neolithic Age (3500–2000 BC). Its has given its name to the Transylvanian regional group of the Vinca culture and is often coupled with that of Vinca to describe a Middle Neolithic culture covering parts of Yugoslavia, Romania, and Hungary. Tordos is the largest Vinca site in Romania and has a collection of incised signs and a range of fired clay figurines. (*syn.* Turdas)

Torihama: An Initial-Early Jomon shell midden site in Fukui Prefecture, Japan, dating to c. 5000–3500 BC. Rich organic remains have been preserved by waterlogging, including a dugout canoe, canoe paddles, hunting bows, ax handles, lacquered wooden comb, basketry, melon rinds and seeds and mung beans, and many bone and wood artifacts.

Toro: A Late Yayoi village in Shizuoka Prefecture, Japan. Excavations have revealed 12 dwellings, two storage houses built on piles and with rat guards, and rice paddies. Artifacts include bronze ornaments, wooden bowls and other kitchen utensils, agricultural tools, and parts of looms.

Torralba: Lower Palaeolithic lakeside site in the Spanish province of Soria. Torralba and the nearby site of Ambrona have Acheulian tools (cleavers, flake tools, hand axes) and the remains of dismembered elephants and horses. The sites are of the Middle Pleistocene, c. 300,000–700,000 BP. Traces of fire are among the earliest known, possibly c. 0.4 million years ago. (*syn.* Torralba and Ambrona)

torre: The name for circular dry-stone towerlike structures built in Corsica (mainly in the south) during the Middle and Late Bronze Ages. They are typically of cyclopean masonry and measure 10–15 meters in diameter and 3–7 meters in height; normally a narrow entrance opens into a central corbelled chamber, sometimes with subsidiary niches. The basic plan was often changed to incorporate natural rock formations or extra corridors. The oldest examples are of the early 2nd millennium BC. Although the torri are superficially similar to the Naragi of Sardinia and the Talayots of the Balearic Islands, they are considerably smaller and not effective as defenses or refuges. (*syn.* pl. torri)

Torre in Pietra: Palaeolithic site just outside Rome with an Acheulian (Riss) and a Mousterian level, both with the bones of hunted mammals.

torsade: A decorative band in which two ribbons twist in a regular pattern around a row of circles. In the double torsade, three ribbons twist around two rows of circles.

tortoise core: In stone toolmaking, a distinctive core having the shape of a tortoise shell and characteristic of the Levalloisian culture. A nodule of flint is prepared to form a core resembling a tortoise, from which flakes are struck.

torus molding: A semicircular or cylindrical band that forms the edge of a stela or the corner of a stone wall; a large convex molding usually semicircular in cross-section, especially at the base of a column. Some are decorated with a pattern that suggests lashings around a pole or reed bundle.

Tószeg: A tell near Szolnok on the River Tisza in eastern Hungary, with a defining sequence for the Early Bronze Age of the region. The succession begins with the Neolithic Tisza culture, followed by the Copper Age Tiszapolgár culture, then the Bronze Age cultures of Nagyrév (Tószeg A), Hatvan (Tószeg B), and Füzesabony (Tószeg C and D). The site provides one of the most important stratigraphies in European prehistory; the settlement layers provide the Nagyrév–Hatvan–Füzesabony sequence of 1800–1300 BC.

total data acquisition: The investigation of all sample units in a population.

total excavation: Complete excavation of an archaeological site, confined mainly to smaller sites, such as burial mounds or campsites.

total system approach: Archaeological research based on the assumption that to reconstruct an ancient culture, all parts of it must be examined.

totem: Any object from the natural world, usually an animal, with which a particular clan or tribe considers itself to have a special association or even a blood relationship. It is also the term for a representation of such in an emblem or badge or a group of people in a Native American nation who share the same totem.

Totonac: A member of a Middle American Indian people of east-central Mexico. The Totonacs occupied the central part of Veracruz in the Post-Classic period and possibly in the Classic period. Artifacts from the ball game, scrolls, and figurines are common. The Totonac lived in two environments—high mesa, cool and rainy (highland Totonac), and coastal lowland, hot and humid (lowland Totonac). In ancient times, both grew corn (maize) and squash as staple crops. Lowland Totonac also kept bees, poultry, and hogs. Highland Totonac kept poultry and raised some livestock. At the time of the Spanish Conquest, Cempoala was the great city of the Totonacs with a population of around 30,000. The Totonacs paid tribute to the Aztecs. Today, this region is dominated by speakers of Totonac, a distant relative of Mayan, and the Totonac themselves claim that they built El Tajín.

toumba: In Greek archaeology, an artificial mound or tell. (*syn.* magoula)

tournette: A turntable that was rotated manually to assist in the manufacture of a pot. It was used in Mesopotamia from about 5000 BC. It was a forerunner of the potter's wheel (c. 3400 BC).

trace: Any physical characteristic of an artifact that can be described.

trace element: Elements present in a mineral in minor proportions (between 0.1–2.0%) but that are frequently characteristic of the original source of the material. Trace elements occur naturally in minerals in soils and sediment and are not added deliberately to a substance. Minute amounts of chemical elements found in minerals emit characteristic wavelengths of light when heated to incandescence. Quantitative analyses of metal, clay, obsidian, and so on, can show the amounts of the trace elements present and may suggest a source. Source identification can lead to further interpretations of trade and economic systems. (*syn.* accessory element, guest element)

trace element analysis: The use of quantitative chemical techniques, such as neutron activation analysis or x-ray fluorescence spectrometry, for determining the elements present in a mineral in minor proportions. These methods are widely used in the identification of raw material sources for metal, clay, obsidian, and so on. Trace elements emit characteristic wavelengths of light when heated to incandescence.

traceology: The study of the traces left by use on the cutting edges of stone tools, with the aid of a microscope.

tracer: A tool for marking out or engraving designs, used to outline the raised areas on a surface. In metalworking, a tracer was frequently used to outline the raised areas on the surface of repoussé metalwork. A tracer is worked by hammering.

trackway: A path beaten by use; an unsurfaced communication route that does not have the status of a road. An exception is the group of timber trackways discovered in boggy areas of the Netherlands and southwest England (c. 4th–3rd millennia BC).

tract: The sampling element in a quadrat sample research design.

trade: The transmission of material objects from one society to another; the buying and selling or exchange of commodities between nations or trading parties. Trade is a descriptive cultural model used in the culture historical approach.

tradition: A term describing the persistence in a given area over a period of individual attributes, artifact types, or technologies; a culture that exists for an extended period and usually over an extended area. An example is the chopping-tool tradition of South Asia. A tradition is also a series of archaeological phases or cultures that share cultural similarities. In American terminology, it is a sequence of cultures or pottery styles that develop out of each other and form a continuum in time. The term is used especially to designate specific New World cultures such as the Arctic Small Tool tradition, Big Game (Hunting) tradition, Mississippi(an) tradition, Woodland tradition, and Desert tradition. The attributes, styles, traits, or technologies develop continuously, thus forming an easily accounted-for series of advancements. There are problems with the use of this term: Where an industry is described as belonging to one culture with the tradition of another (e.g., Mousterian of Acheulian tradition for flint industries), it is unclear as to what is implied about the relation of the two industries.

trait: Any element of human culture—material or nonmaterial—or technology. This term can be used for any individual artifact or aspect of human culture, ranging from monument or artifact types to social or ritual practices.

trait list: A list of characteristics describing an archaeological culture.

Trajan's Column: Tall commemorative column erected in Rome in honor of the emperor Trajan (reigned AD 98–117) and dedicated on 18 May 113 (erected 106–113). The column marks the center of what was once the fabulous Trajan's Forum. Composed of 18 massive drums of marble, the column stands 38 meters, including the statue plinth. The decoration is a continuous spiral relief frieze commemorating the emperor's triumphs in Dacia (101–102, 105–106), and the column contains an internal spiral staircase. The ashes of the emperor and his wife, Plotina, were in its base at one time. The frieze is an invaluable source of information on the Roman and Dacian military.

trajectory: In systems thinking, the series of successive states through which the system proceeds over time, said to represent the long-term behavior of the system.

tranchet: A large Mesolithic or Neolithic chisel-ended flint artifact with a sharp straight cutting edge, produced by the removal of a thick flake at a right angle to the main axis of the tool. The technique was used for the manufacture of axes and adzes and allowed a blunted tool to be resharpened by removing another flake from across the edge. The tranchet technique has two definitions: (1) the removal of a large flat flake from the tip of a biface to form a straight cutting edge from the edge of the tranchet flake scar; or (2) the technique used to create or resharpen the ax or adze's cutting edge. (*syn.* tranchet ax; tranchet axe; tranchet technique; tranchet flake)

transcription: Any rewriting of a text from another script according to the conventions of one's own script.

transect: An arbitrary sample unit that is a linear corridor of uniform specified width. A straight line or narrow section through an archaeological site or feature, along which a series of observations or measurements is made.

transept: In church architecture, the transverse part of a cruciform church at right angles to the nave; a transverse nave, passing in front of the choir, and crossing the longitudinal or central nave of the church.

transepted gallery grave: A type of gallery grave having side chambers resembling transepts; a variant of the megalithic gallery grave in which side chambers (transepts) open from the main burial chamber. These tombs are found only in three areas: near the mouth of the River Loire in France, in the Bristol Channel region (e.g., Severn-Cotswold), and in northwest Ireland. The three are in some way interrelated, and all lie on western seaways linking Atlantic France with the British Isles. Some scholars regard those in France as variant passage graves, unrelated to the British Isles tombs.

transformational process: Any process, natural or human caused, that transforms an abandoned prehistoric settlement into an archaeological site over time. This includes the conditions and events that affect archaeological data from the time of deposition to the time of recovery.

transhumance: A subsistence practice that forms one aspect of seasonality of occupation; the transfer of cattle from summer to winter pasture and vice versa. It consists of the movement of farmers and their herds and flocks away from the winter settlement to upland pasture. Spring to autumn is spent on high pasture, and in winter animals are taken to a main settlement, often in sheltered valleys, where fodder has been collected. This movement of farmers results in the occupation of two sites at different times of the year by the same group of people. In Europe and the Old World, the term is used for pastoralist farmers and livestock. In the New World, the term is used for any animal-and-human migration. Identification of transhumance patterns is a focus of palaeo-economy. (*syn.* Transhumance; Transhumant)

transit: A surveyor's instrument used to produce topographic or planimetric maps through the measurement of horizontal and vertical angles and horizontal distances. It is similar to a level, alidade, and theodolite and is used for the same purposes as a theodolite. (*syn.* transit theodolite)

transliteration: The act or process of rewriting the characters or letters (signary) of one language into those of another used to represent the same sounds; writing in the closest corresponding characters of another alphabet or language. It is possible to reconstruct the original spelling from a transliteration, but not from a transcription.

transmission electron microscopy: A technique used to examine the internal and surface structure and microstructure of materials such as metals, ceramics, and stone. A type of electron microscope is used in which the specimen transmits an electron beam focused on it, image contrasts are formed by the scattering of electrons out of the beam, and various magnetic lenses perform functions analogous to those of ordinary lenses in a light microscope. The sample must be very thin for examination of its internal structure; this is achieved either by grinding and depositing the material onto carbon film, or by preparing thin foils of metallic or nonmetallic material by electropolishing or ion-thinning techniques. It is possible to study in detail such things as the wear arks on stone tools or the techniques of pottery making through examination of the surface.

transposed primary context: In midden formation, a primary context resulting from depositional activities.

transverse flaking: A technique similar to oblique flaking, but the flake scars lie at right angles to the central line of the artifact.

Traprain Law: Cone-shaped rocky hill ("law") east of Edinburgh, Scotland, which was a tribal stronghold of Iron Age peoples before and after the brief Roman occupation of the area. The Wotadini capital was on Traprain Law, but it appears that in about AD 500, after the Roman withdrawal from Britain, the capital was moved to the site of the present Castle. A silver treasure representing loot from the disintegrating Roman provinces, probably Gaul, c. 4th–5th centuries AD, has been found.

travertine: A compact, light-colored limestone (calcite) deposition formed by limestone in solution. It has been much used in architecture. Stalactites and stalagmites in caves are formed from travertine. Fossils and other remains may be found in travertine deposits, and dense travertine may sometimes be dated through uranium series dating and isotopic analysis. (*syn.* tufa)

travois: Native American vehicle consisting of two joined poles (transversely connected wooden shafts) pulled by a horse or dog (dragged at an angle to the ground). Found in North America, it is believed to be the first vehicle used by humans.

TRB culture: Abbreviated name for the Danish Tragterbecker or German Trichterrandbecher culture, alternatively known in English as the Funnel Beaker culture. It is the first Neolithic culture of northern Europe, found in southern Scandinavia, the Low Countries, northern Germany, and northern Poland, in the later 4th and early 3rd millennia BC. It is characterized by the use of a funnel-necked beaker with globular body. It is thought to represent the acculturation of local Mesolithic communities by contact with the Linear

Pottery culture group farther south. Five regional groups have been determined: a western group in the Netherlands, sometimes associated with hunebedden (megalithic burial monuments); a southern group in Germany; a southeastern group in Czechoslovakia; an eastern group in Poland; and a northern group in Denmark and Sweden. Settlement sites are not well known, but burials are abundant, especially Dysser in Scandinavia and Kujavian Graves in Poland; passage graves were eventually used. Other artifacts include ground stone axes and battle axes, and copper tools appear in later phases. The TRB culture is succeeded by—and perhaps developed directly into—the Single Grave culture. (*syn.* Funnel Beaker culture)

treasure trove: In law, treasure found hidden in the ground or elsewhere, but of unknown ownership. In Britain, treasure troves are the property of the State, although sometimes they are in part returned or recompensed to the owner of the land. To be declared treasure trove by a coroner's inquest, the items must be of gold or silver, must have been lost or hidden with the intention of recovery, and by someone who is no longer traceable. In these circumstances, the Crown takes possession, rewarding the finder with the market value or with the object itself if it is not required for the national collections.

treasury: Building used to contain precious objects—annexes of sanctuaries, for storing the offerings and goods of the sanctuaries and of the donor cities to which they belonged.

Trebeniste: Iron Age burial site of the Hallstatt D period, c. 6th–5th centuries BC, in Macedonia near Knoplje. The rich graves contained datable Greek imports and the site is the most northerly penetration of Greek goods during that period in lands adjacent to Greece.

tree line: A line marking the point in the Arctic north where trees do not grow because the subsoil is permanently frozen. Proceeding northward or as the elevation increases, the height of the trees gradually decreases while the spacing between them increases until a point is finally reached where the trees give way to tundra—the tree line.

tree-ring dating: The use of annual growth rings in trees to date archaeological sites. (*syn.* dendrochronology)

Trelleborg: Site in southern Zealand, Denmark, of a well-preserved Viking fortress of AD c. 1000. It is an insular-type Viking military camp with a central circular fortification, substantial earth-and-timber bank, and four timber gates. The internal enclosure is divided into four quadrants each containing four boat-shaped longhouses. Trelleborg has a concentric outer defensive bank and an adjoining enclosure and 13 additional buildings between the two enceintes. Trelleborg was used between the mid-10th and early 11th centuries.

trenching: An excavation technique in which a site is penetrated with long, narrow trenches that reveal the vertical dimension of the area, to explore the horizontal dimension along one axis. (*syn.* trench)

trend surface analysis: A method used to make a generalized map from observed data and used to highlight the main features and important trends of a geographic distribution. Archaeological observations mapped are discontinuous and at isolated points and therefore must be used to give information over a wider area. This is done either by averaging the values at a number of points to produce a general value or by a form of linear regression analysis, which finds the contours that best fit the observations plotted on the map. The map produced then shows a general trend of the distribution, along with localized fluctuations. The technique is most useful for displaying archaeological data in a simplified and generalized form, making it easier to examine and explain the broad regional trends and the local variations. It can be applied to several different artifact distributions at the regional level and has also been used to describe the distribution of artifact types in a site.

trepanation: A surgical practice in which small sections of cranial bone are removed or a hole is made in a living human's head. It was used as an attempt to cure tumors, to relieve the brain of pressure after injury, to cure headaches or epilepsy, or to cure insanity. It is clear that many subjects survived the operation, for in several cases the bone has started to regenerate, while in others there is evidence for successive trepanations. There are many prehistoric records of the practice, especially in Neolithic France and Pre-Columbian Peru. The practice survives among some primitive peoples. (*syn.* trepanning, trephining; trephination)

Tressé: Late Neolithic allée couverte in Ille-et-Vilaine, France. There is a paved chamber roofed by seven capstones and artifacts including coarse ware pottery and blades of Grand Pressigny flint.

Tres Zapotes: Important Late Pre-Classic Olmec ceremonial site, located near the Tuxtla Mountains in southern Veracruz, Mexico. The site has cut-stone facings on its rectangular pyramid and numerous unevenly scattered earthen mounds. It flourished long after the abandonment of La Venta or San Lorenzo and was partly contemporaneous with Middle Pre-Classic Olmec florescence. Occupied from 1000–600 BC, the pottery was flat bottomed and white rimmed and there were colossal stone heads. Later periods showed the increasing presence of Izapan pottery forms and had Maya-influenced stelae. The site's most important find is the epi-Olmec Stele C, which has the earliest Maya Long Count date yet discovered, 31 BC.

Trewhiddle: Site in Cornwall, England, with a hoard of metal objects deposited in the latter part of the 9th century AD. Included were some bronze plaques decorated with niello-inlaid animal ornament, Anglo-Saxon coins, and a silver chalice ornamented with beaded wire.

triad: A term used to describe a group of three gods, usually a divine family of father, mother, and child, worshiped at particular cult centers. It was also a means of linking three formerly independent gods of an area, especially in Egypt's New Kingdom.

Trialeti: Site in southern Georgia in the Caucasus, where kurgans have been excavated and an extensive culture revealed. The Bronze Age burials (c. 2nd millennium BC) were often accompanied by chariots, gold and other metal objects, jewelry, and pottery.

Trianda: Minoan colony site on Rhodes, founded in the 16th century BC, which facilitated trade between Crete and Cyprus. The site was abandoned in the 14th century.

triangulation: A surveying method used to measure a large area of land by establishing a baseline from which a network of triangles is laid out. Triangulation is based on the laws of plane trigonometry: If one side and two angles of a triangle are known, the other two sides and angle can be readily calculated. One side of the selected triangle is measured; this is the baseline. The two adjacent angles are measured by means of a surveying instrument (transit, theodolite), and the entire triangle is established. By constructing a series of such triangles, each adjacent to at least one other, values can be obtained for distances and angles not otherwise measurable. Triangulation can be used to plan features or significant finds whose exact position it is important to record.

tribe: An egalitarian society generally composed of a centrally organized group of bands. Its kinship is more complex than that of the band, and its economy is often agricultural rather than foraging, although they also include nomadic pastoral groups whose economy is based on exploitation of livestock. Individual communities tend to be integrated into the larger society through kinship ties. Political dominance is gained through achieved leadership. Tribes may be aggregated into higher order clusters, called nations.

tribunal: In Roman architecture, a raised platform in a basilica on which the magistrates' seats were placed. It was also the rostrum, or raised platform, from which the commander of a fort spoke to his assembled men or dealt out justice.

triclinium: In Roman architecture, the dining room, often with an arrangement of three couches around a table or placed along the walls of a square room. (*syn.* pl. triclinia)

Trier: Principal Roman city of northeast Gaul, first the capital of the Treveri, a Celto-Germanic tribe. It became the chief city of the Roman province of Belgica in the 2nd century AD and was adopted by Constantius and Constantine in the 4th century AD as an imperial capital. The city's strategic position at a crossroad contributed to its rapid rise as a commercial and administrative center. Remains include an amphitheater (AD c. 100), Constantinian basilica, baths, and Porta Nigra (ornate late Roman gateway). Trier has more preserved Roman monuments than any other German city. A mint was in use from about AD 296. (*syn.* Augusta Treviroum; Roman Augusta Treverorum; Trèves)

triglyph: In the Doric architectural order, the part of an entablature of a building that alternates with a metope. It consisted of three elements separated by two vertical grooves in a Doric frieze.

trigonolith: In the West Indies, a triangular or breast-shaped stone object, with or without decoration, usually representing a zemi. Small pottery or shell examples can also be found. (*syn.* three-cornered stone)

trilithon: A stone structure consisting of two standing stones with a third (the lintel) placed across the top of them, forming an arch or doorway, as at Stonehenge. Trilithons appear in megalithic monuments of various types, but the most impressive examples are Stonehenge's five huge ones of sarsen stones, skillfully joined together with mortice and tenon joints. The island of Tonga has a massive coral trilithon of AD c. 1200. (*syn.* trilith)

Trinil: Site in east-central Java where the first *Homo erectus* fossil skull and the first recorded pre-Neanderthal human fossil were found. The human remains found in the 1890s included a skull cap, some teeth, and five leg bones. The Middle Pleistocene fauna of Java, c. 1.3 million–500,000 BP, are also named for Trinil. They overlie deposits of the Djetis faunal zone, which are about 1,600,000 years old. Djetis deposits have also yielded the fossil remains of hominids that have been related to the australopithecines or to *Homo erectus* or *Homo habilis*; these remains have been assigned to *Meganthropus palaeojavanicus*.

trinomial: The Smithsonian system of archaeological site numbering. The trinomial (three number) consists of the state number (or alpha designation), the county alpha designation, and the site number.

tripartite: The architectural plan used in 'Ubaid houses and early Mesopotamian temples, with a long central room flanked by rows of smaller rooms.

Triple Alliance: A military alliance formed in AD 1428, in the Late Post-Classic Period, between Tenochtitlán, Texcoco, and Tacuba, which became the dominant force in the Lake Texcoco region of the Basin of Mexico. They joined together to overthrow the Tepenacs in the city-state of Azcapotzalco. The Aztecs eventually dominated the alliance, although Texcoco, under the philosopher-king Nezahuacoyotl, became a renowned center of culture and learning.

Tripolye: The type site, in the Balkans near Kiev, of a

Neolithic-Copper Age culture, which formed in the Western Ukraine and east Romania (Cucuteni culture) in the 4th millennium BC. It is best known for its villages of up to 100 timber longhouses, and for fine polychrome vessels painted with curvilinear and geometric designs. There were also copper and gold objects. Tripolye people practiced shifting agriculture, frequently moving their settlements. The Tripolye culture came to an end with the expansion westward of steppe cultures of kurgan or single-grave type. The Cucuteni-Tripolye culture was a Neolithic European culture that arose in the Ukraine between the Seret and Bug Rivers, with an extension to the Dnepr River, about 3000 BC.

trireme: The earliest type of Greek warship, which used a battering ram in the prow as its main weapon and was named for the three banks of oars by which it was propelled.

triumphal arch: In Roman architecture, a form of monument used to commemorate victories, the achievements of emperors, or the restoration of peace. The archway is usually freestanding and decorative, the earliest occurring in the 2nd century BC, and found in all provinces. Consisting of one to three arches, sometimes with intersection, it is commonly decorated with relief panels and attached sculptures. These arches often spanned either a street or a roadway, preferably one used for triumphal processions. Most of the triumphal arches were built during the empire period (27 BC–AD 476).

Trojan War: The legendary conflict between the early Greeks and the people of Troy in western Anatolia, dated by later Greek authors to the 12th or 13th century BC and lasting 10 years. It was described in Homer's *Iliad* and *Odyssey* as occurring when Paris, son of the king of Troy, eloped with Helen, wife of Menelaus, king of Sparta. Menelaus's brother, Agamemnon, king of Mycenae, raised an army and besieged Troy.

Troldebjerg: Middle Neolithic TRB settlement on the island of Langeland, Denmark. There are longhouses divided up into smaller units.

Trondheim: Third largest city of Norway, founded in 997 by King Olaf I Tryggvason as the village of Kaupangr. He built a church and a royal residence, Kongsgård, and it became the great medieval capital of Norway. Located along the ice-free Trondheim Fjord, it commanded land and sea routes to Russia and the rest of Europe. The sagas describe it as a flourishing late Viking trade center with as many as three royal palaces, several churches, and a Thing-place where parliament assembled. Excavations have uncovered only part of the timber-built medieval town: the outlines of a 10th-century hall-type house, 11th-century church, and other smaller buildings. (*syn.* Kaupangr, Nidaros)

trophic levels: Levels in the food chain characterized by similar energy consumption. A trophic level is a step in a food chain of an ecosystem. The organisms of a chain are classified based on their feeding behavior: (1) the producers, green plants; (2) the herbivores, or plant eaters; (3) primary carnivores, or meat eaters, which eat the herbivores; and (4) secondary carnivores which eat the primary carnivores.

troweling: Small-scale, controlled hand excavation, best accomplished with a Marshalltown trowel.

Troy: Ancient city in northwestern Anatolia (Turkey), which holds an enduring place in both literature (the *Iliad*, *Odyssey*, etc.) and archaeology. A large mound, called Hisarlik (or Hissarlik) by the Turks, holds the ruins—as discovered by the German archaeologist Heinrich Schliemann. Between 1870–1890, Schliemann exposed most of the remains of the Early Bronze Age and showed that nine successive cities had stood on the site, of which he considered the second to be that described in Homer's *Iliad*. Wilhelm Dörpfeld, who continued excavations after Schleimann's death, established a chronology for the cities and believed the sixth to be Troy. In Troy VI (c. 1900–1300 BC), there was evidence of the arrival of invaders with horses and superior building techniques—possibly the Luwians. It was devastated by an earthquake c. 1300 BC. Carl William Blegen, who also worked there, argued for the earlier part of the seventh city. Troy VIIa represents a rebuilt city along the plan of Troy VI, but it was destroyed by fire c. 1220 BC, in what may have been the Trojan War. The nine main periods of occupation began in the mid-3rd millennium BC and ended with the Greco-Roman city of Ilion/Ilium. At the end of each period when a settlement was destroyed (usually by fire, or earthquake, or both), the survivors leveled the site and built new houses on it. Priam's gold treasure was found in Troy II, c. 2400–2200 BC. (*syn.* Hisarlik, Hissarlik, Ilion or Ilium)

trumpet: A brass wind musical instrument sounded by lip vibration against a cup mouthpiece. It has been made of horn, conch, reed, or wood, with a horn or gourd bell, as well as the modern brass instrument. The metal trumpet dates from the 2nd millennium BC in Egypt, when it was a small ritual or military instrument sounding only one or two notes. In the Late Bronze Age, it was made by riveting sheet bronze into the shape of a cattle horn.

Trundholm: Site where a bronze wheeled model of a horse pulling a disk, dated to c. 1650 BC, was found in the Trundholm bog in Zealand, Denmark. It probably represented a chariot of the sun and was deposited as a ritual offering.

trunnion: Either of a pair of cylindrical mounting lugs or projections on the sides of a cannon or mortar, by which it is pivoted on its carriage. A trunnion is also one of a pair of laterally projecting knobs on a stone or metal blade (ax, chisel, etc.) to assist in its hafting.

Trusesti: Large settlement and cemetery site of the Late

Neolithic Cucuteni-Tripolye culture, in Moldavia, Romania. The site has almost 100 complete house-plans on a promontory, enclosed on one side by a double ditch, and there were rich pottery assemblages of the Cucuteni A phase.

Truso: Baltic trading port of early medieval times, c. 9th century AD, described by the Anglo-Saxon traveler Wulfstan but not yet definitely located. It is believed to be on the eastern delta of the Vistula River.

Trzciniec: Early and Middle Bronze Age culture of eastern Poland, dating to the mid-2nd millennium BC. The type site near Lublin has a large number of houses with sunken foundations. Burial types are diverse, with inhumation and cremation, flat and barrow graves, occurring in varying combinations. It had ceramics and a flint industry, as well as imported bronze artifacts. The Trzciniec culture is closely related in material culture to the Komarow and Sosnicja groups farther to the east, in the Ukraine.

Tsangli: Neolithic–Bronze Age settlement mound in Thessaly, Greece, with characteristic gray matte-painted pottery.

Tshangula: Cave site in the Matopo Hills of southwestern Zimbabwe, with several layers of archaeological deposits preserving microlithic artifacts and sherds attributed to Bambata ware. The sequence includes Middle Stone Age and Later Stone Age assemblages and is also the name of a Middle Stone Age industry postdating 30,000 BP. This horizon contained backed microliths associated with diminutive implements and ostrich eggshell beads. (*syn.* Umguzan)

Tshikapa: A mining area and village in Zaire on the Kasai River where Early Iron Age pottery vessels of Urewe type were found in an undated context and without further archaeological associations. The discovery has been used as evidence for an early spread of Early Iron Age industries along the southern fringes of the equatorial forest.

Tshitolian: Later Stone Age Industry named after the Tshitolo Plateau in southern Zaire, the microlithic successor to the Lupemban, dated c. 14,000–5000 BP. Tshitolian industries also occur in Angola, Gabon, and Cameroon in equatorial Africa. The characteristic backed microliths are of a flared triangular shape and may have been hafted for use as transverse arrowheads. Other tool types are small picks, small core axes, and foliate points.

Tsodilo Hills: Later Stone Age and Iron Age rock shelters with rock art, in northwest Botswana. Depression Shelter in the Tsodilo Hills has evidence of continuous Khoisan occupation from about 17,000 BC to about AD 1650. There is also evidence of early farming settlement there, alongside Khoisan hunter and pastoralist sites, dated from about AD 550. Archaeologists therefore have difficulty in interpreting the hundreds of rock paintings in the Tsodilo Hills, which were once assumed to be painted by "Bushman" (San)

hunters remote from all pastoralist and farmer contact. (*syn.* Nqoma)

Tsountas, Christos (1857–1934): Greek archaeologist who excavated cemeteries of earlier phases of the Bronze Age on the Cycladic Islands and continued the work begun by Heinrich Schliemann at Mycenae. He also investigated settlement sites in Thessaly (Dhimini, Sesklo).

t-test: In statistics, a univariate test designed to discover differences among relatively small samples of variates. It is a method of testing hypotheses about the mean of a small sample drawn from a normally distributed population when the population standard deviation is unknown.

Tuc d'Audoubert: Deep cave system in the central Pyrenees, southwest France, with a few examples of Palaeolithic cave art. It is known for a bison modeled in clay, preserved deep in the cave.

tufa: A compact, light-colored limestone (calcite) deposition formed by limestone in solution. It has been much used in architecture. Stalactites and stalagmites in caves are formed from travertine. Fossils and other remains may be found in travertine deposits, and dense travertine may sometimes be dated through uranium series dating and isotopic analysis. (*syn.* travertine)

tuff: Solidified volcanic ash or dust; a soft, porous rock consisting of the compacted volcanic ash or dust. Tuffs may be grouped as vitric, crystal, or lithic when they are composed principally of glass, crystal chips, or the debris of pre-existing rocks, respectively. They can often be dated by potassium-argon dating. (*syn.* tuffaceous rock)

Tula: The Toltec capital, located in the modern state of Hidalgo, Mexico, then identified as Tollán. Founded on an already existing settlement in AD c. 960, it grew to cover 11 square kilometers. The site gained importance AD c. 800 after Teotihuacán fell. There was a stepped pyramid on which there was a temple, and the buildings had colonnaded halls. At its height, there were some 1,000 mounds and at least as many low rectangular house mounds, and five ball courts. The monumental civic architecture featured Talud-Tablero architecture. In sculpture, the most diagnostic figures are the Chac Mools, reclining human figures holding offering dishes, and the famous Atlantean statues that supported the roof of Pyramid B. The earliest pre-architectural phases at Tula are characterized by the presence of Coyotlatelco ware, but the dominant ceramic occurring after c. 1000 is Mazapan ware. Imported Plumbate ware also occurs frequently. Although the Toltec are associated with the introduction of metallurgy into central Mexico, no metals have been found. Tula was violently destroyed, probably by a Chichimec group, in either 1156 or 1168 (depending on how one reads the Calendar date). Although its exact location is not certain, an archaeological site near the contemporary town of Tula in Hidalgo state has been the consistent choice of historians. (*syn.* Tollán)

tula adze: In Australia, a hafted chisel made to work hardwoods. It is a thick, round stone flake, usually about 5 centimeters long, with a steeply trimmed working edge opposite an obtuse-angled striking platform. It usually has a prominent bulb and convex bulbar surface. Ethnographic examples are set in gum on the end of a wooden handle or spear thrower. The edge would be resharpened until the flake became elliptical, when it was discarded. In this form, with a heavily step-flaked edge opposite the striking platform, it is termed a "tula adze slug." Tula adzes are restricted to more arid regions, and the oldest examples come from Puntutjarpa (c. 8000–5000 BC) and are exactly like those still used by desert Aborigines. (*syn.* tula)

tulang mawas: Literally, "monkey bone," a long-shafted, socketed iron ax of Iron Age peninsular Malaysia, c. 300 BC.

Tule Springs: Site near Las Vegas, Nevada, with traces of human occupation c. 11,000 BP—in the form of hearths and artifacts.

Tulúm: Post-Classic Maya site on the eastern shores of Yucatán, Mexico, and one of the few walled Maya cities known. The wall stands 3–5 meters high and is 6 meters thick, with a series of civic and residential squat flat-roofed buildings around the ceremonial center. It was an important trading center.

tumbaga: An alloy of gold and copper common in Central and South America during the first millennium AD. It was used for making fine ornaments, particularly in the native cultures of Colombia.

tumulus: A mound of earth or stones built over a burial—most often a large, circular tomb. Tumuli were used for the burial chambers of Etruscan aristocrats in the Archaic period (6th–5th centuries BC), also in the Bronze Age, and later revived by the Roman emperors Augustus and Hadrian. (*syn.* pl. tumuli)

Tumulus culture: A Middle Bronze Age culture of the central Danube region in Czechoslovakia, Austria, and Bavaria, with burials beneath round barrows, dating c. 1500–1200 BC. The heartland of the Tumulus culture was Bavaria, Württemberg, and the area previously occupied by the Únetice culture, but distribution extended into north Germany and west as far as Alsace. With the introduction of urnfield burial, the Tumulus culture and the Middle Bronze Age came to an end. It is defined mainly by the dominant burial rite of inhumation beneath a burial mound, as well as a number of characteristic bronze types, found both in the burials and in hoards. It continued earlier trends in ceramics and metalwork, although more elaborate in form and decoration. (*syn.* Tumulus Bronze Age, Tumulus period)

Tuna el-Gebel: Site of the necropolis of Hermopolis Magna, including a complex of catacombs for the burial of sacred animals and an associated temple of Thoth, located on the west bank of the Nile, near modern Mallawi in Middle Egypt. There are Late Period/Greco-Roman tombs and underground galleries with burials of ibises and baboons.

tundra: An almost treeless region adjacent to polar ice; the region between ice caps and the tree line in lower Arctic latitudes. All but the top few inches of soil are permanently frozen, and only a few plants can grow—mosses, lichens, sedges, grasses, and stunted shrubs. There are two types: on level or rolling ground in polar regions (arctic tundra) or on high mountains (alpine tundra).

Tungus: Ethnolinguistic group of eastern Eurasia and Siberia who spoke Tungusic languages of the Altaic language family. They are believed to have entered the Korean peninsula in the 1st millennium BC (Bronze Age).

tunnel: A method of penetrating excavation that, instead of cutting through strata vertically, follows buried strata or features along one horizontal dimension.

tunnel handle: In pottery, a handle flush with the surface of the pot. It is usually produced by piercing two adjacent holes in the wall of the vessel before firing and adding a pouch of clay inside to prevent the contents from escaping. The feature was widely used around the western Mediterranean c. 3500–2000 BC. (*syn.* subcutaneous handle)

Turdas or Tordos: Site in Transylvania, northwest Romania, the name of a Vinca culture variant.

Turfan: City in the Uygur autonomous ch'ü (region) of Sinkiang, China, long the center of a fertile oasis and an important trade center on the main northern branch of the Silk Road. An oasis city, it was traditionally on the border between the nomadic peoples of the north and settled oasis dwellers of Sinkiang. Under the Han Dynasty (206 BC–AD 220), the Chinese knew it as the Chü-shih Kingdom. In 450, it became the new state of Kao-ch'ang. Eventually taken in the 13th century by the Mongols, Turfan enjoyed a new commercial prosperity as the Central Asian land routes flourished. (*syn.* Chinese: Turpan)

turf line: A layer of soil rich in organic material, which indicates a stratum or buried turf. A turf line may be the remains of a buried land surface or an artificial structure, possibly the cap of a mound or a layer of sod consolidating a barrow or rampart. It may also be the remains of vegetation that grew on the soil before burial. A real turf line indicates a pause in construction long enough for a soil to have developed.

Turin Papyrus: A hieratic manuscript of the 19th Dynasty of Egypt, which lists the kings of Egypt from earliest times to the reign of Ramses II (1279–1213 BC), under whom it was written. The papyrus is now in the Egyptian Museum in Turin, Italy, in very fragmentary condition, but it is still considered the most detailed and reliable of the existing Egyptian king lists. It lists not only names but also regnal years, months, and days and also divides pharaonic history into dynasties and into three major periods—Old Kingdom, Middle Kingdom, and New Kingdom. It was evidently copied from a more complete original. (*syn*. Turin Royal Canon, Turin Papyrus of Kings, Turin Canon)

turquoise: A phosphate gemstone, sky blue to pale green, which forms as veins and nodules in the fissures of sandstone and trachyte. It was mined by the Egyptians from the late Predynastic period onward and was almost as highly prized as jade in Mesoamerica. It was also highly prized for jewelry in western Asia and the American Southwest. Turquoise was obtained from the Sinai Peninsula before the 4th millennium BC in one of the world's first important hard-rock mining operations. It was transported to Europe through Turkey, probably accounting for its name, which is French for "Turkish."

turret: Towers of great height in proportion to their diameter, often with staircases and crowned with small spires. Two were placed between each mile castle on Hadrian's Wall as lookout posts and signal stations.

Turville-Petre, Francis Adrian Joseph (1901–1942): English archaeologist who worked in Palestine, discovering the "Galilee Skull" in Zuttiyeh Cave, the earliest hominid skull in the Levant. He also identified the late Palaeolithic Kebaran culture, c. 20,000–12,500 BP, in Kebara Cave, Mount Carmel.

Tuscan order: The simplest order of architecture, a Roman adaptation of the Doric order. The Tuscan has an unfluted shaft, a simple echinus-abacus capital, and no triglyphs. It is similar in proportion and profile to the Roman Doric but much plainer. The column is 7 diameters high. This order is the most solid in appearance of all the orders.

tussah: A type of strong, coarse, tan-colored silk obtained from the cocoon of wild silkworms in China and India (the products of various Asiatic Saturniidae, such as *Antheraea paphia*).

Tustrup: Neolithic mortuary house in a megalithic tomb cemetery in Jutland, Denmark, c. 2900 BC. Highly decorated pottery vessels accompanied the burial.

Tutankhamun (r. c. 1336–1327 BC): A minor Egyptian pharaoh of the late 18th Dynasty who came into great prominence when his tomb in the Valley of Kings at Thebes was found with minimal disturbance by Howard Carter and Lord Carnarvon in 1922. A son of Amenhotep III, he succeeded the heretic pharaoh Akhenaten. During an undistinguished reign of 9 years, he began the restoration of the worship of Amen (Amun) and returned the capital to Thebes. His more orthodox successors attempted to obliterate him from memory because of the taint of Aten worship, which he apparently never entirely threw off. The tomb, although probably far poorer than those of the greater pharaohs, yielded a remarkable treasure and great detail of the ritual of Egyptian royal burials. The mummy, with a magnificent inlaid gold mask, lay inside three cases—the innermost of pure gold weighing over a ton, the outer two of gilded wood. These were enclosed in a stone sarcophagus within successive shrines also of gilded wood, nearly filling the burial chamber. Three other rooms held chariots, furniture, statues, and other possessions of the king. It took 3 years to clear and preserve the contents of the wealthy tomb. The discovery stirred the public imagination and opened up a great interest in archaeology. (*syn*. Tutankhamen)

Tutishcainyo: One of the oldest sites in the Upper Amazon, South America, with evidence of human occupation on Lake Yarinacocha in eastern Peru. The distinctive sand or shell-tempered pottery was decorated with incision. The Early Tutishcainyo is dated to c. 2500–1300 BC. There is also wattle-and-daub construction.

tuyère: A metal nozzle through which the air is forced into a forge, hearth, kiln, or furnace from the bellows. In antiquity, it was usually of clay and often survives as the only evidence for a metalworking site. This short tube made of clay, through which the air from bellows could be blown into a furnace, was used to produce the high temperatures required for metalworking and smelting.

twining: Basketry made with a horizontal stitch or weft; a technique of textile or basket weaving in which the wefts are inserted in pairs, and twine around one another as they embrace each successive warp. The warp is relatively rigid, and the weft is relatively pliable. (*syn*. twined; twined basketry)

twist: The direction that cordage was rolled in its manufacture—either S-twist or Z-twist.

Ty (c. 2500 BC): Fifth Dynasty official who was overseer of the pyramid complexes and sun temples of the rulers Neferirkara and Nyuserra at Abusir, as well as the sun temples of Sahura and Raneferef. (*syn*. Ti)

Tylissos: Minoan settlement site on Crete with Neopalatial houses.

tympanum: The triangular space in a pediment, or the space between the top of a door and its surrounding arch. It is a vertical face that forms the rear of a pediment. (*syn*. tympanon)

type: A classification of artifacts based on the shared attributes of groups of artifacts or features, such as pottery types, projectile point types, or house types. The class is defined by a consistent clustering of attributes. In pottery, it is part of a standardized taxonomic classification based on stylistic attributes: modes and varieties (minimal units); types, groups, complexes, and spheres (maximal units).

type fossil: A tool characteristic of a particular "archaeological era," a dated concept borrowed from geology. A particular artifact form used to define a specific period or culture, such as an Acheulian hand ax; a specific artifact that serves to represent the taxon of which it is a member. Such an artifact would have a wide distribution in space but a restricted one in time. Its value is for correlating cultural sequences over large areas, as in cross-dating. In archaeology, the time taken for a type to spread by diffusion must be allowed for and, if possible, calculated from outside evidence. (*syn.* fossil directeur)

type series: The arrangement of a particular form of artifact into a series, usually according to a progression of changes in its shape/form. It may provide a form of relative dating for objects as well as a means of classification.

type site: A site that establishes the typical content of a particular culture, taken as characteristic of a given cultural group. Often, it is the site on which that group was first recognized. An example is al-Badari, the type site of the Badarian culture. (*syn.* type-site, typesite)

typological method: The classification of artifacts into types to compare artifacts or features across time and space, or to determine relative dates for sites. (*syn.* typology)

typology: The systematic classification of artifacts or remains according to type, that is, form and decoration. This is the first step in archaeological analysis, necessary in comparing assemblages and in determining time sequences. Groups of pottery, for example, may be assembled according to those with long necks, those with handles, and those with a pedestal base. Within these may be subgroups based on variations in handle shape or decoration. The relations between similar types can sometimes be shown not merely to classify, but also to explain, their development—which is called seriation. It may show increasing complexity or functional improvement, simplification and functional decline, or change based on fashion. Typology may be associated with chronology, in that it may be possible to place groups of the same kind of material in a sequence. A chronometric or stratigraphically produced relative date may help to order such a sequence as it is often hard to tell which direction it goes in. Typology as an aid to relative dating can be useful.

Tyre: Site on the coast of Lebanon of a chief city of the Phoenicians from c. 2000 BC. It occupied a small island off the coast with two harbors. It was the parent city of Carthage and flourished until its destruction by Nebuchadnezzar in 574/572 BC after a long siege. Between 538–332, it was ruled by the Achaemenian kings of Persia. Most famous was its siege by Alexander the Great in 332 BC, which came about only after a causeway was built to the mainland. After its capture, 10,000 of the inhabitants were put to death, and 30,000 were sold into slavery. Alexander's causeway, which was never removed, converted the island into a peninsula. Excavation has found only the Roman and Byzantine levels; most of the remains of the Phoenician period still lie beneath the present town. It is the site of one of the factories for the purple dye "Tyrian Purple," obtained from murex shell and much prized. Hiram, king of Tyre (970–936 BC) was a contemporary of Solomon. (*syn.* modern Sur)

Tzakol: One of the chronological phases or cultures of the lowland Maya civilization, which is Early Classic and began shortly before AD 250. It is characterized by lowland Maya artifacts, including elaborately decorated polychrome pottery, especially a basal flanged bowl. Almost all early Tzakol monuments draw heavily on a heritage from the older Izapan civilization of the Late Formative, with its highly baroque, narrative stylistic content. Because of the Maya penchant for covering older structures with later ones, Tzakol remains must be laboriously dug out from under towering Late Classic.

tzolkin: The sacred 260-day almanac of the Calendar Round of Mesoamerica. There are 20 named days and 13 numbers. (*syn.* Tonalpohualli)

tzompantli: Skull rack on which, in the Aztec and some other Mesoamerican cultures, the skulls of sacrificial victims were displayed.

Tz'u-chou ware: Large group of Chinese stoneware made in Chihli, Hopei, Honan, and Shansi Provinces and decorated in bold designs with contrasting slips and later with enamels. It was produced during the Sung (960–1279), Yuan (1279–1368), and Ming (1368–1644) Dynasties. Vases, bottles, and other vessels are decorated with simple brushwork in brown, black, or gray on a white, cream, buff, or turquoise background; the pale background is achieved by applying a coating of slip to the body of the vessel before firing. Bold strokes, curves, splotches, concentric bands, and animals and birds are typical motifs. Another type of ornamentation consists of incisions in the slip coating, which reveal the contrasting color of the body underneath. (*syn.* Cizhou)

Uu

Uan Muhuggiag: Cave site in the Acacus Mountains, Libya, with rock paintings. Occupations were c. 7500 bp and 4800 bp.

Uaxactún: Maya center in the Guatemalan Petén with most surviving structures of the Classic period (AD 100–900). Occupation of the Uaxactún site began in the Middle Formative period of Mayan culture (900–300 BC), and before the close of the Late Formative period (300 BC–AD 100) a number of ceremonial buildings had been erected, including a temple with giant stucco masks reminiscent of the more ancient Olmec civilization. The site has many usual lowland Maya architectural features, but was a small center in contrast to Tikal, to whom it owed politicoreligious allegiance. The central complex consists of a small plaza flanked by long, low palace- or apartment-style buildings and two temple-pyramids. The site is best known for its Late Chicanel stucco decoration in the Izapan style. Stele 9 has one of the earliest Long Count dates of the Classic Period (AD 328). The terminal Long Count date for the site is AD 889. In the 9th century, Uaxactún declined like other southern lowland Mayan centers and was abandoned in the 10th century. For many years, the pottery sequence (Formative to Classic) at Uaxactún formed the basis for the whole of lowland Maya chronology.

'Ubaid: A small tell of Ur, which has given its name to a culture c. 5000–3000 BC in southern Mesopotamia, where it underlies practically every city of Sumer. It later spread to the north, displacing the Halaf culture and becoming the first culture to cover the whole of Mesopotamia. It is distinguished by a well-made buff pottery, frequently overfired to a greenish color, and painted in dark brown or black. In the south, stone was scarce, but there were terra-cotta pounders, sickles, hoes, and axes. Temples were built (e.g., Eridu, Gawra), ancestral in structure and siting to those of Sumerian times. At Al 'Ubaid are the remains of a temple with copper statues and reliefs and mosaic friezes of the 1st Dynasty of Ur

c. 2600 BC. The period represents the time when the first villages, and later, the first towns and cities, appeared and many of the characteristics of Sumerian civilization emerged. It expanded greatly, and between 4500–3700 BC, it influenced almost the entire Near East, from the coasts of Syria to the Iranian plateau and the Arabian Gulf. It lasted until the beginning of the Uruk period. (*syn.* 'Ubaid period; 'Ubaid culture complex)

Ubayama: Shell midden in Chiba Prefecture, Japan, with pit houses, human skeletons, and Middle and Late Jomon pottery. Radiocarbon dates of the 3rd millennium BC were given to the Jomon material.

Ubeidiyah: Site in the Jordan Valley at Afikim, Israel, where there are a series of Pleistocene deposits with stone tools dated by potassium-argon dates between 1.7–0.7 million years ago. The lower levels are of Oldowan type, while Acheulian types appear above and had a pebble tool and flake industry similar to Olduvai Gorge. Some fragments of *Homo erectus* have been found.

Ucayali sequence: In eastern Peru, a number of sites near Pucallpa, where the many pottery styles have been placed into a 4,000-year sequence.

Ugarit: Important site of an ancient Syrian city, north of Latakia on the Syrian coast, occupied from an aceramic Early Neolithic (7th millennium BC) through the Chalcolithic and Bronze Ages. It was destroyed c. 1200 BC; its fall coincided with the invasion of the Northern and Sea Peoples and earthquakes and famines. In its last three centuries, it was in commercial contact with Egypt, the Hittites, and the Mycenaeans. Temples to Baal and Dagon (2nd millennium BC) and an elaborate palace with archives of cuneiform clay tablets have been excavated. These commercial and administrative documents and religious texts are very important records of the Canaanites. The texts are written either in the Babylonian cuneiform script or in the special alphabetic cuneiform script invented in Ugarit, dating to the 15th–14th centuries BC when it came first under strong Egyptian influence and then under Hittite dominance. Ugarit may be credited with the development of the first true alphabet: Simplified cuneiform signs were used for an alphabet of 30 letters. Bronzes, ivories, stelae, a high priest's library, and built tombs also survive. (*syn.* modern Ras Shamra, Ra's Shamra)

Ugaritic: An extinct Semitic language spoken and written from at least the middle of 2nd millennium BC at Ugarit and the surrounding area. It belonged to a western group of Semitic languages (i.e., Arabic, Hebrew) and was conveyed alphabetically—the earliest alphabet for which we have a complete record. The cuneiform writing system used on the Syrian coast from the 15th–13th centuries BC. It was unique, although possibly patterned after the North Semitic alphabet. Ugaritic was written from left to right; its 30 symbols included 3 syllabic signs for vowels. Documents in Ugaritic are written on clay tablets with a wedge-shaped stylus and date from the 15th–14th centuries BC.

Uhle, Max (1856–1944): Peruvian archaeologist, one of the greatest in South American archaeology. He was one of the first to use artifact style and stratigraphic associations to produce a chronological sequence. Uhle was the first to apply the principles of stratigraphy and seriation to central Andean material, and he carried out more fieldwork in western South America than any scholar before or since. He worked at Tiahuanaco, Pachacamac, several Mochica sites, an early Chimú cemetery, in the valleys of Chincha, Moche, Chancay, and Ica; near Ancon, near Cuzco, and in Chile and Ecuador. He established the Early, Middle, and Late Tiahuanaco and Inca Ceramic sequence, which although corrected and elaborated, still stands today. His more than 130 volumes of unpublished notes and other records are housed at the University of California.

uinal: In the Classic Maya Long Count, a period of time equaling 20 days.

Ujjain: One of seven sacred Hindu cities, the capital (as Ujjayini) of the Aryan Avanti kingdom (6th–4th centuries BC), near Indore on the main route from the Ganges plain to the Bombay coast. In the 2nd century BC, Ujjain was the seat of the emperor Ashoka, the last of the Mauryan rulers and an early influential Buddhist. Greek geographer Ptolemy (2nd century AD) called it Ozene, the capital of the Western Satraps (i.e., the Greek, Scythian, and Parthian rulers of western India). Black-and-red and painted gray wares and the use of iron are associated with the earliest occupation, succeeded by an occupation with Northern Black Polished ware. (*syn.* Ujjayini, Ozene)

Ukhaidir: The ruins of a castle or early Islamic fortified palace in Iraq, assigned to the 8th century on the basis of style

and construction. It was probably built by the Abbasid prince Isa b. Musa in 778. (*syn.* al-Ukhaidir)

Ulalinka: Palaeolithic site on the Ulalinka River in Siberia, with artifacts that may represent a chopping tool industry of the early Pleistocene.

Ullastret: Early Iron Age town in Girona, Spain, founded in the 6th century BC. It consisted of a hilltop enclosure surrounded by a stone wall with circular towers; inside were stone-built houses, cisterns, paved streets, and a market. Greek pottery and coins are among the artifacts. Ullastret was destroyed by fire c. 200 BC.

ulu: A transverse-bladed Arctic knife, crescent shaped and usually of slate. The blade of the knife is the lower element of an inverted T, and the handle is the vertical upright element.

Ulu Leang: Important rock shelter in the Maros region of southern Sulawesi, Indonesia, with a sequence c. 8000–6000 BC in the early Holocene. It illustrates the development of the Toalian microlithic industry, with flake and bone tools.

Uluzzo, Uluzzian: A lithic industry in Palaeolithic caves and open-air sites around the bay of Uluzzo, in Apulia, southern Italy. The most important is Grotta Cavallo, with a series of Mousterian and Upper Palaeolithic levels. The earliest Upper Palaeolithic levels are called the Uluzzian (c. 33,000 bp) and include scrapers, denticulates, small curved backed points, and crescents. It occurred after the final Mousterian and was contemporary with early Aurignacian.

Umayyad: The first great Muslim dynasty of Arab leaders (caliphs) to rule the Empire of the Caliphate, AD 661–750, descended from a Meccan merchant who became a prominent administrator under the Prophet Muhammad. Headed by Abu Sufyan, the Umayyads were a tribe centered in Mecca who initially resisted Islam but finally converted in 627. In the first Muslim civil war (656–661), Abu Sufyan's son Mu'awiyah emerged victorious over 'Ali, Muhammad's son-in-law and fourth caliph; Mu'awiyah then established himself as the first Umayyad caliph. The Umayyads were supplanted by the Abbasids in 750. (*syn.* Omayyad)

umiak: A large, open boat used in Greenland and by other Arctic peoples, made of seal or other animal skins stretched on a wooden (driftwood) or whalebone frame. It was called the woman's boat, as opposed to the kayak, the men's hunting and fishing boat. It was paddled and either round or elongated, like the birchbark canoe. The umiak was used by women for transporting themselves, children, the elderly, and possessions. It was also used by the men for whaling.

Umm an-Nar: Bronze Age settlement and chamber tomb cemetery on the small island of Abu Dhabi on the Oman peninsula. The site has given its name to an early 3rd-millennium BC culture, also found through southeastern Arabia. Characteristic Umm an-Nar pottery, funerary architecture, and other artifacts are dated c. 2500–2000 BC. Evidence suggests that the Umm an-Nar culture might be identified with the land of Magan, mentioned in cuneiform Sumerian documents. (*syn.* Umm an-nar)

Umm Dabaghiyah: Early 6th-millennium BC type site of the Umm Dabaghiyah culture, the earliest-known culture of the northern Iraq plain, a pre-Hassuna occupation of Mesopotamia. The small site has long buildings with rows of small cell-like rooms arranged around a central space. Some wall paintings have been recorded with hunting scenes—something relied on heavily for the economy. Domesticated sheep, goats, cattle, and pigs were also kept, and some domesticated cereals are present, possibly imported. Pottery is abundant in all the four main phases and includes incised, burnished, plain, and painted types similar to "archaic" Hassuna pottery. Other sites of this culture are Yarim Tepe, Telul Thalathat, and Tell es-Sotto (Tell Soto).

umu ti: Large earthen ovens of South Island, New Zealand, used to cook the roots of a cabbage tree.

Unas (fl. 24th century BC): The last ruler of the 5th Dynasty (c. 2465–2325 BC) of Egypt. He was the first pharaoh to inscribe the interior of his pyramid with the Pyramid Texts. According to later king lists, Unas was the last ruler of the 5th Dynasty, but the innovations in his pyramid complex and the use of blocks from his predecessor's monuments in his own pyramid have led some to consider him the founder of the 6th Dynasty or possibly a transitional ruler. Unas' daughter married his successor Teti, whom the ancient sources considered the founder of the 6th Dynasty. (*syn.* Wenis)

unconformity: A surface representing a major period of erosion before new sediments are deposited; a surface of nondeposition that is a break between two rock or sediment units. They may represent substantial periods for which a depositional record is lacking.

underwater archaeology: The study of sites and shipwrecks beneath the surface of the water, much more difficult to recover than material that has been buried. Since the invention of the aqualung in World War II, techniques for overcoming the difficulties have advanced. Specialized techniques have been developed to solve the problems of excavating and recording under water and of raising finds from the sea and lake beds, as well as subsequent problems of conservation of materials previously preserved under water. Underwater archaeology includes the examination of submerged settlement sites under freshwater lakes, in harbors, and shipwrecks under the sea. This branch of archaeology was pioneered in the Mediterranean.

underwater reconnaissance: Geophysical methods of underwater survey. Some of these methods are: (1) towing a proton magnetometer behind a survey vessel to detect iron

and steel objects; (2) using side-scan sonar that transmits sound waves in a fan-shaped beam to produce a graphic image of surface features on the sea bed; and (3) using a subbottom profiler that emits sound pulses that bounce back from features and objects buried beneath the sea floor.

underworld book: Pictorial and textual compositions inscribed in New Kingdom royal tombs, which describe the passage of the sun god through the underworld and the sky. They probably imparted secret knowledge and included hundreds of names of demons and of deities and other beings who accompanied the sun god in his barque on his journey through night and day. The texts are in the present tense and form a description and a series of tableaux rather than a narrative. Private individuals used them in the Late period.

Únetice: Early Bronze Age culture centered on Bohemia, Bavaria, Germany, Poland, and Moravia, named after a type site cemetery north of Prague, Czechoslovakia. Characteristic metal objects include ingot torcs, lock rings, various pins, flanged axes, riveted daggers, and the halberd. Regional groups include Nitra, Adlerberg, Straubing, Marschwitz, and Unterwölbling (Austria). In late Únetice times, there is evidence of commercial contact with the Wessex culture of Britain and, via the amber route, perhaps with southeast Europe and the Mycenaeans. The Veterov culture of Moravia and the Mad'arovce culture of Slovakia, which had links with the Mycenaean would, are sometimes considered to be subgroups in the final Únetice tradition. Innovations of the culture include the two-piece mold and the use of tin to make bronze. The earliest Bronze Age center, Unetician A, consisted of a complex of flat inhumation graves with modest grave goods in copper and bronze. Únetice is an umbrella term for the local groups and is dated to c. 1800–1500 BC. (*syn.* Únetice period; Aunjetitz; Unetician culture)

unguentarium: A container for perfumed oil used in Hellenistic times. It was often of ceramic or glass and is found in tombs.

ungulate: Any hoofed typically herbivorous quadruped mammal—ruminant, swine, camel, hippopotamus, horse, tapir, rhinoceros, elephant, or hyrax.

unidirectional core: A core that has had flakes removed from only one direction.

uniface: A stone tool having only side or surface flaked or chipped. (*syn.* uniface tool)

Uniformitarianism: A fundamental philosophy of geologic science, the principle that the Earth was formed by the same natural geological processes that are still going on today. This principle—that existing processes acting in the same manner and with essentially the same intensity as at present are sufficient to account for all geologic change—provided the cornerstone of modern geology. William Whewell introduced the term in 1832. (*syn.* uniformitarianism)

unilinear cultural evolution: A 19th-century evolutionary theory holding that all human cultures pass through the same sequence of evolutionary changes or stages, from simple hunting and gathering to literate civilization. Lewis H. Morgan described seven stages, or ethnical periods, from lower savagery, barbarism, to civilization. (*syn.* unilinear evolution)

unit: An artificial grouping used for describing artifacts.

unit of stratification: A term that can be applied to any layers, interfaces, or structures found in the recording of the stratification of an excavation.

univallate: Having only a single rampart.

Upper Egypt: A term for that part of the Nile Valley in southern Egypt, generally referring to places between Luxor and Aswan. It thus consists of the entire Nile River valley from Cairo south to Lake Nasser (formed by the Aswan High Dam). This division also includes what some scholars term Middle Egypt (from Lisht to Panopolis). In late predynastic times, Upper Egypt was a political entity separate from Lower Egypt (the delta region), until Menes (fl. 2900 BC) joined them.

Upper Nubia: A term for that part of the Sudanese Nile valley from the second cataract south to Khartoum.

Upper Palaeolithic: The final part of the Palaeolithic period, from about 40,000 years ago to about 10,000 years ago. It was characterized by the development of bladed stone tools and regional stone-tool industries (e.g., Perigordian, Aurignacian, Solutrean, and Magdalenian of Europe), the hunting of large herd animals, human burials, the appearance of cave paintings and other art forms, and the presence of modern humans (Cro-Magnon man) replacing the Neanderthals. There were also localized industries in the Old World and the oldest known cultures of the New World. Upper Palaeolithic industries exhibit greater complexity, specialization, and variety of tool types, and distinctive regional artistic traditions emerged. These include small sculptures (clay and stone figurines, ivory carvings), monumental paintings, incised designs, and reliefs on the walls of caves.

Upper Republican: Culture of the central plains of North America dated to AD 1000–1450 and characterized by cord-roughened pottery and semisubterranean earth lodges. The people grew corn, beans, and squash and were hunter gatherers.

Upper Swan: Site on Swan River, Western Australia, with a date of c. 38,000 bp and an assemblage of quartz and quartzite flakes and flake tools.

upward migration: The movement of previously deposited objects to the soil surface as a result of plowing, bulldozing, or other nonarchaeological processes.

Uqair, Tell: Tell site south of Baghdad, Iraq, with a temple of the Uruk phase with unexpectedly fine wall paintings depicting mythical scenes. The fine polychrome wall paintings had human and animal figures. A small subsidiary chapel, later in date than the temple, contained a collection of pottery and four clay tablets inscribed with pictographic symbols of the kind used in the Jemdet Nasr period (4th millennium BC). The site was occupied from the 'Ubaid period. (*syn.* 'Uqair)

Ur: A site in southern Mesopotamia occupied from 'Ubaid times (6th–5th millennia BC), which grew in importance during the Early Dynastic period (3rd millennium BC) to become an important Sumerian city. 'Ubaid and Uruk levels are separated by a flood level. In the last century of the 3rd millennium, it was the ceremonial center of the Ur III empire, which controlled much of Mesopotamia. Located south of the Euphrates and west of Basra, it has a Royal Cemetery c. 2800. The arch and dome were used in constructing the combs, and they contained precious metal and stones, animal figures; shell, lapis lazuli, and carnelian mosaic inlays; gold and lapis jewelry; and evidence for the sacrifice of human attendants to accompany the dead royal master or mistress. There is also spectacular 3rd millennium BC religious architecture (the ziggurat of Nanna/Sin, the moon god), residential architecture and street plans, and texts from then to the late 1st millennium BC. It was destroyed by Elam and the Amorites, but recovered by the early 2nd millennium BC. The city later declined and was finally abandoned in the 4th century BC. (*syn.* modern Tell el-Muqqayr)

Ur III period: The Third Dynasty of Ur according to the Sumerian king lists, a time when Ur controlled much of Mesopotamia and the Zagros highlands. It began with Ur-nammu (2112–2095 BC), and the period is noted for the numerous economic texts from its administrative centers. Ur III collapsed under attack by the Elamites and Amorites.

uraeus: The coiled cobra of ancient Egypt, worn by the pharaoh on his brow, usually combined with one or other of the royal crowns, as a symbol of his supreme authority. The cobra is associated with the goddess Wadjit or with the sun, whose "eye" it is held to be. It is an agent of destruction and protection of the king, spitting fire.

uranium dating: A method of dating based on measuring the rate of radioactive decay of uranium isotopes in bone and other organic remains to the stable isotope of lead. It has proved particularly useful for the period before 50,000 years ago, which lies outside the time range of radiocarbon dating. Each of the isotopes decays through a series of radioactive daughter isotopes until a stable isotope of lead is reached.

Three daughter isotopes are created and decay with half-lives useful for dating: ionium, proactinium, and radium. Several uranium dating methods exist, and material datable by these methods includes: aragonitic coral, speleothem, travertine, mollusk shell, mars, bone, teeth, caliche, calcretes, peat, wood, and detrital sediment. (*syn.* uranium series dating, uranium series disequilibrium dating)

uranium test: A relative dating method used for bone. Calcium ions in the phosphatic mineral hydroxyapatite are gradually altered after burial into uranium ions as a result of uranium being in solution in the percolating groundwater. The longer bone has been in the ground, the more uranium will have been absorbed. The local environmental conditions affect the rate, and therefore there is no universal rate that yields absolute dates. The uranium is radioactive, and the emitted beta particles are measured by using a Geiger counter. The method is much less destructive than the chemical analyses required for the nitrogen and fluorine tests.

Urartu: A kingdom of the 1st millennium BC in the mountains north of Assyria (northwest Iran, northeast Anatolia, Armenia, in the mountainous region southeast of the Black Sea and southwest of the Caspian Sea), which was the last important Hurrian-speaking state. Its people, relatives of the Hurri, established themselves around Lake Van during the 2nd millennium BC. Mentioned in Assyrian sources from the early 13th century BC, Urartu enjoyed considerable political power in the 9th–8th centuries BC. The citadel of their capital at Van could be entered only by a rock-cut passage, on which are cuneiform inscriptions that supplement the records of the Assyrians, with whom the Urartians were usually at war over access to raw materials, such as metal. A promontory nearby had a temple. Urartu is famous for its metalwork, particularly the great bronze cauldrons on tripod stands, which were traded as far as Etruscan Italy, and for fine, red burnished ware. They adapted a cuneiform script to their own language, a late dialect of Hurrian, which has been deciphered. The language is mainly known from rock-face inscriptions dating from the 8th century BC, in the eastern part of Asia Minor. Pressure from the Cimmerians, Phrygians, and Scythians led to the disappearance of the kingdom c. 590 BC, and they were overcome by invading Armenians. (*syn.* Urartian)

urban revolution: A term applied to a sociocultural type or stage of human development. V. Gordon Childe proposed that the criteria for the urban revolution are: (1) cities, or large, dense settlements; (2) the differentiation of the population into specialized occupational groups; (3) social classes, including a ruling stratum exempt from primary subsistence tasks; (4) mechanisms for extracting a "social surplus," such as taxes or tribute; (5) monumental public buildings and other enterprises; and (6) writing. (*syn.* Urban Revolution)

urbanization: The clustering of large numbers of people into cities, although there is no clear-cut line between large towns and cities, both being characterized by very high population densities. In southeast Europe, urbanization seems to have begun by 4000 BC, in Greece leading eventually to the growth of Mycenaean civilization, in Italy (early 1st millennium BC) to Etruscan civilization, and so on. Many civilizations, such as the Maya, with large ceremonial centers, have wrongly been called "urban."

Urewe ware: Characteristic Early Age pottery type of the interlacustrine region of East Africa: southwest Kenya, northwest Tanzania, Rwanda, east Zaire, and south Uganda. It dates from the last centuries BC to the first centuries AD and is the name of a tradition of the Chifumbaze complex. Urewe ware was ancestral to the varied wares of the Early Iron Age complex farther south. Named after a site in southwest Kenya, Urewe ware's makers were clearly skilled workers of iron.

Urfirnis: Characteristic ware of the Middle Neolithic and Early Helladic periods of Greece and also the name of the glaze-like paint. The pottery has a buff fabric decorated with a dark lustrous slip or glaze. The sauceboat and the askos are the most notable shapes.

urial: A species of wild sheep in Iran, Turkestan, and the Himalayas, with the first record of domestication from Anau c. 5000 BC. It replaced the moufflon to become the ancestor of nearly all modern sheep.

urn: Any large and decorative vase, especially one having an ornamental base and no handles, and often used for storage. It is most often found as a container for the ashes of a cremation burial, the so-called cinerary urn for jar burials. The term is widely used in the European Bronze Age, and the name Urnfield Cultures, given to the Late Bronze Age of much of Central, Eastern and Southern Europe, refers to the characteristic burial rite.

Urnes: The site of an 11th-century church in Norway, one of the oldest stave churches in existence. Some of the staves are decorated with Viking ornament in the form of animals and zoomorphic ribbons; the term "Urnes style" is derived from these decorations. This late Viking art style is a type of ornament that occurs a great deal on Scandinavian metalwork of that time and also on Swedish rune stones.

urnfield: A type of cremation grave or cemetery in which the ashes of individuals were placed in pottery vessels or funerary urns. Sometimes unurned cremations may also be present.

Urnfield period: A widespread group of related Bronze Age cultures practicing burial by cremation in pottery urns, at first in central and eastern Europe and later spreading to northern and western Europe. Such funerary urns were buried in a cemetery of urns (urnfields), and the practice dates from c. 1300 BC to c. 750 BC. Other features of the Urnfield period include coppermining, sheet bronze metalworking, and fortified settlements. At the start of the Iron Age, inhumation once again became the dominant form of burial in many areas. A small pot with holes in it is often found interred with the urn, which may have been the ritual fire igniter or an incense burner. The Urnfield cultures succeeded the Tumulus culture in central Europe and developed into the Hallstatt Iron Age culture. (*syn.* Urnfield period; Urnfield; Urn culture, Urnfield complex)

Uruk: One of the greatest city-states of Sumer, northwest of Ur, which flourished at the beginning of the 3rd millennium BC. It is 250 kilometers south of Bagdad, Iraq. Pottery dating from around 5000 BC has been found there, but the civilization is traditionally dated to c. 3800–3100 BC. Uruk's rulers tried to lead Sumer until Ur became more powerful, but Uruk still remained important as a holy city. It was one of the great Sumerian city-states, developing from the 'Ubaid period. It was the site of numerous innovations, the most important being the invention of writing. It lost importance with the rise of Ur, c. 2100 BC, but remained occupied until the Parthian period. Archaeologists have found very important structures and deposits of the 4th millennium BC, and the site has given its name to the period that succeeded the 'Ubaid and preceded the Jemdet Nasr period. Uruk was Mesopotamia's— and the world's—first true city. There are two large temple complexes—the Anu sanctuary and the Eanna sanctuary— both with several successive temple structures during the Uruk period, including the White Temple in the Anu sanctuary and the Limestone and Pillar Temples in the Eanna sanctuary. A characteristic form of decoration is clay cones with painted tops pressed into the mud plaster—known as clay cone mosaic. A ziggurat laid out by Ur-Nammu in the Ur III period (late 3rd millennium BC) is by the Eanna sanctuary. The earliest clay tablets appear in late Uruk levels; they are simple labels and lists with pictographic symbols. Tablets from slightly later levels, of the Jemdet Nasr phase, show further developments toward the cuneiform script of the Early Dynastic period. There was also mass-produced wheel-made pottery, cylinder seals, and sophisticated art. Uruk was the home of the epic hero Gilgamesh, now thought to be a real king of the city's first dynasty. (*syn.* biblical Erech, modern Warka; Uruk period)

Usatovo: Settlement, barrow cemeteries, and flat-grave cemeteries near Odessa, in the Ukraine—a regional variant of the Eneolithic Cucuteni-Tripolye culture. It is the type site of a copper-using culture with painted pottery and with the kurgan burial of the steppe zone. It is thought to date c. 2600– 2100 BC. One barrow cemetery at Usatovo was one of the richest in the steppe zone and lay next to a stone-built settlement. Crouched inhumations as primary burials were often accompanied by many secondary burials in cists or pits.

Widespread contacts are documented by the presence of Baltic amber and Anatolian silver and antimony, and the existence of corbel-vaulted tombs suggest Aegean affinities. (*syn.* Usatovo culture)

use: The third stage of behavioral processes, in which artifacts are used (the others being acquisition, manufacture, and, later deposition).

uselife or use life: The length of time a tool or artifact is used before it is discarded; the sequence a tool goes through from production to discard. (*syn.* use-life continuum)

use-related primary context: A primary context resulting from abandonment of materials during either manufacturing or use activities.

use-related secondary context: A secondary context resulting from disturbance by human activity after original deposition of materials.

use-wear analysis: The examination and study of the edges and surfaces of artifacts, mainly stone tools, to determine the type of wear they have experienced and thus the tasks for which they were used. Microscopic analysis is used to detect signs of wear on working edges. (*syn.* edge-wear analysis; usewear analysis; microwear analysis)

ushabti: Small wooden or glazed-stone mummiform figurines placed in Egyptian tombs of the Middle Kingdom onward. They were to undertake work on behalf of the deceased, who might be called on to perform manual labor in the afterlife. (*syn.* shabti)

Ushki Lake: Five sites in Kamchatka, Siberia, with Neolithic levels overlying Upper Palaeolithic. Wedge-shaped cores and side scrapers have been dated to the early Holocene, c. 8790 bp. A Dyuktai culture assemblage is dated to c. 10,760–10,360 bp. The lowest layer is c. 14,300–13,600 bp, with stemmed bifacial points and perforated stone ornaments. Hearths and a burial were excavated in this level, with red ocher surviving. This is the only Palaeolithic site in Siberia to represent a tundra rather than a forest adaptation. (*syn.* Ushki)

usnu: On Inca sites, a platform or small mound where the emperor held court.

Ust'-Kan Cave: Middle Palaeolithic site in the Altai region of Siberia with Levallois cores, side scrapers, and points, dated probably just before the last glacial.

Ust'-Kova: Site on the Angara River of central Siberia with artifacts of the Iron and Bronze Ages and Mesolithic and Neolithic remains. Radiocarbon dates range from 32,865 to 14,220 bp.

U-Thong: Large prehistoric and early historic moated settlement in central Thailand, the site of an ancient city that was for a time the capital of the Mon kingdom of Dvaravati (6th–

11th centuries). There was a palace center and a bead-producing industry. U-Thong is also the name of a Buddhist art style of the 12th–15th centuries. It was later annexed by the state of Kambuja. (*syn.* U Thong; now Suphan Buri)

Utica: Traditionally the oldest Phoenician settlement on the coast of North Africa, located near the mouth of the Majardah (Medjerda) River in modern Tunisia. It was founded in the 8th or 7th century BC and grew rapidly, being second only to Carthage among Phoenician settlements in Africa. In the Third Punic War (149–146 BC), Utica sided with Rome against Carthage; after the destruction of Carthage it was made the administrative center of the Roman province of Africa. Utica became a municipium in 36 BC, but lost its primacy when Carthage was refounded as a Roman city in 44 BC. Excavators have found Phoenician graves dating from the 8th century BC onward, Roman bath buildings, and a substantial residential area of the Roman city with houses containing mosaics. (*syn.* modern Utique)

utilized flake: A piece of stone debitage used for cutting or slicing. The edge may be damaged from use, but not deliberately.

Utnur: One of the earliest known settlements of peninsular India, dating to c. 2900 BC. It is a Neolithic site in the central Deccan, with four major phases of occupation. The people were primarily cattle herders, probably living in huts built of branches and brush. Pottery and stone tools were found.

Utqiagvik: Inuit site in Barrow, Alaska, with 60 house remains and bodies, one with a date of 440 bp. The ice preserved the bodies, clothing, and hunting tools.

Utu: Sumerian god, equal to the Akkadian Shamash, god of the sun and light and the god of justice and righteousness.

Uvarov, Count Aleksei Sergeevich (1828–1884): Russian archaeologist who organized the Imperial Russian Archaeological Society in 1864 and worked at Cheronese, the Merian graves, and Karacharovo.

Uxmal: Important Puuc Maya site of the Late Classic period (AD 600–900), located south of Mérida, Yucatán, Mexico. It is the best known site built in Puuc style, with the pyramid of the Magician, palace of the Governor, Nunnery Quadrangle, the House of Turtles, and the House of Pigeons. There are large masonry buildings with a veneer of well-cut stone and decoration on the upper portions. The site was very well planned and flourished c. AD 800–1000. No Long Count dates are associated with the site, and construction ceased c. 1000 after the rise of Chichén Itzá. It was connected by a causeway (sache) to the Puuc site of Kabáh. The ruling family of the city were the Tutul Xius. According to Maya legend, Uxmal continued to be occupied and was a participant in the political League of Mayapán. When the league ended, Uxmal, like the other great cities of the north, was abandoned (c. 1450).

Vv

Vadastra: Middle and Late Neolithic culture of southwest Romania and northern Bulgaria in the late 5th millennium BC. The tell's stratigraphy includes an Aurignacian level, separated by a long hiatus from two Vadastra culture levels and a Salcuta culture level (early 4th millennium BC). There are large grain storage pits and evidence of draft animals pulling plows. (*syn.* Vadastra culture)

Vahangeku'a: Site of one of the largest tohua in the Taipivai Valley of the Marquesas, Polynesia. The artificial terrace is surrounded by massive *pa'epa'e*.

Vailele: Site in Upolu, Samoa, with assemblages from the terminal ceramic phase of Samoan prehistory c. 300 BC–AD 200 stratified beneath later aceramic mounds. The large earthen mounds were built as house platforms and contained plain pottery and stone adzes.

Vaillant, George Clapp (1901–1945): American archaeologist who was an expert on the high plateau of central Mexico and other aspects of Mesoamerican chronology. He was the first to systematically investigate the remains predating the time when the Classical civilizations were at their height. He also established some basic chronologies of the Maya Lowlands and the Basin of Mexico.

Vaisali: A city of the Ganges civilization of northern India, famous as the birthplace of Mahavira, founder of the Jain religion. The earliest occupation belongs to the Iron Age, when Mahavira lived (6th century BC) and has yielded Northern Black Polished ware and iron artifacts.

vaisselle blanche: A type of ceramics made in the Aceramic Neolithic (PPNB) of Syria, Lebanon, and the east bank of the Jordan River. It was white, made from lime mixed with ashes, air dried, and sometimes painted in bands.

Vaito'otia: Important Early Eastern Polynesian settlement on Huahine, Society Islands, AD c. 800. There are rich organic and nonorganic remains of the period c. 850–1100. The material culture has close parallels with that of the first Maori Patu settlers of New Zealand.

Valac: Small hilltop settlement of the Late Vinca phase, c. 3950 BC, near Kosovska Mitrovica, Kosovo, Serbia. The single occupation level has poor ceramics, but each house has a rich ritual assemblage with fired clay zoomorphic figurines known as "centaurs."

Val Camonica: Glaciated Alpine valley in northwest Italy, with an abundance of rock carvings on rock faces. The carvings have four chronological phases—Neolithic, Chalcolithic, Bronze Age, Iron Age—which are often superimposed. What is exceptional about the carvings of the Val Camonica is that they represent a variety of subjects—rituals, battles, hunting, and daily labor—and that these were treated as compositions.

Valders Advance: The final advance of the ice during the Wisconsin Glaciation of the Pleistocene in North America, beginning about 12,000 BP until approximately 10,000 BP. (*syn.* Valders substage; Greaklakean substage)

Valdivia: Early Formative period site in Ecuador's coast, and the name of a Formative period culture c. 3200 BC. The type site flourished beginning sometime before 3800 BC and lasted until c. 1400 BC. Its pottery is among the oldest in the New World. Radiocarbon dates, stratification of midden deposits, and considerable stylistic variation in the highly distinctive ceramic complex have facilitated the construction of a chronology. The periods are: A: 3200–2300 BC; B: 2300–2000 BC; C: 2000–1500 BC; and D: 1500–1400 BC. Characteristically, ceramics have a gray body, are smoothly polished, and decorated with incision, rocker stamping, and appliqué. Decoration is typically only on the upper part of the vessel, and all vessels are utilitarian rather than ritual. Periods C and D contained some traded sherds from Machalilla. Figurines in stone and ceramic appeared after Period B, with the ceramics usually portraying stylized nude females often with a distinctive "page boy" hairstyle. Valdivia sites consist of coastal shell mounds left by fisherman and shellfish collectors, and also villages (Real Alto) of maize farmers.

Valea Lupului: A large settlement site of the Late Neolithic Cucuteni culture, Moldavia, Romania, with a radiocarbon date c. 2750 BC. The single-phase occupation produced domestic assemblages of the Cucuteni B3 phase.

Valencia: Ceramic complex of red-colored jars, one of the best known in Venezuela, found on a number of mound sites in the north-central part of country. The shapes of huge human figurines with flat, wide heads are very distinctive. Typically the pottery is coarse and sand or mica tempered. Decoration may be appliqué work, rectilinear incision, or modeled human faces with coffee-bean eyes. It is AD c. 1000–1500 and is possibly derived from the Arauquim complex or from the La Cabrera phase of the Barrancoid series. (*syn.* Valencoid subtradition)

Valhager: Migration period nucleated settlement of the 5th and 6th centuries on the Baltic island of Gotland just off the coast of Sweden. There were cattle droveways and individual farm dwellings enclosed within stone-walled fields. The buildings are typical longhouses with central hearths.

Valhöll: In Norse mythology, the hall of slain warriors, who live there blissfully under the leadership of the god Odin, ready to defend the gods at Ragnarök. (*syn.* Valhalla)

Valley of Oaxaca: Large highland plateau in Oaxaca, Mexico, with occupation from c. 5500 BC and some of the first cities of the area, including Monte Albán. Zapotec and Mixtec lived there.

Valley of the Kings: Rocky valley in the western desert opposite Thebes and just west of Luxor, on the Nile in Upper Egypt, which was chosen as the royal cemetery during the New Kingdom. From 1580 BC, the tombs of the pharaohs were cut in the limestone of its walls. It actually consists of two separate valleys: the eastern valley is the main cemetery of the 18th–20th Dynasties whereas the western (Cemetery of Monkeys/Apes) has only four tombs: Amenhotep III, Ay, and two others uninscribed (KV24–25). There are 62 in all. One of the main features of the royal tombs at the Valley of the Kings was their separation from the mortuary temples, which were built some distance away, in a long line at the edge of the desert. The discovery of the unspoiled tomb of Tutankhamen in 1922 revealed for the first time just how lavishly these tombs were equipped. (*syn.* Biban el-Muluk)

Valley of the Queens: Cemetery of the royal wives and sons of some of the New Kingdom pharaohs, located on the west bank at Thebes, just northwest of Medinet Habu, Egypt. Late 17th- and early 18th-Dynasty royal families are buried there; most of the 18th-Dynasty rulers' wives were buried with their husbands in the Valley of the Kings. The 19th- and 20th-Dynasty royal wives and offspring were then buried in the Valley of the Queens. There are about 75 tombs at the site. (*syn.* Biban el-Harim)

valley temple: A mortuary temple placed at the edge of the Nile, where the king's body was received for final rites before being transported via a connecting causeway to his pyramid.

Vallonnet: Lower Palaeolithic cave site in Roquebrune-Cap-Martin in the south of France with stone artifacts associated with a fauna datable to c. 0.9 million years ago.

vallum: A Roman defensive rampart of an earthworks, made as a defense obstacle around a camp or fort. It is also the name of the flat-bottomed ditch with two parallel walls running south of Hadrian's Wall in northern Britain.

Valsequillo Reservoir: A site south of Puebla, Mexico, with radiocarbon dates that would be the earliest for man's presence in the New World, c. 36,000 BC. A level containing bifacial and stemmed points has been dated 21,800 BC. These dates are not widely accepted.

Vandals: Germanic people who in the early 5th century set out from central Europe into Gaul and eventually crossed from Spain to invade North Africa, where they quickly annexed most of the major towns. They imposed their Arian religion on the native population, and it appears that they upheld many Roman legal and economic practices. The Vandals maintained a kingdom in North Africa from AD 429–534 and sacked Rome in 455. The Vandal empire was overrun by the Arabs late in the 7th century.

Van-lang: A legendary kingdom of north Vietnam, literally the Land of the Tattooed Men, rule by the Hong Bang Dynasty c. 3rd millennium BC. It was succeeded by the historic kingdom of Au-Lac in 258 BC. Existing archaeological evidence does not support the Vietnamese ancient texts that credit Hung Vuong with establishing, in 2879 BC, the Hong Bang Dynasty, which is said to have survived for 2,621 years. According to available data, the earliest Vietnamese kingdom originated between 1000–500 BC. (*syn.* Van Lang)

Vanuatu: A chain of 13 principal and many smaller islands in the southwestern Pacific Ocean, 500 miles (800 km) west of Fiji and 1,100 miles (1,800 km) east of Australia. Many of the northern islands have been inhabited by Melanesian peoples for at least 3,000 years; the earliest radiocarbon date for settlement on the southern islands is 420 BC on Tanna. It has an Austronesian-speaking population. Important archaeological phenomena include the Mangaasi pottery tradition and the burial site of Roy Mata. (*syn.* New Hebrides)

Vapheio: The site of a Mycenaean tholos tomb in Laconia, Greece, dated to the 15th century BC, and the style of a magnificent gold cup found there. The popular shape had straight or slightly splayed walls widening to the rim and a single handle. The form occurs in pottery from the Middle Minoan period (late 16th–early 15th centuries BC) on Crete and was important to the Mycenaeans in the Late Helladic period. Two examples are decorated with scenes of bulls. Other rich grave goods were bronze weapons and fine jewelry. (*syn.* Vapheio cup)

variable: Any dimension, quality, or measurement that varies.

variety: A group of artifacts in a type with other more specific attributes in common; for example, pottery made over several generations by the same family.

Varna: Late Copper Age cemetery site on the Black Sea coast of eastern Bulgaria, of the Gumennita culture (Karanovo VI), with some of the richest burials of the 4th millennium BC. It is the largest collection of pre-Mycenaean gold in Europe. The cemetery contains over 100 extended inhumations as well as two special grave types: the "mask" grave (where the skull is replaced by a clay mask) and the "cenotaph" grave (where grave goods are arranged as if the missing body were present). These grave categories contained some of the richest grave goods: gold scepters, diadems, pendants, appliqués, copper tools and weapons; stone, shell, and bone jewelry. Foreign items include copper and graphite, spondylus and dentalium shells, carnelian, and marble. Analysis of the Varna gold indicates two sources, probably in the eastern Mediterranean and the Caucasus. Varna was founded as Odessus by Milesian Greeks in the 6th century BC. (*syn.* Odessus)

varve: A sedimentary bed, layer, or sequence of layers deposited in a body of still water within a year's time, and usually during a season, by the melting of glaciers, used in determining the age of geological formations and in archaeological dating, especially in northern Europe. These annual deposits are found in river and lake beds near glaciers, reflecting the fluctuation of the flow of water during periods of freezing and melting and especially useful in measuring recent Pleistocene geological events. The Swedish pioneer Baron Gerard de Geer discovered in the late 19th century that these could be counted and correlated or linked over long distances, which gave him a time scale of 12,000 years and fixed the end of the Ice Age at about 10,000 years ago.

varve dating: A technique for producing chronometric dates based on the annual formation of layers of sediment on lake and river beds in glacial regions. Seasonal fluctuations in particle size and speed of sedimentation take place. During the winter, ice melting is very slow, melt-water streams do not contain much water, and they flow slowly, carrying little material. During the summer, melting accelerates, melt-water streams flow faster and carry more material. The supply of sediment to the ice-marginal lake varies with the season. A varve chronology, similar to a tree-ring chronology may be set up. But as with tree rings (see dendrochronology), the varves vary from year to year, depending on the rapidity

of the thaw, quantity of summer rain, winter snow, the variations showing some correlation with the sunspot cycle. Such varve chronologies have been built up for Scandinavia and are used to date the retreat of the Weichselian ice sheet. Varve dating has a greater significance than just for local dating, because frequently there is enough organic material to allow radiocarbon dates to be calculated. There is therefore the possibility of using the calendrical varve chronology to calibrate radiocarbon dates. Its use for archaeological dating is rather limited in that sites have to be related to the geological changes (the ice-sheet moraines or changing Baltic sea levels) before their dates can be determined. The Swedish pioneer Baron Gerard de Geer discovered in the late 19th century that these could be counted and correlated or linked over long distances, which gave him a time scale of 12,000 years and fixed the end of the Ice Age at about 10,000 years ago.

vase support: A pottery vessel with a hollow cylindrical base, which supports a dishlike upper surface; the name for a pottery pedestal or ring made to support round-based pottery that could not stand by itself on a flat surface. The term is used especially in European prehistory to describe highly decorated incised examples from the French Middle Neolithic Chasséen culture. (*syn.* vase-support)

Vasic, Miloje (1869–1956): Serbian archaeologist who worked at Vinca and recognized its importance in the Neolithic chronology of the western Balkans and in relation to the Aegean area.

Vasíliki: Minoan settlement on Crete with an Early Minoan II prototype palace of c. 2600–2200 BC. Vasiliki pottery was an elaborately made mottled (through uneven firing) red, brown, and black ware.

Vatcha: Lapita site on Ile des Pins, New Caledonia, Melanesia, with two occupations starting c. 2855 bp.

vault: A type of roofing in stone or brick, using the principle of gravity to lock the materials together. The barrel vault is continuous and of semicircular section; in the rib vault, the weight of the roof is carried by ribs. The evolution of the vault begins with the discovery of the arch, because the basic "barrel" form, which appeared first in ancient Egypt and the Near East, is simply a deep, or three-dimensional, arch.

Vedbaek Bogebakken: Danish Mesolithic cemetery on Zealand dated to c. 4800 BC. There are 17 graves of the Ertebolle phase.

Vegas: Sites in the Santa Elena peninsula region of southeast coastal Ecuador with unifacial stone gravers, denticulates, spoke shaves; cobble choppers, and pestles, c. 5000 BC.

vegetational climax: A model that tries to explain vegetational history as a series of phases culminating in a terminal phase of equilibrium. It is maintained that there are points in vegetational history beyond which there can be no progress until the environmental conditions change. The stages leading up to these climaxes (seres) represent the gradual replacement of one ecosystem with another until a stabilized point (equilibrium) is attained. In different areas, these climaxes take different forms depending on climate. A change in the climax vegetation therefore means a change in environmental conditions.

Veii: South Etruscan city just north of Rome, destroyed by Rome in 396 BC. After some intermittent Bronze Age occupation, it was settled in the Villanovan period (9th century BC), occupying a large plateau. The 7th century BC saw early Etruscan chamber tombs, including some painted examples. It was enclosed by a wall and rampart in the 5th century BC and had a temple containing large terra-cotta statues of deities. Veii was the greatest center for the fabrication of terracotta sculptures in Etruria in the 6th century BC. Evidence suggests an irregular street plan, with cisterns and cuniculi indicating the Etruscan hydraulic engineering. The town is surrounded by a number of Villanovan and Etruscan cemeteries. One of the chambered tombs, the Grotta Campana, contains the oldest known Etruscan frescoes. The ashes of the dead were stored in burial urns surmounted by archaic terracotta portrait heads. Nearby are the remains of the temple of Apollo, home of the terra-cotta statue of the ''Apollo of Veii,'' and also a temple shrine dedicated to the neighboring Cremera River. Veii's destruction in 396 BC was not total, however, and the Romans later reconstructed the city. Under Augustus, it was made a municipium, and up to the 3rd century AD it continued as a religious center. (*syn.* modern Veio)

Velatice group: Late Bronze Age regional group of the Urnfield tradition in Moravia, c. 12th century BC; there are settlements and burial grounds.

vellum: Fine parchment from the skins of calves, a term that was broadened in its usage to include any especially fine parchment. In the 4th century AD, vellum or parchment as a material and the codex as a form became dominant.

Vénat: Late Bronze Age metal hoard in Charente, France, c. 700 BC. A large pottery vessel contained 2,720 bronzes, including swords, spear heads, socketed axes, and bracelets.

Vendel period: A term for a main phase of the Migration period, the 7th and 8th centuries AD in Scandinavia, the last phase of the Iron Age before the Viking Age. It takes its name from a site in central Sweden with rich burials. Other cemeteries of the Vendel period are at Valsgarde and Old Uppsala, with burials often in boats with rich treasures.

Venedian: Late Iron Age people of the lower Vistula basin, Poland, c. 1st century BC–6th century AD. Iron and bronze artifacts show the importance of metalworking.

Veneti: An Illyrian people who came from the east and took possession of the region named for them (Venetia) in Italy c. 1000 BC. The Venetic language is known from more than 400 funerary and votive inscriptions and from Classical writings. It is an Indo-European language of Archaic type, bearing similarities to the Latin and the Germanic. The principal centers of the Veneti were Padua and Este. Their culture developed from the 9th century to the period of Romanization, with relations with the Golasecca, Villanovan, and Etruscan cultures and with the transalpine Hallstatt culture. They peaked in the 6th–4th centuries BC and produced figured bronze situlae (conical vessels). The Veneti were horse breeders and peaceful traders and navigators. They were protected by the waters of the lower Po and the lower Adige and preserved their independence against Etruscan expansion and Celtic invasion. In the 3rd century BC, they established a peaceful alliance with Rome.

Venosa: A town in southern Italy, which has a Lower Palaeolithic site with a hand axe or Acheulian level overlying one with abundant side scapers (evolved Clactonian, Tayacian, or Charentian?). Originally a settlement of the Lucanians (an ancient Italic tribe), it was taken by the Romans after the Samnite Wars (291 BC). Its position on the Appian Way made it an important Roman garrison town. The poet Horace was born there, and many of his poems mention it.

Ventana Cave: Rock shelter and stratified site in southwest Arizona occupied from over 11,000 years ago. The stratigraphy starts with remains left by hunters of extinct species of horse, bison, and ground sloth, who also had stone tools—including Clovis/Folsom-like projectile points. It may have been contemporary with the San Dieguito complex of California. After a break, the cave was reoccupied by people of Desert Culture type (especially Cochise, Aramagosa). The firmest date for these upper levels, from geological evidence, is post-5000 BC. The more recent strata contain evidence of the transition from Desert to Hohokam and use of the cave into historic times.

Ventris, Michael (George Francis) (1922–1956): British scholar, architect, and linguist trained in code breaking during war service, who in 1952 deciphered the Linear B script of Minoan and Mycenaean Greece. He showed them to be an early form of Greek, dating from about 1500 to 1200 BC, roughly the period of the Homeric epics. In 1953, he published a historic paper with John Chadwick, ''Evidence for Greek Dialect in the Mycenaean Archives.'' Their *Documents on Mycenaean Greek* (1956; rev. ed., 1973) was published a few weeks after Ventris' death in an auto accident, and Chadwick's *The Decipherment of Linear B* (1958; 2nd ed., 1968) followed.

Venus figurine: Small female statuettes of the Upper Palaeolithic, found from southwest France to European Russia—

statuettes, sculptured in the round, of naked and often obese women. The figures, sometimes with exaggerated abdomen, breasts, and buttocks, were made of clay, stone, antler, bone, limestone, steatite, or mammoth ivory, and have been found on Eastern Gravettian and Upper Périgordian sites from the Pyrenees to eastern Russia. The heads are featureless, and the legs and arms are little emphasized. They mainly date from the period 30,000 to 15,000 years ago; a later series is different in character, more slender and hollow stomached, and is contemporary with the Magdalenian. (*syn.* 'Venus' figurine)

Vergina: Royal capital of Macedonia in northern Greece with a tumulus cemetery of the Early Iron Age. A pair of royal tombs from the fourth century BC contained many objects of gold, silver, bronze, and iron, several wall frescoes, and two caskets of human bones, which may be the remains of the parents of Alexander III, Philip II, and his fourth wife Olympias.

vernacular: The writing, speech, architecture, and so on, common among the indigenous people of a country or region.

vernacular architecture: Buildings belonging to the middle and lower end of the social scale, which fall into three main categories—domestic, agricultural and industrial—and which are characteristic of a period, place, or group. Building styles that remain common over a period in a particular place.

Verona: City in northern Italy at the foot of the Lessini Mountains on the River Adige. The city was founded by an ancient tribe (possibly the Euganei or Raeti) and was later occupied by the Gallic Cenomani. It became a Roman colony in 89 BC and rapidly rose in importance because it was at the junction of main roads between Italy and northern Europe. There are two large gateways dating from 1st century AD, a theater, and the Arena, the third-largest surviving Roman amphitheater.

Vértes, Laszlo (1914–1968): Hungarian archaeologist and expert on the Palaeolithic in Hungary. He worked at Vertesszollos, Istallosko, Szeleta Cave, Tata, and Jankovich.

Vértesszöllös: Lower Palaeolithic quarry site northwest of Budapest, Hungary, near the confluence of the Ataler and Danube Rivers, with artifacts and fauna dating 350,000–175,000 bp (Middle Pleistocene). The pebble chopping tools and flake tools are associated with human skeletal remains, which are intermediate between *Homo erectus* and *Homo sapiens* (Homo (erectus seu sapiens) palaeohungaricus). The principal significance of this specimen, apart from its structure, is that it is dated to a warm phase in the second (Mindel) glaciation, 500,000 to 400,000 years ago.

vertical exposure: Excavation of a site to reveal its vertical extent, with relatively little breadth. This type of excavation is undertaken to establish a chronological sequence, normally covering a limited area. (*syn.* vertical excavation)

vertical photograph: In aerial photography, a photo taken from directly overhead to reveal the plan of a site or object.

Verulamium: Romano-British town across from St. Albans, Hertfordshire, England. Before the Roman conquest, Verulamium was the capital of Tasciovanus, prince of the Catuvellauni; under Roman rule, it soon was made a municipium. Destroyed by Boudicca (or Boadicea; queen of the Iceni) in AD 60–61, it soon regained its prosperity. Among its ruins are the city grid plan, the forum, a theater associated with a temple of Romano-Celtic type, a market hall, two triumphal arches, fragments of the town wall, and many well-appointed houses with fine mosaics and wall paintings. It was still of some importance when it was visited by St. Germanus in 429, but thereafter was replaced by St. Albans. It is thought to be the third largest Roman town in Britain. (*syn.* modern St. Albans)

Veselé: Early Bronze Age site in southwest Slovakia, c. 1800–1700 BC. The fortified area is of the Mad'arovce culture.

Veselinovo: Middle and Late Neolithic tell site of the Karanovo III culture in southern Bulgaria. Dated to the late 5th millennium BC, the culture marks a sharp break from the preceding Starcevo. It is contemporaneous with the early Vinca culture. The pottery is undecorated except for some cordons and is pear shaped or cylindrical with flat bases. The beakers often have a curving handle with an upper knob.

Veterov culture: Early Bronze Age culture of Moravia with a material culture of the Hungarian Early Bronze Age and the Unetice culture of Bohemia.

Vetulonia: Principal Etruscan city and, according to traditional sources, one of the confederation of twelve. The original settlement was probably early Iron Age (Villanovan), and it prospered between the 9th–6th centuries BC. There are Villanovan pits, biconical ossuaries (a type of circular tomb with a tumulus), and some monumental tholos-like vaulted examples. The grave goods are often rich, of gold, silver, and particularly bronze. From the Tomba della Pietrera have come the earliest examples of Etruscan stone statuary, which are flat, rectilinear figurines. (*syn.* Etruscan Vetluna)

Via Maris: Historic road that runs along the Palestine coast, Latin for "way of the sea." It was the most important route from Egypt to Syria (the Fertile Crescent), which followed the coastal plain before crossing over into the plain of Jezreel and the Jordan valley.

Victoria West: A technique for preparing cores by removing a single flake, that is Levallois-like and associated with Earlier Stone Age assemblages of interior South Africa.

Vicús: Early Horizon culture of the Piura basin in north Peru, where deep shaft tombs were discovered. The Vicús tombs have produced abundant metalwork, modeled wares resembling the Gallinazo style, and early Moche ceramics, and a local style of pottery with negative painting. Vicús material covers most of the 1st millennium AD and was eventually replaced by Chimú.

vicus: In Roman times, the smallest division of housing, roughly equivalent to a village or to a suburb. As a village, the vicus would be administered by magistri or aediles elected by the villagers. In military areas, such as along Hadrian's Wall, civilian vici often grew up next to military forts. It would consist of houses used by the families of troops, the shops, inns, civilian workshops, and so on, outside a Roman fort or encampment. (*syn.* pl. vici; village)

Vidra: Middle and Late Neolithic tell settlement near Giurgiu in the lower Danube Valley, southeast Romania. The main occupation horizons include a Boian level, a Boin-Gumelnita transitional level, and three Gumelnita levels. Of the Gumelnita levels, the first two have rich metal finds, including gold pendants and copper pins and earrings.

Vietnam: A distinct Vietnamese ethnolinguistic group began to emerge about 200 BC in the independent kingdom of Nam Viet, which was later annexed to China. In the 1st century AD, the kingdom of Funan occupied much of the Mekong delta area, but it disappeared in the 6th century. Most Vietnamese archaeological sites are in the northern part of the country: Lower Palaeolithic tools, a lithic sequence from the end of the Pleistocene (c. 10,000–4000 BC) with pottery, full Neolithic cultures appearing after 3000 BC and the Bronze Age, terminating in the classic Dong-Son culture (early second millennium BC–AD 200). The Bronze Age-Iron Age in southern Vietnam is associated with the Sa-Huynh culture and Chamic (Austronesian) settlement.

vigesimal mathematics: The base-20 system used in Mesoamerican writing systems and by the Maya for the Long Count calendar.

Viking: The inhabitants of Scandinavia from about AD 700–1100, great boat builders and navigators who settled all over Europe and the Mediterranean. Term embraces the Norse, who raided and settled northern Britain, Iceland, Greenland, and North America; the Swedes, who established a trade route from the Baltic through Russia to Byzantium and beyond; and the Danes, who were a serious threat in England and Ireland. Viking raiders were descended from the native peoples of Migration period Scandinavia. In 865, their raids of England led to their conquest of most of the eastern part of the country, with their capital at York. At the beginning of the 10th century, Iceland was settled, then Greenland, and even the North American coast (Vinland) was reached, culminating in the settlement of Anse au Meadow in Newfoundland.

Some Viking raids even penetrated the Mediterranean by way of Gibraltar. During this time, the many Scandinavian chiefdoms shared a similar material culture and were involved in trading far beyond the Baltic Sea. (*syn.* Norseman, Northman)

Viking Age: The period of Scandinavian history from AD c. 700–1100, which begins with the first Viking raids on western Europe at the end of the 8th century. Therefore, the period is more narrowly defined as the 9th–11th centuries.

Vikletice: Corded Ware culture cemetery in Bohemia.

Vila Nova de São Pedro: Important Chalcolithic site near Santarém, Portugal, with an unenclosed settlement c. 3800 BC, succeeded by one surrounded by at least two bastioned stone walls, c. 3200 BC. The first belonged to the Palmella culture, and the final phase belonged to the Beaker culture, c. 2500 BC. Artifacts include copper axes, chisels, and daggers; pottery included Beaker material and local wares of the 3rd millennium BC. Strongly fortified settlements, such as this, accompanied by cemeteries containing rich collections of prestige goods suggest the appearance of a hierarchically organized society.

Vilcabamba: Inca site in the eastern Andes, north of Cuzco, Peru, established after the Spanish conquest.

Vilcas Guamán: Large Inca administrative center near Ayacucho, Peru, and the symbolic center of the Inca universe. There is a large four-stepped Usnu of dressed stone.

villa: In Roman architecture, the name of a farm or country house or a farming residence with luxurious private, urban, and humble rural dwellings. In the Roman context, the farmstead had ancillary buildings and one main residential structure. In a Minoan context, a villa was a rural residence with some local administrative functions. The residential villas were often in an area of beauty or on the seashore. Many villas existed throughout the Roman Empire, and references to them are common in the works of Roman writers, especially Cicero, who had seven villas, and Pliny, who described his villas in Tuscany and near Laurentum. The most famous villa is Hadrian's Villa at Tivoli (AD c. 120–130).

Villafranchian: A major division of early Pleistocene deposits and a time named for a sequence of terrestrial sediments studied in the region of Villafranca d'Asti, an Italian town near Turin. This was a time when new mammals suddenly appeared in the Lower Pleistocene period. The Villafranchian is also significant because within it the earliest hominids that clearly evolved into modern man (the australopithecines) appeared. The Villafranchian is in part contemporaneous with the Blancan Stage of North America.

Villanovan: Early Iron Age people of the Po Valley, Etruria, and parts of Campania, Italy, c. 900–700 BC. The culture is defined by artifacts from the type site of Villanova: metalwork in gold and bronze. The craftsmen played a major part in the development of the fibula and the technique of sheet metalwork, especially the situla. The cemeteries were urn-fields with decorated biconical urns and bronze objects; subsidiary vessels, fibulae, ornaments, crescentic razors, and so on, frequently accompanied the ashes. The pottery was handmade, dark burnished, decorated with meanders of grooved bands. The Villanovans were replaced culturally by the Etruscans in the south in the 8th century, in the north in the 6th century. This period laid the foundations for the Etruscan culture and city-states of the 8th century BC. (*syn.* Villanovan culture; Villanova period)

Villeneuve-Tolosane: Middle Neolithic village in Haute-Garonne, France, with many pits, ditches, hearths, and Chasséen material c. 4250–3600 BC.

Vinapu: Location of two important Easter Island *ahu*, one with a seaward face of close-fitted blocks of stone, similar to Inca masonry in Peru (AD c. 1516), the other of normal Easter Island type (AD c. 857). Both ahu have a series of *moai*.

Vinca: Large tell just outside Belgrade, Serbia, spanning c. 5000–3500 BC. Its lowest level consisted of Starcevo material; the next of Middle and Late Neolithic are Vinca-Tordos and Vinca-Plocnik. The pottery is typically dark burnished with fluting, channeling, and simple incised decoration. It was a settled farming community that was also important in trade. Many anthropomorphic figurines are found on Vinca sites as well as copper artifacts and evidence of copper mining. It is one of a group of cultures important in the development of copper metallurgy. (*syn.* Vinca culture)

Vindija Cave: Palaeolithic site near Zagreb, Croatia, with occupation from the Middle Palaeolithic (last interglacial) c. 115,000–60,000 bp. Neanderthal remains were in the upper Middle Palaeolithic level; anatomically modern remains in the Gravettian level.

Vindolanda: Roman fort and civilian settlement in Chester-holm, England, of the late 1st–early 2nd centuries AD, just south of Hadrian's Wall. There is a military bathhouse, inn, houses, and mausolea—and thousands of fragments of documents written in ink on wood.

Vinland: Viking name for the part of North America visited by Leif Erikson (Eriksson) AD c. 1000, around L'Anse aux Meadows on the coast of Maine or eastern Canada.

Virú Valley: Valley on the north coast of Peru, which was the scene of the first serious attempt to study a regional settlement pattern in the New World. The aim was to study the relation between site function and location, and between settlement patterns, ecology, and cultural development over a long period. The settlements pattern approach uses locational and environmental interrelations between sites (over a broad region) as a means of interpreting prehistoric cultures. A comprehensive project of survey and excavation has taken place in this valley.

vitrification: The melting and fusion of glassy minerals in clay during the high-temperature firing of pottery (above 1000°C), resulting in loss of porosity. It occurs when clay particles fuse together as glass—a process starting between 800–900 degrees centigrade and completed at about 1200 degrees centigrade.

vitrified fort: A type of Iron Age hill fort where the external walls of stone have become smooth by the heat of the sun or by burning, combined with windy conditions. The walls fuse into a slaggy or glassy mass, becoming vitrified. Dry-stone timber-laced ramparts, especially in Scotland, have timber lacing that has been fired, causing the stone core of the rampart to fuse. They are dated roughly in the last few centuries BC and early centuries AD.

Vix: Iron Age burial mound in Côte-d'Or, France, a rich Celtic burial of the Hallstatt D period (late 6th century BC). In a mortuary house under a barrow, the body of a woman was accompanied by a four-wheeled cart with bronze fittings and by rich offerings, including a gold diadem, bronze and silver bowls, brooches, Etruscan wine flagons, and a Attic Black Figure cup dated c. 520 BC. The most spectacular object is a massive bronze crater with a capacity of nearly 1,300 liters (1.64 m high) and of Greek workmanship. The burial at Vix is associated with the nearby hill fort of Mont Lassois.

vizier: The chief minister or representative of the 'Abbasid caliphs and later a high administrative officer in various Muslim countries and among Arabs, Persians, Turks, Mongols, and other eastern peoples. In Egypt, it was the head of the bureaucratic administration, chief ambassador, supreme civil and criminal judge, and the king's chief minister. (*syn.* Egyptian tjaty)

Vladimirovka: One of the largest sites of the Cucuteni-Tripolye culture in the Ukraine's Bug Valley, dated to the late 4th millennium BC. The settlement consists of over 200 complete huts of the Polshchadki type organized in five concentric rings on a broad promontory. Among the rich domestic assemblages of Cucuteni B pottery were numerous house and shrine models and many fired clay anthropomorphic figurines.

Vlasac: Late Mesolithic fishing-hunting site located in the Iron Gates gorge of the River Danube in Serbia, with occupation dates of 6000–5500 BC. Small circular tents are arranged near stone hearths around a central space or platform. Large numbers of Mesolithic burials are known from the site, mostly Cro-Magnon physical type, with few grave goods.

Vogelherd: Palaeolithic cave in Württemberg, Germany,

with Mousterian layers containing Aurignacian occupation levels and artifacts. There is also a Magdalenian level.

Volga-Oka culture: Mesolithic and Neolithic groups of the central Russian plain, related to Forest Neolithic groups of the Baltic. Pottery was adopted by hunter gatherers who also fished.

Vólos: Site in Thessaly, Greece, occupied from the Early Bronze Age until the Hellenistic period. A large structure of the 14th century BC might be a Mycenaean palace. A tholos tomb was found just north of Vólos. Excavations have been carried out on two Mycenaean palaces in the old town, Áno Vólos. Áno Vólos was the site of ancient Iolcos, inhabited since the beginning of the Bronze Age (c. 2500 BC) and capital of Mycenaean Thessaly. The Neolithic towns of Sesklo and Dimini also stood near present-day Vólos, and just south of it are the ruins of Pagasae, a prominent port from Mycenaean to late Classical times.

Volp Caves: Cave system in Ariège, France, with three sites: Enlène, Le Tuc d'Audoubert, and Les Trois Frères. The portable art is dated c. 12,000–11,000 BC.

Volterra: Ancient Etruscan city (Velathri) and one of the 12 cities of the Etruscan confederation. It supported Rome during the Second Punic War in 205 BC, acquired Roman citizenship after the civil wars between Gaius Marius and Sulla (81–80 BC), and took the name Volaterrae. Occupation began as early as the Copper Age (Rinal-Done culture), and was established by the Iron Age (c. early 1st millennium BC). By the 4th century BC, there was perimeter walling enclosing an extensive area. Volterra is noted for its carved funerary stelae and alabaster urns decorated with mythological scenes. The Roman period itself saw the development of an area to the north of the Etruscan walls, which has left remains of some bath buildings and an Augustan-period theater. There are also two Etruscan-Roman gateways and circular tombs from the 6th century BC, with vaults of concentric rings supported by a central pillar. (*syn.* Etruscan Velathri, Roman Vola-terrae, Volaterrae)

volute: A spiral scroll decorating capitals of the Ionic order.

vomitorium: The way into the cavia of a Roman theater or amphitheater.

Vorbasse: Migration period settlement in southern Jutland, Denmark, of the 4th–5th centuries, a planned village of longhouses. Each house was divided into three rooms, with two or three minor buildings. There was also a series of sunken-floored workshops in the last phase. After its abandonment in the 5th century, the settlement was not reoccupied until the Viking period. In the 10th century, Vorbasse was turned into three major estates, each incorporating a large "Trelleborg type" hall with associated workshops.

votive deposit: An object or group of objects left in a sacred place, an offering to a divinity generally with the intention of securing a favor or expressing gratitude or devotion. Votive deposits were often made at natural sites (cave, river, lake, or peat bog) and, unlike other types of hoard, was not intended to be recovered later.

Vounous: Early Cypriot cemetery in northern Cyprus of the late 3rd millennium BC. The tombs are oval rock-cut chambers entered through a short dromos. Grave goods include terra-cotta models.

V-perforation: A method of making buttons in which two converging holes are drilled to meet at an angle below the surface. The technique was common in Europe in the Copper and Early Bronze Age and was used especially among the Beaker folk.

Vucedol: Late Neolithic tell settlement that is the type site of a Slavonian culture, located by the Drava River in northern Croatia and Slovenia. It is characterized by its pottery, excised and filled with white paste. Some copper was also being worked. The material is related to that from the Ljubljansko Blat and the Eastern Alps and is closely related to the Hungarian Zok culture. It succeeded the Baden culture and the Kostolac group. (*syn.* Vucedol group)

Vulci: City of Etruria in Italy with ruins of an Etruscan temple, Roman houses, Greek pottery, and a production center for bronzes. There are extensive cemeteries and a large network of streets and walls. Vulci grew out of a number of Villanovan villages and flourished chiefly in the 6th–4th centuries BC, largely as a result of trade, the extraction of minerals from nearby Monte Amiata, and the manufacture of bronze jugs and tripods. (*syn.* Velch)

Vyadhapura: Sanskrit for "City of Hunters," capital city of the ancient Hindu kingdom of Funan, which flourished from the 1st–6th centuries AD in an area that includes modern Cambodia and Vietnam. It is 120 miles (190 km) from the mouth of the Mekong River, near a land form called Ba Hill in southern Cambodia.

Ww

wabet: In ancient Egypt, the place where part of the purification or mummification rites took place.

Wace, Alan (1879–1957): British archaeologist who was director of the British School at Athens and excavated in Laconia, Thessaly, and Mycenae. He discovered one of the earliest royal burials at Mycenae, a grave circle consisting essentially of vertical shafts cut into bedrock.

wadi: Arabic term for a channel of a watercourse that is dry except during periods of rainfall; intermittent watercourse.

Wadi Kubbaniya: Series of Egyptian Late Palaeolithic sites on the west bank of the River Nile near Aswan. Artifacts include grinding stones, chipped stone tools, mortars and pestles, and domesticated plant remains (wheat, barley) dated to 18,250–16,960 bp. If confirmed by future research, this might be the earliest evidence for cereal cultivation in the world.

Wadi Shatt er-Rigal: Site of a dried-up watercourse in Upper Egypt with more than 800 predynastic rock engravings and graffiti from Middle Kingdom times.

Wadjet: In ancient Egypt, the cobra goddess, whose cult was associated with the Lower Egyptian town of Buto, dating to the predynastic period. Wadjet and Nekhbet, the vulture goddess if Upper Egypt, were the protective goddesses of the king and were sometimes represented together on the king's diadem, symbolizing his reign over all of Egypt. (*syn.* Edjo, Uto, Wadjit, Buto)

wadjet eye: A symbol common in the New Kingdom, the left eye of Horus, restored by the god Thoth. It symbolized the power of healing and was a powerful protective amulet.

Waira-Jirca: An Initial period phase from the Kotosh site, eastern Andes, central Peru—the earliest ceramic phase, c. 1800–1150 BC. The well-made, dark brown pottery with incised geometric designs resembles early jungle pottery from Ucayali and was ancestral to Kotosh-Kotosh and Chavín. Its most widely occurring forms are the neckless jar and the open bowl, although some spouted forms do occur. (*syn.* Waira-jirca)

Wairau Bar: Archaic Maori burial ground and midden site in the northern South Island, New Zealand, at the mouth of the Wairau River. The site is remarkable for its rich grave goods, including adzes, necklace units, and fishhooks—similar to those from contemporary sites in the Marquesas and Society Islands. Dated to AD c. 1100–1350, Wairau Bar also produced perhaps the richest nonorganic artifact assemblage of any site in New Zealand. It is from the Moa-hunter period.

waisted ax: Large Pleistocene stone tool with a flaked cutting edge and flaked notch on each margin, thereby giving it a waist for hafting. It was made in New Guinea and in Australia.

Wajil: Unglazed earthenware of the Korean Proto-Three Kingdoms period, which was hard fired and reduced.

Waldalgesheim: Chariot burial of the La Tène Iron Age in the Rhineland, Germany, depicting the 4th century BC decorative style of the same name. Funerary offerings included gold ornaments, bronze flagon, imported Italian bronze bucket, and bronze plaques with repoussé human figures. The native pieces (gold torcs, bracelets) are decorated in the Waldalgesheim curvilinear style of ornament based on tendril patterns. After c. 350 BC, metalwork decorated in this Waldalgesheim style made its appearance all over Celtic Europe from Britain to Romania and Bulgaria. (*syn.* Kreis Kreuznach)

Walker Road: Prehistoric site in south-central Alaska with radiocarbon dates c. 11,820–11,010 bp. The assemblage includes Chindadn points and end scrapers of the Nenana complex.

Wallacea: Biogeographical zone of islands between the Southeast Asia Sunda shelf and the Sahul shelf—an area separating Australia from Southeast Asia for 70 million years. It marks the division between two major faunal groups: oriental animals (elephants, tigers, and apes) and the animals of Australia (kangaroos, wombats, and monotremes). Dates of first human settlement are uncertain; the first settlers of Australia before 30,000 years ago had to cross sea gaps of up to 70 kilometers in this zone. The water formed a barrier to the spread of animals and humans into Australia and New Guinea. It is named after the British naturalist A. R. Wallace, who first recognized its significance.

Wandjina figure: A type of anthropomorphic bichrome or polychrome painting made in the Kimberley region of Western Australia, succeeding the Bradshaw style (c. 3000 BC) and persisting to the present. Wandjina takes its name from the ancestor spirits depicted in the paintings. The large white spirit figures are outlined in black and have mouthless, circular faces that are framed in red, rayed halos. The Bradshaw style was a series of bichrome and monochrome figures.

Wando: Site off South Cholla Province, Korea, of a late 11th century AD Koryo shipwreck. There were 30,000 celadon vessels from kilns in Haenam on the ship.

wardum: A slave and servant or official of the king, according to Hammurabi's Code. A threefold division of the populace had been postulated—awilum, muskenum, and wardum—but their descriptions in the Code are problematic. Wardum is the least problematic, however; he was the slave and was able to regain his freedom under certain conditions as a debtor-slave.

ware: Generally, articles made of pottery or ceramic. Specifically, a class of pottery whose members share similar technology, paste, and surface treatment.

Warendorf: Migration period settlement in Westphalia, West Germany, of the 7th–9th centuries. A range of building types is laid out in nucleated groups; other buildings in a typical unit consist of barns and outhouses, stables, octagonal- and hexagonal-shaped silos, haystacks, and a variety of sunken-hut workshops.

Wargata Mina: Limestone cave in Tasmania, Australia, with hand stencils done in human blood and dated to c. 10,730–9240 bp. (*syn.* Judds Cavern)

Warka: Ancient Mesopotamian city northwest of Ur (Tell Al-Muqayyar) in southeastern Iraq, one of the greatest cities of Sumer. Its occupation began in 'Ubaid 2 (c. 5000 BC) and continued through Parthian times (126 BC–AD 224). It was most important during Late Uruk to Early Dynastic times. Urban life in what is known as the Erech–Jamdat Nasr period (c. 3500–2900 BC) is more fully illustrated here than at any other Mesopotamian city. Chief landmarks are the Anu ziggurat crowned by the "White Temple" and the temenos of Eanna, another ziggurat. (*syn.* Erech, Uruk [Sumerian], Orchoë [Greek], Tell al-Warka' [modern])

warp and weft: In weaving, the warp constitutes the foundation threads that run lengthwise over and through which the weft crosses at right angles. The weft are the horizontal threads that interlace through the warp. Warp provides the fairly rigid foundation in basketry, and weft is the more flexible stitching.

warranting argument: An argument used to support assumptions about the way the world works, employed by archaeologists to support interpretations of empirical observations.

Warring States period: A division of the Zhou/Chou Dynasty, 475–221 BC, the latter part of the Eastern Zhou period, made up of six or seven small feuding Chinese kingdoms. The Warring States period saw the rise of many of the great philosophers of Chinese civilization, including the Confucian thinkers Mencius and Hsün-tzu, and the establishment of many of the governmental structures and cultural patterns that were to characterize China for the next 2,000 years. The Warring States period is distinguished from the preceding age, the Spring and Autumn (Ch'un Ch'iu) period (770–476 BC), when the country was divided into many even smaller states. In 223 BC Ch'in defeated Ch'u and two years later established the first unified Chinese empire. (*syn.* Contending States)

Warsaw: City and now capital of Poland, which began as Stare Bródno, a small trading settlement of the 10th and early 11th centuries AD. That settlement's functions were taken over successively by Kamion (c. 1065) and Jazdow (c. 1262). About the end of the 13th century, Jazdow was moved to the north, to a village named Warszowa (Warsaw), and the community was strengthened by the protection of a castle. Medieval Warsaw grew up on the left bank of the River Vistula. Excavations around the royal castle located the earthworks of a proto-urban 10th-century fortress with earth-and-timber ramparts and gateways. The area around the cathedral was the site of the citadel of the 10th-century town. (*syn.* Stare Bródno)

Wasit: Military and commercial city of medieval Iraq, especially important during the Umayyad caliphate (AD 661–750). It was established as a military encampment in 702 on the Tigris River, between Basra and Kufah. A palace and the chief mosque were built, and irrigation and cultivation were encouraged. Because of its location on the Tigris, Wasit became a shipbuilding and commercial center. Even after the caliphal capital was moved from Damascus to Baghdad, the city remained important. The only standing building is a shrine with a monumental portal flanked by minarets, datable to the 13th century. Excavations revealed a congregational mosque with four periods of construction, the earliest with a large courtyard surrounded on three sides by a single arcade and a sanctuary 19 bays wide and 5 bays deep. Adjoining the mosque was the Dar al Imara or governor's palace.

waste flake: A byproduct, eliminated or thrown away as worthless after the making of a stone tool, either a larger piece flaked off from the original stone (primary waste flake) or a smaller piece removed during finishing (secondary waste flake).

waster: A name for the waste product of the pottery manufacturing process. This could occur when the clay choice was bad or there was a problem in the mixing of clays or problems in firing. These finds may suggest the presence of kilns or other pot-firing structures. Any refuse deposit of vessels or fragments of vessels that were cracked, warped, or otherwise damaged and made unusable during firing. (*syn.* waster dump)

Water Newton: The site of a walled Roman-British town situated where the Roman road from the English Channel ports to London crossed the River Medway at the head of its estuary. It was a large and important Roman pottery town, center of production for the Nene Valley color-coated ware. Water Newton grew out of the civilian settlement attached to an early-period Roman fort (AD c. 45). Aerial photography shows a large expanse of industrial development, marking Water Newton as one of the major industrial area of Roman Britain. The hoard of Christian silver plate from the 4th century AD indicates local affluence and is possibly the earliest group of Christian silver. (*syn.* Roman Durobrivae; modern Rochester)

Watling Street: The most famous of the Roman roads in Britain, running from London northwest via St. Albans (Verulamium) to Wroxeter (Viroconium). It was built in the early years of the Roman occupation of Britain and was one of the great arterial roads of Roman and post-Roman Britain. The name came from a group of Anglo-Saxon settlers who called Verulamium by the name of Waetlingaceaster. This local name passed to the whole of the Roman road by the 9th century. (*syn.* Waetlinga Street)

Watom Island: Island off New Britain in the Bismarck Archipelago, Melanesia, with Lapita pottery c. 2767–1787 bp. There is also obsidian from Talasea and Lou and Lapita human skeletal remains.

wattle-and-daub: A building technique in which walls were made by plastering mud (daub, possibly with sand and plant fibers) over a lattice of branches and sticks (wattle). Interwoven twigs or thin split timbers were used. Although the wattle does not normally survive, its imprint is frequently preserved on the daub. It was used for, among other things, house walls, ovens, hurdles, fencing, and simple pottery kilns. (*syn.* wattle; wattle and daub)

Wayland's Smithy: Early Neolithic long barrow in Oxfordshire, southern England, c. 3500 BC. In the first phase of construction, it covered a wooden mortuary house with the remains of 14 individuals. Over this was constructed a much longer trapezoidal (oval) chalk mound with a stone curb and a megalithic passage grave of Severn-Cotswold type.

way station: Name for a small chapel on an avenue in a temple complex, where the shrine of the god might be placed temporarily during processions.

wedge-shaped gallery grave: A megalithic chamber tomb particular to Ireland in the Late Neolithic and sometimes from the Middle–Late Bronze Ages. There is a long narrow chamber of orthostats supporting capstones, which decrease in height toward the back; it would not have a separate entrance passage. The division between antechamber and burial area is marked by a sill slab or by stone jambs. The cairn may be round, oval, or D-shaped, and often has a retaining wall. The earliest grave goods are bucket-shaped pots of the Late Neolithic period, but Beaker pottery is predominant. (*syn.* wedge tomb)

wedge-shaped microcore: A core that is small and keel or wedge shaped and used to make microblades. It has been found in East Europe, Siberia, Mongolia, northern China, Alaska, northwestern North America, and Japan, on Upper Palaeolithic sites from the close of the Pleistocene.

Weeden Island phase: A culture following Middle Woodland and preceding Mississippian, which occupied much of north Florida, southwest Georgia, and southeast Alabama AD c. 200–1000. The pottery is among the finest of the eastern United States.

weed of cultivation: Any plant that is unable to flourish in wooded shady areas but finds its habitat in open regions such as agricultural fields. With the removal of vegetational competition as a result of clearance of woodland, these weeds establish themselves. Where early agriculturists cleared forest for the sowing of crops, these weeds appeared. Pollen evidence from weeds of cultivation is used by palaeobotanists in recognizing phases of agriculture.

Weichselian: The final glacial advance, c. 115,000–10,000 bp, corresponding to the Alpine Würm, American Wisconsinan, and British Devensian. The Weichsel Glacial Stage followed the Eemian Interglacial Stage and marks the last major incursion of Pleistocene continental ice sheets. It is named for the ice sheet of north Germany and other Quaternary glacial deposits in northwest Europe. Most of the Weichselian is within the range of radiocarbon dating. The ice sheets were probably at their maximum size for only a short period, between 30,000–13,000 bp; eight interstadials have been recognized in the Weichselian of northwest Europe. The late Weichsel expansion of the Scandinavian continental ice sheet began about 25,000 years ago; most of the Weichselian sediments over northern Europe are part of this late Weichselian cold period. (*syn.* Weichsel Glaciation; Vistula Glacial Stage)

Weidenreich, Franz (1873–1948): German anatomist and physical anthropologist whose contribution was in the reconstruction of prehistoric human remains and his work on Peking man (*Sinanthropus*) and other hominids, especially from materials at Zhoukoudian, China.

Weipa: Aboriginal site and mining town, northern Queensland, Australia, on the northwestern coast of Cape Fork Peninsula. Matthew Flinders noted the red deposits, which were later identified as bauxite, the ore of aluminum. About 500 shell mounds are dated c. 1200 bp, and they are among the largest and best-preserved examples of shell middens in the world.

welding: The joining together of pieces of metal, especially iron and steel, by heating and hammering or pressure. It was done to combine the different qualities of malleability or hardness of these metals. This method was used in Europe at the end of the Iron Age to produce effective sword blades. Later, welding was done by melting, using local heat provided by an electric arc, oxyacetylene torch, or laser.

Wepwawet: Egyptian jackal god portrayed on the Narmer palette at the end of the fourth millennium BC, the opener of the way for the king's foreign conquests or for the deceased into netherworld. Asyut (Syut) was the center of his worship.

were-jaguar: A creature with human infant and jaguar features, which was important in Olmec art. It has a babylike expression, fangs, snarling mouth, and other feline facial features. The number and unity of the objects in this style first suggested to scholars that they were dealing with a new and previously unknown civilization. There is a whole spectrum of such were-jaguar forms in Olmec art, ranging from the almost purely feline to the human in which only a trace of jaguar can be seen. These Olmec monuments were generally carved in the round, technically very advanced even though the only methods available were pounding and pecking with stone tools. Considerable artistry can also be seen in the pottery figurines of San Lorenzo, which depict nude and sexless individuals with were-jaguar traits. The Olmec also worshiped a rain deity depicted as a were-jaguar.

Wessex: The kingdom of the West Saxons founded by Cerdic in the upper Thames Valley, AD c. 494/495, known from a site with archaeological remains, situated on the upper Thames, probably settled from the northeast. Wessex first spread in influence to the south and west and was one of the last Anglo-Saxon kingdoms to become firmly established. Its nucleus approximated that of the modern counties of Hampshire, Dorset, Wiltshire, Somerset, and southern Avon. At times, its land extended north of the River Thames, and it eventually expanded to cover Devon and Cornwall. It reached its peak in the 9th century. Wessex under Alfred (871–899) became the nucleus of a unified England.

Wessex culture: Early Bronze Age culture of southern England with cemeteries of found barrows of special types (bell, disc, and saucer barrows and enclosures strangely labeled "pond barrows") c. 2650–1400 BC. It developed from the Beaker tradition and was closely related to the Armorican Tumulus culture. The Wessex I period, c. 2650–2000 BC, is associated with the major rebuilding of Stonehenge (III). There are rich grave goods, including bronze daggers and axes, amber and shale beads and buttons, copper, and gold. The pottery is mainly incense cups and the first collared urns. In the Wessex II period, c. 1650–1400 BC, cremation replaced inhumation, and there are faience beads. Bronze was normal in Wessex II and contained up to 17% tin. The culture had contacts with Egypt, Mycenae, and Crete. Unfortunately, no settlements of the Wessex culture are known. (*syn.* Wessex Culture)

Western Chin Dynasty: A phase of the Chin Dynasty, ruling China from AD 265 to 317. Important tombs of this period have been excavated in Kiangsu and Chekiang, provinces in southeastern China, as well as Yüeh ware and rare jewelry items.

Western Neolithic: A main division of the Early and Middle Neolithic cultures of western Europe; it includes the cultures of Chassey, Cortaillod, Lagozza, Windmill Hill, and the Almerian. The local cultures differ in many ways, but have more in common with each other than with cultures of the other major traditions (Danubian, TRB). This can be seen most clearly in the pottery, which shares simple round-based shapes, string-hole lugs rather than handles, and absence of painted decoration or spiral designs. Some scholars feel that these cultures are only loosely connected and that the term Western Neolithic is not useful.

Western Pluvial Lakes Tradition: Culture unit found throughout western North America, characterized by the exploitation of marshes and lakes in the early postglacial period and distinctive artifacts—large, stemmed, lanceolate projectile points and large, leaf-shaped bipoints. These point types immediately followed in time and perhaps derived from the Clovis culture of c. 10,000–9000 BC.

Western Zhou [Chou] period: A division of the Zhou/Chou Dynasty, 1027–771 BC, the earlier part of the Zhou Dynasty, starting with the fall of the Shang Dynasty. The first Zhou/Chou rulers parceled out their expanding territory among feudal lords. As the feudal states rose in power and independence, so did the central Zhou/Chou itself shrink, to be further weakened by the eastward shift of the capital from sites in the Wei River valley near modern-day Sian to Lo-yang in 771 BC. Thereafter, the Zhou/Chou Empire was broken up among rival states. (*syn.* Royal Zhou)

West Kennet: A Neolithic long barrow, the largest of the Severn-Cotswold group of megalithic tombs, in Wiltshire,

England, of c. 3500 BC. The tomb has two pairs of transepts and a terminal chamber; the entrance opens from a crescent-shaped forecourt blocked by a straight facade of sarsen slabs. The burial was of 46 disarticulated inhumations, and the chambers were filled with a mixture of soil, charcoal, sherds of Peterborough ware, and grooved ware and beaker fragments. That material has a date of 2500/2000 BC.

West Slope ware: Pottery of the Hellenistic period decorated with simple designs, found on the west slope of the Athens Akropolis. It evolved from Black-Glossed pottery and was decorated in white and yellow with some incision. Corinth and Crete were also centers of its production.

West Stow: Early Saxon settlement in Suffolk, England, near a Romano-British site, inhabited between the 5th–7th centuries. Pottery production appears to have been carried out at West Stow, and one group of wares has been attributed to the so-called Illington-Lackford potter who operated in the late 6th century.

Wetherill, Richard (1858–1910): American archaeologist whose pioneering work included the location and excavation of some of the most important sites in the American Southwest: Cliff Palace in Mesa Verde and Pueblo Bonito in Chaco Canyon.

wet-rice technology: A type of farming in which rice is grown in paddies, small, level, flooded fields in southern and eastern Asia. Wet-rice cultivation is the most prevalent method of farming in the Far East, where it uses a small fraction of the total land yet feeds the majority of the rural population. Rice was domesticated as early as 3500 BC, and by about 2,000 years ago it was grown predominantly in deltas, floodplains, and coastal plains, and some terraced valley slopes. Although rice can also be grown under dry conditions, wet-rice cultivation in paddy fields is much more productive. The fields can be flooded naturally or by irrigation channels and are kept inundated during the growing season. About a month before harvesting, the water is removed and the field left to dry. (*syn.* wet-rice farming, wet-rice society, wet-rice cultivation, wet-rice growing)

wet sieving: A method used to separate organic material (seeds, snails, insects, etc.) from soil before drying, identification, and analysis. It is a more time-consuming method of extraction than flotation by machine, but has the advantage of being more accurate in its results because there is more control over extraction from the sample. The sample is poured into a sieve in a bowl of water, the lumps of soil are carefully broken up, and the organic material is trapped in the mesh while the soil particles are removed.

Wharram Percy: Deserted medieval village in the valley of Yorkshire Wolds, England, documenting a peasant community between the Early Saxon period and the 16th century.

There are rows of rectangular wattle-and-daub houses, two manor houses, and a 12th century AD church. The village was abandoned by the 14th–15th centuries.

wheat: Cereal grass of the Gramineae (Poaceae) family and of the genus Triticum and its edible grain, one of the oldest and most important of the cereal crops. Two wild forms of wheat are found in the Near East today, wild einkorn (*Triticum boeoticum*) and wild emmer (*Triticum dicoccoides*). Wild einkorn and, less commonly domestic einkorn, appear in the Near East at such early farming sites as Ali Kosh before 7000 BC. Emmer, both wild and domestic, was much more common than einkorn and has been found on most early Neolithic sites in the Near East. Domestic emmer subsequently spread throughout Europe. Hexapolid wheats (club wheat, bread wheat) appear in the Near East before 6000 BC. Spelt wheat was being cultivated at Yarim Tepe in northern Mesopotamia in the 6th millennium BC. In Europe, there are some Neolithic occurrences of spelt, but it became common only in the Iron Age.

wheel: One of man's simplest but most important inventions. A Sumerian (Erech) pictograph, dated about 3500 BC, shows a sledge equipped with wheels. It is also shown in Uruk pictographs, c. 3400 BC, and on the Royal Standard of Ur. Early wheels were solid and unwieldy, made of a single piece of wood or three carved planks clamped together by transverse struts. Spoked wheels appeared about 2000 BC, when they were in use on chariots in Asia Minor. The wheel was not used in Pre-Columbian America, except in Mexico, where small pull-along toys in the form of animals were made in terra-cotta. The use of a wheel (turntable) for pottery had also developed in Mesopotamia by 3500 BC.

Wheeler, Sir Robert Eric Mortimer (1890–1976): English archaeologist who revolutionized excavation standards and invented the stratigraphic grid system technique. Adopting and developing further the methods of General Pitt-Rivers, Wheeler emphasized the vertical site record and its importance in reconstructing the history of a site. He founded Britain's Institute of Archaeology of London University and similar institutions in other countries, especially reorganizing Indian and Pakistani archaeology. He worked at Verulamium, Maiden Castle, Harappa, Arikamedu, St. Albans, Colchester, Stanwick, Taxila, Charsada, Mohenjo-Daro, and Brahmagiri and was the director-general of the Archaeological Survey of India. His most important contribution was in popularizing archaeology, through his writings and especially through television programs.

Wheeler box-grid: An excavation technique developed by Sir Robert Eric Mortimer Wheeler from the work of General Pitt-Rivers. It involved the retaining of intact balks of earth between excavation grid squares so that different stratigraphic layers could be correlated across the site in the vertical profiles.

wheelhouse: A stone-built, circular-plan house with partition walls projecting inward like the spokes of a wheel—a form widespread in western and northern Scotland, the Hebrides, and Shetland Islands in the early centuries AD. It characterizes the later Iron Age culture and survived into the Roman period for dwellings and farmhouses. (*syn.* wheel house, wheel-house)

whetstone: A fine-grained hone stone used to sharpen other tools and to give a smooth edge to cutting tools after grinding.

White, Leslie Alvin (1900–1975): American anthropologist best known for his theories of the evolution of culture and for the scientific study of culture that he called "culturology" (the study of culture as an independent entity). His views were important to the development of processual archaeology—seeing culture as a system and the evolutionary development of societies for the capture of greater amounts of energy, which was facilitated by technological development.

white-ground: Athenian pottery technique, especially of the 5th century BC, where white slip was applied to the vessel surface and the decoration painted on that. The white-ground lekythoi—funerary vases with the figures painted in color against a white background—are the most common shapes employing this technique. It was also used on monumental funerary lekythoi. The white-ground lekythoi are believed to be the most reliable source of information about monumental Greek paintings of the Classical period.

White pottery: Soft white, fairly rare earthenware made only in the Shang period (dates given for the founding of the Shang dynasty vary from about 1760–1520 BC; dates for the dynasty's fall also vary from 1122–1030 BC). Found chiefly at Anyang, China, it was probably made for ritual or mortuary purposes and was decorated with incised geometric patterns. It is made of almost pure kaolin and is very brittle; few pots have survived unbroken.

Whithorn: Site in southwest Scotland on the shore of Solway Firth, of one of the oldest Christian centers in Britain, founded AD c. 397 by Saint Ninian. He built a small whitewashed stone church on the site of which a monastery was built about 1130. St. Ninian's Shrine was a popular place of pilgrimage until the Protestant Reformation.

whorl: Something that whirls, coils, or spirals. It is also the circular object with a central perforation used to weight the end of a spindle and act as a flywheel, giving momentum to its rotation while spinning thread. This drum-shaped section on the lower part of a spindle in spinning or weaving machinery served as a pulley for the tape drive that rotates the spindle.

Wichqana: Type site of a complex on the Ayacucho Valley, central highlands of Peru, c. 1200–800 BC (Early Horizon), a ceremonial center with Chavinoid features. The pottery, typically thin, brown, and pebble polished with little or no decoration, has Paracas and Chavín affinities. The U-shaped ceremonial structure is built of stones of alternating size, similar to Cerro Secchin. Skulls of decapitated females have the fronto-occipital flattening typical of Chavín.

wickerwork: Woven basketry composed of a flexible thin weft and a thick warp; work consisting of interlaced osiers, twigs, or rods.

wickiup: Hut used by the nomadic Indians of the arid regions of the western and southwestern United States, usually with an oval base and a rough domed frame covered with reed mats, grass, or brushwood. A crude temporary shelter or hut sometimes surrounded by circles of stone and covered with pinon tree bark or juniper boughs. (*syn.* Fox [Algonquian language of the Fox, Sauk, and Kickapoo Indians] for wiki-yapi house)

Wietrzychowice: Neolithic Kuyavian long barrows of the Funnel Beaker culture in north-central Poland.

Wilburton: Late Bronze Age village in Cambridgeshire, England, with a metal hoard that gives its name to the Wilburton bronze industry of southern England c. 10th–8th centuries BC. It is distinguished by the replacement of tin bronze by a copper–lead–tin alloy, by the increased use of metal (founders' hoards have broken tools and scrap), and by tools such as the leaf-shaped slashing sword with slotted hilt, socketed spear heads, horse bits, and socketed axes.

Wilkinson, (Sir) John Gardner (1797–1875): British Egyptologist who traveled, surveyed, and excavated such sites as Karnak, Valley of the Kings, and ancient Nubian capital of Gebel Barkal. He was the first to produce a detailed plan of the ancient capital city of Akhenaten at el-Amarnà, and his map of the Theban temples and tombs was the first comprehensive survey of the region. He spent 12 years (1821–1833) copying and collecting material in Egypt, and his copies of monuments and texts were then made available to European scholars.

Willandra Lakes: Sites in New South Wales, Australia, which are now dry lakes filled during times of the Pleistocene. Human activity dates to c. 35,000 years ago, and there are hearths, artifacts, shell middens, extinct megafauna, and burials in the area. Late Pleistocene fossil remains from the Willandra Lakes region include the specimen designated WLH 50, a robust individual.

Willendorf: Upper Palaeolithic site on the River Danube near Krems, Austria, with five Willedorfian or Eastern Gravettian levels (c. 32,000 bp) and lower levels of the Aurignacian (c. 41,700–39,500 bp). The Gravettian yielded art objects, including a famous Venus figurine. Willendorf II had an early Aurignacian settlement and sequence of classic industries in central Europe. (*syn.* Willendorf II)

Williamsburg: In Virginia, a site first settled (by the British) in 1633 as Middle Plantation, originally standing within a 6-mile (10-km) stockade and serving as a refuge from Indian attacks. It is also the site of one of the most extensive restoration projects in North America, a working model of 18th-century life. It became the capital of Virginia in 1699 and was renamed in honor of King William III. The College of William and Mary, founded in 1693, and the Capitol building, begun in 1701, were the earliest public buildings. Structures of brick and wood housed a population of 5,000–6,000. When Williamsburg's tenure as capital ended in 1780, the city went into a general decline, although it was never abandoned as Jamestown was. (*syn.* Middle Plantation)

willow-leaf point: Late Solutrean flake tool—slim, with rounded ends and retouching on one side only—of extremely fine workmanship.

Wilson Butte Cave: Site of long occupation on the Snake River Plain in Idaho, starting c. 14,500 bp—possibly one of the oldest occupations in North America. It is located on what is thought to be one of the major migration routes to the interior. Another date of 12,500 BC from an overlying stratum indicates the presence of man south of the ice at the height of the Wisconsin Glaciation. Six layers covering a period of 10,000 years have been defined, five of which are middle-late Holocene. There are few artifacts, but tool assemblages indicate a hunting and gathering way of life prior to the Clovis specialization. The artifacts are biface, retouched blade, and flake.

Wilson, Daniel (1816–1892): Scottish antiquary who coined the word "prehistoric" in his book *The Archaeology and Prehistoric Annals of Scotland* (1851). He was the first to organize Scotland's artifacts according to the Three-Age System. He also wrote *Prehistoric Man: Researches into the Origin of Civilization in the Old and New World* (1862).

Wilton: Microlithic Later Stone Age industry with its type site in a rock shelter in Cape Province, South Africa, and found in other parts of eastern and southern Africa. It is the African equivalent of the Mesolithic cultures of Europe, although of later date, and in its final stage shows contact with the Iron Age farmers of the 1st millennium AD. It occurred over the last 8,000 years. In the rock shelter area, the characteristic tool is the tiny convex or "thumbnail" scraper; crescent-shaped backed microliths, adzes, and backed blades are also present. There is rock painting, plant remains, and faunal remains of "nongregarious" browsing antelope as well as evidence of fishing. Around the beginning of the Christian era, the descendants of the Wilton folk acquired domestic sheep and possibly cattle and learned the art of

pottery manufacture (called postclimax Wilson or ceramic Wilton). (*syn.* Wiltonian)

Winchester: Town in southwest England, capital of Late Saxon England, and once ruled by Alfred the Great (AD 871–899). It has been documented through Roman and post-medieval times. It first was a walled town, then changed to planned streets with a defensive system. As the capital of Wessex, it continued to thrive during the Middle Ages as an important regional center and seat of a bishopric. It was the seat of the Danish king Canute's government (ruled 1016–1035), and several early kings, including Alfred and Canute II, were buried there. (*syn.* Venta Bulgarum)

Winchester Style: Style of manuscript illumination, ivory carving, stone sculpture, metalwork, embroidery, and architecture from the capital of Late Saxon England, c. 10th century AD. The emphasis was on naturalistic figure design, and acanthus decoration is prominent in manuscripts and the stone angels carved over the chancel arch of Bradford-on-Avon church.

Winckelmann, Johann Joachim (1717–1768): German scholar who was an early contributor to the development of archaeology and art history. His work on the art recovered from Herculaneum and Pompeii was a move toward a study of artifacts as historical documents. His *History of the Art of Antiquity* (1763–1764) covered Classical sculpture and the art of Egypt and Etruria. It was the basis for theories of stylistic development. Winckelmann's visits to Pompeii and Herculaneum led to his "open letters," exposing amateur treasure seekers and encouraging archaeology to become more professional and competent. In Germany, Winckelmann is regarded as the founder of classical archaeology.

Windermere Interstadial: Interstadial of the Devensian Cold Stage, which occurred c. 13,000–11,000 bp. It consisted of a rapid temperature rise to an initial thermal maximum, followed by a slight temperature decline at 12,000 bp. It stabilized until 11,000 bp, when it fell sharply at the start of the Loch Lomond Stadial. The Windermere Interstadial may be correlated with Godwin's Pollen Zone II.

Windmill Cave: Cave site near Kent's Cavern in Brixham, Devon, England, with stone tools associated with extinct animal remains. The site demonstrated the true antiquity of humans in Britain and was occupied until Roman times.

Windmiller Pattern: Culture of central California, c. 2500–2000 BC, characterized by flaked- and ground-stone industries, extensive trade, use of river and marsh resources, a mortuary complex, and shell and stone artifacts.

Windmill Hill: Neolithic causewayed camp north of Avebury, Wiltshire, England, the type site of the culture of the same name. The camp of c. 3350 BC has three ditch circuits, which are part of the Avebury complex of Neolithic ritual monuments. Windmill Hill ware sensu stricto (decorated with grooves and pits) was closely followed by the oldest (Ebbsfleet) variant of Peterborough ware—3330 ± 150. More recent levels have Peterborough styles, grooved ware, and beaker sherds. An earthen long barrow has a radiocarbon date of 4030 ± 150, and there is a cemetery of Bronze Age round barrows. This culture and that of Peterborough were the two first main food-growing and cattle-raising peoples. Stone axes, coarse scrapers, and pressure-flaked leaf-shaped arrowheads were used. They raised pigs, cattle, goats, and had dogs for herding; cereals were grown. The pottery is now divided into separate traditions (Grimston-Lyles Hill, Hembury, Abingdon), and the rest of the cultural content, causewayed camps, long barrows, leaf-shaped arrowheads, and polished flint or other stone axes, is now regarded as simply "British Neolithic." The culture existed until c. 2500 BC. (*syn.* Windmill Hill culture)

Windover: The earliest-known mass burial ground in the United States, located in Florida and dating to c. 7400 bp. The waterlogged site has 168 individuals, many with preserved brain tissue that is being used in DNA studies.

winged disk: A sun disk with an outspread pair of wings attached, found in Egypt from the 1st Dynasty. It is associated with Horus of Behdet (Edfu) and symbolizes the sun, especially in architecture on ceilings, cornices, and stelae. It was often copied outside Egypt—used in the Levant and by the Hittites. In Assyria, it represented the sun god Shamash and perhaps Ashur. It was adopted by the Achaemenid Persians to represent their chief god Ahuramazda. (*syn.* winged disc; Egyptian 'py wer)

Winlock, Herbert Eustis (1884–1950): American Egyptologist who set new standards in field archaeology and in recording excavations, especially at Lisht and Deir el-Bahri. He worked at the temples of Queen Hatshepsut and Mentuhotep II and in the surrounding area of Theban necropolis with important 11th Dynasty tombs. He wrote *Excavations at Deir el Bahri, 1911–1931* (1942).

Wisconsin glaciation: The "age" is a major North American geochronological subdivision of the Pleistocene epoch, c. 75,000–10,000 bp. It was the final glaciation of North America, the fourth and last glacial stage of the Pleistocene. It followed the Sangamon Interglacial and is the North American equivalent of the Würm Glaciation in the Old World; it is broadly correlated with the Weichselian of northwest Europe and the Devensian of Britain. At certain times during this glaciation, enough water was locked up in the form of ice sheets to cause a drop in sea level and the creation of a land bridge between Siberia and Alaska. It was probably during one such period that man colonized America from Asia. As a "stage," it is a chronostratigraphic subdivision of the Pleistocene, with deposits in the upper U.S. Midwest and adjacent areas of Canada. Most of the Wisconsin deposits can be dated by radiocarbon. The sequence has been divided into early Wisconsin (c. 75,000–53,000 bp), Middle Wisconsin (53,000–23,000 bp), and Late Wisconsin (23,000–10,000 bp). The substages have been defined as: Altonian (c. 75,000–25,000 bp), Farmdalian (c. 25,000–22,500 bp), Woodfordian (c. 22,500–12,500 bp), Twocreekan (c. 12,500–11,800 bp), and Greatlakean (c. 11,800–10,000 or 7000 bp). The latter replaced the Valderan substage. (*syn.* Wisconsinan Age, Wisconsinan Stage)

Witów: Upper Palaeolithic site in Poland with artifacts of the Aeolian c. 11,020 bp—including blades, burins, and end scrapers.

Wolstenholme Towne: A palisaded colonial settlement that is part of the tract of land on the James River, Virginia, that includes Jamestown and Williamsburg—Martin's Hundred. It is the earliest palisaded settlement found in North America, dating to 1619. Artifact assemblages have many European imports and a variety of local pottery. The settlement was attacked by Native Americans in 1622, and there is evidence of a massacre.

Wolstonian: In Britain, a penultimate cold stage spanning c. 200,000–125,000 BP. At the type site in the Midlands, Wolstonian deposits overlie interglacial deposits of the Hoxnian. The Wolstonian deposits have Acheulian and Levalloisian artifacts.

womera: A spear-throwing device used by Australian Aborigines.

wood: Hard, fibrous substance that is the principal strengthening and water-conducting tissue found in the stems and roots of trees and shrubs. On archaeological sites, wood may be preserved as a result of waterlogging or as charcoal. (*syn.* xylem)

wood circle: Type of circle erected before megaliths were used. Like stone circles, the smaller ones enclosed burials; the larger, like Woodhenge, near Stonehenge, may have been religious circles or roofed, colonnaded shrines.

wooden-chamber: Large wooden coffins, which are an important form of burial chamber from late Neolithic times in China. A log or board enclosure contained nested wooden coffins and grave goods placed on display ledges in them. Wooden-chambers diffused to Korea and Japan in the early centuries AD.

Woodhenge: Large wood circle, a sacred monument just northeast of Stonehenge in Wiltshire, England, and adjacent to Durrington Walls. It consists of a henge-type earthwork with a wooden structure inside. A central grave was surrounded in turn by six egg-shaped concentric rings of postholes, a ditch, and a bank with a single entrance. The long axis of the oval pointed to the midsummer sunrise; on this axis in the center of the shrine was found buried the skeleton of a 3-year-old child, a ritual sacrifice. The pottery was a variant of the grooved ware style, and Beaker sherds were also found. The monument has a radiocarbon date of c. 2230–1800 BC.

Woodland period: Stage in eastern North America, c. 1000 BC–AD 800, a period in Native American history and culture. It is characterized by hunter gatherers, elaborate burial mounds, beginnings of substantial agriculture (corn, beans, squash), and pottery decorated with cord or fabric impressions. It is a term restricted to the cultures of the Eastern Woodlands (south and east of the Maritime Provinces of Canada to Minnesota and south to Louisiana and Texas), and important sites are Adena, Hopewell, and Effigy Mound. From AD c. 700, the southern part of the Woodland territory shows strong influence from the Mississippian culture, but elsewhere the Woodland tradition continued until the historic period. (*syn.* Woodland tradition)

Woodruff Ossuary: Burial in northwest Kansas with 61 disarticulated individuals and Harlan cord-roughened pottery, Scallorn arrow points, hundreds of disk shell beads, and shell pendants. It belongs to the Keith Focus of the Woodland stage, and the burials are in over 14 pits.

Woolandale: Late Iron Age site in central Zimbabwe and the name of the second phase of Leopard's Kopje Complex, dated to the 13th century AD.

Woolley, Sir (Charles) Leonard (1880–1960): British archaeologist known for his work at Ur, Carchemish, Tell el-Amarnà, Tell Atchana, Al Mina, and Al 'Ubaid. At Ur, he revealed 5,000 years of history and wrote it up in a 10-volume series (*Ur Excavations*). His discovery of geological evidence of a great flood suggested a possible correlation with the deluge described in Genesis, and his findings in the Royal Cemetery brought the astonishing wealth and skills of the Sumerian civilization to the public's attention. He was an exacting excavator, outstanding in interpretation, and published popular accounts of his results. His other books include *The Sumerians* (1928), *Ur of the Chaldees* 1929), and *Digging up the Past* (1930).

Worsaae, Jens Jacob Asmussen (1821–1886): Danish archaeologist who laid the foundations for the study of prehistory. He was the successor to Christian J. Thomsen at the National Museum at Copenhagen, and he applied the Three Age System to stone monuments. He wrote *Danmarks Oldtid oplyst ved Oldsager og Gravhøie* ("The Primeval Antiquities of Denmark," 1843), which introduced such other concepts as nomenclature, typology, and diffusion, and discussed the value and principles of prehistoric research. He focused on the study of excavated artifacts, particularly in their geographic and stratigraphic contexts. His standards and professionalism put him ahead of his time.

wrist clasp: A type of metal object in pagan Saxon graves in the Anglian areas of England and on the European continent. They are flattened rectangular or triangular pieces of bronze, often gilded or inlaid with silver and decorated with animal ornament. They were used to fasten the cuffs of tunics.

wristguard: A rectangular plate of bone or stone, perforated on the ends and strapped to the forearm of an archer to prevent injury when the bowstring recoils. It is sometimes difficult to distinguish a wristguard from a whetstone. They commonly occur in Beaker contexts in Europe. (*syn.* bracer)

writing: Any system for symbolizing the symbols of a language. Writing was developed independently several times in different places, and both the writing materials and the types of script show great variation. The earliest true writing developed in southern Mesopotamia in the 4th millennium BC Uruk culture. The writing material was clay; it was first inscribed and later impressed with a stylus to produce the wedge-shaped cuneiform signs. The earliest signs were pictograms ("picture writing," in which the signs represent stylized pictures of the objects in question), but these rapidly developed into ideograms (the signs indicated not only the original object, but also associated objects or concepts). The Egyptian hieroglyphic script, used for inscriptions on stone, painting on walls, and also writing on papyrus, appears well before 3000 BC. There is dispute as to whether the Egyptians developed writing independently or whether the art was diffused from Mesopotamia. The Harappan civilization of the Indus Valley had a writing system of its own, dated to the second half of the 3rd millennium BC and found almost exclusively on stamp seals and seal impressions. It has not been deciphered. The first true alphabet, with signs for individual letters, seems to have developed in the Levant, probably in the first half of the 2nd millennium BC. The first definite evidence comes from Ugarit in the mid-2nd millennium BC. The Phoenicians spread the alphabet throughout the Mediterranean, and theirs is ancestral to most of the alphabets in use today. In China, writing developed independently, first appearing on oracle bones of the Shang Dynasty. In Europe, the only pre-Classical writing occurs in the Aegean in the 2nd millennium BC—the hieroglyphic and Linear A scripts of the Minoans, as yet undeciphered, and the Linear B of the Mycenaeans, used to record an early form of Greek. The development of writing in the Americas occurred only in Mesoamerica—the glyphic writing of the Maya and related groups, found in inscriptions carved on monuments, and the pictographic writing of Post-Classic groups such as the Mixtecs and Aztecs, found on manuscripts of bark or deerskin known as codices.

Wroxeter: Site of a Roman town in southwestern England, founded in the 1st century AD and from AD c. 90 the tribal capital (civitas) of the Roman province of Cornovii. In 130, it was enlarged to add a grid street plan and a forum in honor of Hadrian. The town became the fourth largest in Roman Britain. There is also a basilica, Roman and Romano-Celtic temples, bath buildings, shops, housing, and an aqueduct. (*syn.* ancient Viroconium; Roman Viroconium Cornoviorum)

Wucheng: Bronze Age site of the mid-2nd millennium BC in Jiangxi Province, China, of the Shang Dynasty. Finds include stone-mold cast bronze weapons and ritual vessels, geometric pottery, and glazed stoneware. The incised marks on the pottery and molds are thought to be an indigenous writing system. (*syn.* Wu-ch'eng)

Würm: The fourth and final Pleistocene glaciation in the European Alps, c. 110,000/70,000–10,000 years ago, ending with the onset of the postglacial Holocene. The Würm Glacial Stage followed the Riss-Würm Interglacial and is correlated with the Weichsel Glacial Stage of northern Europe and the Wisconsin Glacial Stage of North America. It is divided into early, middle, and late phases. The end of the Würm and the retreat of the final glaciers were a complex of minor retreats and advances. (*syn.* Würm Glaciation)

Wuwei: City in Kansu Province, China, situated at the eastern end of the Kansu Corridor through which the Silk Road ran southeast to northwest. Wuwei became an important commandery under the Han Dynasty (206 BC–AD 220). Since T'ang times (618–907), it has been the seat of a prefecture Liang-chou. The 2nd-century tomb of a Han official was discovered, furnished with a procession of miniature bronze cavalry, chariots, and spirited horses including the well-known "flying horse." The ancient city has many monuments. (*syn.* Wu-wei)

Wybalenna: Settlement site on Flinders Island off Tasmania, Australia, where the last Tasmanian Aborigines lived. In 1847, it was closed and the survivors sent to Oyster Cove.

Wylotne: Rock shelter near Krakow, Poland, with Middle Palaeolithic assemblages of the early Glacial, possibly of the Micoquian. Upper Palaeolithic and Neolithic remains were found in upper layers.

Wyrie Swamp: Site in southeast South Australia with the world's oldest-known barbed spears—and the oldest boomerangs yet found in Australia. Gambieran stone artifacts and the boomerangs, barbed and plain spears, and digging sticks occur at the 10,000-year-old site.

Xx

Xanten: Roman legionary camp and civilian settlement on the Rhine near Wesel, Germany, and the confluence with the River Lippe. The Augustan-period camp had earth ramparts, palisades, timber buildings, a hospital, and a quay, with some later stone construction. It was given colonia status by emperor Trajan and subsequently became the principal city of Lower Germany (Germania Inferior). A rectangular grid street system, town walls, gates, bath buildings, amphitheater, porticoed temple, artisans' quarters, and housing have been uncovered. (*syn.* Roman Vetera Castra and Colonia Ulpia Traiana)

Xanthian Marbles: Sculptures found at Xanthus, principal city of ancient Lycia (Turkey), now in the British Museum. The most remarkable ruins of the city are the huge rock-cut pillar tombs. British archaeologist Sir Charles Fellows sent reliefs and sections of the tombs to the British Museum in the 19th century. The figures are Assyrian in character, not later than 500 BC. Sieges, processions, and figures are shown in profile but with the eyes shown in full. On one of the remaining pillar tombs is the longest and most important of inscriptions in the Lycian language.

Xemxija: Rock-cut tombs on the island of Malta of c. 4th millennium BC. The tombs are kidney shaped and have domed roofs and are entered via a circular pit.

xenogram: A word written in another language but read as if it were one's own. For example, we write "lb.," which stands for Latin *libra*, but read it as the English word "pound."

xerophyte: A plant adapted to a very dry climate or habitat. (*syn.* adj. xerophytic, xerophilous)

Xerxes (c. 519–465 BC): The last of the great Persian kings of the Achaemenid Empire, who ruled 486–465 BC, and was the son and successor of Darius I. He is remembered chiefly for his savage destruction of Babylon after a revolt, and for his massive invasion of Greece from across the Hellespont (480 BC), with battles at Thermopylae, Salamis, and Plataea. His ultimate defeat spelled the beginning of the decline of the Achaemenid Empire. (*syn.* Khshayarsha, Xerxes the Great)

X-Group: Culture of Lower Nubia AD c. 350–600, following the Meroitic Kingdom. Cemeteries, especially of chiefs at Ballana and Qustul, and some settlement sites have been found.

Xia: The first of the Chinese dynasties of the Sandai period in China, according to tradition dated c. 2205–1766 BC. It is said to have been overthrown by the Shang (Yin). Some archaeologists regard Erlitou as a Xia site, and archaeological surveys have been undertaken at related sites in western Henan and southern Shanxi. (*syn.* Hsia)

Xiajiadian: Site in Chifeng, Inner Mongolia (China), which lends its name to two cultural entities of the Northern Zone—an early Bronze Age culture, the Lower Xiajiadian; and Upper Xiajiadian, an agricultural and horse-riding aristocracy contemporary with early Zhou/Chou. The Bronze Age culture was contemporary with the Shang in the 2nd millennium BC. (*syn.* [Hsia-chia-tien])

Xiang Khouang: Site just south of the "Plain of Jars" in north-central Laos, with late prehistoric burial and ceremonial sites. There are large stone burial jars, often containing iron knives, arrowheads, spear heads, bronze jewelry, cowrie shells, and imported beads of glass and carnelian. Upright stone slabs (menhirs) mark them, and the site is dated c. 300 BC–AD 300. (*syn.* Xiangkhoang, Xieng Khouang)

Xiaotun: Site of 16 chariot burials in Hebei Province, China, which is also the location of a palace/temple complex of the Late Shang. The chariot burials suggest Indo-European contact with China. The chariot, which probably originated in the Caucasus, entered China via Central Asia and the northern steppe. Animal-headed knives, always associated with chariot burials, are further evidence of a northern connection. (*syn.* [Hsiao-t'un])

Xiasi: Eastern Zhou (Chou) cemetery site in southwestern Honan Province, China. Nine large tombs, five chariot burials, and 16 lesser tombs have been excavated. More than 200 bronze ritual vessels and bells were found in the large tombs and represent Chu bronze-casting. The Xiasi bronzes include the earliest cire perdue castings yet known from China, used to cast the openwork parts of a bronze table and the flamboyant handles, feet, and lid knobs of vessels. Dates are 6th century BC. (*syn.* Hsia-hsu)

Xibeigang: Site in Hebei Province, China, of the Royal Cemetery of the Late Shang, with seven shaft tombs with wooden-chamber burials and human sacrifices. There are also over 2,000 small pit graves with human sacrifices. The hierarchy of burials at this and other cemeteries in the area reflected the social organization of the living. The large pit tombs, some nearly 42 feet deep, were furnished with four ramps and massive grave chambers for the kings. Only a few undisturbed elite burials have been unearthed, the most notable being that of Fu Hao, a consort of Wu-ting. Her relatively small grave contained 468 bronze objects of the Anyang style, 775 jades, carved bone objects, and more than 6,880 cowries—suggesting how great the wealth placed in the far larger royal tombs must have been. (*syn.* [Hsi-pei-kang])

Xinle: Site in Liaoning Province, China, and name of a Neolithic culture of eastern Manchuria dated to the late 6th millennium BC. There are shell middens, textured pottery, and millet agriculture. (*syn.* [Hsin-lo])

Xinyang: City in southern Honan Province, China, traditionally on a cultural divide between the plains and the hilly districts. The area has been settled since early times. Neolithic remains have been discovered in several sites, and important finds from the southern culture of Ch'u (722–220 BC) have also been made in the vicinity. Two large Ch'u tombs of the 4th century BC have been excavated, which included 13 bronze bells and many fine painted lacquers. (*syn.* Hsin-yang)

Xinzheng: Area in central Honan Province, China, with an Eastern Zhou (Chou) tomb that was ransacked. More than a hundred bronze ritual vessels and bells said to belong to the find are now divided among museums in Beijing and Taibei. The vessels, of the 8th–6th centuries BC, show a change to more elegant forms, often decorated with an allover pattern of tightly interlaced serpents; vessels may be set about with tigers and dragons modeled in the round and topped with flaring, petaled lids. The name of the site is now attached to these patterns. A group of monumental vessels found at Xinzheng and affiliated with Ch'u bronzes as not of this style. (*syn.* Hsin-cheng)

Xiongnu: Tribal confederation of mounted nomads who dominated the Mongolian steppes during much of the Han Dynasty and formed c. 5th century BC. They dominated the area for more than 500 years. Their raids on the northern Chinese spurred the building of the Great Wall during the Zhou (Chou) period. Few archaeological remains are definitely assigned to the Xiongnu. Kurgans with horse burials excavated in Noin Ula are thought to be 1st-century AD tombs of Xiongnu nobility. Aristocratic burials in Liaoning Province and in Mongolia have yielded a wealth of gold and silver objects. In 51 BC, the Xiongnu empire split into two bands: an eastern horde, which submitted to the Chinese, and a western horde, which was driven into Central Asia. China's wars against the Xiongnu led to the Chinese exploration and conquest of much of Central Asia. (*syn.* Hsiung-nu)

Xochicalco: Late Classic and Early Post-Classic fortified site in Morelos, Mexico, which benefited on the collapse of Teotihuacán. The site is positioned to control access to the Balsas River drainage. A strong Teotihuacán influence is seen in the cylindrical tripod vases and obsidian objects. After the fall of Teotihuacán, however, the site shows evidence of new cultural influences: architecture in modified Talud-tablero style, a ball court, and Mayan friezes.

x-ray art: A style of prehistoric rock art depicting animals by drawing or painting the skeletal frame and internal organs. The origin of the style can be traced to the Mesolithic art of northern Europe, where the earliest examples were found on fragments of bone in southern France dating from the late Magdalenian. Animals painted in the x-ray motif have also been discovered in the art of hunting cultures in northern Spain, Siberia, the Arctic Circle, North America, western New Guinea, New Ireland, India, and Malaysia. It is found today primarily in the Aboriginal rock, cave, and bark paintings of eastern Arnhem Land, in northern Australia. Figures painted in x-ray style vary in size up to 8 feet (2.5 m) in length and are delicate, polychromed renderings of the interior cavity of the animal. (*syn.* x-ray art, x-ray style, X-ray style)

x-ray diffraction analysis: A technique used to identify minerals present in an artifact's raw materials; it can also be used in geomorphologic contexts to identify particular clay minerals in sediments and thus the source from which the sediment was derived. The technique identifies the major chemical components of an artifact, mainly on pottery, although stone and weathering products on metal have also been analyzed. A sample is powdered and then bombarded with x-rays, and a diffraction pattern is reflected onto and recorded as a series of arcs by photographic film. The patterns are compared with reference standards to identify the minerals present; mineral identification is based on the spacing between the arcs. X-ray diffraction can yield information on the manufacturing processes of pottery and metal, and for this purpose the back-reflection diffraction method is used, which is totally nondestructive. (*syn.* x-ray diffraction analysis)

x-ray emission: A method to determine the elements of a bone by bombarding it with electrons to produce a signature pattern of x-rays. X-ray emission spectrometry is the group of analytical methods in which emitted x-ray radiation is monitored. X-rays are emitted when an electron in an outer orbital falls into a vacancy in an inner orbital. The analytical method that measures the diffraction patterns for the purpose of determining structure is termed x-ray diffraction analysis. (*syn.* x-ray emission; x-ray emission spectrometry)

x-ray fluorescence: A nondestructive physical method used for chemical analyses of solids and liquids. The specimen is irradiated by an intense x-ray beam, and the lines in the spectrum of the resulting x-ray fluorescence are diffracted at various angles by a crystal with known lattice spacing; the elements in the specimen are identified by the wavelengths of their spectral lines, and their concentrations are determined by the intensities of these lines. Constituent elements are identified based on the unique wavelengths of fluorescent x-rays they emit, and concentrations are estimated on the intensity of the released x-rays. It can be used on pottery, obsidian, glass, and some metal and under most circumstances is totally nondestructive. In general terms, the method is more suitable for the analysis of the major elements in a specimen, although trace elements can be determined in some cases. Because automation of recording and sample changing is possible, large numbers of samples can be analyzed at speed, which gives this method a definite advantage over atomic absorption spectrometry and optical emission spectrometry. (*syn.* X-ray fluorescence spectrometry, X-ray fluorimetry; XRF; X-ray fluorescence analysis)

x-ray microscopy: Physical technique used to discover the composition of crystalline substances in an object. The atomic structure is analyzed with a scanning or transmission electron microscope, based on the different rates of absorption and emission of x-rays by different elements.

x-ray milliprobe: A specialized type of x-ray fluorescence spectrometry which satisfies the particular requirements of certain artifacts. The principle is the same as for x-ray fluorescence spectrometry, but an instrument directs a highly focused x-ray beam at a desired point(s) on the sample surface. Secondary x-rays emitted from this point are then directed to a detector and analyzed. The spectrometer is outside the artifact, in contrast to standard x-ray spectrometry where the specimen is inside the spectrometer. The advantage that the x-ray milliprobe has over the electron probe microanalyzer is the ease with which samples can be prepared. The technique has flexibility and the ability to analyze microscopic areas. (*syn.* X-ray milliprobe analysis; x-ray milliprobe analysis)

XTENT modeling: Technique used to generate a settlement hierarchy, which assigns territories to centers based on their scale, assuming that the size of each center is directly proportional to its area of influence. It is said that it overcomes the limitations of both central place theory and Thiessen polygons and that hypothetical political maps may be constructed from survey data.

Yy

Yadin, Yigael (1917–1984): Israeli archaeologist noted for his work on the Dead Sea Scrolls and his excavations at Hazor and Masada. He wrote *The Message of the Scrolls* (1957; new ed. 1962), *Hazor* (3 vols., 1958–1962), *The Art of Warfare in Biblical Lands in the Light of Archaeological Discovery* (2 vols., 1963), and *Masada: Herod's Fortress and the Zealots' Last Stand* (1966).

Yahudiyah, Tell al-: City in the eastern Delta of Egypt, dating from at least the Middle Kingdom until the Roman period, c. 2000 BC–AD 200. During the 19th and 20th Dynasties, the royal palace at Tell al-Yahudiyah was embellished with remarkable polychrome tiles, many of which bear figures of captive foreigners. (*syn.* ancient Naytahut, Leontopolis; Tell el-Yahudiyah)

Yahya, Tepe: Tell site in the Soghun valley of Kirman province, Iran, with a long cultural sequence of seven periods from c. mid-5th millennium BC to early 1st millennium AD. The most important phase was Yahya IV, beginning c. 3000 BC. It was at that time an active trading center, with a cache of tablets inscribed in proto-Elamite, the script of Elam. Jemdet Nasr painted wares and beveled rim bowls have been found. A local source of steatite (chlorite) was worked into distinctive bowls, which were traded to Sumer, the Indus civilization, and the Persian Gulf. The site was on an important trade route between Mesopotamia and the Indus Valley, possibly via Shahr-i-Sokhta and the Persian Gulf via Bampur. Tepe Yahya was also in contact with the Harappan civilization of the Indus Valley and indeed was strategically placed on the overland route between the Indus Valley and Mesopotamia. In the later 3rd millennium BC, the importance of Tepe Yahya declined.

yam: Cultivated tubers originally of Southeast Asia, West Africa, Melanesia, and New Guinea, also grown for food in the Americas. They were domesticated before 3000 BC. These plants occupy a vital place in the social and religious life of some African societies.

Yamatai: A polity of Japan known from Chinese chronicles, the "Wei chih" ("Weizhi") and "Houhanshu," thought to be either in northern Kyushu or in the Kinai district (central Honshu). The site of Yoshinogari is thought to be contemporaneous with the polity, c. 3rd century AD. The queen, Himiko/Pimiko, is the first known ruler of Japan and the supposed originator of the Grand Shrine of Ise, still considered the most important Shinto sanctuary in Japan.

Yamato: The name of a former province in Nara Prefecture, Japan, an emergent state of the Kofun period (2nd–5th centuries AD). When the Tang administrative system of China was adopted in the late 7th century AD, Yamato was made into the Ritsuryo state. The old Yamato Province is rich in archaeological remains of the Yayoi, Kofun, and early historical periods. The period is commonly called the Tumulus or Tomb period from the presence of large burial mounds (kofun), its most common archaeological feature. It is from the very construction of the tombs themselves, from an examination of the grave goods, as well as from increasingly reliable written sources both domestic and foreign, that a picture of the Yamato Kingdom has emerged.

Yamnaya culture: Late Neolithic culture or horizon of the lower Volga and Don steppes, regarded by some as the predecessor to the Corded Ware, Single Grave, or Kurgan culture. (*syn.* Pit-Grave culture)

Yan: A type of Chinese bronze vessel produced during the Shang/Yin (18th–12th centuries BC), and Chou (1111–255 BC) Dynasties. A steamer, or cooking vessel, used particularly for grain, the yen consists of a deep upper bowl with a pierced bottom placed on or attached to a lower, legged vessel similar in shape to the li. The yen is not usually elaborately decorated. The form is derived from a Neolithic (c. 3000–1500 BC) pottery predecessor and is found in the bronze art of the Shang Dynasty and in that of the Chou, especially the early Chou (1111–c. 900 BC). (*syn.* Yen, Hsien)

Yang Shao: The most important Neolithic culture of China, distributed along the middle course of the Yellow River in north-central China and dated to c. 5000–2700 BC. Large open settlements of circular or rectangular houses slightly sunk into the ground cluster along the loess river terraces. It is distinguished by millet agriculture, coarse and painted pottery, sedentary villages, and clans. Some marks on the pottery are thought to be the beginnings of writing; pottery was handmade, painted in black and red on a yellowish slip. At first, the designs were zoomorphic, then later they became abstract, geometric, or curvilinear. Coarser red and gray wares were also common. (*syn.* Yang-shao, Yangshao)

Yanik Tepe: Tell site near Tabriz, Iran, with evidence of the Neolithic, Chalcolithic, Early Bronze Ages, and Iron Age occupations. It is one of the earliest permanent settlement sites in the area, dating from the late 7th millennium BC. The earliest pottery was undecorated, but painted wares appeared in the higher levels. The site was occupied until the beginning of the Islamic period. In the 3rd millennium BC, it was a town surrounded by a stone wall and contained roundhouses and granaries built of mud brick. The latest structure on the mound is massive, perhaps a citadel, built of mud brick and probably of the Sassanian period. The Early Bronze Age settlement consists of a long sequence of Kura-Araxes occupations and many materials of this culture complex.

Yap: Island and archipelago of the western Caroline Islands, part of the Federated States of Micronesia, known for large wheel-shaped discs of stone money. The stone is quarried in the Palau Islands and taken to Yap by canoe. Yap was at the head of a chain of trade and tribute in the Carolines, the so-called Yapese "empire" and in contact with Palau and the Marianas Islands as seen in similar red ware of the 2nd millennium BC. The occurrence of child jar burial suggests later contact with the Philippines. (*syn.* Guap)

yardang: Elongate, eroded land form resembling the hull of an inverted boat. It is created by wind erosion of weakly consolidated rocks and often has smooth, rounded intermittent troughs. They are usually associated with deserts.

Yarim Tepe 1: Tell site of the Hassuna culture, with 13 levels spanning the Archaic through Standard Hassuna phases (6th millennium BC), near the Caspian Sea in northern Iraq. The ceramic sequences give much detail about the Hassuna culture. There is evidence of metallurgy, the smelting of copper and lead, and advanced pottery making. Samarran elements appear, and Halaf and Sassanian burials also occur. The Neolithic settlement was of the Turkmenian Djei-tun culture. (*syn.* Yarim Tepe)

Yarim Tepe 2: Tell site near the Caspian Sea in northern Iraq, occupied in the Halaf period. Many circular houses have been excavated and a rectangular building that may be a shrine. It was then abandoned and reoccupied in the late 4th millennium BC. Yarim 2 is mainly of the Middle Halaf period,

with tholos architecture and painted pottery. Abandoned again in the early 2nd millennium BC, it was reoccupied in the Iron Age (late 1st millennium BC). The site was occupied into the late Parthian period, AD c. 200. (*syn.* Yarim Tepe)

Yarmouth: A major division of Pleistocene deposits and a time in North America, named for deposits in Yarmouth, Iowa, and equivalent to the Mindel-Riss Interglacial Stage of Alpine Europe. In some places, fossil vertebrates are well represented. It was at least as warm as modern times, and, in some regions, the deposits indicate that Yarmouth climates may have been semiarid. The dates are c. 300,000–200,000 BP; the British equivalent is the Hoxnian and the Holsteinian Interglacial in northern Europe. (*syn.* Yarmouth Interglacial Stage)

Yashodharapura: The first city in the Angkor, Cambodia, area founded by King Yashovarman in AD 889. It was Cambodia's capital until it was abandoned in the 15th century. His temple mountain, now called Bakheng, was built on a natural hill that overlooked the city, the rice-growing plain, and the Tonle Sap. Yashovarman built a large reservoir nearby; the city wall of Yashodharapura measured 2.5 miles (4 km) on each side.

Yassi Ada: A graveyard of ancient ships off the Turkish coast near Bodrum, the most important being a Byzantine wreck of the 6th century. The 30-meter vessel was well preserved, and traces of the galley-end and of the cargo holds were found. Amphorae have illustrated trading of later Roman wares and olive oil between North Africa and Anatolia in the Justinian period. Peter Throckmorton, who discovered the site in 1958, developed the mapping of wrecks photogrammetrically with stereophotographs and by using a two-man submarine, the "Asherah," launched in 1964. The "Asherah" was the first submarine ever built for archaeological investigation.

Yasumiba: Late Palaeolithic site in Shizuoka Prefecture, Honshu, Japan, with hearths dated c. 14,300 years ago. Over 400 microblades made from conical cores were found.

Yaxchilán: Major Classic Maya site on the Usumacinta River, Chiapas, Mexico. It has architectural features like Palenque, hieroglyphic inscriptions on stone lintels and stelae, and monuments depicting war. Although there are a number of structures, including palaces with ornamented stucco roof combs and mansard roofing, temple-pyramids, and two ball courts, the site is best known for its more than 125 carved lintels. It flourished AD c. 600–900. Although the site may have been controlled briefly by the Putun just before 750, it was finally abandoned during the general lowland Maya collapse.

Yayoi: Protohistoric period of Japan, 300 BC–AD 300, which replaced the Jomon period and preceded the Kofun. It is marked by the strengthening of mainland influences from Korea and China, as shown by the appearance of bronze and, later, iron, wet-rice growing, the potter's wheel, and cist and jar burials. These changes were absorbed into the Jomon tradition, which was only gradually replaced. Local developments include the great decorated bronze bells, and Late Yayoi mound-burials foreshadow the mounded tombs of the Kofun. Large quantities of bronzes and glass were imported from China. It is generally divided into three parts: Early (300–100 BC), Middle (100 BC–AD 100), and Late (AD 100–300)—dates based mainly on imported Chinese bronze mirrors, because the radiocarbon dates for Yayoi tend to be erratic. Yayoi pottery is less ornate than Jomon ware, but is made and fired in basically the same way. It also incorporates Mumun pottery (from Korea) techniques and is related to the Haji pottery of the Kofun period. Apart from the pottery, the Yayoi culture is characterized by definite evidence of agriculture and the use of metal tools. Yayoi houses were semisubterranean or built at ground level. A series of settlements, a large one with several smaller ones, seem to have formed a community, which was often moated. (*syn.* Yayoi period)

Yaz-depe: Site in the Murghab delta of southern Turkmenia, the type site of the Iron Age Yaz complex. There is a citadel, an extensive irrigation system, and pottery of three phases from mid-2nd to mid-1st millennium BC.

Yazilikaya: (Turkish: "Inscribed Rock") Hittite monument just northeast of Bogazköy; it was the site of the Hittite capital Hattusa in eastern Turkey. In a northeastern recess (open-air gallery) is carved a long procession of mostly male figures. The east gallery contains a relief of a procession of warriors; on the opposite wall is a large relief showing a king in the embrace of his patron god, with a long dagger thrust into the rock before him. The sanctuary was completed by King Tudhaliyas IV during the 13th century BC, the last period of the Hittite Empire, when Hurrian religious and cultural influence were predominant.

year formula: A phase in Mesopotamia when cuneiform documents provide dates for significant events in relation to a given year in a king's reign. Dating by year formula, done from Akkadian through Old Babylonian times, provides a basic framework for the political history of southern Mesopotamia. The Assyrians did not, unlike the Babylonians, use year formulas containing interesting historical details; instead, every year was designated by the name of a high official (eponymic dating). The reconstruction of Hammurabi's rule is based mainly on his date formulas; years were named for a significant act the king had performed in the previous year or at the beginning of the year thus named. (*syn.* date formula; year-name)

Yeavering: Royal seat of Anglo-Saxon Northumbria, England, in the 7th century AD and site of an impressive group of buildings. Great timber halls and a semicircular timber grandstand for meetings and assemblies have been excavated. Of the smaller buildings uncovered, one is thought to have been converted from a pagan temple into a church. It has advanced our knowledge of Saxon timber architecture.

Yeha: Ethiopia's oldest town (3,000 years), where a stone-built temple is the best preserved example of Pre-Axumite architecture. Constructed of well-dressed blocks, it is a double-story building with tiny windows. It was decorated with sculptures in a typical south Arabian-derived style, with inscriptions in the Himyaritic syllabary.

Yengema: Town and cave site in eastern Sierra Leone with one of the few stratified sequences of Palaeolithic and Neolithic stone industries in that country. Crudely flaked picks, choppers, and flake scrapers, hoe-like tools, and backed blades have been found. In another phase, pottery and ground stone tools are found for the first time. Thermoluminescence tests dated the third-phase pottery at c. 2000 BC.

Yenisei: River of Asia, one of the longest rivers on the continent, flowing from south to north across central Russia. The Yenisei valley has yielded much evidence of prehistoric occupation, including more than 50 Palaeolithic sites with radiocarbon dates ranging from c. 19,000–11,000 BC. Sites include Afontova Gora and Verkholenskaia Gora. The first food production appeared probably in the 3rd millennium BC, and a series of Neolithic and Bronze Age cultures is known: Afanasievo, Andronovo, and Karasuk, followed by the Early Nomad period. (*syn.* Yenisey, Enisei)

Yiewsley: Site of a number of gravel pits in West Middlesex, England, with Lower Palaeolithic artifacts—from Clactonian tools to Acheulian bifaces and Levallois flakes and cores. It is dated to c. 250,000–200,000 years ago. There are also Middle Palaeolithic/Mousterian levels with bout coupé-like bifaces. The sequence is one of the longest of its kind in Europe and in part closely parallels Swanscombe.

yoke: Large, heavy U-shaped stone believed to be a ritual copy of a wooden protector worn by players of the Mesoamerican ball game during the Classic period. It was worn on the hips and decorated with carved designs with double-edge scrolls. The term is also used for the wooden crosspiece fastened over the necks of a pair of oxen or horses and attached to the plow, cart, or wagon to be drawn.

Yongnam: Region of South Korea made up of the southeastern provinces of North and South Kyongsang.

York: Legionary fortress in Roman Britain, one of England's best-preserved sites. Of particular interest are the deposits in the Coppergate area, which illustrate the period when the city was an important center of the Vikings. In Roman times, it became a bishopric and was renowned as a center for learning and theology. Remains of the fortress were later incorporated into the medieval walls, and excavations have revealed a large palace-like structure existed. Waterlogged conditions have preserved timber buildings of the Viking period. Certain industries prospered, including bronze, glass, iron and bone working, and wood turning. Recent excavations have also uncovered York's Norman castles, built in 1067–1068. Excavations have shown 10th-century York, a Danish settlement, to have been a center of international trade, economic specialization, and town planning; it was on its way to becoming by 1086 (in the Domesday survey) one of Europe's largest cities, numbering in least 2,000 households. (*syn.* Eboracum, Jorvik)

Yoshinogari: Site in Saga Prefecture, Japan, with a Yayoi-period village. The double-moated village has watchtowers, pit-house remains, storage pits, 2,000 jar burials, and a large oval mound with a jar burial (c. 1st century BC). It is linked to the polity of Yamatai through early Chinese texts and belongs to a time of interaction with China. It is the most important and well-preserved Yayoi site in Japan.

Young, Thomas (1773–1829): English physician, physicist, and Egyptologist who helped decipher the Rosetta Stone. He was the first modern scholar to translate the demotic script. Young began studying the texts of the Rosetta Stone in 1814, and after obtaining additional hieroglyphic writings from other sources, he succeeded in providing a nearly accurate translation within a few years and thus contributed greatly to deciphering the ancient Egyptian language.

Younger Dryas: A stadial of the Weichselian Cold stage, dated to between 11,000–10,000 bp. The last glacial recession (13,000–6,000 years ago) was interrupted by this sharp advance. It takes its name from a tundra plant called *Dryas octopetala*, fossil remains of which are common in deposits of the stadial. It was most evident around the North Atlantic and coincided with an apparent temporary diversion of glacial melt water from the Mississippi River to the St. Lawrence drainage system. It has been postulated that this discharge of cold, fresh water disrupted the Atlantic Ocean circulation system that warms the North Atlantic. (*syn.* Younger Dryas event)

Yüan Dynasty: Dynasty established in China (1206–1368) by Mongol nomads. Yüan rule stretched throughout most of Asia and eastern Europe, although the Yüan emperors were rarely able to exercise much control over their more distant possessions. The dynasty was established by Genghis Khan (c. 1162–1227) and gained control of China under his grandson Kublai Khan (1215–1294). Peking was set up as the capital. The Yüan rebuilt the Grand Canal, and there were new cultural achievements, including the development of the novel as a literary form. A renewed emphasis was placed on traditional craft arts—silver, lacquer, ceramics, and other materials. (*syn.* Mongol Dynasty)

Yuanmou: Early Palaeolithic site in Yunnan Province, China, dated to 700,000 bp; *Homo erectus* dental remains were found.

Yubetsu: Late Palaeolithic microlithic industry of Hokkaido, Japan, dated c. 13,000 bp. Obsidian was worked in the Shirataki technique: A bifacial core has one lateral edge removed, producing a triangular spall. More edge removals make ski spalls of parallel surfaces. The technique was used from Mongolia to Alaska in the later Pleistocene.

Yudinovo: Upper Palaeolithic sites on the Sudost' River in European Russia, with dates c. 15,660–12,300 bp. Three mammoth-bone houses have been found and nonstone artifacts such as perforated shells from the Black Sea.

Yue: Ancient ethnic group of southeastern mainland China during the Han Dynasty, an aboriginal people who in the 5th–4th centuries BC formed a powerful kingdom in present-day Chekiang and Fukien Provinces. The name *Vietnam* means "south of the Yüeh," and some Chinese scholars consider the Vietnamese to be descendants of the Yüeh. It is also the name of an olive-colored glazed stoneware preceding celadon and porcelain and created during the Tang period of the 3rd–10th centuries AD in Kiangsu and Chekiang Provinces. (*syn.* Yüeh)

Yüeh-chih: Nomadic group from Chinese Turkistan, which moved west across Iran and south into the Indus region in the late 2nd century BC. They ruled in Bactria and India from about 128 BC–AD 450. About 128 BC, the Yüeh-chih were recorded living north of the Oxus River (Amu Darya), ruling Bactria as a dependency, but a little later the Great Yüeh-chih kingdom was in Bactria, and Sogdiana was occupied by the Ta-yuan (Tocharians). They gave rise to the Kushan Kingdom of the early 1st millennium AD in northern India and Afghanistan. (*syn.* Yuezhi, Yueh-chi, Indo-Scyth)

Yungang: Series of magnificent Chinese Buddhist cave temples created in the 5th century AD (Six Dynasties period) and located just west of the city of Ta-t'ung (Datong). The caves are among the earliest remaining examples of the first major flowering of Buddhist art in China. A low ridge of soft sandstone was excavated to form about 20 major cave temples and many smaller niches and caves. Activity at Yungang declined after 494, when the Northern Wei capital moved from Datong to Luoyang (Lo-yang). (*syn.* Yun-kang)

Yurovichi: Upper Palaeolithic site on the Pripyat' River, Belarus, dated c. 26,470 bp.

Zz

Zaculeu: Ruins of ancient Maya center in the mountains of highland Guatemala. It is dated from the Classic to Postclassic periods, when it was destroyed by the Spanish (AD 1525). It has architecture different from lowland Maya styles; flat-roofed structures, and far cruder construction techniques.

Zagros: Mountain range of southwest Iran from the Sirvan River (Diyala) to Shiraz, where a number of archaeological sites are located: Jarmo, Ali Kosh, Tepe Ganj Dareh, Tepe Guran, Tepe Sarab, and Zawi Chemi Shangi-Dar.

Zakro: Site of a Minoan palace in eastern Crete. Unlike many of the other Minoan palaces, Zakro did not have a Middle Minoan phase, but was constructed in the Late Minoan period after 1700 BC. The palace was relatively small but had the usual plan grouped around a central court. Among the finds were a collection of fine stone vessels and tablets in Linear A. Zakro was destroyed by fire c. 1450 BC.

Zambian Wilton: Microlithic Later Stone Age industry of Zambia in the drainage of the Kafue and Zambezi Rivers, akin to the Wilton industry. It spans the last 6,000 years.

Zambujal: Village site with megalithic tombs and a Chalcolithic fortress near Lisbon, Portugal. It was a heavily fortified settlement of the Vila Nove De Sao Pedro culture; the walls are up to 10 meters in thickness and have circular towers and a circular citadel. The pottery contains much Beaker material and local wares, c. 2700–2200 BC.

Zaminets: Settlement site of the Krivodol during the Eneolithic, c. 2800 BC.

Zapotec: Mesoamerican cultural and linguistic group centered on the highlands of southern Oaxaca, Mexico, and the culture most clearly associated with Monte Albán and Mitla. Their origins are uncertain, but by AD c. 300 a distinctively Zapotec culture can be recognized. The Early Formative ancestral Zapotec had lived in scattered villages and at least one center of some importance, San José Mogote. Elaborate funerary urns in gray ware are especially characteristic. The Zapotec abandoned their capital in c. 950 and appear to have relocated at other centers, such as Mitla and Lambityeco. In the 14th century AD, the area was infiltrated by Mixtecs who came from the mountains to the north and west and occupied most of the Zapotec sites. Part of the region was never conquered by the Aztecs, and the Zapotecan language has persisted to the present.

Zarzian: Cave in southern Kurdistan, western Iraq, which had an advanced Palaeolithic industry. The industry is based on geometric microliths, notched blades, and backed bladelets and is not widely known. It is dated c. 10,500–6000 BC. (*syn.* Zarzi)

Zaskal'naya: Middle Palaeolithic rock shelters and caves in the Crimea, Ukraine, some with six to seven occupation levels. Some are dated to an interstadial preceding the early cold maximum of the last glacial. Artifacts include bifacial foliates and Ak-Kaya culture side scrapers. Neanderthal fossils have been found.

Závist: Hallstatt D hill fort of c. 600 BC near Praque, of Celt occupation. It was abandoned during the La Tène B, c. 300 BC, but was reconstructed in the 1st century BC and then abandoned again at the end of that century.

Zawi Chemi Shanidar: Village site in northern Iraq near Shanidar Cave, with a terminal epi-Palaeolithic under Iron Age levels. Storage pits and a circular stone structure are dated to the 9th millennium BC. Large numbers of sheep bones are claimed to show signs of domestication at that time. Sickles, grinding stones, and querns testify to the gathering of vegetable products. Occupation was probably seasonal. Other artifacts include stone axes and nonutilitarian objects, such as worked bone with incised or notched decoration. Obsidian from the Lake Van area of Anatolia indicates far-ranging contacts. Burials were associated with a stone platform.

Zawisza, Count Jan (1820–1887): Polish archaeologist

who worked at Mamutowa and revealed the first evidence of Upper Palaeolithic industries with bifacial foliates in that part of Europe.

Zawayet el-Aryan: Site of two unfinished pyramids, a number of mastaba tombs of the Old Kingdom (2686–2181 BC), and a cemetery of the New Kingdom (1550–1069 BC), located on the west bank of the Nile, between Giza and Abusir.

Zazaragi: Palaeolithic site in Miyagi Prefecture, Japan, dated to c. 45,000–40,000 bp, a very early occupation for the islands.

Zebbug: Cemetery of five rock-cut tombs on the island of Malta, which has given its name to the Zebbug phase of the Maltese Islands pre-temple Neolithic, dated c. 4100–3800 BC.

Zeliezovce style: Regional variant of the Linear Pottery culture in Slovakia, Moravia, and southern Poland. The pottery has angular incised lines and lozenge-shaped incisions and is dated c. 4000 BC.

zemi: Religious spirits represented by idols of wood, stones, shell, and bones in the West Indies. Zemis were human or animal in form. Ceremonial centers, ball courts, and caves were associated with the cult, which may have reached the islands from Mesoamerica. The Taino culture was famous for these zemi carvings, which are found in many of the islands, notably Puerto Rico and Hispaniola. A distinctive trait of the Antillean Arawaks was the triangular carved stone zemi that represented the hierarchically ranked individual guardian deities of each household in the society. (*syn.* zemis; Zemi)

Zengövárkony: Large Neolithic settlement and cemetery of the Lengyel culture in Hungary, dated to the 4th millennium BC. The site consists of clusters of graves interspersed with areas of settlement debris, a pattern consistent with family groups buried close to where they lived. Over 360 graves are known, mainly crouched inhumations, including 47 with preserved skeletal material. The grave goods include copper and fine stone artifacts.

Zeuxippos ware: Byzantine pottery named after the baths of Zeuxippos in Istanbul (then Constantinople), Turkey; dated to 12th–13th centuries AD.

Zhangjiapo: Western Zhou/Chou site near the Feng River, southwest of Xi'an, China. Extensive remains may be connected with the Zhou capitals Feng and Hao. Early finds include tombs similar in construction to Shang tombs, some with human sacrifices; chariot burials; bones used in divination, mostly uninscribed; and sherds of glazed stoneware. A bronze hoard, many inscribed, range in date over most of the Western Zhou period. (*syn.* Chang-chia-p'o)

Zhengzhou: A modern city in Honan (Henan) Province, China, the site of a large Bronze Age city, probably a capital

of the Shang Dynasty (Ao) belonging to the Erligang phase. There were also Neolithic settlements in the area. A rammed-earth hangtu foundation of palace buildings is within a walled compound, dated c. 1500 BC. House foundations have been uncovered in the walled enclosure. Outside the wall are workshops for bronze, ceramics, and bone crafts and tombs with bronze ritual vessels. The nearby site of Erligang gives its name to the bronze vessel style at Zengzhou. The settlement declined sharply in importance after the Erligang phase. The Shang, who continually moved their capital, left Ao, perhaps in the 13th century BC. The site, nevertheless, remained occupied; Chou (post-1050 BC) tombs have also been discovered. (*syn.* Cheng-chou)

Zhenla: The name used for an early Khmer state in southeast Cambodia and south Vietnam, probably established during the 6th century AD in the upper-middle reaches of the Mekong River, in what is now Laos. The leaders of Zhenla descended from the Funan. Zhenla was later divided into "Land Chenla" and "Water Chenla," which vied for recognition from China. The Funan-Chenla tradition produced some of the world's most magnificent stone cult images. (*syn.* Chenla)

Zhizo: Early Iron Age culture in western Zimbabwe and Limpopo Valley, c. 8th–10th centuries AD.

Zhob: A valley in north Baluchistan, western Pakistan, with a number of sites of a Chalcolithic culture, c. 4th–3rd millennia BC. Rana Ghundai, Periano Ghundai, and Moghul Ghundai are the best-known sites. The pottery is painted black or red over a red slip; decoration may be stylized humped cattle and buck and groups of vertical lines linking narrow horizontal bands. Other artifacts include female figurines and copper. Buildings were of mud brick, and burials were by cremation. Related material was found stratified beneath that of the Indus civilization at Harappa, and there are similarities to the painted ware of Tepe Hissar in northern Iran. This phase was succeeded by the "Incinerary Pot" phase, with burials placed in vessels under house floors, after disarticulation and some cremation.

Zhongyuan: Literally the "Central Plain" or "Middle Plain," an area of northern China, including the river basins and alluvial plains of the Wei River and the Yellow River east of its confluence with the Wei. Capitals of the Shang, Zhou, Qin, Han, Tang, and Northern Song Dynasties are in this plain, and the Zhongyuan area is traditionally regarded as the birthplace of Chinese civilization. (*syn.* Chung-yüan)

Zhou: Bronze Age ethnic group, which overthrew the Shang c. 1027 BC and established the longest dynasty in Chinese history, surviving until c. 221 BC. The Zhou period is subdivided into Western or Royal Zhou, 1027–771 BC, when the capital was in Shaanxi Province, and Eastern Zhou, with the capital at Louyang, 770–221 BC. It is further divided into the

Spring and Autumn (770–476 BC) and Warring States (475–221 BC) periods. These names come from two historical texts, the "Spring and Autumn Annals of the State of Lu" and the "Discourses of the Warring States." Originating from Qishan as a pastoral people, the Zhou rose to power in the Wei River valley of Shaanxi Province, adopting much of the culture of the Shang they eventually overthrew. From their Shaanxi homeland, the Western Zhou kings ruled through vassal lords, an empire that included most of the former Shang territories and stretched to the northeast beyond Beijing. The period is characterized by small competing states organized into feudal subservience to the Royal Zhou during the early period; stronger states evolved in the later period, and the feudal system broke down. The state of Qin eventually conquered its rivals and united the states in 220 BC. During the Zhou period, the Great Wall was constructed, and iron working and coinage developed. The Warring States period saw a flowering of the arts in many areas. (*syn.* Chou)

Zhoukoudian: Palaeolithic site in Hebei Province, China, with numerous human fossils, including Peking man, found in cave deposits of c. 700,000–400,000 years ago. Over 40 individuals are represented; this has become one of the two fossil populations on which *Homo erectus* is based. In 1941, when the Japanese were about to attack Beijing, the fossils were packed for transport to the United States, but they disappeared; only casts have survived. New investigations have found more skulls and parts, and a pollen sequence is known. Primitive flake tools have been found, along with traces of fire. Remains of *Homo sapiens sapiens* are the first human burials in the East Asian archaeological record. (*syn.* Choukoutien, Chou-k'ou-tien)

ziggurat: A rectangular stepped temple tower in which each story is smaller than the one below, leaving a terrace around each floor—characteristic of Sumerian, Assyrian, Babylonian, and Elamite architecture. It is thought to symbolize a mountain; the tower was the high place of the god, the link between earth and heaven. Its structure was of mud brick with a burnt brick casing, with stairways giving access to a small shrine at its summit. The arrangement of the stairways leading from one stage to another varied greatly from one monument to another. The best known examples are those of Ur, Babylon (the tower of Babel), Eridu, Aqar Quf, Borsippa, Dur Kurigalzu, Uruk, and Choga Zambil (Zanbil) in Elam. It originated with the Sumerians, and the first ziggurats were modest constructions, but, by 2000 BC, more imposing examples dominated the great cities of southern Mesopotamia. (*syn.* zikkurrat)

Zimbabwe: Term applied by Shona speakers in Zimbabwe (country) to many stone-built enclosures located in the plateau between the Zambezi and Limpopo Rivers of southern Africa. It would be the court or house of a chief (*mambo*) and built on a hill. More than 150 are known, including the major site near Fort Victoria, Great Zimbabwe. (*syn.* Dzimbahwe)

Zinjanthropus: Name originally given to a robust Australopithecus found in Bed I at Olduvai Gorge in Tanzania by Louis Leakey, characterized by unusually massive jaws. Potassium-argon dating suggests that he lived about 1.75 million years ago. This fossil is now classified as *Australopithecus boisei* or *Australopithecus robustus*. (*syn.* Australopithecus boisei)

Zincirli Höyük: Site of Samal in the foothills of the Anti-Taurus Mountains, southern Turkey, one of the Late Hittite city-states that perpetuated a Semitized southern Anatolian culture for centuries after the downfall of the Hittite Empire (c. 1190 BC). It was annexed by the Assyrians in the 7th century BC and then abandoned with the downfall of Assyria. The town was surrounded by a wall forming an exact circle and topped by 100 towers; inside there was a fortified citadel with two palaces of the bit hilani type. The palaces and gateways were decorated with relief carvings and inscriptions in the Syro-Hittite hieroglyphic script. The identity with ancient Samal was confirmed by the discovery of a victory inscription of the Assyrian king Esarhaddon from 670 BC. (*syn.* Zenjirli, Senjirli, Zinjerli, Samal)

Ziwiyeh: Tell site in Kurdistan, northwest Iran, with a hoard of gold, silver, and ivory in a coffin of the 7th century BC. It illustrates the workmanship of the local Mannai, strongly influenced by Assyria, Urartu, and the Scythians. The collection is thought by some to have been the property of a Scythian chief who temporarily ruled Mannai. There was also a palace of the Mannaeans on a hilltop fortress. (*syn.* Ziwiye)

Zlota: Settlement and cemetery site of the Neolithic-Copper Age in southern Poland and a culture of the same name. The dead, laid in a contracted position on stone pavements in simple graves, were accompanied by pots whose shape and cord ornament suggest links with the globular amphora and corded ware cultures. Upturned handles of Ansa Lunata type suggest contact with the Baden culture. Other funerary offerings included stone battle axes, copper beads, amber ornaments, and V-perforated plaques. The community lived by farming and the exploitation of nearby flint mines.

zodiac: In astronomy and astrology, a belt around the heavens extending 9 degrees on either side of the ecliptic, the plane of the earth's orbit and of the sun's apparent annual path. The orbits of the moon and of the principal planets (except Pluto) also lie entirely within the zodiac. The 12 astrological signs of the zodiac are each considered to occupy $\frac{1}{12}$ (or 30 degrees) of its great circle. The Babylonian and Greek signs of the zodiac were introduced into Egypt in the Greco-Roman period.

zong: Chinese artifact, a tube of jade with square outer and round inner perimeter, of unknown symbolism to the southern Neolithic cultures of China. Examples vary widely in size and proportions and have also been found at both Shang and Zhou (Chou) sites. They are often decorated with the taotie design. The earliest examples come from the 3rd millennium BC. (*syn.* tsung, ts'ung)

zooarchaeology: The study of animal remains, especially bones, from archaeological contexts, including the identification and analysis of faunal species as an aid to reconstructing human diets, determining the impact of animals on past economies, and understanding the environment at the time of deposition. Animal remains are collected, cleaned, sorted, identified, and measured for their study and interpretation. The study of bones involves calculations of minimum numbers of individuals belonging to each species found; their size, age, sex, stature, dentition, and whether the bones have any marks from implements implying butchering and eating. Archaeologists attempt to answer questions such as how many species of domesticated animals there were, how far wild animals were exploited, how many very young animals there were to determine kill patterns and climate changes, in what way bones were butchered, what the sex ratios were in determining breeding strategies, and if there were any animals of unusual size. By analyzing remains from different parts of a site, it may be possible to understand some of the internal organization of the settlement, while a comparison between sites in a region may show areas of specialization. (*syn.* archaeozoology)

zoomorph: An object, figure, or picture depicting an animal form, such as those found in cave paintings. An animal form used as a symbol in art.

zoomorphic: Having an animal form or appearance, and attributing the form or nature of an animal to something, such as a deity.

zun: Any of a wide range of Chinese vessel types, generally of the Shang Dynasty (18th–12th centuries BC) and early Chou (Zhou) Dynasty (1111–c. 900 BC), probably meant for containing wine. There are two basic varieties: one shaped like a much enlarged ku, tall and somewhat trumpet shaped; the other of various animal shapes, often with animal decoration. (*syn.* tsun)

Zürich-Utoquai: Neolithic lakeside settlement in Switzerland with a Horgen culture occupation c. 3500–2800 BC. It had flat-based flower-pot pottery. A 3rd millennium BC Corded Ware occupation had beakers, polished stone axes, bone and flint tools, and wooden bowls and utensils.

Zvejnieki: Mesolithic and Neolithic cemetery in Latvia next to a settlement. Perforated elk teeth pendants, bone points, and ocher have been found.

Zwolen: Middle Palaeolithic site on the Zwolenka River, Poland, dated c. 115,000–80,000 bp by artifacts (bifacial foliates, side scrapers) and faunal remains (woolly mammoth, horse, reindeer).

Bibliography

Many books were read and researched in the compilation of The *Encyclopedic Dictionary of Archaeology*:

American Museum of Natural History, 1993, *The First Humans*. HarperSanFrancisco, San Francisco.

American Museum of Natural History, 1993, *People of the Stone Age*. HarperSanFrancisco, San Francisco.

American Museum of Natural History, 1994, *New World and Pacific Civilizations*. HarperSanFrancisco, San Francisco.

American Museum of Natural History, 1994, *Old World Civilizations*. HarperSanFrancisco, San Francisco.

Ashmore, W., and Sharer, R. J., 1988, *Discovering Our Past: A Brief Introduction to Archaeology*. Mayfield, Mountain View, CA.

Atkinson, R. J. C., 1985, *Field Archaeology*, 2d ed. Hyperion, New York.

Bacon, E. (ed.), 1976, *The Great Archaeologists*. Bobbs-Merrill, New York.

Bahn, P., 1993, *Collins Dictionary of Archaeology*. ABC-CLIO, Santa Barbara, CA.

Bahn, P. (ed.), 1995, *100 Great Archaeological Discoveries*. Barnes & Noble, New York.

Bahn, P. (ed.), 1996, *Cambridge Illustrated History of Archaeology*. Cambridge University Press, New York.

Baines, J., and Malek, J., 1980, *Atlas of Ancient Egypt*. Facts on File, New York.

Barber, R. J., 1994, *Doing Historical Archaeology: Exercises Using Documentary, Oral, and Material Evidence*. Prentice-Hall, New York.

Barker, P. A., 1983, *Techniques of Archaeological Excavation*, 2d ed. Humanities Press, New York.

Bass, G. F., 1975, *Archaeology Beneath the Sea*. Walker & Co., New York.

Bass, G. F., 1988, *Ships and Shipwrecks of the Americas: A History Based on Underwater Archaeology*. Thames & Hudson, New York.

Biers, W. R., 1987, *The Archaeology of Greece: An Introduction*. Cornell University, Ithaca, NY.

Binford, L. R., 1983, *In Pursuit of the Past, Decoding the Archaeological Record*. Thames and Hudson, London.

Binford, L. R., 1983, *Working at Archaeology*. Academic Press, New York.

Binford, L. R., and Binford, S. R. (eds.), 1968, *New Perspectives in Archaeology*. Aldine, Chicago.

Braidwood, R. J., 1960, *Archaeologists and What They Do*. Franklin Watts, New York.

Branigan, Keith (ed.), 1982, *The Atlas of Archaeology*. St. Martin's, New York.

Bray, W., and Tump, D., 1972, *Penguin Dictionary of Archaeology*. Penguin, New York.

Brennan, L., 1973, *Beginner's Guide to Archaeology*. Stackpole Books, Harrisburg, PA.

Broderick, M., and Morton, A. A., 1924, *A Concise Dictionary of Egyptian Archaeology*. Ares Publishers, Chicago.

Brothwell, D., 1963, *Digging Up Bones: The Excavation, Treatment and Study of Human Skeletal Remains*. British Museum, London.

Brothwell, D., and Higgs, E. (eds.), 1969, *Science in Archaeology*, 2d ed. Thames and Hudson, London.

Budge, E. A. Wallis, 1929, *The Rosetta Stone*. Dover, New York.

Bunson, Margaret, 1991, *A Dictionary of Ancient Egypt*. Oxford University Press, New York.

Bunson, Matthew, 1991, *A Dictionary of the Roman Empire*. Oxford University Press, New York.

Bunson, M. R., and Bunson, S. M., 1996, *Encyclopedia of Ancient Mesoamerica*. Facts on File, New York.

Butzer, K. W., 1972, *Environment and Archaeology*, 2d ed. Aldine, Chicago.

Canfora, L., 1987, *The Vanished Library*. University of California, Los Angeles.

Ceram, C. W., 1967, *Gods, Graves, and Scholars*, 2d ed. Alfred A. Knopf, New York.

Chadwick, J., 1958, *The Decipherment of Linear B*. Cambridge University Press, New York.

Chadwick, J., 1987, *Reading the Past: Linear B and Related Scripts*. University of California and the British Museum, Los Angeles.

Champion, S., 1980, *Dictionary of Terms and Techniques in Archaeology*. Facts on File, New York.

Chaplin, R. E., 1971, *The Study of Animal Bones from Archaeological Sites*. Seminar Press, London.

Charles-Picard, G. (ed.), 1987, *Larousse Encyclopedia of Archaeology*. Crescent, New York.

Childe, V. G., 1956, *Piecing Together the Past*. Praeger, New York.

Clarke, D. L. (ed.), 1972, *Models in Archaeology*. Methuen, London.

Clarke, D. L. (ed.), 1977, *Spatial Archaeology*. Academic Press, London.

Clarke, D. L., and Chapman, B., 1978, *Analytical Archaeology*, 2d ed. Columbia University Press, New York.

Clark, J. G. D., 1960, *Archaeology and Society: Reconstructing the Prehistoric Past*. Methuen, London.

Coe, M. D., 1992, *Breaking the Maya Code*. Thames & Hudson, New York.

Coe, M. D., 1993, *The Maya*. Thames & Hudson, New York.

Coe, M., Snow, D., and Benson, E., 1986, *Atlas of Ancient America*. Facts on File, New York.

Coles, J. M., 1980, *Experimental Archaeology*. Academic Press, New York.

Cook, B. F., 1987, *Reading the Past: Greek Inscriptions*. University of California and the British Museum, Los Angeles.

Cornwall, I. W., 1956, *Bones for the Archaeologist*. Phoenix House, London.

Cornwall, I. W., 1958, *Soils for the Archaeologist*. Macmillan, London.

Cottrell, L. (ed.), 1960, *The Concise Encyclopedia of Archaeology*. Hawthorn Books, New York.

Cottrell, L. (ed.), 1980, *The Penguin Encyclopedia of Ancient Civilizations*. Penguin, New York.

Daniel, G. (ed.), 1975, *Archaeological Atlas of the World*. Thames & Hudson, London.

Daniel, G., 1975, *A Hundred-and-Fifty Years of Archaeology*. Duckworth, London.

Daniel, G., 1977, *The Illustrated Encyclopedia of Archaeology*. Thomas Y. Crowell Company, New York.

Daniel, G., 1981, *A Short History of Archaeology*. Thames & Hudson, London.

Daniels, P. T., and Bright, W., 1996, *The World's Writing Systems*. Oxford University Press, New York.

Daniels, S., and David, N., 1982, *The Archaeology Workbook*. University of Pennsylvania Press, Philadelphia.

Darcy, W. S., 1981, *Archaeological Field Methods: An Introduction*. Burgess Publishing, Minneapolis.

Davies, W. V., 1987, *Reading the Past: Egyptian Hieroglyphs*. University of California and the British Museum, Los Angeles.

Day, Alan E. (ed.), 1978, *Archaeology: A Reference Handbook*. Shoe String Press, New Haven, CT.

Dean, M. (ed.), 1992, *Archaeology Underwater: The NAS Guide to Principles and Practice*. Nautical Archaeological Society/Archetype Publications, London.

Deetz, J., 1967, *Invitation to Archaeology*. Natural History Press, Garden City, NY.

Deetz, J., 1977, *In Small Things Forgotten: The Archaeology of Early American Life*. Anchor/Doubleday, Garden City, NY.

Dilllon, B. D. (ed.), 1985, *The Student's Guide to Archaeological Illustrating (Archaeological Research Tools 1)*. UCLA Institute of Archaeology, Los Angeles.

Dillon, B. D., 1989, *Practical Archaeology: Field and Laboratory Techniques and Archaeological Logistics (Archaeological Research Tools 2)*. UCLA Institute of Archaeology, Los Angeles.

Dimbleby, G. W., 1978, *Plants and Archaeology*, 2d ed. Humanities Press, New York.

Doran, J. E., and Hodson, F. R., 1975, *Mathematics and Computers in Archaeology*. Harvard University Press, Cambridge, MA.

Drucker, J., 1995, *The Alphabetic Labyrinth*. Thames & Hudson, London.

Eddy, F. W., 1984, *Archaeology: A Cultural Evolutionary Approach*. Prentice-Hall, New York.

Ehrich, R. W. (ed.), 1990, *Chronologies in Old World Archaeology*, 3rd ed. University of Chicago Press, Chicago.

Encyclopaedia Britannica Staff, 1997, *Encyclopaedia Britannica: CD97*. Encyclopaedia Britannica, Inc., Chicago.

Evans, J. G., 1978, *An Introduction to Environmental Archaeology*. Cornell University Press, Ithaca, NY.

Fagan, B., 1970, *Introductory Readings in Archaeology*. Little, Brown, Boston.

Fagan, B., 1977, *Elusive Treasure: The Story of Early Archaeologists in the Americas*. Scribner, New York.

Fagan, B., 1987, *The Great Journey: The Peopling of Ancient America*. Thames & Hudson, New York.

Fagan, B., 1988, *Quest for the Past: Great Discoveries in Archaeology*. Waveland Press, Prospect Heights, IL.

Fagan, B., 1989, *The Adventure of Archaeology*. National Geographic Society, Washington, DC.

Fagan, B., 1994, *Archaeology S/E A Brief Introduction*, 5th ed. HarperCollins, New York.

Fagan, B., 1994, *In the Beginning: An Introduction to Archaeology*, 8th ed. HarperCollins, New York.

Fagan, B., 1995, *Ancient North America: The Archaeology of a Continent*. Thames & Hudson, New York.

Fagan, B., 1995, *People of the Earth: An Introduction to World Prehistory*. HarperCollins, New York.

Fagan, B., 1995, *Time Detectives: How Archaeologists Use Technology to Recapture the Past*. Simon & Schuster, New York.

Fagan, B. (ed.), 1996, *The Oxford Companion to Archaeology*. Oxford University Press, New York.

Feder, K. L., 1990, *Frauds, Myths, and Mysteries: Science and Pseudosciences in Archaeology*. Mayfield, Palo Alto, CA.

Feldman, M., 1977, *Archaeology for Everyone*. New York Times Books, New York.

Finley, M. I., 1977, *Atlas of Classical Archaeology*. McGraw Hill, New York.

Fitting, J. E. (ed.), 1973, *The Development of North American Archaeology: Essays in the History of Regional Traditions*. Anchor Press, Garden City, NY.

Fleming, S., 1977, *Dating in Archaeology: A Guide to Scientific Techniques*. St. Martin's, New York.

Folsom, F., and Folsom, M. E., 1993, *America's Ancient Treasures*, 4th ed. University of New Mexico Press, Albuquerque.

Forte, M., and Siliotti, A., 1997, *Virtual Archaeology*. Harry N. Abrams, New York.

Gaur, A., 1992, *A History of Writing*. Cross River Press, New York.

Gelb, I. J., 1963, *A Study of Writing*. University of Chicago, Chicago.

Gibbon, G., 1984, *Anthropological Archaeology*. Columbia University Press, New York.

Goodyear, F. H., 1971, *Archaeological Site Science*. Elsevier, New York.

Gould, R. A., 1980, *Living Archaeology.* Cambridge University Press, New York.

Gould, R. A., and Schiffer, M. B. (eds.), 1981, *Modern Material Culture: The Archaeology of U.S.* Academic Press, New York.

Graham-Campbell, J., 1994, *Cultural Atlas of the Viking World.* Facts on File, New York.

Grant, M., 1990, *The Visible Past: Recent Archaeological Discoveries of Greek and Roman History.* Scribner, New York.

Green, J., 1990, *Maritime Archaeology: A Technical Handbook.* Academic Press, San Diego.

Greene, K. G., 1983, *Archaeology. An Introduction: The History, Principles, and Methods of Modern Archaeology.* Barnes & Noble, New York.

Harris, R., 1995, *Signs of Writing.* Routledge, New York.

Hassan, F., 1981, *Demographic Archaeology.* Academic Press, New York.

Hawkes, J., 1994, *Atlas of Ancient Archaeology.* Barnes & Noble, New York.

Hayden, B., 1992, *Archaeology: The Science of Once and Future Things.* W. H. Freeman, San Francisco.

Healey, J. F., 1990, *Reading the Past: The Early Alphabet.* University of California and the British Museum, Los Angeles.

Heizer, R. F., 1959, *The Archaeologist at Work: A Sourcebook in Archaeological Method and Interpretation.* Harper & Brothers, New York.

Heizer, R. F. (ed.), 1962, *Man's Discovery of His Past: Literary Landmarks in Archaeology.* Prentice-Hall, Englewood Cliffs, NJ.

Hendricks, Rhoda A., 1974, *Discovery of the Past.* Doubleday, New York.

Hester, T. R., Shafer, H. J., and Feder, K., 1997, *Field Methods in Archaeology*, 7th ed. Mayfield, Palo Alto, CA.

Higgs, E., and Brothwell, D. (eds.), 1969, *Science in Archaeology: A Survey of Progress and Research*, 2d ed. Thames & Hudson, London.

Hodder, I. (ed.), 1978, *Simulation Studies in Archaeology.* Cambridge University Press, Cambridge.

Hodder, I., and Orton, C., 1976, *Spatial Analysis in Archaeology.* Cambridge University Press, Cambridge.

Hodges, H., 1964, *Artifacts: An Introduction to Primitive Technology.* Praeger, New York.

Hodges, H., 1992, *Technology in the Ancient World.* Barnes & Noble, New York. 1970/reissue.

Hole, F., and Heizer, R., 1969, *An Introduction to Prehistoric Archaeology.* Henry Holt, New York.

Houston, S. D., 1989, *Reading the Past: Maya Glyphs.* University of California and the British Museum, Los Angeles.

Hume, I. N., 1969, *Historical Archaeology.* Alfred A. Knopf, New York.

Ingersoll, D., Yellen, J. E., and MacDonald, W. (eds.), 1977, *Experimental Archaeology.* Columbia University Press, New York.

Jelinek, J., 1975, *Pictorial Encyclopedia of the Evolution of Man.* Hamlyn, New York.

Jelks, E. B., and Jelks, J. C., 1988, *Historical Dictionary of North American Archaeology.* Greenwood Press, Westport, CT.

Johanson, D., and Johanson, L., 1994, *Ancestors: In Search of Human Origins.* Villard, New York.

Jolly, C., and Plog, F., 1987, *Physical Anthropology and Archaeology*, 4th ed. Random House, New York.

Joukowsky, M., 1980, *A Complete Manual of Field Archaeology: Tools and Techniques of Field Work for Archaeologists.* Prentice-Hall, Englewood Cliffs, NJ.

Leone, M. P., and Silberman, N. A., 1995, *Invisible America: Unearthing Our Hidden History.* Henry Holt, New York.

Levi, P., 1984, *Atlas of the Greek World.* Facts on File, New York.

Libby, W., 1955, *Radiocarbon Dating.* University of Chicago Press, Chicago.

Limbrey, S., 1975, *Soil Science and Archaeology.* Academic Press, London.

Lincoln, R. J., and Boxshall, G. A., 1987, *The Cambridge Illustrated Dictionary of Natural History.* Cambridge University Press, New York.

Little, B. J. (ed.), 1991, *Text-Aided Archaeology.* CRC Press, Boca Raton.

Logsdon, P., 1993, *Ancient Land, Ancestral Places.* Museum of New Mexico Press, Albuquerque.

Lutyk, Carol (ed.), 1985, *The Adventure of Archaeology.* National Geographic Press, Washington, DC.

Lyons, T. R., and Avery, T. E., 1977, *Remote Sensing: A Handbook for Archaeologists and Cultural Resource Managers.* National Park Service, Washington, DC.

McGimsey III, C. R., 1973, *Archaeology and Archeological Resources.* Society for American Archaeology, Washington, DC.

McHargue, G., and Roberts, M., 1977, *A Field Guide to Conservation Archaeology in North America.* J. B. Lippincott, Philadelphia.

McIntosh, J., 1986, *The Practical Archaeologist.* Facts on File, New York.

McMillon, B., 1991, *The Archaeology Handbook.* John Wiley, New York.

Mahdy, Christine El, 1989, *Mummies—Myth and Magic.* Thames & Hudson, London.

Meigham, C. W., 1966, *Archaeology: An Introduction.* Chandler, San Francisco.

Meltzer, D. J., et al. (eds.), 1986, *American Archaeology Past and Future.* Smithsonian Institution Press, Washington, DC.

Michael, H. N., and Ralph, E. K., 1971, *Dating Techniques for the Archaeologist.* MIT Press, Cambridge, MA.

Michels, J. W., 1973, *Dating Methods in Archaeology.* Seminar Press, New York.

Mignon, M. R., 1993, *Dictionary of Concepts in Archaeology.* Greenwood Press, Westport, CT.

Mollett, J. W., 1883/reissued 1994, *Dictionary of Art and Archaeology.* Bracken Books, London.

Moseley, M. E., 1992, *The Incas and Their Ancestors.* Thames & Hudson, New York.

Muckleroy, K., 1978, *Maritime Archaeology.* Cambridge University Press, New York.

Mueller, J. W. (ed.), 1975, *Sampling in Archaeology.* University of Arizona Press, Tucson.

Nakanishi, A., 1980, *Writing Systems of the World.* Charles E. Tuttle, Rutland, VT.

National Geographic Society Book Division, 1994, *Wonders of the Ancient World.* National Geographic Society, Washington, DC.

Norman, B., 1987, *Footsteps: Nine Archaeological Journeys of Romance and Discovery.* Salem House, Topsfield, MA.

Oliphant, M., 1992, *The Atlas of the Ancient World*. Simon & Schuster, New York.

Orme, B., 1981, *Anthropology for Archaeologists*. Cornell University Press, Ithaca, NY.

Orser, C. E., and Fagan, B. M., 1995, *Historical Archaeology: A Brief Introduction*. HarperCollins, New York.

Page, R. I., 1993, *Reading the Past: Runes*. University of California and the British Museum, Los Angeles.

Paor, Liam de, 1971, *Archaeology, an Illustrated Introduction*. Penguin, London.

Patterson, T. C., 1994, *The Theory and Practice of Archaeology: A Workbook*. Prentice-Hall, New York.

Pope, M., 1975, *The Story of Archaeological Decipherment from Egyptian Hieroglyphs to Linear B*. Thames & Hudson, London.

Price, T. D., and Feinman, G. M., 1993, *Images of the Past*. Mayfield, Palo Alto, CA.

Pyddoke, E., 1961, *Stratification for the Archaeologist*. Phoenix House, London.

Radice, B., 1973, *The Penguin Who's Who in the Ancient World*. Penguin, New York.

Rapp, G., and Gifford, J. A. (eds.), 1985, *Archaeological Geology*. Yale University Press, New Haven, CT.

Rathje, W. L., and Schiffer, M. B., 1982, *Archaeology*. Harcourt Brace, San Diego.

Redman, C. L. (ed.), 1973, *Research and Theory in Current Archaeology*. Wiley, New York.

Renfrew, C., 1987, *Archaeology and Language*. Cambridge University Press, New York.

Renfrew, C., and Bahn, P., 1991, *Archaeology: Theories, Methods, and Practice*. Thames & Hudson, New York.

Rexer, L., and Klein, R., 1995, *125 Years of Expedition and Discovery*. Harry N. Abrams and the American Museum of Natural History, New York.

Roaf, M., 1990, *Cultural Atlas of Mesopotamia and the Ancient Near East*. Facts on File, New York.

Robbins, L. H., 1987, *The Archaeologist's Eye: Great Discoveries of Missing Links and Ancient Treasures*. Dodd, New York.

Robbins, L. H., 1992, *Stones, Bones, and Ancient Cities: Great Discoveries in Archaeology and the Search for Human Origins*. St. Martin's, New York.

Robbins, M., and Irving, M. B., 1965, *The Amateur Archaeologist's Handbook*. Thomas Y. Crowell, New York.

Robinson, A., 1995, *The Story of Writing: Alphabets, Hieroglyphs and Pictograms*. Thames & Hudson, London.

Sabloff, J. A., 1990, *The New Archaeology and the Ancient Maya*. W. H. Freeman/Scientific American Library, New York.

Sacks, D., 1995, *A Dictionary of the Ancient Greek World*. Oxford University Press, New York.

Sande, T., 1976, *Industrial Archaeology*. Stephen Green Press, Brattleboro, VT.

Scarre, C. (ed.), 1993, *Smithsonian Timelines of the Ancient World*. Dorling Kindersley, New York.

Scarre, C. (ed.), 1995, *Past Worlds: The Times Atlas of Archaeology*. Crescent Books, Avenel, NJ.

Schele, L., and Freidel, D., 1990, *A Forest of Kings: The Untold Story of the Ancient Maya*. Morrow, New York.

Schick, K. D., and Toth, N., 1993, *Making Silent Stones Speak: Human Evolution and the Dawn of Technology*. Simon & Schuster, New York.

Schiffer, M. B., 1976, *Behavioral Archaeology*. Academic Press, New York.

Schiffer, M. B., 1986, *Advances in Archaeological Method and Theory*. Academic Press, Orlando, FL.

Schiffer, M. B., and Gumerman, G. J. (eds.), 1977, *Conservation Archaeology: A Guide for Cultural Resource Management Studies*. Academic Press, New York.

Schmandt-Besserat, D., 1992, *Before Writing, Volume 1: From Counting to Cuneiform*. University of Texas, Austin, TX.

Schnapp, A., 1997, *The Discovery of the Past*. Harry N. Abrams, New York.

Schuyler, R. L. (ed.), 1978, *Historical Archaeology: A Guide to Substantive and Theoretical Contributions*. Baywood, Farmingdale, NY.

Sease, C., 1994, *A Conservation Manual for the Field Archaeologist (Archaeological Research Tools 4)*. University of California, Los Angeles.

Shackley, M., 1975, *Archaeological Sediments: A Survey of Analytical Methods*. Wiley/Halsted Press, London.

Shanks, M., and Tilley, C., 1987, *Reconstructing Archaeology: Theory and Practice*. Cambridge University Press, New York.

Sharer, R. J., and Ashmore, W., 1993, *Archaeology: Discovering Our Past*, 2d ed. Mayfield, Mountain View, CA.

Shaw, I., and Nicholson, P., 1995, *The Dictionary of Ancient Egypt*. Harry N. Abrams, New York.

Sherratt, A., 1980, *The Cambridge Encyclopedia of Archaeology*. Cambridge University Press, New York.

Smith, G. S., and Ehrenhard, J. E. (eds.), 1991, *Protecting the Past*. CRC Press, Boca Raton, FL.

South, S. A., 1977, *Method and Theory in Historical Archaeology*. Academic Press, New York.

South, S. A., 1977, *Research Strategies in Historical Archaeology*. Academic Press, New York.

Speake, G., 1995, *The Penguin Dictionary of Ancient History*. Penguin, New York.

Stevenson, J. C., 1991, *Dictionary of Concepts in Physical Anthropology*. Greenwood Press, Westport, CT.

Stiebing Jr., W. H., 1993, *Uncovering the Past: A History of Archaeology*. Oxford University Press, New York.

Stuart, G. E., 1983, *People and Places of the Past*. National Geographic Society, Washington, DC.

Sullivan, G., 1980, *Discover Archaeology: An Introduction to the Tools and Techniques of Archaeological Fieldwork*. Doubleday, New York.

Sutton, M. Q., and Arkush, B. S., 1996, *Archaeological Laboratory Methods: An Introduction*. Kendall/Hunt, Dubuque, IA.

Tattersall, I., Delson, E., and Van Couvering, J., 1988, *Encyclopedia of Human Evolution and Prehistory*. Garland, New York.

Taylor, C., 1974, *Fieldwork in Medieval Archaeology*. Batsford, London.

Thomas, D. H., 1974, *Predicting the Past: An Introduction to Anthropological Archaeology*. Henry Holt, New York.

Thomas, D. H., 1979/1991, *Archaeology: Down to Earth*. Henry Holt, New York.

Throckmorton, P., 1970, *Shipwrecks and Archaeology: The Unharvested Sea.* Victor Gollanz, London.

Tite, M., 1972, *Methods of Physical Examination in Archaeology.* Seminar Press, London.

Trigger, B. G., 1978, *Time and Traditions: Essays in Archaeological Interpretation.* Columbia University Press, New York.

Trigger, B. G., 1989, *A History of Archaeological Thought.* Cambridge University Press, New York.

Tylecote, R. F., 1962, *Metallurgy in Archaeology.* Edward Arnold, London.

Walker, C. B. F., 1987, *Reading the Past: Cuneiform.* University of California and the British Museum, Los Angeles.

Watson, P. J., LeBlanc, S. A., and Redman, C. L., 1971, *Explanation in Archaeology: An Explicitly Scientific Approach.* Columbia University Press, New York.

Webster, D. L., Evans, S. T., and Sanders, W. T., 1993, *Out of the Past: An Introduction to Archaeology.* Mayfield, Mountain View, CA.

Webster, G., 1974, *Practical Archaeology: An Introduction to Archaeological Fieldwork and Excavation,* 2d ed. St. Martin's, London.

Weitzman, D., 1980, *Traces of the Past: A Field Guide to Industrial Archaeology.* Scribner, New York.

Wendorf, F., 1966, *A Guide to Salvage Archaeology.* Museum of New Mexico Press, Albuquerque, NM.

Wenke, R. J., 1990, *Patterns in Prehistory: Humankind's First Three Million Years.* Oxford University Press, New York.

Wheeler, R. E. M., 1956, *Archaeology from the Earth.* Penguin, Baltimore.

Whitehouse, Ruth D., 1983, *The Facts on File Dictionary of Archaeology.* Facts on File, New York.

Willey, G. R., 1966, *An Introduction to American Archaeology, Volume One North and Middle America.* Prentice-Hall, Englewood Cliffs, NJ.

Willey, G. R., and Phillips, P., 1958, *Method and Theory in American Archaeology.* University of Chicago Press, Chicago.

Willey, G. R., and Sabloff, J., 1993, *A History of American Archaeology,* 3d ed. W. H. Freeman, London.

Wilson, D., 1975, *The New Archaeology.* Alfred A. Knopf, New York.

Wilson, J., 1980, *The Passionate Amateur's Guide to Archaeology in the United States.* Collier, New York.

Winstone, H. V. F., 1987, *Uncovering the Ancient World.* Facts on File, New York.

Winthrop, R. H., 1991, *Dictionary of Concepts in Cultural Anthropology.* Greenwood Press, Westport, CT.

Wood, M., 1985, *World Atlas of Archaeology.* G. K. Hall, Boston.

Wondall, J. N., 1972, *An Introduction to Modern Archaeology.* Schenkman, Cambridge, MA.

Yellen, J. E., 1977, *Archaeological Approaches to the Present: Models for Reconstructing the Past.* Academic Press, New York.

Zauzich, K-T., 1992, *Hieroglyphs Without Mystery.* University of Texas, Austin, TX.

I also read and researched periodicals with archaeology articles, such as *American Antiquity, American Journal of Archaeology, Antiquity, Archaeology, Historical Archaeology, Journal of Anthropological Archaeology, Journal of Field Archaeology, Journal of World Prehistory, National Geographic, Natural History, Nature, Science, Scientific American, Smithsonian,* and *World Archaeology.*

Supplementary List of Archaeological Sites and Terms

Aacharne   W Syria early tools
Aachen   NW Germany early settlement, Carolingian capital, archbishopric
Ab-yanah   N Persia fire temple
Abadiya   U Egypt ancient temple
Abaj Takalik   S Guatemala early hieroglyphs, Maya settlement
Abbeville   N France early tools
Abdera   NE Greece Greek colony
Aberffraw   N Wales Mesolithic settlement
Abitibi Narrows   C Canada, Ontario Archaic site
Abivard   NE Persia Parthian city
Abri Pataud   C France hunter-gatherer site
Abrigo do Sol   S Brazil early tools
Abu Dulaf   Mesopotamia mosque of Samarra
Abu Ghosh   S Palestine Neolithic site
Abu Rawash   L Egypt pyramid
Abu Salabikh   C Mesopotamia early city, early settlement, palace, early writing
Abu Salem   S Palestine Neolithic site
Abu Seiyal   U Egypt copper mine
Abu Simbel   U Egypt temple
Abu Sir   L Egypt pyramid, early burial
Abydus (a/s Abydos)   U Egypt ancient city, temple
Acacus   N Africa early pottery
Acalan   N Guatemala Aztec trade center
Acancéh   Mexico, Yucatan Maya settlement
Acanthus (a/s Akanthos)   NE Greece Greek colony
Acarí   C Peru Inca center
Acasaguastlán   S Guatemala Maya settlement
Accra   W Africa, Ghanna early port

Acerenza   S Italy archbishopric
Achaea   ancient country of SW Greece
Acharnae   SE Greece Athenian settlement
Achenheim   SW Germany early tools
Achenheim III   W Germany Neanderthal site
Achupallas   C Ecuador Inca tambo
Acigöl   SE Anatolia Neolithic site
Ackman   SW USA Pueblo farming site
Acolman   C Mexico Aztec center
Acrae   E Sicily Greek colony
Acragas (a/s Akragas)   S Sicily Greek colony
Acre   Palestine early port
Adab   C Mesopotamia early city, ancient palace, early writing
Adamgarh   C India Mesolithic site
Adana   SE Anatolia Islamic town
Aden   SW Arabia early trade center, Islamic port, maritime trade
Adena   NE USA, Ohio Adena site
Adichanallur   S India megalithic tomb
Adilcevaz   E Anatolia Uratian fortress
Adloun   Lebanon Neanderthal site
Adramyttium   W Anatolia Byzantine town
Adrar Bous   Africa, Niger Acheulian tools, stone age tools, early cattle, early livestock
Adrar Madet   N Africa, Niger wavy-line pottery
Adrar Tiouëine   N Africa, Algeria early livestock
Adria   N Italy Roman empire
Adulis   Red Sea ancient port, early trade
Adwuku   W Africa, Ghana hunter-gatherers
Aegina (Aiyina)   SE Greece ancient fortress, Greek temple

Aelia Capitolina   (modern Jerusalem): Palestine Roman city
Aenus (modern Enez)   NW Turkey Greek colony
Aerodrome Cave   E Africa, Uganda hunter-gatherers
Aetolia   ancient country of SW Greece
Aexone   SE Greece Athenian settlement
Afalou-bou-Rhummel   N Africa, Algeria Stone Age tools
Afanas'yeva Gora   S Siberia steppe settlement
Afareaitu   Society I. early site
Afikpo   W Africa, Nigeria early food
Afontova Gora   E Russia hunter-gatherer site
Agadès (Agadez)   W Africa, Niger early town
Agano   W Japan Korean pottery
Agathe (modern Agde)   S France Greek colony
Aggersborg   N Denmark Viking fortress
Aggersund   N Denmark shell midden
Aggsbach   Austria hunter-gatherer site
Aghtamar   E Anatolia Byzantine walled town
Agop Atas   NE Borneo Neolithic settlement
Agra   C India Mughal capital
Agris   C France Celtic art
Agua Bendida   C Mexico Pre-Classical site
Agua Blanco   Ecuador early farming settlement
Aguilcourt   NE France Iron Age cemetery
Ahicchatra   N India early city
Ahlât   E Anatolia Sinan mosque
Ahmadabad   W India Mughal mint
Ahraura   NE India rock edict

Ahteut   Alaska Thule site
Ahu Akivi   Easter I. early site
Ahu Ko Te Riku   Easter I. early site
Ahu Te Pito Kura   Easter I. early site
Ahu Tongariki   Easter I. early site
Ahu Vinapu   Easter I. early site
Ahuelican   C Mexico Pre-Classical site
Ahuriri   New Zealand, South I. rock art
Ahutoru   Society Is. early site
Ahwaz   W Persia Sasanian city
Aibunar   C Bulgaria early copper mine
Aila (modern Aqaba)   Jordan Islamic
  town
Aillevans   E France megalithic tomb
Ain Abou Jamaa   NE Syria early tools
Ain el Atrous   N Africa, Tunisia hunter-
  gatherers
Ain Fritissa   NW Africa, Morocco
  Stone Age tools
Ain Hanech   N Africa, Algeria
  Acheulian tools
Ain Maarouf   NW Africa, Morocco
  Stone Age tools
Ain Mallaha   S Syria Natufian site
Ain Tabous   N Syria early tools
Ainu hill forts   N Japan
Air   W Africa early kingdom
Aisne Valley   NE France Iron Age
  farming
Aït Garet   N Algeria megalithic tomb
Aithaia   SW Greece tholos tomb
Aït Raouna   N Algeria megalithic tomb
Aix   S France archbishopric
Ajanta   W India rock-cut temples
Ajbunar   SE Europe early copper mine
Ajdabiya   N Africa, Libya Islamic town
Ak Yum   Cambodia Neolithic settlement
Akan (Akanland)   W Africa early
  kingdom
Akapana   temple complex of
  Tiahuanaco
Akaribaru   SW Japan fishing site
Aké   Mexico, Yucatán Maya settlement
Akhalgori   Caucasus gold and silver
  work
Akhmim   U Egypt noble's tomb, ancient
  city, silk find
Akhshtyr   S Russia Neanderthal site
Akita   N Japan Heian fortress
Akjoujt   W Africa, Mauritania Islamic
  trade, early settlement
Akkermen   SW Russia steppe
  settlement
Akragas (Acragas, Agrigentum,
  Agrigento)   W Sicily Greek temple
Akrai (Acrae)   SE Sicily Greek colony

Akreïjit   W Africa, Mauritania bone
  harpoons
Akroterion   W Greece tholos tomb
Akrotiri   NW Crete sacred cave
Aksha   U Egypt temple
Akshak   C Mesopotamia early city
Aksu   C Asia early trade center,
  Buddhist center
Aktash   SE Russia steppe settlement
Aktobe   C Russia steppe settlement
Akun I.   Aleutian Is. arctic culture
Al Anbar (Peroz Shapur)   N
  Mesopotamia Sasanian city
Al Fustat (Cairo)   Egypt Islamic town
Al Hira   Iraq Islamic town
Al Huraydah   SW Arabia temple remains
Al Kowm   SE Syria early tools,
  Neolithic site
Al Mada'in   Iraq Islamic town
Al Mina   NW Syria ivory, Greek colony
Al Musharrahat   Mesopotamia palace
  of Samarra
Alabanda   SW Anatolia Hellenistic city
alabaster sources   Anatolia and Syria,
  Egypt
Alaca Hüyük   C Anatolia Hittite city
Alaka   Guyana shell midden
Alalakh   N Syria early city
Alalia   Corsica Greek colony
Alamgirpur   N India early city,
  Harappan site
Alandskoye   C Russia barrow burial
Alapraia   C Portugal beaker burial,
  rock-cut tomb and carved ivory
Alborg   N Denmark flint mine, Viking
  center
Alcaide   S Spain rock-cut tomb
Alcalá   S Portugal megalithic tomb
Alcantarilla   E Spain Roman dam
Alcester I.   New Guinea Kula gift
  exchange
Aleksandropol   SW Russia barrow
  burial
Aleksandrovka   S Siberia steppe
  settlement
Aleppo (Beroea)   N Syria early city,
  Islamic town, Sinan mosque
Alexandria   L Egypt Hellenistic city,
  Roman provincial capital, Roman
  empire, early trade, early trading
  capital, early iron, patriarchate, Islamic
  town
Alexandria Areion (modern Herat)
  Afghanistan Hellenistic city
Alexandria Margiana (Merv, Modern
  Mary)   S Russia Hellenistic city

Alexandria Troas   NW Anatolia
  Hellenistic city
Ali Kosh   NW Persia Neolithic site
Ali Murad   NW India Harappan site
Alibates   S USA, Texas Archaic site
Alice Boër   S Brazil early settlement
Alice Springs   C Australia Aboriginal
  site
Aligrama   N India later farming village
Alisar Hüyük   E Anatolia Assyrian
  colony, Hittite city
Aljezur   S Portugal rock-cut tomb
Alkali Ridge   SW USA Pueblo farming
  site
Allahabad/Prayaga   C India pillar edict
Allahdino   NW India early city,
  Harappan site
Almería   S Spain medieval trade
Almizaraque   SE Spain carved ivory
Almondbury   N England medieval town
Almunécar   S Spain Carthaginian
  cemetery
Alpiarca   Portugal early tools
Alta   N Norway rock engraving
Altamira   NW Spain hunter-gatherer art
Altamira   SE Mexico Pre-Classical site
Altamura   SE Italy rock-cut tomb and
  carved ivory
Altar de Sacrificios   E Mexico Maya
  settlement
Altbachtal Trier   W Germany Romano-
  Celtic shrines
Altenburg   N Germany Celtic oppidum
Altendorf   N Germany megalithic tomb
Altenritte   N Germany Celtic site
Altheim   SE Germany defensive
  enclosure
Altintepe   NE Anatolia Uratian fortress,
  Achaemenid city
Altin-X   C Asia Achaemenid palace
Alttrier   W Germany Roman village
Altun Ha   E Mexico Maya center
Altxerri   N Spain hunter-gatherer art
Altyn Tepe   C Asia steppe settlement
Alum Creek   NE USA, Ohio Adena site
Amada   U Egypt temple
Amadzimba   C Africa, Zimbabwe
  hunter-gatherers
Amalfi   S Italy archbishopric
Amalucan   C Mexico early town
Amanzi   S Africa Acheulian tools
Amapa   C Mexico early town
Amara   NW India Harappan site
Amara   U Egypt fortification
Amarapura   C Burma Neolithic
  settlement

Amaravati   S India Buddhist site, early trade center, Buddhist stupa

Amarnà   see El-Amarnà

Amasia (Amasea)   NE Anatolia Byzantine walled town

Amastris   N Anatolia Roman provincial capital

Amatitlán   S Guatemala Maya settlement

Ambilobe   Madagascar Ming pottery

Ambitle I.   Papua New Guinea Lapita site

Amboise   C France Celtic oppidum

Ambon (Amboina)   E Indies, Moluccas maritime trade

Amchitka   Aleutian Is. arctic culture

Amecameca   C Mexico early town, Aztec center

Amekni   S Algeria early pottery, early cereals

Amendola   S Italy defensive enclosure

Amfreville   N France Celtic art

Amida (modern Diyarbakir)   E Anatolia Assyrian provincial capital

Amiens   N France Viking trading emporium

Amiklai   S Greece metal vessels

Amman   Jordan Islamic town

Ammassalik (Angmagssalik)   SE Greenland site

Amnisos   N Crete Linear B tablets

Amose   E Denmark pollen core site

Amoy   SW Norway rock art

Amphiareion   SE Greece theatre, Athenian sanctuary

Amri   NW India Indus Valley settlement, early city, Harappan site

Amrit   Lebanon Neanderthal site

Amsa-dong   C Korea shell mound

Amsterdam   Holland early trade

Amud   N Israel Neanderthal site

An Carra   NW Scotland menhir

An Najaf   S Mesopotamia holy city

An Nhon (Binh Dihn, Vijaya)   S Vietnam early site

Ana   Iraq Islamic town

'Anaeho'omalu   Hawaiian Is. Petroglyph

Anahulu Valley   Hawaiian Is. early site

Anaktuvuk Pass   Alaska Ipiutak site

Ananatuba   E Brazil early horticultural village

Anaphlystus   SE Greece Athenian settlement

Anatolia   early hominids, Neolithic and Palaeolithic settlement, early farming, early pottery, Bronze Age, early civilization, Assyrian empire, early writing, Achaemenid empire, Greek colonies, Hellenistic influence, Roman cities and fortresses, Byzantine empire, Ottoman empire

Anaz   E Anatolia Assyrian stela

Ancón   C Peru early farming, preceramic site, Chavín site, Inca center

Ancona   C Italy Roman city

Ancylus Lake   Baltic

Ancyra (modern Ankara)   C Anatolia Roman provincial capital, Byzantine walled town

Andernach (Antunnacum)   W Germany hunter-gatherer site, hunter-gatherer art, Roman village

Andrews   N USA, Michigan Archaic site

Andronovo   S Siberia steppe settlement

Angel   W USA temple mound

Angers   NW France monastery

Anghelu Ruju   N Sardinia rock-cut tomb

Angkor   Indo-China, Cambodia early monumental site, Khmer capital Buddhist center

Angkor Borei   Cambodia early monumental site

Angkor Wat   Cambodia temple complex

Angles-sur-l'Anglin   C France Neanderthal site, hunter-gatherer art

Aniba   U Egypt fortification

Anjar   Syria Islamic town

Ankara (Ancyra)   W Anatolia Islamic town, Sinan mosque

Anlu   N China early settlement

Annagassan   N Ireland Viking center

Annapolis   E USA, Maryland colonial settlement

Annau   C Asia steppe settlement

Anopolis   N Crete Minoan village

Ano Zakro   E Crete Minoan village

Anta de Marquesa   C Portugal megalithic tomb

Anta dos Gorgions   S Portugal megalithic tomb

Antalaha   Madagascar Ming pottery

Antinoe   L Egypt silk find

Antioch (Antiochia, modern Antakya)   SE Anatolia Hellenistic city, Roman provincial capital, Roman empire, early trading capital, Byzantine walled town

Antium (modern Anzio)   C Italy Roman colony

Antonine Wall   S Scotland

Antwerp (Anvers)   Belgium Viking mint

Anuradhapura   N Ceylon early city, early capital and Buddhist center, Buddhist stupa

Anxi   NW China early trade center

Anxi   SE China Sung kiln

Anyang   N China early city, early writing, Shang capital, steppe bronzes

Anyar   W Java early metal site

Anza   W Bulgaria farming site, early pottery

Aotea   New Zealand, North I. defended settlement

Apa   N Romania metal hoard

Apache Creek   SW USA Pueblo farming site

Apamea   W Syria Hellenistic city

Apan   C Mexico early town

Apatzingán   C Mexico early town

Apaxco   C Mexico Aztec center

Aphidna   SE Greece Athenian settlement

Aphrodisias   SW Anatolia Neolithic site, Roman city

Apizaco   C Mexico early town

Apodhoulou   C Crete Minoan village

Apollo 11 Cave   SW Africa, Namibia Stone Age tools, Stone Age site

Apollonia   NE Africa Greek colony

Apollonia (modern Sozopol)   E Bulgaria Greek colony

Apollonia   NW Greece Greek colony

Apollonis   W Anatolia Hellenistic city

Apologos   S Mesopotamia early trade

Aptera   NW Crete Linear B tablet

Apulum (modern Alba Iulia)   Romania Roman city and legionary fortress

Aquateca   C Guatemala Maya settlement

Aquileia (modern Aglar)   NE Italy Roman city, archbishopric

Aquiles Serdán   SE Mexico Pre-Classical site

Aquincum (modern Budapest)   Hungary Roman provincial capital and legionary fortress, silk find

Arachosians   ancient people of Afghanistan

Aracu   W Brazil early settlement

Aradus (Ruad, Arvad)   W Syria Phoenician city

Arago   SW France early tools and human remains

Arakamchechen I.   E Russia Thule site

Araouane   W Africa, Mali early town
Araphen   SE Greece Athenian sanctuary
Arapuni   New Zealand, North I. rock art
Araxos   C Greece Mycenaean fortress
Araya   C Japan early man
Arbela (Nad Ardashir, modern Arbil)   N Mesopotamia Sasanian city
Arbil (Irbil, Arbela, Arba'ilu)   N Mesopotamia Mitannian city, Assyrian provincial capital
Arcadia   region of S Greece
Archaic Stage culture   N America
Archanes (Arkhanes)   C Crete Minoan village
Arcy-sur-Cure   NE France Neanderthal site, hunter-gatherer site
Ardabil   N Persia Islamic town
Ardales   S Spain hunter-gatherer art
Arelate (modern Arles)   S France Roman city
Arene Candide   NW Italy hunter-gatherer site, hunter-gatherer, farming settlement
Arequipa   S Peru early trade
Argalykty   E Russia barrow burial
Argaru (modern Tiruchchirappalli)   S India early trade
Argentina   early settlement
Argentoratum (modern Strasbourg)   NE France Roman legionary fortress
Argillite   New Zealand
Argissa   N Greece farming site, early pottery
Argoeuvres   N France early tools
Argolis   region of S Greece
Argos   S Greece Mycenae anfortress, Hellenistic city, city-state
Arguin   W Africa, Mauritania early town
Arhus   C Denmark Viking center
Arians   Ancient people of Afghanistan
Arica   N Chile maritime trade
Aridos   C Spain early tools
Ariendorf   NW Germany early tools
Arikamedu (Poduca)   S India early city
Ariminum (Ariminium, modern Rimini)   N Italy Roman city
Arinberd   Armenia Urartian fortress, Achaemenid city
Aristé   NE Brazil early settlement
Arita kilns   W Japan Korean pottery
Ariusd   Romania Cucuteni-Tripolye village
Arkalochori (Arkalokhorion)   C Crete sacred cave

Arkharinskiy   SW Russia steppe settlement
Arkin   U Egypt Archeulian tools
Arkin 5-6A   NE Africa, Egypt Stone Age tools
Arkines   SW Greece tholos tomb
Arklow   E Ireland Viking center
Arkoudiotissa   NW Crete sacred cave
Arku Cave   N Philippines Neolithic settlement
Arles   S France archbishopric
Arlit   N Africa, Niger early livestock
Arlon (Orolaunum)   S Belgium Roman village
Armagh   N Ireland archbishopric
Armant (Hermonthis)   U Egypt ancient cemetery, ancient city
Armavir-Blur   Armenia Urartian fortress
Armenia   Assyrian empire
Armenians   under Achaemenid empire
Armstrong   C Canada, Ontario Archaic site
Aromaton Emporion (Mart of Spices)   NE Africa early trade
Arpa Valley   C Asia steppe settlement
Arpachiyah   N Mesopotamia pottery remains
Arpad (modern Tel Rifaat)   Syria Assyrian provincial capital
Arpi   S Italy Roman empire
Arrapkha (modern Kirkuk)   N Mesopotamia early town, Assyrian provincial capital
Arras   N England Celtic art
Arras   N France Frankish pottery kiln
Arretium (modern Arezzo)   C Italy Etruscan and Roman city
Arslantas   NW Mesopotamia Assyrian city
Artajona   N Spain megalithic tomb
Artemita (Chalasar)   C Mesopotamia Hellenistic city, Parthian city
Artik   SW Russia steppe settlement
Arvad   W Syria Egyptian control
Arvi   S Crete Minoan village
Arzhan Kurgan   E Russia barrow burial
Asabon   SE Arabia early trade
Asahitokoro   N Japan rice farming site
Asejire   W Africa, Nigeria hunter-gatherers
Ashdod   S Palestine early port, Assyrian provincial capital
Ashishik Point   Aleutian Is. arctic culture
Ashkelon (Ashqaluna)   Palestine Egyptian control

Ashur   N Mesopotamia pyramid, early city, early writing, Mitannian city, Assyrian capital, Parthian city
Asikli Hüyük   C Anatolia Neolithic site
Asine   SE Greece Mycenaean tomb
Askitario   E Greece ancient fortress
Askiz   S Siberia steppe settlement
Aspendus   SW Anatolia Hellenistic city, Roman city, aqueduct
Aspero   S Peru pyramid, platform mounds
Asprokhaliko   C Greece Neanderthal site
Aspropirgos   SE Greece Athenian settlement
Assebakte   N Norway Saami settlement
Asselar   N Africa, Algeria bone harpoons
Assos   NW Anatolia Greek temple, Hellenistic city
Astakapra   NW India early trade
Astana   NW China Buddhist center
Asuka-Itabuki   C Japan Yamato palace
Asunción   Paraguay early trade
Aswan (Syene)   U Egypt granite site, ancient mine, Islamic town, gold
Asyut   U Egypt noble's tomb, ancient city
Atapuerca   N Spain early human remains
Atargan   E Russia Thule site
Atashgah   N Persia fire temple
'Atele   Tonga early site
Atfih   U Egypt early capital
Athos   NE Greece Byzantine monastery
Athr   Arabia Islamic town
Athribis   L Egypt ancient city
Atlihuayan   C Mexico Pre-Classical site
Atlixco   C Mexico early town
Atranjikhera   N India early city
Atsinna   SW USA Pueblo farming site
Attalia (modern Antalya)   SW Anatolia Hellenistic city, Roman city
Attica   ancient country of SE Greece
Attigny   N France Viking mint
Attock   NW India Harappan site
Atwetwebooso   W Africa, Ghana Iron Age site
Atzcapotzalco   C Mexico early town, Aztec town
Auch   SW France archbishopric
Auckland   New Zealand, North I. defended settlement
Augusta Praetoria (modern Aosta)   N Italy Roman city
Augusta Treverorum (modern Trier)   N Germany Roman city

Augusta Vindelicorum (modern Augsburg)　S Germany Roman city

Augustodunum (modern Autun)　E France Roman city

Aulnat　E France Celtic site

Aulnay-aux-Planches　NE France Bronze Age settlement

Aurangabad　C India Mughal mint

Aurar　NW India Harappan site

Aurignac　S France hunter-gatherer site

Ausculum (modern Ascoli Satriano)　C Italy Roman empire

Austrheim　W Norway rock art

Austronesian　Language group

Auvernier　W Switzerland corded ware settlement

Auximum　C Italy Roman colony

Ava　N Burma Buddhist center

Avakana　C Ceylon Buddhist site

Avaldsnes　SW Norway early settlement

Avalites (Aualites)　NE Africa, Somalia ancient port, early trade

Avarua　Cook Is. early site

Avdeyevo　C Russia hunter-gatherer art

Avebury　S England stone circle and henge

Avennes　N France flint mine

Avrillé　W France menhir

Avukana　N Ceylon Buddhist remains

Awal　N Mesopotamia early writing

Awamoa　New Zealand, South I. moa bones

Awatobi　SW USA Pueblo farming site

Awdaghost　W Africa, Mauritania Islamic trade, urban center

Awlil　W Africa, Mauritania early settlement

Axim　W Africa, Ghana early port

Axima　SE France Roman provincial capital

Axum　NE Africa, Ethiopia early state, early trade, rock-cut churches

Ayacucho　Peru early farming

Ayaviri　E Peru Inca center

Ayia Gala　S Aegean Neolithic site

Ayia Irini　SE Greece Mycenaean fortress

Ayia Marina　NE Greece Mycenaean fortress

Ayios Ilias　W Greece tholos tomb

Ayios Ioannis　NE Greece Mycenaean fortress

Ayios Nikolaos　SW Greece tholos tomb

Ayios Theodhoros　N Greece tholos tomb

Ayutthaya　C Thailand Buddhist stupa

Azaila　NE Spain native settlement

Azanqaro　C Peru Inca center

Azmak　SW Bulgaria farming site, early pottery

Azmaska Mogila　C Bulgaria tell settlement

Aznavur (Patnos)　E Anatolia Urartian fortress

Aztalan　N USA temple mound

Aztec Ruins　SW USA Pueblo farming site

Azykh Cave　S Russia early tools, Neanderthal site

Ba　W China Han city

Babadan　N Japan early man

Babil　N Mesopotamia Assyrian stela

Babino　SW Russia steppe settlement

Babueski　NW Turkey Sinan mosque

Babylon Fossatum　L Egypt, Roman legionary fortress

Bacare (Bakare, Porakad)　S India early trade

Bac Son　N Indo-China, Vietnam cave site

Bactra (Zariaspa, modern Balkh)　Afghanistan Achaemenid city, Hellenistic city, early trade center

Bad Bertrich　W Germany pagan shrine

Bad Nauheim　C Germany Celtic site

Bada　N Celebes early metal site

Badagri　W Africa, Nigeria early town

Badegoule　C France hunter-gatherer art

Badopal　NW India Harappan site

Badorf　N Germany Rhenish pottery kiln

Bad-tibira　S Mesopotamia early city

Badulla　S Ceylon Buddhist remains

Baeterrae　S France native settlement

Bagarre　N France early tools

Bagh　C India Buddhist center

Baghouz　E Syria pottery remains

Bagneux　NW France megalithic tomb

Bagor　N India Mesolithic site

Bagum　C Mesopotamia pottery remains

Bagumbayan　C Philippines Neolithic settlement

Bahariya Oasis　W Egypt early cultivation

Baia Farta　SW Africa, Angola Acheulian tools

Baijiacun　N China E Chou cemetery

Baile Herculane　Romania Mesolithic settlement

Bailongdong　N China *Homo erectus*

Baimasi　W China E Chou burial, Ming tomb

Baimiaofancun　N China E Chou bronze hoard

Bairat　N India early city

Baishizidi　E China E Chou burial

Baitu　N China Tang kiln

Baker's Hole　SE England early tools

Baksei Chamkrong　Cambodia transitional settlement

Bala　W Egypt temple

Balakot　NW India Indus Valley settlement, early city, Harappan site

Balasore　E India early trade

Balat　W Egypt noble's tomb

Baldegg　Switzerland lake dwelling

Balfarg　NE Scotland stone circle and henge

Balita (modern Varkkallai)　S India early trade

Balkåkra　S Sweden metalwork

Balkh (Bactra, Zariaspa)　Afghanistan Islamic town, early trade

Ballmoos　E Switzerland pollen core site

Ballochroy　W Scotland stone circle

Ballynagilly　N Ireland pollen core site

Ballynoe　NE Ireland stone circle

Ballyscullion　N Ireland pollen core site

Balmori　N Spain shell midden

Balomir　C Romania copper

Baluchistan　Indus civilization

Balve Höhle　W Germany Neanderthal site

Balyma　C Russia steppe settlement

Bamako　W Africa, Mali Islamic trade, early settlement, early town

Bambata Cave　SE Africa, Zimbabwe Stone Age tools, Stone Age site

Bamiyan　Afghanistan Buddhist site, rock-carved temple

Bampur　SE Persia Achaemenid city

Ban Chiang　NE Thailand early plow, transitional settlement, moated site

Ban Don Ta Phet　C Thailand early site

Ban Kao Caves　S Thailand cave site

Ban Kao　C Thailand early metal site

Ban Muang Fai　C Thailand moated site

Ban Na Di　N Thailand transitional settlement

Ban Prasat　N Thailand transitional settlement

Ban Ta Luang　N Thailand transitional settlement

Ban Tamyae　C Thailand transitional settlement, moated site

Ban Thamen Chai　C Thailand moated site

Banahilk　N Mesopotamia pottery remains

Banavali   N India Indus Valley settlement, Harappan site

Banavasi   W India Deccan city

Banbhore   NW India Islamic port

Bandarawela   S Ceylon Mesolithic site

Bandwai   N Mesopotamia Assyrian rock relief

Banepi (Ngalo)   Solomon Is. Lapita site

Banjul   see Bathurst

Banks I.   Solomon Is. Lapita obsidian

Bañolas   N Spain Neanderthal site

Banpo   N China early settlement, early kiln

Bantam   E Indies, Java maritime trade

Banteay Prei Nokor   Cambodia early monumental site

Banting   SE Canada fluted points

Baofeng   N China Sung kiln

Baoji   N China Chou burial

Baozitou   SW China early pottery

Baqitun   N China E Chou cemetery

Bara-Bahou   C France hunter-gatherer art

Barakaccha   NE India Mesolithic site

Barake   NW India early trade

Barapedi cave   S India Mesolithic site

Barasimla   C India Mesolithic site

Barbaricum (Barbarikon)   NW India early trade center

Barbas   C France Neanderthal site

Barbegal   S France Roman water mill

Barca   Czechoslovakia hunter-gatherer site, fortified site

Barca (Barke)   NE Africa Greek colony

Barcelona   NE Spain medieval trade

Barclodiad y Gawres   N Wales megalithic tomb

Bard-i Nishandah   W Persia fire temple

Barger-Oosterveld   N Holland early temple

Bärhorst   E Germany early settlement

Bari   S Italy archbishopric

Baringo   E Africa, Kenya early man

Barium (modern Bari)   S Italy Roman empire

Barleben   E Germany early tools

Barlovento   N Colombia early settlement

Barm-I Dalak   S Persia rock relief

Barnack   E England beaker burial

Barnaul   S Siberia steppe settlement

Barnenez (Barnénès)   NW France megalithic tomb

Baror   NW India Harappan site

Barqa   N Africa, Libya Islamic town

Barrancas   C Venezuela early horticultural village

Barranc Blanc   E Spain hunter-gatherer site

Barton Ramie   Belize Maya settlement

Barumini   Sardinia fortified site

Barus   N Sumatra early port

Barygaza (Eng. Broach, Bharuch)   NW India early trade

Basi   Corsica farming site, early pottery

Basketmaker culture   N America

Basra   S Mesopotamia Islamic port, Sinan mosque

Bass Point   SE Australia early man

Bassae   SW Greece temple

Basse-Yutz   NE France Celtic site

Bastam   E Anatolia Urartian fortress

Bastura Chai   N Mesopotamia tunnel

Bat Cave   SW USA, New Mexico Archaic site, Pueblo farming site

Báta   C Hungary Celtic site

Batavia (Jakarta)   E Indies, Java early trade

Bathurst (Banjul)   W Africa, Sierra Leone early port

Bathurst Head   NE Australia Aboriginal site

Batu Buruk   C Malaya transitional settlement

Batu Ejaya   S Celebes early metal site

Batungan   C Philippines Neolithic settlement

Bau Tro   N Vietnam Neolithic settlement

Bau-de-l'Aubesier   SE France Neanderthal site

Baulmes   Switzerland Mesolithic settlement

Baum   E USA temple mound

Bauma-Bonne   SE France early tools, Neanderthal site

Baumhoff's Rock Shelter   SW USA, Nevada prehistoric diet

Baz-i Hur   NE Persia fire-temple

Bazitou   SW China cave site

Beaker burials   Europe

Bear Is   E Russia Thule site

Beaumetz-lès-Loges   N France early tools

Beaurieux   NE France Iron Age cemetery

Beauvais   N France Viking mint

Becan   E Mexico Maya center

Bédeilhac   SW France hunter-gatherer art

Bedford   C USA, Illinois Hopewell site

Bedsa   S India rock-carved temple

Begho   W Africa, Ghana early city

Beginners Luck Cave   SE Australia early man

Begram (Bagram, Kapisa)   Afghanistan Graeco-Bactrian city, early trade center

Behistun (Bisitun)   NW Persia rock inscription, Hercules relief, rock relief

Beicaogou   E China E Chou burial

Beicaopo   N China Chou burial

Beidha   S Palestine Natufian and Neolithic site

Beisamoun   S Syria Neolithic site

Beishouling   N China early settlement

Beit el-Wali   U Egypt temple

Beixinbao   NE China E Chou cemetery

Beiyinyangying   E China early settlement, Longshan site

Beizhou   N China Tang prefecture

Békásmegyer   E Hungary Copper Age cemetery

Bel'kacha   E Russia arctic culture

Belbasi   SW Anatolia Palaeolithic site, early pottery

Belcher   S USA temple mound

Beldibi   SW Anatolia Palaeolithic site, early pottery

Belevi   W Anatolia Hellenistic mausoleum

Bell   N Canada Thule site

Bella   N England medieval village

Bellefonds   C France Mesolithic settlement

Belle-Roche   Belgium early tools

Bellona I.   Solomon Is. Lapita site

Bellote   E Mexico Maya settlement

Bellows Beach   Hawaiian Is. early site

Bellsås   N Sweden Mesolithic settlement

Belsk   Ukraine Greek imports

Beluga Point   Alaska Pacific Eskimo site

Belur   S India Hindu religious site

Bendemeer   E Australia Aboriginal site

Ben Do   S Vietnam Neolithic settlement

Benevento (Beneventum)   C Italy archbishopric

Beneventum (modern Benevento)   C Italy Roman empire

Benguela   SW Africa, Angola Acheulian tools

Beni Hasan   U Egypt noble's tomb

Bennekom   S Holland corded ware burial

Bent   NE USA, New York Archaic site

Benten   N Japan Ainu Hillfort

Berbati   S Greece tholos tomb

Berdyzh   W Russia hunter-gatherer site

Bërëlëkh   E Russia hunter-gatherer art

Berenice   Red Sea ancient port, early trade center

Berestnyagi   Ukraine Greek imports

Berezan   Ukraine Greek imports

Berezhnovka   C Russia steppe settlement

Berezovka   E Russia barrow burial

Bergamo   N Italy Celtic oppidum

Beringia   Asia-America land bridge

Berkeley Point   NW Canada Thule site

Berkhat-Ram   S Syria early tools

Bern-Engelhalbinsel   C Switzerland Celtic oppidum

Bernifal   C France hunter-gatherer art

Beroea (modern Aleppo)   C Syria Hellenistic city

Berry-au-Bac   NE France Iron Age settlement, defensive enclosure

Berytus (Beruta, modern Beirut)   Lebanon Phoenician city

Berzine   W Syria early tools

Besançon   E France Celtic oppidum, archbishopric

Bechtasheni   SW Russia steppe settlement

Besuki   E Java early metal site

Betatakin   SW US Pueblo farming site

Beth-shan (Beth-shean, Scythopolis)   N Palestine Egyptian fortress, Levantine city and temple

Betijoque   NW Venezuela early settlement

Betulov Spodmol   Yugoslavia Mesolithic settlement

Buene Valley   C France pollen core site

Beverley   N England medieval town

Beycesultan   W Anatolia farming site

Bezeklik   NW China rock-carved temple

Bhagatrav   NW India Harappan site

Bhaja   S India rock-carved temple

Bhimbetka   C India Mesolithic site

Bhogavardhana   W India Deccan city

Biache-Saint-Vaast   N France early tools and human remains

Bianzhou   N China Tang perfecture

Biepi   W Africa, Nigeria early town

Bigo   E Africa, Uganda Iron Age site

Bihourel   N France early tools

Bilbilis (modern Catalayud)   C Spain native settlement

Billig (Belgica)   W Germany Roman village

Bilma   C Africa, Niger Acheulian tools, early settlement, early town

Bilzingsleben   E Germany early tools and human remains

Bingley   N England medieval town

Binglingsi   NW China rock-carved temple

Birbhanpur   E India Mesolithic site

Birch   Michigan Archaic site

Birdlip   W England Celtic oppidium

Birdsall   N England medieval village

Birka   S Sweden Islamic trade, Viking trading emporium

Birkalein   E Anatolia tunnel

Birkenfeld   W Germany Roman village

Birket Habu   U Egypt artificial harbor

Birnin Gazargamu   W Africa, Nigeria early town

Bir Sahara   NE Africa, Egypt Acheulian tools, Stone Age tools

Birsay   Orkney Is. Viking center

Birsmatten   Switzerland Mesolithic settlement, megalithic site

Bir Tarfawi   Egypt Acheulian tools, Stone Age tools

Bisceglie   S Italy, Neanderthal site, megalithic tomb

Bishapur   SW Persia, Sasanian city

Bismantova   N Italy urnfield

Bisovaya   C Russia hunter-gatherer site

Bissau   Guinea-Bissau early port

Bitburg (Beda)   W Germany Roman village

Bitorri Cave   Congo hunter-gatherers

Biysk   S Siberia steppe settlement

Bizen   C Japan pottery kiln

Bizerta   N Tunisia, Carthaginian city

Bjerre   N Denmark flint mine

Black Head   New Zealand, North I. early site

Black Patch   SE England flint mine

Black Rocks   New Zealand, North I. shell midden

Blackburn   S Africa Iron Age site

Blackwater Draw   Texas Palaeo-Indian site

Blaka Kallia   Chad Acheulian tools

Blea Tarn   NW England pollen core site

Blisnietsova Cave   C Russia hunter-gatherer site

Blistrup   E Denmark musical instruments

Bloody Fall   N Canada Thule site

Blucina   W Czechoslovakia fortified site

Bluefish Cave   NW Canada early settlement

Blue Jay   Zimbabwe Iron Age site

Bluff   SW USA Pueblo farming site

Bobo Dioulasso   Burkina early town

Boca del Rio   SE Mexico early farming site

Bockstein   S Germany Neanderthal site

Bodo   Ethiopia *Homo erectus*

Boelkilde   SW Germany bog body

Boeotia   ancient country of C Greece

Bogazköy   C Anatolia Assyrian colony, early writing, Hittite city

Bogdnovka   C Russia barrow burial

Bogong Cave   SE Australia Aboriginal site

Bohai   N China Han city

Boirra   New Caledonia Lapita site

Bois du Rocher   NW France Neanderthal site

Bolkar Dag   S Anatolia Neolithic site

Bol'shaya Rechka   S Siberia steppe settlement

Bol'shoy Ulagan   E Russia barrow burial

Bolton   N England medieval town

Bomaderry   SE Australia Aboriginal site

Bombo Kaburi   Tanzania Iron Age site

Bonampak   E Mexico Maya settlement

Bonna (modern Bonn)   NW Germany Roman legionary fortress

Bono Manso   Ghana early town

Bononia (modern Bologna)   N Italy Roman city

Bonteberg   S Africa Stone Age site

Boomborg-Hatzum   NE Holland terp settlement

Boomplaas   S Africa Stone Age tools

Boone   Iowa Hopewell site

Boppard (Boudobriga)   W Germany Roman village

Boqer Takhtit   Israel Stone Age tools

Borax Lake   California Archaic site

Borazjan   S Persia Achaemenid palace

Borba   C Brazil early settlement

Border Cave   S Africa Stone Age tools

Borg in-Nadur   Malta fortified site

Borj Qinnarit   Lebanon early tools

Borneo   early settlement, early metal sites, early ports

Borno   Nigeria early state

Borodayevka   C Russia steppe settlement

Borodino   SW Russia metal hoard

Boroughbridge   N England medieval town

Borremose   NW Denmark early settlement

Borum Eshoj   W Denmark barrow burial

Bosa   Sardinia Carthaginian city

Bostra (modern Busra)   S Syria Roman provincial capital

Bosumpra Cave   Ghana early food

Bouar   C Africa early settlement
Bouga   C Greece tholos tomb
Bougon   W France megalithic tomb
Boun Marcou   S France beaker burial
Bou Nouara   NE Algeria megalithic tomb
Bouqras   SE Syria Neolithic site, early pottery
Boussargues   S France ancient fortress
Boviolles   NE France Celtic oppidum
Boxgrove   S England early tools
Boy Tepe   E Anatolia Neolithic site
Brahmagiri   S India megalithic tomb
Branc   E Czechoslovakia Copper Age cemetery
Brand   Arkansas Archaic site
Brandskogen   C Sweden rock art
Brankysek   W Czechoslovakia corded ware burial
Brass   Nigeria early town
Brassempouy   SW France hunter-gatherer art
Bratislava   C Czechoslovakia Celtic site
Braughing   E England Celtic oppidum
Braunsberg   E Austria Celtic oppidum
Brauron   SE Greece ancient harbor
Bredmose   NW Denmark bog body
Breisach (Hochstetten)   W Germany Celtic site
Brenig   N Wales barrow burial
Brescia   N Italy Celtic oppidum
Bretteville-le-Rabet   N France flint mine
Brigetio (modern Szony)   Hungary Roman legionary fortress
Brili   SW Russia steppe settlement
Brillenhöhle   W Germany hunter-gatherer site
Brno   Czechoslovakia hunter-gatherer art
Broach (Barygaza)   W India early city
Broadbeach   E Australia Aboriginal site
Brodgar, Ring of   Orkney Is. stone circle and henge
Broederstroom   S Africa Iron Age site
Brohm   Ontario Archaic site
Broken K Pueblo   SW USA early settlement, Pueblo farming site
Bronocice   S Poland corded ware burial
Brooks River   Alaska arctic culture
Broom   S England early tools
Broxbourne   SE England Mesolithic settlement
Brundisium (modern Brindisi)   S Italy Roman city
Bruniquel   SE France hunter-gatherer site

Bryncelli Ddu   N Wales megalithic tomb
Buang Bep   S Thailand early metal site
Bubanj Hum   E Yugoslavia tell settlement
Bubastis   L Egypt ancient city
Buchanan   N Canada Dorset site
Bucy-le-Long   NE France Iron Age settlement
Budakalász   W Hungary Copper Age cemetery
Büdelsdorf   N Germany defensive enclosure
Budino   N Spain early tools
Buhen   U Egypt early city, ancient city, fortification
Bui Ceri Uato   SE Indonesia Timor cave site, Neolithic settlement
Bukit Chuping   N Malaya cave site
Bukit Tengu Lembu   N Malaya early metal site
Bulbjerg   N Denmark Bronze Age settlement
Bull Brook   Massachusetts Paleo-Indian site
Bulltofta   SW Sweden barrow burial
Buni Complex   W Java early metal site
Burdigala (modern Bordeaux)   W France Roman provincial capital
Buret   E Russia hunter-gatherer art
Bürgäschisee-Süd   NW Switzerland farming settlement
Burke's Cave   C Australia Aboriginal site
Burrill Lake   SE Australia early man
Bush Barrow   S England barrow burial
Bushman Rockshelter   S Africa Stone Age tools
Bussa   Nigeria early town
Bust   Afghanistan Parthian/Sasanian city
Buto   L Egypt ancient city
Button Point   NE Canada Dorset site
Buxentum (Pyxous, Pyxus)   S Italy Roman colony
Buzhaozhai   N China Longshan site
Bwana Mkubwa   Zambia Iron Age site
Byblos (Gubla)   SW Syria Neolithic site, Phoenician city, Achaemenid city
Byci Skala   C Czechoslovakia vehicle burial
Bykovo   C Russia steppe settlement
Bynum   Mississippi Hopewell site
Caballito Blanco   C Mexico stone source
Cabeco da Arruda   C Portugal megalithic tomb

Cabeza del Plomo   SE Spain ancient fortress
Cacamahuilpa   C Mexico Pre-Classical site
Cacheu   Guinea-Bissau early port
Caddington   S England early tools
Caere (modern Cerveteri)   C Italy Etruscan city
Caesaraugusta (modern Zaragoza)   NE Spain Roman city
Caesarea (modern Cherchell)   N Algeria Roman provincial capital
Caesarea Cappadociae (modern Kayseri)   C Anatolia Roman provincial capital, Byzantine bishopric
Caesarea Maritima   W Palestine Roman provincial capital
Caf Taht el Ghar   Morocco farming site, beaker burial
Cafer Hüyük   E Anatolia Neolithic site
Cagny-la Garenne   N France early tools
Cahokia   C USA temple mound
Cahuachi   S Peru Paracas site
Cahyup   C Guatemala Maya settlement
Caimito   N Peru early settlement
Cairnpapple   E Scotland stone circle
Cajamarca   N Peru Middle Horizon site, Inca center
Cajamarquilla   C Peru pyramid, Middle Horizon site, Inca center
Caka   E Czechoslovakia barrow burial
Calabar   W Africa, Nigeria early town
Calakmul   Mexico, Yucatán Maya settlement
calcite sources   Egypt
Calico Hills   SW USA early settlement
Calicut (Kozhikode)   SW India Mesolithic site, maritime trade
Calixtlahuaca   C Mexico pyramid, Pre-Classical site, Aztec town
Callanish   NW Scotland stone circle and alignment
Callao   Peru maritime trade
Calleva (modern Silchester)   S England Roman city
Callipolis   S Thrace Byzantine town
Calpulalpan   C Mexico early town
Calydon   C Greece temple
Camargo   NW Spain hunter-gatherer site
Camarina (Kamarina)   S Sicily Greek colony
Cambous   S France farming settlement, early settlement
Cameixa   N Portugal native settlement
Cameron Creek   SW USA Pueblo farming site

Camerota   S Italy Neanderthal site
Caminade   C France Neanderthal site
Caminero   C France Neanderthal site
Camirus   E Mediterranean Hellenistic
city
Camp d'Artus   NW France Celtic
oppidum
Camp de Caledon   NE France Celtic
oppidum
Camp de Laure   SE France ancient
fortress
Camprafaud   SW France farming site
Camster Long   N Scotland megalithic
tomb
**Camulodunum (modern
Colchester)**   SE England Roman city
Camutins   E Brazil early settlement
Can Llobateres   NE Spain Dryopithecus
Can Ponsic   NE Spain Dryopithecus
Canca   E Anatolia Ottoman mint
Cancuén   C Guatemala Maya settlement
Candamo   NW Spain hunter-gatherer art
Çandir   N Anatolia Ramapithecus and
Sivapithecus
Cane   SW Arabia early trade
Canegrate   N Italy urnfield
Cañete   S Peru Paracas site
Cangzhou   N China Tang prefecture
Canhasan   S Anatolia Neolithic site,
farming site
Cannonball Island   NW USA midden
Cañon de la Mano   C Mexico Pre-
Classical site
Cantalouette   C France early tools
Canterbury   New Zealand, South I.
rock art
Canterbury   SE England archbishopric
and pilgrimage center
Canton (Guangzhou)   S China early
trade center, Islamic trade, Buddhist
center, Ming provincial capital
**Canusium (modern Canosa di
Puglia)**   S Italy Roman empire
Canyon de Chelly   SW USA Pueblo
farming site
Caoxieshan   E China early settlement,
rice farming site
Cap Blanc   C France hunter-gatherer
site, hunter-gatherer art
Cap Blanc   N Africa, Tunisia Stone Age
tools
Cap Ragnon   S France early pottery
Capacna   C Mexico early farming site
Cape Andreas   Cyprus Neolithic site
Cape Bol'shoy Baranov   E Russia
Thule site
Cape Bon   N Tunisia Carthaginian site

Cape Coast Castle   W Africa, Ghana
early port
Cape Denbigh   Alaska Thule site
Cape Dorset   E Canada Dorset site
Cape Hangklip   S Africa Acheulian
tools
Cape Kellett   NW Canada Thule site
Cape Krusenstern   Alaska Thule site
Cape Nome   Alaska Thule site
Cape Prince of Wales   Alaska Thule
site
Capelletti   N Africa, Algeria early cattle
Capertee   SE Australia Aboriginal site
Cappadocians   Ancient people of E
Anatolia
Capsa (modern Gafsa)   S Tunisia
Roman city
Capua   C Italy Roman city,
archbishopric
Caracas   Venezuela colonial settlement
Caracol   Belize Maya settlement
Caralis (Carales, modern Cagliari)   S
Sardinia Greek colony
Carapito   N Portugal megalithic tomb
Carchemish   E Anatolia early city,
Assyrian provincial capital
Cardia (Kardia)   NW Turkey Greek
colony
Carenque   W Portugal rock-cut tomb
Caria   ancient country of SW Anatolia
Carians   ancient people of SW Anatolia
Carigüela   S Spain Neanderthal site
Cariüela de Piñar   S Spain farming
settlement
Çark'in   SW Anatolia Palaeolithic site,
early pottery
Carlisle   N England monastery
Carnac   NE France stone circle and
alignment
**Carnuntum (modern
Deutschaltenburg)**   Austria Roman
provincial capital and legionary fortress
Carrhae (modern Harran)   N
Mesopotamia
Carrión de los Condes   N Spain
monastery
Carrowmore   W Ireland megalithic
tomb
Cartagena   Colombia maritime trade
Carthage (Carthago)   N Tunisia
Phoenician city, Carthaginian city,
Roman provincial capital, Roman
aqueduct, early iron, early trade
**Carthago Nova (modern
Cartagena)**   SE Spain Roman city
Casa Grande   SW USA Pueblo farming
site

Casa San Paola   S Italy early pottery
Casainhos   W Portugal megalithic tomb
Casarabe   C Brazil early settlement
Cashel   S Ireland archbishopric
Casma   C Peru Chavín site
Casmenae (Kasmenai)   E Sicily Greek
colony
Casper   W USA, Wyoming bison kill
site
Caspians   ancient people of C Asia
Cassenga   C Africa, Angola Oldowan
tools
Cassington   S England beaker burial
Castelluccio   Sicily rock-cut tomb and
bone artefacts
Castillo   NW Spain early tools, hunter-
gatherer site, hunter-gatherer art
Castillon   N France Celtic oppidum
Castle Cavern   S Africa Iron Age site
Castle Eden   NE England claw beaker
Castle Hill   New Zealand, South I. rock
art
Castlepoint   New Zealand, North I.
shell midden
Castlerigg   NW England stone circle
Castlerock   N Ireland bog body
Castrum Novum   C Italy Roman
empire
Çatal Hüyük   S Anatolia Neolithic site,
early pottery
Çatalca   NW Turkey Sinan mosque
Catana (Katana, modern Catania)   E
Sicily Greek colony
Cathedral Cave   E Australia Aboriginal
site
Catigny   N France Neanderthal site
Cau Sat   S Vietnam Neolithic settlement
Caucasus   Early hominids
Caulonia (Kaulonia)   S Italy Greek
colony
Caúma   C Africa, Angola Oldowan
tools
Caunus   SW Anatolia Hellenistic city
Cave Pompi   C Italy early tools and
human remains
Çavdarhisar   W Anatolia Roman dam
Cave Bay Cave   SE Australia early man
Cave Creek   SW USA Pueblo farming
site
Cave of Hearths   S Africa early man,
Stone Age tools
Ca'Verde   N Italy Neanderthal site
Çavustepe   E Anatolia Urartian fortress
Çayönü   E Anatolia Neolithic site
Cedral   N Mexico early settlement
Ceiba Grande   SE Mexico Pre-Classical
site

Cejkov   Czechoslovakia hunter-gatherer site

Celebes   early settlement, Neolithic settlement

Cellino San Marco   SE Italy rock-cut tomb

Cemenelum   SE France Roman provincial capital

Cempoala   C Mexico pyramid, Aztec town

Centenillo   C Spain Roman mines

Centumcellae (modern Civitavecchia)   C Italy Roman city

Cephisia (Kephissia)   SE Greece Athenian settlement

Cercinitis (Kephissia)   S Russia Hellenistic city

Cernavoda   E Romania Copper Age cemetery

Cernica   C Romania Copper Age cemetery

Cerrig Duon   S Wales stone alignment

Chak Purbane Syal   NW India Harappan site

Chakipamka   S Peru Middle Horizon site

Chalcatzingo   C Mexico Pre-Classical site

Chalcedon (modern Kadiköy)   N Anatolia Greek colony, Byzantine town

Chalchihuites   C Mexico early town

Chalchuapa   El Salvador Pre-Classical site, Maya settlement

Chalcis   SE Greece city-state

Chalco   C Mexico Aztec center

Chale Gar   W Persia early copper mine

Chalk Hollow   S USA, Texas Archaic site

Challans   W France metal hoard

Chalon   E France Celtic site

Chaluka   Aleutian Is. arctic culture

Chamá   C Guatemala Maya settlement

Champ Durand   W France defensive enclosure

Champotón   Mexico, Yucatán Maya settlement, early town

Chan Chan   NW Peru pyramid, Inca capital

Chan Sen   N Thailand transitional settlement, moated site, early site

Chanapata   SE Peru early farming site

Chancelade   C France hunter-gatherer site

Chandragiri   S India Vijayanagara center

Chang'an (Xian)   N China early trade capital, Han city, Islamic trade, Tang capital

Changbong-do   N Korea early settlement

Changge   N China early settlement

Changling   NE China Ming tomb

Changsha   C China Han kingdom, Buddhist center, Tang kiln

Changshan   N China Han city

Changtaiguan   C China E Chou burial

Changzhou   E China Tang prefecture

Chanhu-Daro   NW India early city, Harappan site

Channel Is.   standing stones

Chantsa   NE Greece Mycenaean fortress

Chao'an   SE China cave site, Tang kiln

Chaozhou   S China Sung kiln

Charakopio   SW Greece tholos tomb

Charanke   N Japan Ainu hill fort

Charavines   SE France farming settlement

Charax   S Mesopotamia Hellenistic city

Charleston   E USA, S Carolina colonial settlement

Charlottetown   E Canada, Prince Edward I. colonial settlement

Charsadda (Charsada)   NW India Archaemenid city, Graeco-Bactrian city, early city, early trade center

Chartres   N France archbishopric

Charukorohoi   N Japan Ainu hill fort

Chassemy   NE France Iron Age settlement

Chassey   E France defensive enclosure

Châteauneuf-lès-Martigues   SE France Mesolithic settlement, farming site

Châteauneuf-sur-Charente   C France Neanderthal site

Châtelperron   E France hunter-gatherer site

Chau Say Tevoda   Cambodia Neolithic settlement

Chavez Pass Ruins   SW USA Pueblo farming site

Chavín de Huantar   C Peru pyramid, Chavín site

Chedzurgwe   E Africa, Zimbabwe Iron Age site

Chegitun   E Russia Thule site

Chekka Jdidé   Lebanon Neanderthal site

Chelles   N France early tools

Chelyabinsk   C Russia steppe settlement

Chemagal   E Africa, Kenya Iron Age site

Chemeron   E Africa, Kenya Australopithecus

Chenachane   N Africa, Algeria wavy-line pottery

Chengdu   W China Han city, Buddhist center, Tang prefecture, Ming provincial capital

Chengdufu   W China provincial capital

Chengqiao   E China E Chou burial

Chengzlya   N China Han city

Chenliu   N China Han city

Chercheli   N Algeria Roman aqueduct

Cheremushny   W Russia barrow burial

Chermoozerye   C Russia barrow burial

Chernovaya   S Siberia steppe settlement

Chersonesus (Khersonesos, modern Kherson, Cherson)   S Russia Hellenistic city, Byzantine town

Chertomlyk (Alekseyevka)   SW Russia barrow burial

Chervonyy Yar   SW Russia barrow burial

Chesowanja   E Africa, Kenya *Australopithecus robustus*, Oldowan tools

Chester (Deva)   N England Viking mint

Chetumal   Mexico, Yucatán Aztec trade center

Chevdar   W Bulgaria farming site

Chezarla   S India Buddhist site

Chezieu   E France Celtic site

Chhani Sahnpal   NW India Mughal mint

Chiapa de Corzo   SE Mexico early farming site, Maya settlement, early town

Chiautla   C Mexico Aztec center

Chibuene   SE Africa, Mozambique Islamic trading post

Chicama   N Peru Chavín site

Chichén Itzá   E Mexico sacred cenote, Maya settlement, early town

Chiconautla   C Mexico Aztec center

Chidambaram   S India Hindu religious site

Chiem Son   S Vietnam early site

Chiengmai   N Thailand Buddhist center

Chigna Jota   S Peru Inca center

Chikayevo   E Russia arctic culture

Chikugo   W Japan shogunate provincial capital

Chilca   S Peru early farming, preceramic site

Chilecito   N Argentina Inca tambo

Chilhac   C France early tools

Chiliktinskaya   E Russia barrow burial

Chimalhuacán   C Mexico Aztec center

Chimney Rock Mesa   SW USA Pueblo farming site

Chimú empire   S America

China Lake   NW USA fluted points

Chinguetti   W Africa, Mauritania early town

Chiniot   NW India Mughal mint

Chinkultic   SE Mexico Pre-Classical site, Maya settlement

Chinooka   C Japan Yamato tomb

Chios   C Aegean Greek city

Chiozza   N Italy hunter-gatherer art

Chiquitoy Viejo   N Peru Inca tambo

Chirand   E India later farming village

Chirikof I.   Alaska Pacific Eskimo site

Chitam-ni   N Korea early settlement

Chobi   E Africa, Uganda Iron Age site

Chocolá   S Guatemala Maya settlement

Choga Mami   Mesopotamia pottery remains, irrigation canal

Choga Mish   W Persia early settlement, early kiln, early settlement

Choga Sefid   W Persia early settlement

Choga Zanbil   W Persia pyramid

Chokurcha   S Russia Neanderthal site

Chola empire   S India

Chollerford Bridge   N England Roman water mill

Cholula   C Mexico pyramid, early town

Chondwe   C Africa, Zambia Iron Age site

Chongok-ni   N Korea early Palaeolithic site, early settlement

Chongoyape   N Peru Chavín site

Chopani-Mando   NE India Mesolithic site

Chorasmians   Ancient people of NE Persia

Christos   S Crete Minoan village

Chrysovitsa   NW Greece tholos tomb

Chucalisssa   SE USA temple mound

Chucuito   S Peru Inca center

Chufin   NW Spain hunter-gatherer art

Chugachik   Alaska Pacific Eskimo site

Chukhurkabala   S Russia steppe settlement

Chuluwasi   W Africa, Ghana early settlement

Chumnungwa   E Africa, Zimbabwe Iron Age site

Chup Thmar Pich   Cambodia Neolithic settlement

Chupas   SE Peru early farming site

Chupíuaro   C Mexico early farming site

Chust   C Asia steppe settlement

Chutixtiox   C Guatemala Maya settlement

Chyulu   E Africa, Kenya Iron Age site

Ciftlik   SE Anatolia Neolithic site

Cilicians   ancient people of S Anatolia

Cilvituk   Mexico, Yucatán Maya settlement

Cipolliane di Novaghie   SE Italy Mesolithic settlement

Circeo   C Italy Neanderthal site

Cirta (modern Constantine)   N Algeria Roman provincial capital

Ciry-Salsogne   NE France Iron Age cemetery

Cishan   N China early settlement, early pottery

Cissbury   S England flint mine, Celtic hill fort

Citania de Briteiros   N Portugal native settlement

Cité-de-Limes   NE France Celtic oppidum

Citium (Kition)   Cyprus early port, Assyrian stela

Citrus   SW USA Pueblo farming site

Cizhou (Cixian)   N China Sung kiln

Clacton   SE England early tools

Claiborne   S USA, Mississippi Archaic site

Clairvaux-les-Lacs   E France farming settlement

Clarence River Mouth   New Zealand, South I. defended settlement

Clava   N Scotland megalithic tomb

Clavering I.   NE Greenland Thule site

Clay Mound   E USA temple mound

Claypool   W USA, Colorado Palaeo-Indian site

Clazomenae (Klazomenai)   W Anatolia Greek city

Clermont-Ferrand   C France Celtic site

Clifden   New Zealand, South I. rock art

Clogg's Cave   SE Australia early man, Aboriginal site

Clovis   C USA fluted points

Clunia   C Spain native settlement

Cluny   E France abbey

Clusium (modern Chiusi)   C Italy Etruscan city

Cmielów   C Poland farming settlement

Cnidus (Knidos)   SE Aegean Greek city

Co Loa   N Vietnam transitional settlement, early site

Coari   C Brazil early settlement

Coatepec   C Mexico Aztec center

Coatlinchán   C Mexico Aztec center

Cobá   Mexico, Yucatán Maya settlement, early town

Cochabamba   N Bolivia Inca center

Cochin   SW India maritime trade

Cogull   NE Spain Mesolithic settlement

Cohuna   SE Australia early man

Coimbra   N Portugal monastery

Coincy   N France Mesolithic settlement

Col du Coq   SE France Mesolithic settlement

Colchester (Camulodunum)   E England Celtic oppidum, slik find

Colchi (Kayal, Korkai)   S India early trade

Coles Creek   S USA temple mound

Colless Creek   C Australia Aboriginal site

Coloe   N Ethiopia early trade

Colonai Agrippina (modern Köln, Eng Cologne)   NW Germany Roman city

Colophon (Kolophon)   W Anatolia Greek city

Columbeira   Portugal Neanderthal site

Columnata   NW Africa, Algeria hunter-gatherers

Comalcalco   E Mexico Maya settlement

Combarelles   C France hunter-gatherer art

Combe Capelle   C France hunter-gatherer site

Combe-Grenal   C France early tools, Neanderthal site

Comenda   SE Portugal megalithic tomb

Compiègne   N France Viking mint

Concobar   NW Persia Parthian city

cone mosaics   Mesopotamia

Conelle   C Italy early settlement

Conimbriga (modern Coimbra)   C Portugal native settlement

Con Moong   N Indo-China cave site

Constantine   N Algeria Roman aqueduct

Constantinople (Byzantium)   NW Turkey Roman empire, early trading capital, Byzantine capital, Islamic town

Consuegra   C Spain Roman dam

Conthey   Switzerland silk find

Conza   C Italy archbishopric

Copán   Honduras pyramid, Maya center

Coppa Nevigata   S Italy shell midden, farming site

Coptus (Koptos)   L Egypt early trade

Corbiac   C France hunter-gatherer site

Corcyra (modern Kerkira)   NW Greece Greek colony

Córdoba (Corduba)   S Spain Islamic town

Cordova Ridge   SW USA Pueblo farming site

Cork   S Ireland Viking center, bishopric

Cornelia   S Africa Acheulian tools

Corozal   C Venezuela early settlement

Cortaillod   W Switzerland farming settlement

Cortes de Navarra   N Spain Bronze Age settlement

Cortona   N Italy Etruscan city
Cos (Kos, Asclepius)   SE Aegean Greek city, sanctuary
Cosenza   S Italy archbishopric
Cottingham   N England medieval town
Cotzumalhuapa   E Mexico Maya town
Cougnac   C France hunter-gatherer art
Cova Negra   E Spain early tools and human remains
Coventina's Well   N England Celtic religious site
Coveta de l'Or   E Spain farming site
Cow Point   E Canada, New Brunswick Archaic site
Cowick   N England medieval pottery
Coxcatlán   C Mexico early settlement, early cave settlement
Coyoacán   C Mexico Aztec center
Coyotopec   C Mexico Aztec center
Coyuca de Catalán   C Mexico Pre-Classical site
Cozumel   Mexico, Yucatán early town
Crab Orchard   C USA, Illinois Hopewell site
Cracow   Poland hunter-gatherer site
Crag Point   Alaska Pacific Eskimo site
Craig Harbor   NE Canada Thule site
Cranganore   S India early city
Crayford   S England early tools
Cremona   N Italy Celtic oppidum, Roman city
Cresap   NE USA, Pennsylvania Adena site
Crestaulta   Switzerland Bronze Age settlement
Crewe   N England railway development
Crkvina   N Yugoslavia Neanderthal site
Cro-Magnon   C France hunter-gatherer site
Cromford   C England planned industrial settlement
Crooked Ridge   SW USA Pueblo farming site
Cross River   W Africa, Nigeria monoliths
Crouy   NE France Iron Age cemetery
Crozon   NW France Celtic oppidum
Cruz del Negro   SW Spain Carthaginian cemetery
Crvena Stijena   SW Yugoslavia Mesolithic settlement, farming site
Crystall II   E Canada Thule site
Crystal River   SE USA, Florida Hopewell site
Ctesiphon   C Mesopotamia Parthian/Sasanian capital
Cu Lao Rua   S Vietnam transitional settlement

Cuautitlán   C Mexico Aztec center
Cuautla   C Mexico early town
Cudi Dag   E Anatolia Assyrian rock relief
Cuello   C America, Belize early farming settlement, Maya settlement
Cuernavaca   C Mexico pyramid
Cueva blanca   C Mexico early settlement
Cueva de la Menga   S Spain megalithic tomb
Cueva de la Sarsa   E Spain farming site
Cueva de las Lechuzas   NE Peru early farming site
Cueva de Nerja   S Spain farming site
Cueva de Romeral   S Spain megalithic tomb
Cueva Media Luna   C Mexico Pre-Classical site
Cueva Morin   NW Spain Neanderthal site
Cueva Remigia   E Spain Mesolithic settlement
Cuicuilco   C Mexico Pre-Classical site
Cuina Turcului   Romania Mesolithic settlement
Cuiry-lès-Chaudardes   NE France farming site
Cukurkent   SW Anatolia Neolithic site
Culduthel Mains   N Scotland beaker burial
Culebras   N Peru Preceramic site
Culhuacan   C Mexico Aztec center
Cullalvera   NW Spain hunter-gatherer art
Culverwell   SW England shell midden, megalithic site
Cunani   NE Brazil early settlement
Cuplanique   N Peru Chavín site
Curacchiaghiu   Corsica farming site, early pottery
Curracurrang   SE Australia Aboriginal site
Currarong   SE Australia Aboriginal site
Curuá   E Brazil early settlement
Cusibamba   S Ecuador Inca center
Cuzco   S Peru Paracas site, Inca capital, trade
Cynosura (Kynosoura)   SE Greece Athenian settlement
Cyrene (Kyrene, modern Shahhat)   NE Africa Greek colony, Roman provincial capital
Cyrrhus (Kyrrhos)   SE Anatolia Hellenistic city, Roman city and legionary fortress
Cys-la-Commune   NE France Iron Age cemetery

Cyzicus   NW Anatolia Byzantine town
Da But   N Vietnam Neolithic settlement
Dabaotai   NE China Han burial
Dabarkot   NW India Harappan site
Daboya   W Africa, Ghana early town
Dacun   N China early settlement
Dadianzi   NE China E Chou cemetery
Dadiwan   NW China early pottery
Dadongze   N China early settlement
Dahan-i Ghulaman   E Persia Achaemenid palace
Dahe   N China Han city
Dahecun   N China early settlement
Dahlak Is.   Red Sea monolith
Dahshur   L Egypt pyramids, burial, royal capital
Daigi-gakoi   NE Japan early settlement
Daima   W Africa, Nigeria early livestock, Iron Age site, urban center, early town
Dainzu   SE Mexico early farming site, Pre-Classical site
Dakhla Oasis   NE Africa, Egypt Stone Age tools, early cultivation
Dal'verzin   C Asia steppe settlement
Dali   N China early man
Dalkey I.   E Ireland shell midden
Dalles   NW USA, Washington Archaic site
Dalton   C USA, Missouri Palaeo-Indian site
Daly River   N Australia Aboriginal site
Damascus   S Syria early town, Egyptian control, Assyrian provincial city, Hellenistic city, Roman city, early trade, Islamic town, Sinan mosque
Damb Sadaat   NW India Harappan site
Dambarare   E Africa, Zimbabwe Iron Age site
Dambwa   C Africa, Zimbabwe Iron Age site
Damghan   NE Persia Islamic town
Damingfu   N China provincial capital
Dammwiese   W Austria Celtic site
Dandara (Dendara, Tentyra)   U Egypt ancient cemetery
Danebury   S England Celtic hill fort
Danevirke   S Denmark Frontier dyke
Danger Cave   W USA, Utah Archaic site
Daojali Hading   E India later farming village
Dar es-Soltane   NW Africa, Morocco Stone Age tools
Dara   SW Greece tholos tomb
Dara   U Egypt pyramid
Dara-i-Kur   C Asia later farming village

Darabgird   S Persia Sasanian city

Dariush Kabir   SW Persia remains of bridge

Dastagird   C Mesopotamia Sasanian city

Datong   N China Buddhist center, Sung kiln

Daura   W Africa, Nigeria early town

Davding   W Denmark musical instruments

Davis   USA temple mound

Dawenkou   NE China early settlement, early kiln, Longshan site

Dawu   W Africa, Ghana early town

Daxi   N China early settlement

De Hangen   S Africa hunter-gatherers, Stone Age site

Debert   E Canada, Nova Scotia Palaeo-Indian site

Decelea (Dekeleia)   SE Greece Athenian settlement

Dedan   W Arabia early trade

Deepcar   C England mesolithic settlement

Deh Morasi Ghundai   Afghanistan later farming village

Dehua   SE China Sung kiln

Deir el-Gabrawi   U Egypt noble's tomb

Deir el-Malik   U Egypt noble's tomb

Deir el-Medina   U Egypt workmen's village

Delagoa Day   SE Africa, Mozambique maritime trade

Délébo   C Africa, Chad wavy-line pottery

Delhi   C India Mughal capital

Deling   NE China Ming tomb

Delos   S Aegean harbor and temple, Hellenistic city

Delphi   C Greece theater and temple, sanctuary

Demetrias   N Greece Hellenistic city

Dendenchofu   C Japan mound cemetery

Dendera   U Egypt Ptolemaic temple

Dendra   S Greece Mycenaean fortress

Dengfeng   N China early settlement, Tang kiln, Sung kiln

Dengkil   C Malaya early metal site

Dent   W USA, Colorado Palaeo-Indian site

Deqing   E China Tang kiln

Der (Badra)   E Mesopotamia early city, Assyrian provincial capital

Derby   C England Viking center

Dereivka   SW Russia steppe settlement

Derenberg   N Germany defensive enclosure

Derring   Alaska Ipiutak site

Derry   N Ireland monastery

Derrynahinch   SE Ireland megalithic tomb

Dertona (modern Tortona)   N Italy Roman Empire

Desalpur   NW India early city, Harappan site

Deszk-Olajkút   Hungary farming site

Detzem (Ad Quintum)   W Germany Roman village

Deva (modern Chester)   N England Roman legionary fortress

Deve Hüyük   SE Anatolia cemetery

Devil's Dyke   S England Celtic hill fort

Devil's Lair   SW Australia early man, Aboriginal site

Devil's Tower   Gilbraltar Neanderthal site

Devon Downs   S Australia Aboriginal site

Dewa   N Japan Heian fortress

Dhal   NW India Harappan site

Dharanikota   S India Deccan city

Dhlodhlo   E Africa, Zimbabwe Iron Age site, Ming pottery

Dhokathismata   SE Greece bronze daggers

Dia   N Crete ancient port

Diana Bay   E Canada Dorset site

Diara   W Africa, Mauritania early town and kingdom

Diaurum   SE Brazil early settlement

Díaz Ordaz   C Mexico stone source

Dickson   C USA temple mound

Dictaean   E Crete sacred cave

Didyma   SW Anatolia Greek temple, Hellenistic city

Die Kelders   S Africa Stone Age tools, Stone Age site

Dieng (Dijeng)   W Java early site

Dieng Plateau   C Java early monumental site

Dieskau   N Germany metal hoard

Diji-li-takri   NW India Harappan site

Dikbosch   S Africa Stone Age site

Dimbulagala   N Ceylon Buddhist remains

Dimolit   N Philippines Neolithic settlement

Ding (Dingxian)   N China Sung kiln

Dingcun   NE China early man

Dingling   NE China Ming tomb

Dinorben   N Wales fortified site

Diomede Is.   Alaska/Russia Thule site

Dire Dawa (Porc Epic Cave)   E Africa, Ethiopia Stone Age tools

Direkli Cave   E Anatolia Palaeolithic site

Dishasha   U Egypt noble's tomb

Divostin   C Yugoslavia farming site

Diyarbakir   E Anatolia Sinan mosque

Djado   C Africa early settlement

Djanak   C Asia steppe settlement

Djebila   NW Morocco Carthaginian cemetery

Djeitun   C Asia steppe settlement

Djougou   W Africa, Benin early town

Dobranichevka   W Russia hunter-gatherer site

Doc Chua   S Vietnam transitional settlement

Dodona   NW Greece Greek temple, sanctuary

Doerschuk   SE USA, North Carolina Archaic site

Dog River   Lebanon Assyrian rock relief

Dogubayazit   E Anatolia Urartian fortress

Dogunbaden   SW Persia fire temple

Dölauer Heide   N Germany defensive enclosure

Dolmen de Sota   SW Spain megalithic tomb

Dolní Vestonice   Czechoslovakia hunter-gatherer site, hunter-gatherer art

Domburg   Holland Viking trading emporium

Domebo   S USA, Texas Palaeo-Indian site

Domu s'Orku   S Sardinia dry-stone fortress

Domuztepe   SE Anatolia Neolithic site

Doña Clotilde   E Spain Mesolithic settlement

Doncaster   N England medieval town

Dondo   E Africa, Kenya Ming pottery

Dong   N China Han city

Dong Dau   N Vietnam transitional settlement

Dong Duong   Indo-China, S Vietnam early site, Buddhist center

Dong Lakhon   C Thailand moated site, early site

Dong Son   N Vietnam transitional settlement, early site

Donghai   N China Han city

Dongshankou   NE China E Chou cemetery

Dongsimucun   NE China Ming tomb

Dongsunba   W China E Chou cemetery

Dongxiang   NW China Shang copper source

Dongxing   SW China cave site

Dongyang   E China Tang kiln

Dongzhuangcun   N China early settlement

Donja Slatina   SW Yugoslavia fortified site

Donnersberg   C Germany Celtic oppidum

Doornlaagte   S Africa Acheulian tools

Dorestad   N Holland Viking trading emporium

Dorginarti I.   U Egypt fortress

Dortmund   NW Germany ritual metalwork

Doruthy   SW France hunter-gatherer site

Dostrup   NW Denmark scratch plows

Douara Cave   S Syria early tools

Double Adobe   SW USA, Arizona Archaic site

Dougga   N Tunisia megalithic tomb

Downpatrick   N Ireland Bronze Age settlement, monastery

Dowris   C Ireland metal hoard

Dowth   E Ireland megalithic tomb

Dragonby   E England Celtic site

Dramont   S France Roman shipwreck

Draved   S Denmark pollen core site

Drehem   C Mesopotamia early writing

Drunken Point   C Canada, Ontario Archaic site

Dry Creek   Alaska early settlement

Duandian   N China Tang kiln

Dublin   E Ireland Viking center, archbishopric

Duggleby   N England medieval village

Dülük   E Anatolia early tools

Dunbar   S Scotland Celtic fortress

Dundas Is.   NE Canada Dorset site

Dunhuang   NW China early trade, Han frontier port, rock-carved temple

Dünsberg   C Germany Celtic oppidum

Dur Kurigalzu   C Mesopotamia zigurrat

Dura-Europos (modern Salahiyah)   E Syria early trade center, Roman city, Hellenistic city

Durango   SW USA, Colorado Basketmaker site

Durham   N England monastery

Durkhumid   E Anatolia Assyrian colony

Durostorum (modern Silistra)   N Bulgaria Roman legionary fortress

Durovka   W Russia barrow burial

Durras North   SE Australia Aboriginal site

Durrington Walls   S England stone circle

Dürrnberg   E Austria Celtic site

Dushizi   S China cave site

Dust Devil Cave   SW USA, Utah Archaic site

Dutchess Cave   E USA, New York Palaeo-Indian site

Dutchess Quarry   NE USA fluted points

Dutton   C USA fluted opints

Duvensee   W Germany Mesolithic settlement

Duyong Caves   W Philippines cave site, Neolithic settlement

Dyer   C USA, Indiana Archaic site

Dyrholm   Denmark Mesolithic settlement

Dyrrhachium (Durazzo, modern Durrës)   Albania Roman city, Byzantine walled town

Dzhruchula   S Russia Neanderthal site

Dzibilchaltún   Mexico, Yucatán Maya settlement, early town

Dzibilnocac   Mexico, Yucatán Maya settlement

Dzvonetskaya Balka   SW Russia steppe settlement

Early Khartoum   NE Africa, Sudan hunter-gatherers, early pottery

East Cape   Alaska Thule sites

Ebbou   E France hunter-gatherer art

Ebla   W Syria early city, early writing

Eburacum (modern York)   N England Roman provincial capital & legionary fortress

Ebusus   W Mediterranean Phoenician city

Ecatepec   C Mexico, Aztec center

Echidna Dreaming   NE Australia Aboriginal site

Echigo   N Japan shogunate provincial capital

Echizen   C Japan pottery kiln

Ed Debba   NE Africa, Sudan wavy-line pottery

Ede   S Holland beaker burial

Edfu (Idfu, Appollinopolis)   U Egypt early city, ancient city, Ptolemaic temple

Edinburgh   S Scotland medieval trade

Edirne   NW Turkey Sinan mosque

Edjek   C Philippines Neolithic settlement

Edjeleh   N Africa, Algeria bone harpoons

Eext   N Holland corded ware burial

Effigy Mounds   N USA, Iowa Hopewell site

Eflatun Pinar   S Anatolia spring sanctuary

Egebak   SW Denmark metalwork

Egil   E Anatolia Assyrian rock relief

Egnatian Way (Via Egnatia)   Thrace Byzantine highway

Egolzwil   N Switzerland farming settlement

Egou   N China early settlement

Egrand   W Africa, Ghana early port

Egtved   C Denmark barrow burial

Egusi   N Africa, Chad bone harpoons

Ehi Kournei   N Africa, Chad Acheulian tools

Ehringsdorf   E Germany early tools and human remains

Eiland   S Africa Iron Age site and salt mine

Eilat   Israel ancient port

Eileithyia, Cave of   N Crete sacred cave

Ejsbol   W Germany weapon hoard

Ekain   N Spain Neanderthal cave site, hunter-gatherer art

Ekallatum   N Mesopotamia early town

Ekven   E Russia Thule site

El Abra   W Colombia early settlement

El Aculadero   S Spain early tools

El Alia   E Tunisia megalithic tomb

El Arbolillo   C Mexico early farming site

El Argar   SE Spain fortified site

El Badari   NE Africa, Egypt early cereals

El Barranquete   SE Spain megalithic tomb

El Baúl   S Guatemala Maya settlement

El Bosque   Nicaragua early settlement

El Castillo   NW Spain Neanderthal site

El Cayo   E Mexico Maya town

El Ceibo   S Argentina early settlement

El Chayal   E Mexico Maya town

El Conde   NW Spain Neanderthal site

El Encanto   Ecuador early farming site

El Garcel   SE Spain farming settlement

El Guettar   N Africa, Tunisia Stone Age tools

El Hamel   N Africa, Algeria hunter-gatherers

El Heneal   NW Venezuela early settlement

El Inga   SW Colombia early site

El Jobo   NW Venezuela early settlement

El Jobo   S Guatemala Maya settlement

El Khattara   NE Africa, Egypt early cereals

El Khiam   C Palestine Natufian and Neolithic site

El Khril   NW Africa, Morocco early livestock

El Meco   Mexico, Yucatán Maya settlement

El Mermouta   N Algeria early pottery

El Mirador   N Algeria early pottery

El Mries   N Morocco megalithic tomb

El Oficio   SE Spain fortified site

El Opeño   C Mexico early farming site

El Palito   NW Venezuela early settlement

El Palmar   Mexico, Yucatán Maya settlement

El Paraiso   S Peru early public building

El Pendo   NW Spain Neanderthal site

El Peñón   N Venezuela early settlement

El Pozuelo   SW Spain schist plaques

El Reguerillo   C Spain hunter-gatherer art

El Riego Cave   C Mexico early settlement

El Salvador   Maya settlement

El Tajín   C Mexico pyramids, early town, Aztec town

El Trapiche   C Mexico early farming site, Pre-Classical El'Ubaidios site

El-Amarnà (Tell el-Amarnà)   U Egypt ancient city, early city, noble's tomb, royal capital

El-Amra   U Egypt ancient cemetery

El-Ashmunein   U Egypt ancient city

El-Badari   U Egypt ancient cemetery

El-Ballas   U Egypt ancient cemetery

El-Derr   U Egypt temple

El-Hammamiya   U Egypt noble's tomb

El-Hiba   U Egypt early town

El-Khokha   U Egypt court tombs

El-Kula   U Egypt pyramid

El-Lahun   U Egypt pyramid, royal tomb

El-Lisht   L Egypt pyramid, early burial, royal capital, early capital

El-Mahasna   U Egypt ancient cemetery

El-Masloukh   Lebanon Neanderthal site

El-Matmar   U Egypt ancient cemetery

El-Mo'alla   U Egypt noble's tomb

El-Mustagidda (El-Mostagedda)   U Egypt ancient cemetery

El-Sebua   U Egypt temple

El-Sheikh Ibada   U Egypt temple

El-Tarif   U Egypt royal tombs

El'beidiya   N Israel early tools

Eland's Bay (Elandsbaai)   S Africa Stone Age site

Elandsfontein   S Africa early man

Elandskloof   S Africa Stone Age tools

Elatia   C Greece farming site

Ele Bor   E Africa early food

Elephantine   U Egypt early city, ancient city, early iron

Eleusis   SE Greece Athenian settlement

Eleutherae   SE Greece Athenian fort

Elis   SW Greece theater and temple

Elk Island   C Canada, Manitoba Archaic site

Ellamma   Temple of Vijayanagara

Ellerbek   N Germany megalithic site

Ellerton   N England medieval town

Elliniko   SW Greece Mycenaean fortress

Ellora   C India rock-carved temple

Elmina   W Africa, Ghana early port

Elp   N Holland Bronze Age settlement

Els Antigors   Balearic Is. ancient fortress

Els tudons   Balearic Is. megalithic tomb

Elsloo   S Holland farming site

Elvina   NW Spain native settlement

Emain Macha   E Ireland Celtic religious site

Embrun   SE France archbishopric

Emei Shan   W China holy mountain

Emerald Mound   S USA temple mound

Emmen   N Germany pollen core site

'En Gev   N Palestine Natufian site

Engaruka   E Africa, Tanzania Iron Age site

Engel's (Pokrovsk)   C Russia steppe settlement

Engis   Belgium Neanderthal site, hunter-gatherer site

Enmylyn   E Russia Thule site

Enneri Toboi   N Africa, Chad wavy-line pottery

Enneri Togou   N Africa, Chad wavy-line pottery

Ensérune   S France Celtic oppidum, native settlement

Entzheim   W Germany hunter-gatherer site

Ephesus   W Anatolia Achaemenid city, Greek city, Hellenistic city, Roman provincial capital, aqueduct, Byzantine bishopric

Epidaurus (Asclepius)   SE Greece theater, sanctuary

Episkopi   N Crete Minoan village

Eppelsheim   W Germany Dryopithecus

Er Lannic   NW France stone circle and henge

Erbaba Tepe   S Anatolia Neolithic site, early pottery

Erciyas Dagi   SE Anatolia Neolithic site

Érd   Hungary Neanderthal site

Erebuni   Armenia Urartian fortress

Eregli   S Anatolia Sinan mosque

Erfurt   E Germany farming site

Ergani   SE Anatolia copper source

Erganos   S Crete Minoan village

Ergili   NW Anatolia Achaemenid city

Eridu   S Mesopotamia zigurrat, pottery remains, early city and palace

Erjiacun   N China early settlement

Erlangpo   N China Shang goldwork

Erligang   N China early pottery

Ertebolle   N Denmark shell midden, megalithic site

Erueti   Vanuatu Lapita site

Erzincan   E Anatolia gold and silver work

Es Sinn   SE Syria Neolithic site

Es-Skhul   Israel Stone Age tools

Escoural   Portugal hunter-gatherer site, hunter-gatherer art

Escuintla   E Mexico Maya town

Esh Shaheinab   NE Africa, Sudan harpoons and pottery, early livestock

Eshmoun   SW Syria temples

Eshnunna (modern Tell Asmar)   C Mesopotamia early city and palace, early writing

Esie   W Africa, Nigeria early settlement

Esparragalejo   C Spain Roman dam

Este   N Italy Celtic art

Estonia   Mesolithic settlements

Etiani Kephala   E Crete peak sanctuary

Etia   C Mexico Pre-Classical site

Etowah   SE USA temple mound

Etzná   Mexico, Yucatán Maya settlement

Eudaemon Arabia (modern Aden)   SW Arabia ancient port, early trade

Eutresis (Evtresis)   NE Greece Mycenaean fortress

Eva   C USA, Tennessee Archaic site

Evora   C Portugal archbishopric

Evreux   N France Viking mint

Evron   N Israel early tools

Evtresis   C Greece metal vessels

Exeter   SW England Viking mint, monastery

Exloo   N Holland beaker burial

Eynsham   C England beaker burial

Ezero   E Bulgaria fortified site

Ezerovo   E Bulgaria lake dwelling

Ezinge   N Holland terp settlement

Ezira   W Africa, Nigeria early town

Faaa   Society Is. petroglyph

Faesulae (modern Fiesole)   N Italy early temple

Fafos   S Yugoslavia tell settlement

Failaka (Faylakah)   S Mesopotamia early trade, ancient site

Faiyum   L Egypt early cattle, early agriculture

Faleasi'u   Samoa Lapita site

Falefa   W Samoa early site

Fallahogy   N Ireland pollen core site

False Island   New Zealand, South I. shell midden and moa bones

Faneromeni (Phaneromeni)   SE Greece Athenian fort and sanctuary

Fangel Torp   C Denmark bronze figurines

Fanning I. (Tabuaeran)   C Pacific early site

Faras   U Egypt temple, fortress

Fårdal   NW Denmark bronze figurines

Farnham   SE England Mesolithic settlement

Farrashband   SW Persia fire temple

Fatehpur Sikri   C India Mughal mint

Fatherland   S USA temple mound

Fayda   N Mesopotamia Assyrian rock relief

Faylakah (Failaka)   Kuwait sanctuary

Feddersen Wierde   NW Germany terp settlement

Federsee   S Germany lake dwelling

Feicheng   E China W Chou site

Feigne d'Artimont   SE France pollen core site

Feletoa   Tonga early site

Fell's Cave   S Chile early settlement

Feng-pi-t'ou   Taiwan early settlement, Longshan site

Fengate   E England farming settlement, Bronze Age settlement

Fenghuang Shan   W China Ming tomb

Fenghuangling   E China E Chou bronze hoard

Fenghuangshan   E China E Chou burial

Fenghuangzui   E China E Chou burial

Feniak Lake   Alaska Ipiutak site

Fère-en-Tardenois   N France Mesolithic settlement

Fergana   C Asia steppe settlement, early trade

Fergusson I.   New Guinea Kula gift exchange, Lapita obsidian

Fernando Po (Biyoko)   W Africa, Equatorial Guinea early port

Ferry Berth   Samoa Lapita site

Fez (Fès)   N Africa, Morocco Islamic town, urban center, early town, Ottoman trade

Filitosa   S Corsica fortified site

Fimber   N England medieval village

Finca Arizona   S Guatemala Maya settlement

Finca de Paloma   C Spain metal hoard

Fingira   E Africa Malawi hunter-gatherers

Finsterlohr   S Germany Celtic art

Flagstaff   SW USA Pueblo farming site

Flattop   SW USA Pueblo farming site

Flint Run   E USA, Virginia Palaeo-Indian site

Flögein   NW Germany terp settlement

Flomborn   W Germany farming site

Florence   SE USA temple mound

Florence (Firenze)   N Italy medieval trade, archbishopric

Floreshty   SW Russia farming site, Cucuteni-Tripolye village

Florisbad   S Africa Stone Age tools

Folsom   S USA, Texas bison kill site

Fond-de-Fôret   Belgium Neanderthal site, hunter-gatherer site

Font de Gaume   C France hunter-gatherer art

Font Robert   C France hunter-gatherer site

Fontanaccia   Corsica megalithic tomb

Fontarèches   S France early tools, Neanderthal site

Fontéchevade   C France early tools and human remains

Forbes Quarry   Gibraltar Neanderthal site

Fort Abbas   NW India Harappan site

Fort Ancient   NE USA, Ohio Hopewell site

Fort Center   SE USA, Florida Hopewell site

Fort Harrouard   N France fortified site

Fortaleza   E Brazil early settlement

Fortrose   New Zealand, South I. moa bones

Fosso Conicchio   C Italy beaker burial

Fossum   W Sweden rock art

Fountains Abbey   N England monastery, Cistercian abbey

Fourmile   SW USA Pueblo farming site

Fourneau du Diable   C France hunter-gatherer site, hunter-gatherer art

Foxton   New Zealand, North I. shell midden and moa bones

Fraeer   NW Germany bog body

Fragtrup   NW Denmark Bronze Age settlement

Frankhthi   S Greece shell midden, farming site, early pottery

Frannarp   S Sweden rock art

Frenillot   S France early tools

Fridaythorpe   N England medieval village

Frieze Cave   SW Australia Aboriginal site

Froarp   S Sweden musical instruments

Fromms Landing   S Australia Aboriginal site

Fudodo   C Japan early settlement

Fufeng   N China early settlement

Fuguodun   SE China shell mound

Fuji, Mount   C Japan holy mountain

Fukui   W Japan early man

Fukui Cave   W Japan cave site, early pottery

Fulin   W China early man

Fulinbao   N China Chou burial

Furfooz   Belgium hunter-gatherer art

Furninha   C Portugal farming settlement

Furuichi   C Japan mound cemetery

Fushikokotan   N Japan Ainu hill fort

Fussell's Lodge   S England long barrow

Füzesabony   E Hungary Bronze Age settlement

Fuzhou (Foochow)   SE China early trade center, provincial capital

Fycklinge   C Sweden claw beaker and metalwork

Fyrkat   N Denmark Viking fortress

Gabrong   N Africa, Chad early pottery

Gadamotta   E Africa, Ethiopia Stone Age tools

Gaddesden Row   SE England early tools

Gadeb   NE Africa, Ethiopia early tools

Gades (modern Cádiz)   SW Spain Phoenician city, Roman city

Gagarino   C Russia hunter-gatherer art

Gagraun   C India Mughal mint

Galaz   SW USA Pueblo farming site

Gambell   Alaska Thule sites

Gamble's Cave   E Africa, Kenya hunter-gatherers and pottery

Gangaikondacholapuram   SE India Chola center

Gangguancun   NE China Tang kiln

Gangoh   N India Mughal mint

Gangwayaocun   N China Tang kiln

Ganj Dareh   NW Persia Neolithic site, early pottery

Ganj Nameh   NW Persia rock inscriptions

Gánovce   Czechoslovakia Neanderthal site

Ganties-Montespan   SW France hunter-gatherer art

Gao   W Africa, Mali Iron Age site, Islamic trade, urban center, early town

Gaocheng   N China early city

Gaojiabao   N China W Chou site

Gaozhuang   N China E Chou burial

Gar Cahal   Morocco beaker burial

Garalavouni   SW Greece tholos tomb

Gargamelle Cove   E Canada Dorset site

Gargas   SW France hunter-gatherer art

Gatlin   SW USA Pueblo farming site

Gaudo   S Italy rock-cut tomb

Gavimath   S India rock edict

Gavrinis   NW France megalithic tomb

Gaza (Ghazzati)   Palestine Egyptian fortress, Levantine city, Hellenistic city, early trade

Gazel   S France Mesolithic settlement

Gazi (Gazion)   N Crete Minoan village

Gebel Barkal   NE Africa, Sudan temple, early iron

Gebel el-Silsila   U Egypt ancient mine

Gebel el-Teir   U Egypt noble's tomb

Gebel el-Zeit   Red Sea copper mine

Gebelein (Pathyris)   U Egypt noble's tomb

Gebze   W Anatolia Sinan mosque

Gedebjerg   E Denmark metalwork

Gedi   E Africa, Kenya Islamic trading post, Ming pottery

Gela   S Sicily Greek colony

Gelidonya, Cape   SW Anatolia shipwreck site

Gemeinlebarn   N Austria Bronze Age cemetery

Genay   E France Neanderthal site

Geneva   W Switzerland Celtic site

Genoa (Genva, Genoua)   NW Italy Roman city, medieval trade, archbishopric

Geoksyur Oasis   C Asia steppe settlement

Gerasimovka   SW Russia steppe settlement

Gerf Husein   U Egypt temple

Gerona   NE Spain archbishopric

Gesher Benot Ya'aqov   N Israel early tools

Gezer (Gazri)   Palestine Egyptian control, royal fortress of Israel

Ghadamès (Ghadamis)   N Africa, Libya early settlement, early town

Ghaligari cave   N India later farming village

Ghar Cahal   Morocco farming site

Ghar-i-Asp   Afghanistan early farming village

Ghar-i-Mar   Afghanistan early farming village

Gharmachi   W Syria early tools

Ghat   N Africa, Libya early settlement, early town

Ghazi Shah   NW India Harappan site

Ghent (Gand, Gent)   Belgium Viking mint, medieval trade

Gheo Shih   C Mexico early settlement

Ghiardo Cave   N Italy early tools

Gidalur   S India Mesolithic site

Gila Bend   SW USA Pueblo farming site

Gilgal   N Palestine Neolithic site

Gilgit   NW India Buddhist center, early trade

Gilimanuk   Bali early metal site

Girikihaciyah   N Mesopotamia pottery remains

Girnar   W India Deccan city

Girsu   S Mesopotamia early writing

Giza   L Egypt pyramids, early burial, early writing, temple

Gla   NE Greece Mycenaean settlement

Glanum   C France Roman dam

Glen Elliott   S Africa hunter-gatherers, Stone Age site

Glenaire   S Australia Aboriginal site

Gnewitz   NE Germany megalithic tomb

Go Mun   N Vietnam transitional settlement

Goa   W India maritime trade

Goaréva   NW France Neanderthal site

Gobedra   NE Africa, Ethiopia hunter-gatherers, early cereals

Gobyoyama   C Japan Yamato tomb

Godin Tepe   W Persia early city

Gods Lake   C Canada, Manitoba Archaic site

Gokomere   SE Africa, Zimbabwe Iron Age site

Gol Ba'it   C Malaya rock shelter

Goldberg   S Germany defensive enclosure

Gombe Point   C Africa, Zaire Iron Age site

Gombroon   S Persia maritime trade

Gomolava   C Yugoslavia farming site, Bronze Age settlement

Gongen-yama   C Japan early man

Gongzian   N China rock-carved temple, Tang kiln

Goni   S Sardinia dry-stone fortress

Gonies   N Crete peak sanctuary

Gönnersdorf   N Germany hunter-gatherer site, hunter-gatherer art

Gontsy   W Russia hunter-gatherer site

Goodall   N USA, Indiana Hopewell site

Goodenough I.   New Guinea Kula gift exchange

Gorbunovo   C Russia steppe settlement

Gordium   C Anatolia Achaemenid city

Gordon's Bay   S Africa Stone Age site

Gorée   W Africa, Senegal early port

Gornja Tuzla   C Yugoslavia tell settlement

Gotenyama   N Japan Ainu hill fort

Gough's Cave   S England hunter-gatherer site, hunter-gatherer art

Gouraya   N Algeria Carthaginian cemetery

Gouy   N France hunter-gatherer art

Goyem Barak   W Africa, Mali bone harpoons

Goyet   Belgium hunter-gatherer site, hunter-gatherer art

Goyty (Staryye Atagi)   S Russia barrow burial

Goz Kerki   N Africa, Chad harpoons and pottery

Gozleve (Yevpatoriya)   S Russia Sinan mosque

Grächwil   Switzerland bronze hydria

Gradeshnitsa   W Bulgaria tell settlement

Grado   NE Italy archbishopric

Grafton Regis   C England monastic burial ground

Graham Cave   C USA, Illinois Archaic site

Grai Resh   N Mesopotamia early settlement

Graig Llwyd   N Wales axe factory

Graman   E Australia Aboriginal site

Gramari   SE France Mesolithic settlement

Grammatiko   SE Greece Athenian settlement

Grand Congloué   S France Roman shipwreck

Grand Gulch   SW USA, Utah Basketmaker site

Grand Menhir Brisé   NW France menhir

Grand Pressigny   NW France flint mine

Grand Village   S USA temple mound

Granite Point Rock Shelter   SW USA, Nevada prehistoric diet

Grapevine   SW USA Pueblo farming site

Grasshopper   SW USA Pueblo farming site

Gråträsk   N Sweden Saami site

Grauballe   NW Denmark bog body

Grave Creek   NE USA, Pennsylvania Adena site

Great Barrier Island   New Zealand, North I. shell midden

Great Driffield   N England medieval town

Great Langdale   NW England farming settlement

Great Mercury Island   New Zealand, North I. defended settlement

Great Zimbabwe   E Africa, Zimbabwe Iron Age site, Ming pottery

Green Ant   NE Australia Aboriginal site

Gresik   E Java early port

Grevensvaenge   S Denmark bronze figurines

Grewe   SW USA Pueblo farming site

Grimaldi   N Italy hunter-gatherer site, hunter-gatherer art

Grimes Graves   E England flint mine

Gritille   E Anatolia Neolithic site

Gritsa   N Greece tholos tomb

Gródek Nadbuzny   E Poland farming settlement

Gronhoj   E Denmark megalithic tomb

Gros Guignon   C France vehicle burial

Grosmont   N England medieval town

Grossbrembach   C Germany Bronze Age cemetery

Grosser Plöner See   N Germany pollen core site

Grosser Segeberger See   N Germany pollen core site

Grossmehring   S Germany beaker burial

Grotta Azzurra di Samatorza   Italy Mesolithic settlement

Grotta Corruggi   Sicily Mesolithic settlement

Grotta dei Piccioni   N Italy farming settlement

Grotta dell'Uzzo   Sicily farming site

Grotta della Madonna   S Italy Mesolithic settlement

Grotte Arnaud   S France beaker burial

Grotte des Fées   S France rock-cut tomb

Grotte du Lazaret   S France hunter-gatherer cave

Grotte Dufour   C France hunter-gatherer site

Grotte Gazel   SW France farming site

Gründberg   N Austria Celtic oppidum

Gruta de Furninha   Portugal farming site

Gua Bintong   N Malaya early metal site

Gua Cha   C Malaya rock shelter, early metal site

Gua Kechil   C Malaya cave site, early metal site

Gua Kepah   N Malaya shell midden, Neolithic settlement

Gua Lawa   E Java Neolithic settlement

Gua Musang   C Malaya early metal site

Guajaráa   S Brazil early settlement

Gualupita   C Mexico early farming site, Pre-Classical site

Guangchongcun   S China Tang kiln

Guanghan   W China Han city

Guanyindong   W China early Palaeolithic site

Guarita   E Brazil early settlement

Gudenus-Höhle   Austria early tools, Neanderthal site

Gudzheyli   C Asia steppe settlement

Gué du Plantin   N France defensive enclosure

Guignicourt   NE France Iron Age cemetery, Celtic oppidum

Guilá Naquitz   C Mexico rock shelter

Guilin   S China Ming provincial capital

Guillassou   C France hunter-gatherer site

Guitarrero Cave   N Peru early settlement, early farming

Gujjar   N India rock edict

Gujrat   NW India Mughal mint

Gulåkra Mosse   SW Sweden musical instruments

Guldhoj   SW Denmark barrow burial

Gulf Hazard   E Canada Dorset site

Gumla   NW India early farming village, Harappan site

Gummididurru   S India Buddhist site

Gunda   C Africa, Zambia Iron Age site

Gundeshapur   W Persia Sasanian city

Gundestrup   NW Denmark ritual metalwork

Gunung Kidul   C Java early metal site

Gunung Piring   Bali early metal site

Gure Makeke   NE Africa, Somalia hunter-gatherers

Gure Warbei   NE Africa, Somalia hunter-gatherers

Gurti Aqua   S Sardinia dry-stone fortress

Gussage All Saints   S England Celtic site

Guyana   Early farming

Guyum   S Persia rock relief

Gwalior   N India Mughal mint

Gwato   W Africa, Nigeria early town

Gwisho   C Africa, Zambia hunter-gatherers

Gypsades   C Crete tholos tomb

Gytheum (Gytheion)   S Greece theater

Ha'amonga-a-maui   Tonga early site

Ha'apai   Tonga Lapita site

Ha Long   N Vietnam Neolithic settlement

Ha'ata'live'a   Marquesas Is. early quarry

Ha'atuatua   Marquesas Is. early site

Habuba (Habuba Kebira)   N Syria early kiln, early town

Hacilar   SW Anatolia Neolithic site, farming site

Hackness   N England medieval town

Hadar   E Africa, Ethiopia *Australopithecus afarensis*

Hadda   Afghanistan Gandharan art, Buddhist stupa

Haervej   S Denmark military road

Haftavan Tepe   NW Persia Urartian fortress, Achaemenid city

Håga   E Sweden megalithic tomb, barrow burial

Hagarsa   U Egypt noble's tomb

Hagi Kilns   W Japan Korean pottery

Hahei   New Zealand, North I. shell midden

Haifeng   S China cave site

Haij Creiem   N Africa, Libya Stone Age tools

Hajdusámson   C Hungary metal hoard

Hajii Muhammad   S Mesopotamia pottery remains

Hakatarewa   New Zealand, South I. moa bones

Halakal   Mexico, Yucatán Maya settlement

Halar   NW India Harappan site

Halawa   Hawaiian Is. early site

Halawa Valley   Hawaiian Is. early irrigation

Haldern   NW Germany claw beaker

Haldorf   NW Germany corded ware burial

Haleakala   Hawaiian Is. early quarry

Halele'a   Hawaiian Is. early site

Halicarnassus (Halikarnassos)   SW Anatolia Achaemenid city, Greek city, Hellenistic city, Roman city

Halifax   E Canada, Nova Scotia colonial settlement

Halin   N Burma early monumental site

Halleis   S Greece temple and harbor

Hallstatt   C Austria early cemetery

Hallunda   C Sweden Bronze Age settlement

Halsnoy   W Norway boat burial

Haltwhistle Burn   N England Roman water mill

Hama   W Syria Neolithic site, Roman aqueduct, Islamic town

Hamadan (Ecbatana, Hagamatana)   N Persia Achaemenid palace, Islamic town

Hamadine   C Syria early tools

Hamansumo   NE Japan early settlement

Hamath (modern Hama)   Syria early town, early city, Assyrian provincial capital

Hambledon Hill   S England defensive enclosure

Hamburg   N Germany Viking trading emporium, medieval trade

Hamel   N France Neanderthal site

Hammam Kebir   NW Syria early tools

Hamwic (modern Southampton)   S England Viking trading emporium

Hanatekua   Marquesas Is. early site

Hanaui   Marquesas Is. early site

Hane   Marquesas Is. early site

Hang Chua Cave   N Indo-China, Vietnam cave site

Hang Gon   S Vietnam transitional settlement

Hangenbieten   SW Germany early tools

Hangzhou (Hangchow)   E China plow, early trade center, Buddhist pagoda, Ming provincial capital

Hanzei   C Japan Yamato tomb

Haobi   N China Tang kiln

Har Qedumim   Israel Stone Age tools

Haraldskjaer   W Denmark bog body

Harappa   NW India Indus Valley settlement, early city, early writing

Harar   NE Africa, Ethiopia Iron Age site

Harbaka   S Syria Roman dam

Hard Scrabble   SW USA Pueblo farming site

Hardaway   SE USA, North Carolina Archaic site

Harewood   N England medieval town

Haritalyangar   NW India Ramapithecus and Sivapithecus

Harmony   S Africa Iron Age site

Harness   NE USA, Ohio Hopewell site

Harran (Haran, Carrhae)   N Syria early town, Assyrian provincial city, Islamic town

Harris   SW USA Pueblo farming site

Harting Beacon   S England Celtic hill fort

Hasanli   NW Persia early settlement, ivory

Hashidate   C Japan rock shelter

Hassi Youba   W Africa, Mali bone harpoons

Hassuna   C Mesopotamia pottery remains, early pottery

Hathaway   NE USA, Maine Archaic site

Hatnub   U Egypt alabaster, ancient mine

Hatra   N Mesopotamia Parthian city

Hatun Cañar   C Ecuador Inca tambo

Hatuncolla   S Peru Inca center

Haua Fteah   N Africa, Libya Stone Age tools, hunter-gatherers, early livestock

Hausen   N Germany early tools

Havana   C USA, Illinois Hopewell site

Havelte   Holland Mesolithic settlement, megalithic tomb

Havsa   NW Turkey Sinan mosque

Hawara   U Egypt pyramid, early burial, royal tomb

Hawikuh   SW USA, Pueblo farming site

Hawken   NW USA, Wyoming bison kill site

Hawks Burn   New Zealand, South I. moa bones

Hayaz   E Anatolia Neolithic site

HaYonim   N Anatolia Natufian site

Hazendonk   C Holland megalithic site

Hazor   N Palestine early town, Egyptian control, royal fortress of Israel

Healaugh   N England medieval town

Heaphy River   New Zealand, South I. shell midden and moa bones

Heathrow   SE England Celtic religious site

Hecatompylos (modern Shahr-i Qumis)   N Persia Parthian city, early trade center

Hede   C Sweden ritual metalwork

Hedeby   S Denmark Islamic trade, Viking trading emporium

Hedon   N England medieval town

Hegra   W Arabia early trade

Heidetränk   C Germany Celtic oppidum

Hein   S Norway Mesolithic settlement

Helena Crossing   S USA, Arkansas Hopewell site

Helendorff   SW Russia steppe settlement

Helgö   S Sweden Viking trading emporium

Hélin   Belgium early tools

Heliopolis   L Egypt early city, ancient city, early city and temple

Hell Gap   W USA, Wyoming Palaeo-Indian site

Hellouanndji   N Syria early tools

Helmsdorf   E Germany barrow burial

Hemudu   E China early settlement, lacquer working, rice farming site

Henderson I.   S Pacific early site

Hengistbury Head   S England hunter-gatherer site, Celtic oppidum and hill fort

Hengzhen   N China Longshan site

Hengzhencun   N China early settlement

Herrerías   NW Spain hunter-gatherer art

Hertenritz   Fr. Guyana early settlement

Hesar   NE Persia metal hoard site

Heuneburg   S Germany Hallstatt site

Hidden Cave   SW USA, Nevada prehistoric diet

Hienheim   W Germany farming site, defensive enclosure

Hieraconpolis (Hierakonpolis)   U Egypt early city, ancient city

Higgins Flat   SW USA Pueblo farming site

High Lodge   C England early tools

High Rochester   N Scotland Roman fort

Himmelstalund   E Sweden rock art

Hindana   NW Mesopotamia Assyrian city

Hings Fen   N Germany early settlement

Hio   NW Spain metal hoard

Hiratsuka   C Japan Yamato tomb

Hirschlanden   S Germany Celtic art

Hirsiz Kale (Varto)   E Anatolia Urartian fortress

Hissar   N Persia early settlement

Hiwassee I.   SE USA temple mound

Hjortspring   C Denmark boat burial

Hoa Binh   N Indo-China, N Vietnam early site

Hoa Luu   Indo-China, Vietnam cave site

Hochdorf   C Germany Hallstatt site

Hochdorf (Eberdingen)   SW Germany silk find

Hochob   Mexico, Yucatán Maya settlement

Hockham Mere   E England pollen core site

Hodges   SW USA Pueblo farming site

Hódmezővásárhely   Hungary farming site, Copper Age cemetery

Hoëdic   NW France Mesolithic settlement, megalithic site, megalithic tomb

Hogup Cave   W USA, Utah Archaic site

Hohen Viechein   N Germany Mesolithic settlement

Hohenasperg   C Germany Hallstatt site

Hohmichele   S Germany Hallstatt site, silk find

Hohoupounamu   New Zealand, South I. shell midden

Hokkaido   Ainu hill forts

Hokurikudo   NE Japan early highway

Holborough   SE England silk find

Holingol   N China Han burial

Holme   N England medieval pottery

Holmegård   Denmark Mesolithic settlement

Holmul   N Guatemala Maya settlement

Holyhead   N Wales railway development

Holzgerlingen   C Germany Celtic site

Holzhausen   SE Germany Celtic religious site

Hombori   W Africa, Mali early town

Homolovi Ruins   SW USA Pueblo farming site

Homs (Emesa)   Syria early town, Roman dam, Islamic town

Honaunau   Hawaiian Is. early site

Hong   C Denmark musical instruments

Hong-i Kamalvand   W Persia rock relief

Hong-i Nauruzi   W Persia rock relief

Hong Kong   S China early settlement

Honopue Valley   Hawaiian Is. early irrigation

Hooghly   E India early trade

Hooper Bay   Alaska arctic culture

Hoopper Ranch   SW USA Pueblo farming site

Hope Fountain   C Africa, Zimbabwe Oldowan tools

Horaia   Pakistan early trade

Horby   NW Denmark bog body

Hormuz   S Persia Safavid trade

Horner   NW USA, Montana Palaeo-Indian site

Hornos de la Pena   NW Spain Neanderthal site

Horobetsu   N Japan Ainu hill fort

Hortus   SE France Neanderthal site

Hoshino   C Japan early man

Hoshiriya   N Japan Ainu hill fort

Hostyn   C Czechoslovakia Celtic oppidum

Hot Water Beach   New Zealand, North I. moa bones and shell midden

Hotta   N Japan Heian fortress

Houbirg   C Germany Celtic oppidum

Hougang   N China early settlement, Late Neolithic site

Hougudui   E China E Chou burial

Houhora   New Zealand, North I. early site

Houppeville   N France early tools, Neanderthal site

Hov   N Denmark flint mine

Hove   NW Denmark musical instruments

Hovenweep Sites   SW USA Pueblo farming site

Howard Lake   N USA, Wisconsin Hopewell site

Howieson's Poort   S Africa Stone Age tools

Hoxne   E England early tools

Hoyo de la Mina   S Spain Mesolithic settlement

Hrazany   W Czechoslovakia Celtic oppidum

Huaca Alta   S Peru, Aspero platform mound

Huaca de los Idolos   S Peru, Aspero platform mound

Huaca de los Reyes (Caballo Muerto)   N Peru preceramic site and public building

Huaca de los Sacrificios   S Peru, Aspero platform mound

Huaca Negra   N Peru early farming site

Huaca Prieta   N Peru preceramic site and early agricultural settlement

Huachenggang   C China early kiln

Huacho   S Peru early farming site

Huánuco Pampa   N Peru Inca center

Hualla Tampu   N Bolivia Inca tambo

Huamachuco   N Peru Middle Horizon site, Inca center

Huangdao   N China Tang kiln

Huangniangniangtai   NW China Shang copper source

Huangpi   N China early settlement

Huangtupocun   NE China W Chou burial

Huangxian   NE China early settlement

Huangyan   E China Tang kiln

Huargo   Peru early settlement

Huari   C Peru Middle Horizon site, pre-Inca center

Huaricoto   N Peru early public building

Huarmey   N Peru early farming site

Huating   N China Longshan site

Huatingcun   N China early settlement

Huaymil   Mexico, Yucatán Maya settlement

Hue   Indo-China, N Vietnam early site

Huehuetoca   C Mexico Aztec center

Huelva   SW Spain metal hoard

Huenta   S Peru Paracas site

Huexotla   C Mexico early town, Aztec center

Huexotzingo   C Mexico early town

Hueypoxtla   C Mexico Aztec center

Huggate   N England medieval village

Huitzilopochco   C Mexico Aztec center

Huixian   N China early city, Shang city

Hujra   NW India Mughal mint

Huldremose   NW Denmark bog body

Hull (Kingston upon Hull)   N England medieval town, canal development

Humantia   C Mexico early town

Humboldt Cave   SW USA, Nevada prehistoric diet

Humpata   SW Africa, Angola Oldowan tools

Hunam   C Korea rice farming site

Hundisburg   E Germany early tools

Hungary Hall   C Canada, Ontario Archaic site

Hunguza   E Africa, Zimbabwe Iron Age site

Huon Peninsula   New Guinea early man

Huoxian   N China Sung kiln

Hurst Fen   E England farming settlement

Hurunui River Mouth   New Zealand, South I. moa bones

Hutouliang   E China early man

Hutton   N England medieval town

Huy   Belgium Rhenish pottery kiln

Hvidegård   E Denmark barrow burial

Hvorslev   NW Denmark scratch plows

Hyakkengawa   C Japan rice farming site

Hyrax Hill   E Africa, Kenya Neolithic site, Iron Age site

Iassa Tepe   C Bulgaria tell settlement

Ibarissene   N Algeria megalithic tomb

Ibiza   Balearic Is. Carthaginian site

Ibrakaj   C Russia steppe settlement

Ica   C Peru Inca center

Ichinosawa Cave   NE Japan early settlement

Ichpaatun   Mexico, Yucatán Maya settlement

Idaean Cave   C Crete sacred cave

Idah   W Africa, Nigeria early town

Idanskiy   S Siberia steppe settlement

Idjil   NW Africa, Mauritania salt deposit, early town

Idojiri   C Japan early settlement

Ife   W Africa, Nigeria urban center, early town

Iga   C Japan pottery kiln

Igbaja   W Africa, Nigeria early settlement

Igbo Ukwu   W Africa, Nigeria early settlement

Igloolik   NE Canada Dorset site

Iharana   Madagascar Ming pottery

Ihnasya el-Medina   U Egypt noble's tomb, early town

Ijebu Oda   W Africa, Nigeria early town

Iji   N Japan Heian fortress
Ikaruga   C Japan Yamato palace
Ikegami   C Japan rice farming site
Ikolivrunveen   E Russia Thule site
Ile de Riou   S France early pottery
Ileret   E Africa, Kenya *Australopithecus boisei* and early man, early livestock, Neolithic site
Ilicapinar   C Anatolia Neolithic site
Illerup   W Denmark weapon hoard
Ilmova Pad   E Russia barrow burial
Ilovatka   C Russia steppe settlement
Ilskaya   S Russia Neanderthal site
Ilyintsi   SW Russia barrow burial
In Guezzam   N Africa, Algeria bone harpoons
Inchtuthill   N Scotland Roman legionary fort
Incoronata   S Italy Greek shrine
Independence Fjord   N Greenland Dorset site
Indian Knoll   C USA, Kentucky Archaic site
Indian Point   Alaska Thule site
Indraprastha   N India pillar edict
Ingaladdi Shelter   N Australia Aboriginal site
Ingombe Ilede   C Africa, Zambia Iron Age site
Inkawasi (Incahuasi)   C Peru Inca center
Inugsuk   W Greenland Thule site
Inverhuron   C Canada, Ontario Archaic site
Iolkos   N Greece Mycenaean settlement
Iparu   C Brazil early settlement
Iping Common   SE England Mesolithic settlement
Ipswich   E England Viking trading emporium
Irkutsk   S Siberia steppe settlement, arctic culture
Irmen'   S Siberia steppe settlement
Isamu Pati   C Africa, Zambia Iron Age site
Isca (modern Caerleon)   S Wales Roman legionary fortress
Isernia la Pineta   C Italy early tools
Ishango   C Africa, Zaire hunter-gatherers
Isimila   E Africa, Tanzania Acheulian tools
Isin   C Mesopotamia early city
Isipatana   NE India pillar edict
Isleham   E England metal hoard
Isoyama   C Japan early man
Istállóskő   Hungary hunter-gatherer site

Istanbul (Constantinople)   NW Turkey Ottoman capital
Isturits   SW France hunter-gatherer site, hunter-gatherer art
Itacoatirara   C Brazil early settlement
Itaituba   E Brazil early settlement
Itasuke   C Japan Yamato tomb
Itazuke   W Japan rice farming site
Itford Hill   S England Bronze Age settlement
Ivuna   E Africa, Tanzania Iron Age site and salt mine
Iwafune   N Japan Heian fortress
Iwajuku   C Japan early man
Iwanowice   S Poland barrow burial
Iwatsuchihara   W Japan early settlement
Iwo Eleru   W Africa, Nigeria hunter-gatherers, early food
Ixkun   C Guatemala Maya settlement
Ixtapalapa   C Mexico Aztec center
Ixtapaluca   C Mexico Aztec center
Izamal   Mexico, Yucatán Maya settlement
Izapa   SE Mexico early farming site, Maya settlement
Izawa   N Japan Heian fortress
Izembek Lagoon   Aleutian Is. arctic culture
Izvoare   N Romania Cucuteni-Tripolye village
Izykh   E Russia Han mirror find
Ja 'farabad   W Persia early settlement, early kiln
Jablines   N France flint mine
Jabrud   C Syria Natufian site
Jackrabbit Village   SW USA Pueblo farming site
Jackson   NW Canada Thule site
Jaffna   N Ceylon Mesolithic site
Jaina   Mexico, Yucatán Maya settlement
Jais   NE India Mughal mint
Jaketown   S USA, Mississippi Archaic site, Hopewell site
Jalahalli   S India Mesolithic site
Jalilpur   NW India early farming village, Harappan site
Jamal Garhi   N India Gandharan art
Jambi   S Sumatra cave site, early port, Buddhist center
Janislawice   S Poland Mesolithic settlement
Jarlshof   Shetland Is. Bronze Age settlement, Viking center
Jarmo   N Mesopotamia Neolithic site, early pottery
Jatinga Ramesvara   S India rock edict

Jauari   E Brazil early horticultural village
Jauja   C Peru Inca center
Jaunpur   NE India Mughal mint
Jawsaq al-Khaqani   Mesopotamia palace of Samarra
Jebba   W Africa, Nigeria early settlement, early town
Jebel et Tomat   NE Africa, Sudan early cereals
Jebel Idriss   W Syria early tools
Jebel Irhoud   NW Africa, Morocco Stone Age tools
Jebel Jibtaa   W Syria early tools
Jeitun   C Asia early pottery
Jemdet Nasr (Jamdat Nasr)   C Mesopotamia early settlement, early writing
Jenderam Hilir   S Malaya early metal site
Jenne (Djénné)   W Africa, Mali early cereals, early town
Jenne-jeno   W Africa, Mali Iron Age site, urban center
Jericho   C Palestine Natufian and Neolithic site
Jewett Gap   SW USA Pueblo farming site
Jhang   NW India Harappan site
Jhukar   NW India Harappan site
Jiangchengbao   N China Chou burial
Jiangjiawan   N China early man
Jiangling   C China Han burial, provincial capital
Jiangou   N China Longshan site
Jiangxi'an   SW China cave site
Jiangyin   E China Ming tomb
Jiangzhai   N China early settlement, early kiln
Jianyang   SE China Sung kiln
Jiaozhi   SW China Han city
Jilotzingo   C Mexico Aztec center
Jinan   N China Han city, Ming provincial capital
Jincamocco   C Peru Inca center
Jincun   N China E Chou cemetery
Jingcun   N China early settlement
Jingdezhen   C China Tang kiln, Sung kiln, Ming pottery
Jingjiazhuang   N China Chou burial
Jingling   NE China Ming tomb
Jingshan (Kingshan)   N China early settlement, bronze hoard
Jingzhizhen   N China Longshan site
Jinhua   E China Tang kiln
Jinjan   SW Persia Achaemenid palace
Jinniushan   NE China early Palaeolithic site

Jishiliang   C China E Chou burial

Jiuliandun   W China E Chou bronze hoard

Jiulidun   E China E Chou burial

Jiuyan   E China Tang kiln

Jizhou   C China Sung kiln

Jizhou   N China Tang prefecture

Jonquières   N France defensive enclosure

Jonuta   E Mexico Maya settlement

Joppa (Jaffa, modern Yafo)   Palestine Egyptian fortress

Jordhoj   N Denmark megalithic tomb

Jos Plateau   W Africa, Nigeria Acheulian tools

Joss   N Canada Dorset site

Joubbata   S Syria early tools

Joubbe Jannine   Lebanon early tools

Jourama   NE Australia Aboriginal site

Judeirjo-Daro   NW India Harappan site

Juktas (Yiouktas)   C Crete peak sanctuary

Juli   S Peru Inca tambo

Junapani   C India megalithic tomb

Junín   Peru early farming

Junnar   C India rock-carved temple

Jurjan   NE Persia Islamic fortress

Juxtlahuaca   C Mexico early farming site, Pre-Classical site

Juyan   NW China Han fort

Ka Lae (South Cape)   Hawaiian Is. early site

Kabáh   Mexico, Yucatán Maya settlement

Kabul   Afghanistan Sivapithecus, Islamic town, Mughal mint, early trade

Kabwe   C Africa, Zambia early man

Kada   N Africa, Chad wavy-line pottery

Kadero   NE Africa, Sudan early agriculture

Kaédi   W Africa, Mauritania early town

Kafiavana   E New Guinea swamp site

Kagrak-Kumy   C Asia steppe settlement

Kahana Valley   Hawaiian Is. early site

Kahun   U Egypt early city, early capital

Kaifeng   N China early settlement, provincial capital, Ming provincial capital

Kaikoura   New Zealand, South I. defended settlement

Kaileuna   New Guinea Kula gift exchange

Kailua   Hawaiian Is. early site

Kaingaroa   New Zealand, North I. rock art

Kaipara   New Zealand, North I. rock art

Kaisariani   SE Greece Athenian settlement

Kaitote   New Zealand, North I. defended settlement

Kakimbon   W Africa, Guinea hunter-gatherers

Kakovatos   SW Greece tholos tomb

Kakubetsu   N Japan Heian fortress

Kal-i Jangal   E Persia rock relief

Kalala Island   C Africa, Zambia Iron Age site

Kalambo Falls   E Africa, Tanzania Acheulian tools, hunter-gatherers, Iron Age site

Kalanay   C Philippines early metal site

Kalasasaya   temple complex of Tiahuanaco

Kalathiana   C Crete tholos tomb

Kalibangan   N India Indus Valley settlement, plow marks, early city, Harappan site

Kalinovka   C Russia steppe settlement

Kalliena (modern Kalyan)   W India early trade

Kalmetsky Brod   C Russia steppe settlement

Kaloko   Hawaiian Is. early site

Kalsi   N India rock edict

Kalumpang   C Celebes Neolithic settlement

Kalundu   C Africa, Zambia Iron Age site

Kalyana   W India early city

Kamabai   W Africa, Sierra Leone early food

Kamares Cave   S Crete sacred cave

Kamari   SW Greece tholos tomb

Kambos   SW Greece tholos tomb

Kamenka   SW Russia Greek imports, steppe settlement

Kamenskoye   SW Russia steppe settlement

Kami-Kuroiwa   W Japan cave site, early pottery

Kamilari (Kamilarion)   S Crete tholos tomb

Kaminaljuyú   Guatemala pyramid, Maya center

Kamnama   C Africa, Malawi Iron Age site

Kamo   E Japan early settlement

Kamoa   C Africa, Zaire Acheulian tools

Kampong Sungai Lang   S Malaya transitional settlement

Kanab   SW USA, Utah Basketmaker site

Kanapoi   East Africa, Kenya Australopithecus

Kanchalan   E Russia Thule site

Kanchipuram   S India Pallava center, Buddhist center

Kancikli   E Anatolia Urartian fortress

Kandahar   Afghanistan Achaemenid city, Parthian city, rock edict, Islamic town

Kandana   C Africa, Zimbabwe hunter-gatherers

Kandy   S Ceylon early capital and Buddhist center, Buddhist center

Kangaamiut   SW Greenland Thule site

Kangaba   W Africa, Mali early town

Kangila   C Africa, Zambia Iron Age site

Kangling   NE China Ming tomb

Kanheri   W India Buddhist site, rock-carved temple

Kankan   W Africa, Guinea early town

Kanli Kastelli   C Crete Minoan town

Kano   W Africa, Nigeria urban center, early city

Kansanshi   C Africa, Zaire Iron Age site

Kantharos   SE Greece Athenian fort

Kao Phu Ka   C Thailand transitional settlement

Kapeni   E Africa, Malawi Iron Age site

Kapitan Dimitrievo   C Bulgaria tell settlement

Kapovaya   E Russia hunter-gatherer art

Kapthurin   W Africa, Kenya early man

Kapwirimbwe   C Africa, Zambia Iron Age site

Kara'in   SW Anatolia early tools, Palaeolithic site, early pottery

Kara-Ukok   S Siberia steppe settlement

Karaagach   C Asia Han mirror find

Karabara   W Africa, Mali early town

Karabulak   S Russia Han mirror find

Karabur   Syria Assyrian rock relief

Karadepe   C Asia steppe settlement

Karaganda   SE Russia steppe settlement

Karagodevash   S Russia barrow burial

Karahüyük   C Anatolia Hittite city

Karako   C Japan rice farming site

Karakol   E Russia barrow burial

Karanovo   E Bulgaria farming site, tell settlement

Karaoglan   C Anatolia Neolithic site

Karasuk   S Siberia steppe settlement

Karatepe   E Anatolia Hittite city

Karats   N Norway bear grave

Karatsu   W Japan Korean pottery

Karbuna   SW Russia copper hoard

Karchat   NW India Harappan site

Kariandusi   E Africa, Kenya Acheulian tools

Karim Shahir   N Mesopotamia Neolithic site

Käringsjön   SW Sweden scratch plows

Karitane   New Zealand, South I. defended settlement

Karkarichinkat   W Africa, Mali early livestock

Karlbyneder   N Denmark bog body

Karle   S India rock-carved temple

Kärlich   W Germany early tools

Karistein   W Austria Celtic site

Karluk I.   NE Canada Thule site

Karmis-Blur   Armenia Urartian fortress

Karnak   U Egypt temples

Karos (Keros)   SE Greece cemetery

Karphi (Karfi)   C Crete peak sanctuary

Kartstein   W Germany Neanderthal site

Kashgar (Kashi)   NW China early trade center, Buddhist center, early trade

Kashmir   N India early trade

Kasori   C Japan early settlement, fishing site

Kasserine   C Tunisia Roman dam

Kassope   NW Greece theater and temple

Kastraki   N Greece tholos tomb

Kastri   NE and S Greece Mycenaean fortresses

Kastritsa   C Greece Neanderthal site

Kastro   S Greece Mycenaean fortress

Kasur   NW India Mughal mint

Katakolou   E Greece tholos tomb

Katanda   E Russia barrow burial

Katsambas   N Crete ancient port

Katsina   W Africa, Nigeria early town

Katsurakoi   N Japan Ainu hill fort

Katsusaka   C Japan early settlement

Katuruka   C Africa, Tanzania early iron

Kaupang   S Norway Viking trading emporium

Kaupokonui   New Zealand, North I. defended settlement

Kauri Point   New Zealand, North I. defended settlement

Kausambi   E India early city

Kavalla   N Greece Roman aqueduct

Kavat   C Asia steppe settlement

Kaveripattinam   S India early city

Kavrochori (Kavrokhorion)   N Crete Minoan village

Kawa   NE Africa, Sudan fortress and temple, temple remains, early iron

Kawakawa   New Zealand, North I. early site

Kawela   Hawaiian Is. early site

Kaya   S Korea early state

Kayalidere   E Anatolia Urartian fortress

Kayatha   NW India Harappan site

Kaybely   C Russia steppe settlement

Kayes   W Africa, Mali early town

Kayrakum   C Asia steppe settlement

Kayseri   C Anatolia Sinan mosque

Kazanluk   W Bulgaria farming site

Kazarun   SW Persia fire temple

Kbal Romeas   S Indo-China, Cambodia shell midden

Ke   W Africa, Nigeria early settlement, early town

Kealakekua Bay   Hawaiian Is. early site

Kébibat   NW Africa, Morocco *Homo erectus*

Kedungbrubus   E Java *Homo erectus*

Keet Seel   SW USA Pueblo farming site

Kefar Menahem   C Israel early tools

Kehe   N China early Palaeolithic site

Keilor   SE Australia early man

Kel-a Shin   NE Mesopotamia stela

Kelainai   W Anatolia Achaemenid palace

Kelang   S Malaya transitional settlement

Kelermes   S Russia barrow burial

Kelheim   C Germany Celtic oppidum

Kellali   W Syria early tools

Kemp   E USA temple mound

Kenchraei   S Greece temple and harbor

Kendenglembu   E Java Neolithic settlement

Kenk   SE Anatolia Assyrian rock relief

Kenkol   C Asia barrow burial, Han mirror find

Kenniff Cave   E Australia early man, Aboriginal site

Kents Cavern   S England early tools, hunter-gatherer site

Kephali (Kefali)   S Crete tholos tomb

Kephalos   SE Aegean theater and temple

Keppel Is.   E Australia Aboriginal site

Kerameikos   cemetery of Athens

Keratea   SE Greece Athenian settlement

Kermanshah   N Persia Seleucid inscription

Kernonen   NW France barrow burial

Kervouster   NW France Neanderthal site

Kesslerloch   W Germany hunter-gatherer site, hunter-gatherer art

Kexingzhuang   N China Longshan site

Khafajah   C Mesopotamia early city

Khairla Hill   N India Mesolithic site

Khalandri   SE Greece ancient fortress

Khalandriani   SE Greece ancient fortress

Khami   C Africa, Zimbabwe Iron Age site, Ming pottery

Khania (Chania, Hania, Canea)   NW Crete Minoan town

Khapuz-depe   C Asia steppe settlement

Kharg   SW Persia fire temple

Kharga Oasis   W Egypt Acheulian tools, Stone Age tools, early cultivation

Kharkha   N Mesopotamia Sasanian city

Khartoum   NE Africa, Sudan harpoons and pottery

Khashm el Girba   NE Africa, Sudan wavy-line pottery, early food

Khatanga   E Russia arctic culture

Khattab   W Syria early tools

Khirokitia   Cyprus Neolithic site

Khocho   NW China rock-carved temple

Khodzhasu   C Asia steppe settlement

Khor Abu Anga   NE Africa, Sudan Acheulian tools

Khor Musa   NE Africa Egypt Stone Age tools

Khorsabad (Dur-Sharrukin)   N Mesopotamia zigurrat, Assyrian royal palace, Assyrian capital

Khotan (Hotan)   NW China early trade center, Buddhist center, early trade

Khotnitsa (Chotnica)   C Bulgaria tell settlement

Khotylevo   C Russia hunter-gatherer art

Khrishteni (Hristene)   C Bulgaria early copper mine

Khrisoskalitissa   SW Crete Minoan village

Khristos   SE Greece Athenian settlement

Khurama   E Anatolia Assyrian colony

Khutor Baryshnikovii   C Russia barrow burial

Khutor-Druzhba   S Russia steppe settlement

Khyashchevka   C Russia steppe settlement

Kialegak   Alaska Thule site

Kiatuthlanna   SW USA Pueblo farming site

Kibbanahalli   S India Mesolithic site

Kibiro   E Africa, Uganda Iron Age site and salt mine

Kiffa   W Africa, Mauritania early town

Kiik-Koba   S Russia Neanderthal site

Kilepwa I.   E Africa, Kenya Ming pottery

Kili Gul Muhammad   NW India early farming village

Kilombe   E Africa, Kenya Acheulian tools

Kilwa   E Africa, Tanzania Islamic trade, early trading post, Ming pottery

Kimhae   S Korea rice farming site

Kimmswick   C USA fluted points
Kincaid   E USA temple mound
Kings Mound   SE USA temple mound
Kings Rock   New Zealand, South I. shell midden
King's Table   SE Australia early man
Kinishba   SW USA Pueblo farming site
Kinnarkheda   NW India Harappan site
Kinnikinick   SW USA Pueblo farming site
Kinosoura   SE Greece walled settlement
Kinowa   N Japan Heian fortress
Kinsale Farm   SE Africa, Zimbabwe Iron Age site
Kintampo   W Africa, Ghana early livestock
Kinuni   E Africa, Kenya Ming pottery
Kipushi   C Africa, Zaire Iron Age site
Kirchseeoner Moor   S Germany pollen core site
Kirillovskaya   C Russia hunter-gatherer art
Kiriwina   New Guinea Kula gift exchange
Kisapostag   S Hungary urnfield
Kiseiba   U Egypt early pottery
Kisesse   E Africa, Tanzania hunter-gatherers
Kisesse II   E Africa, Tanzania Stone Age tools
Kish   C Mesopotamia zigurrat, early city, early city and palace, early writing
Kishama   W Japan early settlement
Kit's Coty   SE England megalithic tomb
Kita   W Africa, Mali early town
Kita-Shirakawa   C Japan early settlement
Kitamae   N Japan early man
Kitava   New Guinea Kula gift exchange
Kivik   S Sweden barrow burial, rock art
Kiyevka   SW Russia steppe settlement
Kizil   C Asia rock-carved temple
Kizilkaya   SW Anatolia Neolithic site
Kjelmoj   N Norway Saami settlement
Klasies River Mouth   S Africa caves and rock shelters
Klausennische   S Germany Neanderthal site
Kleine Scheuer   W Germany hunter-gatherer site
Klementowice   NE Poland farming settlement
Klipplaatdrif   S Africa Acheulian tools
Klipriviersberg   S Africa Iron Age site
Klosterlund   Denmark Mesolithic settlement

Knapp Mounds   SE USA temple mounds
Knight   C USA, Illinois Hopewell site
Kobadi   W Africa, Mauritania pottery and harpoons
Kobadian-I   C Asia Achaemenid city
Kobyakovo   SW Russia steppe settlement
Kodak   S Russia Neanderthal site
Kodekal   S India cattle pen site
Koguryo   N Korea early state
Koh Ker   Indo-China, Cambodia early site
Kohika   New Zealand, North I. defended settlement
Kok Charoen   N Thailand Neolithic settlement
Kok Phanom Di   C Thailand Neolithic settlement
Kok Pleb   C Thailand transitional settlement
Kokand   C Asia steppe settlement
Kokcha   C Asia steppe settlement
Kokchetav   SE Russia steppe settlement
Kokkinopolis   C Greece Neanderthal site
Kokonovka   C Russia barrow burial
Kol   SW USA Pueblo farming site
Koldihwa   NE India early farming village
Kolhapur (Brahmapuri)   W India Deccan city
Köln-Lindenthal   W Germany farming site, defensive enclosure
Köln-Müngersdorf   W Germany Roman villa
Kolomoki   SE USA temple mound
Kolomyshchina   W Russia Cucuteni-Tripolye village, steppe settlement
Kolonna   SE Greece Mycenaean fortress
Koltubanka   C Russia steppe settlement
Kolyma River Mouth   E Russia Thule site
Kom el-Hisn   L Egypt ancient city
Kom Medinet Ghurab   U Egypt early town
Kom Ombo   U Egypt Ptolemaic temple
Kommos   S Crete ancient port
Komunmoru   N Korea early Palaeolithic site
Komurhan   E Anatolia Urartian site
Kondapur   W India Deccan city
Kondon   E Russia arctic culture
Kone (Garibaldi)   E Africa, Ethiopia Stone Age tools
Kong   W Africa, Ivory Coast early town
Konin   S Poland Mesolithic settlement

Konya   C Anatolia Ottoman empire
Koobi Fora   E Africa, Kenya *Australopithecus boisei* and early man, Oldowan tools
Koonalda Cave   S Australia ancient flint mine
Kophinas (Kofinas)   S Crete peak sanctuary
Korakou   C Greece Mycenaean fortress
Kore Kore   New Zealand, North I. defended settlement
Korolevskoye   W Russia barrow burial
Koroni   SE Greece fortified camp
Koropi   SE Greece Athenian settlement
Korovinski   Aleutian Is. arctic culture
Korselitse (Corselitze)   SE Denmark bog body
Korshevo   W Russia hunter-gatherer site
Koru   Kenya Proconsul
Körzüt Kalesi (Korzot)   E Anatolia Urartian fortress
Kosegasawa   C Japan cave site
Kosipe   New Guinea early man
Kösk   SE Anatolia Neolithic site
Koster   C USA, Illinois Archaic site
Kostienki   W Russia hunter-gatherer site, hunter-gatherer art
Kostromskaya   S Russia barrow burial
Kotabangun   E Borneo Buddhist center
Kota Cina   N Sumatra port
Kot Diji   NW India Indus Valley settlement, early city, Harappan site
Kota Tongkat   C Malaya rock shelter
Kotasur   NW India Harappan site
Koth   NW India Harappan site
Kothingeichendorf   S Germany defensive enclosure
Kotosh   C Peru preceramic site, Chavín site
Koufonisi   SE Crete ancient port
Koukounara   SW Greece tholos tomb
Koukya   W Africa, Mali early town
Koulen   Indo-China, Cambodia early site
Koumasa   S Crete peak sanctuary
Kouphia Rachi   N Greece tholos tomb
Kourounkorokale   W Africa, Mali bone harpoons, hunter-gatherers, early food
Kouroussa   W Africa, Guinea early town
Kow Swamp   SE Australia early man
Koya, Mt.   C Japan holy mountain
Koyagaugau   New Guinea Kula gift exchange
Kozuke   N Japan shogunate provincial capital
Krabi Cave   S Thailand cave site

Kragehul   C Denmark weapon hoard
Kragelund   W Denmark bog body
Krankmårtenhögen   N Norway Saami grave
Krapina   N Yugoslavia Neanderthal site
Kraske Spilje   Yugoslavia Mesolithic settlement
Krasnaya Gora   SW Russia steppe settlement
Krasnokutsk   SW Russia barrow burial
Krasnopol'ye   W Russia Han mirror find
Krasnoyarsk   S Siberia steppe settlement
Kremikovci   SE Europe farming site
Krepice   E Czechoslovakia iron-working site
Kreshchatyk   SW Russia steppe settlement
Kreuznach   W Germany early tools, Roman village
Krimeng   N Africa, Chad bone harpoons
Krisa   C Greece Mycenaean fortress
Krishna Bridge   S India Mesolithic settlement
Kristel-Jardins   NW Africa farming site, early pottery
Kromdraai   S Africa *Australopithecus robustus*
Krutaya Gora   C Russia hunter-gatherer site
Krzemionki   C Poland flint mine
Ksar Akil   Lebanon Neanderthal site
Ksiaznice Wielkie   SW Poland farming settlement
Ku Bua   Thailand moated site
Kuala Muda   N Malaya early site
Kuala Selinsing   W Malaya early site
Kuala Terengganu   C Malaya transitional settlement
Kucha (Kuqa)   NW China Buddhist center, early trade
Kuchizakai   C Japan rice farming site
Kudaro Cave   S Russia early tools, Neanderthal site
Kudatini   S India cattle pen site
Kudus   Java Islamic trade
Kufa   Iraq Islamic town
Kuh-i Khwaja   S Afghanistan fire temple
Kuizhou   C China provincial capital
Kuk   E Canada Thule site
Kuk   New Guinea early man
Kuk Swamp   E New Guinea early site, Neolithic settlement
Kukak   Alaska Pacific Eskimo site

Kukova   SE Europe burial
Kukulik   Alaska Thule site
Kul Oba (Nevskoye)   S Russia barrow burial
Kulam Mali   S India Islamic trade
Kulchurdo   E Africa, Kenya Stone Age site
Kuldja (Gulja, Yining)   C Asia early trade center
Kuli'ou'ou   Hawaiian Is. early site
Kulli   NW India Indus Valley settlement, Harappan site
Kulna Cave   Czechoslovakia early tools, Neanderthal cave site, hunter-gatherer site
Kültepe   SE Anatolia early trade, early town and palace
Kumara   E India Buddhist site
Kumara-Kaiamo   New Zealand, North I. defended settlement
Kumasi   W Africa, Ghana early town
Kumbakonam   S India Chola center
Kumbi Saleh   W Africa Islamic trade, urban center
Kumgang-san   N Korea holy mountain
Kumidu   Syria Egyptian control
Kumma   U Egypt temple
Kummukh (modern Samsat)   E Anatolia Assyrian provincial capital
Kumtura   C Asia rock-carved temple
Kumul (Hami)   NW China early trade
Kumyer   SW Anatolia road bridge
Kuna   E Mexico Maya settlement
Kunar Siyah   S Persia fire temple
Kunda   NW Russia Mesolithic settlement, megalithic site
Kungsan   N Korea early settlement
Kuningan   W Java early metal site
Kunling Protectorate   C Asia trade with China
Kunming (Yunnanfu)   SW China Ming provincial capital
Kunnattur   S India megalithic tomb
Kuntur Wasi   N Peru Chavín site
Kununurra   NW Australia Aboriginal site
Kupang   NE Borneo early port
Kupgal   S India cattle pen site
Kuratoy   S Siberia steppe settlement
Kurkh   E Anatolia Assyrian stela
Kurkihar   N India Buddhist center
Kürtün Cave   S Anatolia Palaeolithic site
Kuruçay   SW Anatolia Neolithic site
Kusano   W Japan fishing site
Kusinagara   NE India early city, Buddhist center

Kütahya   W Anatolia Sinan mosque
Kuujjua River   N Canada Thule site
Kvarnby   S Sweden Bronze Age settlement
Kwale   E Africa, Kenya Iron Age site
Kwangju   C Korea capital of early state
Kyamil-Tepe   S Russia barrow burial
Kyo-dong   C Korea early settlement
Kyongju   S Korea capital of early state, Islamic trade, Buddhist center
Kyoto   C Japan early capital
Kyozuka   C Japan Yamato tomb
L'Aldène   S France hunter-gatherer art
L'Angle   W France defensive enclosure
L'Escale   S France early tools
La Adam   Romania Mesolithic settlement, megalithic site
La Arboleda   C Mexico Pre-Classical site
La Baume de Gigny   E France Neanderthal site
La Baume de Peyrards   SE France Neanderthal site
La Baume Latrone   S France hunter-gatherer art
La Brèche   N France farming settlement
La Cabrera   NW Venezuela early settlement
La Chaise   C France early tools and human remains
La Chapelle-aux-Saints   C France Neanderthal site
La Chaussée-Tirancourt   N France megalithic tomb
La Clape   S France megalithic tomb
La Cocina   E Spain Mesolithic settlement
La Copa   N Peru Chavín site
La Cotte de St. Brelade   Jersey Neanderthal site
La Couronne   S France early settlement
La Crouzade   S France Mesolithic settlement
La Era   C Mexico Pre-Classical site
La Ferrassie   C France Neanderthal site
La Flecha   NW Spain Neanderthal site
La Florida   S Peru early farming site
La Frebouchère   NW France megalithic tomb
La Galgada   N Peru early public building
La Gravette   C France hunter-gatherer site
La Grive-Saint-Alban   C France Dryopithecus
La Grotta de Broion   N Italy Neanderthal site

La Grotte d'Aldene   C France early tools

La Grotte de l'Observatoire   SE France early tools

La Grotte du Docteur   Belgium Neanderthal site

La Grotte du Prince   SE France early tools and human remains

La Gruta   C Venezuela early horticultural village

La Halliade   SW France megalithic tomb

La Hogue   N France megalithic tomb

La Hoguette   N France megalithic tomb

La Honradez   N Guatemala Maya settlement

La Hoz   C Spain hunter-gatherer art

La Jolla   W USA, California Archaic site

La Madeleine   C France hunter-gatherer site, hunter-gatherer art

La Madeleine   NW France stone alignment

La Magdeleine   SW France hunter-gatherer art

La Mar   E Mexico Maya settlement

La Masque   SE France Neanderthal site

La Micoque   C France early tools

La Mouthe   C France hunter-gatherer art

La Naulette   Belgium Neanderthal site

La Nauterie   C France early tools

La Paya   N Argentina Inca tambo

La Pileta   S Spain hunter-gatherer art

La Pitia   N Colombia early settlement

La Plata (Sucre)   Bolivia colonial settlement

La Quemada   C Mexico early town

La Quercia   S Italy defensive enclosure

La Quina   C France Neanderthal site

La Salpétrière   E France hunter-gatherer site

La Starza   S Italy early settlement

La Tène   C Switzerland Celtic site

La Tranche   NW France farming site

La Venta   C Mexico pyramid, Olmec center

La Victoria   Guatemala early farming site

Laang Spean   S Indo-China, Cambodia cave site, Neolithic settlement

Labastide   SW France hunter-gatherer art

Labna   Mexico-Yucatán Maya settlement

Labraunda   SW Anatolia Hellenistic city

Labwe   WW Syria Neolithic site

Lachish (Lakishi)   S Palestine early town, Egyptian control, Levantine city, Achaemenid palace

Laconia   Ancient country of S Greece

Laetolil   E Africa, Tanzania *Australopithecus afarensis*, early man

Lagash   S Mesopotamia early city, early town, early writing

Lago Agrio   Ecuador early settlement

Lago di Biandronno   N Italy pollen core site

Lago Grande de Vila Franca   E Brazil shell midden

Lagoa Santa   S Brazil early settlement

Lagoon   NW Canada Dorset site

Lagoon Flat   New Zealand, South I. shell midden and moa bones

Lagos   W Africa, Nigeria early town

Lagozza   N Italy farming settlement

Laguna de los Cerros   C Mexico Olmec site

Laguna Francesa   SE Mexico Pre-Classical site

Lahore   NW India Mughal mint

Laish   N Palestine early town

Lake Alakul'   C Russia steppe settlement

Lake Argyle (Miriwun)   NW Australia Aboriginal site

Lake Condah   S Australia Aboriginal site

Lake Hauroko   New Zealand, South I. early site

Lake Jackson   SE USA temple mound

Lake Kerinci   C Sumatra cave site, early metal site

Lake Mangakawere   New Zealand, North I. defended settlement

Lake Mohave   W USA, California Archaic site

Lake Mungo   SE Australia early man

Lake Rusa   E Anatolia Urartian stela

Lake Tytyl'   E Russia Thule site

Lakeba (Lakemba)   Fiji Lapita site

Lalibela   NE Africa, Ethiopia early cereals, rock-cut churches

Lalo   N Philippines Neolithic settlement

Lalomanu   Samoa early site

Lamar   SE USA temple mound

Lamb Spring   W USA early settlement

Lambaesis (Lambèse, modern Tazoult)   N Algeria Roman legionary fortress

Lambourn   S England beaker burial

Lamoka Lake   NE USA, New York Archaic site

Lamphun   N Thailand early site, Buddhist pagoda

Lampsacus (Lampsakos, modern Lâpseki)   NW Anatolia Greek colony, Byzantine town

Lang Ca   N Vietnam transitional settlement

Lang Vac   N Vietnam transitional settlement

Langdon Bay   SE England early shipwreck

Langhnaj   NW India Mesolithic settlement

Långlös Norregård   SE Sweden musical instruments

Langtandong   E China *Homo erectus*

Langton   N England medieval village

Langweiler   W Germany early tools, farming site, defensive enclosure

Lantian   N China *Homo erectus*

Laodicea (Katakia, modern Al Ladhiquyah)   W Syria Hellenistic city, Roman city

Laodicea   S Anatolia Hellenistic city, aqueduct

Laodicea (modern Nihavend)   NW Persia Hellenistic city

Lapakahi   Hawaiian Is. early site

Lapita   New Caledonia Lapita site

Lappland   Saami culture

Lapstone Creek   SE Australia Aboriginal site

Larne   N Ireland Mesolithic settlement, Viking center

Larsa   S Mesopotamia early city, early city and palace

Larzicourt   NE France farming site

Las Bocas   C Mexico Pre-Classical site

Las Flores   C Mexico early town

Las Haldas   N Peru preceramic site

Las Palomas   S Spain hunter-gatherer art

Las Plassas   S Sardinia megalithic tomb

Las Sabanas   C Mexico Pre-Classical site

Lascaux   C France hunter-gatherer art

Lashkari Bazar (Bust)   N India Islamic town

Lassicourt   N France early tools

Lastingham   N England medieval town

Latamne   W Syria early tools

Latma   N Africa, Chad bone harpoons

Latvia   Mesolithic settlements

Laugerie Basse   C France hunter-gatherer site, hunter-gatherer art

Laugerie Haute   C France hunter-gatherer site, hunter-gatherer art

Laura   NE Australia Aboriginal site

Lauricocha   Peru early farming

Laurium (Laureion)   SE Greece silver mines

Lauriya-Araraj   NE India rock edict

Lauriya-Nandangarh   NE India Asokan column

Laus   S Italy Greek colony

Laussel   C France hunter-gatherer art

Lautereck   S Germany Mesolithic settlement, megalithic site

Lazaret   SE France early tools and human remains

Lchashen   Armenia steppe burials, Late Bronze Age

Le Baratin   S France farming site

Le Bernard   W France Celtic religious site

Le Breuil   C France hunter-gatherer site

Le Cerislier   C France hunter-gatherer site

Le Colombare   N Italy early settlement

Le Conquette   S France farming settlement

Le Figuier   E France hunter-gatherer site

Le Flageolet   C France hunter-gatherer site

Le Gabillou   C France hunter-gatherer art

Le Havre   N France early tools

Le Mas   C France hunter-gatherer site

Le Mas d'Azil   SW France hunter-gatherer art, Mesolithic settlement

Le Mas Viel   C France Neanderthal site

Le Menec   NW France stone alignment

Le Moustier   C France Neanderthal site

Le Petit-Puymoyen   C France Neanderthal site

Le Placard   C France hunter-gatherer art

Le Poisson   C France hunter-gatherer art

Le Tillet   N France early tools, Neanderthal site

Le Tuc d'Audoubert   SW France hunter-gatherer art

Le Vallonnet   SE France early tools

Leang Buidane   S Philippines early metal site

Leang Burung   E Indonesia, Celebes cave site, Neolithic settlement

Leang Tuwo Mane's   S Philippines Neolithic settlement

Lebena   Crete marble figurines

Lébous   SW France ancient fortress

Lechaeum   S Greece harbor and temple

Ledro   N Italy lake dwelling

Leeds   N England medieval town, railway development

Lefkanki   E Greece early port

Leggett   SW USA Pueblo farming site

Legio (modern León)   N Spain Roman legionary fortress

Legio   Palestine Roman legionary fortress

Lehner   SW USA, Arizona Palaeo-Indian site

Leicester   C England Viking center

Leigudun   C China E Chou burial

Leipsydrion   SE Greece Athenian fort

Leiria   E Spain native settlement

Leiyang   C China Tang kiln

Lekhahia   NE India Mesolithic settlement

Leki Male   NW Poland barrow burial

Lekka   W Africa, Nigeria early town

Lekkerwater   E Africa, Zimbabwe Iron Age site

Lelang   NE China Han burial

Leles   W Java early site

Leman and Ower   E England Mesolithic settlement

Lemnos   N Aegean Greek theater

Lenderscheid   N Germany early tools

Lengerich   NE Germany ritual metalwork

Leninabad   C Asia Han mirror find

Leonard Rock Shelter   SW USA, Nevada early man

Leoncito   C Chile Inca tambo

Leone   American Samoa early site

Leontini (Leontinoi, modern Lentini)   E Sicily Greek colony

Leontium   S Greece theater

Leopard's Kopje   SE Africa, Zimbabwe Iron Age site

Lepenski Vir   Yugoslavia Mesolithic settlement

Leptis (Leptis Minor, Leptis Parva, modern Lamta)   NE Tunisia Cathaginian city

Leptis Magna (Lepcis, modern Labdah)   N Libya Phoenician city, Roman city, Roman dam, early iron

Lérida   NE Spain monastery

Lerna   S Greece ancient fortress

Les Avaix   C France pollen core site

Les Cornaux   C Switzerland Celtic site

Les Fouaillages   Channel Is. megalithic tomb

Les Hoteaux   E France hunter-gatherer site

Les Lauzières   SE France ancient fortress

Les Matignons   W France defensive enclosure

Les Trois Frères   SW France hunter-gatherer art

Leskovo   Bulgaria early copper mine

Lespugue   C France hunter-gatherer art

Let   Romania farming site

Letoön   SW Anatolia Hellenistic city

Leubingen   C Germany barrow burial

Leuca   S Italy Neanderthal site

Leucaspide   S Italy megalithic tomb

Leucate   SW France farming site

Leucecome   Red Sea ancient port, early trade center

Leucos Limen (modern Quseir el-Qadim)   Red Sea early trade center

Leuluasi   Western Samoa early site

Leuwiliang   W Java early metal site

Levant   Early cities and states

Levanzo   Sicily hunter-gatherer art

Levkas   W Greece bronze daggers

Levroux   C France Celtic site

Lewan   NW India Harappan site

Lezetxiki   N Spain Neanderthal site

Lhasa   Tibet Buddhist center

Li Lolghi   N Sardinia megalithic tomb

Li Muri   Sardinia megalithic tomb

Liangcheng   N China Longshan site

Liangzhu   E China early settlement, Longshan site

Lianjiang   SE China Sung kiln

Liare Valley   E Africa, Kenya Iron Age site

Libenice   W Czechoslovakia Celtic religious site

Licun   N China W Chou burial

Lie Siri   Timor Neolithic settlement

Liepen   NE Germany megalithic tomb

Ligor   SW Thailand early site

Lijiacun   N China Shang burial

Lijialou   N China E Chou bronze hoard

Lilybaeum (modern Marsala)   W Sicily Carthaginian city

Limages   SW Africa, Angola Acheulian tools

Limerick   SW Ireland Viking center

Limnae   NW Anatolia Greek colony

Limonum (modern Poitiers)   C France Roman city

Lincoln (Lindum)   E England Roman Aqueduct, Viking center

Lindenmeier   W USA, Wyoming bison kill site

Lindholm   N Denmark Viking center

Lindisfarne   S Scotland Celtic fortress

Lindos   E Mediterranean Greek city, Hellenistic city

Lindow Moss   NW England bog body

Lindum (modern Lincoln)   E England Roman city

Lingjing   N China early settlement

Lingshan   SW China cave site

Lingshanwei   E China E Chou bronze hoard

Linhai   E China Tang kiln

Linhuai   C China Han city

Linnasaiva   N Sweden Saami site

Lintong   N China Chou site

Linyi   NE China Han burial

Lion Cave   SE Africa, Swaziland Stone Age tools

Lios   SW Ireland stone circle and henge

Lipara (modern Lipari)   SW Italy Greek colony

Lisbon (Lisboa)   C Portugal Islamic town, medieval trade, maritime trade

Liscuis   NW France megalithic tomb

Lishan   N China Han burial

Lishui   E China Sung kiln

Lisnacrogher   N Ireland Celtic art

Little Bighorn   NW USA battle site

Little Kelk   N England medieval pottery

Little Papanui   New Zealand, South I. early site

Little Salt Spring   SE USA fluted points

Little Swanport   Tasmania Aboriginal site

Liuchengqiao   C China E Chou burial

Liufeng   W China Ramapithecus and Sivapithecus

Liujiacha   N China early man

Liujiazhuang   N Japan early settlement

Liulichang   W China Tang kiln

Liulige   N China E Chou cemetery

Liulin   N China early settlement, Longshan site

Lixus (modern Larache)   NW Morocco Carthaginian city

Liyu   NE China E Chou bronze hoard

Liyuan   N China early settlement

Llatas   E Spain Mesolithic settlement

Llyn Cerrig Bach   N Wales Celtic religious site

Loanhead of Daviot   NE Scotland stone circle

Lochard   C Africa, Zimbabwe Acheulian tools

Lochhill   SW Scotland megalithic tomb

Locri   S Italy Greek colony

Locris   Ancient country of C Greece

Löddenköppinge   S Sweden Viking center

Lodenice   W Czechoslovakia iron-working site

Loe Band   N India later farming village

Lofthoj   E Denmark swords

Logan Creek   C USA, Nebraska Archaic site

Lohri   NW India Harappan site

Lohumjo-Daro   NW India Harappan site

Lokri Epizephyril   SW Italy Greek colony

Lolokoka   C Pacific Lapita site

Loltun Cave   Mexico, Yucatán Maya settlement

Loma Larga   C Mexico stone source

Lommersum   N Germany hunter-gatherer site

Londinium (modern London)   SE England Roman provincial capital

Long Meg and her Daughters   NW England stone circle

Long Wittenham   C England Celtic religious site

Long's Drift   E Africa, Kenya early food

Longmen   N China rock-carved temple

Longquan   E China Tang kiln, Sung kiln

Longquanwucun   N China Tang kiln

Longxingfu   C China provincial capital

Lop Buri   C Thailand early site, Buddhist center

Lop Buri artillery center   C Thailand transitional settlement

Lorlyan Tangai   N India Gandharan art

Los Casares   C Spain hunter-gatherer art

Los Higos   Honduras Maya settlement

Los Millares   SE Spain defensive enclosure

Los Morteros   N Peru early farming site

Los Muertos   SW USA Pueblo farming site

Los Murciélagos   S Spain farming settlement

Los Placeres del Oro   C Mexico Pre-Classical site

Los Soldados   C Mexico Olmec site

Los Terrones   C Mexico Pre-Classical site

Los Toldos   S Argentina early settlements

Lothagam (Loktang)   E Africa, Kenya Australopithecus, harpoons and pottery

Lothal   NW India early city, Harappan site

Lotofaga   Western Samoa early site

Lou I.   Papua New Guinea Lapita obsidian

Lough Cur   SW Ireland farming settlement

Loulan   NW China silk find, Buddhist center

Lovelock Cave   SW USA, Nevada prehistoric diet

Low Flat Site   Kermadec Is.

Lowasera   E Africa, Kenya harpoons and pottery, early pottery

Lower Lena Valley   E Russia arctic culture

Lowry Ruins   SW USA Pueblo farming site

Luanza   C Africa, Zaire Iron Age site

Luatuanu'u   Western Samoa early site

Lubaantun   Belize Maya settlement

Lubná   Czechoslovakia hunter-gatherer site

Lubusi   C Africa, Zambia Iron Age site

Luca (modern Lucca)   N Italy Roman colony

Ludérov   C Czechoslovakia beaker burial

Lugdunum (modern Lyon)   E France Roman provincial capital

Lugovoye-Muzhichi   S Russia barrow burial

Luk'yanovka   SW Russia steppe settlement

Luka Vrublevetskaya   W Russia Cucuteni-Tripolye village

Lukenya   E Africa, Kenya hunter-gatherers, Neolithic site, Iron Age site

Lüleburgaz   NW Turkey Sinan mosque

Lululampembele   E Africa, Tanzania hunter-gatherers

Lumbini   NE India pillar edict, Buddhist center

Lumigny   N France Celtic site

Luna   NW India Harappan site

Luna   SW USA Pueblo farming site

Luna (modern Luni)   N Italy Roman colony

Lund   N Denmark Viking center

Lunde   C Denmark rock art

Lundfors   N Sweden Mesolithic settlement

Lundi   E Africa, Zimbabwe Iron Age site

Lunel Viel   C France early tools

Luni   C Italy early settlement

Lunteren   S Holland beaker burial

Luojiajiao   E China rice farming site

Luoyang (Lo-yang)   N China early settlement, early city, Shang city, early trade capital, Han burial, Buddhist center, Tang capital

Luparevo   SW Russia barrow burial
Lupemba   C Africa, Zaire Stone Age
  tools
Luqurmata   N Bolivia early town
Lurin   C Peru Chavín site, Inca center
Lushan   N China Sung kiln
Lutetia (modern Paris)   N France
  Roman city
Luxembourg   Luxembourg Roman
  village, Roman Empire
Luxor   U Egypt temples
Lycia   ancient country of SW Anatolia
Lydenburg   S Africa Iron Age site
Lydia   ancient country of NW Anatolia
Lykkegårdens Mose   N Denmark bog
  body
Lyon (Lugdunum, Lyons)   E France
  Roman aqueduct, medieval trade,
  archbishopric
Lysolaje   W Czechoslovakia corded
  ware burial
Lyubimovka   C Russia barrow burial
Ma'in   SW Arabia early state
Ma'rib   SW Arabia ancient dam
Ma'yan Barukh   N Israel early tools
Maba   S China early man
Mabaruma   Guyana early horticultural
  village
Mablyyat   W Arabia Islamic town
Mablaqah   SW Arabia early trade
Mabo Mosse   S Sweden pollen core site
Maboko Island   Kenya Proconsul and
  Kenyapithecus
Mabveni   SE Africa, Zimbabwe Iron
  Age site
Macao   S China maritime trade
MacArthur Cave   W Scotland
  Mesolithic settlement
Macassar   E Indies, Celebes maritime
  trade
Machalilla   Ecuador early farming site
Machanggou   NE China W Chou
  bronze hoard
Machaquilá   C Guatemala Maya
  settlement
Machu Picchu   C Peru Inca center
Machupo   S Brazil early settlement
Mâcon   E France Celtic oppidum
Macon Plateau   SE USA temple mound
Macun Çay   N Anatolia Palaeolithic site
Madai   NE Borneo cave site, early
  metal site
Madhava   temple of Vijayanagara
Madhavpur   W India Deccan city
Madrague de Gien   France shipwreck
  excavation
Madras   SE India early trade

Madsebakke   E Denmark rock art
Madura (Madurai)   S India early city,
  Pandya capital
Madytus   NW Turkey Greek colony
Maes Howe   N Scotland megalithic
  tomb
Magadha   early state of NE India
Magarida   W Japan rice farming site
Magdalenenberg   C Switzerland
  Hallstatt site
Magdalensberg   S Austria Celtic
  oppidum
Magdeburg   E Germany archbishopric
Magheralin   NE Ireland bog body
Maglehoj   E Denmark barrow burial
Magna Graecia   the Greek colonies of
  S Italy
Magnesia   SW Anatolia Greek temple,
  Hellenistic city
Magosi   E Africa, Uganda Stone Age
  tools, hunter-gatherers
Magoula   SE Greece Athenian
  settlement
Magsuhot   C Philippines early metal
  site
Mahadaha   NE India Mesolithic
  settlement
Mahagama   S Ceylon Buddhist site
Mahagara   C India early farming
  village
Mahana   Hawaiian Is. early site
Mahdia   N Africa, Tunisia Islamic town
Mahismati   C India Deccan city
Mahurjari   C India megalithic tomb
Mai Lumba   W Africa, Nigeria Stone
  Age tools
Maiden Castle   S England defensive
  enclosure
Maidum (Meidum)   U Egypt pyramid,
  early plow, early burial, early town
Maiji Shan   N China rock-carved
  temple
Mailhac   S France urnfield, Celtic
  oppidum
Maininskaya   E Russia hunter-gather art
Mainz (Mogontiacum)   W Germany
  Roman town, archbishopric
Maioro   New Zealand, North I.
  defended settlement
Maisières   Belgium hunter-gatherer site
Maizy   NE France Iron Age cemetery
Majiabang   E China early settlement
Majiabin   E China Longshan site
Majiawan   NW China early settlement
Majiayao   NW China early settlement
Makaha Valley   Hawaiian Is. early
  irrigation

Makapansgat   S Africa
  Australopithecus africanus
Makgwareng   S Africa Iron Age site
Makotukutuku Valley   New Zealand,
  North I. shell midden
Maksyutovo   C Russia steppe settlement
Makwe   C Africa, Zambia hunter-
  gatherers
Malaca (modern Málaga)   S Spain
  Phoenician city and harbor
Malacca   S Malaya Islamic trade,
  maritime trade
Malao (modern Berbera)   NE Africa,
  Somalia ancient port, early trade
Malapati   SE Africa, Zimbabwe Iron
  Age site
Mälaren   E Sweden Bronze Age
  settlement
Malatya   SE Anatolia Islamic town
Malazgirt   E Anatolia Uratian fortress
Malé Kosihy   E Czechoslovakia fortified
  site
Malerualik   N Canada Thule site
Maligawila   S Ceyton Buddhist remains
Malinalco   C Mexico pyramid, Aztec
  town
Malindi   E Africa, Kenya Islamic
  trading post
Malkata   U Egypt royal palace
Mallia (Malia)   N Crete Minoan palace
Malo   Vanuatu Lapita site
Maloye Okulovo   C Russia steppe
  settlement
Malta   ancient temples, Bronze Age
Mal'ta   E Russia hunter-gatherer site,
  hunter-gatherer art
Maltai   N Mesopotamia Assyrian rock
  relief
Maltepe   S Anatolia Neolithic site
Malthi   SW Greece tholos tomb
Malton   N England medieval town
Malyy Koytas   S Siberia steppe
  settlement
Mamallapuram   S India Pallava center
Mamaodong   SW China early man
Mambrui   E Africa, Kenya Ming
  pottery
Mammoth Cave   SW Australia early
  man
Mamutowa   Poland hunter-gatherer site
Manares   E Crete Minoan villa
Mancheng   N China Han burial
Manchester   C England railway
  development
Manching   SE Germany Celtic oppidum
Manda   E Africa, Kenya Islamic trade
Mandagora   W India early trade

Mandalay   N Burma Buddhist center

Mandeure   E France Celtic site

Mandeville   SE USA, Georgia Hopewell site

Mandheera   NE Africa, Somalia hunter-gatherers

Mandra   SW Greece tholos tomb

Manekweni   SE Africa, Mozambique Iron Age site

Mangakino   New Zealand, North I. rock art

Mangueiras   W Brazil early horticultural village

Mangzhang   C China Shang lacquerware

Maní   Mexico, Yucatán Maya settlement

Manika   C Greece rock-cut tomb

Manikpur   NE India Mughal mint

Manikyal   N India Buddhist site

Manila   Philippines maritime trade

Manisa   W Anatolia Sinan mosque

Mann   C USA, Indiana Hopewell site

Manothi   NW India Harappan site

Mansura   N India Islamic town

Mantinea   S Greece theater and temple

Manton Swamp   New Guinea Neolithic settlement

Manukau South Head   New Zealand shell midden and moa bones

Manunu   Society Is. early site

Maodigou   N China early settlement

Maoling   NE China Ming tomb

Mapela   SE Africa Iron Age site

Mapungubwe   S Africa Iron Age site

Marae-Mahaiatea   Society Is. early site

Marande   W Africa, Niger urban center

Maras   E Anatolia Assyrian provincial city

Marash   SE Anatolia Islamic town

Marathon   SE Greece Athenian settlement

Marathus   W Syria Levantine temple

Marcey Creek   E USA, Virginia Archaic site

Marcoing   N France Neanderthal site

Mardan   N India Gandharan art

Mareth   N Africa, Tunisia hunter-gatherers

Mareuil   N France early tools

Mari   N Mesopotamia early city, early city and palace, early writing

Marillac   C France Neanderthal site

Markkleeberg   E Germany early tools

Markopoulon   SE Greece Athenian settlement

Marksville   S USA, Louisiana Hopewell site, temple mound

Marlborough Downs   SW England source of stones

Marmagen (Marcomagus)   W Germany Roman village

Marmariani   N Greece tholos tomb

Marmes   NW USA, Washington Archaic site

Maronea   NE Greece Greek colony

Marquesas Is.   early settlement

Marsala   W Sicily shipwreck, monastery

Marseilles (Marseille)   S France medieval trade

Marsh Pass   SW USA, Arizona Basketmaker site

Marsiliana   N Italy Etruscan city

Marte   W Africa, Nigeria early town

Martelange   S Belgium Roman village

Martinez Rockshelter   C Mexico early settlement

Marton   N England medieval town

Marzabotto   N Italy early temple

Masal Hüyük   N Anatolia Hittite palace

Mashan   C China E Chou burial

Masjid-i Sulaiman (Masjed-e Soleyman)   W Persia religious site, fire temple

Maski   S India megalithic tomb

Massilia (modern Marseille)   S France Greek colony, Roman city, early trade center

Mastyugino   S Russia barrow burial

Masulipatam (Masalia, modern Machilipatnam)   SE India early city, early trade center, maritime trade

Maszycha   Poland hunter-gatherer site, hunter-gatherer art

Matacapan   C Mexico early town

Matala   SW Africa, Angola Acheulian tools

Matara   NE Ethiopia temple remains

Matarrah   C Mesopotamia pottery remains

Matarrubilla   SW Spain ancient fortress

Matauros   S Italy Greek colony

Mathura   C India early city, early trade center, Buddhist center

Matieni   ancient people of NW Persia

Matjiesrivier   S Africa hunter-gatherers, Stone Age site

Matola   SE Africa, Mozambique Iron Age site

Matougang   S China E Chou burial

Matsuoka   C Japan mound cemetery

Mattie Canyon   SW USA Pueblo farming site

Mattocks   SW USA Pueblo farming site

Matupi Cave   C Africa, Zaire hunter-gatherers

Mauer   SW Germany human remains

Mauern   S Germany Neanderthal site, hunter-gatherer site, hunter-gatherer art

Mauna Kea   Hawaiian Is. early quarry

Maungaroa Valley   Cook Is. early site

Maupiti   Society Is. early site

Mavesyn Ridware   C England defensive enclosure

Mawangdui   C China Han burial

Mawudzu   E Africa, Malawi Iron Age site

Maxela   C Mexico Pre-Classical site

Ma'yan Barukh   N Israel early tools

Mayapán   Mexico, Yucatán Maya settlement, early town

Mayen   NW Germany Roman village, Rhenish pottery kiln

Mayenne Sciences   N France hunter-gatherer art

Mayfa'ah   SW Arabia early trade

Maykop   SW Russia steppe settlement, barrow burial

Mayo Louti   W Africa, Cameroon Stone Age tools

Mayor I.   New Zealand, North I. shell midden

Mazagao   E Brazil early settlement

Mazarakata   W Greece tholos tomb

Mazghuna   L Egypt pyramids

Mazorayeh   W Persia early mine

Mazouco   N Portugal hunter-gatherer art

Mazukari   C Japan fishing site

Mbande Hill   E Africa Iron Age site

McConnell   N USA, Ohio Archaic site

McKean   NW USA, Montana Archaic site

Mcquorquodale   S USA, Mississippi Hopewell site

Me'ae Pekia   Marquesas Is. early site

Meadowcroft   NE USA fluted points

Meaux   N England Cistercian abbey

Mecca (Makkah)   W Arabia Islamic town, Sinan mosque

Mechta el Arbi   N Africa, Algeria hunter-gatherers

Medemblik   N Holland Viking trading emporium

Medigiriya   N Ceylon Buddhist remains

Medina (Madinah)   W Arabia trade, Islamic town

Medinet el-Faiyum   early town

Medinet Habu   U Egypt temple

Medinet Ma'adi   U Egypt temple

Mediolanum (modern Milano, Milan)   N Italy Roman city

Mediolanum (modern Saintes) W France Roman city

Medma S Italy Greek colony

Meerut N India pillar edict, Buddhist center

Megalopolis S Greece theatre and temple, Hellenistic city

Megara SE Greece city-state, walled settlement

Megara Hyblaea E Sicily Greek colony

Megaris district of SE Greece

Megiddo C Palestine early town, Egyptian fortress, royal fortress of Israel

Mehi NW India Harappan site

Mehrgarh NW India early farming village, early city, Harappan site

Meinarti, Island of U Egypt fortress

Meir U Egypt noble's tomb

Mejiro W Africa, Nigeria hunter-gatherers

Mejlgård N Denmark shell midden

Melanesia W Pacific early settlement

Meldon Bridge SE Scotland defensive enclosure

Meliddu (Melitene, modern Malatya) E Anatolia Assyrian provincial city

Melilli Sicily ancient fortress

Melitene (Meliddu, modern Malatya) E Anatolia Roman legionary fortress

Melitopol SW Russia barrow burial

Melizeigara W India early trade

Melka Kunture (Kontoure) E Africa, Ethiopia early man, Stone Age tools, hunter-gatherers

Melkhoutboom S Africa Stone Age site

Melolo S Indonesia early metal site

Melos S Aegean Greek city

Melville Koppies S Africa Iron Age site

Memphis L Egypt early city, ancient city, Achaemenid city, Hellenistic city, early iron

Menard S USA temple mound

Mende NE Greece Greek colony

Mendut C Java Buddhist center

Menehune Ditch Hawaiian Is.

Menelaion S Greece Mycenaean settlement

Mengchi Protectorate C Asia trade with China

Mengxi C China Longshan site

Menidi E Greece tholos tomb

Meniet N Africa, Algeria bone harpoons, early livestock

Menneville NE France Iron Age cemetery

Mercin-et-Vaux NE France Iron Age cemetery

Mérida W Spain Roman aqueduct, Islamic town

Merimda NE Africa, Egypt early cereals

Merkour SE Greece Athenian settlement

Meroë NE Africa, Sudan temple remains, early trade, early iron

Merrivale SW England stone alignment and menhir

Merry Maidens (Dawns Men) SW England stone circle

Mersa Gawasis Red Sea temple

Mersin SE Anatolia Neolithic site, farming site, early pottery

Merv (Margush, Alexandria, modern Mary) C Asia Achaemenid city, Parthian/Sasanian city, early trade center, Islamic town

Mesa Verde SW USA Pueblo farming site

Mesas de Asta SW Spain early settlement

Mesembria Bulgaria Greek colony, Byzantine walled town

Meshed NE Persia holy city

Messene S Greece theater and temple

Messenia region of SW Greece

Messina Sicily archbishopric

Mesvin IV Belgium early tools

Metapontum (Metapontion) S Italy Greek colony

Metaurus S Italy Greek colony

Methone NE Greece Greek colony

Metmenge SE Anatolia early tools

Metz E France Roman aqueduct

Mexicaltzingo C Mexico Aztec center

Mextitlán early state of Mexico

Mezcala C Mexico early farming site, Pre-Classical site

Mezhirich' C Russia hunter-gatherer site, hunter-gatherer art

Mezin W Russia hunter-gatherer site, hunter-gatherer art

Miami S USA, Texas Palaeo-Indian site

Miaodigou N China Longshan site

Miaoqiancun N China E Chou cemetery

Mid Clyth NE Scotland stone alignment

Midhen SW Greece tholos tomb

Miesenheim W Germany early tools

Mihintale N Ceyton Buddhist site, Buddhist remains

Mikhaylovka SW Russia steppe settlement

Mikonos (Mykonos) SE Greece ancient fortress

Mikro Kavouri SE Greece Athenian settlement

Mila Mergi N Mesopotamia Assyrian rock relief

Mila NW Greece tholos tomb

Milan (Milano) N Italy Celtic oppidum medieval trade, archbishopric

Miletus W Anatolia Classical state, early port, Achaemenid city, Greek city, Hellenistic city, Roman city

Miller S USA, Mississippi Hopewell site

Millstream W Australia Aboriginal site

Mimasaka C Japan shogunate provincial capital

Mimot Cambodia Neolithic settlement

Mina Perdida S Peru early farming site

Mina E Brazil shell midden

Mindeddu E Sardinia dry-stone fortress

Mindif W Africa, Cameroon Stone Age tools

Minisink E USA, Delaware Palaeo-Indian site

Minoa (Heraclea Minoa) W Sicily Greek colony

Minturnae (modern Minturno) C Italy Roman colony

Mirabib SW Africa, Namibia Stone Age site

Mirador SE Mexico Pre-Classical site

Miran NW China Buddhist center

Mirgissa U Egypt fortification

Miriwun N Australia early man

Mirpur Khas NW India Buddhist site

Misa-ri C Korea early settlement

Mison C Vietnam early monumental site

Miswar SW Arabia early capital

Mitathal (Mitahal) NW India Indus Valley settlement, Harappan site

Mitha Deheno NW India Harappan site

Mitla C Mexico pyramid, Pre-Classical site, Aztec town

Mitla Fortress C Mexico stone source

Mitli NW India Mesolithic settlement

Mitropolis S Crete Minoan villa

Mitterberg W Austria copper mine

Mittimatalik NE Canada Dorset site

Mivath N India Mughal mint

Miwa, Mt. C Japan holy mountain

Mixco Viejo S Guatemala Maya settlement, early town

Mixian N China Tang kiln, Sung kiln

Mixnitz Austria Neanderthal site

Mixquic C Mexico Aztec center

Mizukamidani C Japan early settlement

Mlu Prei Cambodia transitional settlement

Mnarani E Africa, Kenya Ming pottery

Moanalua Hawaiian Is. early irrigation

Mocha SW Arabia, Yemen maritime trade

Moche NW Peru pyramid, pre-Inca center

Mochlos (Mokhlos) NE Crete Minoan town

Modoc C USA, Illinois Archaic site

Moel Ty Uchaf N Wales stone circle

Mogadishu (Muqdisho) E Africa, Somalia Islamic trade, Iron Age site, Ming pottery

Mogador (modern Essaouira) NW Africa, Morocco Phoenician city, early iron

Mogara N India Mesolithic settlement

Mogen S Norway early settlement

Moghogha Sura NW Morocco Carthaginian cemetery

Mogollon Village SW USA Pueblo farming site

Mogontiacum (modern Mainz) W Germany Roman legionary fortress

Mohameriya U Egypt ancient cemetery

Mohelnice Czechoslovakia farming site

Mohenjo-Daro NW India early city, early writing, Buddhist site

Moho Cay E Mexico Maya center

Moikau New Zealand, North I. early site

Mokau New Zealand, North I. rock art

Mokrin NE Yugoslavia Bronze Age cemetery

Molino Casarotto N Italy farming settlement

Molodovo S Russia Neanderthal site, hunter-gatherer site, hunter-gatherer art

Moluccas (Spice Islands) early maritime trade

Mombasa E Africa, Kenya maritime trade

Monagrillo C America, Panama early pottery

Monamore W Scotland megalithic tomb

Monastir NW Africa, Tunisia Islamic fortress

Monastiraki C Crete Minoan villa

Mongolia early civilization, steppe nomads

Mongonu W Africa, Nigeria early town

Monk Bretton N England medieval town

Monks Mound C USA temple mound

Monoo N Japan Heian fortress

Monreale W Sicily archbishopric

Monsempron C France Neanderthal site

Monsheim C Germany defensive enclosure

Mont Auxois E France Celtic oppidum

Mont Bégo SE France rock art

Mont Beuvray E France Celtic oppidum

Mont Lassois E France Hallstatt site

Mont-Dol NW France Neanderthal site

Mont-St. Michel NW France monastery

Montagu Cave S Africa Acheulian tools, Stone Age tools

Montclus S France Mesolithic settlement

Monte Albán C Mexico pyramid, early writing, early farming site, Zapotec site, early town, Aztec town

Monte Alto S Guatemala Maya settlement

Monte Aquilone S Italy defensive enclosure

Monte Bernorio N Spain native settlement

Monte sa Idda S Sardinia metal hoard

Monte Sant'Angelo C Italy archbishopric

Monte Sirai S Sardinia Carthaginian site

Monte Verde C Chile early settlement

Montenegro C Mexico Pre-Classical site

Monteoru NE Romania fortified site

Montgaudier C France hunter-gatherer art

Montières N France early tools

Montmaurin C France early tools

Montpellier S France monastery

Monzú Colombia early pottery

Moor Park S Africa Iron Age site

Moore Creek E Australia Aboriginal site

Moose River Alaska Pacific Eskimo site

Mopti W Africa early settlement

Morales E Mexico Maya settlement

Moravany Czechoslovakia hunter-gatherer site, hunter-gatherer art

Morgedal S Norway iron-working site

Morhana Pahar NE India Mesolithic settlement

Morongo Uta Austral Is. early site

Moroto Uganda Proconsul

Morrisons Islands C Canada, Ontario Archaic site

Mortensnes N Norway Saami grave

Morton E Scotland shell midden, megalithic site

Moscha (Moskha) S Arabia early trade

Moschi ancient people of E Anatolia

Moshebis S Africa Stone Age site

Mosselbaai S Africa Stone Age tools

Mossgiel SE Australia early man

Mostar Yugoslavia Sinan mosque

Mosul (Nud Ardashir) N Mesopotamia Sasanian city, Islamic town

Mosyllon (Mosullon) NE Africa, Somalia ancient port, early trade

Mother Grundy's Parlour C England hunter-gatherer site

Motuopuhi New Zealand, North I. early settlement

Motutapu Island New Zealand, North I. defended settlement

Motya (Motye) W Sicily Phoenician city, Carthaginian city

Mouchi Sounosso N Africa, Chad early man

Mouila W Africa, Gabon early iron

Mouliana E Crete Minoan village

Mound City NE USA, Ohio Hopewell site

Moundville SE USA burial site, temple mound

Mount Burr S Australia Aboriginal site

Mount Caburn S England Celtic hill fort

Mount Camel New Zealand, North I. moa bones

Mount Horeb SE USA, Kentucky Hopewell site

Mount Olo Western Samoa early site

Mount Pleasant S England henge

Mount Rowland Tasmania Aboriginal site

Mount William SE Australia Aboriginal site

Mount's Bay SW England ax factory

Mountain Cow Belize Maya settlement

Mountsandel N Ireland Mesolithic settlement

Mowthorpe N England medieval village

Moxby N England medieval town

Mözs C Hungary early cemetery

Mozu C Japan mound cemetery

Mpulungu C Africa, Zambia hunter-gatherers

Msecké Zehrovice W Czechoslovakia Celtic site

Mt. Darwin   E Africa, Zimbabwe Iron Age site

Mt. Gabriel   S Ireland early copper mine

Mu'a   Tonga petroglyphs

Muaco   NW Venezuela early settlement

Muang Bon   N Thailand moated site

Muang Fa Daet   NE Thailand moated site, early site

Muang Sema   C Thailand moated site

Maura Takus   N Sumatra early site

Mucking   S England early settlement

Müddersheim   W Germany farming site

Mufo   C Africa, Angola Oldowan tools

Muge   S Portugal shell midden

Mughāret el-Aliya   NW Africa, Morocco Stone Age tools

Mughāret el-Wad   C Palestine Natufian site

Mughāret Kebara   C Palestine Natufian site

Mugumamp Swamp   E New Guinea early site

Mugur-Aksy   E Russia Han mirror find

Mukkala   N Finland Saami grave

Mulberry   E USA temple mound

Muldbjerg   W Denmark barrow burial

Mulifanua   Samoa Lapita site

Mulineddu   W Sardinai dry-stone fortress

Mullerup   Denmark Mesolithic settlement

Multan   NW India Mughal mint

Mumbwa   C Africa, Zambia hunter-gatherers

Muminabad   C Asia steppe settlement

Mummy Cave   NW USA, Montana Archaic site

Munda   NW India Harappan site

Mundie   E Africa, Zimbabwe Iron Age site

Mundigak   Afghanistan early farming village, early city, Harappan site

Mundus   NE Africa, Somalia ancient port

Munhata   S Palestine Neolithic site, early pottery

Münsterberg   S Germany Celtic oppidum

Munychia (Mounikhia)   SE Greece harbor of Athens

Murcens   S France Celtic oppidum

Mure   C Japan rice farming site

Mureybat   N Syria Neolithic site

Muringa   E Africa, Kenya Iron Age site

Mursa (modern Osijek)   N Yugoslavia Roman legionary fortress

Mursella (modern Petrijevci)   N Yugoslavia Roman legionary fortress

Muru   W Brazil early settlement

Musa-Khel   NW India Harappan site

Musang Cave   N Philippines cave site, Neolithic settlement

Musawwarat es Sofra   L Egypt temple remains

Muscat   SE Arabia Islamic trade

Mutina (modern Modena)   N Italy Roman city

Muza (Musa, modern Mawza'ah)   SW Arabia ancient port, early trade

Muziris (Mouziris, modern Cranganur)   SW India early trade

Mwamasapa   E Africa, Malawi Iron Age site

My Son (Mison)   Indo-China, S Vietnam early site

Mylae   N Sicily Greek colony

Myndus   SW Anatolia Hellenistic city

Mynydd-bach   SW Wales stone alignment

Mynydd Rhiw   N Wales ax factory

Myos Hormos   Red Sea ancient port, early trade

Myra   SW Anatolia Roman provincial capital

Myrina   N Aegean Greek city

Myrsini (Mirsini)   NE Crete tholos tomb

Myrtos   S Crete Minoan village

Mysia   Ancient country of NW Anatolia

Mysians   ancient people of SW Anatolia

Mytilene (Mitylene)   E Aegean Greek theater and temple

Myus   W Anatolia Classical site

Naachtun   N Guatemala Maya settlement

Naame   Lebanon Neanderthal site

Nabataea   NW Arabia early state

Nabatake   W Japan rice farming site

Nabta   W Egypt wavy-line pottery, early pottery, early agriculture

Nachikufu   C Africa, Zambia hunter-gatherers

Naco   Honduras Maya settlement

Naco   SW USA, Arizona Palaeo-Indian site

Nad-i Ali   E Persia Achaemenid palace

Nadezhdino-Kurakino   C Russia steppe settlement

Nadporizhka   SW Russia steppe settlement

Nag el-Deir   U Egypt noble's tomb

Nag el-Gaziriya   U Egypt noble's tomb

Nagappattinam   S India Hindu religious site, Buddhist center

Nagarjunakonda   S India, Mesolithic village, Buddhist site, Buddhist stupa

Nagaur   C India Mughal mint

Nahal Oren   N Palestine Natufian and Neolithic site

Nahr Ibrahim   Lebanon Neanderthal site

Naibor Soit Inselberg   in Olduvai Gorge

Naikund   C India megalithic tomb

Nainte Sume   Mongolia Han mirror find

Naislusiu   in Olduvai Gorge

Najafenhabad   NW Persia stela

Najran   SW Arabia early trade, Islamic town

Nakamine   N Japan early man

Nakayama   N Japan Heian fortress

Nakhon Pathom   C Thailand moated site, early site, Buddhist stupa

Nakhon Si Thammarat   S Thailand early site

Naknek River Mouth   Alaska arctic culture

Nal'chik   SW Russia steppe settlement

Nalanda   N India Buddhist center

Nalatale   E Africa, Zimbabwe Iron Age site

Nam Tun   N Indo-China, Vietnam cave site

Namazga   C Asia steppe settlement

Nämforsen   N Sweden rock art

Namgoi   E Africa, Kenya Iron Age site

Namur   S Belgium Celtic oppidum

Nan (Linjiang)   C China Han city

Nan-t'ou   Taiwan early settlement

Nana Mode   C Africa Iron Age site

Nanchang   E China Ming tomb

Nanfeng   C China Sung kiln

Nanggu   Solomon Is. Lapita site

Nanhai   S China cave site

Nanhaiya   N China early Palaeolithic site

Nanjing   E China Ming provincial capital

Nannook   E Canada Dorset site

Nanoropus   NE Africa, Sudan bone harpoons

Nanshangen   NE China E Chou cemetery

Nanyang   N China Han city

Nanyuan   NE China Ming provincial capital

Nanzhihui   N China E Chou cemetery

Napak   Uganda Proconsul

Napata   NE Africa, Sudan fortress, early iron

Naqada (Ombos)   U Egypt bone harpoons, ancient cemetery

Naqsh-i Bahram   SW Persia rock relief
Naqsh-i Rajab   S Persia rock relief
Naqsh-i Rustam   SW Persia royal tomb, rock relief
Naqsh-i Rustam Darab   S Persia rock relief
Nara   C Japan Shosho-in temple, Islamic trade, Buddhist pagoda, early capital
Naranjo   N Guatemala Maya settlement
Narbo (modern Narbonne)   S France Roman provincial capital
Narbonne (Narbo)   S France archbishopric
Narce   C Italy Bronze Age settlement
Nargius   W Sardinia dry-stone fortress
Nariokotome   E Africa, Kenya *Homo erectus*
Narosura   E Africa, Kenya early livestock, Neolithic site
Narva   NW Russia mesolithic settlement, megalithic site
Nasera   E Africa, Tanzania hunter-gatherers
Nasik   W India Deccan city
Natal'yevka   SW Russia steppe settlement
Natanz   C Persia fire temple
Native Point   E Canada Dorset site
Natsushima   C Japan shell mound
Natufian sites   Palestine
Natunuku   Fiji Lapita site
Naucratis   Egypt Greek colony
Naujan   E Canada Thule site
Nauloxes   W Anatolia Classical site
Naura (modern Cannanore)   SW India early trade
Naushahro   NW India Harappan site
Navinal   NW India Harappan site
Navish   N Persia fire temple
Naxos   E Sicily Greek colony
Nayin   NE Persia Islamic town
Nazca   N Peru pre-Inca center
Nazlet Aulad el-Sheikh   L Egypt flint
Nazlet Khatir   NE Africa, Egypt Stone Age tools
Ndutu   E Africa, Tanzania early man
Nea Nikomidhia   N Greece farming site, early pottery
Nea Skala   W Greece early tools
Neanderthal   N Germany Neanderthal site
Neapolis (Naples, Napoli)   C Italy Greek colony
Neapolis   NE Greece Greek colony
Neapolis (Piotrovsk)   S Russia steppe settlement

Nebaj   C Guatemala Maya settlement, early town
Nebket Adhoual   W Africa, Mali bone harpoons
Nebo Hill   C USA, Missouri Archaic site
Necker   Hawaiian Is. early site
Negar   S Persia fire temple
Negub   N Mesopotamia tunnel and canal head
Neirab   C Syria cemetery
Nelcynda (Nelkunda, modern Kottayam)   S India early trade
Nelson Bay   S Africa Stone Age site
Nelson Bay Cave   S Africa Stone Age tools, hunter-gatherers
Nemea   S Greece temple
Nemrut Dag   E Anatolia obsidian source
Nenthorn   New Zealand, South I. early site
Nenumbo   Solomon Is. Lapita site
Nepeña   C Peru Chavín site
Nericagua   Venezuela early settlement
Nerja   S Spain hunter-gatherer art, farming settlement
Neshkan   E Russia Thule site
Netiv HaGedud   N Palestine Neolithic site
Nettersheim   W Germany claw beaker
Netzahualcóyotl   C Mexico Aztec dyke
Neubäu   N Austria Celtic site
Neuberg   SE Germany Celtic oppidum
Neumagen (Noviomagus)   W Germany Roman town
Nevalla Çori   E Anatolia Neolithic site
Neville   NE USA Archaic site
Nevsehir   S Anatolia Neolithic site
New Bern   E USA, N Carolina colonial settlement
New Buipe   W Africa, Ghana urban center, early town
New Caledonia   Lapita culture
New Cnidus   SW Anatolia Hellenistic city
New Guinea   Kula gift exchange, early settlement, Lapita culture
New Madrid   SE USA temple mound
New Smyrna   S Anatolia Hellenistic city
Newark   NE USA, Ohio Hopewell site
Newburgh   N England medieval town
Newferry   N Ireland Mesolithic settlement, megalithic site
Newgrange   E Ireland gold
Newstead   S Scotland Celtic religious site

Nexpa   C Mexico Pre-Classical site
Nezviska   W Russia farming site
NFX   New Guinea site of early man
Ng'orora   Kenya early man
Ngandong   Java early man
Ngarradje-Warde-Djobkeng   N Australia Aboriginal site
Nha Trang   Indo-China, S Vietnam early site
Nia   E Persia Parthian/Sasanian city
Niah   N Borneo early metal site
Niah Cave   N Borneo early man, cave site, Neolithic settlement
Niamey   W Africa, Niger early town
Niani   W Africa, Mali early settlement, early city
Niaux   SW France hunter-gatherer art
Nicaea   S France Greek colony
Nicaea   NW Anatolia Hellenistic city, Byzantine town
Nichoria   SW Greece Mycenaean settlement
Nicomedia (modern Izmir)   NW Anatolia, Hellenistic city, Roman provincial capital
Nicopolis   NW Greece Roman provincial capital, aqueduct
Niederanwen (Andethanna)   Luxembourg Roman village
Nieui-sur-'Autize   W France beaker burial
Nigliva   NE India pillar edict
Nihavend   NW Persia Parthian city
Nihoa   Hawaiian Is. early site
Nikinki   Timor Neolithic settlement
Nikki   W Africa, Benin early town
Nikolayevka   SW Russia steppe settlement
Nikon   NE Africa, Somalia early trade
Nillipidji   N Australia Aboriginal site
Nimes (Nemausus)   S France Roman aqueduct
Nimrud (Kalhu, Calah)   N Mesopotamia zigurrat, Assyrian royal palace, Assyrian capital
Nina   S Mesopotamia early city
Nindowari   NW India Indus Valley settlement, early city, Harappan site
Nineveh   N Mesopotamia pottery remains, early city, Mitannian city, Assyrian royal palace, Assyrian capital, Parthian city
Ningbo   E China early trade center, Buddhist center, Tang kiln, Sung kiln
Nintoku Emperor tomb   C Japan
Nioi   N Japan Ainu hill fort
Nioro   W Africa, Mali early settlement

Nippur   C Mesopotamia zigurrat, pottery remains, early city, early writing, Achaemenid city, Hellenistic city, Parthian city

Niriz (Neyriz)   S Persia Islamic town

Nirou Khani   N Crete Minoan village

Nisa   NE Persia Parthian city

Nisanzai   C Japan Yamato tomb

Nishapur (Neyshabur)   NE Persia Sasanian city, Islamic town

Nishinoji   E Japan early settlement

Nishishiga   C Japan rice farming site

Nisibis (modern Nusaybin)   E Anatolia Assyrian provincial capital, Hellenistic city, Roman provincial capital

Nitaro Cave   C Japan early settlement

Nitchie Lake   SE Australia early man

Nitra   Czechoslovakia farming site

Nitriansky Hrádok   SE Czechoslovakia fortified site

Nitta   N Japan Heian fortress

Niya   C Asia Buddhist center

Niyasar   NW Persia fire temple

Njimi   W Africa, Chad early settlement, early town

Njoro River Cave   E Africa, Kenya early food, Neolithic site

Nkope   C Africa, Malawi Iron Age site

Noailles   C France hunter-gatherer site

Nodena   SE USA temple mound

Nogliki   E Russia arctic culture

Nohmul   Belize Maya settlement

Noin Ula (Noyon Uul)   Mongolia barrow burial, silk find

Noisy (-sur-Ecole)   N France megalithic tomb

Nok   W Africa, Nigeria Stone Age tools, Iron Age site

Nokjo-Shahdinzai   NW India Harappan site

Nombe   New Guinea early man

Nombre de Dios   C America maritime trade

Non Chai   N Thailand transitional settlement

Non Nok Tha   N Thailand transitional settlement

Nong Chae Sao   C Thailand early metal site

Nonnebakken   C Denmark Viking fortress

Noola   SE Australia early man

Nora   S Sardinia Greek colony

Nora Velha   S Portugal megalithic tomb

Normanby I.   New Guinea Kula gift exchange

North Brabant   S Africa Stone Age site

North Ferriby   N England medieval town

North Grimston   N England medieval village

North Horr   E Africa, Kenya early food, Stone Age site

North Otago   New Zealand, South I. rock art

Northallerton   N England medieval town

Northcliffe   SW Australia Aboriginal site

Norton Mound   N USA, Michigan Hopewell site

Norwich   E England Viking center, monastery

Notgrove   C England megalithic tomb

Notornis Valley   New Zealand, South I. rock art

Notre Dame d'Or   C France metal hoard

Nottingham   C England Viking center

Novae   N Bulgaria Roman legionary fortress

Noves   S France Celtic art

Novgorod   NW Russia Islamic trade

Noviomagus (modern Nijmegen)   S Holland Roman legionary fortress

Novo-Lipovka   W Russia barrow burial

Novo-Rozanovka   SW Russia barrow burial

Novyye Ruseshty (Novi-Rusesti)   SW Russia Cucuteni-Tripolye village

Noyen (sur-Seine)   N France defensive enclosure

Nsongezi   E Africa, Uganda Acheulian tools, Stone Age tools, hunter-gatherers

Ntereso   W Africa, Ghana early food

Ntusi   E Africa, Uganda Iron Age site

Nueva Cádiz   Venezuela maritime trade

Nuhato   NW India Harappan site

Numantia   N Spain Celtic oppidum, native settlement

Numas Entrance   SW Africa, Namibia Stone Age site

Nun Appleton   N England medieval town

Nun Monkton   N England medieval town

Nunguvik   NE Canada Thule site

Nunivak   Alaska arctic culture

Nunligran   E Russia Thule site

Nunyamo   E Russia Thule site

Nupe   W Africa, Nigeria early kingdom

Nuremberg (Mümberg)   S Germany medieval trade

Nuri   NE Africa, Sudan ancient cemetery, early iron

Nuribda   Palestine Egyptian control

Nutari   N Japan Heian fortress

Nuulliit   NW Greenland Thule site

Nuzi (Nuzu, modern Yorghan Tepe)   N Mesopotamia early city, early town, early writing, Mitannian city

Nydam   SE Denmark weapon hoard

Nyirankuba   E Africa Iron Age site

Nymphaeum (Nymphaion)   Ukraine Greek colony

Nyong   C Malaya Neolithic settlement

Nyrup   NW Denmark musical instruments

Nysa   SW Anatolia Hellenistic city

Nyu   W Japan early man

Nzabi   C Africa, Congo Iron Age site

O'Neil   NE USA, New York Archaic site

Oak Grove   SW USA, California Archaic site

Oakhanger   S England Mesolithic settlement

Oakhurst   S Africa hunter-gatherers, Stone Age site

Oaxaca   C Mexico pyramid

Oberkassel   N Germany hunter-gatherer site, hunter-gatherer art

Oberlarg (Mannlefelsen)   Switzerland Mesolithic settlement

Oberleiservberg   E Austria Celtic oppidum

Obion   SE USA temple mound

Obluang   NW Thailand cave site

Oboda   Sinai temple remains

Obre   C Yugoslavia farming site

Obrero   S Guatemala Maya settlement

Oc Eo   S Vietnam early trade center, moated site

Ocala Cave   SW USA, Nevada early man

Ocelis (Okelis, modern Khawr Ghurayrah)   SW Arabia ancient port, early trade

Ochoz   Czechoslovakia Neanderthal site

Ockov   C Czechoslovakia barrow burial

Ocmulgee   SE USA temple mound

Oconto   N USA, Wisconsin Archaic site

Ocucaje   S Peru Paracas site

Odense   C Denmark Viking center

Odessus (modern Varna)   E Bulgaria Greek colony

Odienné   W Africa, Ivory Coast early town

Odishi   SW Russia steppe settlement

Oeniadae   NW Greece theater and temple

Oenoe   SE Greece Athenian fort

Oenpelli   N Australia Aboriginal site
Oescus   N Bulgaria Roman city
Ofufunbe   N Japan Ainu hill fort
Ogachi   N Japan Heian fortress
Oglakty   E Russia silk find
Ohaba-Ponor   Romania Neanderthal site
Oissel   N France early tools
Ojika   N Japan Heian fortress
Okinohara   C Japan early settlement
Okunev   S Siberia steppe settlement
Öküzlü'in   SW Anatolia Palaeolithic site
Olbia   N Sardinia Carthaginian cemetery
Olbia   S Russia Greek colony, Hellenistic city, barrow burial
Olby   E Denmark barrow burial
Olby Lyng   E Denmark shell midden
Old Beach   Tasmania Aboriginal site
Old Crow   NW Canada early settlement
Old Fort   C USA temple mound
Old Kandahar   Afghanistan Hellenistic city
Old Kiavak   Alaska Pacific Eskimo site
Old Kismayu   E Africa, Somalia Ming pottery
Old Neck   New Zealand, South I. shell midden and moa bones
Old Oyo   W Africa, Nigeria early town
Old Sleaford   E England Celtic site
Old Uppsala   C Sweden barrow burial
Old Winchester Hill   S England Celtic hill fort
Oldbury   S England Neanderthal site
Oldendorf   N Germany megalithic tomb
Olieboompoort   S Africa Stone Age tools, Stone Age site
Olifantspoort   S Africa Iron Age site
Olimbos   SE Greece Athenian settlement
Olinalá   C Mexico Pre-Classical site
Olintepec   C Mexico Pre-Classical site
Ollantaytambo   C Peru Inca center
Olmec Caves   C Mexico Pre-Classical site
Olorgasallie   E Africa, Kenya early man
Olsen-Chubbuck   W USA, Colorado bison kill site
Olszanica   W Poland farming site
Olympia   S Greece temple, sanctuary
Olympus   NE Greece Byzantine bishopric
Omi   C Japan shogunate provincial capital
Omihi   New Zealand, South I. shell midden
Omo   NE Africa, Ethiopia early man, site of modern humans

Omo Basin (Omo Valley)   E Africa, Ethiopia *Australopithecus boisei*, bone harpoons
Omrynskiy   E Russia arctic culture
Omuna   New Zealand, North I. defended settlement
Onayna   U Egypt early town
Ongbah Cave   N Thailand cave site, transitional settlement
Onion Portage   Alaska lpiutak and Thule site
Onnemoto   N Japan Ainu hill fort
Oos (Ausava)   W Germany Roman village
Opatowskie   W Poland flint mine
Opito   New Zealand, North I. defended settlement
Opone (modern Xaafuun)   NE Africa, Somalia ancient port, early trade
Opunohu Valley   Society Is. early site
Oraibi   SW USA Pueblo farming site
Orak   S Siberia steppe settlement
Orangia   S Africa Stone Age tools
Orbliston   N Scotland beaker site
Orchestra Shell Cave   SW Australia Aboriginal site
Orchomenos   C Greece Mycenaean settlement
Orgnac III   C France early tools
Orito   Easter I. early quarry
Oriximiná   E Brazil early horticultural village
Oriéans   N France monastery
Orongo   Easter I. petroglyph
Orongo Bay   New Zealand, North I. shell midden
Oronsay   W Scotland shell midden, megalithic site
Oronsk   S Poland Mesolithic settlement
Oropia   district of SE Greece
Oropou   SE Greece Athenian settlement
Oropus   SE Greece temple
Orsett   SE England defensive enclosure
Oruarangi   New Zealand, North I. defended settlement
Orvieto   N Italy early temple
Osa   NW Russia megalithic site
Osaka   C Japan Buddhist center
Osan-ni   C Korea early settlement
Osare, Mt.   N Japan holy mountain
Osceola   N USA Archaic site
Osiers   N France early tools
Ostermoor   NW Germany terp settlement
Ostia   C Italy Roman city
Ostrów   S Poland Mesolithic settlement

Otakanini   New Zealand, North I. defended settlement
Otatara   New Zealand, North I. defended settlement
Otero   N Spain shell midden
Otley   N England medieval town
Otoe   N Japan Ainu hill fort
Ototara   New Zealand, South I. moa bones
Otranto   S Italy archbishopric
Otsukayama   C Japan Yamato tomb
Otumba   C Mexico Aztec center
Oturehua   New Zealand, South I. rock art
Ouadi Aabet   Lebanon early tools
Ouadi Zeringa   N Africa, Chad Acheulian tools
Ouagadougou (Wagadugu)   W Africa, Burkina early town
Ouahigouya   W Africa, Burkina early town
Ouidah   W Africa, Benin early port
Ounianga   N Africa, Chad wavy-line pottery
Ouroux (sur-Saône)   E France farming settlement
Outeidat   W Africa, Mali wavy-line pottery, early pottery
Ovilava (modern Wels)   N Austria Roman legionary fortress
Owl Creek   SE USA temple mound
Owo   W Africa, Nigeria early town
Oxkintok   Mexico, Yucatán Maya settlement
Oxpemul   Mexico, Yucatán Maya settlement
Oxtotitlán   C Mexico Pre-Classical site
Oyamato-Yanagimoto   C Japan mound cemetery
Ozette   NW USA hunting village
Påarp Karup   SW Sweden musical instruments
Paars   NE France Iron Age cemetery
Pabumath   NW India Harappan site
Pachácamac   C Peru pyramid, Middle Horizon site
Pachamachay   Peru early farming
Pacheco   S Peru Middle Horizon site
Pachmarhi   C India Mesolithic settlement
Pachten (Contiomagus)   W Germany Roman village
Pachuca   C Mexico early town
Pacopampa   N Peru Chavín site
Padah-lin   Burma cave site
Padan Lawas   N Sumatra early site

Padre Piedra   SE Mexico Pre-Classical site
Paekche   S Korea early site
Paengariki   Cook Is. early site
Paethana   C India early trade
Pagan   N Burma temple complex, Buddhist center
Pagar Ruyung   S Sumatra early site
Pagaralam   C Sumatra early metal site
Paharpur (Somapura)   N India Buddhist center
Painsthorpe   N England medieval village
Pair-non-Pair   C France hunter-gatherer art
Pajchiri   N Bolivia early town
Pajón   SE Mexico Pre-Classical site
Palaepatmae (modern Dabhoi)   W India early trade
Palaesimundu   N Ceylon early trade
Palaikastro (Palaiokastro)   NE Crete Minoan town and port
Palanli Caves   E Anatolia Palaeolithic site
Palantio   N Spain native settlement
Palauea   Hawaiian Is. early site
Palembang   S Sumatra early port, Buddhist center
Palenque   C Mexico pyramid, Maya settlement
Palermo   Sicily medieval trade, archbishopric
Palkigunda   S India rock edict
Pallavoy   S India cattle pen site
Palma   W Mediterranean Phoenician city, medieval trade
Palmeirinhas   SW Africa, Angola Oldowan tools
Palmela   C Portugal rock-cut tomb
Palmyra (modern Tadmur)   Syria Roman city, temple remains, early trade, Islamic town
Palpa   S Peru Paracas site
Palu   E Anatolia Uratian inscription
Palugvik   Alaska Pacific Eskimo site
Panactum (Panakton)   SE Greece Athenian fort
Pandi Wahi   NW India Harappan site
Panipat   N India Mughal mint
Panlongcheng   C China early city, Shang city
Panopeus   C Greece Mycenaean fortress
Panopolis   L Egypt silk trade
Panormos   SE Greece ancient fortress
Panormus (modern Palermo)   NW Sicily Phoencian city, Roman city
Pantaleón   S Guatemala Maya settlement

Panther Cave   S USA, Texas Archaic site
Panticapaeum (Pantikapaion, modern Kerch)   S Russia Greek colony, Hellenistic city, Roman city, early trade center
Pantzac   C Guatemala Maya settlement
Panyu   S China Han burial
Paomaling   C China Longshan site
Papatowai   New Zealand, South I. moa bones
Papoura   S Crete tholos tomb
Paracas   S Peru early site
Paramonga   N Peru Inca center
Parc y Meirw   SW Wales stone alignment
Paredao   E Brazil early settlement
Paremata   New Zealand, North I. defended settlement
Pareora Mouth   New Zealand, South I. moa bones
Parga   NW Greece tholos tomb
Paria   N Bolivia Inca tambo
Paricatuba   E Brazil shell midden
Parihasapura (modern Paraspur)   NW India Buddhist stupa
Parikanians (Paricanii)   ancient people of SE Persia
Pariwhakatau   New Zealand, South I. defended settlement
Parkhill   SE Canada fluted points
Parkin   SE USA temple mound
Parma   N Italy Roman city
Paros   S Aegean Greek city
Parpalló   E Spain hunter-gatherer site, hunter-gatherer art, Mesolithic settlement
Parthians   ancient people of N Persia
Pasalar   N Anatolia Ramapithecus and Sivapithecus
Pasargadae   SW persia Achaemenid palace
Paso   E Indonesia, Celebes shell midden
Paso de la Arena   C Mexico Pre-Classical site
Passo di Corvo   S Italy defensive enclosure
Pasterskoye   Ukraine Greek imports
Patallputra (modern Patna)   NE India early city, early trade center
Patavium (modern Padova, Padua)   N Italy Roman empire
Patna (Pataliputra)   N India Buddhist center
Pavagarh Hill   NW India Mesolithic site
Paviken   S Sweden Viking trading emporium

Paviland   S England hunter-gatherer site
Pavlopetri   S Greece Mycenaean settlement
Pavlov   Czechoslovakia hunter-gatherer site, hunter-gatherer art
Pavón   C Mexico early farming site
Payas   SE Anatolia Sinan mosque
Pazyryk   E Russia barrow burial silk find
Peacock's Farm   E England Mesolithic settlement
Pechal   Mexico, Yucatán Maya settlement
Pech-de-l'Azé   C France early tools, Neanderthal site
Pech-Merie   C France hunter-gatherer art
Pedra Branca   S Portugal megalithic tomb
Pedra Coberta   NW Spain megalithic tomb
Pedra Furada   E Brazil early settlement
Peer Sultan   NW India Harappan site
Pegtymel' River   E Russia Thule site
Pegu   S Burma early site, Buddhist center
Peikthano   C Burma early monumental site
Peiligang   N China early settlement, early pottery
Peine Tampu   N Chile Inca tambo
Pella   N Greece Hellenistic city
Pella (Peheli)   Palestine Egyptian control, Hellenistic city, Islamic town
Peloponnese   ancient country of C Greece
Pendeli   SE Greece quarry
Pengkalan Bujang   N Malaya early site
Peninj   E Africa, Tanzania *Australopithecus boisei*, early man
Penukonda   S India Hindu religious site
Penzhina Bay   E Russia Thule sites
Penzhina River   E Russia arctic culture
Pera   E Thrace Byzantine town
Perarine   S France stone circle and menhir
Perati   SE Greece ancient quarry
Perdikaria   C Greece Mycenaean fortress
Perelló   NE Spain Mesolithic settlement
Peres   Yugoslavia Mesolithic settlement
Pergamum (Pergamon, modern Bergama)   NW Anatolia Hellenistic city, Roman provincial capital, ancient aqueduct and water supply, Byzantine town
Perge   SW Anatolia Hellenistic city

Periam   W Romania Bronze Age settlement

Periano Ghundai   NW India Harappan site

Perinthus   NW Turkey Roman provincial capital

Peristeria   SE Greece Athenian fort

Peristeria   SW Greece Mycenaean fortress

Pernant   NE France Iron Age cemetery

Persepolis   SW Persia Achaemenid palace

Perseverancia   SE Mexico Pre-Classical site

Perusia (modern Perugia)   C Italy Etruscan city

Peshawar   Pakistan Mughal mint, Buddhist stupa

Pesse   Holland Mesolithic settlement

Petersfels   W Germany hunter-gatherer site, hunter-gatherer art

Petit-Spiennes   Belgium early tools

Petra   Jordan Roman city, Nabataean capital, early trade

Petralona   N Greece early tools and human remains

Petrkovice   Czechoslovakia hunter-gatherer site, hunter-gatherer art

Petropavlovsk   C Russia steppe settlement

Petsophas (Petsofas)   E Crete peak sanctuary

Peu-Richard   W France defensive enclosure

Pfupi   C Africa, Zimbabwe hunter-gatherers

Phaistos (Phaestos, Lat. Phaestus)   S Crete Minoan palace

Phalaborwa   S Africa Iron Age site

Phaleric Wall   Athens

Phalerum (Faliron)   SE Greece harbor of Athens

Phan Rang   Indo-China, S Vietnam early site

Pharsalus   C Greece Hellenistic city

Phaselis   S Anatolia Greek colony

Philadelphia (modern Amman)   Jordan Hellenistic city

Philadelphia   SW Anatolia Hellenistic city

Philae   U Egypt Ptolemaic temple

Philippi   NE Greece theater

Philippines   early settlement, Neolithic settlement, early metal sites, early maritime trade

Philippopolis (modern Plovdiv)   Bulgaria Hellenistic city, Roman city

Phimai   C Thailand transitional settlement, early site

Phnom Da   Cambodia early monumental site

Phnom Laang   S Indo-china, Cambodia cave site

Phnom Ruung   E Thailand early site

Phocaea (Phokaia)   W Anatolia Greek city

Phocis   ancient country of C Greece

Phoenicia   cities and trade

Phoenicians   ancient people of Palestine

Phopo Hill   C Africa, Malawi Iron Age site

Phra   Afghanistan Parthian/Sasanian city

Phra Vihar (Preah Vihear)   Indo-china, Cambodia early site

Phrygia   ancient country of NW Anatolia

Phu Hoa   S Vietnam transitional settlement

Phung Nguyen   N Vietnam transitional settlement

Phylakopi (Filakopi)   SE Greece ancient fortress, Mycenaean fortress

Phyle   SE Greece Athenian settlement

Pi-Rameses   L Egypt ancient city, early city

Pictograph Grave   NW USA, Montana Archaic site

Piediluco   C Italy metal hoard

Piedra   N Spain monastery

Piedras Negras   Guatemala Maya settlement

Piégu   NW France Neanderthal site

Pietersburg   S Africa Stone Age tools

Pignicourt   NE France Iron Age cemetery

Pijijiapan   SE Mexico Pre-Classical site

Pikes Peak   N USA, Iowa Hopewell site

Pikillaqta   S Peru pre-Inca center

Pikimachay   Peru early settlement

Piksyasi   C Russia steppe settlement

Pilismarót-Baharc   N Hungary Celtic site

Pimenteiras   S Brazil early settlement

Pin Hole   C England hunter-gatherer site

Pinarbasi   SE Anatolia Neolithic site

Pincevent   NE France hunter-gatherer site

Pindal   NW Spain hunter-gatherer art

Pineda   C Mexico Pre-Classical site

Pinedale Ruins   SW USA Pueblo farming site

Pinedo   C Spain early tools

Pine Lawn Valley   SW USA Pueblo farming site

Pingitkalik   E Canada Thule site

Pingliangtai   N China E Chou burial

Pingshan   N China E Chou burial

Pingyuan   N China Han city

Pinson   C USA, Tennessee Hopewell site

Pinto Basin   SW USA, California Archaic site

Pintu Cave   N Philippines cave site

Piquillaqta   S Peru Middle Horizon site

Piraeus   SE Greece ancient harbor, port of Athens

Pirapitinga   W Brazil early settlement

Pirikatai   N Japan Ainu hill fort

Pisác   E Peru Inca center

Pisaurum (modern Pesaro)   N Italy Roman colony

Pita   W Africa, Guinea early town

Pitangalya   W India Buddhist site

Pithecusa (Pithekoussai)   C Italy Greek colony

Placentia (modern Piacenza)   N Italy Roman city

Plainview   S USA, Texas Palaeo-Indian site

Platanos   S Crete tholos tomb

Plateau Parrain   C France hunter-gatherer site

Plati   C Crete Minoan town

Platinum   Alaska arctic culture

Plawangan   C Java early metal site

Plenge   NE USA fluted points

Plocnik   S Yugoslavia tell settlement

Plussulien   NW France ax factory

Plymouth   SW England railway development

Pochampad   S India megalithic tomb

Pocklington   N England medieval town

Poco da Gateira   S Portugal megalithic tomb

Podbaba   W Czechoslovakia iron-working site

Podbornoye   E Russia steppe settlement

Poduca (Arikamedu, modern Pondicherry)   S India early trade

Poetovio (modern Ptuj)   N Yugoslavia Roman legionary fortress

Pohanská   C Czechoslovakia Celtic oppidum

Poike Ditch   Easter I. early site

Point Barrow (Birnik)   Alaska Thule site

Pointe de St-Gildas   NW France Mesolithic settlement

Point Hope   Alaska Ipiutak and Thule sites

Point of Pines   SW USA Pueblo farming site

Polada   N Italy lake dwelling

Poliokhni (Poliochni)   NE Greece ancient fortress

Politotdel'skoye   C Russia steppe settlement

Pololu Valley   Hawaiian Is. early irrigation

Polonnaruwa   N Ceylon early capital and Buddhist center

Polyanitsa   E Bulgaria farming site

Pomata   S Peru Inca tambo

Pomona   Belize Maya settlement

Pomongwe   C Africa, Zimbabwe hunter-gatherers

Pomongwe Cave   SE Africa, Zimbabwe Stone Age tools

Pondicherry   SE India maritime trade

Pong Tuk   C Thailand early site

Ponta de Giraúl   SW Africa, Angola Oldowan tools

Pont d'Ambon   C France hunter-gatherer site

Pont-Arcy   NE France Iron Age cemetery

Ponteau   SE France Mesolithic settlement

Pontefract   N England medieval town

Ponte San Pietro   C Italy rock-cut tomb

Pontnewydd   N Wales early tools and human remains

Ponui Island   New Zealand, North I. shell midden

Poor Hill   New Zealand, North I. defended settlement

Poplar Grove   NW Canada, British Columbia Archaic site

Populonia   N Italy Etruscan city

Port Moller   Aleutian Is. arctic culture

Port Royal   Jamaica underwater excavation

Port-aux-Choix   E Canada Dorset site

Porter   S USA, Mississippi Hopewell site

Porti   S Crete tholos tomb

Portsmouth   NE USA, New Hampshire colonial settlement

Poseidonia (Posidonia, Paestum, modern Pesto)   S Italy Greek colony

Poshankou   E China E Chou burial

Positano   S Italy shell midden

Postoloprty   NW Czechoslovakia Bronze Age settlement

Potchevash   N Russia Han mirror find

Potentia (modern Potenza)   S Italy Roman colony

Potidaea   NE Greece Greek colony

Potonchan   E Mexico early town

Potrero de Payagasta   C Chile Inca tambo

Potrero Nuevo   C Mexico Olmec site

Potter Brompton   N England medieval pottery

Potterton   N England medieval town

Potwar Plateau   NW India Ramapithecus and Sivapithecus

Pouey-Mayou   SW France megalithic tomb

Poulailler   N France Celtic oppidum

Pounawea   New Zealand, South I. moa bones

Pouto   New Zealand, North I. defended settlement

Poverty Point   S USA, Louisiana clay figurine

Poyemau   SW France Mesolithic settlement

Praaspa   NW Persia Parthian city

Prah Khan (Preah Khan)   Indo-China, Cambodia early site

Praia a Mare   C Portugal beaker burial

Praia das Maças   S Italy farming site, early pottery

Prairie de Mauves   NW France metal hoard

Praisos   E Crete Minoan village

Prambanan   C Java temple complex

Prasat Andet   Cambodia early monumental site

Pratisthana   C India Deccan city

Predmosti   Czechoslovakia Neanderthal site, hunter-gatherer site, hunter-gatherer art, beaker burial

Prembanan   C Java Buddhist center

Prescelly Mts.   SW Wales source of standing stones

Priene   W Anatolia Classical site, Greek city, Hellenistic city

Prinias   E Crete peak sanctuary

Priniatiko Pyrgos   E Crete ancient port

Privol'noye   SW Russia steppe settlement

Protorville   E USA temple mound

Prome   S Burma Buddhist pagoda

Prostpect Farm   E Africa, Kenya Stone Age tools, Neolithic site

Prosymna   S Greece tholos tomb

Protesilaos   NW Anatolia metal vessels

Providence   NE USA, Rhode Island colonial settlement

Prusa   NW Anatolia Byzantine town

Psafis   SE Greece Athenian settlement

Pseira (Psira)   E Crete Minoan town and port

Pskent   C Asia Han mirror find

Ptolemais Theron   Red Sea early trade

Puako   Hawaiian Is. petroglyph

Puamau Valley   Marquesas Is. early site

Pucará   S Peru Paracas site, Inca center

Pucará de Andagala   N Argentina Inca center

Pueblito   N Colombia early settlement

Pueblo Bonito   SW USA Pueblo farming site

Pueblo de los Muertos   SW USA Pueblo farming site

Pueblo Viejo   SE Mexico Pre-Classical site

Puerto Hormiga   N Colombia early pottery, early settlement

Puerto Marquez   C Mexico early farming site

Puig Roig   NE Spain megalithic tomb

Pukaki   New Zealand, South I. rock art

Pukearuhe   New Zealand, North I. defended settlement

Pulau Kumpai (Pulau Kompei)   N Sumatra early port

Pulau Tioman   S Malaya early site

Pulemelei   Western Samoa early site

Pulguk-sa   S Korea Buddhist center

Pulicat   SE India early trade

Pulli   NW Russia Mesolithic settlement

Pumpu   N Peru Inca center

Punapau   Easter I. early quarry

Puntutjarpa   N Australia Aboriginal site

Punuk Is.   Alaska Thule site

Purakanui   New Zealand, South I. shell midden

Puritjarra   C Australia early man

Purrón and Abejas Caves   C Mexico early settlement

Purushaddum (Burushattum)   E Anatolia Assyrian colony

Pushkar   N India Mesolithic site

Pushkari   W Russia hunter-gatherer site

Pusilha   Belize Maya settlement

Puteoli (modern Puzzuoli)   C Italy Roman city

Putu   Alaska early settlement

Putuo Shan   E China holy mountain

Puwon   S Korea rice farming site

Puy d'Yssandon   C France Celtic oppidum

Puy de Paulhiac   SW France stone circle and menhir

Puyo   S Korea capital of early state

Pyagina Peninsula   E Russia Thule site

Pylos   SW Greece early port, Mycenaean settlement

Pyolmang   C Korea early settlement

Pyongyang   N Korea capital of early state, Buddhist center

Pyrgi   C Italy Roman empire

Pyrgos   C Crete peak sanctuary

Pyrgos   N Crete Minoan village

Pyrgos   NE Greece Mycenaean fortress

Pyrgos   S Crete Minoan village

Pyrrha   W Anatolia Classical site

Pyxus   S Italy Greek colony

Qadesh   SW Syria Neolithic site, early city

Qal'at Bani Hammad   NW Africa, Algeria Islamic town

Qalat   SW Arabia early trade

Qalatgar   NW Persia Urartian fortress

Qaleh-i Dukhtar   SW Persia rock relief

Qalinj Agha   N Mesopotamia pottery remains, early settlement

Qana   SW Arabia ancient port

Qarnaw   SW Arabia temple remains

Qasr al-'Ashiq   Mesopotamia palace of Samarra

Qasr al Hayr   Syria Islamic port

Qasr al-Ja'fari   Mesopotamia palace of Samarra

Qasr el Mushatta   Jordan Islamic port

Qasr el-Sagha   L Egypt temple

Qasr Ibrim   U Egypt fortress

Qasr Khubbaz   NW Iraq Roman dam

Qasr Shamamok (Kaksu)   Mesopotamia Assyrian provincial capital

Qataban   SW Arabia early state

Qatna   C Syria early city

Qaw el-Kebir (Antaeopolis)   U Egypt noble's tomb

Qazvin   N Persia Islamic town, Safavid capital

Qianshanyang   E China early settlement, Longshan site

Qiaocun   N China E Chou cemetery

Qijiacun   N China W Chou burial and bronze hoard

Qincun   N China E Chou cemetery

Qingchuan   C China E Chou bronze hoard

Qinggongcha   NW China early settlement

Qinghe   N China Han city

Qinglingang   N China early settlement

Qingling   NE China Ming tomb

Qingyanggong   W China Tang kiln

Qingzhou   N China Tang kiln, provincial capital

Qinjiagou   N China Chou bronze hoard

Qinweijia   NW China Shang copper source

Qionglai   W China Tang kiln

Qir   S Persia rock relief

Qishan   NW China early settlement, oracle bones

Qizqapan   NW Persia rock relief

Quad   SE USA, Alabama Archaic site

Quanterness   N Scotland megalithic tomb

Quanzhou   SE China early trade center, Sung kiln

Quban   U Egypt fortress

Qubbat al-Sulaibiyya   Mesopotamia mausoleum of Samarra

Qubbet el-Hawa   U Egypt noble's tomb

Québec   E Canada colonial settlement

Quechula   SE Mexico Pre-Classical site

Quen Santo   C Guatemala Maya settlement

Quenstedt   N Germany defensive enclosure

Quentowic   N France Viking trading emporium

Quereo   N Chile early settlement

Quetta   E Baluchistan Harappan site

Quetzalpapaloti Palace   C Mexico

Quiçama (Kisama)   SW Africa, Angola salt mine

Quinzano   N Italy Neanderthal site

Quiriguá   N Guatemala Maya settlement

Quito   N Ecuador Inca capital, colonial settlement early trade

Qujialing   C China Longshan site, rice farming site

Qum   N Persia Sasanian city, Islamic town, holy city

Qumis   N Persia Islamic town

Qunduz   Afghanistan coin hoard

Quseir Amra   Jordan Islamic port

Quynh Vanh   N Vietnam Neolithic settlement

Rabat   NW Africa, Morocco Islamic town

Rabbit Mount   SE USA, South Carolina Archaic site

Rachgoun   NW Algeria Carthaginian cemetery

Radomyshl   W Russia hunter-gatherer site

Rafter Lake   E Canada, Nova Scotia Archaic site

Raglan   New Zealand, North I. rock art

Ragusa   Sicily medieval trade

Rahapara Pa   New Zealand, North I. defended settlement

Rahman Dheri   NW India Indus Valley settlement, early city, Harappan site

Raisthorpe   N England medieval village

Rajghat   NE India early city

Rajgir   NE India early city

Rajula Mandagiri   S India rock edict

Rakaia River Mouth   New Zealand, South I. shell midden and moa bones

Rakhigarhi   NW India Indus Valley settlement, Harappan site

Rakival   Papua New Guinea Lapita site

Ramachandra   temple of Vijayanagara

Ramatirtha   E India Buddhist site

Rambaban   S Sumatra early site

Rameswaram   S India Hindu religious site

Ramnagar   NW India Ramapithecus and Sivapithecus

Ramp   SW USA Pueblo farming site

Rampurwa   NE India pillar edict

Ramshög   S Sweden megalithic tomb

Rana Ghundai   NW India Indus Valley settlement, early city, Harappan site

Ranchillos   N Argentina Inca tambo

Rancho Peludo   Colombia early pottery

Ranggiloch   Switzerland Mesolithic settlement

Rangoon   S Burma Buddhist pagoda

Rangpur   NW India early city, Harappan site

Rano Raraku   Easter I. early site

Ranviken   S Sweden pollen core site

Raphanea   W Syria Roman legionary fortress

Raqchi   S Peru Inca center

Raqote   L Egypt harbor works

Raqqa   Syria Islamic town

Ras Beyrouth   Lebanon early tools, Neanderthal site

Ras el'Amiya   C Mesopotamia pottery remains

Ras el Ma   W Africa, Mali early settlement

Ras el-Kelb   Lebanon Neanderthal site

Rasel-Lados   Lebanon Neanderthal site

Ras Shamra (Ugarit)   NW Syria Neolithic site, early pottery, Achaemenid burial

Rat Buri   C Thailand early site

Ratiaria (modern Archar)   N Bulgaria Roman legionary fortress

Räuberhöhle   S Germany Neanderthal site

Ravenna   N Italy archbishopric

Ravensburg   NW Germany early tools

Ravnholt   C Denmark bog body

Rawak   C Asia Buddhist center

Ray (Rai, modern Tehran)   N Persia Parthian/Sasanian city

Razet   NE France rock-cut tombs

Real Alto   W Ecuador pyramid, early farming site

Red Mountains   SW USA Pueblo farming site

Redkin Lager   SW Russia steppe settlement

Reggio (di Calabria)   S Italy archbishopric

Regourdou   C France Neanderthal site

Reigh   N USA, Wisconsin Archaic site

Relilaia   N Africa, Algeria hunter-gatherers

Remagen (Rigomagus)   W Germany Roman village

Remedello   N Italy Copper Age cemetery

Remojadas   C Mexico early farming site

René Simard   C France Neanderthal site

Rennell I.   Solomon Is. Lapita site

Renner   C USA, Missouri Hopewell site

Reric   N Germany Viking trading emporium

Resolute   NE Canada Thule site

Retoka   S Pacific burial site

Revheim   SW Norway musical instruments

Rhaedestus   E Thrace Byzantine town

Rhamnus   SE Greece theater and temple, Athenian settlement

Rhegium (Rhegion, modern Reggio di Calabria)   S Italy Greek colony, Roman city

Rheims (Reims)   N France Viking center, archbishopric

Rheindahlen   NW Germany early tools, Neanderthal site

Rheingönheim   W Germany silk trade

Rhodes   E Mediterranean Hellenistic city

Rhos-y-beddau   NW Wales stone alignment

Ribblehead   NE Ireland Viking center

Ribe   W Denmark early settlement, Viking trading emporium

Richmond   N England medieval town

Richu   C Japan Yamato tomb

Rickeby   E Sweden rock art

Rievaulx   N England monastery, Cistercian abbey

Rigabe   SE France early tools, Neanderthal site

Rijkholt (-Sint-Geertruid)   S Holland flint mine

Rim   W Africa Mali hunter-gatherers, Iron Age site

Rinaldone   C Italy Copper Age cemetery

Ringkloster   N Denmark Mesolithic settlement, megalithic site

Rio Azul   N Guatemala Maya settlement

Rio Bec   Mexico, Yucatán Maya settlement

Rio Chiquito   C Mexico Olmec site

Rio de Janeiro   Brazil colonial settlement

Rio Seco   S Peru early public building

Rio Tinto   S Spain early copper mine

Riofrio   N Spain pollen core site

Riol (Rigodulum)   W Germany Roman village

Ripabianca   C Italy farming site

Riparo Blanc   C Italy shell midden

Ripiceni-Izvor   Romania Neanderthal site

Ripoli   C Italy defensive enclosure

Ripon   N England medieval town

Rishahr (Rev Ardashir)   SW Persia Sasanian city

Rissori   Belgium early tools

Rithymna (modern Rethimnon)   N Crete Minoan village

Riverton   C USA, Illinois Archaic site

Riverton   New Zealand, South I. shell midden

Rixheim   E France farming site, urnfield

Roaix   SE France rock-cut tomb

Roanne   E France Celtic site

Robbins   NE USA, Kentucky Adena site

Roberts Drift   S Africa Iron Age site

Robin Hood's Cave   C England hunter-gatherer site

Robinson   NE USA, New York Archaic site

Roc de Marsal   C France Neanderthal site

Roc de Sers   NW France hunter-gatherer site, hunter-gatherer art

Roc-en-Pail   NW France Neanderthal site

Rock Eagle   SE USA temple mound

Rockmarshall   N Ireland shell midden

Rocky Cape   Tasmania Aboriginal site

Rocourt   Belgium Neanderthal site

Rodgers Shelter   C USA, Missouri Archaic site

Roersdam   C Denmark bog body

Rognac   S France native settlement

Rohira   NW India Harappan site

Roi Et Sites   NE Thailand early sites

Rojadi   NW India Harappan site

Rollright Stones   C England stone circle

Roluos   Indo-China, Cambodia early site

Romagnano   N Italy Mesolithic settlement, farming site

Romanelli   S Italy hunter-gatherer site, hunter-gatherer art

Romeral   S Spain megalithic tomb

Renbjerg   NW Denmark bog body

Ronquin   C Venezuela early horticultural village

Rooidam   S Africa Acheulian tools

Roonka Flat   S Australia Aboriginal site

Roosevelt   SW USA Pueblo farming site

Ropp   W Africa, Nigeria hunter-gatherers

Roquepertuse   S France Celtic site

Rorbaek   NW Denmark bog body

Rosh Horesha   S Palestine Natufian site

Rosh Zin   S Palestine Natufian site

Roskilde   N Denmark Viking center

Ross   S Ireland monastery

Rossano   S Italy archbishopric

Rossum Praestegård   S Norway musical instruments

Rotokura   New Zealand, South I. shell midden and moa bones

Roudo   W Syria early tools

Rouen   N France Viking trading emporium, archbishopric

Rouffignac   C France hunter-gatherer art, Mesolithic settlement

Rough I.   N Ireland shell midden

Roum   NW Denmark bog body

Round Green   S England early tools

Roundway   S England beaker burial

Ruahihi   New Zealand, North I. defended settlement

Ruanga   E Africa, Zimbabwe Iron Age site

Ruarangi Pa   New Zealand, North I. defended settlement

Rudabánya   Hungary Dryopithecus

Rudki   W Poland iron-working site

Rudna Glava   C Yugoslavia early copper mine

Rudston   NE England beaker burial

Runan   C China Han city

Runnymede   S England Bronze Age settlement

Runzhou   E China Tang prefecture

Rupar   NW India early city, Harappan site

Rupnath   C India rock edict

Rupununi   Guyana early settlement

Rusahinili   E Anatolia Urartian city

Ruse   N Yugoslavia urnfield

Rusellae   N Italy Etruscan city

Rusinga I.   Kenya Proconsul

Russell Cave   SE USA, Tennessee Archaic site

Rustenburg   S Africa Iron Age site

Sa Huynh   S Vietnam transitional settlement, early site
Saaide   W Syria Natufian site
Saalburg   NW Germany Roman water mill
Saami culture   Scandinavia
Saarbrücken   W Germany Roman village
Sab Champa   C Thailand moated site
Saba'a   NW Mesopotamia Assyrian stela
Sabaea   SW Arabia early state
Sabancheyevo   C Russia steppe settlement
Sabrata   W Libya Roman city
Saccopastore   C Italy Neanderthal site
Sacrificios Island   C Mexico Aztec town
Sacsayhuamán   C Peru Inca fortress
Sadanoyama   C Japan Yamato tomb
Sadhaura   N India Mughal mint
Sado Middens   S Portugal
Sado   N Japan shogunate provincial capital
Saeth Maen   S Wales stone alignment
Sagaholm   S Sweden rock art
Sagartians   ancient people of S Persia
Saguntum (modern Sagunto)   E Spain native settlement
Ságvár   Hungary hunter-gatherer site
Sahul-land   early land bridge
Sai Yok   S Thailand cave site, early metal site
Sai, Island of   U Egypt fortress
Said Qala Tepe   Afghanistan later farming village
Saikaido   C Japan early highway
Saint-Eugène   S France beaker burial
Saint-Gaudens   SW France Dryopithecus
Sais   L Egypt ancient city
Saitobaru   SW Japan mound cemetery
Sakcagözü   SE Anatolia pottery remains, Assyrian city
Saki   C Japan mound cemetery
Sakitama   C Japan mound cemetery
Sal'a   Czechoslovakia Neanderthal site
Saladero   C Venezuela early horticultural village
Salaga   W Africa, Ghana early town
Salamanca   N Spain monastery
Salamis   Cyprus ivory
Salamis   SE Greece Athenian settlement
Salapia   C Italy Roman empire
Salcombe   SW England ancient shipwreck
Saldae (Bougie, modern Bejaia)   NW Africa Phoenician city

Salé   NW Africa, Morocco *Homo erectus*
Salemas   Portugal Neanderthal site
Salerno (Salernum)   S Italy Roman colony, archbishopric
Salgir River   SW Russia steppe settlement
Salinas la Blanca   SE Mexico Maya settlement
Salinelles   SE France flint mine
Salipetaka   E India Buddhist site
Salmas   NW Persia rock relief
Salmendingen   W Germany Dryopithecus
Salonae (modern Solin)   N Yugoslavia Roman provincial capital
Salts Cave   C USA, Kentucky Archaic site
Salzburg   W Austria archbishopric
Saizgitter-Lebenstedt   N Germany Neanderthal site
Samandag Cave   S Anatolia Palaeolithic site
Samanli   W Anatolia Sinan mosque
Samapa   E India rock edict
Samaria   N Palestine Royal fortress of Israel, Achaemenid city, Hellenistic city
Samarkand (Maracanda)   C Asia Achaemenid city, early trade center, Islamic town, early trade
Samarra   C Mesopotamia pottery remains, Abbasid capital, holy city
Sambava   Madagascar Ming pottery
Sambor Prei Kuk   Cambodia Neolithic settlement, early monumental site
Samburu Hills   Kenya Kenyapithecus
Samhar   S Arabia ancient port
Samoa   Lapita culture, early settlement
Samos   SE Aegean Greek city, Greek aqueduct
Samosata (modern Samsat)   E Anatolia Roman legionary fortress
Samothrace   N Aegean sanctuary
Samrong Sen   Cambodia transitional settlement
Samun Dukiya   W Africa, Nigeria Iron Age site
San Antonio   S USA, Texas colonial settlement
San Augustin   E Mexico Maya settlement
San Biagio   S Italy Greek shrine
San Carla   Balearic Is. fortified site
San Cosmos   SW USA Pueblo farming site
San Diego   SW USA early settlement

San Felipe   E Guatemala Maya settlement
San Fernando de Apure   Venezuela early settlement
San Gervasio   Mexico, Yucatán Maya settlement
San Isidro   C Spain early tools
San Isidro   N Mexico early settlement
San Isidro   SE Mexico Pre-Classical site
San Jerónimo   C Mexico early farming site, Pre-Classical site
San Jose   Belize Maya settlement
San Jose Mogote   C Mexico early farming site, early hieroglyphs
San Lorenzo   C Mexico early public building, Olmec center
San Marco   S Italy monastery
San Marcos   C Mexico early settlement
San Martin de Castaneda   NW Spain monastery
San Martín Pajapán   C Mexico Olmec site
San Miguel   E Mexico Maya settlement
San Miguel Amuco   C Mexico Pre-Classical site
San Pablito   C Mexico Pre-Classical site
San Pedro de Atacama   S Bolivia
San Simon   SW USA Pueblo farming site
San Vicenze al Volturno   C Italy monastery
Sana   SW Arabia Islamic town
Sanchi   C India Buddhist site, Buddhist stupa
Sand Hill Point   New Zealand, South I. shell midden
Sandalja   Yugoslavia hunter-gatherer site
Sandhanawaia   NW India Harappan site
Sandouville   N France Celtic oppidum
Sane   NE Greece Greek colony
Sanga   C Africa Zaire Iron Age site
Sanganakallu   S India Mesolithic site
Sangasanga   NE Borneo Neolithic settlement
Sangiran   C Java
Sanindo   C Japan early highway
Sankaram   E India Buddhist site
Sankissa   N India pillar edict
Sanliqiao   N China Longshan site
Sanmenxia   N China early Palaeolithic site
Sansan   SW France Dryopithecus
Sant Andria Priu   W Sardinia rock-cut tomb

Sant'Angelo Vecchio S Italy Greek shrine

Sant'Alvera NW Sardinia dry-stone fortress

Santa Clara W USA, California Archaic site

Santa Cristina N Italy beaker burial

Santa Cruz SE Mexico Pre-Classical site, Maya settlement

Sante Fe SW USA, New Mexico colonial settlement

Santa Fé de Bogotá (Bogatá) Colombia colonial settlement

Santa Maria in Selva N Italy farming settlement

Santa Marta SE Mexico early farming site

Santa Rita Mexico, Yucatán Maya settlement, early town

Santa Rosa SE Mexico early farming site, Pre-Classical site, Maya settlement

Santa Rosa I. SW USA, California Archaic site

Santa Rosa Xtampak Mexico, Yucatán Maya settlement

Santa Sarbana NE Sardinia dry-stone fortress

Santa Severina S Italy archbishopric

Santa Tecchia S Italy farming site, early pottery

Santa Teresa C Mexico Pre-Classical site

Santani-dar S Russia early tools

Santarém E Brazil early settlement

Santiago C Chile Inca tambo, colonial settlement, early trade

Santiago de Compostela NW Spain archbishopric and pilgrimage center

Santimamiñe N Spain hunter-gatherer art, shell midden

Santo Domingo (Ciudad Trujillo) Caribbean maritime trade

Santobong NW Borneo early port

Sanyodo C Japan early highway

Sao Pedro do Estoril C Portugal beaker burial

Sao Vicente S Portugal monastery

Sapanca W Anatolia Sinan mosque

Saphar SW Arabia early trade

Saqqara L Egypt pyramid, early burial, early writing, court cemetery

Sar Mashhad SW Persia rock relief

Sar-i Pul NW Persia rock relief

Sarabit el-Khadim Sinai copper mine

Sarai Khola NW India early farming village, Harappan site

Sarai-Nahar-Rai NE India Mesolithic site

Sarangpur C India Mughal mint

Sarapion NE Africa, Somalia early trade

Sardis (Serdis) W Anatolia Achaemenid city, Hellenistic city, Roman city

Sarepta (Zarephath) Levant ivory

Sarnath N India Buddhist stupa

Sarnowo Poland adoption of plow, megalithic tomb

Sarre S England Viking trading emporium

Sarup SE Denmark defensive enclosure

Sarurab C Sudan early pottery

Sarutaru E India later farming village

Sas Prigionas C Sardinia megalithic tomb

Sasaram NE India rock edict

Saskya (Sa'gya) Tibet Buddhist center

Sassafras SE Australia Aboriginal site

Sasseruwa N Ceylon Buddhist remains

Satala (modern Gümüsane) NE Anatolia Roman city

Sathing Phra S Thailand early site

Satogi W Japan early settlement

Satohama N Japan fishing site

Satsuma W Japan shogunate provincial capital

Saturnia N Italy Roman colony

Satyrion S Italy Greek colony

Saue SW Arabia early trade

Sauniatu Western Samoa early site

Sauveterre-la-Lémance S France Mesolithic settlement

Savannah SE USA, Georgia colonial settlement

Savignano C Italy hunter-gatherer art

Sawa SW Arabia early trade

Sawankhalok N Thailand early site

Sawaris U Egypt noble's tomb

Sayil Mexico, Yucatán settlement

Sazonkin Bugor W Russia barrow burial

Scarborough N England medieval town

Schafstädt E Germany corded ware burial

Schambach S Germany Neanderthal site

Scharmbeck N Germany iron-working site

Schnapper Point E Australia Aboriginal site

Schöfflisdorf N Switzerland corded ware burial

Schötz Switzerland Mesolithic settlement

Schroeder C Mexico early town

Schulerloch S Germany Neanderthal site

Schwanberg C Germany Celtic oppidum

Schwarzenacker W Germany Roman village

Schweizerbild S Germany hunter-gatherer site, hunter-gatherer art

Scidrus (Skidros) S Italy Greek colony

Scione (Skioni) NE Greece Greek colony

Sclayn Belgium Neanderthal site

Scoglio del Tonno S Italy Bronze Age settlement

Scotts Lake E USA temple mound

Scottsbluff W USA, Nebraska Palaeo-Indian site

Scupi (modern Skopje) S Yugoslavia Roman legionary fortress

Scythopolis (Beth-shean) N Palestine Hellenistic city

Seaford Head S England Celtic hill fort

Sebastea E Anatolia Byzantine bishopric

Sebennytus L Egypt ancient city

Sedeinga U Egypt temple

Seelands E Australia Aboriginal site

Segesta W Sicily Greek temple

Segovia C Spain Roman aqueduct

Segu (Ségou) W Africa, Mali early settlement, early town

Segusio (modern Susa) NW Italy Roman provincial capital

Seibal N Guatemala Maya settlement

Seila L Egypt pyramid

Seip NE USA, Ohio Hopewell site

Selby C USA early settlement

Selby N England medieval town

Seleucia (on the Tigris) C Mesopotamia Hellenistic city

Seleucia/Ctesiphon C Mesopotamia early trading capital

Seleucia Pieria SE Anatolia Hellenistic city

Seleucia Sidera SW Anatolia Hellenistic city

Selinus (modern Selinunte) SW Sicily Greek colony

Selsey S England Celtic oppidum

Selymbria E Thrace Byzantine town

Semma U Egypt temple, fortress

Semylla (modern Chaul) W India early trade

Sena E Africa, Mozambique Iron Age site

Sena (modern Siena) N Italy Roman colony

Séneret   C France vehicle burial
Senon   E France Roman village
Senpukuji   W Japan cave site, early pottery
Seoul   S Korea Buddhist center
Serdica (modern Sofiya, Sofia)   C Bulgaria Roman city
Sered'   Czechoslovakia Mesolithic settlement
Serendipity Cave   New Zealand, South I. early site
Sermemiut   W Greenland Dorset and Thule site
Serpent Mound   NE USA, Ohio Adena site
Serpent Mound   SE Canada, Ontario Hopewell site
Seruwawila   N Ceylon Buddhist remains
Ses Paisses   Balaeric Is. fortified site
Sesebi   U Egypt temple
Sesklo   C Greece farming site, early pottery
Sessebi   U Egypt fortress
Sestus   NW Anatolia Greek colony, Roman city
Setaia (Seteia, modern Sitia)   NE Crete Minoan town
Setanai   N Japan Ainu hill fort
Seto   C Japan pottery kiln
Settiva   Corsica megalithic tomb
Settrington   N England medieval village
Sevan   Armenia Urartian inscription
Seven Brothers   S Russia burial, barrow burial
Seville   SW Spain Islamic town, maritime trade
Sexi   SE Spain Phoenician city
Shabik'aschee   SW USA, New Mexico Basketmaker farming village
Shabona   NE Africa, Sudan wavy-line pottery, early pottery
Shabwah   SW Arabia early capital and temple remains
Shag River Mouth   New Zealand, South I. moa bones
Shah-ji-ki-dheri   N India Buddhist stupa
Shahbazgarhi   N India rock edict
Shahjo-Kotiro   NW India Harappan site
Shahr-i Dakyanus   S Persia Achaemenid city
Shahr-i Sokhta   S Persia early trade
Shama   W Africa, Ghana early port
Shami   W Persia fire temple
Shanbiaozhen   N China E Chou cemetery

Shanga   E Africa, Kenya Islamic trading post, Ming pottery
Shangcunling   N China E Chou cemetery
Shangguocun   N China E Chou bronze hoard
Shanghai   E China early settlement, Ming tomb
Shangjiaocun   N China E Chou cemetery
Shangjing   N China Tang kiln
Shanglinhu   E China Sung kiln
Shangmacun   N China E Chou cemetery
Shangwangzhuang   E China E Chou burial
Shangyu   E China Tang kiln, Sung kiln
Shanidar   N Mesopotamia Neanderthal site
Shantou (Swatow)   SE China early settlement
Shaogou   N China E Chou cemetery
Shaqadud   C Sudan early pottery
Sharpovskoye   Ukraine Greek imports
Shawnee-Minisink   NE USA fluted points
Shazhong   C China E Chou burial
She   U Egypt early town
Shechem (Shakmi, modern Nablus)   N Palestine Egyptian control, Levantine city
Sheep Rock   E USA, Pennsylvania Archaic site
Sheikh'Atiya   U Egypt noble's tomb
Sheikh Hammad   N Mesopotamia Assyrian stela
Sheikh Sa'id   U Egypt noble's tomb
Sherda   N Africa, Chad Oldowan tools
Shibam   S Arabia Islamic town
Shibaniba (modern Tell Billa)   N Mesopotamia Assyrian provincial capital
Shibe   E Russia barrow burial
Shibechari   N Japan Ainu hill fort
Shibiki   N Japan early man
Shide   S England Neanderthal site
Shigaraki   C Japan pottery kiln
Shigaste (Xigazê)   Tibet Buddhist center
Shikoma   N Japan Heian fortress
Shilka Cave   E Russia irctic culture
Shilla (Silla)   S Korea early state
Shillacoto   E Peru early public building
Shiloh   SE USA temple mound
Shilongtou Cave   C China early Palaeolithic site
Shilou   N China Shang tomb
Shipovo   W Russia silk find

Shippea Hill   SE England megalithic site
Shirataki   N Japan early man
Shiraz   S Persia Islamic town
Shirjan   SW Arabia ancient dam
Shironoyama   C Japan Yamato tomb
Shiwa   N Japan Heian fortress
Shiyu   NE China early man
Shizhaishan   SW China E Chou cemetery, Han burial
Shkaft-i Gulgul   W Persia Assyrian rock relief
Shongweni   S Africa Stone Age site
Shoop   E USA, Pennsylvania Palaeo-Indian site
Shorttughai (Shortugai)   C Asia early trade, Indus colony
Shotorak   N India Gandharan art
Shouchunfu   N China provincial capital
Shouxian   N China Tang kiln
Show Low   SW USA Pueblo farming site
Shriver   C USA fluted points
Shuidonggou   N China early man
Shuihudi   C China E Chou burial, Han burial
Shungura   NE Africa, Ethiopia early tools
Shuqba   S Palestine Natufian site
Shuruppak   S Mesopotamia early city, early writing
Shusharra (Shemshara, Shimshara)   N Mesopotamia early town
Shushtar   W Persia Sasanian city
Shwezayan   C Burma Neolithic settlement
Si Maha Phot   C Thailand moated site, early site
Si Thep   N Thailand moated site, early site
Siah Damb   NW India early farming village
Sialk (Tepe Sialk)   W Persia early kiln, early trade, early settlement, burial
Sialkot   NW India Mughal mint
Siberia   steppe nomads, arctic cultures
Sidamo   region of S Ethiopia monoliths
Siddapura   S India rock edict
Side   SW Anatolia Greek colony, Hellenistic city, Roman city, aqueduct
Sidhari   NW Greece shell midden, farming site, early pottery
Sidhpura   NE India Mesolithic site
Sidi Abderrahman   NW Africa, Morocco early man
Sidi Mansour   N Africa, Tunisia Stone Age tools

Sidi Zin   N Africa, Tunisia Acheulian tools, Stone Age tools

Sidjilmassa   N Africa, Morocco early town

Sidmant el-Gebel   L Egypt noble's tomb

Sidoarjo (Hujung-Galuh)   E Java early site

Sidon (Siduna, modern Saïda)   Lebanon early port, Phoenician city, Achaemenid palace, Hellenistic city, early trade

Siena   N Italy archbishopric

Sierkavagge   N Norway Saami settlement

Sigatoka (Singatoka)   Fiji Lapita site

Sigeium (Sigeion)   NW Anatolia Greek colony

Sigiriya   N Ceylon palace-fortress, Buddhist center

Sigoukou   N China early man

Siguiri   W Africa, Guinea early settlement

Sigus   N Algeria megalithic tomb

Silversti   NW Ukraine Mesolithic settlement

Sijilmassa   NW Africa, Morocco Islamic town

Silchester   S England Celtic site

Siling   NE China Ming tomb

Silivri   W Anatolia Sinan mosque

Silumiut   E Canada Thule site

Silver Leaves   S Africa Iron Age site

Simmern   W Germany Roman village

Simonsen   C USA, Iowa Archaic site

Simyra   W Syria Egyptian control

Sinai   early trade, bishopric

Sinam-ni   N Korea early settlement

Sinam-ni   S Korea early settlement

Sinap   N Anatolia Ramapithecus and Sivapithecus

Sine-Saloum   W Africa region of Senegal

Singa   NE Africa, Sudan Stone Age tools

Singidunum (modern Beograd, Belgrade)   C Yugoslavia Roman legionary fortress

Sinjar   N Mesopotamia Assyrian stela

Sinope (modern Sinop)   N Anatolia gold and silver work, Greek colony, Hellenistic city, Roman city, Byzantine walled town

Sinuessa   C Italy Roman colony

Sion-Petit Chasseur   Switzerland megalithic tomb

Sipka   Czechoslovakia Neanderthal site

Sipontum   C Italy Roman colony

Sippar   C Mesopotamia early city

Siraf   S Persia Sasanian city, Islamic port

Sireniki   E Russia Thule site

Sirgenstein   W Germany hunter-gatherer site

Sirhind   NW India Mughal mint

Siris   S Italy Greek colony

Sirwah   SW Arabia temple remains

Sisters Creek   Tasmania Aboriginal site

Sisupalgarh   E India early city

Sitagroi   NE Greece farming site

Sitagroi-Fotolivos   NE Greece tell settlement

Sithulpahuwa   S Ceylon Buddhist remains

Sitt Markho   W Syria early tools

Sizma   C Anatolia Neolithic site

Sjörup   S Sweden weapon hoard

Skallerup   S Denmark metalwork

Skatovka   C Russia steppe settlement

Skedemosse Bog   SE Sweden ritual metalwork

Skew Valley   W Australia Aboriginal site

Skipshelleren   S Norway Mesolithic settlement

Sklavokambos   N Crete Minoan village

Skogstorp   E Sweden metalwork

Skoteino (Skotino)   C Crete sacred cave

Skrydstrup   SW Sweden barrow burial

Skudrians   ancient people of SE Europe

Sledmere   N England medieval village

Smilcic   W Yugoslavia farming site

Smyrna (modern Izmir)   W Anatolia Greek city, Roman city, Byzantine bishopric

Snaith   N England medieval town

Snaketown   SW USA Hohokam farming village

Snape   E England boat burial

Snowdrift   NE Canada Thule site

Sobata   W Japan early settlement

Soconusco   S Guatemala Aztec trade center

Socotra   Gulf of Aden frankincense and myrrh

Sodo   NE Africa, Ethiopia monoliths

Soesterberg   S Holland beaker burial

Sofala   E Africa, Mozambique early trading post, maritime trade

Sofia (Serdica)   Bulgaria Sinan mosque

Sogård   NW Denmark bog body

Sogdians   ancient people of C Asia

Sokkuram   S Korea rock-carved temple

Sokoto   W Africa, Nigeria early town

Solbjerg   NW Denmark metalwork

Soldiers Hole   S England hunter-gatherer site

Soleb   U Egypt temple, fortress

Soleilhac   C France early tools

Soloeis   NW Sicily Greek colony

Solola   S Guatemala Maya settlement

Solomon Is.   Lapita culture

Solutré   E France hunter-gatherer site

Solvieux   C France hunter-gatherer site

Somers, Mt.   New Zealand, South I. rock art

Somme-Bionne   NE France vehicle burial

Somnath   NW India Harappan site

Somnathpur   S India Hindu religious site

Songguk   S Korea rice farming site

Songhay Empire   W Africa

Songhor   Kenya Proconsul

Songyuan   NE China E Chou cemetery

Songze   E China early settlement, Longshan site, rice farming site

Songzhou   N China Tang prefecture

Sop'ohang   NE Korea shell mound

Sopatma (Sopattinam, modern Marakkanam)   SE India early trade

Soroki   SW Russia Mesolithic settlement, megalithic site

Sorrento   S Italy archbishopric

Sos   SW France Celtic oppidum

Sosan   S Korea Buddhist center

Sösdala   S Sweden ritual metalwork

Sotka-Koh   NW India Harappan site

Soulabé-las-Maretas   SW France Neanderthal site

Soumont-Saint-Quentin   N France stone alignment

Sound of Mull   SW Scotland shipwreck excavation

Sources de la Seine   E France Celtic religious site

Sous-Balme   SE France Mesolithic settlement

Sousse   N Africa, Tunisia Islamic fortress

Southern Africa   early man, hunter-gatherers, Stone Age sites

Southwark   S England Viking mint

Southwest Cape   Alaska Thule sites

Sovetskoye (Marienthal)   W Russia silk find

Soyo-do   C Korea early settlement

Sozudai   W Japan early man, early settlement

Spasinou Charax   S Mesopotamia Parthian city, early trade

Surkotada NW India early city, Harappan site

Surt N Africa, Libya Islamic town

Susa W Japan Korean pottery

Susa W Persia early settlement, early pottery and kiln, early city, early writing, Assyrian provincial city, Achaemenid palace, Parthian/Sasanian city, Islamic town

Susuga E Russia arctic culture

Sutkagen Dor Baluchistan, NW India early city, Harappan site

Sutton Hoo E England boat burial

Suttukeni S India megalithic tomb

Sutz W Switzerland corded ware settlement

Suurkree S Africa early man

Svaerdborg Denmark Mesolithic settlement

Svilengrad Bulgaria Sinan mosque

Swakopmund SW Africa, Namibia Stone Age site

Swanscombe SE England early tools and human remains

Swartkrans S Africa *Australopithecus robustus*, early man

Swarts SW USA Pueblo farming site

Sweet Track SW England pollen core site

Swieciechów C Poland flint mine

Swift Creek SE USA, Georgia Hopewell site

Swifterbant N Holland megalithic site

Sybaris S Italy Greek colony

Sybrita C Crete Linear B tablets

Syningthwaite N England medieval town

Syracuse (Syracuse, modern Siracusa) E Sicily Greek colony, Roman city, monastery

Százhalombatta C Hungary Celtic site

Szigetszentmárton C Hungary Copper Age cemetery

Taanach Palestine Egyptian control

Tabarin E Africa, Kenya Australopithecus

Tabbat el Hammam W Syria Neolithic site

Tabon Cave SW Philippines early man, cave site, Neolithic settlement, early metal site

Tabriz N Persia Safavid capital

Tabuk NW Arabia Islamic town

Tabun C Israel Neanderthal site

Tachenghit NW Africa, Algeria Acheulian tools

Taehuksan I. SW Korea early settlement

Taepyong S Korea rice farming site

Tafahi I. C Pacific Lapita obsidian

Taferjit N Africa, Niger bone harpoons

Taforalt NW Africa, Morocco Stone Age tools, hunter-gatherers

Taga N Japan Heian fortress

Tagara (modern Thair) C India early trade

Tagdaït W Africa, Niger bone harpoons

Taghaza W Africa, Mali early town

Tagra NE Africa, Sudan bone harpoons, early pottery

Taharoa New Zealand, North I. shell midden

Tahert N Africa Islamic town

Tahunanui New Zealand, South I. shell midden and moa bones

Tai Shan N China holy mountain

Ta'if W Arabia Islamic town

Tailing NE China Ming tomb

Taïmanga C Africa, Chad bone harpoons

Taimataima N Venezuela early settlement

Taipivai Valley Marquesas Is. early site

Tairua New Zealand, North I. shell midden

Tairua New Zealand, South I. moa bones

Taishakukyo W Japan early settlement

Taixicun N China early burial, Shang city

Taiyuan N China Han city, Tang prefecture, Ming provincial capital

Taiyuanfu N China provincial capital

Taizongmiao N China Chou burial

Tajumulco S Guatemala Maya settlement, early town

Takalghat C India megalithic tomb

Takatori W Japan Korean pottery

Takedda W Africa, Niger early settlement

Takeo Indo-China, Cambodia early site

Takht-i Bahi N India gandharan art, buddhist center

Takht-i Kaikaus N Persia fire temple

Takht-i Rustam N Persia fire temple

Takht-i Rustam SW Persia royal tomb

Takht-i Sulaiman (Takht-i Suleyman) NW Persia Parthian/Sasanian city, Islamic town

Takrur Africa, Gambia early settlement

Takua Pa S Thailand early site

Tal-i Ghazir W Persia early city

Tal-i Iblis S Persia early trade

Tal-i Malyan W Persia early city

Talaja W India Buddhist site

Taland Is. S Philippines rock-shelter

Talas C Asia early trade

Talasea Papua New Guinea Lapita site

Talgai E Australia early man

Taliski C Russia hunter-gatherer site

Tall-i Bakun W Persia early kiln

Talus Village SW USA Pueblo farming site

Tam Hang N Indo-China, Laos cave site

Tam Pong N Indo-China, Laos cave site

Tamar Hat N Africa, Algerian hunter-gatherers

Tamatarcha S Russia early town

Tamatsukuri N Japan Heian fortress

Tamaulipas N Mexico early settlement, early farming

Tamaya Mellet W Africa, Niger bone harpoons, early pottery

Tamba C Japan pottery kiln

Tambo Colorado C Peru Inca center

Tamboratra N Peru Inca tambo

Tamluk (Tamralipta) E India early trade center

Tamuin C Mexico early town

Tancáh Mexico, Yucatán Maya settlement

Tanca Manna N Sardinia dry-stone fortress

Tandou Lake SE Australia early man

Tang Dynasty China

Tang-i Chakchak S Persia fire temple

Tang-i Sarvak W Persia rock relief

Tanghu N China E Chou cemetery

Tangiru C Romania tell settlement

Tanis L Egypt early city, early trade

Taniwha Pa New Zealand, North I. defended settlement

Tanjungpura W Borneo Buddhist center

Tannstock S Germany Mesolithic settlement

Tanshishan E China Longshan site

Tantrimalai (Tantirimale) N Ceylon Buddhist religious site

Tanum W Sweden rock art

Tanzania early man, hunter-gatherers, early farming, Iron Age

Tanzhou C China provincial capital

Taoudenni (Taodeni) W Africa, Mali early town

Tapadong NE Borneo early metal site

Ta-p'en-keng Taiwan cave site

Taplow S England claw beaker

Taputapuatea Society Is. early site

Taq-i Bustan W Persia rock relief

Tara   N Ireland Celtic religious site

Tarakai qila   NW India Indus Valley settlement, Harappan site

Taranto   S Italy archbishopric

Taras (Tarentum, modern Taranto)   S Italy Greek colony

Tarascans   early people of C Mexico

Tarata Pa   New Zealand, North I. defended settlement

Tarawera   New Zealand, North I. rock art

Tarentaise   E France archbishopric

Tareyanagi   N Japan rice farming site

Tarila   N India early city

Tarkhan   L Egypt ancient cemetery

Tarkhanawala Dera   NW India Harappan site

Tarma Tambo   Inca center

Tarquinii (modern Tarquinia)   C Italy Etruscan city

Tarraco (modern Tarragona)   NE Spain Roman provincial, capital, Roman aqueduct

Tarsus   SE Anatolia Neolithic site, early trade, Achaemenid city, Hellenistic city, Roman provincial capital, Islamic town

Tartaria   C Romania tell settlement

Taruga   W Africa, Nigeria early iron

Tarxien   Malta bone plaques

Tas Ayir   S Russia Mesolithic settlement

Tas-Khazaa   S Siberia steppe settlement

Tashkent   C Asia steppe settlement

Tasovice   Czechoslovakia Mesolithic settlement

Tastybutak   SE Russia steppe settlement

Tata   Hungary Neanderthal site

Tateyama   N Japan Ainu hill fort

Tateyama, Mt.   N Japan holy mountain

Tauá   E Brazil early settlement

Tauai   C Pacific Lapita site

Tauchira   NE Africa Greek colony

Taung   S Africa *Australopithecus africanus*

Tavola Palatine   S Italy Greek shrine

Taxila (Bhir Mound)   NW India Achaemenid city, Graeco-Bactrian city, early trade center, Buddhist stupa

Taxla   C Mexico early farming site

Tayadirt   N Morocco megalithic tomb

Tayasal   N Guatemala Maya settlement, early town

Tazawa   C Japan early settlement

Te Awanga   New Zealand, North I. defended settlement

Te Ikaamaru   New Zealand, North I. defended settlement

Teayo   C Mexico pyramid, Aztec town

Tebingtinggi   C Sumatra early metal site

Tecorral Cave   C Mexico early settlement

Tehuacán Valley   C Mexico hunter-gatherers, early farming

Tekapo   New Zealand, South I. rock art

Tekedda   W Africa, Niger early town

Tekirdag   W Anatolia Sinan mosque

Telamon   N Italy Etruscan city

Tell 'Abta   N Mesopotamia Assyrian city

Tell Abbada   C Mesopotamia pottery remains

Tell Abu Hassan   C Mesopotamia early settlement

Tell Abu Hureira   E Syria Neolithic site

Tell Agrab (Tell Ajrab)   C Mesopotamia early settlement

Tell Ahmad el-Hatu   N Mesopotamia early settlement

Tell al Oueili   S Mesopotamia pottery remains

Tell Aqab   E Syria pottery remains

Tell Ashara (Tirqa)   NW Mesopotamia Assyrian stela

Tell Asmar (Eshnunna)   N Mesopotamia early city

Tell Aswad   N Mesopotamia Neolithic site, early pottery

Tell Berné (Tall Birnah)   NW Syria Neolithic site, Mitannian city

Tell Brak   E Syria pottery remains, early city, early town and palace, early writing, Mitannian city

Tell Deim   N Mesopotamia Achaemenid palace

Tell el Rimah   N Mesopotamia early town, Assyrian stela

Tell el 'Ubaid   S Mesopotamia pottery remains, early settlement

Tell el-Daba   L Egypt ancient city

Tell el-Far'a   S Palestine burial

Tell el-Rub'a   L Egypt noble's tomb

Tell el-Yahundiya   L Egypt temple

Tell es-Sa'idiyeh   Palestine Egyptian control

Tell es-Sawwan   N Mesopotamia pottery remains

Tell Fakhariyah   N Mesopotamia Neolithic site

Tell Halaf   E Syria pottery remains

Tell Halim Asra Hajin   C Mesopotamia early settlement

Tell Harmal   C Mesopotamia early town

Tell Judeideh   NW Syria Neolithic site

Tell Madhhur   C Mesopotamia pottery remains, early settlement

Tell Magzaliyah   N Mesopotamia Neolithic site

Tell Mismar   S Mesopotamia pottery remains

Tell Nabasha   L Egypt ancient city

Tell Ramad   Lebanon Neolithic site, early pottery

Tell Rubeidheh   N Mesopotamia early settlement

Tell Shemshara   C Mesopotamia pottery remains, early settlement

Tell Sotto   N Mesopotamia Neolithic site, pottery remains

Tell Taya   N Mesopotamia early town

Tell Tayinat   Syria Mitannian city, Assyrian city

Tell Turlu   C Syria pottery remains

Tell 'Uqair   C Mesopotamia early city, early settlement, early writing

Tell Wilaya   S Mesopotamia early settlement, ancient palace

Tellerup   C Denmark musical instruments

Telloh   S Mesopotamia early city

Telmessus   SW Anatolia rock-cut tombs

Telod   NW India Harappan site

Telul eth-Thalathat   N Mesopotamia early pottery

Témara   NW Africa, Morocco *Homo erectus*

Temple Wood   W Scotland stone circle and alignment

Tempsa   S Italy Roman colony

Tenayuca   C Mexico Aztec center

Tenayucán   C Mexico pyramid

Tengdian   C China E Chou burial

Tenochtitlán   C Mexico pyramid, Aztec capital

Tenta   Cyprus Neolithic site

Teojate   S Peru Paracas site

Teopanzolco   C Mexico pyramid

Teos   W Anatolia Greek city, Hellenistic city

Teotitlán   early state of C Mexico

Tepe Abdolhoseyn   NW Persia Neolithic site

Tepe Asiab   NW Persia Neolithic site

Tepe Gawra   N Mesopotamia pottery remains, early city, early settlement

Tepe Giyan   C Persia early settlement

Tepe Guran   NW Persia Neolithic site, early pottery

Tepe Sabz   W Persia early settlement

Tepe Sarab   W Persia early pottery

Tepe Yahya   S Persia early trade, Achaemenid city

Tepeapulco   C Mexico early town

Tepecoacuilco C Mexico Pre-Classical site

Tepetiaoxtoc C Mexico Aztec center

Tepexpán C Mexico Aztec center

Tepotzotlán C Mexico Aztec center

Tepoztlán C Mexico pyramid

Tequixquiac C Mexico Aztec center

Terina S Italy Greek city, Greek colony

Termes C Spain native settlement

Termini Imerses Sicily Mesolithic settlement

Ternate E Indies, Moluccas maritime trade

Ternifine N Africa, Algeria *Homo erectus*

Terra Amata SE France early tools

Terroso N Portugal native settlement

Tertry N France Viking mint

Teshik-Tash C Asia Neanderthal site

Teso dos Bichos E Brazil early settlement

Tesson W France vehicle burial

Tete E Africa, Mozambique Iron Age site

Téviec NW France shell midden, megalithic site, Mesolithic grave

Teviotdale New Zealand, South I. early site

Texcoco C Mexico early town, Aztec town

Teyjat C France hunter-gatherer art

Tezoyuca C Mexico Aztec center

Thair (Tagara) S India Deccan city

Thalassa SE Greece Athenian settlement

Thalia Point E Canada Dorset site

Tham Hoi N Indo-China, Vietnam cave site

Tham Khuyen N Vietnam *Homo erectus*

Thamugadi (modern Timgad) N Algeria Roman city

Thandwe C Africa, Zambia Iron Age site

Thang Long Indo-China, N Vietnam early site

Thanjavur (Tanjuvur, Tanjore) S India Chola center

Thano Bula Khan NW India Harappan site

Thap Cham Indo-China, S Vietnam early site

Thapsus N Africa Phoenician city

Tharro NW India Indus Valley settlement, Harappan site

Tharrus W Sardinia Phoenician city, Carthaginian city

Thasos (Thasus) NE Greece Greek colony, Hellenistic city

Thatcham S England Mesolithic settlement

Thaton S Burma early site, Buddhist center

The Tombs E Australia Aboriginal site

Thebes NE Greece Mycenaean settlement

Thebes U Egypt early city, royal capital, early iron

Theodosian Walls of Constantinople

Theodosiopolis E Anatolia Byzantine walled town

Thera (Santorini, modern Thira) S Aegean fallout from eruption, Greek city

Thermi NE Greece ancient fortress

Thessalonica N Greece Hellenistic city, Roman provincial capital, Byzantine bishopric

Thessaly ancient country of N Greece

Thetford E England Viking center

Thicket N England medieval town

Thiensville N USA, Wisconsin Archaic site

Thiré W France beaker burial

Thirsk N England medieval town

Thixendale N England medieval village

Tholey W Germany Roman village

Thomas Quarries NW Africa, Morocco *Homo erectus*

Thoralby N England medieval village

Thoricus (Thorikos) SE Greece tholos tomb, temple, Athenian settlement

Three Rivers S Africa Acheulian tools

Thrimbokambos SW Crete Minoan village

Thugga (modern Dougga) W Tunisia Roman city

Thule NW Greenland Arctic culture

Thuna N India pillar edict

Thunderbird NE USA fluted points

Ti-n-Torha N Africa early pottery

Tiahuanaco (Tiwanaku) N Bolivia pyramid, early city

Tiandai Shan E China holy mountain

Tianlong Shan N China rock-carved temple

Tianxingguan C China E Chou burial

Tibava N Czechoslovakia Copper Age cemetery

Tibchi W Africa, Nigeria Stone Age tools

Tichitt W Africa, Mauritania early agriculture, early town

Tievebulliagh N Ireland ax factory

Tigaida I. Aleutian Is. arctic culture

Tihna U Egypt early town

Tihna el-Gebel U Egypt noble's tomb

Tihodaïne N Africa, Algeria Acheulian tools

Tihoo Mexico, Yucatán Maya settlement

Tikal N Guatemala pyramid, early writing, Maya center, Maya city

Til Barsib (Til Barsip, modern Tell Ahmar) E Syria Assyrian provincial city, burial

Tilaura-kot NE India early city

Tilcara S Bolivia Inca tambo

Tilki Tepe N Mesopotamia pottery remains

Tiltekin S Algeria early pottery

Timbuktu (Tombouctou) W Africa, Mali Islamic town, urban city, early city

Timna S Israel early copper mine

Timna' SW Arabia early capital and temple remains

Timonovka W Russia hunter-gatherer site

Timor early settlement, early maritime trade

Tindouf NW Africa, Algeria Islamic trade, early settlement

Tingis (Tangiers, modern Tanger) N Morocco Phoenician city, Roman provincial capital

Tingzhou NW China early trade

Tipasa N Algeria Carthaginian cemetery

Tiquisate S Guatemala Maya settlement

Tiraspol SW Russia barrow burial

Tiriyai N Ceylon Buddhist religious site

Tirpesti N Romania farming site, Cucuteni-Tripolye village

Tirunelveli S India Hindu religious site

Tiruvannamalai S India Hindu religious site

Tiruvarur (Thiruvarur) S India Hindu religious site

Tiruvengalanatha temple of Vijayanagara

Tiryns S Greece Mycenaean settlement

Tissamaharama S Ceylon Buddhist site, Buddhist remains

Tiszapolgár N Hungary Copper Age cemetery

Tit Mellil NW Africa, Morocco Stone Age tools

Titelberg NE France Celtic oppidum

Tito Bustillo NW Spain hunter-gatherer art

Tiwai Point   New Zealand, South I. shell midden

Tiwanaku (Tihuanaco)   N Bolivia Inca center

Tijikkiträsk   N Sweden Mesolithic settlement

Tlacopán   C Mexico Aztec town

Tláhuac   C Mexico Aztec center

Tlalmanalco   C Mexico Aztec center

Tlapacoya   C Mexico early farming site, Pre-Classical site

Tlapacoyan   S Mexico early settlement

Tlapanaloya   C Mexico Aztec center

Tlatelolco   C Mexico pyramid, Aztec center

Tlatilco   C Mexico early farming settlement, Pre-Classical site, early town

Tlazcala   C Mexico early town, early state

Tlaxmalac   C Mexico Pre-Classical site

Tlemcen   N Africa, Algeria Islamic town

Toala I.   C Africa Iron Age site

Toca Mai   C Africa, Angola Oldowan tools

Tofting   NW Germany terp settlement

Toftum   E Denmark defensive enclosure

Togariishi   C Japan early settlement

Togiak   Alaska arctic culture

Tojin   SW Japan mound cemetery

Tokaido   C Japan early highway

Tok-Kala   C Russia steppe settlement

Tokmak   C Asia early trade

Tokoname   C Japan pottery kiln

Tokoro   N Japan early settlement, Ainu hill fort

Tokoroa   New Zealand, North I. moa bones

Tokutan   N Japan Heian fortress

Tolaga Bay   New Zealand, North I. rock art

Toledo (Toletum)   C Spain Roman capital, Roman aqueduct, Islamic town, medieval trade

Tollund   N Denmark bog body

Tolosa (modern Toulouse)   SW France Roman city

Tomakovka   Ukraine Greek imports

Tombos   U Egypt fortress

Tombua (Porto Alexandre)   SW Africa, Angola Acheulian tools

Tomebamba   C Ecuador Inca center

Tomerdingen   SE Germany Celtic religious site

Tomi (modern Constanta)   E Romania Roman city

Tomsk   S Siberia steppe settlement

Tonalá   SE Mexico Pre-Classical site, Maya settlement

Tonga   Lapita culture, early settlement

Tonga Bay   New Zealand, South I. rock art

Tong'an   SE China Sung kiln

Tongaporutu   New Zealand, North I. rock art

Tongatapu   Tonga Lapita site

Tongchuan   N China Tang kiln

Tongchuanfu   W China provincial capital

Tonggou   N Korea capital of early state

Tongking   N Indo-China, Vietnam shell middens

Tongliang   W China early man

Tonglushan   NE China early copper mine, E Chou copper mine

Tongmak-tong   N Korea early settlement

Tongsam-dong   S Korea cave site

Tongzi   W China early man

Toniná   E Mexico Maya settlement

Tonopah   W USA, Nevada Palaeo-Indian site

Toolesboro Mounds   N USA, Iowa Hopewell site

Toolondo   S Australia Aboriginal site

Tooya   N Japan Ainu hill fort

Topange Canyon   W USA, California Archaic site

Topoxte   N Guatemala Maya settlement

Toprakkale   E Anatolia Urartian capital, silk trade

Topzawa   NE Mesopotamia stela

Torihama   C Japan shell mound, fishing site

Torkop   S Norway Mesolithic settlement

Toro   C Japan rice farming site

Torone   NE Greece Greek colony

Torralba-Ambrona   NE Spain early tools

Torralbet   Balaeric Is. megalithic tomb

Torre in Pietra   C Italy early tools

Torrente Conca   N Italy early tools

Torsbjerg (Thorsberg)   SW Denmark weapons and metalwork

Torslunda   E Sweden metalwork

Torupgaarde   S Denmark swords

Tosali   E India rock edict

Tosamporo   N Japan early settlement

Tószeg   E Hungary Bronze Age settlement

Tot   E Africa, Kenya Iron Age site

Toterfout   S Holland barrow burial

Toulouse (Tolosa)   SW France medieval trade, bishopric

Toumba   N Greece tholos tomb

Toungour   N Africa, Chad wavy-line pottery

Tournai   NW France monastery

Touro Passo   N Argentina early settlement

Tours   C France archbishopric

Town Creek   E USA temple mound

Towosahgy   SE USA temple mound

Towthorpe   N England medieval village

Tra Kieu   Indo-China, S Vietnam early site

Trakhtemirov   SW Russia steppe settlement

Trani   C Italy archbishopric

Tranquility   SW USA, California Archaic site

Traostalos   E Crete peak sanctuary

Trapezus (Trebizond, modern Trabzon)   NE Anatolia Greek colony, Hellenistic city, Roman city, Byzantine walled town

Trasimeno   C Italy hunter-gatherer art

Trayamar   C Spain Carthaginian cemetery

Tre Erici   C Italy farming settlement

Trebizond (Trapezus)   NE Anatolia Byzantine walled town

Tréissény   NW France early tools

Trelleborg   C Denmark viking fortress

Trempealeau   N USA, Wisconsin Hopewell site

Tremper   NE USA, Ohio Hopewell site

Tres Cabezos   SE Spain farming settlement

Tres Zapotes   C Mexico pyramid, early writing, Olmec center, early town

Tressé   NW France megalithic tomb

Tri Brata   SW Russia steppe settlement

Trialeti   Georgia steppe burials

Trichur   S India Hindu religious site

Tricorythus   SE Greece Athenian settlement

Trier (Augusta Treverorum)   NW Germany Roman city, silk find, Rhenish pottery kiln, archbishopric

Trikkala   C Greece Sinan mosque

Trincomalee   Ceylon maritime trade

Trindhoj   SW Sweden barrow burial

Trinidad   E Mexico Pre-Classical site

Trinil   C Java *Homo erectus*

Tripoli   N Africa, Libya Islamic town, early town

Tripolye   W Russia Cucuteni-Tripolye village

Tripuri   C India Deccan city

Trísov   W Czechoslovakia Celtic oppidum

Trivento   C Italy archbishopric

Trizay   W France beaker burial

Troesmis (modern Iglita)   NE Romania Roman legionary fortress

Tromoy   S Norway barrow burial

Trou du Diable   Belgium Neanderthal site

Trou Magrite   Belgium hunter-gatherer art

Trou Reuviau   Belgium hunter-gatherer site

Troy   NW Anatolia Bronze Age citadel

Trundholm   C Denmark metalwork

Trundle, The   S England Celtic hill fort

Trusesti   N Romania Cucuteni-Tripolye village

Tsarëv   C Russia steppe settlement

Tsareva Mogila   SW Russia steppe settlement

Tsarskaya   SW Russia steppe settlement

Tsona   S Russia Neanderthal site

Tsona Cave   S Russia early tools

Tsopi   S Russia Neanderthal site

Tsukamawari   C Japan Yamato tomb

Tsurashi   N Japan Ainu hill fort

Tsushima   C Japan rice farming site

Tuam   W Ireland archbishopric

Tuban   E Java early port

Tube Tube   New Guinea Kula gift exchange

Tukh (Nubt)   U Egypt pyramid

Tula   C Mexico pyramid, early town, Aztec town

Tulancingo   C Mexico early town

Tularosa Cave   SW USA, New Mexico Archaic site, Pueblo farming site

Tultitlán   C Mexico Aztec center

Tulum   Mexico, Yucatán Maya settlement, early town

Tumbes   S Ecuador Inca center

Tunacunnhee   SE USA, Alabama Hopewell site

Tunip   Syria Egyptian control

Tunis   N Africa, Tunisia Islamic town, early town

Tunisia   Stone Age, Bronze Age, Roman cities and fortresses

Tunsucancha   N Peru Inca tambo

Tunxi   E China W Chou site

Tupiza   C Bolivia Inca tambo

Tura   L Egypt limestone

Turbino   C Russia steppe settlement

Turdas   C Romania tell settlement

Tureng Tepe   NE Persia Achaemenid city

Turfan (Turpan)   NW China early trading center, Buddhist center, early trade

Turkana   NE Africa, Kenya harpoons and pottery

Turkestan   early civilizations, steppe settlements, steppe nomads

Turkey Foot Ridge   SW USA Pueblo farming site

Turner Farm   NE USA, Maine Archaic site

Turner   NE USA, Ohio Hopewell site

Turnstone Beach   NE Canada Thule site

Tus   NE Persia Islamic town

Tushpa   E Anatolia Urartian capital

Tusket Falls   E Canada, Nova Scotia Archaic site

Tustrup   N Denmark megalithic tomb

Tutishcainyo   NE Peru early farming settlement

Tuttul   C Mesopotamia early town

Tutub (modern Khafajah)   C Mesopotamia early city

Twickenham Road   E Africa, Zambia Iron Age site

Ty Isaf   S Wales megalithic tomb

Tyara   E Canada Dorset site

Tybrind Vig   C Denmark megalithic site

Tyimede   N Australia Aboriginal site

Tylissos (Tilisos)   N Crete Minoan town

Tyndis (Tundis)   SW India early trade

Tyras   S Russia Greek colony

Tyre (Surri, modern Soûr)   Lebanon early port, Phoenician city, Achaemenid city, Hellenistic city, early trade

Tzimin Kax   Belize Maya settlement

Tzintzuntzan   C Mexico early town

U Thong   C Thailand moated site, early site

Uai Bobo   Timor Neolithic settlement, metal site

Uan Muhuggiag   N Africa, Libya early cattle

Uaxactún   N Guatemala Maya settlement

Ubulla   S Mesopotamia Sasanian city

Ucanal   C Guatemala Maya settlement

Uch   NW India Mughal mint

Uckange (Caranusca)   E France Roman village

Udal   Hebrides Viking center

Ue'a Valley   Marquesas Is. early site

Uelen   E Russia Thule site

Uerda   NE Spain native settlement

Ugarit (modern Ras Shamra)   W Syria early town, early writing, early city

Ugashik Drainage   Aleutian Is. arctic culture

Ugernum   S France native settlement

Ui-do   C Korea early settlement

Uioara de Sus   N Romania metal hoard

Uitkomsts   S Africa Iron Age site

Uji Byodo-in   C Japan Buddhist center

Ujjain   C India early city

Ukhaidir   Iraq Islamic port

Ulan-Khada   S Siberia steppe settlement

Ulasli   W Anatolia Sinan mosque

Ulkestrup   Denmark Mesolithic settlement

Ulpia Traiana (Sarmizegetusa)   NW Romania Roman provincial capital

Ulu Leang   E Indonesia, Celebes cave site, Neolithic settlement

Ulug Depe   C Asia steppe settlement

Umami   C Japan mound cemetery

Umanak   W Greenland Thule site

Umanoyama   W Japan mound cemetery

Umataka   C Japan early settlement

Umma   S Mesopotamia early city, early writing

Umm an Nar   Persian Gulf early trade

Umm Dabaghiyah   N Mesopotamia Neolithic site, pottery remains

Umm ez-Zuweitina   C Palestine Natufian site

Unalaska Bay   Aleutian Is. arctic culture

Uncleby   N England medieval village

Undelev   S Denmark bog body

Unetice   NW Czechoslovakia Bronze Age cemetery

Ungwana   E Africa, Kenya Ming pottery

Uolantún   N Guatemala Maya settlement

Uppsala   S Sweden Viking center

Upton Lovell   SW England tin and copper mining

Ur   S Mesopotamia early city, Sumerian city, early city and palace, early writing, Assyrian city

Ura-Tyube   C Asia frontier fortress

Uramanat   E Mesopotamia Assyrian rock relief

Urasa   N India rock edict

Urash   SW Arabia ancient dam

Ureia   Society Is. early site

Ureia   Cook Is. early site

Urewe   E Africa, Kenya Iron Age site

Uria   S Italy Roman Empire

Urmitz   NW Germany defensive enclosure

Uronarti   U Egypt temple

Urshu   E Anatolia Assyrian colony
Uruvela   NE India Buddhist site
Usangi   E Africa, Kenya Iron Age site
Usatovo   SW Russia barrow burial, steppe settlement
Ushki   E Russia arctic site
Ushkur   NW India Buddhist center
Uspenka   C Russia steppe settlement
Ust'-Belaya   E Russia arctic culture
Ust'-Mayn   E Russia arctic culture
Usulután   Honduras Maya settlement
Utatián   S Guatemala Maya settlement, early town
Utica   N Tunisia Phoenician city, Carthaginian city
Utnur   S India cattle pen site
Uvinza   E Africa, Tanzania Iron Age site and salt mine
Uxmal   Mexico, Yucatán Maya settlement
Uxul   Mexico, Yucatán Maya settlement
Uyak   Alaska Pacific Eskimo site
Vaihi   Society Is. early site
Vail   SE Canada fluted points
Vailele   Western Samoa early site
Vaisali   NE India early city, Buddhist center
Vaison   S France Roman relief
Vaito'otia   Society Is. early site
Vakenaya   E Russia arctic culture
Vakhsh Valley   C Asia steppe settlement
Vakuta   New Guinea Kula gift exchange
Valdivia   Ecuador early pottery
Valencia   E Spain medieval trade
Vallentigny   N France early tools
Valley of the Kings   U Egypt early burial, royal tombs
Vallhagar   E Sweden early settlement
Valsequillo   S Mexico fluted points
Valsgärde   C Sweden boat burial
Valshni Village   SW USA Pueblo farming site
Valsomagle   C Denmark metalwork
Valuraka   W India Buddhist site
Valverde Huelva   SW Spain Roman mine
Van   E Anatolia rock inscription, Sinan mosque
Vankarem   E Russia Thule site
Vanse   S Norway barrow burial
Vanuatu   Lapita culture
Vaphio   S Greece Mycenaean settlement
Variscourt   NE France Iron Age cemetery
Varjaren   N Norway bear grave
Varna   E Bulgaria Copper Age cemetery
Vasilika   S Russia Neanderthal site

Vasiliki   E Crete Minoan town
Vatcha   New Caledonia Lapita site
Vathypetro (Vathipetro)   C Crete Minoan village
Vatte di Zambana   N Italy Mesolithic settlement
Vattina   W Romania Bronze Age settlement
Vaughn   NW Canada Thule site
Vava'u   Tonga Lapita site
Vedbaek   E Denmark shell midden, megalithic site
Veh Antiokh Khusrau   C Mesopotamia suburb of Ctesiphon
Veh Ardashir (Seleucia)   C Mesopotamia Parthian city
Veh Ardashir (modern Kirman)   SE Persia Sasanian city
Veii   C Italy early temple
Velagiri   S India Buddhist site
Velem Szentvid   W Hungary Celtic oppidum
Velika Pecina   N Yugoslavia Neanderthal site
Vellore   S India Hindu religious site
Venafro   C Italy Roman water mill
Vénat   W France metal hoard
Vendel   C Sweden boat burial
Ventana Cave   SW USA, Arizona Archaic site, Pueblo farming site
Verdelpino   NE Spain farming site, early pottery
Vergennes   NE USA, New Hampshire Archaic site
Vergina   N Greece royal tombs
Vergranne   C France early tools and human remains
Vergunda   SE Aegean Greek harbor and temple
Verkhneye Pogromnoye   W Russia barrow burial
Verlaine   Belgium hunter-gatherer art
Vernonnet   N France Celtic oppidum
Verona   N Italy Roman empire, medieval trade
Verrières-le-Buisson   N France early tools
Vertault   E France Celtic oppidum
Vértesszollos   Hungary early tools and human remains
Vestby   S Norway swords
Vetera (modern Xanten)   NW Germany Roman legionary fortress
Veternica   N Yugoslavia Neanderthal site, hunter-gatherer site
Veterov   N Czechoslovakia fortified site

Vetulonia   N Italy Etruscan city
Vézelay   C France monastery
Vho   N Italy farming site
Viannos   S Crete tholos tomb
Viborg   N Denmark Viking center
Victoria Falls   C Africa, Zimbabwe early tools, hunter-gatherers
Vidisa   C India early city
Vidra   E Romania tell settlement
Vienna   E Austria Celtic site
Vienne   E France Celtic site, archbishopric
Vientiane   Indo-China, Laos Buddhist center
Viet Khe   N Vietnam transitional settlement
Vijayanagara (Hampi)   S India dynastic capital
Vikletice   W Czechoslovakia corded ware burial
Vilcashuamán   C Peru pyramid, Inca center
Villaricos   SE Spain Carthaginian cemetery
Villars-sous-Dampjoux   E France Mesolithic settlement
Villejoubert   C France Celtic oppidum
Villeneuve-Saint-Germain   NE France Iron Age sanctuary
Villeneuve-sur-Verberie   N France Mesolithic settlement
Villeneuve-Tolosane   SW France farming settlement
Villers-en-Prayères   NE France Iron Age cemetery
Villethierry   C France metal hoard
Viminacium (modern Kostolac)   NE Yugoslavia Roman provincial capital and legionary fortress
Vimose   C Denmark weapon hoard
Vimy   N France early tools
Vinca   E Yugoslavia farming site, tell settlement
Vindija   N Yugoslavia Neanderthal site
Vindobona (modern Wien, Vienna)   E Austria Roman legionary fortress
Vinelz   W Switzerland corded ware settlement
Viratanagara   C India Buddhist site
Virobesca (Virovesca)   N Spain native settlement
Virú Valley   Peru Pre-Columbian settlement
Virunum   S Austria Roman provincial capital
Virupaksha   temple of Vijayanagara
Visadi   NW India Mesolithic site

Vistahermosa   SE Mexico Pre-Classical site
Viste Cave   S Norway Mesolithic settlement
Vitaria   Austral Is. early site
Vivallen   N Norway Saami grave
Vix   E France Greek bronze, Hallstatt site
Vladimirovka   SW Russia Cucuteni-Tripolye village, steppe settlement
Vo Canh   S Vietnam early site
Vogelherd   S Germany Neanderthal site, hunter-gatherer art, hunter-gatherer site
Volaterrae (modern Volterra)   N Italy Etruscan city
Voidtofte   S Denmark Bronze Age settlement
Volgu   E France hunter-gatherer site
Volsinii (modern Bolsena)   N Italy Etruscan city
Volturnum   C Italy Roman colony
Vorou   C Crete tholos tomb
Vorukh   C Asia Han mirror find
Vouni   Cyprus Achaemenid palace
Vourvoura   S Greece tholos tomb
Vrana   E Greece tholos tomb, Athenian settlement
Vrevskiy   C Asia Han mirror find
Vromopousi   SE Greece Athenian settlement
Vroue   N Denmark corded ware burial
Vrsnik   S Yugoslavia farming site
Vrysinas (Vrisinas)   W Crete peak sanctuary
Vulci   N Italy Etruscan city
Wa   W Africa, Ghana early town
Wadan (Ouadane)   W Africa, Mauritania early town
Wadi Caam   N Libya Roman dam
Wadi Djidiouia   N Algeria Roman dam
Wadi el Boul   Tunisia Roman dam
Wadi el-Hudi   U Egypt ancient mine
Wadi el-Sheikh   L Egypt flint
Wadi Ganima   N Libya Roman dam
Wadi Garawi   L Egypt calcite
Wadi Labdah   N Libya Roman dam
Wadi Maghara   Sinai graffiti, copper mine
Wadi Megenin   N Libya Roman dam
Wadi Mina   N Algeria Roman dam
Wadi Shaw   N Sudan early pottery
Wadi Wassa'   U Egypt early pottery
Wahlitz   N Germany corded ware burial
Waiahukini   Hawaiian Is. early site
Waihi   New Zealand, North I. rock art
Waikaia (Upper)   New Zealand, South I. moa bones

Waimaru   New Zealand, South I. shell midden
Waimataitai   New Zealand, South I. moa bones
Waimea   Hawaiian Is. early site
Waingongoro   New Zealand, North I. shell midden
Waioneke   New Zealand, North I. defended settlement
Wairau Bar   New Zealand, South I. early site, moa hunter's camp
Waitaki River Mouth   New Zealand, South I. moa bones
Waitore   New Zealand, North I. rock art
Wajak   Java early man
Wakanui   New Zealand, South I. moa bones
Wakapatu   New Zealand, South I. shell midden
Wakefield   N England medieval town
Wakhshushana   E Anatolia Assyrian colony
Walakpa   Alaska Thule site
Walata (Oualata)   W Africa, Mauritania early settlement, early town
Waldalgesheim   N Germany vehicle burial
Valdfischbach   W Germany Roman village
Wales   early hominids, Megalithic Age, standing stones, Bronze Age
Wallacea   E Indies
Walls   SE USA temple mound
Walpi   SW USA Pueblo farming site
Walsingham   S England pilgrimage center
Wanbaoting   NE China early stirrups
Wanfosi   NW China Buddhist center
Wangdu   N China Han burial
Wangshan   C China E Chou burial
Wangwan   N China Longshan site
Wangyandong   S China cave site
Wanlek   E New Guinea swamp site
Waramuri   Guyana early settlement
Warka (Uruk)   S Mesopotamia pottery remains
Warm Mineral Springs   SE USA fluted points
Warri   W Africa, Nigeria early town
Warter   N England medieval town
Washpool   New Zealand, North I. early site
Washshukanni   E Anatolia Mitannian city
Wasit   Iraq Islamic town
Wasserbillig   W Germany Roman village

Wasserburg   S Germany Bronze Age settlement
Wat Phu   Indo-China, Laos monumental site, early site
Wat's Dyke   W England
Waterford   S Ireland Viking center
Watertown Arsenal   NE USA, Massachusetts Archaic site
Watton   N England medieval town
Wawcott   SW England megalithic site
Wei   N China Han city
Weifang   N China Shang pottery
Weipa   NE Australia Aboriginal site
Weis   NW USA, Montana Archaic site
Weizhou   N China Tang prefecture
Weka Pass   New Zealand, South I. rock art
Weligama   S Ceylon Buddhist remains
Wellington, Mount   New Zealand, North I. Maori hill fort
Wells Crater   C USA, Kentucky Palaeo-Indian site
Wenchi   W Africa, Ghana early town
Wengyuan   S China cave site
Wenzhou   E China Tang kiln, Sung kiln
Weris   E Belgium megalithic tomb
West Athens Hill   NE USA, New York Palaeo-Indian site
West Kennet   S England longbarrow
West Point   Tasmania Aboriginal site
West Stow   SE Denmark claw beaker
Westeregeln   E Germany farming site
Western Samoa   early settlement
Westernschouwen   Holland Viking trading emporium
Westness   Orkney Is. Viking center
Westward Ho   SW England shell midden
Wet   SW USA Pueblo farming site
Wetwang   N England medieval village
Wetzikon   Switzerland Mesolithic settlement
Wexford   S Ireland Viking center
Whakamoenga Cave   New Zealand, North I. early site
Whangamata   New Zealand, North I. shell midden and moa bones
Wharetaewa Pa   New Zealand, North I. defended settlement
Wharram Grange   N England medieval village
Wharram Percy   N England medieval village
Wharram-le-Street   N England medieval village
Wheathampstead   N England Celtic site
Whiritoa   New Zealand, North I. rock art

Whitby   N England medieval town

White Mound Village   SW USA Pueblo farming site

Whitipirorua   New Zealand, North I. shell midden

Whitsbury   S England Celtic hill fort

Wichquana   SE Peru early farming settlement

Wicklow   E Ireland Viking center

Wiesbaden (Aquae)   W Germany Roman town

Wietrzychowice   W Poland megalithic tomb

Wilberfoss   N England medieval town

Wildscheuer   N Germany Neanderthal site, hunter-gatherer site

Wilgie Mia   W Australia Aboriginal site

Willendorf   Austria hunter-gatherer site, hunter-gatherer art

Williamsburg   E USA, Virginia colonial settlement

Williamson   E USA, Virginia Palaeo-Indian site

Wilsford   S England Celtic religious site

Wilson Butte   NW USA, Idaho Archaic site

Wilson Butte Cave   NW USA fluted points

Wilson Mound   C USA temple mound

Wilson's Promontory   SE Australia Aboriginal site

Wilton   S Africa hunter-gatherers, Stone Age site

Wimereux   N France early tools

Winay Wayna   S Peru pre-Inca center

Winchester   S England Viking mint

Windeby Bog   N Germany bog body

Windhoek   SW Africa, Namibia Stone Age tools

Windmill Hill   S England defensive enclosure

Winnall Moors   S England pollen core site

Winona and Ridge Ruins   SW USA Pueblo farming site

Winterville   S USA temple mound

Witów   S Poland Mesolithic settlement

Wittnauer Horn   N Switzerland fortified site

Wolstenholme   E USA, Virginia colonial settlement

Wombah   E Australia Aboriginal site

Wonderboom   S Africa Acheulian tools

Woodchuck Cave   SW USA Pueblo farming site

Woodlark I.   New Guinea Kula gift exchange

Wollbury   S England Celtic hill fort

Woollandale   E Africa, Zimbabwe Iron Age site

Worcester   C England monastery

Worms (Borbetomagus)   W Germany Roman town

Wright   NE USA, Kentucky Hopewell site

Wu'an   N China early settlement

Wuchang   E China Ming provincial capital

Wucheng   C China early city, Shang city

Wupatki   SW USA Pueblo farming site

Wuping   SE China Longshan site

Wutai Shan   N China rock-carved temple

Wuwei   NW China early trade center, Han burial

Wuzhou   E China Tang prefecture

Wykeham   N England medieval town

Wyrie Swamp   S Australia Aboriginal site

Xalitla   C Mexico Pre-Classical site

Xaltocán   C Mexico Aztec center

Xanthus   SW Anatolia rock inscription, Hellenistic city

Xcocha   Mexico, Yucátan Maya settlement

Xelhá   Mexico, Yucátan Maya settlement, early town

Xerovrysi   SW Greece tholos tomb

Xi'an (Chang'an)   N China early settlement, Buddhist pagoda, Ming provincial capital

Xiachuan   NE China early man

Xiangyangfu   C China provincial capital

Xiangzhou   N China Tang prefecture

Xianling   NE China Ming tomb

Xianmengcun   N China early settlement

Xianrendong   SE China early settlement, early pottery

Xiaolinding   N China early settlement

Xiaonanhai   NE China early man

Xiaoshan   E China Tang kiln

Xiapanwang   N China early settlement

Xiasi   N China E Chou cemetery

Xiawanggang   N China Longshan site

Xibeigang   N China early burial

Xicalango   E Mexico Maya settlement, Aztec trade center

Xicun   S China Tang kiln, Sung kiln

Xigong   N China E Chou burial

Xihanzhuang   N China early settlement

Xilingxia   N China early settlement

Ximen   E China E Chou burial

Xingtai   N China early city, Shang city

Xingyuan   N China provincial capital

Xingzhou   N China Tang prefecture

Xinxiang   N China Ming tomb

Xishishan   E China E Chou burial

Xixiahou   N China early settlement

Xiyincun   N China early settlement

Xoc   SE Mexico Pre-Classical site

Xochicalco   C Mexico pyramid, early town, Aztec town

Xochimilco   C Mexico Aztec center

Xochipala   C Mexico Pre-Classical site

Xpuhil   Mexico, Yucátan Maya settlement

Xuantu   NE China Han city

Xuanzhou   E China Tang prefecture

Xueguan   N China early man

Xujiayao   NE China early man

Yabrud   Syria Neanderthal site

Yaco (Iiaco)   W Brazil early settlement

Yagala   W Africa, Sierra Leone early food

Yagodnoye   C Russia steppe settlement

Yagul   C Mexico pyramid, early settlement

Yajima-yakata   Japan Samurai mansion

Yakutsk   E Russia arctic culture

Yala Alego   E Africa, Kenya Iron Age site

Yamada-Uenodai   N Japan early man

Yamama   E Arabia Islamic town

Yamato   C Japan early state

Yanagimata   C Japan early settlement

Yandogay   E Russia Thule site

Yangjia   S China E Chou bronze hoard

Yangshao   N China Longshan site

Yangshaocun   N Japan early settlement

Yangzhou   E China Islamic trade, provincial capital

Yanjiamatou   N China early settlement

Yanling   N China early settlement

Yanshi   N China early settlement

Yanuca (Yanutha)   Fiji Lapita site

Yanxiadu   NE China E Chou cemetery

Yaojiagang   N China E Chou bronze hoard

Yaotougou   N China early man

Yaozhou (Yaoxian)   NW China Sung kiln

Yapahuwa   N Ceylon Buddhist remains

Tarang   SW Thailand early site

Yara   N Australia Aboriginal site

Yarim Tepe   N Mesopotamia pottery remains

Yarinocacha   N Peru early horticultural village

Yarkand (Yarkant)   NW China Buddhist center, early trade

Yarm   N England medieval town

Yarnbury   S England Celtic hill fort

Yarumela   Honduras Maya settlement

Yashtukh   S Russia early tools

Yasuni   Ecuador early settlement

Yatsushiro   W Japan Korean pottery

Yauca   S Peru Paracas site

Yaxchilán   E Mexico Maya settlement

Yaxhá   E Mexico Maya center

Yaxuná   Mexico, Yucatán Maya settlement

Yayo   C Africa, Chad Australopithecus

Yayoi culture   Japan

Yayoi-cho   C Japan rice farming site

Yazd   C Persia Sasanian city, Islamic town

Yazd-i Khvast   S Persia fire temple

Yazilikaya   C Anatolia rock sanctuary

Yeavering   S Scotland early settlement

Yecapixtia   C Mexico early town

Yedi   W Africa, Nigeria early town

Yedingham   N England medieval town

Yeha   NE Ethiopia temple remains

Yei Lulu Loga   N Africa, Chad Oldowan tools

Yekia   N Africa, Chad wavy-line pottery

Yelisavetovskaya   W Russia barrow burial

Yeliseyevichi   C Russia hunter-gatherer art

Yelleshwaram   S India megalithic tomb

Yelwe   W Africa, Nigeria Iron Age site

Yengema   W Africa, Sierra Leone early food

Yenitsari   SW Greece tholos tomb

Yerevan   Armenia early tools and human remains

Yerraguddi   S India rock edict

Yinan   NE China Han burial

Ying-p'u   C Taiwan Longshan site

Yingchuan   N China Han city

Yingtianfu   N China provincial capital

Yinxian   E China Tang kiln

Yondo-ri   N Korea early settlement

Yongjil-li   C Korea early settlement

Yongling   NE China Ming tomb

Yopotzingo   early state of Mexico

York (Eburacum)   N England Viking center, archbishopric, medieval town

Yorkshire   feudal villages

Yuanjunmiao   N China early settlement

Yuanmou   W China *Homo erectus*

Yubetsu-Ichikawa   N Japan early settlement

Yucatán   E Mexico Maya empire

Yucuñudahui   C Mexico early settlement

Yudinovo   W Russia hunter-gatherer site, hunter-gatherer art

Yuezhou   C China Tang kiln

Yufufeng   NW China Han city

Yukon I.   Alaska Pacific Eskimo site

Yuku   New Guinea early man

Yukuepira   N Japan Ainu hill fort

Yulin   NW China rock-carved temple

Yuling   NE China Ming tomb

Yunan   S China early settlement

Yungang   N China rock-carved temple

Yunmeng   N China early settlement

Yunus   C Syria pottery remains

Yunxian   N China *Homo erectus*

Yuri   N Japan Heian fortress

Yushi   N China early settlement

Yuxian   N China Sung kiln

Yuzanú   C Mexico early settlement

Zaayfontein (Saaifontein)   S Africa Stone Age site

Zabalan   C Mexico early writing

Zabid   SW Arabia Islamic town

Zacuala Palace   C Mexico

Zacualpa   S Guatemala Maya settlement, early town

Zaculeu   S Guatemala Maya settlement, early town

Zacynthus (Zakynthos, Zante)   SW Greece ancient city

Zafar   SW Arabia early capital

Zaghouan   N Tunisia Roman aqueduct

Zaka   E Africa, Zimbabwe Iron Age site

Zakro (Zakros)   E Crete Minoan village

Zalpa   E Anatolia Assyrian colony

Zaman-Baba   C Asia steppe settlement

Zaman-Baba culture   Steppes

Zambezi, R.   early trade routes

Zambujal   C Portugal ancient fortress

Zancle (Zankle, later Messana, modern Messina)   S Italy Greek colony

Zanja   C Mexico early farming settlement

Zanzibar   E Africa, Tanzania Islamic trade, maritime trade

Zaphon   Palestine Egyptian control

Zaranj   Afghanistan Parthian/Sasanian city

Zarax   SE Greece harbor and theater

Zaria   W Africa, Nigeria early town

Zátyní   Czechoslovakia Mesolithic settlement

Závist   W Czechoslovakia Celtic oppidum

Zawi Chemi   N Mesopotamia Neolithic site

Zawilah   N Africa, Libya Islamic town, early settlement, early town

Zawiyet el-Amwat   U Egypt pyramid

Zawiyet el-Aryan   L Egypt pyramid

Zazaragi   N Japan early man

Zea   SE Greece harbor of Athens

Zeila (Saylac)   E Africa, Somalia monolith

Zenabi   W Africa, Nigeria Stone Age tools

Zencirli (Senjirli, Sama'al)   SE Anatolia ancient provincial capital

Zenebi   W Africa, Nigeria hunter-gatherers

Zengcheng   S China early settlement

Zengovárkony   Hungary farming site

Zengpiyan   W China cave site, early pottery

Zeugma   SE Anatolia Hellenistic city, Roman city and legionary fortress

Zhangjiapo   N China W Chou burial

Zhanjiawan   N China early Palaeolithic site

Zhaobeihu   N China Chou cemetery

Zhaoling   NE China Ming tomb

Zhdanov (Mariupol')   SW Russia steppe settlement

Zhendingfu   N China provincial capital

Zhengzhou   N China early kiln, early city, Shang capital

Zhigalovo   S Siberia steppe settlement

Zhmerinka   W Russia steppe settlement

Zhongxian   N China early settlement

Zhongzhoulu   N China E Chou burial

Zhoukoudian   NE China cave dwelling, early man

Zhujiaji   E China E Chou burial

Zhuwajie   W China W Chou site

Zibo   N China Tang kiln, Sung kiln

Zigouries (Zygouries)   W Greece marble and metal artefacts

Zil'gi   SW Russia steppe settlement

Zimri-Lim   Mesopotamia palace

Zitlaltepec   C Mexico Aztec center

Ziwa   SE Africa Iron Age site

Ziota   SW Poland corded ware burial

Zofengyi   NW China Han city

Zohak (Fasa)   S Persia Achaemenid city

Zombepata   SE Africa, Zimbabwe Stone Age tools

Zou   E Crete Minoan village

Zouxian   NE China Ming tomb

Zumpango   C Mexico Aztec center

Zuojiatang   C China E Chou burial

Zurich-Utoquai   N Switzerland corded ware settlement

Zuttiyen   C Israel Neanderthal site

Zvejnieki   NW Russia Mesolithic settlement

Zwenkau-Harth   E Germany farming site

Resource   Past Worlds: The Times Atlas of Archaeology

Writing and Archaeology: A Timeline

Discoveries, Inventions, Landmarks, Turning Points, Decipherments

The definition of *writing* is any system for symbolizing a language. Writing was developed independently several times in different places, and both the writing materials and the types of script show great variation. The earliest true writing developed in southern Mesopotamia in the 4th millennium BC Uruk culture. The writing material was clay; it was first inscribed and later impressed with a stylus to produce wedge-shaped cuneiform signs. The earliest signs were *pictograms* (picture writing, in which the signs represent stylized pictures of the objects in question), but these rapidly developed into ideograms (the signs indicated not only the original object, but also associated objects or concepts). The Egyptian hieroglyphic script, used for inscriptions on stone, painting on walls, and also writing on papyrus, appears well before 3000 BC. There is a dispute as to whether the Egyptians developed writing independently or whether the art was diffused from Mesopotamia. The Harappan civilization of the Indus Valley had a writing system of its own, dated to the second half of the 3rd millennium BC and found almost exclusively on stamp seals and seal impressions. It has not been deciphered. The first true alphabet, with signs for individual letters, seems to have developed in the Levant, probably in the first half of the 2nd millennium BC. The first definite evidence comes from Ugarit in the mid-2nd millennium BC. The Phoenicians spread the alphabet throughout the Mediterranean, and theirs is ancestral to most of the alphabets in use today. In China, writing developed independently, first appearing on oracle bones of the Shang Dynasty. In Europe, the only Pre-Classical writing occurs in the Aegean in the 2nd millennium BC—the hieroglyphic and Linear A scripts of the Minoans, as yet undeciphered, and the Linear B of the Mycenaeans, used to record an early form of Greek. The development of writing in the Americas occurred only in Mesoamerica—the glyphic writing of the Maya and related groups, found in inscriptions carved on monuments, and the pictographic writing of Post-Classic groups such as the Mixtecs and Aztecs, found on manuscripts of bark or deerskin known as codices.

Archaeology and writing are powerful companions, compelling in their ability to open even the most trivial windows into the past. The voices of the past, once anonymous and indirect, now speak directly through their writings. Their passion for record keeping brings archaeology alive.

Writing and literacy were invented in cities and large settled communities to cope with administrative problems. As previously mentioned, writing was probably invented at least four times in the Old World: Egypt, Mesopotamia, the Indus Valley, and China—and twice in the New World (Mayas, Zapotecs). The origin of writing can be traced to specific stress in a socioeconomic system and a need for some form of record keeping. Writing emerged almost universally as a series of symbols for things and relations and probably arose first among the societies of the Near East as early as 10,000 years ago.

At first the archaeologists' only hope of finding absolute dates came from written history. Greek history went back to about 500 BC, but, as excavation in Egypt proceeded and more and more Egyptian inscriptions were discovered and deciphered, an accurate historical date system was built up for ancient Egypt stretching back to 3000 BC—and correct within 25 years at worst for the 1st and 2nd millennia BC and within 100 years at worst for the third.

Discoveries such as the royal library of clay cuneiform tablets in the Assyrian capital of Nineveh, provided, when the writing had been deciphered, an enormous structure of his-

Note that references are all enclosed in quotation marks (" "), whether they are books or articles. Complete bibliographical references are not attempted in this timeline.

torical events concerning not only Assyria, but its neighbors, which were easily cross-related at several points to Egyptian records. Thus a dated structure for a much wider Middle Eastern history emerged.

One of the most valuable excavations occurred at Ras Shamra in Syria, also known as Ugarit. It has provided a variety of trade and diplomatic documents and records, which have enabled a whole series of states and civilizations to be firmly anchored to Egyptian chronology and therefore given absolute dates of their own. Letters and treaties between Hittite monarchs and Egyptian pharaohs have been discovered, and the first alphabetic script was also found at Ugarit.

The Babylonians' and Akkadians' written records, in turn, have been cross-related to dated Egyptian history. With the Code of Hammurabi inscribed on stone as the most famous of their documents, these Babylonian records have allowed dated history to be pushed back beyond Egyptian times, although with decreasing accuracy and certainty about the dates. That, in turn, allowed the Sumerians to be tied into the dating system, back to the early cultures of Ur and al'Ubaid.

Reconstruction of what happened in Roman Britain is partly based on the writings of Roman authors, partly based on archaeologists' discoveries of sculptured inscriptions on tombstones, altars, and elsewhere, and partly based on pure archaeological work.

Reconstruction of the Maya civilization of Yucatan and Guatemala is partly based on pure archaeology and partly on the translation of the Mayan glyphic writing sculptured on stelae and temples.

Before 4000 BC, however, there is no accurate dating. History, in the sense of a dated time sequence of recorded events, ceases. Therefore, before 4000 BC, there is no hope of obtaining an absolute date anywhere in the world by using the traditional and newer methods of the historian and archaeologist combined. History begins when written records begin. Recorded history began when the first document of writing was set down—a calendar of the ancient Egyptians from 4241 BC.

The invention of computers is a re-enactment of the invention of writing on a more sophisticated level. The processing of information by industrial societies had become so cumbersome that it threatened further advances in cultural complexity.

Writing gives the archaeologist an added measure for the past, although a limited one as so much of writing is sanitized through official sanction. Official records can yield information, but unofficial writings offer the most compelling data. This timeline is offered as a partial description of discoveries, inventions, landmarks, turning points, and decipherments involving writing and archaeology.

BC 60,000–25,000   First traces of visual symbols in the prehistoric Near East (Mousterian).

BC 35,000   Beginnings of European Palaeolithic art, prefigurative period: Mousterian or Chatelperronian incisions on bone or stone slabs. In the Upper Palaeolithic, the use of abstract symbols and primitive notation began. There is evidence in cave art and engraved bones.

BC 25,000   Ice Ages protowriting: pictographic communication, in use. Ice Age bones bear series of neat notches—made with various tools over time—which may have been keeping track of phases of the moon to create useful calendars. Protowriting (signs and other forms of partial writing) long preceded the emergence of full writing in Sumer c. 3300 BC—and it will always exist alongside full writing. Among the oldest forms: tallies. In the 6th century BC, Darius left a thong with 60 knots, to be untied 1 per day when he left to fight the Scythians (according to Herodotus).

BC 20,000   Notational systems go back this far, according to Alexander Marshack.

BC 18,000   Ice Age graffiti, cave in Pech Merle (Lot, southern France)—some consider it art and others consider it writing.

BC 10,000   Prehistoric painting of bison on walls of cave; paint of minerals with blood, fat, and urine.

BC 8000–3000   Plain clay tokens, exact purpose unknown, found at many Middle Eastern archaeological sites. The volume of trade demanded some means of tracking shipments. As early as this, villagers were using carefully shaped clay tokens, which they carried on strings. Substitution of 2-dimensional signs for these tokens, with the signs resembling the tokens, is a first step toward writing. Plain tokens were characterized by mostly geometric shapes and a plain surface. Tokens declined greatly by 3000 BC but continued in use until 1500 BC; pictographic writing in "embryo"—used in Babylonia, Palestine, Anatolia, Iraq, Iran.

BC 8000   One theory claims earliest writing system began at this time in Sumer and evolved into cuneiform script by 3100 BC. It has long been known that the earliest writing system in the world was Sumerian script, which in its later stages was known as cuneiform.

BC 6500   Shrine from Çatal Hüyük in southern Anatolia with walls of frescoes showing bull and deer hunts.

BC 6000   Ancient Berber script.

BC 6000   Maya language begins. The Maya languages are a family of Mesoamerican Indian languages spoken in southern Mexico, Guatemala, and Belize; Maya languages were also formerly spoken in western Honduras and western El Salvador. The family may be subdivided into the Huastec, Yucatec, Western Maya, and Eastern Maya groups. The most important Eastern Maya languages are Quiché and Cakchiquel; others are Mam, Teco, Aguacatec, Ixil, Uspantec, Sacapultec, Sipacapa, Pocomam, Pocomchi, and Kekchí. The largest Western Maya language is Tzeltal, spoken in Chiapas, Mexico; other Western Maya languages include Chontal, Chol, Chortí, Tzotzil, Tojolabal, Chuj, Kanjobal, Acatec, Jacaltec, and Motozintlec. The Yucatec languages, including Yucatec, Lacandón, Itzá, and Mopán, are sometimes also classed as Western Maya languages; Yucatec, the most important, is spoken in Yucatán, northern Guatemala, and Belize. The Huastec group is composed of the Huastec and Chicomuceltec languages.

BC **5300–4300**   Vinca culture's script on religious items.

BC **5000**   By now, commercial transactions of all kinds were so complex that there were endless possibilities for thievery and accounting errors. Some clever officials made small clay tablets and scratched them with signs depicting the objects. From there, it was a short step to simplified, more conventionalized, cuneiform signs.

BC **5000**   In the Halaf period, stamp seals were used in northern Mesopotamia, Iran, and Anatolia (in BC 6000 in Çatal Hüyük).

BC **4800**   Neolithic pottery fragments in China with incised marks, but they are not identifiable with Shang or other Chinese writing; forerunner to writing.

BC **4400–3100**   Complex tokens with more shapes, greater variety of linear and punched markings. Complex series of counters of same shape with variable number of lines or punctuation. The use of seals and writing on clay tablets appeared together in Mesopotamia. Seals were cylindrical with vertical perforation and carved with a design. In Early Dynastic times, carved with the owner's name.

BC **4000**   Discovery of the rebus principle, the idea that a pictographic symbol could be used for its phonetic value—that is, the use of pictographic shapes to evoke in the viewer's mind an underlying sound form rather than the basic notion of the drawn object. This brought about a transition from pure word writing to a partial phonetic script. In Egypt and Sumer, the use of a system of rebus was an extraordinary development in the progress of writing, when signs came to represent the sounds of the spoken language. The representation of sounds lies at the root of all true writing. Pictograms for the sounds made up the pictograms' names. In Sumer, about 1,500 different early pictograms. Distinctive scripts of Babylonia and Egypt (cuneiform and hieroglyphic) may have already been well established.

BC **4000**   Hieroglyphs record the spread of boxing throughout the Nile Valley.

BC **4000–3000**   Clay tablets of Eanna/Uruk.

BC **4000–3000**   Mesopotamian protocuneiform.

BC **4000–2600**   Early Harappan cultures of Baluchistan and Indus Valley used potters' marks but had no real writing.

BC **3700**   New shapes of clay tokens as well as markings to record more data such as units of land; then envelopes (hollow clay balls) to hold the tokens were invented. Groups of tokens representing particular transactions were enclosed in envelopes to be kept in archives. Some envelopes bore on the outside the impressions of the tokens held inside. These envelopes were the turning point between tokens and writing.

BC **3500**   Papyrus is new writing material from tough, reed-like sedge.

BC **3500**   According to the ancient Egyptians, the god Thoth created writing and then bestowed it as a gift on humankind. Hieroglyphic writing developed as a picture or sign used for a noun, then a word or one or more ideas (ideograph) closely associated with it. Then came the use of the same symbol to represent a group of words derived from a common root word, even though there might be differences in meaning. Then a symbol came to indicate a sound rather than a meaning. Because only consonants were represented in hieroglyphics, the same word sign might be used for more than one word despite the fact that their pronunciations and meanings were different and unrelated. Finally, the use of a sign to represent not a word or the stem of a word, but an alphabetic sound.

BC **3500**   Earliest writing dates to at least this time in southwest Asia, for recording business transactions.

BC **3500**   Complex tokens reach climax.

BC **3500–3100**   Tablets displaying impressed markings in the shapes of tokens superseded the envelopes.

BC **3500–3000**   Uruk civilization dawns in Sumer. Cuneiform in Sumer; one of fewer than a dozen instances of the invention of writing that are recorded in human history. Pictograms appear for keeping accounts. In China, writing develops from pictograms to ideograms and phonograms. India sees parallel development, and first early writing appears on stone and copper tablets. Pictograms eventually became so abstract they no longer resembled objects they stood for.

BC **3300**   Sumerian clay tablets with pictographic writing in Uruk (Iraq), linked to dynamic changes in society—this was the invention of writing to record business transactions—receipts, records of crop yields, quantities delivered, and so on. The first texts that can be read and express a language are Sumerian (cuneiform later adapted to write Akkadian and Eblaite). Texts have lists of raw materials and products such as barley and beer; list of laborers and tasks; lists of field areas and their owners; the income and outgoings of temples—all with calculations about production levels, delivery dates, locations, and debts. Writing in Sumer develops as a direct consequence of the compelling demands of an expanding economy. The round end of a reed stylus was either pressed vertically into soft clay to make a circular hole or pressed at an angle to make a fingernail-shaped depression—or a combination of both impressions, superimposed, was used to express a larger numeral. By 2500 BC, these signs had become abstract cuneiform in widespread use for writing Sumerian.

BC **3300**   Sumero-Akkadian cuneiform.

BC **3300–2900**   Tell Brak tablets in Sumer/Babylon.

BC **3300–2200**   Proto-Elamite economic texts in Susa archives (Elam/Persia). Bullae and numerical tablets of Susa and Mesopotamia. System of Sumerian writing taken over by the Semitic Akkadians, later by the Elamites.

BC **3100**   Symbols that inventory objects, even gods and professions, appear at Uruk. Initially the tablets are used only for administrative operations and systematic lists of characters; they are pictographic and ideographic. Sumerians create literate civilization. Mesopotamian cuneiform became the lingua franca of trade and international diplomacy, a written language so complex that learned teachers and scribes traveled and taught widely. Proto-Sumerian pictographic. Pictographic script traced with a stylus on clay tablets marked the true beginning of writing; tokens dwindled.

BC **3100–AD 400**   First Egyptian hieroglyphs in form of short label-texts on stone and pottery objects from various sites; about 700 symbols. The hieroglyphs come into existence virtually fully developed at the beginning of dynastic period. Many designs/signs have been found belonging to the centuries preceding this (the predynastic period)—painted on pottery; worked into weapons, amulets, ornaments, tools—closely resembling or identical with hieroglyphic pictograms of dynastic Egypt. They show topographical features, geographical features, "standards" of tribes and deities, and signs standing for concepts.

BC **3000**   Sumer and Elam, where there is clear written evidence for the existence of two non-Indo-European languages, Sumerian and Elamite.

BC **3000**   Images embossed on seals by people of the Indus Valley (modern Pakistan), who used seals to emboss images of their animals and gods. Indus scribes wrote mostly on perishable material such as wood, which has long since decayed. Material evidence comes from archaeology, and only the barest historical outline can be reconstructed.

BC **3000**   First traces of writing in the Aegean world.

BC **3000**   Egyptian hieratic cursive script developed. Hieratic cursive writing dating almost from invention of hieroglyphs. Hieratic after hieroglyphs but before demotic: a more cursive form of hieroglyphs for the new medium of papyrus. Egypt's uniconsonantal or alphabetic signs system essentially complete. *Hieroglyph* means "writing of the gods" in Greek, from *hieros* (holy) and *gluphein* (to engrave). Hieroglyphs were from the beginning a true form of writing because they could almost completely record the spoken language (which survives as Coptic) and because they could deal with abstract as well as concrete entities.

BC **3000–2000**   Hieroglyphs used in Anatolia (Syria).

BC **3000–2000**   Evolving signs underwent change of orientation. Pictograms on clay tablets became turned through 90 degrees so that they lay on their backs. Instead of being written vertically, it became a horizontally written script (often partitioned into newspaper-like columns). Instead of being written right to left, it was switched to left to right. Date of change is vague and reason unclear.

BC **3000–1000**   Cuneiform, invented between the Tigris and the Euphrates, traveled south to Palestine (Canaanite) and north to Armenia (Urartian).

BC **3000–800**   Chinese script begins with *jiaguwen*, bone writing.

BC **3000–500**   Etruscan inscriptions are brief and similar to each other, dealing with burial or religion. They are not long enough or sufficiently varied to aid decipherment. Ten thousand Etruscan inscriptions, all written in an alphabet similar to early Greek; pronunciation is established, but no one is sure what they say: can be read but have never been translated. The alphabetic link between the Greeks and the Romans was the Etruscans.

BC **3000–AD 75**   Numbers written on cuneiform texts. Fifteen languages in 3,000 years written in cuneiform script.

BC **2950–2770**   Tomb of Hemka at Saqqara: roll of blank papyrus. If papyrus was produced then, then writing must have been in wide use considerably earlier. Very few records survive from this period.

BC **2900**   Narmer palette, Egyptian hieroglyphics—which were used almost unchanged visually for 3,000 years. Participants in the decipherment of hieroglyphics included Thomas Young, Alexander Sayce, and Jean-François Champollion.

BC **2900**   Interesting development—curves in primitive pictographic signs disappeared, probably because it was technically difficult to draw curves on wet clay, so the script rapidly evolved into signs formed purely of straight lines (wedges, from *cuneus*).

BC **2900–2600**   First traces of the discovery of the phonetic value of written signs in the Uruk/Ur archives. First identifiable use of purely phonetic elements and grammar in Sumerian language.

BC **2800**   Pictograms in Jemdet Nasr.

BC **2700–2650**   Hesire, from Saqqara, chief of the royal scribes.

BC **2650–2135**   Language of the inscriptions of the Old Kingdom, the period in which the first continuous texts appear, is Old Egyptian.

BC **2600**   Chinese emperor Huang Che discovered the gift of writing.

BC **2600** At Fa'rah (Shuruppak) and Tell Abu-Salabikh, the first properly literary texts are produced (hymns, incantations, and myths).

BC **2500** Writing had become standardized across Mesopotamian plain and went from economic to literary, religious, and historical records. By this time, Sumerian writing's original 2,000 symbols were reduced to around 600 (Old Sumerian). Stone monuments continued to be written in the orientation of the archaic script.

BC **2500** Old Akkadian, the earliest written Semitic language, in cuneiform. Seen in the Amarna letters—from Syrian, Hittite, Kassite rulers to Egyptian pharaohs. It was gradually replaced by Aramaic, which was written alphabetically on parchment. Ebla is known from Akkadian texts; archive of texts found at Ebla (some in cuneiform Eblaite, earliest-known form of written West Semitic), which shows that by c. 2500 BC, Ebla was prosperous trading city. Fifteen thousand tablets of Early Dynastic period at Ebla; many have 3,000 lines or more. The earliest type of Semitic cuneiform in Mesopotamia is called the Old Akkadian, seen for example in the inscriptions of the ruler Sargon of Akkad (died c. 2279 BC). Sumer, the southernmost part of the country, continued to be a loose agglomeration of independent city-states until it was united by Gudea of Lagash (died c. 2124 BC) in a last brief manifestation of specifically Sumerian culture. The political hegemony then passed decisively to the Akkadians, and King Hammurabi of Babylon (d. 1750 BC) unified all of southern Mesopotamia. In adapting the script to their wholly different language, the Akkadians retained the Sumerian logograms and combinations of logograms for more complex notions but pronounced them as the corresponding Akkadian words. They also kept the phonetic values but extended them far beyond the original Sumerian inventory of simple types (open or closed syllables like *ba* or *ab*). Many more complex syllabic values of Sumerian logograms (of the type *kan, mul, bat*) were transferred to the phonetic level, and polyphony became an increasingly serious complication in Akkadian cuneiform (e.g., the original pictograph for "sun" may be read phonetically as *ud, tam, tú, par, lah, his*). The Akkadian readings of the logograms added new complicated values. Thus the sign for "land" or "mountain range" (originally a picture of three mountain tops) has the phonetic value *kur* on the basis of Sumerian but also *mat* and *sad* from Akkadian *matu* ("land") and *sadû* ("mountain"). No effort was made until very late to alleviate the resulting confusion, and equivalent "graphies" like *ta-am* and *tam* continued to exist side by side throughout the long history of Akkadian cuneiform.

BC **2500** Meroe inscriptions in Egyptian hieroglyphic script.

BC **2500** The Gilgamesh of the poems and of the epic tablets was probably the Gilgamesh who ruled at Uruk in southern Mesopotamia sometime during the first half of the 3rd millennium BC.

BC **2500** Cuneiform similar to Ugaritic used in Palestine. Cuneiform adapted to write Semitic dialects in Mesopotamia and Syria.

BC **2500–2000** Babylonians, then Assyrians, adopted the cuneiform of the Sumerians—about 750 signs in total, 300 in general use. Cuneiform remained in use until the Christian era. Akkadians, who ruled Mesopotamia after the Sumerians, take over the Sumerian cuneiform script, even though Akkadian and Sumerian are dissimilar languages. Other forms of writing coexisted with cuneiform: Proto-Elamite, Indus Valley, Byblos pseudohieroglyphic, and Hittite hieroglyphic. Cuneiform script originated by Sumerians was used to write some 15 languages during its history: languages that borrowed the Sumero-Babylonian signs and syllabary (Hittites, Anatolia) and languages that borrowed only the principle of the clay wedge while inventing new cuneiform script unrelated to the Sumero-Babylonian signs.

BC **2500–1700/1500** Indus script used by Harappan civilization; Indus seals, copper tablets, and inscriptions from 60 sites. Indus Valley script invented independently; later vanished without development. The civilization was literate, and its script, with some 250 to 500 characters, has been partly and tentatively deciphered; the language has been tentatively identified as Dravidian. Generally square or rectangular symbols that probably stood for syllables. Lack of long texts and appearance of inscriptions primarily on seals indicate script was used for limited and special purposes. Script died with civilization.

BC **2500–AD 400** Egyptian hieratic script.

BC **2500–331** Elamite written in cuneiform.

BC **2480–2330** It is in Unas's pyramid that the "Pyramid texts" first make their appearance.

BC **2400** Byblos pseudohieroglyphs.

BC **2400** Classical Sumerian in linear and cuneiform scripts.

BC **2400–1700** Rulers were in the habit of placing inscribed nails in walls of temples or chapels, sometimes by the hundreds. Inscriptions range from simple name tags to recitals of historical and cult events.

BC **2250** Kings had their names stamped into bricks; the stamp was made either of clay or wood. This continued until Nebuchadnezzar II (604–562 BC) of Babylon, then revived in the 1980s in Iraq during "rebuilding" of ancient Babylon.

BC **2200** Proto-Indic pictographic.

BC **2200** Linear Elamite royal inscriptions.

BC **2200** Akkad eclipsed by Sumerian dynasties.

BC **2135–1785** Middle Egyptian used in literary, religious, and monumental inscriptions through Graeco-Roman period.

BC **2112–2004** Puzrish-Dagan and Girsu archives in Sumer/Babylon.

BC **2100** Byblos mentioned in Mesopotamian texts. Archive found at Ugarit contains texts in several languages, some written in cuneiform alphabetic script; also material on Ugaritic religion and myths, which has cast light on Canaanite religious practices.

BC **2100** Semitic consonantal alphabet.

BC **2100–2000** Law books of Ur, earliest Mesopotamian law codes.

BC **2004–1595** Archives from Larsa, Nippur, Eshnunna, Sippar, Tell ed-Der, Ur, Kish in Sumer/Babylon; Old Assyrian archives from Kanesh in Assyria BC 2000: Two pictographic scripts developed at Knossos, Crete, followed by Linear A (not Greek) and Linear B (archaic form of Greek). Linear B indicated that Greek administrators/rulers dominated the Minoan capital. It was used for palace accounts of transactions, trade, inventories. The date of the oldest fragment found at Knossos is 2000–1650 BC. The first phase of Minoan writing was pictorial signs, the script of the seal stones. The development of writing using clay tablets (Linear A) helped to facilitate administration in Aegean world. Most of the inscriptions from Knossos have been ascribed to the period 2000–1500 BC. Sir Arthur Evans listed 140 different signs.

BC **2000** Susa had adopted Mesopotamian cuneiform characters.

BC **2000** On the southern coast (Phoenician) of Ugarit at Byblos, there was an experiment in creating a script—"pseudohieroglyphic" of about 120 signs.

BC **2000** Numerals changed into wedge-shaped signs; numbers then expressed using a place value system as we use today.

BC **2000** Northern Linear (Canaanite).

BC **2000** Easter Island proto-writing.

BC **2000** Hurrians in northern Mesopotamia and Hittites in Anatolia borrowed writing from Akkadians. Hurrians use cuneiform syllabary.

BC **2000** Cuneiform reached its definitive form.

BC **2000** Chinese writing appears; the system is still in use today.

BC **2000** Middle Elamite, Old Babylonian, Old Assyrian, Hurrian scripts.

BC **2000–1800** Cylinder seals used on tablets or clay envelopes in Iran, Anatolia, Syria, and Palestine. Beautifully carved and undeciphered, they probably served as signatures and property markers. Scribes in the Middle East encased clay tablets in clay envelopes for safekeeping. Early examples come from Kanesh in southern Anatolia.

A copy or summary of the document was written on the envelope, and this could be compared to the original inside. Seals were employed as an extra safeguard.

BC **2000–1600** The greatest contribution of the Phoenicians was their alphabetic writing system. First invented by the Canaanites in the second millennium, this simple script was taken abroad by Phoenician merchants wherever they traveled. From them, it was adopted by the Greeks, who made small changes to suit their language. Later, the Romans adapted the Greek alphabet, and it is the Roman alphabet that forms the basis of modern western scripts. A Canaanite source produced Phoenician and Aramaic. East of Syria, alphabets were offshoots of Aramaic and west, derived from Phoenician.

BC **2000–1700** Phaistos Disk (Crete), script unknown and language unknown. First "typewritten" document.

BC **2000–1650** Fairly consistent 700 signs used to write classical stage of hieroglyphics.

BC **2000–1500** Hittite hieroglyphs. Hittites used a picture script; total number of signs between 220–350.

BC **2000–1500** Byblos pseudohieroglyphic script.

BC **2000–1200** Abjad invented during the Middle Bronze Age and came into increasing use during the Late Bronze Age.

BC **1990–1780** Twelfth Dynasty funeral inscriptions were "democratized," and the sarcophagus writings helped the dead reach the realm of Osiris.

BC **1900** Another set of documents provides insight on Assyrian merchants. These tablets were found in Anatolia at the site of an Assyrian trading colony on the edge of Kanesh. This is Old Assyrian, and these tablets relating to commercial transactions represent the oldest vestiges of writing in Anatolia.

BC **1900** Old Babylonian texts.

BC **1900** Proto-Sinaitic/Canaanite script. A number of early Canaanite inscriptions have been found near Byblos, Gezer, Lachish, on seals, daggers, bowls, and pottery. Most Proto-Canaanite inscriptions from Shechem, Gezer, Lachish—meanings unknown—date to 1700–1600 BC.

BC **1894–1595** Middle Elamite.

BC **1800** The earliest known examples of Cretan Linear A. The script is partially known, but its language is unknown.

BC **1800–1200** Consonantal alphabetic script developed among Semitic people on the eastern shore of the Mediterranean between Mesopotamia and Egypt—Canaanites (conventionally includes Phoenicians, early Hebrews, and Semitic speakers of Palestine). The northwestern Semitic languages of Canaanite and Aramaic were both represented by early alphabets. In these proper alphabets, each symbol represents a sound. First, the Phoenicians with 22 letters and no vowels; then Hebrew, Greek (1200 BC), the Etruscans, and the Romans. From unclear origins on the eastern shores of the Mediterranean, writing employing alphabetic principle spread to the west (via Greek) to modern Europe, to the east (probably via Aramaic) to modern India. Today, most peoples write in alphabetic script, except Chinese and Japanese. Most alphabets are 20–30 symbols. The smallest, Rotokas in the Solomon Islands, has 11 letters; the largest, Khmer in Kampuchea, has 74 letters.

BC 1792–1750   Law code of Hammurabi, king of Babylon inscribed on stela. Hammurabi's diplomatic and trading links with other cities are known from a cache of letters found at the site of Mari (Syria). When the city was excavated, 13,000 cuneiform tablets were found. The Amorite ruler of Ashur (Assyria's capital) is also known from the Mari letters as an adversary. Law code is written in cuneiform on a black piece of diorite about 7 feet long. It was likely taken by the Elamites as war booty from Babylon and brought to their capital at Susa (Iran) about 500 years after Hammurabi's reign.

BC 1792–1750   Babylonian literature flourishes; old Sumerian masterpieces copied out, and new literature in Akkadian is born.

BC 1750–1450   The date of the second-oldest fragment of Linear A found at Knossos; 150 clay tablets from Phaistos.

BC 1700   Linear A documented in short inscriptions, mainly at Knossos. At this time, there is also Hurrian cuneiform, Cretan and Helladic linear, Byblos syllabary, Proto-Semitic syllabary, Old Babylonian cuneiform, Hittite cuneiform.

BC 1700   Earliest alphabetic inscriptions in ancient Near East, Byblos (Lebanon), Jordan, Serabit al-Khadim in Sinai.

BC 1700   South Arabian script.

BC 1700–800   Da Zhuan, great seal script, China.

BC 1650–1600   The oldest texts in the Hittite language date to this period (Boghazkoy/Anatolia). They are written in cuneiform, and the most remarkable specimens are the historical annals, the laws, and above all, the political testament of Hattusli I, a unique document in ancient Near eastern literature. The Hittite archives from Mari could date to 1750 BC.

BC 1625–1450   Linear A script has 7,000 signs.

BC 1600   Proto-Phoenician syllabary, Proto-Palestinian syllabary.

BC 1600–1200   Some of the clay tablets found at Knossos are inscribed with a script known as Linear B. This was developed from Linear A for use by mainland Greeks who took control of Crete around 1450 BC, recording Greek dialect of Mycenaeans who occupied Crete from at least 1450–1375 BC. Linear A had been designed for the purposes of Minoan administration and was in use in Crete and parts of the Cyclades by 1650 BC. Linear A has yet to

be deciphered. Mycenaean trading relations became so complex that they found it necessary to establish their own writing system. They refined a simple pictographic script known as Linear A, which had been used by the Minoans (1900–1400 BC) and wrote it in the Greek language, creating what scholars call Linear B. Large numbers of clay tablets from a Mycenaean palace at Pylos in western Greece show that the script was used for administrative purposes.

BC 1600–1000   Over 100,000 oracle bones—made from cattle bones and tortoise shell—were found in storage pits in palace and temple areas of Anyang China. These were a means of divination and were used by the king to consult his ancestors. Engraved with questions, the bones were then heated, and the resulting cracks interpreted as positive or negative answers. The answers and their verification (or otherwise) were also recorded on the bones, which were stored in royal archives. Oracle bones reveal much about Shang Dynasty (1384–1111) society—events, rituals, and sacrifices.

BC 1600–1000   Boundary stones (kudurru) used in Mesopotamia to record land grants and tax concessions. The symbolic motifs of the gods meant they were "witnesses" to the contract.

BC 1550–1070   For most of this period—constant flow of diplomatic correspondence between Kassite dynasty (Mesopotamia) and other Middle Eastern courts. The common language was Akkadian, written in cuneiform.

BC 1550–700   Late Egyptian used, especially in secular documents (1300–1080 BC); also found to some extent in literary and monumental inscriptions.

BC 1500   The first documents in hieroglyphic characters appear southeast of Anatolia. This script, which was a transcription of a Luwian dialect, spreads progressively over a large part of the territory.

BC 1500   Sinai sphinx made, later found by Sir Flinders Petrie, with inscriptions plus hieroglyphs.

BC 1500   Scribes in Babylonia compiled bilingual tablets to help students learn to write Sumerian in cuneiform; clay equivalents of Latin-English dictionaries.

BC 1500   Old Canaanite alphabet, representing consonants.

BC 1500   Horapollo wrote "Hieroglyphics" manuscript.

BC 1500   Hebrew probably existed.

BC 1500   Chinese codified.

BC 1500   Middle Babylonian, Middle Assyrian scripts.

BC 1500–1400   Nuzi archives in Assyria; Alalakh archives.

BC 1500–1400   Ugaritic texts record myths and legends in literary form—using alphabet with 32 symbols. Also at this time, attempts to simplify Egyptian hieroglyphic system.

BC 1500–1200   Cyprus (Cypriote) inscriptions at Enkomi; source was Cretan Linear A.

BC 1500–600   Hittite hieroglyphic system in use (Anatolia,

Syria) until their civilization conquered and absorbed. There were 400 signs not used by any other people.

BC 1450–1200 Linear A replaced by Linear B on Crete and later in parts of Greece. Linear B tablets at Knossos, 3,400 baked by fire; 1,100 at Pylos; now fully deciphered.

BC 1400 Tablet written in Hittite from Boghazkoy, giving indications of the 8th language to be found in the archive there.

BC 1400 Linear B had spread to mainland Greece, possibly to Cyprus, by Mycenaeans.

BC 1400 Armenian pictographic, Ras Shamrah syllabary, Chinese pictographic.

BC 1400 Alphabetic cuneiform developed at Ugarit/Syria (Ras Shamra) north of Byblos (32 signs = 29 consonants, 3 vowels, 1 word separator). This phonetic alphabet using symbols to represent the sounds of individual letters (instead of syllables or words) was widely used in the Levant. It was invented by the Canaanites, a Semitic people, who based their alphabet on Egyptian hieroglyphics.

BC 1400 Egyptians began to stamp their bricks. The stamp block was usually made with the name or device in hieroglyphics. They varied in function.

BC 1400–1350 Important letter in the El-Amarna archives written by king of Mitanni to the Egyptian pharaoh Amenophis III. It was the pharaoh's diplomatic correspondence and tablets written in cuneiform (Babylonian/Akkadian). The tablets showed Alexander Sayce had been right—that the Hittites were a great force in Anatolia.

BC 1400–1200 Hittite archives from Hattusas.

BC 1400–1100 The Minoan civilization. Four thousand clay tablets were preserved by their accidental firing in the blaze that destroyed the Knossos palace.

BC 1400–1100 Canaanite linear alphabet.

BC 1300 South Semitic alphabets took independent direction. From this branch developed many pre-Islamic scripts of the Arabian peninsula and the Sabaean script, which spread into North Africa and became the basis for Ethiopic and then Amharic.

BC 1300 South Arabic scripts.

BC 1300 Pylos' archive room of Mycenaean palace.

BC 1300 North Semitic is the closest immediate antecedent to the Phoenician. Epitaph of King Ahiram put on sarcophagus near Byblos.

BC 1300 Middle Assyrian archives at Ashur.

BC 1300 "Book of the Dead" written.

BC 1300–1200 Cyprus, Syria/Palestine used Ugaritic writing.

BC 1300–1100 Invasions of the Levant by tribes from the north and east promoted rapid spread of writing system and the first adaptations of letter forms to non-Semitic languages. Phoenicians are responsible for the stabilization and spread of the alphabet.

BC 1285 Egyptian inscription/propaganda on eve of battle of Kadesh, the Egyptian pharaoh Ramesses II discussed plan of attack against Hittites—Hittite inscription at Boghazkoy says they won; Egyptian inscription at Karnak says they won.

BC 1200 Ugarit destroyed as well as its cuneiform syllabary. The alphabet's linear and schematic form lent itself to production in ink on papyrus. Ugarit and cuneiform script wiped out by Peoples of the Sea.

BC 1200 Northern Linear abjad has 22 sounds, and Southern Linear abjad has 28 sounds.

BC 1200 Knossos' link with the Greek mainland documents pointed to Linear B as an inflected language related to Greek.

BC 1200 In China, a writing system based on pictographs developed from the early use of distinctive marks on pots to denote numbers or clan names. Shang rulers recorded events on wooden or bamboo slips (the origin of writing in vertical lines). Inscriptions on oracle bones and bronzes include at least 2,000 characters, many of which are related to those in use today.

BC 1200 Cuneiform Hittite dies out.

BC 1200–1100 Destruction of Mycenaean civilization and its syllabary.

BC 1200–800 The Phoenicians' need for a highly accurate record-keeping system played a significant part in the development of the western alphabet. The first noncuneiform alphabet appears in Phoenicia.

BC 1200–800 Olmec elite horizon style (iconography).

BC 1168 The stelae of the Code of Hammurabi was likely taken by the Elamites as war booty from Babylon and brought to their capital at Susa (Iran) about 500 years after Hammurabi's reign.

BC 1100 Earliest known surviving Chinese characters.

BC 1100 Aramaic developed in Syria. Aramaic influential for 1,000 years; official script of later Babylonian, Assyrian, Persian empires. It was the vernacular of Jesus and the Apostles, possibly the original language of the Gospels. (The Dead Sea Scrolls are written in Aramaic.)

BC 1100–800 Site of the earliest recognizable Phoenician inscriptions on the sarcophagus of King Ahiram. Although Phoenician inscriptions are found all around the Mediterranean, the earliest are of this date. The Phoenicians left few records and almost no literature, but their alphabet of 22 letters went with them wherever they ventured. The names of the letters were the same as those in use by the Hebrews—and today in the Hebrew script; there were no vowels. Transmitted to Greek and Aramaic, including Old Hebrew and Punic forms. The new script was much simpler than earlier syllabic or pictographic writing systems and ultimately made writing accessible to many more people. The alphabet was adopted in Greece and adapted to the Greek language with farreaching consequences. One of the earliest uses was in recording Homer's *Iliad* and *Odyssey*.

BC 1100–1050   Phoenician alphabet (22 letters) settles down, right-to-left order fixed.

BC 1050–771   Seal script from the Western Zhou period in China.

BC 1000   West Semitic, early Palestinian, palaeo-Sinaitic writing, Old South Arabian.

BC 1000   Urartians adapted cuneiform script to their own language, which seems to be a late dialect of Hurrian. Bilingual inscriptions found at Kelishin and Topzawa.

BC 1000   The greater part of the Old Testament was written in Hebrew; oldest extant examples date to here.

BC 1000   Normal Hittite syllabary is one used in Syria, especially for cylinder seals.

BC 1000   Ithobaal, King of Byblos, has sarcophagus made for his father Ahiram bearing an inscription that for the first time uses whole Phoenician alphabet except for two letters. Earliest Byblos inscriptions written in system of 22 linear signs. Derived subdivisions of this Semitic writing are Phoenician, Palestinian, and Aramaic.

BC 1000   Gezer agricultural calendar.

BC 1000   First carving of inscriptions in stone in Mesoamerica, for counting time. Amerindian pictograms—best-known form of protowriting; comparatively crude marks and symbols engraved or painted on walls and rocks—commonest known as petroglyphs. The Maya developed a hieroglyphic script for calculating calendars and regulating religious observances. They also used it for recording genealogies, king lists, conquests, and dynastic histories.

BC 1000   Much of what is known about ancient Egypt comes from the writings found in the tombs, preserved by the dry desert conditions.

BC 1000–800   Punic, archaic Greek, Etruscan, and other alphabets made their appearance on the Greek islands or the Italian peninsula. Indo-European speaking Greeks adopted the alphabet from the Phoenicians. Greeks transformed several of the consonants in the Phoenician alphabet into letters to notate essential vowels.

BC 1000–700   Writing of bilingual or trilingual texts (Luwian, Phoenician, Aramaic). Tradition of writing hieroglyphic Luwian continued even after the fall of the Hittite Empire, but writing cuneiform on clay tablets discontinued.

BC 1000–625   Neo-Babylonian in Sumer/Babylon; Neo-Assyrian archives from Ashur, Kalhu, and Nineveh; Urartian inscriptions.

BC 1000–609   Great majority of Assyrian texts written.

BC 1000–100   Cypro-Phoenician version of Phoenician script.

BC 900   Texts of Hebrew in Palestine. Hebrew script used for religious literature and by a small community of Samaritans; evolved from Phoenician script and disappeared in the 6th c BC with dispersion of Jews. First religious literature of Yahweh (prophets).

BC 900–800   Phoenician, Hebrew, Aramaic scripts diverged to some extent.

BC 900–700   Chaldean script.

BC 850   Moabite Stone with script that is an early branch of Canaanite. This black basalt stone was discovered at Dhiban in 1868 and is now in the Louvre Museum in Paris. The stone's text of 34 lines, written in a Canaanite alphabet similar to contemporary Hebrew, is the only written document of any length that survives from Moab and the only royal stela known from Israel's neighbors. In its inscription, Mesha (fl. c. 870 BC) tells of King Omri's reconquest of Moab and ascribes the renewed Israelite domination over Moab to the anger of Chemosh. Mesha then describes his own successful rebellion against Israel, which probably occurred during the reign of Omri's successor, Ahab. Moabite was an eastern subdivision of the Canaanite branch of the early Semitic alphabet, closely related to the early Hebrew alphabet. Until the discovery of the Ahiram inscription in 1923 at Byblos, the Mesha Stone was considered the earliest extant alphabetic inscription.

BC 830–650   Urartian cuneiform in Anatolia.

BC 800   In Syria (Aram), another alphabet was developed—Aramaic—similar to that of the Phoenicians. Aramaic writing and language had a major impact on history as it was in this language that several books of the Old Testament were written. A scribe might write in imperial Aramaic (alphabetic script) with a brush on papyrus; a colleague might write in traditional cuneiform script on a clay or wax-covered tablet.

BC 800   *Iliad* and *Odyssey*, epic poems attributed to Homer, written down. Also, writings of Hesiod. Greek could not be transcribed by any of the existing alphabetic systems, so they borrowed certain signs from the Aramaic alphabet to transcribe their vowel sounds—choosing those signs that represented consonants that did not exist in the Greek language: A alpha, E epsilon, O omicron, Y upsilon, and I iota. The earliest extant inscriptions date from end of 8th or beginning of 7th century BC (scratched on pottery) and include the verse inscription on Bowl of Nestor at Pithecusa (Ischia).

BC 800   Earliest known examples of Etruscan (northern Italy), script known and language partially known. Beautiful Etruscan abecedary preserved, which shows well-developed linear Phoenician alphabet.

BC 800   Assyrians, Babylonians, Persians used alphabet.

BC 800–500   Herodotus calls alphabet *phoinikeia grammata* ("Phoenician letters") and says they were brought to

Greece by Kadmos. The 22 Phoenician consonants were adopted as Greek consonants and vowels. Three new signs were added. Accounts of Greek historians Herodotus and Thucydides and other later authors such as geographer Strabo offer information to supplement archaeological evidence.

BC **800–403**   Dorian script, Greece.

BC **800–200**   Cypriot syllabary, which shares features of Linear B.

BC **750**   Newly invented Greek phi, khi, and psi.

BC **750**   Greek colonists took Euboean to Italy, then taken by Etruscans (with modifications), and later adopted by Romans.

BC **750–700**   Writing reappears on Greek mainland after disappearance of Minoan Crete and Mycenae. Dipylon jug and Nestor's cup are among oldest examples of Greek epigraphy. Earliest known alphabetic Greek inscription (on vase from Athens, "to him who dances most delicately," 730 BC), but there are no practical or business documents for over 200 years after the Greek alphabet's invention.

BC **700**   The legacy of the Aramaeans was their language, which at this date became the common tongue of the Near East until Arabic. The Aramaic script was adapted from the Phoenician alphabet and because it was easy to write, displaced cuneiform. Persian Empire selected it as official language.

BC **700**   Roman/Latin script. Neo-Assyrian cuneiform. Cypriote syllabary, Anatolian alphabet. Etruscan alphabet based on Greek.

BC **700**   Library of Ashubanipal of Assyria at Nineveh— nearly 25,000 tablets recovered. Scribal schools have also yielded many clay copybooks; schools at far-flung outposts helped spread writing to much of southwest Asia. Royal libraries at Nineveh have bilingual texts in Sumerian and Akkadian.

BC **700**   India's 0 and Arabic numerals invented.

BC **700**   In Karatepe (Anatolia), longest-known hieroglyphic Hittite inscription with Phoenician.

BC **700**   Branch that was neither early Aramaic nor derived from Canaanite prototype spread to the non-Semitic languages of the Indian subcontinent.

BC **700–650**   Earliest abecedaria of the Greek alphabet.

BC **700–650**   Demotic (cursive) Egyptian script developed; standard documentary script by the time of the Rosetta Stone. Originally, hieratic was everyday administrative and business script, then ousted by demotic and became a priestly script. Deomtic was quicker, lighter, more ligatured; same demotic signs retained in Coptic script.

BC **700–600**   The Phrygian language, which survived in the Anatolian province of Phrygia in Greek times, is known from 25 inscriptions. Then a hundred or so inscriptions

from the first three centuries AD—written in the Greek alphabet.

BC **700–600**   Parts of the calendar began to be recorded in Mesoamerica.

BC **700–600**   Greek inscription from Egyptian site of Abu Simbel.

BC **700–403**   Laconian script, Greece.

BC **700–400**   Oaxacan script in use: logographic, but became more iconographic. Isolated examples of hieroglyphs, sometimes accompanied by numbers, occur on stone carvings in Oaxaca and parts of Chiapas and Veracruz (some dealing with kings and conquest). Later Maya glyphs deal mainly with a ruler, his birth, accession to throne, death, and anniversaries (sometimes parentage, ancestry). Writing was carved on stone monuments, painted on murals and pottery, preserved in codices (folded manuscript books of bark paper or deerskin). Closely tied to the writing systems were the symbols and numbers used in the complex calendar. Only the elite 2% were able to read the complicated glyphs.

BC **700–100**   Iron Age inscriptions in Aegean.

BC **668–627**   Epic of Gilgamesh anticipates the Greek myths, foreshadows the account in the Bible. Mesopotamian cuneiform confined to those who knew how to inscribe the signs and who understood the various meanings (depending on the context). The fullest extant text of the Gilgamesh epic is on 12 incomplete Akkadian-language tablets found at Nineveh in the library of the Assyrian king Ashurbanipal (reigned 668–627 BC). The gaps that occur in the tablets have been partly filled by various fragments found elsewhere in Mesopotamia and Anatolia. In addition, five short poems in the Sumerian language are known from tablets that were written during the first half of the 2nd millennium BC; the poems have been entitled "Gilgamesh and Huwawa," "Gilgamesh and the Bull of Heaven," "Gilgamesh and Agga of Kish," "Gilgamesh, Enkidu, and the Nether World," and "The Death of Gilgamesh." The Gilgamesh of the poems and of the epic tablets was probably the Gilgamesh who ruled at Uruk in southern Mesopotamia sometime during the first half of the 3rd millennium BC.

BC **664–332**   Generation of new hieroglyphics accelerates.

BC **650**   Late Assyrian cuneiform.

BC **625–539**   Archives from Babylon.

BC **620**   Roman alphabet from Etruscan.

BC **600**   Zapotecs used hieroglyphic elements in pictographs.

BC **600**   Persian syllabary; Thamudic, Lihyanic, Safaitic. Old North Arabic scripts; Ammonite, Neo-Babylonian cuneiform.

BC **600**   Old Testament Deuteronomy and story of creation written down.

BC **600**   Greeks as well as Etruscans began to settle in

Rome. Latin appears for the first time on the "Black Stone" of the Forum.

BC **600–500**   Carian script.

BC **600–332**   Imperial Aramaic; Aramaic spread widely until the breakup of the Persian Empire. Aramaic spawned major branches of national scripts: Syriac, Nabataean, Palmyrene, and Jewish alphabet.

BC **600–AD 500**   South Arabian/Sabaean script.

BC **600–AD 1100**   Rune inscriptions.

BC **597–539**   Hebrew written in linear Hebrew abjad when it was gradually replaced by a form of the Aramaic script.

BC **559–331**   Old Persian inscriptions, Late Elamite tablets.

BC **521–486**   The inscription of Behistun in Media recounts Darius I's (king of Persia) version of events in four languages (Old Persian, Akkadian, Elamite, Aramaic).

BC **520/519**   Behistun—carved on a smoothed rock face of Kuh-i-Parau Mountain, runs along ancient road of Persepolis to Hamadan; appears to be first inscription written in Old Persian, the language of the Achaemenids. Darius I created Behistun inscription (key to decipherment of cuneiform) to record the official version of the controversial events surrounding his accession to the throne.

BC **518**   An extension to the relief damaged the Elamite text, so a second identical Elamite version was added in the language of Susa in SW Iran. It is a language unrelated to its neighbors and is unlike any other language known.

BC **500**   Velianas, King of Caere (Cerveteri) dedicates shrine at Pyrgi (San Severa) to the goddess Astarte—text in Etruscan and Phoenician.

BC **500**   Southeastern script culminating in Mayan writing.

BC **500**   Pindar's descriptions of national games at Olympia, Nemea, Corinth, and Delphi.

BC **500**   Old Persian was written in a cuneiform alphabet derived from the Mesopotamian sign forms. Old Persian cuneiform of 36 characters.

BC **500**   Mesopotamia has many cuneiform documents carrying notation of their substance in the Aramaic alphabet, inked onto tablets with brushes.

BC **500**   Introduction of Byzantine minuscule script in Greek alphabet.

BC **500**   Herodotus said Phoenicians introduced writing into Greece. Herodotus's first-hand, full account of Egypt. Greek alphabet has 17 consonants, 7 vowels. Greek was the forerunner of the complicated Coptic, Armenian, and Georgian alphabets and was the source of the Latin alphabet. Greek writing became the basis for four different families of writing: through Glagolithic to Cyrillic, through Armenian to Georgian, through Etruscan to Latin, and finally Coptic.

BC **500**   Early Sanskrit literature written in accordance with grammarian Panini's code.

BC **500–510**   The Elamite tablets—records of wages paid to workers, peasants, and artisans employed at Persepolis—archive of Achaemenid Persian kings.

BC **500–400**   Lydian alphabet; Lycian script.

BC **500–400**   Earliest known text in the Americas was carved around this time on a monolith (now in 3 pieces) erected in the Zapotec city of Monte Alban in Oaxaca, Mexico. Zapotec is largely undeciphered, but appears to use a native system of writing and calendrical notation.

BC **500–AD 300**   Kharoshthi script.

BC **500–200**   Turdetanian script.

BC **500**   Samaritan script.

BC **500–AD 500**   Brahmi script.

BC **450–430**   Herodotus, subject of Artaxerxes I, describes Persian Empire in his "History."

BC **403**   The Ionian alphabet was adopted as the standard, official form by a decree in Athens (22 letters).

BC **400**   Revival of cuneiform under the Seleucids, Mesopotamia.

BC **400**   Panini, the first grammarian, was able to describe exact functions of the consonants and vowels in Sanskrit. Indian scripts are integrally alphabetic and have a highly structured phonetic system.

BC **400**   Last hieroglyph at Philae.

BC **400**   Iberian script. Hebrew (square) script.

BC **400**   Composed over possibly hundreds of years, "Mahabharata," world's largest epic poem. These encyclopedic Sanskrit epics, together with the Vedas, the Upanishads and so on, make up extraordinary body of literature.

BC **400–AD 900**   Stone majuscule (capital) script, Greece.

BC **400–500**   Brahmi script, Kharoshthi script.

BC **400–300**   Lydian script. Latin, Jewish, later Aramaic scripts.

BC **400–100**   Oscan/Umbrian script.

BC **350**   Koine began to evolve in Greece.

BC **335**   From the time of Alexander the Great, cuneiform was increasingly superseded by Aramaic and eventually disappeared at the beginning of the Christian era. Soon after that, the Coptic alphabet supplanted Egyptian hieroglyphs.

BC **304–282**   The founder of the Ptolemaic Dynasty in Egypt, Ptolemy I Soter, established a Shrine of the Muses in his palace complex at Alexandria—and the Great Library, in which most of the writings of classical antiquity were stored. It grew to ½ million papyrus rolls.

BC **300**   Quadrate form of Greek majuscules became standardized; some rounded forms or uncials found in inscriptions after this time.

BC **300**   Manetho's "Chronicle of Kings" (in Greek), preserved by later writers, lists Egyptian rulers from Menes to the conquest of Egypt by Alexander the Great in 332 BC. Manetho's 31-dynasty system still used today as the basic framework for Egypt's history.

BC **300** Lapidary script flourished on the monuments of the Roman Empire.

BC **300** Iberian, Pahlevi scripts. Achaemenid Elamite, Late Babylonian scripts.

BC **300** Adaptation and modification of an Italic script by migrating Goths in the Alpine region. Writing was possibly introduced to the Goths by Ulphilas, who was the successor of Theophilus as bishop under Emperor Valens.

BC **300** "Hymns of the Rigveda" preserve the oldest form—Vedic Sanskrit—and earliest actual inscriptions from India, dating to Ashoka.

BC **300–200** Northeast Iberian adapted by Celtiberians.

BC **300–AD 700** Pahlavi script.

BC **300–AD 300** Xiao Zhuan, small seal script, China.

BC **273–232** Indian writing first appeared, when edicts of Ashoka (265/273–238/232 BC) were committed to stone. Principal writing systems, Kharosthi and Brahmi, appeared on the Indian subcontinent (not counting variants used to transcribe other languages spoken there). The needs of trade combined with western influences led to the development of the Brahmi script, ancestor to most modern Indian scripts. Two hundred modern Indian scripts derive from Brahmi, including southern/Dravidian and northern/Sanskrit. Brahmi, a totally alphabetic script of consonants and vowels, was the root of the Devanagari script, used to write Sanskrit. Brahmi also lies behind Hindi. All are traced back to the Phoenician alphabet. In the Middle East, the old cuneiform script, composed of wedge-shaped marks, had given way to new alphabetic scripts, Aramaic and Greek.

BC **270–250** Bible translated into Greek.

BC **250** Breakdown of uniformity of Imperial Aramaic script.

BC **221–206** Qin/Ch'in Dynasty reforms Chinese character spelling and introduces Small Seal script (simplified) in China. Chinese writing system fixed in its present form.

BC **210–AD 224** Iranian texts in Aramaic script.

BC **206–AD 220** There were 10,000 characters in writing during the Han Dynasty of China.

BC **200** Square Hebrew became the Hebrew script and was the one most used by Jewish communities.

BC **200** Rosetta Stone written.

BC **200** Numidian/Old Lybian script, which developed into Berber script.

BC **200** Neo-Punic Jewish, Nabatean, Palmyran, Edessan, Hatran, Mandaic, Elymaic.

BC **200** Egypt refused to supply rival Pergamon with papyrus, so they resorted to leather/parchment.

BC **200** Earliest known examples of Meroitic (Meroe/ Sudan), script known and language partially known. Earliest dated text in Meroitic (hieroglyphic temple inscription of Queen Shanakdakhete) around 180/170.

BC **200–AD 100** In China, paper was made from hemp waste or old rags, and fragments have been found in north and northwest China. Solid ink was rubbed onto an ink stone with water, then a brush used to apply the resulting liquid ink.

BC **200–AD 200** Parthian period texts.

BC **200–AD 200** Caoshu, grass script, China.

BC **200–AD 220** Lishu, clerical script, China.

BC **200–AD 300** Thalmudic script.

BC **200–AD 900** Maya hieroglyphs on monuments.

BC **199** X and Y added to the alphabet.

BC **150** Earliest deciphered text from Veracruz, descendants of Olmecs.

BC **146** Greece annexed by Roman Empire—but Greek alphabet adopted by founders of Rome. The letter A, B, E, I, K, M, N, O, T, X, Y, Z adopted almost unchanged. Greek characters altered to form D, G, L, S, P, R. Romans resurrected F, Q, and V.

BC **100** Samaritan script emerged, Hebrew (Paleo), Coptic, Nabatean, Palmyrene.

BC **100** Diodorus Siculus described hieroglyphic writing.

BC **100–AD 100** Old Cursive version of Roman/Latin.

BC **100–AD 300** Carthaginian/Punic version of Phoenician script.

BC **58** Tironian notae script.

BC **40** At this stage, only a few legal and literary texts still written in cuneiform.

AD **1** Classical Ethiopic, Ligyan, Runic, Syriac scripts.

AD **1** Chinese script known in Japan, to a small circle of people.

AD **1–100** The Dead Sea Scrolls were likely written by the Essenes in Aramaic/Hebrew script. These are a collection of documents that include the earliest surviving examples of the books of the Bible. There are sectarian writings among the Dead Sea Scrolls: copies of most of the Hebrew sacred canon, and commentaries on prophets such as Isaiah. List of Dead Sea Scrolls: book of Isaiah in Hebrew, comments on Book of Habakkuh, version of book of Genesis in Aramaic, Psalms of Thanksgiving, The War of the Children of Light Against the Children of Darkness, and Manual of Discipline (rules of the Essenes), as well as two copper scrolls.

AD **75** Latest Babylonian tablet; latest inscription in cuneiform dated to this time; total years cuneiform employed as writing system is 3,000 years. Cuneiform still used along the northern coast where Phoenicians traded and in Mesopotamia.

AD **100** Aramaic is principal language of traders from Egypt and Asia Minor in India.

AD **100** Armazi script; Sinaitic script.

AD **100** People of northern Arabia—the Nabateans—were already using a script that was neither Phoenician nor Arabic.

AD **100**   Pliny's history of obelisks.

AD **100–200**   Earliest inscriptions in runes with some mastery of the script and variety of technique in recording it. Runes bear strong resemblance to early forms of Etruscan and Latin alphabets. Beginning of Christian era was the invention of runic alphabet. Runes were used to record the early stages of Gothic, Danish, Swedish, Norwegian, English, Frisian, Frankish, and tribal tongues of Germany. There are a range of runic scripts and 500 inscriptions found in Nordic countries; most are in Sweden, then Norway, Denmark, Iceland. The earliest finds in eastern Europe are Pietroassa in Rumania, Dahmsdorf in Germany, and Kowel in Russia. The Roman alphabet exercised influence of some kind on the runic script, which was used for over 1,000 years. The runic alphabet has 24 letters in an order called *futhark* after the first 6 letters. Germanic runes perhaps derived from Etruscan.

AD **100–200**   First inscriptions in Sanskrit or Indian alphabet.

AD **100–200**   Latin alphabet spread throughout northern Europe into British Isles under the influence of earlier Roman occupations and subsequent Christian missions.

AD **100–200**   Pausanias, Greek traveler and geographer, detailed an account of what he saw as he traveled around Greece.

AD **100–200**   Pergamon disk with areas associated with 24 letters.

AD **100–200**   Tacitus describes Ramesses inscriptions, Egyptian writing.

AD **100–400**   New Cursive version of Roman/Latin.

AD **100–600**   Rustic script.

AD **100–1500**   Maya writing; 800 known hieroglyphs. Sites with inscriptions: Tikal, Palenque, Copan, Calakmul. Virtually all Maya monuments bear glyphs detailing the exact date when the rituals and events they depict were performed. The Mayan glyphs were copied and transformed by Toltec, Aztec, etc. The Spanish conquest terminated their development.

AD **105**   Chinese legend credits Tsai Lun (c. 50–118) with the invention of paper. The Chinese kept this a secret.

AD **135**   Paleo-Hebrew remained in intermittent use until this date.

AD **150**   Earliest known examples of La Mojarra (Mesoamerica), script unknown and language unknown (no scholarly consensus, however).

AD **163**   Epi-Olmec script, known from two inscriptions at Veracruz.

AD **186**   Introduction of the Chinese script into Vietnam.

AD **200**   Find spots of runes parallel the movements of migrating Goths.

AD **200**   Syriac script.

AD **200**   Xingshu, running script, China.

AD **200–300**   Clement of Alexandria produced "Stromates" on symbology.

AD **200–300**   Coptic, final stage of the Egyptian language, begins and is used till AD c. 900.

AD **200–300**   Jewish script or "square Hebrew" evolved from Aramaic; now used in Israel as national script. Used after the Jews' Babylonian captivity, first for religious literature and then in 19th c for colloquial writing, too.

AD **200–300**   Latest Phoenician inscriptions (in Punic script).

AD **200–300**   Neo-Phyrgian inscriptions.

AD **200–750**   Germanic Runic alphabet of 24 letters in three groups of eight (aettir).

AD **200–900**   Manichaean script.

AD **200–1200**   Champa script.

AD **250–900**   Maya writing's "golden age"—most of the 5,000 Maya texts were carved or painted then. Probably began as early as Epi-Olmec.

AD **300**   Avestan, Ethiopic scripts.

AD **300**   Glyphs of pre-Columbian America.

AD **300**   Plotinus praises hieroglyphs.

AD **300–400**   The increased use of parchment (animal skin prepared for writing) may have led to the adoption of the codex or book, because parchment was less suitable than papyrus for scrolls. In a codex, both sides of each page could be written on.

AD **300–500**   Arabic script originated from the script of the Nabataeans. Earliest inscriptions of Arabic writing.

AD **300–700**   Ogham inscriptions dated to this time, from southern Ireland, Wales, Scotland, and Isle of Man. The Ogham alphabet was probably invented in Ireland and imported to Scotland with the Dalriadic settlers in the 5th century. K. H. Jackson said the inscriptions date from the late-Pictish period.

AD **300–900**   Sogdian script.

AD **300–1000**   Uncial/half uncial version of Roman/Latin.

AD **350**   Alphabet invented by Bishop Wulfila for transcribing holy texts for Visigoths. The earliest extensive Germanic text is the (incomplete) Gothic Bible, translated at this time by the Visigothic bishop Ulfilas (Wulfila), and written in a 27-letter alphabet of the translator's own design.

AD **350**   Ethiopic/Ge'ez, Old Abyssinian scripts.

AD **394**   Latest datable Egyptian hieroglyphic examples in temple inscription, island of Philae. Total number of hieroglyphs about 6,000, although fewer than 1,000 in standard use.

AD **400**   Ammianus Marcellinus discussed obelisks, including a translation of an obelisk inscription by Hermapion.

AD **400**   Gothic, Armenian, Georgian, Ethiopic (OSA) scripts.

AD **400**   Horapollo's hieroglyph treatise from Nilopolis

translated into Greek, then lost until manuscript discovered on a Greek island in 1419.

AD 400   Kaishu, standard script, China.

AD 400–500   Alvan, Arabic, Estranghelo, Samaritan scripts. First Sanskrit inscriptions from Cambodia, Java, Borneo. Georgian, khutsuri or ecclesiastical hand, script.

AD 400–600   Anglo-Saxons brought Germanic Runic script to England, increased the letters to 28 and then 33.

AD 400–600   Japanese/Chinese script. Japanese imported Chinese characters, despite the great disparity between the two languages.

AD 400–700   Runes common in central Germany and then disappear with Christianity. Runes throughout Germanic world (Denmark, Sweden, Norway, England, Germany, Poland, Russia, Hungary). They record different Germanic languages and are cut, stamped, inlaid, or impressed on metal, bone, and stone. There is no standard *futhark* (the peculiar order of the alphabet). What survives to modern times is only a small fragment of the total runic corpus. Inscriptions on stone are uncommon before AD c. 400. Total number of known inscriptions is 5,000, mostly in Sweden, then Norway, Denmark, and Iceland. There are some in Greenland, Faroe, Isle of Man, Orkneys, Shetlands, Ireland, Anglo-Saxon England, Germany, and Frisia. They were used in Scandinavia well into the Middle Ages.

AD 400–800   Proto-Sinhalese script.

AD 400–1000   Gupta script.

AD 400–1300   Syriac/Estrangela script.

AD 400–1400   Grantha script.

AD 408   Last time Etruscan language was spoken. It was faithfully written in Greek alphabet, but the language is still completely unknown. There are 13,000 Etruscan inscriptions in central Italy.

AD 414   Use of Chinese by Koreans on a stone inscription.

AD 500   Samaritan, Sogdian, Arabic, Japanese syllabary.

AD 500–600   Discovery of a script identical to Etruscan on the island of Lemnos; heavy rectangular block has an engraving of what is probably a warrior with one inscription of perhaps 18 words surrounding the head and another of 16 words in three lines on an adjacent side.

AD 500–600   The art of block-book printing is almost certainly of Chinese origin, probably of the 6th century AD. The first examples were produced by hand-rubbing impressions from the block.

AD 500–1000   Chalukya script.

AD 500–1100   Rediscoveries of ancient writers, notably the renaissance of Greek science and philosophy in the Islamic world, saved by translators and passed on later to the Western world.

AD 500–1300   Sephardic script of Hebrew.

AD 500–1400   Khmer/Cambodian script.

AD 512–513   First truly Arabic inscriptions.

AD 540   Chinese book written on methods of cultivation.

AD 580   Great quantities of Maya glyphic texts appear.

AD 600   Earliest runic texts from Frisia.

AD 600   Gaelic, Mandean, Pre-Islamic, Tibetan (*dbu-can*), Tibetan (*dbu-med*) scripts.

AD 600–700   Aramaic was a unifying force of Arabic (whose script descended from Aramaic script) and Islam. Beginning of the Islamic period: several forms of Arabic script, 28 consonants with new ordering based on letter shape.

AD 600–700   The Koreans adopted the Chinese script and later exported it to Japan.

AD 600–700   Tokhaian/Kuchen script.

AD 600–800   Merovingian script.

AD 600–900   At Koucha and Turfan, documents found in two related languages of which no trace had previously been recognized.

AD 600–1200   Visigothic minuscule.

AD 650   Koran dictated to Mohammed by Allah, then transcribed into Arabic script.

AD 650   Tribes from Altay consolidate first Turkic empire and develop ancient Orkhon script.

AD 690   First attempt at creating a syllabic Korean script based entirely on Chinese script signs.

AD 698   Date of Franks Casket, most famous of English runic objects. It was named after the man who donated it to British Museum and has scenes of Wayland the Smith and the Adoration of Christ.

AD 700   Ma'il script (replaced by Kufic). Syriac/Jacobite script.

AD 700   New runes developed in Norse country. Norse inscriptions form the most important epigraphical archive of any Germanic people. Find spots of runes parallel the movements of Anglo-Saxon pilgrims.

AD 700–750   Mashk script.

AD 700–800   Sharada/Kashmir script; Tamil script.

AD 700–900   Tocharian manuscripts largely written in a north Indian alphabet of the Brahmi type—and the material consisted of translations of Sanskrit originals: texts written on palm leaves, occasionally on Chinese paper, and ink on wooden tablets.

AD 700–1300   Beneventan script; Carolingian minuscule script.

AD 700–1500   Vatteluttu script.

AD 700–1700   Uighur script. Mongols wrote in two alphabetic scripts—Uighur and Phags-pa.

AD 700–1800   Thuluth script.

AD 700–1900   Mandaic script.

AD 700–1900   Syriac/Nestorian script, then becomes modified New Syriac script.

AD 700–1928   Runic Old Turkish (Kok Turki).

AD 712 Earliest work of Japanese literature, Kojiki, an ancient history of Japan. Japanese writing is a mix of *kanji* (Chinese characters) and *kana* (Japanese phonetic signs). There are two syllabaries: *hiragana* (easy kana) and *katakana* (side kana).

AD 800 Hiragana script, Japan. Slavonic script.

AD 800–900 Cyrillic alphabet (43 letters, now 30) used in Russia, adapted from Greek alphabet. It became the script for more than 60 languages. Saint Cyril (AD c. 827–869) was entrusted the mission of creating this alphabet by the Byzantine emperor Constantine at the request of the Slav king of Moravia. The Russians had no system of writing before the reign of the Byzantine emperor Michael the Paphlagonian, when they adopted the language and characters of the Slavs (Greek characters).

AD 800–900 Use of runes persisted until this time in England (futhark). Ogham inscriptions found in areas of British Isles where there were Scandinavian settlements (esp. Wales) and were out of use by end of the medieval period.

AD 800–1000 Kufic script.

AD 800–1050 Nordic Runic alphabet, at the time of the Viking expansion, spread over Europe.

AD 800–1100 Persian script.

AD 800–1500 Andalusian script; Muhaqqaq script.

AD 800–1800 Tawqi script.

AD 800–1900 Naskhi script.

AD 807 Book of Kells (in Trinity College Library, Dublin) in Insular script developed by Irish monks from uncial script of official Roman documents of 3rd century AD onward. Each monastery developed its own variant of uncials.

AD 832 Baghdad, translations made from the Greek. A world atlas is made.

AD 850 Muslim mapmakers are active.

AD 860 First Slavic writing.

AD 900 Documentary minuscule script, Greece.

AD 900 Ecclesiastical script created by Cyril and Methodius, missionaries to Slavic Moravians and Bulgarians.

AD 900 Katakana script, Japan; Old Bulgarian script.

AD 900 Mixtecs had developed a script based on pictographs.

AD 900 Recording of Maya texts on architectural monuments ceased.

AD 900–1000 Decorative writing, the Kufic script, was a version of Arabic that came into widespread use in North Africa. It was used on ornamental panels and was easier to carve than the usual flowing script. The Arabic alphabet is derived from earlier Semitic alphabets. The Arabic script had been in use since before the time of Muhammad. Several flowing styles of Arabic writing had developed under the impetus of recording the Koran, and these multiplied dramatically in the 10th century. Abu Ali Ibn Muqlah

devised geometric principles for the six major scripts, a system that has been followed every since. Arabic characters in use today are the invention of Vizier Moclah, AD 933. The oldest Arabic characters are called Kufic (after the town of Kufa).

AD 900–1000 In the Khitan, a kingdom on China's northeastern frontier, a writing system was devised, based on the 3,000 Chinese characters and modified for the Khitan language. The Mongolians did the same. Chinese characters, however, were designed for uninflected language and were unsuited to multisyllabic languages with complicated grammar. In time, these hybrids were abandoned. The Koreans created a new alphabet, and the Mongolians adopted an alphabetic system derived from Aramaic.

AD 900–1000 Rabbinical script of Hebrew; Western Kufic script.

AD 900–1100 Anglo-Saxon script.

AD 900–1500 Old Javanese/Kavi script.

AD 900–1600 Glagolitic script.

AD 916–1125 Kitan scripts introduced, inner Asia.

AD 960 Chinese treatise on the history of technology is written.

AD 1000 Buddhist scribes become important to Chinese civilization.

AD 1000 Continental Celtic (series of languages) written. Sources of information are inscriptions and names; numerous preserved in ancient Gaul, northern Italy, and Iberia—but a lack of long literary texts.

AD 1000 Earliest extant examples of Rongorongo script of Easter Island, of unknown origin and function. Rongorongo, a form of protowriting, used for "chants or recitations" of the language of Easter Island. Script inscribed on wooden boards and tablets—29 examples in museums, containing 14,000 "glyphs" engraved with shark's tooth, obsidian flakes, or sharpened bird bone. One scholar stated there are 120 elements combined to form between 1,800–2,000 compound signs. Yuri Knorosov said "Rongorongo may be compared with the ancient Egyptian hieroglyphs at an early stage of their development."

AD 1000 Nabataean Arabic script, precursor of the Arabic script, replaced Aramaic script. The sequence was Phoenician > Aramaic > Nabataean > Arabic.

AD 1000 Writing system spread to all regions of Europe that were dominated by the Romans and where Latin was written.

AD 1000–1050 Codex Nuttall is an early example of Mixtec pictographic writing. Recorded genealogy and history of 1st, 2nd dynasties of Tilantongo (Oaxaca, Mexico).

AD 1000–1050 Runic script—the Vikings borrowed the practice of writing from France and Britain where Latin script was in use but developed their own script, with characters known as runes. Runic script used by Viking communities in Scandinavia and the British Isles was gradually replaced by the Latin script in the 11th and 12th centuries. Find spots of runes parallel the movements of Viking adventurers.

AD 1000–1100   Nubian script.

AD 1000–1500   Old Kannada script.

AD 1000–1521   Mixtecs, Aztecs write—but restricted to members of the elite.

AD 1036–1227   Tangut/Hsi-hsia script.

AD 1041–1048   The earliest movable type for printing was invented in China. Consisted of individual characters made of clay, which could be fixed onto an iron-framed plate.

AD 1100   Burmese and Devanagari scripts. Bengali script. Bengali script's mix of syllabic letters and vowels is arranged in an order determined by Indian phoneticians well over 2,000 years ago. Calligraphy was most respected art form of China.

AD 1100–1200   Ashkanazi script of Hebrew.

AD 1100–1200   Runic script used by Viking communities in Scandinavia and the British Isles was gradually replaced by the Latin script. By the time of the Norman Conquest (1066), the Roman script had triumphed, and in Britain the runic script had almost disappeared.

AD 1100–1200   The many written documents that have survived from the medieval kingdoms of western Europe testify to the growing complexity of bureaucratic administration. Substantial collections of royal and ecclesiastical records detail expenditure and receipts and were written on sheepskin or parchment by using a stylus. Styli were usually made of bone with a metal tip, but some were entirely metal.

AD 1100–1200   There were 23,000 characters in the Chinese script.

AD 1100–1300   Rayhani script.

AD 1100–1500   Codex Dresden, Madrid, and Paris—the only surviving Maya manuscripts—thought to have been composed at this time, although some suggest slightly earlier dates. Only four codices of thousands survived the early Spanish missionaries to Mesoamerica. There are, however, hundreds of statements on fine clay vessels and monumental inscriptions on stelae and architectural features. Maya glyphs tell about grand historical events, the rise and fall of dynasties, and sophisticated ideology, religion, and cosmology. The Madrid Codex, together with the Paris and Dresden codices, one of several richly illustrated glyphic texts of the pre-Conquest Mayan period to have survived the mass book burnings by the Spanish clergy during the 16th century. The Madrid Codex is believed to be a product of the late Mayan period (AD c. 1400) and is possibly a Post-Classic copy of Classic Mayan scholarship. The figures and glyphs of this codex are poorly drawn and not equal in quality to those of the other surviving codices. The Paris Codex is devoted almost entirely to Mayan ritual and ceremony, such as the ceremony held to celebrate the end of a 20-year period.

AD 1100–1600   Gothic script. In the Middle Ages, Carolingian, Gothic, and humanist scripts recorded Latin while Cyrillic, derived from Greek, also developed. For more than 1,000 years, writing skills were virtually the monopoly of monks. Maya's bark-paper books elaborately painted in color and bound in jaguar skin; the prognostications based on a written calendrical system so sophisticated it extended back 5 billion years.

AD 1100–1650   Yu-chen script.

AD 1120   Jurchin script introduced, inner Asia.

AD 1150   Europeans still used papyrus and parchment while Chinese keep paper a secret.

AD 1155   Anglo-Saxon Chronicle, earliest records of Anglo-Saxon England.

AD 1200   English cursive script; Modern Sinhalese script; Vietnamese (chu nom).

AD 1200–1300   Lao script; Sibo script form Uighur; Sudanese script.

AD 1200–1600   Thai/Siamese script evolves.

AD 1200–1800   Ahom script; Maghribi script.

AD 1272–1350   Passepa script.

AD 1300   Movable type replaced by a wooden-type process.

AD 1300–1500   Maya glyphs in written form/documents.

AD 1300–1600   Aztec script.

AD 1300–1700   Mamluk script.

AD 1300–1800   Sini script.

AD 1300–1900   Moso (Na-khi/Naxi) script.

AD 1310–1400   Kalika/Galik script.

AD 1400   Modern Javanese, Balti, Lolo, Telugu scripts; Aztecs had adapted the Mixtec script for their use.

AD 1400–1600   Batarde, Gothic hybrid, Humanistic book scripts. Philippine script, including Bisaya, Buhil, Tagbanu, and Belarmino.

AD 1400–1700   Bihari script.

AD 1419   Horapollo's book "Hieroglyphics" discovered on island of Andros by Buondelmonte.

AD 1443–1444   Korean Hangul alphabet invented. Riqa, Secretary hands scripts. The development of the Hangul alphabet is traditionally ascribed to Sejong, fourth king of the Yi Dynasty; the system was made the official writing system for the Korean language in the mid-1440s by one of Sejong's decrees. Because of the influence of Confucianism and of Chinese culture, however, Hangul was not used by scholars or Koreans of the upper classes until after 1945, when Korea ceased to be under Japanese rule. The 28 letters introduced are one of the few alphabets that can be dated. Hangul has yet to entirely supplant Chinese characters throughout Korea.

AD **1500**   Inca quipus—knotted arrangement of rope and cords for keeping track of the movement of goods in the empire. Many types of knot, each representing a value in a decimal system, but no zero. Value varies also according to knot's position on cord. Summation cords were used to tie off bunches of strings. Also spelled *quipo*, it was an Incan accounting apparatus consisting of a long rope from which hung 48 secondary cords and various tertiary cords attached to the secondary ones. Knots were made in the cords to represent units, tens, and hundreds; and, in imperial accounting, the cords were differently colored to designate the different concerns of government—such as tribute, lands, economic productivity, ceremonies, and matters relating to war and peace. The quipus were created and maintained as historical records and were kept not only by high officials at the capital of Cuzco—judges, commanders, and important heads of extended families— but also by regional commanders and village headman.

AD **1500**   Balinese, Kannada, Kavi, Khmati, Limbu, Malay/ Jawi scripts.

AD **1500**   Discovery that Dresden Codex, containing Maya dates, was written as an almanac of divination with days linked by complex astronomical calculations. Each god/ goddess is named with a glyph above his or her portrait.

AD **1500–1700**   Attempts to decipher Egyptian hieroglyphs in Europe by Giovanni Pierio Valeriano, Mercati M., Athanasius Kircher, and Sir J. Marshall.

AD **1500–1700**   Modi script.

AD **1500–1800**   Urdu script.

AD **1500–present**   Diwani, Farsi scripts.

AD **1505**   Horapollo's "Hieroglyphs" published, went through 30 editions, one illustrated by Albrecht Durer.

AD **1538**   Gurmukhi script.

AD **1556**   First book on hieroglyphs by Pierius Valerianus.

AD **1561**   Fray Diego de Landa (1524–1579), in Yucatan (later, its bishop, 1572), writes "An Account of Things of Yucatan," which contains the Mayan "alphabet," which proved to be the key to deciphering Mayan glyphs in the 20th century. He burnt most of the surviving codices. In late 1560s, he returned to Spain to face charges, was exonerated, and returned. Realization that Mayan glyphs were partially phonetic.

AD **1563**   Leo Africanus's description of Africa published.

AD **1566**   Diego de Landa's "Relacion de las casas de Yucatan" published. French scholar Brasseur de Bourbourg came across de Landa's colonial dictionary in a Madrid archive and published it in French and Spanish.

AD **1582–1589**   Six ancient Egyptian obelisks were re-sited or re-erected in Rome.

AD **1583**   John Eldred's "The Voyage of M. John Eldred to Trypolis in Syria by Sea and from Thence by Land and River to Babylon and Balsara."

AD **1600s**   There were collectors and students of Coptic manuscripts: Peirsec, Pietro della Valle, Salmasius, Thomas Obicini.

AD **1600–1800**   Old Hungarian script.

AD **1600–1900**   Manchu, Mughal script.

AD **1604**   Pietro della Valle made preliminary drawings of Behistun monument.

AD **1609**   Garcilaso de la Vega's "The Royal Commentaries of the Incas."

AD **1618**   Persepolis (capital of Darius and Persian kings of Achaemenid dynasty) discoverer was Spanish ambassador to Persia, Garcia Silva Figueroa; mysterious inscriptions on ruins in carved black jasper. Persepolis scripts: Old Persian, Elamite (regional variant of Babylonian), and Babylonian.

AD **1621**   Spanish ambassador to Persia correctly identifies site of Persepolis and described an inscription in the language of the Persian Empire: Garcia Silva Figueroa, "De Rerum Persicarum Epistola."

AD **1632**   Mongolian script.

AD **1636**   Athanasius Kircher's "Introduction to Coptic, or Egyptian" published. Kircher assisted in the rescue of Coptic, the language of the last phase of ancient Egypt. Coptic dates to Christian times and was the official language of the Egyptian church but lost ground to Arabic and by late 17th century was headed for extinction.

AD **1643**   Athanasius Kircher's "The Egyptian Language Restored" published.

AD **1646**   John Greaves's "Pyramidographia" about Egyptian pyramids.

AD **1649–1950**   Kalmuck script from Mongolian.

AD **1657**   First published example of a cuneiform inscription, by Pietro della Valle.

AD **1658**   Pietro della Valle described Sumerian system of writing after a visit to Persepolis. Groups of sign lists are found in Sumer, which were used by scribes as an early dictionary and an aid to learning. The number of signs diminished as each sign came to stand for more than its original meaning; eventually no more than 600 signs in common use.

AD **1666**   Athanasius Kircher entrusted with publication of an Egyptian hieroglyphic inscription on obelisk in Rome's Piazza dell Minerva from 6th century BC.

AD **1678**   Jean Tavernier's "The Six Voyages of Tavernier through Turkey into Asia."

AD **1681**   Robert Knox's "An Historical Relation of Ceylon, Together with Somewhat Concerning Remarkable Passages of My Life."

AD **1700**   Gottfried Wilhelm Leibniz (philosopher, mathematician) wanted to invent new written language for universal communication.

AD **1700**   Malayalam script.

AD **1700** Thomas Hyde coined name *cuneiform* meaning wedge-like ("ductuli pyramidales seu cuneiformes," *cuneus* being Latin for wedge).

AD **1700–1800** Attempts to decipher Egyptian hieroglyphs in Europe by: P. Lucas, R. Pococke, C. Niebuhr, F. L. Norden, A. Gordon, N. Freret, P. D'Origny, C. de Gebelin, J. H. Schumacher, J. G. Koch, T. Ch. Tychsen, P. E. Jablonski, A. De Caylus, Bishop Warburton, C. de Guignes, and G. Zoega.

AD **1700–1800** There were 49,000 characters (including many variants and obsolete forms) in the Chinese script.

AD **1700–1900** Takri script.

AD **1707** Edward Lhwyd's "Archaeologia Britannica."

AD **1712** E. Kaempfer published better cuneiform inscriptions from visit to Persepolis in 1686.

AD **1720** Lepcha/Rong script, derived from Tibetan.

AD **1721** Jacob Roggeveen discovered Easter Island statues and wooden writing boards with over 500 signs.

AD **1722** J. Richardson's "Account of Statues, Bas Reliefs, Drawings, and Pictures of Italy."

AD **1723** Sir Thomas Dempster's "De Etruria Regali" published.

AD **1739** Dresden Codex, key to the decipherment of Mayan glyphs, which was painted by Maya scribes, just before the Spanish conquest of Mexico—purchased by the royal library of the court of Saxony in Dresden. It had been taken to Europe by Cortes. At the height of Maya power, AD **250–800**, codices had jaguar-skin covers and were painted by scribes. One of only four surviving "books" of the ancient Maya of Central America, the Dresden Codex has 39 leaves folding out to 12 feet. A series of gods and animals is accompanied by hieroglyphic symbols. Alexander von Humboldt published Dresden Codex in part. The codex was acquired by the Sächsische Landesbibliothek (Saxon State Library), Dresden, Saxony, and was published by Edward King, Viscount Kingsborough, in *Antiquities of Mexico* (1930–48). King erroneously attributed the codex to the Aztecs. The first scientific edition of the codex was made by E. Förstemann (Leipzig, 1880).

AD **1740** William Stuckeley's "Stonehenge, A Temple Restored to the British Druids."

AD **1743** Richard Pococke's "A Description of the East, and Some Other Countries."

AD **1750** Abbe Barthelemy guessed cartouches contain kings' or gods' names.

AD **1750** Albanian/Elbasan script.

AD **1753** Discovery at Herculaneum of 3,000 rolls of charred papyri.

AD **1755** Swinton's Palmyrene abjad.

AD **1757** Frederick Norden's "Travels in Egypt and Nubia."

AD **1759** Abbe Barthelemy's Palmyrene abjad.

AD **1761–1762** Stuart and Revett's "Antiquities of Athens."

AD **1763** Denis Diderot and Jean D'Alembert published "L'Art d'ecrire," which was the first scholarly account of the writing systems of the world.

AD **1763** Ruins of Pompeii identified. Pompeii had handwriting on the walls—graffiti—an amount of writing so prolific that it was an important means of communication. Early Greek alphabetic writing used for recording poetic verse (hexametrical poetry) and also for graffiti (such as that on Thera and in Pompeii).

AD **1764** Abbe Barthelemy's Phoenician abjad.

AD **1764** Johann Winckelmann's "History of Ancient Art."

AD **1765** Carsten Niebuhr's copies of inscriptions at Persepolis.

AD **1765** William Warburton's second edition of the book describing his theory of hieroglyphics and writing in general, including Barthelemy's table of the signs. Warburton's three stages of history of the hieroglyphic class of writing were: (1) by representation (example: Mexican, pictures), (2) by analogy or symbol (example: Egyptian, pictures, contrasted and arbitrarily chosen marks), and (3) by arbitrary institution (example: Chinese, marks only). Warburton was first to suggest that all writing might have evolved from pictures.

AD **1768** Abbe Barthelemy's Imperial Aramaic abjad.

AD **1771** Anquetil-Duperron published translation of sacred literature of Zoroastrians (Avesta).

AD **1772** Carsten Niebuhr (1733–1815) confirmed left-to-right direction of cuneiform writing; first to draw the inscriptions accurately. He showed that there were three different cuneiform scripts at Persepolis.

AD **1772–1778** First decent copies of trilingual Old Persian, Elamite, Akkadian from Persepolis published.

AD **1774** Carsten Niebuhr made a table of hieroglyphs arranged in an order.

AD **1775** James Adair's "History of the American Indian."

AD **1776** James Hutton's "Theory of the Earth."

AD **1784** Sir William Jones first showed that Sanskrit was related to Latin and Greek.

AD **1787–1791** Silvestre de Sacy's Sassanian abjad.

AD **1788** Abbe Barthelemy's "Voyage du jeune Anacharsis en Grece."

AD **1788** First (historical) writing in Australia.

AD **1789** Abbe Lanzi's "Saggio di lingua Etrusca" (Story of the Etruscan Language).

AD **1792–1798** Eckhel's "Doctrina numorum veterum."

AD **1797** Georg Zoeg/Zoega's book "On the Order and Purpose of the Obelisks" suggested some hieroglyphs might be phonetic signs.

AD **1798** Word *cartouche* coined by French soldiers in Egypt who were part of Napoleon's invasion force; the ovals reminded them of the cartridges in guns.

AD **1799** Rosetta Stone discovered in Egypt by demolition

squad of soldiers, probably built into a very old wall in the village of Rashid (Rosetta) on a branch of the Nile. Top register Egyptian hieroglyph, middle register demotic, and bottom register Greek.

AD **1800**   Aymara, Bushman, Chipewyan, Cree, Tamahag, Vai scripts; Miao phonetic script, Chu Yin System.

AD **1800**   Copies of the Rosetta Stone made and distributed to scholars in Europe.

AD **1800**   Danish scholar Zoega said some hieroglyphs might be "phonetic signs" and coined the phrase "notae phoneticae."

AD **1800**   Constantine Samuel Rafinesque discovered Maya bar-and-dot numeration.

AD **1800s**   Attempts to decipher Egyptian hieroglyphs in Europe by: N. G. de Pahlin, J. von Hammer-Purgstall, A. Lenoir, P. Lacour, J. Bailey.

AD **1800s**   Discovery of Franks casket, now in British Museum, most famous of English runic objects.

AD **1800s**   The Mayan numbers were the first part of the writing system to be deciphered; very sophisticated. Place value increased in multiples of 20; had a zero (which Romans and Babylonians did not have).

AD **1800s**   Until archaeological discoveries of this time and later, the decipherment of the Babylonian script, the Mesopotamian area and its history were known only through biased accounts and inaccurate narratives.

AD **1800**   Ernst Förstemann's studies of Dresden Codex and Maya calendrics, unraveling some of the Maya calendrical systems, identifying glyphs of the Long Count, and recognizing some distinctive features of Maya writing. The first scientific edition of the codex was made by E. Förstemann (Leipzig).

AD **1801**   Rosetta Stone moved to Alexandria in attempt to avoid its capture by British forces.

AD **1802**   Georg Grotefend (1775–1853) decided the single slanting wedges of Old Persian cuneiform were word dividers and concluded the system must be alphabetic. Compiled an alphabet of Old Persian, but many of his sign values were wrong because the Persian script was not purely alphabetic but partially syllabic. He deciphered 12 Persian cuneiform signs.

AD **1802**   Count Silvestre de Sacy and Johan Akerblad read "Ptolemy" and "Alexander" off demotic section of Rosetta Stone. Akerblad attempted to transliterate proper names of Rosetta Stone. Silvestre de Sacy's "Lettre a Citoyen Chaptal"—one of the earliest and best articles on the discovery of the Rosetta Stone.

AD **1802**   Rosetta Stone arrived in England; went to British Museum.

AD **1803**   Vivant Denon's "Travels in Upper and Lower Egypt."

AD **1807**   Jean-François Champollion presented paper on

the Coptic etymology of Egyptian placenames preserved in the works of Greek and Latin authors.

AD **1809–1828**   Napoleon Bonaparte's men's reports and monographs were collected in the monumental "Description de l'Égypte" (Description of Egypt), published in parts in Paris.

AD **1812**   John Izard Middleton's "Grecian Remains in Italy."

AD **1814**   Jean-François Champollion's 1st of 3 volumes on Egypt: 1 = geography, 2 = social institutions, 3 = language and letters.

AD **1814**   Thomas Young deciphers the hieroglyphic writing of the names "Cleopatra" and "Ptolemy" by using the Rosetta Stone. Young made an important breakthrough by deducing that hieratic was a kind of cursive for hieroglyphics.

AD **1815**   Claudius Rich's "Memoir on the Ruins of Babylon."

AD **1815**   Obelisk of Philae (island on Nile) found and removed to England (and used as a decoration on an estate).

AD **1816**   William Smith's "Strata Identified by Organized Fossils."

AD **1818–1819**   Encyclopaedia Britannica included articles on Egyptian hieroglyphs. Thomas Young's article in Encyclopaedia Britannica, "Egypt," on his ideas on the Egyptian script, which he first communicated to Jean-François Champollion. W. J. Bankes transported from Egypt an obelisk and base block.

AD **1818**   C. Rich's "Second Memoir on the Ruins of Babylon."

AD **1818**   Thomas Young's Egyptian logosyllabary.

AD **1820**   Caleb Atwater's "Description of the Antiquities Discovered in the State of Ohio and Other Western States."

AD **1821**   Cherokee "alphabet" invented by Sequoya in United States.

AD **1821**   Jean-François Champollion published "De l'ecriture Hieratique des Anciens Egyptiens."

AD **1821**   W. J. Bankes made lithographs of Greek and hieroglyphic texts.

AD **1822, 1828**   Jean-François Champollion announced his decipherment of Egyptian hieroglyphics and exhibited his logosyllabary/hieroglyphic alphabet. Champollion got crucial clue from obelisk excavated at Philae by William J. Bankes (it now stands at Kingston Lacy in Dorset)—copy of bilingual obelisk inscription sent to Champollion by Bankes. The base block inscription was in Greek, the column inscription in hieroglyphic script. Champollion's "Lettre a M. Dacier" with table of demotic and hieroglyphic signs with their Greek equivalents.

AD **1821–1833**   John Gardiner Wilkinson recorded inscriptions, cartouches, and tomb paintings. He filled dozens of notebooks with details of ancient Egyptian life, culled from papyri and other writings.

AD 1822   Antonio Del Rio's "Descriptions of the Ruins of an Ancient City, Discovered Near Palenque."

AD 1822   W. J. Bankes published a copy of his new bilingual inscription from Egyptian obelisk.

AD 1823   Jean-François Champollion's fundamentals explained further: The writing system is a mixture of semantic symbols, i.e., symbols that stand for words and ideas (also called logograms) and phonetic signs, phonograms, that represent one or more sounds (alphabetic or polyconsonantal). Pictogram may function as a phonogram and as a logogram, depending on its context. Champollion accomplished full decipherment of Egyptian hieroglyphs ("Tableau des Signes Phonetiques").

AD 1824   Jean-François Champollion's "Precis du systeme hieroglyphique" (Summary of the Hieroglyphic System of Ancient Egyptians) published.

AD 1826   Frederick Cailliaud's "Voyage a Meroe."

AD 1827   H. Baradere's "Antiquities Mexicaines."

AD 1828   August Bockh began publishing all known examples of Greek inscriptions.

AD 1830   Charles Lyell's "Principles of Geology" and Lord Kingsborough's "Antiquities of Mexico."

AD 1833   Eugene Burnouf's Avestan alphabet.

AD 1834, 1837   James Prinsep's Brahmi abugida. He was the first European scholar to decipher the edicts of the ancient Indian emperor Ashoka.

AD 1835–1837   Sir Henry Creswicke Rawlinson copied great rock inscriptions of King Darius from the cliff at Behistun. Rawlinson's first major step in cuneiform led to the reading of the earliest texts of the Near East, from which the cuneiform system of writing was later deciphered. Rawlinson went to cliff in the Zagros Mountains of western Iran near Behistun (Bisitun) and copied Darius' inscription—leading to the decipherment of Babylonian cuneiform. He never explained how he did it, and study of his notes suggests that he borrowed without attribution from Edward Hincks.

AD 1836–1841   Jean-François Champollion's "Grammaire Egyptienne."

AD 1836   Eugene Burnouf's and Christian Lassen's Old Persian syllabaries.

AD 1836   Claudius Rich's "Narrative of a Residence in Koordistan" and Albert Gallatin's "A Synopsis of the Indian Tribes Within the U.S."

AD 1837   John G. Wilkinson brought his work together in "The Manners and Customs of the Ancient Egyptians." Ancient Egypt offered up a mass of written materials, including some of the world's first literature, the Books of the Dead, medical manuals, school texts, legal documents,

estate papers, lawsuits, narratives, proverbs, teachings, and poetry.

AD 1837   Karl Richard Lepsius's Egyptian logosyllabary.

AD 1837   Sir Henry Rawlinson deciphered and translated first half of the Old Persian cuneiform inscription from Behistun. Inscription of Darius contains Elamite; 2.5 millennia before, a quasipictographic script was used to write the language of Elam, and it is known as Proto-Elamite and is yet undeciphered.

AD 1837   Wilhelm Gesenius published and deciphered full corpus of known examples of Phoenician writing ("Scripturae Linguaquae Phoeniciae Monumenta").

AD 1838   Jean F. Waldeck's "Voyage pittoresque et archaeologique dans . . . Yucatan."

AD 1838   James Prinsep's Kharoshthi's abugida.

AD 1838   William Henry Harrison's "Discourse on the Aborigines of the Valley of the Ohio."

AD 1839   John Lloyd Stephens discovered Maya civilization. Frederick Catherwood (with John Lloyd Stephens) went to Copan and sketched stela after stela, recording exotic glyphs (also Palenque, Chichen Itza, Uxmal, and Cozumel). The decipherment of this complicated script came through teamwork between linguists, epigraphers, and scholars. The published "Incidents of Travel in Central America, Chiapas, and Yucatan." The Cholan language covered Copan, Palenque, and influenced the Dresden Codex. Yucatec had three of four surviving codices.

AD 1839   Sir Henry Rawlinson completed the task of deciphering the Behistun Rock. This opened the way to the reading of Babylonian and the related Assyrian languages so that much of the literature of the early Near East was unlocked.

AD 1839   Samuel G. Morton's "Crania Americana."

AD 1840–1850   George Friedrich Grotefend said that he had deciphered the cuneiform inscriptions of Persepolis. Grotefend tackled the top inscription directly below the sculptured relief on the Behistun Rock (Old Persian). Grotefend identified the names of Hystaspes, Darius, and Xerxes. Rawlinson identified the names of peoples ruled by Darius, mentioned in the Greek histories of the Persian empire. Rawlinson knew to expect consistent relations between words of same meaning in Avestan, Sanskrit, and Old Persian. Investigations were also done by Rasmus C. N. Raske, Eugene Burnouf, Christian Lassen, and Henry Creswicke Rawlinson.

AD 1840   Second Albanian script.

AD 1841   Wilhelm Gesenius's Himyaritic abjad. Gesenius also laid the basis for Semitic epigraphy, collecting and deciphering the Phoenician inscriptions known in his time.

AD 1841   John L. Stephens's "Incidents of Travel in Central America, Chiapas, and Yucatan."

AD 1842 Jens Worsaae's "Danmarks Oldtid."

AD 1843 F. de Saulcy deciphers ancient Berber.

AD 1843 Jean-François Champollion's "Dictionnaire Egyptien."

AD 1843 William Prescott's "History of the Conquest of Mexico" and John L. Stephens's "Incidents of Travel in Yucatan."

AD 1846, 1859 Edward Hincks's Egyptian logosyllabary.

AD 1846 Darius's inscription on the Behistun Rock was used by Sir Henry Rawlinson to complete Grotefend's decipherment.

AD 1846 Discovery in Egypt of papyrus containing three lost orations of Hyperides.

AD 1846 Edward Hincks's and Henry Rawlinson's Old Persian syllabaries. Old Persian cuneiform was deciphered after Babylonian and Susian. Rawlinson's complete translation ("The Persian Cuneiform Inscription of Behistun") of a portion of the Behistun inscription in Old Persian. Also, Christian Lassen noticed certain cuneiform signs occurred only before particular vowels—a mixed alphabet/syllabary. Rawlinson and Hincks, independently, realized that the proportion of syllabic spelling varied from sound to sound.

AD 1846 Edward Hincks's Elamite cuneiform logosyllabary.

AD 1847 Papyri written in an older form of hieratic than any previously known was published in facsimile by Prisse d'Avennes ("Le Papyrus").

AD 1847 William Prescott's "History of the Conquest of Peru."

AD 1848 Edward Hincks moved toward decipherment of Urartian (cuneiform logosyllabary).

AD 1848 George Dennis's "Cities and Cemeteries of Etruria," Austen Layard's "Nineveh and Its Remains," and E. Squier and E. Davis's "Ancient Monuments of the Mississippi Valley."

AD 1849 Jens Worsaae's "Primeval Antiquities of Denmark" and Paul Botta and Eugene Flandin's "Monument de Nineve."

AD 1850, 1856 Edward Hincks's Sumerian cuneiform logosyllabary.

AD 1850–1851, 1857 Sir Henry Rawlinson's Mesopotamian cuneiform logosyllabary.

AD 1850 Hittite hieroglyphs' decipherment assisted by discovery of the Tarkondemos seal, an embossed silver roundel bearing cuneiform and hieroglyphic inscriptions.

AD 1851 Henry C. Rawlinson translated the 112 lines of the third column of the Behistun inscription—which was Semitic Akkadian.

AD 1852 Edwin Norris's Elamite cuneiform logosyllabary.

AD 1853 Britain's Hormuzd Rassasm beat the French to the discovery of the palace and library of Ashurbanipal, including the Gilgamesh Epic, c. 2nd millennium BC.

AD 1853 The Gilgamesh Epic, the first heroic epic known, is discovered in the library of King Ashurbanipal (c. 669–663 BC) of Assyria at the site of Kouyounjik (biblical Nineveh). Sir Austen Henry Layard found some; Paul Botta did some initial work there. Just as some of the ideas in the Code of Hammurabi were restated in the Bible, the Gilgamesh Epic has a flood story similar to Genesis.

AD 1855 Edwin Norris deciphered most of Elamite and entire Behistun inscription.

AD 1856 Sir Clements Markham's "Cuzco: A Journey to the Ancient Capital of Peru."

AD 1857 Cuneiform inscription on a clay cylinder of Tiglath-Pileser I of Assyria (1120–1074 BC) translated, confirming the decipherment of Babylonian cuneiform.

AD 1857 M. Thenou found first inscribed stone of Gortyna law inscription.

AD 1857 Royal Asiatic Society (London) sent recently discovered Behistun inscription to four Assyriologists: Henry Rawlinson, Edward Hincks, William H. Fox Talbot, and Julius Oppert. They were to study it without consulting each other. A month later, they turned in translations, which proved to be essentially the same.

AD 1857 The decipherment of Akkadian cuneiform texts recognized.

AD 1859, 1874 Emmanuel de Rouge's talk suggesting an Egyptian origin for the Phoenician alphabet; and its later publication ("Memoire sur l'origine Egyptienne de l'alphabet Phoenicienne").

AD 1859 Charles Darwin's "Origin of Species."

AD 1863 Charles Lyell's "The Geological Evidences of the Antiquity of Man."

AD 1867 J. Thompson's "The Antiquities of Cambodia."

AD 1867 Typewriter invented. Christopher Latham Sholes constructed what became the first practical typewriter. His second model, patented in 1868, wrote at a speed far exceeding that of a pen.

AD 1868 Bishop Jaussen obtained square board which is now in Congregation of the Sacred Heart in Rome; written boustrophedon where reader has to turn the board 180 degrees at the end of each line. Archaeological evidence supports colonization of Easter Island from the west (Polynesia). Bishop Jaussen of Tahiti tried to get islander to chant Rongorongo texts so he could translate them, but the results were inaccurate. Florentin Etienne Janssen created list of several hundred signs of Rongorongo.

AD 1868 Sindhi, remodeled Landa, script.

AD 1868 The Moabite stone, stelae of King Mesha, found in Dhiban, preserved an archaic form predating the Phoenician letters.

AD **1869**   Heinrich Schliemann's "Ithaka, the Peloponnese and Troy."

AD **1869**   Jules Oppert identified Sumerians through cuneiform tablets.

AD **1870**   Conze's "Zur Geschichte der Anfänge griechischen Kunste."

AD **1870s**   Cypriote script solved by George Smith, as related to Linear B. Sounds of Cypriote script could be deciphered.

AD **1870s**   Archaeologists aware of an undeciphered script from the Indus Valley area.

AD **1871**   Charles Darwin's "The Descent of Man" and Edward Tylor's "Primitive Culture."

AD **1871**   George Smith's work on Cypriot characters.

AD **1872**   Flood story of the Gilgamesh Epic deciphered by George Smith at the British Museum. Shortly thereafter, he found the missing piece at Nineveh.

AD **1873**   Johann Brandis' work on Cypriote characters/syllabary.

AD **1873**   Publication of the discovery of the Moabite stone.

AD **1874**   Heinrich Schliemann at Mycenae at home of Agamemnon, finds dated to 1600 BC.

AD **1874**   Moriz Schmidt's work on Cypriot characters.

AD **1874**   Alexander Sayce's Elamite cuneiform logosyllabary.

AD **1875**   Stamp seal from Harappa, first-known Indus sample, published.

AD **1876**   Leon de Rosny applied the Landa alphabet to the first sign in the glyph for "turkey" in the Madrid Codex. He went on to propose that Mayan writing was a phonetic system, based on syllables.

AD **1877–1878**   Ernest de Sarzee unearthed rich deposits of cuneiform tablets (35,000–40,000 total) at Telloh (Lagash), a royal archive from 3000 BC.

AD **1877**   Lewis Morgan's "Ancient Society: or Researches in the Lines of Human Progress from Savagery through Barbarism to Civilization."

AD **1878**   Paul Haupt's Sumerian cuneiform logosyllabary.

AD **1879**   M. Haussoullier found fragments of Gortyna law inscription.

AD **1879**   Stone Age paintings in cave of Altamira discovered by Sautnola.

AD **1880**   Archibald Henry Sayce made remarkable claim that remains in Turkey and North Syria belonged to a forgotten empire in Anatolia—the Hittites. Also, Sayce's Luwian logosyllabary.

AD **1880**   Ernst Forstemann published "Venus Tables of Dresden Codex."

AD **1880s–1890s**   Englishman Alfred Percival Maudslay recorded many inscriptions in Mesoamerica.

AD **1881**   Sir John Evans's "Ancient Bronze Implements of Great Britain."

AD **1882–1903**   Perrot e Chipiez's "Histoire de l'art antique."

AD **1882**   A. H. Sayce published lengthy study of Urartian.

AD **1883**   I. Taylor's "The Alphabet: An Account of the Origin and Development of Letters."

AD **1884**   Gortyna law inscription discovered.

AD **1885**   Gustav Oscar Montelius's "Sur la Chronologie l'Age du Bronze."

AD **1887**   Tell el'Amarna letters found by peasant woman looking for old bricks, correspondence of Akhenaten and earlier letters probably brought from Thebes when the capital was moved. From the tablets, possible to follow the international events of the time.

AD **1887**   Augustus Pitt Rivers began publishing "Excavations at Cranborne Chase."

AD **1890**   Discovery of Gurob papyrus and one leaf of the "Antiope" of Euripides.

AD **1890s**   First excavations at Susa (the capital of Elam) by J. de Morgan, with clay tablets of cuneiform/Proto-Elamite, but the tablets also occur as far east as the Iranian border with Afghanistan (roughly contemporary with earliest Sumerian tablets of Uruk). Linear Elamite is a half a millennium younger than Proto-Elamite.

AD **1891**   Discovery at El Hibeh in Upper Egypt of papyrus roll containing adventures of Wenamen.

AD **1891**   Flinders Petrie excavated the capital city of Amenophis IV (Akhnaton).

AD **1892**   Alphons Stubel and Max Uhle's "Die Ruin enstatte von Tiahuanaco."

AD **1892**   Yukashir Love Letter, example of pictography, northeastern Siberia, found.

AD **1893–1894**   Vilhelm Thomsen's Orkhon runes alphabet. Orkhon (Orhon) are oldest extant Turkish writings.

AD **1893**   French archaeologists discovered fragments of clay tablets clearly written in unknown Arzawa language at the Boghazkoy site in Anatolia. Arzawa was an unknown land also mentioned in the Amarna tablets.

AD **1893/1972**   G. Mallery's "Picture-Writing of the American Indians."

AD **1893**   Erland Nordenskiold's "The Cliff Dwellers of Mesa Verde, Southwestern Colorado, Their Pottery and Implements."

AD **1894**   Cyrus Thomas's "Report on the Mound Explorations of the Bureau of Ethnology."

AD **1894**   Sir Arthur Evans suggested connection between Cyprus's script and Minoan (from Crete). Evans also discovered two other scripts in Crete: a hieroglyphic script (almost all on seal stones and sealings) and the Linear A script (mainly on clay tablets and fewer than Linear B) evolved from the hieroglyphic script and lasted until the collapse of the Minoan civilization in the 15th century BC. The largest collection of Linear A tablets was found in the

Minoan palace of Ayia Triada, on the Cycladic island of Kea.

AD 1895   Engravings found on a cave wall at La Mouthe, France.

AD 1895   Bernard Grenfell, Arthur Hunt, and David Hogarth began to hunt for papyri in Egypt.

AD 1895   Sir Arthur Evans on Crete, published paper "Cretan Pictographs and the Prae-Phoenician Script."

AD 1895   W. H. Holmes' "Archaeological Studies among the Ancient Cities of Mexico."

AD 1896   G. A. Smith's "The Historical Geography of the Holy Land."

AD 1897   Cave drawings found at Pair-non-Pair, France.

AD 1897   Sir John Evans' "Ancient Stone Implements of Great Britain."

AD 1897–1907   Bernard Grenfell and Arthur Hunt excavated Oxyrhynchus in the Faiyum and found a large number of papyri with sayings (Logia) of Jesus—which have provided much information about life under the Ptolemies and Romans, for many are copies of edicts, petitions, receipts, contracts, and letters. Also contain copies of lost works by classical authors and scholars, including Plato, Aristotle, and Sophocles. Oxyrhynchus was ancient capital of the 19th Upper Egyptian nome (province), on the western edge of the Nile Valley. It is best known for the numerous papyri uncovered there, first by Grenfell and Hunt, and later by Italian scholars early in the 20th century. The papyri—dating from about 250 BC to AD 700 and written primarily in Greek and Latin but also in demotic Egyptian, Coptic, Hebrew, Syriac, and Arabic—include religious texts (e.g., miracles of Sarapis, early copies of the New Testament, and such apocryphal books as the Gospel of Thomas) and also masterpieces of Greek classical literature. Among the papyri were texts once considered lost, including selections of early Greek lyric poetry, Pindar, dramatists such as Menander and Callimachus, and innumerable prose works of oratory or history, such as those of the Oxyrhynchus historian.

AD 1898–1899   In the wake of the Yellow River's flooding, fragments of tortoise shells and deer scapulae were found—which had inscriptions—the oldest known examples of Chinese writing. Early Chinese writing discovered—the "oracle bones" in Anyang. These were turtle shells and ox scapulae with signs scratched on their surfaces. Around this time, the oracle bones were bought up from Chinese medicine shops in Peking where they had been sold as "dragon bones." The Anyang artifacts include divinations by the 12 kings of the later Shang Dynasty (1400–1200 BC). There are drilled or chiseled concavities so that when heat was applied by the diviner, a crack would appear to the left or right, which was then interpreted as the answer to a question. Many of the signs on the oracle bones are recog-

nizable antecedents of modern Chinese characters. There were 4,500 Shang signs, about 1,000 identifiable. There were 10,000 characters in the Han Dynasty (206 BC–AD 220). By the 12th century, there were 23,000 characters, and by the 18th century there were 49,000 characters (including many variants and obsolete forms). Wang-I-Yang (Wang Yirong) purchased some "dragon bones" with ancient Chinese characters inscribed on them.

AD 1899   Isaac Taylor's publication on alphabet history.

AD 1898   J. G. Frazer's "Pausanias' Description of Greece."

AD 1898   Narmer palette uncovered at Kom el-Ahmar (Hierakonpolis) recorded victories, agricultural, ritual events.

AD 1899   A. Mau and F. W. Kelsey's "Pompeii, Its Life and Art."

AD 1899   Publishing of find in Kensington, Minnesota, of a rune stone.

AD 1900   Alaska, Barnum, Chukchi, Landa, Lisu, Malinshi, Mappila, Mende, Miao, Slave/Tinne, Somali scripts.

AD 1900   Archaeologist Sir Arthur Evans (1851–1941) began to dig up and reconstruct Knossos (from *The Odyssey*), discovering what he thought was the palace of King Minos with famous labyrinth. Also discovered caches of over 3,000 clay tablets, but published less than 200. Script did not resemble Egyptian hieroglyphs, Sumerian cuneiform, or Greek. Coined term *Minoan* for it; named unknown writing "Linear Script of Class B." First Linear B tablet published ("The Athenaeum"). Although Evans failed to decipher the script, he did take steps in the right direction. He saw that ancient Crete had hieroglyphic script, Linear A, and Linear B.

AD 1900   Dogri script remodeled from Takri.

AD 1900   First archaic texts of Proto-Elamite from Susa are published.

AD 1900   G. A. Cook and Mark Lidzbarski, noted epigraphists, laid authoritative groundwork for modern Phoenician epigraphy.

AD 1900   Taoist priest Wang Tao-shih found a whole library of ancient documents in one of the Caves of the Thousand Buddhas at Ch'ien Fo Tung. Aurel Stein had the area reopened in 1907 and found Buddhist texts dating to the 5th century BC, written in Chinese and other languages, Tibetan manuscripts, and other works in a variety of scripts and languages.

AD 1900s   Epigraphic revolution began with Heinrich Berlin's decipherment of the names of the different Maya city-states ("emblem glyphs") and recognition by Tatiana Proskouriakoff that the Classic Maya stone inscriptions' dates recorded the birth, accession to power, conquests, anniversaries, deaths of Maya rulers, proving that Maya stelae lined up before pyramids were dynastic records. Proskouriakoff was a pioneer decipherer of Mayan glyphs.

AD **1900–1910** Francis L. Griffith carried out fundamental work on Meroitic.

AD **1900–1925** Avid collecting of oracle bones.

AD **1901** Work undertaken at the Akropolis: produced clay tablets with cuneiform, stone inscriptions, and one Akkadian text in cuneiform—of 3000 BC.

AD **1901–1905** First series of impressed tablets excavated at Susa by Jacques de Morgan.

AD **1901/1902** Code of Hammurabi was discovered by M. de Morgan at Susa excavation. It is now in the Louvre. Its discovery was important because it extended the knowledge of early legal systems to before the ancient Greeks and Romans. Shortly after 1902, Father Vincent Scheil translated it. There are about 300 laws on the stelae, 262 well preserved and classifiable.

AD **1902** Norwegian Assyriologist Jørgen Alexander Knudtzon's study on the Arzawa letters was published; these were two letters exchanged between a king of Arzawa and Pharaoh Amenhotep III that had been found in the Amarna archive. They were written in the Hittite language is cuneiform writing.

AD **1902** Alfred Percival Maudslay's casts, drawings, and photos provide the first raw material for serious decipherment of Mesoamerican writings.

AD **1902** R. M. Hall and W. O. Neal's "The Ancient Ruins of Rhodesia."

AD **1902** W. Doerpfeld's "Troia and Ilion."

AD **1903** First decipherment of oracle bones; most have come from Anyang, the last Shang capital.

AD **1903** Major comparative study by Stanley A. Cook published, "The Laws of Moses and the Code of Hammurabi."

AD **1904–1905** Stone inscriptions found by W. M. Flinders Petrie on Sinai Peninsula, a Proto-Sinaitic writing. Alan H. Gardiner laid the foundations for its decipherment. Also, W. F. Albright contributed toward final decipherment. Flinders Petrie unearthed evidence of Egyptian origin of Semitic alphabet. Found inscriptions in Sinai caves, mine entrances, and temples (Serabit El-Khadem) with links to hieroglyphics, but which demonstrated a Semitic language. Petrie's research provided the basis for investigating an early source for the alphabet, one that preceded the Phoenician dissemination and extended the period in which both development and transmission had occurred. At Serabit el-Khadim in Sinai, found by Flinders Petrie, in turquoise mines active in ancient Egyptian times—a sphinx dated to middle of 18th Dynasty (by Flinders Petrie), now c. 1500 BC. One side has inscriptions plus hieroglyphs—and Petrie guessed that the script was an alphabet because it had less than 30 signs. He thought it was Semitic because Semites from Canaan had worked the mines for the pharaohs.

AD **1905** Drawings of 200+ Proto-Elamite texts published (from Susa/Elam 3000 BC) with similarities to later cuneiform. The earliest Elamite writings are in a figurative or pictographic script and date from the middle of the 3rd millennium BC.

AD **1905** François Thureau-Dangin produced first translation of Sumerian, the earliest identified writing. Sumerologists consulted an enormous corpus of cuneiform texts, and cuneiform laboratories have developed comprehensive computer databases of individual tablets of Sumerian grammar and word usage. The archaeologist and epigrapher can study Sumerian against a backdrop of multidisciplinary research.

AD **1905** Hugo Winkler excavated Boghazkoy (Turkey) and found 34 fragments of clay tablets . . . eventually finding more than 10,000 cuneiform tablets (mostly in Akkadian)—letters between Egypt and King of Hatti. He had unearthed the Hittite royal archive.

AD **1906** Excavation of Hittite capital at Boghazkoy (ancient Hattusas) revealed a royal archive of 10,000 tablets. Many could be read in Babylonian, but majority were in unknown Hittite language. Hittite scribes alternated freely between Hittite, Sumerian, Babylonian, and that provided a good starting point for decipherment of Hittite cuneiform.

AD **1906** Flinders Petrie excavated temples of Hathor's inscriptions (11 texts) with hieroglyphics and Sinaitic script.

AD **1906** Bernard Grenfell and Arthur Hunt found in Egypt a basket of broken rolls including parts of "Paeans" of Pindar, the "Hypsipyle" of Euripides, the "Phaedrus," and a history of Greece.

AD **1906** Hugo Winkler excavated at Boghazkoy and uncovered large Hittite cuneiform archive—10,000 clay tablets, some in Akkadian (Babylonian)—he had discovered the capital city of the empire Sayce had suggested, dated to 1200 BC and having an occupation of 400 years.

AD **1907** Sir Aurel Stein discovered library of early Chinese texts in one of the Caves of the 1000 Buddhas at Ch'ien Fo Tung, China.

AD **1907** Hugo Winkler published his readings of the Hittite cuneiform texts and although he had translated many Akkadian tablets, there remained a large number in a language he could not read.

AD **1908** Discovery of the famous Phaistos Disk by Italian archaeologists in Crete. It remains one of the greatest puzzles in the history of writing. Large clay disk, covered on both faces with 45 signs written in a spiral. Phaistos disk found in ruins of a palace at Phaistos—in an archaeological context suggesting the disk was not later than 1700 BC (contemporary with Linear A). It is baked clay with signs impressed by punch or stamp—"the world's first typewritten document"—resembles no other Minoan signs, nor the hieroglyphic script, nor Linear A or B. Both sides with inscription of 242 signs, first "typewritten" document.

AD **1908** Christos Tsountas's "Prehistoric Acropolis of Dimini and Sesklo."

AD **1908** C. Kahnweiler's translation of A. Michaelis's "A Century of Archaeological Discoveries."

AD **1909–1911** Francis Griffith's Meroitic alphabet and the phonetic values of the script. Although a small number of Meroitic words and a small portion of the grammar are known, the language remains largely undeciphered.

AD **1909** First volume of Minoan inscriptions published by Sir Arthur Evans, "Scripta Minoa I."

AD **1911** Comprehensive classifications of the Mesoamerican Indian languages were presented by the U.S. anthropologists Cyrus Thomas and John R. Swanton in "Indian Languages of Mexico and Central America and Their Geographical Distribution." Cyrus Thomas spoke for phonetic approach to Maya glyphs.

AD **1911–1912** John Myres published volume that Sir Arthur Evans planned and largely compiled.

AD **1912** T. A. Joyce's "South American Archaeology."

AD **1912** W. Flinders Petrie's "The Formation of the Alphabet."

AD **1913** Czech scholar Bedrich Hrozny deciphered the Hittite language Winkler could not read and made the astounding discovery that it belonged to the Indo-European languages and was possibly the oldest.

AD **1913** C. H. Weller's "Athens and Its Monuments."

AD **1913** Zhuyin zimu, national alphabet, China.

AD **1915** Clay tablets found in southern Mesopotamia of proto-cuneiform.

AD **1915** F. Hrozny announced his decipherment of Hittite and published paper "The Solution of the Hittite Problem."

AD **1915** H. R. Hall's "Aegean Archaeology."

AD **1915** S. G. Morley's "An Introduction to the Study of Maya Hieroglyphs."

AD **1916** Sir Alan Gardiner attempted to read Semitic/Sinaitic script that Flinders Petrie found in 1904/05 and succeeded. He studied Proto-Sinaitic signs and noted resemblances to pictographic Egyptian hieroglyphs: Proto-Sinaitic sign | Egyptian sign | Semitic name. The Semitic names are the same as the names of the letters of the Hebrew alphabet (he knew Hebrews had lived in Canaan in the late 2nd millennium BC). Gardiner's hypothesis enabled him to translate one of the inscriptions on the Sinai sphinx.

AD **1917** Dr. Friedrich Hrozny's decipherment of Hittite published in book form.

AD **1920** F. H. Marshall's "Discovery in Greek Lands."

AD **1921** Sir John Marshall (with R. D. Banerji) discovered the Indus Valley civilization of 3000–1800 BC. Most of the inscriptions preserved on seal stones—generally of only a few characters each (400 signs, 53 used commonly)—may be a mixed hieroglyphic and syllabic script. Scholars have attempted decipherment of the Indus script; 3,500 inscriptions are known, mostly on seal stones. Indus script also on terracotta sealings, pottery, copper tablets, bronze implements, ivory and bone rods; scattered in houses and streets (but not on walls, tombs, statues, clay tablets, papyri). The inscriptions average less than four signs in a line. Consisted of signs, animal outlines, and anthropomorphic figures.

AD **1921** Sir Arthur Evans published "The Palace of Minos."

AD **1923** Sarcophagus inscription found near Byblos by Paul Montet, debatably the oldest of the group of north Semitic examples of alphabet, epitaph praising King Ahiram of 13th c BC. Until the discovery of the Ahiram inscription, the Moabite Stone was considered the earliest extant alphabetic inscription.

AD **1924** Alfred Kidder's "An Introduction to the Study of Southwestern Archaeology."

AD **1924** D. Randall-MacIver's "Villanovans and Early Etruscans."

AD **1924** F. J. Haverfield's "The Roman Occupation of Britain" (revised by G. MacDonald).

AD **1924** George G. MacCurdy's "Human Origins."

AD **1924** O. G. S. Crawford's "Air Survey and Archaeology."

AD **1924** University of Michigan worked in Antioch (Pisidia) on 200 fragments; F. W. Kelsey and D. M. Robinson published "Res Gestae Divi Augusti."

AD **1925** Vere Gordon Childe's "The Dawn of European Civilization."

AD **1925** Discovery of 1,000 tablets in Assyrian by American School at Baghdad and Iraq Museum.

AD **1928** About 4,000 clay tablets found in Eanna/Uruk, the oldest written documents in that part of the Near East, if not the oldest in history—from end of 4th, beginning of 3rd millennium.

AD **1928** Excavations at Caerlon in Wales brought to light a dedication inscription to Trajan.

AD **1928** H. R. Hall's "Babylonian and Assyrian Sculpture in the British Museum" and "The Civilization of Greece in the Bronze Age."

AD **1928** Kemal Ataturk officially abandoned Arabic script, replacing it with Latin/Roman script.

AD **1928** Scholars decided to investigate the most productive places for finding oracle bones—near the city of Anyang.

AD **1929** Discovery of the Ras Shamrah/Ugarit tablets, cuneiform unlike any others; the low number of 30 different signs pointed to an alphabetic type. The use of a vertical stroke as word divider facilitated the decipherment, which was based on the correct assumption that an early North Semitic Canaanite dialect was involved. Thus the script was solved with astonishing speed by Hans Bauer, Edouard Dhorme, and Charles Virolleaud, yielding a Semitic dialect named Ugaritic, closely related to Old Phoenician.

This was hard evidence of the existence of an alphabet by 14th century BC, well after Proto-Sinaitic writing. Ten languages and five scripts used at Ugarit; dominant script was Akkadian cuneiform until the alphabet was introduced, written in cuneiform (30 signs) bearing no resemblance to Akkadian cuneiform.

AD 1929 Vere Gordon Childe's "The Danube in Prehistory."

AD 1929 Sir Leonard Woolley found list of Sumerian kings that refer to "the flood." Max Mallowan dated the Mesopotamian flood to 2900 BC.

AD 1930–1931 Impressed tablets in temple of Eanna at Uruk, identified as precursor of pictographic tablets.

AD 1930s Decipherment of Hittite hieroglyphic writing by the combined efforts of Helmuth T. Bossert, Emil O. Forrer, Bedrich Hrozny, Piero Meriggi, and Ignace J. Gelb.

AD 1930s Maurice Dunand found a number of inscriptions on bronze tablets and spatulae—a different form of Old Canaanite script (pseudohieroglyphic). Dunand published inscriptions of Byblos.

AD 1930s–1940s Matthew Stirling and Miguel Covarrubias found evidence of writing and calendar of Olmecs.

AD 1930 Tatiana Proskouriakoff built on Yuri Knosorov's work, obtaining an unrivaled knowledge of the glyphs through architectural reconstruction.

AD 1930 Decipherment of Iberian script by Manual Gomez-Moreno. Also, inscriptions of Gaud, numerous and informative, including calendar of Coligny. Also, a bronze tablet at Botorrita, north-central Spain, bearing on both faces a long inscription written in Celt-Iberian. The discovery of this long text has had a major impact on the understanding of Hispano-Celtic.

AD 1931, 1935, 1942 Ignace J. Gelb's Luwian logosyllabary.

AD 1931 Oberi Okaime script.

AD 1932 Emil Forrer's Luwian logosyllabary.

AD 1933 Complete decipherment of Hittite cuneiform.

AD 1933 Hittite decipherment begun by B. Hrozny.

AD 1934–1935 Khafaje impressed tablets found.

AD 1934 Excavations at Tell Hariri, Syria (ancient Mari), where a great cuneiform archive from the 17th century BC would be found.

AD 1934 Glossary of Hittite hieroglyphics published by Piero Meriggi. In 1936, Lydian was proved to be an Indo-European language by the Italian scholar Piero Meriggi,

and Onofrio Carruba gave strong evidence in 1959 that Lydian should be placed in the Anatolian subgroup of Indo-European languages because Lydian shares many common features with Hittite, Luwian, and Palaic.

AD 1935 Johannes Sundwall copied 38 inscriptions in Crete and published them, offending Sir Arthur Evans.

AD 1936–1952 Michael Ventris (1922–1956) able to compile a promising grid, after suspecting that the Knossos tablets studied by Kober contained place names.

AD 1936 Adam Falkenstein's publication of the first 620 tablets found during first 3 seasons of Uruk.

AD 1936 Vere Gordon Childe's "Man Makes Himself."

AD 1937 Piero Meriggi's Luwian logosyllabary.

AD 1937 Tepe Sialk impressed tablets found.

AD 1938 Thomas Obicini's manuscript notes on Coptic discovered in Vatican Library.

AD 1939 Cache of 600 Linear B tablets found at ancient Pylos, mainland Greece, by Carl Blegen at Epano Englianos (in first season). The fragments dated to 1200 BC; he published them after World War II.

AD 1940–1960 Sir J. Eric Thompson wrote "Maya Hieroglyphic Writing" among 250 publications.

AD 1940 Palaeolithic paintings found in Lascaux Cave, France.

AD 1940s Alice Kober identified five groups of words, with three words in each group (called Kober's triplets by Michael Ventris) which suggested declension. Kober saw beginning of a tentative phonetic pattern. Kober was the first to discover the nature of language (Linear B syllabary) through the barrier of script.

AD 1941 A large number of tablets with Linear B helped Sir Arthur John Evans put forward many theories and suggestions before his death.

AD 1945 Yuri Valentinovich Knorosov considered chief initiator of the decipherment of Mayan glyphs. As a military man, he snatched one book from the burning National Library—the one-volume edition (1933) of the Dresden, Madrid, and Paris codices of the Maya. He discovered Maya writing was mixed script with fundamental phonetic component.

AD 1945 G. Pugliese Carratelli published important series of Linear A.

AD 1946 Second great postwar Maya discovery was murals of Bonampak (three painted rooms) in Chiapas, Mexico, close to Yaxchilan. Murals show life of Classic Maya in late 8th century AD just before civilization's collapse. Many of its glyphs are yet to be deciphered. Murals show narrative of a successful battle, its aftermath, and victory celebrations. Murals were never completed as Bonampak was abandoned. Seem to have been painted for the consecration of a male heir to the throne. Objects looted from various Maya sites have actually helped the decipherment of Maya glyphs.

AD **1946/1947** Nomadic Bedouins herding sheep and goats near the northwest end of the Dead Sea found two holes in a cliff and fell into a cave where they found large pottery jars—three scrolls in one jar. A Hebrew dictionary was used to identify that part of the scrolls were written by Isaiah. AD 33 ± 200 years is the radiocarbon date of the linen wrapping of the Isaiah Scroll.

AD **1947** Luwian/Luvian (Anatolia, Syria) deciphered owing to discovery of bilingual inscription at Karatepe. The importance of Karatepe lies in its inscriptions. At the beginning of the excavations, a long Phoenician text was discovered. The gateways were found to contain extensive versions of the same text in both Phoenician script and Hittite (Luwian) hieroglyphs. By comparing the two inscriptions, archaeologists greatly increased their understanding of the Hittite hieroglyphic script and language.

AD **1948–1949** Tall-i-Ghazir tablets found.

AD **1948** Discovery of abecedary that uses traditional sequence of Semitic alphabet.

AD **1948** Hebrew became national language in Israel.

AD **1948** The Biblical Archaeologist published "A Phenomenal Discovery" about that particular scroll, which was important because it filled a significant gap in knowledge of biblical history—between the Old and New Testaments, near the beginning of Christianity. The original scrolls are now housed in a specially built part of the Israeli Museum called "The Shrine of the Book." Through the years, a large number of scrolls were found at other sites by Bedouins and archaeologists—about 800 are available now, with nearly half from one cave.

AD **1948** Ugarit text found with letters in abecedary order.

AD **1948** Walter Taylor's "A Study of Archaeology."

AD **1948** G. R. Driver's "Semitic Writing."

AD **1948** O. Ogg's "The 26 Letters."

AD **1948** William Albright said he had identified 19 of 25–27 Sinaitic signs, and Sinai inscriptions were vulgar form of Canaanite.

AD **1949** D. Diringer's "The Alphabet."

AD **1949** More scroll fragments discovered in the caves at Kumran by the Dead Sea.

AD **1949** North Korea adopted Hangul; South Korea inching toward Hangul-only.

AD **1950s** Carl Blegen used a tablet, one of 400 found at Pylos, to test Michael Ventris's syllabary and found that it worked. With continued excavation from 1952, more than 1,000 inscribed tablets were found at Pylos, and a fine 13th-century-BC Mycenaean palace was revealed. First Linear B tablet from Mycenae found.

AD **1950s** Heinrich Berlin found each Maya city-state had its own emblem glyph.

AD **1950s** The Chinese Small Seal script used until now. Communist rulers introduced still-controversial simplified script.

AD **1950, 1984** Sir Arthur Evans' unrecorded tablets discovered in Iraklion Museum.

AD **1950** G. Boas's "The Hieroglyphics of Horapollo."

AD **1950** Discovery of arrowheads at El-Khadr showing resemblance to Sinai pictographs midway in evolution to the schematic linear form of the Phoenician letters. This was evidence of the connection between Old Canaanite protoalphabet of Sinai and the Phoenician system.

AD **1950** Emmett L. Bennett demonstrated divergence of systems of measurements in Linear A and Linear B.

AD **1951–1952** Michael Ventris's Linear B syllabary.

AD **1951** Emmett L. Bennett wrote about Blegen's find of tablets near Pylos, "The Pylos Tablets: A Preliminary Transcription."

AD **1951** Excavation of Khirbet Qumran, monastery by the Dead Sea, by G. Lankaster Harding and Pere Roland de Vaux.

AD **1952–1953** With help of John Chadwick, Michael Ventris showed more and more tablets yielding to "Greek solution." It began to seem that Minoans and Mycenaeans had been speaking and writing Greek centuries before Homer. Chadwick believed he has deciphered Linear B.

AD **1952** Archaeological discovery providing breakthrough in decipherment of Mayan script. Mexican archaeologist Alberto Ruz, temple of the Inscriptions at Palenque, found great funerary crypt with treasure trove; compared find to tomb of Tutankhamen.

AD **1952** Yuri Knorosov made the phonetic breakthrough with Maya writing; alphabet was a syllabary. He proposed phonetic readings of many glyphs. Produced a series of such decipherments—his basic approach was sound, and most Mayanists (except Thompson) thought he was onto something important.

AD **1952** A. J. B. Wace found clay tablets at Mycenae, including Linear B, outside the walls of the akropolis and royal castle. Fifty-seven thousand occurrences of signs in Linear B enabled Michael Ventris to decipher it.

AD **1952** John Myres finished and published Sir Arthur Evans's "Scripta Minoa II."

AD **1952** Michael Ventris accomplished decipherment of the whole syllabary of signs and with Chadwick was able to make sense of many of the Pylos and Knossos tablets. Ventris announced decipherment of the Linear B/Mycenaean script.

AD **1952** Yuri Knosorov published "Ancient Writing of South America" and set out to crack the Maya script, phonetic and syllabic hieroglyphs.

AD **1953**   A. C. Moorhouse's "The Triumph of the Alphabet: A History of Writing."

AD **1953**   Confirmation from new tablet find, made at ancient Pylos on Greek mainland, by Carl Blegen. The tablet that clinched the decipherment of Linear B is a simple inventory of tripod cauldrons and of goblets of varying sizes and number of handles.

AD **1955**   Another bilingual broken tablet discovered that lists Ugaritic signs in the abecedary order and adds to each one its Akkadian syllabic equivalent. It allowed definitive decipherment of Ugarit (making clear its alphabetic character).

AD **1955**   Chinese characters simplified by eliminating certain variants and reducing the number of strokes in many of those remaining.

AD **1955/1957**   Earliest Cyprus inscription found on Island of Enkomi; source was Cretan Linear A of 1500 BC. Also, a group of tablets similar to Cretan scripts (12th c BC).

AD **1956**   Michael Ventris and John Chadwick assembled dramatic evidence supporting Ventris' theory. In 1953 they published their historic paper, "Evidence for Greek Dialect in the Mycenaean Archives." Their Documents in Mycenaean Greek (1956; rev. ed., 1973) was published a few weeks after Ventris' death in an auto accident, and Chadwick's "The Decipherment of Linear B" (1958; 2nd ed., 1968) followed.

AD **1957**   Sir A. Gardiner's "Egyptian Grammar: Being an Introduction to the Study of Hieroglyphs."

AD **1958**   Heinrich Berlin's Maya logosyllabary.

AD **1958**   China's Pinyin system permits Chinese language to be written in romanized form. Chinese government introduced romanized Chinese script, Pinyin ("spell sound") as official system for writing sounds and transcribing Chinese characters. Pinyin adopted for the spelling of Chinese names outside China, as Peking > Beijing. Now Pinyin is in chaos and has an uncertain status. China uses two scripts: digraphia. Chinese is older than any other living script.

AD **1959**   A. G. Woodhead's "The Study of Greek Inscriptions."

AD **1959**   R. W. V. Elliott's "Runes: An Introduction."

AD **1959**   Tatiana Proskouriakoff graphed all the Maya dates from the stelae and found they formed distinct patterns—an actual recorded history.

AD **1960**   Documents from the Second Jewish Revolt (AD 132–135) found in Cave of Letters near Dead Sea (Nahal Hever, Israel).

AD **1960**   Tatiana Proskouriakoff's Maya logosyllabary.

AD **1960**   Yigael Yadin got his first clue as to the existence of a new Dead Sea Scroll. The Dead Seal Scrolls contain almost all the books of the Old Testament and a variety of other religious writings. Close to the Dead Sea Scroll caves is a site called Khirbet Qumran, possibly the home of the authors of the scrolls—the Essenses. This link is disputed. The scrolls seem too varied to be linked to one group.

AD **1961**   Hertha Marquardt published bibliography of runic inscriptions in British Isles with appendix of reported runic inscription in North America (40 distinct sites).

AD **1961**   Ignace Gelb developed Old Akkadian syllabary.

AD **1961**   L. H. Jeffery's "The Local Scripts of Archaic Greece."

AD **1962**   J. E. S. Thompson's "A Catalog of Maya Hieroglyphs."

AD **1963**   I. J. Gelb's "A Study of Writing: The Foundations of Grammatology."

AD **1963**   L. R. Palmer's "The Interpretation of Mycenaean Greek Texts."

AD **1964**   Bilingual inscription (c. 500 BC) with Etruscan found at Pyrgi, a major Etruscan seaport near Rome—two gold plaques, one in Phoenician, the other in Etruscan/Greek script. The Greeks borrowed the alphabetic principle from the Phoenicians and then gave it to the Etruscans, including the signs of their alphabet.

AD **1964**   Linear B tablets found in Thebes.

AD **1964**   Mari tablets found.

AD **1965–1966**   Chogha Mish tablets found.

AD **1966**   Linear B tablets found in Tiryns.

AD **1966**   W. F. Albright's "The Proto-Sinaitic Inscriptions and Their Decipherment."

AD **1967**   During the Six-Day War, Yigael Yadin followed up lead about new Dead Sea Scroll. It was 27 feet long (the longest) and contained elaborate plans for building a temple. It also contained many parts of the Old Testament.

AD **1968**   C. Gordon's "Forgotten Scripts: The Story of Their Decipherment."

AD **1968**   D. Diringer's "The Alphabet: A Key to the History of Mankind."

AD **1968–1970**   Proto-Elamite found at Tepe Yahya on southern Iranian plateau, including texts, seals and sealings from 3rd millennium.

AD **1969**   Denise Schmandt-Besserat began investigating when and in what ways clay first came to be used in the Near East. She found tokens all the way from Turkey to the Nile Valley in the Sudan, first used in Neolithic times (9,000 years ago) and up to the first city-states in Mesopotamia. They were used for keeping economic records. Many of their patterns have been shown to closely resemble the incised designs on the earliest clay tablets. Eventually, tokens were put into clay envelopes and sealed with the number and kinds of tokens inscribed on the surface. Subsequently, envelopes developed into the first clay tablets.

AD **1969**   H. Jensen's "Sign, Symbol, and Script."

AD **1970–1971**   Jebel Aruda tablets found.

AD **1970s**   Cuneiform is photo-digitized with a scanner, in which a laser breaks down the image into individual pixels, for computer processing. It becomes a drawing template on electronic canvas. Division lines and discernible signs can be traced on the screen.

AD **1970s**   Ebla (Tell Mardikh) in Syria, where an archive of 15,000 clay tablets has yielded evidence of a previously unknown language and state of the 3rd millennium BC.

AD **1971**   Only four Mayan codices are known to survive: the Dresden Codex, or Codex Dresdensis, probably dating from the 11th or 12th century, a copy of earlier texts of the 5th to 9th century AD; the Madrid Codex, or Codex Tro-Cortesianus, dating from the 15th century; the Paris Codex, or Codex Peresianus, probably slightly older than the Madrid Codex; and the Gorlier Codex, discovered in 1971 and dated to the 13th century AD. The codices were made of fig-bark paper folded like an accordion; their covers were of jaguar skin.

AD **1971**   Michael Coe noticed the sequence of glyphs around rims of many pots was similar: Primary Standard Sequence.

AD **1971**   Asko Parpola has made impressive analysis in attempt to decipher the Indus Valley script. So far, no bilingual inscriptions involving the Indus Valley script have been found, nor can any proper names be read.

AD **1971**   Fragmentary Linear B tablets found at Tiryns.

AD **1972**   Habuba Kabira tablets found.

AD **1973**   Floyd Lounsbury, Linda Schele, Peter Matthews assembled dynastic history of Palenque from early 7th century to its demise. The next year, they teamed up to put together the missing part of Palenque's history, the first 200 years of the dynasty. Lounsbury's Maya logosyllabary.

AD **1973**   Godin Tepe tablets found.

AD **1973**   J. E. S. Thompson's "Maya Hieroglyphic Writing."

AD **1973**   M. Ventris and J. Chadwick's "Documents in Mycenaean Greek."

AD **1973**   Scholars in Palenque realized that the name glyph on the sarcophagus was logographic, while that in the temple was phonographic.

AD **1974**   E. J. W. Barber's "Archaeological Decipherment."

AD **1974**   R. Claiborne's "The Birth of Writing."

AD **1975**   Archive of Early Bronze Age tablets, many in a previously unknown Semitic language, found at Tell Mardikh (ancient Ebla) in Syria. Over 15,000 cuneiform tablets (fragments) discovered in the library by Paolo Matthiae—4500 years old.

AD **1975**   M. Pope's "The Story of Archaeological Decipherment."

AD **1976**   D. Kelley's "Deciphering the Mayan Script."

AD **1976**   Over 80 artifacts discovered in tomb of Fu Hao (a wife of Shang King Wuding, 1324–1266 BC) at Anyang were inscribed with her name or various titles, making hers the earliest tomb in China whose occupant is historically identifiable. She was already known as royalty from oracle bone records.

AD **1976**   R. Caminos and H. G. Fischer's "Ancient Egyptian Epigraphy and Palaeography."

AD **1978**   Tell Brak tablets found.

AD **1980**   A. Nakanishi's "Writing Systems of the World: Alphabets—Syllabaries—Pictograms."

AD **1980s**   Roman alphabet invaded Japanese writing through advertising.

AD **1981**   Denise Schmandt-Besserat deciphered some of the earliest known cuneiform tablets by using the analysis of clay tokens; found evidence of 18 signs on the clay tablets that represent tokens. Tokens were simple clay disks, cones, triangles.

AD **1982**   Copan project exhibited how combination of archaeology and epigraphy produces more complete results.

AD **1985**   Forty years after Yuri Knorosov's first publication, scholars have put together a syllabic chart; now 85% of the Mayan glyphs can be "read" (meaning they can be understood with some precision, and a lot of the pronunciations are done). Without Landa's alphabet, no one would have been able to create the Mayan equivalent of the Linear B grid.

AD **1985**   G. Sampson's "Writing Systems: A Linguistic Introduction."

AD **1985**   One of the earliest hieroglyphically inscribed stone monuments found in Copan.

AD **1987**   C. B. F. Walker's "Cuneiform."

AD **1987**   David Stuart's "Ten Phonetic Glyphs."

AD **1989**   F. Coulmas's "Writing Systems of the World."

AD **1989**   J. Chadwick's "Linear B and Related Scripts."

AD **1989**   J. DeFrancis's "Visible Speech: The Diverse Oneness of Writing Systems."

AD **1989**   S. D. Houston's "Maya Glyphs."

AD **1989**   W. M. Senner's "The Origins of Writing."

AD **1990**   Yuri Knorosov unable to personally visit Maya ruins until this time.

AD **1990**   In the contemporary world, there are several hundred alphabets in use, all of which are derivations of the Canaanite scripts of the Old Semitic language. Thus the Phoenician alphabet is the direct antecedent of the alphabets of western Europe.

AD **1990**   Linda Schele and David Freidel published first Mayan history derived from archaeology and glyphs, "A Forest of Kings," combining archaeology and deciphered inscriptions.

AD **1990**   M. P. Brown's "A Guide to Western Historical Scripts from Antiquity to 1600."

AD **1991**   Maya hieroglyphs fully deciphered.

AD **1992**   A. Gaur's "A History of Writing."

AD **1992**   M. D. Coe's "Breaking the Maya Code."

AD **1996**   British Museum epigrapher Dr. Nikolai Grube announced decipherment of some inscriptions on an 11-foot-high stone monument associated with a royal tomb site in La Milpa (Belize), symbols deciphered give date of AD 406.

AD **1996**   Partially deciphered (in decreasing degree of decipherment) Egyptian hieroglyphs, Linear B, Mayan script, Hittite hieroglyphs. Undeciphered scripts in three categories: (1) unknown script writing a known language (Mayan, until recently), (2) a known script writing an unknown language (Etruscan), and (3) an unknown script writing an unknown language (Indus Valley). Although research continues, neither Linear A nor the Phaistos disk have given up their secrets. That goes for some Maya writing and Rongorongo from Easter Island, too.

AD **2012**   Current Maya Great Cycle of time due to end.